Robert C. Melzi, Author

ROBERT C. MELZI, D. in L., A.M., Ph.D., was trained in Italy, at the University of Padua, and in the United States, at the University of Pennsylvania. He has done extensive linguistic research, traveling frequently to his native country. Now professor of Romance Languages at Widener College, he has contributed articles and reviews to many learned journals, is the author of *Castelvetro's Annotations to the Inferno,* The Hague and Paris, 1966 (Castelvetro was one of Italy's foremost philologists), and is an associate editor of *The Scribner-Bantam English Dictionary* (Scribner's, 1977; Bantam Books, 1979). Professor Melzi is a Cavaliere in the Order of Solidarity of the Republic of Italy.

Edwin B. Williams, General Editor

EDWIN B. WILLIAMS (1891–1975), A.B., A.M., Ph.D., Doct. d'Univ., LL.D., L.H.D., was chairman of the Department of Romance Languages, dean of the Graduate School, and provost of the University of Pennsylvania. He was a member of the American Philosophical Society and the Hispanic Society of America. Among his many lexicographical works are *The Williams Spanish and English Dictionary* (Scribner's, formerly Holt) and *The Bantam New College Spanish and English Dictionary.* He created and coordinated the Bantam series of original dictionaries—English, French, German, Italian, Latin, and Spanish. The University of Pennsylvania named "Williams Hall" in honor of Edwin B. Williams and his wife, Leonore, and is establishing the "Williams Chair in Lexicography," as the first chair in lexicography in an English-speaking country.

THE NEW INTERNATIONAL
WEBSTER'S
ITALIAN &
ENGLISH
DICTIONARY

◆◆◆

ROBERT C. MELZI, Ph.D.
Widener College, Philadelphia

TRIDENT PRESS INTERNATIONAL
1997 EDITION

TRIDENT PRESS INTERNATIONAL
1997 EDITION

All rights reserved.
Copyright © 1976 by Bantam Books.

Reprinted by permission of Bantam Books, a division of
Bantam Doubleday Dell Publishing Group, Inc. Paperback
edition available from Bantam under the title The Bantam
New College Italian & English Dictionary.

ISBN 1-888777-46-X

CONTENTS

CONTENTS

PREFACE

PREFAZIONE

Inasmuch as the basic function of a bilingual dictionary is to provide semantic equivalences, syntactical constructions are shown in both the source and the target languages on both sides of the Dictionary. In performing this function, a bilingual dictionary must fulfill six purposes. That is, an Italian and English dictionary must provide (1) Italian words which an English-speaking person wishes to use in speaking and writing (by means of the English-Italian part), (2) English meanings of Italian words which an English-speaking person encounters in listening and reading (by means of the Italian-English part), (3) the spelling, pronunciation, and inflection of Italian words and the gender of Italian nouns which an English-speaking person needs in order to use Italian words correctly (by means of the Italian-English part), (4) English words which an Italian-speaking person wishes to use in speaking and writing (by means of the Italian-English part), (5) Italian meanings of English words which an Italian-speaking person encounters in listening and reading (by means of the English-Italian part), and (6) the spelling, pronunciation, and inflection of English words which an Italian-speaking person needs in order to use English words correctly (by means of the English-Italian part).

Dato che la funzione principale di un dizionario bilingue è quella di fornire all'utente equivalenze semantiche, le costruzioni sintattiche sono indicate in entrambe le lingue, quella di partenza e quella di arrivo, in entrambe le parti del Dizionario. Per compiere questa funzione, un dizionario bilingue deve raggiungere sei scopi differenti. Cioè, un dizionario italiano e inglese deve fornire (1) nella parte inglese-italiano, le parole italiane che la persona anglofona vuole adoperare parlando e scrivendo l'italiano; (2) nella parte italiano-inglese, il significato in inglese delle parole italiane che tale persona oda nella lingua parlata o legga in libri o giornali; (3) nella parte italiano-inglese, l'ortografia, la pronunzia, la flessione delle parole italiane e il genere dei nomi italiani che la persona anglofona deve conoscere per servirsi correttamente della lingua italiana; (4) nella parte italiano-inglese, le parole inglesi che la persona italofona vuole adoperare parlando o scrivendo l'inglese; (5) nella parte inglese-italiano, il significato in italiano delle parole inglesi che tale persona oda nella lingua parlata o legga in libri o giornali; (6) nella parte inglese-italiano, l'ortografia, la pronunzia figurata e la flessione delle parole inglesi che la persona italofona deve conoscere per servirsi correttamente della lingua inglese.

It may seem logical to provide the pronunciation and inflection of English words and the pronunciation and inflection of Italian words and the gender of Italian nouns where these words appear as target words inasmuch as target words, according to (1) and (4) above, are sought for the purpose of speaking and writing. Thus the user would find not only the words he seeks but all the information he needs about them in one and the same place. But this technique is impractical because target words are not alphabetized and could, therefore, be found only by the roundabout and uncertain way of seeking them through their translations in

A prima vista potrebbe sembrare logico che la pronunzia e la flessione delle parole inglesi e la pronunzia e la flessione delle parole italiane e il genere dei nomi italiani fossero indicati dove queste parole si trovano nella lingua d'arrivo, dato che le parole della lingua d'arrivo, secondo i punti (1) e (4) enunciati più sopra, sono consultate da coloro che vogliono parlare e scrivere in lingua straniera. In questa maniera l'utente troverebbe non solo le parole che cerca, ma tutte le informazioni che gli sono necessarie, nello stesso luogo. Questa tecnica, peraltro, non è pratica poiché le parole della lingua d'arrivo non si trovano in ordine

the other part of the dictionary. And this would be particularly inconvenient for persons using the dictionary for purposes (2) and (5) above. It is much more convenient to provide immediate alphabetized access to pronunciation and inflection where the words appear as source words.

alfabetico e potrebbero quindi essere trovate solo in maniera complicata nella parte opposta del dizionario. E ciò sarebbe specialmente scomodo per coloro che usano il dizionario per gli scopi (2) e (5) menzionati più sopra. È molto più semplice aggiungere la pronuncia e la flessione nella serie alfabetica in cui le parole si trovano nella loro lingua di partenza.

Since Italian is an almost perfectly phonetic language, IPA transcription of Italian words has been omitted. The only elements of pronunciation not shown by standard spelling are the values of tonic e and o (§1; pp. 3, 4) the stress of words stressed on the third syllable from the end (§3,3; p. 5), the value of intervocalic s when unvoiced, and the values of z and zz when voiced (§1; p. 4); these are shown in the entry words themselves.

Dato che l'italiano è una lingua quasi perfettamente fonetica, non si è data la trascrizione delle parole italiane nell'alfabeto dell'Associazione Fonetica Internazionale. Considerando che l'ortografia comune non mostra il vario timbro della e (§1, p. 3) e della o (§1, p. 4) quando esse sono toniche, l'accento delle parole sdrucciole (§3,3, p. 5), la pronunzia della s sorda (§1, p. 4) e la pronunzia delle z e zz sonore (§1, p. 4), si è data tale informazione nell'esponente stesso.

All words are treated in a fixed order according to the parts of speech and the functions of verbs, as follows: adjective, article, substantive, pronoun, adverb, preposition, conjunction, transitive verb, intransitive verb, reflexive verb, auxiliary verb, impersonal verb, interjection.

Ogni singola voce è trattata secondo uno schema fisso che si riferisce alle parti del discorso o alle funzioni del verbo, nel seguente ordine: aggettivo, articolo, sostantivo, pronome, avverbio, preposizione, congiunzione, verbo transitivo, verbo intransitivo, verbo riflessivo, verbo ausiliare, verbo impersonale e interiezione.

Meanings with labels come after more general meanings. Labels (printed in roman and in parentheses) refer to the preceding entry or phrase (printed in boldface).

I significati accompagnati da sigle si trovano dopo quelli di accezione più generale. Tali sigle (che sono sempre stampate in carattere romano e in parentesi) si riferiscono all'esponente precedente, stampato in grassetto, o alla frase precedente, ugualmente stampata in grassetto.

In view of the fact that the users of this Italian and English bilingual dictionary are for the most part English-speaking people, definitions and discriminations are provided in English. They are printed in italics and in parentheses and refer to the English word which they particularize:

Dato che gli utenti di questo dizionario bilingue italiano e inglese sono per lo più anglofoni, definizioni e locuzioni esplicative sono apportate in inglese. Sono stampate in corsivo e in parentesi e si riferiscono sempre alla parola inglese il cui significato cercano di spiegare:

porter ['portər] *s* (*doorman*) portiere *m;* (*man who carries luggage*) facchino; . . .
órdine *m* order; . . . series (*e.g., of years*); college (*e.g., of surgeons*); . . .

English adjectives are always translated by the Italian masculine form

Gli aggettivi inglesi sono sempre tradotti in maschile italiano, anche se il

regardless of whether the translation of the exemplary noun modified would be masculine or feminine:	nome che qualificano sia un femminile italiano:

tough [tʌf] *adj* duro; . . . ; (*luck*) cattivo; . . .

In order to facilitate the finding of the meaning and use sought for, changes within a vocabulary entry in part of speech and function of verb, in irregular inflection, in the use of an initial capital, in the gender of Italian nouns, and in the pronunciation of English words are marked with parallels: ‖, instead of the usual semicolons.	Per facilitare l'uso del Dizionario, i raggruppamenti sono stati fatti secondo le parti del discorso, la funzione del verbo, la flessione irregolare, l'uso della maiuscola iniziale, il genere dei nomi italiani e la pronunzia delle parole inglesi e sono separati da sbarrette verticali: ‖, invece del punto e virgola che è stato generalmente usato.
Since vocabulary entries are not determined on the basis of etymology, homographs are included in a single entry. When the pronunciation of an English homograph changes, this is shown in the proper place after parallels:	Dato che gli esponenti in questo Dizionario non sono stati selezionati su base etimologica, tutti gli omografi sono inclusi sotto il medesimo esponente. Il cambio di pronunzia di un omografo inglese è indicato al posto adatto dopo sbarrette verticali:

frequent ['frikwənt] *adj* frequente ‖ [frɪ'kwɛnt]
or ['frikwənt] *tr* . . .

However, when the pronunciation of an Italian homograph changes, the words are entered separately:	Però, quando la pronunzia di un omografo italiano cambia, si hanno esponenti separati:

retina *f* small net
rètina *f* (anat) retina
tóc•co -ca (-chi -che) *adj* . . . ‖ *m* touch; . . .
tòc•co *m* (-chi) chunk, piece; . . .

Periods are omitted after labels and grammatical abbreviations and at the end of vocabulary entries.	. Il punto è stato omesso dopo sigle, abbreviazioni grammaticali, ed alla fine di ogni articolo.
Proper nouns are listed in their alphabetical position in the main body of the Dictionary. Thus **Svezia** and **svedese** do not have to be looked up in two different sections of the book. And all subentries are listed in strictly alphabetical order.	Tutti i nomi propri sono posti nella loro posizione alfabetica nel corpo del Dizionario: quindi **Svezia** e **svedese** non si trovano in sezioni separate di questo libro. Per la medesima ragione di semplicità d'uso, le parole e frasi contenute sotto ogni esponente sono poste in ordine alfabetico.
The gender of Italian nouns is shown on both sides of the Dictionary, except that the gender of masculine nouns ending in -o, feminine nouns ending in -a and -ione, masculine nouns modified by an adjective ending in -o, and feminine nouns modified by an adjective	Il genere dei nomi italiani è indicato in entrambe le parti del Dizionario, eccezion fatta nella parte inglese-italiano, per le parole maschili che terminano in -o, per le parole femminili che terminano in -a e in -ione, per i nomi maschili accompagnati da un

ending in -a is not shown on the English-Italian side.

aggettivo che termina in -o e per i nomi femminili accompagnati da un aggettivo che termina in -a.

The feminine form of an Italian adjective used as a noun (or an Italian feminine noun having identical spelling with the feminine form of an adjective) which falls alphabetically in a separate position from the adjective is treated in that position and is listed again as a cross reference under the adjective:

Quando un nome femminile italiano ha la medesima grafia della forma femminile di un aggettivo o quando tale forma femminile di aggettivo è usata come nome, lo si trova elencato nella sua posizione alfabetica come nome e poi di nuovo come rinvio interno sotto l'aggettivo:

> **nòta** *f* mark, score, . . .
> **nò·to -ta** *adj* . . . ǁ *m* . . . ǁ *f* see **nota**

The centered period is used in vocabulary entries of inflected words to mark off, according to standard orthographic principles in the two languages, the final syllable that has to be detached before the syllable showing the inflection is added:

Qualora l'esponente italiano o inglese sia un vocabolo a flessione, un punto leggermente elevato sopra il rigo è stato usato per separare, secondo le regole ortografiche di ciascuna delle due lingue, la sillaba finale che dev'essere rimossa prima che la nuova desinenza di flessione possa essere attaccata al corpo dell'esponente, per es.:

> **vèc·chio -chia (-chi -chie)** *adj* . . .
> **put·ty** [ˈpʌti] *s* (**-ties**) . . . ǁ *v* (*pret & pp*
>   **-tied**) . . .
> **hap·py** [ˈhæpi] *adj* (**-pier; -piest**) . . .

If the entry word cannot be divided by a centered period the full form is given in parentheses:

Se l'esponente non può essere scisso a mezzo del suddetto punto, la forma completa è indicata in parentesi:

> **mouse** [maʊs] *s* (**mice** [maɪs]) . . .
> **mouth** [maʊθ] *s* (**mouths** [maʊðz]) . . .
> **die** [daɪ] *s* (**dice** [daɪs]) . . . ǁ *s* (**dies**)
>   . . . ǁ *v* (*pret & pp* **died;** *ger* **dying**) *intr* . . .

Many Italian verbs which take an indirect object have, as their equivalent, English verbs which take a direct object. This is shown on both sides of this Dictionary by the insertion of (with *dat*) after the Italian verb, e.g.,

Molti verbi italiani che reggono un oggetto indiretto hanno come equivalenti inglesi verbi che reggono un oggetto diretto. Questa equivalenza è indicata in entrambe le parti del Dizionario con l'aggiunta di (with *dat*) dopo il verbo italiano, per es.:

> **ubbidire** §176 *intr* . . . ; (with *dat*) to obey
> **obey** [oˈbe] *tr* ubbidire (with *dat*)

On the Italian-English side inflection is shown by: a) numbers that refer to the grammatical tables of articles, pronouns, etc., and to the tables of model verbs; they are placed before the abbreviation indicating the part of speech:

Nella parte italiano-inglese la flessione si indica: a) con numeri che si riferiscono alle tavole grammaticali degli articoli, dei pronomi, ecc., e alle tavole dei verbi modello; questi numeri sono posti innanzi all'abbreviazione indicante la parte del discorso:

> **mì·o -a** §6 *adj & pron poss*
> **lui** §5 *pron pers*
> **congiùngere** §183 *tr & ref*

b) the first person singular of the present indicative of verbs in which the stess falls on either an **e** or an **o** not stressed in the infinitive or on the third syllable from the end, whatever the vowel may be:

b) con la prima persona singolare del presente dell'indicativo dei verbi non sdruccioli all'infinito in cui l'accento tonico cade o su una **e** o su una **o**, o su qualsiasi vocale di una parola sdrucciola:

ritornare (ritórno) *tr ...*
visitare (vìsito) *tr ...*

---

c) the feminine endings of all adjectives which end in **-o:**

c) con la desinenza femminile di tutti gli aggettivi che terminano in **-o** nel maschile:

laborió•so -sa [s] *adj ...*

---

d) the plural endings of nouns and adjectives which are formed irregularly:

d) con la desinenza plurale dei nomi e aggettivi che si formano in maniera irregolare:

bràc•cio *m* (-cia *fpl*) ... ‖ *m* (-ci) ...
cit•tà *f* (-tà) ...
dià•rio -ria (-ri -rie) *adj* ... ‖ *m* ... ‖ *f* ...
fotogram•ma *m* (-mi) ...
fràn•gia *f* (-ge) ...
laburi•sta (-sti -ste) *adj* ... ‖ *mf* ...
la•go *m* (-ghi) ...
òr•co *m* (-chi) ...
òtti•co -ca (-ci -che) *adj* ... ‖ *m* ... ‖ *f* ...

---

e) the full plural forms of all nouns that cannot be divided by a center period or whose plural cannot be shown by such division:

e) con la completa forma plurale di quei nomi che non possono essere scissi col suddetto punto o che hanno mutamenti interni:

re *m* (re) ...
caporeparto *m* (capireparto) ...

I wish to express my gratitude to many persons who helped me in the production of this book and particularly to Dr. Edwin B. Williams who, ever since graduate school, has been a constant inspiration and who has established the principles upon which this book was compiled, to my wife and children, who patiently aided and abetted me through ten years of research and compilation, to Richard J. Nelson, Sebastiano DiBlasi, Walter D. Glanze, and to Giacomo De Voto, Miro Dogliotti, and Michele Ricciardelli.

Labels and abbreviations
Sigle ed abbreviazioni

abbr abbreviation—abbreviazione
(acronym) word formed from the initial letters or syllables of a series of words—parola costituita dalle lettere o sillabe iniziali di una serie di parole
adj adjective—aggettivo
adv adverb—avverbio
(aer) aeronautics—aeronautica
(agr) agriculture—agricoltura
(alg) algebra—algebra
(anat) anatomy—anatomia
(archaic) arcaico
(archeol) archeology—archeologia
(archit) architecture—architettura
(arith) arithmetic—aritmetica
art article—articolo
(astr) astronomy—astronomia
(astrol) astrology—astrologia
(aut) automobile—automobile
aux auxiliary verb—verbo ausiliare
(bact) bacteriology—batteriologia
(baseball) baseball
(basketball) pallacanestro
(bb) bookbinding—legatoria
(Bib) Biblical—biblico
(billiards) biliardo
(biochem) biochemistry—biochimica
(biol) biology—biologia
(bot) botany—botanica
(bowling) bowling
(boxing) pugilato
(bridge) bridge
(Brit) British—britannico
(cards) carte da gioco
(carp) carpentry—falegnameria
(checkers) gioco della dama
(chem) chemistry—chimica
(chess) scacchi
(coll) colloquial—familiare
(com) commercial—commerciale
comb form elemento di parola composta
comp comparative—comparativo
cond conditional—condizionale
conj conjunction—congiunzione
(cricket) cricket
(culin) cooking—cucina
dat dative—dativo
def definite—determinativo, definito
dem demonstrative—dimostrativo
(dentistry) medicina dentaria
(dial) dialectal—dialettale
(dipl) diplomacy—diplomazia

(disparaging) sprezzante
(eccl) ecclesiastical—ecclesiastico
(econ) economics—economia
(educ) education—istruzione
e.g., or *e.g.,* per esempio
(elec) electricity—elettricità
(electron) electronics—elettronica
(ent) entomology—entomologia
(equit) horseback riding—equitazione
f feminine noun—nome femminile
(fa) fine arts—belle arti
fem feminine—femminile
(fencing) scherma
(fig) figurative—figurato
(fin) financial—finanziario
(football) football americano
fpl feminine noun plural—nome femminile plurale
fut future—futuro
(geog) geography—geografia
(geol) geology—geologia
(geom) geometry—geometria
ger gerund—gerundio
(golf) golf
(gram) grammar—grammatica
(herald) heraldry—araldica
(hist) history—storia
(hort) horticulture—orticoltura
(hunt) hunting—caccia
(ichth) ichthyology—ittiologia
i.e., cioè
imperf imperfect—imperfetto
impers impersonal verb—verbo impersonale
impv imperative—imperativo
ind indicative—indicativo
indef indefinite—indefinito, indeterminativo
inf infinitive—infinito
(ins) insurance—assicurazione
interj interjection—interiezione
interr interrogative—interrogativo
intr intransitive verb—verbo intransitivo
invar invariable—invariabile
(Italian cards) carte italiane
(jewelry) gioielleria
(joc) jocular—faceto
(journ) journalism—giornalismo
(law) diritto, legge
(letterword) word in the form of an abbreviation which is pronounced by sounding the names of its letters in

succession and which functions as a part of speech—parola in forma di abbreviazione che si ottiene pronunziando consecutivamente la denominazione di ciascuna lettera e che funziona come parte del discorso

(lexicography) lessicografia
(ling) linguistics—linguistica
(lit) literary—letterario
(log) logic—logica
m masculine noun—nome maschile
(mach) machinery—macchinario
masc masculine—maschile
(math) mathematics—matematica
(mech) mechanics—meccanica
(med) medicine—medicina
(metallurgy) metallurgia
(meteor) meteorology—meteorologia
mf masculine or feminine noun according to sex—nome maschile o nome femminile secondo il sesso
m & f see below between (mythol) and (naut)
(mil) military—militare
(min) mining—lavorazione delle miniere
(mov) moving pictures—cinematografo
mpl masculine noun plural—nome maschile plurale
(mus) music—musica
(mythol) mythology—mitologia
m & f masculine and feminine noun without regard to sex—nome maschile e femminile senza distinzione di sesso
(naut) nautical—nautico
(nav) naval—navale
neut neuter—neutro
num number—numero
(obs) obsolete—in disuso
(obstet) obstetrics—ostetricia
(opt) optics—ottica
(orn) ornithology—ornitologia
(painting) pittura
(pathol) pathology—patologia
(pej) pejorative—peggiorativo
perf perfect—perfetto, passato
pers personal—personale; person—persona
(pharm) pharmacy—farmacia
(philately) filatelia
(philol) philology—filologia
(philos) philosophy—filosofia
(phonet) phonetics—fonetica
(phot) photography—fotografia
(phys) physics—fisica
(physiol) physiology—fisiologia
pl plural—plurale
(poet) poetical—poetico
(poker) poker
(pol) politics—politica
pp past participle—participio passato
poss possessive—possessivo
pref prefix—prefisso
prep preposition—preposizione

prep phrase prepositional phrase—frase preposizionale
pres present—presente
pret preterit—passato remoto
pron pronoun—pronome
(pros) prosody—prosodia
(psychoanal) psychoanalysis—psicanalisi
(psychol) psychology—psicologia
(psychopath) psychopathology—psicopatologia
qlco or *qlco* qualcosa—something
qlcu or *qlcu* qualcuno—someone
(racing) corse
(rad) radio—radio
ref reflexive verb—verbo riflessivo o pronominale
rel relative—relativo
(rel) religion—religione
(rhet) rhetoric—retorica
(rok) rocketry—studio dei razzi
(rowing) canottaggio
(rr) railroad—ferrovia
(rugby) rugby
s substantive—sostantivo
(scornful) sprezzante
(Scot) Scottish—scozzese
(sculp) sculpture—scultura
(sew) sewing—cucito
sg singular—singolare
(slang) gergo
s.o. or *s.o.* someone—qualcuno
(soccer) calcio
spl substantive plural—sostantivo plurale
(sports) sport
ssg substantive singular—sostantivo singolare
s.th or *s.th* something—qualcosa
subj subjunctive—congiuntivo
suf suffix—suffisso
super superlative—superlativo
(surg) surgery—chirurgia
(surv) surveying—agrimensura, topografia
(taur) bullfighting—tauromachia
(telg) telegraphy—telegrafia
(telp) telephone—telefonia
(telv) television—televisione
(tennis) tennis
(tex) textile—tessile
(theat) theater—teatro
(theol) theology—teologia
tr transitive verb—verbo transitivo
(trademark) marchio di fabbrica
(typ) printing—tipografia
(U.S.A.) S.U.A.
v verb—verbo
var variant—variante
(vet) veterinary medicine—medicina veterinaria
(vulg) vulgar—volgare, ordinario
(wrestling) lotta
(zool) zoology—zoologia

PART ONE

Italian-English

Italian Spelling and Pronunciation

§1. The Italian Alphabet. 1. The twenty-one letters of the Italian alphabet are listed below with their names and their sounds in terms of approximate equivalent English sounds. Their gender is masculine or feminine.

LETTER	NAME	APPROXIMATE SOUND
a	a	Like *a* in English *father*, e.g., **facile, padre.**
b	bi	Like *b* in English *boat*, e.g., **bello, abate.**
c	ci	When followed by **e** or **i**, like *ch* in English *cherry*, e.g., **cento, cinque;** if the **i** is unstressed and followed by another vowel, its sound is not heard, e.g., **ciarla, cieco.** When followed by **a, o, u,** or a consonant, like *c* in English *cook*, e.g., **casa, come, cura, credere.** The digraph **ch**, which is used before **e** and **i**, has likewise the sound of *c* in English *cook*, e.g., **chiesa, perché.**
d	di	Like *d* in English *dance*, e.g., **dare, madre.**
e	e	Has two sounds. One like *a* in English *make*, shown on stressed syllables in this DICTIONARY by the acute accent, e.g., **séra, trénta;** and one like *e* in English *met*, shown on stressed syllables in this DICTIONARY by the grave accent, e.g., **fèrro, fèsta.**
f	effe	Like *f* in English *fool*, e.g., **farina, efelide.**
g	gi	When followed by **e** or **i**, like *g* in English *general*, e.g., **gelato, ginnasta;** if the **i** is unstressed and followed by another vowel, its sound is not heard, e.g., **giallo, giorno.** When followed by **a, o, u,** or a consonant, like *g* in English *go*, e.g., **gamba, goccia, gusto, grado.** The digraph **gh**, which is used before **e** and **i**, has likewise the sound of *g* in English *go*, e.g., **gherone, ghisa.** When the combination **gli** (a) is a form of the definite article or the personal pronoun, (b) is final in a word, or (c) is intervocalic, it has the sound of Castilian *ll*, which is somewhat like *lli* in English *million*, e.g., (a) **gli uomini, gli ho parlato ieri,** (b) **battagli,** (c) **figlio, migliore.** When it is (a) initial (except in the word **gli,** above), (b) preceded by a consonant, or (c) followed by a consonant, it is pronounced like *gli* in English *negligence*, e.g., (a) **glioma,** (b) **ganglio,** (c) **negligenza.** The combination **gl** followed by **a, e, o,** or **u** is pronounced like *gl* in English *globe*, e.g., **glabro, gleba, globo, gluteo, inglese, poliglotto.** The digraph **gn** has the sound of Castilian *ñ*, which is somewhat like *ni* in English *onion*, e.g., **signore, gnocco.**
h	acca	Always silent, e.g., **ah, hanno.** See **ch** under **c** above and **gh** under **g** above.
i	i	Like *i* in English *machine*, e.g., **piccolo, sigla.** When unstressed and followed by another vowel, like *y* in English *yes*, e.g., **piatto, piede, fiore, fiume.** For **i** in **ci**, see **c** above, in **gi**, see **g** above, and in **sci**, see **s** below.

3

LETTER	NAME	APPROXIMATE SOUND
l	elle	Like *l* in English *lamb*, e.g., **labbro, lacrima.**
m	emme	Like *m* in English *money*, e.g., **mano, come.**
n	enne	Like *n* in English *net*, e.g., **nome, cane.**
o	o	Has two sounds. One like *o* in English *note*, shown on stressed syllables in this DICTIONARY by the acute accent, e.g., **dópo, sóle;** and one like *ou* in English *ought*, shown on stressed syllables in this DICTIONARY by the grave accent, e.g., **còsa, dònna.**
p	pi	Like *p* in English *pot*, e.g., **passo, carpa.**
q	cu	This letter is always followed by the letter **u** and the combination has the sound of *qu* in English *quart*, e.g., **quanto, questo.**
r	erre	Like *r* in English *rubber*, with a slight trill, e.g., **roba, carta.**
s	esse	Has two sounds. When initial and followed by a vowel, when preceded by a consonant and followed by a vowel, and when followed by **c** [k] **f, p, q,** or **t**, like *s* in English *see*, e.g., **sale, falso, scappare, spazio, stoffa;** and when standing between two vowels and when followed by **b, d, g** [g], **l, m, n, r** or **v**, like *z* in English *zero*, e.g., **paese, sbaglio, svenire.** However, **s** standing between two vowels in some words and initial **s** followed by **b, d, g** [g], **l, m, n, r,** or **v** in some foreign borrowings are pronounced like *s* in *see*, e.g., **casa*, tesa, smoking, slam.** In this DICTIONARY this is indicated by the insertion of [s] immediately after the entry word. However, when initial **s** stands between two vowels in a compound, its pronunciation remains that of initial **s**, e.g., **autoservizio** and this is not indicated. The digraph **sc**, when followed by **e** or **i** has the sound of *sh* in English *shall*, e.g., **scelta, scimmia;** if the **i** is unstressed and followed by another vowel, its sound is not heard, e.g., **sciame, sciopero.** The trigraph **sch** has the sound of *sc* in English *scope*, e.g., **scherzo, schiavo.**
t	ti	Like *t* in English *table*, e.g., **terra, pasto.**
u	u	Like *u* in English *rule*, e.g., **luna, mulo.** When followed by a vowel, like *w* in English *was*, e.g., **quanto, guerra, nuovo.**
v	vu	Like *v* in English *vain*, e.g., **vita, uva.**
z	zeta	Has two sounds. One like *ts* in English *nuts*, e.g., **grazia, zucchero;** and one like *dz* in English *adze*, e.g., **zero, mezzo.** In this DICTIONARY the sound of *dz* in *adze* is indicated by the insertion of [dz] immediately after the entry word. If the sound is long, [ddzz] is inserted

* Intervocalic **s** is generally voiced in the north of Italy.

2. The following five letters are found in borrowings from other languages.

LETTER	NAME	EXAMPLES
j	i lunga	**jazz, jingo**
k	cappa	**kiosco, kodak**
w	doppia vu	**water-polo, whisky**
x	ics	**xenofobo, xilofono**
y	ìpsilon	**yacht, yoghurt**

3. Consonants written double are longer than consonants written single, that is, it takes a longer time to pronounce them, e.g., **camino** *chimney* and **cam-**

4

mino *road*, **capello** *hair* and **cappello** *hat*. Special attention is called to the following double consonants: **cc** followed by **e** or **i** has the sound of *ch ch* in English *beach chair*, that is, a lengthened *ch* (not the sound of *ks*), e.g., **accento**; **cch** has the sound of *kk* in English *bookkeeper*, e.g., **becchino**; **cq** has the sound of *kk* in English *bookkeeper*, e.g., **acqua**; **gg** followed by **e** or **i** has the sound of *ge j* in English *carriage joiner*, e.g., **peggio**; **ggh** has the sound of *g g* in English *tag game*, e.g., **agghindare**.

§2. Division of Syllables.
In the application of the following rules for the syllabic division of words, the digraphs **ch, gh, gl, gn,** and **sc** count as single consonants.

(a) When a single consonant stands between two vowels it belongs to the following syllable, e.g., **ca·sa, fu·mo, ami·che, la·ghi, fi·glio, biso·gno, la·sciare**.

(b) When a consonant group consisting of two consonants of which the second is **l** or **r** stands between two vowels, the group belongs to the following syllable, e.g., **nu·cleo, so·brio, qua·dro**.

(c) When a consonant group consisting of two or more consonants of which the first or the second is **s** stands between two vowels, that part of the group beginning with **s** belongs to the following syllable, e.g., **ta·sca, bo·schi, fine·stra, super·sti·zione, sub·strato**.

(d) When a consonant group consisting of two or three consonants of which the first is **l, m, n,** or **r** stands between two vowels, the **l, m, n,** or **r** belongs to the preceding syllable, the other consonant or consonants to the following syllable, e.g., **al·bero, am·pio, prin·cipe, mor·te, in·flazione, com·pleto**.

(e) When a double consonant stands between two vowels or between a vowel and **l** or **r**, the first belongs to the preceding syllable, the second to the following syllable, e.g., **bab·bo, caval·lo, an·no, car·ro, mez·zo, sup·plica, lab·bro, quat·tro**.

§3. Stress and Accent Marks.
1. Whenever stress is shown as part of regular spelling, it is shown on **a, i,** and **u** by the grave accent mark, e.g., **libertà, giovedì, gioventù**, on close **e** and **o** by the acute accent mark, e.g., **perché**, and on open **e** and **o** by the grave accent mark, e.g., **caffè, parlò**. This occurs (a) in words ending in a stressed vowel, as in the above examples, (b) in stressed monosyllables in which the vocalic element is a diphthong of which the first letter is unstressed **i** or **u**, e.g., **già, più, può**, and (c) on the stressed monosyllable of any pair of monosyllables of which one is stressed and the other unstressed, in order to distinguish one from the other, e.g., **dà** *he gives* and **da** *from*, **è** *is* and **e** *and*, **sé** *himself* and **se** *if*, **sì** *yes* and **si** *himself*.

2. Whenever stress is not shown as part of regular spelling, it is often difficult to determine where it falls.

(a) In words of two syllables, the stress falls on the syllable next to the last, e.g., **ca'sa, mu'ro, ter'ra**. If the syllable next to the last contains a diphthong, that is, a combination of a strong vowel (**a, e,** or **o**) and a weak vowel (**i** or **u**), the strong vowel is stressed, regardless of which vowel comes first, e.g., **da'ino, ero'ico, ne'utro, fia'to, dua'le, sie'pe, fio're, buo'no**.

(b) In words of more than two syllables, the stress may fall on the syllable next to the last, e.g., **anda'ta, canzo'ne, pasto're** or on a preceding syllable, e.g., **fis'sile, gon'dola, man'dorla**. In these positions also the stressed syllable may contain a diphthong, e.g., **inca'uto, idra'ulico, fio'cina**.

(c) If a weak vowel in juxtaposition with a strong vowel is stressed, the two vowels constitute two separate syllables, e.g., **abba·i'no, ero·i'na, pa·u'ra, miri'ade, vi'a**.

(d) Two strong vowels in juxtaposition constitute two separate syllables, e.g., **pa·e'se, aure'ola, ide'a, oce'ano**.

(e) Two weak vowels in juxtaposition generally constitute a diphthong in which the first vowel is stressed in some words, e.g., **flu'ido** and the second vowel in others, e.g., **piu'ma**.

(f) If a word ends in a diphthong, the diphthong is stressed, e.g., **marina'i, parla'i, ero'i**.

3. In this DICTIONARY, stress is understood or shown on all words that do not bear an accent mark as part of regular spelling according to the following principles. In the application of these principles, individual vowels and not diphthongs are counted as units. In some words in which it is not necessary to show stress, an accent mark is used to show the quality of the stressed vowels **e** and **o**.

As in regular Italian spelling, stress is shown on **a, i,** and **u** by the grave accent mark, on close **e** and **o** by the acute accent mark, and on open **e** and **o** by the grave accent mark.

(a) It is understood that in words of more than one syllable in which no accent mark is shown, the stress falls on the vowel next to the last, e.g., **casa**,

fiato, duale, abbaino, paura. In such words as **sièpe, fióre, buòno, paése, fluènte, eròe, nói, pòi,** the accent mark is used to show the quality of the vowel.

(b) An accent mark is placed on the stressed vowel if the word is stressed on the third vowel from the end, e.g., **mùsica, sìmbolo, dàino, incàuto, marinàio, contìnuo, infànzia.** If this vowel is **e** or **o,** the acute or grave accent mark must correspond to the quality of the vowel, e.g., **fiòcina, rómpere, nèutro, eròico, assèdio, filatóio.**

(c) Contrary to the above-mentioned principle of counting vowels, an accent mark is placed on the strong vowel of a final diphthong, e.g., **marinài, assài.**

(d) Contrary to the above-mentioned principle of counting vowels, an accent mark is placed on the **i** of final **ia, ie, ii,** and **io,** e.g., **farmacìa, scìa, farmacìe, mormorìi, gorgoglìo, fìo.**

(e) An accent mark is placed on some borrowings ending in a consonant, e.g., **hàrem, revòlver.**

(f) The loss of the last vowel or last syllable of a word does not alter the position of the stress of the word, e.g., **la maggior parte, in alcun modo, fan bene.**

Grammatical Tables

84. The Definite Article and Combinations with Prepositions.

		MASC BEFORE CONSONANT	MASC BEFORE S IMPURE OR Z[1]	MASC BEFORE VOWEL	FEM BEFORE CONSONANT	FEM BEFORE VOWEL
	SG	il	lo	l'	la	l'
	PL	i	gli	gli[2]	le	le[3]
WITH a	SG	al	allo	all'	alla	all'
	PL	ai	agli	agli[2]	alle	alle[3]
WITH di	SG	del	dello	dell'	della	dell'
	PL	dei	degli	degli[2]	delle	delle[3]
WITH con	SG	col	collo	coll'	colla	coll'
	PL	coi	cogli	cogli[2]	colle	colle[3]
WITH da	SG	dal	dallo	dall'	dalla	dall'
	PL	dai	dagli	dagli[2]	dalle	dalle[3]
WITH in	SG	nel	nello	nell'	nella	nell'
	PL	nei	negli	negli[2]	nelle	nelle[3]
WITH su	SG	sul	sullo	sull'	sulla	sull'
	PL	sui	sugli	sugli[2]	sulle	sulle[3]

[1] Other letters and groups of letters, which occur in a few words, are gn, pn, ps, sc, x, and i before a vowel, sometimes spelled j or y.

[2] These forms may drop the i before words beginning with i, e.g., gl'inglesi.

[3] The e of these forms is not elided, e.g., le erbe.

7

85. Personal and Reflexive Pronouns.

PERSONS	SUBJECT	PERSONAL DIRECT OBJECT	PERSONAL INDIRECT OBJECT	REFLEX. & RECIPROCAL DIRECT & INDIRECT OBJECT	PERSONAL PREPOSITIONAL OBJECT	REFLEX. & RECIPROCAL PREPOSITIONAL OBJECT
SG						
1	io *I*	mi *me*	mi *to me*	mi *myself; to myself*	me *me*	me *myself*
2	tu *you*	ti *you*	ti *to you*	ti *yourself; to yourself*	te *you*	te *yourself*
3 MASC	egli, lui *he*	lo *him or it*	gli *to him*	si *himself; to himself*	lui *him*	sé *himself*
3 FEM	lei, essa *she*	la *her or it*	le *to her*	si *herself; to herself*	lei, essa *her*	sé *herself*
2 FORMAL	Lei *you*	La *you*	Le *to you*	si *yourself; to yourself*	Lei *you*	sé *yourself*
PL						
1	noi *we*	ci *us*	ci *to us*	ci *ourselves; to ourselves; each other; to each other*	noi *us*	noi *ourselves; each other*
2	voi *you*	vi *you*	vi *to you*	vi *yourself; yourselves; to yourself; to yourselves; each other; to each other*	voi *you*	voi *yourself; yourselves; each other*
3 MASC	loro, essi *they*	li *them*	loro *to them*	si *themselves; to themselves; each other; to each other*	loro, essi *them*	sé *themselves; each other*
3 FEM	loro, esse *they*	le *them*	loro *to them*	si *themselves; to themselves; each other; to each other*	loro, esse *them*	sé *themselves; each other*
2 FORMAL	Loro *you*	Li Le } *you*	Loro *to you*	si *yourselves; to yourselves; each other; to each other*	Loro *you*	sé *yourselves; each other*

ci and vi both mean also *here, there, to it, in it, to them, in them, about it.*
ne means *of, from,* or *with him, her, it, them; some, any; from here, from there, thence, about it.*

meco *with me,* teco *with you,* and seco *with him,* and seco *with you,* may be used instead with her, with herself; with you, with yourself, with yourselves; with them, with themselves; with each other may be used instead of con me, con te, and con sé respectively.

8

COMBINATION OF DIRECT AND INDIRECT OBJECT

PERSONS		PERSONS	
1 SG & 3 SG	me lo / me la } *him, her, it to me*	1 PL & 3 SG	ce lo / ce la } *him, her, it to us*
1 SG & 3 PL	me li / me le } *them to me*	1 PL & 3 PL	ce li / ce le } *them to us*
2 SG & 3 SG	te lo / te la } *him, her, it to you*	2 PL & 3 SG	ve lo / ve la } *him, her, it to you*
2 SG & 3 PL	te li / te le } *them to you*	2 PL & 3 PL	ve li / ve le } *them to you*
3 SG & 3 SG	glielo } *him, her, it to him* / gliela } *him, her, it to her*	3 SG & 3 PL	lo / la } VERB loro *him, her, it to them*
3 SG & 3 PL	glieli } *them to him* / gliele } *them to her*	3 PL & 3 PL	li / le } VERB loro *them to them*
2 SG FORMAL & 3 SG	Glielo / Gliela } *him, her, it to you*	3 SG & 2 PL FORMAL	lo / la } VERB Loro *him, her, it to you*
2 SG FORMAL & 3 PL	Glieli / Gliele } *them to you*	3 PL & 2 PL FORMAL	li / le } VERB Loro *them to you*

The form si (third singular and plural reflexive and reciprocal indirect object) changes to se before one of the direct objects lo, la, li, and le, and before ne, e.g., se lo mette he puts it on; se n'è andato he went away.

In combinations, ne occupies the same position as lo, la, li, and le, e.g., me ne, and forms one word with gli, namely, gliene.

9

§6 Possessive Adjectives and Pronouns

PERSON, NUMBER & SEX OF POSSESSOR	GENDER & NUMBER OF POSSESSIVE ADJECTIVE OR PRONOUN ACCORDING TO THE GENDER & NUMBER OF THE PERSON OR THING POSSESSED				MEANING OF ADJECTIVE	MEANING OF PRONOUN
SG	MSG	MPL	FSG	FPL		
1	il mio	i miei	la mia	le mie	*my*	*mine*
2	il tuo	i tuoi	la tua	le tue	*your*	*yours*
3 MASC	il suo	i suoi	la sua	le sue	*his*	*his*
3 FEM	il suo	i suoi	la sua	le sue	*her*	*hers*
3 NEUT	il suo	i suoi	la sua	le sue	*its*	*its*
2 FORMAL	il Suo	i Suoi	la Sua	le Sue	*your*	*yours*
PL						
1	il nostro	i nostri	la nostra	le nostre	*our*	*ours*
2	il vostro	i vostri	la vostra	le vostre	*your*	*yours*
3	il loro	i loro	la loro	le loro	*their*	*theirs*
2 FORMAL	il Loro	i Loro	la Loro	le Loro	*your*	*yours*

The definite article, shown here, is not generally used (a) in direct address, e.g., mio caro amico *my dear friend*, (b) after the verb essere, e.g., la casa è nostra *the house is ours*, and (c) when a singular form modifies the name of a relative, e.g., sua sorella *his sister*. With forms of the indefinite article, the possessive adjective, whether standing before or after the noun, is translated by *of* plus the possessive pronoun, e.g., un amico mio *a friend of mine;* una sua zia *an aunt of his* (or *of hers*). The forms of the possessive pronouns also have the force of nouns, e.g., il mio *my property, my belongings;* i suoi *his people, relatives, followers, troops, retinue*, etc.; la mia *my letter;* la sua *his opinion.*

87. The Demonstrative Adjective.

	MASC BEFORE CONSONANT	MASC BEFORE S IMPURE OR Z (see note 1, p. 7)	MASC BEFORE VOWEL	FEM BEFORE CONSONANT	FEM BEFORE VOWEL
SG	quel *that*	quello	quell'	quella	quell'
PL	quei *those*	quegli	quegli	quelle	quelle
SG	questo *this*	questo	questo or quest'	questa	questa or quest'
PL	questi *these*	questi	questi	queste	queste

11

§8. The Demonstrative Pronoun.

	MASC	FEM	MASC
SG	quello *that one*	quella	quegli *that one; the former*
PL	quelli *those*	quelle	
SG	questo *this one*	questa	questi *this one; the latter*
PL	questi *these*	queste	

The demonstrative pronoun **quello** is often followed by **che, di,** or **da** and the masculine singular form may be shortened to **quel** before these words.

SG	**colui** *that one*	**colei**
PL	**coloro** *those*	**coloro**
SG	**costui** *this one*	**costei**
PL	**costoro** *these*	**costoro**

code·sto -sta -sti -ste and **cote·sto -sta -sti -ste** are demonstrative adjectives and demonstrative pronouns and mean *that (of yours).*

§9. **Indefinite Article and Numeral Adjective.**

MASC BEFORE CONSONANT	MASC BEFORE S IMPURE OR Z (see note 1, p. 7)	MASC BEFORE VOWEL	FEM BEFORE CONSONANT	FEM BEFORE VOWEL
un *a, an; one*	uno	un	una	un'

13

§10. Indefinite Pronoun uno.

MASC	FEM
uno *one*	una

§11. Correlative Indefinite Pronoun.

	MASC	FEM
SG	l'uno . . . l'altro *one . . . the other*	l'una . . . l'altra
PL	gli uni . . . gli altri *some . . . the others*	le une . . . le altre

§12. Reciprocal Indefinite Pronoun.

	MASC	FEM
SG	l'un l'altro *each other, one another*	l'una l'altra
PL	gli uni gli altri	le une le altre

Table of Regular Endings of Italian Verbs

The stem to which the endings of the gerund, past participle, present participle, imperative, present indicative, present subjunctive, imperfect indicative, preterit indicative, and imperfect subjunctive are attached is obtained by dropping the ending of the infinitive, viz., **-are**, **-ere**, **-ire**.

The stem to which the endings of the future indicative and present conditional are attached is obtained by dropping the **-e** of the ending of the infinitive of all conjugations and changing the **a** of the ending of the infinitive of the first conjugation to **e**.

The letters before the names of some of the tenses of this table correspond to the designation of the tenses shown on the following page.

Letters printed in italics have a written accent that is not part of the regular spelling.

TENSE	FIRST CONJUGATION	SECOND CONJUGATION	THIRD CONJUGATION
inf	-are	-*é*re (or *-ere*)	-ire
ger	-ando	-*è*ndo	-*è*ndo
pp	-ato	-uto	-ito
pres part	-ante	-*è*nte	-*è*nte
(a) *impv*	-a -ate	-i -*é*te	-i -ite
(b) *pres ind*	-o -i -a -iamo -ate -ano	-o -i -e -iamo -*é*te -ono	-o -i -e -iamo -ite -ono
(c) *pres subj*	-i -i -i -iamo -iate -ino	-a -a -a -iamo -iate -ano	-a -a -a -iamo -iate -ano
(d) *imperf ind*	-*a*vo -*a*vi -ava -avamo -avate -*à*vano	-*é*vo -*é*vi -*é*va -evamo -evate -*é*vano	-ivo -ivi -iva -ivamo -ivate -*ì*vano
(e) *pret ind*	-*à*i -asti -*ò* -ammo -aste -*à*rono	-*é*i -*é*sti -è -*é*mmo -*é*ste -*é*rono	-*ì*i -isti -*ì* -immo -iste -*ì*rono
imperf subj	-assi -assi -asse -*à*ssimo -aste -*à*ssero	-*é*ssi -*é*ssi -*é*sse -*é*ssimo -*é*ste -*é*ssero	-issi -issi -isse -*ì*ssimo -iste -*ì*ssero
(f) *fut ind*	-er-*ò* -er-*à*i -er-à -er-*é*mo -er-*é*te -er-anno	-*ò* -*à*i -à -*é*mo -*é*te -anno	-*ò* -*à*i -à -*é*mo -*é*te -anno

TENSE	FIRST CONJUGATION	SECOND CONJUGATION	THIRD CONJUGATION
pres cond	-er-*èi* -er-*ésti* -er-*èbbe* -er-*émmo* -er-*éste* -er-*èbbero*	-*èi* -*ésti* -*èbbe* -*émmo* -*éste* -*èbbero*	-*èi* -*ésti* -*èbbe* -*émmo* -*éste* -*èbbero*

MODEL VERBS
ORDER OF TENSES

(a) imperative
(b) present indicative
(c) present subjunctive

(d) imperfect indicative
(e) preterit indicative
(f) future indicative

In addition to the infinitive, gerund, and past participle, which are shown in line one of these tables, all simple tenses are shown if they contain at least one irregular form, except (1) the present conditional, which is always formed on the stem of the future indicative, (2) the imperfect subjunctive, which is always formed on the stem of the *2nd sg* of the preterit indicative, and (3) the present participle, which is generally formed by changing the final -do of the gerund to -te (exceptions being shown in parentheses after the gerund).

Letters printed in italics have a written accent that is not part of the regular spelling.

§100 ACCÈDERE—accedèndo—acceduto
(e) accedètti *or* accedéi *or* accèssi; accedésti; accedètte *or* accedé *or* accèsse; accedémmo; accedéste; accedèttero *or* accedérono *or* accèssero

§101 ACCÈNDERE—accendèndo—accéso
(e) accési, accendésti, accése, accendémmo, accendéste, accésero

§102 ADDURRE—adducèndo—addótto
(b) adduco, adduci, adduce, adduciamo, adducéte, addùcono
(c) adduca, adduca, adduca, adduciamo, adduciate, addùcano
(d) adducévo, adducévi, adducéva, adducevamo, adducevate, adducévano
(e) addussi, adducésti, addusse, adducémmo, adducéste, addùssero

§103 AFFÌGGERE—affiggèndo—affisso
(e) affissi, affiggésti, affisse, affiggémmo, affiggéste, affìssero

17

§104 AFFLÌGGERE—affliggèndo—afflitto
(e) afflissi, affliggésti, afflisse, affliggémmo, affliggéste, afflìssero

§105 ALLÙDERE—alludèndo—alluso
(e) allusi, alludésti, alluse, alludémmo, alludéste, allùsero

§106 ANDARE—andando—andato
(a) va *or* va' *or* vai, andàte
(b) vò *or* vado, vai, va, andiamo, andate, vanno
(c) vada, vada, vada, andiamo, andiate, vàdano
(f) andrò, andràì, andrà, andrémo, andréte, andranno

§107 ANNÈTTERE—annettèndo—annèsso or **annéttere**, annetténdo, annésso
(e) annettéi *or* annèssi *or* annéssi; annettésti; annetté *or* annèsse *or* annésse; annettémmo; annettéste; annettérono *or* annèssero *or* annéssero

§108 APPARIRE—apparèndo—apparso
(a) apparisci *or* appari; apparite
(b) apparisco *or* appàio; apparisci *or* appari; apparisce *or* appare; appariamo; apparite; apparìscono *or* appàiono
(c) apparisca *or* appàia; apparisca *or* appàia; apparisca *or* appàia; appariamo; appariate; apparìscano *or* appàiano
(e) apparvi *or* apparìi *or* apparsi; apparisti; apparve *or* apparì *or* apparse; apparimmo; appariste; appàrvero *or* apparìrono *or* appàrsero

§109 APPÈNDERE—appendèndo—appéso
(e) appési, appendésti, appése, appendémmo, appendéste, appésero

§110 APRIRE—aprèndo—apèrto
(e) aprìi *or* apèrsi; apristi; aprì *or* apèrse; aprimmo; apriste; aprìrono *or* apèrsero

§111 ÀRDERE—ardèndo—arso
(e) arsi, ardésti, arse, ardémmo, ardéste, àrsero

§112 ASPÈRGERE—aspergèndo—aspèrso
(e) aspèrsi, aspergésti, aspèrse, aspergémmo, aspergéste, aspèrsero

§113 ASSÌDERE—assidèndo—assiso
(e) assisi, assidésti, assise, assidémmo, assidéste, assìsero

§114 ASSÌSTERE—assistèndo—assistito
(e) assistéi *or* assistètti; assistésti; assisté *or* assistètte; assistémmo; assistéste; assistérono *or* assistèttero

18

§115 ASSÒLVERE—assolvèndo—assòlto *or* assoluto
(e) assolvéi *or* assolvètti *or* assòlsi; assolvésti; assolvé *or* assolvètte *or* assòlse; assolvémmo; assolvéste; assolvérono *or* assolvèttero *or* assòlsero

§116 ASSÙMERE—assumèndo—assunto
(e) assunsi, assumésti, assunse, assumémmo, assuméste, assùnsero

§117 ASSÙRGERE—assurgèndo—assurto
(e) assursi, assurgésti, assurse, assurgémmo, assurgéste, assùrsero

§118 AVÈRE—avèndo—avuto
(a) abbi, abbiate
(b) ho, hai, ha, abbiamo, avete, hanno
(c) àbbia, àbbia, àbbia, abbiamo, abbiate, àbbiano
(e) èbbi, avésti, èbbe, avémmo, avéste, èbbero
(f) avrò, avrài, avrà, avrémo, avréte, avranno

§119 AVVIARE—avviando—avviato
(b) avvìo, avvìi, avvìa, avviamo, avviate, avvìano
(c) avvìi, avvìi, avvìi, avviamo, avviate, avvìino

§120 BÉRE—bevèndo—bevuto
(a) bévi, bevéte
(b) bévo, bévi, béve, beviamo, bevéte, bévono
(c) béva, béva, béva, beviamo, beviate, bévano
(d) bevévo, bevévi, bevéva, bevevamo, bevevate, bevévano
(e) bévvi *or* bevéi *or* bevètti; bevésti; bévve *or* bevé *or* bevètte; bevémmo; bevéste; bévvero *or* bevérono *or* bevèttero
(f) berrò, berrài, berrà, berrémo, berréte, berranno

§121 CADÉRE—cadèndo—caduto
(e) caddi, cadésti, cadde, cadémmo, cadéste, càddero
(f) cadrò, cadrài, cadrà, cadrémo, cadréte, cadranno

§122 CECARE—cecando—cecato
(a) cièca *or* cèca; cecate
(b) cièco *or* cèco; cièchi *or* cèchi; cièca *or* cèca; cechiamo; cecate; ciècano *or* cècano
(c) cièchi *or* cèchi; cièchi *or* cèchi; cièchi *or* cèchi; cechiamo; cechiate; cièchino *or* cèchino
(f) cecherò, cecherài, cecherà, cecherémo, cecheréte, cecheranno

§123 CÈDERE—cedèndo—ceduto
(e) cedéi *or* cedètti; cedésti; cedé *or* cedètte; cedémmo; cedéste; cedérono *or* cedèttero

19

§124 CHIÈDERE—chiedèndo—chièsto
(e) chièsi, chiedésti, chièse, chiedémmo, chiedéste, chièsero

§125 CHIÙDERE—chiudèndo—chiuso
(e) chiusi, chiudésti, chiuse, chiudémmo, chiudéste, chiùsero

§126 CÌNGERE—cingèndo—cinto
(e) cinsi, cingésti, cinse, cingémmo, cingéste, cìnsero

§127 CÒGLIERE—coglièndo—còlto
(a) cògli, cogliéte
(b) còlgo, cògli, còglie, cogliamo, cogliéte, còlgono
(c) còlga, còlga, còlga, cogliamo, cogliate, còlgano
(e) còlsi, cogliésti, còlse, cogliémmo, cogliéste, còlsero

§128 COMINCIARE—cominciando—cominciato
(b) comìncio, cominci, comìncia, cominciamo, cominciate, comìnciano
(c) cominci, cominci, cominci, cominciamo, cominciate, comìncino
(f) comincerò, comincerài, comincerà, comincerémo, cominceréte, cominceranno

§129 COMPÈTERE—competèndo—*pp* missing

§130 CÒMPIERE—compièndo—compiuto
(a) cómpi, compite
(b) cómpio, cómpi, cómpie, compiamo, compite, cómpiono
(c) cómpia, cómpia, cómpia, compiamo, compiate, cómpiano
(d) compivo, compivi, compiva, compivamo, compivate, compìvano
(e) compiéi *or* compìi; compiésti *or* compisti; compié *or* compì; compiémmo *or* compimmo; compiéste *or* compiste; compiérono *or* compìrono

§131 COMPRÌMERE—comprimèndo—comprèsso
(e) comprèssi, comprimésti, comprèsse, comprimémmo, compriméste, comprèssero

§132 CONCÈDERE—concedèndo—concèsso
(e) concedéi *or* concèssi *or* concedètti; concedésti; concedé *or* concèsse *or* concedètte; concedémmo; concedéste; concedérono *or* concèssero *or* concedèttero

§133 CONCÈRNERE—concernèndo—*pp* missing
(e) concernéi *or* concernètti; concernésti; concerné *or* concernètte; concernémmo; concernéste; concernérono *or* concernèttero

20

§134 CONÓSCERE—conoscèndo—conosciuto
    (e) conóbbi, conoscésti, conóbbe, conoscémmo, conoscéste, conóbbero

§135 CONQUÌDERE—conquidèndo—conquiso
    (e) conquisi, conquidésti, conquise, conquidémmo, conquidéste, conquìsero

§136 CONSÙMERE—*ger* missing—consunto
    (a) missing
    (b) missing
    (c) missing
    (d) missing
    (e) consunsi, consunse, consùnsero
    (f) missing

§137 CONVÈRGERE—convergèndo—convèrso
    (e) convèrsi *or* convergéi; convergésti; convèrse *or* convergé; convergémmo; convergéste; convèrsero *or* convergérono

§138 CONVERTIRE—convertèndo—convertito
    (e) convertìi *or* convèrsi; convertisti; convertì or convèrse; convertimmo; convertiste; convertìrono *or* convèrsero

§139 CÓRRERE—corrèndo—córso
    (e) córsi, corrésti, córse, corrémmo, corréste, córsero

§140 COSTRUIRE—costruèndo—costruito
    (a) costruisci, costruite
    (b) costruisco, costruisci, costruisce, costruiamo, costruite, costruìscono
    (c) costruisca, costruisca, costruisca, costruiamo, costruiate, costruìscano
    (e) costruìi *or* costrussi; costruisti; costruì *or* costrusse; costruimmo; costruiste; costruìrono *or* costrùssero

§141 CRÉDERE—credèndo—creduto
    (e) credéi *or* credètti; credésti; credé *or* credètte; credémmo; credéste; credérono *or* credèttero

§142 CRÉSCERE—crescèndo—cresciuto
    (e) crébbi, crescésti, crébbe, crescémmo, crescéste, crébbero

§143 CUCIRE—cucèndo—cucito
    (b) cùcio, cuci, cuce, cuciamo, cucite, cùciono
    (c) cùcia, cùcia, cùcia, cuciamo, cuciate, cùciano

§144a CUÒCERE—cuocèndo *or* cocèndo (cocènte)—còtto *or* cociuto

(a) cuòci, cocéte
(b) cuòcio, cuòci, cuòce, cociamo, cocéte, cuòciono
(c) cuòcia, cuòcia, cuòcia, cociamo, cociate, cuòciano
(d) cocévo, cocévi, cocéva, cocevamo, cocevate, cocévano
(e) còssi, cocésti, còsse, cocémmo, cocéste, còssero
(f) cocerò, cocerài, cocerà, cocerémo, coceréte, coceranno

§144b DARE—dando—dato
(a) dà or dài or da'; date
(b) dò or dò; dài; dà; diamo; date; danno
(c) dìa, dìa, dìa, diamo, diate, dìano
(e) dièdi or dètti; désti; diède or dètte or diè; démmo; déste; dièdero or dèttero
(f) darò, darài, darà, darémo, daréte, daranno

§145 DECÌDERE—decidèndo—deciso
(e) decisi, decidésti, decise, decidémmo, decidéste, decìsero

§146 DELÌNQUERE—delinquèndo—*pp* missing
(a) missing
(c) missing
(e) missing

§147 DEVÒLVERE—devolvèndo—devoluto
(e) devolvéi or devolvètti; devolvésti; devolvé or devolvètte; devolvémmo; devolvéste; devolvérono or devolvèttero

§148 DIFÈNDERE—difendèndo—diféso
(e) difési, difendésti, difése, difendémmo, difendéste, difésero

§149 DILÌGERE—diligèndo—dilètto
(a) missing
(b) missing
(c) missing
(d) missing
(e) dilèssi, diligésti, dilèsse, diligémmo, diligéste, dilèssero
(f) missing

§150 DIPÈNDERE—dipendèndo—dipéso
(e) dipési, dipendésti, dipése, dipendémmo, dipendéste, dipésero

§151 DIRE—dicèndo—détto
(a) di' or dì; dite
(b) dico, dici, dice, diciamo, dite, dìcono
(c) dica, dica, dica, diciamo, diciate, dìcano
(d) dicévo, dicévi, dicéva, dicevamo, dicevate, dicévano
(e) dissi, dicésti, disse, dicémmo, dicéste, dìssero
(f) dirò, dirài, dirà, dirémo, diréte, diranno

22

§152 DIRÌGERE—dirigèndo—dirètto
(e) dirèssi, dirigésti, dirèsse, dirigémmo, dirigéste, dirèssero

§153 DISCÈRNERE—discernèndo—*pp* missing
(e) discernéi; discernésti; discerné *or* discernètte; discernémmo; discernéste; discernérono *or* discernèttero

§154 DISCÙTERE—discutèndo—discusso
(e) discussi, discutésti, discusse, discutémmo, discutéste, discùssero

§155 DISSÒLVERE—dissolvèndo—dissòlto
(e) dissòlsi *or* dissolvéi *or* dissolvètti; dissolvésti; dissòlse *or* dissolvé *or* dissolvètte; dissolvémmo; dissolvéste; dissòlsero *or* dissolvérono *or* dissolvèttero

§156 DISTÌNGUERE—distinguèndo—distinto
(e) distinsi, distinguésti, distinse, distinguémmo, distinguéste, distìnsero

§157 DIVÈRGERE—divergèndo—*pp* missing
(e) obsolete

§158 DIVÌDERE—dividèndo—diviso
(e) divisi, dividésti, divise, dividémmo, dividéste, divìsero

§159 DOLÉRE—dolèndo—doluto
(a) duòli, doléte
(b) dòlgo, duòli, duòle, doliamo, doléte, dòlgono
(c) dòlga, dòlga, dòlga, doliamo, doliate, dòlgano
(e) dòlsi, dolésti, dòlse, dolémmo, doléste, dòlsero
(f) dorrò, dorrài, dorrà, dorrémo, dorréte, dorranno

§160 DOVÉRE—dovèndo—dovuto
(b) dèbbo *or* dèvo; dèvi; dève; dobbiamo; dovéte; dèbbono *or* dèvono
(c) dèva *or* dèbba; dèva *or* dèbba; dèva *or* dèbba; dobbiamo; dobbiate; dèvano *or* dèbbano
(e) dovéi *or* dovètti; dovésti; dové *or* dovètte; dovémmo; dovéste; dovérono *or* dovèttero

§161 ELÌDERE—elidèndo—eliso
(e) elisi, elidésti, elise, elidémmo, elidéste, elìsero

§162 EMÈRGERE—emergèndo—emèrso
(e) emèrsi, emergésti, emèrse, emergémmo, emergéste, emèrsero

§163 ÉMPIERE & EMPIRE—empièndo—empito *or* empiuto
(a) émpi, empite

23

    (b) émpio, émpi, émpie, empiamo, empite, émpiono
    (c) émpia, émpia, émpia, empiamo, empiate, émpiano
    (d) empivo, empivi, empiva, empivamo, empivate, empìvano
    (e) empiéi *or* empìi; empiésti; *or* empisti; empié *or* empì; empiémmo *or* empimmo; empiéste *or* empiste; empiérono *or* empìrono
    (f) empirò, empirài, empirà, empirémo, empiréte, empiranno

§164 ÈRGERE—ergèndo—èrto
    (e) èrsi, ergésti, èrse, ergémmo, ergéste, èrsero

§165 ESÌGERE—esigèndo—esatto
    (e) esigéi *or* esigètti; esigésti; esigé *or* esigètte; esigémmo; esigéste; esigérono *or* esigèttero

§166 ESÌMERE—esimèndo—*pp* missing
    (e) esiméi *or* esimètti; esimésti; esimé *or* esimètte; esimémmo; esiméste; esimérono *or* esimèttero

§167 ESPÀNDERE—espandèndo—espanso
    (e) espandéi *or* espandètti *or* espansi; espandésti; espandé *or* espandètte *or* espanse; espandémmo; espandéste; espandérono *or* espandèttero *or* espànsero

§168 ESPÈLLERE—espellèndo—espulso
    (e) espulsi, espellésti, espulse, espellémmo, espelléste, espùlsero

§169 ESPLÒDERE—esplodèndo—esplòso
    (e) esplòsi, esplodésti, esplòse, esplodémmo, esplodéste, esplòsero

§170 ÈSSERE—essèndo—stato
    (a) sii, siate
    (b) sóno, sèi, è, siamo, siète, sóno
    (c) sìa, sìa, sìa, siamo, siate, sìano
    (d) èro, èri, èra, eravamo, eravate, èrano
    (e) fui, fósti, fu, fummo, fóste, fùrono
    (f) sarò, sarài, sarà, sarémo, saréte, saranno

§171 ESTÒLLERE—estollèndo—*pp* missing
    (e) missing

§172 EVÀDERE—evadèndo—evaso
    (e) evasi, evadésti, evase, evadémmo, evadéste, evàsero

§173 FARE—facèndo—fatto
    (a) fa *or* fài *or* fa'; fate

(b) fàccio *or* fò; fài; fa; facciamo; fate; fanno
(c) fàccia, fàccia, fàccia, facciamo, facciate; fàcciano
(d) facévo, facévi, facéva, facevamo, facevate, facévano
(e) féci, facésti, féce, facémmo, **facé**ste, fécero
(f) farò, faràì, farà, farémo, faréte, faranno

§174 FÈNDERE—fendèndo—fenduto *or* fésso
(e) fendéi *or* fendètti; fendésti; fendé *or* fendètte; fendémmo; fendéste; fendérono *or* fendèttero

§175 FÈRVERE—fervèndo—*pp* missing
(e) fervéi *or* fervètti; fervésti; fervé *or* fervètte; fervémmo; fervéste; fervérono *or* fervèttero

§176 FINIRE—finèndo—finito
(a) finisci, finite
(b) finisco, finisci, finisce, finiamo, finite, finìscono
(c) finisca, finisca, finisca, finiamo, finiate, finìscano

§177 FLÈTTERE—flettèndo—flèsso
(e) flettéi *or* flèssi; flettésti; fletté *or* flèsse; flettémmo; flettéste; flettérono *or* flèssero

§178 FÓNDERE—fondèndo—fuso
(e) fusi, fondésti, fuse, fondémmo, fondéste, fùsero

§179 FRÀNGERE—frangèndo—franto
(e) fransi, frangésti, franse, frangémmo, frangéste, frànsero

§180 FRÌGGERE—friggèndo—fritto
(e) frissi, friggésti, frisse, friggémmo, friggéste, frìssero

§181 GIACÉRE—giacèndo—giaciuto
(b) giàccio; giaci; giace; giacciamo *or* giaciamo; giacete; giàcciono
(c) giàccia, giàccia, giàccia, giacciamo, giacciate, giàcciano
(e) giàcqui, giacésti, giàcque, giacémmo, giacéste, giàcquero

§182 GIOCARE—giocando—giocato
(a) giuòca *or* giòca; giocate
(b) giuòco *or* giòco; giuòchi *or* giòchi; giuòca *or* giòca; giochiamo; giocate; giuòcano *or* giòcano
(c) giuòchi *or* giòchi; giuòchi *or* giòchi; giuòchi *or* giòchi; giochiamo; giochiate; giuòchino *or* giòchino
(f) giocherò, giocheràì, giocherà, giocherémo, giocheréte, giocheranno

§183 GIÙNGERE—giungèndo—giunto
(e) giunsi, giungésti, giunse, giungémmo, giungéste, giùnsero

25

§184 **GODÉRE**—godèndo—goduto
(e) godéi *or* godètti; godésti; godé *or* godètte; godémmo; godéste; godérono *or* godèttero
(f) godrò, godrài, godrà, godrémo, godréte, godranno

§185 **IMBÉVERE**—imbevèndo—imbevuto
(e) imbévvi, imbevésti, imbévve, imbevémmo, imbevéste, imbévvero

§186 **INCÓMBERE**—incombèndo—*pp* missing
(e) incombéi *or* incombètti; incombésti; incombé *or* incombètte; incombémmo; incombéste; incombérono *or* incombèttero

§187 **INDÙLGERE**—indulgèndo—indulto
(e) indulsi, indulgésti, indulse, indulgémmo, indulgéste, indùlsero

§188a **INFERIRE**—inferèndo—inferito *or* infèrto
(a) inferisci, inferite
(b) inferisco, inferisci, inferisce, inferiamo, inferite, inferìscono
(c) inferisca, inferisca, inferisca, inferiamo, inferiate, inferìscano
(e) inferìi *or* infèrsi; inferisti; inferì *or* infèrse; inferimmo; inferiste; inferìrono *or* infèrsero

§188b **INSTARE**—instando—*pp* missing

§189 **INTRÌDERE**—intridèndo—intriso
(e) intrisi, intridésti, intrise, intridémmo, intridéste, intrìsero

§190 **INTRÙDERE**—intrudèndo—intruso
(e) intrusi, intrudésti, intruse, intrudémmo, intrudéste, intrùsero

§191 **IRE**—*ger* missing—ito
(a) *sg* missing, ite
(b) missing
(c) missing
(d) ivo, ivi, iva, ivamo, ivate, ìvano
(e) *1st sg* missing, isti, *3rd sg* missing, *1st pl* missing, iste, ìrono

§192 **LÈDERE**—ledèndo—léso *or* lèso
(e) lési, ledésti, lése, ledémmo, ledéste, lésero

§193 **LÈGGERE**—leggèndo—lètto
(e) lèssi, leggésti, lèsse, leggémmo, leggéste, lèssero

§194 LIQUEFARE—liquefac*è*ndo—liquefatto
 (a) liquef*à*, liquefate
 (b) liquef*ò* or liquef*à*ccio; liquef*à*i; liquef*à* liquefacciamo; liquefate; liquefanno
 (c) liquef*à*ccia, liquef*à*ccia, liquef*à*ccia, liquefacciamo, liquefacciate, liquef*à*cciano
 (d) liquefac*é*vo, liquefac*é*vi, liquefac*é*va, liquefacevamo, liquefacevate, liquefac*é*vano
 (e) liquef*é*ci, liquefac*é*sti, liquef*é*ce, liquefac*é*mmo, liquefac*é*ste, liquef*é*cero
 (f) liquefar*ò*, liquefar*à*i, liquefar*à*, liquefar*é*mo, liquefar*é*te, liquefaranno

§195 MALEDIRE—maledic*è*ndo—maled*é*tto
 (a) maledici, maledite
 (b) maledico, maledici, maledice, malediciamo, maledite, maled*ì*cono
 (c) maledica, maledica, maledica, malediciamo, malediciate, maled*ì*cano
 (d) maledic*é*vo *or* maledivo; maledic*é*vi *or* maledivi; maledic*é*va *or* malediva; maledicevamo *or* maledivamo; maledicevate *or* maledivate; maledic*é*vano *or* maled*ì*vano
 (e) maled*ì*i *or* maledissi; maledisti *or* maledic*é*sti; maled*ì* *or* maledisse; maledimmo *or* maledic*é*mmo; malediste *or* maledic*é*ste; maled*ì*rono *or* maled*ì*ssero
 (f) maledir*ò*, maledir*à*i, maledir*à*, maledir*é*mo, maledir*é*te, malediranno

§196 MALVOL*É*RE—*ger* missing—malvoluto
 (a) missing
 (b) missing
 (c) missing
 (d) missing
 (e) missing
 (f) missing

§197 MANCARE—mancando—mancato
 (b) manco, manchi, manca, manchiamo, mancate, m*à*ncano
 (c) manchi, manchi, manchi, manchiamo, manchiate, m*à*nchino
 (f) mancher*ò*, mancher*à*i, mancher*à*, mancher*é*mo, mancher*é*te, mancheranno

§198 M*É*TTERE—mett*è*ndo—m*é*sso
 (e) misi, mett*é*sti, mise, mett*é*mmo, mett*é*ste, m*ì*sero

§199 M*Ì*NGERE—mingendo—minto
 (e) minsi, ming*é*sti, minse, ming*é*mmo, ming*é*ste, m*ì*nsero

27

§200 MÒRDERE—mordèndo—mòrso
(e) mòrsi, mordésti, mòrse, mordémmo, mordéste, mòrsero

§201 MORIRE—morèndo—mòrto
(a) muòri, morite
(b) muòio, muòri, muòre, moriamo, morite, muòiono
(c) muòia. muòia, muòia, moriamo, moriate, muòiano
(f) morrò *or* morirò; morràì *or* moriràì; morrà *or* morirà; morrémo *or* morirémo; morréte *or* moriréte; morranno *or* moriranno

§202 MUÒVERE—muovèndo *or* movèndo (movènte)—mòsso
(a) muòvi, movéte
(b) muòvo, muòvi, muòve, moviamo, movéte, muòvono
(c) muòva, muòva, muòva, moviamo, moviate, muòvano
(d) movévo, movévi, movéva, movevamo, movevate, movévano
(e) mòssi, movésti, mòsse, movémmo, movéste, mòssero
(f) moverò, moveràì, moverà, moverémo, moveréte, moveranno

§203 NÀSCERE—nascèndo—nato
(e) nàcqui, nascésti, nàcque, nascémmo, nascéste, nàcquero

§204 NASCÓNDERE—nascondèndo—nascósto
(e) nascósi, nascondésti, nascóse, nascondémmo, nascondéste, nascósero

§205 NEGLÌGERE—negligèndo—neglètto
(a) missing
(b) missing
(c) missing
(e) neglèssi, negligésti, neglèsse, negligémmo, negligéste, neglèssero

§206 NUÒCERE—nuocèndo—nociuto
(a) nuòci, nocéte
(b) nuòccio *or* nòccio; nuòci; nuòce; nociamo; nocéte; nuòcciono *or* nòcciono
(c) nòccia, nòccia, nòccia, nociamo, nociate, nòcciano
(d) nocévo, nocévi, nocéva, nocevamo, nocevate, nocévano
(e) nòcqui, nocésti, nòcque, nocémmo, nocéste, nòcquero
(f) nocerò, noceràì, nocerà, nocerémo, noceréte, noceranno

§207 OFFRIRE—offrèndo (offerènte)—offèrto
(e) offrìi *or* offérsi; offristi; offrì *or* offérse; offrimmo; offriste; offrìrono *or* offèrsero

§208 OTTÙNDERE—ottundèndo—ottuso
(e) ottusi, ottundésti, ottuse, ottundémmo, ottundéste, ottùsero

§209 PAGARE—pagando—pagato
(b) pago, paghi, paga, paghiamo, pagate, pàgano
(c) paghi, paghi, paghi, paghiamo, paghiate, pàghino
(f) pagherò, pagheràì, pagherà, pagherémo, pagheréte, pagheranno

§210 PARÉRE—parèndo (parvènte)—parso
(a) missing
(b) pàio; pari; pare; pariamo or paiamo; paréte; pàiono
(c) pàia; pàia; pàia; pariamo or paiamo; pariate or paiate; pàiano
(e) parvi, parésti, parve, parémmo, paréste, pàrvero
(f) parrò, parràì, parrà, parrémo, parréte, parranno

§211 PÀSCERE—pascèndo—pasciuto
(a) pascéi or pascètti; pascésti; pascé or pascètte; pascémmo; pascéste; pascérono or pascèttero

§212 PÈRDERE—perdèndo—pèrso or perduto
(e) perdéi or pèrsi or perdètti; perdésti; perdé, or pèrse or perdètte; perdémmo; perdéste; perdérono or pèrsero or perdèttero

§213 PERSUADÉRE—persuadèndo—persuaso
(e) persuasi, persuadésti, persuase, persuadémmo, persuadéste, persuàsero

§214 PIACÉRE—piacèndo—piaciuto
(b) piàccio, piaci, piace, piacciamo, piacéte, piàcciono
(c) piàccia, piàccia, piàccia, piacciamo, piacciate, piàcciano
(e) piàcqui, piacésti, piàcque, piacémmo, piacéste, piàcquero

§215 PIÀNGERE—piangèndo—pianto
(e) piansi, piangésti, pianse, piangémmo, piangéste, piànsero

§216 PIÒVERE—piovèndo—piovuto
(e) piòvvi, piovésti, piòvve, piovémmo, piovéste, piòvvero

§217 PÒRGERE—porgèndo—pòrto
(e) pòrsi, porgésti, pòrse, porgémmo, porgéste, pòrsero

§218 PÓRRE—ponèndo—pósto
(a) póni, ponéte
(b) póngo, póni, póne, poniamo, ponéte, póngono
(c) pónga, pónga, pónga, poniamo, poniate, póngano
(d) ponévo, ponévi, ponéva, ponevamo, ponevate, ponévano
(e) pósi, ponésti, póse, ponémmo, ponéste, pósero

§219 POTÉRE—potèndo (potènte or possènte)—potuto
(a) missing
(b) pòsso, puòi, può, possiamo, potéte, pòssono

29

(c) pòssa, pòssa, pòssa, possiamo, possiate, pòssano
(e) potéi *or* potètti; potésti, poté *or* potètte; potémmo; potéste; potérono *or* potèttero
(f) potrò, potrài, potrà, potrémo, potréte, potranno

§220 **PRÈNDERE**—prendèndo—préso
(e) prési, prendésti, prése, prendémmo, prendéste, présero

§221 **PROVVEDÉRE**—provvedèndo—provveduto *or* provvisto
(e) provvidi, provvedésti, provvide, provvedémmo, provvedéste, provvìdero

§222 **PRÙDERE**—prudèndo—*pp* missing
(e) *1st sg* missing; *2nd sg* missing; prudé *or* prudètte; *1st pl* missing; *2nd pl* missing; prudérono *or* prudèttero

§223 **RÀDERE**—radèndo—raso
(e) rasi, radésti, rase, radémmo, radéste, ràsero

§224 **REDÌGERE**—redigèndo—redatto
(e) redassi, redigésti, redasse, redigémmo, redigéste, redàssero

§225 **REDÌMERE**—redimèndo—redènto
(e) redènsi, redimésti, redènse, redimémmo, rediméste, redènsero

§226 **RÈGGERE**—reggèndo—rètto
(e) rèssi, reggésti, rèsse, reggémmo, reggéste, rèssero

§227 **RÈNDERE**—rendèndo—réso
(e) rési *or* rendéi *or* rendètti; rendésti; rése *or* rendé *or* rendètte; rendémmo; rendéste; résero *or* rendérono *or* rendèttero

§228 **RETROCÈDERE**—retrocedèndo—retrocèsso *or* retroceduto
(e) retrocèssi *or* retrocedéi *or* retrocedètti; retrocedésti; retrocèsse *or* retrocedé *or* retrocedètte; retrocedémmo; retrocedéste; retrocèssero *or* retrocedérono *or* retrocedèttero

§229 **RIAVÉRE**—riavèndo—riavuto
(a) riabbi, riabbiate
(b) riò, riài, rià, riabbiamo, riavéte, rianno
(c) riàbbia, riàbbia, riàbbia, riabbiamo, riabbiate, riàbbiano
(e) rièbbi, riavésti, rièbbe, riavémmo, riavéste, rièbbero
(f) riavrò, riavrài, riavrà, riavrémo, riavréte, riavranno

§230 **RIDARE**—ridando—ridato
(a) ridài *or* ridà; ridate
(b) ridò, ridài, ridà, ridiamo, ridate, ridanno
(c) ridìa, ridìa, ridìa, ridiamo, ridiate, ridìano

(e) ridièdi *or* ridètti; ridésti; ridiède *or* ridètte; ridémmo; ridéste; ridièdero *or* ridèttero

(f) ridarò, ridarài, ridarà, ridarémo, ridaréte, ridaranno

§231 RÌDERE—ridèndo—riso
(e) risi, ridésti, rise, ridémmo, ridéste, rìsero

§232 RIFLÈTTERE—riflettèndo—riflèsso *or* riflettuto

§233 RIFÙLGERE—rifulgèndo—rifulso
(e) rifulsi, rifulgésti, rifulse rifulgémmo, rifulgéste, rifùlsero

§234 RILÙCERE—rilucèndo—*pp* missing

§235 RIMANÉRE—rimanèndo—rimasto
(b) rimango, rimani, rimane, rimaniamo, rimanéte, rimàngono
(c) rimanga, rimanga, rimanga, rimaniamo, rimaniate, rimàngano
(e) rimasi, rimanésti, rimase, rimanémmo, rimanéste, rimàsero
(f) rimarrò, rimarrài, rimarrà, rimarrémo, rimarréte, rimarranno

§236 RINCORARE—rincorando—rincorato
(a) rincuòra, rincorate
(b) rincuòro, rincuòri, rincuòra, rincoriamo, rincorate, rincuòrano
(c) rincuòri, rincuòri, rincuòri, rincoriamo, rincoriate, rincuòrino

§237 RISOLARE—risolando—risolato
(a) risuòla, risolate
(b) risuòlo, risuòli, risuòla, risoliamo, risolate, risuòlano
(c) risuòli, risuòli, risuòli, risoliamo, risoliate, risuòlino

§238 RISPÓNDERE—rispondèndo—rispósto
(e) rispósi, rispondésti, rispóse, rispondémmo, rispondéste, rispósero

§239 RÓDERE—rodèndo—róso
(e) rósi, rodésti, róse, rodémmo, rodéste, rósero

§240 RÓMPERE—rompèndo—rótto
(e) ruppi, rompésti, ruppe, rompémmo, rompéste, rùppero

§241 ROTARE—rotando—rotato
(a) ruòta, rotate
(b) ruòto, ruòti, ruòta, rotiamo, rotate, ruòtano
(c) ruòti, ruòti, ruòti, rotiamo, rotiate, ruòtino

31

§242 SALIRE—salèndo—salito
(b) salgo, sali, sale, saliamo, salite, sàlgono
(c) salga, salga, salga, saliamo, saliate, sàlgano

§243 SAPÉRE—sapèndo (sapiènte)—saputo
(a) sappi, sappiate
(b) sò, sai, sa, sappiamo, sapéte, sanno
(c) sàppia, sàppia, sàppia, sappiamo, sappiate, sàppiano
(e) sèppi, sapésti, sèppe, sapémmo, sapéste, sèppero
(f) saprò, saprài, saprà, saprémo, sapréte, sapranno

§244 SCÉGLIERE—sceglièndo—scélto
(a) scégli, scegliéte
(b) scélgo, scégli, scéglie, scegliamo, scegliéte, scélgono
(c) scélga, scélga, scélga, scegliamo, scegliate, scélgano
(e) scélsi, scegliésti, scélse, scegliémmo, scegliéste, scélsero

§245 SCÉNDERE—scendèndo—scéso
(e) scési, scendésti, scése, scendémmo, scendéste, scésero

§246 SCÈRNERE—scernèndo—*pp* missing
(e) scernéi *or* scernètti; scernésti; scerné *or* scernètte; scernémmo; scernéste; scernérono *or* scernèttero

§247 SCÌNDERE—scindèndo—scisso
(e) scissi, scindésti, scisse, scindémmo, scindéste, scìssero

§248 SCOIARE—scoiando—scoiato
(a) scuòia, scoiate
(b) scuòio, scuòi, scuòia, scoiamo, scoiate, scuòiano
(c) scuòi, scuòi, scuòi, scoiamo, scoiate, scuòino

§249 SCÒRGERE—scorgèndo—scòrto
(e) scòrsi, scorgésti, scòrse, scorgémmo, scorgéste, scòrsero

§250 SCRÌVERE—scrivèndo—scritto
(e) scrissi, scrivésti, scrisse, scrivémmo, scrivéste, scrìssero

§251 SCUÒTERE—scotèndo—scòsso
(a) scuòti, scotéte
(b) scuòto, scuòti, scuòte, scotiamo, scotéte, scuòtono
(c) scuòta, scuòta, scuòta, scotiamo, scotiate, scuòtano
(d) scotévo, scotévi, scotéva, scotevamo, scotevate, scotévano
(e) scòssi, scotésti, scòsse, scotémmo, scotéste, scòssero

§252 SEDÉRE—sedéndo—seduto
(a) sièdi, sedéte
(b) sièdo *or* sèggo; sièdi; sième; sediamo; sedéte; sièdono *or* sèggono
(c) sièda *or* sègga; sièda *or* sègga; sièda *or* sègga; sediamo; sediate; sièdano *or* sèggano
(e) sedéi *or* sedètti; sedésti; sedé *or* sedètte; sedémmo; sedéste; sedérono *or* sedèttero

§253 SEPPELLIRE—seppellèndo—sepólto *or* seppellito
  (a) seppellisci, seppellite
  (b) seppellisco, seppellisci, seppellisce, seppelliamo, seppellite, seppellìscono
  (c) seppellisca, seppellisca, seppellisca, seppelliamo, seppelliate, seppellìscano

§254 SODDISFARE—soddisfacèndo—soddisfatto
  (a) soddisfa *or* soddisfài *or* soddisfa'
  (b) soddisfàccio *or* soddisfò *or* soddisfo; soddisfài *or* soddisfi; soddisfà *or* soddisfa; soddisfacciamo; soddisfate; soddisfanno *or* soddìsfano
  (c) soddisfàccia *or* soddisfi; soddisfàccia *or* soddisfi; soddisfàccià *or* soddisfi; soddisfacciamo; soddisfacciate; soddisfàcciano *or* soddìsfino
  (d) soddisfacévo, soddisfacévi, soddisfacéva, soddisfacevamo, soddisfacevate, soddisfacévano
  (e) soddisféci, soddisfacésti, soddisféce, soddisfacémmo, soddisfacéste, soddisfécero
  (f) soddisfarò, soddisfarài, soddisfarà, soddisfarémo, soddisfaréte, soddisfaranno

§255 SOLÉRE—solèndo—sòlito
  (a) missing
  (b) sòglio, suòli, suòle, sogliamo, soléte, sògliono
  (c) sòglia, sòglia, sòglia, sogliamo, sogliate, sògliano
  (e) missing
  (f) missing

§256 SÒLVERE—solvèndo—soluto
  (e) solvéi *or* solvètti; solvésti; solvé *or* solvètte; solvémmo; solvéste; solvérono *or* solvèttero

§257 SONARE—sonando—sonato
  (a) suòna, sonate
  (b) suòno, suòni, suòna, soniamo, sonate, suònano
  (c) suòni, suòni, suòni, soniamo, soniate, suònino

§258 SÓRGERE—sorgèndo—sórto
  (e) sórsi, sorgésti, sórse, sorgémmo, sorgéste, sórsero

§259 SOSPÈNDERE—sospendèndo—sospéso
  (e) sospési, sospendésti, sospése, sospendémmo, sospendéste, sospésero

§260 SPÀNDERE—spandèndo—spanto
  (e) spandéi *or* spandètti *or* spansi; spandésti; spandé *or* spandètte *or* spanse; spandémmo; spandéste; spandérono *or* spandèttero *or* spànsero

§261 SPÀRGERE—spargèndo—sparso
  (e) sparsi, spargésti, sparse, spargémmo, spargéste, spàrsero

§262 SPÈGNERE—spegnèndo—spènto
- (b) spéngo *or* spèngo; spégni *or* spègni; spégne *or* spègne; spegniamo; spegnéte; spéngono *or* spèngono
- (c) spénga *or* spènga; spénga *or* spènga; spénga *or* spènga; spegniamo; spegniate; spéngano *or* spèngano
- (e) spènsi, spegnésti, spènse, spegnémmo, spegnéste, spènsero

§263 STARE—stando—stato
- (a) sta *or* stai *or* sta'; state
- (b) stò, stài, sta, stiamo, state, stanno
- (c) stìa, stìa, stìa, stiamo, stiate, stìano
- (e) stètti, stésti, stètte, stémmo, stéste, stèttero
- (f) starò, starài, starà, starémo, staréte, staranno

§264 STRÌDERE—stridèndo—*pp* missing
- (e) stridéï *or* stridètti; stridésti; stridé *or* stridètte; stridémmo; stridéste; stridérono *or* stridèttero

§265 STRÌNGERE—stringèndo—strétto
- (e) strinsi, stringésti, strinse, stringémmo, stringéste, strìnsero

§266 STRÙGGERE—struggèndo—strutto
- (e) strussi, struggésti, strusse, struggémmo, struggéste, strùssero

§267 SVÈLLERE—svellèndo—svèlto
- (b) svèllo *or* svèlgo; svèlli; svèlle; svelliamo; svelléte; svèllono *or* svèlgono
- (c) svèlla *or* svèlga; svèlla *or* svèlga; svèlla *or* svèlga; svelliamo; svelliate; svèllano *or* svèlgano
- (e) svèlsi, svellésti, svèlse, svellémmo, svelléste, svèlsero

§268 TACÉRE—tacèndo—taciuto
- (b) tàccio, taci, tace, taciamo, tacéte, tàcciono
- (c) tàccia, tàccia, tàccia, taciamo, taciate, tàcciano
- (e) tàcqui, tacésti, tàcque, tacémmo, tacéste, tàcquero

§269 TÀNGERE—tangèndo—*pp* missing
- (a) missing
- (b) *1st sg* missing; *2nd sg* missing; tange; *1st pl* missing; *2nd pl* missing; tàngono
- (c) *1st sg* missing; *2nd sg* missing; tanga; *1st pl* missing; *2nd pl* missing; tàngano
- (d) *1st sg* missing; *2nd sg* missing; tangéva; *1st pl* missing; *2nd pl* missing; tangévano
- (e) missing
- (f) *1st sg* missing; *2nd sg* missing; tangerà; *1st pl* missing; *2nd pl* missing; tangeranno

§270 TÈNDERE—tendèndo—téso
(e) tési, tendésti, tése, tendémmo, tendéste, tésero

§271 TENÉRE—tenèndo—tenuto
(a) tièni, tenéte
(b) tèngo, tièni, tiène, teniamo, tenéte, tèngono
(c) tènga, tèǹga, tènga, teniamo, teniate, tèngano
(e) ténni, tenésti, ténne, tenémmo, tenéste, ténnero
(f) terrò, terrài, terrà, terrémo, terréte, terranno

§272 TÒRCERE—torcèndo—tòrto
(e) tòrsi, torcésti, tòrse, torcémmo, torcéste, tòrsero

§273 TRARRE—traèndo—tratto
(a) trài, traéte
(b) traggo, trài, trae, traiamo, traéte, tràggono
(c) tragga, tragga, tragga, traiamo, traiate, tràggano
(d) traévo, traévi, traéva, traevamo, traevate, traévano
(e) trassi, traésti, trasse, traémmo, traéste, tràssero

§274 UCCÌDERE—uccidèndo—ucciso
(e) uccisi, uccidésti, uccise, uccidémmo, uccidéste, uccìsero

§275 UDIRE—udèndo *or* udièndo—udito
(a) òdi, udite
(b) òdo, òdi, òde, udiamo, udite, òdono
(c) òda, òda, òda, udiamo, udiate, òdano
(f) udirò *or* udrò; udirài *or* udrài; udirà *or* udrà; udirémo *or* udrémo; udiréte *or* udréte; udiranno *or* udranno

§276 ÙRGERE—urgèndo—*pp* missing
(a) missing
(e) missing

§277 USCIRE—uscèndo—uscito
(a) èsci, uscite
(b) èsco, èsci, èsce, usciàmo, uscite, èscono
(c) èsca, èsca, èsca, usciamo, usciate, èscano

§278 VALÉRE—valèndo—valso
(b) valgo, vali, vale, valiamo, valéte, vàlgono
(c) valga, valga, valga, valiamo, valiate, vàlgano
(e) valsi, valésti, valse, valémmo, valéste, vàlsero
(f) varrò, varrài, varrà, varrémo, varréte, varranno

§279 VEDÉRE—vedèndo—veduto *or* visto
(e) vidi, vedésti, vide, vedémmo, vedéste, vìdero
(f) vedrò, vedrài, vedrà, vedrémo, vedréte, vedranno

§280 VEGLIARE—vegliando—vegliato
(b) véglio, végli, véglia, vegliamo, vegliate, végliano
(c) végli, végli, végli, vegliamo, vegliate, véglino

§281 VÉNDERE—vendèndo—venduto
 (e) vendéi *or* vendètti; vendésti; vendé *or* vendètte; vendémmo; vendéste; vendérono *or* vendèttero

§282 VENIRE—venèndo (veniènte)—venuto
 (a) vièni, venite
 (b) vèngo, vièni, vième, veniamo, venite, vèngono
 (c) vènga, vènga, vènga, veniamo, veniate, vèngano
 (e) vénni, venisti, vénne, venimmo, veniste, vénnero
 (f) verrò, verrài, verrà, verrémo, verréte, verranno

§283 VÈRTERE—vertèndo—*pp* missing

§284 VÌGERE—vigèndo—*pp* missing
 (a) missing
 (b) *1st sg* missing; *2nd sg* missing; vige; *1st pl* missing; *2d pl* missing; vìgono
 (c) *1st sg* missing; *2d sg* missing; viga; *1st pl* missing; *2d pl* missing; vìgano
 (d) *1st sg* missing; *2d sg* missing; vigéva; *1st pl* missing; *2d pl* missing; vigévano
 (e) missing

§285 VÌNCERE—vincèndo—vinto
 (e) vinsi, vincésti, vinse, vincémmo, vincéste, vìnsero

§286 VÌVERE—vivèndo—vissuto
 (e) vissi, vivésti, visse, vivémmo, vivéste, vìssero
 (f) vivrò, vivrài, vivrà, vivrémo, vivréte, vivranno

§287 VIZIARE—viziando—viziato
 (b) vìzio, vizi, vìzia, viziamo, viziate, vìziano
 (c) vizi, vizi, vizi, viziamo, viziate, vìzino

§288 VOLÉRE—volèndo—voluto
 (a) vògli, vogliate
 (b) vòglio, vuòi, vuòle, vogliamo, voléte, vògliono
 (c) vòglia, vòglia, vòglia, vogliamo, vogliate, vògliano
 (e) vòlli, volésti, vòlle, volémmo, voléste, vòllero
 (f) vorrò, vorrài, vorrà, vorrémo, vorréte, vorranno

§289 VÒLGERE—volgèndo—vòlto
 (e) vòlsi, volgésti, vòlse, volgémmo, volgéste, vòlsero

§290 VOLTEGGIARE—volteggiando—volteggiato
 (b) voltéggio, voltéggi, voltéggia, volteggiamo, volteggiate, voltéggiano
 (c) voltéggi, voltéggi, voltéggi, volteggiamo, volteggiate, voltéggino
 (f) volteggerò, volteggerài, volteggerà, volteggerémo, volteggeréte, volteggeranno

A

A, a [a] *m* & *f* first letter of the Italian alphabet

a *prep* (**ad** in front of a vowel) to, e.g., **diede il libro a Giovanni** he gave the book to John; in, e.g., **a Milano** in Milan; at, e.g., **a casa** at home; within, e.g., **a tre miglia da qui** within three miles from here; on, e.g., **portare una catena al collo** to wear a chain on one's neck; e.g., **al sabato** on Saturdays; for, e.g., **a vita** for life; by, e.g., **fatto a mano** made by hand; with, e.g., **una gonna a pieghe** a skirt with pleats; as, e.g., **eleggere a presidente** to elect as chairman; into, e.g., **fu gettato a mare** he was thrown into the sea; of, e.g., **un quarto alle due** fifteen minutes of two

àba·co *m* (**-chi**) (archit) abacus

abate *m* abbot

abbacchiare §287 *tr* to knock down (*e.g., olives*); to sell too cheap ‖ *ref* to lose courage; to be dejected

abbacchia·to -ta *adj* (coll) dejected

abbàc·chio *m* (**-chi**) baby lamb (*slaughtered*)

abbacinare (**abbàcino**) *tr* to dazzle; to deceive

abbadéssa *f* var of **badessa**

abbagliante *adj* dazzling ‖ *m* (aut) bright light, high beam

abbagliare §280 *tr* to dazzle; to deceive; to blind (*with the lights of a car*)

abbà·glio *m* (**-gli**) error; **prendere abbaglio** to make a mistake

abbaiaménto *m* bark (*of dog*)

abbaiare §287 *intr* to bark; to yelp

abbaino *m* dormer window; skylight; attic

abbambinare *tr* to walk (*a heavy piece of furniture*)

abbandonare (**abbandóno**) *tr* to abandon; to give up; to let go (*e.g., the reins*); to let fall; (sports) to withdraw from ‖ *ref* to yield; to lose courage

abbandóno *m* abandon, abandonment; desertion; neglect; relaxation; renunciation (*of a right*); cession (*of property*); withdrawal (*from a fight*)

abbarbicare §197 (**abbàrbico**) *intr* & *ref* to cling; to hold on

abbassalin·gua *m* (**-gua**) tongue depressor

abbassaménto *m* lowering; reduction; drop, fall

abbassare *tr* to lower; to dim (*lights*); to turn (*the radio*) lower; **abbassare le armi** to surrender; **abbassare la cresta** to yield ‖ *ref* to lower oneself; to drop

abbas·so *m* (**-so**) angry shout (*of a crowd*) ‖ *adv* down, below; downstairs ‖ *interj* down with!

abbastanza *adj invar* enough ‖ *adv* enough; rather, fairly

abbàttere *tr* to demolish; to fell; to shoot down; to refute (*an argument*); to depress ‖ *ref* to be depressed, be downcast

abbattiménto *m*. demolition; felling; shooting down; chill; (fig) depression; **abbattimento alla base** (econ) basic exemption (*from taxes*)

abbattu·to -ta *adj* dejected, downcast ‖ *f* clearing (*of trees*)

abbazìa *f* abbey; abbacy

abbecedà·rio *m* (**-ri**) speller, primer

abbelliménto *m* embellishment, ornamentation

abbellire §176 *tr* to embellish, adorn; to landscape

abbeverare (**abbévero**) *tr* to water (*animals*) ‖ *ref* to quench one's thirst

abbevera·tóio *m* (**-tói**) watering trough

abbic·cì *m* (**-cì**) alphabet; speller, primer; ABC's, rudiments

abbiènte *adj* well-to-do ‖ *m*—**gli abbienti** the haves; **gli abbienti e nullatenenti** the haves and the have-nots

abbiettézza or **abiettézza** *f* abjectness, baseness

abbièt·to -ta or **abièt·to -ta** *adj* abject, base, low

abbiezióne or **abiezióne** *f* wretchedness, baseness

abbigliaménto *m* attire, wear

abbigliare §280 *tr* & *ref* to dress; to dress up

abbinaménto *m* coupling; merger

abbinare *tr* to couple; to join, merge

abbindolare (**abbìndolo**) *tr* to dupe, deceive

abbiosciare §128 *ref* to fall down; to lose heart, be downcast

abbisognare (**abbisógno**) *intr* to be in need

abboccaménto *m* interview, conversation

abboccare §197 (**abbócco**) *tr* to swallow (*the hook*); to fit (*pipes*) ‖ *intr* to bite (*said of fish*); to fall; to fit (*said of pipes*) ‖ *ref* to confer

abbocca·to -ta *adj* palatable; slightly sweet (*wine*)

abbonacciare §128 *ref* to calm down, abate (*said of weather*)

abbonaménto *m* subscription; **abbonamento postale** mailing permit

abbonare (**abbòno**) *tr* to take out a subscription for (*s.o.*) ‖ *ref* to subscribe ‖ §257 *tr* to remit (*a debt*); to forgive

abbona·to -ta *mf* subscriber; commuter

abbondante *adj* abundant, plentiful; heavy (*rain*)

abbondanza *f* abundance, plenty

abbondare (**abbóndo**) *intr* (ESSERE & AVERE) to abound; to exceed; **abbondare di** or **in** to abound in

abbonire §176 *tr* to calm; to placate ‖ *ref* to calm down

abbordàbile *adj* accessible, approachable; negotiable (*curve*)

abbordàg·gio *m* (-gi) boarding (*of an enemy ship*); **andare all'abbordaggio di** to board

abbordare (abbórdo) *tr* to board (*an enemy ship*); to negotiate (*a curve*); to face (*a problem*); (fig) to button-hole

abborracciare §128 *tr* to botch, bungle

abborracciatura *f* botch, bungle

abbottonare (abbottóno) *tr* to button || *ref* (coll) to keep to oneself

abbottonatura *f* buttoning; row of buttons

abbozzare (abbòzzo) *tr* to sketch; to hew (*e.g., a statue*); (naut) to tie up || *intr* (coll) to take it

abbòzzo *m* sketch, draft

abbracciabò·sco *m* (-schi) (bot) woodbine

abbracciare *m* embrace, embracing || §128 *tr* to embrace, hug; to seize (*an opportunity*); to become converted to (*e.g., Christianity*); to enter (*a profession*); to span, encompass || *ref* to cling; to embrace one another

abbràc·cio *m* (-ci) embrace, hug

abbrancare §197 *tr* to grab; to herd || *ref* to cling; to join a herd

abbreviaménto *m* abbreviation, shortening

abbreviare §287 (abbrèvio) *tr* to abbreviate, shorten, abridge

abbreviatura *f* shortening, abridgment

abbreviazióne *f* abbreviation

abbrivo or **abbrìvio** *m* headway (*of a ship*); **prendere l'abbrivio** to gather momentum

abbronzante [dz] *adj* suntanning || *m* suntan lotion

abbronzare [dz] (abbrónzo) *tr & ref* to bronze; to tan

abbronza·to -ta [dz] *adj* tanned, suntanned

abbronzatura [dz] *f* tan, suntan

abbruciacchiare §287 *tr* to singe

abbrunare *tr* to brown; to hang crepe on || *ref* to wear mourning

abbrunire §176 *tr* to turn brown; to tan; to burnish

abbrustolire §176 *tr* to toast; to singe || *ref* to tan; to become sunburned

abbrutiménto *m* degradation, brutishness

abbrutire §176 *tr* to degrade; to brutalize || *intr & ref* to become brutalized

abbuiare §287 *tr* to darken; to hush up, hide || *ref* to grow dark; to become gloomy || *impers*—**abbuia** it's growing dark

abbuòno *m* allowance, discount; handicap (*in racing*)

abburattaménto *m* sifting

abburattare *tr* to sift, bolt

abdicare §197 (àbdico) *tr & intr* to abdicate; **abdicare a** to give up, renounce; to abdicate (*e.g., the throne*)

abdicazióne *f* abdication

aberrare (abèrro) *intr* to deviate

aberrazióne *f* aberration

abéte *m* fir

abetina *f* forest of fir trees

abiàti·co *m* (-ci) (coll) grandson

abièt·to -ta *adj* abject, base, low

abigeato *m* (law) cattle rustling

àbile *adj* able, clever, capable; (mil) fit

abili·tà *f* (tà) ability, skill

abilitare (abìlito) *tr* to certify (*e.g., a teacher*); to qualify, license

abilita·to -ta *adj* certified (*teacher*)

abilitazióne *f* qualification; certification (*of teachers*)

abissale *adj* abysmal

Abissìnia, l' *f* Abyssinia

abissi·no -na *adj & mf* Abyssinian

abisso *m* abyss; fountain (*of knowledge*); slough (*of degradation*)

abitàbile *adj* inhabitable

abitàcolo *m* (aer) cockpit; (aut) cab, interior; (naut) compass bowl; **abitacolo eiettabile** (aer) ejection capsule

abitante *mf* inhabitant; resident

abitare (àbito) *tr* to inhabit; to occupy || *intr* to dwell, live, reside

abitati·vo -va *adj* living, e.g., **condizioni abitative** living conditions

abita·to -ta *adj* inhabited, populated || *m* built-up area

abita·tóre -trice *mf* dweller

abitazióne *f* dwelling; housing

àbito *m* suit (*for men*); dress (*for women*); garb, attire; habit; **abiti** clothes; **abito da ballo** evening gown; **abito da cerimonia** formal dress; **abito da inverno** winter suit; winter clothes; **levarsi l'abito** to doff the cassock; **prender l'abito** to enter the Church

abituale *adj* habitual

abituare (abìtuo) *tr* to accustom || *ref* to grow accustomed

abitudinà·rio -ria *adj* (-ri -rie) set in his ways

abitùdine *f* habit, custom

abituro *m* (poet) shanty, hut

abiura *f* abjuration

abiurare *tr* to abjure

ablati·vo -va *adj & m* ablative

ablazióne *f* (med) removal; (geol) erosion

abluzióne *f* ablution

abnegare §209 (abnégo & abnègo) *tr* to renounce, abnegate

abnegazióne *f* abnegation, self-denial

abnòrme *adj* abnormal

abolire §176 *tr* to abolish

abolizióne *f* abolition

abominàbile *adj* abominable

abominare (abòmino) *tr* to abominate, detest

abominazióne *f* abomination

abominévole *adj* abominable

aborìge·no -na *adj* aboriginal || *m* aborigine; **aborigeni** aborigines

aborrire §176 & (abòrro) *tr* to abhor, loathe || *intr*—**aborrire da** to shun, shrink from

abortire §176 *intr* to abort

abòrto *m* abortion, miscarriage; **aborto di natura** monstrosity

abrasióne *f* abrasion; erosion

abrasi·vo -va *adj & m* abrasive

abrogare §209 (àbrogo) *tr* to abrogate

abrogazióne *f* abrogation

abruzzése *adj* of the Abruzzi ‖ *mf* person of the Abruzzi ‖ *m* dialect of the Abruzzi

àbside *f* (archit) apse

abusare *intr*—**abusare di** to go to excesses in (*e.g., smoking*); to take advantage of; to impose on

abusi•vo -va *adj* illegal, abusive; unwarranted

abuso *m* abuse, excess

acà•cia *f* (-cie) acacia

acanto *m* acanthus

àcaro *m* (ent) acarus, mite, tick; **acaro della scabbia** itch mite

ac•ca *m* & *f* (-ca or -che) h (*letter*); **non valere un'acca** (coll) to not be worth a fig

accadèmia *f* academy

accadèmi•co -ca (-ci -che) *adj* academic ‖ *mf* academician

accadére §121 *intr* (ESSERE) to happen, occur

accadu•to -ta *adj* happened, occurred ‖ *m* fact, event; what has taken place

accagliare §280 *tr, intr* (ESSERE) & *ref* to curdle, coagulate

accalappia•ni *m* (-ni) dogcatcher

accalappiare §287 *tr* to catch (*a dog*); to snare; (fig) to fool

accalcare §197 *tr* to crowd ‖ *ref* to throng

accaldare *ref* to get hot; to become flushed

accalda•to -ta *adj* hot; perspired

accalorare (accalóro) *tr* to excite ‖ *ref* to get excited

accalora•to -ta *adj* excited, animated

accampaménto *m* encampment, camp; camping

accampare *tr* to encamp; to advance, lay (*a claim*) ‖ *ref* to camp, encamp

accaniménto *m* animosity, bitterness; obstinacy, stubbornness

accanire §176 *ref* to persist; to work doggedly; **accanirsi contro** to harass

accani•to -ta *adj* obstinate, persistent; furious; fierce, ruthless, bitter (*fight*)

accanto *adv* near, nearby; **accanto a** near

accantonaménto *m* tabling (*e.g., of a discussion*); reserve (*of money*); (mil) billeting; (sports) camping

accantonare (accantóno) *tr* to set aside (*money*); (mil) to billet

accaparraménto *m* cornering (*of market*)

accaparrare *tr* to corner (*merchandise*); to hoard; to put a down payment on (*e.g., a house*); (coll) to gain (*somebody's affection*)

accaparra•tóre -trice *mf* monopolizer; hoarder

accapigliare §280 *ref* to pull each other's hair; to scuffle; to come to blows

accapo or **a capo** *m* paragraph

accappa•tóio *m* (-tói) bathrobe

accapponare (accappóno) *tr* to castrate (*a rooster*) ‖ *ref* to wrinkle; **mi si accappona la pelle** I get gooseflesh

accarezzare (accarézzo) *tr* to caress, fondle; to pet; to nurture (*e.g., a*

---

hope); **accarezzare le spalle di** to strike; to club

accartocciare §128 (accartòccio) *tr* to wrap up in a cone ‖ *ref* to curl up

accartoccia•to -ta *adj* curled up

accasare [s] *tr* & *ref* to marry

accasciaménto *m* dejection

accasciare §128 *tr* to weaken, enfeeble; to depress ‖ *ref* to weaken; to lose heart

accasermare [s] (accasèrmo) *tr* to quarter, billet

accatastare *tr* to register (*real estate*); to pile, heap up

accattàbri•ghe *mf* (-ghe) quarrelsome person, scrapper

accattare *tr* to beg for; to borrow (*e.g., ideas*) ‖ *intr* to beg

accattonàg•gio *m* (-gi) begging, mendicancy

accattó•ne -na *mf* mendicant, beggar

accavalcare §197 *tr* to straddle; to go over

accavalciare §128 *tr* to bestride

accavallare *tr* to superimpose; to cross (*one's legs*) ‖ *ref* to pour forward, run high (*said of waves*)

accecaménto *m* blinding

accecare §122 *tr* to blind; to countersink ‖ *intr* (ESSERE) to become blind ‖ *ref* to blind oneself

acceca•tóio *m* (-tói) countersink

accèdere §100 *intr* (ESSERE) to enter, approach; to accede

acceleraménto *m* acceleration

accelerare (accèlero) *tr* & *intr* to accelerate

accelera•to -ta *adj* accelerated; intensive (*course*); local (*train*) ‖ *m* local train

acceleratóre *m* accelerator

accelerazióne *f* acceleration

accèndere §101 *tr* to kindle; to turn on (*e.g., the light*); to light (*e.g., a match, a cigar*) ‖ *ref* to catch fire; to become lit; **accendersi in viso** to become flushed

accendisìgaro *m* lighter

accendi•tóio *m* (-tói) candle lighter

accenditóre *m* lighter

accennare (accénno) *tr* to nod; to point at; to sketch ‖ *intr* to refer; to hint

accénno *m* nod; sign; allusion

accensióne *f* lighting, kindling; (aut) ignition; (law) contraction (*of a debt*); **accensione improvvisa** spontaneous combustion

accentare (accénto) *tr* to accent

accènto *m* accent; stress; (poet) accent (*word*); **accento tonico** stress accent

accentraménto *m* centralization

accentrare (accèntro) *tr* to concentrate, centralize

accentuare (accèntuo) *tr* to accentuate ‖ *ref* to become aggravated

accentuazióne *f* accentuation

accerchiaménto *m* encirclement

accerchiare §287 (accérchio) *tr* to encircle, surround

accertàbile *adj* verifiable

accertaménto *m* ascertainment, verification; determination (*e.g., of taxes*)

accertare (accèrto) *tr* to assure; to ascertain, verify; to determine (*the tax due*) || *ref* to make sure

accè·so -sa [s] *adj* lit; turned on; on (*e.g., radio*); excited, aroused; bright (*color*)

accessìbile *adj* accessible; moderate (*price*)

accessióne *f* accession

accèsso *m* access, approach; admittance, entry; fit (*of anger, of coughing*)

accessò·rio -ria (-ri -rie) *adj* accessory || *m* accessory; (mach) accessory, attachment

accètta *f* hatchet, axe, cleaver; **tagliato con l'accetta** rough-hewn

accettàbile *adj* acceptable

accettare (accètto) *tr* to accept

accettazióne *f* acceptance; receiving room; (econ) acceptance

accèt·to -ta *adj* agreeable; welcome; **male accetto** unwelcome

accezióne *f* meaning, acceptation

acchiappafarfal·le *m* (-le) butterfly net

acchiappamó·sche *m* (-sche) fly catcher

acchiappare *tr* to grab, seize; (coll) to catch in the act

acchito *m* (billiards) break; **di primo acchito** at first

acciaccare §197 *tr* to crush; to trample upon; (coll) to lay low (*e.g., by illness*)

acciac·co *m* (-chi) illness, infirmity, ailment

acciaiare §287 *tr* to convert into steel; to strengthen with steel

acciaierìa *f* steel mill, steelworks

ac·ciàio *m* (-ciài) steel; **acciaio inossidabile** stainless steel

acciaiòlo *m* whetstone

acciambellare (acciambèllo) *tr* to shape in the form of a doughnut || *ref* to curl up

acciarino *m* flintlock; linchpin; (nav) war nose (*of a torpedo*)

accidèmpoli *interj* (slang) darn it!

accidentale *adj* accidental

accidenta·to -ta *adj* paralyzed; uneven, rough (*road*); broken (*ground*)

accidènte *m* accident; crack-up; (coll) paralytic stroke; (coll) hoot, fig; (coll) pest, menace (*child*); (mus) accidental; **accidenti!** (coll) darn!, damn!; **correre come un accidente** to run like the devil; **mandare un accidente a** to wish ill luck to; **per accidente** perchance

accìdia *f* sloth

accidió·so -sa [s] *adj* slothful

accigliare §280 *ref* to frown, knit one's brow

accìngere §126 *ref—***accingersi a** to get ready to

-àccio -àccia *suf adj & mf* (-acci -acce) no good, e.g., **gentaccia** no good people; good-for-nothing, e.g., **ragazzaccio** good-for-nothing boy

acciò or **acciocché** *conj* (poet) so that

acciottolare (acciòttolo) *tr* to pave with cobblestones

acciottola·to -ta *adj* cobblestone || *m* cobblestone pavement

acciottolì·o *m* (-i) clatter (*e.g., of dishes*)

accipìcchia *interj* (coll) darn it!

acciuffare *tr* to seize, grab, pinch (*a thief*)

acciu·ga *f* (-ghe) anchovy

acclamare *tr* to acclaim || *intr* to voice one's approval

acclamazióne *f* acclamation

acclimatare (acclìmato) *tr & ref* to acclimate

acclimatazióne *f* acclimatation

acclive *adj* (poet) steep

acclivi·tà *f* (-tà) acclivity

acclùdere §105 *tr* to enclose

acclu·so -sa *adj* enclosed

accoccare §197 (accòcco & accócco) *tr* (poet) to nock (*the arrow*)

accoccolare (accòccolo) *ref* to squat down

accodare (accódo) *tr* to line up || *ref* to line up, queue

accogliènte *adj* cozy, hospitable, inviting

accogliènza *f* reception, welcome

accògliere §127 *tr* to receive; to welcome; to grant (*a request*) || *ref* (poet) to gather

accoglitrice *f* receptionist

accòlito *m* acolyte, altar boy; follower

accollare (accòllo) *tr* to overload (*a cart*); **accollare qlco a qlcu** to charge s.o. with s.th || *intr* to go up to the neck (*said of a dress*) || *ref* to assume, take upon oneself

accolla·to -ta *adj* high-necked (*dress*); high-cut (*shoes*) || *f* accolade

accollatura *f* neck, neckhole

accòlta *f* (poet) gathering

accoltellare (accoltèllo) *tr* to knife

accomandante *m* limited partner

accomandatà·rio *m* (-ri) (law) general partner

accomàndita *f* (law) limited partnership

accomiatare *tr* to dismiss || *ref* to take leave

accomodaménto *m* arrangement; compromise; settlement

accomodante *adj* accommodating, obliging

accomodare (accòmodo) *tr* to arrange; to fix; to settle || *intr* to be convenient || *ref* to adapt oneself; to agree; to sit down; **si accomodi** have a seat, make yourself comfortable

accomodatura *f* arrangement; repair

accompagnaménto *m* retinue; cortege; (mus) accompaniment; (law) writ of mandamus; (mil) softening-up (*by gunfire*)

accompagnare *tr* to accompany; to escort; to follow; to match || *ref—***accompagnarsi a** or **con** to join

accompagna·tóre -trice *mf* escort; guide; (mus) accompanist

accomunare *tr* to mingle, mix; to unite, associate; to share

acconciaménto *m* arrangement

acconciare §128 (accóncio) *tr* to prepare for use; to arrange; to set (*e.g., the hair*) || *ref* to adorn oneself; to dress one's hair; to adapt oneself

acconcia·tóre -trice *mf* hairdresser

acconciatura _f_ hairdo; headdress
accón·cio -cia _adj_ (**-ci -ce**) proper, fitting
accondiscendènte _adj_ acquiescing, acquiescent
accondiscendènza _f_ acquiescence
accondiscéndere §245 _intr_ to acquiésce, consent; to yield
acconsentire (**acconsènto**) _intr_ to consent, acquiesce
acconsenziènte _adj_ consenting, acquiescing
accontentare (**accontènto**) _tr_ to satisfy, please || _ref_ to be satisfied, be pleased
accónto _m_ installment
accoppare (**accòppo**) _tr_ (coll) to kill; (coll) to beat to death || _ref_ (coll) to get killed
accoppiaménto _m_ pairing; mating; (mach) parallel operation
accoppiare §287 (**accòppio**) _tr_ to couple, pair, cross (_e.g., animals_) || _ref_ to mate, copulate
accoppiata _f_ daily double (_in races_)
accoraménto _m_ sadness, sorrow
accorare (**accòro**) _tr_ to stab to death; to sadden || _ref_ to sadden, grieve
accora·to -ta _adj_ saddened, grieving
accorciare §128 (**accórcio**) _tr_ & _ref_ to shorten; to shrink
accorciatura _f_ shortening; shrinking
accordare (**accòrdo**) _tr_ to harmonize (_colors_); to reconcile (_people_); to tune up; to grant; (gram) to make agree || _ref_ to agree; to match
accorda·to -ta _adj_ tuned up || _m_ (econ) credit limit
accorda·tóre -trice _mf_ (mus) tuner
accordatura _f_ tuning
accòrdo _m_ agreement, accordance; (law) mutual consent; (mus) harmony; **d'accordo** O.K., agreed; **d'accordo con** in accord with; **di comune accordo** with one accord; **essere d'accordo** to agree; **mettersi d'accordo** to come to an agreement
accòrgere §249 _ref_ to perceive, notice; **accorgersi di** to become aware of, realize; **senza accorgersi** inadvertently
accorgiménto _m_ smartness; device, trick
accórrere §139 _intr_ (ESSERE) to run up, rush up
accortézza _f_ alertness; shrewdness, perspicacity
accòr·to -ta _adj_ alert; shrewd, perspicacious
accosciare §128 (**accòscio**) _ref_ to squat
accostàbile _adj_ approachable
accostaménto _m_ approach; combination (_e.g., of colors_)
accostare (**accòsto**) _tr_ to approach; to bring near; to leave (_a door_) ajar || _intr_ to be near; to cling, adhere; (naut) to come alongside; (naut) to maneuver alongside a pier; (naut) to change direction, haul || _ref_ to approach, come near; to cling (_e.g., to a faith_)
accosta·to -ta _adj_ ajar
accò·sto -sta _adj_ (coll) near || _m_ approach; help || **accosto** _adv_ near; **accosto a** near, close to
accovacciare §128 _ref_ to crouch
accovonare (**accovóno**) _tr_ to sheave
accozzàglia _f_ hodgepodge; motley crowd
accozzare (**accòzzo**) _tr_ to jumble up; to collect, gather (_people_) together || _ref_ to collect, congregate
accòzzo _m_ jumble, medley
accreditàbile _adj_ chargeable (_e.g., account_); creditable
accreditaménto _m_ crediting
accreditare (**accrédito**) _tr_ to credit, believe; to accredit (_an ambassador_); to credit (_one's account_)
accredita·to -ta _adj_ confirmed (_news_); accredited
accréscere §142 _tr_ & _ref_ to increase
accresciménto _m_ increase
accucciare §128 _ref_ to curl up (_said of dogs_)
accudire §176 _tr_ (coll) to attend (_a sick person_) || _intr_—**accudire a** to take care of
acculturazióne _f_ acculturation
accumulare (**accùmulo**) _tr, intr_ & _ref_ to accumulate; to gather
accumulatóre _m_ storage battery
accumulazióne _f_ accumulation
accuratézza _f_ care, carefulness
accura·to -ta _adj_ careful, painstaking
accusa _f_ accusation, charge; **pubblica accusa** (law) public prosecutor
accusare _tr_ to accuse, charge; to betray; to acknowledge (_receipt_); (cards) to declare, bid
accusati·vo -va _adj_ & _m_ accusative
accusa·to -ta _adj_ accused || _mf_ defendant
accusatóre -trice _mf_ accuser; **pubblico accusatore** (law) public prosecutor, district attorney
accusatò·rio -ria _adj_ (**-ri -rie**) accusatory, accusing
acèfa·lo -la _adj_ headless; without the first page (_said of a manuscript_)
acèr·bo -ba _adj_ unripe, green, sour
àcero _m_ maple tree, sugar maple
acèrri·mo -ma _adj_ bitter, fierce
acetato _m_ acetate
acèti·co -ca _adj_ (**-ci -che**) acetic
acetificare §197 (**acetifico**) _tr_ to acetify
acetilène _m_ acetylene
acéto _m_ vinegar; **aceto aromatico** aromatic spirits; **sotto aceto** pickled
acetóne _m_ acetone
acetósa [s] _f_ (bot) sorrel
acetosèlla [s] _f_ wood sorrel
acetó·so -sa [s] _adj_ vinegarish || _f_ see **acetosa**
Acherónte _m_ Acheron
Achille _m_ Achilles
acidificare §197 (**acidifico**) _tr_ to acidify
acidi·tà _f_ (**-tà**) acidity; **acidità di stomaco** heartburn
àci·do -da _adj_ acid, sour || _m_ acid; **sapere d'acido** to taste sour
acìdu·lo -la _adj_ acidulous
àcino _m_ berry (_of grapes_); bead (_of rosary_)
acme _f_ acme; crisis
acne _f_ acne

acònito *m* (bot) monkshood

àcqua *f* water; rain; purity (*e.g., of a diamond*); acqua a catinelle pouring rain; acqua alta high water; acqua corrente running water; acqua dolce fresh water; drinking water; acqua in bocca! mum's the word!; acqua morta stagnant water; acqua ossigenata hydrogen peroxide; acqua potabile drinking water; acqua salata salt water; acqua viva spring; all'acqua di rose very mild; avere l'acqua alla gola to be in dire straits; della più bell'acqua of the first water; fare acqua to leak (*said of a boat*); fare un buco nell'acqua to waste one's efforts; portare acqua al mare to carry coals to Newcastle; prendere l'acqua to get wet; sott'acqua (fig) underhand; tirare l'acqua al proprio mulino to be grist to one's mill; versare acqua in un cesto to waste one's efforts

acquafòrte *f* (acquefòrti) etching

acquaforti•sta *mf* (-sti -ste) etcher

ac•quàio -quàia (-quài -quàie) *adj* watering (*trough*) || *m* sink

acquaiò•lo -la *adj* water || *m* water carrier; (sports) water boy

acquamarina *f* (acquemarine) aquamarine

acquaplano *m* aquaplane

acquaràgia *f* turpentine

acquarèllo *m* var of acquerello

acquà•rio *m* (-ri) aquarium || Acquario *m* (astr) Aquarius

acquartierare (acquartièro) *tr* (mil) to quarter || *ref* to be quartered

acquasanta *f* holy water

acquasantièra *f* (eccl) stoup

acquàti•co -ca *adj* (-ci -che) aquatic, water

acquattare *ref* to crouch, squat

acquavite *f* brandy; liquor, rum

acquazzóne *m* downpour, heavy shower

acquedótto *m* aqueduct

àcque•o -a *adj* aqueous, watery

acquerelli•sta *mf* (-sti -ste) watercolorist

acquerèllo *m* watercolor; watered-down wine

acqueràgiola *f* fine drizzle

acquiescènte *adj* acquiescent

acquietare (acquièto) *tr* to pacify, placate || *ref* to quiet down

acquirènte *mf* buyer, purchaser; il miglior acquirente the highest bidder

acquisire §176 *tr* to acquire

acquisi•tóre -trice *mf* salesperson, agent || *m* salesman || *f* saleswoman

acquistare *tr* to purchase, buy; to acquire; to gain (*e.g., ground*) || *intr* to improve

acquisto *m* buy, purchase; acquisition

acquitrino *m* marsh

acquitrinó•so -sa [s] *adj* marshy

acquolina *f*—far venire l'acquolina in bocca a to make one's mouth water

acquó•so -sa [s] *adj* watery

acre *adj* sour; pungent; acrid; bitter (*words*)

acrèdine *f* acrimony, sourness

acrimònia *f* acrimony

acro *m* acre

acròba•ta *mf* (-ti -te) acrobat

acrobàti•co -ca (-ci -che) *adj* acrobatic || *f* acrobatics

acrobatismo *m* acrobatics

acrobazia *f* acrobatics; stunt, feat

acrocòro *m* plateau

acrònimo *m* acronym

acròpo•li *f* (-li) acropolis

acròsti•co *m* (-ci) acrostic

acuire §176 *tr* to sharpen, whet

acuità *f* acuity

acùle•o *m* (-i) quill; prickle, thorn; stinger (*of an insect*)

acume *m* acumen

acuminare (acùmino) *tr* to sharpen, whet

acumina•to -ta *adj* pointed, sharp

acùsti•co -ca (-ci -che) *adj* acoustic(al) || *f* acoustics

acutézza *f* acuteness, sharpness

acutizzare [ddzz] *tr & ref* to sharpen

acu•to -ta *adj* acute, sharp || *m* high note

ad *prep* var of a before words beginning with a vowel

adagiare §290 *tr* to lay down gently; to lower gently || *ref* to lie down; to stretch out

adà•gio *m* (-gi) adage; (mus) adagio || *adv* slowly; gently; (mus) adagio

Adamo *m* Adam

adattàbile *adj* adaptable

adattaménto *m* adaptation; adaptability

adattare *tr* to adapt, fit || *ref* to adapt oneself; to become adapted; adattarsi a to go with; to match; to be becoming to

adat•to -ta *adj* suitable, adequate

addebitaménto *m* debiting

addebitare (addébito) *tr* to debit; addebitare una spesa a qlcu to debit s.o. with an expense

addébito *m* charge; (com) debit; elevare l'addebito di qlco a qlcu (law) to charge s.o. with s.th

addènda *mpl* addenda

addèndo *m* (math) addend

addensare (addènso) *tr* to thicken || *ref* to thicken; to gather, throng

addentare (addènto) *tr* to bite || *ref* (mach) to mesh

addentatura *f* bite; (carp) tongue (*of tongue and groove*)

addentella•to -ta *adj* toothed, notched || *m* chance, occasion; (archit) toothing

addentrare (addéntro) *tr* to penetrate || *ref* to penetrate; to proceed

addèntro *adv* inside; addentro in into; inside of

addestraménto *m* training

addestrare (addèstro) *tr & ref* to train

addestra•tóre -trice *mf* trainer

addét•to -ta *adj* assigned; attached; pertaining || *m* attaché; addetto stampa press secretary

addì *adv* the (+ *a certain date*), e.g., addì 27 gennaio the 27th of January

addiàc•cio *m* (-ci) sheepfold; bivouac

addiètro *m* (naut) stern; per l'addietro in the past || *adv* behind; ago; dare

addietro to back up; **lasciarsi addietro** to delay; **tempo addietro** some time ago; **tirarsi addietro** to back away

addì•o *m* (**-i**) farewell; **dare l'addio to** say good-bye; **dare l'estremo addio to** pay one's last respects; **fare gli addii to** say good-bye || *interj* farewell, good-bye!

addire §151 *tr* (poet) to consecrate || *ref* to be suitable, be becoming; **addirsi a** to be becoming to

addirittura *adv* directly; even, without hesitation; absolutely, positively

addirizzare *tr* to straighten up; **addirizzare le gambe ai cani** to try the impossible

additare *tr* to point out

additi•vo -va *adj & m* additive

addivenire §282 *intr* (ESSERE)—**addivenire a** to come to, reach (*e.g., an agreement*)

addizionale *adj* additional || *f* supplementary tax

addizionare (**addizióno**) *tr & intr* to add

addizionatrice *f* adding machine

addizióne *f* addition

addobbaménto *m* adornment, decoration

addobbare (**addòbbo**) *tr* to adorn, bedeck, decorate

addobba•tóre -trice *mf* decorator

addòbbo *m* adornment, decoration; hangings (*in a church*)

addocilire §176 *tr* to soften up

addolcire §176 *tr* to sweeten; to calm down || *ref* to mellow, soften

addolorare (**addolóro**) *tr & ref* to grieve; **addolorarsi per** to grieve over, lament

addolora•to -ta *adj* sorrowful || **l'Addolorata** *f* (eccl) Our Lady of Sorrows

addòme *m* abdomen

addomesticàbile *adj* tamable

addomesticaménto *m* taming

addomesticare §197 (**addomèstico**) *tr* to tame; to accustom || *ref* to become accustomed

addomestica•to -ta *adj* tame, domesticated

addominale *adj* abdominal

addormentare (**addorménto**) *tr* to put to sleep; to numb || *ref* to fall asleep; to be asleep (*said of a limb*)

addormenta•to -ta *adj* asleep; numbed

addossare (**addòsso**) *tr* to put on; **addossare qlco a qlco** to lean s.th against s.th; **addossare qlco a qlcu** to put s.th on s.o.; (fig) to entrust s.o. with s.th || *ref* to take upon oneself; to crowd together; **addossarsi a** to lean against; to crowd

addossa•to -ta *adj* leaning

addòsso *adv* on; on oneself, on one's back; about oneself; **addosso a** on, upon; against; **avere la sfortuna addosso** to be always unlucky; **dare addosso a qlcu** to assail s.o.; **levarsi d'addosso** to get rid of; **levarsi i panni d'addosso** to take the shirt off one's back

addót•to -ta *adj* adduced, alleged

addottorare (**addottóro**) *tr* to confer the doctor's degree on || *ref* to receive the doctor's degree

addurre §102 *tr* to adduce; to allege; (poet) to bring

Ade *m* Hades

adeguare (**adéguo**) *tr* to equalize; to bring in line || *ref* to conform, adapt oneself

adegua•to -ta *adj* adequate

adeguazióne *f* equalization

adémpiere §163 *tr* to fulfill, accomplish || *ref* to come true

adempiménto *m* fulfillment, discharge (*of one's duty*)

adempire §176 *tr* to fulfill, accomplish || *ref* to come true

adenòide *adj* adenoid || **adenoidi** *fpl* adenoids

adèpto *m* follower; initiate

aderènte *adj* adherent || *mf* adherent, supporter

aderènza *f* adherence; (mach) friction; (pathol) adhesion; **aderenze** connections

aderire §176 *intr* to adhere; to stick; **aderire a** to grant (*e.g., a request*); to concur with; to subscribe to

adescare §197 (**adésco**) *tr* to lure, bait, entice; (mach) to prime (*a pump*)

adesióne *f* adhesion; support; (phys) adherence

adesi•vo -va *adj & m* adhesive

adèsso *adv* now, just now; **da adesso in poi** from now on; **per adesso** for the time being

adiacènte *adj* adjacent

adiacènza *f* adjacency; **adiacenze** vicinity

adianto *m* (bot) maidenhair

adibire §176 *tr* to assign; to use

àdipe *m* fat

adipó•so -sa [s] *adj* adipose

adirare *ref* to get angry

adira•to -ta *adj* angry, mad

adire §176 *tr* to apply to (*the court*); to enter into possession of (*an inheritance*)

adocchiare §287 (**adòcchio**) *tr* to eye; to ogle; to spot

adolescènte *adj & mf* adolescent

adolescènza *f* adolescence

adombrare (**adómbro**) *tr* to shade; to hide, veil || *ref* to shy (*said of a horse*); (fig) to take umbrage

Adóne *m* Adonis

adontare (**adónto**) *tr* (obs) to offend || *ref* to take offense

adoperare (**adòpero & adópero**) *tr* to use, employ || *ref* to exert oneself; to do one's best

adoràbile *adj* adorable

adorare (**adóro**) *tr* to adore; to worship || *intr* (archaic) to pray

adora•tóre -trice *mf* worshiper || *m* (joc) admirer, suitor

adorazióne *f* adoration, worship

adornare (**adórno**) *tr* to adorn || *ref* to bedeck oneself

adór•no -na *adj* adorned, bedecked; (poet) fine, beautiful

adottante *mf* (law) adopter

adottare (adòtto) *tr* to adopt
adotti·vo -va *adj* adoptive; foster *(child)*
adozióne *f* adoption
Adriàti·co -ca *adj* **(-ci -che)** Adriatic
‖ **Adriatico** *m* Adriatic
adulare (àdulo) *tr* to flatter; to fawn on
adula·tóre -trice *mf* flatterer
adulatò·rio -ria *adj* **(-ri -rie)** flattering; fawning
adulazióne *f* adulation; fawning
adulterante *adj & m* adulterant
adulteri·no -na *adj* bastard; adulterated
adultè·rio *m* **(-ri)** adultery
adùlte·ro -ra *adj* adulterous ‖ *m* adulterer ‖ *f* adulteress
adul·to -ta *adj & mf* adult
adunanza *f* assembly
adunare *tr & ref* to assemble, gather
adunata *f* reunion, meeting; (mil) muster
adun·co -ca *adj* **(-chi -che)** hooked, crooked
adunghiare §287 *tr* (poet) to claw
adu·sto -sta *adj* skinny; (poet) burnt
aerare (àero) *tr* to air, ventilate
aerazióne *f* aeration; airing
aère·o -a *adj* aerial; air; overhead; high, lofty; airy, fanciful ‖ *m* airplane; (rad & telv) aerial
aerobrigata *f* (mil) wing
aerocistèrna *f* (aer) tanker
aerodinàmi·co -ca (-ci -che) *adj* aerodynamic(al); streamlined ‖ *f* aerodynamics
aeròdromo *m* airfield, airdrome
aerofaro *m* airport beacon
aerofotogram·ma *m* **(-mi)** aerial photograph
aerogiro *m* helicopter
aerògrafo *m* spray gun *(for painting)*
aerolìnea *f* airline; **aerolinea principale** trunkline
aeròlito *m* aerolite, meteorite
aeromarìtti·mo -ma *adj* air-sea
aeròmetro *m* aerometer
aeromòbile *m* aircraft; **aeromobile senza pilota** drone, pilotless aircraft
aeromodellismo *m* model-airplane building
aeromodelli·sta *mf* **(-sti -ste)** model-airplane builder
aeromodèllo *m* model airplane
aeromotóre *m* windmill; aircraft motor
aeronàu·ta *m* **(-ti)** aeronaut
aeronàuti·co -ca (-ci -che) *adj* aeronautic(al) ‖ *f* aeronautics
aeronave *f* airship, aircraft
aeroplano *m* airplane
aeropòrto *m* airport, airfield
aeroportuale *adj* airport
aerorazzo [ddzz] *m* rocket spaceship
aeroriméssa *f* hangar
aerosbar·co *m* **(-chi)** landing of airborne troops
aeroservì·zio [s] *m* **(-zi)** air service
aerosilurante [s] *f* torpedo plane
aerosiluro [s] *m* aerial torpedo
aerosòl [s] *m* aerosol
aerosostenta·to -ta [s] *adj* airborne
aerospaziale *adj* aerospace
aerospà·zio *m* **(-zi)** aerospace

aerostàti·co -ca (-ci -che) *adj* aerostatic(al) ‖ *f* aerostatics
aeròstato *m* aerostat
aerostazióne *f* air terminal
aerotas·sì *m* **(-sì)** taxiplane
aerotrasportare (aerotraspòrto) *tr* to airlift
aerotrasporta·to -ta *adj* airlifted; airborne
aerovìa *f* (aer) beam *(course indicated by a radio beam)*; (aer) air lane
afa *f* sultriness; **fare afa a** (coll) to be a pain in the neck to
afèresi *f* apheresis
affàbile *adj* affable, agreeable
affaccendare (affaccèndo) *tr* to busy ‖ *ref* to busy oneself, bustle
affaccenda·to -ta *adj* busy, bustling; occupied with busywork
affacciare §128 *tr* to show or display at the window; to bring forward *(e.g., an objection)*; to raise *(a doubt)* ‖ *ref* to show oneself *(at the door or window)*; to present itself *(said of a doubt)*
affaccia·to -ta *adj* facing
affagottare (affagòtto) *tr* to bundle ‖ *ref* to bundle up; to dress sloppily
affamare *tr* to starve
affama·to -ta *adj* starved, ravenous ‖ *mf* starveling; hungry person; wretch
affannare *tr* to worry, to afflict ‖ *intr* to pant; to be out of breath ‖ *ref* to worry; to bustle around
affanna·to -ta *adj* panting; out of breath; worried
affanno *m* shortness of breath; grief, sorrow
affannó·so -sa [s] *adj* panting; wearisome
affardellare (affardèllo) *tr* to bundle together; (mil) to pack
affare *m* affair, matter; business; condition, quality; deal; **affari** business; **affari esteri** foreign affairs; **un buon affare** a good deal; a bargain
affarismo *m* sharp business practice
affari·sta *mf* **(-sti -ste)** unscrupulous operator
affarìsti·co -ca *adj* **(-ci -che)** sharp
affascinante *adj* fascinating, charming
affascinare (affàscino) *tr* to fascinate, charm; to seduce; to spellbind ‖ **(affascino)** *tr* to bundle, to sheave
affascina·tóre -trice *adj* fascinating, charming ‖ *mf* charmer, spellbinder
affastellare (affastèllo) *tr* to fagot *(twigs)*: to sheave, bundle *(e.g., hay)*; to pile, heap *(wood, crops, etc)*; (fig) to jumble up
affaticare §197 *tr* to fatigue, tire, weary ‖ *ref* to get tired; to weary; to toil
affatica·to -ta *adj* weary, tired
affatto *adv* quite, entirely; **niente affatto** not at all; **non . . . affatto** not at all
affatturare *tr* to bewitch; to adulterate *(e.g., food)*
affermare (affèrmo) *tr* to affirm, assert ‖ *intr* to nod assent ‖ *ref* to take hold *(said, e.g., of a new product)*
affermati·vo -va *adj & f* affirmative
affermazióne *f* affirmation; assertion,

statement; success (*e.g., of a new product*); (sports) victory

afferrare (affèrro) *tr* to grab, grasp; to catch, nab || *ref* to cling

affettare (affétto) *tr* to slice; to cut up || (affètto) *tr* to affect

affetta·to -ta *adj* affected || *m* cold cuts

affettatrice *f* slicing machine

affettazióne *f* affectation

affetti·vo -va *adj* emotional

affèt·to -ta *adj* afflicted, burdened || *m* affection, love; feeling

affettuosi·tà [s] *f* (-tà) love, affection

affettuó·so -sa [s] *adj* affectionate, loving, tender

affezionare (affezióno) *tr* to inspire affection in || *ref*—**affezionarsi a** to become fond of

affeziona·to -ta *adj* affectionate, loving; Suo affezionatissimo best regards; tuo affezionatissimo love, as ever

affezióne *f* affection

affiancare §197 *tr* to place next; to favor, help; (mil) to flank

affiatamento *m* harmony; teamwork

affiatare *tr* to harmonize

affibbiare §287 *tr* to buckle, fasten; to deliver (*a blow*); to play (*a trick*); to slap (*a fine*)

affidamento *m* consignment, delivery; trust, confidence; **dare affidamento** to be trustworthy; **fare affidamento su** to rely upon

affidare *tr* to entrust; to commit (*to memory*); **affidare qlco a qlcu** to entrust s.o with s.th || *ref* to trust; **affidarsi a** to trust in

affievolimento *m* weakening

affievolire §176 *tr* to weaken || *ref* to grow weaker

affiggere §103 *tr* to post; to fix (*one's eyes or glance*) || *ref* to gaze, stare

affigliare §280 *tr & ref* var of affiliare

affilacoltèl·li *m* (-li) steel (*for sharpening knives*)

affilara·sóio *m* (-sói) strop

affilare *tr* to sharpen, hone, whet; to make thin || *ref* to become thin

affila·to -ta *adj* sharp, sharpened; thin || *f* sharpening

affila·tóio *m* (-tói) sharpener

affilatrice *f* grindstone

affiliare §287 *tr* to affiliate || *ref* to become affiliated; **affiliarsi a** to become a member of

affilia·to -ta *adj* affiliated || *mf* affiliate; foster child; member of a secret society

affiliazióne *f* affiliation

affinare *tr* to sharpen; to refine, purify; to improve (*e.g., one's style*) || *ref* to improve

affinché *conj* so that, in order that; affinché non lest

affine *adj* akin, related; similar || *mf* in-law || *m* kinsman || *f* kinswoman || *adv*—affine di in order to

affini·tà *f* (-tà) affinity

affiochire §176 *tr* to make hoarse; to weaken || *ref* to become hoarse; to grow dim (*said of a candle*)

affioramento *m* surfacing; (min) outcrop

affiorare (affióro) *intr* to surface, emerge; to appear, to show

affissare *tr* (poet) to fix || *ref* to concentrate; (poet) to gaze

affissióne *f* posting, bill posting

affis·so -sa *adj* fixed; posted || *m* bill, poster; door or window; (gram) affix

affittacàme·re *m* (-re) landlord || *f* landlady

affittanza *f* rent

affittare *tr* to rent || *ref*—si affitta for rent

affitto *m* rent, rental; **dare in affitto** to rent (*to grant by lease*); **prendere in affitto** to rent (*to take by lease*)

affittuà·rio -ria *mf* (-ri -rie) renter; tenant

affliggènte *adj* tormenting, distressing

affliggere §104 *tr* to afflict, distress || *ref* to grieve

afflìt·to -ta *adj* afflicted, grieving || *mf* afflicted person, wretch

afflizióne *f* affliction, distress

afflosciare §128 (afflòscio) *tr* to cause to sag; to weaken || *ref* to droop; to sag; to be deflated; to faint

affloscire §176 *tr & ref* var of afflosciare

affluènte *adj & m* confluent

affluènza *f* confluence; abundance; crowd

affluire §176 *intr* (ESSERE) to flow (*said of river*); to flock (*said of people*); to pour in (*said of earnings*)

afflusso *m* flow

affogamento *m* drowning

affogare §209 (affógo) *tr* to drown; to smother || *intr* (ESSERE) to drown

affoga·to -ta *adj* drowned; poached (*egg*)

affollamento *m* crowd, throng

affollare (affóllo & affòllo) *tr* to crowd; to overcome || *ref* to crowd

affolla·to -ta *adj* crowded

affondamento *m* sinking

affondami·ne *m* (-ne) mine layer

affondare (affóndo) *tr* to sink; to stick || *ref* to sink

affondata *f* (aer) nosedive

affóndo *m* (fencing) lunge || *adv* deeply

afforestare (afforèsto) *tr* to reforest

affossare (affòsso) *tr* to ditch; (fig) to table (*e.g., a proposal*); to hollow out || *ref* to become sunken or hollow (*said, e.g., of cheeks*)

affossatóre *m* ditchdigger; gravedigger

affrancare §197 *tr* to set free; to free; to redeem (*a property*); to stamp || *ref* to free oneself; to take heart

affrancatrice *f* postage meter

affrancatura *f* stamp, stamping

affràngere §179 *tr* to weary; (obs) to break down (*the spirit*)

affran·to -ta *adj* weary; broken down, broken-hearted

affratellamento *m* fraternization

affratellare (affratèllo) *tr* to bind in brotherly love || *ref* to fraternize

affrescare §197 (affrésco) *tr* to fresco; to paint in fresco

affré·sco *m* (**-schi**) fresco
affrettare (**affrétto**) *tr* & *ref* to hurry, hasten
affretta· to -ta *adj* hurried
affrontare (**affrónto**) *tr* to face, confront || *ref* to meet in combat; to come to blows
affronta·to -ta *adj*—**affrontati** (herald) combattant
affrónto *m* affront, offense
affumicare §197 (**affùmico**) *tr* to smoke; to blacken; to smoke out; to smoke (*meat or fish*)
affumica·to -ta *adj* smoked; dark (*glasses*)
affusolare [s] (**affùsolo**) *tr* & *ref* to taper
affusola·to -ta [s] *adj* tapered; slender
affusto *m* gun carriage
afga·no -na *adj* & *mf* Afghan
àfo·no -na *adj* voiceless
afori·sma *m* (**-smi**) aphorism
afó·so -sa [s] *adj* sultry
Africa, l' *f* Africa
africa·no -na *adj* & *mf* African
afrodisìa·co -ca *adj* & *m* (**-ci -che**) aphrodisiac
afta *m* mouth ulcer; **afta epizootica** (vet) foot-and-mouth disease
àgata *f* agate || **Agata** *f* Agatha
agènda *f* notebook; agenda
agènte *adj* active || *m* agent; broker; merchant; officer; **agente delle tasse** tax collector; **agente di cambio** stockbroker; money changer; **agente di commercio** broker, commission merchant; **agente di custodia** jailer; **agente di polizia** police officer, policeman; **agente di spionaggio** informer; **agente provocatore** agent provocateur
agenzìa *f* agency; office, branch; **agenzia immobiliare** real-estate office
agevolare (**agévolo**) *tr* to facilitate, help
agevolazióne *f* facility; **agevolazione di pagamento** easy terms
agévole *adj* easy
agevolézza *f* facility
aggallare *intr* to come to the surface
agganciaménto *m* docking (*in space*); (rr) coupling
agganciare §128 *tr* to hook; (rr) to couple; (mil) to engage (*the enemy*)
aggàn·cio *m* (**-ci**) docking (*in space*); (rr) coupling
aggég·gio *m* (**-gi**) gadget
aggettivale *adj* adjectival
aggettivo *m* adjective
agghiacciaménto *m* freezing
agghiacciante *adj* hair-raising, frightful
agghiacciare §128 *tr* to freeze || *ref* to freeze; to be horrified
agghiaccia·to -ta *adj* frozen, icy
agghindare *tr* & *ref* to preen, primp
àg·gio *m* (**-gi**) agio; **fare aggio** to be at a premium
aggiogare §209 (**aggiógo**) *tr* to yoke
aggiornaménto *m* adjournment (*e.g., of a meeting*); bringing up to date
aggiornare (**aggiórno**) *tr* to bring up to date; to adjourn || *ref* to keep up with the times

aggiraménto *m* surrounding, outflanking
aggirare *tr* to surround, outflank; to swindle || *ref* to roam, wander; **aggirarsi su** to approximate; to be almost
aggiudicare §197 (**aggiùdico**) *tr* to adjudicate, award || *ref* to win
aggiudicazióne *f* adjudication, award
aggiùngere §183 *tr* to add; to join, connect || *ref* to be added; to join
aggiunta *f* addition
aggiuntare *tr* to attach, join
aggiun·to -ta *adj* & *m* associate, assistant, deputy || *f* see **aggiunta**
aggiustàbile *adj* repairable
aggiustaménto *m* settlement; adjustment; (mil) correction (*of fire*)
aggiustare *tr* to fix, repair; to adjust; (mil) to correct (*cannon fire*); **aggiustare per le feste** (coll) to fix; (coll) to give a good beating to || *ref* (archaic) to come closer; (coll) to manage; (coll) to come to an agreement
aggiusta·tóre -trice *mf* repairer, fixer || *m* repairman
aggiustatura *f* fixing, repairing, repair
agglomerare (**agglòmero**) *tr* & *ref* to pile up; to crowd together
agglomerato *m* built-up area; **agglomerato urbano** urban center
agglutinare (**agglùtino**) *tr* & *ref* to agglutinate
agglutinazióne *f* agglutination
aggobbire §176 *tr* to bend, bend over || *intr* (ESSERE) & *ref* to hunch over
aggomitolare (**aggomìtolo**) *tr* to coil || *ref* to curl up
aggradare *intr* (with *dat*) (poet) to please; **come Le aggrada** as you please
aggradire §176 *tr* to appreciate || *intr* (poet) (with *dat*) to please
aggraffare *tr* to hook; to grab; to join (*metal sheets*) with a double seam; to stitch, staple
aggraffatrice *f* folding machine; (mach) can sealer
aggranchire §176 *tr* to benumb; to deaden, stupefy || *intr* to become numb
aggrappare *tr* to grab; to clamp || *ref* to cling
aggravaménto *m* aggravation
aggravante *adj* (law) aggravating (*circumstances*)
aggravare *tr* to aggravate; to overload (*e.g., one's stomach*) || *ref* to get worse
aggrà·vio *m* (**-vi**) burden (*e.g., of taxes*); **fare aggravio a qlcu di qlco** to impute s.th to s.o.
aggraziare §287 *tr* to embellish; to render graceful || *ref* to win, gain; to ingratiate oneself
aggrazia·to -ta *adj* graceful; polite
aggredire §176 *tr* to assail, attack, assault
aggregare §209 (**aggrègo**) *tr* & *ref* to join, unite
aggrega·to -ta *adj* adjunct || *m* aggregation
aggressióne *f* aggression

aggressi·vo -va *adj* aggressive ‖ *m* (mil) poison gas
aggressóre *m* aggressor
aggricciare §128 *tr* to wrinkle; (slang) to knit (*e.g., the brow*) ‖ *ref* (poet) to shiver
aggrinzare *tr & ref* to wrinkle
aggrinzire §176 *tr & ref* var of **aggrinzare**
aggrondare (**aggróndo**) *tr* to knit (*the brow*)
aggrottare (**aggròtto**) *tr* to knit (*the brow*)
aggrovigliare §280 *tr* to tangle, entangle ‖ *ref* to become entangled
aggrumare *tr & ref* to clot; to coagulate
aggruppare *tr* to group
agguagliare §280 *tr* to level; to equalize; to compare
agguantare *tr* to grab; to nab; (coll) to hit; **agguantare per il collo** to grab by the neck ‖ *ref*—**agguantarsi a** to get hold of
agguato *m* ambush; **cadere in un agguato** to fall into a trap; **stare in agguato** to wait in ambush
agguerrire §176 *tr* to train for war; to inure to war; to inure
aghétto *m* shoestring; (mil) lanyard
agiatézza *f* comfort, wealth; **vivere nell'agiatezza** to live in comfort
agia·to -ta *adj* well-to-do, comfortable
àgile *adj* agile, nimble; prompt
agili·tà *f* (-tà) agility, nimbleness; promptness
à·gio *m* (-gi) comfort; opportunity; ease; **agi** conveniences, comforts; **a Suo agio** at your convenience; **aver agio** to have time; **stare a proprio agio** to feel at ease; to be comfortable; **vivere negli agi** to live comfortably
agiografìa *f* hagiography
agiògrafo *m* hagiographer
agire §176 *intr* to act; to work; (theat) to act, perform
agitare (**àgito**) *tr* to agitate, shake; to stir; to stir up; to discuss (*e.g., a problem*) ‖ *ref* to toss; to shake; to stir; to get excited
agita·to -ta *adj* rough, choppy (*sea*); troubled, upset ‖ *mf* violently insane person
agita·tóre -trice *mf* agitator ‖ *m* shaker
agitazióne *f* agitation
agli §4
agliàce·o -a *adj* garlicky
à·glio *m* (-gli) garlic
agnellino *m* little lamb, lambkin
agnèllo *m* lamb
agnizióne *f* recognition
agnòsti·co -ca *adj & mf* (-ci -che) agnostic
a·go *m* (-ghi) needle; pointer (*of scales*); stem (*of valve*)
agognare (**agógno**) *tr* to covet
agóne *m* contest; arena
agonìa *f* agony, death struggle; anguish
agonìsti·co -ca *adj* (-ci -che) competitive, aggressive (*spirit*); athletic (*competition*) ‖ *f* athletics

agonizzare [ddzz] *intr* to agonize, be in agony; (fig) to die out
agopuntura *f* acupuncture
ago·ràio *m* (-rài) needle case
agosta·no -na *adj* August, e.g., **pomeriggio agostano** August afternoon
agostinia·no -na *adj & m* Augustinian
agósto *m* August
agrà·rio -ria (-ri -rie) *adj & m* agrarian ‖ *m* landlord ‖ *f* agriculture
agrèste *adj* country
agrìco·lo -la *adj* agricultural
agricoltóre *m* farmer; agriculturist
agricoltura *f* agriculture
agrifò·glio *m* (-gli) holly
agrimensóre *m* surveyor
agrimensura *f* surveying
a·gro -gra *adj* sour, bitter ‖ *m* citrus juice; sourness, bitterness; surrounding country
agrodólce *adj* sweet and sour; (fig) acidulous (*tone*)
agronomìa *f* agronomy
agrònomo *m* agronomist
agrume *m* citrus (*tree and fruit*); **agrumi** citrus fruit
agucchiare §287 *intr* to knit or sew idly
agùglia *f* spire; top; (ichth) gar; (poet) eagle; (obs) needle
aguzzare *tr* to sharpen; to whet (*the appetite*)
aguzzino [ddzz] *m* slave driver; jailer
aguz·zo -za *adj* sharp, pointed
ah *interj* ah!, aha!; ha!
ahi *interj* ouch!
ahimè *interj* alas!
àia *f* yard, barnyard; threshing floor; governess ‖ **L'Aia** *f* the Hague
Aiace *m* Ajax
àio *m* (-ài) tutor
aiòla *f* lawn; flower bed
àire *m* push; short run (*preparing for a jump*); **dare l'aire a** to start off; **prendere l'aire** to take off
airóne *m* heron
aitante *adj* robust, stalwart
aiuòla *f* (poet) var of **aiola**
aiutante *adj* helping ‖ *mf* assistant ‖ *m* (mil) adjutant; **aiutante di campo** aide-de-camp; **aiutante di sanità** orderly
aiutare *tr* to help ‖ *ref* to strive; to help oneself; to help one another
aiutato *m* first assistant (*e.g., of a surgeon*)
aiuto *m* aid, help; assistant; first assistant (*of a surgeon*)
aizzare (**aìzzo**) *tr* to incite, to incite to riot; to sic (*a dog*)
al §4
a·la *f* (-li & -le) wing; sail, vane (*of windmill*); blade (*e.g., of fan*); brim (*of hat*); (football) end; **ala a freccia** backswept wing; **ala di popolo** throng; **fare ala a** to line up along
alabarda *f* halberd
alabardière *m* halberdier
alabastri·no -na *adj* alabaster; white as alabaster
alabastro *m* alabaster
àlacre *adj* eager, lively
alacrità *f* alacrity

alàg·gio *m* (-gi) hauling, towing
alamaro *m* braid, gimp
alambic·co *m* (-chi) still
alano *m* Great Dane
alare *adj* wing (*e.g., span*) || *m* andiron || *tr* to haul
Alasca, l' *f* Alaska
ala·to -ta *adj* winged, sublime
alba *f* dawn, daybreak
albagìa *f* haughtiness
albanése [s] *adj & mf* Albanian
Albanìa, l' *f* Albania
àlbatro *m* (orn) albatross
albeggiaménto *m* dawning
albeggiare §290 (**albéggio**) *intr* (ESSERE) to dawn; (poet) to sparkle (*said, e.g., of ice*) || *impers* (ESSERE)—**albeggia** the day dawns
alberare (**àlbero**) *tr* to plant (*trees*); to reforest; to hoist (*a mast*); to mast (*a ship*)
albera·to -ta *adj* tree-lined; (naut) masted
alberèllo *m* small tree; apothecary's jar
albergare §209 (**albèrgo**) *tr* to lodge; to put up at a hotel; (fig) to harbor || *intr* to lodge; to put up
alberga·tóre -trice *mf* hotelkeeper
alberghiè·ro -ra *adj* hotel
albèr·go *m* (-ghi) hotel; refuge; hospitality; **albergo diurno** day hostel; **albergo per la gioventù** youth hostel; **àlbero** *m* tree; poplar; (mach) shaft; (naut) mast; **albero a camme** (aut) camshaft; **albero a gomito** (aut) crankshaft; **albero di distribuzione** (aut) camshaft; **albero di Natale** Christmas tree; **albero di trasmissione** (aut) transmission; **albero genealogico** family tree
albicòc·ca *f* (-che) apricot
albicòc·co *m* (-chi) apricot tree
al·bo -ba *adj* (poet) white || *m* album; bulletin board; (law) roll; comic book; **albo d'onore** honor roll || *f* see **alba**
albóre *m* (poet) whiteness; (poet) dawn
album *m* (**album**) album, scrapbook
albume *m* albumen
albumina *f* albumin
àlca·li *m* (-li) alkali
alcali·no -na *adj* alkaline
alce *m* moose; elk
alchìmia *f* alchemy
alchimi·sta *m* (-sti) alchemist
alcióne *m* halcyon
alciò·nio -nia *adj* (-ni -nie) halcyon
àlco·le *m* alcohol
alcolici·tà *f* (-tà) alcoholic content
alcòli·co -ca *adj* (-ci -che) alcoholic || *m* alcoholic beverage
alcolismo *m* alcoholism
alcolizzare [ddzz] *tr* to intoxicate || *ref* to become intoxicated
alcolizza·to -ta [ddzz] *adj* intoxicated || *mf* alcoholic
alcool *m* (**alcool**) var of **alcole**
alcoolici·tà *f* (-tà) var of **alcolicità**
alcoòli·co -ca (-ci -che) *adj & m* var of **alcolico**
alcoolismo *m* var of **alcolismo**
alcoolizzare [ddzz] *tr* var of **alcolizzare**

alcoolizza·to -ta [ddzz] *adj & mf* var of **alcolizzato**
alcòva *f* bedroom; bed; alcove
alcunché *pron* something, anything
alcu·no -na *adj & pron* some; **alcu·ni -ne** some; quite a few, several, a good many
aldilà *m* life beyond, afterlife
àlea *f* chance, hazard; **correre l'alea** to try one's luck
aleggiare §290 (**aléggio**) *intr* to flutter; to flap the wings; to hover
aleróne *m* var of **alettone**
alesàg·gio *m* (-gi) (mach) bore
alesare (**aléso**) *tr* (mach) to bore
alesatóre *m* reamer
alesatrice *s* boring machine
Alessandria d'Egitto *f* Alexandria
alessandri·no -na *adj & mf* Alexandrian || *m* Alexandrine (*verse*)
Alessandro *m* Alexander; **Alessandro Magno** Alexander the Great
alétta *f* small wing; fin (*of fish*); (aer) tab; **aletta di compensazione** trim tab; **aletta parasole** (aut) sun visor
alettóne *m* (aer) aileron, flap
Aleuti·no -na *adj*—**Isole Aleutine** Aleutian Islands
al·fa *m* (-fa) alpha || *f* esparto
alfabèti·co -ca *adj* (-ci -che) alphabetical
alfabetizzazióne [ddzz] *f* teaching to read; learning to read
alfabèto *m* alphabet; code (*e.g., Morse*)
alfière *m* flagbearer, standardbearer; (chess) bishop
alfine *adv* finally, at last
al·ga *f* (-ghe) alga; **alga marina** seaweed
àlgebra *f* algebra
algèbri·co -ca *adj* (-ci -che) algebraic
Algèri *f* Algiers
Algeria, l' *f* Algeria
algeri·no -na *adj & mf* Algerian
aliante *m* (aer) glider
alianti·sta *mf* (-sti -ste) glider pilot
àli·bi *m* (-bi) alibi
alice *f* anchovy
alienàbile *adj* alienable
alienare (**alièno**) *tr* to alienate; to transfer, convey || *ref*—**alienarsi dalla ragione** to go out of one's mind
aliena·to -ta *adj* alienated || *mf* insane person; dispossessed person
alienazióne *f* alienation
alieni·sta *mf* (-sti -ste) alienist
alièno -na *adj* disinclined; (poet) foreign, alien
alimentare *adj* alimentary || **alimentari** *mpl* food, foodstuff || *v* (**aliménto**) *tr* to feed; to fuel
alimentari·sta *mf* (-sti) food merchant; food-industry worker
alimenta·tóre -trice *mf* stoker || *m* (mach) stoker, feeder
alimentazióne *f* nourishment; feeding; (mil) loading; **alimentazione artificiale** intravenous feeding
aliménto *m* food, nourishment; feed; **alimenti** alimony (*maintenance*)
alimònia *f* alimony
alìnea *f* (law) paragraph, section

alìquota *f* share; parcel, quota
aliscafo *m* hydrofoil
alisè·o **-a** *adj* trade (*wind*) ‖ *m* trade wind
alitare (**àlito**) *intr* to breathe; to blow gently; **non alitare** to not breathe a word
àlito *m* breath; (fig) breeze
alìvo·lo **-la** *adj* (poet) winged; (fig) swift
alla §4
allacciaménto *m* binding; connection, linking
allacciare §128 *tr* to bind, tie; to connect; to buckle; (fig) to deceive
allacciatura *f* lacing; buckling
allagare §209 *tr* to flood, overflow
allampana·to **-ta** *adj* tall and lean, lanky
allargare §209 *tr* to broaden, widen; **allargare la mano** to be lenient; to be liberal; **allargare il freno** to give free rein ‖ *ref* to widen, spread out; **mi si allarga il cuore** I feel relieved
allargatura *f* widening
allarmante *adj* alarming
allarmare *tr* to alarm ‖ *ref* to worry, become alarmed
allarme *m* alarm; **allarme aereo** air-raid warning; **cessato allarme** all clear; **falso allarme** false alarm; **stare in allarme** to be alarmed
allascare §197 *tr* (naut) to ease, slacken (*a rope*)
allato *adv* (poet) near; **allato a** near; beside; in comparison with
allattaménto *m* nursing, feeding; **allattamento artificiale** bottle feeding
allattare *tr* to nurse (*at the breast*); to feed (*with a bottle*)
alle §4
alleanza *f* alliance
alleare (**allèo**) *tr* to ally ‖ *ref* to become allied; to be connected
allea·to **-ta** *adj* allied ‖ *mf* ally
allegare §209 (**allégo**) *tr* to enclose; to adduce; to allege; **allegare i denti** to set the teeth on edge ‖ *intr* (hort) to ripen
allega·to **-ta** *adj* enclosed ‖ *m* enclosure
alleggeriménto *m* lightening, easing
alleggerire §176 *tr* to lighten; to alleviate ‖ *ref* to put on lighter clothes; **alleggerirsi di** (naut) to jettison
allegorìa *f* allegory
allegòri·co **-ca** *adj* (**-ci -che**) allegorical
allegraménte *adv* cheerfully, merrily; thoughtlessly
allegrézza *f* joy, cheerfulness
allegrìa *f* cheer, gaiety; **stare in allegria** to be merry ‖ *interj* good cheer!
allé·gro **-gra** *adj* cheerful, merry, gay ‖ *m* (mus) allegro
allelùia *m* hallelujah
allenaménto *m* training
allenare (**alléno**) *tr* & *ref* to train
allena·tóre **-trice** *adj* training ‖ *mf* trainer, coach
allentare (**allènto**) *tr* to loosen, slacken; to mitigate; (coll) to deliver (*a blow*); **essere allentato** to have a hernia ‖ *ref* to slow up; to loosen up; to diminish

allergìa *f* allergy
allèrgi·co **-ca** *adj* (**-ci -che**) allergic
allérta *f* alert ‖ *adv* alert, on the alert
allessare (**allésso**) *tr* to boil
allés·so **-sa** *adj* boiled ‖ *m* boiled meat, boiled beef
allestire §176 *tr* to prepare, make ready; to rig (*e.g., a ship*); to produce (*e.g., a play*)
allettaménto *m* allure, fascination
allettante *adj* alluring, enticing
allettare (**allètto**) *tr* to allure, entice; to confine to bed; to bend (*plants*) to the ground ‖ *ref* to be confined to bed
allevaménto *m* raising, breeding; flock
allevare (**allèvo**) *tr* to raise, breed; to rear
alleva·tóre **-trice** *mf* raiser, breeder
alleviare §287 (**allèvio**) *tr* to alleviate, lighten
allibire §176 *intr* (ESSERE) to turn pale; to be astonished, be dismayed
allibraménto *m* registration, entry; booking (*of bets*)
allibrare *tr* to register, enter; to book (*a bet*) on a horse
allibratóre *m* bookmaker (*at races*)
allietare (**allièto**) *tr* to cheer, enliven
alliè·vo **-va** *mf* pupil, student; follower, disciple ‖ *m* trainee; **allievo ufficiale** cadet
alligatóre *m* alligator
allignare *intr* to take root; to do well, prosper
allineaménto *m* alignment; falling in line
allineare (**allìneo**) *tr* to align; (typ) to justify ‖ *ref* to align oneself, be aligned
allinea·to **-ta** *adj* aligned; **non allineato** nonaligned, uncommitted
allitterazióne *f* alliteration
allo §4
allòc·co *m* (**-chi**) horned owl; (fig) dolt, nincompoop
allocu·tóre **-trice** *mf* (poet) speaker
allocuzióne *f* (poet) speech, address
allòdola *f* lark, skylark
allogare §209 (**allògo**) *tr* to place; to let, lease; to find employment for; to invest (*money*); to marry off (*a daughter*)
allòge·no **-na** *adj* minority ‖ *mf* member of an ethnic minority
alloggiaménto *m* (mil) lodging, quarters; (carp, mach) housing
alloggiare §290 (**allòggio**) *tr* to lodge, put up ‖ *intr* to lodge, stay
allòg·gio *m* (**-gi**) lodging, living quarters; accommodations
allontanaménto *m* removal; estrangement
allontanare *tr* to remove; to send away; to exonerate; to dismiss; to alienate ‖ *ref* to go away; to withdraw; to become estranged
allóra *adj* then ‖ *adv* then; at that time; in that case; **da allora** ever since; **da allora in poi** from that time on; **fino allora** until then; **per allora** at that time

allorché *conj* when

allòro *m* laurel; **riposare sugli allori** to rest on one's laurels

allorquando *conj* (poet) when

àlluce *m* big toe

allucinante *adj* hallucinating; dazzling; deceptive

allucinare (allùcino) *tr* to hallucinate; to dazzle; to deceive

allucinazióne *f* hallucination

allùdere §105 *intr* to allude

allume *m* alum

alluminare (allùmino) *tr* to illuminate (*a manuscript*); (poet) to light

allumìnio *m* aluminum

allunàg·gio *m* (-gi) lunar landing; **allunaggio morbido** soft lunar landing

allunare *intr* to land on the moon

allunga *f* (mach) adapter

allungàbile *adj* extensible; extension (*table*)

allungaménto *m* lengthening

allungare §209 *tr* to lengthen; to stretch out (*e.g., the hand*); to dilute (*e.g., wine*); (coll) to deliver (*e.g., a slap*); (sports) to pass (*the ball*); **allungare il collo** to crane the neck; **allungare il passo** to walk faster || *ref* to grow longer; to stretch; to grow taller

allun·go *m* (-ghi) (sports) sprint; (sports) forward pass

allusióne *f* allusion

alluvióne *m* flood

almanaccare §197 *tr* to dream of || *intr* to dream, muse

almanac·co *m* (-chi) almanac

alméno *adv* at least; if only

alno *m* (bot) alder

àloe *m* & *f* aloe

alògeno *m* halogen

alogenuro *m* halide

alóne *m* halo

alòsa *f* (ichth) shad

alpacca *f* German silver

alpe *f* high mountain, alp || **le Alpi** the Alps

alpèstre *adj* mountainous; (fig) uncouth

alpigia·no -na *adj* mountain, mountainous; (fig) uncouth || *mf* mountaineer

alpinismo *m* mountain climbing

alpini·sta *mf* (-sti -ste) mountain climber

alpinìsti·co -ca *adj* (-ci -che) mountain-climbing

alpi·no -na *adj* alpine; Alpine || *m* alpine soldier

alquan·to -ta *adj* & *pron* some; **alquanti -te** some; quite a few, several, a good many || **alquanto** *adv* somewhat, rather

Alsàzia, l' *f* Alsace

alsazia·no -na *adj* & *mf* Alsacian

alt *m* (alt) halt, stop || *interj* halt!, stop!

altaléna *f* seesaw; swing; (fig) ups and downs; **altalena a bilico** seesaw; **altalena sospesa** swing

altalenare (altaléno) *intr* to seesaw; to swing

altana *f* roof terrace

altare *m* altar

altarino *m* small altar; **svelare gli alta-**

rini (joc) to expose the skeleton in the closet

altèa *f* marsh mallow

alterare (àltero) *tr* to alter; to falsify; to adulterate; to anger || *ref* to alter; to become adulterated; to get angry

altera·to -ta *adj* altered; adulterated; feverish; angry

alterazióne *f* change, alteration; adulteration; slight fever

altercare §197 **(altèrco)** *intr* to dispute, quarrel

altèr·co *m* (-chi) altercation; **venire a un alterco** to get into a quarrel

alterìgia *f* haughtiness

alternare (altèrno) *tr* & *ref* to alternate

alternati·vo -va *adj* alternating || *f* alternative; choice

alterna·to -ta *adj* alternate; alternating (*current*)

alternatóre *m* (elec) alternator

altèr·no -na *adj* alternate

altè·ro -ra *adj* proud, haughty

altézza *f* height; width (*of cloth*); depth (*of water*); pitch (*of sound*); (astr, geom) altitude; (fig) loftiness, nobility; (naut) latitude; (typ) size; **essere all'altezza di** to be up to, be equal to; (naut) to be off || **Altezza** *f* Highness

altezzó·so -sa [s] *adj* haughty

altìc·cio -cia *adj* (-ci -ce) tipsy

altìmetro *m* altimeter

altipiano *m* var of **altopiano**

altisonante [s] *adj* high-sounding

altìssi·mo -ma *adj* very high, highest || **l'Altissimo** *m* the Most High

altitùdine *f* altitude

al·to -ta *adj* high; tall; wide (*cloth*); deep (*water*); upper; full (*day*); late (*e.g., Easter*); deep (*sleep*); early (*Middle Ages*); loud (*voice*); lofty (*peak*) || *m* top; upper part; high quarters; **alti e bassi** ups and downs; **fare alto e basso** to be the undisputed boss; **guardare qlcu dall'alto in basso** to look down one's nose at s.o.; **in alto** up || **alto** *adv* up

altofórno *m* (altifórni) blast furnace

altoloca·to -ta *adj* high-placed, high-ranking

altoparlante *m* loudspeaker

altopiano *m* (altipiani) plateau

altrettan·to -ta *adj* & *pron* as much; the same; **altrettan·ti -te** as many || **altrettanto** *adv* as much; the same

altri *indef pron invar* someone; someone else; **non altri che** no one else but

altrièri *m* & *adv* day before yesterday

altriménti *adv* otherwise

al·tro -tra *adj* other; next (*world*); **altro ieri** day before yesterday; **chi altro?** who else?; **domani l'altro** the day after tomorrow; **fra l'altro** among other things; **ieri l'altro** the day before yesterday; **l'altro anno** last year; **l'altro giorno** the other day; **noi altri** we; **qualcun altro** somebody else; anybody else; **quest'altro** (giorno, mese, anno) next (day, month, year) || *pron* other; anything

else; **altro che!** why yes! || **l'altro** §11
correlative indef pron || **l'altro** §12
reciprocal pron
altrónde *adv* (poet) somewhere else;
d'altronde besides; on the other hand
altróve *adv* elsewhere, somewhere else
altrui *adj invar* somebody else's, other
people's || *pron invar* somebody else
|| *m*—**l'altrui** what belongs to some-
one else
altrui·sta (**-sti -ste**) *adj* altruistic || *mf*
altruist
altura *f* height; (naut) high seas
alun·no -na *mf* pupil, student
alveare *m* beehive
àlveo *m* bed (*of a river*)
alvèolo *m* alveolus; socket (*of tooth*);
cell (*of honeycomb*)
alzabandiè·ra *m* (**-ra**) raising of the flag
alzacristal·li *m* (**-li**) (aut) crank (*to
raise a window*)
alzàia *f* tow line; towpath
alzare *tr* to lift, raise; to cut (*cards*); to
shrug (*one's shoulders*); to set (*sail*);
alzare al cielo to praise to the sky;
alzare i tacchi to show a clean pair
of heels; **alzare la cresta** to get cocky
|| *ref* to rise; to get up; **alzarsi in
piedi** to stand up
alzata *f* raising, lifting; shrugging (*of
shoulders*); standing up; riser (*of
step*); three-tier candy tray; **alzata di
scudi** rebellion; **alzata di testa** whim,
caprice
alzavàlvo·le *m* (**-le**) (aut) valve lifter
alzo *m* gunsight
amàbile *adj* amiable; sweetish (*wine*)
amabili·tà *f* (**-tà**) amiability, kindness
ama·ca *f* (**-che**) hammock
amàlga·ma *m* (**-mi**) amalgam
amalgamare (**amàlgamo**) *tr* to amalga-
mate || *ref* to amalgamate; to blend
amalgamazióne *f* amalgamation
amante *adj* loving, fond || *m* lover || *f*
mistress
amanuènse *m* amanuensis, scribe
amare *tr* to love; to like || *ref* to love
one another
amareggiare §290 (**amaréggio**) *tr* to
make bitter; to sadden || *ref* to be-
come bitter; to sadden
amarèna *f* sour cherry
amarétto *m* macaroon
amarézza *f* bitterness
ama·ro -ra *adj* bitter || *m* bitters; bitter-
ness
amarógno·lo -la *adj* bitterish
amarra *f* (naut) hawser
amarrare *tr* & *intr* var of **ammarrare**
ama·tóre -trice *mf* lover; amateur
amató·rio -ria *adj* (**-ri -rie**) amatory, of
love
amàzzone [ddzz] *f* horsewoman; female
jockey; (obs) riding habit; **cavalcare
all'amazzone** to ride sidesaddle ||
Amazzone *f* (myth) Amazon
ambage *f* winding path; **ambagi** circum-
locutions; **senz'ambagi** without beating about the bush
ambascerìa *f* embassy
ambà·scia *f* (**-sce**) shortness of breath;
grief, sorrow

ambasciata *f* embassy; ambassadorship;
errand, mission
ambasciatóre *m* ambassador
ambasciatrice *f* ambassadress
ambedùe *adj invar*—**ambedue i** or **le**
both || *pron invar* both
ambiare §287 *intr* to amble, pace (*said
of a horse*)
ambiatura *f* pacing (*said of a horse*)
ambidè·stro -stra *adj* ambidextrous
ambidùe *adj* & *pron invar* var of **ambedue**
ambientare (**ambiènto**) *tr* to accustom;
to place (*a story in a certain period*)
|| *ref* to get accustomed to one's sur-
roundings; to orient oneself
ambienta·tóre -trice *mf* interior decorator; (theat) decorator
ambiènte *adj* room, e.g., **temperatura
ambiente** room temperature || *m*
environment; habitat; milieu; room;
trovarsi fuori del proprio ambiente
to be out of one's element
ambigui·tà *f* (**-tà**) ambiguity
ambì·guo -gua *adj* ambiguous
àm·bio *m* (**-bi**) amble, pacing
ambire §176 *tr* to be eager for || *intr*
to be ambitious; **ambire a** to be ambitious for
àmbito *m* range, circle; (mus) range;
nell'ambito di within
ambizióne *f* ambition
ambizióso -sa [s] *adj* ambitious || *mf*
ambitious person
ambo or **am·bi -be** *adj pl*—**ambo i,
ambo le, ambi i, ambe le** both
ambosèssi *adj invar* of both sexes, e.g.,
giovani ambosessi young people of
both sexes
ambra *f* amber; **ambra grigia** amber-
gris
ambròsia *f* ambrosia; (bot) ragweed
ambulante *adj* itinerant; circulating;
ambulant || *m* mail car
ambulanza *f* ambulance
ambulare (**àmbulo**) *intr* (coll) to ambu-
late
ambulatòrio -ria (**-ri -rie**) *adj* ambula-
tory || *m* clinic, first-aid department
Amburgo *m* Hamburg
amèba *f* amoeba
a·men *m* (**-men**) amen || *interj* amen!
ameni·tà *f* (**-tà**) *f* amenity; pleasantry
amèno -na *adj* pleasant, agreeable;
amusing (*fellow*)
Amèrica, l' *f* America; **l'America del
Nord** North America; **l'America del
Sud** South America
americana *f* bicycle race between pairs
americanismo *m* Americanism
americanizzare [ddzz] *tr* to American-
ize || *ref* to become Americanized
america·no -na *adj* & *mf* American ||
m vermouth with bitters || *f* see
americana
ametista *f* amethyst
amianto *m* asbestos
amicale *adj* (poet) friendly
amichévole *adj* friendly; (sports) non-
competitive
amicìzia *f* friendship; **stringere amicizia
con** to make friends with

ami·co -ca (-ci -che) *adj* friendly || *mf* friend; beloved || *m* boy friend; lover, paramour; **amico del cuore** bosom friend || *f* girl friend; mistress

amidàce·o -a *adj* starchy

amidatura *f* starching

àmido *m* starch

Amlèto *m* Hamlet

ammaccare §197 *tr* to crush; to pound; to bruise; to dent

ammaccatura *f* bruise; dent

ammaestraménto *m* instruction, teaching; training

ammaestrare (ammaèstro & ammaéstro) *tr* to teach, to educate; to train (*animals*)

ammainare (ammàino) *tr* to lower (*e.g., a flag*)

ammalare *intr* (ESSERE) to fall ill || *ref* to fall ill; **ammalarsi di** to come down with

ammala·to -ta *adj* ill, sick || *mf* patient

ammaliare §287 *tr* to cast a spell on; to charm, enchant, fascinate; to bewitch

ammalia·tóre -trice *adj* charming, enchanting || *mf* charmer || *m* enchanter, sorcerer || *f* enchantress, sorceress

amman·co *m* (-chi) shortage

ammanettare (ammanétto) *tr* to handcuff

ammaniglia·to -ta *adj* shackled; (fig) closely bound, closely tied

ammannare *tr* to sheave (*grain*)

ammannire §176 *tr* to prepare (*a dish*); to dish up (*a meal*)

ammansare *tr & ref* var of **ammansire**

ammansa·tóre -trice *mf* (poet) tamer

ammansire §176 *tr* to tame; to calm || *ref* to become tamed; to calm down

ammantare *tr* to mantle, clothe; to cover; to hide (*the truth*)

ammanto *m* mantle, cloak; (fig) authority

ammaràg·gio *m* (-gi) landing on water; splashdown (*of a space vehicle*)

ammaraménto *m* var of **ammaraggio**

ammarare *intr* (aer) to land on water; (rok) to splash down

ammarrare *tr* (naut) to moor

ammassare *tr* to amass || *ref* to crowd, throng

ammasso *m* heap, pile; cluster (*of stars*); government stockpile

ammattiménto *m* worry, nuisance

ammattire §176 *intr* (ESSERE) to go crazy; **fare ammattire** to drive crazy

ammattonare (ammattóno) *tr* to floor with bricks

ammattona·to -ta *adj* floored with bricks || *m* brick floor; bricklaying

ammazzare *tr* to kill || *ref* to kill oneself; to get killed

ammazzasèt·te *m* (-te) braggart

ammazza·tóio *m* (-tói) slaughterhouse

ammènda *f* fine; satisfaction (*for injury*); **fare ammenda** to make amends

ammendaménto *m* emendation: improvement (*of land*)

ammendare (ammèndo) *tr* to emendate; to improve (*land*)

ammennìcolo *m* excuse; trifle; **ammennicoli** extras

ammés·so -sa *adj* admitted; **ammesso che** supposing that; **ammesso e non concesso** for the sake of argument

amméttere §198 *tr* to admit; to accept, suppose

ammezzare [ddzz] (ammèzzo) *tr* to leave half-finished (*a piece of work*); to fill halfway; to empty halfway

ammezzato [ddzz] *m* mezzanine

ammiccare §197 *intr* to wink; to cock one's eye

amministrare *tr* to administer, manage

amministra·tóre -trice *mf* administrator, manager; **amministratore delegato** chairman of the board

amministrazióne *f* administration, management: **ordinaria amministrazione** run-of-the-mill business

ammiràbile *adj* admirable

ammiràglia *f* (nav) flagship

ammiragliato *m* admiralty

ammirà·glio *m* (-gli) admiral; **ammiraglio d'armata** admiral; **ammiraglio di divisione** rear admiral; **ammiraglio di squadra** vice admiral; **grande ammiraglio** admiral of the fleet

ammirare *tr* to admire || *intr* to wonder

ammirati·vo -va *adj* admiring; exclamation (*mark*)

ammira·tóre -trice *mf* admirer || *m* suitor

ammirazióne *f* admiration

ammirévole *adj* admirable

ammissìbile *adj* admissible; permissible

ammissióne *f* admission; (mach) intake; **ammissione comune** consensus

ammobiliaménto *m* furnishing; furniture

ammobiliare §287 *tr* to furnish

ammodernare (ammodèrno) *tr* to modernize

ammòdo *adj invar* well-mannered, polite || *adv* properly

ammogliare §280 (ammóglio) *tr* to marry, give in marriage || *ref* to marry, get married

ammoglia·to *adj* married || *m* married man

ammollare (ammòllo) *tr* to soften; to soak; to slacken (*e.g., a hawser*); to deliver (*a slap*) || *ref* to get soaked

ammollire §176 *tr* to soften; to weaken || *ref* to soften; to mellow

ammonìaca *f* ammonia

ammoniménto *m* warning

ammonire §176 *tr* to admonish, reprimand

ammoni·tóre -trice *adj* warning

ammonizióne *f* admonition, warning

ammontare *m* amount, total || *v* (ammónto) *tr* to pile up || *intr* (ESSERE) to amount

ammonticchiare §287 *tr* to pile up, heap up

ammorbare (ammòrbo) *tr* to infect, contaminate

ammorbidènte *m* softener

ammorbidire §176 *tr* to soften; to mitigate || *ref* to soften

ammortaménto *m* amortization; payment, redemption (*of a loan*)

ammortare (ammòrto) *tr* to amortize
ammortire §176 *tr* to deaden; to weaken, soften
ammortizzaménto [ddzz] *m* amortization, amortizement
ammortizzare [ddzz] *tr* to amortize; (aut) to absorb (*shocks*)
ammortizzatóre [ddzz] *m* (aut) shock absorber
ammosciare §128 (ammóscio) *tr, intr &* *ref* var of **ammoscire**
ammoscia·to -ta *adj* (coll) downcast
ammoscire §176 *tr* to make sag; to make flabby || *intr & ref* to sag; to become flabby; to droop
ammucchiare §287 *tr* to heap up, pile up || *ref* to crowd together
ammuffire §176 *intr* (ESSERE) to become moldy
ammusare *tr & intr* to nuzzle
ammutinaménto *m* mutiny, riot
ammutinare (ammùtino & ammutino) *tr* to incite to riot || *ref* to mutiny
ammutinato *m* mutineer
ammutolire §176 *intr* (ESSERE) to become silent; to be dumfounded
amnesìa *f* amnesia
amnistìa *f* amnesty
amnistiare §287 or §119 *tr* to amnesty
amo *m* hook; **abboccare all'amo** to bite, to swallow the hook
amorale *adj* immoral; amoral
amorali·tà *f* (-tà) immorality; amorality
amóre *m* love; eagerness; **amor proprio** amour-propre, self-esteem; **con amore** with pleasure; **d'amore e d'accordo** in perfect agreement; **fare all'amore** to make love; **fare l'amore** to flirt; **per amor del cielo** for heaven's sake; **per amore di** for the sake of; **un amore di bambino** a charming child; **un amore di cappello** a darling hat
amoreggiare §290 (amoréggio) *intr* to flirt; to play around
amorévole *adj* loving; kindly
amòr·fo -fa *adj* amorphous; safety (*match*)
amorino *m* cupid; cute child; love seat; (bot) mignonette
amoró·so -sa [s] *adj* loving; kindly; amorous; love (*e.g., life*) || *mf* lover || *m* fiancé || *f* fiancée
amovìbile *adj* removable
amperàg·gio *m* (-gi) amperage
ampère *m* ampere
amperòmetro *m* ammeter
amperóra *m* ampere-hour
ampiézza *f* width, breadth; trajectory (*of a missile*); amplitude; **ampiezza di vedute** open-mindedness
àm·pio -pia *adj* (-pi -pie) ample; wide; roomy
amplèsso *m* (poet) embrace
ampliaménto *m* amplification, extension
ampliare §287 *tr* to enlarge, widen || *ref* to widen
amplificare §197 (amplìfico) *tr* to amplify; to widen; to exaggerate
amplifica·tóre *m* (rad & telv) amplifier
amplificazióne *f* amplification
amplitùdine *f* amplitude
ampólla *f* cruet; (eccl) ampulla
ampollièra *f* cruet stand

ampollosi·tà [s] *f* (-tà) grandiloquence, turgidity
ampolló·so -sa [s] *adj* grandiloquent, turgid
amputare (àmputo) *tr* to amputate
amputazióne *f* amputation
amulèto *m* amulet, charm
anabbagliante *m* (aut) low beam; **anabbaglianti** (aut) dimmers
anacàr·dio *m* (-di) cashew
ànace *m* var of **anice**
anacorè·ta *m* (-ti) anchorite, hermit
anacronismo *m* anachronism
anacronìsti·co -ca *adj* (-ci -che) anachronistic(al)
anàgrafe *m* bureau of vital statistics; registry of births, deaths, and marriages
anagram·ma *m* (-mi) anagram
analcòli·co -ca (-ci -che) *adj* nonalcoholic; soft (*drink*) || *m* soft drink
analfabè·ta *mf* (-ti -te) illiterate
analfabèti·co -ca *adj* (-ci -che) unalphabetized, unalphabetic
analfabetismo *m* illiteracy
analgèsi·co -ca *adj & m* (-ci -che) analgesic
anàli·si *f* (-si) analysis; breakdown; **analisi grammaticale** parsing; **analisi dell'urina** urinalysis
anali·sta *mf* (-sti -ste) analyst; **analista finanziario** financial analyst; **analista tempi e metodi** efficiency expert, efficiency engineer
analìti·co -ca *adj* (-ci -che) analytic(al)
analizzare [ddzz] *tr* to analyze; to assay (*ores*); (telv) to scan
analogìa *f* analogy
anàlo·go -ga *adj* (-ghi -ghe) analogous; similar
anamnè·si *f* (-si) (med) case history
ananasso *m* pineapple
anarchìa *f* anarchy
anàrchi·co -ca (-ci -che) *adj* anarchical || *m* anarchist
anatè·ma or **anàte·ma** *m* (-mi) anathema
anatomìa *f* anatomy
anatòmi·co -ca *adj* (-ci -che) anatomic(al)
ànatra *f* duck; drake
anatròccolo *m* duckling
an·ca *f* (-che) hip; (coll) thigh (*e.g., of a chicken*); **dare d'anche** to run away; **menare anca** to walk
ancèlla *f* maidservant
ancestrale *adj* ancestral
anche *adv* also, too; even; (poet) yet; **anche a** + *inf* even if + *ind*
anchilosare (anchilòso) *tr* to paralyze || *ref* to become paralyzed
anchilòsto·ma *m* (-mi) hookworm
àn·cia *f* (-ce) (mus) reed
ancillare *adj* servant
ancòra *adv* still, yet; again; more e.g., **ancora cinque minuti** five minutes more
àncora *f* anchor; keeper (*of magnet*); armature (*of buzzer or electric bell*); **ancora di salvezza** last hope; **gettar l'ancora** to cast anchor; **salpare** or **levar l'ancora** to weigh anchor
ancoràg·gio *m* (-gi) anchorage, berth

ancorare (**àncoro**) *tr* to anchor; to tie (*e.g., a currency to gold*) || *ref* to anchor; to hold fast

ancorché *conj* although

andalu·so -sa *adj & mf* Andalusian

andaménto *m* course, progress

andante *adj* ordinary, common; continuous

andare *m* going; gait; **a lungo andare** in the long run || §106 *intr* (ESSERE) to go; to spread (*said of news*); to be (*e.g., proud*); to work (*said of machinery*); (with *dat*) to fit, e.g., **quel vestito non gli va** that suit does not fit him; (with *dat*) to please, e.g. **quel vestito non le va** that dress does not please her; **andare a cavallo** to go horseback riding; **andare a finire** to wind up; **andare a male** to spoil; **andare a picco** to sink; **andare d'accordo** to agree; **andare in cerca di** to seek; **andare in macchina** to be in press; **andare in onda** (rad & telv) to go on the air; **andare per i vent'anni** to be bordering on twenty years; **andare pazzo per** to be crazy about; **andare soldato** to be drafted; **andare via** to go away; **come va?** how are things?; **mi va il vino dolce** I like sweet wine; **ne va della vita** life is at stake; **va da sé** it goes without saying || *ref*—**andarsene** to go away, leave

anda·to -ta *adj* gone, past; finished; (coll) spoiled (*e.g., meat*) || *f* going; journey, trip; **a lunga andata** in the long run; **andata e ritorno** round trip; **dare l'andata a** to give the go-ahead to

andatura *f* gait; pace; **fare l'andatura** to set the pace

andazzo *m* bad practice, bad habit; fad

Ande, le the Andes

andicappare *tr* to handicap

andi·no -na *adj* Andean

andiriviè·ni *m* (**-ni**) coming and going; maze; ado

àndito *m* corridor, hallway

andróne *m* hall, lobby

aneddòti·co -ca *adj* (**-ci -che**) anecdotal

anèddoto *m* anecdote

anelante *adj* panting

anelare (**anèlo**) *tr* to long for || *intr* to yearn; (poet) to pant

anèlito *m* last breath; yearning; (poet) panting; **mandare l'ultimo anelito** to breathe one's last

anellino *m* ringlet

anèllo *m* ring; link (*of a chain*); traffic circle; segment (*of a worm*); (sports) track; **ad anello** ring-shaped; **anello di congiunzione** (fig) link; **anello di fidanzamento** engagement ring || **anella** *fpl* (poet) ringlets; (archaic) rings

anemia *f* anemia

anèmi·co -ca *adj* (**-ci -che**) anemic

anestesìa *f* anesthesia

anestesi·sta *mf* (**-sti -ste**) anesthetist

anestèti·co -ca *adj & m* (**-ci -che**) anesthetic

anestetizzare [ddzz] *tr* to anesthetize

aneuri·sma *m* (**-smi**) aneurysm

anfì·bio -bia (**-bi -bie**) *adj* amphibian; (fig) ambiguous || *m* amphibian

anfiteatro *m* amphitheater

anfitrióne *m* (lit) generous host

anfratto *m* ravine; narrow, winding, rugged spot

anfrattuosi·tà [s] *f* (**-tà**) rough broken ground; winding, rough spot

anfrattuó·so -sa [s] *adj* winding, rough, craggy

angariare §287 *tr* to pester, oppress

angèli·co -ca *adj* (**-ci -che**) angelic(al)

àngelo *m* angel; **angelo custode** guardian angel

angherìa *f* vexation; outrage; imposition

angina *f* quinsy; **angina pectoris** angina pectoris

angipòrto *m* blind alley; narrow lane

anglica·no -na *adj & mf* Anglican

anglicismo *m* Anglicism

anglicizzare [ddzz] *tr* to Anglicize || *ref* to become Anglicized

anglòfo·no -na *adj* English-speaking || *m* English-speaking person

anglosàssone *adj & mf* Anglo-Saxon

angolare *adj* angular; corner (*stone*) || *m* angle iron || *v* (**àngolo**) *tr* to take an angle shot of; (sports) to kick (*the ball*) into the corner of the goal

angolazióne *f* (mov) angle shot

angolièra *f* corner shelving; corner cupboard

àngolo *m* angle; corner

angoló·so -sa [s] *adj* angular

àngora *f* Angora cat; Angora goat

angò·scia *f* (**-sce**) anxiety, distress, anguish

angosciare §128 (**angòscio**) *tr* to distress

angoscia·to -ta *adj* tormented, distressed

angosció·so -sa [s] *adj* agonizing

anguilla *f* eel

anguillé·sco -sca *adj* (**-schi -sche**) as slippery as an eel

angùria *f* watermelon

angùstia *f* narrowness; scarcity; **stare in angustia** to be worried

angustiare §287 *tr* to distress, grieve || *ref* to worry

angu·sto -sta *adj* narrow

ànice *m* anise

anicino *m* anise cookie

anidride *f* anhydride

àni·dro -dra *adj* anhydrous

anilina *f* aniline

ànima *f* soul; life (*e.g., of the party*); core; kernel; bore (*of gun*); mold (*of button*); mind; enthusiasm; pith (*of fruit*); sounding post (*of violin*); web (*of rail*); **anima dannata** evil counselor; **anima mia!** darling!; **anima nera** villain; **anima viva** living soul; **buon'anima** late, e.g., **mio padre, buon'anima** my late father; **dannare l'anima** to lose patience; **la buon'anima di** the late; **rompere l'anima a** to annoy

animale *adj* animal; (poet) of the soul; (poet) animate || *m* animal; (fig) boor, lout

animalé·sco -sca *adj* (**-schi -sche**) animal, bestial
animare (**ànimo**) *tr* to animate, to enliven; to promote || *ref* to become lively or heated
anima·to -ta *adj* animated (*cartoon*); animated, lively; animal
anima·tóre -trice *adj* animating || *m* moving spirit; (mov) animator
animazióne *f* animation
animèlla *f* sweetbread
ànimo *m* mind; heart, affection; courage; **aprire l'animo** to open one's heart; **avere in animo di** to have a mind to; **mal animo** ill will; **mettersi l'animo in pace** to resign oneself; **perdersi d'animo** to lose heart; **serbare nell'animo** to keep in mind
animosi·tà [s] *f* (**-tà**) animosity, ill will
animó·so -sa [s] *adj* bold; spirited (*animal*); hostile
anióne *m* anion
anisétta *f* anisette
ànitra *f* var of **anatra**
anitròccolo *m* var of **anatroccolo**
annacquare (**annàcquo**) *tr* to water; to water down
annaffiare §287 *tr* to sprinkle; to water (*wine*)
annaffia·tóio *m* (**-tói**) sprinkling can
annaffia·tóre -trice *adj* watering, sprinkling
annali *mpl* annals *spl*
annaspare *tr* to reel || *intr* to gesticulate; to grope; to flounder
annata *f* year; year's activity; year's rent; year's issues (*of a magazine*)
annebbiare §287 (**annébbio**) *tr* to befog; to dim || *ref* to become foggy; to become dim
annegaménto *m* drowning
annegare §209 (**annégo**) *tr* & *intr* (ESSERE) to drown
anneriménto *m* blackening
annerire §176 *tr* to blacken || *ref* to turn black
annessióne *f* annexation
annès·so -sa *adj* united, attached || *m* annex; **con tutti gli annessi e connessi** everything included
annèttere §107 *tr* to annex; to attach, enclose; to unite; to ascribe (*importance*)
annichilante *adj* annihilating; devastating (*e.g., reply*)
annichilare (**annìchilo**) *tr* to annihilate || *ref* to destroy oneself; (fig) to humble oneself
annichilire §176 *tr* & *ref* var of **annichilare**
annidare *tr* to nest; (fig) to nourish, cherish || *ref* to nest; to hide; (fig) to settle
annientaménto *m* annihilation
annientare (**annièntο**) *tr* to annihilate; to knock down, demolish; (fig) to crush || *ref* to humble oneself
anniversà·rio -ria *adj* & *m* (**-ri -rie**) anniversary
anno *m* year; **anno bisestile** leap year; **anno luce** light-year; **anno nuovo** New Year; **anno scolastico** school

year; **avere . . . anni** to be . . . years old; **l'anno che viene** next year; **l'anno corrente** this year; **quest'altr'anno** next year; **un anno dopo l'altro** year in, year out
annobilire §176 *tr* to ennoble
annodare (**annòdo**) *tr* to knot, tie; (fig) to tie up || *ref* to get entangled
annoiare §287 (**annòio**) *tr* to bore || *ref* to become bored
annòna *f* food; food-control agency
annonà·rio -ria *adj* (**-ri -rie**) food; rationing (*card*)
annó·so -sa [s] *adj* old, aged
annotare (**annòto**) *tr* to jot down; to chalk up; to annotate; to comment
annotazióne *f* note; notation, annotation
annottare (**annòtta**) *impers* (ESSERE) & *ref* to grow dark, e.g., **si annotta** it's growing dark; **è annottato** it grew dark
annoverare (**annòvero**) *tr* to count, number
annuale *adj* annual || *m* anniversary
annuà·rio *m* (**-ri**) annual, yearbook
annuire §176 *intr* to nod assent; to consent
annullaménto *m* nullification, annulment
annullare *tr* to annul, nullify, cancel; to call off || *ref* to cancel one another
annunciare §128 *tr* var of **annunziare**
Annunciazióne *f* Annunciation
annunziare §287 *tr* to announce; (fig) to forecast, foreshadow
annunzia·tóre -trice *mf* announcer, newscaster
annùn·zio *m* (**-zi**) announcement, notice; **annunzio economico** classified ad; **annunzio pubblicitario** advertisement; **annunzio pubblicitario radiofonico** (rad) commercial
ànnu·o -a *adj* yearly, annual
annusare [s] *tr* to smell; to snuff (*tobacco*)
annuvolaménto *m* cloudiness
annuvolare (**annùvolo**) *tr* to cloud, becloud || *ref* to become cloudy; to turn somber
anòdi·no -na *adj* pain-relieving; ineffective; weak, colorless (*person*)
ànodo *m* anode
anomalìa *f* anomaly
anòma·lo -la *adj* anomalous
anonimìa *f* anonymity
anòni·mo -ma *adj* anonymous || *m* anonymous author; **serbare l'anonimo** to preserve one's anonymity
anormale *adj* abnormal || *m* queer fellow
anormali·tà *f* (**-tà**) abnormality
ansa *f* handle (*of vase*); pretext; bend (*of a river*)
ansante *adj* panting
ansare *intr* to pant
ànsia *f* anxiety; **essere in ansia** to be worried
ansie·tà *f* (**-tà**) anxiety
ansimare (**ànsimo**) *intr* to pant
ansió·so -sa [s] *adj* anxious
antagonismo *m* antagonism

antagoni•sta (-sti -ste) *adj* antagonistic ‖ *mf* antagonist, opponent
antagonìsti•co -ca *adj* (-ci -che) antagonistic
antàrti•co -ca *adj* (-ci -che) antarctic ‖ **Antartico** *m* Antarctic
antecedènte *adj* preceding ‖ *m* antecedent
antecedènza *f* antecedence
antecessóre *m* predecessor
antefatto *m* background, antecedents
anteguèr•ra (-ra) *adj* prewar ‖ *m* prewar period
anteluca•no -na *adj* (poet) predawn
antenato *m* ancestor
anténna *f* lance; (naut) yard; (rad & telv) aerial, antenna; (zool) antenna
antepórre §218 *tr* to prefer; to place before
anteprima *f* (mov & theat) preview
anterióre *adj* fore, front; previous; earlier
antesignano [s] *m* forerunner
anti- *pref adj* anti-, e.g., **anticomunistico** anticommunist; un-, e.g., **antieconomico** uneconomical ‖ *pref mf* anti-, e.g., **anticomunista** anticommunist
antiabbagliante *adj* antiglare ‖ *m* low beam
antiàci•do -da *adj* & *m* antacid
antiaère•o -a *adj* antiaircraft ‖ *f* antiaircraft defense
antibattèri•co -ca (-ci -che) *adj* antibacterial ‖ *m* bactericide
antibiòti•co -ca *adj* & *m* (-ci -che) antibiotic
anticà•glia *f* (-glie) antique, curio; rubbish, junk
anticàmera *f* waiting room, anteroom; **fare anticamera** to cool one's heels
anticarro *adj invar* antitank
antichi•tà *f* (-tà) antiquity; **antichità** *fpl* antiques
anticipare (antìcipo) *tr* to advance; to speed up; to pay in advance; to leak (*news*); to expect, anticipate ‖ *intr* to be early
anticipa•to -ta *adj* in advance (*e.g., payment*)
anticipazióne *f* advance; collateral loan; expectation, anticipation
antìcipo *m* advance; loan (*on accounts receivable*); **in antìcipo** in advance
anti•co -ca *adj* (-chi -che) antique, ancient, old; **all'antica** in the old-fashioned manner; **gli antichi** the ancients; the forefathers; **in antico** in olden times
anticoncezionale *adj* & *f* contraceptive
anticonformi•sta *mf* (-sti -ste) nonconformist
anticonformìsti•co -ca *adj* (-ci -che) unconventional
anticongelante *adj* & *m* antifreeze
anticongiunturale *adj* crisis, emergency
anticòrpo *m* antibody
anticristo *m* Antichrist
antidatare *tr* to predate
antiderapante *adj* nonskid
antidetonante *adj* antiknock ‖ *m* antiknock compound

antidiluvia•no -na *adj* antediluvian
antìdoto *m* antidote
antievanescènza *f* (rad) antifading device
antifecondati•vo -va *adj* & *m* contraceptive
antìfona *f* antiphon; **capire l'antifona** (fig) to get the message
antifurto *adj invar* antitheft ‖ *m* antitheft device
antigàs *adj invar* gas (*e.g., mask*)
antigièni•co -ca *adj* (-ci -che) unsanitary
antìlope *f* antelope
antimeridia•no -na *adj* antemeridian, A.M.
antimìssile *adj invar* antimissile
antimònio *m* antimony
antincèndio *adj invar* fire-fighting; fire, e.g., **scala antincendio** fire escape
antinéb•bia *adj invar* fog ‖ *m* (-bia) fog light
antinéve *adj invar* snow, e.g., **catena antineve** snow chain
antiorà•rio -ria *adj* (-ri -rie) counterclockwise
antipatìa *f* antipathy, dislike
antipàti•co -ca *adj* (-ci -che) antipathetic; disagreeable; uncongenial
antipièga *adj invar* crease-resistant, wrinkle-proof
antìpodi *mpl* antipodes
antipòlio *adj invar* polio (*e.g., vaccine*)
antipòrta *f* stormdoor; corridor
antiquà•rio -ria (-ri -rie) *adj* antiquarian ‖ *m* antiquary, antiquarian
antiqua•to -ta *adj* obsolete; antiquated
antireligió•so -sa [s] *adj* antireligious, irreligious
antirùggine *adj invar* antirust
antirumóre *adj invar* antinoise
antisala [s] *f* anteroom, waiting room
antisassi [s] *adj invar* protecting against falling stones
antischiavi•sta *adj* & *mf* (-sti -ste) abolitionist
antisemi•ta [s] (-ti -te) *adj* anti-Semitic ‖ *mf* anti-Semite
antisemìti•co -ca [s] *adj* (-ci -che) anti-Semitic
antisemitismo [s] *m* anti-Semitism
antisètti•co -ca [s] *adj* & *m* (-ci -che) antiseptic
antisociale [s] *adj* antisocial
antisóle [s] *adj invar* sun (*glasses*); suntan (*lotion*)
antisommergìbile [s] *adj* antisubmarine
antistatale [s] *adj* antigovernment
antitàrmi•co -ca *adj* (-ci -che) mothproof
antitèmpo *adv* early, prematurely
antìte•si *f* (-si) antithesis
antitèti•co -ca *adj* (-ci -che) antithetic(al)
antitossìna *f* antitoxin
antiuòmo *adj invar* (mil) antipersonnel
antivigìlia *f*—**l'antivigilia di** two days before
antologìa *f* anthology
antònimo *m* antonym
antrace *m* anthrax
antracite *f* anthracite

antro *m* cave; den, hovel
antròpi•co -ca *adj* (-ci -che) human
antropofagìa *f* cannibalism
antropòfa•go -ga (-gi -ghe) *adj* cannibalistic || *m* cannibal
antropòide *adj* anthropoid
antropologìa *f* anthropology
antropomòrfi•co -ca *adj* (-ci -che) anthropomorphic
antropomòr•fo -fa *adj* see scimmia
anulare *adj* ring-shaped, annular || *m* ring finger
Anvèrsa *f* Antwerp
anzi *adv* on the contrary, rather; anzi che no rather || *prep* (poet) before
anziani•tà *f* (-tà) seniority
anzia•no -na *adj* old, elderly; senior || *m* senior
anziché *conj* rather than
anzidét•to -ta *adj* aforesaid
anzitutto *adv* above all, first of all
apatìa *f* apathy
apàti•co -ca *adj* (-ci -che) apathetic
ape *f* bee; ape operaia worker; ape regina queen bee
aperitivo *m* apéritif
apèr•to -ta *adj* open; frank, candid || *m* open space; all'aperto in the open
apertura *f* opening; aperture; approach; ad apertura di libro at sight; apertura alare (*of a bird*) wingspread; (aer) wingspan
apià•rio *m* (-ri) apiary
àpice *m* apex, top; climax
apicol•tóre -trice *mf* beekeeper, apiarist
apicoltura *f* beekeeping, apiculture
Apocalisse *f* Apocalypse, Revelation
apocalìtti•co -ca *adj* (-ci -che) apocalyptic(al)
apòcri•fo -fa *adj* apocryphal
apofonìa *f* ablaut
apogèo *m* apogee
apòlide *adj* stateless || *m* man without a country
apolìti•co -ca *adj* (-ci -che) nonpolitical, nonpartisan
apologè•ta *m* (-ti) apologist
apologèti•co -ca *adj* (-ci -che) apologetic
apologìa *f* apology
apòlo•go *m* (-ghi) apologue
apoplessìa *f* apoplexy
apoplètti•co -ca *adj* & *m* (-ci -che) apoplectic
apostasìa *f* apostasy
apòsta•ta *mf* (-ti -te) apostate
apostolato *m* apostolate
apostòli•co -ca *adj* (-ci -che) apostolic(al)
apòstolo *m* apostle
apostrofare (apòstrofo) *tr* to write with an apostrophe; to apostrophize
apòstrofe *f* apostrophe (*to a person*)
apòstrofo *m* (gram) apostrophe
apoteò•si *f* (-si) apotheosis
appagare §209 *tr* to satisfy, gratify || *ref*—appagarsi di to be content with
appaiare §287 *tr* to pair, couple; to match || *ref* to match (*said, e.g., of colors*)
appallottolare (appallòttolo) *tr* to

crumple into a ball || *ref* to become lumpy
appaltare *tr* to contract for
appalta•tóre -trice *mf* contractor
appalto *m* contract; state monopoly; appalto di sali e tabacchi tobacco shop
appannàg•gio *m* (-gi) appanage; (fig) prerogative
appannare *tr* to tarnish; to befog, becloud || *ref* to become clouded (*said, e.g., of one's eyesight*)
apparato *m* decoration; display; appliance; leadership (*of political party*); (rad, telv) set
apparecchiare §287 (apparécchio) *tr* to prepare; to set (*the table*) || *ref* to get ready
apparecchiatura *f* sizing (*of paper; of a wall*); preparation (*of a canvas*); apparatus
apparéc•chio *m* (-chi) apparatus; sizing; preparation; gadget; (rad, telv) set; airplane; apparecchio da caccia fighter plane; apparecchio telefonico telephone
apparentare (apparènto) *tr* to tie, unite (*through marriage*) || *ref* to become related; to become intimate; (pol) to form a coalition
apparènte *adj* apparent, seeming
apparènza *f* appearance; in apparenza seemingly
apparigliare §280 *tr* to pair, team (*horses*)
apparire §108 *intr* (ESSERE) to appear, seem; to look
appariscènte *adj* showy, flashy, gaudy
apparizióne *f* apparition; appearance
appartaménto *m* apartment
appartare *tr* to set aside || *ref* to withdraw, retire
apparta•to -ta *adj* secluded, solitary
appartenènza *f* belonging, membership; appartenenze accessories; annexes
appartenére §271 *intr* (ESSERE & AVERE) to belong; to pertain || *impers* (ESSERE & AVERE)—appartiene a it behooves, it is up to
appassionaménto *m* excitement, interest, enthusiasm
appassionare (appassióno) *tr* to move; to interest; to excite || *ref* to be deeply interested
appassiona•to -ta *adj* impassioned; deep, ardent || *m* fan, amateur
appassire §176 *intr* (ESSERE) to wilt, wither; to decay; to dry up (*said, e.g., of grapes*)
appellare (appèllo) *tr* (law) to appeal; (poet) to call || *ref* to appeal; appellarsi a or contro (law) to appeal
appèllo *m* call, roll call; fare appello a to summon (*e.g., one's strength*); fare l'appello to call the roll; mancare all'appello to be absent
appéna *adv* hardly, scarcely; only; just || *conj* as soon as; non appena as soon as, no sooner
appèndere §109 *tr* to hang
appendice *f* appendix; feuilleton
appendicectomìa *f* appendectomy

appendicite *f* appendicitis
Appennino, l' *m* the Apennines
appesantire [s] §176 *tr* to make heavy; to burden, overwhelm ‖ *ref* to get heavy; to get fat
appestare (appèsto) *tr* to infect; to stink up
appesta·to -ta *adj* plague-ridden ‖ *m* plague victim
appetire §176 *tr* to crave, long for ‖ *intr* (ESSERE & AVERE) to be appetizing
appetito *m* appetite
appetitó·so -sa [s] *adj* appetizing, tempting
appètto *adv* opposite; **appetto a** opposite; **in comparison with**
appezzaménto *m* plot, parcel (*of land*)
appianare *tr* to smooth, level; to settle (*a dispute*); to get around (*a difficulty*)
appiana-tóio *m* (-tói) road grader
appiattare *tr* & *ref* to hide
appiattiménto *m* leveling; equalization
appiattire §176 *tr* & *ref* to flatten, to level
appiccare §197 *tr* to hang; **appiccare il fuoco a** to set on fire; **appiccare una lite** to pick a fight
appicciare §128 *tr* (coll) to string together; (coll) to kindle, light
appiccicare §197 (appìccico) *tr* to stick, glue; **appiccicare uno schiaffo a** to slap ‖ *ref* to stick, adhere
appiccicatíc·cio -cia *adj* (-ci -ce) sticky
appic·co *m* (-chi) grip; steep wall (*of mountain*); (fig) pretext
appiè *adv*—**appiè di** at the foot of; at the bottom of
appiedare (appièdo) *tr* to order (*a cavalryman*) off a horse; to order (*e.g., troops*) off a vehicle; to force out of a car (*said, e.g., of motor trouble*)
appièno *adv* (poet) fully
appigionare (appigióno) *tr* to rent ‖ *ref*—**appigionasi** for rent
appigiónasi [s] *m* for-rent sign
appigliare §280 *ref* to cling, adhere; **appigliarsi a un pretesto** to seize a pretext
appì·glio *m* (-gli) grip; (fig) pretext
appiómbo *m* perpendicular ‖ *adv* plumb, perpendicularly
appioppare (appiòppo) *tr* to plant with poplar trees; to tie (*a vine*) to a poplar tree; (coll) to deliver (*a blow*); (coll) to pass off (*e.g., inferior goods*)
appisolare (appìsolo) *ref* to snooze, doze
applaudire §176 & (applàudo) *tr* to applaud ‖ *intr* to applaud, clap the hands; (with *dat*) to applaud
applàuso *m* applause; **applausi** applause
applicàbile *adj* applicable
applicare §197 (àpplico) *tr* to apply; to attach; to give (*e.g., a slap*); to put into effect (*a law*); to assign ‖ *ref* to apply oneself
applica·to -ta *adj* applied; appliqué ‖ *m* clerk
applicazióne *f* application; appliqué

applique *m* (elec) wall fixture
appoggiaca·po *m* (-po) headrest; **tidy** (*on back of chair*)
appoggiagómi·ti *m* (-ti) elbowrest
appoggiama·no *m* (-no) mahlstick
appoggiare §290 (appòggio) *tr* to lean; to rest; to prop, support; to raise (*the tone of voice*); to give (*a slap*); to second (*a motion*); (fig) to back, support ‖ *intr* to lean; to rest ‖ *ref*—**appoggiarsi a** or **su** to lean on
appoggia-tóio *m* (-tói) support, rest; banister
appoggiatura *f* (mus) grace note
appòg·gio *m* (-gi) support, prop; backer; backing, support; grip; (mach) bearing
appollaiare §287 *ref* to roost
appórre §218 *tr* to affix, append
apportare (appòrto) *tr* to cause; to presage; (poet) to carry
appòrto *m* carrying; contribution; (law) share
appositaménte *adv* expressly, on purpose
appòsi·to -ta *adj* proper, fitting
apposizióne *f* apposition
appòsta *adj invar* suitable ‖ *adv* on purpose, expressly, intentionally
appostaménto *m* ambush
appostare (appòsto) *tr* to ambush ‖ *ref* to lie in ambush
apprèndere §220 *tr* to learn ‖ *ref* (poet) to take hold
apprendi·sta *mf* (-sti -ste) apprentice
apprendistato *m* apprenticeship
apprensióne *f* apprehension, fear
apprensi·vo -va *adj* apprehensive
appressare (apprèsso) *tr* (poet) to approach ‖ *ref* to come near
appresso *adj invar* next, following ‖ *adv* near; later on; **appresso a** near; after
apprestare (apprèsto) *tr* to prepare; to supply, provide (*e.g., help*) ‖ *ref* to prepare, get ready
apprettare (apprètto) *tr* to dress (*leather*); to size (*cloth*)
apprètto *m* tan (*for leather*); sizing (*for cloth*)
apprezzàbile *adj* appreciable
apprezzaménto *m* appreciation; estimation
apprezzare (apprèzzo) *tr* to appreciate
apprezza·to -ta *adj* esteemed
appròc·cio *m* (-ci) approach; **approcci** advances
approdare (appròdo) *intr* (ESSERE & AVERE) to land; (with *dat*) (poet) to benefit; **approdare a** to come to
appròdo *m* landing
approfittare *intr*—**approfittare di** to capitalize on ‖ *ref*—**approfittarsi di** to take advantage of
approfondire §176 *tr* to make deep; to study thoroughly ‖ *ref*—**approfondirsi in** to go deep into
approntare (apprónto) *tr* to prepare, make ready
appropriare §287 (appròprio) *tr* to adapt; to bestow ‖ *ref*—**appropriarsi a** to befit; **appropriarsi di** to appropriate; to embezzle

appropria·to -ta *adj* appropriate
appropriazióne *f* appropriation; **appropriazione indebita** fraudulent conversion, embezzlement
approssimare (appròssimo) *tr* to bring near || *ref* to approach, come near
approssimati·vo -va *adj* approximate
approssimazióne *f* approximation
approvàbile *adj* laudable
approvare (appròvo) *tr* to approve, countenance; to subscribe to (*an opinion*); to pass (*a student; a law*); to confirm
approvazióne *f* approval; confirmation; passage (*of a law*)
approvvigionaménto *m* supply
approvvigionare (approvvigióno) *tr* to supply || *ref* to be supplied
appuntaménto *m* appointment; date; **appuntamento amoroso** assignation
appuntare *tr* to sharpen; to fasten, pin; to stick (*a pin*) in; to point; to jot down, take note of; to prick up (*one's ears*); (fig) to reproach || *ref* to be turned; to aim
appunta·to -ta *adj* sharpened || *m* corporal (*of Italian police*)
appuntellare (appuntèllo) *tr* to shore up, prop up
appuntellatura *f* shoring up, propping up
appuntino *adv* precisely, meticulously
appuntire §176 *tr* to sharpen
appunti·to -ta *adj* sharp, pointed
appunto *m* note; blame, charge; **muovere un appunto a** to blame; **per l'appunto** just, precisely || *adv* exactly, precisely
appurare *tr* to ascertain
appuzzare *tr* to befoul, pollute
apribottì·glie *m* (-glie) bottle opener
apri·co -ca *adj* (-chi -che) (poet) sunny, bright
aprile *m* April
apripi·sta *m* (-sta) blade (*of bulldozer*); bulldozer
aprire §110 *tr* to open; to turn on; to dig (*e.g., a grave*) || *ref* to open; to clear up (*said of the weather*); **aprirsi con** to open one's heart to; **aprirsi il varco tra** to press through
apriscàto·le *m* (-le) can opener
aquà·rio *m* (-ri) aquarium || **Aquario** *m* (astr) Aquarius
aquàti·co -ca *adj* (-ci -che) aquatic
àquila *f* eagle; genius
aquili·no -na *adj* aquiline
aquilóne *m* north wind; kite
aquilòtto *m* eaglet; cadet (*in Italian Air Force Academy*)
Aquinate, l' *m* Saint Thomas Aquinas
ara *f* (poet) altar; are (*100 square meters*)
arabé·sca *f* (-sche) (mus) arabesque
arabesca·to -ta *adj* arabesque
arabé·sco -sca (-schi -sche) *adj* arabesque || *m* arabesque; doodle || *f* see **arabesca**
Aràbia, l' *f* Arabia
aràbi·co -ca *adj* (-ci -che) Arabic
aràbile *adj* tillable

àra·bo -ba *adj* Arabic, Arabian || *mf* Arab (*person*) || *m* Arabic (*language*)
aràchide *f* peanut (*vine*)
aragonése [s] *adj & mf* Aragonese
aragósta *f* (*Palinurus vulgaris*) lobster
aràldi·co -ca (-ci -che) *adj* heraldic || *f* heraldry
araldo *m* herald
arancéto *m* orange grove
aràn·cia *f* (-ce) orange
aranciata *f* orangeade
aràn·cio *adj invar* orange (*in color*) || *m* (-ci) orange tree
arancióne *adj & m* orange (*color*)
arare *tr* to plow; (naut) to drag (*the anchor*)
aratro *m* plow
arazzo *m* tapestry, arras
arbitràg·gio *m* (-gi) (sports) umpiring; (com) arbitrage
arbitrale *adj* judge's, umpire's
arbitrare (àrbitro) *tr* to umpire, referee || *intr* to arbitrate || *ref*—**arbitrarsi di** to take the liberty to
arbitrà·rio -ria *adj* (-ri -rie) arbitrary; wanton
arbitrato *m* arbitration
arbì·trio *m* (-tri) will; abuse, violation; **libero arbitrio** free will
àrbitro *m* arbiter; judge, referee, umpire
arboscèllo *m* small tree
arbusto *m* shrub, bush
ar·ca *f* (-che) sarcophagus; ark; chest; **arca di Noè** Noah's Ark; **arca di scienza** (fig) fountain of knowledge
àrcade *adj & m* Arcadian
Arcàdia *f* Arcadia, Arcady
arcài·co -ca *adj* (-ci -che) archaic
arcaismo *m* archaism
arcàngelo *m* archangel
arca·no -na *adj* mysterious, arcane || *m* mystery
arcata *f* arch; arcade
archeologìa *f* archaeology
archeològi·co -ca *adj* (-ci -che) archaeological
archeòlo·go -ga *mf* (-gi -ghe) archaeologist
archètipo *m* archetype
archétto *m* (archit) small arch; (elec) trolley pole; (mus) bow
archi- *pref adj* archi-, e.g., **architettonico** architectonic || *pref m & f* archi-, e.g., **architettura** architecture
archibù·gio *m* (-gi) harquebus
Archimède *m* Archimedes
architettare (architétto) *tr* to plan (*a building*); (fig) to contrive, plot
architétto *m* architect
architettòni·co -ca *adj* (-ci -che) architectural
architettura *f* architecture
architetturale *adj* architectural
architrave *m* architrave; doorhead, lintel
archiviare §287 *tr* to file; to lay aside, shelve; (law) to throw out
archì·vio *m* (-vi) archives; record office; chancery, public records
archivi·sta *mf* (-sti -ste) archivist, file clerk

arci- *pref adj* archi-, e.g., **arcivescovile** archiepiscopal || *pref m & f* arch-, e.g., **arciprete** archpriest
arcicontèn·to -ta *adj* (coll) very glad
arcidiàcono *m* archdeacon
arcidu·ca *m* (**-chi**) archduke
arciduchéssa *f* archduchess
arcière *m* archer, bowman
arci·gno -gna *adj* gruff, surly
arcióne *m* saddlebow; **montare in arcioni** to mount, to mount a horse
arcipèla·go *m* (**-ghi**) archipelago
arciprète *m* archpriest; dean
arcivescovado *m* archbishopric
arcivéscovo *m* archbishop
ar·co *m* (**-chi**) bow; (archit) arch; (geom, elec) arc; **arco rampante** flying buttress
arcobaléno *m* rainbow
arco·làio *m* (**-lài**) reel; **girare come un arcolaio** to spin like a top
arcuare (**àrcuo**) *tr* to arch; to bend; to camber
arcua·to -ta *adj* bent, curved; bow (*e.g., legs*); **avere le gambe arcuate** to be bowlegged
ardènte *adj* burning; hot; ardent, impassioned
àrdere §111 *tr* to burn || *intr* to burn; to be in full swing (*said, e.g., of a war*)
ardèsia *f* slate
ardiménto *m* boldness, daring
ardire *m* boldness; presumption, impudence || §176 *intr*—**ardire** + *inf* or ardire di + *inf* to dare to + *inf*
arditézza *f* daring; temerity
ardi·to -ta *adj* daring; rash || *m* (hist) shock trooper
ardóre *m* intense heat; ardor
àr·duo -dua *adj* arduous
àrea *f* area, surface; group, camp; **area arretrata** backward area
àrem *m* (**àrem**) harem
arèna *f* arena; **scendere nell'arena** to throw one's hat in the ring
aréna *f* sand
arenare (**aréno**) *intr* (ESSERE) & *ref* to run aground
arenària *f* sandstone
arén·go *m* (**-ghi**) (hist) town meeting
arenile *m* sandy beach
arenó·so -sa [s] *adj* sandy
areòmetro *m* hydrometer
aeronàuti·co -ca *adj & f* (**-ci -che**) var of **aeronautico**
areoplano *m* var of **aeroplano**
areopòrto *m* var of **aeroporto**
areòstato *m* var of **aerostato**
àrgano *m* winch; (naut) capstan
argentare (**argènto**) *tr* to silver; to silver-plate; to back (*a mirror*) with foil
argenta·to -ta *adj* silver; silvery; silver-plated
argentatura *f* silver plating; silver plate; foil (*of mirror*)
argènte·o -a *adj* silver, silvery
argenteria *f* silverware
argentière *m* silversmith; jeweler
argenti·no -na *adj* silver, silvery; Argentine || *mf* Argentine || *f* high-necked sweater || **l'Argentina** *f* Argentina

argènto *m* silver; (archaic) money; **argenti** silverware; **argento vivo** quicksilver
argentóne *m* German silver
argilla *f* clay
argilló·so -sa [s] *adj* clayey
arginare (**àrgino**) *tr* to dam, dike; to hold back, check
àrgine *m* embankment, dam; (fig) defense
ar·go *m* (**-ghi**) (chem) argon; (orn) grouse || **Argo** *m* Argus
argomentare (**argoménto**) *tr & intr* to argue
argomentazióne *f* argumentation, discussion
argoménto *m* argument; pretext; subject; **fuori dell'argomento** beside the point
argonàu·ta *m* (**-ti**) Argonaut
arguire §176 *tr* to deduce, infer; (archaic) to denote
argutézza *f* wit; witty remark
argu·to -ta *adj* keen, acute; witty
argùzia *f* keenness; wit
ària *f* air; climate; look; mien; aria, tune; poem; **all'aria aperta** in the open air; **a mezz'aria** in midair; halfway; **andare all'aria** to fail; **aria condizionata** air conditioning; **avere l'aria di** to seem to; to look like; **dare aria a** to air; **in aria** in the air; **tira un'aria pericolosa** a mean wind is blowing
aria·nó -na *adj & mf* Aryan
aridi·tà *f* (**-tà**) dryness, aridity; dearth
àri·do -da *adj* arid, dry, barren; (fig) dry
arieggiare §290 (**ariéggio**) *tr* to air; to imitate || *ref*—**arieggiarsi a** to give oneself the airs of
ariète *m* ram; (mil) battering ram || **Ariete** *m* (astr) Aries
ariétta *s* breeze; (mus) short aria
arin·ga *f* (**-ghe**) herring; **aringa affumicata** kippered herring, kipper
arin·go *m* (**-ghi**) assembly; field; joust; **scendere nell'aringo** to throw one's hat in the ring
arió·so -sa [s] *adj* airy, breezy; (fig) of wide scope
àrista *f* loin of pork
arista *f* (bot) awn
aristocràti·co -ca (**-ci -che**) *adj* aristocratic || *mf* aristocrat
aristocrazia *f* aristocracy
Aristòtele *m* Aristotle
aristotèli·co -ca *adj & m* (**-ci -che**) Aristotelian
aritmèti·co -ca (**-ci -che**) *adj* arithmetical || *m* arithmetician || *f* arithmetic
arlecchino *adj invar* harlequin; fiesta (*e.g., dishes*) || **Arlecchino** *m* Harlequin
ar·ma *f* (**-mi**) arm, weapon; (fig) army; (mil) corps, service; **alle prime armi** at the beginning; **arma bianca** steel blade; **arma da taglio** cutting weapon; **arma delle trasmissioni** signal corps
armacòllo *m*—**ad armacollo** slung across the shoulders (*said of a rifle*)
armà·dio *m* (**-di**) cabinet; closet; **armadio a muro** built-in closet; **armadio**

d'angolo corner cupboard; **armadio farmaceutico** medicine cabinet; **armadio guardaroba** armoire

armaiòlo *m* gunsmith

armamentà·rio *m* (**-ri**) outfit, set (*of tools*)

armaménto *m* armament; crew; gun crew; crew (*of rowboat*); outfit, equipment

armare *tr* to arm; to dub (*s.o. a knight*); to outfit, commission (*a ship*); to cock (*a gun*); to brace, shore up (*a building*); (rr) to furnish with track || *ref* to arm oneself; to outfit oneself

arma·to -ta *adj* armed; reinforced (*concrete*) || *m* soldier || *f* army; navy; fleet; (nav) task force

arma·tóre -trice *adj* outfitting || *m* shipowner; (min) carpenter; (rr) trackwalker

armatura *f* armor; scaffold; framework, support; reinforcement (*for concrete*); (elec) plate (*of condenser*)

armeggiare §290 (**arméggio**) *intr* to fumble, fool around; to scheme; (archaic) to handle arms; (archaic) to joust

armeggì·o *m* (**-i**) fooling around; scheming, intriguing

armè·no -na *adj & mf* Armenian

arménto *m* herd

armerìa *f* armory

armière *m* (aer) gunner

armìge·ro -ra *adj* warlike, bellicose || *m* warrior; bodyguard

armistiziale *adj* armistice

armistì·zio *m* (**-zi**) *m* armistice

armonìa *f* harmony; **in armonia con** according to

armòni·co -ca (**-ci -che**) *adj* harmonic; resonant; harmonious || *f* harmonica; **armonica a bocca** mouth organ

armonió·so -sa [s] *adj* harmonious

armonizzare [ddzz] *tr & intr* to harmonize

arnése [s] *m* tool, implement; garb, dress; (coll) gadget; **bene in arnese** well-heeled; **male in arnese** down at the heels

àrnia *f* beehive

arò·ma *m* (**-mi**) aroma, odor; zest

aromàti·co -ca *adj* (**-ci -che**) aromatic

aromatizzare [ddzz] *tr* to flavor; to spice

arpa *f* harp

arpeggiare §290 (**arpéggio**) *intr* to play arpeggios; to play a harp; to strum

arpég·gio *m* (**-gi**) arpeggio

arpìa *f* Harpy; (coll) harpy

arpionare (**arpióno**) *tr* to harpoon

arpióne *m* hinge (*of door*); hook; harpoon; spike (*for mountain climbing*)

arpionismo *m* ratchet

arpi·sta *mf* (**-sti -ste**) harpist

arrabattare *ref* to exert oneself, to strive, to endeavor

arrabbiare §287 *intr* (ESSERE) to go mad (*said of dogs*) || *ref* to become angry (*said of people*)

arrabbia·to -ta *adj* mad (*dog*); angry; obstinate; confirmed

arrabbiatura *f* rage; **prendersi un'arrabbiatura** to burn up (*with rage*)

arraffare *tr* to snatch

arrampicare §197 (**arràmpico**) *ref* to climb, climb up

arrampicata *f* climbing

arrampica·tóre -trice *mf* climber; mountain climber; **arrampicatore sociale** social climber

arrancare §197 *intr* to hobble, limp; to struggle, work hard; to row hard

arrangiaménto *m* agreement; (mus) arrangement

arrangiare §290 *tr* to arrange; to fix; (coll) to steal || *ref* to manage, get along

arrecare §197 (**arrèco**) *tr* to cause; to carry, deliver

arredaménto *m* furnishing; furnishings; equipment

arredare (**arrèdo**) *tr* to furnish; to equip

arreda·tóre -trice *mf* interior decorator; upholsterer; (mov) property man

arrèdo *m* furnishings, furniture; piece of furniture; **arredi sacri** church supplies

arrembàg·gio *m* (**-gi**) boarding (*of a ship*)

arrenare (**arréno**) *tr* to sand

arrèndere §227 *tr* (archaic) to surrender || *ref* to surrender; **arrendersi a discrezione** to surrender unconditionally

arrendévole *adj* yielding, compliant, flexible

arrendevolézza *f* suppleness; compliance

arrestare (**arrèsto**) *tr* to stop; to arrest || *ref* to stop, stay

arrèsto *m* arrest; stop; pause; (mach) stop, catch; **arresti** (mil) house arrest; **in stato d'arresto** under arrest

arretrare (**arrètro**) *tr* to withdraw || *intr* (ESSERE & AVERE) & *ref* to withdraw

arretra·to -ta *adj* withdrawn; backward; back (*issue*); overdue || **arretrati** *mpl* arrears

arricchiménto *m* enrichment

arricchire §176 *tr* to enrich || *intr* (ESSERE) & *ref* to get rich

arricchi·to -ta *mf* nouveau riche

arricciacapél·li *m* (**-li**) curler

arricciare §128 *tr* to curl; to wrinkle; to screw up (*one's nose*); **arricciare il pelo** to bristle (*said of a person*); to bristle up (*said of an animal*) || *ref* to curl up

arriccia·to -ta *adj* curled up || *m* first coat (*of cement*)

arricciatura *f* curling (*of hair*); pleating (*of a skirt*); kink (*in a rope*)

arrìdere §231 *tr* (poet) to grant || *intr* to smile

arrìn·ga *f* (**-ghe**) harangue; (law) lawyer's plea

arringare §209 *tr* to harangue; (law) to plead

arrischiare §287 *tr* to endanger; to risk || *ref* to dare, venture

arrischia·to -ta *adj* risky; daring

arrivare *tr* to reach || *intr* (ESSERE) to arrive; to happen; to get along, be successful; **arrivare a** to reach; to succeed in

arriva·to -ta *adj* arrived; successful; **ben arrivato** welcome

arrivedér·ci *m* (**-ci**) good-bye ‖ *interj* good-bye!, so long!

arrivedérla *interj* good-bye!

arrivismo *m* social climbing, ruthless ambition

arrivi·sta *mf* (**-sti -ste**) social climber

arrivo *m* arrival; (sports) goal line; (sports) finishing line

arroccare §197 (**arrócco**) *tr* to put (*e.g.*, flax) on the distaff ‖ §197 (**arròcco**) *tr* to shelter; (chess) to castle ‖ *ref* to seek shelter; (chess) to castle

arròc·co *m* (**-chi**) castling

arrochire §176 *tr* to make hoarse ‖ *intr* (ESSERE) to become hoarse

arrogante *adj* arrogant, insolent

arroganza *f* arrogance, insolence

arrogare §209 (**arrògo**) *tr*—**arrogare a sé** to arrogate to oneself ‖ *ref* to arrogate to oneself

arrolare §237 *tr* var of **arruolare**

arrossare (**arrósso**) *tr* to redden

arrossire §176 *intr* (ESSERE) to blush; to change color

arrostire §176 *tr* to roast; to toast; **arrostire allo spiedo** to barbecue on the spit ‖ *intr* (ESSERE) & *ref* to roast

arrò·sto *m* (**-sto** & **-sti**) roast

arrotare (**arròto**) *tr* to grind, hone; to smooth; to strike, run over; to grit (*one's teeth*) ‖ *ref* to grind (*to work hard*); to sideswipe

arrotatrice *f* floor sander

arrotatura *f* sharpening

arrotino *m* grinder

arrotolare (**arròtolo**) *tr* to roll

arrotondaménto *m* rounding; rounding out; increase (*in salary*)

arrotondare (**arrotóndo**) *tr* to make round; to round out; to supplement (*a salary*) ‖ *ref* to round out, become plump

arrovellare (**arrovèllo**) *tr* to vex ‖ *ref* to become angry; to strive, endeavor; **arrovellarsi il cervello** to rack one's brains

arroventare (**arrovènto**) *tr* to make red-hot ‖ *ref* to become red-hot

arroventire §176 *tr* & *ref* var of **arroventare**

arruffapòpo·li *m* (**-li**) rabble-rouser

arruffare *tr* to tangle; to muss, rumple; to confuse

arruf·fìo *m* (**-fìi**) tangle; confusion, mess

arruffó·ne -na *mf* blunderer; swindler

arrugginire §176 *tr, intr* (ESSERE) & *ref* to rust

arruolaménto *m* enlistment; draft

arruolare (**arruòlo**) *tr* to recruit; to draft ‖ *ref* to enlist

arruvidire §176 *tr* to make rough, roughen ‖ *intr* (ESSERE) to become rough

arsenale *m* arsenal; navy yard

arsèni·co -ca (**-ci -che**) *adj* arsenic, arsenical ‖ *m* arsenic

ar·so -sa *adj* burnt; dry, parched; **arso di** consumed with

arsura *f* sultriness; dryness

arte *f* art; ability; guile; **ad arte** on purpose; **arti e mestieri** arts and crafts

artefare §173 *tr* to adulterate

artefat·to -ta *adj* adulterated; artificial

artéfice *m* craftsman; creator

artèria *f* artery

arterioscleròsi *m* arteriosclerosis

arterió·so -sa [s] *adj* arterial

artesia·no -na *adj* artesian

àrti·co -ca *adj* (**-ci -che**) arctic ‖ **Artico** *m* Arctic

articolare *adj* articular ‖ *v* (**artìcolo**) *tr* & *ref* to articulate

articola·to -ta *adj* articulated; articulate; (gram) combined; jagged (*coast-line*)

articolazióne *f* articulation

articoli·sta *mf* (**-sti -ste**) columnist; feature writer

artìcolo *m* article; item; paragraph; **articolo di fondo** editorial; **articolo di spalla** comment

artificiale *adj* artificial

artificière *m* pyrotechnist; (mil) demolition expert

artifì·cio *m* (**-ci**) artifice; sophistication, affectation; **artificio d'illuminazione** (mil) flare

artificiosi·tà [s] *f* (**-tà**) artfulness, craftiness; artificiality

artifició·so -sa [s] *adj* artful, crafty; artificial, affected

artigianato *m* craftsmanship

artigia·no -na *adj* of craftsmen ‖ *m* craftsman

artigliare §280 *tr* (poet) to claw

artiglière *m* artilleryman

artiglierìa *f* artillery; **artiglieria a cavallo** mounted artillery

artì·glio *m* (**-gli**) claw; **cadere negli artigli di** to fall into the clutches of

arti·sta *mf* (**-sti -ste**) artist; actor

artìsti·co -ca *adj* (**-ci -che**) artistic

ar·to -ta *adj* (poet) narrow ‖ *m* limb

artrite *f* arthritis

artrìti·co -ca *adj* & *mf* (**-ci -che**) arthritic

arturia·no -na *adj* Arthurian

arzigogolare [dz] (**arzigògolo**) *intr* to muse; to cavil

arzigògolo [dz] *m* fantasy; cavil

arzil·lo -la [dz] *adj* lively, sprightly; (coll) sparkling (*wine*)

arzin·ga *f* (**-ghe**) tong (*of a blacksmith*)

asbèsto *m* asbestos

ascèlla *f* armpit

ascendènte *adj* ascendant ‖ *m* upper hand, ascendancy; **ascendenti** forefathers

ascendènza *f* ancestry, lineage

ascéndere §245 *tr* to climb ‖ *intr* (ESSERE & AVERE) to ascend, climb

ascensionale *adj* rising; lifting

ascensióne *f* ascent, climb ‖ **Ascensione** *f* Ascension, Ascension Day

ascensóre *m* elevator

ascésa [s] *f* ascent

ascèsso *m* abscess

ascè·ta *mf* (**-ti -te**) ascetic

ascèti·co -ca *adj* (**-ci -che**) ascetic

ascetismo *m* asceticism

à·scia *f* (**-sce**) adze

asciugacapél·li *m* (-li) hair drier
asciugamano *m* towel; **asciugamano spugna** Turkish towel
asciugante *adj* drying; blotting; soaking ‖ *m* dryer
asciugare §209 *tr* to dry, dry up; to wipe; to drain (*e.g., a glass of wine*) ‖ *ref* to dry oneself; to dry, dry up
asciuga·tóio *m* (-tói) towel; bath towel
asciugatrice *f* dryer
asciut·to -ta *adj* dry; skinny; blunt (*in speech*) ‖ *m* dry land; dry climate; **all'asciutto** pennyless
ascoltare (ascólto) *tr* to listen to ‖ *intr* to listen
ascolta·tóre -trice *mf* listener
ascólto *m* listening; **stare in ascolto** to listen
ascòrbi·co -ca *adj* (-ci -che) ascorbic
ascrit·to -ta *adj* ascribed; belonging ‖ *m* member
ascrìvere §250 *tr* to inscribe, register; to ascribe, attribute
ascultare *tr* to sound (*s.o.'s chest*)
asèpsi [s] *f* asepsis
asètti·co -ca [s] *adj* (-ci -che) aseptic
asfaltare *tr* to tar, pave
asfalto *m* asphalt
asfissìa *f* asphyxia
asfissiante *adj* asphyxiating; poison (*gas*); boring
asfissiare §287 *tr* to asphyxiate; to bore ‖ *intr* (ESSERE) to be asphyxiated
asfodèlo *m* asphodel
Àsia, l' *f* Asia; **l'Asia Minore** Asia Minor
asiàti·co -ca *adj & mf* (-ci -che) Asian, Asiatic
asilo *m* shelter; asylum; home; **asilo di mendicità** poorhouse; **asilo infantile** kindergarten; **asilo per i vecchi** old-age home, nursing home
asimmetrìa [s] *f* asymmetry
asimmètri·co -ca [s] *adj* (-ci -che) asymmetric(al)
asinàggine [s] *f* stupidity, asininity
asi·nàio [s] *m* (-nài) donkey driver
asinata [s] *f* stupidity, folly
asinerìa [s] *f* asininity
asiné·sco -sca [s] *adj* (-schi -sche) asinine
asini·no -na [s] *adj* asinine
àsino [s] *m* ass, donkey; **fare l'asino a** (slang) to play up to; **qui casca l'asino** here is the rub
asma *f* asthma
asmàti·co -ca *adj & mf* (-ci -che) asthmatic
àsola *f* buttonhole; buttonhole hem
aspàra·go *m* (-gi) asparagus; piece of asparagus; **asparagi** asparagus (*as food*)
aspèrgere §112 *tr* to sprinkle
aspersióne *f* aspersing, sprinkling
aspettare (aspètto) *tr* to wait for, await; to expect; **aspettare al varco** to be on the lookout for ‖ *intr* to wait; **fare aspettare** to keep waiting ‖ *ref* to expect
aspettativa *f* expectancy, expectation; leave of absence without pay
aspètto *m* waiting; aspect, look; **al primo aspetto** at first sight

àspide *m* asp
aspirante *adj* suction (*pump*) ‖ *m* aspirant; applicant, candidate; suitor; upperclassman (*in naval academy*)
aspirapólve·re *m* (-re) vacuum cleaner
aspirare *tr* to inhale, breathe in; to suck (*e.g., air*); (phonet) to aspirate ‖ *intr* to aspire
aspiratóre *m* exhaust fan
aspirazióne *f* aspiration; (aut) intake
aspirina *f* aspirin
aspo *m* reel
asportàbile *adj* removable
asportare (aspòrto) *tr* to remove, take away
asportazióne *f* removal
asprézza *f* sourness; roughness, harshness
a·spro -spra *adj* sour; rough, harsh
assaggiare §290 *tr* to taste; to sample, test; **assaggiare il terreno** (fig) to see how the land lies
assaggia·tóre -trice *mf* taster
assàg·gio *m* (-gi) taste, sample; tasting; test, trial
assài *adj invar* a lot of ‖ *m* much ‖ *adv* enough; fairly; very
assale *m* axle
assalire §242 *tr* to attack, assail; (fig) to seize
assali·tóre -trice *mf* assailant
assaltare *tr* to assault; **assaltare a mano armata** to stick up
assalto *m* assault, attack; (law) battery; **cogliere d'assalto** to catch unawares; **prendere d'assalto** to assault
assaporare (assapóro) *tr* to taste; to relish, enjoy
assassinare *tr* to assassinate; (fig) to murder
assassì·nio *m* (-ni) assassination, murder
assassi·no -na *adj* murderous ‖ *mf* assassin, murderer
asse *m* axle; shaft, spindle; (geom, phys) axis; **asse ereditario** estate; **asse stradale** median strip ‖ *f* plank; **asse da stiro** ironing board
assecondare (assecóndo) *tr* to help; to second; to uphold
assediante *adj* besieging ‖ *m* besieger
assediare §287 (assèdio) *tr* to lay siege to, besiege
assè·dio *m* (-di) siege; **assedio economico** economic sanctions; **cingere d'assedio** to besiege
assegnaménto *m* awarding; allowance; faith, reliance; **fare assegnamento su** to rely upon
assegnare (asségno) *tr* to assign; to prescribe; to distribute; to award
assegnatà·rio -ria *mf* (-ri -rie) assignee
assegnazióne *f* assignment; awarding
asségno *m* allowance; check; **assegni fringe benefits; assegni familiari** family allowance; **assegno a copertura garantita** certified check; **assegno a vuoto** worthless check; **assegno di studio** (educ) stipend; **assegno turistico** traveler's check; **assegno vademecum** certified check; **contro asségno** C.O.D.

assemblàg·gio *m* (-gi) (mach) assembling, assembly
assemblèa *f* assembly
assembraménto *m* gathering
assembrare (assémbro) *tr* & *ref* to gather
assennatézza *f* good judgment, discretion
assenna·to -ta *adj* sensible, prudent
assènso *m* approval, consent
assentare (assènto) *ref* to be absent, to absent oneself
assènte *adj* absent || *mf* absentee
assenteìsmo *m* absenteeism
assentire (assènto) *tr* (poet) to grant || *intr* to assent, acquiesce; **assentire con un cenno** to nod assent
assènza *f* absence
assenziènte *adj* consenting, approving
assèn·zio *m* (-zi) absinthe; (bot) wormwood
asserire §176 *tr* to affirm, assert
asserragliare §280 *tr* to barricade || *ref* to barricade oneself
assèrto *m* (poet) assertion
asser·tóre -trice *mf* advocate, supporter
asserviménto *m* enslavement
asservire §176 *tr* to enslave; to subjugate
asserzióne *f* assertion
assessóre *m* councilman; alderman
assestaménto *m* arrangement; settling (*of a building*)
assestare (assèsto) *tr* to arrange; to adapt, regulate; to deliver, deal (*a blow*) || *ref* to become organized; to settle (*said of a building*)
assesta·to -ta *adj* sensible, prudent
assetare (asséto) *tr* to make thirsty; (fig) to inflame
asseta·to -ta *adj* thirsty; parched; eager || *mf* thirsty person
assettare (assètto) *tr* to tidy, straighten up || *ref* to straighten oneself up
assetta·to -ta *adj* tidy
assètto *m* arrangement; order; (naut) trim; **assetto longitudinale** (aer) pitch, attitude; **in assetto di guerra** ready for war; **male in assetto** in poor shape
asseverare (assèvero) *tr* to asseverate, assert
assicèlla *f* roofing board, lath; batten
assicuràbile *adj* insurable
assicurare *tr* to assure; to insure; to protect; to fasten; to deliver (*e.g., a thief*) || *ref* to make sure; to take out insurance
assicura·to -ta *adj* & *mf* insured || *f* insured letter
assicura·tóre -trice *mf* insurer
assicurazióne *f* assurance; insurance; **assicurazione contro gli infortuni sul lavoro** workman's compensation insurance; **assicurazione contro i danni** casualty insurance; **assicurazione incendio** fire insurance; **assicurazione infortuni** accident insurance; **assicurazione per la vecchiaia** old age insurance; **assicurazione sociale** social security; **assicurazione sulla vita** life insurance

assideraménto *m* freezing; frostbite
assiderare (assìdero) *ref* to freeze; to become frostbitten
assìdere §113 *ref* (poet) to take one's seat (*e.g., on the throne*)
assì·duo -dua *adj* assiduous, diligent
assième *m* ensemble || *adv* together; **assieme a** together with
assiepare (assièpo) *tr* & *ref* to crowd
assillante *adj* disturbing, troublesome
assillare *tr* to beset, trouble
assillo *m* gadfly; (fig) stimulus, goad
assimilare (assìmilo) *tr* to assimilate; to compare
assimilazióne *f* assimilation
assiòlo *m* horned owl
assiò·ma *m* (-mi) axiom
assiomàti·co -ca *adj* (-ci -che) axiomatic
assì·ro -ra *adj* & *mf* Assyrian
assisa *f* (poet) uniform, livery; (geol) layer; (archaic) duty, tax; **assise** criminal court; assembly, session; (hist) assises
assistènte *mf* assistant; **assistente sanitario** practical nurse; **assistente sociale** social worker || *m*—**assistente ai lavoro** foreman || *f*—**assistente di volo** (aer) hostess
assistènza *f* assistance, help; intervention; **assistenza pubblica** relief
assistenziale *adj* welfare, charity
assìstere §114 *tr* to assist, help || *intr*—**assistere a** to attend, be present at
assito *m* flooring, boarding
assiuòlo *m* var of assiolo
asso *m* ace; **asso del volante** speed king; **piantare in asso** to walk out on
associare §128 (assòcio) *tr* to associate; **associare alle carceri** to take to prison || *ref* to associate; to become a member; to subscribe; to participate
associa·to -ta *adj* associate || *mf* associate, partner
associazióne *f* association; union; subscription; membership
assodare (assòdo) *tr* to solidify; to strengthen; to ascertain || *ref* to solidify; to strengthen
assoggettare (assoggètto) *tr* to subject, subdue || *ref* to submit
assola·to -ta *adj* sunny, exposed to the sun
assolcare §197 (assólco) *tr* to furrow
assoldare (assòldo) *tr* to hire, recruit
assólo *m* (mus) solo
assolutismo *m* absolutism
assolutìsti·co -ca *adj* (-ci -che) absolutist, despotic
assolu·to -ta *adj* & *m* absolute
assoluzióne *f* absolution
assòlvere §115 *tr* to absolve; to fulfill
assomigliare §280 *tr* to compare; to make similar, make equal || *intr* (ESSERE & AVERE) (with *dat*) to resemble, to look like; to be like || *ref* to resemble each other, look alike; **assomigliarsi a** to resemble
assommare (assómmo) *tr* to add; to be the epitome of; (archaic) to complete || *intr* (ESSERE) to amount
assonna·to -ta *adj* sleepy
assopire §176 *tr* to lull to sleep; to

soothe || *ref* to drowse, to nod; to calm down

assorbènte *adj* absorbent || *m* sanitary napkin

assorbiménto *m* absorption

assorbire §176 & (assòrbo) *tr* to absorb

assorbi·to -ta *adj* absorbed; **assorbito da** consumed with

assordare (assórdo) *tr* to deafen || *ref* to become deaf; to dim; to lessen

assortiménto *m* assortment; **avere in assortimento** (com) to carry, stock

assortire §176 *tr* to assort, sort out; to stock

assorti·to -ta *adj* assorted; **bene assortito** well matched

assòr·to -ta *adj* engrossed, absorbed

assottigliare §280 *tr* to thin; to sharpen; to reduce || *ref* to grow thinner

assuefare §173 *tr* to accustom || *ref* to become accustomed

assuefazióne *f* habit, custom

assùmere §116 *tr* to assume; to hire; to raise, elevate; (law) to accept in evidence

Assunta *f* Assumption

assunto *m* thesis, argument; (poet) task

assun·tóre -trice *mf* contractor

assunzióne *f* assumption; hiring; (law) examination || **Assunzione** *f* Assumption

assurdi·tà *f* (-tà) absurdity

assur·do -da *adj* absurd || *m* absurdity

assùrgere §117 *intr* (ESSERE) (poet) to rise

asta *f* staff; rod; arm (*e.g., of scale*); lance; leg (*of compass*); stroke (*in handwriting*); shaft (*of arrow*); auction; (naut) boom; (naut) mast; (elec) trolley pole; **a mezz'asta** half-mast; **vendere all'asta** to auction, auction off

astante *mf* bystander || *m* physician on duty (*in a hospital*)

astanterìa *f* receiving ward

astato *m* (chem) astatine

astè·mio -mia *adj* abstemious, temperate || *mf* teetotaler

astenére §271 *ref* to abstain

astensióne *f* abstention

astenuto *m* person who abstains from voting; abstention (*vote withheld*)

astèrgere §164 (*pp* astèrso) *tr* to wipe

asteri·sco *m* (-schi) asterisk

asticcìola *f* penholder; rib (*of umbrella*); temple (*of eyeglasses*)

àstice *m* (*Hommarus vulgaris*) lobster

asticèlla *f* (sports) bar

astinènte *adj* abstinent

astinènza *f* abstinence

à·stio *m* (-sti) grudge, rancor

astió·so -sa [s] *adj* full of malice, spiteful

astóre *m* goshawk

astràgalo *m* astragalus, anklebone

astrakàn *m* Persian lamb

astrarre §273 *tr* to abstract || *intr*— **astrarre da** to leave aside, overlook

astrat·to -ta *adj* abstract || *m* abstract

astrazióne *f* abstraction

astringènte *adj* & *m* astringent

-astro -astra *suf adj* -ish, e.g., **verdastro**

greenish || *suf mf* -aster, e.g., **poetastro** poetaster

astro *m* star, heavenly body; (bot) aster; (fig) star

astrologìa *f* astrology

astrològi·co -ca *adj* (-ci -che) astrological

astròlo·go *m* (-gi or -ghi) astrologer

astronàu·ta *mf* (-ti -te) astronaut

astronàuti·co -ca (-ci -che) *adj* astronautic(al) || *f* astronautics

astronautizzare [ddzz] *intr* (ESSERE) to be an astronaut

astronave *f* spaceship, spacecraft

astronomìa *f* astronomy

astrònomo *m* astronomer

astronòmi·co -ca *adj* (-ci -che) astronomic(al)

astruserìa *f* abstruseness

astrusi·tà *f* (-tà) abstruseness

astru·so -sa *adj* abstruse

astùc·cio *m* (-ci) case, box

astu·to -ta *adj* astute, crafty

astùzia *f* astuteness, craftiness

àta·vo -va *mf* ancestor

ateismo *m* atheism

atei·sta *mf* (-sti -ste) atheist

Atène *f* Athens

atenèo *m* athenaeum; university

ateniése [s] *adj* & *mf* Athenian

àte·o -a *adj* atheistic || *mf* atheist

atlante *m* atlas || **Atlante** *m* Atlas

atlànti·co -ca *adj* (-ci -che) Atlantic || **Atlantico** *m* Atlantic

atlè·ta *mf* (-ti -te) athlete

atletéssa *f* female athlete

atlèti·co -ca (-ci -che) *adj* athletic || *f* athletics; **atletica leggera** track and field

atmosfèra *f* atmosphere

atmosfèri·co -ca *adj* (-ci -che) atmospheric

atòllo *m* atoll

atòmi·co -ca *adj* (-ci -che) atomic; (coll) stunning

atomizzare [ddzz] *tr* to atomize

atomizzatóre [ddzz] *m* atomizer

àtomo *m* atom

atòni·co -ca *adj* (-ci -che) (pathol) weak

àto·no -na *adj* (gram) atonic

atout *m* (atouts) trump

à·trio *m* (-tri) entrance hall, lobby

atróce *adj* atrocious

atroci·tà *f* (-tà) atrocity

atrofìa *f* atrophy

atròfi·co -ca *adj* (-ci -che) atrophied

atrofizzare [ddzz] *tr* & *ref* to atrophy

attaccabottó·ni *mf* (-ni) bore, pest, buttonholer

attaccabri·ghe *mf* (-ghe) (coll) quarrelsome person, scrapper

attaccaménto *m* attachment, affection

attaccapan·ni *m* (-ni) coathanger

attaccare §197 *tr* to attach; to bind, unite; to sew on; to stick; to hitch (*a horse*); to hang; to attack; to strike up (*a conversation*); to begin; to communicate (*a disease*); **attaccare un bottone a** (fig) to buttonhole || *intr* to stick; to gain a foothold, take root; to begin || *ref* to stick; to

cling; to spread (*said of a disease*); (fig) to become attached
attaccatìc·cio -cia *adj* (**-ci -ce**) sticky
attacchino *m* billposter
attac·co *m* (**-chi**) attachment; onslaught; fastening; beginning; seizure (*e.g., of epilepsy*); spell (*e.g., of coughing*); (elec) plug; (rad) jack; (sports) forward line; **attacco cardiaco** heart attack
attagliare §280 *ref*—**attagliarsi a** to fit, become
attanagliare §280 *tr* to grip; to seize; to hold (*e.g., with tongs*)
attardare *ref* to tarry, delay
attecchire §176 *intr* to take root; to take hold
atteggiaménto *m* attitude
atteggiare §290 (**attéggio**) *tr* to compose (*e.g., one's face*); to place ‖ *ref* to pose; to strike an attitude
attempa·to -ta *adj* elderly
attendaménto *m* camping; jamboree (*of Boy Scouts*)
attendare (**attèndo**) *ref* to encamp; to pitch one's tent
attendènte *m* (mil) orderly
attèndere §270 *tr* to await; (archaic) to keep; **attendere l'ora propizia** to bide one's time ‖ *intr*—**attendere a** to attend to
attendìbile *adj* reliable
attendismo *m* wait-and-see attitude
attendì·sta (**-sti -ste**) *adj* wait-and-see ‖ *mf* fence-sitter
attenére §271 *tr* (poet) to keep (*a promise*) ‖ *intr*—**attenere** (with *dat*) to concern, e.g., **ciò non gli attiene** this does not concern him ‖ *ref*—**attenersi a** to conform to
attentare (**attènto**) *intr*—**attentare a** to attempt (*s.o.'s life*) ‖ *ref* to make an attempt, dare
attentato *m* attempt
attenta·tóre -trice *mf* would-be murderer; attacker
attèn·ti *m* (**-ti**) attention ‖ *interj* (mil) attention!
attèn·to -ta *adj* attentive; careful
attenuare (**attènuo**) *tr* to extenuate, play down; to attenuate; to mitigate
attenzióne *f* attention; **fare attenzione** to take care; **prestare attenzione** to pay attention
atterràg·gio *m* (**-gi**) landing; **atterraggio di fortuna** emergency landing; **atterraggio senza carrello** crash-landing
atterraménto *m* landing; pinning, pin (*in wrestling*); (boxing) knocking down; **atterramento frenato** (aer) arrested landing
atterrare (**attèrro**) *tr* to fell; to knock down; to pin (*in wrestling*); (fig) to humiliate ‖ *intr* to land; **atterrare scassando** or **atterrare senza carrello** to crash-land
atterrire §176 *tr* to frighten, terrify ‖ *ref* to become frightened
atté·so -sa [s] *adj* awaited, expected; **atteso che** considering that ‖ *f* waiting; expectation; **in attesa (di)** waiting (for)

attestare (**attèsto**) *tr* to certify, attest; to prove; to join; (mil) to deploy ‖ *ref* (mil) to take a stand
attestato *m* certificate
attestazióne *f* testimony; affidavit; attestation, proof
àtti·co -ca (**-ci -che**) *adj* & *mf* Attic ‖ *m* attic
attì·guo -gua *adj* adjacent, contiguous
attillare *tr* & *ref* to preen
attilla·to -ta *adj* tight, close-fitting; tidy, all dressed up
àttimo *m* moment, split second; **di attimo in attimo** any moment
attinènte *adj* related, pertinent
attinènza *f* relation; **attinenze** appurtenances; annexes
attìngere §126 *tr* to draw (*water*); to get; (poet) to attain (*e.g., glory*)
attingi·tóio *m* (**-tói**) ladle
attirare *tr* to draw, attract
attitùdine *f* aptitude; attitude
attivare *tr* to activate; to expedite
attivazióne *f* activation; reassessment
attivi·tà *f* (**-tà**) activity; **attività** *fpl* assets
attì·vo -va *adj* active; profit-making ‖ *m* assets
attizzare *tr* to stir, poke (*a fire*); (fig) to stir up
attizza·tóio *m* (**-tói**) poker
at·to -ta *adj* apt, fit ‖ *m* act, action; gesture; (law) instrument; **all'atto pratico** in reality; **atti** proceedings (*of a learned society*); **atti notarili** legal proceedings; **atto di nascita** birth certificate; **fare atto di presenza** to put in a brief formal appearance; **atto di vendita** bill of sale; **nell'atto** o **sull'atto** in the act
attòni·to -ta *adj* astonished
attorcigliare §280 *tr* to twist ‖ *ref* to wind; to coil up
attóre *m* actor; (law) plaintiff; **attore giovane** (theat) juvenile; **primo attore** (theat) lead
attorniare §287 (**attórnio**) *tr* to surround; (fig) to dupe
attórno *adv* around; **andare attorno** to walk around; **attorno a** around, near; **darsi d'attorno** to busy oneself; **levarsi qlcu d'attorno** to get rid of s.o.
attortigliare §280 *tr* to twist ‖ *ref* to wind; to coil up
attraccare §197 *tr* & *intr* to moor, dock
attrac·co *m* (**-chi**) mooring, docking
attraènte *adj* attractive
attrarre §273 *tr* to attract, draw
attratti·vo -va *adj* attractive; alluring ‖ *f* attraction, charm
attraversaménto *m* crossing; **attraversamento pedonale** pedestrian crossing
attraversare (**attravèrso**) *tr* to cross; to go through; to thwart; **attraversare il passo a** to stand in the way of
attravèrso *adv* across; crosswise; **andare attraverso** to go down the wrong way (*said of food or drink*); (fig) to go wrong; **attraverso a** through, across ‖ *prep* through, across
attrazióne *f* attraction
attrezzare (**attrézzo**) *tr* to outfit, equip

attrezzatura *f* outfit; gear, equipment; **attrezzatura di una nave** rigging; **attrezzature** facilities

attrezzi·sta (-sti -ste) *mf* gymnast ‖ *m* toolmaker; (theat) property man

attrézzo *m* tool, utensil; **attrezzi** gymnastic equipment

attribuire §176 *tr* to award; to attribute; **attribuire qlco a qlcu** to credit s.o. with s.th ‖ *ref* to ascribe to oneself, claim for oneself

attributo *m* attribute

attribuzióne *f* attribution

attrice *f* actress; (law) plaintiff; **prima attrice** (theat) lead

attristare *tr* (poet) to sadden ‖ *ref* to become sad

attri·to -ta *adj* worn, worn-out ‖ *m* attrition; disagreement

attruppare *tr* to band, group ‖ *ref* to mill about, throng

attuàbile *adj* feasible

attuale *adj* present; present-day, current

attuali·tà *f* (-tà) timeliness; reality; **attualità** *fpl* current events; **di viva attualità** newsworthy; timely; in the news

attualizzare [ddzz] *tr* to bring up to date ‖ *ref* to become a reality

attuare (àttuo) *tr* to carry out, make come true ‖ *ref* to come true

attuà·rio -ria (-ri -rie) *adj* (hist) transport (*e.g., ship*) ‖ *m* actuary

attuazióne *f* realization

attutire §176 *tr* to mitigate; to deaden (*a sound, a blow*) ‖ *ref* to diminish (*said of a sound*)

audace *adj* audacious

audàcia *f* audacity

audiofrequènza *f* audio frequency

audiovisi·vo -va *adj* audio-visual

auditi·vo -va *adj* var of **uditivo**

auditóre *m* var of **uditore**

auditò·rio *m* (-ri) auditorium

audizióne *f* program; audition; (law) hearing

àuge *f* acme; **essere in auge** to enjoy a great reputation; to be in vogue; to be on top of the world

augurale *adj* well-wishing; salutatory

augurare (àuguro) *tr* to wish; to bid (*good day*) ‖ *intr* to augur ‖ *ref* to hope; to expect

àugure *m* augur

augù·rio *m* (-ri) wish; augury, omen

augustè·o -a *adj* Augustan

augu·sto -sta *adj* august, venerable

àula *f* hall; classroom; (poet) chamber (*of a palace*)

àuli·co -ca *adj* (-ci -che) courtly; noble, elevated

aumentare (auménto) *tr* to augment, increase ‖ *intr* (ESSERE) to increase, rise

aum100nto *m* increase

àura *f* (poet) breeze; (poet) breath

àure·o -a *adj* golden, gold

aurèola *f* halo

auricolare *adj* ear; first-hand ‖ *m* (telp) receiver; (rad) earphone

auròra *f* dawn; (fig) aurora

ausiliare *adj* auxiliary ‖ *m* collaborator, helper

ausilià·rio -ria (-ri -rie) *adj* auxiliary; (mil) supply ‖ *m* helper; (mil) reserve officer ‖ *f* female member of the armed forces

ausì·lio *m* (-li) (poet) help

auspicare §197 (àuspico) *tr* to wish, augur

àuspice *m* sponsor; (hist) augur

auspì·cio *m* (-ci) sponsorship; (hist, poet) augury, omen; **sotto gli auspici di** under the auspices of

austeri·tà *f* (-tà) austerity

austè·ro -ra *adj* austere

australe *adj* austral, southern

Austràlia, l' *f* Australia

australia·no -na *adj & mf* Australian

Austria, l' *f* Austria

austria·co -ca *adj & mf* (-ci -che) Austrian

autarchìa *f* autarky; autonomy (*of an administration*)

autàrchi·co -ca *adj* (-ci -che) autonomous, independent

autènti·ca *f* (-che) authentication of a signature or a document

autenticare §197 (autèntico) *tr* to authenticate

autentici·tà *f* (-tà) authenticity

autènti·co -ca *adj* (-ci -che) authentic, genuine ‖ *f* see **autentica**

autière *m* (mil) driver

auti·sta *mf* (-sti -ste) (aut) driver

au·to *f* (-to) auto

autoabbronzante [dz] *adj* tanning ‖ *m* tanning lotion

autoaffondaménto *m* scuttling

autoambulanza *f* ambulance

autobiografìa *f* autobiography

autobiogràfi·co -ca *adj* (-ci -che) autobiographical

autoblinda·to -ta *adj* armored

autoblin·do *m* (-do) armored car

autobótte *f* tank truck

àuto·bus *m* (-bus) bus

autocarro *m* truck, motor truck

autocèntro *m* (mil) motor pool

autocistèrna *f* tank truck

autocivétta *f* unmarked police car

autocolónna *f* row of cars

autocombustióne *f* spontaneous combustion

autocontròllo *m* self-control

autocorrièra *f* intercity bus, highway bus

autocrazìa *f* autocracy

autocrìti·ca *f* (-che) self-criticism

autòcto·no -na *adj* autochthonous, independent

autodecisióne *m* free will

autodeterminazióne *f* self-determination

autodidat·ta *mf* (-ti -te) self-taught person

autodidàtti·co -ca *adj* (-ci -che) self-instructional

autodifésa [s] *f* self-defense

autodisciplina *f* self-discipline

autòdromo *m* automobile race track

autoemotè·ca *f* (-che) bloodmobile

autofilettante *adj* self-threading

autofurgóne *m* van; **autofurgone cellu-**

lare police van; **autofurgone funebre** hearse
autogiro *m* autogyro
autogovèrno *m* self-government
autògra·fo -fa *adj* autographic(al) ‖ *m* autograph
auto·grù *f* (-grù) tow truck
autolesioni·sta *mf* (-sti -ste) person who wounds himself to avoid the draft or collect insurance
autoletti·ga *f* (-ghe) ambulance
autolibro *m* bookmobile
autolìnea *f* bus line
autò·ma *m* (-mi) automaton, robot
automàti·co -ca (-ci -che) *adj* automatic ‖ *m* snap
automatizzare [ddzz] *tr* to automate
automazióne *f* automation
automèzzo [ddzz] *m* motor vehicle
automòbile *f* automobile, car; **automobile da corsa** racing car; **automobile di serie** stock car; **automobile fuori serie** custom-made car
automobilismo *m* motoring
automobili·sta *mf* (-sti -ste) motorist
automobilìsti·co -ca *adj* (-ci -che) car, automobile
automo·tóre -trice *adj* self-propelled ‖ *f* (rr) automotive rail car
autolég·gio *m* (-gi) car rental agency
autonomìa *f* autonomy; (aer, naut) cruising radius
autonomi·sta *adj* (-sti -ste) autonomous
autòno·mo -ma *adj* autonomous, independent
autoparchég·gio *m* (-gi) parking; parking lot
autopar·co *m* (-chi) parking; parking lot
autopiano *m* player piano
autopilò·ta *m* (-ti) (aer) automatic pilot
autopómpa *f* fire engine
autopsìa *f* autopsy
autorà·dio *f* (-dio) car radio
autóre *m* author; perpetrator; creator, maker
autoreattóre *m* ramjet engine
autorespiratóre *m* aqualung
autorévole *adj* authoritative
autoriméssa *f* garage
autori·tà *f* (-tà) authority
autorità·rio -ria *adj* (-ri -rie) authoritarian
autoritratto *m* self-portrait
autorizzare [ddzz] *tr* to authorize
autorizzazióne [ddzz] *f* authorization
autoscala *f* hook and ladder; ladder (*of hook and ladder*)
autoscuòla *f* driving school
autoservì·zio *m* (-zi) bus service, bus line; self-service
autosilo *m* parking garage
autostazióne *f* bus station
autostèllo *m* roadside motel
auto·stòp *m* (-stòp) hitchhiking; **fare l'autostop** to hitchhike
autostoppi·sta *mf* (-sti -ste) hitchhiker
autostrada *f* highway, turnpike
autosufficiènte *adj* self-sufficient
autote·làio *m* (-lài) (aut) frame
autotrasportare (**autotraspòrto**) *tr* to truck

autotrasportatóre *m* trucker
autotreni·sta *m* (-sti) truck driver, teamster
autotrèno *m* tractor trailer
autoveìcolo *m* motor vehicle
autovettura *f* car, automobile
autrice *f* authoress
autunnale *adj* autumnal, fall
autunno *m* autumn, fall
avallare *tr* to endorse (*a promissory note*); to guarantee
avallo *m* endorsement (*of a promissory note*)
avambràc·cio *m* (-ci) forearm
avampósto *m* outpost
avancàrica *f*—**ad avancarica** muzzle-loading
avanguàrdia *f* vanguard; avant-garde
avanguardismo *m* avant-garde
avanguardi·sta *m* (-sti) avant-gardist; (hist) member of Fascist youth organization
avannòtto *m* small fry (*young fresh-water fish*)
avanti *adj* preceding ‖ *m* forward ‖ *adv* forward, ahead; **andare avanti** to proceed, to go ahead; **andare avanti negli anni** to be up in years; **avanti a** in front of; **avanti che** rather than; **avanti di** before; **essere avanti** to be advanced (*in work or study*); **in avanti** ahead ‖ *prep*—**avanti Cristo** before Christ; **avanti giorno** before daybreak ‖ *interj* come in!
avantièri *adv* day before yesterday
avantrèno *m* (aut) front-axle assembly; (mil) limber
avanzaménto *m* advancement
avanzare *tr* to advance; to overcome; to be creditor for, e.g., **avanza cento dollari da suo fratello** he is his brother's creditor for one hundred dollars; to save ‖ *intr* (mil) to advance ‖ *intr* (ESSERE) to advance; to stick out; to be abundant; to be left over, e.g., **avanzano due polpette** two meatballs are left over; **avanzare negli anni** to grow older ‖ *ref* to advance, come forward
avanza·to -ta *adj* advanced; progressive ‖ *f* (mil) advance
avanzo *m* remainder; **avanzi** remains
avarìa *f* damage, breakdown; (naut) average
avariare §287 *tr* to damage, spoil ‖ *intr* to spoil
avaria·to -ta *adj* damaged, spoiled
avarìzia *f* avarice, greed
ava·ro -ra *adj* avaricious, stingy ‖ *mf* miser
avellana *f* filbert
avellano *m* filbert tree
avèllo *m* (poet) tomb
avéna *f* oats
avére *m* belongings, property; assets, credit; amount due ‖ §118 *tr* to have; to hold; to wear; to receive, get; to stand (*a chance*); to be, e.g., **avere . . . anni** to be . . . years old; **avere caldo** to be hot; to be warm; **avere fame** to be hungry; **avere freddo** to be cold; **avere fretta** to be in a hurry;

avere paura to be afraid; **avere ragione** to be right; **avere sete** to be thirsty; **avere sonno** to be sleepy; **avere torto** to be wrong; **avere vergogna** to be ashamed; **avere voglia di** to be anxious to; **avere qlco da** + *inf* to have s.th to + *inf*, e.g., **ho molto lavoro da fare** I have a lot of work to do; **averla con** to be angry at; **non avere niente a che fare con** to have nothing to do with || *impers*— **v'ha** there is || *aux* to have, e.g., **ha letto il giornale** he has read the newspaper; **avere da** + *inf* to have to + *inf*, e.g., **avevo da lavorare** I had to work; **to be to** + *inf*, e.g., **ha da venire alle cinque** he is to arrive at five o'clock

avià·rio -ria (-ri -rie) *adj* bird || *m* aviary

avia·tóre -trice *mf* aviator || *f* aviatrix

aviazióne *f* aviation

avicoltóre *m* bird raiser; poultry farmer

avidi·tà *f* (**-tà**) avidity, greediness

àvi·do -da *adj* avid, greedy

avière *m* airman

aviogètto *m* jet plane

aviolìnea *f* airline

aviopista *f* (aer) airstrip

aviorimésso *f* (aer) hangar

aviotrasporta·to -ta *adj* airborne

avi·to -ta *adj* ancestral

a·vo -va *mf* grandparent; ancestor || *m* grandfather || *f* grandmother

avocare §197 (**àvoco**) *tr* to demand (*jurisdiction*); to expropriate

avò·rio *m* (**-ri**) ivory

avul·so -sa *adj* (poet) torn, uprooted; (poet) separated

avvalére §278 *ref*—**avvalersi di** to avail oneself of

avvallaménto *m* sinking, settling

avvallare *tr* (poet) to lower (*e.g., one's eyes*) || *ref* to sink; (lit) to humiliate oneself

avvalorare (**avvalóro**) *tr* to strengthen, confirm || *ref* to gain strength

avvampare *tr* (poet) to inflame || *intr* (ESSERE) to burn

avvantaggiare §290 *tr* to be profitable to; to benefit || *ref* to profit; **avvantaggiarsi su** to overcome; to beat

avvedére §279 *ref*—**avvedersi di** to notice, become aware of

avvedutézza *f* discernment; shrewdness

avvedu·to -ta *adj* prudent; shrewd; **fare qlcu avveduto di** to inform s.o. of

avvelenaménto *m* poisoning

avvelenare (**avveléno**) *tr* to poison || *ref* to take poison; to be poisoned

avveniménto *m* happening, event

avvenire *adj invar* future, to come || *m* future; **in avvenire** in the future || §282 *intr* (ESSERE) to happen, occur; **avvenga quel che vuole** come what may

avventare (**avvènto**) *tr* to hurl; to deliver (*a blow*); to venture (*an opinion*) || *ref* to throw oneself

avventatézza *f* thoughtlessness, heedlessness

avventa·to -ta *adj* thoughtless, heedless; **all'avventata** heedlessly

avventì·zio -zia *adj* (**-zi -zie**) outside, exterior; temporary, occasional

avvènto *m* advent; elevation, rise

avven·tóre -tóra *mf* customer, consumer

avventura *f* adventure

avventuriè·ro -ra *adj* adventurous || *m* adventurer || *f* adventuress

avventuró·so -sa [s] *adj* adventurous, adventuresome

avverare (**avvéro**) *tr* to make true || *ref* to come true

avvèr·bio *m* (**-bi**) adverb

avversà·rio -ria (-ri -rie) *adj* opposing, contrary || *mf* adversary, opponent

avversióne *f* aversion

avversi·tà *f* (**-tà**) adversity

avvèr·so -sa *adj* adverse; (obs) opposite || **avverso** *prep* (law) against

avvertènza *f* prudence, caution; advice; **avvertenze** instructions, directions

avvertiménto *m* caution, warning; advice

avvertire (**avvèrto**) *tr* to caution, warn; to notice

avvezzare (**avvézzo**) *tr* to accustom; to inure; to train; **avvezzar male** to spoil || *ref* to get accustomed

avvéz·zo -za *adj* accustomed

avviaménto *m* starting; introduction; trade school; good shape (*of a business*); (mach) starting; (typ) adjustment (*of printing press*)

avviare §119 *tr* to start, set in motion; to introduce; to initiate; to begin || *ref* to set out

avvia·to -ta *adj* going, thriving (*concern*)

avvicendaménto *m* alteration, rotation (*of crops*)

avvicendare (**avvicèndo**) *tr* & *ref* to alternate

avvicinaménto *m* approach; rapprochement

avvicinare *tr* to bring near or closer; to approach, go or come near to || *ref* to approach, come near; **avvicinarsi a** to come closer, approach

avviliménto *m* discouragment, dejection

avvilire §176 *tr* to degrade; to deject || *ref* to become dejected, become discouraged

avviluppare *tr* to entangle, snarl; to wrap

avvinazza·to -ta *adj* & *mf* drunk

avvincènte *adj* fascinating

avvìncere §285 *tr* to fascinate, charm; (poet) to twine

avvinghiare §287 *tr* to claw; to clasp, clutch || *ref* to grip one another

avvì·o *m* (**-i**) beginning

avvisàglia *f* skirmish; **prime avvisaglie** onset; first signs

avvisare *tr* to inform, advise; (archaic) to observe, notice

avvisa·tóre -trice *mf* announcer, messenger || *m* alarm; (theat) callboy; **avvisatore acustico** (aut) horn; **avvisatore d'incendio** fire alarm

avviso *m* advise; notice, poster; opinion; **avviso di chiamata alle armi**

notice of induction; **sull'avviso** on
one's guard
avvistare *tr* to sight
avvitaménto *m* (aer) tailspin
avvitare *tr* to screw; to fasten || *ref*
(aer) to go into a tailspin
avviticchiare §287 *tr* to entwine || *ref* to
cling
avvivare *tr* to revive; to stir up
avvizzire §176 *tr* & *intr* (ESSERE) to
wither
avvocatéssa *f* woman lawyer
avvocato *m* lawyer, attorney
avvocatura *f* law, legal profession
avvòlgere §289 *tr* to wind; to wrap up;
to spread over, surround || *ref* to
wind around; to wrap oneself up
avvolgiménto *m* winding; wrapping;
(elec) coil; (mil) envelopment
avvol·tóio *m* (-tói) vulture
avvoltolare (avvòltolo) *tr* to roll up ||
ref to roll around, wallow
aziènda [dz] *f* business, firm
azionare (azióno) *tr* to start; to drive,
propel
azionà·rio -ria *adj* (-ri -rie) (com) stock
azióne *f* action, act; (law) suit; (com)
share (*of stock*); **azione legale** prosecution; **azione privilegiata** preferred
stock
azioni·sta *mf* (-sti -ste) stockholder,
shareholder

azòto [dz] *m* nitrogen
azoturo [dz] *m* nitride
aztè·co -ca *adj* & *mf* (-chi -che) Aztec
azzannare *tr* to seize with the fangs
azzardare [ddzz] *tr* to risk; to advance
|| *ref* to dare
azzarda·to -ta [ddzz] *adj* daring
azzardo [ddzz] *m* chance, hazard
azzardó·so -sa [ddzz] [s] *adj* hazardous, risky
azzeccagarbu·gli *m* (-gli) shyster
azzeccare §197 (azzécco) *tr* to hit; to
deliver; to pass off (*counterfeit
money*); **azzeccarla** (coll) to hit the
mark
azzimare [ddzz] (àzzimo) *tr* & *ref* to
spruce up
àzzi·mo -ma [ddzz] *adj* unleavened
(*bread*)
azzittare & **azzittire** §176 *tr* to hush ||
ref to keep quiet
azzoppare (azzòppo) *tr* to cripple || *ref*
to become lame or crippled
Azzòrre [ddzz] *fpl* Azores
azzuffare *ref* to come to blows; to
scuffle
azzur·ro -ra [ddzz] *adj* blue || *m* blue;
Italian athlete (*in international competition*)
azzurrógno·lo -la [ddzz] *adj* bluish

B

B, b [bi] *m* & *f* second letter of the
Italian alphabet
ba·bàu *m* (-bàu) bogey, bugbear
babbè·o -a *adj* foolish || *mf* fool
babbo *m* (coll) daddy, father
babbù·cia *f* (-ce) babouche; bedroom
slipper
babbuino *m* baboon
babèle *f* babel || **Babele** *f* Babel
babilònia *f* confusion || **Babilònia** *f*
Babylon
babórdo *m* (naut) port
bacare §197 *ref* to become worm-eaten
baca·to -ta *adj* worm-eaten; rotten
bac·ca *f* (-che) berry
bacca·là *m* (-là) dried codfish; (coll)
skinny person; (coll) lummox
baccalaureato *m* baccalaureate, bachelor's degree
baccanale *m* bacchanal
baccano *m* noise, hubbub; **fare baccano**
to carry on
baccante *f* bacchant
baccellière *m* (hist) bachelor
baccèllo *m* pod
baccellóne *m* simpleton, fool
bacchétta *f* rod, wand, baton; **bacchetta
magica** magic wand; **bacchette del
tamburo** drumsticks
bacchétto *m* stick; handle (*of a whip*)
bacchettó·ne -na *mf* bigot
bàcchi·co -ca *adj* (-ci -che) Bacchic
Bacco *m* Baccus

bachè·ca *f* (-che) showcase
bachelite *f* bakelite
bacheròzzo *m* worm; earthworm; (coll)
cockroach
bachicoltura *f* silkworm raising
baciama·no *m* (-ni) kissing of the
hand
baciapi·le *mf* (-le) bigot
baciare §128 *tr* to kiss; **baciare la pol-
vere** to bite the dust || *ref* to kiss one
another
bacia·to -ta *adj* kissed; rhymed (*couplet*)
bacile *m* basin
bacillo *m* bacillus
bacinèlla *f* small basin; (phot) tray
bacino *m* basin; reservoir; cove; (anat)
pelvis; **bacino carbonifero** coal field;
bacino di carenaggio drydock; **bacino fluviale** river basin
bà·cio *m* (-ci) kiss; **a bacio** with a
northern exposure
baciucchiare §287 *tr* to keep on kissing
|| *ref* to pet
ba·co *m* (-chi) worm; **baco da seta** silkworm
bacuc·co -ca *adj* (-chi -che)—**vecchio
bacucco** dotard
bada *f*—**tenere a bada** to stave off; to
delay
badare *tr* to tend, take care of || *intr*
to attend; to take care; to pay attention; **badare a** to mind; to watch

over; to attend to; **badare alla salute** to take care of one's health

badéssa f abbess

badìa f abbey

badilata f shovelful

badile m shovel

baffo m whiskers; whisker; **baffi** mustache; whiskers; **baffo di gatto** (rad) cat's whiskers; **leccarsi i baffi** to lick one's chops; **sotto i baffi** up one's sleeve

baga·gliàio m (-gliài) (rr) baggage car; (rr) baggage room; (aut) baggage rack

bagaglièra f baggage room

bagaglière m baggage master

bagà·glio m (-gli) baggage, luggage; (of knowledge) fund

bagagli·sta m (-sti) porter (in a hotel)

bagarinàg·gio m (-gi) profiteering; (theat) scalping

bagarino m profiteer; scalper

bagà·scia f (-sce) harlot, prostitute

bagattèlla f trifle, bauble

baggiano m nitwit, simpleton

bà·glio m (-gli) (naut) beam

baglióre m shine, gleam

bagnante mf bather, swimmer; vacationer at the seashore

bagnare tr to bathe; to wet; to soak; to water, sprinkle; to moisten; (fig) to celebrate || ref to bathe; to wet one another

bagnaròla f (coll) bathtub

bagnasciu·ga f (-ghe) (naut) waterline

bagnino m lifeguard

bagno m bath; bathroom; bathtub; **bagno di luce** diathermy; **bagno di schiuma** bubble bath; **bagno di sole** sun bath; **bagno di vapore** steam bath; **bagno turco** Turkish bath; **essere in un bagno di sudore** to be soaked with perspiration; **fare il bagno** to take a bath

bagnomarìa m (**bagnimarìa**) double boiler; bain-marie; **a bagnomaria** in a double boiler

bagórdo m carousal, revelry; **far bagordi** to carouse, revel

bàio bàia (**bài bàie**) adj & m bay || f bay; jest; trifle; **dare la baia a** to make fun of, tease

baionétta f bayonet; **baionetta in canna** with fixed bayonet

bàita f mountain hut

balaustrata f balustrade

balaùstro m baluster

balbettaménto m stammering

balbettare (**balbétto**) tr to stammer; to speak poorly (a foreign language) || intr to stammer; to babble (said of a baby)

balbettì·o m (-i) babble (of a baby); stammering

balbùzie f stammering

balbuziènte adj stammering || mf stammerer

Balcani, i the Balkans

balcàni·co -ca adj (-ci -che) Balkan

balconata f balcony; (theat) upper gallery

balcóne m balcony

baldacchino m canopy, baldachin

baldanza f boldness; aplomb, assurance

baldanzó·so -sa [s] adj bold; self-assured

bal·do -da adj bold; self-assured

baldòria f carousal, revelry; **fare baldoria** to carouse, revel

baldrac·ca f (-che) harlot, prostitute

baléna f whale

balenare (**baléno**) intr to stagger || intr (ESSERE) to flash, e.g., **gli balena un pensiero** a thought flashes through his mind || impers (ESSERE)—**balena,** it is lightning

balenièra f whaler, whaleboat

baléno m flash; flash of lightning; **in un baleno** in a flash

balenòttera f rorqual

balèstra f crossbow; (aut) spring, leaf spring

balestrière m crossbowman

bàlia f wet nurse; **balia asciutta** dry nurse; **prendere a balia** to wet-nurse

balìa f power; **in balia di** at the mercy of

balìsti·co -ca (-ci -che) adj ballistic || f ballistics

balla f bale; (vulg) lie

ballàbile adj dance || m dance tune

ballare tr to dance || intr to dance; to shake; to be loose; to wobble (said, e.g., of a chair)

ballata f ballad; (mus) ballade

balla·tóio m (-tói) gallery; perch (in birdcage)

balleri·no -na adj dancing || m ballet dancer; dancer; dancing partner || f dancing girl; ballerina; chorus girl; ballet slipper; (orn) wagtail

ballétto m ballet; chorus

ballo m dance; chorus; ball; stake; **ballo di San Vito** Saint Vitus's dance; **ballo in maschera** masked ball; **in ballo** at stake; in question; **tirare in ballo** to drag in

ballonzolare (**ballónzolo**) intr to hop around

ballottàg·gio m (-gi) runoff

ballottare (**ballòtto**) tr to ballot (e.g., a candidate)

balneare adj bathing; water, watering

baloccare §197 (**balòcco**) tr to amuse with toys || ref to play; to trifle, to fool around

balòc·co m (-chi) toy; hobby

balordàggine f silliness

balór·do -da adj silly, foolish

balsàmi·co -ca adj (-ci -che) balmy; antiseptic

balsamina f balsam

bàlsamo m balm, balsam

bàlti·co -ca adj (-ci -che) Baltic

baluardo m bastion, bulwark

baluginare (**balùgino**) intr (ESSERE) to flicker; to flash (through one's mind)

balza f crag, cliff; flounce (on dress); fringe (on curtains, bedspreads, etc.)

balza·no -na adj white-footed (horse); odd, funny || f flounce; fringe; white mark (on horse's foot)

balzare tr to throw (a rider; said of a horse) || intr (ESSERE) to jump, leap;

to bounce; **balzare in mente a** to suddenly dawn on
balzellare (balzèllo) *intr* to hop
balzèllo *m* hop; tribute; tax; toll; **stare a balzello** to lie in wait
balzellóni *adv*—**a balzelloni** leaping, skipping
balzo *m* leap; bounce; **pigliare la palla al balzo** to take time by the forelock
bambàgia *f* cotton wool
bambinàggine *f* childishness
bambinàia *f* nursemaid; **bambinaia ad ore** baby sitter
bambiné·sco -sca *adj* (**-schi -sche**) childish
bambi·no -na *adj* childish || *mf* child
bambòc·cio *m* (**-ci**) fat baby; doll; rag doll
bàmbola *f* doll; **bambola di pezza** ragdoll
bam·bù *m* (**-bù**) bamboo
banale *adj* banal, commonplace
banali·tà *f* (**-tà**) banality, commonplaceness, triviality
banana *f* banana; hair with curls shaped as rolls
baniòra *f* banana boat
banano *m* banana plant
ban·ca *f* (**-che**) bank; embankment
bancàbile *adj* negotiable
bancarèlla *f* cart, pushcart; stall
banca·rio -ria (**-ri -rie**) *adj* bank, banking || *m* bank clerk
bancarótta *f* bankruptcy; **fare bancarotta** to go bankrupt
banchettare (banchétto) *intr* to feast, banquet
banchétto *m* banquet
banchière *m* banker
banchina *f* garden bench; bicycle path; sidewalk; shoulder (*of highway*); dock, pier; (rr) platform; (mil) banquette
ban·co *m* (**-chi**) bench; seat; bank; witness stand; school (*of fish*); **banco di coralli** coral reef; **banco di ghiaccio** ice pack; **banco di nebbia** fog bank; **banco di prova** (mach) bench; **banco di sabbia** sandbar; **banco d'ostriche** oyster bed; **banco lotto** lottery office
bancogiro *m* (com) transfer of funds
bancóne *m* counter; bench
banconòta *f* banknote
banda *f* band; **andare alla banda** (naut) to list; **da ogni banda** from every side; **mettere da banda** to put aside
bandèlla *f* hinge (*of door or window*); hinged leaf (*of table*)
banderuòla *f* banderole; weather vane
bandièra *f* flag; banner; **battere la bandiera** (e.g., **italiana**) to fly the (*e.g Italian*) flag; **mutar bandiera** to change sides
bandierare (bandièro) *tr* (aer) to feather
bandire §176 *tr* to announce (*e.g., a competitive examination*); to banish
bandìsti·co -ca *adj* (**-ci -che**) (mus) band
bandi·to -ta *adj* announced; open (*house*) || *m* bandit || *f* preserve (*for hunting or fishing*)

bandi·tóre -trice *mf* town crier; auctioneer; barker
bando *m* announcement; banishment; **bandi matrimoniali** (eccl) banns; **mandare in bando** to exile, banish
bandolièra *f* bandoleer; **a bandoliera** slung across the shoulders
bàndolo *m* end of a skein; **perdere il bandolo** to lose the thread (*e.g., of a story*)
bara *f* bier, coffin
barac·ca *f* (**-che**) hut, cabin; (fig) household; **fare baracca** to carouse around
baracca·to -ta *adj* lodged in a hut or a cabin; slum (*e.g., section*) || *m* dweller in a hut or a cabin; slum dweller
baraccóne *m* big circus tent
baraónda *f* hubbub; mess
barare *intr* to cheat (*e.g., at cards*)
bàratro *m* abyss, chasm
barattare *tr* to barter; **barattare le carte in mano a unò** to distort someone's words; **barattar parole** to chat, talk || *intr* to barter
barattière *m* grafter
baratto *m* barter
baràttolo *m* can, canister, jar
barba *f* beard; whiskers; barb, vane (*of feather*); (naut) line; **barba a punta** imperial, goatee; **fare la barba (a)** to shave; **farla in barba a qlcu** to act in spite of s.o.; to dupe s.o.; **mettere barbe** to take root; **radersi la barba** to shave
barbabiètola *f* beet; sugar beet
barbafòrte *m* horseradish
barbagian·ni *m* (**-ni**) owl; (fig) jackass
barbà·glio *m* (**-gli**) glitter, dazzle
barbaré·sco -sca (**-schi -sche**) *adj* Barbary || *m* inhabitant of the Barbary States
barbàri·co -ca *adj* (**-ci -che**) barbaric
barbà·rie *f* (**-rie**) barbarism, barbarity
barbarismo *m* barbarism
bàrba·ro -ra *adj* barbarous, barbaric || *m* barbarian
barbazzale *m* curb (*of bit*)
Barberìa, la Barbary States
barbétta *f* fetlock (*tuft of hair on horse*); goatee; (mil) barbette; (naut) painter
barbière *m* barber
barbierìa *f* barbershop
barbì·glio *m* (**-gli**) barb (*of arrow*)
barbi·no -na *adj* shoddy; botched; stingy
bàr·bio *m* (**-bi**) (ichth) barbel
barbiturato *m* barbiturate
barbitùri·co -ca *adj* (**-ci -che**) barbituric || *m* barbiturate
barbo *m* var of **barbio**
barbò·gio -gia *adj* (**-gi -gie**) senile
barbóne *m* long beard, thick beard; poodle; (coll) bum, hobo
barbó·so -sa [s] *adj* boring
barbugliare §280 *tr* to stutter (*e.g., a word*) || *intr* to stutter; to bubble, gurgle
barbu·to -ta *adj* bearded
bar·ca *f* (**-che**) boat; heap; (fig) family

affairs; **barca a motore** motorboat; **barca da pesca** fishing boat; **barca a remi** rowboat

barcàc·cia *f* (**-ce**) (theat) stage box

barcaiòlo *m* boatman

barcamenare (barcaméno) *ref* to manage, get along

barcarizzo *m* (naut) gangway

barcaròla *f* barcarole

barcata *f* boatful

barchéssa *f* tool shed

barchétta *f* small boat; (naut) log chip

barcollare (barcòllo) *intr* to totter, stagger

barcollóni *adv* staggering, tottering

barcóne *m* barge

bardare *tr* to harness ‖ *ref* to get dressed

bardatura *f* harnessing; harness

bardo *m* bard

bardòsso *m* —**a bardosso** (archaic) bareback

barèlla *f* stretcher

barellare (barèllo) *tr* to carry on a stretcher ‖ *intr* to totter, stagger

barenatura *f* (mach) boring

bargèllo *m* (hist) chief of police; (hist) police headquarters

bargì·glio *m* (**-gli**) wattle

baricèntro *m* center of gravity; (fig) essence, gist

barile *m* barrel, cask

barilòtto *m* keg

bàrio *m* barium

bari·sta *mf* (**-sti -ste**) bartender, barkeeper ‖ *m* barman ‖ *f* barmaid

baritonale *adj* baritone

barìto·no -na *adj* barytone ‖ *m* baritone

barlume *m* glimmer, gleam

baro *m* cheat, cardsharp

baròc·co -ca *adj & m* (**-chi -che**) baroque

baròmetro *m* barometer

baróne *m* baron

baronéssa *f* baroness

barra *f* bar; link; rod; sandbar; **andare alla barra** to plead a case; **barra del timone** (naut) tiller; **barra di torsione** (aut) torsion bar; **barra spaziatrice** space bar (*of typewriter*)

barrare *tr* to cross, draw lines across (*a check*)

barrétta *f* bar (*e.g., of chocolate*)

barricare §197 (**bàrrico**) *tr* to barricade ‖ *ref* to barricade oneself

barricata *f* barricade

barrièra *f* barrier; bar; **barriera corallina** barrier reef

barrire §176 *intr* to trumpet (*said of elephant*)

barrito *m* trumpeting, cry of an elephant

barroc·ciàio *m* (**-ciài**) cart driver

barròc·cio *m* (**-ci**) cart

baruffa *f* fight, quarrel

barzellétta [dz] *f* joke

basale *adj* basal

basalto *m* basalt

basaménto *m* foundation (*of building*); baseboard; base (*of column*)

basare *tr* to base ‖ *ref*—**basarsi su** to be based on; to rest on

ba·sco -sca *adj & mf* (**-schi -sche**) Basque

basculla *f* balance, scale

base *f* base, foundation; (fig) basis; **a base di** composed of, made of; **base navale** naval base, naval station; **in base a** according to

basétta *f* sideburns

bàsi·co -ca *adj* (**-ci -che**) (chem) basic

basilare *adj* basic, fundamental

Basilèa *f* Basel

basìli·ca *f* (**-che**) basilica

basìli·co *m* (**-ci**) basil

basilissa *f* (fig) queen bee

bàsolo *m* large paving stone

bassacórte *f* barnyard

bassézza *f* baseness

bas·so -sa *adj* low; shallow; late (*e.g., date*); (fig) base, vile; **basso di statura** short ‖ *m* bottom; hovel (*in Naples*); (mus) basso ‖ **basso** *adv* low; down; **a basso, da basso** or **in basso** downstairs

bassofóndo *m* (**bassifóndi**) (naut) shallows, shallow water; **bassifondi** underworld, slums

bassopiano *m* lowland

bassorilièvo *m* bas-relief

bassòt·to -ta *adj* stocky ‖ *m* basset hound

bassotuba *m* bass horn

bassura *f* lowland; (fig) baseness

basta *f* hem; basting (*with long stitches*) ‖ *interj* enough!

bastante *adj* sufficient, adequate; comfortable (*income*)

bastar·do -da *adj* bastard; irregular ‖ *m* bastard

bastare *intr* to suffice, be enough; **basta!** enough!; **basta che** + *subj* as long as + *ind*; **bastare a sé stesso** to be self-sufficient; **non basta che** + *subj* not only + *ind*

bastévole *adj* sufficient

bastiménto *m* ship; shipload

bastióne *m* bastion; (fig) defense, rampart

basto *m* packsaddle; (fig) burden

bastonare (bastóno) *tr* to club, cudgel; **bastonare di santa ragione** to give a good thrashing to

bastonata *f* clubbing, cudgeling; **darsi bastonate da orbi** to thrash one another soundly

bastoncino *m* small stick; roll; (anat) rod

bastóne *m* stick, cane; pole; club; baton; staff; French bread; **bastone a leva** crowbar; **bastone animato** sword cane; **bastone da golf** club; **bastone da montagna** alpenstock; **bastone da passeggio** walking stick; **bastone da sci** ski pole; **bastoni** suit in Neapolitan cards corresponding to clubs; **mettere il bastone tra le ruote** to throw a monkey wrench into the machinery

batàc·chio *m* (**-chi**) clapper (*of bell*); cudgel

batata *f* sweet potato

batisfèra *f* bathysphere
batista *f* batiste, cambric
batòsta *f* blow; (fig) blow
bàtrace or **batrace** *m* batrachian
battà·glia *f* (-glie) battle; campaign
battagliare §280 *intr* to fight
battagliè·ro -ra *adj* fighting, warlike
battà·glio *m* (-gli) clapper (*of bell*); knocker
battaglióne *m* battalion
battèllo *m* boat; **battello di salvataggio** lifeboat; **battello pneumatico** rubber raft
battènte *m* leaf (*e.g., of door*); knocker; tapper (*of alarm clock*)
bàttere *m*—**in un batter d'occhio** in the twinkling of an eye || *tr* to beat; to hit; to strike; to strike (*the hour; said of a clock*); to click (*teeth, heels*); to clap (*hands*); to stamp (*one's foot*); to mint (*coins*); to fly (*a flag*); to beat (*time*); to scour (*the countryside*); to flap (*the wings*); (sports) to bat; (sports) to kick (*a penalty*); **battere a macchina** to type; **battere il naso in** to chance upon; **battere la fiacca** to goof off; **battere la grancassa per** to ballyhoo; **battere la strada** to be a streetwalker; **senza batter ciglio** without batting an eye || *intr* (ESSERE) to beat down (*said, e.g., of rain*); to beat (*said of the heart*); to chatter (*said of teeth*); to knock (*at the door*); **battere in ritirata** to beat a retreat; **battere in testa** (aut) to knock
batterìa *f* battery; set (*of utensils*); (sports) heat
batterici·da (-di -de) *adj* bactericidal || *m* bactericide
battèri·co -ca *adj* (-ci -che) bacterial
battè·rio *m* (-ri) bacterium
batteriologìa *f* bacteriology
batteriòlo·go -ga *mf* (-gi -ghe) bacteriologist
batteri·sta *mf* (-sti -ste) jazz drummer
battesimale *adj* baptismal
battésimo *m* baptism; **tenere a battesimo** to christen
battezzare (battézzo) [ddzz] *tr* to christen || *ref* to receive baptism; to assume the name of
battibaléno *m*—**in un battibaleno** in the twinkling of an eye
battibéc·co *m* (-chi) squabble
batticuòre *m* palpitation; (fig) trepidation
battilò·ro *m* (-ro) goldsmith; silversmith
battimano *m* applause
battimuro *m*—**giocare a battimuro** to pitch pennies (against a wall)
battipalo *m* pile driver
battipan·ni *m* (-ni) clothes beater
battira·me *m* (-me) coppersmith
battiscó·pa *m* (-pa) washboard, baseboard
batti-sta *adj & mf* (-sti -ste) Baptist
battistèro *m* baptistry
battistra·da *m* (-da) outrider; (sports) leader; (aut) tread
battitappéto *m* carpet sweeper
bàttito *m* beating; palpitation; ticking;

wink; pitter-patter (*of rain*)
batti·tóio *m* (-tói) leaf (*e.g., of door*); casement; cotton beater
battitóre *m* (hunt) beater; (baseball) batter
battitrice *f* threshing machine
battitura *f* thrashing, whipping; threshing (*e.g., of wheat*)
battu·to -ta *adj* beaten; hammered || *m* pavement || *f* beat; stroke, keystroke; meter (*in poetry*); witticism, quip; (hunt) battue; (mus) bar; (tennis) service; (theat) line; (theat) cue; **battuta d'aspetto** (mus) pause; **dare la battuta** to give the cue
batùffolo *m* wad; (fig) bundle
baule *m* trunk; **baule armadio** wardrobe trunk; **fare i bauli** to be on one's way; **fare il baule** to pack one's trunk
baulétto *m* small trunk; handbag; jewel case
bava *f* slobber; foam, froth; burr (*on metal edge*); **avere la bava alla bocca** to be frothing at the mouth; **bava di vento** breath of air, soft breeze
bavaglino *m* bib
bavà·glio *m* (-gli) gag
bavarése [s] *adj & mf* Bavarian || *f* Bavarian cream; chocolate cream
bàvero *m* collar
bavièra *f* beaver (*of helmet*) || **la Bavièra** Bavaria
bavó·so -sa [s] *adj* slobbering, slobbery
bazza [ddzz] *f* protruding chin; windfall
bazzana [ddzz] *f* sheepskin
bazzècola [ddzz] *f* trifle, bauble
bazzicare §197 (**bàzzico**) *tr* to frequent
bazzòt·to -ta [ddzz] *adj* soft-boiled; uncertain (*weather*)
beare (bèo) *tr* to delight || *ref* to be delighted, be enraptured
beatìfico §197 (**beatìfico**) *tr* to beatify
beatitùdine *f* beatitude, bliss
bea·to -ta *adj* blissful, happy; blessed || *mf* blessed
be·bè *m* (-bè) baby
beccàc·cia *f* (-ce) woodcock
beccaccino *m* snipe
beccafì·co *m* (-chi) figpecker, beccafico
bec·càio *m* (-cài) butcher
beccamòr·ti *m* (-ti) gravedigger
beccare §197 (**bécco**) *tr* to peck; to pick; (coll) to catch || *ref* to peck one another; to quarrel
beccata *f* peck
beccheggiare §290 (**becchéggio**) *intr* (naut) to pitch
becchég·gio *m* (-gi) (naut) pitching
beccherìa *f* butcher shop
becchime *m* food for poultry
becchino *m* gravedigger
béc·co *m* (-chi) beak, bill; tip, point; nozzle (*e.g., of teapot*); billy goat; (vulg) cuckold; **bagnarsi il becco** (joc) to wet one's whistle; **mettere il becco in** (coll; joc) to stick one's nose into; **non avere il becco di un quattrino** to not have a red cent
beccùc·cio *m* (-ci) small bill; lip, spout
beccuzzare *tr* to peck || *ref* to bill (*said of doves*)

béce·ro -ra *adj* (coll) boorish ‖ *m* (coll) boor

beduì·no -na *adj & m* Bedouin

befana *f* (coll) Epiphany; old hag

bèffa *f* jest, mockery; **farsi beffa di** to make fun of

beffar·do -da *adj* mocking

beffare (bèffo) *tr* to mock, deride ‖ *ref* **—beffarsi di** to make fun of

beffeggiare §290 (befféggio) *tr* to scoff at, deride

bè·ga *f* (-ghe) quarrel; trouble

beghina *f* Beguine; bigoted woman

begònia *f* begonia

bèl *adj* apocopated form of **bello**, used only before masculine singular nouns beginning with a consonant except impure **s, z, gn, ps,** and **x,** e.g., **bel ragazzo**

belare (bèlo) *tr* to croon ‖ *intr* to bleat, baa; to moan

belato *m* bleat, baa

bèl·ga *adj & mf* (-gi -ghe) Belgian

Bèlgio, il Belgium

bèll' *adj* apocopated form of **bello**, used only before singular nouns of both genders beginning with a vowel, e.g., **bell'amico; bell'epoca**

bèlla *adj fem* of **bello** ‖ *f* belle; girlfriend; final draft; (sports) final game; (sports) rubber match; **alla bell'e meglio** the best one could; **bella di notte** (bot) four-o'clock

belladònna *f* belladonna

bellétto *m* rouge, makeup

bellézza *f* beauty; **che bellezza!** how lovely!; **la bellezza di** as much as

bellici·sta *adj* (-sti -ste) bellicose

bèlli·co -ca *adj* (-ci -che) war, warlike

bellicó·so -sa [s] *adj* bellicose

belligerante *adj & m* belligerent

belligeranza *f* belligerence

bellimbusto *m* fop, dandy, beau

bèl·lo -la (declined like **quello §7**) *adj* beautiful; lovely; handsome; good-looking; pleasing; fine; quite a, e.g., **una bella cifra** quite a sum; fair; pretty; **bell'e fatto** ready-made; taken care of; **farla bella** to start trouble; (coll) to do it, e.g., **l'hai fatta bella** you've done it; **farsi bello** to dress up; **farsi bello di** to appropriate ‖ *m* beauty; beautiful; climax; fine weather; beau; **il bello è** the funny thing is; **sul più bello** just then; **sul più bello che** just when ‖ *f* see **bella** ‖ **bello** *adv*—**bel bello** slowly

bellospirito *m* (**begli spiriti**) wit, bel-esprit

bellui·no -na *adj* wild, fierce

bellumóre *m* (**begli umori**) jolly fellow

bel·tà *f* (-tà) beauty (*woman*); (lit) beauty

bélva *f* wild beast

belvedére *adj* (rr) observation (*car*) ‖ *m* belvedere; (naut) topgallant

Belzebù *m* Beelzebub

bemòlle *m* (mus) flat

benama·to -ta *adj* beloved

benarriva·to -ta *adj* welcome

benché *conj* although, albeit

bènda *f* bandage; band; blindfold; **benda gessata** cast, surgical dressing

bendàg·gio *m* (-gi) bandage

bendare (bèndo) *tr* to bandage; **bendare gli occhi a** to blindfold

bendispó·sto -sta *adj* well-disposed

bène *adj* well; well-born ‖ *m* goal, aim; good; love; sake; **bene dell'anima** profound affection; **beni** (econ) assets, goods; **beni di consumo** consumer goods; **beni immobili** real estate; **beni mobili** personal property, chattels; **beni rifugio** hedge (*e.g., against inflation*); **è un bene** it is a blessing; **fare del bene** to do good; **per il Suo bene** for your sake; **voler bene a** to love, like; to care for ‖ *adv* well; all right; properly; **ben bene** quite carefully; **star bene** to be well; **va bene** O.K., all right

benedetti·no -na *adj & m* Benedictine

benedét·to -ta *adj* blessed; holy

benedire §195 *tr* to bless; to praise; **andare a farsi benedire** (coll) to go to wrack and ruin; **mandare a farsi benedire** (coll) to get rid of, dump

benedizióne *f* benediction; boon

beneduca·to -ta *adj* well-behaved

benefattóre *m* benefactor

benefattrice *f* benefactress

beneficare §197 (benèfico) *tr* to benefit, help

beneficènza *f* welfare; charity; beneficence

beneficiale *adj* beneficial

beneficiare §128 *intr* to benefit

beneficià·rio -ria *adj & mf* (-ri -rie) beneficiary

beneficiata *f* benefit performance; streak of good luck; streak of bad luck

benefì·cio *m* (-ci) benefice; profit; favor; benefit

benèfi·co -ca *adj* (-ci -che) beneficial; beneficent

benemerènte *adj* deserving, well-deserving

benemèri·to -ta *adj* worthy, deserving ‖ *m*—**benemerito della patria** national hero ‖ *f*—**la Benemerita** the Carabinieri

beneplàcito *m* approval, consent; **a beneplacito di** at the pleasure of

benèssere *m* well-being, comfort; prosperity

benestante *adj* well-to-do ‖ *mf* well-to-do person

benestare *m* approval; prosperity; **dare il benestare a** to approve

benevolènte *adj* benevolent

benevolènza *f* benevolence

benèvo·lo -la *adj* well-meaning; benevolent

benfat·to -ta *adj* well-done; well-favored; shapely

benga·la *m* (-li & -la) fireworks

benga·li *adj & m* (-li) Bengalese

beniami·no -na *mf* favorite child; favorite

benigni·tà *f* (-tà) benignity; graciousness; mildness (*of climate*)

beni·gno -gna *adj* benign; gracious; mild (*climate*)
benintenziona·to -ta *adj* well-meaning
benintéso [s] *adv* of course, naturally
bènna *f* bucket, scoop (*e.g., of dredge*)
benna·to -ta *adj* (lit) well-born
benpensante *m* sensible person; conformist
benportante *adj* well-preserved
benservito *m* testimonial, recommendation; **dare il benservito a** to dismiss, fire
bensì *adv* indeed ‖ *conj* but
bentorna·to -ta *adj* & *m* welcome ‖ *interj* welcome back!
benvenu·to -ta *adj* & *m* welcome; **dare il benvenuto a** to welcome
benvi·sto -sta *adj* well-thought-of
benvolére *tr*—**farsi benvolere da qlcu** to enter the good graces of s.o.; **prendere a benvolere qlcu** to be well-disposed toward s.o.
benvolu·to -ta *adj* liked, loved
benzina *f* gasoline, gas; benzine; **far benzina** (coll) to get gas
benzi·nàio *m* (**-nài**) gasoline dealer; gas-station attendant
benzòlo *m* benzene
beóne *m* drunkard, toper
bequadro *m* (mus) natural
berciare §128 (**bèrcio**) *intr* (coll) to yell
bére *m* drink, drinking ‖ §120 *tr* to drink; (fig) to swallow; **bere come una spugna** to drink like a fish; **darla a bere** to make believe
bergamòt·to -ta *adj* bergamot ‖ *m* bergamot orange ‖ *f* bergamot pear
berìllio *m* beryllium
berlina *f* pillory; berlin, coach; (aut) sedan; **mettere alla berlina** to pillory
berlinése [s] *adj* Berlin ‖ *mf* Berliner
Berlino *m* Berlin
bermuda *mpl* Bermuda shorts ‖ **le Bermude** Bermuda
bernòccolo *m* bump, protuberance; (fig) knack
berrétta *f* biretta
berrétto *m* cap; **berretto a sonagli** cap and bells; **berretto da notte** nightcap; **berretto gogliardico** student cap
bersagliare §280 *tr* to harass, pursue; to bomb, bombard
bersà·glio *m* (**-gli**) target; butt (*of a joke*); target (*of criticism*)
bèrta *f* pile driver; **dar la berta a** to ridicule
bertùc·cia *f* (**-ce**) Barbary ape; **fare la bertuccia di** to ape
bestémmia *f* blasphemy
bestemmiare §287 (**bestémmio**) *tr* to blaspheme, curse
bestemmia·tóre -trice *adj* blasphemous ‖ *mf* blasphemer
béstia *f* beast, animal; **andare in bestia** to fly into a rage; **bestia da soma** beast of burden; **bestia nera** pet aversion, bête noire; **bestie grosse** cattle
bestiale *adj* beastly, bestial
bestiali·tà *f* (**-tà**) beastliness; blunder
bestiame *m* livestock; **bestiame da cortile** barnyard animals; **bestiame grosso** cattle

bestino *m* gamy odor; stench of perspiration
bestiòla *f* tiny animal; pet
bestsèl·ler *m* (**-ler**) best seller
Betlèmme *f* Bethlehem
betonièra *f* cement mixer
béttola *f* tavern
bettolière *m* tavern keeper
bettònica *f* betony; **conosciuto più della bettonica** very well-known
betulla *f* birch
bèuta *f* flask
bevanda *f* drink, beverage
beverà·gio *m* (**-gi**) beverage, potion
bevìbile *adj* drinkable
bevi·tóre -trice *mf* drinker
bevuta *f* drink, drinking
bezzicare §197 (**bézzico**) *tr* to peck; to vex ‖ *ref* to fight one another
biacca *f* white lead
biada *f* feed; **biade** harvest
bianca·stro -stra *adj* whitish
biancherìa *f* laundry; linen; underwear; **biancheria da letto** bed linen; **biancheria da tavola** table linen; **biancheria di bucato** freshly laundered clothes; **biancheria intima** underclothes
bianchézza *f* whiteness
bianchire §176 *tr* to blanch; to bleach; to polish
bian·co -ca (**-chi -che**) *adj* white; clean; **bianco come un cencio lavato** as white as a ghost ‖ *m* white; **dare il bianco a** to whitewash; **in bianco** blank (*paper*); **mangiare in bianco** to eat a bland or non-spicy diet; **ricamare in bianco** to embroider
biancóre *m* whiteness
biancospino *m* hawthorn
biascicare §197 (**biàscico**) *tr* to chew with difficulty; to peck at (*one's food*); to mumble
biasimare (**biàsimo**) *tr* to blame
biasimévole *adj* blamable, censurable
biàsimo *m* blame, censure; **dare una nota di biasimo a** to censure
biauricolare *adj* binaural
Bibbia *f* Bible
bibe·rón *m* (**-rón**) nursing bottle
bibita *f* soft drink
bìbli·co -ca *adj* (**-ci -che**) Biblical
bìblio·bus *m* (**-bus**) bookmobile
bibliòfi·lo -la *mf* bibliophile
bibliografìa *f* bibliography
bibliotè·ca *f* (**-che**) library; bookshelf, stack; collection (*of books*); **biblioteca ambulante** walking encyclopedia
bibliotecà·rio -ria *mf* (**-ri -rie**) librarian
bibu·lo -la *adj* absorbent (*e.g., paper*)
bi·ca *f* (**-che**) pile of sheaves
bicarbonato *m* bicarbonate; **bicarbonato di soda** bicarbonate of soda, baking soda
bicchierata *f* glassful; wine party
bicchière *m* glass
bicchierino *m* small glass, liquor glass; **bicchierino da rosolio** whiskey glass, jigger
biciclétta *f* bicycle
bicilìndri·co -ca *adj* (**-ci -che**) two-cylinder

bicìpite *adj* two-headed ‖ *m* biceps
bicòc·ca *f* (-che) castle built on a hill; shanty, hut
bicolóre *adj* two-color
bicòrno *m* two-cornered hat
bidèllo *m* school janitor, caretaker
bidènte *m* two-pronged pitchfork
bidimensionale *adj* two-dimensional
bidóne *m* can (*for milk*); drum (*for gasoline or oil*); jalopy; (slang) fraud
bidon·ville *f* (-ville) shantytown
biè·co -ca *adj* (-chi -che) awry; sullen; cross; fierce; guardar bieco to look askance (at)
bièlla *f* connecting rod
biennale *adj* biennial ‖ *f* biennial show
biènne *adj* biennial
bièn·nio *m* (-ni) biennium
biètola *f* Swiss chard
biétta *f* wedge, chock; (naut) batten
bifase *adj* diphase
biffa *f* (surv) rod
biffare *tr* to cross out; (surv) to level
bìfi·do -da *adj* bifurcate
bifocale *adj* bifocal
bifól·co *m* (-chi) ox driver; clodhopper, boor
biforcaménto *m* bifurcation
biforcare §197 (bifórco) *tr* to bifurcate
biforcazióne *f* bifurcation, branching off; fork (*of a road*)
biforcu·to -ta *adj* forked; cloven (*e.g., hoof*)
bifrónte *adj* two-faced
bi·ga *f* (-ghe) chariot
bigamìa *f* bigamy
bìga·mo -ma *adj* bigamous ‖ *mf* bigamist
bighellonare (bighellóno) *intr* to idle, dawdle, dally
bighelló·ne -na *mf* idler, dawdler
bigino *m* (slang) pony (*used to cheat*)
bì·gio -gia *adj* (-gi -gie) gray, grayish; (fig) undecided
bigiotterìa *f* costume jewelry; costume jewelry store
bigliardo *m* billiards
bigliet·tàio *m* (-tài) ticket agent; (rr) conductor
biglietterìa *f* ticket office; (theat) box office
bigliétto *m* note; card; ticket; biglietto d'abbonamento commutation ticket; season ticket; biglietto d'andata e ritorno round-trip ticket; biglietto di banca banknote; biglietto di lotteria lottery ticket, chance; biglietto d'invito invitation; biglietto di visita calling card; business card; biglietto di Stato banknote; mezzo biglietto half fare
bigné *m* (bigné) puff, creampuff
bigodino *m* curler; roller
bigón·cia *f* (-ce) vat; bucket; a bigonce abundantly
bigón·cio *m* (-ci) vat; tub; (theat) ticket box (*for stubs*)
bigottismo *m* bigotry
bigòt·to -ta *adj* bigoted ‖ *mf* bigot
bilàn·cia *f* (-ce) balance, scale; bilancia commerciale balance of trade; bilan-cia dei pagamenti balance of payments ‖ Bilancia *f* (astr) Libra
bilanciare §128 *tr* & *ref* to balance
bilancière *m* balance; balance wheel; rope-walker's balancing rod
bilàn·cio *m* (-ci) balance; bilancio consuntivo balance sheet; bilancio preventivo budget; fare il bilancio to balance; to strike a balance
bile *f* bile; rodersi dalla bile to burn with anger
bìlia *f* billiard ball; marble; (billiards) pocket
biliardino *m* pocket billiards; pinball machine
biliardo *m* billiards
biliare *adj* bile; gall (*stone*)
bili·co *m* (-chi) balance, equipoise; in bilico in balance; tenere in bilico to balance
bilìngue *adj* bilingual
bilióne *m* billion; trillion (Brit)
bilió·so -sa [s] *adj* bilious
bim·bo -ba *mf* child
bimensile *adj* bimonthly
bimèstre *m* period of two months
bimotóre *adj* twin-engine ‖ *m* twin-engine plane
binà·rio -ria (-ri -rie) *adj* binary ‖ *m* (rr) track; binario morto (rr) siding; uscire dai binari (rr) to run off the track; (fig) to go astray
bina·to -ta *adj* binary; twin (*e.g., guns*)
binda *f* (aut) jack
binòcolo *m* binoculars; binocolo da teatro opera glasses
binò·mio -mia (-mi -mie) *adj* binomial ‖ *m* binomial; couple, pair
biòccolo *m* wad (*of cotton*); flake (*of snow*); flock (*of wool*)
biochìmi·co -ca (-ci -che) *adj* biochemical ‖ *m* biochemist ‖ *f* biochemistry
biodegradàbile *adj* biodegradable
biofisica *f* biophysics
biografìa *f* biography
biogràfi·co -ca *adj* (-ci -che) biographic(al)
biògra·fo -fa *mf* biographer
biologìa *f* biology
biòlo·go *m* (-gi) biologist
biondeggiare §290 (biondéggio) *intr* to be or become blond; to ripen (*said of grain*)
bión·do -da *adj* blond, fair ‖ *m* blond; blondness ‖ *f* blonde
biopsìa *f* biopsy
biòssido *m* dioxide
bipartìti·co -ca *adj* (-ci -che) two-party, bipartisan
biparti·to -ta *adj* bipartite ‖ *m* two-party government
bìpede *adj* & *m* biped
bipenne *f* double-bitted ax
biplano *m* biplane
bipósto *adj* *invar* having seats for two ‖ *m* two-seater
birba *f* rascal, rogue
birbante *m* scoundrel, rascal; (joc) madcap, wild young fellow
birbanterìa *f* knavery; trick
birbonata *f* trick

birbó·ne -na *adj* wicked ‖ *mf* rascal, rogue, scoundrel
bireattóre *m* twin jet
birichinata *f* prank
birichi·no -na *adj* prankish; spirited ‖ *mf* rogue; urchin
birillo *m* pin; **birilli** ninepins; tenpins
Birmània, la Burma
birra *f* beer; **birra chiara** light beer; **birra scura** dark beer
bir·ràio *m* (**-rài**) brewer; beer distributor
birrerìa *f* brewery; tavern; beer saloon
bis *adj invar*—**treno bis** (rr) second section ‖ *m* (**bis**) encore ‖ *interj* encore!
bisàc·cia *f* (**-ce**) knapsack; saddlebag; bag (*of mendicant friar*)
Bisànzio *m* Bysantium
bisa·vo -va *mf* great-grandparent; ancestor ‖ *m* great-grandfather ‖ *f* great-grandmother
bisbèti·co -ca (**-ci -che**) *adj* shrewish; crotchety; cantankerous ‖ *f* (fig) shrew
bisbigliare §280 *tr & intr* to whisper
bisbì·glio *m* (**-gli**) whisper
bisbòccia *f*—**fare bisboccia** to revel
bisboccióne *m* reveler
bis·ca *f* (**-che**) gambling house
Biscàglia *f* Biscay, e.g., **Baia di Biscaglia** Bay of Biscay; **la Biscaglia** Biscay
biscaglina *f* (naut) Jacob's ladder
biscazzière *m* gaming-house operator; habitué of a gaming house; marker (*at billiards*)
bìschero *m* (mus) peg
bì·scia *f* (**-sce**) snake; **biscia d'acqua** water snake
biscottare (**biscòtto**) *tr* to toast
biscotterìa *f* cookie factory; cookie store
biscottièra *f* cookie jar
biscottifì·cio *m* (**-ci**) cookie factory
biscòt·to -ta *adj* twice-baked ‖ *m* cookie
biscròma *f* (mus) demisemiquaver
bisdòsso *m*—**a bisdosso** bareback
bisecare [s] §197 (**bìseco**) *tr* to bisect
bisènso [s] *m* double meaning
bisessuale [s] *adj* bisexual
bisestile *adj* leap (*year*)
bisettimanale [s] *adj* biweekly
bisettrice [s] *f* bisector
bisezióne [s] *f* bisection
bisìlla·bo -ba [s] *adj* disyllabic
bislac·co -ca *adj* (**-chi -che**) queer, extravagant
bislun·go -ga *adj* (**-ghi -ghe**) oblong
bismuto *m* bismuth
bisnòn·no -na *mf* great-grandparent; **bisnonni** ancestors ‖ *m* great-grandfather ‖ *f* great-grandmother
bisógna *f* (lit) task, job
bisognare (**bisógna**) *intr* (with *dat*) to need, e.g., **gli bisognavano tre litri di benzina** he needed three liters of gasoline ‖ *impers*—**bisogna + inf** it is necessary to, e.g., **bisogna partire** it is necessary to leave; **bisogna che + subj** must, to have to, e.g., **bisogna che me ne vada** I must go,

I have to go; **bisognando** if need be; **non bisogna** one should not; **più che non bisogna** more than necessary
bisognévole *adj* needy
bisógno *m* need; want, lack; **aver bisogno di** to need; **c'è bisogno di** there is need of; **se ci fosse bisogno** if need be
bisognó·so -sa *adj* needy ‖ **i bisognosi** the needy
bisolfato [s] *m* bisulfate
bisolfito [s] *m* bisulfite
bisolfuro [s] *m* bisulfide
bisónte *m* bison
bistec·ca *f* (**-che**) beefsteak, steak; **bistecca al sangue** rare steak
bisticciare §128 *intr & ref* to quarrel, bicker
bistìc·cio *m* (**-ci**) quarrel, bickering; play on words, pun
bistrattare *tr* to mistreat
bìstu·ri *m* (**-ri**) bistouri, surgical knife
bisul·co -ca [s] *adj* (**-chi -che**) cloven
bisun·to -ta *adj* greasy
bitagliènte *adj* double-edged
bitórzolo *m* wart (*on humans, plants, or animals*); pimple (*on human face*)
bitta *f* (naut) bollard
bitume *m* bitumen, asphalt
bituminó·so -sa [s] *adj* bituminous
bivaccare §197 *intr* to bivouac; to spend the night
bivac·co *m* (**-chi**) bivouac
bì·vio *m* (**-vi**) fork (*of road*); **essere al bivio** (fig) to be at the crossroads
bizanti·no -na [dz] *adj* Byzantine
bizza [ddzz] *f* tantrum; **fare le bizze** to go into a tantrum
bizzarria [ddzz] *f* extravagance, oddity
bizzar·ro -ra [ddzz] *adj* bizarre, odd; skittish (*e.g., horse*)
bizzèffe [ddzz] *adv*— **a bizzeffe** plenty, in abundance
bizzó·so -sa [ddzz] [s] *adj* irritable
blandire §176 *tr* to blandish, coax; to soothe, mitigate
blandìzie *fpl* blandishment
blan·do -da *adj* bland
blasfemare (**blasfèmo**) *tr & intr* to blaspheme
blasfè·mo -ma *adj* blasphemous
blasona·to -ta *adj* emblazoned
blasóne *m* coat of arms, blazon
blaterare (**blàtero**) *intr* to babble
blatta *f* water bug, cockroach
blenoraggìa *f* gonorrhea
blè·so -sa *adj* lisping
blindàg·gio *m* (**-gi**) armor
blindare *tr* to armor
bloccare §197 (**blòcco**) *tr* to block; to blockade; to stop; to jam; to close up; to freeze (*e.g., prices*); (sports) to block ‖ *intr*—**bloccare su** to vote as a block for ‖ *ref* to stop
blòc·co *m* (**-chi**) block; blockade; notebook, pad; freezing (*e.g., of wages*); **in blocco** in bulk
bloc-notes *m* (**-notes**) notebook
blu *adj invar & m* blue
blua·stro -stra *adj* bluish
bluffare *intr* to bluff
blusa *f* blouse; smock

bò·a *m* (-a) boa || *f* buoy
boà·rio -ria *adj* (-ri -rie) cattle
boa·ro -ra *adj* ox || *m* stable boy
boato *m* roar; boato sonico sonic boom
bobina *f* spool (*of thread*); coil (*of wire*); reel (*of movie film; of magnetic tape*); roll (*of film*); cylinder, bobbin; (elec) coil; bobina d'accensione spark coil
bóc·ca *f* (-che) mouth; nozzle; muzzle (*of gun*); pit (*of the stomach*); opening; straits; pass; a bocca aperta agape; bocca da fuoco cannon; di buona bocca easily pleased; in bocca al lupo! good luck!; per bocca orally; rimanere a bocca asciutta to be foiled; to be left high and dry; tieni la bocca chiusa! shut up!
boccaccé·sco -sca *adj* (-schi -sche) written by or in the style of Boccaccio; bawdy, licentious
boccàc·cia *f* (-ce) ugly mouth; grimace; fare le boccacce to make faces
boccà·glio *m* (-gli) nozzle (*of hose or pipe*); mouthpiece (*of megaphone*)
boccale *adj* oral || *m* jug, tankard
boccapòrto *m* hatch; port; mouth (*of oven or furnace*); chiudere i boccaporti to batten the hatches
boccascè·na *m* (-na) proscenium, front (*of stage*)
boccata *f* mouthful; andare a prendere una boccata d'aria to go out for a breath of fresh air
boccétta *f* small bottle, vial; small billiard ball
boccheggiante *adj* gasping; moribund
boccheggiare §290 (bocchéggio) *intr* to gasp
bocchétta *f* nozzle (*of sprinkling can*); mouthpiece (*of wind instrument*); opening (*of drainage or ventilation system*); bocchetta stradale manhole
bocchino *m* cigarette holder; mouthpiece (*of cigarette or of musical instrument*)
bòc·cia *f* (-ce) decanter; ball (*for bowling*); bocce bowls
bocciare §128 (bòccio) *tr* to score (*at bowling*); to reject (*a proposal*); to flunk (*a student*)
bocciatura *f* failure
boccino *m* jack (*at bowls*)
bocciòlo *m* bud
bóccola *f* buckle; earring; (mach) bushing
bocconcino *m* morsel; (culin) stew
boccóne *m* mouthful; piece; morsel; buttar giù un boccone amaro to swallow a bitter pill; levarsi il boccone di bocca to take the bread out of one's mouth (to help someone); mangiare un boccone to have a bite || bocconi *adv* flat on one's face
boè·mo -ma *adj & mf* Bohemian
boè·ro -ra *adj & m* Boer
bofonchiare §287 (bofónchio) *intr* to snort, grumble
bò·ia *m* (-ia) hangman, executioner
boiata *f* (slang) infamy; (slang) trash
boicottàg·gio *m* (-gi) boycott
boicottare (boicòtto) *tr* to boycott

bòl·gia *f* (-ge) pit (*in hell*)
bólide *m* (astr) bolide, fireball; (aut) racer; (joc) lummox; andare come un bolide to go like a flash
bolina *f* (naut) bowline; di bolina (naut) close-hauled
bolivia·no -na *adj & mf* Bolivian
bólla *f* bubble; blister; ticket; bolla di consegna receipt; bolla di spedizione delivery ticket; bolla di sapone soap bubble; bolla papale papal bull
bollare (bóllo) *tr* to stamp; to brand
bolla·to -ta *adj* stamped; sealed
bollatura *f* stamp; brand; postage
bollènte *adj* boiling, scalding hot
bolletta *f* ticket; receipt; bill; essere in bolletta (coll) to be broke
bollettà·rio *m* (-ri) receipt book
bollettino *m* bulletin; receipt; bollettino dei prezzi correnti price list; bollettino di versamento (com) deposit ticket; bollettino meteorologico weather forecast
bollire (bóllo) *tr & intr* to boil
bolli·to -ta *adj* boiled || *m* boiled beef
bollitura *f* boiling
bóllo *m* mark, cancellation; revenue stamp; postmark; seal; bollo a freddo seal (*embossed*); bollo postale cancellation, postmark
bollóre *m* boiling; sultriness; (fig) passion, excitement; alzare il bollore to begin to boil
bolló·so -sa [s] *adj* blistery
bolscevi·co -ca *adj & mf* (-chi -che) Bolshevik
bolscevismo *m* Bolshevism
ból·so -sa *adj* broken-winded (*horse*); asthmatic
bòma *f* (naut) boom
bómba *f* bomb; bubble gum; fireworks; (aer) double loop; (journ) scandal; bomba a idrogeno hydrogen bomb; bomba a mano hand grenade; bomba antisommergibile depth charge; bomba a orologeria time bomb; bomba atomica atom bomb; bomba H (*acca*) H bomb; tornare a bomba (fig) to get back to the point
bombàg·gio *m* swelling (*of a spoiled can of food*)
bombardaménto *m* bombing, bombardment
bombardare *tr* to bomb, bombard; to besiege (*with questions*)
bombardière *m* (aer) bomber; (mil) artilleryman
bombétta *f* derby (*hat*)
bómbola *f* bottle, cylinder; bombola d'ossigeno oxygen tank
bombonièra *f* candy box
bomprèsso *m* (naut) bowsprit
bonàc·cia *f* (-ce) calm; calm sea; (fig) normalcy; (com) stagnation
bonacció·ne -na *adj* good-hearted, good-natured
bonarie·tà *f* (-tà) kindheartedness, good nature
bonà·rio -ria *adj* (-ri -rie) kindhearted, good-natured
boncinèllo *m* hasp
bonìfi·ca *f* (-che) reclamation; re-

claimed land; improvement (*e.g.*, *of morals*); clearing of mines; (metallurgy) hardening and tempering

bonificare §197 (**bonìfico**) *tr* to reclaim; to discount, make a reduction of; to clear of mines

bonìfi·co *m* (**-ci**) discount

bonomìa *f* good nature; simple-heartedness

bon·tà *f* (**-tà**) goodness; kindness; **avere la bontà di** to be kind enough to; **bontà mia** (**sua, etc.**) through my (his, her, etc.) kindness; **per mia** (**sua, etc.**) **bontà** through my (his, her, etc.) efforts

bòra *f* northeast wind

borace *m* borax

borbogliare §280 (**borbóglio**) *intr* to gurgle; to rumble

borbòni·co -ca (**-ci -che**) *adj* Bourbon || *m* Bourbonist

borbottare (**borbòtto**) *tr* to mutter || *intr* to mutter; to gurgle; to rumble (*said*, *e.g.*, *of thunder*)

borbottì·o *m* (**-i**) mutter; gurgle; rumble

bòrchia *f* upholsterer's nail; boss, stud

bordare (**bórdo**) *tr* to border, hem

bordata *f* (naut) tack; (nav) broadside

bordatura *f* border, hem

bordeggiare §290 (**bordéggio**) *intr* (naut) to tack

bordèllo *m* brothel

borde·rò *m* (**-rò**) list; note; (theat) box office, receipts

bórdo *m* side (*of ship*); border, hem; edge, rim; (naut) tack; (naut) board; **a bordo** on board; **a bordo di** on board; on, in; **bordo d'entrata** (aer) leading edge; **bordo d'uscita** (aer) trailing edge; **d'alto bordo** (naut) big, sea-going; (fig) high-toned; **virare di bordo** (naut) to change course

bordóne *m* staff; bass stop (*of organ*); drone (*of insect*); **tener bordone a** (mus) to accompany; (fig) to hold the bag for

bordura *f* hem, edge; rim

boreale *adj* northern, boreal

borgata *f* hamlet, village

borghése [s] *adj* middle-class || *mf* bourgeois, person of the middle class; civilian; **in borghese** in civilian clothes; in plainclothes

borghesìa *f* bourgeoisie, middle class; **alta borghesia** upper middle class

bór·go *m* (**-ghi**) borough; small town; suburb

borgógna *m* Burgundy (*wine*) || **la Borgogna** Burgundy

borgognóne *m* iceberg

borgomastro *m* burgomaster

bòria *f* haughtiness, vainglory

bòri·co -ca *adj* (**-ci -che**) boric

borió·so -sa [s] *adj* haughty, puffed-up; blustery

bòro *m* boron

borotal·co *m* (**-chi**) talcum powder

bórra *f* flock (*for pillows*); (fig) rubbish, filler

borràc·cia *f* (**-ce**) canteen (*e.g.*, *for carrying water*)

bórro *m* gully

bórsa *f* bag; pouch; bourse, exchange; (sports) purse; **borsa da viaggio** traveling bag; **borsa dell'acqua hot-water bag; **borsa della spesa** shopping bag; **borsa di ghiaccio** ice bag; **borsa di studio** scholarship; **borsa merci** commodity exchange; **borsa nera** black market; **borsa valori** stock exchange; **essere di borsa larga** to be generous; **o la borsa o la vita!** your money or your life!; **pagare di borsa propria** to pay out of one's own pocket

borsaiòlo *m* pickpocket

borsanéra *f* black market

borsaneri·sta *mf* (**-sti -ste**) black marketeer

borseggiare §290 (**borséggio**) *tr* to pick the pocket of; to rob

borseggia·tóre -trice *mf* pickpocket

borség·gio *m* (**-gi**) theft

borsellino *m* purse

borsétta *f* handbag, pocketbook

borsétto *m* man's purse

borsi·sta *mf* (**-sti -ste**) recipient of a scholarship; stockbroker

borsìsti·co -ca *adj* (**-ci -che**) stock-exchange

borsite *f* bursitis

boscàglia *f* thicket, underbrush

boscaiòlo *m* woodcutter

boscheréc·cio -cia *adj* (**-ci -ce**) wood, woodland; rustic; pastoral

boschétto *m* coppice, copse

boschi·vo -va *adj* wooded, wood

bò·sco *m* (**-schi**) woods, forest; **bosco ceduo** or **da taglio** tree farm

boscó·so -sa [s] *adj* wooded, woody

bòsforo *m* (lit) straits || **Bosforo** *m* Bosphorus

bòsso *m* boxwood

bòssolo *m* box; cartridge case

botàni·co -ca (**-ci -che**) *adj* botanic(al) || *m* botanist || *f* botany

bòtola *f* trap door

bòtolo *m* small snarling dog

bòtta *f* hit; bump; rumble (*e.g.*, *of an explosion*); thrust, lunging (*in fencing*); (fig) disaster; **botta dritta** (fencing) lunge; **botta e risposta** give-and-take; **botte da orbi** severe beating

bot·tàio *m* (**-tài**) cooper

bótte *f* barrel, cask, casket

botté·ga *f* (**-ghe**) store, shop; **chiudere bottega** to close up shop

botte·gàio -gàia (**-gài -gàie**) *adj* store, shop || *mf* storekeeper, shopkeeper

botteghino *m* box office; lottery agency

bottìglia *f* bottle; **bottiglia Molotov** Molotov cocktail

bottiglierìa *f* wine store, liquor store

bottino *m* booty, spoil; capture; cesspool; sewage

bòtto *m* hit, bump; explosion; noise; toll (*of bell*); **di botto** all of a sudden

bottoncino *m* small button; cuff button; **bottoncino di rosa** rosebud

bottóne *m* button; stud; bud; **attaccare un bottone a** (fig) to buttonhole; **botton d'oro** (bot) buttercup; **bottone automatico** snap; **bottone della**

luce (elec) pushbutton; **bottoni gemelli** cuff links; **bottoni gustativi** taste buds

bottonièra f row of buttons; buttonhole; (elec) panel (with buttons)

bova·ro -ra adj & m var of **boaro**

bovile m ox stable

bovi·no -na adj cattle, cow; bovine || m bovine

box m (box) locker (e.g., in a station); box stall (for a horse); pit (in auto racing); garage (on the ground floor of a split-level); play pen

boxare (bòxo) intr to box

boxe f boxing

bòzza f stud, boss; bump (caused by blow); rough copy, draft; **bozze** (typ) galleys, galley proof

bozzèllo m (mach) block and tackle

bozzétto m sketch

bòzzolo m cocoon; lump (of flour)

bra·ca f (-che) safety belt; (naut) sling; **brache** (archaic) breeches; (joc) trousers

braccare §197 tr to stalk; to hunt out

braccétto—**a braccetto** arm in arm

bracciale m armlet, armband; arm rest

braccialétto m bracelet

bracciante m laborer

bracciata f armful; stroke (in swimming); **bracciata a rana** breaststroke; **bracciata sul dorso** backstroke

bràc·cio m (-cia fpl) arm (of body); unit of length (about 60 centimeters); **a braccia aperte** with open arms; **avere le braccia legate** to have one's hands tied; **braccia** laborers; **braccio destro** right-hand man; **braccio di ferro** Indian wrestling; **fare a braccio di ferro** to play at Indian wrestling; **sentirsi cascare le braccia** to lose courage || m (-ci) arm (e.g., of sea, chair, lamp, etc.); beam (of balance); **braccio diretto** cutoff (of river)

bracciòlo m arm; arm rest; banister

brac·co m (-chi) hound, beagle

bracconàg·gio m (-gi) poaching

bracconière m poacher

brace f embers; (coll) charcoal; **farsi di brace** to blush

brachétta f flap (of trousers); (bb) joint; **brachette** shorts

brachière m truss (for hernia)

bracière m brazier

bracciòla f chop, cutlet

bra·do -da adj wild, untamed

bra·go m (-ghi) (lit) mud, slime

brama f ardent desire; covetousness; longing

bramare tr to desire intensely; to covet; to long for

bramino m Brahmin

bramire §176 intr to roar; to bell (said of a deer)

bramito m bell (of deer)

bramosìa [s] f covetousness; greed

bramó·so -sa [s] adj (lit) covetous, greedy

bran·ca f (-che) branch (of tree); flight (of stairs); **branche** (poet) clutches

brànchia f gill

brancicare §197 (bràncico) tr to finger, handle || intr to grope

bran·co m (-chi) flock, herd; (pej) crowd

brancolare (bràncolo) intr to grope

branda f cot

brandèllo m tatter, shred

brandire §176 tr to brandish

brando m (lit) sword

brano m shred, bit; excerpt; **cadere a brani** to fall apart; **fare a brani** to tear apart

brasare tr to braze (to solder with brass); (culin) to braise

brasile m brazil (nut) || **il Brasile** Brazil

brasilia·no -na adj & mf Brazilian

bravàc·cio m (-ci) braggart, swaggerer

bravare tr to challenge; to threaten || intr to brag

bravata f swagger, bluster; boast; stunt

bra·vo -va adj good, able; honest; goodhearted; brave; **alla brava** rapidly; **bravo ragazzo** good boy; **fare il bravo** to boast, be a braggart || m mercenary soldier; bravo, hired assassin || **bravo!** interj well done!, bravo!

bravura f ability; bravery; bravura

brèc·cia f (-ce) breach, gap; crushed stone

brefotrò·fio m (-fi) foundling hospital

Bretagna, la Brittany

bretèlla f suspenders; strap, shoulder strap

brètone adj Breton; Arthurian

brève adj brief, short; **in breve** in a nutshell; **per farla breve** in short || m (eccl) brief || adv (lit) in short

brevettare (brevétto) tr to patent

brevétto m patent; (aer) license; (obs) commission

brevià·rio m (-ri) compendium; handbook, vade mecum; (eccl) breviary

brevi·tà f (-tà) brevity

brézza [ddzz] f breeze

brezzare (brézzo) [ddzz] tr to winnow || intr to blow gently

bricchétta f briquet

bric·co m (-chi) kettle, pot

bricconata f rascality

briccó·ne -na mf rascal

bricconerìa f rascality

brìciola f crumb; **ridurre in briciole** to crumb, crumble

brìciolo m bit, fragment; (fig) least bit; **andare in bricioli** to crumble; **mandare in bricioli** to crumble

brì·ga f (-ghe) worry, trouble, attaccar **briga** to pick a fight; **darsi la briga di** to worry about; **trovarsi in una briga** to be in trouble

brigadière m noncommissioned officer (in carabinieri); (hist) brigadier

brigantàg·gio m (-gi) brigandage

brigante m brigand

brigantino m (naut) brig, brigantine; **brigantino goletta** (naut) brigantine

brigare §209 tr to plot; to scheme to get || intr to plot, scheme

brigata f company; (mil) brigade

brì·glia f (-glie) bridle; harness (for holding baby); (naut) bobstay; **a briglia sciolta** at full speed; **tirare le briglie a** to bridle

brillante adj brilliant || m cut diamond

brillare *tr* to husk, hull (*rice*); to explode (*e.g., a mine*) || *intr* to shine, sparkle; **far brillare** to explode, blow up

brillì·o *m* (**-i**) shine, sparkle

bril·lo -la *adj* tipsy

brina *f* frost

brinare *tr* to frost; to turn (*e.g., hair*) gray || *impers* (ESSERE)—**è brinato** there was frost; **brina** there is frost

brinata *f* frost

brindare *intr* to toast; **brindare alla salute di** to toast

brìndisi *m* (**-si**) toast; pledge; **fare un brindisi a** to toast

brì·o *m* (**-i**) sprightliness, liveliness, verve, spirit

briò·scia *f* (**-sce**) brioche

briò·so -sa [s] *adj* sprightly, lively

brìscola *f* briscola (*game*); trump (*card*)

britànni·co -ca *adj* (**-ci -che**) British, Britannic

britan·no -na *adj* British || *mf* Briton

brìvido *m* shake, shiver; thrill; **brivido di freddo** chill, shiver

brizzola·to -ta *adj* grizzled

bròc·ca *f* (**-che**) pitcher; pitcherful; shoot, bud; hobnail

broccatèllo *m* brocatel

broccato *m* brocade

bròc·co *m* (**-chi**) twig; shoot; center pin (*of shield or target*); (coll) nag; **dar nel brocco** to hit the bull's eye

bròccolo *m* (bot) broccoli; **broccoli** broccoli (*as food*)

bròda *f* slop, thin or tasteless soup; mud

brodàglia *f* slop

brodétto *m* fish soup

bròdo *m* broth; **andar in brodo di giuggiole** (fig) to swoon with joy; **brodo in dadi** cube bouillon; **brodo ristretto** consommé

brodó·so -sa [s] *adj* thin, watery (*soup*)

brogliàc·cio *m* (**-ci**) (com) daybook, first draft; (naut) first draft of logbook

bròglio *m* (**-gli**) plot, intrigue; maneuver; **broglio elettorale** political maneuver

bròlo *m* (archaic) garden; (lit) garland

bromìdri·co -ca *adj* (**-ci -che**) hydrobromic

bròmo *m* bromine

bromuro *m* bromide

bronchite *f* bronchitis

brón·cio *m* (**-ci**) pout, pouting; **fare il broncio** to sulk; **tenere il broncio a** to harbor a grudge against

brón·co *m* (**-chi**) bronchial tube; thorny branch; ramification (*of antlers*)

brontolare (**bróntolo**) *tr* to grumble (*to express with a grumble*); to grumble at || *intr* to grumble, mutter; to rumble; to gurgle (*said of water*)

brontolì·o *m* (**-i**) grumble, mutter; rumble; gurgle

brontoló·ne -na *mf* grumbler; curmudgeon

bronzare [dz] (**brónzo**) *tr* to bronze

brónze·o -a [dz] *adj* bronze; tanned

bronzina [dz] *f* little bell; (mach) bearing; (mach) bushing

brónzo [dz] *m* bronze

brossura *f* brochure; **in brossura** paperback

brucare §197 *tr* to browse, graze

bruciacchiare §287 *tr* to singe

bruciante *adj* burning

bruciapélo *m*—**a bruciapelo** point-blank

bruciare §128 *tr* to burn; to burn down; to singe; to scorch; to cauterize (*a wound*); (sports) to overcome with a burst of speed; **bruciare le tappe** to go straight ahead; to press on || *intr* (ESSERE) to burn; to smart, sting || *ref* to burn (*e.g., one's fingers*); to get burnt; to blow (*one's brains*) out; to burn out (*said of an electric light or fuse*); **bruciarsi i vascelli alle spalle** to burn one's bridges behind one

bruciatìc·cio *m* (**-ci**) burnt material; **sapere di bruciaticcio** to taste burnt

brucia·to -ta *adj* burnt; burnt out || *m* burnt taste or smell || *f* roast chestnut

bruciatóre *m* burner; heater; **bruciatore a gas** gas burner; **bruciatore a nafta** oil burner

bruciatori·sta *m* (**-sti**) oil burner mechanic

bruciatura *f* burn

brucióre *m* burning; burn; inflammation; **bruciore agli occhi** eye inflammation; **bruciore di stomaco** heartburn

bru·co *m* (**-chi**) caterpillar; worm

brùffolo *m* (coll) small boil

brughièra *f* waste land; heath

brulicare §197 (**brùlico**) *intr* to crawl; to swarm (*e.g., with bees*); to teem (*with people*)

brulichì·o *m* (**-i**) crawling; swarming; teeming

brul·lo -la *adj* barren, bare

bruma *f* shipworm; (lit) fog; (lit) winter

bruna·stro -stra *adj* brownish

brunire §176 *tr* to burnish

bru·no -na *adj* brown; dark (*bread; complexion*) || *m* brown; dark; brunet; **vestire a bruno** to dress in black || *f* brunette

bru·sca *f* (**-sche**) horse brush; **con le brusche** curtly

bruschézza *f* brusqueness

bruschino *m* scrub brush

bru·sco -sca (**-schi -sche**) *adj* sour; curt, gruff; sharp (*weather*); dangerous; sudden || *m* twig || *f* see **brusca**

brùscolo *m* speck, mote; **fare di un bruscolo una trave** to make a mountain out of a molehill

brusì·o *m* (**-i**) buzz, buzzing; (fig) whispering (*gossip*)

brutale *adj* brutal

brutali·tà *f* (**-tà**) brutality

brutalizzare [ddzz] *tr* to brutalize

bru·to -ta *adj* & *m* brute

brùtta *f* rough copy

bruttare *tr* (lit) to soil

bruttézza *f* ugliness; (fig) lowliness

brut·to -ta *adj* ugly, homely; foul (*weather*); bad (*news*); **alle brutte** at the worst; **con le brutte** harshly; **farla brutta a** to play a mean trick on;

guardare brutto to look irritated; **vedersela brutta** to foresee trouble ‖ *m* worst; bad weather ‖ *f* see **brutta**
bruttura *f* ugliness
bùbbola *f* lie; trifle
bùbbolo *m* jingle bell (*on horse*)
bubbòni·co -ca *adj* (**-ci -che**) bubonic
bu·ca *f* (**-che**) hole; pit; hollow; **buca cieca** trap (*for hunting*); **buca del biliardo** pocket; **buca delle lettere** mailbox; **buca del suggeritore** prompter's box; **buca sepolcrale** grave
bucané·ve *m* (**-ve**) snowdrop
bucanière *m* buccaneer
bucare §197 *tr* to pierce; to prick; to puncture (*a tire*)
bucato *m* wash; laundry; **di bucato** freshly laundered; **fare il bucato in famiglia** (fig) to not air one's family affairs, to not wash one's dirty linen in public
bucatura *f* piercing; puncturing; puncture; **bucatura di una gomma** flat tire
bùc·cia *f* (**-ce**) rind, peel; skin (*of a person; of fruit and vegetables*); tender bark; **fare le bucce a** (coll) to thwart, frustrate
bucherellare (**bucherèllo**) *tr* to riddle
bu·co *m* (**-chi**) hole; **fare un buco nell'acqua** to fail miserably
bucòli·co -ca *adj* (**-ci -che**) bucolic, pastoral
Budda *m* Buddha
buddismo *m* Buddhism
buddi·sta *mf* (**-sti -ste**) Buddhist
budèl·lo *m* (**-la** *fpl*) bowel; **budella** bowels; guts ‖ *m* (**-li**) casing (*for salami*); pipe; blind alley
budino *m* pudding
bùe *m* (**buòi**) ox (*for draft*); steer (*for meat*); **bue muschiato** musk ox
bùfalo *m* buffalo
bufèra *f* storm; **bufera di neve** snowstorm; **bufera di pioggia** rainstorm; **bufera di vento** windstorm
buffa *f* cowl; gust of wind; (archaic) trick, jest
buffare *tr* to huff (*at checkers*) ‖ *intr* to joke; (archaic) to blow
buffetterìa *f* (mil) accouterments
buffétto *m* tap, slight blow
buf·fo -fa *adj* funny, comical ‖ *m* gust of wind; comic ‖ *f* see **buffa**
buffonata *f* buffoonery; antics
buffóne *m* buffoon, clown; (hist) jester; **buffone di corte** court jester
buffonerìa *f* buffoonery
buffoné·sco -sca *adj* (**-schi -sche**) clownish
bugìa *f* lie; candlestick; **bugia ufficiosa** white lie
bugiar·do -da *adj* lying, false ‖ *mf* liar
bugigàttolo *m* cubbyhole
bugna *f* ashlar; (naut) clew
bugnato *m* ashlar; (archit) boss
bù·io -ia (*pl* **-i -ie**) *adj* dark ‖ *m* darkness; **buio pesto** pitch dark
bulbo *m* bulb
bùlga·ro -ra *adj* & *mf* Bulgarian ‖ *m* Russian leather
bulinare *tr* to engrave
bulino *m* burin

bullétta *f* tack
bullonare (**bullóno**) *tr* to bolt
bullóne *m* bolt
buon *adj* apocopated form of **buono**, used before masculine singular nouns except those beginning with impure **s, z, gn, ps**, and **x**
buon' *adj* apocopated form of **buona** used before feminine singular nouns beginning with a vowel, e.g., **buon'ora**
buonagràzia *f* (**buonegràzie**) courtesy, good manners; **con Sua buonagrazia** with your permission
buonamano *f* (**buonemani**) tip, gratuity
buonànima *f* departed; **la buonanima di** the late lamented
buonavò·glia *m* (**-glia**) intern (*in a hospital*); (coll) lazybones ‖ *f* good will
buoncostume *m* morals
buongu·stàio *m* (**-stài**) gourmet; connoisseur
buò·no -na *adj* good; kind; high (*society*); cheap (*price*); **alla buona** plainly; without ceremony; **buono a nulla** good-for-nothing; **con le buone** kindly, gently; **che Dio la mandi buona** a may God be kind with; **essere in buona con** to be on good terms with ‖ *m* good person; bond; ticket; **buono a nulla** ne'er-do-well; **buono del tesoro** government bond; **buono di consegna** delivery order; **buono premio** trading stamp
buonsènso *m* common sense
buontempó·ne -na *adj* jolly ‖ *m* playboy ‖ *f* fun-loving girl; playgirl
buonumóre *m* good humor, good cheer
buonuscita *f* indemnity, bonus; severance pay
burattare *tr* to sift
buratti·nàio *m* (**-nài**) puppeteer; puppet maker
burattinata *f* clowning
burattino *m* puppet
buratto *m* sifter, sifting machine
burbanza *f* haughtiness, arrogance
burbanzó·so -sa [s] *adj* haughty, arrogant
bùrbe·ro -ra *adj* gruff, surly
bùr·chio *m* (**-chi**) (naut) lighter
burgun·do -da *adj* & *mf* Burgundian
burla *f* joke, jest; prank; **mettere in burla** to ridicule; **fuori di burla** joking aside
burlare *tr* to ridicule ‖ *intr* to be joking ‖ *ref*—**burlarsi di** to make fun of
burlé·sco -sca (**-schi -sche**) *adj* funny; mocking; burlesque; jocose ‖ *m* burlesque; mock-heroic
burlétta *f* joke, jest; **mettere in burletta** to ridicule
burló·ne -na *mf* joker, jester
buròcrate *m* bureaucrat
burocràti·co -ca *adj* (**-ci -che**) bureaucratic; clerical (*error*)
burocrazia *f* bureaucracy; red tape
burra·sca *f* (**-sche**) storm
burrascó·so -sa [s] *adj* stormy
burrièra *f* butter dish
burrifì·cio *m* (**-ci**) butter factory, dairy
burro *m* butter
burróne *m* canyon, ravine
burró·so -sa [s] *adj* buttery

buscare §197 *tr* to get; to catch ‖ *intr* to be damaged ‖ *ref*—**buscarsi un malanno** to catch a cold
busécchia *f* casing (*for sausage*)
busillis *m*—**qui sta il busillis** here's the rub, that's the trouble
bussa *f* hit, blow; **venire alle busse to** come to blows
bussare *intr* to knock; **bussare a quattrini** (fig) to hit somebody for a loan
bussata *f* knock (*at the door*)
bussa·tòio *m* (-tòi) knocker
bùssola *f* sedan chair; door; revolving door; swinging door; ballot box; (mach) bushing; (aer & naut) compass; **perdere la bussola** to lose one's bearings
bussolòtto *m* dice box
busta *f* envelope; briefcase; **busta a finestrella** window envelope; **busta primo giorno** first-day cover; **in busta a parte** under separate cover

bustapa·ga *f* (-ga) pay envelope
bustarèlla *f* bribery; kickback
bustina *f* powder, dose; small envelope; (mil) cap, fatigue cap
busto *m* chest, trunk; bust; corset
butirró·so -sa [s] *adj* buttery
buttafuò·ri *m* (-ri) bouncer (*in a night club*); (theat) callboy; (naut) outrigger
buttare *tr* to throw; to waste (*e.g., time*); to give off (*e.g., smoke*); **buttar giù** to demolish; to swallow; (fig) to discredit; to jot down; **buttar via** to throw away; to cast aside ‖ *intr* to secrete, ooze ‖ *ref* to throw oneself; to let oneself fall; **buttarsi giù** (fig) to become downcast
butterare (**bùttero**) *tr* to pock, pit
bùttero *m* pockmark; cowboy
buzzo [ddzz] *m* (vulg) belly; **di buzzo buono** with energy; willingly

C

C, c [tʃi] *m* & *f* third letter of the Italian alphabet
càbala *f* cabala; cabal, intrigue
cabina *f* cabin, stateroom; car, cage (*of elevator*); cockpit (*of airplane*); booth (*of telephone*); cab (*of locomotive*)
cablàg·gio *m* (-gi) (elec) cable (*in auto or radio*)
cablare *tr* to cable
cablografare (**cablògrafo**) *tr* to cable
cablogram·ma *m* (-mi) cablegram, cable
cabotàg·gio *m* (-gi) coasting trade, coastal traffic
cabrare *intr* to zoom
cabrata *f* zoom
cacào *m* cocoa
cacasènno *m* (slang) wiseacre
cacatò·a *m* (-a) cockatoo
càc·cia *m* (-cia) pursuit plane, fighter; (nav) destroyer ‖ *f* chase, hunt; pursuit; **caccia alle streghe** witch hunt
cacciagióne *f* small game; venison; kill (*e.g., of game birds*)
cacciapiè·tre *m* (-tre) (rr) cowcatcher
cacciare §128 *tr* to hunt; to chase; to rout; to send out; to stick, thrust; to utter (*e.g., a cry*); **cacciar fuori** to pull out; **cacciar via** to chase away ‖ *ref* to hide; to intrude; to get; to wind up; to thrust oneself; **cacciarsi negli affari di** to butt into the affairs of
cacciasommergìbi·li *m* (-li) subchaser, submarine chaser
cacciata *f* hunting party; expulsion
cacciatóra *f* hunting jacket; **alla cacciatora** (culin) stewed with herbs
cacciatóre *m* hunter; (aer) fighter pilot; **cacciatore di frodo** poacher; **cacciatore di teste** headhunter
cacciatorpediniè·re *m* (-re) destroyer
cacciatrice *f* huntress

cacciavi·te *m* (-te) screwdriver
càccola *f* gum (*on edge of eyelid*); (slang) snot
caccoló·so -sa [s] *adj* gummy (*eyelid*); (slang) snotty
ca·chi (-chi) *adj* khaki ‖ *m* Japanese persimmon; khaki
cacic·co *m* (-chi) Indian chief; boss (*in Latin America*)
cà·cio *m* (-ci) cheese; **come il cacio sui maccheroni** (coll) at the right moment
cacofóni·co -ca *adj* (-ci -che) cacophonous
cac·tus *m* (-tus) cactus
cadau·no -na *adj* each ‖ *pron* each one
cadàvere *m* corpse, cadaver
cadavèri·co -ca *adj* (-ci -che) cadaverous
cadènte *adj* falling (*star*); rickety (*house*); run-down, decrepit (*person*)
cadènza *f* cadence, rhythm; accent (*peculiar to a region*)
cadére §121 *intr* (ESSERE) to fall; to sink; to slough (*said, e.g., of crust*); to fail; (gram) to end; **cadere a proposito** to come in handy; to come at the right moment; **cadere dalle nuvole** to be dumfounded
cadétto *m* cadet
càdmio *m* cadmium
caducità *f* transiency, brevity
cadu·co -ca *adj* (-ci -che) fleeting; deciduous
cadu·no -na *adj* & *pron* var of **cadauno**
cadu·to -ta *adj* fallen; lost, gone astray; **i caduti** the fallen, the dead ‖ *f* fall; crash (*of stock market*); slump (*of prices*)
caf·fè *m* (-fè) coffee; café
caffeìna *f* caffeine
caffetteria *f* cafeteria
caffettièra *f* coffeepot

cafó·ne -na *adj* loud, gaudy ‖ *m* boor, lout

cagionare (cagióno) *tr* to cause, produce

cagióne *f* cause, reason; **a cagione di** because of

cagionévole *adj* sickly, delicate

cagliare §280 *tr, intr* (ESSERE) & *ref* to curdle, curd

cagliata *f* curd

cà·glio *m* (-gli) rennet

cagna *f* bitch

cagnara *f* barking (*of dogs*); uproar, confusion

cagné·sco -sca (-schi -sche) *adj* dog-like, doggish ‖ *m*—**guardare in cagnesco** to look askance at; **stare in cagnesco con** to be angry with

Caino *m* Cain

Càiro, il Cairo

cala *f* cove; (naut) hold

calabrése [s] *adj & mf* Calabrian

calabróne *m* hornet

calafatare *tr* (naut) to caulk

cala·màio *m* (-mài) inkwell

calamaro *m* squid

calamita *f* magnet; (*mineral*) loadstone; (fig) magnet, attraction

calami·tà *f* (-tà) calamity, disaster

calamitare *tr* to magnetize

calamitó·so -sa [s] *adj* calamitous

càlamo *m* reed, quill

calandra *f* calender; (aut) grille

calandrare *tr* to calender

calante *adj* waning (*moon*)

calàp·pio *m* (-pi) snare; noose

calapran·zi *m* (-zi) dumbwaiter

calare *tr* to lower; to strike (*sails*) ‖ *intr* (ESSERE) to fall, sag (*said, e.g., of prices*); to grow shorter (*said of days*); to come down; to shrink (*said, e.g., of meat*); to lose weight; to set (*said, e.g., of the sun*); to wane (*said of the moon*); (mus) to drop in pitch ‖ *ref* to let oneself down; to dive

calata *f* lowering; descent; invasion; fall; wharf; (coll) intonation; **calata del sole** sunset

cal·ca *f* (-che) crowd, throng

calca·gno *m* (-gni) heel ‖ *m* (-gna *fpl*) (fig) heel; **alle calcagna di** at the heels of

calcare *m* limestone ‖ §197 *tr* to trample; to trace (*on paper*); to tread (*the boards*); to emphasize; **calcare la mano** to exaggerate; **calcare le orme di** to follow in the footsteps of

calce *m*—**in calce** at the foot of the page; **in calce a** at the foot of ‖ *f* lime; **calce viva** quicklime

calcedònio *m* chalcedony

calcestruzzo *m* concrete

calciare §128 *tr & intr* to kick

calciatóre *m* soccer player; football player

calcificare §197 (calcìfico) *tr & ref* to calcify

calcificazióne *f* calcification

calcina *f* mortar; lime

calcinàc·cio *m* (-ci) flake of plaster; **calcinacci** ruins, rubble

calci·nàio *m* (-nài) lime pit

calcinare *tr* to calcine; to lime (*e.g., a field*)

càl·cio *m* (-ci) kick; soccer; calcium; (*e.g., of rifle*) butt; **calcio d'inizio** (sports) kickoff

calciocianamide *m* calcium cyanamide

cal·co *m* (-chi) tracing; cast; imprint

calcografia *f* copper engraving

calcolare (càlcolo) *tr* to calculate; to estimate, reckon; to compute; to consider

calcola·tóre -trice *adj* calculating ‖ *m* calculator; computer; schemer ‖ *f* calculating machine, adding machine

càlcolo *m* calculation; estimate; planning; calculus; (pathol) calculus, stone; **calcolo biliare** gallstone; **calcolo errato** miscalculation; **fare calcolo su** to count upon

calcolò·si *f* (-si) (pathol) stones

calcomanìa *f* decalcomania

caldàia *f* boiler

cal·dàio *m* (-dài) cauldron, boiler

caldalléssa *f* boiled chestnut

caldana *f* flush

caldano *m* brazier

caldarròsta *f* roast chestnut

caldeggiare §290 (caldéggio) *tr* to favor, support; to recommend

calde·ràio *m* (-rài) coppersmith; boilermaker

calderóne *m* cauldron

cal·do -da *adj* warm; hot; rich (*voice*); **caldo, caldo** quite recent ‖ *m* heat; warmth; **aver caldo** to be warm (*said of people*); to be hot (*said of people*); **fa caldo** it is warm; it is hot; **non mi fa nè caldo nè freddo** it leaves me cold, it does not move me

calefazióne *f* heating

caleidoscò·pio *m* (-pi) kaleidoscope

calendà·rio *m* (-ri) calendar

calènde *fpl*—**calende greche** Greek calends

calendimàggio *m* May Day

calèsse *m* buggy, gig

calére *impers*—**non mi cale** (lit) I don't care

calettare (calétto) *tr* to dovetail, mortise ‖ *intr* to fit

calibrare (càlibro) *tr* to gauge, calibrate

càlibro *m* caliber; (mach) calipers; (fig) quality, importance

càlice *m* wine cup; (bot) calyx; (eccl) chalice

cali·cò *m* (-cò) calico

califfo *m* caliph

caligine *f* fog, mist; (fig) darkness

caliginó·so -sa [s] *adj* foggy, misty; (fig) dark, gloomy

calla *f*—**calla dei fioristi** calla lily

calle *f* lane, alley

callìfu·go *m* (-ghi) corn remedy

calligrafia *f* penmanship; handwriting

calli·sta *mf* (-sti -ste) chiropodist

callo *m* corn; callus; **fare il callo a** to get used to; **pestare i calli a qlcu** to step on s.o.'s feet

callosi·tà [s] *f* (-tà) callosity; callus

calló·so -sa [s] *adj* corny; callous; hard

calma *f* calm, tranquillity

calmante *adj* sedative, calming, soothing || *m* sedative

calmare *tr* to calm, soothe, appease || *ref* to calm down; to subside, abate

calmierare (calmièro) *tr* to fix the price of

calmière *m* ceiling price; price control

cal·mo -ma *adj* calm, quiet, still || *f* see **calma**

calo *m* decrease; shrinkage

calomelano *m* calomel

calóre *m* heat; warmth; fervor, ardor; (pathol) rash, inflammation; (vet) rut, mating season

caloria *f* calorie

calòri·co -ca *adj* (**-ci -che**) caloric

calorìfero *m* heater, radiator

caloró·so -sa [s] *adj* warm; hot; cordial; heated

calò·scia *f* (**-sce**) var of **galoscia**

calòtta *f* skullcap; case (*e.g., of watch*); (aut) hubcap; (mach) cap; **calotta cranica** skull

calpestare (calpésto) *tr* to trample

calpestì·o *m* (**-ì**) trampling

calùgine *f* down (*of bird*)

calùnnia *f* calumny, slander

calunniare §287 *tr* to calumniate, slander

calunnia·tóre -trice *mf* slanderer

calunnió·so -sa [s] *adj* slanderous

Calvàrio *m* (Bib) Calvary

calvìzie *f* baldness

cal·vo -va *adj* bald

calza *f* sock; stocking; wick; **calza da donna** stocking; **calze** hose, hosiery; **fare la calza** to knit

calzamàglia *f* tights

calzare *m* footwear || *tr* to wear, put on (*shoes, gloves, or socks*) || *intr* to fit (*said of any garment*); to suit

calzascar·pe *m* (**-pe**) shoehorn

calza·tóio *m* (**-tói**) shoehorn

calzatura *f* footwear; **calzature** footwear

calzaturière *m* shoe manufacturer

calzaturiè·ro -ra *adj* shoe (*e.g., industry*) || *m* shoe worker

calzaturifì·cio *m* (**-ci**) shoe factory

calzeròtto *m* woolen sock

calzet·tàio *m* (**-tài**) hosier

calzettóne *m* knee-high woolen sock (*for mountain boots*)

calzifì·cio *m* (**-ci**) hosiery mill

calzino *m* sock; **calzini corti** socks; half hose; **calzini lunghi** knee-high socks

calzo·làio *m* (**-lài**) shoemaker; cobbler

calzoleria *f* shoemaker's shop; shoe store

calzoncini *mpl* shorts

calzóne *m* trouser leg; **calzoni** trousers, pants; slacks; **calzoni a zampe d'elefante** bell-bottom trousers, flares

camaleònte *m* chameleon

camarilla *f* cabal, clique

cambiadi·schi *m* (**-schi**) record changer

cambiale *f* promissory note, IOU

cambiaménto *m* change, modification

cambiare §287 *tr* to change, exchange; to shift (*gears*) || *intr* to change, switch || *ref* to change (*clothing*); **cambiarsi in** to turn into

cambiavalu·te *m* (**-te**) moneychanger

càm·bio *m* (**-bi**) change; switch; rate of exchange; (mil) relief; **cambio a cloche** shift lever, stick; **cambio di velocità** gearshift; **in cambio di in** exchange for, in place of

cambrètta *f* staple (*to hold a wire*)

cam·brì *m* (**-brì**) cambric

cambusa *f* (naut) galley

cambusière *m* steward

càmera *f* room; bedroom; chamber; **camera ardente** funeral parlor; **Camera dei comuni** House of Commons; **Camera dei deputati** House of Representatives; **camera d'aria** inner tube; **camera di sicurezza** detention cell; vault (*of bank*)

camera·ta *m* (**-ti**) friend, comrade || *f* dormitory; barracks; roomful (*of students or soldiers*)

cameratismo *m* comradeship

camerièra *f* waitress; maid, chambermaid

camerière *m* waiter; steward; valet

camerino *m* small room; toilet, lavatory; (nav) noncommissioned officer's quarters; (theat) dressing room

càmice *m* gown (*of physician*); smock (*of painter*); (eccl) alb

camiceria *f* shirt store; shirt factory

camicétta *f* blouse

camìcia *f* shirt; casing, jacket (*e.g., of boiler*); lining (*e.g., of furnace*); vest (*of sailor*); folder; **camicia da giorno** chemise; **camicia da notte** nightgown; **camicia di forza** strait jacket; **camicia di maglia** coat of mail; **camicia nera** black shirt (*Fascist*); **camicia rossa** red shirt (*Garibaldine*); **dare la camicia** to give the shirt off one's back; **essere nato con la camicia** to be born with a silver spoon in one's mouth; **perdere la camicia** to lose one's shirt

cami·ciàio -ciàia *mf* (**-ciài -ciàie**) shirtmaker, haberdasher

camiciòla *f* sport shirt; undershirt; T-shirt; (obs) vest

camiciòtto *m* smock (*of mechanic*); jumper; sport shirt

caminétto *m* small fireplace; fireplace

camino *m* fireplace; chimney; smokestack; shaft (*in mountain*); mouth (*of volcano*); (naut) funnel

cà·mion *m* (**-mion**) truck

camionale *f* highway

camioncino *m* small truck; panel truck; pickup truck

camionétta *f* small truck; van (*e.g., of police*)

camioni·sta *m* (**-sti**) truckdriver, teamster

camma *f* (mach) cam; (mach) wiper

cammellière *m* camel driver

cammèllo *m* camel

cammèo *m* cameo

camminaménto *m* (mil) communication trench

camminare *intr* to walk; to go, run

camminata *f* walk; gait; (obs) hall with fireplace

cammina·tóre -trice *mf* walker; runner

cammino *m* road, way, route; path (*e.g., of the moon*); course; journey; **cammin facendo** on the way; **cammino battuto** beaten path; **cammino coperto** (mil) covered way; **mettersi in cammino** to set out, start out

camomilla *f* camomile

camòrra *f* underworld

camò·scio *m* (**-sci**) chamois

campagna *f* country; countryside; country property; season (*for harvesting*); campaign; **andare in campagna** to go on vacation (in the country)

campagnò·lo -la *adj* country, rural ǁ *mf* peasant

campale *adj* field (*artillery*); pitched, decisive (*battle*)

campana *f* bell; bell glass, bell jar; lamp shade; (archit) bell; **a campana** bell-bottomed; **campana a martello** alarm bell, tocsin; **campana di vetro** bell glass; **campana pneumatica** caisson

campanàc·cio *m* (**-ci**) cowbell

campanaro *m* bell ringer; (archaic) bell founder

campanèlla *f* small bell; door knocker; curtain ring; (bot) bluebell

campanèllo *m* bell; small bell; doorbell, chimes; **campanello d'allarme** alarm bell

campanile *m* steeple, belfry; native city or town

campanilismo *m* parochialism

campano *m* cowbell

campare *tr* to keep alive; to save; to bring out the details of ǁ *intr* (ESSERE) to live; to survive; **si campa** one ekes out a living

campa·to -ta *adj*—**campato in aria** without any foundation ǁ *f* span

campeggiare §290 (**campéggio**) *intr* to camp, encamp; to stand out

campeggia·tóre -trice *mf* camper

campég·gio *m* (**-gi**) camping, outing; campground; (bot) logwood

campeggi·sta *mf* (**-sti -ste**) camper

campèstre *adj* field, country; (sports) cross-country

campidò·glio *m* (**-gli**) capitol ǁ **Campidoglio** *m* Capitoline (*hill*); Capitol (*temple*)

campionare (**campióno**) *tr* to sample

campionà·rio -ria (**-ri -rie**) *adj* of samples; trade (*exposition*) ǁ *m* sample book, catalogue, pattern book

campionato *m* championship, title

campióne *m* champion; sample; specimen; standard; **campione senza valore** uninsured parcel, sample post

campionéssa *f* championess

campionìssimo *m* world champion, ace

campo *m* field; camp; ground; tennis court; golf course; center (*e.g., for refugees*); **campo addestramento** training camp; **campo d'aviazione** airfield, airport; **campo di battaglia** battlefield; **campo petrolifero** oil field; **lasciare il campo** to retreat; **mettere in campo** to bring up, adduce; **piantare il campo** to pitch camp

camposanto *m* cemetery, churchyard

camuffare *tr* to disguise, mask; to camouflage ǁ *ref* to disguise oneself

camu·so -sa *adj* snub-nosed

Canadà, il Canada

canadése [s] *adj & mf* Canadian

canàglia *f* scoundrel; rabble

canagliata *f* knavery, mean trick

canale *m* canal; irrigation ditch; network (*of communications*); pipe, drain; (anat) duct, tract; (rad, telv) channel; (theat) aisle; **Canale della Manica** English Channel; **Canale di Panama** Panama Canal; **Canale di Suez** Suez Canal

canalizzare [ddzz] *tr* to channel; to install pipes in; (elec) to wire

canalizzazióne [ddzz] *f* channeling; piping; ductwork; (elec) wiring

canalóne *m* ravine

cànapa *f* hemp

cana·pè *m* (**-pè**) sofa, couch; (culin) canapé

cànapo *m* rope, cable

Canàrie, le the Canaries

canarino *m* canary

cancàn *m* noise, racket

cancellare (**cancèllo**) *tr* to cancel, erase; to obliterate; to write off (*a debt*); to scratch (*a horse*) ǁ *ref* to vanish, fade

cancellata *f* railing

cancellatura *f* erasure

cancellazióne *f* cancellation; erasure (*of a tape*)

cancellería *f* chancellery; stationery

cancellière *m* chancellor; court clerk; registrar, recorder

cancèllo *m* gate, railing, grating

canceró·so -sa [s] *adj* cancerous ǁ *mf* cancer victim

cànchero *m* trouble; troublesome person; (coll) cancer

cancrèna *f* gangrene; **andare in cancrena** to become gangrenous

cancrenó·so -sa [s] *adj* gangrenous

cancro *m* cancer; (bot) canker ǁ **Cancro** *m* (astr) Cancer

candeggiante *adj* bleaching ǁ *m* bleaching agent, bleach

candeggiare §290 (**candéggio**) *tr* to bleach

candeggina *f* bleach

candég·gio *m* (**-gi**) bleaching

candéla *f* candle; candlestick; candlepower; (aut) spark plug; **studiare a lume di candela** to burn the midnight oil; **tenere la candela a** to favor the love affair of

candelabro *m* candelabrum

candelière *m* candlestick

candelòra *f* Candlemas

candelòtto *m* big wax candle; **candelotto lacrimogeno** tear-gas canister

candida·to -ta *mf* candidate

candidatura *f* candidature, candidacy

càndi·do -da *adj* white; candid

candire §176 *tr* to candy

candi·to -ta *adj* candied ǁ *m* candied fruit

candóre *m* whiteness; candor

cane *m* dog; hound; hammer, cock (*of gun*); ham actor; **cane barbone**

poodle; **cane bastardo** mongrel; **cane da ferma** setter; **cane da guardia** watchdog; **cane da presa** retriever; **cane da punta** pointer; **cane grosso** big shot; **cane guida per ciechi** seeing eye dog; **cane sciolto** (pol) lone wolf; **come un cane** all alone; **come un cane in chiesa** as an unwelcome guest; **da cani** poorly; **menare il can per l'aia** to beat around the bush; **non c'è un cane** there is nobody there; **raddrizzare le gambe ai cani** to perform an impossible task

canèstro *m* basket
cànfora *f* camphor
cangiante *adj* changeable (*color*); changing, iridescent
canguro *m* kangaroo
canìcola *f* dog days
canile *m* doghouse, kennel
canino *adj* canine || *m* canine tooth
canìzie *f* gray hair; head of gray hair; old age
canna *f* cane, reed; rod (*for fishing or measuring*); pipe (*of organ*); barrel (*of gun*); **canna da zucchero** sugar cane; **canna di caduta** disposal chute; **canna fumaria** chimney; **canna della gola** (coll) windpipe
cannèlla *f* small tube; tap (*of barrel*); cinnamon
cannèllo *m* pipe, tube; stick (*e.g., of licorice*); (chem) pipette; **cannello ossiacetilenico** acetylene torch; **cannello ossidrico** oxyhydrogen blowpipe
cannellóni *mpl* cannelloni
cannéto *m* cane field
cannibale *m* cannibal
cannìc·cio *m* (-ci) wicker frame; shade made out of rushes
cannocchiale *m* spyglass; **cannocchiale astronomico** telescope
cannonata *f* cannonade, cannon shot; (slang) hit
cannoncino *m* small gun; **cannoncino antiaereo** antiaircraft gun
cannóne *m* gun, cannon; pipe, stovepipe; box pleat; shin (*of cattle*); **è un cannone** (coll) he's the tops
cannoneggiare §290 (cannonéggio) *tr* to cannonade, shell
cannonièra *f* gunboat
cannonière *m* gunner, artilleryman; kicker (*in soccer*)
cannùc·cia *f* (-ce) reed; thin tube; stem (*e.g., of pipe*); straw (*for drinking*); (chem) pipette
canòa *f* canoe; launch
canòcchia *f* mantis shrimp
cànone *m* canon; rule; rent; fee, charge (*for use of radio*)
canonicato *m* canonry
canòni·co -ca (-ci -che) *adj* canonical, canon (*law*) || *m* canon; priest || *f* parsonage, rectory
canonizzare [ddzz] *tr* to canonize
canò·ro -ra *adj* song (*bird*); melodious
canottàg·gio *m* (-gi) boating, rowing
canottièra *f* undershirt, T-shirt; skimmer, boater
canottière *m* oarsman
canòtto *m* skiff, scull, shell

canovàc·cio *m* (-ci) dishcloth; embroidery cloth; plot (*of novel or play*)
cantàbile *adj* singable; songlike; cantabile || *m* song
cantamban·co *m* (-chi) jongleur, wandering minstrel; mountebank
cantante *adj* singing, song || *mf* singer
cantare *m* song; chant; laisse, epic strophe || *tr* to sing; to chant || *intr* to sing; to chant; (coll) to squeal
càntaride *f* Spanish fly
càntaro *m* urn
cantastò·rie *mf* (-rie) minstrel
canta·tóre -trice *adj* singing || *mf* singer
cantau·tóre -trice *mf* singer composer
canterano *m* chest of drawers
canterellare (canterèllo) *tr & intr* to sing in a low voice, hum
canteri·no -na *adj* singing, warbling; decoy (*bird*) || *mf* songster, singer
càntero *m* urinal
canticchiare §287 *tr & intr* to hum
cànti·co *m* (-ci) canticle
cantière *m* shipyard, dockyard; navy yard; undertaking, work in progress; **avere in cantiere** to have in hand, be working at; **cantiere edile** building site; builder's yard
cantilèna *f* singsong; **la stessa cantilena** the same old tune
cantimban·co *m* (-chi) var of cantambanco
cantina *f* cellar; wine cellar; wine shop, canteen
cantinière *m* cellarman; butler; wineshop keeper; sommelier
canto *m* song, singing; chant; canto; crow (*of rooster*); chirping (*of grasshopper*); corner, edge; (mus) voice part; **canto del cigno** swan song; **dal canto mio** for my part; **d'altro canto** on the other hand; **da un canto** on the one hand
cantonata *f* corner (*of street*); **prendere una cantonata** to make a blunder
cantóne *m* corner (*of room or building*); canton
cantonièra *f* corner cupboard; (rr) section worker's house
cantonière *m* road laborer; (rr) section hand
cantóre *m* choir singer; cantor; (poet) singer
cantùc·cio *m* (-ci) nook, niche
canutézza *f* hoariness
canutìglia *f* gold thread
canu·to -ta *adj* gray-haired; whitehaired; (poet) white
canzonare (canzóno) *tr* to mock, ridicule
canzonatò·rio -ria *adj* (-ri -rie) mocking
canzonatura *f* mockery, gibe
canzóne *f* song; canzone
canzonétta *f* canzonet; popular song
canzonetti·sta *mf* (-sti -ste) singer (*e.g., in a nightclub*) || *m* songster || *f* songstress
canzonière *m* songbook; collection of poems; song writer
caolino *m* kaolin

caos *m* chaos

caòti•co -ca *adj* (-ci -che) caotic

capace *adj* capacious; capable, intelligent; legally qualified; capace di with a capacity of (*e.g., fifty people*); essere capace di to be able to; fare capace di to convince of

capaci•tà *f* (-tà) capacity; capability

capacitare (capàcito) *tr* to persuade || *ref* to become convinced

capanna *f* hut, cabin; thatched cottage; bathhouse

capannèllo *m* group, crowd

capanno *m* hunting box; cabana, bathhouse

capannóne *m* large shed; hangar

caparbiàggine *f* var of caparbietà

caparbie•tà *f* (-tà) obstinacy, stubborness

capàr•bio -bia *adj* (-bi -bie) stubborn, hard-headed

caparra *f* down payment, deposit; performance bond

capatina *f* short visit

capeggiare §290 (capéggio) *tr* to lead

capeggia•tóre -trice *mf* leader

capellini *mpl* small vermicelli

capéllo *m* hair; averne fin sopra i capelli to have one's fill; capelli hair; capelli a spazzola crew cut; c'è mancato un capello che + *subj* he came close to + *ger*; far rizzare i capelli a qlcu to make s.o.'s hair stand on end

capellóne *m* hippie, beatnik

capellu•to -ta *adj* hairy; long-haired

capelvènere *m* maidenhair

capèstro *m* halter; gallows

capezzale *m* bolster; (fig) bedside

capézzolo *m* nipple, teat; udder

capidò•glio *m* (-gli) var of capodoglio

capiènza *f* capacity (*e.g., of bus*)

capigliatura *f* head of hair

capillare *adj* capillary; (fig) far-reaching

capinéra *f* (orn) blackcap

capintè•sta *m* (-sta) boss; (sports) head, leader

capire §176 *tr* to understand; capire a volo to grasp immediately || *intr*— non capire dalla contentezza to be bursting with joy || *ref* to understand each other; to agree

capitale *adj* capital; mortal (*sin*) || *m* capital; principal; capitale sociale capital stock || *f* capital (*of country*)

capitalismo *m* capitalism

capitali•sta *mf* (-sti -ste) capitalist

capitalìsti•co -ca *adj* (-ci -che) capitalistic

capitalizzare [ddzz] *tr* to capitalize; to compound (*interest*)

capitana *f* flagship

capitanare *tr* to lead, captain

capitanerìa *f* (hist) captaincy; capitaneria di porto harbor-master's office; coast guard office; port authority's office

capitano *m* captain; skipper, master (*of ship*); commander (*in air force*); capitano di corvetta or capitano di fregata (nav) lieutenant commander;

capitano di gran cabotaggio master; capitano di lungo corso master; capitano di porto harbor master; capitano di vascello (nav) commander

capitare (càpito) *intr* (ESSERE) to arrive; to happen, occur; to happen to get, e.g., capitò a casa mia alle tre he happened to get to my house at three; capitare bene to be lucky; dove capita at random

capitazióne *f* poll tax

capitèllo *m* (archit) capital; (bb) headband

capitolare *adj & m* capitular || *v* (capìtolo) *intr* to capitulate, surrender

capitolato *m* (com) specifications

capitolazióne *f* capitulation

capìtolo *m* chapter; article, paragraph (*of contract*)

capitombolare (capitómbolo) *intr* to tumble

capitómbolo *m* tumble; fare un capitombolo (fig) to collapse

capitóne *m* big eel

capitozzare (capitòzzo) *tr* to poll (*a tree*)

capo *m* head; chief; boss, leader; top; (geog) cape; (nav) chief petty officer; a capo scoperto bareheaded; capo d'accusa (law) charge; capo del governo prime minister; capo dello stato president, chief of state; capo di vestiario garment; capo scarico scatterbrain; col capo nel sacco (fig) heedlessly; da capo all over (again); fare capo a to flow into; in capo a at the end of (*e.g., one month*); in capo al mondo at the end of the world; per sommi capi briefly; rompersi il capo to rack one's brain; scoprirsi il capo to take one's hat off; senza capo né coda without rhyme or reason; venire a capo di to come to the end of

capobanda *m* (capibanda) bandmaster; ringleader

capocamerière *m* headwaiter

capocannonière *m* (capicannonièri) petty gunnery officer; (soccer) leader in number of goals

capòcchia *f* head (*e.g., of a match*)

capòc•cia *m* (-ci & -cia) head of household; foreman, boss (*e.g., of roadworkers or farmers*)

capocòmi•co *m* (-ci) head of dramatic company

capocòr•da *m* (capicòrda) (elec) binding post, terminal

capocrònaca *m* (capicrònaca) leading article

capocronista *m* (capicronisti) city editor

capocuòco *m* (capocuòchi & capicuòchi) chef

capodanno *m* (capodanni & capi d'anno) New Year's Day

capodò•glio *m* (-gli) sperm whale

capofàbbrica *m* (capifàbbrica) foreman, superintendent

capofabbricato *m* (capifabbricato) air-raid warden

capofamìglia *m* (capifamìglia) head of the family

capofila *m* (capifila) head of a line || *f* (capofila) head of a line

capofitto *adj invar*—a capofitto headlong

capogiro *m* vertigo, dizziness; da capogiro dizzying, e.g., prezzi da capogiro dizzying prices

capolavó·ro *m* (-ri) masterpiece

capolèttera *m* (capilèttera) letterhead; (typ) first large bold letter of a paragraph

capolìnea *m* (capilìnea) terminal, terminus

capolino *m*—fare capolino to peep

capolista *m* (capilista) first (*of a list*); (sports) leader || *f* (capolista) first (*of a list*)

capoluò·go *m* (-ghi) capital (*of province*); county seat

capomacchini·sta *m* (-sti) chief engineer

capomastro *m* (capomastri & capimastri) foreman; building contractor

capomùsica *m* (capimùsica) bandmaster

capoofficina *m* (capiofficina) superintendent (*of shop*)

capopàgina *m* (capipàgina) heading (*of newspaper*)

capopèzzo *m* (capipèzzo) gunnery sergeant

capopòpolo *m* (capipòpolo) demagogue

caporale *m* corporal

caporeparto *m* (capireparto) department manager, floor walker; shop foreman

caporione *m* ringleader

caposaldo *m* (capisaldi) (fig) main point, basis; (mil) stronghold; (surv) datum

caposezióne *m* (capisezióne) department head

caposquadra *m* (capisquadra) group leader; (sports) team captain

capostazióne *m* (capistazióne) station master

capostìpite *m* founder (*of family*); prototype, archetype

capotaménto *m* var of cappottamento

capotare (capòto) *intr* var of cappottare

capotasto *m* nut (*of violin*)

capotàvola *m* (capitàvola) head of the table, honored guest

capòte *f* (aut) top

capotrèno *m* (capitrèno & capotrèni) (rr) conductor

cappottaménto *m* var of cappottamento

cappottare (capòtto) *intr* var of cappottare

capoufficio *m* (capiufficio) office manager

capovèrso *m* paragraph; (typ) indentation

capovòlgere §289 *tr* to overturn; (fig) to upset || *ref* to overturn; (fig) to be or become reversed

capovolgiménto *m* upset; (fig) reversal

capovòlta *f* overturn; turn (*in swimming*)

cappa *f* cape, cloak; mantle; letter K; shroud (*of clouds*); (naut) trysail;

cappa del cielo vault of heaven; navigare alla cappa (naut) to lay to

cappèlla *f* chapel; cappella mortuaria undertaker's parlor || Cappella Sistina Sistine Chapel

cappel·làio *m* (-lài) hatter, hat maker or dealer

cappellano *m* chaplain

cappellata *f* hatful

cappelleria *f* hat store

cappellièra *f* hatbox

cappèllo *m* hat; bonnet; cap (*of mushroom*); head (*of nail*); cowl (*of chimney*); preamble (*of newspaper article*); cappello a cencio slouch hat; cappello a cilindro top hat; cappello a cono dunce cap; cappello a due punte cocked hat; cappello a tre punte three-cornered hat; cappello del lume lampshade; cappello di feltro felt hat; cappello di paglia straw hat; cappello floscio fedora; fare di cappello to take one's hat off; prendere cappello to take offense

cappellóne *adj invar* Western (*movie*) || *m* big hat; (coll) recruit; (mov) Western character

càppero *m* (bot) caper; capperi! (coll) wow!

càp·pio *m* (-pi) bow; noose; loop

capponàia *f* chicken coop

cappóne *m* capon

cappòtta *f* cape; navy coat; hood (*of car*)

cappottaménto *m* upset, rolling over

cappottare (cappòtto) *intr* to upset, roll over

cappottatura *f* (aer) cowl

cappòtto *m* overcoat; lurch (*at the close of game*); (cards) slam; cappotto da mezza stagione lightweight coat

cappuccino *m* espresso with cream; Capuchin (*friar*)

Cappuccétto *m*—Cappuccetto Rosso Little Red Ridinghood

cappùc·cio *m* (-ci) hood, cowl; cabbage; cap (*of fountain pen*)

capra *f* goat; nanny goat; tripod

ca·pràio -pràia *mf* (-prài -pràie) goatherd

caprét·to -ta *mf* kid

capriata *f* truss (*to support roof*)

capric·cio *m* (-ci) whim, fancy, caprice; tantrum; flirting; (mus) capriccio

capricció·so -sa [s] *adj* whimsical, capricious; naughty; fanciful, bizarre

Capricòrno *m* (astr) Capricorn

caprifò·glio *m* (-gli) honeysuckle

caprimul·go *m* (-gi) (orn) goatsucker

capri·no -na *adj* goatlike, goatish || *m* smell of goat

capriòla *f* female roe deer; caper, somersault; fare capriole to cut capers, to caper

capriòlo *m* roe deer; roebuck

capro *m* he-goat, billy goat; capro espiatorio scapegoat

capróne *m* he-goat, billy goat

càpsula *f* capsule; percussion cap; cap (*of bottle*); (rok) capsule

captare *tr* to captivate; to catch, inter-

cept; to harness (*a waterfall*); (rad, telv) to pick up (*a signal*)
captazióne *f* undue influence (*to secure an inheritance*)
capzió•so -sa [s] *adj* insidious, treacherous
carabàttola *f* (coll) trifle
carabina *f* carbine
carabinière *m* carabineer; Italian military policeman, carabiniere; (*hist*) cavalryman
caracollare (caracòllo) *intr* to caracole, caper; (coll) to trot along
caracòllo *m* caracole, caper
caraffa *f* carafe, decanter
caràmbola *f* carom
carambolare (caràmbolo) *intr* to carom
caramèlla *f* piece of hard candy; taffy; (coll) monocle; caramelle hard candy
caramellare (caramèllo) *tr* to caramel; to candy
caramèllo *m* caramel (*burnt sugar*)
caraménte *adv* affectionately
carati•sta *m* (-sti) shareholder (*in ship or business*)
carato *m* carat; share (*of ship*)
caràttere *m* character; type; handwriting; characteristic; disposition; carattere corsivo (typ) italic; carattere maiuscolo capital; carattere minuscolo small letter, lower case; carattere neretto or grassetto (typ) boldface
caratteri•sta *m* (-sti) character actor || *f* (-ste) character actress
caratteristi•co -ca (-ci -che) *adj* & *f* characteristic
caratterizzare [ddzz] *tr* to characterize
caratura *f* share (*in business or ship*)
cara•vàn *m* (-vàn) trailer, mobile home
caravanserrà•glio *m* (-gli) caravansary
caravèlla *f* caravel; carpenter's glue
carbo•nàio -nàia (-nài -nàie) *adj* coal || *m* coal man, coal dealer || *f* charcoal pit; coalbin, bunker; coal yard
carbonato *m* carbonate
carbón•chio *m* (-chi) (agr) smut (*on wheat*); (jewelry) carbuncle
carboncino *m* charcoal (*pencil and drawing*)
carbóne *m* coal; charcoal; carbon (*of arc light or primary battery*); carbone bianco hydroelectric power; carbone dolce charcoal; carbone fossile coal; fare carbone to coal
carbòni•co -ca *adj* (-ci -che) carbonic
carbonièra *f* coal yard; (naut) collier; (rr) tender
carbonile *m* (naut) bunker
carbònio *m* (chem) carbon
carbonizzare [ddzz] *tr* to carbonize; to char
carbùncolo *m* boil, carbuncle; (archaic) ruby
carburante *m* fuel
carburatóre *m* carburetor
carburazióne *f* (aut) mixture
carburo *m* carbide
carcassa *f* carcass; framework; (aut) jalopy; (fig) wreck
carcerare (càrcero) *tr* to jail
carcerà•rio -ria *adj* (-ri -rie) jail, prison

carcera•to -ta *adj* imprisoned || *mf* prisoner
càrce•re *m* (-ri *fpl*) jail, prison
carcerière *m* jailer, prison guard
carciòfo *m* artichoke
cardàni•co -ca *adj* (-ci -che) universal (*e.g., joint*)
cardano *m* universal joint
cardatrice *f* carding machine
cardellino *m* goldfinch
cardìa•co -ca (-ci -che) *adj* heart, cardiac || *m* heart patient
cardinale *adj* cardinal || *m* (eccl, orn) cardinal
cardinali•zio -zia *adj* (-zi -zie) cardinal, cardinal's
càrdine *m* hinge; (fig) pivot, mainstay (*e.g., of theory*)
càr•dio *m* (-di) cockle (*mollusk*)
cardiochirurgìa *f* heart surgery
cardiogram•ma *m* (-mi) cardiogram
cardiòlo•go *m* (-gi) cardiologist
cardiopalmo *m* tachycardia
cardiopatìa *f* heart disease
cardo *m* (bot) thistle; (bot) cardoon
carèna *f* ship's bottom; (aer) outer cover (*of airship*); (bot) rib
carenàg•gio *m* (-gi) careening a ship; careen
carenare (carèno) *tr* to careen (*a ship*)
carenatura *f* streamlining; carenatura di fusoliera (aer) turtleback
carènza *f* lack, want
carestìa *f* famine; scarcity (*e.g., of manpower*)
carézza *f* caress; fare una carezza a to caress
carezzare (carézzo) *tr* to caress
carezzévole *adj* caressing, fondling; sweet, suave; blandishing
cariare §287 *tr* to cause (*a tooth*) to decay; to corrode || *ref* to decay; to rot
cariàtide *f* caryatid
caria•to -ta *adj* decayed
càri•ca *f* (-che) office, appointment; charge; (fig) insistence
caricaménto *m* loading
caricare §197 (càrico) *tr* to load; to burden; to wind (*a watch*); to fill (*a pipe*); to charge (*a battery*); to deepen (*a color*); caricare la mano to exceed; caricare le dosi to exaggerate || *ref* to burden oneself
carica•to -ta *adj* exaggerated, affected
carica•tóre -trice *adj* loading || *m* clip, magazine (*for rifle*); loader (*of gun*); cassette (*of tape recorder*); charger (*of battery*); longshoreman; (phot) cartridge, cassette
caricatura *f* caricature, cartoon; mettere in caricatura to ridicule
caricaturi•sta *mf* (-sti -ste) cartoonist, caricaturist
càrice *m* (bot) sedge
càri•co -ca (-chi -che) *adj* loaded; burdened; vivid (*color*); strong (*tea*); charged (*battery*) || *m* loading; load, burden; charge; cargo || *f* see carica
càrie *f* caries, decay
cari•no -na *adj* nice, pretty, cute; questa è carina! this is funny!

cari·tà *f* (-tà) charity; alms; (poet) love; per carità please
caritatévole *adj* charitable
caritati·vo -va *adj* (obs) charitable
carlin·ga *f* (-ghe) fuselage
Carlo *m* Charles
Carlomagno *m* Charlemagne
carlóna *f*—alla carlona carelessly, haphazardly
carlòtta *f* charlotte || Carlotta Charlotte
carme *m* poem, lyric poem
carmì·nio *m* (-ni) carmine
carnagióne *f* complexion
car·nàio *m* (-nài) carnage; slaughter house; mass of humanity
carnale *adj* carnal, sensual; full (*e.g.*, brother, cousin)
carname *m* carrion
carne *f* flesh; meat; bene in carne plump; carne da macello cannon fodder; carne suina pork; carne viva open wound; essere solo carne ed ossa to be nothing but skin and bones; in carne ed ossa in person, in the flesh; troppa carne al fuoco too many irons in the fire
carnéfice *m* executioner
carneficina *f* slaughter, carnage
càrne·o -a *adj* fleshy, meaty; flesh-colored
carnet *m* (carnet) notebook; checkbook; backlog
carnevale *m* carnival
carnièra *f* hunting jacket; gamebag
carnière *m* gamebag
carnìvo·ro -ra *adj* carnivorous || *mpl* carnivores; Carnivora
carnò·so -sa [s] *adj* fleshy
ca·ro -ra *adj* dear (*beloved; high in price*) || caro *adv* dear || *m* high price; beloved; i miei cari my parents; my relatives; my friends
carógna *f* carcass; cad, rotter; carogne carrion
carosèllo *m* tournament; carousel, merry-go-round
caròta *f* carrot; (fig) lie
caròtide *f* carotid artery
carovana *f* caravan; group, crowd; union of longshoremen; apprenticeship; (naut, nav) convoy; far carovana to join a tour; fare la carovana to be an apprentice
carovaniè·ro -ra *adj* caravan || *f* desert trail
carovi·ta *m* (-ta) high cost of living; cost-of-living increase
carovive·ri *m* (-ri) high cost of living; cost-of-living increase
carpa *f* (ichth) carp
carpentière *m* carpenter
carpire §176 *tr* to snatch, seize; to extract, worm (*a secret*)
carpóni *adv* on all fours; avanzare carponi to crawl
carradóre *m* cart maker, wheelwright
car·ràio -ràia (-rài -ràie) *adj* passable for vehicles || *f* cart road
carrarèc·cia *f* (-ce) country road; rut
carreggiata *f* paved road; track (*of vehicles*); (fig) right path
carrellare (carrèllo) *intr* (mov, telv) to dolly

carrellata *f* (mov) dolly shot, tracking shot
carrèllo *m* car (*for narrow-gauge track*); carriage (*of typewriter*); cart (*for shopping*); (aer) landing gear; (mach, rr) truck; (mov, telv) dolly; carrello d'atterraggio (aer) undercarriage, landing gear; carrello elevatore fork-lift truck
carrétta *f* cart; tramp steamer
carrettata *f* cartful; a carrettate abundantly
carrettière *m* cart driver, drayman; teamster
carrétto *m* small cart; carretto a mano pushcart
carriàg·gio *m* (-gi) wagon; carriaggi (mil) baggage train
carrièra *f* career; di gran carriera at top speed
carrieri·sta *mf* (-sti -ste) unscrupulous go-getter
carriòla *f* wheelbarrow
carro *m* wagon; cart; wagonload; cartload; carload; (rr) car; (astr) Plough; (poet) chariot; carri armati (mil) armor; carro allegorico float (*in a pageant*); carro armato (mil) tank; carro attrezzi (aut) tow truck; wrecker; carro bestiame (rr) cattle car; carro botte or carro cisterna (aut) tank truck; (rr) tank car; carro di Tespi traveling show; carro funebre hearse; carro gru (rr) wrecking crane; carro marsupio (rr) double decker (*used to transport automobiles*); carro merci (rr) freight car; Gran Carro (astr) Big Dipper; mettere il carro innanzi ai buoi to put the cart before the horse; Piccolo Carro (astr) Little Dipper || *m* (carra *fpl*) carload; wagonload; cartload
carròzza *f* wagon carriage; carrozza letti (rr) sleeping car; carrozza ristorante (rr) dining car; carrozza salone (rr) club car; con la carrozza di S. Francesco on shank's mare; signori, in carrozza! (rr) all aboard!
carrozzàbile *adj* open to vehicular traffic || *f* road open to vehicular traffic
carrozzèlla *f* small wagon; baby carriage; wheelchair; hackney
carrozzino *m* baby carriage; sidecar
carrozzóne *m* wagon; hearse; caravan (*e.g.*, of gypsies); (rr) car
carruba *f* carob
carrubo *m* carob tree
carrùcola *f* pulley
carta *f* paper; document (*e.g.*, of identification*); alla carta à la carte; carta assorbente blotter; carta astronomica astronomical map; carta bianca carte blanche; carta bollata stamped paper (*for official documents*); carta carbone carbon paper; carta catramata tar paper; carta da disegno drawing paper; carta da gioco playing card; carta da giornale newsprint; carta da imballaggio or da impacco wrapping paper; carta da lettera or da lettere writing paper; carta geografica map, chart; carta igienica toilet paper; carta oleata wax paper; carta torna-

sole litmus paper; **carta velina** India paper; tissue paper; **carta vetrata** sandpaper; **carte papers**, writings; **carte francesi** cards in the four suits spades, hearts, diamonds, and clubs; **carte napoletane** cards in the four suits gold coins, cups, swords, and clubs; **fare le carte** to shuffle the cards; **fare le carte a qlcu** to tell s.o.'s fortune with cards

cartacarbóne *f* (**cartecarbóne**) carbon paper

cartàc·cia *f* (**-ce**) waste paper

cartàce·o -a *adj* (**-i -e**) paper

Cartàgine *f* Carthage

car·tàio *m* (**-tài**) papermaker; paper dealer; (cards) dealer

cartamonéta *f* paper money

cartapècora *f* parchment

cartapésta *f* papier-mâché

cartà·rio -ria *adj* (**-ri -rie**) paper

cartastràccia *f* (**cartestracce**) wrapping paper; wastepaper

cartég·gio *m* (**-gi**) correspondence; (aer, naut) reckoning

cartèlla *f* lottery ticket; card (*e.g., of bingo*); page of manuscript; Manila folder; schoolbag; briefcase; binding (*of book*); **cartella clinica** clinical chart; **cartella di rendita** government bond; **cartella esattoriale** tax bill; **cartella fondiaria** bond certificate

cartellino *m* label; nameplate (*on door*); file; (sports) contract; **cartellino di presenza** timecard; **cartellino signaletico** criminal record

cartèllo *m* poster; sign (*on store*); (com) cartel, trust; **cartello di sfida** challenge; **cartello stradale** traffic sign

cartellóne *m* show bill, theater poster; bill (*for advertising*); **tenere il cartellone** to find public favor, make a hit, be the rage

car·ter *m* (**-ter**) chain guard (*of bicycle*); (aut) crankcase

cartièra *f* papermill

cartilàgine *f* cartilage, gristle

cartina *f* dose; cigarette paper; small map

cartòc·cio *m* (**-ci**) paper cone; charge (*of gun*); cornhusk; (archit) scroll

cartògrafo *m* cartographer

carto·làio *m* (**-lài**) stationer

cartolerìa *f* stationery store

cartolina *f* card, post card; **cartolina precetto** induction notice

cartomante *mf* fortuneteller

cartoncino *m* light cardboard, calling card; **cartoncino natalizio** Christmas card

cartóne *m* cardboard, carton; **cartone animato** (mov) animated cartoon

cartùc·cia *f* (**-ce**) cartridge; shot, shell; **mezza cartuccia** (fig) half pint

cartuccièra *f* cartridge belt

casa [s] *f* house; dwelling; home; household; **andare a casa** to go home; **casa base** (baseball) home base; **casa colonica** farm house; **casa da gioco** gambling house; **casa del diavolo** faraway place; **casa di bambole** playhouse, doll's house; **casa di correzione** reform school; **casa di cura**

sanatorium, private clinic; **casa di riposo** convalescent home, nursing home; **casa di spedizione** shipping agency; **casa di tolleranza** bawdyhouse; **casa madre** home office, headquarters; **esser di casa** to be intimate; **fuori casa** (sports) away; **in casa** (sports) home; **metter su casa** to set up housekeeping; **sentirsi a casa** to feel at home; **stare a casa** to stay at home; **star di casa** to dwell, live

casac·ca *f* (**-che**) coat; **voltar casacca** to be a turncoat

casàccio *m*—**a casaccio** at random; heedlessly

casalin·go -ga (**-ghi -ghe**) [s] *adj* home, domestic; stay-at-home; homey; home-made || **casalinghi** *mpl* household articles || *f* housewife

casamatta [s] *f* casemate, bunker

casaménto [s] *m* apartment house, tenement; tenants

casata [s] *f* house, lineage

casato [s] *m* birth, family; (obs) family name

cascame *m* waste; remnants (*e.g., of silk*)

cascante *adj* flabby, loose; (poet) languid, dull

cascare §197 *intr* (ESSERE) to fall, droop; to fit (*said of clothes*); **cascare dalla noia** to be bored to death; **cascare dal sonno** to be overwhelmed with sleep; **cascare diritto** to escape unscathed; **non casca il mondo** the world is not coming to an end

cascata *f* fall, waterfall; necklace (*e.g., of pearls*); **a cascata** flood of, e.g., **telefonate a cascata** flood of telephone calls || **le Cascate del Niagara** Niagara Falls

cascina *f* farm house; dairy barn

ca·sco *m* (**-schi**) helmet, crash helmet; electric hairdrier; cluster (*e.g., of bananas*)

caseggiato [s] *m* built-up zone; block, row of houses; apartment house

caseifi·cio *m* (**-ci**) dairy, creamery, cheese factory

casèlla [s] *f* pigeonhole; square (*of paper*); **casella postale** post-office box

casellante [s] *mf* gatekeeper || *m* (rr) trackwalker

casellà·rio [s] *m* (**-ri**) filing cabinet; row of post-office boxes; **casellario giudiziale** criminal file

casèllo [s] *m* tollgate (*on turnpike*); (rr) trackwalker's house

casèrma *f* barracks; fire station

casino [s] *m* country house; clubhouse; (slang) whorehouse; (slang) noise, racket

casìsti·ca *f* (**-che**) case study; (eccl) casuistry

caso *m* case; chance; fate; vicissitude; opportunity; **a caso** inadvertently; **al caso** eventually; **caso fortuito** (law) act of God; **caso mai** assuming that, in the event that; **è il caso** it is the moment; **far caso a qlco** to notice s.th; **in ogni caso** in any event; **mettere il caso che** suppose; **mi fa caso** I am surprised; **non fare caso a** to make nothing of, pay no attention to; **per caso** perchance

casolare [s] *m* hut, hovel; isolated farmhouse

casòtto [s] *m* cabana, bathhouse; sentry box

Càspio *adj* Caspian

càspita *interj* you don't say!

cassa *f* box; chest; case; stock (*of rifle*); cash; cash register; desk (*e.g., in hotel*); check-out (*in a supermarket*); **a pronta cassa** by cash; **cassa acustica** loudspeaker; **cassa di risparmio** savings bank; **cassa malattia** health insurance; **cassa rurale** farmers' credit cooperative; **in cassa** in hand (*said of money*)

cassafórma *f* (**casseforme**) (archit) form (*for cement*)

cassafòrte *f* (**casseforti**) safe

cassapanca *f* (**cassapanche** & **cassepanche**) wooden chest

cassare *tr* to erase, cancel; to cross off; (law) to annull

cassata *f* Neapolitan ice cream with soft core; Sicilian cake

cassazióne *f* annulment, abolition; cancellation

casserétto *m* (naut) poop

càssero *m* (naut) quarterdeck; **cassero di poppa** (naut) cockpit

casseruòla *f* saucepan

cassétta *f* small box; coach box; (theat) box office; **cassetta dei ferri** workbox; **cassetta delle lettere** mail box; **cassetta di cottura** dish warmer; **cassetta di sicurezza** safe-deposit box; **cassetta per ugnature** miter box

cassettièra *f* chest of drawers

cassétto *m* drawer; **cassetto di distribuzione** (mach) slide valve

cassettóne *m* chest of drawers; (archit) coffer, caisson

cassiè·re -ra *mf* cashier; teller

cassóne *m* large case, large box; chest; caisson (*for underwater construction*); body (*of truck*); (mil) caisson

cassonétto *m* cornice

cast *m* cast (*of actors*)

casta *f* caste

castagna *f* chestnut; **castagna d'India** horse chestnut

castagnéto *m* chestnut grove

castagno *m* chestnut tree; chestnut (*lumber*); **castagno d'India** horse chestnut tree

casta·no -na *adj* chestnut (*color*)

castellana *f* chatelaine

castellano *m* lord of the castle, squire

castellétto *m* scaffold; (min) gallows, headframe

castèl·lo *m* castle; works (*e.g., of watch*); scaffold; jungle gym; hydraulic boom, bucket lift (*on truck*); (naut) forecastle; **castello di menzogne** pack of lies; **castello in aria** castle in Spain ‖ *m* (**-la** *fpl*) (archaic) castle

castigare §209 *tr* to punish; (poet) to correct, castigate

castigatézza *f* purity (*e.g., of style*)

castiga·to -ta *adj* decent, modest; pure (*language*)

Castìglia, la Castile

castiglia·no -na *adj* & *mf* Castilian

casti·go *m* (**-ghi**) punishment; (fig) scourge; **mettere in castigo** (coll) to punish

casti·tà *f* (**-tà**) chastity; (fig) purity

ca·sto -sta *adj* chaste; pure, elegant (*language or style*)

castóne *m* setting (*of stone*)

castòro *m* beaver

castrare *tr* to castrate; to spay; (fig) to expurgate

castra·to -ta *adj* castrated; spayed; (fig) effeminate ‖ *m* mutton (of castrated sheep); eunuch

castróne *m* wether (*sheep*); gelding (*horse*); (fig) nincompoop

castroneria *f* (vulg) stupidity

casuale *adj* fortuitous, casual; sundry (*e.g., expenses*)

casuali·tà *f* (**-tà**) chance, accident

casùpola [s] *f* hut, hovel

catacli·sma *m* (**-smi**) cataclysm

catacómba *f* catacomb

catafal·co *m* (**-chi**) catafalque

catafàscio *adv*—**a catafascio** topsy-turvy

catalès·si *f* (**-si**) catalepsy

catàli·si *f* (**-si**) catalysis

catalizza·tóre -trice [ddzz] *adj* catalytic ‖ *m* catalyst

catalogare §209 (**catàlogo**) *tr* to catalogue

catàlo·go *m* (**-ghi**) catalogue

catapècchia *f* hovel

catapla·sma *m* (**-smi**) poultice, plaster; (fig) bore

catapulta *f* catapult

catapultare *tr* to catapult

cataratta *f* cataract; sluice (*of canal*)

catarro *m* catarrh

catar·si *f* (**-si**) catharsis

catàrti·co -ca *adj* (**-ci -che**) cathartic

catasta *f* pile, heap

catastale *adj* land (*office*)

catasto *m* real-estate register; land office

catàstrofe *f* catastrophe; wreck

catastròfi·co -ca *adj* (**-ci -che**) catastrophic

catechismo *m* catechism

catechizzare [ddzz] *tr* to catechize

categoria *f* category; weight (*in boxing*); (sports) class

categòri·co -ca *adj* (**-ci -che**) categorical; classified (*telephone directory*)

caténa *f* chain; range (*of mountains*); (archit) tie beam; **catene da neve** tire chains; **mordere la catena** to champ the bit

catenàc·cio *m* (**-ci**) bolt; (fig) jalopy; (journ) giant-size headline

catenèlla *f* chain

cateratta *f* var of **cataratta**

catèrva *f* great quantity, large number

catetère *m* catheter

cateterizzare [ddzz] *tr* to catheterize

catinèlla *f* water basin; **piovere a catinelle** (coll) to rain cats and dogs

catino *m* basin

càtodo *m* cathode

Catóne *m* Cato; **Catone il Maggiore** Cato the Elder

catòr·cio *m* (**-ci**) (coll) piece of junk

catramare *tr* to tar
catramatrice *f* asphalt-paving machine
catrame *m* tar, coal tar
càttedra *f* desk (*of teacher*); chair, professorship
cattedrale *adj* & *f* cathedral
cattedràti·co -ca (-ci -che) *adj* pedantic || *m* professor
catte·gù *m* (**-gù**) catgut
cattivare *tr* to captivate
cattivèria *f* wickedness; piece of wickedness
cattivi·tà *f* (**-tà**) captivity
catti·vo -va *adj* bad; wicked; vicious (*animal*); worthless; poor (*reputation; condition*); nasty; naughty; (archaic) cowardly || *mf* wicked person || *m* bad taste; **sapere di cattivo** to taste bad
cattolicità *f* catholicity
cattòli·co -ca (-ci -che) *adj* catholic || *adj* & *mf* Catholic
cattura *f* capture, seizure; arrest
catturare *tr* to capture, seize; to arrest
caucàsi·co -ca *adj* & *mf* (**-ci -che**) Caucasian
caucciù *m* (**caucciù**) rubber
càusa *f* cause, motive; fault; lawsuit, action; **a causa di** on account of; **causa civile** civil suit; **causa penale** criminal suit; **fare causa** to take legal action; **intentare causa a** to bring suit against
causale *adj* causal || *f* cause
causare (**càuso**) *tr* to cause
causìdi·co *m* (**-ci**) amicus curiae; (joc) pettifogger
càusti·co -ca *adj* (**-ci -che**) caustic
cautèla *f* caution; precaution, care
cautelare *adj* guaranteeing, protecting || *v* (**cautèlo**) *tr* to guarantee, protect || *ref* to take precautions
cauterizzare [ddzz] *tr* to cauterize
càu·to -ta *adj* cautious, prudent; cagey
cauzióne *f* security, bail; **dare cauzione** to give bail
cava *f* quarry; cave; (fig) mine
cavadènti *m* (**-ti**) (coll) tooth puller, poor dentist
cavagno *m* (coll) basket
cavalcare §197 *tr* to ride; to cross over (*e.g., a river*) || *intr* to ride; **cavalcare a bisdosso** to ride bareback; **cavalcare all'amazzone** to ride sidesaddle
cavalcata *f* ride; cavalcade
cavalcatura *f* mount
cavalca·vìa *m* (**-vìa**) bridge (*between two buildings*); overpass
cavalcióni *adj*—**a cavalcioni (di)** astride
cavalierato *m* knighthood
cavalière *m* rider (*on horseback*); knight; cavalier; chevalier; **a cavaliere** astride; **cavaliere d'industria** adventurer; **cavaliere errante** knight errant; **essere a cavaliere di** to overlook (*e.g., a valley*); to stretch over (*e.g., two centuries*)
cavalla *f* mare
cavalleggière *m* cavalryman
cavalleré·sco -sca *adj* (**-schi -sche**) chivalrous, knightly

cavallerìa *f* cavalry; chivalry, knighthood; (fig) chivalry
cavallerizza *f* manège, riding school; horsemanship; horsewoman
cavallerizzo *m* horseman; riding master
cavallétta *f* grasshopper
cavallétto *m* tripod; easel; trestle (*of ski lift*); scaffold (*e.g., of stonemason*); sawhorse, sawbuck
cavalli·no -na *adj* horse, horse-like || *m* foal, colt || *f* foal, filly; **correre la cavallina** to be on the loose; to sow one's wild oats
cavallo *m* horse; knight (*in chess*); crotch (*of pants*); **a cavallo** on horseback; **a cavallo di** astride; **andare col cavallo di San Francesco** to ride shank's mare; **cavallo a dondolo** hobbyhorse; **cavallo di battaglia** battle horse; (fig) specialty, forte; **cavallo da corsa** race horse; **cavallo da tiro** draft horse; **cavallo di Frisia** cheval-de-frise; **cavallo di ritorno** confirmed news; **cavallo vapore** metric horsepower; **essere a cavallo** (fig) to have turned the corner
cavallóne *m* big horse; billow
cavallùc·cio *m* (**-ci**) little horse; **a cavalluccio** on one's shoulders; **cavalluccio marino** (ichth) sea horse
cavare *tr* to dig; to extract (*e.g., a tooth*); to pull out (*e.g., money*); to draw; **cavare il cuore a qlcu** to move s.o. to compassion; **cavare una spina dal cuore a qlcu** to ease so.o.'s mind || *ref* to take off (*e.g., one's hat*); **cavarsela** to overcome an obstacle; to get out of trouble; **cavarsi la camicia di dosso** to give the shirt off one's back; **cavarsi la fame** to eat one's fill; **cavarsi la voglia** to satisfy one's wishes
cavastiva·li *m* (**-li**) bootjack
cavatap·pi *m* (**-pi**) corkscrew
cavaturàccio·li *m* (**-li**) corkscrew
cavèrna *f* cave, cavern
cavernó·so -sa [s] *adj* cavernous; deep (*voice*)
cavézza *f* halter; (fig) check
càvia *f* guinea pig; **cavia umana** (fig) guinea pig
caviale *m* caviar
cavìc·chio *m* (**-chi**) peg
cavì·glia *f* (**-glie**) ankle; bolt; pin, dowel, peg
caviglièra *f* ankle support
cavillare *intr* to cavil, quibble
cavillo *m* quibble
cavilló·so -sa [s] *adj* quibbling, captious
cavi·tà *f* (**-tà**) cavity
ca·vo -va *adj* hollow || *m* hollow; cable; trough (*between two waves*); (naut) hawser; **cavo di rimorchio** towline; **cavo telefonico** telephone cable || *f* see cava
cavolfióre *m* cauliflower
càvolo *m* cabbage; **cavolo di Bruxelles** Brussels sprouts (*food*); (bot) Brussels sprout; **non capire un cavolo** (vulg) to not understand a blessed thing
cazzòtto *m* (vulg) punch, sock
cazzuòla *f* trowel

ce §5

cecare §122 *tr* to blind

cèc·ca *f* (-che) magpie; **fare cecca** to misfire

cecchino *m* sniper

céce *m* chickpea

ceci·tà *f* (-tà) blindness

cè·co -ca *adj & mf* (-chi -che) Czech

Cecoslovàcchia, la Czechoslovakia

cecoslovac·co -ca *adj & mf* (-chi -che) Czechoslovak

cèdere §123 *tr* to cede; to give up; to sell at cost; **cedere il passo** to let s.o. through; **cedere la strada** to yield the right of way; **non cederla** to be second to none ‖ *intr* to give in, yield; to give way, succumb; to sag

cedévole *adj* yielding; soft; pliable

cedìglia *f* cedilla

cediménto *m* cave-in; (fig) yielding

cèdola *f* slip; coupon

cedri·no -na *adj* citron; citron-like; cedar, cedar-like

cédro *m* (*Citrus medica*) citron; (*Cedrus*) cedar; **cedro del Libano** cedar of Lebanon

CEE *m* (letterword) (**Comunità Economica Europea**) EEC (*European Economic Community-Common Market*)

cefalèa *f* slight headache; headache

cèfalo *m* (ichth) mullet

cèffo *m* snout; (pej) face; **brutto ceffo** ugly mug

ceffóne *m* slap in the face

celare (**cèlo**) *tr* to hide, conceal

cela·to -ta *adj* hidden ‖ *f* sallet

celebèrri·mo -ma *adj* very famous, renowned

celebrare (**cèlebro**) *tr & intr* to celebrate

celebrazióne *f* celebration

cèlebre *adj* famous, renowned, celebrated

celebri·tà *f* (-tà) celebrity

cèlere *adj* swift, rapid; express (*train*); short, quick; prompt ‖ **Celere** *f* special police

celeri·tà *f* (-tà) swiftness, rapidity; speed (*e.g., of a machine gun*)

celèste *adj* heavenly, celestial; blue, sky-blue ‖ *m* blue, sky blue; **celesti** heavenly spirits; (mythol) gods

celestiale *adj* celestial, heavenly

cèlia *f* jest; **mettere in celia** to deride; **per celia** in jest

celiare §287 (**cèlio**) *intr* to jest, joke

celibatà·rio -ria (-ri -rie) *adj* single ‖ *m* old bachelor

celibato *m* celibacy; bachelorhood

cèlibe *adj* single, unmarried ‖ *m* bachelor

cèlla *f* cell; **cella frigorifera** walk-in refrigerator; **cella campanaria** belfry

cèllofan or **cellofàn** *m* cellophane

cèllula *f* cell; **cellula fotoelettrica** photoelectric cell

cellulare *adj* cellular; ventilated (*fabric*); solitary (*confinement*)

cellulòide *f* celluloid

celluló·so -sa [s] *adj* cell-like, cellular ‖ *f* cellulose

cèl·ta *mf* (-ti -te) Celt

cèlti·co -ca *adj* (-ci -che) Celtic; venereal (*disease*)

cementare (**ceménto**) *tr* to cement

ceménto *m* cement, concrete; **cemento armato** reinforced concrete

céna *f* supper; **Ultima Cena** Last Supper

cenàcolo *m* cenacle

cenare (**céno**) *intr* to sup, have supper

cenciaiò·lo -la *mf* ragpicker

cén·cio *m* (-ci) rag, duster (*for cleaning*)

cénere *adj* ashen ‖ *f* ash; cinder; **andare in cenere** to go up in smoke; **ceneri** ashes (*of a person*); **ridurre in cenere** to burn to ashes ‖ **le Ceneri** Ash Wednesday

cenerèntola *f* (fig) Cinderella ‖ **Cenerèntola** *f* Cinderella (*of the fable*)

cén·gia *f* (-ge) ledge (*of a mountain*)

cénno *m* sign; wave (*with hand*); nod; wag; wink; gesture; hint; notice; **ai cenni di** at the orders of; **fare cenno a** or **di** to mention; **fare cenno di no** to shake one's head; **fare cenno di sì** to nod assent

cenò·bio *m* (-bi) monastery

cenobi·ta *m* (-ti) monk, cenobite

censiménto *m* census

censire §176 *tr* to take the census of

cènso *m* wealth, income; census (*in ancient Rome*)

censóre *m* censor; faultfinder; (educ) proctor

censuà·rio -ria (-ri -rie) *adj* income; tax (*register*) ‖ *m* taxpayer

censura *f* censure; censorship; fault-finding

censurare *tr* to censure; to criticize, find fault with

centàuro *m* centaur

centellinare *tr* to sip; to take a nip of

centellino *m* sip, nip

centenà·rio -ria (-ri -rie) *adj & mf* centenary, centennial ‖ *m* centenary, centennial (*anniversary*)

centèsi·mo -ma *adj* hundredth ‖ *m* hundredth; centime; cent; penny

centìgrado *m* centigrade

centigrammo *m* centigram

centìmetro *m* centimeter; tape measure

cèntina *f* (archit) centering; (aer) rib

centi·nàio *m* hundred; **un centinaio di** about a hundred ‖ *m* (-nàia *fpl*)—a **centinaia** by the hundreds

cènto *adj, m & pron* a hundred, one hundred; **per cento** per cent

centomila *adj, m & pron* a hundred thousand, one hundred thousand

centóne *m* cento

centopiè·di *m* (-di) centipede

centrale *adj* central ‖ *f* headquarters, home office; powerhouse, generating station; telephone exchange; **centrale di conversione** (elec) transformer station; **centrale telefonica** central

centralini·sta *mf* (-sti -ste) telephone operator

centralino *m* telephone exchange

centralizzare [ddzz] *tr* to centralize

centrare (**cèntro**) *tr* to center; to hit the center of

centrattac·co *m* (**-chi**) (sports) center forward
centrìfu·go -ga *adj* (**-ghi -ghe**) centrifugal ‖ *f* centrifuge
centrino *m* centerpiece
centrìpe·to -ta *adj* centripetal
centri·sta *mf* (**-sti -ste**) (pol) centrist
cèntro *m* center; **al centro** downtown; **far centro** to hit the mark
centrocampo *m* (soccer) midfield
centuplicare §197 (**centùplico**) *tr* tо multiply a hundredfold
cèntu·plo -pla *adj* & *m* hundredfold
céppo *m* trunk, stump; log; block (*for beheading*); brake shoe; stock (*of anchor*); **ceppi** stocks, fetters ‖ **il Ceppo** (coll) Christmas
céra *f* wax; face, aspect, air, look; **di cera** waxen; pale; **cera da scarpe** shoe polish; **avere buona cera** to look well; **fare buona cera a** to welcome
ceralac·ca *f* (**-che**) sealing wax
ceràmi·co -ca (**-ci -che**) *adj* ceramic ‖ *f* ceramics
cerare (**céro**) *tr* to wax
Cèrbero *m* Cerberus
cerbiatto *m* fawn
cerbottana *f* blowgun, peashooter
cer·ca *f* (**-che**) search, quest; **in cerca di** in search of
cercare §197 (**cérco**) *tr* to seek, look for; to desire, yearn for; **cercare il pelo nell'uovo** to be a faultfinder, to nitpick ‖ *intr* to try
cerca·tóre -tríce *adj* seeking ‖ *mf* seeker; mendicant ‖ *m* prospector
cérchia *f* coterie; compass, limits (*of a wall*); circle (*of friends*)
cerchiare §287 (**cérchio**) *tr* to hoop (*a barrel*); to circle, encircle
cér·chio *m* (**-chi**) circle; hoop; loop; **fare il cerchio della morte** (aer) to loop the loop; **in cerchio** in a circle ‖ *m* (**-chia** *fpl*) (archaic) circle
cerchióne *m* rim; tire (*of metal*)
cereale *adj* & *m* cereal
cerebrale *adj* cerebral
cère·o -a *adj* waxen; wax-colored, pale
cerfò·glio *m* (**-gli**) chervil
cerimònia *f* ceremony; **fare cerimonie** to stand on ceremony; to make a fuss
cerimoniale *adj* & *m* ceremonial
cerimonière *m* master of ceremonies (*at court*)
cerimonió·so -sa [s] *adj* ceremonious
cerino *m* wax match; taper
cernéc·chio *m* (**-chi**) tuft (*of hair*)
cernièra *f* hinge; clasp (*of handbag*); **a cerniera** hinged; **cerniera lampo** zipper
cèrnita *f* sorting, selection, grading
céro *m* church candle; **offrire un cero** to light a candle
ceróne *m* make-up (*of actor*)
ceròtto *m* adhesive tape; (fig) bore; **cerotto per i calli** corn plaster
certame *m* (poet) combat; competition; contest (*of poets*)
certézza *f* certitude, assurance, conviction, certainty
certificare §197 (**certìfico**) *tr* to certify, certificate

certificato *m* certificate
cèr·to -ta *adj* such, some; convinced; certain; real, positive ‖ *m* certainty; **di certo** or **per certo** for certain ‖ **certi** *pron* some ‖ **certo** *adv* undoubtedly
certósa *f* Carthusian monastery, charterhouse
certosi·no *m* Carthusian monk; chartreuse (*liquor*); **da certosino** with great patience
certu·no -na *adj* (obs) some ‖ **certuni** *pron* some
cerùle·o -a *adj* cerulean
cerume *m* ear wax
cervellétto *m* cerebellum
cervelli·no -na *adj* & *mf* scatterbrain
cervèllo *m* (**cervèlli** & **cervèlla** *fpl*) brain; head; mind; **dare al cervello** to go to one's head
cervellòti·co -ca *adj* (**-ci -che**) queer, extravagant
cervice *f* (anat) cervix; (poet) nape of the neck
cerviè·ro -ra *adj* lynx-like; ‖ *m* lynx
cervi·no -na *adj* deer-like ‖ **Cervino** *m* Matterhorn
cèrvo *m* deer; (ent) stag beetle; **cervo volante** kite
Cèsare *m* Caesar
cesàre·o -a *adj* Caesarean; (poet) courtly
cesellare (**cesèllo**) *tr* to chase, chisel; to carve, engrave; to polish (*e.g., a poem*)
cesella·tóre -trice *mf* chaser, engraver, chiseler
cesellatura *f* chasing, engraving; polished writing
cesèllo *m* burin, graver
cesóia *f* shears, metal shears; **cesoie** shears (*for gardening*)
cesoiatrice *f* shearing machine
cèspite *m* source (*of income*); (poet) tuft
céspo *m* tuft
cespù·glio *m* (**-gli**) bush, shrub, thicket
cèssa *f*—**senza cessa** without letup
cessare (**cèsso**) *tr* to stop, interrupt ‖ *intr* to cease, stop; **cessare di** + *inf* to stop ‖ + *ger*
cessazióne *f* cessation, discontinuance; **cessazione d'esercizio** going out of business
cessionà·rio *m* (**-ri**) assignee
cèsso *m* (vulg) privy, outhouse
césta *f* basket, hamper
cestinare *tr* to throw into the wastebasket; to reject (*a book, article, etc.*)
césto *m* basket; tuft; head (*e.g., of lettuce*)
cesura *f* caesura
cetàceo *m* cetacean
cèto *m* class; **ceto medio** middle class
cétra *f* lyre; cither; inspiration
cetriolino *m* gherkin
cetriòlo *m* cucumber; (fig) dolt
che *adj* what; which; what a, e.g., **che bella giornata!** what a beautiful day! ‖ *pron interr* what ‖ *pron rel* who; whom; that; which; (coll) in which ‖ *m*—**essere un gran che** to be a big

shot, to be somebody || *adv* how, e.g., **che bello!** how nice!; **non . . . che** only, e.g., **non venne che Luigi** only Luigi came; no one but, e.g., **non restò che mio cugino** no one but my cousin stayed || *conj* that; *(after comparatives)* than, as

ché *adv* (coll) why || *conj* (coll) because; (coll) so that

checché *pron* (lit) whatever, no matter what

checchessìa *pron* (lit) anything, everything

chèla *f* claw

che·pì *m* (**-pì**) kepi

cherubino *m* cherub

chetare (**chéto**) *tr* to quiet; to placate || *ref* to quiet down, become quiet

chetichèlla *f*—**alla chetichella** surreptitiously, stealthily

ché·to -ta *adj* quiet, still

chi *pron interr* who; whom || *pron rel* who; whom; **chi . . . chi** some . . . some

chiàcchiera *f* chatter, idle talk; gossip; glibness; **fare quattro chiacchiere** to have a chat

chiacchierare (**chiàcchiero**) *intr* to chat; to gossip

chiacchierata *f* talk, chat; **fare una chiacchierata** to visit

chiacchieri·no -na *adj* talkative, loquacious

chiacchierì·o *m* (**-i**) chattering, jabbering *(of a crowd)*

chiacchieró·ne -na *adj* talkative, loquacious || *mf* chatterbox

chiama *f* roll call; **fare la chiama** to call the roll; **mancare alla chiama** to be absent at the roll call

chiamare *tr* to call; to hail *(a cab)*; to invoke, call upon; **chiamare al telefono** to call up; **esser chiamato a** to have the vocation for || *ref* to be named; **si chiama Giovanni** his name is John

chiamata *f* call; (law) designation *(of an heir)*; (telp) ring; (theat) curtain call; (typ) catchword

chiappa *f* (vulg) buttock; (slang) catch *(e.g., of fish)*

chiarét·to -ta *adj & m* claret

chiarézza *f* clarity, clearness

chiarificare §197 (**chiarìfico**) *tr* to clarify

chiarificazióne *f* clarification

chiariménto *m* explanation

chiarire §176 *tr* to clear up, explain; to unravel || *intr* (ESSERE) to clear, become clear || *ref* to make oneself clear; to assure oneself

chia·ro -ra *adj* clear; bright; light *(color)*; honest; clear-cut; plain *(language)*; illustrious, famous || *m* light; bright color; brightness; **chiaro di luna** moonlight; **con questi chiari di luna** in these troubled times; **mettere in chiaro** to clarify, explain || **chiaro** *adv* plainly; **chiaro e tondo** bluntly, frankly

chiaróre *m* light, glimmer

chiaroveggènte *adj & mf* clairvoyant

chiaroveggènza *f* clairvoyance

chiassata *f* uproar, disturbance, racket; noisy scene

chiasso *m* noise; uproar; alley; **fare chiasso** to cause a sensation

chiassó·so -sa [s] *adj* noisy; gaudy

chiatta *f* barge; pontoon

chiavarda *f* bolt

chiave *f* key; wrench; (archit) keystone; (mus) clef; **avere le chiavi di** to own; **chiave a rollino** adjustable wrench; **chiave a tubo** socket wrench; **chiave di volta** keystone; **chiave inglese** monkey wrench; **fuori chiave** off key; **sotto chiave** under lock and key

chiavétta *f* key; cock; cotter pin

chiàvi·ca *f* (**-che**) sewer

chiavistèllo *m* bolt

chiazza *f* spot, blotch

chiazzare *tr* to spot, blotch; to mottle

chiazza·to -ta *adj* spotted, mottled

chic·ca *f* (**-che**) sweet, candy

chìcchera *f* cup

chicchessìa *pron indef* anyone, anybody

chicchirichì *m* cock-a-doodle-doo

chic·co *m* (**-chi**) grain, seed; bead *(of rosary)*; bean *(of coffee)*; **chicco di grandine** hailstone; **chicco d'uva** grape

chièdere §124 *tr* to ask; to ask for; to beg *(pardon)*; to require; to sue *(for damages or peace)*; **chiedere a qlcu di** + *inf* to ask s.o. to + *inf*; **chiedere in prestito** to borrow; **chiedere qlco a qlcu** to ask s.o. for s.th || *ref* to wonder

chiéri·ca *f* (**-che**) tonsure; priesthood

chiéri·co *m* (**-ci**) clergyman; altar boy; (archaic) clerk

chièsa *f* church

chiesuòla *f* small church; clique, set *(e.g., of artists)*; (naut) binnacle

chì·glia *f* (**-glie**) keel; **chiglia mobile** (naut) centerboard

chilo *m* kilo, kilogram; **fare il chilo** to take a siesta

chilociclo *m* kilocycle

chilogrammo *m* kilogram

chilohèrtz *m* kilohertz

chilomètràg·gio *m* (**-gi**) distance in kilometers

chilomètri·co -ca *adj* (**-ci -che**) kilometric; interminable *(e.g., speech)*

chilòmetro *m* kilometer

chilo·watt *m* (**-watt**) kilowatt

chimèra *f* chimera; daydream, utopia

chimèri·co -ca *adj* (**-ci -che**) chimerical

chìmi·co -ca (**-ci -che**) *adj* chemical || *m* chemist || *f* chemistry

chimòno *m* kimono

china *f* slope, decline; India ink; cinchona

chinare *tr* to bend; to lower *(one's eyes)*; **chinare il capo** to nod assent; **chinare la fronte** to yield, give in || *ref* to bend, stoop

china·to -ta *adj* bent, lowered; bitter; with quinine, e.g., **vino chinato** wine with quinine

chincàglie *fpl* notions, knicknacks, sundries

chincaglière _m_ notions or knicknack dealer
chincaglierìa _f_ knicknack; **chincaglierie** knicknacks, notions
chinina _f_ quinine (_alkaloid_)
chinino _m_ quinine (_salt of the alkaloid_)
chi·no -na _adj_ bent, lowered ‖ _f_ see **china**
chiòc·cia _f_ (-ce) brooding hen
chiocciare §128 (**chiòccio**) _intr_ to cluck; to sit, brood; to crouch
chiocciata _f_ brood
chiòc·cio -cia (-ci -ce) _adj_ hoarse ‖ _f_ see **chioccia**
chiòcciola _f_ snail; (anat) cochlea; (mach) nut
chioccolì·o _m_ (-i) cackle (_of hen_); gurgle (_of water_)
chiodare (**chiòdo**) _tr_ to nail
chioda·to -ta _adj_ nailed shut; hobnailed
chiòdo _m_ nail; spike; obsession; craze; (coll) debt; **chiodi** climbing irons; **chiodo a espansione** expansion bolt; **chiodo da cavallo** horseshoe nail; **chiodo di garofano** clove; **chiodo ribattino** rivet
chiòma _f_ hair; mane; foliage; (astr) coma
chioma·to -ta _adj_ hairy, long-haired; leafy
chiòsa _f_ gloss
chiosare (**chiòso**) _tr_ to gloss, comment on
chiò·sco _m_ (-schi) kiosk, stand, newsstand; pavilion, bandstand
chiòstra _f_ circular range (_of mountains_); (poet) enclosure; (poet) set (_of teeth_); (poet) zone, region
chiòstro _m_ cloister
chiòt·to -ta _adj_ quiet, still; **chiotto chiotto** still as a mouse
chiromante _mf_ palmist
chiromanzìa _f_ palmistry
chiropràtica _f_ chiropractice
chirurgìa _f_ surgery
chirùrgi·co -ca _adj_ (-ci -che) surgical
chirur·go _m_ (-ghi & -gi) surgeon
chissà _adv_ maybe
chitarra _f_ guitar; **chitarra hawaiana** ukulele
chitarri·sta _mf_ (-sti -ste) guitar player
chiùdere §125 _tr_ to shut, close; to lock; to turn off; to fasten; to block (_a road_); to fence in; to nail shut (_a box_); to strike (_a balance_); to conclude, wind up; **chiudere a chiave** to lock; **chiudere bottega** to go out of business; **chiudere il becco** (slang) to shut up ‖ _intr_ to shut, close; to lock ‖ _ref_ to shut, close; to lock; to withdraw; to cloud over
chiùnque _pron indef invar_ anybody, anyone ‖ _pron rel invar_ whoever, whomever; anyone who, anyone whom
chiurlo _m_ (orn) curlew
chiusa [s] _f_ fence; lock (_of canal_); end, conclusion (_e.g., of letter_)
chiusino [s] _m_ manhole
chiu·so -sa [s] _adj_ shut, closed, locked; stuffy (_air_); high-bodiced (_dress_);

close (_vowel_) ‖ _m_ enclosure, corral; **close** ‖ _f_ see **chiusa**
chiusura [s] _f_ closing, end; fastener; lock; **chiusura lampo** zipper, slide fastener
ci §5
ciabatta _f_ slipper; old shoe
ciabat·tàio _m_ (-tài) cobbler
ciabattare _intr_ to shuffle along
ciabattino _m_ cobbler, shoemaker
ciàc _f_ (mov) clappers
cialda _f_ wafer; thin waffle
cialdóne _m_ cone (_for ice cream_)
cialtró·ne -na _mf_ rogue, scoundrel; slovenly person
ciambèlla _f_ doughnut; **ciambella di salvataggio** life saver
ciambellano _m_ chamberlain
ciampicare §197 (**ciàmpico**) _intr_ to stumble along
ciana _f_ (slang) fishwife
cianamide _f_ cyanamide
ciàn·cia _f_ (-ce) chatter, prattle, idle gossip
cianciare §128 (**ciàncio**) _intr_ to chatter, prattle
cianciafrùscola _f_ trifle, bagatelle
cianfrusà·glia _f_ (-glie) trifle, trinket; rubbish, trash, junk
cianìdri·co -ca _adj_ (-ci -che) hydrocyanic
cianògeno _m_ cyanogen
cianuro _m_ cyanide
ciao _interj_ (coll) hi!, hello!; (coll) goodbye!, so long!
ciarla _f_ chatter, prattle, idle talk; gossip
ciarlare _intr_ to chatter, prattle
ciarlatanata _f_ charlatanism, quackery
ciarlatanerìa _f_ charlatanism
ciarlatané·sco -sca _adj_ (-schi -sche) charlatan
ciarlatano _m_ charlatan, quack
ciarliè·ro -ra _adj_ talkative, garrulous
ciarpame _m_ rubbish, junk
ciaschedu·no -na _adj indef_ each ‖ _pron indef_ each one, everyone
ciascu·no -na _adj indef_ each ‖ _pron indef_ each one, everyone
cibare _tr_ & _ref_ to feed
cibà·rio -ria (-ri -rie) _adj_ alimentary ‖ **cibarie** _fpl_ foodstuffs, victuals
cibo _m_ food; meal; (fig) dish
cicala _f_ cicada; grasshopper; locust; (fig) chatterbox; (naut) anchor ring
cicalare _intr_ to prattle, babble; to chatter
cicaléc·cio _m_ (-ci) prattle, babble; chatter
cicatrice _f_ scar
cicatrizzare [ddzz] _tr_ to heal (_a wound_) ‖ _intr_ (ESSERE) & _ref_ to heal, scar
cicatrizzazióne [ddzz] _f_ closing, healing (_of a wound_)
cic·ca _f_ (-che) butt (_of cigar or cigarette_); (slang) chewing gum
ciccare §197 _intr_ to chew tobacco; (coll) to boil with anger
cicchettare (**cicchétto**) _tr_ (slang) to prime (_a carburetor_); (slang) to dress down, reprimand ‖ _intr_ to tipple
cicchétto _m_ nip (_of liquor_); (slang) dressing down

cìc·cia *f* (**-ce**) (joc) flesh; (joc) fat

cicció·ne -na *mf* fatty

ceceróne *m* guide || **Cicerone** *m* Cicero

ciclàbile *adj* open to bicycles; bicycle, e.g., **pista ciclabile** bicycle trail

cìcli·co -ca *adj* (**-ci -che**) cyclic(al)

cicli·sta *mf* (**-sti -ste**) cyclist, bicyclist

ciclo *m* cycle; (coll) bicycle; **ciclo operativo** (econ) turnover

ciclomotóre *m* motorbike

ciclomotori·sta *mf* (**-sti -ste**) driver of motorbike

ciclóne *m* cyclone

ciclòpe *m* cyclops

ciclòpi·co -ca *adj* (**-ci -che**) cyclopean, gigantic

ciclopista *f* bicycle trail

ciclostilare *tr* to mimeograph

ciclostile or **ciclostilo** *m* mimeograph

ciclotróne *m* cyclotron

cicógna *f* stork

cicòria *f* chicory; endive

cicuta *f* hemlock

ciè·co -ca (**-chi -che**) *adj* blind; **alla cieca** blindly || *mf* blind person || *m* blind man; **i ciechi** the blind

cièlo *m* sky; heaven; weather, climate; roof (*e.g., of wagon*); **a ciel sereno** in the open air; **cielo a pecorelle** mackerel or fleecy sky; **dal cielo** from above; **non stare né in cielo né in terra** to be utterly absurd; **per amor del cielo** for heaven's sake; **portare al cielo** to praise to the skies; **santo cielo!** good heavens!; **volesse il cielo che . . .!** would that . . .!

cifra *f* number, figure; Arabic numeral; sum, total; digit; initial, monogram; cipher, code; **cifra d'affari** amount of business, turnover; **cifra tonda** round number

cifrare *tr* to cipher, code; to embroider (*a monogram*)

cifrà·rio *m* (**-ri**) code, cipher

cì·glio *m* (**-glia** *fpl*) eyelash; eyebrow; **a ciglio asciutto** with dry eyes; **ciglia** (zool) cilia; **senza batter ciglio** without batting an eye || *m* (**-gli**) (fig) edge, brow

ciglióne *m* bank, embankment

cigno *m* swan; cob

cigolante *adj* creaky, squeaky

cigolare (**cìgolo**) *intr* to squeak, creak

cigolì·o *m* (**-i**) squeak, creak

Cile, il Chile

cilécca *f*—**fare cilecca** to misfire

cileccare §197 (**cilécco**) *intr* to goof, blunder; to fail

cilè·no -na *adj & mf* Chilean

cilè·stro -stra *adj* (poet) azure, blue

cilì·cio *m* (**-ci**) sackcloth

ciliè·gia *f* (**-gie & -ge**) cherry

ciliè·gio *m* (**-gi**) cherry tree

cilindrare *tr* to calender (*e.g., paper*); to roll (*a road*)

cilindrata *f* (aut) cylinder capacity, piston displacement

cilìndri·co -ca *adj* (**-ci -che**) cylindric(al)

cilindro *m* cylinder; top hat; roll, roller

cima *f* top, summit; tip (*e.g., of a pole*); peak (*of mountain*); edge, end; rope, cable; head (*e.g., of let-*

tuce); (coll) genius; **da cima a fondo** from top to bottom

cimare *tr* to cut the tip off; to shear; (agr) to prune

cimasa *f* (archit) coping

cìmbalo *m* gong; (obs) cymbal; **in cimbali** tipsy; in a tizzy

cimè·lio *m* (**-li**) relic, souvenir, memento

cimentare (**ciménto**) *tr* to risk (*e.g., one's life*); to provoke; (archaic) to assay || *ref* to expose oneself; to venture

ciménto *m* risk, danger; (archaic) assay

cìmice *f* bug; bedbug; (coll) thumbtack

cimièro *m* crest; (poet) helmet

ciminièra *f* chimney (*of factory*); smokestack (*of locomotive*); funnel (*of steamship*)

cimitèro *m* cemetery, graveyard; (fig) ghosttown

cimósa [s] or **cimóssa** *f* selvage; blackboard eraser

cimurro *m* distemper; (joc) cold

Cina, la China

cinabro *m* cinnabar; crimson; red ink

cìn·cia *f* (**-ce**) titmouse

cinciallégra *f* great titmouse

cincilla *f* chinchilla

cincischiare §287 *tr* to shred; to wrinkle, crease; to waste (*time*); to mumble (*words*) || *intr* to wrinkle, crease

cine *m* (coll) cinema

cineamatóre *m* amateur movie maker

cine·asta *m* (**-sti**) motion-picture producer; movie fan; movie actor || *f* movie actress

cinecàmera *f* movie camera

cinedilettante *mf* amateur movie maker

cinegiornale *m* newsreel

cinelàndia *f* movieland

cìne·ma *m* (**-ma**) movies; movie house

cinematografare (**cinematògrafo**) *tr* to film, shoot

cinematografìa *f* cinema, motion pictures, movie industry

cinematogràfi·co -ca *adj* (**-ci -che**) movie, motion-picture; movie-like

cinematògrafo *m* motion picture; movie theater; (fig) hubbub; (fig) funny sight

cineparchég·gio *m* (**-gi**) drive-in movie

cinepar·co *m* (**-chi**) drive-in movie

cineprésa [s] *f* movie camera

cinère·o -a *adj* ashen

cinescò·pio *m* (**-pi**) kinescope, TV tube

cinése [s] *adj & mf* Chinese

cineteatro *m* movie house; **cineteatro all'aperto** outdoor movie

cinetè·ca *f* (**-che**) film library

cinèti·co -ca (**-ci -che**) *adj* kinetic || *f* kinetics

cingallégra *f* var of **cinciallegra**

cìngere §126 *tr* to surround; to gird (*e.g., the head*); to gird on (*e.g., the sword*); **cingere cavaliere** to dub a knight; **cingere d'assedio** to besiege

cìnghia *f* belt, strap; **tirare la cinghia** to tighten one's belt

cinghiale *m* wild boar

cinghiata *f* lash

cingola·to -ta *adj* track-driven, caterpillar

cìngolo *m* endless metal belt, track; girdle, belt (*of a priest*)

cinguettare (cinguétto) *intr* to chirp, twitter; to babble

cinguettì•o *m* (-i) chirp, twitter; (fig) babble

cìni•co -ca (-ci -che) *adj* cynical || *m* cynic

cinìglia *f* chenille

cinismo *m* cynicism

cinòfilo *m* dog lover

cinquanta *adj, m & pron* fifty

cinquantenà•rio -ria (-ri -rie) *adj* fifty-year-old; occurring every fifty years || *m* fiftieth anniversary

cinquantènne *adj* fifty-year-old || *mf* fifty-year-old person

cinquantèn•nio *m* (-ni) period of fifty years, half century

cinquantèsi•mo -ma *adj, m & pron* fiftieth

cinquantina *f* about fifty; sulla cinquantina about fifty years old

cìnque *adj & pron* five; le cinque five o'clock || *m* five; fifth (*in dates*)

cinquecenté•sco -sca *adj* (-schi -sche) sixteenth-century

cinquecènto *adj, m & pron* five hundred || *f* small car || il Cinquecento the sixteenth century

cinquina *f* set of five; five numbers (*drawn at Italian lotto*); (mil) pay

cinta *f* fence, wall; circuit, enclosure; circumference (*of a city*)

cintare *tr* to surround; to fence in; to hold (*in wrestling*)

cin•to -ta *adj* surrounded, girded || *m* belt; girdle; cinto erniario truss || *f* see cinta

cìntola *f* waist; belt; con le mani alla cintola idling, loafing

cintura *f* belt; waist; waistband; lock (*in wrestling*); cintura di salvataggio life preserver; cintura di sicurezza safety belt

cinturare *tr* to surround

cinturino *m* strap (*of watch or shoes*); hem (*e.g., of cuffs*)

cinturóne *m* belt; Sam Browne belt

ciò *pron* this; that; a ciò for that purpose; a ciò che so that; ciò nondimeno or ciò nonostante though, nevertheless; con tutto ciò in spite of everything; per ciò therefore

ciòc•ca *f* (-che) lock (*of hair*); cluster (*e.g., of cherries*)

ciòc•co *m* (-chi) log; dormire come un ciocco to sleep like a log

cioccolata *adj invar* chocolate || *f* chocolate (*beverage*)

cioccolatino *m* chocolate candy

cioccolato *m* chocolate; cioccolato al latte milk chocolate

cioè *adv* that is to say, namely; to wit; rather

ciondolare (cióndolo) *tr* to dangle || *intr* to dawdle; to stroll, saunter

cióndolo *m* pendant, charm

ciondolóne *m* idler || *adv* dangling

ciòtola *f* bowl

ciòttolo *m* pebble, small stone; cobblestone

ciottoló•so -sa [s] *adj* pebbly

cip *m* (cip) chip (*in gambling*)

cipì•glio *m* (-gli) frown

cipólla *f* onion; bulb (*e.g., of a lamp*); nozzle (*of sprinkling can*)

cippo *m* column; bench mark

ciprèsso *m* cypress

cipria *f* face powder; cipria compatta compact

ciprió•ta *adj & mf* (-ti -te) Cypriot

Cipro *m* Cyprus

circa *adv* about, nearly || *prep* concerning, regarding, as to

cir•co *m* (-chi) circus; circo equestre circus; circo glaciale cirque; circo lunare walled plain

circolante *adj* circulating; lending (*library*) || *m* available cash (*of a corporation*)

circolare *adj* circular; cashier's (*check*) || *f* circular (*letter*); (rr) beltline || *v* (cìrcolo) *intr* to circulate

circolazióne *f* circulation; traffic; currency; circolazione sanguigna bloodstream; circulation of blood

cìrcolo *m* circle; circulation (*of blood*); reception (*e.g., at court*); club, set, group

circoncìdere §145 *tr* to circumcise

circoncisióne *f* circumcision

circonci•so -sa *adj* circumcised

circondare (circóndo) *tr* to surround, encircle; to overwhelm (*e.g., with kindness*) || *ref* to surround oneself; to be surrounded

circondà•rio *m* (-ri) district; surrounding territory

circonduzióne *f* rotation (*e.g., of the body in calisthenics*)

circonferènza *f* circumference

circonflès•so -sa *adj* circumflex

circonlocuzióne *f* circumlocution

circonvallazióne *f* city-line road; (rr) beltline

circonvenire §282 *tr* to circumvent; to outwit

circonvenzióne *f* circumvention

circonvici•no -na *adj* neighboring, nearby

circoscrit•to -ta *adj* circumscribed

circoscrìvere §250 *tr* to circumscribe

circoscrizióne *f* district; circuit

circospèt•to -ta *adj* circumspect, cautious

circospezióne *f* circumspection

circostante *adj* neighboring, surrounding, nearby || circostanti *mpl* neighbors; bystanders, onlookers

circostanza *f* circumstance

circonstanziale *adj* circumstantial

circostanziare §287 *tr* to describe in detail; to circumstanciate

circostanzia•to -ta *adj* detailed, circumstantial

circuire §176 *tr* to circumvent

circùito *m* circuit; race (*of automobiles or bicycles*); circuito stampato (rad, telv) printed circuit

circumnavigare §209 (circumnàvigo) *tr* to circumnavigate

circumnavigazióne *f* circumnavigation

cirìlli•co -ca *adj* (-ci -che) Cyrillic

Ciro *m* Cyrus
cirro *m* cirrus
cirrò·si *f* (-si) cirrhosis
cispa *f* gum (*on edge of eyelids*)
cisposità [s] *f* gum; gumminess
cispó·so -sa [s] *adj* gummy
ciste *f* cyst
cistèrna *f* cistern; tank
cisti *f* cyst
cistifèllea *f* gall bladder
citante *mf* (law) plaintiff
citare *tr* to cite, quote; to mention; (law) to summon, subpoena
citazióne *f* citation, quotation; mention; (law) summons, subpoena; (mil) commendation
citillo *m* (zool) gopher
citòfono *m* intercom
citostàti·co -ca *adj* (-ci -che) (biochem) cancer-inhibiting
citrato *m* citrate
cìtri·co -ca *adj* (-ci -che) citric
citrul·lo -la *adj* simple, foolish || *mf* simpleton, fool
cit·tà *f* (-tà) city, town || Città del Capo Cape Town; Città del Messico Mexico City; Città del Vaticano Vatican City; città fungo boom town
cittadèlla *f* citadel
cittadinanza *f* citizenship
cittadi·no -na *adj* city, town, civic || *mf* citizen; city dweller, urbanite || *m* townsman
ciù·co *m* (-chi) (coll) donkey, ass
ciuffo *m* lock, forelock; tuft; (bot) tassel
ciuffolòtto *m* (orn) bullfinch
ciurlare *intr*—ciurlare nel manico to play fast and loose
ciurma *f* crew, gang, mob
ciurmare *tr* (archaic) to charm; (archaic) to trick, inveigle
ciurmatóre *m* swindler, charlatan
civétta *f* barn owl, little owl; unmarked police car; ship used as decoy; (fig) coquette, flirt
civettare (civétto) *intr* to flirt
civetterìa *f* coquettishness, coquetry
civettuò·lo la *adj* coquettish; attractive
cìvi·co -ca *adj* (-ci -che) civic; town, city
civile *adj* civil; civilian || *mf* civilian
civili·sta *mf* (-sti -ste) attorney, solicitor
civilizzare [ddzz] *tr* to civilize || *ref* to become civilized
civilizzazióne [ddzz] *f* civilizing (*e.g., of barbarians*); civilization
civil·tà *f* (-tà) civilization; civility
civismo *m* good citizenship
clac·son *m* (-son) horn (*of a car*)
claire *f* (claire) grating (*in front of a store window*)
clamóre *m* clamor, uproar
clamoró·so -sa [s] *adj* noisy; clamorous
clan *m* (clan) clan; clique
clandesti·no -na *adj* clandestine
clangóre *m* clangor, clang
clarinetti·sta *mf* (-sti -ste) clarinet player
clarinétto *m* clarinet
clarino *m* clarion
classe *f* class

classicheggiante *adj* classicistic
classicismo *m* classicism
classici·sta *mf* (-sti -ste) classicist
classici·tà *f* (-tà) classical spirit; classical antiquity
clàssi·co -ca (-ci -che) *adj* classic(al) || *m* classic
classìfi·ca *f* (-che) rank, rating (*in competitive testing*); classification; (sports) rating
classificare §197 (classìfico) *tr* to classify; to rate, rank || *ref* to score
classificazióne *f* classification
claudicante *adj* lame, limping
claudicare §197 (clàudico) *intr* to limp
clauné·sco -sca *adj* (-schi -sche) clownish
clàusola *f* provision, proviso; clause; close, conclusion (*e.g., of a speech*); clausola rossa instructions for payment (*in bank-credit documents*); clausola verde shipping instructions (*in bank-credit documents*)
clausura *f* (eccl) seclusion; (fig) secluded place
clava *f* club, bludgeon
clavicémbalo *m* harpsicord
clavìcola *f* clavicle, collarbone
clemàtide *f* clematis
clemènte *adj* clement, indulgent; mild (*climate*)
clemènza *f* clemency; mildness
cleptòmane *adj & mf* kleptomaniac
clericale *adj* clerical || *m* clericalist
clericalismo *m* clericalism
clèro *m* clergy
clessidra *f* water clock; sandglass
clicchettì·o *m* (-ì) clicking, click-clack (*e.g., of a typewriter*)
cli·ché *m* (-ché) cliché; stereotype (*plate*)
cliènte *m* client, customer, patron
clientèla *f* clientele, customers; practice (*of a professional man*)
cli·ma *m* (-mi) climate
climatèri·co -ca *adj* (-ci -che) climacteric; crucial
climatè·rio *m* (-ri) climacteric; crucial period
climàti·co -ca *adj* (-ci -che) climatic
climatizzazióne [ddzz] *f* air conditioning
clìni·co -ca (-ci -che) *adj* clinic || *m* clinician; highly skilled physician || *f* clinic; private hospital
cli·sma *m* (-smi) enema
clistère *m* enema; clistere a pera fountain syringe
cloa·ca *f* (-che) sewer
cloche *f* (cloche) woman's wide-brimmed hat; (aer) stick; (aut) floor gearshift
clorare (clòro) *tr* to chlorinate
clorato *m* chlorate
clorìdri·co -ca *adj* (-ci -che) hydrochloric
clòro *m* chlorine
clorofilla *f* chlorophyll
clorofòr·mio *m* (-mi) chloroform
cloroformizzare [ddzz] *tr* to chloroform
cloruro *m* chloride

coabitare (coàbito) *intr* to live together; to cohabit

coabitazióne *f* sharing (*of an apartment*)

coaccusa·to -ta *adj* jointly accused ‖ *m* codefendant

coacèrvo *m* accumulation (*e.g., of interest*)

coadiutóre *m* coadjutor

coadiuvante *adj* helping ‖ *m* helper

coadiuvare (coàdiuvo) *tr* to assist, advise

coagulare (coàgulo) *tr & ref* to coagulate, clot

coagulazióne *f* coagulation, clotting

coàgulo *m* clot

coalescènza *f* coalescence

coalizióne *f* coalition

coalizzare [ddzz] *tr & ref* to unite, rally

coartare *tr* to coerce, force

coartazióne *f* coercion, forcing

coatti·vo -va *adj* forceful, compelling

coat·to -ta *adj* coercive

coautóre *m* coauthor

coazióne *f* coercion

cobalto *m* cobalt

cocaina *f* cocaine

cocainòmane *mf* cocaine addict

coc·ca *f* (**-che**) notch (*of arrow*); corner, edge (*e.g., of a handkerchief*); three-mast galley

coccarda *f* cockade

cocchière *m* coachman, cab driver

còc·chio *m* (**-chi**) coach; chariot

cocchiume *m* bung

còc·cia *f* (**-ce**) sword guard; (coll) head, noggin

còccige *m* coccyx

coccinèlla *f* ladybug

cocciniglia *f* cochineal

còc·cio *m* (**-ci**) earthenware; broken piece of pottery

cocciutàggine *m* stubborness

cocciu·to -ta *adj* stubborn

còc·co *m* (**-chi**) coconut (*tree and nut*); (bact) coccus; (coll) egg; (coll) darling, favorite

cocco·dè *m* (**-dè**) cackle

coccodrillo *m* crocodile

còccola *f* berry (*of cypress*); darling girl

coccolare (còccolo) *tr* to fondle, cuddle ‖ *ref* to nestle, cuddle up; to bask

còcco·lo -la *adj* (coll) nice, darling ‖ *m* darling boy ‖ *f* see **coccola**

coccolóne or **coccolóni** *adv* squatting

cocènte *adj* burning

cocktail *m* (**cocktail**) cocktail; cocktail party

còclea *f* dredge; (anat) cochlea

cocómero *m* watermelon; (coll) simpleton

cocorita *f* parakeet

cocuzza *f* (coll) pumpkin; (coll) head, noggin

cocùzzolo *m* crown (*of hat*); peak (*of mountain*)

códa *f* tail; train (*of skirt*); pigtail (*of hair*); **coda di paglia** (coll) uneasy conscience; **con la coda dell'occhio** out of the corner of the eye; **con la coda tra le gambe** with its tail between its legs; (fig) crestfallen; **di**

coda last; **fare la coda** to stand in line; **in coda** in a row; at the tail end

codardìa *f* (lit) cowardice

codar·do -da *adj* cowardly ‖ *mf* coward

codazzo *m* (pej) trail (*of people*)

codeina *f* codein

codé·sto -sta §7 *adj* ‖ §8 *pron*

còdice *m* code; codex; **codice della strada** traffic laws; **codice di avviamento postale** zip code

codicillo *m* codicil

codificare §197 (**codìfico**) *tr* to codify

codi·no -na *adj* reactionary; conformist ‖ *m* pigtail (*of a man*); (fig) reactionary; conformist ‖ *f* small tail

códolo *m* tang, shank (*e.g., of knife*); handle (*of spoon or knife*); head (*of violin*)

coeducazióne *f* coeducation

coefficiènte *m* coefficient

coerciti·vo -va *adj* coercive

coercizióne *f* coercion

coerède *mf* coheir

coerènte *adj* coherent; consistent

coerènza *f* coherence; consistency

coesióne *f* cohesion

coesistènza *f* coexistence

coesistere §114 *intr* to coexist

coesi·vo -va *adj* cohesive

coetàne·o -a *adj & m* contemporary

coè·vo -va *adj* contemporaneous, coeval

cofanétto *m* small chest, small coffer

còfano *m* chest, coffer; box, case (*for ammunition*); (aut) hood

còffa *f* masthead, crow's-nest

cofirmatà·rio -ria *adj & mf* (**-ri -rie**) cosigner

cogitabón·do -da *adj* (poet & joc) thoughtful, meditative

cogitare (còqito) *tr & intr* (poet & joc) to cogitate

cógli §4

cògliere §127 *tr* to gather; to hit (*the target*); to pluck (*flowers*); to grab, seize; (fig) to guess; **cogliere in flagrante** to catch in the act; **cogliere la palla al balzo** to seize time by the forelock; **cogliere nel giusto** to hit the nail on the head; **cogliere qlcu alla sprovvista** to catch s.o. napping; **cogliere sul fatto** to catch in the act

coglióne *m* (vulg) testicle; (vulg) simpleton, fool

coglionerìa *f* (vulg) great stupidity

cognata *f* sister-in-law

cognato *m* brother-in-law

cògni·to -ta *adj* (poet & law) well-known

cognizióne *f* cognition, knowledge

cognóme *m* surname, family name

coguaro *m* cougar

cói §4

coibènte *adj* nonconducting ‖ *m* nonconductor

coincidènza *f* coincidence; harmony, identity; transfer (*from one streetcar or bus to another*); (rr) connection

coincidere §145 *intr* to coincide

coinquilino *m* fellow tenant

cointeressare (cointerèsso) *tr* to give a share (*of profit*) to

cointeressa·to -ta *adj* jointly interested || *mf* party having a joint interest

cointeressènza *f* interest, share

coinvòlgere §289 *tr* to involve

còito *m* coitus, intercourse

cól §4

colà *adv* over there

colabròdo *m* colander, strainer

colàg·gio *m* (**-gi**) loss, leak

colapa·sta *m* (**-sta**) colander

colare (**cólo**) *tr* to filter, strain; to sift (*wheat*); to cast (*metals*); **colare a picco** to sink || *intr* to leak, drip; to flow (*said of blood*); **colare a picco** to sink

colata *f* casting (*of metal*); stream of lava; slide (*of snow or rocks*)

colatìc·cio *m* (**-ci**) drip, dripping

cola·tóio *m* (**-tói**) colander, strainer

colazióne *f* breakfast; lunch; **colazione al sacco** picnic; **prima colazione** breakfast; **seconda colazione** lunch

colbac·co *m* (**-chi**) busby

colèi §8 *pron dem*

colèn·do -da *adj* (archaic) honorable

colè·ra *m* (**-ra**) cholera

colesterina *f* cholesterol

coli·brì *m* (**-brì**) hummingbird

còli·co -ca *adj & f* (**-ci -che**) colic

colino *m* strainer

cólla §4

còlla *f* glue; paste; **colla di pesce** isinglass

collaborare (**collàboro**) *intr* to collaborate; to contribute (*to newspaper or magazine*)

collaboratóre *m* collaborator; contributor (*to newspaper or magazine*)

collaborazióne *f* collaboration

collaborazioni·sta *mf* (**-sti -ste**) collaborationist

collana *f* necklace; series, collection (*of literary works*)

collante *adj & m* adhesive

collare *m* collar || *v* (**còllo**) *tr* to lift or lower (*with a rope*)

collasso *m* collapse

collaterale *adj & m* collateral

collaudare (**collàudo**) *tr* to test; to approve; to pass

collauda·tóre -trice *mf* tester

collàudo *m* test

collazionare (**collazióno**) *tr* to collate

cólle §4

còlle *m* hill; low peak; mountain pass

collè·ga *mf* (**-ghi -ghe**) colleague, associate

collegaménto *m* connection, telephone connection; contact; (mil) liaison

collegare §209 (**collégo**) *tr* to join, connect || *intr* to agree, be in harmony || *ref* to become allied; to make contact, make connection (*e.g., by phone*)

collegiale *adj* collegiate || *mf* boarding-school student

collegiata *f* collegiate church

collè·gio *m* (**-gi**) college (*e.g., of surgeons*); boarding school, academy

còllera *f* anger, wrath; **montare in collera** to become angry

collèri·co -ca *adj* (**-ci -che**) hot-tempered, choleric

collètta *f* collection; collect (*in church*)

collettivismo *m* collectivism

collettivi·tà *f* (**-tà**) collectivity, community

colletti·vo -va *adj* collective || *m* party worker (*of leftist party*)

collétto *m* collar; flank (*of a tooth*)

collet·tóre -trice *adj* connecting; collecting (*pipe*) || *m* collector; tax collector; manifold; (elec) commutator (*of D.C. device*); (elec) collector (*of A.C. device*); **collettore d'ammissione** intake manifold; **collettore di scarico** exhaust manifold

collettoria *f* tax office; small post office

collezionare (**collezióno**) *tr* to collect (*e.g., stamps*)

collezióne *f* collection; collection, series (*of literary works*)

collezioni·sta *mf* (**-sti -ste**) collector

collìdere §135 *intr* to collide

collimare *tr* to point (*a telescope*) || *intr* to coincide, match; to dovetail

collina *f* hill; **in collina** in the hill country

collinó·so -sa [s] *adj* hilly

collì·rio *m* (**-ri**) eyewash

collisióne *f* collision; (fig) conflict: **entrare in collisione** to collide

cóllo §4

còllo *m* neck; piece (*of baggage*); package, parcel; **al collo** in a sling; (fig) downhill; **collo del piede** instep; **collo d'oca** crankshaft; **in collo** in one's arms (*said of a baby*)

collocaménto *m* placement, employment; **collocamento a riposo** retirement; **collocamento in aspettativa** leave of absence without pay; **collocamento in malattia** sick leave

collocare §197 (**còlloco**) *tr* to place; to find employment for; to sell; **collocare a riposo** to retire; **collocare in aspettativa** to give a leave of absence without pay to; **collocare in malattia** to grant sick leave to

collocazióne *f* location (*of a book in a library*); catalogue card

colloidale *adj* colloidal

collòide *m* colloid

colloquiale *adj* colloquial

collò·quio *m* (**-qui**) talk, conference; colloquy; colloquium, symposium

colló·so -sa [s] *adj* gluey, sticky

collotòrto *m* (**collitòrti**) bigot, hypocrite

collòttola *f* nape or scruff of the neck

collùdere §105 *intr* to be in collusion

collusióne *f* collusion

collutó·rio *m* (**-ri**) mouthwash

colluttare *intr* to scuffle, fight

colluttazióne *f* scuffle, fight

cólma *f* high-water level (*during high tide*)

colmare (**cólmo**) *tr* to fill, fill up; to fill in (*with dirt*); to overwhelm; **colmare una lacuna** to bridge a gap

colmata *f* silting; reclaimed land; sand bank

cól·mo -ma *adj* full, filled up || *m* top, peak, summit; (archit) ridgepole; (fig) acme; **al colmo di** at the height of; **è il colmo** that's the limit ‖ *f* see **colma**

colofóne *m* colophon

colofònia *f* rosin

colombàia *f* dovecot

colombèlla *f* ingenue; **a colombella** vertically

colóm·bo -ba *mf* pigeon, dove ‖ **Colombo** *m* Columbus

colònia *f* colony; cologne; settlement; summer camp; **colonia penale** penal colony; penitentiary ‖ **Colonia** *f* Cologne

coloniale *adj* colonial ‖ *m* colonial; colonist; **coloniali** imported foods

colòni·co -ca *adj* (**-ci -che**) farm (*e.g.*, *house*)

colonizzare [ddzz] *tr* to colonize; to settle

colonizzazióne [ddzz] *f* colonization

colonna *f* column; row; **colonna sonora** sound track; **Colonne d'Ercole** Pillars of Hercules

colonnato *m* colonnade

colonnèllo *m* colonel

colonnétta *f* small column; gasoline pump

colò·no -na *mf* sharecropper; colonist; settler; (poet) farmer

colorante *adj* coloring ‖ *m* dye; stain

colorare (**colóro**) *tr* & *ref* to color; to stain

colora·to -ta *adj* colored; stained (*glass*)

colorazióne *f* coloring

colóre *m* color; paint; suit (*of cards*); flush (*at poker*); shade; character (*of a deal*); **di colore** colored (*man*); **farne di tutti i colori** to be up to all kinds of deviltry; **farsi di tutti i colori** to change countenance

colorifi·cio *m* (**-ci**) paint factory; dye factory

colorire §176 *tr* to color

colori·to -ta *adj* colored, flushed; expressive ‖ *m* color, complexion; (fig) expression

coloritura *f* coloring; characteristic; political complexion

colóro §8

colossale *adj* colossal

Colossèo *m* Coliseum

colòsso *m* colossus

cólpa *f* fault; sin; guilt; (law) injury; **avere la colpa** to be guilty; to be wrong; **essere in colpa** to be guilty

colpévole *adj* guilty ‖ *mf* guilty person, culprit

colpevoli·sta *mf* (**-sti -ste**) person who prejudges s.o. guilty

colpire §176 *tr* to hit, strike; to harm; to impress; **colpire nel segno** to hit the mark

cólpo *m* hit, blow; strike; tip, rap; knock; shot; round (*of gun*); cut, slash (*of knife*); thrust (*e.g.*, *of spear*); lash (*of animal's tail*); toot (*of car's horn*); **andare a colpo sicuro** to know where to hit; **colpo apoplettico** stroke; **colpo da maestro** master stroke; **colpo d'aria** draft; **colpo d'ariete** water hammer; **colpo di fortuna** stroke of luck; **colpo di fulmine** love at first sight; **co₁po di**

grazia coup de grâce; **colpo di mano** surprise attack; **colpo di scena** dramatic turn of events; **colpo di sole** sunstroke; **colpo di spugna** wiping the slate clean; **colpo di stato** coup d'état; **colpo di telefono** telephone call; **colpo di testa** sudden decision, inconsiderate action; **colpo di vento** gust of wind; **colpo d'occhio** view; glance, look; **di colpo** at once; **fallire il colpo** to miss the mark; **fare colpo** to make a hit; **sul colpo** then and there; **tutto in un colpo** all at once

colpó·so -sa [s] *adj* unpremeditated; involuntary (*e.g.*, *manslaughter*)

coltèlla *f* butcher knife; (elec) knife switch

coltellàc·cio *m* (**-ci**) hunting knife; butcher knife; (naut) studding sail

coltellata *f* stab, gash, slash; **fare a coltellate** to fight with knives

coltelleria *f* cutlery

coltelli·nàio *m* (**-nài**) cutler

coltèllo *m* knife; **a coltello** edgewise (*said of bricks*); **avere il coltello per il manico** to have the upper hand; **coltello a serramanico** switchblade knife; pocketknife

coltivare *tr* to cultivate

coltiva·to -ta *adj* cultivated

coltivatóre *m* farmer

coltivazióne *f* cultivation

cól·to -ta *adj* cultivated; learned (*word*) ‖ *m* garden; (archaic) worship

cóltre *f* blanket; comforter; (fig) pall; **coltri** bedclothes

coltróne *m* quilt

coltura *f* cultivation; crop; culture (*e.g.*, *of silkworms, bacteria*)

colubrina *f* culverin

colùi §8 *pron dem*

comandaménto *m* commandment

comandante *m* commanding officer; commandant; (nav) captain; **comandante del porto** harbor master; **comandante in seconda** (naut) first mate

comandare *tr* to command, order; to direct (*employees*); to register (*a letter*); (mach) to regulate; (mach) to control; (poet) to overlook, command the view of (*e.g.*, *a valley*); **comandare a bacchetta** to command in a dictatorial manner ‖ *intr* to command; **comandi!** (mil) at your orders!

comando *m* command, order

comare *f* godmother; (coll) friend, neighbor; (coll) gossip

combaciare §128 *tr* (archaic) to gather ‖ *intr* to fit closely together; to tally, dovetail; to coincide

combattènte *adj* fighting ‖ *m* combatant

combàttere *tr* & *intr* to combat ‖ *ref* to fight one another

combattiménto *m* combat; fight; battle; **fuori combattimento** knockout, K.O.; **fuori combattimento tecnico** technical knockout, T.K.O.; **mettere fuori combattimento** to knock out; (fig) to weaken

combatti·vo -va *adj* pugnacious, combative
combattu·to -ta *adj* heated (*discussion*); overcome (*by doubt*); torn (*between two opposing feelings*)
combinare *tr* to combine; to match (*e.g., colors*); to organize || *intr* to agree; **combinare a** to succeed in || *ref* to agree; to chance, happen; to combine
combinazióne *f* combination; chance; coverall (*for mechanics or flyers*)
combriccola *f* gang
combustibile *adj* combustible || *m* fuel, combustible
combustióne *f* combustion; (poet) upheaval
combutta *f* gang, band; **essere in combutta** to be in cahoots
cóme *m* manner, way; **il come e il perchè** the why and the wherefore || *adv* as; like; as for; how; **come mai?** why?; **e come!** and how!; **ma come?** what?, how is it? || *conj* as; as soon as; while; how; because; since; **come se** as if
comecché *conj* (lit) although; (poet) wherever
comedóne *m* blackhead
cométa *f* comet
comici·tà *f* (-tà) comicalness
còmi·co -ca (-ci -che) *adj* comic(al) || *m* comic; author of comedies; comic actor
comìgnolo *m* chimney pot; ridge (*of roof*)
cominciare §128 *tr & intr* to begin, start, commence
comitato *m* committee
comitiva *f* group, party; (poet) retinue
comì·zio *m* (-zi) (pol) meeting, rally; (hist) comitia
còm·ma *m* (-mi) paragraph, article (*of law or decree*)
commèdia *f* comedy; play, drama; (fig) farce; **commedia di carattere** comedy of character; **commedia d'intreccio** comedy of intrigue; **far la commedia** to pretend, feign; **finire in commedia** to end ludicrously; **finire la commedia** to stop faking
commediante *mf* actor; comedian (*amusing person*); (fig) hypocrite
commediògra·fo -fa *mf* playwright, comedian
commemorare (**commèmoro**) *tr* to commemorate
commemorati·vo -va *adj* commemorative, memorial
commemorazióne *f* commemoration
commènda *f* commandership (*of an order*); (eccl) commendam
commendàbile *adj* commendable
commendare (**commèndo**) *tr* (lit) to commend, praise; (obs) to entrust
commendati·zio -zia (-zi -zie) *adj* introductory || *f* letter of introduction; recommendation
commendatóre *m* commander (*of an order*)
commendévole *adj* commendable
commensale *mf* guest; table companion

commensurare (**commènsuro & commensuro**) *tr* to compare; to proportion, prorate
commentare (**comménto**) *tr* to comment, comment on
commentà·rio *m* (-ri) commentary; diary, journal
commenta·tóre -trice *mf* commentator
comménto *m* comment; **fare commenti** to criticize; **non far commenti!** don't waste your time talking!
commerciàbile *adj* marketable
commerciale *adj* commercial; common, ordinary
commerciali·sta *mf* (-sti -ste) business-administration major; attorney specializing in commercial law
commerciante *mf* merchant, dealer
commerciare §128 (**commèrcio**) *tr* to deal in; to buy and sell || *intr* to deal
commèr·cio *m* (-ci) commerce, trade; illegal traffic; (poet) intercourse; **commercio all'ingrosso** wholesale (trade); **commercio al minuto** retail (trade); **fuori commercio** not for sale; **in commercio** for sale
commés·so -sa *adj* committed || *mf* clerk (*in a store*) || *m* salesman; clerk (*in a court*); janitor (*in a school*); **commesso viaggiatore** traveling salesman || *f* saleslady; order (*of merchandise*)
commestìbile *adj* edible || **commestibili** *mpl* staples, groceries; foodstuffs
commèttere §198 *tr* to join, connect; to commit; to charge, commission; to peg; (poet) to entrust || *intr* to join, fit
commettitura *f* joint, seam
commiato *m* leave; **dare commiato a** to dismiss; **prender commiato** to take one's leave
commilitóne *m* comrade, comrade in arms
comminare *tr* (law) to determine, fix (*a penalty*)
comminatò·rio -ria *adj* threatening
commiserare (**commìsero**) *tr* to pity, feel sorry for
commiserazióne *f* commiseration
commissariale *adj* commissioner's, e.g., **funzioni commissariali** commissioner's functions; commissar's functions
commissariato *m* commissary; inspector's office
commissà·rio *m* (-ri) commissary; inspector; commissioner; **commissario del popolo** commissar; **commissario di bordo** purser; **commissario di pubblica sicurezza** police inspector; **commissario tecnico** (sports) soccer commissioner
commissionare (**commissióno**) *tr* to commission, order
commissionà·rio -ria (-ri -rie) *adj* commission || *m* commission merchant
commissióne *f* commission, agency; order (*of merchandise*); committee; errand; commitment (*of an act*)
commisurare *tr* to proportion (*e.g., crime to punishment*)
committènte *mf* buyer, customer

commodòro m commodore

commòs·so -sa adj moved; moving

commovènte adj moving, touching

commozióne f commotion; emotion; **commozione cerebrale** (pathol) concussion

commuòvere §202 tr to move; to touch; to stir || ref to be moved; to be touched

commutare tr to commute; to switch || ref to turn

commuta·tóre -trice adj commutative || m (elec) change-over switch; (elec) commutator (switch); (telp) plugboard || f converter

commutatori·sta mf (-sti -ste) (telp) operator

commutazióne f commutation; (telp) selection; (elec) switchover

co·mò m (-mò) chest; chest of drawers

còmoda f commode

comodare (còmodo) tr to lend || intr (with dat) to please, e.g., **non le comoda** it doesn't please her

comodino m night table; (theat) bit player; **fare il comodino a** (coll) to follow sheepishly

comodi·tà f (-tà) comfort; convenience; opportunity

còmo·do -da adj comfortable; convenient; easy; loose-fitting; calm || m convenience; ease; advantage; comfort; opportunity; **a Suo comodo** at your convenience; **comodo di cassa** credit (at the bank); **con comodo** without hurrying; **fare comodo** to come in handy; (with dat) to please, e.g., **non gli fa comodo** it doesn't please him; **fare il proprio comodo** to think only of oneself; **stia comodo!** make yourself at home! || f see **comoda**

compaesa·no -na mf fellow citizen || m fellow countryman || f fellow countrywoman

compàgine f strict union; connection; assemblage; (fig) cohesion

compagna f companion, mate; (archaic) company

compagnìa f company; **Compagnia di Gesù** Society of Jesus; **compagnia stabile** (theat) stock company

compa·gno -gna adj like, similar || m fellow; companion, comrade; mate; partner; **compagno d'armi** comrade in arms; **compagno di viaggio** fellow traveler || f see **compagna**

companàti·co m (-ci) food to eat with bread

comparàbile adj comparable

comparati·vo -va adj & m comparative

compara·to -ta adj comparative

comparazióne f comparison

compare m godfather; best man (at wedding); fellow; confederate

comparire §108 intr to appear; to be known; to cut a figure

comparizióne f appearance (in court)

comparsa f appearance; (theat) extra, supernumerary; (law) petition, brief; **far comparsa** to cut a figure

compartecipare (compartécipo) intr to share

compartecipazióne f sharing; **compartecipazione agli utili** profit sharing

compartécipe adj sharing

compartiménto m circle, clique; district; (naut, rr) compartment

compartire §176 & (comparto) tr to divide up, distribute

compassa·to -ta adj measured; stiff, formal; reserved; self-controlled

compassionare (compassióno) tr to pity

compassióne f compassion, pity

compassionévole adj compassionate; pitiful

compasso m compass; **compasso a grossezza** calipers

compatibile adj excusable; compatible

compatiménto m compassion; condescension

compatire §176 tr to pity; to forgive, overlook; to bear with; **farsi compatire** to become an object of ridicule || intr to pity

compatriò·ta mf (-ti -te) compatriot

compattézza f compactness

compat·to -ta adj compact, tight

compendiare §287 (compèndio) tr to epitomize, summarize

compèn·dio m (-di) compendium, summary; **fare un compendio di** to abstract

compendió·so -sa [s] adj compendious, brief, succinct

compenetràbile adj penetrable

compenetrabilità f penetrability

compenetrare (compènetro) tr to penetrate; to permeate; to pervade || ref to be overcome; **compenetrarsi di** to be conscious of

compensare (compènso) tr to compensate, pay; to balance, offset; to clear (checks)

compensa·to -ta adj compensated; laminated || m laminate; plywood

compensazióne f compensation; offset; (com) clearing (of checks)

compènso m reward; retribution, pay; **in compenso** on the other hand

cómpera f var of **compra**

comperare (cómpero) tr & intr var of **comprare**

competènte adj competent

competènza f competence; jurisdiction; **competenze honoraria**

competere §129 intr to compete; to concern; to have jurisdiction

competiti·vo -va adj competitive

competi·tóre -trice mf competitor, contender

competizióne f competition, contest

compiacènte adj complaisant, obliging

compiacènza f complaisance, kindness; pleasure

compiacére §214 tr to gratify || intr (with dat) to please, e.g., **non posso compiacere a tutti** I cannot please everybody || ref to be pleased; **compiacersi con** to congratulate; **compiacersi di** to be kind enough to

compiaciménto m pleasure; congratulation; approval

compiaciu·to -ta *adj* pleased, satisfied
compiàngere §215 *tr* to pity ‖ *ref* to feel sorry
compian·to -ta *adj* lamented (*departed person*) ‖ *m* sympathy; (poet) sorrow; (poet) lament
compiegare §209 **(compiègo)** *tr* to enclose (*in a letter*)
cómpiere §130 *tr* to complete, finish; to fulfill, accomplish; **compiere . . . anni** to be . . . years old; **compiere gli anni** to have a birthday ‖ *ref* to happen; to come true
compilare *tr* to compile
compila·tóre -trice *mf* compiler
compilazióne *f* compilation
compiménto *m* fulfillment, accomplishment
compire §176 *tr* to complete, finish; to fulfill, accomplish; **per compir l'opera** as if it weren't enough ‖ *ref* to happen; to come true
compitare (cómpito) *tr* to syllabify; to read poorly; to spell, spell letter by letter
compitazióne *f* spelling letter by letter
compitézza *f* courtesy, politeness
cómpito *m* task; exercise; homework
compi·to -ta *adj* courteous, polite; (poet) adequate
compiu·to -ta *adj* accomplished
compleanno *m* birthday; **buon compleanno** happy birthday
complementare *adj* complementary; additional (*tax*) ‖ *f* graduated income tax
compleménto *m* complement; (mil, nav) reserve
complessióne *f* build, physique
complessi·tà *f* (-tà) complexity
complessi·vo -va *adj* total, aggregate
complès·so -sa *adj* complex, complicated; compound (*fracture*) ‖ *m* whole; complex; **in complesso** in general
completare (complèto) *tr* to complete, carry through; to supplement, round off
complè·to -ta *adj* complete, full; overall, thoroughgoing; **al completo** full (*e.g., bus*) ‖ *m* set (*of matching items*); suit of clothes; **completo femminile** lady's tailor-made suit; **completo maschile** suit
complicare §197 **(còmplico)** *tr* to complicate ‖ *ref* to become complicated
complica·to -ta *adj* complicated, complex
complicazióne *f* complication
còmplice *mf* accomplice, accessory
complici·tà *f* (-tà) complicity
complimentare (compliménto) *tr* to compliment ‖ *ref*—**complimentarsi con** to congratulate
compliménto *m* compliment; congratulation; favor; **complimenti** regards; **complimenti!** congratulations!; **fare complimenti** to stand on ceremony; **senza complimenti** without ceremony; without any further ado
complimentó·so -sa [s] *adj* ceremonious; complimentary

complottare (complòtto) *intr* to plot
complòtto *m* plot, machination
complù·vio *m* (-vi) valley (*of roof*)
componènte *adj* component ‖ *mf* member ‖ *m* component (*component part*) ‖ *f* component (*force*)
componìbile *adj* sectional (*e.g., bookcase*)
componiménto *m* composition, settlement (*of a dispute*)
compórre §218 *tr* to compose; to arrange; to settle (*a quarrel*); to lay out (*a corpse*); (typ) to set
comportaménto *m* behavior
comportare (compòrto) *tr* to allow, tolerate; to entail ‖ *ref* to behave; to handle (*said, e.g., of a motor*); **comportarsi male** to misbehave
compòrto *m* (com) delay
compòsi·to -ta *adj* composite ‖ **composite** *fpl* (bot) Compositae
composi·tóio *m* (-tói) (typ) composing stick
composi·tóre -trice *mf* compositor, typesetter; composer ‖ *f* typesetting machine
composizióne *f* composition; settlement
compósta *f* compote; **composta di frutta** stewed fruit
compostézza *f* neatness, tidiness; good behavior; orderliness
compostièra *f* compote, compotier
compó·sto -sta *adj* compound; neat, tidy; well-behaved ‖ *m* compound ‖ *f* see **composta**
cómpra *f* purchase; shopping; **compre** shopping
comprare (cómpro) *tr* to buy, purchase; to buy off ‖ *intr* to buy, shop; to trade
compra·tóre -trice *mf* buyer, purchaser
compravéndere §281 *tr* to make a deal in, to transfer (*e.g., a house*)
compravéndita *f* transaction; transfer (*e.g., of real estate*)
comprèndere §220 *tr* to comprehend, include, comprise; to overwhelm; to understand; to forgive
comprendò·nio *m* (-ni) (joc) understanding
comprensìbile *adj* understandable, comprehensible
comprensióne *f* comprehension, understanding
comprensi·vo -va *adj* comprehensive; understanding
comprensò·rio *m* (-ri) land to be reclaimed; area, zone, e.g., **comprensorio turistico** tourist area
comprè·so -sa [s] *adj* comprised, included; understood; deeply touched; immersed
comprèssa *f* compress
compressióne *f* compression
comprès·so -sa *adj* compressed; (fig) repressed; (aut) supercharged ‖ *f* see **compressa**
compressóre *m* compressor; **compressore stradale** road roller
comprimà·rio *m* (-ri) (med) associate chief of staff; (theat) second lead

comprìmere §131 *tr* to compress; to repress, restrain; to tamp

compromés·so **-sa** *adj* jeopardized, in danger || *m* compromise; referral (*to arbitration*)

compromettènte *adj* compromising

comprométtere §198 *tr* to compromise; to endanger; to involve, commit; (law) to refer (*to arbitration*)

comproprie·tà *f* (-tà) joint ownership

comproprietà·rio **-ria** *mf* (-ri -rie) joint owner

compròva *f* confirmation

comprovare (**compròvo**) *tr* to confirm; to circumstantiate

compulsare *tr* to consult, peruse; to summon (*to appear in court*)

compulsi·vo **-va** *adj* compulsive

compun·to **-ta** *adj* contrite, repentant

compunzióne *f* compunction

computàbile *adj* computable

computare (**còmputo**) *tr* to compute

computi·sta *mf* (-sti -ste) bookkeeper

computisterìa *f* bookkeeping

còmputo *m* computation, reckoning

comunale *adj* municipal, town (*e.g., hall*); community-owned; (poet) common

comunanza *f* community; **in comunanza** in common

comune *adj* common || *m* normalcy; commune, municipality, town; town hall; (hist) guild; (nav) common seaman; **in comune** in common || *f* commune (*in communist countries*); (theat) main stage entrance; **andare per la comune** to follow the crowd; **per la comune** commonly

comunèlla *f* cabal, clique; passkey (*in a hotel*); (law) mutual insurance (*of cattlemen*); **fare comunella con** to consort with

comunicàbile *adj* communicable

comunicante *adj* communicant; communicating || *m* priest who gives communion

comunicare §197 (**comùnico**) *tr* to communicate; to administer communion to || *intr* to communicate || *ref* to spread; to receive communion, to commune

comunicati·vo **-va** *adj* communicable, spreading; communicative

comunicato *m* communiqué; **comunicato commerciale** advertisement, ad; **comunicato stampa** press release

comunicazióne *f* communication; statement; (telp) connection; **comunicazioni** communications

comunióne *f* community; (law) community property || **Comunione** *f* Communion

comunismo *m* communism

comuni·sta (-sti -ste) *adj* communist || *mf* communist; (law) joint tenant

comunìsti·co **-ca** *adj* (-ci -che) communistic

comuni·tà *f* (-tà) community

comunità·rio **-ria** *adj* (-ri -rie) community, e.g., **interessi comunitari** community interests

comùnque *adv* however, nevertheless || *conj* however, no matter how

cón §4 *prep* with; by (*e.g., boat*); **con + art + inf** by + *ger*, e.g., **col leggere** by reading

conato *m* effort, attempt

cón·ca *f* (-che) washbowl, washbasin; copper water jug; valley, hollow; (poet) shell; **conca idraulica** drydock

concatenaménto *m* (poet) concatenation

concatenare (**concaténo**) *tr* to link || *ref* to unfold, ensue

concatenazióne *f* concatenation

concàusa *f* joint cause; (law) aggravation

cònca·vo **-va** *adj* concave; hollow || *m* hollow

concèdere §132 *tr* to grant, concede; to stretch (*a point*) || *ref* to let oneself go, give oneself over

concènto *m* harmony; (fig) agreement

concentraménto *m* concentration

concentrare (**concèntro**) *tr* to concentrate; to center || *ref* to concentrate, focus; to center

concentra·to **-ta** *adj* concentrated; condensed (*e.g., milk*) || *m* purée (*e.g., of tomatoes*)

concentrazióne *f* concentration; (chem) condensation

concèntri·co **-ca** *adj* (-ci -che) concentric

concepìbile *adj* conceivable

concepiménto *m* conception; (fig) formulation

concepire §176 *tr* to conceive; (fig) to nurture

concerìa *f* tannery

concèrnere §133 *tr* to concern

concertare (**concèrto**) *tr* to scheme, concert; (mus) to orchestrate, arrange || *ref* to agree

concerta·to **-ta** *adj* agreed upon; (mus) with accompaniment || *m* ensemble (*of orchestra, soloists, and chorus*)

concerta·tóre **-trice** *mf* arranger || *m* plotter, schemer

concertazióne *f* (mus) arrangement

concerti·sta *mf* (-sti -ste) concert performer, soloist

concèrto *m* concert; concerto; (fig) choir

concessionà·rio *m* (-ri) sole agent, concessionaire; dealer; lessee (*of business establishment*)

concessióne *f* concession; dealership; admission

concessi·vo **-va** *adj* concessive

concès·so **-sa** *adj* granted, admitting

concètto *m* concept; opinion

concettó·so **-sa** [s] *adj* concise; full of ideas; full of conceits

concettuale *adj* conceptual

concezióne *f* conception; formulation

conchìglia *f* shell, conch; (sports) jock guard, protective cup

conchiùdere §125 *tr, intr & ref* var of **concludere**

cón·cia *f* (-ce) tanning

conciapèl·li *m* (-li) tanner

conciare §128 (**cóncio**) *tr* to tan; to cure (*e.g., tobacco*); to arrange; to straighten up; to reduce; to cut (*a precious stone*); **conciare per le feste** (coll) to give a good beating to || *ref* to get messed up, get dirty

conciatét·ti *m* (**-ti**) roofer

conciató·re -trice *mf* tanner

conciliàbile *adj* reconcilable

conciliàbolo *m* conventicle, secret meeting

conciliante *adj* conciliatory

conciliare *adj* council || *m* member of an ecclesiastical council || §287 *tr* to conciliate, reconcile; to settle (*a fine*); to promote (*e.g., sleep*); to obtain (*a favor*) || *ref* to become reconciled

concilia·tóre -trice *adj* conciliatory || *mf* conciliator, peacemaker || *m* justice of the peace

conciliazióne *f* conciliation || **la Conciliazione** the Concordat (*of 1929 between Italy and the Vatican*)

concì·lio *m* (**-li**) council; church council

concimàia *f* manure pit

concimare *tr* to manure

concimazióne *f* spreading of manure; chemical fertilization

concime *m* manure; fertilizer

cón·cio -cia (**-ci -ce**) *adj* tanned || *m* ashlar; dung, manure; (archaic) agreement; **concio di scoria** cinder block || *f* see **concia**

conciofossecosaché *conj* (archaic) since

concionare (**concióno**) *intr* (archaic) to harangue

concióne *f* (archaic) harangue; (archaic) assembly

conciossiacosaché *conj* (archaic) since

concisióne *f* concision, brevity

conci·so -sa *adj* concise, brief

concistòro *m* consistory; (fig) assembly

concitare (**còncito**) *tr* to excite, stir up

concita·to -ta *adj* excited; (poet) decisive

concitazióne *f* impetus; excitement

concittadi·no -na *mf* fellow citizen

conclave *m* conclave

conclùdere §105 *tr* to conclude || *intr* to conclude; to be convincing || *ref* to conclude, end; **concludersi con** to end with; to result in

conclusionale *adj* (law) summary

conclusióne *f* conclusion; **conclusioni** (law) summation

conclusi·vo -va *adj* conclusive

conclu·so -sa *adj* concluded; terminated; (poet) closed

concomitante *adj* concomitant

concordanza *f* concordance, agreement; (gram) concord; **concordanze** concordance (*e.g., to the Bible*)

concordare (**concòrdo**) *tr* to agree on; to make agree || *intr* & *ref* to come to an agreement

concordato *m* agreement; concordat; settlement (*with creditors*)

concòrde *adj* in agreement

concòrdia *f* concord, harmony

concorrènte *adj* competitive || *m* (com) competitor; (sports) contestant

concorrènza *f* competition

concorrenziale *adj* competitive (*e.g., price*)

concórrere §139 *intr* to converge; to concur; to compete

concórso *m* attendance; concurrence; combination (*of circumstances*); competition; competitive examination; contest; **concorso di bellezza** beauty contest; **concorso di pubblico** turnout; **fuori concorso** not entering the competition; in a class by itself

concretare (**concrèto**) *tr* to realize (*e.g., a dream*); to conclude, accomplish || *ref* to come true

concretézza *f* concreteness, consistency

concrè·to -ta *adj* concrete, real; practical || *m* practical matter; **in concreto** really, in reality

concubina *f* concubine

concubinàg·gio *m* (**-gi**) concubinage

concubinato *m* var of **concubinaggio**

conculcare §197 *tr* (lit) to trample under foot; (lit) to violate

concupire §176 *tr* (poet) to lust for

concupiscènza *f* concupiscence, lust

concussióne *f* extortion, shakedown; **concussione cerebrale** (pathol) concussion

condanna *f* conviction; sentence; (fig) blame, condemnation

condannare *tr* to condemn; to find guilty, convict; to sentence; to damn (*to eternal punishment*); to declare incurable; to wall up

condanna·to -ta *adj* condemned || *m* convict

condensare (**condènso**) *tr* & *ref* to condense

condensa·to -ta *adj* condensed (*e.g., milk*)

condensatóre *m* condenser

condensazióne *f* condensation

condiménto *m* condiment, seasoning

condire §176 *tr* to season

condiret·tóre -trice *mf* associate manager

condiscendènte *adj* condescending

condiscendènza *f* condescension

condiscéndere §245 *intr* to condescend

condiscépo·lo -la *mf* schoolmate, school companion

condivìdere §158 *tr* to share

condizionale *adj* & *m* conditional || *f* (law) suspended sentence

condizionare (**condizióno**) *tr* to condition; to treat (*to prevent spoilage*)

condizionatóre *m* air conditioner

condizióne *f* condition; term (*of sale*); **a condizione che** provided that; **condizioni** condition, shape (*e.g., of a shipment*); **essere in condizione di** to be in a position to

condoglianza *f* condolence; **fare le condoglianze a** to extend one's sympathy to

condolére §159 *ref* to condole

condomì·nio *m* (**-ni**) condominium

condòmi·no -na *mf* joint owner (*of real estate*)

condonare (**condóno**) *tr* to condone; to remit

condóno *m* pardon, parole

condót·to -ta *adj* country (*doctor*) || *m* duct, canal; conduit || *f* behavior, conduct; district (*of country doctor*); transportation; pipeline; (theat) baggage; **condotta forzata** flume

conducènte *m* driver; bus driver; motorman

condù·plex *mf* (-plex) (telp) party-line user

condurre §102 *tr* to lead; to drive (*a car*); to round up (*cattle*); to pipe (*e.g., gas*); to conduct; to trace (*a line*); to take; to bring; to manage; **condurre a termine** to bring to fruition, realize || *intr* to lead || *ref* to behave; to betake oneself, go; **condursi a** (poet) to be reduced to (*e.g., poverty*)

conduttivi·tà *f* (-tà) conductivity

condutti·vo -va *adj* conductive

condut·tóre -trice *adj* guiding, leading || *m* operator (*of a bus*); driver (*of a car*); (rr) engineer; (rr) ticket collector; (phys) conductor

conduttura *f* conduit, pipeline

conduzióne *f* conduction; leasing

conestàbile *m* constable (*keeper of a castle*)

confabulare (**confàbulo**) *intr* to confabulate, commune; to connive, scheme

confacènte *adj* suitable, appropriate; helpful

confare §173 *ref*—**confarsi a** to agree with, e.g., **le uova non gli si confanno** eggs do not agree with him

confederare (**confèdero**) *tr & ref* to confederate

confedera·to -ta *adj & m* confederate

confederazióne *f* confederation

conferènza *f* conference; lecture; **conferenza illustrata** chalk talk; **conferenza stampa** press conference

conferenziè·re -ra *mf* speaker, lecturer

conferiménto *m* conferring, bestowal

conferire §176 *tr* to confer, bestow; to add; to contribute || *intr* to confer; to contribute; **conferire alla salute** to be healthful

conférma *f* confirmation; **a conferma di** (com) in reply to, confirming

confermare (**confèrmo**) *tr* to confirm; to verify; to retain (*in office*) || *ref* to become more sure of oneself; to prove to be; to remain (*in the conclusion of a letter*)

confessare (**confèsso**) *tr & ref* to confess

confessionale *adj* confessional; church; church-related, parochial (*e.g., school*) || *m* confessional

confessióne *f* confession

confès·so -sa *adj* acknowledged, self-admitted; **confesso e comunicato** having made one's confession and taken communion

confessóre *m* confessor

confetterìa *f* candy store, confectioner's shop

confettièra *f* candy box

confettière *m* candy maker; candy dealer, confectioner

confètto *m* sugar-covered nut, sweetmeat; losenge, drop

confettura *f* candy; preserves, jam; **confetture** confectionery

confezionare (**confezióno**) *tr* to make; to tailor (*a suit*)

confezióne *f* preparation, manufacturing; packaging; **confezioni** ready-made clothes

confezioni·sta *mf* (-sti -ste) ready-made clothier

conficcare §197 *tr* to drive (*a nail*); to thrust (*a knife*) || *ref* to become embedded

confidare *tr* to trust (*a secret*) || *intr* to trust || *ref* to confide

confidènte *adj* confident || *mf* confident; informer

confidènza *f* confidence; secret; familiarity

confidenziale *adj* confidential; friendly

confìggere §104 *tr* to plunge, thrust

configurazióne *f* configuration

confinante *adj* bordering || *mf* neighbor

confinare *tr* to exile; to confine || *intr* to border

confinà·rio -ria *adj* (-ri -rie) border (*e.g., zone*)

Confindùstria *f* (acronym) **Confederazione Nazionale degli Industriali** National Confederation of Industrialists

confine *m* border, boundary line; boundary mark, landmark

confino *m* exile (*in a different town*)

confi·sca *f* (-sche) confiscation

confiscare §197 *tr* to confiscate

confit·to -ta *adj* nailed; bound; tied; **confitto in croce** nailed to the cross

conflagrazióne *f* conflagration

conflitto *m* conflict

conflittualità *f* confrontation; belligerent attitude

confluènte *m* confluent

confluènza *f* confluence

confluire §176 *intr* to flow together, join; to converge

confóndere §178 *tr* to confuse; to overwhelm (*with kindness*); to humiliate; **confondere con** to mistake for || *ref* to mix; to become confused

conformare (**confórmo**) *tr* to shape; to conform || *ref* to conform

conformazióne *f* conformation

confórme *adj* faithful, exact; in agreement; true (*copy*)

conformeménte *adv* in conformity

conformi·sta *mf* (-sti -ste) conformist

conformi·tà *f* (-tà) conformity; **in conformità di** in conformity with, in accord with

confortante *adj* comforting

confortare (**confòrto**) *tr* to comfort

confortévole *adj* comforting, consoling; comfortable

confòrto *m* comfort, solace; convenience; corroboration; **conforti religiosi** last rites

confratèllo *m* brother, confrere

confratèrnita *f* brotherhood

confricare §197 *tr* to rub

confrontare (**confrónto**) *tr* to compare, confront; to consult || *intr* to correspond

confrónto *m* comparison; (law) cross examination; **a confronto di** or **in confronto a** in comparison with; with regard to
confusaménte *adv* vaguely, hazily
confusionale *adj* confusing; confused
confusionà·rio -ria (-ri -rie) *adj* blundering; scatterbrain || *mf* blunderer; scatterbrain
confusióne *f* confusion, disorder; noise; error; embarrassment; shambles
confu·so -sa *adj* confused, mixed; vague, hazy; **in confuso** indistinctly
confutare (confuto) *tr* to confute
confutazióne *f* confutation
congedare (congèdo) *tr* to dismiss; to let (*a tenant*) go; (mil) to discharge || *ref* to take leave
congeda·to -ta *adj* discharged || *m* discharged soldier
congèdo *m* dismissal; leave; permission to leave; (mil) discharge; envoy, envoi; **congedo per motivi di salute** sick leave; **dare il congedo a** to discharge; **prender congedo** to take leave
congegnare (congégno) *tr* to assemble (*machinery*); to contrive, cook up
congégno *m* contrivance, gadget; mechanism; design (*of a play*)
congelaménto *m* freezing; frostbite
congelare (congèlo) *tr & ref* to freeze, congeal
congela·tóre -trice *adj* freezing || *m* freezer; freezer unit; freezing compartment (*of a refrigerator*)
congènere *adj* similar, alike
congeniale *adj* congenial
congèni·to -ta *adj* congenital
congèrie *f* congeries
congestionare (congestióno) *tr* to congest
congestióne *f* congestion
congettura *f* conjecture
congetturare *tr* to conjecture
congiùngere §183 *tr & ref* to unite, join
congiuntiva *f* (anat) conjunctiva
congiuntivite *f* (pathol) conjunctivitis
congiunti·vo -va *adj* conjunctive; subjunctive || *m* subjunctive || *f* see congiuntiva
congiun·to -ta *adj* joined; joint || *m* relative
congiuntura *f* juncture; joint; circumstance, situation; **bassa congiuntura** (econ) unfavorable circumstance; (econ) crisis
congiunzióne *f* conjunction
congiura *f* conspiracy, plot
congiurare *intr* to conspire, plot
congiura·to -ta *adj & m* conspirator
conglobare (conglòbo) *tr* to lump together
conglomerare (conglòmero) *tr & ref* to pile up, conglomerate
conglomera·to -ta *adj & m* conglomerate
congratulare (congràtulo) *intr* to rejoice || *ref*—**congratularsi con** to congratulate
congratulazióne *f* congratulation
congrèga *f* gang; cabal; religious brotherhood

congregare §209 (congrègo) *tr & ref* to congregate
congregazióne *f* congregation
congressi·sta *mf* (-sti -ste) delegate || *m* congressman || *f* congresswoman
congrèsso *m* congress, assembly; conference; convention
congruènte *adj* congruous
congruènza *f* congruence
còn·gruo -grua *adj* congruous; congruent
conguagliare §280 *tr* to adjust; to make up (*what is owed*)
conguà·glio *m* (-gli) balance; adjustment (*of wages*)
coniare §287 (cònio) *tr* to mint, coin
coniatura *f* mintage, coinage
còni·co -ca (-ci -che) *adj* conic(al) || *f* conic section
conifera *f* conifer
coniglièra *f* warren, rabbit hutch
coní·glio *m* (-gli) rabbit
cò·nio *m* (-ni) die (*to mint coins*); mintage; wedge; **dello stesso conio** (fig) of the same feather; **di nuovo conio** newly-minted; new-fangled
coniugale *adj* conjugal
coniugare §209 (còniugo) *tr* to conjugate || *ref* to marry, get married
coniuga·to -ta *adj* coupled, paired || *mf* spouse, consort
coniugazióne *f* conjugation
còniuge *mf* spouse; **coniugi** *mpl* husband and wife
connaturale *adj* inborn, innate
connatura·to -ta *adj* deep-seated, deep-rooted; congenital
connazionale *mf* fellow countryman
connessióne *f* connection
connés·so -sa & connès·so -sa *adj* connected, tied
connéttere & connèttere §107 *tr* to connect, link || *ref* to refer
connetti·vo -va *adj* connective
connivènte *adj* conniving
connivènza *f* connivance
connotare (connòto) *tr* to connote
connotato *m* personal characteristic
connù·bio *m* (-bi) wedding, union
còno *m* cone
conòcchia *f* distaff
conoscènte *mf* acquaintance
conoscènza *f* knowledge; acquaintance; understanding; consciousness; **conoscenza di causa** full knowledge; **essere a conoscenza di** to be acquainted with; **prendere conoscenza di** to take cognizance of
conóscere §134 *tr* to know; to recognize; **conoscere i propri polli** to know one's onions; **conoscere per filo e per segno** to know thoroughly; **conoscere ragioni** to listen to reason; **darsi a conoscere** to make oneself known; to reveal oneself || *intr* to reason || *ref* to acknowledge oneself to be; to know one another
conoscibile *adj* knowable
conosci·tóre -trice *mf* connoisseur, expert
conosciu·to -ta *adj* known, well-known; proven
conquìdere §135 *tr* (poet) to conquer

conquista *f* conquest
conquistare *tr* to conquer, win
conquista·tóre -trice *adj* conquering ‖ *m* conqueror; lady killer
consacrare *tr* to consecrate ‖ *ref* to dedicate oneself
consacrazióne *f* consecration
consanguineità *f* consanguinity
consanguìne·o -a *adj* consanguineous; **fratello consanguineo** half brother on the father's side ‖ *m* kin
consapévole *adj* aware, conscious
consapevolézza *f* awareness, consciousness
còn·scio -scia *adj* (**-sci -sce**) conscious
consecutì·vo -va *adj* consecutive
conségna *f* delivery; (mil) order; (mil) confinement (*to barracks*); **in consegna** (com) on consignment
consegnare (conségno) *tr* to deliver; to entrust; (mil) to confine (*to barracks*)
consegnatà·rio *m* (**-ri**) consignee
conseguènte *adj* consequent; consistent; **conseguente a** resulting from; consistent with
conseguènza *f* consequence; consistency; **in conseguenza di** as a result of
conseguìbile *adj* attainable
conseguiménto *m* attainment
conseguire (conséguo) *tr* to attain; to obtain ‖ *intr* to ensue, result
consènso *m* consent, approval; consensus
consensuale *adj* mutual-consent (*e.g., agreement*)
consentiménto *m* consent
consentire (consènto) *tr* to allow, permit ‖ *intr* to agree, consent; to yield; to admit
consenziènte *adj* consenting
consèr·to -ta *adj* intertwined; folded (*arms*); **di conserto** in agreement
consèrva *f* preserve; purée (*e.g., of tomatoes*); tank (*for water*); sauce (*e.g., of cranberries*); **conserve alimentari** canned goods; **di conserva** together, in a group; **far conserva di** to preserve
conservare (consèrvo) *tr* to preserve; to keep; to cure (*e.g., meat*); to cherish (*a memory*) ‖ *ref* to keep; to remain; to keep in good health
conservatì·vo -va *adj* preserving; conservative ‖ *m* conservative
conserva·tóre -trice *adj* preserving; conservative ‖ *mf* keeper, curator; conservative
conservatorìa *f* registrar's office (*in a court house*)
conservatò·rio *m* (**-ri**) conservatory; girl's boarding school (*run by nuns*)
conservatorismo *m* conservatism
conservazióne *f* conservation; preservation; self-preservation; canning
consèsso *m* assembly
consideràbile *adj* considerable; large, important
considerare (consìdero) *tr* to consider; to rate; (law) to provide for
considera·to -ta *adj* considered; **considerato che** considering that, since;

tutto considerato all in all, considering
considerazióne *f* consideration
considerévole *adj* considerable
consigliare *adj* council, councilmanic ‖ §280 *tr* to advise, counsel ‖ *ref* to consult
consigliè·re -ra *mf* counselor, advisor ‖ *m* chancellor (*of embassy*); councilman; **consigliere delegato** chairman of the board
consì·glio *m* (**-gli**) advice, counsel; will (*of God*); decision, idea; council; **consiglio d'amministrazione** (com) board of directors; **consiglio dei ministri** cabinet; **consiglio municipale** city council; **l'eterno consiglio** the will of God; **venire a più miti consigli** to become more reasonable
consìmile *adj* similar
consistènte *adj* consistent, solid; trustworthy
consistènza *f* consistency, resistance; foundation, grounds
consìstere §114 *intr* to consist; **consistere in** to consist of
consociare §128 (**consòcio**) *tr* to syndicate, unite
consocia·to -ta *adj* syndicated, united
consociazióne *f* syndicate, association, group
consò·cio -cia *mf* (**-ci -cie**) fellow shareholder; associate, partner
consolare *adj* consular ‖ *v* (**consólo**) *tr* to console, cheer, comfort ‖ *ref* to rejoice; to take comfort
consolato *m* consulate
consola·tóre -trice *adj* comforting ‖ *mf* comforter
consolazióne *f* consolation
cònsole *m* consul
consò·le *f* (**-le**) console
consòlida *f*—**consolida maggiore** comfrey; **consolida reale** field larkspur
consolidaménto *m* consolidation
consolidare (consòlido) *tr* to consolidate ‖ *ref* to consolidate; to harden
consolida·to -ta *adj* consolidated; joint (*e.g., balance sheet*); hardened ‖ *m* funded public debt; government bonds
consonante *adj* & *f* consonant
consonànti·co -ca *adj* (**-ci -che**) consonant
consonanza *f* consonance; agreement; (mus) harmony
cònso·no -na *adj* consonant
consorèlla *adj* sister (*e.g., company*) ‖ *f* sister of charity; sister branch; sister firm
consòrte *adj* (poet) equally fortunate; (poet) united ‖ *mf* consort, mate, spouse
consorterìa *f* political clique
consòr·zio *m* (**-zi**) syndicate, consortium; (poet) society
constare (cònsto) *intr* to consist ‖ *impers* to be known; to be proved; to understand, e.g., **gli consta che Lei ha torto** he understands that you are wrong
constatare (constato & cònstato) *tr* to verify, ascertain, establish

constatazióne *f* ascertainment, verification

consuè·to -ta *adj* usual, customary; **consueto a** accustomed to, used to || *m* manner, custom; **di consueto** generally

consuetudinà·rio -ria *adj* (-ri -rie) customary; common (*law*)

consuetùdine *f* custom; common law; (poet) familiarity

consulènte *adj* advising, consulting || *mf* adviser, expert

consulènza *f* expert advice

consulta *f* council

consultare *tr* to consult || *ref* to take counsel; to counsel with one another; **consultarsi con** to take counsel with

consultazióne *f* consultation; reference; **consultazione popolare** referendum

consulti·vo -va *adj* advisory

consulto *m* consultation (*of physicians*); legal conference

consul·tóre -trice *mf* adviser, expert || *m* councilman

consultò·rio *m* (-ri) clinic, dispensary

consumare *tr* to consume; to perform, to consummate || *ref* to be consumed, to waste away

consuma·to -ta *adj* consummate, accomplished; consummated (*marriage*); consumed, worn out

consuma·tóre -trice *adj* consuming || *mf* consumer; customer (*of a restaurant*)

consumazióne *f* consummation (*e.g., of a crime*); consumption (*of food*); food or drink

consumismo *m* consumerism

consumo *m* consumption; wear

consunti·vo -va *adj* end-of-year (*e.g., report*); (econ) consumption || *m* balance sheet

consun·to -ta *adj* worn-out

consunzióne *f* consumption

contàbile *adj* bookkeeping || *mf* accountant; bookkeeper, clerk; **esperto contabile** certified public accountant

contabili·tà *f* (-tà) accounting, bookkeeping; accounts

contachilòme·tri *m* (-tri) odometer; (coll) speedometer

contadiné·sco -sca *adj* (-schi -sche) farm, farmer; rustic

contadi·no -na *adj* rustic || *mf* peasant, farmer

contado *m* country, countryside

contagiare §290 *tr* to infect

contà·gio *m* (-gi) contagion

contagió·so -sa [s] *adj* contagious

contagi·ri *m* (-ri) tachometer

contagóc·ce *m* (-ce) dropper, eyedropper

contaminare (**contàmino**) *tr* to contaminate; to pollute

contaminazióne *f* contamination; pollution

contante *adj* & *m* cash; **in contanti** cash

contare (**cónto**) *tr* to count; to limit; to regard, value; to propose; **contarie grosse** (coll) to tell tall tales || *intr* to count; **contare su** to count on

contasecón·di *m* (-di) watch with second hand

conta·to -ta *adj* limited; numbered (*e.g., days*)

conta·tóre -trice *adj* counting || *mf* counter || *m* meter; **contatore dell'acqua** water meter; **contatore della luce** electric meter

contattare *tr* to contact

contatto *m* contact

cónte *m* count

contèa *f* county

conteggiare §290 (**contéggio**) *tr* to charge (*e.g., a bill*) || *intr* to count

contég·gio *m* (-gi) reckoning, calculation; (sports) count; **conteggio alla rovescia** countdown

contégno *m* behavior; reserve, reserved attitude; air

contegnó·so -sa [s] *adj* reserved, dignified

contemperare (**contèmpero**) *tr* to adapt; to mitigate, moderate

contemplare (**contèmplo**) *tr* to contemplate

contemplati·vo -va *adj* contemplative

contemplazióne *f* contemplation

contèmpo *m*—**nel contempo** meanwhile

contemporaneaménte *adv* at the same time

contemporàne·o -a *adj* contemporaneous || *mf* contemporary

contendènte *adj* fighting || *m* contender, fighter; (law) contestant

contèndere §270 *tr* to contest, oppose || *intr* to contend, fight || *ref* to fight

contenére §271 *tr* to contain || *ref* to restrain oneself; to behave

conteniménto *m* containment

contenitóre *m* container

contentare (**contènto**) *tr* to satisfy, content || *ref* to be satisfied

contentézza *f* gladness, contentedness, contentment

contentino *m* gratuity, makeweight, gift to a customer

contèn·to -ta *adj* contented, glad, happy; satisfied || *m* (poet) happiness, contentedness

contenuto *m* content; contents

contenzióne *f* contention

contenzióso [s] *m* legal matter; legal department (*of a corporation*)

conterìe *fpl* beads, sequins

conterrà·neo -nea *adj* from the same country || *m* fellow countryman || *f* fellow countrywoman

conté·so -sa [s] *adj* coveted || *f* contest; dispute; **venire a contesa** to dispute

contéssa *f* countess

contestare (**contèsto**) *tr* to serve (*e.g., a summons*); to deny; to challenge, contest; **contestare qlco a qlcu** to charge s.o. with s.th

contestazióne *f* notification, summons; dispute, confrontation; challenge

contè·sto -sta *adj* (poet) intertwined || *m* context

contì·guo -gua *adj* contiguous

continentale *adj* continental

continènte *adj* & *m* continent

continènza *f* continence

contingentaménto *m* import quota

contingentare (**contingènto**) *tr* to assign a quota to (*imports*)

contingènte *adj* possible, contingent; (obs) due ‖ *m* contingent; import quota; **contingente di leva** draft quota

contingènza *f* contingency

continuare (continuo) *tr* to continue ‖ *intr* to last, continue; **continuare a** + *inf* to keep on + *ger*

continuazióne *f* continuation

continui·tà *f* (-tà) continuity

contì·nuo -nua *adj* continuous; direct (*current*); **di continuo** continuously

cón·to -ta *adj* (archaic) well-known; (poet) gentle; (poet) narrated ‖ *m* figuring; account; bill, invoice; check (*in a restaurant*); opinion; worth, value; **a conti fatti** everything considered; **chiedere conto di** to call to account; **conto all'indietro** countdown; **di conto** valuable; **estratto conto** (com) statement; **fare conto di** + *inf* to intend to + *inf*; **fare conto su** to count on; **fare di conto** to count; **fare i conti senza l'oste** to reckon without one's host; **il conto non torna** the sums do not jibe; **in conto** on account; **in conto di** in one's position as; **per conto di** in the name of; **per conto mio** as far as I am concerned; **render conto di** to give an account of; **rendersi conto di** to realize, be aware of; **tener conto di** to reckon with; **tener di conto** to treat with care; **torna conto** it is worthwhile

contòrcere §272 *tr* to twist ‖ *ref* to writhe

contorciménto *m* contortion, writhing

contornare (contórno) *tr* to surround

contórno *m* outline; contour; circle (*of people*); side dish (*of vegetables*)

contorsióne *f* contorsion; gyration (*e.g., of a dancer*); squirm

contòr·to -ta *adj* twisted (*e.g., face*)

contrabbandare *tr* to smuggle

contrabbandiè·re -ra *adj* smuggling ‖ *mf* smuggler; bootlegger

contrabbando *m* contraband; smuggling; **di contrabbando** by smuggling; (fig) without paying

contrabbasso *m* contrabass, bass viol

contraccambiare §287 *tr* to reciprocate, return ‖ *intr* to reciprocate

contraccàm·bio *m* (-bi) exchange; **in contraccambio di** in exchange for, in return for

contraccólpo *m* shock, rebound; recoil (*of a rifle*); backlash (*of a machine*)

contrada *f* road; (poet) region

contraddire §151 (*impv sg* contraddici) *tr* to contradict ‖ *ref* to contradict oneself; to contradict one another

contraddistìnguere §156 *tr* to earmark ‖ *ref* to stand out

contraddittò·rio -ria (-ri -rie) *adj* contradictory; incoherent ‖ *m* open discussion, debate

contraddizióne *f* contradiction

contraènte *adj* contracting; acting ‖ *mf* contractor (*person who makes a contract*); (law) party

contraère·o -a *adj* antiaircraft

contraffare §173 *tr* to counterfeit; to fake, sham ‖ *intr* (archaic) to disobey ‖ *ref* to camouflage oneself, disguise oneself

contraffat·to -ta *adj* counterfeit; adulterated; apocryphal

contraffat·tóre -trice *mf* counterfeiter; falsifier

contraffazióne *f* forgery; fake; imitation; piracy (*of book*); mockery (*of justice*)

contraffòrte *m* spur (*of mountain*); crossbar (*to secure door*); (archit) buttress

contraggènio *m*—**a contraggenio** against one's will

contral·to (-to) *adj* alto ‖ *m* contralto (*voice*) ‖ *f* contralto (*singer*)

contrammirà·glio *m* (-gli) rear admiral

contrappasso *m* retributive justice

contrappesare [s] (**contrappéso**) *tr* to counterweight, counterbalance

contrappéso [s] *m* counterweight, counterpoise

contrappórre §218 *tr* to oppose; to compare ‖ *ref*—**contrapporsi a** to oppose

contrappó·sto -sta *adj* opposing ‖ *m* opposite, antithesis

contrappunto *m* counterpoint

contrare (cóntro) *tr* (boxing) to counter; (bridge) to double

contrariare §287 *tr* to oppose, counter; to thwart; to contradict; to bother, vex

contrarie·tà *f* (-tà) contrariety, vexation; setback

contrà·rio -ria (-ri -rie) *adj* contrary, opposite ‖ *m* opposite; **al contrario** on the contrary; **al contrario di** unlike; **avere qlco in contrario** to have some objection, object

contrarre §273 *tr* & *ref* to contract

contrassegnare (contrasségno) *tr* to earmark, mark

contrasségno *m* earmark; proof

contrastare *tr* to oppose; to obstruct; to prevent ‖ *intr* to contrast; to disagree; (poet) to quarrel ‖ *ref* to contend

contrasto *m* contrast; fight, dispute; (telv) contrast knob

contrattàbile *adj* negotiable

contrattaccare §197 *tr* to counterattack

contrattac·co *m* (-chi) counterattack

contrattare *tr* to contract for, negotiate a deal for ‖ *intr* to bargain

contrattèmpo *m* mishap

contrat·to -ta *adj* contracted ‖ *m* contract

contrattuale *adj* contractual

contravveléno *m* antidote

contravvenire §282 *intr* (with *dat*) to contravene; **contravvenire a** to infringe upon

contravvenzióne *f* violation; ticket, fine; **in contravvenzione** in the wrong; **intimare una contravvenzione a** to give a ticket to

contrazióne *f* contraction

contribuènte *mf* taxpayer

contribuire §176 *intr* to contribute

contributo *m* contribution

contribu·tóre -trice *mf* contributor

contribuzióne *f* contribution
contristare *tr* & *ref* to sadden
contri·to -ta *adj* contrite
contrizióne *f* contrition
cóntro *m* con, contrary opinion || *adv* —contro di against, versus; **dar contro a** to oppose; **di contro** opposite, facing; **per contro** on the other hand || *prep* against, versus; at; **contro pagamento** upon payment; **contro vento** into the wind; **contro voglia** unwillingly
controbàttere *tr* (mil) to counterattack; (fig) to contest
controbilanciare §128 *tr* to counterpoise, counterbalance
controcanto *m* (mus) counterpoint
controcarro *adj invar* antitank
controchìglia *f* keelson
controcorrènte *f* countercurrent; undertow; (fig) undercurrent || *adv* upstream
controdado *m* lock nut
controffensiva *f* counteroffensive
controfigura *f* (mov) stand-in; (mov) stuntman
controfilo *m*—a **controfilo** against the grain
controfinèstra *f* storm window
controfirma *f* countersign
controfirmare *tr* to countersign
controfòdera *f* inner facing (*of a suit, between lining and cloth*)
controfuò·co *m* (-chi) backfire (*to check the advance of a forest fire*)
controindicare §197 (controìndico) *tr* to contraindicate
controllare (contròllo) *tr* to control, check || *ref* to control oneself
contròllo *m* control, check; restraint; (rad, telv) knob
controllóre *m* (com) comptroller; (rr) ticket collector, conductor
controluce *f* picture taken against the light || *adv* against the light
contromano *adv* against traffic
contromar·ca *f* (-che) check, stub (*e.g., of ticket*)
contromàr·cia *f* (-ce) countermarch; (aut) reverse, reverse gear
contromezzana [ddzz] *f* (naut) topsail
contronòta *f* countermanding note
contropalo *m* strut
controparte *f* (law) opponent
contropedale *m* foot brake (*of a bicycle*)
contropélo *m* close shave (*in the opposite direction of hair's growth*) || *adv* against the grain; the wrong way (*said of the hair*); against the nap; **accarezzare contropelo** to stroke the wrong way
contropiède *m* counterattack; **cogliere in contropiede** to catch off balance
contropòrta *f* storm door
controproducènte *adj* counterproductive, self-defeating
contropropósta *f* counterproposition
contropròva *f* proof; second balloting
contrórdine *m* countermand
controrèplica *f* retort; (law) rejoinder
controrifórma *f* Counter Reformation

controrivoluzióne *f* counterrevolution
controsènso *m* nonsense; mistranslation
controspallina *f* (mil) epaulet
controspionàg·gio *m* (-gi) counterespionage
controvalóre *m* equivalent
controvènto *m* (archit) strut; (archit) crossbrace || *adv* windward
controvèrsia *f* controversy
controvèr·so -sa *adj* controversial, moot
controvòglia *adv* unwillingly
contumace *adj* (archaic) contumacious; (law) absent from court; (law) guilty of nonappearance
contumàcia *f* quarantine; (archaic) contumacy; (law) nonappearance; **in contumacia** (law) in absentia
contumèlia *f* contumely
contundènte *adj* blunt
conturbante *adj* disturbing, upsetting
conturbare *tr* to disturb, upset || *ref* to become perturbed
contusióne *f* bruise, contusion
contu·so -sa *adj* bruised
contuttoché *conj* although
contuttociò *conj* although
convalescènte *adj* convalescent
convalescènza *f* convalescence
convalescenzià·rio *m* (-ri) convalescent home
convàlida *f* validation; confirmation
convalidare (convàlido) *tr* to validate; to confirm; to strengthen (*e.g., a suspicion*)
convégno *m* meeting, convention
conveniènte *adj* convenient; adequate; useful; profitable (*business*); cheap, reasonable
conveniènza *f* convenience; suitability; fitness; propriety; profit; **convenienze** conventions
convenire §282 *tr* to fix (*e.g., a price*); (law) to summon || *intr* (ESSERE) to convene; to agree; to fit, be appropriate; (poet) to flow together || *ref* to be proper; (with *dat*) to behoove, befit, e.g., **gli si conviene** it behooves him || *impers*—**conviene** it is necessary
convènto *m* convent; monastery
convenu·to -ta *adj* agreed upon || *m* agreement; (law) defendant; **convenuti** conventioners, delegates
convenzionale *adj* conventional
convenzióne *f* convention
convergènte *adj* converging, convergent
convergènza *f* convergence
convèrgere §137 *intr* to converge
convèrsa *f* lay sister; flashing (*on a roof*)
conversare (convèrso) *intr* to converse
conversazióne *f* conversation
conversióne *f* conversion; change of heart; (mil) wheeling
convèrso *m* lay brother
convertìbile *adj* convertible || *m* (aer) fighter-bomber || *f* (aut) convertible
convertibili·tà *f* (-tà) convertibility
convertire §138 *tr* to convert, change; to translate || *ref* to convert, change; (poet) to address oneself

convertì·to -ta *adj* converted || *mf* convert

convertitóre *m* converter

convès·so -sa *adj* convex

convincènte *adj* convincing

convìncere §285 *tr* to convince; to convict || *ref* to become convinced

convinciménto *m* conviction

convìn·to -ta *adj* convinced, confirmed; convicted

convinzióne *f* conviction

convìta·to -ta *adj* invited || *mf* guest (*at a banquet*)

convìto *m* banquet

convitto *m* boarding school

convìt·tóre -trice *mf* boarding-school student

convivènte *adj* living together

convivènza *f* living together; **convivenza illecita** cohabitation; **convivenza umana** human society

convìvere §286 *intr* to live together; to cohabit

conviviale *adj* convivial

convì·vio *m* (**-vi**) banquet

convocare §197 (**cònvoco**) *tr* to summon, convoke; to convene

convocazióne *f* convocation

convogliare §280 (**convòglio**) *tr* to convoy, escort; to convey, carry

convò·glio *m* (**-gli**) convoy; cortege; (**rr**) train

convolare (**convólo**) *intr*—**convolare a nozze** to get married

convòlvolo *m* (bot) morning-glory

convulsióne *f* convulsion

convul·so -sa *adj* convulsive; convulsed; choppy (*style*)

coonestare (**coonèsto**) *tr* to justify, palliate

cooperare (**coòpero**) *intr* to cooperate

cooperatì·vo -va *adj* & *f* cooperative

coopera·tóre -trice *adj* coadjutant, cooperating || *m* coadjutor

cooperazióne *f* cooperation

coordinaménto *m* coordination

coordinare (**coórdino**) *tr* to coordinate; to collect (*ideas*)

coordinatì·vo -va *adj* (gram) coordinate

coordìna·to -ta *adj* & *f* coordinate

coordinazióne *f* coordination

coòrte *f* cohort

copèr·chio *m* (**-chi**) lid, cover; top (*of box*)

copertina *f* small blanket, child's blanket; cover (*of book*)

copèr·to -ta *adj* covered; protected; cloudy; obscure || *m* cover; shelter; **al coperto** under cover; indoors; secure || *f* blanket, cover; seat cover; case, sheath; (naut) deck; **coperta da viaggio** steamer rug, lap robe; **far coperta a** to cover up for

copertóne *m* canvas; casing, shoe (*of tire*); **copertone cinturato** belted tire

copertura *f* covering; cover; coverage; whitewash; (boxing) defensive stance; (archit) roof

còpia *f* copy; (poet) abundance; (archaic) opportunity; **brutta copia** first draft; **copia a carbone** carbon copy; **copia dattiloscritta** typescript; **per**

copia conforme certified copy (*formula appearing on a document*)

copialètte·re *m* (**-re**) letter file; copying press

copiare §287 (**còpio**) *tr* to copy

copiatì·vo -va *adj* indelible; copying

copiatura *f* copying; copy; plagiarism

copìglia *f* cotterpin

copilò·ta *mf* (**-ti -te**) copilot

copióne *m* (theat) script

copiosi·tà [s] *f* (**-tà**) copiousness

copió·so -sa [s] *adj* copious

copì·sta *mf* (**-sti -ste**) scribe; copyist

copisterìa *f* copying office; public typing office

còppa *f* cup, goblet; bowl; pan (*of balance*); trophy; (aut) crankcase; (aut) housing; **coppe** suit of Neapolitan cards corresponding to hearts

coppàia *f* chuck (*of lathe*)

còppia *f* couple; pair; **a coppie** two by two; **far coppia fissa** to go steady

coppière *m* cupbearer

coppìglia *f* var of **copiglia**

cóppo *m* earthenware jar (*for oil*); roof tile

copribu·sto *m* (**-sto**) bodice

copricapo *m* headgear

copricatè·na *m* (**-na**) chain guard (*on bicycle or motorcycle*)

coprifuò·co *m* (**-chi**) curfew

coprinu·ca *m* (**-ca**) havelock

coprire §110 *tr* to cover; to occupy (*a position*); to coat (*e.g., a wall*); to drown (*a noise*) || *ref* to cover oneself; (econ) to hedge

copriteiè·ra *m* (**-ra**) cozy

coprivivan·de *m* (**-de**) dish cover

cò·pto -pta *adj* Coptic || *mf* Copt

còpula *f* copulation; (gram) copula

coque *f* see **uovo**

coràg·gio *m* (**-gi**) courage; effrontery; (obs) heart; **fare coraggio a** to hearten, encourage; **prendere il coraggio a quattro mani** to screw up one's courage

coraggió·so -sa [s] *adj* courageous

corale *adj* choral; (archaic) cordial; (fig) unanimous || *m* chorale

corallì·no -na *adj* coral

corallo *m* coral

corame *m* engraved leather

coramèlla *f* razor strop

Corano *m* Koran

corata *f* haslet

coratèlla *f* giblets

corazza *f* breastplate, cuirass; shoulder pad (*in football*); armor plate; carapace, shell

corazzare *tr* to armor || *ref* to armor, protect oneself

corazza·to -ta *adj* armor-plated, armored; plated; protected || *f* battleship, dreadnought

corazzière *m* cuirassier; mounted carabineer

còrba *f* basket

corbellerìa *f* (coll) blunder

corbèllo *m* basket; basketful

corbézzolo *m* (bot) arbutus; **corbezzoli!** gosh!

còrda *f* rope; tightrope; string (*of an*

instrument); chord; woof; cord; plumbline; **dare la corda a** to wind (*a clock*); **essere con la corda al collo** to have a rope around one's neck; **mostrare la corda** to be threadbare; **tagliare la corda** to take off, leave; **tenere sulla corda** to keep in suspense

cordame *m* cordage

cordata *f* group of climbers tied together

cordellina *f* (mil) braided cord, braid; (mil) lanyard

cordiale *adj & m* cordial

cordiali•tà *f* (-tà) cordiality

cordièra *f* (mus) tailpiece

cordò•glio *m* (-gli) sorrow, grief

cordonata *f* gradient

cordóne *m* cordon; (anat, elec) cord; curbstone; **cordone litorale** sandbar; **cordone sanitario** sanitary cordon

corèa *f* St. Vitus's dance ‖ **Corea** *f* Korea

corea•no -na *adj & mf* Korean

coréggia *f* leather strap

coreografia *f* choreography

coreògrafo *m* choreographer

coriàce•o -a *adj* tough, leathery

coriàndolo *m* (bot) coriander; **coriandoli** confetti

coricare §197 (còrico) *tr* to put to bed ‖ *ref* to lie down, go to bed

corindóne *m* corundum

corìn•zio -zia *adj & mf* (-zi -zie) Corinthian

cori•sta *mf* (-sti -ste) choir singer, choirmaster ‖ *m* chorus man; (mus) tuning fork; (mus) pitch pipe

coriza [dz] *or* **corizza** [ddzz] *f* coryza

cormorano *m* cormorant

cornàcchia *f* rook, crow

cornamusa *f* bagpipe

cornata *f* butt; hook, goring (*by bull*)

còrne•o -a *adj* horn, horn-like ‖ *f* cornea

cornétta *f* (mus) cornet; (mus) cornet player; (telp) receiver; (hist) pennon (*of cavalry*)

cornétto *m* little horn; amulet (*in shape of horn*); crescent (*bread*); ear trumpet

cornice *f* cornice; frame; (typ) box; (archit) pediment

corniscióne *m* (archit) ledge; (archit) cornice

cornificare §197 (cornìfico) *tr* (joc) to cuckold

corniòla *f* carnelian

còrniola *f* (bot) dogberry

còrniolo *m* (bot) dogwood

còrno *m* horn; wing (*of army*); edge, end; (mus) horn; **corno da caccia** hunting horn; **corno da scarpe** shoe horn; **corno dell'abbondanza** horn of plenty; **corno dogale** (hist) Doge's hat; **corno inglese** (mus) English horn; **non capire un corno** to not understand a blessed thing; **non valere un corno** to not be worth a fig; **un corno!** (slang) heck no! ‖ *m* (**còrna** *fpl*) horn (*of animal*); **alzare le corna** to raise one's head; to be-

come rambunctious; **dire corna di** to speak evil of; **fare le corna** to make horns, to touch wood (*to ward off the evil eye*); **mettere le corna a** to cuckold (*one's husband*); to be unfaithful to (*one's wife*); **portare le corna** to be cuckolded; **rompersi le corna** to get the worst of it

cornu•to -ta *adj* horny; horn-shaped; (vulg) cuckolded

còro *m* choir; chorus; chancel

corollà•rio *m* (-ri) corollary

coróna *f* crown; coronet; wreath, garland; range (*of mountains*); collection (*e.g., of sonnets*); stem (*of watch*); felloe (*of wheel*); (astr) corona; (rel) string (*of beads*); (mus) pause; **fare corona a** to surround

coronaménto *m* crowning; (archit) capstone; (naut) taffrail

coronare (coróno) *tr* to crown; to top, surmount

coronà•rio -ria *adj* (-ri -rie) coronary; (hist) rewarded with a garland

corpétto *m* baby's shirt; waistcoat, vest

corpino *m* bodice; vest

còrpo *m* body; substance; staff (*of teachers*); (mil) corps; (typ) em quad; **a corpo a corpo** hand-to-hand (*fight*); (sports) in a clinch; **a corpo morto** heavily; doggedly; **andare di corpo** to have a bowel movement; **avere in corpo** (fig) to have inside; **corpo del reato** corpus delicti; **corpo di Bacco!** good Heavens!; **corpo di ballo** ballet; **corpo di commissariato** (mil) supply corps; **corpo di guardia** guard, guardhouse; **corpo semplice** (chem) simple substance; **prendere corpo** to materialize

corporale *adj* bodily, body ‖ *m* (eccl) corporal, Communion cloth

corporativismo *m* corporatism (*e.g., of Fascist Italy*)

corporati•vo -va *adj* corporative, corporate

corpora•to -ta *adj* corporate

corporatura *f* size, build

corporazióne *f* corporation

corpòre•o -a *adj* corporeal

corpó•so -sa [s] *adj* heavy-bodied

corpulèn•to -ta *adj* corpulent

corpùscolo *m* particle; (phys) corpuscle

Corpus Dòmini *m* (eccl) Corpus Christi

corredare (corrèdo) *tr* to provide, furnish; to annotate, accompany

corredino *m* layette

corrèdo *m* trousseau; outfit, garb; actor's kit; furniture; equipment; apparatus (*e.g., footnotes*)

corrèggere §226 *tr* to correct; to straighten (*e.g., a road*); to rewrite, revise (*news*); to touch up the flavor of ‖ *ref* to reform

corrég•gia *f* (-ge) leather strap

corregionale *adj* fellow ‖ *mf* person of the same section of the country

correità *f* complicity

correlare (corrèlo) *tr* to correlate

correlati•vo -va *adj* correlative

correla•tóre -trice *mf* second reader (*of a doctoral dissertation*) correlazióne *f* correlation; (gram) sequence

corrènte *adj* current; running; fluent; recurring; run-of-the-mill || *m*—essere al corrente di to be acquainted with; to be abreast of; mettere al corrente di to acquaint with || *f* current; draft (*of air*); stream (*of water*); mass (*of lava*); (elec) current; (fig) tide; contro corrente upstream; corrente alternata (elec) alternating current; corrente continua (elec) direct current; corrente di rete (elec) house current

córrere §139 *tr* to travel; to run (*a risk; a race*); correre la cavallina to sow one's wild oats || *intr* (ESSERE & AVERE) to run; to speed; to race; to flow; to fly (*said of time*); to elapse; to be (*e.g., the year 1820*); to be current (*said of coins*); to spread (*said of gossip*); to mature (*said of interest*); to intervene (*said of distance*); to have dealings; ci corre! there is quite a difference!; ci corre poco che cadesse he narrowly escaped falling; correre a gambe levate to run at breakneck speed; corre l'uso it is the fashion; corrono parole grosse they are having words; non corre buon sangue fra loro there is bad blood between them

corresponsàbile *adj* jointly responsible

corresponsióne *f* payment; (fig) gratitude

correttézza *f* correctness

corretti·vo -va *adj* corrective || *m* flavoring

corrèt·to -ta *adj* correct; flavored; spiked

corret·tóre -trice *mf* corrector; correttore di bozze proofreader

correzionale *adj* correctional

correzióne *f* correction

córri córri *m* rush

corri·dóio *m* (-dói) corridor; hallway; (tennis) alley; (theat) aisle

corridóre *adj* running || *m* racer; runner (*in baseball*)

corrièra *f* mail coach; bus

corrière *m* courier; mail; carrier (*of merchandise*)

corrispetti·vo -va *adj* equivalent, proportionate || *m* requital, compensation

corrispondènte *adj* corresponding, equivalent || *mf* correspondent

corrispondènza *f* correspondence

corrispóndere §238 *tr* to pay, compensate || *intr* to correspond

corri·vo -va *adj* rash; indulgent

corroborante *adj* corroborating || *m* tonic

corroborare (corròboro) *tr* to corroborate; to invigorate

corroborazióne *f* corroboration

corródere §239 *tr* to corrode; to erode

corrómpere §240 *tr* to spoil; to corrupt; to suborn || *ref* to putrefy, rot

corrosióne *f* corrosion

corrosi·vo -va *adj* & *m* corrosive

corró·so -sa *adj* corroded; eroded

corrót·to -ta *adj* corrupted, corrupt; putrefied, rotten || *m* (archaic) lament

corrucciare §128 *tr* to anger, vex || *ref* to get angry

corrùc·cio *m* (-ci) anger, vexation

corrugaménto *m* wrinkling; (geol) fold

corrugare §209 *tr* to wrinkle, knit (*one's brow*) || *ref* to frown

corruscare §197 *intr* (poet) to shine

corruttèla *f* corruption

corruttìbile *adj* corruptible

corrut·tóre -trice *adj* corrupting, depraving || *m* seducer; briber

corruzióne *f* corruption; putrefaction, decomposition

córsa *f* race; run; trip; fare; (mach) stroke; (hist) privateering; a tutta corsa at full speed; corsa al galoppo flat race; corsa al trotto harness racing; corsa semplice one-way ticket; corse horse racing; da corsa race, for racing, e.g., cavallo da corsa race horse; di corsa running, in a hurry; fare una corsa to run an errand; prendere la corsa to begin to run

corsalétto *m* corselet

corsa·ro -ra *adj* privateering || *m* privateer, corsair, pirate

corsétto *m* corset

corsìa *f* aisle; ward (*in hospital*); runner (*of carpet*); lane (*of highway*); corsia d'accesso entrance lane; corsia d'uscita exit lane

Còrsica, la Corsica

corsivi·sta *mf* (-sti -ste) (journ) political writer

corsi·vo -va *adj* cursive; (poet) running; (poet) current || *m* cursive handwriting; (typ) italics

córso *m* course; navigation (*by sea*); path (*of stars*); parade; large street; boulevard; tender (*of currency*); current rate, current price (*of stock at the exchange*); corso d'acqua watercourse; fuori corso (*coin*) no longer in circulation; in corso in circulation; in progress; in corso di in the course of; in corso di stampa in press

còr·so -sa *adj* & *mf* Corsican

cor·sóio -sóia (-sói -sóie) *adj* running (*knot*); (mach) on rollers || *m* slide (*of slide rule*); (mach) slide

córte *f* court; corte bandita open house; Corte d'appello appellate court; Corte di cassazione Supreme Court; fare la corte a to pay court to, woo

cortéc·cia *f* (-ce) bark; crust (*of bread*); (fig) appearance; (anat) cortex

corteggiaménto *m* courtship

corteggiatóre *m* wooer, suitor

cortég·gio *m* (-gi) retinue; cortege

cortèo *m* procession; parade; funeral train; wedding party

cortése *adj* courteous, polite; (lit) liberal; (poet & hist) courtly

cortesìa *f* courtesy, politeness; (lit) liberality; (poet & hist) courtliness; per cortesia please

còrtice *f* cortex

cortigia·no -na *adj* flattering; courtly || *mf* courtier; flatterer || *f* courtesan

cortile *m* courtyard; barnyard

cortina *f* curtain; cortina di ferro iron curtain; cortina di fumo smoke screen; oltre cortina behind the iron curtain

cortisóne *m* cortisone

cór·to -ta *adj* short; close (*haircut*); alle corte in short; essere a corto di to be short of; per farla corta in short

cortocircùito *m* short circuit

cortometràg·gio *m* (-gi) (mov) short

cor·vè *f* (-vè) tiresome task, drudgery; corvè di cucina kitchen police

corvétta *f* corvette

corvi·no -na *adj* raven-black

còrvo *m* raven; crow

còsa [s] *f* thing; belle cose! or buone cose! regards!; che cosa what; cosa da nulla a mere trifle, nothing at all; cos'ha? what's the matter with you (him, her)?; cosa pubblica commonweal; cosa strana no wonder; cose belongings; per la qual cosa wherefore; per prima cosa first of all; sopra ogni cosa above all; tante belle cose! best regards!; una cosa something; una cosa nuova a piece of news

cosac·co -ca (-chi -che) *adj* Cossack's || *mf* Cossack

cò·scia *f* (-sce) thigh; haunch; leg (*of gun*); (archit) abutment; coscia di montone leg of lamb

cosciènte *adj* conscious; sensible; aware

cosciènza *f* conscience; consciousness; conscientiousness; awareness

coscienzió·so -sa [s] *adj* conscientious

cosciòtto *m* leg; leg of lamb

coscrit·to -ta *adj* conscript || *m* conscript, recruit, draftee

coscrìvere §250 *tr* to conscript

coscrizióne *f* conscription, draft

così [s] *adj invar*—un così... or un... così such a || *adv* thus; like this; so; così ... come as ... as; così così so so; e così via and so on, and so forth; per così dire so to speak

cosicché [s] *conj* so that

cosiddét·to -ta [s] *adj* so-called

cosiffat·to -ta [s] *adj* such, similar

cosino [s] *m* (coll) little fellow

cosmèti·co -ca *adj & m* (-ci -che) cosmetic

còsmi·co -ca *adj* (-ci -che) cosmic; outer (*space*)

còsmo *m* cosmos; outer space

cosmòdromo *m* space center

cosmologìa *f* cosmology

cosmonàu·ta *mf* (-ti -te) cosmonaut, astronaut

cosmopoli·ta *adj & mf* (-ti -te) cosmopolitan

còso [s] *m* (coll) thing, what-d'you-call-it

cospàrgere §261 *tr* to spread; to sprinkle

cospèrgere §112 *tr* (poet) to wet, sprinkle

cospètto *m* presence; al cospetto di in the presence of

cospì·cuo -cua *adj* distinguished, outstanding; huge, immense; (poet) conspicuous

cospirare *intr* to conspire, plot

cospira·tóre -trice *mf* conspirator

cospirazióne *f* conspiracy, plot

còsta *f* side; rib; coast, seashore; slope; welt (*along seam*); wale (*in fabric*); (naut) frame

costà *adv* there; over there

costaggiù *adj* down there

costante *adj & f* constant

Costantinòpoli *f* Constantinople

costanza *f* constancy || Costanza *f* Constance

costare (còsto) *intr* (ESSERE) to cost; to be expensive; costare caro to cost dear; costare un occhio della testa to cost a fortune

costarica·no -na or costaricènse *adj & mf* Costa Rican

costassù *adv* up there

costata *f* rib roast; side

costeggiare §290 (costéggio) *tr* to sail along; to run along; to border on || *intr* to coast

costèi §8 *pron dem*

costellare (costèllo) *tr* to stud, star

costellazióne *f* constellation

costernare (costèrno) *tr* to dismay, cause consternation to

costernazióne *f* consternation

costì *adv* there

costiè·ro -ra *adj* coast, coastal; offshore || *f* coastline; gentle slope

costipare *tr* to constipate; to heap, pile || *ref* to become constipated

costipazióne *f* constipation

costituènte *adj* constituent; constituting || *m* member of constituent assembly; (chem) constituent

costituire §176 *tr* to constitute; to form || *ref* to form; to become; to appoint oneself; to give oneself up (*to justice*); costituirsi in giudizio (law) to sue (*in civil court*); costituirsi parte civile (law) to appear as a plaintiff (*in civil court*)

costituto *m* (law) pact, agreement; (naut) master's declaration (*to health authorities*)

costituzionale *adj* constitutional

costituzióne *f* constitution; charter; composition; (law) appearance; surrender (*to justice*)

còsto *m* cost; a costo di at the price of; ad ogni costo at any cost; a nessun costo by no means; a tutti i costi at any cost, in any event; costo della vita cost of living; sotto costo below cost

còstola *f* rib; spine (*of book*); back (*of knife*); avere qlcu alle costole to have s.o. at one's heels; rompere le costole a (fig) to break the bones of; stare alle costole di to be at the back of

costolétta *f* chop, cutlet

costolóne *m* (archit) groin

costóro §8 *pron dem*

costó·so -sa [s] *adj* costly

costrìngere §265 *tr* to force, constrain; (poet) to compress

costritti·vo -va *adj* constrictive

costrizióne *f* constriction

costruire §140 *tr* to construct, build

costrut·to -ta *adj* constructed ‖ *m* profit; sense; (gram) construction; dov'è il costrutto? what's the point?

costruttóre *m* builder

costruzióne *f* construction; building

costùi §8 *pron dem*

costumanza *f* custom

costumare *intr* (+ *inf*) to be in the habit of (+ *ger*) ‖ *intr* (ESSERE) to be the custom; to be in use

costumatézza *f* good manners

costuma·to -ta *adj* polite, well-bred

costume *m* custom, manner; costume, dress; bathing suit

costumi·sta *mf* (-sti -ste) (theat) costumer

costura *f* seam

cotale *adj* & *pron* such ‖ *adv* (archaic) thus

cotan·to -ta *adj* & *pron* (poet) so much ‖ cotanto *adv* (poet) such a long time

còte *f* flint

coténna *f* pigskin; rind; (coll) hide, skin

coté·sto -sta §7 *adj dem* ‖ §8 *pron dem*

cóti·ca *f* (-che) (coll) hide, skin (*of porker*)

cotógna *f* quince (*fruit*)

cotognata *f* quince jam

cotógno *m* quince (*tree*)

cotolétta *f* chop, cutlet

cotóne *m* cotton; thread; cotone fulminante guncotton; cotone idrofilo absorbent cotton; cotone silicato mineral wool

cotonière *m* cotton manufacturer

cotoniè·ro -ra *adj* cotton ‖ *mf* cotton worker

cotonifi·cio *m adj* (-ci) cotton mill

cotonó·so -sa [s] *adj* cotton; cottony

còtta *f* cooking; baking; drying (*of bricks*); (sports) exhaustion; (coll) drunkenness; (joc) infatuation, love; (eccl) surplice; cotta d'armi coat of mail

cottimi·sta *mf* (-sti -ste) pieceworker

còttimo *m* piecework

còt·to -ta *adj* cooked; baked; burnt; suntanned; (joc) half-baked; (joc) in love; (sports) exhausted ‖ *m* brick ‖ *f* see cotta

cottura *f* cooking; a punto di cottura (culin) done just right

coutènte *mf* (law) joint user; (telp) party-line user

cóva *f* brooding; nest

covare (cóvo) *tr* to brood, to hatch; to harbor or nurse (*an enmity*); to nurture (*a disease*); covare con gli occhi to look fondly at; covare le lenzuola to loll around ‖ *intr* to smolder (*said of fire or passion*)

covata *f* brood, covey

covile *m* doghouse; den

cóvo *m* shelter; den, lair; farsi il covo (fig) to gather a nestegg; uscire dal covo to stick one's nose out of the house

covóne *m* sheaf; cock (*of hay*)

còzza *f* cockle

cozzare (còzzo) *tr* to hit; to butt (*one's head*) ‖ *intr* to butt; (fig) to clash;

cozzare contro to bump into ‖ *ref* to hit one another; to fight

còzzo *m* butt; clash, conflict

crac *m* crash

crampo *m* cramp

cràni·co -ca *adj* (-ci -che) cranial

crà·nio *m* (-ni) cranium, skull

cràpula *f* excess (*in eating and drinking*)

cras·so -sa *adj* crass, gross; large (*intestine*)

cratère *m* crater; bomb crater

cràuti *mpl* sauerkraut

cravatta *f* tie, necktie; cravatta a farfalla bow tie; fare cravatte to be a usurer

creanza *f* politeness; buona creanza good manners

creare (crèo) *tr* to create; to name, elect

creati·vo -va *adj* creative

crea·to -ta *adj* created ‖ *m* creation, universe

crea·tóre -trice *adj* creative ‖ *mf* creator

creatura *f* creature; baby; povera creatura! poor thing!

creazióne *f* creation; (poet) election

credènte *adj* believing ‖ *mf* believer

credènza *f* credence, faith, belief; sideboard, buffet; (coll) credit

credenziale *f* letter of credit; credenziali credentials

credenzière *m* butler

crédere §141 *tr* to believe; to think; lo credo bene! I should say so! ‖ *intr* to believe; to trust; credere a to believe in; credere in Dio to believe in God ‖ *ref* to believe oneself to be

credìbile *adj* credible

credibilità *f* credibility

crédito *m* credit

credi·tóre -trice *mf* creditor

crèdo *m* credo, creed

credulità *f* credulity

crèdu·lo -la *adj* credulous

crèma *f* cream; custard; crema da scarpe shoe polish; crema di bellezza beauty cream; crema di pomodoro cream of tomato soup; crema evanescente vanishing cream; crema per barba shaving cream

cremaglièra *f* rack; cogway, cograil

cremare (crèmo) *tr* to cremate

crema·tóio *m* (-tói) crematory

crematò·rio *m* (-ri) crematory

cremazióne *f* cremation

cremerìa *f* creamery

crèmisi *adj* & *m* crimson

Cremlino *m* Kremlin

cremlinologìa *f* Kremlinology

cremortàrtaro *m* cream of tartar

cremó·so -sa [s] *adj* creamy

crèn *m* horseradish

creolina *f* creolin

crè·olo -la *adj* & *mf* Creole

creosòto *m* creosote

crèpa *f* crack, crevice; rift

crepàc·cio *m* (-ci) crevasse; fissure

crepacuòre *m* heartbreak

crepapància *m*—mangiare a crepapancia to burst from eating too much

crepapèlle *m*—ridere a crepapelle to split one's sides laughing

crepare (crèpo) *intr* to burst; to crack; to chip; (slang) to croak; **crepare dalla sete** to die of thirst; **crepare dalle risa** to die laughing; **crepare d'invidia** to be green with envy

crepitare (crèpito) *intr* to crackle (*said of fire or weapons*); to rustle (*said of leaves*)

crepitìo *m* (-ìi) crackle; rustle; pitter-patter (*of rain*)

crepuscolare *adj* twilight; (fig) dim

crepùscolo *m* twilight

crescènte *adj* rising, growing; crescent (*moon*) ‖ *m* (astr & heral) crescent

crescènza *f* growth

créscere §142 *tr* to grow, raise; to increase ‖ *intr* (ESSERE) to grow; to increase; to rise (*said, e.g., of prices*); to wax (*said of the moon*); **farsi crescere** to grow (*a beard*)

cresciòne *m* watercress

créscita *f* growth; outgrowth; rise (*of water*)

crèsima *f* confirmation

cresimare (crèsimo) *tr* to confirm

Crèso *m* (mythol) Croesus

cré·spo -spa *adj* crispy, kinky; (archaic) wrinkled ‖ *m* crepe ‖ *f* wrinkle; ruffle

crésta *f* comb (*of chicken*); crest; abbassare **la cresta** to come down a peg or two; **alzare la cresta** to become insolent

crestàia *f* (coll) milliner

créta *f* clay

cretése [s] *adj* & *mf* Cretan

cretinerìa *f* idiocy

creti·no -na *adj* & *mf* idiot, cretin

cribro *m* (poet) sieve

cric·ca *f* (-che) clique, gang; group; crevice

cric·co *m* (-chi) (aut) jack

cricéto *m* hamster

cri crì *m* chirping (*of crickets*)

criminale *adj* criminal; (law) penal ‖ *mf* criminal

criminali·sta *mf* (-sti -ste) penal lawyer, criminal lawyer

criminalità *f* criminality

crìmine *m* crime

criminologìa *f* criminology

criminòlo·go *m* (-gi) criminologist

criminó·so -sa [s] *adj* criminal

crinale *adj* (poet) hair ‖ *m* ridge (*of mountains*)

crine *m* horsehair; (poet) hair; (poet) sunbeam

crinièra *f* mane

crinolina *f* crinoline

cripta *f* crypt

criptocomuni·sta *mf* (-sti -ste) fellow traveler

crisàlide *f* chrysalis

crisantèmo *m* chrysanthemum

cri·si *f* (-si) crisis; shortage (*of houses*); attack (*e.g., of fever*); outburst (*of tears*); (econ) slump; **crisi ancillare** or **domestica** servant problem; **in crisi** in difficulties

cristallerìa *f* glassware; crystal service; glassware shop; glassworks

cristallièra *f* china closet

cristalli·no -na *adj* crystalline ‖ *m* crystalline lens

cristallizzare [ddzz] *tr* & *ref* to crystallize

cristallo *m* crystal; glass; pane (*of glass*); windshield; **cristallo di rocca** rock crystal; **cristallo di sicurezza** (aut) safety glass

cristianaménte *adv* in a Christian manner, like a Christian; (coll) decently; **morire cristianamente** to die in the faith

cristianésimo *m* Christianity

cristianità *f* Christendom

cristia·no -na *adj* & *mf* Christian

Cristo *m* Christ; **avanti Cristo** before Christ (B.C.); **dopo Cristo** after Christ (A.D.); **un povero cristo** (slang) a poor guy

critè·rio *m* (-ri) criterion; judgment

crìti·ca *f* (-che) criticism; critique; slur

criticare §197 (crìtico) *tr* to criticize, censure; to find fault with

crìti·co -ca (-ci -che) *adj* critical ‖ *mf* critic; (coll) faultfinder ‖ *f* see **critica**

crittografìa *f* cryptography

crittogram·ma *m* (-mi) cryptogram

crivellare (crivèllo) *tr* to riddle

crivèllo *m* sieve, riddle

croa·to -ta *adj* & *mf* Croatian

Croàzia, la Croatia

croccante *adj* crisp, crunchy ‖ *m* almond brittle, peanut brittle

crocchétta *f* croquette

cròcchia *f* chignon, topknot

crocchiare §287 (cròcchio) *intr* to crackle; to sound cracked or broken; to cluck (*said of a hen*); to crack (*said of joints*)

cròc·chio *m* (-chi) group (*of people*); **far crocchio** to gather around

cróce *f* cross; **x** (*mark made by illiterate person*); tail (*of coin*); (fig) trial; **Croce del Sud** Southern Cross; **croce di Malta** Maltese cross; **Croce Rossa** Red Cross; **croce uncinata** swastika; **fare una croce sopra** to forget about; **gettare la croce addosso** (fig) to put the blame on; **mettere in croce** to crucify

crocefisso *m* crucifix

crocerossina *f* Red Cross worker

croceségno *m* cross, **x** (*mark made instead of signature*)

crocétta *f* (naut) crosstree

croce·vìa *m* (-vìa) crossroads, intersection

crocia·to -ta *adj* crossed; crusading; see **parola** ‖ *m* crusader ‖ *f* crusade

crocièra *f* cruise; (archit) cross (*vault*); (mach) cross (*of universal joint*)

crocière *m* (orn) crossbill

crocifìggere §104 *tr* to crucify

crocifissióne *f* crucifixion

crocifìs·so -sa *adj* crucified ‖ *m* crucifix

crò·co *m* (-chi) crocus

crogiolare (crògiolo) *tr* to cook on a low fire; to simmer; to temper (*glass*) ‖ *ref* to bask; to snuggle (*e.g., in bed*)

crògiolo *m* cooking on a low fire; simmering; tempering (*of glass*)

crogiòlo *m* crucible; (fig) melting pot

crollare (cròllo) *tr* to shake (*e.g., one's head*) ‖ *intr* (ESSERE) to fall down, collapse ‖ *ref* to shake cròllo *m* shake; fall, collapse

cròma *f* (mus) quaver

cromare (cròmo) *tr* to plate with chromium

croma•to -ta *adj* chromium-plated; chrome || *m* chrome yellow

cromatura *f* chromium plating

cròmo *m* chrome, chromium

cromosfèra *f* chromosphere

cromosò•ma [s] *m* (-mi) chromosome

cròna•ca *f* (-che) chronicle; report, news; **cronaca bianca** news of the day; **cronaca giudiziaria** court news; **cronaca mondana** social column; **cronaca nera** police and accident report; **cronaca rosa** wedding column; stork news

cròni•co -ca (-ci -che) *adj* chronic || *mf* incurable

croni•sta *mf* (-sti -ste) reporter; chronicler

cronistòria *f* chronicle

cronologìa *f* chronology

cronològi•co -ca *adj* (-ci -che) chronologic(al)

cronometrare (cronòmetro) *tr* to time

cronomètri•co -ca *adj* (-ci -che) chronometric(al); split-second

cronometri•sta *m* (-sti) (sports) timekeeper

cronòmetro *m* stopwatch; chronometer

crosciare §128 (cròscio) *tr* (archaic) to heave, throw || *intr* to rustle (*said of dry leaves*); to pitter-patter (*said of rain*)

cròsta *f* crust; bark (*of tree*); scab; slough; shell (*of crustacean*); poor painting

crostàceo *m* crustacean

crostata *f* pie

crostino *m* toast

crostó•so -sa [s] *adj* crusty

croupier *m* (croupier) croupier

crucciare §128 *tr* to worry, vex; to chagrin || *ref* to worry; to become angry

cruccia•to -ta *adj* afflicted; worried; angry; chagrined

cruc•cio *m* (-ci) sorrow; (obs) anger; **darsi cruccio** to fret

cruciale *adj* crucial

crucivèr•ba *m* (-ba) crossword puzzle

crudèle *adj* cruel

crudel•tà *f* (-tà) cruelty

crudézza *f* crudity; harshness

cru•do -da *adj* raw; rare (*meat*); (poet) cruel

cruèn•to -ta *adj* (lit) bloody

crumiro *m* scab (*in strikes*)

cruna *f* eye (*of a needle*)

cru•sca *f* (-sche) bran; (coll) freckles

cruscante *adj* Della-Cruscan; affected || *m* member of the Accademia della Crusca

cruschèllo *m* middlings

cruscòtto *m* (aut) dashboard; (aer) instrument panel

cuba•no -na *adj* & *mf* Cuban

cubatura *f* volume

cùbi•co -ca *adj* (-ci -che) cubic; cube (*root*)

cubitale *adj* very large (*handwriting or type*)

cùbito *m* cubit; (poet) elbow

cubo *m* cube

cuccagna *f* plenty; windfall; Cockaigne

cuccétta *f* berth

cucchiàia *f* large spoon; ladle; trowel; bucket (*of power shovel*); **cucchiaia bucata** skimmer

cucchiaiàta *f* spoonful; tablespoonful

cucchiaino *m* teaspoon; teaspoonful; spoon (*lure*)

cuc•chiàio *m* (-chiài) spoon; spoonful; tablespoon; **cucchiaio da minestra** soupspoon

cucchiaióne *m* ladle

cùc•cia *f* (-ce) dog's bed; **a cuccia!** lie down!

cucciare §128 *intr* (ESSERE) & *ref* to lie down (*said of a dog*)

cucciolata *f* litter (*e.g., of puppies*)

cùcciolo *m* puppy; cub; (fig) greenhorn

cuc•co *m* (-chi) cuckoo; simpleton; darling (*child*)

cuccuru•cù *m* (-cù) cock-a-doodle-doo

cucina *f* kitchen; cuisine; kitchen range; **cucina componibile** kitchen with sectional cabinets; **cucina economica** kitchen range; **fare da cucina** to prepare a meal

cucinare *tr* to cook; (fig) to fix

cucinétta *f* kitchenette

cuciniè•re -ra *mf* cook

cucire §143 *tr* to sew; to stitch || *ref*—**cucirsi la bocca** to keep one's mouth shut

cucirino *m* sewing thread

cuci•tóre -trice *adj* sewing || *mf* sewing machine operator || *f* seamstress; sewing machine (*for bookbinding*); **cucitrice a grappe** stapler

cuci•to -ta *adj* sewn || *m* sewing; needle work

cucitura *f* seam; sewing; stitches

cu•cù *m* (-cù) cuckoo

cuculo or cùculo *m* cuckoo

cùffia *f* bonnet (*for baby*); coif; (rad) headset; (telp) headpiece; (theat) prompter's box

cugi•no -na *mf* cousin

cui *pron* *invar* whose; to which; whom; which; of whom; of which; **per cui** (coll) therefore

culatta *f* breech (*of a gun*)

culinà•rio -ria (-ri -rie) *adj* culinary || *f* gastronomy

culla *f* cradle

cullare *tr* to rock (*a baby*); (fig) to delude || *ref* to have delusions

culminante *adj* highest; culminating

culminare (cùlmino) *intr* to culminate

cùlmine *m* top, summit

culo *m* (vulg) behind; (slang) bottom (*of glass or bottle*): **culi di bicchiere** (coll) fake diamonds

cul•to -ta *adj* cultivated; learned (*e.g., word*) || *m* cult, worship

cul•tóre -trice *mf* devotee

cultura *f* culture; **cultura fisica** physical culture

culturale *adj* cultural

cumino *m* (bot) caraway seed; (bot) cumin

cumulati•vo -va *adj* cumulative

cùmulo *m* heap, pile; concurrence (*of penal sentences*); cumulus

cuna *f* cradle

cùneo *m* wedge; chock; (archit) voussoir

cunétta *f* ditch; gutter

cunìcolo *m* small tunnel; burrow

cuòcere §144a *tr* to cook; to bake (*bricks*); to burn, dry up; (fig) to stew || *intr* to cook; to burn; to dry up; (with *dat*) to grieve, to pain

cuò·co -ca *mf* (-chi -che) cook

cuòio *m* (cuòi) leather; **avere il cuoio duro** to have a tough hide; **cuoio capelluto** scalp || *m* (cuoia *fpl*) (archaic) leather; **tirare le cuoia** (slang) to croak, to kick the bucket

cuòre *m* heart; **avere il cuore da coniglio** to be chicken-hearted; **avere il cuore da leone** to be lion-hearted; **cuorì** (cards) hearts; **di cuore** gladly; heartily; **fare cuore a** to encourage; **stare a cuore** to be important

cupidìgia *f* cupidity, greed, covetousness

Cupido *m* Cupid

cùpi·do -da *adj* greedy, covetous

cu·po -pa *adj* dark; deep (*color, voice*); sad, gloomy

cùpola *f* dome, cupola; crown (*of hat*)

cura *f* care; interest; cure; ministry; (poet) anxiety; **a cura di** edited by (*e.g., text*)

curare *tr* to take care of; to heed || *intr* to see to it || *ref* to take care of oneself; to care; to deign; **curarsi di** to care for

curatèla *f* (law) guardianship

curati·vo -va *adj* curative

cura·to -ta *adj* cured; healed || *m* curate

cura·tóre -trice *mf* curator; trustee; editor (*of critical edition*); receiver (*in bankruptcy*)

curculióne *m* (ent) weevil

cur·do -da *adj* & *mf* Kurd

cùria *f* curia; bar

curiale *adj* curia; legal

curialé·sco -sca *adj* (-schi -sche) hairsplitting, legalistic

curiosare [s] (curióso) *intr* to pry around, snoop; to browse around

curiosi·tà [s] *f* (-tà) curiosity; whim; curio

curió·so -sa [s] *adj* curious; bizarre, quaint

curro *m* roller

cursóre *m* process server; court messenger; slide (*of slide ruler*)

curva *f* curve, bend; sweep; **curva di livello** contour line

curvare *tr* to curve, bend; **curvare la fronte** to bow down, yield || *intr* to curve (*said of a road*); to take a curve, negotiate a curve || *ref* to curve, bend; to bow; to become bent; to warp

curvatura *f* curving, bending; warp; stoop, curvature; camber

cur·vo -va *adj* bent, curved || *f* see **curva**

cuscinétto *m* small pillow; pad (*for ink*); buffer (*zone*); (mach) bearing; **cuscinetto a rulli** roller bearing; **cuscinetto a sfere** ball bearing

cuscino *m* pillow; cushion

cùspide *f* point (*e.g., of arrow*); (archit) steeple

custòde *adj* guardian (*angel*) || *m* custodian; janitor; warden; guard; (coll) policeman, cop

custòdia *f* safekeeping, custody; case (*e.g., of violin*); trust; (mach) housing

custodire §176 *tr* to keep; to protect, guard; to be in charge of (*prisoners*); to take care of; to cherish (*a memory*)

cutàne·o -a *adj* cutaneous

cute *f* (anat) skin

cuticagna *f* (joc) nape of the neck

cutìcola *f* epidermis; cuticle; dentine

cutireazióne *f* skin test (*for allergic reactions*)

cutréttola *f* (orn) wagtail

D

D, d [di] *m* & *f* fourth letter of the Italian alphabet

da *prep* from; to; at; on; through; between; since; with; by, e.g., **è stato arrestato dalla polizia** he was arrested by the police; worth, e.g., **un libro da mille lire** a book worth a thousand lire; worthy of, e.g., **azione da gentiluomo** action worthy of a gentleman; at the house, office, shop, etc., of, e.g., **dal pittore** at the house of the painter; **da Giovanni** at John's; **dall'avvocato** at the lawyer's office; **d'altro lato** on the other hand; **d'ora in poi** from now on

dabbasso *adv* downstairs; down below

dabbenàggine *f* simplicity, foolishness

dabbène *adj invar* honest, upright, e.g., **un uomo dabbene** an honest man;

simple, foolish, e.g., **un dabben uomo** a Simple Simon

daccanto *adv* near, nearby

daccapo *adv* again, all over again; **andar daccapo** to begin a new paragraph; **daccapo a piedi** from top to bottom

dacché *conj* since

dado *m* cube; pedestal (*of column*); (mach) nut; (mach) die (*to cut threads*); **dadi** dice; **giocare ai dadi** to shoot craps; **il dado è tratto** the die is cast

daffare *m* things to do; bustle; **darsi daffare** to bustle, bustle about

da·ga *f* (-ghe) dagger

dagli §4 || *interj*—**dagli al ladro!** stop thief!; **e dagli!** cut it out!

dài §4

dài·no -na *mf* fallow deer ‖ *m* fallow deer; buckskin

dal §4

dàlia *f* dahlia

dalla §4

dallato *adv* aside; sideways

dalle §4

dalli *interj*—dalli al ladro! stop thief!; e dalli! cut it out!

dallo §4

dàlma·ta *adj & mf* (-ti -te) Dalmatian

Dalmàzia, la Dalmatia

daltòni·co -ca *adj* (-ci -che) color-blind

daltonismo *m* color blindness

dama *f* lady; dancing partner; checkers; andare a dama (checkers) to be crowned; dama di compagnia companion; dama di corte lady-in-waiting

damare *tr* (checkers) to crown

damascare §197 *tr* to damask

damaschinare *tr* to damascene

dama·sco *m* (-schi) damask ‖ Damasco *f* Damascus

damerino *m* fop, dandy

damigèlla *f* (lit) damsel; (orn) demoiselle; damigella d'onore bridesmaid

damigiana *f* demijohn

danaro *m* var of denaro

danaró·so -sa [s] *adj* wealthy, rich

dande *fpl* leading strings

danése [s] *adj* Danish ‖ *mf* Dane ‖ *m* Danish (*language*); Great Dane

Danimarca, la Denmark

dannare *tr* to damn; to bedevil ‖ *ref* to be damned; to fret

danna·to -ta *adj* damned; wicked; terrible (*e.g., fear*) ‖ *m* damned soul

dannazióne *f* damnation

danneggiare §290 (dannéggio) *tr* to damage; to injure, impair

danneggia·to -ta *adj* damaged; injured, impaired ‖ *mf* victim

danno *m* damage; injury; (ins) loss; chiedere i danni to ask for indemnification; far danni a to damage; rifare i danni a to indemnify; tuo danno so much the worse for you

dannó·so -sa [s] *adj* damaging, harmful

dante *m*—pelle di dante buckskin

danté·sco -sca *adj* (-schi -sche) Dantean, Dantesque

danti·sta *mf* (-sti -ste) Dante scholar

Danùbio *m* Danube

danza *f* dance; dancing

danzare *tr & intr* to dance

danza·tóre -trice *mf* dancer

dappertutto *adv* everywhere

dappiè *adv*—dappiè di at the foot of

dappiù *adv*—dappiù di more than

dappòco *adj invar* worthless

dappòi *adv* (obs) afterwards, after

dapprèsso *adv* near, nearby, close

dapprima *adv* first, in the first place

dapprincìpio *adv* first, in the beginning; over again

dardeggiare §290 (dardéggio) *tr* to hurl darts at; to beat down on; to look daggers at ‖ *intr* to hurl darts; to beat down

dardo *m* dart, arrow; tip (*of blowtorch*)

da·re *m* (-re) (com) debit; dare e avere

debit and credit ‖ §144b *tr* to give; to set (*fire*); to hand over; to lay down (*one's life*); to render (*e.g., unto Caesar*); to give away (*a bride*); to take (*an examination*); to tender (*one's resignation*); to say (*good night*); to shed (*tears*); dare acqua a to water; dare alla luce to give birth to; to bring out (*e.g., a book*); dare aria a to air; dare . . . anni a qlcu to think that s.o. is . . . years old; dare a ridire to give rise to complaint; dare da intendere to lead to believe; dare fastidio a to bother, annoy; dare fondo a to use up; dare gli otto giorni a to dismiss, fire; dare il benvenuto a to welcome; dare il via a to start (*e.g., a race*); dare la colpa a to declare guilty; to put the blame on; dare la mano a to shake hands with; dare l'assalto a to assault; dare luogo a to give rise to; dare noia a to bother; dare per certo a to assure; dare ragione a to agree with; dare torto a to disagree with; dare via to give away ‖ *intr* to burst; to begin; to beat down (*said of the sun*); dare a to verge on; to face, overlook; dare addosso a to attack, persecute; dare ai or sui nervi di to irritate, irk; dare alla testa a to go to one's head, e.g., il vino gli dà alla testa wine goes to his head; dare contro a to disagree with; dare del ladro a to call (s.o.) a thief; dare del Lei a to address formally; dare del tu a to address familiarly; dare di volta il cervello a to go raving mad, e.g., gli ha dato di volta il cervello he went raving mad; dare giù to abate; dare in to hit; dare in affitto to rent, lease; dare nell'occhio to attract attention; to hit the eye; dare nel segno to hit the target ‖ *ref* to put on, e.g., darsi la cipria to put powder on; darsela a gambe to take to one's heels; darsela per intesa to become convinced; to take for granted; darsele to strike one another; darsi a to give oneself over to; darsi delle arie to put on airs; darsi il vanto di to boast of; darsi un bacio to kiss one another; darsi la mano to shake hands; darsi la morte to commit suicide; darsi pace to resign oneself; darsi pensiero to worry; darsi per malato to declare oneself ill; to fall ill; darsi per vinto to give in, submit; può darsi it's possible, maybe; si dà il caso it happens

dàrsena *f* dock; basin

data *f* date; deal (*of cards*); a . . . data (com) . . . days hence, on or before . . . days; di fresca data new (*e.g., friend*); di vecchia data old (*e.g., friend*)

datare *tr* to date ‖ *intr*—a datare da beginning with

datà·rio *m* (-ri) date stamp

dati·vo -va *adj & m* dative

da·to -ta *adj* inclined, bent; addicted; given; appointed (*date*); dato e non concesso assumed for the sake of argument; **dato che** since || *m* datum || *f* see **data**

da·tóre -trice *mf* giver, donor; **datore di lavoro** employer; **datore di sangue** blood donor; **datori di lavoro** management

dàttero *m* date; (zool) date shell

dattilografare (dattilògrafo) *tr* to typewrite, type

dattilografìa *f* typewriting

dattilògra·fo -fa *mf* typist

dattiloscopìa *f* examination of fingerprints

dattiloscrit·to -ta *adj* typewritten || *m* typescript

dattórno *adv* near, nearby; **darsi dattorno** to strive; **stare dattorno a** to cling to; **togliersi dattorno qlcu** to get rid of s.o.

davanti *adj invar* fore, front || **davan·ti** *m* (-**ti**) front, face || *adv* ahead, in front; **davanti a** in front of; **levarsi davanti a qlcu** to get out of someone's way; **passare davanti a** to pass, outstrip

davanzale *m* window sill

davanzo *adv* more than enough

davvéro *adv* indeed; **dire davvero** to speak in earnest

daziare §287 *tr* to levy a duty on

dà·zio *m* (-**zi**) duty, custom; custom office

dèa *f* goddess

debellare (debèllo) *tr* (lit) to crush

debilitare (debìlito) *tr* to debilitate

debilitazióne *f* debilitation

débi·to -ta *adj* due || *m* debit; debt; **debito pubblico** national debt

debi·tóre -trice *mf* debtor

débole *adj* weak; faint; gentle (*sex*); **debole di mente** feeble-minded || *m* weakness, weak point; weakness, foible; weakling

debolézza *f* weakness, debility

debordare (debórdo) *intr* (ESSERE & AVERE) to overflow

debòscia *f* debauchery

deboscia·to -ta *adj* debauched || *mf* debauchee

debuttante *adj* beginning || *mf* beginner || *f* debutante

debuttare *intr* to come out, make one's debut; (theat) to perform for the first time; (theat) to open

debutto *m* debut; (theat) opening night, opening

dècade *f* ten; period of ten days; (mil) ten days' pay

decadente *adj* & *m* decadent

decadènza *f* decadence; lapse (*of insurance policy*); (law) forfeiture

decadére §121 *intr* (ESSERE) to decline; to lose one's standing; (ins) to lapse; **decadere da** (law) to forfeit

decadiménto *m* decadence; (law) forfeiture

decadu·to -ta *adj* fallen upon hard times

decaffeinizzare [ddzz] *tr* to decaffeinate

decalcificatóre *m* water softener

decalcomanìa *f* decalcomania

decàlo·go *m* (-**ghi**) decalogue

decampare *intr* to decamp; **decampare da** to abandon (*a plan*)

decano *m* dean

decantare *tr* to praise, extol; to decant; (lit) to purify || *intr* to undergo decantation

decapàggio *m* (metallurgy) pickling

decapitare (decàpito) *tr* to behead, decapitate

decapitazióne *f* beheading

decappottàbile *adj* & *f* (aut) convertible

decèdere §123 *intr* (ESSERE) to die; to decease

decelerare (decèlero) *tr* & *intr* to decelerate

decennale *adj* & *m* decennial

decènne *adj* & *mf* ten-year-old

decèn·nio *m* (-**ni**) decade

decènte *adj* decent; proper

decentralizzare [ddzz] *tr* to decentralize

decentrare (decèntro) *tr* to decentralize

decènza *f* decency; propriety

decèsso *m* decease, demise

decìdere §145 *tr* to decide; to persuade || *intr* & *ref* to decide; **deciditi!** make up your mind!

decifràbile *adj* decipherable

decifrare *tr* to decipher, decode; (fig) to puzzle out (*e.g., somebody's intentions*); (mus) to sight-read

dècima *f* tithe

decimale *adj* & *m* decimal

decimare (dècimo) *tr* to decimate

decìmetro *m* decimeter; **doppio decimetro** ruler

dèci·mo -ma *adj, m* & *pron* tenth || *f* see **decima**

decisionale *adj* decision-making

decisióne *f* decision

decisi·vo -va *adj* decisive, conclusive

deci·so -sa *adj* determined, resolute; appointed (*time*)

declamare *tr* to declaim || *intr* to declaim; to inveigh

declamazióne *f* declamation

declaratò·rio -ria *adj* (-**ri -rie**) declarative

declinare *tr* to decline; to declare, show; (gram) to decline; (lit) to bend || *intr* to set (*said, e.g., of a star*); to slope; to diminish

declinazióne *f* declination; (gram) declension

declino *m* decline

declì·vio *m* (-**vi**) declivity, slope

decollàg·gio *m* (-**gi**) take-off; lift-off

decollare (decòllo) *tr* to decapitate || *intr* (aer) to take off; (rok) to lift off

decòllo *m* take-off; lift-off

decolorante *adj* bleaching || *m* bleach

decompórre §218 *tr, intr* & *ref* to decompose

decomposizióne *f* decomposition

decompressióne *f* decompression

decongelare (decongèlo) *tr* to thaw; (com) to unfreeze

decontaminare (decontàmino) *tr* to decontaminate

decorare (decòro) *tr* to decorate

decorati·vo -va *adj* decorative

decora·tóre -trice *mf* decorator

decorazióne _f_ decoration

decòro _m_ decorum, propriety; decor; dignity; decoration

decoró•so -sa [s] _adj_ fitting, decorous, proper; dignified

decorrènza _f_ beginning, effective date; lapse

decórrere §139 _intr_ (ESSERE) to elapse; to begin; (lit) to run; **a decorrere da** effective, beginning with

decór•so -sa _adj_ past || _m_ period, span; course; development; **nel decorso di** in the course of

decòt•to -ta _adj_ (com) insolvent || _m_ decoction

decozióne _f_ (com) insolvency

decrèpi•to -ta _adj_ decrepit

decréscere §142 _intr_ (ESSERE) to decrease

decretare (**decréto**) _tr_ to decree

decréto _m_ decree; **decreto legge** decree law

decùbito _m_ recumbency

decuplicare §197 (**decùplico**) _tr_ to multiply tenfold

dècu•plo -pla _adj_ tenfold || _m_ tenfold part

decurtare _tr_ to diminish, decrease

decurtazióne _f_ decrease

dèda•lo -la _adj_ (lit) ingenious || _m_ maze, labyrinth

dèdi•ca _f_ (-che) dedication; inscription (_in a book_)

dedicare §197 (**dèdico**) _tr_ to dedicate; to inscribe (_a book_) || _ref_ to devote oneself

dèdi•to -ta _adj_ devoted; addicted

dedizióne _f_ devotion; (obs) surrender

dedurre §102 _tr_ to deduce; to deduct; to derive; (hist) to found (_a colony_)

deduzióne _f_ deduction

defalcàbile _adj_ deductible

defalcare §197 _tr_ to deduct, withhold

defal•co _m_ (-chi) deduction, withholding

defecare §197 (**defèco**) _tr_ (chem) to purify || _intr_ to defecate

defenestrare (**defenèstro**) _tr_ to throw out of the window; (fig) to fire; (pol) to unseat

defenestrazióne _f_ defenestration; (fig) firing, dismissal

deferènte _adj_ deferential; (anat) deferent

deferènza _f_ deference

deferire §176 _tr_ to submit; (law) to commit; **deferire il giuramento a qlcu** to put s.o. under oath || _intr_ to defer

defezionare (**defezióno**) _intr_ to desert, defect

defezióne _f_ defection

deficiènte _adj_ deficient, lacking || _mf_ idiot

deficiènza _f_ deficiency; idiocy

dèfi•cit _m_ (-cit) deficit

deficità•rio -ria _adj_ (-ri -rie) lacking; deficit (_e.g., budget_)

defilare _tr_ to defilade || _ref_ to protect oneself

denfinìbile _adj_ definable

definire §176 _tr_ to define; to settle (_an argument_)

definiti•vo -va _adj_ definitive; **in definitiva** after all

defini•to -ta _adj_ definite

definizióne _f_ definition; settlement (_of an argument_)

deflagrare _intr_ to burst into flame; (fig) to burst out

deflazionare (**deflazióno**) _tr_ (com) to deflate

deflazióne _f_ deflation

deflèttere §177 _intr_ to deflect

deflettóre _m_ (aut) vent window; (mach) baffle

deflorare (**deflòro**) _tr_ to deflower

defluire §176 _intr_ (ESSERE) to flow down; (fig) to pour out

deflusso _m_ flow; outflow, outpour; ebbtide

deformare (**defórmo**) _tr_ to deform; to cripple; to alter (_a word_)

defórme _adj_ deformed, crippled

deformi•tà _f_ (-tà) deformity

defraudare (**defràudo**) _tr_ to defraud, bilk

defun•to -ta _adj_ dead; deceased; defunct; late || _mf_ dead person, deceased || _m_ deceased; **i defunti** the deceased

degenerare (**degènero**) _intr_ (ESSERE & AVERE) to degenerate; to worsen

degenera•to -ta _adj_ degenerate, perverted || _mf_ degenerate, pervert

degenerazióne _f_ degeneracy, degeneration

degènere _adj_ degenerate

degènte _adj_ bedridden; hospitalized || _mf_ patient; inpatient

degènza _f_ confinement; hospitalization

dégli §4

deglutire §176 _tr_ to swallow

degnare (**dégno**) _tr_ to honor || _ref_ to deign, condescend

degnazióne _f_ condescension

dé•gno -gna _adj_ worthy; **degno di nota** noteworthy

degradante _adj_ degrading

degradare _tr_ to degrade; to downgrade; (mil) to break || _ref_ to become degraded

degradazióne _f_ degradation

degustare _tr_ to taste

degustazióne _f_ tasting

dèh _interj_ oh!

déi §4

deiezióne _f_ excrement; (geol) detritus

deificare §197 (**deìfico**) _tr_ to deify

dei•tà _f_ (-tà) deity

dél §4

dela•tóre -trice _mf_ informer

delazióne _f_ informing; (law) administration of an oath

dèle•ga _f_ (-ghe) proxy, power of attorney

delegare §209 (**dèlego**) _tr_ to delegate

delega•to -ta _adj_ delegated || _m_ delegate; (eccl) legate

delegazióne _f_ delegation

deletè•rio -ria _adj_ (-ri -rie) deleterious

delfino _m_ dolphin; (hist) dauphin

delibare _tr_ to relish; to touch on; to ratify (_a foreign decree_)

delibazióne *f* ratification (*of a foreign decree*)
deliberare (delìbero) *tr* to deliberate; to decide; to award (*at auction*) || *intr* to deliberate
delibera•to -ta *adj* deliberate; resolved
deliberazióne *f* deliberation; decision
delicatézza *f* delicacy; gentleness; tactfulness; luxury
delica•to -ta *adj* delicate; gentle; tactful
delimitare (delìmito) *tr* to delimit
delineare (delìneo) *tr* to outline, sketch || *ref* to take shape; to appear
delinquènte *m* criminal
delinquènza *f* delinquency; **delinquenza minorile** juvenile delinquency
delìnquere §146 *intr* to commit a crime
delì•quio *m* (**-qui**) fainting spell, swoon; **cadere in deliquio** to faint
delirare *intr* to be delirious; to rave; (lit) to stray
delì•rio *m* (**-ri**) delirium; frenzy; **andare in delirio** to go wild; **cadere in delirio** to become delirious
delitto *m* crime
delittuó•so -sa [s] *adj* criminal
delìzia *f* delight; (hort) Delicious (*variety of apple*)
deliziare §287 *tr & ref* to delight
delizió•so -sa [s] *adj* delicious; delightful
délla §4
délle §4
déllo §4
dèl•ta *m* (**-ta**) delta
delucidare (delùcido) *tr* to elucidate; to remove the sheen from
delucidazióne *f* elucidation; removal of sheen
delùdere §105 *tr* to disappoint; to deceive; to foil
delusióne *f* disappointment; deception
delu•so -sa *adj* disappointed; deceived
demagnetizzare [ddzz] *tr* to demagnetize
demagogìa *f* demagogy
demagò•go *m* (**-ghi**) demagogue
demandare *tr* (law) to commit
demà•nio *m* (**-ni**) state land, state property
demarcare §197 *tr* to demarcate
demarcazióne *f* demarcation
demènte *adj* demented, crazy; idiotic || *mf* insane person; idiot
demènza *f* insanity, madness; idiocy
demèrito *m* demerit
demilitarizzare [ddzz] *tr* to demilitarize
democràti•co -ca (**-ci -che**) *adj* democratic || *mf* democrat
democrazia *f* democracy || **Democrazia Cristiana** Christian Democratic Party
democristia•no -na *adj* Christian Democratic || *mf* Christian Democrat
demogràfi•co -ca *adj* (**-ci -che**) demographic
demolire §176 *tr* to demolish
demoli•tóre -trice *adj* wrecking; destructive || *mf* wrecker
demolizióne *f* demolition
dèmone *m* demon
demonìa•co -ca *adj* (**-ci -che**) fiendish; demoniacal

demò•nio *m* (**-ni**) demon; **avere il demonio addosso** to be full of the devil
demoralizzare [ddzz] *tr* to demoralize || *ref* to become demoralized
demoralizza•to -ta [ddzz] *adj* demoralized, dejected
denaro *m* money; denier (*of nylon thread*); **avere il denaro contato** to be short of money; **denari** suit of Neapolitan cards corresponding to diamonds
denatura•to -ta *adj* denatured
denegare §209 (**dènego** or **denégo**) *tr* to deny
denigrare *tr* to denigrate; to backbite
denominare (denòmino) *tr* to call, designate
denomina•tóre -trice *adj* designating || *m* denominator
denominazióne *f* denomination; designation
denotare (denòto) *tr* to denote
densi•tà *f* (**-tà**) density
dèn•so -sa *adj* dense, thick
dentale *adj & f* dental
dentare (dènto) *tr* to notch, scallop || *intr* to teethe
dentaruòlo *m* teething ring
denta•to -ta *adj* toothed
dentatura *f* set of teeth; teeth (*of gear*)
dènte *m* tooth; peak (*of mountain*); pang (*of jealousy*); fluke (*of anchor*); prong (*of fork*); **battere i denti** to shiver; **dente canino** canine tooth; **dente del giudizio** wisdom tooth; **dente di latte** baby tooth; **dente di leone** (bot) dandelion; **mettere i denti** to teethe
dentellare (dentèllo) *tr* to notch, scallop; to perforate (*stamps*)
dentellatura *f* notch; perforation (*of postage stamps*); (archit) denticulation
dentèllo *m* notch, scallop; lace; (archit) dentil
dentièra *f* denture, plate; cog
dentifrì•cio -cia (**-ci -cie**) *adj* tooth || *m* dentifrice
denti•sta *mf* (**-sti -ste**) dentist
dentizióne *f* teething
déntro *adv* inside, in; **dentro di** inside of; within; **essere dentro** (coll) to be behind bars; **in dentro** inward || *prep* inside of
denuclearizzare [ddzz] *tr* to denuclearize
denudare *tr* to denude; to strip; (lit) to unveil
denunciare §128 *tr* var of **denunziare**
denùnzia *f* denunciation; announcement; report
denunziare §287 *tr* to denounce; to accuse; to announce; to report
denutri•to -ta *adj* undernourished
denutrizióne *f* undernourishment
deodorante *adj & m* deodorant
deodorare (deodóro) *tr* to deodorize
depauperare (depàupero) *tr* to impoverish
depennare (depénno) *tr* to strike out, expunge
deperìbile *adj* perishable

deperiménto m deterioration; decline
deperire §176 intr (ESSERE) to deteriorate; to perish; to decay
depilatò·rio -ria adj & m (-ri -rie) depilatory
deplorare (deplòro) tr to deplore; to reproach
deplorévole adj deplorable; reproachable
depolarizzare [ddzz] tr to depolarize
depórre §218 tr to lay; to lay down (crown, arms); to depose (e.g., a king); to take off (clothes); to give up (hope); to renounce; **deporre l'abito talare** to doff the cassock
deportare (depòrto) tr to deport
deporta·to -ta adj deported || mf deportee
deportazióne f deportation
depositare (depòsito) tr to deposit; to register, check || intr to settle (said, e.g., of sand)
deposità·rio -ria (-ri -rie) adj deposit || mf depositary
depòsito m deposit; checking (e.g., of a suitcase); registration; heap (e.g., of refuse); warehouse; morgue; receiving ward; (mil) depot; **deposito bagagli** baggage room
deposizióne f deposition; Descent from the Cross
deprava·to -ta adj depraved
depravazióne f depravation
deprecare §197 (deprèco) tr to deprecate
depredare (deprèdo) tr to plunder
depredazióne f depredation
depressióne f depression
deprès·so -sa adj depressed
deprezzaménto m depreciation
deprezzare (deprèzzo) tr to depreciate; to underestimate || intr (ESSERE) to depreciate
deprimènte adj depressing
deprìmere §131 tr to humble, discourage; to depress
depurare tr to purify
deputare (dèputo) tr to deputize, delegate
deputa·to -ta mf deputy, delegate; representative
deputazióne f deputation, delegation
deragliaménto m derailment
deragliare §280 intr to be derailed, to run off the track
derapàg·gio m (-gi) skidding
derapare intr to skid
derelit·to -ta adj & mf derelict
derelizióne f dereliction
dereta·no -na adj & m posterior
derìdere §231 tr to deride, mock
derisióne f derision, ridicule
derisò·rio -ria adj (-ri -rie) derisory, derisive
deriva f (aer) vertical stabilizer; (aer, naut) leeway; (naut) drift; **alla deriva** adrift
derivare tr to derive; to branch off (e.g., a canal) || intr (ESSERE) to be derived, arise; to drift
deriva·to -ta adj derivative || m derivative (word) || f (math) derivative

derivazióne f derivation; (elec) shunt; (telp) extension
dermatòlo·go m (-gi) dermatologist
dermòide f imitation leather
dèro·ga f (-ghe) exception; **in deroga a** deviating from
derogare §209 (dèrogo) intr to transgress; **derogare a** to deviate from
derrata f foodstuff; **derrate** foodstuff, produce
derubare tr to rob
dèr·vis m (-vis) or **dervì·scio** m (-sci) dervish
desalazióne [s] f desalinization
desalificare [s] §197 (desalìfico) tr to desalt
dé·sco m (-schi) dinner table; meal
descritti·vo -va adj descriptive
descrìvere §250 tr to describe
descrizióne f description
desegregazióne [s] f desegregation
desensibilizzare [s] [ddzz] tr to desensitize
desèrti·co -ca adj (-ci -che) desert, wild
desèr·to -ta adj deserted; **andare deserto** to be unattended || m desert
desideràbile [s] adj desirable
desiderare (desìdero) [s] tr to desire; **farsi desiderare** to make oneself scarce; to be dilatory
desidè·rio [s] m (-ri) desire; craving; lust; **lasciar desiderio di sé** to be greatly missed
desideró·so -sa [s] adj desirous
designare [s] tr to designate
designazióne [s] f designation
desinare m dinner || intr to dine
desinènza f (gram) ending
desì·o m (-i) (lit) desire
desìstere [s] §114 intr to desist
desolante adj distressing
desolare (dèsolo) tr to distress; (lit) to devastate
desola·to -ta adj desolate; distressed
desolazióne f desolation; distress
dèspo·ta m (-ti) despot
despòti·co -ca adj (-ci -che) var of dispotico
despotismo m var of dispotismo
des·sèrt m (-sèrt) dessert
destare (désto) tr to awaken; to stir up || ref to wake up
destinare tr to destine; to assign; to address
destinatà·rio -ria mf (-ri -rie) consignee; addressee
destinazióne f destination; assignment
destino m destiny; (com) destination
destituire §176 tr to demote; to dismiss; to deprive
destituzióne f demotion; dismissal
dé·sto -sta adj awake; (fig) wide-awake
dèstra f right, right hand
destreggiare §290 (destréggio) intr to maneuver || ref to manage shrewdly
destrézza f skill, dexterity
destrière or **destrièro** m (lit) steed
dè·stro -stra adj right; skillful || f see destra
destròr·so -sa adj clockwise; right-hand; (bot) dextrorse
destròsio m dextrose

desùmere [s] §116 *tr* to obtain; to infer
detecti‧ve *m* (-ve) detective
detèc‧tor *m* (-tor) (rad) detector
detenére §271 *tr* to hold; to detain
deten‧tóre ‧**trice** *mf* holder; receiver (*of stolen goods*)
detenu‧to ‧**ta** *mf* prisoner
detenzióne *f* illegal possession; detention
detergènte *adj* & *m* detergent
detèrgere §164 (*pp* **detèrso**) *tr* to cleanse; to wipe
deterioràbile *adj* perishable
deteriorare (**deterióro**) *tr* to spoil ‖ *intr* (ESSERE) & *ref* to deteriorate, spoil
determinare (**detèrmino**) *tr* to determine; to fix; to decide; to cause ‖ *ref* to decide; to happen
determinatézza *f* determination; precision
determinati‧vo ‧**va** *adj* (gram) definite
determina‧to ‧**ta** *adj* given; resolved, determined
determinazióne *f* determination
deterrènte *adj* & *m* deterrent
detersi‧vo ‧**va** *adj* cleansing ‖ *m* cleanser; detergent
detestàbile *adj* detestable
detestare (**detèsto**) *tr* to detest
detettóre *m* detector; **detettore di bugie** lie detector
detonare (**detòno**) *intr* to explode, detonate
detonatóre *m* blasting cap, detonator
detonazióne *f* detonation; report
detrarre §273 *tr* to take away; (lit) to detract
detrat‧tóre ‧**trice** *mf* detractor
detrazióne *f* detraction; deduction
detriménto *m* detriment
detrito *m* debris; detritus; (fig) outcast, outlaw
detronizzare [ddzz] *tr* to dethrone
détta *f*—**a detta di** according to
dettagliante *m* retailer
dettagliare §280 *tr* to tell in detail; to itemize; to retail ‖ *intr*—**pregasi dettagliare** please send detailed information
dettà‧glio *m* (-gli) detail; retail
dettame *m* (lit) law, norm
dettare (**détto**) *tr* to dictate; (lit) to compose, write; **dettar legge** to impose one's will
dettato *m* dictation; (lit) style
dettatura *f* dictation
dét‧to ‧**ta** *adj* called, named; **detto** (**e**) **fatto** no sooner said than done ‖ *m* saying ‖ *f* see **detta**
deturpare *tr* to disfigure, mar
deturpazióne *f* disfigurement, disfiguration
devalutazióne *f* devaluation
devastare *tr* to devastate, lay waste; (fig) to disfigure
devasta‧tóre ‧**trice** *adj* devastating ‖ *m* devastator
devastazióne *f* devastation
deviaménto *m* switching; derailment; (fig) straying
deviare §119 *tr* to turn aside; to lead astray; (rr) to switch; (rr) to derail

‖ *intr* to deviate; to wander; to go astray; (rr) to run off the track
deviatóre *m* (rr) switchman; (elec) two-way switch
deviazióne *f* deviation; detour; curvature (*of the spine*); (phys) declination; (phys) deflection; (rr) switching
deviazionismo *m* deviationism
deviazioni‧sta *mf* (-sti -ste) deviationist
devoluzióne *f* transfer
devòlvere §147 *tr* to transfer ‖ *intr* & *ref* (lit) to roll down
devò‧to ‧**ta** *adj* devoted; devout, pious ‖ *m* devout person; worshiper
devozióne *f* devotion
di §4 *prep* of; in, e.g., **la più bella della famiglia** the prettiest one in the family; (*with definite article*) some, e.g., **mi occorrono dei fiammiferi** I need some matches; than, e.g., **più veloce del baleno** faster than lightning; from, e.g., **è di Milano** he is from Milan; off, e.g., **smontare di sella** to get off the saddle; about, e.g., **discutere di politica** to talk about politics; with, e.g., **ornare di fiori** to adorn with flowers; made of, e.g., **una casa di mattoni** a house made of bricks; by, e.g., **di notte** by night; for, e.g., **amor di patria** love for one's country; worth, e.g., **casa di dieci milioni** house worth ten million; in the amount of, e.g., **multa di mille lire** fine in the amount of one thousand lire; son of, e.g., **Carlo Giovannini di Filippo** Carlo Giovannini son of Philip; daughter of, e.g., **Anna Ponti di Antonio** Anna Ponti daughter of Anthony; **di corsa** running; **di gran lunga** greatly; by far; **di . . .** **in** from . . . to; **di là da** beyond; **di nascosto** stealthily; **di qua da** on this side of; **di quando in quando** from time to time; **di tre metri** three meters long or wide or high
dì *m* (**dì**) day; **a dì** (e.g., **ventisei**) this (e.g., twenty-sixth) day; **conciare per il dì delle feste** (coll) to beat up
diabète *m* diabetes
diabèti‧co ‧**ca** *adj* & *mf* (-ci -che) diabetic
diabòli‧co ‧**ca** *adj* (-ci -che) diabolic(al)
diàcono *m* deacon
diadè‧ma *m* (-mi) diadem (*of king*); tiara (*of lady*)
diàfa‧no ‧**na** *adj* diaphanous
diafonìa *f* (telp) cross talk
diafram‧ma *m* (-mi) diaphragm; (fig) partition
diàgno‧si *f* (-si) diagnosis
diagnosticare §197 (**diagnòstico**) *tr* to diagnose
diagonale *adj* & *f* diagonal
diagram‧ma *m* (-mi) diagram; chart
diagrammare *tr* to diagram
dialettale *adj* dialectal
dialètti‧co ‧**ca** (-ci -che) *adj* dialectic(al) ‖ *m* dialectician ‖ *f* dialectic; (philos) dialectics
dialètto *m* dialect
dialettòfo‧no ‧**na** *adj* dialect-speaking ‖ *m* dialect-speaking person

dialogare §209 (diàlogo) *intr* to carry on a dialogue

dialoga·to -ta *adj* written in the form of a dialogue || *m* dialogue

diàlo·go *m* (-ghi) dialogue

diamante *m* diamond; **diamante taglia-vetro** glass cutter

diametrale *adj* diametric(al)

diàmetro *m* diameter

diàmine *interj* good heavens!; the devil!; sure!

diana *f* (mil) reveille || **Diana** *f* Diana

dianzi *adv* (lit) a short while ago

diàpa·son *m* (-son) (mus) pitch; (mus) tuning fork

diapositiva *f* (phot) slide, transparency

dià·rio -ria (-ri -rie) *adj* daily || *m* diary; journal; **diario scolastico** homework book || *f* per diem

diarrèa *f* diarrhea

diascò·pio *m* (-pi) slide projector

diaspro *m* jasper

diàstole *f* diastole

diatermìa *f* diathermy

diatriba *f* diatribe

diavolàc·cio *m* (-ci) devil; **buon dia-volaccio** good fellow

diavolerìa *f* deviltry; devilment; evil plot

diavolè·rio *m* (-ri) hubbub, uproar

diavoléto *m* hubbub, uproar

diavolétto *m* little devil, imp

diàvolo *m* devil; **avere il diavolo in corpo** to be nervous; **avere un dia-volo per capello** to be in a horrible mood; **buon diavolo** good fellow; **essere come il diavolo e l'acqua santa** to be at opposite poles; **fare il dia-volo a quattro** to make a racket; to try very hard

dibàttere *tr* to debate || *ref* to struggle; to writhe

dibattiménto *m* debate; (law) pleading, trial

dibàttito *m* debate

dicastèro *m* department, ministry

dicèmbre *m* December

dicerìa *f* rumor, gossip

dichiarare *tr* to declare, state; to find (*guilty*); to proclaim; to nominate, name || *ref* to declare oneself to be; to declare one's love; to plead (*e.g., guilty*)

dichiarazióne *f* declaration; avowal (*of love*); return (*of income tax*); **dichia-razioni** representations

diciannòve *adj & pron* nineteen; **le diciannove** seven P.M. || *m* nineteen; nineteenth (*in dates*)

diciannovèsi·mo -ma *adj, m & pron* nineteenth

diciassètte *adj & pron* seventeen; **le diciassette** five P.M. || *m* seventeen; seventeenth (*in dates*)

diciassettèsi·mo -ma *adj, m & pron* seventeenth

diciottèsi·mo -ma *adj, m & pron* eighteenth

diciòtto *adj & pron* eighteen; **le diciotto** six P.M. || *m* eighteen; eighteenth (*in dates*)

dici·tóre -trice *mf* reciter

dicitura *f* caption, legend; (lit) word-ing, language

dicotomìa *f* dichotomy

didascalìa *f* note, notice; caption; legend (*e.g., on coin*); (mov) sub-title

didascàli·co -ca *adj* (-ci -che) didactic

didàtti·co -ca (-ci -che) *adj* didactic; elementary school (*director, princi-pal*) || *f* didactics

didéntro *m* (coll) inside

didiètro *m* behind; back (*of house*) || *adv* behind

dièci *adj & pron* ten; **le dieci** ten o'clock || *m* ten; tenth (*in dates*)

diecimila *adj, m & pron* ten thousand

diecina *f* about ten

dière·si *f* (-si) dieresis

diè·sis *m* (-sis) (mus) sharp

dièta *f* diet; **dieta idrica** fluid diet

dietèti·co -ca (-ci -che) *adj* dietetic || *f* dietetics

dieti·sta *mf* (-sti -ste) dietitian

diètro *adj invar* back, rear || *m* back, rear || *adv* back, behind; **dal di dietro** from behind; **di dietro** hind (*legs*); back (*side*); behind, back (*e.g., of cupboard*) || *prep* behind; beyond; after; upon; **dietro a** behind; beyond; after; according to; **dietro consegna** on delivery; **dietro domanda** upon application; **dietro versamento** upon payment; **essere dietro a** to be in the process of

dietrofrónt *m* (mil) about face

difatti *adv* indeed

difèndere §148 *tr* to defend, protect || *ref* to protect oneself; (coll) to get along

difensi·vo -va *adj & f* defensive

difen·sóre -sóra or **difenditrice** *adj* de-fense || *mf* defender

difésa [s] *f* defense; bulwark; protec-tion; **legittima difesa** self-defense; **pigliare le difese di** to defend, back up; **venire in difesa di** to go to the defense of

difettare (difètto) *intr* to be lacking; to be defective; **difettare di** to lack

difetti·vo -va *adj* defective

difètto *m* lack; blemish; fault; defect; **essere in difetto** to be at fault; **far difetto a** to lack, e.g., **gli fa difetto il denaro** he lacks money

difettó·so -sa [s] *adj* defective

diffamare *tr* to defame, slander

diffama·tóre -trice *mf* defamer, slan-derer

diffamazióne *f* defamation, slander

differènte *adj* different

differènza *f* difference; spread; vari-ance; **a differenza di** unlike; **c'è una bella differenza** it's a horse of an-other color

differenziale *adj & m* differential

differenziare §287 (differènzio) *tr* to differentiate

differiménto *m* deferment

differire §176 *tr* to postpone, defer || *intr* to be different; to differ

difficile *adj* hard, difficult; awkward (*situation*); hard-to-please; unlikely

‖ *mf* hard-to-please person ‖ *m—* **fare il difficile** to be hard to please; **qui sta il difficile!** here's the trouble!

difficol·tà *f* (**-tà**) difficulty; defect; obstacle; objection

difficoltó·so **-sa** [s] *adj* difficult, troublesome; fastidious

diffida *f* notice; warning

diffidare *tr* to give notice to; to warn ‖ *intr* to mistrust

diffidènte *adj* distrustful

diffidènza *f* mistrust

diffóndere §178 *tr* to spread; to circulate; to broadcast ‖ *ref* to spread; to dwell at length

diffórme *adj* unlike; (obs) deformed

diffrazióne *f* diffraction

diffusióne *f* spreading; circulation (*of a newspaper*); diffusion; (rad) broadcast

diffu·so **-sa** *adj* diffuse; widespread

diffusóre *m* diffuser (*to soften light*); baffle (*of loudspeaker*); (mach) choke

difilato *adv* forthwith, right away

difrónte *adj invar* in front

difterite *f* diphtheria

di·ga *f* (**-ghe**) dike; dam

digerènte *adj* alimentary (*canal*), digestive (*tube*)

digeríbile *adj* digestible

digerire §176 *tr* to digest; to tolerate, stand

digestióne *f* digestion

digesti·vo **-va** *adj* digestive

digèsto *m* digest

digitale *adj* digital ‖ *f* (bot) digitalis

digitalina *f* (pharm) digitalin

digiunare *intr* to fast

digiu·no **-na** *adj* without food; deprived; **digiuno di cognizioni** ignorant; **tenere digiuno** to keep in ignorance ‖ *m* fast; **a digiuno** on an empty stomach; **fare digiuno** to fast

digni·tà *f* (**-tà**) dignity; **dignità** *fpl* dignitaries

dignità·rio *m* (**-ri**) dignitary

dignitó·so **-sa** [s] *adj* dignified

digradare *tr* to shade (*colors*) ‖ *intr* to slope; to fade

digredire §176 *intr* to digress

digressióne *f* digression

digrignare *tr* to show (*one's or its teeth*); to grit (*one's teeth*)

digrossare (**digròsso**) *tr* to rough-hew; to whittle down; (fig) to refine ‖ *ref* to become refined

diguazzare *tr* to beat (*a liquid*) ‖ *intr* to wallow; to splash

dilagare §209 *intr* to flood, to overflow; to spread abroad

dilaniare §287 *tr* to tear to pieces ‖ *ref* to slander one another

dilapidare (**dilàpido**) *tr* to squander

dilatare *tr* to expand; to dilate ‖ *ref* to expand; to spread

dilatazióne *f* expansion; dilation

dilatò·rio **-ria** *adj* (**-ri** **-rie**) delaying; dilatory

dilavare *tr* to wash away, erode

dilava·to **-ta** *adj* dull, flat; wan

dilazionare (**dilazióno**) *tr* to delay, put off; (com) to extend

dilazióne *f* delay; (com) extension

dileggiare §290 (**diléggio**) *tr* to mock

dilég·gio *m* (**-gi**) mockery, scoffing; **mettere in dileggio** to scoff at

dileguare (**diléguo**) *tr* to scatter ‖ *intr* (ESSERE) to disappear, vanish; to melt

dilèm·ma *m* (**-mi**) dilemma

dilettante *mf* amateur; dilettante

dilettanté·sco **-sca** *adj* (**-schi** **-sche**) amateurish

dilettare (**dilètto**) *tr* to delight ‖ *ref* to delight; **dilettarsi a** + *inf* to delight in + *ger*; **dilettarsi di** to pursue as a hobby, e.g., **si diletta di pittura** he pursues painting as a hobby

dilettévole *adj* delectable, delightful

dilèt·to **-ta** *adj* beloved ‖ *m* loved one; pleasure; hobby

diligènte *adj* diligent

diligènza *f* diligence; stagecoach

dilucidare (**dilùcido**) *tr* to elucidate

diluire §176 *tr* to dilute

dilungare §209 *tr* (archaic) to stretch ‖ *ref* to expatiate; to be ahead by several lengths (*said of a race horse*)

dilungo *m*—**a un dilungo** more or less

diluviare §287 *tr* to devour ‖ *intr* (ESSERE & AVERE) to rain (*said, e.g., of bullets*) ‖ *impers* (ESSERE)—**diluvia** it is pouring

dilù·vio *m* (**-vi**) deluge, flood; **diluvio universale** Flood

dimagrante *adj* reducing

dimagrare *tr* to thin down ‖ *intr* (ESSERE) to become thin; to lose weight; to become exhausted (*said of land*); (fig) to become meager

dimagrire §176 *intr* (ESSERE) to become thin; to lose weight, reduce

dimanda *f* var of **domanda**

dimane *adv* (coll) tomorrow

dimani *m & adv* var of **domani**

dimenare (**diméno**) *tr* to wag (*the tail*); to beat (*eggs*); to wave (*one's arms*); to stir up (*a question*) ‖ *ref* to toss; to busy oneself

dimensióne *f* dimension; (fig) nature

dimenticanza *f* oversight, neglect; **andare in dimenticanza** to be forgotten

dimenticare §197 (**diméntico**) *tr* to forget; to forgive ‖ *ref* to forget; **dimenticarsi di** to forget; to neglect

dimenticatóio *m*—**mettere nel dimenticatoio** (coll) to forget

diménti·co **-ca** *adj* (**-chi** **-che**) forgetful; neglectful

dimés·so **-sa** *adj* humble, modest (*demeanor*); low (*voice*); shabby (*clothes*)

dimestichèzza *f* familiarity

diméttere §198 *tr* to dismiss; to release ‖ *ref* to resign

dimezzare [ddzz] (**dimèzzo**) *tr* to halve

diminuire §176 *tr* to lessen, reduce; to lower (*prices*) ‖ *intr* (ESSERE) to diminish

diminuti·vo **-va** *adj & m* diminutive

diminuzióne *f* diminution

dimissionare (**dimissióno**) *tr* to dismiss, discharge ‖ *ref* to resign

dimissionà·rio **-ria** *adj* (**-ri** **-rie**) resigning, outgoing

dimissióne *f* resignation; **dare le dimis-**
~~si ... to .esign~~
dimól·to -ta *adj* & *m* (coll) much ||
dimolto *adv* (coll) much
dimòra *f* stay; residence; (lit) delay;
mettere a dimora to install; to plant
(*trees*); **senza dimora** (lit) without
delay; **senza fissa dimora** vagrant
dimorare (dimòro) *intr* to stay; to reside; (lit) to delay
dimostràbile *adj* demonstrable
dimostrante *m* demonstrator
dimostrare (dimóstro) *tr* to demonstrate; to register (*e.g., anger*); **dimo-**
strare trent'anni to look thirty || *intr*
to demonstrate || *ref* to prove oneself
to be
dimostrati·vo -va *adj* demonstrative;
(mil) diverting
dimostra·tóre -trice *mf* demonstrator
dimostrazióne *f* demonstration
dinàmi·co -ca (-ci -che) *adj* dynamic ||
f dynamics
dinamismo *m* dynamism
dinamite *f* dynamite
dìna·mo *f* (-mo) generator, dynamo
dinanzi *adj invar* front, e.g., **la porta**
dinanzi the front door; preceding,
e.g., **il mese dinanzi** the preceding
month || *adv* ahead; beforehand; (lit)
before; **dinanzi a** before, in front of
dìna·sta *m* (-sti) dynast
dinastìa *f* dynasty
dinàsti·co -ca *adj* (-ci -che) dynastic
dindo *m* (coll) turkey
dindòn *m* ding-dong || *interj* ding-dong!
diniè·go *m* (-ghi) denial
dinoccola·to -ta *adj* gangling; clumsy
(*gait*)
dinosàuro [s] *m* dinosaur
dintórno *m*—**dintorni** surroundings,
neighborhood || *adv* around; **dintorno**
a around
dì·o -a *adj* (-i -e) (poet) godly || *m*
(dèi) god; **gli dei** the gods || **Dio** *m*
God; **che Dio la manda** cats and
dogs (*said of rain*); **come Dio volle**
at long last; **come Dio vuole** botched
(*piece of work*); **Dio ci scampi!** God
forbid!; **Dio santo!** good heavens!;
grazie a Dio God willing; thank God;
voglia Dio God grant
dìòce·si *f* (-si) diocese
dìodo *m* (electron) diode
diomedèa *f* (orn) albatross
diottrìa *f* (opt) diopter
dipanare *tr* to unravel, unwind
dipartiménto *m* department
dipartire §176 *tr* (archaic) to divide ||
intr (diparto) (ESSERE) & *ref* (lit) to
depart
dipartita *f* (lit) departure; (lit) demise
dipendènte *adj* dependent || *mf* em-
ployee
dipendènza *f* dependence; employment;
annex; (com) branch; **in dipendenza**
di as a consequence of
dipèndere §150 *intr* (ESSERE) to depend;
dipendere da to depend on
dipìngere §126 *tr* to paint; **dipingere a**
olio to paint in oils; **dipingere a tem-**
pera to distemper || *ref* to paint one-

self; to put make-up on; to appear,
e.g., **gli si dipinse in volto la paura**
fear appeared on his face
dipin·to -ta *adj* painted || *m* painting,
picture
diplò·ma *m* (-mi) diploma, certificate
diplomare (diplòmo) *tr* to grant a
degree to; to graduate || *ref* to receive
a degree; to graduate
diplomàti·co -ca (-ci -che) *adj* diplo-
matic; true, faithful (*copy*) || *m*
diplomat || *f* diplomatics
diploma·to -ta *adj* graduated || *mf*
graduate || *m* alumnus || *f* alumna
diplomazìa *f* diplomacy
dipòi *adv* after, thereafter
diportare (dipòrto) *ref* (lit) to behave;
(obs) to have a good time
dipòrto *m* recreation; (obs) sport; **an-**
dare a diporto to go on an outing;
to go for a walk
diprèsso *adv*—**a un dipresso** about, approximately
diradare *tr* to thin out (*vegetation*); to
disperse; to space out (*one's visits*)
|| *intr* (ESSERE) & *ref* to diminish; to
disperse
diramare *tr* to prune; to circulate
(*notices*); to issue (*a communiqué*) ||
ref to branch out; to spread
diramazióne *f* branch; ramification;
issuance
dire *m* talk; **per sentito dire** by hearsay; **stando al dire** according to his
words || §151 *tr* & *intr* to say; to tell;
to call (*e.g., s.o. a genius*); to talk;
detto (e) fatto no sooner said than
done; **dica pure!** go ahead!; speak
up!; **dire bene di** to speak well of;
dire di no to say no; **dire di sì** to say
yes; **direi quasi** I dare say; **dire la**
sua to have one's say; **dire male di**
to speak ill of; **dirla grossa** to make
a blunder; to tell a tall tale; **dirlo**
chiaro e tondo to speak bluntly;
dirne un sacco e una sporta a to
pour insults upon; **è tutto dire** that's
all; **non c'è che dire** it's a fact; **non**
fo per dire I do not want to boast;
per così dire so to speak; **per meglio**
dire rather; **trovarci a dire** to find
fault with; **trovare da dire con** to
have words with; **voler ben dire** to be
sure; **voler dire** to mean || *ref*—**dir-**
sela con to connive with; **si dice** it is
said
dirètro *m* & *adv* (archaic) behind, back
direttìssima *f* (rr) high-speed line; **per**
direttìssima straight up (*in mountain*
climbing)
direttìssimo *m* express train
diretti·vo -va *adj* managerial || *m*
board of directors || *f* directive;
direction; guideline
dirèt·to -ta *adj* direct; **diretto a** ad-
dressed to; directed at; bound for ||
m through train
diret·tóre -trice *mf* manager; principal
|| *m* director; **direttore di macchina**
(naut, nav) chief engineer; **direttore**
di tiro (nav) gunnery officer; **direttore**
di un giornale editor; **direttore d'or-**

chestra orchestra leader; **direttore responsabile** publisher; **direttore tecnico** (sports) manager ‖ *f* see **direttrice**

direttò·rio -ria (-ri -rie) *adj* directorial ‖ *m* directory

direttrice *adj fem* directing; guiding; front (*wheels*) ‖ *f* directress; line of action

direzionale *adj* directional; managerial

direzióne *f* direction; management; run (*of events*)

dirigènte *adj* leading; managerial ‖ *m* employer; boss; leader; executive

dirigere §152 *tr* to direct; to turn; to lead ‖ *ref* to address oneself; **dirigersi verso** to head for

dirigìbile *adj & m* dirigible

dirimpètto *adj invar & adv* opposite; **dirimpetto a** opposite to; in comparison with

dirit·to -ta *adj* straight; right; unswerving; (coll) smart ‖ *m* law; obverse, face (*of coin*); fee, dues; (fin) right; **a buon diritto** rightly so; **di diritto** by law; **diritti d'autore** copyright; **diritti di segreteria** registration fee; **diritti doganali** customs duty; **diritti speciali di prelievo** (econ) special drawing rights; **diritto canonico** canon law; **diritto consuetudinario** common law; **diritto internazionale** international law; **in diritto** according to law ‖ *f* right, right hand ‖ **diritto** *adv* straight; **tirare diritto** to go straight ahead

dirittura *f* direction; uprightness; (sports) straightaway, home stretch

dirizzóne *m* blunder

diroccare §197 (**diròcco**) *tr* to knock down ‖ *intr* (ESSERE) (archaic) to fall down

dirocca·to -ta *adj* dilapidated, rickety

dirompènte *adj* fragmentation (*bomb*)

dirottaménto *m* hijacking; skyjacking (*of an airplane*)

dirottare (**dirótto**) *tr* to detour (*traffic*); to hijack (*e.g., a ship*); to skyjack (*an airplane*) ‖ *intr* to change course

dirottatóre *m* hijacker; skyjacker (*of a plane*)

diròt·to -ta *adj* copious, heavy (*rain, tears*); (lit) craggy; **a dirotto** cats and dogs (*said of rain*)

dirozzare [ddzz] (**dirózzo**) *tr* to roughhew; to refine ‖ *ref* to become polished

dirugginire §176 *tr* to take the rust off; to limber up; to gnash (*one's teeth*); to clear (*one's mind*)

dirupa·to -ta *adj* rocky, craggy

dirupo *m* rock; crag, cliff

disabbigliare §280 *tr & ref* to undress, disrobe

disabita·to -ta *adj* uninhabited

disabituare (**disabìtuo**) *tr* to disaccustom ‖ *ref* to become unaccustomed

disaccenta·to -ta *adj* unaccented

disaccòrdo *m* disagreement

disadat·to -ta *adj* unfit

disadór·no -na *adj* unadorned, bare

disaffezionare (**disaffezióno**) *tr* to alien-ate the affection of; to estrange ‖ *ref* to become estranged

disaffezióne *f* dislike

disagévole *adj* troublesome, uncomfortable

disagiare §290 *tr* to trouble, inconvenience

disagia·to -ta *adj* uncomfortable; needy

disà·gio *m* (**-gi**) discomfort; need

disalberare (**disàlbero**) *tr* to dismast

disambienta·to -ta *adj* bewildered, strange

disàmina *f* examination, scrutiny

disaminare (**disàmino**) *tr* to scrutinize; to weigh

disamorare (**disamóro**) *tr* to alienate the affection of; to estrange ‖ *ref* to become estranged

disancorare (**disàncoro**) *intr* to weigh anchor; to leave port ‖ *ref* to weigh anchor; (fig) to free oneself

disanimare (**disànimo**) *tr* to dishearten

disappetènza *f* loss of appetite

disapprovare (**disappròvo**) *tr* to disapprove

disapprovazióne *f* disapproval

disappunto *m* disappointment

disarcionare (**disarcióno**) *tr* to unsaddle, unhorse; to kick out

disarmare *tr* to disarm; to dismantle (*a scaffold*); to ship (*oars*); (naut) to unrig ‖ *ref* to disarm; (fig) to give up

disarma·to -ta *adj* unarmed, defenseless

disarmo *m* disarmament; dismantling; unrigging

disarmonìa *f* discord; contrast

disarmòni·co -ca *adj* (**-ci -che**) discordant

disarticolare (**disartìcolo**) *tr* to limber up; to disjoint ‖ *ref* to become dislocated

disassociare §128 (**disassòcio**) *tr* to disassociate

disastra·to -ta *adj* damaged ‖ *mf* victim

disastro *m* disaster, calamity; wreck

disastró·so -sa [s] *adj* disastrous

disattèn·to -ta *adj* inattentive; careless

disattenzióne *f* inattention; carelessness

disattivare *tr* to deactivate (*e.g., a mine*)

disavanzo *m* (com) deficit

disavvedu·to -ta *adj* heedless

disavventura *f* misfortune

disavvertènza *f* inadvertence

disavvezzare (**disavvézzo**) *tr* to break (*s.o.*) of a habit ‖ *ref*—**disavvezzarsi da** to give up or lose the habit of

disavvéz·zo -za *adj* unaccustomed

disbórso *m* disbursement, outlay

disboscare §197 (**disbòsco**) *tr* to deforest

disbrigare §209 *tr* to dispatch ‖ *ref* to extricate oneself

disbri·go *m* (**-ghi**) prompt execution, dispatch

discacciare §128 *tr* (lit) to chase away

discanto *m* (mus) harmonizing

discàpito *m* damage; **tornare a discapito di** to be detrimental to

discàri·ca *f* (**-che**) discharge (*e.g., of pollutants*); dumping (*of refuse*); unloading (*of a ship*)

discàri·co *m* (**-chi**) exculpation; **a discàrico di** in defense of

discatóre *m* hockey player; discus thrower

discendènte *adj* descending; sloping; down (*train*) || *mf* descendant

discendènza *f* descent; pedigree

discéndere §245 *tr* to go down || *intr* (ESSERE & AVERE) to descend, go down; to slope; to fall (*said, e.g., of thermometer*); to get off; **discendere in picchiata** (aer) to nose-dive

discènte *mf* student, pupil

discépo·lo -la *mf* disciple

discèrnere §153 *tr* to discern

discernìbile *adj* discernible

discerniménto *m* discernment

discésa [s] *f* descent; slope; drop

discettare (**discètto**) *tr* (lit) to discuss

dischiodare (**dischiòdo**) *tr* to take the nails out of

dischiùdere §125 *tr* to open; to reveal

discin·to -ta *adj* scantily dressed; untidy; in disarray

disciògliere §127 *tr* to dissolve, melt; (lit) to untie || *ref* to dissolve, melt

disciplina *f* discipline; whip, scourge

disciplinare *adj* disciplinary || *m* regulation || *tr* to discipline

disciplina·to -ta *adj* obedient

di·sco *m* (**-schi**) disk; (phonograph) record; bob (*of pendulum*); (ice hockey) puck; (sports) discus; (rr) signal; (pharm) tablet; **disco combinatore** (telp) dial; **disco microsolco** microgroove record; **disco volante** flying saucer

discòfilo *m* record lover

discòide *m* (pharm) tablet, pill

dìsco·lo -la *adj* undisciplined, wild || *m* rogue, rascal

discolorare (**discolóro**) *tr* to discolor || *ref* to pale

discolorazióne *f* discoloration; paleness

discólpa *f* defense

discolpare (**discólpo**) *tr* to defend

disconnèttere §107 *tr* to disconnect

disconóscere §134 *tr* to ignore, to disregard; to be ungrateful for

discontinuare (**discontìnuo**) *tr* to perform sporadically || *intr* to lose continuity

discontì·nuo -nua *adj* uneven

disconvenire §282 *intr* (ESSERE) (lit) to disagree || *impers* (ESSERE) (lit) to be improper

discoprire §110 (**discòpro**) *tr* to discover

discordante *adj* discordant

discordare (**discòrdo**) *intr* (ESSERE) to disagree, differ

discòrde *adj* discordant; opposing

discòrdia *f* discord, dissension

discórrere §139 *intr* to talk, chat; (coll) to keep company; **discorrere del più e del meno** to make small talk; **e via discorrendo** and so forth

discórso *m* discourse; conversation; speech; **pochi discorsi!** (coll) cut it out!

discostare (**discòsto**) *tr* to remove || *ref* to withdraw; to differ

discò·sto -sta *adj* distant || **discosto** *adv* far

discotè·ca *f* (**-che**) record library; discotheque

discreditare (**discrédito**) *tr* to discredit

discrédito *m* discredit

discrepanza *f* discrepancy

discretaménte *adv* rather; fairly well

discré·to -ta *adj* discreet; fairly large; fair

discrezióne *f* discretion

discriminante *adj* discriminatory; extenuating || *m* (math) discriminant

discriminare (**discrìmino**) *tr* to discriminate; to extenuate

discriminazióne *f* discrimination

discussióne *f* discussion; argument

discus·so -sa *adj* controversial

discùtere §154 *tr* to discuss || *intr* to discuss; to argue

discutìbile *adj* moot, debatable

disdegnare (**disdégno**) *tr* to disdain, scorn || *ref* (obs) to be angry

disdégno *m* disdain, scorn

disdegnó·so -sa [s] *adj* disdainful

disdétta *f* ill luck; (law) notice

disdicévole *adj* unbecoming, unseemly

disdire §151 *tr* to retract; to belie; to cancel; to countermand; to terminate the contract of || *ref* to retract; **disdire a** to be unbecoming to

disdòro *m* shame; **tornare a disdoro di** to bring shame on

disegnare [s] (**diségno**) *tr* to draw; to sketch; to design; (obs) to elect

disegna·tóre -trice [s] *mf* cartoonist; designer || *m* draftsman

diségno [s] *m* drawing; sketch; outline; plan; design; **disegno animato** (mov) cartoon; **disegno di legge** (law) bill

disellare [s] (**disèllo**) *tr* var of **dissellare**

diserbante *adj* weed-killing || *m* weed-killer

diseredare (**diserèdo**) *tr* to disinherit

diseredà·to -ta *adj* disinherited || **i diseredati** the underprivileged

disertare (**disèrto**) *tr* to desert; (lit) to lay waste || *intr* to desert

disertóre *m* deserter

diserzióne *f* desertion

disfaciménto *m* disintegration

disfare §173 *tr* to undo; to defeat; to melt; to unknit; to break up (*housekeeping*); **disfare il letto** to remove the bedclothes || *ref* to spoil (*said, e.g., of meat*); **disfarsi di** to get rid of

disfatta *f* defeat

disfattismo *m* defeatism

disfatti·sta *mf* (**-sti -ste**) defeatist

disfat·to -ta *adj* undone; defeated; melted; broken up; ravaged || *f* see **disfatta**

disfida *f* (lit) challenge

disfunzióne *f* malfunction

disgelare (**disgèlo**) *tr* & *intr* to thaw

disgèlo *m* thaw

disgiùngere §183 *tr* & *ref* to separate

disgiunti·vo -va *adj* disjunctive

disgràzia *f* disfavor; bad luck, misfortune; accident; **per disgrazia** unfortunately

disgrazia·to -ta *adj* unlucky; wretched
disgregaménto *m* disintegration
disgregare §209 (disgrègo) *tr* & *ref* to disintegrate
disgregazióne *f* disintegration
disguido *m* miscarriage, missending (*of a letter*)
disgustare *tr* to disgust, sicken ‖ *ref* to become disgusted, sicken; to have a falling-out, to part company
disgusto *m* disgust, repugnance
disgustó·so -sa [s] *adj* disgusting
disidratare *tr* to dehydrate
disìlla·bo -ba *adj* disyllabic ‖ *m* disyllable
disillùdere §105 *tr* to delude, deceive ‖ *ref* to become disillusioned
disillusióne *f* disillusion
disimboscare §197 (disimbòsco) *tr* to put back in circulation
disimparare *tr* to unlearn, forget
disimpegnare (disimpégno) *tr* to release; to free, to open; to loosen; to redeem (*a pledge*); to clear; to perform ‖ *ref* to succeed
disimpégno *m* release; redemption; performance; disengagement; **di disimpegno** for every day (*e.g., a suit*); main (*e.g., hallway*)
disimpiè·go *m* (-ghi) unemployment; (mil) withdrawal
disincagliare §280 *tr* to set afloat; (fig) to disentangle
disincantare *tr* disenchant
disinfestare (disinfèsto) *tr* to exterminate
disinfestazióne *f* extermination
disinfettante *adj* & *m* disinfectant
disinfettare (disinfètto) *tr* to disinfect
disingannare *tr* to disillusion ‖ *ref* to become disillusioned
disinganno *m* disillusion
disinnescare §197 (disinnésco) *tr* to defuse
disinnestare (disinnèsto) *tr* to disconnect; to throw out, disengage
disinserire §176 *tr* (elec) to disconnect; (aut) to disengage
disintasare [s] *tr* to unclog
disintegrare (disìntegro) *tr* & *ref* to disintegrate
disintegrazióne *f* disintegration
disinteressare (disinterèsso) *tr* to make (*s.o.*) lose interest ‖ *ref* to lose interest; to take no interest
disinteressa·to -ta *adj* selfless, unselfish
disinterèsse *m* disinterest; unselfishness
disintossicare §197 (disintòssico) *tr* to free of poison; (fig) to clean the air in ‖ *ref* to shake the drug habit
disinvòl·to -ta *adj* free and easy; fresh, forward
disinvoltura *f* naturalness, ease of manners, offhandedness; freshness; impudence
disì·o *m* (-i) (poet) desire
disistima *f* scorn, low regard, disesteem
disistimare *tr* to scorn, hold in low regard
dislivèllo *m* difference of level; disparity
dislocaménto *m* transfer of troops; (naut) displacement

dislocare §197 (dislòco) *tr* to transfer (*troops*); to post (*sentries*); (naut) to displace
dislocazióne *f* (mil) transfer; (geog, naut, psychol) displacement
dismisura *f* excess; **a dismisura** excessively
disobbedire §176 *intr* var of **disubbidire**
disobbligare §209 (disòbbligo) *tr* to free from an obligation ‖ *ref* to repay a favor
disoccupa·to -ta *adj* unemployed, jobless; idle; unoccupied ‖ *m* unemployed person; **i disoccupati** the jobless
disoccupazióne *f* unemployment
disone·stà *f* (-stà) dishonesty; shamelessness
disonè·sto -sta *adj* dishonest; shameless; immoral
disonorante *adj* disgraceful
disonorare (disonóro) *tr* to dishonor, disgrace; to seduce
disonóre *m* dishonor, shame
disonorévole *adj* dishonorable; shameful
disoppilare (disòppilo) *tr* to clear of obstructions
disópra *adj invar* upper ‖ *m* (disópra) upper part, top; **prendere il disopra** to have the upper hand ‖ *adv* above; **al disopra di** above
disordinare (disórdino) *tr* to cancel, countermand; to confuse; to mess up ‖ *intr* to indulge ‖ *ref* to become disorganized
disordina·to -ta *adj* confused; messy; untidy; intemperate
disórdine *m* confusion; mess; disarray; disorder; intemperance
disorganizzare [ddzz] *tr* to disorganize; to disrupt
disorganizzazióne [ddzz] *f* disorganization, disorder; disruption
disorientaménto *m* disorientation; confusion, bewilderment
disorientare (disoriènto) *tr* to cause (*s.o.*) to lose his way; to confuse; to disorient ‖ *ref* to be bewildered; to lose one's bearings
disorienta·to -ta *adj* disoriented; confused, bewildered; lost, astray
disormeggiare §290 (disorméggio) *tr* to unmoor
disossare (disòsso) *tr* to bone ‖ *ref* (lit) to lose weight
disótto [s] *adj invar* below ‖ *m* (disótto) lower part, bottom ‖ *adv* below; **al disotto di** below, underneath
disotturare *tr* to unclog
dispàc·cio *m* (-ci) dispatch; urgent letter; **dispaccio telegrafico** telegram
dispara·to -ta *adj* disparate
disparére *m* disagreement
dispari *adj invar* odd, uneven
dispari·tà *f* (-tà) disparity
dispàrte *adv*—**in disparte** apart, aside; **starsene in disparte** to keep aloof
dispèn·dio *m* (-di) expenditure; waste
dispendió·so -sa [s] *adj* expensive; wasteful

dispènsa *f* cupboard; pantry; distribution; number (*of magazine*); installment (*of book*); dispensation; (naut) storeroom; (coll) store

dispensare (**dispènso**) *tr* to exempt, free; to distribute || *ref*—**dispensarsi da** to get out of

dispensà·rio *m* (**-ri**) dispensary

dispensa·tóre -trice *mf* dispenser

dispensiè·re -ra *mf* dispenser || *m* steward

dispepsìa *f* dyspepsia

dispèpti·co -ca *adj* & *mf* (**-ci -che**) dyspeptic

disperare (**dispèro**) *intr* to despair; **fare disperare** to drive crazy || *ref* to despair

dispera·to -ta *adj* hopeless || *m* poor wretch; **come un disperato** desperately || *f*—**alla disperata** with all one's might

disperazióne *f* desperation, despair

dispèrdere §212 *tr* to scatter; to waste || *ref* to disperse; (fig) to waste one's energies

dispersióne *f* dispersion; loss; (elec) leakage

dispersività *f* tendency toward disorganization

dispersi·vo -va *adj* dispersive; disorganized

dispèr·so -sa *adj* scattered; lost; dispersed; missing in action

dispersóre *m* (elec) leakage conductor

dispètto *m* spite; (lit) haughtiness; **a dispetto di** in spite of; **far dispetto a** to provoke

dispettó·so -sa [s] *adj* pestiferous; spiteful, resentful

dispiacènte *adj* sorry; distressing

dispiacére *m* sorrow, displeasure || §214 *intr* (ESSERE) to be displeasing; to be sorry, e.g., **mi dispiace** I am sorry; (with *dat*) to displease; (with *dat*) to dislike, e.g., **le mie parole gli dispiacciono** he dislikes my words; **Le dispiace?** would you please?; **se non Le dispiace** if you don't mind

dispiegare §209 (**dispiègo**) *tr* to manifest; (lit) to unfurl || *ref* to spread out; to flow out

displù·vio *m* (**-vi**) divide, watershed; ridge (*of roof*)

disponìbile *adj* available; open-minded

disponibili·tà *f* (**-tà**) availability; inactive status; **disponibilità** *fpl* available funds

dispórre §218 *tr* to dispose; to prepare || *intr* to provide; to dispose; **disporre di** to have (*available*) || *ref* to get ready

dispositivo *m* gadget; device; (mil) deployment

disposizióne *f* arrangement; inclination, disposition; disposal; instruction; (law) provision

dispó·sto -sta *adj* arranged; disposed; provided; willing; **ben disposto** disposed || *m* (law) proviso

dispòti·co -ca *adj* (**-ci -che**) despotic

dispotismo *m* despotism

dispregiati·vo -va *adj* disparaging; (gram) pejorative

disprè·gio *m* (**-gi**) contempt; disrepute

disprezzàbile *adj* contemptible; negligible

disprezzare (**disprèzzo**) *tr* to despise

disprèzzo *m* contempt, scorn

dìsputa *f* dispute; debate

disputàbile *adj* debatable

disputare (**dìsputo**) *tr* to contest; to discuss; to vie for (*victory*) || *intr* to dispute, debate; to vie || *ref* to vie for

disqualificare §197 (**disqualìfico**) *tr* to disqualify

disquisizióne *f* disquisition

dissacrare *tr* to desecrate

dissacrazióne *f* desecration

dissaldare *tr* to unsolder

dissanguare (**dissànguo**) *tr* to bleed || *ref* to bleed; to ruin oneself

dissangua·to -ta *adj* bled white; **morire dissanguato** to bleed to death

dissapóre *m* disagreement

disseccare §197 (**dissécco**) *tr* to dry || *ref* to dry; to dry up

disselciare §128 (**dissélcio**) *tr* to remove the cobblestones from

dissellare (**dissèllo**) *tr* to unsaddle

disseminare (**dissémino**) *tr* to disseminate; to scatter

dissenna·to -ta *adj* foolish, unwise; crazy, mad

dissensióne *f* dissension

dissènso *m* dissent; disagreement

dissenterìa *f* dysentery

dissentire (**dissènto**) *intr* to dissent

dissenziènte *adj* dissenting || *mf* dissenter

disseppellire §176 *tr* to exhume

dissertare (**dissèrto**) *intr* to discourse

dissertazióne *f* dissertation

disservì·zio *m* (**-zi**) poor service

dissestare (**dissèsto**) *tr* to unsettle; to disarrange

dissesta·to -ta *adj* financially embarrassed; mentally deranged

dissèsto *m* financial embarrassment; mental derangement

dissetante *adj* thirst-quenching

dissetare (**dissèto**) *tr* to quench the thirst of || *ref* to quench one's thirst

dissezióne *f* dissection

dissidènte *adj* & *m* dissident

dissidènza *f* dissent

dissì·dio *m* (**-di**) dissent; disagreement

dissigillare *tr* to unseal || *ref* (lit) to melt

dissìmile *adj* unlike

dissimulare (**dissìmulo**) *tr* to dissimulate, disguise || *intr* to dissimulate

dissimulazióne *f* dissimulation

dissipare (**dìssipo**) *tr* to dissipate; to squander; to clear up (*a doubt*) || *ref* to dissipate

dissipa·to -ta *adj* & *mf* profligate

dissipa·tóre -trice *mf* squanderer

dissipazióne *f* dissipation

dissociare §128 (**dissòcio**) *tr* to dissociate, disassociate || *ref* to dissociate or disassociate oneself

dissociazióne *f* dissociation

dissodare (dissòdo) *tr* to cultivate

dissolutézza *f* profligacy

dissolu·to -ta *adj* & *mf* profligate

dissoluzióne *f* dissolution

dissolvènza *f* (mov) fade-out; **dissolvenza incrociata** (mov) lap dissolve

dissòlvere §155 *tr* to dissolve; to clear up (*a doubt*); (obs) to untie || *ref* to dissolve

dissomiglianza *f* dissimilarity

dissonanza *f* dissonance

dissotterrare (dissottèrro) *tr* to exhume; to unearth

dissuadére §213 *tr* to dissuade

dissuè·to -ta *adj* (lit) unaccustomed

dissuggellare (dissuggèllo) *tr* to unseal

distaccaménto *m* (mil) detachment

distaccare §197 *tr* to detach; to remove; to transfer; to outdistance || *ref* to stand out; to withdraw, become separated

distacca·to -ta *adj* detached; branch (*office*)

distac·co *m* (-chi) detachment; separation; (sports) spread (*in points*)

distante *adj* distant; aloof; different || *adv* far away

distanza *f* distance; **mantenere le distanze** to keep one's distance; **tenere a distanza** to keep at arm's length

distanzjare §287 *tr* to outdistance

distare *intr* to be distant

distèndere §270 *tr* to stretch; to spread; to unfurl; to relax; to knock down; to write || *ref* to stretch; to spread out; to relax

distensióne *f* relaxation; relaxation of tension

disté·so -sa [s] *adj* stretched out; full (*voice*); lank (*hair*) || *m*—**per disteso** in full || *f* expanse; row; **a distesa** with full voice; at full peal

distillare *tr* to distill; to exude; to pour; to trickle || *intr* (ESSERE) to trickle || *ref*—**distillarsi il cervello** to rack one's brain

distilla·to -ta *adj* distilled || *m* distillate

distilla·tóre -trice *mf* distiller || *m* still

distillerìa *f* distillery

distinguìbile *adj* distinguishable

distìnguere §156 *tr* to distinguish; to make out; to tell (*one thing from another*); to divide

distinta *f* note, list; **distinta di versamento** deposit slip

distintaménte *adj* distinctly; sincerely yours

distinti·vo -va *adj* distinctive || *m* emblem, insignia, badge

distin·to -ta *adj* distinct; distinguished; sincere (*greetings*); reserved (*seat*); **Distinto Signor . . .** (*on an envelope*) Mr. . . . || *f* see **distinta**

distinzióne *f* distinction

distògliere §127 *tr* to dissuade; to deter; to distract; to turn (*one's eyes*) away

distòrcere §272 *tr* to distort; to twist || *ref* to become distorted; to sprain (*e.g., one's ankle*)

distorsióne *f* distortion; sprain; **distorsione acustica** wow

distrarre §273 *tr* to distract; to divert;

to amuse; to pull (*a muscle*) || *ref* to become distracted; to relax

distrat·to -ta *adj* absent-minded

distrazióne *f* absent-mindedness; distraction; diversion (*of money*); pull (*of muscle*)

distrét·to -ta *adj* (obs) close; (obs) hard-pressed || *m* district; precinct (*e.g., of police*); circuit (*of court*); ward (*in city*); **distretto militare** draft board; **distretto postale** postal zone || *f* stricture; necessity

distrettuale *adj* district

distribuire §176 *tr* to distribute; to pass out; to allot; to deploy (*troops*); (theat) to cast (*roles*); (mov) to release; (mil) to issue (*e.g., clothing*)

distribu·tóre -trice *adj* distributing, dispensing || *mf* distributor, dispenser || *m* distributor; **distributore automatico** vending machine; **distributore di benzina** gasoline pump

distribuzióne *f* distribution; issue; delivery; (aut) timing gears; (mov) release; (fig) dispensation

districare §197 *tr* to unravel || *ref* to extricate oneself

distrofìa *f* dystrophy

distrùggere §266 *tr* to destroy; to ruin

distrutti·vo -va *adj* destructive

distruzióne *f* destruction

disturbare *tr* to disturb, bother; **disturbo?** may I come in? || *ref* to bother; to go out of one's way

disturba·tóre -trice *mf* disturber; **disturbatore della quiete pubblica** disturber of the peace

disturbo *m* trouble, bother; disturbance; (rad) interference; **disturbi atmosferici** static, atmospherics; **togliere il disturbo a** to take leave of

disubbidiènte *adj* disobedient

disubbidiènza *f* disobedience

disubbidire §176 *intr* to disobey; (with *dat*) to disobey

disuguaglianza *f* inequality; disparity

disuguale *adj* uneven; unequal

disuma·no -na *adj* inhumane; unbearable

disunióne *f* disunion

disunire §176 *tr* to disunite

disusa·to -ta *adj* obsolete, out of use

disuso *m* disuse; **in disuso** obsolete

disùtile *adj* useless; burdensome || *m* worthless fellow; (com) loss

disvì·o *m* (-ì) miscarriage, missending (*of a letter*)

ditale *m* thimble; fingerstall

ditata *f* poke with a finger; finger mark; dab (*with a finger*)

dito *m* (dita *fpl*) finger; toe; **avere le dita d'oro** to have a magic touch; **dita della mano** fingers; **dita del piede** toes; **legarsela al dito** to never forget || *m* (diti) finger, e.g., **dito indice** index finger; **dito anulare** ring finger; **dito medio** middle finger; **dito mignolo** little finger; **dito pollice** thumb

ditta *f* firm, house; office

dittàfono *m* intercom; dictaphone

dittatóre *m* dictator

dittatura _f_ dictatorship

dittongare §209 (**dittòngo**) _tr_ to diphthongize

dittòn·go _m_ (**-ghi**) diphthong

diurèti·co -ca _adj_ & _m_ (**-ci -che**) diuretic

diur·no -na _adj_ daily; daytime ‖ _f_ (theat) matinée

diutur·no -na _adj_ long-lasting

diva _f_ diva; (mov) star; (lit) goddess

divagare §209 _tr_ to amuse; to distract ‖ _intr_ to digress ‖ _ref_ to relax

divagazióne _f_ distraction; digression; relaxation

divampare _intr_ (ESSERE & AVERE) to blaze, flare

divano _m_ divan; couch, sofa

divaricare §197 (**divàrico**) _tr_ to spread (one's legs); to open up (an incision)

divà·rio _m_ (**-ri**) difference

divèllere §267 _tr_ to eradicate, uproot

diveni·re _m_ (**-re**) (philos) becoming ‖ §282 _intr_ (ESSERE) (lit) to become; (archaic) to come

diventare (**divènto**) _intr_ (ESSERE) to become; **diventare di tutti i colori** to blush; to be embarrassed; **diventare grande** to grow up; **diventare matto** to go mad; **diventare pallido** to turn pale; **diventare piccolo** to grow smaller; **diventare rosso** to blush

divèr·bio _m_ (**-bi**) argument; **venire a diverbio** to have an altercation

divergènza _f_ divergency

divèrgere §157 _intr_ to diverge

diversificare §197 (**diversìfico**) _tr_ to diversify ‖ _ref_ to be diversified; to differ

diversióne _f_ diversion

diversi·tà _f_ (**-tà**) diversity

diversi·vo -va _adj_ diverting ‖ _m_ diversion

diver·so -sa _adj_ different; **diver·si -se** several, e.g., **diverse ragazze** several girls ‖ **diver·si -se** _pron_ several

divertènte _adj_ diverting, amusing

divertiménto _m_ amusement, pastime; fun; (mus) divertimento

divertire (**divèrto**) _tr_ to amuse, entertain; (lit) to turn aside ‖ _ref_ to have fun, enjoy oneself; (lit) to go away

diverti·to -ta _adj_ amused; amusing

divétta _f_ starlet

divezzare (**divèzzo**) _tr_ to wean ‖ _ref_— **divezzarsi da** to get out of the habit of

dividèndo _m_ dividend

divìdere §158 _tr_ to divide; to partition; to split; to share in (e.g., s.o.'s grief) ‖ _ref_ to be divided; to become separated; **dividersi fra** to divide one's time between

diviéto _m_ prohibition; **divieto d'affissione** post no bills; **divieto di parcheggio** no parking; **divieto di sosta** no stopping; **divieto di svolta** no turns; **divieto di transito** no thoroughfare

divinare _tr_ (lit) to divine

divina·tóre -trice _adj_ divining ‖ _m_ diviner

divinazióne _f_ divination

divincolare (**divìncolo**) _tr_ & _ref_ to wriggle

divini·tà _f_ (**-tà**) divinity

divinizzare [ddzz] _tr_ to deify

divi·no -na _adj_ divine

divisa _f_ uniform; motto; part (in hair); **divise foreign exchange**

divisare _tr_ (lit) to intend

divisìbile _adj_ divisible

divisióne _f_ division; partition; (sports) league

divisionismo _m_ (painting) divisionism; (pol) separatism

divismo _m_ (mov) star system; (mov) adulation of stars

divisóre _m_ (math) divisor

divisò·rio -ria (**-ri -rie**) _adj_ dividing ‖ _m_ partition; (math) divisor

di·vo -va _adj_ (lit) divine ‖ _m_ (theat, mov) star; (lit) god ‖ _f_ see **diva**

divolgare §209 (**divólgo**) _tr_ & _ref_ var of **divulgare**

divorare (**divóro**) _tr_ to devour; to gulp down; to consume; **divorare la via** to burn up the road

divora·tóre -trice _adj_ consuming ‖ _mf_ consumer (e.g., of food, books)

divorziare §287 (**divòrzio**) _intr_ to become divorced; **divorziare da** to divorce

divorzia·to -ta _adj_ divorced ‖ _m_ divorcé ‖ _f_ divorcée

divòr·zio _m_ (**-zi**) divorce

divulgare §209 _tr_ to divulge; to publicize; to popularize ‖ _ref_ to spread; to become popular

divulga·tóre -trice _adj_ popularizing ‖ _mf_ popularizer; **divulgatore di calunnie** scandalmonger; **divulgatore di notizie** telltale

divulgazióne _f_ publicizing; popularization

divulsióne _f_ (surg) dilation

dizionà·rio _m_ (**-ri**) dictionary; **dizionario geografico** gazetteer

dizióne _f_ diction; reading (of poetry)

do [dɔ] _m_ (**do**) (mus) do; (mus) C

dóc·cia _f_ (**-ce**) shower; gutter (on roof); spout; (fig) dash of cold water; **fare la doccia** to take a shower

docciare §128 (**dóccio**) _tr, intr_ (ESSERE) & _ref_ to shower

doccióne _m_ trough, gutter; gargoyle

docènte _adj_ teaching ‖ _m_ teacher; **libero docente** certified university teacher

docènza _f_ teaching post; **libera docenza** lectureship

dòcile _adj_ docile; tame; amenable (person); workable (material)

documentare (**documénto**) _tr_ to document ‖ _ref_ to gather information

documentà·rio -ria _adj_ & _m_ (**-ri -rie**) documentary

documénto _m_ document; paper; **documenti di bordo** ship's papers

dodecafonìa _f_ twelve-tone system

dodecasìlla·bo -ba _adj_ twelve-syllable, dodecasyllable

dodicèsi·mo -ma _adj, m_ & _pron_ twelfth

dódici _adj_ & _pron_ twelve; **le dodici**

twelve o'clock ‖ *m* twelve; twelfth (*in dates*)
dó·ga *f* (-ghe) stave
dogale *adj* (hist) of the doge
dogana *f* duty; customs; custom house
doganière *m* customs officer
dòge *m* (hist) doge
dò·glia *f* (-glie) (lit) pain, pang; **doglie** labor pains
dò·glio *m* (-gli) barrel; (lit) large jar
doglió·so -sa [*s*] *adj* (lit) sorrowful
dòg·ma *m* (-mi) dogma
dogmàti·co -ca (-ci -che) *adj* dogmatic ‖ *mf* dogmatist
dogmatismo *m* dogmatism
dólce *adj* sweet; soft; gentle; fresh (*water*); mild (*climate*); delicate (*feet*); **dolce far niente** sweet idleness ‖ *m* sweet; sweet dish; **dolci** candy
dolceama·ro -ra *adj* bittersweet
dolcézza *f* sweetness; mildness; gentleness
dolcia·stro -stra *adj* sweetish
dolcière *m* candy maker; pastry baker
dolcificare §197 (**dolcìfico**) *tr* to sweeten
dolciume *m* sweet; **dolciumi** candy
dolènte *adj* aching; sorrowful; sorry
dolére §159 *intr* (ESSERE & AVERE) to ache, e.g., **gli dolgono i denti** his teeth ache ‖ *ref* to grieve ‖ *impers* (ESSERE) to be sorry, e.g., **mi duole che Lei non possa venire** I am sorry that you won't be able to come
dolicònice *m* bobolink
dòllaro *m* dollar
dòlo *m* fraud, malice, guile
dolomite *f* dolomite ‖ **Dolomiti** *fpl* Dolomites
dolorante *adj* aching
dolorare (**dolóro**) *intr* (lit) to ache
dolóre *m* ache; sorrow; contrition
doloró·so -sa [*s*] *adj* painful; sorrowful
doló·so -sa [*s*] *adj* intentional, fraudulent; (law) felonious
domàbile *adj* tamable
domanda *f* question; application; appeal; (econ) demand; **domanda suggestiva** (com) leading question; **fare una domanda** to ask a question
domandare *tr* to ask; to ask for; **domandare la parola** to ask for the floor ‖ *intr* to inquire ‖ *ref* to wonder; (lit) to be called
doma·ni *m* (-ni) tomorrow ‖ *adv* tomorrow; **a domani** until tomorrow; **domani a otto** a week from tomorrow; **domani l'altro** the day after tomorrow
domare (**dómo**) *tr* to tame; to extinguish; to quell
doma·tóre -trice *mf* tamer
domattina *adv* tomorrow morning
doméni·ca *f* (-che) Sunday
domenicale *adj* Sunday (*e.g., rest*)
domenica·no -na *adj* & *m* Dominican (*e.g., order*)
domesticare §197 (**domèstico**) *tr* to domesticate
domèsti·co -ca (-ci -che) *adj* family; household; familiar; domestic ‖ *mf* domestic, servant ‖ *f* maid; **alla**

domestica family style; **domestica a mezzo servizio** part-time domestic
domiciliare *adj* house ‖ §287 *tr* (com) to draw ‖ *ref* to dwell; to settle
domicilia·to -ta *adj* residing
domicì·lio *m* (-li) domicile, residence; principal office; **domicilio coatto** imprisonment; **franco domicilio** free delivery
dominare (**dòmino**) *tr* to dominate, rule; to master; to overlook ‖ *intr* to prevail; to reign ‖ *ref* to control oneself
domina·tóre -trice *mf* ruler
dominazióne *f* domination; rule
domineddìo *m invar* (coll) the Lord God
dominica·no -na *adj* & *mf* Dominican (*e.g., Republic*)
domì·nio *m* (-ni) dominion; domain
dòmi·no *m* (-no) domino (*cloak*); dominoes (*game*)
dòn *m* (used only before singular Christian name) don (*Spanish title*); Don (*priest*); uncle (*familiar title of elderly man*)
donare (**dóno**) *tr* to donate; to give as a present ‖ *intr*—**donare a** to be becoming to
dona·tóre -trice *mf* donor; **donatore di sangue** blood donor
donazióne *f* gift, donation
donchisciottè·sco -sca *adj* (-schi -sche) quixotic
dónde *adv* wherefrom, whence
dondolare (**dóndolo**) *tr* to swing, rock ‖ *ref* to swing, rock; to loaf around
dondolì·o *m* (-i) swinging, rocking
dóndolo *m*—**a dondolo** rocking (*chair, horse*); **andare a dondolo** to loaf around
dondoló·ne -na *mf* idler, loafer
dongiovan·ni *m* (-ni) Don Juan
dònna *f* woman; ladyship; (lit) lady; (coll) Mrs.; (coll) maid; (cards) queen; **da donna** woman's, e.g., **scarpe da donna** woman's shoes; **donna cannone** fat lady (*of circus*); **donna di casa** housewife; **Nostra Donna** Our Lady
donnaiòlo *m* ladies' man, philanderer
donné·sco -sca *adj* (-schi -sche) womanly, feminine
dònnola *f* weasel
dóno *m* gift; **in dono** as a gift
donzèlla [*dz*] *f* (lit) damsel
donzèllo [*dz*] *m* (coll) doorman; (lit) page
dópo *adv* afterwards, later; **dopo che** after; **dopo di** after ‖ *prep* after; **dopo** + *pp* after having + *pp*
dopobar·ba *adj invar* after-shaving ‖ *m* (-ba) after-shaving lotion
dopodomani *m* & *adv* the day after tomorrow
dopoguèr·ra *m* (-ra) postwar era
dopolavóro *m* government office designed to organize workers' leisure time
dopopranzo *m* afternoon ‖ *adv* in the afternoon
doppiàg·gio *m* (-gi) (mov) dubbing

doppiare §287 (dóppio) *tr* to double; (mov) to dub

doppière *m* candelabrum

doppiétta *f* double-barreled shotgun; (aut) double shift

doppiézza *f* duplicity

dóp·pio -pia (-pi -pie) *adj* double; coupled; double-dealing || *adv* twice, twofold || *m* double; twice as much; (tennis) doubles; (theat) understudy

doppióne *m* duplicate; (philol) doublet

doppiopèt·to *adj invar* double-breasted || *m* (-to) double-breasted suit

dorare (dòro) *tr* to gild; (culin) to brown; **dorare la pillola** to sugar-coat the pill

dora·to -ta *adj* gilt, golden

doratura *f* gilding

dormicchiare §287 *intr* to doze

dormiènte *adj* sleeping || *mf* sleeper

dormiglió·ne -na *mf* sleepyhead

dormire (dòrmo) *tr* & *intr* to sleep; **dormire a occhi aperti** to be overcome with sleep; **dormire della grossa** to sleep profoundly; **dormire tra due guanciali** to be safe and secure

dormita *f* long sleep; **fare una bella dormita** to have a long sleep

dormitò·rio *m* (-ri) dormitory

dormivé·glia *m* (-glia) drowsiness

dorsale *adj* dorsal; back (*bone*) || *m* head (*of bed*); back (*of chair*) || *f* (geog) ridge

dòrso *m* back; (sports) backstroke

dosàg·gio *m* (-gi) dosage

dosare (dòso) *tr* to dose

dosatura *f* dosage

dòse *f* dose

dòsso *m* back; (lit) summit; **levarsi di dosso** to take off; **mettersi in dosso** to put on

dotare (dòto) *tr* to provide with a dowry; to endow; to bless

dotazióne *f* dowry; endowment; supply

dòte *f* dowry; gift; endowment

dòt·to -ta *adj* learned, erudite || *m* scholar; (anat) duct

dottorale *adj* doctoral

dottó·re -réssa *mf* doctor

dottrina *f* doctrine; Christian doctrine

dóve *m* where; **per ogni dove** everywhere || *adv* where; **da dove** or **di dove** from where; which way; **fin dove** up to what point; **per dove** which way || *conj* where; whereas

dovére *m* duty, obligation; homework; **a dovere** properly; **doveri** regards; **farsi un dovere di** to feel duty-bound to; **mettere qlcu a dovere** to put s.o. in his place; **più del dovere** more than one should; **sentirsi in dovere di** to feel duty-bound to || §160 *tr* & *intr* to owe || *aux* (ESSERE & AVERE) must, e.g., **deve farlo** you must do it; to have to, e.g., **dovei partire** I had to leave; ought to, e.g., **dovrebbe lucidare la macchina** he ought to polish the car; should, e.g., **dovresti immaginarti** you should imagine; to be to, e.g., **il treno doveva arrivare alle sei** the train was to arrive at six; to be supposed to, e.g., **deve aver fatto un lungo viaggio** he is supposed to have taken a long journey

doveró·so -sa [s] *adj* proper, right

dovizia *f* (lit) abundance, wealth

dovunque *adv* wherever, anywhere; everywhere

dovu·to -ta *adj* & *m* due

dozzina [ddzz] *f* dozen; room and board; **da** or **di dozzina** common, ordinary; **tenere a dozzina** to board

dozzinale [ddzz] *adj* common, ordinary

dozzinante [ddzz] *mf* boarder

dra·ga *f* (-ghe) dredge

dragàg·gio *m* (-gi) dredging

dragami·ne *m* (-ne) minesweeper

dragare §209 *tr* to dredge

dràglia *f* (naut) stay

dra·go *m* (-ghi) dragon; **drago volante** kite

dragóna *f* sword strap

dragoncèllo *m* (bot) tarragon

dragóne *m* dragon; dragoon

dram·ma *m* (-mi) drama, play; **dramma musicale** (hist) melodrama || *f* drachma; dram

drammàti·co -ca (-ci -che) *adj* dramatic || *f* drama, dramatic art

drammatizzare [ddzz] *tr* to dramatize

drammatur·go *m* (-ghi) playwright, dramatist

drappég·gio *m* (-gi) drape; pleats

drappeggiare §290 (drappéggio) *tr* to drape || *ref* to be draped

drappèlla *f* pennon (*on bugler's trumpet*)

drappèllo *m* squad, platoon

drapperìa *f* dry goods; dry-goods store

drappo *m* cloth, silk cloth; (billiards) green cloth, baize

dràsti·co -ca *adj* (-ci -che) drastic

drenàg·gio *m* (-gi) drainage

drenare (drèno) *tr* to drain

dressàg·gio *m* (-gi) *m* training (*of animals*)

dribblare *tr* & *intr* (sports) to dribble

drit·to -ta *adj* straight; (lit) correct; **dritto come un fuso** straight as a ramrod || *m* (fig) old fox || *f* right; (naut) starboard

drizza *f* (naut) halyard

drizzare *tr* to straighten; to address; to erect; to cock (*the head*); to direct (*a blow*); **drizzare le gambe ai cani** to do the impossible; **drizzare le orecchie** to prick up one's ears || *intr* (naut) to hoist the halyard || *ref* to stand erect

drò·ga *f* (-ghe) drug; spice; seasoning

drogare §209 (drògo) *tr* to drug; to spice, season

drogherìa *f* grocery (store)

droghière *m* grocer

dromedà·rio *m* (-ri) dromedary

dru·do -da *adj* (archaic) faithful; (lit) strong || *m* (obs) vassal; (lit) lover

drùi·da *m* (-di) druid

drupa *f* (bot) drupe, stone fruit

duale *adj* & *m* dual

dualismo *m* dualism

duali·tà *f* duality

dùb·bio -bia (-bi -bie) *adj* doubtful || *m* doubt; misgiving; **mettere in dub-**

bio to question; to risk; **senza dubbio** no doubt

dubbió·so -sa [s] *adj* dubious; doubtful; (lit) dangerous

dubitare (dùbito) *intr* to doubt; to suspect; **dubitare di** to mistrust; to doubt; **non dubitare!** don't worry!

du·ca *m* (-chi) duke; (lit) leader

ducato *m* duchy; ducat

duce *m* leader; duce

duchéssa *f* duchess

duchessina *f* young duchess

duchino *m* young duke

due *adj & pron* two; **le due** two o'clock || *m* two; second (*in dates*) || *f*—**fra le due** between two alternatives

duecenté·sco -sca *adj* (-schi -sche) thirteenth-century

duecentèsi·mo -ma *adj, m & pron* two hundredth

duecènto *adj, m & pron* two hundred || **il Duecento** the thirteenth century

duellante *adj* dueling || *m* duelist

duellare (duèllo) *intr* to duel

duèllo *m* duel; contest; debate; **sfidare a duello** to challenge to a duel

duemila *adj, m & pron* two thousand || **Duemila** *m* twenty-first century

duepèz·zi *m* (-zi) two-piece bathing suit

duétto *m* (mus) duet

dulcamara *f* (bot) bittersweet

dulcina *f* artificial sweetening

duna *f* dune

dunque *m*—**venire al dunque** to come

to the point || *adv* then || *conj* therefore, hence || *interj* well!

duodèno *m* (anat) duodenum

duòlo *m* (lit) grief

duòmo *m* cathedral; dome (*e.g., of a boiler*)

du·plex *m* (-plex) (telp) party line

duplicare §197 **(dùplico)** *tr* to duplicate

duplica·to -ta *adj & m* duplicate

duplicatóre *m* duplicator

dùplice *adj* twofold, double || *f* (racing) daily double

duplici·tà *f* (-tà) duplicity

duràbile *adj* durable, lasting

duràci·no -na *adj* clingstone || *f* clingstone peach

durallumìnio *m* duralumin

durare *tr* to endure, bear || *intr* to last; **durare a** + *inf* to keep on + *ger*; **durare in carica** to remain in office

durata *f* duration; lasting quality; **di lunga durata** long-lasting

durante *prep* during; throughout

duratu·ro -ra *adj* enduring, lasting

durévole *adj* lasting, durable

durézza *f* hardness; toughness; rigidity

du·ro -ra *adj* hard; hard-boiled (*egg*); durum (*wheat*); tough (*skin*); harsh; (phonet) voiceless || *m* hard part; hard floor; hard soil; **il duro sta che . . .** the trouble is that . . . ; **tener duro** to hold out

duróne *m* callousness, callosity

dùttile *adj* ductile; tractable

E

E, e [e] *m & f* fifth letter of the Italian alphabet

e *conj* and

ebani·sta *m* (-sti) cabinetmaker

ebanisterìa *f* cabinetmaking; cabinetmaker's shop

ebanite *f* ebonite, vulcanite

èbano *m* ebony

ebbène *interj* well!

ebbrézza *f* intoxication, drunkenness

èb·bro -bra *adj* intoxicated || *mf* drunk

ebdomadà·rio -ria *adj & m* (-ri -rie) weekly

èbete *adj* stupid, dull, dumb

ebollizióne *f* boil, boiling

ebrài·co -ca (-ci -che) *adj* Hebrew, Hebraic || *m* Hebrew (*language*)

ebrè·o -a *adj & mf* Hebrew || *m* Hebrew (*language*); Jew; **ebreo errante** Wandering Jew

è·bro -bra *adj & mf* var of **ebbro**

ebùrne·o -a *adj* (lit) ivory

ecatòmbe *f* hecatomb, slaughter

eccedènte *adj* exceeding || *m* excess

eccedènza *f* excess, surplus

eccèdere §123 *tr* to exceed || *intr* to go too far

eccellènte *adj* excellent

eccellènza *f* excellence || **Eccellenza** *f* Excellency

eccèllere §162 *intr* (ESSERE) to excel

eccèl·so -sa *adj* unexcelled; very high || **—l'Eccelso** *m* the Most High

eccentrici·tà *f* (-tà) eccentricity

eccèntri·co -ca (-ci -che) *adj* eccentric; suburban || *mf* vaudeville performer || *m* (mach) eccentric

eccepìbile *adj* objectionable

eccepire §176 *tr* (law) to take exception to || *intr* (law) to object

eccessi·vo -va *adj* excessive; overweening (*opinion*)

eccèsso *m* excess; **all'eccesso** excessively; **andare agli eccessi** to go to extremes; **dare in eccessi** to fly into a rage; **eccesso di peso** excess weight

eccètera *adv* and so forth, et cetera

eccètto *prep* except, but; **eccetto che** except that; unless

eccettuare (eccèttuo) *tr* to except

eccettua·to -ta *adj* excepted || **eccettuato** *prep* except

eccezionale *adj* exceptional

eccezióne *f* exception; objection; **ad eccezione di** with the exception of; **d'eccezione** extraordinary; **sollevare un'eccezione** (law) to take exception

ecchimò·si *f* (-si) bruise

eccì·dio *m* (-di) massacre

eccitàbile *adj* excitable

eccitaménto *m* instigation; excitement

eccitante *adj* stimulating ‖ *m* stimulant

eccitare (**èccito**) *tr* to excite ‖ *ref* to become excited or aroused; (sports) to warm up

eccitazióne *f* excitement; (elec) excitation

ecclesiàsti·co -ca (**-ci -che**) *adj* ecclesiastical ‖ *m* clergyman

ècco *tr invar* here is (are), there is (are); **ecco che** here, e.g., **ecco che viene** here he comes; **eccoci** here we are; **ecco fatto** that's it; **eccola** here she is; here it is; **eccomi** here I am; **eccone** here are some ‖ *intr invar* here I am; here it is; **quand'ecco** suddenly ‖ *interj* look!

eccóme *interj* and how!, indeed!

echeggiare §290 (**echéggio**) *intr* (ESSERE & AVERE) to echo

eclètti·co -ca *adj & mf* (**-ci -che**) eclectic

eclissare *tr* to eclipse ‖ *ref* to be eclipsed; (coll) to vanish, sneak away

eclis·si *f* (**-si**) eclipse

eclìtti·ca *f* (**-che**) ecliptic

èclo·ga *f* (**-ghe**) var of egloga

è·co *m & f* (**-chi** *mpl*) echo; **far eco a** to echo

ecogoniòmetro *m* sonar

ecologìa *f* ecology

economato *m* comptroller's or administrator's office

economìa *f* administration; management; economy; economics; **economia aziendale** business management; **economia di mercato** free enterprise; **economia domestica** home economics; **economia politica** political economy; economics; **economie** savings; **fare economia** to save

econòmi·co -ca *adj* (**-ci -che**) economic(al); cheap

economi·sta *mf* (**-sti -ste**) economist

economizzare [ddzz] *tr & intr* to economize, save

ecòno·mo -ma *adj* thrifty ‖ *m* comptroller; administrator

ecosistè·ma [s] *m* (**-mi**) ecosystem

ecumèni·co -ca *adj* (**-ci -che**) ecumenical

eczè·ma [dz] *m* (**-mi**) eczema

édera *f* ivy

edìcola *f* shrine; newsstand

edificante *adj* edifying

edificare §197 (**edìfico**) *tr* to build; to edify ‖ *intr* to build

edifica·tóre -trice *adj* building ‖ *mf* builder

edificazióne *f* building; edification

edifì·cio *m* (**-ci**) building, edifice; pack (*e.g., of lies*); structure

edile *adj* building, construction ‖ *m* builder, construction worker

edilì·zio -zia (**-zi -zie**) *adj* building, construction ‖ *f* building trade

edìpi·co -ca *adj* (**-ci -che**) Oedipus (*e.g., complex*)

Edipo *m* Oedipus

èdi·to -ta *adj* published

edi·tóre -trice *adj* publishing ‖ *mf* publisher; editor (*e.g., of a text*)

editorìa *f* publishing; publishers

editoriale *adj* editorial; publishing ‖ *m* editorial

editoriali·sta *mf* (**-sti -ste**) editorial writer

editto *m* edict

edizióne *f* edition; performance; (fig) vintage

edonismo *m* hedonism

edoni·sta *mf* (**-sti -ste**) hedonist

edòt·to -ta *adj* (lit) informed, acquainted; **rendere qlcu edotto su qlco** (lit) to inform s.o. of s.th

edredóne *m* eider, eider duck

educanda *f* boarding-school girl; convent-school girl

educandato *m* (convent) boarding school for girls

educare §197 (**èduco**) *tr* to educate; to rear, bring up; to train; to accustom, inure; (lit) to grow

educati·vo -va *adj* educational

educa·to -ta *adj* educated; polite, well-bred

educa·tóre -trice *mf* educator

educazióne *f* education; breeding, manners; **educazione civica** civics

edule *adj* edible

efèbo *m* (coll) sissy

efèlide *f* freckle

effeminatézza *f* effeminacy

effemina·to -ta *adj* effeminate; frivolous

efferatézza *f* savagery

effervescènte *adj* effervescent

effervescènza *f* effervescence

effettivamente *adv* really

effetti·vo -va *adj* real, true; effective; full (*e.g., member*); regular (*e.g., army officer*) ‖ *m* effective; total amount; (mil) manpower

effètto *m* effect, result; (com) promissory note; (billiards) English; (sports) spin; **a questo effetto** for this purpose; **effetti** effects, belongings; **effetto di luce** play of light; **effetto ottico** optical illusion; **fare effetto** to make a sensation; **fare l'effetto di** to give the impression of; **in effetto** in fact; **mandare a effetto** to carry out; **porre in effetto** to put into effect

effettuàbile *adj* feasible

effettuare (**effèttuo**) *tr* to bring about; to contrive; to actuate; **effettuare** (**una corsa, un servizio**) to run, e.g., **l'autobus effettua una corsa ogni mezz'ora** the bus runs every half hour

efficace *adj* effective; forceful (*writer*)

efficà·cia *f* (**-cie**) effectiveness, efficacy; (law) validity

efficiènte *adj* efficient

efficiènza *f* efficiency; **in piena efficienza** in full working order; in top condition

effigiare §290 *tr* to portray, represent

effì·gie *f* (**-gie** or **-gi**) effigy; image

effìme·ro -ra *adj* ephemeral

efflusso *m* flow, outflow

efflù·vio *m* (**-vi**) effluvium; emanation (*e.g., of light*)

effrazióne *f* (law) burglary

effusióne *f* effusion; outflow; shedding (*of blood*); effusiveness

egemonìa *f* hegemony

egè•o -a *adj* Aegean
ègida *f* aegis
Egitto, l' *m* Egypt
egizia•no -na *adj* & *mf* Egyptian
eglantina *f* sweetbrier
eglefino *m* haddock
égli §5 *pron pers* he
èglo•ga *f* (-ghe) eclogue
egocèntri•co -ca *adj* & *mf* (-ci -che)
egocentric
egoismo *m* egoism, selfishness
egoi•sta (-sti -ste) *adj* selfish || *mf* egoist
egoìsti•co -ca *adj* (-ci -che) egoistic(al)
egotismo *m* egotism
egoti•sta (-sti -ste) *adj* egotistic || *mf*
egotist
egrè•gio -gia *adj* (-gi -gie) (lit) outstanding; **Egregio Signore** Mr. (*before a man's name in an address on
a letter*); Dear Sir
eguaglianza *f* equality
eguale *adj* var of **uguale**
egualità•rio -ria *adj* & *m* (-ri -rie)
equalitarian
éhi *interj* hey!
éi *pron* (lit) he; (archaic) they
eiaculazióne *f* ejaculation
eiettàbile *adj* ejection (*seat*)
eiezióne *f* ejection
él *pron* (archaic) he
elaborare (elàboro) *tr* to elaborate; to
digest; to secrete
elabora•to -ta *adj* elaborate || *m* written
exercise
elaboratóre *m* computer
elaborazióne *f* elaboration; data processing
elargire §176 *tr* to donate
elargizióne *f* donation
elastici•tà *f* (-tà) elasticity; agility;
(com) oscillation; (com) range
elàsti•co -ca (-ci -che) *adj* elastic || *m*
rubber band; bedspring
élce *m* & *f* holm oak
elefante *m* elephant; **elefante marino**
sea elephant
elefantéssa *f* female elephant
elegante *adj* elegant, fashionable
elegantó•ne -na *mf* fashion plate || *m*
dandy, dude
eleganza *f* elegance, stylishness
elèggere §193 *tr* to elect
eleggìbile *adj* eligible
elegìa *f* elegy
elegìa•co -ca *adj* elegiac
elementare *adj* elementary || **elemen-
tari** *fpl* elementary schools
eleménto *m* element; rudiment; member; cell (*of battery*); **elementi** personnel, e.g., **elementi femminili**
female personnel
elemòsina *f* alms; (eccl) collection;
chiedere l'elemosina to beg; **vivere
d'elemosina** to live on charity
elemosinare (elemòsino) *intr* to beg
Èlena *f* Helen
elencare §197 (elènco) *tr* to list; to
enumerate
elèn•co *m* (-chi) list; **elenco telefonico**
telephone directory
eletti•vo -va *adj* elective
elèt•to -ta *adj* elect; distinguished

(*audience*); precious (*metal*); chosen
(*people*) || *mf* elect
elettorato *m* electorate, constituency
elet•tóre -trice *mf* voter; elector
elettràuto *m* automobile electrician;
automotive electric shop
elettrici•sta *mf* (-sti -ste) electrician
elettrici•tà *f* (-tà) electricity
elèttri•co -ca (-ci -che) *adj* electrical ||
m electrical worker
elettrificare §197 (elettrìfico) *tr* to electrify
elettrizzare [ddzz] *tr* to electrify (*e.g.,
a person*) || *ref* to become electrified
ellètro *m* amber
elettrocalamita *f* electromagnet
elettrocardiògrafo *m* electrocardio-
graph
elettrocardiogram•ma *m* (-mi) electro-
cardiogram
elettrodinàmi•co -ca (-ci -che) *adj* elec-
trodynamic || *f* electrodynamics
elèttrodo *m* electrode
elettrodomèsti•co -ca (-ci -che) *adj* elec-
tric household || *m* electric house-
hold appliance
elettroesecuzióne *f* electrocution
elettròge•no -na *adj* generating (*unit*)
elettròli•si *f* (-si) electrolysis
elettrolìti•co -ca (-ci -che) *adj* electro-
lytic
elettròlito *m* electrolyte
elettromagnèti•co -ca *adj* (-ci -che)
electromagnetic
elettromo•tóre -trice *adj* electromotive
|| *m* electric motor || *f* electric train;
electric railcar
elettróne *m* electron
elettróni•co -ca (-ci -che) *adj* electronic
|| *f* electronics
elettropómpa *f* electric pump
elettrosquasso *m* electroshock
elettrostàti•co -ca (-ci -che) *adj* electro-
static || *f* electrostatics
elettrotècni•co -ca (-ci -che) *adj* electro-
technical || *m* electrician; electrical
engineer || *f* electrical engineering
elettrotrèno *m* electric train
elevaménto *m* elevation
elevare (èlevo & elèvo) *tr* to lift, ele-
vate; (math) to raise || *ref* to rise
elevatézza *f* loftiness, dignity
eleva•to -ta *adj* high, lofty
eleva•tóre -trice *adj* elevating || *m*
elevator
elevazióne *f* elevation; (sports) jump;
(math) raising
elezióne *f* election; choice
èlfo *m* elf
èli•ca *f* (-che) propeller; (geom) helix
elicoidale *adj* helicoidal
elicòttero *m* helicopter
elìdere §161 *tr* to annul; to elide || *ref*
to neutralize one another
eliminare (elìmino) *tr* to eliminate
eliminatò•rio -ria (-ri -rie) *adj* eliminat-
ing || *f* (sports) heat
eliminazióne *f* elimination; extermination
èlio- *comb form adj* helio-, e.g., **elio-
centrico** heliocentric || *comb form*

m & *f* helio-, e.g., **elioterapia** helio-therapy
èlio *m* helium
eliocèntri·co -ca *adj* (**-ci -che**) helio-centric
eliògrafo *m* heliograph
elioteràpi·co -ca *adj* (**-ci -che**) sunshine (*treatment*); sunbathing (*establishment*)
eliotrò·pio *m* (**-pi**) heliotrope; blood-stone
elipòrto *m* heliport
elisabettia·no -na *adj* Elizabethan
elì·sio -sia *adj* (**-si -sie**) Elysian
elisióne *f* elision
eli·sir *m* (**-sir**) elixir
èlitra *f* elytron, shard
élla *pron* (lit) she ‖ **Ella** *pron* (lit) you
ellèboro *m* hellebore
ellèni·co -ca *adj* (**-ci -che**) Hellenic
ellisse *f* ellipse
ellis·si *f* (**-si**) (gram) ellipsis
ellìtti·co -ca *adj* (**-ci -che**) elliptical
-èllo -èlla *suf adj* little, e.g., **poverello** poor little
elmétto *m* helmet; tin hat
élmo *m* helmet
elogiare §290 (**elògio**) *tr* to praise
elò·gio *m* (**-gi**) praise, encomium; write-up; **elogio funebre** eulogy
eloquènte *adj* eloquent
eloquènza *f* eloquence
elò·quio *m* (**-qui**) (lit) speech, diction
élsa *f* hilt
elucidare (**elùcido**) *tr* to elucidate
elùdere §105 *tr* to elude, evade
elusi·vo -va *adj* elusive
elvèti·co -ca *adj* & *mf* (**-ci -che**) Helvetian
elzevi·ro -ra [dz] *adj* Elzevir ‖ *m* Elzevir book; (journ) literary article
emacia·to -ta *adj* emaciated, lean
emanare *tr* to send forth; to issue ‖ *intr* (ESSERE) to emanate; to come forth
emanazióne *f* emanation; issuance
emancipare (**emàncipo**) *tr* to emancipate ‖ *ref* to become emancipated
emancipazióne *f* emancipation
emarginare (**emàrgino**) *tr* to note in the margin; (fig) to put aside, neglect
emarginato *m* marginal note
emàti·co -ca *adj* (**-ci -che**) blood, hematic
ematite *f* hematite
embar·go *m* (**-ghi**) embargo
emblè·ma *m* (**-mi**) emblem
emblemàti·co -ca *adj* (**-ci -che**) emblematic
embolìa *f* embolism
èmbrice *m* flat roof tile; shingle
embriologìa *f* embryology
embrionale *adj* embryonic
embrióne *m* embryo
emendaménto *m* emendation (*of a text*); amendment (*to a law*)
emendare (**emèndo**) *tr* to correct; to emend; to amend (*a law*) ‖ *ref* to reform
emergènza *f* emergence; emergency
emèrgere §162 *intr* (ESSERE) to emerge;

to surface (*said of a submarine*); to loom; to stand out
emèri·to -ta *adj* emeritus (*professor*); famous
emerotè·ca *f* (**-che**) periodical library
emersióne *f* emersion; surfacing
emèr·so -sa *adj* emergent
emèti·co -ca *adj* & *m* (**-ci -che**) emetic
eméttere §198 *tr* to emit, send forth; to utter (*a statement*); (com) to issue
emiciclo *m* hemicycle; floor (*of legislative body*)
emicrània *f* migraine, headache
emigrante *adj* & *mf* emigrant
emigrare *intr* (ESSERE & AVERE) to emigrate
emigra·to -ta *adj* & *mf* emigrant
emigrazióne *f* emigration; migration (*e.g., of birds*)
eminènte *adj* eminent
eminènza *f* eminence; (eccl) Eminence
emisfèro *m* hemisphere
emissà·rio *m* (**-ri**) emissary; outlet (*river or lake*); drain
emissióne *f* emission; issuance; (rad) broadcast
emistì·chio *m* (**-chi**) hemistich
emittènte *adj* emitting; issuing; (rad) broadcasting ‖ *f* (rad) transmitting set; broadcasting station
emofilìa *f* hemophilia
emoglobina *f* hemoglobin
emolliènte *adj* & *m* emollient
emoluménto *m* fee, emolument
emorragìa *f* hemorrhage
emorròidi *fpl* hemorrhoids, piles
emostàti·co -ca *adj* (**-ci -che**) hemostatic ‖ *m* hemostat
emotè·ca *f* (**-che**) blood bank
emotivi·tà *f* (**-tà**) emotionalism
emoti·vo -va *adj* emotional ‖ *mf* emotional person
emottisi *f* (pathol) hemoptysis
emozionante *adj* emotional, moving
emozionare (**emozióno**) *tr* to move, stir; to thrill
emozióne *f* emotion
empiastro *m* var of **impiastro**
émpiere §163 *tr* & *ref* var of **empire**
empie·tà *f* (**-tà**) impiety; cruelty
ém·pio -pia *adj* (**-pi -pie**) impious; pitiless, wicked
empire §163 *tr* to fill; (lit) to fulfill; **empire qlcu di insulti** to heap insults on s.o. ‖ *ref* to get full
empìre·o -a *adj* heavenly, sublime ‖ *m* empyrean
empìri·co -ca (**-ci -che**) *adj* empirical ‖ *mf* empiricist
empirismo *m* empiricism
empiri·sta *mf* (**-sti -ste**) empiricist
émpito *m* (lit) rush; fury
empò·rio *m* (**-ri**) emporium, mart
emulare (**èmulo**) *tr* to emulate
emulazióne *f* emulation, rivalry; (law) evil intent
èmu·lo -la *adj* emulous ‖ *mf* emulator
emulsionare (**emulsióno**) *tr* to emulsify
emulsióne *f* emulsion
encefalite *f* encephalitis
encìcli·ca *f* (**-che**) encyclical
enciclopedìa *f* encyclopedia

enciclopèdi·co -ca *adj* (**-ci -che**) encyclopedic
enclave *f* enclave
enclìti·co -ca *adj & f* (**-ci -che**) enclitic
encomiàbile *adj* praiseworthy
encomiare §287 (**encòmio**) *tr* to praise
encò·mio *m* (**-mi**) encomium, praise
endecasìlla·bo -ba *adj* hendecasyllabic ‖ *m* hendecasyllable
endemìa *f* endemic
endèmi·co -ca *adj* (**-ci -che**) endemic
èndice *m* nest egg; (obs) souvenir
endocàr·dio *m* (**-di**) (anat) endocardium
endocarpo *m* (bot) endocarp
endòcri·no -na *adj* endocrine
endourba·no -na *adj* inner-city
endovenó·so -sa [s] *adj* intravenous
energèti·co -ca (**-ci -che**) *adj* energy (*e.g., crisis*); (med) tonic ‖ *m* (med) tonic
energìa *f* energy, power
enèrgi·co -ca *adj* (**-ci -che**) energetic
energùme·no -na *mf* wild or mad person
ènfa·si *f* (**-si**) emphasis; forcefulness
enfàti·co -ca *adj* (**-ci -che**) emphatic
enfiare §287 (**énfio**) *tr & ref* to swell
enfisè·ma *m* (**-mi**) emphysema
enfitèu·si *f* (**-si**) lease (*of land*)
enig·ma *m* (**-mi**) enigma, riddle, puzzle
enigmàti·co -ca *adj* (**-ci -che**) enigmatic, puzzling
-ènne *suf adj* -year-old, e.g., **ragazzo diciassettenne** seventeen-year-old boy ‖ *suf mf* -year-old person, e.g., **diciassettenne** seventeen-year-old person
ennèsi·mo -ma *adj* nth
-èn·nio *suf m* (**-ni**) period of . . . years, e.g., **ventennio** period of twenty years
enòlo·go -ga *mf* (**-gi -ghe**) oenologist
enórme *adj* enormous
enormeménte *adv* enormously
enormi·tà *f* (**-tà**) enormity; outrage; absurdity
Enrico *m* Henry
ènte *m* being; entity; corporation; agency, body
enterocli·sma *m* (**-smi**) enema
enti·tà *f* (**-tà**) entity; value, importance
entomologìa *f* entomology
entram·bi -be *adj*—**entrambi i** both ‖ *pron* both
entrante *adj* next (*e.g., week*)
entrare (**éntro**) *intr* (ESSERE) to enter; to go (*said of numbers*); to get (*into one's head*); **entrarci** to make it, e.g., **con questi soldi non c'entro** I can't make it with this money; **entrarci come i cavoli a merenda** to be completely out of line; **entrare a** to begin to; **entrare in** to enter (*e.g., a room*); to fit in; to go in (*said of a number*); to get into (*one's head*); **entrare in amore** to be in heat (*said of animals*); **entrare in ballo** to come into play; **entrare in carica** to take up one's duties; **entrare in collera** to get angry; **entrare in collisione** to collide; **entrare in contatto** to establish contact; **entrare in gioco** to come into play; **entrare in guerra** to go to war; **entrare in società** to make one's debut; **entrare nella parte di** (theat)

to play the role of; **entrare in vigore** to become effective; **Lei non c'entra** this is none of your business; **questo non c'entra** this is beside the point
entrata *f* entry; entrance; **entrata di favore** (theat) complimentary ticket; **entrate** income
entratura *f* entry; entrance; assumption (*of a position*); familiarity
éntro *adv* inside ‖ *prep* within; **entro di** within, inside of
entrobórdo *m* inboard motorboat
entrotèrra *f* inland, hinterland
entusiasmare *tr* to carry away, enthuse ‖ *ref* to be carried away, to become enthused
entusiasmo *m* enthusiasm
entusia·sta (**-sti -ste**) *adj* enthusiastic ‖ *mf* enthusiast, devotee
entusiàsti·co -ca *adj* (**-ci -che**) enthusiastic
enucleare (**enùcleo**) *tr* to elucidate; (surg) to remove
enumerare (**enùmero**) *tr* to enumerate
enumerazióne *f* enumeration
enunciare §128 *tr* to enunciate, state
enunciati·vo -va *adj* (gram) declarative
enunciazióne *f* enunciation, statement
enzi·ma [dz] *m* (**-mi**) enzyme
èpa *f* (lit) belly, paunch
epàti·co -ca *adj* (**-ci -che**) hepatic, liver
epatite *f* (pathol) hepatitis
epènte·si *f* (**-si**) epenthesis
eperlano *m* (ichth) smelt
èpi·co -ca *adj & f* (**-ci -che**) epic
epicurè·o -a *adj & m* epicurean
epidemìa *f* epidemic
epidèmi·co -ca *adj* (**-ci -che**) epidemic (al)
epidèrmi·co -ca *adj* (**-ci -che**) epidermal; (fig) superficial, skin-deep
epidèrmide *f* epidermis
Epifanìa *f* Epiphany
epiglòttide *f* (anat) epiglottis
epìgono *m* follower; descendant
epìgrafe *f* epigraph
epigram·ma *m* (**-mi**) epigram
epigrammàti·co -ca *adj* (**-ci -che**) epigrammatic
epilessìa *f* (pathol) epilepsy
epilètti·co -ca *adj & m* (**-ci -che**) epileptic
epìlo·go *m* (**-ghi**) epilogue; conclusion
episcopale *adj* episcopal
episcopalia·no -na *adj & mf* Episcopalian
episcopato *m* episcopate, bishopric
episòdi·co -ca *adj* (**-ci -che**) episodic
episò·dio *m* (**-di**) episode
epìstola *f* epistle
epistolà·rio *m* (**-ri**) letters, correspondence
epitàf·fio *m* (**-fi**) epitaph
epitè·lio *m* (**-li**) epithelium
epìteto *m* epithet; insult
epitomare (**epìtomo**) *tr* to epitomize
epìtome *f* epitome
èpo·ca *f* (**-che**) epoch; period; moment; **fare epoca** to be epoch-making
epopèa *f* epic
eppure *conj* yet, and yet
epsomite *f* Epsom salt

epurare *tr* to cleanse; to purge
epurazióne *f* purification; purge
equànime *adj* calm, composed; impartial
equanimità *f* equanimity; impartiality
equatóre *m* equator
equatoriale *adj* & *m* equatorial
equazióne *f* equation
equèstre *adj* equestrian
equilàte·ro -ra *adj* equilateral
equilibrare *tr* to balance; (aer) to trim || *ref* to balance one another
equilibra·to -ta *adj* level-headed
equilibra·tóre -trice *adj* stabilizing || *m* (aer) horizontal stabilizer
equili·brio *m* (-bri) equilibrium, balance; (fig) proportion; equilibrio politico balance of power
equilibri·sta *mf* (-sti -ste) acrobat, equilibrist
equi·no -na *adj* & *m* equine
equinoziale *adj* equinoctial
equinò·zio *m* (-zi) equinox
equipaggiaménto *m* equipment, outfit
equipaggiare §290 *tr* to equip, outfit; (naut) to fit out; (naut) to man
equipàg·gio *m* (-gi) equipage; (naut) crew, complement; (sports) team; (rowing) crew
equiparare *tr* to equalize (*e.g., salaries*)
équipe *f* team
equipollènte *adj* equivalent
equi·tà *f* (-tà) equity, fair-mindedness
equitazióne *f* horsemanship
equivalènte *adj* & *m* equivalent
equivalére §278 *intr* (ESSERE & AVERE) —equivalere a to be equivalent to || *ref* to be equal
equivocare §197 (equìvoco) *intr*—equivocare su to mistake, misunderstand
equìvo·co -ca (-ci -che) *adj* equivocal; ambiguous || *m* misunderstanding
è·quo -qua *adj* equitable, fair
èra *f* era, age; era spaziale space age
erà·rio *m* (-ri) treasury
èrba *f* grass; erba limoncina lemon verbena; erba medica alfalfa; erbe vegetables; erbe aromatiche herbs; far l'erba to cut the grass; in erba (fig) budding; metter a erba to put to pasture
erbàc·cia *f* (-ce) weed
erbaggi *mpl* vegetables
erbaiò·lo -la *mf* fresh vegetable retailer
erbici·da *m* (-di) weed-killer
erbivéndo·lo -la *mf* fresh fruit and vegetable retailer
erbìvo·ro -ra *adj* herbivorous
erbori·sta *mf* (-sti -ste) herbalist
erbó·so -sa [s] *adj* grassy
Èrcole *m* Hercules
ercùle·o -a *adj* Herculean
erède *m* heir || *f* heiress
eredi·tà *f* (-tà) inheritance; heredity
ereditare (erèdito) *tr* to inherit
eredità·rio -ria *adj* (-ri -rie) hereditary; crown (*prince*)
ereditièra *f* heiress
eremi·ta *m* (-ti) hermit
eremitàg·gio *m* (-gi) hermitage
èremo *m* hermitage
eresìa *f* heresy

eresiar·ca *m* (-chi) heretic
erèti·co -ca (-ci -che) *adj* heretical || *mf* heretic
erèt·to -ta *adj* erect, straight
erezióne *f* erection
ergastola·no -na *mf* lifer
ergàstolo *m* life imprisonment; prison for persons sentenced to life imprisonment
èrgere §164 *tr* (lit) to erect; (lit) to lift || *ref* to rise (*said, e.g., of a mountain*)
èrgo *m invar*—venire all'ergo to come to a conclusion || *adv* thus, hence
èri·ca *f* (-che) heather
erìgere §152 *tr* to erect, build || *ref* to rise; erigersi a to set oneself up as
eritrè·o -a *adj* & *mf* Eritrean
ermafrodi·to -ta *adj* & *m* hermafrodite .
ermellino *m* ermine
ermèti·co -ca *adj* (-ci -che) airtight; watertight; hermetic
èrnia *f* hernia; ernia del disco (pathol) herniated disk
eródere §239 *tr* to erode
cròe *m* hero
erogare §209 (èrogo) *tr* to distribute; to bestow
erogazióne *f* distribution; bestowal
eròi·co -ca *adj* (-ci -che) heroic
eroicòmi·co -ca *adj* (-ci -che) mock-heroic
eroìna *f* heroine; (pharm) heroin
eroismo *m* heroism
erómpere §240 *intr* to erupt, burst out
erosióne *f* erosion
eròti·co -ca *adj* (-ci -che) erotic
erotismo *m* eroticism
èrpete *m* (pathol) herpes, shingles
erpicare §197 (èrpico) *tr* to harrow
érpice *m* harrow
errabón·do -da *adj* (lit) wandering
errante *adj* errant; wandering
errare (èrro) *intr* to wander; to err; (lit) to stray
erra·to -ta *adj* mistaken, wrong
erròne·o -a *adj* erroneous
erróre *m* error, mistake; fault; (lit) wandering; errore di lingua slip of the tongue; errore di scrittura slip of the pen; errore di stampa misprint; errore giudiziario miscarriage of justice; salvo errore od omissione barring error or omission
ér·to -ta *adj* arduous, steep; erect || *f* arduous ascent; all'erta on the alert
erudire §176 *tr* to educate, instruct
erudi·to -ta *adj* erudite, learned || *m* scholar, savant
erudizióne *f* erudition, learning
eruttare *tr* to belch forth (*e.g., lava*); to utter (*obscenities*) || *intr* to belch
erutti·vo -va *adj* eruptive
eruzióne *f* eruption
esacerbare (esacèrbo) *tr* to embitter; to exacerbate || *ref* to become embittered
esagerare (esàgero) *tr* & *intr* to exaggerate
esagera·to -ta *adj* exaggerated, excessive || *mf* exaggerator
esagerazióne *f* exaggeration

esagitare (esàgito) *tr* to perturb
esàgono *m* hexagon
esalare *tr* to exhale; **esalare l'ultimo respiro** to breathe one's last || *intr* to spread (*said of odors*)
esalazióne *f* exhalation; fume, vapor
esaltare *tr* to exalt; to excite || *ref* to glorify oneself; to become excited
esalta·to -ta *adj* frenzied, excited || *mf* hothead
esame *m* examination; checkup, test; **dare gli esami** to take an examination; **esame attitudinale** aptitude test; **esame del sangue** blood test; **esame di riparazione** make-up test; **fare gli esami** to prepare a test (*for a student*); **prendere in esame** to take in consideration
esàmetro *m* hexameter
esaminan·do -da *mf* candidate; examinee
esaminare (esàmino) *tr* to examine; to test
esamina·tóre -trice *mf* examiner
esàngue *adj* bloodless; (fig) pale
esànime *adj* lifeless
esasperante *adj* exasperating
esasperare (esàspero) *tr* to exasperate || *ref* to become exasperated
esasperazióne *f* exasperation
esattézza *f* exactness; punctuality
esat·to -ta *adj* exact; punctual
esattóre *m* tax collector; bill collector
esattorìa *f* tax collector's office; bill collector's office
esaudire §176 *tr* to grant
esauriènte *adj* exhaustive; convincing
esauriménto *m* depletion (*e.g., of merchandise*); (pathol) exhaustion; (naut) drainage
esaurire §176 *tr* to exhaust; to play out (*e.g., a hooked fish*); to use up || *ref* to be exhausted; to be depleted; to be sold out
esauri·to -ta *adj* exhausted; depleted; sold out; out of print
esau·sto -sta *adj* exhausted; empty
esautorare (esàutoro) *tr* to deprive of authority; to discredit (*a theory*)
esazióne *f* exaction; collection
é·sca *f* (-sche) bait; punk (*for lighting fireworks*); tinder (*for lighting powder*): **dare esca a** to foment
escandescènza *f*—**dare in escandescenze** to fly off the handle
escava·tóre -trice *mf* excavator, digger || *m* excavator; **escavatore a vapore** steam shovel || *f* (mach) excavator
escavazióne *f* excavation
eschimése [s] *adj & mf* Eskimo
esclamare *tr & intr* to exclaim
esclamati·vo -va *adj* exclamatory; exclamation (*mark*)
esclùdere §105 *tr* to exclude; to keep or shut out
esclusióne *f* exclusion; **a esclusione di** with the exception of
esclusiva *f* sole right, monopoly; (journ) scoop
esclusivi·sta (-sti -ste) *adj* clannish; bigoted || *mf* bigot; (com) sole agent
esclusi·vo -va *adj* exclusive; intolerant, bigoted || *f* see **esclusiva**

esclu·so -sa *adj* excluded, excepted
escogitare (escògito) *tr* to think up, invent; to think out
escoriare §287 **(escòrio)** *tr & ref* to skin
escoriazióne *f* abrasion
escreménto *m* excrement
escrescènza *f* excrescence
escrè·to -ta *adj* excreted || *m* excreta
escursióne *f* excursion; (mach) sweep; (mil) transfer; **escursione termica** (meteor) temperature range
escursioni·sta *mf* (-sti -ste) excursionist, sightseer
escussióne *f* (law) examination, cross-examination
esecrare (esècro) *tr* to execrate
esecrazióne *f* execration
esecuti·vo -va *adj & m* executive
esecu·tóre -trice *mf* (mus) performer || *m* executor; **esecutore di giustizia** executioner || *f* executrix
esecuzióne *f* accomplishment, completion; performance; execution; **esecuzione capitale** capital punishment
esegè·si *f* (-si) exegesis
eseguire (eséguo) & §176 *tr* to execute, carry out; to perform
esèm·pio *m* (-pi) example; **a mo' d'esempio** as an illustration; **dare il buon esempio** to set a good example; **per esempio** for instance
esemplare *adj* exemplary || *m* copy; specimen || *v* **(esèmplo)** *tr* (lit) to copy
esemplificare §197 **(esemplìfico)** *tr* to exemplify
esentare (esènto) *tr* to exempt
esènte *adj* exempt, free
esenzióne *f* exemption
esèquie *fpl* obsequies, funeral rites
esercènte *adj* practicing || *mf* dealer, merchant
esercire §176 *tr* to practice; to run (*a store*)
esercitare (esèrcito) *tr* to exercise; to tax (*e.g., s.o.'s patience*); to practice, ply (*a trade*); to wield (*e.g., power*) || *ref* to practice
esercitazióne *f* exercise, training; **esercitazioni militari** drilling
esèrcito *m* army; (fig) flock; **Esercito della Salvezza** Salvation Army
esercì·zio *m* (-zi) exercise; practice; training; homework; occupation; drill; **d'esercizio** (com) administrative (*expenses*); **esercizio finanziario** fiscal year; **esercizio provvisorio** (law) emergency appropriation; **esercizio pubblico** establishment open to the public; **esercizio spirituale** (eccl) retreat
esibire §176 *tr* to exhibit || *ref* to show oneself, appear; **esibirsi di** to offer to
esibizióne *f* exhibition
esigènte *adj* demanding, exigent
esigènza *f* demand, requirement, exigency
esìgere §165 *tr* to demand; to require; to exact; to collect
esigìbile *adj* due; collectable
esigui·tà *f* (-tà) meagerness, scantiness
esì·guo -gua *adj* meager, scanty

esilarante *adj* exhilarating; laughing (*gas*)

esilarare (esìlaro) *tr* to amuse || *ref* to be amused

èsile *adj* slender, thin; weak

esiliare §287 *tr* to exile || *ref* to go into exile; to withdraw

esilia·to -ta *adj* exiled || *m* exile (*person*)

esì·lio *m* (-li) exile, banishment

esìmere §166 *tr* to exempt || *ref*—**esimersi da** to avoid (*an obligation*)

esì·mio -mia *adj* (-mi -mie) distinguished, eminent

-èsi·mo -ma *suf adj & pron* -eth, e.g., **ventesimo** twentieth; -th, e.g., **diciannovesimo** nineteenth

esistènte *adj* existent; extant

esistènza *f* existence

esistenzialismo *m* existentialism

esìstere §114 *intr* (ESSERE) to exist

esitante *adj* hesitant

esitare (èsito) *tr* to retail || *intr* to hesitate; (med) to resolve itself

esitazióne *f* hesitation; haw (*in speech*)

èsito *m* result, outcome; sale; outlet; (philol) late form; **dare esito a** (com) to reply

esiziale *adj* ruinous, fatal

èsodo *m* exodus, flight

esòfa·go *m* (-gi) esophagus

esonerare (esònero) *tr* to exempt, release

esònero *m* exemption, release

Esòpo *m* Aesop

esorbitante *adj* exorbitant

esorbitare (esòrbito) *intr*—**esorbitare da** to go beyond

esorcismo *m* exorcism

esorcizzare [ddzz] *tr* to exorcise

esordiènte *adj* beginning, budding || *mf* beginner || *f* debutante

esòr·dio *m* (-di) beginning

esordire §176 *intr* to make a start; (theat) to debut; (theat) to open

esortare (esòrto) *tr* to exhort

esortazióne *f* exhortation

esò·so -sa *adj* greedy, avaricious; hateful; exorbitant (*price*)

esòti·co -ca *adj* (-ci -che) exotic

esotismo *m* exoticism; borrowing (*from a foreign language*)

espàndere §167 *tr* to expand || *ref* to spread out; to confide

espansióne *f* expansion; effusiveness

espansionismo *m* expansionism

espansivi·tà *f* (-tà) effusiveness

espansi·vo -va *adj* expansive; effusive

espan·so -sa *adj* flared; expanded, dilated

espatriare §287 *intr* to emigrate

espà·trio *m* (-tri) emigration

espediènte *m* expedient, makeshift; ruse; **vivere di espedienti** to live by one's wits

espedire §176 *tr* to expedite || *ref*—**espedirsi di** to get rid of

espèllere §168 *tr* to expel, eject

esperiènza *f* experience; experiment

esperiménto *m* experiment; test

espèr·to -ta *adj & m* expert

espettorare (espèttoro) *tr & intr* to expectorate

espiare §119 *tr* to expiate; to placate (*the gods*); **espiare una pena** to serve a sentence

espiató·rio -ria *adj* (-ri -rie) expiatory

espiazióne *f* expiation

espirare *tr & intr* to breath out, to exhale

espirazióne *f* exhaling

espletare (esplèto) *tr* to dispatch, complete

esplicare §197 (**èsplico**) *tr* to carry out; (lit) to explain

esplicati·vo -va *adj* explanatory

esplìci·to -ta *adj* explicit

esplòdere §169 *tr* to shoot; to fire (*a shot*) || *intr* (ESSERE & AVERE) to explode; to burst forth

esploratóre *m* blasting machine

esplorare (esplòro) *tr* to explore; to search, probe; (telv) to scan

esplora·tóre -trice *mf* explorer || *m* (nav) gunboat; **giovane esploratore** boy scout

esplorazióne *f* exploration; (telv) scanning

esplosióne *f* explosion, blast; (fig) outburst

esplosi·vo -va *adj & m* explosive

esponènte *adj* (typ) superior || *m* spokesman; dictionary entry; catchword (*of dictionary*); (math) exponent; (naut) net weight

espórre §218 *tr* to expose, show; to expound; to abandon (*a baby*); to lay out (*a corpse*); to lay open (*to danger*) || *intr* to show, exhibit || *ref* to expose oneself

esportare (espòrto) *tr* to export

esporta·tóre -trice *mf* exporter

esportazióne *f* export, exportation

esposìmetro *m* exposure meter

esposi·tóre -trice *mf* commentator; exhibitor

esposizióne *f* exposition; abandonment (*of a baby*); exhibit, fair; line (*of credit*); exposure (*of a house*); (phot) exposure

espó·sto -sta *adj* exposed; aforementioned || *m* petition, brief; foundling

espressióne *f* expression; feeling

espressi·vo -va *adj* expressive

esprès·so -sa *adj* manifest; express; prepared on the spot || *m* espresso; messenger; special-delivery letter; special-delivery stamp

esprìmere §131 *tr* to express; to convey (*an opinion*); (lit) to squeeze || *ref* to express oneself

espropriare §287 (**espròprio**) *tr* to expropriate || *ref* to deprive onself; **espropriarsi di** to divest oneself of

espròprio *m* (-pri) expropriation

espugnare *tr* to take by storm

espulsióne *f* expulsion; (mach) ejection

espulsóre *m* ejector

espurgare §209 *tr* to expurgate

éssa §5 *pron pers* she; it

ésse §5 *pron pers* they

essènza *f* essence

essenziale *adj* essential || *m* main point

èssere *m* being; existence; condition; (coll) character; **in essere** in good shape || §170 *intr* (ESSERE) to be;

c'è there is; **ci sono** there are; **ci sono!** I get it!; **come sarebbe a dire?** what do you mean?; **come se nulla fosse** as if nothing had happened; **esserci** to have arrived, to be there; **essere di** to belong to; **essere per** to be about to; **può essere** maybe; **sarà** maybe; **sia . . . sia** both . . . and; whether . . . or || *aux* (ESSERE) (to form passive) to be, e.g., **fu investito da un tassametro** he was run over by a taxi; (to form the compound tenses of certain intransitive verbs and all reflexive verbs) to have, e.g., **sono arrivati** they have arrived; **mi sono appena alzato** I have just got up || *impers* (ESSERE) to be, e.g., **è giusto** it is fair

éssi §5 *pron pers* they
essiccare §197 *tr* to dry || *ref* to dry up
essicca·tóio *m* (**-tói**) drier
essiccazióne *f* drying
èsso §5 *pron pers* he; it; **chi per esso** his representative
essudare *intr* to exude
èst *m* east
èsta·si *f* (**-si**) ecstasy; **andare in estasi** to become enraptured
estasiare §287 *tr* to enrapture, delight || *ref* to become enraptured
estate *f* summer
estàti·co -ca *adj* (**-ci -che**) ecstatic, enraptured
estemporàne·o -a *adj* extemporaneous
estèndere §270 *tr* to extend; to broaden (*e.g., one's knowledge*); to draw up (*a document*) || *ref* to extend
estensìbile *adj* applicable; **inviare saluti estensibili a** to send greetings to be extended to (*e.g., another person*)
estensióne *f* extension; extent; expanse (*e.g., of water*); (mus) compass, range
estensi·vo -va *adj* extensive
estèn·so -sa *adj*—**per estenso** fully
estensóre *adj* extensible || *m* compiler (*e.g., of a dictionary*); (sports) exerciser, chest expander
estenuante *adj* exhausting
estenuare (estènuo) *tr* to exhaust || *ref* to become exhausted
esterióre *adj* exterior || *m* outside appearance
esteriori·tà *f* (**-tà**) appearance
esternare (estèrno) *tr* to reveal, manifest || *ref* to confide
estèr·no -na *adj* external; outside; day (*student*) || *m* exterior, outside; (baseball) outfielder; **all'esterno** outside; **in esterno** (mov) on location
èste·ro -ra *adj* foreign || *m* foreign countries; **all'estero** abroad
esterrefat·to -ta *adj* terrified
esté·so -sa [s] *adj* extended, wide; **per esteso** in full
estè·ta *mf* (**-ti -te**) aesthete
estèti·co -ca (**-ci -che**) *adj* aesthetic || *f* aesthetics
esteti·sta *mf* (**-sti -ste**) beautician
estima·tóre -trice *mf* appraiser; admirer
èstimo *m* appraisal; assessment
estìnguere §156 *tr* to extinguish; to quench (*thirst*); to pay off (*a debt*) || *ref* to die out

estinguìbile *adj* extinguishable; payable
estìn·to -ta *adj* extinguished; extinct || *m* deceased, dead person
estintóre *m* fire extinguisher
estirpare *tr* to uproot; to eradicate; to pull (*a tooth*)
estirpa·tóre -trice *mf* eradicator || *m* (agr) weeder
estivare *tr & intr* to summer
esti·vo -va *adj* summer; summery
estòllere §171 *tr* to extol
èstone *adj & mf* Estonian
estòrcere §272 *tr* to extort; **estorcere qlco a qlcu** to extort s.th from s.o.
estorsióne *f* extortion
estradare *tr* (law) to extradite
estradizióne *f* extradition
estràne·o -a *adj* extraneous, foreign; aloof || *mf* outsider
estrapolare (estràpolo) *tr* to extrapolate
estrarre §273 *tr* to extract, draw; to pull (*a tooth*)
estrat·to -ta *adj* extracted || *m* extract; abstract; certified copy; (typ) offprint; **estratto conto** bank statement; **estratto dell'atto di nascita** copy of one's birth certificate
estrazióne *f* extraction; drawing (*of lottery*)
estrèma *f* (sports) wing, end
estremi·sta *adj & mf* (**-sti -ste**) extremist
estremi·tà *f* (**-tà**) end; tip, top; extremity; **le estremità** the extremities
estrè·mo -ma *adj* extreme; **esalare l'estremo respiro** to breath one's last || *m* extremity; end, extreme; **essere agli estremi** to be near the end; **estremi** essentials || *f* see **estrema**
estrìnse·co -ca *adj* (**-ci -che**) extrinsic
èstro *m* horsefly; whim, fancy; inspiration; **estro venereo** heat (*of female animal*)
estrométtere §198 *tr* to oust, expel
estró·so -sa [s] *adj* fanciful, whimsical; inspired
estrovèr·so -sa or **estroverti·to -ta** *adj & mf* extrovert
estrùdere §190 *tr* to extrude
estuà·rio *m* (**-ri**) estuary
esuberante *adj* exuberant; buoyant
esuberanza *f* exuberance; buoyancy; **a esuberanza** abundantly
esulare (èsulo) *intr* (ESSERE & AVERE) to go into exile; **esulare da** to be alien to
esulcerare (esùlcero) *tr* to ulcerate on the surface; (fig) to exacerbate
esulcerazióne *f* superficial ulceration; (fig) exasperation, exacerbation
èsule *mf* exile (*person*)
esultante *adj* exultant, jubilant
esultare *intr* to exult
esumare *tr* to exhume; to revive (*e.g., a custom*)
esumazióne *f* exhumation; revival
e·tà *f* (**-tà**) age; **che età ha?** how old is he (or she)?; **ha la sua età** he (or she) is no longer a youngster; **l'età di mezzo** Middle Ages; **maggiore età** majority; **mezza età** middle age; **minore età** minority
etamine *f* cheesecloth
ètere *m* ether

etère·o -a *adj* ethereal
eternare (etèrno) *tr* to immortalize ‖ *ref* to become immortal
eterni·tà *f* (**-tà**) eternity
etèr·no -na *adj* eternal, everlasting ‖ *m* eternity; **in eterno** forever
eterodòs·so -sa *adj* heterodox
eterogène·o -a *adj* heterogeneous
èti·ca *f* (**-che**) ethics
etichétta *f* label; card (*e.g., of a library*); etiquette; **etichetta gommata** sticker
etichettare (etichétto) *tr* to label
èti·co -ca (**-ci -che**) *adj* ethical; consumptive ‖ *m* consumptive ‖ *f* see **etica**
etile *m* ethyl
etilène *m* ethylene
etìli·co -ca *adj* (**-ci -che**) ethyl
ètimo *m* etymon
etimologìa *f* etymology
etìope *adj* & *mf* Ethiopian
Etiòpia, l' *f* Ethiopia
etiòpi·co -ca *adj* (**-ci -che**) Ethiopian
etisìa *f* tuberculosis
ètni·co -ca *adj* (**-ci -che**) ethnic(al)
etnografìa *f* ethnography
etnologìa *f* ethnology
etru·sco -sca *adj* & *mf* (**-schi -sche**) Etruscan
ettàgono *m* heptagon
èttaro *m* hectare
ètte *m* (coll) particle, jot, whit, tittle
ètto or **ettogrammo** *m* hectogram
-étto -étta *suf adj* rather, e.g., **piccoletto** rather small; -ish, e.g., **rotondetto** roundish
ettòlitro *m* hectoliter
cucalìpto *m* eucalyptus
eucaristìa *f* Eucharist
eufemismo *m* euphemism
eufonìa *f* euphony
eufòni·co -ca *adj* (**-ci -che**) euphonic
euforìa *f* euphoria
eufòri·co -ca *adj* (**-ci -che**) euphoric
eufuismo *m* euphuism
eugenèti·co -ca (**-ci -che**) *adj* eugenic ‖ *f* eugenics
eunu·co *m* (**-chi**) eunuch
europè·o -a *adj* & *mf* European
Euròpa, l' *f* Europe
eurovisióne *f* European television chain
eutanasìa *f* euthanasia
Èva *f* Eve
evacuaménto *m* evacuation
evacuare (evàcuo) *tr* to evacuate ‖ *intr* to evacuate; to have a bowel movement
evacuazióne *f* evacuation; bowel movement

evàdere §172 *tr* to evade; to complete (*a deal*); to answer (*a letter*); to execute (*orders*) ‖ *intr* (ESSERE) to flee, escape
evanescènza *f* evanescence; (rad) fading
evanescènte *adj* evanescent; vanishing
evangèli·co -ca *adj* (**-ci -che**) evangelic (al)
evangeli·sta *m* (**-sti**) evangelist
evangelizzare [ddzz] *tr* to evangelize; to campaign for; to subject to political propaganda
evaporare (evapóro) *tr* & *intr* to evaporate
evaporatóre *m* evaporator; humidifier
evaporazióne *f* evaporation
evasióne *f* evasion, escape; (com) reply; **dare evasione a** to complete (*an administrative matter*)
evasi·vo -va *adj* evasive
eva-so -sa *adj* escaped ‖ *m* escapee
evasóre *m* tax dodger
eveniènza *f* eventuality, contingency; **nell'evenienza che** in the event (that); **per ogni evenienza** just in case
evènto *m* event; **eventi correnti** current events; **fausto** or **lieto evento** happy event
eventuale *adj* contingent
eventuali·tà *f* (**-tà**) eventuality
eversi·vo -va *adj* upsetting; destructive
evidènte *adj* evident; clear
evidènza *f* evidence; clearness; **mettersi in evidenza** to make oneself conspicuous; **tenere in evidenza** (com) to keep active
evirare *tr* to emasculate
evitare (èvito) *tr* to avoid, shun; **evitare qlco a qlcu** to spare s.o. s.th, to save s.o. from s.th
èvo *m* age, era; **evo antico** ancient times; **evo moderno** modern times; **medio evo** Middle Ages
evocare §197 (**èvoco**) *tr* to evoke
evoluire §176 *intr* (aer, nav) to maneuver
evolu·to -ta *adj* developed; progressive; modern
evoluzióne *f* evolution
evòlvere §115 *tr* to develop ‖ *ref* to evolve
evvi·va *m* (**-va**) cheer ‖ *interj* long live!, hurrah for!
èx *adj invar* ex-, e.g., **la sua ex moglie** his ex-wife; ex, e.g., **ex dividendo** ex dividend
ex li·bris *m* (**-bris**) bookplate
extraconiugale *adj* extramarital
extraeuropè·o -a *adj* non-European
ex vó·to *m* (**-to**) votive offering
eziologìa *f* etiology

F

F, f ['ɛffe] *m* & *f* sixth letter of the Italian alphabet
fa *m* (fa) (mus) F, fa
fabbisógno *m invar* need; requirement
fàbbri·ca *f* (**-che**) building, construction; factory, plant

fabbricante *mf* builder, manufacturer
fabbricare §197 (**fàbbrico**) *tr* to manufacture; to fabricate
fabbrica·to -ta *adj* built ‖ *m* building
fabbricazióne *f* building; erection; manufacturing; fabrication (*invention*)

fabbro *m* blacksmith; locksmith; (fig) master; **fabbro ferraio** blacksmith

faccènda *f* business, matter; **faccende domestiche** household chores

faccendiè·re -ra *mf* operator, schemer

faccétta *f* small face; face, facet

facchinàg·gio *m* (**-gi**) porterage; (fig) drudgery

facchino *m* porter; **lavorare come un facchino** to work like a slave

fàc·cia *f* (**-ce**) face; countenance; **avere la faccia di** to have the gall to; **di faccia a** opposite; **faccia da galeotto** (coll) gallows bird; **faccia tosta** cheek, gall; **in faccia a** in front of

facciale *adj* facial

facciata *f* façade; page; (fig) surface appearance

face *f* (lit) torch

facè·to -ta *adj* facetious

facèzia *f* pleasantry, banter; **scambiar facezie** to banter with each other

fachiro *m* fakir

fàcile *adj* easy; inclined; loose (*morals*); glib (*tongue*); **è facile** it is probable ‖ *m* something easy

facili·tà *f* (**-tà**) facility, ease; inclination; **facilità di pagamento** easy payments, easy terms; **facilità di parola** glibness

facilitare (**facìlito**) *tr* to facilitate; to grant (*credit*); to give (*easy terms*)

facilitazióne *f* facilitation; easy terms; cut rate

facinoró·so -sa [*s*] *adj* criminal ‖ *m* hoodlum, thug

facoltà *f* (**-tà**) faculty; power; school (*of a university*); **facoltà** *fpl* means, wealth

facoltati·vo -va *adj* optional

facoltó·so -sa [*s*] *adj* wealthy, affluent

facóndia *f* loquacity, gift of gab

facón·do -da *adj* loquacious

facsìmi·le *m* (**-le**) facsimile

faènza *f* faïence ‖ **Faenza** *f* Faenza

fàg·gio *m* (**-gi**) (bot) beech

fagia·no -na *mf* pheasant

fagiolino *m* string bean

fagiòlo *m* bean; (coll) sophomore; **andare a fagiolo a** (coll) to fit perfectly; **fagiolo bianco** lima bean

fà·glia *f* (**-glie**) (geol) fault

fagòtto *m* bundle; (mus) bassoon; **far fagotto** (coll) to pack up

fàida *f* vengeance, vendetta

faìna *f* stone marten

falange *f* phalanx

fal·bo -ba *adj* tawny

falcata *f* step, stride; bucking

falce *f* scythe; crescent (*of moon*); **falce messoria** sickle

falcétto *m* sickle

falciare §128 *tr* to mow

falcia·tóre -trice *mf* mower ‖ *f* mowing machine

falcidiare §287 *tr* to reduce; to cut down

fal·co *m* (**-chi**) hawk; **falco pescatore** osprey

falcóne *m* falcon

falconerìa *f* falconry

falconière *m* falconer

falda *f* -band, strip; flake (*of snow*); gable (*of roof*); brim (*of hat*); foot (*of mountain*); slab (*of stone*); waist plate (*of armor*); hem (*of suit*); flounce (*of dress*); layer (*of rock*); flap, coattail; **falda della camicia** shirttail; **falde** straps (*to hold a baby*); **mettersi in falde** to wear tails

falegname *m* carpenter; cabinetmaker

falegnamerìa *f* carpentry; cabinetmaking; carpenter shop; woodworker shop

falèna *f* moth

falla *f* hole, leak; (archaic) fault

fallace *adj* fallacious, deceptive

fallà·cia *f* (**-cie**) fallacy

fallare *intr* & *ref* (lit) to be mistaken

fallìbile *adj* fallible

fallimentare *adj* bankrupt; ruinous

falliménto *m* bankruptcy; (fig) collapse, failure

fallire §176 *tr* to miss (*the target*) ‖ *intr* (ESSERE) to go bankrupt; to fail ‖ *intr* (AVERE) (lit) to be mistaken

falli·to -ta *adj* & *mf* bankrupt

fallo *m* error, fault; sin; flaw; phallus; (sports) penalty; (sports) foul; **cadere in fallo** to make the wrong move; to be mistaken; **cogliere in fallo** to catch in the act; **far fallo a** to fail, e.g., **gli faccio fallo** I fail him; **senza fallo** without fail

fa·lò *m* (**-lò**) bonfire

falpa·là *f* (**-là**) flounce, furbelow

falsare *tr* to falsify, alter; (lit) to forge

falsari·ga *f* (**-ghe**) guideline (*for writing*); model, pattern; **seguire la falsariga di** to follow in the footsteps of

falsà·rio *m* (**-ri**) forger; counterfeiter

falsétto *m* falsetto

falsificare §197 (**falsìfico**) to falsify; to forge, fake

falsificazióne *f* falsification; forgery; misrepresentation

falsi·tà *f* (**-tà**) falsehood; falsity

fal·so -sa *adj* false; wrong (*step*); assumed (*name*); bogus, counterfeit, fake (*money*); phony ‖ *m* falsehood; perjury; forgery; **commettere un falso** to perjure oneself; to commit forgery; **giurare il falso** to bear false witness; to perjure oneself

fama *f* fame; reputation; **cattiva fama** notoriety

fame *f* hunger; dearth; **aver fame** to be hungry; **avere una fame da lupo** to be as hungry as a wolf, to be as hungry as a bear; **morire di fame** to starve to death; to be ravenous

famèli·co -ca *adj* (**-ci -che**) starving, famished

famigera·to -ta *adj* notorious

famìglia *f* family; community; **di famiglia** intimate; **in famiglia** at home

famì·glio *m* (**-gli**) beadle, usher; hired man

familiare *adj* family; familiar, intimate; homelike ‖ *m* member of the family

familiari·tà *f* (**-tà**) familiarity; **avere familiarità con** to be familiar with

familiarizzare [ddzz] *tr* to familiarize
famó·so -sa [s] *adj* famous, illustrious
fanale *m* lamp, lantern; (rr) headlight; **fanale di coda** taillight
fanalino *m* small light; (aut) parking light; (aut) tail light
fanàti·co -ca (**-ci -che**) *adj* fanatic, fanatical || *mf* fanatic
fanatismo *m* fanaticism
fanatizzare [ddzz] *tr* to make a fanatic of
fanciulla *f* girl; spinster; bride
fanciullè·sco -sca *adj* (**-schi -sche**) childish; children's
fanciullézza *f* childhood; (fig) infancy
fanciulo·lo -la *adj* childish; childlike || *mf* child || *m* boy || *f* see **fanciulla**
fandònia *f* fib, tale, yarn
fanèllo *m* (orn) linnet; (orn) finch
fanfara *f* military band; fanfare
fanfaróne *m* braggart
fangatura *f* mud bath
fanghìglia *f* mud, slush
fan·go *m* (**-ghi**) mud; **fare i fanghi** to take mud baths
fangó·so -sa [s] *adj* muddy
fannullo·ne -na *mf* idler, loafer
fanóne *m* whalebone
fantaccino *m* infantryman, foot soldier
fantascientìfi·co -ca *adj* (**-ci -che**) science-fiction
fantasciènza *f* science fiction
fantasìa *f* fantasy, fancy, whim; (mus) fantasia; **di fantasia** fancy
fantasió·so -sa [s] *adj* fanciful; imaginative
fanta·sma *m* (**-smi**) ghost, spirit; phantom; **fantasma poetico** poetic fancy
fantasticare §197 (**fantàstico**) *tr* to imagine, dream up || *intr* to daydream
fantasticherìa *f* imagination, daydreaming
fantàsti·co -ca *adj* (**-ci -che**) fantastic || **fantastico** *interj* unbelievable!
fante *m* infantryman, foot soldier; (cards) jack; (obs) youth
fanterìa *f* infantry
fanté·sca *f* (**-sche**) (joc, lit) housemaid
fantino *m* jockey
fantòc·cio *m* (**-ci**) puppet
fantomàti·co -ca *adj* (**-ci -che**) ghostly; mysterious
farabutto *m* scoundrel, heel
faraóna *f* guinea fowl
faraóne *m* Pharaoh; (cards) faro
farcire §176 *tr* to stuff
fardèllo *m* bundle; burden; **far fardello** to pack one's bags
fare *m* doing; break (*of day*); way (*of acting*); **sul far della sera** at nightfall || §173 *tr* to do; to make; to work; to take (*e.g., a walk, a step*); to give (*a sigh*); to deal (*cards*); to suffer (*hunger*); to lead (*a good or bad life*); to render (*service*); to log (*e.g., 15 m.p.h.*); to be, e.g., **tre volte tre fa nove** three times three is nine; to build (*e.g., a house*); to put together (*a collection*); to prepare (*dinner*); to say, utter (*a word*); to have (*a dream*); to give (*fruit*); to pay (*atten-*

tion); to play (*a role*); to stir up (*pity*); to mention (*a name*); **fare il** (or **la**) to be a (*e.g., carpenter*); **fare** + *inf* to have + *inf*, e.g., **gli ho fatto . . .** I had him . . . ; to make + *inf*, e.g., **il medico mi fece** . . . the doctor made me . . .; to have + *pp*, e.g., **farò fare** . . . I shall have . . . done; **fare acqua** to leak, to take in water; to get a supply of water; (coll) to urinate; **fare a metà** to divide in half; **fare a pugni** to come to blows; **fare a tempo** to be on time; **fare benzina** to buy gasoline; **fare caldo a** to keep warm, e.g., **questa coperta gli fa caldo** this blanket keeps him warm; **fare carbone** to coal; **fare . . . che** to have been . . . since, e.g., **fanno tre mesi che siamo in questa città** it has been three months since we have been in this city; **fare che** + *subj* to see to it that + *ind*, e.g., **faccia che comincino a lavorare subito** see to it that they begin to work at once; **fare colpo** to make an impression; **fare corona a** to crown; **fare cuore a** to encourage; **fare del male a** to harm; **fare di** + *inf* to see to it that + *ind;* **fare di tutto** to do one's best; **fare festa a** to cheer; **fare fiasco** to fail; **fare finta di** to pretend to; **fare fronte a** to face, meet; **fare fuoco su** to fire upon; **fare il gioco di** to play into the hands of; **fare il pappagallo** to parrot, ape; **fare il pieno** to fill up (*with gasoline*); **fare la bocca a** to get used to; **fare la calza** to knit; **fare la coda** to queue up, line up; **fare la festa a** to kill; **fare la guardia** to stand guard; **fare la mano a** to get used to; **fare le cose in famiglia** to wash one's dirty linen at home; **fare le cose in grande stile** to splurge; **fare legna** to gather firewood; **fare l'occhio** to become accustomed; **fare mente** to pay attention; **fare onore a** to do honor to; **fare paura a** to frighten; **fare sangue** to bleed; **fare sapere a qlcu** to let s.o. know; **fare scalo** (aer, naut) to make a call; **fare sì che** to act in such a way that; to see to it that; **fare silenzio** to keep silent; **fare specie a** to amaze, e.g., **il tuo comportamento gli fa specie** your behavior amazes him; **fare tesoro di** to prize; **fare una bella figura** to look good; to make a fine appearance; **fare una mala figura** to look bad; to make a bad showing; **fare una malattia** (coll) to get sick; **fare vela** to set sail; **fare venire** to send for; **fare vigilia** to fast; **farla corta** to cut it short; **farla franca** to get off scot-free; **farla grossa** to commit a blunder; **farla in barba a** to outwit; **farne di cotte e di crude,** **farne di tutti i colori,** or **farne più di Carlo in Francia** to engage in all sorts of mischief; to paint the town red; **non fare che** + *ind* to do nothing but + *inf* || *intr*—**averla a che fare con** to have words with; to have to deal with; **fare a coltellate** to have a fight with knives; **fare a girotondo** to play ring-around-the-rosy; **fare al caso di** to fit; to suit; **fare a meno di** to do without; to serve as, e.g., **fare da cuscino** to serve as a pillow; **fare da cena** to fix dinner; **fare di cappello** to take one's hat off; **fare presto** to hurry; **fare per** to be just the thing for; **fare tardi** to be late || *ref* to become; to cut (*e.g., one's hair*); to move, e.g., **farsi in là** to move farther; **farsi avanti** to come forward; **farsi beffe di** to make fun of; **farsi bello** to bedeck oneself; to dress up; **farsi bello di** to boast about; to appropriate; **farsi gioco di** to make fun of; **farsi le labbra** to put lipstick on; **farsi strada** to make one's way; **farsi una ragione di** to rationalize, explain to oneself; **farsi un baffo** to not give a hoot; **si fa giorno** it is getting light; **si fa tardi** it is getting late || *impers*—**che tempo fa?** what's the weather like?; **fa ago**, e.g., **alcune settimane fa** a few weeks ago; **fa estate** it is like summer; **fa fino** it is smart; **fa freddo** it is cold; **fa luna** there is moonlight, the moon is out; **fa nebbia** it is foggy; **fa notte** it is nighttime; it is dark; it is getting dark; **fa sole** it is sunny, the sun is out; **fa tipo** or **fa tono!** that's classy!; **non fa nulla** it doesn't matter, never mind

farètra *f* quiver

farfalla *f* butterfly; bow tie; (mach) butterfly valve; (coll) promissory note

farfallóne *m* large butterfly; blunder; Don Juan

farfugliare §280 *intr* to mumble, mutter

farina *f* flour; **farina d'avena** oatmeal; **farina di legno** sawdust; **farina di ossa** bone meal; **farina gialla** yellow corn meal

farináce·o -a *adj* farinaceous || **farinacei** *mpl* flour-yielding cereals

farinata *f* porridge

faringe *f* pharynx

faringite *f* pharingitis

farinó·so -sa [s] *adj* floury; powdery (*snow*); crumbly, friable

fariseò *m* Pharisee; (fig) pharisee

farmacèuti·co -ca *adj* (-ci -che) pharmaceutical, drug

farmacìa *f* pharmacy; drugstore; medicine cabinet; **farmacia di guardia** or **di turno** drugstore open all night and Sunday

farmaci·sta *mf* (-sti -ste) pharmacist, druggist

fàrma·co *m* (-ci or -chi) remedy, medicine

farneticare §197 (farnètico) *intr* to rave

farnèti·co -ca (-chi -che) *adj* raving || *m* delirium; craze

faro *m* lighthouse, beacon; (aut) headlight; **faro retromarcia** (aut) back-up light

farràgine *f* hodgepodge

farraginó·so -sa [s] *adj* confused, mixed

farsa *f* farce; burlesque

farsè·sco -sca *adj* (-schi -sche) farcical, ludicrous

farsétto *m* sweater; (hist) doublet

fascétta *f* girdle; band; wrapper; clamp; **fascetta editoriale** advertising band (*of book*)

fà·scia *f* (-sce) band; belt; bandage; newspaper wrapper; **fascia del cappello** hatband; **fascia di garza** gauze bandage; **fascia elastica** abdominal supporter; (aut) piston ring; **fasce del neonato** swaddling clothes; **in fasce** newborn; **sotto fascia** in a wrapper

fasciame *m* (naut) planking; (naut) plating

fasciare §128 to bind; to bandage; to wrap; to surround

fasciatura *f* bandaging, dressing

fascìcolo *m* number, issue; pamphlet; file, dossier; (bb) fasciculus

fascina *f* fagot

fascina·tóre -trice *mf* charmer

fàscino *m* fascination, charm

fà·scio *m* (-sci) bundle; sheaf; bunch (*of flowers*); pencil or beam (*of rays*); fascist party

fascismo *m* fascism

fasci·sta *adj* & *mf* (-sti -ste) fascist

fase *f* phase, stage; (aut) cycle; (astr, elec, mach) phase

fastèllo *m* bundle, fagot

fasti *mpl* records, annals; notable events; (hist) Roman calendar

fastì·dio *m* (-di) annoyance; (coll) loathing, nausea; **avere in fastidio** to loathe; **dar fastidio a** to annoy; **fastidi** troubles, worries

fastidió·so -sa [s] *adj* annoying, irksome; irritable; (obs) disgusting

fastì·gio *m* (-gi) top, summit

fa·sto -sta *adj* (lit) propitious || *m invar* pomp, display || *mpl* see **fasti**

fastó·so -sa [s] *adj* pompous, ostentatious

fata *f* fairy; **buona fata** fairy godmother; **Fata Morgana** Fata Morgana (*mirage; Morgan le Fay*)

fatale *adj* fatal; inevitable; irresistible (*woman*)

fatalismo *m* fatalism

fatali·sta *mf* (-sti -ste) fatalist

fatali·tà *f* (-tà) fatality, fate

fatalóna *f* vamp

fata·to -ta *adj* fairy, enchanted; (lit) predestined

fati·ca *f* (-che) fatigue, weariness; labor; **a fatica** with difficulty; **da fatica** draft (*e.g., horse*); of burden (*beast*); **durar fatica a** + *inf* to have trouble in + *ger*

faticare §197 *intr* to toil; **faticare a** to be hardly able to

faticó·so -sa [s] *adj* burdensome, heavy; (lit) weary

fatìdi·co -ca *adj* (-ci -che) fatal

fato *m* fate, destiny

fatta *f* kind, sort; **essere sulla fatta di** to be on the trail of

fattàc·cio *m* (-ci) (coll) crime

fattézze *fpl* features

fattìbile *adj* feasible, possible
fattispècie *f*—nella fattispecie in this particular case
fat·to -ta *adj* made, e.g., fatto a mano handmade; broad (*daylight*); deep (*night*); ready-made (*e.g., suit*); ben fatto well-done; shapely; esser fatto per to be cut out for; fatto di made of; venir fatto a to happen, chance, e.g., gli venne fatto d'incontrarmi he happened to meet me ‖ *m* fact; act, deed; feat; action; business, affair; badare ai fatti propri to mind one's own business; cogliere sul fatto to catch in the act; dire a qlcu il fatto suo to give s.o. a piece of one's mind; fatto compiuto fait accompli; fatto d'arme feat of arms; fatto si è the fact remains that; in fatto di concerning; as of; sapere il fatto proprio to know one's business; venire al fatto to come to the point ‖ *f* see fatta
fat·tóre -tóra or **-toréssa** *mf* farm manager ‖ *m* maker; factor; steward ‖ *f* stewardess; manager's wife
fattorìa *f* farm; stewardship
fattorino *m* delivery boy, messenger boy; conductor (*of streetcar*)
fattrìce *f* (zool) dam
fattucchiè·re -ra *mf* magician ‖ *m* sorcerer ‖ *f* sorceress, witch
fattura *f* preparation; workmanship; bill, invoice; (coll) witchcraft; (lit) creature
fatturare *tr* to adulterate; to invoice, bill
fattura·to -ta *adj* adulterated ‖ *m* (com) turnover
fatturi·sta *mf* (-sti -ste) billing clerk
fà·tuo -tua *adj* fatuous
fàuci *fpl* jaws; (fig) mouth
fàuna *f* fauna
fàuno *m* faun
fàu·sto -sta *adj* propitious, lucky
fau·tóre -trice *mf* supporter, promoter
fava *f* broad bean; pigliare due piccioni con una fava to catch two birds with one stone
favèlla *f* speech; (lit) tongue
favilla *f* spark; far or mandare faville to sparkle
favo *m* honeycomb
fàvola *f* fable; tale; favola del paese talk of the town
favoló·so -sa [s] *adj* fabulous; mythical
favóre *m* favor; help; cover (*e.g., of night*); a favore di for the benefit of; di favore special (*price*); complimentary (*ticket*); favore politico patronage; per favore please; per favore di courtesy of
favoreggiaménto *m* abetting, support
favoreggiare §290 (favoréggio) *tr* to abet, support
favoreggia·tóre -trice *mf* abettor, supporter, backer
favorévole *adj* favorable; propitious
favorire §176 *tr* to favor; to accept; to oblige, accommodate; favorire qlcu di qlco to oblige s.o. with s.th; favorisca + *inf* please + *inf*, be kind

enough to + *inf;* favorisca alla cassa please pay the cashier; favorisca uscire! please leave!; tanto per favorire just to keep you company; vuol favorire? won't you please join us (*at a meal*)?; please help yourself!
favorita *f* royal mistress
favoritismo *m* favoritism
favori·to -ta *adj* & *mf* favorite ‖ *m* protegé; favoriti sideburns ‖ *f* see favorita
fazióne *f* faction; essere di fazione to be on guard duty
fazió·so -sa [s] *adj* factious ‖ *m* partisan
fazzolétto *m* handkerchief; fazzoletto da collo neckerchief
fé *f* var of fede
feb·bràio *m* (-brài) February
fèbbre *f* fever; fever blister; febbre da cavallo (coll) very high fever; febbre da fieno hay fever; febbre dell'oro gold fever
febbricitante *adj* feverish
febbrile *adj* feverish
Fèbo *m* Phoebus
féc·cia *f* (-ce) dregs; (fig) dregs (*of society*); fino alla feccia to the bitter end
fèci *fpl* feces
fècola *f* starch
fecondare (fecóndo) *tr* to fecundate
fecondazióne *f* fecundation; fecondazione artificiale artificial insemination
fecondi·tà *f* (-tà) fecundity
fecón·do -da *adj* fecund, prolific
féde *f* faith; certificate; wedding ring; faithfulness; far fede to bear witness; in fede di che in testimony whereof; in fede mia! upon my word! prestar fede a to put one's faith in; tener fede alla parola data to keep one's word
fedecommésso *m* fideicommissum; trusteeship
fedéle *adj* faithful, devoted ‖ *mf* faithful person; i fedeli the faithful
fedel·tà *f* (-tà) faithfulness, allegiance; fidelity; ad alta fedeltà hi-fi
fèdera *f* pillowcase
federale *adj* federal
federali·sta *mf* (-sti -ste) federalist
federati·vo -va *adj* federative
federa·to -ta *adj* federate, federated
federazióne *f* federation; (sports) league
Federico *m* Frederick
fedìfra·go -ga *adj* (-ghi -ghe) unfaithful, treacherous
fedìna *f* police record; avere la fedina sporca to have a bad record; fedine sideburns
fégato *m* liver; courage; fegato d'oca pâté de foie gras; rodersi il fegato to be consumed with rage
félce *f* fern
feldspato *m* feldspar
felice *adj* happy; blissful; glad; felicitous
felici·tà *f* (-tà) happiness; bliss
felicitare (felìcito) *tr* to make happy; che Dio vi feliciti! God bless you! ‖

ref to rejoice; **felicitarsi con qlcu per qlco** to congratulate s.o. for or on s.th
felicitazióne *f* congratulation
feli·no -na *adj* & *m* feline
fellóne *m* (lit) traitor
félpa *f* plush
felpa·to -ta *adj* covered with plush; soft (*e.g.*, *step*)
féltro *m* felt; felt hat
felu·ca *f* (**-che**) two-cornered hat; (naut) felucca
fémmina *adj* & *f* female
femminile *adj* feminine, female || *m* feminine gender
femminili·tà *f* (**-tà**) femininity, womanliness
femminismo *m* feminism
fèmore *m* femur; thighbone
fendènte *m* slash with a sword
fèndere §174 *tr* to split, cleave; to plow (*water*); to rend (*air*); to make one's way through (*a crowd*) || *ref* to split; to come apart
fenditura *f* split, breach, fissure
fenice *f* phoenix
feni·cio -cia (**-ci -cie**) *adj* & *mf* Phoenician || **la Fenicia** Phoenicia
fèni·co -ca *adj* (**-ci -che**) carbolic
fenicòttero *m* flamingo
fenòlo *m* phenol
fenomenale *adj* phenomenal
fenòmeno *m* phenomenon; freak, monster; **essere un fenomeno** to be unbelievable
ferace *adj* (lit) fertile
ferale *adj* (lit) mortal, deadly
fèretro *m* bier, coffin
feriale *adj* working (*day*); weekday
fèrie *fpl* vacation; **ferie retribuite** vacation with pay
ferire §176 *tr* to wound; to strike; **senza colpo ferire** without striking a blow || *ref* to wound oneself
feri·to -ta *adj* wounded, injured || *m* wounded person; injured person; **i feriti** the wounded; the injured || *f* wound, injury
feritóia *f* loophole; embrasure
feri·tóre -trice *mf* assailant
férma *f* setting (*of setter or pointer*); (mil) service; (mil) enlistment
fermacarro *m* (rr) buffer
fermacar·te *m* (**-te**) paperweight; large paper clip
fermacravat·ta *m* (**-ta**) tiepin
fermà·glio *m* (**-gli**) clasp; buckle; clip; brooch
fermare (**férmo**) *tr* to stop; to pay (*attention*); to fasten; to close, shut; to detain (*in police station*); to set (*game*); to reserve (*seats*) || *ref* to stop; to stay
fermata *f* stop; **fermata a richiesta** or **facoltativa** stop on signal
fermentare (**ferménto**) *tr* & *intr* to ferment
fermentazióne *f* fermentation
ferménto *m* ferment
fermézza *f* firmness; steadfastness
fér·mo -ma *adj* firm; stopped; quiet (*water*); (fig) steadfast; **fermo in**

posta general delivery; **fermo restando che** seeing that; **stare fermo** to be quiet || *m* stop; detention; **mettere il fermo a** to stop (*a check*)
fermopòsta *m* general delivery || *adv* care of general delivery
feróce *adj* fierce; wild
ferò·cia *f* (**-cie**) ferocity, ferociousness, fierceness
feròdo *m* (aut) brake lining
ferragósto *m* Assumption; mid-August holiday
ferrame *m* ironware
ferramén·to *m* (**-ti**) iron or metal bracket; iron or metal trimming || *m* (**-ta** *fpl*)—**ferramenta** hardware
ferrare (**fèrro**) *tr* to shoe (*a horse*); to hoop (*a barrel*)
ferra·to -ta *adj* iron; ironclad; shod (*horse*); spiked (*shoe*); well-versed || *f* pressing, ironing; mark or burn (*caused by ironing*); (coll) iron grate
ferravèc·chio *m* (**-chi**) scrap-iron dealer, junkman
fèrre·o -a *adj* iron; ironclad
ferrièra *f* ironworks; (obs) iron mine
fèrro *m* iron; tool; anchor; sword; **ai ferri** on the grill, broiled (*e.g.*, *steak*); **essere sotto i ferri del chirurgo** to go under the knife; **ferri** shackles; **ferri del mestiere** tools of the trade; **ferro battuto** wrought iron; **ferro da arricciare** curling iron; **ferro da calza** knitting needle; **ferro da cavallo** horseshoe; **ferro da stiro** iron, flatiron; **ferro fuso** cast iron; **ferro grezzo** pig iron; **mettere a ferro e fuoco** to put to fire and sword; **venire ai ferri corti** to get into close quarters
ferromodellismo *m* hobby of model railroads
ferrotranvièri *mpl* transport workers
ferrovìa *f* railroad; **ferrovia a dentiera** rack railway; **ferrovia sopraelevata** elevated railroad
ferrovià·rio -ria *adj* (**-ri -rie**) railroad
ferrovière *m* railroader
fèrtile *adj* fertile
fertilizzante [ddzz] *adj* fertilizing || *m* fertilizer
fertilizzare [ddzz] *tr* to fertilize
fervènte *adj* fervent
fèrvere §175 *intr* to be fervent; to rage (*said, e.g., of a battle*); to go full blast
fèrvi·do -da *adj* fervent
fervóre *m* fervor; (fig) heat
fervorino *m* lecture, sermon
fesserìa *f* (slang) stupidity, nonsense; (slang) trifle
fés·so -sa *adj* cracked; cleft; (slang) dumb || *m* (lit) cranny; **fare fesso qlcu** (slang) to play s.o. for a sucker
fessura *f* crack; cranny
fèsta *f* feast; holiday; birthday; saint's day; **a festa** festively; **buone feste!** happy holiday!; **conciare per le feste** to drub the daylights out of; **fare festa a** to welcome; **fare le feste** to spend the holidays; **far festa** to celebrate; to take the day off; **far la festa**

a to do in, kill; **festa del ceppo** Christmas; **festa da ballo** or **danzante** dancing party; **festa della mamma** Mother's Day; **festa del papà** Father's Day; **festa di precetto** (eccl) day of obligation; **festa nazionale** national holiday; **mezza festa** half holiday

festante adj cheerful

festeggiaménto m celebration

festeggiare §290 (**festéggio**) tr to celebrate, fete; to cheer

festi·no -na adj (lit) rapid || m party

festivi·tà f (**-tà**) festivity

festi·vo -va adj festive, holiday

festóne m festoon

festó·so -sa [s] adj cheerful, merry

festu·ca f (**-che**) straw; (fig) mote

fetènte adj stinking; stink (bomb) || mf (fig) stinker, louse

fetic·cio m (**-ci**) fetish

feticismo m fetishism

fèti·do -da adj stinking, fetid

fèto m fetus

fetóre m stench

fétta f slice; **tagliare a fette** to slice

fettina f thin slice; twist (of lemon); **fettina di vitello** veal cutlet

fettùc·cia f (**-ce**) tape, ribbon

fettuccine fpl noodles

feudale adj feudal

feudalismo m feudalism

feudatà·rio -ria (**-ri -rie**) adj feudatory || m feudal vassal

fèudo m fief

fiaba f fairy tale; tale, yarn

fiacca f tiredness; sluggishness; **batter la fiacca** to loaf, to goof off

fiaccare §197 tr to weaken; to weary; to break || ref to weaken; to break (e.g., one's neck)

fiacche·ràio m (**-rài**) (coll) hackman, cabman

fiacchézza f weakness; sluggishness

fiac·co -ca adj (**-chi -che**) weak; sluggish; slack || f see **fiacca**

fiàccola f torch; **fiaccola della discordia** firebrand

fiaccolata f torchlight procession

fiala f vial, phial

fiamma f flame; blaze; (mil) insignia; (nav) pennant; **alla fiamma** (culin) flaming; **dare alle fiamme** to set on fire; **diventare di fiamma** to blush; **in fiamme** afire

fiammante adj blazing; **nuovo fiammante** brand-new

fiammata f blaze; flare-up

fiammeggiante adj flaming, blazing; (archit) flamboyant

fiammeggiare §290 (**fiamméggio**) tr to singe || intr to flame, blaze

fiammìfero m match

fiammin·go -ga (**-ghi -ghe**) adj Flemish; Dutch (e.g., master) || mf Fleming || m Flemish (language); (orn) flamingo

fiancata f blow with one's hip; dig, sarcastic remark; side, flank; (nav) broadside

fiancheggiare §290 (**fianchéggio**) tr to flank; to border (a road); to support

fiancheggia·tóre -trice mf supporter, backer

fian·co m (**-chi**) flank, side; hip; **di fianco** sideways; **fianco a fianco** side by side; **fianco destr'!** (mil) right face!; **fianco destro** (naut) starboard; **fianco sinistr'!** (mil) left face!; **fianco sinistro** (naut) port; **prestare il fianco a** to leave oneself wide open to; **tenersi i fianchi dal ridere** to split one's sides laughing

Fiandre, le fpl Flanders

fia·sca f (**-sche**) flask

fiaschetteria f tavern, wine shop

fia·sco m (**-schi**) straw-covered wine bottle; flask; fiasco

fiata f (archaic) time

fiatare intr to breathe; **senza fiatare** without breathing a word

fiato m breath; (archaic) stench; **avere il fiato grosso** to be out of breath; **bere d'un fiato** to gulp down; **col fiato sospeso** holding one's breath; **dare fiato a** to blow, sound (a trumpet); **d'un fiato** or **in un fiato** without interruption; in one gulp; **fiati** (mus) winds; **senza fiato** out of breath

fiatóne m—**avere il fiatone** to be out of breath

fibbia f clasp, buckle

fibra f fiber

fibró·so -sa [s] adj fibrous

ficcana·so [s] mf (**-si** mpl **-so** fpl) (coll) busybody, meddler; nosy person

ficcare §197 tr to stick; to drive (e.g., a nail); to push; **ficcare gli occhi addosso a** to gaze at, stare at; **ficcare il naso negli affari degli altri** to poke one's nose in other people's business || ref to hide; to butt in; to get involved

fi·co m (**-chi**) fig; fig tree

ficodìndia m (pl **fichidìndia**) prickly pear

fidanzaménto m engagement, betrothal

fidanzare tr to betroth || ref to become engaged

fidanza·to -ta adj engaged || m fiancé || f fiancée

fidare tr to entrust || intr to trust || ref to have confidence; **fidarsi a** (coll) to dare to; **fidarsi di** to trust, rely on

fida·to -ta adj trustworthy, reliable

fi·do -da adj (lit) faithful, trusted || m loyal follower; credit; **far fido** to extend credit

fidùcia f faith, confidence; (com) credit; **di fiducia** trustworthy

fiducià·rio -ria (**-ri -rie**) adj fiduciary || mf fiduciary, trustee

fidució·so -sa [s] adj confident, hopeful

fièle m invar gall, bile; acrimony

fienile m hayloft

fièno m hay

fierìsti·co -ca adj (**-ci -che**) of a fair, e.g., **attività fieristica** activity of a fair

fiè·ro -ra adj fierce; dignified; proud || f fair; exhibit; wild beast

fièvole *adj* feeble, weak

fifa *f* (coll) scare; **avere la fifa** (coll) to be chicken; **avere una fifa blu** (coll) to be scared stiff

fifó·ne -na *mf* (coll) scaredy-cat

figgere §104 *tr* (lit) to drive, thrust ‖ *ref*—**figgersi in capo** to get into one's head

figlia *f* daughter; (com) stub; **figlia consanguinea** stepdaughter on the father's side

figliare §280 *tr & intr* to whelp (*said of animals*)

figlia·stro -stra *mf* stepchild ‖ *m* stepson ‖ *f* stepdaughter

figliata *f* litter (*e.g., of pigs*)

fi·glio -glia *mf* child, offspring ‖ *m* son; **figli** children; **figlio consanguineo** stepson on the father's side ‖ *f* see **figlia**

figliòc·cio -cia (-ci -ce) *mf* godchild ‖ *m* godson ‖ *f* goddaughter

figliolanza *f* children, offspring

figliò·lo -la *mf* child ‖ *m* son, boy ‖ *f* daughter, girl

figura *f* figure; illustration; figurehead; face card; **far bella figura** to make a good showing; **far cattiva figura** to make a poor showing; **far figura** to look good; **figura retorica** figure of speech

figurante *mf* (theat) extra, super

figurare *tr* to feign; to represent ‖ *intr* to figure; to appear; to make a good showing ‖ *ref* to imagine; **si figuri!** imagine!

figurati·vo -va *adj* (fa) figurative

figura·to -ta *adj* figurative (*speech*); transcribed (*pronunciation*); illustrated (*book*)

figurina *f* figurine; card, picture (*of a series of athletes or entertainment celebrities*)

figurini·sta *mf* (-sti -ste) dress designer; costume designer

figurino *m* fashion plate; fashion magazine

figuro *m* scoundrel; gangster

figuróne *m*—**fare un figurone** to make a very good showing

fila *f* row; file, line; series; **di fila** in a row; **fare la fila** to wait in line; **file ranks**

filàc·cia *f* (-ce) lint

filacció·so -sa [s] or filacció·so -sa [s] *adj* thready, stringy

filaménto *m* filament

filamentó·so -sa [s] *adj* thready, stringy; thread-like

filanda *f* spinning mill; silk spinning mill

filante *adj* spinning; shooting (*star*); thready; flowing (*e.g., line*)

filantropia *f* philanthropy

filantròpi·co -ca *adj* (-ci -che) philanthropic

filàntro·po -pa *mf* philanthropist

filare *m* row, line ‖ *tr* to spin; to drip, ooze; to rest on (*one's oars*); to make (*e.g., ten knots*); (naut) to pay out; (mus) to hold (*a note*); **filare l'amore** to be in love ‖ *intr* to spin (*said of a spider*); to rope, thread (*said of wine*

or *syrup*); to make sense; to drip; **fare filare dritto qlcu** to keep s.o. in line; **filare a** to do (*e.g., twenty miles an hour*); **filare all'inglese** to take French leave; **fila via!** (coll) get out!

filarmòni·co -ca (-ci -che) *adj* philharmonic ‖ *f* philharmonic society

filastròc·ca *f* (-che) rigmarole; nursery rhyme

filatelìa *f* philately

filatèli·co -ca (-ci -che) *adj* philatelic(al) ‖ *mf* philatelist

fila·to -ta *adj* spun; well-constructed (*speech*) ‖ *m* yarn

fila·tóio *m* (-tói) spinning wheel

filatura *f* spinning; spinning mill

filettare (filétto) *tr* to fillet; (mach) to thread

filettatura *f* stripe (*on a cap*); (mach) thread

filétto *m* fillet; stripe; snaffle (*on a horse's bit*); fine stroke (*in handwriting*); (mach) thread; (typ) ornamental line, headband; (typ) rule

filiale *adj* filial ‖ *f* branch office

filiazióne *f* filiation

filibustière *m* filibuster, buccaneer; adventurer

filièra *f* (mach) drawplate; (mach) die (*to cut threads*)

filigrana *f* filigree; watermark (*in paper*)

filippi·no -na *adj* Philippine ‖ *m* Filipino ‖ **le Filippine** the Philippines

Filippo *m* Philip

filistè·o -a *adj & m* philistine; Philistine

Fìllide *f* Phyllis

film *m* (film) film; movie, motion picture; **film parlato** or **sonoro** talking picture

filmare *tr* to film

filmina *f* filmstrip

filmìsti·co -ca *adj* (-ci -che) movie, motion-picture

filmotè·ca *f* (-che) film library

fi·lo *m* (-li) thread; wire; yarn; blade (*of grass*); breath (*of air*); string (*of pearls*); edge (*of razor*); **dare del filo da torcere** to cause trouble; **essere ridotto a un filo** to be only skin and bones; **fil di voce** thin voice; **filo a piombo** plumb line; **filo d'acqua** thin stream; **filo della schiena** or **delle reni** spine; **filo spinato** barbed wire; **passare a fil di spada** to put to the sword; **per filo e per segno** in detail; from beginning to end; **senza fili** wireless; **stare a filo** to stand upright; **tenere i fili** (fig) to pull wires; **tenere in filo** to keep in line; **un filo di** a bit of ‖ *m* (-la *fpl*) string (*e.g., of cooked cheese*); (archaic) file, row

filo·bus *m* (-bus) trolley bus

filodiffusióne *f* wired wireless; cable TV

filodrammàti·co -ca *adj & mf* (-ci -che) (theat) amateur

filogovernati·vo -va *adj* on the government side

filologìa *f* philology

filòlo·go -ga (-gi -ghe) *adj* philologic(al) ‖ *m* philologist

filóne *m* vein (*of ore*); ripple (*of a cur-*

rent); stream; loaf (*of bread*); (lit) mainstream; **filone d'oro** gold lode
filó·so -sa [s] *adj* stringy
filosofìa *f* philosophy
filosòfi·co -ca *adj* (**-ci -che**) philosophic(al)
filòso·fo -fa *mf* philosopher
filovìa *f* trolley bus line
filtrare *tr* to filter; to percolate (*coffee*) || *intr* to filter, permeate
filtrazióne *f* filtering, filtration
filtro *m* filter; philter
filugèllo *m* silkworm
filza *f* string (*of pearls*); series (*of errors*); row; dossier, file; basting (*of dress*)
finale *adj* final, last; consumer (*goods*) || *m* end, ending; (mus) finale; (sports) finish || *f* end, ending; (sports) finals
finali·sta *mf* (**-sti -ste**) finalist
finali·tà *f* (**-tà**) end, purpose
finanche *adv* even
finanza *f* finance
finanziaménto *m* financing
finanziare §287 *tr* to finance
finanzià·rio -ria (**-ri -rie**) *adj* finance, financial || *f* (com) holding company
finanzia·tóre -trice *mf* financial backer
finanzièra *f* frock coat; **alla finanziera** with giblet gravy
finanzière *m* financier; (coll) customs officer
fin·ca *f* (**-che**) column, row (*of ledger*)
finché *conj* until, as long as; **finché non** until
fine *adj* fine, thin; choice, nice || *m* end, purpose; conclusion; (lit) limit, border; **a fin di bene** to good purpose, for the best; **secondo fine** ulterior motive || *f* end, conclusion; **condurre a fine** to bring to fruition; **fine di settimana** weekend; **in fin dei conti** after all; **senza fine** endless
fine-settima·na *m* or *f* (**-na**) weekend
finèstra *f* window; (lit) gash, wound; **finestra a gangheri** casement window; **finestra a ghigliottina** sash window; **finestra panoramica** picture window; **finestre** (lit) eyes
finestrino *m* (aut, rr) window
finézza *f* thinness; delicacy; finesse; kindness
fìngere §126 *tr* to feign, pretend; (lit) to invent || *intr* to feign, pretend || *ref* to pretend to be
finiménto *m* finishing touch; **finimenti** harness
finimóndo *m* fracas, uproar
finire §176 *tr* to end; to put an end to; **finiscila!** cut it out! || *intr* (ESSERE) to end, to be over; to abut; to wind up; **finire con** + *inf* to wind up + *ger*; **finire di** + *inf* to finish + *ger*, e.g., **ho finito di farmi la barba** I have finished shaving
fini·to -ta *adj* finished; accomplished; finite; exhausted; **aver finito** to be through; **falla finita!** cut it out!; **farla finita con** to be through with; **farla finita con la vita** to end one's life
finitura *f* finish, finishing touch

finlandése [s] *adj* Finnish || *mf* Finlander, Finn || *m* Finnish (*language*)
Finlàndia, la Finland
fìnni·co -ca *adj* & *mf* (**-ci -che**) Finnic
fi·no -na *adj* fine, thin; refined; pure; sheer; **fare fino** (coll) to be refined || *adv* even; **fin a quando?** till when?; **fin da domani** beginning tomorrow; **fin da ora** beginning right now; **fin dove?** how far?; **fin in cima** up to the top; **fino a** until; down to; up to; as far as; **fin qui** up to now; up to this point
finòc·chio *m* (**-chi**) fennel; (vulg) fairy, queer
finóra *adv* up to now, heretofore
finta *f* pretense; fly (*of trousers*); (sports) feint; **far finta di** + *inf* to pretend to + *inf*, to feign + *ger*
fintantoché *conj* until
fin·to -ta *adj* false (*teeth*); fake; fictitious; sham (*battle*) || *mf* hypocrite || *f* see **finta**
finzióne *f* pretense; fiction; figment
fìo *m*—**pagare il fio** to pay the piper; **pagare il fio di** to pay the penalty for
fioccare §197 (**fiòcco**) *intr* (ESSERE) to fall (*said of snow*); to flow (*said, e.g., of complaints*) || *impers* (ESSERE) —**fiocca** it is snowing
fiòc·co *m* (**-chi**) bow, knot; flake (*of snow*); flock, tuft (*of wool*); (naut) jib; **coi fiocchi** excellent; made to perfection; **fiocco pallone** (naut) spinnaker
fioccó·so -sa [s] *adj* flaky
fiòcina *f* harpoon
fiò·co -ca *adj* (**-chi -che**) feeble, faint
fiónda *f* sling; slingshot
fio·ràio -ràia (**-rài -ràie**) *mf* florist || *f* flower girl
fiorami *mpl*—**a fiorami** with flower design
fiordaliso *m* fleur-de-lis; (bot) iris; (lit) lily
fiòrdo *m* fjord
fióre *m* flower; prime (*of life*); best, pick; bloom; **a fior d'acqua** on the surface; skimming the water; **a fior di labbra** in a low tone, sottovoce; **a fior di pelle** skin-deep, superficial; **fior di** (coll) a lot of; **fiore di latte** cream; **fiori** (cards) clubs; **primo fiore** down (*soft hairy growth*)
fiorènte *adj* flourishing, thriving
fiorenti·no -na *adj* & *mf* Florentine
fiorettare (**fiorétto**) *tr* (fig) to overembellish
fiorétto *m* little flower; choice, pick; overembellishment; choice passage (*from life of saint*); foil; button of foil
fioricoltóre *m* var of **floricoltore**
fioricoltura *f* var of **floricoltura**
fiorino *m* florin
fiorire §176 *tr* to cause to flower; to adorn with flowers || *intr* (ESSERE) to flower, bloom; to flourish; to break out (*said of skin eruption*); to get moldy
fiori·sta *mf* (**-sti -ste**) florist
fiori·to -ta *adj* flowering; flowery;

mottled; moldy; studded (*e.g.*, *with errors*)

fioritura *f* flowering; flourish; mold; (pathol) eruption

fiorrancino *m* (orn) kinglet, firecrest

fiorràn·cio *m* (-ci) marigold ·

fiòtto *m* gush, surge; (obs) wave

Firènze *f* Florence

firma *f* signature; power of attorney; good reputation; (mil) enlisted man; **buona firma** famous writer; **farci la firma** (coll) to accept quite willingly; **firma di favore** guarantor's signature

firmaiòlo *m* (mil) enlisted man

firmaménto *m* firmament

firmare *tr* to sign

firmatà·rio -ria (-ri -rie) *adj* signatory || *mf* signer, signatory

fisarmòni·ca *f* (-che) accordion

fiscale *adj* fiscal, tax

fischiare §287 *tr* to whistle; to boo || *intr* to whistle; to ring (*said of ears*); to blow (*said, e.g., of a factory whistle*)

fischiettare (fischiétto) *tr* & *intr* to whistle

fischiétto *m* whistle (*instrument*)

fì·schio *m* (-schi) whistle; hiss, boo; blow (*of whistle*); ringing (*in the ears*)

fi·sciù *m* (-sciù) kerchief, fichu

fisco *m invar* treasury; internal revenue service

fisi·co -ca (-ci -che) *adj* physical; bodily || *m* physicist; physique; (obs) physician || *f* physics

fisima *f* whim, fancy, caprice

fisiologìa *f* physiology

fisiològi·co -ca *adj* (-ci -che) physiological

fisionomìa or **fisonomìa** *f* physiognomy; countenance, face; appearance

fisionomi·sta *mf* (-sti -ste) person good at faces; physiognomist

fi·so -sa *adj* (lit) fixed

fissàg·gio *m* (-gi) (phot) fixing

fissare *tr* to fix; to fasten; to gaze at; to reserve; to hire; **fissare lo sguardo** to gaze || *ref* to gaze, stare; to become obsessed; to settle down

fissati·vo -va *adj* fixing

fissa·to -ta *adj* fixed; (coll) cracked || *mf* (coll) crackpot

fissa·tóre -trice *adj* (phot) fixing || *m* fixer; **fissatore per capelli** hair spray; hair dressing

fissazióne *f* fixation; fixed idea

fissile *adj* fissionable

fissionàbile *adj* fissionable

fissióne *f* fission

fis·so -sa *adj* fixed; regular || *m* pay

fistola *f* (pathol) fistula; (lit) pipe

fitta *f* pang, stitch; crowd; great amount; (coll) blow; (obs) quagmire

fittàvolo *m* tenant farmer

fittì·zio -zia *adj* (-zi -zie) fictitious

fit·to -ta *adj* fixed, dug in; thick, dense; pitch (*dark*) || *m* thick; rent; tenancy || *f* see **fitta**

fittóne *m* (bot) taproot

fiuma·no -na *adj* river; from Fiume || *m* person from Fiume || *f* flood, stream

fiumara *f* torrent

fiume *m* river; **a fiumi** like a river

fiutare *tr* to snuff, sniff; to smell

fiutata *f* snuff, sniff

fiuto *m* sense of smell; snuff; flair

flàcci·do -da *adj* flabby

flacóne *m* flacon

flagellare (flagèllo) *tr* to scourge, lash, flagellate

flagèllo *m* whip, scourge; pest, plague; (coll) mess

flagrante *adj* flagrant; **in flagrante (delitto)** in the act

flan *m* (**flan**) pudding; (typ) mat

flanèlla *f* flannel

flàn·gia *f* (-ge) flange

flato *m* gas, flatus

flatulènza *f* flatulence

flautino *m* flageolet

flauti·sta *mf* (-sti -ste) flutist

flàuto *m* flute; **flauto diritto** or **dolce** (mus) recorder

fla·vo -va *adj* (lit) blond, golden

flèbile *adj* mournful

flebite *f* phlebitis

flèmma *f* apathy; coolness; phlegm

flemmàti·co -ca *adj* (-ci -che) phlegmatic(al)

flessìbile *adj* flexible, pliable

flessióne *f* bending; (com) fall, drop; (gram) inflection

flessuó·so -sa [s] *adj* lithe, willowy; winding; flowing (*style*)

flèttere §177 *tr* to flex; (gram) to inflect

flirtare *intr* to flirt

flòra *f* flora

floreale *adj* floral

floricoltóre *m* floriculturist

floricoltura *f* floriculture

flòri·do -da *adj* florid; flourishing

flò·scio -scia *adj* (-sci -sce) flabby; soft (*hat*)

flòtta *f* fleet

flottante *adj* floating || *m* (com) floating stock

flottare (flòtto) *tr* & *intr* to float

flottìglia *f* flottilla

fluènte *adj* flowing

fluidità *f* fluidity

flùi·do -da *adj* & *m* fluid; fluent (*style*)

fluire §176 *intr* (ESSERE) to flow; to pour

fluitazióne *f* log driving

fluorescènte *adj* fluorescent

fluorescènza *f* fluorescence

fluorìdri·co -ca *adj* (-ci -che) hydrofluoric

fluorite *f* fluor, fluorite

fluorizzazióne [ddzz] *f* fluoridation

fluòro *m* fluorine

fluoruro *m* fluoride

flusso *m* flow; flood (*of tide*); high tide; (pathol) flow (*e.g., of blood*); (phys) flux

flutto *m* (lit) wave

fluttuare (flùttuo) *intr* to fluctuate; to bob, toss; to waver; to surge, stream

fluviale *adj* fluvial, river

fobìa *f* phobia

fò·ca *f* (-che) seal; sealskin

focàc·cia *f* (-ce) flat, rounded loaf; cake

focaccina *f* bun

fo·càia *adj fem* (**-càie**) flint
focale *adj* focal
fóce *f* mouth (*of river*)
focèna *f* porpoise
fochi·sta *m* (**-sti**) fireman, stoker; fire-works manufacturer
foco·làio *m* (**-lài**) (pathol) focus; (fig) hotbed
focolare *m* hearth; firebox; fireside, home
focó·so -sa [s] *adj* fiery, high-spirited
fòdera *f* lining (*of suit*); cover, case
foderare (**fòdero**) *tr* to line; to cover
fòdero *m* sheath, scabbard; raft
fó·ga *f* (**-ghe**) ardor, impetus
fòg·gia *f* (**-ge**) fashion, shape; **a foggia di** shaped like
foggiare §290 (**fòggio**) *tr* to shape, fashion
fòglia *f* leaf; petal; foil (*of gold*); **mangiare la foglia** (fig) to get wise, catch on
fogliame *m* foliage
fò·glio *m* (**-gli**) sheet; bill, banknote; folio; newspaper; permit; **foglio d'avviso** notice; **foglio di congedo** (mil) discharge; **foglio d'iscrizione** application; **foglio di via** (mil) travel orders; **foglio modello** blank form; **foglio rosa** (aut) permit; **foglio volante** flier, handbill
fógna *f* sewer, drain
fognatura *f* sewerage
fòla *f* tale, fable
fola·ga *f* (**-ghe**) (zool) coot
folata *f* gust; (lit) flight (*of birds*)
folclóre *m* folklore
folgorante *adj* striking; flashing; meteoric (*career*)
folgorare (**fólgoro**) *tr* to strike (with lightning) || *intr* to flash by || *impers* —**folgora** it is thundering
fólgore *m* (lit) thunderbolt || *f* flash of lightning; thunderbolt
fólla *f* crowd; (fig) flock
follare (**fóllo**) *tr* to full
fòlle *adj* mad, crazy; (aut) neutral; (mach) loose (*pulley*)
folleggiare §290 (**folléggio**) *intr* to act foolishly; to frolic
folleménte *adv* desperately, madly
follétto *m* elf; little imp
follìa *f* madness, lunacy; folly; **alla follia** madly; **far follie per** to be crazy about
follìcolo *m* follicle
fól·to -ta *adj* thick; beetle (*brow*); deep (*night*) || *m* depth (*e.g., of the night*); thick (*e.g., of the battle*)
fomentare (**foménto**) *tr* to foment
fòmite *m* (lit) instigation; impetus
fónda *f* anchorage; lowland; saddlebag; **alla fonda** at anchor
fónda·co *m* (**-chi**) (hist) warehouse
fondale *m* depth (*of river, sea*); (theat) backdrop
fondamentale *adj* fundamental, basic
fondamén·to *m* (**-ti**) ground, foundation; basis; **fare fondamento su** to count on; **fondamenti** elements; **senza fondamento** baseless; without getting anywhere || *m* (**-ta** *fpl*)—**fondamenta** foundations (*of a building*)

fondare (**fóndo**) *tr* to found; to build; to charter || *ref*—**fondarsi su** to rely on; to be based upon
fondatézza *f* basis, ground, foundation
fonda·to -ta *adj* well-founded
fonda·tóre -trice *mf* founder
fondazióne *f* foundation
fondèllo *m* bottom, base
fondènte *m* flux
fóndere §178 *tr* to smelt; to melt; to blow (*a fuse*); to cast (*a statue*); to blend (*colors*) || *intr* to melt; to blend || *ref* to melt; to blend; to burn out
fonderìa *f* foundry
fondià·rio -ria (**-ri -rie**) *adj* real-estate, land || *f* real-estate tax
fondina *f* holster; (coll) soup dish
fondi·sta *mf* (**-sti -ste**) editorialist; (sports) long-distance runner
fóndita *f* (typ) font
fonditóre *m* smelter, founder
fón·do -da *adj* deep || *m* bottom; fund; innermost nature; seat; end; background; land, property; **a doppio fondo** with a false bottom; **a fondo** thoroughly; **a fondo perduto** as an outright grant; **dar fondo** (naut) to cast anchor; **dar fondo a** to exhaust; **di fondo** (journ) editorial; (sports) long-distance; **fondi** funds; lees; **fondi di bottega** remnants; **fondi di caffè** coffee grounds; **fondo comune d'investimento** mutual fund; **fondo d'ammortamento** sinking fund; **fondo di beneficenza** community chest; **fondo tinta** foundation (*in make-up*); **in fondo** in the end; at the bottom; after all
fonè·ma *m* (**-mi**) phoneme
fonèti·co -ca (**-ci -che**) *adj* phonetic || *f* phonetics
fonògeno *m* pickup (*of record player*)
fonògrafo *m* phonograph, Gramophone
fonogram·ma *m* (**-mi**) telegram delivered by telephone
fonologìa *f* phonology
fonorivelatóre *m* pickup (*of record player*)
fonovalìgia *f* portable phonograph
fontana *f* fountain; spring; source
fónte *m* (lit) spring, source; **fonte battesimale** font || *f* spring; fountain; source; **da fonte autorevole** on good authority
foraggiare §290 *tr* to subsidize || *intr* to forage
forà·ggio *m* (**-gi**) forage, provender, fodder
foràne·o -a *adj* rural; outer; (naut) outer (*dock*)
forare (**fóro**) *tr* to pierce; to bore; to puncture || *intr* to have a flat tire || *ref* to be punctured
foratura *f* puncture
fòrbice *f*—**a forbice** (sports) scissors (*e.g., kick*); **forbici** scissors; clippers; **forbici per le unghie** nail clippers
forbire §176 *tr* to wipe; to polish; to shine
fór·ca *f* (**-che**) fork; pitchfork; gallows; mountain pass; **fare la forca a qlcu** (slang) to betray s.o.; (slang) to do s.o. dirt; **fatto a forca** V-shaped

forcèlla *f* fork (*of bicycle or motorcycle*); mountain pass; fork-shaped pole; hairpin; cradle (*of handset*); (coll) wishbone (*of chicken*)

forchétta *f* fork; (coll) wishbone (*of chicken*); **alla forchetta** (culin) cold (*e.g., lunch*)

forchettata *f* forkful; blow with a fork

forchettóne *m* carving fork

forcina *f* hairpin

fòrcipe *m* forceps

forcóne *m* pitchfork

forellino *m* pinhole

forèsta *f* forest

forestale *adj* forest, park

foresterìa *f* guest quarters (*in college or monastery*)

forestierismo *m* borrowing (*from another language*)

forestiè·ro -ra *adj* foreign || *mf* foreigner; stranger; outsider

forfettà·rio -ria *adj* (**-ri -rie**) job, e.g., **contratto forfettario** job contract; all-inclusive, e.g., **combinazione forfettaria** all-inclusive price agreement

fórfora *f* dandruff

fòr·gia *f* (**-ge**) forge; smithy

forgiare §290 (**fòrgio**) *tr* to forge

foriè·ro -ra *adj* forerunning || *mf* forerunner, harbinger

fórma *f* shape; form; mold (*e.g., for cakes*); wheel (*of cheese*); (typ) form; **forma da cappelli** hat block; **forma da scarpe** shoe tree; shoe last (*used by shoemaker*); **forme** shape, body; good manners; **salvare le forme** to save face

formaggièra *f* dish for grated cheese

formàg·gio *m* (**-gi**) cheese

formaldèide *f* formaldehyde

formale *adj* formal; prim

formalismo *m* formality

formali·tà *f* (**-tà**) formality

formalizzare [ddzz] *tr* to scandalize || *ref* to be shocked

formare (**fórmo**) *tr & ref* to form

forma·to -ta *adj* formed || *m* format

formazióne *f* formation

fòrmica *f* (trademark) Formica

formi·ca *f* (**-che**) ant

formi·càio *m* (**-cài**) anthill; (fig) swarm

formichière *m* anteater

formicolare (**formìcolo**) *intr* to swarm; to crawl || *intr* (ESSERE) to creep (*said, e.g., of a leg*)

formicolì·o *m* (**-i**) swarm; creeping sensation, numbness

formidàbile *adj* formidable

formó·so -sa [s] *adj* shapely, buxom

fòrmula *f* formula; (aut) category, class; **formula dubitativa** (law) lack of evidence; **formula piena** (law) acquittal

formulare (**fòrmulo**) *tr* to formulate

formulà·rio *m* (**-ri**) formulary; form

fornace *f* furnace, kiln

for·nàio -nàia *mf* (**-nài -nàie**) baker

fornèllo *m* stove, range; (*of boiler*) firebox; bowl (*of pipe*); (min) shaft; **fornello a gas** gas range; **fornello a spirito** kerosene stove; chafing dish

fornire §176 *tr* to furnish, supply

forni·tóre -trice *mf* supplier, purveyor

fornitura *f* supply; order; delivery

fórno *m* oven; furnace; kiln; bakery; (theat) empty house; **al forno** or **in forno** baked; **alto forno** blast furnace; **forno crematorio** crematorium; **far forno** (theat) to play before an empty house

fóro *m* hole

fòro *m* forum; (law) bar

forosétta [s] *f* (lit) peasant girl

fórse *m* doubt; **mettere in forse** to endanger; to put in doubt || *adv* perhaps, maybe

forsenna·to -ta *adj* mad, insane || *mf* lunatic

fòrte *adj* strong; firm; bad (*cold*); fat, hefty; fast (*color*); offensive (*joke*); hard (*smoker*); main (*dish*); (lit) thick || *m* strong person; fortress; bulk, main body; forte; (lit) thick; **sapere di forte** to have a strong flavor; **farsi forte** to bear up; **farsi forte di** to appropriate, use; to be cocksure of || *adv* hard, strong; much; loud; openly; a lot; fast; swiftly

fortézza *f* fortress; strength; fortitude

fortificare §197 (**fortìfico**) *tr* to fortify || *ref* to be strengthened; to dig in

fortificazióne *f* fortification

fortino *m* blockhouse, redoubt

fortùi·to -ta *adj* fortuitous

fortuna *f* fortune; luck; good luck; fate, destiny; (lit) storm; **avere fortuna** to be lucky; to be a hit; **buona fortuna!** good luck!; **di fortuna** makeshift, emergency; **non aver la fortuna di** to not be fortunate enough to; **per fortuna** luckily

fortunale *m* storm, tempest

fortuna·to -ta *adj* fortunate, lucky

fortunó·so -sa [s] *adj* eventful

forùncolo *m* boil; pimple

forviare §119 *tr* to mislead, lead astray || *intr* to go astray

fòrza *f* strength; force; power; police; (phys) force; **a forza di** by dint of; **a tutta forza** at full speed; **bassa forza** (mil) enlisted personnel; **di forza** by force; **di prima forza** first-rate; **far forza a** to encourage; to force; **fare forza a sé stesso** to restrain oneself; **forza!** courage!; **forza di corpo** (typ) height-to-paper; **forza maggiore** force majeure, act of God; **forza muscolare** brawn; **forza pubblica** police; **forza viva** kinetic energy; **per forza** of course; under duress

forzare (**fòrzo**) *tr* to force; to strain; to rape; to tamper with (*a lock*); **forzare il passo** to hasten one's step; **forzare la consegna** (mil) to violate orders

forza·to -ta *adj* forced; force (*e.g., feed*) || *m* convict

forzière *m* chest, coffer

forzó·so -sa [s] *adj* compulsory; imposed by law

forzu·to -ta *adj* husky, robust

foschìa *f* smog; mist; haze

fó·sco -sca adj (**-schi -sche**) dark; gloomy; misty
fosfato m phosphate
fosforeggiare §290 (**fosforéggio**) intr to phosphoresce; to glow
fosforescènte adj phosphorescent
fòsforo m phosphorus
fòssa f grave; hollow; hole, ditch; moat; pit; den (of lions); **fossa biologica** sewage-treatment plant; **fossa di riparazione** (aut) pit; **fossa settica** septic tank
fossato m ditch; moat
fossétta f dimple
fòssile adj & m fossil
fossilizzare [ddzz] tr to fossilize ‖ ref to become fossilized
fòsso m ditch; moat
fò·to f (**-to**) photo
fotocòpia f photocopy
fotocopiare §287 (**fotocòpio**) tr to photocopy
fotoelèttri·co -ca (**-ci -che**) adj photoelectric ‖ f (mil) searchlight
fotogèni·co -ca adj (**-ci -che**) photogenic
fotogiornale m pictorial magazine
fotografare (**fotògrafo**) tr to photograph
fotografia f photography; photograph
fotogràfi·co -ca adj (**-ci -che**) photographic
fotògrafo m photographer
fotogram·ma m (**-mi**) (phot) frame
fotoincisióne f photoengraving
fotolampo m flashlight
fotòmetro m exposure meter
fotomontàg·gio m (**-gi**) photomontage
fototubo m phototube
fra m invar brother, e.g., **fra Cristoforo** Brother Christopher ‖ prep among; between; in, within
frac m (**frac**) swallow-tailed coat
fracassare tr to crash, smash ‖ ref to crash
fracasso m crash; uproar; (coll) slew
fràdi·cio -cia (**-ci -cie**) adj rotten; soaked ‖ m rotten part; decay; wet ground
fràgile adj fragile; brittle; frail
fragilità f fragility, frailty
fràgola f strawberry
fragóre m din; peal; roar
fragoró·so -sa [s] adj noisy
fragrante adj fragrant
fraintèndere §270 tr to misunderstand
frammassóne m Freemason
frammassonerìa f Freemasonry
frammentare (**framménto**) tr to fragment
frammentà·rio -ria adj (**-ri -rie**) fragmentary
framménto m fragment
framméttere §198 tr to interpose ‖ ref to meddle; **frammettersi in** to intrude in, to butt into
frammèzzo [ddzz] adv in the middle ‖ prep in the midst of
frammischiare §287 tr to mix ‖ ref to concern oneself
frana f landslide; (fig) collapse
franare intr to slide; to collapse

francesca·no -na adj & mf Franciscan
francé·sco -sca (**-schi -sche**) adj (archaic) French ‖ **Francesco** m Francis ‖ **Francesca** f Frances
francése adj French ‖ m French (language); Frenchman (person); **i francesi** the French ‖ f Frenchwoman
francesismo m gallicism
francesizzare [ddzz] tr to Frenchify
franchézza f frankness
franchì·gia f (**-gie**) franchise; exemption; deductible insurance; (naut) shore leave; **franchigia postale** franking privilege
Frància, la France
fran·co -ca (**-chi -che**) adj free; frank; Frankish; **farla franca** to get off scot free; **franco di porto** prepaid, postpaid; **franco domicilio** home delivery, free delivery ‖ m franc ‖ **Franco** m Frank
francobóllo m postage stamp, stamp
frangènte m breaker, surf; **essere nei frangenti** to be in bad straits
fràngere §179 tr to crush; (lit) to break ‖ ref to break, comb (said of waves)
frangétta f bangs
fràn·gia f (**-ge**) fringe; embellishment; shoreline; bangs; **frangia di corallo** coral reef
frangìbile adj breakable
frangiflut·ti m (**-ti**) breakwater
frangi·vènto m (**-vènto**) windbreak
frangizòl·le m (**-le**) disc harrow
Frankfur·ter m (**-ter**) hot dog
fran·tóio m (**-tói**) crusher; **frantoio a mascelle** jawbreaker
frantumare tr to crush; to break to pieces ‖ ref to be crushed; to go to pieces
frantume m fragment; **andare in frantumi** to go to pieces
frappé m (**frappé**) shake; frappé; **frappé alla menta** mint julep; **frappé di latte** milk shake
frappórre §218 tr to interpose ‖ ref to interfere; to intervene
frasà·rio m (**-ri**) language, speech
fra·sca f (**-sche**) branch; bush; ornament; whim; frivolous woman, flirt
frase f sentence; (mus) phrase; **frase fatta** cliché; **frase idiomatica** idiom; **frasi** words; **frasi di commiserazione** condolences
fraseggiare §290 (**fraséggio**) intr to use phrasing; to use big words; (mus) to phrase
fraseologìa f phraseology
fràssino m ash tree
frastagliare §280 tr to cut out (e.g., paper)
frastaglia·to -ta adj indented, jagged; ornamented
frastornare (**frastórno**) tr to disturb; (lit) to prevent
frastuòno m din, roar
frate m friar, monk, brother
fratellanza f brotherhood
fratellastro m stepbrother; half brother
fratèllo m brother; **fratelli** brothers and sisters; **fratello consanguineo** half brother on the father's side; **fratello**

di latte foster brother; **fratello gemello** twin
fraterni·tà f (-tà) fraternity
fraternizzare [ddzz] intr to fraternize
fratèr·no -na adj fraternal, brotherly
fratrici·da (-di -de) adj fratricidal || mf fratricide
fratricì·dio m (-di) fratricide
fratta f brushwood; (coll) hedge
frattàglie fpl giblets, chitterlings, offal
frattanto adv meantime, meanwhile
frattèmpo m—**nel frattempo** meanwhile
frattura f fracture; break; breach
fratturare tr & ref to fracture, break
fraudolènte adj fraudulent
frazionare (**frazióno**) tr to fractionate; to break up
frazionà·rio -ria adj (-ri -rie) fractional
frazióne f fraction; hamlet; (eccl) breaking of the host
fréc·cia f (-ce) arrow, bolt; steeple, spire; clock (on hosiery); (archit) rise; (fig) aspersion; **freccia consensiva** arrow (on traffic light); **freccia direzionale** (aut) turn signal
frecciata f arrow shot; taunt, gibe; **dare una frecciata a** to hit for a loan
freddare (**fréddo**) tr to chill; to kill
freddézza f chill; cold, coldness; coolness, cold shoulder; sang-froid
fréd·do -da adj cold; cool, chilly; frigid || m cold, cold weather; chill; **a freddo** cold; cooly; **avere freddo** to be cold (said of people); **fare freddo** to be cold (said of weather); **freddo cane** biting cold; **sentire freddo** to feel cold; **sudare freddo** to be in a cold sweat
freddoló·so -sa [s] adj chilly (person)
freddura f joke, pun; cold weather
freddurì·sta mf (-sti -ste) punster
fregagióne f rubbing, rubdown, massage
fregare §209 (**frégo**) tr to rub; to strike (a match); (slang) to steal; (slang) to cheat, dupe; (vulg) to make love with || ref to rub (e.g., one's hands); **fregarsene di** (vulg) to not give a hoot about
fregata f rubbing; (nav) frigate; (orn) frigate bird; (slang) cheating
fregatura f (slang) cheating; (slang) hitch, halt
fregiare §290 (**frégio**) tr to decorate; to fret
fré·gio m (-gi) decoration; insignia (on cap of officer); (archit) frieze
fré·go m (-ghi) line, stroke
frégola f rut, heat; (slang) mania, craze
fremènte adj throbbing; thrilling
frèmere §123 tr (lit) to beg insistently || intr to throb; to be thrilled; to shake, tremble, rustle; to shudder (with horror); (fig) to boil; (fig) to fret
frèmito m throb; thrill; shudder; roar; quiver
frenare (**fréno**) tr to brake, stop; to bridle (a horse); to curb (passions); to restrain (e.g., laughter); **frenare la corsa** to slow down || intr to put the brakes on || ref to control oneself

frenatóre m (rr) brakeman
frenesìa f frenzy; (fig) craze, fever; (lit) thought
frenèti·co -ca adj (-ci -che) frenzied; frantic; crazy, enthusiastic
fréno m bit, bridle; brake; (fig) check; (mach) lock; **freno ad aria compressa** air brake; **mordere il freno** to champ the bit; **senza freno** wild, unbridled; **tenere a freno** to keep in check
frenologìa f phrenology
frequentare (**frequènto**) tr to frequent; to attend || intr to associate
frequenta·tóre -trice mf patron, customer; frequenter, habitué
frequènte adj frequent; rapid (pulse); (lit) crowded
frequènza f frequency; attendance; **frequenza ultraelevata** ultrahigh frequency
frèsa f milling cutter; burr (of dentist's drill)
fresatrice f milling machine
fresatura f (mach) milling
freschézza f freshness; coolness
fré·sco -sca (-schi -sche) adj fresh; cool; **fresco di malattia** just recovered; **fresco di stampa** fresh off the press; **fresco di studi** fresh out of school; **star fresco** to be in a fix; to be all wrong || m cool weather; tropical fabric; **di fresco** recently; **fare fresco** to be cool (said of weather); **mettere al fresco** (coll) to put in the clink; **per il fresco** in cool weather
frescó·ne -na mf (slang) dumbell
frescura f coolness, freshness
frétta f hurry, haste; **avere fretta** to be in a hurry; **in fretta** in a hurry; **in fretta e furia** in a rush
frettazzo m plasterer's wooden trowel; steel brush
frettoló·so -sa [s] adj hurried, hasty
freudismo m Freudianism
friàbile adj friable, crumbly
friabilità f friableness
fricassèa f fricassee
frìggere §180 tr to fry; **mandare qlcu a farsi friggere** to tell s.o. to go to the devil || intr to fry; to sizzle; to fret
friggitoria f fried-food shop
frigidézza f frigidity
frigidi·tà f (-tà) coldness; frigidity
frìgi·do -da adj cold; frigid
frì·gio -gia adj (-gi -gie) Phrygian
frignare intr to whimper
frigorìfe·ro -ra adj refrigerating || m refrigerator; (journ) morgue
fringuèl·lo -la mf chaffinch, finch
frinire §176 intr to chirp
frisata f gunnel
frittata f omelet; **fare la frittata** (coll) to make a mess of it
frittèlla f fritter; pancake; (coll) grease spot
frit·to -ta adj fried; cooked, ruined || m fry, fried platter
frittura f frying; fry, fried platter
frivolézza f frivolity
frìvo·lo -la adj frivolous; flighty
frizionare (**frizióno**) tr to massage

frizióne *f* friction; massage; (aut) clutch

frizzante [ddzz] *adj* crisp, brisk (*weather*); sparkling (*wine*)

frizzare [ddzz] *intr* to tingle; to sparkle, fizz (*said of wine*); (fig) to sting

frizzo [ddzz] *m* jest, witticism; gibe, dig

frodare (**fròdo**) *tr* to cheat, swindle

fròde *f* fraud; **frode fiscale** tax evasion or fraud

fròdo *m invar* customs evasion; **di frodo** smuggled

frò·gia *f* (-ge or -gie) nostril (*of horse*)

fròl·lo -**la** *adj* high (*meat*); soft, tender; (fig) weak

frónda *f* branch, bough; political opposition; **fronde** foliage; ornaments

frondó·so -**sa** [s] *adj* leafy

frontale *adj* front; frontal

frónte *m* (mil, pol) front; **far fronte a** to face; to face up to; to meet (*expenses*); **tenere fronte a** to face, resist || *f* forehead, brow; countenance; title page; headline; (fig) face; **a fronte** opposite, facing; **a fronte di** (com) in reference to; **dietro front!** (mil) about face!; **di fronte a** in the face of; facing; **di fronte a tutti** in plain view; **fronte destr'!** (mil) right face!; **mettere a fronte** to compare; **tenere a fronte** to have in front of one's eyes

fronteggiare §290 (**frontéggio**) *tr* to face, front || *ref* to face one another

frontespì·zio *m* (-**zi**) title page

frontièra *f* border, frontier

frontóne *m* (archit) pediment; (archit) gable

frónzolo *m* bauble, gewgaw; **fronzoli** finery, frippery

fròtta *f* crowd; swarm; flock

fròttola *f* fib; popular poem; **frottole** humbug

frugale *adj* frugal (*meal; life*); temperate (*in eating or drinking*)

frugare §209 *tr* to rummage through; to search (*a person*) || *intr* to rummage, poke around

frùgo·lo -**la** *mf* restless child, imp

fruire §176 *tr* to enjoy || *intr*—**fruire di** to enjoy

fruitóre *m* user

frullare *tr* to beat, whip || *intr* to flutter; to spin; **frullare per il capo a** to get into the head of, e.g., **cosa gli è frullato per il capo?** what got into his head?

frulla·to -**ta** *adj* whipped || *m* shake (*drink*)

frullatóre *m* electric beater

frullino *m* egg beater

fruménto *m* wheat

frumentóne *m* corn

frusciare §128 *intr* to rustle

frusci·o *m* (-**i**) rustle, rustling

frusta *f* whip; egg beater

frustare *tr* to whip, lash; (fig) to censure; (coll) to wear out (*clothes*)

frustata *f* lash; (fig) censure

frustino *m* whip, crop

fru·sto -**sta** *adj* worn out, threadbare || *f* see **frusta**

frustrare *tr* to frustrate, baffle; to discomfit

frut·ta *f* (-**ta** & -**te**) fruit; **essere alle frutta** to be at the end of the meal, to be having one's dessert

fruttare *tr* & *intr* to yield

fruttéto *m* orchard

frutticoltóre *m* fruit grower

fruttièra *f* fruit dish

fruttìfe·ro -**ra** *adj* fruit-bearing; fruitful, profitable; (lit) fecund

fruttificare §197 (**fruttìfico**) *intr* to fructify; to yield

fruttivéndo·lo -**la** *mf* fruit dealer

frutto *m* fruit; **frutti di mare** shellfish; **mettere a frutto** to make yield

fruttuó·so -**sa** [s] *adj* fruitful, profitable

fu *adj invar* late (*deceased*); son of the late . . . ; daughter of the late . . .

fucilare *tr* to shoot

fucilata *f* rifle shot

fucilazióne *f* execution by a firing squad

fucile *m* rifle, gun; **fucile ad aria compressa** air gun; **fucile da caccia** shotgun; **un buon fucile** a good shot

fucileria *f* fusillade

fucilière *m* rifleman

fucina *f* forge, smithy

fu·co *m* (-**chi**) (bot) rockweed; (zool) drone

fùcsia *f* fuchsia

fu·ga *f* (-**ghe**) flight; leak; row (*e.g., of rooms*); spurt (*in bicycle race*); (mus) fugue; **di fuga** hastily; **prendere la fuga** to take flight; **volgere in fuga** to put to flight; to take flight

fugace *adj* passing, fleeting

fugare §209 *tr* (lit) to avoid; (lit) to put to flight; (lit) to dispel

fuggènte *adj* passing, fleeting

fuggévole *adj* fleeting

fuggia·sco -**sca** (-**schi** -**sche**) *adj* fleeing, fugitive || *mf* fugitive; refugee

fuggi fug·gi *m* (-**gi**) stampede

fuggire *tr* to flee; to avoid || *intr* (ESSERE) to flee, run away; (sports) to take the lead; **fuggire a** to flee from

fuggiti·vo -**va** *adj* & *mf* fugitive

fulcro *m* fulcrum; (fig) pivot

fulgènte *adj* (lit) resplendent

fùlgi·do -**da** *adj* resplendent

fulgóre *m* resplendency, radiance

fulìggine *f* soot

fuligginó·so -**sa** [s] *adj* sooty

fulmicotóne *m* guncotton

fulminante *adj* crushing (*illness*); withering (*look*); explosive || *m* exploding cap; (coll) match

fulminare (**fùlmino**) *tr* to strike by lightning; to strike down; to confound, dumfound || *ref* (elec) to burn out, to blow out || *impers* (ESSERE)— **fulmina** it is lightning

fùlmine *m* lightning, thunderbolt; **fulmine a ciel sereno** bolt out of the blue

fulmìne·o -**a** *adj* swift, instant

ful·vo -**va** *adj* tawny

fumaiòlo *m* chimney; smokestack; (naut) funnel

fumante *adj* smoking; steaming; dusty
fumare *tr* to smoke; (lit) to exhale ‖ *intr* to smoke; to steam; to fume; **fumare come un turco** to smoke like a chimney
fumata *f* smoking; smoke signal; **fare una fumata** to have a smoke
fuma·tóre -trice *mf* smoker
fumetti·sta *mf* (-sti -ste) cartoonist
fumétto *m* cartoon; **fumetti** comics
fumigare §209 (fùmigo) *tr* (obs) to fumigate ‖ *intr* to steam, smoke
fumigazióne *f* fumigation
fumi·sta *m* (-sti) heater man; joker, hoaxer
fumisterìa *f* fondness for practical jokes; bamboozling
fumo *m* smoke; vapor, steam; smoking; (coll) hot air; **andare in fumo** to go up in smoke; **fumi** vapors, fumes; **mandare in fumo** to squander; to thwart; **sapere di fumo** to taste smoky; **vedere qlcu come il fumo negli occhi** to not be able to stand s.o.; **vender fumo** to peddle influence
fumòge·no -na *adj* smoke, e.g., **cortina fumogena** smoke curtain
fumó·so -sa [s] *adj* smoky; obscure
funambolismo *m* tightrope walking; (fig) acrobatics
funàmbo·lo -la *mf* tightrope walker; (fig) acrobat
fune *f* rope, cable; **fune portante** suspension cable
fùnebre *adj* funeral; funereal, gloomy
funerale *adj* & *m* funeral
funerà·rio -ria *adj* (-ri -rie) funeral
funère·o -a *adj* funereal; funeral
funestare (funèsto) *tr* to afflict
funè·sto -sta *adj* baleful; mournful
fungaia *f* mushroom farm; mushroom bed; flock, swarm
fùngere §183 *intr*—**fungere da** to act as
fun·go *m* (-ghi) mushroom; fungus; **fungo atomico** mushroom cloud; **venir su come i funghi** to mushroom
fungó·so -sa [s] *adj* fungous
funicolare *adj* cable, cable-driven ‖ *f* funicular railway
funivìa *f* cableway
funzionale *adj* functional
funzionalità *f* functionalism
funzionaménto *m* working order; functioning
funzionare (funzióno) *intr* to work; to function; **funzionare da** to act as
funzionà·rio -ria *mf* (-ri -rie) functionary, official; public official
funzióne *f* function; office; duty; (eccl) service; **facente funzione** acting; **mettere in funzione** to make (*s.th*) work
fuò·co *m* (-chi) fire; burner (*of gas range*); focus; (fig) home; (lit) thunderbolt; **al fuoco!** fire! (*warning*); **andare per il fuoco** (culin) to boil over; **cuocere a fuoco lento** (culin) to simmer; **dar fuoco a** to set fire to; **di fuoco** fiery; blushing; **far fuoco** to fire; **fuochi artificiali** fireworks; **fuoco di fila** enfilade; **fuoco!** (mil) fire!; **fuoco di paglia** (fig) flash in the pan; **fuoco di segnalazione** flare; **fuoco fatuo** will-o'-the-wisp; **fuoco**

incrociato cross fire; **fuoco nutrito** drumfire; **mettere a fuoco** to focus; **mettere una mano sul fuoco** to be absolutely sure, to swear by it
fuorché *prep* except; **fuorché di** except to
fuòri *adv* outside, out; aside; e.g., **lasciar fuori** to leave aside; **andar di fuori** (culin) to boil over; **dar fuori** to do away with; to squander; **di fuori** outside; **far fuori** to publish; **fuori di** out of; outside of; beyond (*a doubt*); off (*the road*); beside (*oneself*); **fuori d'uso** out of style; obsolete; **il di fuori** the outside; **in fuori** protruding; forward; **mettere fuori** to throw out; to spread; to exhibit ‖ *prep* beyond; out of; outside; **fuori commercio** not for sale; **fuori concorso** in a class by itself (himself, etc.); **fuori luogo** untimely, out of place; **fuori (di) mano** far away; solitary; **fuori testo** inserted, tipped in
fuoribór·do *m* (-do) outboard; outboard motor
fuoricombattimén·to (-to) *adj* knocked out ‖ *m* knockout
fuorigiò·co *m* (-co) (sports) offside
fuorilég·ge *mf* (-ge) outlaw
fuorisè·rie (-rie) *adj* custom-built ‖ *m* & *f* custom model ‖ *f* custom-built car
fuoristra·da *m* (-da) land rover
fuoriusci·to -ta *adj* exiled ‖ *mf* political exile ‖ *f* leak; flow; protrusion
fuorvia·to -ta *adj* mislead, misguided
furbacchió·ne -na *mf* slippery person
furberìa *f* slyness, cunning
fur·bo -ba *adj* sly, cunning ‖ *mf* knave; **furbo di tre cotte** slicker
furènte *adj* furious
furerìa *f* (mil) company headquarters
furétto *m* ferret
furfante *m* sharper, scoundrel
furfanterìa *f* rascality
furgoncino *m* small delivery van
furgó·ne *m* truck; patrol wagon; hearse; **furgone cellulare** prison van
furgoni·sta *mf* (-sti -ste) truck driver, teamster
fùria *f* fury; strength, violence; hurry; **a furia di** by dint of; **con furia** in a hurry; **far furia a** to urge; **montare in furia** to go berserk; to fly off the handle
furibón·do -da *adj* furious, wild
furière *m* soldier attached to company headquarters
furió·so -sa [s] *adj* furious; fierce; mad
furóre *m* furor, frenzy; violence; longing; **far furore** to be a hit, to be all the rage
furoreggiare §290 (furoréggio) *intr* to be a hit, be all the rage
furti·vo -va *adj* stealthy; furtive; stolen (*e.g., goods*)
furto *m* theft; stolen goods; **di furto** stealthily; **furto con scasso** burglary
fusa [s] *fpl*—**fare le fusa** to purr
fuscèllo *m* twig
fusciac·ca *f* (-che) sash (*around the waist*)

fusèllo [s] *m* spindle; axle, shaft
fusìbile *adj* fusible || *m* (elec) fuse
fusióne *f* fusion; melting; merger; blending (*of colors*)
fu·so -sa *adj* melted; molten
fuso [s] *m* spindle; shank (*of anchor*); shaft (*of column*); (aut) axle; fuso orario time zone
fusolièra *f* (aer) fuselage
fustagno *m* fustian
fustàia *f* adult forest, full-grown forest
fustèlla *f* (perforating) punch; (pharm) price stub

fustigare §209 (fùstigo) *tr* to whip
fusto *m* trunk (*of tree*); stalk; stem (*of key*); beam (*of balance*); butt (*of gun*); trunk, body; frame (*of armchair*); tank (*for holding liquids*); drum (*metal receptacle*); holding stick (*of umbrella*); shaft (*of column*); d'alto fusto full-grown (*tree*)
fùtile *adj* futile, trifling
futilità *f* futility
futurismo *m* futurism
futuri·sta *mf* (-sti -ste) futurist
futu·ro -ra *adj* & *m* future

G

G, g [dʒi] *m* & *f* seventh letter of the Italian alphabet
gabardi·ne *f* (-ne) gabardine; gabardine raincoat or topcoat
gabbamón·do *m* (-do) cheat, sharper
gabbanèlla *f* gown (*of physician or patient*); robe
gabbano *m* cloak; frock; mutare gabbano to be a turncoat
gabbare *tr* to dupe, cheat || *ref*—gabbarsi di to make fun of
gàbbia *f* cage; ox muzzle; dock (*in courtroom*); (mach) housing; (naut) top; (naut) topsail; gabbia d'imballaggio crate; gabbia toracica rib cage
gabbiano *m* sea gull
gabbo *m*—farsi gabbo di to make fun of; prendere a gabbo to make light of
gabèlla *f* (obs) customs, duty
gabellare (gabèllo) *tr* to palm off; to swallow (*e.g., a tall story*); (obs) to tax
gabinétto *m* office (*of doctor, dentist, lawyer*); cabinet; chamber (*of judge*); toilet; closet; laboratory; gabinetto da bagno bathroom; gabinetto di decenza toilet, bathroom
ga·gà *m* (gà) fop, dandy; lounge lizard
gaggia *f* acacia
gagliardétto *m* pennon; pennant
gagliardìa *f* (lit) vigor; (lit) prowess
gagliar·do -da *adj* vigorous; stalwart; hearty (*e.g., voice*)
gagliòf·fo -fa *adj* loutish; rascal || *mf* lout; rascal
gaièzza *f* gaiety, vivacity
gàio gàia *adj* (gài gàie) gay, vivacious
gala *m* & *f* gala; gala affair; di gala formal; mettersi in gala to dress up || *f* frill; bow tie (*for formal attire*); (naut) bunting
galalite *f* casein plastic, galalith
galante *adj* gallant, courtly; amorous; pretty, graceful
galanterìa *f* gallantry, courtliness
galantuò·mo *m* (-mini) honest man; (coll) my good fellow
galàssia *f* galaxy
galatèo *m* good manners
galèna *f* (min) galena
galeóne *m* galleon
galeòt·to -ta *adj* (archaic) intermediary

(*in love affairs*) || *m* galley slave; convict; (archaic) procurer
galèra *f* galley; forced labor
gali·lèo -lèa (-lèi -lèe) *adj* & *m* Galilean
galla *f* (bot) gall; (pathol) blister; a galla afloat; tenersi a galla (fig) to keep alive; to manage; venire a galla to come to the surface
galleggiante *adj* floating || *m* float
galleggiare §290 (galléggio) *intr* to float
galleria *f* tunnel; gallery; balcony; mall, arcade; wind tunnel
Galles, il Wales
gallése [s] *adj* Welsh || *m* Welshman; Welsh (*language*) || *f* Welsh woman
gallétta *f* cracker; hardtack; (naut) ball on top of flagpole
gallétto *m* cockerel; (fig) gallant; (fig) whippersnapper; (mach) wing nut; fare il galletto to swagger
gàlli·co -ca *adj* & *m* (-ci -che) Gallic
gallina *f* hen; gallina faraona guinea fowl
gal·lo -la *adj* Gallic; (sports) Bantam (*weight*) || *m* rooster, cock; weathercock; Gaul; Gallic (*language*); fare il gallo to strut; gallo cedrone wood grouse; gallo d'India turkey
gallòc·cia *f* (-ce) (naut) cleat
gallóne *m* braid; stripe; chevron; gallon
galoppare (galòppo) *intr* to gallop; (fig) to rush around
galoppata *f* gallop
galoppa·tóio *m* (-tói) bridle path
galoppino *m* errand boy; galoppino elettorale ward heeler
galòppo *m* gallop; andare al piccolo galoppo to canter; di gran galoppo at full speed; piccolo galoppo canter
galò·scia *f* (-sce) overshoe, rubber
galvanizzare [ddzz] *tr* to electroplate; (fig) to galvanize
galvanoplàsti·ca *f* (-che) electroplating
gamba *f* leg; stem; (aer) shock strut; a gambe all'aria upside down; a gambe levate at top speed; upside down; darsela a gambe to take to one's heels; essere in gamba to be in good shape; to be on the ball; essere male in gamba to be in bad shape; gamba di legno peg leg; gamba a ciambella bowlegs; le gambe mi fanno giacomo my knees shake;

prendere qlcu sotto gamba to make light of s.o.; raddrizzare le gambe ai cani to try the impossible

gambale *m* legging, gaiter; boot last; leg (*of boot*)

gamberétto *m* shrimp

gàmbero *m* (*Astacus, Cambarus*) crawfish

gambétto *m* stumble; trip; (chess) gambit

gambo *m* stem

gamèlla *f* (mil) mess kit, mess tin

gamma *f* gamut; range; gamma d'onda (rad) wave band

ganà·scia *f* (-sce) jaw; (aut) brake shoe; mangiare a quattro ganasce to eat like a horse

gàn·cio *m* (-ci) hook; clasp; hanger

gan·ga *f* (-ghe) gang; (min) gangue

gànghero *m* hinge; clasp; uscire dai gangheri to fly off the handle

gàn·glio *m* (-gli) ganglion

ganzo [dz] *m* (slang) lover; (coll) slicker

gara *f* competition, match; fare a gara to compete; gara d'appalto competitive bidding

garagi·sta *m* (-sti) garage man

garante *adj* responsible || *m* guarantor; farsi garante per to vouch for

garantire §176 *tr* to guarantee; to secure (*a mortgage*)

garanti·to -ta *adj* guaranteed, warranted; downright, absolute (*liar*)

garanzìa *f* guarantee, warranty; insurance, assurance

garbare *tr* (naut) to shape (*a hull*) || *intr* (ESSERE) (with *dat*) to like, e.g., non gli garbano le Sue parole he does not like your words

garbatézza *f* politeness, courtesy

garba·to -ta *adj* polite, courteous

garbo *m* politeness, good manners; gesture; act; shape (*of a hull*); good cut (*of clothes*); elegance (*in painting or writing*); a garbo correctly

garbù·glio *m* (-gli) tangle, confusion; mess

gardènia *f* gardenia

gareggiare §290 (garéggio) *intr* to compete, vie

garétta *f* var of garitta

garétto *m* var of garretto

garganèlla *f*—bere a garganella to gulp down

gargarismo *m* gargling; gargle

gargarizzare [ddzz] *intr & ref* to gargle

gargaròzzo *m* throat, gullet

garitta *f* railroad-crossing box; (mil) sentry box; (rr) brakeman's box

garòfano *m* carnation, pink

garrése [s] *m* withers

garrétto *m* ankle (*of man*); hock (*of horse*)

garrire §176 *intr* to chirp, twitter; to flap; (archaic) to quarrel

garrito *m* chirp, twitter

garròtta *f* garrote

gàrru·lo -la *adj* garrulous

garza [dz] *f* gauze

garzonato [dz] *m* apprenticeship

garzó·ne -na [dz] *mf* helper || *m* helper, boy; apprentice; (archaic) bachelor; garzone di stalla stableboy

gas *m* (gas) gas; gasoline; gas asfissiante poison gas; gas delle miniere firedamp; gas esilarante laughing gas; gas illuminante illuminating gas; gas lacrimogeno tear gas

gasdótto *m* gas pipeline

gasificare §197 (gasìfico) *tr* var of gassificare

gasòlio *m* Diesel oil

gasòmetro *m* var of gassometro

gassificare §197 (gassìfico) *tr* to gasify

gassi·sta *m* (-sti) gasworker; gas fitter; gas-meter reader

gassòmetro *m* gasholder, gas tank

gassó·so -sa [s] *adj* gaseous, gassy || *f* soda, pop

gastronomìa *f* gastronomy

gatta *f* she-cat, tabby; comprare la gatta nel sacco to buy a pig in a poke; gatta ci cova something is rotten in Denmark; pigliare una gatta da pelare to take on a heavy burden, to get a tiger by the tail

gattabùia *f* (coll) clink, lockup

gattamòrta *f* (gattemòrte) hypocrite

gattino *m* kitten; (bot) catkin

gat·to -ta *mf* cat || *m* tomcat; tamper, pile driver; gatto a nove code cat-o'-nine-tails; gatto soriano tortoiseshell cat; quattro gatti a handful of people || *f* see gatta

gattóni *adv* on all fours

gattopardo *m* (zool) serval; gattopardo americano ocelot

gattùc·cio *m* (-ci) compass saw; (ichth) small dotted dogfish

gaudènte *adj* jovial || *m* bon vivant

gàu·dio *m* (-di) joy, happiness

gavazzare *intr* (lit) to revel

gavétta *f* mess kit, mess gear; venire dalla gavetta to come up through the ranks

gavitèllo *m* buoy

gazza [ddzz] *f* magpie

gazzarra [ddzz] *f* racket, uproar

gazzèlla [ddzz] *f* gazelle

gazzétta [ddzz] *f* newspaper; gazette; newsmonger, gossip; Gazzetta Ufficiale Official Gazette (*in Italy*); Congressional Record (*U.S.A.*)

gazzettino [ddzz] *m* small newspaper; column, e.g., gazzettino rosa social column; newsmonger, gossip

gazzósa [ddzz] *f* var of gassosa

gèl *m* gel

gelare (gèlo) *tr* to freeze; to nip || *intr* (ESSERE) & *ref* to freeze || *impers* (ESSERE & AVERE)—gela it is freezing

gelata *f* frost

gela·tàio -tàia *mf* (-tài -tàie) ice-cream dealer

gelaterìa *f* ice-cream parlor

gelatièra *f* ice-cream freezer

gelatière *m* ice-cream dealer

gelatina *f* gelatin; jelly; gelatina di frutta fruit jelly; gum drop

gelatinizzare [ddzz] *tr & ref* to gelatinize; to jell

gela·to -ta *adj* frozen || *m* ice cream;

gelato da passeggio ice cream on a stick, popsicle

gèli·do -da *adj* icy, ice-cold

gèlo *m* frost; ice; cold; diventare di gelo to remain dumfounded; farsi di gelo to be cold or aloof; sentirsi il gelo addosso to get a chill

gelóne *m* chilblain

gelosìa [s] *f* jealousy; great care; shutter

gelό·so -sa [s] *adj* jealous; solicitous

gèlso *m* mulberry

gelsomino *m* jasmine

gemebόn·do -da *adj* (lit) moaning

gemellàggio *m* sisterhood (*of two cities*)

gemèl·lo -la *adj* twin; sister (*ship*) || *mf* twin || gemelli *mpl* cufflinks || Gemelli *mpl* (astr) Gemini

gèmere §123 *tr* (lit) to lament || *intr* (ESSERE & AVERE) to moan, groan; to suffer; to squeak (*said of a wheel*); to ooze; to coo (*said of a dove*)

gèmito *m* moan; howl (*of wind*)

gèmma *f* gem; (bot) bud

gemma·to -ta *adj* gemmate; jeweled

gendarme *m* gendarme, policeman

genealogìa *f* genealogy

generalato *m* generalship

generale *adj* general || *m* general; generale d'armata (mil) general; generale di brigata brigadier general; generale di corpo d'armata lieutenant general; generale di divisione major general || *f* (mil) assembly; stare sulle generali to speak in vague generalities

generali·tà *f* (-tà) generality; majority; generalità *fpl* personal data

generalizzare [ddzz] *tr* to generalize; to bring into general use || *intr* to generalize, deal in generalities

generare (gènero) *tr* to beget; to generate || *ref* to occur

genera·tóre -trice *adj* generating || *m* generator || *f* generatrix

generazióne *f* generation

gènere *m* genus; kind, type; genre; (gram) gender; del genere similar, alike; farne di ogni genere to commit all sorts of mischief; genere umano mankind; generi alimentari foodstuffs; generi diversi sundries, assorted articles; in genere generally

genèri·co -ca (-ci -che) *adj* generic; vague; all-round; general (*e.g., practitioner*) || *mf* (theat) actor playing bit parts || *m* vagueness, imprecision

gènero *m* son-in-law

generosi·tà [s] *f* (-tà) generosity

generό·so -sa [s] *adj* generous; rich (*wine*)

gène·si *f* (-si) genesis || il Genesi Genesis

genèti·co -ca (-ci -che) *adj* genetic(al) || *f* genetics

genetlìa·co -ca (-ci -che) *adj* birth || *m* birthday

gengiva *f* (anat) gum

genìa *f* set, gang; (lit) breed

geniale *adj* clever; genial; inspired, genius-like

geniali·tà *f* (-tà) cleverness, ingeniousness; genius; (lit) geniality

genière *m* (mil) engineer

gè·nio *m* (-ni) genius; (mil) corps of engineers; andare a genio (with *dat*) to like, e.g., la musica moderna non gli va a genio he does not like modern music; fare qlco di genio to do s.th willingly

genitale *adj* genital || genitali *mpl* genitals

geniti·vo -va *adj* & *m* genitive

geni·tóre -trice *mf* parent

gen·nàio *m* (-nài) January

genocìdio *m* genocide

Gènova *f* Genoa

genovése [s] *adj* & *mf* Genoese

gentàglia *f* riffraff, rabble, scum

gènte *adj* (archaic) gentle || *f* people; nation; family; (nav) crew; gente d'arme soldiers; gente di mal affare riffraff; gente di mare sailors

gentildònna *f* gentlewoman

gentile *adj* gentle; nice; genteel || Gentili *mpl* heathen

gentilézza *f* gentleness; kindness; per gentilezza kindly, please

gentilì·zio -zia *adj* (-zi -zie) of noble family; (lit) ancestral

gentiluò·mo *m* (-mini) gentleman, nobleman

genuflèttere §177 *ref* to kneel down

genui·no -na *adj* genuine

genziana *f* gentian

geofìsi·co -ca (-ci -che) *adj* geophysical || *f* geophysics

geografìa *f* geography

geogràfi·co -ca *adj* (-ci -che) geographic (al)

geògra·fo -fa *mf* geographer

geologìa *f* geology

geòlo·go -ga *mf* (-gi -ghe) geologist

geòme·tra *m* (-tri) geometrician; land surveyor

geometrìa *f* geometry

gerà·nio *m* (-ni) geranium

gerar·ca *m* (-chi) leader

gerarchìa *f* hierarchy

geràrchi·co -ca *adj* (-ci -che) hierarchical; per via gerarchica through proper channels

Geremìa *f* Jeremiah

geremìade *f* jeremiad

gerènte *m* manager, director; gerente responsabile (journ) managing editor

gèr·go *m* (-ghi) jargon

geriatrìa *f* geriatrics

Gèrico *f* Jericho

gèrla *f* pannier (*carried on the back*)

Germània, la Germany

germàni·co -ca *adj* (-ci -che) Germanic

germànio *m* germanium

germanizzare [ddzz] *tr* to Germanize

germa·no -na *adj* german, e.g., fratello germano brother-german; Germanic || *m* (lit) brother-german; germano nero (orn) coot; germano reale (orn) mallard

gèrme *m* germ; (lit) offspring

germici·da (-di) *adj* germicidal || *m* germicide

germinare (gèrmino) *intr* (ESSERE & AVERE) to germinate

germogliare §280 (germóglio) *tr* to put forth || *intr* (ESSERE & AVERE) to bud, sprout

germó·glio *m* (-gli) bud, sprout

geroglìfi·co -ca *adj* & *m* (-ci -che) hieroglyphic

Geròlamo *m* Jerome

gerontocò·mio *m* (-mi) or gerotrò·fio *m* (-fi) old people's home, nursing home

gerùn·dio *m* (-di) gerund

Gerusalèmme *f* Jerusalem

gessare (gèsso) *tr* to plaster; to lime (*a field*)

gèsso *m* gypsum; plaster; chalk; (sculp) plaster cast

gessó·so -sa [s] *adj* plastery, chalky; chalklike

gèsta *f* (archaic) army; gesta *fpl* deeds, exploits

gestante *f* pregnant woman

gestazióne *f* gestation

gesticolare (gestìcolo) *intr* to gesticulate

gestióne *f* management, operation; data processing

gestire §176 *tr* to manage, operate || *intr* to gesticulate; (theat) to make gestures

gèsto *m* gesture; attitude; act, deed

ge·stóre -strice *mf* manager, operator; gestore di stazione (rr) station agent

gestualità *f* bodily movements (*e.g., of an actor*)

Gesù *m* Jesus; Gesù Cristo Jesus Christ

gesui·ta *m* (-ti) Jesuit

gesuìti·co -ca *adj* (-ci -che) Jesuitic(al)

gettare (gètto) *tr* to throw; to cast; to pour; to lay (*e.g., a floor*); to send forth; to yield; to broadcast (*seed*); to risk (*one's life*); gettare la colpa addosso a qlcu to lay the blame on s.o.; gettare le armi to lay down one's arms; gettar giù to fell, knock down; gettar sangue to bleed || *ref* to throw oneself; to plunge; to flow, empty (*said of a river*)

gettata *f* pour, pouring; jetty; shoot, sprout; cast; range (*of a gun*); gettata cardiaca (med) rate of flow of blood

gèttito *m* yield; waste; far gettito di to waste

gètto *m* throw; gush; shoot, sprout; cast; precast concrete slab; (aer) jet; a getto (aer) jet; a getto continuo continuously; di getto spontaneously; far getto di to waste; primo getto first draft

gettonare (gettóno) *tr* (coll) to call up from a pay station; (coll) to make the selection of (*a record in a juke-box*)

gettóne *m* counter, token; attendance fee; (cards) chip

gettopropulsióne *f* jet propulsion

ghepardo *m* cheetah

ghép·pio *m* (-pi) kestrel

gherì·glio *m* (-gli) kernel, meat (*of nut*)

gherlino *m* (naut) warp, line

gherminèlla *f* trick, sleight of hand; trickery

ghermire §176 *tr* to claw; to seize

gheróne *m* gusset

ghétta *f* gaiter; ghette spats

ghétto *m* ghetto

ghiacciàia *f* icebox, cooler

ghiac·ciàio *m* (-ciài) glacier; ghiacciaio continentale polar cap

ghiacciare §128 *tr* to freeze || *intr* (ESSERE) to freeze || *impers* (ESSERE) —ghiaccia it is freezing

ghiaccia·to -ta *adj* iced; ice-cold; frozen || *f* flavored crushed ice

ghiàc·cio -cia (-ci -ce) *adj* icy, ice-cold || *m* ice; ghiaccio secco dry ice

ghiacciò·lo -la *adj* crumbly, breakable || *m* icicle; popsicle

ghiàia *f* gravel, crushed stone

ghianda *f* fringe (*on a curtain*); (bot) acorn; ghiande mast (*for swine*)

ghiandàia *f* (orn) jay

ghiàndola *f* gland

ghibelli·no -na *adj* & *m* Ghibelline

ghièra *f* ferrule; ring

ghigliottina *f* guillotine; a ghigliottina sash (*window*)

ghigliottinare *tr* to guillotine

ghigna *f* (coll) grimace

ghignare *intr* to grimace; to sneer

ghigno *m* sneer, smirk; grin

ghinèa *f* guinea

ghìngheri *m invar*—in ghingheri dressed up

ghiót·to -ta *adj* fond; gluttonous; eager; dainty (*food*) || *f* (culin) dripping pan

ghiottó·ne -na *mf* glutton; (zool) glutton, wolverine

ghiottonerìa *f* gluttony; tidbit; (fig) rarity

ghiòzzo [ddzz] *m* dolt; (ichth) gudgeon

ghirba *f* jar; (coll) skin, life

ghiribizzo [ddzz] *m* (coll) whim, caprice

ghirigòro *m* doodle, curlicue

ghirlanda *f* garland, wreath

ghiro *m* dormouse; dormire come un ghiro to sleep like a log

ghisa *f* cast iron

già *adv* already; once upon a time; formerly || *interj* indeed!

giac·ca *f* (-che) jacket, coat; giacca a due petti double-breasted coat; giacca a vento windbreaker

giacché *conj* since

giacènte *adj* lying; idle (*capital*); unclaimed (*letter*); in abeyance

giacènza *f* lying; stay, abeyance; giacenze di capitali idle capital; giacenze di magazzino unsold stock of merchandise

giacére §181 *intr* (ESSERE) to lie; to be in abeyance; (lit) to be prostrate

giacì·glio *m* (-gli) pallet, cot

giaciménto *m* field, bed; giacimento petrolifero oil field

giacinto *m* hyacinth

Giàcomo *m* James

giaculatòria *f* ejaculation (*prayer*); litany (*monotonous account*); curse

giada *f* jade

giaggiòlo *m* (bot) iris

giaguaro *m* jaguar
giaiétto *m* jet (*black coal*)
gialappa *f* (pharm) jalap
gialla·stro -stra *adj* yellowish
gial·lo -la *adj* yellow; detective (*book or picture*); white (*with fear*) || *m* yellow; detective story, whodunit; suspense movie; giallo dell'uovo egg yolk
giamaica·no -na *adj & mf* Jamaican
giàmbi·co -ca *adj* (-ci -che) iambic
giambo *m* iamb
giammài *adv* never
giansenismo *m* Jansenism
Giappóne, il Japan
giapponése [s] *adj & mf* Japanese
giara *f* crock, jar
giardinàg·gio *m* (-gi) gardening
giardinétta *f* station wagon
giardiniè·re -ra *mf* gardener || *f* jardiniere; mixed pickles; mixed salad; wagonette; station wagon
giardino *m* garden; giardino d'infanzia kindergarten; giardino pensile roof garden; giardino zoologico zoological garden
giarrettièra *f* garter
Giasóne *m* Jason
giavanése [s] *adj & mf* Javanese
giavellòtto *m* javelin
gibbó·so -sa [s] *adj* gibbous, humped; humpbacked; rough (*ground*)
gibèrna *f* cartridge box; cartridge belt
gi·bus *m* (-bus) opera hat
gi·ga *f* (-ghe) gigue, jig
gigante *adj & m* giant
giganté·sco -sca *adj* (-schi -sche) gigantic
gigantéssa *f* giantess
gigióne *m* ham actor
gì·glio *m* (-gli) Madonna lily; fleur-de-lys
gilda *f* guild
gi·lè *f* (-lè) vest, waistcoat
gimnòto *m* electric eel
ginecologìa *f* gynecology
ginecòlo·go -ga *mf* (-gi -ghe) gynecologist
gine·pràio *m* (-prài) juniper thicket; (fig) mess
ginépro *m* juniper
ginèstra *f* (bot) Spanish broom
Ginèvra *f* Geneva
ginevri·no -na *adj & mf* Genevan
gingillare *ref* to trifle; to idle
gingillo *m* trifle, bauble
ginnà·sio *m* (-si) secondary school; gymnasium
ginna·sta *mf* (-sti -ste) gymnast
ginnàsti·co -ca (-ci -che) *adj* gymnastic || *f* gymnastics; ginnastica a corpo libero or ginnastica da camera calisthenics
gìnni·co -ca *adj* (-ci -che) gymnastic
ginocchiata *f* blow with the knee; blow on the knee
ginocchièra *f* kneepad; elastic bandage (*for knee*); kneepiece (*of armor*)
ginòc·chio *m* (-chi) knee; avere il ginocchio valgo to be bowlegged; avere il ginocchio varo to be knock-kneed; in ginocchio on one's knees

|| *m* (-chia *fpl*) knee; fino alle ginocchia knee-deep; gettarsi alle ginocchia di to go down on one's knees to; mettere qlcu in ginocchio to bring s.o. to his knees
ginocchióni *adv* on one's knees
giocare §182 *tr* to play; to stake, bet, risk, gamble; to make a fool of || *intr* to play; to gamble; to circulate (*said of air*); (fig) to play a role; giocare a to play; to wager; giocare a mosca cieca to play blindman's buff; giocare con to risk; giocare d'armi to fence; giocare d'azzardo to gamble; giocare di to use (*e.g., one's wits*); giocare di gomiti to elbow one's way; giocare di mano to steal; giocare sulle parole to play on words; to pun || *ref* to risk (*e.g., one's life*); to gamble away
giocata *f* wager, stake; game, play
gioca·tóre -trice *mf* player; gambler; speculator
giocàttolo *m* toy, plaything
giocherellare (giocherèllo) *intr* to play, trifle
giochétto *m* children's game; child's play; dirty trick
giò·co *m* (-chi) game; gambling; play; wager, stake; set; joke; (cards) hand; entrare in gioco to come into play; fare gioco a to come in handy to; fare il doppio gioco to be guilty of duplicity; fare il gioco di to play into the hands of; giochi di equilibrio balancing act; gioco da ragazzi child's play; gioco d'azzardo gambling; game of chance; gioco dei bussolotti (fig) jugglery; gioco di destrezza game of skill; gioco di parole play on words, pun; gioco di prestigio sleight of hand; gioco di società parlor game; metter in gioco to risk; to stake; per gioco for fun; prendersi gioco di to make fun of
giocofòrza *m*—è giocoforza + *inf* it is necessary + *inf*
giocolière *m* juggler
giocón·do -da *adj* merry, joyful
giocó·so -sa [s] *adj* jocose, jolly
giogàia *f* dewlap; chain of mountains
giò·go *m* (-ghi) yoke; beam (*of balance*); rounded peak; pass
giòia *f* joy, happiness; darling; jewel; darsi alla pazza gioia to have a wild time
gioiellerìa *f* jewelry; jewelry store
gioiellière *m* jeweler
gioièllo *m* jewel
gioió·so -sa [s] *adj* joyful
gioire §176 (*pres part* missing) *intr* to rejoice
Giòna *m* Jonas
Giordània, la Jordan (*country*)
giorda·no -na *adj & mf* Jordanian || Giordano *m* Jordan (*river*)
Giórgio *m* George
giorna·làio -làia *mf* (-lài -làie) newsdealer
giornale *m* newspaper; magazine; (com) journal; giornale di bordo log, logbook; giornale murale poster; giornale radio newscast

giornaliè·ro -ra *adj* daily || *mf* day laborer

giornalismo *m* journalism

giornali·sta *mf* (-sti -ste) journalist; **giornalista pubblicista** free-lance writer || *m* newspaperman || *f* newspaperwoman

giornalménte *adv* daily

giornata *f* day; day's work; birthday; pay, salary; battle; day's march; **giornata campale** pitched battle; **giornata della mamma** Mother's Day; **giornata lavorativa** workday; **vivere alla giornata** to live from hand to mouth

giórno *m* day; **a giorni** within the next few days; **a giorni . . . a giorni** some days . . . others; **a giorno** open, open-work (*needlework*); full (*light*); **ai giorni nostri** nowadays; **al giorno d'oggi** nowadays; **buon giorno** good day; good morning; good-bye; **dare gli otto giorni a** to dismiss, fire; **di ogni giorno** everyday (*e.g., clothes*); **essere a giorno** to be up to date; **giorno dei morti** All Souls' Day; **giorno di lavoro** workday; **giorno di paga** payday; **giorno fatto** broad daylight; **giorno feriale** weekday; **giorno festivo** holiday; **mettere a giorno** to bring up to date; **otto giorni oggi** one week from today; **passare un brutto giorno** to have a bad time; **un giorno o l'altro** one of these days

giòstra *f* joust; merry-go-round

giostrare (**giòstro**) *intr* to joust; to get along, manage; to idle, loiter

Giosuè *m* Joshua

Giotté·sco -sca *adj* (-schi -sche) of the school of Giotto

giovaménto *m* benefit, advantage

gióvane *adj* young; youthful; fresh (*e.g., cheese*); Younger, e.g., **Plinio il Giovane** Pliny the Younger || *m* young man; boy, apprentice; **i giovani** the young || *f* young woman

giovanile *adj* youthful

Giovanni *m* John; **Giovanni Battista** John the Baptist

giovanòtta *f* young woman

giovanòtto *m* young man; (coll) bachelor

giovare (**gióvo**) *tr* (lit) to help || *intr* (with *dat*) to help, to be of use to || *ref* to avail oneself || *impers* (ESSERE) —non **giova** it's no use

Giòve *m* Jupiter

giove·dì *m* (-dì) Thursday; **giovedì santo** Maundy Thursday

giovèn·ca *f* (-che) heifer

gioventù *f* youth

giovévole *adj* helpful, beneficial

gioviale *adj* jovial

giovinézza *f* youth

gip *f* (gip) jeep

gippóne *m* large jeep, panel truck

giràbile *adj* endorsable

giradi·schi *m* (-schi) record player

giradito *m* (pathol) felon

giraffa *f* giraffe; (mov, telv) boom, crane

girafilièra *f* diestock

giramà·schio *m* (-schi) tap wrench

giraménto *m*—**giramento di testa** vertigo, dizziness

giramón·do *m* (-do) globetrotter

giràndola *f* girandole; pinwheel; (fig) weathercock

girandolare (**giràndolo**) *intr* to stroll, saunter

girante *mf* endorser || *f* blade (*e.g., of fan*)

girare *tr* to turn; to tour; to go around, travel over; to switch (*the conversation*); to film, shoot; to transfer (*a phone call*); to endorse; (mil) to surround || *intr* to turn; to circulate; to spin (*said of one's head*) || *ref* to turn; to toss and turn

girarrósto *m* turnspit; **girarrosto a motore** rotisserie

girasóle *m* sunflower

girata *f* turn; walk, ramble; (com) endorsement; (cards) deal; (coll) tongue-lashing

giratà·rio -ria *mf* (-ri -rie) endorsee

giravòlta *f* turn, pirouette; bend; sudden change of mind

girellare (**girèllo**) *intr* to stroll, wander around

girèllo *m* rump; go-cart, walker

girévole *adj* revolving

girino *m* tadpole; bicycle rider competing on the Tour of Italy

giro *m* periphery; turn, revolution; ride; size (*of hat*); edge (*of glass*); round (*of a doctor*); (sports) tour; (sports) lap; (com) transfer; (cards) hand; (theat) tour; **a giro di posta** by return mail; **andare in giro** to poke along; **giro collo** neckline; **giro d'affari** volume of business, turnover; **giro di parole** circumlocution; **fare il giro di** to tour; **mettere in giro** to spread (*news, gossip*); **nel giro di** within (*a period*); **prendere in giro** to poke fun at

girobùssola *f* gyrocompass

girondolare (**giróndolo**) *intr* var of girandolare

giróne *m* (sports) conference; (sports) division; (sports) league; (archaic) circle

gironzolare [dz] (**girónzolo**) *intr* to stroll, saunter

giropilò·ta *m* (-ti) gyropilot

giroscò·pio *m* (-pi) gyroscope

girotóndo *m* ring-around-a-rosy

giròtta *f* weather vane

girovagare §209 (**giròvago**) *intr* to roam, wander

giròva·go -ga (-ghi -ghe) *adj* wandering; strolling (*player*) || *m* vagrant, hobo

gita *f* trip, excursion, outing

gita·no -na *adj* & *mf* Gypsy

gitante *mf* excursionist, vacationist

gittata *f* range (*of gun*)

giù *adv* down; **andar giù** to go down; to deteriorate; to get worse; **buttar giù** to throw down; (culin) to start to cook, e.g., **buttar giù gli spaghetti** to start to cook the spaghetti; (fig) to jot down; **da . . . in giù** for the past . . . ; **dar giù** to look worse (*said* *of a sick person*); **esser giù** to be downcast; **giù di lì** thereabouts; **in giù** down; downstream; **mandar giù** to swallow; **non andar giù** to not be able to stomach or swallow, e.g., **non gli vanno giù i bugiardi** he cannot stomach liars; **venire giù** to come down; to crumble; to collapse

giubba *f* coat, jacket; mane

giubbétto *m* small coat; bodice; jerkin

giubbòtto *m* jacket (*e.g., of a motorcyclist*); **giubbotto salvagente** (aer, naut) life jacket

giubilare (**giùbilo**) *tr* to retire, to pension || *intr* to rejoice

giubilèo *f* jubilee

giùbilo *m* jubilation, exultation

giuda *m* Judas || **Giuda** *m* Judas

giudài·co -ca *adj* (**-ci -che**) Judaic

giudaismo *m* Judaism

giudè·o -a *adj* Judean; Jewish || *mf* Judean; Jew

giudicare §197 (**giùdico**) *tr* to judge; to find (*e.g., s.o. innocent*); to try (*a case*) || *intr* to judge, deem

giudicato *m* (hist) Sardinian region; **passare in giudicato** (law) to become final

giùdice *m* judge; magistrate, justice; **giudice conciliatore** justice of the peace; **giudice popolare** member of the jury

giudizià·rio -ria *adj* (**-ri -rie**) judicial, judiciary

giudì·zio *m* (**-zi**) judgment; wisdom; trial; sentence; **giudizio di Dio** (hist) ordeal; **giudizio finale** Last Judgment; **metter giudizio** to mend one's ways

giudizió·so -sa [s] *adj* judicious, wise

giùggiola *f* jujube; (joc) trifle; **andare in brodo di giuggiole** (joc) to swoon, become ecstatic

giugno *m* June

giugulare *adj* jugular || *v* (**giùgolo**) *tr* to cut the throat of

giulèbbe *m* julep

giuliana *f* (culin) julienne || **Giuliana** Juliana

giuli·vo -va *adj* gay

giullare *m* jongleur; (pej) mountebank

giumén·to -ta *mf* beast of burden || *f* female saddle horse

giun·ca *f* (**-che**) (naut) junk

giunchìglia *f* (bot) jonquil

giun·co *m* (**-chi**) (bot) rush

giùngere §183 *tr* to join (*e.g., one's hands*) || *intr* (ESSERE) to arrive; **giungere a** or **in** to arrive at, reach; **giungere a + inf** to succeed in + *ger*; **mi giunge nuovo** it's news to me

giungla *f* jungle

Giunóne *f* Juno

giunòni·co -ca *adj* (**-ci -che**) Junoesque

giunta *f* addition; makeweight; strip (*of cloth*); junta; committee; **di prima giunta** at the very beginning; **per giunta** in addition

giuntare *tr* to join

giuntatrice *f* (mov) splicer

giunto *m* (mach) joint, coupling;

giunto a sfere ball-and-socket joint; **giunto cardanico** universal joint

giuntura or **giunzióne** *f* joint; juncture, seam

giuò·co *m* (**-chi**) var of **gioco**

giuraménto *m* oath; **deferire il giuramento a** to put under oath

giurare *tr* to swear, pledge || *intr* to swear

giura·to -ta *adj* sworn || *m* juror

giurìa *f* committee; jury

giurìdi·co -ca *adj* (**-ci -che**) juridical

giurisdizióne *f* jurisdiction

giurisprudènza *f* jurisprudence

giuri·sta *mf* (**-sti -ste**) jurist

Giusèppe *m* Joseph

Giuseppina *f* Josephine

giusta *prep* according to; in accordance with

giustappórre §218 *tr* to juxtapose

giustézza *f* correctness, justness; (typ) measure

giustificàbile *adj* justifiable

giustificare §197 (**giustìfico**) *tr* to justify || *ref* to excuse oneself

giustificazióne *f* justification

giustìzia *f* justice; **far giustizia a** to execute; **farsi giustizia da sé** to take the law into one's own hands; **render giustizia a** to do justice to

giustiziare §287 *tr* to execute

giustizière *m* executioner; (obs) judge

giu·sto -sta *adj* just; opportune || *m* just man; just price; rights, due || **giusto** *adv* just, justly

gla·bro -bra *adj* smooth (*face*)

glaciale *adj* glacial; (fig) icy

gladiatóre *m* gladiator

gladiòlo *m* gladiolus

glàndola *f* var of **ghiandola**

glassa *f* glaze, icing

glassare *tr* to glaze, ice

glèba *f* clod, lump of earth

gli §4 *art* || §5 *pers pron*

glicerina *f* glycerin

glìcine *m* wistaria

gliéla; gliéle; gliéli; gliélo; gliéne §5

globale *adj* total, aggregate

glòbo *m* globe; **globo oculare** eyeball

globulare *adj* globular, global

glòbulo *m* globule; (physiol) corpuscle

gloglottare (**gloglòtto**) *intr* to gobble; to gurgle

gloglottì·o *m* (**-i**) gobble, gobbling; gurgle

glòria *f* glory

gloriare §287 (**glòrio**) *tr* (lit) to exalt || *ref* to boast; to glory

glorificare §197 (**glorìfico**) *tr* to glorify

glorió·so -sa [s] *adj* glorious; proud

glòssa *f* gloss

glossà·rio *m* (**-ri**) glossary

glòttide *f* glottis

glottò·go -ga *mf* (**-gi -ghe**) linguist

glucòsio *m* glucose

glùtine *m* gluten

gnòc·co *m* (**-chi**) potato dumpling

gnòmo *m* gnome

gnòrri *m invar*—**fare lo gnorri** to feign ignorance

gòb·bo -ba *adj* hunchbacked || *mf*

hunchback ‖ *f* hump; hunch; hump (*of gibbous moon*); hook (*of nose*)
góc·cia *f* (**-ce**) drop; bead; **avere la goccia al naso** to have a runny nose; **goccia d'acqua** raindrop
góc·cio *m* (**-ci**) drop, swallow
gócciola *f* drop; bead
gocciolare (**gócciolo**) *tr & intr* to drip
gocciola·tóio *m* (**-tói**) dripstone
gocciolì·o *m* (**-i**) drip, trickle
godére §184 *tr* to enjoy ‖ *intr* to take pleasure; to revel; to profit ‖ *ref* to enjoy; **godersela** to have a good time
godìbile *adj* enjoyable
godiménto *m* enjoyment, pleasure
goffàggine *f* clumsiness
gòf·fo -fa *adj* awkward; ill-fitting
gógna *f* pillory; **mettere alla gogna** to pillory
góla *f* throat; neck; gluttony; gorge (*of mountain*); mouth (*of cannon*); flue (*of chimney*); (archit) ogee; **far gola a** to tempt; **mentire per la gola** to lie shamelessly; **tornare a gola** to repeat (*said of food*)
golétta *f* neck (*of shirt*); (naut) schooner
gòlf *m* (**gòlf**) sweater, cardigan; (sports) golf
gólfo *m* gulf; **golfo mistico** orchestra pit ‖ **Golfo Persico** Persian Gulf
Gòlgota, il Golgotha
goliardo *m* goliard; university student
golosi·tà [s] *f* (**-tà**) gluttony; tidbit
goló·so -sa [s] *adj* gluttonous; appetizing
gómena *f* hawser
gomitata *f* blow with the elbow; nudge
gómito *m* elbow; bend; **alzare il gomito** to crook the elbow; **dare di gomito a** to nudge
gomìtolo *m* skein, clew
gómma *f* gum; rubber; eraser; tire; **bucare una gomma** to have a flat tire; **gomma arabica** gum arabic; **gomma a terra** flat tire; **gomma da masticare** chewing gum; **gomma lacca** shellac
gommapiuma *f* foam rubber
gomma·to -ta *adj* gummed; with tires
gommatura *f* gumming; (aut) tires
gommi·sta *m* (**-sti**) tire dealer; tire repairman
gommó·so -sa [s] *adj* gummy
góndola *f* gondola; (aer) pod
gonfalóne *m* gonfalon
gonfiare §287 (**gónfio**) *tr* to inflate, blow up; to bloat; to swell; to exaggerate; to puff up ‖ *intr* (ESSERE) to swell ‖ *ref* to swell; to puff up; to bulge, balloon
gonfiatura *f* inflation; exaggeration
gonfiézza *f* swelling; grandiloquence
gón·fio -fia (**-fi -fie**) *adj* inflated, swollen; conceited ‖ *m* swelling, bulge
gonfióre *m* swelling
gongolare (**góngolo**) *intr* to rejoice; to be elated
goniòmetro *m* goniometer; protractor
gònna *f* skirt; **gonna pantaloni** culottes
gonnèlla *f* skirt; (fig) petticoat
gonnellino *m* kilt; ballerina skirt

gón·zo -za [dz] *mf* simpleton, fool
gòra *f* millpond; marsh; (coll) spot
górbia *f* tip (*of umbrella*)
gorgheggiare §290 (**gorghéggio**) *tr & intr* to warble; to trill
gorghég·gio *m* (**-gi**) warbling; trill
gór·go *m* (**-ghi**) whirlpool; (lit) river
gorgogliàre §280 (**gorgóglio**) *intr* to gurgle
gorgó·glio *m* (**-gli**) gurgle
gorgoglì·o *m* (**-i**) gurgling
goril·la *m* (**-la**) gorilla
gòta *f* cheek; (lit) side
gòti·co -ca *adj & m* (**-ci -che**) Gothic
Gòto *m* Goth
gótta *f* (pathol) gout
gottazza *f* (naut) scoop
gottó·so -sa [s] *adj* gouty
governale *m* fin (*of bomb*); (obs) rudder
governante *adj* governing ‖ *m* ruler ‖ *f* governess; housekeeper
governare (**govèrno**) *tr* to rule, govern; to steer (*a ship*); to tend (*animals*); to wash and dry (*dishes*); to run (*e.g., a bank*) ‖ *intr* to steer
governati·vo -va *adj* government
govèrno *m* government; tending (*e.g., of animals*); running (*of household*); cleaning (*of house*); blending (*of wine*); (archaic) steering
gózzo *m* crop, craw (*of bird*); (pathol) goiter
gozzovigliare §280 *intr* to go on a spree
gracchiare §287 *intr* to caw
gràc·chio *m* (**-chi**) caw; (orn) chough
gracidare (**gràcido**) *intr* to croak; to honk (*said, e.g., of a goose*)
gràcile *adj* weak, frail; thin, delicate
gradasso *m* swaggerer, braggadocio
grada·to -ta *adj* graded; gradual
gradazióne *f* gradation; alcoholic proof; **gradazione vocalica** (phonet) ablaut
gradévole *adj* pleasant
gradiménto *m* pleasure; acceptance (*of a product*); liking
gradinata *f* steps; tier (*of seats*)
gradino *m* step; (fig) stepping stone
gradire §176 *tr* to like; to welcome
gradi·to -ta *adj* agreeable; welcome (*guest*); kind (*letter*)
grado *m* degree; rank; (nav) rating; (archaic) step; **a buon grado o a mal grado** willy-nilly; **a grado a grado** little by little; **a Suo grado** according to your wishes; **di buon grado** willingly; **di secondo grado** secondary (*school*); **essere in grado di** to be in a position to; **saper grado a** (lit) to be grateful to
graduale *adj & m* gradual
graduare (**gràduo**) *tr* to graduate
gradua·to -ta *adj* graduated ‖ *m* noncommissioned officer
graduatòria *f* ranking; rank
graffa *f* clamp; brace, bracket
graffiare §287 *tr* to scratch; (coll) to swipe
graffiétto *m* tiny scratch; marking gage
gràf·fio *m* (**-fi**) scratch
grafìa *f* writing, spelling; (gram) graph

gràfi·co -ca (-ci -che) *adj* graphic || *m* graph, diagram; designer (*for printing industry*); member of printers' union || *f* graphic arts
grafite *f* graphite
grafologìa *f* graphology
gragnòla *f* hail
gramàglia *f* crepe; widow's weeds; **in gramaglie** in mourning
gramigna *f* couch grass; weed
grammàti·co -ca (-ci -che) *adj* grammatical || *m* grammarian || *f* grammar
grammo *m* gram
grammofòni·co -ca *adj* (**-ci -che**) phonograph, recording
grammòfono *m* phonograph, record player
gra·mo -ma *adj* poor, sad; wretched, miserable; frail, sickly
gran *adj* apocopated form of **grande**, used before singular and plural nouns beginning with a consonant sound other than **gn, pn, ps,** impure **s, x,** and **z**
gra·na *m* (**-na**) Parmesan cheese || *f* (**-ne**) cochineal; grain (*of wood, metal, etc*); (slang) dough; (coll) trouble
granàglie *fpl* grain, cereals
gra·nàio *m* (**-nài**) granary, barn
granata *adj invar & m* garnet (*color*) || *f* pomegranate (*fruit*); garnet; broom; grenade
granatière *m* grenadier
granatina *f* grenadine
Gran Bretagna, la Great Britain
grancassa *f* bass drum
grancèvola *f* spider crab
gràn·chio *m* (**-chi**) crab; claw (*of hammer*); (coll) cramp; **prendere un granchio** to make a blunder
grandangolare *adj* wide-angle
grande *adj* big, large; great; tall; high (*mass; voice*); long (*time*); capital (*letter*); full (*speed*); grown-up || *m* grownup; grandeur; grandee; **fare il grande** to show off; **i grandi** the great; **in grande** on a large scale; lavishly
grandézza *f* size; enormity; greatness; quantity; **in grandezza naturale** lifesize; **grandezze** ostentatiousness
grandezzó·so -sa [s] *adj* ostentatious
grandiloquènza *f* grandiloquence
grandinare (**gràndino**) *tr* (obs) to hail || *intr* to hail || *impers* (ESSERE & AVERE)—**grandina** it is hailing
grandinata *f* hailstorm
gràndine *f* hail
grandiosi·tà [s] *f* (**-tà**) grandeur, magnificence
grandió·so -sa [s] *adj* grandiose, grand
grandu·ca *m* (**-chi**) grand duke
granduchéssa *f* grand duchess
granèllo *m* grain, seed; speck
grànfia *f* clutch
granìco·lo -la *adj* grain, wheat
granire §176 *tr* to grain; to stipple; (mus) to make (*the notes*) clear-cut || *intr* to teethe
granita *f* sherbet, water ice

granito *m* granite
granitura *f* knurl, milled edge
grano *m* wheat; grain of wheat; grain; speck; **grano duro** durum wheat; **grano saraceno** buckwheat; **grano turco** corn
granturco *m* corn
granulare *adj* granular || *v* (**grànulo**) *tr* to granulate
granulatóre *m* crusher
grànulo *m* granule, pellet, bud
granuló·so -sa [s] *adj* granular; lumpy; gritty; friable, crumbly
grappa *f* eau de vie; clamp, brace
grappétta *f* staple; crampon
grappino *m* (naut) grapnel
gràppolo *m* bunch, cluster
grassàg·gio *m* (**-gi**) (aut) lubrication
grassatóre *m* highwayman
grassazióne *f* holdup
grassétto *m* boldface
grassézza *f* fatness; richness
gras·so -sa *adj* fat; rich; greasy; risqué || *m* fat, suet; grease; shortening
grassòc·cio -cia *adj* (**-ci -ce**) pudgy, plump
grata *f* grate, grating
gratèlla *f* strainer; sieve; broiler
gratìc·cia *f* (**-ce**) (theat) gridiron
gratìc·cio *m* (**-ci**) lattice, trellis
gratìcola *f* gridiron; grating; graticule
gratìfi·ca *f* (**-che**) bonus
gratificare §197 (**gratìfico**) *tr* to give a bonus to; (fig) to pelt (*with insults*)
gratificazióne *f* bonus
gratis *adv* gratis, free, for nothing
gratitùdine *f* gratitude
gra·to -ta *adj* grateful, appreciative || *f* see **grata**
grattacapo *m* trouble, worry
grattacièlo *m* skyscraper
grattare *tr* to scratch; to scrape; to grate; (slang) to snitch || *intr* to scratch; to grate
grattùgia *f* grater
grattugiare §290 *tr* to grate
gratùi·to -ta *adj* gratuitous, free
gravame *m* burden; tax; (law) appeal; **fare gravame a qlcu di qlco** to impute s.th to s.o.
gravare *tr* to burden, oppress; (obs) to seize || *intr* (ESSERE & AVERE) to weigh; to lie; to be sorry, e.g., **gli grava d'avermi disturbato** he is sorry to have bothered me || *ref*—**gravarsi di** to take upon oneself
grave *adj* heavy; burdensome; grave, serious || *m* (phys) body; **stare sul grave** to put on airs
graveolènte *adj* stinking
gravézza *f* heaviness; burden; oppression; (obs) taxation
gravidanza *f* pregnancy
gràvi·do -da *adj* pregnant; fraught
gravi·tà *f* (**-tà**) gravity
gravitare (**gràvito**) *intr* to gravitate; to weigh, lie
gravitazióne *f* gravitation
gravó·so -sa [s] *adj* heavy; hard, burdensome; oppressive
gràzia *f* grace; pardon, mercy; delicacy; kindness; **di grazia!** please!;

essere nelle grazie di qlcu to be in s.o.'s good graces; **fare grazia di qlco a qlcu** to spare s.o. s.th; **grazia di Dio** abundance, bounty; **grazie!** thank you!; **grazie tante!** thanks a lot!; **in grazia di** thanks to; **male grazie** bad manners; **per grazie** as a favor; **render grazia a** to thank; **saper grazia a** to be thankful to

graziare §287 *tr* to pardon; **graziare qlcu di qlco** to grant s.th to s.o.

grazió·so -sa [s] *adj* graceful, pretty; gracious; (lit) free, gratuitous

Grècia, la Greece

grè·co -ca (-ci -che) *adj* & *mf* Greek || *f* fret, fretwork; bullion (*on Italian general's hat*); tunic

gregà·rio -ria (-ri -rie) *adj* gregarious || *m* private; follower

grég·ge *m* (**-gi** or **-ge** *fpl*) flock, herd

grég·gio -gia (-gi -ge) *adj* coarse; raw, unrefined || *m* crude oil

gregoria·no -na *adj* Gregorian

grembiale *m* var of **grembiule**

grembiule *m* apron; frock; smock

grembiulino *m* pinafore

grèmbo *m* lap; womb; bosom

gremire §176 *tr* to crowd || *ref* to become crowded

gremi·to -ta *adj* overcrowded

gréppia *f* manger, crib

gréto *m* dry gravel bed of a river

grettézza *f* stinginess; narrow-mindedness

grét·to -ta *adj* stingy; narrow-minded

grève *adj* heavy; uncouth; (lit) grievous

gréz·zo -za [ddzz] *adj* raw, crude; coarse

gridare *tr* to cry out; to cry for (*help*); (coll) to scold || *intr* to cry out, shout

grido *m* cry (*of animal*) || *m* (**grida** *fpl*) cry; scream; shout; yell; fame; **di grido** famous; **grido di guerra** war cry; **ultimo grido** latest fashion

grifa·gno -gna *adj* rapacious, fierce

griffa *f* hobnail; (mov, phot) sprocket

grifo *m* snout (*of pig*); (pej) snoot; (lit) griffin

grifóne *m* vulture; (mythol) griffin

grigia·stro -stra *adj* grayish

grì·gio -gia *adj* & *m* (**-gi -gie**) grey

grigiovérde *adj invar* olive-drab || *m* olive-drab uniform

grìglia *f* gridiron, broiler; grate, grille; (elec) grid (*of vacuum tube*)

grillare *tr* to grill, broil || *intr* to sizzle; to bubble (*said of fermenting wine*); to have a sudden whim

grillétto *m* trigger

grillo *m* cricket; whim, fancy

grimaldèllo *m* picklock

grìnfia *f* claw, clutch; **grinfie** clutches

grinta *f* grim or forbidding face

grinza *f* wrinkle; crease; **non fare una grinza** to be perfect

grinzó·so -sa [s] *adj* wrinkled; creased

grippare *intr* & *ref* to bind, jam

grisèlla *f* (naut) ratline

gri·sou *m* (**-sou**) firedamp

grissino *m* breadstick

Groenlàndia, la Greenland

grómma *f* incrustation, deposit

grónda *f* eaves; slope (*of ground*)

grondàia *f* gutter (*of roof*)

grondare (**gróndo**) *tr* to drip || *intr* (ESSERE) to ooze (*said, e.g., of perspiration*); to drip; **grondare di sangue** to stream with blood

gròppa *f* back (*of animal*); top (*of mountain*); **restare sulla groppa a** to be stuck with, e.g., **gli sono restati sulla groppa cento esemplari** he is stuck with one hundred copies

groppata *f* bucking (*of horse*)

gróppo *m* knot, tangle; lump (*in throat*); squall

groppóne *m* back, rump

gròssa *f* gross; **dormire della grossa** to sleep like a log

grossézza *f* bigness; thickness; density; swelling (*of river*); (fig) coarseness; **grossezza d'udito** hardness of hearing

grossi·sta *mf* (**-sti -ste**) wholesaler

gròs·so -sa *adj* big, large; thick; heavy (*seas*); swollen (*river*); hard (*breathing*); offensive (*words*); coarse (*e.g., salt*); pregnant; deep (*voice*); (coll) important; **alla grossa** approximately; **di grosso** a lot, very much; **dirla grossa** to talk nonsense; **farla grossa** to make a blunder; **grosso d'udito** hard of hearing; **in grosso** wholesale; **spararle grosse** to tell tall tales || *m* bulk; main body (*e.g., of an army*) || *f* see **grossa**

grossola·no -na *adj* coarse; boorish, uncouth; big (*blunder*)

gròtta *f* grotto; (coll) inn

grotté·sco -sca (-schi -sche) *adj* & *m* grotesque || *f* (hist) grotesque painting

grovièra *f* Gruyère cheese

grovì·glio *m* (**-gli**) tangle, snarl

gru *f* (**gru**) (orn, mach) crane

grùc·cia *f* (**-ce**) crutch; clothes hanger; (obs) wooden leg

grufolare (**grùfolo**) *intr* to nuzzle || *ref* to wallow (*in mud*)

grugnire §176 *tr* & *intr* to grunt

grugnito *m* grunt

grugno *m* snout; (pej) snoot; **fare il grugno** to sulk

grui·sta *m* (**-sti**) crane operator

grulleria *f* foolishness

grul·lo -la *adj* silly, simple

gruma *f* deposit, incrustation

grumo *m* lump; clot

grùmolo *m* heart (*e.g., of lettuce*); small lump

grumó·so -sa [s] *adj* lumpy; incrusted, scaly

gruppo *m* group; main body (*e.g., of runners*); club; **gruppo elettrogeno** generating unit; **gruppo motore** (aut) power plant

grùzzolo *m* hoard, pile; **farsi il gruzzolo** to feather one's nest

guadagnare *tr* to earn; to win; to gain; to pick up (*speed*); to reach (*port*) || *intr* to win; to look better || *ref* to win; to win over; **guadagnarsi il pane** or **la vita** to earn one's living

guadagno *m* earnings; profit; **a basso**

guadagno (rad, telv) low-gain; **ad
alto guadagno** (rad, telv) high-gain
guadare *tr* to wade, ford
guado *m* ford; (bot) woad; **passare a
guado** to ford
guài *interj* woe!
guaina *f* case; scabbard, sheath; corset;
(aut) seat cover
guàio *m* (guài) trouble || *interj* see **guài**
guaire §176 *intr* to yelp; to whine
guaito *m* yelp, whine
gualcire §176 *tr* to crumple
gualdrappa *f* saddlecloth
Gualtièro *m* Walter
guàn·cia *f* (-ce) cheek; moldboard;
cheek side (*of gunstock*)
guanciale *m* pillow; **dormire tra due
guanciali** to sleep safe and sound
guan·tàio -tàia *mf* (-tài -tàie) glove
maker; glove merchant
guanterìa *f* glove factory
guantièra *f* glove case; tray
guanto *m* glove; **gettare il guanto** to
fling down the gauntlet; **raccogliere
il guanto** to take up the gauntlet;
trattare con i guanti gialli to handle
with kid gloves
guantóne *m* big glove; **guantoni da
pugilato** boxing gloves
guardabarriè·re *m* (-re) (rr) gatekeeper,
crossing watchman
guardabò·schi *m* (-schi) forester
guardacà·cia *m* (-cia) gamekeeper
guardacò·ste *m* (-ste) coast guard;
coast-guard cutter
guardafi·li *m* (-li) (elec) lineman
guardalì·nee *m* (-nee) (rr) trackwalker;
(sports) linesman
guardama·no *m* (-no) guard (*of sabre
or rifle*); work glove; (naut) handrail
guardaportó·ne *m* (-ne) doorman
guardare *tr* to look at; to protect;
watch; to pay attention to; to face,
overlook; (obs) to keep to (*one's
bed*); (obs) to keep (*a holiday*);
guardare a vista to keep under close
watch; **guardare dall'alto in basso**
to look down one's nose at; **guardare
di sotto in su** to leer at || *intr* to
look; to pay attention; **Dio guardi!**
God forbid!; **guardare a** to face
(*said, e.g., of a room*); **guardare di
non** + *inf* to be careful not to +
inf; **guardare in faccia** to face (*e.g.,
danger*); **stare a guardare** to keep on
the sidelines || *ref* to look at one
another; to look at oneself; **guardarsi
da** to keep from; to guard against
guardarò·ba *m* (-ba) wardrobe; linen
closet; checkroom, cloakroom
guardarobiè·re -ra *mf* checkroom at-
tendant || *f* hatcheck girl
guardasigil·li *m* (-li) minister of justice
(*in Italy*); (Brit) Lord Privy Seal;
(U.S.A.) attorney general; (hist)
keeper of the seals
guardaspal·le *m* (-le) bodyguard
guardata *f* quick look, glance
guarda·vìa *m* (-vìa) guardrail; median
strip
guàrdia *f* watch; guard; top water
level; flyleaf; **di guardia** on duty;

fare la guardia a to watch; **guardia
campestre** forester; **guardia carceraria** prison guard; **guardia del corpo**
guard, body guard; **guardia di
finanza** customs officer; **guardia
d'onore** honor guard; **guardia forestale** forester; park guard; **guardia
giurata** private policeman; **guardia
medica** emergency clinic; **guardia
municipale** police officer; **guardia
notturna** night watch; **mettere qlcu
in guardia** to warn s.o.; **montare la
guardia** to be on guard duty, keep
guard; **stare in guardia** to be on one's
guard
guardiamari·na *m* (-na) (nav) ensign
guardiano *m* keeper; warden; watchdog; (eccl) superior; **guardiano notturno** night watchman
guardina *f* lockup; **in guardina** in jail
guardinfante *m* bustle (*worn under the
back of a woman's skirt*)
guardin·go -ga *adj* (-ghi -ghe) wary
guàrdolo *m* welt (*in shoe*)
guardóne *m* peeping tom
guarentì·gia *f* (-gie) guarantee
guarìbile *adj* curable
guarigióne *f* cure, recovery
guarire §176 *tr* to cure; to heal || *intr*
(ESSERE) to recover; to heal
guaritóre *m* healer; quack
guarnigióne *f* (mil) garrison
guarnire §176 *tr* to equip; to rig; to
trim; (naut) to rig; (culin) to garnish
|| *intr* to add beauty
guarnizióne *f* decoration; trimming;
lining; (culin) garniture; (mach)
gasket; (mach) washer
Guascógna, la Gascony
guascó·ne -na *adj & mf* Gascon
guastafè·ste *mf* (-ste) kill-joy
guastare *tr* to ruin, spoil; to undo; to
wreck; (obs) to lay waste; **guastare
le uova nel paniere a** to spoil the
plans of || *ref* to spoil; to worsen
(*said, e.g., of the weather*); (mach)
to break down; **guastarsi con qlcu**
to quarrel with s.o.; **guastarsi il
sangue** to blow one's top
guastatóre *m* commando
gua·sto -sta *adj* ruined, spoiled;
wrecked || *m* breakdown; corrup-
tion; discord
guatare *tr* (lit) to look askance or with
fear at
Guayana, la Guyana
guazza *f* dew
guazzabù·glio *m* (-gli) muddle, mess
guazzare *tr* to make (*an animal*) wade
in a river || *intr* to wallow
guazzétto *m* stew, ragout
guazzo *m* puddle, pool; gouache
guèl·fo -fa *adj & mf* Guelph
guèr·cio -cia (-ci -ce) *adj* cross-eyed;
one-eyed; almost blind || *mf* cross-
eyed person; one-eyed person
guèrra *f* war; warfare; **guerra a coltello**
internecine feud; **guerra di Troia**
Trojan war; **guerra fredda** cold war;
guerra lampo blitzkrieg; **guerra mondiale** world war

guerrafon·dàio -dàia (-dài -dàie) *adj* warmongering || *mf* warmonger
guerreggiare §290 **(guerréggio)** *tr* to fight, war against || *intr* to fight || *ref* to make war on one another
guerré·sco -sca *adj* (-schi -sche) warlike
guerriè·ro -ra *adj* war, warlike || *mf* fighter || *m* warrior
guerrìglia *f* guerrilla
guerriglièro *m* guerrilla (*soldier*)
gufo *m* misanthrope; (orn) horned owl
gùglia *f* spire; peak
gugliata *f* needleful
Guglièlmo *m* William
guida *f* guide; guidance; driving; runner (*rug*); guidebook; manual (*of instruction*); (aut) steering; **guida a destra** right-hand drive; **guide reins** (*of horse*); (mach) slide
guidaiòlo *m* leader (*among animals*)
guidare *tr* to guide, lead; to steer; to drive || *intr* to drive || *ref* to restrain oneself
guida·tóre -trice *mf* driver
guiderdóne *m* (lit) premium, prize
guidóne *m* pennant, pennon
guidoslitta *f* bobsled
guidovìa *f* ski lift

Guinèa, la Guinea
guinzà·glio *m* (-gli) leash; (fig) fetter, shackle
guisa *f* way, manner; **in guisa che** so that; **in guisa di** under the guise of
guìt·to -ta *adj* miserly, niggardly || *m* strolling player
guizzare *intr* to dart; to wriggle; to flash (*said of lightning*); (naut) to yaw || *intr* (ESSERE) to slip away
guizzo *m* dart; wriggle; flash
gù·scio *m* (-sci) shell; pod (*of pea*); tick (*of mattress*); **guscio di noce** nutshell; **guscio d'uovo** eggshell
gustare *tr* to taste; to relish || *intr* (ESSERE & AVERE) to please; to like, e.g., **gli gustano le gite in barca** he likes boat rides
gusto *m* taste; pleasure, fun; whim; style; **di cattivo gusto** tasteless; **di gusto** gladly, with gusto; **prendere gusto per** to take a liking for; **prendersi il gusto di** to relish; **provar gusto** to have fun
gustó·so -sa [s] *adj* tasty
guttapèrca *f* gutta-percha
gutturale *adj* & *f* guttural

H

H, h ['akkɑ] *m* & *f* eighth letter of the Italian alphabet
handicappare *tr* var of **andicappare**
hangar *m* (hangar) hangar
havaia·no -na *adj* & *mf* Hawaiian
henné *m* henna
hertz *m* hertz

hertzia·no -na *adj* Hertzian
hi-fi *f* (coll) hi-fi
hockei·sta *m* (-sti) hockey player
hollywoodia·no -na *adj* Hollywood, Hollywood-like
hurrà *interj* hurrah!

I

I, i, [i] *m* & *f* ninth letter of the Italian alphabet
i §4 *def art* the
iarda *f* yard
iato *m* hiatus
iattanza *f* boasting, bragging
iattura *f* misfortune, calamity
ibèri·co -ca *adj* (-ci -che) Iberian
ibernare (ibèrno) *intr* to hibernate
ibi·sco *m* (-schi) hibiscus
ibridare (ibrido) *tr* & *intr* to hybridize
ìbri·do -da *adj* & *m* hybrid
icàsti·co -ca *adj* (-ci -che) figurative; realistic
-ìccio -ìccia *suf adj* -ish, e.g., **gialliccio** yellowish
iconocla·sta *mf* (-sti -ste) iconoclast
iconografìa *f* iconography
iconoscò·pio *m* (-pi) iconoscope
iddì·o *m* (-i) god || **Iddio** *m* God
idèa *f* idea; goal, purpose; bit, touch; **avere idea di** to have a mind to; **dare l'idea di** to seem; **farsi un'idea di** to

grasp the notion of; **idea fissa** fixed idea; **neanche per idea** not in the least
ideale *adj* & *m* ideal
idealismo *m* idealism
ideali·sta *mf* (-sti -ste) idealist
idealìsti·co -ca *adj* (-ci -che) idealistic
idealizzare [ddzz] *tr* to idealize
ideare (idèo) *tr* to conceive
idea·tóre -trice *mf* inventor
idem *adv* ditto
idènti·co -ca *adj* (-ci -che) identical
identificare §197 **(identìfico)** *tr* to identify || *ref* to resemble each other; **identificarsi con** to identify with
identificazióne *f* identification
identi·tà *f* (-tà) identity
ideologìa *f* ideology
idi *mpl* & *fpl* ides
idillìa·co -ca *adj* (-ci -che) idyllic
idìl·lio *m* (-li) idyll; romance
idiò·ma *m* (-mi) language, idiom
idiomàti·co -ca *adj* (-ci -che) idiomatic

idiosincrasìa *f* aversion; (med) idiosyncrasy
idiò·ta (-**ti** -**te**) *adj* idiotic ‖ *mf* idiot
idiotismo *m* idiom; idiocy
idiozìa *f* idiocy
idolatrare *tr* & *intr* to idolize
idolatrìa *f* idolatry
ìdolo *m* idol
idonei·tà *f* (-**tà**) fitness, aptitude; qualification
idòne·o -**a** *adj* fit; qualified; opportune
idra *f* hydra
idrante *m* hydrant, fireplug
idratante *adj* moisturizing
idratare *tr* & *ref* to hydrate
idrato *m* hydrate
idràuli·co -**ca** (-**ci** -**che**) *adj* hydraulic ‖ *m* plumber ‖ *f* hydraulics
ìdri·co -**ca** *adj* (-**ci** -**che**) water, e.g., **forza idrica** water power
idrocarburo *m* hydrocarbon
idroelèttri·co -**ca** *adj* (-**ci** -**che**) hydroelectric
idròfi·lo -**la** *adj* absorbent
idrofobìa *f* hydrophobia, rabies
idròfo·bo -**ba** *adj* hydrophobic, rabid
idròfu·go -**ga** *adj* (-**ghi** -**ghe**) waterproof
idrogenare (**idrògeno**) *tr* to hydrogenate
idrògeno *m* hydrogen
idròpi·co -**ca** (-**ci** -**che**) *adj* dropsical ‖ *mf* patient suffering from dropsy
idropisìa *f* dropsy
idroplano *m* hydroplane (*boat*)
idropòrto *m* seaplane airport
idrorepellènte *adj* water-repellent
idroscalo *m* seaplane airport
idro·scì *m* (-**scì**) water ski
idroscivolante *m* (naut) hydroplane
idrosilurante *m* torpedo plane
idròssido *m* hydroxide
idroterapìa *f* hydrotherapy
idrovìa *f* inland waterway
idrovolante *m* seaplane, hydroplane
idròvo·ro -**ra** *adj* suction (*pump*) ‖ *f* suction pump
ièna *f* hyena
ièri *m* & *adv* yesterday; **ieri l'altro** the day before yesterday; **ieri notte** last night; **ieri sera** last evening, last night, yesterday evening
ietta·tóre -**trice** *mf* hoodoo
iettatura *f* evil eye; bad luck, jinx
igiène *f* hygiene; sanitation
igièni·co -**ca** *adj* (-**ci** -**che**) hygienic, sanitary
igname *m* yam
igna·ro -**ra** *adj* unaware; inexperienced
igna·vo -**va** *adj* (lit) slothful
ignizióne *f* ignition
ignòbile *adj* (lit) ignoble
ignomìnia *f* ignominy; outrage
ignominió·so -**sa** [s] *adj* ignominious
ignorante *adj* ignorant; illiterate ‖ *mf* ignoramus
ignoranza *f* ignorance
ignorare (**ignòro**) *tr* to not know; to ignore
ignò·to -**ta** *adj* & *m* unknown
ignu·do -**da** *adj* (lit) naked ‖ *m* (lit) naked person
il §4 *def art* the
ìlare *adj* cheerful

ilari·tà *f* (-**tà**) cheerfulness; laughter
ìlice *f* (lit) ilex, holm oak
ìlio *m* (anat) ilium
illanguidire §176 *tr* to weaken ‖ *intr* (ESSERE) to get weak
illazióne *f* inference
illéci·to -**ta** *adj* illicit, unlawful ‖ *m* unlawful act
illegale *adj* illegal
illeggiadrire §176 *tr* to embellish
illeggìbile *adj* illegible
illegìtti·mo -**ma** *adj* illegitimate
illé·so -**sa** *adj* unhurt, unharmed
illettera·to -**ta** *adj* & *mf* illiterate
illiba·to -**ta** *adj* spotless, pure
illimita·to -**ta** *adj* unlimited
illìri·co -**ca** *adj* (-**ci** -**che**) Illyrian
illògi·co -**ca** *adj* (-**ci** -**che**) illogical
illùdere §105 *tr* to delude
illuminare (**illùmino**) *tr* to illuminate; to brighten; to enlighten ‖ *ref* to grow bright
illumina·to -**ta** *adj* illuminated; enlightened; educated
illuminazióne *f* illumination; enlightenment
illuminismo *m* Age of Enlightenment
illusióne *f* illusion; delusion; **farsi illusioni** to indulge in wishful thinking
illusionismo *m* sleight of hand; magic
illusioni·sta *mf* (-**sti** -**ste**) magician
illu·so -**sa** *adj* deluded ‖ *mf* deluded person
illusò·rio -**ria** *adj* (-**ri** -**rie**) illusory, illusive
illustrare *tr* to illustrate; to explain, elucidate ‖ *ref* to become famous
illustra·to -**ta** *adj* illustrated, pictorial
illustra·tóre -**trice** *mf* illustrator
illustrazióne *f* illustration; illustrious person
illustre *adj* illustrious, famous
illustrìssi·mo -**ma** *adj* distinguished; honorable; **Illustrissimo Signore** Dear Sir; Mr. (*addressing a letter*)
imbacuccare §197 *tr* & *ref* to muffle up; to wrap up
imbaldanzire §176 *tr* to embolden ‖ *intr* (ESSERE) & *ref* to grow bold
imballàg·gio *m* (-**gi**) wrapping, packaging
imballare *tr* to wrap up, package; to bale; to race (*the motor*); **imballare in una gabbia** to crate ‖ *ref* to race (*said of a motor*)
imballa·tóre -**trice** *mf* packer
imballo *m* packing; packaging, wrapping; racing (*of motor*)
imbalsamare (**imbàlsamo**) *tr* to embalm; to stuff (*animals*)
imbambola·to -**ta** *adj* gazing, staring; stunned, dumfounded; sleepy-eyed; sluggish
imbandierare (**imbandièro**) *tr* to bedeck with flags
imbandire §176 *tr* to prepare (*food, a meal, a table*) lavishly
imbarazzante *adj* embarrassing, awkward
imbarazzare *tr* to embarrass; to encumber, hamper; to upset (*the stomach*)

imbarazza·to -ta *adj* embarrassed, perplexed; upset (*stomach*); ill-at-ease

imbarazzo *m* embarrassment; annoyance; **imbarazzo di stomaco** upset stomach

imbarbarire §176 *tr* & *ref* to make barbarous; to corrupt (*a language*)

imbarcadèro *m* landing pier

imbarcare §197 *tr* to ship; to load, embark; to ship (*water*) ‖ *ref* to sail; to embark; to curve (*said of furniture*)

imbarca·tóio *m* (-tói) landing pier

imbarcazióne *f* boat; **imbarcazione di salvataggio** lifeboat

imbar·co *m* (-chi) embarkation; port of embarkation

imbardare *intr* & *ref* (aer) to yaw; (aut) to swerve, lurch

imbardata *f* (aer) yaw; (aut) swerve, lurch

imbarilare *tr* to barrel

imbastardire §176 *tr* to corrupt ‖ *ref* to become corrupt

imbastire §176 *tr* (sew) to baste; (fig) to sketch out

imbastitura *f* (sew) basting

imbàttere *ref*—**imbattersi bene** to be lucky; **imbattersi in** to come across; **imbattersi male** to have bad luck

imbattìbile *adj* unbeatable

imbavagliare §280 *tr* to gag

imbeccare §197 (imbécco) *tr* to feed (*a fledgling*); (fig) to prompt

imbeccata *f* beakful; (fig) prompting

imbecillàggine *f* imbecility

imbecille *adj* & *mf* imbecile

imbecilli·tà *f* (-tà) imbecility

imbèlle *adj* unwarlike; cowardly

imbellettare (imbellétto) *tr* to apply rouge to, apply make-up on ‖ *ref* to put on make-up

imbellire §176 *tr* to embellish

imbèrbe *adj* beardless; callow

imbestialire §176 *tr* to enrage ‖ *intr* (ESSERE) & *ref* to become enraged

imbévere §185 *tr* to soak; to soak up; to imbue ‖ *ref* to become soaked; to become imbued

imbiancare §197 *tr* to whiten; to bleach; to whitewash ‖ *intr* (ESSERE) & *ref* to turn white (*said, e.g., of hair*); to clear up (*said of weather*)

imbiancatura *f* bleaching (*of laundry*); whitening; whitewashing

imbianchiménto *m* bleaching

imbianchino *m* whitewasher; house painter; (pej) dauber

imbianchire §176 *tr* to whiten; to bleach ‖ *ref* to turn white

imbiondire §176 *tr* to bleach (*hair*) ‖ *intr* to become blond; to ripen (*said of wheat*)

imbizzarrire [ddzz] *intr* (ESSERE) & *ref* to become skittish (*said of a horse*); to become infuriated

imbizzire [ddzz] §176 *intr* (ESSERE) to get angry

imboccare §197 (imbócco) *tr* to feed by mouth; to put (*an instrument*) in one's mouth; to take, enter (*a road*); to prompt ‖ *intr* (ESSERE) to

flow; to open (*said of a road*); (mach) to fit

imboccatura *f* entrance (*of street*); inlet; opening, top (*e.g., of bottle*); bit (*of bridle*); (mus) mouthpiece; **avere l'imboccatura a** to be experienced in

imbóc·co *m* (-chi) entrance; inlet; opening

imboniménto *m* claptrap

imbonire §176 *tr* to lure, entice (*s.o. to buy or enter*)

imbonitóre *m* barker

imborghesire §176 *tr* to render middle-class ‖ *intr* (ESSERE) to become middle-class

imboscare §197 (imbòsco) *tr* to hide; to hide (*s.o.*) underground ‖ *ref* to shirk; to be a slacker

imbosca·to -ta *adj* (mil) shirking, draft-dodging ‖ *m* (mil) slacker; (mil) goldbrick ‖ *f* ambush; **tendere un'imboscata** to set an ambush

imboscatóre *m* accomplice of a draft dodger; hoarder (*of scarce items*)

imboschire §176 *tr* to forest

imbottare (imbótto) *tr* to barrel

imbottigliare §280 *tr* to bottle; to bottle up ‖ *ref* to get bottled up (*said of traffic*)

imbottire §176 *tr* to pad, fill; to stuff; to pad (*a speech*)

imbottita *f* bedspread, quilt

imbottitura *f* padding

imbra·ca *f* (-che) breeching strap (*of harness*); safety belt; (naut) sling

imbracare §197 *tr* to sling

imbracciare §128 *tr* to fasten (*shield*); to level (*gun*)

imbrancare §197 *tr* & *ref* to herd

imbrattacar·te *mf* (-te) scribbler

imbrattamu·ri *mf* (-ri) dauber

imbrattare *tr* to soil, dirty; to smudge, smear

imbrattaté·le *mf* (-le) dauber

imbratto *m* dirt; smudge, smear; daub; scribble; swill

imbrigliare §280 *tr* to bridle

imbroccare §197 (imbròcco) *tr* to hit (*the target*); to guess right

imbrodare (imbròdo) *tr* to soil

imbrogliare §280 (imbròglio) *tr* to cheat; to mix up; to tangle; to confuse; **imbrogliare le vele** (naut) to take in the reef ‖ *ref* to get tangled up; to get confused; to turn bad (*said of weather*)

imbrò·glio *m* (-gli) cheat; tangle; (naut) reef; **cacciarsi in un imbroglio** to get involved in a mess

imbroglió·ne -na *mf* swindler

imbronciare §128 (imbróncio) *intr* (ESSERE) & *ref* to pout, sulk ‖ *ref* to lower (*said of the weather*)

imbroncia·to -ta *adj* sulky, surly; cloudy, overcast

imbrunire *m*—**sull'imbrunire** at nightfall ‖ §176 *intr* (ESSERE) to turn brown ‖ *impers* (ESSERE)—**imbrunisce** it is growing dark

imbruttire §176 *tr* to mar; to make ugly ‖ *intr* (ESSERE) & *ref* to grow ugly

imbucare §197 *tr* to mail; to put in a hole ‖ *ref* to hide

imburrare *tr* to butter
imbuto *m* funnel
imène *m* (anat) hymen, maidenhead
imitare (ìmito) *tr* to imitate
imita·tóre -trice *mf* imitator; (theat) mimic
imitazióne *f* imitation
immacola·to -ta *adj* immaculate
immagazzinare [ddzz] *tr* to store, store up
immaginare (immàgino) *tr* to imagine; to guess; to invent || *ref*—**si immagini!** of course!; not at all!
immaginà·rio -ria *adj* (-**ri** -**rie**) imaginary
immaginativa *f* imagination
immaginazióne *f* imagination
immàgine *f* image; picture
immaginó·so -sa [s] *adj* imaginative
immalinconire §176 *tr* to sadden || *intr* (ESSERE) & *ref* to become melancholy
immancàbile *adj* unfailing; certain
immane *adj* monstruous; gigantic
immangiàbile *adj* uneatable, inedible
immantinènte *adv* (lit) immediately
immarcescìbile *adj* incorruptible
immateriale *adj* immaterial
immatricolare (immatrìcolo) *tr* to matriculate
immatricolazióne *f* matriculation
immatu·ro -ra *adj* immature; premature
immedesimare (immedésimo) *tr* to identify; to blend || *ref* to identify oneself
immediataménte *adv* immediately
immediatézza *f* immediacy
immedia·to -ta *adj* immediate
immemoràbile *adj* immemorial
immèmore *adj* forgetful
immèn·so -sa *adj* immense, huge
immèrgere §162 *tr* to immerse; to plunge || *ref* to plunge; to become absorbed
immerita·to -ta *adj* undeserved
immeritévole *adj* undeserving
immersióne *f* immersion; submersion (*of a submarine*); (naut) draft
imméttere §198 *tr* to let in; **immettere qlcu nel possesso di** (law) to grant s.o. possession of
immigrante *adj* & *mf* immigrant
immigrare *intr* (ESSERE) to immigrate
immigrazióne *f* immigration; (biol) migration
imminènte *adj* imminent
imminènza *f* imminence
immischiare §287 *tr* to involve || *ref* to meddle; to become involved
immiserire §176 *tr* to impoverish || *intr* (ESSERE) & *ref* to become impoverished; to become debased
immissà·rio *m* (-**ri**) tributary
immissióne *f* letting in, introduction; intake; insertion (*in lunar orbit*)
immòbile *adj* motionless, immobile; real (*property*) || **immobili** *mpl* real estate
immobiliare *adj* real, e.g., **proprietà immobiliare** real estate; real-estate, e.g., **imposta immobiliare** real-estate tax
immobilizzare [ddzz] *tr* to immobilize; to pin down; to tie up (*capital*)

immodè·sto -sta *adj* indecent; immodest
immolare (immòlo) *tr* to immolate
immondézza *f* filth; impurity
immondez·zàio *m* (-**zài**) rubbish heap, dump; garbage can
immondìzia *f* trash; garbage; filth
immón·do -da *adj* filthy, dirty; unclean
immorale *adj* immoral
immorali·tà *f* (-**tà**) immorality
immortalare *tr* to immortalize
immortale *adj* immortal
immortalità *f* immortality
immò·to -ta *adj* (lit) motionless
immune *adj* immune
immunizzare [ddzz] *tr* to immunize
immutàbile *adj* immutable
immuta·to -ta *adj* unchanged
i·mo -ma *adj* (lit) bottom, lowest || *m* (lit) bottom; (lit) depth
impaccare §197 *tr* to pack, wrap up
impacchettare (impacchétto) *tr* to pack, bundle
impacciare §128 *tr* to hamper; to embarrass || *ref* to meddle
impaccia·to -ta *adj* hampered; clumsy
impàc·cio *m* (-**ci**) embarrassment; hindrance; trouble; **essere d'impaccio** to be in the way
impac·co *m* (-**chi**) wrapping; (med) compress
impadronire §176 *ref*—**impadronirsi di** to seize; to take possession of; to master (*a language*)
impagàbile *adj* invaluable, priceless
impaginare (impàgino) *tr* (typ) to make up (*in pages*), paginate
impaginato *m* (typ) page proof
impagliare §280 *tr* to cane (*a chair*); to stuff (*an animal; a doll*); to pack in straw
impalare *tr* to impale; to tie to a pole or stake || *ref* to stiffen up
impala·to -ta *adj* stiff, rigid
impalcatura *f* scaffold; frame, framework
impallidire §176 *intr* to turn pale; to blanch; to grow dim (*said of a star*); (fig) to wane
impalmare *tr* (lit) to wed
impalpàbile *adj* impalpable
impaludare *tr* to make swampy or marshy || *intr* to become marshy
impanare *tr* to bread; to thread (*a screw*) || *intr* to screw in
impaniare §287 *tr* to trap, ensnare || *ref* to fall into the trap
impantanare *tr* to turn into a swamp || *ref* to get stuck, to sink (*in vice*)
impaperare (impàpero) *ref* to fluff, make a slip
impappinare *tr* to confuse || *ref* to blunder; to stammer
imparare *tr* to learn; **imparare a memoria** to learn by heart || *intr* **imparare a** to learn to, to learn how to
impareggiàbile *adj* peerless, unmatched
imparentare (imparènto) *tr* to bring into the family || *ref*—**imparentarsi con** to marry into
ìmpari *adj* odd, uneven
imparrucca·to -ta *adj* bewigged
impartire §176 *tr* to impart
imparziale *adj* impartial

impasse *f* blind alley; deadlock; (cards) finesse

impassìbile *adj* impassible, impassive

impastare *tr* to knead; to mix; to smear with paste

impasta•to -ta *adj* kneaded; smeared; **impastato di** tainted with; overwhelmed with (*sleep*)

impasto *m* paste; pastiche

impastoiare §287 (**impastóio**) *tr* to fetter, hamstring

impataccare §197 *tr* to besmear, soil

impattare *tr* to even up; to tie (*a game*); **impattarla con** to tie (*a person*)

impatto *m* impact

impaurire §176 *tr* to scare || *ref* to get scared

impàvi•do -da *adj* fearless

impaziènte *adj* impatient

impazientire §176 *intr* (ESSERE) & *ref* to get impatient

impaziènza *f* impatience

impazzare *intr* (ESSERE) to be wild with excitement; to go mad; (culin) to curdle

impazzata *f*—**all'impazzata** at top speed; berserk

impazzire §176 *intr* (ESSERE) to go crazy; **fare impazzire** to drive crazy

impeccàbile *adj* impeccable

impeciare §128 (**impécio**) *tr* to tar

impedènza *f* impedance

impedimento *m* hindrance, obstacle, impediment

impedire §176 *tr* to impede, hinder; to obstruct || *intr* to prevent; **impedire** (with *dat*) **di** + *inf* or **che** + *subj* to prevent from + *ger*

impegnare (**impégno**) *tr* to pawn; to reserve (*a room*); to engage (*the enemy*); to keep occupied; to pledge || *ref* to obligate oneself; to go all out; to become entangled

impegnati•vo -va *adj* demanding (*activity*); binding (*promise*)

impegna•to -ta *adj* pawned; pledged; occupied; committed

impégno *m* commitment; obligation; task; zeal; **senza impegno** without promising

impegolare (**impégolo**) *tr* to tar || *ref* to become entangled

impelagare §209 (**impèlago**) *ref* to bog down; to become entangled

impellicciare §128 *tr* to fur; to veneer

impenetràbile *adj* impenetrable

impenitènte *adj* impenitent; confirmed

impennàg•gio *m* (-gi) (aer) empennage

impennare (**impénno**) *tr* to feather; (fig) to give wings to || *ref* to rear (*said of a horse*); to take umbrage; (aer) to zoom

impennata *f* rearing (*of horse*); (aer) zoom

impensàbile *adj* unthinkable

impensa•to -ta *adj* unexpected

impensierire §176 *tr* & *ref* to worry

imperante *adj* prevailing

imperare (**impèro**) *intr* to rule, reign; to prevail; **imperare su** to rule over

imperati•vo -va *adj* & *m* imperative

imperatóre *m* emperor

imperatrice *f* empress

impercettìbile *adj* imperceptible

imperdonàbile *adj* unforgivable

imperfèt•to -ta *adj* & *m* imperfect

imperfezióne *f* imperfection

imperiale *adj* imperial || *m* upper deck (*of bus or coach*); **imperiali** imperial troops

imperiali•sta *adj* & *mf* (-sti -ste) imperialist

impè•rio *m* (-ri) empire; rule

imperió•so -sa [s] *adj* imperious; imperative

imperi•to -ta *adj* (lit) inexperienced

imperitu•ro -ra *adj* immortal; everlasting, imperishable

imperìzia *f* inexperience

imperlare (**impèrlo**) *tr* to bead; to cover with beads (*of perspiration*)

impermalire §176 *tr* to provoke || *ref* to become provoked

impermeàbile *adj* waterproof || *m* raincoat

imperniare §287 (**impèrnio**) *tr* to pivot; (fig) to base

impèro *adj invar* Empire || *m* empire; control, sway

imperscrutàbile *adj* inscrutable

impersonale *adj* impersonal

impersonare (**impersóno**) *tr* to impersonate || *ref*—**impersonarsi in** to be the embodiment of; (theat) to impersonate

impertèrri•to -ta *adj* undaunted

impertinènte *adj* impertinent, pert

impertinènza *f* impertinence

imperturbàbile *adj* imperturbable

imperturba•to -ta *adj* unperturbed

imperversare (**impervèrso**) *intr* to storm, rage; to be the rage

impèr•vio -via *adj* (-vi -vie) impassable

impeto *m* impetus; onslaught; violence; outburst; **d'impeto** rashly

impetrare (**impètro**) *tr* to beg for; to obtain by entreaty || *intr* (ESSERE) (lit) to turn to stone

impetti•to -ta *adj* puffed up with pride

impetuó•so -sa [s] *adj* impetuous

impiallacciare §128 *tr* to veneer

impiallacciatura *f* veneer, veneering

impiantare *tr* to install (*a machine*); to set up (*a business*); to open (*an account*)

impiantito *m* floor, flooring

impianto *m* installation; plant; system

impiastrare *tr* to plaster; to dirty

impiastricciare §128 *tr* to plaster; to daub; to soil

impiastro *m* (med) plaster; (fig) bore

impiccagióne *f* hanging

impiccare §197 *tr* to hang

impicciare §128 *tr* to hinder; to bother || *ref* to meddle, butt in; **impicciarsi degli affari propri** to mind one's own business

impìc•cio *m* (-ci) hindrance; trouble; **essere d'impiccio** to be in the way

impiccio•ne -na *mf* meddler

impiccolire §176 *tr* to reduce in size || *ref* to shrink in size

impiegare §209 (**impiègo**) *tr* to employ;

to use; to devote (*one's energies*); to spend (*time*); to invest (*capital*); to take (*time*) || *ref* to have a job

impiegatì·zio -zia *adj* (**-zi -zie**) employee, white-collar

impiega·to -ta *mf* employee; clerk

impiè·go *m* (**-ghi**) employment; use; job; place of business; investment

impietosire [s] §176 *tr* to move to pity || *ref* to be moved to pity

impietrire §176 *tr, intr* (ESSERE) & *ref* to turn to stone

impigliare §280 *tr* to entangle || *ref* to become entangled

impigrire §176 *tr* to make lazy || *intr* (ESSERE) & *ref* to get lazy

impinguare (**impìnguo**) *tr* & *ref* to fatten

impinzare *tr* to stuff || *ref* to stuff oneself; **impinzarsi il cervello** to stuff one's brain (*with knowledge*)

impiombare (**impiómbo**) *tr* to lead; to plumb, seal with lead; to fill (*a tooth*); (naut) to splice (*a cable*)

impiombatura *f* seal; filling (*of tooth*); (naut) splicing

impipare *ref*—**impiparsi di** (slang) to not give a hoot about

implacàbile *adj* implacable

implicare §197 (**ìmplico**) *tr* to implicate; to imply

implìci·to -ta *adj* implicit, implied

implorare (**implòro**) *tr* to implore

implume *adj* unfledged, featherless

impolìti·co -ca *adj* (**-ci -che**) unpolitical; impolitic, injudicious

impollinare (**impòllino**) *tr* to pollinate

impoltronire §176 *tr* to make lazy || *ref* to get lazy

impolverare (**impólvero**) *tr* to cover with dust || *ref* to get covered with dust

impomatare *tr* to pomade; to smear with pomade

imponderàbile *adj* imponderable; weightless

imponderabilità *f* imponderability; weightlessness

imponènte *adj* imposing; stately

imponìbile *adj* taxable || *m* taxable income

impopolare *adj* unpopular

impopolarità *f* unpopularity

impórre §218 *tr* to place, put; to impose; to order; to compel; to give (*a name*) || *intr* (ESSERE) to be imposing; (with *dat*) to order, command || *ref* to command respect; to win favor; to be necessary

importante *adj* important; sizable || *m* important thing

importanza *f* importance; size; **darsi importanza** to assume an air of importance

importare (**impòrto**) *tr* to import; to imply; to involve || *intr* (ESSERE) to be of consequence || *impers* (ESSERE) —**importa** it matters; **non importa** never mind

importa·tóre -trice *mf* importer

importazióne *f* importation; import

impòrto *m* amount

importunare *tr* to bother, importune

importu·no -na *adj* importunate, bothersome || *mf* bore

imposizióne *f* imposition; giving (*of a name*); order, command; taxation

impossessare (**impossèsso**) *ref*—**impossessarsi di** to seize; to master (*a language*)

impossìbile *adj* & *m* impossible

impossibili·tà *f* (**-tà**) impossibility

impossibilitare (**impossibìlito**) *tr* to make impossible; to make unable or incapable

impossibilita·to -ta *adj* unable

impòsta *f* tax; shutter; (archit) impost; **imposta complementare** surtax; **imposta sul valore aggiunto** value-added tax

impostare (**impòsto**) *tr* to start, begin; to state (*a problem*); to mail; to lay (*a stone*); to open (*an account*); to attune (*one's voice*); to lay the keel of (*a ship*) || *ref* to take one's position, get ready

impostazióne *f* beginning, starting; laying; mail, mailing; (com) posting

impo·stóre -stóra *mf* impostor

impostura *f* imposture

impotènte *adj* weak; impotent

impotènza *f* impotence

impoveriménto *m* impoverishment

impoverire §176 *tr* to impoverish || *intr* (ESSERE) & *ref* to become impoverished

impraticàbile *adj* impracticable; impassable

impratichire §176 *tr* to train, familiarize || *ref* to become familiar (*e.g., with a task*)

imprecare §197 (**imprèco**) *tr* to wish (*e.g., s.o.'s death*) || *intr* to curse

imprecazióne *f* imprecation, curse

imprecisàbile *adj* undefinable

imprecisióne *f* inexactness, inaccuracy

impreci·so -sa *adj* vague, inexact

impregnare (**imprégno**) *tr* to impregnate

impremedita·to -ta *adj* unpremeditated

imprendìbile *adj* impregnable

imprendi·tóre -trice *mf* contractor || *m*—**imprenditore di pompe funebri** undertaker

imprenditoriale *adj* managerial

imprepara·to -ta *adj* unprepared

impreparazióne *f* unpreparedness

imprésa [s] *f* enterprise; undertaking; achievement; firm, concern; (theat) management; **impresa (di) pompe funebri** undertaking establishment

impresà·rio [s] *m* (**-ri**) manager; (theat) impresario

imprescindìbile *adj* essential, indispensable; unavoidable

impresentàbile *adj* unpresentable

impressionàbile *adj* impressionable

impressionante *adj* striking, impressive; frightening

impressionare (**impressióno**) *tr* to impress; (phot) to expose || *ref* to become frightened; (phot) to be exposed

impressióne *f* impression

imprestare (**imprèsto**) *tr* (coll) to lend

imprèstito *m* (philol) borrowing
imprevedìbile *adj* unforeseeable
imprevedu•to -ta *adj* unforeseen
imprevidènte *adj* improvident
imprevi•sto -sta *adj* unforeseen, un-
expected || imprevisti *mpl* unfore-
seen events
imprigionare (imprigióno) *tr* to imprison
imprìmere §131 *tr* to impress; to imprint; to impart (*e.g., motion*)
improbàbile *adj* improbable, unlikely
ìmpro•bo -ba *adj* dishonest; laborious
improdutti•vo -va *adj* unproductive
imprónta *f* print, imprint; mark; impronta digitale fingerprint
improntare (imprónto) *tr* to impress,
imprint; to mark
improntitùdine *f* audacity, impudence
impronunziàbile *adj* unpronounceable
impropè•rio *m* (-ri) insult
improprie•tà *f* (-tà) impropriety; error
imprò•prio -pria *adj* (-pri -prie) improper, inappropriate; (math) improper
improrogàbile *adj* unextendible
improvvi•do -da *adj* improvident
improvvisare *tr* to improvise || *ref* to
suddenly decide to become
improvvisa•to -ta *adj* improvised; im-
promptu || *f* surprise; surprise party
improvvisazióne *f* improvisation
improvvi•so -sa *adj* sudden || *m* (mus)
impromptu; all'improvviso or d'improvviso suddenly
imprudènte *adj* imprudent; rash
imprudènza *f* imprudence; rashness
impudènte *adj* shameless; brazen; impudent
impudènza *f* shamelessness; impudence
impudicizia *f* immodesty
impudi•co -ca *adj* (-chi -che) immodest,
indecent
impugnare *tr* to grip, seize; to take up
(*arms*); to impugn, contest
impugnatura *f* handle; grip, hold; hilt,
haft
impulsi•vo -va *adj* impulsive
impulso *m* impulse; dare impulso a to
promote, foment
impuneménte *adv* with impunity
impunità *f* impunity
impuni•to -ta *adj* unpunished
impuntare *intr* to stumble, trip; to
stutter || *ref* to stutter; to balk; to be
stubborn; impuntarsi a or di + *inf*
to stubbornly insist on + *ger*
impuntigliare §280 *ref* to persist, insist
impuntire §176 *tr* to tuft (*e.g., a pillow*)
impuntura *f* backstitch
impuri•tà *f* (-tà) impurity; unchastity
impu•ro -ra *adj* impure; unchaste
imputàbile *adj* attributable
imputare (ìmputo) *tr* to impute; to
charge, accuse; (com) to post
imputa•to -ta *mf* accused, defendant
imputazióne *f* imputation; charge, accusation; (com) posting
imputridire §176 *tr* & *intr* (ESSERE) to
rot
in *prep* in; at; into; to; on, upon;
through; during; married to, e.g.,

Maria Roberti in Bianchi Marie
Roberti married to Bianchi; as, e.g.,
in premio as a prize; by, e.g., in
automobile by car; of, e.g., studente
in legge student of law; essere in
quattro to be four; in alto up; in
breve soon; in a word; in giù down;
in là there; in qua here; in realtà
really; in seguito a because of
-ina *suf fem* about, e.g., cinquantina
about fifty
inabbordàbile *adj* unapproachable
inàbile *adj* unfit; ineligible; awkward
inabili•tà *f* (-tà) unfitness; awkward-
ness; inability
inabilitare (inabìlito) *tr* to incapacitate;
to render unfit; to disqualify
inabilitazióne *f* disqualification
inabissare *tr* to plunge || *ref* to sink
inabitàbile *adj* uninhabitable
inabita•to -ta *adj* uninhabited
inaccessìbile *adj* inaccessible; unfathomable
inaccettàbile *adj* unacceptable
inacerbire §176 *tr* to exacerbate || *ref*
to grow bitter
inacidire §176 *tr* & *ref* to sour
inadattàbile *adj* unadaptable; maladjusted
inadat•to -ta *adj* inadequate
inadegua•to -ta *adj* inadequate
inadempiènte *adj* not fulfilling; ina-
dempiente agli obblighi di leva draft-
dodging
inafferràbile *adj* that cannot be caught
or captured; incomprehensible; elusive
inalare *tr* to inhale
inalatóre *m* inhaler
inalberare (inàlbero) *tr* to hoist || *ref*
to rear; to fly into a rage
inalteràbile *adj* unalterable
inamidare (inàmido) *tr* to starch
inamida•to -ta *adj* starched; pompous,
starchy
inammissìbile *adj* inadmissible
inamovìbile *adj* irremovable
inamovibili•tà *f* (-tà) irremovability;
tenure
inane *adj* inane; futile
inanella•to -ta *adj* curly; beringed
inanima•to -ta *adj* inanimate; lifeless
inanizióne *f* starvation
inappagàbile *adj* unquenchable
inappaga•to -ta *adj* unsatisfied
inappellàbile *adj* definitive, final
inappetènza *f* lack of appetite
inapprezzàbile *adj* inappreciable, imperceptible; inestimable
inappuntàbile *adj* faultless, impeccable
inarcare §197 *tr* to arch; to raise (*one's
eyebrows*)
inargentare (inargènto) *tr* to silver
inaridire §176 *tr* to dry; to parch || *ref*
to dry up
inarrestàbile *adj* irresistible
inarrivàbile *adj* unattainable; inimitable
inarticola•to -ta *adj* indistinct, inarticulate
inascolta•to -ta *adj* unheeded
inaspetta•to -ta *adj* unexpected
inasprimento *m* exacerbation

inasprire §176 *tr* to aggravate ‖ *ref* to sour; to become embittered; to become sharper; to become fierce or furious

inastare *tr* to hoist (*flag*); to fix (*bayonets*)

inattaccàbile *adj* unattackable; unassailable; **inattacabile da** resistant to

inattendìbile *adj* unreliable

inatté·so -sa [s] *adj* unexpected

inatti·vo -ta *adj* inactive

inaudi·to -ta *adj* unheard-of

inaugurale *adj* inaugural; maiden (*voyage*)

inaugurare (**inàuguro**) *tr* to inaugurate; to usher in (*the New Year*); to open (*e.g., an exhibit*); to unveil (*a statue*); to sport for the first time

inaugurazióne *f* inauguration

inauspica·to -ta *adj* (lit) inauspicious

inavvedu·to -ta *adj* careless, rash

inavvertènza *f* inadvertence, oversight

inavverti·to -ta *adj* unnoticed; inadvertent, thoughtless

inazióne *f* inaction

incagliare §280 *tr* to hamper; to run aground ‖ *intr* (ESSERE) & *ref* to run aground; (fig) to get stuck

incà·glio *m* (-gli) running aground; hindrance, obstacle

incalcinare *tr* to whitewash; to lime (*a field*)

incalcolàbile *adj* incalculable

incallire §176 *tr* to make callous ‖ *intr* (ESSERE) to become callous; to become inured

incalli·to -ta *adj* callous; inveterate

incalzante *adj* pressing

incalzare *tr* to press, pursue ‖ *intr* to be imminent; to be pressing ‖ *ref* to follow one another in rapid succession

incamerare (**incàmero**) *tr* to confiscate

incamminare *tr* to launch; to guide, direct ‖ *ref* to set out; to be on one's way

incanagli·to -ta *adj* vile, despicable

incanalare *tr* to channel ‖ *ref* to flow

incancrenire §176 *tr* to affect with gangrene ‖ *ref* to become gangrenous; (fig) to become callous

incandescènte *adj* incandescent; (fig) red-hot

incandescènza *f* incandescence

incannare *tr* to reel, wind

incantare *tr* to bewitch; to auction off ‖ *ref* to become enraptured; to be spellbound; to jam, get stuck (*said of machinery*)

incanta·tóre -trice *adj* enchanting ‖ *m* enchanter ‖ *f* enchantress

incantésimo *m* enchantment, spell

incantévole *adj* enchanting, charming

incanto *m* enchantment; bewitchery; auction; **d'incanto** marvelously well

incanutire §176 *tr, intr* (ESSERE) & *ref* to turn gray-headed, to turn gray (*said of a person*)

incanuti·to -ta *adj* hoary

incapace *adj* incapable; (law) incompetent ‖ *mf* oaf; (law) incompetent

incapaci·tà *f* (-tà) incapacity; (law) incompetence

incaparbire §176 *intr* (ESSERE) & *ref* to be obstinate; to be determined

incaponire §176 *ref* to get stubborn; to be determined

incappare *intr* (ESSERE) to stumble

incappottare (**incappòtto**) *tr* to cover with a coat ‖ *ref* to wrap oneself in a coat

incappucciare §128 *tr* to cover with a hood

incapricciare §128 *ref*—**incapricciarsi di** to take a fancy to; to become infatuated with

incapsulare (**incàpsulo**) *tr* to encapsulate; to cap

incarcerare (**incàrcero**) *tr* to jail, incarcerate; (fig) to confine

incaricare §197 (**incàrico**) *tr* to charge ‖ *ref*—**incaricarsi di** to take charge of; to take care of

incarica·to -ta *adj* in charge; visiting (*professor*) ‖ *mf* deputy; **incaricato d'affari** chargé d'affaires

incàri·co *m* (-chi) task; appointment, position; **per incarico di** on behalf of

incarnare *tr* to incarnate, embody

incarna·to -ta *adj* incarnate ‖ *m* pink complexion

incarnazióne *f* incarnation

incarnire §176 *intr* (ESSERE) & *ref* to grow in (*said of a toenail*)

incarni·to -ta *adj* ingrown (*toenail*)

incartaménto *m* file, dossier

incartapecori·to -ta *adj* shriveled up

incartare *tr* to wrap up (*in paper*)

incasellare [s] (**incasèllo**) *tr* to file; to sort out

incasellatóre [s] *m* post-office file clerk

incassare *tr* to box up; to put (*a watch*) in a case; to mortise (*a lock*); to channel (*a river*); to cash (*a check*); (fig) to take (*e.g., blows*) ‖ *intr* to fit; to take it

incasso *m* receipts

incastellatura *f* scaffolding

incastonare (**incastóno**) *tr* to set, mount (*a gem*); **incastonare citazioni in un discorso** to stud a speech with quotations

incastrare *tr* to insert; to mortise; (fig) to corner ‖ *intr* to fit ‖ *ref* to fit; to become imbedded; to telescope (*said, e.g., of a train in a collision*)

incastro *m* joint; insertion; (carp) tenon; (carp) mortise

incatenare (**incaténo**) *tr* to chain, put in chains; to tie down, restrain

incatramare *tr* to tar

incàu·to -ta *adj* unwary, careless

incavallatura *f* truss (*to support roof*)

incavare *tr* to hollow out; to groove

incava·to -ta *adj* hollow

incavatura *f* hollow

incavicchiare §287 *tr* to peg

incavigliare §280 *tr* to peg

incavo *m* hollow; cavity; **incavo dell'ascella** armpit

incazzottare (**incazzòtto**) *tr* (naut) to furl

incèdere *m* stately walk || §123 *intr* to walk stately

incendiare §287 (**incèndio**) *tr* to set on fire; (fig) to inflame || *ref* to catch fire

incendià·rio -ria *adj* & *mf* (**-ri -rie**) incendiary

incèn·dio *m* (**-di**) fire; **incendio doloso** arson

incenerire §176 *tr* to reduce to ashes; to wither (*e.g., with a look*) || *ref* to turn to ashes

inceneritóre *m* incinerator

incensare (**incènso**) *tr* (eccl) to incense; (fig) to flatter

incensa·tóre -trice *mf* incense burner; (fig) flatterer

incensière *m* incense burner

incènso *m* incense

incensura·to -ta *adj* uncensured; (law) having no previous record

incentivo *m* incentive

inceppare (**incèppo**) *tr* to hinder; to shackle || *ref* to jam (*said of firearm*)

incerare (**incéro**) *tr* to wax

incerata *f* oilcloth; (naut) raincoat

incernierare (**incernièro**) *tr* to hinge

incertézza *f* uncertainty, incertitude

incèr·to -ta *adj* uncertain; irresolute || *m* uncertainty; **incerti** extras; **incerti del mestiere** cares of office, occupational annoyances, occupational hazards

incespicare §197 (**incéspico**) *intr* to stumble

incessàbile *adj* (lit) ceaseless

incessante *adj* unceasing, incessant

incèsto *m* incest

incestuó·so -sa [s] *adj* incestuous

incètta *f* cornering (*of market*)

incettare (**incètto**) *tr* to corner (*market*)

incetta·tóre -trice *mf* monopolizer

inchiavardare *tr* to key, bolt

inchièsta *f* probe, inquest; (journ) inquiry

inchinare *tr* to bend; to bow (*the head*) || *intr* (lit) to go down (*said of stars*) || *ref* to bow; to yield

inchi·no -na *adj* bent; bowing || *m* bow; curtsy

inchiodare (**inchiòdo**) *tr* to nail; to spike; to rivet; to tie, bind; to stop (*a car*) suddenly; to transfix || *ref* to freeze (*said, e.g., of brakes*); (fig) to be tied down; (fig) to go into debt

inchiostrare (**inchiòstro**) *tr* (typ) to ink

inchiòstro *m* ink; **inchiostro di china** India ink, Chinese ink

inciampare *intr* to trip, stumble

inciampo *m* stumbling block, obstacle; **essere d'inciampo a** to be in the way of

incidentale *adj* incidental

incidènte *adj* incidental || *m* incident; accident; argument, question

incidènza *f* incidence

incidere §145 *tr* to engrave; to cut; to record (*a record, a tape; a song*); **incidere all'acqua forte** to etch || *intr*—**incidere su** to weigh heavily on (*expenses, a budget*); to leave a mark on

incinerazióne *f* incineration; cremation

incinta *adj fem* pregnant

incipiènte *adj* incipient

incipriare §287 *tr* to powder || *ref* to powder oneself

incirca *adv* about; **all'incirca** more or less

incisióne *f* engraving; cutting (*of a record*); recording (*of a tape; of a song*); incision; **incisione all'acquaforte** etching

incisi·vo -va *adj* incisive; sharp (*photograph*) || *m* incisor

inciso *m* (gram) parenthetical clause; (mus) theme; **per inciso** incidentally

incisóre *m* engraver, etcher

incitare *tr* to incite, provoke

incivile *adj* uncivilized; uncouth

incivilire §176 *tr* to civilize || *ref* to become civilized

inclemènte *adj* inclement, harsh

inclemènza *f* inclemency, harshness

inclinare *tr* to tilt; to bow, bend; to incline || *intr* (fig) to lean || *ref* to bend

inclinazióne *f* inclination; slope; **inclinazione laterale** (aer) bank; **inclinazione magnetica** magnetic dip

incline *adj* inclined

incli·to -ta *adj* famous; noble

inclùdere §105 *tr* to enclose, include

inclusi·vo -va *adj* including; **inclusivo di** including

inclu·so -sa *adj* enclosed; included; inclusive || *f* enclosed letter

incoerènte *adj* incoherent

incògliere §127 *tr* (lit) to catch in the act || *intr*—**incogliere a** to happen to

incògni·to -ta *adj* unknown || *m* incognito; unknown; **in incognito** incognito || *f* (math) unknown quantity; (fig) puzzle

incollare (**incòllo**) *tr* to glue, paste; to size (*paper*) || *intr* to stick || *ref* to stick; to take on one's shoulders

incollatura *f* neck (*of horse*); glueing, sticking

incollerire §176 *intr* & *ref* to get angry

incolloca·to -ta *adj* unemployed

incolonnare (**incolónno**) *tr* to set up in columns

incolonnatóre *m* tabulator

incolóre *adj* colorless

incolpàbile *adj* blamable; (lit) guiltless

incolpare (**incólpo**) *tr*—**incolpare di** to charge with

incól·to -ta *adj* uncultivated; unkempt

incòlume *adj* unharmed, unhurt

incolumità *f* safety, security

incombènte *adj* (*danger*) impending; (*duty*) incumbent

incombènza *f* task, charge, incumbency

incómbere §186 *intr* (ESSERE) to be impending; to be incumbent

incombustibile *adj* incombustible

incominciare §128 *tr* & *intr* (ESSERE) to begin

incommensuràbile *adj* immeasurable; (math) incommensurable

incomodare (**incòmodo**) *tr* to bother, disturb || *ref* to bother; **non s'incomodi!** don't bother!

incòmo·do -da *adj* bothersome, inconvenient || *m* inconvenience; ailment;

levare l'incomodo a to get out of the way of
incomparàbile *adj* incomparable
incompatìbile *adj* incompatible; unforgivable
incompetènte *adj & mf* incompetent
incompiu•to -ta *adj* unfinished
incomplè•to -ta *adj* incomplete
incompó•sto -sta *adj* untidy; unkempt; unbecoming (*behavior*)
incomprensìbile *adj* incomprehensible
incomprensióne *f* lack of understanding
incomprè•so -sa [s] *adj* misunderstood
incomprimìbile *adj* irrepressible; incompressible
inconcepìbile *adj* inconceivable
inconciliàbile *adj* irreconcilable
inconcludènte *adj* inconclusive; insignificant
inconcus•so -sa *adj* (lit) unshaken
incondiziona•to -ta *adj* unconditional
inconfessàbile *adj* unspeakable, vile
inconfessa•to -ta *adj* unavowed
inconfondìbile *adj* unmistakable
inconfutàbile *adj* irrefutable
incongruènte *adj* inconsistent
incòn•gruo -grua *adj* incongruous
inconoscìbile *adj* unknowable
inconsapèvole *adj* unaware, unconscious
incòn•scio -scia *adj & m* (-sci -sce) unconscious
inconseguènte *adj* inconsistent, inconsequential
inconsidera•to -ta *adj* inconsiderate
inconsistènte *adj* flimsy; inconsistent
inconsistènza *f* flimsiness; inconsistency
inconsolàbile *adj* inconsolable
inconsuè•to -ta *adj* unusual
inconsul•to -ta *adj* ill-advised, rash
incontamina•to -ta *adj* uncontaminated
incontenìbile *adj* irrepressible
incontentàbile *adj* insatiable; hard to please; exacting
incontinènza *f* incontinence
incontrare (incóntro) *tr* to meet; to encounter, meet with ‖ *intr* (ESSERE) to catch on (*said, e.g., of fashions*) ‖ *ref* to meet; to agree ‖ *impers* (ESSERE) to happen
incontrastàbile *adj* indisputable
incontrasta•to -ta *adj* undisputed
incóntro *m* meeting; encounter; success; meet; game, fight, match; occasion, opportunity; all'incontro on the other hand; opposite; andare incontro a to go towards; to go to meet; to face; to meet (*expenses*); to accommodate; farsi incontro a to advance toward
incontrollàbile *adj* uncontrollable
incontrolla•to -ta *adj* unchecked
incontrovertìbile *adj* incontrovertible
inconveniènte *adj* inconvenient ‖ *m* inconvenience, disadvantage
incoraggiante *adj* encouraging
incoraggiare §290 *tr* to encourage
incorare §257 (incuòro) *tr* to hearten
incordare (incòrdo) *tr* to string (*e.g., a racket*); to tie up (*with a cord*) ‖ *ref* to stiffen (*said of a muscle*)
incornare (incòrno) *tr* (taur) to gore

incorniciare §128 *tr* to frame; (journ) to border; (slang) to cuckold
incoronare (incoróno) *tr* to crown
incoronazióne *f* coronation
incorporàbile *adj* absorbable; adaptable
incorporare (incòrporo) *tr* to incorporate; to absorb ‖ *ref* to incorporate
incorpòre•o -a *adj* incorporeal
incorreggìbile *adj* incorrigible
incórrere §139 *intr* (ESSERE)—incorrere in to incur
incorrót•to -ta *adj* uncorrupt
incosciènte *adj* unconscious; unaware; irresponsible ‖ *mf* irresponsible person
incosciènza *f* unconsciousness; irresponsibility; madness
incostante *adj* inconstant, fickle
incredìbile *adj* incredible, unbelievable
incrèdu•lo -la *adj* incredulous ‖ *mf* disbeliever; doubter
incrementare (increménto) *tr* to increase, boost
increménto *m* increase, increment, boost
increscio•so -sa [s] *adj* disagreeable, unpleasant
increspare (incréspo) *tr* to ripple; to wrinkle; to knit (*the brow*); to pleat ‖ *ref* to ripple
incretinire §176 *tr* to make stupid; (fig) to deafen ‖ *intr* (ESSERE) to become stupid; to lose one's mind
incriminare (incrìmino) *tr* to incriminate
incrinare *tr* to flaw; to ruin
incrinatura *f* crack, flaw
incrociare §128 (incrócio) *tr* to cross ‖ *intr* (naut) to cruise ‖ *ref* to cross one another; to interbreed
incrociatóre *m* (nav) cruiser
incró•cio -cio (-ci) crossing; cross; crossroads; crossbreed
incrollàbile *adj* unshakable
incrostare (incròsto) *tr* to incrust; to inlay (*e.g., with mosaic*) ‖ *ref* to become incrusted
incrostazióne *f* incrustation
incrudelire §176 *tr* to enrage ‖ *intr* to commit cruelties ‖ *intr* (ESSERE) to become cruel; incrudelire su to commit cruelties upon
incruèn•to -ta *adj* bloodless
incubare (ìncubo & incubo) *tr* to incubate
incubatrice *f* incubator; brooder
incubazióne *f* incubation; in incubazione brewing (*said of an infectious disease*)
incubo *m* nightmare
incùdine *f* anvil; essere tra l'incudine e il martello to be between the devil and the deep blue sea
inculcare §197 *tr* to inculcate
incunàbolo *m* incunabulum
incuneare (incùneo) *tr & ref* to wedge
incuràbile *adj & mf* incurable
incurante *adj* careless, indifferent
incùria *f* malpractice; neglect
incuriosire [s] §176 *tr* to intrigue ‖ *ref* to be intrigued
incursióne *f* incursion; incursione aerea air raid

incurvare *tr* to bend; (lit) to lower ‖ *intr* (ESSERE) & *ref* to bend; to warp
incurvatura *f* bend, curve
incustodi·to -ta *adj* unguarded, unwatched
incùtere §154 *tr* to inspire; **incutere terrore a** to strike with terror
ìndaco *adj* & *m* indigo
indaffara·to -ta *adj* busy
indagare §209 *tr* & *intr* to investigate; **indagare su** to investigate
indaga·tóre -trice *adj* probing, searching ‖ *mf* investigator
indàgine *f* investigation, inquiry
iudarno *adv* (lit) in vain
indebitare (indébito) *tr* to burden with debts ‖ *ref* to run into debt
indebita·to -ta *adj* indebted
indébi·to -ta *adj* undue; unjust; fraudulent (*conversion*) ‖ *m* what one does not owe; excess payment
indeboliménto *m* weakening
indebolire §176 *tr*, *intr* (ESSERE) & *ref* to weaken
indecènte *adj* indecent
indecènza *f* indecency; outrage
indecifràbile *adj* indecipherable
indecisióne *f* indecision
indeci·so -sa *adj* uncertain; undecided; indecisive
indecoró·so -sa [s] *adj* indecorous, unseemly
indefès·so -sa *adj* indefatigable
indefinìbile *adj* indefinable
indefini·to -ta *adj* indefinite; undefined
indegni·tà *f* (-tà) indignity
indé·gno -gna *adj* unworthy; disgraceful
indelèbile *adj* indelible
indelica·to -ta *adj* indelicate
indemagliàbile *adj* runproof
indemonia·to -ta *adj* possessed by the devil; restless
indènne *adj* undamaged, unscathed; **tener indenne** to guarantee against harm or damage
indenni·tà *f* (-tà) indemnity; indemnification; **indennità di carica** special emolument; bonus; **indennità di carovita** cost-of-living allowance; **indennità di preavviso** severance pay; **indennità di trasferta** per diem
indennizzare [ddzz] *tr* to indemnify
indennizzo [ddzz] *m* indemnification; indemnity
inderogàbile *adj* inescapable
indescrivìbile *adj* indescribable
indesideràbile *adj* undesirable
indesidera·to -ta *adj* unwished-for; undesirable
indeterminati·vo -va *adj* indefinite
indetermina·to -ta *adj* indeterminate; (gram) indefinite
indi *adv* (lit) then; (lit) thence; **da indi innanzi** (lit) from that moment on
India, l' *f* India; **le Indie Occidentali** the West Indies; **le Indie Orientali** the East Indies
india·no -na *adj* & *mf* Indian; **fare l'indiano** to feign ignorance ‖ *f* printed calico
indiavola·to -ta *adj* devilish, fierce; impish (*child*)

indicare §197 (**ìndico**) *tr* to indicate; to show
indicati·vo -va *adj* & *m* indicative
indica·to -ta *adj* appropriate, fitting; recommended, advisable
indica·tóre -trice *adj* indicating, pointing ‖ *m* indicator; **indicatore di direzione** (aut) turn signal; **indicatore di livello** gauge; **indicatore di pressione** pressure gauge; **indicatore di velocità** (aut) speedometer; **indicatore stradale** road sign; **indicatore telefonico** telephone directory
indicazióne *f* indication; direction; **indicazioni per l'uso** instructions
ìndice *m* index finger; pointer, gauge; indicator; sign, indication; index; (typ) fist; **indice delle materie** table of contents ‖ **Indice** *m* Index; **mettere all'Indice** to put on the Index; to ban, index
indicìbile *adj* inexpressible, unspeakable
indietreggiare §290 (**indietréggio**) *intr* (ESSERE & AVERE) to withdraw
indiètro *adv* back; behind; **all'indietro** backwards; **dare indietro** to return, give back; **domandare indietro** to ask back; **essere indietro** to be slow (*said of a watch*); to be behind; to be backward, be slow; **tirarsi indietro** to withdraw; to step back
indifendìbile *adj* indefensible
indifé·so -sa [s] *adj* defenseless
indifferènte *adj* indifferent; **essere indifferente a** to be the same to; **lasciare indifferente** to leave cold
indifferènza *f* indifference
indìge·no -na *adj* indigenous ‖ *m* native
indigènte *adj* indigent, poor
indigestìbile *adj* indigestible
indigestióne *f* indigestion
indigè·sto -sta *adj* indigestible; (fig) dull, boring
indignare *tr* to anger, shock ‖ *ref* to be aroused, be indignant
indigna·to -ta *adj* indignant, outraged
indignazióne *f* indignation
indigni·tà *f* (-tà) indignity
indimenticàbile *adj* unforgettable
indipendènte *adj* & *m* independent
indipendènza *f* independence
indire §151 *tr* to announce publicly; (lit) to declare (*war*)
indirèt·to -ta *adj* indirect
indirizzare *tr* to direct; to address
indirizzà·rio *m* (-ri) mailing list
indirizzo *m* address; direction
indiscernìbile *adj* indiscernible
indisciplina *f* lack of discipline
indisciplina·to -ta *adj* undisciplined
indiscré·to -ta *adj* indiscreet; tactless
indiscrezióne *f* indiscretion; gossip; news leak
indiscus·so -sa *adj* unquestioned
indiscutìbile *adj* indisputable
indispensàbile *adj* indispensable ‖ *m* essential
indispettire §176 *tr* to annoy ‖ *ref* to get annoyed
indisponènte *adj* vexing, irritating

indispórre §218 *tr* to indispose; to disgust
indisposizióne *f* indisposition
indispó·sto -sta *adj* indisposed
indissolùbile *adj* indissoluble
indistin·to -ta *adj* indistinct
indistruttìbile *adj* indestructible
indisturba·to -ta *adj* undisturbed
indìvia *f* endive
individuàbile *adj* distinguishable
individuale *adj* individual
individuali·tà *f* (-tà) individuality
individuare (indìviduo) *tr* to individuate; to outline; to single out
indivíduo *m* individual; fellow
indivisìbile *adj* indivisible
indivi·so -sa *adj* undivided
indiziare §287 *tr* to cast suspicion on
indizià·rio -ria *adj* (-ri -rie) circumstancial
indì·zio *m* (-zi) clue; token; symptom
indòcile *adj* indocile, unteachable
Indocina, l' *f* Indochina
indocinése [s] *adj* & *mf* Indochinese
indoeuropè·o -a *adj* & *m* Indo-European
indolcire §176 *tr* to sweeten || *ref* to become sweet
ìndole *f* temper, disposition; nature
indolènte *adj* indolent
indolenziménto *m* soreness, stiffness; numbness
indolenzire §176 *tr* to make sore or stiff; to benumb || *ref* to become sore or stiff
indolenzi·to -ta *adj* sore, stiff; numb
indolóre *adj* painless
indomàbile *adj* indomitable
indoma·ni *m* (-ni) morrow, next day; l'indomani di ... the day after ...
indoma·to -ta *adj* (lit) indomitable, untamed
indòmi·to -ta *adj* (lit) indomitable, untamed
Indonèsia l' *f* Indonesia
indonesia·no -na *adj* & *mf* Indonesian
indorare (indòro) *tr* to gild; (culin) to brown; (fig) to sugar-coat
indoratura *f* gilding
indossare (indòsso) *tr* to wear; to put on
indossatrice *f* mannequin, model
indòsso *adv* on, on one's back; **avere indosso** to have on, wear
Indostàn, l' *m* Hindustan
indosta·no -na *adj* & *mf* Hindustani
indòtto *m* (elec) armature (*of motor*)
indottrinare *tr* to indoctrinate
indovinare *tr* to guess; **indovinarla** to guess right; **non indovinarne una** to never hit the mark
indovina·to -ta *adj* felicitous
indovinèllo *m* puzzle, riddle
indovi·no -na *mf* soothsayer, fortune-teller
indù *adj invar* & *mf* Hindu
indùb·bio -bia *adj* (-bi -bie) undoubted, undisputed
indubita·to -ta *adj* undeniable
indugiare §290 *tr* to delay || *intr* to linger; to hesitate || *ref* to linger
indù·gio *m* (-gi) delay; **rompere gli**

indugi to come to a decision; **senza ulteriore indugio** without further delay
indulgènte *adj* indulgent
indulgènza *f* indulgence
indùlgere §187 *tr* to grant; to forgive || *intr* to be indulgent; **indulgere a** to indulge; to yield to
indulto *m* (law) pardon
induménto *m* garment; **indumenti intimi** undergarments, unmentionables
indurire §176 *tr* to harden || *intr* (ESSERE) to harden; to get stiff
indurre §102 *tr* to induce
indùstria *f* industry; **grande industria** heavy industry
industriale *adj* industrial || *m* industrialist
industrializzare [ddzz] *tr* to industrialize
industriare §287 *ref* to try, try hard; **industriarsi a** or **per** + *inf* to try to + *inf*, to do one's best to + *inf*
industrió·so -sa [s] *adj* industrious
indut·tóre -trice *adj* inducing, provoking || *m* (elec) field (*of motor*)
induzióne *f* induction
inebetire §176 *tr* to dull; to stun || *intr* (ESSERE) & *ref* to become dull; to be stunned
inebriare §287 **(inèbrio)** *tr* to intoxicate || *ref* to get drunk
inebriante *adj* intoxicating
ineccepìbile *adj* unexceptionable
inèdia *f* starvation, inanition; boredom
inèdi·to -ta *adj* unpublished; new, novel
ineduca·to -ta *adj* uneducated; ill-mannered
ineffàbile *adj* ineffable
inefficace *adj* ineffectual, ineffective
inefficàcia *f* inefficacy
inefficiènte *adj* inefficient
ineguale *adj* unequal; uneven
inelegante *adj* inelegant; shabby
ineleggìbile *adj* ineligible
ineluttàbile *adj* inevitable, inescapable
inenarràbile *adj* unspeakable
inerènte *adj* inherent
inèrme *adj* unarmed, defenseless
inerpicare §197 **(inérpico)** *ref* to clamber
inèrte *adj* inert
inèrzia *f* inertia; inactivity
inesattézza *f* inaccuracy
inesat·to -ta *adj* inaccurate, inexact; uncollected
inesaudi·to -ta *adj* unanswered
inesauribile *adj* inexhaustible
inescusàbile *adj* inexcusable
inesigìbile *adj* uncollectable
inesistènte *adj* inexistent
inesoràbile *adj* inexorable
inesperiènza *f* inexperience
inespèr·to -ta *adj* inexperienced; unskilled
inesplicàbile *adj* inexplicable
inesplica·to -ta *adj* unexplained
inesplora·to -ta *adj* unexplored
inesplò·so -sa *adj* unexploded
inespressi·vo -va *adj* inexpressive
inesprimìbile *adj* inexpressible

inespugnàbile *adj* impregnable; incorruptible
inespugna·to -ta *adj* unconquered
inestimàbile *adj* priceless, invaluable
inestinguìbile *adj* inextinguishable
inestirpàbile *adj* ineradicable
inestricàbile *adj* inextricable
inèt·to -ta *adj* inept
ineva·so -sa *adj* unfinished (*business*); unanswered (*mail*)
inevitàbile *adj* unavoidable, inevitable
inèzia *f* trifle, bagatelle
infagottare (infagòtto) *tr & ref* to bundle up
infallìbile *adj* infallible
infamante *adj* shameful, disgraceful
infamare *tr* to disgrace; to slander
infame *adj* infamous; villainous; (coll) horrible || *mf* villain
infàmia *f* infamy; (coll) botch, bungle
infangare §209 *tr* to splash with mud; (fig) to stain, spot
infante *adj & mf* infant, baby || *m* infante || *f* infanta
infantile *adj* infantile, childish
infànzia *f* infancy, childhood
infarcire §176 *tr* to cram; (culin) to stuff
infarinare *tr* to sprinkle with flour; to powder; (fig) to cram || *ref* to be covered with flour
infarinatura *f* sprinkling with flour; (fig) smattering
infastidire §176 *tr* to annoy || *ref* to be annoyed, lose one's patience
infaticàbile *adj* indefatigable, tireless
infatti *adv* indeed; really
infatuare (infàtuo) *tr* to infatuate || *ref* to become infatuated
infatua·to -ta *adj* infatuated
infàu·sto -sta *adj* unlucky, fatal
infecón·do -da *adj* barren
infedéle *adj* unfaithful; inaccurate || *mf* infidel
infedel·tà *f* (-tà) unfaithfulness; inaccuracy; infidelity
infelice *adj* unhappy, unfortunate; unfavorable || *mf* wretch
infelici·tà *f* (-tà) unhappiness
inferióre *adj* inferior; lower; **inferiore a** lower than; less than; smaller than
inferiorità *f* inferiority
inferire §188a *tr* to inflict; to infer; (naut) to bend (*a sail*)
infermare (inférmo) *tr* (lit) to weaken || *intr* (ESSERE) to get sick
infermería *f* infirmary
infermiè·re -ra *adj* nursing || *m* male nurse || *f* nurse; **infermiera diplomata** trained nurse
infermierìsti·co -ca *adj* (-ci -che) nursing
infermi·tà *f* (-tà) infirmity
infér·mo -ma *adj* infirm; sick || *m* patient
infernale *adj* infernal
infèr·no -na *adj* (lit) lower (*region*) || *m* hell; inferno
inferocire §176 *tr* to infuriate || *intr*— **inferocire su** to be pitiless to || *intr* (ESSERE) to become infuriated
inferriata *f* grating, grill

infervorare (infèrvoro & infervóro) *tr* to excite, stir up || *ref* to get excited; to become absorbed
infestare (infèsto) *tr* to infest
infettare (infètto) *tr* to infect
infetti·vo -va *adj* infectious
infèt·to -ta *adj* infected; corrupted
infezióne *f* infection
infiacchire §176 *tr* to weaken || *intr* (ESSERE) & *ref* to grow weak
infiammàbile *adj* inflammable
infiammare *tr* to inflame; to ignite || *ref* to catch fire, ignite
infiamma·to -ta *adj* burning; aflame; inflamed, excited
infiammazióne *f* inflammation
infi·do -da *adj* untrustworthy
infierire §176 *intr* to become cruel; to be merciless to; to rage (*said, e.g., of a disease*)
infievolire §176 *tr* to weaken
infìggere §103 *tr* to thrust, stick, sink || *ref*—**infiggersi in** to creep in; to work in
infilare *tr* to thread (*a needle*); to insert (*a key*); to transfix (*with a sword*); to put on (*e.g., a coat*); to pull on (*one's pants*); to slip on (*a dress*); to slip (*e.g., one's arm into a sleeve*); to string (*beads*); to hit (*the target*); to take (*a road*); to enter through (*a door*); **infilare l'uscio** to slip away; **infilarle tutte** to succeed all the time; **non infilarne mai una** to never succeed || *ref* to slip; to sink; to slide (*e.g., through a crowd*)
infilata *f* row; string (*e.g., of insults*); (mil) enfilade; **d'infilata** lengthwise
infiltrare *ref* to infiltrate; to seep; (fig) to creep
infilzare *tr* to pierce; to string; (sew) to baste
infilzata *f* string (*of pearls, of lies, etc.*)
ìnfi·mo -ma *adj* lowest, bottom
infine *adv* finally
infingar·do -da *adj* lazy, slothful
infini·tà *f* (-tà) infinity
infinitèsi·mo -ma *adj & m* infinitesimal
infiniti·vo -va *adj* (gram) infinitive
infini·to -ta *adj* infinite || *m* infinite; infinity; (gram) infinitive; (math) infinity; **all'infinito** ad infinitum
infino *adv* (lit)—**infino a** until; as far as; **infino a che** as long as
infinocchiare §287 (infinòcchio) *tr* (coll) to fool, bamboozle
infioccare §197 (infiòcco) *tr* to adorn with tassels
infiorare (infióro) *tr* to adorn with flowers; (fig) to sprinkle; (fig) tò embellish || *ref* to be covered with flowers
infiorescènza *f* inflorescence
infirmare *tr* to weaken; to invalidate
infischiare §287 *ref*—**infischiarsi di** to not care a hoot about
infisso *m* frame (*e.g., of door*); fixture
infittire §176 *tr, intr* (ESSERE) & *ref* to thicken
inflazionare (inflazióno) *tr* to inflate
inflazióne *f* inflation
inflessìbile *adj* inflexible

inflessióne _f_ inflection
inflèttere §177 _tr_ (lit) to inflect
infliggere §104 _tr_ to inflict
influènte _adj_ influential
influènza _f_ influence; (pathol) influenza
influenzare (influènzo) _tr_ to influence, sway
influire §176 _intr_ to have an influence; **influire su** to influence || _intr_ (ESSERE) —**influire in** to flow into
influsso _m_ influence; (lit) plague
infocare §182 _tr_ to make glow with heat || _ref_ to catch fire; to get excited
infoca·to -ta _adj_ red-hot; sultry
infognare (infógno) _ref_ (coll) to sink (_e.g., in vice_); (coll) to get stuck (_e.g., in debt_)
infoltire §176 _tr_ & _intr_ (ESSERE) to thicken
infonda·to -ta _adj_ unfounded, groundless
infóndere §178 _tr_ to infuse, instill
inforcare §197 (**infórco**) _tr_ to pitch (_hay_); to bestride; to mount (_a horse or bicycle_); to put on (_one's eyeglasses_)
inforcatura _f_ pitching with a fork; crotch
informare (infórmo) _tr_ to inform; (fig) to mold || _ref_ to conform; to inquire; **informarsi da** to seek or get information from; **informarsi di** or **su** to inquire about; to find out about
informati·vo -va _adj_ informative, informational
informa·tóre -trice _adj_ underlying || _mf_ informer; (journ) reporter || _m_ informant (_of a foreign language_)
informazióne _f_ piece of information; **chiedere informazioni sul conto di** to inquire about; **informazioni** information
infórme _adj_ shapeless
informicolire §176 _ref_ to tingle; **informicolirsi a** to go to sleep, _e.g._, **gli si è informicolita la gamba** his leg went to sleep
infornare (infórno) _tr_ to put in the oven; to bake
infornata _f_ batch (_of bread_); (coll) flock
infortunare _ref_ to get hurt
infortuna·to -ta _adj_ injured || _mf_ casualty, victim
infortù·nio _m_ (-**ni**) accident, mishap; **infortunio sul lavoro** job-connected injury
infossare (infòsso) _tr_ to bury || _ref_ to cave in, settle; to become sunken (_said of eyes or cheeks_)
infracidare (infràcido) _tr_ var of **infradiciare**
infracidire §176 _intr_ to rot
infradiciare §128 (**infràdicio**) _tr_ to drench || _ref_ to get drenched; to rot (_said of fruit_)
inframmettènza _f_ interference, meddling
inframméttere §198 _tr_ to interpose || _ref_ to meddle, interfere
inframmezzare [ddzz] (**inframmèzzo**) _tr_ to intersperse

infràngere §179 _tr_ & _ref_ to break
infrangìbile _adj_ unbreakable
infran·to -ta _adj_ broken, shattered
infrarós·so -sa _adj_ & _m_ infrared
infrascrit·to -ta _adj_ mentioned below
infrastruttura _f_ underpinning; infrastructure; (rr) roadbed
infrazióne _f_ infraction, breach
infreddatura _f_ mild cold
infreddolire §176 _ref_ to feel cold, to be chilled
infrenàbile _adj_ irrepressible
infrequènte _adj_ infrequent
infrollire §176 _tr_ to make (_meat_) high || _intr_ (ESSERE) & _ref_ to get high (_said of meat_); (fig) to soften
infruttuó·so -sa [s] _adj_ unprofitable
infuòri _adv_ out; **all'infuori** outward; **all'infuori di** except
infuriare §287 _tr_ to infuriate, enrage || _intr_ to get blustery; to rage || _intr_ (ESSERE) to lose one's temper
infusióne _f_ infusion; sprinkling (_of holy water_)
infuso _m_ infusion
ingabbiare §287 _tr_ to cage; to jail; to corner; to build the framework of
ingabbiatura _f_ frame, framework
ingaggiare §290 _tr_ to hire; to engage || _ref_ to sign up; to get tangled up
ingàg·gio _m_ (-**gi**) engagement; (sports) bonus (_for signing up_)
ingagliardire §176 _tr_ to strengthen || _ref_ to become strong
ingannare _tr_ to deceive; to cheat; to elude; to beguile || _ref_ to be mistaken
inganna·tóre -trice _adj_ deceptive || _mf_ impostor
ingannévole _adj_ deceitful; deceptive
inganno _m_ deception; illusion
ingarbugliare §280 _tr_ to entangle; to jumble || _ref_ to get mixed up; to become embroiled
ingegnare (ingégno) _ref_ to manage; to scheme
ingegnère _m_ engineer
ingegnerìa _f_ engineering; **ingegneria civile** civil engineering; **ingegneria meccanica** mechanical engineering
ingégno _m_ brain, intelligence; talent; genius; expediency; (lit) machinery
ingegnosità [s] _f_ ingeniousness
ingegnó·so -sa [s] _adj_ ingenious; euphuistic
ingelosire [s] §176 _tr_ to make jealous || _intr_ (ESSERE) & _ref_ to become jealous
ingemmare (ingèmmo) _tr_ to adorn or stud with gems
ingenerare (ingènero) _tr_ to engender
ingèni·to -ta _adj_ inborn
ingènte _adj_ huge, vast
ingentilire §176 _tr_ to refine
ingenui·tà _f_ (-**tà**) ingenuousness; ingenuous act
ingè·nuo -nua _adj_ ingenuous, artless || _m_ (theat) artless character || _f_ (theat) ingénue
ingerènza _f_ interference
ingerire §176 _tr_ to ingest, swallow || _ref_ to meddle

ingessare (**ingèsso**) *tr* to put in a plaster cast; to plaster up

ingessatura *f* (surg) plaster cast

inghiaiare §287 *tr* to gravel, cover with gravel

Inghilterra, l' *f* England; **la Nuova Inghilterra** New England

inghiottire (**inghiótto**) & §176 *tr* to swallow; to swallow up; to pocket (*one's pride*)

inghirlandare *tr* to bedeck with garlands; (lit) to encircle

ingiallire §176 *tr* & *intr* (ESSERE) to turn yellow

ingigantire §176 *tr* to exaggerate || *intr* (ESSERE) to grow larger, increase

inginocchiare §287 (**inginòcchio**) *ref* to kneel down

inginocchia·tóio *m* (-tói) prie-dieu

ingioiellare (**ingioièllo**) *tr* to bejewel; (fig) to stud

ingiù *adv* down; **all'ingiù** downwards

ingiùngere §183 *tr* to order, command || *intr* (with *dat*) to order, command, e.g., **il giudice ingiunse all'imputato di rispondere** the judge ordered the accused to answer

ingiunzióne *f* order; (law) injunction

ingiùria *f* insult, abuse; damage, wear

ingiuriare §287 *tr* to insult

ingiurió·so -sa [s] *adj* insulting

ingiustificàbile *adj* unjustifiable

ingiustifica·to -ta *adj* unjustified

ingiustìzia *f* injustice

ingiu·sto -sta *adj* unjust, unfair || *m* unjust person

inglése [s] *adj* English; **all'inglese** in the English fashion; **andarsene all'inglese** to take French leave || *m* Englishman; English (*language*) || *f* Englishwoman

ingoiare §287 (**ingóio**) *tr* to swallow; to gulp down; **ingoiare un rospo** (fig) to swallow one's pride

ingolfare (**ingólfo**) *tr* (aut) to flood || *ref* to form a gulf; to get involved; (aut) to flood

ingollare (**ingóllo**) *tr* to swallow, gulp down

ingolosire [s] §176 *tr* to make the mouth of (*s.o.*) water || *intr* (ESSERE) & *ref* to have a craving

ingombrante *adj* cumbersome

ingombrare (**ingómbro**) *tr* to clutter

ingóm·bro -bra *adj* encumbered, cluttered || *m* encumbrance; **essere d'ingombro** to be in the way

ingommare (**ingómmo**) *tr* to glue

ingordìgia *f* greed

ingór·do -da *adj* greedy, covetous

ingorgare §209 (**ingórgo**) *ref* to get clogged up

ingór·go *m* (-ghi) blocking, congestion; **ingorgo stradale** traffic jam

ingovernàbile *adj* uncontrollable

ingozzare (**ingózzo**) *tr* to gobble, gulp down; to swallow; to cram (*e.g., a goose for fattening*)

ingranàg·gio *m* (-gi) gear, gearwheel; (fig) meshes; **ingranaggio di distribuzione** (aut) timing gear; **ingranaggio elicoidale** worm gear

ingranare *tr* to engage (*a gear*); **ingranare la marcia** to throw into gear || *intr* to be in gear; to succeed

ingrandiménto *m* enlargement; increase

ingrandire §176 *tr* to enlarge; to increase; || *intr* (ESSERE) & *ref* to increase, get larger

ingrassare *tr* to fatten; to lubricate || *intr* (ESSERE) & *ref* to get fat; to get rich

ingrassa·tóre -trice *mf* greaser, lubricator || *f* grease gun; lubricating machine

ingratitùdine *f* ingratitude

ingra·to -ta *adj* ungrateful; thankless || *mf* ingrate

ingraziare §287 *ref* to ingratiate oneself with

ingrediènte *m* ingredient

ingrèsso *m* entrance; admittance, entry; **ingressi** hallway furniture; **primo ingresso** debut

ingrossaménto *m* enlargement; swelling

ingrossare (**ingròsso**) *tr* to enlarge; to swell; to make bigger; to dull (*the mind*); to raise (*one's voice*) || *intr* (ESSERE) & *ref* to swell; to thicken; to become fat; to become pregnant; to become important

ingròsso *m*—**all'ingrosso** wholesale; approximately, more or less

ingrullire §176 *tr* to drive crazy || *intr* (ESSERE) & *ref* to become silly; **fare ingrullire** to drive crazy

inguadàbile *adj* not fordable

inguainare (**inguaìno**) *tr* to sheathe

ingualcìbile *adj* wrinkle-free, wrinkleproof

inguanta·to -ta *adj* with gloves on; **con le mani inguantate** with gloves on

inguarìbile *adj* incurable

inguine *f* (anat) groin

ingurgitare (**ingùrgito**) *tr* to swallow, gulp down

inibire §176 *tr* to inhibit

inibi·tóre -trice *adj* inhibiting || *m* inhibitor

inidòne·o -a *adj* unfit, unqualified

iniettare (**iniètto**) *tr* to inject || *ref* to become bloodshot; **iniettarsi di sangue** to become bloodshot

iniezióne *f* injection

inimicare §197 *tr* to make an enemy of; to alienate || *ref*—**inimicarsi con** to fall out with

inimicìzia *f* enmity

inimitàbile *adj* inimitable, matchless

ininterrót·to -ta *adj* uninterrupted

iniqui·tà *f* (-tà) injustice; iniquity

inì·quo -qua *adj* unjust; wicked

iniziale *adj* & *f* initial

iniziare §287 *tr* to initiate || *ref* to begin

iniziativa *f* initiative; sponsorship; **iniziativa privata** private enterprise

inizia·tóre -trice *adj* initiating || *mf* initiator, promoter

iniziazióne *f* initiation

inì·zio *m* (-zi) beginning, start

innaffiare §287 *tr* var of **annaffiare**

innaffia·tóio *m* (-tói) var of **annaffiatoio**

innalzaménto *m* elevation

innalzare *tr* to raise; to elevate; **innalzare al cielo** to praise to the sky || *ref* to rise; to tower

innamorare (innamóro) *tr* to charm, fascinate; to inspire with love || *ref* to fall in love

innamora·to -ta *adj* in love, enamored; fond || *mf* sweetheart || *m* boyfriend || *f* girl friend

innanzi *adj invar* previous, prior (*e.g., day*) || *adv* ahead, before; **innanzi a** in front of; **innanzi di** + *inf* before + *ger;* **mettere innanzi** to prefer; to place before; to advance (*an excuse*); **per l'innanzi** before, in the past; **tirare innanzi** to get along || *prep* before; above; **innanzi tempo** ahead of time; **innanzi tutto** above all

innà·rio *m* (**-ri**) hymnal

inna·to -ta *adj* inborn, innate

innegàbile *adj* undeniable

inneggiare §290 (**innéggio**) *intr*—**inneggiare a** to sing the praises of

innervosire [s] §176 *tr* to make nervous

innescare §197 (**innésco**) *tr* to bait (*a hook*); to prime (*a bomb*)

inné·sco *m* (**-schi**) primer; detonator

innestare (innèsto) *tr* (hort & surg) to graft; (surg) to implant; (med) to inoculate (*a vaccine*); (mach) to engage; (elec) to plug in (*e.g., a plug*); **innestare la marcia** (aut) to throw into gear || *ref* to be grafted; **innestarsi in** to merge with; **innestarsi su** to connect with

innèsto *m* (hort & surg) graft; (surg) implant; (med) inoculation; (mach) engagement; (mach) coupling; (elec) plug

inno *m* hymn; **inno nazionale** national anthem

innocènte *adj* innocent || *m* innocent; **innocenti** foundlings

innocènza *f* innocence

innò·cuo -cua *adj* innocuous, harmless

innominàbile *adj* unmentionable

innomina·to -ta *adj* unnamed

innovare (innòvo) *tr* to innovate

innovazióne *f* innovation

innumerévole *adj* countless, innumerable

-ino -ina *suf adj* little, e.g., **poverino** poor little; hailing from, e.g., **fiorentino** hailing from Florence, Florentine || *suf f* see **-ina**

inoccupa·to -ta *adj* unoccupied || *m* person looking for his first job

inoculare (inòculo) *tr* to inoculate

inoculazióne *f* inoculation

inodó·ro -ra *adj* odorless

inoffensi·vo -va *adj* inoffensive

inoltrare (inóltro) *tr* (com) to forward (*e.g., a request*) || *ref* to advance

inóltre *adv* besides, in addition

inóltro *m* (com) forwarding

inondare (inóndo) *tr* to inundate, flood; to swamp

inondazióne *f* flood, inundation

inoperosità *f* idleness

inoperó·so -sa [s] *adj* idle

inopina·to -ta *adj* (lit) unexpected

inopportu·no -na *adj* inopportune, untimely

inoppugnàbile *adj* incontestable; indisputable

inorgàni·co -ca *adj* (**-ci -che**) inorganic

inorgoglire §176 *tr* to make proud || *intr* (ESSERE) & *ref* to grow proud

inorridire §176 *tr* to horrify || *intr* (ESSERE) to be horrified

inospitale *adj* inhospitable

inosservante *adj* unobservant

inosserva·to -ta *adj* unnoticed; unperceived

inossidàbile *adj* stainless

inquadrare *tr* to frame; to arrange

inquadratura *f* framing; (mov, phot) frame

inqualificàbile *adj* unspeakable

inquietante *adj* disquieting

inquietare (inquièto) *tr* to worry || *ref* to worry; to get angry

inquiè·to -ta *adj* worried; restless; angry; (lit) stormy

inquietùdine *f* worry; restlessness; preoccupation

inquili·no -na *mf* tenant

inquinaménto *m* pollution

inquinare *tr* to pollute

inquirènte *adj* investigating

inquisi·tóre -trice *adj* inquiring || *m* inquisitor

inquisizióne *f* inquisition

insabbiare §287 *tr* to cover with sand; to pigeonhole; to shelve || *ref* to get covered with sand; to bury oneself in sand; to get stuck

insaccare §197 *tr* to bag; to stuff (*e.g., salami*); (mil) to hem in; (fig) to bundle up; (coll) to gulp down || *ref* to be packed in; to crumple up; to disappear behind a thick bank of clouds (*said, e.g., of the sun*)

insaccato *m* participant in a sack race; **insaccati** cold cuts, lunch meat

insalata *f* salad; (fig) mess

insalatièra *f* salad bowl

insalubre *adj* unhealthy

insaluta·to -ta *adj* unsaluted; **andarsene insalutato ospite** to take French leave

insanàbile *adj* incurable; implacable

insanguinare (insànguino) *tr* to bloody; to cover with blood; to bathe in blood

insa·no -na *adj* insane

insaponare (insapóno) *tr* to soap; to lather; (fig) to soft-soap

insaporire §176 *tr* to flavor || *intr* (ESSERE) to become tasty

insaputa *f*—**all'insaputa di** without the knowledge of, unbeknown to

insaziàbile *adj* insatiable

insazia·to -ta *adj* insatiate, unsatisfied

inscatolare (inscàtolo) *tr* to can

inscenare (inscèno) *tr* to stage

inscindìbile *adj* inseparable

inscrìvere §250 *tr* (geom) to inscribe

inscrutàbile *adj* inscrutable

inscurire §176 *tr, intr* (ESSERE) & *ref* to darken

insecchire §176 *tr* to dry || *intr* (ESSERE) & *ref* to dry up

insediaménto *m* installation (*into an office*); assumption (*of an office*)
insediare §287 (**insèdio**) *tr* to install ‖ *ref* to be installed; to take one's seat; to settle
inségna *f* badge, insignia, emblem; ensign, flag; coat of arms; motto; sign (*e.g., on a restaurant*); traffic sign
insegnaménto *m* education, instruction
insegnante *adj* teaching ‖ *mf* teacher
insegnare (**inségno**) *tr* to teach; to show ‖ *intr* to teach
inseguiménto *m* pursuit
inseguire (**inséguo**) *tr* to pursue, chase; to chase after
insellare (**insèllo**) *tr* to saddle; to put on (*e.g., one's glasses*); to bend
insellatura *f* saddling; bending
insenatura *f* inlet, cove
insensatézza *f* nonsense, folly
insensa·to -ta *adj* nonsensical, foolish ‖ *mf* scatterbrain
insensìbile *adj* insensible; unresponsive; insensitive
inseparàbile *adj* inseparable ‖ *m* (orn) lovebird
insepól·to -ta *adj* unburied
inserire §176 *tr* to insert; to plug in ‖ *ref* to slip in; to butt in
inseri·tóre -trice *adj* (elec) connecting ‖ *m* (elec) connector, plug ‖ *f* sorter (*of punch cards*)
insèrto *m* file, folder; insert; spliced film
inservìbile *adj* useless, worthless
inserviènte *m* attendant, porter; (eccl) server
inserzionare (**inserzióno**) *intr* to advertise
inserzióne *f* insertion; advertisement
inserzioni·sta (**-sti -ste**) *adj* advertising ‖ *mf* advertiser
insettici·da *adj & m* (**-di -de**) insecticide
insettìfu·go *m* (**-ghi**) insect repellent
insètto *m* insect; **insetti** vermin
insìdja *f* trap, ambush; **insidie** lure
insidiare §287 *tr* to ensnare; to try to trap; to try to seduce; to attempt (*someone's life*)
insidió·so -sa [s] *adj* insidious
insième *m* whole, entirety; harmony; ensemble; set; **d'insieme** general, comprehensive; **nell'insieme** as a whole ‖ *adv* together
insigne *adj* famous; notable; arrant (*knave*)
insignificante *adj* insignificant; petty
insignire §176 *tr* to decorate; **insignire qlcu di un titolo** to bestow a title upon s.o.
insignorire §176 *tr* (lit) to invest with a fief ‖ *intr* (ESSERE) to enrich oneself ‖ *ref* to enrich oneself; **insignorirsi di** to seize; to take possession of
insilare *tr* to silo, ensile
insilato *m* ensilage
insincè·ro -ra *adj* insincere
insindacàbile *adj* final, indisputable
insino *adv* (lit) —**insino a** until; as far as; **insino a che** as long as
insinuante *adj* insinuating
insinuare (**insìnuo**) *tr* to stick, thrust;

to insinuate; (law) to register ‖ *ref* to creep, filter; to ingratiate oneself; **insinuarsi in** to worm one's way into
insinuazióne *f* insinuation, hint
insìpi·do -da *adj* insipid, vapid
insistènte *adj* insistent
insìstere §114 *intr* to insist
insì·to -ta *adj* inborn, inherent
insociévole *adj* unsociable
insoddisfat·to -ta *adj* dissatisfied
insofferènte *adj* intolerant
insoffrìbile *adj* unbearable, insufferable
insolazióne *f* sunning; sun bath; sunstroke; sunny exposure
insolènte *adj* insolent
insolentire §176 *tr* to insult, abuse ‖ *intr* to be insolent
insolènza *f* insolence; insult
insòli·to -ta *adj* unusual
insolùbile *adj* insoluble
insolu·to -ta *adj* unsolved; not dissolved; unpaid
insolvènza *f* insolvency
insolvìbile *adj* insolvent; bad (*debt*)
insómma *adv* in conclusion ‖ *interj* well!
insommergìbile *adj* unsinkable
insondàbile *adj* unfathomable
insònne *adj* sleepless
insònnia *f* insomnia
insonnoli·to -ta *adj* sleepy, drowsy
insonorizzazióne [ddzz] *f* soundproofing
insopportàbile *adj* unbearable
insorgènte *adj* appearing ‖ *mf* insurgent
insorgènza *f* appearance (*of illness*)
insórgere §258 *intr* (ESSERE) to rise up, revolt; to appear
insormontàbile *adj* unsurmountable, insurmountable
insór·to -ta *adj & m* insurgent
insospettàbile *adj* above suspicion; unexpected
insospetta·to -ta *adj* not suspect; unexpected
insospettire §176 *tr* to make suspicious ‖ *intr* (ESSERE) & *ref* to become suspicious
insostenìbile *adj* indefensible; unbearable
insostituìbile *adj* irreplaceable
insozzare (**insózzo**) *tr* to soil, sully
inspera·to -ta *adj* unexpected; unhoped-for
inspiegàbile *adj* unexplainable
inspirare *tr* to inhale, breathe in
inspirazióne *f* inhalation
instàbile *adj* unstable
installare *tr* to install; to set up, settle; to induct (*in an office*) ‖ *ref* to settle
installatóre *m* plumber; erector
installazióne *f* installation; plumbing
instancàbile *adj* untiring
instante *adj* insistent; impending ‖ *m* petitioner
instare (*pp missing*) *intr* to insist; to threaten, be imminent
instaurare (**instàuro**) *tr* to establish
instaurazióne *f* establishment
instigare §209 *tr* var of **istigare**
instillare *tr* var of **istillare**
instituire §176 *tr* var of **istituire**

instruire §176 *tr* var of **istruire**
instrumento *m* var of **istrumento**
instupidire §176 *tr* var of **istupidire**
insù *adv* up; **all'insù** up
insubordina·to -ta *adj* insubordinate
insuccèsso *m* failure
insudiciare §128 (**insùdicio**) *tr* to soil, dirty; to sully || *ref* to get dirty
insufficiènte *adj* insufficient; failing (*in school*)
insufficiènza *f* insufficiency; failure (*in school*)
insulare *adj* insular
insulina *f* insulin
insulsàggine *f* silliness, nonsense
insul·so -sa *adj* insipid; simple, silly
insultante *adj* insulting
insultare *tr* to insult || *intr* (with *dat*) to insult
insulto *m* insult; (pathol) attack
insuperàbile *adj* insuperable; unparalleled
insupera·to -ta *adj* unsurpassed
insuperbire §176 *tr, intr* (ESSERE) & *ref* to swell with pride
insurrezióne *f* insurrection
insussistènte *adj* nonexistent, unfounded
intabarrare *tr* to wrap up
intaccare §197 *tr* to notch; to corrode; to scratch; to attack (*said of a disease*); to damage (*e.g., a reputation*); to cut into (*capital*) || *intr* to stutter
intaccatura *f* notch; (carp) mortise
intagliare §280 *tr* to carve; to engrave
intà·glio *m* (-gli) carving; intaglio
intanare *ref* to hide
intangìbile *adj* intangible; inviolable
intanto *adv* meanwhile; (coll) yet; (coll) finally; **intanto che** while; **per intanto** at present; in the meantime
intarsiare §287 *tr* to inlay; (fig) to stud
intarsia·to -ta *adj* inlaid
intàr·sio *m* (-si) inlay; inlaid work
intasare [s] *tr* to clog; to tie up (*traffic*); to stop up || *ref* to be clogged up; to be tied up; to be stopped up (*said of nose*)
intascare §197 *tr* to pocket
intat·to -ta *adj* intact, untouched
intavolare (**intàvolo**) *tr* to start (*a conversation*); to broach (*a subject*); to launch (*negotiations*)
intavolato *m* boarding, planking
integèrri·mo -ma *adj* of the utmost honesty
integrale *adj* integral; whole; wholewheat (*bread*); built-in || *m* integral
integralismo *m* policy of the complete absorption of the body politic by an ideology
integrante *adj* constituent, integral
integrare (**ìntegro**) *tr* to integrate || *ref* to complement each other
integrazióne *f* integration
integrità *f* integrity
ìnte·gro -gra *adj* whole, complete; honest, upright; intact
intelaiatura *f* frame; framework
intellètto *m* intellect, mind; understanding
intellettuale *adj* & *mf* intellectual

intellettuali·tà *f* (-tà) intellectuality; intelligentsia
intellettualòide *mf* highbrow
intelligènte *adj* intelligent; clever
intelligènza *f* intelligence; understanding; **essere d'intelligenza con** to be in collusion with
intellighènzia *f* intelligentsia
intelligìbile *adj* intelligible
intemera·to -ta *adj* pure, spotless || *f* reprimand, scolding; long, boring speech
intemperante *adj* intemperate
intemperanza *f* intemperance
intempèrie *fpl* inclement weather
intempesti·vo -va *adj* untimely
intendènte *m* district director; **intendente di finanza** director of customs office; **intendente militare** commissary, quartermaster
intendènza *f* office of the district director; intendance; **intendenza militare** quartermaster corps
intèndere §270 *tr* to understand; to hear; to intend; to turn (*e.g., one's eyes*); to mean; **dare ad intendere a** to lead (*s.o.*) to believe (*s.th*); **far intendere** to give to understand; **farsi intendere** to force obedience; to make oneself understood; **intender dire che** to hear that; **intendere a rovescio** to misunderstand; **intendere a volo** to catch on quickly (to); **intendere ragione** to listen to reason; **lasciare intendere** to give to understand || *intr* to aim (*toward a goal*) || *ref* to come to an agreement; **intendersela con** to be in collusion with; to have an affair with; **intendersi di** to be a good judge of; to be an expert in
intendiménto *m* understanding, comprehension; aim, goal
intendi·tóre -trice *mf* connoisseur, expert; **a buon intenditore poche parole** a word to the wise is sufficient
intenerire §176 *tr* to soften; (fig) to move || *ref* to soften; (fig) to be moved
intensificare §197 (**intensìfico**) *tr* & *ref* to intensify
intensi·tà *f* (-tà) intensity
intensi·vo -va *adj* intensive
intèn·so -sa *adj* intense
intentare (**intènto**) *tr* (law) to bring (*action*)
intenta·to -ta *adj* unattempted
intèn·to -ta *adj* intent || *m* intent, goal; **coll'intento di** with the purpose of
intenzionale *adj* intentional
intenziona·to -ta *adj*—**bene intenzionato** well-meaning; **essere intenzionato di** to intend to
intenzióne *f* intention; purpose; **con intenzione** on purpose
intepidire §176 *tr* & *ref* var of **intiepidire**
interbase *f* (baseball) shortstop
intercalare *m* refrain; pet word or phrase || *tr* to intercalate; to inset
intercalazióne *f* intercalation; inset
intercapèdine *f* air space
intercèdere §123 *tr* to seek, get (*a par-*

don for s.o.) ‖ *intr* to intercede ‖ *intr* (ESSERE)—**intercedere tra** to intervene or elapse between; to extend between; to exist between

intercettare (intercètto) *tr* to intercept; to tap (*a phone*)

intercetta·tóre -trice *mf* interceptor

intercettóre *m* (aer) interceptor

intercomunale *adj* long-distance (*call*)

intercórrere §139 *intr* (ESSERE) to elapse; to happen; to be, to stand

interdét·to -ta *adj* dumfounded; forbidden ‖ *m* interdict; (coll) dumbell

interdire §151 *tr* to prohibit; (eccl) to interdict; (law) to disqualify

interessaménto *m* interest, concern

interessante *adj* interesting; **in stato interessante** in the family way

interessare (interèsso) *tr* to interest; to concern ‖ *intr* to be of interest ‖ *ref*—**interessarsi a** to take an interest in; **interessarsi di** to concern oneself with

interessa·to -ta *adj* interested; selfish ‖ *m* interested party

interèsse *m* interest; self-interest

interessènza *f* (com) share, interest

interferènza *f* interference

interferire §176 *intr* to interfere

interfogliare §280 **(interfòglio)** *tr* to interleave

interiezióne *f* interjection

interinato *m* temporary office or tenure

interi·no -na *adj* acting ‖ *m* temporary appointee

interióra *fpl* entrails

interióre *adj* interior ‖ **interiori** *mpl* entrails

interlìnea *f* interlining; (typ) leading

interlineare *adj* interlinear ‖ *v* **(interlìneo)** *tr* (typ) to lead

interlocu·tóre -trice *mf* participant (*in a discussion*); person speaking

interloquire §176 *intr* to take part in a discussion; to chime in

interlù·dio *m* (-di) interlude

intermedià·rio -ria (-ri -rie) *adj* & *mf* intermediary ‖ *m* middleman

intermè·dio -dia (-di -die) *adj* intermediate ‖ *mf* supervisor

intermèzzo [ddzz] *m* intermezzo; entr'acte; interval

interminàbile *adj* interminable, endless

intermissióne *f* intermission

intermittènte *adj* intermittent

internaménto *m* internment

internare (intèrno) *tr* to intern; to confine; to commit (*an insane person*) ‖ *ref* to go deep (*into a problem*)

interna·to -ta *adj* interned ‖ *m* internee; inmate; boarder; boarding school

internazionale *adj* international

internazionalizzare [ddzz] *tr* to internationalize

interni·sta *mf* (-sti -ste) internist

intèr·no -na *adj* inside, internal; inland; interior; boarding (*student*) ‖ *m* inside; interior; (med) intern; lining (*of coat*); **all'interno** inside; **interni** (mov) indoor shots ‖ **gli Interni** the Italian Ministry of Internal Affairs

inté·ro -ra *adj* entire, whole; full (*price*); (lit) upright, honest ‖ *m* whole; **per intero** completely

interpellare (interpèllo) *tr* to interpellate; to question; to consult

interpetrare (intèrpetro) *tr* var of **interpretare**

interplanetà·rio -ria *adj* (-ri -rie) interplanetary

interpolare (intèrpolo) *tr* to interpolate

interpolazióne *f* interpolation

interpónte *m* (naut) between-deck

interpórre §218 *tr* to interpose ‖ *ref* to intervene

interpretare (intèrpreto) *tr* to interpret

interpretazióne *f* interpretation

intèrprete *mf* interpreter

interpunzióne *f* punctuation

interrare (intèrro) *tr* to bury, inter; to fill in (*e.g., a marsh*) ‖ *ref* to become silted

interra·to -ta *adj* underground; **piano interrato** basement

interrogare §209 **(intèrrogo)** *tr* to question; to interrogate

interrogati·vo -va *adj* interrogative ‖ *m* why; question

interrogatò·rio -ria (-ri -rie) *adj* questioning ‖ *m* (law) interrogatory; **interrogatorio di terzo grado** third degree

interrogazióne *f* interrogation; quiz, examination; **interrogazione retorica** rhetorical question

interrómpere §240 *tr* to interrupt

interruttóre *m* (elec) switch; **interruttore di linea** (elec) controller

interruzióne *f* interruption

interscàm·bio *m* (-bi) interchange

interscolàsti·co -ca *adj* (-ci -che) interscholastic; intercollegiate

intersecare §197 **(intèrseco)** *tr* & *ref* to intersect

intersezióne *f* intersection

interstellare *adj* interstellar

interstì·zio *m* (-zi) interstice

interurba·no -na *adj* interurban, intercity; (telp) long-distance ‖ *f* (telp) long-distance call

intervallo *m* interval; pause; (educ) recess; (theat) intermission

intervenire §282 *intr* (ESSERE) to intervene; (surg) to operate; **intervenire a** to take part in

interventi·sta *mf* (-sti -ste) interventionist

intervènto *m* intervention; attendance; (surg) operation

intervenzióne *f* intervention

intervista *f* interview; **fare un'intervista a** to interview

intervistare *tr* to interview

inté·so -sa [s] *adj* understood; intended, designed; **bene inteso** of course; **non darsene per inteso** to not pay attention; **rimanere inteso** to agree ‖ *f* understanding, agreement; entente

intèssere (intèsso) *tr* to interweave; to wreathe (*a garland*)

intestardire §176 *ref* to get obstinate; to be determined

intestare (intèsto) *tr* to caption; to label; (typ) to head (*a page*); **intestare qlco a qlcu** to register s.th in the name of s.o.; **intestare una fattura a** to issue a bill in the name of || *ref* to become obstinate; to take it into one's head

intesta‧to -ta *adj* headed; registered (*stock*); obstinate; (law) intestate

intestazióne *f* heading; registration (*of stock*)

intestinale *adj* intestinal

intesti‧no -na *adj & m* intestine; **intestino crasso** large intestine; **intestino tenue** small intestine

intiepidire §176 *tr & ref* to warm up; to cool off

intiè‧ro -ra *adj & m* var of **intero**

intimare (ìntimo & intìmo) *tr* to intimate; to order, command; to declare (*war*); to impose (*a fine*); (law) to enjoin

intimazióne *f* intimation; order; (law) injunction

intimidazióne *f* intimidation

intimidire §176 *tr* to intimidate; to threaten || *ref* to become bashful

intimi‧tà *f* (-tà) intimacy; privacy

ìnti‧mo -ma *adj* intimate; inmost; **biancheria intima** underwear, lingerie || *m* intimate friend; depth (*of one's heart*)

intimorire §176 *tr* to frighten

intìngere §126 *tr* to dip || *intr*—**intingere in** to dip in || *ref*—**intingersi in un affare** to have a finger in the pie

intingolo *m* sauce, gravy; fancy dish

intirizzire [ddzz] §176 *tr* to benumb || *intr* (ESSERE) & *ref* to become numb or stiff; to become stiff and frostbitten

intirizzi‧to -ta [ddzz] *adj* numb

intisichire §176 *tr* to make tubercular; (fig) to weaken || *intr* (ESSERE) to become tubercular; to wither

intitolare (intìtolo) *tr* to title; to dedicate || *ref* to be named; to assume the title of

intoccàbile *adj & m* untouchable

intolleràbile *adj* intolerable

intollerante *adj* intolerant

intonacare §197 (intònaco) *tr* to plaster; to whitewash; to cover (*e.g., with tar*) || *ref*—**intonacarsi la faccia** (joc) to put on one's warpaint

intòna‧co *m* (-chi) plaster; roughcast

intonare (intòno) *tr* to intone; to harmonize; (mus) to tune || *ref* to harmonize, go

intonazióne *f* intonation; harmony

intòn‧so -sa *adj* uncut; (lit) unsheared

intontire §176 *tr* to stun || *intr* (ESSERE) & *ref* to become stunned

intoppare (intòppo) *tr* to stumble upon || *intr* (ESSERE) & *ref* to stumble

intòppo *m* obstacle, hindrance

intorbidare (intórbido) *tr* to cloud; to muddy; to obfuscate; to upset (*friendship*); to stir up (*passions*) || *ref* to become cloudy or muddy; to become obfuscated

intorbidire §176 *tr & ref* to cloud; to muddy

intormentire §176 *tr* to benumb || *intr* (ESSERE) to become numb

intórno *adv* around, about; **all'intorno** all around; **intorno a** around; about; **levarsi qlco d'intorno** to get rid of s.o.

intorpidire §176 *tr* to benumb || *ref* to become numb

intossicare §197 (intòssico) *tr* to poison, intoxicate

intossicazióne *f* poisoning, intoxication

intraducìbile *adj* untranslatable; inexpressible

intrafèrro *m* spark gap; air gap

intralciare §128 *tr* to hamper; to intertwine || *ref* to become hampered

intràl‧cio *m* (-ci) hindrance; **essere d'intralcio** to be in the way; **intralcio del traffico** traffic congestion

intralicciatura *f* lattice truss (*of high-tension tower*)

intrallazzare *intr* to deal in the black market

intrallazza‧tóre -trice *mf* black marketeer

intrallazzo *m* black-market dealing; kickback

intramezzare [ddzz] (intramèzzo) *tr* to alternate

intramontàbile *adj* undying, immortal

intransigènte *adj & mf* intransigent, die-hard

intransitàbile *adj* impassable

intransiti‧vo -va *adj* intransitive

intrappolare (intràppolo) *tr* to entrap

intraprendènte *adj* enterprising

intraprendènza *f* enterprise, initiative

intraprèndere §220 *tr* to undertake

intrattàbile *adj* unmanageable, intractable

intrattenére §271 *tr* to entertain || *ref* to linger; **intrattenersi su** to dwell upon

intratteniménto *m* entertainment

intravedére §279 *tr* to glimpse, catch a glimpse of; to foresee

intraveno‧so -sa [s] *adj* intravenous

intrecciare §128 (intréccio) *tr* to braid; to twine; to cross (*one's fingers*); (fig) to weave; to begin (*a dance*) || *ref* to become embroiled; to become intertwined; to crisscross

intréc‧cio *m* (-ci) knitting; intertwining; plot (*of novel*); (theat) intrigue

intrepidézza *f* intrepidness, intrepidity

intrèpi‧do -da *adj* intrepid

intricare §197 *tr* (lit) to entangle

intrica‧to -ta *adj* tangled; intricate

intrì‧co *m* (-chi) tangle, jumble

intrìdere §189 *tr* to soak; to knead

intrigante *adj* intriguing || *mf* schemer

intrigare §209 *tr* to tangle‧ || *intr* to intrigue || *ref* (coll) to meddle

intri‧go *m* (-g‧.i) intrigue; trouble

intrìnse‧co -ca (-ci -che) *adj* intrinsic; intimate || *m* intimate nature, core

intrì‧so -sa *adj* soaked || *m* mash

intristire §176 *intr* (ESSERE) to wither; to waste away

introdót·to -ta *adj* introduced; well-known; knowledgeable, expert

introdurre §102 *tr* to introduce; to insert; to open (*a speech*); to show in || *ref* to slip in

introdutti·vo -va *adj* introductory

introduzióne *f* introduction

introitare (intròito) *tr* to collect, take in

intròito *m* receipts, collection; (*eccl*) introit

intromèttere §198 *tr* to insert; to introduce; to involve || *ref* to meddle; to pry

intromissióne *f* meddling; intrusion; intervention

intronare (intròno) *tr* to deafen; to stun

intronizzare [ddzz] *tr* to enthrone

introspetti·vo -va *adj* introspective

introspezióne *f* introspection

introvàbile *adj* unobtainable; inaccessible

introvèr·so -sa *adj & mf* introvert

intrùdere §190 *tr* (lit) to slip in || *ref* to intrude; to trespass

intrufolare (intrùfolo) *tr* (coll) to slip (*e.g.*, *one's hand into somebody's pocket*) || *ref* to slip in, intrude

intrù·glio *m* (**-gli**) concoction, brew; hodgepodge; imbroglio; mess

intrusióne *f* intrusion

intru·so -sa *adj* intrusive || *mf* intruder

intuire §176 *tr* to know by intuition; to guess; to sense

intuiti·vo -va *adj* intuitive; obvious

intùito *m* intuition; insight

intuizióne *f* intuition

inturgidire §176 *intr* (ESSERE) & *ref* to swell

inuma·no -na *adj* inhuman; inhumane

inumare *tr* to bury, inhume

inumazióne *f* burial, inhumation

inumidire §176 *tr* to moisten || *ref* to get wet

inurbaménto *m* migration to the city

inurba·no -na *adj* uncouth, unmannerly

inurbare *ref* to move into the city; to become citified

inusa·to -ta *adj* unused; unusual

inusita·to -ta *adj* unusual; out-of-the-way

inùtile *adj* useless; worthless

inutilizzàbile [ddzz] *adj* unusable

inutilizzare [ddzz] *tr* to waste (*e.g.*, *time*)

inutilizza·to -ta [ddzz] *adj* unused

inutilménte *adv* needlessly, to no purpose || *interj* no use!

invadènte *adj* meddlesome, intrusive

invàdere §172 *tr* to invade; to encroach on; to spread over; to overcome

invaghire §176 *tr* to charm || *ref* to fall in love

invalére §278 *intr* (ESSERE) to become established; to prevail

invalicàbile *adj* impassable, unsurmountable

invalidàbile *adj* voidable

invalidaménto *m* invalidity; invalidation

invalidare (invàlido) *tr* to void, invalidate; to negate (*e.g.*, *evidence*)

invalidi·tà *f* (**-tà**) invalidity; invalidation; sickness, disability

invàli·do -da *adj* void, invalid; sick, disabled || *m* disabled person; invalid

inval·so -sa *adj* prevailing

invano *adv* in vain, vainly

invariàbile *adj* invariable

invaria·to -ta *adj* unchanging; unchanged

invasare *tr* to pot (*a plant*); to fill up (*a reservoir*); to possess, obsess

invasa·to -ta *adj* possessed, obsessed

invasióne *f* invasion

inva·so -sa *adj* invaded || *m* potting (*of plant*); capacity (*of reservoir*)

inva·sóre -ditrice *adj* invading || *m* invader

invecchiaménto *m* aging

invecchiare §287 **(invècchio)** *tr & intr* (ESSERE) to· age

invéce *adv* on the contrary, instead; **invece di** instead of

inveire §176 *intr* to inveigh, rail

invelenire §176 *tr* to envenom; to embitter || *intr* (ESSERE) & *ref* to grow bitter

invendìbile *adj* unsalable

invendica·to -ta *adj* unavenged

invendu·to -ta *adj* unsold

inventare (invènto) *tr* to invent

inventariare §287 *tr* to inventory

inventà·rio *m* (**-ri**) inventory

inventi·vo -va *adj* inventive || *f* inventiveness

inven·tóre -trice *adj* inventive || *mf* inventor

invenzióne *f* invention; (lit) find

inverdire §176 *intr* (ESSERE) to turn green

inverecóndia *f* immodesty

inverecón·do -da *adj* immodest

invernale *adj* winter; wintry

inverniciare §128 *tr* to paint; to varnish

invèrno *m* winter

invéro *adv* (lit) truly, indeed

inverosimiglianza [s] *f* unlikelihood

inverosìmile [s] *adj* unlikely

inversióne *f* inversion

invèr·so -sa *adj* inverse, opposite; (coll) cross || *m* inverse

inversóre *m* inverter; **inversore di spinta** (aer) thrust reverser

invertebra·to -ta *adj & m* invertebrate

invertire §176 & **(invèrto)** *tr* to invert; to reverse

inverti·to -ta *adj* inverted || *m* invert

investigare §209 **(invèstigo)** *tr* to investigate

investiga·tóre -trice *adj* investigating || *mf* investigator; detective

investigazióne *f* investigation

investiménto *m* investment; collision

investire (invèsto) *tr* to invest; to collide with; **investire di insulti** to cover with insults || *ref—**investirsi di** to become conscious of (*e.g.*, *one's authority*); (theat) to become identified with (*a character*)

investi·tóre -trice *mf* investor

investitura *f* investiture

invetera·to -ta *adj* inveterate, confirmed

invetria·to -ta *adj* glazed || *f* window; window pane

invettiva *f* invective

inviare §119 *tr* to send

invia·to -ta *mf* envoy; correspondent

invìdia *f* envy

invidiàbile *adj* enviable

invidiare §287 *tr* to envy; to begrudge; **non aver niente da invidiare a** to be just as good as

invidió·so -sa [s] *adj* envious

invigorire §176 *tr* to strengthen, invigorate || *intr* (ESSERE) & *ref* to grow stronger

invilire §176 *tr* to dishearten; to vilify; to lower (*prices*) || *intr* (ESSERE) & *ref* to lose heart; to lose one's reputation

inviluppare *tr* to envelop; to wrap up

invincìbile *adj* invincible

invì·o *m* (-i) dispatch; shipment; remittance; envoy (*of a poem*)

inviolàbile *adj* inviolable

inviperire §176 *ref* to become enraged

invischiare §287 *tr* to smear with birdlime; to ensnare || *ref* to become ensnared

invisìbile *adj* invisible

invi·so -sa *adj* disliked, hated

invitante *adj* attractive, inviting

invitare *tr* to invite; to summon; (*cards*) to bid; (*cards*) to open; (*mach*) to screw (*e.g., a light bulb*) in; to screw (*e.g., a lid*) on

invita·to -ta *adj* invited || *m* guest

invito *m* invitation; inducement; bottom of stairway; (*cards*) opening

invit·to -ta *adj* unvanquished

invocare §197 (invòco) *tr* to invoke

invocazióne *f* invocation

invogliare §280 (invòglio) *tr* to induce, entice || *ref* to yearn, long

involare (invólo) *tr* to steal; to abduct || *intr* (ESSERE) (aer) to take off || *ref* to disappear; to fly away

invòlgere §289 *tr* to wrap, envelop; to involve || *ref* to become entangled

invólo *m* (aer) take-off

involontà·rio -ria *adj* (-ri -rie) involuntary

invòlto *m* bundle; wrapper

invòlucro *m* wrapping; shell (*of boiler*); (aer) envelope

involu·to -ta *adj* (fig) involved; (lit) enveloped

invòlvere §147 (*pret* missing; *pp* also **invòlto**) *tr* (lit) to envelop

invulneràbile *adj* invulnerable

inzaccherare (inzàcchero) *tr* to bespatter

inzeppare (inzéppo) *tr* to cram, stuff

inzuccherare (inzùcchero) *tr* to sweeten

inzuppare *tr* to soak || *ref* to get drenched

ìo *m* ego; self || §5 *pron pers*

iòdio *m* iodine

iodìdri·co -ca *adj* (-ci -che) hydriodic

ioduro *m* iodide

iògurt *m* yogurt

iò·le *f* (-le) (naut) yawl; (sports) shell

ióne *m* ion

iòni·co -ca *adj* & *m* (-ci -che) Ionic

ionizzare [ddzz] *tr* to ionize

iòsa [s] *f*—**a iosa** in abundance

iperacidità *f* hyperacidity

ipèrbole *f* (geom) hyperbola; (rhet) hyperbole

iperbòli·co -ca *adj* (-ci -che) hyperbolic(al)

ipereccita·to -ta *adj* overexcited

ipermercato *m* shopping center

ipersensìbile *adj* hypersensitive; supersensitive

ipersostentatóre *m* landing flap

ipertensióne *f* hypertension

ipnò·si *f* (-si) hypnosis

ipnòti·co -ca *adj* & *m* (-ci -che) hypnotic

ipnotismo *m* hypnotism

ipnotizzare [ddzz] *tr* to hypnotize

ipnotizza·tóre -trice [ddzz] *adj* hypnotizing || *m* hypnotizer

ipocondrìa·co -ca *adj* & *mf* (-ci -che) hypochondriac

ipocrisìa *f* hypocrisy

ipòcri·ta (-ti -te) *adj* hypocritical || *mf* hypocrite

ipodèrmi·co -ca *adj* (-ci -che) hypodermic

iposolfito [s] *m* hyposulfite

ipotè·ca *f* (-che) mortgage

ipotecare §197 (ipotèco) *tr* to mortgage

ipotecà·rio -ria *adj* (-ri -rie) mortgage

ipotenusa *f* hypotenuse

ipòte·si *f* (-si) hypothesis; **nella miglior delle ipotesi** at best; **nell'ipotesi che** in the event; **per ipotesi** by supposition

ipotèti·co -ca *adj* (-ci -che) hypothetic(al)

ipotizzare [ddzz] *tr* to hypothesize

ìppi·co -ca (-ci -che) *adj* horse, horseracing || *f* horse racing

ippocampo *m* sea horse

ippocastano *m* horse chestnut tree

ippòdromo *m* race track

ippoglòsso *m* (ichth) halibut

ippopòtamo *m* hippopotamus

iprite *f* mustard gas

ira *f* wrath, anger, ire

irachè·no -na *adj* & *mf* Iraqi

iracóndia *f* wrath, anger

iracón·do -da *adj* wrathful

irania·no -na *adj* & *mf* Iranian

irascìbile *adj* irascible

ira·to -ta *adj* irate, angry

ire §191 *intr* (ESSERE) (lit) to go

irida·to -ta *adj* rainbow-hued || *m* world bicycle champion

ìride *f* rainbow; (anat, bot) iris

Irlanda, l' *f* Ireland

irlandése [s] *adj* Irish || *m* Irishman; Irish (*language*) || *f* Irishwoman

ironìa *f* irony

iròni·co -ca *adj* (-ci -che) ironic(al)

iró·so -sa [s] *adj* angry, wrathful

irradiare §287 *tr* to illuminate; to irradiate, radiate; to brighten; (rad) to broadcast || *intr* to radiate || *ref* to radiate; to spread

irraggiare §290 *tr* to illuminate; to irradiate, radiate, beam; to brighten; (rad) to broadcast || *intr* to radiate || *ref* to radiate; to spread

irraggiungìbile adj unattainable
irragionévole adj unreasonable
irrancidire §176 intr (ESSERE) & ref to get rancid
irrazionale adj irrational
irreale adj unreal
irreconciliàbile adj irreconcilable
irrecuperàbile adj irretrievable, irrecoverable
irredentismo m irredentism
irredenti·sta mf (-sti -ste) irredentist
irredèn·to -ta adj not yet redeemed
irredimìbile adj irredeemable
irrefrenàbile adj unrestrainable
irrefutàbile adj irrefutable
irregimentare (irregiménto) tr to regiment
irregolare adj irregular
irregolari·tà f (-tà) irregularity
irreligió·so -sa [s] adj irreligious
irremovìbile adj irremovable; obstinate
irreparàbile adj irreparable; unavoidable
irreperìbile adj not to be found; unaccounted for (e.g., soldier)
irreprensìbile adj irreproachable
irreprimìbile adj irrepressible
irrequiè·to -ta adj restless, restive
irresistìbile [s] adj irresistible
irresolùbile [s] adj unbreakable (bond; contract); insoluble; unsolvable
irresolu·to -ta [s] adj irresolute
irrespiràbile adj unbreathable
irresponsàbile adj irresponsible
irrestringìbile adj unshrinkable
irretire §176 tr to ensnare, entrap
irrevocàbile adj irrevocable
irriconoscìbile adj unrecognizable
irriducìbile adj irreducible; stubborn
irriflessi·vo -va adj thoughtless, rash
irrigare §209 tr to irrigate
irrigazióne f irrigation
irrigidire §176 tr to chill || intr & ref to stiffen, harden; to get cool
irrì·guo -gua adj well-watered; irrigating
irrilevante adj irrelevant
irrilevanza f irrelevance
irrimediàbile adj irremediable
irripetìbile adj unrepeatable
irrisióne f (lit) derision, mockery
irrisò·rio -ria adj (-ri -rie) mocking; paltry
irritàbile adj peevish; irritable
irritante adj irritating || m irritant
irritare (ìrrito) tr to irritate; to anger; to chafe || ref to become irritated
irritazióne f irritation
irriverènte adj irreverent
irrobustire §176 tr & ref to strengthen
irrómpere §240 (pp missing) intr to burst
irrorare (irròro) tr to sprinkle; to bathe, wet; to spray
irroratrice f sprayer; **irroratrice a zaino** portable sprayer
irruènte adj impetuous, rash
irruzióne f foray, raid; irruption
irsu·to -ta adj hairy, bristling
ir·to -ta adj prickly; shaggy (hair); **irto di** bristling with
iscrìvere §250 tr to inscribe; to register || ref to register; to sign up

iscrizióne f inscription; registration
Islam, l' m Islam
Islanda, l' f Iceland
islandése [s] adj Icelandic || mf Icelander || m Icelandic (language)
ìsola f island; block; **isola spartitraffico** traffic island
isolaménto m isolation; (elec) insulation
isola·no -na adj island || mf islander
isolante adj insulating || m (elec) insulation
isolare (ìsolo) tr to isolate; (elec) to insulate || ref to keep apart
isola·to -ta adj isolated; (elec) insulated || m city block; (sports) independent
isolatóre m (elec) insulator
isolazionismo m isolationism
isolazioni·sta mf (-sti -ste) isolationist
isolétta f isle
isòscele adj isosceles
isòto·po -pa adj isotopic || m isotope
ispani·sta mf (-sti -ste) Hispanist
ispa·no -na adj Hispanic
ispanoamerica·no -na adj & mf Spanish-American
ispessire §176 tr & ref to thicken
ispettorato m inspectorship
ispet·tóre -trice mf inspector; **ispettore di produzione** (mov) production manager
ispezionare (ispezióno) tr to inspect
ispezióne f inspection
ìspi·do -da adj bristly
ispirare tr to inspire || ref to be inspired
ispirazióne f inspiration
Israèle m Israel
israelia·no -na adj & mf Israeli
israeli·ta adj & mf (-ti -te) Israelite
issare tr to hoist
issòpo m hyssop
istallare tr & ref var of **installare**
istantàne·o -a adj instantaneous || f snapshot
istante m instant, moment; petitioner
istanza f petition; request, application; (law) instance; **in ultima istanza** as a final decision
istèri·co -ca (-ci -che) adj hysteric(al) || mf hysteric
isterilire §176 tr to make barren || ref to become barren
isterismo m hysteria, hysterics
istigare §209 tr to instigate, prompt
istiga·tóre -trice mf instigator
istillare tr to instill, implant; **istillare il collirio negli occhi** to put drops in the eyes
istinti·vo -va adj instinctive
istinto m instinct
istituire §176 tr to institute, found; (lit) to decide
istituto m institute; institution; bank; **istituto di bellezza** beauty parlor
istitu·tóre -trice mf founder; teacher, instructor || m tutor || f governess; nurse
istituzionalizzare [ddzz] tr to institutionalize
istituzióne f institution
istmo m isthmus
istologìa f histology

istoriare §287 (istòrio) *tr* to adorn with historical figures

istradare *tr* to direct ‖ *ref* to wend one's way

ìstrice *m* & *f* (European) porcupine

istrióne *m* ham actor; buffoon

istriòni·co -ca *adj* (-ci -che) histrionic

istrionismo *m* histrionics

istruire §176 *tr* to instruct; to train; (law) to draw up, prepare (*a case*) ‖ *ref* to learn

istrui·to -ta *adj* learned, educated

istruménto *m* (law) instrument

istrutti·vo -va *adj* instructive

istrut·tóre -trice *mf* instructor; (sports) coach

istruttò·rio -ria (-ri -rie) *adj* investigating, preliminary ‖ *f* (law) preliminary investigation

istruzióne *f* instruction; (law) prelimi-

nary investigation; **istruzioni** instructions; directions

istupidire §176 *tr* to make dull; to stupefy

Itàlia, l' *f* Italy

italia·no -na *adj* & *mf* Italian

itàli·co -ca *adj* (-ci -che) italic; Italic; (lit) Italian ‖ *m* italics

italòfo·no -na *adj* Italian-speaking ‖ *m* Italian-speaking person

itinerante *adj* itinerant

itinerà·rio *m* (-ri) itinerary

ittèri·co -ca *adj* (-ci -che) jaundiced

itterìzia *f* jaundice

ittiologìa *f* ichthiology

Iugoslàvia, la Yugoslavia

iugosla·vo -va *adj* & *mf* Yugoslav

iugulare *adj* & *tr* var of **giugulare**

iuta *f* jute

ivi *adv* (lit) there

J
K
L

L, l ['ɛlle] *m* & *f* tenth letter of the Italian alphabet

la §4 *def art* the ‖ *m* (mus) la, A; **dare il la** to set the tone ‖ §5 *pers pron*

là *adv* there; **al di là da venire** to come, future; **al di là (di)** beyond; **andare di là** to go in the next room; **andare troppo in là** to go too far; **farsi in là** to move aside; **in là con gli anni** advanced in years; **l'al di là** the life beyond; **più in là** further; **più in là di** beyond; **va' là!** come on!

lab·bro *m* (-bri) edge (*of wound*); (lit) lip ‖ *m* (-bra *fpl*) lip; **labbro leporino** harelip

labiale *adj* & *f* labial

làbile *adj* (coll) weak; (lit) fleeting

labiolettura *f* lip reading

labirinto *m* labyrinth, maze

laboratò·rio *m* (-ri) laboratory; workshop; **laboratorio linguistico** language laboratory

laborió·so -sa [s] *adj* hard-working, laborious; labored (*e.g., digestion*)

laburi·sta (-sti -ste) *adj* Labour ‖ *mf* Labourite

lac·ca *f* (-che) lacquer

laccare §197 *tr* to lacquer; to japan; to polish (*nails*)

lac·chè *m* (-chè) lackey

lac·cio *m* (-ci) lasso; snare; noose; string; (fig) bond; **laccio delle scarpe** shoelace; **laccio emostatico** tourniquet

lacciòlo *m* snare

lacerare (làcero) *tr* to lacerate; to tear ‖ *ref* to tear

làce·ro -ra *adj* torn; tattered

lacèrto *m* (lit) shred of flesh; (lit) biceps

lacòni·co -ca *adj* (-ci -che) laconic

làcrima *f* tear; drop

lacrimare (làcrimo) *tr* (lit) to weep

over ‖ *intr* to water (*said of the eyes*); (lit) to weep

lacrima·to -ta *adj* (lit) lamented

lacrimévole *adj* pitiful

lacrimòge·no -na *adj* tear (*e.g., gas*)

lacrimó·so -sa [s] *adj* teary, watery (*eyes*); tearful; lachrymose

lacuna *f* gap, lacuna; blank (*in one's mind*); **colmare una lacuna** to bridge a gap

lacustre *adj* lake

laddóve *conj* while, whereas

ladré·sco -sca *adj* (-schi -sche) thievish

la·dro -dra *adj* thieving; foul (*weather*); bewitching (*eyes*) ‖ *mf* thief; **ladro di strada** highwayman ‖ *f* inside pocket (*of suit*)

ladróne *m* thief; highwayman; **ladrone di mare** pirate

ladrùncolo *m* petty thief, pilferer

laggiù *adv* down there

lagnanza *f* complaint

lagnare *ref* to complain; to moan

lagno *m* complaint, lament

la·go *m* (-ghi) lake; pool (*of blood*)

làgrima *f* var of **lacrima**

laguna *f* lagoon

lai *m* (lai) lay; **lai** *mpl* (lit) lamentations

laicato *m* laity

lài·co -ca (-ci -che) *adj* lay ‖ *m* layman

lài·do -da *adj* foul; obscene

la·ma *m* (-ma) llama; lama ‖ *f* (-me) blade (*of knife*); marsh; (lit) lowland

lambiccare §197 *tr* to distill ‖ *ref* to strive; **lambiccarsi il cervello** to rack one's brains

lambic·co *m* (-chi) still

lambire §176 *tr* to lap; to graze, to touch lightly

lamèlla *f* thin sheet

lamentare (laménto) *tr* to bemoan, lament ‖ *ref* to moan; to complain

lamentazióne *f* lamentation

lamentévole *adj* plaintive; lamentable
laménto *m* complaint, lament; moan
lamentó·so -sa [s] *adj* plaintive, doleful
lamétta *f* razor blade
lamièra *f* plate; armor plate
lamierino *m* sheet metal, lamina
làmina *f* sheet, lamina
laminare (làmino) *tr* to laminate; to roll (*steel*)
lamina·tóio *m* (-tói) rolling mill
làmpada *f* lamp, light; **lampada al neon** neon lamp; **lampada a petrolio** oil lamp; **lampada a stelo** pole lamp; **lampada di sicurezza** (min) safety lamp; **lampada fluorescente** fluorescent lamp; **lampada lampo** (phot) flash bulb
lampadà·rio *m* (-ri) chandelier
lampadina *f* bulb; **lampadina tascabile** flashlight
lampante *adj* shiny; clear; lamp (*oil*)
lampeggiare §290 (lampéggio) *tr* (lit) to flash (*a smile*) || *intr* to flash; (aut) to blink; (coll) to flash the turn signals || *impers* (ESSERE & AVERE)— **lampeggia** it lightens, it is lightning
lampeggiatóre *m* (aut) turn signal; (phot) flashlight
lampio·nàio *m* (-nài) lamplighter
lampióne *m* street lamp
lampìride *f* glowworm
lampo *m* lightning; flash of lightning; (fig) flash
lampóne *m* raspberry
lana *f* wool; **buona lana** (coll) rogue, rascal; **lana d'acciaio** steel wool; **lana di vetro** fiberglass, glass wool
lancétta *f* lancet; hand (*of watch*); pointer (*of instrument*)
làn·cia *f* (-ce) lance, spear; nozzle (*of fire hose*); launch; **lancia di salvataggio** lifeboat
lanciabóm·be *m* (-be) trench mortar
lanciafiam·me *m* (-me) flamethrower
lanciamìssi·li (-li) *adj* missile-launching || *m* missile launcher
lanciaraz·zi [ddzz] *m* (-zi) rocket launcher
lanciare §128 *tr* to throw, hurl; to drop (*from an airplane*); to launch (*e.g., an advertising campaign*) || *ref* to hurl oneself; (rok) to blast off; **lanciarsi col paracadute** to parachute, bail out
lanciasilu·ri *m* (-ri) torpedo tube
lancia·to -ta *adj* hurled, flung; flying, *e.g.*, **partenza lanciata** flying start
lancia·tóre -trice *mf* hurler, thrower; (baseball) pitcher
lancière *m* lancer
lancinante *adj* piercing
làn·cio *m* (-ci) throw; publicity campaign; (aer) drop; (aer) release (*of bombs*); (baseball) pitch; (rok) launch; **lancio del peso** shot put
landa *f* moor; wasteland
lanerìe *fpl* woolens
languidézza *f* languidness, languor
làngui·do -da *adj* languid; sad (*eyes*)
languire (lànguo) & §176 *intr* to languish
languóre *m* languor; languishing; weakness; tenderness

laniè·ro -ra *adj* wool (*industry*)
lanifi·cio *m* (-ci) woolen mill
lanó·so -sa [s] *adj* woolly; kinky (*hair*); bushy (*face*)
lantèrna *f* lantern
lanùgine *f* down
lanzichenéc·co *m* (-chi) landsknecht
laónde *conj* (lit) wherefore
laotia·no -na *adj* & *mf* Laotian
lapalissia·no -na *adj* self-evident
lapidare (làpido) *tr* to stone (to death); (fig) to pick to pieces
làpide *f* stone tablet; tombstone
lapillo *m* lapillus
là·pis *m* (-pis) pencil
lappare *intr* to lap
làppola *f* (bot) burdock; (bot) bur
lappóne *adj* Lappish || *mf* Lapp || *m* Lapp (*language*)
Lappónia, la Lapland
lardellare (lardèllo) *tr* to lard; to stuff with bacon
lardo *m* lard; **nuotare nel lardo** to live on easy street
largheggiare §290 (larghéggio) *intr* to be liberal; to be lavish
larghézza *f* width; liberality; abundance; **larghezza di vedute** broadmindedness
largire §176 *tr* (lit) to bestow liberally
largizióne *f* bestowal; donation
lar·go -ga (-ghi -ghe) *adj* broad, wide; ample; liberal; abundant; (phonet) open; **prenderla larga** to keep away || *m* width; open sea; square; (mus) largo; **al largo di** (naut) off; **fare largo a** to open the way to; **farsi largo** to elbow one's way; **prendere il largo** to run away; (naut) to put to sea; **tenersi al largo** to keep at a distance || *f*—**alla larga!** keep away! || *largo adv*—**girare largo** to keep away
làrice *m* larch
laringe *f* larynx
laringite *f* laryngitis
laringoia·tra *mf* (-tri -tre) laryngologist
laringoscò·pio *m* (-pi) laryngoscope
larva *f* (ent) larva; (lit) ghost; (lit) skeleton; (lit) sham
lasagne *fpl* lasagne
lasciapassa·re *m* (-re) safe-conduct; permit
lasciare §128 *tr* to leave; to let; to let go of; **lasciar cadere** to drop; **lasciarci le penne** (coll) to die; (coll) to be skinned alive; **lasciar correre** to let go; **lasciar detto** to leave word; **lasciar fare** to leave alone; **lasciare in pace** to leave alone; **lasciare libero** to let go; **lasciare scritto** to leave in writing || *ref* to abandon oneself; to abandon one another
làscito *m* (law) bequest
lascivia *f* lasciviousness
lasci·vo -va *adj* lascivious
lassati·vo -va *adj* mildly laxative || *m* mild laxative
lassismo *m* laxity
las·so -sa *adj* lax || *m* lasso; **lasso di tempo** period of time
lassù *adv* up there, up above
lastra *f* slab; paving stone; (phot)

plate; exposed X-ray film; **farsi le lastre** (coll) to be X-rayed
lastricare §197 (**làstrico**) *tr* to pave
lastricato *m* paving, pavement
làstri·co *m* (**-ci** or **-chi**) pavement; roadway; **ridursi sul lastrico** to fall into abject poverty
lastróne *m* slab; plate glass
latènte *adj* latent
laterale *adj* lateral ‖ *m* (soccer) halfback
laterì·zio -zia (**-zi -zie**) *adj* brick ‖ **laterizi** *mpl* bricks, tiles
làtice *m* latex
latifondi·sta *mf* (**-sti -ste**) rich landowner
latifóndo *m* large landed estate
lati·no -na *adj* Latin; lateen (*sail*) ‖ *m* Latin
latitante *adj* hiding ‖ *mf* fugitive
latitanza *f* flight from justice
latitùdine *f* latitude
la·to -ta *adj* wide; broad (*meaning*) ‖ *m* side; **d'altro lato** on the other hand
la·tóre -trice *mf* bearer
latrare *intr* to bark
latrato *m* bark
latrina *f* toilet, lavatory, washroom
latta *f* tin; can
lattàia *f* milkmaid
lat·tàio *m* (**-tài**) milkman, dairyman
lattante *adj* & *m* suckling
latte *m* milk; **latte detergente** cleansing cream; **latte di gallina** flip; (bot) star-of-Bethlehem; **latte in polvere** powdered milk; **latte magro** or **scremato** skim milk
lattemièle *m* whipped cream
làtte·o -a *adj* milky
latterìa *f* dairy; creamery
làttice *m* var of **latice**
latticèllo *m* buttermilk
latticì·nio *m* (**-ni**) dairy product
lattiginó·so -sa [s] *adj* milky
lattonière *m* tinsmith
lattu·ga *f* (**-ghe**) lettuce; head of lettuce; frill
làudano *m* paregoric, laudanum
laudati·vo -va *adj* laudatory
làurea *f* wreath; doctorate; doctoral examination
laurean·do -da *mf* candidate for the doctorate
laureare (**làureo**) *tr* to confer the doctorate on; to award (*s.o.*) the title of; (lit) to wreathe ‖ *ref* to receive the doctorate; (sports) to get the tile of
laurea·to -ta *adj* laureate ‖ *m* alumnus, graduate
làuro *m* laurel
làu·to -ta *adj* sumptuous, rich
lava *f* lava
lavabianche·rìa *f* (**-rìa**) washing machine
lavàbile *adj* washable
lavabo *m* washstand; lavatory
lavacristallo *m* windshield washer
lavacro *m* washing; font; purification; **santo lavacro** baptism
lavàg·gio *m* (**-gi**) washing; **lavaggio a secco** dry cleaning; **lavaggio del cervello** brainwashing

lavagna *f* slate; blackboard; **lavagna di panno** felt board; **lavagna luminosa** overhead projector
lavama·no *m* (**-no**) washstand
lavanda *f* washing; pumping (*of stomach*); lavender
lavandàia *f* laundrywoman; **lavandaia stiratrice** laundress (*woman who washes and irons*)
lavan·dàio *m* (**-dài**) laundryman; **lavandaio stiratore** launderer
lavanderìa *f* laundry; **lavanderia a gettone** laundromat; **lavanderia a secco** dry-cleaning establishment
lavandino *m* sink
lavapiat·ti *mf* (**-ti**) dishwasher (*person*)
lavare *tr* to wash; to cleanse; **lavare a secco** to dry-clean; **lavare il capo a** to scold ‖ *ref* to wash oneself; **lavarsi le mani** to wash one's hands
lavastovì·glie *mf* (**-glie**) dishwasher ‖ *m* & *f* dishwasher (*machine*)
lavata *f* washing; **lavata di capo** scolding
lavativo *m* (coll) enema; (coll) bore; (coll) goldbricker
lava·tóio *m* (**-tói**) laundry room; washtub
lava·tóre -trice *mf* washer ‖ *m* washerman; (mach) purifier ‖ *f* washerwoman; washing machine
lavatura *f* washing; **lavatura a secco** dry cleaning; **lavatura di piatti** dishwater; washing of dishes; (fig) watery soup
lavèllo *m* wash basin; sink
lavoràbile *adj* workable
lavorante *mf* helper, apprentice
lavorare (**lavóro**) *tr* to work; to till ‖ *intr* to work; to perform; to be busy; to trade; **lavorare ai ferri** to knit; **lavorare di fantasia** to daydream; **lavorare di ganasce** to eat voraciously; **lavorare di gomiti** to elbow one's way; **lavorare di mano** to pilfer; **lavorare di traforo** to work with a jig saw
lavorati·vo -va *adj* working; workable
lavora·to -ta *adj* wrought; tilled
lavora·tóre -trice *mf* worker ‖ *m* workman; workingman ‖ *f* workingwoman
lavorazióne *f* working; manufacturing; tilling
lavorì·o *m* (**-i**) bustle; steady work; scheming
lavóro *m* work; labor; steady work; homework; piece of work; (coll) trouble; **a lavori ultimati** when the work is finished; **lavori forzati** hard labor; **lavori in economia** time and material contract work; **lavori teatrali** theatrical productions; **lavoro a cottimo** piecework; **lavoro a maglia** knitting; **lavoro di cucito** needlework; **mettere al lavoro** to press into service
lazzarétto [ddzz] *m* lazaretto
lazzaróne [ddzz] *m* cad; (coll) goldbricker
le §4 *def art* the ‖ §5 *pers pron*
leale *adj* loyal; sincere
leali·sta *mf* (**-sti -ste**) loyalist
leal·tà *f* (**-tà**) loyalty; sincerity

lébbra *f* leprosy
lebbró·so -sa [s] *adj* leprous ‖ *mf* leper
lécca-léc·ca *m* (-ca) (coll) lollypop
leccapiat·ti *m* (-ti) glutton; sponger
leccapiè·di *mf* (-di) bootlicker
leccarda *f* dripping pan
leccare §197 (**lécco**) *tr* to lick; to fawn on; (fig) to polish ‖ *ref* to make oneself up
lecca·to -ta *adj* affected; polished ‖ *f* licking
léc·cio *m* (-ci) holm oak
leccornìa *f* dainty morsel, delicacy
léci·to -ta *adj* licit, permissible; **mi sia lecito** may I ‖ *m* right
lèdere §192 *tr* to damage, injure
lé·ga *f* (-ghe) league; alloy; **di bassa lega** poor, in poor taste; **fare lega** to unite
legale *adj* legal; lawyer's; official ‖ *m* lawyer
legali·tà *f* (-tà) legality, lawfulness
legalità·rio -ria *adj* (-ri -rie) (pol) observing the rule of law
legalizzare [ddzz] *tr* to legalize; to authenticate
legame *m* bond; connection; relationship
legaménto *m* tie, bond; ligament; (phonet) liaison
legare §209 (**légo**) *tr* to tie; to bind; to unite; to set (*a stone*); to bequeath; to alloy; (bb) to bind ‖ *intr* to bond; to mix (*said of metals*); to go together ‖ *ref* to unite; **legarsela al dito** to never forget
legatà·rio -ria *mf* (-ri -rie) legatee
lega·to -ta *adj* muscle-bound ‖ *m* legate; bequest; (mus) legato
lega·tóre -trice *mf* bookbinder
legatorìa *f* bookbindery
legatura *f* typing; binding; ligature; bookbinding; (mus) tie
legazióne *f* legation
légge *f* law; act; **dettar legge** to lay down the law; **è fuori della legge** he is an outlaw; **legge stralcio** emergency law
leggènda *f* legend; story, tall tale; (journ) caption
leggendà·rio -ria *adj* (-ri -rie) legendary
lèggere §193 *tr, intr & ref* to read
leggerézza *f* lightness; nimbleness; thoughtlessness; fickleness
leggè·ro -ra *adj* light; nimble; thoughtless; slight; fickle; **alla leggera** lightly ‖ **leggero** *adv* lightly
leggia·dro -dra *adj* graceful, lovely
leggìbile *adj* legible, readable
leggì·o *m* (-i) lectern; music stand
legiferare (**legìfero**) *intr* to legislate
legionà·rio -ria *adj & m* (-ri -rie) legionary
legióne *f* legion
legislati·vo -va *adj* legislative
legisla·tóre -trice *mf* legislator
legislatura *f* legislature
legittimare (**legìttimo**) *tr* to legitimize
legittimi·tà *f* (-tà) legitimacy
legìtti·mo -ma *adj* legitimate; pure; just, right ‖ *f* (law) legitim
lé·gna *f* (-gna & -gne) firewood; (fig) fuel

legnàia *f* woodpile; woodshed
legname *m* timber, lumber
legnata *f* clubbing, thrashing
légno *m* wood; stick; ship; coach; timber; **legno compensato** plywood; **legno dolce** softwood; **legno forte** hardwood
legnòlo *m* ply (e.g., *of a cable*)
legnó·so -sa [s] *adj* wooden; tough (*meat*); dry (*style*)
legu·lèio *m* (-lèi) pettifogger
legume *m* legume; **legumi** vegetables; legumes
leguminósa [s] *f* leguminous plant; **leguminose** legumes
lèi §5 *pron pers;* **dare del Lei a** to address formally
lémbo *m* edge, border; patch (*of land*)
lèm·ma *m* (-mi) entry (*in a dictionary*)
lèmme lèmme *adv* (coll) slowly
léna *f* energy; enthusiasm; (lit) breath
lèndine *m* nit
lène *adj* (lit) light, soft, gentle; (phonet) voiced
lenire §176 *tr* to soothe, assuage
lenóne *m* panderer, procurer
lenóna *f* procuress
lènte *f* lens; bob, pendulum bob; **lente d'ingrandimento** magnifying glass; **lenti** glasses
lentézza *f* slowness
lentìcchia *f* lentil
lentìggine *f* freckle
lentigginó·so -sa [s] *adj* freckly
lèn·to -ta *adj* slow; slack; (lit) loose (*hair*); (lit) loose-fitting (*garment*) ‖ **lento** *adv* slowly
lènza *f* fishline
lenzuò·lo *m* (-li) sheet; (fig) blanket; **lenzuolo a due piazze** double sheet; **lenzuolo funebre** winding sheet, shroud ‖ *m* (-la *fpl*) sheet; **lenzuola** pair of sheets (*in a bed*)
leoncino *m* lion cub
leóne *m* lion; **leone d'America** cougar; **leóne marino** sea lion ‖ **Leone** *m* (astr) Leo
leonéssa *f* lioness
leopardo *m* leopard
lepidézza *f* wit; witticism
lèpi·do -da *adj* witty, facetious
lepisma *f* (ent) silverfish
lèpre *adj invar* rendezvous, e.g., **razzo lepre** rendezvous rocket ‖ *f* hare
leprotto *m* leveret, young hare
lèr·cio -cia *adj* (-ci -ce) filthy
lerciume *m* filth, dirt
lèsbi·co -ca (-ci -che) *adj & mf* Lesbian ‖ *f* Lesbian (*female homosexual*)
lésina *f* awl; stinginess; miser
lesinare (**lésino** & **lèsino**) *tr* to begrudge ‖ *intr* to be miserly
lesionare (**lesióno**) *tr* to damage; to crack open
lesióne *f* damage; injury; lesion
lé·so -sa *adj* damaged; injured
lessare (**lésso**) *tr* to boil
lessicale *adj* lexical
lèssi·co *m* (-ci) lexicon
lessicografìa *f* lexicography
lessicogràfi·co -ca *adj* (-ci -che) lexicographic(al)
lessicògrafo *m* lexicographer

lessicologìa *f* lexicology
lés·so -sa *adj* boiled ‖ *m* boiled meat; soup meat
lè·sto -sta *adj* swift; nimble; quick; alla lesta hastily; lesto di lingua ready-tongued; lesto di mano light-fingered
lestofante *m* swindler
letale *adj* lethal, deadly
leta·màio *m* (-mài) dunghill
letame *m* manure, dung
letàrgi·co -ca *adj* (-ci -che) lethargic
letar·go *m* (-ghi) lethargy; hibernation
letìzia *f* happiness, joy
lèttera *f* letter; alla lettera literally; lettera morta unheeded, e.g., le sue parole rimasero lettera morta his words remained unheeded; lettere literature; lettere credenziali credentials; scrivere in tutte lettere to spell out
letterale *adj* literal
letterà·rio -ria *adj* (-ri -rie) literary; learned (*word*)
lettera·to -ta *adj* literary; literate ‖ *m* man of letters; (coll) literate, learned person
letteratura *f* literature
lettièra *f* litter, bedding
letti·ga *f* (-ghe) sedan chair; stretcher
lètto *m* bed; bedding; di primo letto born of the first marriage; letti gemelli twin beds; letto a castello bunk bed; letto a due piazze double bed; letto a scomparsa Murphy bed; letto a una piazza single bed; letto bastardo oversize bed; letto caldo hot-bed; letto di morte deathbed; letto operatorio operating table
lèttone or lettóne *adj* Lettish ‖ *mf* Lett ‖ *m* Lett, Lettish (*language*)
Lettónia, La Latvia
let·tóre -trice *mf* reader; lecturer; meter reader ‖ *m* reader (*e.g., for microfilm*); lettore perforatore reader (*of punch cards*)
lettura *f* reading; lecture; lettura del pensiero mind reading
letturi·sta *m* (-sti) meter reader
leucemìa *f* leukemia
leucorrèa *f* leucorrhea
lèva *f* lever; (mil) draft; (mil) class; essere di leva to be of draft age; fare leva su to use (*s.o.'s emotions*)
levachio·di *m* (-di) claw hammer
levante *adj* rising ‖ *m* east; Levant
levanti·no -na *adj* & *mf* Levantine
levare (lèvo) *tr* to lift, raise; to weigh (*anchor*); to pull (*a tooth*); to break (*camp*); to collect (*mail*); to remove, take away; to subtract; levare alle stelle to praise to the sky; levare il disturbo a to take leave of ‖ *ref* to arise; to get up; to take off; to satisfy (*e.g., one's hunger*); to rise (*said of wind*); levarsi dai piedi to get out of the way; levarsi dai piedi or di mezzo qlcu to get rid of s.o.
levata *f* rise; reveille; collection (*of mail*); withdrawal (*of merchandise from warehouse*); levata di scudi uprising
levatàc·cia *f* (-ce) getting up at an im-

possible hour; ho dovuto fare una levataccia I had to get up way too early
leva·tóio -tóia *adj* (-tói -tóie)—ponte levatoio drawbridge
levatrice *f* midwife
levatura *f* intellectual breadth
leviatano *m* leviathan
levigare §209 (lèvigo) *tr* to polish
levigatrice *f* sander; buffer
levi·tà *f* (-tà) (lit) levity
levitazióne *f* levitation
levrière *m* greyhound
lezióne *f* lesson; lecture; reading
lezió·so -sa [s] *adj* affected, mincing
lézzo [ddzz] *m* stench; filth
li *def art masc plur* (obs) the; li tre novembre the third of November (*in official documents*) ‖ §5 *pers pron*
lì *adv* there; di lì that way; di lì a un anno a year hence; essere lì lì per to be about to; fin lì up to that point; giù di lì more or less; lì per lì on the spot
libanése [s] *adj* & *mf* Lebanese
Lìbano, il Lebanon
libare *tr* to toast; to taste ‖ *intr* to toast
libazióne *f* libation
libbra *f* pound
libéc·cio *m* (-ci) southwest wind
libèllo *m* libel; (law) brief
libèllula *f* dragonfly
liberale *adj* & *m* liberal
liberali·tà *f* (-tà) liberality
liberare (lìbero) *tr* to free; to pay in full for; to open into (*said, e.g., of a hall opening into a room*); to clear, empty (*a room*) ‖ *ref*—liberarsi da or di to get rid of
libera·tóre -trice *adj* liberating ‖ *mf* liberator
liberismo *m* free trade
lìbe·ro -ra *adj* free; vacant; without a revenue stamp (*document*); open (*syllable; heart*); outspoken
liber·tà *f* (-tà) freedom; release (*e.g., from mortgage*); libertà provvisoria bail, parole; libertà vigilata probation; mettersi in libertà to put comfortable house clothes on; rimettere in libertà to set free
liberti·no -na *adj* & *mf* libertine
Lìbia, la Libya
lìbi·co -ca *adj* & *mf* (-ci -che) Libyan
libìdine *f* lust; greed
libidinó·so -sa [s] *adj* lustful
libido *f* libido
li·bràio *m* (-brài) bookseller
librare *ref* to balance; to soar; (aer) to glide
libratóre *m* (aer) glider
librerìa *f* bookstore; library (*room*); bookshelf; book collection
libré·sco -sca *adj* (-schi -sche) bookish
librétto *m* booklet; card; (mus) libretto; libretto di banca passbook; libretto degli assegni checkbook; libretto di circolazione car registration; libretto ferroviario railroad pass; libretto di risparmio passbook (*of savings bank*)
libro *m* book; ledger; register (*e.g., of births*); a libro folding; libro di

bordo log; **libro in brossura** paperback; **libro mastro** ledger; **libro paga** (com) payroll

liceale *adj* high-school || *mf* high-school student

licènza *f* permit; license; diploma; (mil) leave; **con licenza parlando!** excuse my language!; **dar licenza a** to dismiss; **prender licenza da** to take leave of

licenziaménto *m* dismissal; **licenziamento in tronco** firing on the spot

licenziare §287 (**licènzio**) *tr* to dismiss; to O.K. (*a book to be published*); to graduate || *ref* to take leave; to give notice, resign; to graduate

licenzió·so -sa [s] *adj* licentious

licèo *m* high school; lycée

lichène *m* lichen

licitazióne *f* auction; (bridge) bidding

lido *m* shore; sand bar

liè·to -ta *adj* glad; blessed (*event*)

lième *adj* light; slight

lievitare (**lièvito**) *tr* to leaven || *intr* (ESSERE & AVERE) to rise; to ferment

lièvito *m* yeast; leaven; **lievito in polvere** baking powder

li·gio -gia *adj* (-**gi -gie**) devoted

lignàg·gio *m* (-**gi**) ancestry, lineage

ligustro *m* privet

lil·la (-**la**) *adj invar & m* lilac

lillipuzia·no -na *adj & mf* Lilliputian

lima *f* file; **lima per le unghie** nail file

limacció·so -sa [s] *adj* miry, muddy

limare *tr* to file; to polish (*e.g., a speech*); to gnaw, plague

limatura *f* filing; filings

limbo *m* (lit) edge; (fig) limbo || **Limbo** *m* (theol) Limbo

limétta *f* nail file; (bot) lime

limitare *m* threshold || *v* (**lìmito**) *tr* to limit; to bound

limitazióne *f* limitation

lìmite *m* limit; boundary; check; (soccer) penalty line; **limite di carico** maximum weight; **limite di età** retirement age; **limite di velocità** speed limit; **senza limiti** limitless

limìtro·fo -fa *adj* neighboring (*country*)

limo *m* mud, mire

limonare (**limóno**) *intr* (coll) to spoon

limonata *f* lemonade; (med) citrate of magnesia

limóne *m* lemon tree; lemon

limó·so -sa [s] *adj* slimy

lìmpi·do -da *adj* limpid, clear

lince *f* lynx, wildcat

linciàg·gio *m* (-**gi**) lynching

linciare §128 *tr* to lynch

lin·do -da *adj* neat; clean

lìnea *f* line; degree (*of temperature*); **conservare la linea** to keep one's figure; **in linea** abreast; (telp) connected; **in linea d'aria** as the crow flies; **linea del fuoco** firing line; **linea del cambiamento di data** international date line; **linea di circonvallazione** (rr) beltline; **linea di condotta** policy; **linea di partenza** starting line; **linea laterale** (sports) side line

lineaménti *mpl* lineaments; elements

lineare *adj* linear || *v* (**lìneo**) *tr* to delineate

lineétta *f* dash; hyphen

linfa *f* (anat) lymph; (bot) sap; **dar linfa** (bot) to bleed

lingòtto *m* (metallurgy) pig, ingot; **lingotto d'oro** bullion

lìngua *f* tongue; language; strip (*of land*); **essere di due lingue** to speak with a forked tongue; **in lingua** in the correct language; **lingua di gatto** ladyfinger; **lingua lunga** backbiter; **lingua sciolta** glib tongue; **mala lingua** wicked tongue

linguacciu·to -ta *adj* talkative; sharptongued

linguàg·gio *m* (-**gi**) language

linguèlla *f* (philately) gummed strip

linguétta *f* tongue (*of shoe*); (mach) pin; (mus) reed

linguìsti·co -ca (-**ci -che**) *adj* linguistic || *f* linguistics

linifì·cio *m* (-**ci**) flax-spinning mill

liniménto *m* liniment

lino *m* flax; linen

linósa [s] *f* flaxseed, linseed

linotipi·sta *mf* (-**sti -ste**) linotypist

liocòrno *m* unicorn

liofilizzare [ddzz] *tr* to freeze-dry

liquefare §194 *tr & ref* to liquefy

liquefazióne *f* liquefaction

liquidare (**lìquido**) *tr* to liquidate; to close out; to dismiss; to settle

liquidazióne *f* liquidation; clearance; **liquidazione del danno** (ins) adjustment

liquidità *f* liquidity

lìqui·do -da *adj* liquid; (com) due || *m* liquid; cash || *f* liquid

liqui·gàs *m* (-**gàs**) liquid gas

liquirìzia *f* licorice

liquóre *m* liqueur; (pharm) liquor

liquori·sta *mf* (-**sti -ste**) liqueur manufacturer or dealer

lira *f* lira; pound; (mus) lyre || **Lira** *f* (astr) Lyra

lìri·co -ca (-**ci -che**) *adj* lyric; (mus) operatic || *m* lyric poet || *f* lyric; lyric poetry; opera

lirismo *m* lyricism

Lisbóna *f* Lisbon

li·sca *f* (-**sche**) fishbone; lisp

lisciare §128 *tr* to smooth; **lisciare il pelo a** to butter up, flatter; to beat up || *ref* to preen

lì·scio -scia *adj* (-**sci -sce**) smooth; straight (*drink*); black (*coffee*); **passarla liscia** to get away scot-free

liscìvia *f* lye; bleach

lisciviatrice *f* washing machine

li·so -sa *adj* worn-out, threadbare

lista *f* list; strip, band; stripe; **lista delle spese** shopping list; **lista delle vivande** bill of fare; **lista elettorale** slate (*of candidates*)

listare *tr* to border; to stripe

listèllo *m* lath; (archit) listel

listino *m* price list; market quotation

litanìa *f* litany

lite *f* quarrel; lawsuit

litigante *adj* quarreling || *mf* quarreler; (law) litigant

litigare §209 (lìtigo) *tr*—**litigare qlco a qlcu** to fight with s.o. for s.th ‖ *intr* to quarrel; to litigate ‖ *ref*—**litigarsi qlco** to strive for s.th
litì·gio *m* (-gi) quarrel, litigation
litigió·so -sa [s] *adj* quarrelsome
lìtio *m* lithium
litografia *f* lithography
litògrafo *m* lithographer
litorale *adj* littoral ‖ *m* seashore, coastline
lìtro *m* liter
Lituània, la Lithuania
litua·no -na *adj* & *mf* Lithuanian ‖ *m* Lithuanian (*language*)
liturgìa *f* liturgy
litùrgi·co -ca *adj* (-ci -che) liturgical
liu·tàio *m* (-tài) lute maker
liuto *m* lute
livèlla *f* level; **livella a bolla d'aria** spirit level
livellaménto *m* leveling; equalization
livellare (livèllo) *tr* to level; to equalize; to survey ‖ *intr* (ESSERE) & *ref* to become level
livella·tóre -trice *adj* leveling ‖ *mf* surveyor ‖ *f* bulldozer
livellazióne *f* leveling
livèllo *m* level; **livello delle acque** sea level
lìvi·do -da *adj* livid, black-and-blue ‖ *m* bruise
lividóre *m* bruise
livóre *m* grudge; hatred
Livórno *f* Leghorn
livrèa *f* livery
lizza *f* tilting ground; **entrare in lizza** to enter the lists
lo §4 *def art* the ‖ §5 *pers pron*
lòb·bia *m* & *f* (-bia *mpl* & *fpl*) homburg
lòbo *m* lobe
locale *adj* local ‖ *m* room; place (*of business*); (naut) compartment; **locale notturno** night spot
locali·tà *f* (-tà) locality, spot
localizzare [ddzz] *tr* to localize; to locate ‖ *ref* to become localized
localizzazióne [ddzz] *f* localization; **localizzazione dei guasti** troubleshooting
locanda *f* inn
locandiè·re -ra *mf* innkeeper
locandina *f* playbill; flyer; small poster
locare §197 (lòco) *tr* to rent, lease
locatà·rio -ria *mf* (-ri -rie) lessee, renter
loca·tóre -trice *mf* lessor
locazióne *f* rent; lease; **dare in locazione** to rent
locomotiva *f* locomotive, engine
locomo·tóre -trice *adj* locomotive ‖ *m* & *f* (rr) electric locomotive
locomotori·sta *m* (-sti) (rr) engineer
locomozióne *f* locomotion; transportation
lòculo *m* burial niche
locusta *f* locust
locuzióne *f* locution, expression; phrase; idiom
lodàbile *adj* praiseworthy
lodare (lòdo) *tr* to praise ‖ *ref* to praise oneself, brag; **lodarsi di** (poet) to be pleased with

lodati·vo -va *adj* laudatory
lòde *f* praise; **con la lode** cum laude; **con lode** plus (*on a report card*)
lodévole *adj* praiseworthy, commendable
lòdo *m* arbitration
logaritmo *m* logarithm
lòg·gia *f* (-ge) lodge; (archit) loggia
loggióne *m* (theat) upper gallery
lògi·co -ca (-ci -che) *adj* logical; **esser logico** to think logically ‖ *m* logician ‖ *f* logic
logisti·co -ca (-ci -che) *adj* logistic ‖ *f* logistics
lò·glio *m* (-gli) cockle
logoraménto *m* wear; attrition
logorare (lógoro) *tr* to wear out; to fray ‖ *ref* to wear away; to become threadbare
logorì·o *m* (-i) wear and tear
lógo·ro -ra *adj* worn out; threadbare
lòlla *f* chaff
lombàggine *f* lumbago
lombar·do -da *adj* & *mf* Lombard
lombata *f* loin, sirloin
lómbo *m* loin; hip; (lit) ancestry
lombri·co *m* (-chi) earthworm
londinése [s] *adj* London ‖ *mf* Londoner
Londra *f* London
longànime *adj* patient, forbearing
longanimi·tà *f* (-tà) patience, forbearance
longevità *f* longevity
longè·vo -va *adj* long-lived
longherina *f* beam, girder
longheróne *m* (aer) longeron; (aer) spar; (aut) main frame member
longitùdine *f* longitude
longobar·do -da *adj* & *mf* Lombard
lontananza *f* distance
lonta·no -na *adj* distant, remote; vague; indirect ‖ *m* (lit) far-away place ‖ *f*—**alla lontana** from a distance; vaguely; distant (*e.g., relative*) ‖ **lontano** *adv* far; **da lontano** from afar; **lontano da** away from; far from; **rifarsi da lontano** to start from the very beginning
lóntra *f* otter
lónza *f* pork loin; (poet) leopard
lòppa *f* chaff; skin (*of plant*); slag, dross
loquace *adj* loquacious; (fig) eloquent
loquèla *f* (lit) tongue; (lit) style
lordare (lórdo) *tr* to soil, dirty
lór·do -da *adj* soiled, dirty; gross (*weight*)
lordume *m* dirt, filth
lordura *f* dirt, filth; soil
lóro §5 *pron pers* ‖ §6 *adj poss* & *pron*
losan·ga *f* (-ghe) rhombus; (herald) lozenge
ló·sco -sca *adj* (-schi -sche) squint-eyed; cross-eyed; (fig) shady
lóto *m* mud
lòto *m* lotus
lòtta *f* fight; struggle; wrestling; **essere in lotta** to be at war; **lotta libera** catch-as-catch-can
lottare (lòtto) *intr* to fight; to quarrel; to struggle; to wrestle

lotta·tóre -trice *mf* fighter; wrestler

loitería *f* lottery

lottizzare [ddzz] *tr* to divide into lots

lòtto *m* lotto; parcel, lot

lozióne *f* lotion

lùbri·co -ca *adj* (**-ci -che**) lewd; (lit) slippery

lubrificante *adj & m* lubricant

lubrificare §197 (**lubrìfico**) *tr* to lubricate

lucchétto *m* padlock

luccicare §197 (**lùccico**) *intr* to sparkle; to shine

luccichì·o *m* (**-i**) glittering; shining; sparkle

luccicóne *m* big tear

lùc·cio *m* (**-ci**) pike

lùcciola *f* firefly; usherette (*in movie*); **prendere lucciole per lanterne** to make a blunder; to be seeing things

luce *f* light; sunlight; opening; glass (*of mirror*); leaf (*e.g., of door*); (archit) span; (coll) electricity; **alla luce del sole** in plain view; **fare luce** to shed light on; **luce degli occhi** eyesight; **luce del giorno** daylight; **luce della luna** moonlight; **luce di arresto** (aut) stoplight; **luce di incrocio** (aut) dimmer, low beam; **luce di posizione** (aut) parking light; **luce di profondità** (aut) high beam; **luci** (poet) eyes; **luci della ribalta** (fig) stage, boards; **mettere alla luce** to give birth to; **mettere in luce** to reveal; to publish; **venire alla luce** to be born; to come to light

lucènte *adj* shiny, shining

lucentézza *f* brightness; sheen

lucèrna *f* lamp; light; **lucerne** (lit) eyes || **Lucerna** *f* Lucerne

lucernà·rio *m* (**-ri**) skylight

lucèrtola *f* lizard

lucherino *m* (orn) siskin

Lucìa *f* Lucy

lucidare (**lùcido**) *tr* to shine, polish; to trace (*a figure*)

lucida·tóre -trice *mf* polisher (*person*) || *f* (mach) floor polisher

lucidatura *f* polish; tracing (*on paper*)

lucidi·tà *f* (**-tà**) polish; lucidity

lùci·do -da *adj* bright; lucid || *m* shine; tracing; **lucido per le scarpe** shoe polish

lucìfe·ro -ra *adj* (poet) light-bringing || **Lucifero** *m* Lucifer, morning star

lucìgnolo *m* wick

lucrare *tr* to win, acquire

lucrati·vo -va *adj* lucrative

lucro *m* gain, earnings, lucre; **lucro cessante** (law) loss of earnings

lucró·so -sa [s] *adj* lucrative

ludì·brio *m* (**-bri**) mockery; laughing-stock

lù·glio *m* (**-gli**) July

lùgubre *adj* gloomy, dismal

lui §5 *pron pers*

luìgi *m* louis || **Luigi** *m* Louis

luma·ca *f* (**-che**) snail

lume *m* light; lamp; **lume degli occhi** eyesight; **lume delle stelle** starlight; **lumi di luna** hard times; **perdere il lume degli occhi** to lose one's self-control; **reggere il lume a** to close one's eyes to; **studiare al lume di candela** to burn the midnight oil

lumeggiare §290 (**luméggio**) *tr* to illuminate, to shed light on

lumicino *m* faint light; **essere al lumicino** to be on one's last legs

luminare *m* star; luminary

luminària *f* illumination

lumino *m* night light; votive light; rush light

luminó·so -sa [s] *adj* luminous; bright (*idea*)

luna *f* moon; **andare a lune** to be fickle; **avere la luna a traverso** to be in a bad mood; **luna calante** waning moon; **luna crescente** crescent moon; **luna di miele** honeymoon

lunare *adj* lunar, moon

lunària *f* (min) moonstone; (bot) honesty

lunà·rio *m* (**-ri**) almanac; **sbarcare il lunario** to live from hand to mouth

lunàti·co -ca *adj* (**-ci -che**) moody; whimsical

lune·dì *m* (**-dì**) Monday

lunétta *f* lunette; fanlight

lunga *f*—**alla lunga** in the long run; **alla più lunga** at the latest; **andare per le lunghe** to last a long time, drag on; **di gran lunga** by far; **farla lunga** to dillydally

lungàggine *f* delay, procrastination

lunghézza *f* length; **lunghezza d'onda** wave length; **prendere la lunghezza di** to measure

lungi *adv* (lit) far

lungimirante *adj* (fig) far-sighted

lun·go -ga (**-ghi -ghe**) *adj* long; sharp (*tongue*); nimble (*fingers*); tall; thin (*soup*); (coll) slow; **a lungo** for a long time; at length; **a lungo andare** in the long run; **lungo disteso** sprawling || *m* length; **in lungo e in largo** far and wide; **per il lungo** lengthwise || *f* see **lunga** || **lungo** *prep* along; during

lungofiume *m* river road

lungola·go *m* (**-ghi**) lakeshore road

lungomare *m* seashore road

lungometràg·gio *m* (**-gi**) full-length movie, feature film

lunòtto *m* (aut) rear window

luò·go *m* (**-ghi**) place; passage; site; (geom) locus; **aver luogo** to take place; **aver luogo in** to be laid in (*e.g., a certain place*); **dar luogo a** to give rise to; **del luogo** local; **far luogo** to make room; **fuori luogo** inopportune(ly); **in alto luogo** high-placed; **in luogo di** instead of; **luogo comune** commonplace; **luogo di decenza** toilet; **luogo di nascita** birthplace; **luogo di pena** penitentiary; **non luogo a procedere** (law) no ground for prosecution; (law) **nolle prosequi**; **sul luogo** on the spot; on the premises

luogotenènte *m* lieutenant

lupa *f* she-wolf

lupanare *m* (lit) brothel

lupé·sco -sca adj (**-schi -sche**) wolfish
lupétto m young wolf; cub (in Boy Scouts)
lupinèlla f sainfoin
lupi·no -na adj wolfish
lu·po -pa mf wolf; **lupo cerviero** lynx; **lupo di mare** seadog; **lupo mannaro** werewolf || f see **lupa**
lùppolo m hops
lùri·do -da adj filthy, dirty
lusco m—**tra il lusco e il brusco** at twilight
lusin·ga f (**-ghe**) flattery; illusion
lusingare §209 tr to flatter || ref to be flattered; to hope
lusinghiè·ro -ra adj flattering; promising
lussare tr to dislocate
lussazióne f dislocation

lusso m luxury; **di lusso** de luxe; **lusso di** abundance of
lussuó·so -sa [s] adj luxurious, sumptuous
lussureggiante adj luxuriant
lussùria f lust
lussurió·so -sa [s] adj lustful, lecherous
lustrare tr to polish, shine; to lick (s.o.'s boots) || intr to shine, be shiny
lustrascar·pe m (**-pe**) bootblack
lustrino m sequin; tinsel
lu·stro -stra adj shiny, polished || m shine, polish; period of five years; **dare il lustro a** to shine, polish
lutto m mourning; bereavement; **a lutto** black-edged (e.g., stationery); **lutto stretto** deep mourning
luttuó·so -sa [s] adj mournful

M

M, m ['ɛmme] m & f eleventh letter of the Italian alphabet
ma m but; **ma e se** ifs and buts || conj but; yet || interj who knows?; too bad!
màca·bro -bra adj macabre
maca·co m (**-chi**) macaque; (fig) dumbbell
macadàm m macadam
macadamizzare [ddzz] tr to macadamize
mac·ca f (**-che**) abundance; **a macca** (coll) abundantly; (coll) without paying
maccarèllo m mackerel
maccheróni mpl macaroni
màcchia f spot, stain; brushwood; thicket; (fig) blot; **alla macchia** clandestinely; (painting) done in pointillism; **darsi alla macchia** to join the underground; to escape the law; **macchia solare** sunspot; **senza macchia** spotless
macchiare §287 tr to stain, soil || ref to become stained; **macchiarsi d'infamia** to soil one's reputation
macchiétta f caricature; comedian; **fare la macchietta di** to impersonate, to parody
macchiettare (**macchiétto**) tr to speckle
macchietti·sta mf (**-sti -ste**) cartoonist; comedian; impersonator
màcchina f machine; engine; car, automobile; machination; **andare in macchina** to go to press; **fatto a macchina** machine-made; **macchina da presa** (mov) camera; **macchina da proiezione** projector; **macchina fotografica** camera; **macchina per** or **da cucire** sewing machine; **macchina per** or **da scrivere** typewriter; **scrivere a macchina** to typewrite
macchinale adj mechanical
macchinare (**màcchino**) tr to plot
macchinà·rio m (**-ri**) machinery
macchinazióne f machination

macchinétta f gadget; **macchinetta del caffé** coffee maker
macchini·sta m (**-sti**) engineer; (theat) stagehand
macchinó·so -sa [s] adj heavy, ponderous; complicated
macedònia f fruit salad, fruit cup
macel·làio m (**-lài**) butcher
macellare (**macèllo**) tr to butcher
macellerìa f butcher shop
macèllo m slaughterhouse; butchering; carnage; disaster
macerare (**màcero**) tr to soak; to mortify (the flesh) || ref to waste away
macèria f low wall; **macerie** ruins
màce·ro -ra adj emaciated; skinny || m soaking vat (for papermaking)
machiavèlli·co -ca adj (**-ci -che**) Machiavellian
macigno m boulder
macilèn·to -ta adj emaciated, pale, wan
màcina f millstone; (coll) grind
macinacaf·fè m (**-fè**) coffee grinder
macinapé·pe m (**-pe**) pepper mill
macinare (**màcino**) tr to grind, mill; to burn up (e.g., the road)
macina·to -ta adj ground || m grindings; ground meat || f grinding
macinino m grinder; (coll) jalopy
mà·cis m & f (**-cis**) mace (spice)
maciste m strong man (in circus)
maciullare tr to brake (flax or hemp); to crush
macrocòsmo m macrocosm
màdia f bread bin; kneading trough
màdi·do -da adj wet, perspiring
madònna f lady || **Madonna** f Madonna
madornale adj huge; gross (error)
madre f mother; stub; mold; **madre nubile** unwed mother
madreggiare §290 (**madréggio**) intr to take after one's mother
madrelìngua f mother tongue
madrepàtria f mother country
madrepèrla f mother-of-pearl
madresélva f (coll) honeysuckle

madrevite *f* (mach) nut; die; **madrevite ad alette** wing nut

madrigna *f* stepmother

madrina *f* godmother; **madrina di guerra** war mother

mae·stà *f* (-stà) majesty; **lesa maestà** lese majesty

maestó·so -sa [s] *adj* majestic, stately

maèstra *f* teacher; (fig) master; **maestra giardiniera** kindergarten teacher

maestrale *m* northwest wind (*in Mediterranean*)

maestranze *fpl* workmen

maestrìa *f* skill, mastery

maè·stro -stra *adj* masterly; main || *m* teacher; master; instructor; northwester (*in Mediterranean*); **maestro di cappella** choirmaster || *f* see **maestra**

mafió·so -sa [s] *adj* Mafia || *mf* member of the Mafia; gaudy dresser

ma·ga *f* (-ghe) sorceress

magagna *f* fault, weak spot

magagna·to -ta *adj* spoiled (*fruit*)

magari *adv* even, maybe || *conj* even if || *interj* would that . . . !

magazzinàg·gio [ddzz] *m* (-gi) storage

magazziniè·re -ra [ddzz] *mf* stockroom attendant || *m* warehouseman

magazzino [ddzz] *m* warehouse; store; inventory; (phot, journ) magazine; **grandi magazzini** department store

maggése [s] *adj* May || *m* (agr) fallow

màg·gio *m* (-gi) May; May Day

maggiolino *m* cockchafer

maggiorana *f* sweet marjoram

maggioranza *f* majority

maggiorare (maggióro) *tr* to increase

maggiorazióne *f* increase, appreciation

maggiordòmo *m* butler; majordomo

maggióre *adj* bigger, greater; major; main; higher (*bidder*); older, elder; (mil) master (*e.g., sergeant*); biggest, greatest; highest; oldest, eldest; **andare per la maggiore** to be all the rage; **maggiore età** majority || *m* (mil) major; oldest one; **maggiori** ancestors

maggiorènne *adj* of age || *mf* grown-up, adult

maggiorènte *mf* notable

maggiori·tà *f* (-tà) (mil) C.O.'s office

maggiorità·rio -ria *adj* (-ri -rie) majority

magìa *f* magic

màgi·co -ca *adj* (-ci -che) magic

Magi *mpl* Magi, Wise Men

magióne *f* (lit) home, dwelling

magistèro *m* education, teaching; mastery; (chem) precipitation

magistrale *adj* teacher's; masterly || *f* teacher's college

magistrato *m* magistrate

magistratura *f* judiciary

màglia *f* knitting; stitch; link; undershirt; sports shirt; (hist) mail; (fig) web; **lavorare a maglia** to knit

maglierìa *f* knitting mill; yarn shop; knitwear store

magliétta *f* polo shirt, T-shirt; buckle (*to secure rifle strap*); picture hook; buttonhole

maglifì·cio *m* (-ci) knitwear factory

mà·glio *m* (-gli) sledge hammer; mallet; drop hammer

maglióne *m* heavy sweater, jersey

magnàni·mo -ma *adj* magnanimous

magnano *m* (coll) locksmith

magnate *m* (lit) magnate, tycoon

magnèsio *m* magnesium

magnète *m* magnet; magneto

magnèti·co -ca *adj* (-ci -che) magnetic

magnetismo *m* magnetism

magnetite *f* loadstone

magnetizzare [ddzz] *tr* to magnetize

magnetòfono *m* tape recorder

magnificare §197 (magnìfico) *tr* to extol, praise; to magnify (*to exaggerate*)

magnificènza *f* magnificence

magnìfi·co -ca *adj* (-ci -che) magnificent; munificent; wonderful, splendid

ma·gno -gna *adj* (lit) great; the Great, e.g., **Alessandro Magno** Alexander the Great

magnòlia *f* magnolia

ma·go *m* (-ghi) magician; wizard

magóne *m* (coll) gizzard; (coll) grief; **avere il magone** (coll) to be in the dumps

magra *f* low water; (fig) dearth, want

magrézza *f* leanness; scarcity

ma·gro -gra *adj* lean, thin; meager || *m* lean meat; meatless day || *f* see **magra**

mài *adv* never; ever; **non . . . mai** never, not ever; **come mai?** how come?

maia·le -la *mf* pig; hog || *m* pork || *f* sow

maialé·sco -sca *adj* (-schi -sche) piggish

maiòli·ca *f* (-che) majolica

maionése [s] *f* mayonnaise

mà·is *m* (-is) corn, maize

maiuscolétto *m* (typ) small capital

maiùsco·lo -la *adj* capital || *m*—**scrivere in maiuscolo** to capitalize || *f* capital letter

Malacca, la Malay Peninsula

malaccèt·to -ta *adj* unwelcome

malaccòr·to -ta *adj* imprudent; awkward

malacreanza *f* (malecreanze) instance of bad manners; **malecreanze** bad manners

malafatta *f* (malefatte) defect; **malefatte** evildoings

malaféde *f* (malefédi) bad faith

malaffare *m*—**donna di malaffare** prostitute; **gente di malaffare** underworld

malagévole *adj* rough (*road*); hard (*work*)

malagràzia *f* (malegràzie) rudeness, uncouthness

malalìngua *f* (malelìngue) slanderer, backbiter

malanda·to -ta *adj* run-down; shabby

malandri·no -na *adj* dishonest; bewitching (*eyes*) || *m* highwayman

malànimo *m* ill will; **di malanimo** reluctantly

malanno *m* misfortune; illness; (joc) menace

malaparata *f* (coll) danger, dangerous situation

malapéna *f*—**a malapena** hardly

malària *f* malaria

malatìc·cio -cia *adj* **(-ci -ce)** sickly

mala·to -ta *adj* sick, ill; **essere malato agli occhi** to have sore eyes; **fare il malato** to play sick || *mf* patient; **i malati** the sick

malattìa *f* sickness; illness; disease; **malattie del lavoro** occupational diseases

malaugura·to -ta *adj* unfortunate; ill-omened

malaugù·rio *m* **(-ri)** ill omen

malavita *f* underworld

malavòglia *f* **(malevòglie)** unwillingness; **di malavoglia** reluctantly

malcapita·to -ta *adj* unlucky || *m* unlucky person

malcàu·to -ta *adj* rash, heedless

malcón·cio -cia *adj* **(-ci -ce)** battered

malcontèn·to -ta *adj* dissatisfied, malcontent || *mf* malcontent || *m* dissatisfaction

malcostume *m* immorality; bad practice

malcrea·to -ta *adj* ill-bred

maldè·stro -stra *adj* clumsy, awkward

maldicènte *adj* gossipy, slanderous || *mf* gossip, slanderer, backbiter

maldicènza *f* gossip, slander

male *m* evil; ill; trouble; **andare a male** to go to pot; **aversela a male** to take offense; **di male in peggio** from bad to worse, worse and worse; **fare del male** to do ill; **fare male** to be in error; **fare male a** to hurt; **farsi male** to get hurt; to hurt oneself; **far venire il mal di mare a** to make seasick; (fig) to nauseate; **Lei fa male** you should not; **mal d'aereo** airsickness; **mal di capo** headache; **mal di cuore** heart disease; **mal di denti** toothache; **mal di gola** sore throat; **mal di mare** sea-sickness; **mal di montagna** mountain sickness; **mal di pancia** bellyache; **mal di schiena** backache; **mandare a male** to spoil; **mettere male** to sow discord; **prendere a male** to take amiss; **voler male a** to bear a grudge against || *adv* badly, poorly; **male educato** ill-bred; **meno male!** fortunately!; **restar male** to be disappointed; **sentirsi male** to feel sick; **stare male** to be ill; **star male a** to not fit, e.g., **questo vestito gli sta male** this suit does not fit him; **veder male qlco** to disapprove of s.th; **veder male qlcu** to dislike s.o.

maledettaménte *adv* (coll) damned

maledét·to -ta *adj* cursed, damned

maledire §195 *tr* to curse

maledizióne *f* malediction, curse || *interj* damn it!, confound it!

maleduca·to -ta *adj* ill-bred || *mf* boor

malefatta *f* var of **malafatta**

malefi·cio *m* **(-ci)** curse, spell; witchcraft; wickedness

malèfi·co -ca *adj* **(-ci -che)** maleficent

maleolènte *adj* (lit) malodorous

malèrba *f* weed, weeds

malése *adj* & *mf* Malay

Malésia, la Malaysia

malèssere *m* malaise; uneasiness; worry

malevolènza *f* malevolence; malice

malèvo·lo -la *adj* malevolent; malicious

malfama·to -ta *adj* ill-famed; notorious

malfat·to -ta *adj* botched; misshapen || *m* misdeed

malfat·tóre -trice *mf* malefactor

malfér·mo -ma *adj* wobbly, unsteady

malfi·do -da *adj* untrustworthy

malgarbo *m* bad manners, rudeness

malgovèrno *m* misrule; mismanagement; neglect

malgrado *prep* in spite of; **mio malgrado** in spite of me || *conj* although

malìa *f* spell, charm

maliar·do -da *adj* enchanting, charming || *mf* magician || *f* enchantress, witch

malignare *intr* to gossip

maligni·tà *f* **(-tà)** maliciousness; malevolence; malignancy

mali·gno -gna *adj* malicious, evil; unhealthy; malignant || **il Maligno** the Evil One

malinconìa *f* melancholy; melancholia

malincòni·co -ca *adj* **(-ci -che)** melancholy, wistful

malincuòre *m*—**a malincuore** unwillingly, against one's will

malintenziona·to -ta *adj* evil-minded || *mf* evildoer

malinté·so -sa [s] *adj* misunderstood; misapplied || *m* misunderstanding

malió·so -sa [s] *adj* malicious; cunning; mischievous; bewitching

malìzia *f* malice; trick; mischief

malizió·so -sa [s] *adj* malicious; clever, artful; mischievous

malleàbile *adj* malleable; manageable

malleva·dóre -drice *mf* guarantor

malleverìa *f* surety

mallo *m* hull, husk

mallòppo *m* bundle; (aer) trail cable; (coll) lump (*in one's throat*); (slang) swag, booty

malmenare (malméno) *tr* to manhandle

malmés·so -sa *adj* shabby, seedy; tasteless

malna·to -ta *adj* uncouth; unfortunate; harmful

malnutri·to -ta *adj* undernourished

malnutrizióne *f* malnutrition

ma·lo -la *adj* (lit) bad

malòc·chio *m* **(-chi)** evil eye

malóra *f* ruin; **mandare in malora** to ruin; **va in malora!** go to the devil!

malóre *m* malaise; fainting spell

malpràti·co -ca *adj* **(-ci -che)** inexperienced

malsa·no -na *adj* unhealthy; unsound

malsicu·ro -ra *adj* unsafe; insecure

malta *f* mortar; plaster; (obs) mud

maltèmpo *m* bad weather

malto *m* malt

maltòlto *m* ill-gotten gains

maltrattaménto *m* mistreatment

maltrattare *tr* to mistreat, maltreat

malumóre *m* bad humor; **di malumore** in a bad mood

malva *f* mallow

malvà·gio -gia (-gi -gie) *adj* wicked || *mf* wicked person || **il Malvagio** the Evil One malversare (malvèrso) *tr* to embezzle; to misappropriate

malversazióne *f* embezzlement; misappropriation

malvesti•to -ta *adj* shabby, seedy

malvi•sto -sta *adj* disliked; unpopular

malvivènte *mf* criminal; (lit) profligate

malvolentièri *adv* unwillingly

malvolére *m* malevolence; indolence || §196 *tr* to dislike

mamma *f* mother, mom; (lit) breast; mamma mia dear me!

mammaluc•co *m* (-chi) simpleton

mammèlla *f* breast; udder

mammìfe•ro -ra *adj* mammalian || *m* mammal

màmmola *f* violet; (fig) shrinking violet

mam•mùt *m* (-mut) mammoth

manata *f* slap; handful; dare una manata a to slap

man•ca *f* (-che) left hand, left

mancante *adj* missing, lacking; unaccounted for

mancanza *f* lack; absence; defect; mistake; in mancanza di for lack of

mancare §197 *tr* to miss || *intr* (AVERE) to be at fault; mancare a to break (*e.g.*, *one's word*); mancare di to be wanting; to lack; mancare di parola to break one's word || *intr* (ESSERE) to fail (*said, e.g., of electric power*); to be lacking, e.g., manca il sale nell'arrosto salt is lacking in the roast; to be missing; to be absent, e.g., mancano tre soci three members are absent; to be, e.g., mancano dieci minuti alle quattro it is ten minutes to four; (with *dat*) to lack, e.g., gli mancano le forze he lacks the strength; to miss, e.g., mi manca la sua compagnia I miss his company; mancare a to be absent from (*e.g., the roll call*); to be . . . from, e.g., mancano dieci chilometri all'arrivo we are ten kilometers from the journey's end; mancare ai vivi (lit) to pass away; sentirsi mancare to feel faint || *impers*—mancare poco che + *subj* to narrowly miss + *ger*, e.g., ci mancò poco che fosse investito da un'automobile he narrowly missed being hit by a car; non ci mancherebbe altro! that would be the last straw!, I should say not!

manca•to -ta *adj* unsuccessful; missed (*opportunity*); abortive (*attempt*), e.g., omicidio mancato abortive attempt to murder; manqué, e.g., un poeta mancato a poet manqué

manchévole *adj* faulty

manchevolézza *f* fault, shortcoming

màn•cia *f* (-ce) tip, gratuity; mancia competente reward

manciata *f* handful

manci•no -na *adj* left-handed; underhanded || *mf* left-handed person || *f* left hand, left; (mach) floating crane

man•co -ca (-chi -che) *adj* left; (lit) sinister, ill-omened; (lit) lacking || *m* (lit) lack; senza manco (coll) without fail || manco *adv*—manco male!

(coll) at least!; manco per idea! (coll) not at all! || *f* see manca

mandaménto *m* jurisdiction

mandante *m* (law) principal

mandare *tr* to send; to condemn (*to death*); to commit (*to memory*); to send forth (*e.g., smoke, buds*); to operate (*a machine*); che Dio ce la mandi buona! may God help us!; mandare ad effetto to carry out; mandare all'altro mondo to dispatch, kill; mandare a monte to ruin; mandare a picco to sink; mandare a quel paese to send to the devil; mandare a spasso to fire, dismiss; to get rid of; mandar giù to swallow; mandare in malora to ruin; mandare in pezzi to break to pieces; mandare per le lunghe to delay || *intr*—mandare a chiamare to send for; mandare a dire to send word

mandarino *m* mandarin; (*Citrus nobilis*) tangerine; (*Citrus reticulata*) mandarin orange

mandata *f* sending; delivery (*of merchandise*); group; gang (*e.g., of thieves*); turn (*of key*); chiudere a doppia mandata to double-lock

mandatà•rio *m* (-ri) mandatary, trustee

mandato *m* mandate; order; mandato di cattura arrest warrant; mandato di comparizione subpoena; mandato di perquisizione search warrant

mandìbola *f* jaw

mandolino *m* mandolin

màndorla *f* almond; kernel (*of fruit*)

mandorla•to -ta *adj* almond || *m* nougat

màndorlo *m* almond tree

mandràgola *f* mandrake

màndria *f* herd

mandriano *m* herdsman

mandrillo *m* mandrill

mandrino *m* (mach) mandrel; (mach) driftpin

mandritta *f*—a mandritta to the right

mane *f*—da mane a sera from morning till night

maneggévole *adj* usable; manageable; accessible to small craft (*sea*)

maneggiare §290 (manéggio) *tr* to work (*e.g., clay*); to handle; to wield (*a sword*); to knead (*dough*); to manage; (equit) to train

manég•gio *m* (-gi) handling; intrigue; horsemanship; management; riding school; manège

manè•sco -sca *adj* (-schi -sche) readyfisted; hand (*e.g., weapons*)

manétta *f* throttle (*on a motorcycle*); manette handcuffs, manacles

manforte *f*—dar manforte a to help

manganèllo *m* bludgeon, cudgel

manganése [s] *m* manganese

màngano *m* calender; mangle

mangeréc•cio -cia *adj* (-ci -ce) edible

mangerìa *f* graft, peculation

mangiàbile *adj* edible

mangiana•stri *m* (-stri) tape recorder

mangia-pane *m* (-pane) idler

mangia•prèti *m* (-prèti) priest hater

mangiare *m* eating; food || *v* §290 *tr*

to eat; to bite, gnaw; to erode; to
embezzle, graft; (cards, chess) to
take; **mangiar la foglia** to get wise ‖
intr to eat; **mangiare alle spalle di
qlcu** to eat at the expense of s.o. ‖
ref to eat up; **mangiarsi il fegato** to
be green with envy; **mangiarsi la
parola** to break one's promise; **mangiarsi le unghie** to bite one's nails;
mangiarsi una promessa to break
one's promise
mangiasòldi *adj invar* money-eating,
e.g., **macchina mangiasoldi** money-
eating contraption
mangiata *f* (coll) fill, hearty meal,
bellyful
mangiatóia *f* manger, crib
mangia·tóre -trice *mf* eater
mangime *m* fodder; feed; poultry feed
mangimìsti·co -ca *adj* (-ci -che) feed,
e.g., **attrezzature mangimistiche** feed
machinery
mangió·ne -na *mf* great eater, glutton
mangiucchiare §287 (mangiùcchio) *tr*
to nibble
mangusta *f* mongoose
manìa *f* mania, craze; complex; whim;
mania di grandezza delusions of
grandeur
manìa·co -ca (-ci -che) *adj* maniacal;
enthusiastic ‖ *m* maniac; fan, enthusiast
màni·ca *f* (-che) sleeve; hose; (coll)
crowd, bunch; **essere di manica larga**
to be broad-minded; **essere nelle
maniche di qlcu** to be in the favor of
s.o.; **è un altro paio di maniche** this
is a horse of another color; **in maniche di camicia** in shirt sleeves;
manica a vento air sleeve, windsock;
manica per l'acqua hose ‖ **la Manica**
the English Channel
manicarétto *m* dainty, delicacy
manichino *m* mannequin; cuff; (obs)
handcuff; **fare il manichino** to model
màni·co *m* (-chi & -ci) handle; stock
(*of rifle*); shaft (*of golf club*); stem
(*of spoon*); (mus) neck; **manico di
scopa** broomstick
manicò·mio *m* (-mi) insane asylum,
madhouse
manicòtto *m* muff; (mach) collar;
(mach) nipple; (mach) sleeve
manicu·re *mf* (-re) manicure, manicurist (*person*) ‖ *f* (-re) manicure (*treatment*)
manicuri·sta *mf* (-sti -ste) manicurist
manièra *f* manner, fashion, way; **belle
maniere** good manners; **di maniera**
(lit, painting) Manneristic; **di maniera che** so that; **in nessuna maniera**
by no means; **maniere** bad manners
maniera·to -ta *adj* mannered, affected;
genteel
manìè·ro -ra *adj* tame, gentle ‖ *m*
manor house, mansion ‖ *f* see
maniera
manieró·so -sa [s] *adj* genteel; mannered
manifattura *f* manufacture; factory;
product; ready-made wear
manifestare (manifèsto) *tr* to manifest

‖ *intr* to demonstrate ‖ *ref* to turn
out to be
manifestazióne *f* manifestation; demonstration
manifestino *m* leaflet, handbill
manifè·sto -sta *adj* manifest, clear ‖ *m*
poster, placard; manifest; (pol) manifesto; **manifesto di carico** (naut)
manifest
manìglia *f* handle; knob; (naut) link
(*of chain*)
manigóldo *m* criminal; scoundrel
manipolare (manìpolo) *tr* to concoct;
to adulterate; (telg) to transmit
manipola·tóre -trice *mf* schemer ‖ *m*
telegraph key
manìpolo *m* sheaf; (eccl; hist) maniple;
(fig) handful
maniscal·co *m* (-chi) blacksmith
manna *f* manna; godsend
mannàia *f* axe; knife (*of guillotine*)
mano *f* hand; way (*in traffic*); coat (*of
paint*); (lit) handful; (fig) finger;
fingertip; **alla mano** plain, affable;
a mani nude barehanded; **a mano** by
hand; **a mano a mano** little by little;
a mano armata armed (*e.g., robbery*); at gunpoint; **andare contro
mano** to buck traffic; **a quattro mani**
four-handed; **avere le mani bucate**
to be a spendthrift; **avere le mani in
pasta** to have one's fingers in the pie;
avere le mani lunghe to be light-
fingered; **battere le mani** to clap;
con le mani in mano idle; **dare la
mano a** to shake hands with; **dare
man forte a** to help; **dare una mano**
to pitch in; **dare una mano a** to lend
a hand to; **di lunga mano** beforehand; **essere colto con le mani nel
sacco** to be caught red-handed;
essere svelto di mano to be light-
fingered; **far man bassa (su)** to plunder; **fuori mano** out of the way;
mani di burro butterfingers; **mani in
alto!** hands up!; **man mano (che)** as;
mettere mano a to begin; **mettere le
mani sul fuoco** to guarantee; to
swear; **per mano di** at the hands of;
prendere la mano to balk; to get out
of hand; **tenere la mano a** to abet;
venire alle mani to come to blows
manodòpera *f* labor, manpower; **manodopera qualificata** skilled labor
manòmetro *m* manometer
manométtere §198 *tr* to tamper with
manomissióne *f* tampering
manomòrta *f* (law) mortmain
manòpola *f* mitten; handgrip; strap
(*to hold on to*); (rad, telv) knob;
(hist) gauntlet
manoscrit·to -ta *adj & m* manuscript
manoscrìvere §250 *intr* to write in one's
own handwriting
manovale *m* laborer, helper; hod carrier
manovèlla *f* handle, crank; lever
manòvra *f* maneuver; (rr) shifting; **fare
manovra** to maneuver; (rr) to shift
manovrare (manòvro) *tr* to maneuver;
to handle, drive; (rr) to shift ‖ *intr*
to maneuver; (rr) to shunt, shift;
(fig) to plot

manovratóre *m* motorman; driver; (rr) brakeman; (rr) flagman

manrovè•scio *m* (-sci) backhanded slap

mansalva *f*—**rubare a mansalva** to help oneself freely (*e.g., to the till*)

mansarda *f* mansard

mansióne *f* duty, function

mansuè•to -ta *adj* tame; meek

mansuetùdine *f* tameness; meekness

mantèlla *f* coat; (mil) cape

mantellina *f* (mil) cape

mantèllo *m* woman's coat; coat (*of animal*); (fig) cloak; (mil) cape; (mach) casing

mantenére §271 *tr* to keep; to maintain; to hold (*e.g., a position*) ‖ *ref* to stay alive; to last; to remain, stay, continue

mantenimónto *m* keeping; maintenance

mantenu•to -ta *adj* kept ‖ *m* gigolo ‖ *f* kept woman

màntice *m* bellows; folding top (*of carriage*); (aut) convertible top

manto *m* mantle; coat; cloak

Màntova *f* Mantua

mantovana *f* valance

manuale *adj* & *m* manual

manualizzare [ddzz] *tr* to make (*e.g., a machine*) hand-operated; to include in a manual; to prepare a manual of

manù•brio *m* (-bri) handlebar; handle; dumbbell

manufat•to -ta *adj* manufactured ‖ *m* manufactured product; manufacture

manutèngolo *m* accomplice

manutenzióne *f* maintenance, upkeep

manza [dz] *f* heifer

manzo [dz] *m* steer; beef

maometta•no -na *adj* & *mf* Mahometan, Mohammedan

maomettismo *m* Mahometanism, Mohammedanism

Maométto *m* Mahomet

maóna *f* barge

mappa *f* map; bit (*of key*)

mappamóndo *m* globe; map of the world

marachèlla *f* mischief

maramèo *m*—**fare marameo** to thumb one's nose

mara•sma *m* (-smi) utter confusion; (pathol) decrepitude, feebleness

maratóna *f* marathon

maratonè•ta *m* (-ti) Marathon runner

mar•ca *f* (-che) mark, label; make, brand; token; ticket; (hist, geog) march; **di marca** of quality; **marca da bollo** revenue stamp; **marca di fabbrica** trademark

marcare §197 *tr* to mark; to label; to brand; to keep the score of; to score (*e.g., a goal*); to accentuate

marcatèm•po *m* (-po) timekeeper

marca•to -ta *adj* marked, pronounced

marchésa *f* marchioness, marquise

marchése *m* marquess, marquis

marchia•no -na *adj* gross (*error*)

marchiare §287 *tr* to brand

màr•chio *m* (-chi) brand; initials; characteristic; trademark

màr•cia *f* (-ce) march; operation; pus; (aut) gear, speed; (mil) hike; (sports)

walk; far **marcia indietro** to back up; (naut) to back water; **marcia indietro** (aut) reverse; **marcia nuziale** wedding march

marciapiède *m* sidewalk; (rr) platform

marciare §128 *intr* to march; (mil) to advance; (sports) to walk; (coll) to function; far **marciare qlcu** to keep s.o. in line

màr•cio -cia (-ci -ce) *adj* rotten; infected; corrupt ‖ *m* rotten part; decayed part; corruption ‖ *f* see **marcia**

marcire §176 *intr* (ESSERE) to rot

marciume *m* rot; pus; decay

mar•co *m* (-chi) mark

marconigram•ma *m* (-mi) radiogram

marconi•sta *mf* (-sti -ste) radio operator

mare *m* sea; bunch, heap; **al mare** at the seashore; **alto mare** high sea; fa **mare** the sea is rough; **gettare a mare** to throw overboard; **mare grosso** rough sea; **mare territoriale** territorial waters; **promettere mari e monti** to promise the moon; **tenere il mare** to be seaworthy

marèa *f* tide; sea (*e.g., of mud*); **alta marea** high tide; **bassa marea** low tide; **marea di quadratura** neap tide; **marea di sizigia** spring tide

mareggiata *f* coastal storm

maremòto *m* seaquake

mareògrafo *m* tide-level gauge

maresciallo *m* marshall; warrant officer

marétta *f* choppy sea; instability

margarina *f* margarine

margherita *f* daisy; **margherite** beads

marginale *adj* marginal

marginatóre *m* margin stop (*of typewriter*); (typ) try square

màrgine *m* margin; edge; **margine a scaletta** thumb index

marijuana *f* marijuana, marihuana

marina *f* seashore; seascape; navy; **marina mercantile** merchant marine

mari•nàio *m* (-nài) seaman, sailor

marinara *f* middy blouse

marinare *tr* to marinate; **marinare la scuola** to cut school, play truant

marinaré•sco -sca *adj* (-schi -sche) sailor, seamanlike

marina•ro -ra *adj* sea, sailor; seamanlike; nautical ‖ *m* (coll) sailor ‖ *f* see **marinara**

mari•no -na *adj* marine, nautical ‖ *f* see **marina**

mariòlo *m* rascal

marionétta *f* puppet, marionette

maritale *adj* marital

maritare *tr* to marry ‖ *ref* to get married

marito *m* husband

maritti•mo -ma *adj* maritime, sea ‖ *m* merchant seaman

marmàglia *f* riffraff, rabble

marmellata *f* jam, preserves; **marmellata di arancia** orange marmalade

marmi•sta *m* (-sti) marble worker; marble cutter

marmitta *f* pot, kettle; (aut) muffler

marmittóne *m* (coll) sad sack

marmo *m* marble

marmòc•chio *m* (-chi) brat

marmòre·o -a *adj* marble

marmorizzare [ddzz] *tr* to marble

marmòtta *f* marmot; woodchuck; (fig) sluggard; (rr) switch signal

marmottina *f* salesman's sample case

marna *f* marl

marnare *tr* to marl

marocchi·no -na *adj & mf* Moroccan ‖ *m* morocco leather

Maròcco, il Morocco

maróso [s] *m* billow, surge

marra *f* hoe; fluke (*of anchor*)

marrano *m* Marrano; (fig) scoundrel; (lit) traitor

marronata *f* (coll) blunder, boner

marróne *adj invar* maroon, tan ‖ *m* chestnut; (coll) blunder

Marsìglia *f* Marseille

marsigliése [s] *adj* Marseilles ‖ *m* native or inhabitant of Marseilles ‖ *f* Marseillaise

marsina *f* swallow-tailed coat

Marte *m* Mars

marte·dì *m* (-dì) Tuesday; martedì grasso Shrove Tuesday

martellare (martèllo) *tr* to hammer; to pester (*with questions*) ‖ *intr* to throb; (fig) to insist

martellata *f* hammer blow

martellétto *m* hammer (*of piano or bell*); lever (*of typewriter*)

martèllo *m* hammer; martello dell'uscio knocker; martello perforatore jack-hammer

martinétto *m* jack; martinetto a vite screw jack

martingala *f* half belt (*sewn in back of sports jacket*); martingale (*of harness*)

martinic·ca *f* (-che) wagon brake

martìn pescatóre *m* kingfisher

màrtire *m* martyr

martì·rio *m* (-ri) martyrdom

martirizzare [ddzz] *tr* to martyrize

màrtora *f* marten

martoriare §287 (martòrio) *tr* to torment

marxi·sta *adj & mf* (-sti -ste) Marxist

marzapane *m* marzipan

marziale *adj* martial

marzia·no -na *adj & mf* Martian

marzo *m* March

mas *m* (mas) torpedo boat

mascalzóne *m* cad, rascal

mascèlla *f* jaw; jawbone

màschera *mf* usher ‖ *f* mask; masque; maschera antigas gas mask; maschera di bellezza beauty pack; maschera respiratoria oxygen mask; maschera subacquea diving helmet

mascheraménto *m* camouflage

mascherare (màschero) *tr, intr & ref* to mask; to camouflage

mascherata *f* masquerade

mascherina *f* little mask, loup; tip (*of shoe*); (aut) grille; (phot) mask

maschiare §287 *tr* (mach) to tap

maschiétta *f* tomboy; alla maschietta bobbed (*hair*); tagliare i capelli alla maschietta to bob the hair

maschiétto *m* baby boy; pintle

maschile *adj* masculine; manly; men's;

male (*sex*); boys' (*school*) ‖ *m* masculine

mà·schio -schia *adj* manly, virile; male ‖ *m* male; keep, donjon; tenon; (mach) tap; (carp) tongue

mascolinizzare [ddzz] *tr* to make masculine or mannish ‖ *ref* to act like a man

mascoli·no -na *adj* masculine; mannish (*woman*)

masnada *f* mob, gang; (obs) group

masnadière *m* highwayman

massa *f* mass; body (*of water*); (elec) ground; mettere a massa (elec) to ground; in massa in a body; massa ereditaria (law) estate

massacrante *adj* killing, fatiguing

massacrare *tr* to massacre; to ruin; to wear out, fatigue

massacro *m* massacre

massaggiare §290 *tr* to massage

massaggiatóre *m* masseur

massaggiatrice *f* masseuse

massàg·gio *m* (-gi) massage

massàia *f* housewife

massèllo *m* block (*of stone*); (metallurgy) pig, ingot

masseria *f* farm

masserizie *fpl* household goods

massicciata *f* roadbed; (rr) ballast

massìc·cio -cia (-ci -ce) *adj* massive; bulky; heavy; (fig) gross ‖ *m* massif

màssi·mo -ma *adj* maximum; top ‖ *m* maximum; limit; al massimo at the most ‖ *f* maxim; maximum temperature

massi·vo -va *adj* massive

masso *m* rock, boulder

Massóne *m* Mason

Massoneria *f* Masonry

mastèllo *m* washtub

masticare §197 (màstico) *tr* to chew, masticate; to mumble (*words*); to speak (*a language*) poorly; masticare amaro to grumble

masticazióne *f* mastication

màstice *m* mastic; glue; putty

mastino *m* mastiff

mastodònti·co -ca *adj* (-ci -che) mammoth

ma·stro -stra *adj* master ‖ *m* ledger; master, e.g., mastro meccanico master mechanic

masturbare *tr & ref* to masturbate

matassa *f* skein; trouble

matemàti·co -ca (-ci -che) *adj* mathematical ‖ *m* mathematician ‖ *f* mathematics

materassino *m* (sports) mat; materassino pneumatico air mattress

materasso *m* mattress; (boxing) sparring partner

matèria *f* matter; substance; subject; (coll) pus; dare materia a to give ground for; materia grigia gray matter; materie coloranti dyestuffs; materie prime raw materials

materiale *adj* material; rough, bulky ‖ *m* material; equipment, supplies; (fig) makings, stuff; materiale ferroviario (rr) rolling stock; materiale stabile (rr) permanent way

materni·tà *f* (**-tà**) maternity; maternity hospital; maternity ward
matèr·no -na *adj* maternal; mother (*tongue, country*)
matita *f* pencil; **matita per gli occhi** eye-shadow pencil; **matita per le labbra** lipstick; cosmetic pencil
matrice *f* matrix; stub
matrici·da *mf* (**-di -de**) matricide
matrici·dio *m* (**-di**) matricide
matrìcola *f* register, roll; registration (*number*); registry; beginner, novice; freshman (*in university*); **far la matricola a** to haze
matricola·to -ta *adj* notorious, arrant
matrigna *f* stepmother
matrimoniale *adj* matrimonial; double (*bed*); married (*life*)
matrimonialménte *adv* as husband and wife
matrimò·nio *m* (**-ni**) matrimony, marriage; wedding
matròna *f* matron
matronale *adj* matronly
matta *f* joker, wild card
mattacchió·ne -na *mf* jester, prankster
mattana *f* tantrum; fit of laughter
matta·tóio *m* (**-tói**) slaughterhouse
matteréllo *m* rolling pin
mattina *f* morning; **di prima mattina** early in the morning; **la mattina** in the morning
mattinale *adj* morning || *m* morning report
mattinata *f* morning; (theat) matinée
mattiniè·ro -ra *adj* early-rising
mattino *m* morning; **di buon mattino** early in the morning
mat·to -ta *adj* crazy; whimsical; dull; false (*jewelry*); wild (*desire*); **andare matto per** to be crazy about; **da matti** unbelievable; **fare il matto** to cut a caper; **matto da legare** raving mad || *f* see **matta**
mattòide *adj & mf* madcap
mattonare (**mattóno**) *tr* to pave with bricks
mattonato *m* brick floor; **restare sul mattonato** to be utterly destitute
mattóne *m* brick; (fig) bore
mattonèlla *f* tile; cushion (*of billiard table*)
mattuti·no -na *adj* morning || *m* matins
maturan·do -da *mf* lycée student who has to take the baccalaureate examination
maturare *tr* to ripen; to ponder; to pass (*a lycée pupil*) || *intr* (ESSERE) to ripen, mature; to fall due
maturazióne *f* ripening
maturi·tà *f* (**-tà**) maturity; ripening; lycée final
matu·ro -ra *adj* ripe; mature; due
Matusalèmme *m* Methuselah
mausolèo *m* mausoleum
mazza *f* club; mallet; sledge hammer; cane; mace; golf club; (baseball) bat
mazzacavallo *m* well sweep
mazzapìc·chio *m* (**-chi**) mallet; sledge
mazzata *f* heavy blow, wallop (*with club*)
mazzeran·ga *f* (**-ghe**) (mach) tamper

mazzière *m* macer; (cards) dealer
mazzo *m* bunch; bouquet; deck (*of cards*); **fare il mazzo** to shuffle the cards
mazzuòla *f* sledge hammer
mazzuòlo *m* sledge; mallet; wedge (*of golf club*); drumstick (*for bass drum*)
me §5 *pron pers*
meandro *m* meander; labyrinth
MEC *m* (letterword) (**Mercato Europeo Comune**) European Economic Community, Common Market
Mècca, la Mecca; (fig) the Mecca
meccàni·co -ca (**-ci -che**) *adj* mechanical || *m* mechanic || *f* mechanics; process (*e.g., of digestion*); machinery
meccanismo *m* machinery; mechanism; movement (*of watch*)
meccanizzare [ddzz] *tr* to mechanize || *ref* to become mechanized
mecenate *m* patron (*of the arts*)
méco §5 *prep phrase* (lit) with me
medàglia *f* medal
medaglióne *m* medallion; locket; biographical sketch
medési·mo -ma *adj & pron* same; -self, e.g., **egli medesimo** he himself; very e.g., **la verità medesima** the very truth
mèdia *f* average; secondary school, middle school; (math) mean; **media oraria** average speed || **mèdia** *mpl* media (*of communication*)
mediana *f* median; (soccer) middle line
mediàni·co -ca *adj* (**-ci -che**) medium
media·no -na *adj* median || *m* (sports) halfback || *f* see **mediana**
mediante *prep* by means of
mediare §287 (**mèdio**) *tr & intr* (ESSERE) to mediate
media·to -ta *adj* indirect
media·tóre -trice *adj* mediating || *mf* mediator; broker; commission merchant
mediazióne *f* mediation; brokerage; broker's fee, commission
medicaménto *m* medicine
medicamentó·so -sa [s] *adj* medicinal
medicare §197 (**mèdico**) *tr* to medicate; to treat
medicastro *m* quack
medicazióne *f* medication; dressing
medichéssa *f* (pej) lady doctor
medicina *f* medicine
medicinale *adj* medicinal || *m* medicine
mèdi·co -ca (**-ci -che**) *adj* medical || *m* doctor, physician; healer; **fare il medico** to practice medicine; **medico chirurgo** surgeon; **medico condotto** board-of-health doctor; country doctor; **medico curante** family physician
medievale *adj* medieval
medievali·sta *mf* (**-sti -ste**) medievalist
mè·dio -dia (**-di -die**) *adj* average; median; middle; secondary (*school*); medium || *m* middle finger || *f* see **media**
mediòcre *adj* mediocre
mediocri·tà *f* (**-tà**) mediocrity
medioèvo *m* Middle Ages
medioleggèro *m* welterweight

mediomàssimo *m* light heavyweight
meditabón•do -da *adj* meditative
meditare (mèdito) *tr & intr* to meditate
medita•to -ta *adj* considered
meditazióne *f* meditation
mediterrà•neo -nea *adj* inland (*sea*) ‖
  Mediterraneo *adj & m* Mediterranean
mè•dium *mf* (**-dium**) medium
medusa *f* jellyfish
mefistofèli•co -ca *adj* (**-ci -che**) Mephistophelian
mefìti•co -ca *adj* (**-ci -che**) mephitic
megaciclo *m* megacycle
megàfono *m* megaphone
megalomanìa *f* megalomania
megalòpo•li *f* (**-li**) megalopolis
mega•òhm *m* (**-òhm**) megohm
megèra *f* hag, termagant, vixen
mèglio *adj invar* better; (coll) best ‖
  m—il meglio the best; **nel meglio di**
  (coll) in the middle of ‖ *f*—**avere la**
  meglio to get the upper hand; **avere**
  la meglio di to get the better of
  ‖ *adv* better; best; rather; **stare**
  meglio to feel better; to be becoming; to fit better; **stare meglio a** to
  be becoming; to fit; **tanto meglio!**
  so much the better!
méla *f* apple; nozzle (*of sprinkling*
  can); **mela cotogna** quince (*fruit*);
  mela renetta pippin
melagrana *f* pomegranate
melanzana [dz] *f* eggplant
melassa *f* molasses, treacle
mela•to -ta *adj* honey, honeyed
melèn•so -sa *adj* dull, silly
melissa *f* (bot) balm
mellìflu•o -a *adj* mellifluous
mélma *f* mud, slime
melmó•so -sa [s] *adj* muddy, slimy
mélo *m* apple tree
melodìa *f* melody
melòdi•co -ca *adj* (**-ci -che**) melodic
melodió•so -sa [s] *adj* melodious
melodram•ma *m* (**-mi**) melodrama;
  lyric opera; (fig) melodrama
melodrammàti•co -ca *adj* (**-ci -che**)
  melodramatic
melograno *m* pomegranate tree
melóne *m* melon; cantaloupe; **melone**
  d'acqua watermelon
membrana *f* membrane; parchment;
  diaphragm (*of telephone*); (zool) web
membratura *f* frame
mèm•bro *m* (**-bri,** *considered individ-*
  ually) limb; member; penis ‖ *m*
  (**-bra** *fpl, considered collectively*)
  limb (*of human body*)
membru•to -ta *adj* burly, husky
memoràbile *adj* memorable
memoràn•dum *m* (**-dum**) memorandum;
  agenda, calendar; note; note paper
mèmore *adj* (lit) mindful, grateful
memòria *f* memory; souvenir; memoir;
  dissertation; (law) brief
memoriale *m* memoir; memorial
memorizzare [ddzz] *tr* to memorize
ména *f* intrigue
mena•bò *m* (**-bò**) (typ) layout, dummy
menadito *m*—**a menadito** at one's
  fingertips; perfectly
menare (méno) *tr* to lead; to bring

(*luck*); to wag (*the tail*); to deliver
  (*a blow*); (coll) to hit; **menare a**
  effetto to carry out; **menare buono di**
  to approve of; **menare il can per l'aia**
  to beat around the bush; **menare per**
  le lunghe to delay; **menare vanto** to
  boast
mènda *f* (lit) fault, flaw
mendace *adj* lying, false, mendacious
mendà•cio *m* (**-ci**) (law) falsehood
mendicante *adj & m* mendicant
mendicare §197 (**méndico**) *tr & intr* to
  beg
mendici•tà *f* (**-tà**) indigence, poverty
mendi•co -ca *adj & mf* (**-chi -che**)
  mendicant
menefreghismo *m* I-don't-care attitude
menestrèllo *m* minstrel
méno *adj invar* less ‖ *m* less; least;
  minus (*sign*); **i meno** the few; **per lo**
  meno at least ‖ *adv* less; least;
  minus; **a meno che** unless; **da meno**
  inferior; **fare a meno di** to do without; to spare; **meno . . . di** less . . .
  than; **meno male** fortunately; **meno**
  . . . meno the less . . . the less; **non**
  poter fare a meno di + *inf* to not be
  able to help + *ger*, e.g., **la confe-**
  renza non poteva fare a meno di
  essere un successo the conference
  could not help being a success;
  quanto meno at least; **senza meno**
  without fail; **venir meno** to swoon,
  pass out; to fail; to lose, e.g., **gli**
  venne meno il cuore he lost his
  courage; **venir meno di** to break
  (*one's word*) ‖ *prep* except; less,
  minus; of, e.g., **le sette meno dieci**
  ten minutes of seven
menomare (mènomo) *tr* to lessen, diminish; (fig) to hurt, damage
mèno•mo -ma *adj* least
menopàusa *f* menopause
mènsa *f* (prepared) table; mess, mess
  hall; (eccl) altar; communion table;
  (poet) mass; (poet) altar; **mensa**
  aziendale company cafeteria
mensile *adj* monthly ‖ *m* monthly salary or allowance
mensili•tà *f* (**-tà**) monthly installment
mènsola *f* bracket; corner shelf; neck
  (*of harp*); mantel (*of chimney*); console
ménta *f* mint
mentale *adj* mental; (anat) chin
mentali•tà *f* (**-tà**) mentality, mind
ménte *f* mind; **a mente di** according to;
  avere in mente to mean; to intend;
  di mente mental; **mente direttiva**
  mastermind; **scappare di mente a**
  qlcu to escape s.o.'s mind, e.g., **gli è**
  scappato di mente it escaped his
  mind; **uscire di mente** to go out of
  one's mind; **venire in mente a qlcu**
  to remember, e.g., **non gli è venuto**
  in mente di spedire la lettera he did
  not remember to mail the letter
mentecat•to -ta *adj & mf* lunatic
mentina *f* mint; **mentina digestiva**
  after-dinner mint
mentire §176 & (**mènto**) *intr* to lie;

mentire per la gola to lie through one's teeth

menti•to -ta *adj* false; disguised

menti•tóre -trice *adj* lying ‖ *mf* liar

ménto *m* chin

mentòlo *m* menthol

méntre *m*—in quel mentre at that very moment; nel mentre che at the time when ‖ *conj* while; whereas

me•nù *m* (-nù) menu

menzionare (menzióno) *tr* to mention

menzióne *f* mention

menzógna *f* lie

menzognè•ro -ra *adj* false, deceptive; lying, untruthful

meraviglia *f* marvel, wonder; a meraviglia wonderfully; destare le meraviglie di to amaze; dire meraviglie di to praise to the skies; fare meraviglia (with *dat*) to amaze; far meraviglie to work wonders

meravigliare §280 (meravìglio) *tr* to amaze; to astonish ‖ *ref* to be astonished

meravigliò•so -sa [s] *adj* marvelous, wonderful ‖ *m* (lit) supernatural

mercan•te -téssa *mf* merchant, dealer

mercanteggiare §290 (mercantéggio) *tr* to sell ‖ *intr* to deal; to haggle

mercantile *adj* mercantile; merchant (*marine*) ‖ *m* cargo boat, freighter

mercanzìa *f* merchandise; (coll) junk

mercato *m* market; trafficking; a buon mercato cheap; far mercato di to traffic in; sopra mercato besides; into the bargain

mèrce *f* merchandise, goods; commodity

mercé *f* favor, grace; mercy; alla mercé di at the mercy of; mercé a thanks to; mercé sua thanks to him (her, etc.)

mercéde *f* pay; (lit) reward

mercenà•rio -ria *adj* & *m* (-ri -rie) mercenary

mercerìa *f* notions store; mercerie notions

mercerizzare [ddzz] *tr* to mercerize

mèr•ci *adj invar* freight (*train, car, etc.*) ‖ *m* (-ci) freight train

mer•ciàio -ciàia *mf* (-ciài -ciàie) notions store owner

merciaiòlo *m* small businessman; merciaiolo ambulante peddler

mercole•dì *m* (-dì) Wednesday

mercuriale *f* market report; price ceiling

mercùrio *m* mercury ‖ Mercurio *m* Mercury

merènda *f* afternoon snack, bite

meretrice *f* harlot

meridia•no -na *adj* & *m* meridian ‖ *f* sundial

meridionale *adj* meridional, southern ‖ *mf* southerner

meridióne *m* south; South

merìg•gio *m* (-gi) noon

merin•ga *f* (-ghe) meringue

meritare (mèrito) *tr* to deserve; to win ‖ *intr* (eccl) to merit; bene meritare di to deserve the gratitude of ‖ *impers*—merita it is worth while to

meritévole *adj* deserving, worthy

mèrito *m* merit; in merito a concerning; per merito di thanks to; render merito a to reward

meritò•rio -ria *adj* (-ri -rie) meritorious

merlan•go *m* (-ghi) whiting

merlatura *f* battlement

merlétto *m* lace, needlepoint

mèrlo *m* blackbird; merlon; (fig) simpleton

merluzzo *m* cod

mè•ro -ra *adj* bare, mere; (poet) pure

merovìngi•co -ca (-ci -che) *adj* Merovingian ‖ *f* Merovingian script

mesata [s] *f* month's wages

méscere (*pp* mesciuto) *tr* to pour (*e.g., wine*); (poet) to mix

meschini•tà *f* (-tà) pettiness; narrowmindedness; meanness, stinginess

meschi•no -na *adj* petty; narrowminded; wretched; puny ‖ *mf* wretch

méscita *f* pouring; counter; bar

mescolanza *f* mixture, blend

mescolare (méscolo) *tr* to mix, blend; to shuffle (*cards*); to stir (*e.g., coffee*) ‖ *ref* to mix, blend; to mingle; to consort; mescolarsi in to mind (*somebody else's business*)

mescolatrice *f* mixer, blender

mése [s] *m* month; month's pay

mesétto [s] *m* short month

mesóne *m* (phys) meson

méssa *f* (eccl & mus) Mass; messa a fuoco (phot) focusing; messa a punto adjustment; clear statement, outline of a problem; (aut) tune-up; messa a terra (elec) grounding; messa cantata high mass; messa in marcia or in moto (mach) starting; messa in orbita (rok) orbiting; messa in piega waving (*of hair*); messa in scena staging; messa in vendita putting up for sale

messaggerìe *fpl* delivery service

messaggè•ro -ra *mf* messenger; postal clerk

messàg•gio *m* (-gi) message

messale *m* missal

mèsse *f* harvest; crop

Messìa *m* Messiah

messiàni•co -ca *adj* (-ci -che) Messianic

messica•no -na *adj* & *mf* Mexican

Mèssico, il Mexico

messinscèna *f* staging; faking

mésso *m* clerk; (poet) messenger

mestare (mésto) *tr* to stir ‖ *intr* to intrigue

mesta•tóre -trice *mf* ringleader; schemer

mèstica *f* (painting) filler

mesticare §197 (mèstico) *tr* to prime (*a canvas*); to mix (*colors*)

mestierante *mf* potboiler (*person*); tradesman, craftsman

mestière *m* trade, craft; (archaic) task; di mestiere by trade; habitual; essere del mestiere to be up in one's line

mestièri *m*—essere di or far mestieri to be necessary

mestìzia *f* sadness

mè•sto -sta *adj* sad

méstola *f* ladle; trowel

méstolo *m* kitchen spoon; avere il mestolo in mano to be the boss

mèstruo *m* menses, menstruation

mèta *f* goal, aim; (rugby) goal line

mèta *f* heap, stack (*e.g., of hay*)

me·tà *f* (-tà) half; middle; halfway; better half; **a metà** halfway, in the middle; **aver qlco a metà con qlcu** to go half and half with s.o.

metabolismo *m* metabolism

metafìsi·co -ca (-ci -che) *adj* metaphysical || *m* metaphysician || *f* metaphysics

metafonèsi *f* umlaut, metaphony

metafonìa *f* umlaut, metaphony

metàfora *f* metaphor

metafòri·co -ca *adj* (-ci -che) metaphoric(al)

metàlli·co -ca *adj* (-ci -che) metallic

metallizzare [ddzz] *tr* to cover with metal

metallo *m* metal; timbre (*of voice*); (poet) metal object; **il vile metallo** filthy lucre

metallòide *m* nonmetal

metallurgìa *f* metallurgy

metallùrgi·co -ca (-ci -che) *adj* metallurgic(al) || *m* metalworker

metalmeccàni·co -ca (-ci -che) *adj* metallurgic(al) and mechanical || *m* metalworker

metamòrfo·si *f* (-si) metamorphosis

metanizzare [ddzz] *tr* to provide with methane

metano *m* methane

metanodótto *m* natural gas pipeline

metàte·si *f* (-si) metathesis

metèora *f* meteor; atmospheric phenomenon

meteorite *m & f* meteorite

meteorologìa *f* meteorology

meteorològi·co -ca *adj* (-ci -che) meteorologic(al); weather (*forecast*)

meteoròlo·go -ga *mf* (-gi -ghe) meteorologist

metìc·cio -cia *adj & mf* (-ci -ce) halfbreed

meticoló·so -sa [s] *adj* meticulous

metìli·co -ca *adj* (-ci -che) methyl

metòdi·co -ca (-ci -che) *adj* methodical; subject (*e.g., index*) || *mf* methodical person || *f* methodology

metodi·sta *adj & mf* (-sti -ste) Methodist

mètodo *m* method

metràg·gio *m* (-gi) length in meters; **corto metraggio** short; **lungo metraggio** full-length movie, feature film

metratura *f* length in meters

mètri·co -ca (-ci -che) *adj* metric(al) || *f* metrics, prosody

mètro *m* meter; (fig) yardstick; (lit) words

métro *m* (coll) subway

metrònomo *m* (mus) metronome

metronòt·te *m* (-te) night watchman

metròpo·li *f* (-li) metropolis

metropolita·no -na *adj* metropolitan || *m* policeman, traffic cop || *f* subway

metrovìa *f* subway

méttere §198 *tr* to put, place; to set (*e.g., foot*); to run (*e.g., a nail into a board*); to cause (*fear; fever*); to employ; to admit; to put forth; to give out; (coll) to charge; (coll) to install; (aut) to engage (*a gear*); **metterci** to take (*e.g., an hour*); **mettere a confronto** to compare; **mettere a freno** to check; **mettere a fuoco** (phot) to focus; **mettere al bando** to banish; **mettere all'asta** to auction off; **mettere al mondo** to give birth to; **mettere a nudo** to lay bare; **mettere fuori** to pull out; to give out (*news*); to throw (*s.o.*) out; **mettere giù** to lower; **mettere in onda** to broadcast; **mettere in pericolo** to endanger; **mettere la pulce nell'orecchio a** to put a bug in the ear of; **mettere qlcu alla porta** to show s.o. the door; **mettere su** to set up; (coll) to put (*e.g., a coat*) on; **mettere su qlcu contro qlcu** to excite s.o. against s.o. || *intr* to sprout; to lead (*said, e.g., of a road*) || *ref* to put on, to don; to place oneself, put oneself; to take shape; **mettersi a** to begin to; **mettersi al bello** to clear up (*said of weather*); **mettersi a letto** to go to bed; **mettersi a sedere** to sit down; **mettersi con** to start to work with; **mettersi in ferie** to take one's vacation; **mettersi in malattia** to fall ill; **mettersi in mare** to put to sea; **mettersi in maschera** to wear a masked costume; **mettersi in salvo** to get out of danger; to save oneself; **mettersi in viaggio** to set out on a journey; **mettersi in vista** to make oneself conspicuous || *impers*—**mette conto** it is worth while

mettima·le *mf* (-le) troublemaker

mezzadrìa [ddzz] *f* sharecropping

mezza·dro -dra [ddzz] *mf* sharecropper

mezzaluna [ddzz] *f* (**mezzelune**) halfmoon; crescent (*symbol of Turkey and Islam*); curved chopping knife; lunette (*of fortification*)

mezzana [ddzz] *f* procuress; (naut) mizzen

mezzanave [ddzz] *f*—**a mezzanave** amidships

mezzanino [ddzz] *m* mezzanine

mezza·no -na [ddzz] *adj* median; medium; middle || *m* procurer || *f* see mezzana

mezzanòtte [ddzz] *f* (**mezzenòtti**) midnight

mezzatinta [ddzz] *f* (**mezzetinte**) halftone

méz·zo -za *adj* overripe, rotten

mèz·zo -za [ddzz] *adj* half; middle || *m* half; middle; medium; means; vehicle; **a mezzo (di)** by (*e.g., messenger*); **andar di mezzo** to suffer the consequences; to be the loser; **entrare di mezzo** to interpose oneself; **esserci di mezzo** to be present; to be at stake; **giusto mezzo** happy medium; **in mezzo a** among; in the lap of, *e.g.,* **in mezzo alle delicatezze** in the lap of luxury; **in quel mezzo** meanwhile; **levar di mezzo** to get rid of; **mezzi** means; facilities; **mezzi di comunicazione di massa** mass media; **per mezzo di** by means of

mezzobusto [ddzz] *m* (**mezzibusti**) (sculp) bust; **a mezzobusto** halflength (*e.g., portrait*)

mezzo•dì [ddzz] *m* (**-dì**) noon; south; South

mezzogiórno [ddzz] *m* noon; south; South

mezzùc•cio [ddzz] *m* (**-ci**) expedient

mi §5 *pron*

miagolare (**miàgolo**) *intr* to meow

miagolì•o *m* (**-i**) meow, mew

mi•ca *f* (**-che**) mica; (obs) crumb || *adv*—**mica male** (coll) not too bad!; **non . . . mica** not . . . ever; not at all

mìc•cia *f* (**-ce**) fuse

michelàc•cio *m* (**-ci**) (coll) lazy bum

micidiale *adj* deadly; (fig) unbearable

mì•cio -cia *mf* (**-ci -cie**) (coll) pussy cat

micrò•bio *m* (**-bi**) microbe

microbiologìa *f* microbiology

mìcrobo *m* microbe

microfà•rad *m* (**-rad**) microfarad

microferrovìa *f* model railroad

micro•film *m* (**-film**) microfilm

microfilmare *tr* to microfilm

micròfono *m* microphone

microlettóre *m* microfilm reader

micromotóre *m* small motor; motorcycle

microónda *f* microwave

microschèda *f* microcard

microscòpi•co -ca *adj* (**-ci -che**) microscopic(al)

microscò•pio *m* (**-pi**) microscope

microsól•co *adj invar* microgroove || *m* (**-chi**) microgroove; microgroove, long-playing record

microtelèfono *m* French telephone, handset

midólla *f* crumb; (coll) marrow

midól•lo *m* (**-la** *fpl*) marrow; (bot & fig) pith; **midollo spinale** (anat) spinal cord

mièle *m* honey

mìetere (**mièto**) *tr* to reap; (lit) to kill

mietitrebbiatrice *f* combine

mieti•tóre -trice *mf* reaper, harvester

mietitura *f* harvesting

mi•gliàio *m* (**-gliàia** *fpl*) thousand

mì•glio *m* (**-glia** *fpl*) mile; milestone; **miglio marino** nautical mile; **miglio terrestre** mile || *m* (**-gli**) millet

miglioraménto *m* improvement

migliorare (**miglióro**) *tr, intr* (ESSERE & AVERE) & *ref* to improve

miglióre *adj* better; best

migliorìa *f* improvement (*e.g., of real estate*)

mignatta *f* leech

mìgnolo *adj masc* little (*finger or toe*) || *m* little finger; little toe

migrare *intr* to migrate

migra•tóre -trice *adj* & *m* migrant

migrazióne *f* migration

Milano *f* Milan

miliardà•rio -ria *adj* & *mf* (**-ri -rie**) billionaire

miliardo *m* billion

milionà•rio -ria *adj* & *mf* (**-ri -rie**) millionaire

milióne *m* million

milionèsi•mo -ma *adj* & *m* millionth

militante *adj* & *m* militant

militare *adj* military || *m* soldier || *v* (**mìlito**) *intr* to be a member; to mili-

tate; to be in the armed forces; **militare in** to be a member of (*e.g., a party*)

militaré•sco -sca *adj* (**-schi -sche**) military, soldierly

militarismo *m* militarism

militari•sta (**-sti -ste**) *adj* militaristic || *mf* militarist

militarizzare [ddzz] *tr* to militarize; to fortify

mìlite *m* militiaman; soldier; **milite del fuoco** fireman; **Milite Ignoto** Unknown Soldier

militesènte *adj* exempt from military service || *m* man exempt from military service

milìzia *f* militia; (mil) service; struggle; **milizie celesti** heavenly host

miliziano *m* militiaman

millantare *tr* to boast of || *ref* to brag, boast

millanta•tóre -trice *mf* braggart

millanterìa *f* bragging

mille *adj, m* & *pron* (**mila**) thousand, a thousand, one thousand || **il Mille** the eleventh century; the year one thousand

millecènto *m* eleven hundred || *f* car with a 1100 cc. motor

millefò•glie *m* (**-glie**) puff-paste cake

millenà•rio -ria *adj* (**-ri -rie**) millennial || *m* millennium

millèn•nio *m* (**-ni**) millennium

millepiè•di *m* (**-di**) millipede

millèsi•mo -ma *adj* & *m* thousandth

milliam•père *m* (**-père**) milliampere

milligrammo *m* milligram

millimetra•to -ta *adj* divided into squares of one millimeter square

millìmetro *m* millimeter

milli•vòlt *m* (**-vòlt**) millivolt

milza *f* spleen

mimare *tr* & *intr* to mime

mimetizzare [ddzz] *tr* (mil) to camouflage

mimetizzazióne [ddzz] *f* (mil) camouflage

mìmi•co -ca (**-ci -che**) *adj* mimic; sign (*language*) || *f* mimicry; (theat) gestures; (theat) miming

mi•mo -ma *mf* mime || *m* (orn) mockingbird

mina *f* lead (*of pencil*); (mil) mine; **mina anticarro** antitank mine; **mina antiuomo** antipersonnel mine

minaccévole *adj* (lit) threatening

minàc•cia *f* (**-ce**) threat, menace

minacciare §128 *tr* to threaten, menace

minacció•so -sa [s] *adj* threatening

minare *tr* to mine; to undermine

minaréto *m* minaret

minatóre *m* miner

minatò•rio -ria *adj* (**-ri -rie**) threatening

minchionare (**minchióno**) *tr* (slang) to make a sucker of

minchióne *m* (slang) sucker

minerale *adj* mineral || *m* mineral; ore

mineralogìa *f* mineralogy

minerà•rio -ria *adj* (**-ri -rie**) mining

minèr•va *m* (**-va**) safety match

minèstra *f* vegetable soup

minestróne *m* minestrone; hodgepodge

mìngere §199 *intr* to urinate

mingherli·no -na *adj* frail, thin

miniare §287 *tr* to paint in miniature; to illuminate

miniatura *f* miniature

miniaturizzare [ddzz] *tr* to miniaturize

miniaturizzazióne [ddzz] *f* miniaturization

minièra *f* mine

mini·gòlf *m* (-gòlf) miniature golf

minigònna *f* miniskirt

mìnima *f* lowest temperature; (mus) minim

minimizzare [ddzz] *tr* to minimize

mìni·mo -ma *adj* smallest, least; minimum || *m* minimum; al mìnimo at the least; girare al mìnimo or tenere il minimo (aut) to idle || *f* see minima

mìnio *m* red lead; rouge

ministeriale *adj* ministerial

ministèro *m* ministry; cabinet; department; pubblico ministero public prosecutor

ministra *f* (joc) wife of minister; (joc) female minister; (poet) minister

ministro *m* minister; secretary; administrator; ministro degli Esteri foreign minister; (U.S.A.) Secretary of State

minoranza *f* minority

minorare (minóro) *tr* to lessen; to disable

minora·to -ta *adj* disabled || *mf* disabled person

minorazióne *f* reduction; disability

minóre *adj* smaller, lesser; minor; smallest, least; younger; youngest || *m* minor

minorènne *adj* underage || *mf* minor

minorìle *adj* juvenile (*e.g., court*)

minori·tà *f* (-tà) minority

minuétto *m* minuet

minù·gia *f* (-gia & -gie) (mus) catgut

minùsco·lo -la *adj* small (*letter*); diminutive || *m* & *f* small letter

minuta *f* first draft, rough copy

minutàglia *f* trifles; small fry

minutante *m* secretary; retailer

minuterìa *f* trinkets, notions

minu·to -ta *adj* minute; small (*change*); common (*people*) || *m* minute; al minuto retail; di minuto in minuto at any moment; minuto secondo second; nel minuto in detail; per minuto minutely || *f* see minuta

minùzia *f* trifle; minuzie minutiae

minuzió·so -sa [s] *adj* meticulous

minùzzolo *m* scrap, crumb; small boy

mìo mìa §6 *adj* & *pron poss* (mièi mìe)

mìope *adj* nearsighted || *mf* nearsighted person

miopìa *f* nearsightedness

mira *f* aim; sight; target, goal; prendere di mira to aim at; to torment

miràbile *adj* admirable || *m* wonder

mirabìlia *fpl* wonders; far mirabilia to perform wonders; dir mirabilia di to speak highly of

mirabolante *adj* amazing, astonishing

miracola·to -ta *adj* miraculously cured || *mf* miraculously cured person

miràcolo *m* miracle; wonder; dir mira-

coli di to praise to the skies; per miracolo by mere chance

miracoló·so -sa [s] *adj* miraculous; wonderful

miràg·gio *m* (-gi) mirage

mirare (lit) *tr* to look at; (lit) to aim at || *intr* to aim; mirare a to aim at; mirare a + *inf* to aim to + *inf*; to intend to + *inf*

mirìade *f* myriad

mirino *m* sight (*of gun*); (phot) finder

mirra *f* myrrh

mirtillo *m* blueberry; whortleberry, huckleberry

mirto *m* myrtle

misantropìa *f* misanthropy

misàntro·po -pa *adj* misanthropic || *mf* misanthrope

miscèla *f* mixture, blend

miscelare (miscèlo) *tr* to mix, blend

miscellàne·o -a *adj* miscellaneous || *f* miscellany

mìschia *f* fight; (sports) scrimmage

mischiare §287 *tr* to mix, blend; to shuffle (*cards*) || *ref* to mix

misconóscere §134 *tr* to not appreciate, undervalue

miscredènte *adj* misbelieving || *mf* misbeliever

miscù·glio *m* (-gli) mixture, blend

miseràbile *adj* pitiful, miserable; poor, wretched

miseran·do -da *adj* pitiable

miserère *m* Miserere; essere al miserere to be in one's last hours

miserévole *adj* pitiful; pitiable

misèria *f* destitution, misery; wretchedness; lack, want; trifle; piangere miseria to cry poverty

misericòrdia *f* mercy

misericordió·so -sa [s] *adj* merciful

mìse·ro -ra *adj* unhappy, wretched; poor; meager; mean; too small, too short

misfatto *m* misdeed, misdoing

misiriz·zì *m* (-zì) tumbler (*toy*); (fig) chameleon

misògi·no -na *adj* misogynous || *m* misogynist

mìssile *adj* & *m* missile; missile antimissile antimissile missile; missile intercontinentale I.C.B.M.; missile teleguidato guided missile

missillìsti·co -ca *adj* (-ci -che) missile

missionà·rio -ria *adj* & *m* (-ri -rie) missionary

missióne *f* mission

missiva *f* missive

misterió·so -sa [s] *adj* mysterious

mistèro *m* mystery

mìstica *f* mysticism; mystical literature

misticismo *m* mysticism

mìsti·co -ca (-ci -che) *adj* & *mf* mystic || *f* see mistica

mistificare §197 (mistìfico) *tr* to hoax

mistificazióne *f* hoax

mi·sto -sta *adj* mixed || *m* mixture; mixed train

mistura *f* mixture

misura *f* measure; size; bounds; fitting; a misura che in proportion as; di

misura (sports) with a narrow margin; **su misura** made-to-order
misuràbile adj measurable
misurare tr to measure; to deliver (e.g., a slap); to budget (expenses); to try on (clothes); to weigh (the outcome) || intr to measure || ref to compete; to limit oneself; **misurarsi con** to try conclusions with
misura·to -ta adj moderate; scanty
misurino m measuring spoon or cup
mite adj mild; tame; low (price)
mìti·co -ca adj (-ci -che) mythical
mitigare §209 (mìtigo) tr to mitigate; to assuage, allay || ref to abate
mìtilo m mussel
mito m myth
mitologìa f mythology
mitològi·co -ca adj (-ci -che) mythologic(al)
mitòmane mf compulsive liar
mi·tra m (-tra) submachine gun || f miter
mitràglia f grapeshot; scrap iron; (coll) machine gun
mitragliare §280 (mitràglio) tr to machine-gun
mitragliatrice f machine gun
mitraglièra f heavy machine gun
mitraglière m machine gunner
mittènte mf sender; shipper
mo' m—apocopated form of **modo** by way of; **a mo' d'esempio** as an illustration
mòbile adj movable; personal (property); (fig) fickle; (rr) rolling (stock) || m piece of furniture; cabinet; (phys) body; **mobili** furniture
mobìlia f furniture
mobiliare adj (fin) security; (law) movable || §287 (mobìlio) tr to furnish
mobilière m furniture maker; furniture dealer
mobilità f mobility
mobilitare (mobìlito) tr & intr to mobilize
mobilitazìóne f mobilization
mò·ca m (-ca) mocha; **caffè moca** Mocha coffee
mocassino m mocassin
moccicare §197 (móccico) intr (slang) to snivel; (slang) to run (said of the nose); (slang) to whimper
moccicó·so -sa [s] adj (slang) snotty
móc·cio m (-ci) snot, snivel
mocció·so -sa [s] adj snotty || m brat
mòccolo m end of candle, snuff; (joc) snot; (slang) curse word; **reggere il moccolo a qlcu** to be a third party to a couple's necking
mòda f fashion, vogue; **andar di moda** to be fashionable; to be all the rage; **fuori moda** outdated
modali·tà f (-tà) modality; method
modanatura f molding
mòdano m mold
modèlla f model
modellare (modèllo) tr to model; to mold || ref to pattern oneself
modella·tóre -trice mf pattern maker; molder

modellino m (archit) model, maquette
modèllo adj invar model || m model; fashion; style; pattern
moderare (mòdero) tr to moderate, control
moderatézza f moderation
modera·to -ta adj moderate; (mus) moderato || m middle-of-the-roader
modera·tóre -trice adj moderating || m moderator
modernizzare [ddzz] tr & ref to modernize
modèr·no -na adj & m modern
modèstia f modesty; scantiness, meagerness
modè·sto -sta adj modest; humble
mòdi·co -ca adj (-ci -che) reasonable
modìfi·ca f (-che) modification; alteration
modificare §197 (modìfico) tr to modify; to change; to alter
modiglióne m (archit) modillion
modista f milliner
modisterìa f millinery; millinery shop
mòdo m manner, mode, way; custom; idiom; (gram) mood; (mus) mode; **ad ogni modo** anyhow; nevertheless; **ad un modo** equally; **a modo** proper; properly; **a suo modo** in his own way; **bei modi** good manners; **di modo che** so that; **in malo modo** poorly; **in modo da** so as to; **in nessun modo** by no means; **in ogni modo** anyhow; **in qualche modo** somehow; **modo di dire** idiom; turn of phrase; **modo di fare** behavior; **modo di vedere** opinion; **per modo di dire** so to speak
modulare (mòdulo) tr to modulate
modulazióne f modulation; **modulazione d'ampiezza** amplitude modulation; **modulazione di frequenza** frequency modulation
mòdulo m module; blank, form
moffétta f skunk
mògano m mahogany
mòg·gio m (-gi) bushel
mò·gio -gia adj (-gi -gie) downcast, crestfallen
mó·glie f (-gli) wife
moìne fpl blandishments
mòla f grindstone; (coll) millstone
molare adj grinding; molar || m molar || v (mòlo) tr to grind
molassa f molasse, sandstone
molatóre m grinder (person); sander (person)
molatrice f grinder (machine); sander (machine); **molatrice di pavimenti** floor sander
mòle f size; pile; bulk, mass; huge structure
molècola f molecule
molestare (molèsto) tr to bother, annoy
molèstia f bother, trouble, annoyance
molè·sto -sta adj bothersome, troublesome
molibdèno m molybdenum
molinétto m (naut) winch
mòlla f spring; (fig) mainspring; **molla a balestra** leaf spring; **molle tongs**; **molle del letto** bedspring; **prendere**

qlco con le molle to keep at a reasonable distance from s.th

mollare (mòllo) *tr* to let go; to slacken; to drop (*anchor*); (coll) to soak || *intr* to give up; (coll) to soak; **molla!** (coll) cut it out!

mòlle *adj* wet, soaked; soft; mild; easy (*life*); weak (*character*); flexible || *m* softness; soft ground; **tenere a molle** to soak

mollécca *f* soft-shell crab

molleggiaménto *m* suspension; springiness

molleggiare §290 (mollèggio) *tr* to provide with springs, to make elastic; (aut) to provide with suspension || *intr* to be springy, to have bounce || *ref* to bounce along

mollég·gio *m* (-gi) springs; (aut) suspension; springiness

mollétta *f* hairpin; clothespin; **mollette** sugar tongs

mollettièra *f* puttee

mollettóne *m* swansdown

mollézza *f* softness

molli·ca *f* (-che) crumb (*soft inner portion of bread*); **molliche** crumbs

mollificare §197 (mollìfico) *tr & ref* to mollify; to soften

mòl·lo -la *adj* soft || *m*—**mettere a mollo** to soak || *f* see **molla**

mollu·sco *m* (-schi) mollusk

mòlo *m* pier, wharf

moltéplice *adj* multiple, manifold

moltilaterale *adj* multilateral, many-sided

moltìpli·ca *f* (-che) front sprocket (*of bicycle*)

moltiplicare §197 (moltìplico) *tr & ref* to multiply

moltitùdine *f* multitude, crowd

mól·to -ta *adj* much, a lot of; very, e.g., **ho molta sete** I am very thirsty || *pron* much; a lot; **a dir molto** mostly; **ci corre molto** there is a great difference || **mol·ti -te** *adj & pron* many || **molto** *adv* very; quite; much; a lot; widely; long; **fra non molto** before long; **non ... molto** (coll) not ... at all

momentàne·o -a *adj* momentary

moménto *m* moment; opportune time; (slang) trifle; (phys) momentum; **dal momento che** since; **per il momento** for the time being; **sul momento** this very moment

mòna·ca *f* (-che) nun

monacale *adj* monachal, conventual

monacato *m* monkhood

monachésimo *m* monachism, monasticism

monachina *f* little nun; **monachine** sparks

mòna·co *m* (-ci) monk; (archit) king post || **Monaco** *m* Monaco || *f* Munich

monar·ca *m* (-chi) monarch

monarchìa *f* monarchy

monàrchi·co -ca *adj* (-ci -che) monarchical; monarchist(ic) (*advocating a monarch*) || *mf* monarchist

monastèro *m* monastery

monàsti·co -ca *adj* (-ci -che) monastic(al)

moncherino *m* stump (*without hand*)

món·co -ca (-chi -che) *adj* one-handed; one-armed; incomplete || *mf* cripple

moncóne *m* stump

mondana *f* prostitute

mondani·tà *f* (-tà) worldliness

monda·no -na *adj* mundane; worldly; society; fashionable || *m* playboy || *f* see **mondana**

mondare (móndo) *tr* to peel, pare; to thresh; to weed; to prune; (fig) to cleanse

mondari·so *mf* (-so) rice weeder

mondez·zàio *m* (-zài) dump

mondiale *adj* world, world-wide; (coll) stupendous

mondìglia *f* chaff; trash; refuse

mondina *f* rice weeder

món·do da *adj* clean-peeled; (lit) pure || *m* world; hopscotch; (coll) heap, bunch; **bel mondo** smart set; **cascasse il mondo!** (coll) come what may!; **da che mondo è mondo** since the world began; **essere nel mondo della luna** to be absent-minded; **mandare all'altro mondo** (coll) to send packing; **mettere al mondo** to give birth to; **mondo della luna** world of fancy; **un mondo** a lot; **venire al mondo** to be born || **Mondo** *m*—**Terzo Mondo** Third World

monega·sco -sca *adj & mf* (-schi -sche) Monacan

monellerìa *f* prank

monèl·lo -la *mf* urchin, brat || *f* romp

monéta *f* money; coin; piece of money; purse (*in horse races*); change; **batter moneta** to mint money; **moneta sonante** cash

monetà·rio -ria (-ri -rie) *adj* monetary || *m*—**falso monetario** counterfeiter

monetizzare [ddzz] *tr* to express in money; to transform into cash

mòngo·lo -la *adj & mf* Mongolian

monile *m* necklace; jewel

mònito *m* admonition, warning

monitóre *m* monitor

mònna *f* (obs) lady; (coll) monkey

monoàlbero *adj invar* (aut) single-camshaft, valve-in-head (*distribution*)

monoaurale *adj* monaural

monoblòc·co (-co) *adj* single-block || *m* (aut) cylinder block

monocilìndri·co -ca *adj* (-ci -che) (mach) single-cylinder

monòco·lo -la *adj* one-eyed || *m* monocle

monocolóre *adj invar* one-color; one-party

monofa·se *adj* (-si & -se) single-phase

monogamìa *f* monogamy

monòga·mo -ma *adj* monogamous || *m* monogamist

monografìa *f* monograph

monogram·ma *m* (-mi) monogram

monolìti·co -ca *adj* (-ci -che) monolithic

monolito *m* monolith

monòlo·go *m* (-ghi) monologue

monomanìa *f* monomania

monò·mio *m* (-mi) monomial
monopàttino *m* scooter
monopèt·to (-to) *adj* single-breasted ‖ *m* single-breasted suit
monoplano *m* (aer) monoplane
monopò·lio *m* (-li) monopoly
monopolizzare [ddzz] *tr* to monopolize
monopósto *adj invar* one-man ‖ *m* single-seater
monorotàia *adj invar* single-track ‖ *f* monorail
monoscò·pio *m* (-pi) (telv) test pattern
monosìlla·bo -ba *adj* monosyllabic ‖ *m* monosyllable
monòssido *m* monoxide
monoteìsti·co -ca *adj* (-ci -che) monotheistic
monotipìa *f* monotype
monotipo *m* monotype
monotonìa *f* monotony
monòto·no -na *adj* monotonous
monsignóre *m* monsignor
monsóne *m* monsoon
mónta *f* horseback riding; stud; jockey
montacàri·chi *m* (-chi) freight elevator
montàg·gio *m* (-gi) (mach) assembly; (mov) editing; (mov) montage
montagna *f* mountain; **montagna di ghiaccio** iceberg; **montagne russe** roller coaster
montagnó·so -sa [s] *adj* mountainous
montana·ro -ra *adj* mountain ‖ *mf* mountaineer
monta·no -na *adj* mountain
montante *adj* rising ‖ *m* riser, upright; (football) goal post; (aer) strut; (boxing) uppercut; (com) aggregate amount
montare (mónto) *tr* to mount; to go up (*the stairs*); to set (*jewels*); to frame (*a painting*); to whip (*e.g., eggs*); to excite; to exaggerate (*news*); to decorate (*a house*); to cover (*said of a male animal*); (mach) to assemble; (mov) to edit; **montare la testa a** to excite; to give a swell head to ‖ *intr* (ESSERE) to jump; to climb; to go up; to rise; to swell; **montare alla testa a** to go to the head of; **montare in collera** to get angry ‖ *impers*—**non monta** it doesn't matter, never mind
monta·tóre -trice *mf* (mach) assembler; (mov) editor
montatura *f* assembly; frame (*of glasses*); appliqué; setting (*of gem*); (journ) ballyhoo; (mov) editing; **montatura pubblicitaria** publicity stunt
montavivan·de *m* (-de) dumbwaiter
mónte *m* mountain; bank; mount (*in palmistry*); (cards) discard; **a monte** uphill; upstream; **andare a monte** to fail; **mandare a monte** to cause to fail; **monte di pietà** pawnbroker's; **monte di premi** pot (*in a lottery*)
montenegri·no -na *adj & mf* Montenegrin
montessoria·no -na *adj* Montessori
montóne *m* ram; mutton; rounded stone
montuó·so -sa [s] *adj* mountainous
montura *f* uniform

monumentale *adj* monumental
monuménto *m* monument
moquètte *f* (**moquètte**) wall-to-wall carpeting
mòra *f* mulberry; blackberry; brunette; Moorish woman; arrears; penalty (*for arrears*); (archaic) heap of stones
morale *adj* moral ‖ *m* morale; **giù di morale** downcast; **su di morale** in high spirits ‖ *f* morals, ethics; moral (*of a fable*)
moraleggiare §290 (**moraléggio**) *intr* to moralize
moralismo *m* moralism
morali·tà *f* (-tà) morality; morals
moralizzare [ddzz] *tr & intr* to moralize
moratòria *f* moratorium
morbidézza *f* softness
mòrbi·do -da *adj* soft; sleek; pliable ‖ *m* soft ground
morbillo *m* measles
mòrbo *m* disease; plague
morbó·so -sa [s] *adj* morbid
mòrchia *f* sediment; dregs of oil
mordace *adj* biting, mordacious
mordènte *adj* biting; (chem) mordant; (mach) interlocking ‖ *s* strength; (chem) mordant
mòrdere §200 *tr* to bite; to grab; to corrode; **mordere il freno** to champ the bit
mordicchiare §287 (**mordìcchio**) *tr* to nibble
morèl·lo -la *adj* blackish; black (*horse*) ‖ *m* black horse
morènte *adj* dying ‖ *mf* dying person
moré·sco -sca (-schi -sche) *adj* Moresque, Moorish ‖ *f* Moorish dance
morét·to -ta *adj* brunet ‖ *m* Negro boy; dark-skinned boy; chocolate-covered ice-cream bar ‖ *f* Negro girl; dark-skinned girl; mask; (orn) scaup duck
morfè·ma *m* (-mi) morpheme
morfina *f* morphine
morfinòmane *mf* morphine addict
morfologìa *f* morphology
moria *f* pestilence; high mortality
moribón·do -da *adj* moribund
morigera·to -ta *adj* temperate, moderate
morire §201 *intr* (ESSERE) to die; to die out; to end (*said of a street*); **morire di noia** to be bored to death
moritu·ro -ra *adj* about to die, doomed
mormóne *mf* Mormon
mormorare (mórmoro) *tr* to murmur; to whisper ‖ *intr* to murmur; to whisper; to babble (*said of a brook*); to rustle; to gossip
mormori·o *m* (-i) whisper; murmur
mò·ro -ra *adj* Moorish; dark-skinned; dark-brown ‖ *mf* Moor ‖ *m* mulberry tree ‖ *f* see **mora**
morosi·tà [s] *f* (-tà) delinquency (*in paying one's bills*)
moró·so -sa [s] *adj* delinquent (*in paying one's bills*) ‖ *m* (coll) boyfriend; **i morosi** (coll) the lovers ‖ *f* (coll) girl friend
mòrsa *f* vise; (archit) toothing
morsétto *m* clamp; (elec) binding post

morsicare §197 (mòrsico) *tr* to bite
morsicatura *f* bite
morsicchiare §287 (morsìcchio) *tr* to nibble
mòrso *m* bite; bit
mor·tàio *m* (-tài) mortar
mortale *adj* mortal; deadly || *m* mortal
mortali·tà *f* (-tà) mortality
mortarétto *m* firecracker
mòrte *f* death; end; **averla a morte con** to harbor hatred for; **morte civile** (law) attainder, loss of civil rights
mortèlla *f* myrtle
mortificare §197 (mortìfico) *tr* to mortify || *ref* to feel ashamed
mòr·to -ta *adj* dead; still (*life*); **morto di fame** dying of hunger; **morto di paura** scared to death || *mf* dead person, deceased || *m* hidden treasure; (cards) dummy, widow; **fare il morto** to float on one's back; to play possum; **morto di fame** ne'er-do-well, good-for-nothing; **suonare a morto** to toll
mortò·rio *m* (-ri) funeral
mortuà·rio -ria *adj* (-ri -rie) mortuary
mosài·co -ca (-ci -che) *adj* Mosaic || *m* mosaic
mó·sca *f* (-sche) fly; imperial (*beard*); **mosca bianca** one in a million; **mosca cieca** blindman's buff; **fare venire la mosca al naso a** to make angry || **Mosca** *f* Moscow
moscaiòla *f* fly netting; flytrap
moscardino *m* dandy; (zool) dormouse
moscatèl·lo -la *adj* muscat || *m* muscatel
moscato *m* muscat grape; muscat wine
moscerino *m* gnat
moschèa *f* mosque
moschettière *m* musketeer; Italian National soccer player
moschétto *m* musket
moschettóne *m* snap hook
moschici·da *adj* (-di -de) fly-killing
mó·scio -scia *adj* (-sci -sce) flabby, soft
moscóne *m* big fly; pesky suitor
moscovi·ta *adj* & *mf* (-ti -te) Muscovite
Mosè *m* Moses
mòssa *f* gesture; movement; move; fake; post; **fare la mossa** to sprout (*said of plants*); **mossa di corpo** bowel movement; **prendere le mosse** to begin; **stare sulle mosse** to be about to begin; to be eager to take off (*said of a horse*)
mossière *m* starter (*in a race*)
mòs·so -sa *adj* moved; in motion; plowed; rough (*sea*); blurred (*picture*); wavy (*hair; ground*) || *f* see **mossa**
mostarda *f* mustard; candied fruit
mósto *m* must
móstra *f* show; pretense, simulation; exhibit; display window; lapel; face (*of watch*); sample; (mil) insignia; (obs) military parade; **far mostra di sé** to show off; **mettersi in mostra** to show off
mostrare (móstro) *tr* to show; to put on; **mostrare a dito** to point to;

mostrare la corda to be threadbare || *ref* to show up; to show oneself
mostreggiatura *f* lapel; cuff
mostrina *f* (mil) insignia
móstro *m* monster
mostruó·so -sa [s] *adj* monstruous
mòta *f* mud, mire
mo·tèl *m* (-tèl) motel
motivare *tr* to cause; to justify
motivazióne *f* justification, reason
motivo *m* motive, reason; motif; theme; (coll) tune; **a motivo di** because of; **motivo per cui** wherefore
mò·to *m* (-ti) motion; movement; emotion; riot; **mettere in moto** to start || *f* (-to) (coll) motorcycle
motobar·ca *f* (-che) motorboat
motocannonièra *f* gunboat
motocarro *m* three-wheeler (*truck*)
motocarrozzétta *f* three-wheeler (*vehicle with sidecar*)
motociclétta *f* motorcycle
motocicli·sta *mf* (-sti -ste) motorcyclist
motocorazza·to -ta *adj* armored, panzer
motofalciatrice *f* power mower
motofurgóne *m* delivery truck
motolàn·cia *f* (-ce) motorboat, speedboat
motonàuti·co -ca (-ci -che) *adj* motorboat || *f* motorboating
motonave *f* motor ship
motopescheréc·cio *m* (-ci) motor fishing boat
mo·tóre -trice *adj* motive (*power*); (mach) drive || *m* motor; engine; car; **a motore** motorized, motor; **motore rotativo** (aut) rotary engine; **primo motore** prime mover || *f* see **motrice**
motorétta *f* motor scooter
motorino *m* small motor; motor bicycle; **motorino d'avviamento** (aut) starter
motori·sta *m* (-sti) mechanic
motorìsti·co -ca *adj* (-ci -che) motor
motorizzare [ddzz] *tr* to motorize
motoscafo *m* motorboat; **motoscafo da corsa** speedboat
motosé·ga *f* (-ghe) chain saw
motosilurante *f* torpedo boat
motoveìcolo *m* motor vehicle
motovelièro *m* motor sailer
motrice *f* (rr) engine, motor; (aut) tractor; **motrice a vapore** steam engine
motteggiare §290 (mottéggio) *tr* to mock, jeer at || *intr* to jest
mottég·gio *m* (-gi) mockery, jest
mòtto *m* witticism; motto; (lit) word
movènte *m* stimulus, motive
movènza *f* bearing, carriage; flow (*of a sentence*); cadence
movìbile *adj* movable
movimenta·to -ta *adj* lively; eventful
moviménto *m* motion, movement; traffic; **movimento di cassa** cash turnover
moviòla *f* (mov) viewer and splicer
mozióne *f* motion; (lit) movement
mozzare (mózzo) *tr* to lop off; to sever; **mozzare la testa a** to cut off the head of

mozzicóne *m* stump; butt (*e.g., of cigar*)

móz·zo -za *adj* cut off; truncated; cropped (*ears*); docked (*tail*); hard (*breathing*) || *m* cabin boy; **mozzo di stalla** stable boy

mòzzo [ddzz] *m* hub

muc·ca *f* (-**che**) milch cow

mùc·chio *m* (-**chi**) pile, heap; bunch

mucillàgine *f* mucilage

mu·co *m* (-**chi**) mucus, phlegm

mucó·so -sa [s] *adj* mucous || *f* mucous membrane

muda *f* molt

muffa *f* mold; mildew; **fare la muffa** to be musty

muffire §176 *intr* (ESSERE) to be musty

mùffola *f* mitten; muffle (*of furnace*)

muflóne *m* mouflon

mugghiare §287 (**mùgghio**) *intr* to bellow; to roar

mùggine *m* (ichth) mullet

muggire §176 & (**muggo**) *intr* to moo, low; to roar; to howl

muggito *m* bellow; moo, low; roar

mughétto *m* lily of the valley

mu·gnàio -gnàia *mf* (-**gnài -gnàie**) miller

mugolare (**mùgolo**) *intr* to yelp; to moan

mugolì·o *m* (-**i**) yelp; moan

mugò·lio *m* (-**li**) pine tar

mugugnare *intr* (coll) to mumble; (coll) to grumble

mugugno *m* (coll) grumble

mulattière *m* mule driver, muleteer

mulattiè·ro -ra *adj* mule || *f* mule track

mulat·to -ta *adj & mf* mulatto

muliebre *adj* womanly, feminine

mulinare *tr* to twirl; to scheme || *intr* to whirl; to muse; to buzz (*in the mind*)

mulinèllo *m* twirl; whirlpool; whirlwind; fishing reel; whirligig; **fare mulinello con** to twirl

mulino *m* mill; **mulino ad acqua** water mill; **mulino a vento** windmill

mu·lo -la *mf* mule; (slang) bastard

multa *f* penalty, fine

multare *tr* to fine

multilaterale *adj* multilateral, manysided

mùlti·plo -pla *adj & m* multiple

mùmmia *f* mummy

mummificare §197 (**mummìfico**) *tr* to mummify

mùngere §183 *tr* to milk

mungi·tóre -trice *mf* milker || *f* milking machine; milk maid

mungitura *f* milking

municipale *adj* municipal, city

municipalizzazióne [ddzz] *f* municipalization; city management

municì·pio *m* (-**pi**) municipality; city council; city hall

munificènza *f* munificence

munìfi·co -ca *adj* (-**ci -che**) munificent

munire §176 *tr* to fortify; to provide; **munire di** to equip with || *ref* to provide oneself

munizióne *f* (obs) fortification; **munizioni** ammunition; building supplies

muòvere §202 *tr* to move; to wag; to propel, run; to lift (*one's finger*); to take (*a step*); to pose (*a question*); to stir up (*laughter*); to institute (*a lawsuit*); **muovere accusa a** to reproach || *intr* (ESSERE) to begin; to move, start || *ref* to move; to travel; to stir; to set out; to be moved; **muoviti!** hurry up!

mura *fpl* see **muro**

muràglia *f* wall; (fig) obstacle; **muraglia cinese** Chinese Wall

muraglióne *m* high wall, rampart

murale *adj & m* mural

murare *tr* to wall; to wall in || *intr* to build a wall; **murare a secco** to build a dry wall || *ref* to close oneself in

murata *f* (naut) bulwark

muratóre *m* bricklayer, mason

muratura *f* bricklaying, stonework

muriàti·co -ca *adj* (-**ci -che**) muriatic

mu·ro *m* (-**ri**) wall; **muro del pianto** Wailing Wall; **muro del suono** sound barrier || *m* (-**ra** *fpl*)—**mura** walls (*of a city*)

musa *f* muse

muschia·to -ta *adj* musk (*e.g., ox*)

mù·schio *m* (-**schi**) musk; (coll) moss

mu·sco *m* (-**schi**) moss

mùscolo *m* muscle; (fig) sinew; (coll) mussel

muscoló·so -sa [s] *adj* muscular

muscó·so -sa [s] *adj* (lit) mossy

musèo *m* museum

museruòla *f* muzzle

musétta *f* nose bag

mùsi·ca *f* (-**che**) music; band; **cambiare musica** to change one's tune

musicale *adj* musical

musicante *adj* music-playing (*angels*) || *mf* band player; second-rate musician

musicare §197 (**mùsico**) *tr* to set to music

musicassétta *f* cassette, tape cartridge

music-hall *m* (-**hall**) *m* vaudeville, burlesque

musici·sta *mf* (-**sti -ste**) musician

musicologìa *f* musicology

musicòlo·go *m* (-**gi**) musicologist

muso *m* muzzle, snout; (coll) mug; (fig) nose; **avere il muso lungo** to make a long face; **mettere il muso** to pout

musó·ne -na *mf* pouter, sulker

mussare *tr* to publish with great fanfare (*a piece of news*) || *intr* to foam (*said of wine*)

mùssola or **mussolina** *f* muslin

mussolinia·no -na *adj* of Mussolini

mùssolo *m* mussel

mustàc·chio *m* (-**chi**) shroud (*of bowsprit*); **mustacchi** moustache

musulma·no -na [s] *adj & mf* Moslem

muta *f* change; shift; molt; set (*of sails*); pack (*of hounds*); (mil) watch

mutàbile *adj* changeable

mutande *fpl* shorts, briefs, drawers

mutandine *fpl* panties; **mutandine da bagno** trunks

mutare *tr, intr* (ESSERE) & *ref* to change

mutazióne *f* mutation; (biol) mutation, sport

mutévole *adj* changeable; fickle

mutilare (**mùtilo**) *tr* to mutilate, maim
mutila·to **-ta** *adj* mutilated ‖ *mf* cripple; amputee; **mutilato di guerra** disabled veteran
mutismo *m* silence, willful silence; (pathol) dumbness
mu·to **-ta** *adj* mute; dumb; silent (*movie*); unexpressed ‖ *mf* mute ‖ *f* see **muta**
mùtria *f* sulking attitude; proud demeanor

mùtua *f* mutual benefit society; medical insurance; **mettersi in mutua** to go on sick leave
mutuali·tà *f* (**-tà**) mutuality; mutual benefit institutions
mutuare (**mùtuo**) *tr* to borrow; to lend
mutua·to **-ta** *mf* person insured by mutual benefit society; person insured by medical insurance
mù·tuo **-tua** *adj* mutual; borrowing ‖ *m* loan ‖ *f* see **mutua**

N

N, n [ˈenne] *m & f* twelfth letter of the Italian alphabet
nababbo *m* nabob
Nabucodònosor *m* Nebuchadnezzar
nàcchera *f* castanet
nafta *f* crude oil; naphta; Diesel oil
naftalina *f* naphthalene
nàia *f* cobra; (slang) army discipline; (slang) military service
nàiade *f* naiad
nàilon *m* nylon
nanna *f* sleep (*of child*); **fare la nanna** to sleep (*said of child*)
na·no **-na** *adj & mf* dwarf
nàpalm *m* napalm
napoleòne *m* napoleon (*gold coin*) ‖ **Napoleone** *m* Napoleon
napoleòni·co **-ca** *adj* (**-ci** **-che**) Napoleonic
napoleta·no **-na** *adj & mf* Neapolitan ‖ *f* espresso coffee machine
Nàpoli *f* Naples
nappa tassel; tuft; kid (*leather*)
narciso *m* narcissus
narcòti·co **-ca** *adj & m* (**-ci** **-che**) narcotic
narcotizzare [ddzz] *tr* to drug, dope; to anesthetize
narghi·lè *m* (**-lè**) hookah
narice *f* nostril
narrare *tr* to narrate, tell, recount
narrati·vo **-va** *adj* narrative; fictional ‖ *f* narrative; fiction
narra·tóre **-trice** *mf* narrator, storyteller
narrazióne *f* narration; tale, story; narrative
nasale [s] *adj & f* nasal
nascènte *adj* nascent; budding; rising (*sun*); dawning (*day*)
nàscere *m* beginning, origin ‖ §203 *intr* (ESSERE) to be born; to bud; to shoot; to dawn; to rise; to spring up; **nascere con la camicia** to be born with a silver spoon in one's mouth
nàscita *f* birth; birthday; origin
nascitu·ro **-ra** *adj* unborn, future ‖ *mf* unborn child
nascóndere §204 *tr* to hide; **nascondere a** to hide from ‖ *ref* to hide; to lurk
nascondì·glio *m* (**-gli**) hiding place; hideout; cache
nascondino *m* hide-and-seek; **giocare a nascondino** to play hide-and-seek
nascó·sto **-sta** *adj* hidden, concealed; secret; **di nascosto** secretly

nasèllo [s] *m* catch (*of latch*); (ichth) hake
nasièra [s] *f* nose ring
naso [s] *m* nose; (fig) face; **aver buon naso** to have a keen sense of smell; **ficcare il naso negli affari degli altri** to pry into the affairs of others; **menare per il naso** to lead by the nose; **naso adunco** hooknose; **restare con un palmo di naso** to be duped
nassa *f* pot (*for fishing*); **nassa per aragoste** lobster pot
nastrino *m* ribbon; badge
nastro *m* ribbon; band; tape; streamer; tape measure; **nastro del cappello** hatband; **nastro isolante** friction tape; **nastro per capelli** hair ribbon
nastùr·zio *m* (**-zi**) nasturtium
natale *adj* native, natal ‖ **natali** *mpl* birth; birthday; **dare i natali a** to be the birthplace of ‖ **Natale** *m* Christmas
natali·tà *f* (**-tà**) birth rate
natalì·zio **-zia** (**-zi** **-zie**) *adj* natal; Christmas ‖ *m* birthday
natante *adj* swimming; floating ‖ *m* craft
natatóia *f* fin
natató·rio **-ria** *adj* (**-ri** **-rie**) swimming
nàti·ca *f* (**-che**) buttock
nati·o **-a** *adj* (**-i** **-e**) (poet) native
nativi·tà *f* (**-tà**) birth, nativity ‖ **Natività** *f* Nativity
nati·vo **-va** *adj* native; natural, inborn ‖ *mf* native
N.A.T.O. *f* (acronym) (**North Atlantic Treaty Organization**)—**la N.A.T.O.** NATO
na·to **-ta** *adj* born; **nata** née; **nato e sputato** the spit and image of; **nato morto** stillborn ‖ *mf* child
natura *f* nature; **natura morta** still life; **in natura** in kind
naturale *adj* natural ‖ *m* nature, disposition; **al naturale** life-size
naturalézza *f* naturalness; spontaneity
naturalismo *m* naturalism
naturali·sta *mf* (**-sti** **-ste**) naturalist
naturali·tà *f* (**-tà**) naturalization
naturalizzare [ddzz] *tr* to naturalize ‖ *ref* to become naturalized
naturalizzazióne [ddzz] *f* naturalization
naturalménte *adv* naturally; of course
naufragare §209 (**nàufrago**) *intr* (ESSERE

& AVERE) to be shipwrecked; to sink, to fail

naufrà·gio m (-gi) shipwreck; failure

nàufra·go -ga (-ghi -ghe) adj shipwrecked || mf shipwrecked person; (fig) outcast

nàusea f nausea; disgust; **avere la nausea** to be sick at one's stomach

nauseabón·do -da adj sickening, nauseating; (fig) unsavory

nauseante adj sickening, nauseous

nauseare (nàuseo) tr to nauseate, sicken

nausea·to -ta adj sickened, disgusted

nàuti·co -ca (-ci -che) adj nautical || f sailing, navigation

navale adj naval, navy, sea

navata f nave; **navata centrale** nave; **navata laterale** aisle

nave f ship, vessel, boat; craft; **nave ammiraglia** flagship; **nave a motore** motorboat; **nave appoggio** tender; **nave a vela** sailboat; **nave da carico** freighter; **nave da guerra** warship; **nave petroliera** tanker; **nave portaerei** aircraft carrier; **nave rompighiaccio** icebreaker; **nave traghetto** ferryboat

navétta f shuttle; **fare la navetta** to shuttle

navicèlla f nacelle, cabin (of airship); car (of balloon)

navigàbile adj navigable

navigabili·tà f (-tà) navigability; seaworthiness

navigante adj sailing || m sailor

navigare §209 (nàvigo) tr & intr to navigate, to sail

naviga·to -ta adj seawise; wordly-wise

naviga·tóre -trice mf navigator

navigazióne f navigation

navi·glio m (-gli) ship, craft, boat; fleet; navy; canal; **naviglio mercantile** merchant marine

nazionale adj national || f national team

nazionalismo m nationalism

nazionali·sta mf (-sti -ste) nationalist

nazionalìsti·co -ca adj (-ci -che) nationalistic

nazionali·tà f (-tà) nationality

nazionalizzare [ddzz] tr to nationalize

nazionalizzazióne [ddzz] f nationalization

nazióne f nation

nazi·sta adj & mf (-sti -ste) Nazi

nazzarè·no -na [ddzz] adj & mf Nazarene || **il Nazzareno** the Nazarene

ne §5 pron & adv

né conj neither, nor; **né . . . né** neither . . . nor

neanche adv not even; nor; not . . . either

nébbia f fog, haze, mist; **fa nebbia** it is foggy; **nebbia artificiale** smoke screen

nebbióne m thick fog, pea soup

nebbió·so -sa [s] adj foggy, hazy, misty

nebulare adj nebular

nebulizzare [ddzz] tr to atomize

nebulizzatóre [ddzz] m atomizer

nebulósa [s] f nebula

nebulosi·tà [s] f (-tà) fogginess, haziness, mistiness

nebuló·so -sa [s] adj foggy, hazy, misty || f see **nebulosa**

néces·saire m (-saire) vanity case; sewing kit

necessariaménte adv necessarily

necessà·rio -ria (-ri -rie) adj necessary, needed; essential || m necessity; necessities (of life)

necessi·tà f (-tà) necessity; need, want; **di necessità** necessarily

necessitare (necèssito) tr to require; to force || intr to be in want; to be necessary; **necessitare di** to need

necrologìa f necrology, obituary

necrològi·co -ca adj (-ci -che) obituary

necromanzìa f necromancy

necròsi f necrosis, gangrene

nefan·do -da adj heinous, nefarious

nefa·sto -sta adj ill-fated; ominous

nefrite f nephritis

negare §209 (négo & nègo) tr to deny, negate; to refuse

negati·vo -va adj & f negative

nega·to -ta adj unfit, unsuited

negazióne f negation, denial; (gram) negative

neghittó·so -sa [s] adj lazy, slothful

neglèt·to -ta adj neglected; untidy

négli §4

negligènte adj negligent, careless

negligènza f negligence, carelessness; dereliction (of duty)

neglìgere §205 tr to neglect

negoziàbile adj negotiable

negoziante mf merchant, shopkeeper; dealer; **negoziante all'ingrosso** wholesaler; **negoziante al minuto** retailer; shopkeeper, storekeeper

negoziare §287 (negòzio) tr to negotiate, transact || intr to negotiate, deal

negoziati mpl negotiations

negozia·tóre -trice mf negotiator

negò·zio m (-zi) business; transaction; store, shop; **negozio di cancelleria** stationery store

negrière m slave trader; slave driver

negriè·ro -ra adj slave || m slave trader; slave driver

né·gro -gra adj & mf Negro

negromante m sorcerer

néi §4

nél §4

nélla §4

nélle §4

néllo §4

némbo m rain cloud; cloud (e.g., of dust)

Nembròd m Nimrod

nèmesi f invar nemesis || **Nemesi** f Nemesis

nemi·co -ca (-ci -che) adj inimical, hostile, unfriendly; enemy; (fig) adverse || mf enemy, foe; **Il Nemico** the Evil One

nemméno adv not even; nor; not . . . either

nènia f funeral dirge; lamentation

nenùfaro m water lily

nèo m mole (on the skin); flaw, blemish; neon; beauty spot

neoclassicheggiante adj in the direction of the neoclassical

neòfi·ta *mf* (**-ti -te**) neophite
neolati·no -na *adj* Neo-Latin, Romance
neologismo *m* neologism
neomicina *f* neomycin
nèon *m* neon
neona·to -ta *adj* newborn || *mf* infant, baby; newborn child
neozelandése [dz][s] *adj* New Zealand || *mf* New Zealander
nepènte *f* nepenthe
Nepóte *m* Nepos
neppure *adv* not even; nor; not . . . either
nequìzia *f* iniquity, wickedness
nera·stro -stra *adj* blackish
nerbata *f* heavy blow
nèrbo *m* whip; sinew; bulk; strength (*of an opposing force*)
nerboru·to -ta *adj* muscular, sinewy
nereggiare §290 (**neréggio**) *intr* to look black; to be blackish
nerétto *m* (*typ*) boldface
né·ro -ra *adj* black; dark; gloomy; dark-red (*wine*) || *mf* black; Negro || *m* black
nerofumo *m* lampblack
Neróne *m* Nero
nervatura *f* ribbing
nervi·no -na *adj* nerve (*gas*); nervine (*medicine*)
nèrvo *m* nerve; sinew; **avere i nervi** to be in a bad mood
nervosismo [s] *m* nervousness, irritability
nervó·so -sa [s] *adj* nervous, irritable; sinewy, vigorous (*style*) || *m* bad mood; **avere il nervoso** to be in a bad mood
nèsci *m*—**fare il nesci** to feign ignorance
nèspola *f* medlar; **nespole** (coll) blows
nèspolo *m* medlar tree
nèsso *m* connection, link; **avere nesso** to cohere
nessu·no -na *adj* no, not any || **nessuno** *pron* nobody, no one; none; not anybody; not anyone; **nessuno dei due** neither one
nettapén·ne *m* (**-ne**) penwiper
nettare (**nétto**) *tr* to clean, to cleanse
nèttare *m* nectar
nettézza *f* cleanness, cleanliness; neatness; **nettezza urbana** department of sanitation; garbage collection
nét·to -ta *adj* clean; clear; sharp; net || **netto** *adv* clearly, distinctly
nettùnio *m* neptunium
Nettuno *m* Neptune
netturbino *m* street cleaner
neurologìa *f* neurology
neuró·si *f* (**-si**) neurosis
neuròti·co -ca *adj* (**-ci -che**) neurotic
neutrale *adj* & *mf* neutral
neutrali·sta *adj* & *mf* (**-sti -ste**) neutralist
neutrali·tà *f* (**-tà**) neutrality
neutralizzare [ddzz] *tr* to neutralize
nèu·tro -tra *adj* neuter; neutral
neutróne *m* neutron
ne·vàio *m* (**-vài**) snowfield; snowdrift
néve *f* snow; **neve carbonica** dry ice
nevicare §197 (**névica**) *impers* (ESSERE) —**nevica** it is snowing

nevicata *f* snowfall
nevìschio *m* sleet
nevó·so -sa [s] *adj* snowy
nevralgìa *f* neuralgia
nevrastèni·co -ca *adj* & *mf* (**-ci -che**) neurasthenic
nevvéro (i.e., **n'è vero** for **non è vero**) see **non**
niacina *f* niacin
nib·bio *m* (**-bi**) (orn) kite
nìcchia *f* niche; nook, recess
nicchiare §287 (**nìcchio**) *intr* to waver
nìc·chio *m* (**-chi**) shell; nook
nichel *m* nickel
nichelare (**nìchelo**) *tr* to nickel, to nickel-plate
nichelatura *f* nickel-plating
nichelino *m* nickel (*coin*)
nichèlio *m* var of **nichel**
Nicòla *m* Nicholas
nicotina *f* nicotine
nidiata *f* nestful; brood
nidificare §197 (**nidìfico**) *intr* to build a nest, to nest
nido *m* nest; home; nursery; den (*of thieves*)
niènte *m* nothing; nothingness; **dal niente** from scratch; **di niente** you're welcome || *pron* nothing; not . . . anything; **quasi niente** next to nothing
nientediméno *adv* no less, nothing less
Nilo *m* Nile
ninfa *f* nymph
ninfèa *f* white water lily
ninnananna *f* lullaby, cradlesong
nìnnolo *m* toy; trinket
nipóte *mf* grandchild || *m* grandson; nephew; **nipoti** descendants || *f* granddaughter; niece
nippòni·co -ca *adj* (**-ci -che**) Nipponese
nirvana, il nirvana
nìti·do -da *adj* clear, distinct
nitóre *m* brightness; elegance
nitrato *m* nitrate
nitrire §176 *intr* to neigh
nitrito *m* neigh; (chem) nitrite
nitro *m* niter; **nitro del Cile** Chile saltpeter
nitroglicerina *f* nitroglycerin
nitruro *m* nitride
niu·no -na *adj* (poet) var of **nessuno**
nìve·o -a *adj* snow-white
Nizza *f* Nice
no *adv* no; not; **come no?** why not; certainly; **dire di no** to say no; **no?** is it not so?; **non dir di no** to consent; **proprio no** certainly not
nòbile *adj* noble; second (*floor*) || *m* nobleman || *f* noblewoman
nobiliare *adj* noble, of nobility
nobilitare (**nobìlito**) *tr* to ennoble
nobil·tà *f* (**-tà**) nobility
nòc·ca *f* (**-che**) knuckle
nocchière *m* or **nocchièro** *m* petty officer; (poet) pilot, helmsman
nocchieru·to -ta *adj* knotty
nòc·chio *m* (**-chi**) knot (*in wood*)
nocciòla *adj invar* hazel (*in color*) || *f* hazelnut; filbert
nocciolina *f* little nut; **nocciolina americana** peanut; roasted peanut
nòcciolo *m* stone, pit, kernel; **il noc-**

ciolo della questione the crux of the matter

nocciòlo *m* hazel (*tree*); filbert (*tree*)

nóce *m* walnut tree || *f* walnut (*fruit*); noce del collo Adam's apple; noce di cocco coconut; noce di vitello filet of veal; noce moscata nutmeg

nocévole *adj* harmful

noci•vo -va *adj* harmful, detrimental

nòdo *m* knot; crux, gist (*of a question*); junction; lump (*in one's throat*); (naut) knot; (phys) node; lì è il nodo there's the rub; nodo d'amore true-love knot; nodo ferroviario rail center, junction; nodo scorsoio noose; nodo stradale highway center, cross-roads

nodó•so -sa [s] *adj* knotty

Noè *m* Noah

noi §5 *pron pers* we; us; noi altri we, e.g., noi altri italiani we Italians

nòia *f* boredom; bother, trouble; bug (*in a motor*); venire a noia (with *dat*) to weary; dar noia (with *dat*) to bother

noial•tri -tre *pron* we; us; noialtri italiani we Italians

noió•so -sa [s] *adj* boring, annoying

noleggiare §290 (noléggio) *tr* to rent; to hire, to charter || *ref*—si noleggia, si noleggiano for rent

noleggiatóre *m* hirer; lessor (*e.g., of a car*)

nolég•gio *m* (-gi) rent, lease; car rental; chartering; freightage

nolènte *adj* unwilling

nòlo *m* rent, hire; a nolo for hire

nòmade *adj* nomad, nomadic || *mf* nomad

nóme *m* name; fame; reputation; (gram) noun; a nome di on behalf of; in nome di in the name of; nome commerciale firm name; nome depositato registered name; nome di battesimo Christian name; nome e cognome full name

nomèa *f* name, reputation; notoriety

nomìgnolo *m* nickname; affibbiare un nomignolo a to nickname

nòmina *f* appointment; di prima nomina newly appointed

nominale *adj* nominal; noun

nominare (nòmino) *tr* to name, call; to mention; to elect; to appoint

nominati•vo -va *adj* nominative; with names in alphabetical order; (fin) registered || *m* nominative; name; model number

non *adv* no, not; none, e.g., non troppo presto none too soon; non appena as soon as; non c'è di che you are welcome; non . . . che but, only; non è vero? is it not so?, isn't it so? La traduzione in inglese di questa domanda dipende generalmente dalla proposizione che la precede. Se la proposizione è affermativa, l'interrogazione sarà negativa, p.es. Lei mi scriverà, non è vero? You will write me. Won't you? Se la proposizione è negativa, l'interrogazione sarà positiva, p.es. Lei non beve birra, non è

vero? You do not drink beer. Do you? Se il soggetto della proposizione è un nome sostantivo, sarà rappresentato nell'interrogazione da un pronome personale, p.es. Giovanni ha finito, non è vero? John has finished. Hasn't he?

nonagenà•rio -ria *adj* & *mf* (-ri -rie) nonagenarian

nonagèsi•mo -ma *adj, pron* & *m* ninetieth

nonconformi•sta *mf* (-sti -ste) nonconformist

noncurante *adj* careless, indifferent

noncuranza *f* carelessness, indifference

nondiméno *conj* yet, nevertheless

nòn•no -na *mf* grandparent || *m* grandfather || *f* grandmother

nonnulla *m invar* nothing, trifle

nò•no -na *adj, m* & *pron* ninth

nonostante *prep* in spite of, notwithstanding; nonostante che although, even though

nonpertanto *adv* nevertheless, still, yet

non plus ultra *m* ne plus ultra, acme

nonsènso *m* nonsense

non so ché *adj invar* indefinable || *m invar* something indefinable

nontiscordardi•mé *m* (-mé) forget-me-not

nòrd *m* north

nòrdi•co -ca (-ci -che) *adj* Nordic; northern, north || *mf* northerner

nòrma *f* rule, regulation; a norma di legge according to law; per Sua norma for your guidance

normale *adj* normal; normative; perpendicular || *f* perpendicular line

normali•tà *f* (-tà) normality, normalcy

normalizzare [ddzz] *tr* to normalize, to standardize

Normandìa, la Normandy

norman•no -na *adj* & *mf* Norman || *m* Norseman

normati•vo -va *adj* normative || *f* normativeness

normògrafo *m* stencil

norvegése [s] *adj* & *mf* Norwegian

Norvègia, la Norway

nosocò•mio *m* (-mi) hospital

nossignóra (*i.e.*, no signora) *adv* no, Madam

nossignóre (*i.e.*, no signore) *adv* no, Sir

nostalgìa *f* nostalgia, longing; home-sickness

nostàlgi•co -ca (-ci -che) *adj* nostalgic; homesick || *m* worshiper of the good old days (*esp. of Fascism*)

nostra•no -na *adj* domestic, national; home-grown; regional

nò•stro -stra §6 *adj* & *pron poss*

nostròmo *m* boatswain

nòta *f* mark; score; memorandum; list; bill, invoice; report (*on a subordinate*); (mus) note; note caratteristiche personal folder, efficiency report (*of an employee*); prender nota di to take down

notàbile *adj* notable, noteworthy || *m* notable

no•tàio *m* (-tài) notary (public); lawyer

notare (nòto) *tr* to mark, check; to note, to jot down; to observe; to bring out; **farsi notare** to attract attention, make oneself conspicuous; **nota bene** note well, take notice

notariale or **notarile** *adj* notarial

notazióne *f* notation; annotation; observation

nò•tes *m* (-tes) notebook

notévole *adj* noteworthy, remarkable

notifi•ca *f* (-che) notification, notice; service (*e.g., of a summons*)

notificare §197 **(notìfico)** *tr* to report; to serve (*a summons*); to declare ..(*e.g., one's income*)

notificazióne *f* notification, notice; service (*e.g., of a summons*)

notìzia *f* knowledge; report; piece of news; **aver notizie di** to hear from; **notizie** news; **una notizia** a news item

notizià•rio *m* (-ri) news; news report, news bulletin; (rad) newscast; **notiziario sportivo** sports page; (rad, telv) sports news

nò•to -ta *adj* known, well-known ‖ *m* south wind; (coll) swimming ‖ *f* see **nota**

notorie•tà *f* (-tà) general knowledge; affidavit; notoriety

notò•rio -ria *adj* (-ri -rie) well-known

nottàmbu•lo -la *adj* nighttime; night-wandering ‖ *mf* nightwalker; night owl

nottata *f* night; **far nottata bianca** to spend a sleepless night

nòtte *f* night; **buona notte** good night; **di notte** at night, by night, in the nighttime; **la notte di lunedì** Sunday night; Monday night; **lunedì notte** Monday night; **notte bianca** sleepless night; **notte di San Silvestro** New Year's Eve; watch night

nottetèmpo *adv*—**di nottetempo** at night, in the nighttime

nòttola *f* wooden latch; (zool) bat

nottolino *m* small wooden latch; ratchet, catch

nottur•no -na *adj* nocturnal, night ‖ *m* nocturne

novanta *adj, m & pron* ninety

novantènne *adj* ninety-year-old ‖ *mf* ninety-year-old person

novantèsi•mo -ma *adj, m & pron* nine-tieth

novantina *f* about ninety; **sulla novantina** about ninety years old

nòve *adj & pron* nine; **le nove** nine o'clock ‖ *m* nine; ninth (*in dates*)

novecentismo *m* twentieth-century arts and letters

novecenti•sta (-sti -ste) *adj* twentieth-century ‖ *mf* artist of the twentieth century

novecènto *adj, m & pron* nine hundred ‖ **il Novecento** the twentieth century

novèla *f* short story; (poet) news

novelliè•re -ra *mf* storyteller; short-story writer

novelli•no -na *adj* early, tender; inexperienced, green

novellìstica *f* storytelling; fiction

novèl•lo -la *adj* fresh, young, tender; new ‖ *f* see **novella**

novèmbre *m* November

novenà•rio -ria *adj* (-ri -rie) nine-syllable

noverare (nòvero) *tr* to count; to enumerate; (poet) to remember

nòvero *m* number; class

novilù•nio *m* (-ni) new moon

novìssi•mo -ma *adj* (lit) last, newest

novi•tà *f* (-tà) newness, originality; novelty, innovation; latest idea; late news

noviziato *m* novitiate; apprenticeship

novì•zio -zia (-zi -zie) *mf* novice; apprentice ‖ *f* novice (*in a convent*)

novocaìna *f* novocaine

nozióne *f* notion, conception

nòzze *fpl* wedding, marriage; **nozze d'argento** silver wedding; **nozze d'oro** golden wedding

nube *f* cloud

nubifrà•gio *m* (-gi) cloudburst

nùbile *adj* unmarried, single (*woman*); marriageable ‖ *f* unmarried girl

nu•ca *f* (-che) nape of the neck, scruff

nucleare *adj* nuclear

nùcleo *m* nucleus; group; (elec) core

nudismo *m* nudism

nudi•sta *adj & mf* (-sti -ste) nudist

nudi•tà *f* (-tà) nudity, nakedness

nu•do -da *adj* naked, bare; barren; simple; **mettere a nudo** to lay bare; **nudo e crudo** stark-naked; destitute ‖ *m* nude

nùgolo *m* cloud; throng, swarm

nulla *pron* nothing ‖ *m invar* nothing; nothingness

nulla òsta *m* permission; visa

nullatenènte *adj* poor ‖ *mf* have-not

nullificare §197 **(nullìfico)** *tr* to nullify

nulli•tà *f* (-tà) nothingness; nonentity; invalidity (*of a document*)

nul•lo -la *adj* void, worthless ‖ **nullo** *pron* (poet) none, no one ‖ **nulla** *m & pron* see **nulla**

nume *m* divinity, deity

numerare (nùmero) *tr* to number

numeratóre *m* numerator; numbering machine

numèri•co -ca *adj* (-ci -che) numerical

nùmero *m* number; lottery ticket; size (*of shoes*); **numero dispari** odd number; **numero legale** quorum; **numero pari** even number

numeró•so -sa [s] *adj* numerous, large; harmonious

nùn•zio *m* (-zi) nuncio; (poet) news

nuòcere §206 *intr* to be harmful; (with *dat*) to harm

nuòra *f* daughter-in-law

nuotare (nuòto) *intr* to swim; to float; to wallow (*in wealth*)

nuotata *f* swim, dip, plunge

nuota•tóre -trice *mf* swimmer

nuòto *m* swimming; **gettarsi a nuoto** to jump into the water; **traversare a nuoto** to swim across

nuòva *f* news; late news

Nuòva York *f* New York
Nuova Zelanda, la [dz] New Zealand
nuòvo -va *adj* new; **di nuovo** again; **nuovo di zecca** brand-new; **nuovo fiammante** brand-new; **nuovo venuto** new arrival || *m*—**il nuovo** the new || *f* see **nuova**
nùtria *f* coypu
nutrice *f* wet nurse; (lit) provider
nutriènte *adj* nourishing
nutriménto *m* nourishment
nutrire §176 & (**nutro**) *tr* to nourish;

to nurture; to harbor (*e.g., hatred*) || *ref*—**nutrirsi di** to feed on or upon
nutriti·vo -va *adj* nutritious, nutritive
nutri·to -ta *adj* well-fed; strong; rich (*food*); brisk, heavy (*gunfire*)
nutrizióne *f* nutrition; food
nùvo·lo -la *adj* cloudy || *m* cloudy weather; (lit) cloud; (fig) swarm || *f* cloud
nuvoló·so -sa [s] *adj* cloudy
nuziale *adj* wedding, nuptial
nuzialità *f* marriage rate

O

O, o [o] *m & f* thirteenth letter of the Italian alphabet
o *conj* or; now; **o . . . o** either . . . or; whether . . . or || *interj* oh!
òa·si *f* (-si) oasis
obbediènte *adj* var of **ubbidiente**
obbediènza *f* obedience
obbedire §176 *tr & intr* var of **ubbidire**
obbiettare (**obbiètto**) *tr & intr* var of **obiettare**
obbligare §209 (**òbbligo**) *tr* to oblige; to compel, to force || *ref* to obligate oneself
obbligatìssi·mo -ma *adj* much obliged
obbligatò·rio -ria *adj* (-ri -rie) compulsory, obligatory
obbligazióne *f* obligation; burden; (com) debenture, bond
obbligazioni·sta *mf* (-sti -ste) bondholder
òbbli·go *m* (-ghi) obligation; duty; **d'obbligo** obligatory, mandatory; **fare d'obbligo a qlcu** + *inf* to be necessary for s.o. to + *inf, e.g.,* **gli fa d'obbligo lavorare** it is necessary for him to work
obbrò·brio *m* (-bri) opprobrium, disgrace; **obbrobri** insults
obbrobrió·so -sa [s] *adj* opprobrious, disgraceful
obeli·sco *m* (-schi) obelisk
obera·to -ta *adj* overburdened
obesità *f* obesity
obè·so -sa *adj* obese, stout
òbice *m* howitzer
obiettare (**obiètto**) *tr & intr* to argue; to object
obietti·vo -va *adj & m* objective
obiettóre *m* objector; **obiettore di coscienza** conscientious objector
obiezióne *f* objection
obitò·rio *m* (-ri) morgue
oblare (**òblo**) *tr* to willingly pay (*a fine*)
obla·tóre -trice *mf* donor
oblazióne *f* donation; (eccl) oblation; (law) payment of a fine
obliare §119 *tr* (lit) to forget
oblì·o *m* (-i) (lit) oblivion
oblì·quo -qua *adj* oblique
obliterare (**oblìtero**) *tr to* obliterate, cancel
o·blò *m* (-blò) (naut) porthole; **oblò di accesso** door (*of space capsule*)

oblun·go -ga *adj* (-ghi -ghe) oblong
òbo·e *m* (-e) oboe
oboi·sta *mf* (-sti -ste) oboist
òbolo *m* mite
ò·ca *f* (-che) goose; gander
ocarina *f* ocarina, sweet potato
occasionale *adj* chance; immediate (*cause*)
occasionare (**occasióno**) *tr* to occasion
occasióne *f* occasion; opportunity; ground, pretext; bargain; **all'occasione** on occasion; **d'occasione** second-hand; occasional (*verses*)
occhiàia *f* eye socket; **occhiaie** rings under the eyes
occhia·làio *m* (-lài) optician
occhiale *adj* eye, ocular || **occhiali** *mpl* glasses; goggles; **occhiali antisole** sunglasses; **occhiali a stringinaso** nose glasses
occhialétto *m* lorgnon; monocle
occhiata *f* glance
occhieggiare §290 (**occhiéggio**) *tr* to eye || *intr* to peep
occhièllo *m* buttonhole; boutonniere; eyelet; half title; subhead
occhièra *f* eyecup
òc·chio *m* (-chi) eye; speck of grease (*in soup*); handle (*of scissors*); ring (*of stirrup*); (typ) face; (fig) bit; **a occhio e croce** at a rough guess; **a quattr'occhi** in private; **battere gli occhi** to blink; **cavarsi gli occhi** to strai.n one's eyes; **dar nell'occhio** to attract attention; **di buon occhio** favorably; **fare l'occhio a** to get used to; **fare tanto d'occhi** to be amazed, to open one's eyes wide; **lasciare gli occhi su** to covet; **non chiudere un occhio** not to sleep a wink; **occhio!** watch out!; **occhio della testa** outrageous price; **occhio di bue** (naut) porthole; **occhio di cubia** (naut) hawsehole; **occhio di pavone** (zool) peacock butterfly; **occhio di triglia** sheep's eyes; **occhio pesto** black eye; **occhio pollino** corn (*on toes*); **tenere d'occhio** to keep an eye on
occhiolino *m* small eye; **far l'occhiolino** to wink
occidentale *adj* western, occidental
occidènte *adj* (poet) setting (*sun*) || *m* west, occident

occìpite *m* occipital bone
occlusióne *f* occlusion
occlusi·vo -va *adj* & *f* occlusive
occlu·so -sa *adj* occluded
occorrènte *adj* necessary || *m* necessary; (lit) occurrence
occorrènza *f* necessity; all'occorrenza if need be
occórrere §139 *intr* (ESSERE) to happen; (with *dat*) to need, e.g., gli occorre dell'olio he needs oil || *impers* (ESSERE)—occorre it is necessary
occultaménto *m* concealment
occultare *tr* & *ref* to hide
occul·to -ta *adj* occult; (lit) hidden
occupante *adj* occupying || *m* occupant
occupare (òccupo) *tr* to occupy; to employ || *ref* to take employment; occuparsi di to busy oneself with, to mind; to attend to
occupa·to -ta *adj* occupied; busy
occupazionale *adj* occupational
occupazióne *f* occupation
oceàni·co -ca *adj* (-ci -che) oceanic
ocèano *m* ocean
òcra *f* ocher
oculare *adj* ocular; see testimone || *m* eyepiece
oculatézza *f* circumspection, prudence
ocula·to -ta *adj* circumspect, prudent
oculi·sta *mf* (-sti -ste) oculist
od *conj* or
odali·sca *f* (-sche) odalisque
òde *f* ode
odepòri·co -ca (-ci -che) *adj* (lit) travel || *m* (lit) travelogue
odiare §287 (òdio) *tr* to hate
odièr·no -na *adj* today's, current
ò·dio *m* (-di) hatred; avere in odio to hate; essere in odio a to be hated by
odió·so -sa [s] *adj* hateful, odious
odissèa *f* odyssey || Odissea *f* Odyssey
Odissèo *m* Odysseus
odontoia·tra *mf* (-tri -tre) doctor of dental surgery, dentist
odontoiatrìa *f* odontology, dentistry
odorare (odóro) *tr* & *intr* to smell
odora·to -ta *adj* (poet) fragrant || *m* smell
odóre *m* smell, odor, scent; cattivo odore bad odor; odori herbs, spice
odoró·so -sa [s] *adj* odorous, fragrant
offèndere §148 *tr* & *intr* to offend || *ref* to take offense
offensi·vo -va *adj* & *f* offensive
offensóre *m* offender
offerènte *mf* bidder; miglior offerente highest bidder
offèrta *f* offer; offering, donation; (*at an auction*) bid; (com) supply
offésa [s] *f* offense; wrongdoing; ravage (*of time*); da offesa (mil) offensive; recarsi a offesa qlco to regard s.th as offensive
officina *f* shop, workshop; officina meccanica machine shop
officló·so -sa [s] *adj* helpful, obliging
offrire §207 *tr* to offer; to sponsor (*a radio or TV program*); to dedicate (*a book*); to bid (*at an auction*); (com) to tender || *ref* to offer oneself, to volunteer

offuscare §197 *tr* to darken, obscure; to obfuscate; to dim (*mind; eyes*) || *ref* to grow dark; to grow dim
oftàlmi·co -ca *adj* (-ci -che) opthalmic
oftalmòlo·go -ga *mf* (-gi -ghe) ophthalmologist
oggettività *f* objectivity
oggetti·vo -va *adj* & *m* objective
oggètto *m* object; subject, argument; article; oggetti preziosi valuables
òggi *m* today; dall'oggi al domani suddenly; overnight || *adv* today; d'oggi in poi henceforth; oggi a otto a week hence; oggi come oggi at present; oggi è un anno one year ago
oggidì *m invar* & *adv* nowadays
oggigiórno *m invar* & *adv* nowadays
ogiva *f* ogive, pointed arch; nose cone
ógni *adj indef invar* each; every, e.g., ogni due giorni every two days; ogni cosa everything; ogni tanto every now and then; per ogni dove (lit) everywhere
ogniqualvòlta *conj* whenever
Ognissan·ti *m* (-ti) All Saints' Day
ognitèmpo *adj invar* all-weather
-ógno·lo -la *suf adj* -ish, e.g., giallognolo yellowish
ognóra *adv* (lit) always
ognu·no -na *adj* (obs) each || *pron* each one, everyone
oh *interj* oh!
òhi *interj* ouch!
ohibò *interj* fie!
ohimè *interj* alas!
ohm *m* (ohm) ohm
olanda *f* Dutch linen || l'Olanda *f* Holland
olandése [s] *adj* Dutch || *m* Dutch (*language*); Dutchman; Dutch cheese || *f* Dutch woman
oleandro *m* oleander
oleà·rio -ria *adj* (-ri -rie) oil
olea·to -ta *adj* oiled
oleifì·cio *m* (-ci) oil mill
oleodótto *m* pipeline
oleó·so -sa [s] *adj* oily
olezzare [ddzz] (olézzo) *intr* (lit) to smell sweet
olézzo [ddzz] *m* perfume, fragrance
olfatto *m* smell
oliare §287 (òlio) *tr* to oil
oliatóre *m* oiler, oil can
olìbano *m* frankincense
olièra *f* cruet
oligarchìa *f* oligarchy
olimpìade *f* Olympiad
olìmpi·co -ca *adj* (-ci -che) Olympic; Olympian
olimpiòni·co -ca *adj* (-ci -che) Olympic || *mf* Olympic athlete
ò·lio *m* (-li) oil; ad olio oil, e.g., quadro ad olio oil painting; olio di fegato di merluzzo cod-liver oil; olio di lino linseed oil; olio di ricino castor oil; olio solare sun-tan lotion
oliva *f* olive
oliva·stro -stra *adj* livid; swarthy || *m* wild olive (*tree*)
olivéto *m* olive grove
Olivièro *m* Oliver
olivo *m* olive tree

ólmo *m* elm tree

olocàu·sto -sta *adj* (lit) burnt; (lit) sacrificed ‖ *m* holocaust; sacrifice

ològra·fo -fa *adj* holographic

olóna *f* sailcloth, canvas

oltracciò *adv* besides

oltraggiare §290 *tr* to outrage; to insult

oltràg·gio *m* (-gi) outrage; offense; ravages (*of time*); **oltraggio al pudore** offense to public morals; **oltraggio al tribunale** contempt of court

oltraggió·so -sa [s] *adj* outrageous

oltranza *f*—**a oltranza** to the bitter end

oltranzi·sta *mf* (-sti -ste) (pol) extremist

óltre *adv* beyond; ahead; further; **oltre a** apart from; in addition to; **troppo oltre** too far ‖ *prep* beyond; past; more than

oltrecortina *adj invar* beyond-the-iron-curtain ‖ *m* country beyond the iron curtain

oltremare *m invar* country overseas ‖ *adv* overseas

oltremisura *adv* (lit) beyond measure

oltremòdo *adv* (lit) exceedingly

oltrepassare *tr* to overstep; to cross (*a river*); to be beyond (. . . *years old*); (sports) to overtake

oltretómba *m*—**l'oltretomba** the life beyond

omàg·gio *m* (-gi) homage; compliment; **in omaggio** complimentary; **rendere omaggio a** to pay tribute to

òmaro *m* Norway lobster

ombeli·co *m* (-chi) navel

ómbra *f* shade; shadow; umbrage; form, mass; **nemmeno per ombra** not in the least

ombreggiare §290 (**ombréggio**) *tr* to shade

ombrèlla *f* shade (*of trees*); (bot) umbel; (coll) umbrella

ombrel·làio *m* (-lài) umbrella maker

ombrellino *m* parasol

ombrèllo *m* umbrella

ombrellóne *m* beach umbrella

ombró·so -sa [s] *adj* shady; touchy; skittish (*horse*)

omelette *f* (**omelette**) omelet

omelìa *f* homily

omeopàti·co -ca (-ci -che) *adj* homeopathic ‖ *m* homeopathist

omèri·co -ca *adj* (-ci -che) Homeric

òmero *m* (anat) humerus; (lit) shoulder

omertà *f* code of silence of underworld

ométtere §198 *tr* to omit

ométto *m* little man; (coll) clothes hanger; (billiards) pin; (archit) king post

omici·da (-di -de) *adj* homicidal, murderous ‖ *mf* homicide, murderer

omici·dio *m* (-di) homicide, murder; **omicidio colposo** (law) manslaughter; **omicidio doloso** (law) first-degree murder

ominó·so -sa [s] *adj* (lit) ominous

omissióne *f* omission

òmni·bus *m* (-bus) omnibus; way train

omnisciènte *adj* all-knowing, omniscient

omogène·o -a *adj* homogeneous

omologare §209 (**omòlogo**) *tr* to con-firm, ratify; to probate (*a will*); (sports) to validate

omòni·mo -ma *adj* of the same name ‖ *m* namesake; homonym

omosessuale [s] *adj* & *mf* homosexual

ón·cia *f* (-ce) ounce; **oncia a oncia** little by little

ónda *f* wave; **a onde** wavy; wavily; **essere in onda** (rad, telv) to be on the air; **farsi le onde** to have one's hair waved; **mettere in onda** (rad, telv) to put on the air; **onda crespa** whitecap; **onda portante** (rad, telv) carrier wave

ondata *f* wave, billow; gust (*e.g., of smoke*); rush (*of blood*); wave (*of cold weather*)

ondatra *f* muskrat

ónde *pron* from which; of which ‖ *adv* whereof; hence; (poet) wherefrom ‖ *prep* **onde** + *inf* in order to ‖ *conj* **onde** + *subj* so that

ondeggiante *adj* waving, swaying

ondeggiare §290 (**ondéggio**) *intr* to wave, sway; to waver

ondina *f* mermaid; (mythol) undine; (mythol) mermaid

ondó·so -sa [s] *adj* wavy

ondulare (**óndulo** & **òndulo**) *tr* to wave; to corrugate (*e.g., metal*) ‖ *intr* to sway

ondula·to -ta *adj* wavy (*hair*); corrugated (*e.g., metal*); bumpy (*road*)

ondulazióne *f* undulation; **ondulazione permanente** permanent wave

-óne -óna *suf mf* big, e.g., **librone** big book; **dormigliona** big sleeper ‖ **-óne** *suf m* (applies to both sexes) big, e.g., **donnone** *m* big woman

ònere *m* (lit) onus, burden

oneró·so -sa [s] *adj* onerous, burdensome

onestà *f* honesty; (poet) modesty

onè·sto -sta *adj* honest; fair; (poet) modest ‖ *m* moderate amount; honest gain; honest person

ònice *m* onyx

onnipossènte & **onnipotènte** *adj* almighty, omnipotent

onnisciènte *adj* omniscient

onniveggènte *adj* all-seeing

onnìvo·ro -ra *adj* omnivorous

onomàsti·co -ca (-ci -che) *adj* onomastic ‖ *m* name day ‖ *f* study of proper names

onomatopèi·co -ca *adj* (-ci -che) onomatopeic

onoràbile *adj* honorable

onoranza *f* honor; **onoranze** homage; **onoranze funebri** obsequies

onorare (**onóro**) *tr* to honor ‖ *ref* to deem it an honor

onorà·rio -ria (-ri -rie) *adj* honorary ‖ *m* fee, honorarium

onora·to -ta *adj* honored; honest; honorable

onóre *m* honor; **d'onore** honest, e.g., **uomo d'onore** honest man; **estremi onori** last rites; **fare gli onori di casa** to receive guests; **fare onore a** to honor; **onore al merito** credit where credit is due; **onor del mento** (lit) beard

onorévole *adj* honorable ‖ *m* honorable member (*of parliament*)

onorificènza *f* dignity; decoration

onorìfi•co -ca *adj* (**-ci -che**) honorific; honorary (*e.g., title*)

ónta *f* dishonor, shame; **a onta di** in spite of; **avere onta** to be ashamed; **fare onta a** to bring shame upon; **in onta a** against

ontano *m* alder

O.N.U. (acronym) *f* (**Organizzazione delle Nazioni Unite**) United Nations, U.N.

onu•sto -sta *adj* (poet) laden

opa•co -ca *adj* (**-chi -che**) opaque

opale *m* opal

opali•no -na *adj* opaline ‖ *f* shiny cardboard; luster (*fabric*)

òpera *f* work; organization, foundation; day's work; (mus) opera; **mettere in opera** to install; to start work on; to make ready; to begin using; **opera di consultazione** reference work; **opera morta** (naut) upper works; **opera viva** (naut) quickwork; **per opera di** thanks to

ope•ràio -ràia (**-rài -ràie**) *adj* workman's, worker's; working ‖ *m* workman, worker; **operaio a cottimo** pieceworker; **operaio a giornata** day laborer; **operaio specializzato** craftsman, skilled workman ‖ *f* workwoman

operante *adj* actively engaged; operative

operare (**òpero**) *tr* to operate; to work (*a miracle*); (surg) to operate on ‖ *intr* to operate; to be actively engaged ‖ *ref* to be operated on; to occur, take place

operati•vo -va *adj* operative; operations, e.g., **ricerca operativa** operations research

opera•to -ta *adj* operated; embossed ‖ *m* behavior; patient operated on

opera•tóre -trice *mf* operator ‖ *m* (mov) cameraman

operatò•rio -ria *adj* (**-ri -rie**) surgical (*operation*); operating (*room*); (math) operational

operazióne *f* operation; transaction

operétta *f* short work; (mus) operetta

operìsti•co -ca *adj* (**-ci -che**) operatic

operosi•tà [s] *f* (**-tà**) industry

operó•so -sa [s] *adj* industrious; active

opi•mo -ma *adj* (lit) fat; rich, fertile

opinare *intr* to opine, deem

opinióne *f* opinion

opòs•sum *m* (**-sum**) opossum

oppia•to -ta *adj* opiate (*mixed with opium*); dulled by drugs ‖ *m* opiate (*medicine containing opium*)

òppio *m* opium

oppiòmane *adj* opium-eating; opium-smoking ‖ *mf* opium addict

oppórre §218 *tr* to oppose; to offer, put up (*resistance*) ‖ *ref* to be opposite; **opporsi a** to oppose, to be against

opportuni•sta *mf* (**-sti -ste**) opportunist

opportuni•tà *f* (**-tà**) opportunity; opportuneness

opportu•no -na *adj* opportune

opposi•tóre -trice *mf* opponent

opposizióne *f* opposition; (law) appeal; **fare opposizione a** to object to

oppó•sto -sta *adj* opposite; contrary ‖ *m* opposite; **all'opposto** on the contrary

oppressióne *f* oppression

oppressi•vo -va *adj* oppressive

opprès•so -sa *adj* oppressed; overcome, overwhelmed ‖ **oppressi** *mpl* oppressed people

oppressóre *m* oppressor

opprimènte *adj* oppressive

opprìmere §131 *tr* to oppress; to overcome, overwhelm; to weigh down

oppugnare *tr* to refute, contradict

oppure *adv* otherwise ‖ *conj* or else; or rather

optare (**òpto**) *intr* to choose; (com) to exercise an option

optometri•sta *mf* (**-sti -ste**) optometrist

opulèn•to -ta *adj* opulent

opùscolo *m* booklet, brochure, pamphlet; **opuscolo d'informazioni** instruction manual

opzióne *f* option

ór *adv* now; **or ora** right now; **or sono** ago

óra *f* hour; time; period (*in school*); **alla buon'ora!** finally!; **a ore** by the hour; **a tarda ora** late; **che ora è?** or **che ore sono?** what time is it?; **da un'ora all'altra** from one moment to the next; **dell'ultima ora** up-to-date (*news*); **di buon'ora** early; early in the morning; **di ora in ora** at any moment; **d'ora in avanti** from this moment on; **d'ora in poi** from now on; **far l'ora** to kill time; **fin ora** until now; **non vedere l'ora di** + *inf* to be hardly able to wait until + *ind*; **ora di cena** suppertime; **ora di punta** rush hour, peak hour; **ora legale** daylight-saving time; **ore piccole** late hours; **un'ora di orologio** one full hour ‖ *adv* now

oràcolo *m* oracle

òra•fo -fa *adj* goldsmith's ‖ *m* goldsmith

orale *adj* & *m* oral

oralménte *adv* orally; by word of mouth

oramài *adv* now; already

oran•go *m* (**-ghi**) orangutan

orà•rio -ria (**-ri -rie**) *adj* hourly; per hour; clockwise ‖ *m* timetable; schedule; roster; **essere in orario** to be on time; **orario di lavoro** working hours; **orario d'ufficio** office hours

ora•tóre -trice *mf* orator

oratò•rio -ria (**-ri -rie**) *adj* oratorical ‖ *m* (eccl) oratory; (mus) oratorio ‖ *f* oratory, public speaking

orazióne *f* oration; prayer; **orazione domenicale** Lord's Prayer

orbare (**òrbo**) *tr* (lit) to bereave; (lit) to deprive

òrbe *f* (lit) orb; (lit) world

orbène *adv* well

òrbita *f* orbit; (fig) sphere
orbitare (òrbito) *intr* to orbit
orbitaziòne *f* orbiting
òr·bo -ba *adj* bereaved; deprived; blind || *m* blind man
òrca *f* killer whale
Òrcadi *fpl* Orkney Islands
orchèstra *f* orchestra; band; orchestra pit
orchestrale *adj* orchestral || *mf* orchestra player, orchestra performer
orchestrare (orchèstro) *tr* to orchestrate; (fig) to organize
orchestrina *f* dance band; dance-band music
orchidèa *f* orchid
ór·cio *m* (-ci) jar, jug, crock
orciòlo *m*—a orciolo puckered up (*lips*)
òr·co *m* (-chi) ogre
òrda *f* horde
ordàlia *f* (hist) ordeal
ordigno *m* gadget, contrivance; tool; ordigno esplosivo infernal machine
ordinale *adj* & *m* ordinal
ordinaménto *m* disposition; regulation
ordinanza *f* ordinance; (mil) orderly; d'ordinanza regulation (*e.g.*, uniform*);* in ordinanza (mil) in formation
ordinare (órdino) *tr* to order; to straighten up; to range; to regulate; to ordain; to trim
ordinà·rio -ria (-ri -rie) *adj* ordinary; plain; inferior; workday (*suit*) || *m* ordinary; full professor; d'ordinario ordinarily, usually
ordina·to -ta *adj* orderly, tidy; ordained || *f* ordinate; straightening up; (aer) frame; (naut) bulkhead
ordinazióne *f* order; ordination
órdine *m* order; row; tier; series (*e.g., of years*); college (*e.g., of surgeons*); nature (*of things*); (law) warrant, writ; in ordine a concerning; ordine del giorno order of the day; ordine d'idee train of thought
ordire §176 *tr* to warp (*cloth*); to hatch (*a plot*)
ordi·to -ta *adj* plotted || *m* warp (*of fabric*)
orécchia *f* ear; dog-ear; con le orecchie tese all ears
orecchiale *m* earphone (*of sonar equipment*)
orecchiétta *f* (anat) auricle
orecchino *m* earring
oréc·chio *m* (-chi) ear; hearing; dog-ear; moldboard; fare orecchio da mercante to turn a deaf ear || *m* (orécchia *fpl*) (archaic) ear
orecchióne *m* long-eared bat; (mil) trunnion; orecchioni (pathol) mumps
oréfice *m* goldsmith; jeweler
oreficerìa *f* goldsmith shop; jewelry shop
orfanézza *f* orphanage (*condition*)
òrfa·no -na *adj* orphaned || *mf* orphan
orfanotrò·fio *m* (-fi) orphanage (*institution*)
Orfèo *m* Orpheus
organdi *m* organdy
organétto *m* hand organ; mouth organ; organetto di Barberia hand organ

orgàni·co -ca (-ci -che) *adj* organic || *m* personnel, staff || *f* (mil) organization
organigram·ma *m* (-mi) organization chart
organino *m* hand organ, barrel organ
organismo *m* organism
organi·sta *mf* (-sti -ste) organist
organizzare [ddzz] *tr* to organize
organizza·tóre -trice [ddzz] *mf* organizer
organizzazióne [ddzz] *f* organization; Organizzazione delle Nazioni Unite United Nations
òrgano *m* organ; part (*of a machine*); organo di stampa mouthpiece
orgasmo *m* orgasm; agitation, excitement
òr·gia *f* (-ge) orgy
orgó·glio *m* (-gli) pride
orglió·so -sa [s] *adj* proud
orientale *adj* & *mf* oriental; Oriental
orientaménto *m* orientation; bearing; trend; trim (*of sail*); orientamento scolastico e professionale aptitude test; vocational guidance
orientare (oriènto) *tr* to orient; to guide; to trim (*a sail*) || *ref* to find one's bearings
oriènte *m* orient; grand'oriente grand lodge || Oriente *m* Orient, East; Estremo Oriente Far East; Medio Oriente Middle East; Vicino Oriente Near East
orifi·zio *m* (-zi) orifice, opening
orìgano *m* wild marjoram
originale *adj* original; odd || *mf* queer character, odd person || *m* original; copy (*for printer*)
originare (orìgino) *tr* to originate || *intr* (ESSERE) & *ref* to originate
originà·rio -ria *adj* (-ri -rie) originating; native; original
orìgine *f* origin; source; extraction
origliare §280 *intr* to eavesdrop
origlière *m* (lit) pillow
orina *f* var of urina
orinale *m* chamber pot, urinal
orinare *tr* & *intr* to urinate
orina·tóio *m* (-tói) urinal, comfort station
oriòlo *m* (orn) oriole
oriun·do -da *adj* native || *m* (sports) native son
orizzontale [ddzz] *adj* horizontal || orizzontali *fpl* horizontal words (*in crossword puzzle*)
orizzontare [ddzz] (orizzónto) *tr* to orient || *ref* to get one's bearings
orizzónte [ddzz] *m* horizon
Orlando *m* Roland
orlare (órlo) *tr* to hem, border; orlare a zigzag to pink
órlo *m* edge; brim; hem, border; (fig) brink; orlo a giorno hemstitch
órma *f* footprint; orme remains, vestiges; calcare le orme di to follow the footsteps of
ormeggiare §290 (orméggio) *tr* & *ref* (naut) to moor
ormég·gio *m* (-gi) mooring; mollare gli ormeggi (naut) to cast off
ormóne *m* hormone

ornamentale *adj* ornamental
ornaménto *m* ornament
ornare (órno) *tr* to adorn
orna·to -ta *adj* adorned; ornate ‖ *m* ornament; ornamental design
ornitòlo·go -ga *mf* (-gi -ghe) ornithologist
òro *m* gold; (fig) money; **d'oro** gold, golden; **ori** gold objects; jewels; suit of Neapolitan cards corresponding to diamonds; **oro zecchino** pure gold; **per tutto l'oro del mondo** for all the world
orologerìa *f* watchmaking; clockmaking; watchmaker's shop
orolo·giàio *m* (-giài) watchmaker; clockmaker
orolò·gio *m* (-gi) watch; clock; **orologio a pendolo** clock; **orologio a polvere** sandglass; **orologio a scatto** digital clock; **orologio da polso** wristwatch; **orologio della morte** deathwatch; **orologio solare** sundial
oròscopo *m* horoscope
orpèllo *m* Dutch gold; (fig) tinsel
orrèndo *m* horrible
orrìbile *adj* horrible
òrri·do -da *adj* horrid ‖ *m* horridness; gorge, ravine
orripilante *adj* bloodcurdling, hairraising
orróre *m* horror; awe; **aver in** or **per orrore** to loath; **fare orrore a** to horrify
órsa *f* she-bear ‖ **Orsa** *f*—**Orsa maggiore** Great Bear; **Orsa minore** Little Bear
orsacchiòtto *m* bear cub; Teddy bear
ór·so -sa *mf* bear; **orso bianco** polar bear; **orso grigio** grizzly bear ‖ *f* see **orsa**
orsù *interj* come on!
ortàg·gio *m* (-gi) vegetable
ortàglia *f* vegetable garden; vegetable
ortènsia *f* hydrangea
orti·ca *f* (-che) nettle; hives
orticàrìa *f* hives, nettle rash
orticoltóre *m* truck gardener; horticulturist
òrto *m* garden, vegetable garden; (lit) sunrise; **orto botanico** botanical garden; **orto di guerra** Victory garden
ortodòs·so -sa *adj* orthodox ‖ *m* Greek Catholic
ortografìa *f* orthography; spelling
ortola·no -na *adj* garden ‖ *m* truck farmer, gardener
ortopèdi·co -ca (-ci -che) *adj* orthopedic ‖ *m* orthopedist
òrza *f* bowline; windward; **andare all'orza** to sail close to the wind
orzaiòlo [dz] *m* (pathol) sty
orzare (òrzo) *intr* to sail close to the wind; to luff
orzata [dz] *f* orgeat
orzata *f* (naut) luff
òrzo [dz] *m* barley
osannare *intr* to cry or sing hosanna; **osannare a** to acclaim, applaud
osare (òso) *intr* to dare
osceni·tà *f* (-tà) obscenity
oscè·no -na *adj* obscene; (coll) horrible
oscillante *adj* oscillating

oscillare *intr* to oscillate; to swing; to wobble; to waver, hesitate
oscillazióne *f* oscillation; fluctuation
oscuraménto *m* darkening, dimming; blackout
oscurare *tr* to darken; to blot out; to dim ‖ *ref* to get dark; **oscurarsi in volto** to frown
oscuri·tà *f* (-tà) obscurity; darkness; ignorance
oscu·ro -ra *adj* obscure, dark; opaque (*style*) ‖ *m* obscurity, darkness; **essere all'oscuro di** to be in the dark about
osmòsi *f* osmosis
ospedale *m* hospital
ospedalière *m* hospital worker
ospedaliè·ro -ra *adj* hospital ‖ *m* hospitaler
ospedalizzare [ddzz] *tr* to hospitalize
ospitale *adj* hospitable ‖ *m* hospital
ospitali·tà *f* (-tà) hospitality
ospitare (òspito) *tr* to lodge, shelter, accommodate; to entertain; (sports) to play (*an opposing team*) at home
òspite *mf* host; guest; **andarsene insalutato ospite** to take French leave; **ospiti** company (*guests at home*)
ospì·zio *m* (-zi) hospice; hostel; (lit) hospitality; **ospizio dei vecchi** nursing home; **ospizio di mendicità** poorhouse
ossatura *f* frame, framework; skeleton
òsse·o -a *adj* bony
ossequènte *adj* (lit) respectful; (lit) reverent
ossequiare §287 (**ossèquio**) *tr* to pay one's respects to; to honor
ossè·quio *m* (-qui) respect; reverence; **i miei ossequi** my best regards; **in ossequio a** in conformity with; **porgere i propri ossequi a** to pay one's respects to
ossequió·so -sa [s] *adj* obsequious; respectful
osservante *adj* & *m* observant
osservanza *f* observance; deference
osservare (ossèrvo) *tr* to observe
osserva·tóre -trice *adj* observing, observant ‖ *mf* observer
osservatò·rio *m* (-ri) observatory
osservazióne *f* observation; rebuke
ossessionare (ossessióno) *tr* to obsess; to harass, bedevil
ossessióne *f* obsession
ossès·so -sa *adj* possessed ‖ *mf* person possessed
ossìa *conj* or; to wit
ossidante *adj* oxidizing ‖ *m* oxidizer
ossidare (òssido) *tr* & *ref* to oxidize
òssido *m* oxide; **ossido di carbone** carbon monoxide
ossìdulo *m* protoxide; **ossidulo di azoto** nitrous oxide
ossificare §197 (**ossìfico**) *tr* & *ref* to ossify
ossigenare (ossìgeno) *tr* to oxygenate; to bleach (*the hair*); to infuse strength into ‖ *ref* to bleach (*the hair*)
ossìgeno *m* oxygen; (fig) transfusion, shot in the arm
ossìto·no -na *adj* & *m* oxytone

òs·so *m* (-si) bone (*of animal*); stone (*of fruit*); **osso di balena** whalebone; **osso di seppia** cuttlebone; **osso duro da rodere** hard nut to crack; **osso sacro** sacrum; **rimetterci l'osso del collo** to be thoroughly ruined; **rompersi l'osso del collo** to break one's neck || *m* (-sa *fpl*) bone (*of a person*); **avere le ossa rotte** to be dead-tired

ossu·to -ta *adj* bony; scrawny

ostacolare (**ostàcolo**) *tr* to hinder; to obstruct; **ostacolare l'azione** (sports) to interfere

ostàcolo *m* obstacle; obstruction; (golf) hazard; (sports) hurdle

ostàg·gio *m* (-gi) hostage

ostare (**òsto**) *intr* (lit) to be in the way; (with *dat*) to hinder; **nulla osta** no objection, permission granted

òste ostéssa *mf* innkeeper || **oste** *m* & *f* (lit) army in the field || *m* (poet) enemy

ostèllo *m* hostel; (poet) abode

ostentare (**ostènto**) *tr* to show, display; to affect, feign

ostenta·to -ta *adj* affected, ostentatious

ostentazióne *f* show, ostentation

osteopatìa *f* osteopathy

osterìa *f* tavern, inn, taproom

ostéssa *f* see **oste**

ostètri·ca *f* (-che) midwife

ostetrìcia *f* obstetrics

ostètri·co -ca (-ci -che) *adj* obstetrical || *m* obstetrician || *f* see **ostetrica**

òstia *f* wafer; Host; sacrificial victim

òsti·co -ca *adj* (-ci -che) hard; (lit) repugnant, distasteful

ostile *adj* hostile

ostili·tà *f* (-tà) hostility

ostinare *ref* to be stubborn; to persist

ostina·to -ta *adj* obstinate; persistent

ostinazióne *f* obstinacy

ostracismo *m* ostracism; **dare l'ostracismo a** to ostracize

ostracizzare [ddzz] *tr* (poet) to ostracize

òstri·ca *f* (-che) oyster; **ostrica perlifera** pearl oyster

ostri·càio *m* (-cài) oyster bed; oysterman

ostruire §176 *tr* to obstruct; to stop up

ostruzióne *f* obstruction

Otèllo *m* Othello

otorinolaringoia·tra *mf* (-tri -tre) ear, nose, and throat specialist, otorhinolaryngologist

ótre *f* wineskin; **otre di vento** windbag (*person*)

ottàni·co -ca *adj* (-ci -che) octane

ottano *m* octane

ottanta *adj, m* & *pron* eighty

ottantènne *adj* eighty-year-old || *mf* eighty-year-old person

ottantèsi·mo -ma *adj, m* & *pron* eightieth

ottantina *f* about eighty; **essere sull'ottantina** to be about eighty years old

ottava *f* octave

Ottaviano *m* Octavian

ottavino *m* (mus) piccolo; (com) commission of ⅛ of 1%

otta·vo -va *adj* & *pron* eighth || *m* eighth; octavo || *f* see **ottava**

ottemperare (**ottèmpero**) *intr* (with *dat*) to obey; **ottemperare a** to comply with

ottenebrare (**ottènebro**) *tr* to becloud

ottenére §271 *tr* to obtain, get

ottétto *m* octet

òtti·co \-**ca** (-ci -che) *adj* optic(al) || *m* optician || *f* optics

ottimismo *m* optimism

ottimi·sta *mf* (-sti -ste) optimist

ottimìsti·co -ca *adj* (-ci -che) optimistic

òtti·mo -ma *adj* very good, excellent || *m* best; highest rating

òtto *adj* & *pron* eight; **le otto** eight o'clock || *m* eight; eighth (*in dates*); (sports) racing shell with eight oarsmen; **otto giorni** a week; **otto volante** roller coaster

ottóbre *m* October

ottocenté·sco -sca *adj* (-schi -sche) nineteenth-century

ottocènto *adj, m* & *pron* eight hundred || **l'Ottocento** the nineteenth century

ottoma·no -na *adj* & *m* Ottoman || *m* ottoman (*fabric*) || *f* ottoman (*sofa*)

ottomila *adj, m* & *pron* eight thousand

ottoname *m* brassware

ottonare (**ottóno**) *tr* to coat with brass

ottóne *m* brass; **ottoni** (mus) brasses || **Ottone** *m* Otto

ottuagenà·rio -ria *adj* & *mf* (-ri -rie) octogenerian

ottùndere §208 *tr* (fig) to deaden; (lit) to blunt

otturare *tr* to fill; to plug; to stop; to obstruct, stop up (*e.g., a channel*) || *ref* to clog up

otturatóre *m* breechblock; (phot, mov) shutter; (mach) cutoff (*of cylinder*)

otturazióne *f* filling (*of tooth*)

ottu·so -sa *adj* obtuse; blunt

ovàia *f* ovary

ovale *adj* oval || *m* oval; oval face

ovatta *f* wadding; absorbent cotton

ovattare *tr* to pad, wad; to muffle

ovazióne *f* ovation

óve *adv* (lit) where || *conj* (lit) if; (poet) while

òvest *m* west

Ovìdio *m* Ovid

ovile *m* sheepcote, fold

ovi·no -na *adj* ovine || **ovini** *mpl* sheep

òvo *m* var of **uovo**

ovoidale *adj* egg-shaped

òvulo *m* pill shaped like an egg; (biol) ovum; (bot) ovule

ovùnque *adv* (lit) wherever; (lit) everywhere

ovvéro *conj* or; to wit

ovvìa *interj* come on!

ovviare §119 *intr*—(with *dat*) to obviate

òv·vio -via *adj* (-vi -vie) obvious

oziare §287 *intr* to idle, loiter

ò·zio *m* (-zi) idleness; leisure

oziosi·tà [s] *f* (-tà) idleness

ozió·so -sa [s] *adj* idle; useless, vain

ozòno [dz] *m* ozone

P

P, p [pi] *m & f* fourteenth letter of the Italian alphabet
pacare §197 *tr* (poet) to placate
pacatézza *f* tranquillity, serenity
paca·to -ta *adj* serene, tranquil
pac·ca *f* (-che) slap
pacchétto *m* parcel, package; book (*of matches*); pack (*of cigarettes*)
pàcchia *f* (coll) hearty meal; (coll) godsend, windfall
pacchia·no -na *adj* boorish, uncouth || *mf* boor
pacciamantura *f* mulching
pacciame *m* mulch
pac·co *m* (-chi) package; **pacchi postali** parcel post (*service*); **pacco dono** gift package; **pacco postale** parcel by mail
paccottìglia *f* shoddy goods, junk; trinkets
pace *f* peace; **lasciare in pace** to leave alone; **mettersi il cuore in pace** to resign oneself
pachidèr·ma *m* (-mi) pachyderm
pachista·no -na *adj & mf* Pakistani
paciè·re -ra *mf* peacemaker
pacificare §197 (**pacìfico**) *tr* to pacify; to appease; to mediate || *ref* to make one's peace
pacifica·tóre -trice *adj* pacifying || *mf* peacemaker
pacificazióne *f* pacification; appeasement
pacìfi·co -ca (-ci -che) *adj* peaceful, pacific; **è pacifico che** it goes without saying that || *m* peaceable person || **Pacifico** *adj & m* Pacific
pacifismo *m* pacifism
pacifi·sta *mf* (-sti -ste) pacifist
pacioccó·ne -na *mf* chubby, easygoing person
padèlla *f* frying pan; bedpan; **cadere dalla padella nella brace** to jump from the frying pan into the fire
padiglióne *m* pavilion; hunting lodge; roof (*of car*); ward (*of a hospital*); (naut) rigging, tackle; **padiglione auricolare** (anat) auricle of the ear
Pàdova *f* Padua
padre *m* father; sire; **padre di famiglia** provider; (law) head of household; **Padre Eterno** Heavenly Father
padreggiare §290 (**padréggio**) *intr* to resemble one's father
padrino *m* godfather; second (*in duel*)
padrona *f* owner, boss, mistress; **padrona di casa** lady of the house
padronale *adj* proprietary; private (*e.g., car*)
padronanza *f* command; **padronanza di sé stesso** self-control
padróne *m* owner, boss, master; **essere padrone di** + *inf* to have the right to + *inf*; **padrone di casa** landlord; **padrone di sé** cool and collected
padroneggiare §290 (**padronéggio**) *tr* to master, control
paesàg·gio *m* (-gi) landscape
paesaggi·sta *mf* (-sti -ste) landscapist

paesa·no -na *adj* country || *mf* villager || *m* countryman || *f* countrywoman; **alla paesana** according to local tradition
paése *m* country; village; **i Paesi Bassi** the Netherlands; (hist) the Low Countries; **mandare a quel paese** to send to blazes
paesi·sta *mf* (-sti -ste) landscapist
paffu·to -ta *adj* chubby, plump
pa·ga *f* (-ghe) salary; wages; repayment; **mala paga** poor pay (*person*)
pagàbile *adj* payable
pagàia *f* paddle
pagaménto *m* payment; **pagamento alla consegna** c.o.d.
paganésimo *m* paganism
paga·no -na *adj & mf* pagan, heathen
pagare §209 *tr* to pay; to pay for; **far pagare** to charge; **pagare di egual moneta** to repay in kind; **pagare il fio per** to pay (the penalty) for; **pagare in natura** to pay in kind; **pagare salato** to pay dearly; **pagare un occhio della testa** to pay through the nose || *intr* to pay
paga·tóre -trice *mf* payer
pagèlla *f* report card
pàg·gio *m* (-gi) page (*boy attendant*)
paghe·rò *m* (-rò) promissory note, I.O.U.
pàgina *f* page (*e.g., of book*)
paginatura *f* pagination
pàglia *f* straw; thatch (*for roof*); **paglia di ferro** steel wool; **paglia di legno** excelsior
pagliaccé·sco -sca *adj* (-schi -sche) clownish
pagliaccétto *m* rompers
pagliacciata *f* buffoonery, antics
pagliàc·cio *m* (-ci) clown, buffoon; **fare il pagliaccio** to clown
pa·gliàio *m* (-gliài) heap of straw; haystack
paglierìc·cio *m* (-ci) straw mattress
paglieri·no -na *adj* straw-colored
pagliétta *f* skimmer, boater; steel wool; (coll) pettifogger
pagnòtta *f* loaf of bread; (coll) bread
pa·go -ga *adj* (-ghi -ghe) satisfied || *f* see **paga**
paguro *m* (zool) hermit crab
pà·io *m* (-ia *fpl*) pair, couple; **è un altro paio di maniche** this is a horse of another color; **fare il paio** to match perfectly
paiòlo *m* caldron, kettle; (mil) platform
Pakistan, il Pakistan
pala *f* shovel; blade (*e.g., of turbine*); paddle (*of waterwheel*); peel (*of baker*); **pala d'altare** altarpiece
paladi·no *m* champion || *m* paladin; **farsi paladino di** to champion
palafitta *f* pile dwelling; piles (*to support a structure*)
palafrenière *m* groom
palafréno *m* palfrey
palan·ca *f* (-che) beam, board; (naut)

gangplank; copper coin; **palanche** (coll) money

palanchino *m* palanquin; (naut) pulley

palandrana *f* (joc) long, full coat

palata *f* shovelful; stroke (*of oar*); **a palate** by the bucketful

palatale *adj & f* palatal

palati·no -na *adj* palatine; (anat) palatal

palato *m* palate

palazzina *f* villa

palazzo *m* palace; large office or government building; mansion; **palazzo dello sport** sports arena; **palazzo di città** city hall; **palazzo di giustizia** courthouse

palchetti·sta (-sti -ste) *mf* (theat) boxholder || *m* person who lays floors

palchétto *m* shelf; (theat) small box; (journ) box

pal·co *m* **(-chi)** flooring; scaffold; stand, platform; (theat) box; (theat) stage

palcoscèni·co *m* **(-ci)** (theat) stage

palesare (paléso) *tr* to reveal, manifest || *ref* to show oneself

palése *adj* plain, manifest; **fare palese** to manifest, reveal

palèstra *f* gymnasium; palestra

palétta *f* small shovel, scoop; blade (*of turbine*)

palettata *f* shovelful

palétto *m* stake; bolt (*of door*)

palificazióne *f* pile work (*in the ground for foundation*); line of telephone poles

pà·lio *m* **(-lii)** embroidered cloth (*given as prize*); **metter in palio** to offer as a prize; **palio di Siena** colorful horserace at Siena

palissandro *m* Brazilian rosewood

palizzata *f* palisade; picket fence

palla *f* ball; bullet; sphere; **dar palla nera a** to blackball; **palla da cannone** cannon ball; **palla di neve** snowball; **prendere la palla al balzo** to seize the opportunity

pallabase *f* baseball

pallacanè·stro *f* **(-stro)** basketball

pallamuro *m* handball

pallanuòto *f* water polo

pallavó·lo *f* **(-lo)** volleyball

palleggiare §290 **(palléggio)** *tr* to toss (*e.g., a javelin*); to shift from one hand to another || *intr* (tennis) to knock a few balls; (soccer) to dribble || *ref*—**palleggiarsi la responsabilità** to shift the responsibility

pallég·gio *m* **(-gi)** (tennis) knocking back and forth; (soccer) dribbling

palliati·vo -va *adj & m* palliative

pallidézza *f* paleness

pàlli·do -da *adj* pale; faint

pallina *f* marble; small ball; **pallina antitarmica** mothball

pallino *m* little ball; (bowling) jack; bullet; **a pallini** polka-dot; **avere il pallino di** to be crazy about; **pallini** buckshot; polka dots

palloncino *m* child's balloon; Chinese lantern

pallóne *m* (soccer) ball; (aer) balloon;

pallone di sbarramento barrage balloon; **pallone gonfiato** (fig) stuffed shirt; **pallone sonda** trial balloon

pallonétto *m* (tennis) lob

pallóre *m* pallor, paleness

pallòttola *f* pellet; ball; bullet

pallottolière *m* abacus

pallovale *f* rugby

palma *f* palm; **tenere in palma di mano** to hold in the highest esteem

palmare *adj* evident, plain

palménto *m* millstone; **mangiare a quattro palmenti** (coll) to stuff oneself eating

palméto *m* palm grove

palmìpede *adj* palmate, web-footed

palmì·zio *m* **(-zi)** palm

palmo *m* span; palm (*of hand*); foot (*measure*); **a palmo a palmo** little by little; **restare con un palmo di naso** to be disappointed

palo *m* pole (*of wood or metal*); beam; pile; (soccer, football) goal post; **fare il palo** to be on the lookout (*said of thieves*); **palo indicatore** signpost; **saltare di palo in frasca** to digress

palombaro *m* diver

palómbo *m* dogfish

palpàbile *adj* palpable

palpare *tr* to touch; to palpate

pàlpebra *f* eyelid; **battere le palpebre** to blink

palpeggiare §290 **(palpéggio)** *tr* to finger, touch repeatedly

palpitante *adj* throbbing; burning (*question*); fluttering (*e.g., with love*)

palpitare (pàlpito) *intr* to palpitate, pulsate; (fig) to pine

palpitazióne *f* palpitation

pàlpito *m* heartbeat; (fig) throb

pal·tò *m* **(-tò)** overcoat

paltoncino *m* child's winter coat; lady's topcoat

paludaménto *m* (joc) array, attire

palude *f* marsh, bog

paludó·so -sa [s] *adj* marshy

palustre *adj* marshy

pàmpino *m* grape leaf

panacèa *f* panacea, cure-all

pàna·ma *m* **(-ma)** Panama hat

panamé·gno -gna *adj & mf* Panamenian

panamènse *adj & mf* Panamenian

panare *tr* (culin) to bread

pan·ca *f* **(-che)** bench; **scaldare le panche** (coll) to loaf around; (coll) to waste one's time at school

pancétta *f* potbelly; bacon

panchétto *m* footstool

panchina *f* bench

pàn·cia *f* **(-ce)** belly; **a pancia all'aria** on one's back; **mangiare a crepa pancia** to stuff oneself like a pig; **mettere su pancia** to grow a potbelly; **salvar la pancia per i fichi** to not take any chances; **tenersi la pancia dalle risate** to split one's side laughing

panciata *f* belly flop

pancièra *f* bellypiece; body girth

panciòlle *m*—**in panciolle** frittering one's time away

panciòtto *m* waistcoat; vest; **panciotto a maglia** cardigan
panciu·to -ta *adj* potbellied
pàncre·as *m* (-as) pancreas
pandemò·nio *m* (-ni) pandemonium
pane *m* bread; thread (*of screw*); cake (*e.g., of butter*); loaf (*of sugar*); (metallurgy) pig; **a pane di zucchero** conic(al); **dire pane al pane e vino al vino** to call a spade a spade; **essere come pane e cacio** to be hand and glove; **essere pane per i propri denti** to be a match for s.o.; **guadagnarsi il pane** to earn one's living; **pane a cassetta** sandwich bread; **pane azzimo** unleavened bread, matzoth; **pan di Spagna** angel food cake, sponge cake; **pane integrale** graham bread; **render pan per focaccia** to give tit for tat
panegìri·co *m* (-ci) panegyric
panetterìa *f* bakery
panettière *m* baker
panétto *m* pat (*e.g., of butter)*
pànfilo *m* yacht
panfrutto *m* plum cake
pangrattato *m* bread crumbs
pània *f* birdlime; **cadere nella pania** to fall into the trap
pàni·co -ca (-ci -che) *adj* panicky ‖ *m* panic
pani·co *m* (-chi) (bot) Italian millet
panièra *f* basket; basketful
panière *m* basket; basketful
panificazióne *f* breadmaking
panifì·cio *m* (-ci) bakery
panino *m* roll, bun; **panino imbottito** sandwich
panna *f* cream, heavy cream; **essere in panna** (naut) to lie to; (aut) to have a breakdown; **mettere in panna** (naut) to heave to; **panna montata** whipped cream
panne *f* (aut) breakdown; **essere in panne** (aut) to have a breakdown
pannèllo *m* linen cloth; pane; panel (*of machine*); (archit; elec) panel
pannìcolo *m* (anat) membrane, tissue
panno *m* cloth; woolen cloth; film, membrane; **bianco come un panno** as white as a ghost; **mettersi nei panni di** to put oneself in the boots of; **non stare più nei propri panni** to be beside oneself with joy; **panni** clothes; **panno verde** baize
pannòcchia *f* ear (*of corn*)
pannolino *m* linen cloth; diaper; sanitary napkin
panòplia *f* panoply
panora·ma *m* (-mi) panorama
panoràmi·co -ca *adj* (-ci -che) panoramic ‖ *f* panoramic view; (mov) panoramic scene
pantaloncini *mpl* trunks
pantalóni *mpl* trousers; **pantaloni da donna** slacks
pantano *m* bog, quagmire
panteismo *m* pantheism
pànteon *m* pantheon
pantèra *f* panther; (slang) police car
pantòfola *f* slipper
pantomima *f* pantomine, mimicry

panzana *f* (lit) fib, lie
Pàolo *m* Paul
paonaz·zo -za *adj* & *m* purple
pa·pa *m* (-pi) pope; **ad ogni morte di papa** once in a blue moon; **morto un papa se ne fa un altro** nobody is indispensable
pa·pà *m* (-pà) daddy, papa
papàbile *adj* likely to be elected ‖ *mf* front runner ‖ *m* cardinal likely to be elected to the papacy
papale *adj* papal (*e.g., benediction*); Papal (*States*)
papali·no -na *adj* papal ‖ *m* advocate of papal temporal power ‖ *f* skullcap
paparazzo *m* freelance photographer
papato *m* papacy
papàvero *m* poppy; **alto papavero** (fig) big shot
pàpera *f* young goose; slip of the tongue; spoonerism; **fare una papera** to make a boner
pàpero *m* gander
papiro *m* papyrus
pappa *f* bread soup, farina, pap; **pappa molla** (fig) jellyfish
pappafi·co *m* (-chi) (naut) topgallant; (slang) goatee
pappagallo *m* parrot; bedpan; (slang) masher
pappagòr·gia *f* (-ge) double chin, jowl
pappare *tr* (coll) to gulp; (fig) to gobble up fraudulently
pappata·ci *m* (-ci) gnat
pappina *f* light pap; poultice
pàpri·ca *f* (-che) paprika
para *f* crepe rubber
paràbola *f* parable; (geom) parabola
parabórdo *m* (naut) fender
parabréz·za [ddzz] *m* (-za) windshield
paracadutare *tr* to parachute, airdrop ‖ *ref* to parachute
paracadu·te *m* (-te) parachute
paracadutismo *m* parachute jumping; (sports) sky diving
paracaduti·sta *mf* (-sti -ste) parachutist; skydiver ‖ *m* paratrooper
paracarro *m* spur stone
paracól·pi *m* (-pi) doorstop
paràcqua *m* (paràcqua) umbrella
paradèn·ti *m* (-ti) (sports) mouthpiece
paradisìa·co -ca *adj* (-ci -che) heavenly
paradiso *m* paradise
paradossale *adj* paradoxical
paradòsso *m* paradox
parafa *f* initials
parafan·go *m* (-ghi) fender, mudguard
parafare *tr* to initial
paraffina *f* paraffin
parafiam·ma *m* (-ma) fire-proof partition
parafrasare (paràfraso) *tr* to paraphrase
paràfra·si *f* (-si) paraphrase
parafùlmine *m* lightning rod
parafuò·co *m* (-co) screen, fender (*in front of fireplace*)
paràg·gio *m* (-gi) lineage; **paraggi** neighborhood, vicinity
paragonàbile *adj* comparable
paragonare (paragóno) *tr* to compare
paragóne *m* comparison; **a paragone di**

in comparison with; **mettere a paragone** to compare; **senza paragone** beyond compare

paragrafare (paràgrafo) *tr* to paragraph

paràgrafo *m* paragraph

paraguaia·no -na *adj* & *mf* Paraguayan

paràli·si *f* (**-si**) paralysis

paralìti·co -ca *adj* & *mf* (**-ci -che**) paralytic

paralizzare [ddzz] *tr* to paralyze

parallè·lo -la *adj* & *m* parallel ‖ *f* (geom) parallel line; **parallele** (sports) parallel bars

paralume *m* lamp shade

paramano *m* cuff, wristband; (archit) facing brick

paraménto *s* facing (*of a wall*); (eccl) vestment

parami·ne *m* (**-ne**) (nav) paravane

paramó·sche *m* (**-sche**) fly net

paran·co *m* (**-chi**) tackle

paranin·fo -fa *mf* matchmaker

paranòi·co -ca *adj* & *mf* (**-ci -che**) paranoiac

paraòc·chi *m* (**-chi**) blinker (*on horse*)

parapètto *m* parapet

parapì·glia *m* (**-glia**) hubbub

parapiòg·gia *m* (**-gia**) umbrella

parare *tr* to adorn; to hang; to protect; to parry (*a thrust*); to offer; to drive (*e.g., cattle*) ‖ *intr*—**dove va a parare?** what are you driving at? ‖ *ref* to protect oneself; (eccl) to don the vestments; **pararsi dinanzi a** to loom up in front of

parasóle *m* parasol; (aut) sun visor

paraspal·le *m* (**-le**) (sports) shoulder pad

parassi·ta (-ti -te) *adj* parasitic ‖ *m* parasite

parassità·rio -ria *adj* (**-ri -rie**) parasitic(al)

parassiti·co -ca *adj* (**-ci -che**) parasitic(al)

parastatale *adj* government-controlled ‖ *mf* employee of government-controlled agency

parastin·chi *m* (**-chi**) (sports) shin guard

parata *f* fence, bar; (fencing) parry; (soccer) catch; (mil) parade; **mala parata** dangerous situation

paratìa *f* bulkhead

parato *m* hangings; **parati** hangings; (naut) bilgeways

paratóia *f* sluice gate

paraur·ti *m* (**-ti**) (aut) bumper; (rr) buffer

paravènto *m* screen

Par·ca *f* (**-che**) Fate

parcare §197 *tr* & *intr* to park

parcèlla *f* bill, fee, honorarium; parcel, lot (*of land*)

parcheggiare §290 (**parchéggio**) *tr* & *intr* to park

parchég·gio *m* (**-gi**) parking; parking lot

parchìmetro *m* parking meter

par·co -ca (-chi -che) *adj* frugal; parsimonious ‖ *m* park; parking; parking lot; **parco dei divertimenti** amusement park

paréc·chio -chia (-chi -chie) *adj indef*

a good deal of, a lot of; **parecchi** several ‖ *pron* a good deal, a lot; **parecchi** several ‖ **parecchio** *adv* a lot; rather

pareggiare §290 (**paréggio**) *tr* to level; to equal; to match; to balance; to recognize ‖ *intr* (sports) to tie

pareggia·to -ta *adj* accredited (*school*)

parég·gio *m* (**-gi**) leveling; matching; (sports) tie; **pareggio del bilancio** balancing of the budget

parentado *m* kinsfolk, kindred; relationship; **concludere il parentado di** to arrange for the wedding of

parènte *mf* relative; (lit) parent; **parenti** kin

parentèla *f* relationship; relations

parènte·si *f* (**-si**) parenthesis; break, interval; **fra parentesi** parenthetically; in parentheses; **parentesi quadra** bracket

parére *m* opinion, mind; advice; **a mio parere** in my opinion ‖ §210 *intr* (ESSERE) to seem; **che Le pare?** what is your opinion?; **ma Le pare!** not at all!; **mi pare che + subj** it seems to me that + *ind;* I guess that + *ind;* **non Le pare?** don't you think so?; **non mi pare vero** I can't believe it

paréte *f* wall; **tra le pareti domestiche** within the four walls of the home

pargolét·to -ta *adj* (poet) infantile ‖ *mf* (poet) child

pàrgo·lo -la *adj* (poet) infantile ‖ *mf* (poet) child

pari *adj invar* equal, even; **camminare di pari passo** to walk at the same rate; **essere pari** to be quits; **essere pari al proprio compito** to be equal to the task; **fare un salto a piè pari** to jump with feet together; **pari pari** verbatim; **rimanere pari con** (sports) to be tied with; **saltare a piè pari** to skip (*e.g., a page*); to dodge (*a difficulty*); **trattare da pari a pari** to treat as an equal ‖ *m* peer; **al pari di** as, like; **del pari** also; **in pari** even, leveled; **senza pari** matchless, peerless ‖ *f*—**stare alla pari con** to be an even match for

parìa *f* peerage

pà·ria *m* (**-ria**) pariah

parificare §197 (**parìfico**) *tr* to level; to match; to accredit (*a school*); to balance

Parigi *f* Paris

parigi·no -na *adj* & *mf* Parisian ‖ *f* slow-burning stove; Parisian woman; (rr) switching spur

parìglia *f* pair, couple; team (*of horses*); (cards) two of a kind; **rendere la pariglia** to give tit for tat

pariménti *adv* likewise

pari·tà *f* (**-tà**) parity

paritèti·co -ca *adj* (**-ci -che**) joint (*e.g., committee*)

parlamentare *adj* parliamentary ‖ *mf* member of parliament ‖ *m* (mil) envoy ‖ *v* (**parlaménto**) *intr* to parley

parlaménto *m* parliament

parlante *adj* talking; life-like ‖ *mf* speaker

parlantina *f* glibness

parlare *m* talk, speech; dialect || *tr* to speak (*a language*) || *intr* to speak, talk; to discuss; **chi parla?** (telp) hello!; **far parlare di sé** to be talked about; **parlare chiaro** to speak bluntly; **parlare del più e del meno** to make small talk; **parlare tra sé e sé** to talk to oneself || *ref* to talk to one another

parla·to -ta *adj* spoken; current (*speech*); talking (*movie*) || *m* talkie; (mov) sound track; (theat) dialogue || *f* speech, talk; dialect

parla·tóre -trice *mf* speaker

parlatò·rio *m* (**-ri**) visting room (*e.g., in jail*)

parlottare (**parlòtto**) *intr* to whisper in secret

parmigia·no -na *adj* & *mf* Parmesan || *m* Parmesan cheese

parnaso *m* Parnassus (*poetry, poets*) || **il Parnaso** Mount Parnassus

paro *m*—**in un par d'ore** in a couple of hours || *adv*—**andare a paro** to keep abreast; **mettere a paro** to compare

parodìa *f* parody; **fare la parodia di** to parody

parodiare §287 (**paròdio**) *tr* to parody

paròla *f* word; speech; **avere parole con** to have words with; **buttare la mezza parola** to make an allusion; **dare la parola a** to give the floor to; **di poche parole** of few words; **domandare la parola** to ask for the floor; **essere di parola** to keep one's word; **essere in parola con** to have dealings with; **mangiarsi la parola** to break one's word; **mangiarsi le parole** to slur one's words; **non far parola** to not breathe a word; **parola crociata** crossword puzzle; **parola d'ordine** password; **parola macedonia** acronym **parola sdrucciola** proparoxytone; **parole** lyrics; **parole di circostanza** occasional words; **prendere la parola** to take the floor; **rivolgere la parola a** to address; **venire a parole** to begin to quarrel

paròlàc·cia *f* (**-ce**) dirty word; swearword

paro·làio -làia (**-lài -làie**) *adj* wordy, verbose || *mf* windbag

parolière *m* lyricist

parossismo *m* paroxysm; climax

parossìto·no -na *adj* paroxytone

parotite *f* (pathol) parotitis; **parotite epidemica** (pathol) mumps

parrici·da *mf* (**-di -de**) patricide

parrocchétto *m* parakeet; (naut) fore-topsail; (naut) fore-topmast

parròcchia *f* parish

parrocchia·no -na *mf* parishioner

pàrro·co *m* (**-ci**) rector, parson

parruc·ca *f* (**-che**) wig; (fig) old fogey

parsimònia *f* parsimony

parsimonió·so -sa [s] *adj* parsimonious

partàc·cia *f*—**fare una partaccia** to break one's word; **fare una partaccia a** to make a scene in front of; to rebuke loudly

parte *f* part; share; section; side; party; partiality; (theat) role; **a parte sepa**rately; (theat) aside; **d'altra parte** on the other hand; **da parte** aside; **da parte mia** as for me; **fare le parti** to divide in shares; **gran parte di** a great deal of; **in parte** partially; **la maggior parte di** most of; **parte civile** (law) plaintiff; **parte . . . parte** some . . . some; part . . . part; **prendere in mala parte** to take amiss

partecipante *adj* participating || *mf* participant; (sports) contestant

partecipare (**partécipo**) *tr* to announce; (lit) to share in || *intr*—**partecipare a** to share in; to participate in; **partecipare di** to partake of (*e.g., the nature of an animal*)

partecipazióne *f* announcement; card; announcement (*of a wedding*); share *in a business*); participation (*in some action*)

partécipe *adj* sharing, partaking

parteggiare §290 (**partéggio**) *intr* to side; **parteggiare per** to side with

Partenóne *m* Parthenon

partènte *adj* departing || *mf* person departing, traveler; (sports) starter

partènza *f* departure; sailing; (sports) start; **di partenza** or **in partenza** about to leave; **partenza lanciata** (sports) running start

particèlla *f* particle

partici·pio *m* (**-pi**) participle

particolare *adj* particular; private; **in particolare** especially || *m* detail

particolareggiare §290 (**particolaréggio**) *tr* to detail

particolarismo *m* regionalism, particularism

particolarìsti·co -ca *adj* (**-ci -che**) particularistic; individualistic

particolari·tà *f* (**-tà**) peculiarity; detail

partigianerìa *f* partisanship, factionalism

partigia·no -na *adj* & *mf* partisan

partire §176 *tr* (lit) to divide || *v* (**parto**) *intr* to depart; (fig) to arise; **a partire da** beginning with; **far partire** to start (*e.g., a car*) || *ref* to depart, leave

parti·to -ta *adj* parted || *m* match (*in marriage*); (pol) party; **ridotto a mal partito** in bad shape; **mettere la testa a partito** to reform; **partito preso** parti pris; **prendere partito** to take sides; to make up one's mind; **trarre il miglior partito da** to make the best of || *f* panel (*e.g., of door*); lot (*of goods*); game; match; party; round (*of golf*); (com) entry; **partita di caccia** hunting party; **partita doppia** (com) double entry; **partita semplice** (com) single entry

partitura *f* (mus) score

partizióne *f* partition, division

parto *m* birth, childbirth

partorire §176 *tr* to bear, bring forth

parvènza *f* (lit) appearance

parziale *adj* partial, one-sided

parziali·tà *f* (**-tà**) partiality

pàscere §211 *tr, intr* & *ref* to pasture, graze

pa·scià *m* (**-scià**) pasha

pasciu·to -ta *adj* well-fed

pascolare (pàscolo) *tr & intr* to pasture
pàscolo *m* pasture
Pàsqua *f* Easter; **contento come una Pasqua** as happy as a lark; **Pasqua fiorìta** Palm Sunday
pasquale *adj* paschal (*e.g., lamb*)
passàbile *adj* passable, tolerable
passàg·gio *m* (-gi) passage; transfer; crossing; traffic; passageway; ride; promotion; (sports) pass; **aprirsi il passaggio** to make one's way; **di passaggio** in passing; transient (*visitor*); **essere di passaggio** to be passing by; **passaggio a livello** railroad crossing; **passaggio zebrato** zebra crossing; **vietato il passaggio** no thoroughfare
passamano *m* passing from hand to hand; ribbon; (coll) railing, handrail
passante *adj* passing (*shot*) || *mf* passer-by || *m* strap
passapòrto *m* passport
passare *tr* to cross; to pass; to undergo (*a medical examination*); to move; to hand; to pay; to send (*word*); to pierce; to spend (*time*); to strain; to go over; to let have (*e.g., a slap*); to overstep (*the bounds*); **passare in rassegna** to pass in review; **passare per le armi** to execute; **passare un brutto quarto d'ora** to have a bad ten minutes; **passare un guaio** to have a hard time; **passarla a qlcu** (coll) to forgive s.o.; **passarla liscia** (coll) to get off unscathed; **passarsela bene** (coll) to have a good time || *intr* (ESSERE) to pass; to go; to filter (*said of air, light*); to move; to spoil (*said of food*); to be over-cooked; to be promoted; to become; to enter; (lit) to be over; **fare passare qlcu** to let s.o. come in; **passare a nozze** to get married; **passare a seconde nozze** to remarry; **passare avanti a** to overcome; **passare di mente a** to forget, *e.g.,* **gli è passata di mente la riunione** he forgot the meeting; **passare di moda** to go out of style; **passare in giudicato** (law) to be no longer appealable; **passare per** to pass as; **passare per il rotto della cuffia** to barely make it; **passare sopra qlco** to overlook s.th; **passi!** come in!; **passo!** (rad) over!; **passo** (cards) pass
passata *f* purée; **dare una passata a** to glance at; **dare una passata di straccio a** to rub lightly with a rag; to give a lick and a promise to; **di passata** hurriedly
passatèmpo *m* pastime; hobby
passati·sta *mf* (-sti -ste) traditionalist
passa·to -ta *adj* past; last; overcooked; **essere passato** (coll) to be no longer in one's prime; **passato di moda** out of fashion || *m* past; purée; **passato prossimo** present perfect; **passato remoto** preterit || *f* see **passata**
passatóia *f* runner (*rug*)
passa·tóio *m* (-tói) stepping stone
passeggè·ro -ra *adj* passing || *mf* passenger; **passeggero clandestino** stowaway

passeggiare §290 (passéggio) *tr* to walk (*e.g., a horse*) || *intr* to walk, prome-nade
passeggiata *f* promenade; walk; drive, ride; drive, road; **fare una passeggiata** to take a walk; to take a ride
passeggiatrice *f* streetwalker
passég·gio *m* (-gi) walk; promenade; **andare a passeggio** to take a walk
passerèlla *f* gangway; catwalk; foot-bridge
pàsse·ro -ra *mf* sparrow || *f*—**passera di mare** (ichth) flounder
passìbile *adj*—**passibile di** subject to, liable to
passiflòra *f* passionflower
passino *m* colander, strainer
passióne *f* passion
passivi·tà *f* (-tà) passivity; (com) deficit
passì·vo -va *adj* passive || *m* (com) liabilities; (com) debit side; (gram) passive
pas·so -sa *adj*—see **uva** || *m* step; passage; pass (*in mountain*); pace; footstep; pitch (*of screw, helix, etc.*); (aut) wheelbase; (phot) tread; (phot) size (*of roll*); **a grandi passi** with great strides; **andare al passo** to march in step; to walk (*said of a horse*); **a passi di gigante** by leaps and bounds; **a passo di corsa** run-ning; **a passo d'uomo** walking, at a walk; **aprire il passo** to open the way; **di buon passo** at a good clip; **di pari passo** at the same rate; **fare quattro passi** to take a stroll; **passo doppio** paso doble; **passo d'uomo** manhole; step; **passo falso** misstep; (fig) stumble; **sbarrare il passo** to block the way; **seguire i passi di** to walk in the footsteps of || *interj* (cards) pass!; over!
pasta *f* paste; dough; **di pasta grossa** uncouth, coarse; **pasta alimentare** pasta, macaroni products; **pasta all'uovo** egg noodles; **pasta asciutta** pasta with sauce and cheese; **pasta dentifricia** toothpaste; **una pasta d'uomo** a good-natured man
pastasciutta *f* pasta with sauce and cheese
pasteggiare §290 (pastéggio) *intr* to dine
pastèllo *adj invar & m* pastel || *m* crayon
pastétta *f* batter; (coll) trickery
pastìc·ca *f* (-che) lozenge, tablet; **pasticche per la tosse** cough drops
pasticcerìa *f* pastrymaking; pastry; pastry shop
pasticciare §128 (pastìccio) *tr & intr* to bungle; to scribble
pasticciè·re -ra *mf* pastry cook; con-fectioner
pasticcino *m* cookie; patty
pastìc·cio *m* (-ci) pie (*of meat, maca-roni, etc*); bungle; mess; **cacciarsi nei pasticci** to wind up in the soup
pasticció·ne -na *mf* bungler
pastifì·cio *m* (-ci) spaghetti and maca-roni factory
pastìglia *f* lozenge, tablet; **pastiglia per la tosse** cough drop

pastina·ca *f* (**-che**) parsnip
pa·sto -sta *adj* (archaic) fed ‖ *m* meal; **pasto a prezzo fisso** table d'hôte ‖ *f* see **pasta**
pastóia *f* hobble; (fig) shackle
pastóne *m* mash
pastóra *f* shepherdess
pastorale *adj* pastoral
pastóre *m* shepherd; pastor
pastorì·zio -zia (**-zi -zie**) *adj* shepherd ‖ *f* sheep raising
pastorizzare [ddzz] *tr* to pasteurize
pastó·so -sa [s] *adj* pasty; mellow
pastrano *m* overcoat
pastura *f* pasture; hay; fodder
patac·ca *f* (**-che**) large, worthless coin; fake; (coll) medal; (coll) spot
patata *f* potato
patatràc *m* (**patatràc**) crash
patèlla *f* kneecap; (zool) limpet
patè·ma *m* (**-mi**) affliction; **patema d'animo** anxiety
patenta·to -ta *adj* licensed; (coll) well-known
patènte *adj* patent ‖ *f* license; driver's license; **patente sanitaria** (naut) bill of health
patentino *m* (aut) permit
pateréc·cio *m* (**-ci**) whitlow
paternale *adj* (obs) paternal ‖ *f* reprimand
paterni·tà *f* (**-tà**) paternity; authorship
patèr·no -na *adj* paternal; fatherly
paternòstro *m* Lord's Prayer; **è vero come il paternostro** it is the gospel truth
patèti·co -ca (**-ci -che**) *adj* pathetic; mawkish ‖ *m* pathos; mawkishness
pathos *m* pathos
patìbile *adj* endurable
patibolare *adj* gallows
patìbolo *m* executioner's instrument; scaffold
patiménto *m* suffering
pàtina *f* patina; coating (*on paper*); varnish; fur (*on tongue*)
patinare (**pàtino**) *tr* to gloss, glaze (*e.g., paper*)
patire §176 *tr* to suffer; (gram) to be the recipient of (*an action*) ‖ *intr* to suffer
pati·to -ta *adj* suffering, sickly ‖ *mf* fan ‖ *m* boyfriend ‖ *f* girlfriend
patòge·no -na *adj* pathogenic
patologìa *f* pathology
patològi·co -ca *adj* (**-ci -che**) pathologic(al)
patos *m* var of **pathos**
patrasso *m*—**andare a patrasso** to die; to go to ruin; **mandare a patrasso** to kill; to ruin
pàtria *f* fatherland, native land
patriar·ca *m* (**-chi**) patriarch
patriarcale *adj* patriarchal
patrigno *m* stepfather
patrimoniale *adj* patrimonial; property (*tax*); capital (*e.g., transaction*)
patrimò·nio *m* (**-ni**) patrimony; estate; fortune; (fig) heritage
pà·trio -tria (**-tri -trie**) *adj* paternal; of one's country (*e.g., love*) ‖ *f* see **patria**

patriò·ta *mf* (**-ti -te**) patriot; (coll) fellow citizen
patriòtti·co -ca *adj* (**-ci -che**) patriotic
patriottismo *m* patriotism
patrì·zio -zia (**-zi -zie**) *adj* & *m* patrician ‖ **Patrizio** *m* Patrick
patrocinante *adj* pleading (*lawyer*)
patrocinare *tr* to favor, sponsor; to plead
patrocina·tóre -trice *mf* defender; pleader
patrocì·nio *m* (**-ni**) support; sponsorship; (law) defense; **patrocinio gratuito** public defense
patronato *m* patronage; charitable institution, foundation; **patronato scolastico** state aid fund
patronéssa *f* sponsor; trustee (*of charitable institution*)
patròno *m* patron saint; patron; sponsor; trustee (*of charitable institution*); (law) counsel
patta *f* flap (*of garment*); bill (*of anchor*); (coll) potholder; **essere** or **far patta** to be even, tie
patteggiaménto *m* negotiation
patteggiare §290 (**pattéggio**) *tr* & *intr* to negotiate
pattinàggio *m* skating
pattinare (**pàttino**) *intr* to skate; to skid (*said of a car*)
pattina·tóio *m* (**-tói**) skating rink
pattina·tóre -trice *mf* skater
pàttino *m* skate; guide block (*of an elevator*); (aer) skid, runner; **pattino a rotelle** roller skate
pattino *m* racing shell with outrigger floats
patto *m* pact; **a nessun patto** by no means; **a patto che** provided (that); **patto sociale** social contract; **venire a patti** to come to terms
pattùglia *f* patrol
pattugliare §280 *tr* & *intr* to patrol
pattuire §176 *tr* & *intr* to negotiate
pattuì·to -ta *adj* agreed ‖ *m* agreement
pattume *m* litter, garbage
pattumièra *f* dustpan; trash bin
patùrnie *fpl*—**avere le paturnie** (coll) to be in the dumps
paura *f* fear; **aver paura di** to be afraid of; **da far paura** frightful; **dar** or **metter paura a** to frighten; **per paura che** for fear that, lest
pauró·so -sa [s] *adj* fearful
pàusa *f* pause
pausare (**pàuso**) *tr* (lit) to interrupt ‖ *intr* (lit) to pause
paventare (**pavènto**) *tr* & *intr* to fear
pavesare (**pavéso**) *tr* to deck with flags; to dress (*a ship*)
pavése [s] *adj*—see **zuppa** ‖ *m* pavis (*shield*); (naut) bunting
pàvi·do -da *adj* cowardly, timid
pavimentare (**paviménto**) *tr* to pave
pavimentazióne *f* paving, pavement
paviménto *m* floor; bottom (*of sea*); paving (*of street*)
pavoncèlla *f* lapwing
pavó·ne -na or **-néssa** *mf* peacock
pavoneggiare §290 (**pavonéggio**) *ref* **to** swagger, strut
pazientare (**paziènto**) *intr* to be patient

paziènte *adj & mf* patient

pazienza *f* patience; fare scappare la pazienza a to drive mad; pazienza! too bad!

pazzé·sco -sca *adj* (-schi -sche) crazy, wild

pazzìa *f* madness, insanity; folly; fare pazzie to act like a fool

paz·zo -za *adj* crazy, insane; andar pazzo per to be crazy about || *mf* crazy person

pèc·ca *f* (-che) imperfection

peccaminó·so -sa [s] *adj* sinful

peccare §197 (pècco) *intr* to sin; to be lacking; to be at fault

peccato *m* sin; che peccato! what a pity!; è un peccato it's a shame

pecca·tóre -trice *mf* sinner

pécchia *f* bee

pecchióne *m* drone

péce *f* pitch; pece greca rosin

pechinése [s] *adj & mf* Pekingese

Pechino *f* Peking

pècora *f* sheep

peco·ràio *m* (-rài) shepherd

pecorèlla *f* small sheep, lamb

pecori·no -na *adj* sheep; sheepish || *m* sheep-milk cheese || *f* sheep manure

peculato *m* embezzlement, peculation

peculiare *adj* peculiar

peculiari·tà *f* (-tà) peculiarity

pecù·lio *m* (-li) nest egg, savings; (obs) cattle

pecùnia *m* (lit) money

pecunià·rio -ria *adj* (-ri -rie) pecuniary

pedàg·gio *m* (-gi) toll

pedagogìa *f* pedagogy, pedagogics

pedagògi·co -ca *adj* (-ci -che) pedagogic(al)

pedagò·go -ga *mf* (-ghi -ghe) pedagogue

pedalare *intr* to pedal

pedale *m* trunk (*of tree*); pedal; treadle (*e.g., of sewing machine*)

pedalièra *f* pedals, pedal keyboard; (aer) rudder bar

pedalino *m* (coll) sock, short stocking

pedana *f* footrest; platform; bedside rug; hem (*of skirt*); (aut) running board; (sports) springboard

pedante *adj* pedantic || *m* pedant

pedanterìa *f* pedantry

pedanté·sco -sca *adj* (-schi -sche) pedantic

pedata *f* kick; footprint; tread (*of step*)

pedèstre *adj* pedestrian

pedia·tra *mf* (-tri -tre) pediatrician

pediatrìa *f* pediatrics

pedicu·re *mf* (-re) pedicure

pedicu·ro -ra *mf* var of pedicure

pedilù·vio *m* (-vi) foot bath

pedina *f* (checkers) checker, man; (chess) pawn

pedinare *tr* to shadow, follow about

pedìsse·quo -qua *adj* servile

pedivèlla *f* pedal crank

pedóne *m* pedestrian; (chess) pawn

pedule *m* stocking foot || *fpl* climbing shoes, sneakers

pedùncolo *m* (anat, bot, zool) peduncle

pegamòide *f* imitation leather

pèggio *adj invar* worse; il peggio the worst, e.g., il peggio ragazzo the worst boy; || *m* worst; andare per il peggio to be getting worse || *f* worst; alla peggio if worst comes to worst; averne la peggio to get the worst of it || *adv* worse; worst; at worst; peggio + *pp* less + *pp*; least + *pp*; tanto peggio so much the worse

peggioraménto *m* deterioration, worsening

peggiorare (peggióro) *tr & intr* to worsen

peggió·re (-ri) *adj* worse; worst || *m* worst

pégli §4

pégno *m* pledge, pawn

pégola *f* pitch; (coll) bad luck

péi §4

pél §4

pèla·go *m* (-ghi) (poet) open sea; (coll) mess; pelago di guai sea of trouble

pelame *m* hair, coat

pelandróne *m* (coll) shirker, do-nothing

pelapata·te *m* (-te) potato peeler

pelare (pélo) *tr* to fleece; to pluck; to pare, peel; to clear (*land*); (fig) to strip; to scald, burn || *ref* (coll) to shed; to become bald

pela·to -ta *adj* peeled; hairless, bald; barren || *m* (coll) baldy; pelati peeled tomatoes || *f* fleecing, plucking; (joc) baldness, bald spot

pélla §4

pellàc·cia *f* (-ce) tough hide

pellame *m* skins, hides

pèlle *f* skin, hide; a fior di pelle slightly, superficially; essere nella pelle di to be in the boots of; fare la pelle a to bump off; non stare più nella pelle to be beside oneself with joy; pelle di dante buckskin; pelle d'oca goose skin, goose flesh; pelle d'uovo mull; pelle pelle skin-deep, superficial

pélle §4

pellegrinàg·gio *m* (-gi) pilgrimage

pellegrinare *intr* (lit) to go on a pilgrimage

pellegri·no -na *adj* wandering; (lit) foreign; (lit) strange, quixotic || *mf* pilgrim, traveler

pelleròssa *mf* (pellirosse) redskin

pelletterìa *f* leather goods; leather goods store

pellicano *m* pelican

pelliccerìa *f* furrier's store; furrier's trade, fur industry

pellìc·cia *f* (-ce) fur

pellic·ciàio -ciàia *mf* (-ciài -ciàie) furrier

pelliccióne *m* fur jacket

pellicola *f* film; pellicola in rotolo roll film; pellicola piana film pack; pellicola sonora sound film; pellicola vergine unexposed film

pellirós·sa *mf* (-se) var of pellerossa

pélo *m* hair (*of beard*); pile (*of carpet*); fur; avere pelo sul cuore not to be easily moved; cercare il pelo nell'uovo to split hairs; di primo pelo green, inexperienced; non avere peli sulla lingua to not mince one's words; pelo dell'acqua water surface; per un pelo by a hair's breadth

peloponnesìa·co -ca *adj* (-ci -che) Peloponnesian
peló·so -sa [s] *adj* hairy; self-serving (*e.g., charity*)
péltro *m* pewter
pelùria *f* down, soft hair
péna *f* penalty; concern; compassion; pain, suffering; grief; **a mala pena** barely; **essere in pena per** to worry about; **fare pena** to arouse compassion; **pena infamante** degrading punishment; loss of civil rights; **sotto pena di** under penalty of; **valere la pena** to be worthwhile
penale *adj* penal ‖ *f* penalty
penali·sta *mf* (-sti -ste) criminal lawyer
penali·tà *f* (-tà) penalty
penalizzare [ddzz] *tr* (sports) to penalize
penare (**péno**) *intr* to suffer; to find it difficult
pencolare (**pèncolo**) *intr* to totter; to waver
pendà·glio *m* (-gli) pendant; **pendaglio da forca** gallows bird
pendènte *adj* leaning; hanging; pending ‖ *m* pendant
pendènza *f* inclination, pitch; controversy; balance; **in pendenza** pending
pèndere §123 *intr* to hang; to lean; to slope; to pitch
pendìce *f* slope, declivity
pen·dìo *m* (-dìi) slant; slope
pèndola *f* clock
pendolare *adj* pendulum-like; commuting; transient (*tourist*) ‖ *mf* commuter ‖ *v* (**pèndolo**) *intr* to sway back and forth; to waver; (nav) to cruise back and forth
pèndolo *m* pendulum; clock
pèndu·lo -la *adj* (lit) hanging
penetrante *adj* penetrating, piercing
penetrare (**pènetro**) *tr* to penetrate, pierce ‖ *intr* to penetrate ‖ *ref*— **penetrarsi di** to be convinced of; to become aware of
penicillina *f* penicillin
peninsulare *adj* peninsular
penìsola *f* peninsula
penitènte *adj* & *mf* penitent
penitènza *f* penitence; punishment
penitenzià·rio -ria *adj* & *mf* (-ri -rie) penitentiary
pénna *f* feather; pen; peen (*of hammer*); (mus) plectrum; **penna a sfera** ball-point pen; **penna d'oca** quill; **penna stilografica** fountain pen
pennàc·chio *m* (-chi) panache; plume, tuft; cloud (*of smoke*)
pennaiòlo *m* hack writer
pennarèllo *m* felt-tip pen
pennellare (**pennèllo**) *intr* to brush; (med) to pencil
pennellata *f* brush stroke
pennèllo *m* brush; (naut) signal flag; (naut) kedge; **pennello per la barba** shaving brush; **stare a pennello** to fit to a T
pennino *m* pen; penpoint, nib
pennóne *m* flagpole; (naut) yard; (mil) pennant

pennu·to -ta *adj* feathered ‖ **pennuti** *mpl* birds
penómbra *f* penumbra; semidarkness; faint light; **vivere in penombra** to live in obscurity
penó·so -sa [s] *adj* painful
pensàbile *adj* thinkable
pensante *adj* thinking
pensare (**pènso**) *tr* to think; to think of ‖ *intr* to think; to worry; **dar da pensare a** to cause worry to, e.g., **suo figlio gli dà da pensare** his son causes him worry; **pensa ai fatti tuoi** (coll) mind your own business; **pensa alla salute** (coll) don't worry!; **pensare a** to think of; **pensare di** to plan, intend to
pensata *f* bright idea, brainstorm
pensa·tóre -trice *mf* thinker
pensièro *m* thought; **dare pensiero a** to cause worry to; **darsi pensiero per** to worry about; **essere sopra pensiero** to be absorbed in thought
pensieró·so -sa [s] *adj* thoughtful, pensive
pènsile *adj* hanging, overhead
pensilina *f* marquee
pensionaménto *m* retirement
pensionante *mf* boarder, paying guest
pensionare (**pensióno**) *tr* to pension
pensiona·to -ta *adj* pensioned ‖ *mf* pensioner ‖ *m* boarding school
pensióne *f* pension; boarding house; **in pensione** retired; **tenere a pensione** to board (*a lodger*); **vivere a pensione** to board (*said of a lodger*)
pensó·so -sa [s] *adj* thoughtful, pensive
pentàgono *m* pentagon
pentagram·ma *m* (-mi) (mus) staff, stave
pentàmetro *m* pentameter
Pentecòste, la Pentecost, Whitsunday
pentiménto *m* repentance; correction (*e.g., in a manuscript*); change of heart
pentire (**pènto**) *ref* to repent; to change one's mind; **pentirsi di** to repent
penti·to -ta *adj* repentant, repenting; **pentito e contrito** in sackcloth and ashes
péntola *f* pot, kettle; potful; **pentola a pressione** pressure cooker
penùlti·mo -ma *adj* next to the last ‖ *f* penult
penùria *f* shortage, scarcity
penzolare (**pènzolo**) [dz] *intr* to dangle, hang down
penzolóni [dz] *adv* dangling
peònia *f* peony
pepaiòla *f* pepper shaker; pepper mill
pepare (**pépo**) *tr* to pepper
pepa·to -ta *adj* peppered; peppery
pépe *m* pepper; **pepe della Giamaica** allspice; **pepe di Caienna** red pepper, cayenne pepper
peperóne *m* (bot) pepper
pepita *f* nugget
per *prep* by; through; throughout; for; because of; to, in order to; in favor of; considering; **essere per** to be about to; **per** + *adj* or *adv* + **che** + *subj* however + *adj* or *adv* + *ind*,

e.g., **per intelligente che sia** however intelligent he is; **per caso** perchance; **per che cosa?** what for?; **per l'appunto** exactly, just; **per lungo** lengthwise; **per me** as for me; **per ora** now; **per parte mia** as for me; **per poco** hardly, scarcely, **per quanto** + *adj* or *adv* + *subj* however + *adj* or *adv* + *pres ind*, e.g., **per quanto disperatamente provi** however desperately he attempts; **per tempo** early; **per traverso** diagonally; **per via che** (coll) because; **stare per** to be about to
péra *f* pear (*fruit*); bulb, light bulb; (joc) head
peraltro *adv* besides, moreover
peranco *adv* yet
perbacco *interj* by Jove!
perbène *adj invar* nice, well brought up
percalle *m* percale
percènto *m* percent; percentage
percentuale *adj* percentage || *f* percent; commission, bonus
percepibile *adj* collectable
percepire §176 *tr* to perceive; to receive (*a salary*)
percettibile *adj* perceptible
percetti·vo -va *adj* perceptive
percezióne *f* perception
perché *m* why, reason; **il perché e il percome** the why and the wherefore || *pron rel* for which || *adv* why || *conj* because; so that
perciò *conj* therefore, accordingly
percóme *m & conj* wherefore
percorrènza *f* stretch, distance
percórrere §139 *tr* to cross; to cover, go through
percórso *m* crossing, distance
percòssa *f* hit, blow; contusion
percuòtere §251 *tr* to hit, beat; (fig) to shake || *intr* to strike
percussióne *f* percussion
percussóre *m* firing pin
perdènte *adj* losing || *mf* loser
pèrdere §212 *tr* to lose; to waste; to miss (*e.g., a train*); to ruin; to leak || *intr* to lose; to leak; to be inferior || *ref* to get lost; to waste one's time; **perdersi d'animo** to lose heart; **perdersi in un bicchier d'acqua** to become discouraged for nothing
perdifiato *m*—a **perdifiato** at the top of one's lungs
perdigiór·no *mf* (-no) idler
perdinci *interj* good Heavens!
pèrdita *f* loss; leak; **a perdita d'occhio** as far as the eye can see; **perdite** (mil) casualties
perditèm·po *mf* (-po) idler || *m* waste of time
perdizióne *f* perdition
perdonàbile *adj* pardonable
perdonare (perdóno) *tr* to forgive; to spare; **perdonare a qlcu qlco** or **perdonare qlcu di qlco** to forgive s.o. for s.th || *intr* (with *dat*) to pardon
perdóno *m* forgiveness, pardon
perdurare *intr* (ESSERE & AVERE) to last; to persevere
perdu·to -ta *adj* lost; **andar perduto** to be desperately in love; to get lost

peregrinare *intr* to wander
peregrinazióne *f* wandering
peregri·no -na *adj* far-fetched, outlandish
perènne *adj* everlasting; perennial
perentò·rio -ria *adj* (-ri -rie) peremptory
perequare (perèquo) *tr* to equalize
perequazióne *f* equalization
perfèt·to -ta *adj & m* perfect
perfezionaménto *m* improvement; (educ) specialization
perfezionare (perfezióno) *tr* to improve, polish up; to perfect || *ref* to improve; (educ) to specialize
perfezióne *f* perfection; **a** or **alla perfezione** to perfection
perfidia *f* perfidy
pèrfi·do -da *adj* perfidious, treacherous; (coll) foul, nasty
perfini·re *m* (-re) punch line
perfino *adv* even
perforante *adj* piercing, perforating
perforare (perfóro) *tr* to pierce; to perforate; to punch; to bore
perfora·tóre -trice *mf* key-punch operator || *m* drill || *f* punch; drill; pneumatic drill, rock drill
perforazióne *f* perforation
pergamèna *f* parchment, vellum
pèrgamo *m* (lit) pulpit
pèrgola *f* bower, pergola
pergolato *m* arbor, pergola; grape arbor
pericolante *adj* tottering, unsafe
pericolo *m* danger; **non c'è pericolo** don't worry
pericoló·so -sa [s] *adj* dangerous
periferia *f* periphery; suburbs
perifèri·co -ca *adj* (-ci -che) peripheral
perìfra·si *f* (-si) periphrasis
perìmetro *m* perimeter
periodare *m* writing style || *v* (perìodo) *intr* to turn a phrase
perìodi·co -ca (-ci -che) *adj* periodic(al) || *m* periodical
perìodo *m* period; age; (gram) sentence; (phys) cycle; **il periodo delle feste** holiday time
peripezìa *f* vicissitude
pèriplo *m* circumnavigation
perire §176 *intr* (ESSERE) to perish
periscò·pio *m* (-pi) periscope
peritale *adj* expert
peritare (pèrito) *ref* (lit) to hesitate
peri·to -ta *adj* expert, skilled || *mf* expert; **perito agrario** land surveyor; **perito calligrafo** handwriting expert; **perito chimico** chemist; **perito industriale** industrial engineer
peritonèo *m* peritoneum
perizia *f* skill; survey; appraisal
periziare §287 (perìzio) *tr* to estimate, appraise
pèrla *f* pearl; (med) capsule
perlàce·o -a *adj* pearly
perla·to -ta *adj* pearly, smooth
perlìfe·ro -ra *adj* pearl-producing
perlina *f* bead
perloméno *adv* at least
perlopiù *adv* mostly, generally
perlustrare *tr* to patrol
perlustrazióne *f* patrol, patrolling

permaló·so -sa [s] *adj* touchy, grouchy
permanènte *adj* permanente || *f* permanent wave
permanènza *f* permanence; stay; continuance (*in office*); duration (*of a disease*); **in permanenza** permanent (*employee*); **buona permanenza!** may your stay be happy!
permanére §235 (*pp* **permaso**) *intr* (ESSERE) to remain, stay
permeàbile *adj* permeable
permeare (pèrmeo) *tr* to permeate
permés·so -sa *adj* permitted, allowed; **è permesso?** may I come in? || *m* permit; (mil) pass, leave
perméttere §198 *tr* to permit, allow, let; **permette?** do you mind? || *ref* to take the liberty; to afford
permissìbile *adj* permissible
pèrmuta *f* barter; exchange
permutàbile *adj* tradable, exchangeable
permutare (pèrmuto) *tr* to barter; (math) to permute
pernàcchia *f* (vulg) raspberry
pernice *f* partridge
pernició·so -sa [s] *adj* pernicious || *f* pernicious malaria
pèr·nio *m* (-ni) var of **perno**
pèrno *m* pivot; pin; kingbolt; swivel; heart (*of the matter*); kernel (*of the story*); support (*of the family*); (mach) journal; **fare perno** to pivot
pernottare (pernòtto) *intr* to spend the night, stay overnight
péro *m* pear tree
però *conj* but, yet; however, nevertheless; **e però** (lit) therefore
peróne *m* fibula
peronòspora *f* downy mildew
perorare (pèroro) *tr & intr* to perorate; (law) to plèad
perorazióne *f* peroration; (law) pleading
peròssido *m* peroxide; **perossido d'idrogeno** hydrogen peroxide
perpendicolare *adj & f* perpendicular
perpendìcolo *m* plumb line; **a perpendicolo** perpendicularly
perpetrare (pèrpetro & perpètro) *tr* (lit) to perpetrate
perpètua *f* priest's housekeeper
perpetuare (perpètuo) *tr* to perpetuate
perpè·tuo -tua *adj* perpetual, life || *f* see **perpetua**
perplessi·tà *f* (-tà) perplexity
perplès·so -sa *adj* perplexed; (lit) ambiguous
perquisire §176 *tr* to search
perquisizióne *f* search
persecu·tóre -trice *mf* persecutor, oppressor
persecuzióne *f* persecution
perseguire (perséguo) *tr* to pursue; to persecute; to pester
perseguitare (perséguito) *tr* to persecute; to pursue; to pester
perseveranza *f* perseverance
perseverare (persèvero) *intr* to persevere
persia·no -na *adj* Persian || *m* Persian; Persian lamb || *f* slatted shutter; **persiana avvolgibile** Venetian blind

pèrsi·co -ca (-ci -che) *adj* Persian || *m* (ichth) perch; (obs) peach || *f* (coll) peach
persino *adv* var of **perfino**
persistènte *adj* persistent
persistènza *f* persistence
persìstere §114 *intr* to persist
pèr·so -sa *adj* lost, wasted; (archaic) reddish-brown; **a tempo perso** in one's spare time
persóna *f* person; **per persona** apiece; per capita; **persona di servizio** servant; **persone** people
personàg·gio *m* (-gi) personage; character
personale *adj* personal || *m* figure, body; personnel, staff; crew || *f* one-man show
personali·tà *f* (-tà) personality; personage
personificare §197 (**personìfico**) *tr* to personify
perspicace *adj* perspicacious; far-sighted
perspicàcia *f* perspicacity
perspì·cuo -cua *adj* perspicuous
persuadére §213 *tr* to persuade || *ref* to become convinced
persuasióne *f* persuasion
persuasi·vo -va *adj* persuasive; pleasing || *f* persuasiveness
persua·so -sa *adj* convinced; resigned
pertanto *conj* therefore; **non pertanto** nevertheless
pèrti·ca *f* (-che) perch; pole
pertinace *adj* pertinacious, persistent
pertinà·cia *f* (-cie) pertinacity, obstinacy
pertinènte *adj* pertinent, relevant
pertinènza *f* pertinence; competence
pertósse *f* whooping cough
pertù·gio *m* (-gi) hole
perturbare *tr* to perturb || *ref* to be perturbed
perturbazióne *f* perturbation; disturbance
Perù, il Peru; **valere un Perù** to be worth a king's ransom
peruvia·no -na *adj & mf* Peruvian
pervàdere §172 *tr* (lit) to pervade
pervenire §282 *intr* (ESSERE) to arrive; to come; **pervenire a** to reach
perversióne *f* perversion
perversi·tà *f* (-tà) perversity
pervèr·so -sa *adj* perverse; wicked
pervertiménto *m* perversion
pervertire (pervèrto) *tr* to pervert || *ref* to become perverted
perverti·to -ta *adj* perverted || *mf* pervert
pervicace *adj* (lit) obstinate
pervin·ca *f* (-che) periwinkle
pésa [s] *f* weighing; scale
pesage *m* (pesage) weigh-in; place for weighing in jockeys
pesalètte·re [s] *m* (-re) postal scale
pesante [s] *adj* heavy
pesantézza [s] *f* heaviness; weight
pesare (péso) [s] *tr* to weigh || *intr* to weigh; **pesare a qlcu** to weigh upon s.o.
pesa·tóre -trice [s] *mf* scale or weigh-

bridge operator; **pesatore pubblico** inspector for the department of weights and measures

pesatura [s] _f_ weighing

pé‑sca _f_ (‑sche) fishing; catch (_of fish_) **pesca alla traina** trawling; **pesca d'altura** deep-sea fishing; **pesca di beneficenza** benefit lottery

pè‑sca _f_ (‑sche) peach

pescàg‑gio _m_ (‑gi) (naut) draft

pescàia _f_ dam, weir

pescare §197 (**pésco**) _tr_ to fish; to draw (_a card_); to dig up (_a piece of news_); to dive for (_pearls_); **pescare con la lenza** to angle for (_fish_) || _intr_ to fish; (naut) to displace; **pescare con la lenza** to angle; **pescare di frodo** to poach; **pescare nel torbido** to fish in troubled waters

pesca‑tóre ‑trice _mf_ fisher; **pescatore di canna** angler; **pescatore di frodo** poacher

pésce _m_ fish; (typ) omission; (coll) biceps; **a pesce** headlong; **non sapere che pesci pigliare** to not know which way to turn; **pesce d'aprile** April fool; **pesce gatto** catfish; **pesce martello** hammerhead || **Pesci** _mpl_ (astr) Pisces

pescecane _m_ (**pescecani** & **pescicani**) shark; (fig) war profiteer

pescheréc‑cio ‑cia (‑ci ‑ce) _adj_ fishing || _m_ fishing boat

pescherìa _f_ fish market

peschièra _f_ fishpond; fishpound (_net_)

pescivéndo‑lo ‑la _mf_ fishmonger, fish dealer || _f_ fishwife, fishwoman

pè‑sco _m_ (‑schi) peach tree

pesi‑sta [s] _m_ (‑sti) (sports) weight lifter

péso ‑sa [s] _adj_ (coll) heavy || _m_ weight; burden; bob (_of clock_); (racing) weigh-in; (sports) shot; **di peso** bodily; **peso lordo** gross weight; **peso massimo** (sports) heavyweight; **peso specifico** specific gravity; **rubare sul peso** to give short weight; **usare due pesi e due misure** to have a double standard || _f_ see **pesa**

pessimismo _m_ pessimism

pessimi‑sta _mf_ (‑sti ‑ste) pessimist

pessimìsti‑co ‑ca _adj_ (‑ci ‑che) pessimistic

pèssi‑mo ‑ma _adj_ very bad, very poor

pésta _f_ track, footprint; **lasciar nelle peste** to leave in the lurch; **seguir le peste di** to follow in the footsteps of

pestàggio _m_ beating, clubbing

pestare (**pésto**) _tr_ to pound; to trample; to step on; **pestare le orme di** to follow in the footsteps of; **pestare i piedi** to stamp the feet; **pestare sodo** to beat up

pèste _f_ plague, pest

pestèllo _m_ pestle

pestìfe‑ro ‑ra _adj_ pestiferous

pestilènza _f_ pestilence; stench

pestilenziale _adj_ pestilential; pernicious

pé‑sto ‑sta _adj_ crushed; thick (_darkness_) || _m_ Genoese sauce || _f_ see **pesta**

pètalo _m_ petal

petardo _m_ petard, firecracker

petènte _mf_ petitioner

petizióne _f_ petition; **petizione di principio** begging the question

péto _m_ wind, gas

Petrarca _m_ Petrarch

petrarché‑sco ‑sca _adj_ (‑schi ‑sche) Petrarchan

petrolièra _f_ (naut) tanker

petrolière _adj_ incendiary || _m_ petroleum-industry worker; incendiary; oilman (_producer_)

petrolìfe‑ro ‑ra _adj_ oil-yielding

petrò‑lio _m_ (‑li) petroleum; coal oil, kerosene

petró‑so ‑sa [s] _adj_ (lit) stony

pettegolare (**pettégolo**) _intr_ to gossip

pettegolézzo [ddzz] _m_ gossip, rumor

pettégo‑lo ‑la _adj_ gossipy || _mf_ gossip

pettinare (**pèttino**) _tr_ to comb; to card; (coll) to scold

pettinatóre _m_ carder

pettinatrice _f_ hairdresser; carding machine

pettinatura _f_ coiffure, hairstyling

pèttine _m_ comb; (zool) scallop; **a pettine perpendicular** (_parking_)

pettino _m_ dickey; bib (_of an apron_); plastron

pettirósso _m_ robin redbreast

pètto _m_ breast, chest; bust; bosom; **a un petto** single-breasted; **avere al petto** to feed at the breast; **a due petti** or **a doppio petto** double-breasted; **stare a petto** to be equal

pettorale _adj_ pectoral || _m_ pectoral; breast collar (_of horse_)

pettorina _f_ var of **pettino**

pettorù‑to ‑ta _adj_ strutting, haughty

petulante _adj_ importunate; impertinent

petulanza _f_ importunity; impertinence

petùnia _f_ petunia

pèzza _f_ piece (_of cloth_); diaper; patch (_in suit or tire_); bolt (_of paper or cloth_); **pezza d'appoggio** supporting document, voucher; **trattare come una pezza da piedi** to wipe one's boots on

pezza‑to ‑ta _adj_ spotted, dappled

pezzatura _f_ dapple (_on a horse_); size (_e.g., of a loaf of bread_)

pezzènte _mf_ beggar

pezzétto _m_ little bit; scrap, snip

pèzzo _m_ piece; cut (_of meat_); coin; (journ) article; **andare** or **cadere a pezzi** to fall apart; **a pezzi e bocconi** by fits and starts; **fare a pezzi** to break to pieces; to blow to bits; **pezzo di ricambio** spare part; **pezzo d'uomo** hunk of a man; **pezzo duro** brick ice cream; **pezzo forte** forte; **pezzo fuso** cast, casting; **un bel pezzo** a good while; **un pezzo grosso** a big shot

pezzuòla _f_ small piece of cloth; (coll) handkerchief

phy‑lum _m_ (‑lum) phylum

piacènte _adj_ attractive, pleasant

piacére _m_ pleasure; **a piacere** at will; **a Suo piacere** as you please; **fare piacere a** to do a favor for; to please; **per piacere** please; **piacere!**

pleased to meet you! || §214 *intr* (ESSERE) to please; to be pleasing; (with *dat*) to please, e.g., **come piace a Dio** as it pleases God; to like, e.g., **gli piace il ballo** he likes dancing

piacévole *adj* pleasant, pleasing

piacevolézza *f* pleasantness; off-color joke

pia·ga *f* (-ghe) sore; ulcer; wound; plague; (joc) bore; **piaga di decubito** bedsore

piagare §209 *tr* to make sore, injure

piàg·gia *f* (-ge) (archaic) declivity; (lit) clime, country

piaggiare §290 *tr* (lit) to flatter, blandish || *intr* (archaic) to coast

piagnistèo *m* whining

piagnó·ne -na *mf* (coll) weeper, crybaby

piagnucolare (**piagnùcolo**) *intr* to whimper, whine

piagnucoló·ne -na *mf* whimperer, crybaby

piagnucoló·so -sa [s] *adj* whimpering, whining

pialla *f* (carp) plane

piallàc·cio *m* (-ci) veneer

piallare *tr* (carp) to plane

piallatrice *f* (carp) planer

piallatura *f* (carp) planing

piana *f* plain; wide table

pianale *m* plain; platform; (rr) flatcar, platform car

pianeggiante *adj* plane, level

pianèlla *f* mule (*slipper*); tile

pianeròttolo *m* landing (*of stairs*); ledge

piané·ta *m* (-ti) planet; horoscope || *f* (eccl) chasuble

piàngere §215 *tr* to shed (*tears*); to mourn, lament; **piangere miseria** to cry poverty || *intr* to cry, weep

piangimisè·ria *mf* (-ria) poverty-crying penny pincher

piangiucchiare §287 *intr* to whimper

pianificare §197 (**pianìfico**) *tr* to level; (econ) to plan

pianifica·tóre -trice *mf* planner

pianino *m* (coll) barrel organ

piani·sta *mf* (-sti -ste) pianist

pia·no -na *adj* plane; plain, flat || *m* plain; plane; floor; plateau; plan; map; (mus) piano; **di primo piano** first-class; **in piano** horizontal; **piano di coda** (aer) tail assembly; **piano di studio** curriculum; **piano regolatore** building plan; **piano terra** ground floor; **primo piano** (phot) close-up; (theat) foreground || *f* see **piana** || **piano** *adv* slowly; softly

pianofòrte *m* piano; **pianoforte a coda** grand piano

pianòla *f* player piano

pianòro *m* plateau

pianotèr·ra *m* (-ra) ground floor

pianta *f* plant; sole (*of foot*); plan, map; floor plan; **di sana pianta** wholly; **in pianta stabile** permanent (*employee*); **pianta rampicante** (bot) climber

piantagióne *f* plantation

piantana *f* scaffolding

piantare *tr* to plant; to set up (*e.g., a gun emplacement*); to pitch (*a tent*); **piantala!** (slang) cut it out!; **piantare baracca e burattini** (coll) to clear out; **piantar chiodi** (coll) to go into debt; **piantare gli occhi addosso a** to stare at; **piantare in asso** to leave in the lurch || *ref* to place oneself; to abandon one another

pianta·to -ta *adj* planted; stuck; driven; **bien piantato** well-built (*person*)

pianta·tóre -trice *mf* planter

pianterréno *m* ground floor

piantito *m* (coll) floor

pianto *m* weeping, tears; sadness; (bot) sap; (coll) sight, mess

piantonare (**piantóno**) *tr* to watch, guard

piantóne *m* watchman; (mil) orderly; (mil) sentry; (bot) cutting, shoot; **piantone di guida** (aut) steering wheel column

pianura *f* plain

piastra *f* plate; plaster (*coin*)

piastrèlla *f* tile; small flat stone; bounce (*of an airplane on landing*)

piastrellaménto *m* bump, bounce (*of motorboat or airplane*)

piastrelli·sta *m* (-sti) tiler, tile layer

piastrina *f* or **piastrino** *m* small plate; (mil) dog tag; (biol) platelet

piatire §176 *intr* (lit) to argue; (coll) to beg insistently

piattafórma *f* platform; roadbed (*of highway*); (rr) turntable; (pol) plank; **piattaforma di lancio** launching pad

piattèllo *m* small dish; bobêche; clay pigeon

piattina *f* electric cord; metal band; (min) wagon

piattino *m* saucer

piat·to -ta *adj* flat || *m* dish, plate; pan (*of scale*); pot (*in gambling*); course (*of meal*); cover (*of book*); flat (*e.g., of blade*); **piatti** (mus) cymbals; **piatto del grammofono** turntable; **piatto del giorno** plat du jour; **piatto di lenticchie** (Bib & fig) mess of pottage; **piatto fondo** soup dish; **piatto forte** pièce de résistance

piàttola *f* (zool) crab louse; (coll) cockroach; (vulg) bore

piazza *f* square; plaza; crowd; market; fortress; **andare in piazza** (coll) to become bald; **da piazza** common, ordinary; **di piazza** for hire (*e.g., cab*); **fare la piazza** (com) to canvass for customers; **far piazza pulita di** to get rid of; to clean out; **mettere in piazza** to noise abroad; **piazza d'armi** parade ground; **scendere in piazza** to take to the streets

piazzafòrte *f* (**piazzefòrti**) stronghold, fortress

piazzale *m* large square, esplanade, plaza

piazzaménto *m* placement; (sports) position (*of a team*)

piazzare *tr* to place; to sell || *ref* to place; to show (*said of a racing horse*)

piazza·to -ta *adj* placed; arrived (*at a high position*) ‖ *f* row, brawl

piazzi·sta *m* (**-sti**) salesman; traveling salesman

piazzòla *f* court, place; rest area (*off a highway*); (mil) emplacement; **piazzola di partenza** (golf) tee

pi·ca *f* (**-che**) (orn) magpie

picaré·sco -sca *adj* (**-schi -sche**) picaresque

pic·ca *f* (**-che**) pike; pique; **per picca** out of spite; **picche** (cards) spades; **rispondere picche** (fig) to answer no

piccante *adj* piquant, racy

piccare §197 *tr* (obs) to prick ‖ *ref* to become angry; **piccarsi di** to pride oneself on

pic·chè *f* (**-chè**) piqué

picchettaménto *m* picketing

picchettare (picchétto) *tr* to stake out; to picket

picchétto *m* stake; picket; (mil) detail

picchiare §287 *tr* to hit, strike ‖ *intr* to knock; to strike; to tap (*said, e.g., of rain*); (aer) to nose-dive; **picchiare in testa** (aut) to knock ‖ *ref* to hit one another

picchiata *f* hit, blow; (aer) nose dive

picchia·tóre -trice *mf* hitter ‖ *m* (boxing) puncher

picchierellare (picchierèllo) *tr & intr* to tap

picchiettare (picchiétto) *tr* to tap; to scrape; to speckle ‖ *intr* to tap

picchiet·tìo *m* (**-tìi**) patter (*e.g., of rain*)

pic·chio *m* (**-chi**) knock; (orn) woodpecker; **di picchio** all of a sudden

picchiòtto *m* knocker (*on door*)

piccinerìa *f* pettiness

picci·no -na *adj* little, tiny; petty ‖ *mf* child; baby

picciòlo *m* stem (*e.g., of cherry*); leafstalk, petiole

piccionàia *f* dovecote; loft; attic; (theat) upper gallery

piccióne -na *mf* pigeon; **pigliare due piccioni con una fava** to hit two birds with one stone

pic·co *m* (**-chi**) peak; (naut) gaff; **andare a picco** to sink; to go to ruin; **a picco** vertically; **picco di carico** (naut) derrick

piccolézza *f* smallness; trifle

pìcco·lo -la *adj* small; low (*speed*); short (*distance*); young; petty; **da piccolo** when young; **in piccolo** on a small scale; **nel mio piccolo** with my modest abilities ‖ *mf* child

piccóne *m* pick

piccòzza *f* mattock (*for mountain climbing*)

pidocchierìa *f* stinginess; meanness

pidòc·chio *m* (**-chi**) louse; **pidocchio rifatto** (slang) parvenu

pidocchió·so -sa [s] *adj* lousy; stingy

piè *m* (**piè**) (lit) foot; **ad ogni piè sospinto** on every occasion; **saltare a piè pari** to skip with the feet together; (fig) to skip over

piède *m* foot; leg (*of table*); stalk (*of salad*); bottom (*of column*); trunk (*of tree*); footing; **alzarsi in piedi** to stand up; **a piede libero** free; **a piedi** on foot; **a piedi nudi** barefooted; **con i piedi di piombo** cautiously; **essere in piedi** to be up and around; **fare con i piedi** to botch; **mettere un piede in fallo** to stumble; **piede di porco** crowbar; **prendere piede** to take hold; **puntare i piedi** to balk; **su due piedi** offhand; **tenere il piede in due staffe** to carry water on both shoulders

piedestallo or **piedistallo** *m* pedestal

piedritto *m* buttress

piè·ga *f* (**-ghe**) bend; crease; pleat; crimp; wrinkle; (fig) turn; **prendere una cattiva piega** to take a turn for the worse

piegare §209 (**piègo**) *tr* to bend; to wave (*hair*); to fold; to pleat; to bow (*head*) ‖ *intr* to turn ‖ *ref* to bow; to bend; to buckle; to yield

piega·tóre -trice *mf* folder ‖ *f* folding machine

piegatura *f* fold, crease

pieghettare (pieghétto) *tr* to pleat

pieghévole *adj* folding; pliant; (fig) versatile ‖ *m* folder

pieghevolézza *f* flexibility

piè·go *m* (**-ghi**) folder; bundle of papers

pièna *f* flood; rise (*of river*); crowd; (fig) overflow; **in piena** overflowing

pienézza *f* plenitude, fullness

piè·no -na *adj* full; solid; broad (*daylight*); full (*honors*); **a pieno** or **in pieno** to the full; **colpire nel pieno** to hit the bull's eye; **pieno di** alive with; **pieno di sé** conceited; **pieno zeppo** replete, chock-full ‖ *m* fullness; height (*e.g., of winter*); **fare il pieno** (aut) to fill up ‖ *f* see **piena**

pie·tà *f* (**-tà**) mercy; pity; (lit) piety

pietanza *f* main course

pietó·so -sa [s] *adj* pitiful, piteous; merciful

piètra *f* stone; rock; **pietra angolare** cornerstone; **pietra da affilare** whetstone; **pietra da sarto** French chalk; **pietra dello scandalo** source of scandal; **pietra di paragone** touchstone; **pietra focaia** flint; **pietra miliare** milestone; **pietra tombale** tombstone; **posare la prima pietra** to lay the cornerstone

pietrificare §197 (**pietrìfico**) *tr & ref* to petrify

pietrina *f* flint (*for lighter*)

pietri·sco *m* (**-schi**) rubble; (rr) ballast

Piètro *m* Peter

pietró·so -sa [s] *adj* (lit) stony

pievano *m* parish priest

piffero *m* pipe, fife

pìgia *m*—**pigia pigia** crowd, throng

pigia·ma *m* (**-ma & -mi**) pajamas

pigiare §290 *tr* to squeeze, press ‖ *intr* to insist ‖ *ref* to squeeze

pigia·tóre -trice *mf* presser (*of grapes*) ‖ *f* wine press

pigiatura *f* pressing, squeezing

pigionante *mf* tenant

pigióne *f* rent, rental; **dare a pigione** to rent; to grant the possession of; **prendere a pigione** to rent; to hold for payment

pigliamó·sche *m* (-sche) flypaper; fly-trap; (orn) flycatcher
pigliare §280 *tr* to take, catch; to mis-take; che Le piglia? what's the mat-ter with you? || *ref*—pigliarsela (con) to get angry (at)
pì·glio *m* (-gli) hold; countenance; dar di piglio a to grab
pigménto *m* pigment
pigmè·o -a *adj & mf* pygmy; Pygmy
pigna *f* strainer (*at the end of a suction pipe*); bunch (*of grapes*); (bot) pine cone
pignatta *f* pot
pignò·lo -la *adj* finicky, fussy || *m* pine nut
pignóne *m* pinion; embankment
pignoraménto *m* (law) seizure
pignorare (pìgnoro) *tr* (law) to seize
pigolare (pìgolo) *intr* to peep (*said, e.g., of young birds*)
pigolì·o *m* (-ì) peep (*e.g., of a young bird*)
pigrìzia *f* laziness
pì·gro -gra *adj* lazy; (lit) sluggish
pila *f* pier; buttress (*of bridge*); heap; sink; font; (elec) cell; (elec) battery; pila atomica atomic pile
pilastro *m* pier, pillar
pillàcchera *f* mud splash; (fig) fault
pìllola *f* pill; (slang) bullet; addolcire la pillola to sugar-coat the pill
pilóne *m* pier; pylon
pilò·ta (-ti -te) *adj* pilot || *mf* pilot; (aut) driver
pilotàg·gio *m* (-gi) piloting; steering
pilotare (pilòto) *tr* to pilot; to drive
pilotina *f* (naut) pilot boat
piluccare §197 *tr* to pluck (*e.g., grapes one by one*); to nibble, pick at; to scrounge; (lit) to consume
piménto *m* allspice
pinacotè·ca *f* (-che) picture gallery
pinéta *f* pine grove
pìngue *adj* fat; rich
pinguèdine *f* fatness, corpulence
pinguino *m* penguin
pinna *f* fin (*of fish*); flipper; (zool) pen shell (*mussel*)
pinnàcolo *m* pinnacle
pino *m* pine tree; pino marittimo pi-naster; pino silvestre Scotch fir
pinòlo *m* pine nut
pinta *f* pint
pinza *f* claw (*of lobster*); pinza emo-statica hemostat; pinza tagliafili wire cutter; pinze clippers; pliers; pincers
pinzatrice *f* stapler
pinzétte *fpl* tweezers, pliers
pinzòche·ro -ra *mf* bigot
pì·o -a *adj* (-i -e) pious; charitable || Pio *m* Pius
piòg·gia *f* (-ge) rain
piòlo *m* peg; rung (*of ladder*); picket, stake
piombàggine *f* graphite
piombare (piómbo) *tr* to lead; to seal; to knock down; to fill (*a tooth*) || *intr* to fall; to swoop down
piombatura *f* leading; filling (*of tooth*)
piombino *m* weight; seal; plumb; plumb bob

piómbo *m* lead; a piombo perpendicu-larly; di piombo suddenly
pionerìsti·co -ca *adj* (-ci -che) pioneer-ing
pionière *m* pioneer
piòppo *m* poplar; pioppo tremolo aspen
piorrèa *f* pyorrhea
piotare (piòto) *tr* to sod
piova·no -na *adj* rain (*water*)
piova·sco *m* (-schi) rain squall
piovènte *m* pitch, slope
piòvere §216 *intr* (ESSERE) to rain; to pour; to flock (*said of people*); pio-vere addosso a to rain down on; piovere su to flow down over || *impers* (ESSERE & AVERE)—piove it is raining; it is leaking (*from rain*); piove a catinelle or a dirotto it is raining cats and dogs
piovigginare (piovìggina) *impers* (ES-SERE & AVERE)—pioviggina it is driz-zling
piovigginó·so -sa [s] *adj* drizzling, drizzly
piovór·no -na *adj* (lit) var of piovoso
piovosi·tà [s] *f* (-tà) raininess; rainfall
piovó·so -sa [s] *adj* rainy
piòvra *f* octopus; (fig) leech
pipa *f* pipe; non valere una pipa di tabacco to not be worth a tinker's dam
pipare *intr* to smoke a pipe
pipata *f* pipe, pipeful
pipistrèllo *m* (zool) bat
pipita *f* hangnail; (vet) pip
pira *f* (lit) pyre
piràmide *f* pyramid
pira·ta *adj invar* pirate || *m* (-ti) pirate; pirata dell'aria skyjacker; pirata della strada hit-and-run driver
pirateggiare §290 (piratéggio) *intr* to pirate
pirateria *f* piracy; pirateria letteraria piracy of literary works
Pirenèi *mpl* Pyrenees
pìri·co -ca *adj* (-ci -che) fireworks; polvere pirica gunpowder
pirite *f* pyrite
piroétta *f* pirouette
pirò·ga *f* (-ghe) pirogue
pirolisi *f* (chem) cracking
piróne *m* (mus) tuning pin
piròscafo *m* steamship; piroscafo da carico (naut) freighter; piroscafo da passeggeri passenger ship
piroscissióne *f* (chem) cracking
pirotècni·co -ca (-ci -che) *adj* pyro-tecnic || *m* pyrotecnist || *f* fireworks, pyrotechnics
pisciare §128 *intr* (vulg) to urinate
piscia·tóio *m* (-tói) (vulg) street urinal
piscina *f* swimming pool
pisèllo [s] *m* pea; pisello odoroso sweet pea
pisolare (pìsolo) *intr* (coll) to doze
pìsolo *m* (coll) nap; schiacciare un pisolo (coll) to take a nap
pìsside *f* (eccl) pyx; (bot) pyxidium
pista *f* track; ring (*of circus*); race track, speedway (*for car races*); ski run; (aer) runway; pista ciclabile bicycle trail; pista da ballo dance

floor; **seguire una pista** to follow a clue

pistàc·chio *m* (**-chi**) pistachio

pistillo *m* (bot) pistil

pistòla *f* pistol

pistolettata *f* pistol shot

pistolòtto *m* lecture, talking-to; theatrical peroration

pistóne *m* piston; plunger

pitagòri·co -ca *adj* & *m* (**-ci -che**) Pythagorean

pitale *m* (coll) chamber pot

pitoccare §197 (**pitòcco**) *intr* to beg

pitòc·co *m* (**-chi**) beggar; miser

pitóne *m* python

pìttima *f* plaster; (fig) bore

pit·tóre -trice *mf* painter

pittoré·sco -sca *adj* (**-schi -sche**) picturesque

pittòri·co -ca *adj* (**-ci -che**) pictorial

pittura *f* painting; picture; (coll) paint

pitturare *tr* to paint; to varnish || *ref* to put on make-up

più *adj invar* more; several || *m* (**più**) plus; most; **credersi da più** to believe oneself superior; **dal più al meno** about, more or less; **i più** most, the majority; **parlare del più e del meno** (coll) to make small talk || *adv* more; again; **a più non posso** to the very utmost; **in più** besides; **mai più** never again; **non poterne più** to be exhausted; **per di più** besides; **per lo più** for the most part; **più o meno** more or less; **tanto più** moreover; **tutt'al più** mostly

piuma *f* feather, plume; **piume** (fig) bed

piumàc·cio *m* (**-ci**) feather pillow

piumàg·gio *m* (**-gi**) plumage

piumino *m* down; comforter; puff, powder puff; feather duster

piuttòsto *adv* rather; somewhat

piva *f* bagpipe; **tornare con le pive nel sacco** to return bitterly disappointed

pivèllo *m* greenhorn; whippersnapper

pivière *m* (orn) plover

pizza *f* pizza; (mov) canister; (coll) bore

pizzaiò·lo -la *mf* owner of pizzeria || *m* pizza baker || *f*—**alla pizzaiola** prepared with tomato and garlic sauce

pizzardóne *m* (coll) cop, officer

pizzicàgno·lo -la *mf* grocer; sausage dealer

pizzicare §197 (**pìzzico**) *tr* to pinch; to pluck; to bite, burn; (mus) to pick, twang

pizzicherìa *f* delicatessen, grocery

pìzzi·co *m* (**-chi**) pinch

pizzicóre *m* itch

pizzicòtto *m* pinch; **dar pizzicotti a** to pinch

pizzo *m* peak (*of mountain*); goatee; lace

placare §197 *tr* to placate || *ref* to calm down

plac·ca *f* (**-che**) plate; plaque; tag, badge; (elec, rad) plate; (pathol) blotch, spot

placcare §197 *tr* to plate; (sports) to tackle

plàci·do -da *adj* placid

plafond *m* (**plafond**) ceiling; (aer) ceiling; (com) top credit

pla·ga *f* (**-ghe**) (lit) clime, region

plagiare §290 *tr* to plagiarize

plagià·rio -ria (**-ri -rie**) *adj* plagiaristic || *mf* plagiarist

plà·gio *m* (**-gi**) plagiarism

planare *intr* (aer) to glide

planata *f* (aer) gliding

plàn·cia *f* (**-ce**) (naut) gangplank; (naut) bridge

planetà·rio -ria (**-ri -rie**) *adj* planetary || *m* planetarium; (aut) planetary gear

plantare *m* arch support

pla·sma *m* (**-smi**) plasma

plasmare *tr* to mold, shape

plàsti·ca *f* (**-che**) plastic art; plastics; plastic surgery; plastic

plasticare §197 (**plàstico**) *tr* to mold, shape; to cover with plastic

plàsti·co -ca (**-ci -che**) *adj* plastic || *m* relief map; maquette; plastic bomb || *f* see **plastica**

plastilina *f* modeling clay

plastron *m* (**plastron**) ascot

plàtano *m* plane tree; **platano americano** buttonwood tree

platèa *f* audience; (theat) orchestra; (archit) foundation

plateale *adj* obvious; plebeian

plàtina *f* (typ) platen

platinare (**plàtino**) *tr* to platinize; **to** bleach (*hair*)

plàtino *m* platinum

Platóne *m* Plato

plaudènte *adj* enthusiastic

plàudere (**plàudo**) & **plaudire** (**plàudo**) *intr* to applaud; (with *dat*) to applaud, e.g., **plaudere alla generosità** to applaud the generosity

plausibile *adj* plausible

plàuso *m* (lit) applause, praise

plebàglia *f* rabble

plèbe *f* populace; (lit) crowd

plebè·o -a *adj* & *mf* plebeian

plebiscito *m* plebiscite

plenà·rio -ria *adj* (**-ri -rie**) plenary

plenilù·nio *m* (**-ni**) full moon

plenipotenzià·rio -ria *adj* & *m* (**-ri -rie**) plenipotentiary

plètora *f* plethora

plèttro *m* (mus) pick, plectrum

pleurite *f* (pathol) pleurisy

pli·co *m* (**-chi**) sealed document; bundle of papers; **in plico a parte** or **in plico separato** under separate cover

plotóne *m* platoon; **plotone d'esecuzione** firing squad

plùmbe·o -a *adj* lead, leaden

plurale *adj* & *m* plural; **al plurale** in the plural

plurilingue *adj* multilingual

plurimotóre *adj* multimotored || *m* multimotor

pluristàdio *adj invar* (rok) multistage

plusvalènza *f* unearned increment

plusvalóre *m;* surplus value (*in Marxist economics*)

Plutarco *m* Plutarch

plutocrazìa *f* plutocracy

Plutóne *m* Pluto

plutònio m plutonium
pluviale adj rain || m waterspout
pneumàti·co -ca (-ci -che) adj pneumatic, air || m tire; **pneumatico da neve** snow tire
po' m see **poco**
pochézza f lack, scarcity
pò·co -ca (-chi -che) adj little; short (distance); poor (health; memory); (with collective nouns) few, e.g., **poca gente** few people; (with plural nouns) a few, e.g., **fra pochi mesi** in a few months; (with plural nouns having singular meaning in English) little, e.g., **pochi quattrini** little money || m invar little; short distance; short time; **a ogni poco** often; **da poco** a little while ago; of no account; **da un bel po'** quite a while; quite a while ago; **fra poco** in a little while; **manca poco a** it won't be long till; **manca poco che** (e.g., il ragazzo) **non** + subj (e.g., the boy) almost + ind; **per poco non** almost; **poco di buono** good-for-nothing; **poco fa** a little while ago; **saper di poco** to taste flat; **un poco di** or **un po' di** a little || f—**poca di buono** hussy || **poco** adv little; **poco bene** poorly; **poco dopo** shortly after; **poco male** not too poorly
podagra f gout
podére m farm, country property
poderó·so -sa [s] adj powerful
pode·stà m (-stà) (hist) mayor; (hist) podesta
podia·tra mf (-tri -tre) chiropodist
pò·dio m (-di) podium; platform; (archit) base
podismo m foot racing
podi·sta mf (-sti -ste) foot racer
poè·ma m (-mi) long poem
poesìa f poetry; poem
poè·ta m (-ti) poet
poetéssa f poetess
poèti·co -ca (-ci -che) adj poetic(al) || f poetics
pòg·gia f (-ge) leeward
poggiare §290 (pòggio) tr to lean || intr to be based; (mil) to move; (naut) to sail before the wind; (archaic) to rise
poggiatè·sta m (-sta) headrest; (aut) head restraint
pòg·gio m (-gi) hillock, knoll
poggiòlo m balcony
pòi m future || adv then; later; **a poi** until later; **poi dopo** later on
poiana f buzzard
poiché conj since, as; (lit) after
pòker m poker (game); four of a kind; **poker di re** four kings
polac·co -ca (-chi -che) adj Polish || mf Pole || f (mus) polonaise
polare adj pole, polar
polarizzare [ddzz] tr to polarize
pòl·ca f (-che) polka
polèmi·co -ca (-ci -che) adj polemical || f polemics
polemizzare [ddzz] intr to engage in polemics
polèna f (naut) figurehead
polènta f corn mush

polentina f poultice
poliambulanza f clinic, emergency ward
policlìni·co m (-ci) polyclinic
polifonìa f polyphony
polìga·mo -ma adj polygamous || m polygamist
poliglòt·ta adj & mf (-ti -te) polyglot
poliglòt·to -ta adj & mf polyglot
polìgono m polygon; **poligono di tiro** shooting range
polìgrafo m author skilled in many subjects; multigraph
polinesia·no -na adj & mf Polynesian
polinò·mio m (-mi) polynomial
pòlio f (coll) polio
poliomielite f poliomielitis, infantile paralysis
pòlipo m (pathol, zool) polyp
polisìlla·bo -ba adj polysyllabic || m polysyllable
poli·sta m (-sti) polo player
politea·ma m (-mi) theater
politècni·co -ca (-ci -che) adj polytechnic || m polytechnic institute
politei·sta (-sti -ste) adj polytheistic || mf polytheist
politeìsti·co -ca adj (-ci -che) polytheistic
politézza f smoothness
polìti·ca f (-che) politics; policy
politicante mf petty politician
polìti·co -ca (-ci -che) adj political || m politician || f see **politica**
polìtti·co m (-ci) polyptych
polizìa f police; **polizia sanitaria** health department; **polizia stradale** highway patrol; **polizia tributaria** income-tax investigation department
polizié·sco -sca adj (-schi -sche) police (car); detective (story)
poliziòtto adj masc police (dog) || m policeman; detective; **poliziotto in borghese** plain-clothes man
pòlizza f policy; ticket (e.g., of pawnbroker); **polizza di carico** bill of lading
pólla f spring (of water)
pol·làio m (-lài) chicken coop
pollaiò·lo -la mf chicken dealer
pollame m poultry
pollastra f pullet; (coll) chick
pollerìa f poultry shop
pòllice m thumb; big toe; inch
pollicoltura f poultry raising
pòlline m pollen
pollivéndo·lo -la mf poultry dealer
póllo m chicken; (fig) sucker; **conoscere i propri polli** (fig) to know one's onions; **pollo d'India** turkey
pollóne m (bot) shoot; (fig) offspring
polmóne m lung; **a pieni polmoni** at the top of one lungs; **polmone d'acciaio** iron lung
polmonite f pneumonia
pòlo m pole; polo shirt; (sports) polo
Polònia, la Poland
pólpa f meat; pulp; flesh (of fruit); (fig) gist; **in polpe** (hist) in knee breeches
polpàc·cio m (-ci) calf (of leg); cut of meat; ball of thumb

polpastrèllo *m* finger tip
polpétta *f* meat ball; meat patty, cutlet
polpettóne *m* meat loaf; (fig) hash
pólpo *m* (zool) octopus
polpó·so -sa [s] *adj* pulpy, fleshy
polpu·to -ta *adj* meaty
polsino *m* cuff
pólso *m* pulse; wrist; cuff, wristband; strong hand, energy; **di polso** energetic
poltìglia *f* mash; slush
poltrire §176 *intr* to idle; to loll in bed
poltróna *f* armchair; (theat) orchestra seat; **poltrona a orecchioni** wing chair; **poltrona a sdraio** chaise longue; **poltrona letto** day bed
poltroncina *f* parquet-circle seat
poltró·ne -na *mf* lazybones, sluggard || *f* see **poltrona**
poltronerìa *f* laziness
poltronìssima *f* (theat) first-row seat
pólvere *f* dust; powder; **in polvere** powdered; **polvere da sparo** gunpowder; **polvere di stelle** stardust; **polvere nera** or **pirica** gunpowder; **polveri** gunpowder
polverièra *f* powder magazine; (fig) tinderbox, trouble spot
polverifi·cio *m* (-ci) powder works
polverina *f* (pharm) powder
polverino *m* pounce, sand
polverizzare [ddzz] *tr* to crush, powder; to atomize; to pulverize
polverizza·to -ta [ddzz] *adj* powdered (*sugar*)
polverizzatóre [ddzz] *m* atomizer
polveróne *m* dust cloud
polveró·so -sa [s] *adj* dusty; powdery (*snow*)
pomata *f* ointment; pomade
pomella·to -ta *adj* dapple-grey
pomèllo *m* cheek; cheekbone; pommel, knob
pomeridia·no -na *adj* afternoon, P.M.
pomerìg·gio *m* (-gi) afternoon
pomiciare §128 (**pómicio**) *tr* to pumice || *intr* (slang) to spoon
pomicióne *m* (slang) spooner
pomidòro *m* var of **pomodoro**
pómo *m* apple; knob; pommel (*of saddle*); **pomo della discordia** apple of discord; **pomo di Adamo** Adam's apple; **pomo di terra** potato
pomodòro *m* tomato; **pomodoro di mare** (zool) sea anemone
pómolo *m* (coll) knob, handle
pómpa *f* pump; pomp; state; **in pompa magna** all dressed up; **pompa aspirante** suction pump; **pompa premente** force pump; see **imprenditore** and **impresa**
pompare (**pómpo**) *tr* to pump; to pump up
pompèlmo *m* grapefruit
pompière *m* fireman
pompó·so -sa [s] *adj* pompous
pòn·ce *m* (-ci) punch
ponderare (**pòndero**) *tr* to weigh, ponder; to weight || *intr* to think it over
pondera·to -ta *adj* considerate, careful
ponderó·so -sa [s] *adj* ponderous

ponènte *m* west; west wind; West; West Wind
pónte *m* bridge; metal scaffolding; (aut) axle; (naut) deck; **fare il ponte** to take the day off between two holidays; **fare ponti d'oro a** to offer a good way out to; **ponte aereo** airlift; **ponte delle segnalazioni** (rr) gantry; **ponte di chiatte** pontoon bridge; **ponte di comando** (naut) bridge; **ponte di volo** flight deck; **ponte levatoio** drawbridge; **ponte radio** radio communication; **ponte sospeso** suspension bridge
pontéfice *m* pontiff; (hist) pontifex
pontéggio *m* scaffolding
ponticèllo *m* small bridge; nosepiece (*of eyeglasses*); (mus) bridge
pontière *m* (mil) engineer
pontificale *adj* pontifical || *m* pontifical ' mass
pontifi·cio -cia *adj* (-ci -cie) papal
pontile *m* pier
pontóne *m* pontoon, barge
ponzare (**pónzo**) *tr* (coll) to strain to accomplish || *intr* (coll) to rack one's brains
popeli·ne *f* (-ne) broadcloth
popola·no -na *adj* popular || *mf* commoner
popolare *adj* popular || *v* (**pòpolo**) *tr* to people, populate || *ref* to be inhabited
popolarità *f* popularity
popola·to -ta *adj* peopled; crowded
popolazióne *f* population
pòpolo *m* people; crowd; **popolo grasso** (hist) rich bourgeoisie; **popolo minuto** (hist) artisans, common people
popoló·so -sa [s] *adj* populous
popóne *m* (coll) melon
póppa *f* breast; (naut) stern; (lit) ship; **a poppa** astern, aft
poppante *adj* & *mf* suckling
poppare (**póppo**) *tr* to suckle
poppa·tóio *m* (-tói) nursing bottle
poppavìa *f*—**a poppavia** astern, aft
pòr·ca *f* (-che) ridge (*between furrows*); sow
porcacció·ne -na *m* cad, rake || *f* slut
por·càio *m* (-cài) swineherd; pigsty
porcellana *f* porcelain, china; (bot) purslane
porcellino *m* piggy; **porcellino d'India** guinea pig
porcherìa *f* dirt; (coll) dirty trick; (coll) botch
porchétta *f* roast suckling pig
porcile *m* pigsty
porci·no -na *adj* pig || *m* (bot) boletus
pòr·co -ca *mf* (-ci -che) pig, hog, swine; pork; **porco mondo!** (slang) heck! || *f* see **porca**
porcospino *m* porcupine
pòrfido *m* porphyry
pòrgere §217 *tr* to hand, offer; to relate; **porgere l'orecchio** to lend an ear || *intr* to declaim || *ref* to appear, show up
pornografìa *f* pornography
pòro *m* pore
poró·so -sa [s] *adj* porous
pórpora *f* purple

porpora·to -ta adj purple ‖ m purple; cardinal

porpori·no -na adj purple

pórre §218 tr to put; to repose (trust); to set (a limit; one's foot); to lay (a stone); to pose (a question); to pay (attention); to suppose; to advance (the candidacy); **porre gli occhi addosso a** to lay one's eyes on; **porre in dubbio** to cast doubt on; **porre mano a** to set to work at; **porre termine a** to put an end to; **posto che** since, provided ‖ ref to place oneself; **porsi in cammino** to set out or forth; **porsi in salvo** to reach safety

pòrro m wart; (bot) leek

pòrta f door; gate; (cricket) wicket; (sports) goal; **di porta in porta** door-to-door; **fuori porta** outside the city limits; **mettere alla porta** to dismiss, fire; **porta di servizio** delivery entrance; **porta scorrevole** sliding door; **porta stagna** (naut; theat) safety door

portabagà·gli m (-gli) porter; baggage rack

portabandiè·ra m (-ra) standard-bearer

portàbile adj portable

portàbi·ti m (-ti) coat hanger

portabotti·glie m (-glie) bottle rack

portacar·te adj invar & m (-te) folder

portacati·no adj invar washstand-supporting ‖ m (-no) washstand

portacéne·re m (-re) ashtray

portachia·vi m (-vi) key ring

portacì·pria m (-pria) compact

portadi·schi m (-schi) record cabinet, record rack; turntable

portadól·ci m (-ci) candy dish

portaère·i f (-i) aircraft carrier

portaferi·ti m (-ti) (mil) stretcher bearer

portafinèstra f (portefinèstre) French window

portafió·ri m (-ri) flower vase

portafò·gli m (-gli) or **portafò·glio** m (-gli) billfold, wallet; pocketbook; portfolio

portafortu·na m (-na) charm, amulet

portafrut·ta m (-ta) fruit dish

portafusìbi·li m (-li) fuse box

portagiò·ie m (-ie) jewel box

portaimmondì·zie m (-zie) trash can, garbage can

portainse·gna m (-gna) standard-bearer

portalàmpa·da m (-da) (elec) socket

portale m portal

portalètte·re (-re) mf letter carrier ‖ m postman, mailman

portamaz·ze m (-ze) caddie

portaménto m posture; gait; (fig) behavior

portami·na m (-na) mechanical pencil

portamìssi·li (-li) adj invar missile-carrying ‖ m missile carrier

portamoné·te m (-te) purse

portamùsi·ca m (-ca) music stand

portante adj carrying; (archit) weight-bearing; (aer) lifting; (rad) carrier ‖ m amble

portantina f sedan chair; stretcher

portantino m bearer (of sedan chair); stretcher bearer

portanza f (archit) capacity; (aer) lift

portaombrèl·li m (-li) umbrella stand

portaórdi·ni m (-ni) (mil) messenger

portapac·chi m (-chi) parcel delivery man; basket (on bicycle)

portapén·ne m (-ne) penholder

portapiat·ti m (-ti) dish rack

portaposa·te [s] m (-te) silverware chest

portapran·zi [dz] m (-zi) dinner pail

portaraz·zi (-zi) [ddzz] adj invar missile-carrying ‖ m missile carrier

portare (pòrto) tr to carry; to bring; to take; to carry along; to lead; to herald; to praise; to wear; to drive (car); to run (a candidate); to adduce; to nurture (hatred); (aut) to hold (e.g., five people); **portare a conoscenza di** to let know; **portare avanti** to carry forward; **portare in alto** to lift; **portare via** to steal; to take away ‖ intr to carry (said of a gun) ‖ ref to move; to behave; to be (a candidate)

portaritrat·ti m (-ti) picture frame

portasapó·ne m (-ne) soap dish

portasigarét·te m (-te) cigarette case

portasìga·ri m (-ri) cigar case; humidor

portaspil·li m (-li) pincushion

portata f course (of a meal); capacity; flow (of river); compass (of voice); range (of voice or gun); importance; (naut) burden; (naut) tonnage; **a portata di mano** within reach; **a portata di voce** within call, within earshot

portatès·se·re m (-re) card case

portàtile adj portable

porta·to -ta adj worn; **portato a** leaning toward ‖ m result, effect ‖ f see portata

porta·tóre -trice mf bearer

portatovagliòlo m napkin ring

portauò·vo m (-vo) eggcup

portavó·ce m (-ce) megaphone; (fig) mouthpiece

porte-enfant m (porte-enfant) baby bunting

portèllo m wicket; leaf (of cabinet door); (naut) porthole

portènto m portent

portica·to -ta adj arcaded ‖ m arcade

pòrti·co m (-ci) portico, arcade, colonnade; shed

portiè·re -ra mf concierge ‖ m janitor, doorman; (sports) goalkeeper ‖ f portiere (in church door); (aut) door

porti·nàio -nàia (-nài -nàie) adj door, door-keeping ‖ mf doorkeeper, concierge

portinerìa f janitor's quarters

pòrto m port, harbor; transportation charge; port wine; goal; **condurre a buon porto** to carry to fruition; **franco di porto** prepaid, postpaid; **porto a carico del mittente** postage prepaid; **porto assegnato** charges to be paid by addressee; **porto d'armi** permit to carry arms; **porto franco** free port

Portogallo, il Portugal

portoghése [s] adj & mf Portuguese;

fare il portoghese (theat) to crash the gate
portóne m portal
portorica•no -na adj & mf Puerto Rican
Portorico m Puerto Rico
portuale adj port, harbor || m dock worker, longshoreman
porzióne f portion
pòsa [s] f laying (e.g., of cornerstone); posing (for portrait); posture, affectation, pose; dregs; (phot) exposure; (lit) rest; senza posa relentless; relentlessly
posami•ne (-ne) [s] adj invar mine-laying || f minelayer
posare [s] (pòso) tr to lay, put down || intr to lie; to settle; to pose; posare a to pose as || ref to settle; to alight; (lit) to rest
posata [s] f cover, place (at table); table utensil (knife, fork or spoon); posate knife, fork and spoon
posaterìa [s] f service (of knives, forks, and spoons)
posa•to -ta [s] adj sedate, quiet; placed || f see posata
posa•tóre -trice [s] mf poseur || m layer, installer (of cables or pipes)
pòscia adv then, afterwards; poscia che after
poscritto m postscript
posdatare tr var of postdatare
posdomani adv (lit) day after tomorrow
positivaménte adv for sure
positi•vo -va adj positive || f (phot) positive, print
posizióne f position; status; (fig) stand
pospórre §218 tr to put off, postpone; to put last; posporre qlco a qlco to put or place s.th after s.th
pòssa f (lit) strength, vigor
possanza f (lit) power
possedére §252 tr to possess; to own; to master (a language); essere posseduto da to be enthralled with; to be possessed by
possediménto m possession, property
posseditrice f owner, possessor
possènte adj (lit) powerful
possessióne f possession
possessi•vo -va adj possessive
possèsso m possession
possessóre m owner, possessor
possibile adj possible || m—fare il possibile to do one's best
possibili•sta (-sti -ste) adj pragmatically flexible || mf pragmatically flexible person, possibilist
possibili•tà f (-tà) possibility; opportunity; possibilità fpl means
possidènte mf proprietor, owner; possidente terriero landowner
pòsta f post; mail; post office; box (in stable); ambush; bet; a giro di posta by return mail; a posta on purpose; darsi la posta to set up an appointment; fare la posta a to have under surveillance; fermo in posta general delivery; levare la posta to pick up the mail; posta aerea air mail; posta dei lettori (journ) letters to the editor; poste postal department

pósta f (archaic) planting; (archaic) footprint
postagi•ro m (-ro & -ri) postal transfer of funds
postale adj postal, mail || m mail; mail train (boat, bus, or plane)
postare (pòsto) tr (mil) to post || ref (mil) to take a position
postazióne f (mil) emplacement
postbèlli•co -ca adj (-ci -che) postwar
postbruciatóre m (aer) afterburner
postdatare tr to postdate
posteggiare §290 (postéggio) tr & intr to park
posteggia•tóre -trice• mf parking-lot attendant; customer (in a parking lot); (coll) outdoor merchant; posteggiatore abusivo parking violator
postég•gio m (-gi) parking lot; stand (in outdoor market); posteggio di tassì cabstand
posterióre adj back; subsequent, later
posteri•tà f (-tà) posterity
pòste•ro -ra adj later, subsequent || posteri mpl posterity, descendants
postíc•cio -cia (-ci -ce) adj artificial; false (e.g., tooth); temporary || m wiglet, ponytail || f row of trees
posticipare (postícipo) tr to postpone
posticipa•to -ta adj deferred
postièrla f postern
postiglióne m postilion
postilla f marginal note
postillare tr to annotate
posti•no -na mf letter carrier || m mailman, postman
pósto m place; room; seat; job, position; spot; (mil) post; a posto in order; orderly; al posto di instead of; essere a posto to have a good job; mettere a posto to find a good job for; (coll) to keep quiet; quel posto (coll) seat of the pants; (coll) toilet; posto a sedere seat; posto di blocco road block; (rr) signal tower; posto di guardia (mil) guardhouse; posto di medicazione or di pronto soccorso first-aid station; posto in piedi standing room; posto letto bed (e.g., in hospital); posto telefonico pubblico public telephone, pay station; rimettere a posto to fix, repair; saper stare al proprio posto to know one's place; sul posto on the spot
postrè•mo -ma adj (lit) last
postríbolo m (lit) brothel
postulante adj petitioning || mf petitioner, applicant; (eccl) postulant
postulare (pòstulo) tr to postulate
pòstu•mo -ma adj posthumous || postumi mpl sequel; (pathol) sequelae
potàbile adj drinkable
potare (póto) tr to trim, prune
potassa f potash
potàssio m potassium
potatura f pruning, polling
potentato m (lit) potentate
potènte adj powerful; influential || i potenti the powers that be
potènza f power, might; (math) power; all'ennesima potenza (math) to the nth power; (fig) to the nth degree; in potenza potential; potentially

potenziale *adj* & *m* potential
potére *m* ability; authority, power; **in potere di** in the hands of; **potere d'acquisto** purchasing power; **potere esecutivo** executive; **potere giudiziario** judiciary; **quarto potere** fourth estate || §219 *intr* to be powerful; **non ne posso più** I am at the end of my rope; **si può?** may I come in? || *aux* (ESSERE & AVERE) to be able; **non posso fare a meno di** + *inf* I can't help + *ger;* **non potere fare a meno di** to not be able to do without; **posso,** etc. I can; I may, etc.; **potrei,** etc. I could; I might, etc.
pote·stà *f* (-stà) power, authority
poveràc·cio -cia *mf* (-ci -ce) poor guy, poor soul
pòve·ro -ra *adj* poor; needy, wretched; lean (*gasoline mixture*); **povero in canna** as poor as a church mouse || *mf* pauper; beggar; poor devil || **i poveri** the poor
pover·tà *f* (-tà) poverty; paucity, scantiness
poveruòmo *m* (used only in *sg*) poor devil
pozióne *f* potion, brew
pózza *f* pool, puddle
pozzànghera *f* puddle
pozzétto *m* small well; manhole; forecastle (*in small boat*)
pózzo *m* well; shaft; **pozzo artesiano** artesian well; **pozzo delle catene** (naut) chain locker; **pozzo di scienza** fountain of knowledge; **pozzo di ventilazione** (min) air shaft; **pozzo nero** cesspool; **pozzo petrolifero** oil well; **pozzo trivellato** deep well; **un pozzo di** (fig) a barrel of
Praga *f* Prague
prammàti·co -ca (-ci -che) *adj* pragmatic || *f* social custom; **di prammatica** obligatory, de rigueur
pranzare [dz] *intr* to dine
pranzo [dz] *m* dinner; **dopo pranzo** afternoon
pras·si *f* (-si) practice, praxis
pratería *f* prairie
pràti·ca *f* (-che) practice; knowledge; matter; file, dossier; business; experience; (naut) pratique; **aver pratica con** to be familiar with (*people*); **aver pratica di** to be familiar with (*things*); **far pratica** to be an apprentice; **fare le pratiche** to make an application; **in pratica** practically; **insabbiare una pratica** to pigeonhole a matter
praticàbile *adj* practicable; passable || *m* (theat) raised platform
praticante *adj* practicing || *mf* apprentice; novice; churchgoer
praticare §197 (pràtico) *tr* to practice; to frequent; to be familiar with; to make (*e.g., a hole*); to grant (*a discount*) || *intr* to practice; **praticare in** to frequent
pratici·tà *f* (-tà) utility; practicality
pràti·co -ca (-ci -che) *adj* practical; experienced || *f* see **pratica**
praticó·ne -na *mf* (pej) old hand
prato *m* meadow

pratolina *f* daisy
pra·vo -va *adj* (lit) wicked
preaccennare (preaccénno) *tr* to mention in advance
preaccenna·to -ta *adj* aforementioned
preallarme *m* early warning
Prealpi *fpl* foothills of the Alps
preàmbolo *m* preamble
preannunziare §287 (preannùnzio) *tr* to foretell, forebode
preannùn·zio *m* (-zi) advance information; foreboding
preautunnale *adj* pre-fall
preavvertire (preavvèrto) *tr* to forewarn
preavvisare *tr* to give advance notice to; to forewarn
preavviso *m* forewarning; notification of dismissal
prebèlli·co -ca *adj* (-ci -che) prewar
prebènda *f* prebend; (fig) easy money, sinecure
precà·rio -ria *adj* (-ri -rie) precarious
precauzióne *f* precaution
precedènte *adj* preceding || *m* precedent; **precedenti** background; **precedenti penali** previous offenses, record
precedènza *f* precedence; (aut) right of way; (fig) priority
precèdere §123 *tr* & *intr* to precede
precettare (precètto) *tr* (mil) to call back from furlough
precètto *m* precept; (eccl) obligation
precettóre *m* tutor
precipitare (precìpito) *tr* to precipitate; to hasten; (chem) to precipitate || *intr* (ESSERE) to fall; to fail; to rush (*said of events*); (chem) to precipitate || *ref* to rush
precipitó·so -sa [s] *adj* hasty, headlong
precipì·zio *m* (-zi) precipice, cliff; ruin; **a precipizio** headlong
precì·puo -pua *adj* chief, principal, primary
precisare *tr* to say exactly, specify, clarify; to fix (*a date*)
precisazióne *f* clarification
precisióne *f* precision
precì·so -sa *adj* precise, exact; punctilious; identical, same; sharp, e.g., **alle sette precise** at seven o'clock sharp
precla·ro -ra *adj* (lit) illustrious
preclùdere §105 *tr* to preclude
precòce *adj* precocious, premature
preconcèt·to -ta *adj* preconceived || *m* preconception; prejudice, bias
preconizzare [ddzz] *tr* to foretell, forecast; (eccl) to preconize
precórrere §139 *tr* (lit) to precede || *intr* (lit) to occur before
precursóre *m* precursor
prèda *f* booty, prize; prey
predace *adj* (lit) preying, predatory
predare (prèdo) *tr* to pillage; to prey upon
preda·tóre -trice *adj* predacious, rapacious || *mf* plunderer
predecessóre *m* predecessor
predèlla *f* dais; altar step; platform
predellino *m* footboard
predestinare (predestino & predèstino) *tr* to predestine

predét·to -ta *adj* aforementioned
prediale *adj* field, rural ‖ *f* land tax
prèdi·ca *f* (**-che**) sermon
predicare §197 (**prèdico**) *tr & intr* to preach
predicato *m* predicate; **essere in predicato di** + *inf* to be rumored to + *inf;* **essere predicato per** to be considered for
predica·tóre -trice *mf* preacher
predicazióne *f* preaching; sermon
predicòzzo *m* (coll) lecture, scolding
predilèt·to -ta *adj & m* favorite
predilezióne *f* predilection
predilìgere §149 (*pres part* missing) *tr* to prefer; to like best
predire §151 *tr* to foretell
predispórre §218 *tr* to predispose, prearrange ‖ *ref* to prepare oneself
predisposizióne *f* predisposition
predizióne *f* prediction
predominare (**predòmino**) *tr* to overcome ‖ *intr* to predominate; to prevail
predomì·nio *m* (**-ni**) predominance
predóne *m* marauder; **predone del mare** pirate
preesìstere §114 *intr* (ESSERE) to preexist
prefabbricare §197 (**prefàbbrico**) *tr* to prefabricate
prefazióne *f* preface
preferènza *f* preference; **a preferenza** rather; **usar preferenze a** to favor
preferìbile *adj* preferable
preferire §176 *tr* to prefer
preferi·to -ta *adj* preferred, favored ‖ *mf* favorite; pet
prefètto *m* prefect
prefettura *f* prefecture
prèfi·ca *f* (**-che**) professional mourner, paid mourner; (coll) crybaby
prefìggere §103 *tr* to set, fix; (gram) to prefix ‖ *ref* to plan
prefis·so -sa *adj* appointed; prefixed ‖ *m* (gram) prefix; (telp) area code
prefissòide *m* prefixed combining form
pregare §209 (**prègo**) *tr* to beg, pray; to ask, request; **farsi pregare** to take a lot of asking; **La prego** please; **prego!** please!; beg your pardon!; you are welcome!
pregévole *adj* valuable
preghièra *f* entreaty; prayer
pregiare §290 (**prègio**) *tr* (lit) to praise, esteem ‖ *ref* to be honored, to have the pleasure
pregia·to -ta *adj* precious; esteemed; **la Sua pregiata (lettera)** your favor, your kind letter; **pregiatissimo Signore** (com) dear Sir; **pregiato Signore** (com) dear Sir
prè·gio *m* (**-gi**) value, worth; esteem; **avere in pregio** to value
pregiudicare §197 (**pregiùdico**) *tr* to damage, harm, jeopardize
pregiudica·to -ta *adj* prejudged; prejudiced; compromised; bound to fail ‖ *m* previous offender
pregiudiziale *adj* (law) pretrial; (pol) essential ‖ *f* (law) pretrial
pregiudiziévole *adj* prejudicial, detrimental

pregiudì·zio *m* (**-zi**) prejudice, bias; harm, damage
pregnante *adj* pregnant
pré·gno -gna *adj* pregnant; saturated
prè·go *m* (**-ghi**) (lit) prayer ‖ *interj* please!; beg your pardon!; you are welcome!
pregustare *tr* to foretaste, anticipate with pleasure
preistòri·co -ca *adj* (**-ci -che**) prehistoric(al)
prelato *m* prelate
prelazióne *f* (law) preemption; (obs) privilege
prelevaménto *m* (com) withdrawal
prelevare (**prelèvo**) *tr* to withdraw (*money*); to capture
preliba·to -ta *adj* excellent, delicious
prelièvo *m* withdrawal; (med) specimen
preliminare *adj* preliminary ‖ **preliminari** *mpl* preliminary negotiations
prelùdere §105 *intr* to make an introductory statement; (with *dat*) to precede, usher in
prelù·dio *m* (**-di**) prelude; (*of an opera*) overture
prematu·ro -ra *adj* premature
premeditare (**premèdito**) *tr* to premeditate
premeditazióne *f* premeditation; **con premeditazione** (law) with malice prepense
prèmere §123 *tr* to press; to push; to squeeze ‖ *intr* (ESSERE & AVERE) to press; to be urgent; **premere a** to matter to, e.g., **gli preme** it matters to him; **premere su** to press, put pressure on
premèssa *f* premise; introduction (*to a book*)
preméttere §198 *tr* to state at the onset; to place at the beginning
premiare §287 (**prèmio**) *tr* to award a prize to, reward
premiazióne *f* awarding of prizes
preminènte *adj* prominent, preeminent
prè·mio *m* (**-mi**) prize; premium; bonus; award
prèmito *m* straining (*to defecate*)
premolare *adj & m* premolar
premonire §176 *tr* (lit) to foretell
premonizióne *f* premonition
premorire §201 *intr* (ESSERE) (with *dat*) to predecease
premunire §176 *tr* to fortify ‖ *ref*— **premunirsi contro** to provide against; **premunirsi di** to provide oneself with
premura *f* haste; attention, care; **aver premura (di)** to be in a hurry (to); **di premura** hastily; **far premura** (with *dat*) to urge
premuró·so -sa [s] *adj* attentive, careful
prèndere §220 *tr* to take; to catch; to lift; to pick up; to fetch; to get; to receive; **prendere a calci** to kick; **prendere a pugni** to punch; **prendere a servizio** to employ, hire; **prendere commiato** to take leave; **prendere con le buone** to treat with kid gloves; **prendere in castagna** to catch in the act; **prendere il sole** to sun oneself; **prendere la fuga** to take flight;

prendere la mano to run away (*said of a horse*); **prendere le mosse** to begin (*said, e.g., of a story*); **prendere lucciole per lanterne** to commit a gross error; **prender paura** to get scared; **prendere per** to take for; **prendere per il naso** to lead by the nose; **prendere quota** (aer) to gain altitude; **prendere sonno** to fall asleep; **prendere un granchio** to make a blunder || *intr* to take root; to set (*said of cement*); to catch (*said of fire*); to turn (*left or right*); **prendere a** + *inf* to begin to + *inf* || *ref* to grab one another; to get along together; **prendersela con** to become angry with; to lay the blame on; **prendersi a** to take hold of

prendi·tóre -trice *mf* receiver; payee (*of a note*); margin buyer || *m* (baseball) catcher

prenóme *m* first name, given name

prenotare (prenòto) *tr* to reserve, book || *ref* to register

prenotazióne *f* reservation, booking

preoccupante *adj* worrisome

preoccupare (preòccupo) *tr* to preoccupy; **preoccupare la mente di** to win the favor of || *ref* to worry

preoccupazióne *f* preoccupation, worry

preordinare (preórdino) *tr* to foreordain; to prearrange

preparare *tr* to prepare; to prime; to steep, brew || *ref* to be prepared; to brew (*said, e.g., of a storm*)

peparati·vo -va *adj* preparatory || **preparativi** *mpl* preparations

prepara·to -ta *adj* prepared; well-equipped || *m* patent medicine; (med) preparation; **preparato anatomico** dissection, anatomical specimen

preparatò·rio -ria *adj* (-ri -rie) preparatory

preparazióne *f* preparation

preponderante *adj* preponderant, prevailing

preponderanza *f* preponderance

prepórre §218 *tr* to prefix; to place before; to prefer; **preporre (qlcu) a** to place (*s.o.*) at the head of

preposizióne *f* preposition

prepósto *m* chief; (eccl) provost

prepotènte *adj* arrogant, overbearing; urgent (*desire*) || *m* bully

prepotènza *f* arrogance; outrage; **di prepotenza** by force

prerogativa *f* prerogative

présa [s] *f* hold, grip; handle; potholder; capture; pinch (*e.g., of salt*); setting (*of cement*); intake; (cards) trick; (elec) jack; (mov) take; **a pronta presa** quick-setting (*cement*); **dar presa a** to give rise to; **essere alle prese** to come to grips; **far presa** to stick (*said of glue*); to set (*said of cement*); to take root; **far presa su** to impress; **mettere alle prese** to pit (*e.g., animals*); **presa d'acqua** spigot, faucet; **presa d'aria** outlet (*of air hose*); air shaft; **presa di corrente** (elec) wall socket, outlet, receptacle; **presa di terra** (elec) ground; **presa**

in giro kidding, joke; **venire alle prese** to come to grips

presà·gio *m* (-gi) forecast; portent

presagire §176 *tr* to forecast; to portend

presalà·rio [s] *m* (-ri) (educ) stipend

prèsbite *adj* far-sighted || *mf* far-sighted person

presbiteria·no -na *adj & mf* Presbyterian

prescégliere §244 *tr* to choose, select

prescìndere §247 (*pret* **prescindéi & prescissi**) *intr*—**a prescindere da** except for; **prescindere da** to leave out

prescolàsti·co -ca *adj* (-ci -che) preschool

prescrit·to -ta *adj* prescribed

prescrìvere §250 *tr* to prescribe || *intr* (ESSERE) (law) to prescribe, to lapse

prescrizióne *f* prescription; (law) extinctive prescription

presegnale [s] *m* warning sign

presentàbile *adj* presentable

presentare (presènto) *tr* to present; to introduce; **presentare la candidatura di** to nominate; **presentat'arm!** present arms! || *ref* to show up, appear; to come, arise (*said, e.g., of an opportunity*)

presenta·tóre -trice *mf* presenter; (rad, telv) announcer || *m* master of ceremonies

presentazióne *f* presentation; introduction

presènte *adj* present; **avere presente** to have in mind; **fare presente qlco a qlcu** to bring s.th to s.o.'s attention; **tenere presente** to keep in mind || *m* present; bystander, onlooker; **al presente** at present; **di presente** immediately || *interj* here!

presentiménto [s] *m* presentiment, foreboding

presentire [s] (**presènto**) *tr* to have a presentiment of

presènza *f* presence; attendance; **di presenza** in person; **presenza di spirito** presence of mind

presenziare §287 (**presènzio**) *tr* to attend; to witness || *intr*—**presenziare a** to be present at; to witness

presè·pio *m* (-pi) Nativity, crèche

preservare [s] (**presèrvo**) *tr* to preserve, protect

preservati·vo -va [s] *adj & m* prophylactic

prèside [s] *m* principal (*of secondary school*); **preside di facoltà** dean

presidènte [s] *m* president; chairman; **presidente del Consiglio** premier

presidentéssa [s] *f* president; chairwoman

presidènza [s] *f* presidency; chairmanship

presi·dio [s] *m* (-di) garrison; (fig) defense, help; **presidi medical aids**

presièdere [s] §141 (**presièdo**) *tr* to preside over || *intr* to preside; **presiedere a** to preside over

prèssa *f* crowd; haste; (mach) press; **far pressa** (poet) to urge

pressacar·te *m* (-te) paperweight

pressaforàg·gio *m* (-gio) baler, hay baler

pressante *adj* pressing, urgent

pressappòco *adv* more or less

pressare (**prèsso**) *tr* to press; to urge

pressióne *f* pressure; **far pressione su** to put pressure on; **pressione sanguigna** blood pressure; **sotto pressione** under steam

prèsso *m*—**nei pressi di** in the neighborhood of || *adv* near, nearby; **a un di presso** approximately; **da presso** close; **press'a poco** more or less || *prep* near; about; at; according to; at the house of; at the office of; care of; with, e.g., **godere fama presso** to enjoy popularity with

pressoché *adv* almost, about, nearly

pressurizzare [ddzz] *tr* to pressurize

prestabilire §176 *tr* to preestablish

prestabili·to -ta *adj* appointed

prestanó·me *m* (**-me**) straw man, figurehead

prestante *adj* strong, vigorous; comely

prestanza *f* vigor; (lit) comeliness

prestare (**prèsto**) *tr* to lend; to loan; to give (*ear; help*); to pay (*attention*); to render (*obedience*); to take (*oath*); to keep (*faith*); **prestar man forte** to give aid; **prestar servizio** to work || *ref* to lend oneself; to be suitable; to be willing; to volunteer

presta·tóre -trice *mf* lender; **prestatore d'opera** worker; **prestatori d'opera** labor

prestazióne *f* service; performance

prestigia·tóre -trice *mf* magician, juggler

prestì·gio *m* (**-gi**) prestige; spell, influence; ledgerdemain

prestigió·so -sa [s] *adj* captivating, spellbinding; illusory

prèstito *m* loan; (philol) borrowing; **dare a prestito** to lend; **prendere a prestito** to borrow

prè·sto -sta *adj* (archaic) quick || *m* (mus) presto || **presto** *adv* soon; fast; quick, quickly; early; **al più presto** at the earliest possible time; **ben presto** soon; **far presto** to hurry; **più presto che può** as soon as you can; **presto detto** easy to say

presùmere §116 *tr & intr* to presume

presunti·vo -va *adj* presumptive; budgeted, estimated (*expenditure*)

presun·to -ta *adj* alleged, supposed; estimated (*expenditure*)

presuntuó·so -sa [s] *adj* presumptuous; bumptious

presunzióne *f* presumption; conceit

presuppórre [s] §218 *tr* to presuppose

presuppósto [s] *m* assumption

prète *m* priest; minister; wooden frame (*to hold bed warmer*)

pretendènte *m* suitor; pretender

pretèndere §270 *tr* to demand, claim; **pretenderla a** to pretend to be || *intr*—**pretendere a** to be a suitor for; to claim (*e.g., a throne*)

pretensióne *f* demand; pretention; pretense

pretensió·so -sa [s] or **pretenzió·so -sa** [s] *adj* pretentious

preterintenzionale *adj* (law) unintentional; (law) justifiable

pretèri·to -ta *adj & m* preterit

preté·so -sa [s] *adj* alleged, ostensible; assumed (*name*) || *f* pretense; pretension

pretèsto *m* pretext, excuse; **sotto il pretesto di** under pretense of

pretòni·co -ca *adj* (**-ci -che**) pretonic

pretóre *m* judge, magistrate (*of lower court*)

prèt·to -ta *adj* pure, genuine

pretura *f* lower court

prevalènte *adj* prevalent, prevailing

prevalènza *f* prevalence; **essere in prevalenza** to be in the majority; **in prevalenza** for the most part

prevalére §278 *intr* (ESSERE & AVERE) to prevail || *ref* to take advantage

prevaricare §197 (**prevàrico**) *intr* to transgress; to graft

prevarica·tóre -trice *mf* grafter

prevedére §279 *tr* to foresee; to provide for (*said of a statute*)

prevedìbile *adj* foreseeable

prevenire §282 *tr* to precede; to anticipate; to forewarn; to prejudice

preventivi·sta *mf* (**-sti -ste**) estimator

preventi·vo -va *adj* preventive; prior; estimated (*budget*) || *m* estimate

prevenu·to -ta *adj* forewarned; biased, prejudiced || *m* defendant

prevenzióne *f* prevention; prejudice, bias

providènte *adj* provident, prudent

previdènza *f* providence; foresight; **previdenza sociale** social security

previdenziale *adj* social (*e.g., responsibility*); social-security (*e.g., contribution*)

prè·vio -via *adj* (**-vi -vie**) with previous, e.g., **previo accordo** with previous agreement

previsióne *f* foresightedness; **in previsione di** anticipating; **previsioni del tempo** weather forecast

previ·sto -sta *adj* foreseen, expected || *m* expected time; estimated amount

prezió·so -sa [s] *adj* precious, valuable; affected; **fare il prezioso** (coll) to play hard to get || **preziosi** *mpl* valuables, jewels

prezzare (**prèzzo**) *tr* to care about; to price

prezzémolo *m* parsley

prèzzo *m* price; cost; **mettere a prezzo** (fig) to sell; **prezzo di favore** special price; **prezzo d'ingresso** admission; **tenere in gran prezzo** to value highly, to esteem highly; **ultimo prezzo** rock-bottom price

prezzolare (**prèzzolo**) *tr* to hire (*e.g., a gunman*); to bribe

prigióne *f* prison, jail; (naut) brig

prigionìa *f* imprisonment; bondage

prigioniè·ro -ra *adj* imprisoned || *mf* prisoner || *m* stud bolt

prillare *intr* to spin, whirl

prima *f* first grade (*in school*); (rr) first class; (theat) first night; (aut) first (gear); **alla prima** or **sulle prime** at the outset || *adv* before; first; prior; ahead; **di prima** previous; **prima che** before; **prima di** ahead of; before;

prima o poi sooner or later; **quanto prima** as soon as possible

primàrio -ria (-ri -rie) adj primary ‖ m (elec) primary; (med) chief of staff

primati·sta mf (-sti -ste) (sports) record holder

primato m primacy; (sports) record

primavèra f spring; springtime; (bot) primrose

primaverile adj spring; spring-like

primeggiare §290 (priméggio) intr to excel

primiè·ro -ra adj (lit) prior; (lit) pristine ‖ f (cards) meld

primiti·vo -va adj & m primitive

primìzia f first fruits; scoop, beat

pri·mo -ma adj first; early (dawn); prime (cost); raw (material); **sulle prime** at first ‖ m first; minute; **primo arrivato** first comer ‖ f see **prima**

primogèni·to -ta adj first-born; (fig) beloved ‖ mf first-born child

primòrdi mpl beginning, origin

primordiale adj primordial, primeval

prìmula f primrose ‖ **Primula** f—**la Primula Rossa** the Scarlet Pimpernel

principale adj principal, main ‖ m (coll) boss, chief

principalménte adv chiefly, mainly

principato m principality

prìncipe adj princeps ‖ m prince; **il principe di Galles** the Prince of Wales; **principe ereditario** crown prince

principé·sco -sca adj (-schi -sche) princely

principéssa f princess

principiante adj beginning ‖ mf beginner

principiare §287 tr & intr (ESSERE & AVERE) to begin; **a principiare da** beginning with

princì·pio m (-pi) beginning; principle; **in principio** at the beginning, at first

princisbécco m pinchbeck; **restare or rimanere di princisbecco** to be dumfounded

prióre m prior

priori·tà f (-tà) priority

priorità·rio -ria adj (-ri -rie) priority, e.g., **progetto prioritario** priority project

pri·sma m (-smi) prism

privare tr to deprive; to remove

privativa f government monopoly; salt and tobacco store; patent

priva·to -ta adj private ‖ m private individual

privazióne f privation, loss

privilegiare §290 (privilègio) tr to privilege; (fig) to endow

privilegia·to -ta adj privileged; preferred (stock) ‖ m privileged person

privilè·gio m (-gi) privilege

pri·vo -va adj deprived; **privo di** lacking

prò m (pro) profit, advantage; **a che pro?** what's the use?; **buon pro!** good appetite!; **far pro** to be good for the health; **il pro e il contro** the pros and the cons ‖ prep pro, in favor of

probàbile adj probable

probabili·tà f (-tà) probability; chance; odds

probante adj proving; evidential

probatò·rio -ria adj (-ri -rie) probative, evidential

problè·ma m (-mi) problem

prò·bo -ba adj (lit) honest

procàc·cia mf (-cia) messenger; mail carrier

procacciare §128 tr to get, procure ‖ ref to eke out (a living); to get into (trouble)

procace adj buxom, sexy; saucy, petulant

procèdere §123 (procèdo) intr to proceed, take action ‖ intr (ESSERE) to proceed, go ahead

procediménto m procedure; behavior

procedura f procedure

procèlla f (lit) storm, tempest

procellària f (orn) petrel

processare (procèsso) tr to try, prosecute

processióne f procession

procèsso m process; trial; **processo verbale** minutes

processuale adj trial

procinto m—**in procinto di** on the point of

procióne m raccoon

procla·ma m (-mi) proclamation

proclamare tr to proclaim

proclamazióne f proclamation

proclìti·co -ca adj & f (-ci -che) proclitic

proclive adj inclined, disposed

proclivi·tà f (-tà) proclivity

procrastinare (procràstino) tr to procrastinate, put off ‖ intr to procrastinate

procreare (procrèo) tr to procreate

procura f agency; power of attorney; **Procura della Repubblica** attorney general's office; district attorney's office

procurare tr to procure, to get; to cause; **procurare che** to see to it that; **procurare di** to try to ‖ ref to get, acquire

procura·tóre -trice mf proxy; agent; attorney-at-law; (sports) manager; **Procuratore della Repubblica** district attorney

pròda f shore, bank; (archaic) prow

pròde adj brave ‖ m brave person, hero

prodézza f prowess; accomplishment

prodiè·ro -ra adj prow, e.g., **cannone prodiero** prow gun; preceding (in a row of ships)

prodigare §209 (pròdigo) tr to squander, lavish ‖ ref to do one's best

prodì·gio m (-gi) prodigy; wonder

prodigió·so -sa [s] adj prodigious; wonderful

pròdi·go -ga adj (-ghi -ghe) lavish, prodigal; **prodigo di** profuse in

proditò·rio -ria adj (-ri -rie) traitorous

prodótto m product; result; **prodotti in scatola** canned goods; **prodotti (ortofrutticoli)** produce

produrre §102 tr to produce; to turn out; to yield; to breed; to cause; (lit) to prolong; (law) to exhibit || *ref* (theat) to perform, appear

produtti·vo -va *adj* productive

produttivìsti·co -ca *adj* (-ci -che) productivity, e.g., **fine produttivistico** productivity policy

produt·tóre -trice *adj* producing || *mf* producer; agent; manufacturer's representative || *m* salesman || *f* saleswoman

produzióne *f* production; output; **produzione in massa** or **in serie** mass production

proè·mio *m* (-mi) preamble, proem

profanare *tr* to profane, desecrate

profanazióne *f* profanation, desecration

profa·no -na *adj* profane; lay, uninformed || *m* layman; **il profano** the profane

proferire §176 *tr* (lit) to utter; (lit) to proffer

professare (professo) *tr* to profess; to practice (*e.g., law*) || *intr* to practice || *ref* to profess oneself to be

professionale *adj* professional; occupational (*disease*); trade (*school*)

professióne *f* profession; **fare il ladro di professione** to be a confirmed thief; **fare qlco di professione** to pursue the trade of s.th, e.g., **fa il falegname di professione** he pursues the trade of carpenter

professioni·sta *mf* (-sti -ste) professional

professorale *adj* professorial; pedantic

profes·sóre -soréssa *mf* professor; teacher; **professore d'orchestra** orchestra member

profè·ta *m* (-ti) prophet

profetéssa *f* prophetess

profèti·co -ca *adj* (-ci -che) prophetic

profetizzare [ddzz] *tr* to prophesy

profezìa *f* prophecy

profferire §176 (*pp* **profférto**; *pret* **profferìi** & **proffèrsi**) *tr* to offer; (lit) to utter

profì·cuo -cua *adj* profitable

profilare *tr* to outline; to sketch; to hem; (mach) to shape || *ref* to be outlined; to loom

profilas·si *f* (-si) prophylaxis

profila·to -ta *adj* outlined; hemmed; (mach) shaped || *m* structural piece

profilàtti·co -ca *adj* (-ci -che) prophylactic

profilatura *f* hemming: (mach) shaping

profilo *m* profile; sketch; outline

profittare *intr* to profit, benefit

profitta·tóre -trice *mf* profiteer

profittévole *adj* (lit) profitable

profitto *m* profit; progress; **profitti e perdite** profit and loss

proflù·vio *m* (-vi) overflow; (pathol) discharge

profondare (profóndo) *tr* & *intr* to sink

profóndere §178 *tr* to squander, lavish || *ref* to be profuse

profondi·tà *f* (-tà) depth

profón·do -da *adj* deep; profound; searching (*e.g., investigation*) || *m* bottom; depth; subconscious

pro fórma *adj invar* pro forma; perfunctory || *m* (coll) formality

pròfu·go -ga (-ghi -ghe) *adj* fugitive || *mf* refugee

profumare *tr* to perfume || *intr* to smell

profumataménte *adv* lavishly

profuma·to -ta *adj* perfumed, fragrant

profumerìa *f* perfumery; perfume shop

profumo *m* perfume; bouquet (*of wine*)

profusióne *f* profusion; **a profusione** in profusion

profu·so -sa *adj* profuse

progè·nie *f* (-nie) progeny, offspring; (pej) breed

progeni·tóre -trice *mf* ancestor

progettare (progètto) *tr* to plan; to design

progetti·sta *mf* (-sti -ste) planner; designer; wild dreamer

progètto *m* project; plan; draft (*of law*); **far progetti** to plan; **progetto di scala reale** (cards) possible straight flush

prògno·si *f* (-si) prognosis

program·ma *m* (-mi) program; plan; curriculum; cycle (*of washing machine*); (mov) feature; (theat) playbill; **programma politico** platform

programmare *tr* to program; to plan

programma·tóre -trice *mf* programmer

programmazióne *f* programming

progredire §176 *intr* (ESSERE & AVERE) to progress, advance

progredi·to -ta *adj* advanced

progressióne *f* progression

progressi·sta *adj* & *mf* (-sti -ste) progressive

progressi·vo -va *adj* progressive

progrèsso *m* progress; progression, advance; **fare progressi** to progress

proibire §176 *tr* to prohibit; to prevent

proibi·to -ta *adj* forbidden; **è proibito entrare** no admission; **è proibito fumare** no smoking

proibizióne *f* prohibition

proibizionismo *m* prohibition

proiettare (proiètto) *tr* to project; to cast (*a shadow*) || *intr* to project || *ref* to be projected, project

proièttile *m* projectile, missile

proiet·tóre *m* projector, projection machine; searchlight; (aut) headlight; **proiettore acustico** sonar projector

proiezióne *f* projection; **proiezione rallentata** slow motion

pròle *f invar* offspring, progeny

proletariato *m* proletariat

proletà·rio -ria *adj* & *mf* (-ri -rie) proletarian

proliferare (prolìfero) *intr* to proliferate

prolificare §197 (**prolìfico**) *intr* to proliferate

prolìfi·co -ca *adj* (-ci -che) prolific

prolis·so -sa *adj* prolix, long-winded; long (*e.g., beard*)

pròlo·go *m* (-ghi) prologue; preface

prolun·ga *f* (-ghe) extension

prolungaménto *m* prolongation, extension

prolungare §209 *tr* to prolong, extend || *ref* to extend; to speak at great length

prolunga·to -ta *adj* extended, protracted

prolusióne *f* inaugural lecture

promemò·ria or **pro memò·ria** *m* (**-ria**) reminder

promés·so -sa *adj* promised ‖ *mf* betrothed ‖ *f* promise; promising individual

promettènte *adj* promising

promettère §198 *tr* to promise; to threaten (*e.g., a storm*) ‖ *intr* to promise; **promettere bene** to be very promising ‖ *ref*—**promettersi a Dio** to make a vow to God; **promettersi in matrimonio** to become engaged

prominènte *adj* prominent

promì·scuo -scua *adj* promiscuous; coeducational; mixed (*marriage; races*); (gram) epicene

promontò·rio *m* (**-ri**) promontory, cliff

promo·tóre -trice *adj* promoting ‖ *mf* promoter

promozióne *f* promotion

promulgare §209 *tr* to promulgate

promuòvere §202 *tr* to promote; to pass (*a student*); to initiate (*legal suit*); to induce (*e.g., perspiration*)

pronipóte *mf* great-grandchild ‖ *m* great-grandson; grandnephew; **pronipoti** descendants ‖ *f* great-granddaughter; grandniece

prò·no -na *adj* (lit) prone

pronóme *m* pronoun

pronominale *adj* (gram) pronominal; (gram) reflexive (*verb*)

pronosticare §197 (**pronòstico**) *tr* to prognosticate, forecast

pronòsti·co *m* (**-ci**) prognostication, forecast; sign, omen

prontézza *f* readiness; quickness, promptness

prón·to -ta *adj* ready; first (*aid*); quick; prompt; ready (*cash*) ‖ **pronto** *interj* (telp) hello!

prontuà·rio *m* (**-ri**) handbook

pronùn·cia *f* (**-cie**) or **pronunzia** *f* pronunciaton; (law) judgment

pronunziare §287 *tr* to pronounce; to utter; to pass (*sentence*); to make (*a speech*) ‖ *ref* to pass judgment

pronunzia·to -ta *adj* pronounced, marked; prominent (*nose, chin, beard*) ‖ *m* (law) sentence

propaganda *f* propaganda; advertisement; advertising

propagandi·sta *mf* (**-sti -ste**) propagandist; advertiser; agent; detail man

propagandìsti·co -ca *adj* (**-ci -che**) advertising

propagare §209 *tr* to propagate; to spread ‖ *ref* to spread

propàggine *f* offspring; (geog) spur, counterfort; (hort) layer

propalare *tr* (lit) to spread, divulge

propellènte *adj & m* propellent

propèllere §168 *tr* to propel

propèndere §123 (*pp* **propènso**) *intr* to incline, tend

propensióne *f* propensity, inclination

propèn·so -sa *adj* inclined, bent

propinare *tr* to administer (*e.g., poison*); **propinare qlco a qlcu** to put s.th over on s.o.

propìn·quo -qua *adj* (lit) near; (lit) related

propiziare §287 *tr* to propitiate, appease

propì·zio -zia *adj* (**-zi -zie**) propitious, favorable

proponiménto *m* intention, plan

propórre §218 *tr* to propose, present; to propound; **proporre come candidato** to nominate ‖ *ref*—**proporsi di** to propose to, resolve to

proporzionare (**proporzióno**) *tr* to proportion, prorate

proporzióne *f* proportion

propòsito *m* purpose; **a proposito** opportune; opportunely; proper; by the way; **a proposito di** on the subject of; **di proposito** deliberately; **fuor di proposito** out of place; **parlare a proposito** to speak to the point

proposizióne *f* proposition; (gram) clause; **proposizione subordinata** dependent clause

propósta *f* proposal; **proposta di legge** bill

propriaménte *adv* exactly; properly

proprie·tà *f* (**-tà**) propriety; ownership; property; **la proprietà** property owners; **proprietà immobiliare** real estate; **proprietà letteraria** copyright; **sulla proprietà** on the premises

proprietà·rio -ria *mf* (**-ri -rie**) owner, proprietor

prò·prio -pria (**-pri -prie**) *adj* peculiar, characteristic; proper (*e.g., name*); own, e.g., **il mio proprio libro** my own book ‖ *m* one's own; **i propri** one's folks; **lavorare in proprio** to work for oneself ‖ **proprio** *adv* just, really, exactly; **non . . . proprio** not . . . at all; **proprio adesso** just, just now

propugnare *tr* to advocate; (lit) to fight for

propugna·tóre -trice *mf* (lit) advocate

propulsare *tr* to propel; (lit) to repulse

propulsióne *f* propulsion

propulsóre *m* propeller, motor

pròra *f* prow, bow

proravìa *f*—**a proravia** (naut) fore

pròro·ga *f* (**-ghe**) delay, extension

prorogare §209 (**pròrogo**) *tr* to extend; to put off, delay

prorómpere §240 *intr* to overflow; **to** burst (*into tears*)

prosa *f* prose

prosài·co -ca *adj* (**-ci -che**) prose; prosaic

prosàpia *f* (lit) ancestry

prosa·tóre -trice *mf* prose writer

proscènio *m* (**-ni**) forestage

prosciògliere §127 *tr* to free; to exonerate

prosciugare §209 *tr* to drain, reclaim ‖ *ref* to dry up

prosciutto *m* ham; **prosciutto cotto** boiled ham; **prosciutto crudo** prosciutto

proscrìvere §250 *tr* to proscribe, outlaw

prosecuzióne [s] *f* prosecution, pursuit

proseguiménto [s] *m* prosecution, pursuit

proseguire [s] (**proséguo**) *tr* to follow, pursue ‖ *intr* (ESSERE & AVERE) to continue

prosèlito *m* proselyte
prosodìa *f* prosody
prosopopèa *f* conceit
prosperare (pròspero) *intr* to prosper, thrive
prosperi·tà *f* (-tà) prosperity || *interj* gesundheit!
pròspe·ro -ra *adj* prosperous, thriving; flourishing; successful || *m* (coll) match
prosperó·so -sa [s] *adj* flourishing; healthy; buxom
prospettare (prospètto) *tr* to face, overlook; to outline || *intr*—prospettare su to face || *ref* to look; to appear; to loom up
prospetti·vo -va *adj* prospective || *f* perspective; prospect; view
prospètto *m* prospect, view; front (*of building*); diagram; outline; prospectus
prospettóre *m* prospector
prospiciènte *adj* facing
prossimaménte *adv* shortly
prossimi·tà *f* -tà proximity, nearness; in prossimità di near
pròssi·mo -ma *adj* near, close; next; immediate (*cause*) || *m* neighbor, fellow man
pròstata *f* prostate
prosternare (prostèrno) *ref* to prostrate oneself
prostituire §176 *tr* to prostitute
prostituta *f* prostitute
prostituzióne *f* prostitution
prostrare (pròstro) *ref* to prostrate oneself
prostrazióne *f* prostration
protagoni·sta *mf* (-sti -ste) protagonist
protèggere §193 *tr* to protect; to help, defend; to favor, promote
proteina *f* protein
protèndere §270 *tr & ref* to stretch
pròte·si *f* (-si) (philol) prothesis; (surg) prosthesis
protèsta *f* protest, protestation
protestante *adj & mf* protestant; Protestant
protestare (protèsto) *tr* to protest; to reject (*faulty merchandise*) || *intr & ref* to protest
protestatà·rio -ria (-ri -rie) *adj* protesting || *m* protester
protèsto *m* (com) protest
protèt·to -ta *adj* protected || *m* protegé || *f* protegée
protettorato *m* protectorate
protet·tóre -trice *adj* patron || *mf* protector, guardian || *m* patron || *f* patroness
protezióne *f* protection; patronage
pròto·m (typ) foreman
protocòllo *adj invar* commercial (*size*) || *m* protocol; mettere a protocollo to register, record
protopla·sma *m* (-smi) protoplasm
protòtipo *m* prototype; (fig) epitome
protozòi [dz] *mpl* protozoa
protrarre §273 *tr* to protract, extend || *ref* to continue
protrùdere §190 *intr* to protrude (*said, e.g., of a broken bone*)

protuberante *adj* protruding, bulging
pròva *f* test, examination; proof; try, attempt; probationary period (*of employment*); trial; token (*e.g., of friendship*); (sports) competition, event; (theat) rehearsal; a prova di bomba bombproof; foolproof; a tutta prova thoroughly tested; in prova on approval; mettere a dura prova to test (*e.g., one's patience*); mettere alla prova to test (*e.g., one's ability*); mettere in prova to fit (*a suit*); prova del fuoco trial by fire; prova dell'acido acid test; prova generale dress rehearsal; prova indiziaria circumstantial evidence
provare (pròvo) *tr* to test; to try; to try on; to try out; to taste; to prove; to feel (*e.g., anger*); (theat) to rehearse || *intr* to try || *ref* to compete
proveniènza *f* origin
provenire §282 *intr* (ESSERE) to stem, originate
provènto *m* income, proceeds
provenzale *adj & mf* Provençal
provèr·bio *m* (-bi) proverb; byword
provétta *f* test tube
provèt·to -ta *adj* (lit) masterful
provìn·cia *f* (-ce) province; in provincia outside of the big cities
provinciale *adj* provincial || *mf* small-town person || *f* provincial highway, state highway
provino *m* gauge; (mov) screen test
provocare §197 (pròvoco) *tr* to provoke; to bring about, cause; to arouse; to entice
provoca·tóre -trice *adj* provoking || *mf* provoker
provocatò·rio -ria *adj* (-ri -rie) provoking, provocative
provocazióne *f* provocation; challenge
provvedére §221 *tr* to prepare; to supply; provvedere che to see to it that || *intr* to take the necessary steps; provvedere a to provide for; provvedere a + *inf* to provide for + *ger*; provvedere nei confronti di to take steps against
provvediménto *m* measure, step
provvedi·tóre -trice *mf* provider || *m* superintendent; provveditore agli studi superintendent of schools
provvedu·to -ta *adj* supplied; careful
provvidènza *f* providence; windfall; provvidenze provisions, help
provvidenziale *adj* providential
pròvvi·do -da *adj* (lit) provident
provvigióne *f* (com) commission
provvisò·rio -ria *adj* (-ri -rie) provisional, temporary
provvi·sto -sta *adj* supplied || *f* supply, provision; fare le provviste to shop
prozìa *f* grandaunt
prozì·o *m* (-i) granduncle
prua *f* bow, prow
prudènte *adj* prudent, cautious
prudènza *f* prudence, discretion
prùdere §222 *intr* to itch; sentirsi prudere le mani to feel like giving s.o. a beating
prugna *f* plum; prugna secca prune

prugno *m* plum tree
prùgnola *f* sloe
prùgnolo *m* sloe, blackthorn
pruno *m* thorn
prurito *m* itch
pseudònimo *m* pseudonym; alias; pen name
psicanàlisi *f* psychoanalysis
psicanali•sta *mf* (-sti -ste) psychoanalyst
psicanalizzare [ddzz] *tr* to psychoanalyze
psiche *f* psyche; cheval glass
psichia•tra *mf* (-tri -tre) psychiatrist
psichiatrìa *f* psychiatry
psìchi•co -ca *adj* (-ci -che) psychic
psicologìa *f* psychology
psicològi•co -ca *adj* (-ci -che) psychological
psicòlo•go -ga *mf* (-gi -ghe) psychologist
psicopàti•co -ca (-ci -che) *adj* psychopathic || *mf* psychopath
psicò•si *f* (-si) psychosis
psicosomàti•co -ca *adj* (-ci -che) psychosomatic
psicotècni•co -ca *adj* (-ci -che) psychotechnical || *m* industrial psychologist || *f* industrial psychology
psicòti•co -ca *adj* (-ci -che) psychotic
pubblicare §197 (pùbblico) *tr* to publish
pubblicazióne *f* publication; **pubblicazioni di matrimonio** marriage banns
pubblicismo *m* communications; advertising
pubblici•sta *mf* (-sti -ste) free-lance newspaper writer; publicist
pubblicìsti•co -ca (-ci -che) *adj* advertising; political-science || *f* newspaper business
pubblicità *f* publicity; advertising
pubblicità•rio -ria (-ri -rie) *adj* advertising || *mf* advertising agent
publicizzare [ddzz] *tr* to publicize
publicizzazióne [ddzz] *f* publicizing
pùbbli•co -ca *adj & m* (-ci -che) public; **mettere in pubblico** to publish
pubertà *f* puberty
pudibón•do -da *adj* (lit) modest, bashful; (lit) prudish
pudicìzia *f* modesty; prudery
pudi•co -ca *adj* (-chi -che) modest, chaste; bashful; (lit) reserved
pudóre *m* modesty; decency; shame
puericoltóre *m* pediatrician
puerile *adj* puerile, childish
puerili•tà *f* (-tà) puerility, childishness
puèrpera *f* lying-in patient
pugilato *m* boxing
pugilatóre *m* boxer, prize fighter
pùgile *m* boxer, prize fighter
pugili•sta *m* (-sti) boxer, prize fighter
pù•glia *f* (-glie) stake (in gambling)
pugnace *adj* (lit) pugnacious
pugnalare *tr* to stab
pugnalata *f* stab
pugnale *m* dagger
pugno *m* fist; fistful; punch; **avere in pugno** to have in one's grasp; **di proprio pugno** in one's own hand; **fare a pugni** to fight; to clash

pula *f* chaff
pulce *f* flea; **mettere una pulce nell'orecchio di** to put a bug in the ear of; **pulce tropicale** jigger, chigger
pulcèlla *f* maid, maiden
pulcinèlla *f*—**pulcinella di mare** (orn) Atlantic puffin || **Pulcinel•la** *m* (-la) buffoon; Punch, Punchinello
pulcino *m* chick
pulédra *f* filly
pulédro *m* colt, foal
pulég•gia *f* (-ge) pulley
pulire §176 *tr* to clean; to shine (shoes); to wipe; to polish
puliscipiè•di *m* (-di) doormat
puli•to -ta *adj* clean; polished; clear (conscience) || *f*—**dare una pulita a** to give a lick and a promise to
pulitura *f* cleaning; **pulitura a secco** dry cleaning
pulizìa *f* cleaning; cleanliness; **fare le pulizie** to clean house
pullulare (pùllulo) *intr* to swarm
pùlpito *m* pulpit
pulsante *m* knob; push button
pulsare *intr* to throb; to pulsate
pulvìscolo *m* fine dust; haze
pulzèlla *f* var of pulcella
pu•ma *m* (-ma) cougar
pungènte *adj* pungent; bitter (cold)
pùngere §183 *tr* to sting; (fig) to goad
pungiglióne *m* stinger (of bee); (fig) sting; (obs) goad
pungitòpo *m* (bot) butcher's broom
pungolare (pùngolo) *tr* to goad, prod
punire §176 *tr* to punish
punizióne *f* punishment; penalty
punta *f* point, tip; prong; brad; bit, trifle; needle (of phonograph); avantgarde; point (of dog); (lit) wound; (fig) peak; (mach) broach; **averne fino alla punta dei capelli** to be sick and tired; **fare la punta a** to sharpen; **in punta di penna** elegantly; **prendere di punta** to treat roughly; to face up to; **punta delle dita** fingertip; **punta di piedi** tiptoe
puntale *m* tip, ferrule
puntaménto *m* aiming
puntare *tr* to aim; to aim at; to point; to thrust; to dot; to bet; to stare at; to fix (one's eyes); **puntare i piedi** to stiffen up; (fig) to balk || *intr* to aim; to point; to pin; to bet; **puntare su** to count on; **puntare verso** to march on; to sail toward
puntaspil•li *m* (-li) pincushion
puntata *f* jab (with weapon); excursion; bet; issue, number (of magazine); installment (of story); (mil) incursion
punteggiare §290 (puntéggio) *tr* to dot; (gram) to punctuate
punteggiatura *f* dotting; punctuation
puntég•gio *m* (-gi) score
puntellare (puntèllo) *tr* to prop, brace; to support
puntèllo *m* prop, brace; support
punterìa *f* aiming; aiming gear; (aut) tappet
punteruòlo *m* punch; awl
puntì•glio *m* (-gli) obstinacy, stubbornness; punctilio

puntiglió·so -sa [s] *adj* punctilious, scrupulous; obstinate, stubborn
puntina *f* brad; needle; thumbtack
puntino *m* small dot; G-string; **a puntino** to a T
punto *m* point; period; dot; place, spot; extent; stitch; **dare dei punti a** to be superior to; **di punto in bianco** all of a sudden; **di tutto punto** thoroughly; **due punti** colon; **essere a buon punto** to be well advanced; **essere sul punto di** + *inf* to be about to + *inf*; **fare il punto** (fig; naut) to take one's bearings; **in punto** on the dot; **in punto franco** in bond; **in un punto** together; **mettere a punto** to get in working order; (aut) to tune up; **mettere i punti sulle i** to dot one's i's; **punto assistenza** service agency; **punto di partenza** starting point; **punto di vista** viewpoint; **punto esclamativo** exclamation point; **punto e virgola** semicolon; **punto fermo** full stop; **punto interrogativo** question mark; **punto morto** (mach) dead center; **punto stimato** (naut) dead reckoning; **qui sta il punto!** here's the rub!; **vincere ai punti** (boxing) to win by points, win by decision ‖ *adv—né* **punto né poco** not at all; **non . . . punto** not at all
puntóne *m* rafter
puntuale *adj* punctual, prompt
puntuali·tà *f* (-tà) punctuality, promptness
puntura *f* sting; stitch (*sharp pain*); (coll) injection; **puntura lombare** spinal anesthesia
punzecchiare §287 (**punzécchio**) *tr* to keep on stinging; to tease, torment
punzecchiatura *f* sting, bite
punzonare (**punzóno**) *tr* to mark or stamp with a punch
punzonatrice *f* punch press
punzóne *m* punch; nailset
pupa *f* doll; (zool) pupa
pupazzetti·sta *mf* (-sti -ste) cartoonist
pupazzétto *m* caricature; cartoon; **pupazzetto di carta** paper doll
pupazzo *m* puppet; **pupazzo di stoffa** rag doll

pupil·lo -la *mf* pupil; ward, protégé ‖ *f* pupil (*of eye*); protégée
pupo *m* (coll) baby
purché *conj* provided, providing
pure *adv* too, also; indeed; (lit) only; **pur di** only in order to; **quando pure** even if; **se pure** even if ‖ *conj* though, although; but, yet
pu·rè *m* (-rè) purée; **purè di patate** mashed potatoes
purézza *f* purity
pur·ga *f* (-ghe) laxative; purification; purge
purgante *adj* purging ‖ *m* laxative
purgare §209 *tr* to purge; to purify; to expurgate ‖ *ref* to take a laxative
purgati·vo -va *adj* laxative
purgatò·rio *m* (-ri) purgatory
purificare §197 (**purìfico**) *tr* to purify
purismo *m* purism
purità *f* purity
purita·no -na *adj* & *m* puritan; Puritan
pu·ro -ra *adj* pure; clear; simple, mere
purosàn·gue *adj invar* & *m* (-gue) thoroughbred
purpùre·o -a *adj* (lit) purple
purtròppo *adv* unfortunately
purulèn·to -ta *adj* purulent
pus *m* pus
pusillànime *adj* pusillanimous
pùstola *f* pustule; pimple
puta caso *adv* possibly, maybe
putifè·rio *m* (-ri) hubbub
putrefare §173 *intr* (ESSERE) & *ref* to putrefy, rot
putrefazióne *f* putrefaction
putrèlla *f* I beam
pùtri·do -da *adj* putrid ‖ *m* corruption
putta *f* (coll) girl; (lit) prostitute
puttana *f* (vulg) whore
put·to -ta *adj* (archaic) meretricious ‖ *m* figure of a child ‖ *f* see **putta**
puzza *f* var of **puzzo**
puzzare *intr* to stink, smell
puzzo *m* stench, smell, bad odor
pùzzola *f* polecat, skunk
puzzolènte *adj* stinking, smelly
puzzonata *f* (coll) contemptible action; (coll) botch, bungle
puzzóne *m* (coll) skunk (*person*)

Q

Q, q [ku] *m* & *f* fifteenth letter of the Italian alphabet
qua *adv* here; **da un (giorno, mese, anno) in qua** for the past (day, month, year); **di qua da** on this side of; **in qua** on this side; here
quàcche·ro -ra or **quàcque·ro -ra** *adj* & *mf* Quaker; **alla quacquera** in a plain fashion
quadèrno *m* copybook; **quaderno di cassa** cash book
quadràngo·lo -la *adj* quadrangular ‖ *m* quadrangle
quadrante *m* quadrant; dial; face (*of watch*); **quadrante solare** sundial

quadrare *tr* to square ‖ *intr* (ESSERE & AVERE) to square; **quadrare a** to be satisfactory to; **quadrare con** to fit
quadra·to -ta *adj* square; sound (*mind*) ‖ *m* square; diaper; (boxing) ring; (nav) wardroom
quadratura *f* squaring; concreteness; (astr) quadrature
quadrèl·lo *m* (-li) square ruler; square tile ‖ *m* (-la *fpl*) (lit) bolt, arrow
quadrerìa *f* picture gallery; collection
quadretta·to -ta *adj* checkered
quadrétto *m* small painting; checker, small square; (fig) picture

quadriennale *adj* four-year ‖ *f* quadrennial

quadrifò·glio *m* (**-gli**) four-leaf clover; **a quadrifoglio** cloverleaf

quadrì·glio *m* (**-gli**) (cards) quadrille

quadrimensionale *adj* four-dimensional

quadrimestrale *adj* four-month

quadrimèstre *m* four-month period; four-month payment

quadrimotóre *adj* four-motor ‖ *m* four-motor plane

quadrireattóre *m* four-motor jet

qua·dro -dra *adj* square; (fig) solid ‖ *m* picture; painting; sight; square; table, summary; panel, switchboard; (theat) scene; **quadri** bulletin board; (mil) cadres; (cards) diamonds

quadrùmane *adj* quadrumanous ‖ *m* monkey; ape

quadruplicare §197 (**quadrùplico**) *tr* & *ref* to quadruple

quadrùplice *adj* quadruple; **in quadruplice copia** in four copies

quàdru·plo -pla *adj* & *m* quadruple

quaggiù *adv* down here

quàglia *f* quail

quagliare §280 *tr*, *intr* (ESSERE) & *ref* var of **cagliare**

qualche *adj invar* some, e.g., **qualche giorno** some day; some, e.g., **qualche elefante è bianco** some elephants are white; any, e.g., **ha qualche libro da vendere?** do you have any books to sell?; a few, e.g., **qualche giorno** a few days

qualchedu·no -na *pron indef* var of **qualcuno**

qualcòsa [s] *m* (fig) something; (fig) somebody ‖ *pron indef* something; anything; **qualcosa di buono** something good

qualcu·no -na *pron indef* some; any; somebody; anybody ‖ *m* somebody

quale *adj* which, what; what a, e.g., **quale onore!** what an honor!; as, e.g., **il pane, quale vedi, è fresco** the bread, as you can see, is fresh; **quale che sia** regardless of ‖ *pron* which; what; (archaic) who; **il quale** who, whom; **per la quale** o.k.; well-bred; commendable; terrific; **quale . . . quale** some . . . some ‖ *prep* as, e.g., **quale ministro** as a minister

qualìfi·ca *f* (**-che**) rating; position; quality, qualification

qualificare §197 (**qualìfico**) *tr* to qualify; to classify; to rate, give a rating to ‖ *ref* to introduce oneself; to qualify

qualifica·to -ta *adj* aggravated (*assault*); qualified (*personnel*); specialized (*worker*)

quali·tà *f* (**-tà**) quality; capacity

qualóra *conj* if; (lit) whenever

qualsiasi [s] *adj invar* any; whatever; ordinary

qualunque *adj invar* any; whatever; common, ordinary; **in qualunque modo** anyway, anyhow; **qualunque altro** anybody else; **qualunque cosa** anything; no matter what

qualvòlta *conj* (lit) whenever

quando *m* when ‖ *adv* when; **di quando**

in quando from time to time; **quando . . . quando** sometimes . . . sometimes ‖ *conj* when; whenever; while; **da quando** since

quantìsti·co -ca *adj* (**-ci -che**) quantum

quanti·tà *f* (**-tà**) quantity; number

quantitativo *m* quantity

quan·to -ta *adj* how much; as much; how great; how great a; what a; **quan·ti -te** how many; as many ‖ *m* quantum ‖ *pron* how much; as much; how great; how long; that which; what; whatever; **a quanto si dice** according to what is rumored; **da quanto** from what; for how long; **fra quanto** how soon; **per quanto** io ne sappia as far as I know; **quanto più** (or **meno**) . . . **tanto più** (or **meno**) the more (or the less) . . . the more (or the less); **quan·ti -te** how many; all those; as many as; **quanti ne abbiamo?** what's the date? ‖ **quanto** *adv* how much; as much as; **in quanto** as; **in quanto che** inasmuch as; **per quanto** although; no matter; nevertheless; **quanto a** as to, as for; **quanto mai** as never before; **quanto meno** at least; **quanto prima** as soon as possible

quantunque *conj* although, though

quaranta *adj*, *m* & *pron* forty; **gli anni quaranta** the forties; **i quaranta** the forties (*in age*)

quarantèna *f* quarantine

quarantènne *adj* forty-year-old ‖ *mf* forty-year-old person

quarantèsi·mo -ma *adj*, *m* & *pron* fortieth

quarantina *f* about forty; **essere sulla quarantina** to be about forty years old

quarantòtto *adj* forty-eight ‖ *m* forty-eight; (coll) hubbub, uproar

quarésima *f* Lent

quartabuòno *m* triangle (*in drafting*); **tagliare a quartabuono** to miter

quartétto *m* quartet; **quartetto d'archi** string quartet

quartière *m* quarter, district; (mil) quarters; (coll) apartment; **quartier generale** headquarters; **senza quartiere** (*fight*) without quarter

quar·to -ta *adj* & *pron* fourth ‖ *m* fourth; quarter; quarter of a kilo; quarter of a liter; (naut) watch; **l'una e un quarto** a quarter after one; **l'una meno un quarto** a quarter to one

quarzo *m* quartz

quasi *adv* almost, nearly; **quasi che** as if; **quasi mai** hardly ever; **senza quasi** without any ifs and buts

quassù *adv* up here

quat·to -ta *adj* crouching; squatting; **quatto quatto** stealthy, silent; **starsene quatto quatto** to not make a sound

quattordicènne *adj* fourteen-year-old ‖ *mf* fourteen-year-old person

quattordicèsi·mo -ma *adj*, *m* & *pron* fourteenth

quattórdici *adj* & *pron* fourteen; **le**

quattordici two P.M. ‖ *m* fourteen; fourteenth (*in dates*)

quattrino *m* penny; (fig) bit; **quattrini** money

quattro *adj* four; a few, e.g., **quattro gatti** a few people; **a quattro mani** (mus) for four hands ‖ *pron* four; **dirne quattro a** to upbraid; **farsi in quattro** to go all out; **in quattro e quattr'otto** in a few minutes; **le quattro** four o'clock ‖ *m* four; fourth (*in dates*); racing shell with four oarsmen

quattrocènto *adj, m & pron* four hundred ‖ **il Quattrocento** the fifteenth century

quattromila *adj, m & pron* four thousand

quégli §7 *adj* ‖ §8 *pron*

quéi §7 *adj*

quél §7 *adj* ‖ §8 *pron*

quéll' §7 *adj*

quél·lo -la §7 *adj* ‖ §8 *pron*—**per quello che so io** as far as I know

quèr·cia *f* (**-ce**) oak tree

querci·no -na *adj* oaken

querèla *f* complaint

querelante *adj* complaining ‖ *mf* plaintiff

querelare (**querèlo**) *tr* to sue ‖ *ref* (law) to sue; (lit) to complain

querela·to -ta *adj* accused ‖ *mf* defendant

quèru·lo -la *adj* (lit) plaintive

quesito *m* question; problem; (lit) request

quésti §7 *pron*

questionare (**questióno**) *intr* to quarrel

questionà·rio *m* (**-ri**) questionnaire

questióne *f* question; (coll) quarrel; **questione di gabinetto** call for a vote of confidence; **venire a questione** to quarrel

qué·sto -sta §7 *adj* ‖ §8 *pron*—**e con questo?** so what?; **per questo** therefore; **questa** this matter; **questo . . . quello** the former . . . the latter

questóre *m* police commissioner; sergeant at arms (*of congress*)

quèstua *f* begging; collection of alms; **andare alla questua** to go begging; **vietata la questua** no begging

questura *f* police department; police headquarters

questurino *m* (coll) policeman

què·to -ta *adj* var of **quieto**

qui *adv* here; **di qui** hence, from here; this way; **di qui a un anno** one year hence; **di qui in avanti** from now on; **qui vicino** nearby

quiescènza *f* quiescence; retirement

quietanza *f* receipt

quietanzare *tr* to receipt

quietare (**quièto**) *tr* to quiet, calm; to satisfy (*e.g., thirst*) ‖ *ref* to quiet down

quiète *f* quiet, calmness

quiè·to -ta *adj* quiet, calm; still; **stia quieto!** don't worry! ‖ *m* quiet life

quindi *adv* then; therefore; (archaic) thence, from there

quindicènne *adj* fifteen-year-old ‖ *mf* fifteen-year-old person

quindicèsi·mo -ma *adj, m & pron* fifteenth

quìndici *adj & pron* fifteen; **le quindici** three P.M. ‖ *m* fifteen; fifteenth (*in dates*)

quindicina *f* about fifteen; two weeks, fortnight; semimonthly pay

quindicinale *adj* fortnightly

quinquennale *adj* five-year

quinta *f* (theat) wing; (mus) fifth; **dietro le quinte** behind the scenes

quintale *m* quintal (*100 kilos*)

quintèrno *m* signature of five sheets; (bb) quire

quintessènza *f* quintessence

quintétto *m* quintet

quin·to -ta *adj, m & pron* fifth ‖ *f* see **quinta**

quisquìlia *f* trifle

quivi *adv* (lit) over there; (lit) then

quòrum *m* quorum

quòta *f* quota; share; altitude; elevation; level (*of stock market*); market average; odds (*in betting*); subscription (*to club*); **quota zero** (fig) point of departure

quotare (**quòto**) *tr* to quote (*a price*); to value, esteem ‖ *ref* to sign up for, e.g., **si quotò duemila lire** he signed up for two thousand lire

quotazióne *f* quotation

quotidia·no -na *adj & m* daily

quoziènte *m* quotient; (sports) percentage; **quoziente d'intelligenza** I.Q.

R

R, r ['erre] *m & f* sixteenth letter of the Italian alphabet

rabàrbaro *m* rhubarb

rabberciare §128 (**rabbèrcio**) *tr* (coll) to patch up

ràbbia *f* rage, anger; rabies

rabbino *m* rabbi

rabbió·so -sa [s] *adj* furious; rabid

rabbonire §176 *tr* to pacify ‖ *ref* to calm down

rabbrividire §176 *intr* (ESSERE) to shiver, shudder

rabbuffare *tr* to rebuke; to dishevel

rabbuffo *m* rebuke; **fare un rabbuffo a** to rebuke

rabbuiare §287 *ref* to darken, turn dark

rabdomante *m* dowser, diviner

rabé·sco *m* (**-schi**) arabesque; scrawl, scribble

ràbi·do -da *adj* rabid

raccapezzare (**raccapézzo**) *tr* to put together; to gather (*news*); to find (*one's way*); to make out (*what is* *meant*) ‖ *ref*—non **raccapezzarsi** to not be able to get one's bearings

raccapricciante *adj* bloodcurdling

raccapríc•cio *m* (-ci) horror

raccartocciare §128 (**raccartòccio**) *tr* & *ref* to shrivel

raccattare *tr* to pick up; to gather

racchétta *f* racket; **racchetta da neve** snowshoe; **racchetta da sci** ski pole

ràc•chio -chia *adj* (-chi -chie) (coll) ugly, homely

racchiùdere §125 *tr* to contain, hold

raccògliere §127 *tr* to pick up; to gather; to collect (*e.g., stamps*); to take up (*the gauntlet*); to receive; to reap; to furl (*sail*); to draw in (*a net*); to fold (*the wings*); to shelter (*e.g., foundlings*); **raccogliere i passi** to stop walking ‖ *ref* to gather; to concentrate

raccogliménto *m* concentration; meditation

raccogli•tóre -trice *mf* collector, compiler ‖ *m* folder

raccòl•to -ta *adj* crouched; collected; engrossed; snug, intimate ‖ *m* harvest ‖ *f* harvest; collection; **chiamare a raccolta** to rally

raccomandàbile *adj* recommendable; **poco raccomandabile** unreliable

raccomandare *tr* to recommend; to secure (*e.g., a boat*); to register (*mail*); to exhort ‖ *ref* to recommend oneself; to entreat; **mi raccomando** please; **raccomandarsi a** to beg, implore; **raccomandarsi alle gambe** to take to one's heels

raccomanda•to -ta *adj* recommended; registered ‖ *m* protégé ‖ *f* protégée; registered letter

raccomandazióne *f* recommendation; registration (*of mail*); exhortation

raccomodare (**raccòmodo**) *tr* to fix; to mend

racconciare §128 (**raccóncio**) *tr* to fix; to mend ‖ *ref* to clear up (*said of the weather*); to tidy oneself up

raccontare (**raccónto**) *tr* to tell; **raccontarla bene** to be good at telling lies

raccónto *m* tale; story; narrative

raccorciaménto *m* shortening

raccorciare §128 (**raccòrcio**) *tr* to shorten

raccordare (**raccòrdo**) *tr* to link, connect

raccòrdo *m* link, connection; **raccordo a circolazione rotatoria** traffic circle; **raccordo anulare** (rr) belt line; **raccordo ferroviario** junction; spur; siding; **raccordo stradale** connecting road

raccostare (**raccòsto**) *tr* & *ref* to draw near

raccozzare (**raccòzzo**) *tr* to scrape together

ràchide *m* & *f* backbone; midrib (*of leaf*); shaft (*of feather*)

rachìti•co -ca *adj* (-ci -che) stunted; weak; (pathol) rickety

rachitismo *m* rickets

racimolare (**racìmolo**) *tr* to glean; to scrape together

rada *f* roadstead; cove

ràdar *m* radar

addobbare (**raddòbbo**) *tr* (naut) to refit

raddolcire §176 *tr* & *ref* to sweeten; to mellow

raddoppiare §287 (**raddóppio**) *tr, intr* (ESSERE) & *ref* to double, redouble

raddrizzare *tr* to straighten; (elec) to rectify ‖ *ref* to straighten up

raddrizzatóre *m* (elec) rectifier

ràdere §223 *tr* to shave; to raze; to graze, skim ‖ *ref* to shave

radézza *f* rarity, rareness; thinness; sparsity (*of vegetation*); space, distance (*e.g., between trees*)

radiante *adj* radiating

radiare §287 *tr* to strike off; to expel; to condemn (*a ship*); **radiare dall'albo degli avvocati** to disbar

radiatóre *m* radiator

radiazióne *f* radiation; expulsion

ràdi•ca *f* (-che) brier; (coll) root

radicale *adj* & *mf* radical ‖ *m* & *f* (philol) radical, root ‖ *m* (chem, math) radical

radicare §197 (**ràdico**) *tr* & *intr* to root

radice *f* root; base or foot (*e.g., of a mountain or tower*); **mettere radice** to take root; **svellere dalle radici** to pull up by the roots; to eradicate

rà•dio *adj invar* radio ‖ *m* (-di) (anat) radius; (chem) radium ‖ *f* (-dio) radio; **radio fante** (mil) grapevine

radioabbonato *m* (rad) subscriber (*to radio broadcasting*)

radioama•tóre -trice *mf* radio fan; radio ham

radioannunciatóre *m* radio announcer

radioascolta•tóre -trice *mf* radio listener

radioatti•vo -va *adj* radioactive

radiobùssola *f* radio compass

radiocanale *m* radio channel

radiocomanda•to -ta *adj* radio-controlled

radiocròna•ca *f* (-che) newscast

radiocroni•sta *mf* (-sti -ste) newscaster

radiodiffóndere §178 *tr* to broadcast

radiodiffusióne *f* broadcasting

radiofaro *m* radio beacon

radiofòni•co -ca *adj* (-ci -che) radio

radiofonògrafo *m* radiophonograph

radiofò•to *f* (-to) radiophoto

radiofrequènza *f* radiofrequency

radiologìa *f* radiology

radiomontatóre *m* radio assembler

radioónda *f* radio wave; **radioonde airwaves**

radioricevènte *adj* radio ‖ *f* radio set; radio station

radioriparatóre *m* radio repairman

radiosegnale *m* radio signal

radiosentièro *m* range of a radio beacon

radió•so -sa [s] *adj* radiant

radiosorgènte *f* quasar

radiostazióne *f* radio station

radiostélla *f* quasar

radiotas•sì *m* (-sì) radio-dispatched taxi

radiotelescò•pio *m* (-pi) radiotelescope

radiotrasméttere §198 *tr* & *intr* to broadcast, radio

radiotrasmissióne *f* broadcast

radiotrasmittènte *adj* broadcasting ‖ *f* broadcasting station

ra·do -da *adj* rare; thin; sheer; sparse; scattered; **di rado** seldom, rarely

radunare *tr & ref* to assemble, gather

radunata *f* gathering; (mil) assembly; **radunata sediziosa** unlawful assembly

raduno *m* assembly, gathering

radura *f* clearing, glade

ràfano *m* (bot) radish

raffazzonare (raffazzóno) *tr* to mend, patch up

raffazzonatura *f* patchwork, hodgepodge

raffèrma *f* confirmation; stay (*in office*); return to office; (mil) reenlistment

raffermare (raffèrmo) *tr* to reaffirm; to secure; (coll) to reconfirm; to reappoint, reelect; to return (*e.g., a mayor*) to office ‖ *intr* (ESSERE) & *ref* to reenlist; (coll) to harden

raffèr·mo -ma *adj* stale (bread) ‖ *f* see **rafferma**

ràffi·ca *f* (-che) gust; blast; burst (*e.g., of machine gun*); **a raffiche** gusty

raffigurare *tr* to represent; to symbolize

raffinare *tr* to refine; to polish ‖ *intr* (ESSERE) to become refined

raffinatézza *f* refinement, polish

raffinatura *f* refinement (*of oil*)

raffinazióne *f* refining

raffinerìa *f* refinery

ràf·fio *m* (-fi) hook; grappling iron

rafforzare (raffòrzo) *tr* to strengthen

raffreddaménto *m* cooling

raffreddare (raffréddo) *tr* to make cold; to cool; **raffreddare gli spiriti di qlcu** to dampen s.o.'s enthusiasm ‖ *intr* (ESSERE) & *ref* to get cold; to cool

raffreddóre *m* cold

raffrontare (raffrónto) *tr* to compare; (law) to bring face to face

raffrónto *m* comparison; confrontation

ràfia *f* raffia

raganèlla *f* rattle; (zool) tree frog

ragazza *f* girl; spinster; (coll) girl friend; **ragazza copertina** cover girl; **ragazza squillo** call girl

ragazzata *f* boyish prank

ragaz·zo -za *mf* youth, young person ‖ *m* boy; (coll) boyfriend ‖ *f* see **ragazza**

raggelare (raggèlo) *intr* (ESSERE) to freeze

raggiante *adj* radiant; beaming

raggiare §290 *tr & intr* to radiate

raggièra *f* rayed halo; **a raggiera** radially

ràg·gio *m* (-gi) ray; beam; spoke; (geom) radius; **raggio d'azione** radius, range of action; **raggio di sole** sunbeam

raggiornare (raggiórno) *tr* (coll) to bring up to date ‖ *intr* (ESSERE) to dawn ‖ *impers* (ESSERE)—**raggiorna** it is dawning

raggirare *tr* to trick, swindle ‖ *ref* to roam, wander; **raggirarsi su** to turn on (*e.g., a certain subject*)

raggiro *m* trickery, swindle

raggiungere §183 *tr* to reach; to catch up with, rejoin

raggiungìbile *adj* attainable

raggomitolare (raggomitolo) *tr* to roll up ‖ *ref* to curl up; to cuddle

raggranellare (raggranèllo) *tr* to gather; to scrape together

raggrinzire §176 *tr & ref* to crease, wrinkle

raggrumare *tr & ref* to clot, coagulate

raggruppaménto *m* grouping; group

raggruppare *tr & ref* to group, assemble

ragguagliare §280 *tr* to compare; to balance; to inform in detail; to level

ragguà·glio *m* (-gli) comparison; detailed report

ragguardévole *adj* considerable, notable

ragionaménto *m* reasoning; discussion

ragionare (ragióno) *intr* to reason; to discuss ‖ *impers ref*—**si ragiona** it is rumored

ragióne *f* reason; account; rate; justice; (math) ratio; **a maggior ragione** with all the more reason; **a ragione** within reason; **aver ragione** to be right; **aver ragione di** to get the best of; **dar ragione a qlcu** to admit that s.o. is right; **di santa ragione** hard, a great deal; **farsi ragione** to be resigned; **in ragione di** at the rate of; **ragion per cui** and therefore; **ragione sociale** (com) trade name; **rendere di pubblica ragione** to publicize

ragionerìa *f* accounting; bookkeeping

ragionévole *adj* reasonable

ragioniè·re -ra *mf* accountant; bookkeeper

ragliare §280 *intr* to bray

rà·glio *m* (-gli) bray

ragnatéla *f* spider web

ragno *m* spider

ra·gù *m* (-gù) meat gravy; stew

ràion *m* rayon

rallegraménto *m* congratulation, act of congratulating; **rallegramenti** congratulations

rallegrare (rallégro) *tr* to cheer up; to rejoice, gladden ‖ *ref* to cheer up; to rejoice; **rallegrarsi con** to congratulate

rallentare (rallènto) *tr, intr & ref* to slow down; to lessen

rallentatóre *m* slow-motion projector; **al rallentatore** slow-motion

ra·màio *m* (-mài) tinker, coppersmith

ramaiòlo *m* ladle

ramanzina [dz] *f* reprimand

ramare *tr* to copperplate; (agr) to spray with copper sulfate

ramarro *m* green lizard

ramazza *f* broom; (mil) cleaning detail; (mil) soldier on cleaning detail

rame *m* copper; etching

ramerino *m* (coll) rosemary

ramificare §197 (ramìfico) *intr & ref* to branch; to branch off; to branch out, ramify

ramin·go -ga *adj* (-ghi -ghe) wandering

ramino *m* copper pot; rummy (*card game*)

rammagliare §280 *tr* to reknit; to mend a run in (*a stocking*)

rammaricare §197 (rammàrico) *tr* to afflict ‖ *ref* to be sorry, regret; **rammaricarsi di** to be sorry for

rammàri•co *m* (**-chi**) regret
rammendare (**ramméndo**) *tr* to darn
rammèndo *m* darn
rammentare (**rammènto**) *tr* to remember; to remind || *ref*—**rammentarsi di** to remember
rammenta•tóre -trice *mf* prompter
rammollire §176 *tr* & *ref* to soften
rammolli•to -ta *adj* soft; soft-headed || *m* dodo, jellyfish
ramo *m* branch; bough; point (*of antler*); **ramo di pazzia** streak of madness
ramoscèllo *m* twig; **ramoscello d'olivo** olive branch
rampa *f* ramp; flight (*of stairs*); launching platform
rampicante *adj* climbing || *m* (ichth) perch; (orn) climber
rampino *m* hook; tine, prong; pretext
rampógna *f* (lit) reprimand
rampóllo *m* spring (*of water*); scion; shoot (*of a plant*); (joc) offspring
rampóne *m* harpoon; crampon
rana *f* frog
rànci•do -da *adj* rancid
ràn•cio -cia (**-ci -ce**) *adj* (poet) orange || *m* (mil) mess
rancóre *m* rancor; grudge; **serbar rancore** to bear malice
randa *f* (naut) spanker; (obs) edge
randà•gio -gia *adj* (**-gi -gie**) wandering; stray
randellare (**randèllo**) *tr* to cudgel; to bludgeon; to blackjack
randèllo *m* cudgel; bludgeon
ran•go *m* (**-ghi**) rank; station
rannicchiare §287 *tr* to cause to curl up || *ref* to crouch; to cower; to cuddle up
ranno *m* lye; **buttar via il ranno e il sapone** to waste one's time and effort
rannuvolare (**rannùvolo**) *tr* & *ref* to cloud; to darken
ranòcchia *f* frog
ranòc•chio *m* (**-chi**) frog
rantolare (**ràntolo**) *intr* to wheeze
ràntolo *m* wheezing; death rattle
ranùncolo *m* buttercup
rapa *f* turnip; **valere una rapa** to be not worth a fig
rapace *adj* rapacious || **rapaci** *mpl* birds of prey
rapare *tr* to shave (*s.o.'s head*) || *ref* to shave one's head; to have one's head shaved
rapidi•tà *f* (**-tà**) rapidity, swiftness
ràpi•do -da *adj* rapid, swift || *m* (rr) express || **rapide** *fpl* rapids
rapiménto *m* rape, abduction; rapture
rapina *f* pillage, plunder; misappropriation; prey; (lit) fury; **rapina a mano armata** armed robbery
rapinare *tr* to rob, plunder; to hold up; **rapinare qlco a qlcu** to rob s.o. of s.th
rapina•tóre -trice *mf* robber, plunderer
rapire §176 *tr* to rape, abduct; to kidnap; to enrapture
rapi•tóre -trice *mf* kidnaper
rappacificare §197 (**rappacìfico**) *tr* to reconcile || *ref* to become reconciled
rappezzare (**rappèzzo**) *tr* to patch; to

piece; **rappezzarla** to get out of trouble
rappèzzo *m* patch; patchwork
rapportare (**rappòrto**) *tr* to report; to transfer (*a design*) || *ref* to refer
rapporta•tóre -trice *mf* reporter || *m* protractor
rappòrto *m* report; relation; relationship; (math) ratio; **chiamare a rapporto** to summon; **chiedere di mettersi a rapporto** to ask for a hearing; **fare rapporto** to report; **in rapporto a** concerning; **mettersi a rapporto** to report; **sotto ogni rapporto** in every respect
rapprèndere §220 *tr* & *ref* to coagulate
rappresàglia [s] *f* reprisal; retaliation
rappresentante *adj* representing; representative || *mf* representative; agent; **rappresentante di commercio** agent
rappresentanza *f* delegation; proxy; agency; representation
rappresentare (**rappresènto**) *tr* to represent; to play; to portray
rappresentati•vo -va *adj* representative
rappresentazióne *f* representation; description; (theat) performance; **rappresentazione teatrale diurna** matinée; **sacra rappresentazione** (theat) mystery, miracle play
rapsodìa *f* rhapsody
raraménte *adv* seldom, rarely
rarefare §173 *tr* to rarefy || *ref* to become rarefied
rari•tà *f* (**-tà**) rarity
ra•ro -ra *adj* rare; **di raro** seldom
rasare [s] *tr* to shave; to mow; to trim; to smooth || *ref* to shave
raschiare §287 (**ràschio**) *tr* to scrape; to scratch || *intr* to clear one's throat
raschiétto *m* scraper; erasing knife; footscraper
rà•schio *m* (**-schi**) clearing one's throat; hoarseness; frog in the throat
rasentare (**rasènto**) *tr* to graze; to scrape; to border on; to come close to
rasènte *adv* close; **rasente a** close to || *prep* close to
ra•so -sa [s] *adj* shaved; trimmed; brimful; disreputable (*clothes*); flush || *m* satin || *adv*—**raso terra** down-to-earth; **volare raso terra** to skim the ground; to hedgehop
ra•sóio [s] *m* (**-sói**) razor; **rasoio a mano libera** straight razor; **rasoio di sicurezza** safety razor
raspa *f* rasp
raspare *tr* to rasp; to irritate; to stamp, paw; (coll) to steal || *intr* to rasp; to scratch (*said of a chicken*); to scrawl
raspo *m* grape stalk; scraper; (vet) mange
rasségna *f* review; exposition
rassegnare (**rasségno**) *tr* to resign; **rassegnare le dimissioni** to resign || *ref* to resign oneself; to submit
rassegnazióne *f* resignation
rasserenare (**rasseréno**) *tr* & *ref* to brighten; to cheer up
rassettare (**rassètto**) *tr* & *ref* to tidy up

rassicurare *tr* to reassure ‖ *ref* to be reassured

rassodare (rassòdo) *tr* to harden; to strengthen ‖ *intr* (ESSERE) & *ref* to harden

rassomigliare §280 **(rassomìglio)** *tr* to compare ‖ *intr* (ESSERE) (with *dat*) to resemble ‖ *ref* to resemble each other

rastrellaménto *m* roundup; mop-up operation

rastrellare (rastrèllo) *tr* to rake; to round up; to mop up; to drag (*e.g., the bottom*)

rastrellièra *f* rack; crib

rastrèllo *m* rake

rastremare (rastrèmo) *tr* to taper

rata *f* installment; quota; **a rate** on time; by installments

rateale *adj* installment

rateizzare [ddzz] *tr* to prorate; to divide (*a payment*) into installments

ratifi·ca *f* (-che) ratification

ratificare §197 **(ratìfico)** *tr* to ratify

rat·to -ta *adj* (lit) swift ‖ *m* rat; (lit) rape ‖ **ratto** *adv* (lit) swiftly

rattoppare (rattòppo) *tr* to patch, patch up

rattrappire §176 *tr* to cramp; to make numb, benumb ‖ *ref* to become cramped; to become numb

rattristare *tr* & *ref* to sadden

raucèdine *f* hoarseness

ràu·co -ca *adj* (-chi -che) hoarse, raucous

ravanèllo *m* radish

ravizzóne *m* (bot) rape

ravvedére §279 (*fut* **ravvedrò** & **ravvederò;** *pp* **ravveduto**) *ref* to repent; to mend one's ways

ravvedu·to -ta *adj* repentant; reformed

ravviare §119 *tr* to arrange, adjust; to poke (*fire*) ‖ *ref* to tidy up; (lit) to reform

ravvicinaménto *m* approach; reconciliation; rapprochement

ravvicinare *tr* to bring up; to reconcile ‖ *ref* to approach; to become reconciled; **ravvicinarsi a** to approach

ravviluppare *tr* to wrap up; to wind up; to bamboozle ‖ *ref* to become tangled

ravvisare *tr* to recognize

ravvivare *tr* to revive; to enliven; to brighten; to stir (*fire*) ‖ *ref* to revive

ravvòlgere §289 *tr* to wrap up

razioci·nio *m* (-ni) reasoning; reason; common sense

razionale *adj* rational

razionalizzare [ddzz] *tr* (com, math) to rationalize

razionaménto *m* rationing

razionare (razióno) *tr* to ration

razióne *f* ration; portion

razza *f* race; breed; kind; **di razza** purebred; **far razza** to reproduce; **passare a razza** to go to stud

razza [ddzz] *f* (ichth) ray; **razza cornuta** manta ray

razzìa *f* raid; foray; insect powder

razziale *adj* racial

razziare §119 *tr* & *intr* to foray

razzismo *m* racism

razzi·sta *mf* (-sti -ste) racist

razzo [ddzz] *m* rocket; (coll) spoke; (mil) flare

razzolare (ràzzolo) *intr* to scratch (*said of chickens*); (coll) to rummage

re [e] *m* (re) king

re [ɛ] *m* (re) (mus) re

reagènte *m* reagent

reagire §176 *intr* to react

reale *adj* real, actual; royal, regal

realismo *m* realism; royalism

reali·sta *mf* (-sti -ste) realist; royalist

realìsti·co -ca *adj* (-ci -che) realistic

realizzare [ddzz] *tr* to carry out; to realize; to build ‖ *ref* to come true

realizzazióne [ddzz] *f* realization; **realizzazione scenica** production

realizzo [ddzz] *m* conversion into cash; profit taking; forced sale

realménte *adv* really, indeed

real·tà *f* (-tà) reality; actuality; **realtà romanzesca** truth stranger than fiction

reato *m* crime

reatti·vo -va *adj* reactive

reattóre *m* reactor; jet plane; jet engine

reazionà·rio -ria (-ri -rie) *adj* & *mf* reactionary

reazióne *f* reaction; (mach) backlash; **a reazione** jet-propelled

réb·bio *m* (-bi) prong

recalcitrante *adj* balky, restive; **essere recalcitrante a** to be opposed to, to resist

recalcitrare (recàlcitro) *intr* to be balky; to kick; (with *dat*) to buck, resist

recapitare (recàpito) *tr* to deliver

recàpito *m* address; delivery; **far recapito in** to be domiciled in; **recapiti** (com) notes

recare §197 **(rèco)** *tr* to bring; to cause; **recare ad effetto** to carry out; **recare qlco alla memoria di qlcu** to remind s.o. of s.th; **recare qlco a lode di qlcu** to praise s.o. for s.th ‖ *ref* to go, betake oneself

recèdere §123 *intr* (ESSERE & AVERE) to recede

recensióne *f* book review; collation

recensire §176 *tr* to review; to collate

recensóre *m* reviewer

recènte *adj* recent; **di recente** recently

recessióne *f* recession

recèsso *m* recess; subsiding (*of fever*); ebb tide

recìdere §145 *tr* to cut off; to chop off

recidiva *f* relapse; second offense

recìngere §126 *tr* to enclose, pen in

recinto *m* enclosure; pen, yard; compound; playpen; paddock; **recinto delle grida** floor of the exchange

recipiènte *m* container

reciprocità *f* reciprocity

recìpro·co -ca *adj* (-ci -che) reciprocal

reci·so -sa *adj* cut off; abrupt

rècita *f* show, performance

recitare (rècito) *tr* to recite; to portray, play; **recitare la commedia** to put on an act ‖ *intr* to perform, play; **recitare a soggetto** (theat) to improvise

recitazióne *f* recitation; diction; acting

reclamare *tr* to claim, demand || *intr* to complain

récla·me *f* (-me) advertising; advertisement; **fare réclame a** to advertise; to boost

reclami·sta *mf* (-sti -ste) advertising agent; show-off || *m* advertising man

reclamìsti·co -ca *adj* (-ci -che) advertising

reclamo *m* complaint; **fare reclamo** to complain

reclinare *tr* to bow || *intr* to recline

reclusióne *f* seclusion; imprisonment

reclu·so -sa *adj* recluse || *mf* recluse; prisoner

reclusò·rio *m* (-ri) penitentiary

rècluta *f* recruit; rookie

reclutaménto *m* recruitment

reclutare (**rècluto**) *tr* to recruit

recòndi·to -ta *adj* concealed; inmost; recondite

recriminare (**recrìmino**) *intr* to recriminate

recuperare (**recùpero**) *tr* see **ricuperare**

redarguire §176 *tr* to berate

redat·tóre -trice *mf* compiler; newspaper editor; **redattore capo** managing editor; **redattore pubblicitario** copywriter; **redattore responsabile** publisher; **redattore viaggiante** correspondent

redazionale *adj* editorial, editor's (*e.g., policy*)

redazióne *f* writing; draft; version; (journ) city room

redazza *f* mop; (naut) swab

redditi·zio -zia *adj* (-zi -zie) lucrative

rèddito *m* income, revenue; yield; **reddito nazionale** gross national product

redèn·to -ta *adj* redeemed, set free

reden·tóre -trice *mf* redeemer || **Redentore** *m*—**il Redentore** the Redeemer

redenzióne *f* redemption

redìgere §224 *tr* to compile; to write up, compose

redìmere §225 *tr* to redeem; to ransom; to save

rèdine *f* rein

redivi·vo -va *adj* come back to life

rèduce *adj* back (*from war*) || *mf* veteran

réfe *m* thread

referèn·dum *m* (-dum) referendum; **referendum postale** mail questionnaire

referènza *f* reference

referenziare (**referènzio**) *tr* to give references to; to write references for || *intr* to have good references

referenzia·to -ta *adj* with good references, e.g., **impiegato referenziato** employee with good references

refèrto *m* report (*of a physician*)

refettò·rio *m* (-ri) refectory

refezióne *f* lunch, light meal; **refezione scolastica** school lunch

refrattà·rio -ria *adj* (-ri -rie) refractory

refrigerante *adj* cooling || *m* refrigerator; (chem) condenser

refrigerare (**refrìgero**) *tr* to refrigerate; to cool || *ref* to cool off

refrigè·rio *m* (-ri) relief, comfort

refurtiva *f* stolen goods

refuso *m* misprint

regalare *tr* to present; to deliver (*a slap*); to throw away (*money*); **è regalato** it's a steal

regale *adj* regal; royal; imposing

regalìa *f* gratuity; bonus

regalità *f* regality, royalty

regalo *m* present, gift

regata *f* regatta

reggènte *adj* & *m* regent

reggènza *f* regency

règgere §226 *tr* to hold, hold up; to stand, withstand; to guide; (gram) to govern; **reggere il sacco a** to connive with; **reggere l'animo di** + *inf* to bear or stand + *ger*, e.g., **non gli regge l'animo di vederla piangere** he cannot stand seeing her cry || *intr* to hold; to be valid; to last, hold out (*said of weather*); **reggere** (with *dat*) to withstand (*e.g., the cold*); **reggere al paragone** to bear comparison || *ref* to stand up; to hold; to be ruled; **reggersi a** to hold on to; to be governed as (*e.g., a republic*); **reggersi a galla** to float

règ·gia *f* (-ge) royal palace

reggical·ze *m* (-ze) girdle

reggilibro *m* book end

reggimentale *adj* regimental

reggiménto *m* regiment

reggipètto *m* brassiere

reggisé·no *m* (-ni & -no) brassiere

regìa *f* monopoly; (mov) direction; (theat) production

regici·da *mf* (-di -de) regicide

regicì·dio *m* (-di) regicide

regime *m* regime; diet; flow (*e.g., of river*); government; authoritarian government; (mach) rate; **regime secco** total abstinence

regina *f* queen; **regina claudia** greengage; **regina madre** queen mother

reginétta *f* young queen; queen (*of a beauty contest*)

rè·gio -gia *adj* (-gi -gie) royal || **i regi** the king's soldiers

regióne *f* region

regi·sta *mf* (-sti -ste) coordinator; (theat) producer; (mov) director

registrare *tr* to register, record; to enter; to tally, log; to adjust; to tune up (*a musical instrument*) || *ref* to register

registra·tóre -trice *mf* registrar || *m* recorder; **registratore di cassa** cash register

registrazióne *f* registration; record, entry; adjustment; (aut) tune-up; (telv) videotaping; (telv) video-taping studio; (telv) video-taped program

registro *m* register; registration; classbook; regulator (*of watch*); stop (*of organ*); **cambiar registro** to change one's tune; **dar registro a** to regulate (*a watch*)

regnante *adj* reigning; prevailing || **i regnanti** the rulers

regnare (**régno**) *intr* to reign, rule; to prevail; to take hold (*said of a root*)

régno *m* kingdom; reign

règola *f* rule; regulation; moderation; **a regola d'arte** to a T; **di regola** as a rule; **in regola** in good order; **mettere in regola** to put in order; **regole** menstruation; **secondo le regole** by the book

regolamentare *adj* regulation || *v* (**regolaménto**) *tr* to regulate

regolaménto *m* regulation; settlement; **regolamento edilizio** building code

regolare *adj* regular; steady (*employment*); stock (*material*) || *v* (**règolo**) *tr* to regulate; to adjust; to set (*a watch*); to focus (*a lens*); to settle (*an account*) || *ref* to behave; to control oneself

regolari·tà *f* (-**tà**) regularity

regolarizzare [ddzz] *tr* to regularize

regolatézza *f* regularity; moderation

regola·to -ta *adj* regular, orderly

regola·tóre -trice *adj* regulating; see **piano** || *m* ruler; regulator (*of watch*); (mach) governor; **regolatore dell'aria** register; **regolatore di volume** (rad, telv) volume control

regolazióne *f* regulation

regolìzia *f* (coll) licorice

règolo *m* ruler; slat; (orn, hist) kinglet; **regolo calcolatore** slide rule

regredire §176 (*pres participle* **regrediènte**; *pp* **regredito & regrèsso**) *intr* (ESSERE & AVERE) to retrogress

regrèsso *m* regression; abatement (*of fever*); (com) recourse

reièt·to -ta *adj* rejected || *mf* outcast

reimbarcare §197 *tr* & *ref* to reship; to transship

reimbar·co *m* (-**chi**) reshipment; transshipment

reincarnare *tr* to reincarnate || *ref* to become reincarnated

reincarnazióne *f* reincarnation

reinseriménto *m* integration

reintegrare (**reìntegro**) *tr* to restore; to reinstate; to indemnify

reità *f* guilt

reiterare (**reìtero**) *tr* to reiterate

relativi·tà *f* (-**tà**) relativity

relati·vo -va *adj* relative

rela·tóre -trice *adj* reporting || *mf* relator (*of proceedings*); presenter (*of a bill*); dissertation supervisor

relazióne *f* relation; relationship; report; **relazione amorosa** affair; **relazioni** relations; connections

re·lè *m* (-**lè**) (elec) relay

relegare §209 (**rèlego**) *tr* to banish; to store away

religióne *f* religion

religió·so -sa [s] *adj* religious || *m* clergyman || *f* nun

relìquia *f* relic

relit·to -ta *adj* residual || *m* shipwreck; air crash; derelict; shoal, bar

remare (**rèmo** & **rémo**) *intr* to row

rema·tóre -trice *mf* rower || *m* oarsman

reminiscènza *f* reminiscence

remissióne *f* submissiveness; remission

remissi·vo -va *adj* submissive

rèmo *m* oar; **remo alla battana** paddle

rèmora *f* hindrance; (lit) delay

remò·to -ta *adj* remote; **passato remoto** (gram) preterit

réna *f* sand

Renània, la the Rhineland

Renata *f* Renée

rèndere §227 *tr* to return, give back; to give (*thanks*); to render (*justice*); to yield; to translate; to make (*known*); **render conto di** to give an account of; **rendere di pubblica ragione** to publicize; **rendere l'anima a Dio** to give up the ghost; **rendere pan per focaccia** to give tit for tat || *intr* to pay, yield || *ref* to make oneself; to betake oneself; to become; (lit) to surrender; **rendersi conto di** to realize

rendicónto *m* account; report; **rendiconti** proceedings

rendiménto *m* rendering; yield; output; (mech) efficiency

rèndita *f* private income; yield; Italian Government bond

rène *m* kidney

renèlla *f* (pathol) gravel

renétta *f* pippin

réni *fpl* loins; **spezzare le reni a** to break the back of

renitènte *adj* opposed || *m*—**renitente alla leva** draft dodger

rènna *f* reindeer; reindeer skin

Rèno *m* Rhine

rè·o -a *adj* guilty; (lit) wicked || *m* guilty person; accused

reòstato *m* (elec) rheostat

reparto *m* department; (mil) unit; **reparto d'assalto** shock troops

repèllere §168 *tr* to repel

repentàglio *m* jeopardy; **mettere a repentaglio** to jeopardize

repènte *adj*—**di repente** suddenly

repenti·no -na *adj* sudden

reperìbile *adj* available

reperiménto *m* finding

reperire §176 *tr* to find

repèrto *m* (archeol) find; (law) evidence; (law) exhibit; (med) report

repertò·rio *m* (-**ri**) repertory; catalogue

rèpli·ca *f* (-**che**) repetition; replica; (law) rebuttal; (theat) repeat performance; **in replica** in reply

replicare §197 (**rèplico**) *tr* to repeat; to reply, answer; (theat) to repeat (*a performance*)

reportàg·gio *m* (-**gi**) news coverage; reporting

repòr·ter *m* (-**ter**) reporter

repressióne *f* repression; constraint

repressi·vo -va *adj* repressive; controlling, checking (*e.g., a disease*)

reprìmere §131 *tr* to repress; to hold back (*tears*) || *ref* to restrain oneself

rèpro·bo -ba *adj* & *m* reprobate

repùbbli·ca *f* (-**che**) republic

repubblica·no -na *adj* & *mf* republican

repulisti *m*—**fare repulisti** (coll) to make a clean sweep

repulsióne *f* repulsion

repulsi·vo -va *adj* var of **ripulsivo**

reputare (**rèputo**) *tr* to think, esteem, repute

reputazióne *f* reputation

rèquie *m* & *f* (eccl) requiem || *f* rest, respite

Rèquiem *m* & *f* Requiem

requisire §176 *tr* to requisition, commandeer

requisito *m* requisite, requirement

requisitòria *f* scolding, reproach; (law) summation

requisizióne *f* requisition

résa [s] *f* surrender; rendering (*of an account*); delivery (*of merchandise*); return (*e.g., of newspapers*); yield; **resa a discrezione** unconditional surrender

rescìndere §247 *tr* to rescind

resezióne [s] *f* (surg) resection

residènte [s] *adj & mf* resident

residènza [s] *f* residence

residenziale [s] *adj* residential

residua·to -ta [s] *adj* residual

resì·duo -dua [s] *adj* residual ‖ *m* residue; remainder; balance

rèsina *f* resin

resipiscènza [s] *f* (lit) repentance

resistènte [s] *adj* resistant; strong; fast (*color*) ‖ *mf* member of the Resistance

resistènza [s] *f* resistance ‖ **Resistenza** *f* Resistance

resìstere [s] §114 *intr* to resist; (with *dat*) to withstand; (with *dat*) to endure; (with *dat*) to resist

rèso [s] *m* rhesus

resocónto [s] *m* report, relation

respingènte *m* (rr) bumper, buffer

respìngere §126 *tr* to drive back, beat off; to reject; to fail (*a student*); to vote down

respin·to -ta *adj* rejected ‖ *mf* failure (*pupil*)

respirare *tr & intr* to breathe, respire

respiratò·rio -ria *adj* (**-ri -rie**) respiratory

respirazióne *f* breathing

respiro *m* breath; breathing; respite

responsàbile *adj* responsible; **responsabile di** responsible for

responsabili·tà *f* (**-tà**) responsibility

respònso *m* decision (*of an oracle*); report (*of a physician*); return (*of an election*); (lit) response

rèssa *f* crowd; **far ressa** to crowd

rèsta *f* string (*of garlic or onions*); awn (*e.g., of wheat*); (coll) fishbone; (*for a lance*) (hist) rest

restante *adj* remaining ‖ *m* remainder

restare (**rèsto**) *intr* (ESSERE) to remain; to stay; to be located; (lit) to stop; **non restare a…che** to have no alternative but to, e.g., **non gli resta che andarsene** he has no alternative but to go; **non restare a qlco qlco da** + *inf* to not have s.th + to + *inf*, e.g., **non gli resta molto da finire** he does not have much to finish; **resta a vedere** it remains to be seen; **restare qlco a qlcu** to have s.th left, e.g., **gli restano tre dollari** he has three dollars left; **restare sul colpo** to die on the spot; **resti comodo** please don't get up!

restaurare (**restàuro**) *tr* to restore, renovate

restaurazióne *f* restoration

restàuro *m* restoration (*of a building*)

restì·o -a (**-i -e**) *adj* balky, restive ‖ *m* balkiness

restituire §176 *tr* to give back, return; (lit) to restore ‖ *ref* (lit) to return

restituzióne *f* restitution, return

rèsto *m* remainder; change; balance; **del resto** besides, after all; **resti** remains

restrìngere §265 (*pp* **ristrétto**) *tr* to narrow down; to shrink; to take in (*a suit*); to limit (*expenses*); to tighten (*a knot*); to bind (*the bowels*); to restrict ‖ *ref* to contract; to narrow

restrizióne *f* restriction

retàg·gio *m* (**-gi**) (lit) heritage

retata *f* haul; (fig) roundup

réte *f* net; network; (soccer) goal; **rete a strascico** trawl; **rete da pesca** fishing net; **rete del letto** bedspring; **rete metallica** wire mesh; window screen; **rete per i capelli** hair net; **rete viaria** highway network

reticèlla *f* small net; hair net; mantle (*of gas jet*)

reticènte *adj* secretive, dissembling; evasive, noncommittal

reticènza *f* secretiveness; evasiveness

reticolato *m* grid (*on map*); wire entanglement

retìcolo *m* grid

retina *f* small net

rètina *f* (anat) retina

retino *m* small net; (typ) screen

retòri·co -ca (**-ci -che**) *adj* rhetorical ‖ *m* rhetorician ‖ *f* rhetoric

retràttile *adj* retractile

retribuire §176 *tr* to remunerate

retributi·vo -va *adj* retributive; salary (*e.g., conditions*)

retri·vo -va *adj* backward

rètro *m* back; verso; back of store ‖ *adv* (lit) behind; **retro a** (lit) behind

retroatti·vo -va *adj* retroactive

retrobottè·ga *m & f* (**-ga** *mpl* **-ghe** *fpl*) back of store

retrocàmera *f* back room

retrocàrica *f*—**a retrocarica** breechloading

retrocèdere §228 *tr* to demote; (com) to return; (com) to give a discount to ‖ *intr* (ESSERE & AVERE) to retreat

retrocessióne *f* demotion; (sports) assignment to a lower division

retrodatare *tr* to antedate, predate

retrògra·do -da *adj* backward; retrograde

retroguàrdia *f* rearguard

retromàr·cia *f* (**-ce**) (aut) reverse

retrorazzo [ddzz] *m* retrorocket

retrosapóre *m* aftertaste

retroscè·na *m* (**-na**) intrigue, maneuver ‖ *f* backstage

retrospetti·vo -va *adj* retrospective

retrotèr·ra *m* (**-ra**) hinterland; (fig) background

retrotrèno *m* rear end (*of vehicle*); (aut) rear assembly

retroversióne *f* retroversion; retranslation

retrovìe *fpl* zone behind the front

retrovisi·vo -va *adj* rear-view, e.g., **specchietto retrovisivo** rear-view mirror

retrovisóre *m* rear-view mirror

rètta *f* board and lodging; straight line; **dar retta a** to pay attention to

rettangolare *adj* rectangular

rettàngolo *m* rectangle

rettìfi·ca *f* (**-che**) straightening; rectification; (mach) grinding; (mach) reboring

rettificare §197 (**rettìfico**) *tr* to straighten; to rectify; (mach) to grind; (mach) to rebore

rettifica·tóre **-trice** *adj* rectifying ‖ *mf* rectifier (*person*) ‖ *m* rectifier (*apparatus*)

rettifilo *m* straightaway

rèttile *m* reptile

rettilì·neo **-nea** *adj* rectilinear ‖ *m* straightaway ‖ *f* straight line

rettitùdine *f* straightness; uprightness, rectitude

rèt·to **-ta** *adj* straight; correct; upright; (geom) right ‖ *m* right; recto; (anat) rectum ‖ *f* see **retta**

rettóre *m* rector; president (*of university*)

reumàti·co **-ca** *adj* (**-ci** **-che**) rheumatic

reumatismo *m* rheumatism

reverèn·do **-da** *adj* & *m* reverend

reverènte *adj* var of **riverente**

reverènza *f* var of **riverenza**

revisióne *f* revision; (mach) overhaul

revisionismo *m* revisionism

revisóre *m* inspector; **revisore dei conti** auditor; **revisore di bozze** proofreader

reviviscènza *f* rebirth

rèvo·ca *f* (**-che**) revocation; recall; repeal

revocare §197 (**rèvoco**) *tr* to revoke; to recall; to repeal

revòl·ver *m* (**-ver**) revolver

revolverata *f* gun shot

revulsióne *f* (med) revulsion

ri- *pref* re-, e.g., **rivivere** to relive; again, e.g., **rifare** to do again; back, e.g., **riandare** to go back

riabbonare (**riabbòno**) *tr* to renew the subscription of ‖ *ref* to renew one's subscription

riabbracciare §128 (**riabbràccio**) *tr* to embrace again; to greet again

riabilitare (**riabìlito**) *tr* to rehabilitate ‖ *ref* to reestablish one's good name

riaccèndere §101 *tr* to rekindle ‖ *ref* to become rekindled

riaccompagnare *tr* to take home

riaccostare (**riaccòsto**) *tr* to bring near; to bring together ‖ *ref* to draw near

riacquistare *tr* to buy back; to recover

riaddormentare (**riaddormènto**) *tr* to put back to sleep ‖ *ref* to go back to sleep

riaffacciare §128 (**riaffàccio**) *tr* to present again ‖ *ref* to reappear

riaffermare (**riaffèrmo**) *tr* to reaffirm

riaggravare *tr* to make worse ‖ *ref* to get worse again

rialesare (**rialèso**) *tr* to rebore

riallacciare §128 (**riallàccio**) *tr* to tie again ‖ *ref* to be tied or connected

rialto *m* knoll, height; **fare rialto** (coll) to eat better than usual

rialzare *tr* to lift, raise; to increase ‖ *ref* to rise

rialzi·sta *mf* (**-sti** **-ste**) bull (*in stock market*)

rialzo *m* rise; raise; knoll, height; **giocare al rialzo** to bull the market

riammobiliare §287 *tr* to refurnish

rianimare (**riànimo**) *tr* to revive; to encourage ‖ *ref* to revive; to recover one's spirits, to rally

riapertura *f* reopening

riapparire §108 *intr* (ESSERE) to reappear

riapparizióne *f* reappearance

riaprire §110 *tr* & *ref* to reopen

riarmare *tr* to rearm; to reinforce; to refit ‖ *intr* & *ref* to rearm

riarmo *m* rearmament

riar·so **-sa** *adj* dry, parched

riassaporare (**riassapóro**) *tr* to relish again

riassettare (**riassètto**) *tr* to tidy up

riassicurare *tr* to reinsure; to fasten again; to reassure

riassorbire §176 & (**riassòrbo**) *tr* to reabsorb

riassùmere §116 *tr* to hire again; to summarize, sum up

riassunto *m* précis, abstract; résumé

riassunzióne *f* rehiring; resumption

riattaccare §197 *tr* to attach again; (coll) to begin again; (telp) to hang up

riattare *tr* to repair, fix

riattivare *tr* to reactivate

riavére §229 *tr* to get again; to recover; to get back ‖ *ref* to recover

riavvicinaménto *m* var of **ravvicinamento**

riavvicinare *tr* & *ref* var of **ravvicinare**

ribadire §176 *tr* to clinch (*a nail*); to rivet; to drive home (*an idea*); to back up (*a statement*)

ribaldo *m* scoundrel, rogue

ribalta *f* lid with hinge; trap door; (theat) footlights; (theat) forestage; (fig) limelight; **a ribalta** hinged

ribaltàbile *adj* collapsable (*e.g., seat*) ‖ *m* dump-truck lift; dump truck

ribaltare *tr* & *ref* to upset, turn over

ribassare *tr* & *intr* (ESSERE) to lower

ribassi·sta *mf* (**-sti** **-ste**) bear (*in stock market*)

ribasso *m* fall, decline; discount, rebate; **giocare al ribasso** to be a bear

ribàttere *tr* to clinch (*a nail*); to return (*a ball*); to iron smooth; to belabor (*a point*) ‖ *intr* to answer back

ribattezzare [ddzz] (**ribattézzo**) *tr* to rebaptize

ribattino *m* rivet

ribellare (**ribèllo**) *tr* to rouse to rebellion ‖ *ref* to rebel; **ribellarsi a** to rebel against

ribèlle *adj* rebellious ‖ *mf* rebel

ribellióne *f* rebellion

ri·bes *m* (**-bes**) currant; gooseberry

ribobinazióne *f* rewind (*of a tape*)

riboccare §197 (**ribócco**) *intr* (ESSERE & AVERE) to overflow

ribollire (**ribóllo**) *tr* to boil again ‖

intr to boil over; to simmer; to ferment

ribrézzo [ddzz] *m* repugnance, disgust

ributtare *tr* to return (*a ball*); to throw up; to reject; to push back ‖ *intr* to sprout; (with *dat*) to disgust, nauseate

ricacciare §128 *tr* to drive back ‖ *intr* to sprout ‖ *ref* to sneak away, disappear

ricadére §121 *intr* (ESSERE) to fall back; to fall down; to relapse; **ricadere su** to devolve upon

ricaduta *f* relapse

ricalcare §197 *tr* to transfer (*a design*); to imitate; **ricalcare le orme di** follow in the footsteps of

rical·co *m* (-chi) copy, copying; **a ri-calco** multiple-copy

ricamare *tr* to embroider

ricambiare §287 *tr* to return; to repay ‖ *ref* to change clothes

ricàm·bio *m* (-bi) exchange; spare part; refill; metabolism; **di ricambio** spare (*part*)

ricamo *m* embroidery; needlework; **ricami** (*fig*) embellishments

ricapitolare (**ricapìtolo**) *tr* to recapitulate

ricaricare §197 (**ricàrico**) *tr* to reload; to wind (*a watch*); to charge (*a battery*)

ricattare *tr* to blackmail

ricatta·tóre **-trice** *mf* blackmailer

ricatto *m* blackmail

ricavare *tr* to draw, extract; to obtain, derive

ricavato *m* proceeds; (fig) fruit, yield

ricavo *m* proceeds

ricchézza *f* wealth; **ricchezza mobile** income from personal property; **ricchezze** riches

rìc·cio -cia (-ci -ce) *adj* curly ‖ *m* curl; shaving; burr; scroll (*of violin*); crook (*of crozier*); (zool) hedgehog; **riccio di mare** (zool) sea urchin

rìcciolo *m* curl

ricciolu·to -ta *adj* curly

ricciu·to -ta *adj* curly

ric·co -ca *adj* (-chi -che) rich ‖ **i ricchi** the rich

ricér·ca *f* (-che) search; research; **ri-cerca operativa** operations research

ricercare §197 (**ricérco**) *tr* to search for again; to seek; to investigate; (poet) to pluck (*a musical instrument*)

ricercatézza *f* affectation; sophistication

ricerca·to -ta *adj* sought after, wanted; affected; sophisticated

ricetrasmettitóre *m* two-way radio

ricètta *f* prescription; recipe

ricettàcolo *m* receptacle; depository

ricettare (**ricètto**) *tr* to receive (*stolen goods*); to prescribe

ricetta·rio *m* (-ri) recipe book; prescription pad

ricetta·tóre **-trice** *mf* fence, receiver of stolen goods

ricetti·vo -va *adj* receptive

ricètto *m* (poet) refuge

ricévere §141 *tr* to receive; to get; to contain; to withstand

ricevimento *m* reception; receipt

ricevi·tóre **-trice** *mf* addressee ‖ *m* receiver; collector; registrar of deeds; **ricevitore postale** postmaster

ricevitorìa *f* collection office; **ricevi-toria postale** post office

ricevuta *f* receipt; **accusare ricevuta di** to acknowledge receipt of

ricezióne *f* (rad, telv) reception; **accu-sare ricezione** to acknowledge receipt

richiamare *tr* to call back; to recall; to call (*e.g., attention*); to quote; to chide ‖ *ref* to refer

richiamato *m* soldier recalled to active duty

richiamo *m* call; recall; admonition; cross reference; advertisement

richièdere §124 *tr* to ask again; to demand; to require; to apply for ‖ *ref* to be required

richiè·sto -sta *adj*—**essere richiesto** to be in demand ‖ *f* request; demand; petition, application

richiùdere §125 *tr* & *ref* to shut again

riciclare *tr* to recycle (*e.g., in the chemical industry*)

rìcino *m* castor-oil plant

ricognitóre *m* scout; reconnaissance plane; (law) recognition

ricognizióne *f* recognition; (mil) reconnaissance

ricollegare §209 (**ricollégo**) *tr* to connect ‖ *ref* to be connected; to refer

ricolmare (**ricólmo**) *tr* to fill to the brim; to overwhelm

ricominciare §128 *tr* & *intr* (ESSERE) to begin again, resume

ricomparire §108 *intr* (ESSERE) to reappear

ricomparsa *f* reappearance

ricompènsa *f* compensation, recompense; reward; (mil) award

ricompensare (**ricompènso**) *tr* to compensate, recompense; to reward

ricomperare (**ricómpero**) *tr* var of **ricomprare**

ricompórre §218 *tr* to recompose; to plan again ‖ *ref* to regain one's composure

ricomprare (**ricómpro**) *tr* to buy again; to buy back

riconcentrare (**riconcèntro**) *tr* to concentrate again; to gather (*one's thoughts*) ‖ *ref* to be withdrawn

riconciliare §287 (**riconcìlio**) *tr* to reconcile ‖ *ref* to become reconciled

ricondurre §102 *tr* to bring back; to take back ‖ *ref* to go back

riconfermare (**riconférmo**) *tr* to reconfirm

riconfortare (**riconfòrto**) *tr* to comfort

ricongiùngere §183 *tr* & *ref* to reunite

riconoscènte *adj* grateful

riconoscènza *f* gratitude

riconóscere §134 *tr* to recognize; (mil) to reconnoiter

riconosciménto *m* recognition; **in ri-conoscimento di** in recognition of

riconquistare *tr* to reconquer

riconsegnare (**riconségno**) *tr* to give back, to return

riconsiderare (riconsìdero) *tr* to reconsider

ricontare (ricónto) *tr* to recount, count again

riconversióne *f* reconversion

riconvertire §138 *tr* to reconvert; to recycle

ricopèr·to -ta *adj* covered; coated

ricopertura *f* covering; seat cover

ricopiare §287 **(ricòpio)** *tr* to make a fair copy of; to recopy; to copy

ricoprire §110 *tr* to cover; to coat; to hide ‖ *ref* to become covered

ricordanza *f* (poet) memory

ricordare (ricòrdo) *tr* to remember; to remind; to mention ‖ *ref* to remember; **ricordarsi di** to remember

ricòrdo *m* memory; souvenir; **ricordo marmoreo** marble statue

ricorrènte *adj* recurrent, recurring

ricorrènza *f* recurrence; anniversary

ricórrere §139 *intr* (ESSERE & AVERE) to run again; to run back; to resort; to recur; (law) to appeal; **ricorrere a** to have recourse to

ricórso *m* recurrence; recourse; appeal

ricostituènte *adj* invigorating ‖ *m* tonic

ricostituire §176 *tr* to reconstitute, to reform; to reinvigorate

ricostruire §140 *tr* to rebuild; to reconstruct

ricostruzióne *f* rebuilding; reconstruction

ricòtta *f* Italian cottage cheese; **di ricotta** weak

ricoverare (ricóvero) *tr* to shelter ‖ *ref* to take shelter

ricóvero *m* shelter; nursing home; (med) admission; **ricovero antiaereo** air-raid shelter

ricreare (ricrèo) *tr* to recreate; to refresh ‖ *ref* to relax

ricreati·vo -va *adj* refreshing; recreational

ricreatò·rio -ria (-ri -rie) *adj* recreation, recreational ‖ *m* recreation room; playground

ricreazióne *f* recreation; recess

ricrédere §141 *intr*—**far ricredere qlcu** to make s.o. change his mind ‖ *ref* to change one's mind

ricréscere §142 *intr* (ESSERE) to grow again; to swell

ricucire §143 *tr* to sew up

ricuòcere §144a *tr* to cook again; to anneal

ricuperare (ricùpero) *tr* to recover; (naut) to salvage; (sports) to make up for (*rained-out game*)

ricùpero *m* recovery; salvage; rally; making up (*for lost time or postponed game*)

ricur·vo -va *adj* bent; bent over

ricusare *tr* to refuse

ridacchiare §287 *intr* to titter, giggle

ridancia·no -na *adj* prone to laughter; amusing

ridare §230 (*1st sg pres ind* **ridò**) *tr* to give back; to give again; **ridare fuori** to vomit ‖ *intr* (coll) to reappear, e.g., **gli ha ridato il foruncolo** his boil has reappeared ‖ *intr*

(ESSERE)—**ridare giù** to have a relapse

ridda *f* round; confusion; throng

ridènte *adj* laughing; bright, pleasant

rìdere §231 *tr* (poet) to laugh at ‖ *intr* to laugh; (poet) to shine; **far rìdere i polli** to be utterly ridiculous; **ridere sotto i baffi** to laugh up one's sleeve ‖ *ref*—**ridersi di** to laugh at

ridestare (ridésto) *tr* & *ref* to reawaken

ridicolizzare [ddzz] *tr* to ridicule; to twit

ridìco·lo -la *adj* ridiculous ‖ *m* ridicule; ridiculousness

ridipìngere §126 *tr* to paint again

ridire §151 *tr* to tell again; to repeat; to tell (*to express*); **avere** or **trovare a** or **da ridire (su)** to find fault (with)

ridistribuzióne *f* redistribution

ridivenire §282 or **ridiventare (ridivènto)** *intr* (ESSERE) to become again

ridonare (ridóno) *tr* to give back

ridondante *adj* redundant

ridondare (ridóndo) *intr* (ESSERE & AVERE) (fig) to overflow; **ridondare a** or **in** to redound to

ridòsso *m* back; shelter; **a ridosso** sheltered; as a shelter; behind, close behind

ridót·to -ta *adj* reduced; **mal ridotto** down at the heel ‖ *m* lounge; (theat) foyer ‖ *f* (mil) redoubt

ridurre §102 *tr* to reduce; to adapt; to translate; to lead; to curtail; (mus) to arrange ‖ *ref* to be reduced; to retire

riduttóre *m* (mach) reduction gear

riduzióne *f* reduction; (mus) arrangement

riecheggiare §290 **(riechéggio)** *tr* & *intr* to echo

riedificare §197 **(riedìfico)** *tr* to rebuild

rieducare §197 **(rièduco)** *tr* to reeducate

rielèggere §193 *tr* to reelect

rielezióne *f* reelection

riemèrgere §162 *intr* to resurface

riempiménto *m* fill

riempire §163 *tr* to fill; to stuff

riempiti·vo -va *adj* expletive ‖ *m* expletive; fill-in

rientrante *adj* hollow (*cheeks*); (mil) reentrant

rientranza *f* recess

rientrare (rièntro) *intr* (ESSERE) to reenter; to come back; to recede; (coll) to shrink; **rientrare in** to recover (*one's expenses*); **rientrare in sé** to come to one's senses

rièntro *m* reentry

riepilogare §209 **(riepìlogo)** *tr* to sum up, recapitulate

riepìlo·go *m* (-ghi) recapitulation

riesame *m* reexamination

riesaminare (riesàmino) *tr* to reexamine

riesumare *tr* to exhume; (fig) to dig up; (fig) to bring back

rievocare §197 **(rièvoco)** *tr* to recall

rifaciménto *m* adaptation; recasting

rifare §173 (*3d sg* **rifà**) *tr* to do again, redo; to remake; to imitate; to indemnify; to prepare again; to repeat;

to make (*a bed*) || *ref* to recover; to
become again; to recoup one's losses;
to begin; **rifarsi con** to get even with;
rifarsi da to begin with
rifasciare §128 *tr* to rebind
riferimento *m* reference
riferire §176 *tr* to wound again; to
refer; to relate || *ref*—**riferirsi a** to
refer to; to concern
riffa *f* raffle; lottery; (coll) violence;
di riffa o di raffa by hook or crook
rifilare *tr* to trim; (coll) to reel off
(*a list of names*); (coll) to deal (*a
blow*); (coll) to palm off
rifinire §176 *tr* to give the finishing
touch to; to wear out || *intr* to stop
|| *ref* to wear oneself out
rifiorire §176 *tr* (lit) to revive || *intr*
to bloom again || *intr* (ESSERE) to
flourish; to grow better; to reappear
rifischiare §287 *tr* to whistle again;
(coll) to report || *intr* to talk, gossip
rifiutare *tr* to refuse; (lit) to reject ||
intr (cards) to renege, renounce || *ref*
to refuse, deny
rifiuto *m* refusal; refuse, rubbish; rejection; rebuff, spurn; (fig) wreck;
(cards) renege; **di rifiuto** waste, e.g.,
materiale di rifiuto waste material
riflessióne *f* reflexion
riflessi·vo -va *adj* thoughtful; (gram)
reflexive
riflès·so -sa *adj* reflex, e.g., **azione
riflessa** reflex action || *m* reflection;
(physiol) reflex; **di riflesso** vicarious
riflèttere §177 (*pp* **riflettuto** & **riflèsso**)
tr & *intr* to reflect || *ref* to be re-
flected
riflettóre *m* searchlight; reflector
rifluire §176 *intr* (ESSERE & AVERE) to
flow; to flow back
riflusso *m* flow; ebb, ebb tide
rifocillare *tr* to refresh (*with food*) ||
ref to take refreshment
rifóndere §178 *tr* to melt again; to recast; to refund; to reedit
rifórma *f* reform; (mil) rejection ||
Riforma *f*—**la Riforma** the Reformation
riformare (**rifórmo**) *tr* to reform; to
amend; (mil) to reject
riformati·vo -va *adj* reformatory
riforma·tóre -trice *adj* reforming || *mf*
reformer
riformatò·rio *m* (**-ri**) reform school,
reformatory
rifornimento *m* supply; refueling; **fare
rifornimento di** to fill up with; **rifornimenti** supplies
rifornire §176 *tr* to supply; to restock;
rifornire di benzina to refuel
rifràngere §179 *tr* to crush || *ref* to
break (*said of waves*) || §179 (*pp
rifratto) *tr* to refract || *ref* to be
refracted
rifrat·tóre -trice *adj* refracting || *m*
refractor
rifrazióne *f* refraction
rifrìggere §180 *tr* to fry again; to rehash
|| *intr* to fry too long or in too much
oil
rifrit·to -ta *adj* fried again; (fig) hack-

neyed || *m* taste of stale fat; (fig)
rehash
rifuggire *tr* to avoid || *intr*—**rifuggire
da** to abhor || *intr* (ESSERE) to take
refuge
rifugiare §290 *ref* to take refuge, take
shelter
rifugiato *m* refugee
rifù·gio *m* (**-gi**) refuge; **rifugio alpino**
mountain hut; **rifugio antiaereo** air-
raid shelter; **rifugio antiatomico** fall-
out shelter
rifùlgere §233 *intr* (ESSERE & AVERE) to
shine
rifusióne *f* recast; refund, reimburse-
ment
ri·ga *f* (**-ghe**) line; row; rank; ruler;
part (*in hair*); stripe; (fig) quality
rigàglie *fpl* giblets
rigàgnolo *m* rivulet; gutter (*at the side
of a road*)
rigare §209 *tr* to rule, line; to stripe; to
mark; to rifle (*gun*) || *intr*—**rigare
diritto** to toe the line
rigatino *m* gingham
rigattière *m* second-hand dealer
rigatura *f* ruling; rifling (*of gun*)
rigenerare (**rigènero**) *tr* to regenerate;
to reclaim; to recycle || *ref* to be-
come regenerate
rigenera·tóre *m*—**rigeneratore per i capelli** hair restorer
rigettare (**rigètto**) *tr* to throw back; to
reject; to recast; (slang) to throw up
|| *intr* to sprout
rigètto *m* rejection
righèllo *m* ruler
rigidi·tà *f* (**-tà**) rigidity; rigor; stiffness;
rigidità cadaverica rigor mortis
rìgi·do -da *adj* rigid, stiff; severe
rigirare *tr* to keep turning; to dupe; to
invest; to encircle || *intr* to ramble ||
ref to turn around; to tumble
ri·go *m* (**-ghi**) line; **rigo musicale** (mus)
staff
rigò·glio *m* (**-gli**) luxuriance; bloom;
gurgling
rigonfiare §287 (**rigónfio**) *tr* to inflate
|| *intr* (ESSERE) & *ref* to swell up
rigóre *m* rigor; severity; precision; **a
rigor di termini** strictly speaking;
di rigore de rigueur; (sports) penalty
(*e.g., kick*)
rigorismo *m* rigorism, strictness, severity
rigori·sta *mf* (**-sti -ste**) rigorist || *m*
(soccer) kicker of penalty goal
rigoró·so -sa [s] *adj* rigorous, strict
rigovernare (**rigovèrno**) *tr* to clean,
wash (*dishes*); to groom, tend (*animals*)
riguadagnare *tr* to regain
riguardare *tr* to look again; to look
back; to examine; to consider; to
take care of; to concern || *intr*—
riguardare a to look out for; to face
(*said of a window*) || *ref* to take care
of oneself; **riguardarsi da** to keep
away from
riguardo *m* care; esteem; regard; **a
questo riguardo** in this regard; **ri-**

guardo a as far as . . . is concerned;
senza **riguardo a** irrespective of
riguardó·so -sa [s] *adj* considerate
rigurgitare (rigùrgito) *tr & intr* to
regurgitate
rilanciare §128 *tr* to toss back; to reestablish (*e.g., fashions*); (poker) to
raise
rilasciare §128 *tr* to free, let go; to
relax; to grant || *ref* to relax
rilà·scio *m* (-sci) release; delivery;
granting, issue (*of a document*)
rilassante *adj* relaxing
rilassare *tr & ref* to relax
rilassatézza *f* laxity
rilegare §209 (rilégo) *tr* to tie again;
to bind, rebind (*a book*); to set (*a
stone*)
rilega·tóre -trice *mf* binder
rilegatura *f* binding
rilèggere §193 *tr* to reread
rilènto *m*—a rilento slowly
rilevaménto *m* survey; (naut) bearing
rilevare (rilèvo) *tr* to lift again; to observe; to draw; to bring out; to survey; to take over; to pick up; (mil)
to relieve || *intr* to be delineated;
to be of import || *ref* to rise again;
to recover
rilevatà·rio *m* (-ri) successor; (law)
assignee
rilièvo *m* relief; survey; remark; assumption (*of debts*); taking over (*of
business*); mettere in rilievo to bring
out; to set off
rilò·ga *f* (-ghe) traverse rod
rilucènte *adj* shiny, shining
rilùcere §234 *intr* to shine
riluttante *adj* reluctant
riluttanza *f* reluctance
rima *f* rhyme; slit; crevice; rispondere
per le rime to answer in kind, to
retort
rimandare *tr* to send back; to refer; to
dismiss; to put off, postpone; to refer; rimandare a ottobre to condition
(*a student*)
rimando *m* delay; reference; footnote;
repartee; postponement; (sports) return
rimaneggiare §290 (rimanéggio) *tr* to
rearrange; to reshuffle; to shake up
(*personnel*); to rewrite (*news*)
rimanènte *adj* remaining || *m* remain-
der; remnant; i rimanenti the rest
rimanènza *f* remainder
rimanére §235 *intr* (ESSERE) to remain,
stay; to be in agreement; to have left,
e.g., mi sono rimasti solo tre dollari
I only have three dollars left; to be
located; (poet) to stop; rimanerci
(coll) to be killed; (coll) to be duped;
rimanere da to depend on, e.g.,
questo rimane da Lei this depends on
you
rimangiare §290 *tr* to eat again || *ref*—
rimangiarsi la parola to go back on
one's word
rimarcare §197 *tr* to mark again; to
point out
rimar·co *m* (-chi) remark, notice
rimare *tr & intr* to rhyme

rimarginare (rimàrgino) *tr, intr & ref*
to heal
rimaritare *tr & ref* to marry again
rimasù·glio *m* (-gli) leftover
rima·tóre -trice *mf* poet; rhymster
rimbalzare *intr* (ESSERE & AVERE) to
bounce back, rebound
rimbalzo *m* rebound
rimbambire §176 *intr* (ESSERE) & *ref*
to become feeble-minded (*from old
age*)
rimbambi·to -ta *adj* feeble-minded || *mf*
dotard
rimbeccare §197 (rimbécco) *tr* to peck;
to retort
rimbecilli·to -ta *adj* feeble-minded
rimboccare §197 (rimbócco) *tr* to tuck
up; to tuck in; to fill to the brim
rimbombare (rimbómbo) *intr* (ESSERE &
AVERE) to thunder, boom
rimbómbo *m* thunder, boom
rimborsare (rimbórso) *tr* to reimburse,
pay back
rimborso *m* repayment
rimboscare §197 (rimbòsco) *tr* to re-
forest || *ref* to take to the woods
rimboschiménto *m* reforestation
rimboschire §176 *tr* to reforest || *intr*
(ESSERE) to become wooded
rimbrottare (rimbròtto) *tr* to scold
rimbròtto *m* scolding
rimediare §287 (rimèdio) *tr* (coll) to
scrape together; (coll) to patch up ||
intr (with *dat*) to remedy; to make
up (*lost time*)
rimè·dio *m* (-di) remedy
rimembranza *f* remembrance
rimeritare (rimèrito) *tr* to reward
rimescolare (riméscolo) *tr* to stir; to
shuffle (*cards*)
riméssa *f* remittance; shipment; harvest; store; loss; sprout; carriage
house; garage; (sports) return;
(sports) putting in play; rimessa del
tram carbarn
rimestare (rimésto) *tr* to stir
riméttere §198 *tr* to remit; to put back;
to set back; to sprout; to postpone,
defer; to ship; to vomit; to recover;
to deliver; to straighten up; (sports)
to return; rimetterci to lose; rimettere a nuovo to renovate; rimettere
in ordine to tidy up; rimettere in
piedi to rebuild, restore || *intr* (coll)
to sprout; (coll) to grow; (lit) to
abate || *ref* to recover; to quiet down;
to defer; to be clearing (*said of
weather*); rimettersi a to go back to
(*e.g., bed*); rimettersi a + *inf* to start
+ *ger* + again; rimettersi in cammino to start off again
rimirare *tr* to stare at
rimmel *m* mascara
rimodellare (rimodèllo) *tr* to remodel
rimodernare (rimodèrno) *tr* to modernize; to remodel; to bring up to date
|| *ref* to become modern
rimónta *f* reassembly; return (*of migratory birds*); revamping (*of shoes*);
(mil) remount
rimontare (rimónto) *tr* to rewind; to go
up (*a stream*); to vamp (*shoes*); to

renovate; to regain; to reassemble (*a machine*); (mil) to remount ‖ *intr* (ESSERE & AVERE) to climb again; to go back (*in time*)

rimorchiare §287 (**rimòrchio**) *tr* to tow; to drag along

rimorchiatóre *m* tugboat; tow car

rimòr·chio *m* (**-chi**) tow; trailer; **prendere a rimorchio** to take in tow

rimòrdere §200 *tr* to bite again; to prick (*said, e.g., of conscience*)

rimòrso *m* remorse

rimostranza *f* remonstrance

rimostrare (**rimóstro**) *tr* to show again ‖ *intr* to remonstrate; **rimostrare a** to remonstrate with

rimozióne *f* removal; demotion

rimpannucciare §128 *tr* to outfit better ‖ *ref* to be better dressed; to be better off

rimpastare *tr* to knead again; to reshuffle, remake

rimpasto *m* reshuffling, rearrangement

rimpatriare §287 *tr* to repatriate ‖ *intr* to be repatriated

rimpà·trio *m* (**-tri**) repatriation

rimpètto *adv* opposite; **di rimpetto a** opposite to; in comparison with

rimpiàngere §215 *tr* to regret; to mourn

rimpianto *m* regret

rimpiattare *tr & ref* to hide; **giocare a rimpiattarsi** to play hide-and-seek

rimpiattino *m* hide-and-seek

rimpiazzare *tr* to replace

rimpiazzo *m* replacement, substitute

rimpiccolire §176 *tr* to make smaller ‖ *intr* (ESSERE) to get smaller

rimpinzare *tr* to stuff, cram

rimproverare (**rimpròvero**) *tr* to chide, reproach; **rimproverare qlcu di qlco** or **rimproverare qlco a qlcu** to reproach s.o. for s.th

rimpròvero *m* reproach, rebuke

rimuginare (**rimùgino**) *tr & intr* to rummage; to stir; to ruminate

rimunerare (**rimùnero**) *tr* to reward ‖ *intr* to pay

rimunerati·vo -va *adj* remunerative; rewarding

rimunerazióne *f* remuneration

rimuòvere §202 *tr* to remove; to demote; to move

rinàscere §203 *intr* (ESSERE) to be born again; to grow again; to revive; **far rinascere** to revive

rinasciménto *m* rebirth ‖ **Rinascimento** *m* Renaissance

rinàscita *f* rebirth

rincagna·to -ta *adj* snub (*nose*)

rincalzare *tr* to hill (*plants*); to underpin; to tuck in

rincalzo *m* reinforcement; support

rincantucciare §128 *tr & ref* to hide in a corner

rincarare *tr* to raise the price of; to raise; **rincarare la dose** to add insult to injury ‖ *intr* (ESSERE) to rise, go up (*said of prices*)

rincasare [s] *intr* (ESSERE) to return home

rinchiùdere §125 *tr* to enclose, shut in

rinchiu·so -sa [s] *adj* shut in; musty ‖ *m*—**saper di rinchiuso** to smell musty

rincitrullire §176 *intr* (ESSERE) to grow stupid

rincóntro *m*—**a rincontro** opposite

rincorare §236 *tr* to encourage ‖ *ref* to take heart

rincórrere §139 *tr* to pursue, chase

rincórsa *f*—**prendere la rincorsa** to take off (*for a jump*); to get a running start

rincréscere §142 *intr* (ESSERE) (with *dat*) to displease; to be sorry, e.g., **gli rincresce** he is sorry; to mind, **Le rincresce?** do you mind?

rincresciménto *m* regret

rincrudire §176 *tr* to sharpen; to embitter ‖ *intr* (ESSERE) to become bitter; to get worse

rinculare *intr* (ESSERE & AVERE) to back up; to recoil

rinculo *m* recoil

rinfacciare §128 *tr* to throw in one's face

rinfarcire §176 *tr* to stuff

rinfiancare §197 *tr* to support

rinfocolare (**rinfòcolo**) *tr* to rekindle; to revive

rinfoderare (**rinfòdero**) *tr* sheathe

rinforzare (**rinfòrzo**) *tr* to reinforce; strengthen ‖ *intr* (ESSERE) & *ref* to become stronger

rinfòrzo *m* reinforcement

rinfrancare §197 *tr* to reassure ‖ *ref* to buck up

rinfrescante *adj* refreshing ‖ *m* mild laxative

rinfrescare §197 (**rinfrésco**) *tr* to refresh; to restore; to renew ‖ *intr* (ESSERE & AVERE) to cool off (*said of the weather*) ‖ *ref* to have some refreshments; to cool off

rinfré·sco *m* (**-schi**) refreshment

rinfusa *f*—**alla rinfusa** at random; pellmell; in bulk

ringalluzzire §176 *tr & ref* to perk up

ringhiare §287 *intr* to growl, to snarl

ringhièra *f* railing

rìn·ghio *m* (**-ghi**) growl, snarl

ringiovaniménto *m* rejuvenation

ringiovanire §176 *tr* to rejuvenate ‖ *intr* (ESSERE) to grow or look younger

ringraziaménto *m* thanks

ringraziare §287 *tr* to thank; to dismiss

ringuainare (**ringuàino**) *tr* to sheathe

rinnegare §209 (**rinnègo & rinnégo**) *tr* to forswear; to repudiate

rinnega·to -ta *adj & m* renegade

rinnovaménto *m* renewal; reawakening

rinnovare (**rinnòvo**) *tr* to renew; to renovate; to restore; to replace ‖ *ref* to occur again; to renew

rinnovellare (**rinnovèllo**) *tr* to repeat; (poet) to renew ‖ *intr* (ESSERE) & *ref* to change; to renew

rinnòvo *m* renewal

rinocerónte *m* rhinoceros

rinomanza *f* renown

rinoma·to -ta *adj* renowned, famous

rinsaldare *tr* to starch; (fig) to strengthen ‖ *ref* to become confirmed (*in one's opinion*)

rinsanguare (rinsànguo) *tr* to give new strength to ‖ *ref* to regain strength; to recover

rinsavire §176 *intr* (ESSERE) to return to reason

rintanare *ref* to burrow; to hide

rintóc·co *m* (-chi) toll (*of bell*)

rintontire §176 *tr* to stun, to daze

rintracciare §128 *tr* to track down

rintronare (rintròno) *tr* to deafen; to make rumble ‖ *intr* (ESSERE & AVERE) to thunder; to rumble

rintuzzare *tr* to dull, blunt; to repel; to repress

rinùn·cia *f* (-ce) or **rinùnzia** *f* renunciation

rinunziare §287 *tr* to renounce ‖ *intr* (with *dat*) to give up, renounce, e.g., **rinunziò al trono** he renounced the throne

rinvangare §209 *tr* & *intr* var of **rivangare**

rinvenire §282 *tr* to find ‖ *intr* (ESSERE) to come to; **far rinvenire** to bring to, revive

rinviare §119 *tr* to send back; to postpone; to refer; to adjourn; to remit (*to a lower court*)

rinvigorire §176 *tr* to strengthen ‖ *intr* (ESSERE) & *ref* to regain strength

rinvì·o *m* (-i) return; postponement; adjournment; reference; (law) continuance

rì·o *m* (-i) (lit) sin; (lit) brook; (coll) canal

rioccupare (rioccupo) *tr* to reoccupy

rioccupazióne *f* reoccupation

rionale *adj* neighborhood

rióne *m* district; neighborhood

riordinare (riórdino) *tr* to rearrange; to reorganize; to order again

riorganizzare [ddzz] *tr* to reorganize

riottó·so -sa [s] *adj* (lit) quarrelsome; (lit) unruly, rebellious

ripa *f* (lit) bank (*of river*); (lit) escarpment

ripagare §209 *tr* to repay; to pay again

riparare *tr* to protect; to mend, fix, repair; to make up (*an exam*) ‖ *intr* —**riparare a** to make up for ‖ *intr* (ESSERE) & *ref* to take refuge; to betake oneself

riparazióne *f* repair; reparation; redress; (educ) make-up

riparlare *intr* to speak again; **ne riparleremo!** you will see!

riparo *m* repair; shelter

ripartire §176 *tr* to divide; to distribute; to share ‖ (**riparto**) *intr* (ESSERE) to leave again; to start again ‖ §176 *ref* to split up

ripartizióne *f* division; distribution

riparto *m* division; distribution; allotment

ripassare *tr* to cross again; to brush up, review; to repass; to sift again; to check; to read over; (mach) to overhaul ‖ *intr* (ESSERE) to go by; to come by

ripassata *f* checkup; review; (coll) rebuke

ripassa·tóre -trice *mf* checker

ripasso *m* return (*of birds*); (coll) review

ripensare (ripènso) *intr* to keep thinking; **ripensare a** to think of again; to think over again

ripentire (ripènto) *ref* to repent; **ripentirsi di** to repent

ripercórrere §139 *tr* to retrace

ripercuòtere §251 *tr* to reflect; to strike again ‖ *ref* to reverberate

ripescare §197 (**ripésco**) *tr* to fish again; (fig) to dig up

ripètere *tr* & *intr* to repeat ‖ *ref* to be repeated

ripeti·tóre -trice *mf* repeater; coach; tutor ‖ *m* (rad, telv) rebroadcasting station; (rad) relay

ripetizióne *f* repetition; review; tutoring; **a ripetizione** repeating (*firearm*)

ripiano *m* terrace; ledge; shelf; landing; (com) balancing

ripic·co *m* (-chi) pique; spite

rìpi·do -da *adj* steep

ripiegaménto *m* bend; (mil) withdrawal, retreat

ripiegare §209 (**ripiègo**) *tr* to fold, fold over ‖ *intr* to do better; (mil) to fall back ‖ *ref* to bend over; to withdraw into oneself

ripiè·go *m* (-ghi) expedient

ripiè·no -na *adj* full; stuffed ‖ *m* stuffing; (culin) filling

ripigliare §280 *tr* to reacquire; to catch again; to begin again ‖ *intr* to recover ‖ *ref* to renew a quarrel

ripiombare (ripiómbo) *tr* to make plumb; (fig) to plunge back ‖ *intr* (ESSERE) (fig) to plunge back

ripopolare (ripòpolo) *tr* to repopulate; to restock (*e.g., a pond*)

ripórre §218 *tr* to put back; to place (*one's hope*); to repose (*one's trust*) ‖ *ref* to back down; **riporsi a** + *inf* to start + *ger* again

riportare (ripòrto) *tr* to bring back; to report; to get; to transfer (*a design*); (com) to carry forward; (hunt) to retrieve; (math) to carry ‖ *ref* to go back

ripòrto *m* filler; retrieving; (com) balance carried forward; (math) number carried

riposante [s] *adj* restful

riposare [s] (**ripòso**) *tr, intr* & *ref* to rest

ripòso [s] *m* rest; repose; Requiem; retirement; **buon riposo!** sleep well!; **mettere a riposo** to retire; **riposo!** (mil) at ease

ripostì·glio *m* (-gli) closet

ripó·sto -sta *adj* innermost ‖ *m* (coll) pantry

riprèndere §220 *tr* to take back; to take up again; to get back; to take in (*a garment*); to catch (*s.th thrown in the air*); to take up (*arms*); to get; to reconquer; to start again, resume; to reprehend; to recover; (mov, telv) to shoot; **riprendere moglie** to remarry ‖ *intr* to start again; to recover, improve; to pick up (*said of a* *motor*) ‖ *ref* to recover; **to catch oneself up**

riprésa [s] *f* resumption; (aut) pickup; (theat) revival; (mov) shooting, take; (boxing) round; (soccer) second half; (mus, pros) refrain; **a più riprese** several times

ripresentare (ripresènto) *tr* to present again

ripristinare (ripristino) *tr* to restore; to reestablish

ripristino *m* revival, restoration

riprodurre §102 *tr* to reproduce; to express ‖ *ref* to reproduce; to occur

riprodut·tóre -trice *adj* reproducing ‖ *mf* reproducer ‖ *m* reproducer (*e.g., of sound*)

riproduzióne *f* reproduction; playback (*e.g., of tape*)

ripromèttere §198 *tr* to promise again ‖ *ref* to hope; to propose; to hope for

ripròva *f* new proof; confirmation

riprovare (ripròvo) *tr* to try again; to try on again; to feel, experience again; to flunk; to censure ‖ *ref* to try again

riprovazióne *f* disapproval

ripudiare §287 *tr* to repudiate

ripugnante *adj* repugnant, repulsive

ripugnanza *f* repugnance; aversion

ripugnare *intr* (with *dat*) to disgust, revolt, be repugnant to

ripulire §176 *tr* to clean again; to tidy up; to clean up; to polish ‖ *ref* to be dressed up; to become polished

ripulita *f*—**dare una ripulita a** to give a lick and a promise to; **fare una ripulita** (fig) to clean house

ripulsi·vo -va *adj* repulsive

riquadrare *tr* to square; to decorate (*a room*) ‖ *intr* to measure; to square

riquadro *m* square

risac·ca [s] *f* (-che) undertow; backwash

risàia [s] *f* rice field

risalire [s] §242 *tr* to go up again; to stem (*the tide*); **risalire la corrente** to go upstream ‖ *intr* (ESSERE) to climb again; to reascend; (com) to appreciate; to date back

risaltare [s] *tr* to jump again ‖ *intr* (ESSERE & AVERE) to rebound ‖ *intr* to stand out; **far risaltare** to emphasize

risalto [s] *m* emphasis; prominence; relief; foil

risanare [s] *tr* to heal; to reclaim (*land*); to redevelop (*urban areas*); to reorganize ‖ *intr* (ESSERE) to heal; to improve

risapére [s] §243 *tr* to find out

risapu·to -ta [s] *adj* well-known

risarciménto [s] *m* indemnification, redress

risarcire [s] §176 *tr* to indemnify; to compensate

risata [s] *f* outburst of laughter

risatina [s] *f* chuckle

riscaldaménto *m* heating; inflammation

riscaldare *tr* to heat; to warm up; to inflame ‖ *ref* to warm up; to go in heat; to perspire; to get excited

riscaldo *m* inflammation; prickly heat; padding (*for clothes*)

riscattare *tr* to ransom; to redeem ‖ *intr* (ESSERE) to click again (*said, e.g., of a ratchet*)

riscatto *m* ransom; redemption

rischiarare *tr, intr* (ESSERE) & *ref* to clear, clear up

rischiare §287 *tr* to risk ‖ *intr* to run a risk

rì·schio *m* (-schi) risk

rischió·so -sa [s] *adj* risky

risciacquare (risciàcquo) *tr* to rinse

risciacquatura *f* rinse; swill

risciàcquo *m* rinsing (*of mouth*); mouthwash

riscónto *m* (com) discount

riscontrare (riscóntro) *tr* to compare, collate; to check; to reply to ‖ *intr* to reply; to tally ‖ *ref* to tally

riscóntro *m* comparison; check, control; draft; correspondence; reply; **far riscontro** to correspond; **far riscontro con** to correspond to; **far riscontro di** to check; **mettere a riscontro** to compare; **riscontri** drafts (*of air*); parts (*that fit together*)

riscoprire §110 *tr* to rediscover

riscòssa *f* insurrection; recovery, reconquest; (mil) counterattack

riscossióne *f* collection

riscrìvere §250 *tr* to rewrite; to write back

riscuòtere §251 *tr* to shake; to wake up; to collect; to get; to redeem ‖ *ref* to wake up; to come to one's senses

riseccare [s] §197 **(risécco)** *tr, intr* (ESSERE) & *ref* to dry up

risecchire [s] §176 *intr* (ESSERE) & *ref* to dry up

risentiménto [s] *m* resentment, pique

risentire [s] **(risènto)** *tr* to hear again; to feel ‖ *intr*—**risentire di** to feel the effects of ‖ *ref* to take offense; to wake up; to come to one's senses; (telp) to talk again; **a risentirci!** (telp) until we talk again!; **risentirsi con** to resent (*a person*); **risentirsi di** to feel the effects of; **risentirsi per** to resent (*an act*)

risenti·to -ta [s] *adj* heard again; resentful; strong; swift; incisive

riserbare [s] **(risèrbo)** *tr* var of **riservare**

risèrbo [s] *m* var of **risèrvo**

risèrva [s] *f* preservation; exclusive rights; preserve; reserve; supply; backlog; reservation; circumspection; vintage

riservare [s] **(risèrvo)** *tr* to reserve

riservatézza [s] *f* reservedness

riserva·to -ta [s] *adj* reserved; private; classified

riservista [s] *m* (-sti) reservist

risèrvo [s] *m* discretion

risguardo *m* end paper

risièdere [s] *intr* to reside

risma *f* ream; (fig) type

riso [s] *m* rice ‖ *m* (**risa** *fpl*) laugh; laughter; jest; cheer; (lit) smile

risolare [s] §257 *tr* to resole

risolino [s] *m* smile; giggle

risollevare [s] (**risollèvo**) *tr* to raise again; to lift || *ref* to rise

risolutézza [s] *f* resoluteness

risolu·to -ta [s] *adj* resolved, determined

risoluzióne [s] *f* resolution; resolve; dissolution

risòlvere [s] §256 (*pret ind* **risolvéi** or **risolvètti** or **risòlsi**; *pp* **risòlto**) *tr* to resolve; to solve; to dissolve; to persuade || *ref* to dissolve; to resolve

risolvìbile [s] *adj* solvable

risonante [s] *adj* resounding

risonanza [s] *f* resonance; (fig) sensation

risonare [s] §257 *tr* to ring again; (lit) to repeat || *intr* (ESSERE & AVERE) to resonate; to resound; to ring again; to echo

risórgere [s] §258 *intr* (ESSERE) to rise again; to revive, to come back to life; to recover

risorgiménto [s] *m* renaissance; resurgence || **Risorgimento** *m* Risorgimento

risórsa [s] *f* resource

risór·to -ta [s] *adj* arisen; reborn

risòtto [s] *m* risotto, rice cooked with broth

risparmiare §287 *tr* to save; to spare

rispàr·mio *m* (**-mi**) saving; sparing; savings; **risparmi** savings; **senza risparmio** lavishly

rispecchiare §287 (**rispècchio**) *tr* to reflect

rispedire §176 *tr* to send back; to forward; to reship

rispedizióne *f* reshipment

rispettàbile *adj* respectable

rispettare (**rispètto**) *tr* to respect; **farsi rispettare** to command respect; **rispettare sé stesso** to have self-respect

rispetti·vo -va *adj* respective

rispètto *m* respect; observance; restriction (*e.g., in building*); comparison; regard; **con rispetto parlando** excuse the word; **di rispetto** (naut) spare (*e.g., parts*); **rispetti** regards; **rispetto di sé medesimo** self-respect; **rispetto umano** fear of what people will say

rispettó·so -sa [s] *adj* respectful; respectable (*distance*)

risplendènte *adj* resplendent

risplèndere §281 *intr* (ESSERE & AVERE) to shine

rispóndere §238 *tr* to answer; **risponder picche** (coll) to say no || *intr* to answer; **rispondere a** to answer (*e.g., a letter*); **rispondere con un cenno del capo** to nod assent; **rispondere di** to be responsible for; **rispondere in** to face, overlook

risposare (**rispòso**) *tr* & *ref* to marry again, remarry

rispósta *f* answer, reply, response

rissa *f* scuffle, brawl

rissó·so -sa [s] *adj* quarrelsome

ristabilire §176 *tr* to reestablish || *ref* to recover

ristagnare *tr* to tin; to solder || *intr* to stagnate

ristampa *f* reprint

ristampare *tr* to reprint

ristorante *m* restaurant

ristorare (**ristòro**) *tr* & *ref* to refresh

ristora·tóre -trice *adj* refreshing || *m* restaurant

ristòro *m* refreshment; compensation

ristrettézza *f* narrowness; scarcity; **ristrettezza d'idee** narrow-mindedness

ristrét·to -ta *adj* narrow; limited; **in** straitened circumstances; concentrated, condensed (*e.g., broth*)

ristrutturazióne *f* restructuring

risùc·chio [s] *m* (**-chi**) whirlpool

risultante [s] *adj* resulting || *m* & *f* resultant; (phys) resultant

risultare [s] *intr* (ESSERE) to result; to prove to be, turn out to be; to appear

risultato [s] *m* result

risurrezióne [s] *f* resurrection

risuscitare [s] (**risùscito**) *tr* to resurrect; to revive || *intr* to be resurrected; to be revived

risvegliare §280 (**risvéglio**) *tr* & *ref* to awaken; to reawaken

risvé·glio *m* (**-gli**) awakening, reawakening

risvòlto *m* cuff; lapel; inside flap (*of book*); minor aspect (*of a question*)

ritagliare §280 *tr* to cut again; to clip; to trim

rità·glio *m* (**-gli**) clipping (*of paper*); scrap (*of meat*); cutting (*of fabric*); bit (*of time*); **al ritaglio** retail

ritappezzare (**ritappézzo**) *tr* to repaper

ritardare *tr* to delay; to slow down, retard; || *intr* to tarry; to be late; to be slow (*said of a watch*)

ritardatà·rio -ria *mf* (**-ri -rie**) latecomer; (com) delinquent

ritardo *m* delay; retard; lateness; **essere in ritardo** to be late

ritégno *m* reservation; discretion; **senza ritegno** shamelessly

ritemprare (**ritèmpro**) *tr* to temper again; to invigorate || *ref* to harden

ritenére §271 *tr* to retain; to hold; to withhold; to believe, think || *ref* to restrain oneself; to consider oneself; to be considered

ritentare (**ritènto**) *tr* to try again; (law) to retry

ritirare *tr* to withdraw; to pay (*a note*); to throw back; to shoot again; to accept delivery of; to take back (*a promise*) || *intr* to shrink || *ref* to shrink; to withdraw; to fall back, retreat; to retire

ritirata *f* toilet; (mil) retreat

ritiro *m* withdrawal; retreat; retirement; shrinkage; (metallurgy) shrinking

ritma·to -ta *adj* measured (*step*)

rìtmi·co -ca *adj* (**-ci -che**) rhythmic(al)

ritmo *m* rhythm; **a ritmo serrato** at a quick pace

rito *m* rite; (fig) ritual, ceremony; **di rito** customary

ritoccare §197 (**ritócco**) *tr* to retouch; to brush up

ritóc·co *m* (**-chi**) retouch; improvement; change

ritòrcere §272 *tr* to twist, twine; to wring; to retort

ritornare (**ritórno**) *tr* to return, give back ‖ *intr* (ESSERE) to return, go back, come back; **ritornare in sé** to come back to one's senses

ritornèllo *m* refrain; chorus (*of song*)

ritórno *m* return; reoccurrence; **di ritorno** reoccurring; **essere di ritorno** to be back; **far ritorno** to return; **ritorno di fiamma** backfire

ritòr·to -ta *adj* twisted ‖ *m* twist

ritrarre §273 *tr* to retract; to draw; to portray ‖ *intr*—**ritrarre da** to look like ‖ *ref* to retreat; to portray oneself

ritrasméttere §198 *tr* (rad, telv) to retransmit, rebroadcast

ritrattare *tr* to treat again; to retract; (coll) to portray ‖ *ref* to recant

ritrattazióne *f* retraction

ritratti·sta *mf* (-sti -ste) portrait painter

ritratto *m* portrait, picture; photograph; **ritratto parlante** spit and image

ritri·to -ta *adj* (fig) stale, trite

ritrósa [s] *f* (coll) cowlick

ritrosìa [s] *f* coyness, shyness

ritró·so -sa [s] *adj* coy, shy; **a ritroso** backwards ‖ *f* see **ritrosa**

ritrovare (**ritròvo**) *tr* to discover; to find; to regain; to meet again ‖ *ref* to meet again; to find oneself; to find one's bearings; **non ritrovarcisi** to be out of sorts

ritrovato *m* discovery, find

ritròvo *m* meeting; nightspot; **ritrovo estivo** summer resort; **ritrovo notturno** night club

rit·to -ta *adj* upright; straight; right ‖ *m* face (*of medal*); prop; (sports) post ‖ *f* (lit) right hand

rituale *adj & m* ritual

riunióne *f* reunion; meeting; assembly; **riunione alla sommità** summit conference

riunire §176 *tr* to assemble; to reunite; to reconcile ‖ *ref* to gather together; to meet; to be reunited; to rally

riuscire §277 *intr* (ESSERE) to go out again; to turn out, turn out to be; to lead (*said, e.g., of a door*); to succeed; **riuscire a** + *inf* to succeed in + *ger* ‖ *impers*—**riesce** (with *dat*) **di** + *inf* to succeed in + *ger*, e.g., **non gli è riuscito di farsi ricevere** he did not succeed in being received

riuscita *f* success; result; outlet

riva *f* shore; bank; (naut) board

rivale *adj & mf* rival

rivaleggiare §290 (**rivaléggio**) *intr* to compete; **rivaleggiare con** to rival

rivalére §278 *ref*—**rivalersi di** to use; **rivalersi su qlcu** to resort to s.o. for compensation; to fall back on s.o., to have recourse to s.o.

rivali·tà *f* (-tà) rivalry

rivalsa *f* compensation; revenge; (com) recourse

rivalutare (**rivàluto & rivaluto**) *tr* to revalue

rivalutazióne *f* reassessment

rivangare §209 *tr* to rake up; to mull over ‖ *intr* to reminisce

rivedére §279 *tr* to see again; to review; to check; to reread; to revise; to read (*proof*) ‖ *ref* to see one another; **a rivederci!** good-bye!, au revoir!

rivedìbile *adj* deferred (*for draft*)

rivelare (**rivélo**) *tr* to reveal; to detect; (phot) to develop

rivela·tóre -trice *adj* revealing ‖ *m* (phot) developer; (rad) detector; **rivelatore di mine** mine detector

rivelazióne *f* revelation

rivéndere §281 *tr* to resell; (fig) to surpass

rivendicare §197 (**rivéndico**) *tr* to demand; to claim

rivendicazióne *f* demand; claim

rivéndita *f* resale; shop; **rivendita sali e tabacchi** cigar store

rivendi·tóre -trice *mf* seller, dealer, retailer

rivendùgliolo *m* peddler; huckster

rivèrbero *m* reverberation; reflection; glare; echo

riverènte *adj* reverent

riverènza *f* reverence; curtsy, bow

riverire §176 *tr* to revere; to pay one's respects to

riversare (**rivèrso**) *tr* to pour again; to transfer ‖ *ref* to overflow

rivèr·so -sa *adj* on one's back

rivestiménto *m* coating; covering; lining

rivestire (**rivèsto**) *tr* to dress again; to coat; to line; to cover; to wear; to have (*importance*); to hold (*a rank*) ‖ *ref* to get dressed again; to wear; to be covered

rivièra *f* coast ‖ **Riviera** *f* Riviera

riviera·sco -sca *adj* (-schi -sche) coastal; riverside

rivìncere §285 *tr* to win back

rivìncita *f* revenge; return match; **prendersi la rivincita** to get even

rivista *f* review; parade; magazine, journal; revue; proofreading

rivìvere §286 *tr* to relive ‖ *intr* (ESSERE) to live again; to revive

rivo *m* (lit) rivulet, brook

rivolare (**rivólo**) *intr* (ESSERE & AVERE) to fly again

rivolére §288 *tr* to want back

rivòlgere §289 *tr* to turn again; to revolve; to overturn; to train (*a weapon*); to address; to deter ‖ *ref* to turn; to turn around; **rivolgersi a** to apply to

rivolgiménto *m* turn; revolution; upheaval

rivòlta *f* revolt; cuff

rivoltante *adj* revolting

rivoltare (**rivòlto**) *tr* to overturn; to turn inside out; to toss (*salad*); to upset ‖ *ref* to turn around; to revolt; to toss

rivoltèlla *f* revolver; spray gun

rivoltellata *f* revolver shot

rivoltó·so -sa [s] *adj* rebellious ‖ *m* rioter; rebel

rivoluzionare (**rivoluzióno**) *tr* to revolutionize

rivoluzionà·rio -ria *adj* & *mf* **(-ri -rie)** revolutionary
rivoluzióne *f* revolution
rizza *f* (naut) rigging
rizzare *tr* to raise; to hoist; to pay (*attention*); to build; (naut) to lash || *ref* to rise; to bristle (*said of hair*); to rear up (*said of a horse*)
ròba *f* things, stuff; property
robìnia *f* locust tree
robivèc·chi *m* **(-chi)** junk dealer
robu·sto -sta *adj* robust; burly
róc·ca *f* **(-che)** distaff
ròc·ca *f* **(-che)** fortress
roccafòrte *f* **(rocchefòrti)** stronghold
rocchétto *m* spool; reel; coil; roll (*of film*); pinion, rear sprocket wheel; (eccl) rochet; **rocchetto d'accensione** ignition coil; **rocchetto d'induzione** induction coil
ròc·cia *f* **(-ce)** rock; crag; cliff
rocció·so -sa [s] *adj* rocky
rò·co -ca *adj* **(-chi -che)** hoarse; (poet) faint
rodàg·gio *m* **(-gi)** breaking in, running in; adjustment period (*to a new situation*); **in rodaggio** (aut) being run in
Ròdano *m* Rhone
rodare (ròdo) *tr* to break in; (aut) to run in
ródere §239 *tr* to gnaw; to bite; to corrode || *ref* to worry, to fret
Ròdi *f* Rhodes
rodì·o *m* **(-i)** gnawing
rodi·tóre -trice *adj* gnawing || *mf* rodent
rodomónte *m* braggart
rogare §209 **(rògo)** *tr* to draw up (*a contract*); (law) to request
rògito *m* (law) instrument, deed
rógna *f* mange; itch
rognóne *m* (culin) kidney
rognó·so -sa [s] *adj* scabby, mangy
rò·go *m* **(-ghi)** pyre; stake
rollì·o *m* **(-i)** roll (*of ship*)
Róma *f* Rome
romané·sco -sca *adj* **(-schi -sche)** Roman (*dialect*)
Romanìa, la Rumania
romàni·co -ca *adj* & *m* **(-ci -che)** Romanesque
roma·no -na *adj* & *mf* Roman; **pagare alla romana** to go Dutch
romanticismo *m* romanticism
romànti·co -ca *adj* **(-ci -che)** romantic || *mf* romanticist
romanza *f* romance; ballad
romanzare *tr* to fictionalize
romanzé·sco -sca *adj* **(-schi -sche)** romantic; of chivalry; novelistic
romanzière *m* novelist
roman·zo -za *adj* Romance (*language*) || *m* novel; story; romance; fiction; **romanzi** fiction; **romanzo a fumetti** comic strip; comic book; **romanzo d'appendice** serial story, feuilleton; **romanzo giallo** whodunit; **romanzo rosa** love story
rombare (ròmbo) *intr* to thunder
rómbo *m* thunder, roar
romè·no -na *adj* & *mf* Rumanian

romi·to -ta *adj* (lit) lonely || *m* (coll) hermit
rómpere §240 *tr* to break; to bust; **rompere la testa a** to annoy, pester || *intr* to overflow; to be wrecked; to break; **rompere in pianto** to burst out crying || *ref* to fly to pieces; **rompersi la testa** to rack one's brains
rompicapo *m* annoyance; puzzle; jig-saw puzzle
rompicòllo *m* madcap; **a rompicollo** headlong, rashly; at breakneck speed
rompighiàc·cio *m* **(-cio)** icebreaker; ice pick
rompiscàto·le *m* **(-le)** bore, pest
ronci·glio *m* **(-gli)** (poet) hook
róncola *f* pruning hook
rónda *f* patrol; beat (*of policeman*)
rondèlla *f* (mach) washer
róndine *f* swallow
rondóne *m* European swift
ronfare (rónfo) *intr* (coll) to snore; (coll) to purr
ronzare [dz] **(rónzo)** *intr* to buzz; to hum
ronzino [dz] *m* jade, nag
ronzì·o [dz] *m* **(-i)** buzzing; humming
ròsa *adj invar* & *m* pink || *f* rose; group; rosette; **rosa dei venti** compass card; **rosa del Giappone** (bot) camelia; **rosa delle Alpi** (bot) rhododendron; **rosa di tiro** (mil) dispersion
ro·sàio *m* **(-sài)** rosebush
rosà·rio *m* **(-ri)** rosary; **recitare il rosario** to count one's beads
rosa·to -ta *adj* rosy
ròse·o -a *adj* rosy
roséto *m* rose garden
rosétta *f* rosette; hard roll; (mach) washer
rosicanti [s] *mpl* rodents
rosicchiare [s] §287 *tr* to gnaw; to pick (*a bone*); to bite (*one's fingernails*)
rosmarino *m* (bot) rosemary
rosolare (ròsolo) *tr* (culin) to brown
rosolìa *f* German measles
rosóne *m* (archit) rosette; (archit) rose window
ròspo *m* toad; ugly person; unsociable person; **ingoiare un rospo** to swallow a bitter pill
rossa·stro -stra *adj* reddish
rossétto *m* rouge; **rossetto per le labbra** lipstick
rós·so -sa *adj* red; red-headed; Red; **diventare rosso** to blush || *mf* red-head; Red (*Communist*) || *m* red
rossóre *m* redness; blush
rosticceria *f* grill; rotisserie
rotàbile *adj* open to vehicular traffic (*road*); (rr) rolling (*stock*) || *f* road open to vehicular traffic
rotàia *f* rail; rut; **uscire dalle rotaie** to jump the track; (fig) to go astray
rotare §257 *tr* & *intr* to rotate; to circle
rotativa *f* (typ) rotary press
rotazióne *f* rotation
roteare (ròteo) *tr* to roll (*the eyes*); to flourish (*a sword*) || *intr* to circle
rotèlla *f* small wheel; caster; roller; kneecap; disk (*of ski pole*); **gli**

manca una **rotella** he has a screw loose

rotocal·co *m* **(-chi)** rotogravure

rotolare (ròtolo) *tr & intr* (ESSERE) to roll || *ref* to turn over; to wallow

ròtolo *m* roll; bolt; coil; **a rotoli** to rack and ruin

rotolóne *m* tumble; **a rotoloni** falling down; to rack and ruin

rotón·do -da *adj* round; rotund || *f* rotunda; terrace

rótta *f* break; rout; (aer, naut) course; **a rotta di collo** at breakneck speed; **mettere in rotta** to rout

rottame *m* fragment; wreck; **rottami** scraps, debris; wreckage; **rottami di ferro** scrap iron

rót·to -ta *adj* broken; shattered; inured || *m* break, tear; **e rotti** odd, e.g., **duecento e rotti** two hundred odd; **per il rotto della cuffia** hardly; just about || *f* see **rotta**

rottura *f* break; breakage; rupture; breakdown (*of relations*); crack

ròtula *f* kneecap

rovèllo *m* (lit) anger

rovènte *adj* red-hot

róvere *m & f* oak tree || *m* oak (*lumber*)

rovè·scia *f* **(-sce)** cuff; **alla rovescia** inside out; upside down; the wrong way

rovesciaménto *m* upset; overturn

rovesciare §128 **(rovèscio)** *tr* to overturn; to upset; to throw back (*one's head*); to spill (*liquid*); to pour; to hurl (*insults*); to turn inside out || *intr* to throw up || *ref* to spill; to pour; to upset

rovè·scio -scia (-sci -sce) *adj* reverse; inverse; inside out; upside down; backwards || *m* reverse; wrong side; downpour; upset; (com) crash; (tennis) backhand; **a rovescio** upside down; backwards || *f* see **rovescia**

rovéto *m* bramble; brier patch

rovina *f* ruin; blight; **andare in rovina** to go to ruin; **mandare in rovina** to ruin; **rovine** ruins

rovinare *tr* to ruin || *intr* (ESSERE) to collapse || *ref* to go to ruin

rovinì·o *m* **(-i)** clatter; crash

rovinó·so -sa **[s]** *adj* ruinous

rovistare *tr* to rummage through

róvo *m* bramble

ròzza [ddzz] *f* nag

róz·zo -za [ddzz] *adj* rough; coarse

ruba *f*—**andare a ruba** to sell like hotcakes; **mettere a ruba** to plunder

rubacchiare §287 *tr* to pilfer

rubacuò·ri (-ri) *adj* ravishing || *m* lady-killer || *f* vamp

rubare *tr* to steal; **rubare a man salva** to pillage, loot || *intr* to steal; **rubare sul peso** to give short measure

rubería *f* thieving, stealing

rubicón·do -da *adj* rubicund

rubinétto *m* faucet; cock

rubino *m* ruby; jewel (*of watch*)

rubiz·zo -za *adj* well-preserved (*person*)

rubri·ca *f* **(-che)** title, heading; directory; (journ) section

rude *adj* (lit) rough; (lit) rude

rùdere *m* ruin

rudimentale *adj* rudimentary

rudiménto *m* rudiment

ruffia·no -na *mf* go-between || *m* pimp, panderer || *f* bawd, procuress

ru·ga *f* **(-ghe)** wrinkle; (bot) rocket

rùggine *f* rust; ill-will; (bot) blight

rugginó·so -sa **[s]** *adj* rusty

ruggire §176 *tr & intr* to roar

ruggito *m* roar

rugiada *f* dew

rugó·so -sa **[s]** *adj* wrinkled, wrinkly

rullàg·gio *m* **(-gi)** (aer) taxiing

rullare *tr* to roll || *intr* to roll; to taxi

rullì·o *m* **(-i)** roll; rub-a-dub

rullo *m* roll; platen (*of typewriter*); pin (*in tenpins*); **rullo compressore** road roller

rumè·no -na *adj & mf* var of **romeno**

ruminare (rùmino) *tr & intr* to ruminate

rumóre *m* noise; rumor; ado; **far molto rumore** to create a stir

rumoreggiare §290 **(rumoréggio)** *intr* to rumble

rumoró·so -sa **[s]** *adj* noisy; rumbling; controversial

ruolino *m* roster

ruòlo *m* roll; role; list; **di ruolo** regular, full-time; **fuori ruolo** temporary, part-time

ruòta *f* wheel; paddle wheel; revolving server (*in convent*); **a quattro ruote** four-wheel; **dar la ruota a** to sharpen; **esser l'ultima ruota del carro** to be the fifth wheel to a wagon; **fare la ruota** to spread its tail, strut (*said, e.g., of a peacock*); to turn cartwheels (*said, e.g., of an acrobat*); **ruota dentata** cog, cogwheel; **ruota idraulica** water wheel; **seguire a ruota** to follow closely

rupe *f* cliff

rurale *adj* rural, farm, farmer

ruscèllo *m* brook

ruspa *f* road grader

ruspante *m* barnyard chicken

russare *intr* to snore

Rùssia, la Russia

rus·so -sa *adj & mf* Russian

rustica·no -na *adj* rustic, boorish

rùsti·co -ca (-ci -che) *adj* rustic; coarse || *m* tool shed; cottage; (lit) peasant

rutilante *adj* (lit) shiny

ruttare *tr* (lit) to belch || *intr* (vulg) to belch

rutto *m* (vulg) belch

ruttóre *m* (elec) contact breaker

ruvidézza *f* or **ruvidi·tà** *f* **(-tà)** coarseness; roughness

rùvi·do -da *adj* coarse; rough

ruzzare [ddzz] *intr* to romp

ruzzolare (rùzzolo) *tr* to roll || *intr* (ESSERE) to tumble down; to roll

ruzzolóne *m* tumble; **a ruzzoloni** tumbling down

S

S, s [ˈɛsse] *m & f* seventeenth letter of the Italian alphabet
s- *pref* dis-, e.g., **sleale** disloyal; e.g., **sconto** discount; un-, e.g., **scatenare** to unchain, unleash
sàbato *m* Saturday; (*of Jews*) Sabbath; **sabato inglese** Saturday afternoon off
sabbàti·co -ca *adj* (**-ci -che**) sabbatical
sàbbia *f* sand; **sabbia mobile** quicksand
sabbiatura *f* sand bath; sandblast
sabbièra *f* (rr) sandbox
sabbió·so -sa [s] *adj* sandy
sabotàg·gio *m* (**-gi**) sabotage
sabotare (**sabòto**) *tr* to sabotage
sac·ca *f* (**-che**) bag; satchel; (mil) pocket; **sacca d'aria** (aer) air pocket; **sacca da viaggio** traveling bag; duffel bag
saccarina *f* saccharine
saccènte *mf* wiseacre, know-it-all
saccheggiare §290 (**sacchéggio**) *tr* to pillage, plunder
sacchég·gio *m* (**-gi**) pillage, plunder
sacchétto *m* little bag, pouch
sac·co *m* (**-chi**) bag; sack; sackcloth; pouch; (boxing) punching bag; (fig) heap, lot; **fare sacco** to sag; **mettere a sacco** to sack; **mettere nel sacco** to outwit; **sacco alpino** knapsack; **sacco a pelo** or **a piuma** sleeping bag; **sacco postale** mailbag
saccòc·cia *f* (**-ce**) (coll) pocket
sacerdòte *m* priest; (fig) devotee
sacerdotéssa *f* priestess
sacerdòzio *m* priesthood; ministry
sacramentale *adj* sacramental; (joc) habitual, ritual
sacraménto *m* sacrament
sacrà·rio *m* (**-ri**) memorial; sanctuary, shrine
sacrestìa *f* var of **sagrestia**
sacrificare §197 (**sacrìfico**) *tr* to sacrifice; to waste; to force || *ref* to sacrifice oneself
sacrifì·cio *m* (**-ci**) sacrifice
sacrilè·gio *m* (**-gi**) sacrilege
sacrìle·go -ga *adj* (**-ghi -ghe**) sacrilegious
sacri·sta *m* (**-sti**) sexton
sacristia *f* var of **sagrestia**
sa·cro -cra *adj* sacred
sacrosan·to -ta *adj* sacrosanct; sacred (*truth*)
sàdi·co -ca (**-ci -che**) *adj* sadistic || *mf* sadist
sadismo *m* sadism
saétta *f* stroke of lightning; hand (*of watch*); (mach) bit; (lit) arrow
saettare (**saétto**) *tr* to shoot; **saettare sguardi a** to look daggers at
saettóne *m* (archit) strut
sagace *adj* sagacious, shrewd
sagà·cia *f* (**-cie**) sagacity
saggézza *f* wisdom
saggiare §290 *tr* to assay; to test; (dial) to taste
saggia·tóre -trice *mf* assayer || *m* assay balance
saggina *f* sorghum

sàg·gio -gia (**-gi -ge**) *adj* wise || *m* sage; assay; sample; proof; theme; test; rate (*of interest*); display; **di saggio** examination (*copy*)
saggi·sta *mf* (**-sti -ste**) essayist
sagittària *f* (bot) arrowhead
sagittà·rio *m* (**-ri**) (obs) archer || **Sagittario** *m* Sagittarius
sàgola *f* (naut) halyard
sàgoma *f* outline; target; model, pattern; (joc) character
sagomare (**sàgomo**) *tr* to outline; to mold; to shape
sagomato *m* billboard
sagra *f* anniversary consecration (*of church*); festival
sagrato *m* elevated square in front of a church; churchyard; (coll) curse
sagrestano *m* sexton, sacristan
sagrestìa *f* sacristy, vestry
sàia *f* serge
sàio *m* (**sài**) habit (*of monk or nun*); doublet; frock coat
sala *f* axletree; hall, room; (bot) cattail, reed mace; **sala da ballo** dance hall; **sala da pranzo** dining room; **sala d'aspetto** waiting room; anteroom; **sala operatoria** operating room
salac·ca *f* (**-che**) (coll) sardine; (coll) shad
salace *adj* salacious; pungent
salamandra *f* salamander
salame *m* salami
salamelèc·co *m* (**-chi**) salaam
salamòia *f* brine
salare *tr* to salt; (coll) to cut (*school*)
salaria·to -ta *adj* wage-earning || *m* wage earner
salà·rio *m* (**-ri**) pay, wages
salassare *tr* to bleed
salasso *m* bloodletting
sala·to -ta *adj* salted; salty; dear, expensive; (fig) sharp || *m* salt pork; cold cuts || *f* salting
salda *f* starch solution (*used in laundering*)
saldacón·ti *m* (**-ti**) bookkeeping department; credit department; ledger; bookkeeping machine
saldare *tr* to solder; to set (*a bone*); to weld; to pay, settle || *ref* to knit (*said of a bone*); (lit) to heal
saldatóre *m* solderer; welder; soldering iron
saldatura *f* soldering; setting (*of bones*); joint; continuity; **saldatura autogena** welding
saldézza *f* firmness
sal·do -da *adj* firm; valid (*reason*); flawless || *m* balance; clearance sale; job lot; payment; **saldi** remnants || *f* see **salda**
saldobrasatura *f* soldering
sale *m* salt; wit; (lit) sea; **restare di sale** to be dumbfounded; **sale inglese** Epsom salts; **sali aromatici** smelling salts; **sali da bagno** bath salts
salgèmma *f* rock salt

sàlice *m* willow tree; **salice piangente** weeping willow

salicilato *m* salicylate

saliènte *adj* projecting; (fig) salient || *m* projection

salièra *f* saltcellar, salt shaker

salini·tà *f* (-tà) salinity

sali·no -na *adj* saline; salty || *f* salt bed

salire §242 *tr* to climb || *intr* (ESSERE) to climb; to go up; to rise; **salire in** or su to get on (*e.g., a train*)

saliscén·di *m* (-di) latch; **saliscendi** *mpl* ups and downs

salita *f* climbing; ascent, rise; slope; **in salita** uphill

saliva *f* saliva

salma *f* corpse, body

salma·stro -stra *adj* briny; saltish || *m*— **sapere di salmastro** to smell or taste salty

salmerìe *fpl* wagon train; (mil) supplies

salmì *m*—**in salmì** (culin) in a stew

salmo *m* psalm

salmodiare §287 (salmòdio) *intr* to chant, sing hymns, intone

salmóne *m* salmon

salnitro *m* saltpeter

Salomóne *m* Solomon

salóne *m* hall; salon, drawing room; (naut) saloon; **salone da barbiere** barber shop; **salone dell'automobile** auto show

salòtto *m* drawing room; living room, parlor; reception room

salpare *tr* to weigh (*anchor*) || *intr* (ESSERE) to weigh anchor

salsa *f* sauce

salsapariglia *f* sarsaparilla

salsèdine *f* saltiness

salsìc·cia *f* (-ce) sausage

salsièra *f* gravy boat

sal·so -sa *adj* salty; saline || *m* saltiness || *f* see **salsa**

saltabeccare §197 (saltabécco) *intr* to hop

saltaleóne *m* coil spring

saltare *tr* to jump; to skip; to sauté; (sports) to vault, hurdle; **far saltare** to kick out; to blow up (*e.g., a mine*); **saltare la sbarra** (coll) to go A.W.O.L. || *intr* (ESSERE & AVERE) to jump; to pop off, e.g., **mi è saltato un bottone** one of my buttons has popped off; to blow out (*said of a fuse*); **saltare agli occhi** to be self-evident; **saltare a piè pari** to skip with both feet; **saltar fuori** to pop out (*said of the eyes*); to appear suddenly; **saltare in mente a** to come to the mind of; **saltare il ticchio a (qlcu) di** to feel like + *ger*, e.g., **gli è saltato il ticchio di cantare** he felt like singing; **saltare la mosca al naso a (qlcu)** to blow one's top, e.g., **le è saltata la mosca al naso** she blew her top; **saltare per aria** to blow up; **saltare su** to start (*to make a sudden jerk*); **saltare su a** + *inf* to begin suddenly to + *inf*

salta·tóre -trice *mf* jumper, hurdler

saltellare (saltèllo) *intr* to skip, hop

saltellóni *adv*—**a saltelloni** skipping, hopping

saltimban·co *m* (-chi) acrobat, tumbler; mountebank

salto *m* jump; leap; fall; skip; (*of animals*) mating; (fig) step; **a salti** skipping, jumping; **al salto** sauté; **fare quattro salti** to dance; **fare un salto** to hop, hurry; **salto a pesce** jackknife (*dive*); **salto coll'asta** pole vaulting; **salto in altezza** high jump; **salto in lunghezza** broad jump; **salto mortale** somersault; **salto nel vuoto** leap in the dark

saltuà·rio -ria *adj* (-ri -rie) desultory, occasional

salubre *adj* salubrious, healthy, healthful

salume *m* pork product

salumerìa *f* pork butcher shop

salumiè·re -ra *mf* pork butcher

salutare *adj* healthful || *tr* to greet; to salute; (lit) to proclaim

salute *f* health; salvation; safety || *interj* good luck; to your health!; gesundheit!

saluto *m* salute; greeting; salutation; **distinti saluti** sincerely yours

salva *f* salvo; outburst; **a salve with** blank cartridges, with blanks

salvacondótto *m* safe-conduct

salvada·nàio *m* (-nài) piggy bank

salvagèn·te *m* (-te & -ti) life preserver; fender (*of trolley car*) || *m* (-te) safety island

salvaguardare *tr* to safeguard

salvaguàrdia *f* safeguard

salvaménto *m* safety

salvamotóre *m* circuit breaker; fuse box

salvapun·te *m* (-te) pencil cap; tap (*on sole of shoe*)

salvare *tr* to save; to spare (*a life*); to rescue || *ref* to save oneself; to be rescued; **si salvi chi può!** every man for himself!

salvatàg·gio *m* (-gi) rescue

salvatóre *m* savior, rescuer || **il Salvatore** the Saviour

salvazióne *f* salvation

salve *interj* hello!, hail!

salvézza *f* salvation; safety

sàlvia *f* (bot) sage

salviétta *f* napkin; paper napkin; paper towel

sal·vo -va *adj* safe; saved; secure || *m* —**mettere in salvo** to put in a safe place; **mettersi in salvo** to reach safety || *f* see **salva** || **salvo** *prep* except; **salvo che** unless; **salvo il vero** unless I am mistaken

samarita·no -na *adj* & *mf* Samaritan

sambu·co *m* (-chi) elder tree

san *adj* apocopated and unstressed form of **santo**

sanàbile *adj* curable

sanare *tr* to heal; to remedy; to reclaim (*land*); to normalize

sanatò·rio *m* (-ri) sanatorium

sancire §176 *tr* to ratify, sanction; to establish

sàndalo *m* sandal; sandalwood; flat-bottom boat

sandolino *m* canoe, skiff, kayak

sangue *m* blood; **agitarsi il sangue** to fret; **all'ultimo sangue** (*duel*) to the death; **al sangue** rare (*meat*); **a sangue freddo** in cold blood; cold-blooded; **cavar sangue da una rapa** to draw blood from a stone; **farsi cattivo sangue** to get angry; **il sangue non è acqua** blood is thicker than water; **puro sangue** thoroughbred; **sangue dal naso** nosebleed; **sangue freddo** calmness, composure

sangui·gno -gna *adj* blood (*circulation*); bloody; sanguine, ruddy ‖ *m* (lit) color of blood

sanguinante *adj* bloody, bleeding

sanguinare (**sànguino**) *intr* to bleed; to be rare (*said of meat*)

sanguinà·rio -ria *adj* (**-ri -rie**) sanguinary

sanguinó·so -sa [s] *adj* bloody; bleeding; (fig) stinging

sanguisu·ga [s] *f* (**-ghe**) leech

sani·tà *f* (**-tà**) health; healthfulness; soundness (*of body*); sanity; health department

sanità·rio -ria (**-ri -rie**) *adj* health; sanitary ‖ *m* physician

sa·no -na *adj* healthy; sound; **sano e salvo** safe and sound

sant' *adj* apocopated form of **santo** and **santa**

santa *f* saint

santabàrbara *f* (**santebàrbare**) (nav) powder magazine

santarellina *f* goody-goody girl

santificare §197 (**santìfico**) *tr* to sanctify

santìssi·mo -ma *adj* most holy ‖ *m* Eucharist

santi·tà *f* (**-tà**) sanctity, holiness; sainthood, saintliness

san·to -ta *adj* saintly, holy; sacred; blessed, livelong, e.g., **tutto il santo giorno** all the livelong day ‖ *m* saint; name day; (fig) someone ‖ *f* see **santa**

santorég·gia *f* (**-ge**) (bot) savory

santuà·rio *m* (**-ri**) sanctuary

sanzionare (**sanzióno**) *tr* to sanction; to ratify

sanzióne *f* sanction

sapére *m* knowledge; **sapere fare** savoir-faire ‖ §243 *tr* to know; to find out; to know how to; **far sapere** to let know; **saperla lunga** to know a thing or two; **un certo non so che** a certain something, something vague ‖ *intr*— **sapere di** to know; to taste; to smell; to smack of; **mi sa che** I think that; **non voler più saperne di** to not want to have anything to do with; **sapere male** (with *dat*) to feel sorry, e.g., **gli sa male** he feels sorry ‖ *ref*—**che io mi sappia** as far as I know

sàpido -da *adj* savory; witty

sapiènte *adj* wise; talented; trained (*dog*) ‖ *m* wise man

sapiéntó·ne -na *mf* wiseacre, know-it-all

sapiènza *f* wisdom; knowledge

saponària *f* (bot) soapwort

saponata *f* soapsuds; lather; (fig) soft soap

sapóne *m* soap; **sapone da toletta** toilet soap; **sapone per la barba** shaving soap

saponétta *f* cake of soap

saponière *m* soap maker

saponifi·cio *m* (**-ci**) soap factory

saponó·so -sa [s] *adj* soapy

sapóre *m* taste; savor; flavor

saporire §176 *tr* to savor

saporitaménte *adv* heartily; soundly

sapori·to -ta *adj* tasty; flavorful; salty; expensive

saporó·so -sa [s] *adj* savory; witty

saputèl·lo -la *adj* cocksure ‖ *m* smart aleck

sarac·co *m* (**-chi**) hand saw

saracè·no -na *adj* Saracen, Saracenic ‖ *m* Saracen; quintain

saraciné·sca *f* (**-sche**) metal shutter (*of store*); sluice gate; (hist) portcullis

sarcasmo *m* sarcasm

sarcàsti·co -ca *adj* (**-ci -che**) sarcastic

sarchiare §287 *tr* to weed

sarchia·tóre -trice *mf* weeder ‖ *f* (agr) cultivator

sarchièllo *m* weeding hoe

sàr·chio *m* (**-chi**) hoe

sarcòfa·go *m* (**-gi & -ghi**) sarcophagus

sarcràuti *mpl* sauerkraut

Sardégna, la Sardinia

sardèlla *f* pilchard; sardine

sardina *f* pilchard; sardine

sar·do -da *adj & mf* Sardinian

sardòni·co -ca *adj* (**-ci -che**) sardonic

sarménto *m* vine shoot, running stem

sarta *f* dressmaker

sàrtie *fpl* (naut) shrouds

sarto *m* tailor

sartorìa *f* dressmaker's shop; tailor shop; dressmaking; tailoring

sassaiòla *f* shower of stones

sassata *f* blow with a stone

sasso *m* stone, rock; pebble; (poet) tombstone; **di sasso** stony; **restare di sasso** to be taken aback; **tirare sassi in colombaia** to cut one's nose to spite one's face

sassòfono *m* saxophone

sàssone *adj & mf* Saxon

sassó·so -sa [s] *adj* stony

Sàtana *m* Satan

satanasso *m* Satan; devil

satèllite *m* satellite

sa·tin *m* (**-tin**) sateen

satinare *tr* to gloss

sàtira *f* satire

satireggiare §290 (**satiréggio**) *tr* to satirize, lampoon ‖ *intr* to compose satires

satìri·co -ca *adj* (**-ci -che**) satiric(al) ‖ *m* satirist

sàtiro *m* satyr

satól·lo -la *adj* sated, full

saturare *tr* (**sàturo**) *tr* to saturate; to steep; (fig) to fill; (com) to glut (*a market*)

saturni·no -na *adj* Saturnian; saturnine

Saturno *m* (astr) Saturn

sàtu·ro -ra *adj* saturated; (fig) full; (lit) sated

sàu·ro -ra *adj* & *m* sorrel (*horse*)

Savèrio *m* Xavier

sà·vio -via (-vi -vie) *adj* wise ‖ *m* wise man, sage

savoiar·do -da *adj* & *mf* Savoyard ‖ *m* ladyfinger

saxòfono *m* saxophone

saziare §287 *tr* to satisfy; to cloy, satiate

sazietà *f* satiety, surfeit; **mangiare a sazietà** to eat one's fill

sà·zio -zia *adj* (-zi -zie) sated; full; satisfied

sbaciucchiare §287 (sbaciùcchio) *tr* to kiss again and again ‖ *ref* to neck

sbadatàggine *f* carelessness; oversight

sbada·to -ta *adj* careless; heedless

sbadigliare §280 *intr* to yawn

sbadì·glio *m* (-gli) yawn

sbafa·tóre -trice *mf* sponger

sbafo *m*—a sbafo sponging; **mangiare a sbafo** to sponge

sbagliare §280 *tr* to miss; to mistake; **sbagliarla** to be sadly mistaken ‖ *intr* & *ref* to be mistaken; to make a mistake

sbaglia·to -ta *adj* wrong; mistaken

sbà·glio *m* (-gli) error, mistake

sbalestrare (sbalèstro) *tr* to fling with the crossbow; to send (*an employee*) far away ‖ *intr* to speak amiss; to ramble; to blunder

sbalestra·to -ta *adj* unbalanced; ill-at-ease

sballare *tr* to unpack; **sballarle grosse** to tell tall tales ‖ *intr* to overbid

sballa·to -ta *adj* unpacked; absurd, wild

sballottare (sballòtto) *tr* to toss

sbalordire §176 *tr* to stun; to amaze; to bewilder ‖ *intr* to lose consciousness; to be dumfounded

sbalorditi·vo -va *adj* amazing

sbalzare *tr* to upset; to send far away; to overthrow; to emboss ‖ *intr* (ESSERE) to bounce

sbalzo *m* leap, jump; climb; embossment, relief; **a sbalzi** by leaps and bounds; **di sbalzo** all of a sudden

sbancare §197 *tr* to clear (*ground*) of rocks; to ruin; (cards) to break (*the bank*)

sbandaménto *m* skid; swerve; disbandment; breaking up; (naut) list

sbandare *tr* to disband; (naut) to cause to list ‖ *intr* to list; to skid; to swerve; to deviate ‖ *ref* to disband; to break up

sbanda·to -ta *adj* disbanded; stray; alienated ‖ *mf* alienated person ‖ *m* straggler *f* listing (*of ship*); skidding (*of vehicle*); **prendere una sbandata per** to get a crush on

sbandierare (sbandièro) *tr* to wave (*a flag*); to display

sbaragliare §280 *tr* to rout; to crush

sbarà·glio *m*—mettere allo sbaraglio to endanger

sbarazzare *tr* to clear out; to free ‖ *ref* —sbarazzarsi di to get rid of

sbarazzi·no -na *adj* mischievous ‖ *mf* scamp; **alla sbarazzina** cocked, at an angle (*said of a hat*)

sbarbare *tr* to shave; to uproot ‖ *ref* to shave

sbarbatèllo *m* greenhorn, fledgling

sbarcare §197 *tr* to unload; to discharge; to disembark; to pass; to strew (*fodder*); **sbarcare il lunario** to make ends meet ‖ *intr* (ESSERE) to come ashore, land

sbarca·tóio *m* (-tói) landing pier

sbar·co *m* (-chi) unloading; landing

sbarra *f* bar; (typ) dash

sbarraménto *m* barrage; obstacle

sbarrare *tr* to bar; to block (*the way*); to open (*one's eyes*) wide, e.g., **sbarrò gli occhi** he opened his eyes wide

sbarrétta *f* bar; **sbarrette verticali** (typ) parallels

sbatacchiare §287 *tr* to slam; to flap ‖ *intr* to slam

sbatàc·chio *m* (-chi) shore, prop

sbàttere *tr* to flap; to fling; to slam; to beat; to toss; to send away; to make pale; **sbatter fuori** to throw out ‖ *intr* to flap; to slam

sbattighiàc·cio *m* (-cio) cocktail shaker

sbattitóre *m* electric mixer

sbattiuò·va *m* (-va) egg beater

sbattu·to -ta *adj* haggard, downcast

sbavare *tr* to slobber over; (mach) to trim ‖ *intr* to drivel, slobber; to run (*said of colors*)

sbavatura *f* drivel; run (*of colors*); burr (*of metal*); deckle edge; verbosity

sbeccare §197 (sbécco) *tr* & *ref* to chip

sbeffeggiare §290 (sbefféggio) *tr* to make fun of

sbellicare §197 *ref*—sbellicarsi dalle risa to burst with laughter

sbèrla *f* (coll) slap

sberlèffo *m* scar; grimace; **fare gli sberleffi a** to make faces at

sbevazzare *intr* to guzzle

sbevucchiare §287 *intr* to tipple

sbiadire §176 *tr* & *intr* (ESSERE) to fade

sbiadi·to -ta *adj* faded; dull

sbiancare §197 *tr* to whiten ‖ *ref* to become white; to pale

sbianchire §176 *tr* (culin) to blanch

sbiè·co -ca (-chi -che) *adj* oblique; **di sbieco** on the bias; **guardare di sbieco** to look askance at ‖ *m* cloth cut diagonally

sbigottire §176 *tr* to terrify, dismay ‖ *intr* (ESSERE) & *ref* to be dismayed

sbilanciare §128 *tr* to unbalance; to upset ‖ *intr* to lose one's balance ‖ *ref* to commit oneself

sbilàn·cio *m* (-ci) disequilibrium; (com) deficit

sbilèn·co -ca *adj* (-chi -che) twisted, crooked

sbirciare §128 *tr* to leer at, ogle; to eye closely

sbir·ro -ra *adj* (coll) smart ‖ *m* (pej) cop

sbizzarrire [ddzz] §176 *tr* to cure the whims of ‖ *ref* to indulge one's whims

sbòbba *f* slop, dishwater

sboccare §197 (sbócco) *tr* to break the

mouth of (*a bottle*); to remove a few drops from (*a bottle*) ‖ *intr* (ESSERE) to flow; to open (*said of a street*); **sboccare in** to turn out to be

sbocca·to -ta *adj* foulmouthed; foul (*language*); chipped at the mouth (*said of a bottle*)

sbocciare §128 (**sbòccio**) *intr* (ESSERE) to bud, burgeon, bloom

sbóc·co *m* (**-chi**) outlet; **avere uno sbocco di sangue** to spit blood

sbocconcellare (**sbocconcèllo**) *tr* to nibble at; to chip, nick

sbollentare (**sbollènto**) *tr* to blanch

sbollire §176 *intr* to stop boiling; to calm down

sbolognare (**sbológno**) *tr* (coll) to palm off; (coll) to get rid of

sbórnia *f* (coll) drunk, jag; **smaltire la sbornia** to sober up

sborsare (**sbórso**) *tr* to pay out, disburse

sbórso *m* disbursement, outlay

sbottare (**sbòtto**) *intr*—**sbottare a + inf** to burst out + *ger*

sbottonare (**sbottóno**) *tr* to unbutton ‖ *ref* (fig) to unbosom oneself

sbozzare (**sbòzzo**) *tr* to rough-hew; to sketch, outline

sbraca·to -ta *adj* without pants; slovenly; vulgar

sbracciare §128 *intr* to gesticulate ‖ *ref* to roll up one's sleeves; to wear sleeveless clothes; to gesticulate; to do one's best

sbraccia·to -ta *adj* bare-armed

sbraitare (**sbràito**) *intr* to scream

sbraitó·ne -na *mf* bigmouth

sbranare *tr* to tear to pieces

sbrano *m* tear, rent

sbrattare *tr* to clean; to clear

sbreccare §197 (**sbrécco**) *tr* to chip, nick

sbrecciare §128 (**sbréccio**) *tr* to open a gap in

sbréndolo *m* tatter, rag

sbriciolare (**sbrìciolo**) *tr* to crumb ‖ *ref* to crumble

sbrigare §209 *tr* to transact; to take care of ‖ *ref* to hasten, hurry; **sbrigarsela** to get out of trouble; **sbrigarsi di** or to get rid of; **sbrigati!** make it snappy!, hurry up!

sbrigativ·o -va *adj* quick, brisk; businesslike

sbrigliare §280 *tr* to unbridle; to reduce (*a hernia*); to lance (*an infected wound*) ‖ *ref* to cut loose

sbrinare *tr* to defrost

sbrindella·to -ta *adj* tattered

sbrodolare (**sbròdolo**) *tr* to soil; (fig) to drag out ‖ *ref* to slobber

sbrogliare §280 (**sbròglio**) *tr* to untangle; to clean up ‖ *ref* to extricate oneself; **sbrogliarsela** to get out of a tight spot

sbronzare (**sbrónzo**) *ref* (coll) to get drunk

sbruffare *tr* to squirt out of the mouth; to spatter; to bribe ‖ *intr* to tell tall tales

sbruffo *m* sprinkle, squirt; bribe

sbruffó·ne -na *mf* braggart

sbucare §197 *intr* (ESSERE) to pop out, come out

sbucciare §128 *tr* to peel; to skin ‖ *ref* to slough (*said of snakes*); **sbucciarsela** (coll) to goldbrick

sbucciatura *f* slight abrasion

sbudellare (**sbudèllo**) *tr* to disembowel ‖ *ref*—**sbudellarsi dalle risa** to burst with laughter, split one's sides laughing

sbuffare *tr* & *intr* to puff

sbuffo *m* puff; gust (*of wind*); **a sbuffo** puffed (*sleeve*)

sbullonare (**sbullóno**) *tr* to unbolt

sc- *pref* dis-, e.g., **sconto** discount; es-, e.g., **scalare** to escalate; ex-, e.g., **scusare** to excuse

scàbbia *f* scabies

sca·bro -bra *adj* rough; stony; tight (*style*)

scabró·so -sa [s] *adj* scabrous

scacchièra *f* checkerboard; chessboard

scacchière *m* (mil) sector; (obs) checkerboard; exchequer

scacciaca·ni *m* & *f* (**-ni**) toy gun; gun shooting only blanks

scacciamó·sche *m* (**-sche**) fly swatter

scacciapensiè·ri *m* (**-ri**) jew's-harp

scacciare §128 *tr* to chase away, drive away; to expel

scaccino *m* sexton, sacristan

scac·co *m* (**-chi**) chessman; checker; check; square; **a scacchi** checkered; **dare scacco matto a** to checkmate; **in scacco** or **sotto scacco** in check; **scacchi** chess; **scacco matto** checkmate

scàccoli *mpl* cement piles

scaccomatto *m* checkmate

scadente *adj* inferior, poor, shoddy

scadènza *f* term, maturity; obligation; **a breve scadenza** short-term; **a lunga scadenza** long-term

scadére §121 *intr* (ESSERE) to decay, to decline; to fall due; to expire; (naut) to drift

scafandro *m* diving suit; **scafandro astronautico** space suit

scaffale *m* bookcase; shelf

scafo *m* hull

scagionare (**scagióno**) *tr* to exonerate, exculpate

scàglia *f* scale (*of fish*); chip; plate (*of medieval armor*); flake (*of soap*); tile (*of slate roof*)

scagliare §280 *tr* to hurl, fling, throw; to scale (*fish*) ‖ *ref* to dash, to rush; to flake

scaglionare (**scaglióno**) *tr* to echelon; to stagger (*e.g., payments*)

scaglióne *m* terrace (*of mountain*); echelon; scale; **a scaglioni** graded (*e.g., income tax*)

scala *f* stairs; ladder; scale; (cards) straight; (rad) dial; **a scale** scaled, graded; **fare le scale** to climb the stairs; **scala a chiocciola** spiral stairway; **scala a gradini** or **a libretto** stepladder; **scala mobile** escalator; (econ) sliding scale; **scala porta** aerial ladder; **scala reale** (poker) straight flush; **su larga scala** large-scale; **su scala nazionale** on a national scale

scalandróne *m* (naut) gangway

scalare *adj* graded, scaled; gradual || *m* (com) running balance || *tr* to climb, ascend; to scale, grade; to reduce

scalata *f* climb, ascent; **dar la scalata a** to climb; to climb up to

scalcagna·to -ta *adj* down-at-the-heel

scalcare §197 *tr* to slice, carve

scalciare §128 *intr* to kick

scalcina·to -ta *adj.* (*wall or plaster*) that is peeling off; worn-out; down-at-the-heels

scalda·acqua *m* (**-acqua**) hot-water heater

scaldaba·gno *m* (**-gno**) hot-water heater; **scaldabagno a gas** gas heater

scaldalèt·to *m* (**-ti & -to**) bedwarmer

scaldare *tr* to warm, warm up; to heat, heat up || *intr* (mach) to become hot || *ref* to warm up; to heat up; **scaldarsi la testa** to get excited

scaldavivan·de *m* (**-de**) hot plate

scaldino *m* hand warmer

scalèa *f* flight of stairs, stairway

scalèo *m* stepladder

scalétta *f* small ladder; small stairs; (mov) rough draft

scalfire §176 *tr* to graze, scratch; to cut (*e.g., glass*)

scalfittura *f* graze, scratch

scalinata *f* stairway, perron

scalino *m* step (*of a stair*); (fig) ladder

scalmana *f* chill; flush; **prendere una scalmana per** to take a fancy to

scalmanare *ref* to hustle, bustle; to fuss

scalmana·to -ta *adj* panting; hotheaded

scalmo *m* (naut) oarlock

scalo *m* pier, dock; (naut) ways; (naut) port of call; **fare scalo** (naut) to call, stop; (aer) to land; **scalo di alaggio** (naut) slip; **scalo merci** (rr) freight yard; **senza scalo** (aer, naut) nonstop

scalógna *f* (coll) bad luck

scalógno *m* (bot) scallion

scalòppa *f* veal chop

scaloppina *f* veal cutlet, scallop

scalpellare (**scalpèllo**) *tr* to chisel

scalpellino *m* stone cutter

scalpèllo *m* chisel; (surg) scalpel; **scalpello a taglio obliquo** skew chisel

scalpicciare §128 *tr & intr* to shuffle

scalpitare (**scàlpito**) *intr* to paw the ground

scalpóre *m* scene; **fare scalpore** to raise a fuss

scaltrézza *f* shrewdness, cunning

scaltrire §176 *tr* to polish, refine; to sharpen the wits of || *ref* to catch on; to improve

scal·tro -tra *adj* shrewd, smart

scalzare *tr* to take the shoes or stockings off of; to undermine || *ref* to take off one's shoes or stockings

scal·zo -za *adj* barefoot

scambiare §287 *tr* to exchange; to mistake || *ref* to exchange (*presents*)

scambiévole *adj* mutual

scàm·bio *m* (**-bi**) exchange; (rr) switch;

libero scambio free trade; **scambio di persona** mistaken identity

scamicia·to -ta *adj* in shirt sleeves; extremist || *m* extremist; tunic, waist

scamoscia·to -ta *adj* chamois, suede

scampagnata *f* excursion, outing

scampanare *intr* to peal, chime; to flare (*said of a garment*)

scampanellare (**scampanèllo**) *intr* to ring loud and clear

scampanì·o *m* (**-i**) toll, peal

scampare *tr* to save, rescue; **scamparla bella** to have a narrow escape || *intr* (ESSERE)—**scampare a** to escape from; to take refuge in

scampo *m* escape; safety; (zool) Norway lobster; **non c'è scampo** there is no way out

scàmpolo *m* remnant; **scampoli di tempo** free moments

scanalare *tr* to channel, groove, rabbet || *intr* to overflow

scanalatura *f* channel, groove, rabbet

scandagliare §280 *tr* to sound

scandà·glio *m* (**-gli**) sounding lead; **fare uno scandaglio** to make a sounding or survey

scandalismo *m* scandalmongering, yellow journalism

scandalizzare [ddzz] *tr* to scandalize, shock || *ref* to be scandalized

scàndalo *m* scandal

scandaló·so -sa [s] *adj* scandalous

scandina·vo -va *adj & mf* Scandinavian

scandire §176 *tr* to scan; to syllabize; (telv) to scan

scàndola *f* wood shingle

scannare *tr* to slaughter, butcher

scanna·tóio *m* (**-tói**) slaughterhouse; gyp joint

scanno *m* bench; seat; sand bar

scansafati·che *mf* (**-che**) loafer

scansare *tr* to move; to avoid || *ref* to get out of the way

scansìa *f* shelf; bookcase

scansióne *f* scansion; (telv) scanning

scanso *m*—**a scanso di** in order to avoid

scantinare *intr* to make a blunder; (mus) to be out of tune

scantinato *m* basement

scantonàre (**scantóno**) *tr* to round (*a corner*) || *intr* to duck around the corner

scanzona·to -ta *adj* flippant; unconventional

scapacctóne *m* clout; **dare uno scapaccione a** to clout, slap

scapa·to -ta *adj* scatterbrained || *m* scatterbrain

scapestra·to -ta *adj & m* libertine

scapigliare §280 *tr* to dishevel || *ref* to be disheveled

scapiglia·to -ta *adj* disheveled; libertine; unconventional; free and easy

scapitare (**scàpito**) *intr* to lose

scàpito *m* damage; loss; **a scapito di** to the detriment of

scàpola *f* shoulder blade

scapolare *m* scapular || *v* (**scàpolo**) *tr* (coll) to escape, avoid || *intr*—**scapolare da** to get out of (*danger*) scàpo·lo -la *adj* unmarried ‖ *m* bachelor ‖ *f* see **scapola**

scappaménto *m* escapement (*of watch, of piano*); (aut) exhaust

scappare *tr*—**scapparla bella** to have a narrow escape ‖ *intr* (ESSERE) to flee; to run; to get away; to escape; to stick out; to burst out (*said, e.g., of sun*); **far scappare la pazienza a qlcu** to make s.o. lose his patience, to tax s.o.'s patience; **scappare a gambe levate** to run away, beat it; **scappare da** to burst out, e.g., **gli è scappato da ridere** he burst out laughing; **scappar detto di** to blurt out that, e.g., **gli scappò detto di non poterne più** he blurted out that he could not hold out; **scappare di mente** to escape one's mind; **scappar fuori con** to come out with

scappata *f* excursion; sally; escapade; bolt (*of horse*); **fare una scappata** to take a run; **scappata spiritosa** witticism

scappatóia *f* subterfuge; loophole

scappellare (scappèllo) *ref* to tip one's hat

scappellòtto *m* smack, slap (on the head); **entrare a scappellotto** (coll) to squeeze in; **passare a scappellotto** (coll) to squeeze through with influence

scapricciare §128 *tr* to satisfy the whims of

scarabèo *m* beetle; scarab (*stone*); **scarabeo sacro** scarab; **scarabeo stercorario** dung beetle

scarabocchiare §287 (scarabòcchio) *tr* to scribble; to blot (*with ink*)

scaraboc·chio *m* (-chi) ink blot; scribble; scrawl

scarafàg·gio *m* (-gi) cockroach

scaramanzìa *f* exorcism; **per scaramanzia** to ward off the evil eye, for good luck

scaramazza *adj fem* irregular (*pearl*)

scaramùc·cia *f* (-ce) skirmish

scaraventare (scaravènto) *tr* to hurl, chuck; to transfer suddenly

scarcerare (scàrcero) *tr* to release from jail

scardinare (scàrdino) *tr* to unhinge

scàri·ca *f* (-che) discharge; volley; evacuation; (elec) discharge; (fig) shower

scaricabarili *m*—**giocare a scaricabarili** (fig) to pass the buck

scaricare §197 (scàrico) *tr* to unload; to discharge; to hurl (*insults*); to wreak (*anger*); to free (*from responsibility*) ‖ *ref* to unburden oneself; to flow (*said of a river*); to discharge; to run down (*said of a battery or a watch*)

scaricatóre *m* longshoreman; (elec) lightning arrester

scàri·co -ca (-chi -che) *adj* empty, unloaded; discharged; clear (*sky*); free; run-down (*e.g., clock*) ‖ *m* unloading; discharge; exhaust; waste, refuse; **a mio** (**tuo, etc.**) **scarico** in my (your, etc.) defense ‖ *f* see **scarica**

scarlattina *f* scarlet fever

scarlat·to -ta *adj* & *m* scarlet

scarmigliare §280 *tr* to dishevel

scarnificare §197 (scarnìfico) or **scarnire** §176 *tr* to bone, take the flesh off; to make thin; to wear down to the bone

scarni·to -ta or **scar·no** -na *adj* boned; meager; skinny

scaròla *f* escarole, endive

scarpa *f* shoe; wedge, skid; scarp; **fare le scarpe a** to undercut; **scarpe al sole** violent death; **scarpe da sci** ski boots

scarpata *f* escarp, escarpment; slope (*of embankment*); blow with a shoe; **scarpata continentale** continental slope

scarpétta *f* small shoe; low shoe; **scarpette chiodate** spikes; **scarpette da ginnastica** gym shoes

scarpinare *intr* to trudge

scarpóne *m* heavy boot; clodhopper

scarròc·cio *m* (-ci) (aer, naut) leeway

scarrozzare (scarròzzo) *tr* to take for a ride ‖ *intr* to go for a ride; to go for a walk

scarrozzata *f* ride, drive

scarseggiare §290 (scarséggio) *intr* (ESSERE) to be scarce, be in short supply; **scarseggiare di** to be short of

scarsèlla *f* pocket; (obs) purse

scarsézza *f* or **scarsi·tà** *f* (-tà) scarcity, dearth, lack

scar·so -sa *adj* short; scarce; scanty, scant; weak (*wind*); **scarso a** short of

scartabellare (scartabèllo) *tr* to leaf through (*a book*)

scartafàc·cio *m* (-ci) note pad, notebook; poorly-bound copybook

scartaménto *m* (rr) gauge; **a scartamento ridotto** narrow-gauge; small-size; small-scale

scartare *tr* to unpack, unwrap; to discard (*cards*); to remove; to scrap (*e.g., a machine*); (mil) to reject ‖ *intr* to swerve; to side-step

scartata *f* unwrapping; side step; swerving; (fig) scolding

scartina *f* discard

scarto *m* discard; reject; swerve; (mil) rejected soldier; (sports) difference; **di scarto inferior**

scartocciare §128 (scartòccio) *tr* to unwrap; to unfold; to husk (*corn*)

scartòffie *fpl* old papers, trash

scassare *tr* to uncrate; to plow up; (coll) to ruin, bust ‖ *ref* (coll) to break down

scassinare *tr* to pick (*a lock*); to burglarize; to break open

scassina·tóre -trice *mf* burglar; **scassinatore di casseforti** safe-cracker

scasso *m* plowing, tilling; burglary

scatenare (scaténo) *tr* to unchain; to trigger; to excite, stir up ‖ *ref* to break loose

scàtola *f* box; can; **a scatola chiusa** sight unseen; **in scatola** canned; **rompere le scatole a** (vulg) to bug, pester; **scatola armonica** music box; **scatola a sorpresa** jack-in-the-box;

scatola cranica cranium, skull; **scatola del cambio** (aut) transmission, gear box
scatolame *m* boxes; canned food
scatolifi·cio *m* (-ci) box factory
scattare *tr* to take (*a picture*) || *intr* (ESSERE & AVERE) to jump, spring; to go off (*said of a trap*); to go up (*said of the cost of living*); to go into action, begin
scatto *m* click (*of camera, gun*); outburst; sprint; automatic increase (*in salary*); shutter release; **a scatti** in jerks; **di scatto** suddenly
scaturire §176 *intr* (ESSERE) to spring; to pour, gush; to stem
scavalcare §197 *tr* to jump over; to pass over; to unsaddle; to skip (*a stitch*) || *intr* (ESSERE) to dismount || *ref* (coll) to rush
scavallare *intr* to caper, cavort
scavare *tr* to dig; to dig up, unearth
scava·tóre -trice *adj* excavating || *m* digger || *f* digger, excavator
scavezzacòllo *m* scamp; daredevil; **a scavezzacollo** headlong, at breakneck speed
scavezzare (scavézzo) *tr* to lop; to burst; to break; to take the halter off (*a horse*)
scavo *m* digging, excavation
scazzottare (scazzòtto) *tr* to beat up
scégliere §244 *tr* to choose; to pick out
sceic·co *m* (-chi) sheik
scelleratàggine *f* or **scelleratézza** *f* wickedness, villainy
scellera·to -ta *adj* wicked || *m* villain
scellino *m* shilling
scél·to -ta *adj* choice; selected; (mil) first-class || *f* choice; pick; selection; **di prima scelta** choice
scemare (scémo) *tr* to diminish, reduce; to lower the level of || *intr* (ESSERE) & *ref* to lessen, diminish
scemènza *f* foolishness, stupidity
scé·mo -ma *adj* silly, foolish || *mf* simpleton, fool
scempiàggine *f* silliness, foolishness
scém·pio -pia (-pi -pie) *adj* simple; single; (lit) wicked || *m* ruination; (lit) slaughter; **fare scempio di** to ruin, (lit) to slaughter
scèna *f* scene; stage; acting; scenery; **esser di scena** (theat) to be on; **mettere in scena** (theat) to stage; **scene di prossima programmazione** (mov) coming attractions
scenà·rio *m* (-ri) scenery; scenario, setting
scenari·sta *mf* (-sti -ste) scenarist; script writer
scenata *f* scene (*outbreak of anger*)
scéndere §245 *tr* to descend, go down; to bring down || *intr* (ESSERE) to descend, go down; to get off; to come (*to an agreement*); to step (*into the ring*); to put up (*at a hotel*); to check in (*at a hotel*)
scendilèt·to *m* (-to) scatter rug; bathrobe
sceneggiare §290 (scenéggio) *tr* to write a scenario for; to adapt for the stage

sceneggia·tóre -trice *mf* scenarist
sceneggiatura *f* (mov) screenplay; (rad, telv) continuity
scenètta *f* (theat) sketch
scenògrafo *m* scene designer
scenotècni·ca *f* (-che) stagecraft
sceriffo *m* sheriff
scèrnere §246 *tr* to discern; to distinguish; to select
scervellare (scervèllo) *ref* to rack one's brains
scervella·to -ta *adj* scatterbrained
scésa [s] *f* descent; slope
scespiria·no -na *adj* Shakesperean
scetticismo *m* skepticism
scètti·co -ca (-ci -che) *adj* skeptic(al) || *m* skeptic
scèttro *m* scepter
sceverare (scévero) *tr* (lit) to distinguish
scé·vro -vra *adj* (lit) free, exempt
schèda *f* card; slip, form; **scheda elettorale** ballot; **scheda perforata** punch card
schedare (schèdo) *tr* to file
schedà·rio *m* (-ri) card index, card catalogue; file cabinet
schég·gia *f* (-ge) splinter; chip
scheggiare §290 (schéggio) *tr* & *ref* to splinter
schelètri·co -ca *adj* (-ci -che) skeleton, skeletal; succint
schèletro *m* skeleton
schè·ma *m* (-mi) diagram; draft; model; scheme; **schema di montaggio** (electron) hookup
schérma *f* fencing
schermàglia *f* argument
schermare (schérmo) *tr* to screen; (elec) to shield
schermire §176 *tr* to protect; (obs) to fence with || *ref*—**schermirsi da** to ward off, parry; to protect oneself from
schermi·tóre -trice *mf* fencer
schérmo *m* screen; protection; (elec) shield; **farsi schermo di** to use as protection; **farsi schermo delle mani** to ward off a blow with one's hands
schernire §176 *tr* to deride
schérno *m* derision, ridicule, mockery
scherzare (schérzo) *tr* (coll) to mock || *intr* to play; to joke, trifle
schérzo *m* play; joke, jest; freak (*of nature*); child's play; trick; **neppure per scherzo** under no circumstances; **per scherzo** in jest; **stare allo scherzo** to take a joke
scherzó·so -sa [s] *adj* joking; playful
schiacciaménto *m* crushing; flattening
schiaccianó·ci *m* (-ci) nutcracker
schiacciante *adj* crushing
schiacciapata·te *m* (-te) ricer
schiacciare §128 *tr* to crush; to take (*a nap*); to squelch (*a rumor*); to subdue (*the details of a painting*); to mash (*potatoes*); to tread on, step on (*s.o.'s foot*); to flatten; to run (*s.o.*) over; to make (*s.o.'s figure*) look squatty; to crack (*nuts*); to flunk; (tennis) to smash
schiacciata *f* hot cake; (tennis) smash

schiaffare *tr* (coll) to fling, clap

schiaffeggiare §290 (**schiafféggio**) *tr* to slap; to buffet

schiaffo *m* slap, box

schiamazzare *intr* to squawk, cackle; to honk; to make a racket

schiamazzo *m* squawking, cackle; honk; hubbub

schiantare *tr* to crush, burst || *intr* (ESSERE) (coll) to burst; (coll) to croak || *ref* to break, crack, split

schianto *m* break, crack; crash; bang; knockout (*extraordinary, attractive person or thing*); **di schianto** all of a sudden; **schianto al cuore** heartache

schiappa *f* splinter; (coll) good-for-nothing

schiarimento *m* elucidation

schiarire §176 *tr* to make clearer; to make (*the hair*) light; to clear; to explain; to elucidate || *intr* (ESSERE) to become light || *ref* to clear up (*said of the weather*); to clear (*one's throat*); to fade || *impers* (ESSERE) —**schiarisce** it is getting light

schiarita *f* clearing (*of weather*); improvement (*in relations*)

schiatta *f* race, stock

schiattare *intr* (ESSERE) to burst

schiavi·sta (-**sti** -**ste**) *adj* slave (*e.g., state*) || *mf* antiabolitionist

schiavi·tù *f* (-**tù**) slavery; bondage

schia·vo -va *adj* enslaved || *mf* slave

schiccherare (**schícchero**) *tr* to scribble; to soil; to sketch; to dash off; to blurt out; (coll) to clean out

schidionare (**schidióno**) *tr* to put on the spit

schidióne *m* spit

schiena *f* back; divide; crown (*of road*); **giocare di schiena** to buck

schienale *m* back (*of chair; cut of meat*)

schiera *f* crowd; flock; herd; (mil) rank

schieramento *m* alignment

schierare (**schièro**) *tr* to line up || *ref* to line up; **schierarsi dalla parte di** to side with

schiet·to -ta *adj* pure; frank, honest

schifare *tr* to loathe; to disgust || *ref*— **schifarsi di** to feel disgusted with

schifa·to -ta *adj* disgusted

schifiltó·so -sa [s] *adj* fastidious; squeamish

schifo *m* disgust, loathing; skiff; shell; **fare schifo a** to disgust; to make sick

schifó·so -sa [s] *adj* disgusting; sickening; (slang) tremendous

schioccare §197 (**schiocco**) *tr* to snap (*the fingers*); to click (*the tongue*); to smack (*the lips*); to crack (*a whip*) || *intr* to crack

schiòc·co *m* (-**chi**) crack, snap; click; smack

schiodare (**schiòdo**) *tr* to take the nails out of

schioppettata *f* gunshot; earshot

schiòppo *m* gun, shotgun; **a un tiro di schioppo** within earshot

schiùdere §125 *tr & ref* to open

schiuma *f* foam, froth; lather; head (*of beer*); dregs, scum; meerschaum;

avere la schiuma alla bocca to froth at the mouth

schiumaiòla *f* skimmer

schiumare *tr* to scum; to skim || *intr* to foam, froth; to lather

schiumó·so -sa [s] *adj* foamy

schivare *tr* to avoid; to avert || *ref* to shy

schi·vo -va *adj* averse; bashful, shy

schizzare *tr* to spray; to sprinkle; to ooze (*venom*); to sketch; **schizzare fuoco dagli occhi** to have fire in one's eyes || *intr* (ESSERE) to gush; to squirt; to dart; **gli occhi gli schizzano dall'orbita** his eyes are popping out of his head

schizzétto *m* sprayer; syringe; water pistol

schizzinó·so -sa [s] *adj* finicky, fastidious

schizzo *m* spray; splash; sketch; survey (*e.g., of literature*)

sci *m* (**sci**) ski

scìa *f* wake; track; trail; **scia di condensazione** contrail

sciàbola *f* saber

sciabordare (**sciabórdo**) *tr* to shake, agitate || *intr* to break (*said of waves*)

sciacallo *m* jackal

sciacquadi·ta *m* (-**ta**) finger bowl

sciacquare (**sciàcquo**) *tr* to rinse

sciacquatura *f* rinse

sciacqui·o *m* (-**i**) splash, dash

sciàcquo *m* rinsing (*of the mouth*); mouthwash

sciagura *f* calamity, misfortune

sciagura·to -ta *adj* unfortunate; wretched

scialacquare (**scialàcquo**) *tr* to squander

scialare *tr* to squander || *intr* to be well off; to live it up

scial·bo -ba *adj* pale, faded; wan

scialle *m* shawl; **scialle da viaggio** traveling blanket

scialo *m* squandering; opulence; **a scialo** lavishly

scialuppa *f* launch; lifeboat

sciamanna·to -ta *adj* slovenly

sciamannó·ne -na *mf* slovenly person || *f* slattern

sciamare *intr* (ESSERE & AVERE) to swarm

sciame *m* swarm; flock

sciampagna *f* champagne

scianca·to -ta *adj* cripple, lame; wobbly (*table*)

sciangài *m* pick-up-sticks || **Sciangai** *f* Shanghai

sciarada *f* charade

sciare §119 *intr* to ski; to back water

sciarpa *f* scarf; sash (*e.g., of an officer or of a mayor*)

scias·sì *m* (-**sì**) chassis

sciàtica *f* (pathol) sciatica

scia·tóre -trice *mf* skier

sciatterìa *f* or **sciattézza** *f* slovenliness

sciat·to -ta *adj* slovenly, sloppy

scìbile *m* knowledge

sciènte *adj* conscious; knowing

scientìfi·co -ca *adj* (-**ci** -**che**) scientific

scienza *f* science; knowledge

scienzia•to -ta *mf* scientist

scilinguàgnolo *m* frenum (*of tongue*); avere lo scilinguagnolo sciolto to have a loose tongue

Scilla *f* Scylla; fra Scilla e Cariddi between Scylla and Charibdis

scimitarra *f* scimitar

scìmmia *f* monkey; (coll) drunk; fare la scimmia a to ape; scimmia antropomorfa anthropoid ape

scimmié•sco -sca *adj* (-schi -sche) monkeyish; apish

scimmiottare (scimmiòtto) *tr* to ape

scimpan•zé *m* (-zé) chimpanzee

scimuni•to -ta *adj* idiotic || *mf* idiot

scìndere §247 *tr* (lit) to split; to separate

scintilla *f* spark; sparkle; (fig) scintilla; scintilla elettrica jump spark

scintillare *intr* to spark; to sparkle

scintillì•o *m* (-ì) sparkle, brilliance

scioccare §197 *tr* to shock

sciocchézza *f* silliness; trifle

sciòc•co -ca (-chi -che) *adj* silly, foolish || *mf* fool, blockhead

sciògliere §127 *tr* to loosen; to release; to unfasten, untie; to solve; to disperse; to dissolve; to limber; to fulfill (*a promise*); to unfurl (*sails*) || *ref* to loosen up; to get loose; to dissolve; to melt (*into tears*)

scioglilìn•gua *m*(-gue) tongue twister

sciogliménto *m* melting; dissolution; fulfillment; denouement

sciolina *f* ski wax

scioltézza *f* nimbleness, agility; freedom (*of movement*); ease

sciòl•to -ta *adj* loose; glib; free; blank (*verse*)

scioperante *adj* striking || *mf* striker

scioperare (sciòpero) *intr* to strike

sciopera•to -ta *adj* loafing; lazy || *m* loafer

sciòpero *m* strike; walkout; sciopero a singhiozzo slowdown strike; sciopero bianco sit-down strike; sciopero della fame hunger strike; sciopero di solidarietà sympathy strike; sciopero pignolo slowdown

sciorinare *tr* to display; to tell (*lies*); to air (*laundry*)

sciovìa *f* ski lift

sciovinismo *m* chauvinism, jingoism

scipì•to -ta *adj* insipid

scippo *m* snatching (*e.g., of a bag*)

sciròc•co *m* (-chi) sirocco; southeast

sciròppo *m* syrup

sci•sma *m* (-smi) schism

scismàti•co -ca *adj* (-ci -che) schismatic

scissióne *f* split; (biol, phys) fission

scis•so -sa *adj* split, rent

scisto *m* schist

sciupare *tr* to spoil; to wear out; to waste; to rumple || *ref* to wear; to run down (*said of health*); to get rumpled

sciupa•to -ta *adj* ruined; worn out; wasted; run down

sciupì•o *m* (-ì) waste

sciupó•ne -na *mf* waster, squanderer

sciu•scià *m* (-scià) bootblack; urchin

scìvola *f* chute

scivolare (scìvolo) *intr* (ESSERE & AVERE) to slide, glide; to steal; scivolare d'ala (aer) to sideslip

scivolata *f* slide, glide; scivolata d'ala (aer) sideslip

scìvolo *m* chute; (aer) slip (*for seaplanes*)

scivolóne *m* slip, slide

scivoló•so -sa [s] *adj* slippery

scoccare §197 (scòcco) *tr* to shoot (*an arrow*); to give (*a buss*); to strike (*the hour*) || *intr* (ESSERE) to dart; to spring; to strike (*said of a clock*); to shoot

scocciare §128 (scòccio) *tr* (coll) to break; (coll) to bother; (naut) to unhook || *ref* to be bored

scoccia•tóre -trice *mf* (coll) nuisance

scocciatura *f* (coll) bother, annoyance

scòc•co *m* (-chi) darting; stroke (*e.g., of three*); (naut) hook; scocco di baci bussing, kissing

scodèlla *f* bowl; soup plate

scodellare (scodèllo) *tr* to dish out

scodellino *m* small bowl; (mil) pan (*of musket lock*)

scodinzolare (scodìnzolo) *intr* to wag its tail; to waddle (*said of a woman*)

scoglièra *f* reef (*of rocks*); scogliera corallina coral reef

scò•glio *m* (-gli) rock; reef; cliff; stumbling block

scoiare §248 *tr* to skin

scoiàttolo *m* squirrel

scolabrò•do *m* (-do) colander, strainer

scolafrit•to *m* (-to) strainer

scolapa•sta *m* (-sta) (coll) colander

scolare (scólo) *tr* to drain; (fig) to polish off || *intr* (ESSERE) to drip || *ref* to melt

scolaré•sco -sca (-schi -sche) *adj* school || *f* schoolchildren; student body

scola•ro -ra *mf* pupil; student

scolàsti•co -ca (-ci -che) *adj* school; scholastic || *m* scholastic, schoolman || *f* scholasticism

scola•tóio *m* (-tói) drain; strainer

scolatura *f* drip, drippings; dregs

scollaccia•to -ta *adj* low-necked; wearing a low-cut dress; dirty, obscene

scollare (scòllo) *tr* to cut off at the neck; to unglue || *ref* to wear a low-necked dress; to come unglued

scollatura *f* neckline; ungluing; scollatura a barchetta low neck; scollatura a punta V neck

scòllo *m* neck, neckline

scólo *m* drain; drainage; (slang) clap

scolopèndra *f* centipede

scolorare (scolóro) *tr*, *intr* (ESSERE), & *ref* to fade, discolor; to pale

scolorire §176 *tr*, *intr* (ESSERE), & *ref* to fade, discolor

scolpare (scólpo) *tr* to excuse

scolpire §176 *tr* to sculpture; to engrave; to emphasize

scólta *f* (lit) sentry; fare la scolta to stand guard

scombaciare §128 *tr* to pull apart, separate

scombinare *tr* to disarrange; to upset

scómbro *m* mackerel

scombù·glio *m* (-gli) (coll) disorder
scombussolare (scombùssolo) *tr* to up-set
scomméssa *f* bet, wager
scomméttere §198 *tr* to bet; to separate
scommetti·tóre -trice *mf* bettor
scomodare (scòmodo) *tr* to trouble, disturb || *ref* to take the trouble
scomodi·tà *f* (-tà) trouble, inconvenience
scòmo·do -da *adj* awkward, unwieldy; uncomfortable || *m* inconvenience
scompaginare (scompàgino) *tr* to up-set; (typ) to pi
scompagna·to -ta *adj* odd
scomparire §108 *intr* (ESSERE) to dis-appear; to make a bad showing
scompar·so -sa *adj* disappeared; extinct || *mf* deceased || *f* disappearance; death
scompartiménto *m* compartment; par-tition
scompènso *m* lack of compensation; imbalance
scompigliare §280 *tr* to disarray; to trouble, upset
scompì·glio *m* (-gli) disarray; upset
scompisciare §128 *tr* (vulg) to piss on || *ref* (vulg) to wet oneself; **scom-pisciarsi dalle risa** (coll) to split one's sides laughing
scomplè·to -ta *adj* incomplete
scompórre §218 *tr* to decompose, dis-integrate; to rumple; to dishevel; to upset; to dismantle, take apart; (typ) to pi || *ref* to lose one's composure
scompó·sto -sta *adj* unseemly
scomùni·ca *f* (-che) excommunication
scomunicare §197 (scomùnico) *tr* to ex-communicate; (joc) to ostracize
sconcertare (sconcèrto) *tr* to upset; to disconcert || *ref* to become disconcerted
sconcézza *f* obscenity, indecency
scón·cio -cia (-ci -ce) *adj* dirty, filthy, obscene || *m* obscenity; shame
sconclusiona·to -ta *adj* inconsequential; incoherent; rambling
sconcordanza *f* disagreement; (gram) lack of agreement
scondi·to -ta *adj* unseasoned
sconfessare (sconfèsso) *tr* to disavow; to retract
sconfessióne *f* disavowal
sconfìggere §104 *tr* to defeat, rout; to pull (*a nail*); to unfasten
sconfinare *intr* to cross the border; **sconfinare da** to stray from
sconfina·to -ta *adj* boundless, unlimited
sconfitta *f* defeat, rout
sconfortante *adj* discouraging
sconfortare (sconfòrto) *tr* to discour-age; to distress || *ref* to become dis-couraged
sconfòrto *m* depression; distress
scongelare (scongèlo) *tr* to thaw
scongiurare *tr* to conjure; to implore
scongiuro *m* conjuration; entreaty
sconnès·so -sa *adj* disconnected; inco-herent
sconnèttere §107 *tr* to disconnect; to take apart || *intr* to be incoherent

sconoscènte *adj* unappreciative
sconosciu·to -ta *adj* unknown || *mf* stranger
sconquassare *tr* to smash, shatter
sconquassa·to -ta *adj* broken-down; upset
sconquasso *m* destruction; confusion; smash-up
sconsacrare *tr* to desecrate
sconsideratézza *f* thoughtlessness
sconsidera·to -ta *adj* inconsiderate
sconsigliare §280 *tr* to dissuade, dis-courage
sconsiglia·to -ta *adj* thoughtless
sconsola·to -ta *adj* disconsolate
scontare (scónto) *tr* to expiate; to dis-count; to serve (*time in jail*)
scontentare (scontènto) *tr* to dissatisfy
scontèn·to -ta *adj & m* discontent
scónto *m* discount; part payment; (fig) partial remission
scontrare (scóntro) *tr* to meet; (naut) to turn (*the wheel*) sharply || *ref* to clash; to collide; to come to blows
scontrino *m* check, ticket
scóntro *m* collision; battle, encounter; clash; ward (*of key*)
scontró·so -sa [s] *adj* peevish, cross
sconveniènte *adj* unfavorable; un-seemly, unbecoming; indecent
sconvenire §282 *intr* (ESSERE) to be un-seemly or unbecoming
sconvòlgere §289 *tr* to upset; to dis-concert
sconvolgiménto *m* upsetting; **sconvolgi-mento di stomaco** stomach upset; **sconvolgimento tellurico** upheaval
sconvòl·to -ta *adj* upset; disconcerted; distracted
scópa *f* broom; **scopa per lavaggio** mop
scopare (scópo) *tr* to sweep
scopata *f* sweep
scoperchiare §287 (scopèrchio) *tr* to uncover; to take the lid off
scopèr·to -ta *adj* uncovered; open; bare; exposed; unpaid || *m* open ground; open air; overdraft; (econ) short sale; (com) balance; **allo scoperto** in the open; overdrawn (*check*); short (*sale*) || *f* discovery; **alla scoperta** openly
scòpo *m* purpose, goal, aim
scoppiare §287 (scòppio) *tr* to uncouple || *intr* (ESSERE) to burst; to blow; to explode; to break (*said, e.g., of news*); (fig) to die (*e.g., of over-eating*); **scoppiare a** to burst out (*laughing or crying*)
scoppiettare (scoppiétto) *intr* to crackle
scoppiettì·o *m* (-ìi) crackle
scòp·pio *m* (-pi) burst; explosion; out-break; outburst; blowout (*of tire*); **a scoppio** internal-combustion (*en-gine*); **scoppio di tuono** clap of thunder
scòppola *f* drop (*of plane in air pocket*); (coll) rabbit punch
scopriménto *m* uncovering; unveiling
scoprire §110 *tr* to uncover; to unveil; to discover; to expose || *ref* to take off one's clothes; to take one's hat off; to reveal oneself

scopri•tóre -trice *mf* discoverer
scoraggiaménto *m* discouragement
scoraggiante *adj* discouraging
scoraggiare §290 *tr* to discourage, dishearten ‖ *ref* to be or become discouraged
scoraménto *m* (lit) discouragement
scorbuto *m* scurvy
scorciare §128 (scórcio) *tr* to shorten; to foreshorten ‖ *intr* (ESSERE) to shorten, grow shorter; to look foreshortened ‖ *ref* to shorten, grow shorter
scorciatóia *f* shortcut, cutoff
scór•cio *m* (-ci) foreshortening; end, close (*of a period*); **di scorcio** foreshortened
scordare (scòrdo) *tr* to forget; to put out of tune ‖ *ref* to forget; to get out of tune
scorég•gia *f* (-ge) (vulg) fart
scoreggiare §290 (scoréggio) *intr* (vulg) to fart
scòrgere §249 *tr* to perceive, to discern
scòria *f* slag, dross; (fig) scum, dregs; **scorie atomiche** atomic waste
scorna•to -ta *adj* humiliated, ridiculed; hornless
scòrno *m* humiliation, ridicule
scorpacciata *f* bellyful; **fare una scorpacciata di** to stuff oneself with
scorpióne *m* scorpion ‖ **Scorpione** *m* (astrol) Scorpio
scorrazzare *tr* to wander over ‖ *intr* to run around; to move about; (fig) to ramble; (mil) to raid
scórrere §139 *tr* to raid; to glance over ‖ *intr* (ESSERE) to flow; to run; to glide
scorrerìa *f* raid, foray, incursion
scorrettézza *f* imprecision; impropriety
scorrèt•to -ta *adj* incorrect; improper
scorrévole *adj* sliding; flowing, fluent ‖ *m* slide (*of slide rule*)
scorribanda *f* raid, foray, incursion
scór•so -sa *adj* past, last ‖ *m* error, slip ‖ *f* glance; short stay
scor•sóio -sóia *adj* (-sói -sóie) slip (*knot*)
scòrta *f* escort; provision, stock; **di scorta** spare (*tire*); **fare di scorta a** to escort; **scorta d'onore** (mil) honor guard; **scorte** (com) stockpile; (com) supplies; **scorte morte** agricultural supplies; **scorte vive** livestock
scortare (scòrto) *tr* to escort; to foreshorten
scortecciare §128 (scortéccio) *tr* to strip the bark from; to peel off; to scrape ‖ *ref* to peel off
scortése *adj* discourteous, impolite
scortesìa *f* discourtesy, impoliteness
scorticare §197 (scórtico) *tr* to skin; to be overdemanding with (*students*); to fleece ‖ *ref* to skin (*e.g., one's arm*)
scòrza *f* bark; skin, hide; (fig) appearance; **scorza di limone** lemon peel
scoscendiménto *m* landslide; cliff
scoscé•so -sa [s] *adj* sloping, steep
scòssa *f* shake; jerk; **scossa di pioggia**

downpour; **scossa di terremoto** earth tremor; **scossa elettrica** electric shock; **scossa tellurica** earthquake
scossóne *m* jolt, jerk
scostaménto *m* removal; separation
scostare (scòsto) *tr* to move away; to try to avoid ‖ *intr* (ESSERE) to stand away ‖ *ref* to step aside; to stray
scostuma•to -ta *adj* dissolute, debauched
scotennare (scoténno) *tr* to scalp; to skin (*an animal*)
scòtta *f* whey; (naut) sheet
scottante *adj* burning (*question*); outrageous (*offense*)
scottare (scòtto) *tr* to burn; to scald; to sear; to boil (*eggs*); (fig) to sting ‖ *intr* to burn; to be hot (*said of stolen goods*) ‖ *ref* to get burnt
scottatura *f* burn; (fig) blow, jolt
scòt•to -ta *adj* overcooked, overdone ‖ *m*—**pagare lo scotto** to foot the bill; **pagare lo scotto di** to expiate ‖ *f* see **scotta**
scoutismo *m* scouting
scovare (scóvo) *tr* to rouse (*game*); to find, discover
scovolino *m* pipe cleaner; (mil) small swab
scóvolo *m* (mil) swab
scòzia *f* (archit) scotia ‖ **la Scozia** Scotland
scozzése [s] *adj* Scotch, Scottish ‖ *m* Scotch, Scottish (*language*); Scotchman ‖ *f* Scotchwoman
scozzonare (scozzóno) *tr* to break in (*a horse*); to train
scranna *f* (hist) seat
screanza•to -ta *adj* ill-mannered, rude
screditare (scrédito) *tr* to discredit
scremare (scrèmo) *tr* to cream
scrematrice *f* cream separator
screpolare (scrèpolo) *tr*, *intr* (ESSERE), & *ref* to crack; to chap
screpolatura *f* crack; chap (*of skin*)
screziare §287 (scrèzio) *tr* to mottle, variegate
scrè•zio *m* (-zi) tiff
scri•ba *m* (-bi) scribe (*Jewish scholar*)
scribacchiare §287 *tr* to scribble, scrawl
scribacchino *m* scribbler; hack
scricchiolare (scrìcchiolo) *intr* to crack, creak
scricchiolì•o *m* (-i) crack, creak
scrìcciolo *m* wren
scrigno *m* jewel box
scriminatura *f* part (*in hair*)
scrit•to -ta *adj* written ‖ *m* writing ‖ *f* sign; inscription; contract; **scritta luminosa** electric sign
scrit•tóio *m* (-tói) writing desk
scrit•tóre -trice *mf* writer
scrittura *f* handwriting; penmanship; writing; contract; entry; (theat) booking; **Sacra Scrittura** Holy Scripture; **scrittura privata** contract; **scrittura pubblica** deed, indenture; **scrittura a macchina** typing
scritturale *adj* scriptural ‖ *m* clerk; copyist; fundamentalist
scritturare *tr* (theat) to book, engage
scrivanìa *f* desk

scrivano *m* clerk, copyist, typist
scrìvere §250 *tr* & *intr* to write; **scrivere a macchina** to type
scroccare §197 (**scròcco**) *tr* to sponge (*a meal*); to manage to get (*a prize*) || *intr* to sponge
scrocca·tóre -trice *mf* sponger
scròc·co *m* (-chi) sponging; creaking; **a scrocco** sponging; spring (*lock*); switchblade (*knife*)
scroccó·ne -na *mf* sponger
scròfa *f* sow; slut
scrollare (**scròllo**) *tr* to shake; to shrug (*one's shoulders*) || *ref* to get into action; to pull oneself together
scrollata *f* shake; **scrollata di spalle** shrug
scrosciare §128 (**scròscio**) *intr* (ESSERE & AVERE) to pelt down; (fig) to thunder
scrò·scio *m* (-sci) thunder, roar; **scroscio di pioggia** downpour; **scroscio di tuono** thunderclap
scrostare (**scròsto**) *tr* to pick (*a scab*); to scrape; to peel off || *ref* to peel off
scrosta·to -ta *adj* peeling; scaly
scròto *m* scrotum
scrùpolo *m* scruple; scrupulousness
scrupoló·so -sa [s] *adj* scrupulous
scrutare *tr* to scan, scrutinize
scruta·tóre -trice *adj* inquisitive || *mf* teller (*of votes*)
scrutina·tóre -trice *mf* teller (*of votes*)
scrutì·nio *m* (-ni) poll, vote; evaluation (*of an examination*); count (*of votes*); **scrutinio segreto** secret ballot
scucire §143 *tr* to unstitch; (coll) to cough up || *ref* to come unstitched
scucitura *f* unstitching; rip
scuderìa *f* stable
scudétto *m* badge; escutcheon; (sports) badge of victory
scudièro *m* esquire
scudisciare §128 *tr* to whip
scudì·scio *m* (-sci) whip
scudo *m* shield; escutcheon; **far scudo a** to shield
scùffia *f* (coll) load (*intoxication*); **fare scuffia** to capsize; **prendersi una scuffia per** to fall for, to fall in love with
scugnizzo *m* Neapolitan urchin
sculacciare §128 *tr* to spank
sculacciata *f* spank, spanking
sculaccióne *m* spank, spanking
sculettare (**sculétto**) *intr* to waddle
scul·tóre -trice *mf* sculptor || *f* sculptress
scultura *f* sculpture
scuòla *f* school; **scuola allievi ufficiali** military academy; officers' candidate school; **scuola dell'obbligo** mandatory education; **scuola di danza** dancing school; **scuola di dressaggio** obedience school (*for dogs*); **scuola di guerra** war college; **scuola di guida** driving school; **scuola di perfezionamento per laureati** postgraduate school; **scuola di taglio** sewing school; **scuola materna** kindergarten; **scuola mista** coeducational school

scuòla·bus *m* (-bus) school bus
scuòtere §251 *tr* to shake; to shake up; **scuotere di dosso** to shake off
scure *f* ax; cleaver
scurire §176 *tr, intr* (ESSERE), & *ref* to darken
scu·ro -ra *adj* dark || *m* darkness; dark; shutter; **essere allo scuro** to be in the dark
scurrile *adj* scurrilous
scusa *f* excuse; apology; pretext; **chiedere scusa** to apologize
scusare *tr* to excuse; to pardon; to apologize for; **scusi!** pardon me! || *ref* to apologize; to beg off
sdaziare §287 *tr* to clear through customs
sdebitare (**sdébito**) *tr* to free from debt || *ref* to become free of debt; **sdebitarsi con** to repay a favor to
sdegnare (**sdégno**) *tr* to scorn; to arouse, enrage || *ref* to get mad
sdégno *m* indignation, anger; (lit) scorn
sdegnó·so -sa [s] *adj* indignant; haughty
sdenta·to -ta *adj* toothless
sdilinquire §176 *tr* to weaken || *intr* (ESSERE) & *ref* to swoon; to become mawkish
sdoganare *tr* to clear through customs
sdolcina·to -ta *adj* mawkish
sdolcinatura *f* mush, slobber
sdoppiare §287 (**sdóppio**) *tr* & *ref* to split
sdoppiaménto *m* splitting
sdottoreggiare §290 (**sdottoréggio**) *intr* to pontificate
sdràia *f* chaise longue; deck chair
sdraiare §287 *tr* to lay down || *ref* to stretch out (*e.g., on the ground*)
sdràio *m* (sdrài) stretching out; **mettersi a sdraio** to lie down
sdrucciolare (**sdrùcciolo**) *intr* (ESSERE & AVERE) to slip, slide
sdrucciolévole *adj* slippery
sdrùccio·lo -la *adj* proparoxytone || *m* slip; slope; proparoxytone
sdrucciolóni *adv* slipping, sliding
sdrucire (**sdrùcio**) & §176 *tr* to tear, rend, rip
sdrucitura *f* tear, rend, rip
se *m* (se) if || §5 *pron* || *conj* if; whether; **se mai** in the event; **se no** otherwise; **se non tu** (lui, lei, etc.) nobody else but you (him, her, etc.), e.g., **non puoi essere stato se non tu** it could not have been anyone else but you; **se non altro** at least; **se non che** but; **se pure** even if
sé §5 *pron* himself; herself; itself; yourself; themselves; yourselves; oneself; **di per sé stesso** by itself; **fuori di sé** beside oneself; **rientrare in sé** to come back to one's senses; **uscire di sé** to be beside oneself
sebbène *conj* although, though
sèbo *m* sebum, tallow
séc·ca *f* (-che) sand bank, shoal; drought; **dare in secca** to run aground; **in secca** hard up
seccante *adj* drying; annoying
seccare §197 (**sécco**) *tr* to dry; to bore;

to bother, annoy || *intr* (ESSERE) to dry up || *ref* to dry up; to be annoyed

secca·tóio *m* (-tói) drying room; squeegee (*to remove water from wet decks*)

secca·tóre -trice *mf* bore, pest

seccatura *f* drying; trouble, nuisance

sécchia *f* bucket, pail; **piovere a secchie** to rain cats and dogs

secchièllo *m* little bucket

séc·chio *m* (-chi) bucket, pail; bucketful; **secchio dell'immondezza** trash can

séc·co -ca (-chi -che) *adj* dry; lanky; sharp || *m* dryness; dry land; drought; **a secco** dry (*cleaning*); **dare in secco** to run aground; **in secco** hard up; **lavare a secco** to dry-clean || *f* see **secca**

secenté-sco -sca *adj* (-schi -sche) seventeenth-century

secentèsi·mo -ma *adj, m & pron* six hundredth

secèrnere §153 (*pp* **secrèto**) *tr* to secrete

secessióne *f* secession

séco §5 *prep phrase* (lit) with oneself; along, e.g., **portare seco** to bring along

secolare *adj* secular; century-old; worldly || *m* layman

sècolo *m* century; age; world

secónda *f* second; second-year class; **a seconda** with the wind; **a seconda di** according to; **in seconda** (aut) in second; (mil) second in command

secondare (**secóndo**) *tr* to second

secondà·rio -ria *adj* (-ri -rie) secondary

secondino *m* prison guard, turnkey

secón·do -da *adj* second; (lit) favorable || *m* second; second course; (nav) executive officer || *f* see **seconda** || *pron* second || **secondo** *prep* according to; **secondo me (te, etc.)** in my (your, etc.) opinion

secondogèni·to -ta *adj* second-born

secrezióne *f* secretion

sèdano *m* celery

sedare (**sèdo**) *tr* to calm, placate

sedati·vo -va *adj & m* sedative

sède *f* seat; branch; residence; period; (gram) syllable; (rr) right of way; **in separata sede** in private; (law) with change of venue; **Santa Sede** Holy See; **sede centrale** main office, home office

sedentà·rio -ria *adj* (-ri -rie) sedentary || *m* sedentary person

sedére *m* sitting; rear, backside || *v* §252 *intr* (ESSERE) to sit, to be seated; to be in session; to be located || *ref* to sit down

sèdia *f* chair; seat; see; **sedia a braccioli** armchair; **sedia a dondolo** rocking chair; **sedia a pozzetto** bucket seat; **sedia a sdraio** deck chair; **sedia da posta** (hist) mail coach; **sedia di vimini** wicker chair; **sedia elettrica** electric chair; **sedia girevole** swivel chair

sedicènne *adj* sixteen-year-old || *mf* sixteen-year-old person

sedicènte *adj* so-called, self-styled

sedicèsi·mo -ma *adj, m & pron* sixteenth

sédici *adj & pron* sixteen; **le sedici** four P.M. || *m* sixteen; sixteenth (*in dates*)

sedile *m* seat; bench; bottom (*of chair*); (aut) bucket seat

sediménto *m* sediment

sediòlo *m* sulky

sedizióne *f* sedition

sedizió·so -sa [s] *adj* seditious

seducènte *adj* seductive; alluring

sedurre §102 *tr* to seduce; to allure; to lead astray; to charm, captivate

seduta *f* sitting; session, meeting; **seduta fiume** (pol) uninterrupted session; **seduta stante** on the spot

sedut·tóre -trice *adj* seductive; alluring; charming || *mf* seducer

seduzióne *f* seduction; allurement; charm

sefardi·ta (-ti -te) *adj* Sephardic || *mf* Sephardi

sé·ga *f* (-ghe) saw; **a sega** serrated; **sega a nastro** band saw; **sega circolare** buzz saw; **sega da carpentiere** lumberman's saw; **sega intelaiata a lama** bucksaw; **sega meccanica** power saw

ségala *f* rye

segali·gno -gna *adj* rye; lean, wiry

segare §209 (**ségo**) *tr* to saw; to cut

segatrice *f* power saw; **segatrice a disco** circular saw; **segatrice a nastro** band saw

segatura *f* cutting; sawdust

seggétta *f* commode

sèg·gio *m* (-gi) seat (*e.g., in congress*); **seggio elettorale** voting commission

sèggiola *f* chair; **seggiola a sdraio** deck chair

seggiolino *m* child's chair; stool; bucket seat; **seggiolino eiettabile** (aer) ejection seat

seggiolóne *m* highchair; easy chair

seggiovìa *f* chair lift

segherìa *f* sawmill

seghetta·to -ta *adj* serrated

seghétto *m* hacksaw; **seghetto da traforo** coping saw

segménto *m* segment; **segmento elastico** (aut) piston ring

segnaccénto *m* accent mark

segnàcolo *m* (lit) symbol, sign

segnalare *tr* to signal; to point out || *ref* to distinguish oneself

segnalazióne *f* signaling; sign, signal; nomination; recommendation; **dare la segnalazione a** to notify; **fare segnalazioni** to signal; **segnalazioni stradali** road signs

segnale *m* sign; signal; bookmark; **segnale di allarme** (mil) alarm; **segnale di occupato** (telp) busy signal; **segnale di via libera** (telp) dial tone; **segnale orario** (rad, telv) time signal; **segnali stradali** road signs

segnalèti·co -ca *adj* (-ci -che) identification (*mark*) || *f* road signs

segnalibro *m* bookmark

segnalìne·e *m* (-e) lineman

segnapósto *m* place card

segnapun·ti *m* (-ti) scorekeeper

segnare (ségno) *tr* to mark; to underscore, underline; to jot down; to say (*e.g., five o'clock, said of a watch*); to brand; (sports) to score; segnare a dito to point to || *ref* to cross oneself

segnatas·se *m* (-se) postage-due stamp

segnatura *f* signing; signature; library number; (eccl) chancery; (sports) final score; (typ) signature

segnavèn·to *m* (-to) weather vane

ségno *m* mark; bookmark; symbol; sign; signal; boundary; (mus) signature; a segno che so that; a tal segno to such a point; essere fatto segno di to be the target of; in segno di as a token of; mettere a segno to check, control; segno della Croce sign of the Cross; segno di croce cross (*mark*); segno d'interpunzione, or di punteggiatura, or grafico punctuation mark; segno di riconoscimento identification mark

ségo *m* tallow, suet

segregare §209 (sègrego) *tr* to segregate; to secrete || *ref* to withdraw

segregazióne *f* segregation; segregazione cellulare solitary confinement

segregazioni·sta *mf* (-sti -ste) segregationist

segretariato *m* secretariat

segretà·rio -ria *mf* secretary; clerk

segreterìa *f* secretary's office; secretaryship

segretézza *f* secrecy

segré·to -ta *adj* secret; secretive || *m* secret; secrecy; segreto d'alcova boudoir secret; segreto di Pulcinella open secret

seguace *mf* follower

seguènte *adj* following, next

segù·gio *m* (-gi) bloodhound; (fig) private eye

seguire (séguo) *tr* to follow; to attend || *intr* (ESSERE) to continue; to follow, ensue; (with *dat*) to follow

seguitare (séguito) *intr*—seguitare a + *inf* to keep on + *ger*, e.g., seguitare a parlare to keep on talking; seguiti! go ahead!

séguito *m* following; retinue; followers; sequence; sequel; pursuit; di seguito in succession; far seguito a to refer to; in seguito thereafter; in seguito a as a consequence of

sèi *adj* & *pron* six; le sei six o'clock || *m* six; sixth (*in dates*)

seicènto *adj, m* & *pron* six hundred || *f* car with a motor displacing 600 cubic centimeters || il Seicento the seventeenth century

seimila *adj, m,* & *pron* six thousand

sélce *f* silica; flint; (lit) stone; selci paving blocks

selciare §128 (sélcio) *tr* to pave

selcia·to -ta *adj* paved || *m* paving

seletti·vo -va *adj* selective

selezionare (selezióno) *tr* to select, sort out

selezióne *f* selection; choice

sèlla *f* saddle

sel·làio *m* (-lài) saddler

sellare (sèllo) *tr* to saddle

sellerìa *f* saddler's shop; saddlery; (aut) upholstery

sélva *f* woods, forest

selvaggina *f* game

selvàg·gio -gia (-gi -ge) *adj* savage; vicious (*horse*) || *m* savage; unsociable person

selvàti·co -ca *adj* (-ci -che) wild

selvicoltura *f* forestry

sèlz *m* (sèlz) seltzer, club soda

semàforo *m* traffic light; semaphore

semànti·co -ca (-ci -che) *adj* semantic || *f* semantics

sembiante *m* (lit) look; fare sembianti di to pretend

sembianza *f* look; (lit) similarity

sembrare (sémbro) *intr* (ESSERE) to seem, look, appear || *impers*—sembra it seems

séme *m* seed; stone (*of fruit*); (cards) suit

seménta *f* sowing season; (lit) seed

seménte *f* seed

semènza *f* seed; brads (*used in upholstery*)

semenzà·io *m* (-zài) hotbed, seedbed

semestrale *adj* semiannual, semiyearly

semèstre *m* semester; half year

sèmi- *pref adj* semi-, e.g., semicircolare semicircular; half-, e.g., semichiuso half-closed || *pref mf* semi-, e.g., semicerchio semicircle; half, e.g., semitono half tone; demi-, e.g., semidio demigod

semiapèr·to -ta *adj* half-open; ajar

semiasse *m* (mach) axle (*on each side of differential*)

semicér·chio *m* (-chi) semicircle

semichiu·so -sa [s] *adj* half-closed

semicingola·to -ta *adj* & *m* half-track

semicìrcolo *m* semicircle

semiconduttóre *m* semiconductor

semiconvit·tóre -trice *mf* day student

semicù·pio *m* (-pi) sitz bath

semi·dìo *m* (-dèi) demigod

semidòt·to -ta *adj* semilearned

semifinale *f* semifinal

sémina *f* sowing; sowing season

seminare (sémino) *tr* to sow, seed; to plant; (coll) to leave behind

seminà·rio *m* (-ri) seminary; seminar

seminari·sta *m* (-sti) seminarian

semina·to -ta *adj* sown, seeded || *m* sown land; uscire dal seminato to digress

semina·tóre -trice *mf* sower || *f* (mach) seeder, seeding machine

seminterrato *m* basement

seminu·do -da *adj* half-naked

semioscurità *f* partial darkness

semirìgi·do -da *adj* semirigid; inelastic

semirimòr·chio *m* (-chi) semitrailer

semisè·rio -ria [s] *adj* (-ri -rie) seriocomic

semisfèra *f* (geom) hemisphere

semi·ta (-ti -te) *adj* Semitic || *mf* Semite

semitòno *m* (mus) semitone, half tone

semmài *conj* if ever; in the event that

sémola *f* bran; (coll) freckles

semolino *m* semolina

semovènte *adj* self-propelled

sempitèr·no -na *adj* (lit) everlasting
sémplice *adj* simple; single; plain; mere; (mil) private; (nav) ordinary ‖ *m* medicinal herb; **semplici** simple folk
semplició·ne -na *adj* simple ‖ *mf* simpleton
semplici·tà *f* (-tà) simplicity
semplificare §197 (**semplìfico**) *tr* to simplify ‖ *ref* to become easier or simpler
sèmpre *adv* always; ever; yet; **da sempre** from time immemorial; **di sempre** same, same old; **e poi sempre** ever and ever; **ma sempre** but only; **per sempre** forever; **sempre che** provided; **sempre meglio** better and better; **sempre meno** less and less; **sempre però** but only; **sempre vostro** very truly yours
semprevérde *adj, m & f* evergreen
sènape *f* mustard
senapismo *m* mustard plaster
senato *m* senate
sena·tóre -trice *mf* senator
senése [s] *adj & mf* Sienese
senile *adj* old; of old age
senilismo *m* (pathol) senility
senilità *f* old age
senióre *adj & m* elder, senior
Sènna *f* Seine
sénno *m* wisdom; **far senno** to come back to one's senses; **senno di poi** hindsight; **uscir di senno** to go out of one's mind
séno *m* chest; breast, bosom; cove; (anat) sinus; (math) sine; (fig) heart; **in seno a** within
senonché or **se non che** *conj* but
sensale *m* broker; commission merchant
sensa·to -ta *adj* sensible, reasonable; sane
sensazionale *adj* sensational
sensazióne *f* sensation
sensibile *adj* sensible; perceptible; appreciable; sensitive; responsive (*e.g., to affection*) ‖ *m* world of the senses
sensibili·tà *f* (-tà) sensitivity; sensibility
sensibilizzare [ddzz] *tr* to sensitize
sensiti·vo -va *adj* sensitive ‖ *m* medium
sènso *m* sense; feeling; meaning; aspect; tone, fashion; direction; **ai sensi di legge** according to law; **a senso** free (*translation*); **doppio senso** double entendre; **in senso contrario** in the opposite direction; **perdere i sensi** to lose consciousness; **riprendere i sensi** to come to; **sensi** carnal appetite, flesh; **senso unico** one-way; **senso vietato** no entry, one-way
sensò·rio -ria *adj* (-ri -rie) sensory
sensuale *adj* sensual, carnal; sensuous
sensualità *f* sensuality
sentènza *f* sentence; maxim
sentenziare §287 (**sentènzio**) *tr* to pass sentence upon, sentence ‖ *intr* to pontificate
sentenzió·so -sa [s] *adj* sententious
sentièro *m* path, pathway
sentimentale *adj* sentimental; mawkish
sentimentalismo *m* sentimentalism
sentiménto *m* feeling; sentiment; sense;

uscire di sentimento (coll) to go out of one's mind
sentina *f* bilge; sink (*of vice*)
sentinèlla *f* sentry, sentinel
sentire *m* feeling ‖ *v* (**sènto**) *tr* to feel; to hear; to listen to; to consult (*a doctor*); to smell; to taste **farsi sentire** to make oneself heard ‖ *intr* to feel; to listen; to smell; to taste; **non sentirci di quell'orecchio** to turn a deaf ear; **sentirci bene** to have keen hearing ‖ *ref* to feel; **non sentirsela di** to not have the courage to; **sentirsela** to feel up to it
senti·to -ta *adj* heartfelt
sentóre *m* inkling, feeling; sign; (lit) smell
sènza *prep* without; beyond (*e.g., comparison*); **senza** + *inf* without + *ger;* **senza che** + *subj* without + *ger;* **senza di** + *pron* without + *pron,* e.g., **senza di lui** without him; **senz'altro** without any doubt, of course
senza·dìo *m* (-dìo)—**i senzadio** the godless
senzapà·tria *m* (-tria) man without a country; renegade
senzatét·to *m* (-to) homeless person; **i senzatetto** the homeless
separare *tr & ref* to separate
separazióne *f* separation
sepolcrale *adj* sepulchral
sepolcréto *m* cemetery
sepólcro *m* sepulcher, grave
sepoltura *f* burial; grave
seppellire §253 *tr* to bury
séppia *adj invar* sepia ‖ *f* cuttlefish
seppure *conj* even if
sè·psi *f* (-psi) sepsis
sequèla *f* series
sequènza *f* sequence
sequestrare (**sequèstro**) *tr* to seize, confiscate; to kidnap; to confine; to quarantine; (law) to attach, sequester
sequèstro *m* seizure; attachment; **sequestro di persona** unlawful detention
séra *f* evening; night; **da mezza sera** cocktail (*dress*); dark (*suit*); **da sera** evening (*gown*); formal (*attire*)
serac·co *m* (-chi) serac
serafino *m* seraph
serale *adj* evening; night
seralménte *adv* in the evening; every evening
serata *f* evening; soiree, evening party; **serata d'addio** (theat) farewell performance; **di beneficenza** benefit performance
serbare (**sèrbo**) *tr* to keep; to save (*e.g., a place*); to bear (*a grudge*) ‖ *ref* to keep oneself; to stay
serba·tóio *m* (-tói) tank; reservoir; cartridge clip
sèr·bo -ba *adj & mf* Serbian ‖ *m*—**in serbo** in store
serbocroa·to -ta *adj & mf* Serbo-Croatian
serenata *f* serenade
serenìssi·mo -ma *adj* Serene (*Highness*)
sereni·tà *f* (-tà) serenity

seré·no -na *adj* serene; clear, fair (*weather*)

sergènte *m* sergeant; carpenter's clamp; sergente maggiore first sergeant

sèri·co -ca *adj* (-ci -che) silk

sè·rie *f* (-rie) series; (sports) division; fuori serie (aut) custom-built; in serie (aut) standard; (elec) in series

serietà *f* seriousness; gravity

serigrafìa *f* silkscreen process

sè·rio -ria (-ri -rie) *adj* serious; stern; poco serio unreliable (*man*); loose (*woman*) || *m* seriousness; sul serio in earnest; really, e.g., bello sul serio really beautiful

sermonare (sermóno) *tr & intr* (lit) to sermonize

sermóne *m* sermon

sermoneggiare §290 (sermonéggio) *intr* to preach; to lecture

seròti·no -na *adj* late; (lit) evening

sèrpa *f* coach box

sèrpe *f* snake, serpent; a serpe coiled, in a coil; nutrirsi or scaldarsi la serpe in seno to nourish a viper in one's bosom

serpeggiare §290 (serpéggio) *intr* to zigzag; to wind; to creep, spread

serpènte *m* snake, serpent; serpente a sonagli rattlesnake

serpenti·no -na *adj* serpentine || *m* serpentine; coil (*of pipe*) || *f* zigzag, turn (*of winding road*); coil (*of pipe*)

sérqua *f* dozen; lot, large number

sèrra *f* dike, levee; hothouse; sierra; un serra serra a milling crowd

serrafi·la *m* (-le) rear-guard soldier || *f* rear ship (*of convoy*)

serrafilo *m* electrician's pliers; (elec) binding post

serrà·glio *m* (-gli) menagerie; seraglio

serramànico *m*—a serramanico clasp (*knife*); switchblade (*knife*)

serrame *m* lock

serraménto *m* closing, bolting || serra·mén·ti & -ta *fpl* closing devices, doors, windows, and shutters

serranda *f* shutter (*of store*)

serrare (sèrro) *tr* to shut, close; to pursue (*the enemy*); to increase (*tempo*); to furl (*sails*); to lock; to clench (*one's teeth, one's fists*); to shake (*hands*) || *intr* to shut; to be tight || *ref* to be wrenched, e.g., gli si serrò il cuore his heart was wrenched; serrarsi addosso a to press (*the enemy*)

serrata *f* lockout

serrate *m*—serrate finale (sports) finish

serra·to -ta *adj* shut (*e.g., door*); concise (*style*); tight (*game*); rapid (*gallop*); closed (*ranks*); thick (*crowd*) || *f* see serrata

serratura *f* lock

sèrto *m* (poet) crown, wreath

sèrva *f* (pej) maidservant, maid

servènte *adj* (*gentleman*) in waiting || *m* gunner; (obs) servant

servìbile *adj* usable

serviènte *m* (eccl) server

servì·gio *m* (-gi) service; favor

servile *adj* servile; menial; modal (*auxiliary*)

servire (sèrvo) *tr* to serve; to wait on; in che posso servirLa what can I do for you?; may I help you?; per servirLa at your service || *intr* to serve || *intr* (ESSERE & AVERE) to serve; to answer the purpose; to last; (with *dat*) (coll) to need, e.g., gli serve il martello he needs the hammer; non servire a nulla to be of no use; servire da to act as || *ref* to help oneself; servirsi da to patronize, deal with; servirsi di to avail oneself of, use

servitóre *m* servant; tea wagon; servitor suo umilissimo your humble servant

servi·tù *f* (-tù) servitude; captivity; servants, help; servitù di passaggio (law) easement

serviziévole *adj* obliging, accommodating

servì·zio *m* (-zi) service; favor; turn; a mezzo servizio part-time (*domestic help*); di servizio delivery (*entrance*); for hire (*car*); domestic (*help*); fuori servizio out of commission; in servizio in commission; servizi kitchen and bath; facilities; servizi pubblici public services; public works; servizio attivo active duty; servizio permanente effettivo service in the regular army

sèr·vo -va *adj* (lit) enslaved || *m* slave; servant; servo della gleba serf || *f* see serva

servoassisti·to -ta *adj* servocontrolled

servofréno *m* (aut) power brake

servomotóre *m* servomotor

servostèrzo *m* (aut) power steering

sèsamo *m* sesame; apriti sesamo! open sesame!

sessanta *adj, m & pron* sixty

sessantènne *adj* sixty-year-old || *mf* sixty-year-old person

sessantèsi·mo -ma *adj, m & pron* sixtieth

sessantina *f* about sixty

sessióne *f* session

sèsso *m* sex; il sesso debole the fair sex

sessuale *adj* sexual

sestante *m* sextant

sestétto *m* sextet

sestière *m* district, section

sè·sto -sta *adj & pron* sixth || *m* sixth; curve (*of an arch*); fuori sesto out of sorts; mettere in sesto to arrange; to set in order; sesto acuto (archit) ogive

sèt *m* (sèt) set; set all'aperto (mov) location

séta *f* silk; seta artificiale rayon

setacciare §128 *tr* to sift, sieve

setàc·cio *m* (-ci) sieve

setàce·o -a *adj* silky

séte *f* thirst; aver sete to be thirsty; to lust after; sete di thirst for

seterìa *f* silk mill; seterie silk goods

setifì·cio *m* (-ci) silk mill

sétola *f* bristle; (joc) stubble

sètta *f* sect

settanta *adj, m & pron* seventy

settantènne *adj* seventy-year-old || *mf* seventy-year-old person

settantèsi·mo -ma *adj, m & pron* seventieth

settantina _f_ about seventy
settà·rio -ria _adj_ & _mf_ (**-ri -rie**) sectarian
sètte _adj_ & _pron_ seven; **le sette** seven o'clock || _m_ seven; seventh (_in dates_); V-shaped tear (_in clothing_)
settecentèsi·mo -ma _adj, m_ & _pron_ seven hundredth
settecènto _adj, m_ & _pron_ seven hundred || **il Settecento** the eighteenth century
settèmbre _m_ September
settennale _adj_ seven-year (_e.g., plan_)
settènne _adj_ seven-year-old || _mf_ seven-year-old child
settentrionale _adj_ northern || _mf_ northerner
settentrióne _m_ north; (astr) Little Bear
setticemìa _f_ septicemia
sètti·co -ca _adj_ (**-ci -che**) septic
settimana _f_ week; week's wages; **settimana corta** five-day week
settimanale _adj_ & _m_ weekly
settimi·no -na _adj_ premature (_baby_) || _m_ (mus) septet
sètti·mo -ma _adj, m_ & _pron_ seventh
sètto _m_ septum
settóre _m_ sector; section, branch; dissector, anatomist; coroner's pathologist
sevè·ro -ra _adj_ severe, stern
seviziare §287 _tr_ to torture
sevìzie _fpl_ cruelty
sezionale _adj_ sectional
sezionare (**sezióno**) _tr_ to cut up; to divide up; to dissect
sezióne _f_ section; dissection; chapter (_of club_); department (_of agency_); (geom) cross section
sfaccenda·to -ta _adj_ loafing || _mf_ loafer
sfaccettare (**sfaccétto**) _tr_ to facet
sfacchinare _intr_ (coll) to toil, drudge
sfacchinata _f_ (coll) drudgery, grind
sfacciatàggine _f_ brazenness, impudence
sfaccia·to -ta _adj_ brazen, impudent; loud, gaudy; **fare lo sfacciato** to be fresh
sfacèlo _m_ breakdown, collapse
sfà·glio _m_ (**-gli**) swerve (_e.g., of horse_); (cards) discard
sfaldare _tr_ to exfoliate; to cut into slices || _ref_ to flake, scale; (fig) to collapse, crumble
sfamare _tr_ to feed (_the hungry; the family_) || _ref_ to get enough to eat
sfare §173 _tr_ to undo || _ref_ to spoil (_said, e.g., of meat_)
sfarzo _m_ pomp, display; luxury
sfarzó·so -sa [s] _adj_ sumptuous, luxurious
sfasare _tr_ to throw out of phase; (coll) to depress || _intr_ (ESSERE) (aut) to misfire; (elec) to be out of phase
sfasciare §128 _tr_ to remove the bandage from; to unswathe; to smash, shatter || _ref_ to go to pieces; to lose one's figure
sfatare _tr_ to discredit; to unmask
sfatica·to -ta _adj_ lazy || _mf_ loafer
sfat·to -ta _adj_ overdone; overripe; undone (_bed_); ravaged (_by age_)
sfavillare _intr_ to spark, sparkle
sfavóre _m_ disfavor

sfavorévole _adj_ unfavorable
sfebbra·to -ta _adj_ free of fever
sfegata·to -ta _adj_ (coll) rabid, fanatical
sfèra _f_ sphere; (coll) hand (_of clock_); **a sfera** ball-point (_pen_); **a sfere** ball (_bearing_); **sfera di cuoio** (sports) pigskin
sfèri·co -ca _adj_ (**-ci -che**) spherical
sferrare (**sfèrro**) _tr_ to unshoe (_a horse_); to unchain; to draw (_a weapon from a wound_); to deliver (_a blow_) || _ref_ to hurl oneself
sfèrza _f_ whip, scourge
sferzare (**sfèrzo**) _tr_ to whip, scourge
sfiancare §197 _tr_ to break open; to tire out; to fit (_clothes_) too tight || _ref_ to burst open; to get worn out
sfiatare _intr_ to leak (_said, e.g., of a tire_) || _intr_ (ESSERE) to leak (_said of air or gas_) || _ref_ to waste one's breath
sfiata·tóio _m_ (**-tói**) vent
sfibbiare §287 _tr_ to unbuckle, unfasten; to untie (_a knot_)
sfibrante _adj_ exhausting
sfibrare _tr_ to grind (_wood_) into fibers; to shred (_rags_) into fibers; to weaken, wear out
sfida _f_ challenge
sfidare _tr_ to challenge, dare; to brave, defy; to endure (_the challenge of time_); **sfidare che** to bet that
sfidù·cia _f_ (**-cie**) mistrust; (pol) no confidence
sfiducia·to -ta _adj_ downcast, depressed
sfigurare _tr_ to disfigure || _intr_ to make a bad impression; to lose face
sfilacciare §128 _tr_ & _ref_ to ravel, fray
sfilare _tr_ to unstring; to take off (_one's shoes_); to count (_beads_); to unthread; to dull (_a blade_); to ravel || _intr_ (ESSERE) to march, parade; to follow one another || _ref_ to become unthreaded; to become frayed; to run (_said of knitted work_); to break one's back
sfilata _f_ parade; row; **sfilata di moda** fashion show
sfilza _f_ row, sequence
sfinge _f_ sphinx
sfiniménto _m_ exhaustion
sfinire §176 _tr_ to exhaust, wear out || _ref_ to be worn out
sfintère _m_ sphincter
sfiorare (**sfióro**) _tr_ to graze; to barely touch (_a subject_); to skim; (lit) to barely reach
sfioratóre _m_ spillway
sfiorire §176 _intr_ (ESSERE) to wither, fade
sfit·to -ta _adj_ not rented
sfocare §197 (**sfòco**) _tr_ to put out of focus; to blur
sfociare §128 (**sfócio**) _tr_ to dredge (_the mouth of a river_) || _intr_ (ESSERE) to flow; **sfociare in** (fig) to lead to
sfoderare (**sfòdero**) _tr_ to unsheathe; to show off, sport, display; to take the cover or lining off || _intr_ to be drawn out
sfogare §209 (**sfógo**) _tr_ to vent, give vent to || _intr_ (ESSERE) to flow; to pour out; **sfogare in** to turn into || _ref_—**sfogarsi a** + _inf_ to have one's

fill of + *ger;* **sfogarsi con** to unburden oneself to; **sfogarsi su qlcu**
to take it out on s.o.
sfoga·tóio *m* (-tói) vent
sfoggiare §290 (sfòggio) *tr* to display,
sport; to show off
sfòg·gio *m* (-gi) display, ostentation
sfòglia *f* foil; skin (*of onion*); layer of
puff paste; (ichth) sole
sfogliare §280 (sfòglio) *tr* to pluck (*a
flower*); to defoliate (*a tree*); to leaf
through (*a book*); to deal (*cards*);
to husk (*corn*); to press (*dough*) into
layers || *ref* to shed its leaves; to
flake
sfogliata *f* defoliation; puff paste; **dare
una sfogliata a** to glance through
sfó·go *m* (-ghi) exhaust; outlet; vent;
(coll) eruption (*of skin*)
sfolgorare (sfólgoro) *intr* (ESSERE &
AVERE) to shine, blaze
sfolgorì·o *m* (-i) glittering, blazing
sfollagèn·te *m* (-te) billy
sfollaménto *m* evacuation; layoff
sfollare (sfòllo) *tr* to clear; to cut the
staff of || *intr* (ESSERE & AVERE) to
disperse, evacuate; to cut down the
staff
sfolla·to -ta *adj* driven from home ||
mf evacuee
sfoltire §176 *tr* to thin out
sfondare (sfóndo) *tr* to stave in; to
break through; to be heavy on (*the
stomach*) || *intr* to give || *ref* to
break open
sfóndo *m* background
sfondóne *m* (coll) blunder, error
sforbiciare §128 (sfòrbicio) *tr* to clip,
shear
sforbiciata *f* clipping; (sports) scissors;
(sports) scissors kick
sformare (sfórmo) *tr* to pull out of
shape; to take out of the mold ||
intr to get mad
sforma·to -ta *adj* out of shape || *m*
pudding
sfornare (sfórno) *tr* to take out of the
oven
sfornire §176 *tr* to deprive; to strip
sfortuna *f* bad luck, misfortune
sfortuna·to -ta *adj* unsuccessful; unlucky, unfortunate
sforzare (sfòrzo) *tr* to strain; to force
|| *ref* to strive, endeavor
sforza·to -ta *adj* forced, unnatural
sfòrzo *m* effort; strain; stretch (*of
imagination*); **senza sforzo** effort-
lessly
sfóttere *tr* (vulg) to make fun of
sfracassare *tr* to smash, crash
sfracellare (sfracèllo) *tr & ref* to shatter, smash
sfrangiare §290 *tr* to ravel
sfrattare *tr* to evict; to deport || *intr*
to be evicted
sfratto *m* eviction; notice of eviction
sfrecciare §128 (sfréccio) *intr* (ESSERE
& AVERE) to speed by
sfregaménto *m* rubbing
sfregare §209 (sfrégo) *tr* to rub; to
scrape; to strike (*a match*)
sfregiare §290 (sfrégio & sfrègio) *tr* to
disfigure, slash

sfregia·to -ta *adj* disfigured, slashed ||
m scarface
sfré·gio or **sfrè·gio** *m* (-gi) slash, scar,
gash; insult
sfrenare (sfréno & sfrèno) *tr* to take
the brake off; to give free rein to ||
ref to kick over the traces
sfrìggere §180 *intr* to sizzle
sfrigolì·o *m* (-i) sizzle
sfrondare (sfróndo) *tr* to defoliate; to
lop off; to trim down || *ref* to lose
leaves
sfrontatézza *f* effrontery, impudence
sfronta·to -ta *adj* brazen, impudent
sfrusciare §128 *intr* to rustle
sfruttare *tr* to exploit; to exhaust (*e.g.,
a mine*); to take advantage of
sfrutta·tóre -trice *mf* exploiter, developer (*e.g., of an invention*)
sfuggènte *adj* fleeting; receding (*forehead*); shifty (*glance*)
sfuggire *tr* to avoid, flee || *intr* (ESSERE)
to flee, escape, get away; (with *dat*)
to escape, e.g., **nulla gli sfugge** nothing escapes him; to break, e.g.,
sfuggì a una promessa he broke a
promise; **lasciarsi sfuggire** to let slip
sfuggita *f*—**di sfuggita** hastily; incidentally; **dare una sfuggita** to run
down (*e.g., to the post office*)
sfumare *tr* to shade down; to tone
down; to trim (*hair*) || *intr* (ESSERE)
to vanish; to shade
sfumatura *f* nuance, shade; razor clipping
sfumino *m* stump (*in drawing*)
sfuriare §287 *tr* to vent (*one's anger*) ||
intr to rave
sfuriata *f* outburst of anger; gust (*of
wind*); **fare una sfuriata a** to give a
scolding to
sgabèllo *m* stool, footstool
sgabuzzino *m* cubbyhole
sgambettare (sgambétto) *tr* to trip ||
intr to toddle; to kick (*said of a
baby*); to scamper
sgambétto *m* trip, stumble; **dare lo
sgambetto a** to trip
sganasciare §128 *tr* to dislocate the jaw
of; to break the jaw of; to tear apart
|| *intr* to steal right and left || *ref* to
break one's jaw; **sganasciarsi dalle
risa** to split one's sides laughing
sganciare §128 *tr* to unhook; to lay out
(*money*); to drop (*bombs*) || *intr* to
drop bombs; (coll) to go away || *ref*
to get unhooked; (mil) to disengage
oneself; **sganciarsi da** to get rid of
sgangherare (sgànghero) *tr* to unhinge;
to burst || *ref*—**sgangherarsi dalle
risa** to split one's sides laughing
spanghera·to -ta *adj* unhinged; broken
down; rickety; coarse (*laughter*)
sgarbatéz·za *f* rudeness, incivility;
clumsiness
sgarba·to -ta *adj* rude; clumsy
sgarberia *f* var of **sgarbatezza**
sgarbo *m*—**fare uno sgarbo a** to be rude
to
sgargiante *adj* loud, flashy, showy
sgarrare *intr* to go wrong
sgattaiolare (sgattàiolo) *intr* (ESSERE)
to slip away; to wriggle out

sgelare (sgèlo) *tr* & *intr* to thaw, melt
sgèlo *m* thaw
sghém·bo -ba *adj* crooked; a sghembo askew ‖ sghembo *adv* askew; sideways
sghèrro *m* hired assassin; gendarme
sghiacciare §128 *tr* to thaw
sghignazzare *intr* to guffaw
sghignazzata *f* guffaw
sghimbè·scio -scia *adj*—a or di sghimbescio askew, crooked
sghiribizzo [ddzz] *m* whim, fancy
sgobbare (sgòbbo) *intr* to drudge, plod, plug
sgobbó·ne -na *mf* plugger, plodder, drudge
sgocciolare (sgócciolo) *tr* to let drip ‖ *intr* to drip (*said of container*) ‖ *intr* (ESSERE) to drip (*said of liquid*)
sgocciola·tóio *m* (-tói) dish rack; drip pan
sgocciolatura *f* dripping; drippings
sgócciolo *m* last drop; essere agli sgoccioli to be coming to an end
sgolare (sgólo) *ref* to shout oneself hoarse
sgomberare (sgómbero) *tr* & *intr* var of sgombrare
sgómbero *m* moving
sgombrané·ve *m* (-ve) snowplow (*truck*)
sgombrare (sgómbro) *tr* to clear; to vacate ‖ *intr* to move, vacate
sgóm·bro -bra *adj* clear ‖ *m* moving; (ichth) mackerel
sgomentare (sgoménto) *tr* to frighten; to dismay
sgomén·to -ta *adj* dismayed ‖ *m* dismay; rimanere di sgomento to be dismayed
sgominare (sgòmino) *tr* to rout
sgomma·to -ta *adj* unglued; without tires; with poor tires
sgonfiare §287 (sgónfio) *tr* to deflate; to damn with faint praise (*e.g., a play*); (coll) to bore ‖ *intr* (ESSERE) to boast; to balloon ‖ *ref* to go down (*said of swelling*); to go flat (*said of a tire*); (fig) to collapse
sgón·fio -fia *adj* deflated, flat
sgonfiòtto *m* jelly doughnut; puff (*in clothing*)
sgórbia *f* (carp) gouge
sgorbiare §287 (sgòrbio) *tr* to scribble; (carp) to gouge
sgòr·bio *m* (-bi) ink spot; scribble, scrawl
sgorgare §209 (sgórgo) *tr* to unclog ‖ *intr* (ESSERE) to gush
sgottare (sgótto) *tr* to bail out (*a boat*)
sgozzare (sgózzo) *tr* to slaughter; to slit the throat of; (fig) to bleed, fleece
sgradévole *adj* disagreeable, unpleasant
sgradire §176 *tr* to refuse ‖ *intr* to be displeasing
sgradi·to -ta *adj* unpleasant; unwelcome
sgraffignare *tr* to snitch, snatch
sgrammatica·to -ta *adj* ungrammatical
sgranare *tr* to shell (*e.g., peas*); to count (*one's beads*); to seed (*grapes*); to open (*one's eyes*) wide; (mach) to disengage ‖ *ref* to crumble; to scratch oneself

sgranchire §176 *tr* to stretch (*e.g., one's legs*)
sgranocchiare §287 (sgranòcchio) *tr* to crunch, munch
sgrassare *tr* to remove the grease from; to skim (*broth*); to scour (*wool*)
sgravare *tr* to relieve, lighten ‖ *ref* to be relieved; to give birth
sgrà·vio *m* (-vi) lightening, lessening; a sgravio di coscienza to ease one's conscience
sgrazia·to -ta *adj* gawky, clumsy
sgretolare (sgrétolo) *tr* & *ref* to crumble
sgretola·to -ta *adj* crumbling, falling down
sgridare *tr* to scold, chide
sgridata *f* scolding, reprimand
sgrondare (sgróndo) *tr* to cause to drip ‖ *intr* to drip, trickle
sgroppare (sgròppo) *tr* to wear (*a horse*) out ‖ *intr* to buck (*said of a horse*)
sgroppare (sgróppo) *tr* to untie
sgrossare (sgròsso) *tr* to rough-hew; (fig) to refine
sgrovigliare §280 *tr* to untangle
sguaiatàggine *f* uncouthness
sguaia·to -ta *adj* crude, vulgar; uncouth ‖ *mf* vulgar person; uncouth person
sguainare *tr* to unsheathe; to show (*one's nails*)
sgualcire §176 *tr* to crumple ‖ *ref* to become crumpled
sgualdrina *f* trollop, strumpet
sguardo *m* glance, look; eyes
sguarnire §176 *tr* to untrim; (mil) to strip, dismantle
sguàtte·ro -ra *mf* dishwasher, scullion ‖ *f* kitchenmaid, scullery maid
sguazzare *tr* to waste, squander ‖ *intr* to splash; to wallow; to be lost (*in shoes too big or clothes too loose*)
sguinzagliare §280 *tr* to unleash, let loose
sgusciare §128 *tr* to shell, hull ‖ *intr* (ESSERE) to slip; sgusciare di soppiatto to slip away
shòp·ping *m* (-ping) shopping; shopping bag; fare lo shopping to go shopping
shràpnel *m* (shràpnel) shrapnel
si *m* (-si) (mus) si ‖ §5 *pron*
sì *m* (sì) yes; yea; stare tra il sì e il no to not be able to make up one's mind; un . . . sì e l'altro no every other (*e.g., day*)
sìa *conj* see essere
siamése [s] *adj* & *mf* Siamese
siberia·no -na *adj* & *mf* Siberian
sibilante *adj* & *f* sibilant
sibilare (sìbilo) *intr* to hiss
sibilla *f* sibyl
sibilo *m* hiss, hissing
sicà·rio *m* (-ri) hired assassin
sicché *conj* so that
siccità *f* drought
siccóme *adv* as ‖ *conj* since; as; how
Sicìlia, la Sicily
sicilia·no -na *adj* & *mf* Sicilian
sicomòro *m* sycamore
sicumèra *f* cocksureness, overconfidence
sicura *f* safety lock (*on gun*)

sicurézza *f* security; assurance; safety; certainty; reliability; **di sicurezza** safety; **sicurezza sociale** social security

sicu·ro -ra *adj* sure; safe; steady; **di sicuro** certainly ‖ *m* safety; **camminare sul sicuro** to take no chances ‖ **sicuro** *adv* certainly ‖ *f* see **sicura**

sicur·tà *f* (**-tà**) insurance

siderale *adj* sidereal

sidère·o -a *adj* sidereal

siderùrgi·co -ca (**-ci -che**) *adj* iron-and-steel ‖ *m* iron-and-steel worker

sidro *m* cider, hard cider

sièpe *f* hedge; (fig) wall

sièro *m* serum

sièsta *f* siesta; **fare la siesta** to take a nap, take a siesta

siffat·to -ta *adj* such

sifìlide *f* syphilis

sifóne *m* siphon; siphon bottle; trap

siga·ràio -ràia (**-rài -ràie**) *mf* cigar maker ‖ *m* (ent) grape hopper; ‖ *f* cigarette girl

sigarétta *f* cigarette

sigaro *m* cigar

sigillare *tr* to seal

sigillo *m* seal; **avere il sigillo alle labbra** to have one's lips sealed; **sigillo sacramentale** seal of confession

sigla *f* acronym; initials; abbreviation; letterword; **sigla musicale** theme song

siglare *tr* to initial

significare §197 (**signìfico**) *tr* to mean; to signify; **significare qlco a qlcu** to inform s.o. of s.th

significati·vo -va *adj* significant; meaningful

significato *m* meaning; **senza significato** meaningless

signóra *f* Madam, Mrs.; lady; mistress, owner; wife ‖ **Nostra Signora** Our Lady

signóre *m* sir, Mr.; gentleman; rich man; lord, master, owner; man; **il signore desidera?** what is your pleasure?; **per signori** stag ‖ **Signore** *m* Lord

signoreggiare §290 (**signoréggio**) *tr* to rule over; to master; to tower over; to overshadow ‖ *intr* to be the master

signorìa *f* seigniory; rule; **La Signoria Vostra** your Honor; **Sua Signoria** his Lordship; your Lordship

signorile *adj* seigniorial; gentlemanly; ladylike; elegant, refined

signorina *f* miss; Miss; young lady; spinster

signorino *m* master, young gentleman

signornò *adv* no, Sir

signoró·ne -na *mf* (coll) rich person

signoròtto *m* lordling

signorsì *adv* yes, Sir

silenziatóre *m* silencer (*of firearm*); (aut) muffler

silèn·zio *m* (**-zi**) silence; (mil) taps; **fare silenzio** to be silent; **ridurre al silenzio** (mil) to silence

silenzió·so -sa [s] *adj* silent; noiseless

silfide *f* sylphid

silfo *m* sylph

silhouèt·te *f* (**-te**) silhouette

sìlice *f* silica

silìcio *m* silicon

silicóne *m* silicone

siliquastro *m* redbud

sillaba *f* syllable

sillabare (**sìllabo**) *tr* to syllabify; to spell

sillabà·rio *m* (**-ri**) reader, primer

sìllabo *m* syllabus

silo *m* silo

silòfono *m* xylophone

siluétta *f* silhouette

silurante *adj* torpedoing, torpedo ‖ *f* destroyer; torpedo boat

silurare *tr* to torpedo; (fig) to fire, dismiss; (fig) to undermine

siluro *m* torpedo

silva·no -na *adj* sylvan

silvèstre *adj* (lit) sylvan; (lit) wild; (lit) hard, arduous

simboleggiare §290 (**simboléggio**) *tr* to symbolize

simbòli·co -ca *adj* (**-ci -che**) symbolic

simbolismo *m* symbolism

sìmbolo *m* symbol

similari·tà *f* (**-tà**) similarity

sìmile *adj* similar; such ‖ *m* like; **i propri simili** fellow men

similòro *m* tombac

simmetrìa *f* symmetry

simmètri·co -ca *adj* (**-ci -che**) symmetrical

simonìa *f* simony

simpamina *f* benzedrine

simpatèti·co -ca *adj* (**-ci -che**) sympathetic

simpatìa *f* like, liking; **cattivarsi la simpatia di** to make oneself well liked by

simpàti·co -ca (**-ci -che**) *adj* nice, pleasant, congenial ‖ *m* (anat) sympathetic system

simpatizzante [ddzz] *adj* sympathizing ‖ *mf* sympathizer

simpatizzare [ddzz] *intr* to sympathize; to become friends

simpò·sio *m* (**-si**) symposium

simulare (**sìmulo**) *tr* to simulate

simula·tóre -trice *mf* faker, impostor ‖ *m* simulator

simultàne·o -a *adj* simultaneous

sin- *pref adj* syn-, e.g., **sinonimo** synonymous ‖ *pref m & f* syn-, e.g., **sinonimo** synonym

sin *adv*—**sin da** ever since

sinagò·ga *f* (**-ghe**) synagogue

sincerare (**sincèro**) *tr* (lit) to convince ‖ *ref*—**sincerarsi di** to ascertain

sincè·ro -ra *adj* sincere; pure

sinché *conj* until

sìncope *f* fainting spell; (phonet) syncope; (mus) syncopation

sincronismo *m* syncronism; **sincronismo orrizzontale** (telv) horizontal hold; **sincronismo verticale** (telv) vertical hold

sincronizzare [ddzz] *tr* to syncronize

sìncro·no -na *adj* syncronous

sindacale *adj* mayoral; union

sindacalismo *m* trade unionism

sindacali·sta *mf* (**-sti -ste**) union member; union leader

sindacare §197 (**sìndaco**) *tr* to criticize; to scrutinize

sindaca·to -ta *adj* controlled, scrutinized ‖ *m* control; labor union; syndicate; **sindacato giallo** company union

sìnda·co *m* (**-ci**) mayor; controller; auditor

sinecura *f* sinecure

sinfonìa *f* symphony; (*of an opera*) overture; (coll) racket (*noise*)

sinfòni·co -ca *adj* (**-ci -che**) symphonic

singhiozzare (**singhiózzo**) *intr* to sob; to hiccup; to jerk

singhiózzo *m* sob; hiccups; **a singhiozzo** in jerks; by fits and spurts

singolare *adj* singular ‖ *m* singular; (tennis) singles

sìngo·lo -la *adj* single ‖ *m* individual; shell for one oarsman; (rr) roomette; (telp) private line; (tennis) singles

singulto *m* hiccups; sob

sinistra *f* left hand; left

sinistrare *tr* to ruin; to damage

sinistra·to -ta *adj* injured, damaged, ruined ‖ *mf* victim (*of bombing or flood*)

sinistrismo *m* leftism

sinistri·sta *adj* (**-sti -ste**) leftish, leftist

sini·stro -stra *adj* left; sinister ‖ *m* accident; (boxing) left ‖ *f* see **sinistra**

sinistròide *adj & mf* leftist

sino *adv* var of **fino**

sinologìa *f* Sinology

sinòni·mo -ma *adj* synonymous ‖ *m* synonym

sinò·psi *f* (**-psi**) (mov) synopsis

sinóra *adv* var of **finora**

sinòs·si *f* (**-si**) synopsis

sinòtti·co -ca *adj* (**-ci -che**) synoptic(al)

sintas·si *f* (**-si**) syntax

sìnte·si *f* (**-si**) synthesis

sintèti·co -ca *adj* (**-ci -che**) synthetic(al); concise

sintetizzare [ddzz] *tr* to synthesize

sintogram·ma *m* (**-mi**) (rad) dial

sìntomo *m* symptom

sintonìa *f* harmony; (rad) tuning

sintonizzare [ddzz] *tr* (rad) to tune

sintonizzatóre [ddzz] *m* (rad) tuner

sinuó·so -sa [s] *adj* sinuous, winding

sionismo *m* Zionism

sipà·rio *m* (**-ri**) curtain; **sipario di ferro** iron curtain

sirèna *f* siren; mermaid; **sirena da nebbia** foghorn

Sìria, la Syria

siria·no -na *adj & mf* Syrian

sirin·ga *f* (**-ghe**) panpipe; syringe; catheter; grease gun; (orn) syrinx

siringare §209 *tr* to catheterize

siròcchia *f* (obs) sister

si·sma *m* (**-smi**) earthquake

sismògrafo *m* seismograph

sismologìa *f* seismology

sissignóre *adv* yes, Sir!

sistè·ma *m* (**-mi**) system

sistemare (**sistèmo**) *tr* to arrange; to put in order; to systematize; to settle; to find a job for; to find a husband for; (coll) to fix ‖ *ref* to settle; to get married

sistemazióne *f* arrangement; settlement; job, position

sìstole *f* systole

sitibón·do -da *adj* (lit) thirsty

si·to -ta *adj* (lit) located ‖ *m* (lit) site, spot, location; (mil) sight; (coll) musty odor

situare (**sìtuo**) *tr* to locate, place, situate

situazióne *f* situation; condition

slabbrare *tr* to chip; to open (*a wound*) ‖ *intr* to overflow ‖ *ref* to become chipped; to reopen (*said of a cut*)

slacciare §128 *tr* to untie; to unfasten; to unbutton ‖ *ref* to get undone; to get unbuttoned

sladinare *tr* (sports) to train; (mach) to run in, break in

slanciare §128 *tr* to hurl, throw ‖ *ref* to hurl oneself; to rise (*said, e.g., of a tower*)

slancia·to -ta *adj* slender; soaring

slàn·cio *m* (**-ci**) leap; outburst (*of feeling*); momentum; **di slancio** with a rush; **prendere lo slancio** to get a running start

slargare §209 *tr* to widen; to warm (*the heart*) ‖ *ref* to widen, spread out

slattare *tr* to wean

slava·to -ta *adj* pale, washed out

sla·vo -va *adj* Slav, Slavic ‖ *mf* Slav ‖ *m* Slavic (*language*)

sleale *adj* disloyal; unfair (*competition*)

sleal·tà *f* (**-tà**) disloyalty

slegare §209 (**slégo**) *tr* to untie

slega·to -ta *adj* untied; disconnected

slip *m* (slip) briefs; tank suit, bathing suit (*for men*)

slitta *f* sled, sleigh; (mach) carriage

slittaménto *m* skid; slide

slittare *intr* to sled; to skid; to slide

slogare §209 (**slògo**) *tr* to dislocate ‖ *ref* to become dislocated; to dislocate (*e.g., an arm*)

slogatura *f* dislocation

sloggiare §290 (**slòggio**) *tr* to dislodge; to evict ‖ *intr* to vacate

slòg·gio *m* (**-gi**) moving; eviction

slovac·co -ca *adj & mf* (**-chi -che**) Slovak

smacchiare §287 *tr* to clean; to deforest

smacchia·tóre -trice *mf* cleaner ‖ *m* cleaning fluid; spot remover

smac·co *m* (**-chi**) letdown; slap in the face

smagliante *adj* dazzling, shining

smagliare §280 *tr* to break the links of; to undo the meshes of; to remove (*a fish*) from the net ‖ *intr* to shine, dazzle ‖ *ref* to run (*said, e.g., of knitted fabric*); to free itself from the net

smagliatura *f* run (*in stockings*); (fig) break

smagrire §176 *tr* to impoverish ‖ *intr* (ESSERE) *& ref* to become thin or lean

smaliziare §287 *tr* to make wiser ‖ *ref* to get wiser

smaltare *tr* to enamel; to glaze

smaltire §176 *tr* to digest; to sleep off (*a drunk*); to swallow (*an offense*);

to sell off; to get rid of; to drain off (*water*)

smalti·tóio *m* (-tói) drain, sewer

smalto *m* enamel; **smalto per le unghie** nail polish

smancerìe *fpl* affectation; mawkishness

smanceró·so -sa [s] *adj* prissy

smangiare §290 *tr* to erode, eat away || *ref* to be consumed (*e.g., by hatred*)

smània *f* frenzy; craze, yearning; **dare in smanie** to be in a frenzy

smaniare §287 *intr* to be delirious; to yearn, crave

smanió·so -sa [s] *adj* eager; disturbing

smantellare (**smantèllo**) *tr* to dismantle; to demolish; to disable (*a ship*)

smargias·so -sa *mf* braggart, boaster

smarriménto *m* loss; bewilderment; discouragement

smarrire §176 *tr* to lose || *ref* to get lost; to get discouraged

smascellare (**smascèllo**) *ref*—**smascellarsi dalle risa** to split one's sides laughing

smascherare (**smàschero**) *tr & ref* to unmask

smazzata *f* (cards) deal; (cards) hand

smembraménto *m* dismemberment

smembrare (**smèmbro**) *tr* to dismember

smemoratàggine *f* forgetfulness

smemora·to -ta *adj* absent-minded; forgetful || *mf* absent-minded or forgetful person

smentire §176 *tr* to belie; to refute; to retract; to be untrue to || *ref* to not be consistent, to contradict oneself

smentita *f* denial; retraction

smeraldo *m* emerald

smerciare §128 (**smèrcio**) *tr* to sell, sell out

smèr·cio *m* (-ci) sale

smèr·go *m* (-ghi) (zool) merganser

smerigliare §280 *tr* to grind, polish; to sand

smeriglia·to -ta *adj* polished; sand (*paper*); emery (*cloth*); frosted (*glass*)

smerì·glio *m* (-gli) emery; (orn) merlin; (ichth) porbeagle

smerlare (**smèrlo**) *tr* to scallop

smèrlo *m* scallop (*along the edge of a garment*)

smés·so -sa *adj* hand-me-down, castoff

sméttere §198 *tr* to stop; to stop wearing; to break up (*housekeeping*); **smetterla** to cut it out || *intr*—**smettere di** + *inf* to stop + *ger*

smezzare [ddzz] (**smèzzo**) *tr* to halve

smidollare (**smidóllo**) *tr* to remove the marrow from; (fig) to emasculate

smilitarizzare [ddzz] *tr* to demilitarize

smil·zo -za *adj* slender; poor, worthless

sminare *tr* to remove mines from

sminuire §176 *tr* to belittle

sminuzzare *tr* to crumble; to mince; to expatiate on || *ref* to crumble

smistaménto *m* sorting (*of mail*); (rr) shunting, shifting

smistare *tr* to sort; (rr) to shift; (soccer) to pass; (rad) to unscramble

smisura·to -ta *adj* immense, huge

smitizzante [ddzz] *adj* debunking, demythologizing

smitizzare [ddzz] *tr* to debunk; to demythologize

smobiliare §287 *tr* to remove the furniture from

smobilitare (**smobìlito**) *tr* to demobilize

smobilitazióne *f* demobilization

smoccolare (**smòccolo** & **smóccolo**) *tr* to snuff (*a candle*) || *intr* (slang) to swear, curse

smoda·to -ta *adj* excessive, immoderate

smòg *m* smog

smóking *m* (**smóking**) dinner jacket, tuxedo

smontàbile *adj* dismountable

smontàg·gio *m* (-gi) disassembling, dismantling

smontare (**smónto**) *tr* to take apart; to dismantle; to cause (*e.g., whipped cream*) to fall; to take (*a precious stone*) out of its setting; to dishearten; to dissuade; to drop (*s.o.*) off; **smontare la guardia** to come off guard duty || *intr* (ESSERE) to dismount; to get off or out (*of a conveyance*); to fade; to drop (*said, e.g., of beaten eggs*) || *ref* to become downcast

smòrfia *f* grimace; mawkishness; **fare le smorfie a** to make faces at

smorfió·so -sa [s] *adj* mawkish, prissy

smòr·to -ta *adj* pale, wan; faded

smorzare (**smòrzo**) *tr* to attenuate; to lessen; to tone down; to turn off (*light*); (phys) to dampen

smorzatóre *m* (mus) damper

smòs·so -sa *adj* moved; loose

smottaménto *m* mud slide

smozzicare §197 (**smózzico**) *tr* to crumble; to mince; to clip, mince (*one's words*)

smun·to -ta *adj* emaciated, pale, wan

smuòvere §202 *tr* to budge; to till; (fig) to move || *ref* to budge; to move away; **smuoviti!** get going!

smussare *tr* to blunt; to bevel; (fig) to soften

snaturalizzare [ddzz] *tr* to denaturalize; to denationalize

snaturare *tr* to change the nature of; to distort, misrepresent

snatura·to -ta *adj* distorted; monstrous, unnatural

snebbiare §287 (**snébbio**) *tr* to drive the fog from; to clear (*e.g., one's mind*)

snellézza *f* slenderness; nimbleness

snellire §176 *tr & ref* to slenderize

snèl·lo -la *adj* slender; nimble; lively

snervante *adj* enervating

snervare (**snèrvo**) *tr* to enervate, prostrate || *ref* to become enervated

snidare *tr* to drive out, flush

snòb *adj invar* snobbish || *mf* (**snòb**) snob

snobbare (**snòbbo**) *tr* to snub, slight

snobismo *m* snobbishness, snobbery

snobìsti·co -ca *adj* (-ci -che) snobbish

snocciolare (**snòcciolo**) *tr* to spill (*a secret*); to peel off (*sums of money*); to pit, stone (*fruit*)

snodare (**snòdo**) *tr* to untie; to limber up; to exercise; to loosen up (*e.g.,* *s.o.'s tongue*) || *ref* to become loose; to wind (*said, e.g., of a road*)

snòdo *m* (mach) joint; **a snodo** flexible

soave *adj* sweet, gentle

sobbalzare *intr* to jerk, jolt

sobbalzo *m* jerk, jolt; **di sobbalzo** with a jolt

sobbarcare §197 *tr* to overburden || *ref* —**sobbarcarsi a** to take it upon oneself to

sobbór·go *m* (-**ghi**) suburb

sobillare *tr* to instigate, stir up

sobilla·tóre -trice *mf* instigator

sobrietà *f* sobriety, temperance

sò·brio -bria *adj* sober, temperate; plain

socchiùdere §125 *tr* to half-shut; to leave ajar

socchiu·so -sa [s] *adj* ajar

soccómbere §186 *intr* to succumb

soccórrere §139 *tr* to help || *intr* (lit) to occur

soccórso *m* help, succor; **mancato soccorso** failure to render assistance; hit-and-run driving

sociale *adj* social; company (*e.g., outing*)

socialismo *m* socialism

sociali·sta (-**sti** -**ste**) *adj* socialistic || *mf* socialist

sociali·tà *f* (-**tà**) gregariousness; social responsibility

socie·tà *f* (-**tà**) society; company; **in società in partnership; società anonima** corporation; **società a responsabilità limitata** limited company; **Società delle Nazioni** League of Nations; **società finanziaria** holding company; **società in accomandita** limited partnership; **società per azioni** corporation

sociévole *adj* sociable; gregarious

sò·cio *m* (-**ci**) member; cardholder; partner; shareholder; **socio fondatore** charter member; **socio sostenitore** patron, sustaining member

sociologìa *f* sociology

sociòlo·go -ga *mf* (-**gi** -**ghe**) sociologist

sòda *f* soda

sodalì·zio *m* (-**zi**) society; brotherhood, fraternity; friendship

soddisfacènte *adj* satisfying, satisfactory

soddisfare §173 (*2d sg pres ind* **soddisfài** or **soddìsfi;** *3d pl pres* **soddisfanno** or **soddìsfano;** *1st, 2d & 3d sg pres subj* **soddisfaccia** or **soddìsfi;** *3d pl pres subj* **soddisfàcciano** or **soddìsfino**) *tr* to satisfy || *intr* (with *dat*) to satisfy || *ref* to be satisfied

soddisfat·to -ta *adj* satisfied

soddisfazióne *f* satisfaction

sòdi·co -ca *adj* (-**ci** -**che**) sodium

sòdio *m* sodium

sò·do -da *adj* hard; hard-boiled; stubborn; solid; **prenderle sode** to get a good thrashing || *m* hard ground; untilled soil; solid foundation; **venire al sodo** to come to the point; **mettere in sodo** to ascertain || *f* see **soda** || **sodo** *adv* hard

sodomìa *f* sodomy

so·fà *m* (-**fà**) couch, sofa; **sofà a letto** sofa bed

sofferènte *adj* sickly, ailing; (lit) longsuffering

sofferènza *f* suffering, pain; bad debt; **in sofferenza** overdue

soffermare (**sofférmo**) *tr*—**soffermare il passo** to come to a stop || *ref* to linger, pause

soffiare §287 (**sóffio**) *tr* to blow; to whisper; (checkers) to huff; (coll) to steal || *intr* to blow; to bellow; (slang) to squeal (*about somebody's offense*); **soffiare sul fuoco** to stir up trouble || *ref* to blow (*one's nose*)

soffia·to -ta *adj* blown || *m* soufflé || *f* (slang) squealing, **darsi una soffiata di naso** to blow one's nose

soffiatóre *m* glass blower

sòffice *adj* soft

soffierìa *f* glass factory; blower

soffiétto *m* bellows; hood (*of carriage*); (journ) puff, ballyhoo

sóf·fio *m* (-**fi**) blow; breath; **in un soffio** in a jiffy; **soffio al cuore** heart murmur

soffióne *m* blowpipe; fumarole; (bot) dandelion; (coll) spy

soffitta *f* attic, garret

soffitto *m* ceiling

soffocaménto *m* choking

soffocante *adj* stifling; oppressive

soffocare §197 (**sòffoco**) *tr* to choke; to stifle; to suffocate; to smother; to repress

sòffo·co *m* (-**chi**) sultriness

soffóndere §178 *tr* (lit) to suffuse

soffregare §209 (**soffrégo**) *tr* to rub lightly

soffrìggere §180 *tr* to fry lightly || *intr* to mutter

soffrire §207 *tr* to suffer; to endure; **non poter soffrire** to not be able to stand || *intr* to suffer; to ail; **soffrire di** to be troubled with

soffritto *m* fried onions and bacon

sofistica·to -ta *adj* adulterated; sophisticated, studied

sofìsti·co -ca *adj* (-**ci** -**che**) sophistic; faultfinding || *f* sophistry

soggetti·sta *mf* (-**sti** -**ste**) scriptwriter

soggetti·vo -va *adj* subjective

soggèt·to -ta *adj* subject || *m* subject; (coll) character; (law) person; **cattivo soggetto** hoodlum; **recitare a soggetto** to improvise

soggezióne *f* subjection; awe, embarrassment; **mettere a soggezione** to awe

sogghignare *intr* to sneer

soggiacére §181 *intr* (ESSERE & AVERE) to be subject; to succumb

soggiogare §209 (**soggiógo**) *tr* to subjugate, subdue

soggiornare (**soggiórno**) *intr* to sojourn, stay

soggiórno *m* sojourn, stay; living room; sitting room (*in hotel*)

soggiùngere §183 *tr* to add

soggólo *m* wimple (*of nun*); throatlatch (*on horse*); (mil) chin strap

sòglia *f* doorsill; threshhold

sògliola *f* sole

sognare (**sógno**) *tr* to dream of || *intr*

to dream; **sognare ad occhi aperti** to daydream

sogna·tóre -trice adj dreaming || mf dreamer

sógno m dream; **nemmeno per sogno** (coll) by no means

sòia f (bot) soy

sòl m (sòl) (mus) sol

so·làio m (-lài) attic, loft; (agr) crib

solare adj solar; bright; clear || v §257 tr to sole

solàr·rio m (-ri) solarium

solatì·o -a (-i -e) adj sunny || m—a **solatio** with a southern exposure

solcare §197 (sólco) tr to furrow; to plow (the waves)

sól·co m (-chi) furrow; rut; groove (of phonograph record); (fig) path; (naut) wake

solcòmetro m (naut) log

soldaté·sco -sca (-schi -sche) adj soldier || f soldiery; soldiers; undisciplined troops

soldatino m toy soldier

soldato m soldier; **andare soldato** to enlist; **soldato di ventura** soldier of fortune; **soldato scelto** private first class; **soldato semplice** private

sòldo m soldo (Italian coin); coin; money; (mil) pay; (fig) penny; **a soldo a soldo** a penny at a time; **al soldo di** in the pay of; **tirare al soldo** to be a tightwad

sóle m sun; sunshine; (fig) day, daytime; **sole artificiale** sun lamp; **sole a scacchi** (joc) hoosegow, calaboose

soleggia·to -ta adj sunny

solènne adj solemn; (joc) first-class

solenni·tà f (-tà) solemnity

solennizzare [ddzz] tr to solemnize

solére §255 intr (ESSERE) + inf to be accustomed to + inf, e.g., **suole arrivare alle sette** he is accustomed to arrive at seven || impers (ESSERE) —**suole** + inf it generally + 3d sg ind, e.g., **suole nevicare** it generally snows

solèrte adj (lit) diligent, industrious

solèrzia f (lit) diligence

solét·to -ta adj (lit) alone, lonely || f sole; inner sole; (archit) slab, cement slab

sòlfa f (mus) solfeggio; **la solita solfa** the same old story

solfanèllo m var of **zofanello**

solfara f sulfur mine

solfato m sulfate

solfeggiare §290 (solféggio) tr to sol-fa

solfiè·ro -ra adj sulfur

solfito m sulfite

sólfo m var of **zolfo**

solfòri·co -ca adj (-ci -che) sulfuric

solforó·so -sa [s] adj sulfurous

solfuro m sulfide

solidale adj solidary; (law) joint; (law) jointly responsible; (mach) built-in; **solidale con** integral with

solidarie·tà f (-tà) solidarity; (law) joint liability

solidarizzare [ddzz] intr to make common cause, become united

solidificare §197 (solidìfico) tr to solidify; to settle

solidi·tà f (-tà) solidity; (fig) soundness

sòli·do -da adj solid; (law) joint || m solid; **in solido** jointly

solilò·quio m (-qui) soliloquy

solin·go -ga adj (-ghi -ghe) (lit) lonely; (lit) solitary (enjoying solitude)

solino m detachable collar; **solino duro** stiff collar

soli·sta mf (-sti -ste) soloist

solità·rio -ria (-ri -rie) adj solitary, lonely || m solitaire; solitary

sòli·to -ta adj usual, customary; **esser solito** to be accustomed to || m habit, custom; **come il solito** as usual; **di solito** usually

solitùdine f solitude, loneliness

sollazzare tr to amuse || ref to have a good time, amuse oneself

sollazzo m (lit) amusement; **essere il sollazzo di** to be the laughingstock of

sollecitare (sollécito) tr to solicit; to urge; to induce; (mach) to stress || intr & ref to hasten

sollecitazióne f solicitation; urging; (mach) stress

solléci·to -ta adj quick, prompt; diligent; solicitous, anxious || m (com) solicitation, urging

sollecitùdine f solicitude; promptness; diligence; **cortese sollecitudine** (com) prompt attention

solleóne m dog days

solleticare §197 (sollético) tr to tickle; (fig) to flatter

solléti·co m (-chi) tickling; stimulation; **fare il solletico a** to tickle

sollevaménto m lifting; **sollevamento di pesi** weight lifting

sollevare (sollèvo) tr to lift; to relieve; to pick up; to raise (e.g., a question); to excite; to elevate || ref to rise; to lift oneself; to pick up (said of courage or health)

sollevazióne f uprising

sollièvo m relief

sollùchero m—**andare in solluchero** to become ecstatic; **mandare in solluchero** to thrill

só·lo -la adj lone, lonely, alone; only; single; **fare da solo** to operate all by oneself; **solo soletto** all by myself (yourself, himself, etc.); within oneself; **un solo** only one || m (mus) solo || **solo** adv only || **solo** conj only; **solo che** provided that

solstì·zio m (-zi) solstice

soltanto adv only

solùbile adj soluble

soluzióne f solution; installment; **soluzione di comodo** compromise; **soluzione provvisoria** stopgap

solvènte adj & m solvent

solvènza f solvency

solvìbile adj collectable; solvent

sòma f burden, load

Somàlia, la Somaliland

sòma·lo -la adj & mf Somali

soma·ro -ra mf donkey, ass

someggia·to -ta adj carried by pack animal; carried on mule back

somigliante adj similar; **essere somigliante a** to look like || m same thing

somiglianza f similarity, resemblance

somigliare §280 *tr* to resemble; (lit) to compare || *intr* (ESSERE & AVERE) (with *dat*) to resemble; to seem to be || *ref* to resemble each other

sómma *f* addition; sum; summary

sommare (sómmo) *tr* to add; to consider; tutto sommato all in all || *intr* to amount

sommà·rio -ria (-ri -rie) *adj* summary || *m* summary; abstract; (journ) subheading

sommèrgere §162 *tr* to submerge; (fig) to plunge; (fig) to flood (*with insults*) || *ref* to submerge

sommergibile *adj* & *m* submarine

sommés·so -sa *adj* submissive; subdued (*voice*)

somministrare *tr* to administer; to provide; to deliver (*a blow*); to adduce (*proof*)

somministrazióne *f* administration; provision

sommi·tà *f* (-tà) summit

sóm·mo -ma *adj* highest; supreme || *m* top; peak, summit || *f* see somma

sommòssa *f* insurrection, riot

sommoviménto *m* tremor (*of earth*); arousal (*of passions*); riot

sommozzatóre *m* skin diver; (nav) frogman

sommuòvere §202 *tr* (lit) to agitate; (lit) to stir up, excite

sonaglièra *f* collar with bells

sonà·glio *m* (-gli) bell; rattle; raindrop; pitter-patter (*of the rain*)

sonante *adj* ringing, sounding; ready (*cash*)

sonare §257 *tr* to sound; to play; to strike (*the hour*); to ring (*a bell*); (coll) to dupe, cheat; (coll) to give a sound thrashing to; sonare le campane a distesa to ring a full peal || *intr* (ESSERE & AVERE) to play; to ring (*said of a bell*); to sound; (lit) to spread (*said of reputation*)

sona·to -ta *adj* played; past, e.g., le tre sonate past three o'clock; cinquant'anni sonati past fifty years of age || *f* ring (*of bell*); (mus) sonata; (coll) thrashing; (coll) cheating

sona·tóre -trice *mf* (mus) player

sónda *f* sound; probe; drill

sondàg·gio *m* (-gi) sounding; probe; drilling; sondaggio d'opinioni opinion survey, public opinion poll

sondare (sóndo) *tr* to sound; to probe; to drill; to survey (*public opinion*)

sonerìa *f* alarm (*of clock*)

sonétto *m* sonnet

sonnacchió·so -sa [s] *adj* sleepy, drowsy

sonnàmbu·lo -la *mf* sleepwalker

sonnecchiare §287 (sonnécchio) *intr* to drowse, take a nap; to nap, nod

sonnellino *m* nap

sonnìfe·ro -ra *adj* soporific; narcotic || *m* sleeping medicine; narcotic

sónno *m* sleep; (lit) dream; aver sonno to be sleepy; far venir sonno a to bore; prender sonno to fall asleep

sonnolèn·to -ta *adj* sleepy; lazy

sonnolènza *f* drowsiness; laziness

sonori·tà *f* (-tà) sonority; acoustics

sonorizzare [ddzz] *tr* to voice; (mov) to dub || *ref* to voice

sonò·ro -ra *adj* sound (*wave*); sonorous; (phonet) sonant, voiced

sontuó·so -sa [s] *adj* sumptuous

sopèr·chio -chia *adj* & *m* (-chi -chie) var of soverchio

sopire §176 *tr* to appease, calm

sopóre *m* drowsiness

soporìfe·ro -ra *adj* soporific

soppanno *m* interlining; lining (*of shoes*)

sopperire §176 *intr*—sopperire a to provide for; to make up for

soppesare [s] (soppéso) *tr* to heft; (fig) to weigh

soppiantare *tr* to supplant by scheming; to kick out; to replace; to trick

soppiatto *m*—di soppiatto stealthily

sopportàbile *adj* bearable, tolerable

sopportare (soppòrto) *tr* to bear, support; to suffer, endure

sopportazióne *f* forbearance, endurance

soppressióne *f* suppression, abolition

sopprìmere §131 *tr* to suppress, do away with

sópra *adj invar* upper; above, preceding || *m* upper, upper part; al di sopra above; al di sopra di above, over; beyond; di sopra upper || *adv* above; up; on top || *prep* on; upon; on top of; over; beyond; above; versus; sopra pensiero absorbed in thought

sopràbito *m* overcoat, topcoat

sopraccàri·co -ca (-chi -che) *adj* overburdened || *m* overload; overweight; (naut) supercargo

sopraccenna·to -ta *adj* above-mentioned

sopraccì·glio *m* (-gli & -glia *fpl*) brow, eyebrow; window frame

sopraccita·to -ta *adj* above-mentioned

sopraccopèrta *f* bedspread; book jacket, dust jacket || *adv* (naut) on deck

sopraddét·to -ta *adj* above-mentioned

sopraffare §173 *tr* to overcome, overpower

sopraffazióne *f* overpowering; abuse

sopraffinèstra *f* transom window

sopraffi·no -na *adj* first-class; superfine

sopraggitto *m* (sew) overcasting

sopraggiùngere §183 *intr* (ESSERE) to arrive; to happen

sopraintèndere §270 *tr* var of soprintendere

sopralluò·go *m* (-ghi) inspection, investigation on the spot

sopralzo *m* var of soprelevazione

soprammercato *m*—per soprammercato in addition, to boot

soprammòbile *m* knicknack

soprannaturale *adj* & *m* supernatural

soprannóme *m* nickname

soprannominare (soprannòmino) *tr* to nickname

soprannùmero *adj invar* in excess; overtime || *m* —in soprannumero extra; in excess

sopra·no -na *adj* upper; (lit) supreme

|| **sopra·no** *mf* (**-ni -ne**) soprano (*person*) || *m* soprano (*voice*)

soprappensièro *adj invar & adv* immersed in thought

soprappéso [s] *m*—per soprappeso besides, into the bargain

soprap·più *m* (**-più**) plus, extra; **in soprappiù** besides, into the bargain

soprapprèzzo *m* extra charge, surcharge

soprascarpa *f* overshoe

soprascrit·to -ta *adj* written above || *f* address

soprassalto *m* start, jump; **di soprassalto** with a start

soprassedére §252 *intr* to wait; (with *dat*) to postpone

soprassòldo *m* extra pay; (mil) warzone indemnity

soprastare §263 *intr* (ESSERE) to be the boss

soprattac·co *m* (**-chi**) rubber heel

soprattassa *f* surtax; surcharge

soprattutto *adv* above all, especially

sopravanzare *tr* to overcome || *intr* (ESSERE) to be left over

sopravanzo *m* surplus

sopravvalutare *tr* to overrate

sopravvenire §282 *tr* (lit) to overrun || *intr* (ESSERE) to arrive; to happen, occur; (with *dat*) to befall

sopravvènto *m* windward; **avere il sopravvento** to have the upper hand || *adv* windward

sopravvissu·to -ta *adj* surviving || *mf* survivor

sopravvivènza *f* survival

sopravvìvere §286 *intr* (ESSERE) to survive; (with *dat*) to outlive

soprelevare (**soprelèvo**) *tr* to elevate (*e.g., a railroad*); to increase the height of (*building*)

soprelevazióne *f* elevation; addition of one or more floors

soprintendènte *m* superintendent

soprintendènza *f* superintendency

soprintèndere §270 *tr* to oversee

sopròsso *m* (coll) bony outgrowth

sopruso *m* abuse of power

soqquadro *m*—a **soqquadro** upside down, topsy-turvy

sòrba *f* sorb apple; (coll) hit, blow

sorbettièra *f* ice-cream freezer

sorbétto *m* ice cream; sherbet

sorbire §176 *tr* to sip; (fig) to swallow, endure

sòrbo *m* sorb; service tree

sór·cio *m* (**-ci**) mouse

sòrdi·do -da *adj* sordid; dirty

sordina *f* (mus) sordino, mute; (mus) soft pedal; **in sordina** quietly, stealthily; **mettere in sordina** (mus) to muffle

sór·do -da *adj* deaf; dull (*pain*); deepseated (*hatred*); hollow (*sound*); (phonet) surd, voiceless; **sordo come una campana** stone-deaf || *mf* deaf person

sordomu·to -ta *adj* deaf and dumb || *mf* deafmute

sorèlla *f* sister

sorellastra *f* stepsister

sorgènte *adj* rising || *f* spring; well (*of oil*); (fig) source; **sorgente del fiume** riverhead

sórgere §258 *intr* (ESSERE) to rise; to arise; to spring forth; **sorgere su un'ancora** (naut) to lie at anchor

sorgi·vo -va *adj* spring (*water*)

sór·go *m* (**-ghi**) sorghum

sormontare (**sormónto**) *tr* to surmount; to overcome || *intr* to fit

sornió·ne -na *adj* cunning, sly || *m* sneak

sorpassare *tr* to get ahead of; to surpass; to overstep; to go above

sorpasso *m* (aut) passing

sorprendènte *adj* surprising, astonishing

sorprèndere §220 *tr* to surprise; to catch; **sorprendere la buona fede di** to take advantage of || *ref* to be surprised

sorprésa [s] *f* surprise; surprise investigation; **di sorpresa** suddenly; unprepared; by surprise

sorrèggere §226 *tr* to sustain, support; to bolster

sorrìdere §231 *tr* (lit) to say with a smile || *intr* to smile; **sorridere a** to appeal to, e.g., **le sorride l'idea di questa gita** the idea of this trip appeals to her; to smile upon, e.g., **gli sorrideva la vita** life was smiling upon him

sorriso [s] *m* smile

sorsata *f* gulp, draught

sorseggiare §290 (**sorséggio**) *tr* to sip

sórso *m* sip; **a sorso a sorso** sipping

sòrta *f* kind, sort

sòrte *f* luck, lot, fate; chance; kind; (com) principal; **per sorte** of each kind; by chance; **tirare a sorte** to cast lots

sorteggiare §290 (**sortéggio**) *tr* to choose by lot; to raffle; **sorteggiare un premio** to draw a prize

sortég·gio *m* (**-gi**) drawing

sortilè·gio *m* (**-gi**) sortilege; sorcery, magic

sortire §176 *tr* (lit) to get by lot; (lit) to have (*results*); (lit) to allot || (**sòrto**) *intr* (ESSERE) to come out (*said, e.g., of a newspaper*); (coll) to be drawn (*by lot*); (coll) to go out; (mil) to make a sally

sortita *f* witticism; (mil) sally, sortie; (theat) appearance

sorvegliante *adj* watchful || *mf* overseer, caretaker; guardian || *m* watchman; foreman

sorveglianza *f* surveillance; supervision

sorvegliare §280 (**sorvéglio**) *tr* to oversee, watch over; to check, control

sorvolare (**sorvólo**) *tr* to fly over; to overfly; (fig) to avoid, skip

sorvólo *m* overflight

sò·sia *m* (**-sia**) double, counterpart

sospèndere §259 *tr* to hang; to suspend; (chem) to prepare a suspension of; (law) to stay

sospensióne *f* suspension; suspense; (law) stay; **sospensione cardanica** gimbals

sospensò·rio *m* (**-ri**) jockstrap, supporter

sospé·so -sa [s] *adj* suspended; suspension (*bridge*); **in sospeso** in suspense; in abeyance ‖ *m* employee who has been disciplined by suspension; (com) pending item

sospettare (**sospètto**) *tr* to suspect ‖ *intr*—**sospettare di** to suspect; to fear

sospèt·to -ta *adj* suspected; suspicious ‖ *m* dash; suspicion

sospettó·so -sa [s] *adj* suspicious

sospìngere §126 *tr* (fig) to drive; (lit) to push

sospirare *tr* to long for, crave; **fare sospirare** to keep waiting ‖ *intr* to sigh

sospiro *m* sigh; longing; (lit) breath; **a sospiri** little by little

sossópra *adv* upside down

sòsta *f* stop; reprieve; (rr) demurrage

sostanti·vo -va *adj & m* substantive

sostanza *f* substance; **sostanza grigia** gray matter

sostanziale *adj* substantial

sostanzió·so -sa [s] *adj* substantial

sostare (**sòsto**) *intr* to stop, pause

sostégno *m* prop; (fig) support

sostenére §271 *tr* to support; to sustain; to take (*an examination*); to defend (*a thesis*); to prop up; to stand (*alcohol*); to play (*a role*) ‖ *ref* to support oneself; to hold up (*said, e.g., of a theory*); to take nourishment

sosteni·tóre -trice *mf* backer, supporter

sostentaménto *m* sustenance, support

sostentare (**sostènto**) *tr* to support, keep ‖ *ref* to feed, eat

sostenu·to -ta *adj* reserved, austere; rising (*prices*); bullish (*market*); starchy (*manner*)

sostituìbile *adj* replaceable

sostituire §176 *tr* to replace, substitute for, take the place of; **sostituire** (*qlco* or *qlcu*) **a** to substitute (*s.th* or *s.o.*) for

sostitu·to -ta *adj* acting; associate, assistant ‖ *m* replacement, substitute

sostituzióne *f* replacement, substitution

sostrato *m* substratum

sottàbito *m* slip

sottacére §268 *tr* (lit) to withhold

sottacéto *adj invar* pickled ‖ **sottaceti** *mpl* pickles

sott'àcqua *adv* underwater

sotta·no -na *adj* lower (*town*) ‖ *f* skirt; petticoat; (eccl) cassock; **gettare la sottana alle ortiche** to doff the cassock

sottécchi *adv*—**di sottecchi** stealthily, secretly; **guardare di sottecchi** to peep, look furtively (at)

sottentrare (**sottèntro**) *intr* (ESSERE) (with *dat*) to replace

sotterfù·gio *m* (**-gi**) subterfuge

sottèrra *adv* underground

sotterràne·o -a *adj* subterranean, underground; secret, clandestine ‖ *m* cave, vault; dungeon; underground passage ‖ *f* (rr) subway, underground

sotterrare (**sottèrro**) *tr* to bury

sottigliézza *f* thinness; subtlety

sottile *adj* thin; subtle; (naut) lightweight ‖ *m*—**guardare troppo per il sottile** to split hairs

sottilizzare [ddzz] *intr* to quibble

sottintèndere §270 *tr* to understand ‖ *ref* to be understood, be implied

sottinté·so -sa [s] *adj* understood, implied ‖ *m* innuendo

sótto *adj invar* lower ‖ *m* lower part ‖ *adv* under; underneath; **al di sotto** below; **al di sotto di** under, below; **di sotto** lower; underneath; downstairs; **di sotto a** under, below; **farsi sotto** to sneak up; **metter sotto** to run over (*with a vehicle*); **sotto a** under; **sotto di** under ‖ *prep* under; beneath; below; just before; **prendere sotto gamba** to underestimate; **sotto braccio** arm in arm; **sotto caricó** (naut) being loaded; **sotto i baffi** up one's sleeve; **sotto le armi** in the service; **sotto mano** within reach; **sotto voce** under one's breath, sottovoce

sottoascèl·la *m* (**-la**) underarm pad

sottobanco *adv* under the counter

sottobicchière *m* coaster

sottobò·sco *m* (**-schi**) underbrush, thicket

sottobràccio *adv* arm in arm

sottòcchio *adv* under one's eyes

sottoccupa·to -ta *adj* underemployed

sottochiave *adv* under lock and key

sottocó·da *m* (**-da**) crupper

sottocommissióne *f* subcommittee

sottocopèrta *adv* (naut) below decks

sottocòp·pa *m* (**-pa**) mat; coaster; (aut) oil pan

sottocòsto *adj invar & adv* below cost

sottocutàne·o -a *adj* subcutaneous

sottofà·scia *m* (**-scia**) wrapper; **spedire sottofascia** to mail (*a newspaper*) in a wrapper ‖ *f* (**-sce**) wrapper (*for cigars*)

sottogamba *adv* lightly; **prendere sottogamba** to underestimate

sottogó·la *m & f* (**-la**) chin strap; throatlatch (*of harness*)

sottolineare (**sottolìneo**) *tr* to underline, underscore; to emphasize

sott'òlio *adv* in oil

sottomano *m* writing pad ‖ *adv* underhand; within reach

sottomari·no -na *adj & m* submarine

sottomés·so -sa *adj* conquered; subdued; submissive

sottométtere §198 *tr* to subdue, crush; to defer, postpone; to present (*a bill*); to subject ‖ *ref* to submit, yield

sottomissióne *f* submission

sottopan·cia *m* (**-cia**) bellyband, girth

sottopassàg·gio *m* (**-gi**) underpass; lower level (*of highway*)

sottopiatto *m* saucer

sottopórre §218 *tr* to subject; to submit ‖ *ref* to submit; **sottoporsi a** to submit to; to undergo (*e.g., an operation*)

sottopó·sto -sta *adj* subject; exposed ‖ *m* subordinate

sottoprèzzo *adj invar* cut-rate ‖ *adv* at a cut rate

sottoprodótto *m* by-product

sottórdine *m* suborder; in sottordine secondary

sottosca·la *m* (-la) space under the stairs; closet under the stairs

sottoscrit·to -ta *adj & mf* undersigned

sottoscrit·tóre -trice *mf* subscriber

sottoscrìvere §250 *tr* to subscribe; to sign, undersign; to underwrite ‖ *intr* to subscribe

sottoscrizióne *f* subscription

sottosegretà·rio *m* (-ri) undersecretary

sottosópra *adj invar* upset; mettere sottosopra to upset; to turn upside down ‖ *m* confusion, disorder ‖ *adv* upside down

sottostante *adj* lower; subordinate ‖ *m* subordinate

sottostare §263 *intr* (ESSERE) to be located below; to be subject; to yield, submit; (with *dat*) to undergo (*e.g., an examination*)

sottosuòlo *m* subsoil; cellar

sottosviluppa·to -ta *adj* underdeveloped

sottotenènte *m* second lieutenant; sottotenente di vascello (nav) lieutenant j.g.

sottotèr·ra *m* (-ra) basement ‖ *adv* underground

sottotétto *m* attic, garret

sottotìtolo *m* subtitle; (mov) caption

sottovalutare *tr* to underrate

sottovènto *m & adv* leeward

sottovèste *f* slip (*undergarment*)

sottovóce *adv* sotto voce, under one's breath

sottrarre §273 *tr* to subtract; sottrarre a to take away from, steal from ‖ *ref*—sottrarsi a to avoid; to escape from

sottrazióne *f* subtraction

sottufficiale *m* noncommissioned officer

sovènte *adv* often

soverchiante *adj* overwhelming

soverchiare §287 (sovèrchio) *tr* to overwhelm; to excel; to bully; (lit) to overflow ‖ *intr* to be in excess

soverchia·tóre -trice *adj* overbearing ‖ *mf* overbearing person, oppressor

sovèr·chio -chia (-chi -chie) *adj* excessive; overbearing ‖ *m* overbearing action

sovè·scio *m* (-sci) plowing under (*of green manure*)

sovièti·co -ca (-ci -che) *adj* Soviet ‖ *mf* Soviet citizen

sovrabbondante *adj* superabundant

sovrabbondare (sovrabbóndo) *intr* (ESSERE & AVERE) to be superabundant; to go to excesses

sovraccaricare §197 (sovraccàrico) *tr* to overload

sovraccàri·co -ca (-chi -che) *adj* overburdened ‖ *m* overload; overweight

sovraspó·sto -sta *adj* overexposed

sovraggiùngere §183 *intr* (ESSERE) var of sopraggiungere

sovralimentazióne *f* (aut) supercharging

sovrani·tà *f* (-tà) sovereignty

sovra·no -na *adj & mf* sovereign

sovrappopolare (sovrappòpolo) *tr* to overpopulate

sovrappórre §218 *tr* to overlay; to superimpose; sovrapporre qlco a to lay s.th on ‖ *ref* to be superimposed; to be added; sovrapporsi a to put oneself above

sovrapproduzióne *f* overproduction

sovrastampa *f* overprint

sovrastante *adj* overlooking, overhanging; impending

sovrastare *tr* to tower over; to hang over; to surpass; to excel ‖ *intr* (ESSERE & AVERE)—sovrastare a to tower over; to overlook; to hang over; to surpass; to excel

sovratensióne *f* (elec) surge

sovreccitare (sovrèccito) *tr* to overexcite

sovrespórre §218 *tr* to overexpose

sovrimpòsta *f* surtax

sovrimpressióne *f* double exposure

sovruma·no -na *adj* superhuman

sovvenire §282 *tr* (lit) to help ‖ *intr* (with *dat*) (lit) to help ‖ *impers* (ESSERE)—sovviene (with *dat*) di remember, e.g., gli sovviene spesso dei suoi cari he often remembers his dear ones ‖ *ref*—sovvenirsi di to remember

sovvenzionare (sovvenzióno) *tr* to subsidize, grant a subvention to

sovvenzióne *f* subsidy, subvention

sovversi·vo -va *adj & m* subversive

sovvertire (sovvèrto) *tr* to subvert

sóz·zo -za *adj* dirty, filthy, foul

sozzura *f* dirt, filth

spaccalé·gna *m* (-gna) woodcutter

spaccamón·ti *m* (-ti) braggart

spaccaòs·sa *m* (-sa) butcher's cleaver

spaccare §197 *tr* to break, burst; to crack; to unpack; to chop; to split ‖ *ref* to crack; to break; to split

spacca·to -ta *adj* broken; split; (coll) identical; (coll) true ‖ *f* (sports, theat) splits

spaccatura *f* break; crack; cleavage; split

spacchétto *m* vent (*in jacket*)

spacciare §128 *tr* to sell out; to palm off; to spread (*reports*); to expedite; to abandon (*as hopeless*); (slang) to push (*e.g., dope*) ‖ *ref*—spacciarsi per to pretend to be, pass oneself off as

spaccia·to -ta *adj* (coll) cooked, done for; (coll) hopeless

spaccia·tóre -trice *mf* passer (*of bad currency or stolen goods*); spacciatore di notizie false gossipmonger

spàc·cio *m* (-ci) sale; passing (*of counterfeit money*); spreading (*of false news*); post exchange; tobacco shop

spac·co *m* (-chi) break; split; tear; crack; vent (*in jacket*)

spacconata *f* brag, braggadocio

spaccó·ne -na *mf* braggart, braggadocio

spada *f* sword; a spada tratta doggedly; **spade** suit of Neapolitan cards corresponding to spades

spadaccino *m* swordsman; swashbuckler

spadóne *m* two-handed sword

spadroneggiare §290 (**spadronéggio**) *intr* to be domineering or bossy

spaesa•to -ta *adj* out-of-place

spaghétto *m* (coll) fear, jitters; **avere lo spaghetto** (coll) to be scared stiff; **spaghetti** spaghetti

Spagna, la Spain

spagnòla *f* Spanish woman; Spanish influenza

spagnolétta *f* espagnolette; spool; (coll) cigarette; (coll) peanut

spagnò•lo -la *adj* Spanish || *m* Spaniard (*individual*); Spanish (*language*); **gli spagnoli** the Spanish || *f* see **spagnola**

spa•go *m* (**-ghi**) string, twine; (coll) fear, jitters

spaiare §287 *tr* to break a pair of

spaia•to -ta *adj* unmatched

spalancare §197 *tr* to open wide || *ref* to open up; to gape

spalare *tr* to shovel; to feather (*oar*)

spalla *f* shoulder; back; abutment (*of bridge*); (theat) stooge, straight man; **alle spalle di qlcu** behind s.o.'s back; **a spalla** on one's back; **fare spalla a** to help; **lavorare di spalle** to elbow one's way; (fig) to worm one's way up; **vivere alle spalle di** to sponge on

spallàrm *interj* (mil) shoulder arms!

spallata *f* push with the shoulder; shrug of the shoulders

spalleggiare §290 (**spalléggio**) *tr* to back, support; (mil) to carry on one's back

spallétta *f* parapet, retaining wall; jamb

spallièra *f* back (*of chair*); head (*of bed*); foot (*of bed*); espalier

spallina *f* epaulet; shoulder strap

spallùccia *f*—**fare spallucce** to shrug one's shoulders

spalmare *tr* to spread; to smear

spalto *m* glacis; **spalti** seats (*of a stadium*)

spanare *tr* to strip the thread of || *ref* to be stripped (*said, e.g., of the thread of a nut*)

spanciare §128 *tr* to disembowel, gut || *intr* to belly-flop; to bulge (*said of a wall*) || *ref*—**spanciarsi dalle risa** to split one's sides laughing

spanciata *f* belly flop; bellyful; **fare una spanciata** to stuff oneself

spàndere §260 *tr* to spread; to spill; to shed (*tears*); to squander || *ref* to spread

spanna *f* span

spannare *tr* to skim (*milk*)

spannocchiare §287 (**spannòcchio**) *tr* to husk (*corn*)

spappolare (**spàppolo**) *tr* to crush, squash || *ref* to become mushy

sparadrappo *m* adhesive tape; (obs) plaster, poultice

sparagnare *tr* (coll) to save

sparare *tr* to gut, disembowel; to shoot; to let go with (*a kick*); to remove

the hangings from; **spararne delle grosse** to tell tall tales

sparato *m* shirt front, dickey

sparatòria *f* shooting

sparecchiare §287 (**sparécchio**) *tr* to clear (*the table*); to clear away (*one's tools*); to eat up

sparég•gio *m* (**-gi**) disparity; deficit; (sports) play-off

spàrgere §261 *tr* to spread; to shed; to spill || *ref* to spread

spargiménto *m* spreading; **spargimento di sangue** bloodshed

spargisa•le [s] *m* (**-le**) salt shaker

sparigliare §280 *tr* to break a pair of; to break (*a set*)

spariglia•to -ta *adj* unmatched

sparire §176 *intr* (ESSERE) to disappear

sparlare *intr* to backbite; **sparlare di** to backbite, slander

sparo *m* shot

sparpagliare §280 *tr & intr* to scatter

spar•so -sa *adj* scattered; dotted; speckled; hanging loosely (*e.g., hair*)

sparta•no -na *adj & mf* Spartan

spartiàc•que *m* (**-que**) watershed

spartiné•ve *m* (**-ve**) snowplow

spartire §176 *tr* to divide, share; to separate; **non aver nulla da spartire con** to have nothing to do with

spartito *m* (mus) score; (mus) arrangement

spartitràffi•co *m* (**-co**) median strip

spar•to -ta *adj* (lit) spread || *m* esparto grass

sparu•to -ta *adj* lean, wan; meager

sparvière *m* sparrow hawk; mortarboard

spasimante *m* (joc) lover, wooer

spasimare (**spàsimo**) *intr* to writhe; **spasimare per** to long for; to be madly in love with

spàsimo *m* pang; severe pain; longing

spasmo *m* spasm

spasmòdi•co -ca *adj* (**-ci -che**) spasmodic

spassare *tr* to amuse || *ref*—**spassarsela** to have a good time

spassiona•to -ta *adj* dispassionate, unbiased

spasso *m* fun, amusement; walk; (coll) funny guy; **andare a spasso** to go out for a walk; **essere a spasso** to be out of a job; **mandare a spasso** to fire, dismiss; to get rid of; **per spasso** for fun; **portare a spasso** to lead by the nose; **prendersi spasso di** to make fun of

spassó•so -sa [s] *adj* amusing, droll

spàsti•co -ca *adj & mf* spastic

spato *m* spar

spatofluòre *m* fluorspar

spàtola *f* spatula; putty knife; slapstick (*of harlequin*)

spauràc•chio *m* (**chi**) scarecrow; bugaboo, bugbear

spaurare *tr & ref* (lit) var of **spaurire**

spaurire §176 *tr* to frighten || *ref* to be scared

spaval•do -da *adj* bold, swaggering

spaventapàs•seri *m* (**-ri**) scarecrow

spaventare (spavènto) *tr* to scare, frighten || *ref* to be scared
spaventévole *adj* frightening, dreadful
spavènto *m* fright, fear
spaventó·so -sa [s] *adj* frightful, fearful
spaziale *adj* space
spaziare §287 *tr* (typ) to space || *intr* to soar; to range, rove (*said, e.g., of eye*)
spazia·tóre -trice *adj* spacing || *f* space bar (*of typewriter*)
spaziatura *f* spacing
spazientire §176 *tr* to make (*s.o.*) lose his patience || *intr* (ESSERE) & *ref* to lose patience
spà·zio *m* (-zi) space; (fig) room; **spazio aereo** air space; **spazio cosmico** outer space
spazió·so -sa [s] *adj* spacious, roomy; wide
spazzacamino *m* chimney sweep
spazzami·ne *m* (-ne) mine sweeper
spazzané·ve *m* (-ve) snowplow
spazzare *tr* to sweep; to plow (*snow*); to clean up
spazzata *f*—**dare una spazzata a** to give a lick and a promise to
spazzatrice *f* street sweeper
spazzatura *f* sweeping; sweepings; rubbish, trash
spazzatu·ràio *m* (-rài) or **spazzino** *m* street *›* cleaner; trashman, garbage collector, trash collector
spàzzola *f* brush; **capelli a spazzola** crew cut
spazzolare (spàzzolo) *tr* to brush
spazzolino *m* little brush; (elec) brush; **spazzolino da denti** toothbrush; **spazzolino per le unghie** nailbrush
spazzolóne *m* push broom
specchiare §287 (spècchio) *tr* (lit) to reflect || *ref* to look at oneself (*in a mirror*); to be reflected; **specchiarsi in qlcu** to model oneself on s.o.
specchièra *f* mirror; dressing table; full-length mirror
specchiétto *m* mirror; synopsis; **specchietto retrovisivo** (aut) rear-view mirror
spèc·chio *m* (-chi) mirror; synopsis; shore (*of lake or river*); panel (*of door or window*); sheet (*of water*); (sports) goal line; (sports) board; **specchio di poppa** (naut) transom; **specchio ustorio** burning glass
speciale *adj* special
speciali·sta *mf* (-sti -ste) specialist
speciali·tà *f* (-tà) specialty; (mil) special services; **specialità farmaceutica** patent or proprietary medicine
specializzare [ddzz] *tr* & *ref* to specialize
spè·cie *f* (-cie) species; kind, sort; appearance, semblance; **fare specie** (with *dat*) (coll) to be surprised, e.g., **gli fa specie** he is surprised; **in specie** especially; **sotto specie di** under pretext of
specifi·ca *f* (-che) itemized list; specification
specificare §197 (specìfico) *tr* to specify; to itemize

specìfi·co -ca (-ci -che) *adj* & *m* specific || *f* see **specifica**
specillo *m* (med) probe
speció·so -sa [s] *adj* specious
spè·co *m* (-chi) (lit) cave
spècola *f* observatory
spècolo *m* (med, surg) speculum
speculare (spèculo) *tr* to observe; to meditate on || *intr* to speculate
specula·tóre -trice *adj* speculating || *mf* speculator; **speculatore al rialzo** bull; **speculatore al ribasso** bear
speda·to -ta *adj* footworn
spedire §176 *tr* to expedite; to prepare; to ship, send, forward; (law) to deliver
spedi·to -ta *adj* rapid; free, easy
spedi·tóre -trice *mf* shipper, sender; shipping clerk
spedizióne *f* shipment, shipping; sending, forwarding; expedition; (naut) papers; **di spedizione** expeditionary
spedizionière *m* shipper, forwarder, forwarding agent
spègnere §262 *tr* to extinguish, put out; to turn off; to slake (*lime*); to kill; to mix (*flour*) with water or milk; to quench; to obliterate (*a memory*) || *ref* to burn out; to go out (*said of a light*); to fade, die away; to die
spegni·tóio *m* (-tói) snuffer
spegnitura *f* (theat) blackout
spelacchiare §287 *tr* to strip of hair || *ref* to shed hair or fur
spelacchia·to -ta *adj* mangy; (pej) baldy
spelare (spélo) *tr* to strip of hair; to pluck (*e.g., a chicken*); (fig) to fleece || *ref* to shed hair or fur; to get bald
spellare (spèllo) *tr* to skin; (fig) to skin, fleece
spelón·ca *f* (-che) cave; hovel, den
spème *f* (poet) hope
spendacció·ne -na *mf* spendthrift
spèndere §220 *tr* to spend
spenderéc·cio -cia *adj* (-ci -ce) spendthrift, prodigal
spennacchiare §287 *tr* to pluck; (fig) to fleece || *ref* to lose its feathers
spennare (spénno) *tr* & *ref* var of **spennacchiare**
spennellare (spennèllo) *tr* to dab
spensieratézza *f* thoughtlessness
spensiera·to -ta *adj* thoughtless, careless; carefree, happy-go-lucky
spèn·to -ta *adj* extinguished; turned off; slaked (*lime*); dull (*color*); low (*tone*)
spenzolare [dz] (spènzolo) *tr* & *intr* to hang || *ref*—**spenzolarsi da** to hang out of
speranza *f* hope; prospect, expectation
speranzó·so -sa [s] *adj* hopeful
sperare (spèro) *tr* to candle (*eggs*); to hope for; to expect || *intr* to hope; to trust
spèrdere §212 *tr* (lit) to scatter; (lit) to lose (*one's way*) || *ref* to lose one's way, get lost
sperdu·to -ta *adj* lost, astray; godforsaken (*place*)
sperequazióne *f* disproportion; inequality; unjust distribution

spergiurare *tr & intr* to swear falsely; **giurare e spergiurare** to swear over and over again

spergiu·ro -ra *adj* perjured || *mf* perjurer || *m* perjury

spericola·to -ta *adj* reckless, daring

sperimentale *adj* experimental

sperimentare (speriménto) *tr* to test, try out; to experience

sperimenta·to -ta *adj* experienced

spèr·ma *m* (-mi) sperm

speronare (speróno) *tr* (naut) to ram

speróne *m* spur; abutment; (nav) ram

sperperare (spèrpero) *tr* to squander

spèrpero *m* squandering

spèr·so -sa *adj* lost, stray

spertica·to -ta *adj* too long; too tall; exaggerated, excessive

spésa [s] *f* expense; shopping; buy, purchase; **fare la spesa** to shop; **fare le spese di** to be the butt of; **lavorare per le spese** to work for one's keep; **pagare le spese** to bear the charges; **spese** expenses; room and board; **spese di manutenzione** upkeep; **spese minute** petty expenses; **spese processuali** (law) costs

spesare [s] **(spéso)** *tr* to support

spesa·to -ta [s] *adj* with all expenses paid

spés·so -sa *adj* thick; many (*times*) || **spesso** *adv* often; **spesso spesso** again and again

spessóre *m* thickness

spettàbile *adj* esteemed; **Spettabile Ditta** (com) Gentlemen

spettàcolo *m* spectacle, show; sight; **dar spettacolo di sé** to make a show of oneself; **spettacolo all'aperto** outdoor performance

spettacoló·so -sa *adj* spectacular; (coll) exceptional; (coll) sensational

spettanza *f* concern; pay

spettare (spètto) *intr* (ESSERE)—**spettare a** to belong to || *impers* (ESSERE) —**spetta a** it behooves, it is up to

spetta·tóre -trice *mf* spectator, bystander; **spettatori** public, audience

spettegolare (spettégolo) *intr* to gossip

spettinare (spèttino) *tr* to muss the hair of

spettrale *adj* ghost-like; spectral

spèttro *m* specter, ghost; spectrum

speziale *m* dealer in spices; (coll) pharmacist

spèzie *fpl* spices

spezieria *f* grocery; (coll) drug store, pharmacy; **spezierie** spices

spezzare (spèzzo) *tr* to break; to smash; to interrupt || *ref* to break

spezzatino *m* stew; **spezzatini** change

spezza·to -ta *adj* broken; fragmentary; interrupted || *m* stew; (theat) set piece; **spezzati** change

spezzettare (spezzétto) *tr* to mince

spezzóne *m* small aerial bomb; fragmentation bomb; fragment

spìa *f* spy; indication; peephole; (aut) gauge; (aut) pilot light; **fare la spia** to be an informer

spiaccicare §197 **(spiàccico)** *tr* to squash, crush || *ref* to be squashed

spiacènte *adj* sorry; (lit) disliked

spiacére §214 *intr* (ESSERE) (with *dat*) to dislike, e.g., **queste parole gli spiacciono** he dislikes these words; to mind, e.g., **se non Le spiace** if you don't mind || *ref*—**spiacersi di** to be sorry for || *impers* (ESSERE) (with *dat*)—**gli spiace** he is sorry

spiacévole *adj* unpleasant

spiàg·gia *f* (-ge) beach, shore

spianare *tr* to grade (*land*); to roll (*dough*); to pave (*the way*); to iron (*pleats*); to raze, demolish; to level (*a gun*); **spianare la fronte** to smooth one's brow || *intr* (ESSERE) to be level

spianata *f* esplanade; **dare una spianata a** to level

spianatóia *f* board (*for rolling dough*)

spiana·tóio *m* (-tói) rolling pin

spianatrice *f* grader

spiano *m* leveling; esplanade; **a tutto spiano** at full blast; continuously

spiantare *tr* to uproot; to raze, level; to ruin (*financially*) || *ref* to ruin oneself

spianta·to -ta *adj* ruined || *m* pauper

spiare §119 *tr* to spy on; to keep an eye on

spiattellare (spiattèllo) *tr* to blurt out

spiazzo *m* square; plain; clearing

spiccare §197 *tr* to detach; to pick; to enunciate; to begin; to draw up (*a commercial paper*); to issue (*a warrant*); **spiccare il volo** (aer) to take off || *intr* to stand out || *ref* to separate (*said, e.g., of the stone of a peach*)

spicca·to -ta *adj* clear, distinct; typical; outstanding

spìc·chio *m* (-chi) section (*of fruit*); clove (*of garlic*); slice (*e.g., of apple*); arm (*of cross*)

spicciare §128 *tr* to clear up; to wait on; to dispatch (*business*) || *intr* (ESSERE) to flow forth, gush out || *ref* to hurry up, make haste

spicciati·vo -va *adj* expeditious, quick; straightforward; gruff

spiccicare §197 **(spìccico)** *tr* to unglue; to enunciate; to utter || *ref* to come unglued; **spiccicarsi di** to get rid of

spìc·cio -cia (-ci -ce) *adj* expeditious, quick; unhampered; small (*change*) || **spicci** *mpl* change

spicciolata *adj fem*—**alla spicciolata** little by little; a few at a time

spìcciolo -la *adj* small (change); (coll) plain || **spiccioli** *mpl* small change

spìc·co -ca (-chi -che) *adj* freestone (*e.g., peach*) || *m*—**fare spicco** to stand out

spidocchiare §287 **(spidòcchio)** *tr* to delouse

spièdo *m* spit; **allo spiedo** barbecued

spiegàbile *adj* explainable

spiegaménto *m* (mil) array; (mil) deployment

spiegare §209 **(spiègo)** *tr* to unfold; to let go (*with one's voice*); to unfurl; to spread (*wings*); to deploy (*troops*); to explain; to show, demonstrate; **spiegare il volo** (aer) to take off || *ref* to become unfurled or unfolded;

to make oneself understood; to come to an understanding; to realize

spiega·to -ta *adj* open; full (*voice*)

spiegazióne *f* explanation

spiegazzare *tr* to crumple, rumple

spieta·to -ta *adj* pitiless, ruthless

spifferare (**spìffero**) *tr* (coll) to blurt out || *intr* to blow in (*said of wind*)

spìffero *m* (coll) draft

spi·ga *f* (**ghe**) panicle (*of oats*); (bot) ear, spike; **a spiga** herringbone

spiga·to -ta *adj* herringbone

spighétta *f* braid; (bot) spikelet

spigionare (**spigióno**) *ref* to be or become vacant

spiglia·to -ta *adj* easy, free and easy

spi·go *m* (**-ghi**) lavender

spigolare (**spìgolo**) *tr* to glean

spigola·tóre -trice *mf* gleaner

spìgolo *m* corner; edge; (archit) arris

spilla *f* brooch, pin; **spilla da cravatta** tiepin; **spilla di sicurezza** safety pin

spillare *tr* to draw off, tap; to wheedle, worm (*money*) || *intr* to leak (*said of container*) || *intr* (ESSERE) to leak (*said of liquid*)

spillàti·co *m* (**-ci**) (law) pin money (*for one's wife*)

spillo *m* pin; gimlet; trifle; **a spillo** spikelike; **spillo da balia** or **di sicurezza** safety pin

spillóne *m* hatpin; bodkin

spilluzzicare §197 (**spillùzzico**) *tr* to pick at, nibble; to scrape together

spilorcerìa *f* stinginess

spilòr·cio -cia (**-ci -ce**) *adj* stingy || *mf* miser, tightwad

spilungó·ne -na *mf* lanky person

spina *f* thorn; quill, spine (*of porcupine*); bone (*of fish*); (fig) preoccupation, worry; **alla spina** (*beer*) on tap; **a spina di pesce** herringbone (*fabric*); **con una spina nel cuore** sick at heart; **essere sulle spine** to be on pins and needles; **spina della botte** tap; bunghole; **spina dorsale** spinal column; (fig) backbone; **spina elettrica** plug

spinà·cio *m* (**-ci**) spinach (*plant*); **spinaci** spinach (*as food*)

spinapésce *m*—**a spinapesce** herringbone

spina·to -ta *adj* barbed (*wire*); herringbone (*fabric*)

spìngere §126 *tr* to push, press; to prod, goad || *ref* to push; to reach

spi·no -na *adj* thorny || *m* thorn || *f* see **spina**

spinóne *m* griffon

spinó·so -sa [s] *adj* thorny

spinòtto *m* wrist pin

spinta *f* push; pressure; poke, prod; stress

spinterògeno *m* (aut) distributor unit, ignition system

spin·to -ta *adj* pushed; bent, inclined; (coll) risqué; (coll) far-out, offbeat || *f* see **spinta**

spintóne *m* (coll) push, shove

spionàg·gio *m* (**-gi**) espionage, spying

spioncino *m* peephole

spió·ne -na *mf* spy, stool pigeon

spiovènte *adj* drooping; sloping; falling || *m* slope; drainage area (*of a mountain*)

spiòvere §216 *intr* to fall, to hang down (*said, e.g., of hair*); to flow down || *impers* (ESSERE)—**è spiovuto** it stopped raining

spira *f* turn (*of a coil*); coil (*of serpent*); **a spire** spiral

spirà·glio *m* (**-gli**) small opening; gleam (*of light or hope*)

spirale *adj* spiral || *f* spiral; hairspring; wreath (*of smoke*); **spirale di fumo** smoke ring

spirare *tr* to send forth; (lit) to inspire, infuse; (lit) to show (*kindness*) || *intr* to blow; to emanate; to die; to expire

spirita·to -ta *adj* possessed; wild, mad

spìriti·co -ca *adj* (**-ci -che**) spiritual; spiritualistic

spiritismo *m* spiritualism

spìrito *m* spirit; wit; mind; spirits, alcohol; sprite; **bello spirito** wit (*person*); **fare dello spirito** to be witty; to crack jokes; **l'ultimo spirito** (lit) one's last breath; **spirito di corpo** esprit de corps; **spirito di parte** partisanship; **spirito sportivo** sportsmanship

spiritosàggine [s] *f* witticism

spiritó·so -sa [s] *adj* witty; alcoholic

spirituale *adj* spiritual

spizzi·co *m* (**-chi**)—**a spizzico** or **a spizzichi** little by little; a little at a time

splendènte *adj* resplendent, shining

splèndere §281 *intr* (ESSERE & AVERE) to shine

splèndi·do -da *adj* splendid; gorgeous; bright || *m*—**fare lo splendido** to be a big spender

splendóre *m* splendor; brightness; beauty

splène *m* (anat) spleen

spòcchia *f* haughtiness

spodestare (**spodèsto**) *tr* to dispossess; to dethrone; to oust

spoetizzare [ddzz] *tr* to disillusion

spòglia *f* slough (*of snake*); skin (*of onion*); husk (*of corn*); (lit) body; (lit) outer garment; **sotto mentite spoglie** under false pretense; **spoglie** spoils

spogliare §280 (**spòglio**) *tr* to undress, strip; to strip of armor; to defraud, deprive; to free; to check, examine; to husk (*corn*); to go through (*e.g., correspondence*) || *ref* to undress; to slough (*said, e.g., of a snake*); **spogliarsi di** to get rid of; to divest oneself of; to shake (*a habit*)

spogliarelli·sta *f* (**-ste**) stripteaser

spogliarèllo *m* striptease

spoglia·tóio *m* (**-tói**) dressing room; locker room

spò·glio -glia (**-gli -glie**) *adj* stripped, bare; free || *m* cast-off clothing; sorting; scrutiny; counting (*of votes*); **di spoglio** second-hand (*material*) || *f* see **spoglia**

spòla *f* bobbin; shuttle; **fare la spola** to shuttle

spolétta _f_ bobbin, spool; (mil) fuse

spolmonare (**spolmóno**) _ref_ (coll) to talk, sing, or shout oneself hoarse

spolpare (**spólpo**) _tr_ to gnaw (_a bone_); to eat up (_fruit_); (fig) to fleece

spolverare (**spólvero**) _tr_ to dust off, whisk; to powder, dust; to pounce

spolveratura _f_ dusting; powdering; sprinkling, smattering (_of knowledge_); **dare una spolveratura a** to brush up on

spolverina _f_ (coll) duster

spolverino _m_ duster, smock; powder-sugar duster; pounce; (coll) whisk broom

spolverizzaménto [ddzz] _m_ sprinkling (_with powder_)

spolverizzare [ddzz] _tr_ to dust, powder, pounce

spólvero _m_ dusting; powdering; pounce; smattering, sprinkling (_of knowledge_); display

spónda _f_ bank (_of river_); side; cushion (_of billiard table_)

sponsale _adj_ (lit) wedding ‖ **sponsali** _mpl_ (lit) wedding

spontàne·o -a _adj_ spontaneous; artless

spopolare (**spòpolo**) _tr_ to depopulate ‖ _intr_ to be a hit; to become depopulated or deserted

spoppare (**spóppo**) _tr_ to wean

sporàdi·co -ca _adj_ (-ci -che) sporadic

sporcaccióne·-na _adj_ filthy ‖ _mf_ filthy person; (fig) dirty mouth

sporcare §197 (**spòrco**) _tr_ to dirty; to soil ‖ _ref_ to get dirty; to soil oneself; **sporcarsi la fedina** (coll) to get a black mark on one's record

sporcìzia _f_ dirt, filth

spòr·co -ca (-chi -che) _adj_ dirty, filthy; foul; **farla sporca** to pull a dirty trick ‖ _m_ dirt, filth

sporgènte _adj_ leaning; protruding; beetle (_brow_)

sporgènza _f_ prominence, projection

spòrgere §217 _tr_ to stick out; to stretch out; to lodge (_a complaint_) ‖ _intr_ (ESSERE) to project, jut out ‖ _ref_ to lean out

spòrt _m_ (**spòrt**) sport; game; **per sport** for fun, for pleasure

spòrta _f_ shopping bag; bagful; basket; basketful; shopping; **a sporta** wide-brimmed (_hat_)

sportèllo _m_ door; panel; window (_in bank, station, etc._); wicket; branch (_of a bank_); (theat) box office

sportivi·tà _f_ (-tà) sportsmanship

sporti·vo -va _adj_ sporting; sportsman-like; athletic ‖ _m_ sportsman

spòr·to -ta _adj_ projecting; jutting out ‖ _m_ projection; removable shutter (_on store door or window_) ‖ _f_ see **sporta**

spòsa _f_ bride; wife; **andare in sposa a** to get married to; **sposa promessa** fiancée

sposalì·zio -zia (-zi -zie) _adj_ (lit) nuptial ‖ _m_ wedding

sposare (**spòso**) _tr_ to marry; to unite; to embrace (_a cause_); to fit perfectly; to give in marriage ‖ _ref_ to get married, marry

spòso _m_ bridegroom; **sposi** newlyweds

spossare (**spòsso**) _tr_ to exhaust ‖ _ref_ to become worn out

spossatézza _f_ exhaustion

spostaménto _m_ shift; movement; displacement; change

spostare (**spòsto**) _tr_ to move; to change, shift; to upset ‖ _ref_ to move; to shift; to get out of place; to be upset

sposta·to -ta _adj_ ill-adjusted, out of place ‖ _mf_ misfit

spran·ga _f_ (-ghe) bar, crossbar

sprangare §209 _tr_ to bar, bolt

sprazzo _m_ spray; flash; burst

sprecare §197 (**sprèco**) _tr_ to waste; to miss (_an opportunity_) ‖ _ref_ to waste one's efforts

sprè·co _m_ (-chi) waste; squandering

sprecó·ne -na _adj & mf_ spendthrift

spregévole _adj_ contemptible, despicable

spregiare §290 (**sprègio**) _tr_ to despise

sprè·gio _m_ (-gi) contempt, scorn

spregiudica·to -ta _adj_ open-minded, unbiased ‖ _m_ open-minded person

sprèmere §123 _tr_ to squeeze, press; **spremere le lacrime a** to move to tears ‖ _ref_—**spremersi il cervello** to rack one's brain

spremifrut·ta _m_ (-ta) squeezer

spremilimó·ni _m_ (-ni) lemon squeezer

spremuta _f_ squeezing; **spremuta d'arancia** orange juice

spretare (**sprèto**) _ref_ to doff the cassock

sprezzante _adj_ contemptuous, haughty

sprezzare (**sprèzzo**) _tr_ (lit) to despise

sprèzzo _m_ disdain, contempt

sprigionare (**sprigióno**) _tr_ to exhale, emit; to free from prison ‖ _ref_ to free oneself; to escape, come forth, issue (_said, e.g., of steam_)

sprimacciare §128 _tr_ to beat, fluff (_e.g., a pillow_)

sprizzare _tr_ to spout; to sparkle with (_joy, health_) ‖ _intr_ (ESSERE) to spurt; to fly (_said of sparks_); to sparkle

sprizzo _m_ sprinkle; spurt; spark

sprofondare (**sprofóndo**) _tr_ to send to the bottom; to destroy, ruin; to sink ‖ _intr_ (ESSERE) to sink; to founder; to cave in; to be sunk (_e.g., in meditation_)

sprolò·quio _m_ (-qui) long rigmarole

spronare (**spróno**) _tr_ to spur, goad

spróne _m_ spur; prodding; example; guimpe; buttress; abutment (_of bridge_); **a sprone battuto** at full speed; at once; **dar di sprone a** to spur on; **sprone di cavaliere** (bot) rocket larkspur

sproporziona·to -ta _adj_ out of proportion, disproportionate

sproporzióne _f_ disproportion

sproposita·to -ta _adj_ out of proportion; excessive; gross (_error_)

spropòsito _m_ blunder, gross error; excessive amount; **a sproposito** out of place; inopportunely

sprovvedu·to -ta _adj_ deprived; brainless, witless

sprovvi·sto -sta _adj_ deprived; devoid, lacking; **alla sprovvista** suddenly; unawares, off guard

spruzzabianche·rìa *m* (-rìa) sprinkler (*to sprinkle clothes*)

spruzzare *tr* to sprinkle, spray; to powder (*sugar*)

spruzzatóre *m* sprayer; (aut) nozzle (*of carburetor*)

spruzzo *m* spray; splash (*of mud*)

spudora·to -ta *adj* shameless; impudent

spugna *f* sponge; dare un colpo di spugna to wipe the slate clean; gettare la spugna to throw in the towel

spugnare *tr* to sponge; to swab

spugnatura *f* sponge bath

spugnó·so -sa [s] *adj* spongy

spulciare §128 *tr* to pick the fleas off; to scrutinize, examine minutely

spuma *f* foam, froth

spumante *adj* sparkling || *m* sparkling wine; champagne

spumare *intr* to froth

spumeggiante *adj* sparkling; vaporous; foamy

spumeggiare §290 (spuméggio) *intr* to foam

spumóne *m* spumoni

spumó·so -sa [s] *adj* foamy, frothy

spunta *f* check; check list; check mark

spuntare *tr* to blunt; to unpin; to overcome; to clip, trim; to check off; spuntarla to come out on top; to overcome || *intr* (ESSERE) to appear; to sprout; to rise; to well up (*said of tears*); to pop out; to break through || *ref* to become blunt; to die down

spuntino *m* bite, snack; fare uno spuntino to have a bite

spunto *m* sourness (*of wine*); (theat) cue; (sports) sprint; (fig) starting point, origin

spuntóne *m* spike; pike; crag

spurgare §209 *tr* to purge, clear; to clean up || *ref* to expectorate

spur·go *m* (-ghi) discharge; reject (*e.g., book*)

spù·rio -ria *adj* (-ri -rie) spurious

sputacchiare §287 *tr* to spit upon || *intr* to sputter

sputacchièra *f* spittoon, cuspidor

sputare *tr* to spit; to cough up; (fig) to spew (*venom*); sputare sangue to spit blood; (fig) to sweat blood || *intr* to spit

sputasentènze *mf* (-ze) wiseacre

sputo *m* spit, sputum; spitting

squadernare (squadèrno) *tr* to leaf through; squadernare qlco a qlcu to put s.th under the nose of s.o. || *ref* to come apart (*said of a book*)

squadra *f* square (*for measuring right angles*); squad, group; (mil) squadron; (sports) team; a squadra at right angles; fuori squadra out of kilter; squadra di pompieri fire company; squadra mobile flying squad

squadrare *tr* to square; (fig) to examine, study

squadrìglia *f* (aer, nav) squadron

squadróne *m* squadron (*of cavalry*)

squagliare §280 *tr* to melt || *ref* to melt; squagliarsela to take French leave

squalifi·ca *f* (-che) disqualification

squalificare §197 (squalìfico) *tr* to disqualify || *ref* to disqualify oneself; to prove to be unqualified

squàlli·do -da *adj* wretched, dreary, gloomy; faint (*smile*); (lit) emaciated

squallóre *m* wretchedness, dreariness, gloominess

squalo*m* shark

squama *f* scurf (*shed by the skin*); (bot, pathol, zool) scale

squamare *tr & ref* to scale

squamó·so -sa [s] *adj* scaly

squarciagóla *adv*—a squarciagola at the top of one's voice

squarciare §128 *tr* to rend, tear apart; to dispel (*a doubt*) || *ref* to become torn; to open

squàr·cio *m* (-ci) tear, rip; passage (*of book*)

squartare *tr* to quarter

squartatura *f* quartering

squassare *tr* to shake violently; to wreck

squattrina·to -ta *adj* penniless || *m* pauper

squilibra·to -ta *adj* unbalanced, deranged || *mf* mad or insane person

squili·brio *m* (-bri) lack of balance; squilibrio mentale insanity; unbalanced mental condition

squillante *adj* ringing, shrill; sharp

squillare *intr* to ring; to ring out; to blare

squillo *m* ring; peal; blare, blast (*of horn*); || *f* call girl

squinternare (squintèrno) *tr* to tear (*a book*) to pieces; (fig) to upset

squisi·to -ta *adj* exquisite

squittire §176 *intr* to squeak; to squeal

sradicare §197 (sràdico) *tr* to uproot; to eradicate; to pull (*a tooth*)

sragionare (sragióno) *intr* to talk nonsense

sregola·to -ta *adj* intemperate; dissolute

srotolare (sròtolo) *tr* to unroll

stàb·bio *m* (-bi) pen; manure, dung

stabbiòlo *m* pigpen

stàbile *adj* stable; real (*estate*); permanent; stock (*company*) || *m* building

stabiliménto *m* plant, factory; establishment; settlement, colony; conclusion (*of a deal*)

stabilire §176 *tr* to establish; to decide || *ref* to settle

stabili·tà *f* (-tà) stability, steadiness

stabilito *m* (law) agreement of sale (*drawn up by a broker*)

stabilizzare [ddzz] *tr & ref* to stabilize

stabilizza·tóre -trice [ddzz] *mf* stabilizing person || *m* (aer) stabilizer; (elec) voltage stabilizer

staccare §197 *tr* to detach; to unhitch; to outdistance; to draw (*a check*); to tear off; to take (*one's eyes*) away; to begin; to enunciate (*words*) || *intr* to stand out; (coll) to stop working || *ref* to come off; staccarsi da to come off (*e.g., the wall*); to leave (*one's home; the shore*); (aer) to take off from

stacciare §128 *tr* to sift, sieve

stàc·cio *m* (-ci) sieve

staccionata *f* fence; hurdle; stockade

stac·co *m* (-chi) tearing off; cut of cloth (*for a suit*); interval; **fare stacco** to stand out

stadèra *f* steelyard; **stadera a ponte** weighbridge

stàdia *f* leveling rod

stà·dio *m* (-di) stadium; stage

staffa *f* stirrup; heel (*of sock*); gaiter strap; clamp; (mach) bracket; **perdere le staffe** to lose one's nerve

staffétta *f* courier, messenger; pilot (*car*); **a staffetta** relay

staffière *m* groom, footman; servant

staffilare *tr* to whip, belt, lash

staffilata *f* lash

staffile *m* stirrup strap; whip

stàg·gio *m* (-gi) stay, upright

stagionale *adj* seasonal ǁ *mf* seasonal worker

stagionare (stagióno) *tr* to season, cure

stagiona·to -ta *adj* seasoned, ripe

stagióne *f* season; **da mezza stagione** spring-and-fall (*coat*); **di fine stagione** year-end (*sale*)

stagliare §280 *tr* to hack ǁ *ref* to stand out

staglia·to -ta *adj* sheer (*cliff*)

sta·gnàio *m* (-gnài) tinsmith; plumber

stagnante *adj* stagnant

stagnare *tr* to tin; to solder; to stanch ǁ *intr* to stagnate

stagnaro *m* var of **stagnaio**

stagnina *f* tin can

stagnino *m* (coll) var of **stagnaio**

sta·gno -gna *adj* watertight; airtight ǁ *m* tin; pond, pool

stagnòla *f* tin foil; tin can

stàio *m* (stài) bushel (*container*); **a staio** (coll) top (*hat*) ǁ *m* (stàia *fpl*) bushel (*measure*); **a staia** in abundance

stalla *f* stable

stallìa *f* (com) lay day

stallière *m* stableman, stableboy

stallo *m* seat; stall; (chess) stalemate

stallóne *m* stallion

stamane, stamani or stamattina *adv* this morning

stambéc·co *m* (-chi) ibex

stambèr·ga *f* (-ghe) hovel

stambù·gio *m* (-gi) hole, hovel

stamburare *tr* to puff up, to boast about ǁ *intr* to drum

stame *m* (bot) stamen; thread, yarn

stamigna *f* cheesecloth

stampa *f* printing; print; (fig) print; (fig) mold; **stampe** printed matter

stampàg·gio *m* (-gi) (mach) stamping

stampare *tr* to stamp; to print; to impress; to publish ǁ *ref* (fig) to be ingraved

stampatèllo *m*—**in stampatello** in block letters; **scrivere in stampatello** to print (*with pen or pencil*)

stampa·to -ta *adj* printed; impressed ǁ *m* printed form; **stampati** printed matter

stampa·tóre -trice *mf* printer

stampèlla *f* crutch

stamperìa *f* print shop

stampìglia *f* rubber stamp; billboard; overprint

stampigliare §280 *tr* to stamp; to overprint

stampinare *tr* to stencil

stampino *m* stencil

stampo *m* mold; stencil; stamp, kind; decoy

stanare *tr* to flush (*game*); (fig) to dig up

stancare §197 *tr* to tire, fatigue; to bore ǁ *ref* to tire, weary

stanchézza *f* tiredness, weariness

stan·co -ca *adj* (-chi -che) tired; tired out; (lit) left (*hand*)

standardizzare [ddzz] *tr* to standardize

stan·ga *f* (-ghe) bar; shaft (*of cart*); beam (*of plow*)

stangata *f* blow

stanghétta *f* small bar; bolt (*of lock*); temple (*of spectacles*); (mus) bar

stanòtte *adv* tonight; last night

stante *adj* being; standing; **a sé stante** by itself, independent ǁ *prep* because of; **stante che** since

stan·tìo -tìa *adj* (-tìi; -tìe) stale; musty

stantuffo *m* piston; plunger

stanza *f* room; stanza; **essere di stanza** (mil) to be stationed; **stanza da bagno** bath room; **stanza di compensazione** clearing house; **stanza di soggiorno** living room

stanziare §287 *tr* to allocate; to appropriate; to budget ǁ *ref* to settle

stanzino *m* small room; closet

stappare *tr* to uncork

stare §263 *intr* (ESSERE) to stay; to stand; to live; to be; to be located; to linger; to last; to stick (*e.g., to a rule*); (poker) to stand pat; **come sta?** how are you?; **lasciar stare** to leave alone; **lasciar stare che** to leave aside that; **non stare in sé dalla gioia** to be beside oneself with joy; **sta bene!** O.K.!; **starci** to fit, e.g., **ci stanno trecento persone** three hundred people fit there; **starci di** to be in favor of, e.g., **io ci starei d'andare al cine** I would be in favor of going to the movies; **stare + ger** to be + *ger*, e.g., **stava leggendo** he was reading; **stare a** to be up to; to stand on (*ceremony*); to base oneself on; to take (*a joke*); to cost, e.g., **a quanto sta il prosciutto?** how much does the ham cost?; **stare a + inf** to keep + *ger*, e.g., **stai sempre a sognare** you always keep dreaming; **to take + inf**, e.g., **stette poco a decidere** he took little time to decide; **stare a cuore** (with *dat*) to deem important, e.g., **gli sta a cuore il lavoro** he deems his work important; **stare a pancia all'aria** to not do a stroke of work; **stare al proprio posto** to keep one's place; **stare a segno** to behave properly; **stare a vedere** to be possible, e.g., **sta a vedere che non viene?** could it be possible that he won't come?; **stare bene** to be well; to be well-off; (with *dat*) to fit, to become, e.g., **questo vestito gli sta**

bene this suit fits him well, this suit becomes him; to serve right, e.g., **gli sta bene!** it serves him right!; **stare comodo** to be at ease; to remain seated; **stare con** (fig) to be on the side of; **starsene** to stay apart, e.g., **se ne sta solo soletto** he stays apart or all alone; **stare fermo** to be quiet; to not move; **stare in forse** to doubt; to be doubtful; **stare sulle proprie** to stand aloof; **stare su** to stand erect; **stare su tardi** to stay up late; **stia comodo!** remain seated!

starna f gray partridge

starnazzare intr to flap its wings; to flutter; to cackle

starnutare intr to sneeze

starnuto m sneeze

stasare [s] tr to unplug, unblock

staséra [s] adv tonight, this evening

sta·si f (-si) (com) stagnation; (pathol) stasis

statale adj government; state ‖ mf government employee

stàti·co -ca (-ci -che) static ‖ f statics

stati·no -na adj (coll) migratory ‖ m itemized list; (educ) registration form

stati·sta m (-sti) statesman

statisti·co -ca (-ci -che) adj statistical ‖ m statistician ‖ f statistics; **fare una statistica (di)** to survey; **statistiche** statistics (data)

stati·vo -va adj nonmigratory; permanent ‖ m stand (of microscope)

stato m state; condition; plight; frame (of mind); status; estate (social class); **di stato** public (e.g., school); **essere in stato di arresto** to be under arrest; **stati** extracts from vital statistics; **Stati Pontifici** Papal States; **Stati Uniti** United States; **stato civile** marital status; vital statistics; **stato confessionale** state under ecclesiastical rule; **stato cuscinetto** buffer state; **stato di preallarme** state of emergency; **stato di previsione** preliminary budget; **stato interessante** pregnancy; **stato maggiore** (mil) general staff

statoreattóre m ramjet engine

stàtua f statue

statuà·rio -ria (-ri -rie) adj statuary; statuesque ‖ m sculptor

statunitènse adj & mf American (U.S.A.)

statura f stature; height

statuto m statute

stavòlta adv (coll) this time

stazionaménto m parking; **stazionamento vietato** no parking

stazionare (stazióno) intr to park

stazionà·rio -ria adj (-ri -rie) stationary

stazióne f station; bearing, posture; **stazione balneare** shore resort; **stazione climatica** health resort, spa; **stazione di rifornimento** service station; **stazione di tassametri** cab stand; **stazione estiva** summer resort; **stazione generatrice** power plant; **stazione orbitale** orbiting station; **stazione sanitaria** clinic

stazza f tonnage; (naut) displacement

stazzare tr (naut) to gauge; (naut) to displace

stazzonare (stazzóno) tr to crumple

steatite f French chalk

stéc·ca f (-che) small stick; slat (of shutter); rib (of umbrella); bone (of whale); carton (of cigarettes); rail (of fence); letter opener; chisel (of sculptor); (billiards) cue; (billiards) miscue; (surg) splint; **fare una stecca** (billiards) to miscue; (mus) to sing or play a sour note

steccadèn·ti m (-ti) (coll) toothpick

steccare §197 (stécco) tr to fence; to put in a splint ‖ intr to play or sing a sour note; (billiards) to miscue

steccato m fence; (racing) inside track

stecchétto m small stick; **tenere a stecchetto** to keep on a strict diet; to keep short of money

stecchino m toothpick

stecchi·to -ta adj stiff; lean, lank; dry (twig); dumfounded

stéc·co m (-chi) stick, twig

stecconata f stockade; fence

stélla f star; rowel (of spur); speck of fat (in soup); (fig) sky; **a stella** star-shaped; stellar; **montare alle stelle** to be sky-high (said, e.g., of prices); **portare alle stelle** to praise to the skies; **stella alpina** edelweiss; **stella cadente** shooting star; **stella di mare** starfish; **stella filante** shooting star; confetti; **stella polare** polestar, lodestar

stellare adj stellar; (mach) radial ‖ v (stéllo) tr to spangle with stars; to stud

stella·to -ta adj starry; star-spangled; star-shaped; studded

stellétta f (mil) star; (typ) asterisk; **guadagnarsi le stellette** (mil) to earn a promotion; **portare le stellette** (mil) to be in the service

stellina f starlet

stelloncino m (journ) short paragraph

stèlo m stem, stalk

stèm·ma m (-mi) coat of arms; genealogy (of a manuscript)

stemperare (stèmpero) tr to dilute; to blunt; to untemper; (lit) to waste ‖ ref to melt; to become dull or blunt

stendardo m banner, standard

stèndere §270 tr to stretch; to hang up (laundry); to spread; to draw up (a document); (mil) to deploy; **stendere a terra** to knock down ‖ ref to stretch out

stendibianche·rìa m (-rìa) clothes rack, clotheshorse

stenodattilògra·fo -fa mf shorthand typist

stenografare (stenògrafo) tr to take down in shorthand

stenografìa f shorthand, stenography

stenogràfi·co -ca adj (-ci -che) stenographic, shorthand

stenògra·fo -fa mf stenographer

stenòsi f (pathol) stricture

stenotipìa f stenotypy

stentare (stènto) tr to eke out (a living)

|| *intr* to barely make ends meet; **stentare a** to hardly be able to; to find it hard to

stenta·to -ta *adj* hard; stunted; strained (*smile*)

stènto *m* privation; hardship; **a stento** hardly; with difficulty; **senza stento** without any trouble

stèr·co *m* (**-chi**) dung

stereofòni·co -ca *adj* (**-ci -che**) stereo, stereophonic

stereoscòpi·co -ca *adj* (**-ci -che**) stereoscopic

stereoscò·pio *m* (**-pi**) stereoscope

stereotipa·to -ta *adj* stereotyped

sterilizzare [ddzz] *tr* to sterilize

sterlina *f* pound sterling

sterminare (**stèrmino**) *tr* to exterminate

stermina·to -ta *adj* immense, boundless

stermì·nio *m* (**-ni**) extermination; (coll) large amount, lots

stèrno *m* breastbone

sterpàglia *f* brushwood; undergrowth

stèrpo *m* dry twig; bramble

sterrare (**stèrro**) *tr* to excavate

sterratóre *m* digger

sterzare (**stèrzo**) *tr* to diminish by one third; to thin out (*woodland*); (aut) to steer || *intr* to swerve

sterzata *f* swerve

stèrzo *m* handle bar; (aut) steering gear; (aut) steering wheel

stésa [s] *f* coat (*of paint*); string (*of clothes on line*)

stés·so -sa *adj* same, e.g., **lo stesso mese** the same month; very, e.g., **tuo fratello stesso** your very brother; **essere alle stesse** to be just the same; **io stesso** I myself; **lui stesso** he himself, etc.; **per sé stesso** by himself; by itself || *pron* same; same thing; **fa lo stesso** it's all the same, it makes no difference

stesura [s] *f* drawing up (*of a contract*); **prima stesura** first draft

stetoscò·pio *m* (**-pi**) stethoscope

stìa *f* chicken coop

Stige *m* Styx

stì·gio -gia *adj* (**-gi -gie**) Stygian

stìgmate *fpl* stigmata

stilare *tr* to draft properly

stile *m* style

stilè *adj invar* stylish

stilétto *m* dagger, stiletto

stilizzare [ddzz] *tr* to stylize

stilla *f* (lit) drop, droplet

stillare *tr* to exude; to distill || *intr* (ESSERE) to ooze, drip, exude || *ref*— **stillarsi il cervello** to rack one's brains

stillicì·dio *m* (**-di**) dripping; repetition

stilo *m* stylus; arm (*of steelyard*); dagger; gnomon (*of sundial*); (poet) style || *f* (coll) fountain pen

stilogràfi·ca *f* (**-che**) fountain pen

stima *f* appraisal; esteem; (naut) dead reckoning; **a stima d'occhio** more or less

stimare *tr* to estimate; to deem; to esteem || *ref* (coll) to think a lot of oneself

stima·tóre -trice *mf* appraiser; admirer

stìmmate *fpl* var of **stigmate**

stimolante *adj* & *m* stimulant

stimolare (**stìmolo**) *tr* to stimulate

stìmolo *m* influence; stimulus

stin·co *m* (**-chi**) shinbone; shin; **stinco di santo** saintly person, saint; **rompere gli stinchi a** to annoy

stìngere §126 *tr, intr* (ESSERE) & *ref* to fade

stipa *f* kindling wood, brushwood

stipare *tr* & *ref* to crowd, jam

stipendiare §287 (**stipèndio**) *tr* to employ, hire; to pay a salary to

stipendia·to -ta *adj* salaried || *mf* salaried person

stipèn·dio *m* (**-di**) pay, salary

stipétto *m* (naut) closet, cabinet

stìpite *m* jamb; stock, family; (bot) trunk (*of palm tree*)

stipo *m* cabinet

stipulare (**stìpulo**) *tr* to draw up (*a contract*); to stipulate

stiracchiare §287 *tr* to stretch; to eke out (*a living*); to twist (*a meaning*); to haggle over || *intr* to haggle; to economize || *ref* to stretch out

stirare *tr* to stretch; to iron, press || *intr* to iron || *ref* to stretch out

stira·tóre -trice *mf* ironer, presser

stiratura *f* ironing; stretching

stirerìa *f* ironing shop

stiro *m*—**ferro da stiro** see **ferro**

stirpe *f* family; birth, origin

stitichézza *f* constipation

stìti·co -ca *adj* (**-ci -che**) constipated; (fig) tight

stiva *f* (naut) hold; (lit) beam (*of plow*)

stivàg·gio *m* (**-gi**) stowage

stivale *m* boot; **dei miei stivali** good-for-nothing; **lustrare gli stivali a qlcu** to lick s.o.'s boots

stivalétto *m* high shoe

stivalóne *m* boot; **stivaloni da equitazione** riding boots; **stivaloni da palude** hip boots

stivare *tr* to stow

stivatóre *m* stevedore

stizza *f* anger; irritation

stizzire §176 *tr* to anger, vex || *ref* to get angry

stizzó·so -sa [s] *adj* peevish, irritable

stoccafisso *m* stockfish

stoccata *f* thrust (*with dagger or rapier*); dig, sarcastic remark; touch (*for money*)

stòc·co *m* (**-chi**) dagger; rapier; stalk (*of corn*)

Stoccólma *f* Stockholm

stòffa *f* cloth, material; (fig) stuff, makings

stoicismo *m* stoicism

stòi·co -ca (**-ci -che**) *adj* stoic, stoical || *m* stoic; Stoic

stoino *m* doormat

stòla *f* stole

stòli·do -da *adj* foolish, silly

stoltézza *f* foolishness, silliness

stól·to -ta *adj* silly || *mf* fool

stomacare §197 (**stòmaco**) *tr* to disgust; to nauseate

stomachévole *adj* disgusting, sickening

stòma·co *m* (-ci or -chi) stomach; maw (*of animal*); dare di stomaco to vomit

stonare (stòno) *tr* to sing or play out of tune; to upset ‖ *intr* to sing or play out of tune; to be out of place; to not harmonize

stona·to -ta *adj* out-of-tune; upset; clashing (*color*)

stonatura *f* jarring sound; clash (*of colors*); lack of harmony

stóppa *f* tow; oakum; di stoppa flaxen; weak, trembling; stoppa incatramata oakum

stoppàc·cio *m* (-ci) wad

stóppie *fpl* stubble

stoppino *m* wick

stoppó·so -sa [s] *adj* stubby; stringy

stórcere §272 *tr* to twist; to twitch; to wrench (*one's ankle*); to roll (*one's eyes*) ‖ *ref* to twist; to writhe; to bend

stordiménto *m* bewilderment; dizziness

stordire §176 *tr* to bewilder; to daze ‖ *intr* to be bewildered ‖ *ref* to dull one's senses

storditàggine *f* carelessness; mistake, blunder

stordi·to -ta *adj* careless; bewildered; amazed; dizzy ‖ *mf* scatterbrain

stòria *f* history; story, tale; fact; fare storie to stand on ceremony; un'altra storia a horse of another color

stòri·co -ca (-ci -che) *adj* historical ‖ *m* historian

storièlla *f* tale, short story; joke

storiografìa *f* historiography

storióne *m* sturgeon

stormire §176 *intr* to rustle

stórmo *m* swarm, flock; (aer) group

stornare (stórno) *tr* to ward off; to dissuade; to divert (*funds*); to write off (*as noncollectable*)

stornèllo *m* Italian folksong; (orn) starling

stór·no -na *adj* dapple-gray ‖ *m* (com) transfer; (orn) starling

storpiare §287 (stòrpio) *tr* to cripple; to clip (*one's words*)

stòr·pio -pia (-pi -pie) *adj* crippled ‖ *m* cripple

stòr·to -ta *adj* twisted; crooked; crippled ‖ *f* twist; dislocation; retort

stovìglie *fpl* dishes; lavare le stoviglie to wash the dishes

stra- *pref adj* extra-, e.g., straordinario extraordinary; over-, e.g., stracarico overloaded

stràbi·co -ca *adj* (-ci -che) crosseyed

strabiliante *adj* astonishing, amazing

strabiliare §287 *tr* to amaze ‖ *intr* & *ref* to be amazed

strabismo *m* strabismus, squint

straboccare §197 (strabócco) *intr* to overflow

strabocchévole *adj* overflowing

strabuzzare [ddzz] *tr* (coll) to roll (*one's eyes*)

stracàri·co -ca *adj* (-chi -che) overloaded, overburdened

stracca *f*—pigliare una stracca to be dead tired

straccale *m* breeching (*of harness*); straccali (coll) suspenders

straccare §197 *tr* (coll) to tire

stracciaiò·lo -la *mf* ragpicker

stracciare §128 *tr* to tear, rend; to comb (*natural silk*)

stràc·cio -cia (-ci -ce) *adj* torn, in rags; waste (*paper*) ‖ *m* rag, tatter; tear, rend; combed silk

stracció·ne -na *mf* tatterdemalion

straccivéndo·lo -la *mf* ragpicker; rag dealer

strac·co -ca *adj* (-chi -che) tired; worn-out; alla stracca lazily ‖ *f* see stracca

stracòt·to -ta *adj* overcooked, overdone ‖ *m* stew

stracuòcere §144a *tr* to overcook, overdo

strada *f* roadway; street; da strada vulgar, common; divorare la strada to burn up the road; essere in mezzo a una strada to be in a bad way; fare strada a to pave the way for; farsi strada to make one's way; prender la strada to set forth; strada carrozzabile carriage road; strada dell'orto easy way out; strada ferrata railroad; strada maestra main road; tagliare la strada a to stand in the way of; (aut) to cut in front of

stradale *adj* road; street; traffic (*e.g., accident*); highway (*police*) ‖ *m* avenue ‖ *f* highway patrol

stradà·rio *m* (-ri) street directory

strafalcióne *m* blunder, gross error

strafare §173 *tr* to overdo; to overcook

strafóro *m* drilled hole; di straforo stealthily

strafottènte *adj* unconcerned, nonchalant; arrogant, impudent

strafottènza *f* nonchalance, unconcern; arrogance, impudence

strage *f* butchery, massacre, carnage; (coll) multitude, lot

stragrande *adj* enormous, huge

stralciare §128 *tr* to prune, trim (*grapevines*); to eliminate, remove; (com) to liquidate

stràl·cio *adj invar* interim; emergency (*e.g., law*); liquidating ‖ *m* (-ci) excerpt; clearance sale; a stralcio at a bargain

strale *m* (lit) arrow

strallo *m* (naut) stay

stralunare *tr* to roll (*one's eyes*)

straluna·to -ta *adj* upset; wild-eyed

stramazzare *tr* to fell ‖ *intr* (ESSERE) to fall down

stramazzo *m* sluice; (coll) straw mattress

stramberìa *f* eccentricity

stram·bo -ba *adj* odd, queer, eccentric; crooked (*legs*); squint (*eyes*)

strame *m* litter; fodder

strampala·to -ta *adj* strange; preposterous, absurd

stranézza *f* strangeness; oddity

strangolare (stràngolo) *tr* to strangle; (naut) to furl

strangola·tóre -trice *mf* strangler

straniare §287 *tr* (lit) to draw away ‖ *ref* to become estranged

straniè·ro -ra *adj* foreign, alien; (lit) strange || *mf* foreigner, alien

stra·no -na *adj* strange, odd; (lit) estranged

straordinà·rio -ria (-ri -rie) *adj* extraordinary; extra || *mf* temporary employee || *m* overtime

strapagare §209 *tr* to overpay; to pay too much for

strapazzare *tr* to rebuke, upbraid; to mishandle; to bungle || *ref* to overwork oneself

strapazza·to -ta *adj* crumpled; bungled; scrambled (*eggs*); overworked || *f* upbraiding, rebuke; fatigue

strapazzo *m* misuse; fatigue; excess; **da strapazzo** working (*clothes*); hackneyed, second-rate

strapèrdere §212 *tr* & *intr* to lose hopelessly || *intr* to be wiped out

strapiè·no -na *adj* chock-full

strapiombare (strapiómbo) *intr* to overhang, jut out

strapiómbo *m* overhang; **a strapiombo** sheer (*cliff*)

strapotènte *adj* overpowerful

strappare *tr* to pull; to tear, rend; to wring (*s.o.'s heart*); **strappare le lacrime a qlcu** to move s.o. to tears; **strappare qlco a qlcu** to pry s.th out of s.o.; to snatch s.th from s.o. || *ref* to tear (*e.g., one's hair*)

strappata *f* pull, tug, snatch

strappo *m* pull; tear, rip; infraction, breach; pulling away (*on a bicycle*); patch (*of sky*); **a strappi** in jerks; **strappo muscolare** pulled muscle; sprain

strapuntino *m* folding seat, jump seat; bucket seat; (naut) mattress

straric·co -ca *adj* (**-chi -che**) (coll) immensely rich

straripare *intr* (ESSERE & AVERE) to overflow

strascicare §197 (**stràscico**) *tr* to drag; to shuffle; **strascicare le parole** to drawl

strascichì·o *m* (**-i**) shuffle (*of feet*)

stràsci·co *m* (**-chi**) train (*of skirt*); trail; sequel, aftermath; **a strascico** dragging

strascinare (stràscino) *tr* to drag || *ref* to drag oneself, drag

strascini·o *m* (**-i**) shuffle

stràscino *m* dragnet, trawl

stratagèm·ma *m* (**-mi**) stratagem

strategìa *f* strategy

stratègi·co -ca *adj* (**-ci -che**) strategic

stratè·go *m* (**-ghi**) strategist; general, commander

stratificare §197 (**stratìfico**) *tr* to stratify

strato *m* layer; coat, coating; stratum; (meteor) stratus

stratosfèra *f* stratosphere

strattóne *m* jerk, tug

stravagante *adj* extravagant; whimsical, capricious || *mf* eccentric

stravèc·chio -chia *adj* (**-chi -chie**) aged (*cheese, wine, etc.*); very old

stravincere §285 *tr* to overpower

straviziare §287 *intr* to be intemperate

stravì·zio *m* (**-zi**) intemperance, excess

stravòlgere §289 *tr* to roll (*the eyes*); to distort; to derange

straziante *adj* heartbreaking; excruciating (*pain*); horrible

straziare §287 *tr* to torture; to dismay; to mangle; to murder (*a language*)

strazia·to -ta *adj* torn, stricken

strà·zio *m* (**-zi**) suffering, pain; torture; shame; boredom; **fare strazio di** to squander

stré·ga *f* (**-ghe**) witch; sorceress

stregare §209 (**strégo**) *tr* to bewitch

stregóne *m* sorcerer; witch doctor

stregonerìa *f* witchcraft; sorcery

strègua *f* standard, criterion; **alla stregua di** on the basis of

strema·to -ta *adj* exhausted

strènna *f* Christmas gift, New Year's gift; special New Year's issue

strè·nuo -nua *adj* strenuous

strepitare (strèpito) *intr* to make a noise; to shout, make a racket

strèpito *m* noise, racket; **fare strepito** to make a hit

strepitó·so -sa [s] *adj* loud, noisy; resounding (*success*)

streptomicina *f* streptomycin

stressa·to -ta *adj* under stress

strétta *f* grasp, clench; tightening (*of brakes*); hold; press, crush; pang; mountain pass; **mettere alle strette** to drive into a corner; **stretta dei conti** rendering of accounts; **stretta di mano** handshake; **stretta finale** climax

strettézza *f* narrowness; **strettezze** straits, hardship

strét·to -ta *adj* narrow; tight; bare (*necessities*); pure (*e.g., dialect*); strict; clenched (*fist*); heavy (*heart*); minimum (*price*); (phonet) close || *m* straits, narrows || *f* see **stretta** || **stretto** *adv* tightly

strettóia *f* narrow stretch; hardship; bandage

strìa *f* stripe, streak

striare §119 *tr* to stripe, streak

stricnina *f* strychnine

stridènte *adj* jarring; clashing (*colors*); strident (*sound*)

strìdere §264 *tr* to grit (*one's teeth*) || *intr* to shriek; to squeak; to creak; to clash (*said of colors*); to croak (*said of raven*); to hoot (*said of owl*); to howl (*said of wind*) || *ref* (coll) to be resigned

strido *m* (**-di** & **-da** *fpl*) shriek; squeak

stridóre *m* shriek; creak, squeak; gnashing (*of teeth*)

strìdu·lo -la *adj* shrill

strigare §209 *tr* to disentangle || *ref* to extricate oneself

strìglia *f* currycomb

strigliare §280 *tr* to curry; to upbraid || *ref* to groom oneself

strillare *tr* to shout; (coll) to scold; (coll) to hawk (*newspapers*) || *intr* to scream

strillo *m* shriek; shout, scream

strilló·ne -na *mf* loud-mouthed person || *m* newsdealer; newsboy, paperboy

striminzi·to -ta *adj* shrunken; tight; stunted; skinny

strimpellare (strimpèllo) *tr* to thrum; to thrum on

strinare *tr* to singe; to burn (*with a flatiron*)

strin·ga *f* (-ghe) lace; shoelace

stringa·to -ta *adj* terse, concise

stringere §265 *tr* to tighten; to grip; to shake, clasp (*a hand*); to drive into a corner; to squeeze; to embrace; to close (*an alliance, a deal*); to wring (*one's heart*); to clench (*the fist*); (lit) to gird (*a sword*); (mus) to accelerate; **stringere d'assedio** to besiege; **stringere i freni** to put the brakes on ‖ *intr* to be tight; **il tempo stringe** time is running short; **stringi, stringi** at the very end, in conclusion ‖ *ref* to squeeze close together; to shrink; to coagulate; to draw close; **stringersi a** to snuggle up to; **stringersi addosso a** to attack; **stringersi nelle spalle** to shrug one's shoulders

stringina·so [s] *m* (-so) pince-nez

stri·scia *f* (-sce) strip, band; trail; stripe; line; **a strisce** striped; **striscia d'atterramento** airstrip; **striscia di cuoio** strop

strisciante *adj* crawling; (fig) fawning

strisciare §128 *tr* to shuffle (*feet*); to graze; **strisciare una riverenza** to curtsy ‖ *intr* to creep, crawl; to graze by ‖ *ref* to fawn; **strisciarsi a** to rub one's back against

strisciata or **strisciatura** *f* sliding; trail

stri·scio *m* (-sci) rubbing; shuffling; **ballare di striscio** to shuffle; **da** or **di striscio** superficial (*wound*)

striscióne *m* festoon; festooned sign; flatterer; **striscione d'arrivo** landing (*in gymnastics*); **striscione del traguardo** (sports) tape

striscióni *adv* crawling

stritolare (stritolo) *tr* to crush, smash

strizzalimó·ni *m*(-ni) lemon squeezer

strizzare *tr* to squeeze, press; to wink (*the eye*); **strizzare l'occhio** to wink

strizza·tóio *m* (-tói) wringer

strò·fa or **strò·fe** *f* (-fe) strophe

strofinàc·cio *m* (-ci) dust cloth

strofinare *tr* to rub; to polish ‖ *ref* to rub oneself; to fawn

strofinata *f*—**dare una strofinata a** to give a lick and a promise to

strofinì·o *m* (-i) rubbing; wiping

stròla·ga *f* (-ghe) (orn) loon

strombatura *f* embrasure

strombazzare *tr* to glorify; **strombazzare i propri meriti** to toot one's own horn ‖ *intr* to blast away on the trumpet

strombazza·tóre -trice *mf* show-off

strombettare (strombétto) *tr* to trumpet, toot

stroncare §197 (**strónco**) *tr* to break off; to break down; to eliminate; (fig) to criticize severely

stroncatura *f* devastating criticism

strònzio *m* strontium

strónzo *m* (vulg) turd

stropicciare §128 *tr* to rub (*hands*); to drag, shuffle (*feet*); (coll) to crumple ‖ *ref*—**stropicciarsene** (coll) to not give a hoot

stropicci·o *m* (-i) rubbing; shuffling

stròzza *f* (coll) gullet, throat

strozzare (stròzzo) *tr* to strangle; to stop up; to fleece, swindle ‖ *ref* to choke; to narrow

strozza·to -ta *adj* choked; choking; strangulated (*hernia*)

strozzatura *f* narrowing

strozzinàg·gio *m* (-gi) usury

strozzino *m* usurer, loan shark

strùggere §266 *tr* to melt; to consume ‖ *ref* to melt; to pine away; to be upset; **struggersi di** to be consumed by

struggiménto *m* melting; longing; torment

strumentale *adj* instrument (*flying*); capital (*goods*); instructional (*language, in multi-lingual regions*); (gram, mus) instrumental

strumentali·sta *mf* (-sti -ste) instrumentalist

strumentalizzare [ddzz] *tr* to use, take advantage of

strumentare (struménto) *tr* to orchestrate

struménto *m* instrument; tool, implement; **strumento a corda** stringed instrument; **strumento a fiato** wind instrument; **strumento di bordo** (aer) flight recorder

strusciare §128 *tr* to rub; to shuffle (*feet*); to crumple; to wear out ‖ *ref*—**strusciarsi a** to fawn on

strutto *m* lard, shortening

struttura *f* structure

strutturare *tr* to organize, structure

struzzo *m* ostrich

stuccare §197 *tr* to putty; to stucco; to surfeit ‖ *ref* to grow weary

stucchévole *adj* sickening

stuc·co -ca (-chi -che) *adj* bored; **stucco e ristucco** sick and tired ‖ *m* putty; stucco; plaster of Paris; **rimanere di stucco** to be taken aback

studèn·te -téssa *mf* student

studenté·sco -sca (-schi -sche) *adj* student; student-like ‖ *f* student body

studiare §287 *tr* to study; **studiarle tutte** to consider every angle ‖ *intr* to study; to try ‖ *ref* to try; to gaze at oneself

studia·to -ta *adj* affected, studied

stù·dio *m* (-di) study; school district; office (*of professional man*); studio; (hist) university; (lit) wish; (mus) étude; **a studio** on purpose; **essere allo studio** to be under consideration

studió·so -sa [s] *adj* studious ‖ *m* scholar

stufa *f* stove, heater; hothouse

stufare *tr* to warm up, heat up; to stew; (coll) to bore

stufato *m* stew

stu·fo -fa *adj* (coll) bored, sick and tired ‖ *f* see **stufa**

stuòia *f* mat; matting

stuòlo *m* throng, crowd; flock; (lit) army

stupefacènte *adj* amazing; habit-forming || *m* dope
stupefare §173 *tr* to amaze, astonish
stupefazióne *f* amazement, astonishment; stupefaction
stupèn·do -da *adj* stupendous
stupidàggine *f* stupidity; silliness; child's play, cinch
stùpi·do -da *adj* stupid; silly; (lit) amazed
stupire §176 *tr* to amaze || *ref* to be amazed
stupóre *m* amazement
stuprare *tr* to rape
stura *f* tapping; uncorking; **dar la stura a** to begin (*a speech*)
sturabottì·glie *m* (**-glie**) bottle opener
sturalavandì·ni *m* (**-ni**) plunger (*to open up clogged sink*)
sturare *tr* to uncork; to take the wax out of (*ears*); to open up (*clogged line*)
stuzzicadèn·ti *m* (**-ti**) toothpick
stuzzicare §197 (**stùzzico**) *tr* to pick (*e.g., one's teeth*); to bother; to excite, arouse; to tease; to sharpen (*appetite*)
su *adv* up; on top; upstairs; **da . . . in su** from . . . on, e.g., **dal mese scorso in su** from last month on; **di su** from upstairs; **in su up**; **metter su** to put on the fire; to instigate; **metter su bottega** to set up shop; **metter su casa** to set up housekeeping; **più su** higher; further up; **su!** come on!; let's go!; **su di** on; **su e giù** back and forth; up and down; **su per giù** more or less; **tirarsi su** to lift oneself up; to sit up; to get better, recover; **tirar su** to pick up; to grow, raise; **venir su** to grow; to come up || §4 *prep* on, upon; up; towards; over, above; onto; against; at, e.g., **sul far del giorno** at daybreak; on top of; out of, e.g., **due volte su tre** two times out of three; **mettere su superbia** to become proud; **stare sulle sue** to be reserved; **sul serio** in earnest; **su misura** made to order
suaccenna·to -ta *adj* above-mentioned
sub *m* (**sub**) (coll) skindiver
subàcque·o -a *adj* submarine
subaffittare *tr* to sublet
subaffitto *m* subletting, sublet; **prendere in subaffitto** to sublet
subaltèr·no -na *adj* & *m* subaltern; subordinate
subastare *tr* to auction off
sùbbia *f* stonecutter's chisel
subbù·glio *m* (**-gli**) turmoil, hubbub
subcosciènte *adj* & *m* subconscious
sùbdo·lo -la *adj* treacherous, deceitful
subentrare (**subéntro**) *intr* (ESSERE) (with *dat*) to succeed, follow
subire §176 *tr* to suffer; to undergo
subissare *tr* to ruin; to sink; to overwhelm || *intr* (ESSERE) to sink; to go to rack and ruin
subisso *m* ruin; (coll) lots, plenty
subitàne·o -a *adj* sudden
sùbi·to -ta *adj* (lit) sudden || *m*—**d'un subito** all of a sudden || **subito** *adv*

rapidly; immediately; right away; **subito al principio** at the very beginning; **subito dopo** right after; **subito prima** right before || *interj* right away!
sublima·to -ta *adj* sublimated || *m* **sublimato corrosivo** corrosive sublimate
sublime *adj* & *m* sublime
subodorare (**subodóro**) *tr* to suspect; to get wind of
subordinare (**subórdino**) *tr* to subordinate
subordina·to -ta *adj* & *m* subordinate || *f* subordinate clause
subornare (**subórno**) *tr* to bribe
substrato *m* substratum
suburba·no -na *adj* suburban
subùr·bio *m* (**-bi**) suburb
succedàne·o -a *adj* & *m* substitute
succèdere §132 (*pp* **succeduto** or **succèsso**) *intr* (ESSERE) (with *dat*) to succede, to follow || *ref* to follow one another, follow one after the other || (*pret* **succèssi**; *pp* **succèsso**) *intr* (ESSERE) to happen, to come to pass; (with *dat*) to happen to, to come over, e.g., **che gli è successo?** what happened to him?
successióne *f* succession; **in successione** in succession; in a row
successi·vo -va *adj* successive; next
succèsso *m* success; outcome
successóre *m* successor
successò·rio -ria *adj* (**-ri -rie**) inheritance (*tax*)
succhiare §287 *tr* to suck
succhièllo *m* gimlet
succhiétto *m* pacifier
sùc·chio *m* (**-chi**) suck, sucking; (bot) sap; (coll) gimlet
succiaca·pre *m* (**-pre**) goatsucker, whippoorwill
succin·to -ta *adj* scanty (*clothing*); succinct, concise
suc·co *m* (**-chi**) juice; (fig) gist
succó·so -sa [s] *adj* juicy; pithy
succursale *f* branch, branch office
sud *m* south
sudafrica·no -na *adj* & *mf* South African
sudamerica·no -na *adj* & *mf* South American
sudàmina *f* prickly heat
sudare *tr* to sweat; to ooze; **sudare il pane** to earn one's living by the sweat of one's brow; **sudare sette camicie** to toil very hard || *intr* to perspire, sweat; to reek
sudà·rio *m* (**-ri**) shroud
suda·to -ta *adj* wet with perspiration; hard-earned || *f* sweat, sweating
suddét·to -ta *adj* aforesaid, above
sùddi·to -ta *adj* & *mf* subject
suddivìdere §158 *tr* to subdivide
sud-èst *m* southeast
sudicerìa *f* filth, filthiness; smut
sùdi·cio -cia (**-ci -cie**) *adj* dirty, filthy || *m* dirt, filth
sudiciume *m* dirt, filth
sudi·sta *mf* (**-sti -ste**) Southerner
sudóre *m* sweat, perspiration

sud-òvest *m* southwest
sufficiènte *adj* sufficient, adequate; self-sufficient ‖ *m* sufficient
sufficiènza *f* sufficiency; self-sufficiency; (educ) minimum passing grade
suffisso *m* suffix
suffragare §209 *tr* to support; to pray for
suffragétta *f* suffragette
suffrà·gio *m* (-gi) suffrage
suffumicare §197 (suffùmico) *tr* to fumigate
suffumi·gio *m* (-gi) treatment by inhalation; fumigation
suggellare (suggèllo) *tr* to seal
suggèllo *m* seal
suggeriménto *m* suggestion
suggerire §176 *tr* to suggest; to prompt
suggeri·tóre -trice *mf* prompter ‖ *m* (baseball) coach
suggestionàbile *adj* suggestible
suggestionare (suggestióno) *tr* to influence by suggestion ‖ *ref*—suggestionarsi a + *inf* to talk oneself into + *ger*
suggestióne *f* suggestion; fascination
suggesti·vo -va *adj* suggestive; fascinating; (law) leading (*question*)
sùghero *m* cork
sugli §4
sugna *f* fat; lard
su·go *m* (-ghi) juice; gravy; gist, pith; non c'è sugo it's no fun; there's nothing to it; senza sugo pointless, dull
sugó·so -sa [s] *adj* juicy
sui §4
suici·da (-di -de) *adj* suicidal ‖ *mf* suicide (*person*)
suicidare *ref* to commit suicide
suici·dio *m* (-di) suicide (*act*)
sui·no -na *adj* swinish; see carne ‖ *m* swine
sul §4
sulfamìdi·co -ca (-ci -che) *adj* sulfa ‖ *m* sulfa drug
sulla §4
sulle §4
sulli §4
sullo §4
sulloda·to -ta *adj* above-mentioned
sultano *m* sultan
summentova·to -ta, summenziona·to -ta, sunnomina·to -ta *adj* above-mentioned
sunteggiare §290 (suntéggio) *tr* to summarize
sunto *m* résumé, summary
suo sua §6 *adj* & *pron poss* (suòi sue)
suòcera *f* mother-in-law
suòcero *m* father-in-law; i suoceri the in-laws
suòla *f* sole (*of shoe*); share (*of plow*); (naut) sliding ways; (rr) flange (*of rail*)
suòlo *m* ground; soil; floor ‖ *m* (suola *fpl*) (coll) layer; (coll) sole (*of shoe*)
suonare (suòno) *tr* & *intr* var of sonare
suòno *m* sound; (fig) ring; a suon di bastonate with a sound thrashing; a suon di fischi with loud boos; suono armonico (mus) overtone

suòno·stère·o *m* (-o) stereo tape player
suòra *f* nun, sister
super- *pref adj* & *mf* super-, e.g., supersonico supersonic; over-, e.g., superallenamento overtraining
superaffollaménto *m* overcrowding
superare (sùpero) *tr* to surpass; to cross; to overcome; to pass; to exceed; (cards) to trump
supera·to -ta *adj* out-of-date, passé
supèrbia *f* pride, haughtiness; montare in superbia to get a swelled head
superbió·so -sa [s] *adj* proud, haughty
supèr·bo -ba *adj* proud, haughty; superb; spirited ‖ i superbi the haughty ones
supercarburante *m* high-octane gas
supercolòsso *m* supercolossal film
superdònna *f*—si da arie di superdonna she thinks she's hot stuff
supereterodina *f* superheterodyne
superficiale *adj* superficial; surface; cursory, perfunctory ‖ *m* superficial fellow
superfì·cie *f* (-ci & cie) surface; area; superficie portante airfoil
supèr·fluo -flua *adj* superfluous ‖ *m* surplus
super-ìo *m* (-ìo) superego
superióra *f* (eccl) mother superior
superióre *adj* superior; upper; higher; above; superiore a higher than; more than; larger than ‖ *m* superior
superlati·vo -va *adj* & *m* superlative
superlavóro *m* overwork
supermercato *m* supermarket
supersòni·co -ca *adj* (-ci -che) supersonic
supèrstite *adj* surviving; remaining ‖ *mf* survivor
superstizióne *f* superstition
superstizió·so -sa [s] *adj* superstitious
superstrada *f* superhighway
superuòmo *m* superman
supervisióne *f* supervision
supervisóre *m* supervisor; (mov) director
supi·no -na *adj* supine; on one's back
suppellèttile *f* furnishings; equipment; fixtures; fund (*of knowledge*)
supplementare *adj* supplementary
suppleménto *m* supplement; (mil) reinforcement
supplènte *adj* & *mf* substitute
supplènza *f* substitute assignment
suppleti·vo -va *adj* additional; (gram) suppletive
sùppli·ca *f* (-che) supplication; plea; petition
supplicante *mf* supplicant
supplicare §197 (sùpplico) *tr* to beseech; to plead with; to appeal to
supplichévole *adj* beseeching, imploring
supplire §176 *tr* to replace ‖ *intr* (with *dat*) to supplement, make up for
suppliziare §287 *tr* to torture; to execute
supplì·zlo *m* (-zi) torture, torment; estremo supplizio capital punishment
suppórre §218 *tr* to suppose
suppòrto *m* support, prop
suppositò·rio *m* (-ri) suppository

supposizióne *f* supposition; presumption

suppó·sto -sta *adj* alleged || *m* supposition || *f* suppository

suppurare *intr* (ESSERE & AVERE) to suppurate

supremazìa *f* supremacy

suprè·mo -ma *adj* supreme

surclassare *tr* to outclass

surgelare (surgèlo) *tr* to quick-freeze

surreali·sta *mf* (-sti -ste) surrealist

surrenale *adj* adrenal (*gland*)

surrène *m* (anat) adrenal gland

surriscaldare *tr* to overheat

surrogare §209 (surrògo) *tr* to replace

surroga·to -ta *adj* replaceable || *m* makeshift, substitute, ersatz

suscettìbile *adj* susceptible; touchy

suscitare (sùscito) *tr* to rouse; to give rise to; to provoke

susina *f* plum

susino *m* plum tree

susseguènte *adj* subsequent, following

susseguire (sussèguo) *intr* (ESSERE) (with *dat*) to follow || *ref* to follow one after the other

sussidiare §287 *tr* to subsidize

sussidià·rio -ria (-ri -rie) *adj* subsidiary; (nav) auxiliary || *m* supplementary text book; subsidiary

sussì·dio *m* (-di) subsidy; assistance, relief; **sussidi audiovisivi** audio-visual aids; **sussidi didattici** teaching aids; **sussidio di disoccupazione** unemployment compensation

sussiè·go *m* (-ghi) stiffness, haughtiness

sussistènza *f* substance; subsistence; (mil) quartermaster corps

sussìstere §114 *intr* (ESSERE & AVERE) to subsist; to be, exist

sussultare *intr* to start, jump; to quake

sussulto *m* start, jump; **sussulto di terremoto** earth tremor

sussurrare *tr* to whisper; to murmur, mutter || *intr* to whisper; to rustle || *ref*—**si sussurra** it is rumored

sussurra--tóre -trice *mf* whisperer; grumbler

sussurrì·o *m* (-i) whispering; murmur, rustle

sussurro *m* whisper; murmur

susta *f* temple (*of spectacles*); (coll) spring

suvvìa *interj* come!, come on!

svagare §209 *tr* to entertain; to distract || *ref* to have a good time; to relax

svaga·to -ta *adj* absent-minded; inattentive

sva·go *m* (-ghi) entertainment, diversion; avocation, hobby

svaligiare §290 *tr* to ransack; to rob; to pirate

svaligia·tóre -trice *mf* thief, robber

svalutare (svàluto & svaluto) *tr* to devaluate; to depreciate; to belittle || *ref* to depreciate

svalutazióne *f* depreciation

svanire §176 *intr* (ESSERE) to evaporate; to vanish

svani·to -ta *adj* faded, evaporated; vanished; enfeebled

svantàg·gio *m* (-gi) disadvantage

svantaggió·so -sa [s] *adj* disadvantageous

svaporare (svapóro) *intr* (ESSERE) to evaporate; to vanish

svaria·to -ta *adj* varied; **svaria·ti -te** several

svarióne *m* blunder, gross error

svasare *tr* to transplant from a pot; to make (*e.g., a gown*) flare

svasa·to -ta *adj* bell-mouthed, flaring

svecchiare §287 (svècchio) *tr* to renew; to rejuvenate; to modernize

svedése [s] *adj* Swedish; safety (*match*) || *mf* Swede || *m* Swedish

svéglia *f* awakening; reveille; alarm clock; **dare la sveglia a** to wake up

svegliare §280 *tr* & *ref* to wake up

svegliarino *m* alarm clock; (coll) rebuke

své·glio -glia *adj* (-gli -glie) awake; alert || *f* see **sveglia**

svelare (svélo) *tr* to reveal; to unveil || *ref* to reveal oneself; **svelarsi per** to reveal oneself to be

svèllere §267 *tr* (lit) to eradicate

sveltézza *f* quickness; slenderness

sveltire §176 *tr* to make shrewd; to quicken, accelerate || *ref* to become smart

svèl·to -ta *adj* quick; slender; brisk; quick-witted; **alla svelta** quickly; **svelto di lingua** loose-tongued; **svelto di mano** light-fingered || **svelto** *interj* quick!

svenare (svéno) *tr* to bleed to death; (fig) to bleed || *ref* to bleed to death; (fig) to bleed oneself white

svéndere §281 *tr* to sell below cost; to undersell

svéndita *f* clearance sale

svenévole *adj* maudlin, mawkish

svenevolézza *f* maudlinness, mawkishness

sveniménto *m* faint, swoon

svenire §282 *intr* (ESSERE) to faint

sventagliare §280 *tr* to fan; to flash, display

sventagliata *f* blow with a fan; volley

sventare (svènto) *tr* to foil, thwart; (naut) to spill (*a sail*)

sventa·to -ta *adj* careless, thoughtless

svèntola *f* fan (*to kindle fire*); (coll) box, slap; **a sventola** (*ears*) that stick out

sventolare (svèntolo) *tr* to wave; to fan; to winnow || *intr* to flutter || *ref* to fan oneself

sventolì·o *m* (-i) fluttering, flutter

sventraménto *m* demolition; disembowelment; hernia

sventrare (svèntro) *tr* to demolish; to disembowel; to draw (*a fowl*)

sventura *f* misfortune, mishap; bad luck

sventura·to -ta *adj* unfortunate, unlucky

sverginare (svérgino) *tr* to deflower

svergognare (svergógno) *tr* to put to shame; to unmask

svergogna·to -ta *adj* shameless

svergolare (svérgolo) *tr & ref* to warp; (mach) to twist
svernare (svèrno) *intr* to winter
svérza [dz] *f* big splinter
sverzino [dz] *m* lash, whipcord
svestire (svèsto) *tr* to undress; to hull (*rice*); (fig) to strip || *ref* to undress; **svestirsi di** to shed (*e.g., leaves*)
svettare (svétto) *tr* to pollard, top || *intr* to stand out; to sway (*said of a tree*)
Svè·vo -va *adj & m* Swabian
Svèzia, la Sweden
svezzaménto *m* weaning
svezzare (svézzo) *tr* to wean; **svezzare da** to break (s.o.) of (*e.g., a habit*)
sviare §119 *tr* to turn aside; to lead astray || *intr & ref* to go astray; to straggle; (rr) to run off the track
svignare *intr* (ESSERE) to slip away || *ref*—**svignarsela** to sneak away
svilire §176 *tr* to devaluate
svillaneggiare §290 (svillanéggio) *tr* to insult, abuse
sviluppare *tr* to develop; to cause; (lit) to uncoil || *intr* (ESSERE & AVERE) & *ref* to develop; to break out (*said of fire*)
sviluppo *m* development; puberty
svincolare (svìncolo) *tr* to free; to clear (*at customs*)
svìncolo *m*—**svincolo autostradale**

interchange; **svincolo doganale** customs clearance
svirilizzare [ddzz] *tr* (fig) to emasculate
svisare *tr* to alter, distort
sviscerare (svìscero) *tr* to eviscerate; to examine thoroughly || *ref*—**sviscerarsi per** to be crazy about; to bow and scrape to
sviscera·to -ta *adj* ardent, passionate; obsequious
svista *f* slip, error, oversight
svitare *tr* to unscrew
svìzze·ro -ra *adj & mf* Swiss || **la Svizzera** Switzerland
svocia·to -ta *adj* hoarse
svogliatézza *f* laziness; listlessness
svoglia·to -ta *adj* lazy; listless
svolazzare *intr* to flutter, flit
svolazzo *m* flutter; short flight; curlicue, flourish
svòlgere §289 *tr* to unwrap; to unfold; to unwind; to develop; to pursue (*an activity*); to dissuade || *ref* to unwind; to free oneself; to develop; to take place; to unfold
svolgiménto *m* development; composition
svòlta *f* turn; curve; turning point
svoltare (svòlto) *tr* to unwrap || *intr* to turn
svotare §257 or **svuotare** (svuòto) *tr* to empty

T

T, t [ti] *m & f* eighteenth letter of the Italian alphabet
tabac·càio -càia *mf* (-**cài** -**càie**) tobacconist
tabaccare §197 *intr* to take snuff
tabaccherìa *f* cigar store
tabacchièra *f* snuffbox
tabac·co *m* (-**chi**) tobacco; **tabacco da fiuto** snuff
tabarro *m* winter coat; cloak
tabèlla *f* tablet; list; schedule; (coll) clapper, noisemaker; **tabella di marcia** timetable
tabellare *adj* (typ) on wooden blocks; scheduled
tabellóne *m* board; bulletin board; (basketball) backboard
tabernàcolo *m* tabernacle
ta·bù *adj invar & m* (-**bù**) taboo
tàbula *f*—**far tabula rasa di** to make a clean sweep of
tabulare (tàbulo) *tr* to tabulate
tabulatóre *m* tabulator
tabulatrice *f* printer (*of computer*)
tac·ca *f* (-**che**) notch; size; kind; tally; blemish; (typ) nick; **di mezza tacca** middle-sized; mediocre; **tacca di mira** rear sight (*of firearm*)
tacca·gno -gna *adj* stingy, closefisted || *mf* miser
taccheggia·tóre -trice *mf* shoplifter || *f* prostitute, streetwalker

taccheggiatura *f* or **tacchég·gio** *m* (-**gi**) shoplifting
tacchétto *m* high heel; cleat (*on soccer or football shoe*)
tacchina *f* turkey hen
tacchino *m* turkey
tàc·cia *f* (-**ce**) notoriety
tacciare §128 *tr*—**tacciare di** to accuse of, charge with
tac·co *m* (-**chi**) heel; block; (typ) underlay; **battere i tacchi** to take to one's heels
taccóne *m* (coll) patch; (coll) hobnail; **battere il taccone** to take to one's heels
taccuino *m* pocketbook; notebook
tacére *m* silence; **mettere a tacere** to silence || §268 *tr* to conceal, withhold; to imply, understand || *intr* to keep quiet; to stop playing; to quiet down; to be silent; **far tacere** to silence; **taci!** (coll) shut up!
tachìmetro *m* tachometer; (aut) speedometer
tacitare (tàcito) *tr* to silence, satisfy (*a creditor*); to pay off
tàci·to -ta *adj* silent; tacit
tacitur·no -na *adj* taciturn
tafano *m* horsefly, gadfly
tafferù·glio *m* (-**gli**) scuffle
taffe·tà *m* (-**tà**) taffeta; **taffetà adesivo**

or **inglese** adhesive plaster, court plaster

tàglia *f* ransom, reward; size; build; tally; (mach) tackle

tagliabór·se *m* (**-se**) pickpocket

tagliabò·schi *m* (**-schi**) woodcutter, woodsman

tagliacar·te *m* (**-te**) letter opener, paper knife

tagli·àcque *m* (**-àcque**) cutwater (*of bridge*)

tagliaèrba *adj invar* grass-cutting

tagliafèr·ro *m* (**-ro**) cold chisel

taglialé·gna *m* (**-gna**) woodcutter

tagliama·re *m* (**-re**) cutwater (*of ship*)

tagliando *m* coupon

tagliapiè·tre *m* (**-tre**) stonecutter

tagliare §280 *tr* to cut; to cut down; to cut off; to pick (*a pocket*); to cross (*finish line*); to tailor (*a suit*); to blend (*wine*); to turn off (*e.g., water*); **tagliare a fette** to slice; **tagliare in due** to split; **tagliare i panni addosso a qlcu** to slander s.o.; **tagliare i ponti con** to sever relations with; **tagliare i viveri a** to cut off supplies from; **tagliare la corda** to run away; **tagliare la strada a** to stand in the way of; (aut) to cut in front of; **tagliare le gambe a** to make wobbly (*said of wine*) || *intr* to cut; to bite (*said of cold*); **tagliare per una scorciatoia** to take a shortcut || *ref* to cut oneself; to tear (*said of material*)

tagliasìga·ri *m* (**-ri**) cigar cutter

tagliata *f* cut; clearing; (mil) abatis; **tagliata ai capelli** haircut

tagliatèlle *fpl* noodles

taglia·to -ta *adj* cut; fashioned; **essere tagliato per** to be cut out for; **tagliato all'antica** old-fashioned; **tagliato con l'accetta** rough-hewn || *f* see **tagliata**

taglia·tóre -trice *mf* cutter

tagliènte *adj* cutting || *m* edge

taglière *m* carving board

taglierina *f* paper cutter

tà·glio *m* (**-gli**) cut; cutting; dressmaking; cutting edge; sharpness; blending (*of wines*); size; denomination (*of paper money*); crossing (*of t*); (bb) fore edge; **a due tagli** double-edged; **a tagli** by the slice; **dare un taglio a** to chop; **di taglio** edgewise; **rifare il taglio a** to sharpen; **taglio cesareo** Caesarean section; **taglio d'abito** suiting; **taglio dei capelli** haircut; **venire in taglio** to come in handy

tagliòla *f* trap

tagliuzzare *tr* to shred, cut into shreds

tailandése [s] *adj & mf* Thai

Tailàndia, la Thailand

tailleur *m* (**tailleur**) woman's tailored costume

talal·tro -tra *pron indef* another, some other

tàlamo *m* (lit) nuptial bed

talare *adj* ankle-length || *f* soutane, cassock

talché *conj* so that

talco *m* talcum; talcum powder

tale *adj* such; such a; that; **il tale** such and such a; **u tale** such a; a certain; **un tal quale** such a; a certain || *pron* so-and-so; **il tal dei tali** so-and-so; Mr. so-and-so; **il tale** that fellow; that guy; **quel tale** that fellow, that guy; **tale e quale** like; **tali e quali** exactly, word for word; **un tale** someone, a certain person

talèa *f* (hort) cutting

talènto *m* talent; inclination; **a proprio talento** gladly, willingly; **di mal talento** grudgingly; **andare a talento a** to suit, e.g., **non gli va a talento nulla** nothing suits him

talismano *m* talisman

tallire §176 *intr* (ESSERE & AVERE) to sprout

tallonare (**tallóno**) *tr* (sports) to be at the heels of

talloncino *m* coupon, stub

tallóne *m* heel; coupon, stub; tang (*of knife*); **tallone d'Achille** Achilles heel

talménte *adv* so, so much

talóra *adv* sometimes

talpa *f* mole

talu·no -na *pron indef* some; someone, somebody || **talu·ni -ne** *adj & pron indef* some

talvòlta *adv* sometimes

tamarindo *m* tamarind

tambureggiare §290 (**tamburéggio**) *intr* to drum; to beat down (*said, e.g., of hail*)

tamburèllo *m* tambour (*for embroidering*); (mus) tambourine

tamburino *m* drummer

tamburo *m* drum; barrel (*of watch; of windlass*); **a tamburo battente** on the spot

tamerice *f* tamarisk

Tamigi *m* Thames

tampòco *adv*—**né tampoco** (archaic) nor . . . either

tamponaménto *m* stopping, plugging; rear-end collision

tamponare (**tampóno**) *tr* to tampon, plug; to collide with; to hit from the rear; (surg) to tampon

tampóne *m* plug, tampon; pad; (mus) drumstick; (rr) buffer; (surg) tampon; **tampone di vapore** vapor lock

tana *f* burrow; den; hole; hovel; base (*in children games*)

tanàglie *fpl* var of **tenaglie**

tan·ca *f* (**-che**) can, jerry can; tank

tanfo *m* musty or stuffy smell

tangènte *adj* tangent || *f* tangent; (com) commission

tàngere §269 *tr* (lit) to touch

Tàngeri *f* Tangier

tànghero *m* boor, lout

tangìbile *adj* tangible

tàni·ca *f* (**-che**) var of **tanca**

tantino *m*—**un tantino** a little, e.g., **è un tantino arrabbiato** he is a little angry; a little bit, e.g., **un tantino di dolce** a little bit of cake

tan·to -ta *adj & pron indef* such, such a; so much; as much; **a dir tanto** or **a far tanto** at the most; **ai tanti**

(*del mese*) on such and such a day (*of the month*); **a tanto** to such a point; to such a level; **e tanto** odd, e.g., **mille dollari e tanto** a thousand odd dollars; **è tanto** it has been a long time, e.g., **è tanto che lo conosco** it has been a long time since I made his acquaintance; **fra tanto** meanwhile; **senza tanto chiasso** without any noise; **tan·ti -te** many; so many; as many; a lot, e.g., **grazie tante!** thanks a lot! **tanti ... che** so many ... that; **tanti ... quanti** as many ... as; **tanto di guadagnato** so much the better ‖ **tanto** *adv* so much; so; only, e.g., **tanto per passare il tempo** only to pass the time; anyhow; anyway; **nè tanto nè quanto** at all; **tant'è** it's the same; **tanto che** so much that, e.g., **mi ha annoiato tanto che l'ho mandato via** he bothered me so much that I dismissed him; **tanto ... che** both ... and, e.g., **tanto Maria che Roberto** both Mary and Robert; **so much ... that**; **tanto fa** or **vale** it's all the same; **tanto meglio** so much the better; **tanto meno** so much the less; **tanto per cambiare** as usual; **tanto più ... quanto più** the more ... the more; **tanto ... quanto** as ... as ‖ *s*— **ascoltare con tanto d'orecchie** to be all ears; **di tanto in tanto** from time to time

tapi·no -na *adj* (lit) wretched ‖ *mf* (lit) wretch

tappa *f* stopping place; stop; stage, leg; (sports) lap; **bruciare le tappe** to press on, keep going; **fare tappa** to stop

tappabu·chi *mf* (-chi) makeshift, pinch hitter, substitute

tappare *tr* to cork, plug; to shut up tight ‖ *ref* to shut oneself in; to plug (*e.g., one's ears*)

tapparèlla *f* (coll) inside rolling shutter

tappéto *m* rug, carpet; (sports) canvas, mat; **mettere al tappeto** (boxing) to knock out; **tappeto erboso** lawn, green; **tappeto verde** gambling table

tappezzare (**tappèzzo**) *tr* to paper (*a wall*); to upholster

tappezzerìa *f* wallpaper; upholstery; upholsterer's shop; tapestry; wallflower

tappezzière *m* paperhanger; upholsterer

tappo *m* cork, stopper; cap; plug; **tappo a corona** bottle cap; **tappo a vite** screw cap

tara *f* tare

taràntola *f* tarantula

tarare *tr* to tare; to set, adjust

tara·to -ta *adj* net (*weight*); calibrated (*instrument*); sickly, weak

tarchia·to -ta *adj* stocky, sturdy

tardare *tr* to delay ‖ *intr* to delay; to be late

tardi *adv* late; **al più tardi** at the latest; **a più tardi!** so long! **fare tardi** to be late; **più tardi** later; later on; **sul tardi** in the late afternoon

tardi·vo -va *adj* late; retarded, slow; belated

tar·do -da *adj* slow; late; **di età tarda** of advanced years; **tardo d'ingegno** slow-witted

tardó·ne -na *adj* slow-moving ‖ *mf* slowpoke ‖ *f* old dame, middle-aged vamp

tar·ga *f* (-ghe) plate; nameplate; shield; (aut) license plate; (sports) trophy

targare §209 *tr* (aut) to register

targatura *f* (aut) registration

targhétta *f* nameplate

tariffa *f* tariff; rate; rates

tariffà·rio -ria (-ri -rie) *adj* tariff; rate ‖ *m* price list; rate book

tarlare *tr* to eat (*said of woodworms or moths*) ‖ *intr* (ESSERE) & *ref* to become worm-eaten; to become moth-eaten

tarlo *m* woodworm; moth; bookworm; (fig) gnawing

tarma *f* moth; clothes moth

tarmare *tr* to eat (*said of moths*) ‖ *intr* (ESSERE) & *ref* to become moth-eaten

tarmici·da (-di -de) *adj* moth-repelling ‖ *m* moth repellent

taròc·co *m* (-chi) tarot; tarok

tarpare *tr* to clip; **tarpare le ali a** to clip the wings of

tartagliare §280 *tr* & *intr* to stutter, stammer

tàrta·ro -ra *adj* Tartar ‖ *m* tartar; Tartar ‖ **Tartaro** *m* Tartarus

tartaru·ga *f* (-ghe) turtle, tortoise; tortoise shell

tartassare *tr* to ill-treat; to harass

tartina *f* slice of bread and butter; canapé

tartufo *m* truffle; (fig) tartuffe, hypocrite

ta·sca *f* (-sche) pocket; briefcase; **aver le tasche piene di** to be sick and tired of; **da tasca** pocket; **rompere le tasche a** (vulg) to bother, annoy; **tasca in petto** inside pocket

tascàbile *adj* pocket; vest-pocket

tascapane *m* knapsack, rucksack

tascata *f* pocketful

taschino *m* vest pocket, small pocket

tassa *f* tax; (coll) duty, fee; **tassa complementare** surtax; **tassa di circolazione** road-use tax; **tassa di registro** registration fee; **tassa scolastica** tuition

tassàbile *adj* taxable

tassàmetro *m* taximeter; **tassametro di parcheggio** parking meter

tassare *tr* to tax; to assess ‖ *ref* to pledge money

tassati·vo -va *adj* positive; specific; peremptory

tassazióne *f* taxation; tax

tassèllo *m* dowel; inlay; plug; patch; reinforcement

tas·sì *m* (-sì) taxi, taxicab

tassi·sta *m* (-sti) taxi driver

tasso *m* stake (*anvil*); yew tree; (com) rate (*e.g., of interest*); (zool) badger; **tasso valutario fluttuante** (econ) fluctuation of currency rate

tastare *tr* to touch; to feel; to probe; **tastare il terreno** (fig) to see how the land lies

tastièra *f* keyboard; manual (*of organ*)

tasto *m* touch, feeling, feel; plug (*e.g., in watermellon*); key (*of piano or typewriter*); sample (*in drilling*); **tasto bianco** white key, natural; **toccare un tasto falso** to strike a sour note

tastóni *adv*—**a tastoni** gropingly

tàtti·co -ca (**-ci -che**) *adj* tactical; tactful ‖ *m* tactician ‖ *f* tactics; prudence; tactfulness

tatto *m* touch; tact

tatuàg·gio *m* (**-gi**) tattoo

tatuare (**tàtuo**) *tr* to tattoo

taumatur·go *m* (**-gi & -ghi**) wonderworker

tauri·no -na *adj* taurine, bull-like; bull

tavèrna *f* tavern, inn

tavernière *m* tavernkeeper

tàvola *f* board, plank; slab; table; tablet; bookplate; list; **tavola a ribalta** drop-leaf table; **tavola armonica** (mus) sound board; **tavola calda** cafeteria, snack bar; **tavola da stirare** ironing board; **tavola di salvezza** (fig) last recourse, lifesaver; **tavola imbandita** open house; **tavola nera** blackboard; **tavola operatoria** operating table; **tavola pitagorica** multiplication table; **tavola reale** backgammon; **tavole di fondazione** charter (*of a charitable institution*)

tavolàc·cio *m* (**-ci**) wooden board (*on which soldiers on guard and prisoners used to sleep*)

tavolare (**tàvolo**) *tr* to board up

tavolata *f* tableful

tavolato *m* planking; plateau

tavolétta *f* small table; tablet; bar (*e.g., of chocolate*)

tavolière *m* chessboard table; card table; plateau, tableland

tavolino *m* small table; desk

tàvolo *m* table; desk; **tavolo di gioco** gambling table; **tavolo d'ufficio** office desk

tavolòzza *f* palette

tazza *f* cup; bowl

tazzina *f* demitasse

tazzóna *f* mug

te §5 *pron pers*

tè *m* (**tè**) tea; **tè danzante** tea dance, thé dansant

tèa *adj fem*—**rosa tea** tea rose

teatrale *adj* theatrical

teatro *m* theater; performance; drama; stage; (fig) scene; **che teatro!** what fun!; **teatro dell'opera** or **teatro lirico** opera house; **teatro di posa** (mov) studio; **teatro di prosa** legitimate theater

teatróne *m* large theater; (coll) excellent box office

Tèbe *f* Thebes

tè·ca *f* (**-che**) case; (eccl) reliquary

tecnicismo *m* technicality

tècni·co -ca (**-ci -che**) *adj* technical ‖ *m* technician; engineer ‖ *f* technique; technics

téco §5 *prep phrase* (lit) with you

tedé·sco -sca *adj & mf* (**-schi -sche**) German

tediare §287 (**tèdio**) *tr* to bore ‖ *ref* to get bored

tè·dio *m* (**-di**) dullness, tedium, boredom; **recare tedio a** to annoy, bother

tedió·so -sa [s] *adj* dull, tedious

tegame *m* pan; **al tegame** fried (*e.g., eggs*)

tegamino *m* small pan; **uova al tegamino** fried eggs

téglia *f* pan; baking pan

tégola *f* tile; (fig) blow

tégolo *m* tile

teièra *f* teapot, teakettle

tèk *m* teak

téla *f* linen; cloth; material; canvas, oil painting; (fig) plot, trap; (lit) weft; (theat) curtain; **far tela** (coll) to beat it; **tela batista** batiste; **tela cerata** oilcloth; **tela da imballaggio** burlap; **tela di ragno** cobweb; **tela di sacco** sackcloth; **tela greggia** gunny, burlap; **tela smeriglio** emery cloth

te·làio *m* (**-lài**) loom; frame; embroidery frame; sash; stretcher (*for oil painting*); (aut) chassis; **telaio di finestra** window sash

teleama·tóre -trice *mf* TV viewer

telear·ma *f* (**-mi**) guided missile

telecabina *f* cable car

telecàmera *f* TV camera

telecomanda·to -ta *adj* remote-control

telecomando *m* remote control

telecommentatóre *m* TV newscaster

telecròna·ca *f* (**-che**) TV broadcast; **telecronaca diretta** live broadcast

telecroni·sta *mf* (**-sti -ste**) TV news announcer, TV newscaster

telediffusióne *f* TV broadcasting

teledram·ma *m* (**-mi**) teleplay

telefèri·ca *f* (**-che**) cableway, telpherage

telefonare (**telèfono**) *tr & intr* to telephone ‖ *ref* to call one another

telefonata *f* telephone call

telefòni·co -ca *adj* (**-ci -che**) telephone

telefoni·sta *mf* (**-sti -ste**) telephone operator, central; telephone installer

telèfono *m* telephone; **telefono a gettone** pay telephone (*operated by tokens*); **telefono a moneta** pay telephone; **telefono interno** intercommunication system, intercom

telegèni·co -ca *adj* (**-ci -che**) telegenic, videogenic

telegiornale *m* TV newscast

telegrafare (**telègrafo**) *tr & intr* to telegraph

telegràfi·co -ca *adj* (**-ci -che**) telegraphic

telegrafi·sta *mf* (**-sti -ste**) telegrapher; telegraph installer

telègrafo *m* telegraph; **telegrafo di macchina** (naut) engine-room telegraph; **telegrafo ottico** heliograph; wigwag; **telegrafo senza fili** wireless

telegram·ma *m* (**-mi**) telegram

teleguida *f* remote control

teleguidare *tr* to control from a distance, to operate by remote control

Telèmaco *m* Telemachus

telèmetro *m* telemeter; range finder

teleobbiettivo *m* (phot) telephoto lens

telepatia *f* telepathy

teleproiètto *m* guided missile

telericévere §141 *tr* to receive by TV; to teleview

teleschérmo *m* television screen

telescò·pio *m* (-pi) telescope

telescrivènte *f* teletypewriter; ticker

telescriventi·sta *mf* (-sti -ste) teletype operator

teleselezióne *f* (telp) direct distance dialing

telespetta·tóre -trice *mf* televiewer

teletrasméttere §198 *tr* to televise, telecast

teletrasmissióne *f* telecast

televisióne *f* television, TV

televisi·vo -va *adj* television, **TV**

televisóre *m* television set

tellina *f* sunset shell or clam

télo *m* piece of cloth; yardage, length of material; (mil) side (*of tent*)

tèlo *m* (lit) dart, arrow

telóne *m* canvas; (theat) curtain

tè·ma *m* (-mi) theme; (gram) stem

téma *f* (lit) fear; **per tema di** (lit) for fear of

temerarie·tà *f* (-tà) recklessness, rashness

temerà·rio -ria *adj* (-ri -rie) reckless, rash; ill-founded

temére (**témo** & **tèmo**) *tr* to fear; to respect ‖ *intr* to fear; **temere di** to be afraid to

temeri·tà *f* (-tà) temerity

temìbile *adj* frightening

tèmpera *f* tempera, distemper

temperala·pis *m* (-pis) or **temperamati·te** *m* (-te) pencil sharpener

temperaménto *m* middle course, compromise; temper, temperament

temperante *adj* temperate, moderate

temperanza *f* temperance

temperare (**tèmpero**) *tr* to mitigate; to temper; to sharpen (*a pencil*)

tempera·to -ta *adj* temperate; tempered (*metal*); watered (*wine*)

temperatura *f* temperature; **temperatura ambiente** room temperature

temperino *m* penknife, pocketknife

tempèsta *f* tempest, storm; **tempesta in un bicchier d'acqua** tempest in a teapot

tempestare (**tempèsto**) *tr* to pound; to pepper, pelt; to pester ‖ *intr* to storm

tempesta·to -ta *adj* studded, spangled

tempesti·vo -va *adj* timely

tempestó·so -sa [s] *adj* stormy, tempestuous

tèmpia *f* temple (*side of forehead*); **tempie** (lit) head

tempiale *m* temple (*in loom; of spectacles*)

tempière *m* Templar

tèm·pio *m* (-pi & -pli) temple (*edifice*)

tempi·sta *mf* (-sti -ste) person or athlete showing good timing; (mus) rhythmist

tèmpo *m* time; weather; age; period, stage; cycle (*of internal-combustion engine*); (gram) tense; (mus) tempo, (mus) movement; (sports) period; (theat, mov) part; **ad un tempo** at the same time; **al tempo che Berta filava** long ago; **a suo tempo** in due time; long ago; **a tempo debito** in due time; **a tempo e luogo** at the opportune time; **a tempo perso** in

one's spare time; **aver fatto il proprio tempo** to be outdated; **c'è sempre tempo** we are still in time; **col tempo** in time; **dare tempo al tempo** to allow time to heal things; **darsi del bel tempo** to have a good time; **da tempo** for a long time; **del tempo di** from the time of; **è scaduto il tempo utile** the time is up; **è tanto tempo** it's been a long time; **fa bel tempo** the weather is fine; **il Tempo** Father Time; **lasciare il tempo che trova** to have no effect; **molto tempo dopo** long afterward; **nel tempo che** while; **per tempo** early; **prima del tempo** formerly; **quanto tempo** how long; **sentire il tempo** to feel the weather in one's bones; **senza por tempo in mezzo** without any delay; **tempi che corrono** present times; **tempo fa** some time ago; **tempo legale** legal time limit; **tempo libero** leisure time; **tempo supplementare** (sports) overtime; **tempo un . . .** within (*e.g., one month*); **un tempo** long ago

temporale *adj* temporal ‖ *m* storm

temporàne·o -a *adj* temporary, provisional

temporeggiare §290 (**temporéggio**) *intr* to temporize

tèmpra *f* (metallurgy) tempering, temper; (mus) timbre; (fig) fiber, timber

temprare (**tèmpro**) *tr* to temper (*metal*); to harden, inure ‖ *ref* to become hardened or inured

tenace *adj* tenacious; tough

tenàcia *f* tenacity

tenaci·tà *f* (-tà) strength, resistance; tenacity

tenàglie *fpl* nippers, pincers, pliers; tongs; **a tenaglie** (mil) pincers (*e.g., action*)

tènda *f* curtain; awning; tent

tendènza *f* tendency; trend

tendenzió·so -sa [s] *adj* tendentious

tèn·der *m* (-der) (rr) tender

tèndere §270 *tr* to stretch; to tighten; to draw (*a bow*); to cast (*nets*); to lay (*snares*); to reach out (*one's hand*); to prick up (*one's ears*); to draw (*s.o.'s attention*); to set (*sail*) ‖ *intr* to aim; to lean; to tend; to tend to be

tendina *f* curtain, blind

tèndine *m* (anat) tendon

tendiscar·pe *m* (-pe) shoetree

tenditóre *m* turnbuckle; **tenditore della racchetta** (tennis) press

tendóne *m* big curtain; canvas; tent (*of circus*); (theat) curtain

tendòpo·li *f* (-li) tent city

tènebre *fpl* darkness

tenebró·so -sa [s] *adj* dark, gloomy

tenènte *m* lieutenant; (mil) first lieutenant; (nav) lieutenant junior grade; **tenente colonnello** (mil) lieutenant colonel; **tenente di vascello** (nav) lieutenant senior grade

tenére §271 *tr* to hold; to have; to keep; to stand (*e.g., rough sea*); to wear; to make (*a speech*); to follow

(*a course*); **tenere a battesimo** to
stand for, sponsor; **tenere al corrente**
to keep informed; **tenere a memoria**
to remember; **tenere da conto** to hold
in high esteem; to take good care of
(*s.th*); **tenere d'occhio** to keep an eye
on; **tenere la destra** to keep to the
right; **tenere la strada** (aut) to hug
the road; **tenere la testa a partito**
to mend one's ways; **tenere le distanze** to keep aloof; **tenere mano a**
to connive with; **tenere presente** to
bear in mind; **tenere qlco a conto**
to take good care of s.th || *intr* to
hold; to take root; **tenerci che** to be
anxious for, e.g., **ci tengo che vinca
le elezioni** I am anxious for him to
win the elections; **tenere a destra** to
keep to the right; **tenere alle apparenze** to stand on ceremony; to keep
up appearances; **tenere da** to hail
from; to take after; **tenere dietro a**
to follow; to keep abreast of; **tenere
duro** to hold fast; **tenere per** (sports)
to be a fan of || *ref* to hold; to hold
on; to keep; to keep (*e.g., ready*); to
regard oneself; **tenersi a** to adhere to
(*e.g., a treaty*); to hold on to; to
stick to; to follow; **tenersi a galla**
to stay afloat; **tenersi al largo** (naut)
to keep to the open sea; **tenersi al
vento** (naut) to sail to leeward; (fig)
to follow a safe course; **tenersi in
piedi** to stand up; **tenersi per mano**
to hold hands; **tenersi sulle proprie**
to keep aloof
tenerézza *f* tenderness; fondness, en-
dearment
tène·ro -ra *adj* tender || *m* tender por-
tion
tènia *f* tapeworm
teni·tóre -trice *mf* keeper
tènnis *m* tennis; **tennis da tavolo** table
tennis, ping-pong
tenni·sta *mf* (-sti -ste) tennis player
tennìsti·co -ca *adj* (-ci -che) tennis
tenóne *m* tenon
tenóre *m* character, tone; tenor; alcoholic content; manner (*of living*);
tenore di vita way of life; standard
of living
tensióne *f* tension; **alta tensione** high
tension; **tensione sanguigna** blood
pressure
tentàcolo *m* tentacle
tentare (tènto) *tr* to try, attempt; to
assay; to tempt; (lit) to touch
tentativo *m* attempt; **tentativo di furto**
attempted robbery
tenta·tóre -trice *adj* tempting || *m*
tempter || *f* temptress
tentazióne *f* temptation
tentennare (tenténno) *tr* to shake; to
rock || *intr* to shake; to wobble; to
hesitate; to stagger
tentóne or **tentóni** *adv* blindly; gropingly; at random
tènue *adj* small (*intestine*); (lit) tenuous, thin
tenu·to -ta *adj* bound, obliged || *f* ca-
pacity, volume; estate, farm; uni-
form; outfit; (sports) endurance,

resistance; **a tenuta d'acqua** watertight; **a tenuta d'aria** airtight; **tenuta
dei libri** bookkeeping; **tenuta di gala**
(mil, nav) full-dress uniform; **tenuta
di servizio** (mil) fatigues; **tenuta di
strada** (aut) roadability
tenzóne *f* combat; poetic contest
teologìa *f* theology
teòlo·go *m* (-gi) theologian
teorè·ma *m* (-mi) theorem
teorèti·co -ca *adj* (-ci -che) theoretic(al)
teorìa *f* theory; (lit) series, row
teòri·co -ca (-ci -che) *adj* theoretical ||
m theoretician
tèpi·do -da *adj* var of **tiepido**
tepóre *m* warmth
téppa *f* underworld, rabble
teppi·sta *m* (-sti) hoodlum, hooligan
terapèuti·co -ca (-ci -che) *adj* thera-
peutic || *f* therapeutics
terapìa *f* therapy; **terapia convulsivante**
or **terapia d'urto** shock therapy
Terèsa *f* Theresa
tèrgere §162 *tr* (lit) to wipe
tergicristallo *m* windshield wiper
tergiversare (tergivèrso) *intr* to stall;
to beat around the bush
tèr·go *m* (-ghi) back (*of a coin*); **a
tergo** on the reverse side || *m* (-ga
fpl) (lit) back; **volgere le terga** (lit)
to turn one's back
termale *adj* thermal (*e.g., waters*)
tèrme *fpl* spa, hot spring
tèrmi·co -ca *adj* (-ci -che) thermal;
heat, heating
terminale *adj* & *m* terminal
terminare (tèrmino) *tr* to border; to
end, terminate || *intr* (ESSERE) to end,
terminate
terminazióne *f* termination; completion; (gram) ending
tèrmine *m* border; marker; term; dead-
line; end; goal; boundary, bounds;
(fig) point; **a termini di legge** according to law; **avere termine** to end;
in altri termini in other words;
mezzo termine half measure; **porre
termine a** to put an end to; **portare
a termine** to put through
terminologìa *f* terminology
termistóre *m* (elec) thermistor
tèrmite *f* termite
termoconvettóre *m* baseboard radiator
termocòppia *f* thermocouple
termodinàmi·co -ca (-ci -che) *adj* ther-
modynamic || *f* thermodynamics
termòforo *m* heating pad
termòmetro *m* thermometer
termonucleare *adj* thermonuclear
tèr·mos *m* (-mos) thermos bottle
termosifóne *m* radiator; hot-water
heating system; steam heating system
termòstato *m* thermostat
termovisièra *f* electric defroster
tèrno *m* tern (*in lotto*); **vincere un
terno al lotto** to hit the jackpot
tèrra *f* earth; land; ground; world; city,
town; dirt, soil; clay; **essere a terra**
to be downcast; to be broke; to be
flat (*said of a tire*); **rimanere a terra**
to miss the boat; **sotto terra** underground; **terra bruciata** scorched

earth; **terra di nessuno** no man's land; **terra di Siena** sienna; **terra ferma** terra firma; mainland; **terra terra** skimming the ground; (naut) close to the shore; (fig) mediocre, second-rate

terracòtta f (**terrecòtte**) terra cotta; earthenware

terraférma f mainland (as distinguished from adjacent islands); terra firma (dry land, not air or water)

terràglia f crockery; **terraglie** earthenware

terranò·va m (**-va**) Newfoundland (dog) || **Terranova** f Newfoundland

terrapièno m embankment

terrazza f terrace; **a terrazza** terraced

terrazza·no -na mf villager

terrazzo m balcony; terrace; ledge, shelf; terrazzo

terremota·to -ta adj hit by an earthquake || mf earthquake victim

terremòto m earthquake

terré·no -na adj terrestrial, earthly; ground-floor; first-floor || m ground floor; first floor; ground; soil; land, plot of ground; combat zone, terrain; **preparare il terreno** to work the soil; (fig) to pave the way; **scendere sul terreno** to fight a duel; **tastare il terreno** to feel one's way; **terreno di gioco** (sports) field

tèrre·o -a adj wan, sallow

terrèstre adj terrestrial; ground, land || m earthling

terrìbile adj terrible; awesome, awful

terrìc·cio m (**-ci**) soil; top soil

terriè·ro -ra adj land; landed

terrificare §197 (**terrìfico**) tr to terrify

terrina f tureen

territò·rio m (**-ri**) territory

terróre m terror

terrorismo m terrorism

terrori·sta mf (**-sti -ste**) terrorist

terrorizzare [ddzz] tr to terrorize

terró·so -sa [s] adj dirty (e.g., spinach); dirty-earth (color); (chem) rare-earth (metal)

tèr·so -sa adj clear

tèrza f third grade; (aut) third; (eccl) tierce; (rr) third class

terzaforzì·sta (**-sti -ste**) adj of the third force || m partisan of the third force

terzaròlo m (naut) reef

terzétto m trio

terzià·rio -ria adj (**-ri -rie**) tertiary

terzina f tercet

terzino m (soccer) back

tèr·zo -za adj & pron third || m third; third party || f see **terza**

terzùlti·mo -ma adj third from the end

tésa [s] f brim (of hat); snare, net

tesare [s] (**téso**) tr to pull taut

tè·schio m (**-schi**) skull

tè·si f (**-si**) thesis; dissertation

té·so -sa [s] adj taut, tight; strained; outstretched (hand); **con le orecchie tese** all ears || f see **tesa**

tesorerìa f treasury; liquid assets

tesorière m treasurer

tesòro m treasure; treasury; thesaurus; bank vault; **far tesoro di** to treasure, prize; **tesoro mio!** my darling!

Tèspi m Thespis

tèssera f card; domino (piece); tessera (of mosaic)

tessera·to -ta adj card-carrying; rationed || mf card-carrying member; holder of ration card

tèssere tr to weave; to spin

tèssile adj textile || m textile; **tessili** textile workers

tessilsac·co m (**-chi**) garment bag

tessi·tóre -trice mf weaver

tessitura f weaving; spinning mill; (mus) range; (fig) plot

tessuto m cloth, fabric; tissue

tèsta f head; mind; bulb (of garlic); spindle (of wheel); warhead (of torpedo); row (of bricks); **a testa** apiece; per capita; **a testa a testa** neck and neck; **fare di testa propria** to act on one's own; **fare la testa grossa a** to stun; to annoy; **levarsi di testa** to forget about; **mettersi in testa di** to get it into one's head to; **non avere testa di** + inf to not feel like + ger; **non sapere dove battere la testa** to not know which way to turn; **per una corta testa** by a neck; **rompersi la testa** to rack one's brains; **tenere testa a** to face up to; **testa coda** (aut) spin; **testa di ponte** (mil) bridgehead; **testa di sbarco** beachhead; **testa e croce** head or tails

testaménto m will, testament || **Antico** or **Vecchio Testamento** Old Testament; **Nuovo Testamento** New Testament

testardàggine f stubborness

testar·do -da adj stubborn

testata f headboard (of bed); top; end (e.g., of beam); heading (of newspaper); butt with the head; nose (of rocket)

tèste m witness

testé adv (lit) a short time ago; (lit) presently, in a little while

testìcolo m testicle

testièra f headboard; crown (of harness); battering ram

testimòne m witness; **testimone di nozze** best man; **testimone di veduta** or **testimone oculare** eyewitness

testimonianza f testimony

testimoniare §287 (**testimònio**) tr to attest; to depose, testify; **testimoniare il falso** to bear false witness || intr to bear witness

testimò·nio m (**-ni**) (coll) witness

testina f small head; whimsical person; boiled head of veal; head (e.g., of tape recorder)

tèsto m text; pie dish; (coll) flower vase; **fare testo** to serve as a model

testó·ne -na mf dolt; stubborn person

testuale adj textual; word-for-word

testùggine f turtle; tortoise

tètano m tetanus

tè·tro -tra adj (lit) gloomy, dark

tétta f (coll) teat

tettarèlla f nipple

tétto m roof; ceiling price; home; **senza tetto** homeless; **tetto a capanna** gable roof; **tetto a padiglione** hip

roof; **tetto a una falda** lean-to roof; **tetto di paglia** thatched roof
tettóia *f* shed; pillared roof
tettóia-garage *f* (**tettóie-garage**) carport
tettùc·cio *m* (**-ci**) (aut) roof; (aut) top; **tettuccio a bulbo** dome; **tettuccio rigido** (aut) convertible top
ti §5 *pron*
tìbia *f* tibia, shinbone
tic *m* (**tic**) twitch; habit
ticchettì·o *m* (**-i**) click (*of typewriter*); patter (*of rain*); tick (*of clock*)
tìc·chio *m* (**-chi**) whim; tic; viciousness (*of animal*); blemish
tièpi·do -da *adj* tepid, lukewarm
tifo *m* typhus; **fare il tifo per** to root for; to be a fan of
tifoidèa *f* typhoid fever
tifóne *m* typhoon
tifó·so -sa [s] *adj* rooting || *mf* fan, rooter
tì·glio *m* (**-gli**) linden, lime; bast; fiber
tiglió·so -sa [s] *adj* tough, fibrous
tigna *f* ringworm; (coll) tightwad
tignòla *f* clothes moth
tigra·to -ta *adj* striped; tabby
tigre *f* tiger
timballo *m* pie, meat pie; timbale; (lit) drum
timbrare *tr* to stamp; to cancel (*stamps*)
timbro *m* stamp; character (*of a writer*); (mus) timbre; **timbro di gomma** rubber stamp; **timbro postale** postmark
timidézza *f* shyness, bashfulness; timidity
tìmi·do -da *adj* shy, bashful; timid || *mf* shy person
timo *m* (anat) thymus; (bot) thyme
timóne *m* rudder, helm; shaft, pole (*of cart*); **timone di direzione** (aer) rudder; **timone di profondità** (aer) elevator; (nav) diving plane (*of submarine*)
timonièra *f* (naut) pilot house
timonière *m* helmsman, steersman; coxswain
timoniè·ro -ra *adj* rudder; tail (*feather*) || *f* see **timoniera**
timora·to -ta *adj* conscientious; **timorato di Dio** God-fearing
timóre *m* fear; awe; **avere timore di** to fear
timoró·so -sa [s] *adj* timorous
tìmpano *m* (archit) tympanum; (anat) eardrum; (mus) kettledrum; **rompere i timpani a** to deafen
tin·ca *f* (**-che**) (ichth) tench
tinèllo *m* pantry; breakfast room
tìngere §126 *tr* to dye; to dirty, soil; to color || *ref* to dye (*e.g., one's hair*); to put on make-up; to become colored
tino *m* tub, vat
tinòzza *f* tub, washtub
tinta *f* paint; color; dye; shade; stain; **calcare le tinte** to exaggerate; **mezza tinta** halftone, shade; **vedere qlco a fosche tinte** to take a dim view of s.th; **vedere qlco a tinte rosee** to see s.th through rose-colored glasses
tintarèlla *f* (coll) suntan
tinteggiare §290 (**tintéggio**) *tr* to calci-

mine; to whitewash; to tint; to paint (*e.g., a house*)
tintinnare *intr* (ESSERE & AVERE) to jingle; to clink
tintinnì·o *m* (**-i**) jingling; clink
tin·to -ta *adj* dyed; tinged; soiled; (lit) dark || *f* see **tinta**
tintó·re -ra *mf* dyer; dry cleaner
tintoria *f* dyeworks; dry cleaning establishment; dyeing
tintura *f* dyeing; dyestuff; tincture; smattering; **tintura di iodio** iodine
tìpi·co -ca *adj* (**-ci -che**) typical
tipificare §197 (**tipìfico**) *tr* to standardize
tipizzare [ddzz] *tr* to standardize
tipo *adj invar* typical, e.g., **famiglia tipo** typical family || *m* type; standard, model; fellow, guy; phylum (*in taxonomy*); **bel tipo** (coll) character, card; **coi tipi di** printed in the shop of; **sul tipo di** similar to; **vero tipo** prototype, epitome
tipografìa *f* typography; print shop
tipogràfi·co -ca *adj* (**-ci -che**) typographical
tipògrafo *m* typographer; owner of print shop, printer
tipòmetro *m* (typ) line gauge
tiptologìa *f* table rapping (*during séance*); tapping in code (*among jailbirds*)
tiraba·ci *m* (**-ci**) (coll) spitcurl
tiràg·gio *m* (**-gi**) draft; **a tiraggio forzato** forced-draft
tiralìne·e *m* (**-e**) ruling pen
tirannìa *f* tyranny
tirànni·co -ca *adj* (**-ci -che**) tyrannical
tiran·no -na *adj* tyrannical || *mf* tyrant
tirante *m* brace; rod; strap; trace (*of harness*); **tirante degli stivali** bootstrap
tirapiè·di *m* (**-di**) hangman's assistant; underling
tirapu·gni *m* (**-gni**) brass knuckles
tirare *tr* to pull; to draw; to tug; to suck; to haul in (*nets*); to deserve (*a slap*); to pluck; to throw; to give (*blows*); to utter (*oaths*); to shoot (*arrows, bullets*); to stretch; to tighten (*one's belt*); to print; to make (*an addition*); (sports) to force (*the pace*); **tirare a lucido** to polish; **tirare a sé** to attract; **tirare a sorte** to draw lots for; **tirare fuori** to draw out; to pull out; to get out; **tirare giù** to lower; to jot down; (coll) to gulp down; **tirare gli orecchi a** to punish by yanking the ears of; **tirare il collo a** to wring the neck of; **tirare in ballo** to bring up (*a subject*); **tirare l'acqua al proprio mulino** to look out for number one; **tirare l'anima coi denti** to be at the end of one's rope; **tirare l'aria** to draw (*said of a chimney*); **tirare le cuoia** (slang) to kick the bucket; **tirare per i capelli** to drag by the hair; to drag in; to push, coerce; **tirare per le lunghe** to stretch out; **tirare su** to lift; to raise (*children*); to pull up || *intr* to be too tight (*said of clothes*); to shoot; to blow (*said of wind*); to

draw (*said, e.g., of chimney*); **tirare a** to tend toward, lean toward; **tirare a** + *inf* to try to + *inf;* **tirare a campare** (coll) to goldbrick; **tirare avanti** to go ahead; to manage to get along; **tirare di boxe** to box; **tirare diritto** to go straight ahead; **tirare di scherma** to fence; **tirare in lungo** to delay, linger; to dillydally; **tirare innanzi** to keep on going; to go ahead; **tirare sul prezzo** to haggle; **tirare via** to hurry along || *ref—* **tirarsi addosso** (coll) to bring upon oneself; **tirarsi dietro** to drag along; **tirarsi fuori da** to get out of (*e.g., trouble*); **tirarsi gente in casa** to keep open house; **tirarsi indietro** to move back; **tirarsi in là** to move aside; **tirarsi su** to get up; to recover; to roll up (*one's sleeves*); **tirarsi un colpo di rivoltella** to shoot oneself

tirastiva·li *m* (-li) bootjack
tirata *f* pull; stretch; tirade
tirati·ra *m* (-ra) (coll) yen; **fare a tiratira per** (coll) to scramble for
tira·to -ta *adj* taut; forced (*smile*); drawn (*face*); tight, closefisted; **tirato con** short of || *f* see **tirata**
tira·tóre -trice *mf* shot; **tiratore scelto** sharpshooter; **franco tiratore** sniper
tiratura *f* printing
tirchierìa *f* stinginess
tìr·chio -chia (-chi -chie) *adj* stingy, closefisted || *mf* miser
tirèlla *f* trace (*of harness*)
tirétto *m* (coll) drawer
tiritèra *f* rigmarole
tiro *m* pull; pair, brace (*e.g., of oxen*); throw; fire, shot; trick; **a tiro** within reach; **a un tiro di schioppo** within gunshot; **da tiro** draft; **fuori del tiro dell'orecchio** out of earshot; **tiro alla fune** tug of war; **tiro al piattello** trapshooting; **tiro a quattro** four-in-hand; **tiro a segno** rifle range; shooting gallery
tiroci·nio *m* (-ni) apprenticeship; internship; **tirocinio didattico** practice teaching
tiròide *f* thyroid
tirolése [s] *adj & mf* Tyrolean
tirrèni·co -ca *adj* (-ci -che) Tyrrhenian **Tirrèno** *m* Tyrrhenian Sea
tisana *f* tea, infusion
tisi *f* consumption, tuberculosis
tìsi·co -ca (-ci -che) *adj* consumptive; stunted || *mf* consumptive
titàni·co -ca *adj* (-ci -che) titanic
titànio *m* titanium
titillare *tr* to tickle
titolare *adj* titular; regular, full-time || *m* owner, boss; incumbent || *v* (**titolo**) *tr* to name, call
tìtolo *m* title; heading; name; caption; entry (*in dictionary*); grade; fineness (*of gold*); (chem) titer; (educ) credit; **avere titolo a** to have a right to; **a titolo di** as, by way of; **titoli di testa** (mov) credits; **titolo al portatore** security payable to bearer; **titolo azionario** share; **titolo corrente** subtitle; **titolo di credito** instrument of

credit; certificate; deed; conveyance; **titolo di studio** degree, diploma; credits; **titolo di trasporto** travel document
titubare (**tìtubo**) *intr* to hesitate; to waver
tiziané·sco -sca *adj* (-schi -sche) titian; Titian
tì·zio *m* (-zi) fellow, guy
tizzo or **tizzóne** *m* brand, firebrand
to' *interj* here!; well!
tobò·ga *m* (-ga) toboggan
toccafèrro *m* tag (*game*)
toccamano *m* handshake (*to close a deal*); bribe, under-the-table tip
toccante *adj* touching, moving
toccare §197 (**tócco**) *tr* to touch; to reach; to concern; to push (*a button*); to play (*an instrument*); to feel; to hit (*the target*); to border on (*e.g., the age of forty*); **toccare con mano** to make sure of; **toccare il cielo col dito** to be in seventh heaven; **toccare nel vivo** to touch to the quick; **toccare terra** to land; **toccarne molte** to get a good thrashing; **toccato!** touché! || *intr* (ESSERE) to be touching; **toccare a** to be up to, e.g., **tocca a lui** it's up to him; to have to, e.g., **le tocca partire domani** she has to leave tomorrow; to deserve, e.g., **gli è toccato il premio** he deserved the prize || *ref* to meet, e.g., **gli estremi si toccano** extremes meet
toccasa·na [s] *m* (-na) cure-all, panacea
tocca·to -ta *adj* touché; touched in the head, nutty; **già toccato** abovementioned || *f* (mus) toccata
tóc·co -ca (-chi -che) *adj* touched, nutty; spoiled (*fruit*) || *m* touch; knock; one o'clock (*P.M.*); (coll) stroke
tòc·co *m* (-chi) chunk, piece; mortarboard; toque; **un bel tocco di ragazza** a buxom lass
tò·ga *f* (-ghe) gown, academic gown; (hist) toga
tògliere §127 *tr* to remove, take away; to take; to cut (*telephone connection*); to deduct; to take off; to preclude, prevent; **togliere a** to take away from; **togliere al cielo** (lit) to praise to the skies; **togliere di mezzo** to remove; to do away with; **togliere la parola a** to take the floor from; **togliere l'onore a** to dishonor; **togliere una spina dal cuore a** to relieve the heart and mind of || *intr—* **tolga Dio!** God forbid! || *ref* to take off (*e.g., one's coat*); to have (*e.g., a tooth*) pulled; to satisfy (*a whim*); **togliersi di mezzo** to get out of the way; **togliersi la vita** to take one's life; **togliersi qlcu dai piedi** to get rid of s.o.
tòlda *f* (naut) deck
tolemài·co -ca *adj* (-ci -che) Ptolemaic
tolétta *f* dressing table; dressing room; toilet, washroom; dress, gown; **fare toletta** or **farsi la toletta** to make one's toilet
tolleràbile *adj* tolerable

tollerante *adj* tolerant; liberal
tolleranza *f* tolerance; leeway
tollerare (**tòllero**) *tr* to tolerate; to bear, stand
tòl·to **-ta** *adj* taken; except, leaving out, e.g., **tolta sua figlia** leaving his daughter out ‖ *m*—**il mal tolto** ill-gotten goods
to·màio *m* (**-mài** & **-màia** *fpl*) or **to·màia** *f* (**-màie**) upper (*of shoe*)
tómba *f* tomb, grave
tombale *adj* grave (*e.g., stone*)
tombino *m* sewer inlet
tómbola *f* bingo; (coll) tumble
tombolare (**tómbolo**) *tr* (coll) to tumble down (*the steps*) ‖ *intr* (ESSERE) to fall headlong; (coll) to go to rack and ruin; (aer) to tumble
tómbolo *m* fall, tumble; bolster; lace pillow; (coll) fatso; **fare un tombolo** to go to rack and ruin; to lose one's position
Tommaso *m* Thomas
tòmo *m* volume; (coll) character
tòna·ca *f* (**-che**) (eccl) frock; (eccl) soutane; **gettare la tonaca alle ortiche** to doff the cassock
tonare §257 *intr* to peal; to thunder ‖ *impers* (ESSERE & AVERE)—**tuona** it is thundering
tondeggiante *adj* round; rounded; chubby; curvaceous
tondino *m* coaster; iron rod (*for reinforced concrete*); (archit) molding (*at top or bottom of column*); (archit) astragal
tón·do **-da** *adj* round; (typ) roman ‖ *m* round; circle; plate, dish; (typ) roman; **in tondo** around
tónfo *m* splash; thump
tòni·co **-ca** (**-ci** **-che**) *adj* tonic ‖ *m* tonic (*medicine*) ‖ *f* (mus) tonic
tonificare §197 (**tonìfico**) *tr* to invigorate
tonnara *f* tuna nets
tonnellàg·gio *m* (**-gi**) tonnage
tonnellata *f* ton; **tonnellata di stazza** displacement ton
tónno *m* tuna
tòno *m* tone; tune; hue; style; (mus) pitch; (mus) key; **darsi tono** to put on airs; **di tono** stylish; **fuori di tono** out of tune
tonsilla *f* tonsil
tonsura *f* tonsure
tón·to **-ta** *adj* (coll) dumb, stupid
topàia *f* rat's nest; hovel
topà·zio *m* (**-zi**) topaz
tòpi·co **-ca** (**-ci** **-che**) *adj* topical ‖ *f* topic; (coll) blunder
tòpo *m* mouse; rat; **topo campagnolo** field mouse; **topo d'acqua** water rat; **topo d'albergo** hotel thief; **topo d'auto** car thief; **topo di biblioteca** bookworm
topografia *f* topography
topolino *m* little mouse ‖ **Topolino** *m* Mickey Mouse
toporagno *m* shrew
tòppa *f* patch; keyhole
tòppo *m* stump; headstock (*of lathe*)
torace *m* thorax

tórba *f* peat
tórbi·do **-da** *adj* cloudy; murky ‖ *m* trouble; **pescare nel torbido** to fish in troubled waters; **torbidi** disorder
torbièra *f* peatbog
tòrcere §272 *tr* to twist; to wring; to bend, curve; to curl (*the lips*); to lead astray ‖ *intr* (ESSERE) to bend, curve ‖ *ref* to writhe; to bend over; **torcersi dalle risa** to split with laughter
torchiare §287 (**tòrchio**) *tr* to press
tòr·chio *m* (**-chi**) press; printing press
tòr·cia *f* (**-ce**) torch
torcicòllo *m* stiff neck; (orn) wryneck
torcinaso [s] *m* (vet) twitch
tórdo *m* thrush; simpleton
torèllo *m* young bull; (naut) garboard
torèro *m* bullfighter
tórlo *m* yolk
tórma *f* crowd, throng; herd
torménta *f* blizzard
tormentare (**torménto**) *tr* to torture, torment; to pester, nag ‖ *ref* to worry
torménto *m* torture, torment; pang; bore, pest, annoyance
tornacónto *m* interest, advantage
tornante *m* curve
tornare (**tórno**) *tr* (lit) to restore; (obs) to turn ‖ *intr* (ESSERE) to return; to go back; (coll) to jibe, agree, square; **tornare a** to be profitable to; **tornare a** + *inf* verb + again, e.g., **tornare a essere** to become again; **tornare a fare** to do again; **tornare a bomba** to return to the point; **tornare a galla** to come back to the surface; **tornare a gola** to repeat (*said of food*); **tornare a onore a qlcu** to do credit to s.o.; **tornare a pennello** to fit to a T; **tornare in sé** to come to; **tornare opportuno** or **utile a** to suit, e.g., **non gli tornò opportuno vendere la casa** it did not suit him to sell the house; **tornare utile** to come in handy; **tornare sulle proprie decisioni** to change one's mind
tornasóle *m* litmus
tornèllo *m* turnstile
tornèo *m* tournament, tourney
tór·nio *m* (**-ni**) lathe
tornire §176 *tr* to turn, turn up (*on a lathe*); to polish
tornitóre *m* lathe operator
tórno *m* turn; period (*of time*)*;* **levarsi di torno** to get rid of; **torno torno** all around
tòro *m* bull; (archit, geom) torus; (lit) marital bed ‖ **Toro** *m* (astrol) Taurus
torpèdine *f* torpedo
torpedinièra *f* destroyer escort; torpedo-boat destroyer
torpè·do *f* (**-do**) (aut) touring car
torpedóne *m* bus, motor coach
tòrpi·do **-da** *adj* torpid, sluggish; numb
torpóre *m* torpor, sluggishness; numbness
tórre *f* tower; (chess) castle; (nav) turret; **torre campanaria** bell tower; **torre d'avorio** ivory tower; **torre di**

lancio (rok) gantry; **torre pendente** leaning tower
torrefare §173 *tr* to roast (*coffee*)
torreggiante *adj* towering
torreggiare §290 (**torréggio**) *intr* to tower
torrènte *m* torrent
torrenziale *adj* torrential
torrétta *f* turret; (nav) conning tower (*of submarine*); (archit) bartizan
tòrri·do -da *adj* torrid
torrióne *m* donjon; (nav) conning tower (*of battleship*)
torróne *m* nougat
torsióne *f* torsion
tórso *m* stalk; core (*of fruit*); torso, trunk; **a torso nudo** bare-chested
tórsolo *m* core; stalk; stem; **non vale un torsolo** it's not worth a fig
tórta *f* pie; cake, tart; **torta di mele** apple pie
tòrta *f* twist
tortièra *f* baking pan
tòr·to -ta *adj* twisted; crooked; gloomy (*face*) || *m* wrong; **a torto** unjustly; **avere torto** to be wrong; **avere torto marcio** to be dead wrong; **dar torto a** to lay the blame on; **fare torto a** to wrong, e.g., **fece torto al proprio fratello** he wronged his own brother; to bring discredit upon || *f* see **tòrta** || **torto** *adv* askance
tórtora *f* turtledove
tortuó·so -sa [s] *adj* winding; ambiguous; (fig) devious
tortura *f* torture
torturare *tr* to torture; to pester || *ref* to torment oneself; **torturarsi il cervello** to rack one's brain
tosare (**tóso**) *tr* to clip, crop; to shear; (fig) to fleece
tosa·tóre -trice *mf* clipper, shearer || *f* clippers; lawn mower
tosatura *f* sheepshearing; clip (*of wool*)
tosca·no -na *adj & mf* Tuscan || *m* stogy || **Toscana, la** Tuscany
tósse *f* cough; **tosse asinina** or **canina** whooping cough
tòssi·co -ca (**-ci -che**) toxic || *m* (archaic) poison
tossicòmane *mf* drug addict
tossicomanìa *f* drug addiction
tossina *f* toxin
tossire (**tósso**) & §176 *intr* to cough
tostapa·ne *m* (**-ne**) toaster
tostare (**tòsto**) *tr* to toast; to roast (*e.g., coffee*)
tò·sto -sta *adj* (lit) prompt; (lit) impudent; (lit) brazen (*face*) || **tosto** *adv* (lit) soon; **ben tosto** (lit) very soon; **tosto che** (lit) as soon as
tòt *adj pl invar* so many, that many || *pron invar* so much, that much
totale *adj & m* total
totalità·rio -ria *adj* (**-ri -rie**) total, complete; totalitarian
totalizzare [ddzz] *tr* to add up; to make (*so many points*)
totalizzatóre [ddzz] *m* pari-mutuel; betting window; (mach) totalizator
tòtano *m* squid; (orn) tattler
totocàlcio *m* soccer pool

tovàglia *f* tablecloth
tovagliòlo *m* napkin
tòz·zo -za *adj* stubby, stocky || *m* piece (*of fresh bread*); crust (*of bread*)
tra *prep* among; between
trabàccolo *m* small fishing boat
traballare *intr* to shake; to totter; to wobble; to stagger; to toddle
trabìccolo *m* frame for bedwarmer; jalopy; hulk
traboccante *adj* overflowing
traboccare §197 (**trabócco**) *tr* to knock down || *intr* to overflow (*said of container*) || *intr* (ESSERE) to overflow (*said of liquid*) || *intr* (ESSERE & AVERE) to tip (*said of scales*); **far traboccare** to make (*the scales*) tip
trabocchétto *m* pitfall; trapdoor
trabóc·co *m* (**-chi**)—**trabocco di sangue** internal hemorrhage
tracagnòt·to -ta *adj* stubby, stocky || *mf* stocky person
tracannare *tr* to gulp down
tracchég·gio *m* (**-gi**) delay; (fencing) feint
tràc·cia *f* (**-ce**) track; trace, clue; trail; outline, plan; (lit) line, row; **buona traccia** right track; **fare la traccia a** to open the way for; **in** or **sotto traccia** concealed (*e.g., wiring*); **tracce** tinge; (chem) traces
tracciante *adj* tracer (*bullet*)
tracciare §128 *tr* to trace; to pave (*the way*); to outline; (lit) to track
tracciato *m* tracing, drawing; outline; map; layout
trachèa *f* trachea, windpipe
tracòlla *f* baldric; shoulder strap; **a tracolla** slung across the shoulders
tracòllo *m* collapse, debacle
tracotanza *f* arrogance
tradiménto *m* treason; treachery; **a tradimento** unawares, unexpectedly; treacherously
tradire §176 *tr* to betray; to fail (*a person; said of memory*) || *ref* to give oneself away
tradi·tóre -trice *adj* charming, seductive; treacherous; deceitful, faithless || *mf* traitor; betrayer || *f* traitress
tradizionale *adj* traditional
tradizióne *f* tradition
tradótta *f* military train
tradurre §102 *tr* to translate
tradut·tóre -trice *mf* translator
traduzióne *f* translation
traènte *mf* (com) drawer
trafela·to -ta *adj* breathless, out of breath
trafèrro *m* (elec) air gap; (elec) spark gap
trafficante *m* dealer, trader; trafficker
trafficare §197 (**tràffico**) *tr* to sell; to traffic in || *intr* to trade, deal; to hustle
tràffi·co *m* (**-ci**) traffic
trafficó·ne -na *mf* hustler
trafìggere §104 *tr* to pierce, stab, transfix; to wound
trafila *f* routine; red tape; (mach) drawplate
trafilare *tr* to wiredraw

trafilétto _m_ (journ) short feature, special item; (journ) notice
trafitta _f_ stab wound; shooting pain
trafittura _f_ stab; shooting pain
traforare (**trafòro** & **trafóro**) _tr_ to bore; to pierce; to carve (_wood_); to pink (_leather_); to embroider with open work
trafóro _m_ boring; tunnel; open work
trafugare §209 _tr_ to purloin; to sneak off with
tragèdia _f_ tragedy; **far tragedie** (coll) to make a fuss
traghettare (**traghétto**) _tr_ to ferry
traghétto _m_ ferry; **traghetto spaziale** space shuttle
tràgi·co -ca (**-ci -che**) _adj_ tragic ‖ _m_ tragedian; **il tragico** (fig) the tragic
tragitto _m_ journey; (obs) ferry
traguardo _m_ sight; aim; goal; finish line; (phot) viewfinder; (sports) tape
traiettòria _f_ trajectory; path
tràina _f_ towline; **pescare alla traina** to troll
trainare (**tràino**) _tr_ to drag, tug, pull
tràino _m_ drag; load; trailer
tralasciare §128 _tr_ to interrupt; to omit; **non tralasciare di** to not fail to
tràl·cio _m_ (**-ci**) stem (_of vine_)
tralìc·cio _m_ (**-ci**) ticking, bedtick; trellis; tower (_of high-tension line_)
tralice _m_—**in tralice** askance
tralignare _intr_ (ESSERE & AVERE) to degenerate
tram _m_ (tram) streetcar
trama _f_ woof, weft; plot (_of play_); texture (_of cloth_)
tramà·glio _m_ (**-gli**) trammel net
tramandare _tr_ to hand down
tramare _tr_ & _intr_ to weave; to plot
trambusto _m_ bustle
tramestì·o _m_ (**-i**) bustle, confusion
tramèzza [ddzz] _f_ partition
tramezzare (**tramèzzo**) [ddzz] _tr_ to interpose; to partition
tramezzino [ddzz] _m_ small partition; sandwich; sandwich man
tramèzzo [ddzz] _m_ partition; side dish; (sew) insertion ‖ _adv_ in between; **tramezzo a** among
tràmite _m_ intermediary; (lit) pass; **per tramite di** through ‖ _prep_ (coll) by; by means of
tramòg·gia _f_ (**-ge**) hopper
tramontana _f_ north wind; **perdere la tramontana** to lose one's bearings
tramontare (**tramónto**) _intr_ (ESSERE) to set (_said, e.g., of sun_); to end
tramónto _m_ setting; sunset; decline
tramortire §176 _tr_ to stun ‖ _intr_ (ESSERE) to faint, swoon
trampolière _m_ wading bird; (orn) stilt
tràmpoli _mpl_ stilts
trampolino _m_ diving board; springboard; ski jump; (fig) springboard
tramutare _tr_ to transfer; to transform
tràn·cia _f_ (**-ce**) slice; (mach) shears
tranèllo _m_ trap, snare
trangugiare §290 _tr_ to swallow; to gulp down
tranne _prep_ except, save; **tranne che** unless

tranquillante _m_ tranquilizer
tranquillare _tr_ & _ref_ (lit) to tranquilize; to calm down
tranquilli·tà _f_ (**-tà**) tranquillity
tranquillizzare [ddzz] _tr_ to tranquilize; to reassure ‖ _ref_ to become reassured
tranquil·lo -la _adj_ tranquil, calm; clear (_conscience_)
transatlànti·co -ca _adj_ & ' _m_ (**-ci -che**) transatlantic
transazióne _f_ compromise
transènna _f_ bar, barrier
transètto _m_ (archit) transept
trànsfu·ga _m_ (**-ghi**) (lit) deserter
transìgere §165 _tr_ to settle ‖ _intr_ to compromise
transistóre _m_ transistor
transitàbile _adj_ passable
transitare (**trànsito**) _intr_ to move; to walk
transiti·vo -va _adj_ transitive
trànsito _m_ passage; traffic; (lit) passing; **di transito** transient
transitò·rio -ria _adj_ (**-ri -rie**) temporary; transitory; transitional
transizióne _f_ transition
transoceàni·co -ca _adj_ (**-ci -che**) transoceanic
transòni·co -ca _adj_ (**-ci -che**) transonic
transunto _m_ abstract, summary (_of a document_)
trantràn _m_ routine
tran·vài _m_ (**-vài**) (coll) streetcar
tranvìa _f_ streetcar line
tranvià·rio -ria _adj_ (**-ri -rie**) streetcar
tranvière _m_ streetcar conductor; motorman
trapanare (**tràpano**) _tr_ to drill; (surg) to trephine
tràpano _m_ drill; (surg) trephine; **trapano a vite** automatic drill
trapassare _tr_ to pierce; (fig) to grieve; (poet) to cross; (lit) to pass, spend ‖ _intr_ (ESSERE) to go through; to pass (_said of an inheritance_); (lit) to pass away; **trapassare da, per** or **al di là di** to come through (_said, e.g., of a nail, light_)
trapassato _m_ (lit) deceased; **trapassato prossimo** past perfect
trapasso _m_ crossing; transfer; transition; (lit) passing, death
trapelare (**trapélo**) _intr_ (ESSERE) to ooze; to trickle out; to leak through; (fig) to leak out
trapè·zio _m_ (**-zi**) trapeze; (geom) trapezoid
trapezòide _adj_ trapezoidal ‖ _m_ trapezoid
trapiantare _tr_ to transplant ‖ _ref_ to transfer
trapianto _m_ transplantation; transplant; **trapianto cardiaco** heart transplant
tràppola _f_ trap; (coll) gadget; (fig) lie; **trappola esplosiva** booby trap
trapunta _f_ quilt
trapuntare _tr_ to quilt; to embroider
trapun·to -ta _adj_ quilted; embroidered; studded ‖ _m_ embroidery ‖ _f_ see **trapunta**
trarre §273 _tr_ to pull; to drag; to draw; to bring; to deduct; to lead; to un-

sheathe (*a sword*); to heave (*a sigh*); to spin (*silk, wool,* etc.); **il dado è tratto** the die is cast; **trarre dalla prigione** to free from prison; **trarre d'impaccio** to get (*s.o.*) out of trouble; **trarre fuori** to extract; **trarre in inganno** to deceive; **trarre in rovina** to ruin; **trarre per mano** to lead by the hand ‖ *intr* to kick (*said of a mule*); (lit) to run; (lit) to blow (*said of the wind*) ‖ *ref* to take off (*e.g., one's hat*); **trarsi d'impaccio** to get out of trouble; **trarsi indietro** to pull back; **trarsi in disparte** to move aside

trasalire [s] §176 *intr* (ESSERE & AVERE) to start, jump

trasanda·to -ta *adj* untidy, slovenly

trasbordare (trasbórdo) *tr* to transfer, transship

trasbórdo *m* transfer, transshipment

trascéndere §245 *tr* to transcend ‖ *intr* (ESSERE) to go to excesses

trascinare *tr* to drag; to stir; to enthrall; to lead astray; **trascinare la vita** to barely make ends meet ‖ *ref* to drag oneself; to drag on

trascolorare (trascolóro) *tr* to discolor; to change the color of ‖ *intr* (ESSERE) & *ref* to discolor; to change color

trascórrere §139 *tr* to pass (*time*); to skim through (*e.g., a book*); (lit) to go through ‖ *intr* to go to excesses ‖ *intr* (ESSERE) to elapse, pass

trascórso *m* slip (*e.g., of pen*); peccadillo

trascrìvere §250 *tr* to transcribe

trascrizióne *f* transcription; registration (*e.g., of a deed*)

trascuràbile *adj* negligible

trascurare *tr* to neglect; to fail; to disregard ‖ *ref* to not take care of oneself

trascuratézza *f* negligence, neglect; carelessness; slovenliness

trascura·to -ta *adj* neglected; careless; slovenly

trasecolare (trasècolo) [s] *intr* (ESSERE & AVERE) to marvel, be astonished

trasferìbile *adj* transferable

trasferiménto *m* transfer; conveyance

trasferire §176 *tr* to transfer; to assign, convey ‖ *ref* to move

trasfèrta *f* business trip; traveling expenses, per diem

trasfigurare *tr* to transfigure; to distort (*the truth*) ‖ *ref* to be transfigured; to change countenance

trasfocatóre *m* (phot) zoom lens

trasfóndere §178 *tr* to transfuse; (fig) to instill

trasformàbile *adj* transformable; (aut) convertible

trasformare (trasfórmo) *tr* to transform; to alter ‖ *ref* to transform oneself; to be converted

trasformati·vo -va *adj* (gram) transformational

trasformatóre *m* transformer

trasformazióne *f* transformation

trasformi·sta *mf* (-sti -ste) quick-change artist

trasfusióne *f* transfusion

trasgredire §176 *tr* & *intr* to transgress

trasgressióne *f* transgression

trasgressóre *m* transgressor

trasla·to -ta *adj* figurative; metaphorical; (lit) transferred ‖ *m* figure of speech; metaphor

traslitterare (traslìttero) *tr* to transliterate

traslocare §197 **(traslòco)** *tr* to transfer; to move ‖ *intr* & *ref* to move

traslò·co m (-chi) moving

traslùci·do -da *adj* translucent

trasméttere §198 *tr* to transmit; (rad) to broadcast

trasmetti·tóre -trice *mf* transmitter ‖ *m* (naut) engine-room telegraph; (telg) sender

trasmigrare *intr* (ESSERE & AVERE) to transmigrate ‖ *intr* (ESSERE) to pass, pass on

trasmissióne *f* transmission; conveyance; broadcast; telecast; **trasmissione del pensiero** thought transference

trasmittènte *adj* transmitting; broadcasting ‖ *f* broadcasting station

trasmutare *tr* to transmute; to change

trasogna·to -ta [s] *adj* dreamy; daydreaming; dazed

trasparènte *adj* transparent ‖ *m* transparency

trasparènza *f* transparence; **in trasparenza** against the light

trasparire §108 *intr* (ESSERE) to appear; to shine; to show through; to show, be revealed (*said of feelings*); **far trasparire** to reveal

traspirare *intr* to perspire ‖ *intr* (ESSERE) to show, be revealed

traspirazióne *f* perspiration

traspórre §218 *tr* to transpose

trasportare (traspòrto) *tr* to transport; to carry away; to transfer; to translate; to postpone; (mus) to transpose; **lasciarsi trasportare** to be carried away ‖ *ref* to move; (fig) to go back

trasporta·tóre -trice *mf* carrier ‖ *m* (mach) conveyor belt; (phot) sprocket

traspòrto *m* transportation; transport; transfer; eagerness; moving; (mus) transposition; **trasporto funebre** funeral procession

trasposi·tóre -trice *mf* (mus) transposer

trassa·to -ta *adj* paying ‖ *m* drawee

trastullare *tr* to amuse; to entice ‖ *ref* to have a good time; to loiter

trastullo *m* play, game; fun; plaything

trasudare [s] *tr* to ooze; (fig) to exude ‖ *intr* to ooze (*said of a wall*) ‖ *intr* (ESSERE) to drip (*said of perspiration*)

trasversale *adj* transverse, cross ‖ *f* crossroad

trasvèr·so -sa *adj* transverse ‖ *m* transverse beam

trasvolare (trasvólo) *tr* to fly over, cross by air ‖ *intr*—**trasvolare su** to skip over

trasvolata *f* non-stop flight

tratta *f* tug, pull; (rr) stretch; (com)

draft; (lit) crowd; **tratta dei neri** slave trade; **tratta delle bianche** white slavery

trattàbile *adj* negotiable; friendly, sociable

trattaménto *m* treatment; working conditions; food, spread; reception, welcome; **trattamento di favore** special treatment; **trattamento di quiescenza** retirement benefits

trattare *tr* to treat; to deal with; to transact; to wield; to play (*an instrument*); to work (*e.g., iron*); to deal in; **trattare qlcu da bugiardo** to call s.o. a liar; **trattare da cane** to treat like a dog || *intr* to bargain; **trattare di** to deal with; to take care of; to treat, handle || *ref* to take good care of oneself || *impers* (ESSERE) **si tratta di** it's question of

trattà·rio -ria *mf* (-**ri -rie**) drawee

trattativa *f* negotiation

trattato *m* treatise; treaty

trattazióne *f* treatment

tratteggiare §290 (**trattéggio**) *tr* to sketch; to outline; to hatch

trattég·gio *m* (**-gi**) hatching

trattenére §271 *tr* to keep; to entertain; to withhold; to hold back; to detain || *ref* to stop; to refrain; to remain

tratteniménto *m* entertainment, party; delay

trattenuta *f* withholding; checkoff

trattino *m* dash; hyphen

trat·to -ta *adj* drawn, extracted || *m* stretch; span; passage; tract; gesture; throw (*of dice*); stroke (*of pen*); bearing; section; (chess) move; **a larghi tratti** in broad outline; **a tratti** from time to time; **a un tratto** all of a sudden; at the same time; **dare un tratto alla bilancia** to tip the scales; **tratti** features; **tratti del volto** features; **tratto di corda** strappado; **tratto di unione** hyphen; **tutto d'un tratto** all of a sudden; **un bel tratto** quite a while

trat·tóre -trice *mf* innkeeper; restaurateur || *m* tractor; **trattore a cingoli** caterpillar tractor || *f* tractor (*vehicle*)

trattorìa *f* inn, restaurant

trattùro *m* cow path

traumatizzare [ddzz] *tr* to traumatize

travagliare §280 *tr* to torment; to molest || *intr & ref* to toil, labor

travà·glio *m* (**-gli**) suffering; toil; trave (*to inhibit horse being shod*); **travaglio di parto** labor pains; **travaglio di stomaco** upset stomach

travasare *tr* to pour off; to decant; to transfer || *ref* to spill

travaso *m* pouring off; transfer; **travaso di bile** gall bladder attack; **travaso di sangue** hemorrhage

travatura *f* roof timbers; **travatura maestra** ridgepole

trave *f* beam; joist; **fare una trave d'un fuscello** to make a mountain out of a molehill

travedére §279 *tr* to glimpse || *intr* to be mistaken

travéggole *fpl*—**avere le traveggole** to see things; to see one thing for another

travèrsa *f* crossbar; crossroad; crosspiece; rung; bar (*of goalpost*); dam; rail (*of fence*); transom; slat (*to hold bedspring*); rubber pad; (rr) tie

traversare (**travèrso**) *tr* to cross

traversata *f* passage, crossing

traversìa *f* strong wind; **traversie** misfortunes

traversina *f* (rr) tie

travèr·so -sa *adj* cross; devious || *m* width; crossbar; (naut) beam; (naut) side; **a traverso** (naut) on the beam; **capire a traverso** to misunderstand; **di traverso** askance; crosswise; the wrong way || *f* see **traversa**

traversóne *m* large crossbar; westerly gale; side blow with saber

travestiménto *m* disguise; travesty

travestire (**travèsto**) *tr* to disguise; to travesty, parody || *ref* to disguise oneself

traviare §119 *tr* to lead astray || *intr & ref* to go astray

travicèllo *m* joist

travisare *tr* to distort

travolgènte *adj* impetuous; fascinating; sweeping

travòlgere §289 *tr* to overwhelm; to overturn; to sweep away

trazióne *f* traction

tre [e] *adj & pron* three; **le tre** three o'clock || *m* three; third (*in dates*)

trébbia *f* thresher; threshing

trebbiare §287 (**trébbio**) *tr & intr* to thresh

trebbiatrice *f* thresher, threshing machine

trebbiatura *f* threshing

tréc·cia *f* (-**ce**) plait; braid; **treccia a ciambella** bun, knot

trecentèsi·mo -ma *adj, m & pron* three hundredth

trecènto *adj, m & pron* three hundred || **il Trecento** the fourteenth century

tredicèsi·mo -ma *adj, m & pron* thirteenth || *f* Xmas bonus

trédici *adj & pron* thirteen; **le tredici** one P.M. || *m* thirteen; thirteenth (*in dates*)

trégua *f* truce; respite; **tregua atomica** nuclear test ban; **senza tregua** without letup

tremare (**trèmo**) *intr* to shake, tremble; to quiver; **far tremare** to shake

tremarèlla *f*—**avere la tremarella** (coll) to shake in one's boots

tremebón·do -da *adj* (lit) shaky

tremèn·do -da *adj* tremendous

trementina *f* turpentine

tremila *adj, m & pron* three thousand

trèmito *m* trembling; quivering

tremolare (**trèmolo**) *intr* to shake; to quiver; to flicker

trèmo·lo -la *adj* tremulous || *m* (bot) aspen; (mus) tremolo

trèno *m* train; quarter (*of animal*); set (*of tires*); threnody, lamentation; **treno accelerato** local; **treno di lusso** Pullman train; **treno direttissimo** express; **treno di vita** mode of life; mode of living; **treno merci** freight train; **treno stradale** tractor-trailer

trenodìa *f* threnody

trénta *adj & pron* thirty ‖ *m* thirty; thirtieth (*in dates*)

trentèsi·mo -ma *adj, m & pron* thirtieth

trentina *f* about thirty

Trènto *f* Trent

trepidare (trèpido) *intr* to fear; to worr.'

trepidazióne *f* fear, trepidation

treppiède *m* tripod; trivet

tré·sca *f* (**-sche**) intrigue; liaison

tréspolo *m* stool; pedestal; stand, perch; (coll) jalopy

triàngolo *m* triangle; **triangolo rettangolo** right triangle

tribolare (trìbolo) *tr* to torment, afflict ‖ *intr* to suffer

tribolazióne *f* tribulation, ordeal

tribórdo *m* (naut) starboard

tri·bù *f* (**-bù**) tribe

tribuna *f* rostrum, platform; (sports) grandstand; **tribuna stampa** press box

tribunale *m* court, tribunal; courthouse; **tribunale dei minorenni** juvenile court; **tribunale di prima istanza** court of first instance

tributare *tr* to bestow

tributà·rio -ria (-ri -rie) *adj* tributary; tax ‖ *m* tributary

tributo *m* tribute; tax

trichè·co *m* (**-chi**) walrus

triciclo *m* tricycle

tricolóre *adj & m* tricolor

tricòrno *m* cocked hat, tricorn

tricromìa *f* three-color printing; three-color print

tridènte *m* trident

trifase *adj* three-phase

trifocale *adj* trifocal

trifò·glio *m* (**-gli**) clover; three-leaf clover

trìfola *f* (coll) truffle

trìglia *f* red mullet

trigonometrìa *f* trigonometry

trilióne *m* trillion

trillare *intr* to trill; to vibrate

trillo *m* trill; ringing

trilogìa *f* trilogy

trimestrale *adj* quarterly

trimèstre *m* quarter; quarterly dues; quarterly payment; (educ) quarter, trimester

trimotóre *m* three-engine plane

trina *f* lace

trin·ca *f* (**-che**) (naut) gammoning; **di trinca** clearly, cleanly; **nuovo di trinca** brand-new

trincare §197 *tr* (coll) to gulp down, swill

trincèa *f* trench

trincerare (trincèro) *tr* to dig trenches in ‖ *ref* to entrench oneself

trincétto *m* shoemaker's blade

trinchétto *m* (naut) foremast; (naut) foresail

trinciante *adj* cutting ‖ *m* carving knife

trinciapóllo *m* meat shears

trinciare §128 *tr* to carve; to shred; to advance (*rash opinions*); to cut up

trinciato *m* smoking tobacco

trinciatrice *f* shredder; slicer

Trinità *f* Trinity

trionfale *adj* triumphal

trionfante *adj* triumphant

trionfare (triónfo) *intr* to triumph

triónfo *m* triumph; center piece; tidbit dish with three or four tiers; trump (*in game of tarot*)

triparti·to -ta *adj* tripartite

triplicare §197 (**trìplico**) *tr & ref* to triple

trìplice *adj* threefold

tri·plo -pla *adj & m* triple

trìpode *m* tripod

trippa *f* tripe; (coll) belly

tripudiare §287 *intr* to exult

tripù·dio *m* (**-di**) exultation

tris *m* (tris) (poker) three of a kind

trisàvola *f* great-great-grandmother

trisàvolo *m* great-great-grandfather; **trisavoli** great-great-grandparents

trisma *m* lockjaw

triste *adj* sad; gloomy, bleak

tristézza *f* sadness

tri·sto -sta *adj* wicked; wretched; poor (*figure*); (lit) sad

tritacar·ne *m* (**-ne**) meat grinder

tritaghiàc·cio *m* (**-cio**) ice crusher

tritare *tr* to chop; to grind; to mince, hash; to pound

tri·to -ta *adj* minced, hashed; worn, trite

tritòlo *m* T.N.T.

tritóne *m* (zool) newt; (fig) merman ‖ **Tritone** *m* Triton

trìtti·co *m* (**-ci**) triptych; export document in triplicate; trilogy

trittòn·go *m* (**-ghi**) triphthong

triturare *tr* to mince, hash

trivèlla *f* auger, drill; post-hole digger

trivellare (trivèllo) *tr* to drill, bore

triviale *adj* vulgar

triviali·tà *f* (**-tà**) vulgarity

trì·vio *m* (**-vi**) crossroads; trivium; **da trivio** vulgar

trofèo *m* trophy; (mil) insignia (*on headpiece*)

trògolo *m* trough

tròia *f* sow; slut ‖ **Troia** *f* Troy

troia·no -na *adj & m* Trojan

trómba *f* trumpet; bugle, clarion; trunk (*of elephant*); leg (*of boot*); (anat) tube; (aut, rad) horn; **con le trombe nel sacco** crestfallen, dejected; **tromba d'aria** whirlwind; tornado; **tromba marina** waterspout; **tromba delle scale** stairwell

trombétta *f* trumpet

trombettière *m* (mil) trumpeter

trombetti·sta *m* (**-sti**) trumpet player

trombóne *m* trombone; blunderbuss

trombò·si *f* (**-si**) thrombosis

troncare §197 (**trónco**) *tr* to chop; to cut off; to clip (*words*); to break, sever; to block (*s.o.'s progress*); to apocopate

tronchése [s] *m* wire cutter

trón·co -ca (-chi -che) *adj* truncate; oxytone; apocopated; exhausted, dead-tired; incomplete; **in tronco** in the middle; (*dismissal*) on the spot ‖ *m* trunk; stub (*of receipt book*);

section (*of highway*); log; strain (*of a family*); (rr) branch; **tronco di cono** truncated cone; **tronco maggiore** (naut) lower mast

troncóne *m* stump

troneggiare §290 (**tronéggio**) *intr* to tower; to hold forth; **troneggiare su** to lord it over

trón·fio -fia *adj* (**-fi -fie**) haughty; bombastic

tròno *m* throne

tropicale *adj* tropical

tròpi·co *m* (**-ci**) tropic

troposfèra *f* troposphere

tròp·po -pa *adj* & *pron* too much; **trop·pi -pe** too many ‖ *m* too much; **questo è troppo!** enough is enough! ‖ **troppo** *adv* too; too much; **essere di troppo** to be in the way

tròta *f* trout

trottare (**tròtto**) *intr* to trot

trotterellare (**trotterèllo**) *intr* to trot along; to toddle

tròtto *m* trot; **piccolo trotto** jog trot

tròttola *f* top

trovare (**tròvo**) *tr* to find; to visit; **trovare a** or **da ridire** (**su**) to find fault (with); **trovi?** don't you think so? ‖ *ref* to find oneself; to meet; to be; to be located; to happen, e.g., **mi trovai a passare di fronte a casa sua** I happened to pass in front of his house

trovarò·be *m* (**-be**) (theat) property man ‖ *f* (theat) dresser

trovata *f* find; trick, gimmick

trovatèl·lo -la *mf* foundling, waif

trovatóre *m* troubadour

trovièro *m* trouvère

truccare §197 *tr* to make up; to falsify; (aut) to soup up ‖ *ref* to put on make-up

truccatura *f* make-up; trick, gimmick

truc·co *m* (**-chi**) make-up; trick, gimmick

truce *adj* fierce, cruel; menacing

trucidare (**trùcido**) *tr* to massacre

trùciolo *m* chip, shaving

truculènto *adj* truculent

truffa *f* cheat, fraud, swindle; **truffa all'americana** confidence game

truffare *tr* to cheat, swindle

truffa·tóre -trice *mf* cheat, swindler

truismo *m* truism

truògolo *m* var of **trogolo**

truppa *f* troop; soldiers; **di truppa** (mil) enlisted (*man or woman*); **in truppa** in a flock

tu §5 *pron pers;* **a tu per tu** face to face; **dare del tu a** to address in the familiar form

tuba *f* tuba; (hist) horn, trumpet; (joc) top hat, stovepipe; (anat) tube

tubare *intr* to coo

tubatura *f* piping, tubing; pipe, tube; pipeline

tubazióne *f* tubes, pipes

tubèrcolo *m* tubercle

tubercolosà·rio [s] *m* (**-ri**) tuberculosis sanitarium

tubercolò·si *f* (**-si**) tuberculosis

tubercoló·so -sa [s] *adj* tuberculous ‖ *mf* T.B. patient

tùbero *m* tuber

tubétto *m* tube (*for pills or toothpaste*); spool

tubino *m* small tube; derby (hat)

tubo *m* tube; pipe; (anat) canal, duct; **a tubo** tubular; **tubo di scarico** exhaust pipe; **tubo di troppopieno** overflow; **tubo di ventilazione** air shaft

tubolare *adj* tubular ‖ *m* tire (*for racing bicycle*)

tuffare *tr* to dip; to plunge ‖ *ref* to plunge; to dive

tuffa·tóre -trice *mf* diver ‖ *m* dive bomber

tuffétto *m* (orn) dabchick, grebe

tuffo *m* dive; plunge; throb; **a tuffo** (aer) diving; **scendere a tuffo** (aer) to dive; **tuffo ad angelo** (sports) swan dive; **tuffo d'acqua** downpour

tufo *m* tufa

tu·ga *f* (**-ghe**) (naut) deckhouse

tugù·rio *m* (**-ri**) hovel

tulipano *m* tulip

tumefare §173 *tr* & *ref* to swell

tumefazióne *f* swelling

tùmi·do -da *adj* tumid

tumóre *m* tumor

tùmulo *m* tomb; tumulus

tumulto *m* tumult, riot; commotion

tumultuó·so -sa [s] *adj* tumultuous

tungstèno *m* tungsten

tùni·ca *f* (**-che**) tunic

Tùnisi *f* Tunis

Tunisìa, la Tunisia

tunisì·no -na *adj* & *mf* Tunisian

tuo tua §6 *adj* & *pron poss* (**tuòi tue**)

tuòno *m* thunder

tuòrlo *m* yolk

turàcciolo *m* cork, stopper

turare *tr* to plug, stop; to cork

turba *f* crowd; mob; (pathol) upset

turbaménto *m* commotion, perturbation; disturbance, breach (*of law and order*)

turbante *m* turban

turbare *tr* to muddy; to disturb; to upset ‖ *ref* to become cloudy; to become upset

turba·to -ta *adj* upset; disturbed; distracted

tùrbi·do -da *adj* turbid

turbina *f* turbine

turbinare (**tùrbino**) *tr* to separate in a centrifuge ‖ *intr* to whirl

tùrbine *m* whirlwind; swarm; tumult

turbinó·so -sa [s] *adj* whirling; tumultuous

turboèli·ca *m* (**-ca**) turboprop

turbogètto *m* turbojet

turbolèn·to -ta *adj* turbulent

turbolènza *f* turbulence

turbomotrice *f* (rr) turbine engine

turboreattóre *m* turbojet

turcasso *m* quiver

turchése [s] *m* turquoise

Turchìa, la Turkey

turchinétto *m* bluing

turchi·no -na *adj* dark-blue ‖ *m* dark blue

tur·co -ca (**-chi -che**) *adj* Turkish; **sedere alla turca** to sit cross-legged ‖ *mf* Turk ‖ *m* Turkish (*language*); **bestemmiare come un turco** to swear like a trooper; **fumare come un turco** to smoke like a steam engine

tùrgi·do -da *adj* turgid

turìbolo *m* thurible, censer

turismo *m* tourism

turi·sta *mf* (-sti -ste) tourist

turìsti·co -ca *adj* (-ci -che) tourist; travel (*e.g., bureau*); traveler's (*check*)

turlupinare *tr* to hoodwink, swindle

turlupinatura *f* swindle, confidence game

turno *m* turn; shift; **a turno** in turn; **di turno** on duty; **fare a turno** to take turns

turpe *adj* base, abject; (lit) ugly

turpilò·quio *m* (-qui) foul language

turpitùdine *f* turpitude

tuta *f* overalls; **tuta antigravità** anti-G suit; **tuta da bambini** jumpers; **tuta spaziale** spacesuit

tutèla *f* guardianship; defense, protection

tutelare *adj* tutelary ‖ *v* (**tutèlo**) *tr* to protect, defend

tùtolo *m* corncob

tu·tóre -trice *mf* guardian; protector

tuttavìa *adv* yet, nevertheless; (lit) always, continuously

tut·to -ta *adj* whole; all; full; **con tutto** in spite of, e.g., **con tutto quello che ho fatto per lui** in spite of all I have done for him; **del tutto** fully, completely; **è tutt'uno** it's all the same; **tutt'altro** completely different; on the contrary; **tutt'altro che** anything but; **tutti** every, e.g., **tutti gli scolari** every pupil; **tutti e due** both ‖ *m* everything; whole; **con tutto che** although; **fare di tutto** to do everything possible; **in tutto** altogether ‖ *pron* **tut·ti -te** all, everybody (*of a group*); **tutti** everybody ‖ **tutto** *adv* quite; **tutt'a un tratto** all of a sudden; **tutto al contrario** quite the opposite

tuttofa·re *adj invar* of all trades; of all work ‖ *m* (-re) factotum, jack-of-all-trades ‖ *f* (-re) maid of all work

tuttóra *adv* yet, still

tziga·no -na *adj & mf* var of **zigano**

U

U, u [u] *m & f* nineteenth letter of the Italian alphabet

ubbìa *f* prejudice, bias; complex; whim

ubbidiènte *adj* obedient

ubbidire §176 *tr* to obey ‖ *intr* to obey; to respond (*said of a car*); (with *dat*) to obey, e.g., **gli ubbedì** he obeyed him

ubertó·so -sa [s] *adj* fruitful; fertile

ubicazióne *f* location

ubiquità *f* ubiquity; **non ho il dono dell'ubiquità** I can't be everywhere at the same time

ubi·quo -qua *adj* ubiquitous

ubriacare §197 *tr* to make drunk, intoxicate ‖ *ref* to get drunk

ubriacatura or **ubriachézza** *f* drunkenness, intoxication

ubria·co -ca (-chi -che) *adj* drunk; **ubriaco fradicio** dead drunk ‖ *mf* drunkard

ubriacó·ne -na *mf* drunkard

uccellare (**uccèllo**) *tr* to take in, cajole ‖ *intr* to snare; to fowl; to hunt birds

uccèllo *m* bird; **uccello di bosco** fugitive; **uccello di galera** gallows bird; **uccello di passo** bird of passage

uccella·tóre -trice *mf* live-bird catcher

uccellièra *f* aviary; large birdcage

uccìdere §274 *tr* to kill ‖ *ref* to kill oneself; to get killed; to kill one another

-ùccio -ùccia (-ucci -ucce) *suf adj* not very, e.g., **calduccio** not very hot; rather, e.g., **magruccio** rather thin; poor little, e.g., **caruccio** poor little darling ‖ *suf m & f* small e.g., **cappelluccio** small hat

uccisióne *f* killing; murder

ucci·so -sa *adj* killed ‖ *mf* victim

ucci·sóre -ditrice *mf* killer

ucrai·no -na *adj & mf* Ukrainian ‖ **l'Ucraina** *f* the Ukraine

ʋdìbile *adj* audible

udiènza *f* audience; hearing; **l'udienza è aperta!** the court is now in session!

udire §275 *tr* to hear; to listen to

udito *m* hearing

uditòfono *m* hearing aid

udi·tóre -trice *adj* hearing ‖ *mf* (educ) auditor ‖ *m* magistrate

uditò·rio -ria (-ri -rie) *adj* auditory ‖ *m* audience

ufficiale *adj* official ‖ *m* official; officer; **primo ufficiale** (naut) first officer, mate; **ufficiale di giornata** (mil) officer of the day; **ufficiale di rotta** (aer, naut) navigator; **ufficiale giudiziario** clerk of the court; process server, bailiff; **ufficiale medico** (mil) medical officer

ufficiare §128 *tr* to officiate

uffì·cio *m* (-ci) duty; office; bureau; department (*of agency*); **d'ufficio** ex-officio; public, e.g., **avvocato d'ufficio** public defender; **ufficio di collocamento** placement bureau; **ufficio di compensazione** clearing house; **ufficio d'igiene** board of health

uffició·so -sa [s] *adj* unofficial; kindly; white (*lie*)

uffì·zio *m* (-zi) (eccl) office

ufo *m*—**a ufo** gratis, without paying

ugèllo *m* nozzle

ùg·gia *f* (-ge) darkness; gloom; dislike; **avere in uggia** to dislike

uggiolare (**ùggiolo**) *intr* to whine (*said of a dog*)

uggió·so -sa [s] *adj* gloomy; boring

ugnare *tr* to bevel; to miter

ugnatura _f_ bevel; miter

ùgola _f_ uvula; **bagnarsi l'ugola** (coll) to wet one's whistle

ugonòtto _m_ Huguenot

uguaglianza _f_ equality

uguagliare §280 _tr_ to equal; to make equal; to equalize; to level; to compare || _ref_ to compare oneself; to be equal; to be compared

uguale _adj_ equal; same; even; level; **per me è uguale** it's the same to me || _m_ equal; (math) equal sign

ùlcera _f_ ulcer; sore

ulcerare (**ùlcero**) _tr & ref_ to ulcerate

uliva _f_ var of **oliva**

ulterióre _adj_ further, subsequent, ulterior

ùltima _f_ latest news; last straw

ultimare (**ùltimo**) _tr_ to complete, finish

ultimato _m_ ultimatum

ultimìssima _f_ latest edition (_of newspaper_); **ultimissime** late news

ùlti·mo- ma _adj_ last; final; latest; latter; farthest; ultimate; least; top (_floor_); **all'ultimo, dall'ultimo, nell'ultimo** or **sull'ultimo** lately; finally, at the end || _f_ see **ultima**

ultimogèni·to -ta _adj_ last-born || _mf_ last-born child

ultra- _pref adj_ and _m & f_ ultra-, e.g., **ultraelevato** ultrahigh; super-, e.g., **ultrasonico** supersonic (_speed_)

ultracór·to -ta _adj_ ultrashort

ultrarós·so -sa _adj & m_ infrared

ultraterré·no -na _adj_ ultramundane; unearthly

ultraviolét·to -ta _adj & m_ ultraviolet

ululare (**ùlulo**) _intr_ to howl

ululato _m_ howl

umanésimo _m_ humanism

umani·sta _mf_ (-sti -ste) humanist

umani·tà _f_ (-tà) humanity; **umanità** _fpl_ humanities

umanità·rio -ria _adj & mf_ (-ri -rie) humanitarian

uma·no -na _adj_ human; humane || _m_ human nature; **umani** human beings

um·bro -bra _adj & m_ Umbrian

umettare (**umétto**) _tr_ to moisten, dampen

umidìc·cio -cia _adj_ (-ci -ce) dampish

umidi·tà _f_ (-tà) humidity, dampness

ùmi·do -da _adj_ humid, damp || _m_ humidity, dampness; **in umido** stewed (_e.g., meat_)

ùmile _adj_ humble || **gli umili** _mpl_ the meek

umiliare §287 _tr_ to humiliate, humble || _ref_ to humble oneself

umiliazióne _f_ humiliation

umiltà _f_ humility

umóre _m_ humor, mood, temper; whim; (bot) sap; **un bell'umore** (coll) quite a character

umorismo _m_ humor

umori·sta _mf_ (-sti -ste) humorist

umorìsti·co -ca _adj_ (-ci -che) humorous; amusing, comic, funny

un (apocopated form of **uno**) §9 _indef art_ a, an || §9 _numeral adj_ one || §12 _reciprocal indef pron_—**l'un l'altro** each other, one another

unànime _adj_ unanimous

unanimità _f_ unanimity

unàni·mo -ma _adj_ unanimous

uncinare _tr_ to hook, grapple

uncinétto _m_ small hook; crochet hook

uncino _m_ hook; grapnel; clasp; pothook; (fig) pretext; **a uncino** hooked

undicèsi·mo -ma _adj, m & pron_ eleventh

ùndici _adj & pron_ eleven; **le undici** eleven o'clock || _m_ eleven; eleventh (_in dates_); (soccer) squad

ùngere §183 _tr_ to grease; to oil; to smear; to anoint; to flatter || _ref_ to smear oneself

Ungherìa, l' _f_ Hungary

ungherése [s] _adj & mf_ Hungarian

ùnghia _f_ nail; fingernail; claw; hoof; fluke (_of anchor_); (fig) hairbreadth; **avere le unghie lunghe** to be light-fingered; **unghia del piede** toenail; **unghie** (fig) clutches

unghiata _f_ nail scratch

unguènto _m_ unguent, ointment

ùni·co -ca _adj_ (-ci -che) only, sole; unique; single (_copy_); complete (_text_) || _f_—**l'unica** the only solution

unicòrno _m_ unicorn

unificare §197 (**unìfico**) _tr_ to unify; to standardize

unificazióne _f_ unification; standardization

uniformare (**unifórmo**) _tr_ to make uniform, standardize || _ref_—**uniformarsi a** to conform to; to comply with

unifórme _adj_ uniform; standard || _f_ uniform; **alta uniforme** (mil) full dress

unilaterale _adj_ unilateral

unióne _f_ union; agreement; **unione libera** free love

unire §176 _tr & ref_ to unite

unìsono [s] _m_ unison; **all'unisono** in unison

uni·tà _f_ (-tà) unity; unit; **unità di misura** unit of measurement

unità·rio -ria (-ri -rie) _adj_ unit (_e.g., price_); united || _m_ Unitarian

uni·to -ta _adj_ united; joined; compact; plain (_color_); consolidated

universale _adj_ universal; last (_judgment_)

universi·tà _f_ (-tà) university

università·rio -ria (-ri -rie) _adj_ university; college || _mf_ university or college student; university or college professor

univer·so -sa _adj_ universal || _m_ universe

unno _m_ Hun

u·no -na §9 _indef art_ a, an || §9 _numeral adj_ one || _m_ one || §10 _pron indef_ one; **le una, la una,** or **l'una** one o'clock; **l'uno e l'altro** both; **l'uno o l'altro** either, either one; **per uno** in single file; **uno per uno** one by one; **each other** || §11 _correlative pron_ one

un·to -ta _adj_ greasy || _m_ grease, fat; flattery; anointed one

untuosità [s] _f_ greasiness; unction, unctuousness

untuó·so -sa [s] _adj_ greasy; unctuous

unzióne *f* unction

uò·mo *m* (**-mini**) man; **come un sol uomo** to a man; **uomo d'affari** businessman; **uomo del giorno** man of the hour; **uomo della strada** man of the street; **uomo di chiesa** churchman; **uomo di fatica** laborer; **uomo di fiducia** trusted man; **uomo di mare** seaman; **uomo di paglia** straw man; **uomo di parola** man of his word; **uomo in mare!** man overboard!; **uomo meccanico** automaton; **uomo morto** (rr) deadman brake; **uomo nuovo** nouveau riche; **uomo rana** frogman

uòpo *m*—**all'uopo** if need be; **essere d'uopo** (lit) to be necessary

uòse [s] *fpl* leggings

uò·vo *m* (**-va** *fpl*) egg; **meglio un uovo oggi che una gallina domani** a bird in a hand is worth two in the bush; **rompere le uova nel paniere a qlcu** to spoil s.o.'s plans; **uovo affogato** poached egg; **uovo alla coque** soft-boiled egg; **uovo all'occhio di bue** fried egg; **uovo da tè** tea ball; **uovo strapazzato** scrambled egg

uragano *m* hurricane; storm (*of applause*); **uragano di neve** blizzard

Urali *mpl* Ural Mountains

uranìfe·ro -ra *adj* uranium-bearing

urànio *m* uranium

urbanésimo *m* urbanization, migration toward the cities

urbanìsti·co -ca (**-ci -che**) *adj* city-planning ‖ *f* city planning

urbani·tà *f* (**-tà**) urbanity, civility; city population

urbanizzare [ddzz] *tr* to urbanize

urba·no -na *adj* urban; urbane

urètra *f* urethra

urgènte *adj* urgent, pressing

urgènza *f* urgency; **d'urgenza** urgent; emergency (*e.g., operation*); **fare urgenza a** to urge

ùrgere §276 *tr* to urge, press ‖ *intr* to be urgent

urina *f* urine

urinà·rio -ria *adj* (**-ri -rie**) urinary

urlare *tr* to shout; to shout down ‖ *intr* to howl; to shout, yell

urla·tóre -trice *adj* screaming ‖ *mf* screamer; loud singer

ur·lo *m* howl ‖ *m* (**-la** *fpl*) yell, scream

urna *f* urn; ballot box; (poet) grave; **urne** polls

-uro *suf m* (chem) **-ide**, e.g., **cloruro** chloride

urologìa *f* urology

urrà *interj* hurrah!

ursóne *m* Canada porcupine

urtare *tr* to hit; to bump; to annoy ‖ *intr*—**urtare contro** to hit, strike against; **urtare a** to hit; to stumble into ‖ *ref* to get annoyed; to clash; to bump into one another

urto *m* hit; bump; collision; onslaught; clash, disagreement; **urto di nervi** huff

Uruguai, l' *m* Uruguay

uruguaia·no -na *adj & mf* Uruguayan

usanza *f* usage, custom; habit, practice

usare *tr* to use, employ; to wear out; (lit) to frequent; **usare** + *inf* to be accustomed to + *inf*; **usare di** + *ger* ‖ *intr* to be fashionable; **usare di** to use, employ ‖ *ref* to become accustomed; **si usa** + *inf* it is customary to + *inf*

usa·to -ta *adj* used, second-hand; worn; worn-out; (lit) usual ‖ *m* usage, custom; norm; second-hand goods

usbèr·go *m* (**-ghi**) hauberk; (fig) shield, protection

uscènte *adj* ending, terminating; retiring

uscière *m* receptionist; office boy, errand boy; (coll) court clerk; (coll) bailiff; (coll) tipstaff

ù·scio *m* (**-sci**) door; **infilar l'uscio** to take French leave; **metter tra l'uscio e il muro** (fig) to corner

uscire §277 *intr* (ESSERE) to go out, leave; to come out; to flow out; to escape; to turn out, ensue; **essere uscito** to be out; **uscire da** to leave; to run off (*the track*); **uscire dai gangheri** to get mad; **uscire dal comune** to be out of the ordinary; **uscire dal segno** to go too far; **uscire dal seminato** to go astray; **uscire di mente a** to escape one's mind, e.g., **gli è uscito di mente** it escaped his mind; **uscire di sentimento** to pass out; **uscire di vita** to die; **uscire in** to lead into; **uscire per il rotto della cuffia** to barely make it

uscita *f* exit; outlay; quip, sally; gate (*e.g., in an airport*); (gram) ending; **all'uscita** on the way out; **buona uscita** severance pay; bonus; **libera uscita** day off (*of servant*); (mil) pass; **uscita di sicurezza** emergency exit

usignòlo *m* nightingale

u·so -sa *adj* (lit) accustomed ‖ *m* practice; usage; use; wear; faculty; power (*e.g., of hearing*); (lit) intimate relations; **all'uso di** in the fashion of; **avere per uso di** to be wont to; **come d'uso** as usual; **farci l'uso** to get used to it!; **fuori d'uso** worn-out, out of commission; **uso esterno!** (pharm) not to be taken internally!

ustionare (**ustióno**) *tr* to burn, scorch

ustióne *f* burn

usuale *adj* usual; ordinary, common

usufruire §176 *intr*—**usufruire di** to have the use of; to enjoy

usura *f* usury; (mach) wear and tear; **ad usura** abundantly

usu·ràio -ràia (**-rài -ràie**) *adj* usurious ‖ *mf* usurer, loanshark

usurpare *tr* to usurp

utensile *adj* tool, e.g., **macchina utensile** machine tool ‖ *m* utensil; tool

utènte *m* user; customer, consumer

ùtero *m* uterus, womb

ùtile *adj* useful; usable; workable; legal, prescribed (*e.g., time*); **essere utile a** to help; **venire utile** to come in handy ‖ *m* usefulness; profit, gain

utili·tà *f* (**-tà**) utility, usefulness; profit, gain

utilitària *f* economy car, compact

utilizzare [ddzz] *tr* to utilize

utopìa *f* utopia
utopi·sta *mf* (-sti -ste) utopian
utopìsti·co -ca *adj* (-ci -che) utopian
uva *f* grapes; **un grano di uva passa** a raisin; **uva passa** raisins

uxorici·da *m* (-di) uxoricide ‖ *f* (-de) murderer of one's husband
uxorici·dio *m* (-di) uxoricide; murder of one's husband
ùzzolo [ddzz] *m* whim, fancy, caprice

V

V, v [vu] *m & f* twentieth letter of the Italian alphabet
V. *abbr* (**vostro**) your
vacante *adj* vacant
vacanza *f* vacancy; vacation; **fare vacanza** to be on vacation; **vacanze** vacation
vacanzière *m* vacationer
vac·ca *f* (-che) cow
vac·càio *m* (-cài) cowboy; stable boy
vaccherìa *f* dairy farm
vacchétta *f* cowhide
vaccina *f* cow manure; cow
vaccinare *tr* to vaccinate
vaccinazióne *f* vaccination
vacci·no -na *adj* cow; bovine ‖ *m* vaccine ‖ *f* see **vaccina**
vacillante *adj* vacillating
vacillare *intr* to totter; to vacillate; to shake; to flicker; to fail, e.g., **la memoria gli vacilla** his memory is failing; **far vacillare** to rock
vacui·tà *f* (-tà) vacuity
và·cuo -cua *adj* empty ‖ *m* vacuum
vademè·cum *m* (-cum) almanac, ready-reference handbook
vagabondàg·gio *m* (-gi) vagrancy; wandering; rambling
vagabondare (**vagabóndo**) *intr* to wander, rove
vagabón·do -da *adj* wandering; vagabond ‖ *mf* vagrant, bum, tramp; rover
vagare §209 *intr* to wander, ramble, rove
vagheggiare §290 (**vaghéggio**) *tr* to gaze fondly at; to cherish
vagire §176 *intr* to cry, whimper
vagito *m* cry, whimper
và·glia *m* (-glia) money order ‖ *f—di* **vaglia** worthy, capable
vagliare §280 *tr* to sift, bolt
và·glio *m* (-gli) sieve; **mettere al vaglio** to scrutinize
va·go -ga (-ghi -ghe) *adj* vague; vacant (*stare*); (lit) beautiful; (lit) roving; (poet) desirous ‖ *m* vagueness; (lit) rover; (anat) vagus
vagonata *f* carload
vagóne *m* (rr) car; **vagone frigorifero** (rr) refrigerator car; **vagone letto** (rr) sleeping car, sleeper; **vagone ristorante** (rr) dining car; **vagone volante** (aer) flying boxcar
vàio vàia (**vài vàie**) *adj* dark-grey ‖ *m* dark grey; (heral) vair; (zool) Siberian squirrel
vaiòlo *m* smallpox
valan·ga *f* (-ghe) avalanche
valènte *adj* capable, skillful; clever
valentìa *f* skill; cleverness

valentino *m* Valentine (*sweetheart*)
valènza *f* (chem) valence
valére §278 *tr* to win, get (*e.g., an honor for s.o.*); **che vale?** what's the use?; **valere la pena** to be worthwhile; **valere un Perù** to be worth a king's ransom ‖ *intr* (ESSERE & AVERE) to be worth: to be of avail; to be valid; to mean; to be the equivalent; **far valere** to enforce; **farsi valere** to assert oneself; **tanto vale** it's all the same; **vale a dire** that is to say; **valere meglio** to be better ‖ *ref*—**valersi di** to avail oneself of; to play on; to employ
valévole *adj* valid, good
valicare §197 (**vàlico**) *tr* to cross, pass
vàli·co *m* (-chi) mountain pass; passage; opening (*in a hedge*)
validi·tà *f* (-tà) validity
vàli·do -da *adj* valid; able, able-bodied; strong
valigerìa *f* luggage; luggage store
valigétta *f* valise; **valigetta diplomatica** attaché case
valì·gia *f* (-ge) suitcase; traveling bag; **fare le valige** to pack one's bags; **valigia diplomatica** diplomatic pouch; attaché case; **valigia per abiti** suit carrier
vallata *f* valley
valle *f* valley; **a valle** downhill; downstream
vallétta *f* (telv) assistant
vallétto *m* valet; page; (telv) assistant
valló·ne -na *adj & mf* Walloon ‖ *m* narrow valley
valóre *m* value; valor, bravery; force; (fig) jewel; (math) variable; **mettere in valore** to raise the value of; **valore di mercato** market value; **valore facciale** face value; **valore locativo** rental value; **valori** valuables; securities; **valori mobiliari** securities
valorizzare [ddzz] *tr* to enhance the value of
valoró·so -sa [s] *adj* brave, valiant
valuta *f* currency; (com) effective date; (com) value (*of promissory note*)
valutare *tr* to estimate, appraise; to value, prize; to count, reckon; to take into consideration
valutazióne *f* estimation, appraisal; evaluation
valva *f* (bot, zool) valve
vàlvola *f* (anat, mach) valve; (elec) fuse; (rad, telv) tube, valve; **valvola a galleggiante** ball cock; **valvola di sicurezza** safety valve; **valvola in testa** overhead valve
vàl·zer *m* (-zer) waltz

vamp *f* (vamp) vamp

vampa *f* flame; blaze; flash; flush

vampata *f* burst (*of heat*); blast (*of hot air*); flash, flush

vampiro *m* vampire

vanàdio *m* vanadium

vanaglòria *f* vainglory, boastfulness

vanaglorió·so -sa [s] *adj* vainglorious

vandalismo *m* vandalism

vànda·lo -la *adj & m* vandal || **Vandalo** *m* Vandal

vaneggiare §290 (**vanéggio**) *intr* to rave; to be delirious; (lit) to open, yawn

vanè·sio -sia *adj* (-si -sie) vain

van·ga *f* (-ghe) spade

vangare §209 *tr* to spade up; to dig with a spade

vangèlo *m* gospel || **Vangelo** *m* Gospel

vanghétto *m* spud

vanìglia *f* vanilla

vanilò·quio *m* (-qui) empty talk

vani·tà *f* (-tà) vanity

vanitó·so -sa [s] *adj* vain, conceited

va·no -na *adj* vain; (lit) empty, hollow; **in vano** in vain || *m* empty space; room

vantàg·gio *m* (-gi) advantage; profit; odds, handicap; discount; (coll) extra; (typ) galley; **a vantaggio di** on behalf of

vantaggió·so -sa [s] *adj* advantageous

vantare *tr* to boast of; to set up (*a claim*) || *ref* to boast; **vantarsi di** to brag about, vaunt

vanterìa *f* brag, boast, vaunt

vanto *m* brag, boast; **aver vanto su** (lit) to overcome

vànvera *f*—**a vanvera** at random

vapóre *m* vapor; steam; locomotive; steamship; **a tutto vapore** at full speed

vaporétto *m* small river boat; vaporetto (*in Venice*)

vaporizzare [ddzz] *tr* to vaporize; to spray || *intr* (ESSERE) & *ref* to evaporate

vaporizzatóre [ddzz] *m* vaporizer; sprayer

vaporó·so -sa [s] *adj* vaporous

varaménto *m* assemblage (*of prefab pieces*)

varano *m* monitor lizard

varare *tr* to launch; to pass (*a law*); (coll) to back, promote (*a candidate*)

varcare §197 *tr* to cross || *intr* (poet) to pass (*said of time*)

var·co *m* (-chi) opening; mountain pass; breach; **attendere al varco** to lie in wait for; **cogliere al varco** to catch unawares; **fare varco in** to breach

varechina *f* (laundry) bleach

variàbile *adj & f* variable

variante *f* variant; detour; (aut) model

variare §287 *tr & intr* (ESSERE & AVERE) to vary

variazióne *f* variation

varicèlla *f* chicken pox

varicó·so -sa [s] *adj* varicose

variega·to -ta *adj* variegated

varie·tà *m* (-tà) (theat) vaudeville || *f* variety

và·rio -ria (-ri -rie) *adj* varied; various; variable; different; **va·ri -rie** several || *m* variety || **varie** *fpl* miscellanies || **va·ri -rie** *pron indef* several

variopìn·to -ta *adj* multicolored

varo *m* (naut) launch

vas *m* (vas) subchaser

va·sàio *m* (-sài) potter

va·sca *f* (-sche) tub; basin; pool; **vasca da bagno** bathtub; **vasca dei pesci** aquarium; **vasca navale** (naut) basin

vascèllo *m* vessel, ship

vaselina or **vasellina** *f* vaseline

vasellame *m* dishes; set of dishes; **vasellame da cucina** kitchen ware; **vasellame d'argento** silverware; **vasellame di porcellana** chinaware

vasèllo *m* (lit) vessel

vasi·stas *m* (-stas) transom

vaso *m* vase; vessel; jar, pot; nave (*of church*); hall (*of building*); (naut) shipway; (poet) cup; **vasi vinari** wine containers; **vaso da fiori** flowerpot; **vaso da notte** chamber pot; **vaso d'elezione** (eccl) chosen vessel (*viz., Saint Paul*)

vassallo *m* vassal; (obs) helper

vas·sóio *m* (-sói) tray; mortarboard

vasti·tà *f* (-tà) vastness

va·sto -sta *adj* spacious; vast; (fig) deep

vate *m* (lit) prophet, poet

vatica·no -na *adj* Vatican || **Vaticano** *m* Vatican

vaticinare (**vatìcino** & **vaticino**) *tr* to prophesy

vaticì·nio *m* (-ni) prophecy

ve §5 *pron*

V.E. *abbr* (**Vostra Eccellenza**) Your Excellency

vècchia *f* old woman

vecchiàia *f* old age

vecchiézza *f* old age

vèc·chio -chia (-chi -chie) *adj* old; elder; **vecchio come il cucco** as old as the hills || *m* old man; **vecchi** old people; **vecchio del mestiere** old hand || *f* see **vecchia**

véc·cia *f* (-ce) vetch

véce *f* stead, e.g., **in vece mia** in my stead; (lit) vicissitude; **fare le veci di** to act for or as

vedére *m* seeing; looks; view, opinion || §279 *tr* to see; to review; to look over; **chi s'è visto s'è visto!** good-by and good luck!; **dare a vedere** to make believe; **stare a vedere** to watch; observe; **non poter vedere** to not be able to stand; **non vedere l'ora di** to be hardly able to wait for; **vedere male qlcu** to be ill-disposed toward s.o. || *intr*—**stare a vedere** to wait and see; **vederci bene** to see (*e.g., in the dark*); **vederci chiaro** to look into it; **vedere di** to try to || *ref* to see oneself; to see each other; **vedersela brutta** to anticipate trouble

vedétta *f* lookout; (nav) vedette

védova *f* widow

vedovanza *f* widowhood

vedovile *adj* widow's; widower's || *m* dower

védo·vo ·va *adj* widowed ‖ *m* widower ‖ *f* see **vedova**

veduta *f* view; (lit) eyesight; **di corte vedute** narrowminded; **di larghe vedute** broadminded

veemènte *adj* vehement; violent; impassioned

veemènza *f* vehemence; violence

vegetale *adj* vegetable ‖ *m* plant, vegetable

vegetare (**vègeto**) *intr* to vegetate

vegetaria·no -na *adj* & *mf* vegetarian

vegetazióne *f* vegetation

vège·to -ta *adj* vigorous, spry

veggènte *adj* (obs) seeing ‖ *mf* fortuneteller ‖ *m* seer, prophet; **i veggenti** people having eyesight ‖ *f* seeress, prophetess

véglia *f* vigil, watch; wakefulness; evening party, soirée; party, crowd; **a veglia** unbelievable (*tale*); **veglia danzante** dance; **veglia funebre** wake

vegliardo *m* old man

vegliare §280 (**véglio**) *tr* to keep watch over ‖ *intr* to stay awake; to keep watch; to stay up

vegllóne *m* masked ball

veicolo *m* vehicle; carrier (*of disease*)

véla *f* sail; sailing; **alzare le vele** to set sail; **ammainare le vele** to take in sail; **a vela** under sail; **far vela** to set sail; **vela aurica** lugsail; **vela bermudiana** or **Marconi** jib; **vela maestra** mainsail

ve·làio *m* (-lài) sailmaker

velare *adj* & *f* (phonet) velar ‖ *v* (**vélo**) *tr* to veil; to cover; to muffle (*sound*); to attenuate, reduce (*a shock*); to dim, cloud; to conceal; (phot) to fog ‖ *ref* to cover oneself with a veil; to take the veil; to get dim, e.g., **gli si è velata la vista** his eyesight got dim

velà·rio *m* (-ri) (hist) velarium; (theat) curtain

vela·to -ta *adj* veiled; sheer (*hosiery*)

velatura *f* coating; (aer) airfoil; (naut) sails

veleggiare §290 (**veléggio**) *tr* (lit) to sail over (*the sea*) ‖ *intr* to sail; (aer) to glide

veleggiatóre *m* sailboat; (aer) glider

veléno *m* poison; (fig) venom

velenó·so -sa [s] *adj* poisonous; (fig) venomous

velétta *f* veil; (naut) topgallant

vèli·co -ca *adj* (-ci -che) sail, sailing

velièro *m* sailing ship

veli·no -na *adj* thin (*paper*) ‖ *f* carbon copy; onionskin; slant (*given to a news item*)

velìvo·lo -la *adj* (lit) gliding; (lit) sailing ‖ *m* (lit) airplane, aircraft

vellei·tà *f* (-tà) wild ambition, dream

vellicare §197 (**vèllico**) *tr* to tickle

vèllo *m* (lit) fleece; **vello d'oro** Golden Fleece

velló·so -sa [s] *adj* hairy

velluta·to -ta *adj* velvety

vellutino *m* thin velvet; velvet ribbon; **vellutino di cotone** velveteen

vellu·to -ta *adj* (lit) hairy ‖ *m* velvet; **velluto a coste** corduroy

vélo *m* veil; coating; film; skin (*e.g., of onion*); (anat, bot) velum; (fig) body; **fare velo a** to becloud; to fog

velóce *adj* speedy, quick, fast; fleeting

velocipedastro *m* poor or reckless bicycle rider

veloci·sta *mf* (-sti -ste) (sports) sprinter

veloci·tà *f* (-tà) velocity; speed; (aut) speed; **a grande velocità** by express; **a piccola velocità** by freight; **velocità di crociera** cruising speed; **velocità di fuga** (rok) escape velocity

velòdromo *m* bicycle ring or track

véna *f* vein; grain (*in wood or stone*); mood; streak (*of madness*); **di vena** willingly; **essere in vena di** to be in the mood to

venale *adj* venal

venare (**véno**) *tr* to vein

vena·to -ta *adj* veined; streaked; suffused; **venato di sangue** bloodshot

venatura *f* veining; (fig) streak

vendémmia *f* vintage

vendemmiare §287 (**vendémmio**) *tr* to harvest (*grapes*) ‖ *intr* to gather grapes; (fig) to make a killing

vendemmia·tóre -trice *mf* vintager

véndere §281 *tr* to sell; **da vendere** plenty, more than enough; **vendere allo scoperto** (fin) to sell short; **vendere fumo** to peddle influence ‖ *intr* to sell; **vendere allo scoperto** (fin) to sell short ‖ *ref* to sell; **si vende** for sale

vendétta *f* vengeance; revenge; **gridare vendetta** to cry out for retribution

vendicare §197 (**véndico**) *tr* to avenge ‖ *ref* to get revenge

vendicati·vo -va *adj* vengeful, vindictive

vendica·tóre -trice *adj* avenging ‖ *mf* avenger

vendifu·mo *mf* (-mo) influence peddler

véndita *f* sale; shop; **in vendita** for sale; **vendita allo scoperto** (fin) short sale; **vendita per corrispondenza** catalogue sale

vendi·tóre -trice *mf* seller; clerk (*in store*) ‖ *m* salesman; **venditore ambulante** peddler; **venditore di fumo** influence peddler ‖ *f* saleslady

venefì·cio *m* (-ci) poisoning

venèfi·co -ca (-ci -che) *adj* poisonous; unhealthy ‖ *m* (lit) poisonmaker

veneràbile or **venerando** *adj* venerable

venerare (**vènero**) *tr* to venerate, revere; to worship

venerazióne *f* veneration; worship

vener·dì *m* (-dì) Friday ‖ **Venerdì Santo** Good Friday

Vènere *m* (astr) Venus ‖ *f* (mythol & fig) Venus

venè·reo -rea *adj* (-rei -ree) venereal

Venèzia *f* Venice; Venetia (*province*)

venezia·no -na *adj* & *mf* Venetian ‖ *f* Venetian blind

venezola·no -na *adj* & *mf* Venezuelan

vènia *f* (lit) forgiveness, pardon

venire §282 *intr* (ESSERE) to come; to turn out (*well or badly*); to turn out to be; **che viene** next, e.g., **il mese che viene** next month; **come viene** as it is; **far venire** to send for; to give, cause; **un va e vieni** a backward-and-forward motion; **venire** + *ger* to keep + *ger;* **venire** + *pp* to be + *pp, e.g.,* **il portone viene aperto alle tre** the gate is opened at three; **venire a capo di** to solve; **venire ai ferri corti** to come into open conflict; **venire al dunque** or **al fatto** to come to the point; **venire alle corte** to get down to brass tacks; **venire alle mani** or **alle prese** to come to blows; **venire a parole** to have words; **venire a patti con** to come to terms with; **venire a proposito** to come in handy; **venire incontro a** to go to meet; **venire in possesso di** to come into possession of (*s.th*); to come into the hands of (*s.o.*); **venire meno** to faint; **venir meno a** to fail to keep (*one's word*); **venir su** to grow, come up; **venire via** to give way || *ref*—**venirsene** to stroll along || *impers* (with *dat*)—**viene da** feel the urge to, e.g., **gli venne da starnutire** he felt the urge to sneeze; **gli è venuto da ridere** he felt the urge to laugh; **viene detto** blurt out, e.g., **gli è venuto detto che non gli piaceva quel tipo** he blurted out that he did not like that fellow; **viene fatto di**+*inf* succeed in+*ger*, e.g., **le venne fatto di convincerli** she succeeded in convincing them; happen to + *inf*, e.g., **gli venne fatto di incontrarmi per istrada** he happened to meet me on the way

ventà·glio *m* (-gli) fan; (fig) spread; **a ventaglio** fanlike; **diramarsi a ventaglio** to fan out

ventaròla *f* weather vane

ventata *f* gust of wind; (fig) wave

ventènne *adj* twenty-year-old || *mf* twenty-year-old person

ventèsi·mo -ma *adj, m & pron* twentieth

vénti *adj & pron* twenty; **le venti** eight P.M. || *m* twenty; twentieth (*in dates*)

ventidue *adj & pron* twenty-two **le ventidue** ten P.M. || *m* twenty-two; twenty-second (*in dates*)

ventilare (**vèntilo**) *tr* to air, ventilate; to winnow (*grain*); to discuss minutely; to air (*a subject*); to broach (*a subject*); to unfurl (*a flag*) || *ref* to fan oneself

ventilatóre *m* fan, ventilator; vent; (min) ventilation shaft; (naut) funnel

ventilazióne *f* ventilation; winnowing

ventina *f* score; **una ventina (di)** twenty, about twenty

ventino *m* twenty-cent coin

ventiquattro *adj & pron* twenty-four; **le ventiquattro** twelve P.M. || *m* twenty-four; twenty-fourth (*in dates*)

ventiquattró·re *f* (-re) overnight bag; twenty-four-hour race; **ventiquattrore** *fpl* period of twenty-four hours

ventitré *adj & pron* twenty-three; **le ventitré** eleven P.M.; **portare il cappello alle ventitré** to wear one's hat cocked || *m* twenty-three; twenty-third (*in dates*)

vènto *m* wind; air; guy wire; **presentarsi al vento** to sail into the wind; **farsi vento** to fan oneself; **a vento** windproof; wind-propelled; **col vento in prora** downwind; **col vento in poppa** upwind; favorably, famously

vèntola *f* fireside fan; lampshade; candle sconce; blade (*of fan*)

ventó·so -sa [s] *adj* windy || *f* cupping glass; suction cup; (zool) sucker

vèntre *m* belly; **a ventre a terra** on one's belly; on one's face; at full speed (*said of a horse*)

ventrìcolo *m* ventricle

ventrièra *f* abdominal band or belt

ventrilòquia *f* ventriloquism

ventrìlo·quo -qua *mf* ventriloquist

ventuno *adj & pron* twenty-one; **le ventuno** nine P.M. || *m* twenty-one; twenty-first (*in dates*); (cards) blackjack

ventu·ro -ra *adj* next || *f* (lit) luck, fortune; (lit) good fortune; **alla ventura** at random, at a venture; **di ventura** of fortune, e.g., **soldato di ventura** soldier of fortune

venustà *f* (lit) pulchritude

venu·to -ta *mf*—**nuovo venuto** newcomer; **primo venuto** firstcomer || *f* coming, arrival

véra *f* curbstone (*of well*); (coll) wedding ring

verace *adj* true; truthful, veracious

veraci·tà *f* (-tà) veracity, truthfulness

veranda *f* veranda; porch

verbale *adj* verbal || *m* minutes; ticket (*given by a policeman*); **mettere a verbale** to enter into the record

verbèna *f* verbena

vèrbo *m* verb; (lit) word || **Verbo** *m* (theol) Word

verbosità [s] *f* verbiage, verbosity

verbó·so -sa [s] *adj* windy, long-winded, verbose

verda·stro -stra *adj* greenish

vérde *adj* green; young, youthful || *m* green; **al verde** (coll) broke, penniless; **nel verde degli anni** in the prime of life

verdeggiante *adj* verdant

verderame *m* blue vitriol; verdigris

verdét·to -ta *adj* greenish || *m* verdict

verdógno·lo -la *adj* greenish; sallow (*face*)

verdura *f* vegetables

verecóndia *f* modesty, bashfulness

verecón·do -da *adj* modest, bashful

vér·ga *f* (-ghe) switch; rod; ingot, bar; pole; penis; (eccl) staff, crosier; (naut) yard; **tremare a verga a verga** to shake like a leaf

vergare §209 (**vérgo**) *tr* to switch; to rule (*paper*); to stripe; to write

vergati·no -na *adj* thin (*paper*) || *m* striped cloth

verga·to -ta *adj* striped; watermarked with stripes || *m* (obs) serge

verginale *adj* maidenly, virginal

vérgine *adj & f* virgin || **Vergine** *f* (eccl) Virgin; (astr) Virgo

verginità *f* virginity, maidenhood

vergógna *f* shame; **aver vergogna** to be

ashamed; **vergogne** privates ‖ *interj* for shame!

vergognare (**vergógno**) *ref* to be ashamed; to feel cheap; **vergognati!** shame on you!

vergognó·so -sa [s] *adj* ashamed; bashful; shameful

veridici·tà *f* (**-tà**) veracity

veridi·co -ca *adj* (**-ci -che**) veracious

verìfi·ca *f* (**-che**) verification; control; **verifica fiscale** auditing (*of tax return*)

verificare §197 (**verìfico**) *tr* to verify; to control, check; to audit ‖ *ref* to come true; to happen

verifica·tóre -trice *mf* checker, inspector

verismo *m* verism (*as developed in Italy*)

veri·sta *adj & mf* (**-sti -ste**) verist

veri·tà *f* (**-tà**) truth; **in verità** truthfully, verily

veritiè·ro -ra *adj* truthful

vèrme *m* worm; (mach) thread; **verme solitario** tapeworm

vermì·glio -glia (**-gli -glie**) *adj* vermilion; ruby (*lips*) ‖ *m* vermilion

vèr·mut *m* (**-mut**) vermouth

vernàcolo *m* vernacular

vernice *f* varnish; paint; polish; patina; (painting) private viewing; (fig) veneer; **scarpe di vernice** patent-leather shoes; **vernice a olio** oil paint; **vernice a spruzzo** spray paint; **vernice da scarpe** shoe polish

verniciare §128 *tr* to varnish; to paint

vé·ro -ra *adj* true; real; right; pure; **non è vero?** isn't that so? La traduzione precedente è generalmente rimpiazzata da molte altre frasi. Se la prima espressione è negativa, la domanda equivalente a **non è vero?** sarà affermativa, per esempio, **Lei non lavora, non è vero?** You are not working, are you? Se la prima espressione è affermativa, la domanda sarà negativa, per esempio, **Lei lavora, non è vero?** You are working, are you not? or aren't you? Se la prima espressione contiene un ausiliare, la domanda conterrà l'ausiliare stesso senza infinito o senza participio passato, per esempio, **Arriveranno domani, non è vero?** They will arrive tomorrow, won't they? **Ha finito il compito, non è vero?** He has finished his homework, hasn't he? Se la prima espressione non contiene né un ausiliare, né una delle forme del verbo "to be" in funzione di copula, la domanda conterrà l'ausiliare "do" o "did" senza l'infinito del verbo, per esempio, **Lei è vissuto a Milano, non è vero?** You lived in Milano, did you not? **Lei non va mai al parco, non è vero?** You never go to the park, do you?; **non mi par vero** it seems unbelievable ‖ *m* truth; actuality; **a dire il vero** to tell the truth, as a matter of fact; **dal vero** from nature; **salvo il vero** if I am not mistaken ‖ *f* see **vera**

veróne *m* (lit) balcony

verosimiglianza *f* verisimilitude; probability, likelihood

verosìmile *adj* verisimilar; probable, likely

verricèllo *m* winch, windlass

vèrro *m* boar

verru·ca *f* (**-che**) wart

versaménto *m* spilling; payment; deposit

versante *m* depositor; slope, side

versare (**vèrso**) *tr* to pour; to spill; to shed; to pay; to deposit ‖ *intr* to overflow; **versare in gravi condizioni** to be in a bad way ‖ *ref* to spill; to pour (*said of people*); to empty (*said of a river*)

versàtile *adj* versatile; fickle

versa·to -ta *adj* versed; gifted; fully subscribed to (*e.g., stock of a corporation*)

verseggia·tóre -trice *mf* verse writer

versétto *m* verse (*of Bible*)

versificare §197 (**versìfico**) *tr & intr* to versify

versificazióne *f* versification

versióne *f* version; translation

vèrso *adj invar*—**pollice verso** (hist) thumbs down ‖ *m* verse; local accent; voice, cry; reverse (*of coin*); verso (*of page*); line (*of poetry*); singsong; gesture; direction, way, manner; respect; **andare a verso** (with *dat*) to suit, e.g., **le sue maniere non gli vanno a verso** her manners do not suit him; **a verso** properly; **contro verso** against the grain; **fare un verso** to make faces; **per un verso** on one hand; **rifare il verso** (with *dat*) to mimick; **senza verso** without rhyme or reason; **verso sciolto** blank verse ‖ *prep* toward; near, around; about; for, toward; upon, in return for; as compared with; **verso di** toward

vèrtebra *f* vertebra

vertebrale *adj* vertebral; spinal

vertebra·to -ta *adj & m* vertebrate

vertènza *f* quarrel, dispute; **vertenza sindacale** labor dispute

vèrtere §283 *intr*—**vertere su** to deal with, to turn on

verticale *adj & f* vertical

vèrtice *m* top, summit; vertex; summit conference

vertìgine *f* vertigo, dizziness; **avere le vertigini** to feel dizzy

vertiginó·so -sa [s] *adj* dizzy; breathtaking

vérza [dz] *f* cabbage

verzière [dz] *m* (lit) fruit, vegetable, and flower garden; (coll) produce market

verzura [dz] *f* verdure

vesci·ca *f* (**-che**) bladder; blister; **vescica di vento** (fig) windbag; **vescica gonfiata** swellhead; **vescica natatoria** air bladder

vescichétta *f* blister; vescicle; **veschichetta biliare** gall bladder

vescìcola *f* blister

vescovado *m* bishopric

véscovo *m* bishop

vè·spa f wasp, yellowjacket || f (-spe & -spa) motor scooter

ve·spàio m (-spài) wasp's nest; (fig) hornet's nest

vespasiano m public urinal

Vèspero m Vesper

vesperti·no -na adj (lit) evening

vèspro m (eccl) vespers; (lit) vespertide

vessare (**vèsso**) tr (lit) to oppress

vessatò·rio -ria adj (-ri -rie) vexatious

vessazióne f oppression

vessillo m flag

vestàglia f negligee, dressing gown; **vestaglia da bagno** bathrobe

vèste f dress; cover; (lit) body; **in veste di** in the quality of; as; in the guise of; **veste da camera** negligee, dressing gown; bathrobe; **veste talare** (eccl) long vestment; **vesti** clothes

vestià·rio m (-ri) wardrobe

vestìbolo m vestibule, lobby

vestì·gio m (-gi & -gia fpl) vestige, trace; (lit) footprint

vestire (**vèsto**) tr to dress; to don; to wear; to clothe; to cover, bedeck || intr to dress; to fit || ref to get dressed; to dress; to dress oneself; to buy one's own clothes

vesti·to -ta adj dressed; covered || m dress; suit; clothing; **vestiti** clothes; **vestito da donna** dress; **vestito da festa** Sunday best; **vestito da sera** evening clothes, formal suit; evening gown; **vestito da uomo** suit

Vesùvio, il Vesuvius

vetera·no -na adj & mf veteran

veterinà·rio -ria adj (-ri -rie) veterinary || m veterinarian || f veterinary medicine

vèto m veto; **porre il veto a** to veto

ve·tràio m (-trài) glass manufacturer; glass dealer; glass blower

vetra·to -ta adj glass, glass-enclosed; sand (paper) || m glare ice, glaze || f glass door; glass window; glass enclosure; **vetrata a colori** or **vetrata istoriata** stained-glass window

vetrerìa f glassworks; **vetrerie** glassware

vetria·to -ta adj glassy; glass-covered

vetrificare §197 (**vetrìfico**) tr to vitrify || ref to become vitrified

vetrina f show window; showcase, glass cabinet; **mettersi in vetrina** to show off; **vetrine** (coll) eyeglasses

vetrini·sta mf (-sti -ste) window dresser

vetri·no -na adj glass-like; brittle, fragile || m slide (of microscope) || f see **vetrina**

vetriòlo m vitriol

vétro m glass; glassware; window pane; piece of glass; **vetro aderente** contact lens; **vetro infrangibile** (aut) safety glass; **vetro smerigliato** ground glass, frosted glass

vetrorèsina f fiberglass

vetró·so -sa [s] adj vitreous, glassy

vétta f peak; top, tip; limb (of tree); (naut) end (of hawser); **tremare come una vetta** to shake like a leaf

vet·tóre -trice adj leading, guiding; spreading, carrying || m carrier; (math, phys) vector

vettovagliare §280 tr to supply with food

vettovàglie fpl victuals, food; supplies

vettura f forwarding; coach; car; freight; **in vettura!** (rr) all aboard!; **prendere in vettura** to hire (a conveyance); **vettura belvedere** (rr) observation car; **vettura da turismo** (aut) pleasure car; **vettura di piazza** hack, hackney; **vettura letto** (rr) sleeping car; **vettura ristorante** (rr) diner

vetturétta f economy car, compact

vetturino m hackman, cab driver

vetu·sto -sta adj old, ancient

vezzeggiare §290 (**vezzéggio**) tr to coddle || intr (lit) to strut

vezzeggiati·vo -va adj endearing || m endearing expression; diminutive

vézzo m habit; caress; necklace; bad habit; **vezzi** fondling, petting; mawkish behavior; charms

vezzó·so -sa [s] adj graceful, charming; affected, mincing

vi §5

vìa m (vìa) starting signal; **dare il via a** to give the go-ahead to || f street; road, way; route; career; **dare la via a** to open the way to; **in via confidenziale** in confidence; **in via eccezionale** as an exception; **per via di via**, through; (coll) because of; **per via gerarchica** through administrative channels; **per via orale** orally; **per via rettale** rectally; **prendere la via** to be on one's way; **venire a vie di fatto** to come to blows; **Via Crucis** Way of the Cross; **via d'acqua** waterway; **via di scampo** (fig) way out; **via d'uscita** way out; **Via Lattea** Milky Way; **vie di fatto** assault and battery; **vie legali** legal steps || adv away; (math) times, by; **e così via** and so on; **e via dicendo** and so on; **tirar via** to hurry along; **via via che** as || prep via, by way of

viadótto m viaduct

viaggiare §290 intr to travel; (com) to deal

viaggia·tóre -trice adj traveling; homing (pigeon) || mf traveler || m traveling salesman

viàg·gio m (-gi) travel; journey; trip; **buon viaggio!** bon voyage!; **viaggio d'andata e ritorno** round trip; **viaggio di prova** (naut) trial run, shakedown cruise

viale m boulevard

viandante mf (lit) wayfarer

vià·rio -ria adj (-ri -rie) road, highway

viàti·co m (-ci) viaticum

viavài m coming and going; hustle and bustle

vibrante adj vibrant; wiry; (phonet) vibrant || f (phonet) trill, vibrant

vibrare tr to jar; to deliver (a blow); to vibrate; (lit) to hurl || intr to vibrate

vibra·to -ta adj vibrant; resolute, vigorous || m vibrating sound

vibrazióne f vibration

vicariato m vicarage

vicà·rio m (-ri) vicar

vice- *pref adj* vice-, e.g., **vicereale**
viceroyal ‖ *pref m & f* vice-, e.g.,
viceammiraglio vice-admiral; assistant, e.g., **vicegovernatore** assistant
governor; deputy, e.g., **vicesindaco**
deputy mayor
vicediret·tóre -trice *mf* assistant manager
vicènda *f* vicissitude; rotation (*of
crops*); **a vicenda** in turn
vicendévole *adj* mutual, reciprocal
vicepresidènte [s] *mf* vice president
vice·ré *m* (-ré) viceroy
vicevèrsa *adv* vice versa; (coll) instead,
on the contrary
vichin·go -ga *adj & mf* (-ghi -ghe)
Viking
vicinanza *f* nearness; **in vicinanza di**
in the neighborhood of; **vicinanze**
vicinity, neighborhood
vicinato *m* neighborhood
vici·no -na *adj* near; neighboring; next;
close (*relative*) ‖ *mf* neighbor ‖
vicino *adv* nearby, near; **da vicino**
closely; at close quarters; **vicino a**
near; next to, close to
vicissitùdine *f* vicissitude
vi·co *m* (-chi) alley, lane; village; (lit)
region
vìcolo *m* alley, court, place; **vicolo
cieco** blind alley, dead end
videocassétta *f* video cassette
vidimare (**vìdimo**) *tr* to validate, visa;
to sign
vidimazióne *f* validation, visa; signature
viennése [s] *adj & mf* Viennese
viepiù *adv* (lit) more and more
vietare (**vièto**) *tr* to forbid, prohibit
vieta·to -ta *adj* forbidden; **senso vietato** one way; **sosta vietata** no parking; no stopping; **vietato fumare** no
smoking
Vietnam, il Vietnam
vietnami·ta *adj & mf* (-ti -te) Vietnam-
ese
viè·to -ta *adj* (lit) old-fashioned; (coll)
musty-smelling, rancid
vigènte *adj* current, in force
vìgere §284 *intr* to be in force
vigèsi·mo -ma *adj* twentieth
vigilante *adj* watchful, vigilant ‖ *m*
watchman
vigilanza *f* vigilance; surveillance
vigilare (**vìgilo**) *tr* to watch; to watch
over; to police ‖ *intr* to watch; **vigilare che** to see to it that
vigila·tóre -trice *mf* inspector ‖ *f* camp
counselor; **vigilatrice sanitaria** child
health inspector
vìgile *adj* (lit) watchful ‖ *m* watch;
vigile del fuoco fireman; **vigile urbano** policeman
vigìlia *f* fast; vigil; **la vigilia di** on the
eve of, the night before
vigliacchería *f* cowardice
vigliac·co -ca (-chi -che) *adj* cowardly
‖ *m* coward
vigna *f* vineyard
vignaiòlo *m* vine dresser
vignéto *m* vineyard
vignétta *f* vignette; **vignetta umoristica**
cartoon

vignetti·sta *mf* (-sti -ste) cartoonist
vigógna *f* vicuña
vigóre *m* vigor; **in vigore** in force
vigorìa *f* vigor
vigoró·so -sa [s] *adj* vigorous
vile *adj* cowardly; vile, low, cheap;
base (*metal*)
vilificare §197 (**vilìfico**) *tr* to vilify
vilipèndere §148 *tr* to despise; to show
scorn for
villa *f* villa; country house; one-family
detached house; (lit) country
villàg·gio *m* (-gi) village; **villaggio del
fanciullo** boys' town
villanata *f* boorishness
villanìa *f* boorishness, rudeness; insult
villa·no -na *adj* rude, churlish ‖ *mf*
boor, churl; (lit) peasant
villanzó·ne -na *mf* boor, uncouth person
villeggiante *mf* vacationist
villeggiare §290 (**villéggio**) *intr* to vacation
villeggiatura *f* vacation, summer vacation
villétta *f* or **villino** *m* bungalow
villó·so -sa [s] *adj* hairy
vil·tà *f* (-tà) baseness; cowardice
viluppo *m* tangle, twist
vìmine *m* withe, wicker, osier
vinàcce *fpl* pressed grapes
vi·nàio *m* (-nài) wine merchant
vincènte *adj* winning ‖ *mf* winner
vìncere §285 *tr* to overcome; to win;
to convince; to check; to defeat;
vincere per un pelo to nose out; **vincerla** to come out on top ‖ *ref* to
control oneself
vincetòssi·co *m* (-ci) swallowwort, tame
poison
vincipèr·di *m* (-di) giveaway
vìncita *f* gain; winnings
vinci·tóre -trice *adj* conquering, victorious ‖ *mf* winner; conqueror;
victor
vincolare *adj* binding; bound ‖ *v* (**vìncolo**) *tr* to tie; to bind, obligate; to
restrict the use of (*real-estate property*)
vìncolo *m* tie, bond; (law) entail; (law)
restriction (*in a real-estate deed*)
vinìco·lo -la *adj* wine, wine-producing
vinile *m* vinyl
vino *m* wine; **vin caldo** mulled wine;
vino da pasto table wine; **vino di
marca** vintage wine; **vino di mele**
cider
vin·to -ta *adj* vanquished, overcome,
defeated; victorious (*battle*); **averla
vinta** su to overcome; **darla vinta a
qlcu** to let s.o. get away with murder;
darsi per vinto to give in, yield ‖ *m*
vanquished person; **i vinti** the vanquished
viò·la *adj invar* violet ‖ *m* (-la) violet
(*color*) ‖ *f* violet; (mus) viola; **viola
del pensiero** pansy; **viola mammola**
sweet violet
violacciòc·ca *f* (-che) (bot) wallflower
violà·ceo -cea *adj* violet
violare (**vìolo**) *tr* to violate; to run
(*a blockade*)
violazióne *f* violation; **violazione di**

domicilio housebreaking, burglary; **violazione di proprietà** trespass

violentare (**violènto**) *tr* to violate, force; to do violence to; to rape

violèn·to -ta *adj* violent ‖ *m* violent person

violènza *f* violence; **violenza carnale** rape

violét·to -ta *adj* & *m* violet ‖ *f* (bot) violet

violini·sta *mf* (-sti -ste) violinist

violino *m* violin; **primo violino** concertmaster

violoncelli·sta *mf* (-sti -ste) violoncellist

violoncèllo *m* violoncello, cello

viòttolo *m* path

vìpera *f* viper, adder

viràg·gio *m* (-gi) turn; (aer) banking; (naut) tacking; (phot) toning

virare *tr* to veer; to turn (*a winch*); (aer) to bank; (phot) to tone ‖ *intr* to veer, steer; **virare di bordo** (naut) to put about; (naut) to tack

virata *f* turn, veer; (aer) banking; (naut) tacking

virginale *adj* var of **verginale**

virgi·nia *m* (-nia) Virginia tobacco ‖ *f* (-nia) Virginia cigarette

virgola *f* comma; (*used in Italian to set off the decimal fraction from the integer*) decimal point; **doppia virgola** quotation mark

virgolétta *f* quotation mark

virgulto *m* (lit) shoot; (lit) shrub

virile *adj* virile

virilità *f* virility

viròla *f* (mach) male piece

virologìa *f* virology

vir·tù *f* (-tù) virtue; (lit) valor

virtuale *adj* virtual

virtualménte *adv* virtually, to all intents and purposes

virtuosismo [s] *m* virtuosity; showing off

virtuosità [s] *f* virtuosity

virtuó·so -sa [s] *adj* virtuous ‖ *mf* virtuoso

virulèn·to -ta *adj* virulent

virulènza *f* virulence

vi·rus *m* (-rus) virus

vìsce·re *m* (-ri) internal organ; **visceri** entrails, viscera ‖ **viscere** *fpl* entrails, viscera; (fig) heart, feeling; (fig) bowels (*of the earth*)

vì·schio *m* (-schi) mistletoe; birdlime; (fig) trap

vischió·so -sa [s] *adj* sticky, viscous; (com) steady

vìsci·do -da *adj* viscid; clammy; (fig) unctuous

vìsciola *f* sour cherry

vìsciolo *m* sour cherry tree

viscónte *m* viscount

viscontéssa *f* viscountess

viscó·so -sa [s] *adj* viscous, sticky ‖ *f* viscose

visétto *m* small face; baby face

visìbile *adj* visible; obvious

visibi·lio *m* (-li) (coll) crowd; (coll) bunch; **andare in visibilio** to become ecstatic; **mandare in visibilio** to throw into ecstasy, enrapture

visibilità *f* visibility

visièra *f* visor; fencing mask; eyeshade; **visiera termica** (aut) electric defroster

visigò·to -ta *adj* Visigothic ‖ *mf* Visigoth

visionà·rio -ria *adj* & *mf* (-ri -rie) visionary

visióne *f* vision; sight; (mov, telv) showing; **in visione gratuita** for free examination; **mandare qlco a qlcu in visione** to send s.th to s.o. for his (or her) opinion; **prendere visione di** to examine; to peruse

vi·sìr *m* (-sìr) vizier

vìsita *f* visit; visitation; **fare una visita** to pay a visit; **marcare visita** (mil) to report sick; **visita doganale** customs inspection

visitare (**vìsito**) *tr* to visit; to inspect

visita·tóre -trice *mf* visitor ‖ *f* social worker

visitazióne *f* visitation

visì·vo -va *adj* visual

viso *m* face; **far buon viso a cattivo gioco** to grin and bear it

visóne *m* mink

visóre *m* (phot) viewer; (phot) viewfinder

vi·spo -spa *adj* brisk, lively

vissu·to -ta *adj* wordly-wise

vista *f* sight, eyesight; view; vista; glance; (poet) window; **a vista** exposed, visible; **a vista d'occhio** as far as the eye can see; **essere in vista** to be expected; to be imminent; to be in the limelight; **far vista di** to pretend to; **in vista di** in view of; **mettere in vista** to show off; **vista a volo d'uccello** bird's-eye view; **vista corta** poor eyesight

vistare *tr* to validate, visa

vi·sto -sta *adj*—**visto che** seeing that, inasmuch as ‖ *m* visa; approval ‖ *f* see **vista**

vistó·so -sa [s] *adj* showy, flashy; (fig) considerable

visuale *adj* visual ‖ *f* view; line of sight

visualizzare [ddzz] *tr* to visualize

vita *f* life; livelihood; living; waist; **avere breve vita** to be short-lived; **fare la vita** to be a prostitute; **vita natural durante** for life; during one's lifetime

vitaiòlo *m* man about town; playboy, bon vivant

vitale *adj* vital

vitalità *f* vitality

vitalì·zio -zia (-zì -zie) *adj* life, lifetime ‖ *m* life annuity

vitamina *f* vitamin

vite *f* (bot) grapevine; (mach) screw; **a vite** threaded; (aer) in a tailspin; **vite autofilettante** self-tapping screw; **vite del Canadà** woodbine, Virginia creeper; **vite per legno** wood screw; **vite per metallo** machine screw; **vite perpetua** (mach) endless screw, worm gear; **vite prigioniera** stud bolt

vitèllo *m* calf; veal

vitic·cio *m* (-ci) tendril

vìtre·o -a *adj* vitreous; glassy (*eyes*)

vìttima *f* victim
vitto *m* food; diet; **vitto e alloggio** room and board
vittòria *f* victory; **cantar vittoria** to crow; to crow too soon
vittorió·so -sa [s] *adj* victorious
vituperare (vitùpero) *tr* to vituperate
vituperévole *adj* contemptible, shameful
vitupè·rio *m* (**-ri**) shame, infamy; insult; (lit) blame
viuzza *f* narrow street, lane
viva *interj* long live!
vivacchiare §287 *intr* (coll) to get along || *ref*—**si vivacchia** (coll) so, so
vivace *adj* lively, brisk; brilliant; vivacious
vivacità *f* liveliness, briskness; brilliancy, brightness; vivacity
vivaddìo *interj* yes, of course!; by Jove!
vivagno *m* selvage; edge
vi·vàio *m* (**-vài**) fishpond; fish tank; tree nursery; (fig) seedbed
vivanda *f* food
vivandiè·re -ra *mf* (mil) sutler
vìvere *m* life; living; cost of living; **viveri** food, provisions; allowance || §286 *tr* to live; **vivere un brutto momento** to spend an uncomfortable moment || *intr* (ESSERE) to live; **vive** (typ) stet; **vivere alla giornata** to live from hand to mouth
vivézza *f* liveliness
vìvi·do -da *adj* vivid, lively
vivificare §197 (**vivìfico**) *tr* to vivify
vivisezionare (vivisezióno) *tr* to vivisect; to scrutinize
vivisezióne *f* vivisection
vi·vo -va *adj* alive; living; live, vivacious; lively; vivid; high (*flame*); bright (*light*); raw (*flesh*); sharp, acute (*pain*); hearty (*thanks*); outright (*expense*); gross (*weight*); brute (*strength*); modern (*language*); kinetic (*energy*); running (*water*) || *m* living being; heart (*of a question*); **al vivo** lively; lifelike; **i vivi e i morti** the quick and the dead; **toccare nel vivo** to sting to the quick || **viva** *interj* see viva
viziare §287 *tr* to spoil; to ruin; (law) to vitiate || *ref* to become spoiled
vizia·to -ta *adj* spoiled; ruined; stale (*air*)
vì·zio *m* (**-zi**) vice; defect; flaw; (law) vitiation
vizió·so -sa [s] *adj* vicious; defective || *mf* profligate
viz·zo -za *adj* withered
vocabolà·rio *m* (**-ri**) dictionary; vocabulary
vocàbolo *m* word
vocale *adj* vocal; (lit) sonorous || *f* vowel
vocalizzare [ddzz] *tr & ref* to vocalize
vocativo *m* vocative
vocazióne *f* vocation
vóce *f* voice; noise, roar; word; rumor; entry; tone; **ad alta voce** aloud; **a bassa voce** in a low voice; **a viva voce** by word of mouth; **a voce** orally; **dare una voce a** (coll) to call; **dare sulla voce a** to rebuke; to con-

tradict; **fare la voce grossa** to raise one's voice; **non avere voce in capitolo** to have no say; **schiarirsi la voce** to clear one's throat; **senza voce** hoarse; **sotto voce** in a low tone; **voce bianca** child's voice (*in singing*)
vociare *m* bawl || §128 (**vócio**) *intr* to bawl
vociferare (vocìfero) *intr* to vociferate, shout || *ref*—**si vocifera** it is rumored
vó·ga *f* (**-ghe**) fashion, vogue; energy, enthusiasm; rowing
vogare §209 (**vógo**) *tr & intr* to row
voga·tóre -trice *mf* rower || *m* oarsman; rowing machine
vòglia *f* wish; whim, fancy; willingness; birthmark; **aver voglia di** to feel like, have a notion to; **di buona voglia** willingly; **di mala voglia** unwillingly
voglió·so -sa [s] *adj* fanciful; (lit) desirous
vói §5 *pron pers* you; **voi altri** you, e.g., **voi altri americani** you Americans
voial·tri -tre *pron pl* you, e.g., **voialtri americani** you Americans
volano *m* shuttlecock; (mach) flywheel
volante *adj* flying; loose (*sheet*); free (*agent*) || *m* steering wheel; (mach) hand wheel; shuttlecock
volantino *m* leaflet; fringe; (mach) hand wheel
volare (vólo) *tr* (soccer) to overthrow || *intr* (ESSERE & AVERE) to fly
volata *f* flight; sprint; run; mouth (*of gun*); (tennis) volley; **di volata** in a hurry
volàtile *adj* volatile; flying (*animal*) || **volatili** *mpl* birds
volatilizzare [ddzz] *tr & intr* (ESSERE) to volatilize
volènte *adj*—**Dio volente** God willing; **volente o nolente** willy-nilly
volentièri *adv* gladly, willingly
volére *m* will, wish; **al volere di** at the bidding of || §288 *tr* to will; to want, desire; (lit) to believe, affirm; **l'hai voluto tu** it's your fault; **non vuol dire!** never mind!; **qui ti voglio** here's the rub, that's the trouble; **senza volere** without meaning to; **voglia Dio!** may God grant!; **voler bene** (with *dat*) to like; **volerci** to take, e.g., **ci vorranno due anni per finire questo palazzo** it will take two years to complete this building; **ce ne vogliono ancora tre** it takes three more of them; **voler dire** to mean; to try, e.g., **vuole piovere** it is trying to rain; **volere che** + *subj* to want + *inf*, e.g., **vuole che vengano** he wants them to come; **volere piuttosto** to prefer; **volere è potere** where there is a will there is a way; **voler male** (with *dat*) to dislike; **volerne a** to bear a grudge against; **vorrei** I should like, I'd like; **vuoi . . . vuoi** either . . . or
volgare *adj* vernacular, popular, common; vulgar || *m* vernacular
volgari·tà *f* (**-tà**) vulgarity

volgarizzare [ddzz] *tr* to popularize

vòlgere §289 *tr* to turn; (lit) to translate ‖ *intr* to turn; (lit) to go by; **volgere a** to turn toward; to draw near, to approach; **volgere in fuga** to take to flight ‖ *ref* to turn; to devote oneself

vól·go *m* (**-ghi**) (lit) crowd, mob

volièra *f* aviary

voliti·vo -va *adj* volitional; strong-minded, strong-willed

vólo *m* flight; fall; **al volo** on the spot; on the wing; **a volo d'uccello** as the crow flies; bird's-eye (*e.g.,* view); **di volo** at top speed, immediately; **in volo** aloft, in the air; **prendere il volo** to take flight; **volo a vela** or **volo planato** gliding; **volo strumentale** instrument flying; **volo veleggiato** gliding

volon·tà *f* (**-tà**) will; **di spontanea volontà** of one's own volition; **pieno di buona volontà** eager to please; **ultime volontà** last will and testament

volontariato *m* volunteer work; apprenticeship without pay; (mil) volunteer service

volontà·rio -ria (**-ri -rie**) *adj* voluntary ‖ *m* volunteer

volonteró·so -sa [s] *adj* willing, well-disposed

volpacchiòtto *m* fox cub; (fig) sly fox

vólpe *f* fox; (agr) smut; **volpe argentata** silver fox

volpi·no -na *adj* fox; fox-colored; foxy ‖ *m* Pomeranian

volpó·ne -na *mf* sly fox

vòlt *m* (**vòlt**) (elec) volt

vòl·ta *m* (**-ta**) (elec) volt ‖ *f* turn; time; vault; roof (*of mouth*); **alla volta di** toward; **a volta di corriere** by return mail; **a volte** sometimes; **c'era una volta** once upon a time there was; **certe volte** sometimes; **dare di volta il cervello a** to go crazy, e.g., **gli ha dato di volta il cervello** he went crazy; **dar la volta** to turn sour (*said of wine*); **due volte** twice; **molte volte** often; **per una volta tanto** only once; **poche volte** seldom; **tante volte** often; **tutto in una volta** at one swoop, at one stroke; in one gulp, in one swallow; **una volta** once; **una volta che** (coll) inasmuch as; **una volta per sempre** once and for all; **una volta tanto** for once; **volta a crociera** cross vault; **volta per volta** little by little; **volte** (math) times, e.g., **cinque volte cinque** five times five

voltafàc·cia *m* (**-cia**) volte-face; **fare voltafaccia** to wheel around (*said of a horse*)

voltagabba·na *mf* (**-na**) turncoat

voltàg·gio *m* (**-gi**) voltage

voltài·co -ca *adj* (**-ci -che**) voltaic

voltare (**vòlto**) *tr, intr & ref* to turn

voltastòma·co *m* (**-chi**) (coll) nausea; **fare venire il voltastomaco a qlcu** (coll) to turn s.o.'s stomach

voltata *f* turn; curve

volteggiare §290 (**voltéggio**) *tr* to put (*a horse*) through its paces ‖ *intr* to hover; to flit, flutter; (sports) to vault (*e.g., on horseback or trapeze*)

voltég·gio *m* (**-gi**) (sports) vaulting

vòltmetro *m* voltmeter

vólto *m* (lit) face

voltura *f* (com, law) transfer

volùbile *adj* fickle

volubilità *f* fickleness

volume *m* volume; bulk; mass

voluminó·so -sa [s] *adj* voluminous, bulky

volu·to -ta *adj* desired; intentional ‖ *f* (archit) volute, scroll

volut·tà *f* (**-tà**) pleasure, enjoyment; voluptuousness

voluttuà·rio -ria *adj* (**-ri -rie**) luxury (*goods*)

voluttuó·so -sa [s] *adj* voluptuous, sensuous

vòmere *m* plowshare; trail spade (*of gun*)

vòmi·co -ca *adj* (**-ci -che**) emetic

vomitare (**vòmito**) *tr & intr* to vomit

vomitati·vo -va *adj & m* emetic

vòmito *m* vomit

vóngola *f* clam

vorace *adj* voracious

voraci·tà *f* (**-tà**) voracity

voràgine *f* chasm, gulf, abyss

vòrtice *m* vortex, whirlpool; whirlwind

vorticó·so -sa [s] *adj* whirling, swirling

vò·stro -stra §6 *adj & pron poss*

votare (**vóto**) *tr* to devote; to vote ‖ *intr* to vote ‖ *ref* to devote oneself

votazióne *f* vote, voting, poll; (educ) grades

voti·vo -va *adj* votive

vóto *m* vow; wish; votive offering; vote, ballot; grade, mark; **a pieni voti** with highest honors; **fare un voto** to make a vow; **pronunciare i voti** to take vows; **voto di fiducia** vote of confidence; **voto preferenziale** write-in vote; preferential ballot

vudù *m* voodoo

vudui·sta *mf* (**-sti -ste**) voodoo (*person*)

vulcàni·co -ca *adj* (**-ci -che**) volcanic

vulcanizzare [ddzz] *tr* to vulcanize

vulcano *m* volcano

vulga·to -ta *adj* disseminated ‖ **Vulgata** *f* Vulgate

vulneràbile *adj* vulnerable

vuotare (**vuòto**) *tr* to empty; **vuotare il sacco** to speak one's mind, unburden oneself ‖ *ref* to empty

vuò·to -ta *adj* empty; devoid ‖ *m* vacuum; emptiness; empty space; empty seat; empty feeling; empty (*e.g., container*); **a vuoto** in vain; wide of the mark; (*check*) without sufficient funds; **andare a vuoto** to fail; (mach) to idle; **cadere nel vuoto** to fall on deaf ears; **mandare a vuoto** to thwart; **sotto vuoto** in a vacuum; **vuoto d'aria** (aer) air pocket; **vuoto di cassa** deficit; **vuoto di potere** power vacuum

W

W, w ['doppjo 'vu] *m & f*
wà·fer *m* (-fer) wafer
water-clòset *m* (-clòset) flush toilet
watt *m* (watt) watt

watt·óra *m* (-óra) watt-hour
wèstern *m* (wèstern) (mov) western
whisky *m* (whisky) whiskey
wìgwam *m* (wìgwam) wigwam

X

X, x [ɪks] *m & f*
xèno *m* xenon
xenòfo·bo -ba *mf* xenophobe

xè·res *m* (-res) sherry
xerografia *f* xerography
xerófito *m* xerophyte

Y

Y, y ['ɪpsɪlon] *m & f*
yacht *m* (yachts) yacht
yak *m* (yak) yak

yànkee *m* (yànkees) Yankee
yìddish *adj invar & m* Yiddish

Z

Z, z ['dzeta] *m & f* twenty-first letter of the Italian alphabet
zabaióne [dz] *m* eggnog
zàcchera *f* splash of mud
zaffare *tr* to plug; to bung
zaffata *f* unpleasant whiff, stench; gust
zafferano [dz] *m* saffron
zaffiro [dz] *m* sapphire
zaffo *m* plug; bung; tampon
zàgara [dz] *f* orange blossom
zàino [dz] *m* knapsack; (mil) pack
zampa *f* paw; (culin) leg; **a quattro zampe** on all fours; **zampa di gallina** crow's-foot; illegible scrawl; **zampa di porco** crowbar
zampare *intr* to paw; to stamp
zampettare (zampétto) *intr* to toddle; to scamper
zampillare *intr* (ESSERE & AVERE) to spurt, gush, spring
zampillo *m* spurt, gush, spring
zampino *m* little paw; **metterci lo zampino** to put one's finger in the pie
zampiróne *m* slow-burning mosquito repellent; foul-smelling cigarette
zampógna *f* bagpipe
zampognare (zampógno) *intr* to pipe, play the bagpipe
zampóne *m* Modena salami (*stuffed forepaw of a hog*)
zanèlla *f* gully
zàngola *f* butter churn
zanna *f* tusk; fang; **mostrare le zanne** to show one's teeth
zanzara [dz] [dz] *f* mosquito
zanzarièra [dz] [dz] *f* mosquito net; window screen
zappa *f* hoe; **darsi la zappa sui piedi**

to cut one's nose off to spite one's face
zappare *tr* to hoe
zappatóre *m* hoer, digger; (mil) sapper
zar *m* (zar) czar
zàttera *f* raft; **zattera di salvataggio** life raft
zatterière *m* log driver
zavòrra [dz] *f* ballast; (fig) deadwood
zavorrare [dz] (zavòrro) *tr* to ballast
zàzzera *f* mop (*of hair*)
zèbra [dz] *f* zebra; **zebre** zebra crossing
zebra·to -ta [dz] *adj* zebra-striped
ze·bù [dz] *m* (-bù) zebu
zéc·ca *f* (-che) mint; (ent) tick; **nuovo di zecca** brand-new
zecchino *m* sequin, gold coin
zèfiro [dz] *m* zephyr
zelante [dz] *adj* zealous; studious ‖ *mf* zealot; eager beaver
zèlo [dz] *m* zeal; **zelo pubblico** public spirit
zènit [dz] *m* zenith
zénzero [dz] [dz] *m* ginger
zép·po -pa *adj* crammed, jammed ‖ *f* wedge; (fig) padding
zerbino [dz] *m* doormat; dandy
zerbinòtto [dz] *m* dandy, sporty fellow
zèro [dz] *m* zero
zìa *f* aunt
zibaldóne [dz] *m* notebook; collection of thoughts; (pej) hodgepodge
zibellino [dz] *m* sable
zibétto [dz] *m* civet cat; civet (*substance used in perfumery*)
zibibbo [dz] *m* raisin
ziga·no -na *adj & mf* gypsy
zìgomo [dz] *m* cheekbone

zigrinare [dz] *tr* to grain (*leather*); to mill, knurl (*metal*)

zigrina·to -ta [dz] *adj* shagreened, grained (*leather*); knurled

zigzàg [dz] [dz] *m* (**zigzàg**) zigzag; andare a zigzag to zigzag

zigzagare §209 [dz] [dz] *intr* to zigzag

zimarra [dz] *f* cassock; (obs) overcoat

zimbèllo *m* decoy (*bird*); laughingstock

zincare §197 *tr* to zinc

zinco *m* zinc

zingaré·sco -sca (**-schi -sche**) *adj & mf* gypsy

zìnga·ro -ra *mf* gypsy

zìnnia [dz] *f* zinnia

zìo *m* uncle; **zio d'America** rich uncle

zìpolo *m* peg, bung

zircóne [dz] *m* zircon

zircònio [dz] *m* zirconium

zirlare *intr* to warble; to squeak (*said of mouse*)

zitèlla *f* old maid

zittire §176 *tr & intr* to hoot, hiss

zit·to -ta *adj* silent; **far stare zitto** to hush up; **stare zitto** to keep quiet ‖ *m* whisper ‖ **zitto** *interj* quiet!; hush!; shut up!

zizzània [dz] [ddzz] *f* (bot) darnel; **seminar zizzania** to sow discord

zòccolo *m* clog, sabot; clump, clod; clodhopper; base (*of column*); pedestal; wide baseboard; (zool) hoof

zodìaco [dz] *m* zodiac

zolfanèllo *m* sulfur match

zolfara *f* var of **solfara**

zólfo *m* sulfur

zòlla *f* clod, clump; turf; lump, cube (*of sugar*)

zollétta *f* lump, cube (*of sugar*)

zòna [dz] *f* zone; area; girdle; band, stripe; ticker tape; (pathol) shingles; (telg) tape; **zona glaciale** frigid zone; **zona tropicale** tropics, tropical zone

zónzo [dz] [dz] *m*—andare a zonzo to stroll, loiter along

zoòfito [dz] *m* zoophite

zoologìa [dz] *f* zoology

zoològi·co -ca [dz] *adj* (**-ci -che**) zoological

zoòlo·go -ga [dz] *mf* (**-gi -ghe**) zoologist

zootecnìa [dz] *f* animal husbandry

zootècni·co -ca [dz] (**-ci -che**) *adj* livestock ‖ *m* livestock specialist

zoppicante *adj* limping; halting; shaky

zoppicare §197 (**zòppico**) *intr* to limp; to be shaky (*in one's studies*); to wobble

zoppicatura *f* limp; wobble

zòp·po -pa *adj* crippled; lame; wobbly ‖ *mf* cripple; lame person

zòti·co -ca [dz] (**-ci -che**) *adj* uncouth, boorish ‖ *m* churl, boor

zuc·ca *f* (**-che**) pumpkin; (joc) pate; (coll) empty head

zuccherare (**zùcchero**) *tr* to sweeten, sugar

zuccherièra *f* sugar bowl

zuccherifì·cio *m* (**-ci**) sugar refinery

zuccheri·no -na *adj* sugary ‖ *m* candy; sugar plum; sugar-coated pill

zùcchero *m* sugar; **zucchero filato** cotton candy; **zucchero in polvere** powdered sugar

zuccheró·so -sa [s] *adj* sugary

zucchétto *m* scull cap; zucchetto

zucchi·no -na *m & f* zucchini

zuccó·ne -na *mf* dunce, dumbbell

zuffa *f* brawl, fight

zufolare (**zùfolo**) *tr & intr* to whistle

zùfolo *m* (mus) whistle, pipe

zu·lù (-lù) [dz] *adj & mf* Zulu

zumare [dz] *tr & intr* (mov, telv) to zoom

zumata [dz] *f* (mov, telv) zoom

zuppa *f* soup; (fig) mess; **zuppa inglese** cake with brandy and whipped cream; **zuppa pavese** consommé with toast and eggs

zuppièra *f* tureen

zup·po -pa *adj* drenched, soaked ‖ *f* see **zuppa**

Zurigo *f* Zurich

zuzzurulló·ne -na [dz] [ddzz] *mf* overgrown child, just a big kid

PART TWO

Inglese-Italiano

La pronunzia dell'inglese

I simboli seguenti rappresentano approssimativamente tutti i suoni della lingua inglese.

VOCALI

SIMBOLO	SUONO	ESEMPIO
[æ]	Più chiuso della a in caso.	hat [hæt]
[ɑ]	Come la a in basso.	father ['fɑðər] proper ['prɑpər]
[ɛ]	Come la e in sella.	met [mɛt]
[e]	Più chiuso della e in ché. Specialmente in posizione finale, si pronunzia come se fosse seguita da [ɪ].	fate [fet] they [ðe]
[ə]	Come la seconda e nella parola francese gouvernement.	heaven ['hɛvən] pardon ['pɑrdən]
[i]	Come la i in nido.	she [ʃi] machine [məˈʃin]
[ɪ]	Come la i in ritto.	fit [fɪt] beer [bɪr]
[o]	Più chiuso della o in sole. Specialmente in posizione finale, si pronunzia come se fosse seguito da [ʊ].	nose [noz] road [rod] row [ro]
[ɔ]	Meno chiuso della o in torre.	bought [bɔt] law [lɔ]
[ʌ]	Piuttosto simile alla eu nella parola francese peur	cup [kʌp] come [kʌm] mother ['mʌðər]
[ʊ]	Meno chiuso della u in insulto.	pull [pʊl] book [bʊk] wolf [wʊlf]
[u]	Come la u in acuto.	rude [rud] move [muv] tomb [tum]

DITTONGHI

SIMBOLO	SUONO	ESEMPIO
[aɪ]	Come ai in laico.	night [naɪt] eye [aɪ]
[aʊ]	Come au in causa.	found [faʊnd] cow [kaʊ]
[ɔɪ]	Come oi in poi.	voice [vɔis] oil [ɔɪl]

3

CONSONANTI

SIMBOLO	SUONO	ESEMPIO
[b]	Come la **b** in **bambino**. Suono bilabiale occlusivo sonoro.	**bed** [bɛd] **robber** [ˈrabər]
[d]	Come la **d** in **caldo**. Suono dentale occlusivo sonoro.	**dead** [dɛd] **add** [æd]
[dʒ]	Come la **g** in **gente**. Suono palatale affricato sonoro.	**gem** [dʒɛm] **jail** [dʒel]
[ð]	Come la **d** nella pronuncia castigliana di **nada**. Suono interdentale fricativo sonoro.	**this** [ðɪs] **father** [ˈfɑðər]
[f]	Come la **f** in **fare**. Suono labiodentale fricativo sordo.	**face** [fes] **phone** [fon]
[g]	Come la **g** in **gatto**. Suono velare occlusivo sonoro.	**go** [go] **get** [gɛt]
[h]	Come la **c** aspirata nella pronuncia toscana di **casa**.	**hot** [hɔt] **alcohol** [ˈælkə ˌhɔl]
[j]	Come la **i** in **ieri** o la **y** in **yo-yo**. Semiconsonante di suono palatale sonoro.	**yes** [jɛs] **unit** [ˈjunɪt]
[k]	Come la **c** in **casa** ma accompagnato da un'aspirazione. Suono velare occlusivo sordo.	**cat** [kæt] **chord** [kɔrd] **kill** [kɪl]
[l]	Come la **l** in **latino**. Suono alveolare fricativo laterale sonoro.	**late** [let] **allow** [əˈlaʊ]
[m]	Come la **m** in **madre**. Suono bilabiale nasale sonoro.	**more** [mor] **command** [kəˈmænd]
[n]	Come la **n** in **notte**. Suono alveolare nasale sonoro.	**nest** [nɛst] **manner** [ˈmænər]
[ŋ]	Come la **n** in **manca**. Suono velare nasale sonoro.	**king** [kɪŋ] **conquer** [ˈkɑŋkər]
[p]	Come la **p** in **patto** ma accompagnato da un'aspirazione. Suono bilabiale occlusivo sordo.	**pen** [pɛn] **cap** [kæp]
[r]	La **r** più comune in molte parti dell'Inghilterra e nella maggior parte degli Stati Uniti e del Canadà è un suono semivocalico articolato con la punta della lingua elevata verso la volta del palato. Questa consonante è debolissima in posizione intervocalica o alla fine di una sillaba, e può appena percepirsi. L'articolazione di questa consonante ha la tendenza di influenzare il suono delle vocali contigue. La **r**, preceduta dai suoni [ʌ] o [ə], dà il proprio colorito a questi suoni e sparisce completamente come suono consonantico.	**run** [rʌn] **far** [fɑr] **art** [ɑrt] **carry** [ˈkæri] **burn** [bʌrn] **learn** [lʌrn] **weather** [ˈwɛðər]
[s]	Come la **s** in **sette**. Suono alveolare fricativo sordo.	**send** [sɛnd] **cellar** [ˈsɛlər]
[ʃ]	Come **sc** in **lasciare**. Suono palatale fricativo sordo.	**shall** [ʃæl] **machine** [məˈʃin]
[t]	Come la **t** in **tavolo** ma accompagnato da un'aspirazione. Suono dentale occlusivo sordo.	**ten** [ten] **dropped** [drɑpt]
[tʃ]	Come **c** in **cibo**. Suono palatale affricato sordo.	**child** [tʃaɪld] **much** [mʌtʃ] **nature** [ˈnetʃər]
[θ]	Come la **z** castigliana in **zapato**. Suono interdentale fricativo sordo.	**think** [θɪŋk] **truth** [truθ]
[v]	Come la **v** in **vento**. Suono labiodentale fricativo sonoro.	**vest** [vɛst] **over** [ˈovər] **of** [ɑv]

4

SIMBOLO	SUONO	ESEMPIO
[w]	Come la **u** in **quadro**. Suono labiovelare fricativo sonoro.	**work** [wʌrk] **tweed** [twid] **queen** [kwin]
[z]	Come la **s** in **asilo**. Suono alveolare fricativo sonoro.	**zeal** [zil] **busy** ['bɪzi] **his** [hɪz]
[ʒ]	Come la seconda **g** nella parola francese **garage**. Suono palatale fricativo sonoro.	**azure** ['eʒər] **measure** ['mɛʒər]

ACCENTO

L'accento tonico principale, indicato col segno grafico **'**, e l'accento secondario, indicato col segno grafico **„** precedono la sillaba sulla quale cadono, per es., **fascinate** ['fæsɪ ˌnet].

La pronunzia delle parole composte

Nella parte inglese-italiano di questo Dizionario la pronunzia figurata di tutte le parole inglesi semplici è indicata in parentesi quadre che seguono immediatamente l'esponente, secondo un nuovo adattamento dell'alfabeto fonetico internazionale.

Vi sono tre generi di parole composte in inglese: (1) le parole in cui gli elementi componenti si sono uniti per formare una parola solida, come per es., **steamboat** vapore; (2) la parole in cui gli elementi componenti sono uniti da un trattino, come per es., **high'-grade'** di qualità superiore; (3) le parole in cui gli elementi componenti rimangono graficamente indipendenti gli uni da gli altri, per es., **post card** cartolina postale. La pronunzia delle parole inglesi composte non è indicata in questo Dizionario qualora gli elementi componenti appaiano come esponenti indipendenti nella loro normale posizione alfabetica e mostrano quindi la loro pronunzia figurata. Solo gli accenti principali e secondari di tali parole sono indicati, come per es., **steam'boat'**, **high'-grade'**, **post' card'**. Se i due membri di una parola composta inglese solida non sono separati da un accento grafico, si usa un punto leggermente elevato sopra il rigo per indicarne la divisione, come per es., **la'dy·like'**.

Nei nomi in cui l'accento secondario cade sul membro -man o -men, le vocali di tali membri si pronunziano come nelle parole semplici **man** e **men**, come per es., **mailman** ['mel ˌmæn] e **mailmen** ['mel ˌmɛn]. Nei nomi in cui tali membri componenti non sono accentati, le loro vocali si pronunziano come se fossero un'e muta francese, come per es., **policeman** [pə'lismən] e **policemen** [pə'lismən]. In questo Dizionario la trascrizione fonetica di tali nomi non è stata indicata qualora il primo membro componente appaia come esponente con la sua pronunzia in alfabeto fonetico internazionale. Gli accenti sono ciò nondimeno indicati:

mail'man' *s* (-men')

police'man *s* (-men)

La pronunzia dei participi passati

La pronunzia di una parola la cui desinenza è **-ed** (o **-d** dopo una e muta) non è indicata nel presente Dizionario, purché la pronunzia della parola stessa senza tale suffisso appaia con il suo esponente nella sua posizione alfabetica. In tale caso la pronunzia segue le regole indicate qui sotto. Si osservi che il raddoppiamento della vocale finale dopo una semplice vocale tonica non muta la pronunzia del suffisso **-ed**, per es.: **batted** ['bætɪd], **dropped** [drɑpt], **robbed** [rɑbd].

La desinenza **-ed** (o **-d** dopo una e muta) del preterito, del participio passato e di certi aggettivi ha tre pronunzie differenti, che dipendono dal suono in cui il tema termina:

1) Se il tema termina in suono consonantico sonoro (che non sia [d]), cioè [b], [g], [l], [m], [n], [ŋ], [r], [v], [z], [ð], [ʒ] o [dʒ] o in un suono vocalico, l'**-ed** è pronunziato [d]:

SUONO IN CUI TERMINA IL TEMA	INFINITO	PRETERITO E PARTICIPIO PASSATO
[b]	**ebb** [ɛb] **rob** [rɑb] **robe** [rob]	**ebbed** [ɛbd] **robbed** [rɑbd] **robed** [robd]

5

SUONO IN CUI TERMINA IL TEMA	INFINITO	PRETERITO E PARTICIPIO PASSATO
[g]	egg [ɛg] sag [sæg]	egged [ɛgd] sagged [sægd]
[l]	mail [mel] scale [skel]	mailed [meld] scaled [skeld]
[m]	storm [stɔrm] bomb [bɑm] name [nem]	stormed [stɔrmd] bombed [bɑmd] named [nemd]
[n]	tan [tæn] sign [saɪn] mine [maɪn]	tanned [tænd] signed [saɪnd] mined [maɪnd]
[ŋ]	hang [hæŋ]	hanged [hæŋd]
[r]	fear [fɪr] care [kɛr]	feared [fɪrd] cared [kɛrd]
[v]	rev [rev] save [sev]	revved [revd] saved [sevd]
[z]	buzz [bʌz] fuze [fjuz]	buzzed [bʌzd] fuzed [fjuzd]
[ð]	smooth [smuð] bathe [beð]	smoothed [smuðd] bathed [beðd]
[ʒ]	massage [mə'sɑʒ]	massaged [mə'sɑʒd]
[dʒ]	page [pedʒ]	paged [pedʒd]
suono vocalico	key [ki] sigh [saɪ] paw [pɔ]	keyed [kid] sighed [saɪd] pawed [pɔd]

2) Se il tema termina in un suono consonantico sordo (che non sia [t]), cioè [f], [k], [p], [s], [θ], [ʃ] o [tʃ], l'-ed si pronunzia [t]:

SUONO IN CUI TERMINA IL TEMA	INFINITO	PRETERITO E PARTICIPIO PASSATO
[f]	loaf [lof] knife [naɪf]	loafed [loft] knifed [naɪft]
[k]	back [bæk] bake [bek]	backed [bækt] baked [bekt]
[p]	cap [kæp] wipe [waɪp]	capped [kæpt] wiped [waɪpt]
[s]	hiss [hɪs] mix [mɪks]	hissed [hɪst] mixed [mɪkst]
[θ]	lath [læθ]	lathed [læθt]
[ʃ]	mash [mæʃ]	mashed [mæʃt]
[tʃ]	match [mætʃ]	matched [mætʃt]

3) Se il tema termina in un suono dentale, cioè [t] o [d], l'-ed si pronunzia [ɪd] o [əd]:

SUONO IN CUI TERMINA IL TEMA	INFINITO	PRETERITO E PARTICIPIO PASSATO
[t]	wait [wet] mate [met]	waited ['wetɪd] mated ['metɪd]
[d]	mend [mɛnd] wade [wed]	mended ['mɛndɪd] waded ['wedɪd]

L'-ed di alcuni aggettivi aggiunto ad un tema che termina in suono consonantico (oltre a quelli che terminano in [d] o [t]), è ciò nonostante talvolta pronunziato [ɪd] e tale fenomeno è idicato con la piena pronunzia della parola in simboli dell'alfabeto fonetico internazionale, per es., blessed ['blɛsɪd], crabbed ['kræbɪd].

A, a [e] *s* prima lettera dell'alfabeto inglese

a [e] *art indef* un, uno, una, un'

aback [ə'bæk] *adv* all'indietro; **taken aback** colto alla sprovvista, sconcertato

aba·cus ['æbəkəs] *s* (**-cuses** or **-ci** [,saɪ]) pallottoliere *m;* (archit) abaco

abaft [ə'bæft] or [ə'baft] *adv* a poppa || *prep* dietro a

abandon [ə'bændən] *s* disinvoltura || *tr* abbandonare

abase [ə'bes] *tr* umiliare, degradare

abash [ə'bæʃ] *tr* imbarazzare; sconcertare

abate [ə'bet] *tr* ridurre; omettere; (law) terminare || *intr* diminuire, calmarsi

aba·tis ['æbətɪs] or [ə'bætɪs] *s* (**-tis** or **-tises**) (mil) tagliata

abattoir ['æbə ,twar] *s* macello

abba·cy ['æbəsi] *s* (**-cies**) abbazia

abbess ['æbɪs] *s* badessa

abbey ['æbi] *s* badia, abbazia

abbot ['æbət] *s* abate *m*

abbreviate [ə'brivɪ ,et] *tr* abbreviare, raccorciare

abbreviation [ə ,brivɪ'eʃən] *s* (*abbreviated form*) abbreviazione; (*shortening*) abbreviamento

A B C [,e ,bi'si] *s* (letterword) abbicci *m;* **A B C's** abbecedario

abdicate ['æbdɪ ,ket] *tr* abdicare a || *intr* abdicare

abdomen ['æbdəmən] or [æb'domən] *s* addome *m*

abduct [æb'dʌkt] *tr* rapire

abed [ə'bɛd] *adv* a letto

abet [ə'bɛt] *v* (*pret & pp* **abetted;** *ger* **abetting**) *tr* favoreggiare

abeyance [ə'be·əns] *s* sospensione; **in abeyance** in sospeso

ab·hor [æb'hɔr] *v* (*pret & pp* **-horred;** *ger* **-horring**) *tr* aborrire

abhorrent [æb'harənt] or [æb'hɔrənt] *adj* detestabile

abide [ə'baɪd] *v* (*pret & pp* **abode** or **abided**) *tr* aspettare; tollerare || *intr* —**to abide by** attenersi a; rimanere fedele a

abili·ty [ə'bɪlɪti] *s* (**-ties**) abilità *f,* bravura

abject ['æbdʒɛkt] or [æb'dʒɛkt] *adj* abietto, turpe

abjure [æb'dʒʊr] *tr* abiurare

ablative ['æblətɪv] *adj & s* ablativo

ablaut ['æblaʊt] *s* apofonia

ablaze [ə'blez] *adj* in fiamme; risplendente

able ['ebəl] *adj* abile, esperto; **to be able to** + *inf* potere + *inf*

able-bodied ['ebəl'badɪd] *adj* sano; forte

abloom [ə'blum] *adj & adv* in fiore

abnormal [æb'nɔrməl] *adj* anormale

aboard [ə'bord] *adv* a bordo; **all aboard!** (rr) signori, in vettura!; **to go aboard** imbarcarsi; **to take aboard** imbarcare || *prep* a bordo di; (*a bus, train, etc.*) in, su

abode [ə'bod] *s* abitazione, dimora

abolish [ə'balɪʃ] *tr* abolire

A-bomb ['e ,bam] *s* bomba atomica

abominable [ə'bamənəbəl] *adj* abominevole

abomination [ə ,bamɪ'neʃən] *s* abominazione

aborigenes [,æbə'rɪdʒɪ ,niz] *spl* aborigeni *mpl*

abort [ə'bɔrt] *tr* terminare prematuramente; provocare un aborto in || *intr* abortire

abortion [ə'bɔrʃən] *s* aborto

abound [ə'baʊnd] *intr* abbondare; **to abound in** or **with** abbondare di

about [ə'baʊt] *adv* circa, press'a poco; qua intorno; qua e là; in direzione opposta; (coll) quasi; **to be about to** star sul punto di || *prep* intorno a; circa a; addosso a; tutt'intorno a; riguardo a

about'-face' *interj* (mil) dietro front!

about'-face' or **about'-face'** *s* voltafaccia; (mil) dietro front *m* || **about'-face'** *intr* fare dietro front

above [ə'bʌv] *adj* soprammenzionato; superiore || *s*—**from above** dal cielo; dall'alto || *adv* in alto; su; più sopra || *prep* sopra, sopra a; più di; al di là di, oltre; **above all** soprattutto

above-mentioned [ə'bʌv'mɛnʃənd] *adj* summenzionato, sunnominato

abrasive [ə'bresɪv] or [ə'brezɪv] *adj & s* abrasivo

abreast [ə'brɛst] *adj & adv* in fila, in linea; **to keep abreast of** tenersi alla pari con; essere al corrente di

abridge [ə'brɪdʒ] *tr* compendiare; ridurre

abroad [ə'brɔd] *adv* all'estero; all'aria aperta; **to be abroad** (*said of news*) circolare

abrupt [ə'brʌpt] *adj* brusco, improvviso; (*very steep*) scosceso

abscess ['æbsɛs] *s* ascesso

abscond [æb'skand] *intr* scappare; **to abscond with** svignarsela con

absence ['æbsəns] *s* assenza; **in the absence of** in mancanza di

absent ['æbsənt] *adj* assente || [æb- ,sɛnt] *tr*—**to absent oneself** assentarsi

absentee [,æbsən'ti] *s* assente *mf*

absent-minded ['æbsənt'maɪndɪd] *adj* distratto, assente

absinth ['æbsɪnθ] *s* assenzio

absolute ['æbsə ,lut] *adj & s* assoluto

absolutely ['æbsə ,lutli] *adv* assolutamente, certamente || [,æbsə'lutli] *interj* certamente!

absolve [æb'salv] *tr* assolvere

absorb [æb'sɔrb] *tr* assorbire; **to be or become absorbed** essere assorto

absorbent [æb'sɔrbənt] *adj* assorbente; (*cotton*) idrofilo || *s* sostanza assorbente

absorbing [æb'sɔrbɪŋ] *adj* interessantissimo

abstain [æb'sten] *intr* astenersi

abstemious [æb'stimɪ·əs] *adj* astemio

abstention [æb'stenʃən] *s* astensione; astenuto (*vote withheld*)

abstinent [ˈæbstɪnənt] *adj* astinente

abstract [ˈæbstrækt] *adj* astratto ‖ *s* compendio, sommario ‖ *tr* compendiare ‖ (æbˈstrækt) *tr* astrarre; (*to steal*) sottrarre

abstruse [æbˈstrus] *adj* astruso

absurd [æbˈsʌrd] or [æbˈzʌrd] *adj* assurdo

absurdi·ty [æbˈsʌrdɪti] or [æbˈzʌrdɪti] *s* (-ties) assurdità *f*

abundant [əˈbʌndənt] *adj* abbondante

abuse [əˈbjus] *s* (*misuse*) abuso; maltrattamento; insulto ‖ [əˈbjuz] *tr* (*to misuse, take unfair advantage of*) abusare di; maltrattare; insultare

abusive [əˈbjusɪv] *adj* abusivo; insultante

abut [əˈbʌt] *v* (*pret & pp* **abutted;** *ger* **abutting**) *intr*—to abut on confinare con

abutment [əˈbʌtmənt] *s* rinfianco; (*at either end of bridge*) spalla; (*of buttresses of bridge*) sprone *m*

abysmal (əˈbɪzməl) *adj* abissale; (*e.g., ignorance*) spropositato

abyss [əˈbɪs] *s* abisso

academic [ˌækəˈdɛmɪk] *adj* accademico

ac'ademic cos'tume *s* toga accademica

academician [ə,kædəˈmɪʃən] *s* accademico

ac'adem'ic year' *s* anno scolastico

acade·my [əˈkædəmi] *s* (-mies) accademia

accede [ækˈsid] *intr* accedere; **to accede to** salire a; accedere a

accelerate [ækˈsɛlə‚ret] *tr & intr* accelerare

accelerator [ækˈsɛlə‚retər] *s* acceleratore *m*

accent [ˈæksɛnt] *s* accento ‖ [ˈæksɛnt] or [ækˈsɛnt] *tr* accentare; (*to accentuate*) accentuare

ac'cent mark' *s* segnaccento, accento grafico

accentuate [ækˈsɛntʃu‚et] *tr* accentuare

accept [ækˈsɛpt] *tr* accettare

acceptable [ækˈsɛptəbəl] *adj* accettabile

acceptance [ækˈsɛptəns] *s* accettazione

access [ˈæksɛs] *s* accesso

accessible [ækˈsɛsɪbəl] *adj* accessibile; (*person*) abbordabile

accession [ækˈsɛʃən] *s* accessione, acquisto; (*e.g., to the throne*) adito

accesso·ry [ækˈsɛsəri] *adj* accessorio ‖ *s* (-ries) accessorio; (*to a crime*) complice *m*

accident [ˈæksɪdənt] *s* accidente *m;* **by accident** accidentalmente, per caso

accidental [ˌæksɪˈdɛntəl] *adj* accidentale ‖ *s* (mus) accidente *m*

acclaim [əˈklem] *s* acclamazione, applauso ‖ *tr & intr* acclamare, applaudire

acclimate [ˈæklɪ‚met] *tr* acclimatare ‖ *intr* acclimatarsi

accolade [ˌækəˈled] *s* accollata; (fig) elogio

accommodate [əˈkamə‚det] *tr* (*to adjust, make fit*) accomodare; (*to pro-*

vide with a loan) venire incontro a; (*to supply with lodging*) alloggiare; (*to oblige*) favorire; (*to have room for*) aver posto per

accommodating [əˈkamə‚detɪŋ] *adj* servizievole, compiacente

accommodation [ə‚kaməˈdeʃən] *s* (*favor*) favore *m;* (*loan*) prestito; (*adaptation*) adattamento; (*reconciliation*) conciliazione; (*compromise*) accomodamento; **accommodations** (*traveling space*) posto; (*in a hotel*) alloggio

accommoda'tion train' *s* treno accelerato

accompaniment [əˈkʌmpənɪmənt] *s* accompagnamento

accompanist [əˈkʌmpənɪst] *s* accompagnatore *m*

accompa·ny [əˈkʌmpəni] *v* (*pret & pp* **-nied**) *tr* accompagnare

accomplice [əˈkamplɪs] *s* complice *mf*

accomplish [əˈkamplɪʃ] *tr* compiere

accomplished [əˈkamplɪʃt] *adj* (*completed*) compiuto, terminato; (*skilled*) finito, compiuto

accomplishment [əˈkamplɪʃmənt] *s* (*completion*) esecuzione, realizzazione; (*something accomplished*) opera; (*acquired ability*) talento; (*military achievement*) prodezza; (*social skill*) compitezza

accord [əˈkɔrd] *s* accordo; **in accord with** in conformità con; **of one's own accord** spontaneamente; **with one accord** di comune accordo ‖ *tr* concedere ‖ *intr* accordarsi

accordance [əˈkɔrdəns] *s* accordo; **in accordance with** in conformità con

according [əˈkɔrdɪŋ] *adv*—**according as** a seconda che; **according to** secondo, a seconda di

accordingly [əˈkɔrdɪŋli] *adv* per conseguenza, perciò; in conformità

accordion [əˈkɔrdɪ‚ən] *s* fisarmonica

accost [əˈkɔst] or [əˈkast] *tr* accostare, abbordare

accouchement [əˈkuʃmənt] *s* parto

account [əˈkaunt] *s* (*explanation*) versione; (*report*) resoconto; conto; (*statement*) estratto conto; **by all accounts** secondo la voce comune; **of account** d'importanza; **of no account** senza importanza; **on account** in acconto; **on account of** a causa di; per l'amor di; **on all accounts** in ogni modo; **on no account** in nessuna maniera; **to call to account** chiedere conto di; **to give a good account of oneself** comportarsi bene; **to take account of** prendere in considerazione; **to turn to account** trarre profitto da ‖ *intr*—**to account for** render conto di; essere responsabile per

accountable [əˈkauntəbəl] *adj* responsabile; (*explainable*) spiegabile

accountant [əˈkauntənt] *s* contabile *mf*, ragioniere *m*

accounting [əˈkauntɪŋ] *s* contabilità *f*, ragioneria

accouterments [əˈkutərmənts] *spl* (mil)

buffetterie *fpl;* (*trappings*) ornamenti *mpl*

accredit [ə'kredɪt] *tr* accreditare; **to accredit s.o. with s.th** ascrivere qlco a credito di qlcu

accrue [ə'kru] *intr* accumularsi; (*said of interest*) maturare

acculturation [ə,kʌltʃə'reʃən] *s* acculturazione

accumulate [ə'kjumjə,let] *tr* accumulare || *intr* accumularsi

accuracy ['ækjərəsi] *s* esattezza, precisione; fedeltà *f*

accurate ['ækjərɪt] *adj* esatto, preciso; fedele

accursed [ə'kʌrsɪd] or [ə'kʌrst] *adj* maledetto

accusation [,ækjə'zeʃən] *s* accusa

accusative [ə'kjuzətɪv] *adj* & *s* accusativo

accuse [ə'kjuz] *tr* accusare

accustom [ə'kʌstəm] *tr* abituare

ace [es] *s* asso; **to be within an ace of** essere quasi sul punto di

ace' in the hole' *s* asso nella manica

acetate ['æsɪ,tet] *s* acetato

ace'tic ac'id [ə'sitɪk] *s* acido acetico

aceti•fy [ə'setɪ,faɪ] *v* (*pret* & *pp* -**fied**) *tr* acetificare || *intr* acetificarsi

acetone ['æsɪ,ton] *s* acetone *m*

acetylene [ə'setɪ,lin] *s* acetilene *m*

acet'ylene torch' *s* cannello ossiacetilenico

ache [ek] *s* dolore *m* || *intr* dolere, e.g., **my tooth aches** mi duole il dente

Acheron ['ækə,rɑn] *s* Acheronte *m*

achieve [ə'tʃiv] *tr* compiere, conseguire

achievement [ə'tʃivmənt] *s* compimento; successo; (*exploit*) impresa, prodezza

Achil'les heel' [ə'krliz] *s* tallone *m* d'Achille

acid ['æsɪd] *adj* & *s* acido

acidi•fy [ə'sɪdɪ,faɪ] *v* (*pret* & *pp* -**fied**) *tr* & *intr* acidificare

acidity [ə'sɪdɪti] *s* acidità *f*

acid' test' *s* prova del fuoco

ack-ack ['æk'æk] *s* (slang) cannone antiaereo

acknowledge [æk'nɑlɪdʒ] *tr* riconoscere; (*receipt of a letter*) accusare; (*a claim*) ammettere; mostrare la gratitudine per; (law) certificare

acknowledgment [æk'nɑlɪdʒmənt] *s* riconoscimento; (*of receipt of a letter*) accusa, cenno

acme ['ækmi] *s* acme *f*

acolyte ['ækə,laɪt] *s* accolito

acorn ['ekɔrn] or ['ekərn] *s* ghianda

acoustic [ə'kustɪk] *adj* acustico || **acoustics** *s* acustica

acquaint [ə'kwent] *tr* mettere al corrente; **to be acquainted with** conoscere; essere al corrente di; **to become acquainted** (*with each other*) conoscersi

acquaintance [ə'kwentəns] *s* conoscenza; (*person*) conoscente *mf*, conoscenza

acquiesce [,ækwɪ'es] *intr* acconsentire, accondiscendere

acquiescence [,ækwɪ'esəns] *s* accondiscendenza

acquire [ə'kwaɪr] *tr* acquistare

acquisition [,ækwɪ'zɪʃən] *s* acquisto

acquit [ə'kwɪt] *v* (*pret* & *pp* **acquitted;** *ger* **acquitting**) *tr* (*to pay*) ripagare; (*to declare not guilty*) assolvere; **to acquit oneself** condursi

acquittal [ə'kwɪtəl] *s* assoluzione

acre ['ekər] *s* acro

acrid ['ækrɪd] *adj* acrido, pungente

acrobat ['ækrə,bæt] *s* acrobata *mf*

acrobatic [,ækrə'bætɪk] *adj* acrobatico || **acrobatics** *ssg* (e.g., *of a stunt pilot*) acrobazie *fpl;* **acrobatics** *spl* (*gymnastics*) acrobatica

acronym ['ækrənɪm] *s* acronimo, parola macedonia

acropolis [ə'krɑpəlɪs] *s* acropoli *f*

across [ə'krɔs] or [ə'krɑs] *adv* dall'altra parte; **to get an idea across to** farsi capire da || *prep* attraverso; (*on the other side of*) al di là di, dall'altra parte di; **to come across** (*a person*) imbattersi in; **to go across** attraversare

across'-the-board' *adj* generale

act [ækt] *s* atto; legge *f;* rappresentazione; **in the act** in flagrante || *tr* (*a drama*) rappresentare; (*a role*) recitare || *intr* (*on the stage*) recitare; (*to behave*) comportarsi; (*to perform special duties; to reach a decision*) agire; (*to have an effect*) reagire; **to act as** fungere da; **to act for** rimpiazzare; **to act on** eseguire; **to act up** (coll) fare il matto; non funzionare bene (*said, e.g., of a motor*); **to act up to** (coll) fare festa a

acting ['æktɪŋ] *adj* facente funzione, interino || *s* recita

action ['ækʃən] *s* azione; (*moving parts*) meccanismo; **to take action** iniziare azione; (law) intentare causa

activate ['æktɪ,vet] *tr* attivare

active ['æktɪv] *adj* & *s* attivo

activi•ty [æk'tɪvɪti] *s* (-**ties**) attività *f*

act' of God' *s* forza maggiore

actor ['æktər] *s* attore *m*

actress ['æktrɪs] *s* attrice *f*

actual ['æktʃu·əl] *adj* reale

actually ['æktʃu·əli] *adv* realmente, in realtà

actuar•y ['æktʃu,eri] *s* (-**ies**) attuario

actuate ['æktʃu,et] *tr* attuare, mettere in azione; (*to motivate*) stimulare

acuity [ə'kju·ɪti] *s* acuità *f*

acumen [ə'kjumən] *s* acume *m*

acupuncture ['ækju,pʌŋktʃər] *s* agopuntura

acute [ə'kjut] *adj* acuto

ad [æd] *s* (coll) inserzione pubblicitaria

Adam ['ædəm] *s* Adamo; **not to know from Adam** non conoscere affatto

adamant ['ædəmənt] *adj* saldo, inflessibile

Ad'am's ap'ple *s* pomo d'Adamo

adapt [ə'dæpt] *tr* adattare

adaptation [,ædæp'teʃən] *s* adattamento; (*e.g., of a play*) rifacimento

add [æd] *tr* aggiungere; (*numbers*)

sommare || *intr* aggiungere; far di conto; **to add up to** ammontare a; (coll) voler dire

adder ['ædər] *s* vipera

addict ['ædɪkt] *s* (*to drugs*) tossicomane *mf;* (*to a sport*) tifoso || [ə'dɪkt] *tr* abituare; rendere propenso alla tossicomania; **to addict oneself to** darsi a, abbandonarsi a

addiction [ə'dɪkʃən] *s* dedizione; (*to drugs*) tossicomania; (*to sports*) tifo

add'ing machine' *s* calcolatrice *f*

addition [ə'dɪʃən] *s* addizione; (*building*) annessi *mpl;* **in addition** inoltre, per di più; **in addition to** oltre a

additive ['ædɪtɪv] *adj & s* additivo

address [ə'drɛs] or ['ædrɛs] *s* (*speech*) discorso; (*place and destination of mail*) indirizzo; (*skill*) destrezza; (*formal request*) petizione; **to deliver an address** pronunciare un discorso || [ə'drɛs] *tr* indirizzare; (*to speak to*) rivolgere la parola a

addressee [,ædrɛ'si] *s* destinatario

address'ing machine' *s* macchina per indirizzi

adduce [ə'djus] or [ə'dus] *tr* addurre

adenoids ['ædə,nɔɪds] *spl* vegetazioni *fpl* adenoidi, adenoidi *fpl*

adept [ə'dɛpt] *adj & s* esperto

adequate ['ædɪkwɪt] *adj* sufficiente; (*suitable*) conveniente

adhere [æd'hɪr] *intr* aderire

adherence [æd'hɪrəns] *s* aderenza

adherent [æd'hɪrənt] *adj & s* aderente *m*

adhesion [æd'hiʒən] *s* adesione; (pathol) aderenza

adhesive [æd'hisɪv] or [æd'hizɪv] *adj & s* adesivo

adhe'sive tape' *s* tela adesiva, cerotto

adieu [ə'dju] or [ə'du] *s* (**adieus** or **adieux**) addio || *interj* addio!

adjacent [ə'dʒesənt] *adj* adiacente

adjective ['ædʒɪktɪv] *adj* aggettivale; accessorio, secondario || *s* aggettivo

adjoin [ə'dʒɔɪn] *tr* confinare con || *intr* essere confinanti

adjoining [ə'dʒɔɪnɪŋ] *adj* confinante; vicino, attiguo

adjourn [ə'dʒʌrn] *tr* aggiornare, rinviare || *intr* rinviarsi

adjournment [ə'dʒʌrnmənt] *s* aggiornamento, rinvio

adjust [ə'dʒʌst] *tr* accomodare; regolare; (ins) liquidare || *intr* abituarsi

adjustable [ə'dʒʌstəbəl] *adj* regolabile

adjustment [ə'dʒʌstmənt] *s* aggiustamento; accomodamento; (ins) liquidazione del danno

adjutant ['ædʒətənt] *s* aiutante *mf*

ad·lib [,æd'lɪb] *v* (*pret & pp* -**libbed;** *ger* -**libbing**) *tr & intr* improvvisare

administer [æd'mɪnɪstər] *tr* amministrare; (*medicine*) somministrare; (*an oath*) dare || *intr*—**to administer to** ministrare, prestare aiuto a

administrator [æd'mɪnɪs,tretər] *s* amministratore *m*

admirable ['ædmɪrəbəl] *adj* ammirabile, ammirevole

admiral ['ædmɪrəl] *s* ammiraglio

admiral·ty ['ædmɪrəlti] *s* (-**ties**) ammiragliato

admire [æd'maɪr] *tr* ammirare

admirer [æd'maɪrər] *s* ammiratore *m*

admissible [æd'mɪsɪbəl] *adj* ammissibile

admission [æd'mɪʃən] *s* ammissione; confessione; (*entrance fee*) prezzo d'ingresso; **to gain admission** arrivare a entrare

ad·mit [æd'mɪt] *v* (*pret & pp* -**mitted;** *ger* -**mitting**) *tr* ammettere; confessare || *intr* dare l'ingresso; **to admit of** permettere, ammettere; consentire

admittance [æd'mɪtəns] *s* ammissione; permesso di entrare; **no admittance** divieto d'ingresso

admonish [æd'manɪʃ] *tr* ammonire

ado [ə'du] *s* confusione, trambusto; **much ado about nothing** molto rumore per nulla; **to make a big ado** fare cerimonie

adobe [ə'dobi] *s* mattone crudo

adolescence [,ædə'lɛsəns] *s* adolescenza

adolescent [,ædə'lɛsənt] *adj & s* adolescente *mf*

adopt [ə'dapt] *tr* adottare

adoption [ə'dapʃən] *s* adozione

adorable [ə'dorəbəl] *adj* adorabile

adore [ə'dor] *tr* adorare

adorn [ə'dɔrn] *tr* adornare

adornment [ə'dɔrnmənt] *s* ornamento

adre'nal gland' [æd'rinəl] *s* glandola surrenale

Adriatic [,edrɪ'ætɪk] or [,ædrɪ'ætɪk] *adj* adriatico || *adj & s* Adriatico

adrift [ə'drɪft] *adj & adv* alla deriva

adroit [ə'drɔɪt] *adj* destro

adult [ə'dʌlt] or ['ædʌlt] *adj & s* adulto

adulterate [ə'dʌltə,ret] *tr* adulterare

adulterer [ə'dʌltərər] *s* adultero

adulteress [ə'dʌltərɪs] *s* adultera

adulter·y [ə'dʌltəri] *s* (-**ies**) adulterio

advance [æd'væns] or [æd'vans] *adj* avanzato || *s* avanzata; (*increase in price*) aumento; (*of money*) anticipo; **advances** approcci *mpl;* **in advance** in anticipo || *tr* avanzare; aumentare; (*to make earlier*) anticipare; (*money*) anticipare; (*a clock*) mettere avanti || *intr* avanzare; (*said, e.g., of prices*) aumentare

advanced [æd'vænst] or [æd'vanst] *adj* avanzato, progredito

advanced' stand'ing *s* trasferimento di voti scolastici

advancement [æd'vænsmənt] or [æd'vansmənt] *s* progresso; promozione; (mil) avanzata

advance' public'ity *s* pubblicità *f* di lancio

advantage [æd'væntɪdʒ] or [æd'vantɪdʒ] *s* vantaggio; **to advantage** in maniera favorevole; **to take advantage of** approfittarsi di; abusare di || *tr* avantaggiare

advantageous [,ædvən'tedʒəs] *adj* vantaggioso

advent ['ædvɛnt] *s* avvento

adventure [æd'vɛntʃər] s avventura ‖ *tr* avventurare ‖ *intr* avventurarsi

adventurer [æd'vɛntʃərər] s avventuriero

adventuresome [æd'vəntʃərsəm] *adj* avventuroso

adventuress [æd'vɛntʃərɪs] s avventuriera

adventurous [æd'vɛntʃərəs] *adj* avventuroso

adverb ['ædvʌrb] s avverbio

adversar·y ['ædvər‚sɛri] s (**-ies**) avversario

adverse [æd'vʌrs] or ['ædvʌrs] *adj* avverso, contrario

adversi·ty [æd'vʌrsɪti] s (**-ties**) avversità *f*

advertise ['ædvər‚taɪz] or [‚ædvər-'taɪz] *tr* propagandare; reclamizzare ‖ *intr* fare la pubblicità; inserire un annunzio; inserzionare

advertisement [‚ædvər'taɪzmənt] or [æd'vʌrtɪsmənt] s annuncio pubblicitario, inserzione

advertiser ['ædvər‚taɪzer] or [‚ædvər-'taɪzər] s inserzionista *mf*

advertising ['ædvər‚taɪzɪŋ] s pubblicità *f*, pubblicismo

ad'vertising a'gent s pubblicista *mf*

ad'vertising campaign' s campagna pubblicitaria

ad'vertising man' s agente *m* di pubblicità, reclamista *m*

advice [æd'vaɪs] s consiglio; **a piece of advice** un consiglio

advisable [æd'vaɪzəbəl] *adj* consigliabile

advise [æd'vaɪz] *tr* consigliare; informare ‖ *intr*—**to advise with** chiedere il consiglio di; avere una conferenza con

advisement [æd'vaɪzmənt] s considerazione; **to take under advisement** prendere in considerazione

adviser [æd'vaɪzər] s consigliere *m*

advisory [æd'vaɪzəri] *adj* consultivo

advocate ['ædvə‚ket] s difensore *m;* (*lawyer*) avvocato ‖ *tr* sostenere, propugnare

adze [ædz] s ascia

Aege'an Sea' [ɪ'dʒi·ən] s mare Egeo

aegis ['idʒɪs] s egida

Aeneid [i'ni·ɪd] s Eneide *f*

aerate ['eret] or ['e·ə‚ret] *tr* aerare

aerial ['ɛrɪ·əl] or [e'ɪrɪ·əl] *adj* aereo ‖ ['ɛrɪ·əl] s (rad & telv) antenna

aer'ial pho'tograph s aerofotogramma *m*

aerodrome ['ɛrə‚drom] s aerodromo

aerodynamic [‚ɛrodaɪ'næmɪk] *adj* aerodinamico ‖ **aerodynamics** *ssg* aerodinamica

aeronaut ['ɛrə‚nɔt] s aeronauta *m*

aeronautic [‚ɛrə'nɔtɪk] *adj* aeronautico ‖ **aeronautics** *ssg* aeronautica

aerosol ['ɛrə‚sol] s aerosol *m*

aerospace ['ɛro‚spes] *adj* aerospaziale ‖ s aerospazio

Aesop ['isap] s Esopo

aesthete ['ɛsθit] s esteta *mf*

aesthetic [ɛs'θɛtɪk] *adj* estetico ‖ **aesthetics** *ssg* estetica

afar [ə'fɑr] *adv* lontano; **from afar** da lontano

affable ['æfəbəl] *adj* affabile

affair [ə'fɛr] s affare *m;* (*romance*) relazione amorosa

affect [ə'fɛkt] *tr* influenzare; (*to touch the heart of*) commuovere; (*to pretend to have*) affettare

affectation [‚æfɛk'teʃən] s affettazione

affected [ə'fɛktɪd] *adj* affettato

affection [ə'fɛkʃən] s affezione

affectionate [ə'fɛkʃənɪt] *adj* affettuoso, affezionato

affidavit [‚æfɪ'devɪt] s affidavit *m*, dichiarazione sotto giuramento

affiliate [ə'fɪlɪ‚et] *adj* & s affiliato ‖ *tr* affiliare ‖ *intr* affiliarsi

affini·ty [ə'fɪnɪti] s (**-ties**) affinità *f*

affirm [ə'fʌrm] *tr* affermare; confermare

affirmative [ə'fʌrmətɪv] *adj* affermativo ‖ s affermativa

affix ['æfɪks] s affisso ‖ [ə'fɪks] *tr* affiggere; (*a signature*) apporre; (*e.g., blame*) attribuire

afflict [ə'flɪkt] *tr* affliggere

affliction [ə'flɪkʃən] s afflizione

affluence ['æflʊ·əns] s opulenza, abbondanza

affluent ['æflʊ·ənt] *adj* opulento, abbondante; ricco ‖ s affluente *m*

afford [ə'ford] *tr* permettersi il lusso di; (*to furnish*) provvedere; (*to give*) dare

affray [ə'fre] s rissa

affront [ə'frʌnt] s affronto ‖ *tr* fare un affronto a

afghan ['æfgən] or ['æfgæn] s coperta di lana all'uncinetto ‖ **Afghan** *adj* & s afgano

afield [ə'fild] *adv* sul campo; **far afield** lontano

afire [ə'faɪr] *adj* ardente; in fuoco, in fiamme

aflame [ə'flem] *adj* in fiamme

afloat [ə'flot] *adj* & *adv* a galla; a bordo; (*drifting*) alla deriva; (*said of a rumor*) in circolazione

afoot [ə'fut] *adj* & *adv* a piedi; in movimento, in moto

aforementioned [ə'for‚mɛnʃənd] or **aforesaid** [ə'for‚sed] *adj* suddetto

afoul [ə'faul] *adj* & *adv* in collisione; **to run afoul of** finire nelle mani di, impigliarsi con

afraid [ə'fred] *adj* impaurito, spaventato; **to be afraid (of)** aver paura (di)

African ['æfrɪkən] *adj* & s africano

aft [æft] or [ɑft] *adv* a poppa; indietro

after ['æftər] or ['ɑftər] *adj* seguente; di poppa ‖ *adv* dopo; (*behind*) dietro ‖ *prep* dopo; dopo di; (*in the manner of*) secondo; **to run after** correre dietro a ‖ *conj* dopo che

afterburner ['æftər‚bʌrnər] or ['ɑftər-‚bʌrnər] s (aer) postbruciatore *m*

af'ter-din'ner *adj* dopo la cena

aftereffect ['æftərɪ‚fɛkt] òr ['ɑftərɪ-‚fɛkt] s conseguenza

af'ter-hours' *adj* dopo le ore di ufficio

af'ter·life' s aldilà *m*; vita susseguente

aftermath ['æftər‚mæθ] or ['aftər‚mæθ] s consequenze *fpl;* gravi conseguenze *fpl*

af'ter·noon' *adj* pomeridiano ‖ s pomeriggio

after-shaving ['æftər‚ʃevɪŋ] or ['aftər‚ʃevɪŋ] *adj* dopobarba

af'ter·taste' s retrosapore *m*

af'ter·thought' s pensiero tardivo

afterward ['æftərwərd] or ['aftərwərd] *adv* dopo; **long afterward** molto tempo dopo

af'ter·while' *adv* fra un po'

again [ə'gɛn] *adv* di nuovo; ancora; un'altra volta; **again and again** ripetutamente; **as much again** due volte tanto, altrettanto; **to + *inf* + again** tornare a + *inf,* e.g., **to cook again** tornare a cuocere

against [ə'gɛnst] *prep* contro; (*opposite*) in faccia a; **to be against** opporsi a; **to go against the grain** ripugnare

agape [ə'gep] *adj & adv* a bocca aperta

age [edʒ] s età *f;* (*old age*) vecchiaia; (*full term of life*) vita; (*historical or geological period*) evo; generazione; **of age** maggiorenne; **to come of age** diventare maggiorenne; **under age** minorenne ‖ *tr & intr* invecchiare

aged [edʒd] *adj* dell'età di ‖ ['edʒɪd] *adj* vecchio, invecchiato

ageless ['edʒlɪs] *adj* eternamente giovane, che non invecchia mai

agen·cy ['edʒənsɪ] s (**-cies**) azione; agenzia; mediazione; (*of government*) ente *m*

agenda [ə'dʒɛndə] s agenda, ordine *m* del giorno

agent ['edʒənt] s agente *m;* (coll) commesso viaggiatore, agente *m* di commercio; (rr) gestore *m*

Age' of Enlight'enment s illuminismo

agglomeration [ə‚glɑmə'reʃən] s agglomerazione

aggrandizement [ə'grændɪzmənt] s aumento, innalzamento

aggravate ['ægrə‚vet] *tr* aggravare; (coll) irritare, esasperare

aggregate ['ægrɪ‚get] *adj & s* aggregato, totale *m;* **in the aggregate** nel complesso ‖ *tr* aggregare; ammontare a

aggression [ə'grɛʃən] s aggressione

aggressive [ə'grɛsɪv] *adj* aggressivo, attivo

aggressor [ə'grɛsər] s aggressore *m*

aggrieve [ə'griv] *tr* affliggere

aghast [ə'gæst] or [ə'gɑst] *adj* atterrito

agile ['ædʒɪl] *adj* agile

agitate ['ædʒɪ‚tet] *tr* agitare ‖ *intr* agitarsi

agitator ['ædʒɪ‚tetər] s agitatore *m*

aglow [ə'glo] *adj* splendente

agnostic [æg'nɑstɪk] *adj & s* agnostico

ago [ə'go] *adv* fa, e.g., **a year ago** un anno fa; **long ago** molto tempo fa

agog [ə'gɑg] *adj & adv* ansioso; **to set agog** riempire di ansietà

agonize ['ægə‚naɪz] *intr* soffrire straziantemente; (*to struggle*) dibattersi

ago·ny ['ægəni] s (**-nies**) agonia

agrarian [ə'grɛrɪ·ən] *adj* agrario ‖ s membro del partito agrario

agree [ə'gri] *intr* aderire, andar d'accordo; (*to consent*) acconsentire; (gram) concordare; **to agree with** confarsi a, e.g., **eggs do not agree with him** le uova non gli si confanno

agreeable [ə'gri·əbəl] *adj* gentile; gradevole; (*willing to agree*) consenziente

agreement [ə'grimənt] s accordo; **in agreement** d'accordo

agriculture ['ægrɪ‚kʌltʃər] s agricoltura

agriculturist [‚ægrɪ'kʌltʃərɪst] s (*farmer*) agricoltore *m;* perito in agricoltura, agronomo

agronomy [ə'grɑnəmɪ] s agronomia

aground [ə'graʊnd] *adv* alla riva; **to run aground** andare or dare in secca

ague ['egju] s (*chill*) brivido; febbre *f*

ahead [ə'hɛd] *adv* davanti, avanti; **to get ahead** (coll) andare avanti, aver successo; **to get ahead of** sorpassare; **to go ahead** avanzare; continuare

ahoy [ə'hɔɪ] *interj*—**ship ahoy!** ehi della barca!

aid [ed] s aiuto; assistente *m;* (mil) aiutante *m* di campo ‖ *tr* aiutare; **to aid and abet** essere complice di

aide [ed] s assistente *m*

aide-de-camp ['eddə'kæmp] s (**aides-de-camp**) aiutante *m* di campo

ail [el] *tr* affliggere; **what ails you?** che ha? ‖ *intr* soffrire, essere malato

aileron ['elə‚rɑn] s alerone *m*

ailing ['elɪŋ] *adj* ammalato

ailment ['elmənt] s malattia, indisposizione; (*chronic*) acciacco

aim [em] s mira; intento ‖ *tr* (*a gun*) puntare; (*words*) dirigere ‖ *intr* mirare; **to aim to** cercare di, aver l'intenzione di

air [ɛr] *adj* (e.g., *pocket*) d'aria; (e.g., *show*) aeronautico ‖ s aria; **by air** per via aerea; **in the open air** all'aria aperta; **to be in the air** circolare; **to be on the air** (rad, telv) essere in onda; **to go on the air** (rad, telv) andare in onda; **to put on airs** darsi delle arie; **to take the air** andar fuori; **up in the air** incerto; (slang) arrabbiato ‖ *tr* aerare, ventilare

airborne ['ɛr‚bɔrn] or ['ɛr‚born] *adj* aerosostentato; aerotrasportato

air' brake' s freno ad aria compressa

air' cas'tle s castello in aria

air'-condi'tion *tr* climatizzare

air' condi'tioner s condizionatore *m*

air' condi'tioning s aria condizionata, climatizzazione

air·'cool' *tr* raffreddare con aria

air' corps' s aviazione, arma aeronautica

air'craft' s (**-craft**) aeromobile *m*

air'craft car'rier s portaerei *f*

airdrome ['ɛr‚drom] s aerodromo

air'drop' *tr* paracadutare

air'field' s campo d'aviazione

air'foil' s superficie *f* portante, velatura

air' force' s forza aerea

air' gap' s (elec) intraferro

airing ['ɛrɪŋ] *s* aerazione; passeggiata all'aria aperta; pubblica discussione

air' jack'et *s* (aer, naut) giubbotto salvagente

air' lane' *s* aerovia

air'lift' *s* ponte aereo, aerotrasporto ‖ *tr* aerotrasportare

air'line' *s* linea aerea; tubo dell'aria

air' mail' *s* posta aerea

air'-mail' *adj* per via aerea ‖ *s* lettera per posta aerea ‖ *adv* per posta aerea ‖ *tr* spedire per posta aerea

air'-mail let'ter *s* lettera per posta aerea

air'-mail stamp' *s* francobollo posta aerea

air'man *s* (-men) aviatore *m*, aviere *m*

air' mat'tress *s* materassino pneumatico

air'plane' *s* aeroplano, aereo

air'plane car'rier *s* portaerei *f*

air' pock'et *s* vuoto d'aria

air' pollu'tion *s* contaminazione atmosferica, inquinamento atmosferico

air' port' *s* aeroporto

air' pump' *s* pompa pneumatica

air' raid' *s* incursione aerea

air'-raid shel'ter *s* rifugio antiaereo

air'-raid warn'ing *s* allerta

air' ri'fle *s* fucile *m* ad aria compressa

air' serv'ice *s* aeroservizio

air' shaft' *s* tubo di ventilazione

air'ship' *s* aeronave *f*

airsickness ['ɛr,sɪknɪs] *s* male *m* d'aria

air' sleeve' *s* manica a vento

airspace ['ɛr,spes] *s* aerospazio

air'strip' *s* aviopista

air' ter'minal *s* aerostazione

air'tight' *adj* impermeabile all'aria, ermetico

air'waves' *spl* onde *fpl*, radioonde *fpl*

air'way' *s* aerovia; **airways** (rad) onda, onde *fpl*

air·y ['ɛri] *adj* (-ier; -iest) arioso; leggero; aereo

aisle [aɪl] *s* (*between rows of seats*) corsia; (*of a church*) navata laterale; (theat) canale *m*

ajar [ə'dʒar] *adj* socchiuso; in disaccordo

akimbo [ə'kɪmbo] *adj* & *adv*—**with arms akimbo** con le mani sui fianchi

akin [ə'kɪn] *adj* affine; congiunto

alabaster ['ælə,bæstər] or ['ælə-,bastər] *s* alabastro

à la carte [,alə'kart] *adv* alla carta

à la mode [,alə'mod] or [,ælə'mod] *adv* alla moda; servito con gelato

alarm [ə'larm] *s* allarme *m* ‖ *tr* allarmare

alarm' clock' *s* sveglia

alas [ə'læs] or [ə'las] *interj* ahimé!; povero me!

Albanian [æl'bɛnɪ·ən] *adj* & *s* albanese *mf*

albatross ['ælbə,trɔs] or ['ælbə,tras] *s* albatro, diomedea

album ['ælbəm] *s* album *m*

albumen [æl'bjumən] *s* albume *m*

alchemy ['ælkəmi] *s* alchimia

alcohol ['ælkə,hɔl] or ['ælkə,hal] *s* alcole *m*

alcoholic [,ælkə'hɔlɪk] or [,ælkə'ha-lɪk] *adj* alcolico ‖ *s* alcolizzato

alcove ['ælkov] *s* (*recess*) alcova; (*in a garden*) chiosco, padiglione *m*; cameretta attigua

alder ['ɔldər] *s* ontano, alno

al'der·man *s* (-men) assessore *m* municipale, consigliere *m* municipale

ale [el] *s* birra amara

alembic [ə'lembɪk] *s* alambicco

alert [ə'lʌrt] *adj* attento; vispo ‖ *s* allerta; **to be on the alert** stare allerta ‖ *tr* dare l'allerta a

Aleu'tian Is'lands [ə'luʃən] *spl* Isole Aleutine

Alexander [,ælɪg'zændər] or [,ælɪg-'zandər] *s* Alessandro

Alexan'der the Great' *s* Alessandro Magno

Alexandrine [,ælɪg'zændrɪn] *adj* & *s* alessandrino

alfalfa [æl'fælfə] *s* (bot) erba medica

algae ['ældʒi] *spl* alghe *fpl*

algebra ['ældʒɪbrə] *s* algebra

algebraic [,ældʒɪ'bre·ɪk] *adj* algebrico

Algeria [æl'dʒɪrɪ·ə] *s* l'Algeria

Algerian [æl'dʒɪrɪ·ən] *adj* & *s* algerino

Algiers [æl'dʒɪrz] *s* Algeri *f*

alias ['elɪ·əs] *s* pseudonimo ‖ *adv* alias

ali·bi ['ælɪ,baɪ] *s* (-bis) alibi *m*

alien ['eljən] or ['elɪ·ən] *adj* straniero; (*strange*) strano ‖ *s* straniero; (*outsider*) estraneo

alienate ['eljə,net] or ['elɪ·ə,net] *tr* alienare

alight [ə'laɪt] *v* (*pret* & *pp* **alighted** or **alit** [ə'lɪt]) *intr* scendere; **to alight on** or **upon** posarsi su

align [ə'laɪn] *tr* allineare ‖ *intr* allinearsi

alike [ə'laɪk] *adj* uguali; **to look alike** assomigliarsi ‖ *adv* nello stesso modo

alimen'tary canal' [,ælɪ'mentəri] *s* tubo digestivo

alimony ['ælɪ,moni] *s* alimonia

alive [ə'laɪv] *adj* vivo, in vita; (*lively*) vivace; **alive to** conscio di; **alive with** brulicante di, pieno zeppo di; **look alive!** fa presto!

alka·li ['ælkə,laɪ] *s* (-lis or -lies) alcali *m*

alkaline ['ælkə,laɪn] or ['ælkəlɪn] *adj* alcalino

all [ɔl] *adj indef* tutto, tutto il, ogni ‖ *s* tutto ‖ *pron* tutto; tutti; **all of** tutti ‖ *adv* completamente; **all but** quasi; **all in** (slang) stanco morto; **all in all** tutto considerato; **all the better** tanto meglio; **all the worse** tanto peggio; **far all that** per quello che, e.g., **for all that I know** per quello che io ne sappia; **in all** tutto contato; **it's all right!** va bene!; **not at all** niente affatto; prego

allay [ə'le] *tr* calmare, mitigare

all' clear' *s* fine *f* dell'allarme, cessato allarme

allegation [,ælɪ'geʃən] *s* asserzione, affermazione

allege [ə'ledʒ] *tr* asserire, affermare; addurre

allegiance [ə'lidʒəns] *s* fedeltà *f*, lealtà *f*

allegoric(al) [ˌælɪˈgɑrɪk(əl)] or [ˌælɪ-ˈgɔrɪk(əl)] *adj* allegorico

allego·ry [ˈælɪˌgori] *s* (**-ries**) allegoria

aller·gy [ˈælərdʒi] *s* (**-gies**) allergia

alleviate [əˈlivɪˌet] *tr* alleviare

alley [ˈæli] *s* vicolo, calle *f*; (*for bowling*) pista; (*tennis*) corridoio

All' Fools' Day' *s* primo d'aprile

all' fours' *spl*—**on all fours** a quattro gambe

alliance [əˈlaɪ·əns] *s* alleanza

alligator [ˈælɪˌgetər] *s* alligatore *m*

alliteration [əˌlɪtəˈreʃən] *s* allitterazione

all-knowing [ˈɔlˈno·ɪŋ] *adj* onnisciente

allocate [ˈæləˌket] *tr* assegnare; (*funds*) stanziare; (*to fix the place of*) allogare

allot [əˈlɑt] *v* (*pret & pp* **allotted;** *ger* **allotting**) *tr* distribuire, assegnare

all'-out' *adj* completo; (*ruthless*) acerrimo

allow [əˈlaʊ] *tr* permettere; ammettere; concedere ‖ *intr* **to allow for** prendere in considerazione

allowance [əˈlaʊ·əns] *s* (*limited share*) assegno; concessione; (*reduction in price*) sconto; tolleranza; **to make allowance for** prendere in considerazione

alloy [ˈælɔɪ] or [əˈlɔɪ] *s* lega; impurezza ‖ [əˈlɔɪ] *tr* far lega di, legare; adulterare

all-powerful [ˈɔlˈpaʊ·ərfəl] *adj* onnipotente

all' right' *adj* esatto; bene; in buona salute; (slang) dabbene

All' Saints'' Day' *s* Ognissanti *m*

All' Souls'' Day' *s* giorno dei morti

all'spice' *s* pimento, pepe *m* della Giamaica

all'-star game' *s* partita sportiva in cui tutti i giocatori sono scelti fra i migliori

allude [əˈlud] *intr* alludere

allure [əˈlur] *s* fascino, incanto ‖ *tr* affascinare, incantare

alluring [əˈlurɪŋ] *adj* affascinante, seducente

allusion [əˈluʃən] *s* allusione

al·ly [ˈælaɪ] or [əˈlaɪ] *s* (**-lies**) alleato ‖ [əˈlaɪ] *v* (*pret & pp* **-lied**) *tr* alleare; associare; **to become allied** allearsi; imparentarsi ‖ *intr* allearsi

almanac [ˈɔlməˌnæk] *s* almanacco

almighty [ɔlˈmaɪti] *adj* onnipotente

almond [ˈɑmənd] or [ˈæmənd] *s* (*nut*) mandorla; (*tree*) mandorlo

al'mond brittle' *s* croccante *m*

almost [ˈɔlmost] or [ɔlˈmost] *adv* quasi

alms [ɑmz] *s* elemosina

aloe [ˈælo] *s* aloe *m*

aloft [əˈlɔft] or [əˈlɑft] *adv* in alto, sopra; (aer) in volo; (naut) nell'alberatura

alone [əˈlon] *adj* solo; **let alone** senza menzionare; **to leave alone** non disturbare ‖ *adv* solo, solamente

along [əˈlɔŋ] or [əˈlɑŋ] *adv* (*lengthwise*) per il lungo; (*onward*) avanti; **all along** tutto il tempo; **along with**

con; **to get along** andar d'accordo; andarsene; avanzare; aver successo; **to take along** prendere con sè ‖ *prep* lungo

along'side' *adv* a lato; **alongside of** a lato di ‖ *prep* a lato di, vicino a

aloof [əˈluf] *adj* riservato, freddo; **to keep** or **stand aloof from** tenersi a distanza da ‖ *adv* lontano; da solo

aloud [əˈlaʊd] *adv* ad alta voce

alphabet [ˈælfəˌbɛt] *s* alfabeto

alpine [ˈælpaɪn] *adj* alpino

Alps [ælps] *spl* Alpi *fpl*

already [ɔlˈrɛdi] *adv* già

Alsace [ælˈses] or [ˈælsæs] *s* l'Alsazia

Alsatian [ælˈseʃən] *adj & s* alsaziano

also [ˈɔlso] *adv* anche

altar [ˈɔltər] *s* altare *m*

al'tar boy' *s* accolito, chierico

al'tar·piece' *s* pala d'altare

alter [ˈɔltər] *tr* alterare; (*a male animal*) castrare ‖ *intr* diventare differente, cambiare

alteration [ˌɔltəˈreʃən] *s* alterazione, modifica

alternate [ˈɔltərnɪt] or [ˈæltərnɪt] *s* sostituto, supplente *mf* ‖ [ˈɔltərˌnet] or [ˈæltərˌnet] *tr* alternare ‖ *intr* alternarsi, avvicendarsi

al'ternating cur'rent *s* corrente alternata

alternator [ˈɔltərˌnetər] or [ˈæltər-ˌnetər] *s* alternatore *m*

although [ɔlˈðo] *conj* benchè, per quanto, malgrado

altimeter [ælˈtɪmɪtər] or [ˈæltəˌmitər] *s* altimetro

altitude [ˈæltɪˌtjud] or [ˈæltɪˌtud] *s* altitudine *f*

al·to [ˈælto] *s* (**-tos**) contralto

altogether [ˌɔltəˈgɛðər] *adv* completamente, affatto, tutt'insieme

altruist [ˈæltru·ɪst] *s* altruista *mf*

altruistic [ˌæltruˈɪstɪk] *adj* altruistico

alum [ˈæləm] *s* allume *m*

aluminum [əˈlumɪnəm] *s* alluminio

alum·na [əˈlʌmnə] *s* (**-nae** [ni]) diplomata, laureata

alum·nus [əˈlʌmnəs] *s* (**-ni** [nai]) diplomato, laureato

alveo·lus [ælˈvi·ələs] *s* (**-li** [ˌlai]) alveolo

always [ˈɔlwɪz] or [ˈɔlwez] *adv* sempre

amalgam [əˈmælgəm] *s* amalgama *m*

amalgamate [əˈmælgəˌmet] *tr* amalgamare ‖ *intr* amalgamarsi

amass [əˈmæs] *tr* ammassare

amateur [ˈæmətˌʃər] *adj* da dilettante ‖ *s* amatore *m*, dilettante *mf*

amaze [əˈmez] *tr* stupire, meravigliare

amazing [əˈmezɪŋ] *adj* straordinario

Amazon [ˈæməˌzɑn] or [ˈæməzən] *s* rio delle Amazzoni; (myth) Amazzone *f*

ambassador [æmˈbæsədər] *s* ambasciatore *m*

ambassadress [æmˈbæsədrɪs] *s* ambasciatrice *f*

amber [ˈæmbər] *s* ambra

ambigui·ty [ˌæmbɪˈgjuˌiti] *s* (**-ties**) ambiguità *f*

ambiguous [æmˈbɪgju·əs] *adj* ambiguo

ambition [æm'bɪʃən] s ambizione
ambitious [æm'bɪʃəs] adj ambizioso
amble ['æmbəl] s ambio || intr ambiare
ambulance ['æmbjələns] s ambulanza
ambush ['æmbuʃ] s imboscata; to lie in ambush tendere un'imboscata || tr appostare || intr appostarsi
amelioration [ə,miljə're/ən] s miglioramento
amen ['e'men] or ['ɑ'men] s amen m || interj amen!
amenable [ə'minəbəl] or [ə'menəbəl] adj docile, aperto; (accountable) responsabile
amend [ə'mend] tr emendare || amends spl ammenda, contravvenzione; to make amends for fare ammenda per
amendment [ə'mendmənt] s emendamento
ameni·ty [ə'miniti] or [ə'meniti] s (-ties) amenità f
American [ə'merikən] adj & s americano
Americanize [ə'merikə,naiz] tr americanizzare
amethyst ['æmɪθɪst] s ametista
amiable ['emi·əbəl] adj amabile
amicable ['æmikəbəl] adj amichevole
amid [ə'mɪd] prep in mezzo a, fra, tra
amidship [ə'mɪdʃɪp] adv a mezzanave
amiss [ə'mɪs] adj erroneo, sbagliato || adv erroneamente; to take amiss offendersi, prendere in mala parte
ami·ty ['æmiti] s (-ties) amicizia
ammeter ['æm,mitər] s amperometro
ammonia [ə'moni·ə] s ammoniaca; acqua ammoniacale
ammunition [,æmjə'nɪʃən] s munizione, munizioni fpl
amnes·ty ['æmnɪsti] s (-ties) amnistia || v (pret & pp -tied) tr amnistiare
amoeba [ə'mibə] s ameba
among [ə'mʌŋ] prep fra, tra, in mezzo a
amorous ['æmərəs] adj amoroso; erotico
amortize ['æmər,taiz] tr ammortare
amount [ə'maunt] s ammontare m || intr—to amount to ammontare a
ampere ['æmpir] s ampere m
am'pere-hour' s amperora m
amphibious [æm'fɪbi·əs] adj anfibio
amphitheater ['æmfɪ,θi·ətər] s anfiteatro
ample ['æmpəl] adj ampio
amplifier ['æmpli,faɪ·ər] s amplificatore m
ampli·fy ['æmpli,faɪ] v (pret & pp -fied) tr amplificare
amplitude ['æmpli,tjud] or ['æmpli,tud] s ampiezza
am'plitude modula'tion s modulazione d'ampiezza
amputate ['æmpjə,tet] tr amputare
amputee [,æmpjə'ti] s chi ha subito l'amputazione di un arto
amuck [ə'mʌk] adv freneticamente; to run amuck dare in un accesso di pazzia; attaccare alla cieca
amulet ['æmjələt] s amuleto
amuse [ə'mjuz] tr divertire

amusement [ə'mjuzmənt] s divertimento
amuse'ment park' s parco dei divertimenti, luna park m
amusing [ə'mjuzɪŋ] adj divertente
an [æn] or [ən] art indef var of a, used before words beginning with vowel or mute h
anachronism [ə'nækrə,nɪzəm] s anacronismo
anaemia [ə'nimi·ə] s var of anemia
anaesthesia [,ænɪs'θiʒə] s anestesia
anaesthetic [,ænɪs'θetɪk] adj & s anestetico
anaesthetize [æ'nesθɪ,taɪz] tr anestetizzare
analogous [ə'næləgəs] adj analogo
analo·gy [ə'nælədʒi] s (-gies) analogia
analy·sis [ə'nælɪsɪs] s (-ses [,siz]) analisi f
analyst ['ænəlɪst] s analista mf
analytic(al) [,ænə'lɪtɪk(əl)] adj analitico
analyze ['ænə,laɪz] tr analizzare
anarchist ['ænərkɪst] s anarchico
anarchy ['ænərki] s anarchia
anathema [ə'næθɪmə] s anatema m
anatomic(al) [,ænə'tɑmɪk(əl)] adj anatomico
anato·my [ə'nætəmi] s (-mies) anatomia
ancestor ['ænsɛstər] s antenato
ances·try ['ænsɛstri] s (-tries) lignaggio, prosapia
anchor ['æŋkər] s ancora; to cast anchor gettare l'ancora; to ride at anchor stare all'ancora; to weigh anchor salpare l'ancora, salpare || tr ancorare || intr ancorarsi, stare all'ancora
ancho·vy ['æntʃovi] s (-vies) acciuga
ancient ['enʃənt] adj antico || s vecchio, anziano; the ancients gli antichi
ancillary ['ænsɪ,lɛri] adj dipendente; ausiliario, ausiliare
and [ænd] or [ənd] conj e, ed; and so on, and so forth e così via
Andean [æn'di·ən] or ['ændi·ən] adj andino || s abitante mf della regione andina
Andes ['ændiz] spl Ande fpl
andiron ['ænd,aɪ·ərn] s alare m
anecdote ['ænɪk,dot] s aneddoto
anemia [ə'nimi·ə] s anemia
anemic [ə'nimɪk] adj anemico
an'eroid barom'eter ['ænə,rɔɪd] s barometro aneroide
anesthesia [,ænɪs'θiʒə] s anestesia
anesthetic [,ænɪs'θetɪk] adj & s anestetico
anesthetize [æ'nesθɪ,taɪz] tr anestetizzare
aneurysm ['ænjə,rɪzəm] s aneurisma m
anew [ə'nju] or [ə'nu] adv di nuovo, nuovamente
angel ['endʒəl] s angelo; (financial backer) (coll) finanziatore m
angelic(al) [æn'dʒelɪk(əl)] adj angelico
anger ['æŋgər] s ira, collera || tr adirare || intr adirarsi, incollerirsi
angle ['æŋgəl] s angolo; punto di vista

‖ *intr* intrigare; **to angle for** darsi da fare per

an'gle i'ron *s* cantonale *m*, angolare *m*

angler [ˈæŋglər] *s* pescatore *m* alla lenza; (fig) intrigante *m*

Anglo-Saxon [ˈæŋgloˈsæksən] *adj & s* anglosassone *mf*

an·gry [ˈæŋgri] *adj* (**-grier; -griest**) arrabbiato; (pathol) infiammato; **to become angry** incollerirsi per; **to become angry with** adirarsi con

anguish [ˈæŋgwɪʃ] *s* angoscia, pena

angular [ˈæŋgjələr] *adj* angolare

anhydrous [ænˈhaɪdrəs] *adj* anidro

aniline [ˈænɪlɪn] or [ˈænɪˌlaɪn] *s* anilina

animal [ˈænɪməl] *adj & s* animale *m*

an'imated cartoon' [ˈænɪˌmetɪd] *s* cartone animato

animation [ˌænɪˈmeʃən] *s* animazione

animosi·ty [ˌænɪˈmɑsɪti] *s* (**-ties**) animosità *f*

animus [ˈænɪməs] *s* odio, malanimo

anion [ˈænˌaɪ·ən] *s* anione *m*

anise [ˈænɪs] *s* anice *f*

anisette [ˌænɪˈzet] *s* anisetta

ankle [ˈæŋkəl] *s* caviglia

an'kle·bone' *s* malleolo

an'kle support' *s* cavigliera

anklet [ˈæŋklɪt] *s* calzino corto; bracciale *m* da caviglia

annals [ˈænəlz] *spl* annali *mpl*

annex [ˈæneks] *s* annesso, dipendenza ‖ [əˈneks] *tr* annettere, appropriarsi di

annihilate [əˈnaɪ·ɪˌlet] *tr* annientare

anniversa·ry [ˌænɪˈvʌrsəri] *adj* anniversario ‖ *s* (**-ries**) anniversario

annotate [ˈænəˌtet] *tr* annotare

announce [əˈnaʊns] *tr* annunciare

announcement [əˈnaʊnsmənt] *s* annuncio, partecipazione

announcer [əˈnaʊnsər] *s* annunziatore *m*

annoy [əˈnɔɪ] *tr* annoiare, seccare

annoyance [əˈnɔɪ·əns] *s* fastidio, seccatura

annoying [əˈnɔɪ·ɪŋ] *adj* noioso

annual [ˈænjʊ·əl] *adj* annuale ‖ *s* annuario; pianta annuale

annui·ty [əˈnju·ɪti] or [əˈnu·ɪti] *s* (**-ties**) annualità *f*; (*for life*) vitalizio

an·nul [əˈnʌl] *v* (*pret & pp* **-nulled;** *ger* **-nulling**) *tr* annullare, cassare

annunciation [əˌnʌnsɪˈeʃən] *s* annunzio ‖ **Annunciation** *s* Annunciazione

anode [ˈænod] *s* anodo

anoint [əˈnɔɪnt] *tr* ungere

anomalous [əˈnɑmələs] *adj* anomalo

anoma·ly [əˈnɑməli] *s* (**-lies**) anomalia

anonymi·ty [ˌænəˈnɪmɪti] *s* (**-ties**) anonimia; **to preserve one's anonymity** serbare l'anonimo

anonymous [əˈnɑnɪməs] *adj* anonimo

another [əˈnʌðər] *adj & pron indef* un altro

answer [ˈænsər] or [ˈɑnsər] *s* risposta; (*to a problem*) soluzione ‖ *tr* rispondere a; **this will answer your purpose** questo fa per Lei; **to answer back** (slang) dare una rispostaccia a; **to answer the door** andare a rispondere

‖ *intr* rispondere; corrispondere; essere responsabile; **to answer back** (slang) dare una rispostaccia

ant [ænt] *s* formica

antagonism [ænˈtægəˌnɪzəm] *s* antagonismo

antagonize [ænˈtægəˌnaɪz] *tr* opporsi a; creare antagonismo in

antarctic [æntˈɑrktɪk] *adj* antartico ‖ **the Antarctic** la regione antartica

anteater [ˈæntˌitər] *s* formichiere *m*

antecedent [ˌæntɪˈsidənt] *adj & s* antecedente *m;* **antecedents** antenati *mpl*

antechamber [ˈæntɪˌtʃembər] *s* anticamera

antedate [ˈæntɪˌdet] *tr* antidatare; (*to happen before*) antecedere

antelope [ˈæntɪˌlop] *s* antilope *f*

anten·na [ænˈtenə] *s* (**-nae** [ni]) (*of insect*) antenna ‖ *s* (**-nas**) (rad, telv) antenna

antepenult [ˌæntɪˈpinʌlt] *s* terzultima sillaba

anteroom [ˈæntɪˌrum] or [ˈæntɪˌrʊm] *s* anticamera, sala d'aspetto

anthem [ˈænθəm] *s* inno

ant'hill' *s* formicaio

antholo·gy [ænˈθɑlədʒi] *s* (**-gies**) antologia

anthracite [ˈænθrəˌsaɪt] *s* antracite *f*

anthrax [ˈænθræks] *s* antrace *m*

anthropoid [ˈænθrəˌpɔɪd] *adj* antropoide, antropomorfo

anthropology [ˌænθrəˈpɑlədʒi] *s* antropologia

antiaircraft [ˌæntɪˈer ˌkræft] or [ˌæntɪˈer ˌkrɑft] *adj* antiaereo

antibiotic [ˌæntɪbaɪˈɑtɪk] *adj & s* antibiotico

antibod·y [ˈæntɪˌbɑdi] *s* (**-ies**) anticorpo

anticipate [ænˈtɪsɪˌpet] *tr* anticipare, prevedere; ripromettersi

anticipation [ænˌtɪsɪˈpeʃən] *s* anticipazione, previsione

antics [ˈæntɪks] *spl* pagliacciate *fpl,* buffonate *fpl*

antidote [ˈæntɪˌdot] *s* antidoto

antifreeze [ˈæntɪˌfriz] *s* anticongelante *m*

antiglare [ˌæntɪˈgler] *adj* antiabbagliante

anti-G' suit' *s* tuta antigravità

antiknock [ˌæntɪˈnɑk] *adj* antidetonante

antimissile [ˌæntɪˈmɪsɪl] *adj* antimissile

antimony [ˈæntɪˌmoni] *s* antimonio

antinoise [ˌæntɪˈnɔɪz] *adj* antirumore

antipa·thy [ænˈtɪpəθi] *s* (**-thies**) antipatia

antipersonnel [ˌæntɪˌpʌrsəˈnel] *adj* (*e.g., mine*) antiuomo

antiquarian [ˌæntɪˈkwerɪ·ən] *adj & s* antiquario

antiquar·y [ˈæntɪˌkweri] *s* (**-ies**) antiquario

antiquated [ˈæntɪˌkwetɪd] *adj* antiquato

antique [ænˈtik] *adj* antico, vecchio; antiquato ‖ *s* oggetto d'epoca, antichità *f*

antique' deal'er s antiquario
antique' store' s negozio d'antiquariato
antiqui·ty [æn'tɪkwɪti] s (-ties) antichità f
anti-Semitic [,æntɪsɪ'mɪtɪk] adj anti-
semita
antiseptic [,æntɪ'sɛptɪk] adj & s anti-
settico
antislavery [,æntɪ'slevəri] adj anti-
schiavista
antitank [,æntɪ'tæŋk] adj anticarro
antitheft [,æntɪ'θɛft] adj antifurto
antithe·sis [æn'tɪθɪsɪs] s (-ses [,siz])
antitesi f
antitoxin [,æntɪ'taksɪn] s antitossina
antitrust [,æntɪ'trʌst] adj antitrust
antler ['æntlər] s corno di cervo
antonym ['æntənɪm] s antonimo
Antwerp ['æntwərp] s Anversa
anvil ['ænvɪl] s incudine m
anxie·ty [æŋ'zaɪ.əti] s (-ties) ansietà f;
(psychol) angoscia
anxious ['æŋkʃəs] adj ansioso; anxious
about sollecito di; anxious for desideroso di
any ['eni] adj indef ogni, qualunque,
qualsiasi; qualche, e.g., do you know
any boy who could help me? conosce
qualche ragazzo che possa aiutarmi?;
di + art, e.g., do you want any
cheese? vuole del formaggio?; not
. . . any non . . . nessuno, e.g., he
does not read any newspaper non
legge nessun giornale || adv un po',
e.g., do you want any? ne vuole un
po'?; not . . . any longer non . . .
più; not . . . any more non . . . più
|| pron ne, e.g., do you want any? ne
vuole?
an'y·bod'y pron indef chiunque; (in
interrogative sentences) qualcuno;
not . . . anybody non . . . nessuno
an'y·how' adv in qualunque modo, comunque; in ogni caso; (haphazardly)
alla rinfusa
an'y·one' pron indef chiunque; (in interrogative sentences) qualcuno; not
. . . anyone non . . . nessuno
an'y·thing' s qualunque cosa || pron
indef qualcosa; qualunque cosa; tutto
quanto; checchessia; anything at all
qualunque cosa; not . . . anything
non . . . niente; not . . . anything at
all non . . . niente affatto, non . . .
nulla; not . . . anything else non . . .
nient'altro
an'y·way' adv in qualunque modo, comunque; in ogni caso; (haphazardly)
alla rinfusa
an'y·where' adv dovunque, in qualsiasi
luogo; not . . . anywhere non . . . in
nessun luogo
apace [ə'pes] adv presto, rapidamente
apart [ə'part] adv a parte, a pezzi;
separatamente; apart from a parte
da; oltre a; to come apart andare a
pezzi, cadere a pezzi; to set apart
mettere in disparte; to take apart
smontare; to tear apart fare a pezzi;
to tell apart distinguere
apartment [ə'partmənt] s appartamento; (single room) stanza

apart'ment house' s casa d'appartamenti
apathetic [,æpə'θɛtɪk] adj apatico
apathy ['æpəθi] s apatia
ape [ep] s scimmia antropomorfa;
scimmia || tr imitare, scimmiottare
Apennines ['æpə,naɪnz] spl Appennini
mpl
aperture ['æpərtʃər] s apertura
apex ['epɛks] s (apexes or apices
['æpɪ,siz]) apice m
apheresis [ə'fɛrɪsɪs] s aferesi f
aphorism ['æfə,rɪzəm] s aforisma m
aphrodisiac [,æfrə'dɪzɪ,æk] adj & s
afrodisiaco
apiar·y ['epɪ,ɛri] s (-ies) apiario
apiece [ə'pis] adv a testa, per persona;
ciascuno
apish ['epɪʃ] adj scimmiesco; da scimmia
aplomb [ə'plam] s disinvoltura, baldanza
apocalypse [ə'pakə,lɪps] s apocalisse f
apogee ['æpə,dʒi] s apogeo
apologetic [ə,palə'dʒɛtɪk] adj pieno di
scuse
apologize [ə'palə,dʒaɪz] intr chiedere
scusa, scusarsi
apolo·gy [ə'palədʒi] s (-gies) scusa;
(makeshift) surrogato
apoplectic [,æpə'plɛktɪk] adj & s apoplettico
apoplexy ['æpə,plɛksi] s apoplessia
apostle [ə'pasəl] s apostolo
apostrophe [ə'pastrəfi] s (mark) apo-
strofo; (rhet) apostrofe f
apothecar·y [ə'paθɪ,kɛri] s (-ies) farmacista mf
appall [ə'pəl] tr sgomentare, sbigottire
appalling [ə'pəlɪŋ] adj sconcertante
appara·tus [,æpə'retəs] or [,æpə-
'rætəs] s (-tus or -tuses) apparato
apparel [ə'pærəl] s confezioni fpl, vestiario
apparent [ə'pærənt] or [ə'pɛrənt] adj
apparente; chiaramente visibile
apparition [,æpə'rɪʃən] s apparizione
appeal [ə'pil] s appello; (attraction) at-
trattiva, fascino || tr (a sentence) ap-
pellare contro || intr dare nell'occhio;
to appeal from (law) appellarsi contro; to appeal to supplicare, pregare;
piacere a, e.g., his idea appeals to
me la sua idea mi piace
appear [ə'pɪr] intr apparire; (to seem)
sembrare; (said of a book) uscire;
(before the public) presentarsi; (law)
comparire
appearance [ə'pɪrəns] s apparizione;
(of a book) pubblicazione; (outward
look) apparenza; (law) comparizione;
to keep up appearances salvare le
app. renze
appease [ə'piz] tr pacificare, placare;
(a desire) soddisfare
appeasement [ə'pizmənt] s pacifica-
zione, tranquillizzazione
appel'late court' [ə'pɛlɪt] s corte f
d'appello
appellation [,æpə'leʃən] s denominazione, nome m
append [ə'pɛnd] tr allegare, aggiungere

appendage [ə'pɛndɪdʒ] *s* appendice *f*

appendicitis [ə‚pɛndɪ'saɪtɪs] *s* appendicite *f*

appen·dix [ə'pɛndɪks] *s* (**-dixes** or **-dices** [dɪ‚siz]) appendice *f*

appertain [‚æpər'ten] *intr* spettare, riferirsi

appetite ['æpɪ‚taɪt] *s* appetito

appetizer ['æpɪ‚taɪzər] *s* (*drink*) aperitivo; (*food*) stimulante *m* dell'appetito

appetizing ['æpɪ‚taɪzɪŋ] *adj* appetitoso

applaud *tr* applaudire, applaudire (with *dat*) || *intr* applaudire

applause [ə'plɔz] *s* applauso, applausi *mpl*

apple ['æpəl] *s* mela, pomo; (*tree*) melo, pomo

ap′plejack′ *s* acquavite *f* di mele

ap′ple of dis′cord *s* pomo della discordia

ap′ple of one′s eye′ *s* pupilla degli occhi di qlcu, beniamino di qlcu

ap′ple pie′ *s* torta di mele

ap′ple pol′isher *s* leccapiedi *mf*

ap′ple·sauce′ *s* marmellata di mele; (slang) scemenza

appliance [ə'plaɪ·əns] *s* apparecchio, apparato; (*complicated instrument*) congegno; (*for domestic chores*) utensile *m;* (*act of applying*) applicazione

applicant ['æplɪkənt] *s* postulante *mf*, aspirante *m*, candidato

application [‚æplɪ'keʃən] *s* applicazione; uso; richiesta, domanda

ap·ply [ə'plaɪ] *v* (*pret & pp* **-plied**) *tr* applicare; (*the brakes*) mettere; (*e.g.*, *a nickname*) affibbiare || *intr* (*said of a rule*) essere applicabile; fare richiesta; **to apply for** sollecitare

appoint [ə'pɔɪnt] *tr* nominare; assegnare; (*to furnish*) ammobiliare

appointee [‚æpɔɪn'ti] *s* persona nominata a una carica

appointive [ə'pɔɪntɪv] *adj* a nomina

appointment [ə'pɔɪntmənt] *s* nomina; (*position*) ufficio; (*agreement to meet*) appuntamento; **appointments** mobilia, arredamento; **by appointment** previo appuntamento

apportion [ə'pɔrʃən] *tr* spartire, dividere proporzionatamente

appraisal [ə'prezəl] *s* stima, valutazione; (*of real estate*) estimo

appraise [ə'prez] *tr* stimare, valutare

appreciable [ə'priʃɪ·əbəl] *adj* apprezzabile, notevole

appreciate [ə'priʃɪ‚et] *tr* apprezzare, valutare; (*to be grateful for*) gradire; (*to be aware of*) rendersi conto di; (*to raise in value*) valorizzare || *intr* aumentare di valore

appreciation [ə‚priʃɪ'eʃən] *s* apprezzamento, valutazione; (*grateful recognition*) gradimento, riconoscenza; valorizzazione

appreciative [ə'priʃɪ‚etɪv] *adj* grato, riconoscente

apprehend [‚æprɪ'hɛnd] *tr* (*to fear*) temere; (*to understand*) comprendere; (*to arrest*) arrestare

apprehension [‚æprɪ'hɛnʃən] *s* timore *m*, apprensione; comprensione; arresto

apprehensive [‚æprɪ'hɛnsɪv] *adj* apprensivo

apprentice [ə'prɛntɪs] *s* apprendista *mf*, novizio || *tr* mettere in apprendistato; accettare in apprendistato

apprenticeship [ə'prɛntɪs‚ʃɪp] *s* apprendistato, carovana

apprise or **apprize** [ə'praɪz] *tr* avvertire, avvisare; stimare, valutare

approach [ə'protʃ] *s* (*a coming near*) avvicinamento; (*of night*) avvicinarsi *m*, far *m;* approssimazione; (*access*) via d'accesso; (*to a problem*) impostazione; **approaches** approcci *mpl* || *tr* avvicinarsi a, avvicinare; fare approcci con || *intr* avvicinarsi, approssimarsi

approbation [‚æprə'beʃən] *s* approvazione

appropriate [ə'proprɪ·ɪt] *adj* appropriato, acconcio || [ə'proprɪ‚et] *tr* (*to take*) appropriarsi di; (*to set aside for some specific use*) stanziare

approval [ə'pruvəl] *s* approvazione; consenso; **on approval** in prova

approve [ə'pruv] *tr & intr* approvare

approximate [ə'praksɪmɪt] *adj* approssimato, approssimativo || [ə'praksɪ‚met] *tr* approssimarsi a || *intr* approssimarsi

apricot ['epri‚kat] or ['æpri‚kat] *adj* color albicocca || *s* (*fruit*) albicocca; (*tree*) albicocco

April ['eprɪl] *s* aprile *m*

A′pril fool′ *s* pesce *m* d'aprile

A′pril Fools′′ Day′ *s* primo d'aprile

apron ['eprən] *s* grembiale *m*, grembiule *m;* **tied to the apron strings of** attaccato alle sottane di

apropos [‚æprə'po] *adj* opportuno || *adv*—**apropos of** a proposito di

apse [æps] *s* abside *f*

apt [æpt] *adj* atto, appropriato; (*quick*) pronto; **to be apt to** essere propenso a, portato a

aptitude ['æptɪ‚tjud] or ['æptɪ‚tud] *s* attitudine *f*

ap′titude test′ *s* esame *m* attitudinale

Apulia [ə'pjulɪ·ə] *s* la Puglia

aqualung ['ækwə‚lʌŋ] *s* autorespiratore *m*

aquamarine [‚ækwəmə'rin] *s* acquamarina

aquaplane ['ækwə‚plen] *s* acquaplano || *intr* andare in acquaplano

aquari·um [ə'kwɛrɪ·əm] *s* (**-ums** or **-a** [ə]) acquario, vasca dei pesci

Aquarius [ə'kwɛrɪ·əs] *s* (astr) Acquario

aquatic [ə'kwætɪk] or [ə'kwatɪk] *adj* acquatico || *s* animale acquatico; pianta acquatica; **aquatics** sport acquatici

aqueduct ['ækwə‚dʌkt] *s* acquedotto

aqueous ['ekwɪ·əs] or ['ækwɪ·əs] *adj* acquoso

aq′uiline nose′ ['ækwɪ‚laɪn] *s* naso aquilino

Arab ['ærəb] *adj & s* arabo

Arabic ['ærəbɪk] *adj & s* arabo

arbiter ['ɑrbɪtər] s arbitro
arbitrary [ˈɑrbɪ ˌtreri] adj arbitrario
arbitrate ['ɑrbɪ ˌtret] tr arbitrare || intr fare l'arbitro
arbitration [ˌɑrbɪ'treʃən] s arbitrato
arbitrator ['ɑrbɪ ˌtretər] s arbitro
arbor ['ɑrbər] s pergola, pergolato; (mach) albero, asse m
arbore·tum [ˌɑrbə'ritəm] s (-tums or -ta [tə]) arboreto
arbutus [ɑr'bjutəs] s (Arbutus unedc) corbezzolo
arc [ɑrk] s arco; (elec) arco voltaico || intr (elec) formare un arco
arcade [ɑr'ked] s arcata, portico
arch [ɑrtʃ] adj malizioso || s arco; (anat) arco del piede || tr attraversare; arcuare || intr inarcarsi
archaeology [ˌɑrkɪ'ɑlədʒi] s archeologia
archaic [ɑr'ke·ɪk] adj arcaico
archaism ['ɑrke ˌɪzəm] or ['ɑrki ˌɪzəm] s arcaismo
archangel ['ɑrk ˌendʒəl] s arcangelo
archbishop ['ɑrtʃ'bɪʃəp] s arcivescovo
archduke ['ɑrtʃ'djuk] or ['ɑrtʃ'duk] s arciduca m
archene·my ['ɑrtʃ'ɛnɪmi] s (-mies) nemico giurato
archer ['ɑrtʃər] s arciere m
archery ['ɑrtʃəri] s tiro con l'arco
archetype ['ɑrkɪ ˌtaɪp] s archetipo, prototipo
archipela·go [ˌɑrkɪ'pɛləgo] s (-gos or -goes) arcipelago
architect ['ɑrkɪ ˌtɛkt] s architetto
architectural [ˌɑrkɪ'tɛkt/ərəl] adj architetturale, architettonico
architecture ['ɑrkɪ ˌtɛkt/ər] s architettura
archives ['ɑrkaɪvz] spl archivio
arch'way' s arcata
arc' lamp' s lampada ad arco
arctic ['ɑrktɪk] adj artico || the Arctic la regione artica
arc' weld'ing s saldatura ad arco
ardent ['ɑrdənt] adj ardente
ardor ['ɑrdər] s ardore m
arduous ['ɑrdʒʊ·əs] or ['ɑrdju·əs] adj arduo
area ['ɛrɪ·ə] s area
ar'ea code' s prefisso
Argentina [ˌɑrdʒən'tinə] s l'Argentina
Argentine ['ɑrdʒən ˌtin] or ['ɑrdʒən ˌtaɪn] adj & s argentino || the Argentine l'Argentina
Argonaut ['ɑrgə ˌnɔt] s argonauta m
argue ['ɑrgju] tr dibattere; (to indicate) indicare, provare; to argue out of dissuadere da; to argue s.o. into s.th persuadere qlcu di qlco || intr argomentare, discutere
argument ['ɑrgjəmənt] s discussione, argomentazione; (theme) argomento
argumentative [ˌɑrgjə'mɛntətɪv] adj litigioso
aria ['ɑrɪ·ə] or ['ɛrɪ·ə] s aria
arid ['ærɪd] adj arido
aridity [ə'rɪdɪti] s aridità f
Aries ['ɛriz] or ['ɛri ˌiz] s (astr) Ariete m

aright [ə'raɪt] adv correttamente; to set aright rettificare
arise [ə'raɪz] v (pret arose [ə'roz]; pp arisen [ə'rɪzən]) intr alzarsi; (to originate) provenire, trarre origine; (to occur) succedere, avvenire; (to be raised, as objections) avanzarsi
aristocra·cy [ˌærɪs'tɑkrəsi] s (-cies) aristocrazia
aristocrat [ə'rɪstə ˌkræt] s aristocratico
aristocratic [ə ˌrɪstə'krætɪk] adj aristocratico
Aristotelian [ˌærɪstə'tilɪ·ən] adj & s aristotelico
Aristotle ['ærɪ ˌstatəl] s Aristotele m
arithmetic [ə'rɪθmətɪk] s aritmetica
arithmetical [ˌærɪθ'mɛtɪkəl] adj aritmetico
arithmetician [ˌærɪθmə'tɪ/ən] or [ə ˌrɪθmə'tɪ/ən] s aritmetico
ark [ɑrk] s arca
ark' of the cov'enant s arca dell'alleanza
arm [ɑrm] s braccio; (e.g., of a bear) zampa; (of a chair) bracciolo; (weapon) arma; arm in arm a braccetto; to be up in arms essere in armi; essere indignato; to lay down one's arms deporre le armi; to rise up in arms levarsi in armi; with open arms a braccia aperte || tr armare || intr armarsi
armament ['ɑrməmənt] s armamento
armature ['ɑrmə ˌt/ər] s (of an animal) corazza; (of motor or dynamo) indotto; (of a buzzer or electric bell) ancora
arm'chair' s poltrona
Armenian [ɑr'minɪ·ən] adj & s armeno
armful ['ɑrm ˌfʊl] s bracciata
arm'hole' s giro manica
armistice ['ɑrmɪstɪs] s armistizio
armlet ['ɑrmlɪt] s bracciale m
armor ['ɑrmər] s armatura, corazza || tr corazzare, blindare
ar'mored car' s carro armato
ar'mor plate' s lamiera di corazza
armor·y ['ɑrməri] s (-ies) armeria; arsenale m
arm'pit' s ascella
arm'rest' s bracciolo
ar·my ['ɑrmi] adj dell'esercito, militare || s (-mies) esercito; (two or more army corps) armata
ar'my corps' s corpo d'armata
aromatic [ˌærə'mætɪk] adj aromatico
around [ə'raʊnd] adv intorno; all'intorno; dappertutto; to turn around voltarsi || prep intorno a; (coll) vicino a; (approximately) (coll) circa
arouse [ə'raʊz] tr eccitare, incitare; svegliare
arpeg·gio [ɑr'pɛdʒo] s (-gios) arpeggio
arraign [ə'ren] tr citare, portare in giudizio; accusare
arrange [ə'rendʒ] tr disporre, sistemare; (a dispute) comporre, accomodare; (mus) ridurre, arrangiare
arrangement [ə'rendʒmənt] s disposizione, sistemazione; composizione; accomodamento; (mus) riduzione,

arrangiamento; **arrangements** preparazione, preparativi *mpl*

array [ə're] *s* ordine *m; (clothes)* abbigliamento; (mil) spiegamento, schiera || *tr* disporre; abbigliare, adornare; (mil) spiegare, schierare

arrears [ə'rırz] *spl* arretrati *mpl;* **in arrears** in arretrato

arrest [ə'rest] *s* arresto; **under arrest** in arresto || *tr* arrestare; *(the attention)* attrarre

arresting [ə'rɛstɪŋ] *adj* interessante, che fa colpo

arrival [ə'raɪvəl] *s* arrivo; persona arrivata

arrive [ə'raɪv] *intr* arrivare

arrogance ['ærəgəns] *s* arroganza

arrogant ['ærəgənt] *adj* arrogante

arrogate ['ærə,get] *tr (to take without right)* arrogare per sé, arrogarsi; *(to claim for another)* attribuire ingiustamente

arrow ['æro] *s* freccia, saetta

ar'row•head' *s* punta di freccia; (bot) sagittaria

arsenal ['ɑrsənəl] *s* arsenale *m*

arsenic ['ɑrsɪnɪk] *s* arsenico

arson ['ɑrsən] *s* incendio doloso

art [ɑrt] *s* arte *f*

arter•y ['ɑrtəri] *s* (-ies) arteria

artful ['ɑrtfəl] *adj* artificioso; *(clever)* destro; *(crafty)* astuto

arthritic [ɑr'θrɪtɪk] *adj & s* artritico

arthritis [ɑr'θraɪtɪs] *s* artrite *f*

artichoke ['ɑrtɪ,tʃok] *s* carciofo

article ['ɑrtɪkəl] *s* articolo

articulate [ɑr'tɪkjəlɪt] *adj* articolato; facile di parola || ['ɑrtɪkjə,let] *tr* articolare || *intr* pronunziare in modo articolato

articulation [ɑr,tɪkjə'leʃən] *s* articolazione

artifact ['ɑrtɪ,fækt] *s* manufatto

artifice ['ɑrtɪfɪs] *s* artificio

artificial [,ɑrtɪ'fɪʃəl] *adj* artificiale

artillery [ɑr'tɪləri] *s* artiglieria

artil'lery•man *s* (-men) artigliere *m*, cannoniere *m*

artisan ['ɑrtɪzən] *s* artigiano

artist ['ɑrtɪst] *s* artista *mf*

artistic [ɑr'tɪstɪk] *adj* artistico

artistry ['ɑrtɪstri] *s* abilità artistica

artless ['ɑrtlɪs] *adj* ingenuo, naturale; ignorante; *(clumsy)* grossolano

arts' and crafts' *spl* arti *fpl* e mestieri *mpl*

art•y ['ɑrti] *adj* (-ier; -iest) (coll) interessato nell'arte con ostentazione

Aryan ['ɛrɪ•ən] *or* ['ɑrjən] *adj & s* ariano

as [æz] *or* [əz] *pron rel* che; **the same as** lo stesso che || *adv* come; per esempio; **as . . . as** così . . . come; **as far as** fino a; **as far as I know** per quanto mi consta; **as for** in quanto a, per quanto concerne; **as is** (slang) com'è, nelle condizioni in cui si trova; **as long as** tanto che, mentre che; **as per** secondo; **as soon as** appena, non appena, non appena che; **as to** per quanto concerne; **as well** pure, anche; **as yet** ancora || *prep* come; da; **as a rule** come regola ||

conj come; mentre; dato che; per quanto; **as if** come se; **as it were** per così dire; **as though** come se

asbestos [æs'bɛstəs] *s* asbesto, amianto

ascend [ə'sɛnd] *tr* ascendere, scalare || *intr* ascendere, salire

ascension [ə'sɛnʃən] *s* ascensione, scalata || **Ascension** *s* Ascensione

ascent [ə'sɛnt] *s* scalata; salita; *(slope)* erta

ascertain [,æsər'ten] *tr* sincerarsi di, verificare

ascertainable [,æsər'tenəbəl] *adj* verificabile

ascetic [ə'sɛtɪk] *adj* ascetico || *s* asceta *m*

ascor'bic ac'id [ə'skɔrbɪk] *s* acido ascorbico

ascribe [ə'skraɪb] *tr* attribuire, imputare

aseptic [ə'sɛptɪk] *or* [e'sɛptɪk] *adj* asettico

ash [æʃ] *s* cenere *f;* (bot) frassino

ashamed [ə'ʃemd] *adj* vergognoso; **to be** *or* **feel ashamed** vergognarsi

ash'can' *s* pattumiera; (coll) bomba antisommergibile

ashen ['æʃən] *adj* cinereo

ashlar ['æʃlər] *s* bugna, bugnato

ashore [ə'ʃor] *adv* a terra; **to come ashore** andare a terra, sbarcare; **to run ashore** arenarsi

ash'tray' *s* portacenere *m*

Ash' Wednes'day *s* le Ceneri

Asia ['eʒə] *or* ['eʃə] *s* l'Asia *f*

A'sia Mi'nor *s* l'Asia *f* Minore

Asian ['eʒən] *or* ['eʃən] *or* **Asiatic** [,eʒɪ'ætɪk] *or* [,eʃɪ'ætɪk] *adj & s* asiatico

aside [ə'saɪd] *s* parola detta a parte; (theat) a parte *m* || *adv* da parte; a parte; **aside from** (coll) eccetto; separato da; **to step aside** farsi da un lato

asinine ['æsɪnaɪn] *adj (like an ass)* asinino; *(stupid)* asinesco

ask [æsk] *or* [ɑsk] *tr* chiedere (with *dat*), domandare (with *dat*); invitare; *(a question)* fare; **to ask s.o. for s.th** chiedere *or* domandare qlco a qlcu; **to ask s.o. to**+*inf* chiedere a qlcu di+*inf* || *intr* chiedere; **to ask about** chiedere informazioni di; **to ask for** chiedere, domandare; **to ask for it** (coll) andare in cerca di disgrazie; (coll) volerlo, e.g., **he asked for it** l'ha voluto

askance [ə'skæns] *adv* di traverso, di sbieco; (fig) con sospetto

asleep [ə'slip] *adj* addormentato; **to fall asleep** addormentarsi

asp [æsp] *s* aspide *m*

asparagus [ə'spærəgəs] *s* asparago; *(as food)* asparagi *mpl*

aspect ['æspɛkt] *s* aspetto; *(direction anything faces)* esposizione

aspen ['æspən] *s* pioppo tremolo, tremolo

aspersion [ə'spʌrʒən] *or* [ə'spʌrʃən] *s* diffamazione, calunnia; (eccl) aspersione

asphalt ['æsfɔlt] *or* ['æsfælt] *s* asfalto || *tr* asfaltare

asphyxiate [æsˈfɪksɪ ˌet] *tr* asfissiare
aspirant [əˈspaɪrənt] or [ˈæspɪrənt] *s* aspirante *mf*
aspire [əˈspaɪr] *intr* aspirare
aspirin [ˈæspɪrɪn] *s* aspirina
ass [æs] *s* asino
assail [əˈsel] *tr* assalire, assaltare
assassin [əˈsæsɪn] *s* assassino
assassinate [əˈsæsɪ ˌnet] *tr* assassinare
assassination [ə ˌsæsɪˈneʃən] *s* assassinio
assault [əˈsɔlt] *s* assalto || *tr* assaltare
assault' and bat'tery *s* vie *fpl* di fatto
assay [əˈse] or [ˈæse] *s* saggio, esame *m* || [əˈse] *tr* saggiare
assemblage [əˈsɛmblɪdʒ] *s* assemblea; (mach) montaggio
assemble [əˈsɛmbəl] *tr* riunire; (mach) montare, mettere insieme || *intr* assembrarsi, riunirsi
assembler [əˈsɛmblər] *s* montatore *m*
assem·bly [əˈsɛmblɪ] *s* (-blies) assemblea, riunione; (mach) montaggio
assem'bly hall' *s* sala di riunioni
assem'bly line' *s* catena di montaggio
assem'bly·man *s* (-men) membro dell'assemblea legislativa
assent [əˈsɛnt] *s* assenso || *intr* assentire
assert [əˈsʌrt] *tr* asserire; **to assert oneself** far valere i propri diritti
assertion [əˈsʌrʃən] *s* asserzione
assess [əˈsɛs] *tr* stimare, valutare; (*for taxation or fine*) tassare
assessment [əˈsɛsmənt] *s* valutazione; tassazione
assessor [əˈsɛsər] *s* agente *m* delle tasse
asset [ˈæsət] *s* vantaggio; persona di valore; **assets** (com) attivo; (law) beni *mpl*
assiduous [əˈsɪdʒʊ·əs] or [əˈsɪdjʊ·əs] *adj* assiduo
assign [əˈsaɪn] *s* cessionario || *tr* assegnare; (*e.g., a date*) fissare; (*a right*) trasferire
assignation [ˌæsɪgˈneʃən] *s* assegnazione; trasferimento; (*date*) appuntamento amoroso
assignment [əˈsaɪnmənt] *s* assegnamento; (*of rights*) trasferimento; (*schoolwork*) compito
assimilate [əˈsɪmɪ ˌlet] *tr* assimilare || *intr* essere assimilato; assimilarsi
assist [əˈsɪst] *s* aiuto || *tr* aiutare, assistere
assistance [əˈsɪstəns] *s* assistenza, aiuto
assistant [əˈsɪstənt] *adj & s* assistente *m*
associate [əˈsoʃɪ·ɪt] or [əˈsoʃɪ ˌet] *adj* associato || *s* associato; membro limitato || [əˈsoʃɪ ˌet] *tr* associare || *intr* associarsi
association [ə ˌsoʃɪˈeʃən] *s* associazione
assort [əˈsɔrt] *tr* assortire || *intr* associarsi
assortment [əˈsɔrtmənt] *s* assortimento
assuage [əˈswedʒ] *tr* alleviare
assume [əˈsum] or [əˈsjum] *tr* assumere; (*to appropriate*) usurpare; (*to pretend*) fingere; (*to suppose*) supporre
assumed [əˈsumd] or [əˈsjumd] *adj* supposto, immaginario

assumption [əˈsʌmpʃən] *s* (*arrogance*) aria, arroganza; (*thing taken for granted*) supposizione; (*of an undertaking*) assunzione
assurance [əˈʃʊrəns] *s* assicurazione, certezza; baldanza, fiducia in sè; (*too much boldness*) sicumera
assure [əˈʃʊr] *tr* assicurare
assuredly [əˈʃʊrɪdli] *adv* sicuramente
astatine [ˈæstə ˌtin] *s* astato
asterisk [ˈæstə ˌrɪsk] *s* asterisco, stelloncino
astern [əˈstʌrn] *adv* a poppa, a poppavia
asthma [ˈæzmə] or [ˈæsmə] *s* asma
astonish [əˈstɑnɪʃ] *tr* meravigliare, stupefare
astonishing [əˈstɑnɪʃɪŋ] *adj* stupefacente, sorprendente
astound [əˈstaʊnd] *tr* stupefare, sbalordire
astounding [əˈstaʊndɪŋ] *adj* stupefacente
astraddle [əˈstrædəl] *adv* a cavaliere, a cavalcioni
astray [əˈstre] *adv* sulla cattiva via; **to go astray** traviarsi; **to lead astray** traviare
astride [əˈstraɪd] *adj & adv* a cavaliere; (*said of a person*) a cavalcioni || *prep* a cavaliere di; a cavalcioni di
astrology [əˈstrɑlədʒɪ] *s* astrologia
astronaut [ˈæstrə ˌnɔt] *s* astronauta *mf*
astronautic [ˌæstrəˈnɔtɪk] *adj* astronautico || **astronautics** *ssg* astronautica
astronomer [əˈstrɑnəmər] *s* astronomo
astronomic(al) [ˌæstrəˈnɑmɪk(əl)] *adj* astronomico
astronomy [əˈstrɑnəmɪ] *s* astronomia
astute [əˈstjut] or [əˈstut] *adj* astuto
asunder [əˈsʌndər] *adv* a pezzi; **to tear asunder** separare, fare a pezzi
asylum [əˈsaɪləm] *s* asilo
asymmetry [əˈsɪmɪtri] *s* asimmetria
at [æt] or [ət] *prep* a; in; a casa di, e.g., **at John's** a casa di Giovanni; da, e.g., **at Mary's** da Maria; di, e.g., **to be surprised at** essere sorpreso di; **to laugh at** ridersi di
atheist [ˈeθɪ·ɪst] *s* ateista *mf*
Athenian [əˈθinɪ·ən] *adj & s* ateniese *mf*
Athens [ˈæθɪnz] *s* Atene *f*
athirst [əˈθʌrst] *adj* assetato
athlete [ˈæθlit] *s* atleta *mf*
athletic [æθˈlɛtɪk] *adj* atletico || **athletics** *ssg & spl* atletica
Atlantic [ætˈlæntɪk] *adj* atlantico || *adj & s* Atlantico
atlas [ˈætləs] *s* atlante *m* || **Atlas** *s* Atlante *m*
atmosphere [ˈætməs ˌfɪr] *s* atmosfera
atmospheric [ˌætməsˈfɛrɪk] *adj* atmosferico || **atmospherics** *spl* disturbi atmosferici
atom [ˈætəm] *s* atomo
at'om bomb' *s* bomba atomica
atomic [əˈtɑmɪk] *adj* atomico
atom'ic age' *s* era atomica
atom'ic sub'marine *s* sommergibile *m* nucleare
atomize [ˈætə ˌmaɪz] *tr* atomizzare

atomizer ['ætə ,maɪzər] s nebulizzatore *m*

at'om smash'er s acceleratore *m* di particelle

atone [ə'ton] *intr*—**to atone for** espiare

atonement [ə'tonmənt] s riparazione; espiazione

atop [ə'tɑp] *adv* in cima ‖ *prep* in cima a

atrocious [ə'troʃəs] *adj* atroce

atroci·ty [ə'trɑsɪti] s (**-ties**) atrocità *f*

atro·phy ['ætrəfi] s atrofia ‖ *v* (*pret & pp* **-phied**) *tr* atrofizzare ‖ *intr* atrofizzarsi

attach [ə'tætʃ] *tr* attaccare; (*to affix*) apporre; (*to attribute*) attribuire; (law) sequestrare; **to be attached to** essere legato a; fare parte di ‖ *intr*— **to attach to** essere pertinente a

attaché [,ætə'ʃe] or [ə'tæʃe] s attaché *m.*, addetto

attaché' case' s valigetta diplomatica

attachment [ə'tætʃmənt] s attacco, unione; affezione; (mach) accessorio; (law) sequestro

attack [ə'tæk] s attacco ‖ *tr & intr* attaccare

attain [ə'ten] *tr* raggiungere ‖ *intr*—**to attain to** raggiungere, conseguire

attainder [ə'tendər] s morte *f* civile

attainment [ə'tenmənt] s raggiungimento, realizzazione; (*accomplishment*) dote *f*

attempt [ə'tempt] s tentativo; (*attack*) attentato ‖ *tr* tentare; (*s.o.'s life*) attentare a

attend [ə'tɛnd] *tr* (*to be present at*) presenziare, presenziare a, assistere a; (*to accompany*) accompagnare; (*to take care of; to pay attention to*) assistere ‖ *intr*—**to attend to** occuparsi di, attendere a

attendance [ə'tɛndəns] s (*attending*) presenza; (*company present*) concorso; **to dance attendance** essere al servizio completo

attendant [ə'tɛndənt] *adj* assistente; (*accompanying*) concomitante ‖ s (*servant*) inserviente *mf*; presente *m*

attention [ə'tɛnʃən] s attenzione; (mil) attenti *m*; **attentions** attenzioni *fpl*; **to call s.o.'s attention to s.th** fare presente qlco a qlcu; **to stand at attention** stare sull'attenti ‖ *interj* attenti!

attentive [ə'tɛntɪv] *adj* attento, premuroso

attenuate [ə'tɛnju ,et] *tr* attenuare

attest [ə'tɛst] *tr* attestare ‖ *intr*—**to attest to** attestare, testimoniare

attic ['ætɪk] s attico, solaio ‖ **Attic** *adj & s* attico

attire [ə'taɪr] s vestiti *mpl*, vestiario ‖ *tr* vestire

attitude ['ætɪ ,tjud] or ['ætɪ ,tud] s atteggiamento, attitudine *f*; **to strike an attitude** atteggiarsi

attorney [ə'tʌrni] s avvocato; (*proxy*) procuratore *m*

attor'ney gen'eral s (**attor'neys gen'eral** or **attor'ney gen'erals**) procuratore

m generale ‖ **Attorney General** s (U.S.A.) ministro di grazia e giustizia

attract [ə'trækt] *tr* attrarre; (*attention*) chiamare

attraction [ə'trækʃən] s attrazione

attractive [ə'træktɪv] *adj* attrattivo

attribute ['ætrɪ ,bjut] s attributo ‖ [ə'trɪbjut] *tr* attribuire

attrition [ə'trɪʃən] s attrito; diminuzione di numero

auburn ['ɔbərn] *adj & s* biondo fulvo, rosso tizianesco

auction ['ɔkʃən] s asta, incanto ‖ *tr* vendere all'asta

auctioneer [,ɔkʃə'nɪr] s banditore *m* ‖ *tr & intr* vendere all'asta

audacious [ɔ'deʃəs] *adj* audace

audaci·ty [ɔ'dæsɪti] s (**-ties**) audacia

audience ['ɔdɪ-əns] s (*hearing*) udienza; uditorio, pubblico

au'dio fre'quency ['ɔdɪ ,o] s audiofrequenza

au'dio-vis'ual aids' *spl* sussidi audiovisivi

audit ['ɔdɪt] s verifica or esame *m* dei conti ‖ *tr* esaminare i conti di; (*a class*) assistere a, come uditore ‖ *intr* assistere a una classe come uditore

audition [ɔ'dɪʃən] s audizione ‖ *tr* dare un'audizione a

auditor ['ɔdɪtər] s revisore *m* dei conti; (educ) uditore *m*

auditorium [,ɔdɪ'tɔrɪ-əm] s auditorio

auger ['ɔgər] s succhiello, trivella

aught [ɔt] s zero; **for aught I know** per quanto ne so ‖ *adv* affatto

augment [ɔg'mɛnt] *tr & intr* aumentare

augur ['ɔgər] s augure *m* ‖ *tr & intr* vaticinare

augu·ry ['ɔgəri] s (**-ries**) augurio

august [ɔ'gʌst] *adj* augusto ‖ **August** ['ɔgəst] s agosto

aunt [ænt] or [ɑnt] s zia

aurora [ə'rorə] s aurora

auspice ['ɔspɪs] s auspicio; **under the auspices of** sotto gli auspici di

austere [ɔs'tɪr] *adj* austero

Australia [ɔ'streljə] s l'Australia *f*

Australian [ɔ'streljən] *adj & s* australiano

Austria ['ɔstrɪ-ə] s l'Austria *f*

Austrian ['ɔstrɪ-ən] *adj & s* austriaco

authentic [ɔ'θɛntɪk] *adj* autentico

authenticate [ɔ'θɛntɪ ,ket] *tr* autenticare

author ['ɔθər] s autore *m*

authoress ['ɔθərɪs] s autrice *f*

authoritarian [ɔ ,θɑrɪ'tɛrɪ-ən] or [ɔ- ,θɔrɪ'tɛrɪ-ən] *adj* autoritario ‖ s persona autoritaria

authoritative [ɔ'θɑrɪ ,tetɪv] or [ɔ'θɔrɪ- ,tetɪv] *adj* autorevole; autoritario

authori·ty [ɔ'θɑrɪti] or [ɔ'θɔrɪti] s (**-ties**) autorità *f*; **on good authority** da buona fonte, da fonte autorevole

authorize ['ɔθə ,raɪz] *tr* autorizzare

authorship ['ɔθər ,ʃɪp] s paternità letteraria

au·to ['ɔto] s (**-tos**) (coll) auto *f*

autobiogra·phy [,ɔtobaɪ'ɑgrəfi] or [,ɔtobɪ'ɑgrəfi] s (**-phies**) autobiografia

autobus ['ɔto ,bʌs] s autobus m
autocratic(al) [,ɔtə'krætɪk(əl)] adj autocratico
autograph ['ɔtə ,græf] or ['ɔtə ,graf] adj & s autografo ‖ tr porre l'autografo su, firmare con firma autografa
automat ['ɔtə ,mæt] s ristorante m self-service a distribuzione automatica
automate ['ɔtə ,met] tr automatizzare
automatic [,ɔtə'mætɪk] adj automatico ‖ s pistola automatica
automat'ic transmis'sion s trasmissione automatica
automation [,ɔtə'meʃən] s automazione
automa·ton [ɔ'tɑmə ,tɑn] s (**-tons** or **-ta** [tə]) automa m
automobile [,ɔtəmo'bil] or [,ɔtə'mobil] adj & s automobile f
automobile' show' s salone m dell'automobile
automotive [,ɔtə'motɪv] adj (self-propelled) automotore; automobilistico
autonomous [ɔ'tɑnəməs] adj autonomo
autonomy [ɔ'tɑnəmi] s autonomia
autop·sy ['ɔtɑpsi] s (**-sies**) autopsia
au'to trans'port rig' s autotreno per trasporto di automobili
autumn ['ɔtəm] s autunno
autumnal [ɔ'tʌmnəl] adj autunnale
auxilia·ry [ɔg'zɪljəri] adj & s (**-ries**) ausiliare m
avail [ə'vel] s utilità f; **of no avail** che non serve a nulla ‖ tr servire (with dat); **to avail oneself of** servirsi di; approfittare di ‖ intr servire
available [ə'veləbəl] adj disponibile; **to make available to** mettere alla disposizione di
avalanche ['ævə ,læntʃ] or ['ævə ,lantʃ] s valanga
avant-garde [əvɑ̃'gard] adj d'avanguardia
avant-gardism [ə'vɑ̃'gardɪzəm] s avanguardismo
avarice ['ævərɪs] s avarizia
avaricious [,ævə'rɪʃəs] adj avaro
avenge [ə'vendʒ] tr vendicare; **to avenge oneself on** vendicarsi di
avenue ['ævə ,nju] or ['ævənu] s viale m, corso
aver [ə'vʌr] v (pret & pp **averred**; ger **averring**) tr asserire, affermare
average ['ævərɪdʒ] adj medio ‖ s media; (naut) avaria; (e.g., of goals) (sports) quoziente m; **on the average** di media ‖ tr fare la media di; fare . . . di media, e.g., **he averages one hundred dollars a week** fa cento dollari di media alla settimana
averse [ə'vʌrs] adj avverso
aversion [ə'vʌrʒən] s avversione
avert [ə'vʌrt] tr (to ward off) evitare; (to turn away) distogliere
aviar·y ['əvɪ ,ɛri] s (**-ies**) aviario, voliera
aviation [,evɪ'eʃən] s aviazione
aviator ['evɪ ,etər] s aviatore m
avid ['ævɪd] adj avido
avidity [ə'vɪdɪti] s avidità f

avocation [,ævə'keʃən] s svago, passatempo
avoid [ə'vɔɪd] tr evitare
avoidable [ə'vɔɪdəbəl] adj evitabile
avow [ə'vaʊ] tr confessare, ammettere
avowal [ə'vaʊ·əl] s confessione, ammissione
await [ə'wet] tr aspettare, attendere
awake [ə'wek] adj sveglio ‖ v (pret & pp **awoke** [ə'wok] or **awaked**) tr svegliare ‖ intr svegliarsi
awaken [ə'wekən] tr svegliare ‖ intr svegliarsi
awakening [ə'wekənɪŋ] s risveglio
award [ə'wɔrd] s (prize) premio; (decision by judge) sentenza ‖ tr aggiudicare
aware [ə'wɛr] adj conscio, consapevole; **to become aware of** rendersi conto di
awareness [ə'wɛrnɪs] s coscienza
awash [ə'waʃ] or [ə'wɔʃ] adj & adv a fior d'acqua
away [ə'we] adj distante, assente ‖ adv lontano; via; continuamente; **away back** (coll) molto tempo fa; **away from** lontano da; **to do away with** disfarsi di, sopprimere; **to get away** scappare, sfuggire; **to go away** andarsene; **to run away** fuggire; **to send away** mandar via; **to take away** portar via
awe [ɔ] s estremo rispetto; sacro timore ‖ tr infondere rispetto a; infondere un sacro timore a
aweigh [ə'we] adj (anchor) levato
awesome ['ɔsəm] adj grandioso, imponente
awestruck ['ɔ ,strʌk] adj pieno di sacro timore
awful ['ɔfəl] adj terribile; imponente ‖ adv (coll) terribilmente
awfully ['ɔfəli] adv tremendamente, terribilmente; (coll) molto
awhile [ə'hwaɪl] adv un po', un po' di tempo
awkward ['ɔkwərd] adj (clumsy) goffo, maldestro; (unwieldly) scomodo; (embarrassing) imbarazzante
awl [ɔl] s punteruolo
awning ['ɔnɪŋ] s tenda; (in front of a store) tendone m
A.W.O.L. ['ewɔl] (acronym) or ['e-'dʌbəl ,ju'o'ɛl] (letterword) adj (mil) assente al contrappello
awry [ə'raɪ] adv—**to go awry** andare a capovescio; **to look awry** guardare di sbieco
ax or **axe** [æks] s scure f; **to have an axe to grind** (coll) avere un interesse speciale
axiom ['æksɪ·əm] s assioma m
axiomatic [,æksɪ·ə'mætɪk] adj assiomatico
axis ['æksɪs] s (**axes** ['æksiz]) asse m
axle ['æksəl] s assale m, asse m
ax'le·tree' s assale m
ay [aɪ] s & adv sì m
Azores [ə'zɔrz] or ['ezɔrz] spl Azzorre fpl
azure ['æʒər] or ['eʒər] adj & s azzurro, blu m

B

B, b [bi] s seconda lettera dell'alfabeto inglese

baa [bɑ] s belato ‖ intr belare

babble ['bæbəl] s (murmuring sound) mormorio; (senseless prattle) balbettio ‖ tr (e.g., a secret) divulgare ‖ intr mormorare; balbettare; (to talk idly) parlare a vanvera

babe [beb] s bebè m, bambino; persona inesperta; (slang) ragazza

baboon [bæ'bun] s babbuino

ba·by ['bebi] s (-bies) bebè m, neonato; bambino; (the youngest child) piccolo ‖ v (pret & pp -bied) tr coccolare, ninnare

ba'by car'riage s carrozzella

ba'by grand' s piano a mezza coda

babyhood ['bebi ,hud] s infanzia

babyish ['bebi·ɪʃ] adj infantile

Babylon ['bæbɪlən] or ['bæbɪ ,lɑn] s Babilonia

ba'by sit'ter s bambinaia ad ore

ba'by teeth' spl denti mpl di latte

baccalaureate [,bækə'lɔrɪ·ɪt] s baccalaureato; servizio religioso prima del baccalaureato

bacchanal ['bækənəl] adj bacchico ‖ s baccanale m; (person) ubriacone m, bisboccione m

bachelor ['bætʃələr] s (unmarried man) scapolo, celibe m; (holder of bachelor's degree) diplomato; (apprentice knight) bacceliere m

bachelorhood ['bætʃələr ,hud] s celibato

bacil·lus [bə'sɪləs] s (-li [laɪ]) bacillo

back [bæk] adj di dietro, posteriore; arretrato; contrario ‖ s dorso, schiena; parte f posteriore, didietro; (of a sheet or coin) tergo; (of a knife) costola; (of a room) fondo; (of a book) fine f; (of a chair) schienale m; **behind one's back** dietro le spalle di uno; **to turn one's back on** volgere la schiena a ‖ adv dietro; indietro; **a few weeks back** alcune settimane fa; **as far back as** sino da; **back of** dietro, dietro a; **to go back on one's word** mancare di parola; **to go back to** ritornare a; **to pay back** ripagare; **to send back** restituire ‖ tr appoggiare; far indietreggiare ‖ intr indietreggiare; rinculare; **to back down** rinunciarci; **to back off** or **out** ritirarsi; **to back up** (said of a car) fare marcia indietro

back'ache' s mal m di schiena

back'bite' v (pret -bit; pp -bitten or -bit) tr sparlare di ‖ intr sparlare

back'bit'er s maldicente mf

back'board' s (basketball) tabellone m

back'bone' s spina dorsale; (of a book) costola, dorso; (fig) fermezza

back'break'ing adj sfiancante

back'door' adj segreto, clandestino

back' door' s porta di dietro; (fig) mezzo clandestino

back'drop' s (theat) fondale m

backer ['bækər] s sostenitore m, difensore m; (com) finanziatore m

back'fire' s (for firefighting) controfuoco; (aut) ritorno di fiamma ‖ intr (aut) avere un ritorno di fiamma; (fig) raggiungere l'effetto opposto

back'ground' s fondo, sfondo; precedenti mpl; origine f

back'ground mu'sic s musica di fondo

backhand ['bæk ,hænd] adj obliquo ‖ s scrittura inclinata a sinistra; (tennis) rovescio

back'hand'ed adj obliquo; sarcastico; insincero

backing ['bækɪŋ] s appoggio; sostegno; (bb) dorso

back'ing light' s (aut) faro retromarcia; (theat) luce f per il fondale

back'lash' s reazione; contraccolpo; (mach) gioco

back'log' s ceppo; (fig) riserva

back' num'ber s numero arretrato; (coll) persona all'antica

back' pay' s paga arretrata, arretrati mpl

back' scratch'er s manina per grattare la schiena; (coll) leccapiedi m

back' seat' s (aut) sedile m posteriore; (fig) posizione secondaria

back'side' s dorso; didietro

back'slide' v (pret & pp -slid [,slɪd]) intr ricadere

back'spac'er s tasto ritorno

back'spin' s effetto

back'stage' adj dietro alle quinte ‖ s retroscena m ‖ adv a retroscena, dietro alle quinte

back'stairs' adj indiretto, segreto

back' stairs' spl scala di servizio

back'stitch' s impuntura ‖ tr & intr impunturare

back'stroke' s (swimming) bracciata sul dorso

back'swept wing' s ala a freccia

back' talk' s risposta impertinente

back'track' intr ritornare sulle proprie tracce; (fig) fare macchina indietro

back'up light' s (aut) faro retromarcia

backward ['bækwərd] adj ritroso; poco progredito, retrogrado ‖ adv a ritroso, all'indietro; verso il passato; alla rovescia; **backward and forward** (coll) completamente, perfettamente; **to go backward and forward** andare avanti e indietro

back'wash' s risacca

back'wa'ter s gora, ristagno; (fig) eremo

back'woods' spl zona boscosa lontana dai centri popolati

back'yard' s cortile m posteriore

bacon ['bekən] s pancetta

bacteria [bæk'tɪrɪ·ə] spl batteri mpl

bacterial [bæk'tɪrɪ·əl] adj batterico

bacteriologist [bæk ,tɪrɪ'ɑlədʒɪst] s batteriologo

bacteriology [bæk ,tɪrɪ'ɑlədʒi] s batteriologia

bad [bæd] adj (worse [wʌrs]; worst [wʌrst]) cattivo; (coin) falso; (weather) brutto; (debt) insolvibile; severo ‖ s male m; **from bad to**

worse da male in peggio || *adv* male; **to be too bad** essere peccato; **to feel bad** esser spiacente; sentirsi male; **to look bad** aver brutta cera

bad′ breath′ *s* fiato cattivo

bad′ egg′ *s* (slang) cattivo soggetto

badge [bædʒ] *s* divisa; decorazione; simbolo, placca

badger [ˈbædʒər] *s* tasso || *tr* molestare

badly [ˈbædli] *adv* male; gravemente; molto

bad′ly off′ *adj* in cattive condizioni

badminton [ˈbædmɪntən] *s* badminton *m*

baffle [ˈbæfəl] *s* (mach) deflettore *m*; (rad) schermo acustico || *tr* frustrare, confondere

baffling [ˈbæflɪŋ] *adj* sconcertante

bag [bæg] *s* sacco; borsetta; (*of a marsupial*) borsa; (hunt) presa; **bag and baggage** con armi e bagagli; **to be in the bag** (slang) averlo nel sacco; **to be left holding the bag** (coll) essere piantato in asso || *v* (*pret* & *pp* **bagged**; *ger* **bagging**) *tr* insaccare; (hunt) pigliare || *intr* (*to hang loosely*) far pieghe

baggage [ˈbægɪdʒ] *s* bagaglio

bag′gage car′ *s* bagagliaio

bag′gage check′ *s* scontrino del bagaglio

bag′gage room′ *s* deposito bagagli

bag·gy [ˈbægi] *adj* (**-gier**; **-giest**) come un sacco

bag′pipe′ *s* cornamusa, zampogna

bag′pip′er *s* zampognaro

bail [bel] *s* cauzione; libertà provvisoria sotto cauzione; (*bucket*) sassola || *tr* liberare sotto cauzione; **to bail out** (*a boat*) sgottare || *intr*—**to bail out** (aer) gettarsi col paracadute

bailiwick [ˈbeliwɪk] *s* (fig) sfera di competenza

bait [bet] *s* esca; (fig) allettamento || *tr* adescare; (fig) allettare

baize [bez] *s* panno verde

bake [bek] *tr* cuocere al forno || *intr* cuocersi al forno; abbrustolirsi

bakelite [ˈbekəˌlaɪt] *s* bachelite *f*

baker [ˈbekər] *s* fornaio, panettiere *m*

bak′er's doz′en *s* tredici per ogni dozzina

baker·y [ˈbekəri] *s* (**-ies**) panetteria

bak′ing pan′ [ˈbekɪŋ] *s* tortiera

bak′ing pow′der *s* lievito in polvere

bak′ing so′da *s* bicarbonato di soda

balance [ˈbæləns] *s* (*scales*) bilancia; equilibrio; armonia; (*of watch*) bilanciere *m*; (*remainder; amount due*) resto; (*of budget*) pareggio; **in the balance** in bilico; **to lose one's balance** perdere l'equilibrio; **to strike a balance** fare il bilancio || *tr* bilanciare, pesare; (com) bilanciare, pareggiare || *intr* bilanciarsi

bal′ance of pay′ments *s* bilancia dei pagamenti

bal′ance of pow′er *s* equilibrio politico

bal′ance of trade′ *s* bilancia commerciale

bal′ance sheet′ *s* bilancio

balco·ny [ˈbælkəni] *s* (**-nies**) balcone *m*; (theat) galleria

bald [bɔld] *adj* calvo; (*bare*) nudo; (*unadorned*) semplice

bald′ ea′gle *s* aquila col capo bianco dell'America del Nord

baldness [ˈbɔldnɪs] *s* calvizie *f*

baldric [ˈbɔldrɪk] *s* tracolla

bale [bel] *s* balla; collo || *tr* imballare

baleful [ˈbelfəl] *adj* minaccioso, funesto

balk [bɔk] *tr* ostacolare || *intr* intestarsi, impuntarsi

Balkan [ˈbɔlkən] *adj* balcanico || **the Balkans** i Balcani

balk·y [ˈbɔki] *adj* (**-ier; -iest**) caparbio, ostinato

ball [bɔl] *s* palla; pallone *m*; sfera; (*of the thumb*) polpastrello; (*of wool*) gomitolo; (*projectile*) palla, pallottola; (*dance*) ballo; **on the ball** (slang) capace, efficiente; (slang) in gamba; **to play ball** giocare alla palla; **to play ball with** essere in cooperazione con || *tr*—**to ball up** (slang) confondere

ballad [ˈbæləd] *s* ballata

ball′ and chain′ *s* palla di piombo; (fig) impedimento; (slang) moglie *f*

ball′-and-sock′et joint′ [ˈbɔlənˈsakɪt] *s* giunto a sfere

ballast [ˈbæləst] *s* zavorra; (rr) pietrisco || *tr* zavorrare

ball′ bear′ing *s* cuscinetto a sfere

ballet [ˈbæle] *s* balletto

ballistic [bəˈlɪstɪk] *adj* balistico || **ballistics** *ssg* balistica

balloon [bəˈlun] *s* pallone *m*; (*for children*) palloncino; (*in comic strip*) fumetto

ballot [ˈbælət] *s* scheda elettorale; voto || *intr* votare, ballottare

bal′lot box′ *s* bussola, urna

ball′play′er *s* giocatore *m* di palla, giocatore *m* di baseball

ball′-point pen′ *s* penna a sfera

ball′room′ *s* salone *m* da ballo

ballyhoo [ˈbælɪˌhu] *s* chiasso; montatura || *tr* far chiasso a favore di

balm [bɑm] *s* balsamo

balm·y [ˈbɑmi] *adj* (**-ier; -iest**) balsamico; salubre; (slang) pazzo

balsam [ˈbɔlsəm] *s* balsamo; (*plant*) balsamina

Baltic [ˈbɔltɪk] *adj* baltico

baluster [ˈbæləstər] *s* balaustro

balustrade [ˌbæləsˈtred] *s* balaustrata

bamboo [bæmˈbu] *s* bambù *m*

bamboozle [bæmˈbuzəl] *tr* ingannare, raggirare

bamboozler [bæmˈbuzlər] *s* raggiratore *m*

ban [bæn] *s* bando; (*of marriage*) pubblicazione matrimoniale; (eccl) interdetto, scomunica || *v* (*pret* & *pp* **banned**; *ger* **banning**) *tr* proibire

banal [ˈbenəl] or [bəˈnæl] *adj* banale

banana [bəˈnænə] *s* banana; (*tree*) banano

band [bænd] *s* banda, striscia; (*of thin cloth*) benda; (*of metal, rubber*) fascia, nastro; (*of hat*) nastro; (mus) banda, fanfara; **to beat the band** fortemente; abbondantemente || *tr* unire || *intr*—**to band together** unirsi

bandage ['bændɪdʒ] *s* benda, bendaggio || *tr* fasciare

bandanna [bæn'dænə] *s* fazzolettone colorato

band'box' *s* cappelliera

bandit ['bændɪt] *s* bandito

band'mas'ter *s* capomusica *m*

bandoleer [,bændə'lɪr] *s* bandoliera

band' saw' *s* sega a nastro

band'stand' *s* chiosco della banda

band'wag'on *s* carrozzone *m* da circo; **to jump on the bandwagon** prendere le parti del vincitore

baneful ['benfəl] *adj* nocivo; funesto

bang [bæŋ] *s* rumore *m*, scoppio; (coll) energia; (*pleasure*) (slang) piacere *m*, eccitazione; **bangs** frangetta || *adv* tutto d'un colpo || *tr* sbattere || *intr* rimbombare || *interj* bum!

bang'-up' *adj* (slang) eccellente, di prim'ordine

banish ['bænɪʃ] *tr* sbandire, mettere al bando

banishment ['bænɪʃmənt] *s* bando, esilio

banister ['bænɪstər] *s* balaustra; **banisters** balaustrata

bank [bæŋk] *s* (*of fish; of fog*) banco; (*of a river*) sponda; (*for coins*) salvadanaio; (*financial institution*) banca, banco; (*of earth, snow*) mucchio, banco; (*of clouds*) cumulo; (aer) inclinazione laterale; (billiards) sponda || *tr* (*a fire*) coprire di cenere; (*to pile up*) ammonticchiare; (*a curve*) sopraelevare; (*money*) depositare || *intr* depositare denaro; (aer) inclinarsi lateralmente; **to bank on** (coll) contare su (di)

bank'book' *s* libretto bancario, libretto di deposito

banker ['bæŋkər] *s* banchiere *m*

banking ['bæŋkɪŋ] *adj* bancario || *s* attività bancaria; professione di banchiere

bank' note' *s* biglietto di banca

bank'roll' *s* rotolo di carta moneta; soldi *mpl* || *tr* (slang) finanziare

bankrupt ['bæŋkrʌpt] *adj & s* fallito; **to go bankrupt** andare in fallimento || *tr* dichiarare in fallimento; far fallire

bankrupt·cy ['bæŋkrʌptsi] *s* (-cies) fallimento

banner ['bænər] *adj* importante || *s* bandiera, stendardo; (journ) titolo in grassetto

banns [bænz] *spl* bandi *mpl* matrimoniali

banquet ['bæŋqwɪt] *s* banchetto || *tr* dar un banchetto a || *intr* banchettare

bantam ['bæntəm] *adj* piccolo || *s* pollo nano

ban'tam·weight' *s* peso gallo, bantam *m*

banter ['bæntər] *s* scherzo, facezia || *intr* scherzare, celiare

baptism ['bæptɪzəm] *s* battesimo

baptismal [bæp'tɪzməl] *adj* battesimale; (*certificate*) di battesimo

Baptist ['bæptɪst] *adj & s* battista *mf*

baptister·y ['bæptɪstəri] *s* (-ies) battistero

baptize [bæp'taɪz] *or* ['bæptaɪz] *tr* battezzare

bar [bɑr] *s* barra; sbarra; (*of soap*) saponetta; (*of chocolate*) tavoletta; (*of sand*) banco; (*obstacle*) barriera; bar *m*; (*of public opinion*) tribunale *m*; (*legal profession*) avvocatura; (*of door or window*) spranga; (*of lead*) (typ) lingotto; (mus) battuta; **behind bars** in guardina; **to be admitted to the bar** diventare avvocato; **to tend bar** fare il barista || *prep* eccetto, salvo; **bar none** senza eccezione || *v* (*pret & pp* **barred;** *ger* **barring**) *tr* sbarrare; sprangare; bloccare; escludere

bar' associa'tion *s* associazione dell'ordine degli avvocati

barb [bɑrb] *s* (*of arrow*) barbiglio

barbarian [bɑr'bɛrɪ·ən] *s* barbaro

barbaric [bɑr'bærɪk] *adj* barbaro

barbarism ['bɑrbə,rɪzəm] *s* barbarismo

barbari·ty [bɑr'bærɪti] *s* (-ties) barbarie *f*

barbarous ['bɑrbərəs] *adj* barbaro, crudele

Bar'bary ape' ['bɑrbəri] *s* bertuccia

barbecue ['bɑrbɪ,kju] *s* arrosto allo spiedo || *tr* arrostire allo spiedo

barbed [bɑrbd] *adj* irto di punte; mordace, pungente

barbed' wire' *s* filo spinato

barber ['bɑrbər] *s* barbiere *m*; (*who cuts and styles hair*) parrucchiere *m*

bar'ber·shop' *s* barbieria, negozio di barbiere; negozio di parrucchiere

barbiturate [bɑr'bɪtʃə,ret] *s* barbiturato, barbiturico

bard [bɑrd] *s* bardo, poeta *m*

bare [bɛr] *adj* nudo; (*head*) a capo scoperto; (*unconcealed*) palese; (*empty*) vuoto; (*wire*) senza isolante; (*unadorned*) semplice; **to lay bare** mettere a nudo || *tr* denudare, scoprire

bare'back' *adj & adv* senza sella

barefaced ['bɛr,fest] *adj* impudente, sfacciato, spudorato

bare'foot' *adj* scalzo

barehanded ['bɛr,hændɪd] *adj & adv* a mani nude

bareheaded ['bɛr,hɛdɪd] *adj* a capo scoperto

barelegged ['bɛr,lɛgɪd] *adj* a gambe nude

barely ['bɛrli] *adv* appena, soltanto

bargain ['bɑrgɪn] *s* affare *m*, buon affare *m*; contrattazione; **at a bargain** a buon prezzo; **into the bargain** in soprappiù || *tr*—**to bargain away** vendere a buonissimo prezzo || *intr* contrattare, mercanteggiare; **to bargain for** aspettarsi

bar'gain sale' *s* vendita sottoprezzo

barge [bɑrdʒ] *s* barcone *m*, chiatta || *intr*—**to barge in** entrare senza chiedere permesso

baritone ['bɛrɪ,ton] *adj* di baritono || *s* baritono *m*

barium ['bɛrɪ·əm] *s* bario

bark [bɑrk] *s* corteccia, scorza; (*of dog*) abbaiamento, latrato || *tr* (*e.g.,*

insults) lanciare ‖ *intr* abbaiare, latrare
bar'keep'er *s* barista *mf*
barker ['bɑrkər] *s* banditore *m*, imbonitore *m*
barley ['bɑrli] *s* orzo
bar' mag'net *s* calamita a forma di barra allungata
bar'maid' *s* barista *f*
bar'man *s* (-men) barista *m*
barn [bɑrn] *s* granaio; (*for hay*) fienile *m*; (*for livestock*) stalla
barnacle ['bɑrnəkəl] *s* cirripede *m*
barn' owl' *s* civetta
barn'yard' *s* bassacorte *f*, aia
barn'yard fowl' *s* animale *m* da cortile ‖ *spl* animali *mpl* da cortile
barometer [bə'rɑmɪtər] *s* barometro
baron ['bærən] *s* barone *m*; (*industrialist*) cavaliere *m* d'industria
baroness ['bærənɪs] *s* baronessa
baroque [bə'rok] *adj* & *s* barocco
bar'rack-room' *adj* da caserma ‖ *s* camerata
barracks ['bærəks] *spl* caserma; camerata
barrage [bə'rɑʒ] *s* (mil) fuoco di sbarramento
barrel ['bærəl] *s* barile *m*, botte *f*; (*of gun*) canna; (mach) cilindro
bar'rel or'gan *s* organetto di Barberia
barren ['bærən] *adj* sterile; (*without vegetation*) brullo
barricade [,bærɪ'ked] *s* barricata ‖ *tr* barricare
barrier ['bærɪ-ər] *s* barriera
bar'rier reef' *s* barriera corallina
barring ['bɑrɪŋ] *prep* eccetto, salvo
barrister ['bærɪstər] *s* (Brit) avvocato
bar'room' *s* bar *m*, cantina, mescita
bar'tend'er *s* barista *mf*, barman *m*
barter ['bɑrtər] *s* baratto ‖ *tr* & *intr* barattare, permutare
basalt [bə'sɔlt] *s* basalto
base [bes] *adj* basale; basso; servile; (*morally low*) turpe; (*metal*) vile, non prezioso ‖ *s* base *f*; (*in children's games*) tana; (*of a word*) radice *f* basale ‖ *tr* basare
base'ball' *s* baseball *m*, pallabase *f*
base'board' *s* basamento; (*of wall*) zoccolo
Basel ['bɑzəl] *s* Basilea
baseless ['beslɪs] *adj* infondato
basement ['besmənt] *s* scantinato, piano interrato
bashful ['bæʃfəl] *adj* timido
basic ['besɪk] *adj* fondamentale; (chem) basico
ba'sic commod'ities *spl* articoli *mpl* di prima necessità
basilica [bə'sɪlɪkə] *s* basilica
basin ['besɪn] *s* catino; vasca; (*of balance*) piatto; (*of river*) bacino; (*of harbor*) darsena
ba·sis ['besɪs] *s* (-ses [siz]) base *f*
bask [bæsk] or [bɑsk] *intr* crogiolarsi
basket ['bæskɪt] or ['bɑskɪt] *s* cesta; (sports) cesto
bas'ket·ball' *s* pallacanestro *f*
Basque [bæsk] *adj* & *s* basco
bas-relief [,bɑrɪ'lif] or [,bærɪ'lif] *s* bassorilievo

bass [bes] *adj* & *s* (mus) basso ‖ [bæs] *s* (ichth) pesce persico
bass' drum' *s* grancassa
bass' horn' *s* bassotuba *m*
bassinet ['bæsə,net] or [,bæsə'net] *s* culla a forma di cesto; carrozzina a forma di cesto
bas·so ['bæso] or ['bɑso] *s* (-sos or -si [si]) basso
bassoon [bə'sun] *s* fagotto
bass' vi'ol ['vaɪ·əl] *s* contrabbasso
bastard ['bæstərd] *adj* & *s* bastardo
baste [best] *tr* (*to sew*) imbastire; (*meat*) inumidire con acqua o grasso
bastion ['bæstʃən] or ['bæstɪ·ən] *s* bastione *m*
bat [bæt] *s* mazza; (*in cricket*) maglio; (coll) colpo; (zool) pipistrello ‖ *v* (*pret & pp* batted; *ger* batting) *tr* colpire con la mazza; **without batting an eye** (coll) senza batter ciglio
batch [bætʃ] *s* (*of bread*) infornata; gruppo, numero
bath [bæθ] or [bɑθ] *s* bagno; **to take a bath** fare il bagno
bathe [beð] *tr* bagnare, lavare ‖ *intr* bagnarsi, fare il bagno
bather ['beðər] *s* bagnante *mf*
bath'house' *s* (*individual*) cabina; spogliatoio
bath'ing beau'ty *s* bellezza in costume da bagno
bath'ing cap' *s* cuffia da bagno
bath'ing resort' *s* stazione balneare
bath'ing suit' *s* costume *m* da bagno
bath'ing trunks' *spl* mutandine *fpl* da bagno
bath'robe' *s* accappatoio
bath'room' *s* stanza da bagno
bath' salts' *spl* sali *mpl* da bagno
bath'tub' *s* bagno, vasca da bagno
baton [bæ'tɑn] or ['bætən] *s* bastone *m*; (mus) bacchetta
battalion [bə'tæljən] *s* battaglione *m*
batten ['bætən] *tr* assicella; piccola traversa; (naut) bietta ‖ *tr*—**to batten down the hatches** chiudere ermeticamente i boccaporti
batter ['bætər] *s* pasta, farina pastosa; (baseball) battitore *m* ‖ *tr* battere, tempestare di colpi; (*to wear out*) logorare
bat'tering ram' *s* ariete *m*
batter·y ['bætəri] *s* (-ies) (*primary cell*) pila; (*secondary cell*) accumulatore *m*; (*group of batteries*) batteria; (law) assalto; (mil & mus) batteria
battle ['bætəl] *s* battaglia; **to do battle** dar battaglia ‖ *tr* combattere contro ‖ *intr* combattere
bat'tle cry' *s* grido di guerra
battledore ['bætəl,dor] *s* racchetta; **battledore and shuttlecock** gioco del volano
bat'tle·field' *s* campo di battaglia
bat'tle-front' *s* fronte *m* di combattimento
battlement ['bætəlmənt] *s* merlatura
bat'tle roy'al *s* baruffa generale, zuffa generale
bat'tle·ship' *s* corazzata
battue [bæ'tu] or [bæ'tju] *s* (hunt) battuta

bat·ty ['bæti] *adj* (-tier; -tiest) (slang) pazzo, eccentrico

bauble ['bɔbəl] *s* bazzecola, gingillo

Bavaria [bə'vɛrɪ·ə] *s* la Baviera

Bavarian [bə'vɛrɪ·ən] *adj & s* bavarese *mf*

bawd [bɔd] *s* ruffiano; ruffiana

bawd·y ['bɔdi] *adj* (-ier; -iest) indecente, osceno

bawd'y·house' *s* casa di malaffare

bawl [bɔl] *s* grido; (coll) pianto || *tr*— **to bawl out** (slang) fare una ramanzina a || *intr* strillare; (coll) piangere

bay [be] *adj* baio || *s* baia; vano, alcova; (*recess in wall*) apertura nel muro; finestra sporgente; (*of dog*) latrato; cavallo baio; (bot) lauro; **at bay** in una posizione disperata || *intr* latrare

bayonet ['be·ənɪt] *s* baionetta || *tr* dare baionettate a || *intr* dare baionettate

bay' win'dow *s* finestra sporgente; (slang) pancia

bazooka [bə'zukə] *s* bazooka *m*

be [bi] *v* (*pres am* [æm], *is* [ɪz], *are* [ɑr]; *pret was* [wɑz] *or* [wʌz], *were* [wʌr]; *pp* **been** [bɪn]) *intr* essere; fare, e.g., **to be a mason** fare il muratore; fare, e.g., **3 times 3 is 9** tre volte tre fa nove; **be as it may be** comunque sia; **here is** *or* **here are** ecco; **there are** ci sono; **there is** c'è; **to be** futuro, e.g., **my wife to be** la mia futura sposa; **to be ashamed** aver vergogna; **to be cold** aver freddo; **to be hot** aver caldo; **to be hungry** aver fame; **to be in** stare a casa; **to be in a hurry** aver fretta; **to be in with** (coll) essere amico intimo di; **to be off** andarsene; **to be out** essere fuori; **to be out of** (coll) non aver più; **to be right** aver ragione; **to be sleepy** aver sonno; **to be thirsty** avere sete; **to be up** essere alzato; **to be up to** essere all'altezza di; toccare, e.g., **it's up to you** tocca a Lei; **to be warm** avere caldo; **to be wrong** avere torto; sbagliarsi; **to be . . . years old** avere . . . anni || *aux* stare, e.g., **to be waiting** stare aspettando; essere, e.g., **the murder has been committed** l'omicidio è stato commesso; dovere, e.g., **he is to clean the stables tomorrow** domani deve pulire la stalla || *impers* essere, e.g., **it is necessary** è necessario; fare, e.g., **it is cold** fa freddo; **it is hot** fa caldo

beach [bitʃ] *s* spiaggia || *tr* (*a boat*) arenare || *intr* arenarsi

beach'comb' *intr* raccogliere relitti sulla spiaggia

beach'comb'er *s* girellone *m* di spiaggia

beach'head' *s* testa di sbarco

beach' robe' *s* accappatoio

beach' shoe' *s* sandalo da spiaggia

beach' umbrel'la *s* ombrellone *m* da spiaggia

beacon ['bikən] *s* faro || *tr* rischiarare; fare da guida a || *intr* brillare

bead [bid] *s* perlina; grano, chicco; (*drop*) goccia; **beads** (*in a necklace or rosary*) conterie *fpl*; **to count one's beads** recitare il rosario

beagle ['bigəl] *s* segugio, bracco

beak [bik] *s* becco; promontorio

beam [bim] *s* trave *f*; (*of balance*) braccio; (*of light*) raggio; (*ship's breadth*) larghezza; (*smile*) sorriso; (*radio signal*) fascio direttore; (*course indicated by radio beam*) aerovia; (naut) traverso || *tr* (*a radio signal*) dirigere; (e.g., *light*) irraggiare || *intr* raggiare

bean [bin] *s* fagiolo; (*of coffee*) chicco; (slang) testa

beaner·y ['binəri] *s* (-ies) (slang) gargotta, taverna di secondo ordine

bean'pole' *s* puntello per i fagioli; (coll) palo del telegrafo

bear [bɛr] *s* orso; (astr) orsa; (com) ribassista *m*, giocatore *m* al ribasso || *v* (*pret* **bore** [bor]; *pp* **borne** [born]) *tr* (*to carry*) portare; (*to give birth to*) partorire; (*to sustain*) sostenere; (*to withstand*) sopportare; (*a grudge*) serbare; (*in mind*) tenere; (*interest*) produrre; (*to pay*) pagare; **to bear the date** aver la data; **to bear out** confermare; **to bear witness** testimoniare || *intr* (*to be productive*) fruttificare; (*to move*) dirigersi; (*to be oppressive*) fare pressione; **to bear down on** fare pressione su; avvicinarsi a; **to bear up** resistere; **to bear with** tollerare

bearable ['bɛrəbəl] *adj* tollerabile

beard [bɪrd] *s* barba; (e.g., *in wheat*) arista

bearded *adj* barbuto

beardless ['bɪrdlɪs] *adj* imberbe

bearer ['bɛrər] *s* portatore *m*

bearing ['bɛrɪŋ] *s* portamento; relazione; importanza; (mach) bronzina, cuscinetto; **bearings** orientamento; **to lose one's bearings** perdere la bussola; perdere l'orientamento

bearish ['bɛrɪʃ] *adj* (*like a bear*) orsino; (e.g., *prices*) in ribasso; (*market*) al ribasso; (*speculator*) ribassista

bear'skin' *s* pelle *f* dell'orso; (mil) colbacco

beast [bist] *s* bestia

beast·ly ['bistli] *adj* (-lier; -liest) bestiale || *adv* (coll) malissimo

beast' of bur'den *s* bestia da soma

beast' of prey' *s* animale *m* da rapina

beat [bit] *s* (*of heart*) battito; (*of policeman*) ronda; (*stroke*) colpo; (*habitual route*) cammino battuto; (mus) tempo; (phys) battimento || *v* (*pret* **beat**; *pp* **beat** *or* **beaten**) *tr* battere; percuotere; (*eggs*) frullare; (*to whip*) frustare; (coll) confondere; **beat it!** (slang) vattene!; **to beat a retreat** battere in ritirata; **to beat back** respingere; **to beat down** sopprimere; **to beat off** respingere; **to beat up** (*eggs*) frullare; (*people*) dargliene a || *intr* battere; pulsare; **to beat around the bush** (coll) menare il can per l'aia

beat'en path' ['bitən] *s* cammino battuto

beater ['bitər] *s* frullino

beati·fy [bɪ'ætɪ ˌfaɪ] *v* (*pret & pp* -fied) *tr* beatificare

beating ['bitɪŋ] *s* battitura; (*whipping*) frustatura; (*throbbing*) pulsazione, battito; (*defeat*) sconfitta

beau [bo] *s* (**beaus** or **beaux** [boz]) (*dandy*) bellimbusto; (*girl's sweetheart*) spasimante *m*

beautician [bju'tɪʃən] *s* estetista *mf*

beautiful ['bjutɪfəl] *adj* bello

beauti·fy ['bjutɪ,faɪ] *v* (*pret & pp* -fied) *tr* abbellire

beau·ty ['bjuti] *s* (-ties) bellezza

beau'ty con'test *s* concorso di bellezza

beau'ty par'lor *s* istituto di bellezza

beau'ty sleep' *s* primo sonno

beau'ty spot' *s* neo; posto pittoresco

beaver ['bivər] *s* castoro; pelle *f* di castoro; cappello a cilindro

because [bɪ'kɔz] *conj* perchè; **because of** a causa di

beck [bɛk] *s* gesto; **at the beck and call of** agli ordini di

beckon ['bɛkən] *s* gesto || *tr* fare gesto a || *intr* fare gesto

becloud [bɪ'klaud] *tr* annebbiare; oscurare

be·come [bɪ'kʌm] *v* (*pret* -came; *pp* -come) *tr* convenire a; stare bene a, e.g., **this hat becomes you** questo cappello Le sta bene || *intr* diventare; farsi; convertirsi, e.g., **water became wine** l'acqua si convertì in vino; succedere, e.g., **what became of my coat?** che è successo del mio pastrano?; essere, e.g., **what will become of me?** che sarà di me?; **to become accustomed** abituarsi; **to become angry** entrare in collera; **to become crazy** impazzire; **to become ill** ammalarsi

becoming [bɪ'kʌmɪŋ] *adj* conveniente; appropriato; acconcio; **this is very becoming to you** questo Le sta molto bene

bed [bɛd] *s* letto; (*layer*) strato; giacimento; **to go to bed** andare a letto; **to take to one's bed** mettersi a letto

bed' and board' *s* vitto e alloggio; pensione completa

bed'bug' *s* cimice *f*

bed'clothes' *spl* lenzuola *fpl* e coperte *fpl*, biancheria da letto

bed'cov'er *s* coperta da letto

bedding ['bɛdɪŋ] *s* lenzuola *fpl* e coperte *fpl*; (*litter*) lettiera; (*foundation*) fondamenta *fpl*

bedeck [bɪ'dɛk] *tr* ornare, adornare

bedev·il [bɪ'dɛvɪl] *v* (*pret & pp* -iled or -illed; *ger* -iling or -illing) *tr* tormentare diabolicamente; confondere

bed'fast' *adj* confinato a letto

bed'fel'low *s* compagno di letto; compagno di stanza; compagno

bedlam ['bɛdləm] *s* manicomio; pandemonio

bed' lin'en *s* biancheria da letto

bed'pan' *s* padella

bedridden ['bɛd,rɪdən] *adj* degente a letto

bed'room' *s* stanza da letto, camera da letto

bed'room slip'per *s* babbuccia, pantofola

bed'side' *s* capezzale *m*

bed'side man'ner *s* maniera di fare coi pazienti

bed'sore' *s* piaga da decubito

bed'spread' *s* coperta da letto

bed'spring' *s* rete *f* del letto; molla del letto

bed'stead' *s* fusto del letto

bed'tick' *s* traliccio

bed'time' *s* ora di coricarsi

bed'warm'er *s* scaldaletto

bee [bi] *s* ape *f*

beech [bitʃ] *s* faggio

beech'nut' *s* faggiola

beef [bif] *s* bue *m*, manzo; carne *f* di manzo; (coll) forza; (slang) lamentela || *tr*—**to beef up** (coll) rinforzare || *intr* (slang) lamentarsi

beef' cat'tle *s* manzi *mpl* da carne

beef'steak' *s* bistecca

beef' stew' *s* stufato di manzo

bee'hive' *s* alveare *m*

bee'keep'er *s* apicoltore *m*

bee'line' *s*—**to make a beeline for** (coll) andare direttamente verso

beer [bɪr] *s* birra

beer' saloon' *s* birreria

beeswax ['biz,wæks] *s* cera d'api

beet [bit] *s* barbabietola

beetle ['bitəl] *adj* sporgente, folto || *s* scarafaggio

bee'tle-browed' *adj* dalle sopracciglia folte

beet' su'gar *s* zucchero di barbabietola

be·fall [bɪ'fɔl] *v* (*pret* -fell ['fɛl]; *pp* -fallen ['fɔlən]) *tr* succedere a || *intr* succedere

befitting [bɪ'fɪtɪŋ] *adj* appropriato

before [bɪ'for] *adv* prima, prima d'ora || *prep* (*in time*) prima di; (*in place*) dinnanzi a, davanti a; **before Christ** avanti Cristo || *conj* prima che

before'hand' *adv* in anticipo; precedentemente

befriend [bɪ'frɛnd] *tr* diventare amico di, proteggere, favorire; aiutare

befuddle [bɪ'fʌdəl] *tr* confondere

beg [bɛg] *v* (*pret & pp* begged; *ger* begging) *tr* chiedere; implorare; (*alms*) mendicare; **I beg your pardon** Le chiedo scusa; **to beg s.o. for s.th** chiedere qlco a qlcu || *intr* chiedere la carità; **to beg for** sollecitare; **to beg off** scusarsi; **to go begging** rimanere invenduto

be·get [bɪ'gɛt] *v* (*pret* -got ['gɑt]; *pp* -gotten or -got; *ger* -getting) *tr* generare

beggar ['bɛgər] *s* accattone *m*, mendicante *m*

be·gin [bɪ'gɪn] *v* (*pret* -gan ['gæn]; *pp* -gun ['gʌn]; *ger* -ginning) *tr & intr* cominciare, iniziare; **beginning with** a partire da; **to begin with** per cominciare

beginner [bɪ'gɪnər] *s* principiante *mf*

beginning [bɪ'gɪnɪŋ] *s* inizio, origine *f*, principio, esordio

begrudge [bɪ'grʌdʒ] *tr* invidiare; concedere con riluttanza

beguile [bɪ'gaɪl] *tr* ingannare; sedurre; (*to delight*) divertire

behalf [bɪ'hæf] or [bɪ'haf] *s*—**on behalf of** nell'interesse di; a nome di

behave [bɪ'hev] *intr* comportarsi; comportarsi bene

behavior [bɪ'hevjər] *s* comportamento, condotta; funzionamento

behead [bɪ'hɛd] *tr* decapitare

behest [bɪ'hɛst] *s* ordine *m*, comando

behind [bɪ'haɪnd] *s* didietro; (slang) sedere *m* ‖ *adv* dietro; (*in arrears*) in arretrato; **from behind** dal didietro ‖ *prep* dietro a, dietro di; **behind time** in ritardo

be·hold [bɪ'hold] *v* (*pret & pp* **-held** ['hɛld]) *tr* contemplare; ammirare ‖ *interj* guarda!

behoove [bɪ'huv] *impers*—**it behooves him to** gli conviene di

being ['bi·ɪŋ] *adj* esistente; **for the time being** per ora ‖ *s* essere *m*, ente *m*

belabor [bɪ'lebər] *tr* attaccare; (fig) ribattere, confutare; (fig) insistere su

belated [bɪ'letɪd] *adj* tardivo

belch [bɛltʃ] *s* rutto ‖ *tr* eruttare, vomitare ‖ *intr* ruttare

beleaguer [bɪ'ligər] *tr* assediare

bel·fry ['bɛlfri] *s* (**-fries**) (*tower*) campanile *m*; (*site of bell*) cella campanaria; (slang) testa

Belgian ['bɛldʒən] *adj & s* belga *mf*

Belgium ['bɛldʒəm] *s* il Belgio

be·lie [bɪ'laɪ] *v* (*pret & pp* **-lied** ['laɪd]; *ger* **-lying** ['laɪ·ɪŋ]) *tr* (*to misrepresent*) tradire; (*to prove false*) smentire

belief [bɪ'lif] *s* fede *f*, credenza

believable [bɪ'livəbəl] *adj* credibile

believe [bɪ'liv] *tr* credere ‖ *intr* credere, aver fede; **to believe in** credere in

believer [bɪ'livər] *s* credente *mf*

belittle [bɪ'lɪtəl] *tr* menomare

bell [bɛl] *s* campana; (*for a door*) campanello; (*sound*) rintocco; (*on cattle*) campanaccio; (*of deer*) bramito ‖ *intr* bramire

belladonna [ˌbɛlə'dɑnə] *s* belladonna

bell'-bot'tom *adj* a campana

bell'boy' *s* cameriere *m*, ragazzo

belle [bɛl] *s* bella

belles-lettres [ˌbɛl'lɛtrə] *spl* belle lettere

bell' glass' *s* campana di vetro

bell'hop' *s* cameriere *m*, ragazzo

bellicose ['bɛlɪˌkos] *adj* bellicoso

belligerent [bɛ'lɪdʒərənt] *adj & s* belligerante *m*

bellow ['bɛlo] *s* muggito; **bellows** mantice *m*; (*of camera*) soffietto ‖ *tr* gridare ‖ *intr* muggire

bell' ring'er ['rɪŋər] *s* campanaro

bellwether ['bɛlˌwɛðər] *s* pecora guida

bel·ly ['bɛli] *s* (**-lies**) ventre *m*, pancia ‖ *v* (*pret & pp* **-lied**) *intr* far pancia

bel'ly·ache' *s* (coll) mal *m* di pancia ‖ *intr* (slang) lamentarsi

bel'ly·but'ton *s* (coll) ombelico

bel'ly dance' *s* (coll) danza del ventre

bel'ly flop' *s* panciata

bellyful ['bɛlɪˌful] *s*—**to have a bellyful** (slang) averne fino agli occhi

bel'ly·land' *intr* (aer) atterrare sul ventre

belong [bɪ'lɔŋ] or [bɪ'lɑŋ] *intr* appartenere; stare bene, e.g., **this chair belongs in this room** questa sedia sta bene in questa stanza

belongings [bɪ'lɔŋɪŋz] or [bi'lɑŋɪŋz] *spl* effetti *mpl* personali

beloved [bɪ'lʌvɪd] or [bɪ'lʌvd] *adj & s* diletto, amato

below [bɪ'lo] *adv* sotto; più sotto; sotto zero, e.g., **ten below** dieci gradi sotto zero ‖ *prep* sotto, sotto di

belt [bɛlt] *s* cintura, cinghia; (mach) nastro; (mil) cinturone *m*; (geog) fascia, zona; **to tighten one's belt** far cintura ‖ *tr* cingere; (slang) staffilare

belt'ed tire' *s* copertone cinturato

belt' line' *s* linea di circonvallazione

beltway ['bɛltˌwe] *s* raccordo anulare

bemoan [bɪ'mon] *tr* lamentare; compiangere

bench [bɛntʃ] *s* banco, panca; tribunale *m*; (mach) banco di prova; **to be on the bench** (law) essere giudice

bend [bɛnd] *s* curva; (*e.g., of pipe*) gomito, angolo ‖ *v* (*pret & pp* **bent** [bɛnt]) *tr* curvare; piegare; far piegare ‖ *intr* deviare; piegare, piegarsi; **to bend over** inchinarsi

beneath [bɪ'niθ] *adv* sotto; più sotto ‖ *prep* sotto, sotto di

benediction [ˌbɛnɪ'dɪkʃən] *s* benedizione

benefactor ['bɛnɪˌfæktər] or [ˌbɛnɪ'fæktər] *s* benefattore *m*

benefactress ['bɛnɪˌfæktrɪs] or [ˌbɛnɪ'fæktrɪs] *s* benefattrice *f*

beneficence [bɪ'nɛfɪsəns] *s* beneficenza

beneficent [bɪ'nɛfɪsənt] *adj* caritatevole; benefico

beneficial [ˌbɛnɪ'fɪʃəl] *adj* benefico

beneficiar·y [ˌbɛnɪ'fɪʃiˌɛri] *s* (**-ies**) beneficiario

benefit ['bɛnɪfɪt] *s* beneficio; festa di beneficenza; **for the benefit of** a beneficio di ‖ *tr & intr* beneficiare

ben'efit perfor'mance *s* beneficiata

benevolence [bɪ'nɛvələns] *s* benevolenza; carità *f*

benevolent [bɪ'nɛvələnt] *adj* benevolo; (*institution*) benefico

benign [bɪ'naɪn] *adj* benigno

bent [bɛnt] *adj* curvo; **bent on** deciso a ‖ *s* curva; tendenza, propensità *f*

Benzedrine ['bɛnzɪˌdrin] (trademark) *s* benzedrina

benzene ['bɛnzin] *s* benzolo

benzine [bɛn'zin] *s* benzina

bequeath [bɪ'kwiθ] or [bɪ'kwið] *tr* legare, lasciare in eredità

bequest [bɪ'kwest] *s* legato, lascito

berate [bɪ'ret] *tr* redarguire

be·reave [bɪ'riv] *v* (*pret & pp* **-reaved** or **-reft** ['rɛft]) *tr* spogliare

bereavement [bɪ'rivmənt] *s* lutto, perdita

beret [bə're] or ['bɛre] *s* berretto

Berlin [bər'lɪn] *adj* berlinese ‖ *s* Berlino

Berliner [bər'lɪnər] *s* berlinese *mf*

Bermuda [bər'mjudə] *s* le Bermude

ber·ry ['bɛri] *s* (**-ries**) (*dry seed*) chicco; (*fruit*) bacca

berserk [bʌr'sʌrk] *adj* infuriato || *adv* —to go berserk impazzire

berth [bʌrθ] *s* (*for a ship*) posto di ormeggio; (*bed*) cuccetta; (coll) posto

beryllium [bə'rɪlɪ·əm] *s* berillio

be·seech [bɪ'sitʃ] *v* (*pret & pp* -sought ['sɔt] or -seeched) *tr* supplicare

be·set [bɪ'sɛt] *v* (*pret & pp* -set; *ger* -setting) *tr* assediare, circondare; (*e.g., with problems*) assillare

beside [bɪ'saɪd] *adv* oltre, inoltre || *prep* vicino a; in confronto di; oltre a; **beside oneself** fuori di sé; **beside the point** fuori del seminato

besides [bɪ'saɪdz] *adv* inoltre; d'altronde || *prep* oltre a

besiege [bɪ'sidʒ] *tr* assediare; (*with questions*) bombardare

besmear [bɪ'smɪr] *tr* imbrattare, sgorbiare; sporcare

besmirch [bɪ'smʌrtʃ] *tr* insudiciare

bespatter [bɪ'spætər] *tr* inzaccherare

be·speak [bɪ'spik] *v* (-spoke ['spok]; -spoken) *tr* chiedere anticipatamente a; (*to show*) dimostrare

best [bɛst] *adj super* (il) migliore; ottimo || *s* meglio; **at best** nella miglior delle ipotesi; **to do one's best** fare del proprio meglio; **to get the best of** avere la meglio di; **to make the best of** adattarsi a || *adv super* meglio; **had best,** e.g., **I had best** dovrei || *tr* battere, riuscire superiore a

bestial ['bɛstjəl] or ['bɛstʃəl] *adj* bestiale

be·stir [bɪ'stʌr] *v* (*pret & pp* -stirred; *ger* -stirring) *tr* eccitare; **to bestir oneself** darsi da fare

best' man' *s* testimone *m* di nozze

bestow [bɪ'sto] *tr* accordare; conferire

best' sell'er *s* best-seller *m*

bet [bɛt] *s* scommessa || *v* (*pret & pp* bet or betted; *ger* betting) *tr & intr* scommettere; **I bet** ci scommetto; **you bet** (coll) evidentemente

be·take [bɪ'tek] *v* (*pret* -took ['tuk]; *pp* -taken) *tr*—**to betake oneself** andare, dirigersi

be·think [bɪ'θɪŋk] *v* (*pret & pp* -thought ['θɔt]) *tr* **to bethink oneself** pensare; ricordarsi

Bethlehem ['bɛθlɪ·əm] or ['bɛθlɪ‚hɛm] *s* Betlemme *f*

betide [bɪ'taɪd] *tr* accadere a || *intr* accadere

betoken [bɪ'tokən] *tr* indicare, presagire

betray [bɪ'tre] *tr* tradire, ingannare; (*to reveal*) rivelare

betroth [bɪ'troð] or [bɪ'troθ] *tr* promettere in matrimonio a

betrothal [bɪ'troðəl] or [bɪ'trɔθəl] *s* fidanzamento

betrothed [bɪ'troðd] or [bɪ'trɔθt] *adj* fidanzato || *s* promesso sposo, fidanzato

better ['bɛtər] *adj comp* migliore; **to grow better** migliorare || *s*—betters superiori *mpl*; ottimati *mpl*; **to get the better of** avere la meglio di || *adv* meglio; **had better** dovere, e.g., **I had** better dovrei; **to be better off** stare meglio; **to think better of** riconsiderare; **you ought to know better** dovrebbe vergognarsi || *tr* sorpassare; migliorare; **to better oneself** migliorare la propria situazione

bet'ter half' *s* metà *f*

betterment ['bɛtərmənt] *s* miglioramento

bettor ['bɛtər] *s* scommettitore *m*

between [bɪ'twin] *adv* in mezzo; **in between** in mezzo, fra i piedi || *prep* fra, tra

between'-decks' *s* interponte *m*

bev·el ['bɛvəl] *s* (*instrument*) falsa squadra; (*sloping part*) augnatura || *v* (*pret & pp* -eled or -elled; *ger* -eling or -elling) *tr* augnare

beverage ['bɛvərɪdʒ] *s* bevanda

bev·y ['bɛvi] *s* (-ies) (*of women*) gruppo; (*of birds*) stormo

bewail [bɪ'wel] *tr* lamentare

beware [bɪ'wɛr] *tr* fare attenzione a, guardarsi da || *intr* fare attenzione, guardarsi

bewilder [bɪ'wɪldər] *tr* lasciar perplesso, confondere, disorientare

bewilderment [bɪ'wɪldərmənt] *s* perplessità *f*, disorientamento

bewitch [bɪ'wɪtʃ] *tr* stregare

beyond [bɪ'jɑnd] *s*—**the beyond** l'aldilà *m* || *adv* più lontano || *prep* al di là di; oltre a; più tardi di; **beyond a doubt** fuori dubbio; **beyond repair** irreparabile

bias ['baɪ·əs] *s* linea diagonale; pregiudizio; **on the bias** diagonalmente || *tr* prevenire

bib [bɪb] *s* bavaglino

Bible ['baɪbəl] *s* Bibbia

Biblical ['bɪblɪkəl] *adj* biblico

bibliogra·phy [‚bɪblɪ'ɑgrəfi] *s* (-phies) bibliografia

bibliophile ['bɪblɪ·ə‚faɪl] *s* bibliofilo

bicarbonate [baɪ'kɑrbə‚net] *s* bicarbonato

biceps ['baɪsɛps] *s* bicipite *m*

bicker ['bɪkər] *s* bisticcio, disputa || *intr* bisticciare, disputare

bicycle ['baɪsɪkəl] *s* bicicletta

bid [bɪd] *s* offerta; (*cards*) dichiarazione; (coll) invito || *v* (*pret* bade [bæd] or bid; *pp* bidden ['bɪdən] or bid; *ger* bidding) *tr & intr* offrire; comandare; (*cards*) dichiarare

bidder ['bɪdər] *s* offerente *mf*; (*cards*) dichiarante *mf*; **the highest bidder** il miglior offerente

bidding ['bɪdɪŋ] *s* ordine *m*; offerte *fpl*; (*cards*) dichiarazione

bide [baɪd] *tr*—**to bide one's time** attendere l'ora propizia

biennial [baɪ'ɛnɪ·əl] *adj* biennale

bier [bɪr] *s* catafalco

bifocal [baɪ'fokəl] *adj* bifocale || **bifocals** *spl* occhiali *mpl* bifocali

big [bɪg] *adj* (bigger; biggest) grande; (coll) importante; (coll) stravagante; **big with child** incinta || *adv*—**to talk big** (coll) parlare con iattanza

bigamist ['bɪgəmɪst] *s* bigamo

bigamous ['bɪgəməs] *adj* bigamo

big-bellied ['bɪg ,bɛlid] *adj* panciuto

Big' Dip'per *s* Gran Carro

big' game' *s* caccia grossa

big-hearted ['bɪg ,hɑrtɪd] *adj* magnanimo, generoso

big' mouth' *s* (slang) sbraitone *m*

bigot ['bɪgət] *s* bigotto, bacchettone *m*

bigoted ['bɪgətɪd] *adj* (*in religion*) bigotto; intransigente

bigot·ry ['bɪgətri] *s* (*-ries*) bigottismo; intransigenza

big' shot' *s* (slang) pezzo grosso, (un) qualcuno

big' slam' *s* (bridge) grande slam *m*

big'-time op'erator *s* (slang) grosso trafficante

big' toe' *s* alluce *m*

big' wheel' *s* (slang) pezzo grosso

bike [baɪk] *s* (coll) bicicletta

bile [baɪl] *s* bile *f*

bilge [bɪldʒ] *s* sentina; (*of barrel*) ventre *m*

bilge'ways' *spl* parati *mpl*

bilingual [baɪ'lɪŋgwəl] *adj* bilingue

bilious ['bɪljəs] *adj* bilioso

bilk [bɪlk] *tr* defraudare

bill [bɪl] *s* (*of bird*) becco; (*statement of charges*) conto; (*e.g., for electricity*) bolletta; (*menu*) lista; (*money*) biglietto; (*proposed law*) disegno di legge; (*handbill*) annunzio; (law) atto; (theat) cartellone *m;* to fill the bill (coll) riempire i requisiti; to foot the bill (coll) pagare lo scotto ‖ *tr* fare una lista di; mettere in conto a ‖ *intr* (*said of doves*) beccuzzarsi; (*said of lovers*) baciucchiarsi

bill'board' *s* cartellone *m;* (rad, telv) titolo di testa

billet ['bɪlɪt] *s* (mil) alloggiamento; (mil) ordine *m* d'alloggiamento ‖ *tr* (mil) alloggiare, accasermare

bill'fold' *s* portafoglio

bill'head' *s* intestazione di fattura

billiards ['bɪljərdz] *s* bigliardo

bil'ling clerk' *s* fatturista *mf*

billion ['bɪljən] *s* (U.S.A.) miliardo; (Brit) bilione *m*

bill' of exchange' *s* tratta

bill' of fare' *s* menu *m,* lista delle vivande

bill' of lad'ing ['ledɪŋ] *s* polizza di carico

bill' of rights' *s* dichiarazione dei diritti

bill' of sale' *s* atto di vendita

billow ['bɪlo] *s* ondata, cavallone *m*

bill'post'er *s* attacchino

bil·ly ['bɪli] *s* (*-lies*) manganello

bil'ly goat' *s* capro, caprone *m*

bimonthly [baɪ'mʌnθli] *adj* (*occurring every two months*) bimestrale; (*occurring twice a month*) bimensile

bin [bɪn] *s* cassone *m;* (*for bread*) madia; (*e.g., for coal*) deposito

binaural [baɪ'nɔrəl] *adj* biauricolare

bind [baɪnd] *v* (*pret & pp* bound [baund]) *tr* legare; allacciare; (*to bandage*) fasciare; (*to constipate*) costipare; (*a book*) rilegare; (*to oblige*) obbligare; (mach) grippare

binder ['baɪndər] *s* rilegatore *m;* (*cover*) cartella

binder·y ['baɪndəri] *s* (*-ies*) rilegatoria

binding ['baɪndɪŋ] *adj* obbligatorio ‖ *s* (*of book*) rilegatura; legatura; fasciatura

bind'ing post' *s* (elec) capocorda; (*e.g., of battery*) (elec) serrafilo

binge [bɪndʒ] *s*—to go on a binge (coll) far baldoria

bingo ['bɪŋgo] *s* tombola

binnacle ['bɪnəkəl] *s* abitacolo

binoculars [bɪ'nɑkjələrz] *or* [baɪ'nɑkjələrz] *spl* binocolo

biochemical [,baɪ·ə'kɛmɪkəl] *adj* biochimico

biochemist [,baɪ·ə'kɛmɪst] *s* biochimico

biochemistry [,baɪ·ə'kɛmɪstri] *s* biochimica

biodegradable [,baɪ·odɪ'gredəbəl] *adj* biodegradabile

biographer [baɪ'ɑgrəfər] *s* biografo

biographic(al) [,baɪ·ə'græfɪk(əl)] *adj* biografico

biogra·phy [baɪ'ɑgrəfi] *s* (*-phies*) biografia

biologist [baɪ'ɑlədʒɪst] *s* biologo

biology [baɪ'ɑlədʒi] *s* biologia

biophysics [,baɪ·ə'fɪzɪks] *s* biofisica

biop·sy ['baɪ ,ɑpsi] *s* (*-sies*) biopsia

bipartisan [baɪ'pɑrtɪzən] *adj* (*system*) bipartitico; (*government*) bipartito

biped ['baɪpɛd] *adj & s* bipede *m*

birch [bʌrtʃ] *s* betulla ‖ *tr* scudisciare

bird [bʌrd] *s* uccello; a bird in the hand is worth two in the bush un uovo oggi vale meglio di una gallina domani; birds of a feather gente *f* della stessa risma; to kill two birds with one stone pigliare due piccioni con una fava

bird' cage' *s* gabbia

bird' call' *s* richiamo

birdie ['bʌrdi] *s* uccellino; (golf) giocata di un colpo sotto la media

bird'lime' *s* pania

bird' of pas'sage *s* uccello di passo

bird' of prey' *s* uccello da preda

bird'seed' *s* becchime *m*

bird's'-eye view' *s* vista a volo d'uccello

bird' shot' *s* pallini *mpl* da caccia

birth [bʌrθ] *s* nascita; to give birth to dare i natali a; mettere alla luce

birth' certif'icate *s* certificato di nascita

birth' control' *s* limitazione delle nascite

birth'day' *s* natalizio, compleanno; (*of an event*) anniversario

birth'mark' *s* voglia

birth'place' *s* patria; (*e.g., city*) luogo di nascita; to be the birthplace of dare i natali a

birth' rate' *s* natalità *f*

birth'right' *s* diritto acquisito sin dalla nascita

biscuit ['bɪskɪt] *s* panino soffice; (Brit) biscotto

bisect [baɪ'sɛkt] *tr* bisecare ‖ *intr* (*said of roads*) incrociarsi

bisection [baɪ'sɛkʃən] *s* bisezione

bishop ['bɪʃəp] *s* vescovo; (chess) alfiere *m*

bishopric ['bɪʃəprɪk] *s* vescovado

bismuth ['bɪzməθ] s bismuto
bison ['baɪsən] or ['baɪzən] s bisonte m
bisulfate [baɪ'sʌlfet] s bisolfato
bisulfite [baɪ'sʌlfaɪt] s bisolfito
bit [bɪt] s (of bridle) morso; (of key) mappa; (tool) punta, trivella; (small piece) briciolo; **a bit** un po'; (coll) un momento; **a good bit** una buona quantità; **bit by bit** poco a poco; **to blow to bits** fare a pezzi; **to champ the bit** mordere il freno; **two bits** (slang) quarto di dollaro, cinque soldi
bitch [bɪtʃ] s cagna; (vulg) donnaccia || intr (slang) lamentarsi
bite [baɪt] s morso; (mouthful) boccone m; **to take a bite** fare uno spuntino; mangiare un boccone || v (pret **bit** [bɪt]; pp **bit** or **bitten** ['bɪtən]) tr mordere, addentare; pungere; (the dust) baciare || intr mordere; (said of insects) pungere; (said of fish) abboccare
biting ['baɪtɪŋ] adj mordace; pungente
bitter ['bɪtər] adj amaro; (e.g., fight) accanito; (cold) pungente || s amaro; **bitters** amaro
bit'ter end' s—**to the bitter end** fino alla fine; fino alla morte
bit'ter·en'der s (coll) intransigente mf
bitterness ['bɪtərnɪs] s amarezza
bit'ter·sweet' adj dolceamaro; (fig) agrodolce || s dulcamara
bitumen [bɪ'tjumən] or [bɪ'tumən] s bitume m
bivou·ac ['bɪvu ˌæk] or ['bɪvwæk] s bivacco || v (pret & pp -acked; ger -acking) intr bivaccare
biweekly [baɪ'wikli] adj bisettimanale; quindicinale || adv ogni due settimane
biyearly [baɪ'jɪrli] adj semestrale || adv semestralmente
bizarre [bɪ'zɑr] adj bizzarro
blab [blæb] s chiacchierone m || v (pret & pp **blabbed;** ger **blabbing**) tr rivelare || intr chiacchierare
black [blæk] adj nero; (without light) buio || s nero; **to wear black** vestire a lutto, vestire di nero || intr—**to black out** perdere i sensi
black'-and-blue' adj livido e pesto
black'-and-white' adj in bianco e nero
black'ball' s palla nera, voto contrario || tr dare la palla nera a
black'ber'ry s (-ries) mora
black'bird' s merlo
black'board' s lavagna, tavola nera
black'cap' s capinera
black'damp' s putizza
Black' Death' s peste bubbonica
blacken ['blækən] tr annerire; (shoes) lucidare; (reputation) sporcare
black' eye' s occhio pesto; (fig) cattiva reputazione
blackguard ['blægɑrd] s canaglia
black'head' s comedone m
blackish ['blækɪʃ] adj nerastro
black'jack' s randello; (cards) ventuno || tr randellare
black' mag'ic s magia nera

black'mail' s ricatto || tr ricattare
blackmailer ['blæk ˌmelər] s ricattatore m
Black' Mari'a [mə'raɪ·ə] s (coll) furgone m cellulare
black' mar'ket s borsa nera
black' marketeer' [ˌmɑrkɪ'tɪr] s borsanerista mf
blackness ['blæknɪs] s nerezza
black'out' s oscuramento; (theat) spegnitura; (pathol) svenimento passeggero
black' sheep' s (fig) pecora nera
black'smith' s fabbro
black' tie' s cravatta da smoking; smoking m
bladder ['blædər] s vescica
blade [bled] s (of a leaf) pagina; (of grass) stelo, filo; (of oar) pala; (of turbine) paletta; (of fan) ventola; (of knife) lama; (coll) caposcarico
blame [blem] s colpa; **to be to blame for** aver la colpa di; **to put the blame on s.o. for s.th** attribuire a qlcu la colpa di qlco; **you are to blame** è colpa Sua || tr biasimare, incolpare
blameless ['blemlɪs] adj innocente, senza colpa
blanch [blæntʃ] or [blɑntʃ] tr bianchire || intr impallidire
bland [blænd] adj blando; (weather) mite
blandish ['blændɪʃ] tr blandire
blank [blæŋk] adj (not written on) in bianco; (e.g., stare) vuoto; (utter) completo || s (printed form) modulo; (cartridge) cartuccia a salve; (of the mind) lacuna; **to draw a blank** (coll) non avere alcun successo || tr—**to blank out** cancellare
blank' check' s assegno in bianco; (fig) carta bianca
blanket ['blæŋkɪt] adj generale, combinato || s coperta; (of snow) cappa || tr coprire con una coperta; oscurare
blank' verse' s verso sciolto
blare [bler] s squillo || tr proclamare; fare echeggiare || intr squillare; echeggiare
blaspheme [blæs'fim] tr & intr bestemmiare
blasphemous ['blæsfɪməs] adj bestemmiatore
blasphe·my ['blæsfɪmi] s (-mies) bestemmia
blast [blæst] or [blɑst] s (of air) raffica; (of a horn) squillo; (blight) rovina; scoppio, esplosione; **at full blast** a piena velocità || tr rovinare; fare scoppiare, far saltare || intr —**to blast off** (rok) lanciarsi
blast' fur'nace s altoforno
blast'off' s lancio di missile or di nave spaziale
blatant ['bletənt] adj (noisy) rumoroso; (obtrusive) palmare; (flashy) chiassoso
blaze [blez] s fiammata; splendore m; (on a horse's head) stella; **in a blaze** in fiamme || tr proclamare; **to blaze a**

trail marcare il cammino ‖ *intr* divampare

bleach [blitʃ] *s* candeggio, candeggina ‖ *tr* imbiancare, candeggiare

bleachers ['blitʃərz] *spl* posti *mpl* allo scoperto or di gradinata

bleak [blik] *adj* nudo, deserto; (*cold*) freddo; (*gloomy*) triste

blear·y ['bliri] *adj* (**-ier; iest**) (*sight*) cisposo; confuso; offuscato

bleat [blit] *s* belato ‖ *intr* belare

bleed [blid] *v* (*pret & pp* **bled** [blɛd]) *tr* (*to draw blood from*) salassare; (*a tree*) estrare linfa da; (coll) sfruttare ‖ *intr* sanguinare; (*said of a tree*) dar linfa; **to bleed to death** morire dissanguato

blemish ['blɛmɪʃ] *s* difetto; macchia ‖ *tr* danneggiare; macchiare

blend [blɛnd] *s* mescolanza, miscuglio; (*of gasoline*) miscela ‖ *v* (*pret & pp* **blended** or **blent** [blɛnt]) *tr* mescolare, miscelare ‖ *intr* mescolarsi, miscelarsi; armonizzare; fondersi

bless [blɛs] *tr* benedire; (*to endow*) dotare; (*to make happy*) allietare

blessed ['blɛsɪd] *adj* benedetto; beato; fortunato; dotato

bless'ed event' *s* lieto evento

blessing ['blɛsɪŋ] *s* benedizione

blight [blaɪt] *s* (*insect; disease*) piaga; rovina; (*fungus*) ruggine *f* ‖ *tr* rovinare, guastare

blimp [blɪmp] *s* piccolo dirigibile

blind [blaɪnd] *adj* cieco; (slang) ubriaco ‖ *s* persiana; tendina; (*decoy*) mascheratura; preteso ‖ *adv* alla cieca ‖ *tr* accecare

blind' al'ley *s* vicolo cieco

blinder ['blaɪndər] *s* paraocchi *m*

blind' fly'ing *s* (aer) volo senza visibilità

blind'fold' *adj* bendato, cogli occhi bendati ‖ *s* benda ‖ *tr* bendare gli occhi a

blindly ['blaɪndli] *adv* alla cieca

blind' man' *s* cieco

blind'man's buff' *s* mosca cieca

blindness ['blaɪndnɪs] *s* cecità *f*

blind' spot' *s* (anat) punto cieco; (rad) zona di silenzio; (fig) debole *m*

blink [blɪŋk] *s* batter *m* di ciglio; (*glimpse*) occhiata; (*glimmer*) barlume *m;* **on the blink** (slang) fuori servizio ‖ *tr*—**to blink one's eyes** batter il ciglio ‖ *intr* occhieggiare; (*to wink*) ammiccare; (*to flash on and off*) lampeggiare; **to blink at** ignorare; far finta di non vedere

blinker ['blɪŋkər] *s* (*at a crossing*) luce *f* intermittente; (*on a horse*) paraocchi *m*

blip [blɪp] *s* guizzo sullo schermo radar

bliss [blɪs] *s* beatitudine *f*, felicità *f*

blissful ['blɪsfəl] *adj* beato, felice

blister ['blɪstər] *s* vescica, bolla ‖ *tr* coprire di vesciche; (fig) bollare ‖ *intr* coprirsi di vesciche

blithe [blaɪð] *adj* gaio, giocondo

blitzkrieg ['blɪts,krig] *s* guerra lampo

blizzard ['blɪzərd] *s* tormenta, ventoneve *m*

bloat [blot] *tr* gonfiare ‖ *intr* gonfiarsi

blob [blɑb] *s* (*lump*) zolla; (*of liquid*) macchia

block [blɑk] *s* (*e.g., of wood*) blocco; (*for chopping*) ceppo; (*pulley*) puleggia; ostacolo; (*of houses*) isolato; (typ) cliché *m* ‖ *tr* bloccare; (*a hat*) mettere in forma; **to block up** tappare

blockade [blɑ'ked] *s* blocco; **to run a blockade** forzare il blocco ‖ *tr* bloccare

block' and tack'le *s* bozzello

block'bust'er *s* (coll) superbomba

block'head' *s* imbecille *mf*

block' let'ter *s* carattere *m* stampatello

block' sig'nal *s* (rr) segnale di blocco

blond [blɑnd] *adj & s* biondo

blonde [blɑnd] *s* bionda

blood [blʌd] *s* sangue *m;* **in cold blood** a sangue freddo; **to draw blood** ferire, fare sanguinare

blood' bank' *s* emoteca

bloodcurdling ['blʌd,kʌrdlɪŋ] *adj* orripilante

blood' do'nor *s* donatore *m* di sangue

blood'hound' *s* segugio

bloodless ['blʌdlɪs] *adj* esangue; (*e.g., revolution*) senza effusione di sangue

blood'mobile' [mo,bil] *s* autoemoteca

blood' poi'soning *s* avvelenamento del sangue

blood' pres'sure *s* pressione sanguigna

blood' rela'tion *s* consanguineo

blood'shed' *s* spargimento di sangue, carneficina

blood'shot' *adj* iniettato di sangue

blood'stained' *adj* macchiato di sangue

blood'stream' *s* circolazione sanguigna

blood'suck'er *s* sanguisuga

blood' test' *s* esame *m* del sangue

blood'thirst'y *adj* assetato di sangue

blood' transfu'sion *s* trasfusione di sangue

blood' type' *s* gruppo sanguigno

blood' ves'sel *s* vaso sanguigno

blood·y ['blʌdi] *adj* (**-ier; -iest**) sanguinoso; (*bloodthirsty*) avido di sangue ‖ *v* (*pret & pp* **-ied**) *tr* macchiare di sangue

bloom [blum] *s* fiore *m;* (*state of having open buds*) sboccio; (*youthful glow*) incarnato ‖ *intr* fiorire; sbocciare

bloomers ['blumərz] *spl* pantaloni *mpl* femminili larghi fermati sotto il ginocchio

blossom ['blɑsəm] *s* fiore *m;* sboccio ‖ *intr* sbocciare

blot [blɑt] *s* macchia ‖ *v* (*pret & pp* **blotted;** *ger* **blotting**) *tr* macchiare; (*with blotting paper*) asciugare; **to blot out** cancellare; oscurare ‖ *intr* macchiarsi; (*to be absorbent*) essere assorbente; (*said of a pen*) fare macchie

blotch [blɑtʃ] *s* chiazza, macchia ‖ *tr* chiazzare

blotter ['blɑtər] *s* carta asciugante, carta assorbente; (*book*) registro

blouse [blaus] *s* blusa

blow [blo] *s* colpo; (*blast*) folata; (*of*

horn) squillo; (*sudden reverse*) batosta; **at one blow** d'un sol colpo; **to come to blows** venire alle mani; **without striking a blow** senza colpo ferire ‖ *v* (*pret* **blew** [blu]; *pp* **blown**) *tr* soffiare, soffiare su; (*an instrument*) suonare; (*one's nose*) soffiarsi; **to blow in** sfondare; **to blow one's brains out** bruciarsi le cervella; **to blow open** aprire completamente; **to blow out** (*e.g., a candle*) spegnere; (*a fuse*) fondere; **to blow up** (*e.g., a mine*) far brillare; (*phot*) ingrandire ‖ *intr* soffiare; (*to pant*) ansimare; (*with an instrument*) suonare; (*to puff*) sbuffare; (*slang*) andarsene; **to blow hot and cold** cambiare d'opinione ogni cinque minuti; **to blow in** (*coll*) arrivare inaspettatamente; **to blow out** (*said, e.g., of a candle*) spegnersi; (*said of a fuse*) saltare, fondersi; (*said of a tire*) scoppiare; **to blow over** passare; **to blow up** saltar per aria; (*said of a storm*) scoppiare; (*coll*) perdere la pazienza, scoppiare d'ira

blow'out' *s* scoppio di un pneumatico
blow'pipe' *s* (*tube*) soffione *m;* (*peashooter*) cerbottana
blow'torch' *s* saldatrice *f* a benzina
blubber ['blʌbər] *s* grasso di balena ‖ *intr* piangere, lamentarsi
bludgeon ['blʌdʒən] *s* randello ‖ *tr* randellare
blue [blu] *adj* blu, azzurro; (*gloomy*) triste; (*e.g., laws*) puritanico ‖ *s* blu *m*, azzurro; **out of the blue** inaspettatamente; **the blues** la malinconia; (*mus*) blues *m;* **to have the blues** essere giù di morale ‖ *tr* tingere di azzurro; (*a metal*) brunire
blue'ber'ry *s* (**-ries**) mirtillo
blue'bird' *s* uccello azzurro
blue' blood' *s* sangue *m* blu
blue' cheese' *s* gorgonzola americano
blue' chip' *s* (fin) azione di prim'ordine
blue' jay' *s* ghiandaia azzurra
blue' moon' *s*—**once in a blue moon** ad ogni morte di papa
blue'-pen'cil *v* (*pret & pp* **-ciled** or **-cilled**; *ger* **-ciling** or **-cilling**) *tr* correggere col lapis blu
blue'print' *s* riproduzione cianografica; (*plan*) piano ‖ *tr* riprodurre in cianografia; preparare dettagliatamente
blue'stock'ing *s* saccente *f*, sapientona
blue' streak' *s*—**like a blue streak** (coll) come un razzo
bluff [blʌf] *adj* scosceso; brusco, burbero ‖ *s* promontorio scosceso; bluff *m;* bluffatore *m* ‖ *intr* bluffare
bluing ['bluɪŋ] *s* turchinetto
bluish ['blu·ɪʃ] *adj* bluastro
blunder ['blʌndər] *s* errore *m* madornale ‖ *intr* pigliare un granchio
blunt [blʌnt] *adj* ottuso; (*plain-spoken*) franco ‖ *tr* rendere ottuso
bluntness ['blʌntnɪs] *s* ottusità *f;* franchezza
blur [blʌr] *s* macchia; offuscamento; confusione ‖ *v* (*pret & pp* **blurred**;

ger **blurring**) *tr* macchiare; (*the view*) offuscare
blurb [blʌrb] *s* annuncio pubblicitario
blurt [blʌrt] *tr*—**to blurt out** prorompere a dire, lasciarsi sfuggire
blush [blʌʃ] *s* rossore *m;* (*pinkish natural tinge*) incarnato ‖ *intr* arrossire; **to blush at** vergognarsi di
bluster ['blʌstər] *s* frastuono; (fig) boria ‖ *intr* (*said of the wind*) infuriare; fare il bravaccio
blustery ['blʌstəri] *adj* tempestuoso; violento; (*swaggering*) borioso
boar [bor] *s* verro; (*wild hog*) porco selvatico, cinghiale *m*
board [bord] *s* asse *m;* (*notice*) cartello; (*pasteboard*) cartone *m;* (*table*) tavola; (*meals*) vitto; (*group of administrators*) consiglio; (naut) bordo; **above board** franco; **in boards** rilegato; **on board** a bordo; (rr) in vettura; **to go by the board** andare in rovina; **to tread the boards** fare l'attore ‖ *tr* chiudere con assi; (*to provide with meals*) dare pensione a, tenere a dozzina; (*a ship*) salire a bordo di; (*a train*) salire su; (naut) abbordare ‖ *intr* essere a pensione
board' and lodg'ing *s* pensione completa
boarder ['bordər] *s* pensionante *mf*
board'ing house' *s* pensione di famiglia
board'ing school' *s* collegio di pensionanti
board' of direc'tors *s* consiglio d'amministrazione
board' of health' *s* ufficio d'igiene
board' of trade' *s* camera di commercio
board'walk' *s* passeggiata a mare
boast [bost] *s* millanteria, vanteria ‖ *intr* vantarsi
boastful ['bostfəl] *adj* millantatore
boat [bot] *s* nave *f*, battello; (*small ship*) barca, imbarcazione; (*dish*) salsiera; **in the same boat** nella stessa situazione
boat' hook' *s* alighiero
boat'house' *s* capannone *m* per i canotti
boating ['botɪŋ] *s* escursione in barca
boat'man *s* (**-men**) barcaiolo
boat' race' *s* regata
boatswain ['bosən] or ['bot,swen] *s* nostromo
bob [bab] *s* (*plumb*) piombino; (*short haircut*) taglio alla bebè; coda mozza (di cavallo); (*jerky motion*) strattone *m;* (*on pendulum of clock*) lente *f;* (*on fishing line*) sughero ‖ *v* (*pret & pp* **bobbed**; *ger* **bobbing**) *tr* tagliare alla bebè; far muovere a scatti ‖ *intr* muoversi a scatti; fare mossa; **to bob up** apparire
bobbin ['babɪn] *s* bobina
bob'by pin' ['babi] *s* forcina
bob'by·socks' *spl* (coll) calzini *mpl* da ragazza
bobbysoxer ['babɪ,saksər] *s* (coll) ragazzina
bobolink ['babə,lɪŋk] *s* doliconice *m*
bob'sled' *s* guidoslitta
bode [bod] *tr & intr* presagire
bodice ['badɪs] *s* giubbetto, copribusto

bodily ['bɑdɪli] *adj* fisico, corporeo || *adv* fisicamente, corporeamente; di persona; in massa

bodkin ['bɑdkɪn] *s* punteruolo; (*for lady's hair*) spillone *m*

bod·y ['bɑdi] *s* (-ies) corpo; (*corpse*) cadavere *m;* (*of water*) massa; (*of people*) gruppo; (*of a liquid*) sostanza; (*of truck*) cassone *m;* (*of car*) carrozzeria; (*of tree*) tronco; (*coll*) persona; **in a body** in massa

bod'y·guard' *s* (*of a high official*) guardia del corpo; (*e.g., of a movie star*) guardaspalle *m*

bod'y suit' *s* calzamaglia

bog [bɑg] *s* pantano, palude *m* || (*pret & pp* **bogged;** *ger* **bogging**) *intr*—**to bog down** impelagarsi

bogey·man ['bogi ‚mæn] *s* (-men [men]) babau *m*

bogus ['bogəs] *adj* (coll) falso, finto

Bohemian [bo'himi·ən] *adj* boemo; da boḣémien || *s* boemo; (fig) bohémien *m*

boil [bɔɪl] *s* bollore *m*, ebollizione; (pathol) foruncolo; **to come to a boil** cominciare a bollire || *tr* bollire; **to boil down** condensare || *intr* bollire; **to boil away** evaporare completamente; **to boil down** condensarsi; **to boil over** andare per il fuoco

boiled' ham' *s* prosciutto cotto

boiler ['bɔɪlər] *s* caldaia; (*for cooking*) caldaio

boil'er·mak·er *s* calderaio

boiling ['bɔɪlɪŋ] *adj* bollente || *s* bollore *m*, ebollizione

boisterous ['bɔɪstərəs] *adj* (*storm*) violento; (*loud*) rumoroso

bold [bold] *adj* (*daring*) coraggioso; (*impudent*) sfacciato; (*steep*) scosceso; (*clear, sharp*) netto

bold'face' *s* (typ) neretto, grassetto

boldness ['boldnɪs] *s* coraggio, audacia; sfacciataggine *f*, impudenza

boll' wee'vil [bol] *s* antonomo del cotone

bologna [bə'lonə] *or* [bə'lonjə] *s* mortadella

Bolshevik ['bɑlʃəvɪk] *or* ['bolʃəvɪk] *adj & mf* bolscevico

bolster ['bolstər] *s* cuscino; cuscinetto; (*support*) sostegno || *tr* sorreggere; **to bolster up** sostenere

bolt [bolt] *s* (*arrow*) freccia; (*of lightning*) fulmine *m;* (*sliding bar*) chiavistello; (*threaded rod*) bullone *m;* (*of paper or cloth*) pezza, rotolo || *adv*— **bolt upright** dritto come un fuso || *tr* (*to swallow hurriedly*) ingollare; (*to fasten, e.g., a door*) sprangare; (*to fasten, e.g., two metal parts*) bullonare; (*e.g., a political party*) abbandonare || *intr* (*said of people*) spiccare un salto; (*said of a horse*) prendere la mano; precipitarsi

bolt' from the blue' *s* fulmine *m* a ciel sereno

bomb [bɑm] *s* bomba; (*e.g., for spraying*) bombola || *tr* bombardare

bombard [bɑm'bɑrd] *tr* bombardare; (*with questions*) bersagliare

bombardment [bɑm'bɑrdmənt] *s* bombardamento

bombast ['bɑmbæst] *s* ampollosità *f*

bombastic [bɑm'bæstɪk] *adj* ampolloso

bomb' cra'ter *s* cratere *m*

bomber ['bɑmər] *s* bombardiere *m*

bomb'proof' *adj* a prova di bomba

bomb'shell' *s* bomba; (fig) colpo di bomba, colpo di sorpresa

bomb' shel'ter *s* rifugio antiaereo

bomb'sight' *s* traguardo aereo

bona fide ['bonə ‚faɪdə] *adj* sincero || *adv* in buona fede

bonanza [bə'nænzə] *s* (min) ricca vena; (coll) fortuna

bond [bɑnd] *s* legame *m*, vincolo; (*contractual obligation*) obbligazione; (*interest-bearing certificate*) buono, obbligazione; (*surety*) cauzione; **bonds** catene *fpl;* **in bond** sotto cauzione; (*said of goods*) in punto franco || *tr* unire, connettere

bondage ['bɑndɪdʒ] *s* schiavitù *f*

bond'ed ware'house *s* deposito in punto franco

bond'hold'er *s* obbligazionista *mf*

bonds'man *s* (-men) garante *m*

bone [bon] *s* osso; (*of fish*) spina; (*of whale*) stecca; **bones** ossa *fpl;* **to have a bone to pick with** avere un conto da regolare con; **to make no bones about** (coll) ammettere; (coll) parlare esplicitamente || *tr* disossare; cavare le spine a || *intr*—**to bone up on** (coll) ripassare

bone'head' *s* (coll) testa dura

boneless ['bonlɪs] *adj* senz'osso; (*fish*) senza spine

boner ['bonər] *s* (slang) errore *m* madornale

bonfire ['bɑn ‚faɪr] *s* falò *m*

bonnet ['bɑnɪt] *s* cappello da donna; (*of child*) berrettino

bonus ['bonəs] *s* gratifica; indennità *f;* (*to an outgoing employee*) buonuscita

bon·y ['boni] *adj* (-ier; -iest) (*having bones*) osseo; (*emaciated*) scarno; (*fish*) spinoso

boo [bu] *s* fischio, urlaccio || *tr & intr* fischiare, disapprovare

boo·by ['bubi] *s* (-bies) stupido

boo'by hatch' *s* (naut) portello; (slang) manicomio; (slang) prigione *f*

boo'by prize' *s* premio dato al peggior giocatore

boo'by trap' *s* (mil) trappola esplosiva; (fig) tranello

boogie-woogie ['bugi'wugi] *s* bughi-bughi *m*

book [buk] *s* libro; (*e.g., of matches*) pacchetto; (mus) libretto; (fig) regole *fpl;* **the Book** la Bibbia; **to be in one's book** essere nelle grazie di; **to bring s.o. to book** fare una ramanzina a || *tr* registrare; (*e.g., on a horse*) allibrare; (*e.g., a room*) prenotare; (*an actor*) scritturare

book'bind'er *s* rilegatore *m*

book'bind'er·y *s* (-ies) rilegatoria

book'bind'ing *s* rilegatura

book'case' *s* scaffale *m*

book' end' *s* reggilibri *m*

bookie ['bʊkɪ] s (coll) allibratore m
booking ['bʊkɪŋ] s (of a trip) prenotazione; (of an actor) scrittura
book'ing clerk' s impiegato alla biglietteria
bookish ['bʊkɪʃ] adj studioso; libresco
book'keep'er s contabile mf
booklet ['bʊklɪt] s libretto; (pamphlet) opuscolo
book'keep'ing s contabilità f
book'mak'er s (one who accepts bets) allibratore m
book'mark' s segnalibro
bookmobile ['bʊkmo,bil] s bibliobus m
book'plate' s ex libris m
book' review' s rassegna, recensione
book'sell'er s libraio
book'shelf' s (-shelves) scaffale m
book'stand' s (rack) scansia; (stall) edicola
book'store' s libreria
book'worm' s (zool) tarlo dei libri; (fig) topo da biblioteca
boom [bum] s (of crane) braccio; (barrier) barriera galleggiante; (noise) bum m; (fin) boom m; (naut) boma; (mov, telv) giraffa || intr rimbombare; essere in condizioni floride
boomerang ['bumə,ræŋ] s bumerang m
boom' town' s città f fungo
boon [bun] s fortuna, benedizione
boon' compan'ion s compagnone m
boor [bʊr] s bifolco, zotico
boorish ['bʊrɪʃ] adj grossolano
boost [bust] s aumento; (coll) spinta || tr spingere in su; sostenere; (prices) alzare; parlare a favore di
booster ['bustər] s (backer) sostenitore m; propulsore m a razzo; (rok) propulsore m del primo stadio; (med) seconda iniezione
boot [but] s stivale m; (kick) calcio; (patch) (aut) pezza; **the boot is on the other foot** la situazione è rovesciata; **to be in the boots of** essere nella pelle di; **to boot** per di più; **to get the boot** (coll) essere messo sulla strada; **to lick the boots of** leccare i piedi a; **to wipe one's boots on** trattare come una pezza da piedi || tr dare un calcio a; **to boot out** (slang) buttar fuori
boot'black' s lustrascarpe m
booth [buθ] s (stall) banco da mercato; (for telephoning, voting) cabina
boot'jack' s tirastivali m
boot'leg' adj di contrabbando || s liquore m di contrabbando || v (pret & pp -legged; ger -legging) tr vendere di contrabbando || intr vendere alcol di contrabbando
bootlegger ['but,legər] s contrabbandiere m di liquori
boot'lick'er [,lɪkər] s (coll) leccapiedi mf
boot'strap' s tirante m degli stivali
boo·ty ['buti] s (-ties) bottino
booze [buz] s (coll) bevanda alcolica || intr (coll) ubriacarsi
borax ['boræks] s borace m
border ['bordər] adj confinario, con-

finante || s bordo, margine m; (between two countries) confine m || tr bordare; confinare con || intr confinare
bor'der clash' s incidente m ai confini
bor'der·line' adj incerto || s frontiera
bore [bor] s (drill hole) buco, foro; (hollow part of gun) anima; (caliber) calibro; (dull person) seccatore m; (annoyance) seccatura; (mach) alesaggio || tr bucare, forare; seccare; (mach) alesare
boredom ['bordəm] s noia, tedio
boring ['borɪŋ] adj noioso || s trivellazione
born [born] adj nato, partorito; **to be born** nascere; **to be born again** rinascere; **to be born with a silver spoon in one's mouth** nascere con la camicia
borough ['bʌro] s borgata, comune m
borrow ['baro] or ['boro] tr chiedere a or in prestito; prendere a or in prestito; ricevere a or in prestito; (to adopt) adottare; **to borrow trouble** preoccuparsi per nulla
borrower ['baro·ər] or ['boro·ər] s chi riceve a prestito; (law) comodatario, prestatario
borrowing ['baro·ɪŋ] or ['boro·ɪŋ] s prestito; prestito linguistico, forestierismo
bosom ['bʊzəm] s petto, seno; (e.g., of the family) grembo, seno; (of shirt) pettorina
bos'om friend' s amico del cuore
Bosporus ['baspərəs] s Bosforo
boss [bas] or [bas] s (coll) padrone m; (coll) direttore m; (coll) capintesta m; (coll) principale m; (archit) bugna, bozza || tr fare da padrone a || intr fare da padrone
boss·y ['basi] or ['basi] adj (-ier; -iest) autoritario
botanical [bə'tænɪkəl] adj botanico
botanist ['batənɪst] s botanico
botany ['batəni] s botanica
botch [batʃ] s abborracciatura || tr abborracciare
both [boθ] adj entrambi i, tutti e due i || pron entrambi, tutti e due || conj del pari, al medesimo tempo; **both ... and** tanto ... quanto
bother ['baðər] s (worry) noia, seccatura; (person) seccatore m || tr dar noia a, seccare || intr preoccuparsi; **to bother about** or **with** occuparsi di; **to bother to** + inf molestarsi di + inf
bothersome ['baðərsəm] adj incomodo
bottle ['batəl] s bottiglia, fiasco || tr imbottigliare; **to bottle up** imbottigliare
bot'tle cap' s tappo a corona
bot'tle·neck' s collo di bottiglia; (of traffic) congestione, imbottigliamento
bot'tle o'pener ['opənər] s apribottiglie m
bottom ['batəm] adj basso; (price, dollar) ultimo; infimo || s fondo; (of chair) sedile m; base f; (of bottle) culo; (of ship) scafo; **at bottom** in realtà; **to begin at the bottom** comin-

ciare dalla gavetta; **to get at the bottom of** andare a fondo di; **to go to the bottom** andare a picco
bottomless ['batəmlɪs] *adj* senza fondo
boudoir [bu'dwɑr] *s* gabinetto di toletta (da signora)
bough [bau] *s* ramo
bouillon ['bujɑn] *s* brodo schietto
boulder ['boldər] *s* masso, roccia
boulevard ['bulə,vɑrd] *s* corso
bounce [bauns] *s* balzo; salto; elasticità *f;* (*of boat or plane*) piastrellamento; (fig) spirito; **to get the bounce** (slang) essere licenziato || *tr* far balzare; (slang) buttar fuori || *intr* rimbalzare; saltare; (aer, naut) piastrellare
bouncer ['baunsər] *s* (*in night club*) (slang) buttafuori *m*
bouncing ['baunsɪŋ] *adj* forte, vigoroso; grande, rumoroso
bound [baund] *adj* legato; collegato; obbligato; (bb) rilegato; (coll) risoluto; **bound for** destinato a, diretto per; **bound up in** or **with** in strette relazioni con; assorto in || *s* salto; rimbalzo; limite *m;* **bounds** zona limitrofa; **out of bounds** fuori limiti; al di là delle convenienze || *tr* delimitare
bounda·ry ['baundəri] *s* (**-ries**) confine *m*, limite *m*
bound'ary stone' *s* pietra di confine
boundless ['baundlɪs] *adj* illimitato, sconfinato
bountiful ['bauntɪfəl] *adj* generoso; abbondante
boun·ty ['baunti] *s* (**-ties**) dono generoso; generosità *f*, abbondanza; (*reward*) premio
bouquet [bu'ke] or [bo'ke] *s* mazzo, mazzolino; profumo, aroma *m*
bourgeois ['burʒwɑ] *adj* & *s* borghese *mf*
bourgeoisie [,burʒwɑ'zi] *s* borghesia
bout [baut] *s* lotta, contesa; (*of illness*) attacco
bow [bau] *s* inchino, riverenza; (naut) prua; **to take a bow** ricevere gli applausi || *tr* chinare, piegare || *intr* inchinarsi; sottomettersi; **to bow and scrape** fare riverenze || [bo] *s* (*weapon*) arco; (*knot*) nodo; (mus) archetto; (*stroke of bow*) (mus) arcata || *tr* & *intr* (mus) suonare con l'archetto
bowdlerize ['baudlə,raɪz] *tr* espurgare
bowel ['bau·əl] *s* budello; **bowels** viscere *fpl*
bow'el move'ment *s* evacuazione; **to have a bowel movement** andar di corpo
bower ['bau·ər] *s* pergolato
bowery ['bau·əri] *adj* frondoso
bowknot ['bo,nɑt] *s* nodo scorsoio
bowl [bol] *s* (*dish*) ciotola, tazza; (*of pipe*) fornello; (*basin*) catino; (*amphitheater*) arena; (*ball*) boccia; (*delivery of ball*) bocciata; **bowls** bocce *fpl* || *tr* bocciare; **to bowl down** or **over** abbattere || *intr* giocare alle bocce

bowlegged ['bo,lɛgd] or ['bo,lɛgɪd] *adj* con le gambe storte
bowler ['bolər] *s* giocatore *m* di bocce
bowling ['bolɪŋ] *s* bocce *fpl;* bowling *m*, birilli *mpl*
bowl'ing al'ley *s* pista per il bowling; bowling *m*
bowl'ing green' *s* campo di bocce erboso
bowshot ['bo,ʃɑt] *s* tiro d'arco
bowsprit ['bausprit] or ['bosprɪt] *s* (naut) bompresso
bow' tie' [bo] *s* cravatta a farfalla
bowwow ['bau,wau] *interj* bau bau!
box [bɑks] *s* scatola; cassa; (*for jury*) banco; (*for sentry*) garitta; (*on coach*) cassetta; (*in stable*) posta; (*slap*) ceffone *m;* (*with fist*) pugno; (bot) bosso; (theat) palco, barcaccia; (baseball) posto del battitore; (typ) riquadratura || *tr* mettere in scatola; (*to slap*) schiaffeggiare; (*to hit with fist*) fare a pugilato con; **to box in** or **up** rinchiudere || *intr* fare a pugni, combattere
box'car' *s* vagone *m* merci coperto
boxer ['bɑksər] *s* pugile *m*
box'hold'er *s* palchettista *mf*
boxing ['bɑksɪŋ] *s* pugilato
box'ing gloves' *spl* guantoni *mpl* da pugilato
box' of'fice *s* sportello, biglietteria; (theat) incasso; (theat) successo
box'-of'fice hit' *s* grande successo
box' pleat' *s* (*of skirt*) cannone *m*
box' seat' *s* posto in palco
box'wood' *s* bosso
boy [bɔɪ] *s* ragazzo, giovane *m* || *interj* accidempoli!
boycott ['bɔɪkɑt] *s* boicottaggio || *tr* boicottare
boy'friend' *s* innamorato, amico
boyhood ['bɔɪhud] *s* fanciullezza
boyish ['bɔɪ·ɪʃ] *adj* giovanile
boy' scout' *s* giovane esploratore *m*
bra [brɑ] *s* (coll) reggiseno
brace [bres] *s* (*couple*) paio; (*device for maintaining tension*) tirante *m;* (*prop*) sostegno; (*tool*) trapano; (typ) graffa; **braces** (Brit) bretelle *fpl* || *tr* legare; serrare; puntellare; sostenere; invigorare; **to brace oneself** pigliare animo || *intr*—**to brace up** (coll) pigliare animo
brace' and bit' *s* menarola, trapano
bracelet ['breslɪt] *s* braccialetto
bracer ['bresər] *s* (coll) bicchierino
bracket ['brækɪt] *s* mensola; (*for lamp*) braccio; angolo; classifica; (typ) parentesi quadra || *tr* sostenere con mensola; mettere tra parentesi quadra; classificare
brackish ['brækɪʃ] *adj* salmastro
brad [bræd] *s* chiodino, punta
brag [bræg] *s* vanto || *v* (*pret & pp* **bragged;** *ger* **bragging**) *intr* vantare
braggart ['brægərt] *s* millantatore *m*
Brah·man ['brɑmən] *s* (**-mans**) bramino
braid [bred] *s* treccia; (*strip of cloth*) spighetta; (mil) cordellina || *tr* intrecciare; decorare con spighette

brain [bren] *s* cervello; **brains** cervello, intelligenza; **to rack one's brains** rompersi la testa || *tr* far saltare le cervella di

brain'child' *s* (coll) parto dell'ingegno, idea geniale

brain' drain' *s* (coll) fuga di cervelli

brainless ['brenlɪs] *adj* senza testa

brain' pow'er *s* intelligenza

brain'storm' *s* (coll) ispirazione

brain' trust' *s* consiglio d'esperti

brain'wash'ing *s* lavaggio del cervello

brain' wave' *s* onda encefalica; (coll) idea geniale

brain'work' *s* lavoro intellettuale

brain·y ['breni] *adj* (**-ier; -iest**) intelligente

braise [brez] *tr* (culin) brasare

brake [brek] *s* freno; (*thicket*) macchia || *tr & intr* frenare

brake' drum' *s* tamburo del freno

brake' lin'ing *s* ferodo

brake'man *s* (**-men**) frenatore *m*

brake' shoe' *s* ganascia

bramble ['bræmbəl] *s* rovo

bran [bræn] *s* crusca

branch [bræntʃ] *s* (*of tree*) branca, ramo; (*of river*) braccio; (*of a family*) ramo; (*of business*) filiale *f*; (rr) diramazione || *intr* biforcarsi; **to branch off** or **out** ramificarsi, diramarsi

branch' line' *s* ferrovia di diramazione

branch' of'fice *s* succursale *f*

brand [brænd] *s* (*burning stick*) tizzone *m*; (*mark; stigma*) marchio; (*label; make*) marca || *tr* (*to mark with a brand*) marchiare; (*to put a stigma on*) bollare; **to brand as** tacciare di

brandied ['brændid] *adj* conservato in acquavite

brand'ing i'ron *s* ferro da marchio

brandish ['brændɪʃ] *tr* brandire

brand'-new' *adj* nuovo fiammante

bran·dy ['brændi] *s* (**-dies**) cognac *m*, acquavite *f*

brash [bræʃ] *adj* (*too hasty*) avventato; (*insolent*) impudente || *s* frammenti *mpl;* attacco (di malattia), indigestione

brass [bræs] or [brɑs] *s* ottone *m;* (coll) faccia tosta; (slang) alti ufficiali; **brasses** (mus) ottoni *mpl*

brass' band' *s* fanfara

brassiere [brə'zir] *s* reggiseno

brass' knuck'les *spl* tirapugni *m*

brass' tack' *s* chiodino or borchia d'ottone; **to get down to brass tacks** (coll) venire al sodo

brass·y ['bræsi] or ['brɑsi] *adj* (**-ier; -iest**) fatto d'ottone; sfacciato, impudente

brat [bræt] *s* marmocchio, monello

brava·do [brə'vɑdo] *s* (**-does** or **-dos**) bravata

brave [brev] *adj* coraggioso || *s* persona coraggiosa; guerriero indiano || *tr* (*to defy*) sfidare; (*to meet with courage*) affrontare

bravery ['brevəri] *s* coraggio

bra·vo ['brɑvo] *s* (**-vos**) bravo; applauso || *interj* bravo!

brawl [brɔl] *s* zuffa, rissa || *intr* azzuffarsi, rissare

brawn [brɔn] *s* forza muscolare

brawn·y ['brɔni] *adj* (**-ier; -iest**) muscoloso

bray [bre] *s* raglio || *intr* ragliare

braze [brez] *s* brasatura || *tr* brasare

brazen ['brezən] *adj* d'ottone; (*shameless*) sfrontato; (*sound*) penetrante || *tr*—**to brazen out** or **through** affrontare sfacciatamente

brazier ['breʒər] *s* caldano, braciere *m;* (*workman*) ottonaio

Brazil [brə'zɪl] *s* il Brasile

Brazilian [brə'zɪljən] *adj & s* brasiliano

Brazil' nut' *s* noce *f* del Brasile

breach [britʃ] *s* (*gap*) breccia; (*failure to observe a law*) infrazione || *tr* fare breccia su, fare varco in

breach' of faith' *s* abuso di confidenza

breach' of prom'ise *s* rottura di promessa di matrimonio

breach' of the peace' *s* violazione dell'ordine pubblico

bread [brɛd] *s* pane *m;* **to break bread with** sedersi a tavola con || *tr* impannare

bread' and but'ter *s* pane *m* e burro; (coll) pane quotidiano

bread' crumbs' *spl* pangrattato

breaded ['brɛdɪd] *adj* impannato

bread' knife' *s* coltello da pane

bread' line' *s* coda del pane

bread' stick' *s* grissino

breadth [brɛdθ] *s* (*width*) larghezza; (*scope*) ampiezza

bread'win'ner *s* sostegno della famiglia

break [brek] *s* interruzione; intervallo; omissione; (*breaking*) rottura; (*of bones*) frattura; (*of day*) fare *m,* spuntare *m;* (*sudden change*) mutamento; (*from jail*) evasione; (*luck*) (coll) fortuna; **to give s.o. a break** dare a qlcu l'opportunità || *v* (*pret* **broke** [brok]; *pp* **broken**) *tr* (*to smash*) rompere, spezzare; (*to tame*) domare; (*to demote*) destituire; (*a record*) superare; (*to violate*) violare; (*to make bankrupt*) mandare al fallimento; (*to interrupt*) interrompere; (*to reduce the effects of*) attutire; (*to disclose*) rivelare; (*to bring to an end by force*) battere; (*a banknote*) cambiare; (*one's word*) mancare (with *dat*); (*a law*) rompere; **to break asunder** separare; **to break down** analizzare; **to break in** forzare; **to break open** forzare, scassinare; **to break up** dissolvere || *intr* (*to divide*) rompersi; (*to burst*) scoppiare; (*said of voice of youngster*) cambiare; (*said of voice*) indebolirsi; (*said of a crowd*) disperdersi; (*said of weather*) rischiararsi; (*said of prices*) ribassare; (*to come into being*) scoppiare; (boxing) separarsi; **to break asunder** separarsi; **to break away** scappare; **to break down** abbattersi; (aut) essere or rimanere in panna; **to break even** fare patta; **to break in** irrompere; interrompere; **to break into** forzare; **to break into a run** incominciare a correre; **to break loose** liberarsi; (*said of a storm*) scatenarsi; **to break off** interrompere; **to break out** (*said of the skin*) avere un'eruzione; (*said, e.g., of war*) scoppiare; **to break through** aprirsi il varco; **to break up** disperdersi; **to break with** rompere le relazioni con

breakable ['brekəbəl] *adj* fragile

breakage ['brekɪdʒ] *s* rottura

break'down' *s* (*in negotiations*) rottura; (aut) panna; (chem) analisi *f;* (pathol) colasso

breaker ['brekər] *s* (*wave*) frangente *m*

breakfast ['brɛkfəst] *s* prima colazione || *intr* fare prima colazione

break'neck' *adj* pericoloso; **at breakneck speed** a rotta di collo, a rompicollo

break' of day' *s* alba

break'through' *s* (mil) penetrazione; (fig) scoperta sensazionale

break'up' *s* dispersione; dissoluzione; (*of a friendship*) rottura

break'wa'ter *s* diga, frangiflutti *m*

breast [brɛst] *s* petto; (*of female*) seno; (*source of emotions*) animo; **to make a clean breast of** fare una piena confessione di

breast'bone' *s* sterno

breast' drill' *s* trapano da petto

breast'feed' *v* (*pret & pp* -fed [fɛd]) *tr* allattare

breast'pin' *s* spilla

breast'stroke' *s* bracciata a rana

breath [brɛθ] *s* respiro, respirazione; (*odor*) alito; (*breeze*) soffio; (*whisper*) sussurro; (fig) vita; **out of breath** ansimante; **short of breath** corto di respiro; **to gasp for breath** respirare affannosamente; **under one's breath** sottovoce

breathe [brið] *tr* respirare; (*to whisper*) sussurrare; **to breathe one's last** esalare l'ultimo sospiro; **to not breathe a word** non dire una parola || *intr* respirare; **to breathe in** inspirare; **to breathe out** espirare

breath'ing spell' *s* attimo di respiro

breathless ['brɛθlɪs] *adj* senza fiato, ansimante; soffocante

breath'tak'ing *s* emozionante, commovente

breech [britʃ] *s* (*buttocks*) natiche *fpl;* (*rear part*) parte *f* posteriore; (*of gun*) culatta; **breeches** ['brɪtʃɪz] pantaloni *mpl* al ginocchio; pantaloni *mpl* da cavallo; **to wear the breeches** (coll) portare le brache

breed [brid] *s* razza; tipo; (*stock*) origine *f* || *v* (*pret & pp* bred [brɛd]) *tr* produrre; (*to raise*) allevare

breeder ['bridər] *s* allevatore *m;* riproduttore *m*

breeding ['bridɪŋ] *s* (*e.g., of livestock*) allevamento; educazione

breeze [briz] *s* brezza

breez·y ['brizi] *adj* (-ier; -iest) ventilato; (*brisk*) vivace, brioso

brethren ['brɛðrɪn] *spl* fratelli *mpl*

brevi·ty ['brɛvɪti] *s* (-ties) brevità *f*

brew [bru] *s* pozione; bevanda || *tr* (*beer*) fabbricare; (*to steep*) preparare; (*to plot*) complottare || *intr* (*said of beer*) fermentare; (*said of a storm*) prepararsi

brewer ['bruər] *s* birraio

brew'er's yeast' *s* lievito di birra

brewer·y ['bruəri] *s* (-ies) birreria, fabbrica di birra

bribe [braɪb] *s* subornazione, bustarella || *tr* subornare, dare la bustarella a

briber·y ['braɪbəri] *s* (-ies) subornazione, corruzione

bric-a-brac ['brɪkə‚bræk] *s* bric-a-brac *m,* cianfrusaglia, cianfrusaglie *fpl*

brick [brɪk] *s* mattone *m* || *tr* mattonare

brick'bat' *s* pezzo di mattone; (coll) insulto

brick'kiln' *s* fornace *f* per mattoni

bricklayer ['brɪk‚le·ər] *s* muratore *m*

brick'yard' *s* deposito di mattoni

bridal ['braɪdəl] *adj* nuziale, da sposa

brid'al wreath' *s* serto nuziale

bride [braɪd] *s* sposa

bride'groom' *s* sposo

bridesmaid ['braɪdz‚med] *s* damigella d'onore

bridge [brɪdʒ] *s* ponte *m;* (*of violin*) ponticello; (*on a ship*) ponte *m* di comando || *tr* gettare un ponte su; congiungere; **to bridge a gap** colmare una lacuna

bridge'head' *s* testa di ponte

bridle ['braɪdəl] *s* briglia || *tr* mettere la briglia a; (fig) frenare || *intr* drizzare il capo, insuperbirsi

bri'dle path' *s* strada cavalcabile

brief [brif] *adj* breve || *s* sommario; (law) esposto; (eccl) breve *m;* **briefs** slip *m* || *tr* dare istruzíoni a, mettere al corrente

brief' case' *s* cartella, borsa d'avvocato

brier ['braɪ·ər] *s* radica; pipa di radica

brig [brɪg] *s* (naut) brigantino; (naut) prigione

brigade [brɪ'ged] *s* brigata

brigadier [‚brɪgə'dir] *s* (coll) brigadier generale *m,* generale *m* di brigata

brigand ['brɪgənd] *s* brigante *m*

brigantine ['brɪgən‚tin] or ['brɪgən‚taɪn] *s* (naut) brigantino goletta

bright [braɪt] *adj* (*shining*) lucido; (*light*) brillante; (*lively*) vivo; intelligente; famoso; (*idea*) luminoso

brighten ['braɪtən] *tr* illuminare; ravvivare || *intr* illuminarsi; ravvivarsi; rischiararsi

bright' lights' *spl* luci *fpl* abbaglianti; (aut) fari *mpl* abbaglianti

brilliance ['brɪljəns] or **brilliancy** ['brɪljənsi] *s* splendore *m,* scintillio

brilliant ['brɪljənt] *adj* brillante

brim [brɪm] *s* (*e.g., of cup*) orlo, bordo; (*of hat*) ala, tesa || *v* (*pret & pp* brimmed; *ger* brimming) *intr* essere pieno sino all'orlo

brim'stone' *s* zolfo

brine [braɪn] *s* salamoia; acqua di mare

bring [brɪŋ] *v* (*pret & pp* **brought**

[brɔt]) *tr* far venire; provocare; (*to carry along*) portare con sè; **to bring about** causare; **to bring around** persuadere; **to bring back** restituire; **to bring down** far abbassare; (fig) umiliare; **to bring forth** dare alla luce; **to bring forward** (*an excuse*) addurre; (math) riportare; **to bring in** introdurre; far entrare; **to bring off** compiere; **to bring on** causare; **to bring oneself to** rassegnarsi a; **to bring out** (*to expose*) rivelare; (*to offer to the public*) presentare al pubblico; (*a book*) far uscire; **to bring to** far rinvenire; (*a ship*) fermare; **to bring together** riunire; **to bring up** (*children*) allevare, tirar su; (*to introduce*) allegare; (*to cough up*) rigettare

bringing-up [ˈbrɪŋɪŋˌʌp] *s* educazìone
brink [brɪŋk] *s* orlo
briquet [brɪˈket] *s* bricchetta
brisk [brɪsk] *adj* (*quick*) svelto; (*sharp*) acuto; (*invigorating*) frizzante; (*gunfire*) nutrito
bristle [ˈbrɪsəl] *s* setola ‖ *intr* (*to be stiff*) irrigidirsi; (*said of hair*) rizzarsi; (*with anger*) adirarsi
bris·tly [brɪsli] *adj* (**-tlier; -tliest**) irto di setole
British [ˈbrɪtɪʃ] *adj* britannico ‖ **the British** i britannici, gl'inglesi
Britisher [ˈbrɪtɪʃər] *s* britannico
Briton [ˈbrɪtən] *s* britannico
Brittany [ˈbrɪtəni] *s* la Bretagna
brittle [ˈbrɪtəl] *adj* fragile, friabile; (*crisp*) croccante
broach [brotʃ] *s* (*pin*) spilla; (*spit*) spiedo; (mach) alesatore *m* ‖ *tr* perforare; (*a subject*) intavolare
broad [brɔd] *adj* largo; tollerante, liberale; (*daylight*) pieno; (*story*) grossolano; (*extensive*) lato; (*accent*) pronunciato
broad'cast' *s* disseminazione; (rad) radiodiffusione ‖ *v* (*pret & pp* **-cast**) *tr* disseminare, diffondere ‖ (*pret & pp* **-cast** or **-casted**) *tr* radiodiffondere
broad'casting sta'tion *s* stazione radiotrasmittente
broad'cloth' *s* (*wool*) panno di lana; (*cotton*) popeline *f*
broaden [ˈbrɔdən] *tr* allargare, estendere ‖ *intr* allargarsi, estendersi
broad' jump' *s* salto in lunghezza
broadloom [ˈbrɔdˌlum] *adj* tessuto su telaio largo
broad-minded [ˈbrɔdˈmaɪndɪd] *adj* di ampie vedute, liberale
broad-shouldered [ˈbrɔdˈʃoldəred] *adj* largo di spalle
broad'side' *s* (nav) bordo; (nav) bordata; (*verbal criticism*) (coll) sfuriata; (*written criticism*) (coll) attacco violento
broad'sword' *s* spada da taglio
brocade [broˈked] *s* broccato
broccoli [ˈbrɑkəli] *s* broccoli; (*as food*) broccoli *mpl*
brochure [broˈʃur] *s* opuscolo, libriccino

brogue [brog] *s* accento irlandese; scarpa forte e comoda
broil [brɔɪl] *s* cottura alla graticola; carne *f* cotta alla graticola; (*quarrel*) rissa, zuffa ‖ *tr* cucinare alla graticola; bruciare ‖ *intr* cucinare alla graticola; (*to quarrel*) rissare, azzuffarsi
broiler [ˈbrɔɪlər] *s* graticola, gratella; (*chicken*) pollo da cucinare alla gratella or allo spiedo
broke [brok] *adj* (coll) al verde
broken [ˈbrokən] *adj* rotto; fratturato; (*e.g., English*) parlato male; (*tamed*) domato
bro'ken-down' *adj* avvilito; rovinato
broken-hearted [ˈbrokənˈhɑrtɪd] *adj* affranto
broker [ˈbrokər] *s* sensale *m;* (*on the stock exchange*) agente *m* di cambio
brokerage [ˈbrokərɪdʒ] *s* mediazione
bromide [ˈbromaɪd] *s* bromuro; (coll) banalità *f*
bromine [ˈbromin] *s* bromo
bronchitis [brɑŋˈkaɪtɪs] *s* bronchite *f*
bron·co [ˈbrɑŋko] *s* (**-cos**) puledro brado
broncobuster [ˈbrɑŋkoˌbʌstər] *s* domatore *m* di puledri bradi
bronze [brɑnz] *adj* bronzeo ‖ *s* bronzo ‖ *tr* bronzare ‖ *intr* abbronzarsi
brooch [brotʃ] or [brutʃ] *s* spilla
brood [brud] *s* covata, nidiata ‖ *tr* covare ‖ *intr* chiocciare; meditare; **to brood on** or **over** meditare con tristezza (su)
brook [bruk] *s* ruscello ‖ *tr—***to brook no** non sopportare
broom [brum] or [brum] *s* scopa; (*shrub*) saggina
broom'corn' *s* sorgo
broom'stick' *s* manico di scopa
broth [brɔθ] or [brɑθ] *s* brodo
brothel [ˈbrɑθəl] or [ˈbrɑðəl] *s* postribolo, bordello
brother [ˈbrʌðər] *s* fratello
brotherhood [ˈbrʌðərˌhud] *s* fratellanza; (*association*) confraternita
broth'er-in-law' *s* (**brothers-in-law**) cognato
brotherly [ˈbrʌðərli] *adj* fraterno ‖ *adv* fraternamente
brow [brau] *s* ciglio; (*forehead*) fronte *f;* **to knit one's brow** aggrottare la fronte
brow'beat' *v* (*pret* **-beat;** *pp* **-beaten**) *tr* intimidire, intimorire
brown [braun] *adj* bruno; (*tanned*) abbronzato ‖ *s* color bruno ‖ *tr* colorare di bruno; abbronzare; (*metal*) brunire; (culin) dorare ‖ *intr* colorarsi di bruno; abbronzarsi; brunirsi; (culin) dorarsi
brownish [ˈbraunɪʃ] *adj* brunastro
brown' stud'y *s—***in a brown study** assorto in fantasticherie
brown' sug'ar *s* zucchero greggio
browse [brauz] *intr* (*said of cattle*) brucare; sfogliare; **to browse around** curiosare
bruise [bruz] *s* ammaccatura, contu-

sione || *tr* ammaccare || *intr* ammaccarsi
brunet [bru'nɛt] *adj* bruno
brunette [bru'nɛt] *adj & s* bruna
brunt [brʌnt] *s* forza; scontro; peso
brush [brʌʃ] *s* pennello; spazzola; (*stroke*) pennellata; (*light touch*) tocco; (*brushwood*) macchia; (*brief encounter*) scaramuccia; (elec) spazzola || *tr* spazzolare; pennellare; **to brush aside** rigettare; **to brush up** ritoccare || *intr*—**to brush by** passar vicino; **to brush up on** ripassare
brush'-off' *s* (slang) scortesia; **to give the brush-off to** (slang) snobbare
brush'wood' *s* macchia, fratta
brusque [brʌsk] *adj* brusco
brusqueness ['brʌsknɪs] *s* bruschezza
Brussels ['brʌsəlz] *s* Bruxelles *f*
Brus'sels sprouts' *spl* cavolini *mpl*
brutal ['brutəl] *adj* brutale
brutali·ty [bru'tælɪti] *s* (-ties) brutalità *f*
brute [brut] *adj & s* bruto
brutish ['brutɪʃ] *adj* bruto
bubble ['bʌbəl] *s* bolla; (fig) chimera || *intr* bollire; (*to make a bubbling sound*) barbugliare; **to bubble over** traboccare
bub'ble bath' *s* bagno di schiuma
buccaneer [,bʌkə'nɪr] *s* bucaniere *m*
buck [bʌk] *s* (*deer*) cervo; (*goat*) caprone *m*; (*sawhorse*) cavalletto; (*rabbit*) coniglio maschio; (*bucking*) groppata; (*dandy*) damerino; (slang) dollaro; **to pass the buck** (coll) giocare a scaricabarile || *tr* resistere accanitamente || *intr* (*said of a horse*) fare salti da caprone; **to buck for** (slang) cercare di ottenere; **to buck up** (coll) rianimarsi, prender animo
bucket ['bʌkɪt] *s* secchio; bigoncia; (*e.g., of dredge*) benna; **to kick the bucket** (slang) tirare le cuoia
buck'et seat' *s* sedile *m*, strapuntino
buckle ['bʌkəl] *s* (*clasp*) fibbia, boccola; piega || *tr* affibbiare || *intr* piegarsi, curvarsi; **to buckle down to** (coll) mettersi di buzzo buono a
buck' pri'vate *s* (slang) soldato semplice
buckram ['bʌkrəm] *s* tela da fusto
buck'saw' *s* cavalletto
buck'shot' *s* pallini *mpl* da caccia
buck'tooth' *s* (-teeth) dente *m* in fuori, dente *m* sporgente
buck'wheat' *s* grano saraceno
bud [bʌd] *s* bocciolo, gemma; **to nip in the bud** troncare sul nascere || *v* (*pret & pp* budded; *ger* budding) *intr* sbocciare; nascere
Buddhism ['budɪzəm] *s* buddismo
bud·dy ['bʌdi] *s* (-dies) (coll) amico, compare *m*
budge [bʌdʒ] *tr* smuovere || *intr* muoversi
budget ['bʌdʒɪt] *s* bilancio || *tr* stanziare, preventivare; (*to schedule*) anticipare; (*time*) calcolare in anticipo
budgetary ['bʌdʒɪ,tɛri] *adj* preventivo, di bilancio
buff [bʌf] *adj* bruno giallastro; di pelle || *s* (*leather*) pelle gialla; dilet-

tante *m*; (mil) giacca di pelle gialla; (coll) pelle nuda || *tr* lucidare; (*to reduce the force of*) ammortizzare
buffa·lo ['bʌfə,lo] *s* (-loes or -los) bufalo || *tr* (coll) intimidire
buffer ['bʌfər] *s* ammortizzatore *m*; cuscinetto; (*worker*) lucidatore *m*; (mach) lucidatrice *f*; (rr) respingente *m*
buff'er state' *s* stato cuscinetto
buffet [bu'fe] *s* (*piece of furniture*) credenza; (*counter*) buffet *m* || ['bʌfɪt] *s* pugno; schiaffo || *tr* dar pugni a; schiaffeggiare; lottare con; (*to push about*) sballottare
buffet' car' [bu'fe] *s* vagone *m* ristorante
buffoon [bə'fun] *s* buffone *m*
buffoner·y [bə'funəri] *s* (-ies) buffoneria
bug [bʌg] *s* insetto; (coll) germe *m*; (*in motor*) (slang) noia; (slang) pazzo; **to put a bug in the ear of** mettere una pulce nell'orecchio di || *v* (*pret & pp* bugged; *ger* bugging) *tr* (slang) installare un sistema d'ascolto nel telefono di; (*to annoy*) (slang) seccare || *intr*—**to bug out** (slang) andarsene
bug'bear' *s* spauracchio
bug·gy ['bʌgi] *adj* (-gier; -giest) pieno di cimici; (slang) pazzo || *s* (-gies) carrozzino
bug'house' *adj* (slang) pazzo || *s* (slang) manicomio
bugle ['bjugəl] *s* tromba, cornetta
bugler ['bjuglər] *s* trombettiere *m*
build [bɪld] *s* corporatura, taglia || *v* (*pret & pp* built [bɪlt]) *tr* costruire, edificare; fondare, basare; **to build up** sviluppare
builder ['bɪldər] *s* costruttore *m*; costruttore *m* edile
building ['bɪldɪŋ] *s* edificio, stabile *m*; costruzione; edilizia
build'ing and loan' associa'tion *s* società *f* di credito fondiario
build'ing lot' *s* (coll) terreno da costruzioni
build'ing trades' *spl* edilizia
build'-up' *s* concentrazione; sviluppo; processo di preparazione; propaganda favorevole
built'-in' *adj* (*in a wall*) murato; (*in a cabinet*) incassato, incorporato
built'-in clos'et *s* armadio a muro
built'-up' *adj* armato; popolato
bulb [bʌlb] *s* bulbo; (*lamp*) lampadina; (*of a lamp*) globo, cipolla
Bulgarian [bʌl'gɛri·ən] *adj & s* bulgaro
bulge [bʌldʒ] *s* protuberanza, sporgenza || *intr* sporgere, gonfiarsi
bulk [bʌlk] *s* volume *m*, massa; **in bulk** in blocco; sciolto || *intr* avere importanza; aumentare d'importanza
bulk'head' *s* diga; (naut) paratia
bulk·y ['bʌlki] *adj* (-ier; -iest) voluminoso
bull [bul] *s* toro; (*in the stockmarket*) rialzista *mf*; (slang) scemenza; (eccl) bulla || *tr*—**to bull the market** giocare al rialzo
bull'dog' *s* molosso

bulldoze [ˈbul‚doz] *tr* intimidire; (*land*) livellare

bulldozer [ˈbul‚dozər] *s* livellatrice *f*, appripista *m*

bullet [ˈbulɪt] *s* palla, pallottola

bulletin [ˈbulətɪn] *s* bollettino; (*of a school*) albo; (journ) comunicato

bul′letin board′ *s* tabellone *m*

bul′let-proof′ *adj* blindato

bull′fight′ *s* corrida

bull′fight′er *s* torero

bull′finch′ *s* (orn) ciuffolotto

bull′frog′ *s* rana americana

bull-headed [ˈbul‚hɛdɪd] *adj* testardo

bullion [ˈbuljən] *s* lingotti *mpl* d'oro or d'argento; frangia d'oro; (*on an Italian general's hat*) greca

bullish [ˈbulɪʃ] *adj* ostinato; (*market*) al rialzo; (*speculator*) rialzista

bullock [ˈbulək] *s* manzo

bull′ring′ *s* arena

bull's-eye [ˈbulz‚aɪ] *s* centro, tiro in pieno sul bersaglio; **to hit the bull's-eye** fare centro

bul·ly [ˈbuli] *adj* (coll) eccellente ‖ *s* (-lies) bravaccio ‖ *v* (*pret & pp* -lied) *tr* intimidire

bulrush [ˈbul‚rʌʃ] *s* giunco; (Bibl) papiro

bulwark [ˈbulwərk] *s* baluardo; protezione ‖ *tr* proteggere

bum [bʌm] *adj* (slang) pessimo ‖ *s* (slang) vagabondo; **on the bum** (slang) rotto, fuori servizio ‖ *v* (*pret & pp* **bummed**; *ger* **bumming**) *tr* (slang) scroccare ‖ *intr* (slang) oziare; (slang) vivere d'elemosina; (slang) fare lo scroccatore

bumble [ˈbʌmbəl] *tr* abborracciare ‖ *intr* abborracciare; (*to stagger*) barcollare; (*to stumble*) balbettare; (*said of a bee*) ronzare

bum′blebee′ *s* calabrone *m*

bump [bʌmp] *s* botta, botto; (*collision*) colpo, urto; (*swelling*) bernoccolo ‖ *tr* urtare; **to bump off** (slang) uccidere ‖ *intr* urtare, cozzare; **to bump into** incontrarsi con; cozzare contro

bumper [ˈbʌmpər] *adj* (coll) abbondante ‖ *s* bicchiere pieno fino all'orlo; (aut) paraurti *m;* (rr) respingente *m*

bumpkin [ˈbʌmpkɪn] *s* beota *m*

bumptious [ˈbʌmpʃəs] *adj* vanitoso, presuntuoso

bump·y [ˈbʌmpi] *adj* (-ier; -iest) (*road*) irregolare, ondulato; (*air*) agitato

bun [bʌn] *s* panino; (*of hair*) crocchia, treccia a ciambella

bunch [bʌntʃ] *s* (*of grapes*) grappolo; (*of keys*) mazzo; (*of grass*) ciuffo; (*of people*) gruppo; (*of twigs*) fastello; (*of animals*) branco ‖ *tr* (*things*) ammonticchiare; (*people*) raggruppare ‖ *intr* raggrupparsi

bundle [ˈbʌndəl] *s* fascio, fastello; (*package*) pacco; (*large package*) collo; (*bunch*) mucchio ‖ *tr* affastellare; impacchettare; ammucchiare; **to bundle off** or **out** cacciare precipitosamente; **to bundle up** infagottare ‖ *intr*—**to bundle up** infagottarsi

bung [bʌŋ] *s* spina, cannella

bungalow [ˈbʌŋgə‚lo] *s* casetta, villino, bungalow *m*

bung′hole′ *s* spina, foro della botte

bungle [ˈbʌŋgəl] *s* abborracciatura ‖ *tr* abborracciare ‖ *intr* lavorare alla carlona

bungler [ˈbʌŋglər] *s* abborraccione *m*

bungling [ˈbʌŋglɪŋ] *adj* goffo; mal fatto ‖ *s* abborracciatura

bunion [ˈbʌnjən] *s* gonfiore *m* dell'alluce

bunk [bʌŋk] *s* letto a castello; (nav) cuccetta; (slang) sciocchezza ‖ *intr* dormire in cuccetta

bunk′ bed′ *s* letto a castello

bunker [ˈbʌŋkər] *s* (*bin*) carbonile *m;* (mil) casamatta; (golf) ostacolo

bun·ny [ˈbʌni] *s* (-nies) coniglietto

bunting [ˈbʌntɪŋ] *s* ornamento di bandiere; (nav) gala; (orn) zigolo

buoy [bɔɪ] or [ˈbu·i] *s* boa; (*life preserver*) salvagente *m* ‖ *tr*—**to buoy up** tenere a galla; (fig) rincuorare

buoyancy [ˈbɔɪ·ənsi] or [ˈbujənsi] *s* galleggiabilità *f;* (*cheerfulness*) allegria, esuberanza

buoyant [ˈbɔɪ·ənt] or [ˈbujənt] *adj* galleggiante; allegro, esuberante

bur [bʌr] *s* riccio, aculeo

burble [ˈbʌrbəl] *s* gorgoglio ‖ *intr* gorgogliare

burden [ˈbʌrdən] *s* carico, peso, fardello; (*of a speech*) tema *m;* (*chorus*) ritornello; (naut) portata ‖ *tr* caricare

bur′den of proof′ *s* onere *m* della prova

burdensome [ˈbʌrdənsəm] *adj* oneroso

burdock [ˈbʌrdak] *s* lappa, lappola

bureau [ˈbjuro] *s* comò *m;* (*agency*) ufficio, servizio

bureaucra·cy [bjuˈrakrəsi] *s* (-cies) burocrazia

bureaucrat [ˈbjurə‚kræt] *s* burocrate *m*

burglar [ˈbʌrglər] *s* scassinatore *m*

bur′glar alarm′ *s* campanello antifurto

burglarize [ˈbʌrglə‚raɪz] *tr* scassinare

bur′glar-proof′ *adj* a prova di furto

burgla·ry [ˈbʌrgləri] *s* (-ries) furto con scasso, scassinatura

Burgundy [ˈbʌrgəndi] *s* la Borgogna; (*wine*) borgogna *m*

burial [ˈbɛri·əl] *s* sepoltura

bur′ial ground′ *s* cimitero

burin [ˈbjurɪn] *s* burino, cesello

burlap [ˈbʌrlæp] *s* tela di iuta

burlesque [bʌrˈlɛsk] *adj* burlesco ‖ *s* farsa, burlesque *m* ‖ *tr* parodiare

burlesque′ show′ *s* spettacolo di varietà, music-hall *m*

bur·ly [ˈbʌrli] *adj* (-lier; -liest) membruto, robusto

Burma [ˈbʌrmə] *s* la Birmania

burn [bʌrn] *s* bruciatura, scottatura ‖ *v* (*pret & pp* **burned** or **burnt** [bʌrnt]) *tr* bruciare; (*to set on fire*) dar fuoco a; (*bricks*) cuocere; **to burn down** radere al suolo; **to burn up** consumare; (*the road*) divorare; (coll) fare arrabbiare ‖ *intr* bruciare, bruciarsi; (*said of lights*) essere acceso, e.g., **the lights were burning** la luce era accesa; **to burn out** (*said of an electric bulb or a fuse*) bruciarsi;

to burn to (fig) agognare di; **to burn up** (coll) essere arrabiato; **to burn with** (*e.g., envy*) ardere di

burner ['bʌrnər] *s* (*of gas fixture or lamp*) becco; (*of furnace*) bruciatore *m*

burning ['bʌrnɪŋ] *adj* bruciante, scottante || *s* incendio; (*ceramic*) cottura finale

burn'ing ques'tion *s* questione di attualità palpitante

burnish ['bʌrnɪʃ] *s* lucidatura || *tr* brunire

burnt' al'mond [bʌrnt] *s* mandorla tostata

burp [bʌrp] *s* (coll) rutto || *intr* (coll) ruttare

burr [bʌr] *s* riccio, aculeo; (*rough edge*) bava; (*dentist's drill*) fresa

burrow ['bʌro] *s* tana, buca || *intr* imbucarsi, rintanarsi

bursar ['bʌrsər] *s* tesoriere universitario

burst [bʌrst] *s* esplosione; (*e.g., of machine gun*) raffica; (*break*) crepa; (*of passion*) accesso; (*of speed*) slancio || *tr* far scoppiare || *intr* scoppiare, esplodere; **to burst into** (*e.g., a room*) irrompere in; (*e.g., angry words*) esplodere in; **to burst out crying** scoppiare in lacrime; **to burst with laughter** scoppiare dalle risa

bur·y ['beri] *v* (*pret & pp* -ied) *tr* sotterrare; **to be buried in thought** essere immerso nel pensiero; **to bury the hatchet** fare la pace

bus [bʌs] *s* (**buses** or **busses**) bus *m*, autobus *m* || *v* (*pret & pp* **bused** or **bussed**; *ger* **busing** or **bussing**) *tr* trasportare con autobus

bus'boy' *s* secondo cameriere

bus·by ['bʌzbi] *s* (-**bies**) colbacco

bus' driv'er *s* conducente *mf* di autobus

bush [buʃ] *s* cespuglio, arbusto; **to beat around the bush** menare il can per l'aia

bushed [buʃt] *adj* (coll) stanco morto

bushel ['buʃəl] *s* staio

bushing ['buʃɪŋ] *s* (mach) bronzina

bush·y ['buʃi] *adj* (-**ier; -iest**) ricco di arbusti; (*face*) barbuto

business ['bɪznɪs] *adj* commerciale || *s* occupazione; commercio; affare *m*, negozio; faccenda; impiego; **it is not your business** non è affare Suo; **to know one's business** sapere il fatto proprio; **to make it one's business to** proporsi di; **to mean business** (coll) farla sul serio; **to mind one's own business** impicciarsi degli affari propri

businesslike ['bɪznɪs‚laɪk] *adj* metodico; serio; efficace

busi'ness·man' *s* (-**men'**) commerciante *m*, uomo d'affari

busi'ness suit' *s* abito da passeggio

busi'ness·wom'an *s* (**wom'en**) commerciante *f*

bus'man *s* (-**men**) guidatore *m* d'autobus

buss [bʌs] *s* (coll) bacione sonoro || *tr* (coll) baciare sonoramente

bus' stop' *s* fermata degli autobus

bust [bʌst] *s* busto; petto; (slang) fallimento; (slang) pugno || *tr* (slang) rompere; (slang) far fallire; (slang) colpire, dare pugni a; (mil) degradare

buster ['bʌstər] *s* (coll) ragazzo; (coll) rompitore *m*

bustle ['bʌsəl] *s* (*on a dress*) guardinfante *m*; attività *f* || *intr* affrettarsi

bus·y ['bɪzi] *adj* (-**ier; -iest**) occupato || *v* (*pret & pp* -**ied**) *tr* occupare, tenere occupato; **to busy oneself with** occuparsi di

bus'y·bod'y *s* (-**ies**) ficcanaso

bus'y sig'nal *s* (telp) segnale *m* d'occupato

but [bʌt] *s* ma *m* || *adv* solo, solamente; **but for** se non . . . per || *prep* eccetto, ad eccezione di, meno, se non; **all but** quasi || *conj* ma; che non, e.g., **I never go out in the rain but I catch a cold** non esco mai con la pioggia che non mi pigli un raffreddore

butcher ['butʃər] *s* macellaio || *tr* macellare; massacrare

butch'er knife' *s* coltello da cucina, coltella

butch'er shop' *s* macelleria

butcher·y ['butʃəri] *s* (-**ies**) macello; carneficina

butler ['bʌtlər] *s* cantiniere *m*, credenziere *m*

butt [bʌt] *s* (*butting*) cornata; (*of rifle or gun*) calcio; (*of cigar*) mozzicone *m*; (*target*) bersaglio; (*end*) estremità *f*; (*of ridicule*) zimbello; (*cask*) botte *f* || *tr* dare cornate a; cozzare contro || *intr*—**to butt into** (slang) intromettersi in

butter ['bʌtər] *s* burro || *tr* imburrare; **to butter up** (coll) adulare

but'ter·cup' *s* (bot) bottone *m* d'oro, ranuncolo

but'ter dish' *s* piattino per il burro, burriera

but'ter·fat' *s* grasso nel latte

but'ter·fly' *s* (-**flies**) farfalla

but'ter knife' *s* coltello per il burro

but'ter·milk' *s* latticello

but'ter sauce' *s* burro fuso

but'ter·scotch' *s* caramella al burro

buttocks ['bʌtəks] *spl* chiappe *fpl*, natiche *fpl*

button ['bʌtən] *s* bottone *m* || *tr* abbottonare

but'ton·hole' *s* occhiello, asola || *tr* attaccare un bottone a

but'ton·hook' *s* allacciabottoni *m*

buttress ['bʌtrɪs] *s* contrafforte *m*; piedritto || *tr* rinforzare

buxom ['bʌksəm] *adj* avvenente, procace

buy [baɪ] *s* compra || *v* (*pret & pp* **bought** [bɔt]) *tr* comprare; **to buy off** corrompere; **to buy out** comprare la parte di

buyer ['baɪ·ər] *s* compratore *m*

buzz [bʌz] *s* brusio, ronzio || *tr* volare a bassa quota sopra; (coll) fare una telefonata a || *intr* ronzare

buzzard ['bʌzərd] *s* (*hawk*) poiana; avvoltoio americano

buzzer ['bʌzər] *s* suoneria ronzante

buzz′ saw′ *s* sega circolare, segatrice *f* a disco

by [baɪ] *adv* oltre, e.g., **to speed by** correre velocemente oltre; **by and by** fra poco; **by and large** generalmente ‖ *prep* vicino a; di, durante, e.g., **by night** di notte, durante la notte; a, e.g., **they work by the hour** lavorano all'ora; (*not later than, through*) per; (*past*) in fronte a; (*through the agency of*) da; (*according to*) secondo; (math) per, volte; **by far** di molto; **by the way** a proposito

bygone [′baɪ ˌgɔn] or [′baɪ ˌgɑn] *adj & s* passato; **to let bygones be bygones** dimenticare il passato

bylaw [′baɪ ˌlɔ] *s* legge *f* locale, regolamento di una società

by′-line′ *s* (journ) firma

by′pass′ *s* linea secondaria; (*detour*) deviazione ‖ *tr* fare una deviazione oltre a; (*a difficulty*) evitare

by′path′ *s* sentiero secondario; sentiero privato

by′prod′uct *s* sottoprodotto

bystander [′baɪ ˌstændər] *s* astante *m*, spettatore *m*

byway [′baɪ ˌwe] *s* via traversa

byword [′baɪ ˌwʌrd] *s* proverbio; oggetto di obbrobrio

Byzantium [bɪ′zænʃɪ·əm] or [bɪ′zæntɪ·əm] *s* Bisanzio

C

C, c [si] *s* terza lettera dell'alfabeto inglese

cab [kæb] *s* vettura di piazza; tassì *m;* (*of truck or locomotive*) cabina

cabbage [′kæbɪdʒ] *s* cavolo, verza

cab′ driv′er *s* autista *m* di piazza; (*of horse-drawn cab*) vetturino

cabin [′kæbɪn] *s* (*shed*) capanna; (*hut*) baracca; (aer, naut) cabina

cab′in boy′ *s* mozzo

cabinet [′kæbɪnɪt] *s* (*piece of furniture*) vetrina; (*for a radio*) armadietto; (*small room; ministry of a government*) gabinetto

cab′inet-mak′er *s* ebanista *m*

cab′inet-mak′ing *s* ebanisteria

cable [′kebəl] *s* cavo; cablogramma; (elec) cablaggio ‖ *tr* cablare, mandare un cablogramma a

ca′ble address′ *s* indirizzo telegrafico

ca′ble car′ *s* funicolare *f*, teleferica

cablegram [′kebel ˌgræm] *s* cablogramma *m*

caboose [kə′bus] *s* (rr) vagone *m* di coda

cab′stand′ *s* stazione di tassametri

cache [kæʃ] *s* nascondiglio ‖ *tr* mettere in un nascondiglio

cachet [kæ′ʃe] *s* sigillo; (*distinguishing feature*) impronta

cackle [′kækəl] *s* (*of chickens*) coccodè *m;* (*of people*) chiaccherio ‖ *intr* fare coccodè; ciarlare

cac·tus [′kæktəs] *s* (-tuses or -ti [taɪ]) cactus *m*

cad [kæd] *s* mascalzone *m*

cadaver [kə′dævər] *s* cadavere *m*

cadaverous [kə′dævərəs] *adj* cadaverico

caddie [′kædi] *s* portamazze *m*

cadence [′kedəns] *s* cadenza

cadet [kə′dɛt] *s* cadetto

cadmium [′kædmɪ·əm] *s* cadmio

cadres [′kædriz] *spl* (mil) quadri *mpl*

Caesar′ean sec′tion [sɪ′zɛrɪ·ən] *s* taglio cesareo

café [kæ′fe] *s* caffè *m*, bar *m*, ristorante *m*

ca′fé soci′ety *s* bel mondo

cafeteria [ˌkæfə′tɪrɪ·ə] *s* mensa, tavola calda, caffetteria

caffeine [kæ′fin] or [′kæfi·ɪn] *s* caffeina

cage [kedʒ] *s* gabbia; (*of elevator*) cabina ‖ *tr* ingabbiare

ca·gey [′kedʒi] *adj* (-gier; -giest) (coll) astuto, cauto

cahoots [kə′huts] *s*—**to be in cahoots** (slang) far lega, essere in combutta; **to go cahoots** (slang) dividere in parti eguali

Cain [ken] *s* Caino; **to raise Cain** (slang) arrabbiarsi; (slang) fare una sfuriata

Cairo [′kaɪro] *s* il Cairo

caisson [′kesən] *s* cassone *m;* (archit) cassettone *m*

cajole [kə′dʒol] *tr* lusingare; persuadere con lusinghe

cajoler·y [kə′dʒoləri] *s* (-ies) lusinga

cake [kek] *s* dolce *m;* torta, pasta; (*with bread-like dough*) focaccia; (*of soap*) saponetta; (*of earth*) zolla; **to take the cake** (coll) essere il colmo ‖ *tr* incrostare ‖ *intr* indurirsi; incrostarsi

calabash [′kælə ˌbæʃ] *s* zucca a fiasca

calaboose [′kælə ˌbus] *s* (coll) gattabuia

calamitous [kə′læmɪtəs] *adj* calamitoso

calami·ty [kə′læmɪti] *s* (-ties) calamità *f*

calci·fy [′kælsɪ ˌfaɪ] *v* (pret & pp -fied) *tr* calcificare ‖ *intr* calcificarsi

calcium [′kælsɪ·əm] *s* calcio

calculate [′kælkjə ˌlet] *tr* calcolare ‖ *intr* calcolare; **to calculate on** contare su

cal′culating machine′ *s* (macchina) calcolatrice

calcu·lus [′kælkjələs] *s* (-luses or -li [ˌlaɪ]) (math, pathol) calcolo

calendar [′kæləndər] *s* calendario; (*agenda*) ordine *m* del giorno

calf [kæf] or [kɑf] *s* (calves [kævz] or [kɑvz]) vitello; (*of shoes or binding*) pelle *f* di vitello; (*of the leg*) polpaccio

calf′skin′ *s* pelle *f* di vitello

caliber ['kælɪbər] *s* calibro
calibrate ['kælɪ,bret] *tr* calibrare
cali·co ['kælɪ,ko] *s* (**-coes** or **-cos**) cotone stampato, calico
California [,kælɪ'fɔrnɪ·ə] *s* la California
calipers ['kælɪpərz] *spl* compasso a grossezze, calibro
caliph ['kelɪf] or ['kælɪf] *s* califfo
calisthenic [,kælɪs'θenɪk] *adj* ginnastico || **calisthenics** *spl* ginnastica a corpo libero
calk [kɔk] *tr* var of **caulk**
call [kɔl] *s* chiamata; visita; (*shout*) grido, richiamo; (*of bugle*) squillo; (*of telephone*) colpo; (*of ship*) scalo; obbligo; vocazione; (*com*) richiesta; **on call** disponibile; **within call** a portata di voce || *tr* chiamare; convocare; (*to awaken*) svegliare; **to call back** richiamare; **to call in** (*e.g., an expert*) fare venire; (*e.g., currency*) domandare, esigere; **to call off** annullare; **to call out** chiamare; **to call together** convocare; **to call up** chiamare per telefono || *intr* chiamare; visitare; **to call at** passare per la casa di; (*naut*) fare scalo a; **to call for** venire a prendere; **to call out** gridare; **to go calling** andare a fare visite
cal'la lil'y ['kælə] *s* (*Zantedeschia aethiopica*) calla dei fioristi
call'boy' *s* (*in a hotel*) fattorino; (*theat*) buttafuori *m*
caller ['kɔlər] *s* visitatore *m*
call' girl' *s* ragazza squillo
calling ['kɔlɪŋ] *s* appello; professione
call'ing card' *s* biglietto da visita
call' num'ber *s* numero telefonico; numero di biblioteca
callous ['kæləs] *adj* calloso; insensibile
callow ['kælo] *adj* inesperto, immaturo
call' to arms' *s* chiamata alle armi
call' to the col'ors *s* chiamata sotto la bandiera
callus ['kæləs] *s* callo
calm [kɑm] *adj* calmo, tranquillo || *s* calma || *tr* calmare, tranquillizzare || *intr*—**to calm down** calmarsi; (*said of weather*) abbonacciarsi
calmness ['kɑmnɪs] *s* calma, placidità *f*, tranquillità *f*
calomel ['kælə,mel] *s* calomelano
calorie ['kæləri] *s* caloria
calum·ny ['kæləmni] *s* (**-nies**) calunnia
Calvary ['kælvəri] *s* (Bib) Calvario
cam [kæm] *s* camma
camber ['kæmbər] *s* curvatura; convessità *f* || *tr* arcuare || *intr* curvarsi
cambric ['kembrɪk] *s* cambrì *m*
camel ['kæməl] *s* cammello
came·o ['kæmi,o] *s* (**-os**) cammeo
camera ['kæmərə] *s* macchina fotografica; (mov) cinepresa
cam'era·man' *s* (**-men'**) operatore *m*
camomile ['kæmə,maɪl] *s* camomilla
camouflage ['kæmə,flɑʒ] *s* mascheramento || *tr* mascherare, camuffare
camp [kæmp] *s* accampamento, campo || *intr* accamparsi
campaign [kæm'pen] *s* campagna || *intr* fare una campagna

campaigner [kæm'penər] *s* veterano; (pol) propagandista *mf*
camp' bed' *s* letto da campo, branda
camper ['kæmpər] *s* campeggiatore *m*, campeggista *mf*
camp'fire' *s* fuoco di accampamento
camp'ground' *s* terreno per campeggio
camphor ['kæmfər] *s* canfora
camp'stool' *s* seggiolino pieghevole
campus ['kæmpəs] *s* campo, terreno dell'università
cam'shaft' *s* albero di distribuzione, albero a camme
can [kæn] *s* lattina, barattolo; (*of gasoline or oil*) bidone *m* || *v* (*pret & pp* **canned;** *ger* **canning**) *tr* inscatolare; (slang) licenziare || *v* (*pret & cond* **could**) *aux* I **can speak English** so parlare inglese; **can he go now?** se ne può andare ora?
Canada ['kænədə] *s* il Canadà
Canadian [kə'nedɪ·ən] *adj & s* canadese *mf*
canal [kə'næl] *s* canale *m*
canar·y [kə'nɛri] *s* (**-ies**) canarino || **Canaries** *spl* Canarie *fpl*
can·cel ['kænsəl] *v* (*pret & pp* **-celed** or **-celled;** *ger* **-celing** or **-celling**) *tr* cancellare; annullare; revocare; (*stamps*) timbrare, annullare
cancellation [,kænsə'leʃən] *s* cancellazione, annullamento; cassazione; (*of a stamp*) bollo
cancer ['kænsər] *s* cancro || **Cancer** *s* Cancro
cancerous ['kænsərəs] *adj* canceroso
candela·brum [,kændə'lɑbrəm] *s* (**-bra** [brə] or **-brums**) candelabro
candid ['kændɪd] *adj* candido; sincero, franco
candida·cy ['kændɪdəsi] *s* (**-cies**) candidatura
candidate ['kændɪ,det] *s* candidato; (*for a degree*) laureando
can'did cam'era *s* camera fotografica indiscreta
candied ['kændid] *adj* candito
candle ['kændəl] *s* candela || *tr* (*eggs*) sperare
can'dle·hold'er *s* var of **candlestick**
can'dle·light' *s* luce *f* or lume *m* di candela
can'dle·pow'er *s* (phys) candela
can'dle·stick' *s* (*ornate*) candeliere *m;* (*plain*) bugia
candor ['kændər] *s* candore *m;* ingenuità *f*
can·dy ['kændi] *s* (**-dies**) dolciumi *mpl;* **a piece of candy** un bombon || *v* (*pret & pp* **-died**) *tr* candire
can'dy box' *s* bomboniera
can'dy dish' *s* bomboniera; (*three-tier-high*) alzata
can'dy store' *s* confetteria
cane [ken] *s* canna, giunco; (*for walking*) bastone *m* || *tr* bastonare; (*chairs*) impagliare
cane' seat' *s* sedia impagliata
cane' sug'ar *s* zucchero di canna
canine ['kenaɪn] *adj* canino || *s* (*tooth*) canino; (*dog*) cane *m*
canister ['kænɪstər] *s* barattolo

canned' goods' *spl* conserve *fpl* alimentari; prodotti *mpl* in scatola

canned' mu'sic *s* (slang) musica su dischi

canner·y ['kænəri] *s* (-ies) fabbrica di conserve alimentari

cannibal ['kænɪbəl] *adj & s* cannibale *mf*, antropofago

canning ['kænɪŋ] *s* conservazione

cannon ['kænən] *s* cannone *m*

cannonade [,kænə'ned] *s* cannonata || *tr* cannoneggiare

can'non·ball' *s* palla da cannone

can'non fod'der *s* carne *f* da cannone

can·ny ['kæni] *adj* (-nier; -niest) astuto, fino; malizioso

canoe [kə'nu] *s* canoa, piroga

canon ['kænən] *s* canone *m*; (*priest*) canonico

canonical [kə'nɑnɪkəl] *adj* canonico || **canonicals** *spl* paramenti liturgici

canonize ['kænə,naɪz] *tr* canonizzare

can'on law' *s* diritto canonico

canon·ry ['kænənri] *s* (-ries) canonicato

can' o'pener ['opənər] *s* apriscatole *m*

cano·py ['kænəpi] *s* (-pies) tenda; baldacchino; (*of sky*) (fig) volta

cant [kænt] *adj* ipocrita || *s* linguaggio ipocrita; gergo; (*slope*) inclinazione

cantaloupe ['kæntə,lop] *s* melone *m*

cantankerous [kæn'tæŋkərəs] *adj* bisbetico, attaccabrighe

canteen [kæn'tin] *s* cantina, spaccio; (*metal bottle*) borraccia

canter ['kæntər] *s* piccolo galoppo || *intr* andare al piccolo galoppo

cantiliver ['kæntɪ,livər] *adj* a cantiliver || *s* trave *f* a sbalzo; (architt) trave *f* a mensola

cantle ['kæntəl] *s* arcione *m* posteriore

canton [kæn'tɑn] *s* cantone *m*; regione || *tr* accantonare

cantonment [kæn'tɑnmənt] *s* accantonamento

cantor ['kæntər] or ['kæntɔr] *s* cantore *m*

canvas ['kænvəs] *s* (*cloth*) olona; (*e.g. on open truck*) copertone *m*; (*painting*) tela; (naut) vela; **under canvas** (naut) a vele spiegate

canvass ['kænvəs] *s* discussione; dibattito; (pol) sollecitazione di voti || *tr* discutere; (*votes*) sollecitare; (*to investigate*) indagare; (com) fare la piazza a || *intr* discutere; sollecitare voti; indagare; (com) fare la piazza

canyon ['kænjən] *s* cañon *m*

cap [kæp] *s* berretto; cuffia; (*of academic costume*) berrettone *m*; (*of bottle*) tappo, capsula; (*e.g., of fountain pen*) cappuccio || *v* (*pret & pp* **capped;** *ger* **capping**) *tr* (*a person*) coprire il capo di; (*s.o.'s head*) coprire con il berretto; (*a bottle*) mettere il tappo a; terminare; **to cap the climax** essere il colmo

capabili·ty [,kepə'bɪlɪti] *s* (-ties) capacità *f*, abilità *f*

capable ['kepəbəl] *adj* capace, abile

capacious [kə'peʃəs] *adj* ampio, capace

capaci·ty [kə'pæsɪti] *s* (-ties) capacità *f;* **filled to capacity** pieno zeppo; **in the capacity of** in veste di

cap' and bells' *spl* berretto a sonagli; scettro di buffone

cap' and gown' *s* costume accademico, toga e tocco

caparison [kə'pærɪsən] *s* bardatura || *tr* bardare

cape [kep] *s* cappa, mantello; (mil) mantella; (geog) capo

Cape' of Good' Hope' *s* Capo di Buona Speranza

caper ['kepər] *s* capriola; (bot) cappero; **to cut capers** far capriole; (fig) fare monellerie || *intr* fare capriole; saltellare

Cape' Town' *s* Città *f* del Capo

capital ['kæpɪtəl] *adj* capitale || *s* (*money*) capitale *m*; (*city*) capitale *f;* (*of column*) capitello

cap'ital expen'ditures *spl* spese *fpl* d'impianto

cap'ital goods' *spl* beni *mpl* strumentali

capitalism ['kæpɪtə,lɪzəm] *s* capitalismo

capitalize ['kæpɪtə,laɪz] *tr* capitalizzare; scrivere con la maiuscola || *intr*—**to capitalize on** approfittare di

cap'ital let'ter *s* lettera maiuscola

cap'ital pun'ishment *s* pena capitale

cap'ital stock' *s* capitale *m* sociale

capitol ['kæpɪtəl] *s* campidoglio

capitulate [kə'pɪtʃə,let] *intr* capitolare

capon ['kepɑn] *s* cappone *m*

caprice [kə'pris] *s* capriccio, ghiribizzo

capricious [kə'prɪʃəs] *adj* capriccioso, estroso

Capricorn ['kæprɪ,kɔrn] *s* Capricorno

capsize ['kæpsaɪz] *tr* capovolgere || *intr* capovolgersi

capstan ['kæpstən] *s* argano

cap'stone' *s* (archit) coronamento

capsule ['kæpsəl] *adj* in miniatura; riassuntivo || *s* capsula

captain ['kæptən] *s* capitano; (naut) comandante *m*; || *tr* capitanare

caption ['kæpʃən] *s* titolo; (mov) didascalia; (journ) leggenda

captivate ['kæptɪ,vet] *tr* cattivare, affascinare

captive ['kæptɪv] *adj & s* prigioniero

captivi·ty ['kæp'tɪvɪti] *s* (-ties) cattività *f*, prigionia

captor ['kæptər] *s* persona che cattura

capture ['kæptʃər] *s* cattura, presa; (*person*) prigioniero; (*thing*) bottino || *tr* catturare; prendere

car [kɑr] *s* (*of train*) vagone *m*, vettura; (*automobile*) automobile *m* & *f*, macchina, vettura; (*of elevator*) cabina; (*of balloon*) navicella; (*for narrow-gauge track*) carrello

carafe [kə'ræf] *s* caraffa

caramel ['kærəməl] or ['kɑrməl] *s* (*burnt sugar*) caramello; (*candy*) caramella appiccicaticcia

carat ['kærət] *s* carato

caravan ['kærə,væn] *s* carovana; (*covered vehicle*) furgone *m*

caravansa·ry [,kærə'vænsəri] *s* (-ries) caravanserraglio

caraway ['kærə,we] *s* cumino

car'barn' *s* rimessa del tram

carbide ['karbaɪd] s carburo
carbine ['karbaɪn] s carabina
carbol'ic ac'id [kar'balɪk] s acido fenico
carbon ['karbən] s (in arc light, battery, auto cylinder) carbone m; carta carbone; (chem) carbonio
car'bon cop'y s copia a carbone, velina
car'bon diox'ide s anidride carbonica
car'bon monox'ide s ossido di carbonio, monossido di carbonio
car'bon pa'per s carta carbone
carbuncle ['karbʌŋkəl] s (stone; boil) carbonchio; (boil) foruncolo
carburetor ['karbə‚retər] or ['karbjə‚retər] s carburatore m
carcass ['karkəs] s carcassa; (in state of decay) carogna
card [kard] s (file) scheda; (post card) cartolina; (personal card) biglietto; (announcement) partecipazione; (playing card) carta da gioco; (coll) tipo divertente, bel tipo
card'board' s cartone m
card'-car'rying mem'ber s tesserato
card' case' s portatessere m
card' cat'alogue s schedario
card'hold'er s socio, tesserato
cardiac ['kardɪ‚æk] adj & s cardiaco
cardigan ['kardɪgən] s panciotto a maglia
cardinal ['kardɪnəl] adj cardinale, fondamentale || s cardinale m
card' in'dex s schedario
cardiogram ['kardɪ‚o‚græm] s cardiogramma m
card' par'ty s riunione per giocare a carte
card'sharp' s baro
card' ta'ble s tavoliere m, tavolino da gioco
card' trick' s gioco di prestigio colle carte
care [ker] s cura, custodia; inquietudine f, preoccupazione; cautela; care of presso, e.g., R. Smith care of Jones R. Smith presso Jones; to take care fare attenzione; to take care of prendersi cura di, badare a; to take care of oneself badare alla salute || intr curarsi, badare; I don't care non m'importa; to care about preoccuparsi di; to care for voler bene a; curarsi di; to care to volere
careen [kə'rin] s carenaggio || intr sbandare
career [kə'rir] adj di carriera || s carriera
care'free' adj spensierato
careful ['kerfəl] adj attento; diligente; premuroso; careful! faccia attenzione!
careless ['kerlɪs] adj trascurato; imprudente; indifferente
carelessness ['kerlɪsnɪs] s trascuratezza; imprudenza; indifferenza
caress [kə'res] s carezza || tr carezzare, accarezzare
caretaker ['ker‚tekər] adj interinale, provvisorio || s custode m; guardiano; (of school) bidello
care'taker gov'ernment s governo interinale

care'worn' adj accasciato dalle preoccupazioni
car'fare' s passaggio, denaro per il tram; (small sum of money) spiccioli mpl
car·go ['kargo] s (-goes or -gos) carico mercantile
car'go boat' s battello da carico
Caribbean [‚kærɪ'bi·ən] or [kə'rɪbɪ·ən] s Mare m dei Caraibi
caricature ['kærɪkətʃər] s caricatura || tr mettere in caricatura
carillon ['kærɪ‚lɑn] or [kə'rɪljən] s carillon m || intr suonare il carillon
car'load' s vagone completo, vagonata
carnage ['karnɪdʒ] s carnaio, carneficina
carnal ['karnəl] adj carnale
carnation [kar'neʃən] adj incarnato || s garofano; (color) incarnato
carnival ['karnɪvəl] adj carnevalesco || s carnevale m; festa, spettacolo all'aperto
carob ['kærəb] s (fruit) carruba; (tree) carrubo
car·ol ['kærəl] s canzone f popolare; pastorella di Natale || v (pret & pp -oled or -olled; ger -oling or -olling) tr cantare
carom ['kærəm] s carambola || intr carambolare
carousal [kə'rauzəl] s baldoria, gozzoviglia
carouse [kə'rauz] intr fare baldoria, gozzovigliare
carousel [‚kærə'zel] or [‚kæru'zel] s giostra, carosello
carp ['karp] s carpa || intr lagnarsi, criticare
carpenter ['karpəntər] s falegname m
carpentry ['karpəntri] s falegnameria
carpet ['karpɪt] s tappeto || tr coprire con un tappeto, tappetare
carpetbagger ['karpɪt‚bægər] s avventuriero; (hist) politicante m
car'pet sweep'er s spazzolone elettrico per tappeti
car'port' s tettoia-garage f
car'-ren'tal serv'ice s servizio di autonoleggi
carriage ['kærɪdʒ] s carrozza; (of gun) affusto; (of typewriter) carrello; (bearing) portamento; (mach) slitta
carrier ['kærɪ·ər] s portatore m; (person or organization in business of carrying goods) spedizioniere m; (of mail) postino; (e.g., on top of station wagon) portabagagli m; (of a disease) veicolo
car'rier pig'eon s piccione m viaggiatore
car'rier wave' s (rad) onda portante
carrion ['kærɪ·ən] s carogne fpl
carrot ['kærət] s carota
car·ry ['kæri] v (pret & pp -ried) tr portare; trasportare; (a burden) sopportare; (an election) guadagnare; (to keep in stock) avere in assortimento; to carry along portare con sé; to carry away trasportare; entusiasmare; to carry forward riportare; to carry out eseguire; to carry

through completare; **to carry weight** aver importanza ‖ *intr* avere la portata (di), e.g., **this gun carries two miles** questo cannone ha la portata di due miglia; **to carry on** continuare; (coll) fare baccano

cart [kɑrt] *s* carro, carretto; (*for shopping*) carrello; **to put the cart before the horse** mettere il carro davanti ai buoi ‖ *tr* trasportare col carro

carte blanche ['kɑrt'blɑnʃ] *s* carta bianca

cartel [kɑr'tɛl] *s* cartello

Carthage ['kɑrθɪdʒ] *s* Cartagine *f*

cart' horse' *s* cavallo da tiro

cartilage ['kɑrtɪlɪdʒ] *s* cartilagine *f*

carton ['kɑrtən] *s* cartone *m;* scatola di cartone; (*of cigarettes*) stecca

cartoon [kɑr'tun] *s* disegno; caricatura; (*comic strip*) fumetto; (mov) disegno animato ‖ *tr* fare caricature di

cartoonist [kɑr'tunɪst] *s* disegnatore *m;* caricaturista *mf*

cartridge ['kɑrtrɪdʒ] *s* cartuccia; (*e.g., of camera*) caricatore *m*

car'tridge belt' *s* cartucciera; (mil) giberna

car'tridge clip' *s* serbatoio

cart'wheel' *s* ruota di carro; **to turn cartwheels** fare la ruota

carve [kɑrv] *tr* (*meats*) trinciare; scolpire, intagliare

carv'ing knife' *s* trinciante *m*

car' wash'er *s* lavamacchine *m*

cascade [kæs'ked] *s* cascata ‖ *intr* cadere a mo' di cascata

case [kes] *s* (*box*) cassetta; (*of watch*) calotta; (*outer covering*) astuccio; (*instance*) caso; (gram) caso; (law) causa; (typ) cassa; **in case** in caso, nel caso; **in no case** in nessun modo ‖ *tr* rinchiudere; (*to package*) impaccare; (slang) ispezionare

casement ['kesmənt] *s* telaio di finestra; finestra a gangheri

case' stud'y *s* casistica

cash [kæʃ] *s* contante *m;* **cash on delivery** spedizione contro assegno; **for cash** in contanti; a pronta cassa ‖ *tr* (*a check*) cambiare, incassare ‖ *intr* —**to cash in on** (coll) trarre profitto da

cash' box' *s* cassa

cashew ['kæʃu] *s* (*tree*) anacardio; (*nut*) mandorla indiana

cashier [kæ'ʃɪr] *s* cassiere *m* ‖ *tr* (*to dismiss*) silurare

cashier's' check' *s* assegno circolare

cash' reg'ister *s* registratore *m* cassa

casing ['kesɪŋ] *s* rivestimento; tubo di rivestimento; (*for salami*) budello; (*of tire*) copertone *m*

cask [kæsk] or [kɑsk] *s* barile *m*, botte *f*

casket ['kæskɪt] or ['kɑskɪt] *s* scrigno, cofanetto; (*coffin*) bara, cassa da morto

casserole ['kæsə,rol] *s* tegame *m* di terracotta or vetro; (*food*) pasticcio, timballo

cassette [kə'sɛt] *s* (mus) musicassetta; (mus & phot) caricatore *m*

cassock ['kæsək] *s* sottana, tonaca; **to doff the cassock** gettar la tonaca alle ortiche

cast [kæst] or [kɑst] *s* getto; lancio; forma; (mach) pezzo fuso; (surg) gesso; (theat) complesso artistico, cast *m* ‖ *v* (*pret & pp* cast) *tr* gettare; fondere; (*a ballot*) dare; (*the roles*) distribuire; (*actors*) scegliere; **to cast aside** abbandonare; **to cast down** deprimere; **to cast lots** tirare a sorte; **to cast off** abbandonare; **to cast out** buttar fuori ‖ *intr* tirare i dadi; **to cast off** (naut) mollare gli ormeggi

castanets [,kæstə'nɛts] *spl* nacchere *fpl*

cast'a·way' *adj & s* naufrago; (fig) reprobo

caste [kæst] or [kɑst] *s* casta; **to lose caste** perdere prestigio

caster ['kæstər] or ['kɑstər] *s* ampollina, saliera, pepaiola; (*roller*) rotella per i mobili

castigate ['kæstɪ,get] *tr* castigare, punire; correggere

Castile [kæs'til] *s* (la) Castiglia

Castilian [kæs'tɪljən] *adj & s* castigliano

casting ['kæstɪŋ] or ['kɑstɪŋ] *s* getto; getto fuso; (*in fishing*) pesca a getto

cast' i'ron *s* ghisa

cast'-i'ron *adj* fatto di ghisa; (*e.g., stomach*) fatto d'acciaio, di struzzo

castle ['kæsəl] or ['kɑsəl] *s* castello; (chess) torre *f* ‖ *tr & intr* (chess) arroccare

cas'tle in Spain' or **cas'tle in the air'** *s* castello in aria

cast'off' *adj* abbandonato ‖ *s* rigetto; persona abbandonata; (typ) stima

cas'tor oil' ['kæstər] or ['kɑstər] *s* olio di ricino

castrate ['kæstret] *tr* castrare

casual ['kæʒʊ·əl] *adj* casuale, fortuito; (*clothing*) semplice, sportivo

casually ['kæʒʊ·əli] *adv* con disinvoltura; (*by chance*) fortuitamente

casual·ty ['kæʒʊ·əlti] *s* (-ties) accidente *m*, disastro; vittima; **casualties** (*in war*) perdite *fpl*

casuist·ry ['kæʒʊ·ɪstri] *s* (-ries) (*specious reasoning*) speciosità *f;* (philos) casistica

cat [kæt] *s* gatto; donna perfida; **to let the cat out of the bag** lasciarsi scappare il segreto

cataclysm ['kætə,klɪzəm] *s* cataclisma *m*

catacomb ['kætə,kom] *s* catacomba

catalogue ['kætə,lɔg] or ['kætə,lɑg] *s* catalogo ‖ *tr* catalogare

cat'alogue sale' *s* vendita per corrispondenza

catalyst ['kætəlɪst] *s* catalizzatore *m*

catapult ['kætə,pʌlt] *s* catapulta ‖ *tr* catapultare

cataract ['kætə,rækt] *s* cataratta

catarrh [kə'tɑr] *s* catarro

catastrophe [kə'tæstrəfi] *s* catastrofe *f*, disastro

cat'call' s urlo di disapprovazione
catch [kætʃ] s presa; cattura; (of door) paletto; (in marriage) partito; (trick) inganno; (of fish) pesca; (mach) nottolino || v (pret & pp **caught** [kɔt]) tr prendere, acchiappare; (a cold) pigliare, buscarsi; **to catch hold of** afferrare; **to catch it** (coll) prendersele; **to catch oneself** contenersi; **to catch up** sorprendere sul fatto || intr agganciarsi; (said of a disease) trasmettersi; **to catch on** capire l'antifona; **to catch up** mettersi al corrente; **to catch up with** raggiungere
catch'-as-catch'-can' s lotta libera americana
catch' ba'sin s ricettacolo di fogna
catcher [ˈkætʃər] s ricevitore m, catcher m
catching [ˈkætʃɪŋ] adj (alluring) seducente; (infectious) contagioso
catch'word' s slogan m; (typ) chiamata; (typ) esponente m in testa di pagina
catch·y [ˈkætʃi] adj (-ier; -iest) attraente, vivo; (tricky) insidioso
catechism [ˈkætɪˌkɪzəm] s catechismo
catego·ry [ˈkætɪˌgori] s (-ries) categoria
cater [ˈketər] intr provvedere cibo; **to cater to** servire
cater-cornered [ˈkætərˌkɔrnərd] adj diagonale || adv diagonalmente
caterer [ˈketərər] s provveditore m
caterpillar [ˈkætərˌpɪlər] s bruco
cat'erpillar trac'tor s trattore m a cingoli
cat'fish' s pesce m gatto
cat'gut' s (mus) corda di minugia; (surg) catgut m, cattegù m
cathartic [kəˈθɑrtɪk] adj & s catartico
cathedral [kəˈθidrəl] s cattedrale f
catheter [ˈkæθɪtər] s catetere m
catheterize [ˈkæθɪtəˌraɪz] tr cateterizzare
cathode [ˈkæθod] s catodo
catholic [ˈkæθəlɪk] adj cattolico; (e.g., mind) liberale || **Catholic** adj & s cattolico
catkin [ˈkætkɪn] s (bot) amento, gattino
cat'nap' s corta siesta, sonnellino
cat-o'-nine-tails [ˌkætəˈnaɪnˌtelz] s gatto a nove code
cat's'-paw' s gonzo; (breeze) brezzolina
catsup [ˈkætsəp] or [ˈketʃəp] s salsa piccante di pomodoro, ketchup m
cat'tail' s stiancia
cattle [ˈkætəl] s bestiame grosso
cat'tle·man s (-men) allevatore m di bestiame
cat·ty [ˈkæti] adj (-tier; -tiest) malizioso, maligno; felino, gattesco
cat'walk' s passerella, ballatoio
Caucasian [kɔˈkeʒən] or [kɔˈkeʃən] adj & s caucasico
caucus [ˈkɔkəs] s comitato elettorale; conciliabolo politico
cauldron [ˈkɔldrən] s calderone m
cauliflower [ˈkɔlɪˌflau·ər] s cavolfiore m
caulk [kɔk] tr calafatare, stoppare
cause [kɔz] s causa, cagione || tr causare, cagionare; **to cause to** + inf

fare + inf, e.g., **she caused him to fall** l'ha fatto cadere
cause'way' s strada rialzata, scarpata
caustic [ˈkɔstɪk] adj caustico
cauterize [ˈkɔtəˌraɪz] tr cauterizzare
caution [ˈkɔʃən] s cautela, prudenza; ammonizione || tr ammonire
cautious [ˈkɔʃəs] adj prudente
cavalcade [ˈkævəlˌked] or [ˌkævəlˈked] s cavalcata
cavalier [ˌkævəˈlir] or [ˈkævəˌlir] adj altero, sdegnoso; disinvolto || s cavaliere m
caval·ry [ˈkævəlri] s (-ries) cavalleria
cav'alry·man' or **cav'alry·man** s (-men' or -men) cavalleggero, soldato di cavalleria
cave [kev] s caverna, grotta || intr— **to cave in** sprofondarsi; (to give in) (coll) cedere; (to become exhausted) (coll) diventare spossato
cave'-in' s sprofondamento
cave' man' s troglodita m
cavern [ˈkævərn] s caverna
caviar [ˈkævɪˌɑr] or [ˌkævɪˈɑr] s caviale m
cav·il [ˈkævɪl] v (pret & pp -iled or -illed; ger -iling or -illing) intr cavillare
cavi·ty [ˈkævɪti] s (-ties) cavità f; (in tooth) carie f
cavort [kəˈvɔrt] intr far capriole
caw [kɔ] s gracchiamento || intr gracchiare
cease [sis] tr cessare, interrompere || intr cessare, interrompersi; **to cease** + ger cessare di + inf
cease'-fire' s sospensione delle ostilità
ceaseless [ˈsislɪs] adj incessante
cedar [ˈsidər] s cedro; legno di cedro
cede [sid] tr cedere, trasferire
ceiling [ˈsilɪŋ] s soffitto; (aer) altezza massima; **to hit the ceiling** (slang) uscire dai gangheri
ceil'ing price' s calmiere m, tetto
celebrate [ˈsɛlɪˌbret] tr celebrare || intr celebrare; far festa
celebrated [ˈsɛlɪˌbretɪd] adj celebre, famoso
celebration [ˌsɛlɪˈbreʃən] s celebrazione
celebri·ty [sɪˈlɛbrɪti] s (-ties) celebrità f
celery [ˈsɛləri] s sedano
celestial [sɪˈlɛstʃəl] adj celestiale, celeste
celibacy [ˈsɛləbəsi] s celibato
celibate [ˈsɛləˌbet] or [ˈsɛləbɪt] adj & s celibe m; nubile f
cell [sɛl] s (e.g., of jail) cella; (of electric battery) elemento; (biol, phys, pol) cellula
cellar [ˈsɛlər] s cantina; (partly above ground) seminterrato
cellist or **'cellist** [ˈtʃɛlɪst] s violoncellista mf
cel·lo or **'cel·lo** [ˈtʃɛlo] s (-los) violoncello
cellophane [ˈsɛləˌfen] s cellofan m
celluloid [ˈsɛljəˌlɔɪd] s celluloide f
Celtic [ˈsɛltɪk] or [ˈkɛltɪk] adj celtico || s lingua celtica

cement [sɪ'mɛnt] s cemento ‖ tr cementare

cemete·ry ['sɛmɪ ˌtɛri] s (-ries) cimitero

censer ['sɛnsər] s turibolo

censor ['sɛnsər] s censore m ‖ tr censurare

censure ['sɛnʃər] s censura, critica ‖ tr censurare, criticare

census ['sɛnsəs] s censo, censimento

cent [sɛnt] s centesimo di dollaro, cent m; **not to have a red cent to one's name** non avere il becco di un quattrino

centaur ['sɛntɔr] s centauro

centennial [sɛn'tɛnɪ-əl] adj & s centenario

center ['sɛntər] s centro ‖ tr centrare, concentrare ‖ intr—**to center on** concentrarsi su

cen'ter·board' s chiglia mobile

cen'ter·piece' s centro tavola

cen'ter punch' s punzone m, punteruolo

centigrade ['sɛntɪ ˌgred] adj centigrado

centimeter ['sɛntɪ ˌmitər] s centimetro

centipede ['sɛntɪ ˌpid] s centopiedi m

cento ['sɛnto] s centone m

central ['sɛntrəl] adj centrale ‖ s centrale f, centrale telefonica; (operator) telefonista mf

Cen'tral Amer'ica s l'America Centrale

centralize ['sɛntrə ˌlaɪz] tr centralizzare ‖ intr centralizzarsi

centu·ry ['sɛntʃəri] s (-ries) secolo

ceramic [sɪ'ræmɪk] adj ceramico ‖ **ceramics** ssg ceramica; spl oggetti mpl di ceramica

cereal ['sɪrɪ-əl] adj cerealicolo ‖ s (grain) cereale m; (uncooked breakfast food, e.g., cornflakes) fiocchi mpl; (breakfast food to be cooked) farina

cerebral ['sɛrɪbrəl] adj cerebrale

ceremonious [ˌsɛrɪ'monɪ-əs] adj cerimonioso

ceremo·ny ['sɛrɪ ˌmoni] s (-nies) cerimonia; **to stand on ceremony** fare cerimonie

certain ['sʌrtən] adj certo; **for certain** di or per certo; **to be certain to** + inf non mancare di + inf

certainly ['sʌrtənli] adv certamente; (gladly) con piacere

certain·ty ['sʌrtənti] s (-ties) certezza

certificate [sər'tɪfɪkɪt] s certificato; (com) titolo ‖ [sər'tɪfɪ ˌket] tr certificare

cer'tified check' s assegno a copertura garantita

cer'tified cop'y s estratto; (as a formula on a document) per copia conforme

cer'tified pub'lic account'ant s esperto contabile

certi·fy ['sʌrtɪ ˌfaɪ] v (pret & pp -fied) tr certificare, garantire

cervix ['sʌrvɪks] s (cervices [sər'vaɪsiz] cervice f

cessation [sɛ'seʃən] s cessazione

cesspool ['sɛs ˌpul] s pozzo nero

Ceylo·nese [ˌsilə'niz] adj & s (-nese) singalese mf

chafe [tʃef] s irritazione ‖ tr (the hands) strofinare; irritare; (to wear away) logorare ‖ intr irritarsi; logorarsi

chaff [tʃæf] or [tʃɑf] s lolla; pula; (joke) burla; (fig) loppa

chaf'ing dish' s fornello a spirito

cha·grin [ʃə'grɪn] s cruccio, dispiacere m ‖ v (pret -grined or -grinned; ger -grining or -grinning) tr crucciare, affliggere

chain [tʃen] s catena; (e.g., for necklace) catenella ‖ tr incatenare

chain' gang' s catena di forzati

chain' reac'tion s reazione a catena

chain' saw' s motosega

chain'-smoke' intr fumare come un turco

chain' store' s negozio a catena

chair [tʃɛr] s sedia, seggiola; (of important person) seggio; (at a university) cattedra; (chairman) presidente m, presidenza; **to take the chair** cominciare una riunione ‖ tr (a meeting) presiedere

chair' lift' s seggiovia

chair'man s (-men) presidente m

chair'man·ship' s presidenza

chair'wom'an s (-wom'en) presidentessa

chalice ['tʃælɪs] s calice m

chalk [tʃɔk] s gesso ‖ tr marcare or scrivere col gesso; **to chalk up** prendere appunti di; attribuire

chalk' talk' s conferenza illustrata

chalk·y ['tʃɔki] adj (-ier; -iest) gessoso

challenge ['tʃælɪndʒ] s sfida; (law) ricusazione; (mil) chi va là m ‖ tr sfidare; (a juror) (law) ricusare; (mil) dare il chi va là a

chamber ['tʃembər] s camera, stanza; (of a palace) aula; (of a judge) gabinetto

chamberlain ['tʃembərlɪn] s ciambellano

cham'ber·maid' s cameriera

cham'ber of com'merce s camera di commercio

cham'ber pot' s orinale m

chameleon [kə'mili-ən] s camaleonte m

cham·ois ['ʃæmi] s (-ois) camoscio

champ [tʃæmp] s (slang) campione m ‖ tr masticare rumorosamente; (the bit) mordere ‖ intr masticare rumorosamente

champagne [ʃæm'pen] s champagne m, spumante m

champion ['tʃæmpɪ-ən] s campione m ‖ tr difendere; farsi paladino di

championship ['tʃæmpɪ-ən ˌʃɪp] s campionato

chance [tʃæns] or [tʃɑns] adj casuale, fortuito ‖ s occasione; caso; probabilità f; rischio; biglietto di lotteria; **by chance** per caso; **not to stand a chance** non avere la probabilità di riuscita; **to take one's chances** arrischiarsi; **to wait for a chance** attendere l'opportunità ‖ intr succedere; **to chance upon** imbattersi in

chancel ['tʃænsəl] or ['tʃɑnsəl] s presbiterio, coro

chanceller·y ['tʃænsələri] or ['tʃɑnsələri] s (-ies) cancelleria

chancellor [ˈtʃænsələr] or [ˈtʃɑnsələr] s cancelliere m

chandelier [ˌʃændəˈlir] s lampadario

change [tʃendʒ] s cambiamento; (of clothes) muta; (of currency) cambio; (coins) spiccioli mpl; for a change tanto per cambiare; to keep the change tenere il resto || tr cambiare, rimpiazzare; (clothes) cambiare, cambiarsi di || intr cambiare, mutare

changeable [ˈtʃendʒəbəl] adj mutevole, variabile, incostante

change' of heart' s pentimento, conversione

change' of life' s menopausa

chan·nel [ˈtʃænəl] s canale m; tubo, passaggio; stretto; (of river) alveo; (groove) solco; (rad, telv) canale m; through channels per via gerarchica || v (pret & pp -neled or -nelled; ger -neling or -nelling) tr incanalare; (a river) incassare || the Channel il Canale della Manica

chant [tʃænt] or [tʃɑnt] s canto; salmodia; canzone f || tr & intr cantare

chanticleer [ˈtʃæntɪˌklɪr] s il gallo

chaos [ˈke·ɑs] s caos m

chaotic [keˈɑtɪk] adj caotico

chap [tʃæp] s (fellow) individuo, tipo; (of skin) screpolatura; chaps pantaloni mpl di cuoio || v (pret & pp chapped; ger chapping) tr screpolare || intr screpolarsi

chapel [ˈtʃæpəl] s cappella

chaperon or **chaperone** [ˈʃæpəˌron] s accompagnatrice f (di signorina) || tr accompagnare

chaplain [ˈtʃæplɪn] s cappellano

chaplet [ˈtʃæplɪt] s (wreath) corona, ghirlanda; rosario

chapter [ˈtʃæptər] s capitolo; (of a club) sezione

chap'ter and verse' s—to give chapter and verse citare le autorità

char [tʃɑr] v (pret & pp charred; ger charring) tr carbonizzare; bruciare

character [ˈkærɪktər] s carattere m; lettera, scrittura; indole f; (theat) personaggio; (coll) tipo; in character caratteristico di lui (lei, loro, etc.)

char'acter ac'tor s caratterista m

char'acter ac'tress s caratterista f

char'acter assassina'tion s linciaggio morale

characteristic [ˌkærɪktəˈrɪstɪk] adj caratteristico || s caratteristica

characterize [ˈkærɪktəˌraɪz] tr caratterizzare

char'coal' s carbone m di legna, carbone m dolce; (for sketching) carboncino; (sketch) disegno al carboncino

charge [tʃɑrdʒ] s carica; incarico; responsibilità f; (indictment) accusa; costo; prezzo; debito; in charge in comando; in charge of a cura di; to take charge of prendersi cura di || tr caricare; comandare; accusare; (a price) fare pagare; mettere in conto; to charge s.o. with s.th addebitare qlco a qlcu; accusare qlcu di qlco || intr fare una carica

charge' account' s conto corrente

chargé d'affaires [ʃɑrˈʒe dəˈfɛr] s (chargés d'affaires) incaricato d'affari

charger [ˈtʃɑrdʒər] s cavallo di battaglia; (of a battery) caricatore m

chariot [ˈtʃærɪ·ət] s cocchio

charioteer [ˌtʃærɪ·əˈtɪr] s auriga m

charis·ma [kəˈrɪzmə] s (-mata [mətə]) fascino personale; (theol) carisma m

charitable [ˈtʃærɪtəbəl] adj (person) caritatevole; (institution) caritativo

chari·ty [ˈtʃærɪti] s (-ties) carità f; associazione di beneficenza

charlatan [ˈʃɑrlətən] s ciarlatano

charlatanism [ˈʃɑrlətənˌɪzəm] s ciarlataneria

Charlemagne [ˈʃɑrləˌmen] s Carlomagno

Charles [tʃɑrlz] s Carlo

char'ley horse' [ˈtʃɑrli] s (coll) crampo

charlotte [ˈʃɑrlət] s charlotte f || Charlotte s Carlotta

charm [tʃɑrm] s fascino; amuleto; portafortuna m || tr incantare, stregare

charming [ˈtʃɑrmɪŋ] adj affascinante

charnel [ˈtʃɑrnəl] adj orribile || s ossario

chart [tʃɑrt] s carta geografica; lista; diagramma m || tr tracciare

charter [ˈtʃɑrtər] s statuto; privilegio || tr (a company) fondare; (a conveyance) noleggiare

char'ter mem'ber s socio fondatore

char'wom'an s (-wom'en) domestica per la pulizia

chase [tʃes] s inseguimento; caccia; (typ) telaio || tr inseguire; cacciare; (to chisel) cesellare; to chase away scacciare || intr—to chase after inseguire

chaser [ˈtʃesər] s cacciatore m; (coll) bibita da bersi dopo un liquore

chasm [ˈkæzəm] s abisso, baratro

chas·sis [ˈtʃæsi] s (-sis [siz]) telaio

chaste [tʃest] adj casto

chasten [ˈtʃesən] tr castigare

chastise [tʃæsˈtaɪz] tr castigare

chastity [ˈtʃæstɪti] s castità f

chat [tʃæt] s chiacchierata || v (pret & pp chatted; ger chatting) intr chiacchierare

chatelaine [ˈʃætəˌlen] s castellana

chattels [ˈtʃætəlz] spl beni mpl mobili

chatter [ˈtʃætər] s cicaleccio; balbettio; (of teeth) battito || intr cicalare; balbettare; (said of teeth) battere

chat'ter·box' s chiacchierone m

chauffeur [ˈʃofər] or [ʃoˈfʌr] s autista mf || intr fare l'autista

cheap [tʃip] adj a buon mercato, economico; (of poor quality) scadente; to feel cheap vergognarsi || adv a buon mercato

cheapen [ˈtʃipən] tr deprezzare; avvilire; rendere di cattivo gusto

cheapness [ˈtʃipnəs] s buon mercato, prezzo basso

cheat [tʃit] s truffa; truffatore m || tr imbrogliare, truffare || intr truffare; (at cards) barare

check [tʃɛk] s arresto, pausa; ostacolo;

esame *m;* verifica, controllo; (*of bank*) assegno; (*for baggage*) tagliando, scontrino; (*square pattern*) quadretto; (*fabric in squares*) tessuto a scacchi; (*in a restaurant*) conto; **in check** controllato, sotto controllo; (chess) sotto scacco || *tr* fermare; confrontare; ispezionare; marcare; (*e.g., a coat*) depositare; disegnare a quadretti; (chess) dare scacco a; **to check off** controllare marcando; **to check on** controllare, verificare || *intr* fermarsi; corrispondere perfettamente; **to check in** scendere (a un albergo); **to check out** andar via; pagare il conto; **to check up on** controllare

check'book' *s* libretto d'assegni

checker ['tʃɛkər] *s* ispettore *m;* quadretto; (*in game of checkers*) pedina; **checkers** dama || *tr* variegare; marcare a quadretti

check'er·board' *s* scacchiera

check'ered *adj* (*e.g., career*) pieno di vicissitudini; (*marked with squares*) a scacchi; (*in color*) variegato

check'ing account' *s* conto corrente

check'mate' *s* scacco matto || *tr* dare scacco matto a || *interj* scacco matto!

check'off' dues' *spl* trattenute *fpl* sindacali

check'-out' *s* (*from hotel room*) partenza; (*time*) ora della partenza; (*examination*) esame *m* di controllo; (*in a supermarket*) cassa

check'point' *s* punto di ispezione

check'room' *s* guardaroba *m*

check'up' *s* (*of car*) ispezione; (*of patient*) esame *m* (fisico)

cheek [tʃik] *s* guancia, gota; (coll) faccia tosta

cheek'bone' *s* zigomo

cheek·y ['tʃiki] *adj* (**-ier; -iest**) (coll) impudente, sfacciato

cheer [tʃɪr] *s* gioia, allegria; applauso; **of good cheer** di buon umore || *tr* riempire di gioia, rallegrare; applaudire; ricevere con applausi || *intr* rallegrarsi; **cheer up!** animo!, coraggio!

cheerful ['tʃɪrfəl] *adj* allegro, di buon umore; (*willing*) volonteroso

cheerless ['tʃɪrlɪs] *adj* tetro, triste

cheese [tʃiz] *s* formaggio || *intr*— **cheese it!** (slang) scappa via!

cheese' cake' *s* torta di formaggio; (slang) pin-up girl *f*

cheese'cloth' *s* etamine *f*, stamigna

chees·y [tʃisi] *adj* (**-ier; -iest**) di formaggio; come il formaggio; (slang) meschino, di cattiva qualità

chef [ʃef] *s* chef *m*, capocuoco

chemical ['kɛmɪkəl] *adj* chimico || *s* prodotto chimico

chemise [ʃə'miz] *s* sottoveste *f*

chemist ['kɛmɪst] *s* chimico

chemistry ['kɛmɪstri] *s* chimica

cherish ['tʃerɪʃ] *tr* accarezzare; (*a memory*) custodire; (*a hope*) nutrire

cher·ry ['tʃeri] *s* (**-ries**) (*tree*) ciliegio; (*fruit*) ciliegia

cher·ub ['tʃerəb] *s* (**-ubim** [əbɪm] & **-ubs**) cherubino

chess [tʃes] *s* scacchi *mpl*

chess'board' *s* scacchiera

chess'man' or **chess'man** *s* (**-men'** or **-men**) scacco

chest [tʃest] *s* petto; (*box*) cassapanca; (*furniture with drawers*) cassettone *m;* (*for money*) forziere *m*

chestnut ['tʃesnət] *s* (*tree, wood, color*) castagno; (*nut*) castagna

chest' of drawers' *s* cassettone *m*

cheval' glass' [ʃə'væl] *s* psiche *f*

chevalier [ˌʃevə'lɪr] *s* cavaliere *m*

chevron ['ʃevrən] *s* gallone *m*

chew [tʃu] *tr* masticare; **to chew the cud** ruminare; **to chew the rag** (slang) chiacchierare || *intr* masticare

chew'ing gum' *s* gomma da masticare

chic [ʃik] *adj* & *s* chic

chicaner·y [ʃɪ'kenəri] *s* (**-ies**) trucco, rigiro

chick [tʃɪk] *s* pulcino; (slang) ragazza

chicken ['tʃɪkən] *s* pollo, pollastro; (coll) giovane *mf;* **to be chicken** (slang) avere la fifa || *intr*—**to chicken out** (coll) indietreggiare

chick'en coop' *s* pollaio

chick'en feed' *s* (slang) spiccioli *mpl*

chicken-hearted ['tʃɪkən ˌhartɪd] *adj* timido, fifone

chick'en pox' *s* varicella

chick'en store' *s* polleria

chick'en wire' *s* rete metallica esagonale

chick'pea' *s* cece *m*

chico·ry ['tʃɪkəri] *s* (**-ries**) cicoria

chide [tʃaɪd] *v* (*pret* **chided** or **chid** [tʃɪd]; *pp* **chided, chid,** or **chidden** ['tʃɪdən]) *tr* & *intr* rimproverare, correggere

chief [tʃif] *adj* principale, sommo, supremo || *s* capo, comandante supremo; (slang) padrone *m*

chief' exec'utive *s* capo del governo

chief' jus'tice *s* presidente *m* di una corte; presidente *m* della corte suprema

chiefly ['tʃifli] *adv* principalmente

chief' of staff' *s* capo di stato maggiore

chief' of state' *s* capo dello stato

chieftain ['tʃiftən] *s* capo

chiffon [ʃɪ'fɑn] *s* velo trasparente, chiffon *m;* **chiffons** trine *fpl*

chiffonier [ˌʃɪfə'nɪr] *s* mobile *m* a cassettini, chiffonier *m*

chilblain ['tʃɪl ˌblen] *s* gelone *m*

child [tʃaɪld] *s* (**children** ['tʃɪldrən]) bebè *mf*, bambino; figlio; discendente *mf;* **with child** incinta

child'birth' *s* parto

childhood ['tʃaɪldhʊd] *s* infanzia

childish ['tʃaɪldɪʃ] *adj* infantile

childishness ['tʃaɪldɪʃnɪs] *s* puerilità *f*, infanzia

child' la'bor *s* lavoro dei minorenni

childless ['tʃaɪldlɪs] *adj* senza figli

child'like' *adj* infantile, innocente

child's' play' *s* un gioco

child' wel'fare *s* protezione dell'infanzia

Chile ['tʃɪli] *s* il Cile

Chilean ['tʃɪlɪ·ən] *adj* cileno

chil'i sauce' ['tʃɪli] s salsa di pomo-doro con peperoni

chill [tʃɪl] adj freddo || s freddo; bri-vido di freddo; freddezza; (depres-sion) abbattimento || tr raffreddare; (a metal) temprare; (fig) scoraggiare || intr raffreddarsi

chill·y ['tʃɪli] adj (-ier; -iest) fresco, freddiccio; (reception) freddo

chime [tʃaɪm] s scampanio; chimes campanello || intr scampanare; to chime in cominciare a cantare al-l'unisono; (coll) intromettersi

chime' clock' s orologio con carillon

chimney ['tʃɪmni] s .camino; (of fac-tory) ciminiera; to smoke like a chimney fumare come un turco

chim'ney flue' s tubo di stufa, canna del camino

chim'ney pot' s testa della canna fu-maria, comignolo

chim'ney sweep' s spazzacamino

chimpanzee [tʃɪm'pænzi] or [ˌtʃɪm-pæn'zi] s scimpanzé m

chin [tʃɪn] s mento; to keep one's chin up (coll) non perdersi di coraggio; to take it on the chin (slang) subire una sconfitta || v (pret & pp chinned; ger chinning) tr—to chin oneself sol-levarsi fino al mento (ai manubri) || intr (slang) chiacchierare

china ['tʃaɪnə] s porcellana || China s la Cina

chi'na clos'et s armadio per le stoviglie

chi'na·ware' s porcellana, stoviglie fpl

Chi·nese [tʃaɪ'niz] adj cinese || s (-nese) cinese mf

Chi'nese lan'tern s lampioncino alla veneziana

Chi'nese puz'zle s rebus m

chink [tʃɪŋk] s fessura

chin' strap' s sottogola

chintz [tʃɪnts] s chintz m

chip [tʃɪp] s scheggia; frammento; (in card games) gettone m; (of wood) truciolo; chip off the old block vero figlio di suo padre (di sua madre); chip on one's shoulder propensità f a attaccar brighe || v (pret & pp chipped; ger chipping) tr scheggiare; to chip in contribuire || intr scheg-giarsi

chipmunk ['tʃɪp͵mʌŋk] s tamia

chipper ['tʃɪpər] adj (coll) allegro, vivo

chiropodist [kaɪ'rɑpədɪst] or [kɪ'rɑpə-dɪst] s callista mf, pedicure mf

chiropractice ['kaɪrə͵præktɪs] s chiro-pratica

chirp [tʃʌrp] s (of birds) cinguettio; (of crickets) cri cri m || intr cinguet-tare; fare cri cri

chis·el ['tʃɪzəl] s (for wood and metal) scalpello; (for metal) cesello || v (pret & pp -eled or -elled; ger -eling or -elling) tr scalpellare; cesellare; (slang) imbrogliare || intr (slang) imbrogliare, fare l'imbroglione

chiseler ['tʃɪzələr] s scalpellino; cesel-latore m; (slang) imbroglione m

chit-chat [ˈtʃɪt ͵tʃæt] s chiacchierata

chivalrous ['ʃɪvəlrəs] adj cavalleresco

chivalry ['ʃɪvəlri] s cavalleria

chive [tʃaɪv] s cipolla porraia

chloride ['klɔraɪd] s cloruro

chlorine ['klɔrin] s cloro

chloroform ['klɔrə ͵fɔrm] s cloroformio || tr cloroformizzare

chlorophyll ['klɔrəfɪl] s clorofilla

chock [tʃɑk] s (wedge) bietta, cuneo

chock-full ['tʃɑk'fʊl] adj colmo, pieno zeppo

chocolate ['tʃɔkəlɪt] or ['tʃɑkəlɪt] s (candy) cioccolato; (drink) ciocco-lata

choc'olate bar' s barretta di cioccolato

choice [tʃɔɪs] adj di prima scelta, su-periore || s scelta; (variety) assorti-mento

choir [kwaɪr] s coro

choir'boy' s ragazzo cantore

choir' loft' s coro

choir'mas'ter s maestro di cappella

choke [tʃok] s strozzatura; (aut) far-falla del carburatore || tr strozzare; ostruire; (an internal-combustion en-gine) arricchire la miscela di; to choke back trattenere; to choke up tappare, ostruire || intr soffocarsi; to choke up tapparsi; (coll) soffocarsi

choker ['tʃokər] s (necklace) (coll) collana; (scarf) (coll) foulard m

cholera ['kɑlərə] s colera m

choleric ['kɑlərɪk] adj collerico

cholesterol [kə'lɛstə͵rol] or [kə'lɛstə-͵rɑl] s colesterina

choose [tʃuz] v (pret chose [tʃoz]; pp chosen ['tʃozən]) tr scegliere || intr —to choose to decidere di

choos·y ['tʃuzi] adj (-ier; -iest) (coll) di difficile contentatura

chop [tʃɑp] s colpo; (of meat) coto-letta; chops labbra fpl, bocca || v (pret & pp chopped; ger chopping) tr tagliare; (meat) tritare; to chop off troncare; to chop up sminuzzare

chopper ['tʃɑpər] s (man) tagliatore m; interruttore automatico; coltello da macellaio; (slang) elicottero; choppers (slang) i denti

chop'ping block' s tagliere m

chop·py ['tʃɑpi] adj (-pier; -piest) (wind) variabile; (sea) agitato; (style) instabile

choral ['korəl] adj & s corale m

chorale [ko'ral] s corale m

chord [kɔrd] s corda; (mus) accordo

chore [tʃor] s lavoro; lavoro spiace-vole; chores faccende domestiche

choreography [͵korɪ'ɑgrəfi] s coreo-grafia

chorine [ko'rin] s (slang) ballerina

chorus ['korəs] s coro; (group of dancers) corpo di ballo; (of a song) ritornello

cho'rus girl' s ballerina

cho'rus man' s (men') corista m

chow [tʃau] s (dog) chow chow m; (slang) cibo, pappa

chowder ['tʃaudər] s zuppa di vongole; zuppa di pesce

Christ [kraɪst] s Cristo

christen ['krɪsən] tr battezzare

Christendom ['krɪsəndəm] s cristianità f

christening ['krɪsənɪŋ] s battesimo
Christian ['krɪstʃən] adj & s cristiano
Christianity [ˌkrɪstʃɪ'ænɪti] s (*Christendom*) cristianità f; (*religion*) cristianesimo
Chris'tian name' s nome m di battesimo
Christmas ['krɪsməs] adj natalizio || s Natale m; **Merry Christmas!** Buon Natale!
Christ'mas card' s cartoncino natalizio
Christ'mas car'ol s pastorella di Natale
Christ'mas Eve' s vigilia di Natale
Christ'mas gift' s strenna natalizia
Christ'mas tree' s albero di Natale
chrome [krom] adj cromato || s cromo || tr cromare
chromium ['kromɪ·əm] s cromo
chromosome ['kromə ˌsom] s cromosoma m
chronic ['krɑnɪk] adj cronico
chronicle ['krɑnɪkəl] s cronaca || tr fare la storia di
chronicler ['krɑnɪklər] s cronista mf
chronolo·gy [krə'nɑlədʒi] s (-gies) cronologia
chronometer [krə'nɑmɪtər] s cronometro
chrysanthemum [krɪ'sænθɪməm] s crisantemo
chub·by ['tʃʌbi] adj (-bier; -biest) paffuto
chuck [tʃʌk] s buffetto sotto il mento; (*cut of meat*) reale m; (*of lathe*) coppaia || tr accarezzare sotto il mento; (*to throw*) (coll) gettare
chuckle ['tʃʌkəl] s risatina || intr ridacchiare
chum [tʃʌm] s (coll) amico intimo; (coll) compagno di stanza || v (pret & pp **chummed**; ger **chumming**) intr (coll) essere amico intimo; essere compagno di stanza
chum·my ['tʃʌmi] adj (-mier; -miest) (coll) intimo, amicone
chump [tʃʌmp] s ciocco, ceppo; (coll) sciocco
chunk [tʃʌŋk] s grosso pezzo
church [tʃʌrtʃ] s chiesa
churchgoer ['tʃʌrtʃ ˌgo·ər] s praticante mf
church'man s (-men) parrocchiano; (*clergyman*) sacerdote m
Church' of Eng'land s chiesa anglicana
church'yard' s camposanto
churl [tʃʌrl] s zotico, villano
churlish ['tʃʌrlɪʃ] adj villano
churn [tʃʌrn] s zangola || tr agitare violentemente, sbattere || intr (said of water) ribollire
chute [ʃut] s piano inclinato, canna; (*in a river*) cascata, rapida; paracadute m; (*into a swimming pool*) toboga m
Cicero ['sɪsə ˌro] s Cicerone m
cider ['saɪdər] s sidro
cigar [sɪ'gɑr] s sigaro
cigar' case' s portasigari m
cigar' cut'ter s tagliasigari m
cigarette [ˌsɪgə'rɛt] s sigaretta
cigarette' butt' s cicca
cigarette' case' s portasigarette m
cigarette' hold'er s bocchino

cigarette' light'er s accendisigaro, accendino
cigarette' pa'per s cartina da sigarette
cigar' store' s tabaccheria, rivendita di sali e tabacchi
cinch [sɪntʃ] s (on a horse) sottopancia m; (hold) (coll) presa; (slang) giochetto || tr legare con una cinghia; (slang) agguantare
cinder ['sɪndər] s tizzone m; (slag) scoria; **cinders** cenere f
cin'der block' s concio di scoria
Cinderella [ˌsɪndə'rɛlə] s (la) Cenerentola
cinema ['sɪnəmə] s cine m, cinema m
cinnabar ['sɪnə ˌbɑr] s cinabro
cinnamon ['sɪnəmən] s cannella
cipher ['saɪfər] s zero; cifra; codice m; monogramma m || tr calcolare; (to write in code) cifrare
circle ['sʌrkəl] s cerchio; (of theater) prima galleria; (of friends) cerchia || tr cerchiare, compiere una rotazione intorno a
circuit ['sʌrkɪt] s circuito; (district) circoscrizione
cir'cuit break'er s salvamotore m, interruttore automatico
circuitous [sər'kju·ɪtəs] adj tortuoso
circuitry ['sʌrkɪtri] s (plan) schema m di montaggio; (components) elementi mpl di un circuito
circular ['sʌrkjələr] adj & s circolare f
circulate ['sʌrkjə ˌlet] tr mettere in circolazione, diffondere || intr circolare
cir'culating li'brary s biblioteca circolante
circulation [ˌsʌrkjə'leʃən] s circolazione; (of newspaper) diffusione
circumcise ['sʌrkəm ˌsaɪz] tr circoncidere
circumference [sər'kʌmfərəns] s circonferenza
circumflex ['sʌrkəm ˌflɛks] adj circonflesso || s accento circonflesso
circumscribe [ˌsʌrkəm'skraɪb] tr circoscrivere
circumspect ['sʌrkəm ˌspɛkt] adj circospetto
circumstance ['sʌrkəm ˌstæns] s circostanza; (fact) dettaglio; solennità f; **circumstances** condizioni fpl; dettagli mpl; condizioni economiche; **under no circumstances** a nessuna condizione; **under the circumstances** le cose essendo come sono
circumstantial [ˌsʌrkəm'stænʃəl] adj circostanziale, indiziario; (incidental) secondario; (complete) circostanziato
cir'cumstan'tial ev'idence s prova indiziaria
circumstantiate [ˌsʌrkəm'stænʃɪ ˌet] tr (to support with particulars) comprovare; (to describe in detail) circonstanziare
circumvent [ˌsʌrkəm'vɛnt] tr (to surround) accerchiare; (to outwit) circuire; (a difficulty) eludere, scansare
circus ['sʌrkəs] s circo equestre
cistern ['sɪstərn] s cisterna, serbatoio
citadel ['sɪtədəl] s cittadella
citation [saɪ'teʃən] s citazione

cite [saɪt] *tr* citare

cither ['sɪðər] *s* cetra

citizen ['sɪtɪzən] *s* cittadino; *(civilian)* civile *mf*

citizenship ['sɪtɪzən ‚ʃɪp] *s* cittadinanza

citric ['sɪtrɪk] *adj* citrico

citron ['sɪtrən] *s* cedro; cedro candito

cit′rus fruit′ ['sɪtrəs] *s* agrumi *mpl*

cit·y ['sɪti] *s* (-ies) città *f*

cit′y counc′il *s* consiglio municipale

cit′y ed′itor *s* capocronista *m*

cit′y fa′thers *spl* maggiorenti *mpl;* consiglieri *mpl* municipali

cit′y hall′ *s* municipio

cit′y plan′ning *s* urbanistica

cit′y room′ *s* (journ) redazione

civic ['sɪvɪk] *adj* civico || **civics** *s* educazione civica

civil ['sɪvɪl] *adj* civile

civ′il engineer′ing *s* genio civile

civilian [sɪ'vɪljən] *adj & s* civile *mf,* borghese *mf*

civili·ty [sɪ'vɪlɪti] *s* (-ties) cortesia; **civilities** ossequi *mpl*

civilization [‚sɪvɪlɪ'zeʃən] *s* civilizzazione, civiltà *f*

civilize ['sɪvɪ ‚laɪz] *tr* civilizzare

civ′il law′ *s* diritto civile

civ′il serv′ant *s* impiegato statale

civ′il war′ *s* guerra civile || **Civil War** *s* *(of the U.S.A.)* guerra di secessione

claim [klem] *s* pretesa; richiesta; (min) concessione || *tr (one′s rights)* rivendicare; *(one′s property)* richiedere; dichiarare; **to claim to be** pretendere d′essere

claim′ check′ *s* tagliando

clairvoyance [klɛr'vɔɪ·əns] *s* chiaroveggenza

clairvoyant [klɛr'vɔɪ·ənt] *adj* chiaroveggente || *s* veggente *mf,* chiaroveggente *mf*

clam [klæm] *s* vongola || *intr—***to clam up** (coll) essere muto come un pesce

clamber ['klæmər] *intr* arrampicarsi

clam·my ['klæmi] *adj* (-mier; -miest) coperto di sudore freddo; morbido

clamor ['klæmər] *s* clamore *m* || *intr* fare clamore

clamorous ['klæmərəs] *adj* clamoroso

clamp [klæmp] *s* graffa, morsetto; *(e.g., to hold a hose)* fascetta || *tr* assicurare con graffa, aggrappare; *(a tool)* montare || *intr—***to clamp down on** (coll) fare pressione su, mettere i freni a

clan [klæn] *s* clan *m*

clandestine [klæn'dɛstɪn] *adj* clandestino

clang [klæŋ] *s* clangore *m* || *intr* risonare con clangore

clannish ['klænɪʃ] *adj* esclusivista, partigiano

clap [klæp] *s* applauso; *(of thunder)* scoppio || *v (pret & pp* **clapped);** *ger* **clapping)** *tr (the hands)* battere; *(e.g., in jail)* schiaffare; **to clap shut** sbattere || *intr* applaudire

clapper ['klæpər] *s* applauditore *m;* (of bell) batacchio

clap′trap′ *s* imbonimento

claret ['klærɪt] *adj & s* chiaretto

clari·fy ['klærɪ ‚faɪ] *v (pret & pp* **-fied)** *tr* chiarificare, chiarire

clarinet [‚klærɪ'nɛt] *s* clarinetto

clarion ['klærɪ·ən] *adj* chiaro e metallico || *s* tromba, clarino

clash [klæʃ] *s* cozzo, urto; conflitto di opinioni || *intr* cozzare, urtarsi; essere in conflitto

clasp [klæsp] *or* [klɑsp] *s* gancio, fermaglio; *(hold)* presa; *(grip)* stretta || *tr* agganciare; *(to hold in the arms)* abbracciare; *(to grip)* stringere

class [klæs] *or* [klɑs] *s* classe *f* || *tr* classificare

class′book′ *s* registro

classic ['klæsɪk] *adj & s* classico

classical ['klæsɪkəl] *adj* classico

classicism ['klæsɪ ‚sɪzəm] *s* classicismo

classicist ['klæsɪsɪst] *s* classicista *mf*

classified ['klæsɪ ‚faɪd] *adj* segreto

clas′sified ad′ *s* annunzio economico

classi·fy ['klæsɪ ‚faɪ] *v (pret & pp* **-fied)** *tr* classificare

class′mate′ *s* compagno di scuola

class′room′ *s* aula scolastica

class′ strug′gle *s* lotta di classe

class·y ['klæsi] *adj* (-ier; -iest) (slang) di lusso, di prim′ordine

clatter ['klætər] *s* *(of dishes)* acciottolio; vocio, schiamazzo || *tr* acciottolare || *intr* fare schiamazzo

clause [klɔz] *s* clausola; (gram) proposizione

clavicle ['klævɪkəl] *s* clavicola

claw [klɔ] *s* artiglio; *(of lobster)* pinza; *(tool)* raffio; *(of hammer)* granchio; (coll) dita *fpl* || *tr* aggraffiare; artigliare

claw′ ham′mer *s* levachiodi *m*

clay [kle] *s* argilla, creta

clay′ pipe′ *s* pipa di terracotta

clean [klin] *adj* pulito; *(precise)* netto; *(e.g., break)* completo || *adv* completamente || *tr* pulire; **to clean out** pulire, fare repulisti di; (slang) ripulire; **to clean up** pulire completamente; mettere in ordine || *intr* pulirsi, fare pulizia

clean′ bill′ of health′ *s* patente sanitaria; (fig) esonero completo

clean′-cut′ *adj* ben delineato, deciso

cleaner ['klinər] *s* pulitore *m,* smacchiatore *m;* *(machine)* pulitrice *f,* smacchiatrice *f;* **to send to the cleaners** (slang) spolpare

clean′ing fluid′ *s* smacchiatore *m*

clean′ing wom′an *s* donna di servizio per fare la pulizia

clean·ly ['klɛnli] *adj* (-lier; -liest) pulito, netto

cleanse [klɛnz] *tr* pulire; detergere; purificare

cleanser ['klɛnzər] *s* detergente *m*

clean′-sha′ven *adj* sbarbato di fresco

clean′up′ *s* pulizia; (slang) guadagno enorme

clear [klɪr] *adj* chiaro; evidente; completo; innocente; *(profit)* netto; **clear of** libero da || *s* posto libero; **in the clear** libero; esonerato; non in codice || *adv* chiaramente; completamente || *tr (e.g., trees)* rischiarare; *(e.g., peo-*

ple) sgombrare; (the table) sparecchiare; (an obstacle) superare; (from
guilt) discolpare; (a profit) guadagnare; (goods at customs) svincolare;
(a ship through customs) dichiarare
il carico di; (checks) compensare; **to
clear away** or **off** liberare; **to clear
out** sgomberare, sbarazzare; **to clear
up** spiegare; (a doubt) dissipare ‖
intr rasserenarsi; (said of a ship)
partire; **to clear away** or **off** sparire;
to clear out (coll) andarsene; **to clear
up** rasserenarsi
clearance ['klɪrəns] s liberazione; (of
a ship) partenza; (of goods through
customs) sdoganamento; (of checks)
compensazione; (of goods) liquidazione; (mach) gioco
clear'ance sale' s liquidazione
clear'-cut' adj chiaro, distinto
clearing ['klɪrɪŋ] s (open space) radura; (of checks) compensazione
clear'ing house' s stanza di compensazione
cleat [klit] s bietta, cuneo; (on the sole
of shoe) tacchetto; (naut) galloccia
cleavage ['klivɪdʒ] s divisione; fessura
cleave [kliv] v (pret & pp **cleft** [klɛft]
or **cleaved**) tr dividere, fendere ‖ intr
aderire, essere fedele
cleaver ['klivər] s scure f, accetta; (of
butcher) spaccaossa m, fenditoio
clef [klɛf] s (mus) chiave f
cleft [klɛft] adj diviso, fesso ‖ s fessura, crepaccio
cleft' pal'ate s palato spaccato, gola
lupina
clematis ['klɛmətɪs] s clematide f
clemen·cy ['klɛmənsi] s (-cies) cle-
menza
clement ['klɛmənt] adj clemente
clench [klɛntʃ] s stretta ‖ tr stringere;
afferrare
clergy ['klɛrdʒi] s clero
cler'gy·man s (-men) ecclesiastico
cleric ['klɛrɪk] s ecclesiastico, sacerdote m
clerical ['klɛrɪkəl] adj da impiegato;
(error) burocratico; (of clergy) cleri-
cale ‖ s ecclesiastico; **clericals** abiti
ecclesiastici
cler'ical work' s lavoro d'ufficio
clerk [klʌrk] s impiegato, commesso;
(accountant) contabile mf; (e.g., in
a record office) ufficiale m; cancelliere m; (copyist, typist) scrivano
clever ['klɛvər] adj intelligente; bravo,
abile; destro
cleverness ['klɛvərnɪs] s intelligenza;
bravura, abilità f
clew [klu] s indizio, traccia; (of yarn)
gomitolo; (naut) bugna
cliché [kli'ʃe] s cliché m, luogo comune
click [klɪk] s (of camera or gun)
scatto; (of typewriter) battito, ticchettio ‖ tr (the tongue) schioccare;
(the heels) battere ‖ intr ticchettare;
(slang) andare d'accordo; (slang)
avere fortuna
client ['klaɪ·ənt] s cliente mf
clientele [ˌklaɪ·ən'tɛl] s clientela

cliff [klɪf] s rupe f, precipizio
climate ['klaɪmɪt] s clima m
climax ['klaɪmæks] s apice m; (acute
phase) parossismo
climb [klaɪm] s salita; (of a mountain)
scalata, ascensione ‖ tr (the stairs)
salire; (a mountain) scalare, ascen-
dere ‖ intr salire, arrampicarsi; **to
climb down** discendere a carponi;
(coll) ritirarsi
climber ['klaɪmər] s scalatore m;
pianta rampicante; (ambitious person) (coll) arrampicatore m
clinch [klɪntʃ] s stretta, presa; (boxing) corpo a corpo m ‖ tr (nails)
ribattere, ribadire
clincher ['klɪntʃər] s chiodo per riba-
ditura; argomento decisivo
cling [klɪŋ] v (pret & pp **clung** [klʌŋ])
intr avviticchiare, attaccarsi; aderire,
rimanere attaccato
cling'stone' peach' s pesca duracino
clinic ['klɪnɪk] s clinica
clinical ['klɪnɪkəl] adj clinico
clinician [klɪ'nɪʃən] s clinico
clink [klɪŋk] s tintinnio; (slang) gattabuia ‖ tr (glasses) toccare ‖ intr
tintinnare
clinker ['klɪŋkər] s clinker m; mattone
vetrificato; (slang) sbaglio
clip [klɪp] s (of hair) taglio; (of wool)
tosatura; (speed) passo rapido; clip
f, fermaglio; (large clip) fermacarte
m; (for cartridges) caricatore m;
(coll) colpo ‖ v (pret & pp **clipped**;
ger **clipping**) tr tagliare, tosare;
(words) mangiare, storpiare; (paper)
ritagliare; ritenere; (coll) battere ‖
intr andare di buon passo
clipper ['klɪpər] s tagliatore m; (aer,
naut) clipper m; **clippers** (for hair)
tosatrice f; (for nails) pinze fpl per
le unghie
clipping ['klɪpɪŋ] s taglio; (from newspaper) ritaglio
clique [klik] s cricca, chiesuola
cloak [klok] s mantello, manto; (fig)
velo, maschera ‖ tr ammantare, velare
cloak'-and-dag'ger adj d'avventura
cloak'-and-sword' adj di cappa e spada
cloak'room' s guardaroba m
clock [klɑk] s orologio; (with pendulum) pendolo, pendola; (on stocking)
freccia ‖ tr registrare, cronometrare
clock'mak'er s orologiaio
clock' tow'er s torre f dell'orologio
clock'wise' adj & adv nella direzione
delle lancette dell'orologio
clock'work' s movimento d'orologeria;
like clockwork come un orologio
clod [klɑd] s zolla; (fig) tonto
clod'hop'per s (shoe) scarpone m; (fig)
villano, bifolco
clog [klɑg] s intoppo; (to impede
movement) pastoia; scarpone m, zoccolo ‖ v (pret & pp **clogged**; ger
clogging) tr intoppare; (to hold back)
impastoiare ‖ intr otturarsi, ostruirsi
cloister ['klɔɪstər] s chiostro ‖ tr rinchiudere in un chiostro
close [klos] adj vicino; (translation)

fedele; (*air in room*) male arieggiato; (*weather*) soffocante; (*stingy*) avaro; limitato, senza gioco; (*haircut*) corto; (*friend*) intimo; (*hit*) preciso; (*enclosed*) chiuso; (*narrow*) stretto || *adv* da vicino; **close to** vicino a || [kloz] *s* fine *f*, conclusione; **to bring to a close** concludere || *tr* chiudere; otturare; concludere; **to close down** chiudere completamente; **to close out** vendere in liquidazione; **to close up** bloccare || *intr* chiudersi; serrarsi; **to close down** chiudersi completamente; **to close in on** venire alle prese con; **to close up** bloccarsi; (*said of a wound*) rimarginarsi

close′ call′ [klos] *s* rischio scampato per miracolo

closed′ chap′ter *s* affare chiuso

closed′ cir′cuit *s* circuito chiuso

closed′ sea′son *s* periodo di caccia o pesca vietata

closefisted [ˈklosˈfɪstɪd] *adj* taccagno

close-fit′ing [klos] *adj* attillato

close-lipped [ˈklosˈlɪpt] *adj* riservato

closely [ˈklosli] *adv* da vicino; strettamente; fedelmente; attentamente

close′ quar′ters [klos] *spl* (*cramped space*) pigia pigia *m;* **at close quarters** a corpo a corpo

close′ quote′ [kloz] *s* fine *f* della citazione

close′ shave′ [klos] *s*—**to have a close shave** farsi fare la barba a contropelo; (coll) scamparla per un pelo

closet [ˈklɑzɪt] *s* armadio a muro; (*small private room*) gabinetto; (*for keeping clothing*) ripostiglio || *tr*—**to be closeted with** essere in conciliabolo con

close′-up′ [klos] *s* (mov) primo piano

closing [ˈklozɪŋ] *s* fine *f*, conclusione

clos′ing price′ *s* ultimo corso

clot [klɑt] *s* grumo, coagulo || *v* (*pret & pp* **clotted;** *ger* **clotting**) *intr* raggrumarsi, coagularsi

cloth [klɔθ] *or* [klɑθ] *s* panno, tessuto, stoffa; abito; (*for binding books*) tela; **the cloth** il clero

clothe [kloð] *v* (*pret & pp* **clothed** *or* **clad** [klæd]) *tr* vestire, rivestire, coprire

clothes [kloz] *or* [kloðz] *spl* vestiti *mpl*, abiti *mpl;* (*for a bed*) coltre *f;* **to change clothes** cambiarsi

clothes′bas′ket *s* cesto della biancheria

clothes′brush′ *s* spazzola per vestiti

clothes′ dry′er *s* asciugatrice *f*

clothes′ hang′er *s* attaccapanni *m*

clothes′horse′ *s* cavalletto per stendere il bucato; elegantone *m*

clothes′line′ *s* corda per stendere il bucato

clothes′ moth′ *s* tarma, tignola

clothes′pin′ *s* molletta

clothes′ tree′ *s* attaccapanni *m*

clothier [ˈkloðjər] *s* negoziante *m* di confezioni; mercante *m* di panno

clothing [ˈkloðɪŋ] *s* vestiti *mpl*, vestiario

cloud [klaud] *s* nuvola, nube *f;* (*great number*) nuvolo; macchia; sospetto

|| *tr* annuvolare; offuscare || *intr* annuvolarsi; offuscarsi

cloud′ bank′ *s* banco di nubi

cloud′burst′ *s* acquazzone *m*, nubifragio

cloud′-capped′ *adj* coperto di nubi

cloudless [ˈklaudlɪs] *adj* senza nubi

cloud·y [ˈklaudi] *adj* (-ier; -iest) nuvoloso, annuvolato; confuso; tenebroso

clout [klaut] *s* (coll) schiaffo || *tr* (coll) schiaffeggiare

clove [klov] *s* chiodo di garofano; (*of garlic*) spicchio

cloven-hoofed [ˈklovənˈhuft] *adj* dal piede biforcuto; demoniaco

clover [ˈklovər] *s* trifoglio; **in clover** come un papa

clo′ver-leaf′ *s* (-leaves [ˌlivz]) foglia di trifoglio; incrocio stradale a quadrifoglio

clown [klaun] *s* pagliaccio, buffone *m* || *intr* fare il pagliaccio

clownish [ˈklaunɪʃ] *adj* buffonesco, clownesco, claunesco

cloy [klɔɪ] *tr* saziare fino alla nausea

club [klʌb] *s* bastone *m;* circolo, società *f;* (*playing card*) fiore *m* || *v* (*pret & pp* **clubbed;** *ger* **clubbing**) *tr* bastonare || *intr*—**to club together** unirsi

club′ car′ *s* vagone *m* con servizio di buffet

club′house′ *s* sede *f* di un circolo

club′man′ *s* (-men′) frequentatore *m* di circoli

club′room′ *s* sala delle riunioni

club′ sand′wich *s* sandwich *m* a tre fette di pane con insalata

club′wom′an *s* (-wom′en) frequentatrice *f* di circoli

cluck [klʌk] *s* (il) chiocciare || *intr* chiocciare

clue [klu] *s* traccia, indizio

clump [klʌmp] *s* gruppo, massa; (*of earth*) zolla || *intr* camminare con passo pesante

clum·sy [ˈklʌmzi] *adj* (-sier; -siest) goffo, malaccorto, sgraziato

cluster [ˈklʌstər] *s* gruppo; (*of grapes*) grappolo; (*of bees*) sciame *m;* (*of stars*) ammasso; (*of people*) folla || *tr* raggruppare || *intr* raggrupparsi

clutch [klʌtʃ] *s* presa; (*claw*) grinfia; (*of chickens*) covata; (mach) innesto; (aut) frizione; **clutches** grinfie *fpl;* **to throw the clutch in** innestare la marcia; **to throw the clutch out** disinnestare la marcia || *tr* afferrare, aggrappare || *intr*—**to clutch at** aggrapparsi a

clutter [ˈklʌtər] *tr*—**to clutter up** ingombrare alla rinfusa

coach [kotʃ] *s* carrozza, vettura; vagone *m;* (*automobile*) berlina, autobus *m;* (*trainer*) allenatore *m;* (*teacher*) ripetitore *m* || *tr* allenare; preparare

coach′ house′ *s* rimessa

coaching [ˈkotʃɪŋ] *s* suggerimento; (*in school*) ripetizione; (sports) allenamento

coach′man *s* (-men) cocchiere *m*

coagulate [ko'ægjə ,let] *tr* coagulare || *intr* coagularsi

coal [kol] *s* carbone *m*; (*piece of burning wood*) tizzone *m*; **to call** or **haul over the coals** rimproverare || *tr* rifornire di carbone || *intr* rifornirsi di carbone; (*naut*) fare carbone

coal'bin' *s* carbonaia

coal' deal'er *s* (*wholesale*) negoziante *m* di carbone; (*retail*) carbonaio

coal' field' *s* bacino carbonifero

coal' gas' *s* gas *m* illuminante

coalition [,ko·ə'lɪʃən] *s* coalizione

coal' mine' *s* miniera di carbone

coal' oil' *s* cherosene *m*

coal' scut'tle *s* secchio del carbone

coal' tar' *s* catrame *m*

coal' yard' *s* carbonaia, carboniera

coarse [kors] *adj* (*manners*) volgare, ordinario; (*unrefined*) greggio; (*lacking refinement in manners*) rozzo, grossolano

coast [kost] *s* costa; discesa a ruota libera; **the coast is clear** la via è libera || *tr* costeggiare || *intr* costeggiare; scendere a ruota libera

coastal ['kostəl] *adj* costiero

coaster ['kostər] *s* nave *f* di cabotaggio; (*amusement*) otto volante, montagna russa; (*small tray*) sottobicchiere *m*

coast'er brake' *s* freno a contropedale

coast' guard' *s* guardacoste *m*

coast'-guard cut'ter *s* guardacoste *m*

coast'ing trade' *s* cabotaggio

coast'land' *s* costa

coast'line' *s* linea costiera, litorale *m*

coast'wise' *adv* lungo la costa

coat [kot] *s* soprabito; cappotto; (*jacket*) giacca; (*hide of man and animals*) mantello; (*of paint*) mano *f*; (*layer*) strato || *tr* vestire, proteggere; ricoprire, coprire

coat'ed ['kotɪd] *adj* rivestito; (*tongue*) patinato

coat' hang'er *s* attaccapanni *m*

coating ['kotɪŋ] *s* rivestimento; (*of paint*) mano *f*; (*of cement*) strato; (*cloth*) tessuto per abiti

coat' of arms' *s* scudo, stemma *m*

coat'room' *s* guardaroba *m*

coat'tail' *s* falda

coax [koks] *tr* blandire; ottenere con lusinghe

cob [kab] *s* spiga di granturco; (*horse*) cavallo da tiro; (*swan*) cigno maschio

cobalt ['kobəlt] *s* cobalto

cobble ['kabəl] *s* ciottolo || *tr* acciottolare; (*to mend*) raccomodare, riparare

cobbler ['kablər] *s* calzolaio, ciabattino; (*pie*) torta di frutta

cob'ble·stone' *s* ciottolo

cob'web' *s* tela di ragno, ragnatela

cocaine [ko'ken] *s* cocaina

cock [kak] *s* gallo; (*faucet*) rubinetto; (*of gun*) cane *m*; (*of the eye*) ammicco; (*of nose*) angolo (del naso) rivolto all'insù; (*of hay*) covone *m* || *tr* (*a gun*) armare; (*the head*) drizzare

cockade [ka'ked] *s* coccarda

cock-a-doodle-doo ['kakə ,dudəl'du] *s* chicchirichì *m*

cock'-and-bull' sto'ry *s* racconto incredibile

cocked' hat' *s* tricorno, cappello tricorno; **to knock into a cocked hat** (slang) distruggere completamente

cockeyed ['kak ,aɪd] *adj* strabico; (slang) sbilenco; (slang) sciocco, scemo

cockle ['kakəl] *s* (*mollusk*) cardio; (*weed*) loglio; (*boat*) barchetta; (*wrinkle*) grinza; **to warm the cockles of one's heart** far bene al cuore || *intr* raggrinzirsi

cock' of the walk' *s* gallo del pollaio

cock'pit' *s* (*of boat*) cabina; (aer) carlinga; (naut) cassero di poppa

cock'roach' *s* scarafaggio, blatta

cocks'comb' *s* cresta di gallo; berretto da buffone

cock'sure' *adj* ostinato; troppo sicuro di sé stesso

cock'tail' *s* cocktail *m*

cock'tail par'ty *s* cocktail *m*

cock·y ['kaki] *adj* (**-ier**; **-iest**) impudente, presuntuoso

cocoa ['koko] *s* (*bean*) cacao; (*drink*) cioccolata; (*tree*) cocco

coconut ['kokə ,nʌt] *s* noce *f* di cocco

co'conut palm' or **tree'** *s* cocco

cocoon [kə'kun] *s* bozzolo

cod [kad] *s* merluzzo

C.O.D. ['si'o'di] *s* (letterword) (**Collect on Delivery**) contro assegno

coddle ['kadəl] *tr* vezzeggiare

code [kod] *s* codice *m*, cifra; **in code** in codice, in cifra || *tr* mettere in codice or in cifra; cifrare

codex ['kodɛks] *s* (**codices** ['kodɪ ,siz] or ['kadɪ ,siz]) codice *m*

cod'fish' *s* merluzzo

codger ['kadʒər] *s—*old codger (coll) vecchietto

codicil ['kadɪsɪl] *s* codicillo

codi·fy ['kadɪ ,faɪ] or ['kodɪ ,faɪ] *v* (*pret & pp* **-fied**) *tr* codificare

cod'-liver oil' *s* olio di fegato di merluzzo

coed ['co ,ɛd] *s* studentessa di scuola mista

coeducation [,ko ,ɛdʒə'keʃən] *s* coeducazione

co'educa'tional school' [,ko·ɛdʒə'keʃənəl] *s* scuola mista

coefficient [,ko·ɪ'fɪʃənt] *s* coefficiente *m*

coerce [ko'ʌrs] *tr* forzare, costringere

coercion [ko'ʌrʃən] *s* coercizione

coexist [,ko·ɪg'zɪst] *intr* coesistere

coffee ['kɔfi] or ['kafi] *s* caffè *m*; **ground coffee** caffè macinato; **roasted coffee** caffè torrefatto

cof'fee bean' *s* chicco di caffè

cof'fee·cake' *s* pasticcino (da mangiarsi con il caffè)

cof'fee grind'er *s* macinino da caffè, macinacaffè *m*

cof'fee grounds' *spl* fondi *mpl* di caffè

cof'fee house' *s* caffè *m*

cof'fee mak'er *s* macchinetta del caffè

cof'fee mill' s macinino del caffè, macinacaffè m

cof'fee•pot' s caffettiera

cof'fee shop' s caffè m

coffer ['kɔfər] or ['kafər] s forziere m; (ceiling) soffitto a cassettoni; (archit) cassettone m; coffers tesoro

coffin ['kɔfɪn] or ['kafɪn] s bara

cog [kag] s dente m d'ingranaggio; ruota dentata; to slip a cog fare un errore

cogent ['kodʒənt] adj convincente, persuasivo

cogitate ['kadʒɪ‚tet] tr & intr cogitare, ponzare

cognac ['konjæk] or ['kanjæk] s cognac m

cognate ['kagnet] adj consanguineo, parente, affine || s parola dello stesso ceppo linguistico; consanguineo, parente mf

cognizance ['kagnɪzəns] or ['kanɪzəns] s conoscenza; to take cognizance of prendere conoscenza di

cognizant ['kagnɪzənt] or ['kanɪzənt] adj informato, al corrente

cog'wheel' s ruota dentata

cohabit [ko'hæbɪt] intr convivere; (archaic) coabitare

coheir [ko'er] s coerede mf

cohere [ko'hɪr] intr aderire; (fig) avere nesso

coherent [ko'hɪrənt] adj coerente

coiffeur [kwɑ'fʌr] s parrucchiere m per signora; (Brit) parrucchiere m

coiffure [kwɑ'fjur] s pettinatura || tr pettinare

coil [kɔɪl] s (of rope) rotolo; (of pipe) serpentino; (of wire) bobina, avvolgimento || tr arrotolare || intr arrotolarsi

coil' spring' s molla a spirale, molla elicoidale

coin [kɔɪn] s moneta; to pay back in one's own coin pagare della stessa moneta; to toss a coin giocare a testa o croce || tr (money) coniare, battere; (words) inventare, creare; to coin money battere moneta; (coll) fare soldoni

coincide [‚ko-ɪn'saɪd] intr coincidere

coincidence [ko'ɪnsɪdəns] s coincidenza

coke [kok] s coke m, carbone m coke

colander ['kʌləndər] or ['kaləndər] s colabrodo, colapasta m

cold [kold] adj freddo; it is cold (said of weather) fa freddo; to be cold (said of a person) avere freddo || s freddo; (ailment) raffreddore m; out in the cold solo soletto; to catch cold pigliare freddo, pigliarsi un raffreddore

cold' blood' s—in cold blood a sangue freddo

cold'-blood'ed adj insensibile; (sensitive to cold) freddoloso; (animal) a sangue freddo

cold' chis'el s tagliaferro

cold' com'fort s magra consolazione

cold' cream' s crema emolliente

cold' cuts' spl salumi mpl, affettato

cold' feet' spl—to get cold feet (coll) perdersi d'animo

cold'-heart'ed adj—to be coldhearted avere il cuore duro

coldness ['koldnɪs] s freddezza

cold' shoul'der s—to get the cold shoulder (coll) essere trattato con freddezza; to turn a cold shoulder on (coll) trattare con freddezza

cold' snap' s freddo breve e improvviso

cold' stor'age s conservazione a freddo

cold' war' s guerra fredda

cold' wave' s ondata di freddo

coleslaw ['kol‚slɔ] s insalata di cavolo cappuccio

colic ['kalɪk] adj colico || s colica

coliseum [‚kalɪ'si-əm] s stadio, arena || Coliseum s Colosseo

collaborate [kə'læbə‚ret] intr collaborare

collaborationist [kə‚læbə'reʃənɪst] s collaborazionista mf

collaborator [kə'læbə‚retər] s collaboratore m

collapse [kə'læps] s (of business) fallimento; (e.g., of a roof) caduta; (of a person) collasso || tr piegare || intr (to shrink) restringersi, sgonfiarsi; (said of a business) fallire; (said of health) venir meno; (said, e.g., of a roof) cadere, crollare

collapsible [kə'læpsɪbəl] adj pieghevole, smontabile

collar ['kalər] s (of shirt) colletto; (for dog or horse) collare m; (ring) anello; (short piece of pipe) manicotto || tr afferrare per il collo, catturare

col'lar•band' s cinturino della camicia

col'lar•bone' s clavicola

collate [kə'let] or ['kalet] tr collazionare, confrontare

collateral [kə'lætərəl] adj collaterale; accessorio, addizionale || s collaterale m

colleague ['kalig] s collega mf

collect ['kalɛkt] s (eccl) colletta || [kə'lɛkt] adv contro assegno; (telp) pagamento all'abbonato chiamato || tr raccogliere, riunire; (e.g., stamps) collezionare; (mail) levare; (bills) incassare; (ideas) coordinare; (thoughts) riordinare; (e.g., classroom papers) raccogliere; (taxes) riscuotere; to collect oneself riprendersi, riprendere il controllo di sé stesso || intr (for the poor) fare la colletta; riunirsi, raccogliersi

collected [kə'lɛktɪd] adj raccolto; equilibrato, padrone di sè

collection [kə'lɛkʃən] s collezione; (for the poor) colletta; (of mail) levata; (heap) deposito; (of taxes) esazione; (of bills) riscossione

collec'tion a'gency s agenzia di riscossione

collective [kə'lɛktɪv] adj collettivo

collector [kə'lɛktər] s (of stamps) collezionista mf; (of taxes) esattore m; (of tickets) controllore m

college ['kalɪdʒ] s scuola superiore,

università *f;* (*e.g., of medicine*) facoltà *f;* (*electoral*) collegio
collide [kə'laɪd] *intr* collidere, scontrarsi
collie ['kɑli] *s* collie *m*
collier ['kɑljər] *s* (*ship*) carboniera; (min) minatore *m* di carbone
collier·y ['kɑljəri] *s* (-ies) miniera di carbone
collision [kə'lɪʒən] *s* collisione
colloid ['kɑlɔɪd] *adj* colloidale || *s* colloide *m*
colloquial [kə'lokwɪ·əl] *adj* familiare, colloquiale
colloquialism [kə'lokwɪ·ə,lɪzəm] *s* espressione familiare
collo·quy ['kɑləkwi] *s* (-quies) colloquio
collusion [kə'luʒən] *s* collusione; **to be in collusion with** essere d'intelligenza con
cologne [kə'lon] *s* acqua di colonia, colonia || **Cologne** *s* Colonia
colon ['kolən] *s* (anat) colon *m;* (gram) due punti *mpl*
colonel ['kʌrnəl] *s* colonnello
colonist ['kɑlənɪst] *s* colono, coloniale *m*
colonize ['kɑlə,naɪz] *tr & intr* colonizzare
colonnade [,kɑlə'ned] *s* colonnato
colo·ny ['kɑləni] *s* (-nies) colonia
color ['kʌlər] *s* colore *m;* **off color** sbiadito, scolorito; (slang) sporco, volgare; **the colors** i colori, la bandiera; **to call to the colors** chiamare in servizio militare; **to change color** cambiar colore; arrossire; impallidire; **to give or lend color to** far parere probabile; **to lose color** impallidire; **to show one's colors** mostrarsi come si è; **under color of** sotto il pretesto di || *tr* colorare; (fig) colorire || *intr* arrossire
col'or-blind' *adj* daltonico
colored ['kʌlərd] *adj* colorato; (*person*) di colore; esagerato
colorful ['kʌlərfəl] *adj* colorito, espressivo
col'or guard' *s* guardia d'onore alla bandiera
coloring ['kʌlərɪŋ] *s* colorazione; colore *m;* pigmento; (fig) specie *f*
colorless ['kʌlərlɪs] *adj* incolore, incoloro
col'or photog'raphy *s* fotografia a colori
col'or ser'geant *s* sergente *m* portabandiera
col'or tel'evision *s* televisione a colori
colossal [kə'lɑsəl] *adj* colossale
colossus [kə'lɑsəs] *s* colosso
colt [kolt] *s* puledro
Columbus [kə'lʌmbəs] *s* Colombo
column ['kɑləm] *s* colonna
columnist ['kɑləmɪst] *s* giornalista incaricato di una colonna speciale; articolista *mf*
coma ['komə] *s* coma *m*
comb [kom] *s* pettine *m;* (*for horse*) striglia; (*of hen or wave*) cresta; (*honeycomb*) favo || *tr* pettinare;

(fig) esaminare minuziosamente || *intr* (*said of waves*) frangersi
com·bat ['kɑmbæt] *s* combattimento || ['kɑmbæt] or [kəm'bæt] *v* (*pret & pp* -bated or -batted; *ger* -bating or -batting) *tr & intr* combattere
combatant ['kɑmbətənt] *s* combattente *mf*
com'bat du'ty *s* servizio in zona di guerra
combination [,kɑmbɪ'neʃən] *s* combinazione
combine ['kɑmbaɪn] *s* consorzio; (pol) coalizione; mieto-trebbiatrice *f* || [kəm'baɪn] *tr* combinare || *intr* combinarsi
combin'ing form' *s* membro di parola composta
combo ['kɑmbo] *s* orchestrina
combustible [kəm'bʌstɪbəl] *adj & s* combustibile *m*
combustion [kəm'bʌstʃən] *s* combustione
come [kʌm] *v* (*pret* came [kem]; *pp* come) *intr* venire; arrivare; (*to become*) diventare; (*to amount*) ammontare; **come!** macchè!; **come along!** andiamo!; **come in!** avanti!, entri!; **come on!** andiamo!; avanti!, coraggio!; **to come about** accadere, succedere; **to come across** incontrarsi con; (slang) pagare; **to come around** cedere; mettersi d'accordo; (*said of health*) rimettersi; **to come at** raggiungere; (*to attack*) attaccare; **to come back** ritornare; **to come between** mettersi fra; **to come by** ottenere; **to come down** scendere; decadere; essere trasmesso; **to come down with** ammalarsi di; **to come forward** farsi avanti; **to come in** entrare, passare; **to come in for** ricevere; **to come into** ricevere; ereditare; **to come off** succedere; riuscire; **to come on** mostrarsi; migliorare; incontrarsi; **to come out** uscire; debuttare in società; andare a finire; **to come out with** uscire con; mostrare; **to come over** succedere a, e.g., **what came over him?** che gli è successo?; **to come through** riuscire; **to come to** riprendere i sensi; **to come under** essere di competenza di; appartenere a; **to come up** salire; **to come up to** salire fino a; avvicinarsi a; **to come up with** raggiungere; produrre, fornire; proporre
come'back' *s* (coll) ritorno; (slang) pronta risposta; **to stage a comeback** (coll) ritornare in auge
comedian [kə'midɪ·ən] *s* attore comico; (*author*) commediografo; (*amusing person*) commediante *mf*
comedienne [kə,midɪ'ɛn] *s* attrice comica
come'down' *s* (coll) rovescio di fortuna
come·dy ['kɑmədi] *s* (-dies) commedia
come·ly ['kʌmli] *adj* (-lier; -liest) bello, grazioso
comet ['kɑmɪt] *s* cometa
comfort ['kʌmfərt] *s* conforto, sollievo;

(ease) benessere *m* || *tr* confortare, alleviare

comfortable [ˈkʌmfərtəbəl] *adj* comodo, agiato; *(e.g., income)* (coll) bastante || *s* coltre *f*

comforter [ˈkʌmfərtər] *s* consolatore *m; (bedcover)* coltre *f;* sciarpa di lana || **the Comforter** lo Spirito Santo, lo Spirito Consolatore

comforting [ˈkʌmfərtɪŋ] *adj* confortante

com'fort sta'tion *s* latrina pubblica

comic [ˈkɑmɪk] *adj* comico || *s (actor)* comico; comicità *f;* **comics** fumetti *mpl*

comical [ˈkɑmɪkəl] *adj* comico

com'ic book' *s* libretto a fumetti

com'ic op'era *s* opera buffa

com'ic strip' *s* racconto umoristico a fumetti

coming [ˈkʌmɪŋ] *adj* venturo, prossimo; promettente || *s* venuta

com'ing out' *s* debutto in società; *(e.g., of stock)* emissione

comma [ˈkɑmə] *s* virgola

command [kəˈmænd] or [kəˈmɑnd] *s* comando; *(e.g., of a language)* padronanza || *tr* comandare, ordinare; *(to overlook)* dominare; *(to be able to have)* disporre di || *intr* avere il comando

commandant [ˌkɑmənˈdænt] or [ˌkɑmənˈdɑnt] *s* comandante *m*

commandeer [ˌkɑmənˈdɪr] *tr* requisire

commander [kəˈmændər] or [kəˈmɑndər] *s (of knighthood)* commendatore *m;* (mil) comandante *m;* (nav) capitano di vascello

command'er in chief' *s* comandante *m* in capo

command'ing of'ficer *s* comandante *m*

commandment [kəˈmændmənt] or [kəˈmɑndmənt] *s* comandamento

command' mod'ule *s* (rok) modulo di comando

commando [kəˈmændo] *s* guastatore *m*

commemorate [kəˈmɛməˌret] *tr* commemorare, celebrare

commence [kəˈmɛns] *tr & intr* cominciare

commencement [kəˈmɛnsmənt] *s* inizio, esordio; *(in a school)* cerimonia per la distribuzione dei diplomi

commend [kəˈmɛnd] *tr* lodare; *(to entrust)* raccomandare, affidare

commendable [kəˈmɛndəbəl] *adj (person)* lodevole; *(act)* commendevole

commendation [ˌkɑmənˈdeʃən] *s* lode *f;* raccomandazione; (mil) citazione

comment [ˈkɑmɛnt] *s* commento || *tr* commentare || *intr* fare commenti; **to comment on** fare commenti su

commentar·y [ˈkɑmənˌtɛri] *s* (-ies) commentario

commentator [ˈkɑmənˌtetər] *s* commentatore *m*

commerce [ˈkɑmərs] *s* commercio

commercial [kəˈmɜrʃəl] *adj* commerciale || *s* (rad, telv) programma *m* di pubblicità; (rad, telv) annunzio pubblicitario

commiserate [kəˈmɪzəˌret] *intr—to*

commiserate with commiserare, compiangere

commissar [ˈkɑmɪˌsɑr] or [ˌkɑmɪˈsɑr] *s* commissario del popolo

commissar·y [ˈkɑmɪˌseri] *s* (-ies) *(store)* economato; *(deputy)* commissario; *(in army)* intendente *m*

commission [kəˈmɪʃən] *s* commissione; *(e.g., in army)* nomina, brevetto; autorità *f; (of a crime)* perpetrazione; (il) fare; **in commission** in servizio, in uso; **out of commission** fuori servizio || *tr* nominare, dare un brevetto a; autorizzare; *(a ship)* armare

commis'sioned of'ficer *s* (mil, nav) ufficiale *m*

commissioner [kəˈmɪʃənər] *s* commissario; membro di una commissione

commis'sion mer'chant *s* sensale *m*

com·mit [kəˈmɪt] *v (pret & pp* -mitted; *ger* -mitting) *tr* commettere, perpetrare; *(to deliver)* affidare, consegnare; *(to imprison)* mandare in prigione; *(an insane person)* internare; *(to refer)* rinviare; *(to involve)* compromettere; **to commit oneself** compromettersi; **to commit to memory** imparare a memoria; **to commit to writing** mettere in iscritto

commitment [kəˈmɪtmənt] *s (act of committing)* commissione; *(to an asylum)* internamento; promessa; (law) mandato

committal [kəˈmɪtəl] *s* consegna; promessa

committee [kəˈmɪti] *s* comitato, commissione

commode [kəˈmod] *s (chest of drawers)* cassettone *m;* (washstand) lavabo; seggetta, comoda

commodious [kəˈmodɪ-əs] *adj* spazioso; conveniente

commodi·ty [kəˈmɑdɪti] *s* (-ties) merce *f;* articolo di prima necessità

commod'ity exchange' *s* borsa merci

common [ˈkɑmən] *adj* comune || *s* fondo comunale; pascolo comune; **commons** gente *f* non nobile; refettorio; **in common** in comune || **the Commons** la Camera dei Comuni

com'mon car'rier *s* impresa di trasporti pubblici

commoner [ˈkɑmənər] *s* plebeo, borghese *m;* membro della Camera dei Comuni

com'mon law' *s* consuetudine *f,* diritto consuetudinario

com'mon-law mar'riage *s* matrimonio basato sulla mera convivenza

commonly [ˈkɑmənli] *adv* generalmente

com'mon·place' *adj* banale, ordinario || *s* banalità *f,* cosa ordinaria

com'mon sense' *s* senso comune

com'mon-sense' *adj* giudizioso

com'mon stock' *s* azione ordinaria; azioni ordinarie

commonweal [ˈkɑmənˌwil] *s* bene pubblico

com'mon·wealth' *s (citizens of a state)* cittadinanza; repubblica; *(one of the*

50 states of the U.S.A.) stato; comunità *f*, federazione

commotion [kə'moʃən] *s* agitazione

commune [kə'mjun] *s* comune *m* ‖ *intr* confabulare; (eccl) comunicarsi

communicate [kə'mjunɪ‚ket] *tr & intr* comunicare

communicating [kə'mjunɪ‚ketɪŋ] *adj* comunicante

communication [kə‚mjunɪ'keʃən] *s* comunicazione; **communications** sistema *m* di comunicazione; mezzi *mpl* di comunicazione

communicative [kə'mjunɪ‚ketɪv] *adj* comunicativo

Communion [kə'mjunjən] *s* Comunione; **to take Communion** comunicarsi

communiqué [kə‚mjunɪ'ke] or [kə-'mjunɪ‚ke] *s* comunicato

communism ['kamjə‚nɪzəm] *s* comunismo

communist ['kamjənɪst] *s* comunista *mf*

communi·ty [kə'mjunɪti] *s* (-ties) (*people living together*) comunità *f*; (*sharing together*) comunanza; (*neighborhood*) circondario

commu'nity cen'ter *s* centro sociale

commu'nity chest' *s* fondo di beneficenza

commuta'tion tick'et [‚kamjə'teʃən] *s* biglietto d'abbonamento

commutator ['kamjə‚tetər] *s* (*switch*) commutatore *m*; (*of dynamo or motor*) collettore *m*

commute [kə'mjut] *tr* commutare ‖ *intr* commutare; fare il pendolare

commuter [kə'mjutər] *s* pendolare *mf*

compact [kəm'pækt] *adj* compatto ‖ ['kampækt] *s* (*small case for face powder*) portacipria *m*; (*agreement*) accordo; (*small car*) utilitaria

companion [kəm'pænjən] *s* compagno; (*one of two items*) pendant *m*; (*lady*) dama di compagnia

compan'ion·ship' *s* cameratismo

compan'ion·way' *s* (naut) scaletta per andare sottocoperta

compa·ny ['kʌmpəni] *s* (-nies) compagnia; (coll) ospite *m* or ospiti *mpl*; (naut) equipaggio; **to bear company** accompagnare; **to be good company** essere simpatico; **to keep company** (*said of a couple*) andare insieme; **to keep company with** accompagnare; (coll) fare la corte a; **to part company** separarsi

comparable ['kampərəbəl] *adj* comparabile, paragonabile

comparative [kəm'pærətɪv] *adj* comparativo; (*e.g., anatomy*) comparato ‖ *s* (gram) comparativo

compare [kəm'per] *s*—**beyond compare** incomparabile ‖ *tr* confrontare; **compared to** a confronto di, in confronto a

comparison [kəm'pærɪsən] *s* confronto; (gram) comparazione; **in comparison with** in confronto a, a confronto di

compartment [kəm'partmənt] *s* com-

partimento; (naut) compartimento stagno; (rr) compartimento

compass ['kʌmpəs] *s* (*instrument for showing direction*) bussola; (*boundary*) limite *m*; (*range*) ambito; (*range of voice*) portata; (*of a wall*) cerchia; (*circuit*) circuito; (*drawing instrument*) compasso; **compasses** (*drawing instrument*) compasso ‖ *tr* girare intorno a; comprendere; **to compass about** accerchiare

com'pass card' *s* rosa dei venti

compassion [kəm'pæʃən] *s* compassione

compassionate [kəm'pæʃənɪt] *adj* compassionevole

com'pass saw' *s* gattuccio

com·pel [kəm'pɛl] *v* (*pret & pp* -**pelled;** *ger* -**pelling**) *tr* forzare, obbligare

compelling [kəm'pɛlɪŋ] *adj* imperioso, coercitivo

compendious [kəm'pɛndɪ·əs] *adj* compendioso, conciso

compensate ['kampən‚set] *tr & intr* compensare

compensation [‚kampən'seʃən] *s* compensazione; (*pay*) pagamento; (*something given to offset a loss*) risarcimento, indennità *f*

compete [kəm'pit] *intr* competere

competence ['kampɪtəns] or **competency** ['kampɪtənsi] *s* (*fitness*) abilità *f*; (*money*) agiatezza; (*authority*) competenza

competent ['kampɪtənt] *adj* abile; competente

competition [‚kampɪ'tɪʃən] *s* competizione, gara; (*in business*) concorrenza

competitive [kəm'pɛtɪtɪv] *adj* competitivo; (*based on competition*) di concorso

compet'itive pric'es *spl* prezzi *mpl* di concorrenza

competitor [kəm'pɛtɪtər] *s* competitore *m*, concorrente *mf*; rivale *mf*

compilation [‚kampɪ'leʃən] *s* compilazione

compile [kəm'paɪl] *tr* compilare

complacence [kəm'plesəns] or **complacency** [kəm'plesənsi] *s* compiacenza; compiacenza di sé stesso

complacent [kəm'plesənt] *adj* compiaciuto or soddisfatto con sé stesso

complain [kəm'plen] *intr* lagnarsi

complainant [kəm'plenənt] *s* (law) querelante *mf*

complaint [kəm'plent] *s* lagnanza, reclamo; (*sickness*) malattia; (law) querela

complaisance [kəm'plezəns] or ['kampli‚zæns] *s* compiacenza

complaisant [kəm'plezənt] or ['kampli‚zænt] *adj* compiacente, cortese

complement ['kamplɪmənt] *s* complemento; (naut) equipaggio ‖ ['kamplɪ‚mɛnt] *tr* completare

complete [kəm'plit] *adj* completo; (*done*) finito ‖ *tr* completare, finire

completion [kəm'pliʃən] *s* completamento, compimento

complex [kəm'plɛks] or ['kamplɛks]

adj complesso, complicato ‖ ['kamplɛks] *s* complesso

complexion [kəm'plɛkʃən] *s* (*of skin*) carnagione; (*appearance*) aspetto; (*viewpoint*) punto di vista

compliance [kəm'plaɪ·əns] *s* condiscendenza, arrendevolezza; **in compliance with** in conformità di

complicate ['kamplɪ,ket] *tr* complicare

complicated ['kamplɪ,ketɪd] *adj* complicato

compli·ty [kəm'plɪsɪti] *s* (**-ties**) complicità *f*

compliment ['kamplɪmənt] *s* complimento, omaggio ‖ ['kamplɪ,mɛnt] *tr*—**to compliment s.o. on s.th** felicitarsi con qlcu per qlco; **to compliment s.o. with s.th** regalare qlco a qlcu

complimentary [,kamplɪ'mɛntəri] *adj* complimentoso, lusinghiero; (*free*) in omaggio, gratis; (*ticket*) di favore

com·ply [kəm'plaɪ] *v* (*pret & pp* **-plied**) *intr* acconsentire, accondiscendere; **to comply with** accedere a

component [kəm'ponənt] *adj* componente, costituente ‖ *s* (*component part*) componente *m*; (*force*) componente *f*

compose [kəm'poz] *tr* comporre; **to be composed of** essere composto di; **to compose oneself** calmarsi

composed [kəm'pozd] *adj* calmo, tranquillo

composer [kəm'pozər] *s* (*peacemaker*) conciliatore *m*; (mus) compositore *m*

compos'ing stick' *s* (typ) compositoio

composite [kəm'pazɪt] *adj & s* composto, composito

composition [,kampə'zɪʃən] *s* composizione; (*agreement*) compromesso

compositor [kəm'pazɪtər] *s* compositore *m*

compost ['kampost] *s* concime *m* naturale

composure [kəm'pozər] *s* calma

compote ['kampot] *s* (*stewed fruit*) composta; (*dish*) compostiera

compound ['kampaund] *adj* composto; (*fracture*) complesso; (archit, bot) composito ‖ *s* composto; parola composta; (*yard*) recinto ‖ [kam'paund] *tr* (*to mix*) combinare; (*to settle*) comporre; (*interest*) capitalizzare

comprehend [,kamprɪ'hɛnd] *tr* comprendere

comprehensible [,kamprɪ'hɛnsɪbəl] *adj* comprensibile

comprehension [,kamprɪ'hɛnʃən] *s* comprensione

comprehensive [,kamprɪ'hɛnsɪv] *adj* comprensivo

compress ['kamprɛs] *s* compressa ‖ [kəm'prɛs] *tr* comprimere

compressed' air' *s* aria compressa

compression [kəm'prɛʃən] *s* compressione

comprise [kəm'praɪz] *tr* comprendere, includere; **to be comprised of** consistere di

compromise ['kamprə,maɪz] *s* compromesso ‖ *tr* (*a dispute*) transigere, comporre; (*to put in danger*) compromettere ‖ *intr* transigere, fare un compromesso

comptroller [kən'trolər] *s* economo, amministratore *m*, controllore *m*

compulsive [kəm'pʌlsɪv] *adj* obbligatorio, coercitivo; (psychol) compulsivo

compulsory [kəm'pʌlsəri] *adj* obbligatorio

compute [kəm'pjut] *tr & intr* computare, calcolare

computer [kəm'pjutər] *s* calcolatore *m*; elaboratore *m*

comrade ['kamræd] or ['kamrɪd] *s* camerata *m*, compagno

com'rade in arms' *s* compagno d'armi

con [kan] *s* contro ‖ *v* (*pret & pp* **conned;** *ger* **conning**) *tr* imparare a memoria; (slang) imbrogliare

concave ['kankev] or [kan'kev] *adj* concavo

conceal [kən'sil] *tr* nascondere; (*to keep secret*) celare

concealment [kən'silmənt] *s* occultamento; (*place*) nascondiglio

concede [kən'sid] *tr* concedere

conceit [kən'sit] *s* (*high opinion of oneself*) presunzione; (*fanciful notion*) concetto sottile

conceited [kən'sitɪd] *adj* vanitoso

conceivable [kən'sivəbəl] *adj* concepibile

conceive [kən'siv] *tr & intr* concepire

concentrate ['kansən,tret] *s* concentrato ‖ *tr* concentrare ‖ *intr* concentrarsi; **to concentrate on** concentrarsi in

concentra'tion camp' [,kansən'treʃən] *s* campo di concentrazione

concept ['kansept] *s* concetto

conception [kən'sepʃən] *s* concezione

concern [kən'sʌrn] *s* interesse *m*; (*worry*) ansietà *f*; (*firm*) ditta, compagnia; **of concern** d'interesse ‖ *tr* concernere; **as concerns** circa; **to concern oneself** interessarsi; **to whom it may concern** a chiunque possa averne interesse

concerning [kən'sʌrnɪŋ] *prep* riguardo a

concert ['kansərt] *s* concerto ‖ [kən'sʌrt] *tr & intr* concertare

con'cert·mas'ter *s* primo violino

concer·to [kən'tʃɛrto] *s* (**-tos** or **-ti** [ti]) concerto

concession [kən'sɛʃən] *s* concessione

conciliate [kən'sɪlɪ,et] *tr* conciliare, conciliarsi con

concise [kən'saɪs] *adj* conciso

conclude [kən'klud] *tr* concludere ‖ *intr* concludersi, terminare

conclusion [kən'kluʒən] *s* conclusione; **in conclusion** per finire; **to try conclusions with** misurarsi con

conclusive [kən'klusɪv] *adj* decisivo, convincente

concoct [kən'kakt] *tr* preparare, confezionare; (*a story*) inventare

concoction [kan'kakʃən] *s* preparazione, mescolanza; (*unpleasant in taste*) intruglio

concomitant [kən'kɑmɪtənt] *adj* concomitante || *s* fatto or sintomo concomitante

concord ['kɑŋkərd] *s* concordia, armonia; (*treaty*) accordo; (gram) concordanza

concourse ['kɑŋkors] *s* confluenza; (*crowd*) affluenza, concorso; (*boulevard*) viale *m;* (rr) salone *m* principale

concrete ['kɑnkrit] or [kɑn'krit] *adj* concreto; fatto di cemento; solido || *s* cemento, calcestruzzo || *tr* (*e.g., a sidewalk*) cementare

con'crete mix'er *s* betoniera

con·cur [kən'kʌr] *v* (*pret & pp* -curred; *ger* -curring) *intr* (*to work together*) concorrere; (*to agree*) essere d'accordo, aderire

concurrence [kən'kʌrəns] *s* concorso; (*agreement*) accordo

concurrent [kən'kʌrənt] *adj* concomitante, simultaneo; cooperante; armonioso

concussion [kən'kʌʃən] *s* scossa, urto; (*of brain*) commozione cerebrale

condemn [kən'dɛm] *tr* condannare; (*to take for public use*) espropriare

condemnation [ˌkɑndɛm'neʃən] *s* condanna

condense [kən'dɛns] *tr* condensare || *intr* condensarsi

condescend [ˌkɑndɪ'sɛnd] *intr* condiscendere, degnarsi

condescending [ˌkɑndɪ'sɛndɪŋ] *adj* condiscendente

condescension [ˌkɑndɪ'sɛnʃən] *s* condiscendenza, degnazione

condiment ['kɑndɪmənt] *s* condimento

condition [kən'dɪʃən] *s* condizione; clausola; **on condition that** a condizione che || *tr* condizionare; mettere in buone condizioni fisiche

conditional [kən'dɪʃənəl] *adj & s* condizionale *m*

condole [kən'dol] *intr* condolersi

condolence [kən'doləns] *s* condoglianza

condone [kən'don] *tr* condonare

conduce [kən'djus] or [kən'dus] *intr* contribuire, indurre

conducive [kən'djusɪv] or [kən'dusɪv] *adj* contribuente

conduct ['kɑndʌkt] *s* condotta; direzione || [kən'dʌkt] *tr* condurre; (*an orchestra*) dirigere; **to conduct oneself** condursi, comportarsi || *intr* dirigere

conductor [kən'dʌktər] *s* direttore *m;* (*of a streetcar*) fattorino, conduttore *m;* (phys) conduttore *m;* (rr) capotreno

conduit ['kɑndɪt] or ['kɑndu·ɪt] *s* condotto

cone [kon] *s* cono; (bot) pigna

Con'estoga wag'on ['kɑnɪ'stogə] *s* carriaggio coperto

confectioner [kən'fɛkʃənər] *s* confettiere *m*, pasticcere *m*

confec'tioners' sug'ar *s* zucchero in polvere finissimo

confectioner·y [kən'fɛkʃəˌnɛri] *s* (-ies) confetteria, pasticceria; (*candies*) confetture *fpl*

confedera·cy [kən'fɛdərəsi] *s* (-cies) confederazione; lega

confederate [kən'fɛdərɪt] *s* alleato; (*in crime*) complice *mf* || [kən'fɛdəˌret] *tr* confederare || *intr* confederarsi

con·fer [kən'fʌr] *v* (*pret & pp* -ferred; *ger* -ferring) *tr* conferire || *intr* conferire, abboccarsi

conference ['kɑnfərəns] *s* conferenza

confess [kən'fɛs] *tr* confessare, ammettere || *intr* confessare, confessarsi

confession [kən'fɛʃən] *s* confessione

confessional [kən'fɛʃənəl] *s* confessionale *m*

confes'sion of faith' *s* professione di fede

confessor [kən'fɛsər] *s* confessore *m*

confetti [kən'fɛti] *s* coriandoli *mpl*

confide [kən'faɪd] *tr* confidare; (*to entrust*) affidare || *intr* confidarsi

confidence ['kɑnfɪdəns] *s* fiducia; sicurezza di sé; (*boldness*) baldanza; (*secrecy*) confidenza

confident ['kɑnfɪdənt] *adj* fiducioso; baldanzoso || *s* confidente *mf*

confidential [ˌkɑnfɪ'dɛnʃəl] *adj* confidenziale

confine ['kɑnfaɪn] *s* confine *m* || [kən'faɪn] *tr* limitare; confinare; **to be confined** essere in altro stato; **to be confined to bed** dover stare a letto

confinement [kən'faɪnmənt] *s* confino; (*childbirth*) parto; (*imprisonment*) prigionia

confirm [kən'fʌrm] *tr* confermare; (eccl) cresimare

confirmed [kən'fʌrmd] *adj* (*e.g., piece of news*) confermato; (*bachelor; drunkard*) impenitente; inveterato; (*e.g., invalid*) cronico

confiscate ['kɑnfɪsˌket] *tr* confiscare

conflagration [ˌkɑnfləˈgreʃən] *s* conflagrazione

conflict ['kɑnflɪkt] *s* conflitto || [kən'flɪkt] *intr* lottare; essere in conflitto

conflicting [kən'flɪktɪŋ] *adj* contrastante; contraddittorio

confluence ['kɑnflu·əns] *s* confluenza

conform [kən'fɔrm] *tr* conformare || *intr* conformarsi

conformi·ty [kən'fɔrmɪti] *s* (-ties) conformità *f;* **in conformity with** in conformità di

confound [kɑn'faʊnd] *tr* confondere || ['kɑn'faʊnd] *tr* maledire; **confound it!** accidenti!

confounded [kɑn'faʊndɪd] or ['kɑn'faʊndɪd] *adj* maledetto; (*hateful*) odioso

confront [kən'frʌnt] *tr* affrontare, opporsi a; (*to bring face to face*) raffrontare; (*to compare*) confrontare

confrontation [ˌkɑnfrən'teʃən] *s* contestazione

confuse [kən'fjuz] *tr* confondere; **to get confused** confondersi

confusion [kən'fjuʒən] *s* confusione

congeal [kən'dʒil] *tr* congelare; coagulare || *intr* congelarsi; (*said, e.g., of blood*) coagularsi

congenial [kən'dʒinjəl] *adj* (*agreeable*) simpatico; (*having similar tastes*) affine; (*suited to one's needs or tastes*) congeniale

congenital [kən'dʒenɪtəl] *adj* congenito

con'ger eel' ['kaŋgər] *s* grongo

congest [kən'dʒest] *tr* congestionare || *intr* essere congestionato

congestion [kən'dʒestʃən] *s* congestione

conglomerate [kən'glamərɪt] *adj & s* conglomerato || [kən'glamə,ret] *tr* conglomerare || *intr* conglomerarsi

congratulate [kən'grætʃə,let] *tr* congratularsi con

congratulation [kən,grætʃə'leʃən] *s* congratulazione, felicitazione

congregate ['kaŋgrɪ,get] *intr* congregarsi

congregation [,kaŋgrɪ'geʃən] *s* congregazione; fedeli *mpl* di una chiesa

congress ['kaŋgrɪs] *s* parlamento; congresso

con'gress•man *s* (-men) deputato al congresso degli S.U.

con'gress•wom'an *s* (-wom'en) deputatessa al congresso degli S.U.

conical ['kanɪkəl] *adj* conico

conjecture [kən'dʒektʃər] *s* congettura || *tr & intr* congetturare

conjugate ['kandʒə,get] *tr* coniugare

conjugation [,kandʒə'geʃən] *s* coniugazione

conjunction [kən'dʒʌŋkʃən] *s* congiunzione

conjure [kən'dʒur] *tr* (*to entreat*) scongiurare || ['kandʒər] or ['kʌndʒər] *tr* evocare, stregare; **to conjure up** evocare || *intr* fare delle stregonerie

conk [kaŋk] *intr*—**to conk out** (slang) essere in panna; (slang) svenire

connect [kə'nekt] *tr* connettere, unire || *intr* connettersi, essere associato; (*said of public conveyances*) operare in coincidenza

connect'ing rod' [kə'nektɪŋ] *s* (mach) biella

connection [kə'nekʃən] *s* connessione; unione, associazione; (*of trains*) coincidenza; (*relative*) parente *mf*; (*e.g., of a water pipe*) allacciamento; **in connection with** rispetto a

con'ning tow'er ['kanɪŋ] *s* (nav) torretta

conniption [kə'nɪpʃən] *s* (slang) attacco di rabbia

connive [kə'naɪv] *intr* essere connivente; **to connive at** chiudere un occhio su

connote [kə'not] *tr* indicare, suggerire

conquer ['kaŋkər] *tr & intr* conquistare

conqueror ['kaŋkərər] *s* conquistatore *m*

conquest ['kaŋkwest] *s* conquista

conscience ['kanʃəns] *s* coscienza; **in all conscience** a prezzo onesto; certamente

conscientious [,kanʃɪ'enʃəs] *adj* coscienzioso

conscien'tious objec'tor [ab'dʒektər] *s* obiettore *m* di coscienza

conscious ['kanʃəs] *adj* (*aware of one's existence*) cosciente; (*aware*) conscio, consapevole; (*lie*) consapevole; **to become conscious** riprendere i sensi

consciousness ['kanʃəsnɪs] *s* coscienza, conoscenza; **to lose consciousness** perdere la conoscenza

conscript ['kanskrɪpt] *s* coscritto || [kən'skrɪpt] *tr* coscrivere, arruolare

conscription [kən'skrɪpʃən] *s* coscrizione

consecrate ['kansɪ,kret] *tr* consacrare

consecutive [kən'sekjətɪv] *adj* consecutivo; di seguito

consensus [kən'sensəs] *s* consenso

consent [kən'sent] *s* consenso; **by common consent** per comune consenso || *intr* consentire

consequence ['kansɪ,kwens] *s* conseguenza

consequential [,kansɪ'kwenʃəl] *adj* conseguente; importante, d'importanza; pomposo, pieno di sé

consequently ['kansɪ,kwentli] *adv* conseguentemente, per conseguenza

conservation [,kansər'veʃən] *s* conservazione; preservazione delle foreste

conservatism [kən'sʌrvə,tɪzəm] *s* conservatorismo

conservative [kən'sʌrvətɪv] *adj* conservatore; (*cautious*) cauto; (*preserving*) conservativo; (*free from fads*) tradizionale || *s* conservatore *m*

conservato•ry [kən'sʌrvə,tori] *s* (-ries) (*greenhouse*) serra; (mus) conservatorio

conserve [kən'sʌrv] *tr* conservare

consider [kən'sɪdər] *tr* considerare

considerable [kən'sɪdərəbəl] *adj* (*fairly large*) considerevole; (*worth thinking about*) considerabile

considerate [kən'sɪdərɪt] *adj* riguardoso, premuroso

consideration [kən,sɪdə'reʃən] *s* considerazione; (*reason*) motivo; (*money*) pagamento; **in consideration of** a cagione di; in cambio di; **on no consideration** in nessuna maniera, mai; **under consideration** in considerazione, sotto esame; **without due consideration** senza riflessione, alla leggera

considering [kən'sɪdərɪŋ] *adv* tutto considerato || *prep* per, visto || *conj* considerando che, visto che

consign [kən'saɪn] *tr* consegnare; (*to send*) inviare; (*to set apart*) assegnare

consignee [,kansaɪ'ni] *s* consegnatario

consignment [kən'saɪnmənt] *s* consegna; **on consignment** in consegna

consist [kən'sɪst] *intr*—**to consist in** consistere in; **to consist of** consistere in, constare di

consisten•cy [kən'sɪstənsi] *s* (-cies) (*firmness, amount of firmness*) consistenza; (*logical connection*) coerenza

consistent [kən'sɪstənt] *adj* (*holding firmly together*) consistente; (*agree-*

ing with itself or oneself) conseguente, coerente; compatibile

consolation [,kɑnsə'leʃən] *s* consolazione

console ['kɑnsol] *s* (*table*) console *f;* (rad, telv) mobile *m;* (mus) console *f* || [kən'sol] *tr* consolare

consonant ['kɑnsənənt] *adj* consonante, armonioso; (gram) consonantico || *s* consonante *f*

consort ['kɑnsɔrt] *s* consorte *mf* || [kən'sɔrt] *intr* associarsi; (*to agree*) concordarsi

conspicuous [kən'spɪkju·əs] *adj* visibile, manifesto; notevole; (*too noticeable*) appariscente; **to make oneself conspicuous** farsi notare

conspira·cy [kən'spɪrəsi] *s* (-cies) cospirazione, congiura

conspire [kən'spaɪr] *intr* cospirare, congiurare; (*to act together*) cooperare

constable ['kɑnstəbəl] or ['kʌnstəbəl] *s* poliziotto; (*keeper of a castle*) conestabile *m*

constancy ['kɑnstənsi] *s* costanza

constant ['kɑnstənt] *adj & s* costante *f*

constellation [,kɑnstə'leʃən] *s* costellazione

constipate ['kɑnstɪ ,pet] *tr* costipare

constipation [,kɑnstɪ'peʃən] *s* costipazione

constituen·cy [kən'stɪtʃu·ənsi] *s* (-cies) (*voters*) elettorato; (*district*) circoscrizione elettorale

constituent [kən'stɪtʃu·ənt] *adj* costituente || *s* (*component*) parte *f* costituente; (*voter*) elettore *m;* (*of a chemical substance*) costituente *m*

constitute ['kɑnstɪ ,tjut] or ['kɑnstɪ ,tut] *tr* costituire

constitution [,kɑnstɪ'tjuʃən] or [,kɑnstɪ'tuʃən] *s* costituzione

constrain [kən'stren] *tr* (*to force*) costringere; (*to restrain*) restringere, comprimere

constrict [kən'strɪkt] *tr* stringere, comprimere

construct [kən'strʌkt] *tr* costruire

construction [kən'strʌkʃən] *s* costruzione; (*meaning*) interpretazione

construe [kən'stru] *tr* (*to interpret*) interpretare; (*to translate*) tradurre; (gram) analizzare

consul ['kɑnsəl] *s* console *m*

consular ['kɑnsələr] or ['kɑnsjələr] *adj* consolare

consulate ['kɑnsəlɪt] or ['kɑnsjəlɪt] *s* consolato

consult [kən'sʌlt] *tr* consultare || *intr* consultarsi

consultation [,kɑnsəl'teʃən] *s* consultazione, conferenza

consume [kən'sum] or [kən'sjum] *tr* consumare; distruggere; **consumed with** (*passion*) arso di; (*curiosity*) assorbito da

consumer [kən'sumər] or [kən'sjumər] *s* consumatore *m*

consum'er goods' *spl* beni *mpl* di consumo

consumerism [kən'sumər ,ɪzem] *s* consumismo

consummate [kən'sʌmɪt] *adj* consumato || ['kɑnsə ,met] *tr* consumare

consumption [kən'sʌmpʃən] *s* (*decay*) consunzione; (*using up*) consumo; (pathol) consunzione

consumptive [kən'sʌmptɪv] *adj* tubercolotico, tisico; (*wasteful*) logorante || *s* tisico, etico

contact ['kɑntækt] *s* contatto; (elec) contatto; (elec) presa di corrente || *tr* (coll) mettersi in contatto con || *intr* (coll) mettersi in contatto

con'tact break'er *s* ruttore *m*

con'tact lens' *s* lente *f* a contatto

contagion [kən'tedʒən] *s* contagio

contagious [kən'tedʒəs] *adj* contagioso

contain [kən'ten] *tr* contenere; **to contain oneself** frenarsi

container [kən'tenər] *s* recipiente *m*, contenitore *m*

contaminate [kən'tæmɪ ,net] *tr* contaminare

contamination [kən ,tæmɪ'neʃən] *s* contaminazione

contemplate ['kɑntəm ,plet] *tr* contemplare; (*to think about*) meditare; (*to have in mind*) progettare, avere in mente || *intr* meditare

contemplation [,kɑntəm'pleʃən] *s* contemplazione; (*intention*) intenzione

contemporaneous [kən ,tempə'reni·əs] *adj* contemporaneo, coevo

contemporar·y [kən'tempə ,reri] *adj* contemporaneo, coevo || *s* (-ies) contemporaneo

contempt [kən'tempt] *s* (*despising*) disprezzo; (*condition of being despised*) dispregio; (*of the law*) disprezzo

contemptible [kən'temptɪbəl] *adj* disprezzabile, spregevole

contempt' of court' *s* (law) offesa alla magistratura, oltraggio al tribunale

contemptuous [kən'temptʃu·əs] *adj* sprezzante, sdegnoso

contend [kən'tend] *tr* dichiarare || *intr* (*to argue*) disputare, contendere; (*to fight*) lottare

contender [kən'tendər] *s* competitore *m*, concorrente *m*

content [kən'tent] *adj* contento; (*willing*) pronto || *s* contentezza || ['kɑntent] *s* contenuto; **contents** contenuto || [kən'tent] *tr* contentare

contented [kən'tentɪd] *adj* soddisfatto

contention [kən'tenʃən] *s* disputa, litigio; contenzione

contentious [kən'tenʃəs] *adj* litigioso

contentment [kən'tentmənt] *s* contentezza

contest ['kɑntest] *s* contesa, controversia; (*game*) gara || [kən'test] *tr* disputare, contestare || *intr* combattere, fare resistenza

contestant [kən'testənt] *s* concorrente *m;* (law) contendente *m*

context ['kɑntekst] *s* contesto

contiguous [kən'tɪgju·əs] *adj* contiguo

continence ['kɑntɪnəns] *s* continenza

continent ['kɑntɪnəns] *adj & s* continente *m;* **on the Continent** nel continente europeo

continental [ˌkɑntɪˈnɛntəl] *adj* & *s* continentale *mf*

contingen·cy [kənˈtɪndʒənsi] *s* (-cies) contingenza, congiuntura; *(chance)* eventualità *f*

contingent [kənˈtɪndʒənt] *adj* eventuale; imprevisto; (philos) contingente; **to be contingent upon** dipendere da

continual [kənˈtɪnjʊ·əl] *adj* continuo

continuance [kənˈtɪnjʊəns] *s* continuazione; *(in office)* permanenza; (law) rinvio

continue [kənˈtɪnjʊ] *tr* continuare; *(to cause to remain)* mantenere; (law) rinviare ‖ *intr* continuare; rimanere

continui·ty [ˌkɑntɪˈnju·iti] or [ˌkɑntɪˈnu·iti] *s* (-ties) continuità *f;* (mov & telv) sceneggiatura; (rad) copione *m*

continuous [kənˈtɪnjʊ·əs] *adj* continuo

contin'uous show'ing *s* (mov) spettacolo permanente

contortion [kənˈtɔrʃən] *s* contorsione; *(of facts)* distorsione

contour [ˈkɑntur] *s* contorno

con'tour line' *s* curva di livello, isoipsa

contraband [ˈkɑntrəˌbænd] *adj* di contrabbando ‖ *s* contrabbando

contrabass [ˈkɑntrəˌbes] *s* contrabasso

contraceptive [ˌkɑntrəˈsɛptɪv] *adj* & *s* antifecondativo

contract [ˈkɑntrækt] *s* contratto ‖ [ˈkɑntrækt] or [kənˈtrækt] *tr (a business deal)* contrattare; *(marriage)* contrarre ‖ *intr (to shrink)* contrarsi; **to contract for** contrattare, appaltare

contraction [kənˈtrækʃən] *s* contrazione

contractor [kənˈtræktər] *s (person who makes a contract)* contraente *m; (person who contracts to supply material)* appaltatore *m,* imprenditore *m; (in building)* capomastro

contradict [ˌkɑntrəˈdɪkt] *tr* contraddire

contradiction [ˌkɑntrəˈdɪkʃən] *s* contraddizione

contradictory [ˌkɑntrəˈdɪktəri] *adj* contraddittorio

contrail [ˈkɑnˌtrel] *s* (aer) scia di condensazione

contral·to [kənˈtrælto] *s* (-tos) *(person)* contralto *mf; (voice)* contralto *m*

contraption [kənˈtræpʃən] *s* (coll) aggeggio

contra·ry [ˈkɑntreri] *adj* contrario ‖ [kənˈtreri] *adj* ostinato, caparbio ‖ [ˈkɑntreri] *s* (-ries) contrario; **on the contrary** al contrario ‖ *adv* contrariamente

contrast [ˈkɑntræst] *s* contrasto ‖ [kənˈtræst] *tr* confrontare ‖ *intr* contrastare

contravene [ˌkɑntrəˈvin] *tr* contraddire; *(a law)* contravvenire (with *dat)*

contribute [kənˈtrɪbjut] *tr* contribuire ‖ *intr* contribuire; *(to a newspaper)* collaborare

contribution [ˌkɑntrɪˈbjuʃən] *s* contribuzione; *(to a newspaper)* collaborazione

contributor [kənˈtrɪbjutər] *s* contributore *m; (to a newspaper)* collaboratore *m*

contrite [kənˈtraɪt] *adj* contrito

contrition [kənˈtrɪʃən] *s* contrizione

contrivance [kənˈtraɪvəns] *s* dispositivo, congegno; *(faculty)* invenzione; *(scheme)* artificio, piano

contrive [kənˈtraɪv] *tr* inventare; *(to scheme up)* macchinare; *(to bring about)* effettuare; **to contrive to** trovare il modo di

con·trol [kənˈtrol] *s* controllo; *(check)* freno; **controls** comandi *mpl;* **to get under control** riuscire a controllare ‖ *v (pret & pp* **-trolled;** *ger* **-trolling)** *tr* controllare

controller [kənˈtrolər] *s* controllore *m;* analista *mf* di gestione; economo; (mach) regolatore *m;* (elec) interruttore *m* di linea

control'ling in'terest *s* maggioranza delle azioni

control' stick' *s* leva di comando

controversial [ˌkɑntrəˈvɑrʃəl] *adj* controverso, polemico, discusso

controver·sy [ˈkɑntrəˌvɑrsi] *s* (-sies) controversia

controvert [ˈkɑntrəˌvɑrt] or [ˌkɑntrəˈvɑrt] *tr* contraddire

contumacious [ˌkɑntjʊˈmeʃəs] or [ˌkɑntuˈmeʃəs] *adj* ribelle, contumace

contuma·cy [ˈkɑntjuməsi] or [ˈkɑntuməsi] *s* (-cies) contumacia

contusion [kənˈtjuʒən] or [kənˈtuʒən] *s* contusione

conundrum [kəˈnʌndrəm] *s* indovinello

convalesce [ˌkɑnvəˈlɛs] *intr* essere convalescente

convalescence [ˌkɑnvəˈlɛsəns] *s* convalescenza

convalescent [ˌkɑnvəˈlɛsənt] *adj* & *s* convalescente *mf*

con'vales'cent home' *s* convalescenziario

convene [kənˈvin] *tr* convocare ‖ *intr* convenire

convenience [kənˈvinjəns] *s* convenienza; *(comfort)* agio; *(anything that saves work)* conforto; **at your earliest convenience** quanto prima

convenient [kənˈvinjənt] *adj* conveniente, adatto; comodo; **convenient to** *(near)* (coll) vicino a

convent [ˈkɑnvɛnt] *s* convento di religiose

convention [kənˈvɛnʃən] *s* convenzione, assemblea; **conventions** *(customs)* convenzioni *fpl*

conventional [kənˈvɛnʃənəl] *adj* convenzionale

converge [kənˈvʌrdʒ] *intr* convergere

conversant [kənˈvʌrsənt] *adj* versato, esperto, dotto

conversation [ˌkɑnvərˈseʃən] *s* conversazione

converse [ˈkɑnvʌrs] *adj* & *s* contrario ‖ [kənˈvʌrs] *intr* conversare

conversion [kən'vʌrʒən] *s* conversione; (*unlawful appropriation*) malversazione

convert ['kʌnvʌrt] *s* convertito || [kən'vʌrt] *tr* convertire; misappropriare || *intr* convertirsi

convertible [kən'vʌrtɪbəl] *adj & s* convertibile *f;* (aut) trasformabile *f*, decappottabile *f*

convex ['kʌnvɛks] *or* [kɑn'vɛks] *adj* convesso

convey [kən'vei] *tr* (*to carry*) trasportare; (*liquids*) convogliare; (*sounds*) trasmettere; (*to express*) esprimere; (*e.g., property*) trasferire

conveyance [kən've-əns] *s* trasporto; veicolo; comunicazione; (*of property*) trasferimento; (*deed*) titolo di proprietà

convey'or belt' [kən've-ər] *s* trasportatore *m*

convict ['kʌnvɪkt] *s* condannato || [kən'vɪkt] *tr* convincere, condannare

conviction [kən'vɪkʃən] *s* condanna; (*belief*) convinzione, convincimento

convince [kən'vɪns] *tr* convincere

convincing [kən'vɪnsɪŋ] *adj* convincente

convivial [kən'vɪvɪ-əl] *adj* (*festive*) conviviale; gioviale, bonaccione

convocation [ˌkʌnvə'keʃən] *s* convocazione, assemblea

convoke [kən'vok] *tr* convocare

convoy ['kʌnvɔɪ] *s* (*of ships*) convoglio; (*of vehicles*) carovana || *tr* convogliare

convulse [kən'vʌls] *tr* (*to shake*) scuotere; (*to throw into convulsions*) mettere in convulsioni; (*to cause to shake with laughter*) far torcere dalle risa

coo [ku] *intr* tubare, gemere

cook [kʊk] *s* cuoco || *tr* cuocere; **to cook up** (coll) preparare, macchinare || *intr* (*said of food*) cuocere; (*said of a person*) fare il cuoco

cook'book' *s* libro di cucina

cookie ['kʊki] *s* var of **cooky**

cooking ['kʊkɪŋ] *s* culinaria

cook'out' *s* picnic *m*, spuntino all'aperto

cook'stove' *s* cucina economica

cook-y ['kʊki] *s* (-ies) pasticcino, biscotto

cool [kul] *adj* fresco; calmo; (*not cordial*) freddo; (*bold*) sfacciato || *s* fresco || *tr* rinfrescare; **to cool one's heels** fare anticamera || *intr* rinfrescarsi; **to cool off** rinfrescarsi; calmarsi

coolant ['kulənt] *s* miscela refrigerante

cooler ['kulər] *s* ghiacciaia; (slang) prigione

cool'-head'ed *adj* calmo, imperturbabile

coolish ['kulɪʃ] *adj* freschetto

coon [kun] *s* procione *m*

coop [kʊp] *s* pollaio; conigliera; **to fly the coop** (slang) scapparsene || *tr*—**to coop up** rinchiudere tra quattro mura

cooper ['kupər] *s* bottaio

cooperate [ko'apə,ret] *intr* cooperare

cooperation [ko,apə're/ən] *s* cooperazione

cooperative [ko'apə,retɪv] *adj* cooperativo || *s* cooperativa

coordinate [ko'ɔrdɪnɪt] *adj* coordinato; (gram) coordinativo || *s* (math) coordinata || [ko'ɔrdɪ,net] *tr & intr* coordinare

coot [kut] *s* (zool) folaga; (slang) vechio pazzo

cootie ['kuti] *s* (slang) pidocchio

cop [kɑp] *s* (slang) poliziotto || *v* (*pret & pp* **copped;** *ger* **copping**) *tr* (slang) rubare

copartner [ko'pɑrtnər] *s* consocio, socio

cope [kop] *intr*—**to cope with** tener testa a

cope'stone' *s* pietra da cimasa

copier ['kɑpɪ-ər] *s* (*person*) copista *mf;* imitatore *m;* (*machine*) duplicatore *m*

copilot ['ko,paɪlət] *s* copilota *mf*

coping ['kopɪŋ] *s* coronamento, cimasa

cop'ing saw' *s* seghetto da traforo

copious ['kopɪ-əs] *adj* copioso

copper ['kɑp'ər] *s* rame *m;* (*coin*) soldo; (*boiler*) calderone *m;* (slang) poliziotto

cop'per·head' *s* vipera (*Ancistrodon contortrix*)

cop'per·smith' *s* battirame *m*, calderaio

coppice ['kɑpɪs] *or* **copse** [kɑps] *s* boschetto

copulate ['kɑpjə,let] *intr* copularsi, congiungersi carnalmente

cop·y ['kɑpi] *s* (**-ies**) copia; modello; manoscritto || *v* (*pret & pp* **-ied**) *tr* copiare, imitare || *intr* copiare; **to copy after** imitare

cop'y·book' *s* quaderno

copyist ['kɑpɪ-ɪst] *s* copista *mf;* imitatore *m*

cop'y·right' *s* copyright *m*, diritto di proprietà letteraria || *tr* registrare; proteggere con copyright

cop'y·writ'er *s* copy-writer *m*, redattore *m* pubblicitario

coquet·ry ['kokətri] *or* [ko'ketri] *s* (**-ries**) civetteria

coquette [ko'ket] *s* civetta

coquettish [ko'ketɪʃ] *adj* civettuolo

coral ['kɑrəl] *or* ['kɔrəl] *adj* corallino || *s* corallo

cor'al reef' *s* banco di coralli

cord [kɔrd] *s* corda, fune *f;* (*corduroy*) tessuto cordonato; (elec) cordone *m* || *tr* legare con corda

cordial ['kɔrdʒəl] *adj & s* cordiale *m*

corduroy ['kɔrdə,rɔɪ] *s* velluto a coste; **corduroys** pantaloni *mpl* alla cacciatora

core [kor] *s* (*of fruit*) torsolo; (*central part*) centro; (*of problem*) nocciolo; (*of earth*) barisfera, nucleo centrale; (phys) nucleo; **rotten to the core** guasto nelle ossa

corespondent [ˌkorɪs'pɑndənt] *s* coimputato in un processo di divorzio

cork [kɔrk] *s* (*bark*) sughero; (*stopper*) tappo, tappo di sughero || *tr* tappare

cork' oak' *s* sughero

cork'screw' s cavatappi m

cormorant ['kɔrmərənt] s cormorano

corn [kɔrn] s granturco, mais m; (ker- nel) chicco; (thickening of skin) callo; (whiskey) whisky m di gran- turco; (Brit) grano; (Scot) avena; (slang) banalità f

corn' bread' s pane m di farina gialla

corn' cake' s omelette f di granturco

corn'cob' s tutolo

corn'cob pipe' s pipa fatta di un tutolo di pannocchia

corn'crib' s granaio per le pannocchie

corn' cure' s callifugo

cornea ['kɔrnɪ·ə] s cornea

corner ['kɔrnər] s angolo; (of street) cantonata; situazione difficile; (of the eye) coda dell'occhio; (com) acca- parramento, incetta, bagarinaggio; **to cut corners** tagliare le spese; **to turn the corner** passare il punto più peri- coloso || tr mettere in una situazione difficile; (the màrket) incettare, acca- parrare

cor'ner cup'board s cantoniera, arma- dio d'angolo

cor'ner stone' s pietra angolare; (of new building) prima pietra

cornet [kɔr'nɛt] s cornetta

corn' exchange' s borsa dei cereali

corn'field' s (in U.S.A.) campo di gran- turco; (in England) campo di grano; (in Scotland) campo di avena

corn'flakes' spl fiocchi mpl di granturco

corn' flour' s farina di granturco

corn'flow'er s fiordaliso

corn'husk' s brattea, cartoccio

cornice ['kɔrnɪs] s (of house) corni- cione m; (of room) cornice f

corn' liq'uor s whisky m di granturco

corn' meal' s farina di granturco

corn' on the cob' s granturco servito in pannocchia

corn' plas'ter s cerotto per i calli

corn' silk' s barba del granturco

corn'stalk' s fusto di granturco

corn'starch' s amido di granturco

corn·y ['kɔrni] adj (-ier; -iest) (slang) banale, trito, triviale

coronation [,karə'neʃən] or [,kɔrə- 'neʃən] s incoronazione

coroner ['karənər] or ['kɔrənər] s magistrato inquirente

cor'oner's in'quest s inchiesta giudi- ziaria dinanzi a giuria

coronet ['karə,nɛt] or ['kɔrə,nɛt] s corona (non reale); diadema m

corporal ['kɔrpərəl] adj caporalesco || s caporale m

corporation [,kɔrpə'reʃən] s società anonima

corps [kor] s (corps [korz]) corpo

corps' de bal'let s corpo di ballo

corpse [kɔrps] s cadavere m

corpulent ['kɔrpjələnt] adj corpulento

corpuscle ['kɔrpəsəl] s (anat) globulo; (phys) corpuscolo

cor·ral [kə'ræl] s recinto per bestiame || v (pret & pp -ralled; ger -ralling) tr mettere in un recinto; catturrare

correct [kə'rɛkt] adj corretto || tr cor- reggere

correction [kə'rɛkʃən] s correzione

corrective [kə'rɛktɪv] adj & s corret- tivo

correctness [kə'rɛktnɪs] s correttezza

correlate ['karə,lɛt] or ['kɔrə,lɛt] tr correlare || intr essere in correlazione

correlation [,karə'leʃən] or [,kɔrə- 'leʃən] s correlazione

correspond [,karɪ'spand] or [,kɔrɪ- 'spand] intr corrispondere

correspondence [,karɪ'spandəns] or [,kɔrɪ'spandəns] s corrispondenza

correspond'ence school' s scuola per corrispondenza

correspondent [,karɪ'spandənt] or [,kɔrɪ'spandənt] adj & s corrispon- dente mf

corridor ['karɪdər] or ['kɔrɪdər] s corridoio

corroborate [kə'rabə,ret] tr corrobo- rare

corrode [kə'rod] tr corrodere || intr corrodersi

corrosion [kə'roʒən] s corrosione

corrosive [kə'rosɪv] adj & s corrosivo

corrugated ['karə,getɪd] or ['kɔrə- ,getɪd] adj ondulato

corrupt [kə'rʌpt] adj corrotto || tr cor- rompere; (a language) imbarbarire || intr corrompersi

corruption [kə'rʌpʃən] s corruzione

corsage [kɔr'saʒ] s (bodice) corpetto; (bouquet) mazzolino di fiori da ap- puntarsi al vestito

corsair ['kɔr,sɛr] s corsaro

corset ['kɔrsɪt] s corsetto

Corsican ['kɔrsɪkən] adj & s corso

cortege [kɔr'teʒ] s corteggio

cor·tex ['kɔr,tɛks] s (-tices [tɪ,siz]) cortice f

cortisone ['kɔrtɪ,son] s cortisone m

corvette [kɔr'vɛt] s corvetta

cosmetic [kaz'mɛtɪk] adj & s cosme- tico

cosmic ['kazmɪk] adj cosmico

cosmonaut ['kazmə,nɔt] s cosmonauta mf

cosmopolitan [,kazmə'palɪtən] adj & s cosmopolita mf

cosmos ['kazməs] s cosmo

cost [kɔst] or [kast] s costo, prezzo; **at all costs** or **at any cost** ad ogni costo; **costs** (law) spese fpl proces- suali || v (pret & pp cost) intr costare

cost·ly ['kɔstli] or ['kastli] adj (-lier; -liest) costoso; (sumptuous) lussuoso

cost' of liv'ing s costo della vita

costume ['kastjum] or ['kastum] s costume m

cos'tume ball' s ballo in costume

cos'tume jew'elry s gioielli falsi

cot [kat] s (narrow bed) branda; (cot- tage) capanna, cabina

coterie ['kotəri] s gruppo; (clique) chiesuola

cottage ['katɪdʒ] s casetta, villino

cot'tage cheese' s ricotta americana

cot'ter pin' [katər] s copiglia, coppi- glia

cotton ['katən] s cotone m || intr—**to cotton up to** (coll) cominciare a pro- vare della simpatia per; (coll) andare d'accordo con

cot'ton can'dy s zucchero filato

cot'ton gin' *s* sgranatrice *f*

cot'ton pick'er ['pɪkər] *s* chi raccoglie il cotone; macchina che raccoglie il cotone

cot'tonseed oil' *s* olio di semi di cotone

cot'ton waste' *s* cascame *m* di cotone

cot'ton·wood' *s* pioppo deltoide

couch [kaut̪ʃ] *s* canapè *m*, sofà *m*, divano ‖ *tr* esprimere

couch' grass' *s* gramigna

cougar ['kugər] *s* puma *m*

cough [kɔf] or [kɑf] *s* tosse *f* ‖ *tr—to* **cough up** sputare, sputare tossendo; (*slang*) dare, pagare ‖ *intr* tossire

cough' drop' *s* pastiglia per la tosse

cough' syr'up *s* sciroppo per la tosse

could [kud] *v aux—***I could not come yesterday** non ho potuto venire ieri; **I could not see you tomorrow** non potrei vederLa domani; **it could not be so** non potrebbe essere così

council ['kaunsəl] *s* consiglio; (*eccl*) concilio

coun'cil·man *s* (-men) consigliere *m* or assessore *m* municipale

coun·sel ['kaunsəl] *s* consiglio; (*lawyer*) avvocato; **to keep one's counsel** essere riservato; **to take counsel with** consultarsi con ‖ *v* (*pret & pp* -seled or -selled; *ger* -seling or -selling) *tr* consigliare ‖ *intr* consigliare; consigliarsi

counselor ['kaunsələr] *s* consigliere *m;* avvocato

count [kaunt] *s* conto; (*nobleman*) conte *m;* (law) capo d'accusa ‖ *tr* contare; **to count off by** (*twos, threes*) contare per (*due, tre*); **to count out** escludere; (boxing) contare ‖ *intr* contare; (*to be worth*) valere; **to count on** contare su

count'down' *s* conteggio alla rovescia

countenance ['kauntɪnəns] *s* espressione; (*face*) faccia; (*approval*) approvazione ‖ *tr* approvare, incoraggiare

counter ['kauntər] *adj* contrario ‖ *s* contatore *m;* (*token*) gettone *m;* (*table in store*) banco; (*opposite*) contrario ‖ *adv* contro, contrariamente ‖ *tr* contrariare, opporre ‖ *intr* (boxing) rispondere

coun'ter·act' *tr* contrariare, neutralizzare

coun'ter·attack' *s* contrattacco ‖ coun'ter·attack' *tr & intr* contrattaccare

coun'ter·bal'ance *s* contrappeso ‖ coun'ter·bal'ance *tr* controbilanciare

coun'ter·clock'wise' *adj* antiorario ‖ *adv* in senso antiorario

coun'ter·es'pionage' *s* controspionaggio

counterfeit ['kauntərfɪt] *adj* contraffatto ‖ *s* contraffazione; moneta falsa ‖ *tr & intr* contraffare

counterfeiter ['kauntər͵fɪtər] *s* contraffattore *m*

coun'ter·feit mon'ey *s* moneta falsa

countermand ['kauntər͵mænd] or ['kauntər͵mɑnd] *tr* (*troops*) dare un contrordine a; (*an order; a payment*) cancellare

coun'ter·march' *s* contromarcia ‖ *intr* fare contromarcia

coun'ter·offen'sive *s* controffensiva

coun'ter·pane' *s* sopraccoperta

coun'ter·part' *s* copia; (*person*) sosia

coun'ter·point' *s* (mus) contrappunto; (mus) controcanto

Coun'ter Reforma'tion *s* controriforma

coun'ter·rev'olu'tion *s* controrivoluzione

coun'ter·sign' *s* (*password*) parola d'ordine; (*signature*) controfirma ‖ *tr* controfirmare

coun'ter·sink' *v* (*pret & pp* -sunk) *tr* incassare, accecare

coun'ter·spy' *s* (-spies) membro del controspionaggio

coun'ter·stroke' *s* contraccolpo

coun'ter·weight' *s* contrappeso

countess ['kauntɪs] *s* contessa

countless ['kauntlɪs] *adj* innumerevole

countrified ['kʌntrɪ͵faɪd] *adj* rustico, rurale

coun·try ['kʌntri] *s* (-tries) (*land*) terreno; (*nation*) paese *m;* (*land of one's birth*) patria; (*rural region*) campagna

coun'try club' *s* circolo privato sportivo situato nei sobborghi

coun'try cous'in *s* campagnolo

coun'try estate' *s* tenuta

coun'try·folk' *s* campagnoli *mpl*

coun'try gen'tleman *s* proprietario terriero, signorotto di campagna

coun'try house' *s* casa di campagna

coun'try jake' *s* (coll) zoticone *m*

coun'try life' *s* vita rustica

coun'try·man *s* (-men) paesano, compaesano

coun'try·peo'ple *s* gente *f* di campagna

coun'try·side' *s* campagna

coun'try-wide' *adj* nazionale

coun'try·wom'an *s* (-wom'en) *s* paesana, compaesana

coun·ty ['kaunti] *s* (-ties) contea, distretto

coun'ty seat' *s* capoluogo di contea

coup [ku] *s* colpo; colpo di stato

coup de grâce [ku də 'grɑs] *s* colpo di grazia

coup d'état [ku de'ta] *s* colpo di stato

coupe [kup] or coupé [ku'pe] *s* coupé *m*

couple ['kʌpəl] *s* (*of people or animals*) paio, coppia; (*of things*) paio; (*link*) unione ‖ *tr* accoppiare; (*to link*) unire, agganciare ‖ *intr* accoppiarsi

couplet ['kʌplɪt] *s* coppia di versi; (mus) couplet *m*

coupling ['kʌplɪŋ] *s* unione; (mach) giunto

coupon ['kupɑn] or ['kjupɑn] *s* coupon *m*, tagliando

courage ['kʌrɪdʒ] *s* coraggio; **to have the courage of one's convictions** avere il coraggio delle proprie opinioni

courageous [kə'redʒəs] *adj* coraggioso

courier ['kʌrɪ·ər] or ['kurɪ·ər] *s* corriere *m*

course [kors] *s* corso; (*part of meal*) portata; (*place for games*) campo;

(*row*) fila; **in due course** a tempo debito; **in the course of** durante, nel corso di; **of course** certamente, senza dubbio

court [kort] *s* (*uncovered place surrounded by walls*) corte *f,* cortile *m;* (*royal residence; courtship*) corte *f;* (*short street*) vicolo; (*playing area*) campo; (law) corte *f* ‖ *tr* corteggiare; (*e.g., disaster*) andare in cerca di

courteous [ˈkʌrtɪ·əs] *adj* cortese

courtesan [ˈkʌrtɪzən] or [ˈkortɪzən] *s* cortigiana, meretrice *f*

courte·sy [ˈkʌrtɪsi] *s* (-sies) cortesia, gentilezza; **through the courtesy of** con il gentile permesso di

court'house' *s* palazzo di giustizia

courtier [ˈkortɪ·ər] *s* cortigiano

court' jest'er *s* buffone *m* di corte

court·ly [ˈkortli] *adj* (-lier; -liest) cortese, cortigiano; ossequioso

court'-mar'tial *s* (courts-martial) corte *f* marziale ‖ *v* (*pret & pp* -tialed or -tialled; *ger* -tialing or -tialling) *tr* sottomettere a corte marziale

court' plas'ter *s* taffettà *m*

court'room' *s* aula di giustizia

courtship [ˈkortʃɪp] *s* corte *f,* corteggiamento

court'yard' *s* corte *f,* cortile *m*

cousin [ˈkʌzɪn] *s* cugino

cove [kov] *s* piccola baia, cala

covenant [ˈkʌvənənt] *s* convenzione, patto ‖ *tr* promettere solennemente

cover [ˈkʌvər] *s* (*lid*) coperchio; (*tablecloth; shelter*) coperto; (*of book*) copertina; **to take cover** nascondersi; **under cover** in segreto, segretamente; **under cover of** sotto la protezione di; **under separate cover** in busta a parte, in plico a parte ‖ *tr* coprire; puntare un'arma verso; (journ) riferire, riportare; **to cover up** coprire completamente ‖ *intr* (*said of paint*) spandersi

coverage [ˈkʌvərɪdʒ] *s* copertura; (journ) servizio giornalistico; (rad, telv) raggio di udibilità

coveralls [ˈkʌvər ˌɔlz] *spl* tuta

cov'er charge' *s* coperto

cov'ered wag'on *s* carro coperto da tendone

cov'er girl' *s* ragazza-copertina

covering [ˈkʌvərɪŋ] *s* copertura; involucro

covert [ˈkʌvərt] *adj* nascosto, segreto

cov'er-up' *s* dissimulazione; sotterfugio

covet [ˈkʌvɪt] *tr* desiderare, agognare

covetous [ˈkʌvɪtəs] *adj* cupido

covey [ˈkʌvi] *s* covata

cow [kau] *s* vacca; (*of seal, elephant, etc.*) femmina ‖ *tr* spaventare, intimidire

coward [ˈkau·ərd] *s* codardo, vile *m*

cowardice [ˈkau·ərdɪs] *s* codardia, viltà *f*

cowardly [ˈkau·ərdli] *adj* codardo, vile ‖ *adv* vilmente

cow'bell' *s* campano, campanaccio

cow'boy' *s* cowboy *m*

cow'catch'er *s* (rr) cacciapietre *m*

cower [ˈkau·ər] *intr* rannicchiarsi

cow'herd' *s* guardiano d'armenti

cow'hide' *s* pelle *f* di vacca

cowl [kaul] *s* (*hood*) cappuccio; (*monk's cloak*) cappa; (*of car*) sostegno del cofano; (*of chimney*) cappello; (aer) cappottatura

cow'lick' *s* ritrosa

cow'pox' *s* (vet) vaiolo bovino

coxcomb [ˈkaks ˌkom] *s* zerbinotto

coxwain [ˈkaksən] or [ˈkak ˌswen] *s* timoniere *m*

coy [kɔɪ] *adj* timido, ritroso

co·zy [ˈkozi] *adj* (-zier; -ziest) comodo ‖ *s* (-zies) copriteiera *m*

C.P.A. [ˈsiˈpiˈe] *s* (letterword) (**certified public accountant**) esperto contabile

crab [kræb] *s* granchio; (aer) scarroccio; (*complaining person*) (coll) scontroso ‖ *v* (*pret & pp* **crabbed;** *ger* **crabbing**) *intr* (coll) lamentarsi

crab' apple' *s* mela selvatica; (*tree*) melo selvatico

crabbed [ˈkræbɪd] *adj* sgarbato; (*handwriting*) da gallina; (*style*) oscuro, ermetico

crab' louse' *s* piattola

crab·by [ˈkræbi] *adj* (-bier; -biest) scontroso, sgarbato

crack [kræk] *adj* (slang) di prim'ordine, eccellente ‖ *s* (*noise*) schiocco; (*break*) rottura, screpolatura, crepa; (*opening*) fessura; (slang) tentativo; (slang) barzelletta ‖ *tr* (*e.g., a whip*) schioccare; (*to break*) rompere, screpolare; (*oil*) ridurre con distillazione; (coll) risolvere; (*a safe*) (slang) forzare; (*a joke*) (slang) dire; **cracked up to be** (slang) avendo fama di ‖ *intr* (*to make a noise*) scricchiolare; (*to break*) rompersi, screpolarsi; (*said of voice*) diventare fesso; (slang) avere un esaurimento nervoso; **to crack down** (slang) essere severo; **to crack up** (slang) andare a pezzi

cracked [krækt] *adj* rotto, spezzato; (*voice*) fesso; (coll) pazzo

cracker [ˈkrækər] *s* cracker *m,* galletta

crack'er·bar'rel *adj* in piccolo, alla buona

crack'er·jack' *adj* (slang) di prim'ordine ‖ *s* (slang) persona di prim'ordine

cracking [ˈkrækɪŋ] *s* piroscissione

crackle [ˈkrækəl] *s* crepitio, crepito ‖ *intr* crepitare

crack'pot' *adj & s* (coll) mattoide *mf*

crack'-up' *s* accidente *m;* collisione; (*breakdown in health or in relations*) (coll) colasso; (aer) accidente *m* d'atterraggio

cradle [ˈkredəl] *s* culla; (*of handset*) forcella ‖ *tr* cullare

crad'le·song' *s* ninnananna

craft [kræft] or [kraft] *s* (*skill*) abilità *f;* (*trade*) mestiere *m;* (*guile*) astuzia, furberia; (*ship*) nave *f;* aeronave

craftiness [ˈkræftɪnɪs] or [ˈkraftɪnɪs] *s* astuzia, furberia

crafts'man *s* (-men) operaio specializzato, artigiano

craft′ un′ion s artigianato, sindacato artigiano

craft‧y ['kræfti] or ['krɑfti] adj (-ier; -iest) astuto, furbo

crag [kræg] s roccia scoscesa, rupe f

cram [kræm] v (pret & pp **crammed;** ger **cramming**) tr (to pack full) riempire fino all'orlo; (to stuff with food) rimpinzare || intr rimpinzarsi; (coll) preparare un esame alla svelta

cramp [kræmp] s (painful contraction) crampo; (bar with hooks) grappa; (fig) ostacolo || tr ostacolare, restringere

cranber‧ry ['kræn‚bɛri] s (-ries) mirtillo

crane [kren] s (orn, mach) gru f; (boom) (telv, mov) giraffa || tr (one's neck) allungare || intr allungare il collo

crani‧um ['krenɪ-əm] s (-a [ə]) cranio

crank [kræŋk] s manovella; (aut) alzacristalli m; (coll) eccentrico || tr girare con la manovella; mettere in moto con la manovella

crank′case′ s coppa dell'olio, carter m

crank′shaft′ s albero a gomito

crank‧y ['kræŋki] adj (-ier; -iest) irritabile; eccentrico

cran‧ny ['kræni] s (-nies) (crevice) crepaccio; (crack) fessura

crape [krep] s crespo

crape′hang′er s (slang) pessimista uggioso, guastafeste mf

craps [kræps] s gioco dei dadi; **to shoot craps** giocare ai dadi

crash [kræʃ] adj (coll) d'emergenza || s (noise) scoppio, schianto; accidente m; (collapse of business) crac m, rovescio; (bad landing) atterraggio senza carrello || tr fracassare; **to crash the gate** (coll) entrare senza invito || intr fracassarsi; (com) fallire; **to cash into** investire, cozzare contro; **to cash through** sfondare

crash′ dive′ s immersione rapida di un sottomarino

crash′ hel′met s casco

crass [kræs] adj crasso

crate [kret] s gabbia d'imballaggio || tr imballare in una gabbia

crater ['kretər] s cratere m

cravat [krə'væt] s cravatta

crave [krev] tr anelare; (to beg) implorare || intr—**to crave for** desiderare ardentemente

craven ['krevən] adj & s codardo

craving ['krevɪŋ] s anelito, desiderio

craw [krɔ] s gozzo

crawl [krɔl] s strisciamento, avanzata striscioni; (sports) crawl m || intr strisciare, avanzare striscioni; (said of worms) brulicare; (said of insects) formicolare; (to feel creepy) sentirsi il formicolio

crayfish ['krefɪʃ] s (Palinurus vulgaris) aragosta; (Astacus; Cambarus) gambero

crayon ['kre‧ən] s pastello; disegno a pastello || tr disegnare a pastello

craze [krez] s mania, moda || tr fare impazzire

cra‧zy ['krezi] adj (-zier; -ziest) pazzo, matto; **to be crazy about** (coll) esser matto per; **to drive crazy** fare impazzire

cra′zy bone′ s osso rabbioso (del gomito)

creak [krik] s scricchiolio, cigolio || intr scricchiolare, cigolare

creak‧y ['kriki] adj (-ier; -iest) stridente, cigolante

cream [krim] s crema, panna; (finest part) fior fiore m || tr rendere di consistenza cremosa; (to remove cream from) scremare; prendere il meglio di

creamer‧y ['kriməri] s (-ies) (factory) caseificio; (store) cremeria

cream′ puff′ s bignè m

cream‧y ['krimi] adj (-ier; -iest) cremoso; butirroso

crease [kris] s piega, grinza || tr piegare, raggrinzire || intr piegarsi, raggrinzirsi, far pieghe

crease′-resis′tant adj antipiega

create [kri'et] tr creare

creation [kri'eʃən] s creazione; **the Creation** il creato

creative [kri'etɪv] adj creativo

creator [kri'etər] s creatore m

creature ['kritʃər] s creatura

credence ['kridəns] s credenza

credentials [krɪ'dɛnʃəlz] spl lettere fpl credenziali; documento d'autorizzazione

credible ['krɛdɪbəl] adj credibile

credit ['krɛdɪt] s credito; (in a school) unità f di promozione; (com) avere m; **credits** (mov, telv) titoli mpl di testa || tr accreditare; **to credit s.o. with s.th** attribuire qlco a qlcu

creditable ['krɛdɪtəbəl] adj lodevole

cred′it card′ s carta di credito

creditor ['krɛdɪtər] s creditore m

cre‧do ['krido] or ['kredo] s (-dos) credo

credulous ['krɛdʒələs] adj credulo

creed [krid] s credo

creek [krik] s fiumicello

creep [krip] v (pret & pp **crept** [krɛpt]) intr strisciare, avanzare striscioni; (to grow along a wall) arrampicarsi; (to feel creepy) sentirsi il formicolio

creeper ['kripər] s strisciante m; (plant) rampicante f

creeping ['kripɪŋ] adj lento; (plant) rampicante

cremate ['krimet] tr cremare

cremato‧ry ['krimə‚tori] adj crematorio || s (-ries) forno crematorio

Creole ['kri‧ol] adj & s creolo

crescent ['krɛsənt] s (of Islam) mezzaluna; (of moon) crescente m; (roll) cornetto

cress [krɛs] s crescione m

crest [krɛst] s cresta; (heral) stemma m, insegna

crestfallen ['krɛst‚fələn] adj depresso

Cretan ['kritən] adj & s cretese mf

cretin ['kritən] s cretino

crevice ['krɛvɪs] s fessura, fenditura

crew [kru] s (group working together) personale m; (group of workmen;

mob) ciurma; (*of a ship* or *racing boat*) equipaggio; (sports) canottaggio

crew' cut' *s* capelli *mpl* a spazzola

crib [krɪb] *s* (*bed*) lettino; (*rack*) rastrelliera; (*building*) capanna, granaio; (coll) bigino ǁ *v* (*pret & pp* **cribbed; ger cribbing**) *tr* (coll) usare un bigino in ǁ *intr* (coll) usare un bigino; (coll) commettere un plagio

cricket [ˈkrɪkɪt] *s* grillo; (sports) cricket *m*, palla a spatola

crier [ˈkraɪ·ər] *s* banditore *m*

crime [kraɪm] *s* delitto, crimine *m*

criminal [ˈkrɪmɪnəl] *adj* criminale; (*code*) penale ǁ *s* delinquente *mf*

crimp [krɪmp] *s* piega, pieghettatura; **to put a crimp in** (slang) mettere i bastoni fra le ruote a ǁ *tr* pieghettare; (*the hair*) arricciare

crimson [ˈkrɪmzən] *adj & s* cremisi *m* ǁ *intr* imporporarsi

cringe [krɪndʒ] *intr* rannicchiarsi; (*to fawn*) umiliarsi

crinkle [ˈkrɪŋkəl] *tr* arricciare ǁ *intr* (*to rustle*) sfrusciare

cripple [ˈkrɪpəl] *s* zoppo, sciancato ǁ *tr* storpiare; (*e.g., business*) paralizzare

cri·sis [ˈkraɪsɪs] *s* (-ses [siz]) crisi *f*

crisp [krɪsp] *adj* (*brittle*) croccante, friabile; (*air*) frizzante; (*sharp and clear*) acuto

criteri·on [kraɪˈtɪrɪ·ən] *s* (-a [ə] or -ons) criterio

critic [ˈkrɪtɪk] *s* critico

critical [ˈkrɪtɪkəl] *adj* critico

criticism [ˈkrɪtɪˌsɪzəm] *s* critica

criticize [ˈkrɪtɪˌsaɪz] *tr & intr* criticare

critique [krɪˈtik] *s* critica

croak [krok] *s* (*of frogs*) gracidio; (*of crows*) gracchiamento ǁ *intr* gracidare; gracchiare; (slang) crepare

Croat [ˈkro·æt] *s* croato

Croatian [kroˈeʃən] *adj & s* croato

cro·chet [kroˈʃe] *s* lavoro all'uncinetto ǁ *v* (*pret & pp* -**cheted** [ˈʃed]; *ger* -**cheting** [ˈʃe·ɪŋ]) *tr & intr* lavorare all'uncinetto

crock [krak] *s* vaso di terracotta, giara, orcio

crockery [ˈkrakəri] *s* vasellame *m* di terracotta, terracotta

crocodile [ˈkrakəˌdaɪl] *s* coccodrillo

croc'odile tears' *spl* lacrime *fpl* di coccodrillo

crocus [ˈkrokəs] *s* croco

crone [kron] *s* vecchia incartapecorita

cro·ny [ˈkroni] *s* (-nies) amicone *m*, compare *m*

crook [kruk] *s* (*hook*) uncino; (*staff*) pastorale *m*; (*bend*) curva; (*bend of pipe*) gomito; (coll) imbroglione *m* ǁ *tr* piegare ǁ *intr* piegarsi

crooked [ˈkrukɪd] *adj* uncinato; curvo, piegato; (coll) disonesto

croon [krun] *intr* canterellare; cantare in modo sentimentale

crop [krap] *s* (*of bird*) gozzo; (*agricultural product, growing or harvested*) messe *f*; (*agricultural product harvested*) raccolto; (*riding whip*) fru-

stino; (*hair cut close*) capelli corti; gruppo ǁ *v* (*pret & pp* **cropped**; *ger* **cropping**) *tr* (*to cut the ends off of*) spuntare; (*to reap*) raccogliere; (*to cut short*) tosare ǁ *intr*—**to crop out** or **up** apparire inaspettatamente

crop'-dust'ing *s* fumigazione aerea

cropper [ˈkrapər] *s* mietitore *m*; (*sharecropper*) mezzadro; **to come a cropper** (coll) fare una cascataccia; (coll) andare in rovina

croquet [kroˈke] *s* croquet *m*, pallamaglio *m & f*

croquette [kroˈkɛt] *s* crocchetta

crosier [ˈkroʒər] *s* pastorale *m*

cross [krɔs] or [kras] *adj* trasversale, contrario, obliquo; (*irritable*) bisbetico, di cattivo umore; (*of mixed breed*) incrociato ǁ *s* croce *f*; (*crossing of breeds*) incrocio; **to take the cross** farsi crociato ǁ *tr* crociare, segnare con una croce; (*the street*) attraversare; (*e.g., the legs*) incrociare; (*to draw a line across*) barrare; (*to thwart*) ostacolare; **to cross oneself** farsi il segno della croce; **to cross one's mind** venire in mente a uno; **to cross out** cancellare ǁ *intr* incrociarsi

cross'bones' *spl* teschio e tibie incrociate (*simbolo della morte*)

cross'bow' *s* balestra

cross'breed' *v* (*pret & pp* -**bred** [ˌbred]) *tr* incrociare, ibridare

cross'-coun'try *adj* campestre; attraverso il paese

cross'-examina'tion *s* (law) confronto, interrogatorio in contraddittorio

cross-eyed [ˈkrɔsˌaɪd] or [ˈkrasˌaɪd] *adj* guercio, strabico

crossing [ˈkrɔsɪŋ] or [ˈkrasɪŋ] *s* incrocio; ostacolo; (*of the sea*) traversata; (*of a river*) guado; (rr) passaggio a livello

cross'patch' *s* (coll) bisbetico

cross'piece' *s* traversa

cross' ref'erence *s* richiamo, rimando

cross'road' *s* strada trasversale; **at the crossroads** al bivio; **crossroads** crocicchio

cross' sec'tion *s* sezione trasversale

cross' street' *s* traversa

cross' talk' *s* conversazione; (telp) diafonia

cross'word puz'zle *s* cruciverba *m*, parole incrociate

crotch [kratʃ] *s* inforcatura; (*of pants*) cavallo

crotchety [ˈkratʃɪti] *adj* bisbetico

crouch [krautʃ] *intr* accoccolarsi

croup [krup] *s* (pathol) crup *m*

crouton [ˈkrutɑn] *s* crostino

crow [kro] *s* corvo, cornacchia; (*cry of rooster*) chicchirichì *m*; **as the crow flies** in linea retta, a volo d'uccello; **to eat crow** (coll) rimangiarsi le parole ǁ *intr* fare chicchirichì; **to crow over** vantarsi di, esultare per

crow'bar' *s* bastone *m* a leva

crowd [kraud] *s* folla; (*common people*) masse *fpl*; (coll) gruppo ǁ *tr* affollare; (*to push*) spingere || *intr* affollarsi; (*to press forward*) spingersi

crowded ['kraudɪd] *adj* affollato

crown [kraun] *s* corona; (*of hat*) cupola; (*highest point*) sommo || *tr* coronare; (*checkers*) damare; **to crown s.o.** (coll) battere qlcu sulla testa

crown′ prince′ *s* principe ereditario

crown′ prin′cess *s* principessa ereditaria

crow′s′-foot′ *s* (-feet) zampa di gallina

crow′s′-nest′ *s* coffa, gabbia

crucial ['kruʃəl] *adj* cruciale, critico

crucible ['krusɪbəl] *s* crogiolo

crucifix ['krusɪfɪks] *s* crocefisso

crucifixion [,krusɪ'fɪkʃən] *s* crocifissione

cruci•fy ['krusɪ,faɪ] *v* (*pret & pp* -**fied**) *tr* crocifiggere

crude [krud] *adj* (*raw*) grezzo; (*unripe*) acerbo; (*roughly made; uncultured*) rozzo

crudi•ty ['krudɪti] *s* (-ties) rozzezza

cruel ['kru·əl] *adj* crudele

cruel•ty ['kru·əlti] *s* (-ties) crudeltà *f*

cruet ['kru·ɪt] *s* oliera

cruise [kruz] *s* crociera || *tr* navigare, || *intr* andare in crociera; andare avanti e indietro

cruiser ['kruzər] *s* (nav) incrociatore *m*

cruising ['kruzɪŋ] *adj* di crociera

cruis′ing ra′dius *s* autonomia di crociera

cruller ['krʌlər] *s* frittella

crumb [krʌm] *s* briciola || *tr* sbriciolare; (*e.g., a cutlet*) impannare || *intr* sbriciolarsi

crumble ['krʌmbəl] *tr* sbriciolare, polverizzare || *intr* andare a pezzi, polverizzarsi, sbriciolarsi

crum•my ['krʌmi] *adj* (-**mier; -miest**) (slang) sporco; (*miserable*) (slang) schifoso; (*e.g., joke*) (slang) povero

crumple ['krʌmpəl] *tr* sgualcire, spiegazzare; **to crumple into a ball** appallottolare || *intr* spiegazzarsi

crunch [krʌntʃ] *s* crocchio; (coll) stretta, morsa || *tr* sgranocchiare || *intr* crocchiare

crusade [kru'sed] *s* crociata || *intr* crociarsi; (*to take up a cause*) farsi paladino

crusader [kru'sedər] *s* crociato; (*of a cause*) paladino

crush [krʌʃ] *s* pigiatura, schiacciatura; (*crowd*) calca; (coll) infatuazione || *tr* schiacciare; (*to grind*) frantumare; (*to subdue*) sottomettere; (*to extract by squeezing*) pigiare

crust [krʌst] *s* crosta; (slang) faccia tosta || *tr* incrostare || *intr* incrostare, incrostarsi

crustacean [krʌs'teʃən] *s* crostaceo

crust•y ['krʌsti] *adj* (-**ier; -iest**) crostoso; duro; rude

crutch [krʌtʃ] *s* gruccia, stampella; (fig) sostegno

crux [krʌks] *s* difficoltà *f*, busillis *m*; (*crucial point*) punto cruciale

cry [kraɪ] *s* (**cries**) (*shout*) grido; (*fit of weeping*) pianto; (*entreaty*) richiamo; (*of animal*) urlo; **a far cry** ben lontano, ben distinto; **to have a good cry** sfogarsi, piangere a calde lacrime || *tr* gridare; (*to proclaim*) bandire; **to cry down** disprezzare; **to cry one's heart out** piangere a calde lacrime; **to cry out** proclamare; **to cry up** elogiare || *intr* gridare, urlare; piangere; **to cry for** implorare

cry′ba′by *s* (-**bies**) piagnucolone *m*

crypt [krɪpt] *s* cripta

cryptic(al) ['krɪptɪk(əl)] *adj* segreto, occulto, misterioso

crystal ['krɪstəl] *s* cristallo

crys′tal ball′ *s* globo di cristallo

crystalline ['krɪstəlɪn] or ['krɪstə,laɪn] *adj* cristallino

crystallize ['krɪstə,laɪz] *tr* cristallizzare || *intr* cristallizzarsi

cub [kʌb] *s* cucciolo; (*of lion*) leoncino; (*of fox*) volpicino, volpacchiotto

cubbyhole ['kʌbɪ,hol] *s* sgabuzzino, bugigattolo

cube [kjub] *adj* cubico || *s* cubo; (*of sugar*) zolla || *tr* elevare al cubo; (*to shape*) tagliare in quadretti

cubic ['kjubɪk] *adj* cubico

cub′ report′er *s* giornalista novello

cuckold ['kʌkəld] *adj & s* cornuto, becco || *tr* cornificare

cuckoo ['kuku] *adj* (slang) pazzo || *s* cuculo

cuck′oo clock′ *s* orologio a cucù

cucumber ['kjukʌmbər] *s* cetriolo

cud [kʌd] *s* mangime masticato; **to chew the cud** ruminare

cuddle ['kʌdəl] *tr* abbracciare affettuosamente || *intr* (*to lie close*) giacere vicino; (*to curl up*) rannicchiarsi, raggomitolarsi

cudg•el ['kʌdʒəl] *s* manganello, randello; **to take up the cudgels for** farsi paladino di || *v* (*pret & pp* -**eled** or -**elled**; *ger* -**eling** or -**elling**) *tr* bastonare, randellare; **to cudgel one's brains** rompersi la testa

cue [kju] *s* suggerimento, imbeccata; (billiards) stecca; **to miss a cue** (theat) mancare la battuta; (coll) non capire l'antifona || *tr*—**to cue s.o. (in) on** (coll) dare a qlcu informazioni su

cuff [kʌf] *s* (*of shirt*) polsino; (*of trousers*) risvolto; (*slap*) schiaffo || *tr* schiaffeggiare

cuff′ links′ *spl* bottoni doppi, gemelli *mpl*

cuirass [kwɪ'ræs] *s* corazza

cuisine [kwɪ'zin] *s* cucina

culinary ['kjulɪ,nɛri] *adj* culinario

cull [kʌl] *s* scarto || *tr* (*to gather, pluck*) cogliere; selezionare, scegliere

culminate ['kʌlmɪ,net] *tr* culminare

culottes [ku'lɑts] *spl* gonna pantaloni

culpable ['kʌlpəbəl] *adj* colpevole

culprit ['kʌlprɪt] *s* colpevole *m*, imputato

cult [kʌlt] *s* culto

cultivate ['kʌltɪ,vet] *tr* coltivare

cultivated ['kʌltɪ‚vetɪd] *adj* colto, coltivato

cultivation [‚kʌltɪ'veʃən] *s* coltivazione, cultura

culture ['kʌltʃər] *s* cultura

cultured ['kʌltʃərd] *adj* colto

cul'tured pearl' *s* perla coltivata

culvert ['kʌlvərt] *s* chiavica

cumbersome ['kʌmbərsəm] *adj* ingombrante, incomodo; (*clumsy*) goffo

cumulative ['kjumjə‚letɪv] *adj* cumulativo

cunning ['kʌnɪŋ] *adj* (*sly*) astuto; (*skillful*) abile; (*pretty*) bello; (*created with skill*) ben fatto, fine ‖ *s* astuzia; abilità *f*, destrezza

cup [kʌp] *s* tazza; (mach, sports) coppa; (eccl) calice *m;* **in one's cups** ubriaco ‖ *v* (*pret & pp* **cupped;** *ger* **cupping**) *tr* mettere ventose a; **to cup one's hands** foggiare le mani a mo' di conca

cupboard ['kʌbərd] *s* armadio a muro, dispensa; (*buffet*) credenza

Cupid ['kjupɪd] *s* Cupido

cupidity [kju'pɪdɪti] *s* cupidigia

cup' of tea' *s* tazza di tè; (coll) forte *m,* e.g., **physics is not my cup of tea** la fisica non è il mio forte

cupola ['kjupələ] *s* cupola

cur [kʌr] *s* cane bastardo; (*despicable fellow*) canaglia, gaglioffo

curate ['kjurɪt] *s* curato

curative ['kjurətɪv] *adj* curativo

curator [kju'retər] *s* conservatore *m*

curb [kʌrb] *s* (*of bit*) barbazzale *m;* (*of pavement*) orlo del marciapiede; (*check*) freno ‖ *tr* frenare

curb'stone' *s* cordone *m;* (*of well*) sponda del pozzo

curd [kʌrd] *s* cagliata ‖ *tr* cagliare ‖ *intr* cagliarsi

curdle ['kʌrdəl] *tr* cagliare; (*the blood*) far gelare ‖ *intr* cagliarsi; (*said of custard*) impazzare

cure [kjur] *s* cura ‖ *tr* curare; (*e.g., meat*) conservare; (*wood*) stagionare

cure'-all' *s* panacea

curfew ['kʌrfju] *s* coprifuoco

curi·o ['kjurɪ‚o] *s* (-os) curiosità *f*

curiosi·ty [‚kjurɪ'ɑsɪti] *s* (-ties) curiosità *f*

curious ['kjurɪ·əs] *adj* curioso

curl [kʌrl] *s* (*of hair*) ricciolo; (*anything curled*) rotolo, spirale *f* ‖ *tr* arricciare; arrotolare; (*the lips*) torcere ‖ *intr* arricciarsi; arrotolarsi; **to curl up** raggomitolarsi

curlicue ['kʌrlɪ‚kju] *s* ghirigoro

curl'ing i'ron *s* ferro da arricciare

curl'pa'per *s* bigodino

curl·y ['kʌrli] *adj* (-ier; -iest) ricciuto

curmudgeon [kər'mʌdʒən] *s* bisbetico

currant ['kʌrənt] *s* (*seedless raisin*) uva passa di Corinto, uva sultanina; (*shrub and berry of genus Ribes*) ribes *m*

curren·cy ['kʌrənsi] *s* (-cies) (*circulation*) circolazione; (*money*) denaro circolante; (*general use*) corso

current ['kʌrənt] *adj & s* corrente *f*

cur'rent account' *s* conto corrente

cur'rent events' *spl* attualità *fpl,* eventi *mpl* correnti

curricu·lum [kə'rɪkjələm] *s* (-lums or -la [lə]) programma *m;* piano educativo

cur·ry ['kʌri] *s* (-ries) (*spice*) curry *m* ‖ *v* (*pret & pp* -ried) *tr* (*a horse*) strigliare; (*leather*) conciare; **to curry favor** cercare di compiacere

cur'ry·comb' *s* striglia ‖ *tr* strigliare

curse [kʌrs] *s* maledizione; bestemmia ‖ *tr* maledire ‖ *intr* imprecare, bestemmiare

cursed ['kʌrsɪd] *or* [kʌrst] *adj* maledetto; (*hateful*) odiato

cursive ['kʌrsɪv] *adj & s* corsivo

cursory ['kʌrsəri] *adj* rapido, superficiale

curt [kʌrt] *adj* (*rude*) brusco, sgarbato; (*short*) breve, conciso

curtail [kər'tel] *tr* ridurre, restringere

curtain ['kʌrtən] *s* (*in front of stage*) sipario; (*for window*) tendina; (fig) cortina ‖ *tr* coprire con tenda; separare con tenda; coprire, nascondere

cur'tain call' *s* (theat) chiamata

cur'tain rais'er ['rezər] *s* (theat) avanspettacolo; (sports) incontro preliminare

cur'tain ring' *s* campanella

cur'tain rod' *s* bastone *m* su cui si fissano le tende

curt·sy ['kʌrtsi] *s* (-sies) riverenza, inchino ‖ *v* (*pret & pp* -sied) *intr* fare la riverenza, inchinarsi

curve [kʌrv] *s* curva ‖ *tr* curvare ‖ *intr* curvarsi

curved [kʌrvd] *adj* curvo, curvato

cushion ['kuʃən] *s* cuscino; (*of billiard table*) mattonella ‖ *tr* proteggere, ammortizzare, attutire

cuspidor ['kʌspɪ‚dɔr] *s* sputacchiera

cuss [kʌs] *s* (coll) bestemmia; (coll) tipo perverso ‖ *tr* maledire ‖ *intr* bestemmiare

custard ['kʌstərd] *s* crema

custodian [kəs'todɪ·ən] *s* (*caretaker*) custode *m,* guardiano *m;* (*person who is entrusted with s.th*) conservatore *m;* (*janitor of school*) bidello

custo·dy ['kʌstədi] *s* (-dies) custodia; (*imprisonment*) arresto; **in custody** in prigione; **to take into custody** arrestare

custom ['kʌstəm] *s* costume *m;* (*customers*) clientela; **customs** dogana; **diritti** *mpl* doganali

customary ['kʌstə‚mɛri] *adj* consueto, abituale

custom-built ['kʌstəm'bɪlt] *adj* fatto su misura; (*car*) fuori serie

customer ['kʌstəmər] *s* cliente *mf*

cus'tom·house' *adj* doganale ‖ *s* dogana

custom-made ['kʌstəm'med] *adj* fatto su misura

cus'toms inspec'tion *s* visita doganale

cus'toms of'ficer *s* doganiere *m*

cus'tom work' *s* lavoro fatto su misura

cut [kʌt] *adj* (*prices*) ridotto; **to be cut out for** essere tagliato per ‖ *s* taglio; (*reduction*) ribasso; (typ) cliché *m;*

(snub) (coll) affronto; **(coll)** assenza non autorizzata; **(coll)** parte *f*; **a cut above (coll)** un po' meglio di ‖ *tr* tagliare; **(cards)** alzare; **(prices)** ridurre; **(coll)** far finta di non riconoscere; **(coll)** marinare; **cut it out!** basta!; **to cut back** ridurre; **to cut off** tagliare; diseredare; **(surg)** amputare; **to cut short** interrompere; **to cut teeth** fare i denti; **to cut up** sminuzzare; criticare ‖ *intr* tagliare, tagliarsi; **to cut across** attraversare; **to cut in** interrompere; **to cut under** vendere sottoprezzo; **to cut up** **(slang)** fare il pagliaccio

cut-and-dried ['kʌtən'draɪd] *adj* monotono, stantio; bell'e fatto, fatto in anticipo

cutaneous [kju'tenɪ·əs] *adj* cutaneo

cut'away' coat' ['kʌtə‚we] *s* marsina da giorno

cut'back' *s* riduzione; eliminazione; **(mov)** ritorno dell'azione a un'epoca anteriore

cute [kjut] *adj* **(coll)** carino, grazioso; **(shrewd) (coll)** furbo

cut' glass' *s* cristallo intagliato

cuticle ['kjutɪkəl] *s* cuticola

cutlass ['kʌtləs] *s* sciabola

cutler ['kʌtlər] *s* coltellinaio

cutlery ['kʌtləri] *s* coltelleria

cutlet ['kʌtlɪt] *s* cotoletta; **(flat croquette)** polpetta

cut'off' *s* taglio; **(road)** scorciatoia; **(of cylinder)** otturatore *m*, chiusura dell'ammissione; **(of river)** braccio di retto

cut'out' *s* ritaglio; **(aut)** valvola di scappamento libero

cut'-rate' *adj* a prezzo ridotto

cutter ['kʌtər] *s* tagliatore *m*; **(naut)** cutter *m*

cut'throat' *adj* spietato; **(relentless)** senza posa ‖ *s* assassino

cutting ['kʌtɪŋ] *adj* tagliente ‖ *s* taglio; **(from a newspaper)** ritaglio;

(e.g., of prices) riduzione; **(hort)** talea

cut'ting board' *s* tagliere *m*; **(of dishwasher)** piano d'appoggio

cut'ting edge' *s* taglio

cuttlefish ['kʌtəl‚fɪʃ] *s* seppia

cut'wat'er *s* **(of bridge)** tagliacque *m*; **(of boat)** tagliamare *m*

cyanamide [saɪ'ænə‚maɪd] *s* cianamide *f*; cianamide *f* di calcio

cyanide ['saɪə‚naɪd] *s* cianuro

cycle ['saɪkəl] *s* ciclo; bicicletta; **(of internal combustion engine)** tempo; **(phys)** periodo ‖ *intr* andare in bicicletta

cyclic(al) ['saɪklɪk(əl)] *or* ['sɪklɪk(əl)] *adj* ciclico

cyclone ['saɪklon] *s* ciclone *m*

cyclops ['saɪklɑps] *s* ciclope *m*

cyclotron ['saɪklo‚trɑn] *or* ['sɪklo‚trɑn] *s* ciclotrone *m*

cylinder ['sɪlɪndər] *s* cilindro; **(container)** bombola

cyl'inder block' *s* monoblocco

cyl'inder bore' *s* alesaggio

cyl'inder head' *s* testa

cylindric(al) [sɪ'lɪndrɪk(əl)] *adj* cilindrico

cymbals ['sɪmbəls] *spl* piatti *mpl*

cynic ['sɪnɪk] *adj & s* cinico

cynical ['sɪnɪkəl] *adj* cinico

cynicism ['sɪnɪ‚sɪzəm] *s* cinismo

cynosure ['saɪnə‚ʃur] *or* ['sɪnə‚ʃur] *s* centro dell'attenzione

cypress ['saɪprəs] *s* cipresso

Cyprus ['saɪprəs] *s* Cipro

Cyrus ['saɪrəs] *s* Ciro

cyst [sɪst] *s* ciste *f*, cisti *f*

czar [zɑr] *s* zar *m*

czarina [zɑ'rinə] *s* zarina

Czech [tʃɛk] *adj & s* ceco

Czecho-Slovak ['tʃɛko'slovæk] *adj & s* cecoslovacco

Czecho-Slovakia [‚tʃɛkoslo'vækɪ·ə] *s* la Cecoslovacchia

D

D, d [di] *s* quarta lettera dell'alfabeto inglese

dab [dæb] *s* tocco; **(of mud)** schizzo; **(e.g., of butter)** spalmata ‖ *v* **(pret & pp dabbed; ger dabbing)** *tr* toccare leggermente; **(to apply a substance to)** spennellare

dabble ['dæbəl] *tr* spruzzare ‖ *intr* diguazzare; **to dabble in** occuparsi di; **(stocks)** speculare in

dad [dæd] *s* **(coll)** papà *m*

dad-dy ['dædi] *s* **(-dies) (coll)** papà *m*

daffodil ['dæfədɪl] *s* trombone *m*

daff·y ['dæfi] *adj* **(-ier; -iest) (coll)** pazzo

dagger ['dægər] *s* daga, pugnale *m*; **(typ)** croce *f*; **to look daggers at** fulminare con lo sguardo

dahlia ['dæljə] *s* dalia

dai·ly ['deli] *adj* quotidiano, diurno ‖ *s* **(-lies)** quotidiano ‖ *adv* giornalmente

dai'ly dou'ble *s* duplice *f*, accoppiata

dain·ty ['denti] *adj* **(-tier; -tiest)** delicato ‖ *s* **(-ties)** manicaretto

dair·y ['dɛri] *s* **(-ies) (store)** latteria; **(factory)** caseificio

dair'y farm' *s* vaccheria

dair'y·man *s* **(-men)** lattaio

dais ['de·ɪs] *s* predella

dai·sy ['dezi] *s* **(-sies)** margherita

dal·ly ['dæli] *v* **(pret & pp -lied)** *intr* **(to loiter)** bighellonare; **(to trifle)** scherzare

dam [dæm] *s* diga; **(for fishing)** pescaia; **(zool)** fattrice *f* ‖ *v* **(pret & pp dammed; ger damming)** *tr* arginare; ostruire; tappare

damage ['dæmɪdʒ] *s* danno, scapito; (fig) menomazione; (com) avaria; **damages** danni *mpl* ‖ *tr* danneggiare, ledere; sinistrare

damascene ['dæmə,sin] *or* [,dæmə-'sin] *adj* damasceno ‖ *s* damaschinatura ‖ *tr* damaschinare

dame [dem] *s* dama, signora; (slang) donna

damn [dæm] *s*—**I don't give a damn** (slang) me ne impipo; **that's not worth a damn** (slang) non vale un fico ‖ *tr* dannare, condannare ‖ *intr* maledire ‖ *interj* maledizione!

damnation [dæm'neʃən] *s* dannazione; (theol) condanna

damned [dæmd] *adj* dannato, maledetto ‖ **the damned** i dannati ‖ *adv* maledettamente

damp [dæmp] *adj* umido ‖ *s* umidità *f*; (firedamp) grisou *m* ‖ *tr* inumidire; umettare; (to muffle) smorzare; (waves) (elec) smorzare; **to damp s.o.'s enthusiasm** raffreddare gli spiriti di qlcu; scoraggiare qlcu

dampen ['dæmpən] *tr* inumidire; umettare; smorzare; (s.o.'s enthusiasm) raffreddare

damper ['dæmpər] *s* (of chimney) valvola di tiraggio; (fig) doccia fredda; (mus) smorzatore *m;* (mus) sordina

damsel ['dæmzəl] *s* damigella

dance [dæns] *or* [dɑns] *s* ballo, danza ‖ *tr & intr* ballare, danzare

dance' band' *s* orchestrina

dance' floor' *s* pista da ballo

dance' hall' *s* sala da ballo

dancer ['dænsər] *or* ['dɑnsər] *s* danzatore *m;* (expert or professional) ballerino

danc'ing part'ner *s* cavaliere *m;* dama

danc'ing par'ty *s* festa da ballo

dandelion ['dændɪ,laɪ-ən] *s* dente *m* di leone, soffione *m*

dandruff ['dændrəf] *s* forfora

dan·dy ['dændɪ] *adj* (**-dier; -diest**) (coll) eccellente, magnifico ‖ *s* (**-dies**) damerino, elegantone *m*

Dane [den] *s* danese *mf*

danger ['dendʒər] *s* pericolo

dangerous ['dendʒərəs] *adj* pericoloso

dangle ['dæŋgəl] *tr* dondolare ‖ *intr* penzolare, ciondolare

Danish ['denɪʃ] *adj & s* danese *m*

dank [dæŋk] *adj* umido

Danube ['dænjʊb] *s* Danubio

dapper ['dæpər] *adj* azzimato

dapple ['dæpəl] *adj* pezzato ‖ *tr.* chiazzare

dap'ple-gray' *adj* storno

dare [dɛr] *s* sfida ‖ *tr* sfidare ‖ *intr* osare; **I dare say** oserei dire; forse, e.g., **I dare say we will be done at seven** forse avremo finito alle sette; **to dare to** (to have the courage to) osare di, fidarsi a

dare'dev'il *s* scavezzacollo

daring ['dɛrɪŋ] *adj* temerario, spericolato ‖ *s* audacia, temerarietà *f*

dark [dɑrk] *adj* scuro; (complexion) bruno; oscuro, segreto; (gloomy) tetro, fosco ‖ *s* oscurità *f*, scuro; tenebre *fpl;* **in the dark** al buio

Dark' Ag'es *spl* alto medio evo

dark-complexioned ['dɑrkkəm'plɛkʃənd] *adj* bruno

darken ['dɑrkən] *tr* scurire, oscurare ‖ *intr* scurirsi, oscurarsi

dark' horse' *s* vincitore imprevisto, outsider *m*

darkly ['dɑrkli] *adv* oscuramente; segretamente

dark' meat' *s* gamba o anca (di pollo o tacchino)

darkness ['dɑrknɪs] *s* oscurità *f*

dark'room' *s* camera oscura

darling ['dɑrlɪŋ] *adj & s* caro, amato

darn [dɑrn] *s* rammendo ‖ *tr* rammendare ‖ *interj* (coll) accidenti!

darned [dɑrnd] *adj* (coll) maledetto ‖ *adv* maledettamente; (coll) tremendamente

darnel ['dɑrnəl] *s* zizzania

darning ['dɑrnɪŋ] *s* rammendo

darn'ing nee'dle *s* ago da rammendo

dart [dɑrt] *s* freccia, dardo; (game) frecciolo ‖ *intr* dardeggiare; lanciarsi, precipitarsi

dash [dæʃ] *s* sciacquio; piccola quantità, sospetto; (spirit) brio; (typ, telg) trattino, lineetta ‖ *tr* lanciare; mescolare; (s.o.'s hopes) frustrare; deprimere; **to dash off** gettar giù; **to dash to pieces** fare a pezzi ‖ *intr* precipitarsi; **to dash against** gettarsi contro; **to dash by** passare a gran velocità; **to dash in** entrare come un razzo; **to dash off** *or* **out** andarsene in fretta; lanciarsi fuori

dash'board' *s* cruscotto; (in an open carriage) parafango

dashing ['dæʃɪŋ] *adj* impetuoso; vistoso ‖ *s* (of waves) sciacquio

dastard ['dæstərd] *adj & s* vile *mf*, codardo

da'ta proc'essing *s* elaborazione

date [det] *s* (time) data; (palm) palma da datteri; (fruit) dattero; (appointment) (coll) appuntamento; **out of date** fuori moda; **to date** sinora; **up to date** a giorno ‖ *tr* datare; (coll) avere un appuntamento con ‖ *intr*— **to date from** partire da

date' line' *s* linea del cambiamento di data

dative ['detɪv] *adj & s* dativo

datum ['detəm] *or* ['dætəm] *s* (data ['detə] *or* ['dætə]) dato

daub [dɔb] *s* imbratto ‖ *tr* imbrattare

daughter ['dɔtər] *s* figlia, figliola

daughter-in-law ['dɔtərɪn,lɔ] *s* (**daughters-in-law**) nuora

daunt [dɔnt] *tr* spaventare; intimidire

dauntless ['dɔntlɪs] *adj* intrepido

dauphin ['dɔfɪn] *s* delfino

davenport ['dævən,port] *s* sofà *m*, sofà *m* letto

davit ['dævɪt] *s* gru *f* per lancia

daw [dɔ] *s* cornacchia

dawdle ['dɔdəl] *intr* bighellonare

dawn [dɔn] *s* alba ‖ *intr* (said of the day) farsi, nascere, spuntare; **to dawn on** cominciare a apparire nella mente di

day [de] *adj* diurno; (student) esterno ‖ *s* giorno; (of travel, work, etc.)

giornata; **a few days ago** giorni fa; **any day now** da un giorno all'altro; **by day** di giorno; **the day after** il giorno dopo; **the day after tomorrow** dopodomani; **the day before yesterday** ieri l'altro; **to call it a day** (coll) finire di lavorare

day′ bed′ s sofà m letto

day′book′ s brogliaccio

day′break′ s far m del giorno

day′dream′ s fantasticheria || intr fantasticare

day′ la′borer s giornaliero

day′light′ s luce f del giorno; alba; **in broad daylight** alla luce del sole; **to see daylight** comprendere; vedere la fine

day′light-sav′ing time′ s ora legale, ora estiva

day′ nurs′ery s asilo infantile

day′ off′ s giorno di vacanza; (of servant) libera uscita

day′ of reck′oning s giorno di rendiconto; (last judgment) giorno del giudizio

day′ shift′ s turno diurno

day′time′ adj diurno || s giornata

daze [dez] s stordimento; **in a daze** stordito || tr stordire

dazzle ['dæzəl] s abbagliamento || tr abbagliare

dazzling ['dæzlɪŋ] adj abbagliante

deacon ['dikən] s diacono

dead [dɛd] adj morto || s—**in the dead of** (e.g., night) nel pieno di; **the dead** i morti || adv (coll) completamente; (abruptly) (coll) di colpo

dead′ beat′ adj (coll) stanco morto

dead′beat′ s (coll) scroccone m

dead′ cen′ter s punto morto

dead′drunk′ adj ubriaco fradicio

deaden ['dɛdən] tr attutire; (e.g., s.o.'s senses) ottundere

dead′ end′ s vicolo cieco

dead′ let′ter s lettera morta; lettera non reciamata

dead′line′ s termine m

dead′lock′ s punto morto || tr portare al punto morto || intr giungere al punto morto

dead·ly ['dɛdli] adj (-lier; -liest) mortale; insopportabile

dead′ pan′ s (slang) faccia senza espressione

dead′pan′ adj senza espressione

dead′ reck′oning s (naut) stima

dead′wood′ s legna secca; (fig) zavorra

deaf [dɛf] adj sordo; **to turn a deaf ear** fare orecchio di mercante

deaf′-and-dumb′ adj sordomuto

deafen ['dɛfən] tr assordare, intronare

deafening ['dɛfənɪŋ] adj assordante

deaf′-mute′ s sordomuto

deafness ['dɛfnɪs] s sordità f

deal [dil] s accordo; quantità f; (cards) mano, girata; (coll) affare m; (coll) trattamento; **a good deal (of)** or **a great deal (of)** moltissimo || v (pret & pp dealt [dɛlt]) tr (a blow) menare; (cards) fare, sfogliare; **to deal s.o. in** (coll) includere || intr mercanteggiare, commerciare; fare le

carte; **to deal with** trattare con; trattare di

dealer ['dilər] s commerciante mf, esercente mf; (cards) mazziere m

dean [din] s decano

dear [dir] adj (beloved; expensive) caro; **dear me!** povero me!; **Dear Sir** egregio Signore || s caro

dearie ['dɪri] s (coll) caro

dearth [dʌrθ] s scarsezza; insufficienza

death [dɛθ] s morte f; **to bleed to death** morire dissanguato; **to burn to death** morire bruciato; **to choke to death** morire di soffocazione; **to freeze to death** morire di gelo; **to put to death** dare la morte a; **to shoot to death** uccidere a fucilate; **to stab to death** scannare; **to starve to death** far morire di fame; morire di fame

death′bed′ s letto di morte

death′blow′ s colpo mortale

deathless ['dɛθlɪs] adj immortale, eterno

deathly ['dɛθli] adj mortale || adv mortalmente; assolutamente

death′ pen′alty s pena di morte

death′ rate′ s mortalità f

death′ rat′tle s rantolo della morte

death′ ray′ s raggio della morte

death′ sen′tence s pena di morte

death′ war′rant s pena di morte; fine f di ogni speranza

death′watch′ s veglia mortuaria; (zool) orologio della morte

debacle [de'bakəl] s disastro; (downfall) tracollo; (in a river) sgelo repentino

de·bar [dɪ'bar] v (pret & pp -barred; ger -barring) tr escludere; proibire (with dat)

debark [dɪ'bark] tr & intr sbarcare

debarkation [,dibar'keʃən] s sbarco

debase [dɪ'bes] tr degradare; adulterare

debatable [dɪ'betəbəl] adj discutibile

debate [dɪ'bet] s discussione || tr & intr discutere

debauch [dɪ'bɔtʃ] s dissolutezza, corruzione || tr corrompere

debauchee [,dɛbɔ'ʃi] or [,dɛbɔ'tʃi] s degenerato, vizioso

debaucher·y [di'bɔtʃəri] s (-ies) dissolutezza, corruzione

debenture [dɪ'bɛntʃər] s (bond) obbligazione; (voucher) buono

debilitate [dɪ'bɪlɪ,tet] tr debilitare

debili·ty [dɪ'bɪlɪti] s (-ties) debolezza

debit ['dɛbɪt] s debito; (debit side) (com) dare m || tr addebitare

debonair [,dɛbə'nɛr] adj gioviale; cortese

debris [de'bri] s detrito, rottami mpl

debt [dɛt] s debito; **to run into debt** indebitarsi

debtor ['dɛtər] s debitore m

debut [de'bju] or ['debju] s debutto; **to make one's debut** debuttare || intr debuttare

debutante [,dɛbju'tant] or ['dɛbjə,tænt] s debuttante f, esordiente f

decade ['dɛked] s decennio

decadence [dɪ'kedəns] s decadenza

decadent [dɪ'kedənt] *adj & s* decadente *mf*

decanter [dɪ'kæntər] *s* boccia

decapitate [dɪ'kæpɪ,tet] *tr* decapitare

decay [dɪ'ke] *s* (*decline*) decadimento; (*rotting*) marciume *m*, putredine *f*; (*of teeth*) carie *f* || *tr* imputridire || *intr* imputridire, marcire; (*said of teeth*) cariarsi

decease [dɪ'sis] *s* decesso || *intr* decedere

deceased [dɪ'sist] *adj & s* defunto

deceit [dɪ'sit] *s* inganno, frode *f*

deceitful [dɪ'sitfəl] *adj* ingannatore, menzognero, subdolo

deceive [dɪ'siv] *tr & intr* ingannare

decelerate [dɪ'sɛlə,ret] *tr & intr* decelerare

December [dɪ'sɛmbər] *s* dicembre *m*

decen·cy ['disənsi] *s* (*-cies*) decenza, pudore *m;* **decencies** convenienze *fpl*

decent ['disənt] *adj* decente; (*proper*) conveniente

decentralize [dɪ'sɛntrə,laɪz] *tr* decentrare

deception [dɪ'sɛpʃən] *s* inganno

deceptive [dɪ'sɛptɪv] *adj* ingannevole

decide [dɪ'saɪd] *tr* decidere || *intr* decidere, decidersi

decimal ['dɛsɪməl] *adj & s* decimale *m*

dec'imal point' *s* (*in Italian the comma is used to separate the decimal fraction from the integer*) virgola

decimate ['dɛsɪ,met] *tr* decimare

decipher [dɪ'saɪfər] *tr* decifrare

decision [dɪ'sɪʒən] *s* decisione

decisive [dɪ'saɪsɪv] *adj* decisivo; (*resolute*) fermo

deck [dɛk] *s* (*of cards*) mazzo; (*naut*) coperta, tolda, ponte *m;* **on deck** (coll) pronto; (coll) prossimo || *tr—* **to deck out** adornare; (*with flags*) imbandierare

deck' chair' *s* sedia a sdraio

deck' hand' *s* marinaio di coperta

deck'house' *s* (naut) tuga

deck'le edge' ['dɛkəl] *s* sbavatura

declaim [dɪ'klem] *tr & intr* declamare

declaration [,dɛklə'reʃən] *s* dichiarazione

declarative [dɪ'klærətɪv] *adj* declaratorio; (gram) enunciativo

declare [dɪ'klɛr] *tr* dichiarare || *intr* dichiararsi

declension [dɪ'klɛnʃən] *s* declinazione

declination [,dɛklɪ'neʃən] *s* declinazione

decline [dɪ'klaɪn] *s* decadenza; (*in prices*) ribasso; (*in health*) deperimento; (*of sun*) tramonto || *tr* declinare || *intr* declinare; decadere, scadere

declivi·ty [dɪ'klɪvɪti] *s* (*-ties*) declivio, pendice *f*

decode [di'kod] *tr* decifrare

décolleté [,dɛkɑl'te] *adj* scollato

decompose [,dɪkəm'poz] *tr* decomporre || *intr* decomporsi

decomposition [,dikɑmpə'zɪʃən] *s* decomposizione

décor [de'kɔr] *s* decorazione; (*of a room*) stile *m;* (theat) scenario

decorate ['dɛkə,ret] *tr* decorare

decoration [,dɛkə'reʃən] *s* decorazione

decorator ['dɛkə,retər] *s* decoratore *m*

decorous ['dɛkərəs] or [dɪ'korəs] *adj* corretto, decoroso

decorum [dɪ'korəm] *s* decoro, correttezza

decoy [dɪ'kɔɪ] or ['dikɔɪ] *s* richiamo; (*for birds*) zimbello; (*person*) adescatore *m* || *tr* (*to lure*) adescare; (*to deceive*) abbindolare

decrease ['dikris] or [dɪ'kris] *s* diminuzione; (*of salary*) decurtazione || [dɪ'kris] *tr* decurtare || *intr* diminuire

decree [dɪ'kri] *s* decreto || *tr* decretare

de·cry [dɪ'kraɪ] *v* (*pret & pp* **-cried**) *tr* denigrare, screditare

dedicate ['dɛdɪ,ket] *tr* dedicare

dedication [,dɛdɪ'keʃən] *s* dedizione; (*inscription in a book*) dedica

deduce [dɪ'djus] or [dɪ'dus] *tr* dedurre

deduct [dɪ'dʌkt] *tr* dedurre, defalcare

deductible [dɪ'dʌktɪbəl] *adj* defalcabile || *s* (ins) franchigia

deduction [dɪ'dʌkʃən] *s* deduzione

deed [did] *s* fatto; (*exploit*) prodezza; (law) titolo || *tr* trasferire legalmente

deem [dim] *tr & intr* credere, giudicare

deep [dip] *adj* profondo; basso; (*woods*) folto; (*friendship*) intimo; **deep in debt** carico di debiti; **deep in thought** assorto in pensieri || *adv* profondamente; **deep into the night** a notte fatta; **to go deep into** approfondirsi in

deepen ['dipən] *tr* approfondire || *intr* approfondirsi

deep'-freeze' *tr* (*pret* **-froze** [froz]; *pp* **-frozen** [frozən]) *tr* surgelare

deep-laid ['dip,led] *adj* preparato astutamente

deep' mourn'ing *s* lutto stretto

deep-rooted ['dip,rutɪd] *adj* profondo

deep'-sea' fish'ing *s* pesca d'alto mare or d'altura

deep-seated ['dip,sitɪd] *adj* profondo, connaturato

Deep' South' *s* Profondo Sud

deer [dɪr] *s* cervo

deer'skin' *s* pelle *f* di daino

deface [dɪ'fes] *tr* sfigurare

defamation [,dɛfə'meʃən] or [,difə'meʃən] *s* diffamazione

defame [dɪ'fem] *tr* diffamare

default [dɪ'fɔlt] *s* mancanza; (*failure to act*) inadempienza; **in default of** per mancanza di; **to lose by default** dichiarare forfeit. || *tr* essere inadempiente a || *intr* essere inadempiente; (sports) dichiarare forfeit

defeat [dɪ'fit] *s* sconfitta, disfatta || *tr* sconfiggere, vincere

defeatism [dɪ'fitɪzəm] *s* disfattismo

defeatist [dɪ'fitɪst] *adj & s* disfattista *mf*

defecate ['dɛfɪ,ket] *intr* defecare

defect [dɪ'fɛkt] or ['difɛkt] *s* vizio, difetto || [dɪ'fɛkt] *intr* defezionare

defection [dɪ'fɛkʃən] *s* defezione

defective [dɪ'fɛktɪv] *adj* difettivo, difettoso

defend [dɪ'fɛnd] *tr* difendere, proteggere

defendant [dɪ'fɛndənt] *s* (law) imputato, querelato

defender [dɪ'fɛndər] *s* difensore *m*

defense [dɪ'fɛns] *s* difesa

defenseless [dɪ'fɛnslɪs] *adj* indifeso

defensive [dɪ'fɛnsɪv] *adj* difensivo || *s* difensiva

de·fer [dɪ'fʌr] *v* (*pret* & *pp* **-ferred;** *ger* **-ferring**) *tr* differire, rinviare || *intr* rimettersi

deference ['dɛfərəns] *s* deferenza

deferential [,dɛfə'rɛnʃəl] *adj* deferente

deferment [dɪ'fʌrmənt] *s* differimento

defiance [dɪ'faɪ·əns] *s* opposizione; sfida; **in defiance of** a dispetto di

defiant [dɪ'faɪ·ənt] *adj* provocante, ostile

deficien·cy [dɪ'fɪʃənsi] *s* (**-cies**) deficienza; (com) ammanco

deficient [dɪ'fɪʃənt] *adj* deficiente

deficit ['dɛfɪsɪt] *adj* deficitario || *s* deficit *m*, disavanzo

defile [dɪ'faɪl] or ['difaɪl] *s* gola, passo || [dɪ'faɪl] *tr* profanare || *intr* marciare in fila

define [dɪ'faɪn] *tr* definire

definite ['dɛfɪnɪt] *adj* definito; (gram) determinativo, determinato

definition [,dɛfɪ'nɪʃən] *s* definizione

definitive [dɪ'fɪnɪtɪv] *adj* definitivo

deflate [dɪ'flet] *tr* sgonfiare; (*s.o.'s hopes*) deprimere; (*e.g., currency*) deflazionare

deflation [dɪ'fleʃən] *s* sgonfiamento; (*of prices*) deflazione

deflect [dɪ'flɛkt] *tr* far deflettere || *intr* deflettere

deflower [dɪ'flaʊ·ər] *tr* privare dei fiori; (*a woman*) deflorare

deforest [di'farɛst] or [di'fɔrɛst] *tr* disboscare, smacchiare

deform [dɪ'fɔrm] *tr* deformare

deformed [dɪ'fɔrmd] *adj* deforme

deformi·ty [dɪ'fɔrmɪti] *s* (**-ties**) deformità *f*

defraud [dɪ'frɔd] *tr* defraudare

defray [dɪ'fre] *tr* pagare

defrost [di'frɔst] or [di'frɑst] *tr* sgelare, sbrinare

defroster [di'frɔstər] or [di'frɑstər] *s* (aut) visiera termica

deft [dɛft] *adj* destro, lesto

defunct [dɪ'fʌŋkt] *adj* defunto

de·fy [dɪ'faɪ] *v* (*pret* & *pp* **-fied**) *tr* sfidare, provocare

degeneracy [dɪ'dʒɛnərəsi] *s* degenerazione

degenerate [dɪ'dʒɛnərɪt] *adj* & *s* degenerato || [dɪ'dʒɛnə,ret] *intr* degenerare, tralignare

degrade [dɪ'gred] *tr* degradare

degrading [dɪ'gredɪŋ] *adj* degradante

degree [dɪ'gri] *s* grado; titolo accademico; **by degrees** a grado a grado; **to a degree** fino a un certo punto; troppo; **to take a degree** ricevere un titolo di studio

dehydrate [di'haɪdret] *tr* disidratare

deice [di'aɪs] *tr* sgelare

dei·fy ['di·ɪ,faɪ] *v* (*pret* & *pp* **-fied**) *tr* deificare

deign [den] *intr* degnarsi

dei·ty ['di·ɪti] *s* (**-ties**) deità *f;* **the Deity** Dio

dejected [dɪ'dʒɛktɪd] *adj* demoralizzato

dejection [dɪ'dʒɛkʃən] *s* (*in spirits*) demoralizzazione; (*evacuation*) deiezione

delay [dɪ'le] *s* ritardo, proroga; dilazione; **without further delay** senza ulteriore indugio || *tr* tardare; (*to put off*) differire || *intr* tardare, ritardare

delayed'-ac'tion *adj* a azione differita

delectable [dɪ'lɛktəbəl] *adj* dilettevole

delegate ['dɛlɪ,get] or ['dɛlɪgɪt] *s* delegato, incaricato; (*to a convention*) congressista *mf* || ['dɛlɪ,get] *tr* delegare, incaricare

delegation [,dɛlɪ'geʃən] *s* delegazione

delete [dɪ'lit] *tr* cancellare, sopprimere

deletion [dɪ'liʃən] *s* cancellazione

deliberate [dɪ'lɪbərɪt] *adj* meditato; (*slow in deciding*) cauto; (*slow in moving*) lento || [dɪ'lɪbə,ret] *tr* & *intr* deliberare

deliberately [dɪ'lɪbərɪtli] *adv* (*on purpose*) deliberatamente; (*without hurrying*) con ponderatezza

delica·cy ['dɛlɪkəsi] *s* (**-cies**) delicatezza; (*choice food*) leccornia

delicatessen [,dɛlɪkə'tɛsən] *s* negozio di salumerie || *spl* salumerie *fpl,* articoli alimentari scelti

delicious [dɪ'lɪʃəs] *adj* delizioso

delight [dɪ'laɪt] *s* gioia, delizia || *tr* dilettare || *intr* dilettarsi

delightful [dɪ'laɪtfəl] *adj* delizioso

delinquen·cy [dɪ'lɪŋkwənsi] *s* (**-cies**) colpa; (*offense*) delinquenza; (*in payment of a debt*) morosità *f*

delinquent [dɪ'lɪŋkwənt] *adj* colpevole; (*in payment*) moroso; non pagato || *s* delinquente *m;* debitore moroso

delirious [dɪ'lɪrɪ·əs] *adj* in delirio

deliri·um [dɪ'lɪrɪ·əm] *s* (**-ums** or **-a** [ə]) delirio

deliver [dɪ'lɪvər] *tr* consegnare; (*a blow*) affibbiare; (*a speech*) fare; (*a letter*) recapitare; (*electricity or gas*) erogare; (*said of a pregnant woman*) partorire; (*said of a doctor*) assistere durante il parto

deliver·y [dɪ'lɪvəri] *s* (**-ies**) consegna; (*of mail*) distribuzione; (*of merchandise*) fornitura; (*of a speech*) dizione; (*childbirth*) parto; (sports) lancio

deliv'ery·man' *s* (**-men'**) fattorino

deliv'ery room' *s* sala parto

deliv'ery truck' *s* furgoncino

dell [dɛl] *s* valletta

delouse [di'laʊs] or [di'laʊz] *tr* spidocchiare

delude [dɪ'lud] *tr* illudere, ingannare

deluge ['dɛljudʒ] *s* diluvio, inondazione || **the Deluge** il diluvio universale || *tr* inondare

delusion [dɪ'luʒən] *s* illusione, inganno; (psychopath) allucinazione;

(psychopath) idea fissa; **delusions of grandeur** mania di grandezza

de luxe [dɪ'luks] or [dɪ'lʌks] *adj* di lusso || *adv* in gran lusso

delve [dɛlv] *intr* frugare; **to delve into** approfondirsi in

demagnetize [di'mægnɪ,taɪz] *tr* smagnetizzare

demagogue ['dɛmə,gag] *s* demagogo

demand [dɪ'mænd] or [dɪ'mand] *s* esigenza; (com) richiesta, domanda; **to be in demand** essere in richiesta || *tr* esigere

demanding [dɪ'mændɪŋ] or [dɪ'mandɪŋ] *adj* esigente, impegnativo

demarcate [dɪ'market] or ['dimar,ket] *tr* demarcare

démarche [de'marʃ] *s* progetto, piano

demean [dɪ'min] *tr* degradare; **to demean oneself** comportarsi; degradarsi

demeanor [dɪ'minər] *s* condotta, contegno

demented [dɪ'mɛntɪd] *adj* demente

demigod ['dɛmɪ,gad] *s* semidio

demijohn ['dɛmɪ,dʒan] *s* damigiana

demilitarize [di'mɪlɪtə,raɪz] *tr* smilitarizzare

demimonde ['dɛmɪ,mand] *s* donne *fpl* della società equivoca

demise [dɪ'maɪz] *s* decesso

demitasse ['dɛmɪ,tæs] or ['demi,tas] *s* tazzina da caffè; (contents) caffè nero

demobilize [di'mobɪ,laɪz] *tr* smobilitare

democra·cy [dɪ'makrəsi] *s* (-cies) democrazia

democrat ['dɛmə,kræt] *s* democratico

democratic [,dɛmə'krætɪk] *adj* democratico

demolish [dɪ'malɪʃ] *tr* demolire

demolition [,dɛmə'lɪʃən] or [,dimə'lɪʃən] *s* demolizione

demon ['dimən] *s* demonio

demoniacal [,dimə'naɪ·əkəl] *adj* demoniaco

demonstrate ['dɛmən,stret] *tr & intr* dimostrare

demonstration [,dɛmən'streʃən] *s* dimostrazione

demonstrative [dɪ'manstrətɪv] *adj* dimostrativo; (giving open exhibition of emotion) espansivo

demonstrator ['dɛmən,stretər] *s* (of a product) dimostratore *m*; (in a public gathering) dimostrante *m*; (product) prodotto usato da dimostratori

demoralize [dɪ'marə,laɪz] or [dɪ'mɔrə,laɪz] *tr* demoralizzare

demote [dɪ'mot] *tr* retrocedere

demotion [dɪ'moʃən] *s* retrocessione

de·mur [dɪ'mʌr] *v* (pret & pp -murred; ger -murring) *intr* sollevare obiezioni

demure [dɪ'mjur] *adj* modesto; sobrio

demurrage [dɪ'mʌrɪdʒ] *s* (com) controstallie *fpl*; (rr) sosta

den [dɛn] *s* (of animals, thieves) tana; (little room) bugigattolo; (little room for studying or writing) studiolo; (of lions) (Bib) fossa

denaturalize [di'nætʃərə,laɪz] *tr* snaturare; privare della nazionalità

dena'tured al'cohol [dɪ'netʃərd] *s* alcole denaturato

denial [dɪ'naɪ·əl] *s* diniego; (disavowal) smentita

denim ['dɛnɪm] *s* tessuto di cotone per tuta; **denims** tuta; (trousers) jeans *mpl*

denizen ['dɛnɪzən] *s* abitante *mf*

Denmark ['dɛnmark] *s* la Danimarca

denomination [dɪ,namɪ'neʃən] *s* denominazione; categoria; (com) taglio; (eccl) confessione

denote [dɪ'not] *tr* denotare, significare

denouement [denu'mã] *s* scioglimento

denounce [dɪ'nauns] *tr* denunziare

dense [dɛns] *adj* denso; stupido

densi·ty ['dɛnsɪti] *s* (-ties) densità *f*

dent [dɛnt] *s* ammaccatura; (in a gearwheel) tacca, dente *m*; **to make a dent** fare progresso; fare impressione || *tr* ammaccare; (fig) ferire

dental ['dɛntəl] *adj* dentale, dentario || *s* dentale *f*

den'tal floss' *s* filo cerato dentario

dentifrice ['dɛntɪfrɪs] *s* dentifricio

dentist ['dɛntɪst] *s* dentista *mf*

dentistry ['dɛntɪstri] *s* odontoiatria

denture ['dɛntʃər] *s* dentiera

denunciation [dɪ,nʌnsɪ'eʃən] or [dɪ,nʌnʃɪ'eʃən] *s* denunzia

de·ny [dɪ'naɪ] *v* (pret & pp -nied) *tr* (to declare not to be true) negare; (to refuse) rifiutare; **to deny oneself to callers** sottrarsi alle visite || *intr* negare; rifiutare

deodorant [di'odərənt] *adj & s* deodorante *m*

deo'dorant spray' *s* deodorante *m* spray

deodorize [di'odə,raɪz] *tr* deodorare

depart [dɪ'part] *intr* partire, andarsene; (to diverge) dipartire

departed [dɪ'partɪd] *adj* morto, defunto || **the departed** i defunti

department [dɪ'partmənt] *s* dipartimento; (of government) ministero; (e.g., of a hospital) reparto; (of agency) sezione, ufficio

depart'ment store' *s* grandi magazzini *mpl*

departure [dɪ'partʃər] *s* partenza; divergenza, deviazione

depend [dɪ'pɛnd] *intr* dipendere; **to depend on** (to rely on) contare su; dipendere da

dependable [dɪ'pɛndəbəl] *adj* sicuro, fidato

dependence [dɪ'pɛndəns] *s* dipendenza; (trust) fiducia

dependen·cy [dɪ'pɛndənsi] *s* (-cies) dipendenza; (territory) possessione

dependent [dɪ'pɛndənt] *adj* dipendente; a carico; **to be dependent on** dipendere da la || *s* persona a carico

depend'ent clause' *s* proposizione subordinata

depict [dɪ'pɪkt] *tr* descrivere, dipingere

deplete [dɪ'plit] *tr* esaurire

depletion [dɪ'pliʃən] *s* esaurimento

deplorable [dɪ'plorəbəl] *adj* deplorevole

deplore [dɪ'plor] *tr* deplorare

deploy [dɪ'plɔɪ] *tr* (mil) spiegare, stendere

deployment [dɪ'plɔɪmənt] *s* (mil) dispositivo, spiegamento

depolarize [di'polə‚raɪz] *tr* depolarizzare

depopulate [di'pɑpjə‚let] *tr* spopolare

deport [dɪ'port] *tr* deportare; **to deport oneself** comportarsi

deportation [‚dipor'teʃən] *s* deportazione

deportee [‚dipor'ti] *s* deportato

deportment [dɪ'portmənt] *s* condotta, comportamento

depose [dɪ'poz] *tr* & *intr* deporre

deposit [dɪ'pɑzɪt] *s* deposito; (*down payment*) caparra ‖ *tr* depositare ‖ *intr* depositarsi

depos'it account' *s* conto corrente

depositor [dɪ'pɑzɪtər] *s* versante *mf*; (*to the credit of an established account*) correntista *mf*

deposito·ry [dɪ'pɑzɪ‚tori] *s* (**-ries**) deposito; (*person*) depositario

depos'it slip' *s* distinta di versamento

depot [ˈdipo] *or* [ˈdɛpo] *s* magazzino; (mil) deposito; (rr) stazione

depraved [dɪ'prevd] *adj* depravato

depravi·ty [dɪ'prævɪti] *s* (**-ties**) depravazione

deprecate [ˈdɛprɪ‚ket] *tr* deprecare

depreciate [dɪ'priʃɪ‚et] *tr* svalutare, deprezzare ‖ *intr* deprezzarsi

depreciation [dɪ‚priʃɪ'eʃən] *s* (*drop in value*) deprezzamento; (*disparagement*) disprezzo

depredation [‚dɛprɪ'deʃən] *s* depredazione

depress [dɪ'prɛs] *tr* deprimere; avvilire; (*prices*) far abbassare

depression [dɪ'prɛʃən] *s* depressione; (*gloom*) sconforto; (*slump*) crisi *f*

deprive [dɪ'praɪv] *tr* privare; **to deprive oneself** espropriarsi

depth [dɛpθ] *s* profondità *f*; (*of a house or room*) lunghezza; (*of sea*) fondale *m*; (fig) vastità *f*; **in the depth of** nel cuor di; **to go beyond one's depth** non toccare più; (fig) andare oltre le proprie possibilità

depth' bomb' *s* (aer) bomba antisommergibile

depth' charge' *s* (nav) granata antisommergibile

depth' of hold' *s* (naut) puntale *m*

deputation [‚dɛpjə'teʃən] *s* deputazione

deputize [ˈdɛpjə‚taɪz] *tr* deputare

depu·ty [ˈdɛpjəti] *s* (**-ties**) deputato

derail [dɪ'rel] *tr* far deragliare ‖ *intr* deragliare, deviare

derailment [dɪ'relmənt] *s* deragliamento, deviamento

derange [dɪ'rendʒ] *tr* (*to disarrange*) dissestare; (*to make insane*) squilibrare, render pazzo

derangement [dɪ'rendʒmənt] *s* (*disorder*) disordine *m*; (*insanity*) squilibrio mentale, pazzia

der·by [ˈdɑrbi] *s* (**-bies**) bombetta; (*race*) derby *m*

derelict [ˈdɛrɪlɪkt] *adj* derelitto; negligente ‖ *s* derelitto; (naut) relitto

dereliction [‚dɛrɪ'lɪkʃən] *s* (*in one's duty*) negligenza; (law) derelizione

deride [dɪ'raɪd] *tr* deridere, schernire, farsi beffe di

derision [dɪ'rɪʒən] *s* derisione, scherno

derisive [dɪ'raɪsɪv] *adj* derisorio

derivation [‚dɛrɪ'veʃən] *s* derivazione

derivative [dɪ'rɪvətɪv] *adj* & *s* derivato

derive [dɪ'raɪv] *tr* & *intr* derivare

dermatology [‚dɑrmə'tɑlədʒi] *s* dermatologia

derogatory [dɪ'rɑgə‚tori] *adj* dispregiativo

derrick [ˈdɛrɪk] *s* gru *f;* (naut) picco di carico

dervish [ˈdʌrvɪʃ] *s* dervis *m*

desalinization [di‚selɪnɪ'zeʃən] *s* desalazione

desalt [di'sɔlt] *tr* desalificare

descend [dɪ'sɛnd] *tr* discendere ‖ *intr* discendere; **to descend on** calare su, gettarsi su

descendant [dɪ'sɛndənt] *adj* & *s* discendente *mf*

descendent [dɪ'sɛndənt] *adj* discendente

descent [dɪ'sɛnt] *s* (*slope*) china; (*decline*) declino; discesa; (*lineage*) stirpe *f*, discendenza; (*sudden raid*) calata

Descent' from the Cross' *s* Deposizione dalla Croce

describe [dɪ'skraɪb] *tr* descrivere

description [dɪ'skrɪpʃən] *s* descrizione

descriptive [dɪ'skrɪptɪv] *adj* descrittivo

de·scry [dɪ'skraɪ] *v* (*pret & pp* **-scried**) *tr* avvistare

desecrate [ˈdɛsɪ‚kret] *tr* profanare, dissacrare

desecration [‚dɛsɪ'kreʃən] *s* profanazione, dissacrazione

desegregate [di'sɛgrɪ‚get] *intr* sopprimere la segregazione razziale

desegregation [di‚sɛgrɪ'geʃən] *s* desegregazione

desensitize [di'sɛnsɪ‚taɪz] *tr* desensibilizzare

desert [ˈdɛzərt] *adj* & *s* deserto ‖ [dɪ'zʌrt] *s* merito; **he received his just deserts** ricevette quanto meritava ‖ *tr* & *intr* disertare

deserter [dɪ'zʌrtər] *s* disertore *m*

deserted [dɪ'zɛrtɪd] *adj* (*person*) abbandonato; (*place*) deserto

desertion [dɪ'zʌrʃən] *s* diserzione; abbandono del coniuge

deserve [dɪ'zʌrv] *tr* & *intr* meritare

deservedly [dɪ'zʌrvɪdli] *adv* meritatamente, meritevolmente

design [dɪ'zaɪn] *s* disegno; (*of a play*) congegno; **to have designs on** aver mire su ‖ *tr* disegnare; progettare ‖ *intr* disegnare; **designed for** destinato a

designate [ˈdɛzɪg‚net] *tr* designare

designer [dɪ'saɪnər] *s* disegnatore *m*

designing [dɪ'zaɪnɪŋ] *adj* intrigante, macchinatore ‖ *s* disegnazione

desirable [dɪ'zaɪrəbəl] *adj* desiderabile

desire [dɪ'zaɪr] *s* desiderio ‖ *tr* desiderare

desirous [dɪ'zaɪrəs] *adj* desideroso

desist [di'zɪst] *intr* desistere

desk [dɛsk] *s* scrittoio; tavolo d'ufficio;

(*lectern*) leggio; (*of professor*) cattedra; (*of pupil*) banco; (com) cassa

desk'bound' *adj* sedentario; legato al tavolino

desk' pad' *s* blocco da tavolo; blocco per appunti

desolate ['dɛsəlɪt] *adj* desolato, deserto; (*hopeless*) disperato; (*dismal*) lugubre ‖ ['dɛsə,let] *tr* desolare; devastare

desolation [,dɛsə'leʃən] *s* desolazione; devastazione

despair [dɪ'spɛr] *s* disperazione; **to be in despair** disperarsi ‖ *intr* disperare, disperarsi

despairing [dɪ'spɛrɪŋ] *adj* disperato

despera·do [,dɛspə'redo] or [,dɛspə-'rɑdo] *s* (-**does** or -**dos**) fuorilegge disposto a tutto

desperate ['dɛspərɪt] *adj* disposto a tutto; (*hopeless*) disperato; (*very bad*) atroce, terribile; (*bitter, excessive*) accanito; (*remedy*) estremo

desperation [,dɛspə'reʃən] *s* disperazione

despicable ['dɛspɪkəbəl] *adj* spregevole, incanaglito

despise [dɪ'spaɪz] *tr* sprezzare, disprezzare, vilipendere

despite [dɪ'spaɪt] *prep* malgrado

despoil [dɪ'spɔɪl] *tr* spogliare

desponden·cy [dɪ'spɑndənsi] *s* (-**cies**) scoraggiamento, abbattimento

despondent [dɪ'spɑndənt] *adj* scoraggiato, abbattuto

despot ['dɛspɑt] *s* despota *m*

despotic [des'pɑtɪk] *adj* dispotico

despotism ['dɛspə,tɪzəm] *s* dispotismo

dessert [dɪ'zʌrt] *s* dessert *m*

dessert' spoon' *s* cucchiaio or cucchiaino da dessert

destination [,dɛstɪ'neʃən] *s* destinazione

destine ['dɛstɪn] *tr* destinare

desti·ny ['dɛstɪni] *s* (-**nies**) destino

destitute ['dɛstɪ,tjut] or ['dɛstɪ,tut] *adj* (*poverty-stricken*) indigente; (*lacking*) privo

destitution [,dɛstɪ'tjuʃən] or [,dɛstɪ-'tuʃən] *s* indigenza, miseria

destroy [dɪ'strɔɪ] *tr* distruggere

destroyer [dɪ'strɔɪ·ər] *s* (nav) cacciatorpediniere *m*

destruction [dɪ'strʌkʃən] *s* distruzione

destructive [dɪ'strʌktɪv] *adj* distruttivo

desultory ['dɛsəl,tori] *adj* saltuario, sconnesso

detach [dɪ'tætʃ] *tr* staccare, distaccare; (mil) distaccare

detachable [dɪ'tætʃəbəl] *adj* staccabile; separabile

detached [dɪ'tætʃt] *adj* (*e.g., stub*) staccato; (*e.g., house*) discosto; (*aloof*) riservato, freddo; imparziale

detachment [dɪ'tætʃmənt] *s* distacco; imparzialità *f*; (mil) distaccamento

detail [dɪ'tel] or ['ditel] *s* dettaglio, ragguaglio; (mil) distaccamento ‖ [dɪ'tel] *tr* dettagliare; (mil) distaccare

detain [dɪ'ten] *tr* detenere, trattenere

detect [dɪ'tɛkt] *tr* scoprire, discernere; (rad) rivelare

detection [dɪ'tɛkʃən] *s* scoperta; (rad) rivelazione

detective [dɪ'tɛktɪv] *s* detective *m*

detec'tive sto'ry *s* romanzo poliziesco, romanzo giallo

detector [dɪ'tɛktər] *s* (rad) detector *m*, rivelatore *m*

detention [dɪ'tɛnʃən] *s* detenzione

de·ter [dɪ'tʌr] *v* (*pret & pp* -**terred;** *ger* -**terring**) *tr* distogliere, impedire

detergent [dɪ'tʌrdʒənt] *adj & s* detergente *m*

deteriorate [dɪ'tɪrɪ·ə,ret] *tr* deteriorare ‖ *intr* deteriorarsi, andar giù

determination [dɪ,tʌrmɪ'neʃən] *s* determinazione

determine [dɪ'tʌrmɪn] *tr* determinare

determined [dɪ'tʌrmɪnd] *adj* determinato, risoluto

deterrent [dɪ'tʌrənt] *s* deterrente *m*

detest [dɪ'tɛst] *tr* detestare, odiare

dethrone [dɪ'θron] *tr* detronizzare

detonate ['dɛtə,net] or ['dɪtə,net] *tr* far scoppiare ‖ *intr* detonare

detonator ['dɛtə,netər] *s* innesco

detour ['ditur] or [dɪ'tur] *s* deviazione ‖ *tr* far deviare ‖ *intr* deviare

detract [dɪ'trækt] *tr* detrarre ‖ *intr*— **to detract from** diminuire

detractor [dɪ'træktər] *s* detrattore *m*

detriment ['dɛtrɪmənt] *s* detrimento; **to the detriment of** a danno di

detrimental [,dɛtrɪ'mɛntəl] *adj* pregiudizievole

deuce [djus] or [dus] *s* (cards) due *m*; **the deuce!** diavolo!

devaluate [di'vælju,et] *tr* svalutare

devaluation [di,vælju'eʃən] *s* devalutazione, svalutazione

devastate ['dɛvəs,tet] *tr* devastare

devastating ['dɛvəs,tetɪŋ] *adj* devastatore, devastante; (*e.g., reply*) schiacciante, annichilante

devastation [,dɛvəs'teʃən] *s* devastazione

develop [dɪ'vɛləp] *tr* sviluppare; (phot) sviluppare, rivelare ‖ *intr* svilupparsi; manifestarsi

developer [dɪ'vɛləpər] *s* (*e.g., of a new engine*) sfruttatore *m;* (*in real estate*) specialista *mf* in lottizzazione; (phot) sviluppatore *m*, rivelatore *m*

development [dɪ'vɛləpmənt] *s* sviluppo; valorizzazione; sfruttamento; (phot) rivelazione

deviate ['divi,et] *tr* sviare ‖ *intr* deviare, sviarsi

deviation [,divi'eʃən] *s* deviazione

deviationism [,divi'eʃə,nɪzəm] *s* deviazionismo

deviationist [,divi'eʃənɪst] *s* deviazionista *mf*

device [dɪ'vaɪs] *s* dispositivo, congegno; (*trick*) stratagemma *m;* (*motto*) divisa, emblema *m;* **to leave s.o. to his own devices** lasciare che qlcu faccia come gli pare e piace

dev·il ['dɛvəl] *s* diavolo; **between the devil and the deep blue sea** fra l'incudine e il martello; **to raise the devil** (slang) fare diavolo a quattro ‖ *v* (*pret & pp* -**iled** or -**illed;** *ger*

-iling or **-illing**) *tr* condire con spezie or con pepe; (coll) infastidire

devilish ['dɛvəlɪʃ] *adj* diabolico

devilment ['dɛvəlmənt] *s* (*mischief*) diavoleria; (*evil*) cattiveria

devil·try ['dɛvəltri] *s* (**-tries**) malvagità *f*, crudeltà *f*; (*mischief*) diavoleria

devious ['divɪ·əs] *adj* (*tricky*) traverso; (*roundabout*) tortuoso

devise [dɪ'vaɪz] *tr* ideare, inventare; (law) legare, disporre per testamento

devoid [dɪ'vɔɪd] *adj* sprovvisto

devolve [dɪ'valv] *intr*—**to devolve on** ricadere su

devote [dɪ'vot] *tr* dedicare

devoted [dɪ'votɪd] *adj* devoto; dedito, dedicato

devotee [,dɛvə'ti] *s* devoto; (*fan*) fanatico, tifoso, entusiasta *mf*

devotion [dɪ'voʃən] *s* devozione; (*e.g., to work*) dedizione; **devotions** orazioni *mpl*, preghiere *fpl*

devour [dɪ'vaur] *tr* divorare

devout [dɪ'vaut] *adj* devoto; sincero

dew [dju] or [du] *s* rugiada

dew'drop' *s* goccia di rugiada

dew'lap' *s* giogaia

dew·y ['dju·i] or ['du·i] *adj* (**-ier; -iest**) rugiadoso

dexterity [dɛks'tɛrɪti] *s* destrezza

diabetes [,daɪ·ə'bitɪs] or [,daɪ·ə'bitiz] *s* diabete *m*

diabetic [,daɪ·ə'bɛtɪk] or [,daɪ·ə-'bitɪk] *adj & s* diabetico

diabolic(al) [,daɪ·ə'balɪk(əl)] *adj* diabolico

diadem ['daɪ·ə,dɛm] *s* diadema *m*

diaere·sis [daɪ'ɛrɪsɪs] *s* (**-ses** [,siz]) dieresi *f*

diagnose [,daɪ·əg'nos] or [,daɪ·əg-'noz] *tr* diagnosticare

diagno·sis [,daɪ·əg'nosɪs] *s* (**-ses** [siz]) diagnosi *f*

diagonal [daɪ'ægənəl] *adj & s* diagonale *f*

dia·gram ['daɪ·ə,græm] *s* diagramma *m;* (*drawing*) schema *m;* (*plan*) prospetto ‖ *v* (*pret & pp* **-gramed** or **-grammed**) *ger* **-graming** or **-gramming**) *tr* diagrammare

dial ['daɪ·əl] *s* (*of watch*) quadrante *m;* (rad) tabella graduata, sintogramma *m;* (telp) disco combinatore ‖ *tr* (rad) sintonizzare; (*a person*) (telp) chiamare; (*a number*) (telp) comporre; (*the phone*) (telp) comporre il numero di ‖ *intr* (telp) comporre il numero

dialect ['daɪ·ə,lɛkt] *s* dialetto

dialing ['daɪ·əlɪŋ] *s* composizione del numero

dialogue ['daɪ·ə,lɔg] or ['daɪ·ə,lɑg] *s* dialogo

di'al tel'ephone *s* telefono automatico

di'al tone' *s* (telp) segnale *m* di via libera

diameter [daɪ'æmɪtər] *s* diametro

diametric(al) [,daɪ·ə'mɛtrɪk(əl)] *adj* diametrico, diametrale

diamond ['daɪmənd] *s* diamante *m;* (*figure of a rhombus*) losanga; (baseball) diamante *m;* **diamonds** (cards) quadri *mpl*

diaper ['daɪ·pər] *s* pannolino

diaphanous [daɪ'æfənəs] *adj* diafano

diaphragm ['daɪ·ə,fræm] *s* diaframma *m;* (teip) membrana

diar·rhea [,daɪ·ə'ri·ə] *s* diarrea

dia·ry ['daɪ·əri] *s* (**-ries**) diario

diastole [daɪ'æstəli] *s* diastole *f*

diathermy ['daɪ·ə,θʌrmi] *s* diatermia

dice [daɪs] *spl* dadi *mpl;* (*small cubes*) cubetti *mpl;* **no dice** (slang) niente da fare; (slang) risposta a picche

dice' cup' *s* bussolotto

dichloride [daɪ'klɔraɪd] *s* bicloruro

dichoto·my [daɪ'katəmi] *s* (**-mies**) ditomia

dickey ['dɪki] *s* camiciola; (*starched insert*) sparato; (*bib*) bavaglino

dictaphone ['dɪktə,fon] *s* dittafono

dictate ['dɪktet] *s* dettato ‖ ['dɪktet] or [dɪk'tet] *tr* dettare

dictation [dɪk'teʃən] *s* dettato; (*act of ordering*) ordine *m;* **to take dictation** scrivere sotto dettatura

dictator ['dɪktetər] or [dɪk'tetər] *s* dittatore *m*

dictatorship ['dɪktetər,ʃɪp] or [dɪk-'tetər/ɪp] *s* dittatura

diction ['dɪkʃən] *s* dizione

dictionar·y ['dɪkʃən,ɛri] *s* (**-ies**) dizionario, vocabolario

dic·tum ['dɪktəm] *s* (**-ta** [tə]) detto, sentenza

didactic(al) [daɪ'dæktɪk(əl)] or [dɪ-'dæktɪk(əl)] *adj* didattico

die [daɪ] *s* (**dice** [daɪs]) dado; **the die is cast** il dado è tratto ‖ *s* (**dies**) (*for stamping coins, medals, etc.*) stampo; (*for cutting threads*) filiera ‖ *v* (*pret & pp* **died;** *ger* **dying**) *intr* morire; **to die hard** morire lentamente; morire lottando; **to die laughing** morire dalle risa; **to die off** morire uno per uno

die'-hard' *adj & s* intransigente *m*

die'sel oil' ['dizəl] *s* nafta, gasolio

die'stock' *s* girafiliera

diet ['daɪ·ət] *s* dieta, regime *m* ‖ *intr* stare a dieta

dietetic [,daɪ·ə'tɛtɪk] *adj* dietetico ‖ **dietetics** *ssg* dietetica

dietitian [,daɪ·ə'tɪ/ən] *s* dietista *mf*

differ ['dɪfər] *intr* (*to be different*) differire, differenziarsi; **to differ with** dissentire da

difference ['dɪfərəns] *s* differenza; **to make no difference** fare lo stesso; **to split the difference** dividere la differenza; (fig) venire a un compromesso

different ['dɪfərənt] *adj* differente

differential [,dɪfə'rɛn/əl] *adj & s* differenziale *m*

differentiate [,dɪfə'rɛn/ɪ,et] *tr* differenziare ‖ *intr* differenziarsi

difficult ['dɪfɪ,kʌlt] *adj* difficile

difficul·ty ['dɪfɪ,kʌlti] *s* (**-ties**) difficoltà *f*

diffident ['dɪfɪdənt] *adj* timido, imbarazzato

diffuse [dɪ'fjus] *adj* diffuso ‖ [dɪ'fjuz] *tr* diffondere ‖ *intr* diffondersi

dig [dɪg] *s* (*poke*) botta, spintone *m;* (*jibe*) stoccata, fiancata ‖ *v* (*pret & pp* **dug** [dʌg];* ger* **digging**) *tr* scavare, sterrare; **to dig up** dissodare; (*to uncover*) dissotterrare ‖ *intr* scavare; **to dig in** (mil) fortificarsi; **to dig into** (coll) sprofondarsi in

digest ['daidʒest] *s* compendio; (law) digesto ‖ [dɪ'dʒest] or [daɪ'dʒest] *tr & intr* digerire

digestible [dɪ'dʒestɪbəl] or [daɪ'dʒestɪbəl] *adj* digeribile, digestibile

digestion [dɪ'dʒestʃən] or [daɪ'dʒestʃən] *s* digestione

digestive [dɪ'dʒestɪv] or [daɪ'dʒestɪv] *adj* (*tube*) digerente ‖ *s* digestivo

digit ['dɪdʒɪt] *s* cifra, unità *f;* (*finger*) dito; (*toe*) dito del piede

dig'ital clock' *s* orologio a scatto

digitalis [,dɪdʒɪ'tælɪs] or [,dɪdʒɪ-'telɪs] *s* (bot) digitale *f;* (pharm) digitalina

dignified ['dɪgnɪ,faɪd] *adj* dignitoso, fiero, contegnoso

digni·fy ['dɪgnɪ,faɪ] *v* (*pret & pp* -fied) *tr* (*to ennoble*) nobilitare; onorare, esaltare; dare la dignità a

dignitar·y ['dɪgnɪ,teri] *s* (-ies) dignitario; **dignitaries** dignità *fpl*

digni·ty ['dɪgnɪti] *s* (-ties) dignità *f,* decoro; **to stand on one's dignity** mantenere la propria dignità

digress [dɪ'gres] or [daɪ'gres] *intr* digredire, divagare

digression [dɪ'greʃən] or [daɪ'greʃən] *s* digressione, divagazione

dike [daɪk] *s* diga; (*in a river*) argine *m;* (*ditch*) fosso; scarpata

dilapidated [dɪ'læpɪ,detɪd] *adj* dilapidato, decrepito

dilate [daɪ'let] *tr* dilatare ‖ *intr* dilatarsi

dilatory ['dɪlə,tori] *adj* lento, tardivo; (*e.g., strategy*) dilatorio

dilemma [dɪ'lemə] *s* dilemma *m*

dilettan·te [,dɪlə'tænti] *adj* dilettantesco ‖ *s* (-tes or -ti [ti]) dilettante *mf*

diligence ['dɪlɪdʒəns] *s* diligenza

diligent ['dɪlɪdʒənt] *adj* diligente

dill [dɪl] *s* (bot) aneto

dillydal·ly ['dɪlɪ,dæli] *v* (*pret & pp* -lied) *intr* farla lunga

dilute [dɪ'lut] or [daɪ'lut] *adj* diluito ‖ [dɪ'lut] *tr* diluire ‖ *intr* diluirsi

dilution [dɪ'luʃən] *s* diluizione

dim [dɪm] *adj* (**dimmer; dimmest**) (*light*) fioco; (*sight*) debole; (*memory*) vago; (*color*) smorzato; (*sound*) sordo; **to take a dim view of** avere una visione pessimistica di ‖ *v* (*pret & pp* **dimmed; ger dimming**) *tr* (*lights*) smorzare; **to dim the headlights** abbassare i fari

dime [daɪm] *s* moneta di dieci centesimi di dollaro

dimension [dɪ'menʃən] *s* dimensione

diminish [dɪ'mɪnɪʃ] *tr & intr* diminuire, scemare

diminutive [dɪ'mɪnjətɪv] *adj* (*tiny*) minuscolo; (gram) diminutivo ‖ *s* diminutivo

dimly ['dɪmli] *adv* indistintamente

dimmer ['dɪmər] *s* smorzatore *m;* (aut) luce *f* di incrocio; **dimmers** fari *mpl* antiabbaglianti

dimple ['dɪmpəl] *s* fossetta

dimwit ['dɪm,wɪt] *s* (slang) stupido, cretino

din [dɪn] *s* fragore *m,* frastuono ‖ *v* (*pret & pp* **dinned; ger dinning**) *tr* assordare; **to din s.th into s.o.'s ears** rintronare qlco nelle orecchie di qlcu

dine [daɪn] *tr* offrire un pranzo a; offrire una cena a ‖ *intr* pasteggiare; cenare; **to dine out** mangiare fuori di casa

diner ['daɪnər] *s* commensale *m;* (rr) vettura ristorante; (U.S.A.) ristorante *m* a forma di vagone

ding-dong ['dɪŋ,dɒŋ] or ['dɪŋ,dɑŋ] *s* dindon *m*

din·gy ['dɪndʒi] *adj* (**-gier; -giest**) sporco, sbiadito

din'ing car' *s* vagone *m* ristorante

din'ing room' *s* sala da pranzo

dinner ['dɪnər] *s* cena; pranzo; (*formal meal*) banchetto

din'ner coat' or **jack'et** *s* smoking *m*

din'ner knife' *s* coltello da tavola

din'ner set' *s* servizio da tavola

din'ner ta'ble *s* desco

din'ner time' *s* ora di pranzo or di cena

dinosaur ['daɪnə,sɔr] *s* dinosauro

dint [dɪnt] *s* tacca, ammaccatura; **by dint of** a forza di ‖ *tr* ammaccare

diocese ['daɪ·ə,sis] or ['daɪ·əsis] *s* diocesi *f*

diode ['daɪ·od] *s* diodo

dioxide [daɪ'aksaɪd] *s* biossido

dip [dɪp] *s* immersione; (*brief swim*) tuffo, nuotata; (*in a road*) depressione; inclinazione magnetica ‖ *v* (*pret & pp* **dipped; ger dipping**) *tr* immergere, tuffare; (*the flag*) abbassare; (*bread*) inzuppare ‖ *intr* immergersi, tuffarsi; inclinarsi; (*to drop down*) sparire subitamente; **to dip into** (*a book*) sfogliare; (*business*) mettersi in; (*a container of liquids*) intingere; **to dip into one's purse** spendere soldi

diphtheria [dɪf'θɪrɪ·ə] *s* difterite *f*

diphthong ['dɪfθɔŋ] or ['dɪfθɑŋ] *s* dittongo

diphthongize ['dɪfθɔŋ,gaɪz] or ['dɪfθɑŋ,gaɪz] *tr & intr* dittongare

diploma [dɪ'plomə] *s* diploma *m*

diploma·cy [dɪ'ploməsi] *s* (-cies) diplomazia

diplomat ['dɪplə,mæt] *s* diplomatico

diplomatic [,dɪplə'mætɪk] *adj* diplomatico

dip'lomat'ic pouch' *s* valigia diplomatica

dipper ['dɪpər] *s* mestolo

dip'stick' *s* asta di livello

dire [daɪr] *adj* terribile, orrendo

direct [dɪ'rekt] or [daɪ'rekt] *adj* diretto; sincero ‖ *tr* dirigere; ordinare

direct' cur'rent *s* corrente continua

direct' dis'course *s* discorso diretto

direct' dis'tance di'aling *s* (telp) teleselezione *f*

direct' hit' *s* colpo centrato

direction [dɪ'rekʃən] or [daɪ'rekʃən] *s* direzione; **directions** istruzioni *fpl;* (*for use*) indicazioni *fpl* per l'uso

directional [dɪ'rɛkʃənəl] or [daɪ-'rɛkʃənəl] *adj* direzionale

directive [dɪ'rɛktɪv] or [daɪ'rɛktɪv] *s* direttiva

direct' ob'ject *s* (gram) complemento diretto, complemento oggetto

director [dɪ'rɛktər] or [daɪ'rɛktər] *s* direttore *m*, gerente *m;* (*member of a governing body*) consigliere *m*

directorship [dɪ'rɛktər‚ʃɪp] or [daɪ-'rɛktər‚ʃɪp] *s* direzione; amministrazione

directo·ry [dɪ'rɛktəri] or [daɪ'rɛktəri] *s* (**-ries**) (*board of directors*) direzione, direttorio; (*list of names and addresses*) rubrica, elenco; (telp) elenco dei telefoni, guida telefonica

dirge [dʌrdʒ] *s* canto funebre

dirigible ['dɪrɪdʒɪbəl] *adj & s* dirigibile *m*

dirt [dʌrt] *s* (*soil*) terra, suolo; (*dust*) polvere *m;* (*mud*) fango; (*accumulation of dirt*) sudiciume *m*, lerciume *m;* (*moral filth*) porcheria, sozzura; (*gossip*) pettegolezzi *mpl;* **to do s.o. dirt** (slang) calunniare qlcu

dirt'-cheap' *adj* a prezzo bassissimo

dirt' road' *s* strada di terra battuta

dirt·y ['dʌrti] *adj* (**-ier; -iest**) sporco, sudicio; fangoso; polveroso; (*e.g., spinach*) terroso; (*obscene*) sconcio, lurido; immondo‚ || *v* (*pret & pp* **-ied**) *tr* sporcare, insudiciare, imbrattare

dir'ty lin'en *s* roba sporca; **to air one's dirty linen in public** mettere i panni al sole

dir'ty trick' *s* brutto tiro

disabili·ty [‚dɪsə'bɪlɪti] *s* (**-ties**) incapacità *f*, invalidità *f*

disabil'ity insur'ance *s* assicurazione invalidità

disable [dɪs'ebəl] *tr* mutilare, storpiare; (*a ship*) smantellare; (law) invalidare

disabuse [‚dɪsə'bjuz] *tr* disingannare

disadvantage [‚dɪsəd'væntɪdʒ] or [‚dɪsəd'vɑntɪdʒ] *s* svantaggio

disadvantageous [dɪs‚ædvən'tedʒəs] *adj* svantaggioso

disagree [‚dɪsə'gri] *intr* discordare, disconvenire; (*to quarrel*) litigare, altercare; **to disagree with** non essere del parere di

disagreeable [‚dɪsə'gri·əbəl] *adj* sgradevole

disagreement [‚dɪsə'grimənt] *s* sconcordanza, dissidio, dissenso

disallow [‚dɪsə'lau] *tr* non permettere, rifiutare

disappear [‚dɪsə'pɪr] *intr* sparire, scomparire

disappearance [‚dɪsə'pɪrəns] *s* scomparsa

disappoint [‚dɪsə'pɔɪnt] *tr* deludere, disilludere; **to be disappointed** rimanere deluso

disappointment [‚dɪsə'pɔɪntmənt] *s* delusione, disinganno, disappunto

disapproval [‚dɪsə'pruvəl] *s* disapprovazione, riprova

disapprove [‚dɪsə'pruv] *tr & intr* disapprovare

disarm [dɪs'ɑrm] *tr* disarmare || *intr* disarmare, disarmarsi

disarmament [dɪs'ɑrməmənt] *s* disarmo

disarming [dɪs'ɑrmɪŋ] *adj* ingraziante, simpatico

disarray [‚dɪsə're] *s* disordine *m*, scompiglio; (*of apparel*) sciatteria || *tr* scomporre, scompigliare

disassemble [‚dɪsə'sɛmbəl] *tr* smontare, sconnettere

disassociate [‚dɪsə'soʃɪ‚et] *tr* dissociare, disassociare

disaster [dɪ'zæstər] or [dɪ'zɑstər] *s* disastro, sinistro

disastrous [dɪ'zæstrəs] or [dɪ'zɑstrəs] *adj* disastroso

disavow [‚dɪsə'vau] *tr* sconfessare

disavowal [‚dɪsə'vau·əl] *s* sconfessione

disband [dɪs'bænd] *tr* (*an assembly*) sciogliere; (*troops*) congedare; (*any group*) sbandare || *intr* sbandarsi

dis·bar [dɪs'bɑr] *v* (*pret & pp* **-barred;** *ger* **-barring**) *tr* (law) radiare dall'albo degli avvocati

disbelief [‚dɪsbɪ'lif] *s* incredulità *f*

disbelieve [‚dɪsbɪ'liv] *tr* rifiutarsi di credere a || *intr* rifiutarsi di credere

disburse [dɪs'bʌrs] *tr* sborsare

disbursement [dɪs'bʌrsmənt] *s* sborso, disborso

discard [dɪs'kɑrd] *s* scarto, scartina; **to put into the discard** scartare || *tr* scartare

discern [dɪ'zʌrn] or [dɪ'sʌrn] *tr* scernere, discernere, severare

discernible [dɪ'zʌrnɪbəl] or [dɪ'sʌrnɪbəl] *adj* discernibile

discerning [dɪ'zʌrnɪŋ] or [dɪ'sʌrnɪŋ] *adj* perspicace, oculato

discernment [dɪ'zʌrnmənt] or [dɪ-'sʌrnmənt] *s* discernimento

discharge [dɪs'tʃɑrdʒ] *s* (*of a load*) scarico; (*of a gun; of electricity*) scarica; (*of a prisoner*) liberazione; (*of a duty*) adempimento; (*of a debt*) pagamento; (*from a job*) licenziamento; (mil) foglio di congedo; (pathol) spurgo || *tr* scaricare; (*a duty*) adempiere; (*a prisoner*) liberare; (*a debt*) pagare; (*an employee*) licenziare; (*a patient*) lasciar uscire; (*a passenger from a ship*) sbarcare; (*a battery*) scaricare; (mil) congedare || *intr* (*said, e.g., of a liquid*) sboccare; (*said of a gun or a battery*) scaricarsi

disciple [dɪ'saɪpəl] *s* discepolo

disciplinarian [‚dɪsɪplɪ'nɛrɪ·ən] *s* disciplinatore *m;* partigiano di una forte disciplina

disciplinary ['dɪsɪplɪ‚nɛri] *adj* disciplinare

discipline ['dɪsɪplɪn] *s* disciplina; castigo || *tr* disciplinare; castigare

disclaim [dɪs'klem] *tr* non riconoscere, negare

disclose [dɪs'kloz] *tr* rivelare, scoprire

disclosure [dɪs'kloʒər] *s* rivelazione, scoperta; divulgazione

discolor [dɪs'kʌlər] *tr* scolorare, scolorire || *intr* scolorirsi

discoloration [dɪs‚kʌlə'reʃən] *s* discolorazione

discomfit [dɪs'kʌmfɪt] *tr* sconcertare, turbare; frustrare, battere, mettere in fuga

discomfiture [dɪs'kʌmfɪtʃər] *s* sconcerto, turbamento; frustrazione; disfatta

discomfort [dɪs'kʌmfərt] *s* disagio || *tr* incomodare

disconcert [,dɪskən'sʌrt] *tr* sconcertare

disconnect [,dɪskə'nɛkt] *tr* sconnettere; (elec) disinserire

disconsolate [dɪs'kɑnsəlɪt] *adj* sconsolato, desolato

discontent [,dɪskən'tɛnt] *adj* & *s* scontento || *tr* scontentare

discontented [,dɪskən'tɛntɪd] *adj* scontento

discontinue [,dɪskən'tɪnju] *tr* cessare, interrompere

discord ['dɪskərd] *s* discordia, dissidio

discordance [dɪs'kɔrdəns] *s* discordanza

discotheque [,dɪsko'tɛk] *s* discoteca

discount ['dɪskaunt] *s* sconto || ['dɪskaunt] *or* [dɪs'kaunt] *tr* scontare; (*news*) fare la tara a

dis'count rate' *s* tasso di sconto

discourage [dɪs'kʌrɪdʒ] *tr* scoraggiare, sconfortare; (*to dissuade*) sconsigliare

discouragement [dɪs'kʌrɪdʒmənt] *s* scoraggiamento; disapprovazione

discourse ['dɪskors] *or* [dɪs'kors] *s* discorso || [dɪs'kors] *intr* discorrere

discourteous [dɪs'kʌrtɪ·əs] *adj* scortese

discourte·sy [dɪs'kʌrtəsi] *s* (-sies) scortesia

discover [dɪs'kʌvər] *tr* scoprire

discoverer [dɪs'kʌvərər] *s* scopritore *m*

discover·y [dɪs'kʌvəri] *s* (-ies) scoperta

discredit [dɪs'krɛdɪt] *s* discredito || *tr* screditare

discreditable [dɪs'krɛdɪtəbəl] *adj* indegno, disonorevole

discreet [dɪs'krit] *adj* discreto

discrepan·cy [dɪs'krɛpənsi] *s* (-cies) discrepanza, divario

discretion [dɪs'krɛʃən] *s* discrezione

discriminate [dɪs'krɪmɪ,net] *tr* discriminare || *intr*—**to discriminate against** fare delle discriminazioni contro

discrimination [dɪs,krɪmɪ'neʃən] *s* discriminazione

discriminatory [dɪs'krɪmɪnə,tori] *adj* discriminante

discuss [dɪs'kʌs] *tr* & *intr* discutere

discussion [dɪs'kʌʃən] *s* discussione

discus thrower ['dɪskəs 'θro·ər] *s* discobolo

disdain [dɪs'den] *s* disdegno || *tr* disdegnare, sdegnare

disdainful [dɪs'denfəl] *adj* sdegnoso

disease [dɪ'ziz] *s* malattia

diseased [dɪ'zizd] *adj* malato

disembark [,dɪsɛm'bark] *tr* & *intr* sbarcare

disembarkation [dɪs,ɛmbar'keʃən] *s* sbarco

disembowel [,dɪsɛm'bau·əl] *tr* sbudellare, sventrare

disenchant [,dɪsɛn'tʃænt] *or* [,dɪsɛn'tʃɑnt] *tr* disincantare

disenchantment [,dɪsɛn'tʃæntmənt] *or* [,dɪsɛn'tʃɑntmənt] *s* disinganno

disengage [,dɪsɛn'gedʒ] *tr* (*from a pledge*) svincolare; (*to disconnect*) sgranare, disinnestare; (mil) sganciare

disengagement [,dɪsɛn'gedʒmənt] *s* liberazione; disinnesto; svincolamento

disentangle [,dɪsɛn'tæŋgəl] *tr* disincagliare, districare

disentanglement [,dɪsɛn'tæŋgəlmənt] *s* districamento

disestablish [,dɪsɛs'tæblɪʃ] *tr* (*the Church*) separare dallo Stato

disfavor [dɪs'fevər] *s* disfavore *m*

disfigure [dɪs'fɪgjər] *tr* sfigurare, deturpare

disfigurement [dɪs'fɪgjərmənt] *s* deturpazione

disfranchise [dɪs'fræntʃaɪz] *tr* privare dei diritti civili

disgorge [dɪs'gɔrdʒ] *tr* vomitare; (*something illicitly obtained*) restituire; (*said of a river*) scaricare || *intr* vomitare; scaricarsi

disgrace [dɪs'gres] *s* vergogna; disgrazia || *tr* disonorare; privare del favore

disgraceful [dɪs'gresfəl] *adj* infamante, disonorante

disgruntle [dɪs'grʌntəl] *tr* scontentare, irritare

disgruntled [dɪs'grʌntəld] *adj* irritato, di cattivo umore

disguise [dɪs'gaɪz] *s* travestimento || *tr* travestire, dissimulare

disgust [dɪs'gʌst] *s* disgusto, schifo || *tr* disgustare, fare schifo a

disgusting [dɪs'gʌstɪŋ] *adj* disgustoso, schifoso

dish [dɪʃ] *s* piatto, **dishes** vasellame *m*; **to wash the dishes** fare i piatti || *tr* scodellare; (*to defeat*) (slang) sconfiggere; **to dish out** (slang) distribuire

dish'cloth' *s* canovaccio, strofinaccio

dishearten [dɪs'hartən] *tr* scoraggiare, disanimare, desolare

dishev·el [dɪ'ʃɛvəl] *v* (*pret* & *pp* **-eled** *or* **-elled**; *ger* **-eling** *or* **-elling**) *tr* scomporre, scarmigliare, scapigliare

dishonest [dɪs'anɪst] *adj* disonesto

dishones·ty [dɪs'anɪsti] *s* (-ties) disonestà *f*

dishonor [dɪs'anər] *s* disonore *m* || *tr* disonorare; (com) rifiutare di pagare

dishonorable [dɪs'anərəbəl] *adj* disonorevole, disonorante

dish'pan' *s* bacinella per lavare i piatti

dish'rack' *s* portapiatti *m*, sgocciolatoio

dish'rag' *s* canovaccio, strofinaccio

dish'towel' *s* canovaccio per le stoviglie

dish'wash'er *s* (*person*) sguattero, lavapiatti *m;* (*machine*) lavastoviglie *m* & *f*

dish'wa'ter *s* lavatura di piatti

disillusion [,dɪsɪ'luʒən] *s* disillusione || *tr* disilludere

disillusionment [,dɪsɪ'luʒənmənt] *s* disillusione

disinclination [dɪs,ɪnklɪ'neʃən] *s* riluttanza, avversione

disinclined [,dɪsɪn'klaɪnd] *adj* riluttante, avverso

disinfect [,dɪsɪn'fɛkt] *tr* disinfettare
disinfectant [,dɪsɪn'fɛktənt] *adj* & *s* disinfettante *m*
disingenuous [,dɪsɪn'dʒɛnjʊ·əs] *adj* poco schietto, insincero
disinherit [,dɪsɪn'hɛrɪt] *tr* diseredare
disintegrate [dɪs'ɪntɪ ,gret] *tr* disintegrare, disgregare || *intr* disintegrarsi, disgregarsi
disintegration [dɪs ,ɪntɪ'greʃən] *s* disintegrazione, disgregamento
disin·ter [,dɪsɪn'tʌr] *v* (*pret* & *pp* -terred; *ger* -terring) *tr* dissotterrare
disinterested [dɪs'ɪntə ,rɛstɪd] or [dɪs-'ɪntrɪstɪd] *adj* disinteressato
disjunctive [dɪs'dʒʌŋktɪv] *adj* disgiuntivo
disk [dɪsk] *s* disco; (*of ski pole*) rotella
disk' jock'ey *s* presentatore *m* di un programma radiodiffuso di dischi
dislike [dɪs'laɪk] *s* antipatia, avversione; **to take a dislike for** prendere in uggia || *tr* non piacere (with *dat*), e.g., **he dislikes wine** non gli piace il vino
dislocate ['dɪslo ,ket] *tr* spostare, mettere fuori posto; (*a bone*) slogare
dislodge [dɪs'lɑdʒ] *tr* sloggiare
disloyal [dɪs'lɔɪ·əl] *adj* sleale
disloyal·ty [dɪs'lɔɪ·əlti] *s* (-ties) slealtà *f*
dismal ['dɪzməl] *adj* tetro, triste; cattivo, orribile
dismantle [dɪs'mæntəl] *tr* smontare, smantellare; (*a fortress*) sguarnire
dismay [dɪs'me] *s* costernazione || *tr* costernare
dismember [dɪs'mɛmbər] *tr* smembrare
dismiss [dɪs'mɪs] *tr* congedare; (*to fire*) licenziare; (*a subject*) scartare; (*from the mind*) scacciare
dismissal [dɪs'mɪsəl] *s* congedo; licenziamento
dismount [dɪs'maunt] *tr* disarcionare || *intr* scendere, smontare
disobedience [,dɪsə'bidɪ·əns] *s* disubbidienza
disobedient [,dɪsə'bidɪ·ənt] *adj* disubbidiente
disobey [,dɪsə'be] *tr* disubbidire (with *dat*) || *intr* disubbidire
disorder [dɪs'ɔrdər] *s* disordine *m* || *tr* disordinare, confondere
disorderly [dɪs'ɔrdərli] *adj* disordinato, confuso; (*unruly*) turbolento
disor'derly con'duct *s* contegno contrario all'ordine pubblico
disor'derly house' *s* bordello, lupanare *m*
disorganize [dɪs'ɔrgə ,naɪz] *tr* disorganizzare
disoriented [dɪs'ori ,ɛntid] *adj* disorientato
disown [dɪs'on] *tr* disconoscere
disparage [dɪs'pærɪdʒ] *tr* svilire, deprezzare
disparagement [dɪs'pærɪdʒmənt] *s* discredito, deprezzamento
disparate ['dɪspərɪt] *adj* disparato
dispari·ty [dɪs'pærɪti] *s* (-ties) disparità *f*, spareggio
dispassionate [dɪs'pæʃənɪt] *adj* spassionato

dispatch [dɪs'pætʃ] *s* dispaccio || *tr* spedire; (*to dismiss*) congedare; uccidere; (*a meal*) (coll) liquidare
dis·pel [dɪs'pɛl] *v* (*pret* & *pp* -pelled; *ger* -pelling) *tr* dissipare
dispensa·ry [dɪs'pɛnsəri] *s* (-ries) dispensario
dispensation [,dɪspɛn'seʃən] *s* (*dispensing*) distribuzione, dispensa; (*exemption*) dispensa
dispense [dɪs'pɛns] *tr* (*medicines*) distribuire; (*justice*) amministrare; (*to distribute*) dispensare; (*to exempt*) esimere || *intr* —**to dispense with** fare a meno di; esimersi da
dispenser [dɪ'spɛnsər] *s* dispensatore *m*; (*automatic*) distributore *m*
disperse [dɪs'pʌrs] *tr* disperdere || *intr* disperdersi
dispersion [dɪ'spʌrʒən] or [dɪ'spɛrʃən] *s* dispersione
dispersive [dɪ'spʌrsɪv] *adj* dispersivo
dispirit [dɪ'spɪrɪt] *tr* scoraggiare
displace [dɪs'ples] *tr* muovere; costringere a lasciare il proprio paese; (*to supplant*) rimpiazzare; (naut) dislocare
displaced' per'son *s* rifugiato politico
displacement [dɪs'plesmənt] *s* spostamento; sostituzione; (*of a piston*) cilindrata; (naut) dislocamento
display [dɪs'ple] *s* sfoggio, mostra || *tr* mostrare; (*e.g., in a store window*) mettere in mostra; (*to unfold*) spiegare; (*to show ostentatiously*) sfoggiare, ostentare; (*ignorance*) rivelare
display' cab'inet *s* bacheca
display' win'dow *s* mostra, vetrina
displease [dɪs'pliz] *tr* dispiacere (with *dat*)
displeasing [dɪs'plizɪŋ] *adj* spiacevole
displeasure [dɪs'plɛʒər] *s* dispiacere *m*; sfavore *m*
disposable [dɪs'pozəbəl] *adj* (*available*) disponibile; (*made to be thrown away after use*) scartabile, da gettarsi via, usa e getta
disposal [dɪs'pozəl] *s* disposizione; eliminazione; **to have at one's disposal** disporre di
dispose [dɪs'poz] *tr* disporre; **to dispose of** disporre di; (*to get rid of*) sbarazzarsi di; vendere
disposed [dɪ'spozd] *adj* —**to be disposed to** essere disposto a
disposition [,dɪspə'zɪʃən] *s* disposizione; (*mental outlook*) indole *f*; tendenza; (mil) ordinamento
dispossess [,dɪspə'zɛs] *tr* spodestare, bandire; (*to evict*) sfrattare
disproof [dɪs'pruf] *s* confutazione
disproportionate [,dɪsprə'porʃənɪt] *adj* sproporzionato
disprove [dɪs'pruv] *tr* confutare
dispute [dɪs'pjut] *s* disputa; **beyond dispute** incontestabile; **in dispute** in discussione || *tr* & *intr* disputare
disquali·fy [dɪs'kwɑlɪ ,faɪ] *v* (*pret* & *pp* -fied) *tr* squalificare
disquiet [dɪs'kwaɪ·ət] *s* inquietudine *f* || *tr* inquietare, turbare
disquisition [,dɪskwɪ'zɪʃən] *s* disquisizione

disregard [ˌdɪsrɪ'gɑrd] s (of a rule) inosservanza; (of danger) disprezzo, noncuranza ‖ tr non fare attenzione a

disrepair [ˌdɪsrɪ'pɛr] s cattivo stato, rovina

disreputable [dɪs'rɛpjətəbəl] adj malfamato; disonorevole; (in bad condition) raso, logoro

disrepute [ˌdɪsrɪ'pjut] s cattiva fama; **to bring into disrepute** rovinare la reputazione di

disrespect [ˌdɪsrɪ'spɛkt] s mancanza di rispetto ‖ tr mancare di rispetto a

disrespectful [ˌdɪsrɪ'spɛktfəl] adj non rispettoso, irriverente

disrobe [dɪs'rob] tr svestire ‖ intr svestirsi, spogliarsi

disrupt [dɪs'rʌpt] tr disorganizzare; interrompere

disruption [dɪs'rʌpʃən] s rottura; disorganizzazione

dissatisfaction [ˌdɪssætɪs'fækʃən] s scontento, malcontento

dissatisfied [dɪs'sætɪsˌfaɪd] adj scontento, malcontento; insoddisfatto

dissatis·fy [dɪs'sætɪsˌfaɪ] v (pret & pp -fied) tr scontentare

dissect [dɪ'sɛkt] tr sezionare

dissemble [dɪ'sɛmbəl] tr & intr dissimulare

disseminate [dɪ'sɛmɪˌnet] tr disseminare, divulgare

dissension [dɪ'sɛnʃən] s dissensione

dissent [dɪ'sɛnt] s dissenso; (nonconformity) dissidio ‖ intr dissentire

dissenter [dɪ'sɛntər] s dissenziente m

dissertation [ˌdɪsər'teʃən] s dissertazione

disservice [dɪ'sʌrvɪs] s danno; cattivo servizio

dissidence ['dɪsɪdəns] s dissidenza

dissident ['dɪsɪdənt] adj & s dissidente m

dissimilar [dɪ'sɪmɪlər] adj dissimile

dissimilate [dɪ'sɪmɪˌlet] tr dissimilare ‖ intr dissimilarsi

dissimulate [dɪ'sɪmjəˌlet] tr & intr dissimulare

dissipate ['dɪsɪˌpet] tr dissipare ‖ intr dissiparsi; (to indulge oneself) darsi alla dissipatezza

dissipated ['dɪsɪˌpetɪd] adj dissipato

dissipation [ˌdɪsɪ'peʃən] s dissipazione

dissociate [dɪ'soʃɪˌet] tr dissociare ‖ intr dissociarsi

dissolute ['dɪsəˌlut] adj dissoluto

dissolution [ˌdɪsə'luʃən] s dissoluzione

dissolve [dɪ'zɑlv] tr sciogliere, disciogliere ‖ intr sciogliersi, disciogliersi

dissonance ['dɪsənəns] s dissonanza

dissuade [dɪ'swed] tr dissuadere

dissyllabic [ˌdɪsɪ'læbɪk] adj disillabo

dissyllable [dɪ'sɪləbəl] s disillabo

distaff ['dɪstæf] or ['dɪstɑf] s rocca

dis'taff side' s ramo femminile di una famiglia

distance ['dɪstəns] s distanza; **a long distance** (fig) moltissimo; **in the distance** in lontananza; **to keep at a distance** or **to keep one's distance** mantenere le distanze ‖ tr distanziare

distant ['dɪstənt] adj distante; (relative) lontano; (aloof) freddo, riservato

distaste [dɪs'test] s ripugnanza

distasteful [dɪs'testfəl] adj ripugnante, sgradevole

distemper [dɪs'tɛmpər] s cimurro; (painting) tempera ‖ tr dipingere a tempera

distend [dɪs'tɛnd] tr stendere, distendere; gonfiare ‖ intr stendersi, distendersi; gonfiarsi

distension [dɪs'tɛnʃən] s distensione; gonfiamento

distill [dɪs'tɪl] tr distillare

distillation [ˌdɪstɪ'leʃən] s distillazione

distiller·y [dɪs'tɪləri] s (-ies) distilleria

distinct [dɪs'tɪŋkt] adj distinto, chiaro; (not blurred) nitido

distinction [dɪs'tɪŋkʃən] s distinzione

distinctive [dɪs'tɪŋktɪv] adj distintivo

distinguish [dɪs'tɪŋgwɪʃ] tr distinguere

distinguished [dɪs'tɪŋgwɪʃt] adj distinto

distort [dɪs'tɔrt] tr distorcere; (the truth) svisare, snaturare

distortion [dɪs'tɔrʃən] s deformazione; (of the truth) alterazione, svisamento; (rad) distorsione

distract [dɪs'trækt] tr distrarre

distracted [dɪs'træktɪd] adj distratto; (irrational) turbato, sconvolto

distraction [dɪs'trækʃən] s distrazione

distraught [dɪs'trɔt] adj turbato, stordito

distress [dɪs'trɛs] s pena, dispiacere m; pericolo; (naut) difficoltà f ‖ tr sconfortare, affliggere

distressing [dɪs'trɛsɪŋ] adj penoso

distress' mer'chandise s merce f sotto costo

distress' sig'nal s segnale m di soccorso

distribute [dɪs'trɪbjut] tr distribuire

distribution [ˌdɪstrɪ'bjuʃən] s distribuzione, erogazione

distributor [dɪs'trɪbjətər] s distributore m; (aut) distributore m d'accensione

district ['dɪstrɪkt] s regione; (of a city) rione m, quartiere m; (administrative division) distretto ‖ tr dividere in distretti

dis'trict attor'ney s procuratore m generale

distrust [dɪs'trʌst] s diffidenza ‖ tr diffidare di

distrustful [dɪs'trʌstfəl] adj diffidente

disturb [dɪs'tʌrb] tr disturbare, turbare; disordinare

disturbance [dɪs'tʌrbəns] s disturbo, turbamento, perturbazione; disordine m

disuse [dɪs'jus] s disuso

ditch [dɪtʃ] s fossa, fossato ‖ tr scavare un fosso in; (rr) far deragliare; (slang) piantare in asso ‖ intr fare un ammaraggio forzato

dither ['dɪðər] s agitazione; **to be in a dither** (coll) essere agitato

dit·to ['dɪto] s (-tos) lo stesso; (ditto symbol) virgolette fpl ‖ adv ugualmente, idem ‖ tr copiare, duplicare

dit'to marks' spl virgolette fpl

dit·ty ['dɪtɪ] *s* (**-ties**) canzonetta

diva ['divə] *s* (mus) diva

divan ['daɪvæn] or [dɪ'væn] *s* divano

dive [daɪv] *s* tuffo; (*of a submarine*) immersione; (aer) picchiata; (coll) taverna; (com) discesa || *v* (*pret & pp* **dived** or **dove** [dov]) *intr* tuffarsi; (*said of submarine*) immergersi; (*to plunge*) lanciarsi; (aer) scendere in picchiata; **to dive for** (*e.g., pearls*) pescare

dive'-bomb' *tr* bombardare in picchiata || *intr* scendere a tuffo

dive' bomb'ing *s* bombardamento in picchiata

diver ['daɪvər] *s* tuffatore *m;* (*person who works under water*) palombaro; (orn) tuffetto

diverge [dɪ'vʌrdʒ] or [daɪ'vʌrdʒ] *intr* divergere

divers ['daɪvərz] *adj* diversi, vari

diverse [dɪ'vʌrs], [daɪ'vʌrs] or ['daɪvʌrs] *adj* (*different*) diverso; (*of various kinds*) multiforme

diversification [dɪ‚vʌrsɪfɪ'keʃən] or [daɪ‚vʌrsɪfɪ'keʃən] *s* diversificazione

diversi·fy [dɪ'vʌrsɪ‚faɪ] or [daɪ'vʌrsɪ‚faɪ] *v* (*pret & pp* **-fied**) *tr* diversificare || *intr* diversificarsi

diversion [dɪ'vʌrʒən] or [daɪ'vʌrʒən] *s* diversione; (*pastime*) svago

diversi·ty [dɪ'vʌrsɪtɪ] or [daɪ'vʌrsɪtɪ] *s* (**-ties**) diversità *f*

divert [dɪ'vʌrt] or [daɪ'vʌrt] *tr* deviare; (*to entertain*) divertire; (*money*) stornare, distrarre

diverting [dɪ'vʌrtɪŋ] or [daɪ'vʌrtɪŋ] *adj* divertente

divest [dɪ'vest] or [daɪ'vest] *tr* spogliare; spossessare; **to divest oneself of** spogliarsi di, espropriarsi di

divide [dɪ'vaɪd] *s* spartiacque *m* || *tr* dividere || *intr* dividersi

dividend ['dɪvɪ‚dend] *s* dividendo

dividers [dɪ'vaɪdərz] *spl* compasso a punte fisse

divination [‚dɪvɪ'neʃən] *s* divinazione

divine [dɪ'vaɪn] *adj* divino || *s* sacerdote *m*, prete *m* || *tr* divinare

diviner [dɪ'vaɪnər] *s* divinatore *m*

diving ['daɪvɪŋ] *s* tuffo, immersione

div'ing bell' *s* campana da palombaro

div'ing board' *s* trampolino

div'ing suit' *s* scafandro

divin'ing rod' [dɪ'vaɪnɪŋ] *s* bacchetta rabdomantica

divini·ty [dɪ'vɪnɪtɪ] *s* (**-ties**) divinità *f;* teologia; **the Divinity** Dio

divisible [dɪ'vɪsɪbəl] *adj* divisibile

division [dɪ'vɪʒən] *s* divisione

divisor [dɪ'vaɪzər] *s* divisore *m*

divorce [dɪ'vors] *s* divorzio; **to get a divorce** divorziare || *tr* (*a married couple*) divorziare; (*one's spouse*) divorziare da || *intr* divorziare

divorcé [dɪvor'se] *s* divorziato

divorcee [dɪvor'si] *s* divorziata

divulge [dɪ'vʌldʒ] *tr* divulgare

dizziness ['dɪzɪnɪs] *s* vertigine *f*, stordimento; confusione

diz·zy ['dɪzɪ] *adj* (**-zier; -ziest**) (*causing dizziness*) vertiginoso; (*suffering dizziness*) preso da vertigine, stordito; (coll) stupido

do [du] *v* (*3rd pers* **does** [dʌz]; *pret* **did** [dɪd]; *pp* **done** [dʌn]; *ger* **doing** ['du·ɪŋ]) *tr* fare; (*a problem*) risolvere; (*a distance*) percorrere; (*to study*) studiare; (*to explore*) attraversare; (*to tire*) stancare; **to do one's best** fare del proprio meglio; **to do over** tornare a fare; ripetere; **to do right by** trattare bene; **to do s.o. out of s.th** (coll) portare via qlco a qlcu; **to do to death** mettere a morte; **to do up** (coll) impacchettare; stancare; (*one's hair*) farsi; vestire; (*a shirt*) lavare e stirare; **to have done** far fare || *intr* fare; agire; comportarsi; servire; bastare; stare; succedere; **how do you do?** come sta?; **that will do** basta; è sufficiente; **to have done with** non aver più nulla a che fare con; **to have nothing to do with** non aver nulla a che vedere con; **to have to do with** aver a che fare con, trattarsi di; **to do away with** togliere di mezzo; **to do for** servire da; **to do well** crescere bene; **to do without** fare a meno di || *v aux* used 1) in interrogative sentences: **Do you speak Italian?** Parla italiano?; 2) in negative sentences: **I do not speak Italian** Non parlo italiano; 3) to avoid repetition of a verb or full verbal expression: **Did you go to church this morning? Yes, I did.** È stato in chiesa questa mattina? Sì, ci sono stato; 4) to lend emphasis to a principal verb: **I do believe what you told me** Ci credo a quello che mi ha detto; 5) in inverted constructions after certain adverbs: **Seldom does he come to see me** Mi viene a vedere di raro; 6) in a supplicating tone with imperatives: **Do come in** entri per favore

docile ['dɑsɪl] *adj* docile

dock [dɑk] *s* (*wharf*) molo; (*waterway between two piers*) darsena; (*area including piers and waterways*) scalo portuario; (law) gabbia degli imputati || *tr* (*to deduct from the wages of*) fare una deduzione a; (*to deduct s.o.'s salary*) dedurre da; (*an animal*) scodare; (naut) attraccare || *intr* (aer) agganciarsi; (naut) attraccare

dockage ['dɑkɪdʒ] *s* attracco; (*charges*) diritti *mpl* di porto

docket ['dɑkɪt] *s* ordine *m* del giorno; (law) ruolo delle sentenze; **on the docket** (coll) pendente, in sospeso

dock' hand' *s* portuale *m*

docking ['dɑkɪŋ] *s* (aer) aggancio; (naut) attracco

dock'yard' *s* cantiere *m* navale

doctor ['dɑktər] *s* dottore *m;* (*physician*) medico || *tr* curare; aggiustare; falsificare; adulterare || *intr* esercitare la medicina; (coll) curarsi, prendere medicine

doctorate ['dɑktərɪt] *s* dottorato

doctrine ['dɑktrɪn] *s* dottrina

document ['dɑkjəmənt] *s* documento || ['dɑkjə‚ment] *tr* documentare

documenta·ry [ˌdɑkjə'mɛntəri] *adj* & *s* (**-ries**) documentario

documentation [ˌdɑkəmɛn'teʃən] *s* documentazione

doddering ['dɑdərɪŋ] *adj* tremante, rimbambito

dodge [dɑdʒ] *s* scarto, schivata; (fig) stratagemma *m* ‖ *tr* schivare, evitare ‖ *intr* schivarsi; (fig) rispondere evasivamente; **to dodge around the corner** scantonare

do·do ['dodo] *s* (**-dos** or **-does**) (coll) rimbecillito

doe [do] *s* (*of deer*) cerva; (*of goat*) capretta; (*of rabbit*) coniglia

doeskin ['do ˌskɪn] *s* pelle *f* di daino, pelle *f* di dante; lana finissima

doff [dɑf] or [dɔf] *tr* (*one's hat*) togliersi; (*clothing*) deporre

dog [dɔg] or [dɑg] *s* cane *m;* **to go to the dogs** (coll) andare in malora; **to put on the dog** (coll) darsi delle arie ‖ *v* (*pret* & *pp* **dogged;** *ger* **dogging**) *tr* seguire; perseguitare

dog'catch'er *s* accalappiacani *m*

dog' days' *s* solleone *m*, canicola

doge [dodʒ] *s* doge *m*

dog'-ear' *s* orecchia, orecchio

dog'fight' *s* duello aereo

dogged ['dɔgɪd] or ['dɑgɪd] *adj* accanito

doggerel ['dɔgərəl] or ['dɑgərəl] *s* versi *mpl* da colascione

dog·gy ['dɔgi] or ['dɑgi] *adj* (**-gier; -giest**) vistoso; canino ‖ *s* (**-gies**) cagnolino

dog'house' *s* canile *m;* **to be in the dog-house** (slang) essere in disgrazia

dog' Lat'in *s* latino maccheronico

dogma ['dɔgmə] or ['dɑgmə] *s* dogma *m*

dogmatic [dɔg'mætɪk] or [dɑg'mætɪk] *adj* dogmatico

dog' rac'ing *s* corse *fpl* dei cani

dog' show' *s* mostra canina

dog's' life' *s* vita da cani

Dog' Star' *s* canicola

dog' tag' *s* (mil) piastrina, piastrino

dog'-tired' *adj* (coll) stanco morto

dog'tooth' *s* (**-teeth** [ˌtiθ]) canino

dog' track' *s* cinodromo

dog'watch' *s* (naut) quarto di solo due ore, gaettone *m*

dog'wood' *s* corniolo

doi·ly ['dɔili] *s* (**-lies**) centrino

doings ['du·ɪŋz] *spl* azioni *fpl*, fatti *mpl*

do'-it-your·self' *s* il fare tutto da sé

doldrums ['dɑldrəmz] *spl* calma equatoriale; inattività *f;* depressione

dole [dol] *s* elemosina; (*to the jobless*) sussidio di disoccupazione ‖ *tr*—**to dole out** distribuire parsimoniosamente

doleful ['dolfəl] *adj* lugubre, triste

doll [dɑl] *s* bambola ‖ *intr*—**to doll up** (slang) agghindarsi

dollar ['dɑlər] *s* dollaro

dol'lar·wise' *adv* in termini finanziari

dol·ly ['dɑli] *s* (**-lies**) pupattola; (*low, wheeled frame for moving heavy loads*) carrello; (mov, telv) carrello

‖ *v* (*pret* & *pp* **-lied**) *intr* (mov, telv) carrellare

dol'ly shot' *s* (mov, telv) carrellata

dolphin ['dɑlfɪn] *s* delfino

dolt [dolt] *s* gonzo, balordo

doltish ['doltɪʃ] *adj* gonzo, balordo

domain [do'men] *s* dominio; (law) proprietà *f;* (fig) campo, orbita

dome [dom] *s* cupola

dome' light' *s* lampadario

domestic [də'mɛstɪk] *adj* & *s* domestico

domesticate [də'mɛstɪ ˌket] *tr* domesticare

domicile ['dɑmɪsɪl] or ['dɑmɪ ˌsaɪl] *s* domicilio ‖ *tr* domiciliare

dominance ['dɑmɪnəns] *s* dominio

dominant ['dɑmɪnənt] *adj* & *s* dominante *f*

dominate ['dɑmɪ ˌnet] *tr* & *intr* dominare

domination [ˌdɑmɪ'neʃən] *s* dominazione

domineer [ˌdɑmɪ'nɪr] *intr* spadroneggiare

domineering [ˌdɑmɪ'nɪrɪŋ] *adj* dispotico, tirannico

Dominican [də'mɪnɪkən] *adj* & *s* dominicano; (*eccl*) domenicanó

dominion [də'mɪnjən] *s* dominio

domi·no ['dɑmɪ ˌno] *s* (**-noes** or **-nos**) (*costume and person*) domino; (*piece*) tessera di domino; **dominoes** (*game*) domino

don [dɑn] *s* signore *m;* don *m;* membro di un collegio universitario inglese ‖ *v* (*pret* & *pp* **donned;** *ger* **donning**) *tr* (*clothes*) mettersi, vestire

donate ['donet] *tr* donare, dare

donation [do'neʃən] *s* donazione

done [dʌn] *adj* fatto; finito; stanco; (culin) ben cotto, ben rosolato

done' for' *adj* (coll) stanco morto; (coll) rovinato; (coll) fuori combattimento; (coll) morto

donjon ['dʌndʒən] or ['dɑndʒən] *s* torrione *m*, maschio

Don Juan [dɑn 'wɑn] or [dɔn 'hwɑn] *s* Don Giovanni

donkey ['dɑŋki] or ['dʌŋki] *s* asino, somaro

donnish ['dɑnɪʃ] *adj* pedante

donor ['donər] *s* donatore *m*

doodle ['dudəl] *tr* & *intr* scarabocchiare, riempire di ghirigori

doom [dum] *s* destino; morte *f*, rovina; sentenza di morte; giudizio finale ‖ *tr* destinare; condannare; condannare a morte

doomsday ['dumz ˌde] *s* giorno del giudizio

door [dor] *s* porta; (*of a carriage or automobile*) portiera, sportello; (*one part of a double door*) battente *m;* **behind closed doors** a porte chiuse; **to see to the door** accompagnare alla porta; **to show s.o. the door** mettere qlcu alla porta

door'bell' *s* campanello della porta

door' check' *s* chiusura automatica di porta, scontro

door'frame' *s* cornice *f*

door'head' s architrave m
door'jamb' s stipite m
door'keep'er s portinaio
door'knob' s maniglia della porta
door' knock'er s battente m
door' latch' s paletto
door'man' s (-men') portiere m, portinaio; (of large apartment house) guardaportone m
door'mat' s stoino, zerbino
door'nail' s borchione m; **dead as a doornail** morto e ben morto
door'post' s stipite m
door' scrap'er s raschietto
door'sill' s soglia
door'step' s gradino davanti la porta
door'stop' s paracolpi m
door'-to-door' adj (shipment) diretto; (selling) di porta in porta
door'way' s vano della porta; porta
dope [dop] s lubrificante m; (aer) vernice f; (slang) stupido, scemo; (slang) informazioni fpl; (slang) narcotico || tr (slang) narcotizzare; **to dope out** (slang) indovinare, decifrare, immaginare
dope' fiend' s (slang) tossicomane mf
dope'sheet' s giornaletto con le previsioni della corse ippiche
dormant ['dɔrmənt] adj dormente; latente
dor'mer win'dow ['dɔrmər] s abbaino
dormito·ry ['dɔrmɪ‚tori] s (-ries) dormitorio
dor·mouse ['dɔr‚maʊs] s (-mice [‚maɪs]) ghiro
dosage ['dosɪdʒ] s dosatura
dose [dos] s dose f; (coll) boccone amaro || tr dosare; somministrare
dossier ['dɑsɪ‚e] s incartamento
dot [dɑt] s punto; **on the dot** (coll) in punto || v (pret & pp dotted; ger dotting) tr punteggiare; **to dot one's i's** mettere i punti sulle i
dotage ['dotɪdʒ] s rimbecillimento; **to be in one's dotage** essere rimbambito
dotard ['dotərd] s vecchio rimbambito
dote [dot] intr rimbambirsi; **to dote on** essere pazzo per
doting ['dotɪŋ] adj che ama alla follia; (from old age) rimbambito, rimbecillito
dots' and dash'es spl (telg) punti mpl e tratti mpl
dot'ted line' s linea punteggiata; **to sign on the dotted line** firmare inconsideratamente
double ['dʌbəl] adj doppio || s doppio; (bridge) contre m; **doubles** (tennis) doppio || tr raddoppiare; (bridge) contrare || intr raddoppiarsi; (bridge) contrare; (mov, theat) sostenere due ruoli; (mov) doppiare; **to double up** (said of two people) dividere la stessa camera, dividere lo stesso letto; piegarsi in due
double-barreled ['dʌbəl'bærəld] adj a due canne; (fig) a doppio fine
dou'ble bass' s contrabbasso
dou'ble bed' s letto matrimoniale
dou'ble boil'er s bagnomaria m

double-breasted ['dʌbəl'brɛstɪd] adj a doppio petto, doppiopetto
dou'ble chin' s pappagorgia
dou'ble-cross' tr (coll) tradire
dou'ble date' s (coll) appuntamento amoroso di due coppie
dou'ble-deal'ing adj doppio
dou'ble-deck'er s (bed) letto a castello; (sandwich) tramezzino doppio; autobus m a due piani; (naut) nave f due ponti; (aer) aereo due ponti
double-edged ['dʌbəl'ɛdʒd] adj a due tagli, a doppio taglio
dou'ble en'try s (com) partita doppia
dou'ble fea'ture s (mov) programma m di due lungometraggio
double-header ['dʌbəl'hɛdər] s treno con due locomotive; due partite di baseball giocate successivamente
double-jointed ['dʌbəl'dʒɔɪntɪd] adj snodato
dou'ble-park' tr & intr parcheggiare in doppia fila
dou'ble-quick' adj & adv a passo di carica
dou'ble stand'ard s—**to have a double standard** usare due pesi e due misure
doublet ['dʌblɪt] s (close-fitting jacket) farsetto; (philol) doppione m
dou'ble-talk' s discorso incomprensibile; **to give s.o. double-talk** parlare evasivamente a qlcu || intr parlare evasivamente
dou'ble time' s paga doppia; (mil) passo di carica
doubleton ['dʌbəltən] s doppio
doubly ['dʌbli] adv doppiamente
doubt [daʊt] s dubbio; **beyond doubt** senza dubbio; **if in doubt** in caso di dubbio; **no doubt** senza dubbio || tr dubitare di || intr dubitare
doubter ['daʊtər] s incredulo
doubtful ['daʊtfəl] adj incerto; dubbioso
doubtless ['daʊtlɪs] adj indubitabile || adv senza dubbio; probabilmente
douche [duʃ] s irrigazione f; (instrument) irrigatore m || tr irrigare || intr fare irrigazioni
dough [do] s pasta di pane; (money) (slang) soldi mpl, quattrini mpl
dough'boy' s fantaccino americano
dough'nut' s ciambella; (with filling) sgonfiotto
dough·ty ['daʊti] adj (-tier; -tiest) forte, coraggioso
dough·y ['do·i] adj (-ier; -iest) pastoso, molle
dour [daʊr] or [dʊr] adj triste, severo
douse [daʊs] tr immergere; bagnare; (the light) (coll) spegnere
dove [dʌv] s colomba, tortora
dovecote ['dʌv‚kot] s piccionaia
dove'tail' s coda di rondine || tr calettare a coda di rondine; (to make fit) adattare, far combaciare || intr (to fit) combaciare; corrispondere
dowager ['daʊ·ədʒər] s vedova titolata; vecchia signora austera; **queen dowager** regina madre
dow·dy ['daʊdi] adj (-dier; -diest) trasandato

dow·el ['dau·əl] *s* caviglia, tassello ǁ *v (pret & pp* -eled *or* -elled; *ger* -eling *or* -elling) *tr* tassellare

dower ['dau·ər] *s (widow's portion)* legittima, vedovile *m; (marriage portion; natural gift)* dote *f* ǁ *tr* dotare; assegnare un vedovile a

down [daun] *adj* che discende; basso; *(train)* che va al centro; depresso; finito; *(money, payment)* anticipato; *(storage battery)* esaurito ǁ *s (of fruit and human body)* lanugine *f; (of birds)* piumino; *(upset)* rovescio; discesa; *(sandhill)* duna ǁ *adv* giù; all'ingiù, in giù; dabbasso; a terra; al sud; *(in cash)* a contanti; **down and out** rovinato; senza una soldo; **down from** da; **down on one's knees** in ginocchio; **down to** fino a; **down under** agli antipodi; **down with . . . !** abasso . . . !; **to get down to work** mettersi seriamente al lavoro; **to go down** scendere; **to lie down** sdraiarsi; andare a letto; **to sit down** sedersi ǁ *prep* giù per; **down the river** a valle; **down the street** giù per la strada ǁ *tr* abbattere; (coll) buttar giù, tracannare

down'cast' *adj* mogio, sfiduciato

down'fall' *s* rovina, rovescio

down'grade' *adj & adv* in declivio, a valle ǁ *s* discesa; **to be on the downgrade** essere in declino ǁ *tr* attribuire minor importanza a; degradare

downhearted ['daun,hartɪd] *adj* scoraggiato, abbattuto

down'hill' *adj & adv* in declivio; **to go downhill** declinare

down' pay'ment *s* acconto

down'pour' *s* acquazzone *m*, rovescio

down'right' *adj* assoluto; completo; franco, diretto ǁ *adv* completamente

down'stairs' *adj* del piano di sotto ǁ *s* il piano di sotto; i piani di sotto ǁ *adv* dabbasso, di sotto, giù

down'stream' *adv* a valle

down'stroke' *s* corsa discendente

down'town' *adj* centrale ǁ *s* centro della città ǁ *adv* al centro della città

down' train' *s* treno discendente, treno che va al centro

down'trend' *s* tendenza al ribasso

downtrodden ['daun,tradən] *adj* calpestato, oppresso

downward ['daunwərd] *adj & adv* all'ingiù

down·y ['dauni] *adj* (-ier; -iest) piumoso, lanuginoso; *(soft)* molle, morbido

dow·ry ['dauri] *s* (-ries) dote *f*

doze [doz] *s* pisolo ǁ *intr* dormicchiare; **to doze off** appisolarsi

dozen ['dʌzən] *s* dozzina

dozy ['dozi] *adj* sonnolento

drab [dræb] *adj* (**drabber; drabbest**) grigiastro; *(dull)* scialbo ǁ *s* colore grigiastro; *(fabric)* tela naturale; donna di malaffare

drach·ma ['drækmə] *s* (-mas *or* -mae [mi]) dramma

draft [dræft] *or* [draft] *s* corrente *f* d'aria; *(pulling)* tiro; *(in a chimney)* tiraggio; *(sketch, outline)* schizzo; *(first form of a writing)* prima stesura; *(drink)* sorso, bicchiere *m;* (com) tratta, lettera di credito; (law) progetto, disegno; (naut) pesca; (mil) coscrizione *f*, leva; **on draft** alla spina ǁ *tr* disegnare; fare uno schizzo di; *(a document)* stendere; (mil) coscrivere; **to be drafted** essere di leva, andar coscritto

draft' age' *s* età *f* di leva

draft' beer' *s* birra alla spina

draft' board' *s* consiglio di leva

draft' dodg'er ['dadʒər] *s* renitente *m* alla leva, imboscato

draftee [,dræf'ti] *or* [,draf'ti] *s* coscritto

draft' horse' *s* cavallo da tiro

drafts'man *s* (-men) disegnatore *m; (man who draws up documents)* redattore *m*

draft' trea'ty *s* progetto di trattato

draft·y ['dræfti] *or* ['drafti] *adj* (-ier; -iest) pieno di correnti d'aria

drag [dræg] *s (sledge for conveying heavy bodies)* traino, treggia; *(on a cigarette)* boccata; (aer) resistenza aerodinamica; (naut) pressione idrostatica; (naut) draga; (fig) noia; *(influence)* (slang) aderenze *fpl; (a bore)* (slang) rompiscatole *m* ǁ *v (pret & pp* dragged; *ger* dragging) *tr* strascinare, strascicare; (naut) rastrellare ǁ *intr* strascicare, strascicarsi; dilungarsi; **to drag on** andare per le lunghe

drag'net' *s* paranza; (fig) retata

dragon ['drægən] *s* drago, dragone *m*

drag'on·fly' *s* (-flies) libellula

dragoon [drə'gun] *s* (mil) dragone *m* ǁ *tr* forzare, costringere

drain [dren] *s* scolo; prosciugamento; (geog) spiovente *m;* (surg) drenaggio; (fig) salasso ǁ *tr (a liquid)* scolare; prosciugare; *(humid land; a wound)* drenare ǁ *intr* scolare; prosciugarsi; (geog) defluire

drainage ['drenɪdʒ] *s* drenaggio; (geog) displuvio, spartiacque *m*

drain'board' *s* scolatoio per le stoviglie

drain' cock' *s* rubinetto di scarico

drain'pipe' *s* tubo di scarico

drake [drek] *s* anatra maschio

dram [dræm] *s* dramma; bicchierino di liquore

drama ['dramə] *or* ['dræmə] *s* dramma *m;* (art and genre) drammatica

dramatic [drə'mætɪk] *adj* drammatico ǁ **dramatics** *ssg* drammatica; *spl* rappresentazione dilettantesca; comportamento drammatico

dramatist ['dræmətɪst] *s* drammaturgo

dramatize ['dræmə,taɪz] *tr* drammatizzare

drape [drep] *s* tenda, cortina; *(of a curtain)* drappeggio; *(of a skirt)* taglio ǁ *tr* drappeggiare

draper·y ['drepəri] *s* (-ies) drapperia; negozio di tessuti; **draperies** tendaggi *mpl*

drastic ['dræstɪk] *adj* drastico

draught [dræft] or [drɑft] *s & tr* var of **draft**

draught' beer' *s* birra alla spina

draw [drɔ] *s* (*in a game*) patta; (*in a lottery*) sorteggio; (*act of drawing*) tiro; (*of chimney*) tiraggio; (*attraction*) attrazione; (*of a drawbridge*) ala || *v* (*pret* **drew** [dru]; *pp* **drawn** [drɔn]) *tr* (*a line*) tirare; (*to attract*) richiamare; (*butter*) fondere; (*a sword*) sguainare; (*a nail*) estrarre; (*people*) attrarre; (*a sigh*) emettere; (*a curtain*) far scorrere; (*a salary*) pigliare; (*a prize*) ricevere; (*a game*) impattare; (*in card games*) pescare; (*a drawbridge*) sollevare; (*said of a ship*) pescare; (*a comparison*) fare; (*a profit*) ricavare; (*a chicken*) sventrare; (*e.g., a picture*) disegnare, ritrarre; (*to sketch in words*) descrivere; (*a contract*) stipulare; (*interest*) ricevere; (*com*) spiccare, staccare; **to draw forth** far uscire; **to draw off** estrarre; (*a liquid*) spillare; **to draw** (*shoes*) **on** mettersi; **to draw** (*money*) **on** ritirare da; **to draw** (*a draft*) **on** domiciliare presso; **to draw oneself up** raddrizzarsi; **to draw out** (*to persuade to talk*) far parlare, tirar fuori le parole a; **to draw up** (*a document*) estendere; (*mil*) schierare || *intr* (*said of chimney*) tirare; impattare; sorteggiare un premio; aver attrazione; disegnare; **to draw aside** scostarsi; **to draw back** retrocedere, ritirarsi; **to draw near** avvicinarsi; volgere a; **to draw to a close** essere quasi finito; **to draw together** unirsi

draw'back' *s* inconveniente *m*

draw'bridge' *s* ponte levatoio

drawee [ˌdrɔˈi] *s* trattario, trassato

drawer [ˈdrɔˌər] *s* disegnatore *m;* (*com*) traente *m* || [drɔr] *s* cassetto; **drawers** mutande *fpl*

drawing [ˈdrɔˌɪŋ] *s* disegno; (*in a lottery*) sorteggio

draw'ing board' *s* tavolo da disegno

draw'ing card' *s* attrazione

draw'ing room' *s* salotto, salottino

draw'knife' *s* (-knives [ˌnaɪvz]) coltello a petto

drawl [drɔl] *s* accento strascicato || *tr* dire con accento strascicato || *intr* strascicare le parole

drawn' but'ter *s* burro fuso

drawn' work' *s* lavoro a giorno

dray [dre] *s* carro pesante; slitta, treggia; autocarro

drayage [ˈdreˌɪdʒ] *s* carreggio

dray'man *s* (-men) carrettiere *m*

dread [dred] *adj* spaventoso, terribile || *s* spavento, terrore *m* || *tr & intr* temere

dreadful [ˈdrɛdfəl] *adj* spaventevole, terribile; (*coll*) orribile

dread'nought' *s* corazzata

dream [drim] *s* sogno; illusione, fantasticheria; **dream come true** sogno fatto realtà || *v* (*pret & pp* **dreamed** or **dreamt** [drɛmt]) *tr* sognare; **to dream up** (*coll*) immaginare, fantasticare || *intr* sognare

dreamer [ˈdrimər] *s* sognatore *m*

dream'land' *s* paese *m* dei sogni

dream·y [ˈdrimi] *adj* (-ier; -iest) sognante; (*visionary*) trasognato; vago

drear·y [ˈdrɪri] *adj* (-ier; -iest) squallido; triste; (*boring*) noioso

dredge [drɛdʒ] *s* draga || *tr* dragare; (*culin*) infarinare

dredger [ˈdrɛdʒər] *s* (*boat*) draga; (*container*) spolverino

dredging [ˈdrɛdʒɪŋ] *s* dragaggio

dregs [drɛgz] *spl* feccia

drench [drɛntʃ] *tr* infradiciare, inzuppare

dress [drɛs] *s* vestito; vestiti *mpl;* vestito da donna; abito; abito da cerimonia; (*of a bird*) piumaggio || *tr* vestire; adornare, decorare; (*hair*) pettinare; (*a wound*) medicare; (*leather*) conciare; (*food*) condire; (*a boat*) pavesare; **to dress down** (*coll*) rimproverare; **to get dressed** vestirsi || *intr* vestire; vestirsi; (*mil*) schierarsi; **to dress up** vestirsi da sera; farsi bello, mettersi in gala

dress' ball' *s* ballo di gala

dress' coat' *s* frac *m*

dresser [ˈdrɛsər] *s* toletta; (*sideboard*) credenza; **to be a good dresser** vestire con eleganza

dress' goods' *spl* stoffa per abiti

dressing [ˈdrɛsɪŋ] *s* ornamento; (*for food*) condimento, salsa; (*stuffing for fowl*) ripieno; (*fertilizer*) concime *m;* (*for a wound*) medicazione

dress'ing down' *s* ramanzina

dress'ing gown' *s* vestaglia

dress'ing room' *s* spogliatoio, toletta; (*theat*) camerino

dress'ing sta'tion *s* posto di pronto soccorso

dress'ing ta'ble *s* toletta, specchiera

dress'mak'er *s* sarta, sarto per donna

dress'mak'ing *s* taglio, sartoria

dress' rehears'al *s* prova generale

dress' shirt' *s* camicia inamidata

dress' suit' *s* marsina

dress' u'niform *s* (mil) alta uniforme

dress·y [ˈdrɛsi] *adj* (-ier; iest) (coll) elegante, ricercato

dribble [ˈdrɪbəl] *s* goccia || *tr* (sports) palleggiare, dribblare || *intr* gocciolare; (*at the mouth*) sbavare; (sports) dribblare

driblet [ˈdrɪblɪt] *s* piccola quantità; **in driblets** col contagocce

dried' beef' [draɪd] *s* carne seccata

dried' fruit' *s* frutta secca

drier [ˈdraɪˌər] *s* (for hair) asciugacapelli *m;* (for clothes) asciugatrice *f*

drift [drɪft] *s* movimento; (of sand, snow, etc.) cumulo; (snowdrift) neve accumulata dal vento; tendenza, corrente *f;* intenzione; (aer, naut) deriva; (rad, telv) deviazione || *intr* andare alla deriva; (said of snow) accumularsi; (aer, naut) derivare, scadere

drift' ice' *s* ghiaccio alla deriva

drift'pin' *s* (mach) mandrino

drift'wood' *s* legname andato alla deriva

drill [drɪl] s esercizio; (fabric) tela cruda; (agr) seminatrice f; (mach) trapano, trivella; (mil) esercitazioni fpl militari ‖ tr trivellare; istruire; (mil) insegnare gli esercizi militari a ‖ intr addestrarsi; (mil) fare gli esercizi militari

drill'mas'ter s istruttore m

drill' press' s trapano a colonna

drink [drɪŋk] s bevanda; **the drinks are on the house!** paga il proprietario! ‖ v (pret **drank** [dræŋk]; pp **drunk** [drʌŋk]) tr bere; assorbire; **to drink down** tracannare; **to drink in** bere, assorbire; (air) aspirare ‖ intr bere; **to drink out of** bere da; **to drink to the health of** bere alla salute di

drinkable ['drɪŋkəbəl] adj bevibile, potabile

drinker ['drɪŋkər] s bevitore m

drinking ['drɪŋkɪŋ] s (il) bere

drink'ing foun'tain s fontanella pubblica

drink'ing song' s canzone bacchica

drink'ing straw' s cannuccia

drink'ing trough' s abbeveratoio

drink'ing wa'ter s acqua potabile

drip [drɪp] s sgocciolo, sgocciolatura ‖ v (pret & pp **dripped**; ger **dripping**) intr sgocciolare, stillare; (said of perspiration) trasudare

drip' cof'fee s caffè fatto con la macchinetta

drip'-dry' adj non-stiro

drip' pan' s (culin) ghiotta; (mach) coppa

dripping ['drɪpɪŋ] s gocciolio; **drippings** grasso che cola dall'arrosto

drive [draɪv] s scarrozzata; strada; passeggiata; impulso; forza, iniziativa; urgenza; spinta; campagna; (aut) trazione; (mach) trasmissione ‖ v (pret **drove** [drov]; ger **driven** ['drɪvən]) tr (a nail) ficcare, piantare; (e.g., cattle) condurre, parare; (s.o. in a carriage or auto) condurre, portare; spingere; stimulare; forzare; spingere a lavorare; (sports) colpire molto forte; **to drive away** scacciare; **to drive back** respingere; **to drive mad** far impazzire; **to drive out** scacciare ‖ intr fare una scarrozzata; **to drive at** parare a; voler dire; **to drive hard** lavorare sodo; **to drive in** entrare in automobile; (a place) entrare in automobile in; **to drive on the right** guidare a destra; **to drive out** uscire in macchina; **to drive up** arrivare in macchina

drive'-in' mov'ie the'ater s cineparco

drive'-in' res'taurant s ristorante m con servizio alla portiera

driv·el ['drɪvəl] s (slobber) bava; (nonsense) scemenza ‖ v (pret **-eled** or **-elled**; ger **-eling** or **-elling**) intr sbavare; dire scemenze

driver ['draɪvər] s guidatore m; (of a carriage) cocchiere m; (of a locomotive) macchinista m; (of pack animals) carrettiere m, mulattiere m

driv'er's li'cense s patente automobilistica

driv'er's seat' s posto di guida

drive' shaft' s albero motore

drive'way' s strada privata d'accesso; carrozzabile f

drive' wheel' s ruota motrice

driv'ing school' ['draɪvɪŋ] s autoscuola, scuola guida

drizzle ['drɪzəl] s pioviggine f ‖ intr piovigginare

droll [drol] adj buffo, spassoso

dromedar·y ['drɑmə,dɛri] s (-ies) dromedario

drone [dron] s fuco, pecchione m; (hum) ronzio; (of bagpipe) bordone m; areoplano teleguidato ‖ tr dire in tono monotono ‖ intr (to live in idleness) fare il fannullone; (to buzz, hum) ronzare

drool [drul] s (slobber) bava; (slang) scemenza ‖ intr sbavare; (slang) dire scemenze

droop [drup] s accasciamento ‖ intr (to sag) pendere; (to lose spirit) accasciarsi; (said, e.g., of wheat) avvizzire

drooping ['drupɪŋ] adj (eyelid) abbassato; (shoulder) spiovente; (fig) accasciato

drop [drɑp] s goccia; (slope) pendenza; (earring) pendente m; (in temperature) discesa; (from an airplane) lancio; (trap door) botola; (gallows) trabocchetto della forca; (lozenge) pastiglia; (slit for letters) buca; (curtain) tela; (in prices) calo; **a drop in the bucket** una goccia nell'oceano ‖ v (pret & pp **dropped**; ger **dropping**) tr lasciar cadere; (a letter) imbucare; (a curtain) abbassare; (a remark) lasciar scappare; (a note) scrivere; omettere; abbandonare; (anchor) gettare; (from an airplane) lanciare; (from an automobile) lasciare; (from a list) cancellare ‖ intr cadere; lasciarsi cadere; terminare; **to drop dead** cader morto; **to drop in** entrare un momento; **to drop off** sparire; addormentarsi; morire improvvisamente; **to drop out** scomparire; ritirarsi; dare le dimissioni

drop' cur'tain s telone m

drop' ham'mer s maglio

drop'-leaf' ta'ble s tavola a ribalta

drop'light' s lampada sospesa

drop'out' s studente m che abbandona permanentemente la scuola media

dropper ['drɑpər] s contagocce m

dropsical ['drɑpsɪkəl] adj idropico

dropsy ['drɑpsi] s idropisia

dross [drɔs] or [drɑs] s scoria; (fig) feccia

drought [draut] s siccità f; (shortage) mancanza

drove [drov] s branco; folla; **in droves** in massa

drover ['drovər] s mandriano

drown [draun] tr & intr affogare, annegare

drowse [drauz] intr sonnecchiare

drow·sy ['drauzi] adj (-sier; -siest) sonnolento, insonnolito

drub [drʌb] v (pret & pp **drubbed**; ger **drubbing**) tr bastonare; battere

drudge [drʌdʒ] *s* sgobbone *m* || *intr* sgobbare, sfacchinare

drudger·y ['drʌdʒəri] *s* (**-ies**) lavoro ingrato, sfacchinata

drug [drʌg] *s* droga, medicina; narcotico; **drug on the market** merce *f* invendibile || *v* (*pret* & *pp* **drugged;** *ger* **drugging**) *tr* drogare, narcotizzare

drug' ad'dict *s* tossicomane *mf*

drug' addic'tion *s* tossicomania

druggist ['drʌgɪst] *s* farmacista *mf*

drug' hab'it *s* tossicomania

drug'store' *s* farmacia

drug' traf'fic *s* traffico in stupefacenti

druid ['dru·ɪd] *s* druida *m*

drum [drʌm] *s* (*cylinder; instrument*) tamburo; (*container*) fusto || *v* (*pret* & *pp* **drummed;** *ger* **drumming**) *tr* stamburare; **to drum up** (*customers*) farsi; (*enthusiasm*) creare || *intr* tambureggiare; (*with the fingers*) tamburellare

drum'beat' *s* rullo di tamburi

drum' corps' *s* banda di tamburi

drum'fire' *s* fuoco nutrito

drum'head' *s* membrana del tamburo

drum' ma'jor *s* tamburo maggiore

drummer ['drʌmər] *s* (*salesman*) agente *m* viaggiatore; (mus) tamburo; (mil) tamburino

drum'stick' *s* bacchetta del tamburo; (*of cooked fowl*) coscia

drunk [drʌŋk] *adj* ubriaco; **to get drunk** ubriacarsi || *s* ubriaco; (*spree*) sbornia; **to go on a drunk** (coll) ubriacarsi

drunkard ['drʌŋkərd] *s* ubriacone *m*

drunken ['drʌŋkən] *adj* ubriaco

drunk'en driv'ing *s*—**to be arrested for drunken driving** esser arrestato per aver guidato in stato di ubriachezza

drunkenness ['drʌŋkənnɪs] *s* ubriachezza, ebbrezza

dry [draɪ] *adj* (**drier; driest**) secco; (*boring*) arido; **to be dry** aver sete || *s* (**drys**) abolizionista *mf* || *v* (*pret* & *pp* **dried**) *tr* seccare; (*to wipe dry*) asciugare || *intr* seccarsi; **to dry up** prosciugarsi, essiccarsi; (slang) star secco

dry' bat'tery *s* pila a secco; (*group of dry cells*) batteria a secco

dry' cell' *s* pila a secco

dry'-clean' *tr* lavare a secco, pulire a secco

dry' clean'er *s* tintore *m*

dry' clean'ing *s* lavaggio a secco, pulitura a secco

dry'-clean'ing estab'lishment *s* tintoria

dry' dock' *s* bacino di carenaggio

dryer ['draɪ·ər] *s* var of **drier**

dry'-eyed' *adj* a occhi asciutti

dry' farm'ing *s* coltivazione di terreno arido

dry' goods' *spl* tessuti *mpl*; aridi *mpl*

dry'-goods store' *s* drapperia, negozio di tessuti

dry' ice' *s* neve carbonica, ghiaccio secco

dry' law' *s* legge *f* proibizionista

dry' meas'ure *s* misura per solidi

dryness ['draɪnɪs] *s* siccità *f*; (*e.g., of a speaker*) aridità *f*

dry' nurse' *s* balia asciutta

dry' run' *s* esercizio di prova; (mil) esercitazione senza munizioni

dry' sea'son *s* stagione arida

dry' wash' *s* roba lavata e asciugata ma non stirata

dual ['dju·əl] or ['du·əl] *adj* & *s* duale *m*

duali·ty [dju'ælɪti] or [du'ælɪti] *s* (**-ties**) dualità *f*

dub [dʌb] *s* (slang) giocatore inesperto || *v* (*pret* & *pp* **dubbed;** *ger* **dubbing**) *tr* chiamare, affibbiare il nome di; (*a knight*) armare; (mov) doppiare

dubbing ['dʌbɪŋ] *s* doppiaggio

dubious ['djubɪ·əs] or ['dubɪ·əs] *adj* dubbioso; incerto

ducat ['dʌkət] *s* ducato

duchess ['dʌtʃɪs] *s* duchessa

duch·y ['dʌtʃi] *s* (**-ies**) ducato

duck [dʌk] *s* anatra; mossa rapida; (*in the water*) tuffo; (*dodge*) schivata; **ducks** pantaloni *mpl* di tela cruda || *tr* (*one's head*) abbassare rapidamente; (*in water*) tuffare; (*a blow*) schivare || *intr* tuffarsi; **to duck out** (coll) svignarsela

duckling ['dʌklɪŋ] *s* anatroccolo

ducks' and drakes' *s*—**to play ducks and drakes with** buttar via, sperperare

duck' soup' *s* (slang) cosa facilissima

duct [dʌkt] *s* tubo, condotto

ductile ['dʌktɪl] *adj* duttile

duct'less gland' ['dʌktlɪs] *s* ghiandola a secrezione interna

duct'work' *s* condotto, canalizzazione

dud [dʌd] *s* (slang) bomba inesplosa; (*person*) (slang) fallito; (*enterprise*) (slang) fallimento; **duds** (coll) vestito; roba

dude [djud] or [dud] *s* elegantone *m*

due [dju] or [du] *adj* dovuto; atteso, debito; pagabile; **due to** dovuto a; **to fall due** scadere; **when is the train due?** a che ora arriva il treno? || *s* spettanza; debito; **dues** (*of a member*) quota sociale; **to get one's due** ricevere quanto uno merita; **to give the devil his due** trattare ognuno con giustizia || *adv* in direzione, e.g., **due north** in direzione nord

duel ['dju·əl] or ['du·əl] *s* duello; **to fight a duel** battersi a duello || *v* (*pret* & *pp* **dueled** or **duelled;** *ger* **dueling** or **duelling**) *intr* duellare

duelist or **duellist** ['dju·əlɪst] or ['du·əlɪst] *s* duellante *mf*

dues-paying ['djuz ,pe·ɪŋ] or ['duz ,pe·ɪŋ] *adj* regolare, effettivo

duet [dju'ɛt] or [du'ɛt] *s* duetto

duf'fel bag' ['dʌfəl] *s* sacca da viaggio

duke [djuk] or [duk] *s* duca *m*

dukedom ['djukdəm] or ['dukdəm] *s* ducato

dull [dʌl] *adj* (*not sharp*) spuntato, senza filo; (*color*) spento, sbiadito; (*sound, pain*) sordo; (*stupid*) ebete, tonto; (*business*) inattivo; (*boring*) noioso, melenso; (*flat*) opaco, appannato || *tr* spuntare; sbiadire; inebetire; ottundere; (*enthusiasm*) raffreddare; (*pain*) alleviare || *intr* spuntarsi; sbiadirsi; inebetirsi; raf-freddarsi

dullard ['dʌlərd] s stupido

duly ['djuli] or ['duli] adv debitamente

dumb [dʌm] adj (lacking the power to speak) muto; (coll) tonto, stupido

dumb'bell' s manubrio; (slang) zuccone m, stupido

dumb' crea'ture s animale m, bruto

dumb' show' s pantomima

dumb'wai'ter s montavivande m

dumfound [,dʌm'faund] tr interdire, lasciare esterrefatto

dum·my ['dʌmi] adj copiato; falso ‖ s (-mies) (dress form) manichino; (in card games) morto; (figurehead) uomo di paglia, prestanome m; (skeleton copy of a book) menabò m; copia; (slang) stupido, tonto

dump [dʌmp] s immondezzaio; mucchio di spazzature; (mil) deposito munizioni; (min) montagnetta di scarico; **to be down in the dumps** (coll) avere le paturnie ‖ tr scaricare; (to tip over) rovesciare; (com) scaricare sul mercato; (com) vendere sottocosto

dumping ['dʌmpɪŋ] s scarico; (com) dumping m

dumpling ['dʌmplɪŋ] s gnocco

dump' truck' s ribaltabile m

dump·y ['dʌmpi] adj (-ier; -iest) grassoccio, tarchiato

dun [dʌn] adj bruno grigiastro ‖ s creditore importuno; (demand for payment) sollecitazione di pagamento ‖ v (pret & pp **dunned;** ger **dunning**) tr sollecitare

dunce [dʌns] s ignorante mf, zuccone m

dunce' cap' s berretto d'asino

dune [djun] or [dun] s duna

dung [dʌŋ] s sterco, letame m ‖ tr concimare con il letame

dungarees [,dʌŋgə'riz] spl tuta di cotone blu

dungeon ['dʌndʒən] s carcere sotterraneo; (fortified tower) torrione m, maschio

dung'hill' s letamaio

dunk [dʌŋk] tr inzuppare

du·o ['dju·o] or ['du·o] s (-os) duo

duode·num [,dju·ə'dinəm] or [,du·ə-'dinəm] s (-na [nə]) duodeno

dupe [djup] or [dup] s gonzo ‖ tr gabbare, ingannare

du'plex house' ['djuplɛks] or ['du-plɛks] s casa di due appartamenti

duplicate ['djuplɪkɪt] or ['duplɪkɪt] adj & s duplicato ‖ ['djuplɪ,ket] or ['duplɪ,ket] tr duplicare

du'plicating machine' s duplicatore m

duplici·ty [dju'plɪsɪti] or [du'plɪsɪti] s (-ties) duplicità f, doppiezza

durable ['djurəbəl] or ['durəbəl] adj durabile, duraturo

du'rable goods' spl beni mpl durevoli

duration [dju're ʃən] or [du're ʃən] s durata

during ['djurɪŋ] or ['durɪŋ] prep durante

du'rum wheat' ['durəm] or ['djurəm] s grano duro

dusk [dʌsk] s crepuscolo

dust [dʌst] s polvere f ‖ tr (to free of dust) spolverare; (to sprinkle with dust) spolverizzare; **to dust off** (slang) rimettere in uso; (slang) spolverare le spalle a

dust' bowl' s regione polverosissima

dust'cloth' s strofinaccio

dust' cloud' s polverone m

duster ['dʌstər] s (cloth) cencio; (light overgarment) spolverino

dust' jack'et s sopraccoperta

dust'pan' s pattumiera

dust' rag' s strofinaccio

dust·y ['dʌsti] adj (-ier; -iest) polveroso; grigiastro

Dutch [dʌtʃ] adj olandese; (slang) tedesco ‖ s (language) olandese m; (language) (slang) tedesco m; **in Dutch** (slang) in disgrazia; (slang) nei pasticci; **the Dutch** gli olandesi; (slang) i tedeschi; **to go Dutch** (coll) pagare alla romana

Dutch'man s (-men) olandese m; (slang) tedesco

Dutch' treat' s invito alla romana

dutiable ['djutɪ·əbəl] or ['dutɪ·əbəl] adj soggetto a dogana

dutiful ['djutɪfəl] or ['dutɪfəl] adj obbediente, doveroso

du·ty ['djuti] or ['duti] s (-ties) dovere m; (task) funzione; dazio, dogana; **off duty** libero; in libera uscita; **on duty** in servizio; di guardia; **to do one's duty** fare il proprio dovere; **to take up one's duties** entrare in servizio

du'ty-free' adj esente da dogana

dwarf [dwɔrf] adj & s nano ‖ tr rimpiccolire ‖ intr rimpiccolire; apparire più piccolo

dwarfish ['dwɔrfɪʃ] adj nano, da nano

dwell [dwɛl] v (pret & pp **dwelled** or **dwelt** [dwɛlt]) intr dimorare, abitare; **to dwell on** or **upon** intrattenersi su

dwelling ['dwɛlɪŋ] s abitazione, residenza

dwell'ing house' s casa d'abitazione

dwindle ['dwɪndəl] intr diminuire; restringersi, consumarsi

dye [daɪ] s tinta, colore m ‖ v (pret & pp **dyed;** ger **dyeing**) tr tingere

dyed-in-the-wool ['daɪdɪnðə,wul] adj tinto prima della tessitura; completo, intransigente

dyeing ['daɪ·ɪŋ] s tintura

dyer ['daɪ·ər] s tintore m

dye'stuff' s tintura, materia colorante

dying ['daɪ·ɪŋ] adj morente

dynamic [daɪ'næmɪk] or [dɪ'næmɪk] adj dinamico

dynamite ['daɪnə,maɪt] s dinamite f ‖ tr far saltare con la dinamite

dyna·mo ['daɪnə,mo] s (-mos) dinamo f

dynast ['daɪnæst] s dinasta m

dynas·ty ['daɪnəsti] s (-ties) dinastia f

dysentery ['dɪsən,tɛri] s dissenteria

dyspepsia [dɪs'pɛpsɪ·ə] or [dɪs'pɛpʃə] s dispepsia

E

E, e [i] *s* quinta lettera dell'alfabeto inglese

each [itʃ] *adj indef* ogni ‖ *pron indef* ognuno, ciascuno; **each other** ci; vi; si; l'un l'altro ‖ *adv* l'uno; a testa

eager [ˈigər] *adj* (*enthusiastic*) ardente; **eager for** avido di; **eager to** + *inf* desideroso di + *inf*

ea′ger bea′ver *s* zelante *mf*

eagerness [ˈigərnɪs] *s* ardore *m;* brama

eagle [ˈigəl] *s* aquila

ea′gle owl′ *s* gufo reale

eaglet [ˈiglɪt] *s* aquilotto

ear [ir] *s* orecchio; (*of corn*) pannocchia; (*of wheat*) spiga; **to be all ears** essere tutt'orecchi; **to prick up one's ears** tendere l'orecchio; **to turn a deaf ear** far l'orecchio di mercante

ear′ache′ *s* mal *m* d'orecchi

ear′drop′ *s* pendente *m*

ear′drum′ *s* timpano

ear′flap′ *s* paraorecchi *m*

earl [ʌrl] *s* conte *m*

earldom [ˈʌrldəm] *s* contea

ear·ly [ˈʌrli] **(-lier; -liest)** *adj* (*occurring before customary time*) di buon'ora; (*first in a series*) primo; (*far back in time*) remoto, antico; (*occurring in near future*) prossimo ‖ *adv* presto; per tempo, di buon'ora; **as early as** (*a certain time of day*) già a; (*a certain time or date*) fin da, già in; **as early as possible** quanto prima possibile; **early in** (*e.g., the month*) all'inizio di; **early in the morning** di mattina presto, di buon mattino; **early in the year** all'inizio dell'anno

ear′ly bird′ *s* persona mattiniera

ear′ly mass′ *s* prima messa

ear′ly ris′er *s* persona mattiniera

ear′mark′ *s* contrassegno ‖ *tr* contrassegnare; assegnare a scopo speciale

ear′muff′ *s* paraorecchi *m*

earn [ʌrn] *tr* guadagnare, guadagnarsi; (*to get one's due*) meritarsi; (*interest*) (com) produrre ‖ *intr* trarre profitto, rendere

earnest [ˈʌrnɪst] *adj* serio; fervente; **in earnest** sul serio ‖ *s* caparra

ear′nest mon′ey *s* caparra

earnings [ˈʌrnɪŋz] *s* guadagno; salario

ear′phone′ *s* (*of sonar*) orecchiale *m;* (rad, telp) cuffia

ear′piece′ *s* (*of eyeglasses*) susta; (telp) ricevitore *m*

ear′ring′ *s* orecchino

ear′shot′ *s* tiro dell'orecchio; **within earshot** a portata di voce

ear′split′ting *adj* assordante

earth [ʌrθ] *s* terra; **to come back to** or **down to earth** scendere dalle nuvole

earthen [ˈʌrθən] *adj* di terra; di terracotta

ear′then·ware′ *s* coccio, terraglie *fpl,* terracotta

earthling [ˈʌrθlɪŋ] *s* terrestre *mf*

earthly [ˈʌrθli] *adj* terreno, terrestre; **to be of no earthly use** non servire assolutamente a niente

earthmover [ˈʌrθˌmuvər] *s* ruspa

earth′quake′ *s* terremoto

earth′work′ *s* terrapieno

earth′worm′ *s* lombrico

earth·y [ˈʌrθi] *adj* (**-ier; -iest**) terroso; (*coarse*) rozzo; pratico; sincero, diretto

ear′ trum′pet *s* corno acustico

ear′wax′ *s* cerume *m*

ease [iz] *s* facilità *f;* (*naturalness*) spigliatezza, disinvoltura; (*comfort*) benestare *m;* tranquillità *f;* **at ease!** (mil) riposo!; **with ease** con facilità ‖ *tr* facilitare; (*a burden*) alleggerire; (*to let up on*) rallentare; mitigare; **to ease out** licenziare con le buone maniere ‖ *intr* alleviarsi, mitigarsi, diminuire; rallentare

easel [ˈizəl] *s* cavalletto

easement [ˈizmənt] *s* attenuamento; (law) servitù *f*

easily [ˈizɪli] *adv* facilmente; senza dubbio; probabilmente

easiness [ˈizɪnɪs] *s* facilità *f;* disinvoltura; grazia, agilità *f;* indifferenza

east [ist] *adj* orientale, dell'est ‖ *s* est *m* ‖ *adv* verso l'est

Easter [ˈistər] *s* Pasqua

East′er egg′ *s* uovo di Pasqua

East′er Mon′day *s* lunedì *m* di Pasqua

eastern [ˈistərn] *adj* orientale

East′er·tide′ *s* tempo pasquale

eastward [ˈistwərd] *adv* verso l'est

eas·y [ˈizi] *adj* (**-ier; -iest**) facile; (*conducive to ease*) comodo, agiato; (*free from worry*) tranquillo; (*easygoing*) disinvolto, spigliato; (*not tight*) ampio; (*not hurried*) lento, moderato ‖ *adv* (coll) facilmente; (coll) tranquillamente; **to take it easy** (coll) riposarsi; (coll) non prendersela; (coll) andar piano

eas′y chair′ *s* poltrona

eas′y·go′ing *adj* (*person*) comodone; (*horse*) sciolto nell'andatura

eas′y mark′ *s* (coll) gonzo

eas′y mon′ey *s* denaro fatto senza fatica; soldi rubati

eas′y terms′ *spl* facilitazioni *fpl* di pagamento

eat [it] *v* (*pret* **ate** [et]; *pp* **eaten** [ˈitən]) *tr* mangiare; **to eat away** smangiare; **to eat up** mangiarsi ‖ *intr* mangiare

eatable [ˈitəbəl] *adj* mangiabile ‖ **eatables** *spl* commestibili *mpl*

eaves [ivz] *spl* gronda

eaves′drop′ *v* (*pret & pp* **-dropped;** *ger* **-dropping**) *intr* origliare

ebb [ɛb] *s* riflusso; decadenza ‖ *intr* (*said of the tide*) ritirarsi; decadere

ebb′ and flow′ *s* flusso e riflusso

ebb′ tide′ *s* riflusso, deflusso

ebon·y [ˈɛbəni] *s* (**-ies**) ebano

ebullient [ɪˈbʌljənt] *adj* bollente

eccentric [ɛkˈsɛntrɪk] *adj & s* eccentrico

eccentrici·ty [ˌɛksɛn'trɪsɪti] s (-ties) eccentricità f, originalità f
ecclesiastic [ɪˌklizɪ'æstɪk] adj & s ecclesiastico
echelon ['ɛʃəˌlɑn] s scaglione m; (mil) scaglione m || tr scaglionare
ech·o ['ɛko] s (-oes) eco || tr far eco a || intr echeggiare, rieccheggiare
éclair [e'klɛr] s dolce ripieno di crema
eclectic [ɛk'lɛktɪk] adj & s eclettico
eclipse [ɪ'klɪps] s eclisse f, eclissi f || tr eclissare
eclogue ['ɛklɔg] or ['ɛklɑg] s egloga
ecology [ɪ'kɑlədʒi] s ecologia
economic(al) [ˌikə'nɑmɪk(əl)] or [ˌɛkə'nɑmɪk(əl)] adj economico
economics [ˌikə'nɑmɪks] or [ˌɛkə'nɑmɪks] s economia (politica)
economist [ɪ'kɑnəmɪst] s economista mf
economize [ɪ'kɑnəˌmaɪz] tr & intr economizzare
econo·my [ɪ'kɑnəmi] s (-mies) economia
ecosystem ['ɛkoˌsɪstəm] s ecosistema m
ecsta·sy ['ɛkstəsi] s (-sies) estasi f
ecstatic [ɛk'stætɪk] adj estatico
ecumenic(al) [ˌɛkjə'mɛnɪk(əl)] adj ecumenico
eczema ['ɛksɪmə] or [ɛg'zimə] s eczema m
ed·dy ['ɛdi] s (-dies) turbine m || v (pret & pp -died) tr & intr turbinare
edelweiss ['edəlˌvaɪs] s stella alpina
edge [ɛdʒ] s (of knife, sword, etc) filo, tagliente m; (border at which a surface terminates) orlo, bordo; (of a wound) labbro, margine m; (of a book) taglio; (of a tumbler) giro; (of clothing) vivagno; (of a table) spigolo; (slang) vantaggio; **on edge** nervoso; **to have the edge on** (coll) avere il vantaggio su; **to set the teeth on edge** far allegare i denti || tr affilare, aguzzare; orlare, bordare; **to edge out** riuscire ad eliminare || intr avanzare lentamente
edgeways ['ɛdʒˌwez] adv di taglio; **to not let s.o. get a word in edgeways** non lasciar dire una parola a qlcu
edging ['ɛdʒɪŋ] s orlo, bordo
edg·y ['ɛdʒi] adj (-ier; -iest) acuto, angolare; nervoso, ansioso
edible ['ɛdɪbəl] adj mangereccio, mangiabile || **edibles** spl commestibili mpl
edict ['idɪkt] s editto
edification [ˌɛdɪfɪ'keʃən] s edificazione
edifice ['ɛdɪfɪs] s edificio
edi·fy ['ɛdɪˌfaɪ] v (pret & pp -fied) tr edificare
edifying ['ɛdɪˌfaɪ·ɪŋ] adj edificante
edit ['ɛdɪt] tr redigere; (e.g., a manuscript) correggere; (an edition) curare; (a newspaper) dirigere; (mov) montare
edition [ɪ'dɪʃən] s edizione
editor ['ɛdɪtər] s (of a newspaper or magazine) direttore m, gerente mf; (of an editorial) redattore m, cronista mf; (of a critical edition) editore m; (of a manuscript) revisore m

editorial [ˌɛdɪ'tɔrɪ·əl] adj editoriale || s capocronaca m, articolo di fondo
editorial staff s redazione
editor in chief' s gerente mf responsabile
educate ['ɛdʒuˌket] tr educare, erudire
education [ˌɛdʒu'keʃən] s educazione; istruzione, insegnamento
educational [ˌɛdʒu'keʃənəl] adj educativo
educa'tional institu'tion s istituto di magistero
educator ['ɛdʒuˌketər] s educatore m
eel [il] s anguilla; **to be as slippery as an eel** guizzare di mano come un'anguilla
ee·rie or **ee·ry** ['ɪri] adj (-rier; -riest) spettrale, pauroso
efface [ɪ'fes] tr cancellare; **to efface oneself** eclissarsi, mettersi in disparte
effect [ɪ'fɛkt] s effetto; (main idea) tenore m; **in effect** in vigore; in realtà; **to go into effect** or **to take effect** andare in vigore; **to put into effect** mandare ad effetto || tr effettuare
effective [ɪ'fɛktɪv] adj efficace; (actually in effect) effettivo; (striking) che colpisce; **to become effective** entrare in vigore
effectual [ɪ'fɛktʃu·əl] adj efficace
effectuate [ɪ'fɛktʃuˌet] tr effettuare
effeminacy [ɪ'fɛmɪnəsi] s effemminatezza
effeminate [ɪ'fɛmɪnɪt] adj effemminato
effervesce [ˌɛfər'vɛs] intr essere in effervescenza
effervescence [ˌɛfər'vɛsəns] s effervescenza
effervescent [ˌɛfər'vɛsənt] adj effervescente
effete [ɪ'fit] adj esausto, sterile
efficacious [ˌɛfɪ'keʃəs] adj efficace
effica·cy ['ɛfɪkəsi] s (-cies) efficacia
efficien·cy [ɪ'fɪʃənsi] s (-cies) efficienza; (mech) rendimento, efficienza
effi'ciency engineer' s analista mf tempi e metodi
efficient [ɪ'fɪʃənt] adj efficiente; (person) abile; (me h) efficiente
effi·gy ['ɛfɪdʒi] s (-gies) effigie f
effort ['ɛfərt] s sforzo
effronter·y [ɪ'frʌntəri] s (-ies) sfrontatezza, sfacciataggine f
effusion [ɪ'fjuʒən] s effusione
effusive [ɪ'fjusɪv] adj espansivo
egg [ɛg] s uovo; (slang) bravo ragazzo || tr—**to egg on** incitare
egg'beat'er s frullino, sbattiuova m
egg' cup' s portauovo
egg'head' s (coll) intellettuale mf
eggnog ['ɛgˌnɑg] s zabaione m
egg'plant' s melanzana, petonciano
egg'shell' s guscio d'uovo
egoism ['ɛgoˌɪzəm] or ['igoˌɪzəm] s egoismo
egoist ['ɛgo·ɪst] or ['igo·ɪst] s egoista mf
egotism ['ɛgoˌtɪzəm] or ['igoˌtɪzəm] s egotismo
egotist ['ɛgotɪst] or ['igotɪst] s egotista mf

egregious [ɪ'gridʒəs] *adj* gigantesco, tremendo, marchiano

egress ['igrɛs] *s* uscita

Egypt ['idʒɪpt] *s* l'Egitto

Egyptian [ɪ'dʒɪpʃən] *adj* & *s* egiziano

ei'der down' ['aɪdər] *s* piumino

ei'der duck' *s* edredone *m*

eight [et] *adj* & *pron* otto || *s* otto; **eight o'clock** le otto

eighteen ['et'tin] *adj, s* & *pron* diciotto

eighteenth ['et'tinθ] *adj, s* & *pron* diciottesimo || *s* (*in dates*) diciotto

eighth [etθ] *adj* & *s* ottavo || *s* (*in dates*) otto

eight' hun'dred *adj, s* & *pron* ottocento

eightieth ['etɪ·ɪθ] *adj, s* & *pron* ottantesimo

eight·y ['eti] *adj* & *pron* ottanta || *s* (*-ies*) ottanta *m;* **the eighties** gli anni ottanta

either ['iðər] or ['aɪðər] *adj* l'uno o l'altro; l'uno e l'altro; ciascuno; entrambi i, tutti e due i || *pron* l'uno o l'altro; l'uno e l'altro; entrambi || *adv*—**not either** nemmeno || *conj*—**either . . . or** o . . . o

ejaculate [ɪ'dʒækjə‚let] *tr* esclamare; (*physiol*) emettere || *intr* esclamare; (*physiol*) avere un'eiaculazione

eject [ɪ'dʒɛkt] *tr* espellere, gettar fuori; (*to evict*) sfrattare

ejection [ɪ'dʒɛkʃən] *s* espulsione; (*of a tenant*) sfratto

ejec'tion seat' *s* sedile *m* eiettabile

eke [ik] *tr*—**to eke out a living** sbarcare il lunario

elaborate [ɪ'læbərɪt] *adj* (*done with great care*) elaborato; (*detailed*) minuzioso; (*ornate*) ornato || [ɪ'læbə‚ret] *tr* elaborare || *intr*—**to elaborate on** or **upon** circonstanziare, particolareggiare

elapse [ɪ'læps] *intr* passare, trascorrere

elastic [ɪ'læstɪk] *adj* & *s* elastico

elasticity [ɪ‚læs'tɪsɪti] or [‚ilæs'tɪsɪti] *s* elasticità *f*

elated [ɪ'letɪd] *adj* esultante, gongolante

elation [ɪ'leʃən] *s* esultanza, gaudio

elbow ['ɛlbo] *s* gomito; (*in a river*) ansa; (*of a chair*) braccio; **at one's elbow** sotto mano; **out at the elbows** coi gomiti logori; **to crook the elbow** alzare il gomito; **to rub elbows** stare gomito a gomito; **up to the elbows** fino al collo || *tr*—**to elbow one's way** aprirsi il passo a gomitate || *intr* dar gomitate

el'bow grease' *s* (coll) olio di gomiti

el'bow patch' *s* toppa al gomito

el'bow rest' *s* bracciolo

el'bow·room' *s* spazio sufficiente; libertà *f* d'azione

elder ['ɛldər] *adj* seniore, maggiore || *s* (bot) sambuco; (eccl) maggiore *m*

el'der·ber'ry *s* (*-ries*) sambuco; (*fruit*) bacca del sambuco

elderly ['ɛldərli] *adj* attempato, anziano

eld'er states'man *s* uomo di stato esperto

eldest ['ɛldɪst] *adj* (il) maggiore; (il) più vecchio

elect [ɪ'lɛkt] *adj* & *s* eletto; **the elect** gli eletti || *tr* eleggere

election [ɪ'lɛkʃən] *s* elezione

electioneer [ɪ‚lɛkʃə'nɪr] *intr* fare una campagna elettorale

elective [ɪ'lɛktɪv] *adj* elettivo || *s* corso facoltativo

electorate [ɪ'lɛktərɪt] *s* elettorato

electric(al) [ɪ'lɛktrɪk(əl)] *adj* elettrico

elec'tric blend'er *s* frullatore *m*

elec'tric chair' *s* sedia elettrica

elec'tric cord' *s* piattina, filo elettrico

elec'tric eel' *s* gimnoto

elec'tric eye' *s* occhio elettrico

electrician [ɪ‚lɛk'trɪʃən] or [‚ɛlɛk'trɪʃən] *s* elettricista *m*

electricity [ɪ‚lɛk'trɪsɪti] or [‚ɛlɛk'trɪsɪti] *s* elettricità *f*

elec'tric me'ter *s* contatore *m* della luce

elec'tric per'cola'tor *s* caffettiera elettrica

elec'tric shav'er *s* rasoio elettrico

elec'tric shock' *s* scossa elettrica, elettrosquasso

elec'tric tape' *s* nastro isolante

elec'tric train' *s* elettrotreno

electri·fy [ɪ'lɛktrɪ‚faɪ] *v* (*pret* & *pp* -fied) *tr* (*to provide with electric power*) elettrificare; (*to communicate electricity to; to thrill*) elettrizzare

electrocute [ɪ'lɛktrə‚kjut] *tr* fulminare con la corrente; far morire sulla sedia elettrica

electrode [ɪ'lɛktrod] *s* elettrodo

electrolysis [ɪ‚lɛk'trɑlɪsɪs] or [‚ɛlɛk'trɑlɪsɪs] *s* elettrolisi *f*

electrolyte [ɪ'lɛktrə‚laɪt] *s* elettrolito

electromagnet [ɪ‚lɛktrə'mægnɪt] *s* elettrocalamita

electromagnetic [ɪ‚lɛktrəmæg'nɛtɪk] *adj* elettromagnetico

electromotive [ɪ‚lɛktrə'motɪv] *adj* elettromotore

electron [ɪ'lɛktrɑn] *s* elettrone *m*

electronic [ɪ‚lɛk'trɑnɪk] or [‚ɛlɛk'trɑnɪk] *adj* elettronico || **electronics** *s* elettronica

electroplating [ɪ'lɛktrə‚pletɪŋ] *s* galvanostegia

electrostatic [ɪ‚lɛktrə'stætɪk] *adj* elettrostatico

electrotype [ɪ'lɛktrə‚taɪp] *s* stereotipia || *tr* stereotipare

eleemosynary [‚ɛlɪ'mɑsɪ‚nɛri] *adj* caritatevole, di beneficenza

elegance ['ɛlɪgəns] *s* eleganza

elegant ['ɛlɪgənt] *adj* elegante

elegiac [‚ɛlɪ'dʒaɪ·æk] *adj* elegiaco

ele·gy ['ɛlɪdʒi] *s* (*-gies*) elegia

element ['ɛlɪmənt] *s* elemento; **to be out of one's element** essere fuori del proprio ambiente

elementary [‚ɛlɪ'mɛntəri] *adj* elementare

elephant ['ɛlɪfənt] *s* elefante *m*

elevate ['ɛlɪ‚vet] *tr* elevare, innalzare

elevated ['ɛlɪ‚vetɪd] *adj* elevato || *s* ferrovia soprelevata, metropolitana soprelevata

elevation [‚ɛlɪ'veʃən] *s* elevazione; (surv) quota

elevator ['ɛlɪ‚vetər] *s* ascensore *m;*

(*for freight*) montacarichi *m;* (*for hoisting grain*) elevatore *m* di grano; (*warehouse for storing grain*) deposito granaglie; (aer) timone *m* di profondità

eleven [ɪ'lɛvən] *adj & pron* undici || *s* undici *m;* **eleven o'clock** le undici

eleventh [ɪ'lɛvənθ] *adj, s & pron* undicesimo || *s* (*in dates*) undici *m*

elev'enth hour' *s* ultimo momento

elf [ɛlf] *s* (**elves** [ɛlvz]) elfo

elicit [ɪ'lɪsɪt] *tr* cavare, sottrarre

elide [ɪ'laɪd] *tr* elidere

eligible ['ɛlɪdʒɪbəl] *adj* eleggibile; accettabile

eliminate [ɪ'lɪmɪ‚net] *tr* eliminare

elision [ɪ'lɪʒən] *s* elisione

elite [e'lit] *adj* eletto, scelto || *s*—**the elite** l'élite *f*

elk [ɛlk] *s* alce *m*

ellipse [ɪ'lɪps] *s* (geom) ellisse *f*

ellip·sis [ɪ'lɪpsɪs] *s* (**-ses** [siz]) (gram) ellissi *f*

elliptic(al) [ɪ'lɪptɪk(əl)] *adj* ellittico

elm [ɛlm] *s* olmo

elongate . [ɪ'lɔŋget] or [ɪ'laŋget] *tr* allungare, prolungare

elope [ɪ'lop] *intr* fuggire con un amante

elopement [ɪ'lopmənt] *s* fuga con un amante

eloquence ['ɛləkwəns] *s* eloquenza

eloquent ['ɛləkwənt] *adj* eloquente

else [ɛls] *adj*—**nobody else** nessun altro; **nothing else** nient'altro; **somebody else** qualcun altro; **something else** qualcosa d'altro; **what else** che altro; **who else** chi altro; **whose else** di che altra persona || *adv*—**how else** in che altra maniera; **or else** se no; altrimenti; **when else** in che altro momento; in che altro periodo; **where else** dove mai, da che parte

else'where' *adv* altrove

elucidate [ɪ'lusɪ‚det] *tr* dilucidare

elude [ɪ'lud] *tr* eludere

elusive [ɪ'lusɪv] *adj* elusivo; (*evasive*) fugace, sfuggente

emaciated [ɪ'meʃɪ‚etɪd] *adj* smunto, emaciato, maciento

emanate ['ɛmə‚net] *tr & intr* emanare

emancipate [ɪ'mænsɪ‚pet] *tr* emancipare

embalm [ɛm'bɑm] *tr‚* imbalsamare

embankment [ɛm'bæŋkmənt] *s* terrapieno

embar·go [ɛm'bɑrgo] *s* (**-goes**) embargo || *tr* mettere l'embargo a

embark [ɛm'bɑrk] *intr* imbarcarsi

embarkation [‚ɛmbɑr'keʃən] *s* imbarco

embarrass [ɛm'bærəs] *tr* imbarazzare, mettere a disagio; (*to impede*) imbarazzare, impacciare; mettere in difficoltà economiche

embarrassing [ɛm'bærəsɪŋ] *adj* sconcertante; imbarazzante

embarrassment [ɛm'bærəsmənt] *s* imbarazzo, disagio, confusione; impaccio; difficoltà finanziaria, dissesto

embas·sy ['ɛmbəsi] *s* (**-sies**) ambasciata

em·bed [ɛm'bɛd] *s* (*pret & pp* **-bedded;** *ger* **-bedding**) *tr* incastrare, incassare

embellish [ɛm'bɛlɪʃ] *tr* imbellire

embellishment [ɛm'bɛlɪʃmənt] *s* abbellimento; (fig) fioretto

ember ['ɛmbər] *s* brace *f;* **embers** braci *fpl*

Em'ber days' *spl* tempora *fpl*

embezzle [ɛm'bɛzəl] *tr* appropriare, malversare || *intr* appropriarsi

embezzlement [ɛm'bɛzəlmənt] *s* appropriazione indebita, malversazione; (*of public funds*) peculato

embezzler [ɛm'bɛzlər] *s* malversatore *m*

embitter [ɛm'bɪtər] *tr* amareggiare

emblazon [ɛm'blezən] *tr* blasonare; celebrare

emblem ['ɛmbləm] *s* emblema *m*

emblematic(al) [‚ɛmblə'mætɪk(əl)] *adj* emblematico

embodiment [ɛm'bɑdɪmənt] *s* incarnazione, personificazione

embod·y [ɛm'bɑdi] *v* (*pret & pp* **-ied**) *tr* incarnare, personificare; incorporare

embolden [ɛm'boldən] *tr* imbaldanzire

embolism ['ɛmbə‚lɪzəm] *s* embolia

emboss [ɛm'bɔs] or [ɛm'bɑs] *tr* (*metal*) sbalzare; (*paper*) goffrare

embrace [ɛm'bres] *s* abbraccio || *tr* abbracciare || *intr* abbracciarsi

embrasure [ɛm'breʒər] *s* (archit) strombatura; (mil) feritoia

embroider [ɛm'brɔɪdər] *tr* ricamare, trapuntare

embroider·y [ɛm'brɔɪdəri] *s* (**-ies**) ricamo, trapunto

embroil [ɛm'brɔɪl] *tr* ingarbugliare; (*to involve in contention*) coinvolgere

embroilment [ɛm'brɔɪlmənt] *s* imbroglio; (*in contention*) disaccordo

embry·o ['ɛmbrɪ‚o] *s* (**-os**) embrione *m*

embryology [‚ɛmbrɪ'alədʒi] *s* embriologia

embryonic [‚ɛmbrɪ'anɪk] *adj* embrionale

emcee ['ɛm'si] *s* presentatore *m* || *tr* presentare

emend [ɪ'mɛnd] *tr* emendare

emendation [‚imɛn'deʃən] *s* emendamento

emerald ['ɛmərəld] *s* smeraldo

emerge [ɪ'mʌrdʒ] *intr* emergere

emergence [ɪ'mʌrdʒəns] *s* emergenza

emergen·cy [ɪ'mʌrdʒənsi] *s* (**-cies**) emergenza

emer'gency brake' *s* freno a mano

emer'gency ex'it *s* uscita di sicurezza

emer'gency land'ing *s* atterragio di fortuna

emer'gency ward' *s* sala d'urgenza

emeritus [ɪ'mɛrɪtəs] *adj* emerito

emersion [ɪ'mʌrʒən] or [ɪ'mʌrʃən] *s* emersione

emery ['ɛməri] *s* smeriglio

em'ery cloth' *s* tela smeriglio

em'ery wheel' *s* mola a smeriglio

emetic [ɪ'mɛtɪk] *adj & s* emetico

emigrant ['ɛmɪgrənt] *adj & s* emigrante *mf*

emigrate ['ɛmɪ‚gret] *intr* emigrare

émigré [emi'gre] or ['ɛmɪ‚gre] *s* emigrato

eminence ['ɛmɪnəns] *s* eminenza; (eccl) Eminenza

eminent ['ɛmɪnənt] *adj* eminente

emissar·y ['ɛmɪ‚sɛri] *s* (**-ies**) emissario

emission [ɪ'mɪʃən] *s* emissione

emit [ɪ'mɪt] *v* (*pret & pp* **emitted; ger emitting**) *tr* emettere

emolument [ɪ'maljəmənt] *s* emolumento

emotion [ɪ'moʃən] *s* emozione

emotional [ɪ'moʃənəl] *adj* emotivo

emperor ['ɛmpərər] *s* imperatore *m*

empha·sis ['ɛmfəsɪs] *s* (**-ses** [‚siz]) enfasi *f*. risalto

emphasize ['ɛmfə‚saɪz] *tr* dar rilievo a, sottolineare

emphatic [ɛm'fætɪk] *adj* enfatico

emphysema [‚ɛmfɪ'simə] *s* enfisema *m*

empire ['ɛmpaɪr] *s* impero

empiric(al) [ɛm'pɪrɪk(əl)] *adj* empirico

empiricist [ɛm'pɪrɪsɪst] *s* empirista *mf*

emplacement [ɛm'plesmənt] *s* piazzola, postazione

employ [ɛm'plɔɪ] *s* impiego ‖ *tr* impiegare, usare; valersi di

employee [ɛm'plɔɪ·i] *or* [‚ɛmplɔɪ'i] *s* impiegato, dipendente *mf*

employer [ɛm'plɔɪ·ər] *s* dirigente *mf*, datore *m* di lavoro

employment [ɛm'plɔɪmənt] *s* impiego, occupazione

employ'ment a'gency *s* agenzia di collocamento

empower [ɛm'pau·ər] *tr* autorizzare; permettere

empress ['ɛmprɪs] *s* imperatrice *f*

emptiness ['ɛmptɪnɪs] *s* vuoto

emp·ty ['ɛmpti] *adj* (**-tier; -tiest**) vuoto; (*gun*) scarico; (*hungry*) (coll) digiuno; (fig) esausto ‖ *v* (*pret & pp* **-tied**) *tr* vuotare ‖ *intr* vuotarsi

empty-handed ['ɛmpti'hændɪd] *adj* a mani vuote

empty-headed ['ɛmpti'hɛdɪd] *adj* dalla testa vuota, balordo

empyrean [‚ɛmpɪ'ri·ən] *adj & s* empireo

emulate ['ɛmjə‚let] *tr* emulare

emulator ['ɛmjə‚letər] *s* emulo

emulous ['ɛmjələs] *adj* emulo

emulsi·fy [ɪ'mʌlsɪ‚faɪ] *v* (*pret & pp* **-fied**) *tr* emulsionare

emulsion [ɪ'mʌlʃən] *s* emulsione

enable [ɛn'ebəl] *tr* abilitare; permettere (with *dat*)

enact [ɛn'ækt] *tr* decretare; (*a role*) rappresentare

enactment [ɛn'æktmənt] *s* legge *f*; (*of a law*) promulgazione; (*of a play*) rappresentazione

enam·el [ɪn'æməl] *s* smalto ‖ *v* (*pret & pp* **-eled** *or* **-elled; ger -eling** *or* **-elling**) *tr* smaltare

enam'el·ware' *s* utensili *mpl* di cucina di ferro smaltato

enamor [ɛn'æmər] *tr* innamorare; **to become enamored of** innamorarsi di

encamp [ɛn'kæmp] *tr* accampare ‖ *intr* accamparsi

encampment [ɛn'kæmpmənt] *s* campeggio; (mil) accampamento

encase [ɛn'kes] *tr* incassare

encephalitis [ɛn‚sɛfə'laɪtɪs] *s* encefalite *f*

enchain [ɛn'tʃen] *tr* incatenare

enchant [ɛn'tʃænt] *or* [ɛn'tʃɑnt] *tr* incantare

enchantment [ɛn'tʃæntmənt] *or* [ɛn'tʃɑntmənt] *s* incanto, malia

enchanting [ɛn'tʃæntɪŋ] *or* [ɛn'tʃɑntɪŋ] *adj* incantatore, incantevole

enchantress [ɛn'tʃæntrɪs] *or* [ɛn'tʃɑntrɪs] *s* incantatrice *f*, maliarda

enchase [ɛn'tʃes] *tr* incastonare

encircle [ɛn'sʌrkəl] *tr* rigirare, girare intorno a; (mil) circondare

enclave ['ɛnklev] *s* enclave *f*

enclitic [ɛn'klɪtɪk] *adj* enclitico ‖ *s* enclitica

enclose [ɛn'kloz] *tr* rinchiudere; (*in a letter*) accludere, includere; **to enclose herewith** accludere alla presente

enclosure [ɛn'kloʒər] *s* (*land surrounded by fence*) recinto, chiuso; (*e.g., letter*) allegato

encomi·um [ɛn'komɪ·əm] *s* (**-ums** *or* **-a** [ə]) encomio, elogio

encompass [ɛn'kʌmpəs] *tr* circondare; racchiudere, contenere

encore ['aŋkor] *s* bis *m* ‖ *tr* (*a performance*) chiedere il bis di; (*a performer*) chiedere il bis a ‖ *interj* bis!

encounter [ɛn'kauntər] *s* (*casual meeting*) incontro; (*combat*) scontro ‖ *tr* incontrare ‖ *intr* scontrarsi

encourage [ɛn'kʌrɪdʒ] *tr* incoraggiare; (*to foster*) favorire

encouragement [ɛn'kʌrɪdʒmənt] *s* incoraggiamento; favoreggiamento

encroach [ɛn'krotʃ] *intr*—**to encroach on** *or* **upon** invadere; usurpare; occupare il territorio di

encumber [ɛn'kʌmbər] *tr* imbarazzare; ingombrare; (*to load with debts, etc*) gravare

encumbrance [ɛn'kʌmbrəns] *s* imbarazzo; ingombro; gravame *m*

encyclical [ɛn'sɪklɪkəl] *or* [ɛn'saɪklɪkəl] *s* enciclica

encyclopedia [ɛn‚saɪklə'pidɪ·ə] *s* enciclopedia

encyclopedic [ɛn‚saɪklə'pidɪk] *adj* enciclopedico

end [ɛnd] *s* (*extremity; concluding part*) fine *f*; (*e.g., of the week*) fine *f*; (*purpose*) fine *m*; (*part adjacent to an extremity*) lembo; (*small piece*) pezza, avanzo; (*of a beam*) testata; (sports) estrema; **at the end of** in capo a; in fondo a; **in the end** alla fine, all'ultimo; **no end** (coll) moltissimo; **no end of** (coll) un mucchio di; **to make both ends meet** sbarcare il lunario; **to no end** senza effetto; **to stand on end** mettere in piedi, drizzare; mettersi diritto; (*said of hair*) drizzarsi; **to the end that** affinché ‖ *tr* finire, terminare; **to end up** andare a finire ‖ *intr* finire, terminare; **to end up** finire

endanger [ɛn'dendʒər] *tr* mettere in pericolo

endear [ɛn'dɪr] *tr* affezionare; **to endear oneself to** rendersi caro a

endeavor [ɛn'dɛvər] *s* tentativo, sforzo || *intr* tentare, sforzarsi

endemic [ɛn'dɛmɪk] *adj* endemico || *s* endemia

ending ['ɛndɪŋ] *s* fine *f*, conclusione; (gram) terminazione, desinenza

endive ['ɛndaɪv] *s* indivia

endless ['ɛndlɪs] *adj* interminabile; sterminato; (mach) senza fine

end'most' *adj* estremo, ultimo

endorse [ɛn'dɔrs] *tr* girare; (fig) approvare, confermare

endorsee [ˌɛndɔr'si] *s* giratario

endorsement [ɛn'dɔrsmənt] *s* girata; approvazione, conferma

endorser [ɛn'dɔrsər] *s* girante *mf*

endow [ɛn'dau] *tr* dotare

endowment [ɛn'daumənt] *adj* dotale || *s* (*of an institution*) dotazione; (*gift, talent*) dote *f*

end' pap'er *s* risguardo

endurance [ɛn'djurəns] or [ɛn'durəns] *s* sopportazione, tolleranza; (*ability to hold out*) resistenza, forza; (*lasting time*) durata

endure [ɛn'djur] or [ɛn'dur] *tr* sopportare, tollerare; resistere (with *dat*) || *intr* durare, resistere

enduring [ɛn'djurɪŋ] or [ɛn'durɪŋ] *adj* duraturo, durevole; paziente

enema ['ɛnəmə] *s* clistere *m*

ene•my ['ɛnəmi] *adj* nemico || *s* (-**mies**) nemico

en'emy al'ien *s* straniero nemico

energetic [ˌɛnər'dʒɛtɪk] *adj* energetico, vigoroso

ener•gy ['ɛnərdʒi] *s* (-**gies**) energia

enervate ['ɛnərˌvet] *tr* snervare

enfeeble [ɛn'fibəl] *tr* indebolire

enfold [ɛn'fold] *tr* avvolgere; abbracciare

enforce [ɛn'fors] *tr* far osservare; ottenere per forza; (*e.g., obedience*) imporre; (*an argument*) far valere

enforcement [ɛn'forsmənt] *s* imposizione; (*of a law*) esecuzione

enfranchise [ɛn'fræntʃaɪz] *tr* liberare; concedere il diritto di voto a

engage [ɛn'gedʒ] *tr* occupare; riservare; (*s.o.'s attention*) attrarre; (*a gear*) ingranare; (*the enemy*) ingaggiare; (*to hire*) assumere; (theat) scritturare; **to be engaged, to be engaged to be married** essere fidanzato; **to engage s.o. in conversation** intavolare una conversazione con qlcu || *intr* essere occupato; essere impiegato; assumere un'obbligazione; (mil) impegnarsi; (mach) ingranare, incastrarsi

engaged [ɛn'gedʒd] *adj* fidanzato; occupato, impegnato; (*column*) murato

engagement [ɛn'gedʒmənt] *s* accordo; fidanzamento; impegno, contratto; (*appointment*) appuntamento; (mil) azione; (mach) innesto

engage'ment ring' *s* anello di fidanzamento

engaging [ɛn'gedʒɪŋ] *adj* attrattivo

engender [ɛn'dʒɛndər] *tr* ingenerare

engine ['ɛndʒɪn] *s* macchina; (aut) motore *m*; (rr) locomotiva, motrice *f*

engineer [ˌɛndʒə'nɪr] *s* ingegnere *m*; (rr) macchinista *m*; (mil) zappatore *m*, geniere *m* || *tr* costruire; progettare

engineering [ˌɛndʒə'nɪrɪŋ] *s* ingegneria

en'gine house' *s* stazione dei pompieri

en'gine•man' *s* (-**men**) (rr) macchinista *m*

en'gine room' *s* sala macchine

en'gine-room' tel'egraph *s* (naut) telegrafo di macchina, trasmettitore *m*

England ['ɪŋglənd] *s* l'Inghilterra

Englander ['ɪŋgləndər] *s* nativo dell'Inghilterra

English ['ɪŋglɪʃ] *adj* inglese || *s* inglese *m*; (billiards) effetto; **the English** gli inglesi

Eng'lish Chan'nel *s* Canale *m* della Manica

Eng'lish dai'sy *s* margherita

Eng'lish horn' *s* (mus) corno inglese

Eng'lish•man *s* (-**men**) inglese *m*

Eng'lish-speak'ing *adj* di lingua inglese, anglofono

Eng'lish•wom'an *s* (-**wom'en**) inglese *f*

engraft [ɛn'græft] or [ɛn'graft] *tr* (hort) innestare; (fig) inculcare

engrave [ɛn'grev] *tr* incidere

engraver [ɛn'grevər] *s* incisore *m*

engraving [ɛn'grevɪŋ] *s* incisione

engross [ɛn'gros] *tr* preoccupare, assorbire; redigere ufficialmente, scrivere a grandi caratteri; monopolizzare

engrossing [ɛn'grosɪŋ] *adj* assorbente

engulf [ɛn'gʌlf] *tr* sommergere, inondare

enhance [ɛn'hæns] or [ɛn'hans] *tr* valorizzare; far risaltare

enigma [ɪ'nɪgmə] *s* enigma *m*

enigmatic(al) [ˌɪnɪg'mætɪk(əl)] *adj* enigmatico

enjambment [ɛn'dʒæmmənt] or [ɛn'dʒæmbmənt] *s* inarcatura

enjoin [ɛn'dʒɔɪn] *tr* ingiungere, intimare

enjoy [ɛn'dʒɔɪ] *tr* godere; **to enjoy+ ger** provar piacere in + *inf;* **to enjoy oneself** divertirsi

enjoyable [ɛn'dʒɔɪ•əbəl] *adj* gradevole

enjoyment [ɛn'dʒɔɪmənt] *s* (*pleasure*) piacere *m*; (*pleasurable use*) godimento

enkindle [ɛn'kɪndəl] *tr* infiammare

enlarge [ɛn'lardʒ] *tr* aumentare; ingrossare; (phot) ingrandire || *intr* aumentare; **to enlarge on** or **upon** dilungarsi su

enlargement [ɛn'lardʒmənt] *s* aumento; ingrossamento; (phot) ingrandimento

enlighten [ɛn'laɪtən] *tr* illustrare, illuminare

enlightenment [ɛn'laɪtənmənt] *s* spiegazione, schiarimento || **Enlightenment** *s* illuminismo

enlist [ɛn'lɪst] *tr* (*e.g., s.o.'s favor*) guadagnarsi; (*the help of a person*) ottenere; (mil) ingaggiare || *intr* (mil) ingaggiarsi, arruolarsi; **to enlist**

in (a cause) dare il proprio appoggio a

enlistment [ɛn'lɪstmənt] s arruolamento, ingaggio

enliven [ɛn'laɪvən] tr ravvivare

enmesh [ɛn'mɛʃ] tr irretire

enmi·ty ['ɛnmɪti] s (-ties) inimicizia

ennoble [ɛn'nobəl] tr nobilitare

ennui ['ɑnwi] s noia, tedio

enormous [ɪ'nɔrməs] adj enorme

enormously [ɪ'nɔrməsli] adv enormemente

enough [ɪ'nʌf] adj abbastanza || s il sufficiente || adv abbastanza || interj basta!

enounce [ɪ'naʊns] tr enunciare; (to declare) affermare

enrage [ɛn'redʒ] tr infuriare, irritare

enrapture [ɛn'ræptʃər] tr mandare in visibilio, estasiare

enrich [ɛn'rɪtʃ] tr arricchire

enroll [ɛn'rol] tr arruolare, ingaggiare; (a student) iscrivere || intr arruolarsi, ingaggiarsi; (said of a student) iscriversi

enrollment [ɛn'rolmənt] s arruolamento, ingaggio; (of a student) iscrizione

en route [ɑn 'rut] adv in cammino; **en route to** in via per

ensconce [ɛn'skɑns] tr nascondere; **to esconce oneself** rannicchiarsi, istallarsi comodamente

ensemble [ɑn'sɑmbəl] s insieme m; (mus) concertato

ensign ['ɛnsaɪn] s (standard) bandiera, insegna; (badge) distintivo || ['ɛnsən] or ['ɛnsaɪn] s guardamarina m

ensilage ['ɛnsəlɪdʒ] s (preservation of fodder) insilamento; (preserved fodder) insilato

ensile ['ɛnsaɪl] or [ɛn'saɪl] tr insilare

enslave [ɛn'slev] tr fare schiavo, asservire

enslavement [ɛn'slevmənt] s asservimento

ensnare [ɛn'snɛr] tr irretire

ensue [ɛn'su] or [ɛn'sju] intr risultare; seguire, conseguire

ensuing [ɛn'su·ɪŋ] or [ɛn'sju·ɪŋ] adj risultante, conseguente; seguente

ensure [ɛn'ʃʊr] tr assicurare, garantire

entail [ɛn'tel] s (law) obbligo || tr provocare, comportare; (law) obbligare

entangle [ɛn'tæŋgəl] tr intricare, imbrogliare, impigliare

entanglement [ɛn'tæŋgəlmənt] s groviglio, garbuglio

enter ['ɛntər] tr (a house) entrare in; (in the customhouse) dichiarare; (to make a record of) registrare; (a student) iscrivere; iscriversi a; fare membro; (to undertake) intraprendere; **to enter s.o.'s head** passare per la testa a qlcu || intr entrare; (theat) entrare in scena; **to enter into** entrare in; (a contract) impegnarsi in; **to enter on** or **upon** intraprendere

enterprise ['ɛntər‚praɪz] s (undertak-

ing) impresa; (spirit, push) intraprendenza

enterprising ['ɛntər‚praɪzɪŋ] adj intraprendente

entertain [‚ɛntər'ten] tr divertire, intrattenere; (guests) ospitare; (a hope) accarezzare; (a proposal) considerare || intr ricevere

entertainer [‚ɛntər'tenər] s (host) ospite mf; (in public) attore m, cantante mf, fine dicitore m

entertaining [‚ɛntər'tenɪŋ] adj divertente

entertainment [‚ɛntər'tenmənt] s trattenimento, svago; spettacolo, attrazione; buon trattamento

enthrall [ɛn'θrɔl] tr affascinare, incantare; (to subjugate) asservire, soggiogare

enthrone [ɛn'θron] tr mettere sul trono, intronizzare; esaltare, innalzare

enthuse [ɛn'θuz] or [ɛn'θjuz] tr (coll) entusiasmare || intr (coll) entusiasmarsi

enthusiasm [ɛn'θuzɪ‚æzəm] or [ɛn'θjuzɪ‚æzəm] s entusiasmo

enthusiast [ɛn'θuzɪ‚æst] or [ɛn'θjuzɪ‚æst] s entusiasta mf, maniaco

enthusiastic [ɛn‚θuzɪ'æstɪk] or [ɛn‚θjuzɪ'æstɪk] adj entusiastico

entice [ɛn'taɪs] tr attrarre, provocare; tentare

enticement [ɛn'taɪsmənt] s attrazione, provocazione; tentazione

entire [ɛn'taɪr] adj intero

entirely [ɛn'taɪrli] adv interamente; (solely) solamente

entire·ty [ɛn'taɪrti] s (-ties) interezza; totalità f

entitle [ɛn'taɪtəl] tr dar diritto a; (to give a name to) intitolare

enti·ty ['ɛntɪti] s (-ties) (something real; organization, institution) ente m; (existence) entità f

entomb [ɛn'tum] tr seppellire

entombment [ɛn'tummənt] s sepoltura

entomology [‚ɛntə'mɑlədʒi] s entomologia

entourage [‚ɑntu'rɑʒ] s seguito

entrails ['ɛntrelz] or ['ɛntrəlz] spl visceri mpl

entrain [ɛn'tren] tr far salire sul treno || intr imbarcarsi sul treno

entrance ['ɛntrəns] s entrata, ingresso || [ɛn'træns] or [ɛn'trɑns] tr ipnotizzare, incantare

en'trance exam'ina'tion s esame m d'ammissione

entrancing [ɛn'trænsɪŋ] or [ɛn'trɑn-sɪŋ] adj incantatore

entrant ['ɛntrənt] s nuovo membro; (sports) concorrente mf

en·trap [ɛn'træp] v (pret & pp -trapped; ger -trapping) tr intrappolare, irretire

entreat [ɛn'trit] tr implorare

entreat·y [ɛn'triti] s (-ies) implorazione, supplica

entree ['ɑntre] s entrata, ingresso; (culin) prima portata

entrench [ɛn'trɛntʃ] tr trincerare || intr
—**to entrench on** or **upon** violare

entrust [ɛn'trʌst] *tr* affidare, confidare

en·try ['ɛntri] *s* (**-tries**) entrata; (*item*) partita, registrazione; (*in a dictionary*) lemma, esponente *m;* (*sports*) concorrente *mf*

entwine [ɛn'twaɪn] *tr* intrecciare ‖ *intr* intrecciarsi

enumerate [ɪ'njumə‚ret] or [ɪ'numə‚ret] *tr* enumerare

enunciate [ɪ'nʌnsɪ‚et] or [ɪ'nʌnʃɪ‚et] *tr* enunciare, staccare

envelop [ɛn'vɛləp] *tr* involgere

envelope ['ɛnvə‚lop] or ['ɑnvə‚lop] *s* (*for a letter*) busta; (*wrapper*) involucro

envenom [ɛn'vɛnəm] *tr* avvelenare

enviable ['ɛnvɪ‚əbəl] *adj* invidiabile

envious ['ɛnvɪ‚əs] *adj* invidioso

environment [ɛn'vaɪrənmənt] *s* ambiente *m;* condizioni *fpl* ambientali

environs [ɛn'vaɪrənz] *spl* dintorni *mpl*, sobborghi *mpl*

envisage [ɛn'vɪzɪdʒ] *tr* considerare, immaginare

envoi ['ɛnvɔɪ] *s* (pros) congedo

envoy ['ɛnvɔɪ] *s* inviato; (mil) parlamentare *m;* (pros) congedo

en·vy ['ɛnvi] *s* (**-vies**) invidia ‖ *v* (*pret & pp* **-vied**) *tr* invidiare

enzyme ['ɛnzaɪm] or ['ɛnzɪm] *s* enzima *m*

epaulet or **epaulette** ['ɛpə‚lɛt] *s* spallina

epenthe·sis [ɛ'pɛnθɪsɪs] *s* (**-ses** [‚siz]) epentesi *f*

ephemeral [ɪ'fɛmərəl] *adj* effimero

epic ['ɛpɪk] *adj* epico ‖ *s* epica

epicure ['ɛpɪ‚kjʊr] *s* epicureo

epicurean [‚ɛpɪkju'ri‚ən] *adj & s* epicureo

epidemic [‚ɛpɪ'dɛmɪk] *adj* epidemico ‖ *s* epidemia

epidermis [‚ɛpɪ'dʌrmɪs] *s* epidermide *f*

epiglottis [‚ɛpɪ'glɑtɪs] *s* epiglottide *f*

epigram ['ɛpɪ‚græm] *s* epigramma *m*

epilepsy ['ɛpɪ‚lɛpsi] *s* epilessia

epileptic [‚ɛpɪ'lɛptɪk] *adj & s* epilettico

epilogue ['ɛpɪ‚lɔg] or ['ɛpɪ‚lɑg] *s* epilogo

Epiphany [ɪ'pɪfəni] *s* Epifania

Episcopalian [ɪ‚pɪskə'peli‚ən] *adj & s* episcopaliano

episode ['ɛpɪ‚sod] *s* episodio

epistle [ɪ'pɪsəl] *s* epistola

epitaph ['ɛpɪ‚tæf] *s* epitaffio

epithet ['ɛpɪ‚θɛt] *s* epiteto

epitome [ɪ'pɪtəmi] *s* epitome *f;* (fig) prototipo, personificazione

epitomize [ɪ'pɪtə‚maɪz] *tr* epitomare; (fig) incarnare, personificare

epoch ['ɛpək] or ['ipak] *s* epoca

epochal ['ɛpəkəl] *adj* memorabile

ep'och-mak'ing *adj*—**to be epoch-making** fare epoca

Ep'som salt' ['ɛpsəm] *s* sale *m* inglese

equable ['ɛkwəbəl] or ['ikwəbəl] *adj* uniforme; tranquillo

equal ['ikwəl] *adj* uguale; **equal to** pari a, all'altezza di ‖ *s* uguale *m* ‖ *v* (*pret & pp* **equaled** or **equalled**; *ger* **equaling** or **equalling**) *tr* uguagliare

equali·ty [ɪ'kwɑlɪti] *s* (**-ties**) uguaglianza

equalize ['ikwə‚laɪz] *tr* uguagliare; (*to make uniform*) perequare, pareggiare

equally ['ikwəli] *adv* ugualmente

equanimity [‚ikwə'nɪmɪti] *s* equanimità *f*

equate [i'kwet] *tr* mettere in forma di equazione; considerare uguale or uguali

equation [i'kweʒən] or [i'kweʃən] *s* equazione

equator [i'kwetər] *s* equatore *m*

equatorial [‚ikwə'tɔrɪ‚əl] *adj* equatoriale

equer·ry ['ɛkwəri] or [ɪ'kwɛri] *s* (**-ries**) scudiero

equestrian [ɪ'kwɛstrɪ‚ən] *adj* equestre ‖ *s* cavallerizzo

equilateral [‚ikwɪ'lætərəl] *adj* equilatero

equilibrium [‚ikwɪ'lɪbrɪ‚əm] *s* equilibrio

equinoctial [‚ikwɪ'nakʃəl] *adj* equinoziale

equinox ['ikwɪ‚naks] *s* equinozio

equip [ɪ'kwɪp] *v* (*pret & pp* **equipped;** *ger* **equipping**) *tr* equipaggiare; **to equip** (*e.g., a ship*) **with** munire di

equipment [ɪ'kwɪpmənt] *s* equipaggiamento; (*skill*) attitudine *f*, capacità *f*

equipoise ['ikwɪ‚pɔɪz] or ['ɛkwɪ‚pɔɪz] *s* equilibrio ‖ *tr* equilibrare

equitable ['ɛkwɪtəbəl] *adj* equo

equi·ty ['ɛkwɪti] *s* (**-ties**) (*fairness*) equità *f;* valore *m* al netto; (*in a corporation*) interessenza azionaria

equivalent [ɪ'kwɪvələnt] *adj* equivalente ‖ *s* equivalente *m;* (com) controvalore *m*

equivocal [ɪ'kwɪvəkəl] *adj* equivoco

equivocate [ɪ'kwɪvə‚ket] *intr* giocare sulle parole, parlare in maniera equivoca

equivocation [ɪ‚kwɪvə'keʃən] *s* equivocità *f;* equivoco

era ['ɪrə] or ['irə] *s* era, evo

eradicate [ɪ'rædɪ‚ket] *tr* sradicare

erase [ɪ'res] *tr* cancellare

eraser [ɪ'resər] *s* gomma da cancellare; (*for blackboard*) spugna

erasure [ɪ'reʃər] or [ɪ'reʒər] *s* cancellatura; (*of a tape*) cancellazione

ere [ɛr] *prep* (lit) prima di ‖ *conj* (lit) prima che

erect [ɪ'rɛkt] *adj* dritto, eretto; (*hair*) irto ‖ *tr* (*to set in upright position*) drizzare; (*a building*) erigere, costruire; (*a machine*) montare

erection [ɪ'rɛkʃən] *s* erezione

ermine ['ʌrmɪn] *s* ermellino; (fig) carica di giudice, toga, magistratura

erode [ɪ'rod] *tr* erodere ‖ *intr* corrodersi, consumarsi

erosion [ɪ'roʒən] *s* erosione

erotic [ɪ'rɑtɪk] *adj* erotico

err [ʌr] *intr* errare; (*to be incorrect*) sbagliarsi

errand ['ɛrənd] *s* corsa, commissione; **to run an errand** fare una commissione

er'rand boy' *s* fattorino, galoppino

erratic [ɪ'rætɪk] *adj* erratico; strano, eccentrico

erra·tum [ɪ'retəm] or [ɪ'ratəm] *s* (-ta [tə]) errore *m* di stampa

erroneous [ɪ'ronɪ·əs] *adj* erroneo

error ['erər] *s* errore *m*, sbaglio

erudite ['eru̇ˌdaɪt] or ['erju̇ˌdaɪt] *adj* erudito, dotto

erudition [ˌeru̇'dɪʃən] or [ˌerju̇'dɪʃən] *s* erudizione

erupt [ɪ'rʌpt] *intr* (*said of a volcano*) eruttare; (*said of a skin rash*) fiorire; (*said of a tooth*) spuntare; (fig) erompere

eruption [ɪ'rʌpʃən] *s* eruzione

escalate ['eskəˌlet] *tr & intr* aumentare

escalation [ˌeskə'leʃən] *s* aumento

escalator ['eskəˌletər] *s* scala mobile

escallop [ɛs'kæləp] *s* (*on edge of cloth*) dentellatura, festone *m*; (*mollusk*) pettine *m* ‖ *tr* cuocere in conchiglia; cuocere al forno con salsa e pane grattugiato

escapade [ˌeskə'ped] *s* scappatella

escape [ɛs'kep] *s* (*getaway*) fuga; (*from responsibility, duties, etc.*) scampo ‖ *tr* sottrarsi a, eludere; **to escape s.o.** scappare da qlcu; scappar di mente a qlcu ‖ *intr* scappare; sprigionarsi; **to escape from** (*a person*) sfuggire a; (*jail*) evadere da

escapee [ˌeskə'pi] *s* evaso

escape' lit'erature' *s* letteratura di evasione

escapement [ɛs'kepmənt] *s* scappamento

escape' veloc'ity *s* (rok) velocità *f* di fuga

escarpment [ɛs'karpmənt] *s* scarpata

eschew [ɛs't/u] *tr* evitare, rifuggire da

escort ['eskɔrt] *s* scorta; (*of a woman or girl*) compagno, cavaliere *m* ‖ [ɛs'kɔrt] *tr* scortare

escutcheon [ɛs'kʌt/ən] *s* scudo; (*plate in front of lock on door*) bocchetta

Esk·imo ['eskɪˌmo] *adj* eschimese ‖ *s* (-mos or -mo) eschimese *mf*

esopha·gus [i'safəgəs] *s* (-gi [ˌdʒaɪ]) esofago

espalier [ɛs'pæljər] *s* spalliera

especial [ɛs'pe/əl] *adj* speciale

espionage ['espɪ·ənɪdʒ] or [ˌespɪ·ə'naʒ] *s* spionaggio

esplanade [ˌesplə'ned] or [ˌesplə'nad] *s* spianata, piazzale *m*

espousal [ɛs'pauzəl] *s* sposalizio; (*of a cause*) adozione

espouse [ɛs'pauz] *tr* sposare; (*to advocate*) abbracciare, adottare

esquire [ɛs'kwaɪr] or ['eskwaɪr] *s* scudiero ‖ **Esquire** *s* titolo di cortesia usato generalmente con persone di riguardo

essay ['ese] *s* saggio

essayist ['ese·ɪst] *s* saggista *mf*

essence ['esəns] *s* essenza

essential [ɛ'sɛn/əl] *adj & s* essenziale *m*

establish [ɛs'tæblɪ/] *tr* stabilire

establishment [ɛs'tæblɪ/mənt] *s* stabilimento; fondazione; **the Establishment** l'autorità costituita

estate [ɛs'tet] *s* stato; condizione sociale; (*landed property*) tenuta; (*a person's possessions*) patrimonio; (*left by a decedent*) massa ereditaria

esteem [ɛs'tim] *s* stima ‖ *tr* stimare

esthete ['ɛsθit] *s* esteta *mf*

esthetic [ɛs'θɛtɪk] *adj* estetico ‖ **esthetics** *ssg* estetica

estimable ['ɛstɪməbəl] *adj* stimabile

estimate ['ɛstɪˌmet] or ['ɛstɪmɪt] *s* stima, valutazione; (*statement of cost of work to be done*) preventivo ‖ ['ɛstɪˌmet] *tr* stimare, valutare; preventivare

estimation [ˌɛstɪ'meʃən] *s* stima; **in my estimation** a mio parere

estimator ['ɛstɪˌmetər] *s* preventivista *mf*

estrangement [ɛs'trendʒmənt] *s* alienazione, disaffezione

estuar·y ['ɛst/u̇ˌeri] *s* (-ies) estuario

etch [ɛt/] *tr & intr* incidere all'acquaforte

etcher ['ɛt/ər] *s* acquafortista *mf*

etching ['ɛt/ɪŋ] *s* acquaforte *f*

eternal [ɪ'tʌrnəl] *adj* eterno

eterni·ty [ɪ'tʌrnɪti] *s* (-ties) eternità *f*

ether ['iθər] *s* etere *m*

ethereal [ɪ'θɪrɪ·əl] *adj* etereo

ethical ['ɛθɪkəl] *adj* etico

ethics ['ɛθɪks] *ssg* etica

Ethiopian [ˌiθɪ'opɪ·ən] *adj & s* etiope *mf*

ethnic(al) ['ɛθnɪk(əl)] *adj* etnico

ethnography [ɛθ'nagrəfi] *s* etnografia

ethnology [ɛθ'nalədʒi] *s* etnologia

ethyl ['ɛθɪl] *s* etile *m*

ethylene ['ɛθɪˌlin] *s* etilene *m*

etiquette ['ɛtɪˌkɛt] *s* etichetta

étude [e'tjud] *s* (mus) studio

etymology [ˌɛtɪ'malədʒi] *s* etimologia

ety·mon ['ɛtɪˌman] *s* (-mons or -ma [mə]) etimo

eucalyp·tus [ˌjukə'lɪptəs] *s* (-tuses or -ti [taɪ]) eucalipto

Eucharist ['jukərɪst] *s* Eucaristia

eugenics [ju̇'dʒɛnɪks] *ssg* eugenetica

eulogistic [ˌjulə'dʒɪstɪk] *adj* elogiativo

eulogize ['juləˌdʒaɪz] *tr* elogiare

eulo·gy ['julədʒi] *s* (-gies) elogio; elogio funebre

eunuch ['junək] *s* eunuco

euphemism ['jufɪˌmɪzəm] *s* eufemismo

euphemistic [ˌjufɪ'mɪstɪk] *adj* eufemistico

euphonic [ju̇'fanɪk] *adj* eufonico

eupho·ny ['jufəni] *s* (-nies) eufonia

euphoria [ju̇'forɪ·ə] *s* euforia

euphuism ['jufju̇ˌɪzəm] *s* eufuismo

Europe ['ju̇rəp] *s* l'Europa

European [ˌju̇rə'pi·ən] *adj & s* europeo

euthanasia [ˌjuθə'neʒə] *s* eutanasia

evacuate [ɪ'vækju̇ˌet] *tr & intr* evacuare

evacuation [ɪˌvækju̇'eʃən] *s* evacuazione

evacuee [ɪ'vækju̇ˌi] or [ɪˌvækju̇'i] *s* sfollato

evade [ɪ'ved] *tr* eludere ‖ *intr* evadere

evaluate [ɪ'vælju̇ˌet] *tr* valutare

evaluation [ɪˌvælju̇'eʃən] *s* valutazione

Evangel [ɪ'vændʒəl] *s* Vangelo

evangelic(al) [ˌivæn'dʒɛlɪk(əl)] or [ˌevən'dʒɛlɪk(əl)] *adj* evangelico

Evangelist [ɪˈvændʒəlɪst] *s* evangelista *m*

evaporate [ɪˈvæpəˌret] *tr & intr* evaporare

evasion [ɪˈveʒən] *s* evasione; (*subterfuge*) scappatoia

evasive [ɪˈvesɪv] *adj* evasivo

eve [iv] *s* vigilia; **on the eve of** la vigilia di

even [ˈivən] *adj* (*smooth*) piano, regolare; (*number*) pari; uguale, uniforme; (*temperament*) calmo, placido; **even with** a livello di; **to be even** mettersi in pari; **to get even** prendersi la rivincita || *adv* anche; fino, perfino; pure; esattamente; magari; **even as** proprio mentre; **even if** anche se, quando pure; **even so** anche se così; **even though** quantunque; **even when** anche quando; **not even** neppure, nemmeno; **to break even** impattare || *tr* spianare; **to even up** bilanciare

evening [ˈivnɪŋ] *adj* serale || *s* sera, serata; **all evening** tutta la sera; **every evening** tutte le sere; **in the evening** la sera

eve'ning clothes' *spl* vestito da sera

eve'ning gown' *s* vestito da sera da signora

eve'ning star' *s* espero

e'ven·song' *s* (eccl) vespro

event [ɪˈvent] *s* avvenimento; (*outcome*) evenienza; (*public function*) manifestazione; (sports) prova; **at all events or in any event** in ogni caso; **in the event that** in caso che, se mai

eventful [ɪˈventfəl] *adj* ricco di avvenimenti; movimentato

eventual [ɪˈventʃʊ·əl] *adj* finale

eventuali·ty [ɪˌventʃʊˈælɪti] *s* (**-ties**) eventualità *f*, evenienza

eventually [ɪˈventʃʊ·əli] *adv* finalmente, alla fine

eventuate [ɪˈventʃʊˌet] *intr* risultare; accadere

ever [ˈevər] *adv* (*at all times*) sempre; (*at any time*) mai; **as ever** come sempre; **as much as ever** tanto come prima; **ever since** (*since that time*) sin da; da allora in poi; **ever so** molto; **ever so much** moltissimo; **hardly ever or scarcely ever** quasi mai; **not ... ever** non ... mai

ev'er·glade' *s* terreno paludoso coperto di erbe

ev'er·green' *adj & s* sempreverde *m & f*; **evergreens** decorazione di sempreverdi

ev'er·last'ing *adj* eterno; incessante; (*lasting indefinitely*) duraturo; (*wearisome*) noioso || *s* eternità *f*; (bot) semprevivo

ev'er·more' *adv* eternamente; **for evermore** per sempre

every [ˈevri] *adj* tutti i; (*each*) ogni, ciascuno; (*being each in a series*) ogni, e.g., **every three days** ogni tre giorni; **every bit** (coll) in tutto e per tutto, e.g., **every bit a man** un uomo in tutto e per tutto; **every now and then** di quando in quando; **every once in a while** una volta ogni tanto;

every other day ogni secondo giorno; **every which way** (coll) da tutte le parti; (coll) in disordine

ev'ery·bod'y *pron indef* ognuno, tutti

ev'ery·day' *adj* di ogni giorno; quotidiano; ordinario

ev'ery·man' *s* l'uomo qualunque || *pron* chiunque

ev'ery·one' or **ev'ery one'** *pron indef* ciascuno, tutti

ev'ery·thing' *pron indef* tutto, ogni cosa, tutto quanto

ev'ery·where' *adv* dappertutto, dovunque

evict [ɪˈvɪkt] *tr* sfrattare, sloggiare

eviction [ɪˈvɪkʃən] *s* sfratto, sloggio

evidence [ˈevɪdəns] *s* evidenza; (law) prova

evident [ˈevɪdənt] *adj* evidente

evil [ˈivəl] *adj* cattivo, malvagio || *s* male *m*; disgrazia

evildoer [ˈivəlˌdu·ər] *s* malfattore *m*, malvagio

e'vil·do'ing *s* malafatta, malvagità *f*

e'vil eye' *s* iettatura, malocchio

evil-minded [ˈivəlˈmaɪndɪd] *adj* malintenzionato

e'vil one', **the** il nemico

evince [ɪˈvɪns] *tr* mostrare, manifestare

evoke [ɪˈvok] *tr* evocare

evolution [ˌevəˈluʃən] *s* evoluzione

evolve [ɪˈvalv] *tr* sviluppare || *intr* evolversi

ewe [ju] *s* pecora

ewer [ˈju·ər] *s* brocca

ex [eks] *prep* senza includere

exacerbation [ɪgˌzæsərˈbeʃən] *s* esulcerazione, esacerbazione

exacerbate [ɪgˈzæsərˌbet] *tr* esacerbare, esulcerare

exact [egˈzækt] *adj* esatto || *tr* esigere

exacting [egˈzæktɪŋ] *adj* esigente

exaction [egˈzækʃən] *s* esazione

exactly [egˈzæktli] *adv* esattamente; (*sharp, on the dot*) in punto

exactness [egˈzæktnɪs] *s* esattezza

exaggerate [egˈzædʒəˌret] *tr* esagerare

exalt [egˈzɔlt] *tr* elevare, esaltare

exam [egˈzæm] *s* (coll) esame *m*

examination [egˌzæmɪˈneʃən] *s* esame *m*; **to take an examination** sostenere un esame

examine [egˈzæmɪn] *tr* esaminare

examiner [egˈzæmɪnər] *s* esaminatore *m*

example [egˈzæmpəl] or [egˈzampəl] *s* esempio; (*precedent*) precedente *m*; (*of mathematics*) problema *m*; **for example** per esempio

exasperate [egˈzæspəˌret] *tr* esasperare

excavate [ˈekskəˌvet] *tr* scavare

exceed [ekˈsid] *tr* eccedere

exceedingly [ekˈsidɪŋli] *adv* estremamente, sommamente

ex·cel [ekˈsel] *v* (*pret & pp* **-celled**; *ger* **-celling**) *tr* sorpassare || *intr* eccellere

excellence [ˈeksələns] *s* eccellenza

excellen·cy [ˈeksələnsi] *s* (**-cies**) eccellenza; **Your Excellency** Sua Eccellenza

excelsior [ekˈselsɪ·ər] *s* trucioli *mpl* per imballaggio

except [ekˈsept] *prep* eccetto; **except**

for tranne, ad eccezione di; **except that** eccetto che || *tr* eccettuare
exception [ɛk'sɛpʃən] s eccezione; **to take exception** obiettare; scandalizzarsi; **with the exception of** a esclusione di, eccetto
exceptional [ɛk'sɛpʃənəl] *adj* eccezionale
excerpt ['ɛksʌrpt] or [ɛk'sʌrpt] *s* brano, selezione || [ɛk'sʌrpt] *tr* scegliere, selezionare
excess ['ɛksɛs] or [ɛk'sɛs] *adj* eccedente || [ɛk'sɛs] *s* (*amount or degree by which one thing exceeds another*) eccedente *m*, eccedenza; (*excessive amount; immoderate indulgence; unlawful conduct*) eccesso; **in excess of** più di
ex'cess bag'gage *s* bagaglio eccedente
ex'cess fare' *s* (rr) supplemento
excessive [ɛk'sɛsɪv] *adj* eccessivo
ex'cess-prof'its tax' *s* tassa sui sopraprofitti
exchange [ɛks'tʃendʒ] *s* scambio; (*place for buying and selling*) borsa; (*transactions in the currencies of two different countries*) cambio; (telp) centrale *f*, centralino; **in exchange for** in cambio di || *tr* scambiare, scambiarsi; **to exchange blows** venire alle mani; **to exchange greetings** salutarsi
exchequer [ɛks'tʃɛkər] or ['ɛkstʃɛkər] *s* erario, tesoro
ex'cise tax' [ɛk'saɪz] or ['ɛksaɪz] *s* imposta sul consumo
excitable [ɛk'saɪtəbəl] *adj* eccitabile
excite [ɛk'saɪt] *tr* eccitare
excitement [ɛk'saɪtmənt] *s* eccitazione
exciting [ɛk'saɪtɪŋ] *adj* emozionante; (*stimulating*) eccitante
exclaim [ɛks'klem] *tr & intr* esclamare
exclamation [,ɛksklə'meʃən] *s* esclamazione
exclama'tion mark' or **point'** *s* punto esclamativo
exclude [ɛks'klud] *tr* escludere
excluding [ɛks'kludɪŋ] *prep* a esclusione di, senza contare
exclusion [ɛks'kluʒən] *s* esclusione; **to the exclusion of** tranne, salvo
exclusive [ɛks'klusɪv] *adj* esclusivo; **exclusive of** escluso, senza contare || *s* (journ) esclusiva
excommunicate [,ɛkskə'mjunɪ,ket] *tr* scomunicare
excommunication [,ɛkskə,mjunɪ'keʃən] *s* scomunica
excoriate [ɛks'korɪ,et] *tr* criticare aspramente, vituperare
excrement ['ɛkskrəmənt] *s* escremento
excruciating [ɛks'kruʃɪ,etɪŋ] *adj* (*e.g., pleasure*) estremo; (*e.g., pain*) atroce, lancinante, straziante
exculpate ['ɛkskʌl,pet] or [ɛks'kʌlpet] *tr* scolpare, scagionare
excursion [ɛks'kʌrʒən] or [ɛks'kʌrʃən] *s* escursione, gita
excursionist [ɛks'kʌrʒənɪst] or [ɛks'kʌrʃənɪst] *s* escursionista *mf*
excusable [ɛks'kjuzəbəl] *adj* scusabile
excuse [ɛks'kjus] *s* scusa || [ɛks'kjuz] *tr* scusare; esentare; (*a debt*) rimettere
execute ['ɛksɪ,kjut] *tr* (*to carry out; to produce*) eseguire; (*to put to death*) giustiziare; (law) rendere esecutorio
execution [,ɛksɪ'kjuʃən] *s* esecuzione; (*e.g., of a criminal*) esecuzione capitale
executioner [,ɛksɪ'kjuʃənər] *s* giustiziere *m*, boia *m*, carnefice *m*
executive [ɛg'zɛkjətɪv] *adj* esecutivo || *s* esecutivo; (*of a school, business, etc.*) dirigente *mf*
Exec'utive Man'sion *s* palazzo del governatore; residenza del capo del governo statunitense
executor [ɛg'zɛkjətər] *s* (law) esecutore testamentario
executrix [ɛg'zɛkjətrɪks] *s* (law) esecutrice testamentaria
exemplary [ɛg'zɛmpləri] or ['ɛgzəm,pləri] *adj* esemplare
exempli•fy [ɛg'zɛmplɪ,faɪ] *v* (*pret & pp* **-fied**) *tr* esemplificare
exempt [ɛg'zɛmpt] *adj* esente || *tr* esimere, esentare
exemption [ɛg'zɛmpʃən] *s* esenzione
exercise ['ɛksər,saɪz] *s* esercizio; cerimonia; **to take exercise** fare del moto || *tr* esercitare; (*care*) usare; (*to worry*) preoccupare || *intr* esercitarsi
exert [ɛg'zʌrt] *tr* (*e.g., power*) esercitare; **to exert oneself** sforzarsi
exertion [ɛg'zʌrʃən] *s* sforzo, tentativo; (*active use*) uso, esercizio
exhalation [,ɛks·hə'leʃən] *s* (*of gas, vapors*) esalazione; (*of air from lungs*) espirazione
exhale [ɛks'hel] or [ɛg'zel] *tr* (*gases, vapors, etc.*) esalare; (*air from lungs*) espirare || *intr* esalare; espirare
exhaust [ɛg'zɔst] *s* scarico, scappamento; tubo di scarico or scappamento || *tr* (*to wear out*) spossare, finire; (*to use up*) esaurire, dar fondo a; vuotare
exhaust' fan' *s* aspiratore *m*
exhaustion [ɛg'zɔstʃən] *s* esaurimento; estenuazione; (sports) cotta
exhaustive [ɛg'zɔstɪv] *adj* esauriente
exhaust' man'ifold *s* collettore *m* di scarico
exhaust' pipe' *s* tubo di scarico
exhaust' valve' *s* valvola di scappamento
exhibit [ɛg'zɪbɪt] *s* esposizione; (law) documento in giudizio || *tr* esibire
exhibition [,ɛksɪ'bɪʃən] *s* esibizione
exhibitor [ɛg'zɪbɪtər] *s* espositore *m*
exhilarating [ɛg'zɪlə,retɪŋ] *adj* esilarante
exhort [ɛg'zɔrt] *tr* esortare
exhume [ɛks'hjum] or [ɛg'zjum] *tr* esumare, dissotterrare
exigen•cy ['ɛksɪdʒənsi] *s* (**-cies**) esigenza
exigent ['ɛksɪdʒənt] *adj* esigente
exile ['ɛgzaɪl] or ['ɛksaɪl] *s* esilio; (*person*) esule *mf* || *tr* esiliare
exist [ɛg'zɪst] *intr* esistere
existence [ɛg'zɪstəns] *s* esistenza
existing [ɛg'zɪstɪŋ] *adj* esistente
exit ['ɛgzɪt] or ['ɛksɪt] *s* uscita || *intr* uscire

exodus ['ɛksədəs] s esodo
exonerate [ɛg'zɑnə,ret] tr (from an obligation) esonerare; (from blame) scagionare
exorbitant [ɛg'zɔrbɪtənt] adj esorbitante
exorcise ['ɛksɔr,saɪz] tr esorcizzare
exotic [ɛg'zɑtɪk] adj esotico
expand [ɛks'pænd] tr (a metal) dilatare; (gas) espandere; (to enlarge) allargare, ampliare; (to unfold) spiegare; (math) svolgere, sviluppare || intr dilatarsi; espandersi; allargarsi, ampliarsi; spiegarsi, estendersi
expanse [ɛks'pæns] s vastità f
expansion [ɛks'pænʃən] s espansione
expansive [ɛks'pænsɪv] adj espansivo
expatiate [ɛks'peʃɪ,et] intr dilungarsi
expatriate [ɛks'petrɪ·ɪt] adj esiliato || s esule mf || [ɛks'petrɪ,et] tr esiliare; **to expatriate oneself** espatriare
expect [ɛks'pɛkt] tr aspettare, attendere; (coll) credere, supporre; **to expect it** aspettarselo, aspettarsela
expectan·cy [ɛks'pɛktənsi] s (-cies) aspettativa, aspettazione
expect'ant moth'er [ɛks'pɛktənt] s futura madre
expectation [,ɛkspɛk'teʃən] s aspettativa
expectorate [ɛks'pɛktə,ret] tr & intr espettorare
expedien·cy [ɛks'pidɪ·ənsi] s (-cies) industria, ingegno; opportunismo, vantaggio personale
expedient [ɛks'pidɪ·ənt] adj conveniente; vantaggioso; (acting with self-interest) opportunista || s espediente m
expedite ['ɛkspɪ,daɪt] tr sbrigare, accelerare; (a document) dar corso a
expedition [,ɛkspɪ'dɪʃən] s spedizione; (speed) celerità f
expeditionary [,ɛkspɪ'dɪʃən,ɛri] adj (e.g., corps) di spedizione
expeditious [,ɛkspɪ'dɪʃəs] adj spicciativo, spiccio
ex·pel [ɛks'pɛl] v (pret & pp **-pelled; ger -pelling**) tr espellere, scacciare
expend [ɛks'pɛnd] tr spendere, consumare
expendable [ɛks'pɛndəbəl] adj spendibile; da buttarsi via; (mil) da sacrificare
expenditure [ɛks'pɛndɪtʃər] s spesa
expense [ɛks'pɛns] s spesa; **at the expense of** al costo di; **expenses** spese fpl; **to meet expenses** far fronte alle spese
expense' account' s conto delle spese risarcibili
expensive [ɛks'pɛnsɪv] adj caro, costoso
experience [ɛks'pɪrɪ·əns] s esperienza || tr sperimentare, provare
experienced [ɛks'pɪrɪ·ənst] adj esperto, sperimentato
experiment [ɛks'pɛrɪmənt] s esperimento || [ɛks'pɛrɪ,mɛnt] intr sperimentare
expert ['ɛkspərt] adj & s esperto
expertise [,ɛkspər'tiz] s maestria

expiate ['ɛkspɪ,et] tr espiare
expiation [,ɛkspɪ'eʃən] s espiazione
expire [ɛks'paɪr] tr espirare || intr (to breathe out) espirare; (said of a contract) scadere; (to die) morire
explain [ɛks'plen] tr spiegare; **to explain away** giustificare; dar ragione di || intr spiegare, spiegarsi
explainable [ɛks'plenəbəl] adj spiegabile
explanation [,ɛksplə'neʃən] s spiegazione, delucidazione
explanatory [ɛks'plænə,tori] adj esplicativo
explicit [ɛks'plɪsɪt] adj esplicito
explode [ɛks'plod] tr far scoppiare; (a theory) smontare || intr scoppiare
exploit [ɛks'plɔɪt] or ['ɛksplɔɪt] s impresa, prodezza || [ɛks'plɔɪt] tr utilizzare, sfruttare
exploitation [,ɛksplɔɪ'teʃən] s utilizzazione, sfruttamento
exploration [,ɛksplə'reʃən] s esplorazione
explore [ɛks'plor] tr esplorare
explorer [ɛks'plorər] s esploratore m
explosion [ɛks'ploʒən] s esplosione, scoppio; (of a theory) confutazione
explosive [ɛks'plosɪv] adj & s esplosivo
exponent [ɛks'ponənt] s esponente m
export ['ɛksport] adj di esportazione || s esportazione, articolo di esportazione || [ɛks'port] or ['ɛksport] tr & intr esportare
exportation [,ɛkspor'teʃən] s esportazione
exporter ['ɛksportər] or [ɛks'portər] s esportatore m
expose [ɛks'poz] tr esporre; (to unmask) smascherare
exposé [,ɛkspo'ze] s rivelazione scandalosa, smascheramento
exposition [,ɛkspə'zɪʃən] s esposizione; interpretazione, commento
expostulate [ɛks'pɑstʃə,let] intr protestare; **to expostulate with** lagnarsi con
exposure [ɛks'poʒər] s (disclosure) rivelazione; (situation with regard to sunlight) esposizione; (phot) esposizione
expo'sure me'ter s (phot) fotometro, esposimetro
expound [ɛks'paund] tr esporre
express [ɛks'prɛs] adj espresso || s (rr) celere m, rapido, direttissimo; **by express** per espresso, a grande velocità || adv per espresso, a grande velocità || tr esprimere; mandare per espresso; (to squeeze out) spremere; **to express oneself** esprimersi
ex'press com'pany s servizio corriere
expression [ɛks'prɛʃən] s espressione
expressive [ɛks'prɛsɪv] adj espressivo
expressly [ɛks'prɛsli] adv espressamente
express'man s (-men) fattorino di servizio corriere
express'way' s autostrada
expropriate [ɛks'propri,et] tr espropriare
expulsion [ɛks'pʌlʃən] s espulsione

expunge [ɛks'pʌndʒ] *tr* espungere
expurgate ['ɛkspər͵get] *tr* espurgare
exquisite ['ɛkskwɪzɪt] or [ɛks'kwɪzɪt] *adj* squisito; intenso
ex'serv'ice-man' *s* (-men') ex combattente *m*
extant ['ɛkstənt] or [ɛks'tænt] *adj* ancora esistente
extemporaneous [ɛks͵tɛmpə'renɪ·əs] *adj* estemporaneo; (*made for the occasion*) improvvisato
extempore [ɛks'tɛmpəri] *adj* improvvisato || *adv* senza preparazione
extemporize [ɛks'tɛmpə͵raɪz] *tr* & *intr* improvvisare
extend [ɛks'tɛnd] *tr* allungare; estendere; (*e.g., aid*) offrire; (*payment of a debt*) dilazionare || *intr* estendersi
extended [ɛks'tɛndɪd] *adj* esteso; prolungato
extension [ɛks'tɛnʃən] *s* estensione; prolungamento; (com) proroga; (telp) derivazione
exten'sion lad'der *s* scala porta, scala a prolunga
exten'sion ta'ble *s* tavola allungabile
exten'sion tel'ephone' *s* telefono interno
extensive [ɛks'tɛnsɪv] *adj* (*wide*) vasto; (*lengthy*) lungo; (*characterized by extention*) estensivo
extent [ɛks'tɛnt] *s* estensione; **to a certain extent** fino a un certo punto; **to a great extent** in larga misura; **to the full extent** all'estremo limite
extenuate [ɛks'tɛnju͵et] *tr* (*to make seem less serious*) attenuare; (*to underrate*) sottovalutare
exterior [ɛks'tɪrɪ·ər] *adj* & *s* esteriore *m*
exterminate [ɛks'tʌrmɪ͵net] *tr* sterminare
external [ɛks'tʌrnəl] *adj* esterno || **externals** *spl* esteriorità *f*, di fuori *m*
extinct [ɛks'tɪŋkt] *adj* estinto
extinction [ɛks'tɪŋkʃən] *s* estinzione
extinguish [ɛks'tɪŋgwɪʃ] *tr* estinguere
extinguisher [ɛks'tɪŋgwɪʃər] *s* estintore *m*
extirpate ['ɛkstər͵pet] or [ɛks'tʌrpet] *tr* estirpare
ex·tol [ɛks'tol] or [ɛks'tɑl] *v* (*pret* & *pp* -tolled; *ger* -tolling) *tr* inneggiare
extort [ɛks'tɔrt] *tr* estorcere
extortion [ɛks'tɔrʃən] *s* estorsione
extra ['ɛkstrə] *adj* extra; (*spare*) di scorta || *s* (*of a newspaper*) edizione straordinaria; (*something additional*) soprappiù *m*; (theat) figurante *mf* || *adv* straordinariamente
ex'tra charge' *s* supplemento
extract ['ɛkstrækt] *s* estratto || [ɛks'trækt] *tr* (*to pull out*) estrarre; (*to take from a book*) scegliere, selezionare
extraction [ɛks'trækʃən] *s* estrazione
extracurricular [͵ɛkstrəkə'rɪkjələr] *adj* fuori del programma normale
extradition [͵ɛkstrə'dɪʃən] *s* estradizione
ex'tra·dry' *adj* molto secco, brut
ex'tra fare' *s* supplemento al biglietto

ex'tra·mar'ital *adj* extraconiugale
extramural [͵ɛkstrə'mjurəl] *adj* fuori della scuola, interscolastico; fuori delle mura
extraneous [ɛks'trenɪ·əs] *adj* estraneo
extraordinary [͵ɛkstrə'ɔrdɪ͵nɛri] or [ɛks'trɔrdɪ͵nɛri] *adj* straordinario
extrapolate [ɛks'træpə͵let] *tr* & *intr* estrapolare
extrasensory [͵ɛkstrə'sɛnsəri] *adj* extrasensoriale
extravagance [ɛks'trævəgəns] *s* prodigalità *f*; (*wildness, folly*) stravaganza
extravagant [ɛks'trævəgənt] *adj* prodigo; (*wild, foolish*) stravagante
extreme [ɛks'trim] *adj* & *s* estremo; **in the extreme** in massimo grado; **to go to extremes** andare agli estremi
extremely [ɛks'trimli] *adv* estremamente, in sommo grado
extreme' unc'tion *s* Estrema Unzione
extremist [ɛks'trimɪst] *adj* & *s* estremista *mf*
extremi·ty [ɛks'trɛmɪti] *s* (-ties) estremità *f*; (*great want*) estrema necessità; **extremities** estremi *mpl*; (*hands and feet*) estremità *fpl*
extricate ['ɛkstrɪ͵ket] *tr* districare
extrinsic [ɛks'trɪnsɪk] *adj* estrinseco
extrovert ['ɛkstrə͵vʌrt] *s* estroverso
extrude [ɛks'trud] *tr* estrudere || *intr* protrudere
exuberant [ɛg'zubərənt] or [ɛg'zjubərənt] *adj* esuberante
exude [ɛg'zud] or [ɛk'sud] *tr* & *intr* trasudare, stillare
exult [ɛg'zʌlt] *intr* esultare, tripudiare
exultant [ɛg'zʌltənt] *adj* esultante
eye [aɪ] *s* occhio; (*of hook and eye*) occhiello; **to catch one's eye** attirare l'attenzione di qlcu; **to feast one's eyes on** deliziarsi la vista con; **to lay eyes on** riuscire a vedere; **to make eyes at** fare gli occhi dolci a; **to roll one's eyes** stralunare gli occhi; **to see eye to eye** andare perfettamente d'accordo; **to shut one's eyes to** chiudere un occhio a; far finta di non vedere; **without batting an eye** senza batter ciglio || *v* (*pret* & *pp* eyed; *ger* eying or eyeing) *tr* occhieggiare; **to eye up and down** guardare da capo a piedi
eye'ball' *s* globo oculare
eye'bolt' *s* bullone *m* ad anello
eye'brow' *s* sopracciglio; **to raise one's eyebrows** inarcare le sopracciglia
eye'cup' *s* occhiera
eye'drop'per *s* contagocce *m*
eyeful ['aɪ͵ful] *s* vista, colpo d'occhio; (coll) bellezza
eye'glass' *s* (*of optical instrument*) lente *f*, oculare *m*; (*eyecup*) occhiera; **eyeglasses** occhiali *mpl*
eye'lash' *s* ciglio
eyelet ['aɪlɪt] *s* occhiello, maglietta, asola; (*hole to look through*) feritoia
eye'lid' *s* palpebra
eye' o'pener ['opənər] *s* affare *m* che apre gli occhi; (coll) bicchierino bevuto di mattina presto

eye'piece' s oculare *m*
eye'shade' s visiera
eye' shad'ow s rimmel *m*
eye'shot' s—**within eyeshot** a portata di vista
eye'sight' s vista; (*range*) capacità visiva
eye' sock'et s occhiaia, orbita
eye'sore' s pugno in un occhio

eye'strain' s vista affaticata
eye'-test chart' s tabella optometrica
eye'tooth' s (-**teeth**) dente canino; **to cut one's eyeteeth** (coll) fare esperienza; **to give one's eyeteeth for** (coll) dare un occhio della testa per
eye'wash' s (*flattery*) burro, lusinga; (pharm) collirio; (slang) balla
eye' wit'ness s testimone *m* oculare

F

F, f [ɛf] s sesta lettera dell'alfabeto inglese
fable ['febəl] s favola
fabric ['fæbrɪk] s stoffa, tessuto; fabbrica, struttura
fabricate ['fæbrɪ ˌket] tr fabbricare
fabrication [ˌfæbrɪ'keʃən] s fabbricazione; falsificazione, invenzione
fabulous ['fæbjələs] adj favoloso
façade [fə'sad] s facciata
face [fes] s volto, viso, faccia; (*surface*) superficie *f;* (*of coin*) diritto; (*of precious stone*) faccetta; (*of watch*) mostra; (*grimace*) smorfia; (*of building*) facciata; (typ) occhio; **in the face of** di fronte a; **to have a long face** fare il muso lungo; **to keep a straight face** contenere le risa; **to show one's face** farsi vedere ‖ tr far fronte a, fronteggiare; (*a wall*) ricoprire; (*a suit*) foderare; **facing** di fronte a ‖ intr—**to face about** voltarsi, fare dietro front; **to face on** dare a; **to face up to** guardare in faccia
face' card' s figura
face' lift'ing s plastica facciale
face' pow'der s cipria
facet ['fæsɪt] s faccetta; (fig) faccia
facetious [fə'siʃəs] adj faceto
face' val'ue s valore *m* facciale
facial ['feʃəl] adj facciale ‖ s massaggio facciale
fa'cial tis'sue s velina detergente
facilitate [fə'sɪlɪ ˌtet] tr facilitare
facili•ty [fə'sɪlɪti] s (-**ties**) facilità *f;* **facilities** (*installations*) attrezzature *fpl;* (*for transportation*) mezzi *mpl;* (*services*) servizi *mpl*
facing ['fesɪŋ] s rivestimento
facsimile [fæk'sɪmɪli] s facsimile *m*
fact [fækt] s fatto; **in fact** in realtà; **the fact is that** il fatto si è che
faction ['fækʃən] s fazione; discordia
factional ['fækʃənəl] adj fazioso; (*partisan*) partigiano
factionalism ['fækʃənə ˌlɪzəm] s partigianeria; parzialità *f*
factor ['fæktər] s fattore *m* ‖ tr scomporre in fattori
facto•ry ['fæktəri] s (-**ries**) fabbrica
factual ['fæktʃu•əl] adj effettivo, reale
facul•ty ['fækəlti] s (-**ties**) facoltà *f*
fad [fæd] s moda passeggera
fade [fed] tr stingere ‖ intr (*said of colors*) stingersi, sbiadire; (*said of*

sounds, sight, radio signals, memory, etc.) svanire, affievolirsi; (*said of beauty*) sfiorire
fade'-out' s affievolimento, affievolirsi *m;* (mov) chiusura in dissolvenza; (rad, telv) evanescenza
fading ['fedɪŋ] s affievolimento; (mov) dissolvenza; (rad, telv) evanescenza
fag [fæg] s schiavo del lavoro; (coll) sigaretta ‖ tr—**to fag out** stancare
fagot ['fægət] s fascina, fastello
fail [fel] s—**without fail** senza meno ‖ tr mancare (with *dat*); (*a student*) riprovare; (*an examination*) farsi bocciare in ‖ intr fallire, venire a meno; (*said of a student*) farsi riprovare; (*said of a motor*) rompersi, fermarsi; (com) cadere in fallimento; **to fail to** mancare di
failure ['feljər] s insuccesso; insufficienza; (*student*) bocciato; (com) fallimento
faint [fent] adj debole; **to feel faint** sentirsi mancare ‖ s svenimento ‖ intr svenire
faint-hearted ['fent'hartɪd] adj codardo, timido
fair [fer] adj giusto, onesto; (*moderately large*) discreto; (*even*) liscio; (*civil*) gentile; (*hair*) biondo; (*complexion*) chiaro; (*sky, weather*) sereno ‖ s (*exhibition*) fiera; (*carnival*) sagra ‖ adv direttamente; **to play fair** agire onestamente
fair'ground' s terreno dell'esposizione, campo della fiera
fairly ['ferli] adv giustamente, imparzialmente; discretamente, abbastanza; completamente
fair-minded ['fer'maindɪd] adj equanime, equo, giusto
fairness ['fernɪs] s giustizia, imparzialità *f;* bellezza; (*of complexion*) bianchezza
fair' play' s comportamento leale
fair' sex' s bel sesso
fair'-weath'er adj—**a fair-weather friend** un amico del tempo felice
fair•y ['feri] adj fatato ‖ s (-**ies**) fata; (slang) finocchio
fair'y god'mother s buona fata
fair'y•land' s terra delle fate
fair'y tale' s fiaba, racconto delle fate
faith [feθ] s fede *f;* **to break faith with** venir meno alla parola data a; **to keep faith with** tener fede alla parola

data a; **to pin one's faith** on porre tutte le proprie speranze su; **upon my faith!** in fede mia!

faithful ['feθfəl] *adj* fedele ‖ **the faithful** i fedeli

faithless ['feθlɪs] *adj* infedele, sleale

fake [fek] *adj* falso, finto ‖ *s* contraffazione; (*person*) imbroglione *m* ‖ *tr* & *intr* contraffare, falsificare

faker ['fekər] *s* (coll) imbroglione *m*

falcon ['fɔkən] or ['fɔlkən] *s* falcone *m*

falconer ['fɔkənər] or ['fɔlkənər] *s* falconiere *m*

falconry ['fɔkənri] or ['fɔlkənri] *s* falconeria

fall [fɔl] *adj* autunnale ‖ *s* caduta; (*of water*) cataratta, cascata; (*of prices*) ribasso; (*autumn*) autunno; **falls** cataratta, cascate *fpl* ‖ *v* (*pret* **fell** [fɛl]; *pp* **fallen** ['fɔlən]) *intr* cadere; discendere; **to fall apart** farsi a pezzi; **to fall back** (mil) ripiegare; **to fall behind** rimanere indietro; **to fall down** cadere; stramazzare; **to fall due** scadere; **to fall flat** stramazzare; essere un insuccesso; **to fall for** (slang) lasciarsi abbindolare da; (slang) innamorarsi di; **to fall in** (*said of a building*) crollare; (mil) allinearsi; **to fall in with** imbattersi in; mettersi d'accordo con; **to fall off** ritirarsi; diminuire; **to fall out** accadere; essere in disaccordo; (mil) rompere i ranghi; **to fall out of** cadere da; **to fall out with** inimicarsi con; **to fall over** cadere; (coll) adulare; **to fall through** fallire; **to fall to** cominciare; (coll) cominciare a mangiare; (*said, e.g., of an inheritance*) ricadere su; **to fall under** rientrare in

fallacious [fə'leʃəs] *adj* fallace

falla·cy ['fæləsi] *s* (-cies) fallacia

fall' guy' *s* (slang) testa di turco

fallible ['fælɪbəl] *adj* fallibile

fall'ing star' *s* stella cadente

fall'out' *s* pulviscolo radioattivo

fall'out shel'ter *s* rifugio antiatomico

fallow ['fælo] *adj* incolto; **to lie fallow** rimanere incolto ‖ *s* maggese *m* ‖ *tr* maggesare

false [fɔls] *adj* falso; (*hair, teeth, etc.*) posticcio, finto ‖ *adv* falsamente; **to play false** tradire

false' bot'tom *s* doppio fondo

false' col'ors *spl* apparenze mentite

false' face' *s* maschera; (*ugly false face*) mascherone *m*

false'-heart'ed ['fɔls'hɑrtɪd] *adj* perfido

falsehood ['fɔls·hʊd] *s* falsità *f*, falso

false' pretens'es *spl* falso, impostura; **under false pretenses** allegando ragioni false

falset·to [fɔl'sɛto] *s* (-tos) (*voice*) falsetto; (*person*) cantante *m* in falsetto

falsi·fy ['fɔlsɪ,faɪ] *v* (*pret* & *pp* **-fied**) *tr* falsificare; (*to disprove*) smentire ‖ *intr* mentire

falsi·ty ['fɔlsɪti] *s* (-ties) falsità *f*

falter ['fɔltər] *s* vacillamento; (*in

speech) balbettio ‖ *intr* vacillare; balbettare

fame [fem] *s* fama

famed [femd] *adj* famoso

familiar [fə'mɪljər] *adj* familiare; intimo; **to be familiar with** (*people*) aver pratica con; (*things*) aver pratica di

familiari·ty [fə,mɪlɪ'ærɪti] *s* (-ties) familiarità *f*, dimestichezza

familiarize [fə'mɪljə,raɪz] *tr* far conoscere

fami·ly ['fæmɪli] *adj* familiare; **in the family way** (coll) in altro stato ‖ *s* (-lies) famiglia

fam'ily man' *s* (**men'**) padre *m* di famiglia

fam'ily name' *s* cognome *m*

fam'ily tree' *s* albero genealogico

famine ['fæmɪn] *s* carestia

famished ['fæmɪʃt] *adj* famelico; **to be famished** avere una fame da lupo

famous ['feməs] *adj* famoso; (coll) eccellente

fan [fæn] *s* ventaglio; (elec) ventilatore *m*; (coll) tifoso, patito ‖ *v* (*pret* & *pp* **fanned**) *ger* **fanning**) *tr* sventagliare; (*to winnow*) vagliare; (*fire, passions*) attizzare ‖ *intr* sventagliarsi; **to fan out** (*said of a road*) diramarsi a ventaglio

fanatic [fə'nætɪk] *adj* & *s* fanatico

fanatical [fə'nætɪkəl] *adj* fanatico

fanaticism [fə'nætɪ,sɪzəm] *s* fanatismo

fan' belt' *s* (aut) cinghia del ventilatore

fancied ['fænsid] *adj* immaginario

fancier ['fænsɪ·ər] *s* maniaco, tifoso; (*of animals*) conoscitore *m*, allevatore *m*

fanciful ['fænsɪfəl] *adj* fantasioso, estroso; immaginario

fan·cy ['fænsi] *adj* (-cier; -ciest) immaginario; immaginativo; ornamentale; di lusso; fantasioso, estroso ‖ *s* fantasia; (*whim*) grillo, estro; **to take a fancy to** prendere una passione per ‖ *v* (*pret* & *pp* **-cied**) *tr* immaginare

fan'cy ball' *s* ballo in costume

fan'cy dress' *s* costume *m*

fan'cy foods' *spl* cibi *mpl* di lusso

fan'cy-free' *adj* libero dai lacci dell'amore

fan'cy skat'ing *s* pattinaggio artistico

fan'cy·work' *s* (sew) ricamo ornamentale

fanfare ['fænfər] *s* fanfara

fang [fæŋ] *s* zanna; (*of reptile*) dente velenoso

fan'light' *s* lunetta

fantastic(al) [fæn'tæstɪk(əl)] *adj* fantastico

fanta·sy ['fæntəzi] or ['fæntəsi] *s* (-sies) fantasia

far [fɑr] *adj* distante; **on the far side of** dall'altra parte di ‖ *adv* lontano; **as far as** fino a; **as far as I am concerned** per quanto mi riguardi; **as far as I know** per quanto io sappia; **by far** di gran lunga; **far and near** in lungo e in largo; **far away** molto lontano; **far be it from me** Dio me ne scampi e liberi; **far better** molto meglio; molto migliore; **far different** molto differente; **far from** lontano da; **far from it** tutto al contrario; **far into** fino al fondo di; **far into the night** fino a tarda ora; **far more** molto più; **far off** lontanissimo; **how far** quanto lontano; **how far is it?** a che distanza è da qui?; **in so far as** in quanto; **thus far** sinora; **to go far towards** contribuire molto a

faraway ['farə,we] *adj* distante, lontano; distratto

farce [fɑrs] *s* farsa

farcical ['fɑrsɪkəl] *adj* farsesco

fare [fer] *s* prezzo della corsa; passeggero; (*food*) vitto || *intr* andare, e.g., **how did you fare?** come Le è andata?

Far' East' *s* Estremo Oriente

fare'well' *s* congedo, commiato; **to bid farewell to** or **to take farewell of** prender commiato da || *interj* addio!

far-fetched ['far'fetʃt] *adj* peregrino, campato in aria

far-flung ['far'flʌŋ] *adj* ampio; d'ampia distribuzione

farm [fɑrm] *adj* agricolo || *s* fattoria, tenuta || *tr* (*land*) coltivare || *intr* fare l'agricoltore or l'allevatore

farmer ['farmər] *s* agricoltore *m*, contadino

farm' hand' *s* bracciante *m*

farm'house' *s* casa colonica, masseria

farming ['farmɪŋ] *s* agricoltura, coltivazione

farm'yard' *s* aia

far'-off' *adj* lontano

far-reaching ['far'ritʃɪŋ] *adj* di grande portata

far-sighted ['far'saɪtɪd] *adj* lungimirante; perspicace; presbite

farther ['farðər] *adj* più lontano; addizionale || *adv* più lontano, più in là; inoltre; **farther on** più oltre

farthest ['farðɪst] *adj* (il) più lontano; ultimo || *adv* al massimo

farthing ['farðɪŋ] *s* (Brit) quarto di centesimo

Far' West' *s* (U.S.A.) lontano Occidente

fascinate ['fæsɪ,net] *tr* affascinare

fascinating ['fæsɪ,netɪŋ] *adj* incantatore, affascinante

fascism ['fæsɪzəm] *s* fascismo

fascist ['fæsɪst] *adj* & *s* fascista *mf*

fashion ['fæʃən] *s* voga, moda; foggia, maniera; alta società; **after a fashion** in certo modo; **in fashion** di moda; **out of fashion** fuori moda; **to go out of fashion** passare di moda || *tr* fare, foggiare

fashionable ['fæʃənəbəl] *adj* elegante, alla moda

fash'ion design'ing *s* alta moda

fash'ion plate' *s* figurino

fash'ion show' *s* sfilata di moda

fast [fæst] or [fast] *adj* veloce; (*clock*) che corre, in anticipo; dissoluto; ben legato; (*color*) solido; (*friend*) fedele || *s* digiuno; **to break fast** rompere il digiuno || *adv* rapidamente; fortemente; (*asleep*) profondamente; **to hold fast** tenersi saldo; **to live fast**

condurre una vita dissoluta || *intr* digiunare, fare vigilia

fast' day' *s* giorno di magro

fasten ['fæsən] or ['fasən] *tr* fissare; attaccare; (*a door*) sbarrare; (*a nickname; blows*) affibbiare; (*a dress*) allacciarsi || *intr* attaccarsi

fastener ['fæsənər] or ['fasənər] *s* legaccio, laccio; (*snap, clasp*) fermaglio; (*for papers*) fermacarte *m*

fastidious [fæs'tɪdɪ·əs] *adj* schizzinoso; meticoloso

fasting ['fæstɪŋ] or ['fastɪŋ] *s* digiuno

fat [fæt] *adj* (**fatter; fattest**) grasso; (*productive*) forte, ricco, pingue; **to get fat** ingrassare || *s* grasso, unto; (*of pork*) sugna

fatal ['fetəl] *adj* fatale

fatalism ['fetə,lɪzəm] *s* fatalismo

fatalist ['fetəlɪst] *s* fatalista *mf*

fatali·ty [fə'tælɪti] *s* (**-ties**) (*in an accident*) morte *f;* accidente *m* mortale; fatalità *f*

fate [fet] *s* fato; **the Fates** le Parche || *tr* predestinare

fated ['fetɪd] *adj* destinato

fateful ['fetfəl] *adj* fatidico, fatale

fat'head' *s* (coll) zuccone *m*

father ['faðər] *s* padre *m;* (*male ancestor*) antenato || *tr* procreare; creare; assumere la paternità di

fatherhood ['faðər,hud] *s* paternità *f*

fa'ther-in-law' *s* (**fathers-in-law**) suocero

fa'ther·land' *s* patria

fatherless ['faðərlɪs] *adj* orfano di padre; senza padre

fatherly ['faðərli] *adj* paterno

Fa'ther's Day' *s* festa del papà

Fa'ther Time' *s* il Tempo

fathom ['fæðəm] *s* braccio || *tr* sondare

fathomless ['fæðəmlɪs] *adj* senza fondo; imponderabile

fatigue [fə'tig] *s* fatica, strapazzo; (mil) comandata || *tr* stancare, affaticare

fatigue' clothes' *spl* (mil) tenuta di servizio, tenuta di fatica

fatten ['fætən] *tr* & *intr* ingrassare

fat·ty ['fæti] *adj* (**-tier; -tiest**) grasso; (pathol) adiposo || *s* (**-ties**) (coll) tombolo

fatuous ['fætʃu·əs] *adj* fatuo

faucet ['fɔsɪt] *s* rubinetto

fault [fɔlt] *s* (*misdeed, blame*) colpa; (*defect*) difetto, magagna; (geol) faglia; (sports) fallo; **it's your fault** è colpa Sua; **to a fault** all'eccesso; **to find fault with** trovare a ridire sul conto di

fault'find'er *s* ipercritico, criticone *m*

fault'find'ing *adj* criticone || *s* ipercritica

faultless ['fɔltlɪs] *adj* perfetto, inappuntabile

fault·y ['fɔlti] *adj* (**-ier; -iest**) manchevole, difettuoso

faun [fɔn] *s* fauno

fauna ['fɔnə] *s* fauna

favor ['fevər] *s* favore *m;* (*letter*) pregiata; **do me the favor to** mi faccia il piacere di; **by your favor** col Suo permesso; **favors** regali *mpl* di festa; **to be in favor with** essere nelle grazie di; **to be out of favor** cadere in disgrazia || *tr* favorire; (coll) assomigliare (with *dat*)

favorable ['fevərəbəl] *adj* favorevole

favorite ['fevərɪt] *adj* & *s* favorito

favoritism ['fevərɪ‚tɪzəm] *s* favoritismo

fawn [fɔn] *s* cerbiatto || *intr*—**to fawn on** adulare, strusciarsi a

faze [fez] *tr* (coll) perturbare

fear [fɪr] *s* paura; **for fear of** per paura di; **for fear that** per paura che; **no fear** non c'è pericolo; **to be in fear of** aver timore di || *tr* & *intr* temere

fearful ['fɪrfəl] *adj* pauroso, timorato; (coll) spaventoso

fearless ['fɪrlɪs] *adj* impavido

feasible ['fizɪbəl] *adj* fattibile, possibile

feast [fist] *s* festa; (*sumptuous meal*) festino, banchetto || *tr* intrattenere ; *intr* banchettare; **to feast on** rallegrarsi alla vista di

feat [fit] *s* fatto, prodezza

feather ['feðər] *s* penna; (*soft and fluffy structure covering bird*) piuma; (*type*) qualità *f*, conio; (*tuft*) pennacchio; **in fine feather** di buon umore; **in buona salute** || *tr* impennare; coprire di piume; (naut) spalare; (aer) bandierare; **to feather one's nest** arricchirsi

feath'er bed' *s* letto di piume

feath'er‑bed'ding *s* impiego di mano d'opera non necessaria richiesto da un sindacato operaio

feath'er‑brain' *s* cervello di gallina

feath'er‑edge' *s* (*of board*) augnatura; (*of sharpened tool*) filo morto

feath'er‑weight' *s* peso piuma

feathery ['feðəri] *adj* piumato; leggero

feature ['fit/ər] *s* fattezza; caratteristica; (journ) articolo principale; (mov) attrazione; **features** fattezze *fpl* || *tr* caratterizzare; mettere in evidenza; (coll) immaginare

fea'ture film' *s* lungometraggio

fea'ture sto'ry *s* articolo di spalla

February ['febru‚eri] *s* febbraio

feces ['fisiz] *spl* feci *fpl*

feckless ['feklɪs] *adj* debole; inetto

federal ['fedərəl] *adj* federale || *s* federalista *mf*

federate ['fedə‚ret] *adj* federato || *tr* federare || *intr* federarsi

federation [‚fedə'reʃən] *s* federazione

federative ['fedə‚retɪv] or ['fedərətɪv] *adj* federativo

fedora [fɪ'dorə] *s* cappello floscio di feltro

fed' up' [fed] *adj* stanco e stufo; **to be fed up with** averne fin sopra gli occhi di

fee [fi] *s* onorario; (*charge allowed by law*) diritto; (*tip*) mancia; (*for tuition*) tassa; (*for admission*) ingresso || *tr* pagare

feeble ['fibəl] *adj* debole, fievole

feeble‑minded ['fibəl'maɪndɪd] *adj* rimbecillito; debole, vacillante

feed [fid] *s* mangime *m;* (coll) mangiata; (mach) dispositivo d'alimentazione || *v* (*pret* & *pp* **fed** [fed]) *tr* nutrire; (*a machine*) alimentare; (*cattle*) pascere; (theat) imbeccare || *intr* mangiare; **to feed upon** nutrirsi di

feed'back' *s* (*of a computer*) ritorno d'informazioni; (electron) reazione

feed' bag' *s* musetta

feed' pump' *s* pompa di alimentazione

feed' trough' *s* (*for cattle*) vasca; (*for hogs*) trogolo

feed' wire' *s* cavo di alimentazione

feel [fil] *s* sensazione; (*touch*) tocco; (*vague mental impression*) senso || *v* (*pret* & *pp* **felt** [felt]) *tr* sentire; (*e.g., with the hands*) palpare, toccare; (*s.o.'s pulse*) tastare || *intr* (*sick, tired, etc.*) sentirsi; **to feel bad** sentirsi male; (*to be unhappy*) essere spiacente; **to feel cheap** vergognarsi; **to feel comfortable** sentirsi a proprio agio; **to feel for** cercare di toccare; avere compassione per; **to feel like** aver voglia di; **to feel safe** sentirsi al sicuro; **to feel sorry** essere spiacente; pentirsi; **to feel sorry for** aver compassione di; pentirsi di

feeler ['filər] *s* (*hint*) sondaggio; **feelers** (*of insect*) antenne *fpl;* (*of mollusk*) tentacoli *mpl;* **to put out feelers** (fig) tastare il terreno

feeling ['filɪŋ] *s* (*with senses*) senso; (*impression, emotion*) sentimento, sensazione; opinione

feign [fen] *tr* fingere; inventare; imitare || *intr* far finta; **to feign to be** fingersi

feint [fent] *s* finta || *intr* fare una finta

feldspar ['feld‚spar] *s* feldspato

felicitate [fə'lɪsɪ‚tet] *tr* felicitarsi con

felicitous [fə'lɪsɪtəs] *adj* felice, indovinato; eloquente

fell [fel] *adj* crudele, mortale || *tr* (*trees*) abbattere

felloe ['felo] *s* cerchione *m;* (*part of the rim*) gavello

fellow ['felo] *s* compagno; collega *m;* (*of a society*) membro, socio; (*holder of fellowship*) borsista *mf;* (coll) tipo, tizio; (coll) innamorato; **good fellow** buon diavolo; galantuomo

fel'low cit'izen *s* concittadino

fel'low coun'try‑man *s* (**‑men**) concittadino

fel'low crea'ture *s* prossimo

fel'low‑man' *s* (**‑men'**) prossimo

fel'low mem'ber *s* consocio

fellowship ['felo‚ʃɪp] *s* compagnia; (*for study*) borsa di studio

fel'low trav'eler *s* simpatizzante *mf;* criptocomunista *mf;* compagno di viaggio

felon ['felən] *s* criminale *mf;* (pathol) patereccio, giradito

felo‑ny ['feləni] *s* (**‑nies**) delitto doloso

felt [felt] *s* feltro

felt' board' *s* lavagna di panno

felt'‑tip pen' *s* pennarello

female ['fimel] *adj* (*sex*) femminile;

(animal, plant, piece of a device) femmina || *s* femmina

feminine ['fɛmɪnɪn] *adj & s* femminile *m*

feminism ['fɛmɪ ˌnɪzəm] *s* femminismo

fence [fɛns] *s* steccato, staccionata; *(for stolen goods)* ricettatore *m;* (carp) squadra di guida; (sports) scherma; **on the fence** (coll) indeciso || *tr* recingere || *intr* tirare di scherma

fencing ['fɛnsɪŋ] *s* scherma; (fig) schermaglia

fenc'ing mask' *s* visiera

fend [fɛnd] *tr*—**to fend off** parare || *intr*—**to fend for oneself** (coll) badare a sé stesso

fender ['fɛndər] *s (of trolley car)* salvagente *m; (of fireplace)* parafuoco; (aut) parafango; (naut) parabordo

fennel ['fɛnəl] *s* finocchio

ferment ['fʌrment] *s* fermento || [fər-'ment] *tr & intr* fermentare

fern [fʌrn] *s* felce *f*

ferocious [fə'roʃəs] *adj* feroce

ferocity [fə'rɑsɪti] *s* ferocia

ferret ['fɛrɪt] *s* furetto || *tr*—**to ferret out** scovare || *intr* indagare

Fer'ris wheel' ['fɛrɪs] *s* ruota (del parco dei divertimenti)

fer·ry ['fɛri] *s* (-ries) traghetto; nave *f* traghetto || *v (pret & pp* -ried) *tr* traghettare || *intr* attraversare

fer'ry·boat' *s* nave *f* traghetto, ferryboat *m*

fertile ['fʌrtɪl] *adj* fertile

fertilize ['fʌrtɪ ˌlaɪz] *tr* fertilizzare; *(to impregnate)* fecondare

fertilizer ['fʌrtɪ ˌlaɪzər] *s* fertilizzante *m; (e.g., of flowers)* fecondatore *m*

fervent ['fʌrvənt] *adj* fervente, fervido

fervid ['fʌrvɪd] *adj* fervido

fervor ['fʌrvər] *s* fervore *m*

fester ['fɛstər] *s* ulcera, piaga || *tr* corrompere || *intr* suppurare; (fig) corrompersi

festival ['fɛstɪvəl] *adj* festivo || *s* festa; *(of music)* festival *m*

festive ['fɛstɪv] *adj* festivo

festivi·ty [fɛs'tɪvɪti] *s* (-ties) festività *f*

festoon [fɛs'tun] *s* festone *m* || *tr* ornare di festoni

fetch [fɛtʃ] *tr* andare a prendere; *(a price)* fruttare, vendersi per

fetching ['fɛtʃɪŋ] *adj* (coll) cattivante, attraente

fete [fet] *s* festa || *tr* festeggiare

fetid ['fɛtɪd] *or* ['fitɪd] *adj* fetido

fetish ['fitɪʃ] *or* ['fɛtɪʃ] *s* feticcio

fetlock ['fɛtlɑk] *s* nocca; *(tuft of hair)* barbetta

fetter ['fɛtər] *s* ceppo, catena || *tr* mettere ai ceppi, incatenare

fettle ['fɛtəl] *s* stato, condizione; **in fine fettle** in buone condizioni

fetus ['fitəs] *s* feto

feud [fjud] *s* antagonismo; odio ereditario || *intr* essere in lotta

feudal ['fjudəl] *adj* feudale

feudalism ['fjudə ˌlɪzəm] *s* feudalismo

fever ['fivər] *s* febbre *f*

feverish [fivərɪʃ] *adj* febbrile

few [fju] *adj & pron* pochi; **a few** alcuni; **quite a few** molti

fiancé [ˌfi·ɑn'se] *s* fidanzato

fiancée [ˌfi·ɑn'se] *s* fidanzata

fias·co [fɪ'æsko] *s* (-cos or -coes) fiasco

fib [fɪb] *s* menzogna, frottola || *v (pret & pp* **fibbed;** *ger* **fibbing)** *intr* raccontar frottole

fiber ['faɪbər] *s* fibra; (fig) tempra

fi'ber·glass' *s* vetroresina

fibrous ['faɪbrəs] *adj* fibroso

fickle ['fɪkəl] *adj* volubile, incostante, mobile

fiction ['fɪkʃən] *s (invention)* finzione; *(branch of literature)* novellistica

fictional ['fɪkʃənəl] *adj* immaginario

fictionalize ['fɪkʃənə ˌlaɪz] *tr* romanzare

fictitious [fɪk'tɪʃəs] *adj* fittizio

fiddle ['fɪdəl] *s* violino; **fit as a fiddle** in perfetta salute || *tr* (coll) suonare sul violino; **to fiddle away** (coll) sprecare || *intr* (coll) suonare il violino; **to fiddle with** (coll) giocherellare con

fiddler ['fɪdlər] *s* (coll) violinista *mf*

fiddling ['fɪdlɪŋ] *adj* triviale, futile, insignificante

fideli·ty [faɪ'dɛlɪti] *or* [fɪ'dɛlɪti] *s* (-ties) fedeltà *f*

fidget ['fɪdʒɪt] *intr* agitarsi; **to fidget with** giocherellare con

fidgety ['fɪdʒɪti] *adj* irrequieto

fiduciar·y [fɪ'djuʃɪ ˌɛri] *or* [fɪ'duʃɪ- ˌɛri] *adj* fiduciario || *s* (-ies) fiduciario

fie [faɪ] *interj* vergogna!

fief [fif] *s* feudo

field [fild] *adj* (mil) da campagna || *s* campo; (sports) terreno; (min) giacimento; *(of motor or dynamo)* (elec) induttore *m;* (phys) campo

fielder ['fildər] *s (outfielder)* giocatore *m* del campo esterno

field' glass'es *spl* binocolo

field' hock'ey *s* hockey *m* su prato

field' mag'net *s* induttore *m*, calamita induttrice

field' mar'shal *s* (mil) maresciallo di campo

field' mouse' *s* topo di campagna

field'piece' *s* pezzo da campagna

fiend [find] *s* diavolo; (coll) addetto, tifoso

fiendish ['findɪʃ] *adj* diabolico

fierce [fɪrs] *adj* fiero, feroce; *(wind)* furioso; (coll) maledetto

fierceness ['fɪrsnɪs] *s* ferocia

fier·y ['faɪri] *or* ['faɪ·əri] *adj* (-ier; -iest) ardente, focoso

fife [faɪf] *s* piffero

fifteen ['fɪf'tin] *adj, s & pron* quindici *m*

fifteenth ['fɪf'tinθ] *adj, s & pron* quindicesimo || *s (in dates)* quindici *m*

fifth [fɪfθ] *adj, s & pron* quinto || *s (in dates)* cinque *m*

fifth' col'umn *s* quinta colonna

fiftieth ['fɪftɪ·ɪθ] *adj, s & pron* cinquantesimo

fif·ty ['fɪfti] *adj & pron* cinquanta || *s* (-ties) cinquanta *m;* **the fifties** gli anni cinquanta

fif'ty-fif'ty *adv*—**to go fifty-fifty** fare a metà

fig [fɪg] *s* fico

fight [faɪt] *s* lotta; baruffa; combattimento; spirito combattivo; (sports) incontro; **to pick a fight with** attaccar briga con ‖ *v* (*pret & pp* **fought** [fɔt]) *tr* lottare con; combattere contro; opporsi a ‖ *intr* lottare; combattere; **to fight shy of** cercar di evitare

fighter ['faɪtər] *s* lottatore *m;* (*warrior*) combattente *m;* (aer) caccia *m*

fig' leaf' *s* foglia di fico

figment ['fɪgmənt] *s* finzione

figurative ['fɪgjərətɪv] *adj* (fa) figurativo; (rhet) figurato

figure ['fɪgjər] *s* figura; numero; prezzo; **to be good at figures** far bene di conto; **to cut a figure** fare una buona figura; **to keep one's figure** conservare la linea ‖ *tr* figurare; immaginare; raffigurare; supporre, calcolare; **to figure out** calcolare; decifrare ‖ *intr* apparire; **to figure on** (coll) contare su

fig'ure·head' *s* uomo di paglia, prestanome *m;* (naut) polena

fig'ure of speech' *s* figura retorica

fig'ure skat'ing *s* pattinaggio artistico

figurine [ˌfɪgjə'rin] *s* figurina

filament ['fɪləmənt] *s* filamento

filbert ['fɪlbərt] *s* (*tree*) nocciolo, avellano; (*nut*) nocciola, avellana

filch [fɪltʃ] *tr* rubacchiare

file [faɪl] *s* (*row*) fila; (*tool*) lima; (*folder*) filza; (*room*) archivio; (*of cards*) schedario ‖ *tr* mettere in fila; limare; archiviare, schedare; (journ) trasmettere ‖ *intr* sfilare; **to file for** fare domanda di

file' clerk' *s* schedarista *mf*

filet [fɪ'le] or ['fɪle] *s* filetto ‖ *tr* tagliare in filetti

filial ['fɪlɪ·əl] or ['fɪljəl] *adj* filiale

filiation [ˌfɪlɪ'eʃən] *s* filiazione

filibuster ['fɪlɪˌbʌstər] *s* (*tactics*) ostruzionismo; (*speech*) discorso ostruzionista; (*person making such a speech*) ostruzionista *mf;* (*buccaneer*) filibustiere *m* ‖ *tr* fare ostruzionismo contro ‖ *intr* fare dell'ostruzionismo

filigree ['fɪlɪˌgri] *s* filigranato ‖ *s* filigrana ‖ *tr* lavorare in filigrana

filing ['faɪlɪŋ] *s* (*of documents*) schedatura; limatura; **filings** limatura

fil'ing cab'inet *s* schedario

fil'ing card' *s* cartellino, scheda

fill [fɪl] *s* sazietà *f;* (*place filled with earth*) terrapieno; **to have or get one's fill** mangiare a sazietà ‖ *tr* riempire; (*an order*) eseguire; (*a hole*) otturare; (*a tooth*) piombare; (*a tire*) gonfiare; (*a place*) occupare; (*with sand*) interrare; **to fill out** (*a form*) riempire; **to fill up** (aut) fare il pieno di ‖ *intr* riempirsi; **to fill in** prendere il posto; **to fill up** riempirsi

filler ['fɪlər] *s* ripieno; (*person*) riempitore *m;* (painting) mestica; (journ) articolo riempitivo

fillet ['fɪlɪt] *s* nastro, fascia; (*for hair*) nastro; (archit) listello ‖ *tr* filettare

‖ ['frle] or ['fɪlɪt] *s* (*of meat or fish*) filetto ‖ *tr* tagliare a filetti

filling ['fɪlɪŋ] *s* (*of a tooth*) impiombatura; (*of turkey*) ripieno

fill'ing sta'tion *s* stazione di rifornimento

fillip ['fɪlɪp] *s* stimolo; colpetto col dito ‖ *tr* dare un colpetto col dito a; (fig) stimulare

fil·ly ['fɪli] *s* (-**lies**) puledra

film [fɪlm] *s* pellicola; (mov, phot) pellicola, film *m* ‖ *tr* filmare

film' li'brary *s* cineteca, filmoteca

film'strip' *s* filmina

film·y ['fɪlmi] *adj* (-**ier;** -**iest**) sottile, delicato; (*look*) annebbiato

filter ['fɪltər] *s* filtro ‖ *tr & intr* filtrare

filtering ['fɪltərɪŋ] *s* filtrazione

fil'ter pa'per *s* carta da filtro

fil'ter tip' *s* filtro, bocchino filtro

filth [fɪlθ] *s* sporco, sporcizia

filth·y ['frlθi] *adj* (-**ier;** -**iest**) sporco, sudicio

filth'y lu'cre ['lukər] *s* il vile metallo

filtrate ['fɪltret] *s* liquido filtrato ‖ *tr & intr* filtrare

fin [fɪn] *s* pinna; (slang) biglietto da cinque dollari

final ['faɪnəl] *adj* finale; (*last in a series*) ultimo; definitivo, insindacabile ‖ *s* esame *m* finale; **finals** (sports) finale *f*

finale [fɪ'nɑli] *s* (mus) finale *m*

finalist ['faɪnəlɪst] *s* finalista *mf*

finally ['faɪnəli] *adv* finalmente

finance [fɪ'næns] or ['faɪnæns] *s* finanza; **finances** finanze *fpl* ‖ *tr* finanziare

financial [fɪ'næn(ə)l] or [faɪ'næn(əl] *adj* finanziario

financier [ˌfɪnən'sɪr] or [ˌfaɪnən'sɪr] *s* finanziere *m*

financing [fɪ'nænsɪŋ] or ['faɪnænsɪŋ] *s* finanziamento

finch [fɪntʃ] *s* fringuello

find [faɪnd] *s* trovata ‖ *v* (*pret & pp* **found** [faʊnd]) *tr* trovare; rinvenire; (*s.o. innocent or guilty*) dichiarare; **to find out** venire a sapere ‖ *intr* (law) sentenziare; **to find out about** informarsi su

finder ['faɪndər] *s* (phot) mirino; (astr) cannochiale cercatore

finding ['faɪndɪŋ] *s* scoperta; (law) sentenza

fine [faɪn] *adj* buono; bello; fino, fine ‖ *s* multa ‖ *adv* (coll) benissimo; **to feel fine** (coll) sentirsi benissimo ‖ *tr* multare

fine' arts' *spl* belle arti

fineness ['faɪnnɪs] *s* finezza; (*of metal*) titolo

fine' print' *s* testo in caratteri minuti

finer·y ['faɪnəri] *s* (-**ies**) ornamenti *mpl*, fronzoli *mpl;* abito vistoso

fine-spun ['faɪnˌspʌn] *adj* sottile

finesse [fɪ'nɛs] *s* finezza; (bridge) impasse *f* ‖ *tr* fare l'impasse a ‖ *intr* fare l'impasse

fine'-tooth comb' *s* pettine fitto; **to go over with a fine-tooth comb** esaminare minuziosamente

finger ['fɪŋgər] s dito; **to have a finger in the pie** avere le mani in pasta; **to put one's finger on the spot** mettere il dito nella piaga; **to slip between the fingers** sfuggire di tra le dita; **to snap one's fingers at** infischiarsi di; **to twist around one's little finger** fare ciò che si vuole di ‖ tr toccare con le dita; (*to pilfer*) rubacchiare; (slang) mostrare a dito

fin'ger board' s (mus) tastiera
fin'ger bowl' s sciacquadita m
fingering ['fɪŋgərɪŋ] s palpeggiamento; (mus) diteggiatura
fin'ger mark' s ditata
fin'ger-nail' s unghia
fin'ger-print' s impronta digitale ‖ tr prendere le impronte digitali di
fin'ger-tip' s polpastrello; **to have at one's fingertips** avere sulla punta delle dita, sapere a menadito
finical ['fɪnɪkəl] or **finicky** ['fɪnɪki] adj pignolo, schizzinoso
finish ['fɪnɪʃ] s fine f; finitura; (sports) finale m ‖ tr finire; **to finish off** distruggere ‖ intr finire; **to finish** + ger finire di + inf; **to finish by** + ger finire per + inf
fin'ishing school' s scuola di perfezionamento per signorine
fin'ishing touch' s ultimo tocco
finite ['faɪnaɪt] adj finito
Finland ['fɪnlənd] s la Finlandia
Finlander ['fɪnləndər] s finlandese mf
Finn [fɪn] s (*member of a Finnish-speaking group of people*) finnico; (*native or inhabitant of Finland*) finlandese mf
Finnic ['fɪnɪk] adj & s finnico
Finnish ['fɪnɪʃ] adj finlandese ‖ s (*language*) finlandese m
fir [fʌr] s abete m
fire [faɪr] s fuoco; (*destructive burning*) incendio; **to be on fire** ardere; **to be under enemy fire** essere sotto tiro nemico; **to catch fire** infiammarsi; **to hang fire** essere in sospeso; **to open fire** aprire il fuoco; **to set on fire, to set fire to** dar fuoco a; **under fire** sotto fuoco nemico; accusato ‖ tr accendere; (*an oven*) scaldare; (*bricks*) cuocere; (*a weapon*) sparare; (*the imagination*) riscaldare; (*an employee*) (coll) licenziare ‖ intr accendersi; **to fire on** far fuoco su; **to fire up** attivare una caldaia
fire' alarm' s avvisatore m d'incendio
fire'arm' s arma da fuoco
fire'ball' s palla da cannone esplosiva; (*lightning*) lampo a forma di globo infocato; meteorite m a forma di globo infocato; globo infocato
fire'boat' s lancia dei pompieri
fire'box' s (*of a boiler*) fornello; (*to give alarm*) stazione d'allarme
fire'brand' s tizzone m; (fig) fiaccola della discordia
fire'brick' s mattone refrattario
fire' brigade' s corpo di pompieri volontari
fire'bug' s (coll) incendiario
fire' com'pany s corpo dei pompieri;

compagnia d'assicurazioni contro gli incendi
fire'crack'er s mortaretto
fire'damp' s grisou m
fire' depart'ment s corpo dei pompieri
fire'dog' s alare m
fire' drill' s esercitazione in caso d'incendio
fire' en'gine s autopompa
fire' escape' s scala di sicurezza
fire' extin'guisher s estintore m
fire'fly' s (-flies) lucciola
fire'guard' s parafuoco
fire' hose' s manichetta
fire'house' s caserma dei pompieri
fire' hy'drant s bocca d'incendio
fire' insur'ance s assicurazione contro gli incendi
fire' i'rons spl arnesi mpl del camino
fire'man s (-men) (*man who extinguishes fires*) pompiere m, vigile m del fuoco; (*stoker*) fochista m
fire'place' s camino
fire'plug' s bocca da incendio, idrante m
fire'proof' adj incombustibile ‖ tr rendere incombustibile
fire' sale' s vendita di merce avariata dal fuoco
fire' screen' s parafuoco
fire' ship' s brulotto
fire'side' s focolare m
fire'trap' s edificio senza mezzi adeguati per combattere incendi
fire' wall' s paratia antincendio
fire'wa'ter s (coll) acquavite f
fire'wood' s legna
fire'works' spl fuochi mpl artificiali
firing ['faɪrɪŋ] s (*of furnace*) alimentazione; (*of bricks*) cottura; (*of a gun*) sparo; (*of soldiers*) tiro; (*of an internal-combustion engine*) accensione; (*of an employee*) (coll) licenziamento
fir'ing line' s linea del fuoco
fir'ing or'der s (aut) ordine m d'accensione
fir'ing pin' s percussore m
fir'ing squad' s (*for saluting at a burial*) plotone m d'onore; (*for executing*) plotone m d'esecuzione
firm [fʌrm] adj forte, fermo ‖ s ditta, compagnia
firmament ['fʌrməmənt] s firmamento
firm' name' s ragione f sociale
firmness ['fʌrmnɪs] s fermezza
first [fʌrst] adj primo ‖ s primo; (aut) prima; (mus) voce f principale; **at first** sulle prime; **from the first** da bel principio ‖ adv prima; **first of all** per prima cosa
first' aid' s pronto soccorso
first'-aid' kit' s cassetta farmaceutica d'urgenza
first'-aid' sta'tion s posto di pronto soccorso
first'-born' adj & s primogenito
first'-class' adj di prim'ordine, sopraffino ‖ adv in prima classe
first' cous'in s cugino primo
first'-day cov'er s busta primo giorno
first' draft' s brutta copia

first' fin'ger s dito indice
first' floor' s pianoterra m
first' fruits' spl primizie fpl
first' lieuten'ant s tenente m
firstly ['fʌrstli] adv in primo luogo
first' mate' s (naut) primo ufficiale, comandante m in seconda, secondo
first' name' s nome m di battesimo
first' night' s (theat) prima
first' of'ficer s (naut) primo ufficiale, comandante m in seconda, secondo
first'-rate' adj di prima forza; eccellente || adv (coll) benissimo
first'-run' adj di prima visione
fiscal ['fɪskəl] adj (pertaining to public treasury) fiscale; finanziario || s avvocato fiscale
fis'cal year' s esercizio finanziario
fish [fɪʃ] s pesce m; to be like a fish out of water essere come un pesce fuor d'acqua; to be neither fish nor fowl non essere né carne né pesce; to drink like a fish bere come una spugna || tr pescare || intr pescare; to fish for compliments cercare di farsi fare dei complimenti; to go fishing andare alla pesca; to take fishing portare con sé alla pesca
fish'bone' s lisca, spina di pesce
fish'bowl' s vaschetta per i pesci rossi
fisher ['fɪʃər] s pescatore m; (zool) martora canadese
fish'er·man s (-men) pescatore m; (boat) peschereccio
fisher·y ['fɪʃəri] s (-ies) (activity) pesca; (business) pescheria; (grounds) riserva di pesca, luogo dove si pesca
fish' glue' s colla di pesce
fish'hook' s amo
fishing ['fɪʃɪŋ] adj da pesca || s pesca
fish'ing reel' s mulinello
fish'ing rod' s canna da pesca
fish'ing tack'le s attrezzatura da pesca
fish'line' s lenza
fish' mar'ket s pescheria
fish'pool' s peschiera
fish' spear' s fiocina
fish' sto'ry s (coll) fandonia; to tell fish stories spararle grosse
fish'tail' s (aut) imbardata (aer) spedalata || intr (aut) imbardare; (aer) compiere una spedalata
fish'wife' s (-wives') pescivendola; (foul-mouthed woman) ciana
fish'worm' s lombrico
fish·y ['fɪʃi] adj (-ier; -iest) che sa di pesce; (coll) dubbioso, inverosimile
fission ['fɪʃən] s (biol) scissione; (phys) fissione
fissionable ['fɪʃənəbəl] adj fissionabile
fissure ['fɪʃər] s fenditura; (in rock) crepaccio
fist [fɪst] s pugno; (typ) indice m; to shake one's fist at mostrare i pugni a
fist'fight' s scontro a pugni
fist'ful' s pugno, manciata
fisticuff ['fɪsti,kʌf] s pugno; fisticuffs scontro a pugni
fit [fɪt] adj (fitter; fittest) indicato; idoneo, adatto; in buona salute; fit to be tied (coll) infuriato, arrabbia-

tissimo; fit to eat mangiabile; to feel fit sentirsi in buona salute; to see fit giudicare conveniente || s equipaggiamento; (of a suit) taglio; (of one piece with another) incastro; (of coughing) accesso; (of anger) attacco; by fits and starts a pezzi e a bocconi || v (pret & pp fitted; ger fitting) tr adattare; quadrare a; andar bene a; equipaggiare; preparare; servire a; esser d'accordo con; to fit out or up attrezzare, equipaggiare || intr stare; incastrare; (said of clothes) cascare; entrare; to fit in entrarci
fitful ['fɪtfəl] adj capriccioso; incostante, irregolare
fitness ['fɪtnɪs] s convenienza; idoneità f; buona salute
fitter ['fɪtər] s aggiustatore m; (of machinery) montatore m; (of clothing) sarto che mette in prova
fitting ['fɪtɪŋ] adj appropriato, adatto, conveniente || s adattamento; (of a garment) prova; tubo adattabile; (carp) incastro; fittings accessori mpl; utensili mpl; (iron trimmings) ferramenta fpl
five [faɪv] adj & pron cinque || s cinque m; five o' clock le cinque
five' hun'dred adj, s & pron cinquecento
five'-year plan' s piano quinquennale
fix [fɪks] s—in a tight fix (coll) nei pasticci; to be in a fix (coll) star fresco, essere nei guai || tr riparare; fissare; (a meal) preparare; (a bayonet) inastare; (attention) attrarre, fermare; (hair) mettere a posto; (coll) arrangiare || intr fissarsi, stabilirsi; to fix on scegliere
fixed [fɪkst] adj fisso; (time) improrogabile; (coll) arrangiato
fixing ['fɪksɪŋ] adj fissativo || s (fastening) attacco; (phot) fissaggio; with all the fixings (coll) con tutti i contorni
fix'ing bath' s bagno di fissaggio
fixture ['fɪkstʃər] s infisso; accessorio; (of a lamp) guarnizione; fixtures (e.g., of a store) suppellettili fpl
fizz [fɪz] s effervescenza; gazosa; (Brit) spumante m || intr frizzare
fizzle ['fɪzəl] s (coll) fiasco || intr crepitare; (coll) fare fiasco
flabbergast ['flæbər,gæst] tr (coll) sbalordire, lasciare stupefatto
flab·by ['flæbi] adj (-bier; -biest) floscio, flaccido, cascante
flag [flæg] s bandiera || v (pret & pp flagged; ger flagging) tr imbandierare; segnalare; (rr) far fermare || intr ammosciarsi, afflosciarsi
flageolet [,flædʒə'lɛt] s flautino
flag'man s (-men) (rr) manovratore m
flag' of truce' s bandiera parlamentaria
flag'pole' s pennone m
flagrant ['flegrənt] adj flagrante; scandaloso
flag'ship' s nave ammiraglia
flag'staff' s pennone m
flag' sta'tion s (rr) stazione facoltativa
flag'stone' s lastra di pietra

flag' stop' s (rr) fermata facoltativa
flail [flel] s correggiato || tr battere col correggiato; battere
flair [fler] s fiuto, istinto
flak [flæk] s fuoco antiaereo
flake [flek] s falda; (of snow) fiocco, falda; (of cereal) fiocco; || tr sfaldare; (fish) scagliare || intr sfaldarsi
flak·y ['fleki] adj (-ier; -iest) a falde, faldoso
flamboyant [flæm'bɔɪ·ənt] adj sgargiante; (archit) fiammeggiante
flame [flem] s fiamma || tr & intr fiammeggiare
flamethrower ['flem ,θro·ər] s lanciafiamme m
flaming ['flemɪŋ] adj fiammeggiante; appassionato; (culin) alla fiamma
flamin·go [flə'mɪŋgo] s (-gos or -goes) fenicottero, fiammingo
flammable ['flæməbəl] adj infiammabile
Flanders ['flændərz] s le Fiandre
flange [flændʒ] s (e.g., on a pipe) flangia; (on I beam) bordo; (of a wheel) cerchione m
flank [flæŋk] s fianco || tr fiancheggiare
flannel ['flænəl] s flanella
flap [flæp] s (in clothing) falda; (of hat) tesa; (of book) risvolto; (of pocket) patta; (of shoe) linguetta; (blow) colpo; (of a table) pannello; (of the counter in a store) ribalta; (of wings) alata || v (pret & pp flapped; ger flapping) tr battere, sbattere; (to move violently) sbatacchiare || intr penzolare
flare [fler] s vampa; scintillio; (of a dress) svasatura; (mil) fuoco di segnalazione; **flares** (trousers) calzoni mpl a zampe d'elefante || tr svasare || intr scintillare; (said of a garment) scampanare; **to flare up** divampare; (said of an illness) aggravarsi, infiammarsi
flare'-up' s vampa, fiammata; (of an illness) recrudescenza; scoppio d'ira, accesso di collera
flash [flæʃ] s (of light) sprazzo; (of lightning) lampo, baleno; (of hope) raggio; (of joy) accesso; (journ, phot) flash m; (fig) lampo; **flash in the pan** fuoco di paglia || tr (powder) accendere; (a sword) brandire; (journ) diffondere; (e.g., money) (coll) ostentare || intr lampeggiare, balenare, folgorare; **to flash by** passare come un lampo
flash'back' s flashback m
flash' bulb' s lampada lampo
flash' cube' s cuboflash m
flash' flood' s inondazione torrenziale
flashing ['flæʃɪŋ] s metallo per coprire la conversa; commessura metallica fra tetto e comignolo
flash'light' s lampadina tascabile; (of a lighthouse) luce f intermittente; (phot) fotolampo, lampeggiatore m
flash'light bulb' s lampada per fotolampo
flash·y ['flæʃi] adj (-ier; -iest) sgargiante, chiassoso, vistoso

flask [flæsk] or [flɑsk] s fiasco, fiasca; (for laboratory use) beuta
flat [flæt] adj (flatter; flattest) piano; (nose) camuso; (boat) a fondo piatto; (surface) liscio; (beer) svanito; (tire) sgonfio; (denial) deciso; (mus) bemolle; (coll) al verde || s (flat surface) piatto; (flat area) piano; (apartment) appartamento; (mus) bemolle m; (coll) gomma a terra || adv—**to fall flat** fallire
flat'boat' s chiatta
flat'car' s (rr) pianale m
flat-footed ['flæt ,fʊtɪd] adj dai piedi piatti; (coll) inflessibile
flat'head' s (of a bolt) testa piatta; (coll) testa di legno
flat'i'ron s ferro da stiro
flat' race' s corsa piana
flatten ['flætən] tr schiacciare; distendere || intr appiattirsi; indebolirsi; **to flatten out** appiattirsi; (aer) porsi in linea orizzontale di volo
flatter ['flætər] tr adulare, lusingare; (to make seem more attractive) favorire || intr adulare
flatterer ['flætərər] s adulatore m, lusingatore m
flattering ['flætərɪŋ] adj lusinghiero
flatter·y ['flætəri] s (-ies) lusinga
flat' tire' s gomma a terra
flat'top' s portaerei f
flatulence ['flætʃələns] s flatulenza
flat'ware' s argenteria, vasellame m
flaunt [flɔnt] or [flɑnt] tr sfoggiare, ostentare
flautist ['flɔtɪst] s flautista mf
flavor ['flevər] s sapore m, gusto; condimento || tr insaporire; condire; aromatizzare, profumare
flavoring ['flevərɪŋ] s condimento, sapore m
flaw [flɔ] s difetto, menda, fallo; (crack) incrinatura
flawless ['flɔlɪs] adj senza difetti
flax [flæks] s lino
flaxen ['flæksən] adj di lino; biondo
flax'seed' s linosa
flay [fle] tr scorticare, scoiare
flea [fli] s pulce f
flea'bite' s morso di pulce; (fig) inezia, seccatura secondaria
fleck [flɛk] s macchia; efelide f || tr chiazzare, macchiare
fledgling ['flɛdʒlɪŋ] s uccellino appena nato; (fig) pivello
flee [fli] v (pret & pp fled [flɛd]) tr & intr fuggire, sfuggire
fleece [flis] s vello; (e.g., of clouds) bioccolo || tr tosare; (fig) pelare
fleec·y ['flisi] adj (-ier; -iest) lanoso; (sky) a pecorelle
fleet [flit] adj rapido || s flotta
fleeting ['flitɪŋ] adj fugace, passeggero
Fleming ['flemɪŋ] s fiammingo
Flemish ['flemɪʃ] adj & s fiammingo
flesh [flɛʃ] s carne f; (of fruit) polpa; **in the flesh** in carne ed ossa; **to lose flesh** dimagrire; **to put on flesh** ingrassare
flesh' and blood' s (relatives) carne f della carne, i miei, i suoi, etc.; il corpo umano

flesh-colored [ˈflɛʃ ˌkʌlərd] *adj* color carne

fleshiness [ˈflɛʃɪnɪs] *s* carnosità *f*

fleshless [ˈflɛʃlɪs] *adj* scarno

flesh'pot' *s* piatto di carne; locale *m* di dissoluzione; **fleshpots** vita dissoluta

flesh' wound' *s* ferita superficiale

flesh·y [ˈflɛʃi] *adj* (**-ier; -iest**) carnoso; polposo

flex [flɛks] *tr* piegare ‖ *intr* piegarsi

flexible [ˈflɛksɪbəl] *adj* flessibile; (*joint*) a snodo

flick [flɪk] *s* schiocco; (slang) pellicola cinematografica ‖ *tr* schioccare

flicker [ˈflɪkər] *s* fiamma tremolante; (*of eyelids*) battito; (*of hope*) bagliore *m* ‖ *intr* tremolare; vacillare

flier [ˈflaɪ·ər] *s* aviatore *m;* (*venture*) (coll) impresa rischiosa; (coll) foglio volante

flight [flaɪt] *s* fuga; (*of an airplane*) volo; (*of birds*) stormo; (*of stairs*) rampa; (*of fancy*) slancio; **to put to flight** mettere in fuga; **to take flight** prendere la fuga

flight' deck' *s* ponte *m* di volo

flight·y [ˈflaɪti] *adj* (**-ier; -iest**) frivolo; volubile

flim-flam [ˈflɪm ˌflæm] *s* (coll) imbroglio, truffa ‖ *v* (*pret & pp* **-flammed;** *ger* **-flamming**) *tr* (coll) imbrogliare, truffare

flim·sy [ˈflɪmzi] *adj* (**-sier; -siest**) leggero; (*material*) di scarsa consistenza; (*excuse*) inconsistente

flinch [flɪntʃ] *intr* indietreggiare; **without flinching** senza scomporsi

fling [flɪŋ] *s* tiro; ballo scozzese; **to go on a fling** darsi alla pazza gioia; **to have a fling at** tentare di fare; **to have one's fling** correre la cavallina ‖ *v* (*pret & pp* **flung** [flʌŋ]) *tr* sbattere, scagliare; (*e.g., in jail*) schiaffare; **to fling open** spalancare; **to fling shut** chiudere improvvisamente

flint [flɪnt] *s* selce *f*, pietra focaia

flint'lock' *s* fucile *m* a pietra focaia

flint·y [ˈflɪnti] *adj* (**-ier; -iest**) pietroso; (*unmerciful*) spietato; duro come un macigno

flip [flɪp] *adj* (**flipper; flippest**) impertinente ‖ *s* buffetto; salto mortale ‖ *v* (*pret & pp* **flipped;** *ger* **flipping**) *tr* sbattere in aria; muovere d'un tratto **to flip a coin** giocare a testa e croce; **to flip shut** (*e.g., a fan*) chiudere improvvisamente

flippancy [ˈflɪpənsi] *s* leggerezza

flippant [ˈflɪpənt] *adj* scanzonato, leggero

flirt [flʌrt] *s* (*woman*) civetta; (*man*) vagheggino ‖ *intr* (*said of a woman*) civettare; (*said of a man*) fare il damerino; **to flirt with** flirtare con; (*an idea*) accarezzare; (*death*) giocare con

flit [flɪt] *v* (*pret & pp* **flitted;** *ger* **flitting**) *intr* svolazzare, volteggiare; passare rapidamente, volare

flitch [flɪtʃ] *s* fetta di pancetta

float [flot] *s* (*raft*) galleggiante *m;* (*of mason*) cazzuola; carro allegorico ‖ *tr* far galleggiare; (*a business*) lan-

ciare; (*stocks, bonds*) emettere ‖ *intr* galleggiare, tenersi a galla

floating [ˈflotɪŋ] *adj* galleggiante

flock [flɑk] *s* (*of birds*) stormo; (*of sheep*) gregge *m;* (*of people*) stuolo; (*of wool*) fiocco; (fig) mucchio ‖ *intr* affollarsi, riunirsi, radunarsi

floe [flo] *s* tavola di ghiaccio

flog [flɑg] *v* (*pret & pp* **flogged;** *ger* **flogging**) *tr* battere, fustigare

flood [flʌd] *s* (*caused by rain*) diluvio; (*sudden rise of river*) piena, fiumana; (*of tide*) flusso ‖ *tr* inondare; (aut) ingolfare ‖ *intr* straripare; (aut) ingolfarsi ‖ **the Flood** il diluvio universale

flood'gate' *s* (*of a canal*) chiusa; (*of a dam*) saracinesca

flood'light' *s* riflettore *m*

flood' tide' *s* flusso

floor [fior] *s* (*inside bottom surface of room*) pavimento; (*story of building*) piano; (*of the sea, a swimming pool, etc.*) fondo; (*of the exchange*) recinto delle grida; (*of an assembly hall*) emiciclo; (naut) madiere *m;* **to ask for the floor** chiedere la parola; **to have the floor** avere la parola; **to take the floor** prendere la parola ‖ *tr* pavimentare; abbattere, gettare al suolo; (coll) confondere; (coll) vincere

flooring [ˈflorɪŋ] *s* palco, impiantito

floor' mop' *s* redazza

floor' plan' *s* pianta

floor' show' *s* spettacolo di caffè concerto

floor'walk'er *s* direttore *m* di sezione

floor' wax' *s* cera da pavimenti

flop [flɑp] *s* (coll) fiasco ‖ *v* (*pret & pp* **flopped;** *ger* **flopping**) *tr* lasciar cadere; sbattere ‖ *intr* lasciarsi cadere; (coll) fare fiasco; **to flop over** (*to change sides*) cambiare casacca

flora [ˈflorə] *s* flora

floral [ˈflorəl] *adj* floreale

Florence [ˈflɒrəns] *or* [ˈflɑrəns] *s* Firenze *f*

Florentine [ˈflɒrən ˌtin] *or* [ˈflɑrən-ˌtin] *adj & s* fiorentino

florescence [floˈrɛsəns] *s* inflorescenza

florid [ˈflɒrɪd] *or* [ˈflɑrɪd] *adj* florido

florist [ˈflɒrɪst] *s* fiorista *mf*, fioraio

floss [flɒs] *or* [flɑs] *s* lanugine *f;* (*of corn*) barba

floss·y [ˈflɒsi] *or* [ˈflɑsi] *adj* (**-ier; -iest**) serico; (*downy*) lanuginoso; (coll) vistoso

flotsam [ˈflɑtsəm] *s* relitti gettati a mare

flot'sam and jet'sam *s* relitti *mpl* di naufragio; (*trifles*) cianfrusaglie *fpl;* gentaglia, vagabondi *mpl*

flounce [flɑuns] *s* balza, falda, falpalà *m* ‖ *tr* ornare di falpalà ‖ *intr*—**to flounce out** andarsene irosamente

flounder [ˈflɑundər] *s* (ichth) passera ‖ *intr* dibattersi

flour [flaur] *adj* farinoso ‖ *s* farina ‖ *tr* infarinare

flourish [ˈflʌrɪʃ] *s* (*with the sword*) mulinello; (*with the pen*) ghirigoro; (*as part of signature*) svolazzo; (mus) fioritura || *tr* (*one's sword*) roteare || *intr* rifiorire, prosperare

flourishing ['flʌrɪʃɪŋ] *adj* prosperoso

flour' mill' *s* mulino per grano

floury ['flaʊri] *adj* farinoso; infarinato

flout [flaʊt] *tr* burlarsi di || *intr* burlare, motteggiare

flow [flo] *s* flusso; (*of a river*) regime *m* || *intr* fluire; (*said of tide*) montare; (*said of hair in the air*) ondeggiare; **to flow into** gettarsi in, sfociare in; **to flow over** traboccare; **to flow with** abbondare di

flower ['flaʊ·ər] *s* fiore *m* || *tr* infiorare || *intr* fiorire

flow'er bed' *s* aiola fiorita

flow'er gar'den *s* giardino

flow'er girl' *s* fioraia; (*at a wedding*) damigella d'onore

flow'er·pot' *s* vaso da fiori

flow'er shop' *s* negozio di fiori

flow'er show' *s* esposizione di fiori

flow'er·stand' *s* portafiori *m*

flowery ['flaʊ·əri] *adj* fiorito

flowing ['flo·ɪŋ] *adj* (*water*) corrente; (*language*) scorrevole; (*e.g., hair*) fluente; (*e.g., lines of a dress*) filante

flu [flu] *s* influenza

fluctuate ['flʌktʃʊ‚et] *intr* fluttuare, ondeggiare; (*said of prices*) oscillare

flue [flu] *s* gola, fumaiolo

fluency ['flu·ənsi] *s* facilità *f* di parola

fluent ['flu·ənt] *adj* (*speaker*) facondo; (*style*) fluido

fluently ['flu·əntli] *adv* correntemente

fluff [flʌf] *s* lanugine *f;* vaporosità *f;* (*of an actor*) papera || *tr* sprimacciare || *intr* sprimacciarsi; (*coll*) impaperarsi

fluff·y ['flʌfi] *adj* (**-ier; -iest**) lanuginoso; vaporoso

fluid ['flu·ɪd] *adj & s* fluido

flu'id drive' *s* trasmissione idraulica

fluidity [flu'ɪdɪti] *s* fluidità *f*

fluke [fluk] *s* (*of anchor*) marra, dente *m;* (*in billiards*) colpo fortunato; (ichth) passera

flume [flum] *s* gora; condotta forzata

flunk [flʌŋk] *s* (coll) bocciatura || *tr* (coll) bocciare; (*a course*) (coll) farsi bocciare in || *intr* (coll) fare fiasco; **to flunk out** (coll) farsi bocciare

flunk·y ['flʌŋki] *s* (**-ies**) valletto; parassita *m*

fluor ['flu·ɔr] *s* fluorite *f*

fluorescence [‚flu·ə'rɛsəns] *s* fluorescenza

fluorescent [‚flu·ə'rɛsənt] *adj* fluorescente

fluoridation [‚flu·ərɪ'deʃən] *s* fluorizzazione

fluoride ['flu·ə‚raɪd] *s* fluoruro

fluorine ['flu·ə‚rin] *s* fluoro

fluoroscope ['flu·ərə‚skop] *s* schermo fluorescente

fluorspar ['flu·er‚spɑr] *s* spatofluore *m*

flur·ry ['flʌri] *s* (**-ries**) agitazione; (*of wind*) raffica; (*of rain*) acquazzone *m;* (*of snow*) turbine *m* || *v* (*pret & pp* **-ried**) *tr* agitare

flush [flʌʃ] *adj* livellato; contiguo; prospero, ben provvisto; abbondante; vigoroso; (*full to overflowing*) rigurgitante; arrossito; **flush with** allo stesso livello che || *s* (*of water*) flusso improvviso; (*in the cheeks*) caldana, scalmana; (*of spring*) germogliare *m;* (*of joy*) ebbrezza; (*of youth*) rigoglio; (*in poker*) colore *m* || *adv* rasente, raso || *tr* (*to cause to blush*) far arrossire; lavare con un getto d'acqua; (*e.g., a rabbit*) snidare || *intr* essere accaldato; (*to blush*) arrossire; (*to gush*) zampillare

flush' tank' *s* sciacquone *m*

flush' toi'let *s* gabinetto a sciacquone

fluster ['flʌstər] *s* nervosismo, eccitazione || *tr* innervosire, eccitare

flute [flut] *s* (*of a column*) scanalatura; (mus) flauto || *tr* scanalare

flutist ['flutɪst] *s* flautista *mf*

flutter ['flʌtər] *s* svolazzo; agitazione; sensazione || *intr* frullare; svolazzare; agitarsi; (*said of the heart*) palpitare; (*said of the heartbeat*) essere irregolare

flux [flʌks] *s* (*flow*) flusso; (*for fusing metals*) fondente *m*

fly [flaɪ] *s* (*flies*) mosca; (*of trousers*) finta; (*for fishing*) mosca artificiale || *v* (*pret* **flew** [flu]; *pp* **flown** [flon]) *tr* (*an airplane*) pilotare, far volare; trasportare a volo; (*e.g., an ocean*) trasvolare; (*a flag*) battere || *intr* volare; fuggire, scappare; (*said of a flag*) ondeggiare; **to fly away** involarsi; **to fly into a rage** andare in eccessi; **to fly off** volare via; scappare; **to fly over** trasvolare; **to fly shut** chiudersi improvvisamente

fly'blow' *s* uovo di mosca

fly-by-night' *adj* poco raccomandabile; di breve durata

fly'catch'er *s* (orn) pigliamosche *m*

flyer ['flaɪ·ər] *s* var of **flier**

fly'-fish' *intr* pescare con le mosche artificiali

flying ['flaɪ·ɪŋ] *adj* volante; rapido; in fuga; (*start*) lanciato || *s* volo

fly'ing boat' *s* idrovolante *m* a scafo centrale

fly'ing but'tress *s* contrafforte *m*

fly'ing col'ors *spl* successo; **with flying colors** a bandiere spiegate

fly'ing field' *s* campo d'aviazione

fly'ing sau'cer *s* disco volante

fly'ing sick'ness *s* male *m* d'aria

fly'ing squad' *s* squadra mobile

fly'ing time' *s* ore *fpl* di volo

fly'leaf' *s* (**-leaves'**) (bb) guardia

fly' net' *s* (*for a bed*) moschettiera; (*for a horse*) scacciamosche *m*

fly'pa'per *s* carta moschicida

fly'speck' *s* macchia di mosca; macchiolina

fly' swat'ter ['swatər] *s* scacciamosche *m*

fly'trap' *s* pigliamosche *m*

fly'wheel' *s* volano

foal [fol] *s* puledro || *intr* (*said of a mare*) figliare

foam [fom] *s* schiuma || *intr* schiumare

foam' rub'ber *s* gommapiuma

foam·y ['fomi] *adj* (**-ier; -iest**) spumoso, schiumeggiante

fob [fab] *s* taschino per l'orologio; (*chain*) catenina per l'orologio || *v* (*pret & pp* **fobbed; ger fobbing**) *tr*—**to fob off s.th on s.o.** rifilare qlco a qlcu

f.o.b. or **F.O.B.** [,ɛf ,o'bi] *adv* (letter-word) (**free on board**) franco

focal ['fokəl] *adj* focale

fo·cus ['fokəs] *s* (**-cuses** or **-ci** [saɪ]) fuoco; (*of a disease*) focolaio || *v* (*pret & pp* **-cused** or **-cussed; ger -cusing** or **-cussing**) *tr* mettere a fuoco; (*attention*) concentrare || *intr* convergere

fodder ['fadər] *s* foraggio

foe [fo] *s* nemico

fog [fag] or [fɔg] *s* nebbia; (phot) velo || *v* (*pret & pp* **fogged; ger fogging**) *tr* annebbiare; (phot) velare || *intr* annebbiarsi; (phot) velarsi

fog' bank' *s* banco di nebbia

fog'bound' *adj* avvolto nella nebbia

fog·gy ['fagi] or ['fɔgi] *adj* (**-gier; -giest**) annebbiato; nebbioso; (*idea*) vago; (phot) velato; **it is foggy** fa nebbia

fog'horn' *s* sirena da nebbia

foible ['fɔɪbəl] *s* debolezza, debole *m*

foil [fɔɪl] *s* (*thin sheet of metal*) foglia; (*of mirror*) argentatura; contrasto, risalto; (*sword*) fioretto || *tr* sventare; (*a mirror*) argentare

foist [fɔɪst] *tr*—**to foist s.th on s.o.** rifilare qlco a qlcu

fold [fold] *s* piega; drappeggio; (*for sheep*) ovile *m*; (*of sheep; of the faithful*) gregge *m*; (geol) corrugamento || *tr* piegare; (*the arms*) incrociare; **to fold up** ripiegare || *intr* piegarsi; **to fold up** (coll) fare fallimento

folder ['foldər] *s* (*pamphlet*) pieghevole *m*; (*cover*) portacarte *m*

folding ['foldɪŋ] *adj* pieghevole

fold'ing cam'era *s* macchina fotografica a soffietto

fold'ing chair' *s* sedia pieghevole

fold'ing cot' *s* branda

fold'ing door' *s* porta a libro

fold'ing seat' *s* strapuntino

foliage ['folɪ·ɪdʒ] *s* fogliame *m*

foli·o ['folɪ,o] *adj* in-folio || *s* (**-os**) foglio; (*book*) in-folio || *tr* numerare

folk [fok] *adj* popolare || *s* (**folk** or **folks**) gente *f;* **your folks** i Suoi

folk'lore' *s* folclore *m*

folk' mu'sic *s* musica folcloristica

folk' song' *s* canzone *f* tradizionale

folk·sy ['foksi] *adj* (**-sier; -siest**) socievole; alla buona, alla mano

folk'ways' *spl* costumi *mpl* tradizionali

follicle ['falɪkəl] *s* follicolo

follow ['falo] *tr* seguire; (*to keep up with*) interessarsi di; **to follow suit** seguire l'esempio; (cards) rispondere al colore || *intr* seguire; derivare; **as follows** come segue; **it follows** ne risulta

follower ['falo·ər] *s* seguace *m;* discepolo; partigiano

following ['falo·ɪŋ] *adj* susseguente || *s* seguito; aderenti *mpl*

fol'low-up' *adj* susseguente; ricordativo; da continuarsi || *s* prosecuzione; lettera ricordativa

fol·ly ['fali] *s* (**-lies**) follia; **follies** rivista di varietà

foment [fo'mɛnt] *tr* fomentare

fond [fand] *adj* appassionato; (*of food*) ghiotto; **to become fond of** appassionarsi di

fondle ['fandəl] *tr* accarezzare, vezzeggiare

fondness ['fandnɪs] *s* tenerezza; passione

font [fant] *s* acquasantiera, pila; fonte *f* battesimale; (typ) fondita

food [fud] *adj* alimentare || *s* cibo, vitto; (*for animals*) mangiare *m;·* **food for thought** materia di che pensare

food' store' *s* negozio di commestibili

food'stuffs' *spl* commestibili *mpl*

fool [ful] *s* scemo, sciocco; (*jester*) buffone *m;* (*person imposed on*) vittima, zimbello; **to make a fool of** beffarsi di; **to play the fool** fare lo stupido || *tr* infinocchiare, ingannare; **to fool away** sprecare || *intr* giocare, fare per gioco; **to fool around** perdere il proprio tempo; **to fool with** giocherellare con

fooler·y ['fuləri] *s* (**-ies**) pazzia, buffonata

fool'har'dy *adj* (**-dier; -diest**) temerario

fooling ['fulɪŋ] *s* scherzo; **no fooling** senza scherzi, parlando sul serio

foolish ['fulɪʃ] *adj* sciocco; matto

fool'proof' *adj* a tutta prova; infallibile

fools'cap' *s* berretto a sonagli; carta formato protocollo

fool's' er'rand *s* impresa inutile

fool's' par'adise *s* felicità immaginaria

foot [fut] *s* (**feet** [fit]) piede *m;* (*of an animal*) zampa; (*of horse*) zoccolo; **to drag one's feet** procedere a passo di lumaca; **to put one's best foot forward** fare del proprio meglio; **to put one's foot down** farsi valere, imporsi; **to put one's foot in it** (coll) fare una topica; **to stand on one's own two feet** agire indipendentemente; **to tread under foot** calcare || *tr* (*the bill*) pagare; **to foot it** andare a piedi; ballare

footage ['futɪdʒ] *s* distanza or lunghezza in piedi; (*of film measured in meters*) metraggio

foot'-and-mouth' disease' *s* (vet) afta epizootica

foot'ball' *s* (*ball*) pallone *m;* (*game*) pallovale *f;* (*soccer*) calcio, football *m*

foot'board' *s* (*support for foot*) predellino; (*of bed*) spalliera

foot' brake' *s* freno a pedale

foot'bridge' *s* passerella, ponte riservato ai pedoni

foot'fall' *s* passo

foot'hill' *s* collina ai piedi di una montagna

foot'hold' s stabilità f; **to gain a foot-hold** prender piede

footing ['futɪŋ] s piede m, e.g., **he lost his footing** perse piede; **on a friendly footing** in relazioni amichevoli; **on an equal footing** su un piede di parità; **on a war footing** su un piede di guerra

foot'lights' spl luci fpl della ribalta; (fig) ribalta, scena

foot'loose' adj completamente libero

foot'man s (-men) staffiere m

foot'mark' s orma

foot'note' s rimando, rinvio

foot'path' s sentiero

foot'print' s orma, pesta

foot' race' s corsa podistica

foot'rest' s pedana

foot' rule' s regolo di un piede

foot' soldier' s fante m, fantaccino

foot'sore' adj coi piedi stanchi

foot'step' s passo; **to follow in the footsteps of** seguire le orme di

foot'stone' s pietra tombale a piè di un sepolcro; (archit) pietra di sostegno

foot'stool' s sgabello

foot' warm'er s scaldino

foot'wear' s calzature fpl

foot'work' s allenamento delle gambe; (fig) manovra delicata

foot'worn' adj (road) battuto; (person) spedato

foozle ['fuzəl] s schiappinata ‖ tr & intr mancare completamente

fop [fɑp] s bellimbusto, gagà m

for [fɔr] prep per; malgrado, e.g., **for all his wealth** malgrado tutta la sua ricchezza; come, e.g., **he uses his house for an office** adopera la casa come ufficio; di, e.g., **time for bed** ora di andare a letto; da, e.g., **he has been here for three days** è qui da tre giorni; per amor di; **to go for a walk** andare a fare una passeggiata ‖ conj perchè, poichè

forage ['fɑrɪdʒ] or ['fɔrɪdʒ] adj foraggero ‖ s foraggio ‖ tr foraggiare ‖ intr andare in cerca di foraggio

foray ['fɑre] or ['fɔre] s razzia, scorreria ‖ intr razziare

for·bear [fɔr'bɛr] v (pret -bore ['bor]; pp -borne ['born]) tr astenersi da ‖ intr essere longanime

forbearance [fɔr'bɛrəns] s longanimità f, tolleranza; astensione

for·bid [fɔr'bɪd] v (pret -bade ['bæd] or -bad ['bæd]; pp -bidden ['bɪdən]; ger -bidding) tr proibire, vietare ‖ intr—**God forbid!** Dío ci scampi!

forbidding [fɔr'bɪdɪŋ] adj severo, sinistro

force [fors] s forza; (staff of workers) forza, personale m; (phys) forza; **by force of** a forza di; **by main force** con tutte le sue forze; **in force** vigente; in gran numero; **to join forces** allearsi ‖ tr forzare; obbligare; **to force back** respingere; **to force open** forzare; **to force s.th on s.o.** obbligare qlcu a accettare qlco

forced ['forst] adj forzato; studiato

forced' air' s aria sotto pressione

forced' draft' s tiraggio forzato

forced' land'ing s atterraggio forzato

forced' march' s marcia forzata

forceful ['forsfəl] adj vigoroso, energico

for·ceps ['fɔrsəps] s (-ceps or -cipes [sɪ‚piz]) (dent, surg) pinze fpl; (obstet) forcipe m

force' pump' s pompa premente

forcible ['forsɪbəl] adj impetuoso, energico; efficace

ford [ford] s guado ‖ tr guadare

fore [for] adj davanti; (naut) prodiero ‖ s davanti m; (naut) prua; **to the fore** alla ribalta; d'attualità ‖ adv prima; (naut) a proravia ‖ interj attenzione!

fore' and aft' adv a poppa e a prua

fore'arm' s avambraccio ‖ **fore·arm'** tr premunire; prevenire

fore'bears' spl antenati mpl

forebode [for'bod] tr (to portend) preannunziare; (to have a presentiment of) presentire

foreboding [for'bodɪŋ] s preannunzio; presentimento

fore'cast' s pronostico ‖ v (pret & pp -cast or -casted) tr pronosticare

forecastle ['foksəl], ['for‚kæsəl] or ['for‚kasəl] s castello, pozzetto

fore·close' tr escludere, precludere; (a mortgage) (law) precludere il riscatto di

fore·doom' tr condannare all'insuccesso

fore' edge' s (bb) taglio

fore'fa'ther s antenato

fore'fin'ger s dito indice

fore'front' s—**in the forefront** all'avanguardia

fore·go' v (pret -went; pp -gone') tr & intr precedere

fore·go'ing adj precedente, anteriore

fore'gone' conclu'sion s conclusione inevitabile; decisione già scontata

fore'ground' s primo piano

forehanded ['for‚hændɪd] adj previdente; (thrifty) risparmiatore

forehead ['fɑrɪd] or ['fɔrɪd] s fronte f

foreign ['fɑrɪn] or ['fɔrɪn] adj straniero; (product; affairs) estero; **foreign to** estraneo a

for'eign affairs' spl affari esteri

for'eign-born' adj nato all'estero

foreigner ['fɑrɪnər] or ['fɔrɪnər] s straniero, forestiero

for'eign exchange' s divise fpl; (money) valuta

for'eign min'ister s ministro degli affari esteri

for'eign of'fice s ministero degli affari esteri

for'eign serv'ice s servizio diplomatico e consolare; (Brit) servizio militare in paesi d'oltremare

fore'leg' s zampa anteriore

fore'lock' s ciuffo sulla fronte; **to take time by the forelock** acchiappare l'occasione

fore'man s (-men) sorvegliante m, capomastro; presidente m dei giurati

foremast ['formæst], ['for‚mæst] or ['for‚mast] s trinchetto

foremost ['for‚most] adj primo, principale, più importante

fore'noon' *adj* mattinale ‖ *s* mattina
fore'part' *s* parte *f* anteriore; prima parte
fore'paw' *s* zampa anteriore
fore'quar'ter *s* quarto anteriore
fore'run'ner *s* precursore *m*, predecessore *m*, foriero
fore·sail ['forsəl] or ['for‚sel] *s* trinchetto
fore·see' *v* (*pret* -saw'; *pp* -seen') *tr* prevedere
foreseeable [for'si·əbəl] *adj* prevedibile
fore·shad'ow *tr* presagire
fore·short'en *tr* scorciare
fore'sight' *s* (*prudence*) previdenza; (*foreknowledge*) previsione
fore'sight'ed *adj* previdente
fore'skin' *s* prepuzio
forest ['farɪst] or ['fɔrɪst] *adj* forestale ‖ *s* foresta, bosco
fore·stall' *tr* prevenire; anticipare; (*to buy up*) accapparrare
for'est rang'er ['rendʒər] *s* guardaboschi *m*, guardia forestale
forestry ['farɪstri] or ['fɔrɪstri] *s* selvicoltura
fore'taste' *s* pregustazione ‖ *tr* pregustare
fore·tell' *v* (*pret & pp* -told') *tr* predire, presagire, preannunziare
fore'thought' *s* premeditazione; previdenza
forever [for'evər] *adv* per sempre; continuamente
fore·warn' *tr* prevenire, preavvertire
fore'word' *s* avvertenza, prefazione
forfeit ['fɔrfɪt] *adj* perduto ‖ *s* perdita, confisca; multa; (*article deposited*) pegno; **forfeits** (*game*) pegni *mpl* ‖ *tr* decadere da
forfeiture ['fɔrfɪtʃər] *s* perdita di un pegno
forgather [for'gæðər] *intr* riunirsi; incontrarsi
forge [fordʒ] *s* fucina, forgia ‖ *tr* forgiare; (*a lie*) inventare; (*e.g., handwriting*) falsificare ‖ *intr* forgiare; commettere un falso; **to forge ahead** farsi strada
forger·y ['fordʒəri] *s* (-ies) falsificazione, falso, contraffazione
for·get [for'get] *v* (*pret* -got ['gat]; *pp* -got or -gotten ['gatən]) *tr* dimenticare; **forget it!** non si preoccupi!; **to forget oneself** venir meno alla propria dignità; **to forget to** passare di mente a (qlcu) di, e.g., **he forgot to turn off the lights** gli è passato di mente di spegnere la luce
forgetful [for'getfəl] *adj* (*apt to forget*) smemorato; (*neglectful*) dimentico, immemore
forgetfulness [for'getfəlnɪs] *s* (*inability to recall*) smemorataggine *f*; (*neglectfulness*) dimenticanza
for·get'-me-not' *s* nontiscordardimé *m*
forgivable [for'gɪvəbəl] *adj* perdonabile
for·give [for'gɪv] *v* (*pret* -gave'; *pp* -giv'en) *tr* perdonare
forgiveness [for'gɪvnɪs] *s* perdono
forgiving [for'gɪvɪŋ] *adj* clemente
for·go [for'go] *v* (*pret* -went; *pp* -gone) *tr* rinunciare (with *dat*)

fork [fɔrk] *s* (*pitchfork*) forca, forcone *m*; (*of a bicycle*) forcella; (*for eating*) forchetta; (*of a tree or road*) biforcazione, diramazione ‖ *tr* muovere col forcone; inforcare; **to fork out** (slang) cacciar fuori ‖ *intr* biforcarsi, diramarsi
forked [fɔrkt] *adj* biforcuto
fork'-lift truck' *s* carrello elevatore a forca
forlorn [for'lɔrn] *adj* abbandonato; disperato; miserabile
forlorn' hope' *s* impresa disperata
form [fɔrm] *s* forma; (*paper to be filled out*) formulario; (*construction to give shape to cement*) cassaforma ‖ *tr* formare ‖ *intr* formarsi
formal ['fɔrməl] *adj* formale; di gala, da sera, da etichetta
for'mal attire' *s* vestito da cerimonia
for'mal call' *s* visita di prammatica
formali·ty [for'mælɪti] *s* (-ties) formalità *f*; (*excessive adherence to rules*) formalismo
for'mal par'ty *s* ricevimento di gala
for'mal speech' *s* discorso ufficiale
format ['fɔrmæt] *s* formato
formation [for'meʃən] *s* formazione
former ['fɔrmər] *adj* (*preceding*) anteriore; (*long past*) passato, antico; (*having once been*) già, ex; (*of two*) primo; **the former** quello
formerly ['fɔrmərli] *adv* già, prima, in tempi passati
form'fit'ting *adj* aderente al corpo
formidable ['fɔrmɪdəbəl] *adj* formidabile
formless ['fɔrmlɪs] *adj* informe
form' let'ter *s* lettera a formulario, stampato
formu·la ['fɔrmjələ] *s* (-las or -lae [‚li]) formula
formulate ['fɔrmjə‚let] *tr* formulare
for·sake [for'sek] *v* (*pret* -sook ['suk]; *pp* -saken ['sekən]) *tr* abbandonare
fort [fort] *s* forte *m*, fortezza
forte [fort] *s* forte *m*
forth [forθ] *adv* avanti; **and so forth** e così via; **from this day forth** da oggi in poi; **to go forth** uscire
forth'com'ing *adj* prossimo; immediatamente disponibile
forth'right' *adj* diretto ‖ *adv* direttamente; senza ambagi; immediatamente
forth'with' *adv* immediatamente
fortieth ['fɔrti·ɪθ] *adj*, *s & pron* quarantesimo
fortification [‚fɔrtɪfɪ'keʃən] *s* fortificazione
forti·fy ['fɔrtɪ‚faɪ] *v* (*pret & pp* -fied) *tr* fortificare; aumentare il livello alcolico di
fortitude ['fɔrtɪ‚tjud] or ['fɔrtɪ‚tud] *s* fortezza, fermezza
fortnight ['fɔrtnaɪt] or ['fɔrtnɪt] *s* quindicina, due settimane
fortress ['fɔrtrɪs] *s* fortezza, forte *m*
fortuitous [for'tju·ɪtəs] or [for'tu·ɪtəs] *adj* fortuito, occasionale
fortunate ['fɔrtʃənɪt] *adj* fortunato
fortune ['fɔrtʃən] *s* fortuna; **to make a fortune** farsi un patrimonio; **to tell**

s.o. his fortune leggere il futuro a qlcu

for'tune hunt'er *s* cacciatore *m* di dote

for'tune·tel'ler *s* indovino, cartomante *mf*

for·ty ['fɔrti] *adj & pron* quaranta ‖ *s* (-ties) quaranta *m;* **the forties** gli anni quaranta

fo·rum ['forəm] *s* (-rums or -ra [rə]) foro

forward ['fɔrwərd] *adj* avanzato; precoce; impertinente ‖ *s* (soccer) avanti *m* ‖ *adv* avanti; **to bring forward** mettere in luce; riportare; **to come forward** avanzare; **to look forward to** anticipare il piacere di ‖ *tr* inoltrare, trasmettere; promuovere

fossil ['fasɪl] *adj & s* fossile *m*

foster ['fastər] or ['fɔstər] *adj* adottivo; di latte ‖ *tr* allevare; promuovere

fos'ter home' *s* famiglia adottiva

foul [faul] *adj* sporco; (*air*) viziato; (*wind*) contrario; (*weather; breath*) cattivo; (baseball) fuori linea di gioco ‖ *s* (*of boats*) urto, collisione; (baseball) palla colpita fuori linea di gioco; (boxing) colpo basso; (sports) fallo ‖ *adv* slealmente; (baseball) fuori linea di gioco; **to fall foul of** entrare in collisione con; urtarsi con; **to run foul of** avere una controversia con ‖ *tr* sporcare; otturare; (baseball) colpire fuori linea di gioco ‖ *intr* (*said of two boats*) entrare in collisione; (*said, e.g., of a rope*) imbrogliarsi

foul-mouthed ['faul'mauðd] or ['faul-'mauθt] *adj* sboccato, osceno

foul' play' *s* reato; (sports) gioco sleale

found [faund] *tr* fondare; (*to melt, to cast*) fondere

foundation [faun'deʃən] *s* fondazione; (*endowment*) dotazione; (*charitable*) patronato; (*masonry support*) platea, fondamenta *fpl;* (*make-up*) fondo tinta; (fig) fondatezza

founder ['faundər] *s* fondatore *m;* (*of family*) capostipite *m;* (*of metals*) fonditore *m* ‖ *intr* (*said of a ship*) affondare; (*said of a horse*) azzopparsi; (*to fail*) fare fiasco

foundling ['faundlɪŋ] *s* trovatello

found'ling hos'pital *s* brefotrofio

found·ry ['faundri] *s* (-ries) fonderia

found'ry·man *s* (-men) fonditore *m*

fount [faunt] *s* fonte *f*

fountain ['fauntən] *s* fonte *f*, fontana; (*of knowledge*) pozzo

foun'tain·head' *s* sorgente *f*

foun'tain pen' *s* penna stilografica

foun'tain syringe' *s* clistere *m* a pera

four [for] *adj & pron* quattro ‖ *s* quattro; **four o'clock** le quattro; **on all fours** gattoni, carponi

four'-cy'cle *adj* a quattro tempi

four'-cyl'inder *adj* a quattro cilindri

four'-flush' *intr* (coll) millantarsi

fourflusher ['for ˌflʌʃər] *s* (coll) millantatore *m*

four-footed ['for'futɪd] *adj* quadrupede

four' hun'dred *adj, s & pron* quattro-

cento ‖ **the Four Hundred** l'alta società

four'-in-hand' *s* cravatta a cappio; tiro a quattro

four'-lane' *adj* a quattro corsie

four'-leaf clo'ver *s* quadrifoglio

four-legged ['for'lɛgɪd] or ['for'lɛgd] *adj* a quattro zampe; (*schooner*) (coll) a quattro alberi

four'-letter word' *s* parolaccia di quattro lettere

four'-mo'tor plane' *s* quadrimotore *m*

four'-o'clock' *s* (bot) bella di notte

four' of a kind' *s* (cards) poker *m*

four'post'er *s* letto a baldacchino

four'score' *adj* ottanta

foursome ['forsəm] *s* gruppo di quattro giocatori

fourteen ['for'tin] *adj, s & pron* quattordici *m*

fourteenth ['for'tinθ] *adj, s & pron* quattordicesimo ‖ *s* (*in dates*) quattordici *m*

fourth [forθ] *adj, s & pron* quarto ‖ *s* (*in dates*) quattro

fourth' estate' *s* quarto potere

four'-way' *adj* a quattro orifizi; fra quattro persone; quadruplice

fowl [faul] *s* pollo ‖ *intr* uccellare

fowl'ing piece' *s* fucile *m* da caccia

fox [faks] *s* volpe *f* ‖ *tr* (coll) ingannare

fox'glove' *s* digitale *f*

fox'hole' *s* buca ricovero

fox'hound' *s* segugio

fox' hunt' *s* caccia alla volpe

fox' ter'rier *s* fox-terrier *m*

fox'-trot' *s* (*of a horse*) piccolo trotto; (*dance*) fox-trot *m*

fox·y ['faksi] *adj* (-ier; -iest) volpino, astuto

foyer ['fɔɪ·ər] *s* (*of a private house*) ingresso, vestibolo; (theat) ridotto

fracas ['frekəs] *s* lite *f*, tumulto

fraction ['frækʃən] *s* frazione; frammento

fractional ['frækʃənəl] *adj* frazionario; insignificante

fractious ['frækʃəs] *adj* litigioso, permaloso; indisciplinato

fracture ['fræktʃər] *s* frattura ‖ *tr* fratturare; (*e.g., an arm*) fratturarsi, rompersi ‖ *intr* fratturarsi

fragile ['frædʒɪl] *adj* fragile

fragment ['frægmənt] *s* frammento; (*e.g., of a movie*) spezzone *m* ‖ *tr* frammentare, spezzare

fragmenta'tion bomb' [ˌfrægmən'teʃən] *s* bomba dirompente

fragrant ['fregrənt] *adj* fragrante

frail [frel] *adj* (*not robust*) gracile; (*easily broken*) fragile; (*morally weak*) debole ‖ *s* canestro di giunco

frail·ty ['frelti] *s* (-ties) fragilità *f;* (*of a person*) debolezza

frame [frem] *s* (*of picture*) cornice *f;* (*of glasses*) montatura; (*structure*) ossatura; (*of a building*) ingabbiatura, impalcatura; (*for embroidering*) telaio; (*of a window*) intelaiatura; (*of mind*) stato; (*of government*) sistema *m;* (mov) inquadratura; (phot) fotogramma *m;* (aer) ordinata (naut) costa ‖ *tr* (*to put in a frame*) incorniciare; montare; costruire; inventare; esprimere; (slang) architettare un' accusa contro

frame′ house′ *s* casa con l'ossatura di legno

frame′-up′ *s* (slang) complotto per incriminare un innocente

frame′work′ *s* intelaiatura, impalcatura; palificazione

franc [fræŋk] *s* franco

France [fræns] or [frɑns] *s* la Francia

Frances ['frænsɪs] or ['frɑnsɪs] *s* Francesca

franchise ['fræntʃaɪz] *s* diritto di voto; concessione; (*privilege*) franchigia

Francis ['frænsɪs] or ['frɑnsɪs] *s* Francesco

Franciscan [fræn'sɪskən] *adj & s* francescano

frank [fræŋk] *adj* sincero, schietto ‖ *s* affrancatura postale; lettera affrancata; (*franking privilege*) franchigia postale ‖ *tr* affrancare ‖ **Frank** *s* (*member of Frankish tribe*) franco; (*masculine name*) Franco

frankfurter ['fræŋkfərtər] *s* salsiccia di Francoforte, Frankfurter *m*

frankincense ['fræŋkɪn,sɛns] *s* olibano

Frankish ['fræŋkɪʃ] *adj & s* franco

frankness ['fræŋknɪs] *s* franchezza

frantic ['fræntɪk] *adj* frenetico

frappé [fræ'pe] *adj & s* frappé *m*

frat [fræt] *s* (slang) associazione di studenti

fraternal [frə'tʌrnəl] *adj* fraterno

fraterni·ty [frə'tʌrnɪti] *s* (-ties) (*brotherliness*) fraternità *f*; sodalizio; (eccl) confraternita; (U.S.A.) associazione di studenti

fraternize ['frætər,naɪz] *intr* fraternizzare

fraud [frɔd] *s* truffa, frode *f*; (*person*) (coll) truffatore *m*

fraudulent ['frɔdjələnt] *adj* fraudolento; (*conversion*) indebito

fraught [frɔt] *adj*—**fraught with** carico di, gravido di

fray [fre] *s* zuffa, rissa, lotta ‖ *intr* sfilacciarsi, logorarsi

freak [frik] *s* (*sudden fancy*) capriccio, ticchio; (*person, animal*) fenomeno

freakish ['frikɪʃ] *adj* capriccioso; strano, grottesco

freckle ['frɛkəl] *s* lentiggine *f*, efelide *f*

freckle-faced ['frɛkəl,fest] *adj* lentigginoso

freckly ['frɛkli] *adj* lentigginoso

Frederick ['frɛdərɪk] *s* Federico

free [fri] *adj* (**freer** ['fri·ər]; **freest** ['fri·ɪst]) libero; gratis; franco; sciolto; esente; generoso; **to be free with** essere prodigo di; **to set free** liberare ‖ *adv* liberamente; in libertà; gratis ‖ *v* (*pret & pp* **freed** [frid]; *ger* **freeing** ['fri·ɪŋ]) *tr* liberare; (*from customs*) svincolare; esimere

freebooter ['fri,butər] *s* pirata *m*

free′born′ *adj* nato in libertà; proprio di un popolo libero

freedom ['fridəm] *s* libertà *f*

free′dom of speech′ *s* libertà *f* di parola

free′dom of the press′ *s* libertà *f* di stampa

free′dom of the seas′ *s* libertà *f* di navigazione

free′dom of wor′ship *s* libertà religiosa

free′ en′terprise *s* economia libera

free′-for-all′ *s* rissa, tafferuglio

free′ hand′ *s* libertà assoluta

free′-hand′ *adj* a mano libera

freehanded ['fri'hændɪd] *adj* liberale, generoso

free′ lance′ *s* giornalista *mf* pubblicista; scrittore *m* che lavora senza contratto; soldato di ventura

free′load′er ['lodər] *s* (coll) mangiatore *m* a sbafo

free′man *s* (-men) uomo libero; cittadino

Free′ma′son *s* frammassone *m*

Free′ma′sonry *s* frammassoneria

free′ of charge′ *adj* gratis, senza spese

free′ port′ *s* porto franco

free′ serv′ice *s* manutenzione gratuita

free′-spo′ken *adj* franco, aperto

free′stone′ *adj* spiccagnolo ‖ *s* pesca spicca

free′think′er *s* libero pensatore

free′ thought′ *s* libero pensiero

free′ trade′ *s* libero scambio

free′trad′er *s* liberoscambista *mf*

free′way′ *s* autostrada

free′ will′ *s* libero arbitrio

freeze [friz] *s* gelo, gelata; (*e.g., of prices*) blocco ‖ *v* (*pret* **froze** [froz]; *pp* **frozen**) *tr* gelare; (*credits, rentals, etc.*) bloccare ‖ *intr* gelarsi; (*said of brakes*) inchiodarsi; morire assiderato; (*to become immobilized*) irrigidirsi

freeze′-dry′ *v* (*pret & pp* **-dried′**) *tr* liofilizzare

freezer ['frizər] *s* congelatore *m*; (*for making ice cream*) sorbettiera

freight [fret] *s* carico; (*charge*) porto; (naut) nolo; **by freight** come carico mercantile; (rr) a piccola velocità ‖ *tr* spedire come carico

freight′ car′ *s* vagone *m* or carro merci

freighter ['fretər] *s* speditore *m*; nave *f* da carico

freight′ plat′form *s* (rr) banchina adibita al traffico merci

freight′ sta′tion *s* (rr) stazione merci

freight′ train′ *s* treno merci, merci *m*

freight′ yard′ *s* (rr) scalo merci

French [frɛntʃ] *adj & s* francese *m*; **the French** i francesi

French′ bread′ *s* pane *m* a bastone

French′ chalk′ *s* pietra da sarto

French′ door′ *s* porta a vetri

French′ dress′ing *s* salsa verde con aceto

French′ fried′ pota′toes *spl* patate fritte affettate

French′ horn′ *s* (mus) corno

French′ leave′ *s*—**to take French leave** andarsene all'inglese, filare all'inglese

French′man *s* (-men) francese *m*

French′ tel′ephone *s* microtelefono

French′ toast′ *s* pane dorato al salto

French′ win′dow *s* portafinestra

French′wom′an *s* (-wom′en) francese *f*

frenzied ['frɛnzid] *adj* frenetico
fren·zy ['frɛnzi] *s* (**-zies**) frenesia
frequen·cy ['frikwənsi] *s* (**-cies**) frequenza
fre'quency modula'tion *s* modulazione di frequenza
frequent ['frikwənt] *adj* frequente || [frɪ'kwɛnt] *or* ['frikwənt] *tr* frequentare, praticare
frequently ['frikwəntli] *adv* frequentemente
fres·co ['frɛsko] *s* (**-coes** or **-cos**) affresco || *tr* affrescare
fresh [frɛʃ] *adj* fresco; (*water*) dolce; (*new*) nuovo; (*wind*) moderato; (*inexperienced*) novizio; (*cheeky*) (slang) sfacciato || *adv* recentemente, di recente; **fresh in** (coll) appena arrivato; **fresh out** (coll) appena esaurito
freshen ['frɛʃən] *tr* rinfrescare || *intr* rinfrescarsi
freshet ['frɛʃɪt] *s* piena, crescita
fresh'man *s* (**-men**) (*newcomer*) novizio; (educ) matricola
freshness ['frɛʃnɪs] *s* freschezza; (*of air*) frescura; (*cheek*) (slang) sfacciataggine *f*
fresh'-wa'ter *adj* d'acqua dolce; poco conosciuto; piccolo
fret [frɛt] *s* (*interlaced design*) fregio, greca; irritazione; (mus) tasto || *v* (*pret* & *pp* **fretted;** *ger* **fretting**) *tr* fregiare || *intr* fremere, trepidare, agitarsi
fretful ['frɛtfəl] *adj* irritabile, permaloso
fret'work' *s* greca
Freudianism ['frɔɪdɪ·ə‚nɪzəm] *s* freudismo
friar ['fraɪ·ər] *s* frate *m*
friar·y ['fraɪ·əri] *s* (**-ies**) convento di frati
fricassee [‚frɪkə'si] *s* fricassea
friction ['frɪkʃən] *s* frizione; disaccordo, dissenso
fric'tion tape' *s* nastro isolante
Friday ['fraɪdi] *s* venerdì *m*
fried [fraɪd] *adj* fritto
fried' egg' *s* uovo al tegame, uovo occhio di manzo
friend [frɛnd] *s* amico; **to be friends with** essere amico di; **to make friends** allacciare amicizie; **to make friends with** fare l'amicizia di
friend·ly ['frɛndli] *adj* (**-lier; -liest**) amico, amichevole
friendship ['frɛndʃɪp] *s* amicizia
frieze [friz] *s* (archit) fregio
frigate ['frɪgɪt] *s* fregata
fright [fraɪt] *s* spavento; **to take fright at** spaventarsi di
frighten ['fraɪtən] *tr* intimorire, spaventare; **to frighten away** mettere in fuga, sgomentare || *intr* spaventarsi
frightful ['fraɪtfəl] *adj* spaventevole, orribile; (coll) enorme
frightfulness ['fraɪtfəlnɪs] *s* spavento; terrorismo
frigid ['frɪdʒɪd] *adj* freddo; (*zone*) glaciale
frigidity [frɪ'dʒɪdɪti] *s* (fig) frigidezza; (pathol) frigidità *f*
frill [frɪl] *s* pieghettatura; (*of birds and*

other animals) collarino; (*in dress, speech, etc.*) affettazione
fringe [frɪndʒ] *s* frangia; (*in dressmaking*) volantino; (*on curtains*) balza; **on the fringe of** all'orlo di || *tr* orlare
fringe' ben'efits *spl* assegni *mpl*, benefici *mpl* marginali
fripper·y ['frɪpəri] *s* (**-ies**) (*finery*) fronzoli *mpl*; ostentazione; (*trifles*) cianfrusaglie *fpl*
frisk [frɪsk] *tr* perquisire; (slang) derubare || *intr* fare capriole
frisk·y ['frɪski] *adj* (**-ier; -iest**) gaio, vivace
fritter ['frɪtər] *s* frittella; frammento || *tr*—**to fritter away** sprecare
frivolous ['frɪvələs] *adj* frivolo
friz [frɪz] *s* (**frizzes**) ricciolo || *v* (*pret* & *pp* **frizzed;** *ger* **frizzing**) *tr* arricciare
frizzle ['frɪzəl] *s* ricciolo || *tr* arricciare || *intr* arricciarsi
friz·zly ['frɪzli] *adj* (**-zlier; -zliest**) crespo, riccio
fro [fro] *adv*—**to and fro** avanti e indietro; **to go to and fro** andare e venire
frock [frɑk] *s* gabbano; (*smock*) grembiule *m*; blusa; (*of priest*) tonaca
frock' coat' *s* finanziera
frog [frɑg] *or* [frɔg] *s* rana; (*button and loop on a garment*) alamaro; (*in throat*) raschio
frog'man' *s* (**-men'**) sommozzatore *m*, uomo rana
frol·ic ['frɑlɪk] *s* scherzo, monelleria || *v* (*pret* & *pp* **-icked;** *ger* **-icking**) *intr* scherzare, folleggiare
frolicsome ['frɑlɪksəm] *adj* scherzoso
from [frʌm], [frɑm] *or* [frəm] *prep* da; di, e.g., **I am from New York** sono di New York; da parte di; a, e.g., **to take s.th away from s.o.** portar via qlco a qlcu
front [frʌnt] *adj* frontale, anteriore; di fronte || *s* fronte *m* & *f*; (*of a building*) prospetto; (*of a book*) principio; (*of a shirt*) sparato; (*e.g., of wealth*) apparenza; (theat) boccascena *m*; (mil) fronte *m*; **in front of** dinanzi a; **to put on a front** (coll) fare ostentazione; **to put up a bold front** (coll) farsi coraggio || *tr* (*to face*) fronteggiare; (*to confront*) affrontare; (*to supply with a front*) coprire; servire da facciata a || *intr*—**to front on** dare su
frontage ['frʌntɪdʒ] *s* facciata, veduta; terreno di fronte alla casa
front' door' *s* porta d'entrata
front' drive' *s* (aut) trazione anteriore
frontier [frʌn'tɪr] *adj* limitrofo || *s* frontiera
fron'tiers'man *s* (**-men**) pioniere *m*
frontispiece ['frʌntɪs‚pis] *s* (*of book*) pagina illustrata di fronte al frontispizio; (*of building*) facciata
front' mat'ter *s* (*of book*) parte *f* preliminare
front'-page' *tr* stampare in prima pagina
front' porch' *s* porticato

front' room' s stanza con vista sulla strada

front' row' s prima fila

front' seat' s posto in una delle file davanti; (aut) sedile m anteriore

front' steps' spl scalinata d'ingresso

front' view' s vista sulla strada

frost [frɔst] or [frɑst] s gelo, brina, gelata; (fig) freddezza; (slang) fiasco ‖ tr agghiacciare; (with sugar) glassare; (glass) smerigliare

frost'bite' s congelamento

frost'ed glass' s vetro smerigliato

frosting ['frɔstɪŋ] or ['frɑstɪŋ] s glassatura; (of glass) smerigliatura

frost·y ['frɔsti] or ['frɑsti] adj (-ier; -iest) brinato; (hair) canuto; (fig) gelido

froth [frɔθ] or [frɑθ] s schiuma; (fig) frivolezza ‖ intr schiumare; (at the mouth) avere la schiuma

froth·y ['frɔθi] or ['frɑθi] adj (-ier; -iest) spumoso; frivolo

froward ['frowərd] adj indocile

frown [fraun] s aggrottare m delle ciglia; (of disapproval) cipiglio ‖ intr aggrottare le ciglia; **to frown at** or **on** disapprovare

frows·y or **frowz·y** ['frauzi] adj (-ier; -iest) sporco; puzzolente

fro'zen foods' ['frozən] spl cibi congelati; cibi surgelati

frugal ['frugəl] adj parsimonioso; (in food and drink) frugale

fruit [frut] adj (tree) fruttifero; (dish) da frutta ‖ s (such as apple) frutto; (collectively) frutta, e.g., **I like fruit** mi piace la frutta; (fig) frutto

fruit' cake' s torta con noci e canditi

fruit' cup' s macedonia di frutta

fruit' dish' s fruttiera, portafrutta m

fruit' fly' s moscerino del vino

fruitful ['frutfəl] adj fruttuoso

fruition [fru'ɪʃən] s realizzazione; **to come to fruition** giungere a buon fine

fruit' jar' s vaso da frutta

fruit' juice' s sugo or spremuta di frutta

fruitless ['frutlɪs] adj infruttuoso

fruit' sal'ad s macedonia di frutta

fruit' stand' s bancarella da fruttivendolo

fruit' store' s negozio di frutta

frumpish ['frʌmpɪʃ] adj trasandato

frustrate ['frʌstret] tr frustrare

fry [fraɪ] s (fries) fritto ‖ v (pret & pp **fried**) tr & intr friggere

fry'ing pan' s padella; **out of the frying pan into the fire** dalla padella nella brace

fudge [fʌdʒ] s dolce m di cioccolato

fuel ['fju·əl] s combustibile m; (fig) cibo ‖ v (pret & pp **fueled** or **fuelled;** ger **fueling** or **fuelling**) tr rifornire di carburante ‖ intr rifornirsi di carburante

fuel' cell' s cellula elettrogena

fu'el oil' s nafta, olio pesante

fu'el tank' s serbatoio del carburante

fugitive ['fjudʒɪtɪv] adj & s fuggiasco, fuggitivo

fugue [fjug] s (mus) fuga

ful·crum ['fʌlkrəm] s (-crums or -cra [krə]) fulcro

fulfill [ful'fɪl] tr (to carry out) eseguire; (an obligation) mantenere; (to bring to an end) completare

fulfillment [ful'fɪlmənt] s adempimento; realizzazione

full [ful] adj pieno; (speed) tutto; (garment) ampio; (voice) spiegato; (of food) sazio; (member) effettivo; **full of aches and pains** pieno d'acciacchi; **full of fun** divertentissimo; **full of play** pieno di vita ‖ s pieno; colmo; **in full** per esteso, in pieno; **to the full** completamente ‖ adv completamente; **full many (a)** moltissimi; **full well** perfettamente ‖ tr follare

full-blooded ['ful'blʌdɪd] adj vigoroso; purosangue

full-blown ['ful'blon] adj completamente sbocciato; maturo

full-bodied ['ful'badɪd] adj forte, ricco

full' dress' s vestito da sera; (mil) tenuta di gala, alta uniforme

full-faced ['ful'fest] adj paffuto; (view) intero; (typ) grassetto

full-fledged ['ful'fledʒd] adj completamente sviluppato; vero, autentico

full-grown ['ful'gron] adj completamente sviluppato, adulto

full' house' s (theat) piena; (poker) full m

full'-length' mir'ror s specchiera

full'-length mo'vie s lungometraggio

full' moon' s luna piena

full' name' s nome m e cognome m

full'-page' adj di tutta una pagina

full' pow'ers spl pieni poteri

full' sail' adv a vele spiegate

full'-scale' adj in grandezza naturale; completo

full-sized ['ful'saɪzd] adj in grandezza naturale

full' speed' adv a tutta velocità

full' stop' s fermata; (gram) punto

full' swing' s piena attività

full' tilt' adv a tutta forza

full'-time' adj a orario completo

fully ['fuli] or ['fulli] adv completamente, del tutto

fulsome ['fulsəm] or ['fʌlsəm] adj basso, volgare; nauseante

fumble ['fʌmbəl] tr (a ball) lasciar cadere ‖ intr titubare; andare a tentoni; (in one's pocket) cercare alla cieca

fume [fjum] s fumo, vapore m, esalazione ‖ tr affumicare ‖ intr fumare, esalare fumo; (to show anger) irritarsi

fumigate ['fjumɪ,get] tr fumigare

fumigation [,fjumɪ'geʃən] s fumigazione

fun [fʌn] s divertimento, spasso; **to be fun** essere divertente; **to have fun** divertirsi; **to make fun of** prendersi gioco di

function ['fʌŋkʃən] s funzione ‖ intr funzionare, marciare, camminare

functional ['fʌŋkʃənəl] adj funzionale

functionalism ['fʌŋkʃənəl,ɪzəm] s funzionalismo

functionar·y ['fʌŋkʃə,nɛri] s (-ies) funzionario

fund [fʌnd] *s* fondo; (*of knowledge*) suppellettile *f* || *tr* (*debts*) consolidare

fundamental [,fʌndə'mentəl] *adj* fondamentale || *s* fondamento

fundamentalist [,fʌndə'mentəlɪst] *adj & s* scritturale *m*

funeral ['fjunərəl] *adj* funebre, funerario || *s* funerale *m*, trasporto funebre; **it's not my funeral** (slang) non sono affari miei

fu'neral direc'tor *s* imprenditore *m* di pompe funebri

fu'neral home' or **par'lor** *s* impresa di pompe funebri

fu'neral serv'ice *s* ufficio dei defunti

funereal [fju'nɪrɪ·əl] *adj* funebre

fungous ['fʌŋgəs] *adj* fungoso

fungus ['fʌŋgəs] *s* (**funguses** or **fungi** ['fʌndʒaɪ]) *s* fungo

funicular [fju'nɪkjələr] *adj & s* funicolare *f*

funk [fʌŋk] *s* (coll) paura; (čoll) codardo; **in a funk** (coll) con una paura matta

fun·nel ['fʌnəl] *s* imbuto; (*smokestack*) fumaiolo; (*for ventilation*) manica a vento || *v* (*pret & pp* **-neled** or **-nelled**; *ger* **-neling** or **-nelling**) *tr* incanalare

funnies ['fʌniz] *spl* pagine *fpl* fumetti

fun·ny ['fʌni] *adj* (**-nier**; **-niest**) comico, buffo; (coll) strano; **to strike as funny** parere strano or buffo a

fun'ny bone' *s* osso rabbioso (del gomito); **to strike s.o.'s funny bone** far ridere qlcu

fur [fʌr] *s* pelo; (*garment*) pelliccia; (*on the tongue*) patina

furbelow ['fʌrbə ,lo] *s* falpalà *m*

furbish ['fʌrbɪʃ] *tr* lustrare; mettere a nuovo; **to furbish up** rinfrescare

furious ['fjurɪ·əs] *adj* furioso

furl [fʌrl] *tr* (*a flag*) incazzottare; (naut) raccogliere, strangolare

fur-lined ['fʌr ,laɪnd] *adj* foderato di pelliccia

furlong ['fʌrlɔŋ] or ['fʌrlɑŋ] *s* un ottavo di miglio terrestre

furlough ['fʌrlo] *s* licenza || *tr* licenziare

furnace ['fʌrnɪs] *s* fornace *f*; (*to heat a house*) caldaia del calorifero

furnish ['fʌrnɪʃ] *tr* fornire; ammobiliare

furnishings ['fʌrnɪʃɪŋz] *spl* mobilia; (*things to wear*) accessori *mpl* da uomo

furniture ['fʌrnɪtʃər] *s* mobili *mpl*, mobilia; (naut) attrezzatura; **a piece of furniture** un mobile

fur'ni·ture deal'er *s* mobiliere *m*

furor ['fjurər] *s* furore *m*

furrier ['fʌrɪ·ər] *s* pellicciaio

furrier·y ['fʌrɪ·əri] *s* (**-ies**) pellicceria

furrow ['fʌro] *s* solco || *tr* solcare

further ['fʌrðər] *adj* più lontano; ulteriore || *adv* oltre; più; inoltre || *tr* favorire, incoraggiare

furtherance ['fʌrðərəns] *s* avanzamento, incoraggiamento

furthermore ['fʌrðər ,mor] *adv* inoltre

furthest ['fʌrðɪst] *adj* (il) più lontano || *adv* al massimo

furtive ['fʌrtɪv] *adj* furtivo

fu·ry ['fjuri] *s* (**-ries**) furia

furze [fʌrz] *s* ginestra spinosa

fuse [fjuz] *s* (*for igniting an explosive*) miccia; (*for detonating an explosive*) spoletta; (elec) fusibile *m;* **to burn out a fuse** bruciare un fusibile || *tr* fondere || *intr* fondersi; (elec) saltare

fuse' box' *s* valvoliera

fuselage ['fjuzəlɪdʒ] or [,fjuzə'lɑʒ] *s* fusoliera

fusible ['fjuzɪbəl] *adj* fusibile

fusillade [,fjuzɪ'led] *s* fucileria; (fig) gragnola || *tr* attaccare con fuoco di fucileria

fusion ['fjuʒən] *s* fusione

fuss [fʌs] *s* agitazione inutile; (coll) alterco per nulla; **to make a fuss** accogliere festosamente; fare molte storie; **to make a fuss over** aver un alterco su || *tr* disturbare || *intr* agitarsi per un nonnulla

fuss·y ['fʌsi] *adj* (**-ier**; **-iest**) (*person*) pignolo, meticoloso; (*object*) carico di fronzoli; (*writing*) complicato

fustian ['fʌstʃən] *s* fustagno; (fig) verbosità *f*, magniloquenza

fust·y ['fʌsti] *adj* (**-ier**; **-iest**) ammuffito, che sa di muffa; antico, sorpassato

futile ['fjutɪl] *adj* (*unproductive*) sterile; (*unimportant*) futile

futili·ty [fju'tɪlɪti] *s* (**-ties**) sterilità *f*; futilità *f*

future ['fjutʃər] *adj* futuro || *s* futuro; **futures** contratto con consegna a termine; **in the near future** nel prossimo avvenire

fuze [fjuz] *s* (*for igniting an explosive*) miccia; (*for detonating an explosive*) spoletta; (elec) fusibile *m* || *tr* innestare la spoletta a

fuzz [fʌz] *s* lanugine *f*, peluria; (*in corners*) polvere *f*; (slang) poliziotto; (slang) polizia

fuzz·y ['fʌzi] *adj* (**-ier**; **-iest**) lanuginoso; coperto di polvere; (*indistinct*) confuso

G

G, g [dʒi] *s* settima lettera dell'alfabeto inglese

gab [gæb] *s* (coll) parlantina || *v* (*pret & pp* **gabbed**; *ger* **gabbing**) *intr* (coll) chiacchierare

gabardine ['gæbər ,din] *s* gabardine *f*

gabble ['gæbəl] *s* barbugliamento || *intr* barbugliare

gable ['gebəl] *s* (archit) timpano

ga'ble roof' *s* tetto a due falde, tetto a capanna

gad [gæd] *v* (*pret & pp* **gadded**; *ger* **gadding**) *intr* bighellonare

gad'about' *adj* ozioso || *s* vagabondo, bighellone *m;* fannullone *m*

gad'fly' *s* (**-flies**) tafano, moscone *m*

gadget ['gædʒɪt] *s* congegno, dispositivo, macchinetta

Gaelic ['gelɪk] *adj* & *s* gaelico

gaff [gæf] *s* arpione *m;* (naut) picco; **to stand the gaff** (slang) aver pazienza

gag [gæg] *s* bavaglio; *(joke)* barzelletta; (theat) battuta improvvisata || *v (pret* & *pp* **gagged; ger gagging)** *tr* imbavagliare; soffocare || *intr* sentirsi venire la nausea

gage [gedʒ] *s (pledge)* pegno; *(challenge)* sfida

gaie·ty ['ge·ɪti] *s* **(-ties)** gaiezza

gaily ['geli] *adv* allegramente

gain [gen] *s* profitto; *(increase)* aumento || *tr* guadagnare; *(to reach)* raggiungere; *(altitude)* prendere || *intr (said of a patient)* migliorare; *(said of a watch)* correre; **to gain on** guadagnare terreno su; sorpassare

gainful ['genfəl] *adj* rimunerativo

gain'say' *v (pret* & *pp* **-said** [,sed] or [,sed]) *tr* disdire, misconoscere; negare

gait [get] *s* portamento, andatura

gaiter ['getər] *s* ghetta

gala ['gælə] or ['gelə] *adj* di gala || *s* gala *m* & *f,* festa

galax·y ['gæləksi] *s* **(-ies)** galassia

gale [gel] *s (of wind)* bufera; *(of laughter)* scoppio; **to weather the gale** resistere alla tempesta

gall [gɔl] *s* fiele *m;* bile *f;* cistifellea; scorticatura; *(gallnut)* galla; *(audacity)* (coll) faccia tosta || *tr* irritare || *intr* irritarsi; (naut) logorarsi

gallant ['gælənt] or [gə'lænt] *adj* galante || ['gælənt] *adj (brave)* valoroso; *(grand)* magnifico; *(showy)* festivo || *s* prode *m;* (man attentive to women) galante *m*

gallant·ry ['gæləntri] *s* **(-ries)** galanteria; valore *m*

gall' blad'der *s* vescichetta biliare

gall'-blad'der attack' *s* travaso di bile

galleon ['gælɪ·ən] *s* galeone *m*

galler·y ['gæləri] *s* **(-ies)** galleria; tribuna; *(cheapest seats in theater)* loggione *m*

galley ['gæli] *s (vessel)* galera; *(kitchen)* (aer) cucina; *(kitchen)* (naut) cambusa; *(galley proof)* (typ) bozza in colonna; *(tray)* (typ) vantaggio

gal'ley proof' *s* bozza in colonna

gal'ley slave' *s* galeotto

Gallic ['gælɪk] *adj* gallo, gallico

galling ['gɔlɪŋ] *adj* irritante

gallivant ['gælɪ ,vænt] *intr* andare a spasso; fare il galante

gall'nut' *s* galla

gallon ['gælən] *s* gallone *m*

galloon [gə'lun] *s* gallone *m,* nastro

gallop ['gæləp] *s* galoppo; **at a gallop** al galoppo || *tr* far galoppare || *intr* galoppare

gal·lows ['gæloz] *s* **(-lows** or **-lowses)** forca; (min) castelletto

gal'lows bird' *s* (coll) remo di galera, pendaglio da forca

gall'stone' *s* calcolo biliare

galore [gə'lor] *adv* in abbondanza

galosh [gə'lɑʃ] *s* stivaletto di gomma

galvanize ['gælvə ,naɪz] *tr* galvanizzare

gal'vanized i'ron *s* ferro zincato

gambit ['gæmbɪt] *s* gambetto

gamble ['gæmbəl] *s* azzardo; *(game)* gioco d'azzardo || *tr* giocare; **to gamble away** giocarsi || *intr* giocare d'azzardo; (com) speculare

gambler ['gæmblər] *s* giocatore *m;* speculatore *m*

gambling ['gæmblɪŋ] *s* gioco (d'azzardo)

gam'bling den' *s* bisca

gam'bling house' *s* casa da gioco

gam·bol ['gæmbəl] *s* salto, capriola || *v (pret* & *pp* **-boled** or **-bolled; ger -boling** or **-bolling)** *intr* saltare, far capriole

gambrel ['gæmbrəl] *s* garretto

gam'brel roof' *s* tetto a mansarda

game [gem] *adj* da caccia; coraggioso; *(leg)* (coll) zoppo; (coll) pronto || *s (amusement)* gioco; *(contest)* partita; *(any sport)* sport *m; (wild animals hunted)* selvaggina; *(any pursuit)* attività *f; (object of pursuit)* bersaglio; (bridge) manche *f;* **the game is up il** gioco è fallito; **to make game of** farsi gioco di; **to play the game** giocare onestamente

game' bag' *s* carniere *m*

game'cock' *s* gallo da combattimento

game'keep'er *s* guardacaccia *m*

game' of chance' *s* gioco d'azzardo

game' preserve' *s* bandita di caccia

game' war'den *s* guardacaccia *m*

gamut ['gæmət] *s* (mus, fig) gamma

gam·y ['gemi] *adj* **(-ier; -iest)** coraggioso; (culin) che sa di selvatico

gander ['gændər] *s* papero, oca

gang [gæŋ] *adj* multiplo || *s (of workers)* ganga; *(of thugs)* cricca || *intr*—**to gang up** riunirsi; **to gang up against** or **on** (coll) gettarsi insieme contro

gangling ['gæŋglɪŋ] *adj* dinoccolato

gangli·on ['gæŋglɪ·ən] *s* **(-ons** or **-a** [ə])** ganglio

gang'plank' *s* palanca, plancia

gangrene ['gæŋgrin] *s* cancrena || *tr* far andare in cancrena || *intr* andare in cancrena

gangster ['gæŋstər] *s* gangster *m*

gang'way' *s (passageway)* corridoio; *(gangplank)* passerella, scalandrone *m; (in ship's side)* barcarizzo || *interj* lasciar passare!

gan·try ['gæntri] *s* **(-tries)** *(of crane)* cavalletto; (rr) ponte *m* delle segnalazioni; (rok) piattaforma verticale, torre *f* di lancio

gap [gæp] *s (pass)* passo; *(in a wall)* breccia; *(interval)* lacuna; *(between two points of view)* abisso; (mach) gioco

gape [gep] or [gæp] *s* apertura; *(yawn)* sbadiglio; sguardo di meraviglia || *intr* stare a bocca aperta; **to gape at** guardare a bocca aperta

garage [gə'rɑʒ] *s* rimessa

garb [gɑrb] *s* veste *f* || *tr* vestire

garbage ['gɑrbɪdʒ] *s* pattume *m,* immondizia, immondizie *fpl*

gar'bage can' *s* portaimmondizie *m*

gar'bage collec'tor s spazzaturaio, spazzino, netturbino

garble ['garbəl] tr falsare, mutilare

garden ['gardən] s (of vegetables) orto; (of flowers) giardino

gardener ['gardnər] s (of vegetables) ortolano; (of flowers) giardiniere m

gardenia [gar'dinı·ə] s gardenia

gardening ['gardnıŋ] s orticoltura; giardinaggio

gar'den par'ty s trattenimento in giardino

gargle ['gargəl] s gargarismo || intr gargarizzare

gargoyle ['gargɔıl] s doccione m, gargolla

garish ['gerıʃ] or ['gærıʃ] adj appariscente; abbagliante

garland ['garlənd] s ghirlanda || tr inghirlandare

garlic ['garlık] s aglio

garment ['garmənt] s capo di vestiario

gar'ment bag' s tessilsacco

garner ['garnər] tr mettere in granaio; (to get) acquistarsi; (to hoard) incettare

garnet ['garnıt] adj & s granata

garnish ['garnıʃ] s guarnizione; || tr guarnire; (law) sequestrare

garret ['gærıt] s sottotetto, soffitta

garrison ['gærısən] s guarnigione, presidio || tr presidiare

garrote [gə'rat] or [gə'rot] s strangolamento; garrotta || tr strangolare; giustiziare con la garrotta

garrulous ['gærələs] or ['gærjələs] adj garrulo, loquace

garter ['gartər] s giarrettiera

gas [gæs] s gas m; (coll) benzina; (slang) successo; (slang) chiacchiere fpl || v (pret & pp gassed; ger gassing) tr fornire di gas; (mil) gassare; (slang) divertire || intr emettere gas; (slang) chiacchierare; to gas up fare il pieno

gas'bag' s involucro per il gas; (coll) chiacchierone m

gas' burn'er s becco a gas; (on a stove) fornello a gas

Gascony ['gæskəni] s la Guascogna

gaseous ['gæsı·əs] adj gassoso

gas' fit'ter s gassista m

gash [gæʃ] s sfregio || tr sfregiare

gas' heat' s calefazione a gas

gas'hold'er s gassometro

gasi·fy ['gæsı‚faı] v (pret & pp -fied) tr gassificare || intr gassificarsi

gas' jet' s fornello a gas; fiamma

gasket ['gæskıt] s guarnizione

gas'light' s luce f del gas

gas' main' s tubatura principale del gas

gas' mask' s maschera antigas

gas' me'ter s contatore m del gas

gasoline ['gæsə‚lin] or [‚gæsə'lin] s benzina

gas'oline' deal'er s benzinaio

gas'oline' pump' s colonnetta, distributore m di benzina

gasp [gæsp] or [gasp] s respirazione affannosa; (of death) rantolo || tr dire affannosamente || intr boccheggiare

gas' range' s cucina a gas, fornello a gas

gas'-sta'tion attend'ant s benzinaio

gas' stove' s cucina a gas

gas' tank' s gassometro; (aut) serbatoio di benzina

gastric ['gæstrık] adj gastrico

gastronomy [gæs'tranəmi] s gastronomia

gas' works' s officina del gas

gate [get] s porta; (in fence or wall) cancello; (of sluice) saracinesca; (in an airport or station) uscita; (rr) barriera; (sports, theat) incasso totale; **to crash the gate** (coll) fare il portoghese

gate'keep'er s portiere m; (rr) guardiabarriere m

gate'way' s passaggio, entrata

gather ['gæðər] tr raccogliere, cogliere; (news) raccapezzare; (dust) coprirsi di; (e.g., a shawl) avvolgere; (speed) aumentare (di); con:ludere, dedurre; (signatures) (bb) riunire; (sew) increspare || intr riunirsi; raccogliersi; accumularsi

gathering ['gæðərıŋ] s riunione; (bb) raccolta e piegatura; (pathol) ascesso; (sew) pieghettatura

gaud·y ['gɔdi] adj (-ier; -iest) chiassoso, vistoso

gauge [gedʒ] s misura; calibro; (for liquids) indicatore m di livello; (of carpenter) graffietto; indice m; diametro; (aut) spia; (rr) scartamento || tr misurare; calibrare; (naut) stazzare

Gaul [gɔl] s gallo

gaunt [gɔnt] or [gant] adj magro, emaciato; (e.g., landscape) desolato

gauntlet ['gɔntlıt] or ['gantlıt] s guanto; guanto di ferro; guantone m, manopola; **to run the gauntlet** (fig) esporsi alla critica; **to take up the gauntlet** raccogliere il guanto; **to throw down the gauntlet** gettare il guanto

gauze [gɔz] s garza

gavel ['gævəl] s martello, martelletto

gavotte [gə'vat] s gavotta

gawk [gɔk] s sciocco || intr guardare a bocca aperta

gawk·y ['gɔki] adj (-ier; -iest) sgraziato, goffo

gay [ge] adj gaio; brillante; dissipato; (slang) omosessuale

gaye·ty ['ge·ıti] s (-ties) gaiezza

gaze [gez] s sguardo fisso || intr fissare lo sguardo

gazelle [gə'zɛl] s gazzella

gazette [gə'zɛt] s gazzetta

gazetteer [‚gæzə'tır] s dizionario geografico

gear [gır] s utensili mpl, attrezzi mpl; (mechanism) meccanismo, dispositivo; (aut) marcia; (mach) ingranaggio **out of gear** disingranato; (fig) disturbato; **to throw into gear** ingranare; **to throw out of gear** disingranare; (fig) disturbare || tr adattare || intr adattarsi

gear' box' s scatola del cambio

gear'shift' s cambio di velocità

gear'shift lev'er *s* leva del cambio
gear'wheel' *s* ruota dentata
gee [dʒi] *interj* oh!; che bellezza!; **gee up!** (*command to a draft animal*) arri!
Gei'ger count'er ['gaɪgər] *s* contatore *m* Geiger
gel [dʒɛl] *s* gel *m.* ‖ *v* (*pret & pp* **gelled;** *ger* **gelling**) *intr* gelatinizzarsi
gelatine ['dʒɛlətɪn] *s* gelatina
geld [gɛld] *v* (*pret & pp* **gelded** or **gelt** [gɛlt]) *tr* castrare
gem [dʒɛm] *s* gemma, gioia
Gemini ['dʒɛmɪ ˌnaɪ] *spl* i Gemelli
gender ['dʒɛndər] *s* (gram) genere *m;* (coll) sesso
gene [dʒin] *s* (biol) gene *m*
genealo·gy [ˌdʒɛnɪ'ælədʒi] or [ˌdʒɪnɪ'ælədʒi] *s* (-gies) genealogia
general ['dʒɛnərəl] *adj & s* generale *m*
gen'eral deliv'ery *s* fermo in posta, fermo posta *m*
generalissi·mo [ˌdʒɛnərə'lɪsɪmo] *s* (-mos) generalissimo
generali·ty [ˌdʒɛnə'rælɪti] *s* (-ties) generalità *f*
generalize ['dʒɛnərə ˌlaɪz] *tr & intr* generalizzare
generally ['dʒɛnərəli] *adv* in genere, generalmente
gen'eral part'ner *s* accomandatario
gen'eral practi'tioner *s* medico generico
generalship ['dʒɛnərəl ˌʃɪp] *s* generalato; strategia, abilità *f* militare; abilità amministrativa
gen'eral staff' *s* stato maggiore
generate ['dʒɛnə ˌret] *tr* (*offspring; electricity*) generare; (math) originare
gen'erat'ing sta'tion *s* centrale elettrica
generation [ˌdʒɛnə're/ən] *s* generazione
generative ['dʒɛnə ˌretɪv] *adj* generativo
gen'erative gram'mar *s* grammatica generativa
generator ['dʒɛnə ˌretər] *s* generatore *m;* (elec) generatrice *f*
generic [dʒɪ'nɛrɪk] *adj* generico
generous ['dʒɛnərəs] *adj* generoso; abbondante, copioso
gene·sis ['dʒɛnɪsɪs] *s* (-ses [ˌsiz]) genesi *f* ‖ **Genesis** *s* (Bib) Genesi *m*
genetic [dʒɪ'nɛtɪk] *adj* genetico ‖ **genetics** *ssg* genetica
Geneva [dʒɪ'nivə] *s* Ginevra
Genevan [dʒɪ'nivən] *adj & s* ginevrino
genial ['dʒiniˌəl] *adj* affabile, geniale
genie ['dʒini] *s* genio
genital ['dʒɛnɪtəl] *adj* genitale ‖ **genitals** *spl* genitali *mpl*
genitive ['dʒɛnɪtɪv] *adj & s* genitivo
genius ['dʒinjəs] or ['dʒiniˌəs] *s* (**geniuses**) genio ‖ *s* (**genii**) ['dʒiniˌaɪ] (*spirit; deity*) genio
Genoa ['dʒɛnoˌə] *s* Genova
genocide ['dʒɛnə ˌsaɪd] *s* (*act*) genocidio; (*person*) genocida *mf*
Geno·ese [ˌdʒɛno'iz] *adj* genovese ‖ *s* (-ese) genovese *mf*
genre ['ʒanrə] *adj* (*e.g., painting*) di genere ‖ *s* genere *m*

genteel [dʒɛn'til] *adj* (*well-bred*) beneducato; (*affectedly polite*) manieroso, manierato
gentian ['dʒɛn/ən] *s* genziana
gentile ['dʒɛntɪl] or ['dʒɛntaɪl] *adj* gentilizio ‖ ['dʒɛntaɪl] *adj & s* non circonciso; non ebreo; cristiano; (*pagan*) gentile
gentili·ty [dʒɛn'tɪlɪti] *s* (-ties) distinzione, raffinatezza
gentle ['dʒɛntəl] *adj* (*e.g., manner*) gentile; (*e.g., wind*) dolce, soave; (*wellborn*) bennato; (*tap*) leggero
gen'tle·folk' *s* gente *f* per bene
gen'tle·man *s* (-men) signore *m;* (*attendant to a person of high rank*) gentiluomo; (*well-mannered man*) gentleman *m*
gen'tleman in wait'ing *s* gentiluomo di camera
gentlemanly ['dʒɛntəlmənli] *adj* signorile
gen'tleman of the road' *s* brigante *m;* vagabondo
gen'tlemen's agree'ment *s* accordo fondato sulla buona fede
gen'tle sex' *s* gentil sesso
gentry ['dʒɛntri] *s* gente *f* per bene
genuine ['dʒɛnjuˌɪn] *adj* genuino
genus ['dʒinəs] *s* (**genera** ['dʒɛnərə] or **genuses**) genere *m*
geographer [dʒi'agrəfər] *s* geografo
geographic(al) [ˌdʒiˌə'græfɪk(əl)] *adj* geografico
geogra·phy [dʒi'agrəfi] *s* (-phies) geografia
geologic(al) [ˌdʒiˌə'ladʒɪk(əl)] *adj* geologico
geologist [dʒi'alədʒɪst] *s* geologo
geolo·gy [dʒi'alədʒi] *s* (-gies) geologia
geometric(al) [ˌdʒiˌə'mɛtrɪk(əl)] *adj* geometrico
geometrician [dʒi ˌamɪ'trɪ/ən] *s* geometra *mf*
geome·try [dʒi'amɪtri] *s* (-tries) geometria
George [dʒɔrdʒ] *s* Giorgio
geranium [dʒɪ'reniˌəm] *s* geranio
geriatrics [ˌdʒɛri'ætrɪks] *ssg* geriatria
germ [dʒʌrm] *s* germe *m*
German ['dʒʌrmən] *adj & s* tedesco
germane [dʒər'men] *adj* pertinente
Germanize ['dʒʌrmə ˌnaɪz] *tr* germanizzare
Ger'man mea'sles *s* rosolia, rubeola
Ger'man sil'ver *s* alpacca
Germany ['dʒʌrməni] *s* la Germania
germ' car'rier *s* portatore *m* di germi
germ' cell' *s* cellula germinale
germicidal [ˌdʒʌrmɪ'saɪdəl] *adj* germicida
germicide ['dʒʌrmɪ ˌsaɪd] *s* germicida *m*
germinate ['dʒʌrmɪ ˌnet] *intr* germinare
germ' war'fare *s* guerra batteriologica
gerontology [ˌdʒɛrən'talədʒi] *s* gerontologia
gerund ['dʒɛrənd] *s* gerundio
gestation [dʒɛs'te/ən] *s* gestazione
gesticulate [dʒɛs'tɪkjə ˌlet] *intr* gesticolare

gesticulation [dʒɛs͵tɪkjə'leʃən] s gesticolazione

gesture ['dʒɛstʃər] s gesto ‖ intr gestire, gesticolare

get [gɛt] v (pret **got** [gɑt]; pp **got** or **gotten** ['gɑtən]; ger **getting**) tr ottenere; ricevere; prendere; andare a comprare; procacciare; riportare; procurarsi; riscuotere; guadagnare; **to get across** far capire; **to get back** riacquistare; **to get down** staccare; (to swallow) trangugiare; **to get off** togliere, cavare; **to get s.o. to** + inf indurre che qlcu + subj; **to get done** far fare; **to have got** (coll) avere; **to have got to** + inf (coll) dovere + inf ‖ intr (to become) diventare, farsi; (to arrive) arrivare, venire; **to get out** (said of a convalescent) alzarsi; **to get along** andarsene; andare avanti; tirare avanti, giostrare; aver successo; **to get along in years** essere avanti con gli anni; **to get along with** andare d'accordo con; **to get angry** arrabbiarsi; **to get around** uscire; divulgarsi; rigirare; **to get away** scappare, darsela a gambe; **to get away with s.th** scappare con qlco; (coll) farla franca; **to get back** ritornare; ricuperare; **to get back at** (coll) vendicarsi di; **to get behind** rimanere indietro; (to support) appoggiare, patrocinare; **to get better** migliorare; **to get by** passare oltre; (to succeed) arrivare a farcela; passare inosservato; **to get even with** rifarsi con, prendersi la rivincita con; **to get going** mettersi in moto; **to get in** entrare; rientrare; arrivare; **to get in deeper and deeper** cacciarsi nei pasticci; **to get in with** diventare amico di; **to get married** sposarsi **to get off** andarsene; smontare da; **to get old** invecchiare; **to get on** andare avanti; andare d'accordo; **to get out** uscire; propagarsi; **to get out of** (a car) uscire da; (trouble) trarsi di; **to get out of the way** togliersi di mezzo; **to get run over** essere investito; **to get through** finire; arrivare; farsi capire; **to get to be** finire per essere; **to get under way** mettersi in cammino; **to get up** alzarsi; **to not get over it** (coll) non arrivare a rassegnarsi

get'a·way' s fuga; (sports) partenza

get'-to·geth'er s riunione, crocchio

get'up' s (coll) stile m, presentazione; (coll) costume m, abbigliamento

gewgaw ['gjugɔ] s cianfrusaglia

geyser ['gaɪzər] s geyser m

ghast·ly ['gæstli] or ['gɑstli] adj (-lier; -liest) orribile, orrendo; spettrale

gherkin ['gʌrkɪn] s cetriolino

ghet·to ['gɛto] s (-tos or -toes) ghetto

ghost [gost] s spettro, fantasma m; **not a ghost of** nemmeno l'ombra di; **to give up the ghost** rendere l'anima

ghost·ly ['gostli] adj (-lier; -liest) spettrale, fantomatico

ghost' sto'ry s storia di fantasmi

ghost' town' s città morta

ghost' writ'er s collaboratore anonimo

ghoul [gul] s spirito necrofago; ladro di tombe

ghoulish ['gulɪʃ] adj demoniaco, macabro

GI ['dʒi'aɪ] (letterword) (**General Issue**) s (**GI's**) soldato degli Stati Uniti

giant ['dʒaɪ·ənt] adj & s gigante m

giantess ['dʒaɪ·əntɪs] s gigantessa

gibberish ['dʒɪbərɪʃ] or ['gɪbərɪʃ] s linguaggio inintelligibile

gibbet ['dʒɪbɪt] s forca ‖ tr impiccare sulla forca; (to hold up to scorn) mettere alla berlina

gibe [dʒaɪb] s scherno, frecciata ‖ intr schernire; **to gibe at** beffarsi di

giblets ['dʒɪblɪts] spl rigaglie fpl

giddiness ['gɪdɪnɪs] s vertigine f; frivolezza

gid·dy ['gɪdi] adj (-dier; -diest) vertiginoso; preso dalle vertigini; frivolo

gift [gɪft] s regalo; (natural ability) dono, dote f; (for Christmas) strenna

gifted ['gɪftɪd] adj dotato

gift' horse' s—never look a gift horse in the mouth a caval donato non si guarda in bocca

gift' of gab' s (coll) facondia; **to have the gift of gab** (coll) avere la lingua sciolta

gift' pack'age s pacco-dono

gift' shop' s negozio di regali

gift'-wrap' v (pret & pp **-wrapped;** ger **-wrapping**) tr incartare in carta speciale per regali

gigantic [dʒaɪ'gæntɪk] adj gigantesco

giggle ['gɪgəl] s risolino ‖ intr ridere scioccamente, ridacchiare

gigo·lo ['dʒɪgə͵lo] s (-los) gigolo

gild [gɪld] v (pret & pp **gilded** or **gilt** [gɪlt]) tr dorare, indorare

gilding ['gɪldɪŋ] s doratura

gill [gɪl] s (of fish) branchia ‖ [dʒɪl] s quarto di pinta

gilt [gɪlt] adj & s dorato

gilt-edged ['gɪlt͵ɛdʒd] adj a bordo dorato; di primissima qualità

gimcrack ['dʒɪm͵kræk] adj di nessun valore ‖ s cianfrusaglia

gimlet ['gɪmlɪt] s succhiello

gimmick ['gɪmɪk] s (slang) trucco

gin [dʒɪn] s (liquor) gin m; (trap) trappola; (mach) arganello; (tex) sgranatrice f di cotone ‖ v (pret & pp **ginned;** ger **ginning**) tr ginnare, sgranare

ginger ['dʒɪndʒər] s zenzero; (coll) energia, vivacità f

gin'ger ale' s gazosa allo zenzero

gin'ger·bread' s pan di zenzero; ornamento di cattivo gusto

gingerly ['dʒɪndʒərli] adj cauto ‖ adv con cautela

gin'ger·snap' s biscotto allo zenzero

gingham ['gɪŋəm] s rigatino

giraffe [dʒɪ'ræf] or [dʒɪ'rɑf] s giraffa

girandole ['dʒɪrən͵dol] s girandola

gird [gʌrd] v (pret & pp **girt** [gʌrt] or **girded**) tr cingere; (to equip) dotare; (to prepare) preparare; (to surround) circondare

girder ['gʌrdər] s longherina

girdle ['gʌrdəl] s reggicalze m, zona, fascetta ‖ tr fasciare; circondare

girl [gʌrl] s fanciulla; ragazza

girl' friend' s amica, innamorata

girlhood ['gʌrlhʊd] s adolescenza, giovinezza

girlish ['gʌrlɪʃ] adj fanciullesco; da ragazza

girl' scout' s giovane esploratrice f

girth [gʌrθ] s circonferenza; fascia; (to hold a saddle) sottopancia m

gist [dʒɪst] s sugo, nocciolo, essenza

give [gɪv] s elasticità f ‖ v (pret **gave** [gev]; pp **given** ['gɪvən]) tr dare; (trouble) causare; (a play) rappresentare; (a speech; fruit; a sigh) fare; **to give away** distribuire gratuitamente; (to reveal) lasciarsi sfuggire; (a bride) accompagnare all'altare; (coll) tradire; **to give back** restituire; **to give forth** (odors) emettere; **to give oneself up** darsi; **to give up** cedere; (a position) abbandonare ‖ intr dare; cedere; (said, e.g., of a rope) rompersi; **to give in** cedere; darsi per vinto; **to give out** esaurirsi; venir meno; **to give up** darsi per vinto

give'-and-take' s compromesso; conversazione briosa

give'a·way' s premio gratuito; rivelazione involontaria; (game) vinciperdi m; (rad, telv) programma m a premi

given ['gɪvən] adj dato; **given that** dato che, concesso che

giv'en name' s nome m di battesimo

giver ['gɪvər] s donatore m; dispensatore m

gizzard ['gɪzərd] s magone m

glacial ['gleʃəl] adj glaciale

glacier ['gleʃər] s ghiacciaio

glad [glæd] adj (**gladder**; **gladdest**) felice, lieto, contento; **to be glad (to)** essere felice (di)

gladden ['glædən] tr rallegrare

glade [gled] s radura

glad' hand' s (coll) accoglienza calorosa

gladiator ['glædɪ,etər] s gladiatore m

gladiola [,glædɪ'olə] or [glə'daɪ·ələ] s gladiolo

gladly ['glædli] adv volentieri, di buon grado

gladness ['glædnɪs] s contentezza

glad' rags' s (coll) panni mpl da festa; (coll) vestito da sera

glamorous ['glæmərəs] adj affascinante, attraente

glamour ['glæmər] s fascino, malia

glam'our girl' s ragazza sci-sci

glance [glæns] or [glɑns] s occhiata, guardata; **at first glance** a prima vista ‖ intr lanciare uno sguardo; **to glance at** dare un'occhiata a; **to glance off** sorvolare su; deviare da; **to glance over** dare una scorsa a

gland [glænd] s ghiandola

glanders ['glændərz] spl morva

glare [gler] s splendore m, luce f abbagliante; sguardo minaccioso ‖ intr risplendere; lanciare occhiatacce; **to glare at** fare la faccia feroce a

glare' ice' s vetrato

glaring ['glerɪŋ] adj risplendente, abbagliante; (look) torvo; evidente

glass [glæs] or [glɑs] s vetro; (tumbler) bicchiere m; (mirror) specchio; (glassware) cristalleria; **glasses** occhiali mpl

glass' blow'er ['blo·ər] s vetraio

glass' case' s vetrinetta

glass' cut'ter s tagliatore m di cristallo; (tool) diamante m tagliavetro

glass' door' s porta a vetri

glassful ['glæsful] or ['glɑsful] s bicchiere m

glass'house' s vetreria; (fig) casa di vetro

glass'ware' s vetreria, cristalleria

glass' wool' s vetro filato

glass'work'er s vetraio

glass'works' s vetreria, cristalleria

glass·y ['glæsi] or ['glɑsi] adj (**-ier; -iest**) vetriato, vetroso

glaze [glez] s vernice vitrea; smalto; (of ice) superficie invetriata; (culin) glassa ‖ tr smaltare; invetriare; (culin) glassare

glazier ['gleʒər] s vetraio

gleam [glim] s barlume m, raggio ‖ intr baluginare

glean [glin] tr spigolare, racimolare; (to gather facts) raccogliere

glee [gli] s gioia, esultanza

glee' club' s società f corale

glib [glɪb] adj (**glibber; glibbest**) loquace; (tongue) facile, sciolto

glide [glaɪd] s scivolata; (aer) volo a vela, volo planato; (mus) legamento ‖ intr scivolare; (aer) librarsi, planare; **to glide away** scorrere

glider ['glaɪdər] s (aer) libratore m, veleggiatore m

glimmer ['glɪmər] s barlume m ‖ intr brillare, luccicare; tralucere

glimmering ['glɪmərɪŋ] adj tenue, tremulo ‖ s luce fioca; barlume m

glimpse [glɪmps] s occhiata; **to catch a glimpse of** intravedere ‖ tr travedere

glint [glɪnt] s scintillio ‖ intr scintillare

glisten ['glɪsən] s scintillio, luccichio ‖ intr scintillare, luccicare

glitter ['glɪtər] s luccichio ‖ intr rilucere, sfolgorare

gloaming ['glomɪŋ] s crepuscolo (vespertino)

gloat [glot] intr guardare con maligna soddisfazione; **to gloat over** godere di

global ['globəl] adj globale; universale; globulare

globe [glob] s globo; (with map of earth) mappamondo

globe-trotter ['glob,trɑtər] s giramondo

globule ['glɑbjul] s globulo

glockenspiel ['glɑkən,spil] s vibrafono

gloom [glum] s oscurità f; malinconia, uggia

gloom·y ['glumi] adj (**-ier; -iest**) lugubre, triste, tetro

glori·fy ['glorɪ,faɪ] v (pret & pp **-fied**) tr glorificare; (to enhance) esaltare

glorious ['glorɪ·əs] *adj* glorioso; magnifico, splendido

glo·ry ['glori] *s* (-ries) gloria; **to go to glory** morire ‖ *v* (*pret & pp* -ried) *intr* gloriarsi

gloss [glɔs] or [glɑs] *s* lucentezza, patina; (*commentary*) glossa ‖ *tr* satinare, patinare; (*to annotate*) glossare; **to gloss over** nascondere, discolpare

glossa·ry ['glɑsəri] *s* (-ries) glossario

gloss·y ['glɔsi] or ['glɑsi] *adj* (-ier; -iest) lucido; (*paper*) satinato

glottal ['glɑtəl] *adj* articolato alla glottide

glottis ['glɑtɪs] *s* glottide *f*

glove [glʌv] *s* guanto

glove' compart'ment *s* cassetto portaoggetti

glow [glo] *s* fuoco, incandescenza; splendore *m*, scintillio; calore *m;* colorito acceso ‖ *intr* essere incandescente; (*said of cheeks*) avvampare; (*said of cat's eyes*) fosforeggiare

glower ['glau·ər] *s* sguardo torvo ‖ *intr* guardare col viso torvo

glowing ['glo·ɪŋ] *adj* incandescente; acceso; entusiasta, entusiastico

glow'worm' *s* lucciola; lampiride *m*

glucose ['glukos] *s* glucosio

glue [glu] *s* colla, mastice *m* ‖ *tr* incollare, ingommare

glue'pot' *s* pentolino per la colla

gluey ['glu·i] *adj* (gluier; gluiest) attaccaticcio; (*smeared with glue*) incollato

glum [glʌm] *adj* (glummer; glummest) tetro, accigliato

glut [glʌt] *s* abbondanza; eccesso; **there is a glut on the market** il mercato è saturo ‖ *v* (*pret & pp* glutted; *ger* glutting) *tr* saziare; (*the market*) saturare; (*a channel*) otturare

glutton ['glʌtən] *adj & s* ghiottone *m*

gluttonous ['glʌtənəs] *adj* ghiotto

glutton·y ['glʌtəni] *s* (-ies) ghiottoneria, golosità *f*

glycerine ['glɪsərɪn] *s* glicerina

G'-man' *s* (-men') agente *m* federale

gnarl [nɑrl] *s* nodo ‖ *tr* torcere ‖ *intr* ringhiare

gnarled [nɑrld] *adj* nodoso; (*wrinkled*) grinzoso

gnash [næʃ] *tr* digrignare ‖ *intr* digrignare i denti

gnat [næt] *s* moscerino, pappataci *m*

gnaw [nɔ] *tr* rosicchiare, rodere ‖ *intr* —**to gnaw at** (fig) rimordere

gnome [nom] *s* gnomo

go [go] *s* (goes) andata; energia; (*for traffic*) via libera; **it's a go** è un affare fatto; **it's all the go** (coll) è all'ultimo grido; **it's no go** (coll) è impossibile; **on the go** in continuo andare e venire; **to make a go of** (coll) aver successo con ‖ *v* (*pret* went [went], *pp* gone [gɔn] or [gɑn]) *tr* (coll) sopportare; (coll) scommettere; (coll) pagare; **to go it alone** fare da sé ‖ *intr* andare; (*to operate*) camminare, funzionare; (*e.g., mad*) diventare; (*said of numbers*) entrare; **gone!** venduto!; **so it goes** così va il mondo; **to**

be going to + *inf* andare a + *inf*, e.g., **I am going to New York to see him** vado a New York a vederlo; (*to express futurity*) use *fut ind*, e.g., **I am going to stay home today** starò a casa oggi; **to be gone** essere andato; esser morto; **to go against** opporsi a; **to go ahead** andar avanti; tirare avanti; **to go around** andare in giro; **to go away** andarsene; **to go back** tornare; **to go by** passare per; regolarsi su; (*said of time*) passare; **to go down** discendere; (*said of a boat*) affondare; **to go fishing** andare a pescare; **to go for** vendersi per; andare a pigliare; attaccare; favorire; **to go get** andare a pigliare; **to go house hunting** andare in cerca di una casa; **to go hunting** andare a caccia; **to go in** entrare in; (*to fit in*) starci in; **to go in for** dedicarsi a; **to go into** investigare; darsi a, dedicarsi a; (*gear*) (aut) ingranare; **to go in with** associarsi con; **to go off** andarsene; aver luogo; (*said of a bomb*) esplodere; (*said of a rifle*) sparare; (*said of a trap*) scattare; **to go on** continuare, protrarsi; **to go on** + *ger* continuare a + *inf*; **to go out** uscire; passare di moda; (*said, e.g., of fire*) spegnersi; (*to strike*) mettersi in sciopero; **to go over** aver successo; leggere; esaminare; **to go over to** passare ai ranghi di; **to go skiing** andare a sciare; **to go swimming** andare a nuotare, andare al bagno; **to go through** esperimentare; (*to examine carefully*) rovistare; (*said, e.g., of a plan or a project*) aver successo; (*a fortune*) dissipare; **to go through a red light** passare la strada col semaforo rosso; **to go with** andare con, accompagnare; (*a girl*) essere l'amico di; **to go without** fare a meno di

goad [god] *s* pungolo ‖ *tr* pungolare; (fig) spronare

go'-ahead' *adj* intraprendente ‖ *s* via *m*

goal [gol] *s* meta; (football) gol *m*

goalie ['goli] *s* portiere *m*

goal'keep'er *s* portiere *m*

goal' line' *s* linea di porta

goal' post' *s* montante *m*

goat [got] *s* capra; (*male*) becco; (coll) capro espiatorio; **to get the goat of** (coll) irritare

goatee [go'ti] *s* barbetta, pizzo

goat'herd' *s* capraio

goat'skin' *s* pelle *f* di capra

goat'suck'er *s* caprimulgo

gob [gab] *s* massa informe; **gobs** (coll) mucchio, quantità *f* enorme

gobble ['gabəl] *s* gloglottio ‖ *tr* ingozzare; **to gobble up** (coll) trangugiare; (coll) impadronirsi di ‖ *intr* trangugiare; (*said of a turkey*) gloglottare

gobbledegook ['gabəldɪ‚guk] *s* linguaggio oscuro

go'-between' *s* intermediario; (*pander*) mezzano; (poet) pronubo

goblet ['gablɪt] *s* coppa

goblin ['gablɪn] *s* folletto

go'-by' *s*—**to give s.o. the go-by** (coll) schivare qlcu

go'-cart' *s* carrettino; (*walker*) girello

god [gɑd] *s* dio; **God forbid** Dio ci scampi; **God grant** voglia Dio; **God willing** se Dio vuole

god'-child' *s* (**-chil'dren**) figlioccio

god'daugh'ter *s* figlioccia

goddess ['gɑdɪs] *s* dea, diva

god'fa'ther *s* padrino

God'-fear'ing *adj* timorato di Dio

God'for·sak'en *adj* miserabile; (*place*) sperduto, fuori di mano

god'head' *s* deità *f* || **Godhead** *s* Ente Supremo, Dio

godless ['gɑdlɪs] *adj* ateo; malvagio || **the godless** i senza Dio

god·ly ['gɑdli] *adj* (**-lier; -liest**) devoto, pio

god'moth'er *s* madrina

God's' a'cre *s* camposanto

god'send' *s* manna, provvidenza

god'son' *s* figlioccio

God'speed' *s* successo, buona fortuna

go-getter ['go ˌgetər] *s* (coll) persona intraprendente

goggle ['gɑgəl] *intr* stralunare gli occhi

goggle-eyed ['gɑgəl ˌaɪd] *adj* dagli occhi sporgenti

goggles ['gɑgəlz] *spl* occhiali *mpl* da protezione

going ['go·ɪŋ] *adj* in moto, in funzione; **going on** quasi, e.g., **it is going on seven o'clock** sono quasi le sette || *s* andata; progresso

go'ings on' *s* (coll) comportamento, contegno; (coll) avvenimenti *mpl*

goiter ['gɔɪtər] *s* gozzo

gold [gold] *adj* aureo, d'oro || *s* oro

gold'beat'er *s* battiloro

gold'brick' *s* imitazione, frode *f*; (slang) fannullone *m*

gold' dig'ger ['dɪgər] *s* cercatore *m* d'oro; (coll) donna unicamente interessata nel denaro

golden ['goldən] *adj* aureo, d'oro; (*gilt*) dorato; (fig) splendido

gold'en age' *s* età *f* dell'oro

gold'en calf' *s* vitello d'oro

Gold'en Fleece' *s* vello d'oro

gold'en mean' *s* aurea mediocrità

gold'en·rod' *s* (bot) verga d'oro

gold'en rule' *s* regola della carità cristiana

gold'en wed'ding *s* nozze *fpl* d'oro

gold-filled ['gold ˌfɪld] *adj* otturato in oro

gold'finch' *s* cardellino

gold'fish' *s* pesce rosso

goldilocks ['goldɪ ˌlɑks] *s* bionda; (bot) ranuncolo

gold' leaf' *s* oro in foglia

gold' mine' *s* miniera d'oro

gold' plate' *s* vasellame *m* d'oro

gold'-plate' *tr* dorare

gold' rush' *s* febbre *f* dell'oro

gold'smith' *s* orefice *m*

gold' stand'ard *s* regime aureo

golf [gɑlf] *s* golf *m* || *intr* giocare a golf

golf' cart' *s* mini-auto *f* per campi da golf

golf' club' *s* mazza; associazione di giocatori di golf

golfer ['gɑlfər] *s* giocatore *m* di golf

golf' links' *spl* campo di golf

Golgotha ['gɑlgəθə] *s* il Golgota

gondola ['gɑndələ] *s* gondola

gondolier [ˌgɑndə'lɪr] *s* gondoliere *m*

gone [gɔn] *or* [gɑn] *adj* partito; rovinato; andato; morto; **gone on** (coll) innamorato di

gong [gɔŋ] *or* [gɑŋ] *s* gong *m*

goo [gu] *s* (coll) sostanza appiccicaticcia

good [gud] *adj* (**better; best**) buono; **good and . . .** (coll) molto, e.g., **good and cheap** molto a buon mercato; **good for** buono per; responsabile per; (*equivalent*) valido per; **to be good at** esser bravo a; **to be no good** (coll) non servire a nulla; (coll) essere un perdigiorno; **to make good** avere successo; (*one's promise*) mantenere; (*a debt*) pagare; (*damages*) indennizzare || *s* bene *m*; utile *m*, profitto; **for good** per sempre; **for good and all** una volta per sempre; **goods** merce *f*, mercanzia; **the good** il bene; i buoni; **to catch with the goods** (coll) cogliere in flagrante; **to deliver the goods** (slang) mantenere le promesse; **to do good** fare del bene; **to the good** come profitto; come attivo; **what is the good of . . .?** a che serve . . .?

good' afternoon' *s* buon pomeriggio

good'-by' [ˌgud'baɪ] *s* addio || *interj* addio!; arrivederci!

good' day' *s* buon giorno

good' deed' *s* buona azione

good' egg' *s* (slang) bonaccione *m*, gran brava persona

good' eve'ning *s* buona sera; buona notte

good' fel'low *s* buon ragazzo

good'-fel'low·ship' *s* cameratismo

good'-for-noth'ing *adj* inutile, senza valore || *s* pelandrone *m*, inetto

Good' Fri'day *s* Venerdì Santo

good' grac'es *spl* buone grazie

good-hearted ['gud'hɑrtɪd] *adj* di buon cuore

good'-hum'ored *adj* di buon umore

good'-look'ing *adj* bello

good' looks' *s* bellezza

good·ly ['gudli] *adj* (**-lier; -liest**) bello; di buona qualità; ampio, considerevole

good' morn'ing *s* buon giorno

good-natured ['gud'netʃərd] *adj* bonaccione, affabile

goodness ['gudnɪs] *s* bontà *f*; **for goodness sake!** per amor di Dio!; **goodness knows!** chi sa mai! || *interj* Dio mio!

good' night' *s* buona notte

good'-sized' *adj* piuttosto grande

good' speed' *s* buona fortuna

good'-tem'pered *adj* di carattere mite, gioviale

good' time' *s* periodo gradevole; **to have a good time** divertirsi; **to make good time** andare di buon passo

good' turn' *s* favore *m*, servizio

good' will' *s* buona volontà; (com) reputazione; (com) clientela

good·y ['gudi] *adj* (coll) troppo buono || *s* (**-ies**) (coll) santerello; **goodies**

(coll) ghiottonerie *fpl* || *interj* (coll) bene!, benissimo!

gooey ['gu·i] *adj* (**gooier; gooiest**) (slang) attaccaticcio

goof [guf] *s* (slang) sciocco || *tr* (slang) rovinare; **to goof up** (*an opportunity*) (slang) mancare || *intr* (slang) pigliare un granchio; **to goof off** (slang) battere la fiacca; **to goof up** (slang) farla grossa

goof·y ['gufi] *adj* (**-ier; -iest**) (slang) sciocco

goon [gun] *s* (slang) scemo; (coll) crumiro, gaglioffo, terrorista *m*

goose [gus] *s* (**geese** [gis]) oca; **the goose hangs high** tutto va per il meglio; **to cook one's goose** rompere le uova nel paniere di qlcu; **to kill the goose that lays the golden eggs** uccidere la gallina delle uova d'oro || *s* (**gooses**) ferro da stiro per sarto

goose'ber'ry *s* (**-ries**) uva spina; (*berry*) bacca d'uva spina

goose' egg' *s* (slang) zero; (*lump on the head*) (coll) bernoccolo

goose' flesh' *s* pelle *f* d'oca

goose'neck' *s* collo d'oca

goose' pim'ples *spl* pelle *f* d'oca

goose' step' *s* passo dell'oca

gopher ['gofər] *s* scoiattolo di terra, citillo

gore [gor] *s* sangue coagulato; (*in a garment*) gherone *m* || *tr* (*with a horn*) incornare; inserire gheroni in

gorge [gɔrdʒ] *s* gola, burrone *m;* (*meal*) mangiata || *tr* rimpinzare || *intr* rimpinzarsi

gorgeous ['gɔrdʒəs] *adj* splendido, magnifico

gorilla [gə'rɪlə] *s* gorilla *m*

gorse [gɔrs] *s* gineprone *m*

gor·y ['gori] *adj* (**-ier; -iest**) sanguinolento

gosh [gɑʃ] *interj* perbacco!

goshawk ['gas‚hɔk] *s* sparviere *m,* astore *m*

gospel ['gɑspəl] *s* vangelo || **Gospel** *s* Vangelo

gos'pel truth' *s* santissima verità

gossamer ['gɑsəmər] *s* ragnatela; (*variety of gauze*) garza finissima; tessuto impermeabile finissimo

gossip ['gɑsɪp] *s* maldicenza; (*person*) pettegolo; **piece of gossip** maldicenza || *intr* spettegolare

gossipy ['gɑsɪpi] *adj* pettegolo

Goth [gɑθ] *s* Goto

Gothic ['gɑθɪk] *adj & s* gotico

gouge [gaudʒ] *s* (*cut made with a gouge*) scanalatura; (*tool*) sgorbia; (coll) truffa || *tr* sgorbiare; (coll) truffare

goulash ['gulɑʃ] *s* gulasch *m*

gourd [gord] *or* [gurd] *s* zucca

gourmand ['gurmənd] *s* ghiottone *m*

gourmet ['gurme] *s* buongustaio

gout [gaut] *s* gotta, podagra

gout·y ['gauti] *adj* (**-ier; -iest**) gottoso

govern ['gʌvərn] *tr* governare; (gram) reggere

governess ['gʌvərnɪs] *s* governante *f,* istitutrice *f*

government ['gʌvərnmənt] *s* governo; (gram) reggenza

governmental [‚gʌvərn'mɛntəl] *adj* governativo

governor ['gʌvərnər] *s* governatore *m;* (mach) regolatore *m*

governorship ['gʌvərnər‚ʃɪp] *s* governatorato

gown [gaun] *s* (*of a woman*) vestito; (*academic*) toga; (*of a physician or patient*) gabbanella; (*of a priest*) veste *f* talare

grab [græb] *s* presa; **up for grabs** (coll) pronto a esser pigliato || *v* (*pret & pp* **grabbed;** *ger* **grabbing**) *tr* pigliare, afferrare

grace [gres] *s* (*charm; favor*) grazia; (*pardon*) mercé *f;* (*prayer*) benedicite *m;* (com) dilazione; **to say grace** recitare il benedicite; **with good grace** di buona voglia || *tr* adornare

graceful ['gresfəl] *adj* grazioso, vezzoso, leggiadro

grace' note' *s* (mus) appoggiatura

gracious ['greʃəs] *adj* grazioso; misericordioso || *interj* Dio buono!

gradation [gre'deʃən] *s* gradazione; (*step in a series*) passo

grade [gred] *s* grado; (*slope*) pendenza; (*mark in school*) voto; **to make the grade** raggiungere la meta || *tr* selezionare; (*a student*) dare un voto a; (*land*) spianare

grade' cros'sing *s* (rr) passaggio a livello

grade' school' *s* scuola elementare

gradient ['gredɪ·ənt] *adj* in pendenza || *s* pendenza; (phys) gradiente *m*

gradual ['grædʒu·əl] *adj* graduale

graduate ['grædʒu·ɪt] *adj* graduato; superiore; (*student*) laureato; (*candidate for degree*) laureando || ['grædʒu‚et] *tr* graduare; laureare, diplomare || *intr* laurearsi, diplomarsi

grad'uate school' *s* facoltà *f* di studi avanzati

graduation [‚grædʒu'eʃən] *s* graduazione; laurea; cerimonia della consegna delle lauree

graft [græft] *or* [grɑft] *s* (hort) innesto; (surg) trapianto; (coll) prevaricazione || *tr* (hort) innestare; (surg) trapiantare || *intr* (coll) prevaricare

gra'ham bread' ['gre·əm] *s* pane *m* integrale

grain [gren] *s* chicco; (*of sand*) granello; (*cereal seeds*) granaglie *fpl;* (*in wood*) venatura; (*in stone*) grana; **against the grain** di cattivo verso || *tr* granulare; (*leather*) zigrinare; (*metal*) granire

grain' el'evator *s* elevatore *m* di grano; (*building*) deposito di cereali

graining ['grenɪŋ] *s* venatura

gram [græm] *s* grammo

grammar ['græmər] *s* grammatica

grammarian [grə'mɛrɪ·ən] *s* grammatico

gram'mar school' *s* scuola elementare

grammatical [grə'mætɪkəl] *adj* grammatico

gramophone ['græmə ,fon] s (trade-mark) grammofono

grana·ry ['grænəri] s (-ries) granaio

grand [grænd] adj grandioso; grande, famoso

grand'aunt' s prozia

grand'child' s (-chil'dren) nipote mf

grand'daugh'ter s nipote f

grand' duch'ess s granduchessa

grand' duke' s granduca m

grandee [græn'di] s grande m

grandeur ['grændʒər] or ['grændʒur] s grande m, grandiosità f

grand'fa'ther s nonno; (forefather) antenato

grand'father's clock' s grande orologio a pendolo

grandiose ['grændɪ ,os] adj grandioso

grand' ju'ry s giuria investigativa

grand' lar'ceny s furto importante

grand' lodge' s grande oriente m

grandma ['grænd ,ma], ['græm,ma] or ['græmə] s (coll) nonna

grand'moth'er s nonna

grand'neph'ew s pronipote m

grand'niece' s pronipote f

grand' op'era s opera, opera lirica

grandpa ['grænd ,pa], ['græn ,pa] or ['græmpə] s (coll) nonno

grand'par'ent s nonno, nonna

grand' pian'o s pianoforte m a coda

grand'son' s nipote m

grand'stand' s tribuna

grand' to'tal s somma totale; importo globale

grand'un'cle s prozio

grand' vizier' s gran visir m

grange [grendʒ] s (farm) fattoria; (organization of farmers) sindacato di agricoltori

granite ['grænɪt] s granito

grant [grænt] or [grant] s concessione; (sum of money) sovvenzione; trapasso di proprietà || tr concedere; (a wish) esaudire; (a permit) rilasciare; (law) trasferire; to take for granted ammettere come vero; trattare con indifferenza

grantee [græn'ti] or [gran'ti] s concessionario; beneficiario

grant'-in-aid' s (grants'-in-aid') sussidio governativo a'un ente pubblico; borsa di studio

grantor [græn'tor] or [gran'tor] s concedente m, concessore m

granular ['grænjələr] adj granulare

granulate ['grænjə ,let] tr granulare || intr diventare granulato

gran'ulated sug'ar s zucchero cristallizzato

granule ['grænjul] s granulo

grape [grep] s chicco d'uva; (vine) vite f; grapes uva

grape' ar'bor s pergolato

grape'fruit' s pompelmo

grape' juice' s succo d'uva

grape'shot' s mitraglia

grape'vine' s vite f; by the grapevine di bocca in bocca; (mil) attraverso la radio fante

graph [græf] or [graf] s (diagram) grafico; (gram) segno grafico

graphic(al) ['græfɪk(əl)] adj grafico

graphite ['græfaɪt] s grafite f

graph' pa'per s carta millimetrata

grapnel ['græpnəl] s uncino; (anchor) grappino

grapple ['græpəl] s uncino; lotta corpo a corpo || tr uncinare || intr combattere; to grapple with lottare con

grap'pling i'ron s raffio, grappino

grasp [græsp] or [grasp] s impugnatura; (power) possesso; to have a good grasp of sapere a fondo; within the grasp of nei limiti della comprensione di || tr (with hand) impugnare; (to get control of) impadronirsi di; (fig) capire || intr—to grasp at cercare di afferrare

grasping ['græspɪŋ] or ['graspɪŋ] adj tenace; avido, cupido

grass [græs] or [gras] s erba; (pasture land) pastura; (lawn) tappeto erboso; to go to grass (said of cattle) andare al pascolo; andare in vacanza; ritirarsi; andare in rovina; morire; to not let the grass grow under one's feet non dormire in piuma

grass' court' s campo da tennis d'erba

grass'hop'per s cavalletta

grass'-roots' adj popolare

grass' seed' s semente f d'erba

grass' wid'ow s donna separata dal marito

grass·y ['græsi] or ['grasi] adj (-ier; -iest) erboso

grate [gret] s (for cooking) griglia; (at a window) grata || tr mettere una grata a; (one's teeth) digrignare; (e.g., cheese) grattugiare || intr stridere, cigolare; to grate on one's nerves dare sui nervi di qlcu

grateful ['gretfəl] adj riconoscente; (pleasing) piacevole, gradito

grater ['gretər] s grattugia

grati·fy ['grætɪ ,faɪ] v (pret & pp -fied) tr gratificare, soddisfare

gratifying ['grætɪ ,faɪ·ɪŋ] adj soddisfacente, piacevole

grating ['gretɪŋ] adj irritante; (sound) stridente || s inferriata

gratis ['gretɪs] or ['grætɪs] adj gratuito || adv gratis

gratitude ['grætɪ ,tjud] or ['grætɪ ,tud] s gratitudine f, riconoscenza

gratuitous [grə'tju·ɪtəs] or [grə'tu·ɪtəs] adj gratuito

gratui·ty [grə'tju·ɪti] or [grə'tu·ɪti] s (-ties) mancia, regalia

grave [grev] adj grave || s tomba, sepolcro, fossa

gravedigger ['grev ,dɪgər] s becchino

gravel ['grævəl] s ghiaia; (pathol) renella

grav'en im'age ['grevən] s idolo

grave'stone' s pietra tombale

grave'yard' s cimitero, camposanto

gravitate ['grævɪ ,tet] intr gravitare

gravitation [,grævɪ'teʃən] s gravitazione

gravi·ty ['grævɪti] s (-ties) gravità f

gravure [grə'vjur] or ['grevjur] s foto-incisione

gra·vy ['grevi] s (-vies) (juice from

cooking meat) sugo; (*sauce made with it*) salsa, intingolo; (slang) guadagni *mpl* facili

gra'vy boat' *s* salsiera

gra'vy train' *s* (slang) greppia, mangiatoia

gray [gre] *adj* grigio; (*gray-haired*) canuto ‖ *s* grigio; cavallo grigio ‖ *intr* incanutire

gray'beard' *s* vecchio

gray-haired ['gre ˌherd] *adj* canuto

gray'hound' *s* levriere *m*

grayish ['gre·ɪʃ] *adj* grigiastro

gray' mat'ter *s* materia grigia

graze [grez] *tr* (*to touch lightly*) sfiorare; (*to scratch lightly*) scalfire; (*grass*) brucare; (*cattle*) pascere, pascolare ‖ *intr* pascere, brucare

grease [gris] *s* grasso, unto ‖ [gris] or [griz] *tr* ingrassare, ungere

grease' cup' [gris] *s* coppa dell'olio

grease' gun' [gris] *s* ingrassatore *m*

grease' lift' [gris] *s* piattaforma di lubrificazione

grease' paint' [gris] *s* cerone *m*

grease' pit' [gris] *s* fossa di riparazione

greas·y ['grisi] or ['grizi] *adj* (-ier; -iest) grasso, unto, untuoso

great [gret] *adj* grande; (coll) eccellente ‖ **the great** i grandi

great'-aunt' *s* prozia

Great' Bear' *s* Orsa Maggiore

Great' Brit'ain ['brɪtən] *s* la Gran Bretagna

Great' Dane' *s* danese *m*, alano

Great'er New York' *s* Nuova York e i suoi sobborghi

great'-grand'child' *s* (-chil'dren) pronipote *mf*

great'-grand'daught'er *s* pronipote *f*

great'-grand'fa'ther *s* bisnonno

great'-grand'moth'er *s* bisnonna

great'-grand'par'ent *s* bisnonno, bisnonna

great'-grand'son' *s* pronipote *m*

greatly ['gretli] *adj* molto

great'-neph'ew *s* pronipote *m*

greatness ['gretnɪs] *s* grandezza

great'-niece' *s* pronipote *f*

great'-un'cle *s* prozio

Grecian ['griʃən] *adj* & *s* greco

Greece [gris] *s* la Grecia

greed [grid] *s* avarizia, avidità *f*

greediness ['gridɪnɪs] *s* bramosia

greed·y ['gridi] *adj* (-ier; -iest) avaro; ingordo, bramoso

Greek [grik] *adj* & *s* greco

green [grin] *adj* verde; (fig) verde, inesperto ‖ *s* verde *m*; (*lawn*) tappeto erboso; **greens** verdura, insalata

green'back' *s* (U.S.A.) biglietto di banca

green' earth' *s* verdaccio

greener·y ['grinəri] *s* (-ies) (*foliage*) vegetazione; (*hothouse*) serra

green'-eyed' *adj* dagli occhi verdi; (coll) geloso

green'gage' *s* regina claudia

green'horn' *s* (slang) pivello, sempliciotto

green'house' *s* serra

greenish ['grinɪʃ] *adj* verdastro

Greenland ['grinlənd] *s* la Groenlandia

green' light' *s* semaforo verde; (coll) via *m*

greenness ['grinnɪs] *s* verdore *m*, verdezza; inesperienza

green' pep'per *s* peperone *m* verde

greensward ['grin ˌsword] *s* tappeto erboso

green' thumb' *s* abilità *f* speciale per il giardinaggio

green' veg'etables *spl* verdura

green'wood' *s* bosco verde

greet [grit] *tr* salutare; ricevere; (*e.g., one's ears*) offrirsi a

greeting ['gritɪŋ] *s* saluto; accoglienza ‖ **greetings** *interj* saluti!

greet'ing card' *s* cartolina d'auguri

gregarious [grɪ'gɛrɪ·əs] *adj* (*living in the midst of others*) gregario; (*sociable*) sociale

Gregorian [grɪ'gorɪ·ən] *adj* gregoriano

grenade [grɪ'ned] *s* granata

grenadier [ˌgrɛnə'dɪr] *s* granatiere *m*

grenadine [ˌgrɛnə'din] *s* granatina

grey [gre] *adj*, *s* & *intr* var of **gray**

grid [grɪd] *s* (*network*) rete *f*; (*on map*) reticolato; (electron) griglia

griddle ['grɪdəl] *s* tegame *m*

grid'dle·cake' *s* frittella cotta in teglia, crêpe *m*

grid'i'ron *s* griglia; campo di football; (theat) graticcia

grief [grif] *s* affanno, dolore *m*; disgrazia; **to come to grief** andare in rovina

grievance ['grivəns] *s* lagnanza; motivo di lagnanza

grieve [griv] *tr* affliggere ‖ *intr* affliggersi, dolersi; **to grieve over** soffrire per

grievous ['grivəs] *adj* doloroso, penoso; (*error*) grave; (*deplorable*) deplorevole

griffin ['grɪfɪn] *s* grifo, grifone *m*

grill [grɪl] *s* griglia ‖ *tr* mettere alla griglia; (coll) interrogare insistentemente

grille [grɪl] *s* inferriata; (aut) mascherina, calandra

grill'room' *s* grill-room *m*, rosticceria

grim [grɪm] *adj* (grimmer; grimmest) (*stern*) accigliato; (*fierce*) feroce; (*sinister*) sinistro; (*unyielding*) implacabile

grimace ['grɪməs] or [grɪ'mes] *s* smorfia, sberleffo ‖ *intr* fare le boccacce

grime [graɪm] *s* sporco; (*soot*) fuliggine *f*

grim·y ['graɪmi] *adj* (-ier; -iest) sporco; fuligginoso

grin [grɪn] *s* sorriso; (*malicious in intent*) ghigno ‖ *v* (*pret & pp* grinned; *ger* grinning) *intr* sorridere; ghignare

grind [graɪnd] *s* macinata; (*laborious work*) (coll) macina; (slang) sgobbone *m* ‖ *v* (*pret & pp* ground [graʊnd]) *tr* macinare; (*to sharpen*) molare; (*lenses*) smerigliare; (*meat*) tritare; opprimere; (*a crank*) girare; (mach) rettificare ‖ *intr* macinare; frantumarsi; cigolare; (coll) sgobbare

grinder ['graɪndər] *s* (*to sharpen tools*) mola; (*to grind coffee*) macinino;

(*back tooth*) molare *m;* (*person*) molatore *m*

grind'stone' *s* mola; **to keep one's nose to the grindstone** lavorare senza posa

grin·go ['grɪŋgo] *s* (-gos) (disparaging) gringo

grip [grɪp] *s* (*grasp*) presa; (*with hand*) stretta; (*handle*) impugnatura; **to come to grips** venire alle prese ‖ *v* (*pret & pp* **gripped;** *ger* **gripping**) *tr* stringere; impugnare; attirare l'attenzione di

gripe [graɪp] *s* (coll) lamentela; (naut) rizza; **gripes** colica ‖ *intr* (coll) lamentarsi, brontolare

grippe [grɪp] *s* influenza

gripping ['grɪpɪŋ] *adj* interessantissimo, affascinante

gris·ly ['grɪzli] *adj* (-lier; -liest) orribile, spaventoso

grist [grɪst] *s* (*grain td be ground*) macinata; (*ground grain*) farina; (coll) mucchio; **to be grist to the mill of** (coll) fare comodo a

gristle ['grɪsəl] *s* cartilagine *f*

gris·tly ['grɪsli] *adj* (-tlier; -tliest) cartilaginoso

grist'mill' *s* mulino

grit [grɪt] *s* sabbia, arenaria; (fig) forza d'animo ‖ *v* (*pret & pp* **gritted;** *ger* **gritting**) *tr* (*one's teeth*) far stridere, digrignare

grit·ty ['grɪti] *adj* (-tier; -tiest) sabbioso, granuloso; (fig) forte, coraggioso

griz·zly ['grɪzli] *adj* (-zlier; -zliest) brizzolato, canuto ‖ *s* (-zlies) orso grigio

groan [gron] *s* gemito ‖ *intr* gemere; (*to be overburdened*) essere sovraccarico

grocer ['grosər] *s* droghiere *m;* pizzicagnolo; proprietario di negozio di generi alimentari

grocer·y ['grosəri] *s* (-ies) (*store selling spices, soap, etc.*) drogheria; (*store selling cheese, cold cuts, etc.*) negozio di pizzicagnolo; negozio di generi alimentari; **groceries** generi *mpl* alimentari, commestibili *mpl*

grog [grɑg] *s* grog *m*

grog·gy ['grɑgi] *adj* (-gier; -giest) (coll) groggy, intontito

groin [grɔɪn] *s* (anat) inguine *m;* (archit) costolone *m*

groom [grum] *s* mozzo di stalla; (*bridegroom*) sposo ‖ *tr* rassettare; (*horses*) rigovernare; (pol) preparare per le elezioni

grooms'man *s* (-men) compare *m* di nozze

groove [gruv] *s* scanalatura; (*of a pulley*) gola; (*of a phonograph record*) solco; (fig) routine *f* ‖ *tr* scanalare, incavare

grope [grop] *intr* brancicare; (*for words*) cercare; **to grope for** cercare a tastoni

gropingly ['gropɪŋli] *adv* a tastoni

gross [gros] *adj* (*thick*) spesso; (*coarse*) volgare; (*fat*) grosso; (*error*) mar-

chiano; (*without deductions*) lordo ‖ *s* grossa ‖ *tr* fare un incasso lordo di

grossly ['grosli] *adv* approssimativamente; totalmente

gross' na'tional prod'uct *s* reddito nazionale

grotesque [gro'tɛsk] *adj & s* grottesco

grot·to ['grɑto] *s* (-toes or -tos) grotta

grouch [graʊtʃ] *s* (coll) malumore *m;* (coll) persona stizzosa ‖ *intr* (coll) brontolare

grouch·y ['graʊtʃi] *adj* (-ier; -iest) (coll) stizzoso, brontolone

ground [graʊnd] *s* (*earth, soil, land*) terra; (*piece of land*) terreno; (*basis*) causa, fondatezza; (elec) terra, massa; (fig) occasione, motivo; **grounds** giardini *mpl*, terreno; (*of coffee*) fondi *mpl;* **on the ground of** per motivo di; **to break ground** dare la prima palata; (fig) mettere la prima pietra; **to fall to the ground** cadere al suolo; (fig) fallire; **to gain ground** guadagnar terreno; **to give ground** ceder terreno; **to lose ground** perder terreno; **to stand one's ground** non indietreggiare ‖ *tr* fondare; (elec) mettere a massa; **to be grounded** (*said of an airplane*) essere forzato di rimanere a terra; **to be well grounded** essere bene al corrente ‖ *intr* incagliarsi

ground' connec'tion *s* messa a terra

ground' crew' *s* (aer) personale *m* di servizio

ground' floor' *s* pianterreno

ground' glass' *s* vetro smerigliato

ground' hog' *s* marmotta americana

ground' lead' [lid] *s* (elec) collegamento a massa

groundless ['graʊndlɪs] *adj* infondato

ground' meat' *s* carne tritata

ground' plan' *s* progetto, pianta

ground' swell' *s* mareggiata

ground' wire' *s* filo di terra, filo di massa

ground'work' *s* fondamento, base *f*

group [grup] *adj* collettivo ‖ *s* gruppo; (aer) stormo ‖ *tr* raggruppare ‖ *intr* raggrupparsi

grouse [graʊs] *s* gallo cedrone; (slang) brontolio ‖ *intr* (slang) brontolare

grout [graʊt] *s* stucco ‖ *tr* stuccare

grove [grov] *s* boschetto

grov·el ['grʌvəl] or ['grɑvəl] *v* (*pret & pp* **-eled** or **-elled;** *ger* **-eling** or **-elling**) *intr* umiliarsi

grow [gro] *v* (*pret* **grew** [gru]; *pp* **grown** [gron]) *tr* (*plants*) coltivare; (*animals*) allevare; (*a beard*) farsi crescere ‖ *intr* crescere; svilupparsi; nascere; venir su; (*to become*) diventare; farsi; **to grow angry** arrabbiarsi; **to grow old** invecchiare; **to grow out of** (*fashion*) passare di; originare da; **to grow up** svilupparsi

growing ['gro·ɪŋ] *adj* crescente; (*pains*) di crescenza; (*child*) in crescita

growl [graʊl] *s* ringhio; brontolio ‖ *intr* (*said of animals*) ringhiare; brontolare

grown'-up' *adj* adulto, grande ‖ *s* (**grown-ups**) adulto

growth [groθ] *s* crescita, sviluppo; aumento; (pathol) escrescenza

growth' stock' *s* azione *f* che promette di aumentare di valore

grub [grʌb] *s* (*drudge*) sgobbone *m;* larva di coleottero; (coll) mangiare *m* ‖ *v* (*pret & pp* **grubbed; ger grubbing**) *tr* scavare, zappare, dissodare ‖ *intr* cercare assiduamente; scavare; sgobbare

grub·by ['grʌbi] *adj* (**-bier; -biest**) sporco; bacato; infestato di larve

grudge [grʌdʒ] *s* rancore *m;* **to have a grudge against** nutrire rancore contro ‖ *tr* (*to spend unwillingly*) lesinare; invidiare

grudgingly ['grʌdʒɪŋli] *adv* di cattiva voglia

gru·el ['gru·əl] *s* farinata d'avena ‖ *v* (*pret & pp* **-eled** or **-elled; ger -eling** or **-elling**) *tr* estenuare

gruesome ['grusəm] *adj* raccapricciante

gruff [grʌf] *adj* brusco, burbero; (*voice*) rauco, roco

grumble ['grʌmbəl] *s* brontolio ‖ *intr* brontolare, borbottare

grump·y ['grʌmpi] *adj* (**-ier; -iest**) di cattivo umore, scontroso

grunt [grʌnt] *s* grugnito ‖ *intr* grugnire

G-string ['dʒi‚strɪŋ] *s* (*loincloth*) perizoma *m;* (*worn by a female entertainer*) triangolino di stoffa; (mus) corda di sol

guarantee [‚gærən'ti] *s* garanzia; (*guarantor*) garante *mf* ‖ *tr* garantire

guarantor ['gærən‚tɔr] *s* garante *mf*

guaran·ty ['gærənti] *s* (**-ties**) garanzia ‖ *v* (*pret & pp* **-tied**) *tr* garantire

guard [gard] *s* guardia; (*safeguard*) protezione; (*in a prison*) guardia carceraria; (*of a sword*) guardamano; (football) mediano; **off guard** alla sprovvista; **on guard** in guardia; di fazione; **to mount a guard** montare la guardia; **under guard** ben custodito ‖ *tr* guardare ‖ *intr* fare la sentinella; **to guard against** guardarsi da

guarded ['gardɪd] *adj* (*remark*) prudente

guard'house' *s* locale *m* di detenzione; (mil) corpo di guardia

guardian ['gardɪ·ən] *adj* tutelare ‖ *s* guardiano; (law) tutore *m*

guard'ian an'gel *s* angelo custode

guardianship ['gardɪ·ən‚ʃɪp] *s* protezione; (law) tutela

guard'rail' *s* guardavia *m;* (naut) parapetto

guard'room' *s* (mil) corpo di guardia

guards'man *s* (**-men**) guardia

guerrilla [gə'rɪlə] *s* guerrigliero

guerril'la war'fare *s* guerriglia

guess [gɛs] *s* congettura, supposizione ‖ *tr & intr* congetturare, supporre; (*to estimate correctly*) indovinare; (coll) credere; **I guess so** credo di sì

guess'work' *s* congettura

guest [gɛst] *s* invitato, ospite *m;* (*of a hotel*) cliente *mf;* (*of a boarding house*) pensionante *mf*

guest' book' *s* albo d'onore; (*in a hotel*) registro

guffaw [gə'fɔ] *s* sghignazzata ‖ *intr* sghignazzare

Guiana [gɪ'ɑnə] or [gɪ'ænə] *s* la Guayana

guidance ['gaɪdəns] *s* guida, governo; **for your guidance** per Sua norma

guide [gaɪd] *s* guida ‖ *tr* guidare

guide'board' *s* indicatore *m* stradale

guide'book' *s* guida

guid'ed mis'sile ['gaɪdɪd] *s* telearma, teleproietto, missile teleguidato

guide' dog' *s* cane *m* conduttore di un cieco

guide'line' *s* falsariga; corda fissa; linea di condotta, direttiva

guide'post' *s* indicatore *m* stradale

guide' word' *s* esponente *m* in testa di pagina

guidon ['gaɪdən] *s* guidone *m*

guild [gɪld] *s* associazione mutua; (hist) gilda

guild'hall' *s* palazzo delle corporazioni

guile [gaɪl] *s* astuzia, frode *f*

guileful ['gaɪlfəl] *adj* astuto, insidioso

guileless ['gaɪllɪs] *adj* sincero, innocente

guillotine ['gɪlə‚tin] *s* ghigliottina ‖ [‚gɪlə'tin] *tr* ghigliottinare

guilt [gɪlt] *s* colpa, reità *f*

guiltless ['gɪltlɪs] *adj* innocente

guilt·y ['gɪlti] *adj* (**-ier; -iest**) colpevole, reo

guimpe [gɪmp] or [gæmp] *s* sprone *m*

guinea ['gɪni] *s* ghinea; gallina faraona ‖ **Guinea** *s* la Guinea

guin'ea fowl' *s* gallina faraona

guin'ea pig' *s* porcellino d'India, cavia; (fig) cavia

guise [gaɪz] *s* aspetto; veste *f;* **under the guise of** in guisa di

guitar [gɪ'tar] *s* chitarra

guitarist [gɪ'tarɪst] *s* chitarrista *mf*

gulch [gʌltʃ] *s* burrone *m*

gulf [gʌlf] *s* golfo; abisso

Gulf' Stream' *s* corrente *f* del Golfo

gull [gʌl] *s* gabbiano; (coll) credulone *m* ‖ *tr* darla a bere a

gullet ['gʌlɪt] *s* gargarozzo; esofago

gullible ['gʌlɪbəl] *adj* credulone

gul·ly ['gʌli] *s* (**-lies**) borro, zanella

gulp [gʌlp] *s* sorsata ‖ *tr*—**to gulp down** (*food*) ingoiare; (*drink*) tracannare; (fig) ingoiare, tranguggiare

gum [gʌm] *s* gomma; (*mucus on eyelids*) cispa; **gums** (anat) gengive *fpl* ‖ *v* (*pret & pp* **gummed; ger gumming**) *tr* ingommare; **to gum up** (slang) guastare ‖ *intr* secernere gomma

gum' ar'abic *s* gomma arabica

gum'boil' *s* flemmone *m* gengivale

gum' boot' *s* stivale *m* da palude

gum'drop' *s* caramella alla gelatina di frutta, pasticca di gomma, drop *m*

gum·my ['gʌmi] *adj* (**-mier; -miest**) gommoso, vischioso; (*eyelid*) cisposo

gumption ['gʌmpʃən] *s* (coll) iniziativa; (coll) coraggio, fegato

gum'shoe' *s* caloscia; (slang) poliziotto ‖ *v* (*pret & pp* **-shoed; ger -shoeing**) *intr* (slang) camminare silenziosamente

gun [gʌn] *s* (*rifle*) fucile *m;* (*revolver*) revolver *m;* (*pistol*) rivoltella; (*e.g., for spraying*) rivoltella; **to stick to one's guns** tener duro ‖ *v* (*pret & pp* **gunned;** *ger* **gunning**) *tr* far fuoco su, freddare; (*a motor*) (slang) accelerare rapidamente ‖ *intr* andare a caccia; sparare; **to gun for** andare a caccia di

gun'boat' *s* cannoniera, esploratore *m*

gun' car'riage *s* affusto

gun'cot'ton *s* fulmicotone *m*

gun'fire' *s* fuoco, tiro

gun'man *s* (-men) bandito, sicario

gun' met'al *s* bronzo da cannoni; acciaio brunito

gunnel ['gʌnəl] *s* (naut) frisata

gunner ['gʌnər] *s* artigliere *m*, servente *m*

gunnery ['gʌnəri] *s* artiglieria, tiro

gunnysack ['gʌni ˌsæk] *s* sacco di tela greggia

gunpoint ['gʌn ˌpɔint] *s* mirino; **at gunpoint** a mano armata, e.g., **he was held up at gunpoint** subì una rapina a mano armata

gun'pow'der *s* polvere nera or pirica

gun'run'ner *s* contrabbandiere *m* di armi da fuoco

gun'shot' *s* schioppettata; revolverata; **within gunshot** a tiro di schioppo

gun'shot' wound' *s* schioppettata

gun'smith' *s* armaiolo

gun'stock' *s* cassa del fucile

gunwale ['gʌnəl] *s* frisata

gup•py ['gʌpi] *s* (-pies) lebiste *m*

gurgle ['gʌrgəl] *s* gorgoglio, borboglio ‖ *intr* gorgogliare, borbogliare; (*said of a human being*) barbugliare

gush [gʌʃ] *s* getto, fiotto ‖ *intr* zampillare, sgorgare; (coll) dare in effusioni

gusher ['gʌʃər] *s* pozzo di petrolio; (coll) persona espansiva

gushing ['gʌʃɪŋ] *adj* zampillante, sgorgante; (coll) espansivo ‖ *s* zampillo; (coll) espansione, effusione

gush•y ['gʌʃi] *adj* (-ier; -iest) (coll) espansivo, effusivo

gusset ['gʌsɪt] *s* gherone *m*

gust [gʌst] *s* (*of wind*) raffica; (*of smoke*) ondata, zaffata; (*of noise*) esplosione; (*of anger*) sfuriata

gusto ['gʌsto] *s* gusto; entusiasmo

gust•y ['gʌsti] *adj* (-ier; -iest) a raffiche, burrascoso

gut [gʌt] *s* budello; **guts** budello; (slang) fegato, coraggio ‖ *v* (*pret & pp* **gutted;** *ger* **gutting**) *tr* sparare, spanciare; distruggere l'interno di

gutta-percha ['gʌtə 'pʌrtʃə] *s* guttaperca

gutter ['gʌtər] *s* (*on side of road*) cunetta; (*in street*) rigagnolo; (*of roof*) doccia, grondaia; (fig) bassifondi *mpl*

gut'ter•snipe' *s* monello

guttural ['gʌtərəl] *adj & s* gutturale *f*

guy [gai] *s* cavo di sicurezza; (coll) tipo, tizio ‖ *tr* burlarsi di

guzzle ['gʌzəl] *tr & intr* trincare, bere a garganella

guzzler ['gʌzlər] *s* ubriacone *m*

gym [dʒɪm] *s* (coll) palestra

gymnasi•um [dʒɪm 'nezɪ-əm] *s* (-ums or -a [ə]) palestra

gymnast ['dʒɪmnæst] *s* ginnasta *mf*

gymnastic [dʒɪm 'næstɪk] *adj* ginnastico ‖ **gymnastics** *spl* ginnastica

gynecologist [ˌgaɪnə 'kɑlədʒɪst], [ˌdʒaɪnə 'kɑlədʒɪst] or [ˌdʒɪnə 'kɑlədʒɪst] *s* ginecologo

gyp [dʒɪp] *s* (coll) imbroglio; (*person*) (coll) imbroglione *m* ‖ *v* (*pret & pp* **gypped;** *ger* **gypping**) *tr* imbrogliare

gypsum ['dʒɪpsəm] *s* gesso

gyp•sy ['dʒɪpsi] *adj* zingaresco, zingaro ‖ *s* (-sies) zingaro ‖ **Gypsy** *s* (*language*) zingaresco

gypsyish ['dʒɪpsɪ-ɪʃ] *adj* zingaresco

gyrate ['dʒaɪret] *intr* turbinare

gyrocompass ['dʒaɪro ˌkʌmpəs] *s* girobussola

gyroscope ['dʒaɪrə ˌskop] *s* giroscopio

H

H, h [etʃ] *s* ottava lettera dell'alfabeto inglese

haberdasher ['hæbər ˌdæʃər] *s* camiciaio; (*dealer in notions*) merciaio

haberdasher•y ['hæbər ˌdæʃəri] *s* (-ies) camiceria; merceria

habit ['hæbɪt] *s* abitudine *f;* (*addiction*) vizio; (*garb*) saio; **to be in the habit of** aver l'usanza di

habitat ['hæbɪ ˌtæt] *s* habitat *m*

habitation [ˌhæbɪ 'teʃən] *s* abitazione

habit-forming ['hæbɪt ˌfɔrmɪŋ] *adj* (*e.g., drugs*) stupefacente; (*e.g., T.V.*) assuefacente, che fa venire il vizio

habitual [hə 'bɪtʃʊ-əl] *adj* abituale

habitué [hə ˌbɪtʃʊ 'e] *s* habitué *m*

hack [hæk] *s* (*cut*) taglio; (*notch*) tacca; (*cough*) tosse secca; cavallo da nolo; vettura di piazza; (*nag*) ronzino; (*poor writer*) scribacchino ‖ *tr* tagliare; stagliare

hack'man *s* (-men) vetturino

hackney ['hækni] *s* cavallo da sella; vettura di piazza

hackneyed ['hæknid] *adj* banale, trito

hack'saw' *s* seghetto per metalli

haddock ['hædək] *s* eglefino

haft [hæft] or [hɑft] *s* impugnatura

hag [hæg] *s* (*ugly old woman*) megera; (*witch*) strega

haggard ['hægərd] *adj* sparuto, macilento; (*wild-looking*) stralunato

haggle ['hægəl] *intr* mercanteggiare
hagiographer [ˌhægi'ɑgrəfer] or [ˌhedʒi'ɑgrəfər] *s* agiografo
hagiography [ˌhægi'ɑgrəfi] or [ˌhedʒi'ɑgrəfi] *s* agiografia
Hague, The [heg] *s* L'Aia *f*
hail [hel] *s* (*precipitation*) grandine *f;* (*greeting*) saluto; **within hail** a portata di voce || *tr* salutare; accogliere; chiamare; (*e.g., blows*) far cadere || *intr* grandinare; **to hail from** venire da || *interj* salute!; salve!
hail'-fel'low *adj* gioviale
Hail' Mar'y *s* Ave Maria, avemaria
hail'stone' *s* chicco di grandine
hail'storm' *s* grandinata
hair [her] *s* capelli *mpl;* (*of animals*) pelame *m* or pelo; **a hair** (*a single filament*) un capello or un pelo; **to a hair** a perfezione; **to get in one's hair** (slang) dare sui nervi a qlcu; **to let one's hair down** (slang) parlare francamente; (slang) comportarsi alla buona; **to make one's hair stand on end** far rizzare i capelli a qlcu; **to not turn a hair** non scomporsi; **to split hairs** cercare il pelo nell'uovo
hair'breadth' *s* spessore *m* di un capello; **to escape by a hairbreadth** scamparla per un pelo
hair'brush' *s* spazzola per i capelli
hair'cloth' *s* cilicio
hair'cut' *s* taglio dei capelli; **to get a haircut** farsi tagliare i capelli
hair'do' *s* (**-dos**) acconciatura
hair'dress'er *s* parrucchiere *m* per signora; pettinatrice *f*
hair' dri'er *s* asciugacapelli *m*
hair' dye' *s* tintura per i capelli
hairless ['herlɪs] *adj* pelato, calvo
hair' net' *s* rete *f* per i capelli
hair'pin' *s* forcella, forcina, molletta
hair-raising ['her ˌrezɪŋ] *adj* orripilante
hair' re·mov'er *s* depilatorio
hair' restor'er [rɪ'storər] *s* rigeneratore *m* per i capelli
hair' rib'bon *s* nastro per i capelli
hairsplitting ['her ˌsplɪtɪŋ] *adj* meticoloso, pignolo
hair'spring' *s* spirale *f*
hair' styl'ing *s* pettinatura per signora
hair-y ['heri] *adj* (**-ier; -iest**) peloso, villoso, irsuto
hake [hek] *s* merluzzo, nasello
halberd ['hælbərd] *s* alabarda
halberdier [ˌhælbər'dɪr] *s* alabardiere *m*
halcyon ['hælsɪ·ən] *adj* calmo, pacifico
hale [hel] *adj* sano, robusto || *tr* trascinare a viva forza
half [hæf] or [hɑf] *adj* mezzo; **a half** or **half a** mezzo; **half the** la metà di || *s* (**halves** [hævz] or [hɑvz]) metà *f;* (arith) mezzo; **in half** a metà; **to go halves** fare a metà || *adv* mezzo, e.g., **half asleep** mezzo addormentato; a metà, e.g., **half finished** a metà finito; **half past** e mezzo or e mezza, e.g., **half past three** le tre e mezzo or le tre e mezza; **half ... half** metà ... metà
half'-and-half' *adj* mezzo e mezzo || *s* mezza crema e mezzo latte; mezza

birra chiara e mezza scura || *adv* a metà, in parti uguali
half'back' *s* (football) mediano; (soccer) laterale *m*
half-baked ['hæf ˌbekt] or ['hɑf ˌbekt] *adj* mezzo cotto; (*ideas*) infondato, inesperto
half' bind'ing *s* rilegatura in mezza pelle
half'-blood' *s* meticcio; fratellastro; sorellastra
half'-breed' *s* meticcio
half' broth'er *s* fratellastro
half-cocked ['hæf ˌkɑkt] or ['hɑf ˌkɑkt] *adj* immaturo, precipitato || *adv* (coll) precipitatamente
half' fare' *s* mezza corsa
half'-full' *adj* mezzo pieno
half-hearted ['hæf ˌhɑrtɪd] or ['hɑf ˌhɑrtɪd] *adj* indifferente, freddo
half'-hol'iday *s* mezza festa
half' hose' *s* calzini *mpl* corti
half'-hour' *s* mezz'ora; **on the half-hour** ogni trenta minuti allo scoccare dell'ora e della mezz'ora
half'-length' *adj* a mezzo busto || *s* ritratto a mezzo busto
half'life' *s* (phys) vita media
half'-mast' *s*—**at half-mast** a mezz'asta
half'moon' *s* mezzaluna
half' mourn'ing *s* mezzo lutto
half' note' *s* (mus) minima
half' pay' *s* mezza paga
halfpen·ny ['hepəni] or ['hepni] *s* (**-nies**) mezzo penny
half' pint' *s* mezza pinta; (slang) mezza cartuccia, mezza calzetta
half'-seas o'ver *adj*—**to be half-seas over** (slang) essere sbronzato
half' shell' *s*—**on the half shell** in conchiglia
half' sis'ter *s* sorellastra
half' sole' *s* mezza suola
half'-sole' *tr* mettere la mezza suola a
half'-staff' *s*—**at half-staff** a mezz'asta
half-timbered ['hæf ˌtɪmbərd] or ['hɑf ˌtɪmbərd] *adj* in legno e muratura
half' ti'tle *s* occhiello, occhietto
half'tone' *s* mezzatinta
half'-track' *s* semicingolato
half'truth' *s* mezza verità, mezza bugia
half'way' *adj* a metà strada; parziale, mezzo || *adv* a metà strada; **halfway through** nel mezzo di; **to meet halfway** fare concessioni mutue
half-witted ['hæf ˌwɪtɪd] or ['hɑf ˌwɪtɪd] *adj* mezzo scemo
halibut ['hælɪbət] *s* ippoglosso
halide ['hælaɪd] or ['helaɪd] *s* alogenuro
halitosis [ˌhælɪ'tosɪs] *s* alito cattivo, fiato puzzolente
hall [hɔl] *s* (*passageway*) corridoio; (*entranceway*) vestibolo; (*large meeting room*) salone *m;* (*assembly room of a university*) aula magna; (*building of a university*) edificio
halleluiah or **hallelujah** [ˌhælɪ'lujə] *s* alleluia *m* || *interj* alleluia!
hall'mark' *s* punzone *m* di garanzia; (fig) contrassegno, caratteristica
hal·lo [hə'lo] *s* (**-los**) grido || *interj* ehi!
hallow ['hælo] *tr* santificare

hallowed ['hælod] *adj* consacrato
Halloween or **Hallowe'en** [,hælo'in] *s* vigilia di Ognissanti
hallucination [hə ,lusɪ'neʃən] *s* allucinazione
hall'way' *s* corridoio; entrata
ha·lo ['helo] *s* (-los or -loes) alone *m*
halogen ['hælədʒən] *s* alogeno
halt [hɔlt] *adj* zoppicante || *s* fermata; **to call a halt** dare ordine di fermarsi; **to come to a halt** fermarsi || *tr* fermare || *intr* fermarsi, esitare || *interj* altolà!
halter ['hɔltər] *s* (*for leading horse*) cavezza; (*noose*) capestro; (*hanging*) impiccagione; corpino bagno di sole
halting ['hɔltɪŋ] *adj* zoppicante; esitante
halve [hæv] or [hɑv] *tr* dimezzare
halyard ['hæljərd] *s* (naut) drizza
ham [hæm] *s* (*part of leg behind knee*) polpaccio; (*thigh and buttock*) coscia; (*cured meat from hog's hind leg*) prosciutto; (slang) istrione *m;* (slang) radioamatore *m;* **hams** natiche *fpl*
ham' and eggs' *spl* uova *fpl* col prosciutto
hamburger ['hæm ,bʌrgər] *s* hamburger *m*
hamlet ['hæmlɪt] *s* frazione, paese *m* || **Hamlet** *s* Amleto
hammer ['hæmər] *s* martello; (*of gun*) cane *m;* (*of piano*) martelletto; **under the hammer** all'asta pubblica || *tr* martellare; **to hammer out** battere; portare a fine faticosamente || *intr* martellare; **to hammer away** lavorare accanitamente
hammock ['hæmək] *s* amaca
hamper ['hæmpər] *s* cesta || *tr* imbarazzare, intralciare
hamster ['hæmstər] *s* criceto
ham·string ['hæm ,strɪŋ] *v* (*pret & pp* -strung) *tr* azzoppare; tagliare i garretti a; (fig) impastoiare
hand [hænd] *adj* manuale; fatto a mano || *s* mano *f;* (*workman*) garzone *m,* operaio; (*way of writing*) scrittura; (*signature*) firma; (*clapping of hands*) applauso; (*of clock or watch*) lancetta; (*all the cards in one's hand*) gioco; (*a round of play*) smazzata, mano *f;* (*player*) giocatore *m;* (*skill*) destrezza; (*side*) lato; **all hands** (naut) tutto l'equipaggio; (coll) tutti *mpl;* **at first hand** direttamente; **at hand** a portata di mano; **hand in glove** in perfetta unione; **hand in hand** tenendosi per mano; **hands up!** le mani in alto!; **hand to hand** corpo a corpo; **in hand** tra le mani; **in his own hand** di proprio pugno; **on hand** disponibile; **on hands and knees** (*crawling*) a gattoni; (*beseeching*) in ginocchio; **on the one hand** da un canto; **on the other hand** per contro; **to change hands** cambiare di mano; **to clap hands** battere le mani; **to eat out of one's hand** essere sottomesso a qlcu; **to get out of hand** diventare incontrollabile; **to have a hand in** prender parte a; **to have one's hands**

full essere occupatissimo; **to hold hands** tenersi per mano; **to hold up one's hands** (*as a sign of surrender*) alzare le mani; **to join hands** darsi la mano; **to keep one's hands off** non mettere il naso in; **to lend a hand** dare una mano; **to live from hand to mouth** vivere alla giornata; **to not lift a hand** non alzare un dito; **to play into the hands of** fare il gioco di; **to shake hands** darsi la mano; **to show one's hand** scoprire il proprio gioco; **to take in hand** prendere in mano; (*a matter*) prendere in esame; **to throw up one's hands** darsi per vinto; **to try one's hand** mettere la propria abilità alla prova; **to turn one's hand to** dedicarsi a; **to wash one's hands of** lavarsi le mani di; **under my hand** di mia firma autografa; **under the hand and seal of** firmato di pugno da || *tr* dare, porgere; **to hand down** tramandare; **to hand in** consegnare; **to hand on** trasmettere; **to hand out** distribuire
hand'bag' *s* borsetta
hand' bag'gage *s* valigie *fpl* a mano
hand'ball' *s* palla a mano
hand'bill' *s* manifestino, foglio volante
hand'book' *s* manuale *m;* guida; (*of a particular field*) prontuario
hand'breadth' *s* palmo
hand'car' *s* (rr) carrello a mano
hand'cart' *s* carretto a mano
hand'cuffs' *spl* manette *fpl* || *tr* mettere le manette a
handful ['hænd ,fʊl] *s* manata, manciata
hand' glass' *s* lente *f* di ingrandimento; specchietto
hand' grenade' *s* bomba a mano
handi·cap ['hændɪ ,kæp] *s* svantaggio; (sports) handicap *m* || *v* (*pret & pp* -capped; *ger* -capping) *tr* andicappare
handicraft ['hændɪ ,kræft] or ['hændɪ ,krɑft] *s* destrezza manuale; artigianato
handiwork ['hændɪ ,wʌrk] *s* lavoro fatto a mano; opera, lavoro
handkerchief ['hæŋkərtʃɪf] or ['hæŋkər ,tʃif] *s* fazzoletto
handle ['hændəl] *s* manico; (*of a sword*) impugnatura; (*of a door*) maniglia; (*of a drawer*) pomolo; (*of a hand organ*) manovella; espediente *m;* **to fly off the handle** (slang) uscire dai gangheri || *tr* maneggiare; manovrare, dirigere; commerciare in || *intr* comportarsi
handle'bar' *s* manubrio
handler ['hændlər] *s* (sports) allenatore *m*
hand'made' *adj* fatto a mano
hand'maid' or **hand'maid'en** *s* domestica, serva; (fig) ancella
hand'-me-down' *adj* smesso || *s* vestito smesso or di seconda mano
hand' or'gan *s* organetto, organino, organetto di Barberia
hand'out' *s* elemosina di cibo; articolo distribuito gratis; comunicato stampa
hand-picked ['hænd ,pɪkt] *adj* colto a mano; scelto specialmente

hand′rail′ *s* guardamano, passamano
hand′saw′ *s* sega a mano
hand′set′ *s* microtelefono
hand′shake′ *s* stretta di mano
handsome [ˈhænsəm] *adj* bello; considerevole; generoso
hand′spring′ *s* capriola, salto mortale fatto toccando il terreno con le mani
hand′-to-hand′ *adj* corpo a corpo
hand′-to-mouth′ *adj* precario, da un giorno all′altro
hand′work′ *s* lavoro fatto a mano
hand′writ′ing *s* scrittura
hand′wrought′ *adj* lavorato a mano
hand·y [ˈhændi] *adj* (**-ier; -iest**) (*easy to handle*) maneggevole; (*within easy reach*) vicino; (*skillful*) destro, abile; **to come in handy** tornare utile
hand′y·man′ *s* (**-men′**) factotum *m*
hang [hæŋ] *s* maniera di cadere; **to get the hang of** (coll) imparare a adoperare; **to not give a hang** (coll) non importare un fico a || *v* (*pret & pp* **hung** [hʌŋ]) *tr* sospendere; (*laundry*) stendere; (*to attach*) attaccare; (*a door or window*) mettere sui cardini; (*one′s head*) abbassare; **hang it!** (coll) al diavolo!; **to hang up** appendere; sospendere il progesso di || *intr* pendere, penzolare; esitare; essere sospeso; essere attaccato; **to hang around** ciondolare, oziare, gironzolare; **to hang on** essere sospeso a; dipendere da; persistere; (*s.o.′s words*) pendere; **to hang out** sporgersi; (slang) raccogliersi; (slang) vivere; **to hang over** esser sospeso; (*to threaten*) minacciare; **to hang together** mantenersi uniti; **to hang up** (telp) riattaccare || *v* (*pret* **hanged** or **hung**) *tr* (*to execute*) impiccare || *intr* impiccarsi
hangar [ˈhæŋər] or [ˈhæŋɑr] *s* rimessa; (aer) aviorimessa, hangar *m*
hanger [ˈhæŋər] *s* gancio, uncino; (*for clothes*) attaccapanni *m*
hang′er-on′ *s* (**hangers-on**) seguace *mf;* seccatore *m;* (*sponger*) parassita *m*
hanging [ˈhæŋɪŋ] *adj* pendente, pensile || *s* impiccagione; **hangings** parati *mpl*
hang′man *s* (**-men**) boia *m*
hang′nail′ *s* pipita delle unghie
hang′out′ *s* (coll) ritrovo abituale
hang′o′ver *s* mal *m* di testa dopo una sbornia
hank [hæŋk] *s* matassa
hanker [ˈhæŋkər] *intr* agognare
Hannibal [ˈhænɪbəl] *s* Annibale *m*
haphazard [ˌhæpˈhæzərd] *adj* fortuito, a caso || *adv* a caso; alla carlona
hapless [ˈhæplɪs] *adj* sfortunato
happen [ˈhæpən] *intr* succedere; **to happen along** sopravvenire; **to happen on** incontrarsi per caso con; **to happen to** + *inf* per caso + *ind*, e.g., **I happened to see her at the theater** l′ho incontrata per caso a teatro
happening [ˈhæpənɪŋ] *s* avvenimento, fatto
happily [ˈhæpɪli] *adv* felicemente; fortunatamente

happiness [ˈhæpɪnɪs] *s* felicità *f;* gioia, piacere *m*
hap·py [ˈhæpi] *adj* (**-pier; -piest**) lieto, felice, contento; **to be happy to** avere il piacere di
hap′py-go-luck′y *adj* spensierato
hap′py me′dium *s* giusto mezzo
Hap′py New Year′ *interj* buon anno!, felice anno nuovo!
harangue [həˈræŋ] *s* arringa, concione || *tr & intr* arringare
harass [ˈhærəs] or [həˈræs] *tr* bersagliare; tartassare, tormentare
harbinger [ˈhɑrbɪndʒər] *s* foriero; annunzio || *tr* annunziare
harbor [ˈhɑrbər] *adj* di porto, portuario || *s* porto || *tr* albergare; (*love or hatred*) nutrire; (*e.g., a criminal*) dare ricetto a
har′bor mas′ter *s* capitano di porto
hard [hɑrd] *adj* duro; (*difficult*) difficile; (*work*) improbo; (*solder*) forte; (*hearing or breathing*) grosso; (*drinker*) impenitente; (*liquor*) fortemente alcolico; **to be hard on** essere severo con; (*to wear out fast*) logorare rapidamente || *adv* duro; forte; molto; **hard upon** subito dopo
hard′-and-fast′ *adj* inflessibile
hard-bitten [ˈhɑrdˈbɪtən] *adj* duro, incallito
hard-boiled [ˈhɑrdˈbɔɪld] *adj* (*egg*) sodo; (coll) duro
hard′ can′dy *s* caramelle *fpl;* **piece of hard candy** caramella
hard′ cash′ *s* denaro contante
hard′ ci′der *s* sidro fermentato
hard′ coal′ *s* antracite *f*
hard′-earned′ *adj* guadagnato a stento
harden [ˈhɑrdən] *tr* indurire || *intr* indurirsi
hardening [ˈhɑrdənɪŋ] *s* indurimento; (metallurgy) tempra
hard′ facts′ *spl* realtà *f*
hard-fought [ˈhɑrdˈfɔt] *adj* accanito
hard-headed [ˈhɑrdˈhedɪd] *adj* astuto; ostinato, caparbio
hard-hearted [ˈhɑrdˈhɑrtɪd] *adj* dal cuore duro
hardihood [ˈhɑrdɪˌhʊd] *s* forza, coraggio; insolenza
hardiness [ˈhɑrdɪnɪs] *s* ardire *m;* vigore *m*, robustezza fisica
hard′ la′bor *s* lavori forzati
hard′ luck′ *s* mala sorte
hard′-luck′ sto′ry *s* storia delle proprie disgrazie
hardly [ˈhɑrdli] *adv* appena, quasi no; (*with great difficulty*) a malapena, a fatica; **hardly ever** quasi mai
hardness [ˈhɑrdnɪs] *s* durezza
hard′-of-hear′ing *adj* duro d′orecchio
hard-pressed [ˈhɑrdˈprest] *adj* oppresso; **to be hard-pressed for** essere a corto di
hard′ rub′ber *s* ebanite *f*
hard′ sauce′ *s* miscela di burro e zucchero
hard′-shell crab′ *s* granchio con la corazza
hardship [ˈhɑrdʃɪp] *s* pena, privazione; **hardships** privazioni *fpl*, strettezze *fpl*

hard'tack' *s* galletta

hard' times' *spl* strettezze *fpl*

hard' to please' *adj* di difficile contentatura

hard' up' *adj* (coll) in urgente bisogno; **to be hard up for** (coll) essere a corto di

hard'ware' *s* ferramenta *fpl;* macchinario

hard'ware store' *s* negozio di ferramenta

hard-won ['hard ,wʌn] *adj* (*victory, battle*) conquistato con molti sforzi; (*money*) acquistato con molti sforzi

hard'wood' *s* legno forte

hard'wood floor' *s* pavimento di legno, parquet *m*

har·dy ['hardi] *adj* (**-dier; -diest**) forte, resistente; (*rash*) temerario; (hort) resistente al freddo

hare [hɛr] *s* lepre *f*

harebrained ['hɛr ,brend] *adj* scervellato, sventato

hare'lip' *s* labbro leporino

harem ['hɛrəm] *s* arem *m*

hark [hark] *intr* ascoltare; **to hark back** (*said of hounds*) ritornare sulla pista; riandare col pensiero || *interj* ascolta!

harken ['harkən] *intr* ascoltare

harlequin ['harləkwɪn] *s* arlecchino

harlot ['harlət] *s* meretrice *f*, baldracca

harm [harm] *s* danno || *tr* rovinare; nuocere (with *dat*), fare del male (with *dat*)

harmful ['harmfəl] *adj* nocivo

harmless ['harmlɪs] *adj* innocuo

harmonic [har'manɪk] *adj* armonico || *s* (phys) armonica || **harmonics** *ssg* armonica; *spl* suoni armonici

harmonica [har'manɪkə] *s* armonica a bocca

harmonious [har'monɪ·əs] *adj* armonioso

harmonize ['harmə ,naɪz] *tr* intonare; (mus) armonizzare || *intr* intonarsi; (mus) cantare all'unisono

harmo·ny ['harməni] *s* (**-nies**) armonia

harness ['harnɪs] *s* bardatura, finimenti *mpl;* (fig) routine *f;* **to die in the harness** morire sulla breccia || *tr* bardare, imbrigliare; (*a waterfall*) captare

har'ness mak'er *s* sellaio

har'ness race' *s* corsa al trotto, corsa di cavalli col sulky

harp [harp] *s* arpa || *intr*—**to harp on** ripetere ostinatamente

harpist ['harpɪst] *s* arpista *mf*

harpoon [har'pun] *s* rampone *m* || *tr* & *intr* arpionare

harpsichord ['harpsɪ ,kɔrd] *s* arpicordo, clavicembalo

har·py ['harpi] *s* (**-pies**) arpia

harrow ['hæro] *s* erpice *m* || *tr* (agr) erpicare; (fig) tormentare

harrowing ['hæro·ɪŋ] *adj* straziante

har·ry ['hæri] *v* (*pret* & *pp* **-ried**) *tr* saccheggiare; tormentare

harsh [harʃ] *adj* (*to touch*) ruvido; (*to taste or hearing*) aspro; inclemente

harshness ['harʃnɪs] *s* ruvidezza; asprezza; inclemenza

hart [hart] *s* cervo

harum-scarum ['hɛrəm 'skɛrəm] *adj* & *s* scervellato

harvest ['harvɪst] *s* raccolta, mietitura || *tr* raccogliere, mietere

harvester ['harvɪstər] *s* (*person*) mietitore *m;* (*machine*) mietitrice *f*

har'vest home' *s* fine *f* della mietitura; festa dei mietitori; canzone *f* dei mietitori

har'vest moon' *s* luna di settembre

has-been ['hæz ,bɪn] *s* (*person*) fallito; (*thing*) anticaglia

hash [hæʃ] *s* polpettone *m* || *tr* tritare

hash' house' *s* osteria di terz'ordine

hashish ['hæʃɪʃ] *s* ascisc *m*

hasp [hæsp] or [hasp] *s* boncinello

hassle ['hæsəl] *s* (coll) rissa, disputa

hassock ['hæsək] *s* cuscino poggiapiedi

haste [hest] *s* premura; **in haste** di premura; **to make haste** fare presto

hasten ['hesən] *tr* affrettare || *intr* affrettarsi

hast·y ['hesti] *adj* (**-ier; -iest**) frettoloso; precipitato

hat [hæt] *s* cappello; **to keep under one's hat** (coll) mantenere il segreto su; **to throw one's hat in the ring** (coll) dichiarare la propria candidatura

hat'band' *s* nastro del cappello

hat' block' *s* forma da cappelli

hat'box' *s* cappelliera

hatch [hætʃ] *s* (*brood*) nidiata; (*shading line*) tratteggio; (*trap door*) porta a ribalta; (*lower half of door*) mezza porta; (naut) boccaporto || *tr* (*eggs*) covare; (*a drawing*) tratteggiare; complottare, tramare || *intr* schiudersi

hat'check' girl' *s* guardarobiera

hatchet ['hætʃɪt] *s* accetta; **to bury the hatchet** fare la pace

hatch'way' *s* (*trap door*) porta a ribalta; (naut) boccaporto

hate [het] *s* odio || *tr* & *intr* odiare

hateful ['hetfəl] *adj* odioso

hat'pin' *s* spillone *m*

hat'rack' *s* attaccapanni *m*

hatred ['hetrɪd] *s* odio, livore *m*

hatter ['hætər] *s* cappellaio

haughtiness ['hɔtɪnɪs] *s* superbia

haugh·ty ['hɔti] *adj* (**-tier; -tiest**) superbo, sprezzante

haul [hɔl] *s* (*tug*) tiro; (*amount caught*) retata; (*distance transported*) percorso, pezzo || *tr* trasportare; tirare; (naut) alare

haunch [hɔntʃ] or [hantʃ] *s* fianco; anca; (*hind quarter of an animal*) coscia; (*same used for food*) cosciotto

haunt [hɔnt] or [hant] *s* ritrovo, nido || *tr* frequentare assiduamente; perseguitare

haunt'ed house' *s* casa frequentata dai fantasmi

haute couture [ot ku'tyr] *s* alta moda

have [hæv] *s*—**the haves and the have-nots** gli abbienti e i nullatenenti || *v* (*pret* & *pp* **had** [hæd]) *tr* avere; (*a dream*) fare; (*to get, take*) prendere, ottenere, ricevere; **to have got** (coll) avere; **to have got to** + *inf* (coll) dovere + *inf;* **to have it in for** (coll) serbar rancore per; **to have it out with** avere a che dire con; **to have on** portare; **to have (s.th) to do with** avere (qlco) a che fare con, e.g., **I don't want to have anything to do with him** non voglio aver nulla a che fare con lui; **to have** + *inf* fare + *inf*, e.g., **I had him pay the bill** gli ho fatto pagare il conto; **to have** + *pp* fare + *inf,* e.g., **I had my watch repaired** ho fatto aggiustare l'orologio || *intr*—**to have at** attaccare, mettersi di buzzo buono con; **to have to** + *inf* dovere + *inf;* **to have to do with** avere a che fare con; trattare di, e.g., **this book has to do with superstition** questo libro tratta di superstizione || *v aux* avere, e.g., **he has studied his lesson** ha studiato la sua lezione

havelock ['hævlɑk] *s* coprinuca *m*

haven ['hevən] *s* porto; asilo

haversack ['hævər‚sæk] *s* bisaccia; (mil) zaino

havoc ['hævək] *s* rovina; **to play havoc with** rovinare; scompigliare

haw [hɔ] *s* (*of hawthorn*) bacca; (*in speech*) esitazione || *intr* voltare a sinistra || *interj* voltare a sinistra!

hawk [hɔk] *s* falco; (*mortarboard*) sparviere *m;* (coll) persona rapace || *tr* imbonire; (*newspapers*) strillare; **to hawk up** sputare raschiandosi la gola || *intr* fare il merciaiolo ambulante; schiarirsi la gola

hawker ['hɔkər] *s* merciaiolo ambulante

hawse [hɔz] *s* (naut) cubia; (*hole*) (naut) occhio di cubia; (naut) altezza di cubia

hawse'hole' *s* occhio di cubia

hawser ['hɔzər] *s* cavo, gomena

haw'thorn' *s* biancospino

hay [he] *s* fieno; **to hit the hay** (slang) andare a letto; **to make hay while the sun shines** battere il ferro fin ch'è caldo

hay' fe'ver *s* febbre *f* da fieno, raffreddore *m* da fieno

hay'field' *s* prato seminato a fieno

hay'fork' *s* forcone *m;* (mach) rastrello

hay'loft' *s* fienile *m*

haymow ['he‚mau] *s* fienile *m*

hay'rack' *s* rastrelliera

hay'ride' *s* gita notturna in carro da fieno

hay'seed' *s* semente *f* d'erba; (coll) semplicione *m,* campagnolo

hay'stack' *s* meta, pagliaio

hay'wire' *adj* (coll) disordinato, in confusione; (coll) impazzito || *s* filo per legare il fieno

hazard ['hæzərd] *s* pericolo; (*chance*) rischio; (golf) ostacolo || *tr* rischiare; (*an opinion*) arrischiare

hazardous ['hæzərdəs] *adj* pericoloso

haze [hez] *s* foschia; (fig) confusione || *tr* far la matricola a

hazel ['hezəl] *adj* nocciola || *s* (*tree*) nocciolo; (*fruit*) nocciola

ha'zel·nut' *s* nocciola

hazing ['hezɪŋ] *s* vessazione, angheria; (*at university*) matricola

ha·zy ['hezi] *adj* (**-zier; -ziest**) nebbioso; confuso

H-bomb ['etʃ‚bɑm] *s* bomba **H**

he [hi] *s* (**hes**) maschio || *pron pers* (**they**) lui, egli, esso

head [hed] *s* testa, capo; (*of bed*) testiera; (*caption*) testata; (*of a nail*) cappello; (*on a glass of beer*) schiuma; (*of a boil*) punta purulenta; (*e.g., of cattle*) capo; **at the head of** a capo di; **from head to foot** da capo a piedi; **head over heels** a gambe levate; completamente; **heads or tails** testa o croce; **over one's head** al di sopra della capacità intellettuale di qlcu; (*going to a higher authority*) al di sopra di qlcu; **to be out of one's head** (coll) esser matto; **to bring to a head** far giungere alla crisi; **to come into one's head** passar per la mente a qlcu; **to go to one's head** dare al cervello a qlcu; **to keep one's head** non perdere la testa; **to keep one's head above water** arrivare a sbarcare il lunario; **to not make head or tail of** non riuscire a raccappezzarsi su || *tr* dirigere, comandare; essere alla testa di || *intr*—**to head towards** dirigersi verso

head'ache' *s* mal di capo, emicrania

head'band' *s* fascia sul capo; (bb) capitello; (typ) filetto

head'board' *s* testiera del letto

head' cheese' *s* salame *m* di testa

head'dress' *s* acconciatura

header ['hedər] *s*—**to take a header** (coll) gettarsi a capofitto

head'first' *adv* a capofitto

head'gear' *s* copricapo; (*for protection*) casco

head'hunt'er *s* cacciatore *m* di teste

heading ['hedɪŋ] *s* intestazione; (*of a chapter of a book*) titolo; (journ) testata, capopagina *m*

headland ['hedlənd] *s* promontorio

headless ['hedlɪs] *adj* senza testa

head'light' *s* (naut, rr) fanale *m;* (aut) faro

head'line' *s* (*of a page of a book*) titolo; (journ) testata || *tr* intestare; fare pubblicità a

head'lin'er *s* (slang) attrazione principale

head'long' *adj* precipitoso || *adv* a precipizio; a capofitto

head'man *s* (**-men**) capo; giustiziere *m*

head'mas'ter *s* direttore *m* di un collegio per ragazzi

head'most' *adj* primo, più avanzato

head' of'fice *s* sede *f* centrale

head' of' hair' *s* capigliatura

head'-on' *adj* frontale || *adv* di fronte, frontalmente

head'phones' *spl* cuffia

head'piece' *s* (*any covering for the head*) copricapo; (*helmet*) elmo; (*brains, judgment*) testa; (*of bed*) spalliera; (*headset*) cuffia; (typ) testata

head'quar'ters *s* sede *f* centrale, direzione; (mil) quartier *m* generale

head'rest' *s* poggiatesta *m*, testiera

head'set' *s* cuffia

head'ship' *s* direzione

head'stone' *s* pietra angolare; (*on a grave*) pietra tombale

head'stream' *s* affluente *m* principale

head'strong' *adj* testardo, ostinato

head'wait'er *s* capocameriere *m*

head'wa'ters *spl* fonti *fpl* or sorgenti *fpl* d'un fiume

head'way' *s* progresso; **to make headway** progredire

head'wear' *s* copricapo

head'wind' *s* vento di prua

head'work' *s* lavoro intellettuale

head·y ['hedi] *adj* (**-ier; -iest**) eccitante; impetuoso; violento; (*clever*) astuto; intossicante

heal [hil] *tr* sanare, guarire; purificare ‖ *intr* risanarsi, guarire; (*said of a wound*) rimarginare

healer ['hilər] *s* guaritore *m*

health [helθ] *s* salute *f;* **to radiate health** sprizzare salute da tutti i pori; **to your health!** alla Sua salute!

health' depart'ment *s* sanità *f*

healthful ['helθfəl] *adj* salutare

health' insur'ance *s* assicurazione malattia

health·y ['helθi] *adj* (**-ier; -iest**) sano; salubre

heap [hip] *s* mucchio; (coll) insalata, mare *m* ‖ *tr* ammucchiare; **to heap s.th upon s.o.** colmare qlcu di qlco; **to heap with** colmare di

hear [hɪr] *v* (*pret & pp* heard [hʌrd]) *tr* udire; **to hear it said** sentirlo dire ‖ *intr* udire; **hear!, hear!** bravo!; **to hear about** sentir parlare di; **to hear from** aver notizie di; **to hear of** sentir parlare di; **to hear that** sentir dire che

hearer ['hɪrər] *s* ascoltatore *m*

hearing ['hɪrɪŋ] *s* (*sense*) udito, orecchio; (*act*) udienza; **in the hearing of** in presenza di; **within hearing** a portata d'orecchio

hear'ing aid' *s* uditofono

hear'say' *s* diceria; **by hearsay** per sentito dire

hearse [hʌrs] *s* carro, carrozzone *m*, or furgone *m* funebre

heart [hart] *s* cuore *m;* (*e.g., of lettuce*) grumolo; **after one's heart** di gusto di qlcu; **by heart** a memoria; **heart and soul** di tutto cuore; **to break the heart of** spezzare il cuore di; **to die of a broken heart** morire di crepacuore; **to eat one's heart out** piangere silenziosamente; **to get to the heart of** sviscerare il nocciolo di; **to have one's heart in one's work** lavorare di buzzo buono; **to have one's heart in the right place** avere buone intenzioni; **to lose heart** scoraggiarsi; **to open one's heart to** aprire il cuore a; **to take heart** prender coraggio; **to take to heart** prendersi a cuore; **to**

wear one's heart on one's sleeve parlare a cuore aperto; **with one's heart in one's mouth** col cuore in bocca

heart'ache' *s* angustia, angoscia

heart' attack' *s* attacco cardiaco

heart'beat' *s* battito del cuore

heart'break' *s* angoscia straziante

heart'break'er *s* rubacuori *m*

heartbroken ['hart,brokən] *adj* col cuore spezzato

heart'burn' *s* bruciore *m* di stomaco

heart' disease' *s* mal *m* di cuore

hearten ['hartən] *tr* rincuorare

heart' fail'ure *s* (*death*) arresto cardiaco; collasso cardiaco

heartfelt ['hart,felt] *adj* sentito

hearth [harθ] *s* focolare *m*

hearth'stone' *s* pietra del focolare

heartily ['hartɪli] *adv* di cuore, cordialmente; saporitamente

heartless ['hartlɪs] *adj* senza cuore, insensibile

heart' mur'mur *s* soffio al cuore

heart-rending ['hart,rendɪŋ] *adj* da far male al cuore

heart'sick' *adj* afflitto, sconsolato

heart'strings' *spl* precordi *mpl*

heart'-to-heart' *adj* cuore a cuore

heart' trans'plant *s* trapianto cardiaco

heart'wood' *s* cuore *m* del legno

heart·y ['harti] *adj* (**-ier; -iest**) cordiale, di cuore; abbondante; (*eater*) grande

heat [hit] *adj* termico ‖ *s* calore *m;* (*of room, house, etc.*) riscaldamento; (zool) fregola; (sports) batteria; (fig) fervore *m;* **in heat** (zool) in amore ‖ *tr* scaldare, riscaldare; (fig) eccitare ‖ *intr* riscaldarsi; (fig) accalorarsi

heated ['hit:d] *adj* accalorato

heater ['hitər] *s* riscaldatore *m;* (*for central heating*) calorifero; (*to heat hands or bed*) scaldino; (*to heat water in tub*) scaldabagno

heath [hiθ] *s* (*shrub*) brugo, erica; (*tract of land*) brughiera

hea·then ['hiðən] *adj* pagano; irreligioso ‖ *s* (**-then** or **-thens**) pagano

heathendom ['hiðəndəm] *s* (*worship*) paganesimo; (*land*) pagania

heather ['heðər] *s* erica, brugo

heating ['hitɪŋ] *adj* di riscaldamento ‖ *s* riscaldamento

heat'ing pad' *s* termoforo

heat' light'ning *s* lampo di caldo

heat' shield' *s* (rok) scudo termico

heat'stroke' *s* colpo di calore

heat' wave' *s* ondata di caldo

heave [hiv] *s* sollevamento, sforzo; **heaves** (vet) bolsaggine *f* ‖ *v* (*pret & pp* heaved or hove [hov]) *tr* sollevare, alzare; rigettare; (*a sigh*) emettere ‖ *intr* alzarsi e abbassarsi; (*said of one's chest*) palpitare; avere conati di vomito

heaven ['hevən] *s* cielo; **for heaven's sake!** or **good heavens!** per amor del cielo!; **heavens** (*firmament*) cielo ‖ Heaven *s* cielo

heavenly ['hevənli] *adj* celeste

heav'enly bod'y *s* corpo celeste

heav·y ['hevi] *adj* (**-ier; -iest**) (*of great*

weight) pesante; (*liquid*) denso; (*cloth, sea*) grosso; (*traffic*) forte; (*serious*) grave; (*crop*) abbondante; (*rain*) dirotto; (*features*) grossolano; (*heart*) stretto; (*ponderous*) macchinoso; (*industry*) grande; (*stock market*) abbattuto ‖ *adv* (coll) pesantemente; **to hang heavy** (*said of time*) passar lentamente

heav'y-du'ty *adj* extraforte

heavy-hearted ['hɛvɪ'hɑrtɪd] *adj* afflitto, triste

heav'y·set' *adj* forte, corpulento

heav'y·weight' *s* peso massimo

Hebrew ['hibru] *adj & s* ebreo; (*language*) ebraico

hecatomb ['hɛkə,tom] or ['hɛkə,tum] *s* ecatombe *f*

heckle ['hɛkəl] *tr* interrompere con domande imbarazzanti

hectic ['hɛktɪk] *adj* febbrile

hedge [hɛdʒ] *s* barriera; (*of bushes*) siepe *f*; (*in stock market*) operazione controbilanciante ‖ *tr* circondare con siepe; **to hedge in** circondare ‖ *intr* evitare di compromettersi; (com) coprirsi

hedge'hog' *s* (zool) riccio; (*porcupine*) (zool) porcospino

hedge'hop' *v* (*pret & pp* -hopped; *ger* hopping) *intr* volare a volo radente

hedgehopping ['hɛdʒ,hɑpɪŋ] *s* volo radente

hedge'row' [ro] *s* siepe *f*

heed [hid] *s* attenzione; **to take heed** fare attenzione ‖ *tr* badare a ‖ *intr* fare attenzione, badare

heedless [hidlɪs] *adj* sbadato

heehaw ['hi,hɔ] *s* (*of donkey*) raglio d'asino; risata ‖ *intr* ragliare; ridere fragorosamente

heel [hil] *s* (*of shoe, of foot*) calcagno, tallone *m*; (*of stocking or shoe*) tallone *m*; (*raised part of shoe below heel*) tacco; (coll) farabutto; **down at the heel** mal ridotto; **to cool one's heels** aspettare a lungo; **to kick up one's heels** darsi alla pazza gioia; **to show a clean pair of heels** or **to take to one's heels** battere i tacchi

heeler ['hilər] *s* politicante *mf*

heft·y ['hɛfti] *adj* (-ier; -iest) (*heavy*) pesante; (*strong*) forte

hegemon·y [hɪ'dʒɛməni] or ['hɛdʒɪ,moni] *s* (-ies) egemonia

hegira [hɪ'dʒaɪrə] or ['hɛdʒɪrə] *s* fuga

heifer ['hɛfər] *s* manza, giovenca

height [haɪt] *s* altezza; (*of a person*) altezza, statura; (*e.g., of folly*) colmo

heighten ['haɪtən] *tr* innalzare; (*to increase the amount of*) accrescere, aumentare ‖ *intr* aumentare

heinous ['henəs] *adj* nefando, odioso

heir [er] *s* erede *m*

heir' appar'ent *s* (**heirs' appar'ent**) erede necessario

heirdom ['ɛrdəm] *s* eredità *f*

heiress ['ɛrɪs] *s* ereditiera, erede *f*

heirloom ['ɛr,lum] *s* cimelio di famiglia

Helen ['hɛlən] *s* Elena

helicopter ['hɛlɪ,kɑptər] *s* elicottero

heliport ['hɛlɪ,port] *s* eliporto

helium ['hilɪ·əm] *s* elio

helix ['hilɪks] *s* (**helixes** or **helices** ['hɛlɪ,siz]) spirale *f*; (geom) elica

hell [hɛl] *s* inferno

hell-bent ['hɛl'bɛnt] *adj* (coll) risoluto; **to be hell-bent on** (coll) avere un chiodo in testa di

hell'cat' *s* arpia, megera

hellebore ['hɛlɪ,bor] *s* elleboro

Hellene ['hɛlin] *s* greco

Hellenic [hɛ'lɛnɪk] or [hɛ'linɪk] *adj* ellenico

hell'fire' *s* fuoco dell'inferno

hellish ['hɛlɪʃ] *adj* infernale

hel·lo [hɛ'lo] *s* saluto ‖ *interj* ciao!; (*on telephone*) pronto!

helm [hɛlm] *s* barra del timone; ruota del timone; timone *m* ‖ *tr* dirigere

helmet ['hɛlmɪt] *s* (mil) elmetto; (sports) casco; (hist) elmo

helms'man *s* (-men) timoniere *m*

help [hɛlp] *s* aiuto; (*relief*) rimedio, e.g., **there's no help for it** non c'è rimedio; servitù *f*; impiegati *mpl*; operai *mpl*; **to come to the help of** venire in aiuto di ‖ *tr* aiutare; soccorrere, mitigare; (*to wait on*) servire; **it can't be helped** non c'è rimedio; **so help me God!** Dio mi sia testimonio!; **to help down** aiutare a scendere; **to help s.o. with his coat** aiutare qlcu a mettersi il cappotto; **to help oneself** servirsi da solo; **to help up** aiutare a salire; aiutare ad alzarsi; **to not be able to help** + *ger* non poter fare a meno di + *inf*, e.g., **he can't help laughing** non può fare a meno di ridere ‖ *intr* aiutare ‖ *interj* aiuto!

helper ['hɛlpər] *s* aiutante *m*; (*in a shop*) garzone *m*, lavorante *m*

helpful ['hɛlpfəl] *adj* utile, servizievole

helping ['hɛlpɪŋ] *s* (*of food*) razione

helpless ['hɛlplɪs] *adj* (*weak*) debole; (*powerless*) impotente; senza risorse; (*confused*) perplesso; (*situation*) irrimediabile

help'mate' *s* compagno; (*wife*) compagna

helter-skelter ['hɛltər'skɛltər] *adj & adv* in fretta e furia; alla rinfusa

hem [hɛm] *s* (*any edge*) orlo; (*of skirt*) basta, pedana; (*of suit*) falda ‖ *v* (*pret & pp* hemmed; *ger* hemming) *tr* orlare, bordare; **to hem in** insaccare ‖ *intr* esitare; **to hem and haw** esitare; essere evasivo

hemisphere ['hɛmɪ,sfɪr] *s* emisfero

hemistich ['hɛmɪ,stɪk] *s* emistichio

hem'line' *s* orlo della gonna

hem'lock' *s* (*herb and poison*) cicuta; (*Tsuga canadensis*) abete *m* del Canada

hemoglobin [,hɛmə'globɪn] or [,himə-'globɪn] *s* emoglobina

hemophilia [,hɛmə'fɪlɪ·ə] or [,himə-'fɪlɪ·ə] *s* emofilia

hemorrhage ['hɛmərɪdʒ] *s* emorragia

hemorrhoids ['hɛmə,rɔɪdz] *spl* emorroidi *fpl*

hemostat ['hɛmə,stæt] or ['himə,stæt] *s* pinza emostatica

hemp [hɛmp] *s* canapa

hemstitch ['hɛm‚stɪtʃ] s orlo a giorno || tr & intr orlare a giorno
hen [hɛn] s gallina
hence [hɛns] adv di qui; da ora; quindi; di qui a, e.g., **three weeks hence** di qui a tre settimane
hence'forth' adv d'ora innanzi
hench·man ['hɛntʃmən] s (**-men** [mən]) accolito; politicante m
hen'house' s pollaio
henna ['hɛnə] s henna || tr tingere con la henna
hen'peck' tr (a husband) trovare a ridire con
hen'pecked' hus'band s marito dominato dalla moglie
her [hʌr] adj poss suo, il suo || pron pers la, lei; **to her** le, a lei
herald ['hɛrəld] s araldo; annunziatore m || tr annunziare
heraldic [hɛ'rældɪk] adj araldico
herald·ry ['hɛrəldri] s (-ries) (office) consulta araldica; (science) araldica; (coat of arms) blasone m
herb [ʌrb] or [hʌrb] s erba; erba medicinale
herbaceous [hʌr'beʃəs] adj erbaceo
herbage ['ʌrbɪdʒ] or ['hʌrbɪdʒ] s erba; (law) erbatico
herbalist ['hʌrbəlɪst] or ['ʌrbəlɪst] s erborista m
herbari·um [hʌr'bɛrɪ·əm] s (-ums or -a [ə]) erbario
herb' doc'tor s erborista mf
herculean [hʌr'kjulɪ·ən] or [‚hʌrkju-'li·ən] adj erculeo
herd [hʌrd] s (of sheep) gregge m; (of cattle) mandria; (of men) torma || tr & intr imbrancare
herds'man s (-men) (of cattle) mandriano, vaccaio; (of sheep) pastore m
here [hɪr] adj presente || s—**the here and the hereafter** la vita presente e l'aldilà || adv qui, qua; **here and there** qua e là; **here is** or **here are** ecco; **that's neither here not there** ciò non ha nulla a che vedere || interj presente!
hereabouts ['hɪrə‚bauts] adv qua vicino
here·af'ter s aldilà m || adv d'ora innanzi; nel futuro
here·by' adv con la presente
hereditary [hɪ'rɛdɪ‚tɛri] adj ereditario
heredi·ty [hɪ'rɛdɪti] s (-ties) eredità f
here·in' adv qui; in questo posto
here·of' adv di questo
here·on' adv in questo; su questo
here·sy ['hɛrəsi] s (-sies) eresia
heretic ['hɛrətɪk] adj & s eretico
heretical [hɪ'rɛtɪkəl] adj eretico
heretofore [‚hɪrtu'for] adv sinora
here·u·pon' adv su questo; in questo; immediatamente dopo
here·with' adv accluso; con la presente
heritage ['hɛrɪtɪdʒ] s eredità f
hermetic(al) [hʌr'mɛtɪk(əl)] adj ermetico
hermit ['hʌrmɪt] s eremita m
hermitage ['hʌrmɪtɪdʒ] s eremitaggio
herni·a ['hʌrnɪ·ə] s (-as or -ae [‚i]) ernia
he·ro ['hɪro] s (-roes) eroe m

heroic [hɪ'ro·ɪk] adj eroico || **heroics** spl linguaggio altisonante
heroin ['hɛro·ɪn] s (pharm) eroina
heroine ['hɛro·ɪn] s eroina
heroism ['hɛro‚ɪzəm] s eroismo
heron ['hɛrən] s airone m
herring ['hɛrɪŋ] s aringa
her'ring·bone' s (in fabrics) spina di pesce; (in hardwood floors) spiga
hers [hʌrz] pron poss il suo; **of hers** suo
herself [hʌr'sɛlf] pron pers lei stessa; sé stessa; si, e.g., **she enjoyed herself** si divertì; **with herself** con sé
hertz [hʌrts] s hertz m
hesitan·cy ['hɛzɪtənsi] s (-cies) titubanza, esitanza
hesitant ['hɛzɪtənt] adj esitante
hesitate ['hɛzɪ‚tet] intr esitare, titubare; (to stutter) balbettare
hesitation [‚hɛzɪ'teʃən] s esitazione
heterodox ['hɛtərə‚dɑks] adj eterodosso
heterodyne ['hɛtərə‚daɪn] s eterodina
heterogeneous [‚hɛtərə'dʒinɪ·əs] adj eterogeneo
hew [hju] v (pret **hewed**; pp **hewed** or **hewn**) tr tagliare; (a passage) aprirsi; (a statue) abbozzare; **to hew down** abbattere || intr—**to hew close to the line** (coll) filare diritto
hex [hɛks] s strega; incantesimo || tr stregare, incantare
hexameter [hɛks'æmɪtər] s esametro
hey [he] interj ehi!
hey'day' s apogeo
hia·tus [haɪ'etəs] s (-tuses or -tus) (gap) lacuna; (gram) iato
hibernate ['haɪbər‚net] intr ibernare; (said of people) svernare
hibiscus [hɪ'bɪskəs] or [haɪ'bɪskəs] s ibisco
hic·cup ['hɪkəp] s singhiozzo || v (pret & pp -cuped or -cupped; ger -cuping or -cupping) intr singhiozzare
hick [hɪk] adj & s (coll) rustico
hicko·ry ['hɪkəri] s (-ries) hickory m
hidden ['hɪdən] adj nascosto
hide [haɪd] s cuoio, pelle f; **hides** cuoio; **neither hide nor hair** nemmeno una traccia; **to tan s.o.'s hide** (coll) dargliele sode a qlcu || v (pret **hid** [hɪd]; pp **hid** or **hidden** ['hɪdən]) tr nascondere || intr nascondersi; **to hide out** (coll) rintanarsi
hide'-and-seek' s rimpiattino; **to play hide-and-seek** giocare a rimpiattino or a nascondino
hide'bound' adj retrogrado, conservatore
hideous ['hɪdɪ·əs] adj orribile, brutto
hide'out' s nascondiglio
hiding ['haɪdɪŋ] s nascondere m; (place) nascondiglio; **in hiding** nascosto
hid'ing place' s nascondiglio
hie [haɪ] v (pret & pp **hied**; ger **hieing** or **hying**) tr—**hie thee home** affrettati a tornare a casa || intr affrettarsi
hierar·chy ['haɪ·ə‚rɑrki] s (-chies) gerarchia
hieroglyphic [‚haɪ·ərə'glɪfɪk] adj & s geroglifico

hi-fi ['haɪ'faɪ] *adj* di alta fedeltà || *s* alta fedeltà
higgledy-piggledy ['hɪgəldɪ'pɪgəldɪ] *adj* confuso || *adv* alla rinfusa
high [haɪ] *adj* alto; (*color*) forte; (*merry*) allegro; (*luxurious*) lussuoso; (coll) ubriaco; (culin) frollo; **high and dry** abbandonato; **high and mighty** (coll) arrogante || *adv* molto; riccamente; **to aim high** mirare in alto; **to come high** essere caro || *s* (aut) quarta, diretta; **on high** in cielo
high' al'tar *s* altare *m* maggiore
high'ball' *s* whiskey con ghiaccio e gazosa || *intr* (slang) andare di carriera
high' blood' pres'sure *s* ipertensione
high'born' *adj* di nobile lignaggio
high'boy' *s* cassettone alto
high'brow' *s* intellettuale *mf;* (coll) intellettualoide *mf*
high'chair' *s* seggiolino per bambini
high' command' *s* comando supremo
high' cost' of liv'ing *s* carovita *m*, caro-viveri *m*
high'er educa'tion *s* insegnamento universitario, istruzione superiore
higher-up [,haɪ·ər'ʌp] *s* (coll) superiore *m*
high' explo'sive *s* esplosivo ad alta potenza
highfalutin [,haɪfə'lutən] *adj* (coll) pomposo, pretenzioso
high' fidel'ity *s* high fidelity, alta fedeltà
high'-fre'quency *adj* ad alta frequenza
high' gear' *s* (aut) presa diretta
high'-grade' *adj* di qualità superiore
high-handed ['haɪ'hændɪd] *adj* arbitrario
high' hat' *s* cappello a cilindro
high'-hat' *adj* (coll) snob *m* || *v* (*pret* & *pp* **-hatted;** *ger* **-hatting**) *tr* (coll) snobbare
high'-heeled' shoe' ['haɪ,hild] *s* scarpa coi tacchi alti
high' horse' *s* comportamento arrogante; **to get up on one's high horse** darsi delle grandi arie
high' jinks' ['dʒɪŋks] *s* (slang) pagliacciata, gazzarra
high' jump' *s* salto in altezza
highland ['haɪlənd] *adj* montagnoso || **highlands** *spl* regione montagnosa
high' life' *s* high-life *f*, alta società
high'light' *s* punto culminante || *tr* mettere in risalto
highly ['haɪlɪ] *adv* altamente, molto; (*paid*) profumatamente; **to speak highly of** parlar molto bene di
High' Mass' *s* messa cantata
high-minded ['haɪ'maɪndɪd] *adj* magnanimo
highness ['haɪnɪs] *s* altezza || **Highness** *s* Altezza
high' noon' *s* mezzogiorno in punto; (fig) sommo
high-pitched ['haɪ'pɪtʃt] *adj* acuto; intenso, emozionante
high-powered ['haɪ'pau·ərd] *adj* ad alta potenza; (*binoculars*) ad alto ingrandimento

high'pres'sure *adj* ad alta pressione || *tr* sollecitare con insistenza
high-priced ['haɪ'praɪst] *adj* caro, di alto prezzo
high' priest' *s* sommo sacerdote
high' rise' *s* edificio di molti piani
high'road' *s* strada principale
high'school' *s* scuola media; (*in Italy*) liceo
high' sea' *s* alto mare; **high seas** alto mare
high' soci'ety *s* l'alta società
high'-sound'ing *adj* altisonante
high'-speed' *adj* ad alta velocità
high-spirited ['haɪ'spɪrɪtɪd] *adj* fiero, vivace, focoso
high' spir'its *spl* allegria, vivacità *f*
high-strung ['haɪ'strʌŋ] *adj* teso, nervoso
high'-test' fuel' *s* supercarburante *m*
high' tide' *s* alta marea; punto culminante
high' time' *s* ora, e.g., **it is high time for you to go** è proprio ora che Lei se ne vada; (coll) baldoria
high' trea'son *s* (*against the sovereign*) lesa maestà; (*against the state*) alto tradimento
high' wa'ter *s* alta marea; (*in a river*) straripamento
high'way' *adj* autostradale || *s* autostrada
high'way'man *s* (**-men**) grassatore *m*
hijack ['haɪ,dʒæk] *tr* rubare; (*e.g., an airplane*) dirottare || *intr* effettuare un dirottamento
hijacker ['haɪ,dʒækər] *s* ladro a mano armata; (*e.g., of an airplane*) dirottatore *m*
hijacking ['haɪ,dʒækɪŋ] *s* furto a mano armata; dirottamento
hike [haɪk] *s* (*for pleasure*) gita, camminata; (*increase*) aumento; (mil) marcia || *tr* tirar su; aumentare || *intr* fare una gita; (mil) fare una marcia
hiker ['haɪkər] *s* camminatore *m*
hilarious [hɪ'lɛrɪ·əs] or [haɪ'lɛrɪ·əs] *adj* ilare; (*e.g., joke*) allegro, divertente
hill [hɪl] *s* collina || *tr* rincalzare
hillbil·ly ['hɪl,bɪli] *s* (**-lies**) (coll) montanaro rustico
hillock ['hɪlək] *s* poggio, collinetta
hill'side' *s* pendio
hill'top' *s* cima
hill·y ['hɪli] *adj* (**-ier; -iest**) collinoso; ripido
hilt [hɪlt] *s* impugnatura, elsa; **up to the hilt** completamente
him [hɪm] *pron pers* lo; lui; **to him** gli, a lui
himself [hɪm'sɛlf] *pron pers* lui stesso; sé stesso; si, e.g., **he enjoyed himself** si è divertito; **with himself** con sé
hind [haɪnd] *adj* posteriore, di dietro || *s* cerva
hinder ['hɪndər] *tr* ostacolare, impedire
hindmost ['haɪnd,most] *adj* ultimo
hind'quar'ter *s* quarto posteriore
hindrance ['hɪndrəns] *s* ostacolo, impedimento

hind'sight' s senno di poi
Hindu ['hɪndu] adj & s indù mf
hinge [hɪndʒ] s cardine m; (bb) cerniera; (philately) listello gommato; punto principale || tr munire di cardini || intr—**to hinge on** dipendere da
hin·ny ['hɪni] s (-nies) bardotto
hint [hɪnt] s insinuazione; **to take the hint** capire l'antifona || tr & intr insinuare; **to hint at** alludere a
hinterland ['hɪntər‚lænd] s retroterra m, entroterra m
hip [hɪp] adj—**to be hip to** (slang) essere al corrente di || s anca, fianco; (of a roof) spigolo
hip'bone' s ileo, osso iliaco
hipped [hɪpt] adj (livestock) zoppicante; (roof) a padiglione; **hipped on** (coll) ossessionato per
hippie ['hɪpi] s capellone m
hip·po ['hɪpo] s (-pos) (coll) ippopotamo
hippodrome ['hɪpə‚drom] s ippodromo
hippopota·mus [‚hɪpə'pɑtəməs] s (-muses or -mi [‚maɪ]) ippopotamo
hip' roof' s tetto a padiglione
hire [haɪr] s paga, salario; nolo; **for hire** a nolo || tr (help) impiegare; (a conveyance) noleggiare || intr—**to hire out** mettersi a servizio
hired' girl' s lavorante f di campagna
hired' hand' s lavorante mf
hired' man' s (men') lavorante m di campagna
hireling ['haɪrlɪŋ] adj venale || s persona prezzolata
his [hɪz] adj poss suo, il suo || pron poss il suo
Hispanic [hɪs'pænɪk] adj ispano
Hispanist ['hɪspənɪst] s ispanista mf
hiss [hɪs] s (of fire, serpent, etc.) sibilo; (of disapproval) fischio, zittio || tr zittire || intr zittire; sibilare; (said of a kettle) fischiare
histology [hɪs'tɑlədʒi] s istologia
historian [hɪs'tɔri·ən] s storico
historic(al) [hɪs'tɑrɪk(əl)] or [hɪs'tɔrɪk(əl)] adj storico
histo·ry ['hɪstəri] s (-ries) storia
histrionic [‚hɪstrɪ'ɑnɪk] adj teatrale; (artificial, affected) istrionico, teatrale || **histrionics** s istrionismo, teatralità f
hit [hɪt] s colpo; successo; (sarcastic remark) frecciata; **to be a hit** far furore; **to make a hit with** fare ottima impressione con || v (pret & pp hit; ger hitting) tr colpire; (to bump) cozzare; (the target) toccare, imbroccare, infilare; (with a car) metter sotto; (a certain speed) andare a || intr battere; **to hit on** (s.th new) imbroccare; **to hit out at** attaccare
hit'-and-run' adj (driver) colpevole di mancato soccorso
hit'-and-run' driv'er s pirata m della strada
hitch [hɪtʃ] s (jerk) strattone m; (knot) nodo; difficoltà f, ostacolo; || tr (to tie) attaccare; (oxen) aggiogare; (slang) sposare
hitch'hike' intr fare l'autostop

hitch'hik'er s autostoppista mf
hitch'ing post' s palo per attaccare un cavallo
hither ['hɪðər] adv qua, qui; **hither and thither** qua e là
hith'er·to' adv sinora
hit'-or-miss' adj fatto alla carlona
hit' rec'ord s disco di grande successo
hive [haɪv] s (box for bees) alveare m; (swarm) sciame m; **hives** orticaria || tr (bees) raccogliere
hoard [hord] s cumulo; (of money) gruzzolo || tr & intr custodire gelosamente; tesaurizzare
hoarding ['hordɪŋ] s ammassamento, tesaurizzazione
hoarfrost ['hor‚frɔst] s brina
hoarse [hors] adj rauco, svociato
hoarseness ['horsnɪs] s raucedine f
hoar·y ['hori] adj (-ier; -iest) canuto, incanutito
hoax [hoks] s mistificazione || tr mistificare
hob [hɑb] s mensola del focolare; **to play hob with** (coll) mettere a soqquadro
hobble ['hɑbəl] s zoppicamento; (to tie legs of animal) pastoia || tr far zoppicare; imbarazzare; mettere le pastoie a || intr zoppicare
hob·by ['hɑbi] s (-bies) svago, passatempo; **to ride a hobby** dedicarsi troppo alla propria occupazione favorita
hob'by-horse' s cavallo a dondolo
hob'gob'lin s folletto
hob'nail' s brocca, bulletta
hob·nob ['hɑb‚nɑb] v (pret & pp -nobbed; ger -nobbing) intr essere amiconi; **to hobnob with** essere intimo di
ho·bo ['hobo] s (-bos or -boes) girovago, vagabondo
Hob'son's choice' ['hɑbsənz] s scelta fra quanto viene offerto o niente
hock [hɑk] s garretto; (coll) pegno; **in hock** (coll) impegnato, al monte di pietà || tr tagliare i garretti a; (coll) impegnare
hockey ['hɑki] s hockey m
hock'ey play'er s hockeista m, discatore m
hock'shop' s (coll) negozio di prestiti su pegno
hocus-pocus ['hokəs'pokəs] s (meaningless formula) abracadabra m; gherminella
hod [hɑd] s vassoio; secchio per il carbone
hod' car'rier s manovale m
hodgepodge ['hɑdʒ‚pɑdʒ] s farragine f
hoe [ho] s marra, zappa || tr & intr zappare
hog [hɑg] or [hɔg] s suino, porco, maiale m || v (pret & pp hogged; ger hogging) tr (slang) mangiarsi il meglio di
hoggish ['hɑgɪʃ] or ['hɔgɪʃ] adj maialesco; egoista
hogs'head' s barilozzo di sessantatrè galloni
hog'wash' s broda da maiali

hoist [hɔɪst] *s* montacarichi *m;* *(lift)* spinta ‖ *tr* alzare, rizzare; *(a flag)* inastare; *(naut)* issare

hoity-toity [ˈhɔɪtiˈtɔɪti] *adj* arrogante, altezzoso

hokum [ˈhokəm] *s* (coll) fandonie *fpl;* (coll) sentimentalismo volgare

hold [hold] *s* presa, piglio; *(handle)* impugnatura; autorità *f*, ascendente *m;* (wrestling) presa; (aer) cabina bagagli; (mus) corona; (naut) cala, stiva; **to take hold of** afferare; impossessarsi di ‖ *v* (*pret & pp* **held** [hɛld]) *tr* tenere; (*to hold up*) sostenere; (*e.g., with a pin*) assicurare; (*a rank*) rivestire; contenere; (*a meeting*) avere; (*a note*) (mus) filare; **to hold back** trattenere; **to hold in** trattenere; **to hold one's own** non perdere terreno; **to hold over** differire; **to hold up** reggere, sostenere; (*to rob*) (coll) derubare, rapinare ‖ *intr* stare; (*to cling*) reggere; restare valido; **hold on!** un momento!; **to hold back** frenarsi; **to hold forth** fare un discorso; **to hold off** astenersi; mantenersi a distanza; **to hold on** continuare; **to hold on to** attaccarsi a; **to hold out** tener duro, resistere; **to hold out for** mantenersi fermo per

holder [ˈholdər] *s* possessore *m*, detentore *m;* (*e.g., for a cigar*) bocchino; (*e.g., for a pot*) manico, impugnatura

holding [ˈholdɪŋ] *s* possesso; **holdings** valori *mpl*, patrimonio

hold'ing com'pany *s* società finanziaria

hold'up' *s* (*delay*) interruzione; (coll) rapina a mano armata; (fig) furto

hold'up man' *s* grassatore *m*

hole [hol] *s* buco; (*in cheese*) occhio; (*in a road*) buca; (*den*) tana; (*burrow*) fossa; **in a hole** in grane, in difficoltà; **to burn a hole in one's pocket** (*said of money*) scorrere attraverso le mani bucate di qlcu; **to pick holes in** trovare a ridire su ‖ *intr*—**to hole up** (coll) imbucarsi

holiday [ˈhɑlɪˌde] *s* giorno festivo, festa; vacanza

holiness [ˈholɪnɪs] *s* santità *f;* **his Holiness** sua Santità

Holland [ˈhɑlənd] *s* l'Olanda *f*

Hollander [ˈhɑləndər] *s* olandese *mf*

hollow [ˈhɑlo] *adj* vuoto; (*sound*) sordo; (*eyes, cheeks*) infossato; vano, futile ‖ *s* buca, cavità *f;* (*small valley*) valletta ‖ *adv*—**to beat all hollow** (coll) battere completamente ‖ *tr* scavare

hol·ly [ˈhɑli] *s* (-lies) agrifoglio

holly'hock' *s* altea, malvone *m*

holm' oak' [hom] *s* leccio

holocaust [ˈhɑləˌkɔst] *s* olocausto

holster [ˈholstər] *s* fondina

ho·ly [ˈholi] *adj* (-lier; -liest) santo; (*writing*) sacro; (*water*) benedetto

Ho'ly Ghost' *s* Spirito Santo

ho'ly or'ders *spl* ordini sacri; **to take holy orders** entrare in un ordine religioso

Ho'ly Rood' [rud] *s* Santa Croce

Ho'ly Scrip'ture *s* Sacra Scrittura

Ho'ly See' *s* Santa Sede

Ho'ly Sep'ulcher *s* Santo Sepolcro

Ho'ly Thurs'day *s* l'Ascensione; il giovedì santo

ho'ly wa'ter *s* acqua benedetta, acquasanta

Ho'ly Writ' *s* Sacra Scrittura

homage [ˈhɑmɪdʒ] or [ˈɑmɪdʒ] *s* omaggio

homburg [ˈhɑmbʌrg] *s* lobbia *m & f*

home [hom] *adj* casalingo, domestico; nazionale ‖ *s* casa, dimora; (*fatherland*) patria; (*for the sick, aged, etc.*) ricovero; (sports) meta, traguardo; **at home** a casa; (*at ease*) a proprio agio; (sports) nel proprio campo; **away from home** fuori di casa; **make yourself at home** stia comodo; **to be at home** (*to receive callers*) ricevere ‖ *adv* a casa; **to see home** accompagnare a casa; **to strike home** toccare nel vivo

home'bod'y *s* (-ies) persona casalinga

homebred [ˈhomˌbrɛd] *adj* domestico; rozzo; semplice

home'brew' *s* bevanda fatta in casa

home-coming [ˈhomˌkʌmɪŋ] *s* ritorno a casa

home' coun'try *s* paese *m* natale

home' deliv'ery *s* trasporto a domicilio

home' front' *s* fronte domestico

home'land' *s* paese natio

homeless [ˈhomlɪs] *adj* senza tetto

home' life' *s* vita familiare

home-loving [ˈhomˌlʌvɪŋ] *adj* casalingo

home·ly [ˈhomli] *adj* (-lier; -liest) (*not goodlooking*) brutto; (*not elegant*) semplice, scialbo

homemade [ˈhomˈmed] *adj* fatto in casa

homemaker [ˈhomˌmekər] *s* casalinga

home' of'fice *s* sede *f* centrale ‖ **Home Office** *s* (Brit) ministero degli interni

homeopath [ˈhomɪ·əˌpæθ] or [ˈhɑmɪ·əˌpæθ] *s* omeopatico

home' plate' *s* casa base

home' port' *s* porto d'iscrizione (nel registro marittimo)

home' rule' *s* autogoverno

home' run' *s* colpo che permette al battitore di percorrere tutte le basi del diamante fino alla casa base

home'sick' *adj* nostalgico; **to be homesick for** sentire la nostalgia per

home'sick'ness *s* nostalgia

homespun [ˈhomˌspʌn] *adj* filato a casa; semplice

home'stead *s* casa e terreno

home'stretch' *s* (sports) dirittura d'arrivo; (fig) fase *f* finale

home'town' *s* città *f* natale

homeward [ˈhomwərd] *adj* di ritorno ‖ *adv* verso casa; verso la patria

home'work' *s* lavoro a domicilio; (*of a student*) dovere *m*, esercizio

homey [ˈhomi] *adj* (**homier; homiest**) intimo, comodo

homicidal [ˌhɑmɪˈsaɪdəl] *adj* omicida

homicide [ˈhɑmɪˌsaɪd] *s* (*act*) omicidio; (*person*) omicida *mf*

homi·ly [ˈhɑmɪli] *s* (-lies) omelia

homing ['homɪŋ] *adj* (*pigeon*) viaggiatore; (*weapon*) cercatore del bersaglio

hominy ['hamɪnɪ] *s* granturco macinato

homogenei·ty [ˌhoməd͡ʒɪ'ni·ɪtɪ] or [ˌhaməd͡ʒɪ'ni·ɪtɪ] *s* (**-ties**) omogeneità *f*

homogeneous [ˌhomə'd͡ʒɪnɪ·əs] or [ˌhamə'd͡ʒɪnɪ·əs] *adj* omogeneo

homogenize [hə'mad͡ʒə ˌnaɪz] *tr* omogeneizzare

homonym ['hamənɪm] *s* omonimo

homonymous [hə'manɪməs] *adj* omonimo

homosexual [ˌhomə'sekʃʊ·əl] *adj & s* omosessuale *mf*

hone [hon] *s* cote *f* || *tr* affilare

honest ['anɪst] *adj* onesto; guadagnato onestamente; integro, schietto

honesty ['anɪstɪ] *s* onestà *f;* (bot) lunaria

hon·ey ['hʌnɪ] *adj* melato, dolce || *s* miele *m;* nettare *m;* (coll) caro || *v* (*pret & pp* **-eyed** or **-ied**) *tr* dire parole melate a

hon'ey·bee' *s* ape domestica

hon'ey·comb' *s* favo || *tr* crivellare

honeyed ['hʌnɪd] *adj* melato

hon'eydew mel'on *s* melone *m* dolce dalla scorza liscia

hon'ey lo'cust *s* acacia a tre spine

hon'ey·moon' *s* luna di miele || *intr* andare in viaggio di nozze

honeysuckle ['hʌnɪ ˌsʌkəl] *s* caprifoglio

honk [haŋk] or [hɔŋk] *s* (*of wild goose*) schiamazzo; (*of automobile horn*) suono del clacson || *tr* (aut) suonare || *intr* schiamazzare; (aut) suonare

honkytonk ['haŋki ˌtaŋk] or ['hɔŋki- ˌtɔŋk] *s* (coll) locale notturno rumoroso

honor ['anər] *s* onore *m* || *tr* onorare; (com) accettare e pagare

honorable ['anərəbəl] *adj* (*upright*) onorato; (*bringing honor; worthy of honor*) onorevole

honorari·um [ˌanə'rerɪ·əm] *s* (**-ums** or **-a** [ə]) onorario

honorary ['anə ˌrerɪ] *adj* onorario

honorific [ˌanə'rɪfɪk] *adj* onorifico || *s* titolo onorifico; formula di gentilezza

hon'or sys'tem *s* sistema scolastico basato sulla parola d'onore

hood [hʊd] *s* cappuccio; cappuccio di toga universitaria; (*of carriage*) soffietto; (aut) cofano; (slang) gangster *m* || *tr* incappucciare

hoodlum ['hʊdləm] *s* (slang) facinoroso, gangster *m*, teppista *m*

hoodoo ['hʊdū] *s* (*body of primitive rites*) vuduismo; (*bad luck*) iettatura; (*person who brings bad luck*) iettatore *m* || *tr* iettare

hood'wink' *tr* turlupinare, imbrogliare

hooey ['hu·i] *s* (coll) sciocchezze *fpl*

hoof [huf] or [hʊf] *s* zoccolo, unghia; **on the hoof** (*cattle*) vivo || *tr—*to **hoof it** (slang) camminare; ballare

hoof'beat' *s* rumore *m* degli zoccoli

hook [hʊk] *s* gancio; (*for fishing*) amo; (*to join two things*) agganciamento; (*for pulling*) raffio, rampino; (*curve*) curva; (*of hook and eye*) uncinello; (boxing) hook *m*, gancio; **by hook or by crook** di riffa o di raffa; **to swallow the hook** abboccare all'amo || *tr* agganciare; (*to bend*) curvare; (*fish*) pigliare; (*to wound with the horns*) incornare; **to hook up** agganciare; (*e.g., a loudspeaking system*) montare || *intr* agganciarsi; curvarsi

hookah ['hʊkə] *s* narghilè *m*

hook' and eye' *s* uncinello e occhiello

hook' and lad'der *s* autoscala

hooked' rug' *s* tappeto fatto all'uncinetto

hook'nose' *s* naso gobbo

hook'up' *s* (electron) diagramma *m*, schema *m* di montaggio; (rad, telv) rete *f*

hook'worm' *s* anchilostoma *m*

hooky ['hʊki] *s—*to **play hooky** marinare la scuola

hooligan ['hʊlɪgən] *s* teppista *m*

hooliganism ['hʊlɪgən ˌɪzəm] *s* teppismo

hoop [hup] or [hʊp] *s* cerchio || *tr* cerchiare

hoop' skirt' *s* crinolina

hoot [hut] *s* grido della civetta; grido di derisione || *tr* zittire || *intr* stridere; **to hoot at** fischiare

hoot' owl' *s* allocco

hop [hap] *s* salto, saltello; (aer) breve volo; (bot) luppolo; (coll) corsa; **hops** (*dried flowers of hop vine*) luppolo || *v* (*pret & pp* **hopped;** *ger* **hopping**) *tr* saltare su; (aer) trasvolare || *intr* saltellare; saltellare su un piede; **to hop over** saltare su; fare una corsa a

hope [hop] *s* speranza || *tr & intr* sperare; **to hope for** sperare

hope' chest' *s* corredo da sposa

hopeful ['hopfəl] *adj* (*feeling hope*) fiducioso; (*giving hope*) promettente

hopeless ['hoplɪs] *adj* disperato

hopper ['hapər] *s* tramoggia

hop'scotch' *s* gioco del mondo

horde [hord] *s* orda

horehound ['hor ˌhaund] *s* marrubio; pastiglie *fpl* per la tosse al marrubio

horizon [hə'raɪzən] *s* orizzonte *m*

horizontal [ˌharɪ'zantəl] or [ˌhɔrɪ- 'zantəl] *adj & s* orizzontale *f*

hormone ['hɔrmon] *s* ormone *m*

horn [hɔrn] *s* corno; (aut) clacson *m*, avvisatore acustico; (mus) corno; (*trumpet*) (slang) tromba; **to blow one's horn** cantare le proprie lodi; **to lock horns** lottare, disputare; **to pull in one's horns** battere in ritirata || *intr—*to **horn in** (slang) intromettersi (in)

horned' owl' [hɔrned] *s* allocco

hornet ['hɔrnɪt] *s* calabrone *m*

hor'net's nest' *s* vespaio; **to stir up a hornet's nest** suscitare un vespaio

horn' of plen'ty *s* corno dell'abbondanza

horn'pipe' *s* clarinetto contadinesco inglese fatto di corno di bue

horn'-rimmed glass'es ['hɔrn'rɪmd] *spl* occhiali cerchiati di corno or con la montatura di corno

horn·y ['hɔrni] *adj* (**-ier; -iest**) corneo; (*callous*) calloso; (*having hornlike projections*) cornuto; (slang) preso da desiderio lussurioso

horoscope ['harə,skop] or ['hɔrə-,skop] *s* oroscopo

horrible ['harɪbəl] or ['hɔrɪbəl] *adj* orrendo, orribile

horrid ['harɪd] or ['hɔrɪd] *adj* orrido, orribile

horri·fy ['harɪ,faɪ] or ['hɔrɪ,faɪ] *v* (*pret & pp* **-fied**) *tr* inorridire

horror ['harər] or ['hɔrər] *s* orrore *m*; **to have a horror of** provare orrore per

hors d'oeuvre [ɔr 'dʌrv] *s* (**hors d'oeuvres** [ɔr 'dʌrvz]) *s* antipasto

horse [hɔrs] *s* cavallo; (*of carpenter*) cavalletto; **hold your horses!** (coll) aspetti un momento!; **to back the wrong horse** (coll) puntare sul perdente; **to be a horse of another color** (coll) essere un altro paio di maniche || *intr*—**to horse around** (slang) giocherellare; (slang) fare tiri burloni

horse'back' *s*—**on horseback** a cavallo || *adv*—**to ride horseback** montare a cavallo

horse' block' *s* montatoio

horse'break'er *s* domatore *m* di cavalli

horse'car' *s* tram *m* a cavalli

horse' chest'nut *s* (*tree*) ippocastano; (*nut*) castagna d'India

horse' deal'er *s* mercante *m* di cavalli

horse' doc'tor *s* veterinario

horse'fly' *s* (**-flies**) tafano

horse'hair' *s* crine *m* di cavallo; (*fabric*) cilicio

horse'hide' *s* cuoio di cavallo

horse'laugh' *s* risataccia

horse'man *s* (**-men**) cavallerizzo

horsemanship ['hɔrsmən,ʃɪp] *s* equitazione, maneggio

horse' meat' *s* carne equina

horse' op'era *s* western *m*

horse' pis'tol *s* pistola da sella

horse'play' *s* gioco violento, tiro burlone

horse'pow'er *s* cavallo vapore inglese

horse' race' *s* corsa ippica

horse'rad'ish *s* cren *m*, barbaforte *m*

horse' sense' *s* (coll) senso comune

horse'shoe' *s* ferro di cavallo

horse'shoe mag'net *s* calamita a ferro di cavallo

horse'shoe nail' *s* chiodo da cavallo

horse' show' *s* concorso ippico

horse' thief' *s* ladro di cavalli

horse'-trade' *intr* trafficare

horse'whip' *s* staffile *m* || *v* (*pret & pp* **-whipped**; *ger* **-whipping**) *tr* staffilare

horse'wom'an *s* (**-wom'en**) amazzone *f*

hors·y ['hɔrsi] *adj* (**-ier; -iest**) equestre; (*interested in horses*) appassionato ai cavalli; (coll) goffo

horticulture ['hɔrtɪ,kʌltʃər] *s* orticoltura

horticulturist [,hɔrtɪ'kʌltʃərɪst] *s* orticoltore *m*

hose [hoz] *s* (*stocking*) calza; (*sock*) calzino corto; (*flexible tube*) manica || **hose** *spl* calze *fpl*

hosier ['hoʒər] *s* calzettaio

hosiery ['hoʒəri] *s* calze *fpl*; calzificio

hospice ['haspɪs] *s* ospizio

hospitable ['haspɪtəbəl] or [has'pɪtəbəl] *adj* ospitale

hospital ['haspɪtəl] *s* ospedale *m*

hospitali·ty [,haspɪ'tælɪti] *s* (**-ties**) ospitalità *f*

hospitalize ['haspɪtə,laɪz] *tr* ospedalizzare

host [host] *s* ospite *m*; (*at an inn*) oste *m*; (*army*) milizia; (*crowd*) folla || **Host** *s* (eccl) ostia

hostage ['hastɪdʒ] *s* ostaggio

hostel ['hastəl] *s* ostello della gioventù

hostel·ry ['hastəlri] *s* (**-ries**) albergo

hostess ['hostɪs] *s* ospite *f*, padrona di casa; (*e.g., on a bus*) accompagnatrice *f*, guida *f*; (aer) assistente *f* di volo

hostile ['hastɪl] *adj* ostile

hostili·ty [has'tɪlɪti] *s* (**-ties**) ostilità *f*

hostler ['haslər] or ['aslər] *s* stalliere *m*

hot [hat] *adj* (**hotter; hottest**) caldo; (*reception*) caloroso; (*e.g., pepper*) piccante; (*fresh*) fresco; (*pursuit*) impetuoso; (*in rut*) in calore; (coll) radioattivo; **to be hot** (*said of a person*) aver caldo; (*said of the weather*) fare caldo; **to make it hot for** (coll) dare del filo da torcere a

hot' air' *s* aria calda; (slang) fumo

hot'-air fur'nace *s* impianto di riscaldamento ad aria calda

hot' baths' *spl* terme *fpl*

hot'bed' *s* (*e.g., of revolt*) focolaio; (hort) semenzaio, letto caldo

hot'-blood'ed *adj* ardente; impetuoso

hot' cake' *s* frittella; **to sell like hot cakes** vendersi come se fosse regalato

hot' dog' *s* Frankfurter *m*, Würstel *m*

hotel [ho'tel] *adj* alberghiero || *s* albergo

ho·tel'keep'er *s* albergatore *m*

hot'head' *s* testa calda

hotheaded ['hat,hɛdɪd] *adj* esaltato, scalmanato

hot'house' *s* serra

hot' plate' *s* fornello elettrico, scaldavivande *m*

hot' springs' *spl* terme *fpl*

hot-tempered ['hat'tɛmpərd] *adj* impulsivo, irascibile

hot' wa'ter *s*—**to be in hot water** (coll) essere nei guai

hot'-wa'ter boil'er *s* caldaia del termosifone

hot'-wa'ter bot'tle *s* borsa dell'acqua calda

hot'-wa'ter heat'er *s* scaldabagno

hot'-wa'ter heat'ing *s* riscaldamento a circolazione di acqua calda

hound [haund] *s* bracco; **to follow the hounds** or **to ride to hounds** andare a caccia alla volpe || *tr* perseguitare

hour [aur] *s* ora; **by the hour** a ore; **in an evil hour** in un brutto momento; **on the hour** ogni ora al suonar del-

l'ora; **to keep late hours** andare a letto tardi
hour′glass′ *s* clessidra
hour′ hand′ *s* lancetta delle ore
hourly [′aʊrli] *adj* orario ‖ *adv* ogni ora; spesso
house [haʊs] *s* (**houses** [′haʊzɪz]) casa; (*legislative body*) camera; (*size of audience*) concorso di pubblico; teatro; **to keep house** fare le faccende domestiche; **to put one′s house in order** migliorare il proprio comportamento; accomodare le próprie faccende ‖ [haʊz] *tr* allogare
house′ arrest′ *s* arresto a domicilio
house′boat′ *s* casa galleggiante
house′break′er *s* scassinatore *m*
housebreaking [′haʊs ,brekɪŋ] *s* violazione di domicilio, scasso
housebroken [′haʊs ,brokən] *adj* (e.g., *cat*) che è stato addestrato a tenersi pulito
house′clean′ing *s* pulizia della casa; (fig) pulizia, repulisti *m*
house′coat′ *s* vestaglia da casa
house′ cur′rent *s* corrente *f* di rete
house′fly′ *s* (**-flies**) mosca domestica
houseful [′haʊs ,fʊl] *s* casa piena
house′ fur′nishings *spl* arredi domestici
house′hold′ *adj* domestico ‖ *s* famiglia
house′hold′er *s* capo della famiglia
house′-hunt′ *intr*—**to go house-hunting** andare in cerca di casa
house′keep′er *s* governante *f*
house′keep′ing *s* faccende domestiche; **to set up housekeeping** metter su casa
house′keeping apart′ment *s* appartamentino
house′maid′ *s* domestica
house′ me′ter *s* contatore domestico
house′moth′er *s* maestra in pensionato per studenti
house′ of cards′ *s* castello di carte
house′ of ill′ repute′ *s* casa di malaffare
house′ paint′er *s* imbianchino
house′ physi′cian *s* medico residente
house′top′ *s* tetto; **to shout from the housetops** proclamare ai quattro venti
housewarming [′haʊs ,wɔrmɪŋ] *s* festa per l'inaugurazione di una casa
house′wife′ *s* (**-wives′**) donna di casa
house′work′ *s* faccende domestiche
housing [′haʊzɪŋ] *s* (*of a horse*) gualdrappa; (*dwelling*) abitazioni *fpl*; (carp) alloggiamento; (mach) gabbia, custodia; (aut) coppa; (*of transmission*) (aut) scatola
hous′ing short′age *s* crisi *f* degli alloggi
hovel [′hʌvəl] or [′havəl] *s* catapecchia, stamberga; (*shed*) baracca
hover [′hʌvər] or [′havər] *intr* librarsi; (*on the lips*) trapelare; (fig) ondeggiare, esitare
how [haʊ] *adv* come; (*at what price*) a quanto; **how early** quando, a che ora; **how else** in che altro modo; **how far** fino a dove; quanto, e.g., **how far is it to the station?** quanto c'è da qui alla stazione?; **how long** quanto tempo; **how many** quanti; **how much**

quanto; **how often** quante volte; **how old are you?** quanti anni ha?; **how soon** quando, a che ora; **how + adj** quanto + *adj*, e.g., **how beautiful she is!** quanto è bella!
how·ev′er *adv* comunque; in qualunque modo; per quanto . . . , e.g., **however wrong he may be** per quanto torto possa avere ‖ *conj* come, e.g., **do it however you want** lo faccia come vuole
howitzer [′haʊ·ɪtsər] *s* obice *m*
howl [haʊl] *s* ululato, urlo; scoppio di risa ‖ *tr* gridare; **to howl down** sopraffare a grida; ‖ *intr* ululare, urlare
howler [′haʊlər] *s* urlatore *m;* (coll) strafalcione *m,* topica
hoyden [′hɔɪdən] *s* ragazzaccia
hub [hʌb] *s* mozzo; (fig) centro
hubbub [′hʌbəb] *s* putiferio, fracasso
hub′cap′ *s* (aut) calotta della ruota
huckleber·ry [′hʌkəl ,beri] *s* (**-ries**) mirtillo
huckster [′hʌkstər] *s* venditore *m* ambulante; trafficante *m*
huddle [′hʌdəl] *s* conferenza segreta ‖ *intr* affollarsi, accalcarsi
hue [hju] *s* tono, tinta; **hue and cry** grido d'indignazione
huff [hʌf] *s* stizza; **in a huff** di cattivo umore ‖ *tr* (checkers) buffare
hug [hʌg] *s* abbraccio ‖ *v* (*pret & pp* **hugged;** *ger* **hugging**) *tr* abbracciare; (*e.g., a wall*) costeggiare ‖ *intr* abbracciarsi
huge [hjudʒ] *adj* smisurato, immane
huh [hʌ] *interj* eh!
hulk [hʌlk] *s* scafo, carcassa; (*unwieldy object*) trabiccolo
hulking [′hʌlkɪŋ] *adj* grosso e goffo
hull [hʌl] *s* (*of ship or hydroplane*) scafo; (*of dirigible*) intelaiatura; (*of airplane*) fusoliera; (*e.g., of a nut*) guscio ‖ *tr* sgusciare; (*rice*) brillare
hullabaloo [′hʌləbə ,lu] or [,hʌləbə′lu] *s* fracasso, baccano
hum [hʌm] *s* canterellio; (*of bee, machine, etc.*) ronzio ‖ *v* (*pret & pp* **hummed;** *ger* **humming**) *tr* canterellare ‖ *intr* canterellare; (*to buzz*) ronzare; (coll) vibrare, essere attivo
human [′hjumən] *adj* umano
hu′man be′ing *s* essere umano
humane [hju′men] *adj* umano; compassionevole
humanist [′hjumənɪst] *adj* umanistico ‖ *s* umanista *mf*
humanitarian [hju ,mænɪ′terɪ·ən] *adj &* *s* umanitario
humani·ty [hju′mænɪti] *s* (**-ties**) umanità *f;* **humanities** (*of Greece and Rome*) studi umanistici; (*literature, art, philosophy*) scienze umanistiche
hu′man·kind′ *s* genere umano
humble [′hʌmbəl] or [′ʌmbəl] *adj* umile ‖ *tr* umiliare
hum′ble pie′ *s*—**to eat humble pie** accettare un'umiliazione
hum′bug′ *s* frottola; (*person*) impostore *m* ‖ *v* (*pret & pp* **-bugged;** *ger*

-bugging) *tr* imbrogliare ‖ *intr* fare l'imbroglione

hum'drum' *adj* noioso, monotono

humer·us ['hjumərəs] *s* (-i [ˌaɪ]) omero

humid ['hjumɪd] *adj* umido

humidifier [hju'mɪdɪ ˌfaɪ·ər] *s* evaporatore *m*

humidi·fy [hju'mɪdɪ ˌfaɪ] *v* (*pret & pp* -fied) *tr* inumidire

humidity [hju'mɪdɪti] *s* umidità *f*

humiliate [hju'mɪlɪ ˌet] *tr* umiliare

humiliating [hju'mɪlɪ ˌetɪŋ] *adj* umiliante

humility [hju'mɪlɪti] *s* umiltà *f*

hummingbird ['hʌmɪŋ ˌbʌrd] *s* colibrì *m*

humor ['hjumər] or ['jumər] *s* umore *m;* umorismo; **out of humor** di cattivo umore ‖ *tr* adattarsi alle fisime di, assecondare

humorist ['hjumərɪst] or ['jumərɪst] *s* umorista *mf*

humorous ['hjumərəs] or ['jumərəs] *adj* umoristico

hump [hʌmp] *s* gobba; (*in the ground*) monticello

hump'back' *s* gobba; (*person*) gobbo

humus ['hjuməs] *s* humus *m*

hunch [hʌntʃ] *s* gobba; (*premonition*) (coll) sospetto ‖ *tr* piegare ‖ *intr* accovacciarsi

hunch'back' *s* gobba; (*person*) gobbo

hundred ['hʌndrəd] *adj, s & pron* cento; **a hundred** or **one hundred** cento; **by the hundreds** a centinaia

hundredth ['hʌndrədθ] *adj, s & pron* centesimo

hun'dred·weight' *s* cento libbre

Hungarian [hʌŋ'gɛrɪ·ən] *adj & s* ungherese *mf*

Hungary ['hʌŋgəri] *s* l'Ungheria *f*

hunger ['hʌŋgər] *s* fame *f* ‖ *intr* aver fame; **to hunger for** aver un desiderio ardente di, agognare

hun'ger strike' *s* sciopero della fame

hun·gry ['hʌŋgri] *adj* (-grier; -griest) affamato; **to be hungry** aver fame; **to go hungry** andare digiuno

hunk [hʌŋk] *s* (coll) bel pezzo

hunt [hʌnt] *s* caccia; **on the hunt for** a caccia di ‖ *tr* cacciare; (*to look for*) cercare ‖ *intr* andare a caccia; cercare; **to go hunting** andare a caccia; **to hunt for** cercare

hunter ['hʌntər] *s* cacciatore *m;* (*dog*) cane *m* da caccia

hunting ['hʌntɪŋ] *adj* da caccia ‖ *s* caccia

hunt'ing box' *s* capanno

hunt'ing dog' *s* cane *m* da caccia

hunt'ing ground' *s* terreno di caccia

hunt'ing horn' *s* corno da caccia

hunt'ing jack'et *s* cacciatora

hunt'ing lodge' *s* (*hut*) capanno; villino da caccia

hunt'ing sea'son *s* stagione della caccia

huntress ['hʌntrɪs] *s* cacciatrice *f*

hunts'man *s* (-men) cacciatore *m*

hurdle ['hʌrdəl] *s* (*hedge*) siepe *f;* (*wooden frame*) barriera; (sports, fig) ostacolo; **hurdles corsa ad ostacoli** ‖ *tr* saltare, superare

hur'dle race' *s* corsa agli ostacoli

hurl [hʌrl] *s* lancio ‖ *tr* lanciare; **to hurl back** respingere

hurrah [hu'rɑ] or **hurray** [hu're] *s* viva *m* ‖ *tr* applaudire ‖ *intr* gridare urrà ‖ *interj* evviva!, urrà!; **hurrah for . . . !** viva . . . !

hurricane ['hʌrɪ ˌken] *s* uragano

hurried ['hʌrɪd] *adj* frettoloso

hur·ry ['hʌri] *s* (-ries) fretta; **to be in a hurry** avere fretta ‖ *v* (*pret & pp* -ried) *tr* affrettare, sollecitare ‖ *intr* affrettarsi; **to hurry after** correr dietro a; **to hurry away** andarsene di furia; **to hurry back** ritornare presto; **to hurry up** spicciarsi

hurt [hʌrt] *adj* (*injured*) ferito; (*offended*) risentito ‖ *s* (*harm*) danno; (*injury*) ferita; (*pain*) dolore *m* ‖ *v* (*pret & pp* hurt) *tr* (*to harm*) fare male a; (*to injure*) ferire; (*to offend*) offendere; (*to pain*) dolere (with *dat*) ‖ *intr* fare male, dolere; aver male, e.g., **my head hurts** ho male alla testa

hurtle ['hʌrtəl] *intr* sferrarsi, scagliarsi, precipitarsi

husband ['hʌzbənd] *s* marito ‖ *tr* amministrare con economia

hus'band·man *s* (-men) agricoltore *m*

husbandry ['hʌzbəndri] *s* agricoltura; (*management of domestic affairs*) governo, economia domestica

hush [hʌʃ] *s* silenzio ‖ *tr* far tacere; **to hush up** (*a scandal*) soffocare ‖ *intr* tacere ‖ *interj* zitto!

hushaby ['hʌʃə ˌbaɪ] *interj* fa' la nanni!

hush'-hush' *adj* segretissimo

hush' mon'ey *s* prezzo del silenzio

husk [hʌsk] *s* guscio; (*of corn*) spoglia ‖ *tr* sgusciare; (*rice*) brillare; (*corn*) scartocciare, spogliare

husk·y ['hʌski] *adj* (-ier; -iest) forte; (*voice*) rauco

hus·sy ['hʌzi] or ['hʌsi] *s* (-sies) poca di buono; ragazza impudente

hustle ['hʌsəl] *s* vigore *m;* (slang) traffico ‖ *tr* forzare, spingere ‖ *intr* affrettarsi, scalmanarsi; (slang) trafficare; (*said of a prostitute*) (slang) accostare un cliente

hustler ['hʌslər] *s* (*go-getter*) persona intraprendente; (slang) trafficone *m*, imbroglione *m;* (slang) passeggiatrice *f*

hut [hʌt] *s* casolare *m*, casupola

hyacinth ['haɪ·əsɪnθ] *s* giacinto

hybrid ['haɪbrɪd] *adj & s* ibrido

hybridize ['haɪbrɪ ˌdaɪz] *tr & intr* ibridare

hy·dra ['haɪdrə] *s* (-dras or -drae [dri]) idra

hydrant ['haɪdrənt] *s* idrante *m;* (*water faucet*) rubinetto

hydrate ['haɪdret] *s* idrato ‖ *tr* idratare ‖ *intr* idratarsi

hydraulic [haɪ'drɔlɪk] *adj* idraulico ‖ **hydraulics** *s* idraulica

hydrau'lic ram' *s* pompa idraulica

hydriodic [ˌhaɪdrɪ'ɑdɪk] *adj* iodidrico

hydrobromic [ˌhaɪdrə'brɒmɪk] *adj* bromidrico

hydrocarbon [ˌhaɪdrə'kɑrbən] s idro-carburo
hydrochloric [ˌhaɪdrə'klorɪk] adj cloridrico
hydroelectric [ˌhaɪdro·ɪ'lɛktrɪk] adj idroelettrico
hydrofluoric [ˌhaɪdrəflu'ɑrɪk] or [ˌhaɪdrəflu'ɔrɪk] adj fluoridrico
hydrofoil ['haɪdrə,fɔɪl] s superificie idrodinamica; (winglike member) aletta idrodinamica; (vessel) aliscafo, idroplano
hydrogen ['haɪdrədʒən] s idrogeno
hy'drogen bomb' s bomba all'idrogeno
hy'drogen perox'ide s perossido d'idrogeno, acqua ossigenata
hy'drogen sul'fide s solfuro d'idrogeno
hydrometer [haɪ'drɑmɪtər] s areometro
hydrophobia [ˌhaɪdrə'fobɪ·ə] s idrofobia
hydroplane ['haɪdrə,plen] s (aer) idrovolante m; (naut) idroscivolante m, idroplano
hydroxide [haɪ'drɑksaɪd] s idrossido
hyena [haɪ'inə] s iena
hygiene ['haɪdʒin] or ['haɪdʒɪ,in] s igiene f
hygienic [ˌhaɪdʒɪ'ɛnɪk] or [haɪ'dʒinɪk] adj igienico
hymn [hɪm] s inno
hymnal ['hɪmnəl] s innario
hyperacidity [ˌhaɪpərə'sɪdɪti] s iperacidità f
hyperbola [haɪ'pʌrbələ] s (geom) iperbole f
hyperbole [haɪ'pʌrbəli] s (rhet) iperbole f

hyperbolic [ˌhaɪpər'bɑlɪk] adj iperbolico
hypersensitive [ˌhaɪpər'sɛnsɪtɪv] adj ipersensibile
hypertension [ˌhaɪpər'tɛnʃən] s ipertensione
hyphen ['haɪfən] s trattino
hyphenate ['haɪfə,net] tr unire con trattino; scrivere con trattino
hypno·sis [hɪp'nosɪs] s (-ses [siz]) ipnosi f
hypnotic [hɪp'nɑtɪk] adj & s ipnotico
hypnotism ['hɪpnə,tɪzəm] s ipnotismo
hypnotize ['hɪpnə,taɪz] tr ipnotizzare
hypochondriac [ˌhaɪpə'kɑndrɪ,æk] or [ˌhɪpə'kɑndrɪ,æk] s ipocondriaco
hypocri·sy [hɪ'pɑkrəsi] s (-sies) ipocrisia
hypocrite ['hɪpəkrɪt] s ipocrita mf
hypocritical [ˌhɪpə'krɪtɪkəl] adj ipocrita
hypodermic [ˌhaɪpə'dʌrmɪk] adj ipodermico
hyposulfite [ˌhaɪpə'sʌlfaɪt] s iposolfito
hypotenuse [haɪ'pɑtɪ,nus] or [haɪ'pɑtɪ,njus] s ipotenusa
hypothesis [haɪ'pɑθɪsɪs] s (-ses [,siz]) ipotesi f
hypothesize [haɪ'poθɪ,saɪz] tr ipotizzare
hypothetic(al) [ˌhaɪpə'θɛtɪk(əl)] adj ipotetico
hyssop ['hɪsəp] s issopo
hysteria [hɪs'tɪrɪ·ə] s isterismo
hysteric [hɪs'tɛrɪk] adj isterico || **hysterics** s isterismo
hysterical [hɪs'tɛrɪkəl] adj isterico

I

I, i [aɪ] s nona lettera dell'alfabeto inglese
I [aɪ] pron pers (we [wi]) io; **it is I** sono io
iambic [aɪ'æmbɪk] adj giambico
iam·bus [aɪ'æmbəs] s (-bi [baɪ]) giambo
I'-beam' s putrella
Iberian [aɪ'bɪrɪ·ən] adj iberico || s abitante mf dell'Iberia; lingua iberica
ibex ['aɪbɛks] s (ibexes or ibices ['ɪbɪ,siz]) stambecco
ice [aɪs] s ghiaccio; **to break the ice** rompere il ghiaccio; **to cut no ice** (coll) non avere importanza; **to skate on thin ice** cacciarsi in una situazione delicata || tr gelare; (to cover with icing) glassare || intr gelarsi
ice' age' s epoca glaciale
ice' bag' s borsa di ghiaccio
iceberg ['aɪs,bʌrg] s borgognone m, montagna di ghiaccio
ice'boat' s slitta a vela; (icebreaker) rompighiaccio
icebound ['aɪs,baund] adj chiuso dal ghiaccio
ice'box' s ghiacciaia
ice'break'er s rompighiaccio

ice' buck'et s secchiello da ghiaccio
ice'cap' s calotta glaciale
ice'-cold' adj gelido, ghiacciato
ice' cream' s gelato, sorbetto
ice'-cream cone' s cono gelato
ice'-cream freez'er s gelatiera
ice'-cream par'lor s gelateria
ice' cube' s cubetto di ghiaccio
ice' hock'ey s hockey m su ghiaccio
Iceland ['aɪslənd] s l'Islanda f
Icelander ['aɪs,lændər] or ['aɪsləndər] s islandese mf
Icelandic [aɪs'lændɪk] adj islandese || s (language) islandese m
ice'man' s (-men') venditore m di ghiaccio
ice' pack' s banco di ghiaccio; (ice bag) borsa di ghiaccio
ice' pick' s rompighiaccio
ice' shelf' s tavolato di ghiaccio
ice' skate' s pattino da ghiaccio
ice' wa'ter s acqua gelata
ichthyology [ˌɪkθɪ'ɑlədʒi] s ittiologia
icicle ['aɪsɪkəl] s ghiacciolo
icing ['aɪsɪŋ] s glassa; (meteor) gelo
iconoclast [aɪ'kɑnə,klæst] s iconoclasta mf

iconoscope [aɪ'kanə,skop] *s* (trademark) iconoscopio

icy ['aɪsi] *adj* (**icier; iciest**) ghiacciato; (*e.g., wind, hands*) gelido; (fig) glaciale

idea [aɪ'di·ə] *s* idea

ideal [aɪ'di·əl] *adj* & *s* ideale *m*

idealist [aɪ'di·əlɪst] *adj* & *s* idealista *mf*

idealistic [aɪ,dɪ·əl'ɪstɪk] *adj* idealistico

idealize [aɪ'di·ə,laɪz] *tr* idealizzare

identic(al) [aɪ'dentɪk(əl)] *adj* identico

identification [aɪ,dentɪfɪ'keʃən] *s* identificazione, riconoscimento

identifica'tion card' *s* carta d'identità

identifica'tion tag' *s* piastrina

identi·fy [aɪ'dentɪ,faɪ] *v* (*pret* & *pp* **-fied**) *tr* identificare

identi·ty [aɪ'dentiti] *s* (**-ties**) identità *f*

ideolo·gy [,aɪdɪ'alədʒi] or [,ɪdɪ'alədʒi] *s* (**-gies**) ideologia

ides [aɪdz] *spl* idi *mpl* & *fpl*

idio·cy ['ɪdi·əsi] *s* (**-cies**) idiozia

idiom ['ɪdi·əm] *s* (*expression that is contrary to the usual patterns of the language*) locuzione idiomatica, idiotismo; (*style of language*) lingua, idioma *m*; (*style of an author*) stile *m*; (*character of a language*) indole *f*

idiomatic [,ɪdɪ·ə'mætɪk] *adj* idiomatico

idiosyncra·sy [,ɪdɪ·ə'sɪnkrəsi] *s* (**-sies**) eccentricità *f*, originalità *f*; (med) idiosincrasia

idiot ['ɪdi·ət] *s* idiota *mf*

idiotic [,ɪdɪ'atɪk] *adj* idiota

idle ['aɪdəl] *adj* (*unemployed*) disoccupato; (*machine*) fermo; (*capital*) giacente; (*time*) perso; (*talk*) vano; (*lazy*) fannullone, ozioso; **to run idle** girare a vuoto ‖ *tr*—**to idle away** (*time*) sprecare ‖ *intr* poltrire, fare il fannullone; (aut) girare al minimo

idleness ['aɪdəlnɪs] *s* ozio

idler ['aɪdlər] *s* fannullone *m*

idling ['aɪdlɪŋ] *s* (*of motor*) minimo

idol ['aɪdəl] *s* idolo

idola·try [aɪ'dalətri] *s* (**-tries**) idolatria

idolize ['aɪdə,laɪz] *tr* idolatrare

idyll ['aɪdəl] *s* idillio

idyllic [aɪ'dɪlɪk] *adj* idilliaco

if [ɪf] *conj* se; **as if** come se; **even if** anche se; **if so** se è così; **if true** se è vero

ignis fatuus ['ɪgnɪs'fætʃu·əs] *s* (**ignes fatui** ['ɪgniz'fætʃu,aɪ]) fuoco fatuo

ignite [ɪg'naɪt] *tr* infiammare ‖ *intr* infiammarsi

ignition [ɪg'nɪʃən] *s* ignizione; (aut) accensione

igni'tion switch' *s* (aut) chiavetta dell'accensione

igni'tion sys'tem *s* (aut) apparecchiatura d'accensione

ignoble [ɪg'nobəl] *adj* ignobile

ignominious [,ɪgnə'mɪnɪ·əs] *adj* ignominioso

ignoramus [,ɪgnə'reməs] *s* ignorante *mf*

ignorance ['ɪgnərəns] *s* ignoranza

ignorant ['ɪgnərənt] *adj* ignorante; **to be ignorant of** ignorare

ignore [ɪg'nor] *tr* (*a person; a person's kindness*) ignorare

ill [ɪl] *adj* (**worse** [wʌrs]; **worst** [wʌrst]) malato; **to take ill** cadere malato ‖ *adv* male; **to take ill** prendere in mala parte

ill-advised ['ɪləd'vaɪzd] *adj* inconsulto, sconsiderato

ill'-at-ease' *adj* imbarazzato, spaesato

ill-bred ['ɪl'bred] *adj* maleducato

ill-considered ['ɪlkən'sɪdərd] *adj* sconsiderato

ill-disposed ['ɪldɪs'pozd] *adj* maldisposto, malintenzionato

illegal [ɪ'ligəl] *adj* illegale

illegible [ɪ'ledʒɪbəl] *adj* illeggibile

illegitimate [,ɪlɪ'dʒɪtɪmɪt] *adj* illegittimo

ill' fame' *s* pessima fama

ill-fated ['ɪl'fetɪd] *adj* infausto

ill-gotten ['ɪl'gatən] *adj* male acquistato

ill-humored ['ɪl'hjumərd] *adj* di cattivo umore

illicit [ɪ'lɪsɪt] *adj* illecito

illitera·cy [ɪ'lɪtərəsi] *s* (**-cies**) analfabetismo; (*mistake*) solecismo; ignoranza

illiterate [ɪ'lɪtərɪt] *adj* (*uneducated*) illetterato; (*unable to read or write*) analfabeta ‖ *s* analfabeta *mf*

ill-mannered ['ɪl'mænərd] *adj* screanzato, ineducato

illness ['ɪlnɪs] *s* malattia

illogical [ɪ'ladʒɪkəl] *adj* illogico

ill-spent ['ɪl'spent] *adj* sprecato

ill-starred ['ɪl'stard] *adj* nato sotto una cattiva stella; sfortunato, funesto

ill-tempered ['ɪl'tempərd] *adj* di cattivo umore

ill-timed ['ɪl'taɪmd] *adj* inopportuno

ill'-treat' *tr* maltrattare, tartassare

illuminate [ɪ'lumɪ,net] *tr* illuminare; (*a manuscript*) miniare

illumination [ɪ,lumɪ'neʃən] *s* illuminazione; (*in manuscript*) miniatura

illusion [ɪ'luʒən] *s* illusione

illusive [ɪ'lusɪv] *adj* illusorio

illusory [ɪ'lusəri] *adj* illusorio

illustrate ['ɪləs,tret] or [ɪ'lʌstret] *tr* illustrare

illustration [,ɪləs'treʃən] *s* illustrazione

illustrator ['ɪləs,tretər] *s* illustratore *m*

illustrious [ɪ'lʌstrɪ·əs] *adj* illustre

ill' will' *s* astio, ruggine *f*, malevolenza

image ['ɪmɪdʒ] *s* immagine *f*; **the very image of** il ritratto parlante di

image·ry ['ɪmɪdʒri] or ['ɪmɪdʒəri] *s* (**-ries**) (*mental images*) fantasia; (*images collectively*) immagini *fpl*; (rhet) linguaggio figurato

imaginary [ɪ'mædʒɪ,neri] *adj* immaginario

imagination [ɪ,mædʒɪ'neʃən] *s* immaginazione

imagine [ɪ'mædʒɪn] *tr* & *intr* immaginare; (*to conjecture*) immaginarsi; **imagine!** si figuri!

imbalance [ɪm'bæləns] *s* scompenso

imbecile ['ɪmbɪsɪl] *adj* & *s* imbecille *mf*

imbecili·ty [ˌɪmbɪ'sɪlɪti] s (-ties) imbecillità f, imbecillaggine f
imbibe [ɪm'baɪb] tr (to drink) bere; assorbire ‖ intr bere
imbue [ɪm'bju] tr imbevere
imitate ['ɪmɪ ˌtet] tr imitare
imitation [ˌɪmɪ'teʃən] adj (e.g., jewelry) falso ‖ s imitazione
imitator ['ɪmɪ ˌtetər] s imitatore m
immaculate [ɪ'mækjəlɪt] adj immacolato
immaterial [ˌɪmə'tɪrɪ·əl] adj immateriale; poco importante; **it's immaterial to me** a me fa lo stesso
immature [ˌɪmə'tjʊr] or [ˌɪmə'tʊr] adj immaturo
immeasurable [ɪ'mɛʒərəbəl] adj incommensurabile, smisurato
immediacy [ɪ'midɪ·əsi] s immediatezza
immediate [ɪ'midɪ·ɪt] adj immediato
immediately [ɪ'midɪ·ɪtli] adv immediatamente
immemorial [ˌɪmɪ'morɪ·əl] adj immemorabile
immense [ɪ'mɛns] adj immenso
immerge [ɪ'mʌrdʒ] intr sommergersi
immerse [ɪ'mʌrs] tr immergere
immersion [ɪ'mʌrʃən] or [ɪ'mʌrʒən] s immersione
immigrant ['ɪmɪgrənt] adj & s immigrante mf
immigrate ['ɪmɪ ˌgret] intr immigrare
immigration [ˌɪmɪ'greʃən] s immigrazione
imminent ['ɪmɪnənt] adj imminente
immobile [ɪ'mobɪl] or [ɪ'mobil] adj immobile
immobilize [ɪ'mobɪ ˌlaɪz] tr immobilizzare
immoderate [ɪ'madərɪt] adj smodato, sregolato
immodest [ɪ'madɪst] adj immodesto
immoral [ɪ'marəl] or [ɪ'mɔrəl] adj immorale
immortal [ɪ'mɔrtəl] adj & s immortale mf
immortalize [ɪ'mɔrtə ˌlaɪz] tr eternare, immortalare
immune [ɪ'mjun] adj immune
immunize ['ɪmjə ˌnaɪz] or [ɪ'mjunaɪz] tr immunizzare
imp [ɪmp] s diavoletto; (child) frugolo
impact ['ɪmpækt] s impatto
impair [ɪm'pɛr] tr danneggiare; (to weaken) indebolire
impan·el [ɪm'pænəl] v (pret & pp -eled or -elled; ger -eling or -elling) tr iscrivere nella lista dei giurati; (a jury) selezionare
impart [ɪm'part] tr (a secret) far conoscere; (knowledge) impartire; (motion) imprimere
impartial [ɪm'parʃəl] adj imparziale
impassable [ɪm'pæsəbəl] or [ɪm'pasəbəl] adj impraticabile, intrans:tabile
impasse [ɪm'pæs] or ['ɪmpæs] s vicolo cieco, impasse f
impassible [ɪm'pæsɪbəl] adj impassibile
impassioned [ɪm'pæʃənd] adj caloroso, veemente
impassive [ɪm'pæsɪv] adj impassibile

impatience [ɪm'peʃəns] s impazienza
impatient [ɪm'peʃənt] adj impaziente
impeach [ɪm'pitʃ] tr accusare; (a public official) sottoporre a un'inchiesta; (a statement) mettere in dubbio
impeachment [ɪm'pitʃmənt] s accusa; inchiesta
impeccable [ɪm'pɛkəbəl] adj impeccabile
impecunious [ˌɪmpɪ'kjunɪ·əs] adj indigente
impedance [ɪm'pidəns] s impedenza
impede [ɪm'pid] tr impedire, intralciare
impediment [ɪm'pɛdɪmənt] s impedimento; ostacolo
im·pel [ɪm'pɛl] v (pret & pp -peled or -pelled; ger -peling or -pelling) tr spingere, forzare
impending [ɪm'pɛndɪŋ] adj imminente, incombente
impenetrable [ɪm'pɛnətrəbəl] adj impenetrabile
impenitent [ɪm'pɛnɪtənt] adj impenitente ‖ s persona impenitente
imperative [ɪm'pɛrɪtɪv] adj (commanding) imperativo; (urgent) imperioso ‖ s imperativo
imperceptible [ˌɪmpər'sɛptɪbəl] adj impercettibile
imperfect [ɪm'pʌrfɪkt] adj & s imperfetto
imperfection [ˌɪmpər'fɛkʃən] s imperfezione
imperial [ɪm'pɪrɪ·əl] adj imperiale ‖ s (goatee) barbetta, mosca; (top of coach) imperiale m
imperialist [ɪm'pɪrɪ·əlɪst] adj & s imperialista mf
imper·il [ɪm'pɛrɪl] v (pret & pp -iled or -illed; ger -iling or -illing) tr mettere in pericolo
imperious [ɪm'pɪrɪ·əs] adj imperioso
imperishable [ɪm'pɛrɪ/əbəl] adj imperituro, duraturo
impersonate [ɪm'pʌrsə ˌnet] tr (to pretend to be) spacciarsi per; (on the stage) impersonare
impertinence [ɪm'pʌrtɪnəns] s impertinenza
impertinent [ɪm'pʌrtɪnənt] adj impertinente
impetuous [ɪm'pɛtʃʊ·əs] adj impetuoso
impetus ['ɪmpɪtəs] s impeto, foga
impie·ty [ɪm'paɪ·əti] s (-ties) empietà f
impinge [ɪm'pɪndʒ] intr—**to impinge on** or **upon** violare; (said, e.g., of the sun) ferire; (the imagination) colpire
impious ['ɪmpɪ·əs] adj empio
impish ['ɪmpɪʃ] adj indiavolato
implant [ɪm'plænt] tr innestare; instillare, istillare
implement ['ɪmplɪmənt] s utensile m, strumento ‖ ['ɪmplɪ ˌmɛnt] tr completare, mettere in opera; (to provide with implements) attrezzare
implicate ['ɪmplɪ ˌket] tr implicare
implicit [ɪm'plɪsɪt] adj implicito; (unquestioning) assoluto, cieco
implied [ɪm'plaɪd] adj implicito
implore [ɪm'plor] tr (a person; pardon)

implorare; (to entreat) raccomandarsi a

im·ply [ɪm'plaɪ] v (pret & pp -plied) tr voler dire, significare; implicare, sottintendere

impolite [ˌɪmpə'laɪt] adj scortese

import ['ɪmpɔrt] s importazione; articolo d'importazione; importanza || [ɪm'pɔrt] or ['ɪmpɔrt] tr importare; significare || intr importare

importance [ɪm'pɔrtəns] s importanza

important [ɪm'pɔrtənt] adj importante

importation [ˌɪmpɔr'teʃən] s importazione

importer [ɪm'pɔrtər] s importatore m

importunate [ɪm'pɔrtʃənɪt] adj importuno

importune [ˌɪmpɔr'tjun] or [ˌɪmpɔr'tun] tr importunare

impose [ɪm'poz] tr imporre || intr—to impose on or upon abusare di; abusare della gentilezza di

imposing [ɪm'pozɪŋ] adj imponente

imposition [ˌɪmpə'zɪʃən] s imposizione; abuso; abuso della gentilezza; inganno

impossible [ɪm'pɑsɪbəl] adj impossibile

impostor [ɪm'pɑstər] s impostore m

imposture [ɪm'pɑstjər] s impostura

impotence ['ɪmpətəns] s impotenza

impotent ['ɪmpətənt] adj impotente

impound [ɪm'paʊnd] tr rinchiudere, recintare; (water) raccogliere; (law) sequestrare, confiscare

impoverish [ɪm'pɑvərɪʃ] tr impoverire

impracticable [ɪm'præktɪkəbəl] adj impraticabile; (intractable) intrattabile

impractical [ɪm'præktɪkəl] adj poco pratico

impregnable [ɪm'prɛgnəbəl] adj inespugnabile, imprendibile

impregnate [ɪm'prɛgnet] tr impregnare

impresari·o [ˌɪmprɪ'sɑrɪ͵o] s (-os) impresario

impress [ɪm'prɛs] tr (to affect in mind or feelings) impressionare; (to produce by pressure; to fix on s.o.'s mind) imprimere; (mil) arruolare

impression [ɪm'prɛʃən] s impressione

impressionable [ɪm'prɛʃənəbəl] adj impressionabile

impressive [ɪm'prɛsɪv] adj impressionante, imponente

imprint ['ɪmprɪnt] s impronta; (typ) indicazione dell'editore || [ɪm'prɪnt] tr imprimere

imprison [ɪm'prɪzən] tr imprigionare

imprisonment [ɪm'prɪzənmənt] s prigione, prigionia

improbable [ɪm'prɑbəbəl] adj improbabile

impromptu [ɪm'prɑmptju] or [ɪm'prɑmptu] adj improvvisato || s improvvisazione; (mus) impromptu m || adv all'improvviso

improper [ɪm'prɑpər] adj (erroneous) improprio; (inappropriate; unseemly) scorretto; (math) improprio

improve [ɪm'pruv] tr migliorare; (an opportunity) approfittare di || intr migliorare; to improve on or upon perfezionare

improvement [ɪm'pruvmənt] s miglioramento, perfezionamento; (in real estate) miglioria; (e.g., of time) buon uso

improvident [ɪm'prɑvɪdənt] adj improvvido, imprevidente

improvise ['ɪmprə͵vaɪz] tr & intr improvvisare

imprudence [ɪm'prudəns] s imprudenza

imprudent [ɪm'prudənt] adj imprudente

impudence ['ɪmpjədəns] s impudenza, sfrontatezza, sfacciataggine f

impudent ['ɪmpjədənt] adj sfrontato, sfacciato, spudorato

impugn [ɪm'pjun] tr impugnare

impulse ['ɪmpʌls] s impulso

impulsive [ɪm'pʌlsɪv] adj impulsivo

impunity [ɪm'pjunɪti] s impunità f

impure [ɪm'pjʊr] adj impuro

impuri·ty [ɪm'pjʊrɪti] s (-ties) impurità f

impute [ɪm'pjut] tr imputare

in [ɪn] adj interno; (coll) moderno, alla moda || s relazione; the ins and outs tutti i dettagli || adv dentro; a casa; in ufficio; in here qui dentro; in there lì dentro; to be in essere a casa; to be in for essere destinato a; to be in with essere in intimità con || prep in; (within) dentro a; (over, through) per; di, e.g., the best in the class il migliore della classe; dressed in vestito di; in so far as per quanto; in that per quanto, dato che

inability [ˌɪnə'bɪlɪti] s inabilità f

inaccessible [ˌɪnæk'sɛsɪbəl] adj inaccessibile

inaccura·cy [ɪn'ækjərəsi] s (-cies) inesattezza, imprecisione

inaccurate [ɪn'ækjərɪt] adj inesatto

inaction [ɪn'ækʃən] s inazione

inactive [ɪn'æktɪv] adj inattivo

inadequate [ɪn'ædɪkwɪt] adj inadeguato, inadatto

inadvertent [ˌɪnəd'vʌrtənt] adj disattento; inavvertito

inadvisable [ˌɪnəd'vaɪzəbəl] adj poco consigliabile

inane [ɪn'en] adj insensato, assurdo

inanimate [ɪn'ænɪmɪt] adj inanimato

inappreciable [ˌɪnə'priʃɪ͵əbəl] adj inapprezzabile

inappropriate [ˌɪnə'proprɪ͵ɪt] adj non appropriato, improprio

inarticulate [ˌɪnɑr'tɪkjəlɪt] adj (sounds, words) inarticolato; (person) incapace di esprimersi

inasmuch as [ˌɪnəs'mʌtʃ ͵æz] conj dato che, visto che, in quanto che

inattentive [ˌɪnə'tɛntɪv] adj disattento

inaugural [ɪn'ɔgjərəl] adj inaugurale || s discorso inaugurale

inaugurate [ɪn'ɔgjə͵ret] tr inaugurare

inauguration [ɪn͵ɔgjə'reʃən] s inaugurazione; (investiture of a head of government) assunzione dei poteri

inborn ['ɪn͵bɔrn] adj innato, ingenito

inbreeding ['ɪn͵bridɪŋ] s incrocio fra animali o piante affini

incandescent [ˌɪnkən'dɛsənt] adj incandescente

incapable [ɪn'kepəbəl] *adj* incapace
incapacitate [ˌɪnkə'pæsɪ ˌtet] *tr* inabilitare; (law) interdire
incapaci·ty [ˌɪnkə'pæsɪti] *s* (**-ties**) incapacità *f*
incarcerate [ɪn'kɑrsə ˌret] *tr* incarcerare
incarnate [ɪn'kɑrnɪt] *or* [ɪn'kɑrnet] *adj* incarnato || [ɪn'kɑrnet] *tr* incarnare
incarnation [ˌɪnkɑr'neʃən] *s* incarnazione
incendiarism [ɪn'sendɪ·ə ˌrɪzəm] *s* incendio doloso; (*agitation*) sobillazione
incendiar·y [ɪn'sendɪ ˌeri] *adj* incendiario || *s* (**-ies**) incendiario; (fig) sobillatore *m*
incense ['ɪnsens] *s* incenso || *tr* (*to burn incense for*) incensare || [ɪn'sens] *tr* irritare, esasperare
in'cense burn'er *s* (*person*) incensatore *m;* (*vessel*) incensiere *m*
incentive [ɪn'sentɪv] *adj & s* incentivo
inception [ɪn'sepʃən] *s* principio
incertitude [ɪn'sʌrtɪ ˌtjud] *or* [ɪn'sʌrtɪ ˌtud] *s* incertezza
incest ['ɪnsest] *s* incesto
incestuous [ɪn'sestʃʊ·əs] *adj* incestuoso
inch [ɪntʃ] *s* pollice *m;* **to be within an inch of** essere a due dita da || *intr—* **to inch ahead** spingersi avanti poco a poco
incidence ['ɪnsɪdəns] *s* incidenza
incident ['ɪnsɪdənt] *adj* incidente, incidentale || *s* incidente *m*
incidental [ˌɪnsɪ'dentəl] *adj* incidentale || *s* elemento incidentale; **incidentals** piccole spese
incidentally [ˌɪnsɪ'dentəli] *adv* incidentalmente, per inciso; a proposito
incinerator [ɪn'sɪnə ˌretər] *s* inceneritore *m*
incision [ɪn'sɪʒən] *s* incisione
incisive [ɪn'saɪsɪv] *adj* incisivo
incite [ɪn'saɪt] *tr* incitare, stimulare
inclemen·cy [ɪn'klemənsi] *s* (**-cies**) inclemenza
inclination [ˌɪnklɪ'neʃən] *s* inclinazione
incline ['ɪnklaɪn] *or* [ɪn'klaɪn] *s* declivio || [ɪn'klaɪn] *tr* inclinare || *intr* inclinarsi
inclose [ɪn'kloz] *tr* includere, accludere; **to inclose herewith** accludere alla presente
inclosure [ɪn'kloʒər] *s* (*land surrounded by fence*) recinto; (*e.g., letter*) allegato
include [ɪn'klud] *tr* includere; **including** incluso, e.g., **three books including the grammar** tre libri inclusa la grammatica
inclusive [ɪn'klusɪv] *adj* incluso, e.g., **until next Friday inclusive** fino a venerdì prossimo incluso; **inclusive of** inclusivo di, e.g., **price inclusive of freight** prezzo inclusivo delle spese di trasporto
incogni·to [ɪn'kɑgnɪ ˌto] *adj* incognito || *s* (**-tos**) incognito || *adv* in incognito

incoherent [ˌɪnko'hɪrənt] *adj* incoerente
incombustible [ˌɪnkəm'bʌstɪbəl] *adj* incombustibile
income ['ɪnkʌm] *s* reddito, provento
in'come tax' *s* imposta sul reddito
incoming ['ɪn ˌkʌmɪŋ] *adj* entrante; futuro; (*tide*) ascendente || *s* entrata
incomparable [ɪn'kɑmpərəbəl] *adj* incomparabile, impareggiabile
incompatible [ˌɪnkəm'pætɪbəl] *adj* incompatibile
incomplete [ˌɪnkəm'plit] *adj* incompleto, tronco, scompleto
incomprehensible [ˌɪnkɑmprɪ'hensɪbəl] *adj* incomprensibile
inconceivable [ˌɪnkən'sivəbəl] *adj* inconcepibile
inconclusive [ˌɪnkən'klusɪv] *adj* inconcludente
incongruous [ɪn'kɑŋgru·əs] *adj* incongruo
inconsequential [ɪn ˌkɑnsɪ'kwenʃəl] *adj* (*lacking proper sequence of thought or speech*) inconseguente; (*trivial*) di poca importanza
inconsiderate [ˌɪnkən'sɪdərɪt] *adj* inconsiderato, sconsiderato
inconsisten·cy [ˌɪnkən'sɪstənsi] *s* (**-cies**) inconsistenza
inconsistent [ˌɪnkən'sɪstənt] *adj* inconsistente, inconseguente
inconsolable [ˌɪnkən'soləbəl] *adj* inconsolabile, sconsolato
inconspicuous [ˌɪnkən'spɪkju·əs] *adj* poco appariscente, poco apparente
inconstant [ɪn'kɑnstənt] *adj* incostante
incontinence [ɪn'kɑntɪnəns] *s* incontinenza
incontrovertible [ˌɪnkɑntrə'vʌrtɪbəl] *adj* incontrovertibile
inconvenience [ˌɪnkən'vini·əns] *s* scomodo, incomodo || *tr* scomodare
inconvenient [ˌɪnkən'vini·ənt] *adj* incomodo, inconveniente
incorporate [ɪn'kɔrpə ˌret] *tr* incorporare; costituire in società anonima || *intr* incorporarsi; costituirsi in società anonima
incorrect [ˌɪnkə'rekt] *adj* scorretto
increase ['ɪnkris] *s* aumento; crescita; **to be on the increase** essere in aumento || [ɪn'kris] *tr* aumentare; (*by propagation*) moltiplicare || *intr* aumentare; moltiplicarsi
increasingly [ɪn'krisɪŋli] *adv* sempre più
incredible [ɪn'kredɪbəl] *adj* incredibile
incredulous [ɪn'kredʒələs] *adj* incredulo
increment ['ɪnkrɪmənt] *s* aumento, incremento
incriminate [ɪn'krɪmɪ ˌnet] *tr* incriminare
incrust [ɪn'krʌst] *tr* incrostare
incubate ['ɪnkjə ˌbet] *tr* incubare || *intr* essere in incubazione; (*said, e.g., of a hen*) covare; (fig) covare
incubator ['ɪnkjə ˌbetər] *s* incubatrice *f*
inculcate [ɪn'kʌlket] *or* ['ɪnkʌl ˌket] *tr* inculcare

incumben·cy [ɪn'kʌmbənsi] *s* (**-cies**) incombenza

incumbent [ɪn'kʌmbənt] *adj*—**to be incumbent on** incombere a, spettare a || *s* titolare *mf*

incunabula [ˌɪnkjuˈnæbjələ] *spl* (*beginnings*) origini *fpl*; (*early printed books*) incunaboli *mpl*

in·cur [ɪn'kʌr] *v* (*pret & pp* **-curred**) *ger* **-curring**) *tr* incorrere in; (*a debt*) assumere, contrarre

incurable [ɪn'kjurəbəl] *adj & s* incurabile *mf*

incursion [ɪn'kʌrʒən] or [ɪn'kʌrʃən] *s* incursione, scorreria

indebted [ɪn'dɛtɪd] *adj* indebitato; obbligato

indecen·cy [ɪn'disənsi] *s* (**-cies**) indecenza, sconcezza

indecent [ɪn'disənt] *adj* indecente, sconveniente

indecisive [ˌɪndɪ'saɪsɪv] *adj* indeciso; (*e.g., event*) non decisivo

indeed [ɪn'did] *adv* difatti, infatti || *interj* davvero!

indefatigable [ˌɪndɪ'fætɪgəbəl] *adj* indefesso, infaticabile

indefensible [ˌɪndɪ'fɛnsɪbəl] *adj* indifendibile, insostenibile

indefinable [ˌɪndɪ'faɪnəbəl] *adj* indefinibile

indefinite [ɪn'dɛfɪnɪt] *adj* indefinito

indelible [ɪn'dɛlɪbəl] *adj* indelebile

indemnification [ɪnˌdɛmnɪfɪ'keʃən] *s* indennità *f*, indennizzo

indemni·fy [ɪn'dɛmnɪˌfaɪ] *v* (*pret & pp* **-fied**) *tr* indennizzare

indemni·ty [ɪn'dɛmnɪti] *s* (**-ties**) indennità *f*, indennizzo

indent [ɪn'dɛnt] *tr* frastagliare, dentellare; (typ) far rientrare

indentation [ˌɪndɛn'teʃən] *s* frastaglio, dentellatura; (typ) accapo

indenture [ɪn'dɛntʃər] *s* scrittura pubblica; contratto di apprendista || *tr* obbligare per contratto

independence [ˌɪndɪ'pɛndəns] *s* indipendenza

independent [ˌɪndɪ'pɛndənt] *adj & s* indipendente *mf*

indescribable [ˌɪndɪ'skraɪbəbəl] *adj* indescrivibile

indestructible [ˌɪndɪ'strʌktɪbəl] *adj* indistruttibile

indeterminate [ˌɪndɪ'tʌrmɪnɪt] *adj* indeterminato

index ['ɪndɛks] *s* (**indexes** or **indices** ['ɪndɪˌsiz]) indice *m*; (typ) indice *m* indicatore || *tr* mettere un indice a; mettere all'indice || **Index** *s* Indice *m*

in'dex card' *s* scheda di catalogo

in'dex fin'ger *s* dito indice

India ['ɪndɪ·ə] *s* l'India *f*

In'dia ink' *s* inchiostro di china

Indian ['ɪndɪ·ən] *adj & s* indiano

In'dian club' *s* clava di ginnastica

In'dian corn' *s* granoturco

In'dian file' *s* fila indiana || *adv* in fila indiana

In'dian O'cean *s* Oceano Indiano

In'dian sum'mer *s* estate *f* di San Martino

In'dian wres'tling *s* braccio di ferro

In'dia pa'per *s* carta bibbia, carta d'India

In'dia rub'ber *s* caucciù *m*

indicate ['ɪndɪˌket] *tr* indicare

indication [ˌɪndɪ'keʃən] *s* indicazione

indicative [ɪn'dɪkətɪv] *adj & s* indicativo

indicator ['ɪndɪˌketər] *s* indicatore *m*, indice *m*

indict [ɪn'daɪt] *tr* accusare

indictment [ɪn'daɪtmənt] *s* accusa, atto d'accusa

indifferent [ɪn'dɪfərənt] *adj* indifferente; (*not particularly good*) passabile

indigenous [ɪn'dɪdʒɪnəs] *adj* indigeno

indigent ['ɪndɪdʒənt] *adj* indigente || **the indigent** gli indigenti

indigestion [ˌɪndɪ'dʒɛstʃən] *s* indigestione

indignant [ɪn'dɪgnənt] *adj* indignato

indignation [ˌɪndɪg'neʃən] *s* indignazione

indigni·ty [ɪn'dɪgnɪti] *s* (**-ties**) indignità *f*

indi·go ['ɪndɪˌgo] *adj* indaco || *s* (**-gos** or **-goes**) indaco

indirect [ˌɪndɪ'rɛkt] or [ˌɪndaɪ'rɛkt] *adj* indiretto

in'direct dis'course *s* discorso indiretto

indiscernible [ˌɪndɪ'zʌrnɪbəl] or [ˌɪndɪ'sʌrnɪbəl] *adj* indiscernibile

indiscreet [ˌɪndɪs'krit] *adj* indiscreto

indispensable [ˌɪndɪs'pɛnsəbəl] *adj* indispensabile, imprescindibile

indispose [ˌɪndɪs'poz] *tr* indisporre

indisposed [ˌɪndɪs'pozd] *adj* (*disinclined*) mal disposto; (*slightly ill*) indisposto

indissoluble [ˌɪndɪ'saljəbəl] *adj* indissolubile

indistinct [ˌɪndɪ'stɪŋkt] *adj* indistinto

indite [ɪn'daɪt] *tr* redigere

individual [ˌɪndɪ'vɪdʒu·əl] *adj* individuale || *s* individuo

individuali·ty [ˌɪndɪˌvɪdʒu'ælɪti] *s* (**-ties**) individualità *f*; (*person of distinctive character*) individuo

Indochina ['ɪndo'tʃaɪnə] *s* l'Indocina *f*

Indo-Chi·nese ['ɪndotʃə'niz] *adj* indocinese || *s* (**-nese**) indocinese *mf*

Indo-European ['ɪndoˌjurə'pi·ən] *adj & s* indoeuropeo

indolent ['ɪndələnt] *adj* indolente

Indonesia [ˌɪndo'niʃə] or [ˌɪndo'niʒə] *s* l'Indonesia *f*

Indonesian [ˌɪndo'niʃən] or [ˌɪndo'niʒən] *adj & s* indonesiano

indoor ['ɪnˌdor] *adj* situato in casa; da farsi in casa

indoors ['ɪn'dorz] *adv* dentro, a casa, al coperto

indorse [ɪn'dors] *tr* (com) girare; (fig) appoggiare, approvare

indorsee [ˌɪndor'si] *s* giratario

indorsement [ɪn'dorsmənt] *s* (com) girata; (fig) appoggio, approvazione

indorser [ɪn'dorsər] *s* girante *mf*

induce [ɪn'djus] or [ɪn'dus] *tr* indurre

inducement [ɪn'djusmənt] or [ɪn'dusmənt] *s* stimolo, incentivo

induct [ɪn'dʌkt] *tr* installare; iniziare; (mil) arruolare

induction [ɪn'dʌkʃən] *s* iniziazione; (elec & log) induzione; (mil) arruolamento

indulge [ɪn'dʌldʒ] *tr* indulgere (with *dat*) || *intr* cedere, lasciarsi andare; **to indulge in** abbandonarsi a; permettersi il lusso di

indulgence [ɪn'dʌldʒəns] *s* compiacenza; intemperanza, abbandono; (*leniency*) indulgenza

indulgent [ɪn'dʌldʒənt] *adj* indulgente

industrial [ɪn'dʌstrɪəl] *adj* industriale

industrialist [ɪn'dʌstrɪəlɪst] *s* industriale *m*

industrialize [ɪn'dʌstrɪə,laɪz] *tr* industrializzare

industrious [ɪn'dʌstrɪəs] *adj* industrioso, laborioso

indus·try ['ɪndʌstrɪ] *s* (**-tries**) industria

inebriation [ɪn,ibrɪ'eʃən] *s* ubriachezza

inedible [ɪn'edɪbəl] *adj* immangiabile

ineffable [ɪn'efəbəl] *adj* ineffabile

ineffective [,ɪnɪ'fektɪv] *adj* inefficace; (*person*) incapace

ineffectual [,ɪnɪ'fektʃʊəl] *adj* inefficace

inefficient [,ɪnɪ'fɪʃənt] *adj* inefficiente

ineligible [ɪn'elɪdʒɪbəl] *adj* ineleggibile

inequali·ty [,ɪnɪ'kwɑlɪtɪ] *s* (**-ties**) disuguaglianza

inequi·ty [ɪn'ekwɪtɪ] *s* (**-ties**) ingiustizia

ineradicable [,ɪnɪ'rædɪkəbəl] *adj* inestirpabile

inertia [ɪn'ʌrʃe] *s* inerzia

inescapable [,ɪnes'kepəbəl] *adj* ineluttabile, inderogabile

inevitable [ɪn'evɪtəbəl] *adj* inevitabile

inexact [,ɪneg'zækt] *adj* inesatto

inexcusable [,ɪneks'kjuzəbəl] *adj* inescusabile

inexhaustible [,ɪneg'zɔstɪbəl] *adj* inesauribile

inexorable [ɪn'eksərəbəl] *adj* inesorabile

inexpedient [,ɪnek'spidɪ·ənt] *adj* inopportuno

inexpensive [,ɪnek'spensɪv] *adj* poco costoso, a buon mercato

inexperience [,ɪnek'spɪrɪ·əns] *s* inesperienza

inexplicable [ɪn'eksplɪkəbəl] *adj* inesplicabile

inexpressible [,ɪnek'spresɪbəl] *adj* indicibile, inesprimibile

infallible [ɪn'fælɪbəl] *adj* infallibile

infamous ['ɪnfəməs] *adj* infame

infa·my ['ɪnfəmi] *s* (**-mies**) infamia

infan·cy ['ɪnfənsi] *s* (**-cies**) infanzia

infant ['ɪnfənt] *adj* infantile; (*in the earliest stage*) (fig) nascente || *s* neonato, bebè *m*

infantile ['ɪnfən,taɪl] or ['ɪnfəntɪl] *adj* infantile

infan·try ['ɪnfəntri] *s* (**-tries**) fanteria

in'fantry·man *s* (**-men**) fante *m*

infatuated [ɪn'fætʃʊ,etɪd] *adj* infatuato

infect [ɪn'fekt] *tr* infettare

infection [ɪn'fekʃən] *s* infezione

infectious [ɪn'fekʃəs] *adj* infettivo

in·fer [ɪn'fʌr] *v* (*pret & pp* **-ferred;** *ger* **-ferring**) *tr* inferire; (coll) dedurre, supporre

inferior [ɪn'fɪrɪ·ər] *adj & s* inferiore *m*

inferiority [ɪn,fɪrɪ'ɑrɪti] *s* inferiorità *f*

inferior'ity com'plex *s* complesso di inferiorità

infernal [ɪn'fʌrnəl] *adj* infernale

infest [ɪn'fest] *tr* infestare

infidel ['ɪnfɪdəl] *adj & s* infedele *mf*

infideli·ty [,ɪnfɪ'delɪti] *s* (**-ties**) infedeltà *f*

in'field' *s* campo interno, diamante *m*

infiltrate [ɪn'fɪltret] or ['ɪnfɪl,tret] *tr* infiltrarsi in || *intr* infiltrarsi

infinite ['ɪnfɪnɪt] *adj & s* infinito

infinitive [ɪn'fɪnɪtɪv] *adj* infinitivo || *s* infinito

infini·ty [ɪn'fɪnɪti] *s* (**-ties**) infinità *f*; (math) infinito

infirm [ɪn'fʌrm] *adj* infermo; (*not firm*) debole

infirma·ry [ɪn'fʌrməri] *s* (**-ries**) infermeria

infirmi·ty [ɪn'fʌrmɪti] *s* (**-ties**) infermità *f*

inflame [ɪn'flem] *tr* infiammare || *intr* infiammarsi

inflammable [ɪn'flæməbəl] *adj* infiammabile

inflammation [,ɪnflə'meʃən] *s* infiammazione

inflate [ɪn'flet] *tr* gonfiare; (*currency, prices*) inflazionare || *intr* gonfiarsi

inflation [ɪn'fleʃən] *s* inflazione; (*of a tire*) gonfiatura

inflect [ɪn'flekt] *tr* curvare; (*voice*) modulare; (gram) flettere

inflection [ɪn'flekʃən] *s* inflessione; (gram) flessione

inflexible [ɪn'fleksɪbəl] *adj* inflessibile

inflict [ɪn'flɪkt] *tr* infliggere, inferire

influence ['ɪnflu·əns] *s* influenza || *tr* influire su, influenzare

influential [,ɪnflu'enʃəl] *adj* influente

influenza [,ɪnflu'enzə] *s* influenza

inform [ɪn'fɔrm] *tr* informare || *intr* dare informazioni; **to inform on** denunziare, fare la spia contro

informal [ɪn'fɔrməl] *adj* non ufficiale, ufficioso; (*unceremonious*) alla buona, familiare

informant [ɪn'fɔrmənt] *s* informatore *m*; (*informer*) delatore *m*; (ling) fonte *f* orale, informatore *m*

information [,ɪnfər'meʃən] *s* informazioni *fpl*; conoscenze *fpl*

informational [,ɪnfər'meʃənəl] *adj* informativo

informed' sour'ces *spl* fonti *fpl* attendibili

informer [ɪn'fɔrmər] *s* (*informant*) informatore *m*; (*spy*) delatore *m*

in·fraction [ɪn'frækʃən] *s* infrazione

infrared [,ɪnfrə'red] *adj & s* infrarosso

infrequent [ɪn'frikwənt] *adj* infrequente

infringe [ɪn'frɪndʒ] *tr* violare || *intr*— **to infringe on** or **upon** violare, contravvenire a

infringement [ɪn'frɪndʒmənt] *s* infrazione

infuriate [ɪn'fjʊrɪ,et] *tr* infuriare
infuse [ɪn'fjuz] *tr* infondere
infusion [ɪn'fjuʒən] *s* infusione
ingenious [ɪn'dʒinjəs] *adj* ingegnoso
ingenui·ty [,ɪndʒɪ'nu·ɪti] or [,ɪndʒɪ-'nju·ɪti] *s* (-ties) ingegnosità *f*
ingenuous [ɪn'dʒɛnjʊ·əs] *adj* ingenuo
ingenuousness [ɪn'dʒɛnjʊ·əsnɪs] *s* ingenuità *f*
ingest [ɪn'dʒɛst] *tr* ingerire
ingoing ['ɪn,goɪŋ] *adj* entrante
ingot ['ɪngət] *s* lingotto, massello
ingraft [ɪn'græft] or [ɪn'grɑft] *tr* (hort & surg) innestare; (fig) inculcare
ingrate ['ɪngret] *s* ingrato
ingratiate [ɪn'greʃɪ,et] *tr—to ingratiate oneself with* ingraziarsi
ingratiating [ɪn'greʃɪ,etɪŋ] *adj* attraente, affascinante, insinuante
ingratitude [ɪn'grætɪ,tjud] or [ɪn-'grætɪ,tud] *s* ingratitudine *f*
ingredient [ɪn'gridɪ·ənt] *s* ingrediente *m*
in'grown nail' ['ɪngron] *s* unghia incarnita
ingulf [ɪn'gʌlf] *tr* sommergere, inondare
inhabit [ɪn'hæbɪt] *tr* abitare, popolare
inhabitant [ɪn'hæbɪtənt] *s* abitante *mf*
inhale [ɪn'hel] *tr & intr* inspirare
inherent [ɪn'hɪrənt] *adj* inerente
inherit [ɪn'hɛrɪt] *tr & intr* ereditare
inheritance [ɪn'hɛrɪtəns] *s* eredità *f*
inheritor [ɪn'hɛrɪtər] *s* erede *mf*
inhibit [ɪn'hɪbɪt] *tr* inibire
inhospitable [ɪn'hɑspɪtəbəl] or [,ɪn-hɑs'pɪtəbəl] *adj* inospitale
inhuman [ɪn'hjumən] *adj* inumano
inhumane [,ɪnhju'men] *adj* inumano
inimical [ɪ'nɪmɪkəl] *adj* nemico
iniqui·ty [ɪ'nɪkwɪti] *s* (-ties) iniquità *f*
ini·tial [ɪ'nɪʃəl] *adj & s* iniziale *f* ‖ *v* (*pret* -tialed or -tialled; *ger* -tialing or -tialling) *tr* siglare
initiate [ɪ'nɪʃɪ,et] *tr* iniziare
initiation [ɪ,nɪʃɪ'eʃən] *s* iniziazione
initiative [ɪ'nɪʃɪ·ətɪv] or [ɪ'nɪʃətɪv] *s* iniziativa
inject [ɪn'dʒɛkt] *tr* iniettare; introdurre
injection [ɪn'dʒɛkʃən] *s* iniezione
injudicious [,ɪndʒu'dɪʃəs] *adj* avventato, sconsiderato
injunction [ɪn'dʒʌŋkʃən] *s* ingiunzione
injure ['ɪndʒər] *tr* (*to harm*) danneggiare; (*to wound*) ferire; (*to offend*) offendere, ingiuriare
injurious [ɪn'dʒʊrɪ·əs] *adj* dannoso; offensivo, ingiurioso
inju·ry ['ɪndʒərɪ] *s* (-ries) (*harm*) danno; (*wound*) ferita, lesione; offesa, ingiuria
injustice [ɪn'dʒʌstɪs] *s* ingiustizia
ink [ɪŋk] *s* inchiostro ‖ *tr* inchiostrare
inkling ['ɪŋklɪŋ] *s* sentore *m*, indizio
ink'stand' *s* (*container*) calamaio; (*stand*) calamaiera
ink'well' *s* calamaio
ink·y ['ɪŋki] *adj* (-ier; -iest) nero come l'inchiostro; nero d'inchiostro
inlaid ['ɪn,led] or [,ɪn'led] *adj* intarsiato, incrostato

inland ['ɪnlənd] *adj & s* interno ‖ *adv* verso l'interno
in'-law' *s* affine *mf*
in·lay ['ɪn,le] *s* intarsio, tassello ‖ [ɪn'le] or ['ɪn,le] *v* (*pret & pp* -laid) *tr* intarsiare
in'let *s* (*of the shore*) insenatura; (*entrance*) ammissione
in'mate' *s* (*patient, e.g., in an insane asylum*) internato; (*in a jail*) prigioniero
inn [ɪn] *s* taverna, osteria
innate [ɪ'net] or ['ɪnet] *adj* innato
inner ['ɪnər] *adj* interno, interiore; intimo, profondo
in'ner·spring' mat'tress *s* materasso a molle
in'ner tube' *s* camera d'aria
inning ['ɪnɪŋ] *s* (baseball) turno
inn'keep'er *s* locandiere *m*, oste *m*
innocence ['ɪnəsəns] *s* innocenza
innocent ['ɪnəsənt] *adj & s* innocente *mf*
innovate ['ɪnə,vet] *tr* innovare
innovation [,ɪnə've ʃən] *s* innovazione
innuen·do [,ɪnju'ɛndo] *s* (-does) sottinteso, insinuazione
innumerable [ɪ'njumərəbəl] or [ɪ'numərəbəl] *adj* innumerevole
inoculate [ɪn'akjə,let] *tr* inoculare; (*e.g., with hatred*) inoculare; permeare
inoculation [ɪn,akjə'le ʃən] *s* inoculazione
inoffensive [,ɪnə'fɛnsɪv] *adj* inoffensivo
inopportune [ɪn,apər'tjun] or [ɪn,apər'tun] *adj* inopportuno
inordinate [ɪn'ɔrdɪnɪt] *adj* smoderato
inorganic [,ɪnɔr'gænɪk] *adj* inorganico
in'pa'tient *s* degente *mf*
in'put' *s* entrata; (elec, mach) energia immessa
inquest ['ɪnkwɛst] *s* inchiesta
inquire [ɪn'kwaɪr] *tr* domandare, chiedere ‖ *intr—to inquire about, after,* or *for* chiedere di; *to inquire into* investigare
inquir·y [ɪn'kwaɪrɪ] or ['ɪnkwɪri] *s* (-ies) indagine *f*, inchiesta
inquisition [,ɪnkwɪ'zɪʃən] *s* inquisizione
inquisitive [ɪn'kwɪzɪtɪv] *adj* indagatore, curioso
in'road' *s* incursione, invasione
insane [ɪn'sen] *adj* pazzo, matto
insane' asy'lum *s* manicomio
insani·ty [ɪn'sænɪti] *s* (-ties) pazzia, follia, demenza
insatiable [ɪn'seʃəbəl] *adj* insaziabile
inscribe [ɪn'skraɪb] *tr* iscrivere; (*a book*) dedicare; (geom) inscrivere
inscription [ɪn'skrɪpʃən] *s* scritta, iscrizione; (*of a book*) dedica
inscrutable [ɪn'skrutəbəl] *adj* imperscrutabile
insect ['ɪnsɛkt] *s* insetto
insecticide [ɪn'sɛktɪ,saɪd] *adj & s* insetticida *m*
insecure [,ɪnsɪ'kjur] *adj* malsicuro
inseparable [ɪn'sɛpərəbəl] *adj* inseparabile

insert ['insʌrt] s inserzione; (circular) inserto || [in'sʌrt] tr inserire

insertion [in'sʌrʃən] s inserzione; (in lunar orbit) immissione; (of lace) tramezzo

in·set ['in ˌset] s intercalazione || [in-'set] or ['in ˌset] v (pret & pp -set; ger -setting) tr intercalare

in'shore' adj & adv vicino alla spiaggia

in'side' adj interno; privato, confidenziale || s interno; **insides** (coll) interiora fpl; **to be on the inside** avere informazioni confidenziali || adv dentro; all'interno; **inside of** dentro, dentro a, dentro di; **to turn inside out** rovesciare, voltare il diritto al rovescio || prep dentro, dentro a

in'side flap' s (bb) risvolto

insider [ˌin'saidər] s persona informata

in'side track' s (racing) steccato; **to have the inside track** (coll) trovarsi in una situazione vantaggiosa

insidious [in'sidi·əs] adj insidioso

in'sight' s intuito, penetrazione

insigni·a [in'signi·ə] s (-a or -as) distintivo; (distinguishing sign) segno

insignificant [ˌinsig'nifikənt] adj insignificante

insincere [ˌinsin'sir] adj insincero

insinuate [in'sinju ˌet] tr insinuare

insist [in'sist] intr insistere

insofar as [ˌinso'far ˌæz] conj per quanto

insolence ['insələns] s insolenza

insolent ['insələnt] adj insolente

insoluble [in'saljəbəl] adj insolubile

insolven·cy [in'salvənsi] s (-cies) insolvenza

insomnia [in'samni·ə] s insonnia

insomuch [ˌinso'mʌtʃ] adv fino al punto; **insomuch as** giacché, visto che; **insomuch that** fino al punto che

inspect [in'spekt] tr ispezionare

inspection [in'spekʃən] s ispezione

inspector [in'spektər] s ispettore m

inspiration [ˌinspi'reʃən] s ispirazione

inspire [in'spair] tr & intr ispirare

install [in'stɔl] tr istallare

installment [in'stɔlmənt] s rata; (of a book) dispensa; **in installments** a rate

install'ment plan' s pagamento rateale; **on the installment plan** con facilitazioni di pagamento

instance ['instəns] s esempio; (law) istanza; **for instance** per esempio

instant ['instənt] adj istantaneo || s istante m; mese m corrente

instantaneous [ˌinstən'teni·əs] adj istantaneo

instantly ['instəntli] adv immediatamente, istantaneamente

instead [in'sted] adv invece; **instead of** invece di

in'step' s collo del piede

instigate ['insti ˌget] tr istigare

instigation [ˌinsti'geʃən] s istigazione

in·still' tr instillare, istillare

instinct ['instiŋkt] s istinto

instinctive [in'stiŋktiv] adj istintivo

institute ['insti ˌtjut] or ['insti ˌtut] s istituto || tr istituire

institution [ˌinsti'tjuʃən] or [ˌinsti-'tuʃən] s istituzione

institutionalize [ˌinsti'tjuʃənə ˌlaiz] or [ˌinsti'tuʃənə ˌlaiz] tr istituzionalizzare

instruct [in'strʌkt] tr istruire

instruction [in'strʌkʃən] s istruzione

instructive [in'strʌktiv] adj istruttivo

instructor [in'strʌktər] s istruttore m

instrument ['instrəmənt] s strumento; (law) istrumento || ['instrə ˌment] tr strumentare

instrumental [ˌinstrə'mentəl] adj strumentale; **to be instrumental in** contribuire a

instrumentalist [ˌinstrə'mentəlist] s strumentista mf

instrumentali·ty [ˌinstrəmən'tæliti] s (-ties) mediazione, aiuto

in'strument fly'ing s volo strumentale

in'strument pan'el s (aut) cruscotto

insubordinate [ˌinsə'bɔrdinit] adj insubordinato

insufferable [in'sʌfərəbəl] adj insoffribile

insufficient [ˌinsə'fiʃənt] adj insufficiente

insular ['insələr] or ['insjulər] adj insulare; (e.g., attitude) gretto

insulate ['insə ˌlet] tr isolare

in'sulating tape' ['insəletiŋ] s nastro isolante

insulation [ˌinsə'leʃən] s isolamento

insulator ['insə ˌletər] s isolatore m

insulin ['insəlin] s insulina

insult ['insʌlt] s insulto || [in'sʌlt] tr insultare, insolentire

insulting [in'sʌltiŋ] adj insultante

insurance [in'ʃurəns] s assicurazione

insure [in'ʃur] tr assicurare

insurer [in'ʃurər] s assicuratore m

insurgent [in'sʌrdʒənt] adj & s insorgente mf

insurmountable [ˌinsər'mauntəbəl] adj insormontabile

insurrection [ˌinsə'rekʃən] s insurrezione

insusceptible [ˌinsə'septibəl] adj non suscettibile

intact [in'tækt] adj intatto, integro

in'take' s (place of taking in) entrata; (act of taking in) ammissione; (mach) presa, immissione, aspirazione

in'take man'ifold' s collettore m d'ammissione

intangible [in'tændʒibəl] adj intangibile; (fig) vago, inafferrabile

integer ['intidʒər] s numero intero

integral ['intigrəl] adj integrale; (part of a whole) integrante || s (math) integrale m

integration [ˌinti'greʃən] s integrazione

integrity [in'tegriti] s integrità f

intellect ['intə ˌlekt] s intelletto

intellectual [ˌintə'lekt/u·əl] adj & s intellettuale mf

intelligence [in'telidʒəns] s intelligenza; informazione, conoscenza

intel'ligence bu'reau s ufficio spionaggi
intel'ligence quo'tient s quoziente m d'intelligenza
intelligent [ɪn'telɪdʒənt] adj intelligente
intelligentsia [ɪn ‚telɪ'dʒentsɪ‑ə] or [ɪn‑ ‚telɪ'gentsɪ‑ə] s intelighenzia, intellettualità f
intelligible [ɪn'telɪdʒɪbəl] adj intelligibile, comprensibile
intemperance [ɪn'tempərəns] s intemperanza, sregolatezza
intemperate [ɪn'tempərɪt] adj intemperante; (climate) rigoroso
intend [ɪn'tend] tr intendere, prefiggersi; (to mean for a particular purpose) destinare; (to signify) voler dire
intendance [ɪn'tendəns] s intendenza
intendant [ɪn'tendənt] s intendente m
intended [ɪn'tendɪd] adj & s (coll) promesso, promessa
intense [ɪn'tens] adj intenso
intensi·fy [ɪn'tensɪ‑faɪ] v (pret & pp ‑fied) tr intensificare, rinforzare; (phot) rinforzare ‖ intr intensificarsi, rinforzarsi
intensi·ty [ɪn'tensɪti] s (‑ties) intensità f
intensive [ɪn'tensɪv] adj intensivo
intent [ɪn'tent] adj intento, attento; **intent on** deciso a ‖ s (purpose) intento, scopo; (meaning) significato; **to all intents and purposes** virtualmente, in realtà
intention [ɪn'tenʃən] s intenzione
intentional [ɪn'tenʃənəl] adj intenzionale, deliberato
intentionally [ɪn'tenʃənəli] adv apposta, deliberatamente
in·ter [ɪn'tʌr] v (pret & pp ‑terred; ger ‑terring) tr interrare, inumare
interact [‚ɪntər'ækt] intr esercitare un'azione reciproca
interaction [‚ɪntər'ækʃən] s azione reciproca
inter·breed [‚ɪntər'brid] s (pret & pp ‑bred ['bred]) tr incrociare ‖ intr incrociarsi
intercalate [ɪn'tʌrkə‚let] tr intercalare
intercede [‚ɪntər'sid] intr intercedere
intercept [‚ɪntər'sept] tr intercettare
interceptor [‚ɪntər'septər] s (person) intercettatore m; (aer) intercettore m
interchange ['ɪntər‚tʃendʒ] s interscambio; (on a highway) svincolo autostradale ‖ [‚ɪntər't/əndʒ] tr scambiare ‖ intr scambiarsi
intercollegiate [‚ɪntərkə'lidʒɪ‑ɪt] adj interscolastico, fra università
intercom ['ɪntər‚kɑm] s citofono
intercourse ['ɪntər‚kors] s comunicazione; (of products, ideas, etc.) scambio; (copulation) copula, coito; **to have intercourse** accoppiarsi sessualmente
intercross [‚ɪntər'krɔs] or [‚ɪntər‑ 'krɑs] tr incrociare ‖ intr incrociarsi
interdict ['ɪntər‚dɪkt] s interdetto ‖ [‚ɪntər'dɪkt] tr interdire; **to interdict s.o. from** + ger interdire a qlcu di + inf
interest ['ɪntərɪst] or ['ɪntrɪst] s in

teresse m; **the interests** i potenti ‖ ['ɪntərɪst], ['ɪntrɪst] or ['ɪntə‚rest] tr interessare
interested ['ɪntrɪstɪd] or ['ɪntə‚restɪd] adj interessato
interesting ['ɪntrɪstɪŋ] or ['ɪntə‚restɪŋ] adj interessante
interfere [‚ɪntər'fɪr] intr interferire; (sports) ostacolare l'azione; **to interfere with** interferire in
interference [‚ɪntər'fɪrəns] s interferenza
interim ['ɪntərɪm] adj interino ‖ s interim m; **in the interim** frattanto
interior [ɪn'tɪrɪ‑ər] adj & s interno
interject [‚ɪntər'dʒekt] tr interporre ‖ intr interporsi
interjection [‚ɪntər'dʒekʃən] s interposizione; esclamazione; (gram) interiezione
interlard [‚ɪntər'lɑrd] tr infiorare, lardellare
interline [‚ɪntər'laɪn] tr scrivere nell'interlinea di; (a garment) foderare con ovattina
interlining ['ɪntər‚laɪnɪŋ] s soppanno
interlink [‚ɪntər'lɪŋk] tr concatenare
interlock [‚ɪntər'lɑk] tr connettere ‖ intr connettersi
interlope [‚ɪntər'lop] intr intromettersi; trafficare senza permesso
interloper [‚ɪntər'lopər] s intruso
interlude ['ɪntər‚lud] s interludio; (theat) intermezzo
intermarriage [‚ɪntər ‚mærɪdʒ] s matrimonio tra consanguinei; matrimonio fra membri di razze diverse
intermediar·y [‚ɪntər'midɪ‚eri] adj intermediario ‖ (‑ies) s intermediario
intermediate [‚ɪntər'midɪ‑ɪt] adj intermedio
interment [ɪn'tʌrmənt] s inumazione
intermingle [‚ɪntər'mɪŋgəl] tr mescolare ‖ intr mescolarsi
intermission [‚ɪntər'mɪʃən] s interruzione; (theat) intervallo
intermittent [‚ɪntər'mɪtənt] adj intermittente
intermix [‚ɪntər'mɪks] tr mₑscolare ‖ intr mescolarsi
intern ['ɪntʌrn] s interno ‖ [ɪn'tʌrn] tr internare
internal [ɪn'tʌrnəl] adj interno
inter'nal-combus'tion en'gine s motore m a combustione interna, motore m a scoppio
inter'nal rev'enue s fisco
international [‚ɪntər'næʃənəl] adj internazionale
in'terna'tional date' line' s linea del cambiamento di data
internationalize [‚ɪntər'næʃənə‚laɪz] tr internazionalizzare
internecine [‚ɪntər'nisɪn] adj micidiale, sanguinario
internee [‚ɪntʌr'ni] s internato
internist [ɪn'tʌrnɪst] s internista mf
internment [ɪn'tʌrnmənt] s internamento
internship ['ɪntʌrn‚ʃɪp] s tirocinio **in** un ospedale, internato

interpellate [ˌɪntərˈpɛlet] or [ɪnˈtʌrpɪˌlet] *tr* interpellare
interplanetary [ˌɪntərˈplænəˌtɛri] *adj* interplanetario
interplay [ˈɪntərˌple] *s* azione reciproca
interpolate [ɪnˈtʌrpəˌlet] *tr* interpolare
interpose [ˌɪntərˈpoz] *tr* frapporre
interpret [ɪnˈtʌrprɪt] *tr* interpretare
interpreter [ɪnˈtʌrprətər] *s* interprete *mf*
interrogate [ɪnˈtɛrəˌget] *tr* & *intr* interrogare
interrogation [ɪnˌtɛrəˈgeʃən] *s* interrogazione
interroga'tion mark' or **point'** *s* punto interrogativo
interrupt [ˌɪntəˈrʌpt] *tr* interrompere
interruption [ˌɪntəˈrʌpʃən] *s* interruzione
interscholastic [ˌɪntərskəˈlæstɪk] *adj* interscolastico
intersect [ˌɪntərˈsɛkt] *tr* intersecare ‖ *intr* intersecarsi
intersection [ˌɪntərˈsɛkʃən] *s* (*of streets, roads, etc.*) crocevia *m;* (geom) intersezione
intersperse [ˌɪntərˈspʌrs] *tr* cospargere, inframezzare
interstellar [ˌɪntərˈstɛlər] *adj* interstellare
interstice [ɪnˈtʌrstɪs] *s* interstizio
intertwine [ˌɪntərˈtwaɪn] *tr* intrecciare ‖ *intr* intrecciarsi
interval [ˈɪntərvəl] *s* intervallo; **at intervals** a intervalli; di tanto in tanto
intervene [ˌɪntərˈvin] *intr* intervenire; (*to happen*) succedere
intervening [ˌɪntərˈvinɪŋ] *adj*—**in the intervening time** nel frattempo
intervention [ˌɪntərˈvɛnʃən] *s* intervenzione
interview [ˈɪntərˌvju] *s* intervista ‖ *tr* intervistare
inter·weave [ˌɪntərˈwiv] *v* (*pret* -**wove** [ˈwov] or -**weaved;** *pp* -**wove, -woven** or -**weaved**) *tr* intessere
intestate [ɪnˈtɛstet] or [ɪnˈtɛstɪt] *adj* intestato
intestine [ɪnˈtɛstɪn] *s* intestino
inthrall [ɪnˈθrɔl] *tr* affascinare, incantare; (*to subjugate*) asservire, soggiogare
inthrone [ɪnˈθron] *tr* mettere sul trono, intronizzare; esaltare, innalzare
intima·cy [ˈɪntɪməsi] *s* (**-cies**) intimità *f*
intimate [ˈɪntɪmɪt] *adj* & *s* intimo ‖ [ˈɪntɪˌmet] *tr* insinuare
intimation [ˌɪntɪˈmeʃən] *s* insinuazione
intimidate [ɪnˈtɪmɪˌdet] *tr* intimidire
into [ˈɪntu] or [ˈɪntʊ] *prep* in; verso; contro
intolerant [ɪnˈtalərənt] *adj* & *s* intollerante *mf*, insofferente *mf*
intomb [ɪnˈtum] *tr* inumare, seppellire
intombment [ɪnˈtummənt] *s* sepoltura
intonation [ˌɪntoˈneʃən] *s* intonazione
intone [ɪnˈton] *tr* intonare ‖ *intr* salmodiare
intoxicant [ɪnˈtaksɪkənt] *s* bevanda alcoolica

intoxicate [ɪnˈtaksɪˌket] *tr* ubriacare; esilarare; (*to poison*) avvelenare, intossicare
intoxication [ɪnˌtaksɪˈkeʃən] *s* ubriachezza; ebbrezza, allegria; (*poisoning*) avvelenamento, intossicazione
intractable [ɪnˈtræktəbəl] *adj* intrattabile
intransigent [ɪnˈtrænsɪdʒənt] *adj* & *s* intransigente *mf*
intransitive [ɪnˈtrænsɪtɪv] *adj* intransitivo
intravenous [ˌɪntrəˈvinəs] *adj* intravenoso, endovenoso
intrench [ɪnˈtrɛntʃ] *tr* & *intr* var of **entrench**
intrepid [ɪnˈtrɛpɪd] *adj* intrepido
intrepidity [ˌɪntrɪˈpɪdɪti] *s* intrepidezza
intricate [ˈɪntrɪkɪt] *adj* intricato
intrigue [ɪnˈtrig] or [ˈɪntrig] *s* intrigo; tresca, intrigo amoroso; (theat) intreccio ‖ [ɪnˈtrig] *tr* incuriosire ‖ *intr* intrigare; trescare
intrinsic(al) [ɪnˈtrɪnsɪk(əl)] *adj* intrinseco
introduce [ˌɪntrəˈdjus] or [ˌɪntrəˈdus] *tr* introdurre; (*a product*) lanciare; (*a person*) presentare
introduction [ˌɪntrəˈdʌkʃən] *s* introduzione; presentazione
introductory [ˌɪntrəˈdʌktəri] *adj* introduttivo
introit [ˈɪntro·ɪt] *s* (eccl) introito
introspective [ˌɪntrəˈspɛktɪv] *adj* introspettivo
introvert [ˈɪntrəˌvʌrt] *adj* & *s* introverso
intrude [ɪnˈtrud] *intr* intrudersi, intrufolarsi
intruder [ɪnˈtrudər] *s* intruso; importuno
intrusion [ɪnˈtruʒən] *s* intrusione
intrusive [ɪnˈtrusɪv] *adj* invadente
intrust [ɪnˈtrʌst] *tr* affidare, confidare
intuition [ˌɪntuˈɪʃən] or [ˌɪntjuˈɪʃən] *s* intuizione, intuito
inundate [ˈɪnənˌdet] *tr* inondare
inundation [ˌɪnənˈdeʃən] *s* inondazione
inure [ɪnˈjur] *tr* indurire, assuefare ‖ *intr* entrare in vigore; **to inure to** ridondare in favore di
invade [ɪnˈved] *tr* invadere
invader [ɪnˈvedər] *s* invasore *m*
invalid [ɪnˈvælɪd] *adj* (*non valid*) invalido ‖ [ˈɪnvəlɪd] *adj* (*person*) invalido; (*thing*) povero; (*diet*) per malati ‖ [ˈɪnvəlɪd] *s* invalido
invalidate [ɪnˈvæliˌdet] *tr* invalidare
invalidity [ˌɪnvəˈlɪdɪti] *s* invalidità *f*
invaluable [ɪnˈvælju·əbəl] *adj* inestimabile, inapprezzabile
invariable [ɪnˈvɛri·əbəl] *adj* invariabile
invasion [ɪnˈveʒən] *s* invasione
invective [ɪnˈvɛktɪv] *s* invettiva
inveigh [ɪnˈve] *intr*—**to inveigh against** inveire contro
inveigle [ɪnˈvegəl] or [ɪnˈvigəl] *tr* sedurre, abbindolare
invent [ɪnˈvɛnt] *tr* inventare
invention [ɪnˈvɛnʃən] *s* invenzione

inventiveness [ɪn'vɛntɪvnɪs] *s* inventiva
inventor [ɪn'vɛntər] *s* inventore *m*
inven·to·ry ['ɪnvən,tori] *s* (-ries) inventario || *v* (*pret* & *pp* -ried) *tr* inventariare
inverse [ɪn'vʌrs] *adj* & *s* inverso
inversion [ɪn'vʌrʒən] or [ɪn'vʌrʃən] *s* inversione
invert ['ɪnvʌrt] *s* invertito || [ɪn'vʌrt] *tr* invertire
invertebrate [ɪn'vʌrtɪ,bret] or [ɪn'vʌrtɪbrɪt] *adj* & *s* invertebrato
invest [ɪn'vɛst] *tr* investire || *intr* fare un investimento; fare investimenti
investigate [ɪn'vɛstɪ,get] *tr* investigare
investigation [ɪn,vɛstɪ'geʃən] *s* investigazione
investigator [ɪn'vɛstɪ,getər] *s* investigatore *m*
investment [ɪn'vɛstmənt] *s* (*of money*) investimento; (*e.g., with an office*) investitura; (*siege*) assedio
investor [ɪn'vɛstər] *s* investitore *m*
inveterate [ɪn'vɛtərɪt] *adj* inveterato
invidious [ɪn'vɪdɪ·əs] *adj* irritante, odioso
invigorate [ɪn'vɪgə,ret] *tr* invigorire
invigorating [ɪn'vɪgə,retɪŋ] *adj* ritemprante, ricostituente, rinforzante
invincible [ɪn'vɪnsɪbəl] *adj* invincibile
invisible [ɪn'vɪzɪbəl] *adj* invisibile
invis'ible ink' *s* inchiostro simpatico
invitation [,ɪnvɪ'teʃən] *s* invito
invite [ɪn'vaɪt] *tr* invitare
inviting [ɪn'vaɪtɪŋ] *adj* invitante, attrattivo; (*food*) appetitoso; accogliente
invoice ['ɪnvɔɪs] *s* fattura; **as per invoice** secondo fattura || *tr* fatturare
invoke [ɪn'vok] *tr* invocare; (*a spirit*) evocare
involuntary [ɪn'valən,tɛri] *adj* involontario
involve [ɪn'valv] *tr* involvere, includere; occupare; (*to bring unpleasantness upon*) implicare, coinvolgere; complicare
invulnerable [ɪn'vʌlnərəbəl] *adj* invulnerabile
inward ['ɪnwərd] *adj* interno || *adv* al di dentro, verso l'interno
iodide ['aɪ·ə,daɪd] *s* ioduro
iodine ['aɪ·ə,din] *s* iodio || ['aɪ·ə,daɪn] *s* tintura di iodio
ion ['aɪ·ən] or ['aɪ·an] *s* ione *m*
ionize ['aɪ·ə,naɪz] *tr* ionizzare
IOU ['aɪ,o'ju] *s* (letterword) (**I owe you**) cambiale *f*, pagherò *m*
I.Q. ['aɪ'kju] *s* (letterword) (**intelligence quotient**) quoziente *m* d'intelligenza
Iranian [aɪ'renɪ·ən] *adj* & *s* iraniano
Ira·qi [ɪ'raki] *adj* iracheno || *s* (-qis) iracheno
irate ['aɪret] or [aɪ'ret] *adj* irato
ire [aɪr] *s* ira, collera
Ireland ['aɪrlənd] *s* l'Irlanda *f*
iris ['aɪrɪs] *s* iride *f*
I'rish·man *s* (-men) irlandese *m*
I'rish stew' *s* stufato all'irlandese
I'rish·wom'an *s* (-wom'en) irlandese *f*
irk [ʌrk] *tr* infastidire, annoiare

irksome ['ʌrksəm] *adj* fastidioso
iron ['aɪ·ərn] *adj* ferreo || *s* ferro; (*to press clothes*) ferro da stiro; **irons** ferri *mpl*; **strike while the iron is hot** batti il ferro fin ch'è caldo || *tr* (*clothes*) stirare; **to iron out** (*a difficulty*) (coll) appianare
i'ron·bound' *adj* ferrato; (*unyielding*) ferreo, inflessibile; (*rock-bound*) roccioso, scabroso
ironclad ['aɪ·ərn,klæd] *adj* corazzato, blindato; inflessibile, ferreo
i'ron constitu'tion *s* salute *f* di ferro
i'ron cur'tain *s* cortina di ferro
i'ron horse' *s* locomotiva a vapore
ironic(al) [aɪ'ranɪk(əl)] *adj* ironico
ironing ['aɪ·ərnɪŋ] *s* stiratura; **roba** stirata; roba da stirare
i'roning board' *s* tavolo or asse *m* da stiro
i'ron lung' *s* polmone *m* d'acciaio
i'ron·ware' *s* ferrame *m*
i'ron will' *s* volontà *f* di ferro
i'ron·work' *s* lavoro in ferro; **ironworks** *ssg* ferriera
i'ron-work'er *s* ferraio; metalmeccanico, siderurgico
iro·ny ['aɪrəni] *s* (-nies) ironia
irradiate [ɪ'redɪ,et] *tr* irradiare || *intr* irradiare, irradiarsi
irrational [ɪ'ræʃənəl] *adj* irrazionale
irrecoverable [,ɪrɪ'kʌvərəbəl] *adj* irrecuperabile
irredeemable [,ɪrɪ'diməbəl] *adj* irredimibile
irrefutable [,ɪrɪ'fjutəbəl] *adj* irrefutabile
irregular [ɪ'rɛgjələr] *adj* irregolare || *s* (mil) irregolare *m*
irrelevance [ɪ'rɛləvəns] *s* irrilevanza
irrelevant [ɪ'rɛləvənt] *adj* irrilevante
irreligious [,ɪrɪ'lɪdʒəs] *adj* irreligioso
irremediable [,ɪrɪ'midɪ·əbəl] *adj* irrimediabile
irremovable [,ɪrɪ'muvəbəl] *adj* irremovibile, inamovibile
irreplaceable [,ɪrɪ'plesəbəl] *adj* insostituibile
irrepressible [,ɪrɪ'prɛsɪbəl] *adj* irreprimibile, incontenibile
irreproachable [,ɪrɪ'protʃəbəl] *adj* irreprensibile
irresistible [,ɪrɪ'zɪstɪbəl] *adj* irresistibile
irrespective [,ɪrɪ'spɛktɪv] *adj*—**irrespective of** senza riguardo a
irresponsible [,ɪrɪ'spansɪbəl] *adj* irresponsabile
irretrievable [,ɪrɪ'trivəbəl] *adj* irrecuperabile
irreverent [ɪ'rɛvərənt] *adj* irriverente
irrevocable [ɪ'rɛvəkəbəl] *adj* irrevocabile
irrigate ['ɪrɪ,get] *tr* irrigare
irrigation [,ɪrɪ'geʃən] *s* irrigazione
irritant ['ɪrɪtənt] *adj* & *s* irritante *m*
irritate ['ɪrɪ,tet] *tr* irritare
irritation [,ɪrɪ'teʃən] *s* irritazione
irruption [ɪ'rʌpʃən] *s* irruzione
isinglass ['aɪzɪŋ,glæs] or ['aɪzɪŋ,glas] *s* (*gelatine*) colla di pesce; mica
Islam ['ɪsləm] or [ɪs'lam] *s* l'Islam *m*

island ['aɪlənd] *adj* isolano || *s* isola; (*for safety of pedestrians*) salvagente *m*

islander ['aɪləndər] *s* isolano

isle [aɪl] *s* isoletta

isolate ['aɪsə‚let] or ['ɪsə‚let] *tr* isolare

isolation [‚aɪsə'leʃən] or [‚ɪsə'leʃən] *s* isolamento

isolationist [‚aɪsə'leʃənɪst] or [‚ɪsə'leʃənɪst] *s* isolazionista *mf*

isosceles [aɪ'sɑsə‚liz] *adj* isoscele

isotope ['aɪsə‚top] *s* isotopo

Israel ['ɪzrɪ‚əl] *s* l'Israele *m*

Israe·li [ɪz'reli] *adj* israeliano || *s* (**-lis** [liz]) israeliano

Israelite ['ɪzrɪ‚ə‚laɪt] *adj & s* israelita *mf*

issuance ['ɪʃu‚əns] *s* (*of stamps, stocks, bonds, etc.*) emissione; (*e.g., of clothes*) distribuzione; (*of a law*) emanazione

issue ['ɪʃu] *s* (*outlet*) uscita; distribuzione; (*result*) conseguenza; (*offspring*) prole *f;* (*of a magazine*) puntata, fascicolo; (*of a bond*) emissione; (*yield*) prodotto; (*of a law*) promulgazione; (pathol) flusso; **at issue** in discussione; **to face the issue** affrontare la situazione; **to force the issue** forzare la soluzione; **to take issue with** non essere d'accordo con, dissentire da || *tr* (*e.g., a book*) pubblicare; (*bonds, orders*) emettere; (*a communiqué*) diramare; (*e.g., food*) distribuire || *intr* uscire; **to issue from** provenire da

isthmus ['ɪsməs] *s* istmo

it [ɪt] *pron pers* esso, essa; lo, la; **it is**

I sono io; **it is raining** piove; **it is four o'clock** sono le quattro

Italian [ɪ'tæljən] *adj & s* italiano

Ital'ian-speak'ing *adj* italofono

italic [ɪ'tælɪc] *adj* (typ) corsivo || **italics** *s* (typ) corsivo || **Italic** *adj* italico

italicize [ɪ'tælɪ‚saɪz] *tr* stampare in carattere corsivo; sottolineare

Italy ['ɪtəli] *s* l'Italia *f*

itch [ɪtʃ] *s* prurito; (pathol) rogna; (*eagerness*) (fig) pizzicore *m* || *tr* prudere, e.g., **his foot itches him** gli prude il piede || *intr* (*said of a part of body*) prudere; (*said of a person*) avere il prurito; **to itch to** avere il pizzicore di

itch·y ['ɪtʃi] *adj* (**-ier; -iest**) che prude; (pathol) rognoso

item ['aɪtəm] *s* articolo; notizia; (*on the agenda*) questione; (slang) notizia scottante

itemize ['aɪtə‚maɪz] *tr* dettagliare, specificare

itinerant [aɪ'tɪnərənt] or [ɪ'tɪnərənt] *adj* itinerante, ambulante || *s* viaggiatore *m*, viandante *m*

itinerar·y [aɪ'tɪnə‚reri] or [ɪ'tɪnə‚reri] *adj* itinerario || *s* (**-ies**) itinerario

its [ɪts] *adj & pron poss* il suo

itself [ɪt'sɛlf] *pron pers* sé stesso; si, e.g., **it opened itself** si è aperto

ivied ['aɪvid] *adj* coperto di edera

ivo·ry ['aɪvəri] *adj* d'avorio || *s* (**-ries**) avorio; **ivories** (slang) tasti *mpl* del piano; (slang) palle *fpl* da bigliardo; (*dice*) (slang) dadi *mpl;* (slang) denti *mpl*

i'vory tow'er *s* torre *f* d'avorio

ivy ['aɪvi] *s* (**ivies**) edera

J

J, j [dʒe] *s* decima lettera dell'alfabeto inglese

jab [dʒæb] *s* puntata; (*prick*) puntura; (*with elbow*) gomitata || *v* (*pret & pp* **jabbed;** *ger* **jabbing**) *tr* pugnalare; pungere; dare una gomitata a || *intr* dare colpi

jabber ['dʒæbər] *s* borbottamento, ciarla || *tr & intr* borbottare, ciarlare

jack [dʒæk] *s* (*for lifting heavy objects*) cricco, martinetto; (*jackass*) asino; (*device for turning a spit*) girarrosto; (*to remove a boot*) cavastivali *m;* (*cards*) fante *m;* (*bowling*) pallino; (*rad & telv*) jack *m;* (*elec*) presa; (slang) soldi *mpl;* **every man jack** ognuno, tutti *mpl* || **Jack** *s* marinaio; (*coll*) buonuomo || *tr*—**to jack up** alzare col cricco; (*prices*) (coll) alzare

jackal ['dʒækəl] *s* sciacallo

jack'ass' *s* asino

jack'daw' *s* cornacchia

jacket ['dʒækɪt] *s* giacca; (*of boiled*

potatoes) buccia; (*of book*) sopraccoperta; (*metal casing*) camicia

jack'ham'mer *s* martello perforatore

jack'-in-the-box' *s* scatola a sorpresa

jack'knife' *s* (**-knives**) coltello a serramanico; (*sports*) salto a pesce

jack'-of-all'-trades' *s* factotum *m*

jack-o'-lantern ['dʒækə‚læntərn] *s* lanterna a forma di testa umana fatta con una zucca; fuoco fatuo

jack'pot' *s* monte *m* premi; **to hit the jackpot** (slang) vincere un terno al lotto

jack' rab'bit *s* lepre nordamericana di taglia grande

jack'screw' *s* cricco a verme

jack'-tar' *s* (coll) marinaio

jade [dʒed] *adj* di giada, come la giada || *s* (*ornamental stone*) giada; (*wornout horse*) ronzino; (*disreputable woman*) donnaccia || *tr* logorare

jad'ed ['dʒedɪd] *adj* logoro, stanco; (*appetite*) stucco

jag [dʒæg] *s* slabbratura; **to have a jag on** (slang) avere la sbornia

jagged ['dʒægɪd] *adj* dentato, slabbrato

jaguar ['dʒægwɑr] *s* giaguaro

jail [dʒel] *s* prigione *f;* **to break jail** evadere dal carcere || *tr* carcerare

jail'bird' *s* galeotto, remo di galera

jail'break' *s* evasione *f* dal carcere

jailer ['dʒelər] *s* carceriere *m*

jalop·y [dʒə'lɑpi] *s* (-ies) carcassa, trespolo, trabiccolo

jam [dʒæm] *s* stretta, compressione; *(in traffic)* imbottigliamento; *(preserve)* marmellata, confettura; *(difficult situation)* (coll) pasticcio || *v (pret & pp* **jammed;** *ger* **jamming)** *tr* stipare; *(e.g., one's finger)* schiacciare, schiacciarsi; (rad) disturbare; **to jam on the brakes** bloccare i freni || *intr* schiacciarsi; *(said of firearms)* incepparsi; (mach) grippare

jamb [dʒæm] *s* stipite *m*

jamboree [,dʒæmbə'ri] *s* riunione nazionale di giovani esploratori; (coll) riunione

James [dʒemz] *s* Giacomo

jamming ['dʒæmɪŋ] *s* radiodisturbo

jam-packed ['dʒæm'pækt] *adj* gremito, pieno fino all'orlo

jangle ['dʒæŋgəl] *s* suono stridente; *(quarrel)* baruffa || *tr* fare suoni stridenti con || *intr* stridere; litigare

janitor ['dʒænɪtər] *s* portiere *m*

janitress ['dʒænɪtrɪs] *s* portinaia

January ['dʒænju,ɛri] *s* gennaio

ja·pan [dʒə'pæn] *s* lacca giapponese; oggetto di lacca || *v (pret & pp* **-panned;** *ger* **-panning)** *tr* laccare || **Japan** *s* il Giappone

Japa·nese [,dʒæpə'niz] *adj* giapponese || *s* (**-nese**) giapponese *mf*

Jap'anese bee'tle *s* scarabeo giapponese

Jap'anese lan'tern *s* lampioncino alla veneziana

Jap'anese persim'mon *s* cachi *m*

jar [dʒɑr] *s* barattolo; *(earthenware container)* orcio, giara; discordanza; *(jolt)* scossa; (fig) brutta sorpresa; **on the jar** *(said of a door)* socchiuso || *v (pret & pp* **jarred;** *ger* **jarring)** *tr* scuotere; far stridere || *intr* vibrare; stridere; essere in conflitto; **to jar on** irritare

jardiniere [,dʒɑrdɪ'nɪr] *s* *(pot)* vaso da fiori; giardiniera

jargon ['dʒɑrgən] *s* gergo

jasmine ['dʒæsmɪn] *or* ['dʒæzmɪn] *s* gelsomino

jasper ['dʒæspər] *s* diaspro

jaundice ['dʒɔndɪs] *or* ['dʒɑndɪs] *s* itterizia; (fig) invidia

jaundiced ['dʒɔndɪst] *or* ['dʒɑndɪst] *adj* itterico; (fig) invidioso

jaunt [dʒɔnt] *or* [dʒɑnt] *s* passeggiata, gita

jaun·ty ['dʒɔnti] *or* ['dʒɑnti] *adj* (-tier; -tiest) disinvolto; elegante

Java·nese [,dʒævə'niz] *adj* giavanese || *s* (**-nese**) giavanese *m*

javelin ['dʒævlɪn] *or* ['dʒævəlɪn] *s* giavellotto

jaw [dʒɔ] *s* mascella, mandibola; (mach) ganascia; **jaws** fauci *fpl;* gola, stretta || *tr* (slang) rimproverare ||

intr (slang) chiacchierare; (slang) fare la predica

jaw'bone' *s* mascella, mandibola

jaw'break'er *s* (coll) parola difficile da pronunciare; (coll) caramella durissima; (mach) frantoio a mascelle

jay [dʒe] *s* (orn) ghiandaia; (coll) sempliciotto

jay'walk' *intr* attraversare la strada contro la luce rossa del semaforo

jay'walk'er *s* (coll) pedone distratto che attraversa la strada contro la luce rossa del semaforo

jazz [dʒæz] *s* jazz *m;* (slang) spirito || *tr*—**to jazz up** (slang) dar vita a

jazz' band' *s* orchestra jazz

jealous ['dʒɛləs] *adj* geloso; *(envious)* invidioso; vigilante

jealous·y ['dʒɛləsi] *s* (-ies) gelosia; invidia; vigilanza

jean [dʒin] *s* tela cruda; **jeans** pantaloni *mpl* di tela cruda

jeep [dʒip] *s* gip *f,* jeep *f*

jeer [dʒɪr] *s* beffa || *tr* beffare || *intr* beffarsi; **to jeer at** motteggiare

Jeho'vah's Wit'nesses [dʒɪ'hovəs] *spl* Testimoni *mpl* di Geova

jell [dʒɛl] *s* gelatina || *intr* *(to congeal)* gelatinizzarsi; *(to become substantial)* cristallizzarsi

jel·ly ['dʒɛli] *s* (-lies) gelatina || *v (pret & pp* **-lied)** *tr* gelatinizzare || *intr* gelatinizzarsi

jel'ly·fish' *s* medusa; *(weak person)* (coll) fiaccone *m*

jeopardize ['dʒɛpər,daɪz] *tr* compromettere, mettere a repentaglio

jeopardy ['dʒɛpərdi] *s* pericolo, repentaglio

jeremiad [,dʒɛrɪ'maɪ·æd] *s* geremiade *f*

Jericho ['dʒɛrɪ,ko] *s* Gerico *f*

jerk [dʒʌrk] *s* strattone *m,* scatto; tic *m;* *(stupid person)* scempio, sciocco; **by jerks** a scatti || *tr* tirare a strattoni; *(meat)* essiccare || *intr* sobbalzare

jerked' beef' *s* fetta di carne di bue essiccata

jerkin ['dʒʌrkɪn] *s* giubbetto

jerk'wa'ter *adj* di scarsa importanza

jerk·y ['dʒʌrki] *adj* (-ier; -iest) sussultante; *(style)* disuguale

Jerome [dʒə'rom] *s* Gerolamo

jersey ['dʒʌrzi] *s* jersey *m,* maglione *m*

Jerusalem [dʒɪ'rusələm] *s* Gerusalemme *f*

jest [dʒɛst] *s* scherzo, burla; **in jest** per celia || *intr* scherzare

jester ['dʒɛstər] *s* motteggiatore *m,* burlone *m;* (hist) buffone *m*

Jesuit ['dʒɛʒu·ɪt] *or* ['dʒɛzju·ɪt] *adj & s* gesuita *m*

Jesuitic(al) [,dʒɛʒu'ɪtɪk(əl)] *or* [,dʒɛzju'ɪtɪk(əl)] *adj* gesuitico

Jesus ['dʒizəs] *s* Gesù *m*

Je'sus Christ' *s* Gesù *m* Cristo

jet [dʒɛt] *adj* di giaietto || *s (of a fountain)* zampillo; *(stream shooting forth from nozzle)* getto; *(mineral; lustrous black)* giaietto; (aer) aereo a getto || *v (pret & pp* **jetted;** *ger* **jetting)** *tr* spruzzare || *intr* zampillare; volare in aereo a getto

jet' age' *s* era dell'aviogetto

jet'-black' *adj* nero come il carbone

jet' bomb'er *s* bombardiere *m* a reazione

jet' coal' *s* carbone *m* a lunga fiamma

jet' en'gine *s* motore *m* a reazione

jet' fight'er *s* caccia *m* a reazione

jet'lin'er *s* aviogetto da trasporto passeggeri

jet' plane' *s* aviogetto

jet' propul'sion *s* gettopropulsione

jetsam ['dʒɛtsəm] *s* relitto

jet' stream' *s* corrente *f* a getto; scappamento di motore a razzo

jettison ['dʒɛtɪsən] *s* (naut) alleggerimento || *tr* (naut) alleggerirsi di; (fig) disfarsi di

jet·ty ['dʒɛti] *s* (**-ties**) gettata; (*wharf*) molo, imbarcadero

Jew [dʒu] *s* giudeo

jewel ['dʒu·əl] *s* pietra preziosa; (*valuable personal ornament*) gioia, gioiello; (*of a watch*) rubino; (*costume jewelry*) gioia finta; (fig) valore *m*, gioiello

jew'el case' *s* scrigno, portagioie *m*

jeweler or **jeweller** ['dʒu·ələr] *s* gioielliere *m*, orefice *m*

jewelry ['dʒu·əlri] *s* gioielli *mpl*

jew'elry shop' *s* gioielleria

Jewess ['dʒu·ɪs] *s* giudea

Jewish ['dʒu·ɪʃ] *adj* giudeo

jews'-harp or **jew's-harp** ['dʒuz ˌharp] *s* scacciapensieri *m*

jib [dʒɪb] *s* (*of a crane*) (mach) braccio (di gru); (naut) fiocco, vela Marconi

jib' boom' *s* asta di fiocco

jibe [dʒaɪb] *s* burla, beffa || *intr* beffarsi; accordarsi; **to jibe at** beffarsi di

jif·fy ['dʒɪfi] *s*—**in a jiffy** (coll) in men che non si dica

jig [dʒɪg] *s* (*dance*) giga; **the jig is up** (slang) tutto è perduto

jigger ['dʒɪgər] *s* bicchierino di liquore d'un'oncia e mezza; (*flea*) pulce *f* tropicale; (*gadget*) (coll) aggeggio; (naut) bozzello; (min) crivello

jiggle ['dʒɪgəl] *s* scossa || *tr* scuotere, agitare || *intr* scuotersi

jig' saw' *s* sega da traforo

jig'saw puz'zle *s* gioco di pazienza, rompicapo

jilt [dʒɪlt] *tr* piantare

jim·my ['dʒɪmi] *s* (**-mies**) piccolo piede di porco || *v* (*pret* & *pp* **-mied**) *tr* scassinare; **to jimmy open** scassinare

jingle ['dʒɪŋgəl] *s* sonaglio, bubbolo; (*sound*) rumore *m* di sonagliera; cantilena, rima infantile || *tr* far suonare || *intr* tintinnare

jin·go ['dʒɪŋgo] *adj* sciovinista || *s* (**-goes**) sciovinista *mf*; **by jingo!** perbacco!

jingoism ['dʒɪŋgo ˌɪzəm] *s* sciovinismo

jinx [dʒɪŋks] *s* iettatura; (*person*) iettatore *m* || *tr* portare la iettatura a

jitters ['dʒɪtərz] *spl* (coll) nervosismo; **to have the jitters** (coll) essere nervoso

jittery ['dʒɪtəri] *adj* nervoso

job [dʒab] *s* (*piece of work*) lavoro;

(*task*) mansione; (*employment*) posto, impiego; (slang) furto; **by the job** a cottimo; **on the job** (slang) attento, sollecito; **to be out of a job** essere disoccupato; **to lie down on the job** (slang) dormire sul lavoro

job' anal'ysis *s* valutazione delle mansioni

jobber ['dʒabər] *s* grossista *mf*; (*pieceworker*) lavoratore *m* a cottimo; funzionario disonesto

job'hold'er *s* impiegato; (*in the government*) burocrate *m*

jobless ['dʒablɪs] *adj* disoccupato

job' lot' *s* (com) saldo

job' print'er *s* piccolo tipografo non specializzato

job' print'ing *s* piccolo lavoro tipografico

jockey ['dʒaki] *s* fantino || *tr* (*a horse*) montare; manovrare; (*to trick*) abbindolare

jockstrap ['dʒak ˌstræp] *s* sospensorio

jocose [dʒo'kos] *adj* giocoso

jocular ['dʒakjələr] *adj* scherzoso

jog [dʒag] *s* spinta; piccolo trotto || *v* (*pret* & *pp* **jogged**; *ger* **jogging**) *tr* spingere leggermente; (*the memory*) rinfrescare || *intr* barcollare; **to jog along** continuare col solito tran tran

jog' trot' *s* piccolo trotto; (fig) tran tran *m*

John [dʒan] *s* Giovanni *m*

John' Bull' *s* il tipico inglese; gli inglesi, il popolo inglese

John' Han'cock ['hænkak] *s* (coll) la firma

johnnycake ['dʒani ˌkek] *s* pane *m* di granturco

John'ny-come'-late'ly *s* (coll) ultimo arrivato

John'ny-jump'-up' *s* violetta, viola del pensiero

John'ny-on-the-spot' *s* (coll) persona sempre pronta

John' the Bap'tist *s* San Giovanni Battista

join [dʒɔɪn] *tr* giungere, congiungere; associarsi a; unire; (*e.g., a party*) farsi membro di; (*the army*) arruolarsi in; (*battle*) ingaggiare; (*to empty into*) sfociare in || *intr* congiungersi, unirsi; (*said, e.g., of two rivers*) confluire

joiner ['dʒɔɪnər] *s* falegname *m*; membro di molte società

joint [dʒɔɪnt] *adj* congiunto || *s* (*in a pipe*) giuntura; (*of bones*) giuntura, articolazione; (*hinge of book*) brachetta; (*in woodwork*) incastro, commettitura; (*of meat*) taglio; (mach) snodo; (*gambling den*) (slang) bisca; (elec) innesto; (slang) bettola; **out of joint** slogato; (fig) fuori luogo; **to throw** (*e.g., one's arm*) **out of joint** slogarsi

joint' account' *s* conto in comune

joint' commit'tee *s* commissione mista

jointly ['dʒɔɪntli] *adv* unitamente

joint' own'er *s* condomino

joint'-stock' com'pany *s* società *f* per azioni a responsabilità illimitata

joist [dʒɔɪst] *s* trave *f*

joke [dʒok] *s* burla, barzelletta; (*trifling matter*) cosa da nulla; (*person laughed at*) zimbello; **to tell a joke** raccontare una barzelletta; **to play a joke on** fare uno scherzo a || *tr*—**to joke one's way into** ottenere dicendo barzellette || *intr* burlare, dire storielle; **joking aside** senza scherzi

joker ['dʒokər] *s* burlone *m*, fumista *m*; (*wise guy*) saputello; (*hidden provision*) clausola ingannatrice; (*cards*) matta

jol·ly ['dʒali] *adj* (**-lier; -liest**) allegro, gaio || *adv* (coll) molto || *v* (*pret & pp* **-lied**) *tr* (coll) prendersi gioco di

jolt [dʒolt] *s* scossa || *tr* scuotere || *intr* sobbalzare

Jonah ['dʒonə] *s* Giona; (fig) uccello di mal augurio

jongleur ['dʒaŋglər] *s* giullare *m*

jonquil ['dʒaŋkwɪl] *s* giunchiglia

Jordan ['dʒordən] *s* (*country*) la Giordania; (*river*) Giordano

Jordanian [dʒor'denɪ·ən] *adj & s* giordano

josh [dʒaʃ] *tr & intr* (coll) canzonare

jostle ['dʒasəl] *s* spintone *m* || *tr* spingere || *intr* scontrarsi; farsi strada a gomitate

jot [dʒat] *s*—**I don't care a jot for** non mi importa un fico di || *v* (*pret & pp* **jotted;** *ger* **jotting**) *tr*—**to jot down** notare, gettar giù

jounce [dʒauns] *s* scossa || *tr* scuotere || *intr* sobbalzare

journal ['dʒarnəl] *s* (*newspaper*) giornale *m*; (*magazine*) rivista; (*daily record*) diario; (com) giornale *m*; (mach) perno; (naut) giornale *m* di bordo

journalese [ˌdʒarnə'liz] *s* linguaggio giornalistico

journalism ['dʒarnəˌlɪzəm] *s* giornalismo

journalist ['dʒarnəlɪst] *s* giornalista *mf*

journey ['dʒarni] *s* viaggio || *intr* viaggiare

jour'ney·man *s* (**-men**) operaio specializzato

joust [dʒast] *or* [dʒust] *or* [dʒaust] *s* giostra || *intr* giostrare

jovial ['dʒovɪ·əl] *adj* gioviale

jowl [dʒaul] *s* (*cheek*) guancia; (*jawbone*) mascella; (*of cattle*) giogaia; (*of fowl*) bargiglio; (*of fat person*) pappagorgia

joy [dʒɔɪ] *s* gioia, allegria; **to leap with joy** ballare dalla gioia

joyful ['dʒɔɪfəl] *adj* gioioso, festoso; **joyful over** lieto di

joyless ['dʒɔɪlɪs] *adj* senza gioia

joyous ['dʒɔɪ·əs] *adj* gioioso

joy' ride' *s* (coll) gita in auto; (coll) gita all'impazzata in auto

jubilant ['dʒubɪlənt] *adj* esultante

jubilation [ˌdʒubɪ'leʃən] *s* giubilo

jubilee ['dʒubɪˌli] *s* (*jubilation*) giubilo; (eccl) giubileo

Judaism ['dʒudeˌɪzəm] *s* giudaismo

judge [dʒaʤ] *s* giudice *m* || *tr & intr* giudicare; **judging by** a giudicare da

judge' ad'vocate *s* avvocato militare; avvocato della marina da guerra

judgeship ['dʒaʤʃɪp] *s* carica di giudice

judgment ['dʒaʤmənt] *s* giudizio; (*legal decision*) sentenza

judg'ment day' *s* giorno del giudizio

judg'ment seat' *s* banco dei giudici; tribunale *m*

judicature ['dʒudɪkətʃər] *s* carica di giudice

judicial [dʒu'dɪʃəl] *adj* giudiziario; (*becoming a judge*) giudizioso

judiciar·y [dʒu'dɪʃɪˌɛri] *adj* giudiziario || *s* (**-ies**) (*judges collectively*) magistratura; (*judicial branch*) potere giudiziario

judicious [dʒu'dɪʃəs] *adj* giudizioso

jug [dʒag] *s* brocca, boccale *m*; (*narrow-necked vessel*) orcio; (*jail*) (slang) prigione

juggle ['dʒagəl] *s* gioco di prestigio || *tr* fare il giocoliere con; (*documents, facts*) alterare frodolentamente; **to juggle away** ghermire, trafugare || *intr* fare il giocoliere; fare l'imbroglione

juggler ['dʒaglər] *s* giocoliere *m*, prestigiatore *m*; impostore *m*

juggling ['dʒaglɪŋ] *s* giochi *mpl* di prestigio

Jugoslav ['jugo'slav] *adj & s* iugoslavo, jugoslavo

Jugoslavia ['jugo'slavɪ·ə] *s* la Iugoslavia, la Jugoslavia

jugular ['dʒagjələr] *or* ['dʒugjələr] *adj & s* giugulare *f*

juice [dʒus] *s* sugo; (*natural fluid of an animal body*) succo; (slang) elettricità *f*; (slang) benzina; **to stew in one's own juice** (coll) annegarsi nel proprio sugo

juic·y ['dʒusi] *adj* (**-ier; -iest**) sugoso, succoso; (*spicy*) piccante

jukebox ['dʒukˌbaks] *s* grammofono a gettone, juke-box *m*

julep ['dʒulɪp] *s* bibita di menta col ghiaccio; (pharm) giulebbe *m*

julienne [ˌdʒulɪ'ɛn] *s* giuliana

July [dʒu'laɪ] *s* luglio

jumble ['dʒambəl] *s* intrico, garbuglio || *tr* ingarbugliare

jum·bo ['dʒambo] *adj* (coll) enorme || *s* (**-bos**) (*person*) (coll) elefante *m*; (*thing*) (coll) oggetto enorme

jump [dʒamp] *s* salto; (*in a parachute*) lancio; (*of prices*) sbalzo; (*start*) soprassalto; **on the jump** in moto; **to get** *or* **to have the jump on** (coll) avere il vantaggio su || *tr* saltare; (*a horse*) far saltare; (*prices*) alzare; uscire da, e.g., **the train jumped the track** il treno uscì dalle rotaie; (*to attack*) (coll) balzare su; (*checkers*) suffiare || *intr* saltare; (*from surprise*) trasalire; (*said of prices*) salire; (*in a parachute*) lanciarsi; **to jump at** (*e.g., an offer*) afferrare; **to jump on** saltare su; (coll) sgridare, arrabbiarsi con; **to jump over** oltrepassare; (*a page*) saltare; **to jump to a conclusion** arrivare precipitosamente a una conclusione

jumper ['dʒampər] *s* saltatore *m*; camiciotto; **jumpers** tuta da bambini

jump'ing jack' ['dʒʌmpɪŋ] *s* marionetta

jump'ing-off' place' *s* fine *f* del mondo; (fig) trampolino, punto di partenza

jump' seat' *s* strapuntino

jump' spark' *s* scintilla elettrica; (*of induction coil*) (elec) scintilla d'intraferro

jump' wire' *s* filo elettrico di contatto

jump·y ['dʒʌmpi] *adj* (**-ier; -iest**) nervoso, eccitato

junction ['dʒʌŋktʃən] *s* congiunzione; (*of two rivers*) confluenza; (carp) commettitura; (rr) raccordo ferroviario

juncture ['dʒʌŋktʃər] *s* giuntura; (*occasion*) congiuntura; (*moment*) momento

June [dʒun] *s* giugno

jungle ['dʒʌŋgəl] *s* giungla

junglegym ['dʒʌŋgəl,dʒɪm] *s* (trademark) castello

junior ['dʒunjər] *adj* minore, di minore età; giovane; (*in American university*) del penultimo anno; figlio, e.g., **John H. Smith, Junior** Giovanni H. Smith, figlio ‖ *s* minore *m;* socio secondario; studente *m* del penultimo anno

jun'ior col'lege *s* scuola universitaria unicamente di primo biennio

jun'ior high' school' *s* scuola media; ginnasio

juniper ['dʒunɪpər] *s* ginepro

ju'niper ber'ry *s* coccola di ginepro

junk [dʒʌŋk] *s* roba vecchia, ferro vecchio; (*Chinese ship*) giunca; (naut) carne salata ‖ *tr* (slang) gettar via

junk' deal'er *s* robivecchi *m*

junket ['dʒʌŋkɪt] *s* budino di giuncata; (*outing*) viaggio di piacere; viaggio pagato a spese del tesoro ‖ *intr* far un viaggio di piacere; far un viaggio a spese del tesoro

junk'man' *s* (**-men'**) ferravecchio; rigattiere *m*

junk' room' *s* ripostiglio

junk' shop' *s* negozio di robivecchi

junk'yard' *s* cantiere *m* di ferravecchio

juridical [dʒu'rɪdɪkəl] *adj* giuridico

jurisdiction [,dʒurɪs'dɪkʃən] *s* giurisdizione

jurisprudence [,dʒurɪs'prudəns] *s* giurisprudenza

jurist ['dʒurɪst] *s* giurista *mf*

juror ['dʒurər] *s* giurato

ju·ry ['dʒuri] *s* (**-ries**) giuria

ju'ry box' *s* banco della giuria

ju'ry·man *s* (**-men**) giurato

just [dʒʌst] *adj* giusto ‖ *adv* giustamente, giusto; appena; proprio; **just as** come, proprio come; **just beyond** un po' più in là (di); **just now** poco fa, or ora; **just out** appena uscito, appena pubblicato

justice ['dʒʌstɪs] *s* giustizia; (*judge*) giudice *m;* **to bring to justice** arrestare e condannare; **to do justice to** render giustizia a; apprezzare bastantemente

jus'tice of the peace' *s* giudice *m* conciliatore

justifiable ['dʒʌstɪ,faɪ·əbəl] *adj* giustificabile

justi·fy ['dʒʌstɪ,faɪ] *v* (*pret & pp* **-fied**) *tr* giustificare; (typ) giustificare

justly ['dʒʌstli] *adj* giustamente

jut [dʒʌt] *v* (*pret & pp* **jutted;** *ger* **jutting**) *intr*—**to jut out** strapiombare, sporgere

jute [dʒut] *s* iuta ‖ **Jute** *s* Juto

juvenile ['dʒuvənɪl] *or* ['dʒuvə,naɪl] *adj* giovanile; minorile ‖ *s* giovane *mf;* libro per la gioventù; (theat) amoroso

ju'venile court' *s* tribunale *m* per i minorenni

ju'venile delin'quency *s* delinquenza minorile

juvenilia [,dʒuvə'nɪlɪ·ə] *spl* opere *fpl* giovanili; libri *mpl* per ragazzi

juxtapose [,dʒʌkstə'poz] *tr* giustapporre

K

K, k [ke] *s* undicesima lettera dell'alfabeto inglese

kale [kel] *s* verza; (slang) cocuzza soldi *mpl*

kaleidoscope [kə'laɪdə,skop] *s* caleidoscopio

kangaroo [,kæŋgə'ru] *s* canguro

katydid ['ketɪdɪd] *s* grossa cavalletta verde nordamericana

kedge [kɛdʒ] *s* (naut) ancorotto

keel [kil] *s* chiglia ‖ *intr*—**to keel over** (naut) abbattersi in carena, capovolgersi; (fig) svenire

keelson ['kɛlsən] *or* ['kɪlsən] *s* (naut) controchiglia

keen [kin] *adj* (*sharpened*) affilato; (*wind; wit*) tagliente, mordente; (*eyes*) penetrante; (*ears; mind*) acuto;

fine; (*eager*) entusiasta; intenso, vivo; (slang) meraviglioso; **to be keen on** essere appassionato per

keep [kip] *s* mantenimento; (*of medieval castle*) torrione *m*, maschio; **for keeps** (coll) seriamente; (coll) per sempre; **to earn one's keep** guadagnarsi la vita ‖ *v* (*pret & pp* **kept** [kɛpt]) *tr* mantenere; (*watch*) fare; (*one's word*) mantenere; (*to withhold*) trattenere; (*accounts*) tenere; (*servants, guests*) avere; (*a garden*) coltivare; (*a business*) esercitare; (*a holiday*) festeggiare; (*to support*) sostentare; (*a secret; one's seat*) serbare; (*to decide to purchase*) prendere; **to keep away** tener lontano; **to keep back** trattenere; (*a secret*) mantenere; **to keep down** reprimere; (*expenses*) ridurre al minimo; **to keep s.o. from** + *ger* impedire a qlcu di + *inf;* **to keep in** tener chiuso; **to keep off** tenere a distanza; (*e.g., moisture*) non lasciar penetrare; **to keep s.o. informed about s.th** tenere qlcu al corrente di qlco; **to keep s.o. waiting** fare aspettare qlcu; **to keep up** mantenere, sostenere ‖ *intr* **to keep** + *ger* continuare a + *inf;* **to keep away** tenersi lontano; **to keep from** + *ger* evitare di + *inf;* **to keep informed (about)** tenersi al corrente (di); **to keep in with** (coll) stare nelle buone grazie di; **to keep off** stare lontano (da); (*the grass*) non calpestare; **to keep on** + *ger* seguitare a + *inf;* **to keep out** star fuori, non entrare; **to keep out of** non entrare in; (*danger*) stare lontano da; non immischiarsi in; **to keep quiet** stare tranquillo; **to keep to** (*left or right*) tenere; **to keep to oneself** stare in disparte; **to keep up** continuare; **to keep up with** stare alla pari con; (*e.g., the news*) tenersi al corrente di

keeper ['kipər] *s* (*of a shop*) tenitore *m;* guardiano; (*of a game preserve*) guardacaccia *m;* (*of a magnet*) ancora

keeping ['kipɪŋ] *s* custodia; (*of a holiday*) celebrazione; **in keeping with** in armonia con; **in safe keeping** in luogo sicuro; **out of keeping with** in cattivo accordo con

keep'sake' *s* ricordo

keg [kɛg] *s* barilotto, botticella

ken [kɛn] *s* portata; **beyond the ken of** al di là dell'ambito di

kennel ['kɛnəl] *s* canile *m*

kep·i ['kepi] *or* ['kɛpi] *s* (-**is**) chepì *m*

kept' wo'man [kɛpt] *s* (**wom'en**) mantenuta

kerchief ['kʌrtʃɪf] *s* fisciù *m*

kernel ['kʌrnəl] *s* (*of a nut*) gheriglio; (*of wheat*) chicco; (fig) nucleo

kerosene ['kɛrə‚sin] *or* [‚kɛrə'sin] *s* cherosene *m*, petrolio da illuminazione

kerplunk [kər'plʌŋk] *interj* patapum!

ketchup ['ketʃəp] *s* salsa piccante di pomodoro, ketchup *m*

kettle ['ketəl] *s* marmitta, paiolo; (*teakettle*) bricco, teiera

ket'tle·drum' *s* timpano

key [ki] *adj* a chiave; chiave ‖ *s* chiave *f;* (*of piano, typewriter, etc.*) tasto; (*cotter pin*) chiavetta, coppiglia; (*reef*) isolotto; (*tone of voice*) tono; (fig, mus) chiave *f;* (bot) samara; (telg) tasto trasmettitore, manipolatore *m;* **off key** stonato ‖ *tr* aggiustare; inchiavardare; **to key up** eccitare, portare al parossismo

key'board' *s* tastiera

key'hole' *s* toppa, buco della serratura; (*of a clock*) buco della chiave

key'note' *s* (mus) tono; (fig) principio informatore

key'note address' *s* discorso d'apertura

key'punch op'era'tor *s* perforatore *m*

key' ring' *s* portachiavi *m*

key'stone' *s* chiave *f* di volta

key' word' *s* parola chiave

kha·ki ['kɑki] *or* ['kæki] *adj* cachi ‖ *s* (-**kis**) cachi *m*

khedive [kə'div] *s* kedivè *m*

kibitz ['kɪbɪts] *intr* (coll) dare consigli non richiesti

kibitzer ['kɪbɪtsər] *s* (*at a card game*) (coll) consigliere *m* importuno; (coll) ficcanaso *mf*

kibosh ['kaɪbɑʃ] *or* [kɪ'bɑʃ] *s* (coll) sciocchezza; **to put the kibosh on** (coll) impossibilitare

kick [kɪk] *s* calcio, pedata; (*of a gun*) rinculo; (*complaint*) (slang) protesta; (*of liquor*) (slang) forza; **to get a kick out of** (slang) pigliar piacere da ‖ *tr* prendere a calci; (*a ball*) calciare; (*one's feet*) battere; **to kick out** (coll) sbatter fuori a pedate; **to kick up a row** scatenare un putiferio ‖ *intr* calciare; (*said of an animal*) scalciare, trarre; (*said of a firearm*) rinculare; (coll) lamentarsi; **to kick against the pricks** dar calci al vento; **to kick off** (football) dare il calcio d'inizio

kick'back' *s* (coll) contraccolpo; (coll) intrallazzo, bustarella

kick'off' *s* calcio d'inizio

kid [kɪd] *s* capretto; (coll) piccolo; **kids** guanti *mpl or* scarpe *fpl* di capretto ‖ *v* (*pret & pp* **kidded;** *ger* **kidding**) *tr* (coll) prendere in giro; **to kid oneself** (coll) farsi illusioni ‖ *intr* (coll) dirlo per scherzo

kidder ['kɪdər] *s* (coll) burlone *m*

kid' gloves' *spl* guanti *mpl* di capretto; **to handle with kid gloves** trattare con la massima cautela

kid'nap' *v* (*pret & pp* -**naped** *or* -**napped;** *ger* -**naping** *or* -**napping**) *tr* rapire, sequestrare

kidnaper *or* **kidnapper** ['kɪd‚næpər] *s* rapitore *m* a scopo d'estorsione

kidnaping *or* **kidnapping** ['kɪd‚næpɪŋ] *s* rapimento a scopo di estorsione

kidney ['kɪdni] *s* rene *m;* (culin) rognone *m;* (*temperament*) carattere *m;* (*kind*) tipo

kid'ney bean' *s* fagiolo

kid'ney stone' *s* calcolo renale

kill [kɪl] *s* uccisione; (*game killed*) cacciagione; (coll) fiumicello; **for the kill** per il colpo finale ‖ *tr* uccidere; eliminare; (*a bill*) bocciare; (fig) opprimere

killer ['kɪlər] *s* uccisore *m*

kill'er whale' *s* orca

killing ['kɪlɪŋ] *adj* mortale; (*exhausting*) opprimente; (coll) molto divertente ‖ *s* uccisione; (*game killed*) cacciagione; (coll) fortuna; **to make a killing** (coll) fare una fortuna da un giorno all'altro

kill'-joy' *s* guastafeste *mf*

kiln [kɪl] *or* [kɪln] *s* forno, fornace *f*

kil·o ['kɪlo] *or* ['kilo] *s* (-**os**) chilogrammo; chilometro

kilocycle ['kɪlə‚saɪkəl] *s* chilociclo

kilogram ['kɪlə‚græm] *s* chilogrammo

kilo·hertz ['kɪlə‚hʌrts] *s* (-**hertz**) chilohertz

kilometer ['kɪlə‚mitər] or [kɪ'lɑmɪtər] s chilometro

kilowatt ['kɪlə‚wɑt] s kilowatt m, chilowatt m

kilowatt-hour ['kɪlə‚wɑt'aʊr] s (kilowatt-hours) chilowattora m

kilt [kɪlt] s gonnellino

kilter ['kɪltər] s—to be out of kilter (coll) essere fuori squadra

kimo·no [kɪ'monə] or [kɪ'mono] s (-nos) chimono

kin [kɪn] s (family relationship) parentela; (relatives) parenti mpl; of kin parente, affine; the next of kin il parente più prossimo, i parenti più prossimi

kind [kaɪnd] adj gentile; kind to buono con || s genere m, specie f; a kind of una specie di; all kinds of (coll) ogni sorta di; in kind in natura; kind of (coll) quasi, piuttosto; of a kind dello stesso stampo; (mediocre) di poco valore

kindergarten ['kɪndər‚gɑrtən] s scuola materna, giardino d'infanzia

kindergartner ['kɪndər‚gɑrtnər] s allievo della scuola d'infanzia; (teacher) maestra giardiniera

kind-hearted ['kaɪnd'hɑrtɪd] adj gentile, di buon cuore

kindle ['kɪndəl] tr accendere || intr accendersi

kindling ['kɪndlɪŋ] s accensione; legna minuta

kin'dling wood' s legna minuta per accendere il fuoco

kind·ly ['kaɪndli] adj (-lier; -liest) gentile; (climate) benigno; favorevole || adv gentilmente; cordialmente; per gentilezza; to not take kindly to non accettare di buon grado

kindness ['kaɪndnɪs] s gentilezza; have the kindness to abbia la bontà di

kindred ['kɪndrɪd] adj imparentato; affine || s parentela; affinità f

kinescope ['kɪnɪ‚skop] s (trademark) cinescopio

kinetic [kɪ'nɛtɪk] or [kaɪ'nɛtɪk] adj cinetico || kinetics s cinetica

kinet'ic en'ergy s forza viva, energia cinetica

king [kɪŋ] s re m; (checkers) dama; (cards, chess) re m

king'bolt' s perno

kingdom ['kɪŋdəm] s regno

king'fish'er s martin pescatore m

king·ly ['kɪŋli] adj (-lier; -liest) reale; (stately) maestoso || adv regalmente

king'pin' s birillo centrale; (aut) perno dello sterzo; (fig) figura principale

king' post' s (archit) ometto, monaco

king's' e'vil s scrofola

kingship ['kɪŋʃɪp] s regalità f

king'-size' adj extra-grande

king's' ran'som s ricchezza di Creso

kink [kɪŋk] s (in a rope) arricciatura; (in hair) crespatura; (soreness in neck) torcicollo; (flaw) ostacolo; (mental twist) ghiribizzo || tr attorcigliare || intr attorcigliarsi

kink·y ['kɪŋki] adj (-ier; -iest) attorcigliato; (hair) crespo

kinsfolk ['kɪnz‚fok] s parentado

kinship ['kɪnʃɪp] s parentela; affinità f

kins'man s (-men) parente m

kins'wom'an s (-wom'en) parente f

kipper ['kɪpər] s aringa affumicata || tr (herring or salmon) affumicare

kiss [kɪs] s bacio; (billiards) rimpallo leggerissimo; (confection) meringa || tr baciare; to kiss away (tears) asciugare con baci || intr baciare, baciarsi; (billiards) rimpallare leggermente

kit [kɪt] s (case) cassetta dei ferri; (tools) ferri mpl del mestiere; (set of supplies) corredo; (of small tools) astuccio; (of a traveler) borsa da viaggio; (pail) secchio; the whole kit and caboodle (coll) tutti quanti

kitchen ['kɪtʃən] s cucina

kitchenette [‚kɪtʃə'nɛt] s cucinetta

kitch'en gar'den s orto

kitch'en-maid' s sguattera

kitch'en police' s (mil) corvè f di cucina

kitch'en range' s cucina economica

kitch'en sink' s acquaio

kitch'en-ware' s utensili mpl di cucina

kite [kaɪt] s cervo volante, aquilone m; (orn) nibbio

kith' and kin' [kɪθ] spl amici mpl e parenti mpl

kitten ['kɪtən] s gattino

kittenish ['kɪtənɪʃ] adj giocattolone; civettuolo

kit·ty ['kɪti] s (-ties) gattino; (cards) piatto || interj micio!

kleptomaniac [‚klɛptə'meni‚æk] s cleptomane mf

knack [næk] s abilità f, destrezza

knapsack ['næp‚sæk] s zaino

knave [nev] s furfante m; (cards) fante m

knaver·y ['nevəri] s (-ies) furfanteria

knead [nid] tr maneggiare, intridere; (a muscle) massaggiare

knee [ni] s ginocchio; (of trousers) ginocchiera; (mach) gomito; to bring s.o. to his knees ridurre qlcu all'obbedienza; to go down on one's knees (to) gettarsi in ginocchio (davanti a)

knee' breech'es [‚brɪtʃ'ɪz] spl calzoni mpl al ginocchio

knee'cap' s rotula, patella; (protective covering) ginocchiera

knee'-deep' adj fino al ginocchio

knee'-high' adj fino al ginocchio

knee' jerk' s riflesso patellare

kneel [nil] v (pret & pp knelt [nɛlt] or kneeled) intr inginocchiarsi

knee'pad' s ginocchiera

knee'pan' s rotula, patella

knell [nɛl] s rintocco funebre, campana a morto; to toll the knell of annunciare la morte di || intr suonare a morte

knickers ['nɪkərz] spl knickerbockers mpl, calzoni mpl alla zuava

knickknack ['nɪk‚næk] s soprammobile m; gingillo, ninnolo

knife [naɪf] s (knives [naɪvz]) coltello; (of a paper cutter) mannaia; (of a milling machine) fresa; to go under the knife essere sulla tavola operatoria || tr accoltellare; mettere il coltello nella schiena di

knife' sharp'ener s affilatoio

knife' switch' s (elec) coltella
knight [naɪt] s cavaliere m; (chess) cavallo || tr armare cavaliere
knight-errant ['naɪt'ɛrənt] s (knights-errant) cavaliere m errante
knighthood ['naɪt·hʊd] s cavalleria
knightly ['naɪtli] adj cavalleresco
knit [nɪt] v (pret & pp knitted or knit; ger knitting) tr lavorare a maglia; (to join) unire; (e.g., the brow) corrugare || intr lavorare a maglia; fare la calza; unirsi; (said of a bone) saldarsi
knitting ['nɪtɪŋ] s maglia, lavoro a maglia
knit'ting machine' s macchina per maglieria
knit'ting mill' s maglieria
knit'ting nee'dle s ferro da calza
knit'wear' s maglieria
knit'wear store' s maglieria
knob [nɑb] s (lump) bozza, protuberanza; (of a door) maniglia; (on furniture) pomolo; (hill) collinetta rotondeggiante; (rad, telv) manopola, pulsante m
knock [nɑk] s colpo; (on a door) tocco; (slang) attacco, critica || tr battere; (repeatedly) sbatacchiare; (slang) attaccare, criticare; **to knock down** (with a punch) stendere a terra; (a wall) diroccare; (to the highest bidder) aggiudicare; (e.g., a machine) smontare; **to knock off** (work) (slang) sospendere; (slang) terminare; (slang) uccidere; **to knock out** mettere fuori combattimento || intr battere; (aut) battere in testa; (slang) criticare; **to knock about** (slang) gironzolare; **to knock against** urtare contro; **to knock at** (e.g., a door) battere a, bussare a; **to knock off** (slang) cessare di lavorare
knock'down' adj (blow) knock down, che atterra; (dismountable) smontabile || s (blow) colpo che atterra; (discount) sconto
knocker ['nɑkər] s (on a door) battaglio, bussatoio; (coll) criticone m
knock-kneed ['nɑk,nid] adj con le gambe a X [iks]
knock'out' s pugno che mette fuori combattimento; fuori combattimento; (coll) pezzo di giovane
knock'out drops' spl (slang) narcotico
knoll [nol] s poggio, rialzo
knot [nɑt] s nodo; (worn as an ornament) fiocco; (in wood) nocchio; gruppo; protuberanza; (tie) nodo;

(naut) nodo; **to tie the knot** (coll) sposarsi || v (pret & pp knotted; ger knotting) tr annodare; (the brow) corrugare || intr annodarsi
knot'hole' s buco lasciato da un nodo (nel legno)
knot·ty ['nɑti] adj (-tier; -tiest) nodoso; (fig) spinoso
know [no] s—**to be in the know** (coll) essere al corrente || v (pret knew [nju] or [nu]; pp known) tr & intr (by reasoning or learning) sapere; (by the senses or by perception; through acquaintance or recognition) conoscere; **as far as I know** per quanto io ne sappia; **to know about** essere al corrente di; **to know best** essere il miglior giudice; **to know how to** + inf sapere + inf; **to know it all** (coll) sapere tutto; **to know what's what** (coll) saperla lunga; **you ought to know better** dovresti vergognarti
knowable ['no·əbəl] adj conoscibile
know'-how' s sapere m, abilità f
knowingly ['no·ɪŋli] adv con conoscenza di causa; (on purpose) apposta
know'-it-all' adj & s (coll) saputello
knowledge ['nɑlɪdʒ] s (faculty) scibile m, sapere m, sapienza; (awareness, acquaintance, familiarity) conoscenza; **to have a thorough knowledge of** conoscere a fondo; **to my knowledge** per quanto io ne sappia; **with full knowledge** con conoscenza di causa; **without my knowledge** a mia insaputa
knowledgeable ['nɑlɪdʒəbəl] adj intelligente, bene informato
knuckle ['nʌkəl] s nocca; foro del cardine, cardine m; **knuckles** pugno di ferro || intr—**to knuckle down** (coll) lavorare di impegno; **to knuckle under** (coll) darsi per vinto
knurl [nʌrl] s granitura || tr godranare, zigrinare
Koran [ko'ran] or [ko'ræn] s Corano
Korea [ko'ri·ə] s la Corea
Korean [ko'ri·ən] adj & s coreano
kosher ['koʃər] adj kasher, casher, puro secondo la legge giudaica; (coll) autentico
kowtow ['kau'tau] or ['ko'tau] intr inchinarsi servilmente
Kremlin ['krɛmlɪn] s Cremlino
Kremlinology [,krɛmlɪ'nɑlədʒi] s Cremlinologia
kudos ['kjudɑs] or ['kudɑs] s (coll) gloria, fama, approvazione

l

L, l [ɛl] s dodicesima lettera dell'alfabeto inglese
la·bel ['lebəl] s marca, etichetta; (descriptive word) qualifica || v (pret & pp -beled or -belled; ger -beling or -belling) tr etichettare; qualificare
labial ['lebɪ·əl] adj & s labiale f

labor ['lebər] adj operaio || s lavoro; (toil) fatica; (childbirth) parto; (body of wage earners) manodopera; (class as contrasted with management) prestatori mpl d'opera, lavoro; **labors** fatiche fpl; **to be in labor** avere le doglie || intr lavorare; (to exert one-

self) travagliare; (*said of a ship*) rollare e beccheggiare; **to labor for** lottare per; **to labor under** soffrire di

laborato·ry [ˈlæbərəˌtori] *s* (**-ries**) laboratorio

la'bor dispute' *s* vertenza sindacale

labored [ˈlebərd] *adj* elaborato, artificiale; penoso, difficile

laborer [ˈlebərər] *s* lavoratore *m*; (*unskilled worker*) bracciante *m*, manovale *m*, uomo di fatica

laborious [ləˈborɪ·əs] *adj* laborioso

la'bor un'ion *s* sindacato

Labourite [ˈlebəˌraɪt] *s* laburista *mf*

labyrinth [ˈlæbɪrɪnθ] *s* labirinto

lace [les] *s* (*cord or string*) stringa; (*netlike ornament*) trina, merletto; (*braid*) gallone *m* || *tr* stringare; merlettare; (coll) fustigare

lace'work' *s* trina, merletto, pizzo

lachrymose [ˈlækrɪˌmos] *adj* lacrimoso

lacing [ˈlesɪŋ] *s* stringa, cordone *m*; gallone *m*; (coll) battuta, frustata

lack [læk] *s* mancanza, scarsezza, difetto || *tr* mancare di, scarseggiare di || *intr* mancare, scarseggiare, difettare

lackadaisical [ˌlækəˈdezɪkəl] *adj* letargico, indifferente

lackey [ˈlæki] *s* lacchè *m*

lacking [ˈlækɪŋ] *prep* privo di

lack'lus'ter *adj* smorto, spento

laconic [ləˈkɑnɪk] *adj* laconico

lacquer [ˈlækər] *s* lacca || *tr* laccare

lac'quer spray' *s* lacca spray

lac'quer ware' *s* oggetti *mpl* laccati

lacu·na [leˈkjunə] *s* (**-nas** or **-nae** [ni]) lacuna

lac·y [ˈlesi] *adj* (**-ier; -iest**) simile al merletto

lad [læd] *s* ragazzo, fanciullo

ladder [ˈlædər] *s* scala; (*stepladder hinged on top*) scaleo; (*stepping stone*) (fig) scalino

lad'der truck' *s* autocarro di pompieri munito di scale

la'dies' man' *s* beato fra le donne

la'dies' room' *s* gabinetto per signore

ladle [ˈledəl] *s* ramaiolo, mestolo; (*of tinsmith*) cucchiaio || *tr* scodellare

la·dy [ˈledi] *s* (**-dies**) signora, dama

la'dy-bug' *s* coccinella

la'dy·fin'ger *s* savoiardo, lingua di gatto

la'dy-in-wait'ing *s* (**ladies-in-waiting**) dama di corte

la'dy-kil'ler *s* rubacuori *m*

la'dy-like' *adj* signorile; **to be ladylike** comportarsi come una signora

la'dy-love' *s* amata

la'dy of the house' *s* padrona di casa

ladyship [ˈlediˌʃɪp] *s* signoria

la'dy's maid' *s* cameriera personale della signora

lag [læg] *s* ritardo || *v* (*pret & pp* **lagged;** *ger* **lagging**) *intr* ritardare; **to lag behind** rimanere indietro

la'ger beer' [ˈlɑgər] *s* birra invecchiata

laggard [ˈlægərd] *s* tardo, pigro

lagoon [ləˈgun] *s* laguna

laid' pa'per [led] *s* carta vergata

laid' up' *adj* messo da parte; (naut) disarmato; (coll) costretto a letto

lair [lɛr] *s* tana, covo

laity [ˈle·ɪti] *s* laicato

lake [lek] *adj* lacustre || *s* lago

lamb [læm] *s* agnello

lambaste [læmˈbest] *tr* (*to thrash*) sferzare; (*to reprimand*) riprovare

lamb' chop' *s* cotoletta d'agnello

lambkin [ˈlæmkɪn] *s* agnellino; (fig) innocente *mf*

lamb'skin' *s* (*leather*) pelle *f* d'agnello; (*skin with its wool*) agnello

lame [lem] *adj* zoppo; difettoso; (*disabled*) invalido; (*excuse*) debole || *tr* azzoppare

lament [ləˈmɛnt] *s* lamento; lamento funebre || *tr* lamentare || *intr* lamentarsi

lamentable [ˈlæməntəbəl] or [ləˈmɛntəbəl] *adj* lamentevole

lamentation [ˌlæmənˈteʃən] *s* lamentazione

laminate [ˈlæmɪˌnet] *tr* laminare

lamp [læmp] *s* lampada

lamp'black' *s* nerofumo

lamp' chim'ney *s* tubo di vetro di lampada a petrolio

lamp'light' *s* luce *f* di lampada

lamp'light'er *s* lampionaio

lampoon [læmˈpun] *s* satira || *tr* satireggiare

lamp'post' *s* colonna del lampione

lamp'shade' *s* paralume *m*, ventola

lamp'wick' *s* lucignolo

lance [læns] or [lɑns] *s* lancia; (surg) lancetta || *tr* (*with an oxygen lance*) tagliare col cannello ossidrico; (surg) sbrigliare, incidere col bisturi

lance' rest' *s* resta

lancet [ˈlænsɪt] or [ˈlɑnsɪt] *s* (surg) lancetta

land [lænd] *adj* terrestre; (*wind*) di terra || *s* terra; **on land, on sea, and in the air** per mare, per terra e nel cielo; **to make land** toccare terra; **to see how the land lies** tastare terreno || *tr* sbarcare; (aer) fare atterrare; (coll) pigliare || *intr* sbarcare; (*to come to rest*) andare a finire; (naut) toccar terra; (aer) atterrare; **to land on one's feet** cadere in piedi; **to land on one's head** andare a gambe all'aria; **to land on the moon** allunare; **to land on the water** ammarare

land' breeze' *s* vento di terra

landed [ˈlændɪd] *adj* (*owning land*) terriero; (*real estate*) immobile

land'fall' *s* (*sighting land*) avvistamento; terra avvistata; (*landslide*) frana

land' grant' *s* terreno ricevuto in dono dallo stato

land'hold'er *s* proprietario terriero

landing [ˈlændɪŋ] *s* (*of passengers*) sbarco; (*place where passengers and goods are landed*) imbarcadero; (*of stairway*) pianerottolo; (aer, naut) atterraggio

land'ing bea'con *s* radiofaro d'atterraggio

land'ing card' *s* cartoncino di sbarco

land'ing craft' *s* imbarcazione da sbarco

land'ing field' *s* campo d'atterraggio

land'ing flap' s (aer) iposostentatore m
land'ing gear' s (aer) carrello d'atterraggio
land'ing strip' s (aer) pista d'atterraggio
land'la'dy s (**-dies**) (*of an apartment*) padrona di casa; (*of a lodging house*) affittacamere *f*; (*of an inn*) ostessa
landlocked ['lænd ,lakt] *adj* circondato da terra
land'lord' s (*of an apartment*) padrone m di casa; (*of a lodging house*) affittacamere m; (*of an inn*) oste m
land•lubber ['lænd ,lʌbər] s marinaio d'acqua dolce
land'mark' s (*boundary stone*) pietra di confine; (*distinguishing landscape feature*) punto di riferimento; (fig) pietra miliare
land' of'fice s ufficio del catasto
land'-office busi'ness s (coll) sacco d'affari
land'own'er s proprietario terriero
landscape ['lænd ,skep] s paesaggio || *tr* abbellire
land'scape gar'dener s giardiniere m ornamentale
land'scape paint'er s paesista *mf*
landscapist ['lænd ,skepɪst] s paesista *mf*
land'slide' s frana; (fig) vittoria strepitosa
landward ['lændwərd] *adv* verso terra, verso la costa
land' wind' s vento di terra
lane [len] s (*narrow street*) vicolo, viuzza; (*of a highway*) corsia; (naut) rotta; (aer) corridoio
langsyne [,læŋ'saɪn] s (Scotch) tempo passato || *adv* (Scotch) molto tempo fa
language ['læŋgwɪdʒ] s lingua; (*style of language*) linguaggio; (*of a special group of people*) gergo
lan'guage lab'oratory s laboratorio linguistico
languid ['læŋgwɪd] *adj* languido
languish ['læŋgwɪʃ] *intr* languire; affettare languore
languor ['læŋgər] s languore m
languorous ['læŋgərəs] *adj* languido; (*causing languor*) snervante
lank [læŋk] *adj* scarnito, sparuto
lank•y ['læŋki] *adj* (**-ier; -iest**) scarnito, sparuto
lantern ['læntərn] s lanterna
lan'tern slide' s diapositiva
lanyard ['lænjərd] s (naut) drizza; (mil) aghetto, cordellina
lap [læp] s (*of human body or clothing*) grembo; (*with the tongue*) leccata; (*of the waves*) sciacquio; (sports) giro, tappa; **in the lap of** in mezzo a, e.g., **in the lap of luxury** in mezzo alle delicatezze || *v* (*pret & pp* **lapped**; *ger* **lapping**) *tr* lappare; (*said, e.g., of waves*) lambire; (*to fold*) piegare; (*to overlap*); sovrapporre; **to lap up** lappare; (coll) accettare con entusiasmo || *intr* sovrapporsi; **to lap against** (*said of the waves*) lambire; **to lap over** traboccare

lap'board' s tavolino da lavoro da tenersi sulle ginocchia
lap' dissolve' s (mov) dissolvenza incrociata
lap' dog' s cagnolino da salotto
lapel [lə'pel] s risvolto
Lap'land' s la Lapponia
Laplander ['læp ,lændər] s lappone *mf*
Lapp [læp] s lappone *mf*; (*language*) lappone m
lap' robe' s coperta da viaggio
lapse [læps] s (*interval*) spazio di tempo; (*fall, decline*) caduta; (*of memory*) perdita; errore m; (ins) risoluzione; (law) decadenza || *intr* cadere, ricadere; cadere in disuso; (*said of time*) passare; (ins) risolversi; (law) decadere
lap'wing' s pavoncella
larce•ny ['larsəni] s (**-nies**) furto
larch [lartʃ] s larice m
lard [lard] s strutto || *tr* lardellare
larder ['lardər] s dispensa
large [lardʒ] *adj* grande, grosso || **s—at large** in libertà
large' intes'tine s intestino crasso
largely ['lardʒli] *adv* in gran parte
large'-scale' *adj* su larga scala
lariat ['læri·ət] s lazo, laccio
lark [lark] s allodola; (coll) burla; **to go on a lark** (coll) far festa
lark'spur' s (*rocket larkspur*) sprone m di cavaliere; (*field larkspur*) consolida reale
lar•va ['larvə] s (**-vae** [vi]) larva
laryngitis [,lærɪn'dʒaɪtɪs] s laringite *f*
laryngoscope [lə'rɪŋgə ,skop] s laringoscopio
larynx ['lærɪŋks] s (**larynxes** or **larynges** [lə'rɪndʒiz]) laringe *f*
lascivious [lə'sɪvɪ·əs] *adj* lascivo
lasciviousness [lə'sɪvɪ·əsnɪs] s lascivia
laser ['lesər] s (acronym) (**light amplification by stimulated emission of radiation**) laser m
lash [læʃ] s (*cord on end of whip*) sverzino; (*blow with whip; scolding*) staffilata; (*of animal's tail*) colpo; (*eyelash*) ciglio; (fig) assalto || *tr* (*to whip*) frustare; (*to bind*) legare; (*to shake*) agitare; (*to attack with words*) staffilare || *intr* lanciarsi; **to lash out at** attaccare violentemente
lashing ['læʃɪŋ] s legatura; (*severe scolding*) staffilata; (*fastening with a rope*) (naut) rizza
lass [læs] s ragazza, giovane *f*; innamorata
las•so ['læso] or [læ'su] s (**-sos** or **-soes**) lasso, lazo || *tr* pigliare col lasso
last [læst] or [last] *adj* ultimo, passato; (*most recent*) scorso; **before last** ierlaltro, e.g., **the night before last** ierlaltro notte; **every last one** tutti senza eccezione; **last but one** penultimo || *s* ultima persona; ultima cosa; fine *f*; (*for holding shoes*) forma; **at last** alla fine; **at long last!** finalmente!; **stick to your last!** fa' il mestiere tuo!; **the last of the month** alla fine del mese; **to breathe one's last** dare l'ultimo sospiro; **to see the last of s.o.** vedere qlcu per l'ultima

volta; **to the last** fino alla fine ‖ *adv* ultimo, per ultimo, alla fine ‖ *intr* durare, continuare

lasting ['læstɪŋ] or ['lɑstɪŋ] *adj* duraturo, durevole

lastly ['læstli] or ['lɑstli] *adv* finalmente, in conclusione

last'-min'ute news' *s* notizie *fpl* dell'ultima ora

last' name' *s* cognome *m*

last' night' *adv* ieri sera; la notte scorsa

last' quar'ter *s* ultimo quarto

last' sleep' *s* ultimo sonno

last' straw' *s* ultima, colmo

Last' Sup'per *s* Ultima Cena

last will' and tes'tament *s* ultime volontà *fpl*

last' word' *s* ultima parola; (*latest style*) ultima novità, ultimo grido

latch [lætʃ] *s* saliscendi *m; (wooden)* nottola ‖ *tr* chiudere col saliscendi

latch'key' *s* chiave *f* per saliscendi

latch'string' *s*—**the latchstring is out** faccia come fosse a casa Sua

late [let] *adj* (*happening after the usual time*) tardo; (*person*) in ritardo; (*hour of the night*) avanzato; (*news*) dell'ultima ora, recente; (*incumbent of an office*) predecessore, ex, passato; (*coming toward the end of a period*) tardivo; (*deceased*) defunto, fu; **in the late 30's, 40's, etc.** verso la fine del decennio che va dal 1930, 1940, etc. al 1940, 1950, etc.; **of late** recentemente; **to be late in +** *ger* essere in ritardo a + *inf*; **to grow late** farsi tardi; **to keep late hours** fare le ore piccole ‖ *adv* tardi; in ritardo; **late in** (*the week, the month, etc.*) alla fine di; **late in life** a un'età avanzata

latecomer ['let ˌkʌmər] *s* ritardatario

lateen' sail' [læ'tin] *s* vela latina

lately ['letli] *adv* recentemente

latent ['letənt] *adj* latente

later ['letər] *adj comp* più tardi; (*event*) susseguente; **later than** posteriore a ‖ *adv comp* più tardi; **later on** più tardi; **see you later** (coll) arrivederci, a ben presto

lateral ['lætərəl] *adj* laterale

lath [læθ] or [lɑθ] *s* listello, striscia di legno ‖ *tr* mettere listelli su

lathe [leð] *s* tornio

lather ['læðər] *s* schiuma di sapone; schiuma ‖ *tr* insaponare; (coll) bastonare ‖ *intr* schiumare

lathery ['læðəri] *adj* schiumoso

lathing ['læθɪŋ] or ['lɑθɪŋ] *s* costruzione con listelli

Latin ['lætɪn] or ['lætən] *adj & s* latino

Lat'in Amer'ica *s* l'America latina

Lat'in-Amer'ican *adj* dell'America latina

Lat'in Amer'ican *s* abitante *mf* dell'America latina

latitude ['lætɪˌtjud] or ['lætɪˌtud] *s* latitudine *f*

latrine [lə'trin] *s* latrina militare

latter ['lætər] *adj* (*more recent*) posteriore; (*of two*) secondo; **the latter** questo; **the latter part of** la fine di

lattice ['lætɪs] *s* graticcio ‖ *tr* munire di graticcio, graticciare

lat'tice gird'er *s* trave *f* a traliccio

lat'tice-work' *s* graticcio, traliccio

Latvia ['lætvɪˌə] *s* la Lettonia

laud [lɔd] *tr* lodare

laudable ['lɔdəbəl] *adj* lodevole

laudanum ['lɔdənəm] or ['lɔdnəm] *s* laudano

laudatory ['lɔdəˌtori] *adj* lodativo

laugh [læf] or [lɑf] *s* riso ‖ *tr*—**to laugh away** dissipare ridendo; **to laugh off** prendere sotto gamba, non dare importanza a ‖ *intr* ridere, ridersi; **to laugh at** ridersi di; **to laugh up one's sleeve** ridere sotto i baffi

laughable ['læfəbəl] or ['lɑfəbəl] *adj* risibile

laughing ['læfɪŋ] or ['lɑfɪŋ] *adj* che ride; **to be no laughing matter** non esserci niente da ridere ‖ *s* riso

laugh'ing gas' *s* gas *m* esilarante

laugh'ing-stock' *s* ludibrio, zimbello

laughter ['læftər] or ['lɑftər] *s* riso

launch [lɔntʃ] or [lɑntʃ] *s* (*of a ship*) varo; (*of a rocket*) lancio; (naut) lancia, scialuppa ‖ *tr* (*to throw; to send forth*) lanciare; (naut) varare ‖ *intr* lanciarsi

launching ['lɔntʃɪŋ] or ['lɑntʃɪŋ] *s* lancio; (*of a ship*) varo

launch'ing pad' *s* piattaforma di lancio

launder ['lɔndər] or ['lɑndər] *tr* lavare e stirare ‖ *intr* riuscire dopo il lavaggio

launderer ['lɔndərər] or ['lɑndərər] *s* lavandaio stiratore *m*

laundress ['lɔndrɪs] or ['lɑndrɪs] *s* lavandaia stiratrice *f*

laundromat ['lɔndrəˌmæt] or ['lɑndrəˌmæt] *s* (trademark) lavanderia a gettone

laun·dry ['lɔndri] or ['lɑndri] *s* (-**dries**) lavanderia; (*clothing*) bucato

laun'dry·man' *s* (-**men'**) lavandaio

laun'dry·wom'an *s* (-**wom'en**) lavandaia

laureate ['lɔri·ɪt] *adj* laureato ‖ *s* laureato; poeta laureato

lau·rel ['lɔrəl] or ['lɑrəl] *s* lauro, alloro; **laurels** (fig) alloro; **to rest or sleep on one's laurels** dormire sugli allori ‖ *v* (*pret & pp* -**reled** or -**relled**; *ger* -**reling** or -**relling**) *tr* laureare

lava ['lɑvə] or ['lævə] *s* lava

lavato·ry ['lævəˌtori] *s* (-**ries**) (*room*) gabinetto da bagno; (*bowl*) lavabo; (*toilet*) gabinetto di decenza, cesso

lavender ['lævəndər] *s* lavanda

lavish ['lævɪʃ] *adj* prodigo ‖ *tr* prodigare, profondere

law [lɔ] *s* (*of man, of nature, of science*) legge *f*; (*study, profession of law*) diritto; **to enter the law** farsi avvocato; **to go to law** ricorrere alla legge; **to lay down the law** dettar legge; **to maintain law and order** mantenere la pace interna; **to practice law** fare l'avvocato

law-abiding ['lɔ·əˌbaɪdɪŋ] *adj* osservante della legge

law'break'er *s* violatore *m* della legge

law' court' s tribunale m di giustizia
lawful ['lɔfəl] adj legale, legittimo
lawless ['lɔlɪs] adj illegale; (unbridled) sfrenato
law'mak'er s legislatore m
lawn [lɔn] s tappeto erboso; (fabric) batista
lawn' mow'er s tosatrice f
law' of'fice s ufficio d'avvocato
law' of na'tions s diritto delle genti
law' of the jun'gle s legge f della giungla
law' stu'dent s studente m di legge
law'suit' s causa, lite f, processo
lawyer ['lɔjər] s avvocato, legale m
lax [læks] adj (in morals) lasso, rilassato; (rope) lento; (negligent) trascurato; vago, indeterminato
laxative ['læksətɪv] adj purgativo || s purga, purgante m
lay [le] adj (not belonging to the clergy) laico; (not having special training) non dotto, profano || s configurazione, disposizione || v (pret & pp laid [led]) tr mettere, collocare; (snares) tendere; (one's eyes; a stone) porre; (blame) dare, gettare; (a bet) fare; (for consideration) presentare; (the table) imbandire; (said of a hen) deporre; (plans) impostare; (to locate) disporre; **to be laid in** (said of a scene) aver luogo in; **to lay aside** mettere da parte; **to lay down** dichiarare; (one's life) dare; (one's arms) deporre; **to lay low** abbattere; uccidere; **to lay off** (workers) licenziare; (to measure) marcare; (slang) lasciare in pace; **to lay open** rivelare; (to a danger) esporre; **to lay out** estendere; preparare, disporre; (a corpse) comporre; (money) (coll) sborsare; **to lay over** posporre; **to lay up** mettere da parte; obbligare a letto; (naut) disarmare || intr (said of a hen) fare le uova; **to lay about** dar botte da orbi; **to lay for** (slang) attendere al varco; **to lay off** (coll) cessare di lavorare; **to lay over** trattenersi, fermarsi; **to lay to** (naut) navigare alla cappa
lay' broth'er s frate m secolare; converso
lay' day' s (com) stallia
layer ['le·ər] s (of paint) mano f; (of bricks) testa; (e.g., of rocks) strato, falda; (anat) pannicolo; (hort) propaggine f || tr (hort) propagginare
lay'er cake' s dolce m a strati
layette [le'ɛt] s corredino
lay' fig'ure s manichino
laying ['le·ɪŋ] s posa; (of eggs) deporre m; (of a wire) tendere m
lay'man s (-men) (member of the laity) laico, secolare m; (not a member of a special profession) laico, profano
lay'off' s (dismissal of workers) licenziamento; (period of unemployment) disoccupazione
lay' of the land' s andamento generale
lay'out' s piano; (sketch) tracciato; (of tools) armamentario; (coll) residenza; (typ) menabò m; (coll) banchetto, festino

lay'o'ver s fermata in un viaggio
lay' sis'ter s suora al secolo; conversa
laziness ['lezɪnɪs] s pigrizia
la·zy ['lezi] adj (-zier; -ziest) pigro
la'zy·bones' s (coll) poltrone m
lea [li] s (fallow land) maggese m; (meadow) prato
lead [lɛd] adj plumbeo || s piombo; (of lead pencil) mina; (for sounding depth) (naut) scandaglio; (typ) interlinea || [lɛd] v (pret & pp leaded; ger leading) tr impiombare; (typ) interlineare || [lid] s (foremost place) primato; (guidance) guida, direzione; (leash) guinzaglio; (journ) testata; (cards) mano f, prima mano; (elec) conduttore m; (mach) passo; (min) filone m; (rad, telv) filo d'entrata; (theat) ruolo principale; (theat) primo attore; (theat) prima attrice; **to take the lead** prendere il comando || [lid] v (pret & pp led [lɛd]) tr condurre, portare; (to command) comandare, essere alla testa di; (an orchestra) dirigere; (a good or bad life) fare; (s.o. into vice) trascinare; (cards) cominciare a giocare; (elec, mach) anticipare; **to lead astray** forviare || intr essere in testa, guidare; prendere l'offensiva; (said of a road) condurre; (cards) cominciare a giocare; **to lead to** risultare in; **to lead up to** andare a condurre a
leaden ['lɛdən] adj (of lead; like lead) plumbeo; (sluggish) tardo; (with sleep) carico; triste
leader ['lidər] s capo, comandante m; (ringleader) capobanda m; (of an orchestra) direttore m; (among animals) guidaiolo; (in a dance) ballerino guidaiolo; (sports) capintesta m; (journ) articolo di fondo
lead'er dog' s cane m guida di ciechi
leadership ['lidər‚ʃɪp] s comando, direzione; doti fpl di comando
leading ['lidɪŋ] adj principale; primo; dirigente, preeminente
lead'ing ar'ticle s articolo di fondo
lead'ing edge' s (aer) bordo d'attacco
lead'ing la'dy s prima attrice
lead'ing man' s (men') primo attore
lead'ing ques'tion s domanda suggestiva, domanda orientatrice
lead'ing strings' spl dande fpl
lead'-in wire' ['lid‚ɪn] s filo d'antenna
lead' pen'cil [lɛd] s lapis m, matita
leaf [lif] s (leaves [livz]) (of plant) foglia; (of vine) pampino; (of paper) foglio; (of double door) battente m; (of table) asse m a ribalta; **to turn over a new leaf** ricominciare una nuova vita || intr fogliare; **to leaf through** sfogliare
leafless ['liflɪs] adj senza foglie
leaflet ['liflɪt] s manifestino, volantino; (of plant) foglietta
leaf' spring' s molla a balestra
leaf'stalk' s picciolo
leaf·y ['lifi] adj (-ier; -iest) foglioso, frondoso
league [lig] s lega || tr associare || intr associarsi

League' of Na'tions s Società f delle Nazioni

leak [lik] s (in a roof) stillicidio; (in a ship) falla; (of water, gas, steam) fuga; (of electricity) dispersione; buco, fessura; (of news) filtrazione; **to spring a leak** avere una perdita; (naut) cominciare a far acqua || tr (gas, liquids) perdere, lasciar scappare; (news) lasciar trapelare || intr (said of water, gas etc.,) perdere, scappare; (said of a barrel) spillare; (naut) fare acqua; **to leak away** (said of money) andarsene; **to leak out** (said of news) trapelare

leakage ['likɪdʒ] s perdita, fuoruscita, fuga; (elec) dispersione; (com) colaggio

leak·y ['liki] adj (-ier; -iest) che perde; (naut) che fa acqua; (coll) indiscreto

lean [lin] adj magro, secco; (gasoline mixture) povero || v (pret & pp **leaned** or **leant** [lɛnt]) tr inclinare; appoggiare || intr pendere, inclinarsi; (fig) inclinare, tendere; **to lean against** appoggiarsi a, addossarsi a; **to lean back** sdraiarsi; **to lean on** appoggiarsi su; **to lean out (of)** sporgersi (da); **to lean over backwards** fare di tutto; **to lean toward** (fig) tendere a, avere un'inclinazione per

leaning ['linɪŋ] adj inclinato, pendente || s inclinazione

lean'ing tow'er s torre f pendente

lean'-to' s (-tos) tetto a una falda

leap [lip] s salto, balzo; **by leaps and bounds** a passi da gigante; **leap in the dark** salto nel vuoto || v (pret & pp **leaped** or **leapt** [lɛpt]) tr saltare || intr saltare; (said of one's heart) balzare

leap'frog' s cavallina; **to play leapfrog** giocare alla cavallina

leap' year' s anno bisestile

learn [lʌrn] s (pret & pp **learned** or **learnt** [lʌrnt]) tr imparare; imparare a memoria; (news) apprendere || intr istruirsi, apprendere

learned ['lʌrnɪd] adj dotto; (word) colto

learn'ed jour'nal s rivista scientifica

learn'ed soci'ety s associazione di eruditi

learn'ed word' s parola dotta

learn'ed world' s mondo di dotti

learner ['lʌrnər] s apprendista mf; studente m; (beginner) principiante mf

learning ['lʌrnɪŋ] s istruzione; (scholarship) erudizione

lease [lis] s locazione, contratto d'affitto; **a new lease on life** nuove prospettive di felicità; vita nuova (dopo una malattia) || tr locare; prendere in affitto || intr affittare

lease'hold' adj affittato || s beni mpl sotto locazione

leash [liʃ] s guinzaglio; **to strain at the leash** mordere il freno || tr frenare, controllare

least [list] adj minore, menomo, minimo || s (il) meno; **at least** or **at the least** per lo meno, quanto meno;

not in the least nient'affatto || adv meno

leather ['lɛðər] s cuoio

leath'er·back tur'tle s tartaruga di mare

leath'er goods' store' s pelletteria

leathery ['lɛðəri] adj coriaceo

leave [liv] s (permission) permesso; (permission to be absent) licenza; (farewell) commiato; **on leave** in licenza; **to take French leave** andarsene all'inglese; **to take leave (of)** prender congedo (da) || v (pret & pp **left** [lɛft]) tr (to go away from) lasciare, uscire da; (to let stay) lasciare; (to bequeath) lasciare in testamento; **leave it to me!** lasciami fare!; **to be left** restare, e.g., **the door was left open** la porta restò aperta; esserci, e.g., **there is no bread left** non c'è più pane; **to leave alone** lasciare in pace; **to leave no stone unturned** cercare ogni possibilità; **to leave off** abbandonare, lasciare; **to leave out** omettere; **to leave things as they are** lasciar stare le cose || intr andarsene; (said of a conveyance) partire

leaven ['lɛvən] s lievito || tr lievitare; (fig) impregnare, permeare

leavening ['lɛvənɪŋ] s lievito

leave' of ab'sence s licenza; (without pay) aspettativa

leave'-tak'ing s commiato

leavings ['livɪŋz] spl rifiuti mpl

Leba·nese [,lɛbə'niz] adj libanese || s (-nese) libanese mf

Lebanon ['lɛbənən] s il Libano

lecher ['lɛtʃər] s libertino

lecherous ['lɛtʃərəs] adj libidinoso

lechery ['lɛtʃəri] s lussuria

lectern ['lɛktərn] s leggio

lecture ['lɛktʃər] s conferenza; (tedious reprimand) pistolotto || tr dare una conferenza a; sermoneggiare || intr fare una conferenza; sermoneggiare

lecturer ['lɛktʃərər] s conferenziere m

ledge [lɛdʒ] s cornice f, cornicione m

ledger ['lɛdʒər] s (com) libro mastro

ledg'er line' s (mus) rigo supplementare

lee [li] s (shelter) rifugio; (naut) parte f sottovento; **lees** feccia

leech [litʃ] s mignatta, sanguisuga; **to stick like a leech** attaccarsi come una sanguisuga

leek [lik] s porro

leer [lɪr] s occhiata lussuriosa or maligna || intr—**to leer at** guardare di sbieco, sbirciare

leer·y ['lɪri] adj (-ier; -iest) sospettoso

leeward ['liwərd] or ['lu·ərd] adj di sottovento || s sottovento, poggia || adv sottovento

lee'way' s (aer, naut) deriva, scarroccio; (in time) (coll) tolleranza; (coll) libertà f d'azione

left [lɛft] adj sinistro; (pol) di sinistra || s sinistra; (boxing) sinistro || adv alla sinistra

left' field' s fuoricampo di sinistra

left'-hand' drive' s guida a sinistra

left-handed ['lɛft'hændɪd] adj (individual) mancino; (awkward) goffo;

(*compliment*) ambiguo; (mach) sinistrorso

leftish ['lɛftɪʃ] *adj* sinistrista

leftist ['lɛftɪst] *adj* di sinistra ‖ *s* membro della sinistra

left'o'ver *adj* & *s* rimanente *m*; **leftovers** resti *mpl*

left'-wing' *adj* di sinistra

left-winger ['lɛft'wɪŋər] *s* (coll) membro dell'estrema sinistra; (coll) membro della sinistra

leg [lɛg] *s* (*of man, animal, table, chair; of trousers*) gamba; (*of fowl; of lamb*) coscia; (*of boot*) gambale *m*; (*of a journey*) tappa; **to be on one's last legs** essere agli estremi, essere ridotto alla disperazione; **to not have a leg to stand on** (coll) non avere la minima giustificazione; **to pull the leg of** (coll) prendere in giro, burlarsi di; **to shake a leg** (coll) affrettarsi; (*to dance*) (coll) ballare; **to stretch one's legs** sgranchirsi le gambe

lega·cy ['lɛgəsi] *s* (-cies) legato

legal ['ligəl] *adj* legale

legali·ty [lɪ'gælɪti] *s* (-ties) legalità *f*

legalize ['ligə,laɪz] *tr* legalizzare

le'gal ten'der *s* denaro a corso legale

legate ['lɛgɪt] *s* legato

legatee [,lɛgə'ti] *s* legatario

legation [lɪ'geʃən] *s* legazione

legend ['lɛdʒənd] *s* leggenda

legendary ['lɛdʒən,dɛri] *adj* leggendario

legerdemain [,lɛdʒərdɪ'men] *s* gioco di prestigio; (*trickery*) imbroglio

legging ['lɛgɪŋ] *s* gambale *m*

leg·gy ['lɛgi] *adj* (-gier; -giest) dalle gambe lunghe

leg'horn' *s* cappello di paglia di Firenze; gallina bianca livornese ‖ **Leghorn** *s* Livorno

legible ['lɛdʒɪbəl] *adj* leggibile

legion ['lidʒən] *s* legione *f*

legislate ['lɛdʒɪs,let] *tr* ordinare per mezzo di legge ‖ *intr* legiferare

legislation [,lɛdʒɪs'leʃən] *s* legislazione

legislative ['lɛdʒɪs,letɪv] *adj* legislativo

legislator ['lɛdʒɪs,lɛtər] *s* legislatore *m*

legislature ['lɛdʒɪs,lɛtʃər] *s* legislatura; corpo legislativo

legitimacy [lɪ'dʒɪtɪməsi] *s* legittimità *f*

legitimate [lɪ'dʒɪtɪmɪt] *adj* legittimo ‖ [lɪ'dʒɪtɪ,met] *tr* legittimare

legit'imate dra'ma *s* teatro serio

legitimize [lɪ'dʒɪtɪ,maɪz] *tr* legittimare

leg' of lamb' *s* cosciotto d'agnello

legume ['lɛgjum] *or* [lɪ'gjum] *s* (*pod*) legume *m*; (*table vegetables*) legumi *mpl*; (bot) leguminose *fpl*

leg'work' *s* lavoro che involve molto cammino

leisure ['liʒər] *or* ['lɛʒər] *s* ozio; **at leisure** senza fretta; disoccupato; **at one's leisure** quando si abbia un po' di tempo libero

lei'sure class' *s* gente agiata

lei'sure hours' *spl* ore *fpl* d'ozio

leisurely ['liʒərli] *or* ['lɛʒərli] *adj* lento ‖ *adv* lentamente, a tempo perso

lei'sure time' *s* tempo libero

lemon ['lɛmən] *s* limone *m*; (*car*) (coll) catorcio

lemonade [,lɛmə'ned] *s* limonata

lem'on squeez'er *s* spremilimoni *m*

lend [lɛnd] *s* (*pret* & *pp* **lent** [lɛnt]) *tr* prestare; (*a hand*) dare

lender ['lɛndər] *s* prestatore *m*

lend'ing li'brary *s* biblioteca circolante

length [lɛŋθ] *s* lunghezza; (*of time*) durata; **at length** finalmente; **to go to any lengths** fare quanto è possibile; essere disposto a tutto; **to keep at arm's length** (*someone else*) tenere a distanza (qlcu); (*said of oneself*) tenere la distanza

lengthen ['lɛŋθən] *tr* allungare ‖ *intr* allungarsi

length'wise' *adj* longitudinale ‖ *adv* per il lungo

length·y ['lɛŋθi] *adj* (-ier; -iest) lungo, prolungato

lenien·cy ['lini·ənsi] *s* (-cies) indulgenza

lenient ['lini·ənt] *adj* indulgente, clemente

lens [lɛnz] *s* lente *f*; (*of the eye*) cristallino

Lent [lɛnt] *s* quaresima

Lenten ['lɛntən] *adj* quaresimale

lentil ['lɛntəl] *s* lenticchia

Leo ['li·o] *s* (astr) il Leone

leopard ['lɛpərd] *s* leopardo

leotard ['li·ə,tɑrd] *s* calzamaglia

leper ['lɛpər] *s* lebbroso

leprosy ['lɛprəsi] *s* lebbra

leprous ['lɛprəs] *adj* lebbroso; (*of an animal or plant*) squamoso

Lesbian ['lɛzbɪ·ən] *adj* lesbico ‖ *s* lesbico; (*female homosexual*) lesbica

lesbianism ['lɛzbɪ·ə,nɪzəm] *s* lesbismo

lese majesty ['liz'mædʒɪsti] *s* delitto di lesa maestà

lesion ['liʒən] *s* lesione

less [lɛs] *adj* minore ‖ *adv* meno; **less and less** sempre meno; **less than** meno che; (*followed by numeral or personal pron*) meno di; (*followed by verb*) meno di quanto ‖ *s* meno

lessee [lɛs'i] *s* locatario; (*of business establishment*) concessionario

lessen ['lɛsən] *tr* diminuire, ridurre ‖ *intr* diminuire, ridursi

lesser ['lɛsər] *adj comp* minore

lesson ['lɛsən] *s* lezione

lessor ['lɛsər] *s* locatore *m*

lest [lɛst] *conj* per paura che

let [lɛt] *v* (*pret* & *pp* **let**; *ger* **letting**) *tr* permettere; (*to rent*) affittare; **let +** *inf* che + *subj*, e.g., **let him go** che vada; **let alone** tanto meno; senza menzionare; **let good enough alone** essere contento dell'onesto; **let us +** *inf* = *1st pl impv*, e.g., **let us sing** cantiamo; **to let** da affittare; **to let alone** lasciare in pace; **to let be** lasciar stare; **to let by** lasciar passare; **to let down** far scendere; deludere; tradire; abbandonare; **to let fly** (*insults*) lanciare; **to let go** lasciar libero; vendere; **to let in** fare entrare; **to let it go at that** non parlarne più; **to let know** far sapere;

let loose sciogliere; **to let out** lasciar uscire; (*a secret*) divulgare; (*a scream*) lasciarsi scappare; (*to enlarge*) allargare; affittare; **to let through** lasciar passare; **to let up** lasciar salire; lasciar alzare ‖ *intr* affittare; **to let down** diminuire gli sforzi; **to let go of** disfarsi di; **to let on** (coll) fare finta; **to not let on** (coll) non lasciar trapelare; **to let out** (said, *e.g., of school*) terminare; **to let up** (coll) cessare; (coll) diminuire

let'down' *s* diminuzione; smacco, umiliazione; delusione

lethal ['liðəl] *adj* letale

lethargic [lɪ'θɑrdʒɪk] *adj* letargico

lethar·gy ['lɛθərdʒi] *s* (-gies) letargo

Lett [lɛt] *s* lettone *mf*; (*language*) lettone *m*

letter ['lɛtər] *s* lettera; **letters** (*literature*) lettere *fpl*, letteratura; **to the letter** alla lettera ‖ *tr* marcare con lettere

let'ter box' *s* cassetta delle lettere

let'ter car'rier *s* postino

let'ter drop' *s* buca delle lettere

let'ter·head' *s* capolettera *m*; (*paper with printed heading*) carta da lettera intestata

lettering ['lɛtərɪŋ] *s* iscrizione; lettere *fpl*

let'ter of cred'it *s* lettera di credito

let'ter o'pener ['opənər] *s* tagliacarte *m*

let'ter pa'per *s* carta da lettere

let'ter-per'fect *adj* alla lettera; che sa alla perfezione

let'ter·press' *s* stampato in tipografia ‖ *adv* a stampa tipografica

let'ter scales' *spl* pesalettere *m*

let'ter·word' *s* sigla

Lettish ['lɛtɪʃ] *adj* & *s* lettone *m*

lettuce ['lɛtɪs] *s* lattuga

let'up' *s* (coll) pausa, sosta; (coll) tregua; **without letup** (coll) senza posa

leucorrhea [,lukə'ri·ə] *s* leucorrea

leukemia [lu'kimɪ·ə] *s* leucemia

Levant [lɪ'vænt] *s* levante *m*

levee ['lɛvi] *s* (*embankment*) argine *m*; (*reception*) ricevimento

lev·el ['lɛvəl] *adj* piano; livellato; equilibrato; **level with** a livello di; **one's level best** (coll) il proprio meglio ‖ *s* (*instrument*) livella; (*degree of elevation*) livello; (*flat surface*) spianata, pianura; **on the level** (slang) onesto; onestamente; **to find one's level** trovare il proprio ambiente ‖ *v* (*pret & pp* -**eled** or -**elled**; *ger* -**eling** or -**elling**) *tr* livellare; (*to flatten out*) spianare; (*e.g., prices*) pareggiare, ragguagliare; (*a gun*) puntare; (coll) gettare a terra; (fig) dirigere ‖ *intr*— **to level off** (aer) volare orizzontalmente

level-headed ['lɛvəl'hɛdɪd] *adj* equilibrato

lev'eling rod' *s* stadia

lever ['livər] or ['lɛvər] *s* leva ‖ *tr* far leva su ‖ *intr* far leva

leverage ['livərɪdʒ] or ['lɛvərɪdʒ] *s* azione di una leva; (fig) potere *m*

leviathan [lɪ'vaɪ·əθən] *s* leviatano

levitation [,lɛvɪ'teʃən] *s* levitazione

levi·ty ['lɛvɪti] *s* (-ties) leggerezza

lev·y ['lɛvi] *s* (-ies) (*of taxes*) esazione; (*of money*) tributo; (*of troops*) leva ‖ *v* (*pret & pp* -**ied**) *tr* (*a tax*) imporre; (*soldiers*) reclutare; (*war*) fare

lewd [lud] *adj* (*lustful*) lascivo; osceno

lexical ['lɛksɪkəl] *adj* lessicale

lexicographer [,lɛksɪ'kɑgrəfər] *s* lessicografo

lexicographic(al) [,lɛksɪko'græfɪk(əl)] *adj* lessicografico

lexicography [,lɛksɪ'kɑgrəfi] *s* lessicografia

lexicology [,lɛksɪ'kɑlədʒi] *s* lessicologia

lexicon ['lɛksɪkən] *s* lessico

liabili·ty [,laɪ·ə'bɪlɪti] *s* (-ties) svantaggio; responsabilità *f*; (*e.g., to disease*) tendenza; (com) passivo; **liabilities** debiti *mpl*; (com) passivo

liabil'ity insur'ance *s* assicurazione sulla responsabilità civile

liable ['laɪ·əbəl] *adj* (*e.g., to disease*; *e.g., to make mistakes*) soggetto; responsabile; probabile; (*e.g., to a fine*) passibile

liaison ['li·ə,zɑn] or [li'ezən] *s* legame *m*; relazione illecita; (mil, nav) collegamento; (phonet) legamento

li'aison of'ficer *s* ufficiale *m* di collegamento

liar ['laɪ·ər] *s* bugiardo, mentitore *m*

libation [laɪ'beʃən] *s* (joc) libazione, bevuta

li·bel ['laɪbəl] *s* diffamazione; (*defamatory writing*) libello ‖ *v* (*pret & pp* -**beled** or -**belled**; *ger* -**beling** or -**belling**) *tr* diffamare

libelous ['laɪbələs] *adj* diffamatorio

liberal ['lɪbərəl] *adj* liberale; (*translation*) libero ‖ *s* liberale *mf*

liberali·ty [,lɪbə'rælɪti] *s* (-ties) liberalità *f*; (*breadth of mind*) ampiezza di vedute

liberal-minded ['lɪbərəl'maɪndɪd] *adj* liberale, tollerante

liberate ['lɪbə,ret] *tr* liberare

liberation [,lɪbə'reʃən] *s* liberazione

liberator ['lɪbə,retər] *s* liberatore *m*

libertine ['lɪbər,tin] *adj* & *s* libertino

liber·ty ['lɪbərti] *s* (-ties) libertà *f*; **to take the liberty to** permettersi di

liberty·loving ['lɪbərti'lʌvɪŋ] *adj* amante della libertà

libidinous [lɪ'bɪdɪnəs] *adj* libidinoso

libido [lɪ'bido] or [lɪ'baɪdo] *s* libidine *f*; (psychoanal) libido *f*

Libra ['librə] or ['laɪbrə] *s* (astr) Bilancia

librarian [laɪ'brɛrɪ·ən] *s* bibliotecario

librar·y ['laɪ,brɛri] or ['laɪbrɛri] *s* (-ies) biblioteca; (*room in a house*; *collection of books*) libreria

li'brary num'ber *s* segnatura

li'brary sci'ence *s* biblioteconomia

libret·to [lɪ'brɛto] *s* (-tos) (mus) libretto

Libya ['lɪbɪ·ə] *s* la Libia

license ['laɪsəns] *s* licenza; (aut) patente *f* ‖ *tr* dare la licenza a li'cense num'ber *s* numero di targa di circolazione

li'cense plate' or tag' *s* targa di circolazione

licentious [laɪ'sɛnʃəs] *adj* licenzioso

lichen ['laɪkən] *s* lichene *m*

lick [lɪk] *s* leccata, leccatura; (coll) esplosione di energia; (coll) velocità *f;* (coll) battitura; (coll) ripulita; **to give a lick and a promise to** (coll) fare rapidamente e con poca attenzione ‖ *tr* leccare; (*said of waves, flames, etc.*) lambire; (*to defeat*) (*coll*) battere, vincere; (*e.g., with a stick*) (coll) bastonare

licorice ['lɪkərɪs] *s* liquirizia

lid [lɪd] *s* coperchio; (*eyelid*) palpebra; (*curb*) (coll) restrizione, freno; (*hat*) (slang) cappello

lie [laɪ] *s* menzogna; **to catch in a lie** pigliare in castagna; **to give the lie to** smentire ‖ *v* (*pret & pp* lied; *ger* lying) *tr*—**to lie oneself out of** or **to lie one's way out of** trarsi fuori da (*un impaccio*) con una menzogna ‖ *intr* mentire ‖ *v* (*pret* lay [le]; *pp* lain [len]; *ger* lying) *intr* essere sdraiato; trovarsi; (*in the grave*) giacere; **to lie down** sdraiarsi

lie' detec'tor *s* macchina della verità

lien [lin] or ['li·ən] *s* diritto di pegno, diritto di garanzia

lieu [lu] *s*—**in lieu of** in luogo di

lieutenant [lu'tɛnənt] *s* luogotenente *m;* (mil) tenente *m;* (nav) tenente *m* di vascello

lieuten'ant colo'nel *s* (mil) tenente *m* colonnello

lieuten'ant command'er *s* (nav) capitano di corvetta

lieuten'ant gen'eral *s* (mil) generale *m* di corpo d'armata

lieuten'ant gov'ernor *s* (USA) vicegovernatore *m*

lieuten'ant jun'ior grade' *s* (nav) sottotenente *m* di vascello

life [laɪf] *adj* (*animate*) vitale; (*lifelong*) perpetuo; (*annuity*) vitalizio; (*working from nature*) dal vero ‖ *s* (lives [laɪvz]) vita; (*of an insurance policy*) forza; **for life** a vita; **for the life of me** per quanto io provi; **the life and soul of** (*e.g., the party*) l'anima di; **to come to life** tornare a sé; riprender vita; **to depart this life** passar a miglior vita; **to run for one's life** scappare a tutta corsa

life' annu'ity *s* rendita vitalizia

life' belt' *s* cintura di salvataggio

life'boat' *s* imbarcazione di salvataggio, lancia di salvataggio

life' buoy' *s* salvagente *m*

life' float' *s* zattera di salvataggio

life'guard' *s* bagnino

life' impris'onment *s* ergastolo

life' insur'ance *s* assicurazione sulla vita

life' jack'et *s* cintura or giubbotto di salvataggio

lifeless ['laɪflɪs] *adj* inanimato; (*in a faint*) esanime; senza vita

life'like' *adj* (*e.g., portrait*) parlante; naturale

life' line' *s* sagola di salvataggio; (fig) linea di comunicazioni vitale

life'long' *adj* perpetuo, a vita

life' of Ri'ley ['raɪli] *s* vita del michelaccio

life' of the par'ty *s* anima della festa

life' preserv'er [prɪ'zʌrvər] *s* salvagente *m*

lifer ['laɪfər] *s* (slang) ergastolano

life' raft' *s* zattera di salvataggio

life'sav'er *s* salvatore *m* della vita; (*something that saves from a predicament*) ancora di salvezza

life' sen'tence *s* condanna all'ergastolo

life'-size' *adj* in grandezza naturale

life'time' *adj* vitalizio ‖ *s* corso della vita

life' vest' *s* (air, naut) giubbotto salvagente or di salvataggio

life'work' *s* lavoro di tutta una vita

lift [lɪft] *s* sollevamento; (*act of helping*) aiuto; (*ride*) passaggio; (*apparatus*) elevatore *m;* (aer) portanza ‖ *tr* sollevare, alzare; (*one's hat*) levarsi; rimuovere; (coll) plagiare; (coll) rubare; (*fire*) (mil) sospendere ‖ *intr* sollevare, sollevarsi; (*said, e.g., of fog*) dissiparsi

lift'-off' *s* (aer) decollo verticale

lift' truck' *s* carrello elevatore

ligament ['lɪgəmənt] *s* legamento

ligature ['lɪgətʃər] *s* legatura

light [laɪt] *adj* (*in weight*) leggero; (*hair*) biondo; (*complexion*) chiaro; (*oil*) fluido; (naut) con poco carico; (*room*) chiaro, illuminato; (*beer*) chiaro; **light in the head** (*dizzy*) allegro; (*silly*) scimunito; **to make light of** prendere sotto gamba ‖ *s* luce *f;* (*to light a cigarette*) fuoco; (*to control traffic*) segnale *m;* (*shining example*) luminare *m;* (*lighthouse*) faro; (*window*) luce *f;* **according to one's lights** secondo l'intelligenza che il buon Dio gli (le) ha dato; **against the light** controluce; **in this light** sotto questo punto di vista; **lights** esempio; (*of sheep*) polmone *m;* **to come to light** venire alla luce; **to shed** or **throw light on** mettere in luce; **to strike a light** accendere un fiammifero ‖ *v* (*pret & pp* lighted or lit [lɪt]) *tr* (*to furnish with illumination*) illuminare; (*to ignite*) accendere; **to light up** illuminare ‖ *intr* illuminarsi; accendersi; (*said, e.g., of a bird*) posarsi; (*from a car*) scendere; **to light into** (coll) gettarsi contro; **to light out** (slang) darsela a gambe; **to light upon** imbattersi in ‖ *adv* senza bagagli; senza carico

light' bulb' *s* lampadina

light-complexioned ['laɪtkəm'plɛkʃənd] *adj* dal colorito chiaro

lighten ['laɪtən] *tr* alleggerire, sgravare; illuminare; (*to cheer up*) rallegrare ‖ *intr* alleggerirsi; (*to become less dark*) illuminarsi; (*to give off flashes of lightning*) lampeggiare

lighter ['laɪtər] *s* accenditore *m;* (naut) burchio

light-fingered ['laɪt'fɪŋgərd] *adj* svelto di mano, con le mani lunghe

light-footed ['laɪt'futɪd] *adj* agile
light-headed ['laɪt'hɛdɪd] *adj* (*dizzy*) allegro; (*simple*) scemo
light-hearted ['laɪt'hɑrtɪd] *adj* allegro
light'house' *s* faro
lighting ['laɪtɪŋ] *s* illuminazione
lightly ['laɪtli] *adv* alla leggera
light' me'ter *s* esposimetro
lightness ['laɪtnɪs] *s* (*in weight*) leggerezza; (*in illumination*) chiarezza
light·ning ['laɪtnɪŋ] *s* lampo, fulmine *m* ‖ *v* (*ger* -**ning**) *intr* lampeggiare
light'ning arrest'er [ə'rɛstər] *s* scaricatore *m*
light'ning bug' *s* lucciola
light'ning rod' *s* parafulmine *m*
light' op'era *s* operetta
light'ship' *s* battello faro
light-struck ['laɪt ,strʌk] *adj* che ha preso luce
light'weight' *adj* leggero; da mezza stagione, e.g., **lightweight coat** cappotto da mezza stagione
light'-year' *s* anno luce
likable ['laɪkəbəl] *adj* simpatico
like [laɪk] *adj* uguale, simile; uguale a, simile a, e.g., **this hat is like mine** questo cappello è simile al mio; (elec) di segno uguale; **like father like son** tale il padre quale il figlio; **to feel like** + *ger* aver voglia di + *inf;* **to look like** assomigliare a; sembrare, e.g., **it looks like rain** sembra che pioverà ‖ *s* (*liking*) preferenza; (*fellow man*) simile *m;* **and the like** e cose dello stesso genere; **to give like for like** rendere pane per focaccia ‖ *adv* come; **like enough** (coll) probabilmente ‖ *prep* come ‖ *conj* (coll) come; come se; (coll) che, e.g., **it seems like he is afraid** sembra che abbia paura ‖ *tr* voler bene (with *dat*), e.g., **I like her very much** le voglio molto bene; trovar piacere in, e.g., **I like music** trovo piacere nella musica; piacere (with *dat*), e.g., **John likes apples** le mele piacciono a Giovanni; **to like best** or **better** preferire; **to like it** in trovarsi a proprio agio in; **to like to** + *inf* piacere (with *dat*) + *inf*, e.g., **she likes to dance** le piace ballare; gradire che + *subj*, e.g., **I should like him to pay a visit to my parents** gradirei che facesse una visita ai miei genitori ‖ *intr* volere, desiderare, e.g., **as you like** come desidera; **if you like** se vuole
likelihood ['laɪklɪ ,hud] *s* probabilità *f*
like·ly ['laɪkli] *adj* (-**lier**; -**liest**) probabile; verosimile; a proposito; promettente; **to be likely to** + *inf* essere probabile che + *fut*, e.g., **Mary is likely to get married in the spring** è probabile che Maria si sposerà in primavera ‖ *adv* probabilmente
like-minded ['laɪk'maɪndɪd] *adj* dello stesso parere, della stessa opinione
liken ['laɪkən] *tr* paragonare
likeness ['laɪknɪs] *s* (*picture*) ritratto; (*similarity*) rassomiglianza; apparenza
like'wise' *adv* ugualmente; inoltre; **to do likewise** fare lo stesso

liking ['laɪkɪŋ] *s* simpatia; **to be to the liking of** essere di gusto di; **to have a liking for** (*things*) prendere gusto per; (*people*) affezionarsi a
lilac ['laɪlək] *adj* & *s* lilla *m*
Lilliputian [,lɪlɪ'pju∫ən] *adj* & *s* lillipuziano
lilt [lɪlt] *s* canzone *f* a cadenza; movimento a cadenza; (*in verse*) cadenza
lil·y ['lɪli] *s* (-**ies**) giglio; **to gild the lily** cercare di migliorare quanto è già perfetto
lil'y of the val'ley *s* mughetto
li'ma bean' ['laɪmə] *s* fagiolo bianco
limb [lɪm] *s* (*of body*) membro, arto; (*of tree*) ramo; (*of cross*) braccio; **to be out on a limb** (coll) essere nei guai
limber ['lɪmbər] *adj* agile ‖ *intr*—**to limber up** sciogliersi i muscoli, sgranchirsi le gambe
lim·bo ['lɪmbo] *s* (-**bos**) esilio; dimenticatoio; (theol) limbo
lime [laɪm] *s* (*calcium oxide*) calce *f;* (*Citrus aurantifolia*) limetta agra; (*linden tree*) tiglio ‖ *tr* gessare
lime'kiln' *s* fornace *f* da calce
lime'light' *s*—**to be in the limelight** essere in vista
limerick ['lɪmərɪk] *s* canzoncina umoristica di cinque versi
lime'stone' *s* calcare *m*
limit ['lɪmɪt] *s* limite *m;* (coll) colmo; **to go to the limit** andare agli estremi ‖ *tr* limitare
limitation [,lɪmɪ'te∫ən] *s* limitazione
lim'ited-ac'cess high'way ['lɪmɪtɪd] *s* autostrada, strada con corsia d'accesso
lim'ited com'pany *s* società *f* a responsabilità limitata
lim'ited mon'archy *s* monarchia costituzionale
limitless ['lɪmɪtlɪs] *adj* illimitato
limousine ['lɪmə ,zin] or [,lɪmə'zin] *s* berlina
limp [lɪmp] *adj* floscio; debole ‖ *s* zoppicatura ‖ *intr* zoppicare
limpid ['lɪmpɪd] *adj* limpido
linage ['laɪnɪdʒ] *s* (typ) numero di linee
linchpin ['lɪnt∫ ,pɪn] *s* acciarino
linden ['lɪndən] *s* tiglio
line [laɪn] *s* linea; (*e.g., of people*) fila; (*of trees*) filare *m;* (*for fishing*) lenza; (*written or printed*) rigo, riga; (*wrinkle*) ruga; (*of goods*) ramo; (naut) gherlino; **all along the line** su tutta la linea; **in line** allineato; sotto controllo; **in line with** secondo; **out of line** fuori d'allineamento; (slang) in disaccordo; **to bring into line** far filare; **to draw the line at** fermarsi a; stabilire il limite a; **to fall in line** conformarsi; allinearsi; **to have a line on** (coll) aver informazioni su; **to read between the lines** leggere fra le righe; **to stand in line** fare la coda; **to toe the line** filare diritto; **to wait in line** fare la fila ‖ *tr* rigare; (*e.g., the street*) schierare lungo; (*a suit*) foderare; (*a brake*) rivestire; **to line up** allineare; trovare, scovare ‖ *intr*

—**to line up** mettersi in fila; fare la coda

lineage ['lɪnɪ·ɪdʒ] s lignaggio

lineaments ['lɪnɪ·əmənts] spl lineamenti mpl

linear ['lɪnɪ·ər] adj lineare

line'man s (-men) (elec) guardafili m; (sports) guardalinee m; (surv) assistente geometra m

linen ['lɪnən] adj di tela di lino ‖ s (fabric) tela di lino, lino; (yarn) filo di lino; biancheria

lin'en clos'et s guardaroba m per la biancheria

line' of fire' s (mil) linea di tiro

line' of least' resist'ance s principio del minimo sforzo; **to follow the line of least resistance** prendere la via più facile

line' of sight' s visuale f; (mil) linea di mira

liner ['laɪnər] s transatlantico

line'-up' s disposizione; (of prisoners) allineamento; (sports) formazione

linger ['lɪŋgər] intr indugiare, soffermarsi; (to be tardy) tardare; rimanere in vita; **to linger over** contemplare

lingerie [,læn ʒə'rɪ] s biancheria intima

lingering ['lɪŋgərɪŋ] adj prolungato

lingual ['lɪŋgwəl] adj linguale ‖ s suono linguale

linguist ['lɪŋgwɪst] s poliglotto; (specialist in linguistics) glottologo

linguistic [lɪŋ'gwɪstɪk] adj linguistico ‖ **linguistics** s linguistica, glottologia

lining ['laɪnɪŋ] s (of a coat) fodera; (of auto brake) guarnizione; (of a furnace) rivestimento interno; (of wall) rivestimento

link [lɪŋk] s anello, maglia; unione; (of sausage) nocco; **links** campo di golf ‖ tr connettere ‖ intr connettersi

linnet ['lɪnɪt] s fanello

linotype ['laɪnə,taɪp] s linotype f ‖ tr comporre in linotipia

lin'otype op'erator s linotipista mf

linseed ['lɪn,sid] s linosa

lin'seed oil' s olio di lino

lint [lɪnt] s peluria, sfilacciatura; (for dressing wounds) filaccia

lintel ['lɪntəl] s architrave m

lion ['laɪ·ən] s leone m; celebrità f; **to beard the lion in his den** affrontare l'avversario a casa sua; **to put one's head in the lion's mouth** cacciarsi nei pericoli

lioness ['laɪ·ənɪs] s leonessa

lion-hearted ['laɪ·ən,hɑrtɪd] adj cuor di leone, coraggioso

lionize ['laɪ·ə,naɪz] tr festeggiare come una celebrità

li'ons' den' s fossa dei leoni

li'on's share' s parte f del leone

lip [lɪp] s labbro; (of a jar) beccuccio; (slang) linguaggio insolente; **to smack one's lips** leccarsi le labbra

lip'read' v (pret & pp -read [,rɛd]) tr leggere le labbra di ‖ intr leggere le labbra

lip' read'ing s labiolettura

lip' serv'ice s omaggio non sentito

lip'stick' s rossetto per le labbra, matita per le labbra

lique·fy ['lɪkwɪ,faɪ] v (pret & pp -fied) tr & intr liquefare

liqueur [lɪ'kʌr] s liquore m

liquid ['lɪkwɪd] adj liquido ‖ s liquido; (phonet) liquida

liquidate ['lɪkwɪ,det] tr & intr liquidare

liquidity [lɪ'kwɪdɪti] s liquidità f

liq'uid meas'ure s misura di capacità per liquidi

liquor ['lɪkər] s distillato alcolico, bevanda alcolica; (broth) brodo

Lisbon ['lɪzbən] s Lisbona

lisp [lɪsp] s pronuncia blesa ‖ intr parlare bleso

lissome ['lɪsəm] adj flessibile, agile

list [lɪst] s lista, elenco; (border) orlo; (selvage) cimossa, vivagno; (naut) sbandamento; **lists** lizza; **to enter the lists** entrare in lizza ‖ tr elencare, listare ‖ intr (naut) sbandare, andare alla banda

listen ['lɪsən] intr ascoltare; obbedire; **to listen in** ascoltare una conversazione; (rad) captare una comunicazione; **to listen to** ascoltare; obbedire a, prestare attenzione a; **to listen to reason** intendere ragione

listener ['lɪsənər] s ascoltatore m; radioascoltatore m

lis'tening post' s (mil) posto di ascolto

listless ['lɪstlɪs] adj svogliato

list' price' s prezzo di catalogo

lita·ny ['lɪtəni] s (-nies) litania

liter ['lɪtər] s litro

literacy ['lɪtərəsi] s abilità f di leggere e scrivere; istruzione

literal ['lɪtərəl] adj letterale

literary ['lɪtə,reri] adj letterario; (individual) letterato

literate ['lɪtərɪt] adj che sa leggere e scrivere; (educated) istruito; (well-read) letterato ‖ s persona che sa leggere e scrivere; letterato

literature ['lɪtərət/ər] s letteratura; (printed matter) opuscoli pubblicitari

lithe [laɪð] adj flessibile, agile

lithium ['lɪθɪ·əm] s litio

lithograph ['lɪθə,græf] or ['lɪθə,graf] s litografia ‖ tr litografare

lithographer [lɪ'θagrəfər] s litografo

lithography [lɪ'θagrəfi] s litografia

Lithuania [,lɪθu'enɪ·ə] s la Lituania

Lithuanian [,lɪθu'enɪ·ən] adj & s lituano

litigant ['lɪtɪgənt] adj & s litigante mf

litigate ['lɪtɪ,get] tr & intr litigare

litigation [,lɪtɪ'geʃən] s litigio; (lawsuit) lite f, causa

litmus ['lɪtməs] s tornasole m

lit'mus pa'per s cartina al tornasole

litter ['lɪtər] s disordine m; (scattered rubbish) pattume m; (young brought forth at one birth) figliata; (of puppies) cucciolata; (bedding for animals) strame m; (stretcher; bed carried by men or animals) lettiga, portantina ‖ tr mettere in disordine; spargere rifiuti per; coprire di strame ‖ intr partorire

lit'ter·bug' s sparpagliatore m di rifiuti
littering ['lɪtərɪŋ] s—**no littering** vietato gettare rifiuti
little ['lɪtəl] adj (in size) piccolo; (in amount) poco, e.g., **little salt** poco sale; **a little** un po' di, e.g., **a little salt** un po' di sale; **the little ones** i piccini ‖ s poco; **a little** un po'; **to make little of** farsi gioco di; non pigliar sul serio; **to think little of** non tener di conto ‖ adv poco; **little by little** poco a poco, mano a mano
Lit'tle Bear' s Orsa minore
Lit'tle Dip'per s Piccolo Carro
lit'tle fin'ger s mignolo; **to twist around one's little finger** maneggiare come un fantoccio
lit'tle·neck' s piccola vongola (Venus mercenaria)
lit'tle owl' s civetta
lit'tle peo'ple spl fate fpl; folletti mpl
Lit'tle Red Rid'inghood' ['raɪdɪŋ ,hud] s Cappuccetto Rosso
lit'tle slam' s (bridge) piccolo slam
liturgic(al) [lɪ'tʌrdʒɪk(əl)] adj liturgico
litur·gy ['lɪtərdʒi] s (-gies) liturgia
livable ['lɪvəbəl] adj abitabile; socievole; tollerabile
live [laɪv] adj vivo; (flame) ardente; di attualità; (elec) sotto tensione; (telv) in diretta ‖ [lɪv] tr vivere; **to live down** (one's past) far dimenticare; **to live it up** (coll) darsi alla bella vita, scialare; **to live out** (e.g., a war) sopravvivere (with dat) ‖ intr vivere; **to live from hand to mouth** vivere alla giornata; **to live high** darsi alla bella vita; **to live on** continuare a vivere; (e.g., vegetables) vivere di; vivere alle spalle di; **to live up to** (one's promises) compiere; (one's earnings) spendere
live' coal' [laɪv] s brace f
livelihood ['laɪvlɪ ,hud] s vita; **to earn one's livelihood** guadagnarsi la vita
livelong ['lɪv ,lɔŋ] or ['lɪv ,lɑŋ] adj— **all the livelong day** tutto il santo giorno
live·ly ['laɪvli] adj (-lier; -liest) vivo, vivace; (color) vivido; (resilient) elastico; (tune) brioso
liven ['laɪvən] tr animare ‖ intr animarsi, rianimarsi
liver ['lɪvər] s abitante mf; (anat) fegato
liver·y ['lɪvəri] s (-ies) livrea
liv'ery·man s (-men) stalliere m
liv'ery sta'ble s stallaggio
livestock ['laɪv ,stɑk] adj zootecnico ‖ s bestiame m
live' wire' [laɪv] s (elec) filo carico di corrente; (slang) persona energica
livid ['lɪvɪd] adj livido; (with anger) incollerito
living ['lɪvɪŋ] adj vivo; (conditions) abitativo ‖ s vivere m; **to earn a living** guadagnarsi la vita
liv'ing quar'ters spl abitazione, alloggio
liv'ing room' s stanza di soggiorno
liv'ing wage' s salario sufficiente per vivere
lizard ['lɪzərd] s lucertola

load [lod] s peso, carico; **loads of** (coll) un mucchio di; **to get a load of** (slang) stare a vedere; (slang) stare a sentire; **to have a load on** (slang) essere ubriaco ‖ tr caricare ‖ intr caricarsi
loaded ['lodɪd] adj caricato; (slang) ubriaco fradicio; (slang) ricchissimo
load'ed dice' spl dadi truccati
load'stone' s magnetite f; (fig) calamita
loaf [lof] s (loaves [lovz]) pane m; (molded mass) forma; (of sugar) pane m; (long and thin loaf) filone m ‖ intr batter fiacca, oziare
loafer ['lofər] s fannullone m
loam [lom] s ricca argilla sabbiosa; terra da fonderia
loan [lon] s prestito; **to hit for a loan** (coll) dare una stoccata a ‖ tr prestare
loan' shark' s (coll) strozzino
loan' word' s (ling) prestito
loath [loθ] adj poco disposto; **nothing loath** molto volentieri
loathe [loð] tr detestare, aborrire
loathsome ['loðsəm] adj abominevole, disgustoso
lob [lab] s (tennis) pallonetto ‖ v (pret & pp lobbed; ger lobbing) tr (tennis) dare un pallonetto a
lob·by ['labi] s (-bies) anticamera, vestibolo; sollecitazione di voti ‖ v (pret & pp -bied) intr sollecitare voti, influenzare il voto dietro le quinte
lobbyist ['labɪ ·ɪst] s politicante m che cerca di influenzare il voto dietro le quinte
lobe [lob] s lobo
lobster ['labstər] s (Palinurus vulgaris) aragosta; (Hommarus vulgaris) astice m
lob'ster pot' s nassa per aragoste
local ['lokəl] adj locale ‖ s treno accelerato; notizia di interesse locale; (of a union) sezione
locale [lo'kæl] s località f
locali·ty [lo'kælɪti] s (-ties) località f
localize ['lokə ,laɪz] tr localizzare
lo'cal op'tion s referendum m locale sulla vendita di alcolici
locate [lo'ket] or ['loket] tr (to discover the location of) localizzare; (to place, settle) situare, stabilire; (to ascribe a location to) individuare ‖ intr stabilirsi
location [lo'keʃən] s localizzazione; posizione; sito; **on location** (mov) in esterno
lock [lak] s serratura; (of a canal) chiusa; (of hair) ciocca; (of a firearm) percussore m; (mach) freno; **lock, stock, and barrel** (coll) completamente; **under lock and key** sotto chiave ‖ tr chiudere a chiave; serrare; (a boat) far passare per una chiusa; unire; abbracciare; **to lock in** chiudere sotto chiave; **to lock out** chiudere fuori; (workers) sbarrare dal lavoro; **to lock up** chiudere a chiave; incarcerare
locker ['lakər] s armadietto a chiave; (in the form of a chest) bauletto

lock'er room' s spogliatoio
locket ['lɑkɪt] s medaglione m
lock'jaw' s tetano, trisma m
lock' nut' s controdado
lock'out' s serrata
lock'smith' s magnano, fabbro
lock' step' s—**to march in lock step** marciare a passo serrato
lock' stitch' s punto a filo doppio
lock' ten'der s guardiano di chiusa
lock'up' s prigione; (typ) messa in forma
lock' wash'er s rondella di sicurezza
locomotive [ˌlokə'motɪv] s locomotiva
lo·cus ['lokəs] s (-ci [saɪ]) luogo
locust ['lokəst] s (ent) locusta; (cicada) (ent) cicala; (bot) robinia
lode [lod] s filone m, vena
lode'star' s stella polare; guida
lodge [lɑdʒ] s casetta; padiglione m da caccia; albergo; (e.g., of Masons) loggia || tr alloggiare, ospitare; depositare; contenere; (a complaint) sporgere || intr alloggiare; essere contenuto, trovarsi; andar a finire
lodger ['lɑdʒər] s inquilino
lodging ['lɑdʒɪŋ] s alloggio
loft [lɔft] or [lɑft] s (attic) solaio; (hayloft) fienile m; (in theater or church) galleria
loft·y ['lɔfti] or ['lɑfti] adj (-ier; -iest) alto, elevato; (haughty) orgoglioso
log [lɔg] or [lɑg] s ceppo, ciocco; (naut) solcometro; (aer, naut) giornale m di bordo; **to sleep like a log** dormire della grossa || v (pret & pp logged; ger logging) tr registrare; (a speed) fare; (a distance) percorrere
logarithm ['lɔgəˌrɪðəm] or ['lɑgəˌrɪðəm] s logaritmo
log'book' s (aer, naut) libro di bordo
log' cab'in s capanna di tronchi
log' chip' s (naut) barchetta
log' driv'er s zatteriere m
log' driv'ing ['draɪvɪŋ] s fluitazione
logger ['lɔgər] or ['lɑgər] s taglialegna m; trattore m per trasporto tronchi
log'ger·head' s testone m; **at loggerheads** in lite
loggia ['lodʒə] s loggia
logic ['lɑdʒɪk] s logica
logical ['lɑdʒɪkəl] adj logico
logician [lo'dʒɪʃən] s logico
logistic(al) [lo'dʒɪstɪk(əl)] adj logistico
logistics [lo'dʒɪstɪks] s logistica
log'jam' s ingorgo fluviale dovuto a ammasso di tronchi; (fig) ristagno
log' line' s (naut) sagola
log'roll' intr barattare favori politici
log'wood' s campeggio
loin [lɔɪn] s lombo; **to gird up one's loins** prepararsi per l'azione
loin'cloth' s perizoma m, copripudende m
loiter ['lɔɪtər] tr—**to loiter away** (time) sprecare in ozio || intr bighellonare, trastullarsi
loiterer ['lɔɪtərər] s perdigiorno
loll [lɑl] intr sdraiarsi pigramente, adagiarsi pigramente; pendere
lollipop ['lɑliˌpɑp] s caramella sullo stecchetto, lecca-lecca m

Lombard ['lɑmbɑrd] or ['lɑmbərd] adj & s lombardo; (hist) longobardo
Lom'bardy pop'lar s pioppo italico
London ['lʌndən] adj londinese || s Londra
Londoner ['lʌndənər] s londinese mf
lone [lon] adj solo; solitario
loneliness ['lonlinɪs] s solitudine f
lone·ly ['lonli] adj (-lier; -liest) solingo, solo, solitario
lonesome ['lonsəm] adj solitario
lone' wolf' s (coll) orso, solitario
long [lɔŋ] or [lɑŋ] (**longer** ['lɔŋgər] or ['lɑŋgər]; **longest** ['lɔŋgɪst] or ['lɑŋgɪst]) adj lungo; **three meters long** lungo tre metri || adv molto, molto tempo; **as long as** mentre; (provided) fin tanto che; (inasmuch as) dato che; **before long** fra poco; **how long?** quanto?; **long ago** molto tempo fa; **long before** molto prima; **long since** molto tempo fa; **no longer** non più; **so long!** (coll) ciao!, arrivederci!; **so long as** fino a che, finché || intr anelare; **to long for** sviscerarsi per, sospirare per
long'boat' s (naut) lancia
long'-dis'tance adj (telp) interurbano, intercomunale; (sports) di fondo; (aer) a distanza
long'-drawn'-out' adj prolungato
longeron ['lɑndʒərən] s longherone m
longevity [lɑn'dʒɛviti] s longevità f
long' face' s (coll) faccia triste, muso lungo
long'hair' adj & s (coll) intellettuale mf; (coll) musicomane mf
long'hand' adj (scritto) a mano || s scrittura a mano; **in longhand** scritto a mano
longing ['lɔŋɪŋ] or ['lɑŋɪŋ] adj bramoso, anelante || s brama, anelito
longitude ['lɑndʒɪˌtjud] or ['lɑndʒɪˌtud] s longitudine f
long·lived ['lɔŋ'laɪvd], ['lɔŋ'lɪvd], ['lɑŋ'laɪvd] or ['lɑŋ'lɪvd] adj (person) longevo, di lunga vita; (e.g., rumor) di lunga durata
long'-play'ing rec'ord s disco di grande durata
long'-range' adj a lunga portata
long'shore'man s (-men) portuale m, scaricatore m
long'stand'ing adj vecchio, che esiste da lungo tempo
long'-suf'fering adj paziente, longanime
long' suit' s (cards) serie lunga; (fig) forte m
long'-term' adj a lunga scadenza
long'-wind'ed adj verboso; (speech) chilometrico
look [luk] s (appearance) aspetto; (glance) sguardo; (search) ricerca; **looks** aspetto, apparenza; **to take a look at** dare un'occhiata a || tr guardare; (one's age) mostrare; **to look daggers at** fulminare con lo sguardo; **to look up** (e.g., in a dictionary) cercare; andare a visitare; venire a visitare || intr guardare; cercare; parere; **look out!** attenzione!; **to look after** badare a; occuparsi di; **to look at** guardare; **to look back** riguardare

(fig) guardare al passato; **to look down on** s.o. guardare qlcu dall'alto in basso; **to look for** cercare; aspettarsi; **to look forward to** anticipare il piacere di; **to look ill** avere una brutta cera; **to look in on** passare per la casa di; **to look into** esaminare a fondo; **to look like** sembrare, parere; **to look out** fare attenzione; **to look out for** aver cura di; **to look out of** guardare da; **to look out on** dare su; **to look through** guardare per; (*a book*) sfogliare; **to look toward** dare su; **to look up to** ammirare, guardare con ammirazione; **to look well** avere una buona cera; fare figura

looker-on [,lʊkər'an] or [,lʊkər'ɔn] *s* (**lookers-on**) astante *m*

look'ing glass' ['lʊkɪŋ] *s* specchio

look'out' *s* guardia; (*person; watch kept; place from which a watch is kept*) vedetta; (*concern*) (coll) affare *m;* **to be on the lookout** stare in guardia; **to be on the lookout for** essere in cerca di

loom [lum] *s* telaio ‖ *intr* apparire indistintamente; pararsi dinanzi; apparire

loon [lun] *s* scemo; fannullone *m;* (orn) (*Gavia*) strolaga

loon·y ['luni] *adj* (**-ier; -iest**) (slang) pazzo ‖ *s* (**-ies**) (slang) pazzo

loop [lup] *s* cappio; (*e.g., of a road*) tortuosità *f;* (*for fastening a button*) occhiello; (aer) cerchio or giro della morte; (phys) ventre *m;* ‖ *tr* fare cappi in; annodare; **to loop the loop** (aer) fare il giro della morte ‖ *intr* avanzare tortuosamente, girare

loop'hole' *s* (*narrow opening*) feritoia; (*means of evasion*) scappatoia

loose [lus] *adj* libero, sciolto; (*available*) disponibile; (*not firm*) rilasciato; (*tooth*) che balla; (*unchaste*) facile; (*garment*) ampio; (*soil*) smosso; (*translation*) libero; (*rein*) lento; **to become loose** sciogliersi; **to break loose** mettersi in libertà; **to have loose bowels** avere la diarrea; **to turn loose** liberare ‖ *s*—**to be on the loose** (coll) essere in libertà; (coll) correre la cavallina ‖ *tr* sciogliere; slegare; lanciare

loose' change' *s* spiccioli *mpl*

loose' end' *s* capo sciolto; **at loose ends** indeciso; disoccupato, senza nulla da fare

loose'-leaf' *adj* a fogli mobili

loosen ['lusən] *tr* snodare; rilasciare; smuovere; allentare; (*the bowels*) liberare dalla stitichezza ‖ *intr* snodarsi; rilasciarsi; smuoversi; allentarsi

looseness ['lusnɪs] *s* scioltezza; (*in morals*) rilassamento

loose-tongued ['lus'tʌŋd] *adj* sciolto di lingua; linguacciuto, maldicente

loot [lut] *s* bottino ‖ *tr* saccheggiare

lop [lap] *v* (*pret & pp* **lopped**) *ger* **lopping**) *tr* lasciar cadere, lasciar penzolare; **to lop off** mozzare; (*a tree*) potare; (*a vine*) stralciare ‖ *intr* penzolare

lopsided ['lap'saɪdɪd] *adj* che pende da una parte; asimmetrico, sproporzionato

loquacious [lo'kweʃəs] *adj* loquace

lord [lɔrd] *s* signore *m;* (Brit) lord *m* ‖ *tr*—**to lord it over** signoreggiare su

lord·ly ['lɔrdli] *adj* (**-lier; -liest**) signorile, magnifico; altero, disdegnoso, arrogante

Lord's' Day', the la domenica, il giorno del Signore

lordship ['lɔrdʃɪp] *s* signoria

Lord's' Prayer' *s* paternostro

Lord's' Sup'per *s* Eucarestia; Ultima Cena

lore [lor] *s* tradizioni *fpl* popolari; cognizioni *fpl*

lorgnette [lɔrn'jɛt] *s* occhialetto, lorgnette *f;* binocolo da teatro col manico

lor·ry ['lari] or ['lɔri] *s* (**-ries**) (rr) vagoncino; (Brit) camion *m*

lose [luz] *v* (*pret & pp* **lost** [lɔst] or [last]) *tr* perdere; (*said of a physician*) non riuscire a salvare; **to lose heart** perdersi d'animo; **to lose oneself** perdersi, smarrirsi ‖ *intr* perdere; (*said of a watch*) ritardare; **to lose out** rimetterci

loser ['luzər] *s* perdente *mf*

losing ['luzɪŋ] *adj* perdente ‖ **losings** *spl* perdite *fpl*

loss [lɔs] or [las] *s* perdita; **to be at a loss** essere perplesso; **to be at a loss to** + *inf* non saper come + *inf;* **to sell at a loss** vendere in perdita

loss' of face' *s* perdita di faccia

lost [lɔst] or [last] *adj* perduto; **lost in thought** assorto in sè stesso; **lost to** perso per; insensibile a

lost'-and-found' depart'ment *s* ufficio degli oggetti smarriti

lost' sheep' *s* percorella smarrita

lot [lat] *s* (*for building*) lotto; (*fate*) sorte *f;* (*parcel, portion*) partita; (*of people*) gruppo; (coll) grande quantità *f;* (coll) tipo, soggetto; **a lot (of)** or **lots of** (coll) molto, molti; **to cast** or **to throw in one's lot with** condividere la sorte di; **to draw** or **to cast lots** tirare a sorte

lotion ['loʃən] *s* lozione

lotter·y ['latəri] *s* (**-ies**) lotteria, riffa

lotto ['lato] *s* tombola, lotto

lotus ['lotəs] *s* loto

loud [laʊd] *adj* forte; (*noisy*) rumoroso; (*voice*) alto; (*garish*) sgargiante, chiassoso, appariscente; (*foul-smelling*) puzzolente ‖ *adv* a voce alta; rumorosamente

loud-mouthed ['laʊd,maʊθt] or ['laʊd,maʊðd] *adj* chiassone

loud'speak'er *s* altoparlante *m*

lounge [laʊndʒ] *s* divano, sofà *m;* sala soggiorno; ridotto ‖ *intr* oziare, star senza far niente; bighellonare; **to lounge around** bighellonare

lounge' liz'ard *s* (slang) damerino, bellimbusto, gagà *m*

louse [laʊs] *s* (**lice** [laɪs]) pidocchio ‖ *tr*—**to louse up** (slang) rovinare

lous·y ['laʊzi] *adj* (**-ier; -iest**) pidocchioso; (*mean; bungling*) (coll) schifoso; (*filthy*) (coll) sporco; **lousy with** (*e.g., money*) (slang) pieno di

lout [laut] *s* gaglioffo, tanghero

louver ['luvər] *s* sportello girevole di persiana; (aut) feritoia per ventilazione

lovable ['lʌvəbəl] *adj* amabile

love [lʌv] *s* amore *m;* (tennis) zero; **not for love nor money** a nessun prezzo; **to be in love (with)** essere innamorato (di); **to make love to** fare l'amore con || *tr* amare; voler bene a; piacere (with *dat*), e.g., **she loves short skirts** le piacciono le sottane corte

love' affair' *s* passione, amori *mpl*

love'bird' *s* (orn) inseparabile *m;* **lovebirds** (slang) amanti appassionati

love' child' *s* figlio naturale

love' feast' *s* agape *f*

loveless ['lʌvlɪs] *adj* senza amore

lovelorn ['lʌv,lɔrn] *adj* abbandonato dalla persona amata

love·ly ['lʌvli] *adj* (-lier; -liest) bello; (coll) delizioso

love' match' *s* matrimonio d'amore

love' po'tion *s* filtro d'amore

lover ['lʌvər] *s* amante *m;* (*e.g., of music*) amico, appassionato

love' seat' *s* amorino

love'sick' *adj* malato d'amore

love'sick'ness *s* mal *m* d'amore

love' song' *s* canzone *f* d'amore

loving ['lʌvɪŋ] *adj* affezionato, amoroso; **your loving son** il vostro affezionato figlio

lov'ing-kind'ness *s* tenera sollecitudine

low [lo] *adj* basso; (*deep*) profondo; (*diet*) magro; (*visibility*) cattivo; (*dress*) scollato; (*dejected*) abbattuto; (*fire*) lento; (*flame; speed*) piccolo; **to lay low** ammazzare; abbattere; **to lie low** rimanere nascosto; attendere || *s* punto basso; prezzo minimo; (*of cow*) muggito; (aut) prima velocità; (meteor) depressione || *adv* basso, a basso, in basso || *intr* (*said of a cow*) muggire

low'born' *adj* di umili origini

low'boy' *s* cassettone basso con le gambe corte

low'brow' *adj & s* (coll) ignorante *mf*

low'-cost hous'ing *s* case *fpl* popolari

Low' Coun'tries, the i Paesi Bassi

low'-down' *adj* (coll) basso, vile || **low'-down'** *s* (coll) semplice verità *f*, notizie *fpl* confidenziali

lower ['lo·ər] *adj* inferiore, disotto || *tr* abbassare; (*prices*) ribassare || *intr* diminuire; discendere || ['lau·ər] *intr* aggrottare le ciglia; (*said of the weather*) imbronciarsi

low'er berth' ['lo·ər] *s* cuccetta inferiore

low'er case' ['lo·ər] *s* (typ) cassa inferiore

lower-case ['lo·ər ,kes] *adj* (typ) minuscolo

low'er mid'dle class' ['lo·ər] *s* piccola borghesia

lowermost ['lo·ər ,most] *adj* (il) più basso, (l') infimo

low'-fre'quency *adj* a bassa frequenza

low' gear' *s* prima velocità, prima

lowland ['loland] *s* pianura || **Lowlands** *spl* Scozia meridionale, bassa Scozia

low·ly ['loli] *adj* (-lier; -liest) umile

Low' Mass' *s* messa bassa

low-minded ['lo'maɪndɪd] *adj* vile, basso

low-necked ['lo'nɛkt] *adj* scollato

low-pitched ['lo'pɪtʃt] *adj* (*sound*) basso, grave; (*roof*) poco inclinato

low'-pres'sure *adj* a bassa pressione

low-priced ['lo'praɪst] *adj* a buon mercato, a basso prezzo

low' shoe' *s* scarpa bassa

low'-speed' *adj* di piccola velocità

low-spirited ['lo'spɪrɪtɪd] *adj* depresso

low' tide' *s* bassa marea; (fig) punto più basso

low' visibil'ity *s* scarsa visibilità

low' wa'ter *s* (*low tide*) bassa marea; (*of a river*) magra

loyal ['lɔɪ·əl] *adj* leale

loyalist ['lɔɪ·əlɪst] *s* lealista *mf*

loyal·ty ['lɔɪ·əlti] *s* (-ties) lealtà *f*

lozenge ['lazɪndʒ] *s* losanga; (*candy cough drop*) pasticca, pastiglia

LP ['ɛl'pi] *s* (letterword) (trademark) disco di grande durata

lubricant ['lubrɪkənt] *adj & s* lubrificante *m*

lubricate ['lubrɪ ,ket] *tr* lubrificare; (*e.g., one's hands*) ungersi

lubrication [,lubrɪ'keʃən] *s* lubrificazione

lubricous ['lubrɪkəs] *adj* lubrico; incerto, incostante

lucerne [lu'sʌrn] *s* erba medica

lucid ['lusɪd] *adj* lucido

Lucifer ['lusɪfər] *s* Lucifero

luck [lʌk] *s* (*good or bad*) sorte *f;* (*good*) sorte *f*, fortuna; **down on one's luck** in cattive condizioni; **in luck** fortunato; **out of luck** sfortunato; **to bring luck** portare (buona) fortuna; **to try one's luck** tentare la sorte; **worse luck** disgraziatamente

luckily ['lʌkɪli] *adv* fortunatamente

luckless ['lʌklɪs] *adj* sfortunato

luck·y ['lʌki] *adj* (-ier; -iest) fortunato; (*supposed to bring luck*) portafortuna; (*foretelling good luck*) di buon augurio; **to be lucky** aver fortuna

luck'y hit' *s* (coll) colpo di fortuna

lucrative ['lukrətɪv] *adj* lucrativo

ludicrous ['ludɪkrəs] *adj* ridicolo

lug [lʌg] *s* manico; (*pull*) tiro; **to put the lug on s.o.** (slang) batter cassa a qlcu || *v* (*pret & pp* lugged; *ger* lugging) *tr* tirarsi dietro; (coll) introdurre a sproposito

luggage ['lʌgɪdʒ] *s* (*used in traveling*) bagaglio; (*found in a store*) valigeria

lug'gage store' *s* valigeria

lugubrious [lu'gubrɪ·əs] *or* [lu'gjubrɪ·əs] *adj* lugubre

lukewarm ['luk ,wɔrm] *adj* tiepido

lull [lʌl] *s* momento di calma, calma || *tr* calmare, pacificare; addormentare

lulla·by ['lʌlə ,baɪ] *s* (-bies) ninnananna

lumbago [lʌm'bego] *s* lombaggine *f*

lumber ['lʌmbər] *s* legname *m*, legno da costruzione; cianfrusaglie *fpl* ‖ *intr* muoversi pesantemente

lum'ber•jack' *s* boscaiolo

lum'ber jack'et *s* giaccone *m*

lum'ber•man *s* (-men) (*dealer*) commerciante *m* in legname; (*man who cuts down lumber*) boscaiolo

lum'ber room' *s* ripostiglio

lum'ber•yard' *s* deposito legnami

luminar•y ['lumɪ,nɛri] *s* (-ies) luminare *m*

luminous ['lumɪnəs] *adj* luminoso

lummox ['lʌməks] *s* (coll) scimunito

lump [lʌmp] *s* grumo; mucchio; cumulo; (*swelling*) bernoccolo; (*of sugar*) zolletta; (*in one's throat*) groppo; (coll) stupidone *m; in the lump* in blocco; nell'insieme ‖ *tr* mescolare; (*to make into lumps*) raggrumare; **to lump it** (coll) mandarla giù

lumpish ['lʌmpɪʃ] *adj* grumoso; goffo; balordo

lump' sum' *s* ammontare unico, somma globale

lump•y ['lʌmpi] *adj* (-ier; -iest) grumoso; (*person*) pesante, ottuso; (*sea*) agitato

luna•cy ['lunəsi] *s* (-cies) pazzia

lunar ['lunər] *adj* lunare

lu'nar land'ing *s* allunaggio

lu'nar mod'ule *s* modulo lunare

lu'nar rov'er *s* auto *f* lunare

lunatic ['lunətɪk] *adj & s* demente *mf*

lu'natic asy'lum *s* manicomio

lu'natic fringe' *s* estremisti *mpl* fanatici

lunch [lʌntʃ] *s* (*regular midday meal*) seconda colazione; (*light meal*) spuntino, merenda ‖ *intr* fare colazione; fare uno spuntino

lunch' bas'ket *s* portavivande *m*

luncheon ['lʌntʃən] *s* seconda colazione; pranzo ufficiale

luncheonette [,lʌntʃə'nɛt] *s* tavola calda

lunch'eon meat' *s* insaccati *mpl*

lunch'room' *s* tavola calda

lung [lʌŋ] *s* polmone *m*

lunge [lʌndʒ] *s* slancio; (*fencing*) affondo ‖ *intr* slanciarsi

lurch [lʌrtʃ] *s* barcollamento; (*at close of a game*) cappotto; (naut) sbandata; **to leave in the lurch** piantare

in asso ‖ *intr* barcollare; (naut) sbandare

lure [lur] *s* esca; (fig) insidie *fpl* ‖ *tr* adescare; **to lure away** distogliere, sviare

lurid ['lurɪd] *adj* (*fiery*) ardente, acceso; sensazionale; (*gruesome*) orripilante

lurk [lʌrk] *intr* stare in agguato, nascondersi; (fig) essere latente

luscious ['lʌʃəs] *adj* delizioso; lussuoso, lussureggiante; voluttuoso

lush [lʌʃ] *adj* lussureggiante, lussuoso

lust [lʌst] *s* desiderio sfrenato; libidine *f*, lussuria ‖ *intr*—**to lust after or for** aver sete di

luster ['lʌstər] *s* (*gloss*) lustro, lucentezza; (*glory*) lustro, onore *m*

lus'ter•ware' *s* ceramiche smaltate

lustful ['lʌstfəl] *adj* lussurioso

lustrous ['lʌstrəs] *adj* lucido

lust•y ['lʌsti] *adj* (-ier; -iest) vigoroso, gagliardo

lute [lut] *s* (mus) liuto; (chem) luto

Lutheran ['luθərən] *adj & s* luterano

luxuriance [lʌg'ʒurɪ•əns] *s* rigoglio

luxuriant [lʌg'ʒurɪ•ənt] *adj* lussureggiante; (*imagery*) ridondante

luxuriate [lʌg'ʒurɪ,et] *or* [lʌk'ʃurɪ,et] *intr* lussureggiare; trovare piacere

luxurious [lʌg'ʒurɪ•əs] *or* [lʌk'ʃurɪ•əs] *adj* lussuoso, fastoso

luxu•ry ['lʌkʃəri] *or* ['lʌgʒəri] *s* (-ries) lusso, sfarzo

lye [laɪ] *s* ranno, liscivia

lying ['laɪ•ɪŋ] *adj* menzognero ‖ *s* il mentire

ly'ing-in' hos'pital *s* clinica ostetrica, maternità *f*

lymph [lɪmf] *s* linfa

lymphatic [lɪm'fætɪk] *adj* linfatico

lynch [lɪntʃ] *tr* linciare

lynching ['lɪntʃɪŋ] *s* linciaggio

lynx [lɪŋks] *s* lince *f*

lynx-eyed ['lɪŋks,aɪd] *adj* dagli occhi di lince

lyonnaise [,laɪ•ə'nez] *adj* (culin) alla maniera di Lione

lyre [laɪr] *s* lira

lyric ['lɪrɪk] *adj* lirico ‖ *s* lirica; (*words of a song*) parole *fpl*

lyrical ['lɪrɪkəl] *adj* lirico

lyricism ['lɪrɪ,sɪzəm] *s* lirismo

lyricist ['lɪrɪsɪst] *s* (*writer of words for songs*) paroliere *m*; (*poet*) lirico

M

M, m [ɛm] *s* tredicesima lettera dell'alfabeto inglese

ma'am [mæm] *or* [mɑm] *s* (coll) signora

macadam [mə'kædəm] *s* macadàm *m*

macadamize [mə'kædə,maɪz] *tr* macadamizzare

macaroni [,mækə'roni] *s* maccheroni *mpl*

macaroon [,mækə'run] *s* amaretto

macaw [mə'kɔ] *s* ara

mace [mes] *s* mazza; (*spice*) macis *m & f*

mace' bear'er *s* mazziere *m*

machination [,mækɪ'neʃən] *s* macchinazione, macchina

machine [mə'ʃin] *s* macchina ‖ *tr* fare a macchina

machine' gun' *s* mitragliatrice *f*

machine'-gun' *v* (*pret & pp* -gunned; *ger* -gunning) *tr* mitragliare

machine'-made' *adj* fatto a macchina

machiner·y [mə'ʃinəri] *s* (**-ies**) macchinario, meccanismo

machine' screw' *s* vite *f* per metallo

machine' shop' *s* officina meccanica

machine' tool' *s* macchina utensile

machinist [mə'ʃinɪst] *s* meccanico; (nav) secondo macchinista

mackerel ['mækərəl] *s* maccarello

mack'erel sky' *s* cielo a pecorelle

mackintosh ['mækɪn,taʃ] *s* impermeabile *m*

mad [mæd] *adj* (**madder; maddest**) (*angry; rabid*) arrabbiato; (*insane; foolish*) pazzo, folle; furioso; **to be mad about** (coll) andar pazzo per; **to drive mad** far impazzire; **to go mad** impazzire; (*said of a dog*) diventare idrofobo

madam ['mædəm] *s* signora

mad'cap' *s* mattoide *m*, rompicollo

madden ['mædən] *tr* (*to make angry*) inferocire; (*to make insane*) fare impazzire

made-to-order ['medtə'ɔrdər] *adj* fatto apposta; (*clothing*) fatto su misura

made'-up' *adj* inventato; (*using cosmetics*) truccato

mad'house' *s* manicomio

mad'man' *s* (**-men'**) pazzo

madness ['mædnɪs] *s* rabbia; pazzia

Madonna lily [mə'danə] *s* giglio

maelstrom ['melstrəm] *s* vortice *m*

magazine ['mægə,zin] or [,mægə'zin] *s* (*periodical*) rivista, giornale *m*; (*warehouse*) magazzino; (*for cartridges*) caricatore *m*; (*for powder*) polveriera; (naut) santabarbara; (phot) magazzino

maggot ['mægət] *s* larva di dittero

Magi ['medʒaɪ] *spl* Re Magi

magic ['mædʒɪk] *adj* magico ‖ *s* magia; illusionismo; **as if by magic** come per incanto

magician [mə'dʒɪʃən] *s* (*entertainer*) illusionista *mf;* (*sorcerer*) mago

magistrate ['mædʒɪs,tret] *s* magistrato

magnanimous [mæg'nænɪməs] *adj* magnanimo

magnesium [mæg'niʃɪ·əm] or [mæg'niʒɪ·əm] *s* magnesio

magnet ['mægnɪt] *s* calamita, magnete *m*

magnetic [mæg'nɛtɪk] *adj* magnetico

magnetism ['mægnɪ,tɪzəm] *s* magnetismo

magnetize ['mægnɪ,taɪz] *tr* calamitare, magnetizzare

magne·to [mæg'nito] *s* (**-tos**) magnete *m*

magnificent [mæg'nɪfɪsənt] *adj* magnifico

magni·fy ['mægnɪ,faɪ] *v* (*pret & pp* **-fied**) *tr* ingrandire; (*to exaggerate*) magnificare

mag'nifying glass' *s* lente *f* d'ingrandimento

magnitude ['mægnɪ,tjud] or ['mægnɪ,tud] *s* grandezza

magpie ['mæg,paɪ] *s* gazza

mahlstick ['mal,stɪk] or ['mɔl,stɪk] *s* appoggiamano

mahoga·ny [mə'hagəni] *s* (**-nies**) mogano

Mahomet [mə'hamɪt] *s* Maometto

maid [med] *s* (*girl*) ragazza; (*servant*) cameriera, domestica

maiden ['medən] *s* pulzella

maid'en·hair' *s* (bot) capelvenere *m*

maid'en·head' *s* imene *m*

maidenhood ['medən,hud] *s* verginità *f*

maid'en la'dy *s* zitella

maid'en name' *s* nome *m* da signorina

maid'en voy'age *s* viaggio inaugurale

maid'-in-wait'ing *s* (**maids-in-waiting**) (*of a princess*) damigella d'onore; (*of a queen*) dama d'onore

maid' of hon'or *s* (*attendant at a wedding; attendant of a princess*) damigella d'onore; (*attendant of a queen*) dama d'onore

maid'serv'ant *s* domestica, ancella

mail [mel] *s* posta; (*of armor*) maglia; **by return mail** a volta di corriere ‖ *tr* impostare

mail'bag' *s* sacco postale

mail'boat' *s* battello postale

mail'box' *s* cassetta or buca delle lettere

mail' car' *s* vagone *m* postale

mail' car'rier *s* postino, portalettere *m*

mail'ing list' *s* indirizzario

mail'ing per'mit *s* abbonamento postale

mail'man' *s* (**-men'**) portalettere *m*

mail' or'der *s* ordinazione per corrispondenza

mail'-order house' *s* ditta che fa affari unicamente per corrispondenza

mail'plane' *s* areoplano postale

mail' train' *s* treno postale

maim [mem] *tr* mutilare

main [men] *adj* principale, maggiore ‖ *s* condotta principale; **in the main** principalmente, per lo più

main' clause' *s* proposizione principale

main' course' *s* piatto forte

main' deck' *s* ponte *m* principale

mainland ['men,lænd] or ['menlənd] *s* terra ferma, continente *m*

main' line' *s* (rr) linea principale

mainly ['menli] *adv* principalmente

mainmast ['menməst], ['men,mæst] or ['men,mast] *s* albero maestro

mainsail ['mensəl] or ['men,sel] *s* vela maestra

main'spring' *s* molla motrice; (fig) molla

main'stay' *s* (naut) strallo di maestra; (fig) cardine *m*

main' street' *s* strada principale

maintain [men'ten] *tr* mantenere

maintenance ['mentɪnəns] *s* mantenimento; (*upkeep*) manutenzione

maître d'hôtel [,metər do'tɛl] *s* (*butler*) maggiordomo; (*headwaiter*) capocameriere *m*

maize [mez] *s* mais *m*

majestic [mə'dʒɛstɪk] *adj* maestoso

majes·ty ['mædʒɪsti] *s* (**-ties**) maestà *f*

major ['medʒər] *adj* maggiore ‖ *s* (educ) specializzazione; (mil) maggiore *m* ‖ *intr* (educ) specializzarsi

major·do·mo [,medʒər'domo] *s* (**-mos**) maggiordomo

ma'jor gen'eral *s* generale *m* di divisione

majori·ty [mə'dʒɑrɪti] or [mə'dʒɔrɪti] *adj* maggioritario || *s* (-ties) (*being of full age*) maggiore età *f;* (*larger number or part*) maggioranza; (mil) grado di maggiore

make [mek] *s* (*brand*) marca; (*form*) stile *m;* produzione; **on the make** (slang) tirando l'acqua al proprio mulino || *v* (*pret & pp* **made** [med]) *tr* fare; (*a train*) pigliare; (*a circuit*) chiudere; essere, e.g., **she will make a good typist** sarà una buona dattilografa; **to make** + *inf* fare + *inf*, e.g., **she made him study** lo fece studiare; **to make into** trasformare in; **to make known** far sapere; **to make of** pensare di; **to make oneself known** darsi a conoscere; **to make out** decifrare; (*a prescription*) scrivere, preparare; (*a check*) riempire; **to make over** convertire; (com) trasferire; **to make up** preparare, comporre; (*a story*) inventare; (*lost time*) riguadagnare; (typ) impaginare; (theat) truccare || *intr* essere fatto; **to make away with** rubare; disfarsi di; **to make believe that** + *ind* far finta di + *inf*, e.g., **he made believe (that) he was sleeping** fece finta di dormire; **to make for** avvicinarsi a; attaccare; (*better relations*) contribuire a cementare; **to make much of** (coll) fare le feste a; **to make off** andarsene; **to make off with** svignarsela con; **to make out** (coll) farcela; **to make toward** incamminarsi verso; **to make up** truccarsi; fare la pace; **to make up for** compensare per, supplire a; **to make up to** (coll) ingraziarsi; (coll) fare la corte a

make'-be·lieve' *adj* immaginario || *s* finzione, sembianza

maker ['mekər] *s* fabbricante *mf*, costruttore *m* || **Maker** *s* Fattore *m*

make'shift' *adj* improvvisato, di fortuna || *s* espediente *m*, ripiego; (*person*) tappabuchi *mf*

make'-up' *s* composizione, costituzione; truccatura, cosmetico; (typ) impaginazione; (journ) caratteristica

make'-up man' *s* truccatore *m*

make'-up test' *s* esame *m* di riparazione

make'weight' *s* giunta, contentino; (fig) supplemento, di più *m*

making ['mekɪŋ] *s* fabbricazione; costituzione; causa del successo; **makings** materiale *m;* (*potential*) stoffa

maladjusted [,mælə'dʒʌstɪd] *adj* spostato

mala·dy ['mælədi] *s* (-dies) malattia

malaise [mæ'lez] *s* malessere *m*

malapropos [,mæləprə'po] *adj* inopportuno || *adv* a sproposito

malaria [mə'lɛrɪ·ə] *s* malaria

Malay ['mele] or [mə'le] *adj & s* malese *mf*

malcontent ['mælkən,tɛnt] *adj & s* malcontento

male [mel] *adj & s* maschio

malediction [,mælɪ'dɪkʃən] *s* maledizione

malefactor ['mælɪ,fæktər] *s* malfattore *m*

male' nurse' *s* infermiere *m*

malevolent [mə'lɛvələnt] *adj* malevolo

malfeasance [mæl'fizəns] *s* reato di pubblico funzionario

malice ['mælɪs] *s* malizia; (law) dolo; **to bear malice** serbar rancore; **with malice prepense** (law) con premeditazione

malicious [mə'lɪʃəs] *adj* malizioso, maligno

malign [mə'laɪn] *adj* maligno || *tr* calunniare

malignan·cy [mə'lɪgnənsi] *s* (-cies) malignità *f;* (pathol) malignità *f*

malignant [mə'lɪgnənt] *adj* maligno

maligni·ty [mə'lɪgnɪti] *s* (-ties) malignità *f*

malinger [mə'lɪŋgər] *intr* fingersi ammalato, darsi malato (per sottrarsi al proprio dovere)

mall [mɔl] or [mæl] *s* viale *m;* (*strip of land in a boulevard*) aiola

mallet ['mælɪt] *s* maglio; (*of a stone cutter*) mazzuolo

mallow ['mælo] *s* malva

malnutrition [,mælnju'trɪʃən] or [,mælnu'trɪʃən] *s* malnutrizione

malodorous [mæl'odərəs] *adj* puzzolente

malpractice [mæl'præktɪs] *s* incuria, negligenza; (*of physician or lawyer*) negligenza colposa

malt [mɔlt] *s* malto

maltreat [mæl'trit] *tr* maltrattare

mamma ['mɑmə] or [mə'mɑ] *s* (coll) mamma

mammal ['mæməl] *s* mammifero

mammalian [mæ'melɪ·ən] *adj & s* mammifero

mammoth ['mæməθ] *adj* mastodontico || *s* mammut *m*

man [mæn] *s* (**men** [mɛn]) uomo; (*in chess*) pedina; (*in checkers*) pezzo; **a man** uno, e.g., **a man can get lost in this town** uno può perdersi in questa città; **as one man** come un sol uomo; **man alive!** accidenti!; **man and wife** marito e moglie; **to be one's own man** essere completamente indipendente || *v* (*pret & pp* **manned;** *ger* **manning**) *tr* (*a boat*) equipaggiare; (*a fortress*) guarnire; (*a cannon*) maneggiare

man' about town' *s* vitaiolo

manacle ['mænəkəl] *s*—**manacles** manette *fpl* || *tr* ammanettare

manage ['mænɪdʒ] *tr* (*a business*) gestire; (*e.g., a tool*) maneggiare || *intr* sbrogliarsela; **to manage to** fare in modo di; ingegnarsi a; **to manage to get along** barcamenarsi

manageable ['mænɪdʒəbəl] *adj* maneggevole

management ['mænɪdʒmənt] *s* direzione, gestione; (*executives collectively*) classe *f* dirigente; direzione; (*college course*) economia aziendale

manager ['mænədʒər] *s* direttore *m*, gerente *mf;* (theat) impresario; (sports) procuratore *m*, manager *m*

managerial [,mænə'dʒɪrɪ·əl] *adj* direttoriale, imprenditoriale

man'aging ed'itor *s* gerente *m* responsabile, redattore *m* in capo

mandate ['mændet] *s* mandato || *tr* dare in mandato a

mandatory ['mændə‚tori] *adj* obbligatorio

mandolin ['mændəlɪn] *s* mandolino

mandrake ['mændrek] *s* mandragola

mandrel ['mændrəl] *s* (mach) mandrino

mane [men] *s* criniera

maneuver [mə'nuvər] *s* manovra || *tr* manovrare || *intr* manovrare; (aer, nav) evoluire; (fig) intrigare

manful ['mænfəl] *adj* maschile, risoluto

manganese ['mæŋgə‚nis] or ['mæŋgə‚niz] *s* manganese *m*

mange [mendʒ] *s* rogna

manger ['mendʒər] *s* presepio

mangle ['mæŋgəl] *tr* straziare, lacerare

man·gy ['mendʒi] *adj* (-gier; -giest) rognoso; (squalid) misero

man'han'dle *tr* malmenare, maltrattare

man'hole' *s* passo d'uomo, pozzetto

manhood ['mænhud] *s* virilità *f*; uomini *mpl*, umanità *f*

man'hunt' *s* caccia all'uomo

mania ['menɪ‚ə] *s* mania

maniac ['menɪ‚æk] *adj & s* maniaco

manicure ['mænɪ‚kjur] *s* (treatment) manicure *f*; (manicurist) manicure *mf* || *tr* (a person) curare le mani di; (the hands) curare

manicurist ['mænɪ‚kjurɪst] *s* manicurista *mf*, manicure *mf*

manifest ['mænɪ‚fɛst] *adj* manifesto || *s* (naut) manifesto di carico || *tr* manifestare

manifes·to [‚mænɪ'fɛsto] *s* (-toes) manifesto

manifold ['mænɪ‚fold] *adj* molteplice || *s* copia; carta velina; (aut, mach) collettore *m*

manikin ['mænɪkɪn] *s* manichino; (dwarf) nano

man' in the moon' *s* faccia di uomo che appare nella luna piena

man' in the street' *s* uomo qualunque, uomo della strada

manipulate [mə'nɪpjə‚let] *tr* manipolare

man'kind' *s* genere umano || **man'kind'** *s* il sesso maschile

manliness ['mænlɪnɪs] *s* virilità *f*

man·ly ['mænli] *adj* (-lier; -liest) maschio, virile

manned' space'ship *s* astronave pilotata

mannequin ['mænɪkɪn] *s* (figure) manichino; (person) indossatrice *f*

manner ['mænər] *s* maniera; **by all manner of means** in tutti i modi; **in a manner of speaking** in una certa maniera, in certo modo; **in the manner of** alla moda di; **manners** maniere, *fpl*, educazione; **to the manner born** avvezzo sin dalla nascita

mannish ['mænɪʃ] *adj* maschile; (woman) mascolino

man' of God' *s* santo; profeta *m*; (priest) uomo al servizio di Dio

man' of let'ters *s* letterato

man' of means' *s* uomo danaroso

man' of parts' *s* uomo di talento

man' of straw' *s* uomo di paglia

man' of the world' *s* uomo di mondo

man-of-war [‚mænəv'wɔr] *s* (**men-of-war** [‚menəv'wɔr] nave *f* da guerra

manor ['mænər] *s* maniero; feudo

man'or house' *s* maniero, palazzo

man' o'verboard *interj* uomo in mare!

man'pow'er *s* manodopera; (mil) effettivo

mansard ['mænsard] *s* mansarda

man'serv'ant *s* (**men'serv'ants**) servo, servitore *m*

mansion ['mænʃən] *s* palazzo, palazzina; (manor house) maniero

man'slaugh'ter *s* omicidio colposo

mantel ['mæntəl] *s* parte *f* anteriore dei pilastri del camino; (shelf above it) mensola

man'tel·piece' *s* mensola del camino

man'tis shrimp' ['mæntɪs] *s* canocchia

mantle ['mæntəl] *s* mantello, cappa || *tr* ammantare; (to conceal) nascondere || *intr* (to blush) arrossire

manual ['mænju‚əl] *adj* manuale || *s* (book) manuale *m*; (mil) esercizio; (mus) tastiera d'organo

man'ual train'ing *s* istruzione nelle arti e mestieri

manufacture [‚mænjə'fæktʃər] *s* fabbricazione; (thing manufactured) manufatto || *tr* fabbricare

manufacturer [‚mænjə'fæktʃərər] *s* fabbricante *mf*, industriale *m*

manure [mə'njur] or [mə'nur] *s* letame *m* || *tr* concimare

manuscript ['mænjə‚skrɪpt] *adj & s* manoscritto

many ['mɛni] *adj & pron* molti; **a good many** or **a great many** un buon numero; **as many . . . as** tanti . . . quanti; **as many as** fino a, e.g., **they sell as many as five thousand dozen** vendono fino a cinquemila dozzine; **how many** quanti; **many a** molti, e.g., **many a day** molti giorni; **many another** molti altri; **many more** molti di più; **so many** tanti; **too many** troppi; **twice as many** altrettanti, il doppio

many-sided ['mɛni‚saɪdɪd] *adj* multilaterale; versatile

map [mæp] *s* mappa; (of a city) piano || *v* (pret & pp **mapped;** ger **mapping**) *tr* tracciare la mappa di; mostrare sulla mappa; **to map out** fare il piano di

maple ['mepəl] *s* acero

maquette [ma'kɛt] *s* plastico

mar [mar] *v* (pret & pp **marred;** ger **marring**) *tr* deturpare, sfigurare

maraud [mə'rɔd] *tr & intr* predare

marauder [mə'rɔdər] *s* predone *m*

marble ['marbəl] *adj* marmoreo || *s* marmo; (little ball of glass) bilia; **marbles** bilie *fpl*; **to lose one's marbles** (slang) mancare una rotella a qlcu || *tr* marmorizzare

march [martʃ] *s* marcia; (hist) marca; **to steal a march on** guadagnare il vantaggio su || *tr* far marciare || *intr* marciare || **March** *s* marzo

marchioness ['mɑrʃənɪs] *s* marchesa

mare [mer] *s* (*female horse*) cavalla; (*female donkey*) asina

margarine ['mɑrdʒərɪn] *s* margarina

margin ['mɑrdʒɪn] *s* margine *m*; (econ) scoperto

mar'gin stop' *s* marginatore *m*

marigold ['mærɪ,gold] *s* fiorrancio

marihuana or **marijuana** [,mɑrɪ-'hwɑnə] *s* marijuana

marina [mə'rinə] *s* porto turistico di imbarcazioni, porticciolo turistico

marinate ['mærɪ,net] *tr* marinare

marine [mə'rin] *adj* marino, marittimo || *s* marina; soldato di fanteria da sbarco; **marines** fanteria da sbarco; **tell that to the marines!** (coll) va a raccontarlo ai frati!

mariner ['mærɪnər] *s* marinaio

marionette [,mærɪ·ə'nɛt] *s* marionetta

mar'ital sta'tus ['mærɪtəl] *s* stato civile

maritime ['mærɪ,taɪm] *adj* marittimo

marjoram ['mɑrdʒərəm] *s* origano; (*sweet marjoram*) maggiorana

mark [mɑrk] *s* segno; (*brand*) marca; (*of punctuation*) punto; (*in an examination*) voto; (*sign made by illiterate person*) croce *f*; (*landmark*) segnale *m*; (*target*) bersaglio; (*spot*) macchia; (*starting point in a race*) linea di partenza; (*of confidence*) voto; (*coin*) marco; impronta; **to be beside the mark** essere fuori del seminato; **to hit the mark** colpire il bersaglio; **to leave one's mark** lasciare la propria impronta; **to make one's mark** raggiungere il successo; **to miss the mark** fallire il colpo; **to toe the mark** mettersi in fila; filare diritto || *tr* marcare, segnare, contrassegnare; (*a student*) dar il voto a; (*a test*) esaminare; improntare; notare, avvertire; **to mark down** mettere in iscritto; ribassare il prezzo di

mark'down' *s* riduzione di prezzo

market ['mɑrkɪt] *s* mercato; **to bear the market** giocare al ribasso; **to bull the market** giocare al rialzo; **to play the market** giocare in borsa; **to put on the market** lanciare sul mercato || *tr* mettere sul mercato

marketable ['mɑrkɪtəbəl] *adj* commerciabile, vendibile

marketing ['mɑrkɪtɪŋ] *s* compravendita; marketing *m*

mar'ket·place' *s* piazza del mercato

mar'ket price' *s* prezzo corrente

mark'ing gauge' ['mɑrkɪŋ] *s* graffietto

marks'man (**-men**) tiratore *m*; **a good marksman** un tiratore scelto

marksmanship ['mɑrksmən,ʃɪp] *s* qualità *f* di tiratore scelto

mark'up' *s* margine *m* di rivendita

marl [mɑrl] *s* marna || *tr* marnare

marmalade ['mɑrmə,led] *s* marmellata d'arance

marmot ['mɑrmət] *s* marmotta

maroon [mə'run] *adj* & *s* marrone *m* || *tr* abbandonare (*in un luogo deserto*)

marquee [mɑr'ki] *s* pensilina

marquess ['mɑrkwɪs] *s* marchese *m*

marque·try ['mɑrkətri] *s* (**-tries**) intarsio

marquis ['mɑrkwɪs] *s* marchese *m*

marquise [mɑr'kiz] *s* marchesa; (Brit) pensilina

marriage ['mærɪdʒ] *s* matrimonio

marriageable ['mærɪdʒəbəl] *adj* adatto al matrimonio; (*woman*) nubile

mar'riage por'tion *s* dote *f*

mar'riage rate' *s* nuzialità *f*

mar'ried life' *s* vita coniugale

marrow ['mæro] *s* midollo

mar·ry ['mæri] *v* (*pret* & *pp* **-ried**) *tr* sposare; **to get married to** sposarsi con || *intr* sposarsi; **to marry into** (*e.g., a noble family*) imparentarsi con; **to marry the second time** risposarsi

Mars [mɑrz] *s* Marte *m*

Marseilles [mɑr'selz] *s* Marsiglia

marsh [mɑrʃ] *s* palude *f*, lama

mar·shal ['mɑrʃəl] *s* direttore *m* di una sfilata; maestro di cerimonie; (mil) maresciallo; (U.S.A.) ufficiale *m* di giustizia || *v* (*pret* & *pp* **-shaled** or **-shalled**; *ger* **-shaling** or **-shalling**) *tr* introdurre cerimoniosamente; mettere in buon ordine

marsh' mal'low *s* (bot) altea

marsh'mal'low *s* dolce *m* di gelatina e zucchero

marsh·y ['mɑrʃi] *adj* (**-ier; -iest**) paludoso, palustre

marten ['mɑrtən] *s* (*Martes martes*) martora; (*Martes zibellina*) zibellino

martial ['mɑrʃəl] *adj* marziale

mar'tial law' *s* legge *f* marziale

Martian ['mɑrʃən] *adj* & *s* marziano

martin ['mɑrtɪn] *s* rondicchio

martinet [,mɑrtɪ'nɛt] or ['mɑrtɪ,nɛt] *s* pignolo

martyr ['mɑrtər] *s* martire *mf*

martyrdom ['mɑrtərdəm] *s* martirio

mar·vel ['mɑrvəl] *s* meraviglia || *v* (*pret* & *pp* **-veled** or **-velled**; *ger* **-veling** or **-velling**) *intr* meravigliarsi; **to marvel at** stupirsi di, meravigliarsi di

marvelous ['mɑrvələs] *adj* meraviglioso

Marxist ['mɑrksɪst] *adj* & *s* marxista *mf*

mascara [mæs'kærə] *s* bistro, rimmel *m*

mascot ['mæskɑt] *s* mascotte *f*

masculine ['mæskjəlɪn] *adj* & *s* maschile *m*

mash [mæʃ] *s* (*crushed mass*) poltiglia; (*to form wort*) decotto d'orzo germinato; (*e.g., for poultry*) intriso || *tr* schiacciare; impastare

mashed' pota'toes *spl* purè *m* di patate

masher ['mæʃər] *s* utensile *m* per schiacciare; (slang) pappagallo

mask [mæsk] or [mɑsk] *s* maschera; (phot) mascherina || *tr* mascherare; (phot) mettere una mascherina a || *intr* mascherarsi

masked' ball' *s* ballo in maschera

mason ['mesən] *s* muratore *m* || **Mason** *s* massone *m*

mason·ry ['mesənri] *s* (**-ries**) arte *f* del

muratore; muratura || **Masonry** s massoneria

masquerade [ˌmæskəˈred] or [ˌmɑskə-ˈred] s mascherata; (disguise) maschera; (pretense) finzione || intr mascherarsi; **to masquerade as** mascherarsi da; farsi passare per

mass [mæs] s massa; (celebration of the Eucharist) messa; **in the mass** nell'insieme; **the masses** le masse || tr ammassare || intr ammassarsi, accumularsi

massacre [ˈmæsəkər] s massacro, strage f || tr massacrare, trucidare

massage [məˈsɑʒ] s massaggio || tr massaggiare

masseur [mæˈsœr] s massaggiatore m

masseuse [mæˈsœz] s massaggiatrice f

massive [ˈmæsɪv] adj massiccio; (e.g., dose) massivo; solido

mass′ me′dia [ˈmɪdɪ·ə] s mezzi mpl di comunicazione di massa

mass′ meet′ing s assemblea popolare; adunanza in massa

mass′ produc′tion s produzione in serie

mast [mæst] or [mɑst] s (post) palo; (agr) ghiande fpl, faggiole fpl; (naut) albero; **before the mast** come marinaio semplice

master [ˈmæstər] or [ˈmɑstər] s (employer) padrone m; (male head of household) capo di casa; (man who possesses some special skill) maestro; (title of respect for a boy) signorino; (naut) capitano || tr dominare; (a language) possedere

mas′ter bed′room s camera da letto padronale

mas′ter blade′ s foglia maestra (di una balestra)

mas′ter build′er s capomastro

masterful [ˈmæstərfəl] or [ˈmɑstərfəl] adj autoritario; provetto, magistrale

mas′ter key′ s chiave maestra

masterly [ˈmæstərli] or [ˈmɑstərli] adj magistrale || adv magistralmente

mas′ter mechan′ic s mastro meccanico

mas′ter·mind′ s mente direttiva || tr organizzare, dirigere

mas′ter of cer′emonies s maestro di cerimonia; (in a night club, radio, etc.) presentatore m

mas′ter·piece′ s capolavoro

mas′ter ser′geant s (mil) sergente m maggiore

mas′ter stroke′ s colpo da maestro

mas′ter·work′ s capolavoro

master·y [ˈmæstəri] or [ˈmɑstəri] s (-ies) (command of a subject) dominio; (skill) maestria

mast′head′ s (journ) titolo; (naut) testa d'albero

masticate [ˈmæstɪ ˌket] tr masticare

mastiff [ˈmæstɪf] or [ˈmɑstɪf] s mastino

masturbate [ˈmæstər ˌbet] tr masturbare || intr masturbarsi

mat [mæt] s (for floor) tappeto, stuoia; (under a dish) tondo, sottocoppa, centrino; (before a door) stoino, zerbino; (around a picture) bordo di cartone; (sports) materas-

sino; (typ) flan m; flano || v (pret & pp matted; ger matting) tr coprire di stuoie; arruffare || intr arruffarsi

match [mætʃ] s (counterpart) uguale m; (suitably associated pair) paio; (light) fiammifero; (wick) miccia; (prospective mate) partito; (sports) partita, gara; **to be a match for** essere pari a, fare fronte a; **to meet one's match** trovare un degno rivale || tr uguagliare, pareggiare; (colors) combinare; (in pairs) appaiare; giocarsi, e.g., **to match s.o. for the drinks** giocarsi le bevande con qlcu || intr corrispondersi, fare il paio

match′box′ s scatola di fiammiferi; (of wax matches) scatola di cerini

matchless [ˈmætʃlɪs] adj incomparabile, senza pari

match′mak′er s paraninfo

mate [met] s compagno; (husband or wife) consorte mf; (to a female) maschio; (to a male) femmina; (chess) scacco matto; (naut) primo ufficiale || tr appaiare; (chess) dar scacco matto a; **to be well mated** esser ben appaiato || intr accoppiarsi

material [məˈtɪrɪ·əl] adj materiale; importante || s materiale m, materia; (cloth, fabric) tela, stoffa; **materials** occorrente m

materialist [məˈtɪrɪ·əlɪst] s materialista mf

materialize [məˈtɪrɪ·ə ˌlaɪz] intr materializzarsi

matériel [mə ˌtɪrɪˈɛl] s materiale m; materiale bellico

maternal [məˈtʌrnəl] adj materno

maternity [məˈtʌrnɪti] s maternità f

mater′nity ward′ s maternità f

mathematical [ˌmæθɪˈmætɪkəl] adj matematico

mathematician [ˌmæθɪməˈtɪʃən] s matematico

mathematics [ˌmæθɪˈmætɪks] s matematica

matinée [ˌmætɪˈne] s mattinata, diurna

mat′ing sea′son s calore m

matins [ˈmætɪnz] spl mattutino

matriarch [ˈmetrɪ ˌark] s matrona dignitosa; donna che possiede l'autorità matriarcale

matricidal [ˌmetrɪˈsaɪdəl] or [ˌmætrɪ-ˈsaɪdəl] adj matricida

matricide [ˈmetrɪ ˌsaɪd] or [ˈmætrɪ-ˌsaɪd] s (act) matricidio; (person) matricida mf

matriculate [məˈtrɪkjə ˌlet] tr immatricolare || intr immatricolarsi

matriculation [mə ˌtrɪkjəˈleʃən] s immatricolazione, iscrizione

matrimonial [ˌmætrɪˈmonɪ·əl] adj matrimoniale

matrimo·ny [ˈmætrɪ ˌmoni] s (-nies) matrimonio

ma·trix [ˈmetrɪks] or [ˈmætrɪks] s (-trices[trɪ ˌsiz] or -trixes) matrice f

matron [ˈmetrən] s matrona; direttrice f; guardiana

matronly [ˈmetrənli] adj matronale

matter [ˈmætər] s (physical substance) materia; (pus) materia; (affair, busi-

ness) faccenda; (*material of a book*) contenuto; (*reason*) motivo; (*copy for printer*) manoscritto; (*printed material*) stampati *mpl;* **a matter of** un caso di; **for that matter** per quanto riguarda ciò; **in the matter** al soggetto; **no matter** non importa; **no matter how** non importa come; **no matter when** non importa quando; **no matter where** non importa dove; **what is the matter?** cosa succede?; **what is the matter with you?** cosa ha? || *intr* importare

mat'ter of course' *s*—**as a matter of course** come se nulla fosse, come se fosse una cosa naturale

mat'ter of fact' *s*—**as a matter of fact** in realtà, a onor del vero

matter-of-fact ['mætərəv ‚fækt] *adj* prosaico, pratico

mattock ['mætək] *s* piccone *m*

mattress ['mætrɪs] *s* materasso

mature [mə'tʃʊr] *or* [mə'tʊr] *adj* maturo; (*due*) scaduto || *tr* maturare || *intr* maturare; (com) scadere

maturity [mə'tʃʊrɪti] *or* [mə'tʊrɪti] *s* maturità *f;* (com) scadenza

maudlin ['mɔdlɪn] *adj* sentimentale, lagrimoso; piagnucoloso e ubriaco

maul [mɔl] *tr* maltrattare, bistrattare

maulstick ['mɔl ‚stɪk] *s* appoggiamano

maundy ['mɔndi] *s* lavanda

Maun'dy Thurs'day *s* giovedì santo

mausole·um [‚mɔsə'li·əm] *s* (**-ums** or **-a** [ə]) mausoleo

maw [mɔ] *s* (*e.g., of a hog*) stomaco; (*of carnivorous mammal*) fauci *fpl;* (*of fowl*) gozzo; (fig) bocca, fauci *fpl*

mawkish ['mɔkɪʃ] *adj* (*sickening*) nauseante; (*sentimental*) svenevole

maxim ['mæksɪm] *s* massima

maximum ['mæksɪməm] *adj & s* massimo

may [me] *v aux*—**it may be** può essere; **may I come in?** si può?; **may you be happy!** possa tu essere felice! || **May** *s* maggio

maybe ['mebi] *adv* forse

May' Day' *s* primo maggio; festa della primavera; (hist) calendimaggio (*in Florence*)

mayhem ['mehɛm] *or* ['me·əm] *s* mutilazione dolosa

mayonnaise [‚me·ə'nez] *s* maionese *f*

mayor ['me·ər] *or* [mɛr] *s* sindaco

mayoress ['me·ərɪs] *or* ['mɛrɪs] *s* donna sindaco

May'pole' *s* maio, maggio, palo per le danze di calendimaggio

May'pole dance' *s* ballo figurato con nastri per la festa di primavera

May' queen' *s* reginetta di maggio

maze [mez] *s* dedalo, labirinto

me [mi] *pron* me; mi; **to me** mi; **a me**

meadow ['mɛdo] *s* prato

mead'ow·land' *s* prateria

meager ['migər] *adj* magro

meal [mil] *s* (*food*) pasto; (*unbolted grain*) farina

meal'time' *s* ora del pasto

mean [min] *adj* (*intermediate*) medio;

(*low in rank*) basso, umile; (*shabby*) misero; (*of poor quality*) inferiore; (*stingy*) taccagno; (*nasty*) villano; (*vicious, as a horse*) intrattabile; (coll) indisposto; (coll) vergognoso; (slang) splendido; **no mean** eccellente || *s* media, termine medio; **by all means** certamente, senza dubbio; **by means of** per mezzo di; **by no means** in nessuna maniera; **means** beni *mpl;* (*agency*) mezzo, maniera; **to live on one's means** vivere di rendita || *v* (*pret & pp* **meant** [ment]) *tr* significare, voler dire; **to mean to** pensare || *intr*—**to mean well** aver buone intenzioni

meander [mɪ'ændər] *s* meandro || *intr* serpeggiare, vagare

meaning ['minɪŋ] *s* senso, significato

meaningful ['minɪŋfəl] *adj* significativo

meaningless ['minɪŋlɪs] *adj* senza senso, senza significato

meanness ['minnɪs] *s* viltà *f,* bassezza; (*stinginess*) meschinità *f;* (*lowliness*) umiltà *f,* povertà *f*

mean'time' *s*—**in the meantime** nel frattempo || *adv* frattanto, intanto

mean'while' *s & adv* var of **meantime**

measles ['mizəlz] *s* morbillo; (*German measles*) rosolia

mea·sly ['mizli] *adj* (**-slier; -sliest**) col morbillo; (coll) miserabile

measurable ['mɛʒərəbəl] *adj* misurabile

measure ['mɛʒər] *s* misura; (*legislative bill*) progetto di legge; (mus) battuta; **in a measure** in un certo senso; **to take the measure of** prendere le misure di; giudicare accuratamente || *tr* misurare; (*a distance*) percorrere; **to measure out** somministrare || *intr* misurare; **to measure up to** essere all'altezza di

measurement ['mɛʒərmənt] *s* misura; **to take s.o.'s measurements** prendere le misure di qlcu

meas'uring cup' *s* vetro graduato

meat [mit] *s* carne *f;* (*food in general*) cibo; (*of nut*) gheriglio; (fig) sostanza, midollo

meat'ball' *s* polpetta

meat' grind'er *s* tritacarne *m*

meat' loaf' *s* polpettone *m*

meat' mar'ket *s* macelleria

meat·y ['miti] *adj* (**-ier; -iest**) carnoso, polputo; (fig) sostanzioso

Mecca ['mɛkə] *s* la Mecca; **the Mecca** (fig) la Mecca

mechanic [mɪ'kænɪk] *s* meccanico; (aut) motorista *m*

mechanical [mɪ'kænɪkəl] *adj* meccanico; (*machinelike*) (fig) macchinale

mechan'ical engineer'ing *s* ingegneria meccanica

mechan'ical pen'cil *s* matita automatica

mechanics [mɪ'kænɪks] *s* meccanica

mechanism ['mɛkə ‚nɪzəm] *s* meccanismo, congegno

mechanize ['mɛkə ‚naɪz] *tr* meccanizzare

medal ['mɛdəl] *s* medaglia

medallion [mɪ'dæljən] *s* medaglione *m*

meddle ['mɛdəl] *intr* intromettersi

meddler ['mɛdlər] *s* ficcanaso

meddlesome ['mɛdəlsəm] *adj* invadente, indiscreto

median ['midɪ·ən] *adj* medio, mediano || *s* punto medio, numero medio

me'dian strip' *s* spartitraffico

mediate ['midɪ ,et] *tr* (*a dispute*) comporre; (*parties*) pacificare || *intr* (*to be in the middle*) mediare; fare da paciere

mediation [,midɪ'eʃən] *s* mediazione

mediator ['midɪ ,etər] *s* mediatore *m*

medical ['mɛdɪkəl] *adj* medico; (*student*) di medicina

medicinal [mə'dɪsɪnəl] *adj* medicinale

medicine ['mɛdɪsɪn] *s* medicina

med'icine cab'inet *s* armadietto farmaceutico

med'icine kit' *s* cassetta farmaceutica

med'icine man' *s* (**men'**) stregone indiano

medieval [,midɪ'ivəl] or [,mɛdɪ'ivəl] *adj* medievale

medievalist [,midɪ'ivəlɪst] or [,mɛdɪ'ivəlɪst] *s* medievalista *mf*

mediocre ['midɪ ,okər] or [,midɪ'okər] *adj* mediocre

mediocri·ty [,midɪ'akrɪti] *s* (-ties) mediocrità *f*

meditate ['mɛdɪ ,tet] *tr & intr* meditare

meditation [,mɛdɪ'teʃən] *s* meditazione

Mediterranean [,mɛdɪtə'renɪ·ən] *adj & s* Mediterraneo

medi·um ['midɪ·əm] *adj* medio; (*heat*) moderato; (*meat*) cotto moderatamente || *s* (-ums or -a [ə]) (*middle state; mean*) media; mezzo; (*in spiritualism*) medium *m;* **media** (*of communication*) media *mpl;* **through the medium of** per mezzo di

medlar ['mɛdlər] *s* (*tree*) nespolo; (*fruit*) nespola

medley ['mɛdli] *s* farragine *f*, mescolanza; (*mus*) pot-pourri *m*

medul·la [mɪ'dʌlə] *s* (-lae [li]) midollo

meek [mik] *adj* mansueto, umile

meekness ['miknɪs] *s* mansuetudine *f*

meerschaum ['mɪrʃəm] or ['mɪrʃəm] *s* schiuma; pipa di schiuma

meet [mit] *adj* conveniente || *s* incontro || *v* (*pret & pp* **met** [mɛt]) *tr* incontrare, incontrarsi con; (*to become acquainted with*) fare la conoscenza di; riunirsi con; (*to cope with*) sopperire a; (*said of a public carrier*) fare coincidenza con; andar incontro a; (*one's obligations*) far fronte a; (*bad luck*) avere; **to meet the eyes of** presentarsi agli occhi di || *intr* incontrarsi; riunirsi; conoscersi; **till we meet again** arrivederci; **to meet with** incontrare, incontrarsi con; (*an accident*) avere; (*said of a public carrier*) fare coincidenza con

meeting ['mitɪŋ] *s* riunione, ritrovo; seduta, convegno; (*political*) comizio; (*e.g., of two rivers*) confluenza; duello

meet'ing of the minds' *s* accordo, consonanza di voleri

meet'ing place' *s* luogo di riunione

megacycle ['mɛgə ,saɪkəl] *s* megaciclo

megaphone ['mɛgə ,fon] *s* megafono, portavoce *m*

megohm ['mɛg ,om] *s* megaohm *m*

melancholia [,mɛlən'kolɪ·ə] *s* melanconia, malinconia

melanchol·y ['mɛlən ,kali] *adj* malinconico || *s* (-ies) malinconia

melee ['mele] or ['mɛle] *s* (*fight*) mischia; confusione

mellow ['mɛlo] *adj* (*fruit*) maturo; (*wine*) pastoso; (*voice*) soave, melodioso || *tr* raddolcire || *intr* raddolcirsi

melodic [mɪ'ladɪk] *adj* melodico

melodious [mɪ'lodɪ·əs] *adj* melodioso

melodramatic [,mɛlədrə'mætɪk] *adj* melodrammatico

melo·dy ['mɛlədi] *s* (-dies) melodia

melon ['mɛlən] *s* melone *m*, popone *m*

melt [mɛlt] *tr* sciogliere; (*metals*) fondere; (*fig*) intenerire || *intr* sciogliersi; fondersi; (*fig*) intenerirsi; **melt away** svanire; **to melt into** convertirsi in, diventare; (*tears*) struggersi in

melt'ing pot' *s* crogiolo

member ['mɛmbər] *s* membro

membership ['mɛmbər ,ʃɪp] *s* associazione; numero di membri

membrane ['mɛmbren] *s* membrana

memen·to [mɪ'mɛnto] *s* (-tos or -toes) oggetto ricordo

mem·o ['mɛmo] *s* (-os) (coll) memorandum *m*

memoir ['mɛmwar] *s* memoria, memoriale *m;* biografia; **memoirs** memorie *fpl*

memoran·dum [,mɛmə'rændəm] *s* (-dums or -da [də]) memorandum *m*

memorial [mɪ'morɪ·əl] *adj* commemorativo || *s* sacrario; (*petition*) memoriale *m*

Memo'rial Day' *s* giorno dei caduti

memorialize [mɪ'morɪ·ə ,laɪz] *tr* commemorare

memorize ['mɛmə ,raɪz] *tr* imparare a memoria

memo·ry ['mɛməri] *s* (-ries) memoria; **to commit to memory** imparare a memoria

menace ['mɛnɪs] *s* minaccia || *tr & intr* minacciare

ménage [me'naʒ] *s* casa; (*housekeeping*) economia domestica

menagerie [mə'næʒəri] or [mə'nædʒəri] *s* serraglio

mend [mɛnd] *s* riparo; **to be on the mend** migliorare || *tr* (*to repair*) raccomodare, riparare; (*to patch*) rammendare; (*fig*) correggere || *intr* correggersi

mendacious [mɛn'deʃəs] *adj* mendace

mendicant ['mɛndɪkənt] *adj & s* mendicante *mf*

menfolk ['mɛn ,fok] *spl* uomini *mpl*

menial ['minɪ·əl] *adj* basso, servile || *s* servitore *m*, servo

menses ['mɛnsiz] *spl* mestruazione, mestrui *mpl*

men's' fur'nishings *spl* articoli *mpl* d'abbigliamento maschile

men's' room' *s* gabinetto per signori

menstruate ['mɛnstru ,et] *intr* avere le mestruazioni
men'tal arith'metic ['mɛntəl] *s* calcolo mentale
men'tal hos'pital *s* manicomio
men'tal ill'ness *s* malattia mentale
men'tal reserva'tion *s* riserva mentale
men'tal test' *s* test *m* mentale
mention ['mɛnʃən] *s* menzione ‖ *tr* menzionare; **don't mention it** non c'è di che
menu ['mɛnju] or ['menju] *s* menu *m*, lista
meow [mɪ'au] *s* miagolio ‖ *intr* miagolare
Mephistophelian [,mɛfɪstə'filɪ·ən] *adj* mefistofelico
mercantile ['mʌrkən ,til] or ['mʌrkən- ,tail] *adj* mercantile
mercenar·y ['mʌrsə ,nɛri] *adj* mercenario ‖ *s* (**-ies**) mercenario
merchandise ['mʌrtʃən ,daɪz] *s* mercanzia, merce *f*
merchant ['mʌrtʃənt] *adj* mercantile ‖ *s* mercante *m*, commerciante *mf*
mer'chant-man *s* (**-men**) mercantile *m*
mer'chant marine' *s* marina mercantile
merciful ['mʌrsɪfəl] *adj* misericordioso
merciless ['mʌrsɪlɪs] *adj* spietato
mercu·ry ['mʌrkjəri] *s* (**-ries**) mercurio ‖ **Mercury** *s* Mercurio
mer·cy ['mʌrsi] *s* (**-cies**) misericordia; **at the mercy of** alla mercé di
mere [mɪr] *adj* mero, puro
meretricious [,mɛrɪ'trɪʃəs] *adj* vistoso, chiassoso, sgargiante; artificiale, falso, finto
merge [mʌrdʒ] *tr* fondere ‖ *intr* fondersi; (*said of two roads*) convergere; **to merge into** convertirsi lentamente in
merger ['mʌrdʒər] *s* fusione
meridian [mə'rɪdɪ·ən] *adj* meridiano; culminante ‖ *s* meridiano; apogeo
meringue [mə'ræŋ] *s* meringa
merit ['mɛrɪt] *s* merito ‖ *tr* meritare
meritorious [,mɛrɪ'torɪ·əs] *adj* meritorio
merlon ['mʌrlən] *s* merlo
mermaid ['mʌr ,med] *s* sirena
mer'man' *s* (**-men'**) tritone *m*
merriment ['mɛrɪmənt] *s* allegria
mer·ry ['mɛri] *adj* (**-rier; -riest**) allegro, giocondo; **to make merry** divertirsi
Mer'ry Christ'mas *interj* Buon Natale!
mer'ry-go-round' *s* giostra, carosello; (*of parties*) serie ininterrotta
mer'ry·mak'er *s* festaiolo
mesh [mɛʃ] *s* (*network*) rete *f*; (*each open space of net*) maglia; (mach) ingranaggio; **meshes** rete *f* ‖ *tr* irretire; (mach) ingranare ‖ *intr* irretirsi; (mach) ingranarsi
mess [mɛs] *s* (*dirty condition*) disordine *m*; (*meal for a group of people*) mensa, rancio; porzione; **to get into a mess** mettersi nei pasticci; **to make a mess of** rovinare ‖ *tr* sporcare; disordinare; rovinare ‖ *intr* mangiare in comune; **to mess around** (coll) perdersi in cose inutili
message ['mɛsɪdʒ] *s* messaggio

messenger ['mɛsəndʒər] *s* messaggero; (*person who goes on an errand*) fattorino; (mil) portaordini *m*
mess' hall' *s* mensa
Messiah [mə'saɪ·ə] *s* Messia *m*
mess' kit' *s* gavetta, gamella
mess'mate' *s* compagno di rancio
mess' of pot'tage ['patɪdʒ] *s* (Bib & fig) piatto di lenticchie
Messrs. ['mɛsərz] *pl* of **Mr.**
mess·y ['mɛsi] *adj* (**-ier; -iest**) disordinato; sporco
metal ['mɛtəl] *adj* metallico ‖ *s* metallo
metallic [mɪ'tælɪk] *adj* metallico
metallurgy ['mɛtə ,lʌrdʒi] *s* metallurgia
met'al pol'ish *s* lucido per metalli
met'al·work' *s* lavoro di metallo
metamorpho·sis [,mɛtə'mɔrfəsɪs] *s* **-ses** [,siz]) metamorfosi *f*
metaphony [mə'tæfəni] *s* metafonia, metafonesi *f*
metaphor ['mɛtəfər] or ['mɛtə ,fɔr] *s* metafora
metaphorical [,mɛtə'farɪkəl] or [,mɛtə'fɔrɪkəl] *adj* metaforico
metathe·sis [mɪ'tæθɪsɪs] *s* (**-ses** [,siz]) metatesi *f*
mete [mit] *tr*—**to mete out** distribuire
meteor ['mitɪ·ər] *s* meteora
meteoric [,mitɪ'arɪk] or [,mitɪ'ɔrɪk] *adj* meteorico; (fig) rapidissimo, folgorante
meteorite ['mitɪ·ə ,raɪt] *s* meteorite *m* & *f*
meteorology [,mitɪ·ə'ralədʒi] *s* meteorologia
meter ['mitər] *s* (*unit of length; verse*) metro; (*instrument for measuring gas, water, etc.*) contatore *m*; (mus) tempo ‖ *tr* misurare col contatore
me'ter read'er *s* lettore *m*, letturista *m*
methane ['mɛθen] *s* metano
method ['mɛθəd] *s* metodo
methodic(al) [mɪ'θadɪk(əl)] *adj* metodico
Methodist ['mɛθədɪst] *adj* & *s* metodista *mf*
Methuselah [mɪ'θuzələ] *s* Matusalemme *m*
meticulous [mɪ'tɪkjələs] *adj* meticoloso
metric(al) ['mɛtrɪk(əl)] *adj* metrico
metronome ['mɛtrə ,nom] *s* metronomo
metropolis [mɪ'trapəlɪs] *s* metropoli *f*
metropolitan [,mɛtrə'palɪtən] *adj* & *s* metropolitano
mettle ['mɛtəl] *s* disposizione, temperamento; brio, animo; **to be on one's mettle** impegnarsi a fondo
mettlesome ['mɛtəlsəm] *adj* brioso
mew [mju] *s* miagolio; (orn) gabbiano; **mews** scuderie *fpl*
Mexican ['mɛksɪkən] *adj* & *s* messicano
Mexico ['mɛksɪ ,ko] *s* il Messico
mezzanine ['mɛzə ,nin] *s* mezzanino
mica ['maɪkə] *s* mica
microbe ['maɪkrob] *s* microbio
microbiology [,maɪkrəbaɪ'alədʒi] *s* microbiologia
microcard ['maɪkrə ,kard] *s* microscheda

microfarad [ˌmaɪkrə'færæd] s microfarad m

microfilm ['maɪkrə͵fɪlm] s microfilm m || tr microfilmare

microgroove ['maɪkrə͵gruv] adj microsolco || s microsolco; disco microsolco

microphone ['maɪkrə͵fon] s microfono

microscope ['maɪkrə͵skop] s microscopio

microscopic [ˌmaɪkrə'skɑpɪk] adj microscopico

microwave ['maɪkrə͵wev] s microonda

mid [mɪd] adj mezzo, la metà di, e.g., **mid October** la metà di ottobre

mid'day' adj di mezzogiorno || s mezzogiorno

middle ['mɪdəl] adj medio, mezzo || s mezzo, metà f; (of human body) cintura; **about the middle of** verso la metà di; **in the middle of** nel mezzo di

mid'dle age' s mezza età || **Middle Ages** spl Medio Evo

mid'dle class' s ceto medio, borghesia

Mid'dle East' s Medio Oriente

Mid'dle Eng'lish s inglese m medievale parlato fra il 1150 e il 1500

mid'dle fin'ger s dito medio

mid'dle-man' s (-men') intermediario

middling ['mɪdlɪŋ] adj mediocre, passabile || s (coarsely ground wheat) farina grossa integrale; **middlings** articoli mpl di qualità mediocre || adv moderatamente

mid·dy ['mɪdi] s (-dies) aspirante m di marina

mid'dy blouse' s marinara

midget ['mɪdʒɪt] s nano

midland ['mɪdlənd] adj centrale, interno || s regione centrale

mid'night' adj di mezzanotte; **to burn the midnight oil** studiare a lume di candela || s mezzanotte f

midriff ['mɪdrɪf] s diaframma m; (middle part of body) cintura, vita

mid'ship'man s (-men) aspirante m di marina

midst [mɪdst] s mezzo, centro; **in the midst of** in mezzo a

mid'stream' s—**in midstream** in mezzo al fiume

mid'sum'mer s cuore m dell'estate

mid'way' adj situato a metà strada || s metà strada; viale m principale di un' esposizione || adv a metà strada

mid'week' s mezzo della settimana

mid'wife' s (-wives') levatrice f

mid'win'ter s cuore m dell'inverno

mid'year' adj nel mezzo dell'anno || s mezzo dell'anno; **midyears** (coll) esami mpl nel mezzo dell'anno scolastico

mien [min] s aspetto, portamento

miff [mɪf] s (coll) battibecco || tr (coll) offendere

might [maɪt] s forza, potenza; **with might and main** a tutta forza || v aux used to form the potential, e.g., he might change his mind è possibile che cambi opinione

might·y ['maɪti] adj (-ier; -iest) po-

tente; (huge) grandissimo || adv (coll) moltissimo, grandemente

migraine ['maɪgren] s emicrania

migrate ['maɪgret] intr migrare

migratory ['maɪgrə͵tori] adj migratore

milch [mɪltʃ] adj lattifero

mild [maɪld] adj dolce, mite, gentile; (disease) leggero

mildew ['mɪl͵dju] or ['mɪl͵du] s (mold) muffa; (plant disease) peronospora

mile [maɪl] s miglio terrestre; **miglio marino**

mileage ['maɪlɪdʒ] s distanza in miglia

mile'age tick'et s biglietto calcolato in miglia simile al biglietto chilometraggio

mile'post' s colonnina miliare

mile'stone' s pietra miliare

milieu [mɪl'ju] s ambiente m

militancy ['mɪlɪtənsi] s bellicismo; spirito militante

militant ['mɪlɪtənt] adj & s militante mf

militarism ['mɪlɪtə͵rɪzəm] s militarismo

militarist ['mɪlɪtərɪst] adj & s militarista mf

militarize ['mɪlɪtə͵raɪz] tr militarizzare

military ['mɪlɪ͵teri] adj militare || s— **the military** le forze armate

mil'itary acad'emy s scuola allievi ufficiali, accademia militare

mil'itary police' s polizia militare

militate ['mɪlɪ͵tet] intr militare

militia [mɪ'lɪʃə] s milizia

mili'tia·man s (-men) miliziano

milk [mɪlk] adj lattifero; di latte; al latte || s latte m || tr mungere; (fig) spillare || intr dare latte

milk' can' s bidone m per il latte

milk' choc'olate s cioccolato al latte

milk' diet' s regime latteo

milking ['mɪlkɪŋ] s mungitura

milk'maid' s lattaia

milk'man' s (-men') lattaio

milk' of hu'man kind'ness s grande compassione

milk' pail' s secchio da latte

milk' shake' s frappé m or frullato di latte

milk'sop' s effeminato

milk'weed' s vincetossico

milk·y ['mɪlki] adj (-ier; -iest) latteo; (whitish) lattiginoso

Milk'y Way' s Via Lattea

mill [mɪl] s (for grinding grain) mulino; (for making fabrics) filanda; (for cutting wood) segheria; (for refining sugar) zuccherificio; (for producing steel) acciaieria; (to grind coffee) macinino; (part of a dollar) millesimo; **to put through the mill** mettere a dura prova || tr (grains) macinare; (coins) zigrinare; (steel) laminare; (ore) frantumare; (with a milling machine) fresare; (chocolate) frullare || intr—**to mill about or around** girare intorno

millennial [mɪ'lɛnɪəl] adj millenario

milleni·um [mɪ'lɛnɪ·əm] s (-ums or -a [ə]) millennio

miller ['mɪlər] s mugnaio; (ent) tignola notturna

millet ['mɪlɪt] s panico, miglio

milliampere [ˌmɪlɪ'æmpɪr] s milliampere m

milliard ['mɪljərd] or ['mɪljɑrd] s (Brit) miliardo, bilione m

milligram ['mɪlɪ ˌgræm] s milligrammo

millimeter ['mɪlɪ ˌmitər] s millimetro

milliner ['mɪlɪnər] s modista

milliner·y ['mɪlɪ ˌnɛri] or ['mɪlɪnəri] s (-ies) cappelli mpl per signora; modisteria; articoli mpl di modisteria

mil'linery shop' s modisteria

milling ['mɪlɪŋ] s (of grain) macinatura; (of coins) granitura; (mach) fresatura

mill'ing machine' s fresatrice f

million ['mɪljən] adj milione di, milioni di || s milione m

millionaire [ˌmɪljən'ɛr] s milionario

millionth ['mɪljənθ] adj, s & pron milionesimo

millivolt ['mɪlɪ ˌvolt] s millivolt m

mill'pond' s gora

mill'race' s corrente f che aziona il mulino; canale m di presa

mill'stone' s mola, macina, palmento; (fig) peso, gravame m

mill' wheel' s ruota del mulino

mill'work' s lavoro di falegnameria; lavoro di falegnameria fatto a macchina

mime [maɪm] s mimo || tr mimare

mimeograph ['mɪmɪ·ə ˌgræf] or ['mɪmɪə ˌgrɑf] s (trademark) ciclostile m || tr ciclostilare

mim·ic ['mɪmɪk] s mimo, imitatore m || v (pret & pp -icked; ger -icking) tr imitare, scimmiottare

mimic·ry ['mɪmɪkri] s (-ries) mimica; (biol) mimetismo

minaret [ˌmɪnə'rɛt] or ['mɪnə ˌrɛt] s minareto

mince [mɪns] tr tagliuzzare, triturare; (words) pronunziare con affettazione; **to not mince one's words** non aver peli sulla lingua

mince'meat' s carne tritata; **to make mincemeat of** annientare completamente

mince' pie' s torta di frutta secca e carne tritata

mind [maɪnd] s mente f; opinione; **to bear in mind** tener presente; **to be not in one's right mind** essere fuori di senno; **to be of one mind** essere d'accordo; **to be out of one's mind** essere impazzito; **to change one's mind** cambiare d'opinione; **to go out of one's mind** impazzire; **to have a mind to** aver voglia di; **to have in mind to** pensare a; **to have on one's mind** avere in mente; **to lose one's mind** uscire di mente; **to make up one's mind** decidersi; **to my mind a** mio modo di vedere; **to say whatever comes to one's mind** dire quanto salta in testa, e.g., **John always says whatever comes to his mind** Gio-

vanni dice sempre quanto gli salta in testa; **to set one's mind on** risolversi a; **to slip one's mind** scappare di mente (with dat), e.g., **it slipped his mind** gli è scappato di mente; **to speak one's mind** dire la propria opinione; **with one mind** unanimamente || tr (to take care of) occuparsi di; obbedire (with dat); **do you mind the smoke?** Le disturba il fumo?; **mind your own business** si occupi degli affari Suoi || intr osservare, fare attenzione; rincrescere, e.g., **do you mind if I go?** Le rincresce se vado?; **never mind** non si preoccupi

mindful ['maɪndfəl] adj memore

mind' read'er s lettore m del pensiero

mind' read'ing s lettura del pensiero

mine [maɪn] s (e.g., of coal) miniera; (mil & nav) mina || pron poss il mio; mio || tr minare; (earth) scavare; (ore) estrarre || intr lavorare una miniera; (mil & nav) minare

mine' detec'tor s rivelatore m di mine

mine'field' s campo minato

mine'lay'er s posamine m

miner ['maɪnər] s minatore m

mineral ['mɪnərəl] adj & s minerale m

mineralogy [ˌmɪnə'rælədʒi] s mineralogia

min'eral wool' s cotone m or lana minerale

mine' sweep'er s dragamine m

mingle ['mɪŋgəl] tr mescolare; unire || intr mescolarsi, associarsi

miniature ['mɪnɪ·ətʃər] or ['mɪnɪtʃər] s miniatura; **to paint in miniature** miniare, dipingere in miniatura

min'iature golf' s minigolf m

miniaturization [ˌmɪnɪ·ətʃərɪ'zeʃən] or [ˌmɪnɪtʃərɪ'zeʃən] s miniaturizzazione

minimal ['mɪnɪməl] adj minimo

minimize ['mɪnɪ ˌmaɪz] tr minimizzare

minimum ['mɪnɪməm] adj & s minimo

min'imum wage' s salario minimo

mining ['maɪnɪŋ] adj minerario || s estrazione di minerali; (nav) posa di mine

minion ['mɪnjən] s servo; favorito, beniamino

min'ion of the law' s poliziotto

miniskirt ['mɪnə ˌskʌrt] s minigonna

minister ['mɪnɪstər] s ministro; pastore m protestante || tr & intr ministrare

ministerial [ˌmɪnɪs'tɪrɪ·əl] adj ministeriale

minis·try ['mɪnɪstri] s (-tries) ministero; sacerdozio

mink [mɪŋk] s visone m

minnow ['mɪno] s pesciolino; (ichth) ciprino

minor ['maɪnər] adj minore || s minore m, minorenne mf; (educ) corso secondario

minori·ty [mɪ'nɑrɪti] or [mɪ'nɔrɪti] adj minoritario || s (-ties) (smaller number or part; group differing in race, etc., from majority) minoranza; (under legal age) minorità f

minstrel ['mɪnstrəl] s (hist) menestrello; (U.S.A.) comico vestito da nero

minstrel·sy ['mɪnstrəlsi] *s* (-sies) giulleria; poesia giullaresca

mint [mɪnt] *s* zecca; (*plant*) menta; (*losenge*) mentina; (fig) miniera d'oro ‖ *tr* coniare

minuet [,mɪnju'ɛt] *s* minuetto

minus ['maɪnəs] *adj* meno ‖ *s* meno, perdita ‖ *prep* meno, senza

minute [maɪ'njut] or [maɪ'nut] *adj* minuto ‖ ['mɪnɪt] *adj* fatto in un minuto ‖ *s* minuto; momento; **minutes** processo verbale; **to write up the minutes** tenere i verbali; **up to the minute** al corrente; dell'ultima ora

min·ute hand′ ['mɪnɪt] *s* sfera or lancetta dei minuti

minutiae [mɪ'njuʃɪ,i] or [mɪ'nuʃɪ,i] *spl* minuzie *fpl*

minx [mɪŋks] *s* sfacciata, civetta

miracle ['mɪrəkəl] *s* miracolo

mir′acle play′ *s* sacra rappresentazione

miraculous [mɪ'rækjələs] *adj* miracoloso

mirage [mɪ'rɑʒ] *s* miraggio

mire [maɪr] *s* limo, mota

mirror ['mɪrər] *s* specchio ‖ *tr* specchiare, riflettere

mirth [mʌrθ] *s* allegria, gioia

mir·y ['maɪri] *adj* (-ier; -iest) fangoso, limaccioso

misadventure [,mɪsəd'vɛntʃər] *s* disavventura, contrattempo

misanthrope ['mɪsən,θrop] *s* misantropo

misanthropy [mɪs'ænθrəpi] *s* misantropia

misapprehension [,mɪsæprɪ'hɛnʃən] *s* malinteso

misappropriation [,mɪsə,propri'eʃən] *s* malversazione

misbehave [,mɪsbɪ'hev] *intr* comportarsi male

misbehavior [,mɪsbɪ'hevɪ·ər] *s* cattiva condotta

miscalculation [,mɪskælkjə'leʃən] *s* calcolo errato

miscarriage [mɪs'kærɪdʒ] *s* (*of justice*) errore *m;* (*of a letter*) disguido; (pathol) aborto

miscar·ry [mɪs'kæri] *v* (*pret & pp* -ried) *intr* (*said of a project*) fallire; (*said of a letter*) smarrirsi; (pathol) abortire

miscellaneous [,mɪsə'lenɪ·əs] *adj* miscellaneo

miscella·ny ['mɪsə,leni] *s* (-nies) miscellanea

mischief ['mɪstʃɪf] *s* (*harm*) danno; (*disposition to annoy*) malizia; (*prankishness*) birichinata

mis′chief·mak′er *s* mettimale *mf*

mischievous ['mɪstʃɪvəs] *adj* dannoso; malizioso; birichino

misconception [,mɪskən'sɛpʃən] *s* concetto erroneo, fraintendimento

misconduct [mɪs'kɑndəkt] *s* cattiva condotta; (*of a public official*) malgoverno ‖ [,mɪskən'dʌkt] *tr* male amministrare; **to misconduct oneself** comportarsi male

misconstrue [,mɪskən'stru] or [mɪs'kɑnstru] *tr* fraintendere

miscount [mɪs'kaunt] *s* conteggio erroneo ‖ *tr & intr* contare male

miscue [mɪs'kju] *s* sbaglio; (*in billiards*) stecca ‖ *intr* steccare; (theat) sbagliarsi di battuta

mis·deal ['mɪs,dil] *s* distribuzione sbagliata ‖ [mɪs'dil] *v* (*pret & pp* -dealt** [dɛlt]) *tr & intr* distribuire erroneamente

misdeed [mɪs'did] or ['mɪs,did] *s* misfatto, malfatto

misdemeanor [,mɪsdɪ'minər] *s* cattiva condotta; (law) delitto colposo

misdirect [,mɪsdɪ'rɛkt] or [,mɪsdaɪ'rɛkt] *tr* dare un indirizzo sbagliato a; (*a letter*) mettere un indirizzo sbagliato su

misdoing [mɪs'du·ɪŋ] *s* misfatto

miser ['maɪzər] *s* avaro, spilorcio

miserable ['mɪzərəbəl] *adj* miserabile, miserevole; (coll) malissimo; (coll) schifoso

miserly ['maɪzərli] *adj* spilorcio

miser·y ['mɪzəri] *s* (-ies) miseria

misfeasance [mɪs'fizəns] *s* infrazione della legge; abuso di autorità commesso da pubblico funzionario

misfire [mɪs'faɪr] *s* difetto di esplosione; (aut) difetto d'accensione ‖ *intr* (*said of a gun*) fare cilecca; (aut) dare accensione irregolare; (fig) fallire

mis·fit ['mɪs,fɪt] *s* vestito che non va bene; (*person*) spostato, pesce *m* fuor d'acqua ‖ [mɪs'fɪt] *v* (*pret & pp* -fitted; *ger* -fitting) *intr* andar male

misfortune [mɪs'fɔrtʃən] *s* disgrazia

misgiving [mɪs'gɪvɪŋ] *s* dubbio, timore *m,* cattivo presentimento

misgovern [mɪs'gʌvərn] *tr* amministrare male

misguided [mɪs'gaɪdɪd] *adj* fuorviato; (*e.g., kindness*) sconsigliato

mishap ['mɪshæp] or [mɪs'hæp] *s* accidente *m,* infortunio

misinform [,mɪsɪn'fɔrm] *tr* dare informazioni errate a

misinterpret [,mɪsɪn'tɛrprɪt] *tr* interpretare male, trasfigurare

misjudge [mɪs'dʒʌdʒ] *tr & intr* giudicare male

mis·lay [mɪs'le] *v* (*pret & pp* -laid [,led]) *tr* (*e.g., tile*) applicare in maniera sbagliata; (*e.g., papers*) smarrire, mettere al posto sbagliato

mis·lead [mɪs'lid] *v* (*pret & pp* -led [,led]) *tr* sviare, traviare

misleading [mɪs'lidɪŋ] *adj* ingannatore

mismanagement [mɪs'mænɪdʒmənt] *s* malgoverno

misnomer [mɪs'nomər] *s* termine improprio

misplace [mɪs'ples] *tr* mettere fuori di posto; (*trust*) riporre erroneamente

misprint ['mɪs,prɪnt] *s* errore *m* di stampa, refuso ‖ [mɪs'prɪnt] *tr* stampare erroneamente

mispronounce [,mɪsprə'nauns] *tr* pronunciare in modo erroneo

mispronunciation [,mɪsprə,nʌnsɪ-

'eʃən] or [ˌmɪsprəˌnʌnʃɪ'eʃən] s errore m di pronuncia

misquote [mɪs'kwot] tr citare incorrettamente

misrepresent [ˌmɪsreprɪ'zent] tr travisare, snaturare; (pol) rappresentare slealmente

miss [mɪs] s sbaglio, omissione; tiro fuori bersaglio; signorina || tr (a train, an opportunity) perdere; (the target) fallire; (an appointment) mancare; (the point) non vedere, non capire; per poco, e.g., **the car missed hitting him** l'automobile non l'ha investito per poco || intr sbagliare, fallire; mancare il bersaglio || Miss s signorina, la signorina

missal ['mɪsəl] s messale m

misshapen [mɪs'ʃepən] adj deforme, malfatto

missile ['mɪsɪl] adj missilistico || s missile m

mis'sile launch'er s lanciamissili m

missing ['mɪsɪŋ] adj mancante; assente; (in action) disperso

mis'sing link' s anello di congiunzione

miss'ing per'son s disperso

mission ['mɪʃən] s missione

missionar·y ['mɪʃənˌerɪ] adj missionario || s (-ies) (eccl) missionario; (dipl) incaricato in missione

missive ['mɪsɪv] s missiva

mis·spell [mɪs'spel] v (pret & pp -spelled or -spelt ['spelt]) tr & intr scrivere male

misspelling [mɪs'spelɪŋ] s errore m di ortografia

misspent [mɪs'spent] adj sprecato

misstatement [mɪs'stetmənt] s dichiarazione inesatta

misstep [mɪs'step] s passo falso

miss·y ['mɪsɪ] s (-ies) (coll) signorina

mist [mɪst] s caligine f, foschia; (of tears) velo; (of smoke, vapors, etc.) nuvola

mis·take [mɪs'tek] s errore m, sbaglio; **and no mistake** (coll) di sicuro; **by mistake** per sbaglio; **to make a mistake** sbagliarsi || v (pret -took ['tuk]; pp -taken) tr fraintendere; **to be mistaken for** essere preso per; **to mistake for** pigliare per

mistaken [mɪs'tekən] adj errato, sbagliato; **to be mistaken** essere in errore, sbagliarsi

mister ['mɪstər] s (mil, nav) signore m; (coll) marito || interj (coll) signore!; (coll) Lei!; (coll) buonuomo! || Mister s Signore m

mistletoe ['mɪsəlˌto] s vischio

mistreat [mɪs'trit] tr maltrattare

mistreatment [mɪs'tritmənt] s maltrattamento

mistress ['mɪstrɪs] s (of a household) signora, padrona; (paramour) amante f, ganza; (Brit) maestra di scuola

mistrial [mɪs'traɪəl] s processo viziato da errore giudiziario

mistrust [mɪs'trʌst] s diffidenza || tr diffidare di || intr diffidarsi

mistrustful [mɪs'trʌstfəl] adj diffidente

mist·y ['mɪstɪ] adj (-ier; -iest) fosco, brumoso; (fig) vago, confuso

misunder·stand [ˌmɪsʌndər'stænd] v (pret & pp -stood ['stud] tr fraintendere, equivocare

misunderstanding [ˌmɪsʌndər'stændɪŋ] s malinteso

misuse [mɪs'jus] s abuso; (of funds) malversazione || [mɪs'juz] tr abusare di; (funds) malversare

misword [mɪs'wʌrd] tr comporre male

mite [maɪt] obolo; (ent) acaro

miter ['maɪtər] s (carp) ugnatura; (carp) giunto a quartabuono; (eccl) mitra || tr tagliare a quartabuono, ugnare; giungere a quartabuono

mi'ter box' s cassetta per ugnature

mi'ter joint' s giunto a quartabuono

mitigate ['mɪtɪˌget] tr mitigare

mitten ['mɪtən] s manopola, muffola

mix [mɪks] tr mescolare; (colors) mesticare; (dough) impastare; (salad) condire; **to mix up** confondere || intr confondersi, mescolarsi

mixed [mɪkst] adj misto; (candy) assortito; (coll) confuso

mixed' com'pany s riunione f di ambo i sessi

mixed' drink' s miscela di liquori diversi

mixed' feel'ing s sentimento ambivalente

mixed' met'aphor s metafora incongruente

mixer ['mɪksər] s (mach) mescolatrice f; **to be a good mixer** essere socievole

mixture ['mɪkstʃər] s mistura, mescolanza; (aut) miscela, carburazione

mix'-up' s confusione; (coll) baruffa

mizzen ['mɪzən] s mezzana

moan [mon] s gemito || intr gemere

moat [mot] s fosso, fossato

mob [mab] s turba || v (pret & pp mobbed; ger mobbing) tr assaltare; affollarsi intorno a; (a place) affollare

mobile ['mobɪl] or ['mobil] adj mobile

mo'bile home' s caravan m, roulotte f

mobility [mo'bɪlɪtɪ] s mobilità f

mobilization [ˌmobɪlɪ'zeʃən] s mobilitazione

mobilize ['mobɪˌlaɪz] tr & intr mobilitare

mob' rule' s legge f della teppa

mobster ['mabstər] s gangster m

moccasin ['makəsɪn] s mocassino

Mo'cha cof'fee ['mokə] s caffè m moca

mock [mak] adj finto, imitato || s dileggio, burla || tr deridere, canzonare; ingannare || intr motteggiare; **to mock at** farsi gioco di

mocker·y ['makərɪ] s (-ies) dileggio, scherno; (subject of derision) zimbello; (poor imitation) contraffazione

mock'-hero'ic adj eroicomico

mockingbird ['makɪŋˌbʌrd] s mimo

mock' or'ange s gelsomino selvatico

mock' tur'tle soup' s finto brodo di tartaruga

mock'-up' s modello dimostrativo

mode [mod] s modo, maniera; (fashion) moda; (gram) modo

mod·el ['madəl] adj modello, e.g., **model student** studente modello || s modello; (*woman serving as subject for artists*) modello *f;* (*woman wearing clothes at fashion show*) indossatrice *f* ‖ *v* (*pret & pp* **-eled** or **-elled; ger -eling** or **-elling**) *tr* modellare ‖ *intr* modellarsi; fare il manichino

mod'el air'plane *s* aeromodello

mo'del-air'plane build'er *s* aeromodellista *mf*

mod'eling clay' *s* plastilina

moderate ['mɑdərɪt] *adj* moderato ‖ ['mɑdə,ret] *tr* moderare; (*a meeting*) presiedere a ‖ *intr* moderarsi

moderator ['mɑdə,retər] *s* moderatore *m;* (*mediator*) arbitro; (phys) moderatore *m*

modern ['mɑdərn] *adj* moderno

modernize ['mɑdər,naɪz] *tr* modernizzare, rimodernare

modest ['mɑdɪst] *adj* modesto

modes·ty ['mɑdɪsti] *s* (**-ties**) modestia

modicum ['mɑdɪkəm] *s* piccola quantità

modi·fy ['mɑdɪ,faɪ] *v* (*pret & pp* **-fied**) *tr* modificare; (gram) determinare

modish ['mɑdɪʃ] *adj* alla moda

modulate ['mɑdʒə,let] *tr & intr* modulare

modulation [,mɑdʒə'leʃən] *s* modulazione

mohair ['mo,hɛr] *s* mohair *m*

Mohammedan [mo'hæmɪdən] *adj & s* maomettano

Mohammedanism [mo'hæmɪdə,nɪzəm] *s* maomettismo

moist [mɔɪst] *adj* umido; lacrimoso

moisten ['mɔɪsən] *tr* inumidire ‖ *intr* inumidirsi

moisture ['mɔɪstʃər] *s* umidità *f*

molar ['molər] *s* molare *m*

molasses [mə'læsɪz] *s* melassa

mold [mold] *s* stampo, forma; (*fungus*) muffa; humus *m;* (fig) indole *f* ‖ *tr* plasmare, conformare; (*to make moldy*) fare ammuffire ‖ *intr* ammuffire

molder ['moldər] *s* modellatore *m* ‖ *intr* sgretolarsi; polverizzarsi

molding ['moldɪŋ] *s* modellato; (archit, carp) modanatura

mold·y ['moldi] *adj* (**-ier; -iest**) ammuffito

mole [mol] *s* (*pier*) molo; (*harbor*) darsena; (*spot on skin*) neo; (*small mammal*) talpa

molecule ['mɑlɪ,kjul] *s* molecola

mole'hill' *s* mucchio di terra sopra la tana di talpe

mole'skin' *s* pelle *f* di talpa; (*fabric*) fustagno di prima qualità

molest [mə'lɛst] *tr* molestare; fare proposte disoneste a

moll [mɑl] *s* (slang) ragazza della malavita; (slang) puttana

molli·fy ['mɑlɪ,faɪ] *v* (*pret & pp* **-fied**) *tr* pacificare, placare

mollusk ['mɑləsk] *s* mollusco

mollycoddle ['mɑlɪ,kɑdəl] *s* effeminato ‖ *tr* viziare, coccolare

Mo'lotov cock'tail ['mɑlə,tɔf] *s* bottiglia Molotov

molt [molt] *s* muda ‖ *intr* andare in muda

molten ['moltən] *adj* fuso

molybdenum [mə'lɪbdɪnəm] or [,mɑlɪb'dinəm] *s* molibdeno

moment ['momənt] *s* momento; **at any moment** da un momento all'altro

momentary ['momən,tɛri] *adj* momentaneo

momentous [mo'mɛntəs] *adj* grave, importante

momen·tum [mo'mɛntəm] *s* (**-tums** or **-ta** [tə]) slancio; (mech) momento

monarch ['mɑnərk] *s* monarca *m*

monarchic(al) [mə'nɑrkɪk(əl)] *adj* monarchico

monarchist ['mɑnərkɪst] *adj & s* monarchico

monar·chy ['mɑnərki] *s* (**-chies**) monarchia

monaster·y ['mɑnəs,tɛri] *s* (**-ies**) monastero

monastic [mə'næstɪk] *adj* monastico, monacale

monasticism [mə'næstɪ,sɪzəm] *s* monachesimo

Monday ['mʌndi] *s* lunedì *m*

monetary ['mɑnɪ,tɛri] *adj* monetario; pecuniario

money ['mʌni] *s* denaro; **to be in the money** esser carico di soldi; **to make money** far quattrini

mon'ey·bag' *s* borsa per denaro; **moneybags** (coll) riccone sfondato

moneychanger ['mʌnɪ,tʃendʒər] *s* cambiavalute *m*

moneyed ['mʌnid] *adj* danaroso

moneylender ['mʌni,lɛndər] *s* prestatore *m* di denaro

mon'ey·mak'er *s* capitalista *mf;* affare vantaggioso

mon'ey or'der *s* vaglia *m*

Mongolian [mɑŋ'golɪən] *adj & s* mongolo

mon·goose ['mɑŋgus] *s* (**-gooses**) mangusta

mongrel ['mʌŋgrəl] or ['mɑŋgrəl] *adj* ibrido ‖ *s* ibrido; cane bastardo

monitor ['mɑnɪtər] *s* (educ) capoclasse *mf;* (rad, telv) monitore *m* ‖ *tr* osservare; (*a signal*) controllare; (*broadcast*) ascoltare

monk [mʌŋk] *s* monaco

monkey ['mʌŋki] *s* scimmia; **to make a monkey of** farsi gioco di ‖ *intr*—**to monkey around** (coll) oziare; **to monkey around with** (coll) giocherellare con

mon'key·shines' *spl* (slang) monellerie *fpl*, pagliacciate *fpl*

mon'key wrench' *s* chiave *f* inglese

monkhood ['mʌŋkhʊd] *s* monacato

monkshood [mʌŋks,hʊd] *s* (bot) aconito

monocle ['mɑnəkəl] *s* monocolo

monogamy [mə'nɑgəmi] *s* monogamia

monogram ['mɑnə,græm] *s* monogramma *m*

monograph ['mɑnə,græf] or ['mɑnə,grɑf] *s* monografia

monolithic [,mɑnə'lɪθɪk] *adj* monolitico

monologue ['manə‚lɔg] or ['manə‚lag] s monologo
monomania [‚manə'menɪ·ə] s monomania
monomial [mə'nomɪ·əl] s monomio
monopolize [mə'napə‚laɪz] tr monopolizzare, accaparrare
monopo·ly [mə'napəli] s (-lies) monopolio, privativa
monorail ['manə‚rel] s monorotaia
monosyllable ['manə‚sɪləbəl] s monosillabo
monotheist ['manə‚θi·ɪst] adj & s monoteista mf
monotonous [mə'natənəs] adj monotono
monotype ['manə‚taɪp] s (method) monotipia; (typ) monotipo
monoxide [mə'naksaɪd] s monossido
monseigneur [‚mansen'jœr] s monsignore m
monsignor [man'sinjər] s (-monsignors or -monsignori [‚mɔnsi'njori]) (eccl) monsignore m
monsoon [man'sun] s monsone m
monster ['manstər] adj mostruoso ‖ s mostro
monstrance ['manstrəns] s ostensorio
monstrosi·ty [man'strasɪti] s (-ties) mostruosità f
monstrous ['manstrəs] adj mostruoso
month [mʌnθ] s mese m
month·ly ['mʌnθli] adj mensile ‖ s (-lies) rivista mensile; **monthlies** (coll) mestruazione ‖ adv mensilmente
monument ['manjəmənt] s monumento
moo [mu] s muggito ‖ intr muggire
mood [mud] s umore m, vena; (gram) modo; **moods** luna, malumore m
mood·y ['mudi] adj (-ier; -iest) triste, malinconico; lunatico, capriccioso
moon [mun] s luna; **once in a blue moon** ad ogni morte di papa ‖ tr—**to moon away** (time) (coll) sprecare ‖ intr—**to moon about** (coll) gingillarsi, baloccarsi; (to daydream about) (coll) sognarsi di
moon'beam' s raggio di luna
moon'light' s chiaro m di luna
moon'light'ing s secondo lavoro notturno
moon'shine' s chiaro di luna; (coll) chiacchiere fpl, balle fpl; (coll) whisky m distillato illegalmente
moon'shot' s lancio alla luna
moon'stone' s lunaria
moor [mur] s brughiera, landa ‖ tr ormeggiare ‖ intr ormeggiarsi ‖ **Moor** s moro
Moorish ['murɪʃ] adj moresco
moor'land' s brughiera, landa
moose [mus] s (moose) alce americano
moot [mut] adj controverso, discutibile
mop [map] s scopa di filacce; (naut) redazza; (of hair) zazzera ‖ v (pret & pp **mopped**; ger **mopping**) tr (a floor) pulire, asciugare; (one's brow) asciugarsi; **to mop up** rastrellare
mope [mop] intr andare rattristato
mopish ['mopɪʃ] adj triste, avvilito

moral ['marəl] or ['mɔrəl] adj morale ‖ s (of a fable) morale f; **morals** (ethics) morale f; (modes of conduct) costumi mpl
morale [mə'ræl] or [mə'ral] s morale m
morali·ty [mə'rælɪti] s (-ties) moralità f
mor'als charge' s accusa di oltraggio al pudore
morass [mə'ræs] s palude f
moratori·um [‚mɔrə'tɔrɪ·əm] or [‚marə'tɔrɪ·əm] s (-ums or -a [ə]) moratoria
morbid ['mɔrbɪd] adj (gruesome) orribile; (feelings; curiosity; pertaining to disease; pathologic) morboso
mordacious [mɔr'deʃəs] adj mordace
mordant ['mɔrdənt] adj & s mordente m
more [mor] adj & s più m ‖ adv più; **more and more** sempre più; **more than** più di; (followed by verb) più di quanto; **the more . . . the less** tanto più . . . quanto meno
more·o'er adv per di più, inoltre
Moresque [mo'rɛsk] adj moresco
morgue [mɔrg] s deposito, obitorio; (journ) archivio di un giornale, frigorifero
moribund ['mɔrɪ‚bʌnd] or ['marɪ‚bʌnd] adj moribondo
morning ['mɔrnɪŋ] adj mattiniero ‖ s mattina, mattino; **good morning** buon giorno; **in the morning** di mattina
morn'ing coat' s giacca nera a code
morn'ing-glo'ry s (-ries) convolvolo; (Ipomea) campanella; (Convolvolus tricolor) bella di giorno
morn'ing sick'ness s vomito di gravidanza
morn'ing star' s Lucifero, stella del mattino
Moroccan [mə'rakən] adj & s marocchino
morocco [mə'rako] s (leather) marocchino ‖ **Morocco** s il Marocco
moron ['marən] s deficiente mf
morose [mə'ros] adj tetro, imbronciato
morphine ['mɔrfin] s morfina
morphology [mɔr'falədʒi] s morfologia
morrow ['maro] or ['mɔro] s—**on the morrow** l'indomani, il giorno seguente; domani
morsel ['mɔrsəl] s boccone m, bocconcino; pezzetto
mortal ['mɔrtəl] adj & s mortale m
mortality [mɔr'tælɪti] s mortalità f; (death or destruction on a large scale) moria
mortar ['mɔrtər] s (mixture of lime or cement) malta, calcina; (bowl) mortaio; (mil) mortaio, lanciabombe m
mor'tar·board' s sparviere m; (cap) tocco accademico
mortgage ['mɔrgɪdʒ] s ipoteca ‖ tr ipotecare
mortgagee [‚mɔrgɪ'dʒi] s creditore m ipotecario
mortgagor ['mɔrgɪdʒər] s debitore m ipotecario

mortician [mɔr'tɪʃən] s impresario di pompe funebri

morti·fy ['mɔrtɪ,faɪ] v (pret & pp -fied) tr mortificare; **to be mortified** vergognarsi

mortise ['mɔrtɪs] s intaccatura, incastro || tr incassare, incastrare

mor'tise lock' s serratura incastrata

mortuar·y ['mɔrtʃʊ,ɛri] adj mortuario || s (-ies) camera mortuaria

mosaic [mo'ze·ɪk] s mosaico

Moscow ['mɑskaʊ] or ['mɑsko] s Mosca

Moses ['moziz] or ['mozɪs] s Mosè m

Mos·lem ['mɑzləm] or ['mɑsləm] adj musulmano || s (-lems or -lem) musulmano

mosque [mɑsk] s moschea

mosqui·to [məs'kito] s (-toes or -tos) zanzara

mosqui'to net' s zanzariera

moss [mɔs] or [mɑs] s musco

moss'back' s (coll) ultraconservatore m, fossile m

moss·y ['mɔsi] or ['mɑsi] adj (-ier; -iest) muscoso

most [most] adj il più di, la maggior parte di || s la maggioranza, i più; **most of** la maggior parte di; **to make the most of** trarre il massimo da || adv più, maggiormente, al massimo

mostly ['mostli] adv per lo più, maggiormente, al massimo

motel [mo'tɛl] s motel m, autostello

moth [mɔθ] or [mɑθ] s falena; (clothes moth) tarma

moth'ball' s pallina antitarmica

moth-eaten ['mɔθ,itən] or ['mɑθ,itən] adj tarmato; antiquato

mother ['mʌðər] adj (love, tongue) materno; (country) natio; (church, company) madre || s madre f; (elderly woman) (coll) zia || tr fare da madre a; creare; procreare; assumere la maternità di

moth'er coun'try s madrepatria

Moth'er Goose' s supposta autrice di una raccolta di favole infantili

motherhood ['mʌðər,hʊd] s maternità f

moth'er-in-law' s (moth'ers-in-law') suocera

moth'er·land' s madrepatria

motherless ['mʌðərlɪs] adj orfano di madre, senza madre

mother-of-pearl ['mʌðərəv'pʌrl] adj madreperlaceo || s madreperla

motherly ['mʌðərli] adj materno

Moth'er's Day' s giorno della madre, festa della mamma

moth'er supe'rior s madre superiora

moth'er tongue' s madrelingua; (language from which another language is derived) lingua madre

moth'er wit' s intelligenza nativa

moth' hole' s tarlatura

moth·y ['mɔθi] or ['mɑθi] adj (-ier; -iest) tarmato

motif [mo'tif] s motivo

motion ['moʃən] s movimento; (e.g., of a dancer) movenza, mossa; (in parliamentary procedure) mozione; **in motion** in moto || intr fare cenno

motionless ['moʃənlɪs] adj immobile

mo'tion pic'ture s pellicola cinematografica; **motion pictures** cinematografia

mo'tion-picture' adj cinematografico

motivate ['moti,vet] tr animare, incitare

motive ['motɪv] adj motivo; (producing motion) motore || s motivo; (incentive) movente m

mo'tive pow'er s forza motrice; impianto motore; (rr) insieme m di locomotive

motley ['mɑtli] adj eterogeneo; variato, variopinto

motor ['motər] adj motore; (operated by motor) motorizzato; (pertaining to motor vehicles) motoristico || s motore m; (aut) macchina || intr viaggiare in macchina

mo'tor·boat' s motobarca, motoscafo

mo'tor·bus' s torpedone m; autobus m

motorcade ['motər,ked] s carovana di automobili

mo'tor·car' s automobile f

mo'tor·cy'cle s motocicletta

motorist ['motərɪst] s automobilista mf

motorize ['motə,raɪz] tr motorizzare

mo'torman s (-men) guidatore m di tram; guidatore m di locomotore

mo'tor sail'er s motoveliero

mo'tor scoot'er s motoretta

mot'or ship' s motonave f

mo'tor truck' s autocarro, camion m

mo'tor ve'hicle s motoveicolo

mottle ['mɑtəl] tr chiazzare, screziare

mot·to ['mɑto] s (-toes or -tos) motto, divisa

mould [mold] s, tr, & intr var of **mold**

mound [maʊnd] s monticello, collinetta

mount [maʊnt] s monte m, montagna; (horse for riding) cavalcatura, monta; (setting for a jewel) montatura; supporto; (for a picture) incorniciatura || tr montare; (a wall) scalare; (theat) allestire || intr montare; (to climb) salire

mountain ['maʊntən] s montagna; **to make a mountain out of a molehill** fare di un bruscolo una trave, fare d'una mosca un elefante

moun'tain climb'ing s alpinismo

mountaineer [,maʊntə'nɪr] s montanaro

mountainous ['maʊntənəs] adj montagnoso

moun'tain rail'road s ferrovia a dentiera

moun'tain range' s catena di montagne

moun'tain sick'ness s mal m di montagna

mountebank ['maʊntɪ,bæŋk] s ciarlatano

mounting ['maʊntɪŋ] s (act) il montare, montaggio; (setting) montatura; (mach) supporto

mourn [morn] tr (the loss of s.o.) piangere; (a misfortune) lamentare || intr piangere; vestire a lutto

mourner ['mornər] s persona in lutto; (penitent sinner) penitente mf;

(woman hired to attend a funeral or funerals) prefica

mourn′er's bench′ s banco dei penitenti

mournful ['mɔrnfəl] adj luttuoso, funesto; (gloomy) lugubre

mourning ['mɔrnɪŋ] s lutto; **to be in mourning** portare il lutto

mourn′ing band′ s bracciale m a lutto

mouse [maʊs] s (**mice** [maɪs]) topo, sorcio

mouse′hole′ s topaia; piccolo buco

mouser ['maʊzər] s cacciatore m di topi

mouse′trap′ s trappola per topi

moustache [məs'tæʃ] or [məs'tɑʃ] s baffi mpl, mustacchi mpl

mouth [maʊθ] s (**mouths** [maʊðz]) bocca; **by mouth** per via orale; **to be born with a silver spoon in one's mouth** essere nato con la camicia; **to make one's mouth water** fare venire a qlcu l'acquolina in bocca

mouthful ['maʊθ‚fʊl] s boccata

mouth′ or′gan s armonica a bocca

mouth′piece′ s (of wind instrument) bocchetta; (of bridle) imboccatura; (of megaphone) boccaglio; (of cigarette) bocchino; (of telephone) imboccatura; (spokesman) portavoce m

mouth′wash′ s sciacquo, risciacquo

movable ['muvəbəl] adj mobile, movibile; (law) mobiliare

move [muv] s movimento; (change of residence) trasloco; (step) passo; (e.g., in chess) mossa; **on the move** in moto, in movimento; **to get a move on** (coll) affrettarsi || tr muovere; (the bowels) provocare l'evacuazione di; (to prompt) spingere; (to stir the feelings of) emozionare, commuovere; (law) proporre; (com) svendere; **to move up** (a date) anticipare || intr muoversi; passare; (to another house) traslocare; (to another city) trasferirsi; (said of goods) avere una vendita; (said of the bowels) evacuare; procedere; (law) presentare una mozione; (coll) andarsene; **to move away** andarsene; trasferirsi; **to move back** tirarsi indietro; **to move in** avanzare; (society) frequentare; **to move off** allontanarsi

movement ['muvmənt] s movimento; (of a watch) meccanismo; (of the bowels) evacuazione; (mus) movimento, tempo

movie ['muvi] s (coll) film m, pellicola

movie•goer ['muvi‚goər] s frequentatore m del cinema

mov′ie house′ s (coll) cinematografo

mov′ie•land′ s (coll) cinelandia

moving ['muvɪŋ] adj commovente, emozionante || s trasporto; (from one house to another) trasloco

mov′ing pic′ture s film m, pellicola

mov′ing stair′case′ s scala mobile

mow [mo] v (pret **mowed**; pp **mowed** or **mown**) tr & intr falciare

mower ['mo•ər] s falciatore m; (mach) falciatrice f

Mr. ['mɪstər] s (**Messrs.** ['mɛsərz]) Signore m

Mrs. ['mɪsɪz] s Signora

much [mʌtʃ] adj & pron molto; **as much . . . as** tanto . . . quanto; **too much** troppo || adv molto; **however much** per quanto; **how much** quanto; **too much** troppo; **very much** moltissimo

mucilage ['mjusɪlɪdʒ] s colla; (gummy secretion in plants) mucillagine f

muck [mʌk] s letame m; (dirt) sudiciume m; (min) materiale m di scoria

muck′rake′ intr (coll) sollevare scandali

mucous ['mjukəs] adj mucoso

mucus ['mjukəs] s muco

mud [mʌd] s fango, melma, limo; **to sling mud at** calunniare

muddle ['mʌdəl] s confusione, guazzabuglio || tr confondere, intorbidire || intr—**to muddle through** arrangiarsi; cavarsela alla meno peggio in

mud′dle•head′ s (coll) semplicione m

mud•dy ['mʌdi] adj (-dier; -diest) fangoso, melmoso; (obscure) torbido || v (pret & pp -died) tr turbare, intorbidare; (to soil with mud) infangare

mud′guard′ s parafango

mud′hole′ s pozzanghera, fangaia

mud′ slide′ s smottamento

mudslinger ['mʌd‚slɪŋər] s calunniatore m

muff [mʌf] s manicotto || tr (coll) mancare; (to handle badly) (coll) abborracciare; (sports) mancare di pigliare

muffin ['mʌfɪn] s panino soffice

muffle ['mʌfəl] tr infagottare, imbacuccare; (a sound) velare, smorzare

muffler ['mʌflər] s sciarpa; (aut) silenziatore m, marmitta

mufti ['mʌfti] s—**in mufti** in borghese

mug [mʌg] s tazzona; (slang) muso, grugno || v (pret & pp **mugged**; ger **mugging**) tr (slang) fotografare; (slang) attaccare proditoriamente || intr fare le smorfie

mug•gy ['mʌgi] adj (-gier; -giest) afoso, opprimente

mulat•to [mju'læto] or [mə'læto] s (-toes) mulatto

mulber•ry ['mʌl‚bɛri] s (-ries) (tree) gelso; (fruit) mora di gelso

mulct [mʌlkt] tr defraudare

mule [mjul] s mulo; (slipper) pianella

muleteer [‚mjulə'tɪr] s mulattiere m

mulish ['mjulɪʃ] adj testardo

mull [mʌl] tr (wine) scaldare aggiungendo spezie || intr—**to mull over** pensarci sopra, rinvangare

mulled′ wine′ s vino caldo

mullion ['mʌljən] s colonnina che divide una bifora

multigraph ['mʌltɪ‚græf] or ['mʌltɪ‚grɑf] s (trademark) poligrafo || tr poligrafare

multilateral [‚mʌltɪ'lætərəl] adj multilaterale

multimotor [‚mʌltɪ'motər] s plurimotore m

multiple ['mʌltɪpəl] adj & s multiplo

multiplici•ty [‚mʌltɪ'plɪsɪti] s (-ties) molteplicità f

multi•ply ['mʌltɪ‚plaɪ] v (pret & pp -plied) tr moltiplicare || intr moltiplicarsi

multistage ['mʌltɪ ‚stedʒ] *adj* (rok) pluristadio

multitude ['mʌltɪ ‚tjud] or ['mʌltɪ‚tud] s moltitudine *f*

mum [mʌm] *adj* zitto; **mum's the word!** acqua in bocca!; **to keep mum** stare zitto ‖ *interj* zitto!

mumble ['mʌmbəl] *tr* biascicare ‖ *intr* farfugliare

mummer·y ['mʌməri] *s* (-ies) buffonata, mascherata

mum·my ['mʌmi] *s* (-mies) mummia

mumps [mʌmps] *s* orecchioni *mpl*

munch [mʌntʃ] *tr* sgranocchiare

mundane ['mʌnden] *adj* mondano

municipal [mju'nɪsɪpəl] *adj* municipale

municipali·ty [mju‚nɪsɪ'pælɪti] *s* (-ties) municipio

munificent [mju'nɪfɪsənt] *adj* munifico

munition [mju'nɪʃən] *s* munizione ‖ *tr* fornire di munizioni

muni′tion dump′ *s* deposito munizioni

mural ['mjʊrəl] *adj* murale ‖ *s* pittura murale

murder ['mʌrdər] *s* omicidio ‖ *tr* assassinare

murderer ['mʌrdərər] *s* omicida *m*

murderess ['mʌrdərɪs] *s* omicida *f*

murderous ['mʌrdərəs] *adj* omicida, crudele, sanguinario

murk·y ['mʌrki] *adj* (-ier; -iest) fosco, tenebroso; brumoso, nebbioso

murmur ['mʌrmər] *s* mormorio ‖ *tr & intr* mormorare

Mur′phy bed′ ['mʌrfi] *s* letto a scomparsa

muscle ['mʌsəl] *s* muscolo

muscular ['mʌskjələr] *adj* muscolare; (*having well-developed muscles*) muscoloso

muse [mjuz] *s* musa; **the Muses** le Muse ‖ *intr* meditare, rimuginare

museum [mju'zi·əm] *s* museo

mush [mʌʃ] *s* pappa, polentina; (fig) leziosaggine *f*, sdolcinatura

mush′room *s* fungo ‖ *intr* venir su come i funghi; **to mushroom into** diventare rapidamente

mush′room cloud′ *s* fungo atomico

mush·y ['mʌʃi] *adj* (-ier; -iest) polposo, spappolato; (fig) sdolcinato, sentimentale

music ['mjuzɪk] *s* musica; **to face the music** (coll) affrontare le conseguenze; **to set to music** mettere in musica

musical ['mjuzɪkəl] *adj* musicale

mu′sical com′edy *s* operetta, commedia musicale

musicale [‚mjuzɪ'kæl] *s* serata musicale

mu′sic box′ *s* scatola armonica

mu′sic cab′inet *s* scaffaletto per la musica

mu′sic hall′ *s* salone *m* da concerti; (Brit) teatro di varietà, music-hall *m*

musician [mju'zɪʃən] *s* musicista *mf*

musicianship [mju'zɪʃən ‚ʃɪp] *s* abilità *f* musicale, virtuosismo

musicologist [‚mjuzɪ'kalədʒɪst] *s* musicologo

musicology [‚mjuzɪ'kalədʒi] *s* musicologia

mu′sic stand′ *s* portamusica *m*

musk [mʌsk] *s* muschio

musk′ deer′ *s* mosco

musket ['mʌskɪt] *s* moschetto

musketeer [‚mʌskɪ'tɪr] *s* moschettiere *m*

musk′mel′on *s* melone *m*

musk′ ox′ *s* bue muschiato

musk′rat′ *s* ondatra, topo muschiato

muslin ['mʌzlɪn] *s* mussolina

muss [mʌs] *tr* (*the hair*) scompigliare, arruffare; (*clothing*) (coll) sciupare

mussel ['mʌsəl] *s* mussolo

Mussulman ['mʌsəlmən] *adj & s* musulmano

muss·y ['mʌsi] *adj* (-ier; -iest) (coll) arruffato, scompigliato

must [mʌst] *s* (*new wine*) mosto; (*mold*) muffa; (coll) cosa assolutamente indispensabile ‖ *v aux*—**I must go now** devo andarmene ora; **it must be Ann** deve essere Anna; **she must be ill** dev'essere malata; **they must have known it** devono averlo saputo

mustache [məs'tæʃ], [məs'taʃ] or ['mʌstæʃ] *s* baffi *mpl,* mustacchi *mpl*

mustard ['mʌstərd] *s* mostarda

mus′tard plas′ter *s* senapismo

muster ['mʌstər] *s* adunata, rivista; **to pass muster** passar ispezione ‖ *tr* chiamare a raccolta; riunire; **to muster in** arruolare; **to muster out** congedare; **to muster up courage** prendere coraggio a quattro mani

mus′ter roll′ *s* ruolo; (naut) appello

mus·ty ['mʌsti] *adj* (-tier; -tiest) (*moldy*) ammuffito; (*stale*) stantio; (fig) ammuffito, stantio

mutation [mju'teʃən] *s* mutazione

mute [mjut] *adj & s* muto ‖ *tr* mettere la sordina a

mutilate ['mjutɪ ‚let] *tr* mutilare

mutineer [‚mjutɪ'nɪr] *s* ammutinato

mutinous ['mjutɪnəs] *adj* ammutinato

muti·ny ['mjutɪni] *s* (-nies) ammutinamento ‖ *v* (*pret & pp* -nied) *intr* ammutinarsi

mutt [mʌt] *s* (slang) cane bastardo; (slang) scemo

mutter ['mʌtər] *tr & intr* borbottare

mutton ['mʌtən] *s* montone *m*

mut′ton chop′ *s* cotoletta di montone

mutual ['mutʃʊ·əl] *adj* mutuo, vicendevole

mu′tual aid′ *s* mutualità *f*

mu′tual fund′ *s* fondo comune di investimento

muzzle ['mʌzəl] *s* (*of animal*) muso; (*device to keep animal from biting*) museruola; (*of firearm*) bocca ‖ *tr* mettere la museruola a; (fig) imbavagliare

my [maɪ] *adj poss* mio, il mio ‖ *interj* (coll) corbezzoli!

myriad ['mɪrɪ·əd] *s* miriade *f*

myrrh [mʌr] *s* mirra

myrtle ['mʌrtəl] *s* mirto, mortella

myself [maɪ'self] *pron pers* io stesso; me, me stesso; mi, e.g., **I hurt myself** mi sono fatto male

mysterious [mɪs'tɪrɪ·əs] *adj* misterioso
myster·y ['mɪstəri] *s* (**-ies**) mistero
mystic ['mɪstɪk] *adj & s* mistico
mystical ['mɪstɪkəl] *adj* mistico
mysticism ['mɪstɪ‚sɪzəm] *s* misticismo
mystification [‚mɪstɪfɪ'keʃən] *s* mistificazione
mysti·fy ['mɪstɪ‚faɪ] *v* (*pret & pp*

-fied) *tr* avvolgere nel mistero; (*to hoax*) mistificare
myth [mɪθ] *s* mito
mythical ['mɪθɪkəl] *adj* mitico
mythological [‚mɪθə'lɑdʒɪkəl] *adj* mitologico
mytholo·gy [mɪ'θɑlədʒi] *s* (**-gies**) mitologia

N

N, n [ɛn] *s* quattordicesima lettera dell'alfabeto inglese
nab [næb] *v* (*pret & pp* **nabbed; ger nabbing**) *tr* (slang) afferrare, agguantare
nag [næg] *s* ronzino ‖ *v* (*pret & pp* **nagged; ger nagging**) *tr & intr* tormentare, infastidire
naiad ['ne·æd] *or* ['naɪ·æd] *s* naiade *f*
nail [nel] *s* (*of finger or toe*) unghia; (*of metal*) chiodo; **to hit the nail on the head** cogliere nel giusto ‖ *tr* inchiodare
nail'brush' spazzolino per le unghie
nail' file' *s* lima per le unghie
nail' pol'ish *s* smalto per le unghie
nail' set' *s* punzone *m*
naïve [nɑ'iv] *adj* candido, ingenuo
naked ['nekɪd] *adj* nudo, ignudo; **to strip naked** denudare; denudarsi; **with the naked eye** a occhio nudo
name [nem] *s* nome *m;* (*first name*) nome *m;* (*last name*) cognome *m;* fama, reputazione; titolo; lignaggio; **in the name of** nel nome di; **to call s.o. names** coprire qlco di ingiurie; **to go by the name of** essere conosciuto sotto il nome di; **to make a name for oneself** farsi un nome; **what is your name?** come si chiama Lei? ‖ *tr* nominare; menzionare; battezzare; (*a price*) fissare
name' day' *s* onomastico
nameless ['nemlɪs] *adj* senza nome, anonimo
namely ['nemli] *adv* cioè, vale a dire
name'plate' *s* targa, targhetta
namesake ['nem‚sek] *s* omonimo; persona chiamata in onore di qualcun altro
nan'ny goat' ['næni] *s* capra
nap [næp] *s* lanugine *f;* (*pile*) pelo; pisolino, sonnellino; **to take a nap** schiacciare un sonnellino ‖ *v* (*pret & pp* **napped; ger napping**) *intr* sonnecchiare; **to catch napping** cogliere alla sprovvista
napalm ['nepɑm] *s* napalm *m*
nape [nep] *s* nuca
naphtha ['næfθə] *s* nafta
napkin ['næpkɪn] *s* tovagliolo
nap'kin ring' *s* portatovagliolo
Naples ['nepləz] *s* Napoli *f*
Napoleonic [nə‚polɪ'ɑnɪk] *adj* napoleonico
narcissus [nɑr'sɪsəs] *s* narciso
narcotic [nɑr'kɑtɪk] *adj & s* narcotico
narrate [næ'ret] *tr* narrare

narration [næ'reʃən] *s* narrazione
narrative ['nærətɪv] *adj* narrativo ‖ *s* narrazione; (*genre*) narrativa
narrator [næ'retər] *s* narratore *m*
narrow ['næro] *adj* stretto; limitato; (*illiberal*) meschino, ristretto ‖ **narrows** *spl* stretti *mpl* ‖ *tr* limitare, restringere ‖ *intr* limitarsi, restringersi
nar'row escape' *s*—**to have a narrow escape** scamparla bella
nar'row-gauge' *adj* a scartamento ridotto
narrow-minded ['næro'maɪndɪd] *adj* gretto, ristretto d'idee
nasal ['nezəl] *adj & s* nasale *f*
nasturtium [nə'stʌrʃəm] *s* nasturzio
nas·ty ['næsti] *or* ['nɑsti] *adj* (**-tier; -tiest**) brutto, cattivo; sgradevole, orribile; sudicio; (*foul*) perfido
natatorium [‚netə'torɪ·əm] *s* piscina
nation ['neʃən] *s* nazione
national ['næʃənəl] *adj & s* nazionale *mf*
na'tional an'them *s* inno nazionale
na'tional debt' *s* debito pubblico
na'tional hol'iday *s* festa nazionale
nationalism ['næʃənə‚lɪzəm] *s* nazionalismo
nationali·ty [‚næʃən'ælɪti] *s* (**-ties**) nazionalità *f*
nationalize ['næʃənə‚laɪz] *tr* nazionalizzare
na'tion·wide' *adj* su scala nazionale
native ['netɪv] *adj* nativo, indigeno, oriundo; (*language*) materno ‖ *s* indigeno, nativo
na'tive land' *s* patria, paese natio
nativi·ty [nə'tɪvɪti] *s* (**-ties**) nascita, natività *f* ‖ **Nativity** *s* Natività *f*
Nato ['neto] *s* (acronym) (**North Atlantic Treaty Organization**) la N.A.T.O.
nat·ty ['næti] *adj* (**-tier; -tiest**) accurato, elegante
natural ['nætʃərəl] *adj* naturale ‖ *s* imbecille *mf;* (*mus*) bequadro; (*mus*) tono naturale; (*mus*) tasto bianco; **a natural** (coll) proprio quello che ci vuole
naturalism ['nætʃərə‚lɪzəm] *s* naturalismo
naturalist ['nætʃərəlɪst] *s* naturalista *mf*
naturalization [‚nætʃərəlɪ'zeʃən] *s* naturalizzazione
nat'uraliza'tion pa'pers *spl* documenti *mpl* di naturalizzazione

naturalize ['nætʃərə,laɪz] *tr* naturalizzare

naturally ['nætʃərəli] *adv* naturalmente

nature ['netʃər] *s* natura; **from nature** dal vero

naught [nɔt] *s* niente *m;* zero; **to come to naught** ridursi al nulla; **to set at naught** disprezzare

naugh·ty ['nɔti] *adj* (**-tier; -tiest**) cattivo, disubbidiente; (*joke*) di cattivo genere

nausea ['nɔʃɪ·ə] or ['nɔsɪ·ə] *s* nausea

nauseate ['nɔʃɪ,et] or ['nɔsɪ,et] *tr* nauseare ‖ *intr* essere nauseato

nauseating ['nɔʃɪ,etɪŋ] or ['nɔsɪ,etɪŋ] *adj* nauseabondo, stomachevole

nauseous ['nɔʃɪ·əs] or ['nɔsɪ·əs] *adj* nauseabondo

nautical ['nɔtɪkəl] *adj* nautico, marittimo, marino

naval ['nevəl] *adj* navale

na'val acad'emy *s* accademia navale

na'val of'ficer *s* ufficiale *m* di marina

na'val sta'tion *s* base *f* navale

nave [nev] *s* navata centrale; (*of a wheel*) mozzo

navel ['nevəl] *s* ombelico

na'vel or'ange *s* arancia (con depressione alla sommità)

navigability [,nævɪgə'bɪlɪti] *s* navigabilità *f;* (*of a ship*) manovrabilità *f*

navigable ['nævɪgəbəl] *adj* (*river*) navigabile; (*ship*) manovrabile

navigate ['nævɪ,get] *tr & intr* navigare

navigation [,nævɪ'geʃən] *s* navigazione

navigator ['nævɪ,getər] *s* navigatore *m;* (*in charge of navigating ship or plane*) ufficiale *m* di rotta

na·vy ['nevi] *adj* blu marino ‖ *s* (**-vies**) marina (da guerra)

na'vy bean' *s* fagiolo secco

na'vy blue' *s* blu marino

na'vy yard' *s* arsenale *m*

nay [ne] *s* no; voto negativo ‖ *adv* no; anzi

Nazarene [,næzə'rin] *adj & s* nazzareno; **the Nazarene** il Nazzareno

Nazi ['nɑtsi] or ['nætsi] *adj & s* nazista *mf*

N-bomb ['ɛn,bɑm] *s* bomba al neutrone

Neapolitan [,ni·ə'pɑlɪtən] *adj & s* napoletano

neap' tide' [nip] *s* marea di quadratura

near [nɪr] *adj* vicino, prossimo; intimo; esatto ‖ *adv* vicino, da vicino ‖ *prep* vicino a, accanto a; **to come near** avvicinarsi a ‖ *tr* avvicinarsi a ‖ *intr* avvicinarsi

nearby ['nɪr,baɪ] *adj* vicino ‖ *adv* vicino, qui vicino

Near' East' *s* Medio Oriente

nearly ['nɪrli] *adv* quasi; (*a little more or less*) press'a poco; per poco non, e.g., **he nearly died** per poco non morì

near-sighted ['nɪr'saɪtɪd] *adj* miope

near'-sight'ed·ness *s* miopia

neat [nit] *adj* netto, pulito; elegante, accurato; puro

neat's'-foot oil' *s* olio di piede di bue

Nebuchadnezzar [,nɛbjəkəd'nɛzər] *s* Nabucodonosor *m*

nebu·la ['nɛbjələ] *s* (**-lae** [,li] or **-las**) nebulosa

nebular ['nɛbjələr] *adj* nebulare

nebulous ['nɛbjələs] *adj* nebuloso

necessary ['nɛsɪ,sɛri] *adj* necessario

necessitate [nɪ'sɛsɪ,tet] *tr* necessitare, esigere

necessitous [nɪ'sɛsɪtəs] *adj* bisognoso

necessi·ty [nɪ'sɛsɪti] *s* (**-ties**) necessità *f*

neck [nɛk] *s* collo; (*of a horse*) incollatura; (*of violin*) manico; (*of mountain*) gola, passo; **neck and neck** testa a testa; **to stick one's neck out** (coll) esporsi al pericolo; **to win by a neck** vincere per una corta testa ‖ *intr* (slang) abbracciarsi, sbaciucchiarsi

neck'band' *s* colletto

neckerchief ['nɛkər,tʃɪf] *s* fazzoletto da collo

necklace ['nɛklɪs] *s* collana

neck'line' *s* giro collo, scollatura

necktie ['nɛk,taɪ] *s* cravatta

neck'tie pin' *s* spilla da cravatta

necrolo·gy [nɛ'krɑlədʒi] *s* (**-gies**) necrologia

necromancy ['nɛkrə,mænsi] *s* necromanzia

nectar ['nɛktər] *s* nettare *m*

née or **nee** [ne] *adj* nata

need [nid] *s* necessità *f,* bisogno; povertà *f;* **if need be** se ci fosse bisogno; **in need** in strettezze ‖ *tr* aver bisogno di ‖ *intr* necessitare, essere in necessità ‖ *v aux*—**to need (to)** + *inf* dovere + *inf*

needful ['nidfəl] *adj* necessario

needle ['nidəl] *s* ago; (*of phonograph*) puntina; **to look for a needle in a haystack** cercare l'ago nel pagliaio ‖ *tr* cucire; (fig) aguzzare, eccitare

nee'dle bath' *s* bagno a doccia filiforme

nee'dle·case' *s* agoraio

nee'dle·point' *s* merletto; ricamo su canovaccio

needless ['nidlɪs] *adj* inutile

nee'dle·work' *s* lavoro di cucito; (*embroidery*) ricamo; (*needlepoint*) merletto

needs [nidz] *adv* necessariamente; **it must needs be** dev'essere proprio così

need·y ['nidi] *adj* (**-ier; -iest**) bisognoso, indigente ‖ **the needy** i bisognosi

ne'er-do-well ['nɛrdu,wɛl] *adj & s* buono a nulla

negate ['nɛget] or [nɪ'get] *tr* invalidare; negare

negation [nɪ'geʃən] *s* negazione

negative ['nɛgətɪv] *adj* negativo ‖ *s* negativa; (elec) polo negativo; (gram) negazione ‖ *tr* respingere, votare contro; neutralizzare

neglect [nɪ'glɛkt] *s* negligenza, trascuratezza ‖ *tr* trascurare; **to neglect to** trascurare di; dimenticarsi di

neglectful [nɪ'glɛktfəl] *adj* negligente, trascurato

négligée or **negligee** [,nɛglɪ'ʒe] *s* veste *f* da camera or vestaglia per signora

negligence ['nɛglɪdʒəns] *s* negligenza, trascuratezza

negligent ['nɛglɪdʒənt] *adj* negligente, trascurato

negligible ['nɛglɪdʒɪbəl] *adj* trascurabile, insignificante

negotiable [nɪ'goʃɪ·əbəl] *adj* negoziabile; (*security*) al portatore; (*road*) transitabile

negotiate [nɪ'goʃɪ ,et] *tr* negoziare; (*to overcome*) superare ‖ *intr* negoziare

negotiation [nɪ ,goʃɪ'eʃən] *s* negoziazione, negoziato

Ne·gro ['nigro] *adj* negro ‖ *s* (-groes) negro, nero

neigh [ne] *s* nitrito ‖ *intr* nitrire

neighbor ['nebər] *adj* vicino, adiacente ‖ *s* vicino; (*fellow man*) prossimo ‖ *tr* essere vicino a ‖ *intr* essere vicino

neighborhood ['nebər ,hʊd] *s* vicinanza, vicinato; **in the neighborhood of** nei pressi di; (coll) a un dipresso, all'incirca

neighboring ['nebərɪŋ] *adj* vicino, attiguo; (*country*) limitrofo

neighborly ['nebərli] *adj* da buon vicino, socievole

neither ['niðər] or ['naɪðər] *adj indef* nessuno dei due, e.g., **neither boy** nessuno dei due ragazzi ‖ *pron indef* nessuno dei due, nè l'uno nè l'altro ‖ *conj* neppure, nemmeno, e.g., **neither do I** nemmeno io; **neither . . . nor** nè . . . nè

neme·sis ['nɛmɪsɪs] *s* (-ses [,siz]) nemesi *f* ‖ **Nemesis** *s* Nemesi *f*

neologism [ni'ɑlə ,dʒɪzəm] *s* neologismo

neomycin [,ni·ə'maɪsɪn] *s* neomicina

ne'on lamp' ['ni·ɑn] *s* lampada al neon

neophyte ['ni·ə ,faɪt] *s* neofita *mf*

nepenthe [nɪ'pɛnθi] *s* nepente *f*

nephew ['nɛfju] or ['nɛvju] *s* nipote *m*

Nepos ['nipɑs] or ['nɛpɑs] *s* Nipote *m*

Neptune ['nɛptʃun] or ['nɛptjun] *s* Nettuno

neptunium [nɛp'tʃunɪ·əm] or [nɛp'tjunɪ·əm] *s* (chem) nettunio

Nero ['nɪro] *s* Nerone *m*

nerve [nʌrv] *adj* nervoso ‖ *s* nervo; (*courage*) coraggio; (*boldness*) (coll) faccia tosta; **to get on one's nerves** dare ai nervi di qlcu; **to lose one's nerve** perdere le staffe

nerve-racking ['nʌrv ,rækɪŋ] *adj* irritante, esasperante

nervous ['nʌrvəs] *adj* nervoso

nerv'ous break'down *s* esaurimento nervoso

nervousness ['nʌrvəsnɪs] *s* nervosismo

nerv·y ['nʌrvi] *adj* (-ier; -iest) (*strong*) forte, vigoroso; audace; (coll) insolente, sfacciato

nest [nɛst] *s* nido; (*of hen*) cova; (*retreat*) rifugio; (*hangout*) tana; (*brood*) nidiata; **to feather one's nest** farsi il gruzzolo ‖ *tr* (*e.g., tables*) mettere l'uno nell'altro ‖ *intr* nidificare

nest' egg' *s* endice *m;* (fig) gruzzolo

nestle ['nɛsəl] *tr* annidare ‖ *intr* annidarsi, nidificare; (*to cuddle up*) rannicchiarsi

net [nɛt] *adj* netto ‖ *s* rete *f;* (*snare*) laccio, trappola; guadagno netto ‖

tr prendere con la rete; (*a sum of money*) fare un guadagno netto di

nether ['nɛðər] *adj* inferiore, infero

Netherlander ['nɛðər ,lændər] or ['nɛðərləndər] *s* olandese *mf*

Netherlands, The ['nɛðərləndz] *spl* i Paesi Bassi

netting ['nɛtɪŋ] *s* rete *f*

nettle ['nɛtəl] *s* ortica ‖ *tr* irritare, provocare

net'work' *s* rete *f*

neuralgia [nju'rældʒə] or [nu'rældʒə] *s* nevralgia

neurology [nju'rɑlədʒi] or [nu'rɑlədʒi] *s* neurologia

neuro·sis [nju'rosɪs] or [nu'rosɪs] (-ses [siz]) *s* neurosi *f*

neurotic [nju'rɑtɪk] or [nu'rɑtɪk] *adj* & *s* neurotico

neuter ['njutər] or ['nutər] *adj* neutro ‖ *s* genere neutro

neutral ['njutrəl] or ['nutrəl] *adj* neutro; (*not aligned*) neutrale ‖ *s* neutrale *m;* (mach) folle *m*

neutralist ['njutrəlɪst] or ['nutrəlɪst] *adj* & *s* neutralista *mf*

neutrality [nju'trælɪti] or [nu'trælɪti] *s* neutralità *f*

neutralize ['njutrə ,laɪz] or ['nutrə ,laɪz] *tr* neutralizzare

neutron ['njutrɑn] or ['nutrɑn] *s* neutrone *m*

neu'tron bomb' *s* bomba al neutrone

never ['nɛvər] *adv* mai, giammai; non . . . mai; **never mind** non importa

nev'er·more' *adv* mai più

nevertheless [,nɛvərðə'lɛs] *adv* ciò nonostante, ciò nondimeno, tuttavia

new [nju] or [nu] *adj* nuovo; **what's new?** che c'è di nuovo?

new' arri'val *s* nuovo venuto; (*baby*) neonato

new'born' *adj* neonato; (*e.g., faith*) rinato

New'cas'tle *s*—**to carry coals to Newcastle** portare l'acqua al mare, portare vasi a Samo

newcomer ['nju ,kʌmər] or ['nu ,kʌmər] *s* nuovo venuto

New' Eng'land *s* la Nuova Inghilterra

newfangled ['nju ,fæŋgəld] or ['nu ,fæŋgəld] *adj* all'ultima moda; di nuovo conio, di nuova invenzione

Newfoundland ['ʼjufənd ,lænd] or ['nufənd ,lænd] *s* la Terranova ‖ [nju'faʊndlənd] or [nu'faʊndlənd] *s* (*dog*) terranova *m*

newly ['njuli] or ['nuli] *adv* di recente, di fresco

new'ly·wed' *s* sposino or sposina; **the newlyweds** gli sposi

new' moon' *s* luna nuova, novilunio

news [njuz] or [nuz] *s* notizie *fpl;* **a news item** una notizia; **a piece of news** una notizia

news' a'gency *s* agenzia d'informazioni

news'beat' *s* colpo giornalistico

news'boy' *s* strillone *m*

news'cast' *s* notiziario

news'cast'er *s* annunziatore *m*, radiocommentatore *m*, telecommentatore *m*

news' con'ference *s* conferenza stampa

news' cov'erage *s* reportaggio

news'deal'er *s* venditore *m* di giornali

news'man' *s* (-men') (*reporter*) giornalista *m;* giornalaio

newsmonger ['njuz ,mʌŋgər] or ['nuz ,mʌŋgər] *s* persona pettegola, gazzettino

news'pa'per *adj* giornalistico || *s* giornale *m*

news'pa'per·man' *s* (-men') giornalista *m*

news'print' *s* carta da giornale

news'reel' *s* cinegiornale *m*

news'stand' *s* chiosco, edicola

news'week'ly *s* (-lies) settimanale *m* d'informazione

news·y ['njuzi] or ['nuzi] *adj* (-ier; -iest) (coll) informativo

New' Tes'tament *s* Nuovo Testamento

New' Year's' card' *s* cartolina d'auguri di capodanno

New' Year's' Day' *s* il capo d'anno, il capodanno

New' Year's' Eve' *s* la vigilia di capodanno, la sera di San Silvestro

New' York' [jɔrk] *adj* nuovayorchese || *s* New York *f,* Nuova York

New' York'er ['jɔrkər] *s* nuovayorchese *mf*

New' Zea'land ['zilənd] *adj* neozelandese || *s* la Nuova Zelanda

New' Zea'lander ['ziləndər] *s* neozelandese *mf*

next [nɛkst] *adj* prossimo, seguente; (*month*) prossimo, entrante || *adv* la prossima volta; dopo, in seguito; next to vicino a; next to nothing quasi nulla; to come next essere il prossimo

next'-door' *adj* della casa vicina || next'-door' *adv* nella casa vicina

next' of kin' *s* (next' of kin') parente più prossimo

niacin ['naɪ·əsɪn] *s* niacina

Niag'ara Falls' [naɪ'ægərə] *spl* le Cascate del Niagara

nib [nɪb] *s* becco; punta; his nibs (slang & pej) sua eccellenza

nibble ['nɪbəl] *s* piccolo morso || *tr & intr* mordicchiare, sbocconcellare; (*said of a fish*) abboccare

nice [naɪs] *adj* (*pleasant*) simpatico, gentile; (*requiring skill*) buono, bello; (*fine*) sottile; (*refined*) raffinato, per bene; (*fussy*) esigente, difficile; rispettabile; (*weather*) bello; (*attractive*) bello; nice . . . and (coll) bello, e.g., it is nice and warm fa un bel caldo

nice-looking ['naɪs'lukɪŋ] *adj* bello, attraente

nicely ['naɪsli] *adv* precisamente, esattamente; (coll) benissimo

nice·ty ['naɪsəti] *s* (-ties) esattezza, precisione; to a nicety con la massima precisione

niche [nɪtʃ] *s* nicchia

Nicholas ['nɪkələs] *s* Nicola *m*

nick [nɪk] *s* intaccatura; (*of a dish*) slabbratura; in the nick of time al

momento giusto || *tr* intaccare; (*to cut*) tagliare; (*a dish*) slabbrare

nickel ['nɪkəl] *s* nichel *m;* moneta americana di cinque cents || *tr* nichelare

nick'el plate' *s* nichelatura

nick'el-plate' *tr* nichelare

nicknack ['nɪk ,næk] *s* soprammobile *m;* gingillo, ninnolo

nick'name' *s* nomignolo, soprannome *m* || *tr* soprannominare

nicotine ['nɪkə ,tin] *s* nicotina

niece [nis] *s* nipote *f*

nif·ty ['nɪfti] *adj* (-tier; -tiest) (coll) elegante; (coll) eccellente

niggard ['nɪgərd] *adj & s* spilorcio

night [naɪt] *adj* notturno || *s* notte *f;* at or by night di notte; the night before last l'altra notte; to make a night of it (coll) fare le ore piccole

night'cap' *s* berretto da notte; bicchierino di liquore che si beve prima di coricarsi

night' club' *s* night-club *m*

night' driv'ing *s* il guidare di notte

night'fall' *s* crepuscolo; at nightfall sul cader della notte, all'imbrunire

night'gown' *s* camicia da notte

nightingale ['naɪtən ,gel] *s* usignolo

night' latch' *s* serratura a molla

night' let'ter *s* telegramma notturno

night'long' *adj* di tutta la notte || *adv* tutta la notte

nightly ['naɪtli] *adj* di notte; di ogni notte || *adv* di notte; ogni notte

night'mare' *s* incubo

nightmarish ['naɪt ,merɪʃ] *adj* raccapricciante

night' owl' *s* (coll) nottambulo

night' school' *s* scuola serale

night'shirt' *s* camicia da notte

night'time' *s* notte *f*

night'walk'er *s* nottambulo; vagabondo notturno; (*prostitute*) passeggiatrice *f*

night' watch' *s* guardia notturna

night' watch'man *s* (-men) guardiano notturno

nihilist ['naɪ·ɪlɪst] *s* nichilista *mf*

nil [nɪl] *s* nulla *m,* niente *m*

Nile [naɪl] *s* Nilo

nimble ['nɪmbəl] *adj* agile, svelto

Nimrod ['nɪmrɑd] *s* Nembrod *m*

nincompoop ['nɪnkəm ,pup] *s* babbeo, tonto, semplicione *m*

nine [naɪn] *adj & pron* nove || *s* nove *m;* nine o' clock le nove

nine' hun'dred *adj, s & pron* novecento

nineteen ['naɪn'tin] *adj, s & pron* diciannove *m*

nineteenth ['naɪn'tinθ] *adj & s* diciannovesimo; (*century*) decimonono || *s* (*in dates*) diciannove *m* || *pron* diciannovesimo

ninetieth ['naɪntɪ·ɪθ] *adj, s & pron* novantesimo

nine·ty ['naɪnti] *adj & pron* novanta || *s* (-ties) novanta *m;* the gay nineties il decennio scapestrato dal 1890 al 1900

ninth [naɪnθ] *adj, s & pron* nono || *s* (*in dates*) nove *m*

nip [nɪp] *s* morso, pizzicotto; freddo pungente; (*of liquor*) bicchierino,

sorso; **nip and tuck** testa a testa || *v*
(*pret & pp* **nipped; *ger* nipping**) *tr*
pizzicare, mordere; (*to squeeze*) spremere; (*to freeze*) gelare; (*liquor*) sorseggiare; **to nip in the bud** arrestare
di bel principio || *intr* bere a sorsi
nipple ['nɪpəl] *s* capezzolo; (*of rubber*)
tettarella; (*mach*) corto tubo filet-
tato a entrambe le estremità, manicotto, cappuccio
Nippon [nɪ'pɑn] or ['nɪpɑn] *s* il Giap-
pone
Nippon·ese [ˌnɪpə'niz] *adj* nipponico
|| *s* (-ese) Giapponese *mf*
nip·py ['nɪpi] *adj* (-pier; -piest) mordente, pizzicante; gelato
nirvana [nɪr'vɑnə] *s* il nirvana
nit [nɪt] *s* lendine *m;* pidocchio
niter ['naɪtər] *s* nitro
nit'-pick' *intr* (coll) cercare il pelo nel-
l'uovo
nitrate ['naɪtret] *s* nitrato; (agr) nitrato di soda; (agr) nitrato di potassio
ni'tric ac'id ['naɪtrɪk] *s* acido nitrico
nitride ['naɪtraɪd] *s* azoturo, nitruro
nitrogen ['naɪtrədʒən] *s* azoto
nitroglycerin [ˌnaɪtrə'glɪsərɪn] *s* nitroglicerina
ni'trous ox'ide ['naɪtrəs] *s* ossidulo di
azoto
nitwit ['nɪt ˌwɪt] *s* (slang) baggiano
no [no] *adj* nessuno; **no admittance**
vietato l'ingresso; **no doubt** senza
dubbio; **no matter** non importa; **no
parking** divieto di sosta; **no smoking**
vietato fumare; **no thoroughfare** divieto di transito; **no use** inutilmente;
with no senza || *s* no; voto negativo
|| *adv* no; non; **no longer** non . . .
più; **no sooner** non appena
Noah ['no·ə] *s* Noè *m*
nob·by ['nɑbi] *adj* (-bier; -biest)
(slang) elegante; (slang) eccellente
nobili·ty [no'bɪlɪti] *s* (-ties) nobiltà *f*
noble ['nobəl] *adj & s* nobile *m*
no'ble·man *s* (-men) nobile *m*, nobi-
luomo
no'ble·wom'an *s* (-wom'en) nobile *f*,
nobildonna
nobod·y ['no ˌbɑdi] or ['nobədi] *s*
(-ies) nessuno, illustre sconosciuto ||
pron indef nessuno; **nobody but** nessun altro che; **nobody else** nessun
altro
nocturnal [nɑk'tʌrnəl] *adj* notturno
nod [nɑd] *s* cenno d'assenso, cenno
del capo; (*of person going to sleep*)
crollo del capo || *v* (*pret & pp*
nodded; *ger* nodding) *tr* (*one's head*)
inclinare; **to nod assent** fare cenno
di sì || *intr* inclinare il capo; (*to
drowse*) assopirsi
node [nod] *s* nodo; protuberanza;
(phys) nodo
no'-good' *adj & s* (coll) buono a nulla
nohow ['no ˌhaʊ] *adv* (coll) in nessuna
maniera
noise [nɔɪz] *s* rumore *m* || *tr* divulgare
noiseless ['nɔɪzlɪs] *adj* silenzioso
nois·y ['nɔɪzi] *adj* (-ier; -iest) rumoroso, chiassoso

nomad ['nomæd] *adj & s* nomade *m*
no' man's' land' *s* terra di nessuno
nominal ['nɑmɪnəl] *adj* nominale; simbolico
nominate ['nɑmɪ ˌnet] *tr* presentare la
candidatura di; (*to appoint*) nominare, designare
nomination [ˌnɑmɪ'neʃən] *s* candidatura; nomina
nominative ['nɑmɪnətɪv] *adj & s* nomi-
nativo
nominee [ˌnɑmɪ'ni] *s* candidato desi-
gnato
nonbelligerent [ˌnɑnbə'lɪdʒərənt] *adj
& s* non belligerante *m*
nonbreakable [nɑn'brekəbəl] *adj* infrangibile
nonce [nɑns] *s—for the nonce* per
l'occasione
nonchalance ['nɑnʃələns] or [ˌnɑnʃə-
'lɑns] *s* disinvoltura, indifferenza
nonchalant ['nɑnʃələnt] or [ˌnɑnʃə-
'lɑnt] *adj* disinvolto, indifferente
noncom ['nɑn ˌkɑm] *s* (coll) sottufficiale *m*
noncombatant [nɑn'kɑmbətənt] *adj*
non combattente || *s* persona non
combattente
non'commis'sioned of'ficer [ˌnɑnkə-
'mɪʃənd] *s* sottufficiale *m*
noncommittal [ˌnɑnkə'mɪtəl] *adj* ambiguo, evasivo
non compos mentis ['nɑn'kɑmpəs'mɛn-
tɪs] *adj* pazzo; (law) incapace
nonconformist [ˌnɑnkən'fɔrmɪst] *s*
anticonformista *mf*, nonconformista
mf
nondelivery [ˌnɑndɪ'lɪvəri] *s* mancata
consegna
nondescript ['nɑndɪ ˌskrɪpt] *adj* indefinibile, inclassificabile
none [nʌn] *pron indef* nessuno; **none
of** nessuno di; **none other** nessun
altro || *adv* non; affatto, niente af-
fatto; **none the less** ciò nonostante,
nondimeno
nonenti·ty [nɑn'entɪti] *s* (-ties) inesi-
stenza; (*person*) nullità *f*
nonfiction [nɑn'fɪkʃən] *s* letteratura
non romanzesca
nonfulfillment [ˌnɑnfʊl'fɪlmənt] *s*
mancanza di esecuzione
nonintervention [ˌnɑnɪntər'vɛnʃən] *s*
non intervento
nonmetal ['nɑn ˌmɛtəl] *s* metalloide *m*
nonpayment [nɑn'pemənt] *s* mancato
pagamento
non·plus ['nɑnplʌs] or [nɑn'plʌs] *s*
perplessità *f* || *v* (*pret & pp* -plussed
or plused; *ger* -plussing or -plusing)
tr lasciare perplesso
nonprofit [nɑn'prɑfɪt] *adj* senza scopo
lucrativo
nonrefillable [ˌnɑnri'fɪləbəl] *adj* (*prescription*) non ripetibile; (*e.g., bottle*) non ricaricabile
nonresident [nɑn'rɛzɪdənt] *s* persona
di passaggio, non residente *mf*
nonresidential [nɑn ˌrɛzi'dɛnʃəl] *adj*
commerciale, non residenziale
nonscientific [nɑn ˌsaɪ·ən'tɪfɪk] *adj* non
scientifico

nonsectarian [ˌnɑnsɛkˈtɛrɪ‧ən] *adj* che non segue nessuna confessione religiosa

nonsense [ˈnɑnsɛns] *s* sciocchezza, assurdità *f*, nonsenso

nonsensical [nɑnˈsɛnsɪkəl] *adj* sciocco, assurdo, illogico

nonskid [ˈnɑnˈskɪd] *adj* antiderapante

nonstop [ˈnɑnˈstɑp] *adj & adv* senza scalo

nonsupport [ˌnɑnsəˈport] *s* mancato pagamento degli alimenti

noodle [ˈnudəl] *s* (slang) scemo; (slang) testa; **noodles** tagliatelle *fpl*

noo′dle soup′ *s* tagliatelle *fpl* in brodo

nook [nʊk] *s* angolo, cantuccio

noon [nun] *s* mezzogiorno; **at high noon** a mezzogiorno in punto

no one or no-one [ˈno ˌwʌn] *pron indef* nessuno; **no one else** nessun altro

noontime [ˈnun ˌtaɪm] *s* mezzogiorno

noose [nus] *s* laccio, nodo scorsoio

nor [nɔr] *conj* nè

Nordic [ˈnɔrdɪk] *adj* nordico

norm [nɔrm] *s* norma, media, tipo

normal [ˈnɔrməl] *adj* normale ‖ *s* condizione normale; norma; (geom) normale *f*

Norman [ˈnɔrmən] *adj & s* normanno

Normandy [ˈnɔrməndi] *s* la Normandia

Norse [nɔrs] *adj* norvegese; scandinavo ‖ *s* (*ancient Scandinavian language*) scandinavo; (*language of Norway*) norvegese *m;* **the Norse** gli scandinavi; i norvegesi

Norse′man *s* (-men) normanno

north [nɔrθ] *adj* del nord, settentrionale ‖ *s* nord *m* ‖ *adv* al nord, verso il nord

North′ Amer′ica *s* l'America del Nord

North′ Amer′ican *adj & s* nordamericano

north′east′ *adj* di nord-est ‖ *s* nord-est *m* ‖ *adv* al nord-est

north′east′er *s* vento di nord-est

northern [ˈnɔrðərn] *adj* settentrionale; (*Hemisphere*) boreale

North′ Kore′a *s* la Corea del Nord

North′ Pole′ *s* polo nord

northward [ˈnɔrθwərd] *adv* verso il nord

north′west′ *adj* di nord-ovest ‖ *s* nord-ovest *m* ‖ *adv* al nord-ovest

north′ wind′ *s* vento del nord, aquilone *m*

Norway [ˈnɔrwe] *s* la Norvegia

Norwegian [nɔrˈwidʒən] *adj & s* norvegese *mf* ‖ *s* (*language*) norvegese *m*

nose [noz] *s* naso; (*of missile*) testata; **to blow one's nose** soffiarsi il naso; **to count noses** contare il numero dei presenti; **to follow one's nose** andare a lume di naso; **to lead by the nose** menare per il naso; **to look down one's nose at** (coll) guardare dall'alto in basso; **to pay through the nose** pagare un occhio della testa; **to pick one's nose** mettersi le dita nel naso; **to speak through the nose** parlare nel naso; **to thumb one's nose at** fare marameo a; **to turn up one's nose at** guardare dall'alto in basso, guardare

con disprezzo ‖ *tr* fiutare; **to nose out** vincere per un pelo ‖ *intr* fiutare; **to nose about** curiosare

nose′ bag′ *s* musetta

nose′band′ *s* museruola di cavallo

nose′bleed′ *s* sangue *m* dal naso

nose′ cone′ *s* ogiva

nose′ dive′ *s* (*of prices*) subita discesa; (aer) discesa in picchiata

nose′-dive′ *intr* discendere in picchiata

nosegay [ˈnoz ˌge] *s* mazzolino di fiori

nose′ glass′es *spl* occhiali *mpl* a stringinaso

nose′ ring′ *s* nasiera

nose′wheel′ *s* (aer) ruota del carrello anteriore

no′-show′ *s* (coll) passeggero che si è prenotato e non parte

nostalgia [nɑˈstældʒə] *s* nostalgia

nostalgic [nɑˈstældʒɪk] *adj* nostalgico

nostril [ˈnɑstrɪl] *s* narice *f*

nos‧y [ˈnozi] *adj* (-ier; -iest) (coll) curioso

not [nɑt] *adv* no; non; **not at all** niente affatto; **not yet** non ancora; **to think not** credere di no; **why not?** come no?

notable [ˈnotəbəl] *adj* notevole, notabile ‖ *s* notabile *m*

notarize [ˈnotə ˌraɪz] *tr* munire di fede notarile

nota‧ry [ˈnotəri] *s* (-ries) notaio

notch [nɑtʃ] *s* tacca; (*in mountain*) passo; (coll) tantino; **notches** (coll) di gran lunga, e.g., **notches above** di gran lunga migliore ‖ *tr* intaccare

note [not] *s* nota, annotazione; (*currency*) banconota; (*communication*) memorandum *m;* (*of bird*) canto; (*tone of voice*) tono; (*reputation*) riguardo; (*short letter*) biglietto, letterina; (mus) nota; (com) cambiale *f* ‖ *tr* notare, annotare; osservare

note′book′ *s* (*for school*) quaderno; taccuino, notes *m*

noted [ˈnotɪd] *adj* ben noto, eminente

note′ pa′per *s* carta da lettera

note′wor′thy *adj* notevole

nothing [ˈnʌθɪŋ] *s* niente *m*, nulla; **for nothing** gratis; inutilmente; **next to nothing** quasi niente ‖ *pron indef* niente, nulla, non . . . niente, non . . . nulla; **nothing else** nient'altro; **to make nothing of it** non farne caso ‖ *adv* per nulla; **nothing less** non meno

notice [ˈnotɪs] *s* attenzione; notizia, notifica; annunzio, preavviso; (*in newspaper*) trafiletto; (law) disdetta; **on short notice** senza preavviso; (com) a breve scadenza; **to escape the notice of** passare inavvertito a; **to serve notice to** far sapere a, far constatare a ‖ *tr* osservare, notare, prendere nota di

noticeable [ˈnotɪsəbəl] *adj* notevole; (*e.g., difference*) percettibile

noti‧fy [ˈnotɪ ˌfaɪ] *v* (*pret & pp* -**fied**) *tr* informare, far sapere

notion [ˈnoʃən] *s.* nozione; (*whim*) capriccio; **notions** mercerie *fpl;* **to have a notion to** aver voglia di

notorie‧ty [ˌnotəˈraɪ‧ɪti] *s* (-ties) (*state*

of being well known) notorietà *f;* cattiva fama

notorious [no'tori·əs] *adj* (*generally known*) notorio; (*unfavorably known*) famigerato

no'-trump' *adj & s* senza atout *m*

notwithstanding [ˌnɑtwɪð'stændɪŋ] or [ˌnɑtwɪθ'stændɪŋ] *adv* ciò nonostante ‖ *prep* malgrado ‖ *conj* sebbene

nougat ['nugət] *s* torrone *m*

noun [naun] *s* nome *m*, sostantivo

nourish ['nʌrɪʃ] *tr* nutrire

nourishing ['nʌrɪʃɪŋ] *adj* nutriente

nourishment ['nʌrɪʃmənt] *s* nutrimento

novel ['nɑvəl] *adj* nuovo, novello, insolito, originale ‖ *s* romanzo

novelist ['nɑvəlɪst] *s* romanziere *m*

novel·ty ['nɑvəlti] *s* (**-ties**) novità *f;* **novelties** chincaglierie *fpl*

November [no'vɛmbər] *s* novembre *m*

novice ['nɑvɪs] *s* novizio

novitiate [no'vɪʃɪ·ɪt] *s* noviziato

novocaine ['novə ˌken] *s* novocaina

now [nau] *s* presente *m* ‖ *adv* adesso; **from now on** d'ora in poi; **just now** un momento fa; **now and then** di tempo in tempo; **now that** visto che ‖ *conj* visto che, dato che

nowadays ['nau·ə ˌdez] *adv* al giorno d'oggi, oggidì

no'way' *adv* in nessun modo; nient'affatto

no'where' *adv* da nessuna parte; **nowhere else** da nessun'altra parte, in nessun altro luogo

noxious ['nɑkʃəs] *adj* nocivo

nozzle ['nɑzəl] *s* (*of hose or pipe*) boccaglio; (*of tea pot, gas burner*) becco; (*of gun*) bocca; (*of sprinkling can*) bocchetta; (aut, mach) becco; (slang) naso

nth [ɛnθ] *adj* ennesimo; **to the nth degree** all'ennesima potenza

nuance [nju'ans] or ['nju·ans] *s* sfumatura

nub [nʌb] *s* protuberanza; (*of coal*) pezzo; (coll) nocciolo, cuore *m*

nuclear ['njuklɪ·ər] or ['nuklɪ·ər] *adj* nucleare

nu'clear fis'sion *s* fissione nucleare

nu'clear fu'sion *s* fusione nucleare

nu'clear test' ban' *s* accordo per la tregua atomica

nucle·us ['njuklɪ·əs] or ['nuklɪ·əs] *s* (**-i** [ˌaɪ] or **-uses**) nucleo

nude [njud] or [nud] *adj* nudo ‖ *s*—**in the nude** nudo

nudge [nʌdʒ] *s* gomitatina ‖ *tr* dare di gomito a

nudist ['njudɪst] or ['nudɪst] *adj & s* nudista *mf*

nudi·ty ['njudɪti] or ['nudɪti] *s* (**-ties**) nudità *f*

nugget ['nʌgɪt] *s* pepita

nuisance ['njusəns] or ['nusəns] *s* noia, seccatura; (*person*) seccatore *m*, pittima *mf*

null [nʌl] *adj* nullo; **null and void** invalido

nulli·fy ['nʌlɪ ˌfaɪ] *v* (*pret & pp* **-fied**) *tr* annullare, invalidare

nulli·ty ['nʌlɪti] *s* (**-ties**) nullità *f*

numb [nʌm] *adj* intorpidito; (*from cold*) intirizzito; **to become numb** intorpidirsi ‖ *tr* intorpidire

number ['nʌmbər] *s* numero; (*for sale*) articolo di vendita; (*publication*) fascicolo; (*of a serial*) dispensa, puntata; **a number of** parecchi; **beyond** or **without number** senza numero, infiniti ‖ *tr* numerare, contare; **his days are numbered** i suoi giorni sono contati ‖ *intr*—**to number among** essere tra

numberless ['nʌmbərlɪs] *adj* innumerevole

numeral ['njumərəl] or ['numərəl] *adj* numerale ‖ *s* numero

numerical [nju'mɛrɪkəl] or [nu'mɛrɪkəl] *adj* numerico

numerous ['njumərəs] or ['numərəs] *adj* numeroso

numskull ['nʌm ˌskʌl] *s* (coll) stupido

nun [nʌn] *s* monaca, religiosa

nuptial ['nʌpʃəl] *adj* nuziale ‖ **nuptials** *spl* nozze *fpl*

nurse [nʌrs] *s* infermiera; (*to suckle a child*) nutrice *f;* (*to take care of a child*) bambinaia ‖ *tr* (*to minister to*) curare; allattare; allevare; (*e.g., hatred*) covare ‖ *intr* fare l'infermiera

nurser·y ['nʌrsəri] *s* (**-ies**) stanza dei bambini; (*shelter for children*) asilo infantile; (hort) vivaio

nurs'ery·man *s* (**-men**) orticoltore *m*

nurs'ery rhyme' *s* canzoncina per i più piccini

nurs'ery school' *s* scuola materna

nursing ['nʌrsɪŋ] *adj* infermieristico ‖ *s* allattamento; professione d'infermiera

nurs'ing bot'tle *s* biberon *m*, poppatoio

nurs'ing home' *s* convalescenziario; ospizio dei vecchi, gerontocomio

nurture ['nʌrtʃər] *s* allevamento; nutrimento ‖ *tr* allevare; alimentare; (*e.g., hope*) accarezzare

nut [nʌt] *s* noce *f;* (*eccentric*) (slang) esaltato, pazzoide *m;* (mus) capotasto; (mach) madrevite *f*, dado; **a hard nut to crack** un osso duro da rodere; **to be nuts for** (coll) essere pazzo per

nut'crack'er *s* schiaccianoci *m*

nutmeg ['nʌt ˌmɛg] *s* noce moscata

nutrition [nju'trɪʃən] or [nu'trɪʃən] *s* (*process*) nutrizione; (*food*) nutrimento

nutritious [nju'trɪʃəs] or [nu'trɪʃəs] *adj* nutriente

nut'shell' *s* guscio di noce; **in a nutshell** in breve, in poche parole

nut·ty ['nʌti] *adj* (**-tier; -tiest**) che sa di noci; (slang) pazzo; **nutty about** (slang) pazzo per

nuzzle ['nʌzəl] *tr* toccare col muso, ammusare ‖ *intr* (*said of swine*) grufolare; (*said of other animals*) stare muso a muso, ammusare; (*to snuggle*) rannicchiarsi

nylon ['naɪlɑn] *s* nailon *m*

nymph [nɪmf] *s* ninfa

O

O, o [o] *s* quindicesima lettera dell'alfabeto inglese

O *interj* o!, oh!

oaf [of] *s* balordo, scemo, imbecille *mf*

oak [ok] *s* quercia

oaken ['okən] *adj* di quercia, quercino

oakum ['okəm] *s* stoppa incatramata

oar [or] *s* remo; **to lie** or **rest on one's oars** dormire sugli allori; non lavorare più ‖ *tr* spingere coi remi ‖ *intr* remare

oar'lock' *s* scalmo

oars'man *s* (-men) rematore *m*

oa·sis [o'esɪs] *s* (-ses [siz]) oasi *f*

oat [ot] *s* avena; **oats** (*seeds*) avena; **to feel one's oats** (coll) essere pieno di vita; (coll) sentirsi importante; **to sow one's wild oats** correre la cavallina

oath [oθ] *s* giuramento; **on oath** sotto giuramento; **to take an oath** giurare, prestar giuramento

oat'meal' *s* (*breakfast food*) fiocchi *mpl* d'avena; farina d'avena

obdurate ['abdjərɪt] *adj* indurito, inesorabile; impenitente, incallito

obedience [o'bidɪ·əns] *s* obbedienza, ubbidienza

obedient [o'bidɪ·ənt] *adj* ubbidiente

obeisance [o'besəns] or [o'bisəns] *s* saluto rispettoso; omaggio

obelisk ['abəlɪsk] *s* obelisco

obese [o'bis] *adj* obeso

obesity [o'bisɪti] *s* obesità *f*

obey ['obe] *tr* ubbidire (with *dat*), ubbidire ‖ *intr* ubbidire

obfuscate [ab'fʌsket] or ['abfəs,ket] *tr* offuscare

obituar·y [o'bɪt/ʊ,ɛri] *adj* necrologico ‖ *s* (-ies) necrologia

object ['abdʒɪkt] *s* oggetto ‖ [ab'dʒɛkt] *tr* obiettare ‖ *intr* fare obiezioni, obiettare

objection [ab'dʒɛk/ən] *s* obiezione

objectionable [ab'dʒɛk/ənəbəl] *adj* reprensibile; (*e.g., odor*) sgradevole; offensivo

objective [ab'dʒɛktɪv] *adj & s* obiettivo

obligate ['ablɪ,get] *tr* obbligare

obligation [,ablɪ'ge/ən] *s* obbligo, obbligazione

oblige [ə'blaɪdʒ] *tr* obbligare; favorire; **much obliged** obbligatissimo

obliging [ə'blaɪdʒɪŋ] *adj* compiacente, accomodante, servizievole

oblique [ə'blik] *adj* obliquo; indiretto

obliterate [ə'blɪtə,ret] *tr* obliterare; spegnere, distruggere

oblivion [ə'blɪvɪ·ən] *s* oblio

oblivious [ə'blɪvɪ·əs] *adj* (*forgetful*) dimentico; (*unaware*) ignaro

oblong ['ablɔŋ] or ['ablaŋ] *adj* oblungo

obnoxious [əb'nak/əs] *adj* detestabile

oboe ['obo] *s* oboe *m*

oboist ['obo·ɪst] *s* oboista *mf*

obscene [ab'sin] *adj* osceno

obsceni·ty [ab'sɛnɪti] or [ab'sɪnɪti] *s* (-ties) oscenità *f*, sconcezza

obscure [əb'skjʊr] *adj* oscuro ‖ *tr* oscurare

obscuri·ty [əb'skjʊrɪti] *s* (-ties) oscurità *f*

obsequies ['absɪkwiz] *spl* esequie *fpl*

obsequious [əb'sikwɪ·əs] *adj* ossequioso, servile

observance [əb'zʌrvəns] *s* osservanza; **observances** pratiche *fpl;* cerimonie *fpl*

observation [,abzər've/ən] *s* osservazione; osservanza

observa'tion car' *s* (rr) vettura belvedere

observato·ry [əb'zʌrvə,tori] *s* (-ries) osservatorio

observe [əb'zʌrv] *tr* osservare

observer [əb'zʌrvər] *s* osservatore *m*

obsess [əb'sɛs] *tr* ossessionare

obsession [əb'sɛ/ən] *s* ossessione

obsolescent [,absə'lɛsənt] *adj* che sta cadendo in disuso

obsolete ['absə,lit] *adj* disusato

obstacle ['abstəkəl] *s* ostacolo

obstetrical [ab'stɛtrɪkəl] *adj* ostetrico

obstetrics [ab'stɛtrɪks] *s* ostetricia

obstina·cy ['abstɪnəsi] *s* (-cies) ostinazione

obstinate ['abstɪnɪt] *adj* ostinato

obstreperous [ab'strɛpərəs] *adj* turbolento; rumoroso

obstruct [əb'strʌkt] *tr* ostruire

obstruction [əb'strʌk/ən] *s* ostruzione

obtain [əb'ten] *tr* ottenere ‖ *intr* prevalere, essere in voga

obtrusive [əb'trusɪv] *adj* intruso, importuno; sporgente

obtuse [əb'tjus] or [əb'tus] *adj* ottuso

obviate ['abvɪ,et] *tr* ovviare (with *dat*)

obvious ['abvɪ·əs] *adj* ovvio, palmare

occasion [ə'keʒən] *s* occasione; **on occasion** di quando in quando ‖ *tr* occasionare

occasional [ə'keʒənəl] *adj* saltuario; (*e.g., verses*) d'occasione

occasionally [ə'keʒənəli] *adv* occasionalmente, di tanto in quanto

occident ['aksɪdənt] *s* occidente *m*

occidental [,aksɪ'dɛntəl] *adj & s* occidentale *mf*

occlud'ed front' [ə'kludɪd] *s* fronte occluso

occlusion [ə'kluʒən] *s* occlusione

occlusive [ə'klusɪv] *adj* occlusivo ‖ *s* occlusiva

occult [ə'kʌlt] or ['akʌlt] *adj* occulto

occupancy ['akjəpənsi] *s* occupazione, presa di possesso; (*tenancy*) locazione

occupant ['akjəpənt] *s* occupante *m;* (*tenant*) inquilino

occupation [,akjə'pe/ən] *s* occupazione

occupational [,akjə'pe/ənəl] *adj* occupazionale; (*e.g., disease*) professionale, del lavoro

occu·py ['akjə,paɪ] *v* (*pret & pp* -**pied**) *tr* occupare; (*to dwell in*) abitare

oc·cur [ə'kʌr] *v* (*pret & pp* -**curred**;

ger -**curring**) *intr* accadere, succedere; incontrarsi; (*to come to mind*)
venir in mente, e.g., **it occurs to me**
mi viene in mente

occurrence [əˈkʌrəns] *s* evento, avvenimento; apparizione

ocean [ˈoʃən] *s* oceano

o'cean lin'er *s* transatlantico

o'clock [əˈklɑk] *adv* secondo l'orologio; **it is one o'clock** è la una; **it is
two o'clock** sono le due

octane [ˈɑkten] *adj* ottanico || *s* ottano

octave [ˈɑktɪv] or [ˈɑktev] *s* ottava

Octavian [ɑkˈtevɪ·ən] *s* Ottaviano

October [ɑkˈtobər] *s* ottobre *m*

octo·pus [ˈɑktəpəs] *s* (**-puses** or **-pi**
[ˌpaɪ]) (*small*) polpo; (*large*) piovra;
(fig) piovra

ocular [ˈɑkjələr] *adj* & *s* oculare *m*

oculist [ˈɑkjəlɪst] *s* oculista *mf*

odd [ɑd] *adj* (*number*) dispari;
strambo, bizzarro; (*not matching*)
scompagnato, spaiato; strano; e rotti,
e.g., **three hundred odd** tre cento e
rotti || **odds** *ssg* or *spl* probabilità *f;*
(*advantage*) vantaggio, superiorità *f;*
at odds in disaccordo; **by all odds**
senza dubbio; **it makes no odds** fa lo
stesso; **the odds are** la quota è; **to
set at odds** seminare zizzania fra

oddi·ty [ˈɑdɪti] *s* (**-ties**) stranezza

odd' jobs' *spl* lavori saltuari

odd' lot' *s* (fin) compravendita di meno
di cento unità

odds' and ends' *spl* un po' di tutto

odious [ˈodɪ·əs] *adj* odioso

odor [ˈodər] *s* odore *m;* **to be in bad
odor** aver cattiva fama

odorless [ˈodərlɪs] *adj* inodoro

odorous [ˈodərəs] *adj* odoroso

Odysseus [oˈdɪsjus] or [oˈdɪsɪ·əs] *s*
Odisseo

Odyssey [ˈɑdɪsi] *s* Odissea

Oedipus [ˈɛdɪpəs] or [ˈidɪpəs] *s* Edipo

of [ɑv] or [əv] *prep* di, e.g., **the lead
of the pencil** la mina della matita; a,
e.g., **to think of** pensare a; meno,
e.g., **a quarter of ten** le dieci meno
un quarto

off [ɔf] or [ɑf] *adj* (*wrong*) sbagliato;
(*slightly abnormal*) matto, pazzo; inferiore; (*electricity*) tagliato; (*agreement*) sospeso; libero, in libertà; di-
stante; destro; (*season*) morto || *adv*
via; fuori, lontano, distante; **to be
off** mettersi in marcia || *prep* da;
fuori da; al disotto di; lontano da;
distolto da, e.g., **his eyes were off the
target** i suoi occhi erano distolti dal
bersaglio; (naut) al largo di

offal [ˈɑfəl] or [ˈɔfəl] *s* (*of butchered
animal*) frattaglie *fpl;* rifiuti *mpl*

off' and on' *adv* di tempo in tempo

off'beat' *adj* insolito; originale

off'-chance' *s* possibilità remota

off'-col'or *adj* scolorito; indisposto;
(*joke*) di dubbio gusto

offend [əˈfɛnd] *tr* & *intr* offendere

offender [əˈfɛndər] *s* offensore *m*

offense [əˈfɛns] *s* offesa; **to take offense
(at)** offendersi (di)

offensive [əˈfɛnsɪv] *adj* offensivo || *s*
offensiva

offer [ˈɔfər] or [ˈɑfər] *s* offerta || *tr*
offrire; (*thanks*) porgere; (*resistance*)
opporre || *intr* offrirsi

offering [ˈɔfərɪŋ] or [ˈɑfərɪŋ] *s* offerta

off'hand' *adj* fatto all'improvviso; sbri-
gativo, alla buona || *adv* all'improv-
viso; bruscamente

office [ˈɔfɪs] or [ˈɑfɪs] *s* ufficio; funzione, incombenza; (*of a doctor*) gabinetto; (*of a lawyer*) studio; (eccl)
uffizio; **through the good offices of**
per tramite di

of'fice boy' *s* fattorino

of'fice-hold'er *s* pubblico funzionario

of'fice hours' *spl* orario d'ufficio

officer [ˈɔfɪsər] or [ˈɑfɪsər] *s* (*in a
corporation*) funzionario; (*policeman*) agente *m;* (mil, nav, naut)
ufficiale *m;* **officer of the day** (mil)
ufficiale *m* di giornata

of'fice seek'er [ˈsikər] *s* aspirante *m* a
un ufficio pubblico

of'fice supplies' *spl* articoli *mpl* di
cancelleria

official [əˈfɪʃəl] *adj* ufficiale || *s* fun-
zionario, ufficiale *m*

officiate [əˈfɪʃɪˌet] *intr* ufficiare

officious [əˈfɪʃəs] *adj* invadente, infra-
mettente; **to be officious** essere un
impiccione

offing [ˈɔfɪŋ] or [ˈɑfɪŋ] *s*—**in the
offing** al largo; (fig) in preparazione,
probabile

off'-lim'its *adj* proibito; **off-limits to**
ingresso proibito a

off'-peak' heat'er *s* (elec) scaldabagno
azionato unicamente in periodi di
consumo minimo

off'-peak' load' *s* (elec) carico di consumo minimo

off'print' *s* estratto

off'set' *s* compensazione; (typ) offset *m*
|| **off'set'** *v* (*pret* & *pp* **-set**; *ger*
-setting) *tr* compensare; stampare in
offset

off'shoot' *s* (*of plant*) germoglio; (*of
family or race*) discendente *mf;*
(*branch*) ramo; (fig) conseguenza

off'shore' *adj* (*wind*) di terra; (*fishing*)
vicino alla costa; (*island*) costiero ||
adv al largo

off'side' *adv* (sports) fuori gioco

off'spring' *s* discendente *m;* prole *f;*
figlio; figli *mpl*

off'stage' *adv* tra le quinte

off'-the-rec'ord *adj* confidenziale || *adv*
confidenzialmente

often [ˈɔfən] or [ˈɑfən] *adv* sovente,
spesso; **how often?** quante volte?;
once too often una volta di troppo

ogive [ˈodʒaɪv] or [oˈdʒaɪv] *s* ogiva

ogle [ˈogəl] *tr* adocchiare, occhieggiare

ogre [ˈogər] *s* orco

ohm [om] *s* ohm *m*

oil [ɔɪl] *adj* (*pertaining to edible oil*)
oleario; (*e.g., well*) di petrolio; (*e.g.,
lamp*) a olio; (*tanker*) petroliero;
(*field*) petrolifero || *s* olio; petrolio;
to burn the midnight oil studiare a
lume di candela; **to pour oil on troubled waters** pacificare; **to strike oil**
trovare petrolio || *tr* oliare; lubrifi-

care; ungere ‖ *intr* (*said of a motor-ship*) fare petrolio
oil' burn'er *s* bruciatore *m* a gasolio
oil'can' *s* oliatore *m*
oil'cloth' *s* incerata, tela cerata
oil' field' *s* giacimento petrolifero
oil' lamp' *s* lampada a petrolio
oil'man *s* (-**men**) (*retailer*) mercante *m* di petrolio; (*operator*) petroliere *m*
oil' paint'ing *s* quadro a olio
oil' slick' *s* macchia d'olio
oil' tank'er *s* petroliera
oil' well' *s* pozzo di petrolio
oil·y ['ɔɪli] *adj* (-**ier**; -**iest**) oleoso; untuoso
ointment ['ɔɪntmənt] *s* unguento
O.K. ['o'ke] *adj* (coll) corretto ‖ *s* (coll) approvazione ‖ *adv* (coll) benissimo, d'accordo ‖ *v* (*pret & pp* **O.K.'d**; *ger* **O.K.'ing**) *tr* (coll) dare l'approvazione a ‖ *interj* benissimo!
okra ['okrə] *s* (bot) ibisco esculento; (bot) baccello dell'ibisco esculento
old [old] *adj* vecchio; antico, vetusto; **how old is . . . ?** quanti anni ha . . . ?; **of old** anticamente; **to be . . . years old** avere . . . anni
old' age' *s* vecchiaia
old' boy' *s* vecchietto arzillo; (Brit) vecchio mio
old'-clothes'man' *s* (-**men'**) rigattiere *m*
old' coun'try *s* madre patria
old-fashioned ['old'fæʃənd] *adj* all'antica; fuori moda
old' fo'gey *or* **old' fo'gy** ['fogi] *s* (-**gies**) uomo di idee antiquate, reazionario
Old' Glo'ry *s* la bandiera degli Stati Uniti
Old' Guard' *s* (U.S.A.) parte *f* più conservatrice di un partito
old' hand' *s* vecchio del mestiere
old' maid' *s* zitella
old' mas'ter *s* grande maestro; quadro di un gran maestro
old' moon' *s* luna calante
old' salt' *s* lupo di mare
old' school' *s* gente *f* all'antica
old' school' tie' *s* (Brit) cravatta coi colori della propria scuola; (fig) tradizionalismo
Old' Tes'tament *s* Antico Testamento
old'-time' *adj* all'antica; del tempo antico
old-timer ['old'taɪmər] *s* (coll) veterano; (coll) vecchio
old' wives'' tale' *s* superstizione da donnicciole; racconto di vecchie comari
Old' World' *s* mondo antico
oleander [‚olɪ'ændər] *s* oleandro
oligar·chy ['alɪ‚gɑrki] *s* (-**chies**) oligarchia
olive ['alɪv] *adj* oleario; (*color*) olivastro ‖ *s* (*tree*) olivo; (*fruit*) oliva
ol'ive branch' *s* ramoscello d'olivo
ol'ive grove' *s* oliveto
ol'ive oil' *s* olio d'oliva
Oliver ['alɪvər] *s* Oliviero
ol'ive tree' *s* olivo
Olympiad [o'lɪmpɪ‚æd] *s* olimpiade *f*
Olympian [o'lɪmpɪ‚ən] *adj* olimpico ‖ *s* deità olimpica; giocatore olimpico

Olympic [o'lɪmpɪk] *adj* olimpico, olimpionico
omelet *or* **omelette** ['aməlɪt] *or* ['amlɪt] *s* frittata, omelette *f*
omen ['omən] *s* augurio
ominous ['amɪnəs] *adj* infausto, ominoso
omission [o'mɪʃən] *s* omissione
omit [o'mɪt] *v* (*pret & pp* **omitted**; *ger* **omitting**) *tr* omettere
omnibus ['amnɪ‚bʌs] *or* ['amnɪbəs] *adj* di interesse generale ‖ *s* bus *m*; volume collettivo
omnipotent [am'nɪpətənt] *adj* onnipotente
omniscient [am'nɪʃənt] *adj* onnisciente
omnivorous [am'nɪvərəs] *adj* onnivoro
on [an] *or* [ɔn] *adj* addosso, e.g., **with his hat on** col cappello addosso; in uso, in funzione; (*light*) acceso; (*deal*) fatto, concluso; (*e.g., game*) già cominciato; **what is on at the theater?** che cosa si dà al teatro? ‖ *adv* su; avanti; dietro, e.g., **to drag on** tirarsi dietro; **and so on** e così via; **come on!** va via!; **farther on** più in là; **later on** più tardi; **to be on to s.o.** (coll) scoprire il gioco di qlcu; **to have on** avere addosso; **to . . . on** continuare a, e.g., **the band played on** la banda continuò a suonare; **to put on** mettersi ‖ *prep* su, sopra; a, e.g., **on foot** a piedi; **on his arrival** al suo arrivo; sotto, e.g., **on my responsibility** sotto la mia responsabilità; contro, e.g., **an attack on the government** un attacco contro il governo; da, e.g., **on good authority** da buona fonte; **on all sides** da tutte le parti; verso, e.g., **to march on the capital** marciare verso la capitale; dopo, e.g., **victory on victory** vittoria dopo vittoria
on' and on' *adv* senza cessa
once [wʌns] *s* una volta; volta, e.g., **this once** questa volta ‖ *adv* una volta; mai, e.g., **if this once becomes known** se questo si risapesse mai; **all at once** repentinamente; **at once** subito; allo stesso tempo; **for once** almeno una volta; **once and again** ripetutamente; **once in a blue moon** ad ogni morte di papa; **once in a while** di tanto in tanto; **once upon a time there was** c'era una volta ‖ *conj* se appena; una volta che
once'-o'ver *s* (coll) occhiata rapida; **to give s.th the once-over** (coll) esaminare qlco rapidamente; (coll) pulire qlco superficialmente
one [wʌn] *adj* uno; un certo, e.g., **one Smith** un certo Smith; unico e.g., **one price** prezzo unico ‖ *s* uno ‖ *pron* uno, e.g., **how can one live here?** come è possibile che uno viva qui?; si, e.g., **how does one go to the museum?** come si va al·museo?; **I for one** per lo meno io; **it's all one and the same to me** per me fa lo stesso; **my little one** piccolo mio; **one and all** tutti; **one another** si, e.g., **they wrote one another** si scrissero;

l'un(o) l'altro, e.g., **they looked at one another** si guardarono l'un l'altro; **one o'clock** la una; **one's** il suo, il proprio; **the blue hat and the red one** il cappello blu e quello rosso; **the one and only** l'unico; **the one that** chi, quello che; **this one** questo; **that one** quello; **to make one** unire

one'-eyed' *adj* monocolo

one'-horse' *adj* a un solo cavallo; (coll) da nulla, poco importante

one'-man' show' *s* personale *f*

onerous ['anərəs] *adj* oneroso

one-self' *pron* sé stesso; se; si; **to be oneself** essere normale; comportarsi normalmente

one-sided ['wʌn'saɪdɪd] *adj* unilaterale; ingiusto, parziale

one'-track' *adj* a un solo binario; (coll) unilaterale, limitato

one'-way' *adj* a senso unico; (ticket) semplice, d'andata

onion ['ʌnjən] *s* cipolla; **to know one's onions** (coll) conoscere i propri polli

on'ion-skin' *s* carta pelle aglio, carta velina

on'look'er *s* presente *m*, spettatore *m*

only ['onlɪ] *adj* solo, unico || *adv* solo, soltanto, non . . . più di; **not only . . . but also** non solo . . . ma anche || *conj* ma; se non che

on'set' *s* attacco; (beginning) inizio; **at the onset** dapprincipio

onslaught ['an,slɔt] or ['on,slɔt] *s* attacco

on'to *prep* su, sopra a; **to be onto** (coll) rendersi conto del gioco di

onward ['anwərd] or **onwards** ['anwərdz] *adv* avanti, più avanti

onyx ['anɪks] *s* onice *m*

ooze [uz] *s* trasudazione; liquido per concia || *tr* sudare || *intr* trasudare; (said, e.g., of blood) stillare; (said, e.g., of air) filtrare; (fig) trapelare

opal ['opəl] *s* opale *m*

opaque [o'pek] *adj* opaco; (writer's style) oscuro; stupido

open ['opən] *adj* aperto, scoperto; (job) vacante; (time) libero; (hunting season) legale; indeciso; manifesto; (hand) liberale; (needlework) a giorno; **to break** or **to crack open** forzare; **to throw open** aprire completamente || *s* apertura; (in the woods) radura; **in the open** all'aperto; all'aria aperta; in alto mare; apertamente || *tr* aprire; (an account) impostare; **to open up** spalancare; (one's eyes) sbarrare || *intr* aprire, aprirsi; (theat) esordire; **to open into** sboccare in; **to open on** dare su; **to open up** sbottonarsi

o'pen-air' *adj* all'aria aperta

open-eyed ['opən,aɪd] *adj* con gli occhi aperti; meravigliato; fatto con piena conoscenza

open-handed ['opən'hændɪd] *adj* generoso, liberale

open-hearted ['opən'hartɪd] *adj* franco, sincero; gentile

o'pen house' *s* tavola imbandita; **to keep open house** aver sempre ospiti

opening ['opənɪŋ] *s* apertura; (of dress) giro collo; (e.g., of sewer) imbocco; (in the woods) radura; (vacancy) posto vacante; (beginning) inizio; (chance to say something) occasione

o'pening night' *s* debutto, prima

o'pening num'ber *s* primo numero

o'pening price' *s* prezzo d'apertura

open-minded ['opən'maɪndɪd] *adj* di larghe vedute; imparziale

o'pen se'cret *s* segreto di Pulcinella

o'pen shop' *s* officina che impiega chi non è membro del sindacato

o'pen-work' *s* traforo

opera ['apərə] *s* opera

op'era glass'es *spl* binocolo da teatro

op'era hat' *s* gibus m

op'era house' *s* teatro dell'opera

operate ['apə,ret] *tr* (a machine) far funzionare; (a shop) gestire; operare || *intr* funzionare; operare; **to operate on** (surg) operare

operatic [,apə'rætɪk] *adj* operistico

op'erating expens'es *spl* spese *fpl* di ordinaria amministrazione

op'erating room' *s* sala operatoria

op'erating ta'ble *s* tavola operatoria

operation [,apə'reʃən] *s* operazione; funzionamento, marcia

opera'tions research' *s* ricerca operativa

operator ['apə,retər] *s* operatore *m*; (of a conveyance) conduttore *m*, conducente *mf*; (com) gestore *m*; (telp) telefonista *mf*; (surg) chirurgo operatore; (slang) faccendiere *m*

opiate ['opɪ-ɪt] or ['opɪ,et] *adj* & *s* oppiato

opinion [ə'pɪnjən] *s* opinione; **in my opinion** a mio modo di vedere; **to have a high opinion of** avere una grande stima di

opinionated [ə'pɪnjə,netɪd] *adj* ostinato, testardo, dogmatico

opium ['opɪ-əm] *s* oppio

o'pium den' *s* fumeria d'oppio

opossum [ə'pasəm] *s* opossum *m*

opponent [ə'ponənt] *s* avversario

opportune [,apər'tjun] or [,apər'tun] *adj* opportuno

opportunist [,apər'tjunɪst] or [,apər-'tunɪst] *s* opportunista *mf*

opportuni-ty [,apər'tjunɪtɪ] or [,apər-'tunɪtɪ] *s* (-ties) opportunità *f*, occasione

oppose [ə'poz] *tr* opporsi a

opposite ['apəsɪt] *adj* opposto; di rimpetto, e.g., **the house opposite** la casa di rimpetto || *s* contrario || *prep* di faccia a, di rimpetto a

op'posite num'ber *s* persona di grado corrispondente

opposition [,apə'zɪʃən] *s* opposizione

oppress [ə'pres] *tr* opprimere

oppressive [ə'presɪv] *adj* oppressivo; opprimente, soffocante

oppressor [ə'presər] *s* oppressore *m*

opprobrious [ə'probrɪ-əs] *adj* obbrobrioso

opprobrium [ə'probrɪ·əm] s obbrobrio
optic ['aptɪk] adj ottico || **optics** ssg ottica
optical ['aptɪkəl] adj ottico
optician [ap'tɪʃən] s ottico, occhialaio
optimism ['aptɪ ,mɪzəm] s ottimismo
optimist ['aptɪmɪst] s ottimista mf
optimistic [,aptɪ'mɪstɪk] adj ottimistico
option ['apʃən] s opzione
optional ['apʃənəl] adj facoltativo
optometrist [ap'tamɪtrɪst] s optometrista mf
opulent ['apjələnt] adj opulento
or [ɔr] conj o; (or else) oppure
oracle ['arəkəl] or ['ɔrəkəl] s oracolo
oracular [o'rækjələr] adj profetico; ambiguo; misterioso; sentenzioso
oral ['orəl] adj orale
orange ['arɪndʒ] or ['ɔrɪndʒ] adj di arance; arancio || s arancia
orangeade [,arɪndʒ'ed] or [,ɔrɪndʒ-'ed] s aranciata
or'ange blos'som s zagara
or'ange grove' s aranceto
or'ange juice' s sugo d'arancia
or'ange squeez'er s spremiagrumi m
or'ange tree' s arancio
orang-outang [o'ræŋʊ,tæŋ] s orango
oration [o're ʃən] s orazione, discorso
orator ['arətər] or ['ɔrətər] s oratore m
oratorical [,arə'tarɪkəl] or [,ɔrə'tɔrɪkəl] adj oratorio
oratori·o [,arə'torɪ ,o] or [,ɔrə'tɔrɪ ,o] s (-os) (mus) oratorio
orato·ry ['arə ,tori] or ['ɔrə ,tori] s (-ries) oratoria; (eccl) oratorio
orb [ɔrb] s orbe m
orbit ['ɔrbɪt] s orbita; **to go into orbit** entrare in orbita || tr mettere in orbita; orbitare intorno a || intr orbitare
or'biting sta'tion s stazione orbitale
orchard ['ɔrtʃərd] s frutteto
orchestra ['ɔrkɪstrə] s orchestra; (parquet) platea
orchestral [ɔr'kɛstrəl] adj orchestrale
or'chestra pit' s golfo mistico
or'chestra seat' s poltrona di platea
orchestrate ['ɔrkɪs ,tret] tr orchestrare
orchid ['ɔrkɪd] s orchidea
ordain [ɔr'den] tr predestinare; decretare; (eccl) ordinare
ordeal [ɔr'dil] or [ɔr'di·əl] s sfacchinata; (hist) ordalia
order ['ɔrdər] s ordine m; compito, e.g., **a big order** un compito difficile; (com) commessa, ordinazione; (mil) consegna; **in order that** affinché; **in order to** + inf per + inf; **made to order** fatto su misura; **to get out of order** guastarsi; **to give an order** dare un ordine; (com) fare una commessa || tr (e.g., a drink) ordinare; (a person) ordinare (with dat); (e.g., a suit of clothes) far fare; **to order around** mandare attorno; **to order s.o. away** mandar via qlcu
or'der blank' s cedola d'ordinazione
order·ly ['ɔrdərli] adj ordinato; disciplinato || s (-lies) (in a hospital) in-

serviente mf; (mil) ordinanza, attendente m
ordinal ['ɔrdɪnəl] adj & s ordinale m
ordinance ['ɔrdɪnəns] s ordinanza
ordinary ['ɔrdɪ ,nɛri] adj ordinario
ordnance ['ɔrdnəns] s artiglieria; bocche fpl da fuoco; munizionamento
ore [or] s minerale m (metallifero)
organ ['ɔrgən] s organo
organ·dy ['ɔrgəndi] s (-dies) organdi m
or'gan grind'er s suonatore m d'organetto
organic [ɔr'gænɪk] adj organico
organism ['ɔrgə ,nɪzəm] s organismo
organist ['ɔrgənɪst] s organista mf
organization [,ɔrgənɪ'zeʃən] s organizzazione
organize ['ɔrgə ,naɪz] tr organizzare
organizer ['ɔrgə ,naɪzər] s organizzatore m
or'gan loft' s palco, galleria per l'organo
orgasm ['ɔrgæzəm] s orgasmo
or·gy ['ɔrdʒi] s (-gies) orgia
orient ['orɪ·ənt] s oriente m || **Orient** s Oriente m || **orient** ['orɪ ,ɛnt] tr orientare, orizzontare
oriental [,orɪ'ɛntəl] adj orientale || **Oriental** s orientale mf
orifice ['arɪfɪs] or ['ɔrɪfɪs] s orifizio
origin ['arɪdʒɪn] or ['ɔrɪdʒɪn] s origine f, provenienza
original [ə'rɪdʒɪnəl] adj & s originale mf
originate [ə'rɪdʒɪ ,net] tr originare || intr originare, originarsi
oriole ['orɪ ,ol] s oriolo, rigogolo
Ork'ney Is'lands ['ɔrkni] spl Orcadi fpl
ormolu ['ɔrmə'lu] s (alloy) similoro; (gold powder) polvere f d'oro; (gilded metal) bronzo dorato
ornament ['ɔrnəmənt] s ornamento || ['ɔrnə ,mɛnt] tr ornamentare
ornamental [,ɔrnə'mɛntəl] adj ornamentale
ornate [ɔr'net] or ['ɔrnet] adj ornato; (style) elaborato
ornithologist [,ɔrnɪ'θalədʒɪst] s ornitologo
orphan ['ɔrfən] adj & s orfano || tr rendere orfano
orphanage ['ɔrfənɪdʒ] s (institution) orfanotrofio; (condition) orfanezza
Orpheus ['ɔrfjus] or ['ɔrfɪ·əs] s Orfeo
orthodox ['ɔrθə ,daks] adj ortodosso
orthogra·phy [ɔr'θagrəfi] s (-phies) ortografia
oscillate ['asɪ ,let] intr oscillare
osier ['oʒər] s vimine m; (bot) vinco
osmosis [az'mosɪs] or [as'mosɪs] s osmosi f
osprey ['aspri] s falco pescatore
ossi·fy ['asɪ ,faɪ] v (pret & pp -fied) tr ossificare || intr ossificarsi
ostensible [as'tɛnsɪbəl] adj apparente, preteso
ostentatious [,asten'teʃəs] adj ostentato
osteopathy [,astɪ'apəθi] s osteopatia
ostracism ['astrə ,sɪzəm] s ostracismo

ostracize ['ɑstrə‚saɪz] *tr* dare l'ostra-cismo a, ostracizzare

ostrich ['ɑstrɪtʃ] *s* struzzo

Othello [o'θɛlo] *or* [ə'θɛlo] *s* Otello

other ['ʌðər] *adj & pron indef* altro ‖ *adv*—**other than** diversamente che

otherwise ['ʌðər‚waɪz] *adv* altrimenti; differentemente

otter ['ɑtər] *s* lontra

ottoman ['ɑtəmən] *s* (*fabric*) otto-mano; (*sofa*) ottomana; cuscino per i piedi ‖ **Ottoman** *adj & s* ottomano

ouch [aʊtʃ] *interj* ahi!

ought [ɔt] *s* qualcosa; zero; **for ought I know** per quanto io sappia ‖ *v aux* is rendered in Italian by the condi-tional of *dovere*, e.g., **you ought to be ashamed** dovresti vergognarti

ounce [aʊns] *s* oncia

our [aʊr] *adj poss* nostro, il nostro

ours [aʊrz] *pron poss* il nostro

ourselves [aʊr'sɛlvz] *pron pers* noi stessi; ci, e.g., **we enjoyed ourselves** ci siamo divertiti

oust [aʊst] *tr* espellere; (*a tenant*) sfrattare

out [aʊt] *adj* erroneo; esterno; fuori pratica; svenuto; ubriaco; finito; (*book*) pubblicato; (*lights*) spento; fuori moda; introvabile; palmare; di permesso, e.g., **my night out** la mia serata di permesso; (*e.g., at the knees*) frusto; (sports) fuori gioco ‖ *s* via d'uscita; **to be on the outs or at outs with** (coll) essere in disac-cordo con ‖ *adv* fuori, all'infuori; all'aria libera; **out for** in cerca di; **out of** fuori, fuori di; di; da; (*e.g., money*) a corto di, senza; su, e.g., **two students out of three** due stu-denti su tre ‖ *prep* fuori di; per, lungo ‖ *interj* fuori!

out' and away' *adv* di gran lunga

out'-and-out' *adj* perfetto, completo ‖ *adv* perfettamente, completamente

out'bid' *v* (*pret* -**bid**; *pp* -**bid** *or* -**bidden**; *ger* -**bidding**) *tr* fare un'of-ferta migliore di; (bridge) fare una dichiarazione più alta di

out'board mo'tor *s* fuoribordo, motore *m* fuoribordo

out'break' *s* insurrezione; (*of hives*) eruzione; (*of anger; of war*) scoppio

out'build'ing *s* dipendenza

out'burst' *s* (*of tears; of laughter*) scop-pio; (*of energy*) impeto, slancio

out'cast' *s* vagabondo reietto

out'come' *s* risultato

out'cry' *s* (-**cries**) grido, chiasso

out'dat'ed *adj* fuori moda

out'dis'tance *tr* distanziare

out'do' *v* (*pret* -**did**; *pp* -**done**) *tr* sor-passare; **to outdo oneself** sorpassare sé stesso

out'door' *adj* all'aria aperta

out'doors' *s* aria libera, aperta cam-pagna ‖ *adv* all'aria aperta, fuori di casa

out'er space' ['aʊtər] *s* spazio cosmico

out'field' *s* (baseball) campo esterno

out'field'er *s* (baseball) esterno

out'fit' *s* equipaggiamento; (*female cos-*

tume) insieme *m*; (*of bride*) corredo; (*group*) (coll) corpo; (com) compa-gnia ‖ *v* (*pret & pp* -**fitted**; *ger* -**fitting**) *tr* equipaggiare

out'flow' *s* efflusso

out'go'ing *adj* in partenza; (*tide*) de-crescente; (*character*) espansivo ‖ *s* efflusso

out'grow' *v* (*pret* -**grew**; *pp* -**grown**) *tr* essere troppo grande per; sorpassare in statura; perdere l'interesse per ‖ *intr* protrudere

out'growth' *s* risultato, conseguenza; crescita

outing ['aʊtɪŋ] *s* gita, scampagnata

outlandish [aʊt'lændɪʃ] *adj* strano, bizzarro; dall'aspetto straniero; (*re-mote, far away*) in capo al mondo

out'last' *tr* sopravvivere (with *dat*)

out'law' *s* fuorilegge *mf* ‖ *tr* proscri-vere; dichiarare illegale

out'lay' *s* disborso ‖ **out·lay'** *v* (*pret & pp* -**laid**) *tr* sborsare

out'let *s* uscita; (*e.g., of river*) sbocco; (com) mercato; (elec) presa di cor-rente; (fig) sfogo

out'line' *s* contorno; traccia, tracciato; sagoma, profilo; prospetto ‖ *tr* de-lineare; tracciare, tratteggiare; sago-mare, profilare; prospettare

out'live' *tr* sopravvivere (with *dat*)

out'look' *s* prospettiva; (*watch*) guar-dia; (*mental view*) modo di vedere, opinione

out'ly'ing *adj* lontano, fuori di mano; periferico

outmoded [‚aʊt'modɪd] *adj* fuori moda, antiquato

out'num'ber *tr* superare in numero

out'-of-date' *adj* fuori moda

out'-of-door' *adj* all'aria aperta

out'-of-doors' *adj* all'aria aperta ‖ *s* aria aperta ‖ *adv* all'aria aperta; fuori di casa

out'-of-print' *adj* esaurito

out'-of-the-way' *adj* appartato, fuori mano; inusitato, strano

out' of tune' *adj* stonato ‖ *adv* fuori di tono

out' of work' *adj* disoccupato

out'pa'tient *s* paziente *mf* esterno

out'post' *s* (mil) posto avanzato

out'put' *s* produzione; (elec) uscita; (mach) rendimento, potenza utile

out'rage *s* oltraggio, indecenza ‖ *tr* oltraggiare; (*a woman*) violare

outrageous [aʊt'redʒəs] *adj* oltrag-gioso; (*excessive*) eccessivo; atroce, feroce

out'rank' *tr* superare in grado

out'rid'er *s* battistrada *m*

out'right' *adj* completo, intero ‖ *adv* completamente; apertamente; sul colpo, sull'istante

out'set' *s* inizio, principio

out'side' *adj* esterno; (*unlikely*) impro-babile; (*price*) massimo ‖ *s* esterno, di fuori *m*; aspetto esteriore; vita fuori del carcere ‖ *adv* fuori, di fuori; **outside of** fuori di ‖ *prep* fuori di; (coll) all'infuori di

outsider [,aut'saɪdər] *s* estraneo, intruso; (sports) outsider *m*

out'skirts' *spl* sobborghi *mpl*, periferia

out'spo'ken *adj* franco, esplicito

out'stand'ing *adj* saliente, eminente; (*debt*) arretrato, non pagato

outward ['autwərd] *adj* esterno, superficiale || *adv* al di fuori

out'weigh' *tr* pesare più di; eccedere in importanza

out'wit' *v* (*pret* & *pp* **-witted;** *ger* **-witting**) *tr* farla in barba di; (*a pursuer*) far perdere la traccia or la pista a

oval ['ovəl] *adj* & *s* ovale *m*

ova•ry ['ovəri] *s* (**-ries**) ovaia

ovation [o've∫ən] *s* ovazione

oven ['ʌvən] *s* forno

over ['ovər] *adj* superiore; esterno; finito, concluso || *adv* su, sopra; dall'altra parte; dall'altra sponda; al rovescio; di nuovo; (*at the bottom of a page*) continua; qui, e.g., **hand over the money** dammi qui il denaro; **over again** di nuovo; **over against** contro; **over and over** ripetutamente; **over here** qui; **over there** là || *prep* su, sopra; dall'altra parte di; attraverso, per; (*a certain number*) più di; a causa di; **over and above** in eccesso di

o'ver•all' *adj* completo, totale || **overalls** *spl* tuta

o'ver•bear'ing *adj* arrogante, prepotente

o'ver•board' *adv* in acqua; **man overboard!** uomo in mare!; **to go overboard** andare agli estremi

o'ver•cast' *adj* annuvolato || *s* cielo annuvolato || *v* (*pret* & *pp* **-cast**) *tr* coprire, annuvolare

o'ver•charge' *s* prezzo eccessivo; sovraccarico; (elec) carica eccessiva || **o'ver•charge'** *tr* far pagare eccessivamente; sovraccaricare

o'ver•coat' *s* soprabito, pastrano

o'ver•come' *v* (*pret* **-came;** *pp* **-come**) *tr* vincere, sopraffare; (*e.g., passions*) frenare; opprimere

o'vercon'fidence *s* sicumera

o'ver•crowd' *tr* gremire

o'ver•do' *v* (*pret* **-did;** *pp* **-done**) *tr* esagerare; strafare; esaurire; (*meat*) stracuocere || *intr* esaurirsi

o'ver•dose' *s* dose eccessiva

o'ver•draft' *s* assegno allo scoperto

o'ver•draw' *v* (*pret* **-drew;** *pp* **-drawn**) *tr* (*a check*) emettere allo scoperto; (*a character*) esagerare la descrizione di

o'ver•due' *adj* in ritardo; (com) in sofferenza, scaduto

o'ver•eat' *v* (*pret* **-ate;** *pp* **-eaten**) *tr* & *intr* mangiare troppo

o'ver•exer'tion *s* sforzo eccessivo

o'ver•expose' *tr* sovresporre

o'ver•expo'sure *s* sovresposizione

o'ver•flow' *s* (*of a river*) piena, straripamento; (*excess*) sovrabbondanza; (*e.g., of a fountain*) trabocco; (*outlet*) tubo di troppopieno || **o'ver•flow'** *intr* (*said of a river*) straripare; (*said of a container*) traboccare

o'ver•fly' *v* (*pret* **-flew;** *pp* **-flown**) *tr* sorvolare; (*a target*) oltrepassare

o'ver•grown' *adj* cresciuto troppo; coperto, denso

o'ver•hang' *s* strapiombo || **o'ver•hang'** *v* (*pret* & *pp* **-hung**) *tr* sovrastare (with *dat*); sovrastare; (*to threaten*) minacciare; pervadere, permeare || *intr* sovrastare, strapiombare

o'ver•haul' *s* riparazione; esame *m*, revisione || *tr* riparare; esaminare, ripassare, rivedere; raggiungere, mettersi alla pari con

o'ver•head' *adj* in alto, sopra la testa; aereo; elevato, pensile; generale || **o'ver•head'** *adv* in alto, di sopra **o'ver•head'** *s* spese *fpl* generali

o'ver•head projec'tor *s* lavagna luminosa

o'ver•head valve' *s* valvola in testa

o'ver•hear' *v* (*pret* & *pp* **-heard**) *tr* sentire per caso, udire per caso

o'ver•heat' *tr* surriscaldare || *intr* surriscaldarsi; eccitarsi

overjoyed [,ovər'dʒɔɪd] *adj* felicissimo; **to be overjoyed** non stare in sé dalla contentezza

overland ['ovər ,lænd] or ['ovərlənd] *adj* & *adv* per via di terra

o'ver•lap' *v* (*pret* & *pp* **-lapped;** *ger* **-lapping**) *tr* sovrapporre, estendersi sopra || *intr* sovrapporsi, estendersi; coincidere parzialmente

o'ver•load' *s* sovraccarico || **o'ver•load'** *tr* sovraccaricare, stracaricare

o'ver•look' *tr* sovrastare su, dominare; ispezionare, sorvegliare; passare sopra, trascurare; dare su, e.g., **the window overlooks the street** la finestra dà sulla strada

o'ver•lord' *s* dominatore *m* || *tr* dominare despoticamente

overly ['ovərli] *adv* eccessivamente

o'ver•night' *adj* per la notte, per solo una notte || **o'ver•night'** *adv* durante la notte; la notte prima

o'vernight bag' *s* astuccio di toletta per la notte

o'ver•pass' *s* cavalcavia, viadotto

o'ver•pop'ulate' *tr* sovrappopolare

o'ver•pow'er *tr* sopraffare

o'ver•pow'ering *adj* schiacciante

o'ver•produc'tion *s* sovrapproduzione

o'ver•rate' *tr* sopravvalutare

o'ver•run' *v* (*pret* **-ran;** *pp* **-run;** *ger* **-running**) *tr* invadere, infestare; inondare; (*one's time*) oltrepassare, eccedere

o'ver•sea' or **o'ver•seas'** *adj* di oltremare || **o'ver•sea'** or **o'ver•seas'** *adv* oltremare, al di là dei mari

o'ver•see' *v* (*pret* **-saw;** *pp* **-seen**) *tr* sorvegliare

o'ver•seer' *s* sorvegliante *mf*

o'ver•shad'ow *tr* oscurare, eclissare

o'ver•shoe' *s* soprascarpa

o'ver•shoot' *v* (*pret* & *pp* **-shot**) *tr* (*the target*) oltrepassare; (*said of water*) scorrere sopra; **to overshoot oneself** andare troppo in là || *intr* (aer) atterrare lungo e richiamare

o'ver•sight' *s* sbadataggine *f*, svista; sorveglianza, supervisione

o'ver·sleep' v (pret & pp -slept) tr (a certain hour) dormire oltre || intr dormire troppo a lungo

o'ver·step' v (pret & pp -stepped; ger -stepping) tr eccedere, oltrepassare

o'ver·stock' tr riempire eccessivamente

o'ver·sup·ply' s (-plies) fornitura superiore alla richiesta || o'ver·sup·ply' v (pret & pp -plied) tr fornire in quantità superiore alla richiesta

overt ['ovərt] or [o'vʌrt] adj palmare, chiaro, manifesto

o'ver·take' v (pret -took; pp -taken) tr raggiungere, sorpassare; sorprendere

o'ver-the-count'er adj (securities) venduto direttamente al compratore

o'ver·throw' s rovesciamento; disfatta || o'ver·throw' s (pret -threw; pp -thrown) tr rovesciare, sconfiggere

o'ver·time' adj supplementare, fuori orario || s straordinario; (sports) tempo supplementare || adv fuori orario

o'ver·tone' s (mus) suono armonico; (fig) sottinteso

o'ver·trump' s taglio con atout più alto || o'ver·trump' tr & intr tagliare con atout più alto

overture ['ovərtʃər] s apertura; (mus) preludio, sinfonia

o'ver·turn' s rovesciamento || o'ver·turn' tr rovesciare, travolgere || intr rovesciarsi, ribaltarsi

overweening [,ovər'winɪŋ] adj presuntuoso, vanitoso; esagerato, eccessivo

o'ver·weight' adj troppo grasso; oltrepassante i limiti di peso || o'ver·weight' s sovraccarico; preponderanza; eccesso di peso

overwhelm [,ovər'hwɛlm] tr schiacciare, debellare; coprire; (e.g., with kindness) colmare, ricolmare

o'ver·work' s lavoro straordinario; superlavoro || o'ver·work' tr far lavorare eccessivamente || intr lavorare eccessivamente

Ovid ['avɪd] s Ovidio

ow [au] interj ahi!

owe [o] tr dovere || intr essere in debito

owing ['o·ɪŋ] adj dovuto; owing to a causa di

owl [aul] s gufo, barbagianni m

own [on] adj proprio, e.g., my own brother il mio proprio fratello || s il proprio; on one's own (coll) per proprio conto; (without anybody's advice) di testa propria; to come into one's own entrare in possesso del proprio; essere riconosciuto per quanto si vale; to hold one's own non perdere terreno; essere pari || tr possedere; riconoscere || intr—to own up to confessare

owner ['onər] s padrone m, proprietario, titolare m

ownership ['onər,ʃɪp] s proprietà f

own'er's li'cence s permesso di circolazione

ox [aks] s (oxen ['aksən]) bue m

ox'cart' s carro tirato da buoi

oxide ['aksaɪd] s ossido

oxidize ['aksɪ,daɪz] tr ossidare || intr ossidarsi

oxygen ['aksɪdʒən] s ossigeno

ox'ygen mask' s maschera respiratoria

ox'ygen tent' s tenda ad ossigeno

oxytone ['aksɪ,ton] adj tronco, ossitono || s ossitono

oyster ['ɔɪstər] adj di ostriche || s ostrica

oys'ter bed' s ostricaio, banco di ostriche

oys'ter cock'tail s ostriche fpl servite in valva

oys'ter fork' s forchettina da ostriche

oys'ter·house' s ristorante m per la vendita delle ostriche

oys'ter·knife' s coltello per aprire le ostriche

oys'ter·man s (-men) ostricaio

oys'ter shell' s conchiglia d'ostrica

oys'ter stew' s brodetto d'ostriche

ozone ['ozon] s ozono

P

P, p [pi] s sedicesima lettera dell'alfabeto inglese

pace [pes] s passo, andatura; (of a horse) ambio; to keep pace with andare di pari passo con; to put s.o. through his paces mettere qlcu a dura prova; to set the pace for fare l'andatura per; dare l'esempio a || tr misurare a passi, percorrere; to pace the floor andare avanti e indietro per la stanza || intr camminare lentamente; andare al passo; (said of a horse) ambiare

pace'mak'er s battistrada m; (in races) chi stabilisce il passo; (med) pacemaker m

pacific [pə'sɪfɪk] adj pacifico || Pacific adj & s Pacifico

pacifier ['pæsɪ,faɪ·ər] s paciere m; (teething ring) succhietto, tettarella

pacifism ['pæsɪ,fɪzəm] s pacifismo

pacifist ['pæsɪfɪst] adj & s pacifista mf

paci·fy ['pæsɪ,faɪ] v (pret & pp -fied) tr pacificare

pack [pæk] s fardello, pacco; (of merchandise) balla; (of lies) mucchio; (of cards) mazzo; (of thieves) banda; (of dogs) muta; (of animals) branco; (of birds) stormo; (of cigarettes) pacchetto; (of ice) banchiglia; (of people) turba || tr affardellare, impaccare; (to wrap) imballare; ammucchiare; (in cans) mettere in conserva; (people) stipare; (a trunk) fare; to pack in stipare; to pack off mandare via || intr ammucchiarsi, pigiarsi, accalcarsi; **to pack up** fare il baule

package ['pækɪdʒ] *s* pacco, collo; (*small*) pacchetto || *tr* impacchettare

pack' an'imal *s* bestia da soma

packer ['pækər] *s* imballatore *m;* (*of canned goods*) proprietario (di fabbrica di conserve alimentari)

packet ['pækɪt] *s* pacchetto; (*boat*) vapore *m* postale

packing ['pækɪŋ] *s* imballaggio; (*on shoulders of suit*) spallina; (mach) stoppa; (*ring*) (mach) guarnizione

pack'ing box' or **case'** *s* cassa d'imballaggio

pack'ing house' *s* fabbrica di conserve alimentari; fabbrica di carne in conserva

pack'ing slip' *s* foglio d'imballaggio

pack'sad'dle *s* basto

pack'thread' *s* spago d'imballaggio

pack'train' *s* fila di animali da soma

pact [pækt] *s* patto

pad [pæd] *s* cuscinetto, tampone *m;* imbottitura; (*of writing paper*) blocco da annotazioni; (*of an animal*) superficie *f* plantare, zampa; (*of a water lily*) foglia, (rok) piattaforma || *v* (*pret & pp* **padded;** *ger* **padding**) *tr* imbottire, ovattare; (*e.g., a speech*) infarcire || *intr* camminare pesantemente

pad'ding *s* imbottitura

paddle ['pædəl] *s* pagaia; (*of waterwheel*) pala || *tr* remare; (*to spank*) bastonare || *intr* remare; (*to splash*) diguazzare

pad'dle wheel' *s* ruota a pale

paddock ['pædək] *s* prato d'allenamento, paddock *m*

pad'lock' *s* lucchetto || *tr* chiudere col lucchetto

pagan ['pegən] *adj & s* pagano

paganism ['pegə,nɪzəm] *s* paganesimo

page [pedʒ] *s* (*of a book*) pagina; (*at court*) paggio; (*in hotels*) fattorino, valletto || *tr* impaginare; (*in hotels*) chiamare, far chiamare

pageant ['pædʒənt] *s* parata, corteo, spettacolo

pageant·ry ['pædʒəntri] *s* (**-ries**) pompa, fasto

paginate ['pædʒɪ,net] *tr* impaginare

pail [pel] *s* secchio

pain [pen] *s* dolore *m;* **on pain of** sotto pena di; **to take pains to** prendersi cura di; **to take pains not to** guardarsi da || *tr & intr* dolere

painful ['penfəl] *adj* doloroso, penoso

pain'kill'er *s* (coll) analgesico

painless ['penlɪs] *adj* indolore

painstaking ['penz,tekɪŋ] *adj* meticoloso

paint [pent] *s* (*for pictures*) colore *m;* (*for a house*) vernice *f;* (*make-up*) trucco || *tr* dipingere; (*a house*) verniciare, tinteggiare || *intr* (*with make-up*) dipingersi; essere pittore

paint'box' *s* scatola da colori

paint'brush' *s* pennello

painter ['pentər] *s* (*of pictures*) pittore *m;* (*of a house*) verniciatore *m;* (naut) barbetta

painting ['pentɪŋ] *s* pittura, dipinto

paint' remov'er [rɪ'muvər] *s* solvente *m* per levar la vernice

paint' thin'ner *s* diluente *m*

pair [pɛr] *s* paio; (*of people*) coppia || *tr* appaiare, accoppiare || *intr* appaiarsi, accoppiarsi

pair' of scis'sors *s* forbici *fpl*

pair' of trou'sers *s* calzoni *mpl*

pajamas [pə'dʒɑməz] or [pə'dʒæməz] *spl* pigiama *m*

Pakistan [,pɑkɪ'stɑn] *s* il Pakistan

Pakistani [,pɑkɪ'stɑni] *adj & s* pachistano

pal [pæl] *s* (coll) compagno || *v* (*pret & pp* **palled;** *ger* **palling**) *intr* (coll) essere compagni

palace ['pælɪs] *s* palazzo

palatable ['pælətəbəl] *adj* gustoso, appetitoso; accettabile

palatal ['pælətəl] *adj & s* palatale *f*

palate ['pælɪt] *s* palato

pale [pel] *adj* pallido || *s* palo; (*enclosure*) recinto; (fig) ambito || *intr* impallidire

pale'face' *s* faccia pallida

palette ['pælɪt] *s* tavolozza

palfrey ['pɔlfri] *s* palafreno

palisade [,pælɪ'sed] *s* palizzata; (*line of cliffs*) dirupo

pall [pɔl] *s* panno mortuario; (*of smoke*) cappa || *tr* saziare, infastidire || *intr* saziarsi, perdere l'appetito

pall'bear'er *s* chi accompagna il feretro; chi porta il feretro

palliate ['pælɪ,et] *tr* attenuare, alleviare

pallid ['pælɪd] *adj* pallido

pallor ['pælər] *s* pallore *m*

palm [pɑm] *s* (*tree and leaf*) palma; (*of hand; measure*) palmo; **to carry off the palm** riportare la palma; **to grease the palm of** ungere le ruote a || *tr* far sparire nella mano; nascondere; **to palm off s.th on s.o.** rifilare qlco a qlcu

palmet·to [pæl'mɛto] *s* (**-tos** or **-toes**) palmeto

palmist ['pɑmɪst] *s* chiromante *mf*

palmistry ['pɑmɪstri] *s* chiromanzia

palm' leaf' *s* palma, foglia di palma

palm' oil' *s* olio di palma

Palm' Sun'day *s* Domenica delle Palme

palpable ['pælpəbəl] *adj* palpabile

palpitate ['pælpɪ,tet] *intr* palpitare

pal·sy ['pɔlzi] *s* (**-sies**) paralisi *f* || *v* (*pret & pp* **-sied**) *tr* paralizzare

pal·try ['pɔltri] *adj* (**-trier; -triest**) vile, meschino, irrisorio

pamper ['pæmpər] *tr* viziare; (*the appetite*) saziare

pamphlet ['pæmflɪt] *s* opuscolo, libello

pan [pæn] *s* padella, casseruola; (*of a balance*) coppa, piatto; (phot) bacinella || *v* (*pret & pp* **panned;** *ger* **panning**) *tr* friggere; (*gold*) vagliare in padella; (*salt*) estrarre in salina; (coll) criticare || *intr* essere estratto; **to pan out** (coll) riuscire || **Pan** *s* Pan *m*

panacea [,pænə'si·ə] *s* panacea

Pan'ama Canal' ['pænə,mɑ] *s* Canale *m* di Panama

Pan'ama hat' s panama m
Panamanian [ˌpænəˈmenɪ-ən] or [ˌpænəˈmɑnɪ-ən] adj & s panamegno
pan'cake' s frittella || intr (aer) atterrare a piatto
pan'cake land'ing s atterraggio a piatto
pancreas [ˈpænkrɪ-əs] s pancreas m
pander [ˈpændər] s mezzano || intr ruffianeggiare; **to pander to** favorire, assecondare i desideri di
pane [pen] s pannello, vetro di finestra
pan·el [ˈpænəl] s pannello; gruppo che discute in faccia al pubblico, telequiz m; discussione pubblica; (of door or window) specchio; (law) lista di giurati || v (pret & pp -eled or -elled; ger -eling or -elling) tr coprire di pannelli
pan'el discus'sion s colloquio di esperti in faccia al pubblico
panelist [ˈpænəlɪst] s partecipante mf a una discussione in faccia al pubblico
pan'el lights' spl luci fpl del cruscotto
pan'el truck' s camioncino
pang [pæŋ] s (sharp pain) spasimo; (of remorse) tormento
pan'han'dle s manico della padella || intr accattare, mendicare
pan·ic [ˈpænɪk] adj & s panico || v (pret & pp -icked; ger -icking) . tr riempire di panico || intr essere colto dal panico
pan'ic·strick'en adj morto di paura, in preda al panico
pano·ply [ˈpænəpli] s (-plies) panoplia; abbigliamento in pompa magna
panorama [ˌpænəˈræmə] or [ˌpænəˈrɑmə] s panorama m
pan·sy [ˈpænzi] s (-sies) viola del pensiero
pant [pænt] s anelito, affanno; **pants** pantaloni mpl, calzoni mpl; **to wear the pants** portare i calzoni || intr ansare; (said of heart) palpitare
pantheism [ˈpænθɪˌɪzəm] s panteismo
pantheon [ˈpænθɪˌan] or [ˈpænθɪ-ən] s panteon m, pantheon m
panther [ˈpænθər] s pantera
panties [ˈpæntiz] spl mutandine fpl
pantomime [ˈpæntəˌmaɪm] s pantomima
pan·try [ˈpæntri] s (-tries) dispensa
pap [pæp] s pappa
papa·cy [ˈpepəsi] s (-cies) papato
Pa'pal States' [ˈpepəl] spl Stati mpl pontifici
paper [ˈpepər] adj di carta, cartaceo || s carta; (newspaper) giornale m; (of a student) tema m, saggio; (of a scholar) dissertazione; **on paper** per iscritto || tr (a wall) tappezzare
pa'per·back' s libro in brossura
pa'per·boy' s giornalaio, strillone m
pa'per clip' s fermaglio per le carte, clip m
pa'per cone' s cartoccio
pa'per cut'ter s rifilatrice f
pa'per doll' s pupazzetto di carta
pa'per·hang'er s tappezziere m
pa'per knife' s tagliacarte m
pa'per mill' s cartiera
pa'per mon'ey s carta moneta

pa'per prof'its spl guadagni mpl non realizzati su valori non venduti
pa'per tape' s (of teletype) nastro di carta; (of computer) nastro perforato
pa'per·weight' s fermacarte m
pa'per work' s lavoro a tavolino
papier-mâché [ˌpepərməˈʃe] s cartapesta
paprika [pæˈprikə] or [ˈpæprɪkə] s paprica
papy·rus [pəˈpaɪrəs] s (-ri [raɪ]) papiro
par [pɑr] adj alla pari, nominale; normale || s parità f, valore m nominale; **at par** alla pari
parable [ˈpærəbəl] s parabola
parabola [pəˈræbələ] s parabola
parachute [ˈpærəˌʃut] s paracadute m || intr lanciarsi col paracadute
par'a·chute jump' s lancio col paracadute
parachutist [ˈpærəˌʃutɪst] s paracadutista mf
parade [pəˈred] s parata, sfilata; ostentazione, sfoggio || tr ostentare, sfoggiare; disporre in parata || intr fare mostra di sé; (mil) sfilare
paradise [ˈpærəˌdaɪs] s paradiso
paradox [ˈpærəˌdaks] s paradosso
paradoxical [ˌpærəˈdaksɪkəl] adj paradossale
paraffin [ˈpærəfɪn] s paraffina
paragon [ˈpærəˌgan] s paragone m
paragraph [ˈpærəˌgræf] or [ˈpærəˌgrɑf] s paragrafo, capoverso; (in a newspaper) trafiletto; (of law) comma m
parakeet [ˈpærəˌkit] s parrocchetto
paral·lel [ˈpærəˌlɛl] adj parallelo || s (geog, fig) parallelo; (geom) parallela; parallels (typ) sbarrette fpl verticali || v (pret & pp -leled or -lelled; ger -leling or -lelling) tr collocare parallelamente; correre parallelo a; confrontare
par'allel bars' spl parallele fpl
paraly·sis [pəˈrælɪsɪs] s (-ses [ˌsiz]) paralisi f
paralytic [ˌpærəˈlɪtɪk] adj & s paralitico
paralyze [ˈpærəˌlaɪz] tr paralizzare
paramount [ˈpærəˌmaunt] adj capitale, supremo
paramour [ˈpærəˌmur] s amante mf
paranoiac [ˌpærəˈnɔɪˌæk] adj & s paranoico
parapet [ˈpærəˌpɛt] s parapetto
paraphernalia [ˌpærəfərˈnelɪ-ə] spl roba, cose fpl; attrezzi mpl, aggeggi mpl
parasite [ˈpærəˌsaɪt] s parassita m
parasitic(al) [ˌpærəˈsɪtɪk(əl)] adj parassitico, parassitario
parasol [ˈpærəˌsɔl] or [ˈpærəˌsɑl] s parasole m, ombrellino da sole
par'a·troop'er s paracadutista mf
par'a·troops' spl truppe fpl paracadutiste
parboil [ˈpɑrˌbɔɪl] tr bollire parzialmente; (fig) far bollire
parcel [ˈpɑrsəl] s pacchetto; (of land) appezzamento || v (pret & pp -celed or -celled; ger -celing or -celling) tr

impacchettare; **to parcel out** dividere, distribuire

par′cel post′ s servizio pacchi postali

parch [partʃ] tr bruciare; (land) inaridire; (e.g., beans) essiccare; **to be parched** bruciare dalla sete ‖ intr arrostirsi: inaridire

parchment [ˈpartʃmənt] s pergamena

pardon [ˈpardən] s perdono, grazia; **I beg your pardon** scusi ‖ tr perdonare; (an offense) graziare

pardonable [ˈpardənəbəl] adj perdonabile, veniale

par′don board′ s ufficio per la decisione delle grazie

pare [per] tr (fruit, potatoes) sbucciare, pelare; (nails) tagliare; (expenses) ridurre

parent [ˈperənt] adj madre, principale ‖ s genitore m or genitrice f; (fig) origine f; **parents** genitori mpl

parentage [ˈperəntɪdz] s discendenza, lignaggio

parenthesis [pəˈrenθɪsɪs] s (-ses [ˌsiz]) parentesi f; **in parenthesis** tra parentesi

parenthetically [ˌpærənˈθetɪkəli] adv tra parentesi

parenthood [ˈperəntˌhud] s paternità f or maternità f

pariah [pəˈraɪ·ə] or [ˈparɪ·ə] s paria m

pari-mutuel [ˈpærɪˈmjutʃu·əl] s totalizzatore m

par′ing knife′ [ˈperɪŋ] s coltello per sbucciare

Paris [ˈpærɪs] s Parigi f

parish [ˈpærɪʃ] s parrocchia

parishioner [pəˈrɪʃənər] s parrocchiano

Parisian [pəˈrɪʒən] adj & s parigino

parity [ˈpærɪti] s parità f

park [park] s parco ‖ tr parcare, parcheggiare ‖ intr parcare, parcheggiare, stazionare

parking [ˈparkɪŋ] s posteggio, parcheggio; **no parking** divieto di parcheggio

park′ing lights′ spl luci fpl di posizione

park′ing lot′ s posteggio, parcheggio

park′ing me′ter s parchimetro

park′ing tick′et s contravvenzione per parcheggio abusivo

park′way′ s boulevard m

parlay [ˈparli] or [parˈle] tr rigiocare

parley [ˈparli] s trattativa, conferenza ‖ intr parlamentare

parliament [ˈparlɪmənt] s parlamento

parlor [ˈparlər] s salotto; (of beautician or undertaker) salone m; (of convent) parlatorio

par′lor car′ s vettura salone

par′lor game′ s gioco di società

par′lor pol′itics s politica da caffè

Parmesan [ˌparmɪˈzæn] adj & s parmigiano

Parnassus [parˈnæsəs] s (poetry; poets) parnaso; **il Parnaso**

parochial [pəˈrokɪ·əl] adj parrocchiale; ristretto, limitato; (school) confessionale

parody [ˈpærədi] s (-dies) parodia ‖ v (pret & pp -died) tr parodiare

parole [pəˈrol] s parola d'onore; libertà f condizionale, condizionale f ‖ tr mettere in libertà condizionale

paroxytone [pærˈaksɪˌton] adj parossitono ‖ s parola parossitona

parquet [parˈke] s pavimento di legno tassellato, tassellato; (theat) platea ‖ v (pret & pp -queted [ˈked]; ger -queting [ˈke·ɪŋ]) tr pavimentare in legno tassellato

par′quet cir′cle s poltroncine fpl

parricide [ˈpærɪˌsaɪd] s (act) patricidio, parricidio; (person) patricida mf, parricida mf

parrot [ˈpærət] s pappagallo ‖ tr scimmiottare, fare il pappagallo a

parry [ˈpæri] s (-ries) parata ‖ v (pret & pp -ried) tr parare; (fig) evitare

parse [pars] tr (gram) analizzare grammaticalmente

parsimonious [ˌparsɪˈmoni·əs] adj parsimonioso

parsley [ˈparsli] s prezzemolo

parsnip [ˈparsnɪp] s pastinaca

parson [ˈparsən] s parroco; pastore m protestante

part [part] s parte f; (of a machine) pezzo, organo; (of hair) riga; **for my part** per parte mia; **on the part of** da parte di; **part and parcel** parte f integrante; **parts** abilità f, dote f; regione f, paesi mpl; **to do one's part** fare il proprio dovere ‖ adv parzialmente, in part ‖ tr dividere, separare; **to part company** separarsi; **to part one's hair** farsi la riga ‖ intr separarsi; **to part from** separarsi da, dividersi da; **to part with** rinunciare a

partake [parˈtek] v (pret -took [ˈtuk]; pp -taken) tr condividere ‖ intr—**to partake in** partecipare a; **to partake of** condividere

parterre [parˈter] s aiola; (theat) platea

Parthenon [ˈparθɪˌnan] s Partenone m

partial [ˈparʃəl] adj parziale

participate [parˈtɪsɪˌpet] intr partecipare; **to participate in** partecipare a

participation [parˌtɪsɪˈpeʃən] s partecipazione

participle [ˈpartɪˌsɪpəl] s participio

particle [ˈpartɪkəl] s particella

particular [pərˈtɪkjələr] adj (belonging to a single person) particolare; (exacting) esigente, fastidioso ‖ s particolare m; **in particular** specialmente, particolarmente

parting adj (words) di commiato; (last) ultimo ‖ s commiato; separazione

partisan [ˈpartɪzən] adj & s partigiano

partition [parˈtɪʃən] s partizione, divisione; (or house) tramezzo ‖ tr dividere; tramezzare

partner [ˈpartnər] s (in sports) compagno; (in dancing) cavaliere m, dama; (husband or wife) consorte mf; (com) socio

partnership [ˈpartnərˌʃɪp] s associazione; (com) società f

part′ of speech′ s parte f del discorso

partridge [ˈpartrɪdʒ] s pernice f

part′ time′ adj a orario ridotto, a ore

party [ˈparti] adj comune; di gala ‖ s (-ties) festa, ricevimento, trattenimento; (of people) gruppo; (indi-

vidual) persona; (pol) partito; (law) contraente *mf;* (mil) distaccamento; **to be a party to** prendere parte a; essere complice di

par'ty girl' *s* ragazza che fa la vita

par'ty-go'er *s* frequentatore *m* di trattenimenti

part'y line' *s* (*boundary*) linea di confine; (*of Communist party*) politica del partito; (telp) linea in coutenza

pass [pæs] or [pɑs] *s* passaggio; (*state*) stato, situazione; (*free ticket*) ingresso gratuito; (*leave of absence given to a soldier*) congedo, permesso; (*of a hypnotist*) gesto; (*between mountains*) passo; (slang) tentativo d'abbraccio; **a pretty pass** (coll) un bell'affare || *tr* (*a course in school*) passare; (*to promote*) promuovere; (*a law*) approvare; (*a sentence*) pronunciare; (*an opinion*) esprimere, avanzare; (*to excrete*) evacuare; far muovere; **to pass by** non fare attenzione a; **to pass off** (*e.g., bogus money*) azzeccare; **to pass on** trasmettere; **to pass out** distribuire; **to pass over** omettere || *intr* (*to go*) passare; (*said of a law*) essere approvato; (*said of a student*) essere promosso; (*to be accepted*) farsi passare; (*said, e.g., of two trains*) incrociarsi; **to come to pass** accadere, succedere; **to pass as** passare per; **to pass away** morire; **to pass out** (slang) svenire; **to pass over** or **through** attraversare, passare per

passable ['pæsəbəl] or ['pɑsəbəl] *adj* praticabile; (*by boat*) navigabile; (*adequate*) passabile; (*law*) promulgabile

passage ['pæsɪdʒ] *s* passaggio; (*of a law*) approvazione; (*ticket*) biglietto di passaggio; (*of the bowels*) evacuazione

pass'book' *s* libretto di banca; libretto della cassa di risparmio

passenger ['pæsəndʒər] *s* passeggero

passer-by ['pæsər'baɪ] or ['pɑsər'baɪ] *s* (**passers-by**) passante *mf*

passing ['pæsɪŋ] or ['pɑsɪŋ] *adj* (*fleeting*) fuggente; (*casual*) incidentale; (*grade*) che concede la promozione || *s* passaggio; (*death*) morte *f*; promozione

passion ['pæʃən] *s* passione

passionate ['pæʃənɪt] *adj* appassionato; (*hot-tempered*) collerico; veemente, ardente

passive ['pæsɪv] *adj & s* passivo

pass'key' *s* chiave maestra; (*for use of hotel help*) comunella

Pass'o'ver *s* Pasqua ebraica

pass'port' *s* passaporto

pass'word' *s* parola d'ordine

past [pæst] or [pɑst] *adj* passato, scorso; ex, e.g., **past president** ex presidente || *s* passato || *adv* oltre; al di fuori; al di là || *prep* oltre; al di là di; dopo (di); **past belief** incredibile; **past cure** incurabile; **past hope** senza speranza; **past recovery** incurabile; **past three o'clock** le tre passate

paste [pest] *s* (*dough*) pasta; (*adhesive*) colla; diamante *m* artificiale || *tr* incollare; (slang) dare pugni a

paste'board' *s* cartone *m*

pastel [pæs'tel] *adj & s* pastello

pasteurize ['pæstə,raɪz] *tr* pastorizzare

pastime ['pæs,taɪm] or ['pɑs,taɪm] *s* diversione, passatempo

pastor ['pæstər] or ['pɑstər] *s* pastore *m*, sacerdote *m*

pastoral ['pæstərəl] or ['pɑstərəl] *adj* pastorale || *s* (*poem, letter*) pastorale *f*; (*crosier*) pastorale *m*

pas·try ['pestri] *s* (**-tries**) pasticceria

pas'try cook' *s* pasticciere *m*

pas'try shop' *s* pasticceria

pasture ['pæst/ər] or ['pɑst/ər] *s* pastura, pascolo || *tr* condurre al pascolo || *intr* brucare

past·y ['pesti] *adj* (**-ier; -iest**) pastoso; flaccido

pat [pæt] *s* colpetto; (*of butter*) panetto || *v* (*pret & pp* **patted;** *ger* **patting**) *tr* accarezzare leggermente; battere leggermente; **to pat on the back** elogiare, incoraggiare battendo sulla spalla

patch [pæt/] *s* (*on a suit or shoes*) toppa; (*in a tire*) pezza; (*on wound*) benda; (*of ground*) appezzamento; (*small area*) lembo || *tr* rammendare; **to patch up** (*an argument*) comporre; (*to produce crudely*) raffazzonare

patent ['petənt] *adj* patente, palmare || ['pætənt] *adj* brevettato || *s* (*of invention*) brevetto; (*sole right*) privativa || *tr* brevettare

pat'ent leath'er ['pætənt] *s* copale *m & f*, pelle *f* di vernice

pat'ent med'icine ['pætənt] *s* specialità *f* medicinale

pat'ent right' ['pætənt] *s* proprietà brevettata

paternal [pə'tʌrnəl] *adj* paterno

paternity [pə'tʌrnɪti] *s* paternità *f*

path [pæθ] or [pɑθ] *s* via battuta, sentiero; (fig) via

pathetic [pə'θɛtɪk] *adj* patetico

path'find'er *s* esploratore *m*

pathology [pə'θɑlədʒi] *s* patologia

pathos ['peθɑs] *s* patos *m*, pathos *m*

path'way' *s* sentiero, cammino

patience ['peʃəns] *s* pazienza

patient ['peʃənt] *adj & s* paziente *mf*

patriarch ['petri,ɑrk] *s* patriarca *m*

patrician [pə'trɪʃən] *adj & s* patrizio

patricide ['pætri,saɪd] *s* (*act*) parricidio; (*person*) parricida *mf*

Patrick ['pætrɪk] *s* Patrizio

patrimo·ny ['pætri,moni] *s* (**-nies**) patrimonio

patriot ['petri·ət] or ['pætri·ət] *s* patriota *mf*

patriotic [,petri'ɑtɪk] or [,pætri'ɑtɪk] *adj* patriottico

patriotism ['petri·ə,tɪzəm] or ['pætri·ə,tɪzəm] *s* patriottismo

pa·trol [pə'trol] *s* (*group*) pattuglia; (*individual*) soldato o agente *m* di pattuglia || *v* (*pret & pp* **-trolled;** *ger* **-trolling**) *tr & intr* pattugliare

patrol'man *s* (**-men**) agente *m*, poliziotto

patrol' wag'on s carrozzone m cellulare, cellulare m

patron ['petrən] or ['pætrən] s patrono, sostenitore m; (customer) cliente mf

patronize ['petrə‚naɪz] or ['pætrə‚naɪz] tr (to support) sostenere; trattare con condiscendenza; essere cliente abituale di

pa'tron saint' s patrono

patter ['pætər] s (e.g., of rain) battito; (of feet) scalpiccio; (speech) chiaccherio ‖ intr battere, picchiettare; chiaccherare

pattern ['pætərn] s modello; disegno; (of flight) procedura ‖ tr modellare

pat·ty ['pæti] s (-ties) pasticcino; (meat cake) polpetta

paucity ['pɔsɪti] s pochezza, scarsità f, insufficienza

Paul [pɔl] s Paolo

paunch [pɔntʃ] s pancia

paunch·y ['pɔntʃi] adj (-ier; -iest) panciuto

pauper ['pɔpər] s povero, indigente mf

pause [pɔz] s pausa; (of a tape recorder) arresto momentaneo; **to give pause (to)** dar di che pensare (a) ‖ intr far pausa, fermarsi; (to hesitate) esitare, vacillare

pave [pev] tr pavimentare, lastricare; **to pave the way (for)** aprire il cammino (a)

pavement ['pevmənt] s pavimentazione, lastricato; (sidewalk) marciapiede m

pavilion [pə'vɪljən] s padiglione m; (of circus) tendone m

paw [pɔ] s zampa ‖ tr (to touch with paws) dar zampate a; (to handle clumsily) maneggiare goffamente; (coll) palpeggiare ‖ intr zampare

pawn [pɔn] s (security) pegno; (tool of another person) pedina; (chess) pedina, pedone m; (fig) ostaggio ‖ tr dare in pegno, impegnare

pawn'bro'ker s prestatore m su pegno

pawn'shop' s agenzia di prestiti su pegno, monte m di pietà

pawn' tick'et s ricevuta di pegno, polizza del monte di pietà

pay [pe] s pagamento; (wages) paga, salario; (mil) soldo ‖ v (pret & pp **paid** [ped]) tr pagare; (wages) conguagliare; (one's respects) presentare; (a visit) fare; (a bill) saldare; (attention) fare, presentare; **to pay back** ripagare; (fig) pagare pan per focaccia a; **to pay for** pagare; **to pay off** liquidare; (in order to discharge) pagare e licenziare; **to pay up** saldare ‖ intr pagare; valere la pena; **pay as you enter** pagare all'ingresso; **pay as you go** pagare le tasse per trattenuta; **pay as you leave** pagare all'uscita

payable ['pe·əbəl] adj pagabile

pay' boost' s aumento di salario

pay'check' s assegno in pagamento del salario; salario, paga

pay'day' s giorno di paga

payee [pe'i] s beneficiario

pay' en'velope s bustapaga

payer ['pe·ər] s pagatore m

pay'load' s peso utile

pay'mas'ter s ufficiale m pagatore

payment ['pemənt] s pagamento

pay'off' s pagamento, regolamento; (coll) conclusione

pay' phone' s telefono a moneta

pay'roll' s lista degli impiegati; libro paga

pay' sta'tion s telefono pubblico

pea [pi] s pisello

peace [pis] s pace f; **to hold one's peace** tacere, stare zitto

peaceable ['pisəbəl] adj pacifico

peaceful ['pisfəl] adj pacifico

peace'mak'er s paciere m

peace' of mind' s serenità f d'animo

peace' pipe' s calumet m della pace

peach [pitʃ] s pesca; (coll) persona or cosa stupenda

peach' tree' s pesco

peach·y ['pitʃi] adj (-ier; -iest) (coll) stupendo

pea'cock' s pavone m

peak [pik] s picco; (of traffic) punta; (of one's career) sommo

peak' hour' s ora di punta

peak' load' s carico delle ore di punta, carico massimo

peal [pil] s (of bells) squillo; (of gun) rombo; (of laughter) scoppio; (of thunder) scroscio ‖ intr scampanare, squillare

pea'nut' s nocciolina americana; (plant) arachide f

pea'nut but'ter s pasta d'arachidi

pear [pɛr] s (fruit) pera; (tree) pero

pearl [pʌrl] s perla; (mother-of-pearl) madreperla; colore perlaceo

pearl' oys'ter s ostrica perlifera

pear' tree' s pero

peasant ['pɛzənt] adj & s contadino

pea'shoot'er s cerbottana

pea' soup' s minestra di piselli; (coll) nebbione m

peat [pit] s torba

pebble ['pɛbəl] s ciottolo

peck [pɛk] s beccata; misura di due galloni; **a peck of trouble** un mare di guai ‖ tr beccare ‖ intr beccare; **to peck at** beccucciare

peculation [‚pɛkjə'leʃən] s malversazione, peculato

peculiar [pɪ'kjuljər] adj peculiare; (odd) strano

pedagogue ['pɛdə‚gɑg] s pedagogo

pedagogy ['pɛdə‚godʒi] or ['pɛdə‚gadʒi] s pedagogia

ped·al ['pɛdəl] s pedale m ‖ v (pret & pp **-aled** or **-alled;** ger **-aling** or **-alling**) tr spingere coi pedali ‖ intr pedalare

pedant ['pɛdənt] s pedante mf

pedantic [pɪ'dæntɪk] adj pedantesco

pedant·ry ['pɛdəntri] s (-ries) pedanteria

peddle ['pɛdəl] tr vendere di porta in porta ‖ intr fare il venditore ambulante

peddler ['pɛdlər] s venditore m or merciaiolo ambulante

pedestal ['pɛdɪstəl] s piedistallo
pedestrian [pɪ'dɛstrɪ•ən] adj pedestre || s pedone m
pediatrics [,pidɪ'ætrɪks] or [,pɛdɪ-'ætrɪks] s pediatria
pedigree ['pɛdɪ ,gri] s albero genealogico; discendenza, lignaggio
pediment ['pɛdɪmənt] s frontone m
peek [pik] s sbirciata || intr sbirciare
peel [pil] s scorza, buccia; (of baker) pala || tr sbucciare; **to keep one's eyes peeled** (slang) tenere gli occhi aperti || intr pelarsi
peep [pip] s sbirciata; (sound) pigolio || intr guardare attraverso una fessura; (said of birds) pigolare; (to begin to appear) fare capolino
peep'hole' s spioncino
Peep'ing Tom' s guardone m
peep' show' s cosmorama m
peer [pɪr] s pari m, uguale m; (Brit) pari m || intr guardare da vicino
peerless ['pɪrlɪs] adj senza pari
peeve [piv] s (coll) seccatura, irritazione || tr (coll) seccare, irritare
peevish ['pivɪʃ] adj irritabile
peg [pɛg] s (to plug holes) zipolo; (pin) cavicchio; (mus) bischero; (coll) grado; **to take down a peg** (coll) fare abbassare la testa a || v (pret & pp pegged; ger pegging) tr fissare con cavicchi; (prices) stabilizzare || intr—**to peg away** lavorare di lena
peg' leg' s gamba di legno
Peking ['pi'kɪŋ] s Pechino f
Peking•ese [,pikɪ'niz] adj pechinese || s (-ese) pechinese mf
pelf [pɛlf] s (pej) denaro rubacchiato, maltolto
pelican ['pɛlɪkən] s pellicano
pellet ['pɛlɪt] s pallottola; (for shotgun) pallino; (pill) pillola
pell-mell ['pɛl'mɛl] adj confuso, disordinato || adv alla rinfusa
Peloponnesian [,pɛləpə'niʃən] adj & s peloponnesiaco
pelt [pɛlt] s pelle grezza; (blow) colpo || tr scagliare contro; (to beat) battere violentemente || intr battere, scrosciare
pen [pɛn] s (enclosure) recinto; (for writing) penna; (pen point) pennino || v (pret & pp penned) tr scrivere a penna; (to compose) redigere || v (pret & pp penned or pent; ger penning) tr recintare
penalize ['pinə ,laɪz] tr punire; (sports) penalizzare
penal•ty ['pɛnəlti] s (-ties) punizione; (fine) multa; (for late payment) penale f; **under penalty of** sotto pena di
pen'alty goal' s calcio di rigore
penance ['pɛnəns] s penitenza
penchant ['pɛnʃənt] s propensione
pen•cil ['pɛnsəl] s matita; (of rays) fascio || v (pret & pp -ciled or -cilled; ger -ciling or -cilling) tr scrivere a matita; (med) pennellare
pen'cil sharp'ener s temperalapis m
pendent ['pɛndənt] adj pendente, sospeso || s pendente m; ciondolo

pending ['pɛndɪŋ] adj imminente; in sospeso || prep durante; fino a
pendulum ['pɛndʒələm] s pendolo
pen'dulum bob' s lente f
penetrate ['pɛnɪ ,tret] tr & intr penetrare
penguin ['pɛŋgwɪn] s pinguino
pen'hold'er s portapenne m
penicillin [,pɛnɪ'sɪlɪŋ] s penicillina
peninsula [pɛ'nɪnsələ] s penisola
peninsular [pə'nɪnsələr] adj & s peninsulare
penitence ['pɛnɪtəns] s penitenza
penitent ['pɛnɪtənt] adj & s penitente mf
pen'knife' s (-knives) temperino
penmanship ['pɛnmən ,ʃɪp] s calligrafia
pen' name' s nome m di penna, pseudonimo
pennant ['pɛnənt] s pennone m
penniless ['pɛnɪlɪs] adj povero in canna, senza un soldo
pennon ['pɛnən] s pennone m
pen•ny ['pɛni] s (-nies) (U.S.A.) centesimo || s (**pence** [pɛns]) (Brit) penny m
pen'ny pinch'er ['pɪntʃər] s spilorcio
pen' pal' s amico corrispondente
pen'point' s pennino; (of ball-point pen) punta
pension ['pɛnʃən] s pensione || tr pensionare, mettere in pensione
pensioner ['pɛnʃənər] s pensionato
pensive ['pɛnsɪv] adj pensieroso
Pentecost ['pɛntɪ ,kɔst] or ['pɛntɪ ,kɑst] s la Pentecoste
penthouse ['pɛnt ,haʊs] s appartamento di lusso sul tetto; tettoia
pent-up ['pɛnt ,ʌp] adj represso
penult ['pinʌlt] s penultima
penum•bra [pɪ'nʌmbrə] s (-brae [bri] or -bras) penombra
penurious [pɪ'nʊrɪ•əs] adj taccagno, meschino; indigente
penury ['pɛnjəri] s taccagneria; estrema povertà, miseria
pen'wip'er s nettapenne m
people ['pipəl] spl popolo, gente f; (relatives) famiglia; gente f del popolo; si, e.g., **people say** si dice || ssg (**peoples**) nazione, popolazione || tr popolare
pep [pɛp] s (coll) animo, brio || v (pret & pp pepped; ger pepping) tr—**to pep up** (coll) dar animo a
pepper ['pɛpər] s pepe m || tr pepare; (to pelt) tempestare
pep'per•box' s pepaiola
pep'per•mint' s menta piperita
per [pʌr] prep per; (for each) il, e.g., **three dollars per meter** tre dollari il metro; **as per** secondo
perambulator [pər'æmbjə ,letər] s carrozzella, carrozzino
per capita [pər 'kæpɪtə] per persona, a testa
perceive [pər'siv] tr percepire
percent [pər'sɛnt] s percento, per cento
percentage [pər'sɛntɪdʒ] s percento, percentuale f; (coll) vantaggio
perception [pər'sɛpʃən] s percezione

perch [pʌrtʃ] s (*roost*) posatoio; (*horizontal rod*) ballatoio; (ichth) pesce persico || *intr* appollaiarsi

percolator ['pʌrkə‚letər] s caffettiera filtro a circolazione

percus'sion cap' [pər'kʌʃən] s capsula di percussione

per diem [pər 'daɪ‧əm] s assegno giornaliero

perdition [pər'dɪʃən] s perdizione

perennial [pə'rɛnɪ‧əl] *adj* perenne || s pianta perenne

perfect ['pʌrfɪkt] *adj* & s perfetto || [pər'fɛkt] *tr* perfezionare

perfidious [pər'fɪdɪ‧əs] *adj* perfido

perfi‧dy ['pʌrfɪdi] s (-dies) perfidia

perforate ['pʌrfə‚ret] *tr* perforare

perforation [‚pʌrfə'reʃən] s perforazione; (*of postage stamp*) dentellatura

perforce [pər'fɔrs] *adv* per forza, necessariamente

perform [pər'fɔrm] *tr* (*a task*) eseguire; (*a promise*) adempiere; (*to enact*) rappresentare || *intr* recitare; (*said, e.g., of a machine*) funzionare

performance [pər'fɔrməns] s esecuzione; (*of a machine*) funzionamento; (*deed*) atto di prodezza; (theat) rappresentazione

performer [pər'fɔrmər] s esecutore m; attore m; acrobata mf

perform'ing arts' spl arti fpl dello spettacolo

perfume ['pʌrfjum] s profumo || [pər'fjum] *tr* profumare

perfumer‧y [pər'fjuməri] s (-ies) profumeria

perfunctory [pər'fʌŋktəri] *adj* superficiale, pro forma; indifferente

perhaps [pər'hæps] *adv* forse

per‧il ['pɛrəl] s pericolo || *v* (*pret & pp* -iled or -illed; *ger* -iling or -illing) *tr* mettere in pericolo

perilous ['pɛrɪləs] *adj* pericoloso

period ['pɪrɪ‧əd] s periodo; mestruazione; (*in school*) ora; (sports) tempo; (gram) punto

pe'riod cos'tume s costume m dell'epoca

periodic [‚pɪrɪ'ɑdɪk] *adj* periodico

periodical [‚pɪrɪ'ɑdɪkəl] *adj* & s periodico

peripher‧y [pə'rɪfəri] s (-ies) periferia

periscope ['pɛrɪ‚skop] s periscopio

perish ['pɛrɪʃ] *intr* perire

perishable ['pɛrɪʃəbəl] *adj* deteriorabile

periwig ['pɛrɪ‚wɪg] s parrucca

perjure ['pʌrdʒər] *tr*—**to perjure oneself** spergiurare, giurare il falso

perju‧ry ['pʌrdʒəri] s (-ries) spergiuro

perk [pʌrk] *tr* (*the head, the ears*) alzare; **to perk oneself up** agghindarsi || *intr*—**to perk up** ringalluzzirsi

permanence ['pʌrmənəns] s permanenza

permanen‧cy ['pʌrmənənsi] s (-cies) permanenza

permanent ['pʌrmənənt] *adj* permanente || s permanente f, ondulazione permanente

per'manent fix'ture s cosa or persona permanente

per'manent ten'ure s inamovibilità f

per'manent way' s (rr) sede f stradale ed armamento

permeate ['pʌrmɪ‚et] *tr* permeare || *intr* permearsi

permissible [pər'mɪsɪbəl] *adj* permissibile

permission [pər'mɪʃən] s permesso

per‧mit ['pʌrmɪt] s permesso; patente f, licenza || [pər'mɪt] *v* (*pret & pp* -mitted; *ger* -mitting) *tr* permettere

permute [pər'mjut] *tr* permutare

pernicious [pər'nɪʃəs] *adj* pernicioso

pernickety [pər'nɪkɪti] *adj* (coll) incontentabile, meticoloso

perorate ['pɛrə‚ret] *intr* perorare

peroxide [pər'ɑksaɪd] s perossido; perossido d'idrogeno

perox'ide blonde' s bionda ossigenata

perpendicular [‚pʌrpən'dɪkjələr] *adj* & s perpendicolare f

perpetrate ['pʌrpɪ‚tret] *tr* (*a crime*) perpetrare; (*a blunder*) commettere

perpetual [pər'pɛtʃu‧əl] *adj* perpetuo

perpetuate [pər'pɛtʃu‚et] *tr* perpetuare

perplex [pər'plɛks] *tr* lasciare perplesso

perplexed [pər'plɛkst] *adj* perplesso

perplexi‧ty [pər'plɛksɪti] s (-ties) perplessità f

per se [pər 'si] di per se

persecute ['pʌrsɪ‚kjut] *tr* perseguitare

persevere [‚pʌrsɪ'vɪr] *intr* perseverare

Persian ['pʌrʒən] *adj* & s persiano

Per'sian Gulf' s Golfo Persico

persimmon [pər'sɪmən] s diospiro virginiano; cachi m

persist [pər'sɪst] or [pər'zɪst] *intr* persistere

persistent [pər'sɪstənt] or [pər'zɪstənt] *adj* persistente

person ['pʌrsən] s persona; **no person** nessuno

personage ['pʌrsənɪdʒ] s personaggio; persona

personal ['pʌrsənəl] *adj* personale; (*goods*) mobile || s inserzione personale; trafiletto di società

personali‧ty [‚pʌrsə'nælɪti] s (-ties) personalità f; offesa personale

personal'ity cult' s culto della personalità

per'sonal prop'erty s beni mpl mobili

personi‧fy [pər'sɑnɪ‚faɪ] *v* (*pret & pp* -fied) *tr* personificare

personnel [‚pʌrsə'nɛl] s personale m

per'son-to-per'son call' s (telp) chiamata con preavviso

perspective [pər'spɛktɪv] s prospettiva

perspicacious [‚pʌrspɪ'keʃəs] *adj* perspicace

perspire [pər'spaɪr] *intr* sudare

persuade [pər'swed] *tr* persuadere

persuasion [pər'sweʒən] s persuasione; fede religiosa

pert [pʌrt] *adj* impertinente, sfacciato; vivace

pertain [pər'ten] *intr* appartenere; (*to have reference*) riferirsi

pertinacious [‚pʌrtɪ'neʃəs] *adj* pertinace

pertinent ['pʌrtɪnənt] *adj* pertinente
perturb [pər'tʌrb] *tr* perturbare
Peru [pə'ru] *s* il Perù
perusal [pə'ruzəl] *s* attenta lettura
peruse [pə'ruz] *tr* leggere attentamente
pervade [pər'ved] *tr* pervadere
perverse [pər'vʌrs] *adj* perverso; (*obstinate*) ostinato
perversion [pər'vʌrʒən] *s* perversione
perversi·ty [pər'vʌrsɪti] *s* (**-ties**) perversità *f;* contrarietà *f*
pervert ['pʌrvərt] *s* pervertito, degenerato || [pər'vʌrt] *tr* pervertire, degenerare
pes·ky ['pɛski] *adj* (**-kier; -kiest**) (coll) noioso, molesto
pessimism ['pɛsɪ ,mɪzəm] *s* pessimismo
pessimist ['pɛsɪmɪst] *s* pessimista *mf*
pessimistic [,pɛsɪ'mɪstɪk] *adj* pessimistico
pest [pɛst] *s* peste *f,* pestilenza; insetto; animale nocivo; (*person*) peste *f,* seccatore *m*
pester ['pɛstər] *tr* seccare, annoiare
pest'house' *s* lazzaretto
pesticide ['pɛstɪ ,saɪd] *s* insetticida *m*
pestiferous [pɛst'tɪfərəs] *adj* pestifero
pestilence ['pɛstɪləns] *s* pestilenza
pestle ['pɛsəl] *s* pestello
pet [pɛt] *s* animale favorito; beniamino || *v* (*pret & pp* **petted;** *ger* **petting**) *tr* accarezzare || *intr* (coll) pomiciare
petal ['pɛtəl] *s* petalo
petard [pɪ'tard] *s* petardo
pet'cock' *s* chiavetta
Peter ['pitər] *s* Pietro; **to rob Peter to pay Paul** fare un buco per tapparne un altro || *intr*—**to peter out** (coll) affievolirsi
petition [pɪ'tɪʃən] *s* petizione || *tr* rivolgere un'istanza a
pet' name' *s* nomignolo vezzeggiativo
Petrarch ['pitrark] *s* Petrarca *m*
petri·fy ['pɛtrɪ ,faɪ] *v* (*pret & pp* **-fied**) *tr* pietrificare || *intr* pietrificarsi
petrol ['pɛtrəl] *s* (Brit) benzina
petroleum [pɪ'trolɪ·əm] *s* petrolio
pet' shop' *s* negozio di animali domestici
petticoat ['pɛtɪ ,kot] *s* sottoveste *f;* (coll) sottana, gonnella
pet·ty ['pɛti] *adj* (**-tier; -tiest**) insignificante, minore; meschino
pet'ty cash' *s* cassa delle piccole spese
pet'ty lar'ceny *s* furterello
pet'ty of'ficer *s* (nav) sottufficiale *m* di marina
petulant ['pɛtjələnt] *adj* stizzoso, irritabile
pew [pju] *s* banco di chiesa
pewter ['pjutər] *s* peltro; oggetti *mpl* di peltro
phalanx ['felæŋks] or ['fælæŋks] *s* falange *f*
phantasm ['fæntæzəm] *s* fantasma *m*
phantom ['fæntəm] *s* fantasma *m*
Pharaoh ['fɛro] *s* Faraone *m*
pharisee ['færɪ ,si] *s* fariseo || **Pharisee** *s* fariseo
pharmaceutical [,farmə'sutɪkəl] *adj* farmaceutico

pharmacist ['farməsɪst] *s* farmacista *mf*
pharma·cy ['farməsi] *s* (**-cies**) farmacia
pharynx ['færɪŋks] *s* faringe *f*
phase [fez] *s* fase *f* || *tr* mettere in fase; sincronizzare; **to phase in** mettere in operazione gradualmente; **to phase out** eliminare gradualmente
pheasant ['fɛzənt] *s* fagiano
phenobarbital [,fino'barbɪ ,tæl] *s* acido fenil-etilbarbiturico, barbiturato
phenomenal [fɪ'namɪnəl] *adj* fenomenale
phenome·non [fɪ'namɪ ,nan] *s* (**-na** [nə]) fenomeno
phial ['faɪ·əl] *s* fiala
philanderer [fɪ'lændərər] *s* donnaiolo
philanthropist [fɪ'lænθrəpɪist] *s* filantropo
philanthro·py [fɪ'lænθrəpi] *s* (**-pies**) filantropia
philatelist [fɪ'lætəlɪst] *s* filatelico
philately [fɪ'lætəli] *s* filatelia
Philip ['fɪlɪp] *s* Filippo
Philippine ['fɪlɪ ,pin] *adj* filippino || **Philippines** *spl* isole *fpl* Filippine
Philistine [fɪ'lɪstin], ['fɪlɪ ,stin] or ['fɪlɪ ,staɪn] *adj & s* filisteo
philologist [fɪ'laləd3ɪst] *s* filologo
philology [fɪ'laləd3i] *s* filologia
philosopher [fɪ'lasəfər] *s* filosofo
philosophic(al) [,fɪlə'safɪk(əl)] *adj* filosofico
philoso·phy [fɪ'lasəfi] *s* (**-phies**) filosofia
philter ['fɪltər] *s* filtro
phlebitis [flɪ'baɪtɪs] *s* flebite *f*
phlegm [flɛm] *s* (*secretion*) muco, catarro; (*self-possession*) flemma; apatia
phlegmatic(al) [flɛg'mætɪk(əl)] *adj* flemmatico
Phoebus ['fibəs] *s* Febo
Phoenician [fɪ'nɪʃən] or [fɪ'niʃən] *adj & s* fenicio
phoenix ['finɪks] *s* fenice *f*
phone [fon] *s* (coll) telefono || *tr & intr* (coll) telefonare
phone' call' *s* chiamata telefonica
phonetic [fo'nɛtɪk] *adj* fonetico || **phonetics** *s* fonetica
phonograph ['fonə ,græf] or ['fonə ,graf] *s* fonografo
phonology [fə'naləd3i] *s* fonologia
pho·ny ['foni] *adj* (**-nier; -niest**) (coll) falso || *s* (**-nies**) (coll) frode *f;* (*person*) (coll) impostore *m*
phosphate ['fasfet] *s* fosfato
phosphorescent [,fasfə'rɛsənt] *adj* fosforescente
phospho·rus ['fasfərəs] *s* (**-ri** [,raɪ]) fosforo
pho·to ['foto] *s* (**-tos**) (coll) foto *f*
photo·cop·y ['fotə ,kapi] *s* (**-ies**) fotocopia || *tr* fotocopiare
pho'toelec'tric cell' [,foto·ɪ'lɛktrɪk] *s* cellula fotoelettrica
photoengraving [,foto·ɛn'grevɪŋ] *s* fotoincisione
pho'to fin'ish *s* photofinish *m,* arrivo con fotografia

photogenic [ˌfotoˈdʒɛnɪk] *adj* fotogenico
photograph [ˈfotəˌgræf] or [ˈfotəˌgraf] *s* fotografia ‖ *tr* fotografare ‖ *intr*—**to photograph well** riuscire in fotografia
photographer [fəˈtɑgrəfər] *s* fotografo
photography [fəˈtɑgrəfi] *s* fotografia
photojournalism [ˌfotəˈdʒʌrnəˌlɪzəm] *s* giornalismo fotografico
pho'to·play' *s* dramma adattato per il cinematografo
photostat [ˈfotəˌstæt] *s* (trademark) copia fotostatica ‖ *tr* riprodurre fotostaticamente
phototube [ˈfotəˌtjub] or [ˈfotəˌtub] *s* fototubo
phrase [frez] *s* (gram) locuzione; (mus) frase *f* ‖ *tr* esprimere, formulare ‖ *intr* (mus) fraseggiare
phrenology [frɪˈnɑlədʒi] *s* frenologia
Phyllis [ˈfɪlɪs] *s* Fillide *f*
phy·lum [ˈfaɪləm] *s* (-la [lə]) phylum *m*, tipo
phys·ic [ˈfɪzɪk] *s* purgante *m* ‖ *v* (*pret* & *pp* -icked; *ger* -icking) *tr* dare il purgante a, purgare
physical [ˈfɪzɪkəl] *adj* fisico
physician [fɪˈzɪʃən] *s* medico
physicist [ˈfɪzɪsɪst] *s* fisico
physics [ˈfɪzɪks] *s* fisica
physiognomy [ˌfɪzɪˈɑgnəmi] or [ˌfɪziˈɑnəmi] *s* fisionomia
physiological [ˌfɪzɪəˈlɑdʒɪkəl] *adj* fisiologico
physiology [ˌfɪzɪˈɑlədʒi] *s* fisiologia
physique [fɪˈzɪk] *s* fisico
pi [paɪ] *s* (math) pi greco; (typ) tipi scartati ‖ *v* (*pret* & *pp* **pied;** *ger* **piing**) *tr* (typ) scompaginare, scomporre
pian·o [pɪˈæno] *s* (-os) piano
picaresque [ˌpɪkəˈrɛsk] *adj* picaresco
picayune [ˌpɪkəˈjun] *adj* meschino, minore, di poca importanza
picco·lo [ˈpɪkəˌlo] *s* (-los) ottavino
pick [pɪk] *s* (*tool*) piccone *m;* (*choice*) scelta; (*the best*) fiore *m;* (mus) plettro ‖ *tr* scavare; (*to scratch at*) grattare; (*to gather*) cogliere; (*to pluck*) spennare; (*to pull apart*) separare; (*one's teeth*) stuzzicarsi; (*a bone*) rosicchiare; (*to choose*) scegliere; (*a lock*) scassinare; (*a pocket*) tagliare, rubare; (mus) pizzicare; **to pick a fight** attaccare briga; **to pick faults** trovare a ridire; **to pick out** scegliere; distinguere; discriminare; **to pick s.o. to pieces** (coll) tagliare i panni addosso a qlcu; **to pick up** sollevare; (*to find*) trovare; (*to learn*) arrivare a sapere; (*a radio signal*) captare; (*speed*) acquistare ‖ *intr* usare il piccone; **to pick at** (*food*) spilluzzicare; (coll) criticare; **to pick on** (coll) scegliere; (coll) criticare; **to pick up** (coll) migliorarsi
pick'ax' *s* piccone *m*
picket [ˈpɪkɪt] *s* picchetto ‖ *tr* rinchiudere con palizzata; (*to hitch*) legare; (*to post*) (mil) mettere di picchetto; (*e.g., a factory*) picchettare

pick'et fence' *s* steccato
pick'et line' *s* corteo di scioperanti; corteo di dimostranti
pickle [ˈpɪkəl] *s* salamoia, sottaceto; (*cucumber*) cetriolo sottaceto; **to get into a pickle** (coll) cacciarsi in un imbroglio ‖ *tr* mettere sottaceto; (metallurgy) decapare
pick-me-up [ˈpɪkmiˌʌp] *s* (coll) spuntino; (coll) bevanda stimulante
pick'pock'et *s* borseggiatore *m*, borsaiolo
pick'up' *s* sollevamento; (*in speed*) accelerazione; (*of phonograph*) pick-up *m*, fonorivelatore *m;* (aut) camioncino; (coll) persona conosciuta per caso; (coll) miglioramento
pick'-up-sticks' *spl* sciangai *m*
pic·nic [ˈpɪknɪk] *s* picnic *m* ‖ *v* (*pret* & *pp* -nicked; *ger* -nicking) *intr* fare merenda all'aperto
pictorial [pɪkˈtorɪəl] *adj* pittorico; illustrato; vivido ‖ *s* rivista illustrata
picture [ˈpɪktʃər] *s* illustrazione, disegno; (*painting*) quadro, dipinto; (*of a person*) ritratto; fotografia; film *m*, pellicola ‖ *tr* fare il ritratto di; disegnare; dipingere; fotografare; descrivere; immaginare, immaginarsi
pic'ture frame' *s* cornice *f*
pic'ture gal'lery *s* pinacoteca, galleria di quadri, quadreria
pic'ture post' card' *s* cartolina illustrata
pic'ture show' *s* cinematografo; mostra di quadri
picturesque [ˌpɪktʃəˈrɛsk] *adj* pittoresco
pic'ture tube' *s* tubo televisivo
pic'ture win'dow *s* finestra panoramica
piddling [ˈpɪdlɪŋ] *adj* insignificante
pie [paɪ] *s* (*with fruit*) torta; (*with meat*) timballo; (orn) pica ‖ *v* (*pret* & *pp* **pied;** *ger* **pieing**) *tr* (typ) scompaginare, scomporre
piece [pis] *s* pezzo; (*e.g., of cloth*) pezza; **a piece of advice** un consiglio; **a piece of baggage** un collo; **a piece of furniture** un mobile *m;* **a piece of news** una notizia; **by the piece** a cottimo; **to break to pieces** frantumare; frantumarsi; **to cut to pieces** fare a pezzi; **to fall to pieces** cadere a pezzi; **to fly to pieces** rompersi in mille pezzi; **to give s.o. a piece of one's mind** dirne a qlcu di tutti i colori; **to go to pieces** perdere il controllo di sé stesso; **to take to pieces** confutare punto per punto ‖ *tr* rappezzare, mettere insieme ‖ *intr* (coll) mangiucchiare
piece'meal' *adv* poco a poco
piece'work' *s* lavoro a cottimo
piece'work'er *s* cottimista *mf*
pier [pɪr] *s* (*of a bridge*) pila; (*over water*) molo; (archit) pilastro, pilone *m*
pierce [pɪrs] *tr* forare, bucare; penetrare; (*to stab*) trapassare ‖ *intr* penetrare
piercing [ˈpɪrsɪŋ] *adj* acuto; (*eyes*) penetrante; (*pain*) lancinante

pier' glass' *s* specchiera
pie·ty ['paɪ·əti] *s* (**-ties**) pietà *f*
piffle ['pɪfəl] *s* (coll) fesserie *fpl*
pig [pɪg] *s* maiale *m*, porco; (metallurgy) lingotto, massello; **to buy a pig in the poke** comprare il gatto nel sacco
pigeon ['pɪdʒən] *s* piccione *m*
pi'geon·hole' *s* nicchia nella piccionaia; (*for filing*) casella || *tr* (*to lay aside for later time*) archiviare; (*to shelve, e.g., an application*) insabbiare
pi'geon house' *s* colombaia, piccionaia
piggish ['pɪgɪʃ] *adj* porcino, maialesco
pig'gy·back' ['pɪgɪˌbæk] *adv* sulle spalle, sulla schiena; (rr) su carrello stradale per trasporto carri
pig'head'ed *adj* ostinato, cocciuto
pig' i'ron *s* ghisa, ferro grezzo
pigment ['pɪgmənt] *s* pigmento || *tr* pigmentare || *intr* pigmentarsi
pig'pen' *s* porcile *m*
pig'skin' *s* pelle *f* di maiale; (coll) pallone *m* da football, sfera di cuoio
pig'sty' *s* (**-sties**) porcile *m*
pig'tail' *s* codino; (*of girl*) treccia; treccia di tabacco
pike [paɪk] *s* (*weapon*) picca; (*road*) autostrada; (ichth) luccio
piker ['paɪkər] *s* (coll) uomo piccino
pile [paɪl] *s* (*heap*) pila; (*for burning a corpse*) pira; (*large building*) mole *f*; (*beam*) palo; (*of carpet*) pelo; (*of money*) (slang) gruzzolo; (coll) mucchio; **piles** emorroidi *fpl* || *tr* ammucchiare, accumulare; **to pile up** ammonticchiare || *intr* accumularsi; **to pile into** pigiarsi in; **to pile up** accumularsi
pile' driv'er *s* battipalo, berta
pilfer ['pɪlfər] *tr & intr* rubacchiare
pilgrim ['pɪlgrɪm] *s* pellegrino
pilgrimage ['pɪlgrɪmɪdʒ] *s* pellegrinaggio
pill [pɪl] *s* pillola; amara pillola; (coll) rompiscatole *mf*; **to sugar-coat the pill** addolcire la pillola
pillage ['pɪlɪdʒ] *s* saccheggio, rapina || *tr & intr* saccheggiare, rapinare
pillar ['pɪlər] *s* pilastro, colonna; **from pillar to post** da Erode a Pilato
pill'box' *s* scatoletta per le pillole; (mil) casamatta
pillo·ry ['pɪləri] *s* (**-ries**) gogna, berlina || *v* (*pret & pp* **-ried**) *tr* mettere alla berlina
pillow ['pɪlo] *s* cuscino, guanciale *m*
pil'low·case' *s* federa
pilot ['paɪlət] *adj* pilota || *s* pilota *m*; (*of locomotive*) respingente *m* || *tr* pilotare
pi'lot light' *s* fiammella automatica
pimp [pɪmp] *s* ruffiano, lenone *m*
pimple ['pɪmpəl] *s* bitorzolo
pim·ply ['pɪmpli] *adj* (**-plier; -pliest**) bitorzoluto
pin [pɪn] *s* (*of metal*) spillo; (*peg*) caviglia; (*adornment*) spilla; (*linchpin*) acciarino; (*of key*) mappa; (*clothespin*) molletta; (*bowling pin*) birillo; **to be on pins and needles** stare sulle spine || *tr* appuntare; (*to hold*) im-

mobilizzare; **to pin s.o. down** forzare qlcu a rivelare i propri piani to **pin s.th on s.o.** (coll) dare la colpa a qlcu per qlco
pinafore ['pɪnəˌfor] *s* grembiulino
pinaster [paɪ'næstər] *s* pino marittimo
pin'ball machine' *s* biliardino
pince-nez ['pæns ˌne] *s* occhiali *mpl* a stringinaso
pincers ['pɪnsərz] *ssg* or *spl* tenaglie *fpl*; (zool) pinze *fpl*
pinch [pɪntʃ] *s* (*squeeze*) pizzicotto; (*of tobacco*) presa; (*of salt*) pizzico; (*hardship*) strettoia; **in a pinch** in caso di necessità || *tr* stringere, pizzicare; (*to press*) comprimere; ridurre alle strettezze; (slang) rubare; (slang) arrestare || *intr* stringere; (*to be stingy*) fare l'avaro
pin'cush'ion *s* puntaspilli *m*
pine [paɪn] *s* pino || *intr*—**to pine away** struggersi; **to pine for** spasimare per
pine'ap'ple *s* ananas *m*
pine' cone' *s* pigna
pine' nee'dle *s* ago del pino
ping [pɪŋ] *s* rumore secco; rumore metallico || *intr* fare un rumore secco or metallico
pin'head' *s* capocchia di spillo; (slang) testa quadra
pin'hole' *s* forellino
pink [pɪŋk] *adj* rosa || *s* color *m* rosa; condizione perfetta; (bot) garofano || *tr* orlare a zig-zag; (*to stab*) perforare
pin' mon'ey *s* denaro per le piccole spese
pinnacle ['pɪnəkəl] *s* pinnacolo
pin'point' *adj* di precisione || *s* punta di spillo || *tr* mettere in rilievo
pin'prick' *s* puntura di spillo
pint [paɪnt] *s* pinta
pintle ['pɪntəl] *s* maschietto
pin'up' *s* pin-up-girl *f*
pin'wheel' *s* girandola
pioneer [ˌpaɪ·ə'nɪr] *s* pioniere *m* || *tr* aprire la via a || *intr* fare il pioniere
pioneering [ˌpaɪ·ə'nɪrɪŋ] *adj* pioneristico
pious ['paɪ·əs] *adj* pio, devoto
pip [pɪp] *s* (*seed*) seme *m*; (vet) pipita
pipe [paɪp] *s* tubo, canna; (*of stove*) cannone *m*; (*for smoking*) pipa; (mus) legno; (mus) cornamusa || *tr* suonare; cantare ad alta voce; fischiare; condurre in una tubatura; munire di tubatura || *intr* suonare la zampogna; **to pipe down** (slang) stare zitto
pipe' clean'er *s* scovolino
pipe' dream' *s* castello in aria
pipe' line' *s* oleodotto; (fig) fonte *f* (d'informazioni)
pipe' or'gan *s* organo a canne
piper ['paɪpər] *s* zampognaro; **to pay the piper** pagare lo scotto
pipe' wrench' *s* chiave *f* per tubi
piping ['paɪpɪŋ] *adj* (*voice*) acuto; (*sound*) di cornamusa || *s* tubatura; suono di cornamuse; suono acuto; (*on cakes*) fregio; (*on garments*) cor-

doncino ornamentale || *adv*—**piping hot** scottante, bollente

pippin ['pɪpɪn] *s* mela renetta; (*seed*) seme *m;* (fig) gran brava persona

piquant ['pikənt] *adj* piccante

pique [pik] *s* picca, ripicco || *tr* offendere, eccitare

pira‧cy ['paɪrəsi] *s* (**-cies**) pirateria

pirate ['paɪrɪt] *s* pirata *mf* || *tr* derubare; (*a book*) svaligiare, pubblicare illegalmente || *intr* pirateggiare

pirouette [,pɪru'ɛt] *s* piroetta || *intr* piroettare

Pisces ['paɪsiz] or ['pɪsɪz] *s* (astr) Pesci *mpl*

pistol ['pɪstəl] *s* pistola

piston ['pɪstən] *s* pistone *m*

pis'ton displace'ment *s* cilindrata

pis'ton ring' *s* segmento elastico

pis'ton rod' *s* (*of a steam engine*) biella d'accoppiamento; (*of a motor*) asta del pistone, biella

pis'ton stroke' *s* corsa dello stantuffo

pit [pɪt] *s* (*in the ground*) buca; (*trap*) trappola; (*of fruit*) nocciolo; (*of stomach*) bocca; (*scar*) buttero; (*in exchange*) recinto delle grida; (*for fights*) arena; (theat) platea; (min) miniera; (aut) fossa di riparazione || *v* (*pret & pp* **pitted;** *ger* **pitting**) *tr* infossare; butterare; opporre; (*to remove pits from*) snocciolare

pitch [pɪtʃ] *s* (*black sticky substance*) pece *f;* (*throw*) lancio; (*of a roof*) pendenza, inclinazione; (*of a boat*) beccheggio; (*of a screw*) passo; (*of sound*) altezza || *tr* lanciare; (*a tent*) rizzare || *intr* beccheggiare; **to pitch in** (coll) mettersi al lavoro; (coll) cominciare a mangiare

pitch' ac'cent *s* accento di altezza

pitch' at'titude *s* assetto longitudinale

pitch'-dark' *adj* nero come la pece

pitched' bat'tle *s* battaglia campale

pitcher ['pɪtʃər] *s* brocca; (baseball) lanciatore *m*

pitch'fork' *s* forca, tridente *m;* **to rain pitchforks** (coll) piovere a dirotto

pitch' pipe' *s* (mus) corista *m*

pit'fall' *s* trappola, trabocchetto

pith [pɪθ] *s* midollo; (*strength*) (fig) forza; (fig) succo, essenza

pith‧y ['pɪθi] *adj* (**-ier; -iest**) midolloso; succoso, essenziale

pitiful ['pɪtɪfəl] *adj* pietoso

pitiless ['pɪtɪlɪs] *adj* spietato

pit‧y ['pɪti] *s* (**-ies**) pietà *f;* **it is a pity that** è un peccato che; **what a pity!** che peccato! || *v* (*pret & pp* **-ied**) *tr* aver pietà di

Pius ['paɪ‧əs] *s* Pio

pivot ['pɪvət] *s* asse *m,* perno; (fig) asse *m* || *tr* imperniare || *intr* imperniarsi; **to pivot on** fare perno su; dipendere da

placard ['plækɑrd] *s* manifesto, affisso || *tr* affiggere

place [ples] *s* luogo; locale *m;* (*court*) piazzetta; (*short street*) vicolo; residenza; sito, luogo, località *f;* (*space occupied*) posto; (*office*) posto, impiego; **in no place**

da nessuna parte; **in place** a posto; **in place of** al posto di, invece di; **in the first place** in primo luogo; **in the next place** in secondo luogo; **to know one's place** saper stare al proprio posto; **to take place** aver luogo || *tr* piazzare, mettere; (*to find employment for*) collocare; (*to identify*) ravvisare || *intr* (sports) piazzarsi

place‧bo [plə'sibo] *s* (**-bos** or **-boes**) rimedio fittizio

place' card' *s* segnaposto

placement ['plesmənt] *s* (*e.g., of furniture*) collocazione; (*employment*) collocamento

place' name' *s* toponimo

place' of busi'ness *s* ufficio, negozio

placid ['plæsɪd] *adj* placido

plagiarism ['pledʒə‧rɪzəm] *s* plagio

plagiarize ['pledʒə‧raɪz] *tr* plagiare

plague [pleg] *s* peste bubbonica; (*widespread affliction*) piaga, flagello || *tr* infestare, appestare; tormentare

plaid [plæd] *s* tessuto scozzese

plain [plen] *adj* piano; aperto; evidente, esplicito; semplice; (*undyed*) naturale; comune, ordinario; **in plain English** senz'ambagi; **in plain view** di fronte a tutti || *s* pianura

plain'-clothes' man' *s* (**-men'**) agente *m* in borghese

plains'man *s* (**-men**) abitante *m* della pianura

plaintiff ['plentɪf] *s* querelante *mf*

plaintive ['plentɪv] *adj* lamentevole

plan [plæn] *s* piano, progetto || *v* (*pret & pp* **planned;** *ger* **planning**) *tr & intr* progettare

plane [plen] *adj* piano || *m* piano; (*tool*) pialla; (aer) aeroplano; (aer) ala d'aeroplano; (bot) platano || *tr* piallare || *intr* andare in areoplano

plane' sick'ness *s* male *m* d'aria

planet ['plænɪt] *s* pianeta *m*

plane' tree' *s* platano

plan'ing mill' *s* officina di piallatura

plank [plæŋk] *s* tavola, asse *m;* (*of political party*) piattaforma || *tr* coprire d'assi; cucinare sulla graticola e servire sul tagliere; **to plank down** (*e.g., money*) (coll) snocciolare

plant [plænt] or [plɑnt] *s* (*factory*) impianto, stabilimento; (*e.g;, of a college*) complesso di edifici; (bot) pianta; (mach) apparato motore; (slang) trappola || *tr* (*e.g., a tree*) piantare; (*seeds*) seminare; (*to stock*) fornire

plantation [plæn'teʃən] *s* piantagione

planter ['plæntər] *s* piantatore *m;* (mach) piantatrice *f*

plaster ['plæstər] or ['plɑstər] *s* (*gypsum*) gesso; (*mixture to cover walls*) intonaco, malta; (*poultice*) impiastro || *tr* ingessare; intonacare; impiastrare; (*with posters*) affiggere, ricoprire

plas'ter‧board' *s* cartone *m* di gesso

plas'ter cast' *s* (sculp) gesso; (surg) ingessatura

plas'ter of Par'is *s* gesso, stucco

plastic ['plæstɪk] *adj & s* plastico

plate 237 plug

plate [plet] *s* (*dish*) piatto; (*sheet of metal*) placca, piastra; (*thin sheet of metal*) lamina; (*of vacuum tube*) placca; (*of auto license*) targa; (*of condenser*) armatura; (*tableware*) vasellame *m* d'argento, vasellame *m* d'oro; dentiera; (*baseball*) casa base; (phot) lastra; (typ) cliché *m* ‖ *tr* (*with gold or silver*) placcare; (*with armor*) blindare, corazzare

plateau [plæ'to] *s* altipiano

plate′ glass′ *s* lastrone *m*

platen ['plætən] *s* rullo

platform ['plæt,fɔrm] *s* piattaforma; (*for speaker*) tribuna, palco; (*for passengers*) (rr) marciapiede *m;* (*at end of car*) (rr) piattaforma

plat′form car′ *s* (rr) pianale *m*

platinum ['plætɪnəm] *s* platino

plat′inum blonde′ *s* bionda platinata

platitude ['plætɪ,tjud] or ['plætɪ,tud] *s* trivialità *f*, banalità *f*

Plato ['pleto] *s* Platone *m*

platoon [plə'tun] *s* plotone *m*

platter ['plætər] *s* piatto di portata; (slang) disco di grammofono

plausible ['plɔzɪbəl] *adj* plausibile; (*person*) credibile, attendibile

play [ple] *s* gioco; libertà *f* d'azione; recreazione; turno, volta; (theat) dramma *m;* (mach) gioco ‖ *tr* giocare; giocare contro; causare, produrre; (*a drama*) rappresentare; (*a character*) fare la parte di; (*to wield*) esercitare; (mus) suonare; **to play back** (*e.g., a tape*) riprodurre; **to play down** diminuire l'importanza di; **to play one off against another** mettere uno contro l'altro; **to play up** dare importanza a ‖ *intr* giocare; (*to act*) giocare, comportarsi; (theat) recitare; (mus) suonare; (mach) aver gioco; **to play on** continuare a giocare; continuare a suonare; valersi di; **to play safe** non prendere rischi; **to play sick** fare il malato; **to play up to** fare la corte a

play′back′ *s* riproduzione; apparechiatura di riproduzione

play′bill′ *s* (theat) programma *m*

play′boy′ *s* playboy *m*, gaudente *m*

player ['ple·ər] *s* giocatore *m;* (theat) attore *m;* (mus) suonatore *m*

play′er pian′o *s* pianola

playful ['plefəl] *adj* giocoso

playgoer ['ple,go·ər] *s* frequentatore *m* del teatro

play′ground′ *s* parco di ricreazione; (*resort*) posto di villeggiatura

play′house′ *s* teatro; casa di bambole

play′ing card′ ['ple·ɪŋ] *s* carta da gioco

play′ing field′ *s* campo da gioco

play′mate′ *s* compagno di gioco

play′-off′ *s* (sports) spareggio

play′pen′ *s* recinto, box *m*

play′thing′ *s* giocattolo

play′time′ *s* ricreazione

playwright ['ple,raɪt] *s* drammaturgo, commediografo

play′writ′ing *s* drammaturgia

plaza ['plæzə] or ['plɑzə] *s* piazzale *m*

plea [pli] *s* scusa; richiesta, domanda; (law) dichiarazione

plead [plid] *v* (*pret* & *pp* **pleaded** or **pled** [pled]) *tr* (*ignorance*) dichiarare; (*a case*) perorare ‖ *intr* supplicare; argomentare; **to plead guilty** dichiararsi colpevole

pleasant ['plɛzənt] *adj* piacevole; (*person*) simpatico

pleasant·ry ['plɛzəntri] *s* (-ries) facezia, motto

please [pliz] *tr* piacere (with *dat*) ‖ *intr* piacere; **as you please** come vuole; **if you please** per favore; **please** per cortesia; **to be pleased to** avere il piacere di; **to be pleased with** essere soddisfatto con; **to do as one pleases** fare come par e piace

pleasing ['plizɪŋ] *adj* piacevole

pleasure ['plɛʒər] *s* piacere *m;* desiderio; **what is your pleasure?** cosa desidera?

pleas′ure car′ *s* vettura da turismo

pleat [plit] *s* piega ‖ *tr* piegare, pieghettare

plebeian [plɪ'bi·ən] *adj* & *s* plebeo

plebiscite ['plɛbɪ,saɪt] *s* plebiscito

pledge [plɛdʒ] *s* pegno; promessa; voto; (*person*) ostaggio; (*toast*) brindisi *m;* **as a pledge** in pegno; **to take the pledge** giurare d'astenersi dal bere ‖ *tr* dare in pegno; (*to bind*) far promettere a

plentiful ['plentɪfəl] *adj* abbondante

plenty ['plenti] *s* abbondanza ‖ *adv* (coll) abbastanza

pleurisy ['plurɪsi] *s* pleurite *f*

pliable ['plaɪ·əbəl] *adj* flessibile, pieghevole; docile

pliers ['plaɪ·ərz] *ssg* or *spl* pinze *fpl*

plight [plaɪt] *s* condizione or situazione precaria ‖ *tr*—**to plight one's troth** fidanzarsi

plod [plɑd] *v* (*pret* & *pp* **plodded;** *ger* **plodding**) *tr* percorrere pesantemente ‖ *intr* camminare pesantemente; (*to drudge*) sgobbare

plot [plɑt] *s* (*of ground*) appezzamento; (*of a play*) trama, intreccio; (*evil scheme*) cospirazione, trama ‖ *v* (*pret* & *pp* **plotted;** *ger* **plotting**) *tr* fare il piano di; macchinare; preparare la trama di; (aer, naut) fare il punto di ‖ *intr* tramare, cospirare

plover ['plʌvər] or ['plovər] *s* piviere *m*

plow [plau] *s* aratro; (*for snow*) spazzaneve *m* ‖ *tr* arare; (*e.g., water*) solcare; (*snow*) spazzare; **to plow back** reinvestire ‖ *intr* arare; aprirsi la via; camminare pesantemente

plow′man *s* (-men) aratore *m;* contadino

plow′share′ *s* vomere *m*

pluck [plʌk] *s* strattone *m;* coraggio; (*giblets*) frattaglie *fpl* ‖ *tr* (*to snatch*) tirare; (*e.g., fruit*) svellere; (*a fowl*) spennare; (mus) pizzicare ‖ *intr* tirare; **to pluck up** farsi coraggio

pluck·y ['plʌki] *adj* (-ier; -iest) coraggioso

plug [plʌg] *s* tappo, zaffo; tavoletta di

tabacco; bocca da incendi; (elec) spina; (*horse*) (slang) ronzino; (slang) raccomandazione ‖ *v* (*pret & pp* **plugged;** *ger* **plugging**) *tr* tappare, otturare; colpire; inserire; (slang) fare la pubblicità di; **to plug in** (elec) innestare, connettere ‖ *intr* (coll) sgobbare

plum [plʌm] *s* (*fruit*) susina; (*tree*) susino; (slang) cosa bellissima; (slang) colpo di fortuna

plumage ['plumɪdʒ] *s* piumaggio

plumb [plʌm] *adj* appiombo ‖ *s* piombino ‖ *adv* appiombo; (coll) completamente ‖ *tr* determinare la verticale col piombino; assodare

plumb' bob' *s* piombino

plumber ['plʌmər] *s* installatore *m*, idraulico

plumbing ['plʌmɪŋ] *s* impianto idraulico; mestiere *m* d'idraulico; sondaggio

plumb'ing fix'tures *spl* rubinetteria, impianti *mpl* sanitari

plumb' line' *s* filo a piombo

plum' cake' *s* panfrutto

plume [plum] *s* piuma; (*tuft of feathers*) pennacchio ‖ *tr* coprire di piume; **to plume oneself on** piccarsi di; **to plume one's feathers** pulirsi le penne

plummet ['plʌmɪt] *s* piombino ‖ *intr* cadere a piombo

plump [plʌmp] *adj* grassoccio, paffuto; franco ‖ *s* caduta ‖ *adv* francamente ‖ *intr* cadere a piombo

plum' pud'ding *s* budino con uva passa

plum' tree' *s* susino

plunder ['plʌndər] *s* (*act*) saccheggio; (*loot*) bottino ‖ *tr* & *intr* saccheggiare

plunge [plʌndʒ] *s* (*fall*) caduta; (*dive*) nuotata, tuffo ‖ *tr* gettare; tuffare; (*e.g., a knife*) configgere ‖ *intr* (*to rush*) precipitarsi; (*to gamble*) (coll) darsi al gioco; (fig) ripiombare

plunger ['plʌndʒər] *s* tuffatore *m*; (*for clearing clogged drains*) sturalavandini *m*; (mach) stantuffo; (coll) giocatore temerario

plunk [plʌŋk] *adv* (coll) proprio; (coll) con un colpo secco ‖ *tr* (coll) gettare; lasciar cadere; (mus) pizzicare ‖ *intr* (coll) lasciarsi cadere

plural ['plurəl] *adj* & *s* plurale *m*

plus [plʌs] *adj* superiore; (elec) positivo; (coll) con lode ‖ *s* più *m*; soprappiù *m* ‖ *prep* più

plush [plʌʃ] *adj* di lusso ‖ *s* peluche *f*, felpa

Plutarch ['plutark] *s* Plutarco

Pluto ['pluto] *s* Plutone *m*

plutonium [plu'tonɪ·əm] *s* plutonio

ply [plaɪ] *s* (**plies**) spessore *m*; (*layer*) strato; (*of rope*) legnolo ‖ *v* (*pret & pp* **plied**) *tr* (*a trade*) esercitare; (*a tool*) maneggiare; (*to assail*) premere, incalzare ‖ *intr* lavorare assiduamente; **to ply between** fare la spola tra

ply'wood' *s* legno compensato

pneumatic [nju'mætɪk] or [nu'mætɪk] *adj* pneumatico

pneumat'ic drill' *s* martello perforatore or pneumatico

pneumonia [nju'monɪ·ə] or [nu'monɪ·ə] *s* polmonite *f*

poach [potʃ] *tr* (*eggs*) affogare ‖ *intr* cacciare or pescare di frodo

poacher ['potʃər] *s* bracconiere *m*; pescatore *m* di frodo

pock [pak] *s* buttero

pocket ['pakɪt] *adj* tascabile ‖ *s* tasca; (billiards) buca; (aer) vuoto; (min) deposito ‖ *tr* intascare; (*e.g., one's pride*) ingoiare

pock'et·book' *s* portafoglio; (*woman's purse*) borsetta

pock'et book' *s* libro tascabile

pock'et·hand'kerchief *s* fazzoletto

pock'et·knife' *s* (**-knives**) temperino

pock'et mon'ey *s* spiccioli *mpl*

pock'mark' *s* buttero

pod [pad] *s* baccello; (aer) contenitore *m*

poem ['po·ɪm] *s* poesia; (*of some length*) poema *m*

poet ['po·ɪt] *s* poeta *m*

poetess ['po·ɪtɪs] *s* poetessa

poetic [po'etɪk] *adj* poetico ‖ **poetics** *ssg* poetica

poetry ['po·ɪtri] *s* poesia

pogrom ['pogrəm] *s* pogrom *m*

poignancy ['pɔɪnjənsi] or ['pɔɪnənsi] *s* strazio; intensità *f*

poignant ['pɔɪnjənt] or ['pɔɪnənt] *adj* straziante; intenso

point [pɔɪnt] *s* (*sharp end*) punta; (*something essential*) essenziale *m*; (*hint*) suggerimento; (*dot, decimal point, spot, degree, instant, position of compass*) punto; (coll) costrutto; **beside the point** fuori del seminato; **in point of** per quanto concerne; **to come to the point** venire al sodo; **to get the point** capire l'antifona; **to make a point of** dar importanza a; insistere di; **to stretch a point** fare un'eccezione, fare uno strappo alla regola; **to the point** a proposito ‖ *tr* (*e.g., a weapon*) puntare; (*to sharpen*) aguzzare; (*to dot*) punteggiare; (*to give force to*) dare enfasi a; (*with mortar*) rinzaffare ‖ *intr* puntare; **to point at** puntare il dito a; **to point to** mostrare a dito

point'blank' *adj* & *adv* a bruciapelo

pointed ['pɔɪntɪd] *adj* appuntito; personale, diretto, acuto

pointer ['pɔɪntər] *s* (*rod*) bacchetta; indice *m*, indicatore *m*; cane *m* da punta, pointer *m*; (coll) direttiva

poise [pɔɪz] *s* equilibrio, stabilità *f*; dignità *f* ‖ *tr* equilibrare ‖ *intr* equilibrarsi, stare in equilibrio

poison ['pɔɪzən] *s* veleno ‖ *tr* avvelenare

poi'son i'vy *s* edera del Canada, tossicodendro

poisonous ['pɔɪzənəs] *adj* velenoso

poke [pok] *s* spinta, urto; (*with elbow*) gomitata; (slang) polentone *m* ‖ *tr* (*to prod*) spingere, urtare; (*the head*) sporgere; (*the fire*) attizzare; **to poke fun at** burlarsi di; **to poke one's nose into** ficcare il naso in ‖ *intr* (*to jab*) urtare; (*to thrust oneself*) ficcarsi; (*to pry*) ficcare il naso; **to poke around** gironzolare; **to poke out** spuntare, protrudere

poker ['pokər] *s* (*game*) poker *m;* (*bar*) attizzatoio

pok'er face' *s* faccia impassibile

pok·y ['poki] *adj* (**-ier; -iest**) (coll) lento; (coll) meschino, modesto ‖ (**-ies**) *s* (slang) gattabuia

Poland ['polənd] *s* la Polonia

po'lar bear' ['polər] *s* orso bianco

polarize ['polə,raɪz] *tr* polarizzare

pole [pol] *s* palo; (*long rod*) pertica; (*of wagon*) timone *m;* (*for jumping*) asta; (astr, biol, elec, geog, math) polo ‖ *tr* (*a boat*) spingere con un palo ‖ *intr* spingere una barca con un palo ‖ **Pole** *s* polacco

pole'cat' *s* puzzola

pole' lamp' *s* lampada a stelo

pole'star' *s* stella polare

pole' vault' *s* salto coll'asta

police [pə'lis] *s* polizia ‖ *tr* vigilare, proteggere; (mil) pulire

police'man *s* (**-men**) agente *m* di polizia, vigile urbano

police' state' *s* governo poliziesco

police' sta'tion *s* commissariato di polizia

poli·cy ['palɪsi] *s* (**-cies**) politica; (ins) polizza

polio ['polɪ,o] *s* (coll) polio *f*

polish ['palɪʃ] *s* lustro, lucentezza; (*for shoes or furniture*) cera; (fig) raffinatezza, eleganza ‖ *tr* pulire; (*e.g., a stone*) levigare; **to polish off** (slang) finire; **to polish up** (slang) migliorare ‖ *intr* pulirsi; diventar lucido ‖ **Polish** ['polɪʃ] *adj* & *s* polacco

polisher ['palɪʃər] *s* lucidatore *m;* (mach) lucidatrice *f*

polite [pə'laɪt] *adj* raffinato, cortese

politeness [pə'laɪtnɪs] *s* cortesia

politic ['palɪtɪk] *adj* prudente; (*expedient*) diplomatico

political [pə'lɪtɪkəl] *adj* politico

politician [,palɪ'tɪʃən] *s* politico; (pej) politicante *m*, politicastro

politics ['palɪtɪks] *ssg* or *spl* politica

poll [pol] *s* votazione; (*registering of votes*) scrutinio; lista elettorale; (*analysis of public opinion*) referendum *m*, sondaggio; (*head*) testa; **to go to the polls** andare alle urne; **to take a poll** fare un'inchiesta ‖ *tr* ricevere i voti di; contare i voti di; (*a tree*) potare; fare un'inchiesta di

pollen ['palən] *s* polline *m*

pollinate ['palɪ,net] *tr* fecondare col polline

poll'ing booth' ['polɪŋ] *s* cabina elettorale

polliwog ['palɪ,wag] *s* girino

poll' tax' *s* capitazione

pollute [pə'lut] *tr* insudiciare; (*to defile*) desecrare, profanare; (*e.g., the environment*) inquinare, contaminare

pollution [pə'luʃən] *s* inquinamento, contaminazione

poll' watch'er *s* rappresentante *m* di lista

polo ['polo] *s* polo

po'lo play'er *s* giocatore *m* di polo, polista *m*

po'lo shirt' *s* maglietta, polo

polygamist [pə'lɪgəmɪst] *s* poligamo

polygamous [pə'lɪgəməs] *adj* poligamo

polyglot ['palɪ,glat] *adj* & *s* poliglotto

polygon ['palɪ,gan] *s* poligono

polynomial [,palɪ'nomɪ·əl] *adj* polinomiale ‖ *s* polinomio

polyp ['palɪp] *s* (pathol, zool) polipo

polytheist ['palɪ,θi·ɪst] *s* politeista *mf*

polytheistic [,palɪθi'ɪstɪk] *adj* politeistico

pomade [pə'med] or [pə'mad] *s* pomata

pomegranate ['pam,grænɪt] *s* (*shrub*) melograno; (*fruit*) melagrana

pom·mel ['pʌməl] or ['paməl] *s* (*of sword*) pomello; (*of saddle*) arcione *m* ‖ *v* (*pret* & *pp* **-meled** or **-melled;** *ger* **-meling** or **-melling**) *tr* prendere a pugni

pomp [pamp] *s* pompa

pompadour ['pampə,dor] or ['pampə,dur] *s* acconciatura a ciuffo

pompous ['pampəs] *adj* pomposo

pon·cho ['pantʃo] *s* (**-chos**) poncho

pond [pand] *s* stagno

ponder ['pandər] *tr* & *intr* ponderare; **to ponder over** pensare sopra

ponderous ['pandərəs] *adj* ponderoso

poniard ['panjərd] *s* pugnale *m*

pontiff ['pantɪf] *s* pontefice *m*

pontifical [pan'tɪfɪkəl] *adj* pontificale

pontoon [pan'tun] *s* (*boat*) chiatta, pontone *m;* (aer) galleggiante *m*

po·ny ['poni] *s* (**-nies**) pony *m;* (*glass and drink*) bicchierino; (*for cheating*) (slang) bigino

poodle ['pudəl] *s* barbone *m*, cane *m* barbone

pool [pul] *s* (*pond*) stagno; (*puddle*) pozza; (*for swimming*) piscina; (*game*) biliardo; (com) cartello, consorzio; (com) fondo comune ‖ *tr* mettere in un fondo comune ‖ *intr* formare un cartello or un consorzio

pool'room' *s* sala da biliardo

pool' ta'ble *s* tavolo da biliardo

poop [pup] *s* poppa; (deck) casseretto

poor [pur] *adj* povero; (*inferior*) scadente ‖ **the poor** *spl* i poveri

poor' box' *s* cassetta per l'elemosina

poor'house' *s* asilo dei poveri

poorly ['purli] *adv* male

pop [pap] *s* scoppio; (*soda*) gazzosa ‖ *v* (*pret* & *pp* **popped;** *ger* **popping**) *tr* far scoppiare; **to pop the question** (coll) fare la domanda di matrimonio ‖ *intr* esplodere con fragore; **to pop in** fare una capatina; entrare all'improvviso

pop'corn' *s* pop-corn *m*

pope [pop] *s* papa *m*

popeyed ['pap,aɪd] *adj* con gli occhi sporgenti; con gli occhi fuori dalle orbite

pop'gun' *s* fucile *m* ad aria compressa

poplar ['paplər] *s* pioppo

pop·py ['papi] *s* (**-pies**) papavero

pop'py·cock' *s* (coll) scemenza

popsicle ['pɑpsɪkəl] *s* (trademark) gelato da passeggio
populace ['pɑpjəlɪs] *s* gente *f*, popolino
popular ['pɑpjələr] *adj* popolare
popularize ['pɑpjələ ˌraɪz] *tr* divulgare, volgarizzare
populate ['pɑpjə ˌlet] *tr* popolare
population [ˌpɑpjə'leʃən] *s* popolazione
populous ['pɑpjələs] *adj* popoloso
porcelain ['pɔrsəlɪn] or ['pɔrslɪn] *s* porcellana
porch [portʃ] *s* portico
porcupine ['pɔrkjə'paɪn] *s* (*Hystrix cristata*) istrice *m* & *f*, porcospino; (*Erethizon dorsatum*) ursone *m*, porcospino americano
pore [por] *s* poro ‖ *intr*—to pore over studiare minutamente
pork [pork] *s* carne *f* di maiale
pork′ butch′er shop′ *s* salumeria
pork′chop′ *s* cotoletta di maiale
porous ['porəs] *adj* poroso
po′rous plas′ter *s* cataplasma *m*
porphy·ry ['pɔrfɪri] *s* (-ries) porfido
porpoise ['pɔrpəs] *s* focena; (*dolphin*) delfino
porridge ['pɑrɪdʒ] or ['pɔrɪdʒ] *s* pappa, farinata
port [port] *adj* portuario ‖ *s* (*harbor; wine*) porto; (naut) babordo, sinistra; (*opening in side of ship*) portello; (*round opening*) ˏ(naut) oblò *m*
portable ['portəbəl] *adj* portabile
portal ['portəl] *s* portale *m*
portend [por'tɛnd] *tr* presagire
portent ['portɛnt] *s* presagio
portentous [por'tɛntəs] *adj* sinistro, funesto, premonitore; (*amazing*) portentoso
porter ['portər] *s* (*doorman*) portiere *m*; (*man who carries luggage*) facchino; (*of a sleeper*) conduttore *m*; (*in a store*) inserviente *mf*; (*beverage*) birra scura e amara
portfoli·o [port'foli ˌo] *s* (-os) cartella; (*office; holdings*) portafoglio
port′hole′ *s* (*opening in side of ship*) portello; (*round opening*) (naut) oblò *m*
porti·co ['portɪ ˌko] *s* (-cos or -coes) portico
portion ['porʃən] *s* porzione; (*dowry*) dote *f* ‖ *tr*—to portion out dividere, ripartire
port·ly ['portli] *adj* (-lier; -liest) obeso, corpulento
port′ of call′ *s* scalo
portrait ['portret] or ['portrɪt] *s* ritratto
portray [por'tre] *tr* ritrarre
portrayal [por'tre·əl] *s* delineazione; ritratto
Portugal ['portʃəgəl] *s* il Portogallo
Portu·guese ['portʃə ˌgiz] *adj* portoghese ‖ *s* (-guese) portoghese *mf*
pose [poz] *s* posa ‖ *tr* (*a question*) avanzare; (*a model*) mettere in posa ‖ *intr* posare; **to pose as** posare a, atteggiarsi a
posh [pɑʃ] *adj* (coll) di lusso
position [pə'zɪʃən] *s* posizione; rango;

impiego, posto; **to be in a position to** essere in grado di
positive ['pɑzɪtɪv] *adj* positivo ‖ *s* positivo; (phot) positiva
possess [pə'zɛs] *tr* possedere
possession [pə'zeʃən] *s* possedimento; (*of mental faculties*) possesso; **possessions** (*wealth*) beni *mpl*
possessive [pə'zɛsɪv] *adj* possessivo; (*e.g., mother*) opprimente, soffocante
possible ['pɑsɪbəl] *adj* possibile
possum ['pɑsəm] *s* opossum *m*; **to play possum** (coll) fare il morto
post [post] *s* (*mail*) posta; (*pole*) palo; (*in horse racing*) linea di partenza; posizione, rango; (*job*) posto; (mil) presidio ‖ *tr* mettere in una lista; impostare; tenere al corrente; **post no bills** divieto d'affissione
postage ['postɪdʒ] *s* affrancatura
post′age me′ter *s* affrancatrice *f*
post′age stamp′ *s* francobollo
postal ['postəl] *adj* postale
post′al card′ *s* cartolina postale
pos′tal per′mit *s* abbonamento postale
post′al sav′ings bank′ *s* cassa di risparmio postale
post′al scale′ *s* pesalettere *m*
post′ card′ *s* cartolina illustrata; cartolina postale
post′date′ *tr* postdatare
poster ['postər] *s* cartellone *m*, manifesto pubblicitario
posterity [pɑs'tɛrɪti] *s* posterità *f*
postern ['postərn] *adj* posteriore ‖ *s* postierla
post′ exchange′ *s* spaccio militare
post′haste′ *adv* al più presto possibile
posthumous ['pɑstʃuməs] *adj* postumo
post′man *s* (-men) portalettere *m*
post′mark′ *s* bollo, timbro postale ‖ *tr* bollare, timbrare
post′mas′ter *s* ricevitore *m* postale
post′master gen′eral *s* (**postmasters general**) ministro delle poste
post-mortem ['post'mɔrtəm] *adj* postumo ‖ *s* autopsia
post′ of′fice *s* ufficio postale
post′-office box′ *s* casella postale
postpaid ['post ˌped] *adj* franco di porto
postpone [post'pon] *tr* differire, posporre
postscript ['post ˌscrɪpt] *s* poscritto
postulant ['postʃələnt] *s* postulatore *m*, postulante *mf*
posture ['pɑstʃər] *s* portamento; posa ‖ *intr* posare
post′war′ *adj* del dopoguerra
po·sy ['pozi] *s* (-sies) fiore *m*; (*nosegay*) mazzolino di fiori
pot [pɑt] *s* pentola, pignatta; pitale *m*, orinale *m*; (*in gambling*) (coll) piatto; **to go to pot** andare a gambe all'aria
potash ['pɑt ˌæʃ] *s* potassa
potassium [pə'tæsɪ·əm] *s* potassio
pota·to [pə'teto] *s* (-toes) patata
pota′to om′elet *s* omelette *f* con patate
potbellied ['pɑt ˌbɛlɪd] *adj* panciuto
poten·cy ['potənsi] *s* (-cies) potenza
potent ['potənt] *adj* potente

potentate ['potən‚tet] *s* potentato
potential [pə'tenʃəl] *adj* & *s* potenziale *m*
pot'hold'er *s* patta, presa
pot'hook' *s* uncino
potion ['poʃən] *s* pozione
pot'luck' *s*—**to take potluck** mangiare quello che passa il convento
pot' shot' *s* colpo sparato a casaccio
potter ['potər] *s* vasaio
pot'ter's clay' *s* argilla per stoviglie
pot'ter's field' *s* cimitero dei poveri
potter·y ['potəri] *s* (-ies) vasellame *m;* fabbrica di vasellame; ceramica
pouch [pautʃ] *s* sacchetto, borsa; *(of kangaroo)* borsa
poultice ['poltɪs] *s* cataplasma *m*
poultry ['poltri] *s* pollame *m*
poul'try·man *s* (-men) pollivendolo
pounce [pauns] *intr*—**to pounce on** balzare su
pound ['paund] *s* libbra; lira sterlina; *(for stray animals)* recinto ‖ *tr* battere, picchiare; tempestare di colpi; *(to crush)* polverizzare ‖ *intr* battere
pound' cake' *s* dolce *m* fatto con una libbra di burro, una di zucchero ed una di farina
pound' ster'ling *s* lira sterlina
pour [por] *tr* versare; *(e.g., tea)* servire; *(wine)* mescere; *(stones upon an enemy)* far piovere ‖ *intr* fluire; *(to rain)* diluviare; **to pour in** affluire; **to pour out** uscire in massa
pout [paut] *s* broncio ‖ *intr* tenere il broncio
poverty ['povərti] *s* povertà *f*
POW ['pi'o'dʌbl‚ju] *s* (letterword) **(prisoner of war)** prigioniero di guerra
powder ['paudər] *s* polvere *f; (for the face)* cipria; (med) polverina ‖ *tr* incipriare; *(to sprinkle with powder)* spolverizzare
pow'dered sug'ar *s* zucchero in polvere
pow'der puff' *s* piumino
pow'der room' *s* toletta
powdery ['paudəri] *adj* polveroso; fragile; *(snow)* farinoso
power ['pau·ər] *s* *(ability, authority)* potere *m;* forza, energia; *(nation)* potenza; (math, phys) potenza; **in power** al potere; **the powers that be** i potenti ‖ *tr* azionare
pow'er·boat' *s* barca a motore
pow'er brake' *s* (aut) servofreno
pow'er com'pany *s* compagnia di elettricità
pow'er drive' *s* picchiata
powerful ['pau·ərfəl] *adj* poderoso
pow'er·house' *s* centrale elettrica
powerless ['pau·ərlɪs] *adj* impotente
pow'er line' *s* elettrodotto
pow'er mow'er *s* motofalciatrice *f*
pow'er of attor'ney *s* procura legale
pow'er plant' *s* stazione *f* generatrice; (aut) gruppo motore
pow'er steer'ing *s* servosterzo
pow'er tool' *s* apparecchiatura a motore
pow'er vac'uum *s* vuoto di potere
practical ['præktɪkəl] *adj* pratico

prac'tical joke' *s* scherzo da prete
practically ['præktɪkəli] *adv* (in a practical manner; virtually, really) praticamente; più o meno, quasi
practice ['præktɪs] *s* pratica; *(of a profession)* esercizio; *(e.g., of a doctor)* clientela; *(process of doing something)* prassi *f; (habitual performance)* abitudine *f* ‖ *tr* praticare, esercitare ‖ *intr* esercitarsi, praticare; *(to be active in a profession)* esercitare; **to practice as** esercitare la professione di
practitioner [præk'tɪʃənər] *s* professionista *mf*
Prague [prɑg] or [preg] *s* Praga
prairie ['preri] *s* prateria
prai'rie dog' *s* cinomio
prai'rie wolf' *s* coyote *m*
praise [prez] *s* lode *f,* elogio ‖ *tr* lodare, elogiare; **to praise to the skies** levare alle stelle
praise'wor'thy *adj* lodevole
pram [præm] *s* (coll) carrozzella
prance [præns] or [prɑns] *s* caracollo ‖ *intr* caracollare; *(to caper)* ballonzolare
prank [præŋk] *s* burla, tiro
prate [pret] *intr* cianciare
prattle ['prætəl] *s* ciancia, chiacchierio ‖ *intr* cianciare, parlare a vanvera
pray [pre] *tr* & *intr* pregare
prayer [prer] *s* preghiera
prayer' book' *s* libro di preghiere
preach [pritʃ] *tr* & *intr* predicare
preacher ['pritʃər] *s* predicatore *m*
preamble ['pri‚æmbəl] *s* preambolo
precarious [prɪ'kɛrɪ·əs] *adj* precario
precaution [prɪ'kɔʃən] *s* precauzione
precede [prɪ'sid] *tr* & *intr* precedere
precedent ['presɪdənt] *s* precedente *m*
precept ['prisept] *s* precetto
precinct ['prisɪŋkt] *s* distretto; circoscrizione elettorale; **precincts** dintorni *mpl*
precious ['preʃəs] *adj* prezioso ‖ *adv*— **precious little** (coll) molto poco
precipice ['presɪpɪs] *s* precipizio
precipitate [prɪ'sɪpɪ‚tet] *adj* precipitoso ‖ *s* precipitato ‖ *tr* & *intr* precipitare
precipitous [prɪ'sɪpɪtəs] *adj* precipitoso, a precipizio
precise [prɪ'sais] *adj* preciso
precision [prɪ'sɪʒən] *s* precisione
preclude [prɪ'klud] *tr* precludere; escludere
precocious [prɪ'koʃəs] *adj* precoce
predatory ['predə‚tori] *adj* da preda, predatore
predicament [prɪ'dɪkəmənt] *s* situazione critica or imbarazzante
predict [prɪ'dɪkt] *tr* predire
prediction [prɪ'dɪkʃən] *s* predizione
predispose [‚pridɪs'poz] *tr* predisporre
predominant [prɪ'dɑmɪnənt] *adj* predominante
preeminent [prɪ'ɛmɪnənt] *adj* preminente
preempt [prɪ'ɛmpt] *tr* occupare or acquistare in precedenza
preen [prin] *tr* *(feathers, fur)* lisciarsi;

to preen oneself agghindarsi, attillarsi

prefabricate [pri'fæbri ,ket] *tr* prefabbricare

preface ['prefis] *s* prefazione || *tr* prefazionare; essere la prefazione di

pre·fer [pri'fʌr] *v* (*pret & pp* -**ferred**; *ger* -**ferring**) *tr* preferire; (*to advance*) promuovere; (*law*) presentare, avanzare

preferable ['prefərəbəl] *adj* preferibile

preference ['prefərəns] *s* preferenza

preferred' stock' *s* azioni *fpl* privilegiate

prefix ['prifiks] *s* prefisso || *tr* prefiggere

pregnan·cy ['pregnənsi] *s* (-**cies**) gravidanza

pregnant ['pregnənt] *adj* incinta, gravida; (fig) gravido

prehistoric [,prihis'tarik] or [,prihis-'tɔrik] *adj* preistorico

prejudice ['predʒədis] *s* pregiudizio; preconcetto; **without prejudice** senza detrimento || *tr* (*to harm*) pregiudicare; predisporre; **to prejudice against** prevenire contro

prejudicial ['predʒə'dɪʃəl] *adj* pregiudizievole

prelate ['prelit] *s* prelato

preliminar·y [pri'limi ,neri] *adj* preliminare || *s* (-**ies**) preliminare *m*

prelude ['preljud] or ['prilud] *s* preludio || *tr* preludere a || *intr* preludere

premeditate [pri'medi ,tet] *tr* premeditare

premier [pri'mir] or ['primi·ər] *s* primo ministro, presidente *m* del consiglio

premiere [prə'mjer or [pri'mir] *s* prima; prima attrice

premise ['premis] *s* premessa; **on the premises** nella proprietà, sul luogo; **premises** proprietà *f*

premium ['primi·əm] *s* premio; **at a premium** in gran richiesta; a prezzo altissimo

premonition [,primə'niʃən] *s* presentimento; indizio

preoccupation [pri ,akjə'peʃən] *s* preoccupazione

preoccu·py [pri'akjə ,pai] *v* (*pret & pp* -**pied**) *tr* preoccupare; (*to occupy beforehand*) occupare prima

prepaid [pri'ped] *adj* pagato in anticipo; franco di porto

preparation [,prepə'reʃən] *s* preparazione; (*for a trip*) preparativo; (pharm) preparato

preparatory [pri'pærə ,tori] *adj* preparatorio

prepare [pri'per] *tr* preparare || *intr* prepararsi

preparedness [pri'peridnəs] or [pri-'perdnis] *s* preparazione; preparazione militare

pre·pay [pri'pe] *v* (*pret & pp* -**paid**) *tr* pagare anticipatamente

preponderant [pri'pandərənt] *adj* preponderante

preposition [,prepə'ziʃən] *s* preposizione

prepossessing [,pripə'zesiŋ] *adj* simpatico, attraente, piacevole

preposterous [pri'pastərəs] *adj* assurdo, ridicolo

prep' school' [prep] *s* (coll) scuola preparatoria

prerecorded [,priri'kɔrdid] *adj* (rad & telv) a registrazione differita

prerequisite [pri'rekwizit] *s* requisito

prerogative [pri'ragətiv] *s* prerogativa

presage ['presidʒ] *s* presagio || [pri-'sedʒ] *tr* presagire

Presbyterian [,prezbi'tiri·ən] *adj & s* presbiteriano; Presbiteriano

prescribe [pri'skraib] *tr & intr* prescrivere

prescription [pri'skripʃən] *s* prescrizione; (pharm) ricetta

presence ['prezəns] *s* presenza; **in the presence of** alla presenza di

present ['prezənt] *adj* presente || *s* presente *m*, regalo || [pri'zent] *tr* presentare; **present arms!** presentat'arm!; **to present s.o. with s.th** regalare qlco a qlcu

presentable [pri'zentəbəl] *adj* presentabile

presentation [,prezən'teʃən] or [,prizən'teʃən] *s* presentazione; (theat) rappresentazione

presenta'tion cop'y *s* copia d'omaggio

presentiment [pri'zentimənt] *s* presentimento

presently ['prezəntli] *adv* fra poco; attualmente

preserve [pri'zʌrv] *s* (*for hunting*) riserva; **preserves** conserva, marmellata || *tr* preservare; conservare

preserved' fruit' *s* frutta in conserva

preside [pri'zaid] *intr* presiedere; **to preside over** presiedere, presiedere a

presiden·cy ['prezidənsi] *s* (-**cies**) presidenza

president ['prezidənt] *s* presidente *m*; (*of a university*) rettore *m*

press [pres] *s* pressione; (*crowd*) folla; (*closet*) armadio; (mach) pressa; (typ) stampa; **to go to press** andare in macchina || *tr* (*to push*) spingere, premere; (*to squeeze*) spremere; (*to embrace*) abbracciare; forzare; costringere; urgere, sollecitare; (*to iron*) stirare || *intr* premere; avanzare

press' a'gent *s* agente pubblicitario

press' con'ference *s* conferenza stampa

pressing ['presiŋ] *adj* pressante, urgente || *s* (*of records*) incisione

press' release' *s* comunicato stampa

pressure ['preʃər] *s* pressione; tensione; urgenza || *tr* pressare, incalzare con insistenza

pres'sure cook'er ['kukər] *s* pentola a pressione

pressurize ['preʃə ,raiz] *tr* pressurizzare

prestige [pres'tiʒ] or ['prestidʒ] *s* prestigio

prestigious [pre'stidʒi·əs] or [pre-'stidʒəs] *adj* onorato, stimato

presumably [pri'zuməbli] or [pri'zjuməbli] *adv* presumibilmente

presume [pri'zum] or [pri'zjum] *tr* presumere; **to presume to** prendersi

la libertà di || *intr* assumere; **to presume on** or **upon** abusare di
presumption [prɪ'zʌmpʃən] *s* presunzione; supposizione
presumptuous [prɪ'zʌmptʃu·əs] *adj* presuntuoso
presuppose [ˌprisə'poz] *tr* presupporre
pretend [prɪ'tɛnd] *tr* fingere, fare finta di || *intr* fingere; **to pretend to** (*e.g., the throne*) pretendere a
pretender [prɪ'tɛndər] *s* pretendente *mf;* impostore *m*
pretense [prɪ'tɛns] or ['pritɛns] *s* pretesa; finzione; **under false pretenses** allegando ragioni false; **under pretense of** sotto l'apparenza di
pretentious [prɪ'tɛnʃəs] *adj* pretenzioso
preterit ['prɛtərɪt] *adj* passato, preterito || *s* passato remoto, preterito
pretext ['pritɛkst] *s* pretesto
pretonic [pri'tɑnɪk] *adj* pretonico
pret·ty ['prɪti] *adj* (**-tier; -tiest**) grazioso, carino; (*e.g., sum of money*) (coll) bello || *adv* abbastanza; molto; **sitting pretty** (slang) ben messo
prevail [prɪ'vel] *intr* prevalere; **to prevail on** or **upon** persuadere
prevailing [prɪ'velɪŋ] *adj* prevalente
prevalent ['prɛvələnt] *adj* comune
prevaricate [prɪ'værɪˌket] *intr* mentire
prevent [prɪ'vɛnt] *tr* impedire; **to prevent from** + *ger* impedire (with *dat*) di + *inf* or che + *subj*
prevention [prɪ'vɛnʃən] *s* prevenzione
preventive [prɪ'vɛntɪv] *adj* preventivo || *s* rimedio preventivo
preview ['pri ˌvju] *s* indizio; (*private showing*) (mov) anteprima; (*showing of brief scenes for advertising*) (mov) scene *fpl* di prossima programmazione
previous ['privɪ·əs] *adj* previo, precedente || *adv* precedentemente; **previous to** prima di
prewar ['pri ˌwɔr] *adj* anteguerra
prey [pre] *s* preda; **to be prey to** essere preda di || *intr* predare; **to prey on** or **upon** predare, sfruttare; preoccupare
price [praɪs] *s* prezzo; **at any price** a qualunque costo || *tr* chiedere il prezzo di; fissare il prezzo di
price' control' *s* calmiere *m*
price' cut'ting *s* riduzione di prezzo
price' fix'ing *s* regolamento dei prezzi
price' freez'ing *s* congelamento dei prezzi
priceless ['praɪslɪs] *adj* inestimabile; (coll) molto divertente
price' list' *s* listino prezzi
price' tag' *s* cartellino del prezzo
price' war' *s* guerra dei prezzi
prick [prɪk] *s* punta; puntura; **to kick against the pricks** tirare calci al vento || *tr* bucare, forare; pungere; (*to goad*) spronare; (*the ears*) ergere; (*said, e.g., of the conscience*) rimordere (with *dat*)
prick·ly ['prɪkli] *adj* (**-lier; -liest**) spinoso, pungente
prick'ly heat' *s* sudamina
prick'ly pear' *s* ficodindia *m*
pride [praɪd] *s* orgoglio; arroganza; **the**

pride of il fiore di || *tr*—**to pride oneself on** or **upon** inorgoglirsi di
priest [prist] *s* prete *m*, sacerdote *m*
priesthood ['prist·hud] *s* sacerdozio
priest·ly ['pristli] *adj* (**-lier; -liest**) sacerdotale
prig [prɪg] *s* pedante *mf*, moralista *mf*
prim [prɪm] *adj* (**primmer; primmest**) formale, corretto, compito
prima·ry ['praɪˌmɛri] or ['praɪmɛri] *adj* primario || *s* (**-ries**) elezione preferenziale; (elec) bobina primaria; (elec) primario
prime [praɪm] *adj* primo; originale; di prima qualità || *s* (*earliest part*) inizio; (*best period*) fiore *m;* (*choicest part*) fior fiore *m;* (math) numero primo; (*mark*) (math) primo || *tr* preparare; (*a pump*) adescare; (*a firearm*) innescare; (*a canvas*) mesticare; (*a wall*) dare la prima mano a; (*to supply with information*) istruire
prime' min'ister *s* primo ministro
primer ['prɪmər] *s* sillabario, abbecedario || ['praɪmər] *s* innesco, detonatore *m*
primeval [praɪ'mivəl] *adj* primordiale
primitive ['prɪmɪtɪv] *adj* primitivo
primp [prɪmp] *tr* agghindare || *intr* agghindarsi
prim'rose' *s* primula
prim'rose path' *s* sentiero dei piaceri
prince [prɪns] *s* principe *m;* **to live like a prince** vivere da principe
prince' roy'al *s* principe ereditario
princess ['prɪnsɪs] *s* principessa
principal ['prɪnsɪpəl] *adj* principale || *s* (*chief*) padrone *m*, principale *m;* (*of school*) direttore *m*, preside *m;* (*actor*) primo attore; (com) capitale *m;* (law) mandante *mf*
principle ['prɪnsɪpəl] *s* principio; **on principle** per principio
print [prɪnt] *s* stampa; (*cloth*) tessuto stampato; (*printed matter*) stampato; (*newsprint*) giornale *m;* (*mark made by one's thumb*) impronta; (phot) positiva; **in print** stampato; disponibile; **out of print** esaurito || *tr* stampare, tirare; (*to write in print*) scrivere in stampatello; (*in the memory*) imprimere
print'ed cir'cuit *s* circuito stampato
print'ed mat'ter *s* stampati *mpl*
printer ['prɪntər] *s* stampatore *m;* (*of computer*) tabulatrice *f*
print'er's dev'il *s* apprendista *m* tipografo
print'er's ink' *s* inchiostro da stampa
printing ['prɪntɪŋ] *s* stampa; stampato; tiratura, edizione; (*writing in printed letters*) stampatello
prior ['praɪ·ər] *adj* anteriore, precedente || *s* priore *m* || *adv* prima; **prior to** prima di
priori·ty [praɪ'ɑrɪti] or [praɪ'ɔrɪti] *s* (**-ties**) priorità *f*
prism ['prɪzəm] *s* prisma *m*
prison ['prɪzən] *s* prigione, carcere *m*
prisoner ['prɪzənər] or ['prɪznər] *s* prigioniero
pris'on van' *s* furgone *m* cellulare

pris·sy ['prɪsi] *adj* (**-sier; -siest**) smanceroso, smorfioso

priva·cy ['praɪvəsi] *s* (**-cies**) ritiro; segreto; **to have no privacy** non esser mai lasciato in pace

private ['praɪvɪt] *adj* privato, personale || *s* soldato semplice; **in private** privatamente; **privates** pudende *fpl*

pri'vate eye' *s* poliziotto privato

pri'vate first' class' *s* soldato scelto

pri'vate hos'pital *s* clinica

priv'ate view'ing *s* (mov) anteprima; (painting) vernice *f*

privet ['prɪvɪt] *s* ligustro

privilege ['prɪvɪlɪdʒ] *s* privilegio

priv·y ['prɪvi] *adj* privato; **privy to** segretamente a conoscenza di || *s* (**-ies**) latrina

prize [praɪz] *s* premio; (nav) preda || *tr* valutare, stimare

prize' fight' *s* incontro di pugilato

prize' fight'er *s* pugile *m*, pugilista *m*

prize' ring' *s* ring *m*, quadrato

pro [pro] *s* (**pros**) pro; voto favorevole; argomento favorevole; (coll) professionista *m;* **the pros and the cons** il pro e il contro

probabili·ty [ˌprabə'bɪlɪti] *s* (**-ties**) probabilità *f*

probable ['prabəbəl] *adj* probabile

probate ['probet] *s* omologazione di un testamento; copia autentica di un testamento || *tr* (*a will*) omologare

probation [pro'beʃən] *s* prova; periodo di prova; (law) condizionale *f*, libertà vigilata; (educ) provvedimento disciplinare

probe [prob] *s* inchiesta; (surg) sonda || *tr* indagare; sondare

problem ['prabləm] *s* problema *m*

procedure [pro'sidʒər] *s* procedura

proceed ['prosid] *s*—**proceeds** provento || [pro'sid] *intr* procedere

proceeding [pro'sidɪŋ] *s* procedimento; **proceedings** atti *mpl;* (law) procedimenti *mpl*

process ['proses] *s* processo; **in the process of time** in processo di tempo || *tr* trattare

procession [pro'sɛʃən] *s* processione

proc'ess serv'er *s* ufficiale giudiziario

proclaim [pro'klem] *tr* proclamare

proclitic [pro'klɪtɪk] *adj* proclitico || *s* parola proclitica

procrastinate [pro'kræstɪˌnet] *tr & intr* procrastinare

procure [pro'kjʊr] *tr* ottenere || *intr* ruffianeggiare

prod [prad] *s* pungolo, stimolo || *v* (*pret & pp* **prodded;** *ger* **prodding**) *tr* stimulare, pungolare, incitare

prodigal ['pradɪgəl] *adj & s* prodigo

prodigious [pro'dɪdʒəs] *adj* prodigioso

prodi·gy ['pradɪdʒi] *s* (**-gies**) prodigio

produce ['prodjus] or ['produs] *s* produzione; prodotti *mpl* agricoli || [pro'djus] or [pro'dus] *tr* produrre; (theat) presentare

producer [pro'djusər] or [pro'dusər] *s* produttore *m;* (*of a play*) impresario; (mov) produttore *m*

product ['pradəkt] *s* prodotto

production [pro'dʌkʃən] *s* produzione

profane [pro'fen] *adj* profano; blasfemo || *tr* profanare

profani·ty [pro'fænɪti] *s* (**-ties**) bestemmia

profess [pro'fɛs] *tr & intr* professare

profession [pro'fɛʃən] *s* professione

professor [pro'fɛsər] *s* professore *m*

proffer ['prafər] *s* offerta || *tr* offrire

proficient [pro'fɪʃənt] *adj* abile, competente

profile ['profaɪl] *s* profilo || *tr* profilare

profit ['prafɪt] *s* profitto; vantaggio; **at a profit** con guadagno || *tr* avvantaggiare; giovare (with *dat*) || *intr* avvantaggiarsi; **to profit by** approfittare di

profitable ['prafɪtəbəl] *adj* vantaggioso

prof'it and loss' *s* profitti *mpl* e perdite *fpl*

profiteer [ˌprafɪ'tɪr] *s* profittatore *m* || *intr* fare il profittatore

prof'it shar'ing *s* cointeressenza, partecipazione agli utili

prof'it tak'ing *s* realizzo

profligate ['praflɪgɪt] *adj & s* dissoluto; prodigo

pro for'ma in'voice ['fɔrmə] *s* fattura fittizia

profound [pro'faund] *adj* profondo

profuse [prə'fjus] *adj* profuso, abbondante; **profuse in** prodigo di

proge·ny ['pradʒəni] *s* (**-nies**) prole *f*

progno·sis [prag'nosɪs] *s* (**-ses** [siz]) prognosi *f*

prognostic [prag'nastɪk] *s* pronostico

prognosticate [prag'nastɪˌket] *tr* pronosticare

pro·gram ['progræm] *s* programma *m* || *v* (*pret & pp* **-gramed** or **-grammed;** *ger* **-graming** or **-gramming**) *tr* programmare

programmer ['progræmər] *s* pannellista *mf*, programmatore *m*

progress ['pragres] *s* progresso; **in progress** in corso; **to make progress** fare dei progressi || [prə'gres] *intr* progredire; migliorare

progressive [prə'gresiv] *adj* (*proceeding step by step*) progressivo; progressista || *s* progressista *mf*

prohibit [pro'hɪbɪt] *tr* proibire

prohibition [ˌpro·ə'bɪʃən] *s* proibizione; (hist) proibizionismo

project ['pradʒɛkt] *s* progetto || [prə'dʒɛkt] *tr* (*to propose, plan*) progettare; (*light, a shadow, etc.*) proiettare || *intr* sporgere, protrudere

projectile [prə'dʒɛktɪl] *s* proiettile *m*

projection [prə'dʒɛkʃən] *s* proiezione, sporgenza

projector [prə'dʒɛktər] *s* (*apparatus*) proiettore *m;* (*person*) progettista *mf*

proletarian [ˌprolɪ'tɛrɪ·ən] *adj & s* proletario

proliferate [prə'lɪfəˌret] *intr* proliferare

prolific [prə'lɪfɪk] *adj* prolifico

prolix ['prolɪks] or [pro'lɪks] *adj* prolisso

prologue ['prolɔg] or ['prolag] *s* prologo

prolong [pro'lɔŋ] or [pro'laŋ] *tr* prolungare
promenade [ˌprɑmɪ'ned] or [ˌprɑmɪ'nɑd] *s* passeggiata; ballo di gala ‖ *tr & intr* passeggiare
promenade' deck' *s* ponte *m* passeggiata
prominent ['prɑmɪnənt] *adj* prominente
promise ['prɑmɪs] *s* promessa ‖ *tr & intr* promettere
prom'ising young' man' *s* giovane *m* di belle speranze
prom'issory note' ['prɑmɪˌsori] *s* cambiale *f*, pagherò *m*
promonto·ry ['prɑmənˌtori] *s* (**-ries**) promontorio
promote [prə'mot] *tr* promuovere
promotion [prə'moʃən] *s* promozione
prompt [prɑmpt] *adj* pronto ‖ *tr* incitare, istigare; (theat) suggerire
prompter ['prɑmptər] *s* suggeritore *m*, rammentatore *m*
prompt'er's box' *s* buca del suggeritore
promptness ['prɑmptnɪs] *s* prontezza
promulgate ['prɑməlˌget] or [pro'mʌlget] *tr* promulgare
prone [pron] *adj* prono
prong [prɔŋ] or [praŋ] *s* punta; (*of fork*) dente *m*; (*of pitchfork*) rebbio
pronoun ['pronaun] *s* pronome *m*
pronounce [prə'nauns] *tr* pronunziare
pronounced [prə'naunst] *adj* pronunziato, marcato
pronouncement [prə'naunsmənt] *s* dichiarazione ufficiale
pronunciamen·to [prəˌnʌnsɪ·ə'mɛnto] *s* (**-tos**) pronunciamento
pronunciation [prəˌnʌnsɪ'eʃən] or [prəˌnʌnʃɪ'eʃən] *s* pronunzia
proof [pruf] *adj*—**proof against** a prova di ‖ *s* prova; (*of alcoholic beverages*) gradazione; (typ) bozza
proof'read'er *s* correttore *m* di bozze
prop [prɑp] *s* sostegno, puntello; (*pole*) palo; **props** attrezzi *mpl* teatrali ‖ *v* (*pret & pp* **propped;** *ger* **propping**) *tr* sostenere, puntellare
propaganda [ˌprɑpə'gændə] *s* propaganda
propagate ['prɑpəˌget] *tr* propagare ‖ *intr* propagarsi
pro·pel [prə'pɛl] *v* (*pret & pp* **-pelled;** *ger* **-pelling**) *tr* propulsare, spingere, azionare; (*a rocket*) propellere
propeller [prə'pɛlər] *s* elica
propensi·ty [prə'pɛnsɪti] *s* (**-ties**) propensione
proper ['prɑpər] *adj* appropriato, corretto; decente, convenevole; (gram) proprio, **proper to** proprio di
proper·ty ['prɑpərti] *s* (**-ties**) proprietà *f*; **properties** attrezzi *mpl* teatrali
prop'erty man' *s* trovarobe *m*, attrezzista *m*
prop'erty own'er *s* proprietario fondiario
prophe·cy ['prɑfɪsi] *s* (**-cies**) profezia
prophe·sy ['prɑfɪˌsaɪ] *v* (*pret & pp* **-sied**) *tr* profetizzare
prophet ['prɑfɪt] *s* profeta *m*
prophetess ['prɑfɪtɪs] *s* profetessa

prophylactic [ˌprofɪ'læktɪk] *adj* profilattico ‖ *s* rimedio profilattico; preservativo
propitiate [prə'pɪʃɪˌet] *tr* propiziare
propitious [prə'pɪʃəs] *adj* propizio
prop'jet' *s* turboelica *m*
proportion [prə'porʃən] *s* proporzione; **in proportion as** a misura che; **in proportion to** in proporzione a; **out of proportion** sproporzionato ‖ *tr* proporzionare, commensurare
proportionate [prə'porʃənɪt] *adj* proporzionato
proposal [prə'pozəl] *s* proposta; proposta di matrimonio
propose [prə'poz] *tr* proporre ‖ *intr* fare una proposta di matrimonio; **to propose to** chiedere la mano di; proporsi di + *inf*
proposition [ˌprɑpə'zɪʃən] *s* proposizione, proposta; (coll) progetto ‖ *tr* fare delle proposte indecenti a
propound [prə'paund] *tr* proporre
proprietary [prə'praɪ·əˌtɛri] *adj* padronale; esclusivo, patentato
proprietor [prə'praɪ·ətər] *s* proprietario
proprietress [prə'praɪ·ətrɪs] *s* proprietaria
proprie·ty [prə'praɪ·əti] *s* (**-ties**) correttezza, decoro; **proprieties** convenzioni *fpl* sociali
propulsion [prə'pʌlʃən] *s* propulsione
prorate [pro'ret] *tr* rateizzare
prosaic [pro'ze·ɪk] *adj* prosaico
proscribe [pro'skraɪb] *tr* proscrivere
prose [proz] *adj* prosaico ‖ *s* prosa
prosecute ['prɑsɪˌkjut] *tr* eseguire; (law) processare
prosecutor ['prɑsɪˌkjutər] *s* esecutore *m*; (law) querelante *m*; (law) avvocato d'accusa
proselyte ['prɑsɪˌlaɪt] *s* proselito
prose' writ'er *s* prosatore *m*
prosody ['prɑsədi] *s* prosodia, metrica
prospect ['prɑspɛkt] *s* vista; prospettiva; candidato; probabile cliente *m*; **prospects** speranze *fpl* ‖ *intr* fare il cercatore; **to prospect for** fare il cercatore di
prospectus [prə'spɛktəs] *s* prospetto
prosper ['prɑspər] *tr & intr* prosperare
prosperi·ty [prɑs'pɛriti] *s* (**-ties**) prosperità *f*, benessere *m*
prosperous ['prɑspərəs] *adj* prospero
prostitute ['prɑstɪˌtjut] or ['prɑstɪˌtut] *s* prostituta ‖ *tr* prostituire
prostrate ['prɑstret] *adj* prostrato ‖ *tr* prostrare
prostration [prɑs'treʃən] *s* prostrazione
protagonist [pro'tægənɪst] *s* protagonista *mf*
protect [prə'tɛkt] *tr* proteggere
protection [prə'tɛkʃən] *s* protezione
protégé ['protəˌʒe] *s* protetto, favorito
protégée ['protəˌʒe] *s* protetta, favorita
protein ['proti·ɪn] or ['protin] *s* proteina
pro tempore [pro'tɛmpəˌri] *adj* provvisorio, interinale
protest ['protɛst] *s* protesta; (com)

protesto ‖ [proˈtɛst] *tr* & *intr* protestare

Protestant [ˈprɑtɪstənt] *adj* & *s* protestante *mf*

protester [prəˈtɛstər] *s* protestatario

prothonotar·y [proˈθɑnəˌteri] *s* (**-ies**) (law) cancelliere *m* capo

protocol [ˈprotəˌkɑl] *s* protocollo

protoplasm [ˈprotəˌplæzəm] *s* protoplasma *m*

prototype [ˈprotəˌtaɪp] *s* prototipo

proto·zoon [ˌprotəˈzoˌɑn] *s* (**-zoa** [ˈzo·ə]) protozoo

protract [proˈtrækt] *tr* prolungare

protractor [proˈtræktər] *s* rapportatore *m*

protrude [proˈtrud] *intr* sporgere

proud [praʊd] *adj* fiero; arrogante; maestoso, magnifico

proud′ flesh′ *s* tessuto di granulazione

prove [pruv] *v* (*pret* **proved;** *pp* **proved** or **proven**) *tr* provare; (*ore*) analizzare; (law) omologare; (math) fare la prova di ‖ *intr* risultare

proverb [ˈprɑvərb] *s* proverbio

provide [prəˈvaɪd] *tr* provvedere ‖ *intr*—**to provide for** provvedere a; (*to be ready for*) prepararsi a

provided [prəˈvaɪdɪd] *conj* a condizione che, purché; **provided that** a condizione che, purché

providence [ˈprɑvɪdəns] *s* provvidenza

providential [ˌprɑvɪˈdɛnʃəl] *adj* provvidenziale

providing [prəˈvaɪdɪŋ] *conj* var of **provided**

province [ˈprɑvɪns] *s* provincia; (fig) pertinenza, competenza

provision [prəˈvɪʃən] *s* provvedimento; clausola; **provisions** viveri *mpl*

provi·so [prəˈvaɪzo] *s* (**-sos** or **-soes**) stipulazione, clausola

provoke [prəˈvok] *tr* provocare; contrariare, irritare

prow [praʊ] *s* prora, prua

prowess [ˈprau·ɪs] *s* prodezza; maestria

prowl [praʊl] *intr* andare in cerca di preda; vagabondare

prowler [ˈpraʊlər] *s* vagabondo; ladro

proximity [prakˈsɪmɪti] *s* prossimità *f*

prox·y [ˈpraksi] *s* (**-ies**) procura; (*person*) procuratore *m*

prude [prud] *s* pudibondo

prudence [ˈprudəns] *s* prudenza

prudent [ˈprudənt] *adj* prudente

pruder·y [ˈprudəri] *s* (**-ies**) attitudine pudibonda

prudish [ˈprudɪʃ] *adj* pudibondo

prune [prun] *s* prugna secca ‖ *tr* potare

pry [praɪ] *v* (*pret* & *pp* **pried**) *tr*—**to pry open** forzare con una leva; **to pry s.th out of s.o.** strappare qlco à çlcu ‖ *intr* intromettersi, cacciarsi

psalm [sɑm] *s* salmo

pseudo [ˈsudo] or [ˈsjudo] *adj* falso, finto, sedicente

pseudonym [ˈsudənɪm] or [ˈsjudənɪm] *s* pseudonimo

psychiatrist [saɪˈkaɪ·ətrɪst] *s* psichiatra *mf*

psychiatry [saɪˈkaɪ·ətri] *s* psichiatria

psychic [ˈsaɪkɪk] *adj* psichico ‖ *s* medium *mf*

psychoanalysis [ˌsaɪko·əˈnælɪsɪs] *s* psicanalisi *f*

psychoanalyze [ˌsaɪkoˈænəˌlaɪz] *tr* psicanalizzare

psychologic(al) [ˌsaɪkoˈlɑdʒɪk(əl)] *adj* psicologico

psychologist [saɪˈkɑlədʒɪst] *s* psicologo

psycholo·gy [saɪˈkɑlədʒi] *s* (**-gies**) psicologia

psychopath [ˈsaɪkəˌpæθ] *s* psicopatico

psycho·sis [saɪˈkosɪs] *s* (**-ses** [siz]) psicosi *f*

psychotic [saɪˈkɑtɪk] *adj* psicotico

pub [pʌb] *s* (Brit) taverna, bar *m*

puberty [ˈpjubərti] *s* pubertà *f*

public [ˈpʌblɪk] *adj* & *s* pubblico

pub′lic-address′ sys′tem *s* sistema *m* d'amplificazione per discorsi in pubblico

publication [ˌpʌblɪˈkeʃən] *s* pubblicazione

pub′lic convey′ance *s* veicolo di servizi pubblici

publicity [pʌbˈlɪsɪti] *s* pubblicità *f*

publicize [ˈpʌblɪˌsaɪz] *tr* pubblicare, divulgare

pub′lic li′brary *s* biblioteca comunale

pub′lic-opin′ion poll′ *s* sondaggio d'opinioni

pub′lic pros′ecutor *s* pubblico ministero

pub′lic school′ *s* (U.S.A.) scuola dell'obbligo; (Brit) scuola privata, collegio

pub′lic serv′ant *s* funzionario pubblico

pub′lic speak′ing *s* oratoria

pub′lic spir′it *s* civismo

pub′lic toi′let *s* gabinetto pubblico

pub′lic util′ity *s* impresa di servizio pubblico; **public utilities** azioni emesse da imprese di servizi pubblici

publish [ˈpʌblɪʃ] *tr* pubblicare

publisher [ˈpʌblɪʃər] *s* editore *m;* (journ) direttore *m* responsabile

pub′lishing house′ *s* casa editrice

pucker [ˈpʌkər] *s* grinza ‖ *tr* raggrinzire ‖ *intr* raggrinzirsi

pudding [ˈpʊdɪŋ] *s* budino, torta

puddle [ˈpʌdəl] *s* pozza, pozzanghera ‖ *intr* diguazzare

pudg·y [ˈpʌdʒi] *adj* (**-ier; -iest**) grassoccio

puerile [ˈpju·ərɪl] *adj* puerile

Puerto Rican [ˈpwɛrtoˈrikən] *adj* & *s* portoricano

puff [pʌf] *s* soffio, sbuffo; (*e.g., of cigar*) boccata; (*pad*) piumino; (*exaggerated praise*) pistolotto; (culin) bigné *m* ‖ *tr* sbuffare; gonfiare; adulare ‖ *intr* soffiare, sbuffare; (*to breathe heavily*) ansimare, ansare; gonfiarsi; tirare boccate

puff′ paste′ *s* pasta sfoglia

pugilist [ˈpjudʒɪlɪst] *s* pugile *m*

pug-nosed [ˈpʌgˌnozd] *adj* camuso

puke [pjuk] *tr* & *intr* (slang) vomitare

pull [pʊl] *s* tiro; (*act of drawing in*) tirata; (*handle*) tirante *m;* (slang) influenza, appoggi *mpl* ‖ *tr* tirare; (*a tooth*) cavare; (*a muscle*) strappare;

(*a punch*) (coll) limitare la forza di; **to pull apart** fare a pezzi; **to pull down** abbattere; degradare; **to pull on** (*e.g., one's pants*) infilarsi; **to pull oneself together** ricomporsi; **to pull s.o.'s leg** beffarsi di qlcu || *intr* tirare; **to pull apart** andare a pezzi; **to pull at** tirare; **to pull away** andarsene; **to pull for** (coll) fare il tifo per; **to pull in** (*said of a train*) arrivare, entrare in stazione; **to pull out** (*said of a train*) partire; **to pull through** guarire, riuscire a cavarsela; **to pull up to** avanzare fino a

pullet ['pʊlɪt] *s* pollastra

pulley ['pʊli] *s* puleggia, carrucola

pulp [pʌlp] *s* polpa; (*for making paper*) pasta

pulpit ['pʊlpɪt] *s* pulpito

pulsate ['pʌlset] *intr* pulsare

pulsation [pʌl'seʃən] *s* pulsazione

pulse [pʌls] *s* polso; **to feel** or **take the pulse of** tastare il polso a

pulverize ['pʌlvə‚raɪz] *tr* polverizzare

pum'ice stone' *s* ['pʌmɪs] *s* pomice *f*, pietra pomice

pum·mel ['pʌməl] *v* (*pret & pp* -meled or -melled; *ger* -meling or -melling) *tr* prendere a pugni

pump [pʌmp] *s* pompa; (*slipper*) scarpina || *tr* pompare; (coll) cavare un segreto a; **to pump up** pompare

pumpkin ['pʌmpkɪn] or ['pʊŋkɪn] *s* zucca

pump-priming ['pʌmp‚praɪmɪŋ] *s* stimolo governativo per sostentare l'economia

pun [pʌn] *s* gioco di parole || *v* (*pret & pp* **punned**; *ger* **punning**) *intr* fare giochi di parole

punch [pʌntʃ] *s* pugno; (*tool*) punteruolo, punzone *m;* (*drink*) ponce *m;* (coll) forza || *tr* dare un pugno a; (*metal*) punzonare; (*a ticket*) perforare || **Punch** *s* Pulcinella *m;* **pleased as Punch** soddisfattissimo

punch' bowl' *s* vaso per il ponce

punch' card' *s* scheda perforata

punch' clock' *s* orologio di controllo

punch'-drunk' *adj* stordito

punched' tape' *s* nastro perforato

punch'ing bag' *s* sacco

punch' line' *s* perfinire *m*, motto finale

punctilious [pʌŋk'tɪlɪ·əs] *adj* cerimonioso, pignolo

punctual ['pʌŋktʃʊ·əl] *adj* puntuale

punctuate ['pʌŋktʃʊ‚et] *tr* punteggiare

punctuation [‚pʌŋktʃʊ'eʃən] *s* punteggiatura

punctua'tion mark' *s* segno d'interpunzione

puncture ['pʌŋktʃər] *s* puntura; (*hole*) bucatura; **to have a puncture** avere una gomma a terra || *tr* bucare, perforare || *intr* essere bucato

punct'ure-proof' *adj* antiperforante

pundit ['pʌndɪt] *s* esperto, autorità *f*

pungent ['pʌndʒənt] *adj* pungente

punish ['pʌnɪʃ] *tr* punire

punishment ['pʌnɪʃmənt] *s* punizione, castigo

punk [pʌŋk] *adj* (slang) di pessima

qualità || *s* esca; (*decayed wood*) legno marcio; (slang) malandrino

punster ['pʌnstər] *s* freddurista *mf*

punt [pʌnt] *s* (football) calcio dato al pallone prima che tocchi il terreno

pu·ny ['pjuni] *adj* (**-nier; -niest**) insignificante, meschino; (*weak*) debole

pup [pʌp] *s* cucciolo

pupil ['pjupəl] *s* allievo, scolaro; (anat) pupilla

puppet ['pʌpɪt] *s* marionetta, burattino; (fig) fantoccio

pup'pet gov'ernment *s* governo fantoccio or pupazzo

pup'pet show' *s* spettacolo di marionette

pup·py ['pʌpi] *s* (**-pies**) cucciolo

pup'py love' *s* amore *m* giovanile

purchase ['pʌrtʃəs] *s* compra, acquisto; (*grip*) presa, leva || *tr* comprare, acquistare

pur'chasing pow'er *s* potere *m* d'acquisto

pure [pjʊr] *adj* puro

purgative ['pʌrgətɪv] *adj* purgativo || *s* purga

purge [pʌrdʒ] *s* purga || *tr* purgare

puri·fy ['pjʊrɪ‚faɪ] *v* (*pret & pp* -fied) *tr* purificare || *intr* purificarsi

puritan ['pjʊrɪtən] *adj & s* puritano || **Puritan** *adj & s* puritano

purity ['pjʊrɪti] *s* purezza

purloin [pər'lɔɪn] *tr & intr* rubare

purple ['pʌrpəl] *adj* purpureo || *s* porpora

purport ['pʌrport] *s* senso, significato || [pər'port] *tr* significare; **to purport to** + *inf* pretendere di + *inf*

purpose ['pʌrpəs] *s* scopo, fine *m;* **on purpose** apposta; **to good purpose** con buoni risultati; **to no purpose** inutilmente; **to serve one's purpose** fare al caso proprio

purposely ['pʌrpəsli] *adv* a bella posta, apposta

purr [pʌr] *s* ronfare *m* || *intr* fare le fusa

purse [pʌrs] *s* borsa; (*woman's handbag*) borsetta; (*for men*) borsetto || *tr* (*one's lips*) arricciare

purser ['pʌrsər] *s* commissario di bordo

purse' snatch'er ['snætʃər] *s* borsaiolo

purse' strings' *spl* cordini *mpl* della borsa; **to hold the purse strings** controllare le spese

purslane ['pʌrslen] or ['pʌrslɪn] *s* (bot) porcellana

pursue [pər'su] or [pər'sju] *tr* perseguire; (*to harass*) perseguitare; (*a career*) proseguire

pursuit [pər'sut] or [pər'sjut] *s* inseguimento, caccia; occupazione, esercizio

pursuit' plane' *s* caccia *m*

purvey [pər've] *tr* provvedere, fornire

pus [pʌs] *s* pus *m*

push [pʊʃ] *s* spinta; (*advance*) avanzata; (coll) impulso, energia || *tr* premere, spingere; (*a product*) promuovere la vendita di; dare impulso a; (*narcotics*) (slang) spacciare; **to**

push around (coll) dare spintoni a; (fig) fare pressione su; **to push back** ricacciare ‖ *intr* spingere; **to push ahead** avanzarsi a spintoni, avanzarsi; **to push on** avanzare

push' but'ton *s* pulsante *m*, bottone *m*

push'-button con'trol *s* controllo a pulsanti

push'cart' *s* carretto a mano

pusher ['puʃər] *adj* spingente; (aer) propulsivo ‖ *s* spingitore *m*; (aer) aeroplano a elica propulsiva; (slang) spacciatore *m* di stupefacenti

pushing ['puʃɪŋ] *adj* aggressivo, intraprendente

puss [pus] *s* micio

puss' in the cor'ner *s* gioco dei quattro cantoni

puss·y ['pusi] *s* (-ies) micio

puss'y wil'low *s* salice americano a gattini

pustule ['pʌstʃul] *s* pustola

put [put] *v* (*pret & pp* **put;** *ger* **putting**) *tr* mettere; (*to estimate*) stimare; (*a question*) rivolgere; (*to throw*) lanciare; imporre; **to put across** (slang) far accettare; **to put aside, away** or **by** mettere da parte; **to put down** annotare; (*to suppress*) reprimere; **to put off** differire; evadere; **to put on** (*clothes*) mettersi; (*a brake*) azionare; (*to assume*) fingere; (*airs*) darsi; **to put out** spegnere; imbarazzare; incomodare; deludere; annoiare, irritare; (*of a game*) espellere; **to put it over on** s.o. fargliela a qlcu; **to put off** rinviare; **to put over** mandare ad effetto; **to put to flight** mettere in fuga; **to put to shame** svergognare; **to put through** portare a

termine; **to put up** offrire; mettere in conserva; alloggiare; costruire; (*money*) contribuire; (coll) incitare ‖ *intr* dirigersi; **to put to sea** mettersi in mare; **to put up** prendere alloggio; **to put up with** tollerare

put'-out' *adj* sconcertato, seccato

putrid ['pjutrɪd] *adj* putrido

Putsch [putʃ] *s* tentativo di sollevazione, sollevazione

putter ['pʌtər] *intr* occuparsi di inezie; **to putter about** andare avanti e indietro

put·ty ['pʌti] *s* (-ties) stucco, mastice *m* ‖ *v* (*pret & pp* -**tied**) *tr* stuccare

put'ty knife' *s* spatola

put'-up' *adj* (coll) complottato

puzzle ['pʌzəl] *s* enigma *m;* (*toy*) indovinello ‖ *tr* rendere perplesso, confondere; **to puzzle out** decifrare ‖ *intr* essere perplesso

puzzler ['pʌzlər] *s* enigma *m*

puzzling ['pʌzlɪŋ] *adj* enigmatico

pyg·my ['pɪgmi] *s* (-mies) pigmeo

pylon *s* pilone *m*

pyramid ['pɪrəmɪd] *s* piramide *f* ‖ *tr* (*e.g., costs*) aumentare gradualmente; (*one's money*) aumentare giocando in margine

pyre [paɪr] *s* pira

Pyrenees ['pɪrɪ ˌniz] *spl* Pirenei *mpl*

pyrites [paɪ'raɪtiz] or ['paɪraɪts] *s* pirite *f*

pyrotechnics [ˌpaɪrə'tɛknɪks] *spl* pirotecnica

python ['paɪθan] or ['paɪθən] *s* pitone *m*

pythoness ['paɪθənɪs] *s* pitonessa

pyx [pɪks] *s* (eccl) pisside *f*

Q

Q, q [kju] *s* diciassettesima lettera dell'alfabeto inglese

quack [kwæk] *adj* falso ‖ *s* medicastro; ciarlatano; qua qua *m* ‖ *intr* (*said of a duck*) fare qua qua

quacker·y ['kwækəri] *s* (-ies) ciarlataneria

quadrangle ['kwad ˌræŋgəl] *s* quadrangolo

quadrant ['kwadrənt] *s* quadrante *m*

quadruped ['kwadru ˌpɛd] *adj & s* quadrupede *m*

quadruple ['kwadrupəl] or [kwa'drupəl] *adj* quadruplo; (*alliance*) quadruplice ‖ *s* quadruplo ‖ *tr* quadruplicare ‖ *intr* quadruplicarsi

quaff [kwaf] or [kwæf] *s* lungo sorso ‖ *tr & intr* bere a lunghi sorsi

quail [kwel] *s* quaglia ‖ *intr* sgomentarsi

quaint [kwent] *adj* strano, strambo, originale; all'antica ma bello

quake [kwek] *s* terremoto ‖ *intr* tremare, sussultare

Quaker ['kwekər] *adj & s* quacchero, quacquero

Quak'er meet'ing *s* riunione di quaccheri; (coll) riunione in cui si parla poco

quali·fy ['kwalɪ ˌfaɪ] *v* (*pret & pp* -**fied**) *tr* qualificare; (*for a profession*) abilitare ‖ *intr* qualificarsi; abilitarsi

quali·ty ['kwalɪti] *s* (-ties) qualità *f;* (*of a sound*) timbro

qualm [kwam] *s* scrupolo di coscienza; preoccupazione; nausea

quanda·ry ['kwandəri] *s* (-ries) incertezza, perplessità *f*

quanti·ty ['kwantɪti] *s* (-ties) quantità *f*

quan·tum ['kwantəm] *adj* quantistico ‖ *s* (-ta [tə]) quanto

quarantine ['kwarən ˌtin] or ['kworən ˌtin] *s* quarantena ‖ *tr* mettere in quarantena

quar·rel ['kwarəl] or ['kworəl] *s* litigio, diverbio; **to have no quarrel with** non essere in disaccordo con; **to pick a quarrel with** venire a diverbio con ‖ *v* (*pret & pp* -**reled** or -**relled;** *ger* -**reling** or -**relling**) *intr* litigare

quarrelsome ['kwɑrəlsəm] or ['kwɔrəl-səm] *adj* litigioso, rissoso

quar·ry ['kwɑri] or ['kwɔri] *s* (-ries) cava; (*game*) selvaggina, cacciagione || *v* (*pret & pp* -ried) *tr* cavare

quart [kwɔrt] *s* quarto di gallone

quarter ['kwɔrtər] *adj* quarto || *s* quarto; moneta di un quarto di dollaro; (*three months*) trimestre *m;* (*of town*) quartiere *m;* **a quarter after one** l'una e un quarto; **a quarter of an hour** un quarto d'ora; **a quarter to one** l'una meno un quarto; **at close quarters** corpo a corpo; **quarters** quartiere *m* || *tr* squartare; (*soldiers*) accasermare

quar'ter-deck' *s* cassero

quar'ter-hour' *s* quarto d'ora; **on the quarter-hour** ogni quindici minuti allo scoccare del quarto d'ora

quarter·ly ['kwɔrtərli] *adj* trimestrale || *s* (-lies) pubblicazione trimestrale || *adv* trimestralmente

quar'ter·mas'ter *s* (mil) intendente *m* militare; (nav) secondo capo

quartet [kwɔr'tɛt] *s* quartetto

quartz [kwɔrts] *s* quarzo

quasar ['kwesɑr] *s* (astr) radiostella

quash [kwɑʃ] *tr* sopprimere; annullare

quaver ['kwevər] *s* tremito; (mus) tremolo; (mus) croma || *intr* tremare

quay [ki] *s* molo

queen [kwin] *s* regina; (*in cards*) donna; (chess) regina

queen' bee' *s* ape regina; (fig) basilessa

queen' dow'ager *s* regina vedova

queen·ly ['kwinli] *adj* (-lier; -liest) da regina; regio

queen' moth'er *s* regina madre

queen' post' *s* monaco

queen's' Eng'lish *s* inglese corretto

queer [kwɪr] *adj* strano, curioso; poco bene, indisposto; falso; (slang) omosessuale || *s* (slang) finocchio || *tr* rovinare, mettere in pericolo

quell [kwɛl] *tr* soffocare, domare; (*pain*) calmare

quench [kwɛntʃ] *tr* (*fire, thirst*) spegnere, estinguere; (*rebellion*) soffocare; (elec) ammortizzare

que·ry ['kwɪri] *s* (-ries) domanda; punto interrogativo; dubbio || *v* (*pret & pp* -ried) *tr* interrogare; (typ) apporre punto interrogativo a

quest [kwɛst] *s* ricerca; **in quest of** in cerca di

question ['kwɛstʃən] *s* domanda; problema *m*, quesito; (*matter*) questione; **beyond question** senza dubbio; **out of the question** impossibile; **this is beside the question** questo non c'entra; **to ask a question** fare una domanda; **to be a question of** trattarsi di; **to call in** or **into question** mettere in dubbio; **without question** senza dubbio || *tr* interrogare; mettere in dubbio; (pol) interpellare

questionable ['kwɛstʃənəbəl] *adj* discutibile

ques'tion mark' *s* punto interrogativo

questionnaire [ˌkwɛstʃən'ɛr] *s* questionario

queue [kju] *s* (*of hair*) codino; (*of people*) coda || *intr* fare la coda

quibble ['kwɪbəl] *intr* sottilizzare

quick [kwɪk] *adj* pronto, sollecito; sbrigativo; veloce, rapido; vivo || *s*— **the quick and the dead** i vivi e i morti; **to cut to the quick** toccare nel vivo

quicken ['kwɪkən] *tr* sveltire; animare; ravvivare

quick'lime' *s* calce viva

quick' lunch' *s* tavola calda

quickly ['kwɪkli] *adv* svelto, alla svelta; presto

quick'sand' *s* sabbia mobile

quick'-set'ting *adj* a presa rapida

quick'sil'ver *s* argento vivo

quick'work' *s* (naut) opera viva

quiet ['kwaɪ·ət] *adj* quieto; silenzioso; (com) calmo; **to keep quiet** stare zitto || *s* quiete *f*, tranquillità *f*; pace *f*, calma || *tr* quietare; calmare || *intr*— **to quiet down** quietarsi, calmarsi

quill [kwɪl] *s* penna d'oca; (*basal part of feather*) calamo; (*e.g., of porcupine*) aculeo

quilt [kwɪlt] *s* trapunta, imbottita || *tr* trapuntare

quince [kwɪns] *s* cotogna; (*tree*) cotogno

quinine ['kwaɪnaɪn] *s* (*alkaloid*) chinina; (*salt of the alkaloid*) chinino

quinsy ['kwɪnzi] *s* angina

quintessence [kwɪn'tɛsəns] *s* quintessenza

quintet [kwɪn'tɛt] *s* quintetto

quintuplet [kwɪn'tjuplɛt] or [kwɪn'tuplɛt] *s* gemello nato da un parto quintuplice

quip [kwɪp] *s* frizzo, uscita || *v* (*pret & pp* quipped; *ger* quipping) *tr & intr* uscire a dire, dire come battuta

quire [kwaɪr] *s* ventiquattro fogli; (bb) quinterno

quirk [kwʌrk] *s* stranezza, manierismo; (*quibble*) cavillo; (*sudden turn*) mutamento improvviso

quit [kwɪt] *adj* libero; **to be quits** esser pari; **to call it quits** finirla, farla finita || *v* (*pret & pp* quit or quitted; *ger* quitting) *tr* abbandonare || *intr* andarsene; abbandonare l'impiego; smettere (di + *inf*)

quite [kwaɪt] *adv* completamente; molto, del tutto

quitter ['kwɪtər] *s* persona che abbandona facilmente

quiver ['kwɪvər] *s* fremito; (*to hold arrows*) faretra, turcasso || *intr* fremere, tremare

quixotic [kwɪks'ɑtɪk] *adj* donchisciottesco

quiz [kwɪz] *s* (quizzes) esame *m;* interrogatorio || *v* (*pret & pp* quizzed; *ger* quizzing) *tr* esaminare; interrogare

quiz' game' *s* quiz *m*

quiz' pro'gram *s* programma *m* di quiz

quiz' sec'tion *s* (educ) classe *f* a base di esercizi (e non di conferenze)

quizzical ['kwɪzɪkəl] *adj* strano, curioso; (*derisive*) canzonatore

quoin [kɔɪn] or [kwɔɪn] *s* cantone *m*,

píetra angolare; (*piece of wood*) zeppa; (typ) serraforme *m* ‖ *tr* fissare con serraforme

quoit [kwɔɪt] or [kɔɪt] *s* anello di corda o di metallo da lanciarsi come gioco; **quoits** *ssg* gioco consistente nel lancio di anelli su di un piolo

quondam ['kwɑndæm] *adj* quondam

quorum ['kworəm] *s* quorum *m*

quota ['kwotə] *s* (*share*) quota; (*of*

imports) contingentamento; (*of persons*) contingente *m*

quotation [kwo'teʃən] *s* (*from a book*) citazione; (*of prices*) quotazione

quota′tion mark′ *s* doppia virgola, virgoletta

quote [kwot] *s* citazione, richiamo ‖ *tr & intr* citare, richiamare; (com) quotare; **quote** cito

quotient ['kwoʃənt] *s* quoziente *m*

R

R, r [ɑr] *s* diciottesima lettera dell'alfabeto inglese

rabbet ['ræbɪt] *s* scanalatura, incastro ‖ *tr* scanalare, incastrare

rab·bi ['ræbaɪ] *s* (-bis) rabbino

rabbit ['ræbɪt] *s* coniglio

rab′bit ears′ *spl* (telv) doppia antenna a stilo

rabble ['ræbəl] *s* gentaglia, marmaglia

rab′ble-rous′er ['rauzər] *s* arruffapopoli *m*

rabies ['rebiz] or ['rebɪ‚iz] *s* rabbia

raccoon [ræ'kun] *s* procione *m*

race [res] *s* (*branch of human stock*) razza; (*contest in speed*) corsa; (*contest of any kind*) gara; (*channel*) canale *m* di adduzione ‖ *tr* far correre; gareggiare (in velocità) con; (*a motor*) imballare ‖ *intr* correre; fare le corse; (*said of a motor*) imballarsi; (naut) fare le regate

race′ horse′ *s* cavallo da corsa

race′ ri′ot *s* contestazione di razza

race′ track′ *s* pista

racial ['reʃəl] *adj* razziale

rac′ing car′ *s* automobile *f* da corsa

rack [ræk] *s* (*to hang clothes*) attaccapanni *m*; (*framework to hold fodder, baggage, guns, etc.*) rastrelliera; (mach) cremagliera; **to go to rack and ruin** andare a rotoli ‖ *tr* tormentare, torturare; **to rack off** (*wine*) travasare; **to rack one's brains** rompersi il capo, lambiccarsi il cervello

racket ['rækɪt] *s* racchetta; (*noise*) chiasso, gazzarra; (coll) racket *m*; **to raise a racket** fare gazzarra

racketeer [‚rækɪ'tɪr] *s* chi è nel racket; (*engaged in extortion*) ricattatore *m* ‖ *intr* essere nel racket; fare il ricattatore

rack′ rail′way *s* ferrovia a cremagliera

rac·y ['resi] *adj* (-ier; -iest) pungente, vigoroso; piccante

radar ['redar] *s* radar *m*

radiant ['redɪ·ənt] *adj* raggiante, radioso

radiate ['redɪ‚et] *tr* irradiare ‖ *intr* irradiarsi

radiation [‚redɪ'eʃən] *s* radiazione

radia′tion sick′ness *s* malattia causata da radiazione atomica

radiator ['redɪ‚etər] *s* radiatore *m*

ra′diator cap′ *s* tappo del radiatore

radical ['rædɪkəl] *adj* radicale ‖ *s*

radicale *mf;* (chem, math) radicale *m*

radi·o ['redɪ‚o] *s* (-os) radio *f;* radiogramma *m* ‖ *tr* radiotrasmettere

radioactive [‚redɪ·o'æktɪv] *adj* radioattivo

ra′dio am′ateur *s* radioamatore *m*

ra′dio announc′er *s* radioannunciatore *m*

ra′dio bea′con *s* radiofaro

ra′dio·broad′cast *s* radiodiffusione ‖ *tr* radiodiffondere

ra′dio com′pass *s* radiobussola

ra′dio-fre′quency *s* radiofrequenza

ra′dio lis′tener *s* radioascoltatore *m*

radiology [‚redɪ'alədʒi] *s* radiologia

ra′dio net′work *s* rete *f*

ra′dio news′caster *s* radiocronista *mf*

ra′dio·pho′to *s* (-tos) (coll) radiofoto *f*

ra′dio set′ *s* radioricevente *f*

ra′dio sta′tion *s* stazione radio

radish ['rædɪʃ] *s* ravanello

radium ['redɪ·əm] *s* radio

radi·us ['redɪ·əs] *s* (-i [‚aɪ] or -uses) (anat) radio; (fig, geom) raggio; **within a radius of** entro un raggio di

raffle ['ræfəl] *s* riffa ‖ *tr* sorteggiare

raft [ræft] or [rɑft] *s* zattera; (coll) mucchio

rafter ['ræftər] or ['rɑftər] *s* puntone *m*

rag [ræg] *s* straccio; **to chew the rag** (slang) chiacchierare

ragamuffin ['rægə‚mʌfɪn] *s* straccione *m*

rag′ doll′ *s* bambola di pezza

rage [redʒ] *s* rabbia; **to be all the rage** furoreggiare; **to fly into a rage** montare in bestia ‖ *intr* infuriare

ragged ['rægɪd] *adj* cencioso; (*torn*) stracciato; (*edge*) rozzo, scabroso

ragpicker ['ræg‚pɪkər] *s* cenciaiolo, straccivendolo

rag′weed′ *s* (bot) ambrosia

raid [red] *s* irruzione, razzia ‖ *tr* scorrere ‖ *intr* scorrazzare

rail [rel] *s* (*of fence*) stecca, traversa; (*fence*) stecconata; (*railing*) ringhiera; (rr) rotaia; **by rail** per ferrovia; **rails** titoli *mpl* ferroviari ‖ *intr* inveire; **to rail at** inveire contro

rail′car′ *s* automotrice *f*

rail′ fence′ *s* stecconata fatta di traverse piallate alla buona

rail'head' *s* fine *f* della linea ferroviaria
railing ['reliŋ] *s* ringhiera
rail'road' *adj* ferroviario || *s* ferrovia || *tr* trasportare in ferrovia; (*a bill*) far passare precipitosamente; (coll) imprigionare falsamente
rail'road cros'sing *s* passaggio a livello
rail'road'er *s* ferroviere *m*
rail'way' *s* ferrovia, strada ferrata
raiment ['remənt] *s* (lit) abbigliamento
rain [ren] *s* pioggia; **rain or shine** con qualunque tempo || *tr* fare piovere; (lit) piovere; **to rain cats and dogs** piovere a catinelle; **to rain out** far sospendere per via della pioggia || *intr* piovere
rainbow ['ren ‚bo] *s* arcobaleno
rain'coat' *s* impermeabile *m*
rain'fall' *s* acquazzone *m;* piovosità *f*
rain·y ['reni] *adj* (-ier; -iest) piovoso, piovano
rain'y day' *s* giorno piovoso; (fig) tempi *mpl* difficili
raise [rez] *s* aumento || *tr* levare, rialzare; (*children, animals*) allevare; (*to build*) tirare su; (*a question*) sollevare; (*the dead*) risollevare; (*to increase*) aumentare; (*money*) raccogliere; (*a siege*) togliere; (*at cards*) rilanciare; (*anchor*) salpare; (math) elevare
raisin ['rezən] *s* grano d'uva passa, grano d'uva secca; **raisins** uva passa, uva secca
rake [rek] *s* rastrello; (*person*) porcaccione *m*, libertino || *tr* rastrellare; **to rake in money** far soldoni
rake'-off' *s* (coll) compenso illecito, bustarella; (coll) sconto
rakish ['rekɪʃ] *adj* libertino; brioso, vivace; **to wear one's hat at a rakish angle** portare il cappello sulle ventitré
ral·ly ['ræli] *s* (-lies) riunione, comizio; adunata; ricupero || *v* (*pret & pp* -lied) *tr* riunire, chiamare a raccolta; rianimare || *intr* riunirsi; rianimarsi; (*said of stock prices*) rialzarsi; rimettersi in forze; **to rally to the side of** correre all'aiuto di
ram [ræm] *s* (*male sheep*) montone *m;* (mil) ariete *m;* (nav) sperone *m;* (mach) maglio del battipalo || *v* (*pret & pp* **rammed;** *ger* **ramming**) *tr* battere, sbattere contro; cacciare, conficcare; forzare; (nav) speronare || *intr*—**to ram into** sbattere contro
ramble ['ræmbəl] *s* girata || *intr* (*to wander around*) gironzolare; vagare; (*said of a vine*) crescere disordinatamente; (*said, e.g., of a river*) serpeggiare; (fig) scorrazzare, divagare
rami·fy ['ræmɪ ‚faɪ] *v* (*pret & pp* -fied) *tr* ramificare || *intr* ramificarsi
ram'jet en'gine *s* statoreattore *m*
ramp [ræmp] *s* rampa
rampage ['ræmpedʒ] *s* stato d'eccitazione; **to go on a rampage** infierire, comportarsi furiosamente
rampart ['ræmpɑrt] *s* baluardo, muraglione *m*

ram'rod' *s* (*for ramming*) (mil) bacchetta; (*for cleaning*) (mil) scovolo
ram'shack'le *adj* cadente, in rovina
ranch [rænt∫] *s* fattoria agricola
rancid ['rænsɪd] *adj* rancido
rancor ['ræŋkər] *s* rancore *m*
random ['rændəm] *adj* fortuito; **at random** alla rinfusa, a casaccio
range [rendʒ] *s* (*row*) fila; (*rank*) classe *f;* (*distance*) portata; campo di tiro a segno; raggio d'azione; (*scope*) gamma; (*for grazing*) pascolo; (*stove*) fornello, cucina economica; **within range of** alla portata di || *tr* allineare; ordinare; passare attraverso; mandare al pascolo || *intr* variare, fluttuare; estendersi; trovarsi; (mil) portare; **to range over** percorrere; (fig) trattare
range' find'er *s* telemetro
rank [ræŋk] *adj* esuberante; grossolano; denso, spesso; puzzolente; eccessivo; completo, assoluto || *s* rango, grado; (*row*) fila, schiera; **ranks** truppe *fpl*, ranghi *mpl* || *tr* arrangiare, allineare; classificare; avere rango superiore a || *intr* avere il massimo rango; **to rank high** avere un'alta posizione; **to rank low** avere una posizione bassa; **to rank with** essere allo stesso livello di
rank' and file' *s* truppa; massa
rankle ['ræŋkəl] *tr* irritare || *intr* inasprirsi
ransack ['rænsak] *tr* (*to search thoroughly*) frugare, rovistare; (*to pillage*) svaligiare, saccheggiare
ransom ['rænsəm] *s* taglia, riscatto || *tr* riscattare
rant [rænt] *intr* farneticare, parlare a vanvera
rap [ræp] *s* colpo, colpetto; **I don't care a rap** non m'importa un fico; **to take the rap** (slang) prendersi la colpa || *v* (*pret & pp* **rapped;** *ger* **rapping**) *tr* dare colpi a; battere; **to rap out** (*e.g., a command*) lanciare || *intr* dare colpi, bussare
rapacious [rə'peʃəs] *adj* rapace
rape [rep] *s* rapimento; (*of a woman*) stupro; (bot) ravizzone *m* || *tr* rapire; forzare, violentare
rapid ['ræpɪd] *adj* rapido || **rapids** *spl* rapide *fpl*
rap'id-fire' *adj* a tiro rapido
rapidity [rə'pɪdəti] *s* rapidità *f*
rapier ['repɪ-ər] *s* spada, stocco
rapt [ræpt] *adj* assorto; estatico
rapture ['ræpt∫ər] *s* rapimento, estasi *f*
rare [rɛr] *adj* raro; (*thinly distributed*) rado; (*gas*) rarefatto; (*meat*) al sangue; (*gem*) prezioso
rare'-earth' met'al *s* metallo delle terre rare
rare·fy ['rɛrɪ ‚faɪ] *v* (*pret & pp* -fied) *tr* rarefare || *intr* rarefarsi
rarely ['rɛrli] *adv* di rado, raramente
rascal ['ræskəl] *s* briccone *m*, birbante *m*
rash [ræ∫] *adj* temerario, precipitato || *s* eruzione; (fig) mucchio
rasp [ræsp] or [rɑsp] *s* raspa; rumore

m di raspa || *tr* raspare; irritare; dire con voce roca || *intr* fare rumore raspante

raspber·ry ['ræz,bɛri] or ['rɑz,bɛri] *s* (-ries) lampone *m;* (slang) pernacchia

rat [ræt] *s* ratto; (*to give fullness to hair*) posticcio; (slang) traditore *m;* **to smell a rat** (coll) subodorare un inganno

ratchet ['rætʃɪt] *s* nottolino

rate [ret] *s* (*of interest*) saggio, tasso; prezzo; costo; velocità *f;* (*degree of action*) ragione; tariffa; **at any rate** ad ogni modo; **at the rate of** in ragione di || *tr* valutare, classificare || *intr* essere considerato; essere classificato

rate' of exchange' *s* corso del cambio

rather ['ræðər] or ['rɑðər] *adv* piuttosto; a preferenza; per meglio dire; bensì; discretamente; **rather than** piuttosto di || *interj* e come!

rati·fy ['rætɪ,faɪ] *v* (*pret & pp* -fied) *tr* ratificare, sancire

rating ['retɪŋ] *s* classifica; (nav) grado; (com) valutazione

ra·tio ['reʃo] or ['reʃɪ,o] *s* (-tios) ragione, rapporto; proporzione

ration ['reʃən] or ['ræʃən] *s* razione || *tr* razionare

rational ['ræʃənəl] *adj* razionale

ra'tion book' *s* tessera di razionamento

rat' poi'son *s* veleno per i topi

rat' race' *s* (coll) corsa dei barberi

rattle ['rætəl] *s* (*sharp sounds*) fracasso; (*child's toy*) sonaglio; (*noise-making device*) raganella; (*in throat*) rantolo || *tr* scuotere; (*to confuse*) sconcertare; **to rattle off** dire rapidamente, snocciolare || *intr* risuonare; scuotersi; cianciare

rat'tle·snake' *s* serpente *m* a sonagli

rat'trap' *s* trappola per topi; (*hovel*) topaia; (*jam*) (fig) frangente *m*

raucous ['rɔkəs] *adj* rauco

ravage ['rævɪdʒ] *s* distruzione; **ravages** (*of time*) oltraggio || *tr* distruggere, disfare

rave [rev] *intr* farneticare, delirare; infuriare; andare in estasi; **to rave about** levare alle stelle

raven ['revən] *s* corvo

ravenous ['rævənəs] *adj* famelico

ravine [rə'vin] *s* canalone *m*, burrone *m*

ravish ['rævɪʃ] *tr* incantare, entusiasmare; rapire; (*a woman*) stuprare

raw [rɔ] *adj* crudo; (*e.g., silk*) grezzo; (*flesh*) vivo; inesperto

raw' deal' *s* trattamento brutale e ingiusto

raw'hide' *s* pelle greggia

raw' mate'rial *s* materia prima

ray [re] *s* raggio; (*fish*) razza

rayon ['re·ɑn] *s* raion *m*

raze [rez] *tr* radere al suolo

razor ['rezər] *s* rasoio

ra'zor blade' *s* lametta

ra'zor strop' *s* coramella

razz [ræz] *s* (slang) pernacchia || *tr* (slang) prendere in giro

reach [ritʃ] *s* portata; estensione; **out**

of reach (of) fuori della portata (di); oltre alle possibilità (di); fuori tiro (di); **within reach of** alla portata di || *tr* raggiungere; toccare; (*customers*) guadagnare || *intr* estendere la mano; **to reach for** cercare di raggiungere

react [rɪ'ækt] *intr* reagire

reaction [rɪ'ækʃən] *s* reazione

reactionar·y [rɪ'ækʃə,nɛri] *adj* reazionario || *s* (-ies) reazionario

reactor [rɪ'æktər] *s* reattore *m*

read [rid] *v* (*pret & pp* read [rɛd]) *tr* leggere; (*s.o.'s thoughts*) leggere in; **to read over** ripassare || *intr* leggere; saper leggere; essere concepito, e.g., **your cable reads thus** il vostro telegramma è concepito così; leggersi, e.g., **this books reads easily** questo libro si legge facilmente; **to read on** continuare a leggere

reader ['ridər] *s* lettore *m;* libro di lettura, sillabo

readily ['rɛdɪli] *adv* velocemente; facilmente; di buona voglia

reading ['ridɪŋ] *s* lettura; dizione

read'ing desk' *s* leggio

read'ing glass' *s* lente *f* d'ingrandimento; **reading glasses** occhiali *mpl* per la lettura

read'ing lamp' *s* lampada da scrittoio

read'ing room' *s* sala di lettura

read·y ['rɛdi] *adj* (-ier; -iest) pronto; disponibile; **to make ready** preparare; prepararsi || *v* (*pret & pp* -ied) *tr* preparare || *intr* prepararsi

read'y cash' *s* denaro contante

read'y-made cloth'ing *s* confezioni *fpl*

read'y-made suit' *s* vestito già fatto

reaffirm [,ri·ə'fʌrm] *tr* riaffermare

reagent [ri'edʒənt] *s* reagente *m*

real ['ri·əl] *adj* effettivo, reale

re'al estate' *s* beni *mpl* immobili, proprietà *f* immobiliare

re'al-estate' *adj* immobiliare, fondiario

realism ['ri·ə,lɪzəm] *s* realismo

realist ['ri·əlɪst] *s* realista *mf*

realistic [,ri·ə'lɪstɪk] *adj* realistico

reali·ty [ri'ælɪti] *s* (-ties) realtà *f*

realize ['ri·ə,laɪz] *tr* rendersi conto di; concretare; realizzare || *intr* convertire proprietà in contanti

realm [rɛlm] *s* regno

realtor ['ri·əl,tɔr] or ['ri·əltər] *s* (trademark) agente *m* d'immobili membro dell'associazione nazionale

realty ['ri·əlti] *s* proprietà *f* immobiliare

ream [rim] *s* risma; **reams** pagine *fpl* e pagine || *tr* alesare

reamer ['rimər] *s* (mach) alesatore *m;* (dentistry) fresa

reap [rip] *tr & intr* (*to cut*) mietere; (*to gather*) raccogliere

reaper ['ripər] *s* (*person*) mietitore *m;* (mach) mietitrice *f*

reappear [,ri·ə'pɪr] *intr* ricomparire, riapparire

reappearance [,ri·ə'pɪrəns] *s* riapparizione, ricomparsa

reapportionment [,ri·ə'pɔrʃənmənt] *s* ridistribuzione

rear [rɪr] *adj* posteriore, di dietro || *s*

retro, di dietro; posteriore *m;* (mil)
retroguardia || *tr* alzare, elevare;
allevare, educare || *intr* (*said of a
horse*) impennarsi
rear′ ad′miral *s* contrammiraglio
rear′ drive′ *s* trazione posteriore
rear′ end′ *s* retro, di dietro; (coll)
posteriore *m;* (aut) retrotreno
rearmament [ri'ɑrməmənt] *s* riarmo
rear′-view mir′ror *s* specchietto retrovisivo
rear′ win′dow *s* (aut) lunetta posteriore
reason ['rizən] *s* ragione; **by reason of**
per causa di; **to bring s.o. to reason**
indurre qlcu alla ragione; **to stand
to reason** esser logico || *tr & intr*
ragionare
reasonable ['rizənəbəl] *adj* ragionevole
reassessment [ˌri·ə'sesmənt] *s* rivalu-
tazione
reassure [ˌri·ə'ʃur] *tr* rassicurare, riassicurare
reawaken [ˌri·ə'wekən] *tr* risvegliare ||
intr risvegliarsi
rebate ['ribet] *or* [rɪ'bet] *s* ribasso ||
tr ribassare
rebel ['rɛbəl] *adj & s* ribelle *mf* ||
re•bel [rɪ'bɛl] *v* (*pret & pp* -belled;
ger -belling) *intr* ribellarsi
rebellion [rɪ'bɛljən] *s* ribellione
rebellious [rɪ'bɛljəs] *adj* ribelle
re•bind [ri'baɪnd] *v* (*pret & pp*- bound
['baʊnd]) *tr* rifasciare; (bb) rilegare
rebirth ['ribʌrθ] *or* [ri'bʌrθ] *s* rinascita
rebore [ri'bor] *tr* rialesare, rettificare
rebound ['rɪˌbaʊnd] *or* [ri'baʊnd] *s*
rimbalzo || [ri'baʊnd] *intr* rimbal-
zare
rebroad′casting sta′tion *s* stazione ripe-
titrice
rebuff [rɪ'bʌf] *s* rifiuto || *tr* respingere,
rifiutare
rebuild [ri'bɪld] *v* (*pret & pp* -built
['bɪlt]) *tr* ricostruire, riedificare
rebuke [rɪ'bjuk] *s* rabbuffo || *tr* rab-
buffare
re•but [rɪ'bʌt] *v* (*pret & pp* -butted;
ger -butting) *tr* confutare
rebuttal [rɪ'bʌtəl] *s* confutazione
recall [rɪ'kɔl] *or* ['rikəl] *s* richiamo;
revoca || [rɪ'kɔl] *tr* richiamare; ri-
cordare, ricordarsi di; richiamare
alla memoria
recant [rɪ'kænt] *tr* ritrattare || *intr*
ritrattarsi
re•cap ['riˌkæp] *or* [ri'kæp] *v* (*pret &
pp* -capped; *ger* -capping) *tr* ricapitolare, riepilogare; (*a tire*) rifare il
battistrada a
recapitulation [ˌrikəˌpɪtʃə'leʃən] *s* ri-
capitolazione, riepilogo
re•cast ['riˌkæst] *or* ['riˌkɑst] *s* rifu-
sione || [ri'kæst] *or* [ri'kɑst] *v* (*pret
& pp* -cast) *tr* rifondere
recede [rɪ'sid] *intr* ritirarsi, allontanarsi; recedere, retrocedere; (*said,
e.g., of chin*) sfuggire
receipt [rɪ'sit] *s* ricevimento; (*acknowledgment of payment*) ricevuta;
(*recipe*) ricetta; **receipts** incasso, in-
troito || *tr* quietanzare
receive [rɪ'siv] *tr* ricevere; (*stolen*

goods) ricettare; (*to have inflicted
upon one*) subire || *intr* ricevere
receiver [rɪ'sivər] *s* ricevitore *m;* ricet-
tatore *m;* (law) curatore *m* fallimentare; (telp) auricolare *m*
receiv′ing set′ *s* apparecchio radioricevente
receiv′ing tell′er *s* cassiere *m* incaricato
delle riscossioni
recent ['risənt] *adj* recente
recently ['risəntli] *adv* recentemente,
di recente
receptacle [rɪ'sɛptəkəl] *s* recipiente *m;*
(elec) presa
reception [rɪ'sɛpʃən] *s* accoglienza;
(*function*) ricevimento
recep′tion desk′ *s* ufficio informazioni,
bureau *m*
receptionist [rɪ'sɛpʃənɪst] *s* accoglitrice *f;* (*male*) usciere *m*
receptive [rɪ'sɛptɪv] *adj* ricettivo
recess [rɪ'sɛs] *or* ['risɛs] *s* intermezzo,
interludio; ora di ricreazione; (*in a
line*) rientranza; (*in a wall*) nicchia,
alcova; (fig) recesso || [rɪ'sɛs] *tr*
aggiornare, dare vacanza a; incas-
sare, mettere in una nicchia || *intr*
aggiornarsi, prendersi vacanza
recession [rɪ'sɛʃən] *s* ritirata; processione finale; (com) recessione
recipe ['rɛsɪˌpi] *s* ricetta
reciprocal [rɪ'sɪprəkəl] *adj* reciproco
reciprocity [ˌrɛsɪ'prɑsɪti] *s* reciprocità
f
recital [rɪ'saɪtəl] *s* narrazione; (*of
music or poetry*) recital *m*
recite [rɪ'saɪt] *tr* raccontare; (*music or
poetry*) recitare
reckless ['rɛklɪs] *adj* temerario, spericolato
reckon ['rɛkən] *tr* calcolare; conside-
rare; (coll) supporre || *intr* contare;
to reckon with prevedere, tener
conto di
reclaim [rɪ'klem] *tr* (*land*) sanare, prosciugare; (*substances*) rigenerare;
(fig) rigenerare
recline [rɪ'klaɪn] *tr* reclinare || *intr*
reclinarsi, adagiarsi
recluse [rɪ'klus] *or* ['rɛklus] *adj & s*
recluso
recognition [ˌrɛkəg'nɪʃən] *s* riconoscimento
recognize ['rɛkəgˌnaɪz] *tr* riconoscere
recoil [rɪ'kɔɪl] *s* indietreggiamento;
(*of a firearm*) rinculo || *intr* indie-
treggiare; rinculare
recollect [ˌrɛkə'lɛkt] *tr & intr* ricordare
recollection [ˌrɛkə'lɛkʃən] *s* ricordo
recommend [ˌrɛkə'mɛnd] *tr* raccomandare
recompense ['rɛkəmˌpɛns] *s* ricom-
pensa || *tr* ricompensare
reconcile ['rɛkənˌsaɪl] *tr* riconciliare;
to reconcile oneself rassegnarsi
reconnaissance [rɪ'kɑnɪsəns] *s* ricogni-
zione
reconnoiter [ˌrɛkə'nɔɪtər] *or* [ˌrikə-
'nɔɪtər] *tr & intr* perlustrare
reconsider [ˌrikən'sɪdər] *tr* riconsiderare

reconstruct [ˌrikən'strʌkt] *tr* ricostruire

reconversion [ˌrikən'vʌrʒən] *s* riconversione

record ['rɛkərd] *s* registrazione; annotazione; (*official report*) verbale *m*, protocollo; (*criminal*) fedina sporca; (*of a phonograph*) disco; (educ) documenti *mpl* scolastici; (sports) record *m*, primato; **off the record** confidenziale; confidenzialmente; **records** annali *mpl*, documenti *mpl*; **to break a record** battere un record ‖ [rɪ'kɔrd] *tr* registrare; mettere a verbale; (*e.g.*, *a song*) incidere

rec'ord break'er *s* (sports) primatista *mf*

rec'ord chang'er ['tʃɛndʒər] *s* cambiadischi *m*

recorder [rɪ'kɔrdər] *s* (*apparatus*) registratore *m;* (law) cancelliere *m;* (mus) flauto a imboccatura a tubo

rec'ord hold'er *s* (sports) primatista *mf*

recording [rɪ'kɔrdɪŋ] *s* registrazione; (*of a record*) incisione; (*record*) disco

record'ing sec'retary *s* cancelliere *m*

rec'ord play'er *s* giradischi *m*

recount ['ri ˌkaʊnt] *s* nuovo conteggio ‖ [ri'kaʊnt] *tr* (*to count again*) ricontare ‖ [rɪ'kaʊnt] *tr* (*to narrate*) raccontare

recourse [rɪ'kors] *or* ['rikors] *s* ricorso; (com) rivalsa; **to have recourse to** ricorrere a

recover [rɪ'kʌvər] *tr* ricuperare, riacquistare; (*a substance*) rigenerare; **to recover consciousness** riaversi, riprendere conoscenza ‖ *intr* rimettersi; guadagnare una causa

recover•y [rɪ'kʌvəri] *s* (**-ies**) ricupero; guarigione; **past recovery** incurabile

recreant ['rɛkrɪ·ənt] *adj & s* codardo; traditore *m*

recreation [ˌrɛkrɪ'eʃən] *s* ricreazione

recruit [rɪ'krut] *s* recluta ‖ *tr & intr* reclutare

rectangle ['rɛkˌtæŋgəl] *s* rettangolo

rectifier ['rɛktəˌfaɪ·ər] *s* rettificatore *m;* (elec) raddrizzatore *m*

recti•fy ['rɛktɪˌfaɪ] *v* (*pret & pp* **-fied**) *tr* rettificare; (elec) raddrizzare

rectitude ['rɛktɪˌtud] *or* ['rɛktɪˌtjud] *s* rettitudine *f*

rec•tum ['rɛktəm] *s* (**-tums** *or* **-ta** [tə]) retto

recumbent [rɪ'kʌmbənt] *adj* sdraiato

recuperate [rɪ'kjupə·ˌret] *tr* ricuperare ‖ *intr* ristabilirsi, rimettersi

re•cur [rɪ'kʌr] *v* (*pret & pp* **-curred;** *ger* **-curring**) *intr* ricorrere; ritornare; tornare a mente

recurrent [rɪ'kʌrənt] *adj* ricorrente

recycle [ri'saɪkəl] *tr* riconvertire; (*e.g.*, *in chemical industry*) riciclare

red [rɛd] *adj* (**redder; reddest**) rosso ‖ *s* rosso; **in the red** in debito , in rosso ‖ **Red** *adj & s* (*Communist*) rosso

red'bait' *tr* dare del comunista a

red'bird' *s* cardinale *m*

red-blooded ['rɛdˌblʌdɪd] *adj* sanguigno; vigoroso

red'breast' *s* pettirosso

red'bud' *s* siliquastro

red'cap' *s* (Brit) poliziotto militare; (U.S.A.) facchino

red' cell' *s* globulo rosso

red' cent' *s*—**to not have a red cent** (coll) non avere il becco di un quattrino

Red' Cross' *s* Croce Rossa

redden ['rɛdən] *tr* arrossare ‖ *intr* arrossire

redeem [rɪ'dim] *tr* redimere; (*a promise*) disimpegnare

redeemer [rɪ'dimər] *s* redentore *m*

redemption [rɪ'dɛmpʃən] *s* redenzione; disimpegno

red-handed ['rɛd'hændɪd] *adj*—**to be caught red-handed** esser colto sul fatto or con le mani nel sacco

red'head' *s* persona dai capelli rossi

red' her'ring *s* argomento usato per sviare l'attenzione; aringa affumicata

red'-hot' *adj* rovente, incandescente; fresco fresco, appena uscito

rediscover [ˌridɪs'kʌvər] *tr* riscoprire

red'-let'ter *adj* memorabile

red'-light' dis'trict *s* quartiere *m* delle case di tolleranza

red' man' *s* pellerossa *m*

re•do ['ri'du] *v* (*pret* **-did** ['dɪd]; *pp* **-done** ['dʌn]) *tr* rifare

redolent ['rɛdələnt] *adj* fragrante, profumato; **redolent of** che sa di

redoubt [rɪ'daʊt] *s* (mil) ridotta

redound [rɪ'daʊnd] *intr* ridondare

red' pep'per *s* pepe *m* di Caienna

redress [rɪ'drɛs] *or* ['ridrɛs] *s* riparazione, risarcimento ‖ [rɪ'drɛs] *tr* riparare, risarcire

red'skin' *s* pellerossa *mf*

red' tape' *s* trafila, burocrazia

reduce [rɪ'djus] *or* [rɪ'dus] *tr* ridurre; diluire; (mil) retrocedere; (*a hernia*) (surg) sbrigliare ‖ *intr* ridursi; (*to lose weight*) dimagrire

reducing [rɪ'djusɪŋ] *or* [rɪ'dusɪŋ] *adj* dimagrante; (chem) riducente

reduction [rɪ'dʌkʃən] *s* riduzione

redundant [rɪ'dʌndənt] *adj* ridondante

red'wood' *s* sequoia

reed [rid] *s* (*stalk*) calamo; (*plant*) canna; (mus) linguetta; (mus) strumento a linguetta

reedit [ri'edit] *tr* rifondere

reef [rif] *s* scoglio, barriera; (naut) terzarolo; (min) vena, filone *m* ‖ *tr* (*sail*) imbrogliare

reefer ['rifər] *s* giacchetta a doppio petto; (slang) sigaretta di marijuana

reek [rik] *intr* puzzare; sudare, evaporare, fumare

reel [ril] *s* (*spool*) bobina; (*sway*) vacillamento; (*for fishing*) mulinello; **off the reel** senza esitazione ‖ *tr* bobinare; **to reel off** rifilare ‖ *intr* barcollare

reelection [ˌri·ɪ'lɛkʃən] *s* rielezione

reenlist [ˌri·ɛn'lɪst] *tr* arruolare di nuovo ‖ *intr* arruolarsi di nuovo

reen•try [rɪ'ɛntri] *s* (**-tries**) rientro

reexamination [ˌri·ɛgˌzæmɪ'neʃən] *s* riesame *m*

re·fer [rɪ'fʌr] v (pret & pp -ferred; ger -ferring) tr riferire || intr riferirsi

referee [ˌrɛfə'ri] s arbitro || tr & intr arbitrare

reference ['rɛfərəns] s riferimento; (testimonial) referenza; (e.g., in a book) rinvio, rimando

ref'erence book' s libro di consultazione

referen·dum [ˌrɛfə'rɛndəm] s (-dums or -da [də]) referendum m

refill ['rifɪl] s ricambio || [rɪ'fɪl] tr riempire di nuovo

refine [rɪ'faɪn] tr raffinare

refinement [rɪ'faɪnmənt] s raffinatezza; (of oil) raffinatura

refiner·y [rɪ'faɪnəri] s (-ies) raffineria

reflect [rɪ'flɛkt] tr riflettere || intr riflettere, riflettersi

reflection [rɪ'flɛkʃən] s riflessione

reflex ['riflɛks] adj riflesso || s riflesso; (camera) reflex m

reflexive [rɪ'flɛksɪv] adj riflessivo

reforestation [ˌrifɔrɪs'teʃən] or [ˌrifɔrɪs'teʃən] s rimboschimento

reform [rɪ'fɔrm] s riforma || tr riformare || intr correggersi

reformation [ˌrɛfər'meʃən] s riforma || **Reformation** s—**the Reformation** la Riforma

reformato·ry [rɪ'fɔrməˌtori] adj riformativo || s (-ries) riformatorio

reformer [rɪ'fɔrmər] s riformatore m

reform' school' s riformatorio

refraction [rɪ'frækʃən] s rifrazione

refrain [rɪ'fren] s ritornello, intercalare m || intr astenersi

refresh [rɪ'frɛʃ] tr rinfrescare; ristorare || intr ristorarsi

refreshing [rɪ'frɛʃɪŋ] adj rinfrescante; ristoratore; ricreativo

refreshment [rɪ'frɛʃmənt] s rinfresco

refrigerate [rɪ'frɪdʒəˌret] tr refrigerare

refrigerator [rɪ'frɪdʒəˌretər] s refrigerante m, frigorifero

refrig'erator car' s vagone frigorifero

re·fuel [ri'fjul] v (pret & pp -fueled or -fuelled; ger -fueling or -fuelling) tr rifornire di carburante || intr rifornirsi di carburante

refuge ['rɛfjudʒ] s rifugio; scampo; **to take refuge (in)** rifugiarsi (in)

refugee [ˌrɛfju'dʒi] s rifugiato

refund ['rifʌnd] s rifusione || [rɪ'fʌnd] tr (to repay) rifondere || [ri'fʌnd] tr (bonds) consolidare; (to fund anew) rifondere

refurnish [ri'fʌrnɪʃ] tr riammobiliare

refusal [rɪ'fjuzəl] s rifiuto

refuse ['rɛfjus] s rifiuto, spazzatura || [rɪ'fjuz] tr rifiutare; **to refuse to** rifiutarsi di

refute [rɪ'fjut] tr smentire, confutare

regain [rɪ'gen] tr riguadagnare; **to regain consciousness** tornare in sé

regal ['rigəl] adj reale, regale

regale [rɪ'gel] tr intrattenere, rallegrare

regalia [rɪ'gelɪ·ə] spl (of royalty) prerogative fpl reali; alta uniforme

regard [rɪ'gard] s riguardo; (look) sguardo; (esteem) rispetto; **in regard to** rispetto a; **regards** rispetti mpl; **warm regards** cordiali saluti mpl; **without regard to** senza considerare || tr considerare; osservare; concernere; **as regards** per quanto concerne

regarding [rɪ'gardɪŋ] prep per quanto concerne

regardless [rɪ'gardlɪs] adj incurante || adv ciò nonostante; costi quello che costi; **regardless of** malgrado

regatta [rɪ'gætə] s regata

regen·cy ['ridʒənsi] s (-cies) reggenza

regenerate [rɪ'dʒɛnəˌret] tr rigenerare || intr rigenerarsi

regent ['ridʒənt] s reggente mf

regicide ['rɛdʒɪˌsaɪd] s (act) regicidio; (person) regicida mf

regiment ['rɛdʒɪmənt] s reggimento || ['rɛdʒɪˌmɛnt] tr irregimentare

regimental [ˌrɛdʒɪ'mɛntəl] adj reggimentale || **regimentals** spl uniforme f reggimentale

region ['ridʒən] s regione

register ['rɛdʒɪstər] s registro; (for controlling the flow of air) regolatore m dell'aria || tr registrare; (e.g., a student) iscrivere; (e.g., anger) dimostrare; (a letter) raccomandare || intr registrarsi; iscriversi; fare impressione

reg'istered let'ter s raccomandata

reg'istered nurse' s infermiera diplomata

registrar ['rɛdʒɪsˌtrar] s registratore m, archivista mf; (of deeds) ricevitore m

registration [ˌrɛdʒɪs'treʃən] s registrazione; (e.g., of a student) iscrizione; (of mail) raccomandazione

registra'tion fee' s diritto di segreteria

re·gret [rɪ'grɛt] s pentimento, rammarico; **regrets** scuse fpl || v (pret & pp -gretted; ger -gretting) tr rimpiangere; **to regret to** essere spiacente di

regrettable [rɪ'grɛtəbəl] adj deplorevole

regular ['rɛgjələr] adj regolare; (life) regolato; (coll) vero || s cliente m abituale; (mil) effettivo

regularity [ˌrɛgjə'lɛriti] s regolarità f

regularize ['rɛgjələˌraɪz] tr regoralizzare

regulate ['rɛgjəˌlet] tr regolare

regulation [ˌrɛgjə'leʃən] s regolazione; (rule) regolamento

rehabilitate [ˌrihə'bɪlɪˌtet] tr riabilitare

rehearsal [rɪ'hʌrsəl] s prova

rehearse [rɪ'hʌrs] tr provare || intr fare le prove

rehiring [ri'haɪrɪŋ] s riassunzione

reign [ren] s regno || intr regnare

reimburse [ˌri·ɪm'bʌrs] tr rimborsare

rein [ren] s redine f; **to give full rein to** dare briglia sciolta a || tr guidare con le redini; frenare

reincarnation [ˌri·ɪnkar'neʃən] s reincarnazione

reindeer ['ren ˌdɪr] s renna

reinforce [ˌri·ɪn'fors] tr rinforzare; (a wall) armare

re'inforced con'crete s cemento armato

reinforcement [ˌri·ɪnˈforsmənt] *s* rinforzo

reinstate [ˌri·ɪnˈstet] *tr* reintegrare

reiterate [riˈɪtəˌret] *tr* reiterare

reject [ˈridʒɛkt] *s* rigetto, rifiuto; **rejects** scarti *mpl* ‖ [riˈdʒɛkt] *tr* rigettare; (*to refuse*) rifiutare

rejection [riˈdʒɛkʃən] *s* rigetto; rifiuto

rejoice [riˈdʒɔɪs] *intr* rallegrarsi

rejoin [riˈdʒɔɪn] *tr* raggiungere; (*to reunite*) riunire; (*to reply*) rispondere

rejoinder [riˈdʒɔɪndər] *s* risposta; (law) controreplica

rejuvenation [riˌdʒuvɪˈneʃən] *s* ringiovanimento

rekindle [riˈkɪndəl] *tr* riaccendere

relapse [riˈlæps] *s* ricaduta ‖ *intr* ricadere

relate [riˈlet] *tr* mettere in relazione; (*to tell*) narrare

relation [riˈleʃən] *s* relazione; (*account*) resoconto; (*relative*) parente *mf;* (*kinship*) parentela; **in relation to** or **with** in relazione a

relationship [riˈleʃənˌʃɪp] *s* rapporto, relazione; (*kinship*) parentela

relative [ˈrɛlətɪv] *adj* relativo ‖ *s* congiunto, parente *mf*

relativity [ˌrɛləˈtɪvɪti] *s* relatività *f*

relax [riˈlæks] *tr* rilasciare, rilassare ‖ *intr* rilasciarsi, rilassarsi

relaxation [ˌrilæksˈeʃən] *s* distensione; (*entertainment*) ricreazione

relaxa′tion of ten′sion *s* distensione

relaxing [riˈlæksɪŋ] *adj* rilassante; divertente

relay [ˈrile] or [riˈle] *s* (elec) relè *m;* (rad) ripetitore *m;* (mil, sports) staffetta; (sports) corsa a staffetta ‖ *v* (*pret & pp* **-layed**) *tr* trasmettere, ritrasmettere ‖ [riˈle] *v* (*pret & pp* **-laid**) *tr* rimettere, porre di nuovo

re′lay race′ *s* corsa a staffetta

release [riˈlis] *s* (*e.g., from jail*) liberazione; (*from obligation*) disimpegno; (*for publication*) autorizzazione; (mov) distribuzione; (journ) comunicato; (aer) lancio; (mach) scappamento ‖ *tr* liberare; disimpegnare; autorizzare la pubblicazione di; (mov) distribuire; (*a bomb*) (aer) lanciare; **to release s.o. from a debt** rimettere un debito a qlcu

relent [riˈlent] *intr* placarsi

relentless [riˈlentlɪs] *adj* implacabile

relevant [ˈrɛlɪvənt] *adj* pertinente

reliable [riˈlaɪ·əbəl] *adj* (*person*) fidato; (*source*) attendibile

reliance [riˈlaɪ·əns] *s* fiducia, fede *f*

relic [ˈrɛlɪk] *s* reliquia

relief [riˈlif] *s* sollievo; sussidio; (*prominence; projection*) rilievo; (mil) cambio; **in relief** in rilievo; **on relief** sotto sussidio

relieve [riˈliv] *tr* (*e.g., pain*) alleviare; (*e.g., a load*) sgravare; (mil) rilevare

religion [riˈlɪdʒən] *s* religione

religious [riˈlɪdʒəs] *adj* religioso

relinquish [riˈlɪŋkwɪʃ] *tr* abbandonare

relish [ˈrɛlɪʃ] *s* piacere *m,* gusto; sapore *m,* aroma *m;* (culin) condimento ‖ *tr* gustare, apprezzare; dare gusto a

reluctance [riˈlʌktəns] *s* riluttanza

reluctant [riˈlʌktənt] *adj* riluttante

re·ly [riˈlaɪ] *v* (*pret & pp* **-lied**) *intr* fare assegnamento; **to rely on** fidarsi di, fondarsi su

remain [riˈmen] *s*—**remains** resti *mpl;* resti *mpl* mortali ‖ *intr* restare, rimanere

remainder [riˈmendər] *s* resto, restante *m;* (*unsold books*) fondi *mpl* di libreria ‖ *tr* vendere come rimanenza

re·make [riˈmek] *v* (*pret & pp* **-made** [ˈmed]) *tr* rifare

remark [riˈmark] *s* osservazione, rimarco ‖ *tr & intr* osservare; **to remark on** fare osservazioni su

remarkable [riˈmarkəbəl] *adj* notevole

remar·ry [riˈmæri] *v* (*pret & pp* **-ried**) *intr* riprendere moglie, risposarsi

reme·dy [ˈrɛmɪdi] *s* (**-dies**) rimedio ‖ *v* (*pret & pp* **-died**) *tr* rimediare (with *dat*)

remember [riˈmembər] *tr* ricordarsi di; (*to send greetings to*) ricordare ‖ *intr* ricordare, ricordarsi

remembrance [riˈmembrəns] *s* rimembranza, ricordo

remind [riˈmaɪnd] *tr* rammentare

reminder [riˈmaɪndər] *s* promemoria

reminisce [ˌrɛmɪˈnɪs] *intr* ricordare il passato

reminiscence [ˌrɛmɪˈnɪsəns] *s* reminiscenza

remiss [riˈmɪs] *adj* negligente

re·mit [riˈmɪt] *v* (*pret & pp* **-mitted;** *ger* **-mitting**) *tr* rimettere; (*to a lower court*) (law) rinviare

remittance [riˈmɪtəns] *s* rimessa

remnant [ˈrɛmnənt] *s* (*remaining quantity*) rimanente *m;* (*of cloth*) scampolo; vestigio; **remnants** (*of merchandise*) rimanenze *fpl,* fondi *mpl* di magazzino

remod·el [riˈmadəl] *v* (*pret & pp* **-eled** or **-elled;** *ger* **-eling** or **-elling**) *tr* rimodellare; ricostruire

remonstrance [riˈmanstrəns] *s* rimostranza

remonstrate [riˈmanstret] *intr* protestare, rimostrare; **to remonstrate with** rimostrare a

remorse [riˈmɔrs] *s* rimorso

remorseful [riˈmɔrsfəl] *adj* tormentato dal rimorso, pentito

remote [riˈmot] *adj* remoto

remote′ control′ *s* telecomando

removable [riˈmuvəbəl] *adj* amovibile

removal [riˈmuvəl] *s* rimozione; trasferimento; (*dismissal*) destituzione

remove [riˈmuv] *tr* rimuovere; (*one's jacket*) togliersi, cavarsi; (*from office*) destituire; eliminare ‖ *intr* trasferirsi; andarsene

remuneration [riˌmjunəˈreʃən] *s* rimunerazione

renaissance [ˌrenəˈsans] or [riˈnesəns] *s* rinascimento, rinascita ‖ **Renaissance** *s* Rinascimento

rend [rend] *v* (*pret & pp* **rent** [rent]) *tr* (*to tear*) stracciare; (*to split*) fendere, squarciare

render [ˈrendər] *tr* (*justice*) rendere;

(*a service*) fare; (*aid*) prestare; (*a bill*) presentare; (*to translate*) tradurre; (*a piece of music*) interpretare; (*e.g., fat*) struggere

rendez·vous ['rɑndə,vu] *s* (**-vous** [,vuz]) appuntamento; (*in space*) incontro ‖ *v* (*pret & pp* **-voused** [,vud]; *ger* **-vousing** [,vu·ɪŋ]) *intr* incontrarsi

rendition [rɛn'dɪʃən] *s* restituzione, resa; traduzione; interpretazione

renege [rɪ'nɪg] *s* rifiuto ‖ *intr* rifiutare; (coll) venire meno

renew [rɪ'nju] *or* [rɪ'nu] *tr* rinnovare ‖ *intr* rinnovarsi

renewal [rɪ'nju·əl] *or* [rɪ'nu·əl] *s* rinnovo, rinnovamento

renounce [rɪ'nauns] *tr* rinunziare (*with dat*); ripudiare

renovate ['rɛnə,vet] *tr* rinnovare; (*a building*) restaurare; (*a room*) rimettere a nuovo

renown [rɪ'naun] *s* rinomanza

renowned [rɪ'naund] *adj* rinomato

rent [rɛnt] *adj* scisso ‖ *s* fitto, pigione; (*tear*) squarcio ‖ *tr* locare, dare a pigione ‖ *intr* prendere a pigione

rental ['rɛntəl] *s* affitto

renter ['rɛntər] *s* affittuario, locatario

renunciation [rɪ,nʌnsɪ'eʃən] *or* [rɪ,nʌnʃɪ'eʃən] *s* rinunzia

reopen [ri'opən] *tr* riaprire ‖ *intr* riaprirsi

reopening [ri'opənɪŋ] *s* riapertura

reorganize [ri'ɔrgə,naɪz] *tr* riorganizzare ‖ *intr* riorganizzarsi

repair [rɪ'pɛr] *s* riparazione; **in good repair** in buono stato ‖ *tr* riparare ‖ *intr* riparare, dirigersi

repair'man' *s* (**-men'**) aggiustatore *m*

repaper [ri'pepər] *tr* ritappezzare

reparation [,rɛpə'reʃən] *s* riparazione

repartee [,rɛpɑr'ti] *s* replica arguta, rimando

repast [rɪ'pæst] *or* [rɪ'pɑst] *s* pasto

repatriate [ri'petri,et] *tr* rimpatriare

re·pay [rɪ'pe] *v* (*pret & pp* **-paid** ['ped]) *tr* ripagare

repayment [rɪ'pemənt] *s* rimborso; risarcimento, compensazione

repeal [rɪ'pil] *s* revoca, abrogazione ‖ *tr* revocare, abrogare

repeat [rɪ'pit] *s* ripetizione ‖ *tr* ripetere ‖ *intr* ripetere; (*said of food*) tornare a gola

re·pel [rɪ'pɛl] *v* (*pret & pp* **-pelled**; *ger* **-pelling**) *tr* respingere, ricacciare; ripugnare (*with dat*)

repent [rɪ'pɛnt] *tr* pentirsi di ‖ *intr* pentirsi, ravvedersi

repentance [rɪ'pɛntəns] *s* pentimento

repentant [rɪ'pɛntənt] *adj* pentito

repercussion [,ripər'kʌʃən] *s* ripercussione

reperto·ry ['rɛpər,tori] *s* (**-ries**) (com) magazzino; (theat) repertorio

repetition [,rɛpɪ'tɪʃən] *s* ripetizione

repine [rɪ'paɪn] *intr* lamentarsi

replace [rɪ'ples] *tr* (*to put back*) rimettere; (*to take the place of*) rimpiazzare

replaceable [rɪ'plesəbəl] *adj* sostituibile

replacement [rɪ'plesmənt] *s* rimpiazzo, sostituzione; **as a replacement for** al posto di

replenish [rɪ'plɛnɪʃ] *tr* rifornire

replete [rɪ'plit] *adj* pieno zeppo

replica ['rɛplɪkə] *s* replica

re·ply [rɪ'plaɪ] *s* (**-plies**) risposta ‖ *v* (*pret & pp* **-plied**) *tr & intr* rispondere

report [rɪ'port] *s* rapporto, informazione; voce *f*, rumore *m*; (*of a physician*) responso; (*of a firearm*) detonazione ‖ *tr* riportare, rapportare; denunziare ‖ *intr* fare un rapporto; fare il cronista; presentarsi; **to report sick** (mil) marcare visita

report' card' *s* pagella

reportedly [rɪ'portɪdli] *adv* secondo la voce comune

reporter [rɪ'portər] *s* cronista *mf*, reporter *m*

reporting [rɪ'portɪŋ] *s* reportage *m*

repose [rɪ'poz] *s* riposo ‖ *tr* posare, riporre ‖ *intr* riposare

reprehend [,riprɪ'hɛnd] *tr* riprovare, rimproverare

represent [,riprɪ'zɛnt] *tr* rappresentare

representation [,riprɪzɛn'teʃən] *s* rappresentazione; protesta; **representations** dichiarazioni *fpl*

representative [,riprɪ'zɛntətɪv] *adj* rappresentativo ‖ *s* rappresentante *mf*; (pol) deputato

repress [rɪ'prɛs] *tr* reprimere

repression [rɪ'prɛʃən] *s* repressione

reprieve [rɪ'priv] *s* tregua temporanea; sospensione della pena capitale ‖ *tr* accordare una tregua a; sospendere l'esecuzione di

reprimand ['rɛprɪ,mænd] *or* ['rɛprɪ,mɑnd] *s* sgridata, ramanzina ‖ *tr* sgridare, rimproverare

reprint ['ri,prɪnt] *s* ristampa; (*offprint*) estratto ‖ [ri'prɪnt] *tr* ristampare

reprisal [rɪ'praɪzəl] *s* rappresaglia

reproach [rɪ'protʃ] *s* rimprovero; vituperio ‖ *tr* rimproverare; **to reproach s.o. for s.th** rimproverare qlcu di qlco, rimproverare qlco a qlcu

reproduce [,riprə'djus] *or* [,riprə'dus] *tr* riprodurre ‖ *intr* riprodursi

reproduction [,riprə'dʌkʃən] *s* riproduzione

reproof [rɪ'pruf] *s* rimprovero

reprove [rɪ'pruv] *tr* rimproverare; disapprovare

reptile ['rɛptɪl] *s* rettile *m*

republic [rɪ'pʌblɪk] *s* repubblica

republican [rɪ'pʌblɪkən] *adj & s* repubblicano

repudiate [rɪ'pjudi,et] *tr* ripudiare; rinnegare

repugnant [rɪ'pʌgnənt] *adj* ripugnante

repulse [rɪ'pʌls] *s* rifiuto; sconfitta ‖ *tr* rifiutare; (*e.g., an enemy*) sconfiggere

repulsive [rɪ'pʌlsɪv] *adj* ripulsivo

reputation [,rɛpjə'teʃən] *s* reputazione

repute [rɪ'pjut] *s* reputazione, fama ‖ *tr* reputare

reputedly [rɪ'pjutɪdli] *adv* secondo l'opinione corrente

request [rɪ'kwɛst] *s* domanda, richiesta; **at the request of** su domanda di ‖ *tr* richiedere

Requiem ['rikwɪ ˌɛm] or ['rɛkwɪ ˌɛm] *adj* di Requiem ‖ *s* Requiem *m* & *f;* Messa di Requiem

require [rɪ'kwaɪr] *tr* richiedere

requirement [rɪ'kwaɪrmənt] *s* requisito; richiesta, fabbisogno

requisite ['rɛkwɪzɪt] *adj* requisito, richiesto ‖ *s* requisito

requisition [ˌrɛkwɪ'zɪʃən] *s* requisizione

requital [rɪ'kwaɪtəl] *s* contraccambio

requite [rɪ'kwaɪt] *tr* (*e.g., an injury*) contraccambiare; (*a person*) contraccambiare (with *dat*)

re·read [ri'rid] *v* (*pret & pp* -read ['rɛd]) *tr* rileggere

resale ['ri ˌsel] or [ri'sel] *s* rivendita

rescind [rɪ'sɪnd] *tr* annullare, cancellare; (law) rescindere

rescue ['rɛskju] *s* salvataggio, liberazione; **to go to the rescue of** andare al soccorso di ‖ *tr* salvare, liberare, soccorrere

research [rɪ'sʌrtʃ] or ['risʌrtʃ] *s* ricerca, indagine *f* ‖ *intr* investigare

re·sell [ri'sel] *v* (*pret & pp* -sold ['sold]) *tr* rivendere

resemblance [rɪ'zɛmbləns] *s* somiglianza

resemble [rɪ'zɛmbəl] *tr* somigliare (with *dat*), rassomigliare (with *dat*); **to resemble one another** rassomigliarsi

resent [rɪ'zɛnt] *tr* (*a remark*) risentirsi per; (*a person*) risentirsi con

resentful [rɪ'zɛntfəl] *adj* risentito

resentment [rɪ'zɛntmənt] *s* risentimento

reservation [ˌrɛzər'veʃən] *s* riserva; (*e.g., for a room*) prenotazione

reserve [rɪ'zʌrv] *s* riserva; (*self-restraint*) riserbo, contegno ‖ *tr* riservare; prenotare

reservist [rɪ'zʌrvɪst] *s* riservista *m*

reservoir ['rɛzər ˌvwɑr] *s* serbatoio, cisterna; (*large storage place for supplying community with water*) bacino di riserva; (fig) pozzo

re·set [ri'sɛt] *v* (*pret & pp* -set; *ger* -setting) *tr* rimettere a posto; (*a watch*) regolare; (*a gem*) incastonare di nuovo; (*a machine*) rimontare

re·ship [ri'ʃɪp] *v* (*pret & pp* -shipped; *ger* -shipping) *tr* rispedire; (*on a ship*) reimbarcare ‖ *intr* reimbarcarsi

reshipment [ri'ʃɪpmənt] *s* rispedizione; (*on a ship*) reimbarco

reside [rɪ'zaɪd] *intr* risiedere

residence ['rɛzɪdəns] *s* residenza

resident ['rɛzɪdənt] *adj* & *s* residente *mf*

residential [ˌrɛzɪ'dɛnʃəl] *adj* residenziale

residue ['rɛzɪ ˌdju] or ['rɛsɪ ˌdu] *s* residuo

resign [rɪ'zaɪn] *tr* rassegnare, abbandonare; **to be resigned to** rassegnarsi a ‖ *intr* dimettersi, rassegnare le dimissioni

resignation [ˌrɛzɪg'neʃən] *s* (*from a job*) dimissione; (*submission*) rassegnazione

resin ['rɛzɪn] *s* resina

resist [rɪ'zɪst] *tr* resistere (with *dat*) ‖ *intr* resistere

resistance [rɪ'zɪstəns] *s* resistenza

resole [ri'sol] *tr* risolare

resolute ['rɛzə ˌlut] *adj* risoluto

resolution [ˌrɛzə'luʃən] *s* risoluzione; **good resolutions** buoni propositi

resolve [rɪ'zɒlv] *s* risoluzione ‖ *tr* risolvere ‖ *intr* risolversi

resonance ['rɛzənəns] *s* risonanza

resort [rɪ'zɔrt] *s* (*appeal*) ricorso; (*for vacation*) centro di villeggiatura ‖ *intr* ricorrere

resound [rɪ'zaund] *intr* risonare

resounding [rɪ'zaundɪŋ] *adj* risonante; (*success*) strepitoso

resource [rɪ'sors] or ['risors] *s* risorsa

resourceful [rɪ'sorsfəl] *adj* ingegnoso

respect [rɪ'spɛkt] *s* rispetto; **respects** rispetti *mpl*, ossequi *mpl;* **with respect to** rispetto a ‖ *tr* rispettare

respectable [rɪ'spɛktəbəl] *adj* rispettabile; onesto, per bene

respectful [rɪ'spɛktfəl] *adj* rispettoso

respecting [rɪ'spɛktɪŋ] *prep* rispetto a

respective [rɪ'spɛktɪv] *adj* rispettivo

respiratory ['rɛspɪrə ˌtori] or [rɪ'spaɪrə ˌtori] *adj* respiratorio

respire [rɪ'spaɪr] *tr* & *intr* respirare

respite ['rɛspɪt] *s* tregua, requie *f;* (*reprieve*) proroga, dilazione

resplendent [rɪ'splɛndənt] *adj* risplendente

respond [rɪ'spɒnd] *intr* rispondere

response [rɪ'spɒns] *s* risposta

responsibili·ty [rɪ ˌspɒnsɪ'bɪlɪti] *s* (-ties) responsibilità *f*

responsible [rɪ'spɒnsɪbəl] *adj* responsabile; (*job*) di fiducia; **responsible for** responsabile di

responsive [rɪ'spɒnsɪv] *adj* rispondente; (*e.g., to affection*) sensibile; (*e.g., motor*) che risponde

rest [rɛst] *s* riposo; (*what remains*) resto; (mus) pausa; **at rest** in riposo; tranquillo, in pace; (*dead*) morto; **the rest** il resto, gli altri; **to come to rest** andare a finire; **to lay to rest** sotterrare ‖ *tr* riposare; (*to direct one's eyes*) dirigere; (*faith*) porre ‖ *intr* riposarsi, riposare; appoggiarsi; **to rest assured (that)** esser sicuro (che); **to rest on** aver fiducia in; basarsi su; (*one's laurels*) dormire su

restaurant ['rɛstərənt] or ['rɛstə ˌrɑnt] *s* ristorante *m*

restful ['rɛstfəl] *adj* riposante, tranquillo

rest' home' *s* casa di riposo

rest'ing place' *s* luogo di riposo; (*of a staircase*) pianerottolo; (*of the dead*) ultima dimora

restitution [ˌrɛstɪ'tjuʃən] or [ˌrɛstɪ'tuʃən] *s* restituzione

restive ['rɛstɪv] *adj* irrequieto; (*e.g.*, *horse*) recalcitrante

restless ['rɛstlɪs] *adj* irrequieto; (*night*) insonne, in bianco

restock [ri'stɑk] *tr* rifornire; (*e.g.*, *with fish*) ripopolare

restoration [,rɛstə'reʃən] *s* restaurazione

restore [rɪ'stor] *tr* restaurare, ripristinare

restrain [rɪ'stren] *tr* ritenere, frenare; limitare

restraint [rɪ'strent] *s* restrizione; controllo, ritegno; detenzione

restrict [rɪ'strɪkt] *tr* restingere, limitare

restriction [rɪ'strɪkʃən] *s* restrizione

rest' room' *s* toletta; gabinetto di decenza

restructuring [rɪ'strʌktʃərɪŋ] *s* ristrutturazione

result [rɪ'zʌlt] *s* risultato ‖ *intr* risultare; **to result in** risolversi in, concludersi con

resume [rɪ'zum] *or* [rɪ'zjum] *tr* riprendere ‖ *intr* ricominciare

résumé [,rɛzu'me] *or* [,rɛzju'me] *s* sunto, riassunto

resumption [rɪ'zʌmpʃən] *s* ripresa

resurface [ri'sʌrfɪs] *tr* mettere copertura nuova a ‖ *intr* riemergere

resurrect [,rɛzə'rɛkt] *tr* & *intr* risuscitare

resurrection [,rɛzə'rɛkʃən] *s* risurrezione

resuscitate [rɪ'sʌsɪ,tet] *tr* rendere alla vita

retail ['ritel] *adj* & *adv* al dettaglio, al minuto ‖ *s* dettaglio ‖ *tr* dettagliare, vendere al minuto ‖ *intr* vendere *or* vendersi al minuto

retailer ['ritelər] *s* dettagliante *mf*

retain [rɪ'ten] *tr* ritenere; (*a lawyer*) assicurarsi i servizi di

retaliate [rɪ'tælɪ,et] *intr* fare rappresaglie; **to retaliate for** ricambiare

retaliation [rɪ,tælɪ'eʃən] *s* rappresaglia

retard [rɪ'tɑrd] *s* ritardo ‖ *tr* ritardare

retch [rɛtʃ] *intr* avere sforzi di vomito

reticence ['rɛtɪsəns] *s* riservatezza

reticent ['rɛtɪsənt] *adj* riservato, taciturno

retina ['rɛtɪnə] *s* retina

retinue ['rɛtɪ,nju] *or* ['rɛtɪ,nu] *s* seguito, corteggio

retire [rɪ'taɪr] *tr* ritirare; (*an employee*) giubilare, mettere a riposo ‖ *intr* ritirarsi; andare a riposo; (*to go to bed*) andare a letto

retired [rɪ'taɪrd] *adj* (*employee*) in pensione; (*officer*) a riposo

retirement [rɪ'taɪrmənt] *s* ritiro; (*of an employee*) pensionamento, quiescenza

retort [rɪ'tɔrt] *s* risposta per le rime; controreplica; (*chem*) storta ‖ *tr* rispondere per le rime a ‖ *intr* rispondere per le rime

retouch [ri'tʌtʃ] *tr* ritoccare

retrace [rɪ'tres] *tr* ripercorrere; **to retrace one's steps** ritornare sui propri passi

retract [rɪ'trækt] *tr* ritrattare, disdire ‖ *intr* disdirsi

re·tread ['ri,trɛd] *s* pneumatico col copertone ricostruito ‖ [ri'trɛd] *v* (*pret* & *pp* **-treaded**) *tr* ricostruire il copertone di ‖ *v* (*pret* **-trod** ['trɑd]; *pp* **-trod** *or* **-trodden**) *tr* ripercorrere ‖ *intr* rimettere il piede

retreat [rɪ'trit] *s* (*seclusion*) ritiro; (mil) ritirata; (eccl) esercizio spirituale; **to beat a retreat** battere in ritirata ‖ *intr* ritirarsi

retrench [rɪ'trɛntʃ] *tr* ridurre, tagliare; (mil) trinccrare ‖ *intr* ridurre le spese; (mil) trincerarsi

retribution [,rɛtrɪ'bjuʃən] *s* ricompensa; (theol) giudizio finale

retributive [rɪ'trɪbjətɪv] *adj* retributivo

retrieve [rɪ'triv] *tr* riguadagnare, riconquistare; (*to repair*) risarcire; (hunt) riportare ‖ *intr* riportare la presa

retriever [rɪ'trivər] *s* cane *m* da presa

retroactive [,rɛtro'æktɪv] *adj* retroattivo

retrofiring [,rɛtro'faɪrɪŋ] *s* accensione dei retrorazzi

retrogress ['rɛtrə,grɛs] *intr* regredire; retrocedere

retrorocket [,rɛtro'rɑkɪt] *s* retrorazzo

retrospect ['rɛtrə,spɛkt] *s* esame retrospettivo; **in retrospect** retrospettivamente

retrospective [,rɛtrə'spɛktɪv] *adj* retrospettivo

re·try [ri'traɪ] *v* (*pret* & *pp* **-tried**) *tr* (*a person*) riprocessare; (*a case*) ritentare

return [rɪ'tʌrn] *adj* di ritorno; ripetuto ‖ *s* restituzione; ritorno; profitto; (*of income tax*) dichiarazione; risposta; rapporto ufficiale; (*of an election*) responso; (sports) rimando, rimessa; **in return (for)** in cambio (di); **many happy returns of the day!** cento di questi giorni!; **returns** (*of an election*) responso, risultato ‖ *tr* tornare, ritornare restituire; (*a favor*) contraccambiare; (*a profit*) dare; (*thanks; a decision*) rendere; (sports) ribattere ‖ *intr* tornare; rispondere

return' ad'dress *s* indirizzo del mittente

return' bout' *s* (boxing) rivincita

return' mail' *s—***by return mail** a volta di corriere, a giro di posta

return' tick'et *s* biglietto di ritorno; (Brit) biglietto di andata e ritorno

reunification [ri,junɪfɪ'keʃən] *s* riunione, unificazione

reunion [ri'junjən] *s* riunione

reunite [,riju'naɪt] *tr* riunire ‖ *intr* riunirsi

rev [rɛv] *s* (coll) giro ‖ *v* (*pret* & *pp* **revved;** *ger* **revving**) *tr—***to rev up** (coll) imballare ‖ *intr* (coll) accelerare, imballarsi

revamp [ri'væmp] *tr* rinnovare, rappezzare

reveal [rɪ'vil] *tr* rivelare, svelare

reveille ['rɛvəli] *s* sveglia, levata

rev·el ['rɛvəl] *s* baldoria ‖ *v* (*pret* &

pp **-eled** or **-elled;** *ger* **-eling** or
-elling) *intr* gozzovigliare; bearsi
revelation [ˌrevə'leʃən] *s* rivelazione
‖ **Revelation** *s* (Bib) Apocalisse *f*
revel·ry ['revəlri] *s* (**-ries**) baldoria
revenge [rɪ'vendʒ] *s* vendetta ‖ *tr* vendicare
revengeful [rɪ'vendʒfəl] *adj* vendicativo
revenue ['revəˌnju] or ['revəˌnu] *s*
entrata, profitto; (*government income*) entrate *fpl* erariali
rev'enue cut'ter *s* motobarca della
guardia di finanza
rev'enue stamp' *s* marca da bollo
reverberate [rɪ'vʌrbəˌret] *intr* river-
berarsi; (*said, e.g., of sound*) riper-
cuotersi, risonare; (*said of an echo*)
rimbalzare
revere [rɪ'vɪr] *tr* venerare, riverire
reverence ['revərəns] *s* riverenza ‖ *tr*
ossequiare
reverend ['revərənd] *adj & s* reverendo
reverent ['revərənt] *adj* reverente
reverie ['revəri] *s* sogno, fantasticheria
reversal [rɪ'vʌrsəl] *s* inversione, cambio; (law) annullamento
reverse [rɪ'vʌrs] *adj* rovescio, contrario; (mach) di retromarcia ‖ *s*
contrario; (*rear*) dietro; (*misfortune;
side of a coin not bearing principal
design*) rovescio; (mach) retromarcia
‖ *tr* invertire; rovesciare; mettere in
marcia indietro; **to reverse oneself**
cambiare d'opinione; **to reverse the
charges** far pagare al destinatario;
(telp) far pagare al numero chiamato
‖ *intr* invertirsi
revert [rɪ'vʌrt] *intr* ritornare
review [rɪ'vju] *s* (*critical article*) recensione; (*magazine*) rivista; (educ)
ripasso, ripetizione; (mil) rivista ‖
tr recensire; rivedere; (*a lesson*) ripassare; (mil) passare in rassegna
revile [rɪ'vaɪl] *tr* insultare, offendere
revise [rɪ'vaɪz] *s* revisione; (typ) seconda bozza ‖ *tr* rivedere; correggere
revision [rɪ'vɪʒən] *s* revisione
revisionism [rɪ'vɪʒəˌnɪzəm] *s* revisionismo
revival [rɪ'vaɪvəl] *s* ripresa delle forze;
(*restoration*) ripristino; (*of learning*) rinascimento; risveglio religioso;
(theat, mov) ripresa
revive [rɪ'vaɪv] *tr* ravvivare; (*a custom*) ripristinare; (theat) dare la
ripresa di ‖ *intr* ravvivarsi; risorgere
revoke [rɪ'vok] *tr* revocare
revolt [rɪ'volt] *s* rivolta ‖ *tr* rivoltare
‖ *intr* rivoltarsi
revolting [rɪ'voltɪŋ] *adj* rivoltante
revolution [ˌrevə'luʃən] *s* rivoluzione
revolutionar·y [ˌrevə'luʃəˌneri] *adj* rivoluzionario ‖ *s* (**-ies**) rivoluzionario
revolve [rɪ'valv] *tr* far rotare; (*in one's
mind*) rivolgere ‖ *intr* girare, rotare
revolver [rɪ'valvər] *s* rivoltella
revolv'ing book'case *s* scaffale *m* girevole
revolv'ing cred'it *s* credito rotativo
revolv'ing door' *s* porta girevole

revolv'ing fund' *s* fondo rotativo
revue [rɪ'vju] *s* rivista
revulsion [rɪ'vʌlʃən] *s* ripugnanza, **avversione**; (med) revulsione
reward [rɪ'word] *s* premio, ricompensa; (*money offered for capture*)
taglia; (*for return of articles lost*)
mancia competente ‖ *tr* premiare,
ricompensare
rewarding [rɪ'wordɪŋ] *adj* rimunerativo; gradevole
re·wind [rɪ'waɪnd] *s* (*of a tape*) ribo-
binazione ‖ *v* (*pret & pp* **-wound**
[waund]) *tr* ribobinare
re·write [rɪ'raɪt] *v* (*pret* **-wrote** ['rot];
pp **-written** ['rɪtən]) *tr* riscrivere;
(*news*) rimaneggiare, correggere
rhapso·dy ['ræpsədi] *s* (**-dies**) rapsodia
rheostat ['riˌəˌstæt] *s* reostato
rhesus ['risəs] *s* reso
rhetoric ['retərɪk] *s* retorica
rhetorical [rɪ'tarɪkəl] or [rɪ'tɔrɪkəl]
adj retorico
rheumatic [ru'mætɪk] *adj & s* reuma-
tico
rheumatism ['ruməˌtɪzəm] *s* reumatismo
Rhine [raɪn] *s* Reno
Rhineland ['raɪnˌlænd] *s* la Renania
rhine'stone' *s* gemma artificiale
rhinoceros [raɪ'nasərəs] *s* rinoceronte
m
Rhodes [rodz] *s* Rodi *f*
Rhone [ron] *s* Rodano
rhubarb ['rubarb] *s* rabarbaro; (slang)
baruffa
rhyme [raɪm] *s* rima; **without rhyme or
reason** senza capo né coda ‖ *tr &
intr* rimare
rhythm ['rɪðəm] *s* ritmo
rhythmic(al) ['rɪðmɪk(əl)] *adj* ritmico
rial·to [rɪ'ælto] *s* (**-tos**) mercato ‖ **the
Rialto** il ponte di Rialto; il centro
teatrale di New York
rib [rɪb] *s* costola; (*cut of meat*) costata; (*of umbrella*) stecca; (*of leaf*)
nervatura; (aer, archit) centina;
(naut) costa ‖ (*pret & pp* **ribbed;**
ger **ribbing**) *tr* (slang) prendersi
gioco di
ribald ['rɪbəld] *adj* volgare, indecente
ribbon ['rɪbən] *s* nastro; (*decoration*)
nastrino; **ribbons** (*shreds*) brandelli
mpl
rice [raɪs] *s* riso
rich [rɪtʃ] *adj* ricco; (*food*) nutrito,
grasso; (*wine*) generoso; (*voice*)
caldo; (*color*) vivo; (*odor*) forte;
(coll) divertente; (coll) assurdo; **to
strike it rich** trovare la miniera d'oro
‖ **riches** *spl* ricchezze *fpl;* **the rich** i
ricchi
rickets ['rɪkɪts] *s* rachitismo
rickety ['rɪkɪti] *adj* (*object*) sganghe-
rato; (*person*) vacillante; (*suffering
from rickets*) rachitico
rid [rɪd] *v* (*pret & pp* **rid;** *ger* **ridding**)
tr liberare, sbarazzare; **to get rid of**
liberarsi di, sbarazzarsi di
riddance ['rɪdəns] *s* liberazione; **good
riddance!** che sollievo!
riddle ['rɪdəl] *s* enigma *m*, indovi-

nello; (sieve) crivello || tr crivellare;
(to sift) vagliare; (s.o.'s reputation)
rovinare; **to riddle with** crivellare di
ride [raɪd] s scarrozzata; cavalcata;
gita || v (pret **rode** [rod]; pp **ridden**
['rɪdən]) tr cavalcare, montare, montare su; (e.g., a bus) andare in; (the
waves) galleggiare su; attraversare;
tiranneggiare; farsi gioco di; **to ride
down** travolgere; sorpassare; **to ride
out** uscire felicemente da || intr ca-
valcare; fare una passeggiata, fare
una gita; (to float) galleggiare; **to let
ride** lasciar correre; **to ride on** dipendere da
rider ['raɪdər] s cavallerizzo; ciclista
mf; viaggiatore m, passeggero
ridge [rɪdʒ] s (of mountains) crinale
m, dorsale f; (of roof) displuvio;
(agr) porca
ridge'pole' s trave maestra, colmo
ridicule ['rɪdɪ‚kjul] s ridicolo; **to ex-
pose to ridicule** porre in ridicolo ||
tr ridicolizzare
ridiculous [rɪ'dɪkjələs] adj ridicolo
rid'ing boot' s stivalone m d'equitazione
rid'ing school' s maneggio
rife [raɪf] adj comune, prevalente; **rife
with** pieno di
riffraff ['rɪf‚ræf] s gentaglia
rifle ['raɪfəl] s fucile m; cannone ri-
gato || tr (a place) svaligiare; (a
person) derubare; (a gun) rigare
rifle' range' s tiro a segno
rift [rɪft] s crepa, fessura; disaccordo
rig [rɪg] s attrezzatura, equipaggio;
impianto di sondaggio (per il petro-
lio); (outfit) tenuta || v (pret & pp
rigged; ger **rigging**) tr attrezzare,
equipaggiare; guarnire; abbigliare in
maniera strana
rigging ['rɪgɪŋ] s (naut) padiglione m;
(tackle) (naut) rizza; (coll) vestiti
mpl
right [raɪt] adj giusto; corretto; (mind)
sano; destro, diritto; (geom) retto;
(geom) perpendicolare; **right or
wrong** a torto o a ragione; **to be all
right** star bene di salute; **to be right**
aver ragione || s diritto; quanto è
giusto, (il) giusto; (in a company)
interessenza; (right hand) destra;
(turn) giro a destra; (boxing) diritto;
(tex) dritto; (pol) destra; **by right** in
giustizia; **on the right** alla destra; **to
be in the right** aver ragione || adv
direttamente; completamente; immediatamente; proprio, precisamente;
correttamente, giustamente; bene;
alla destra; (coll) molto; **all right**
benissimo || tr drizzare; correggere;
rimettere a posto || intr drizzarsi
righteous ['raɪtʃəs] adj retto; virtuoso
right' field' s (baseball) campo destro
rightful ['raɪtfəl] adj giusto; legittimo
right'-hand drive' s guida a destra
right-handed ['raɪt'hændɪd] adj che
usa la destra; destrorso
right'-hand man' s braccio destro
rightist ['raɪtɪst] adj conservatore || s
conservatore m, membro della destra

rightly ['raɪtli] adv correttamente; giustamente; **rightly or wrongly** a torto
o a ragione
right' mind' s—**in one's right mind** nel
pieno possesso delle proprie facoltà,
con la testa a posto
right' of way' s precedenza; (law) servitù f di passaggio; (rr) sede f
rights' of man' s diritti mpl dell'uomo
right'-wing' adj della destra
right-winger ['raɪt'wɪŋər] s membro
della destra, conservatore m
rigid ['rɪdʒɪd] adj rigido
rigmarole ['rɪgmə‚rol] s sproloquio
rigorous ['rɪgərəs] adj rigoroso
rile [raɪl] tr irritare, esasperare
rill [rɪl] s rigagnolo
rim [rɪm] s orlo, bordo; (of a wheel)
cerchione m
rime [raɪm] s brina; (in verse) rima ||
tr brinare; rimare || intr rimare
rind [raɪnd] s (of animals) cotenna;
(of fruit or cheese) scorza
ring [rɪŋ] s (for finger) anello; (anything round) cerchio; (circular
course) pista; (of people) crocchio;
(of evildoers) combriccola; (of anchor) anello; (sound of bell) squillo;
(loud sound of bell) scampanellata;
(of small bell; of glassware) tintinnio; (act of ringing) sonata; (telp)
chiamata; (fig) suono; (boxing) quadrato; (mach) ghiera; (fig, taur)
arena; **to run rings around** essere
molto migliore di || v (pret & pp
ringed) tr accerchiare; mettere un
anello a || intr formare cerchi || v
(pret **rang** [ræŋ]; pp **rung** [rʌŋ]) tr
sonare; squillare; tintinnare; chiamare al telefono; **to ring up** chiamare
al telefono; (a sale) battere sul regi-
stratore di cassa || intr sonare; squil-
lare; tintinnare; chiamare; (said of
one's ears) fischiare; **to ring for**
chiamare col campanello; **to ring off**
terminare una conversazione telefonica; **to ring up** chiamare al telefono
ring-around-a-rosy ['rɪŋə‚raundə'rozi]
s girotondo
ringing ['rɪŋɪŋ] adj alto, sonoro || s
accerchiamento; squillo; tintinnio;
(in the ears) fischio
ring'lead'er s capobanda m
ringlet ['rɪŋlɪt] s anellino
ring'mas'ter s direttore m di circo
equestre
ring'side' s posto vicino al quadrato
ring'worm' s tigna
rink [rɪŋk] s pattinatoio
rinse [rɪns] s risciacquatura || tr ri-
sciacquare
riot ['raɪ‚ət] s sommossa, tumulto;
profusione; **to be a riot** (coll) essere
divertentissimo; **to run riot** sfrenarsi;
(said of plants) crescere disordinata-
mente || intr tumultuare; darsi alle
gozzoviglie
rioter ['raɪ‚ətər] s rivoltoso
rip [rɪp] s sdrucitura; (open seam)
scucitura || v (pret & pp **ripped**; ger
ripping) tr sdrucire; (to open the

ripe 262 rogue

seam of) scucire ‖ *intr* sdrucirsi; scucirsi; **to rip out with insults** (coll) prorompere in improperi
ripe [raɪp] *adj* maturo; (*lips*) turgido; (*cheese*) stagionato; pronto
ripen ['raɪpən] *tr & intr* maturare
ripple ['rɪpəl] *s* increspatura; (*sound*) mormorio ‖ *tr* increspare ‖ *intr* incresparsi; mormorare
rise [raɪz] *s* (*of prices, temperature*) aumento; (*of a road*) salita; (*of ground*) elevazione; (*of a heavenly body*) levata; (*in rank*) ascesa; (*of a step*) alzata; (*of a stream*) sorgente *f*; (*of water*) crescita; **to get a rise out of** (coll) farsi rispondere per le rime da; **to give rise to** dar origine a ‖ *v* (*pret* **rose** [roz]; *pp* **risen** ['rɪzən]) *intr* (*said of the sun*) sorgere; rialzarsi; (*said of plants*) crescere; (*said of the wind*) alzarsi; (*said of a building*) ergersi; (*to return from the dead*) risorgere; (*to increase*) aumentare; **to rise above** alzarsi al di sopra di; essere al di sopra di; **to rise to** sorgere all'altezza di
riser ['raɪzər] *s* (*of step*) alzata; (*upright*) montante *m*; **early riser** persona mattiniera; **late riser** dormiglione *m*
risk [rɪsk] *s* rischio; **to run or take a risk** correre un rischio ‖ *tr* rischiare
risk·y ['rɪski] *adj* (**-ier; -iest**) rischioso
risqué [rɪs'ke] *adj* audace, spinto
rite [raɪt] *s* rito; **last rites** riti *mpl* funebri
ritual ['rɪtʃu·əl] *adj & s* rituale *m*
ri·val ['raɪvəl] *s* rivale *mf* ‖ *v* (*pret & pp* **-valed** or **-valled**; *ger* **-valing** or **-valling**) *tr* rivaleggiare con
rival·ry ['raɪvəlri] *s* (**-ries**) rivalità *f*
river ['rɪvər] *s* fiume *m*; **down the river** a valle; **up the river** a monte
riv'er ba'sin *s* bacino fluviale
riv'er·bed' *s* letto di fiume
riv'er front' *s* riva di fiume
riv'er·head' *s* sorgente *f* di fiume
riv'er·side' *adj* rivierasco ‖ *s* riva del fiume
rivet ['rɪvɪt] *s* ribattino; (*of scissors*) perno ‖ *tr* ribadire; (*s.o.'s attention*) concentrare
roach [rotʃ] *s* scarafaggio
road [rod] *adj* stradale ‖ *s* strada; via; (naut) rada; **to be in the road of** ostacolare il cammino a; **to burn up the road** divorare la strada; **to get out of the road** togliersi di mezzo
roadability [ˌrodə'bɪlɪti] *s* tenuta di strada
road'bed' *s* (*of highway*) piattaforma; (rr) massicciata, infrastruttura
road'block' *s* (mil) barricata; (fig) impedimento
road'house' *s* taverna su autostrada
road' la'borer *m* cantoniere *m*
road' map' *s* carta stradale
road' roll'er *s* compressore *m* stradale, rullo compressore
road' serv'ice *s* servizio di assistenza stradale
road'side' *s* bordo della strada

road'side inn' *s* taverna posta su autostrada
road' sign' *s* indicatore *m* stradale
road'stead' *s* rada
road'way' *s* carreggiata; strada
roam [rom] *s* vagabondaggio ‖ *tr* girovagare per ‖ *intr* girovagare
roar [ror] *s* ruggito, muggito; boato, fragore *m* ‖ *intr* muggire; **to roar with laughter** fare una risata
roast [rost] *s* arrosto; torrefazione ‖ *tr* arrostire; (*coffee*) tostare, torrefare; (coll) farsi beffe di ‖ *intr* arrostirsi
roast' beef' *s* rosbif *m*
roast'ed pea'nut *s* nocciolina americana abbrustolita
roast' pork' *s* arrosto di maiale
rob [rab] *v* (*pret & pp* **robbed**; *ger* **robbing**) *tr & intr* derubare
robber ['rabər] *s* ladro, malandrino
robber·y ['rabəri] *s* (**-ies**) furto
robe [rob] *s* (*of a woman*) vestito; (*of a professor*) toga; (*of a priest*) abito talare; (*dressing gown*) vestaglia; (*for lap*) coperta da viaggio; **robes** vestiti *mpl* ‖ *tr* vestire ‖ *intr* vestirsi
robin ['rabɪn] *s* pettirosso
robot ['robat] *s* robot *m*
robust [ro'bʌst] *adj* robusto
rock [rak] *s* roccia; (*any stone*) pietra; (*sticking out of water*) scoglio; (*one that is thrown*) sasso; (*hill*) rocca; (slang) pietra preziosa; **on the rocks** (coll) in rovina; (coll) al verde; (*said, e.g., of whiskey*) sul ghiaccio ‖ *tr* far vacillare; dondolare ‖ *intr* vacillare; dondolare
rock'-bot'tom *adj* (l') ultimo; (il) minimo
rock' can'dy *s* zucchero candito
rock' crys'tal *s* cristallo di rocca
rocker ['rakər] *s* (*curved piece at bottom of rocking chair*) dondolo; sedia a dondolo; (mach) bilanciere *m*; **off one's rocker** (slang) matto
rocket ['rakɪt] *s* razzo ‖ *intr* partire come un razzo
rock'et launch'er ['lɔntʃər] or ['lantʃər] *s* lanciarazzo
rock' gar'den *s* giardino piantato fra le rocce
rock'ing chair' *s* sedia a dondolo
rock'ing horse' *s* cavallo a dondolo
rock' salt' *s* salgemma *m*
rock' wool' *s* cotone *m* or lana minerale
rock·y ['raki] *adj* (**-ier; -iest**) roccioso; traballante; (coll) debole
rod [rad] *s* verga, bacchetta; scettro; punizione; (*bar*) asta; (*for fishing*) canna da pesca; (anat, biol) bastoncino; (mach) biella; (surv) biffa; (Bib) razza, tribù *f*; (slang) pistola; **spare the rod and spoil the child** la madre pietosa fa la piaga cancrenosa
rodent ['rodənt] *adj & s* roditore *m*
rod'man *s* (**-men**) *s* aiutante *m* geometra
roe [ro] *s* capriolo; (*of fish*) uova *fpl*
rogue [rog] *s* furfante *m*; (*scamp*) picaro

rogues"' gal'lery *s* collezione di fotografie di malviventi

rôle or **role** [rol] *s* ruolo, parte *f;* **to play a role** fare la parte

roll [rol] *s* (*of film, paper, etc.*) rotolo, bobina; (*of fat*) strato; (*roller*) rotella; (*of bread*) panino; ondulazione; (*noise*) rullio, rullo; (*of a boat*) rollio; (*of thunder*) rombo; (*list*) ruolo; (*of money*) (slang) fascio; **to call the roll** fare la chiama || *tr* far rotolare; (*one's r's*) arrotare; (*one's eyes*) stralunare; (*e.g., dough*) spianare; (*steel*) laminare; (*to wrap*) arrotolare; (*a drum*) rullare; **to roll back** (*prices*) ridurre; **to roll out** spianare; srotolare; **to roll up** (*one's sleeves*) arrotolarsi; accumulare; aumentare || *intr* rotolare; rullare; arrotolarsi; raggomitolarsi; **to roll on** passare; **to roll out** srotolarsi; (*to get out of bed*) (slang) alzarsi

roll' call' *s* chiama, appello

roller ['rolər] *s* rotella; (*for hair*) bigodino; rotolo; (*wave*) ondata lunga

roll'er bear'ing *s* cuscinetto a rotolamento

roll'er coast'er *s* montagne russe

roll'er skate' *s* pattino a rotelle

roll'er-skate' *intr* pattinare coi pattini a rotelle

roll'er tow'el *s* bandinella

roll'ing mill' ['roliŋ] *s* laminatoio

roll'ing pin' *s* matterello

roll'ing stock' *s* (rr) materiale *m* rotabile

roll'-top desk' *s* scrivania a piano scorrevole

roly-poly ['roli'poli] *adj* grassoccio

roman ['romən] *adj* (typ) romano, tondo || *s* (typ) carattere romano, tondo || **Roman** *adj & s* romano

Ro'man can'dle *s* candela romana

Ro'man Cath'olic Church' *s* Chiesa Cattolica Apostolica Romana

romance [ro'mæns] or ['romæns] *s* romanzo; sentimentalità *f;* idillio, intrigo amoroso; (mus) romanza || [ro'mæns] *intr* scrivere romanzi; raccontare romanzi; fare il romantico || **Romance** ['romæns] or [ro-'mæns] *adj* romanzo, neolatino

Ro'man Em'pire *s* Impero Romano

romanesque [,romən'ɛsk] *adj* romantico || **Romanesque** *adj & s* romanico

Ro'man nose' *s* naso aquilino

romantic [ro'mæntɪk] *adj* romantico

romanticism [ro'mæntɪ,sɪzəm] *s* romanticismo

romanticist [ro'mæntɪsɪst] *s* romantico

romp [rɑmp] *intr* ruzzare

rompers ['rɑmpərz] *spl* pagliaccetto

roof [ruf] or [ruf] *s* (*of house*) tetto; (*of heaven*) volta; (*of car*) tetto, padiglione *m;* **to hit the roof** (slang) andare fuori dai gangheri; **to raise the roof** (slang) fare molto chiasso; (slang) protestare violentemente || *tr* ricoprire con tetto

roofer ['rufər] or ['rufər] *s* conciatetti *m*

roof' gar'den *s* giardino pensile

rook [ruk] *s* (*bird*) cornacchia; (*in chess*) torre *f* || *tr* truffare

rookie ['ruki] *s* novizio; (mil) recluta

room [rum] or [rum] *s* stanza, camera; vano, locale *m;* posto, spazio; opportunità *f;* **to make room** far luogo || *intr* alloggiare

room' and board' *s* vitto e alloggio

room' clerk' *s* impiegato d'albergo assegnato alle prenotazioni

roomer ['rumər] or ['rumər] *s* inquilino

room'ing house' *s* casa con camere d'affittare

room'mate' *s* compagno di stanza

room·y ['rumi] or ['rumi] *adj* (**-ier; -iest**) ampio, spazioso

roost [rust] *s* (*perch*) ballatoio; (*house for chickens*) pollaio; (*place for resting*) posto di riposo; **to rule the roost** essere il gallo del pollaio || *intr* appollaiarsi; andare a dormire

rooster ['rustər] *s* gallo

root [rut] *cr* [rut] *s* radice *f;* **to get to the root of** andare al fondo di; **to take root** metter radici || *tr* inchiodare, piantare || *intr* radicare; (*said of swine*) grufolare; **to root for** fare il tifo per

rooter ['rutər] or ['rutər] *s* tifoso

rope [rop] *s* fune *f,* corda; (*of a hangman*) capestro; laccio, lasso; **to know the ropes** (coll) conoscere la faccenda a fondo, saperla lunga || *tr* legare con, fune; prendere al laccio; **to rope in** (slang) imbrogliare

rope'danc'er or **rope'walk'er** *s* funambolo

rosa·ry ['rozəri] *s* (**-ries**) rosario

rose [roz] *adj & s* rosa

rose'bud' *s* bottoncino di rosa

rose'bush' *s* rosaio

rose'-col'ored *adj* color di rosa

rose'-colored glass'es *spl* occhiali *mpl* rosa

rose' gar'den *s* roseto

rosemar·y ['roz,mɛri] *s* (**-ies**) rosmarino

rose' of Shar'on *s* altea

rosette [ro'zɛt] *s* rosetta; (archit) rosone *m*

rose' win'dow *s* rosone *m*

rose'wood' *s* palissandro

rosin ['rɑzɪn] *s* colofonia

roster ['rɑstər] *s* ruolino; orario scolastico

rostrum ['rɑstrəm] *s* tribuna

ros·y ['rozi] *adj* (**-ier; -iest**) rosa, roseo

rot [rɑt] *s* marcio; (coll) stupidaggine *f* || *v* (*pret & pp* **rotted;** *ger* **rotting**) *tr & intr* imputridire

ro'tary en'gine ['rotəri] *s* motore rotativo

ro'tary press' *s* rotativa

rotate ['rotet] or [ro'tet] *tr & intr* rotare

rotation [ro'tefən] *s* rotazione; **in rotation** in successione, a turno

rote [rot] *s* ripetizione macchinale; **by rote** a memoria

rot'gut' *s* (slang) acquavite *f* di infima qualità

rotisserie [ro'tɪsəri] *s* girarrosto a motore

rotten ['rɑtən] *adj* marcio, fradicio; corrotto

rotund [ro'tʌnd] *adj* (*plump*) rotondetto; (*voice*) profondo; (*speech*) enfatico

rouge [ruʒ] *s* belletto, rossetto ‖ *tr* dare il belletto a ‖ *intr* darsi il belletto

rough [rʌf] *adj* scabroso; (*sea*) agitato; (*crude*) rozzo, rude; (*road*) accidentato; approssimativo ‖ *tr*—**to rough it** vivere primitivamente; **to rough up** malmenare

rough'cast' *s* intonaco; modello disgrossato ‖ *v* (*pret & pp* -**cast**) *tr* (*a wall*) intonacare; disgrossare, dirozzare

rough' cop'y *s* brutta copia

rough-hew ['rʌf'hju] *tr* digrossare, dirozzare

roughly ['rʌfli] *adv* aspramente; rozzamente; approssimativamente

round [raund] *adj* rotondo ‖ *s* tondo; (*of applause; of guns*) salva; (*of a single gun*) colpo, tiro; (*of a chair*) piolo; (*of a doctor*) giro; (*of a policeman*) ronda; serie *f;* (*of golf*) partita; (*e.g., of bridge*) mano *f;* cerchio; (*boxing*) ripresa ‖ *adv* intorno; dal principio alla fine ‖ *prep* intorno a; attraverso ‖ *tr* (*to make round*) arrotondare; circondare; (*a corner*) scantonare; **to round off** arrotondare; completare, perfezionare; **to round up** raccogliere; (*cattle*) condurre

roundabout ['raundə,baut] *adj* indiretto ‖ *s* giacca attillata; via traversa; giro di parole; (Brit) giostra; (Brit) anello stradale

round'house' *s* rimessa per locomotive

round-shouldered ['raund'ʃoldərd] *adj* dalle spalle spioventi

round'-trip tick'et *s* biglietto d'andata e ritorno

round'up' *s* (*of cattle*) riunione; (*of criminals*) retata; (*of facts*) riassunto

rouse [rauz] *tr* svegliare; suscitare; (*game*) scovare ‖ *intr* svegliarsi

rout [raut] *s* sconfitta, rotta ‖ *tr* sconfiggere, mettere in rotta ‖ *intr* grufolare

route [rut] or [raut] *s* via, rotta; itinerario ‖ *tr* istradare

routine [ru'tin] *adj* ordinario ‖ *s* trafila, routine *f*

rove [rov] *intr* vagabondare, vagare

rover ['rovər] *s* vagabondo

row [rau] *s* piazzata, scenata; (*clamor*) (coll) baccano; **to raise a row** (coll) fare baccano ‖ [ro] *s* fila; (*of figures*) finca; (*e.g., of trees*) filare *m;* **in a row** in continuazione, di seguito ‖ *tr* vogare ‖ *intr* remare, vogare

rowboat ['ro,bot] *s* barca a remi

row·dy ['raudi] *adj* (-**dier**; -**diest**) turbolento ‖ *s* (-**dies**) attaccabrighe *mf*

rower ['ro·ər] *s* rematore *m*

rowing ['ro·ɪŋ] *s* (*action*) voga; (*sport*) canottaggio

royal ['rɔɪ·əl] *adj* reale, regio

royalist ['rɔɪ·əlɪst] *adj* sostenitore del re ‖ *s* realista *mf*

royal·ty ['rɔɪ·əlti] *s* (-**ties**) regalità *f;* membro della famiglia reale; nobiltà *f;* diritto d'autore; diritto d'inventore; percentuale *f* sugli utili

rub [rʌb] *s* frizione; difficile *m;* **here's the rub** qui sta il busillis ‖ *v* (*pret & pp* **rubbed**; *ger* **rubbing**) *tr* fregare; **to rub elbows with** stare giunto a gomiti con; **to rub out** cancellare con la gomma; (slang) togliere di mezzo ‖ *intr* sfregare; **to rub off** venir via sfregando; cancellarsi

rubber ['rʌbər] *s* gomma, caucciù *m;* gomma da cancellare; (*overshoe*) caloscia; (*in cards*) rubber *m;* (sports) bella

rub'ber band' *s* elastico

rub'ber·neck' *s* (coll) ficcanaso; (coll) turista curioso ‖ *intr* (coll) allungare il collo

rub'ber plant' *s* albero del cauccià

rub'ber stamp' *s* timbro di gomma; (coll) persona che approva inconsultamente

rub'ber-stamp' *tr* timbrare; (coll) approvare inconsultamente

rubbish ['rʌbɪʃ] *s* spazzatura; immondizia; (fig) detrito; (coll) sciocchezza

rubble ['rʌbəl] *s* (*broken stone*) pietrisco; (*masonry*) mistura di malta e pietrame; (*broken bits*) calcinacci *mpl*

rub'down' *s* fregagione

rube [rub] *s* (slang) contadino gonzo

ru·by ['rubi] *adj* vermiglio ‖ (-**bies**) *s* rubino

rudder ['rʌdər] *s* timone *m;* (aer) timone *m* di direzione

rud·dy ['rʌdi] *adj* (-**dier**; -**diest**) rubicondo

rude [rud] *adj* rude, sgarbato

rudiment ['rudɪmənt] *s* rudimento

rue [ru] *tr* lamentare, rimpiangere

rueful ['rufəl] *adj* lamentevole; triste

ruffian ['rʌfɪ·ən] *s* ribaldo

ruffle ['rʌfəl] *s* increspatura; (*of drum*) rullo; (sew) gala, crespa ‖ *tr* increspare; arruffare; irritare; (*a drum*) far rullare; (sew) guarnire di gala or crespa

rug [rʌg] *s* tappeto

rugged ['rʌgɪd] *adj* aspro, irregolare; rugoso; rozzo; forte; tempestuoso

ruin ['ru·ɪn] *s* rovina ‖ *tr* rovinare, mandare in rovina

rule [rul] *s* regola; dominazione; (*reign*) regno; (law) ordinanza; (typ) filetto; **as a rule** in generale ‖ *tr* governare; dominare; (*with lines*) rigare; (law) deliberare; **to rule out** escludere ‖ *intr* governare; regnare; **to rule over** governare

rule' of thumb' *s* regola basata sull'esperienza; **by rule of thumb** secondo la propria esperienza

ruler ['rulər] *s* governante *m*, dominatore *m;* (*for ruling lines*) riga, regolo

ruling ['rulɪŋ] *adj* dirigente ‖ *s* (*ruled lines*) rigatura; (law) decisione

rum [rʌm] *s* rum *m;* (*any alcoholic drink*) acquavite *f*

Rumanian [ru'menɪ·ən] *adj* & *s* rumeno

rumble ['rʌmbəl] *s* rimbombo; (*of the intestines*) gorgoglio; (*slang*) rissa fra ganghe rivali ‖ *intr* rimbombare; gorgogliare

ruminate ['rumɪ ˌnet] *tr* & *intr* ruminare

rummage ['rʌmɪdʒ] *tr* & *intr* rovistare, frugare

rum'mage sale' *s* vendita di cianfrusaglie

rumor ['rumər] *s* voce *f*, diceria ‖ *tr* vociferare; **it is rumored that** corre voce che

rump [rʌmp] *s* anca; posteriore *m*; (*of beef*) quarto posteriore

rumple ['rʌmpəl] *s* piega ‖ *tr* spiegazzare, sgualcire ‖ *intr* sgualcirsi

rumpus ['rʌmpəs] *s* tumulto; rissa; **to raise a rumpus** fare baccano

run [rʌn] *s* corsa; percorso; produzione; (*e.g., in a stocking*) smagliatura; direzione; (*spell*) serie *f*; (*in cards*) scala; (*of goods*) richiesta; (*on a bank*) afflusso; **in the long run** a lungo andare; **on the run** (coll) di corsa; in fuga; **the common run of men** la media della gente; **to give s.o. a run for his money** dare il filo da torcere; essere denaro ben speso per qlcu, e.g., **that sweater gave me a run for my money** quello sweater è stato denaro ben speso per me; **to have a long run** tenere il cartellone per lungo tempo; **to have the run of** avere la libertà di andare e venire per ‖ *v* (*pret* ran [ræn]; *pp* run; *ger* running) *tr* muovere; (*a horse*) far correre; (*the street*) vivere liberamente in; (*game*) inseguire; trasportare; (*a machine*) far camminare; (*a store*) esercire; (*a candidate*) portare; (*a risk*) correre; (*a blockade*) violare; mettere, ficcare; (*a line*) tirare; **to run down** cacciare; esaminare; trovare; (*a pedestrian*) investire; denigrare, criticare; **to run in** (*a machine*) rodare; (*slang*) schiaffare in prigione; **to run off** creare di getto; cacciare; (*typ*) tirare; **to run up** ammassare ‖ *intr* correre; scappare; (*in a race*) arrivare; (*said of a candidate*) portarsi; passare; (*said of knitted material*) smagliarsi; (*said of a liquid*) scorrere; (*said of a color*) sbavare; (*said of fish*) migrare; funzionare; (*to become*) diventare; (*to be worded*) essere del tenore; (com) decorrere; (theat, mov) durare in cartellone; **to run across** imbattersi in; **to run aground** incagliarsi; **to run away** fuggire; (*said of a horse*) prendere la mano; **to run down** (*said of a liquid*) scorrere; (*said of a battery, a watch*) scaricarsi; (*in health*) sciuparsi; **to run for** presentarsi candidato per; **to run in the family** essere una caratteristica familiare; **to run into** imbattersi in; ammontare a; (*to follow*) succedersi a; **to run off the track** (rr) uscire dalle rotaie; **to run out** aver termine; scadere; esaurirsi;

to run out of rimanere senza; **to run over** oltrepassare; (*e.g., with a car*) investire; **to run through** trapassare; (*a fortune*) dilapidare; esaminare rapidamente

run'a·way' *adj* fuggiasco; (*horse*) che ha preso la mano ‖ *s* fuggiasco; cavallo che ha preso la mano; fuga

run'-down' *adj* esausto; negletto, cadente; (*watch, battery*) scarico

rung [rʌŋ] *s* (*of chair or ladder*) piolo

runner ['rʌnər] *s* corridore *m*; messaggero; fattorino, messo; (*of sleigh*) pattino; (*of ice skate*) lama; (*rug*) guida; (*on a table*) striscia di pizzo; (*in stocking*) smagliatura

run'ner-up' *s* (**runners-up**) finalista *mf* secondo

running ['rʌnɪŋ] *adj* in corsa; da corsa; (*water*) corrente; (*vine*) rampicante; (*knot*) scorsoio; (*sore*) purulento; (*writing*) corsivo; consecutivo; (*start*) (sports) lanciato ‖ *s* corsa; (*of a business*) esercizio; direzione; funzionamento; **to be in the running** avere possibilità di vittoria

run'ning board' *s* (aut) pedana

run'ning head' *s* titolo corrente

run·ny ['rʌni] *adj* (**-nier; -niest**) (*liquid*) scorrevole; (*color*) sbavante; **to have a runny nose** avere la goccia al naso

run'off' *s* ballottaggio

run-of-the-mill ['rʌnəvðə'mɪl] *adj* ordinario, corrente

run'proof' *adj* indemagliabile

runt [rʌnt] *s* nanerottolo; animale deperito

run'way' *s* pista; (*of a stream*) letto; (*for animals*) chiusa; (aut) corsia

rupture ['rʌptʃər] *s* rottura; (pathol) ernia ‖ *tr* rompere; causare un'ernia a ‖ *intr* rompersi; soffrire di ernia

ru'ral free' deliv'ery ['rurəl] *s* distribuzione postale campestre

ruse [ruz] *s* astuzia, stratagemma *m*

rush [rʌʃ] *adj* urgente ‖ *s* fretta; slancio, corsa; (*of blood*) ondata; (*rushing of persons to a new mine*) febbre *f*; (bot) giunco; **in a rush** in fretta e furia ‖ *tr* affrettare; portare di fretta; spingere; (coll) fare la corte a; **to rush through** fare di fretta; (*e.g., a bill through Congress*) far approvare di fretta ‖ *intr* lanciarsi; affrettarsi; passare velocemente; **to rush through** (*a book*) leggere velocemente; (*one's work*) fare in fretta; (*a town*) attraversare velocemente

rush'-bot'tomed chair' *s* sedia di giunchi

rush' can'dle *s* lumicino con lo stoppino fatto di midollo di giunco

rush' hour' *s* ora di punta

russet ['rʌsɪt] *adj* color cannella

Russia ['rʌʃə] *s* la Russia

Russian ['rʌʃən] *adj* & *s* russo

rust [rʌst] *s* ruggine *f*; (fig) torpore *m* ‖ *tr* arrugginire ‖ *intr* arrugginirsi

rustic ['rʌstɪk] *adj* & *s* rusti·co

rustle ['rʌsəl] *s* fruscio; (*of leaves*) stormire *m* ‖ *tr* far frusciare; far stormire; (*cattle*) (coll) rubare ‖ *intr* frusciare; stormire; (coll) lavorare di buzzo buono

rust·y ['rʌsti] *adj* (**-ier; -iest**) rugginoso; color ruggine; fuori pratica

rut [rʌt] *s* (*track*) solco, carrareccia; (*of animals*) fregola; (il) solito tran tran

ruthless ['ruθlɪs] *adj* spietato

rye [raɪ] *s* segala; whiskey *m* di segala

S

S, s [ɛs] *s* diciannovesima lettera dell'alfabeto inglese

Sabbath ['sæbəθ] *s* (*of Jews*] sabato; (*of Christians*) domenica; **to keep the Sabbath** osservare il riposo domenicale

sabbat'ical year' [sə'bætɪkəl] *s* anno di congedo; (Bib) anno sabbatico

saber ['sebər] *s* sciabola

sa'ber rat'tling *s* minacce *fpl* di guerra

sable ['sebəl] *adj* nero ‖ *s* zibellino; **sables** vestiti di lutto

sabotage ['sæbə,taʒ] *s* sabotaggio ‖ *tr* & *intr* sabotare

saccharin ['sækərɪn] *s* saccarina

sachet ['sæʃe] or [sæ'ʃe] *s* sacchetto profumato (per la biancheria)

sack [sæk] *s* sacco; (*of an employee*) (slang) licenziamento; (slang) letto ‖ *tr* insaccare; (*to lay waste*) saccheggiare, mettere a sacco; (slang) licenziare

sack'cloth' *s* tela di sacco; (*for penitence*) sacco, cilicio; **in sackcloth and ashes** pentito e contrito

sacrament ['sækrəmənt] *s* sacramento

sacramental [,sækrə'mɛntəl] *adj* sacramentale

sacred ['sekrəd] *adj* sacro

sacrifice ['sækrɪ,faɪs] *s* sacrificio; **at a sacrifice** in perdita ‖ *tr* sacrificare; (com) svendere

sacrilege ['sækrɪlɪdʒ] *s* sacrilegio

sacrilegious [,sækrɪ'lɪdʒəs] or [,sækrɪ'lidʒəs] *adj* sacrilego

sacristan ['sækrɪstən] *s* sagrestano

sacris·ty ['sækrɪsti] *s* (**-ties**) sagrestia

sad [sæd] *adj* (**sadder; saddest**) triste; (*bad*) cattivo; (*color*) tetro

sadden ['sædən] *tr* rattristare ‖ *intr* rattristarsi

saddle ['sædəl] *s* sella ‖ *tr* insellare; **to saddle with** gravare di

saddle'bag' *s* fonda

saddlebow ['sædəl,bo] *s* arcione *m* anteriore

sad'dle·cloth' *s* gualdrappa

saddler ['sædlər] *s* sellaio

sad'dle·tree' *s* arcione *m*

sadist ['sædɪst] or ['sedɪst] *s* sadico

sadistic [sæ'dɪstɪk] or [se'dɪstɪk] *adj* sadico

sadness ['sædnɪs] *s* tristezza

sad' sack' *s* (coll) marmittone *m*

safe [sef] *adj* sicuro; cauto; (*distance*) rispettoso; **safe and sound** sano e salvo ‖ *s* cassaforte *f*

safe'-con'duct *s* salvacondotto

safe'-depos'it box' *s* cassetta di sicurezza

safe'guard' *s* salvaguardia ‖ *tr* salvaguardare

safe·ty ['sefti] *adj* di sicurezza ‖ *s* (**-ties**) sicurezza; (*of a gun*) sicura; **to reach safety** mettersi in salvo

safe'ty belt' *s* (*of a worker*) imbraca; (aer, aut) cintura di sicurezza; (naut) cintura di salvataggio

safe'ty glass' *s* vetro infrangibile

safe'ty is'land *s* salvagente *m*

safe'ty match' *s* fiammifero svedese

safe'ty pin' *s* spillo di sicurezza

safe'ty ra'zor *s* rasoio di sicurezza

safe'ty valve' *s* valvola di sicurezza

saffron ['sæfrən] *s* zafferano

sag [sæg] *s* cedimento; depressione; (*of a rope*) allentamento ‖ *v* (*pret* & *pp* **sagged;** *ger* **sagging**) *intr* curvarsi; cedere, afflosciarsi; allentarsi; (*said of prices*) calare

sagacious [sə'geʃəs] *adj* sagace

sage [sedʒ] *adj* saggio, savio ‖ *s* saggio, savio; (bot) salvia

sage'brush' *s* artemisia

Sagittarius [,sædʒɪ'teri·əs] *s* Sagittario

sail [sel] *s* vela; (*of windmill*) ala; gita a vela; **to set sail** far vela; **under full sail** a piena velatura ‖ *tr* veleggiare, navigare; (*a boat*) far navigare ‖ *intr* veleggiare, navigare; far vela; volare; (*said of a vessel*) partire; **to sail into** (coll) attaccare

sail'boat' *s* nave *f* a vela, veliero

sail'cloth' *s* tela di olona

sailing ['selɪŋ] *adj* in partenza ‖ *s* partenza; navigazione; navigazione a vela

sail'ing ship' *s* veliero

sail'mak'er *s* velaio

sailor ['selər] *s* marinaio

saint [sent] *adj* & *s* santo ‖ *tr* santificare, canonizzare

saint'hood *s* santità *f*

saintliness ['sentlɪnɪs] *s* santità *f*

Saint' Vi'tus's dance' ['vaɪtəsəz] *s* (pathol) ballo di San Vito

sake [sek] *s* causa, interesse *m*; **for the sake of** per il bene di, per l'amor di

salaam [sə'lɑm] *s* salamelecco ‖ *tr* fare salamelecchi a

salable ['seləbəl] *adj* vendibile

salacious [sə'leʃəs] *adj* salace

salad ['sæləd] *s* insalata

sal'ad bowl' *s* insalatiera

sal'ad oil' *s* olio da tavola

sala·ry ['sæləri] *s* (**-ries**) stipendio

sale [sel] *s* vendita; (*at reduced prices*) svendita, saldo; **for sale** in vendita; **si vende, si vendono**

sales'clerk' *s* commesso, impiegato

sales'la'dy *s* (-dies) commessa, impiegata

sales'man *s* (-men) venditore *m;* commesso; (*traveling*) piazzista *m*

sales'man·ship' *s* arte *f* di vendere

sales' promo'tion *s* promozione delle vendite, promotion *f*

sales'room' *s* sala di esposizione; sala vendite

sales' talk' *s* discorso da venditore; (*e.g., of a barker*) imbonimento

sales' tax' *s* imposta sulle vendite

saliva [sə'laɪvə] *s* saliva

sallow ['sælo] *adj* giallastro, olivastro

sal·ly ['sæli] *s* (-lies) escursione, gita; (*outburst*) esplosione; (*witty remark*) uscita; (mil) sortita || *v pret & pp* -lied) *intr* fare una sortita; **to sally forth** balzar fuori

salmon ['sæmən] *s* salmone *m*

salon [sæ'lɑn] *s* salone *m*

saloon [sə'lun] *s* taverna; (*on a passenger vessel*) salone *m*

saloon' keep'er *s* taverniere *m*

salt [sɔlt] *s* sale *m;* **to be worth one's salt** valere il pane che si mangia || *tr* salare; (*cattle*) dare sale a; **to salt away** (coll) metter via, conservare

salt' bed' *s* salina

salt'cel'lar *s* saliera

saltine [sɔl'tin] *s* galletta salata

saltish ['sɔltɪʃ] *adj* salmastro

salt'pe'ter *s* (*potassium nitrate*) salnitro; (*sodium nitrate*) nitro del Cile

salt' shak'er *s* saliera

salt·y ['sɔlti] *adj* (-ier; -iest) salato

salubrious [sə'lubrɪ·əs] *adj* salubre

salutation [ˌsæljə'teʃən] *s* saluto

salute [sə'lut] *s* saluto || *tr* salutare

salvage ['sælvɪdʒ] *s* ricupero || *tr* ricuperare

salvation [sæl'veʃən] *s* salvezza

Salva'tion Ar'my *s* Esercito della Salvezza

salve [sæv] *or* [sɑv] *s* unguento || *tr* lenire, alleviare

sal·vo ['sælvo] *s* (-vos *or* -voes) salva

Samaritan [sə'mærɪtən] *adj & s* samaritano

same [sem] *adj & pron indef* medesimo, stesso; **it's all the same to me** a me fa lo stesso; **just the same** lo stesso, ugualmente; ciò nonostante; **same . . . as** lo stesso . . . che

sameness ['semnɪs] *s* uniformità *f;* monotonia

sample ['sæmpəl] *s* campione *m,* saggio || *tr* (*to take a sample of*) campionare; (*to taste*) assaggiare; provare

sam'ple cop'y *s* esemplare *m* di campione

sancti·fy ['sæŋktɪˌfaɪ] *v* (*pret & pp* -fied) *tr* santificare

sanctimonious [ˌsæŋktɪ'monɪ·əs] *adj* che affetta devozione ipocrita

sanction ['sæŋkʃən] *s* sanzione || *tr* sanzionare

sanctuar·y ['sæŋktʃuˌeri] *s* (-ies) santuario; **to take sanctuary** prendere asilo, rifugiarsi

sand [sænd] *s* sabbia || *tr* insabbiare;

(*to polish*) smerigliare; cospergere di sabbia

sandal ['sændəl] *s* sandalo

san'dal·wood' *s* sandalo

sand'bag' *s* sacchetto a terra

sand'bank' *s* banco di sabbia

sand' bar' *s* cordone *m* litorale, banco di sabbia

sand'blast' *s* sabbiatura || *tr* pulire con sabbiatura, sabbiare

sand'box' *s* cassone *m* pieno di sabbia; (rr) sabbiera

sand'glass' *s* orologio a polvere *or* a sabbia

sand'pa'per *s* carta vetrata || *tr* pulire con carta vetrata

sand'stone' *s* arenaria

sandwich ['sændwɪtʃ] *s* panino imbottito, tramezzino || *tr* inserire

sand'wich man' *s* tramezzino, uomo sandwich

sand·y ['sændi] *adj* (-ier; -iest) sabbioso; (*hair*) biondo rossiccio

sane [sen] *adj* sensato

sanguinary ['sæŋgwɪnˌɛri] *adj* sanguinario

sanguine ['sæŋgwɪn] *adj* fiducioso; (*complexion*) sanguigno

sanitary ['sænɪˌteri] *adj* sanitario

san'itary nap'kin *s* pannolino igienico

sanitation [ˌsænɪ'teʃən] *s* sanità *f*

sanity ['sænɪti] *s* sanità *f* di mente

Santa Claus ['sæntəˌklɔz] *s* Babbo Natale

sap [sæp] *s* linfa, succhio; (mil) trincea; (coll) scemo || *v* (*pret & pp* **sapped;** *ger* **sapping**) *tr* scavare; insidiare, minare; (*to weaken*) indebolire

sapling ['sæplɪŋ] *s* alberello; (*youth*) giovanetto

sapphire ['sæfaɪr] *s* zaffiro

Saracen ['særesən] *adj & s* saraceno

sarcasm ['sɑrkæzəm] *s* sarcasmo

sarcastic [sɑr'kæstɪk] *adj* sarcastico

sardine [sɑr'din] *s* sardina; **packed in like sardines** pigiati come le acciughe

Sardinia [sɑr'dɪnɪ·ə] *s* la Sardegna

Sardinian [sɑr'dɪnɪ·ən] *adj & s* sardo

sarsaparilla [ˌsɑrsəpə'rɪlə] *s* salsapariglia

sash [sæʃ] *s* sciarpa; (*around one's waist*) fusciacca; (*of window*) telaio

sash' win'dow *s* finestra a ghigliottina

sas·sy ['sæsi] *adj* (-sier; -siest) (coll) impertinente; (*pert*) (coll) vivace

satchel ['sætʃəl] *s* sacca; (*of schoolboy*) cartella

sateen [sæ'tin] *s* satin *m*

satellite ['sætəˌlaɪt] *s* satellite *m*

satiate ['seʃɪˌet] *tr* saziare

satin ['sætən] *s* raso

satire ['sætaɪr] *s* satira

satiric(al) [sə'tɪrɪk(əl)] *adj* satirico

satirist ['sætɪrɪst] *s* satirico

satirize ['sætɪˌraɪz] *tr* satireggiare

satisfaction [ˌsætɪs'fækʃən] *s* soddisfazione

satisfactory [ˌsætɪs'fæktəri] *adj* soddisfacente

satis·fy ['sætɪsˌfaɪ] *v* (*pret & pp* -fied) *tr & intr* soddisfare

saturate ['sætʃəˌret] *tr* saturare

Saturday ['sætərdi] s sabato
Saturn ['sætərn] s (astr) Saturno
sauce [sɔs] s salsa; (of fruit) conserva; (of chocolate) crema; (coll) insolenza, impertinenza ‖ tr condire; rendere piccante ‖ [sɔs] or [sæs] tr (coll) rispondere con impertinenza a
sauce'pan' s casseruola
saucer ['sɔsər] s piattino
sau·cy ['sɔsi] adj (-cier; -ciest) impertinente; (pert) vivace
sauerkraut ['saʊr‚kraʊt] s sarcrauti mpl, crauti mpl
saunter ['sɔntər] s giro, bighellonata ‖ intr girandolare, bighellonare
sausage ['sɔsɪdʒ] s salsiccia
savage ['sævɪdʒ] adj & s selvaggio
savant ['sævənt] s erudito
save [sev] prep tranne, salvo ‖ tr salvare; (money) risparmiare; (to set apart) serbare; **to save face** salvare le apparenze ‖ intr fare economia
saving ['sevɪŋ] adj economico; che redime ‖ **savings** spl risparmi mpl, economie fpl ‖ **saving** prep eccetto, salvo
sav'ings account' s conto di risparmio
sav'ings and loan' associa'tion s cassa di risparmio che concede mutui
sav'ings bank' s cassa di risparmio
savior ['sevjər] s salvatore m
Saviour ['sevjər] s Salvatore m
savor ['sevər] s sapore m ‖ tr assaporare; (to flavor) saporire ‖ intr odorare; **to savor of** sapere di; odorare di
savor·y ['sevəri] adj (-ier; -iest) saporoso; piccante; delizioso ‖ s (-ies) (bot) santoreggia
saw [sɔ] s (tool) sega; detto, proverbio ‖ tr segare
saw'buck' s cavalletto
saw'dust' s segatura
saw'horse' s cavalletto
saw'mill' s segheria
Saxon ['sæksən] adj & s sassone m
saxophone ['sæksə‚fon] s sassofono
say [se] s dire m; **to have no say** non aver voce in capitolo; **to have one's say** esprimere la propria opinione; **to have the say** avere l'ultima parola ‖ v (pret & pp said [sed]) tr dire; **I should say so!** certamente!; **it is said** si dice; **no sooner said than done** detto fatto; **that is to say** vale a dire; **to go without saying** essere ovvio
saying ['se·ɪŋ] s detto, proverbio
scab [skæb] s crosta; (strikebreaker) crumiro
scabbard ['skæbərd] s guaina, fodero
scab·by ['skæbi] adj (-bier; -biest) crostoso; (animal) rognoso; (slang) vile
scabrous ['skæbrəs] adj scabroso
scads [skædz] spl (slang) un mucchio
scaffold ['skæfəld] s impalcatura; (to execute a criminal) patibolo
scaffolding ['skæfəldɪŋ] s incastellatura, ponteggio
scald [skɔld] tr scottare; (e.g., milk) cuocere al disotto del punto d'ebollizione
scale [skel] s (e.g., of map) scala;

piatto della bilancia; (of fish) squama; **on a large scale** in grande scala; **scales** bilancia; **to tip the scales** far inclinare la bilancia ‖ tr squamare; (to incrust) incrostare; (to weigh) pesare; scalare; graduare; ridurre a scala ‖ intr squamarsi; scrostarsi
scallion ['skæljən] s scalogno
scallop ['skɑləp] or ['skæləp] s (for cooking) conchiglia; (mollusk) pettine m; (slice of meat) scaloppina; (on edge of cloth) dentello, smerlo ‖ tr (fish) cuocere in conchiglia; dentellare, smerlare
scalp [skælp] s cuoio capelluto ‖ tr scotennare; (tickets) fare il bagarinaggio di
scalpel ['skælpəl] s scalpello
scalper ['skælpər] s bagarino
scal·y ['skeli] adj (-ier; -iest) squamoso; scrostato
scamp [skæmp] s cattivo soggetto, briccone m
scamper ['skæmpər] intr sgambettare; **to scamper away** darsela a gambe
scan [skæn] v (pret & pp scanned; ger scanning) tr scrutare; dare un'occhiata a; (verse) scandire; (telv) analizzare, scandire, esplorare
scandal ['skændəl] s scandalo
scandalize ['skændə‚laɪz] tr scandalizzare
scandalous ['skændələs] adj scandaloso
Scandinavian [‚skændɪ'nevɪ·ən] adj & s scandinavo
scanning ['skænɪŋ] s (telv) esplorazione
scan'ning line' s (telv) riga di analisi
scant [skænt] adj scarso; corto ‖ tr diminuire; lesinare
scant·y ['skænti] adj (-ier; -iest) appena sufficiente; povero, magro; (clothing) succinto
scapegoat ['skep‚got] s capro espiatorio
scar [skɑr] s cicatrice f; (fig) sfregio ‖ v (pret & pp scarred; ger scarring) tr segnare, marcare; sfregiare ‖ intr cicatrizzarsi
scarce [skɛrs] adj scarso, raro; **to make oneself scarce** (coll) non farsi vedere
scarcely ['skɛrsli] adv appena; a mala pena; non ... affatto; **scarcely ever** raramente; non ... affatto
scarci·ty ['skɛrsiti] s (-ties) scarsità f, scarsezza; carestia
scare [skɛr] s spavento ‖ tr spaventare, impaurire; **to scare away** fare scappare per lo spavento; **to scare up** (money) (coll) metter insieme
scare'crow' s spaventapasseri m
scarf [skɑrf] s (scarfs or scarves [skɑrvz]) sciarpa; cravattone m; (cover for table) centro, striscia
scarf'pin' s spilla da cravatta
scarlet ['skɑrlɪt] adj scarlatto
scar'let fe'ver s scarlattina
scar·y ['skɛri] adj (-ier; -iest) (timid) (coll) fifone; (causing fright) (coll) spaventevole

scathing [ˈskeðɪŋ] *adj* severo, bruciante

scatter [ˈskætər] *tr* disperdere, sparpagliare ‖ *intr* disperdersi, sparpagliarsi

scatterbrained [ˈskætər‚brend] *adj* scervellato, stordito

scenari·o [sɪˈnɛrɪ‚o] or [sɪˈnɑrɪ‚o] *s* (-os) scenario

scenarist [sɪˈnɛrɪst] or [sɪˈnɑrɪst] *s* scenarista *mf*, sceneggiatore *m*

scene [sin] *s* (*view*) paesaggio; (*place*) scena; (theat) scena, quadro; **behind the scenes** dietro le quinte; **to make a scene** fare una scenata

scener·y [ˈsinəri] *s* (-ies) paesaggio; (theat) scenario

scenic [ˈsinɪk] or [ˈsɛnɪk] *adj* pittoresco; (*pertaining to the stage*) scenico

scent [sɛnt] *s* odore *m;* profumo; (*sense of smell*) fiuto, odorato; (*trail*) traccia, pista ‖ *tr* profumare; (*to detect*) fiutare, annusare

scepter [ˈsɛptər] *s* scettro

sceptic [ˈskɛptɪk] *adj* & *s* scettico

sceptical [ˈskɛptɪkəl] *adj* scettico

scepticism [ˈskɛptɪ‚sɪzəm] *s* scetticismo

schedule [ˈskɛdjʊl] *s* lista; programma *m;* (*of trains, planes, etc.*) orario ‖ *tr* programmare; mettere in orario

scheme [skim] *s* schema *m;* piano, progetto; (*plot*) trama ‖ *tr* progettare; tramare

schemer [ˈskimər] *s* progettista *mf;* (*underhanded*) manipolatore *m*, concertatore *m*

scheming [ˈskimɪŋ] *adj* intrigante, scaltro

schism [ˈsɪzəm] *s* scisma *m*

schist [ʃɪst] *s* scisto

scholar [ˈskɑlər] *s* (*pupil*) alunno; detentore *m* di una borsa di studio; (*learned person*) dotto, studioso

scholarly [ˈskɑlərli] *adj* erudito, studioso

scholarship [ˈskɑlər‚ʃɪp] *s* erudizione; (*money*) borsa di studio

scholasticism [skəˈlæstɪ‚sɪzəm] *s* scolastica

school [skul] *s* scuola; (*of a university*) facoltà *f;* (*of fish*) banco ‖ *tr* istruire, insegnare

school′ age′ *s* età scolastica

school′bag′ *s* cartella

school′ board′ *s* comitato scolastico

school′boy′ *s* alunno, scolaro

school′ bus′ *s* scuolabus *m*

school′ day′ *s* giorno di scuola; durata della giornata scolastica

school′girl′ *s* alunna, scolara

school′house′ *s* scuola, edificio scolastico

schooling [ˈskulɪŋ] *s* istruzione

school′mas′ter *s* maestro di scuola; direttore scolastico

school′mate′ *s* compagno di scuola, condiscepolo

school′room′ *s* aula scolastica

school′teach′er *s* maestro

school′ year′ *s* anno scolastico

schooner [ˈskunər] *s* goletta

sciatica [saɪˈætɪkə] *s* (pathol) sciatica

science [ˈsaɪ·əns] *s* scienza

sci′ence fic′tion *s* fantascienza

sci′ence-fic′tion *adj* fantascientifico

scientific [‚saɪ·ənˈtɪfɪk] *adj* scientifico

scientist [ˈsaɪ·əntɪst] *s* scienziato

scimitar [ˈsɪmɪtər] *s* scimitarra

scintillate [ˈsɪntɪ‚let] *intr* scintillare

scion [ˈsaɪ·ən] *s* rampollo, discendente *m*

scissors [ˈsɪzərz] *ssg* or *spl* forbici *fpl*

scoff [skɔf] or [skɑf] *s* dileggio, beffa ‖ *intr* burlarsi; **to scoff at** burlarsi di, dileggiare

scold [skold] *s* megera ‖ *tr* & *intr* sgridare, rimproverare

scoop [skup] *s* (*ladlelike utensil*) paletta; (*kitchen utensil*) cucchiaio, cucchiaione *m;* cucchiaiata; palettata; (*of dredge*) benna; (*hollow*) buco; (naut) gottazza; (journ) primizia, esclusiva; (coll) colpo ‖ *tr* vuotare a cucchiaiate; (journ) battere; (naut) gottare; **to scoop out** (*e.g., sand*) scavare; (*soup*) scodellare

scoot [skut] *s* (coll) corsa ‖ *intr* (coll) correre precipitosamente

scooter [ˈskutər] *s* monopattino

scope [skop] *s* ampiezza; lunghezza; **to give full scope to** dare piena libertà d'azione a

scorch [skɔrtʃ] *s* scottatura ‖ *tr* bruciacchiare; bruciare, inaridire; (fig) ferire ‖ *intr* bruciarsi

scorching [ˈskɔrtʃɪŋ] *adj* bruciante

score [skor] *s* (*in a game*) punteggio; (*in an examination*) nota; linea, segno, marca; (*twenty*) ventina; (mus) partitura; **scores** un mucchio; **to keep score** segnare il punteggio; **to settle a score** (fig) saldare un conto ‖ *tr* raggiungere il punteggio di, fare; marcare; guadagnare; (*to censure*) sgridare, rimproverare; (mus) orchestrare

score′board′ *s* quadro del punteggio

score′keep′er *s* segnapunti *m*

scorn [skɔrn] *s* disdegno, disprezzo ‖ *tr* & *intr* disdegnare, disprezzare

scornful [ˈskɔrnfəl] *adj* disdegnoso

Scorpio [ˈskɔrpɪ‚o] *s* Scorpione *m*

scorpion [ˈskɔrpɪ·ən] *s* scorpione *m*

Scot [skɑt] *s* scozzese *mf*

Scotch [skɑtʃ] *adj* scozzese ‖ *s* scozzese *m;* whisky *m* scozzese; **the Scotch** gli scozzesi

Scotch′man *s* (-men) scozzese *m*

Scotch′ pine′ *s* pino silvestre

Scotch′ tape′ *s* (trademark) nastro autoadesivo Scotch

scot′-free′ *adj* impune; **to get off scot-free** farla franca

Scotland [ˈskɑtlənd] *s* la Scozia

Scottish [ˈskɑtɪʃ] *adj* scozzese ‖ *s* scozzese *mf;* **the Scottish** gli scozzesi

scoundrel [ˈskaundrəl] *s* birbante *m*, farabutto, manigoldo

scour [skaur] *tr* sgrassare fregando, pulire fregando; (*the countryside*) battere

scourge [skʌrdʒ] *s* sferza; (fig) flagello ‖ *tr* sferzare

scout [skaut] *s* esplorazione; giovane esploratore *m;* giovane esploratrice *f;* (mil) ricognitore *m;* (nav) esploratore *m;* (slang) tipo ‖ *tr* esplorare, riconoscere; cercar di trovare; disdegnare

scouting ['skautɪŋ] *s* scoutismo

scowl [skaul] *s* cipiglio ‖ *intr* aggrottare le ciglia; guardare torvamente

scram [skræm] *v* (*pret & pp* **scrammed;** *ger* **scramming**) *intr* (coll) tagliare la corda; **scram!** (coll) vattene!, (coll) escimi di tra i piedi!

scramble ['skræmbəl] *s* ruffa, gara ‖ *tr* (*to grab up*) arraffare; confondere, mescolare; (*eggs*) strapazzare ‖ *intr* arrampicarsi; (*to struggle*) azzuffarsi

scram'bled eggs' *spl* uova strapazzate

scrap [skræp] *s* pezzetto, frammento; ritaglio, rottame *m;* (coll) baruffa; **scraps** avanzi *mpl;* ‖ *v* (*pret & pp* **scrapped;** *ger* **scrapping**) *tr* scartare ‖ *intr* (coll) fare baruffa

scrap'book' *s* album *m* di ritagli (di giornale o fotografie)

scrape [skrep] *s* impiccio, imbroglio; baruffa ‖ *tr* raschiare, graffiare; **to scrape together** racimolare ‖ *intr* raschiare; **to scrape along** vivacchiare; **to scrape through** passare per il rotto della cuffia

scraper ['skrepər] *s* raschietto

scrap' i'ron *s* rottami *mpl* di ferro

scrap' pa'per *s* carta straccia; carta da appunti

scratch [skrætʃ] *s* graffio, scalfittura; scarabocchio; (billiards) punto perduto; (sports) linea di partenza; **from scratch** da bel principio; dal niente; **up to scratch** soddisfacente ‖ *tr* graffiare, grattare; (*e.g., a horse*) cancellare ‖ *intr* graffiare; (*said of a chicken*) raspare; (*said of a pen*) grattare

scratch' pad' *s* quaderno per appunti

scratch' pa'per *s* carta da appunti

scrawl [skrɔl] *s* scarabocchio ‖ *tr & intr* scarabocchiare

scraw·ny ['skrɔni] *adj* (**-nier; -niest**) ossuto, scarno

scream [skrim] *s* grido, strillo; cosa divertentissima; persona divertentissima ‖ *intr* gridare, strillare

screech [skritʃ] *s* stridio ‖ *intr* stridere

screech' owl' *s* gufo; (*barn owl*) barbagianni *m*

screen [skrin] *s* (*movable partition*) paravento; (*in front of fire*) parafuoco; rete metallica; (*sieve*) vaglio; (mov; phys) schermo; (telv) teleschermo ‖ *tr* schermare; riparare, proteggere; (*to sieve*) vagliare; (*a film*) proiettare; (*to adapt*) (mov) sceneggiare

screen' grid' *s* (rad, telv) griglia schermo

screen' test' *s* provino

screw [skru] *s* vite *f;* giro di vite; (*of a boat*) elica; **to have a screw loose** (slang) avere una rotella fuori di posto; **to put the screws on** far pressione su ‖ *tr* avvitare; (*to twist*)

torcere; **to screw up** (slang) rovinare; **to screw up one's courage** prendere il coraggio a quattro mani ‖ *intr* avvitarsi

screw'ball' *s* (slang) pazzoide *m,* svitato

screw'driv'er *s* cacciavite *m*

screw' eye' *s* occhiello a vite

screw' jack' *s* martinetto a vite

screw' propel'ler *s* elica

screw·y ['skru·i] *adj* (**-ier; -iest**) (slang) pazzo; (slang) fuori di posto, strano

scribble ['skrɪbəl] *s* scarabocchio ‖ *tr & intr* scarabocchiare

scribe [skraɪb] *s* (*Jewish scholar*) scriba *m;* copista *mf* ‖ *tr* tracciare, incidere

scrimmage ['skrɪmɪdʒ] *s* ruffa; (*football*) azione

scrimp [skrɪmp] *tr & intr* lesinare

script [skrɪpt] *s* scrittura, scrittura a mano; manoscritto; testo; (*e.g., of a play*) copione *m;* (typ) carattere *m* inglese

scriptural ['skrɪptʃərəl] *adj* scritturale, biblico

scripture ['skrɪptʃər] *s* scrittura ‖ **Scripture** *s* Scrittura

script'writ'er *s* soggettista *mf*

scrofula ['skrɑfjələ] *s* scrofola

scroll [skrol] *s* rotolo di carta, rotolo di pergamena; (*of violin*) riccio; (archit) voluta, cartoccio

scroll'work' *s* ornamentazione a voluta

scro·tum ['skrotəm] *s* (**-ta** [tə] or **-tums**) scroto

scrub [skrʌb] *s* boscaglia; alberelli *mpl;* animale bastardo; persona di poco conto; (*act of scrubbing*) fregata; (sports) giocatore *m* di riserva ‖ *v* (*pret & pp* **scrubbed;** *ger* **scrubbing**) *tr* pulire, fregare

scrub' oak' *s* rovere basso

scrub'wom'an *s* (**-wom'en**) lavatrice *f,* donna a giornata

scruff [skrʌf] *s* nuca, collottola

scruple ['skrupəl] *s* scrupolo

scrupulous ['skrupjələs] *adj* scrupoloso

scrutinize ['skrutɪ,naɪz] *tr* scrutare, disaminare

scruti·ny ['skrutɪni] *s* (**-nies**) attento esame, disamina

scuff [skʌf] *s* graffio, logorio ‖ *tr* logorare, graffiare

scuffle ['skʌfəl] *s* zuffa, rissa ‖ *intr* azzuffarsi, colluttare

scull [skʌl] *s* (*oar*) remo a bratto; (*boat*) canotto ‖ *tr* spingere a bratto ‖ *intr* vogare a bratto

sculler·y ['skʌləri] *s* (**-ies**) retrocucina

scul'lery maid' *s* sguattera

scullion ['skʌljən] *s* sguattero

sculptor ['skʌlptər] *s* scultore *m*

sculptress ['skʌlptrɪs] *s* scultrice *f*

sculpture ['skʌlptʃər] *s* scultura ‖ *tr & intr* scolpire

scum [skʌm] *s* schiuma; (*slag*) scoria; (*rabble*) feccia, gentaglia ‖ *v* (*pret & pp* **scummed;** *ger* **scumming**) *tr & intr* schiumare

scum·my ['skʌmi] *adj* (**-mier; -miest**) spumoso; (coll) vile, schifoso

scurf [skʌrf] *s* (*shed by the skin*) squama; incrostazione

scurrilous ['skʌrɪləs] *adj* scurrile

scur·ry ['skʌri] *v* (*pret & pp* **-ried**) *intr* affrettarsi; **to scurry around** dimenarsi

scur·vy ['skʌrvi] *adj* (**-vier; -viest**) spregevole, meschino || *s* scorbuto

scuttle ['skʌtəl] *s* (*for coal*) secchio; (*trap door*) botola; corsa, fuga; (naut) boccaporto || *tr* aprire una falla in, affondare || *intr* affrettarsi, darsi alla corsa

scut'tle·butt' *s* (naut) barilozzo dell'acqua; (coll) rumore *m*, diceria

scuttling ['skʌtlɪŋ] *s* autoaffondamento

Scylla ['sɪlə] *s* Scilla; **between Scylla and Charybdis** fra Scilla e Cariddi

scythe [saɪð] *s* falce *f*

sea [si] *s* mare *m*; (*wave*) maroso; **at sea** in alto mare; **by the sea** a mare, sulla costa; **to follow the sea** farsi marinaio; **to put to sea** prendere il largo

sea'board' *adj* costiero || *s* litorale *m*

sea' breeze' *s* brezza marina

sea'coast' *s* costa, litorale *m*

sea' dog' *s* (*seal*) foca; (*sailor*) lupo di mare

seafarer ['si‚ferər] *s* marinaio; viaggiatore marittimo

sea'food' *s* pesce *m*; (*shellfish*) frutti *mpl* di mare

seagoing ['si‚go·ɪŋ] *adj* di alto mare

sea' gull' *s* gabbiano

seal [sil] *s* sigillo; (*sea animal*) foca; (fig) suggello || *tr* sigillare, apporre i sigilli a; (fig) suggellare

sea' legs' *spl*—**to have good sea legs** avere piede marino

sea' lev'el *s* livello del mare

seal'ing wax' *s* ceralacca

seal'skin' *s* pelle *f* di foca

seam [sim] *s* (*abutting of edges*) giuntura; (*stitches*) costura, cucitura; (*scar*) cicatrice *f*; (*wrinkle*) ruga; (*in metal*) commettitura; (min) filone *m*, vena

sea'man *s* (**-men**) marinaio

sea' mile' *s* miglio marino

seamless ['simlɪs] *adj* senza giuntura; (*stockings*) senza cucitura

seamstress ['simstrɪs] *s* cucitrice *f*

seam·y ['simi] *adj* (**-ier; -iest**) pieno di cuciture; basso, sordido; (*unpleasant*) spiacevole

séance ['se·ɑns] *s* seduta spiritica

sea'plane' *s* idrovolante *m*

sea'port' *s* porto di mare

sea' pow'er *s* potenza navale

sear [sɪr] *adj* secco || *s* scottatura || *tr* scottare, bruciare; (*to brand*) marcare a fuoco; inaridire; (fig) indurire

search [sʌrtʃ] *s* ricerca, investigazione; (*frisking a person*) perquisizione; **in search of** in cerca di || *tr* cercare, investigare; perquisire, frugare || *intr* investigare; **to search for** cercare; **to search into** investigare

searching ['sʌrtʃɪŋ] *adj* (e.g., *inspec-*

tion) profondo; (e.g., *glance*) indagatore, penetrante

search'light' *s* proiettore *m*, riflettore *m*; (mil) fotoelettrica

search' war'rant *s* mandato di perquisizione

sea'scape' *s* vista del mare; (*painting*) marina

sea' shell' *s* conchiglia

sea'shore' *s* costa, marina, mare *m*

sea'sick' *adj*—**to be seasick** aver mal di mare

sea'sick'ness *s* mal *m* di mare

sea'side' *s* costa, riviera, marina

season ['sizən] *s* stagione; **in season** di stagione; **in season and out of season** sempre, continuamente; **out of season** fuori stagione || *tr* (*food*) condire; (*to mature*) stagionare; (e.g., *wood*) stagionare

seasonal ['sizənəl] *adj* stagionale

seasoning ['sizənɪŋ] *s* condimento; (*of wood*) stagionamento

sea'son's greet'ings *spl* migliori auguri *mpl* per le feste natalizie

sea'son tick'et *s* biglietto d'abbonamento

seat [sit] *s* sedia; (*part of chair*) sedile *m*; (*of human body*) sedere *m*; (*of pants*) fondo; sito, posto; (e.g., *of government*) sede *f*; (*in parliament*) seggio; (e.g., *of learning*) centro; (rr, theat) posto || *tr* far sedere; aver posti per; (*a chair*) mettere il sedile a; (*pants*) mettere il fondo a; (*an official*) insediare; (mach) installare; **to be seated** essere seduto; **to seat oneself** sedersi

seat' belt' *s* cintura di sicurezza

seat' cov'er *s* guaina, foderina

seat'ing room' *s* posti *mpl* a sedere

sea' wall' *s* diga

sea'way' *s* via marittima; alto mare; mare grosso; rotta percorsa; via di fiume accessibile a navi da trasporto

sea'weed' *s* alga marina; pianta marina

sea'wor'thy *adj* atto a tenere il mare

secede [sɪ'sid] *intr* separarsi, distaccarsi

secession [sɪ'seʃən] *s* secessione

seclude [sɪ'klud] *tr* appartare; isolare

seclusion [sɪ'kluʒən] *s* reclusione; solitudine *f*, intimità *f*

second ['sekənd] *adj & pron* secondo; **to be second to none** non cederla a nessuno || *s* secondo; (*in a duel*) padrino; (*in dates*) due *m*; (aut, mus) seconda; **seconds** (com) articoli *mpl* di seconda qualità; **to have seconds on** servirsi una seconda volta di || *tr* assecondare; (*a motion*) appoggiare || *adv* in secondo luogo

secondar·y ['sekən‚deri] *adj* secondario || *s* (**-ies**) (elec) secondario

sec'ond-best' *adj* (il) migliore dopo il primo; **to come off second-best** arrivare secondo

sec'-ond-class' *adj* di seconda qualità; (aer, naut, rr) di seconda classe

sec'ond hand' *s* lancetta dei secondi

sec'ond-hand' *adj* di seconda mano, d'occasione

sec'ond lieuten'ant *s* sottotenente *m*
sec'ond-rate' *adj* di seconda categoria; (*inferior*) da strapazzo
sec'ond sight' *s* chiaroveggenza
sec'ond wind' [wɪnd] *s*—**to get one's second wind** riprendere fiato
secre·cy ['sikrəsi] *s* (**-cies**) segretezza; **in secrecy** in segreto
secret ['sikrɪt] *adj* & *s* segreto; **in secret** in segreto
secretar·y ['sɛkrɪ,tɛri] *s* (**-ies**) segretario; (*desk*) scrittoio
se'cret bal'lot *s* scrutinio segreto
secrete [sɪ'krit] *tr* nascondere; (physiol) secernere
secretive ['sikrɪtɪv] or [sɪ'kritɪv] *adj* riservato, poco comunicativo
sect [sɛkt] *s* setta
sectarian [sɛk'tɛrɪ-ən] *adj* & *s* settario
section ['sɛktʃən] *s* sezione; (*of city*) rione *m;* (*of fruit*) spicchio; (*of highway*) tronco; (rr) tratta ‖ *tr* sezionare
sectional ['sɛkʃənəl] *adj* (e.g., *bookcase*) componibile; sezionale; locale, regionale
secular ['sɛkjələr] *adj* & *s* secolare *m*
secularism ['sɛkjələ,rɪzəm] *s* laicismo
secure [sɪ'kjur] *adj* salvo, sicuro ‖ *tr* ottenere; assicurare; fissare; (law) garantire
securi·ty [sɪ'kjurɪti] *s* (**-ties**) sicurezza; protezione; garanzia; (*person*) garante *m;* **securities** valori *mpl,* titoli *mpl*
sedan [sɪ'dæn] *s* (aut) berlina
sedan' chair' *s* bussola, portantina
sedate [sɪ'det] *adj* calmo, posato
sedation [sɪ'deʃən] *s* ritorno alla calma; stato di calma mentale
sedative ['sɛdətɪv] *adj* & *s* sedativo
sedentary ['sɛdən,tɛri] *adj* sedentario
sedge [sɛdʒ] *s* carice *m*
sediment ['sɛdɪmənt] *s* sedimento
sedition [sɪ'dɪʃən] *s* sedizione
seditious [sɪ'dɪʃəs] *adj* sedizioso
seduce [sɪ'djus] or [sɪ'dus] *tr* sedurre
seducer [sɪ'djusər] or [sɪ'dusər] *s* seduttore *m,* corruttore *m*
seduction [sɪ'dʌkʃən] *s* seduzione
seductive [sɪ'dʌktɪv] *adj* seduttore
sedulous ['sɛdjələs] *adj* diligente
see [si] *s* (eccl) sede *f* ‖ *v* (*pret* **saw** [sɔ]; *pp* **seen** [sin]) *tr* vedere; **to see off** andare ad accompagnare; **to see through** portare a termine ‖ *intr* vedere; **see here!** faccia attenzione!; **to see after** prender cura di; **to see through** conoscere il gioco di
seed [sid] *s* seme *m,* semenza; **to go to seed** andare in semenza; deteriorarsi ‖ *tr* seminare; (*fruit*) togliere i semi da ‖ *intr* seminare; produrre semi
seed'bed' *s* semenzaio; (fig) vivaio
seeder ['sidər] *s* (*person*) seminatore *m;* (*machine*) seminatrice *f*
seedling ['sidlɪŋ] *s* piantina da trapianto
seed·y ['sidi] *adj* (**-ier; -iest**) pieno di semi; (*unkempt*) malmesso, malvestito
seeing ['si·ɪŋ] *conj* visto che, dato che

See'ing Eye' dog' *s* cane *m* guida per ciechi
seek [sik] *v* (*pret* & *pp* **sought** [sɔt]) *tr* cercare, ricercare; **to be sought after** essere ricercato; **to seek to** cercare di
seem [sim] *intr* parere, sembrare
seemingly ['simɪŋli] *adv* apparentemente
seem·ly ['simli] *adj* (**-lier; -liest**) decoroso; appropriato
seep [sip] *intr* colare, filtrare
seer [sɪr] *s* profeta *m,* veggente *m*
see'saw' *s* altalena; (*motion*) viavai *m* ‖ *intr* altalenare
seethe [sið] *intr* bollire
segment ['sɛgmənt] *s* segmento
segregate ['sɛgrɪ,get] *tr* segregare
segregation [,sɛgrɪ'geʃən] *s* segregazione
segregationist [,sɛgrɪ'geʃənɪst] *s* segregazionista *mf*
Seine [sen] *s* Senna
seismograph ['saɪzmə,græf] or ['saɪzmə,graf] *s* sismografo
seismology [saɪz'malədʒi] *s* sismologia
seize [siz] *tr* afferrare; impossessarsi di; (*with one's clenched fist*) impugnare; comprendere; (law) sequestrare, confiscare
seizure ['siʒər] *s* conquista, cattura; (*of an illness*) attacco; (law) sequestro, pignoramento
seldom ['sɛldəm] *adj* di raro, raramente
select [sɪ'lɛkt] *adj* scelto, selezionato ‖ *tr* prescegliere, selezionare
selectee [sɪ,lɛk'ti] *s* (mil) recluta
selection [sɪ'lɛkʃən] *s* selezione, scelta
selective [sɪ'lɛktɪv] *adj* selettivo
self [sɛlf] *adj* stesso ‖ *s* (**selves** [sɛlvz]) sé stesso; io, personalità *f;* **all by one's self** senza aiuto altrui ‖ *pron* sé stesso
self'-abuse' *s* abuso delle proprie forze; masturbazione
self'-addressed' *adj* col nome e l'indirizzo del mittente
self'-cen'tered *adj* egocentrico
self'-con'scious *adj* imbarazzato, vergognoso, timido
self'-control' *s* padronanza di sé stesso, autocontrollo
self'-defense' *s* autodifesa; **in self-defense** in legittima difesa
self'-deni'al *s* abnegazione
self'-deter'mina'tion *s* autodeterminazione
self'-dis'cipline *s* autodisciplina
self'-ed'ucat'ed *adj* autodidatta
self'-employed' *adj* che lavora in proprio
self'-ev'i·dent *adj* evidente, lampante
self'-ex·plan'a·tor'y *adj* ovvio, che si spiega da sé
self'-gov'ernment *s* autogoverno; controllo sopra sé stesso
self'-im·por'tant *adj* presuntuoso
self'-in·dul'gence *s* intemperanza
self'-in'terest *s* egoismo, interesse *m*
selfish ['sɛlfɪʃ] *adj* egoista
selfishness ['sɛlfɪʃnɪs] *s* egoismo

selfless ['sɛlflɪs] *adj* disinteressato; altruista
self'-liq'ui·dat'ing *adj* autoammortizzabile
self'-love' *s* amor proprio
self'-made' *adj* che si è fatto da sé
self'-por'trait *s* autoritratto
self'-pos·sessed' *adj* calmo, padrone di sé
self'-pres'er·va'tion *s* conservazione
self'-pro·pelled' *adj* semovente
self'-re·li'ant *adj* pieno di fiducia in sé stesso
self'-re·spect' *s* rispetto di sé stesso
self'-right'eous *adj* che si considera più morale degli altri, ipocrita
self'-sac'ri·fice' *s* sacrificio di sé, spirito di sacrifico
self'-same' *adj* stesso e medesimo
self'-sat'is·fied' *adj* contento di sé
self'-seek'ing *adj* egoista ǁ *s* egoismo
self'-serv'ice *s* autoservizio
self'-start'er *s* motorino d'avviamento
self'-styled' *adj* sedicente
self'-support' *s* indipendenza economica
self'-tap'ping screw' *s* vite *f* autofilettante
self'-taught' *adj* autodidatta
self-threading ['sɛlf'θrɛdɪŋ] *adj* autofilettante
self'-willed' *adj* ostinato, caparbio
self'-wind'ing *adj* a carica automatica
sell [sɛl] *v* (*pret & pp* **sold** [sold]) *tr* vendere; (*an idea*) fare accettare; **to sell off** svendere, liquidare; **to sell out** smerciare; vendere a stralcio; (coll) tradire ǁ *intr* vendere, vendersi; fare il venditore; **to sell off** (*said of the stock market*) essere in ribasso; **to sell out** vendere a stralcio; vendersi
seller ['sɛlər] *s* venditore *m*
Selt'zer wa'ter ['sɛltsər] *s* selz *m*
selvage ['sɛlvɪdʒ] *s* cimosa, vivagno
semantic [sɪ'mæntɪk] *adj* semantico ǁ **semantics** *s* semantica
semaphore ['sɛmə,for] *s* semaforo
semblance ['sɛmbləns] *s* apparenza, specie *f*; apparizione
semen ['simən] *s* sperma *m*
semester [sɪ'mɛstər] *adj* semestrale ǁ *s* semestre *m*
semicircle ['sɛmɪ,sʌrkəl] *s* semicircolo
semicolon ['sɛmɪ,kolən] *s* punto e virgola
semiconductor [,sɛmɪkən'dʌktər] *s* semiconduttore *m*
semiconscious [,sɛmi'kɑnʃəs] *adj* mezzo cosciente
semifinal [,sɛmi'faɪnəl] *s* semifinale *f*
semilearned [,sɛmi'lʌrnɪd] *adj* semidotto
semimonth·ly [,sɛmi'mʌnθli] or [,sɛmaɪ'mʌnθli] *adj* quindicinale ǁ *s* (-lies) rivista quindicinale
seminar ['sɛmɪ,nɑr] or [,sɛmɪ'nɑr] *s* seminario
seminar·y ['sɛmɪ,nɛri] *s* (-ies) seminario
Semite ['sɛmaɪt] or ['simaɪt] *s* semita *mf*

Semitic [sɪ'mɪtɪk] *adj* semitico ǁ *s* lingua semitica; (*family of languages*) semitico
semitrailer ['sɛmɪ,trelər] *s* semirimorchio
semiweek·ly [,sɛmi'wikli] or [,sɛmaɪ'wikli] *adj* bisettimanale ǁ *s* (-lies) periodico bisettimanale
semiyearly [,sɛmi'jɪrli] or [,sɛmaɪ'jɪrli] *adj* semestrale ǁ *adv* due volte all'anno
senate ['sɛnɪt] *s* senato
senator ['sɛnətər] *s* senatore *m*
send [sɛnd] *v* (*pret & pp* **sent** [sɛnt]) *tr* inviare, mandare; spedire; (*e.g., a punch*) lanciare; **to send back** rimandare; **to send forth** emettere; **to send packing** licenziare su due piedi ǁ *intr* (rad) trasmettere; **to send for** mandare a chiamare, far venire .
sender ['sɛndər] *s* speditore *m*, mittente *m*; (telg) trasmettitore *m*
send'-off' *s* (coll) addio affettuoso; (coll) lancio
senility [sɪ'nɪlɪti] *s* (pathol) senilismo
senior ['sinjər] *adj* maggiore, più anziano; seniore, di grado più elevato; dell'ultimo anno, laureando; senior, il vecchio ǁ *s* maggiore *m*; seniore *m*, persona di grado più elevato; studente *m* dell'ultimo anno, laureando
sen'ior cit'izen *s* vecchio, pensionato
seniority [sin'jɑrɪti] or [sin'jɔrɪti] *s* anzianità *f*
sensation [sɛn'seʃən] *s* sensazione
sensational [sɛn'seʃənəl] *adj* sensazionale
sense [sɛns] *s* senso; **in a sense** in un certo senso; **to come to one's senses** riprendere il giudizio; **to make sense out of** arrivare a capire; **to take leave of one's senses** perdere il ben dell'intelletto ǁ *tr* intuire; comprendere
senseless ['sɛnslɪs] *adj* (*unconscious*) privo di sensi; (*meaningless*) insensato, privo di senso
sense' or'gan *s* organo di senso
sensibili·ty [,sɛnsɪ'brɪlɪti] *s* (-ties) sensibilità *f*; **sensibilities** suscettibilità *f*
sensible ['sɛnsɪbəl] *adj* sensato; (*keenly aware*) sensibile; cosciente
sensitive ['sɛnsɪtɪv] *adj* sensitivo, sensibile; delicato
sensitize ['sɛnsɪ,taɪz] *tr* sensibilizzare
sensory ['sɛnsəri] *adj* sensorio
sensual ['sɛnʃu·əl] *adj* sensuale
sensuous ['sɛnʃu·əs] *adj* sensuale
sentence ['sɛntəns] *s* (gram) frase; (law) sentenza, condanna ǁ *tr* sentenziare, condannare
sentiment ['sɛntɪmənt] *s* sentimento
sentimental [,sɛntɪ'mɛntəl] *adj* sentimentale
sentimentalism [,sɛntɪ'mɛntəl,ɪzəm] *s* sentimentalismo
sentinel ['sɛntɪnəl] *s* sentinella; **to stand sentinel** montare di sentinella
sen·try ['sɛntri] *s* (-tries) sentinella
sen'try box' *s* garitta, casotto
separate ['sɛpərɪt] *adj* separato ǁ

['sɛpə,ret] *tr* separare ‖ *intr* separarsi

separation [,sɛpə'reʃən] *s* separazione

Sephardic [sɪ'fɑrdɪk] *adj* sefardita

September [sɛp'tɛmbər] *s* settembre *m*

septic ['sɛptɪk] *adj* settico

sep'tic tank' *s* fossa settica

sepulcher ['sɛpəlkər] *s* sepolcro

sequel ['sikwəl] *s* seguito

sequence ['sikwəns] *s* serie *f*, sequenza, successione; conseguenza; (cards, eccl, mov) sequenza; (gram) correlazione

sequester [sɪ'kwɛstər] *tr* isolare, appartare; (law) sequestrare

sequin ['sikwɪn] *s* lustrino

ser·aph ['sɛrəf] *s* (**-aphs** or **-aphim** [əfɪm]) serafino

Serbian ['sʌrbɪ·ən] *adj & s* serbo

Serbo-Croatian [,sʌrbokro'eʃən] *adj & s* serbocroato

sere [sɪr] *adj* secco, appassito

serenade [,sɛrə'ned] *s* serenata ‖ *tr* fare la serenata a ‖ *intr* fare la serenata

serene [sɪ'rin] *adj* sereno

serenity [sɪ'rɛnɪti] *s* serenità *f*

serf [sʌrf] *s* servo della gleba

serfdom ['sʌrfdəm] *s* servitù *f* della gleba

serge [sʌrdʒ] *s* saia

sergeant ['sɑrdʒənt] *s* sergente *m*

ser'geant at arms' *s* (**ser'geants at arms'**) ufficiale *m* delegato a mantenere l'ordine

ser'geant ma'jor *s* (**sergeants major** or **sergeant majors**) (*in U.S. Army*) sergente *m* maggiore; (*in Italian Army*) maresciallo

serial ['sɪrɪ·əl] *adj* a puntate, a dispense ‖ *s* periodico; romanzo a puntate; programma *m* a serie

se'rial num'ber *s* matricola; (*of a book*) segnatura; (aut) matricola di telaio

se·ries ['sɪriz] *s* (**-ries**) serie *f*; (*works dealing with the same topic*) collana; **in series** (elec) in serie

serious ['sɪrɪ·əs] *adj* serio

seriousness ['sɪrɪ·əsnɪs] *s* serietà *f*; **in all seriousness** molto sul serio

sermon ['sʌrmən] *s* sermone *m*

sermonize ['sʌrmə,naɪz] *tr & intr* sermonare

serpent ['sʌrpənt] *s* serpente *m*

se·rum ['sɪrəm] *s* (**-rums** or **-ra** [rə]) siero

servant ['sʌrvənt] *s* servo, domestico; (*civil servant*) funzionario; (fig) servitore *m*

serv'ant girl' *s* serva, domestica

serv'ant prob'lem *s* crisi *f* ancillare

serve [sʌrv] *s* (*in tennis*) servizio ‖ *tr* servire; (*a sentence*) espiare; (*to suffice*) bastare (with *dat*); (*a writ*) notificare; **to serve s.o. right** stare bene (with *dat*), e.g., **it serves him right** gli sta bene ‖ *intr* servire; **to serve as** fare da

service ['sʌrvɪs] *s* servizio; (*of a writ*) notifica; (*branch of the armed forces*) arma; **at your service** per servirLa ‖ *tr* rifornire, riparare

serviceable ['sʌrvɪsəbəl] *adj* utile; durevole; pratico; riparabile

serv'ice club' *s* casa del soldato

serv'ice·man' *s* (**-men'**) militare *m*; riparatore *m*, aggiustatore *m*

serv'ice mod'ule *s* modulo di servizio

serv'ice rec'ord *s* stato di servizio

serv'ice sta'tion *s* stazione di servizio or di rifornimento

serv'ice-sta'tion attend'ant *s* benzinaio

serv'ice stripe' *s* gallone *m*

servile ['sʌrvɪl] *adj* servile

servitude ['sʌrvɪ,tjud] or ['sʌrvɪ,tud] *s* servitù *f*; lavori forzati

sesame ['sɛsəmi] *s* sesamo; **open sesame** apriti sesamo

session ['sɛʃən] *s* sessione *f*, seduta

set [sɛt] *adj* determinato, preordinato; abituale; fisso, rigido; (*ready*) pronto; meditato, studiato ‖ *s* (*e.g., of books*) collezione, serie *f*; (*e.g., of chess*) gioco; set *m*, insieme *m*, completo; (*of tires*) treno; (*of horses*) pariglia; (*of tennis*) partita; (*of dishes*) servizio; (*of kitchen utensils*) batteria; posizione, atteggiamento; (*of a garment*) linea; (*e.g., of cement*) presa; (*of people*) gruppo; (*of thieves*) genia; (*of sails*) muta; (*of lines*) (geom) fascio; (rad, telv) apparato; (theat, mov) set *m* ‖ *v* (*pret & pp* **set**; *ger* **setting**) *tr* porre, deporre; mettere; (*fire*) dare; (*the table*) imbandire; (*a watch*) regolare; (*s.o. a certain number of tricks*) far cadere di; (*a price*) fissare; (*a gem*) incastonare; (*a fracture*) mettere a posto; (*a saw*) allicciare; (*a trap*) tendere; (*hair*) acconciare; stabilire; insediare; (*to plant*) piantare; (*a sail*) tendere; (*e.g., milk*) rapprendere; calibrare, tarare; (*cement*) solidificare; (typ) comporre; **to set back** ritardare; (*a clock*) mettere indietro; **to set forth** descrivere; **to set one's heart on** desiderare ardentemente; **to set store by** tenere in gran conto; **to set up** metter su; impiantare; (*drinks*) (slang) pagare ‖ *intr* (*said, e.g., of the sun*) tramontare; (*said of a liquid*) solidificarsi; (*said of cement*) fare presa; (*said of milk*) rapprendersi; (*said of a hen*) covare; (*said of a garment*) cascare; (*said of hair*) prendere la piega; **to set about** mettersi a; **to set out** porsi in cammino; **to set out to** mettersi a; **to set to work** mettersi a lavorare; **to set upon** attaccare

set'back' *s* rovescio, contrarietà *f*

set'screw' *s* vite *f* di pressione

setting ['sɛtɪŋ] *s* (*environment*) ambiente *m*; (*of a gem*) montatura; (*of cement*) presa; (*e.g., of the sun*) tramonto; (theat) scenario; (mus) arrangiamento

set'ting-up' ex'ercises *spl* ginnastica da camera

settle ['sɛtəl] *tr* determinare, risolvere; sistemare, regolare; (*a bill*) liquidare; installarsi in, colonizzare; calmare; (*a liquid*) far depositare; (law) conciliare ‖ *intr* mettersi d'accordo; saldare un conto; stanziarsi, domiciliarsi; fermarsi, posare; (*said of a liquid*) depositare, calmarsi; solidificarsi; **to settle down to work** mettersi a lavorare di buzzo buono; **to settle on** scegliere, fissare

settlement ['sɛtəlmənt] *s* stabilimento; sistemazione, regolamento; colonia, comunità *f;* (*of a building*) infossamento; agenzia di beneficenza

settler ['sɛtlər] *s* fondatore *m;* colono; conciliatore *m*

set'up' *s* portamento; (*e.g., of tools*) disposizione; quanto è necessario per mescolare una bibita alcolica; (coll) incontro truccato

seven ['sɛvən] *adj & pron* sette ‖ *s* sette *m;* **seven o'clock** le sette

sev'en hun'dred *adj, s & pron* settecento

seventeen ['sɛvən'tin] *adj, s & pron* diciassette *m*

seventeenth ['sɛvən'tinθ] *adj, s & pron* diciassettesimo ‖ *s* (*in dates*) diciassette *m*

seventh ['sɛvənθ] *adj, s & pron* settimo ‖ *s* (*in dates*) sette *m*

seventieth ['sɛvəntɪ·ɪθ] *adj, s & pron* settantesimo

seven·ty ['sɛvənti] *adj & pron* settanta ‖ *s* (**-ties**) settanta *m;* **the seventies** gli anni settanta

sever ['sɛvər] *tr* tagliare, mozzare; (*relations*) troncare ‖ *intr* separarsi

several ['sɛvərəl] *adj* parecchi, vari; rispettivi ‖ *spl* parecchi *mpl*

sev'erance pay' ['sɛvərəns] *s* buonuscita, indennità *f* di licenziamento

severe [sɪ'vɪr] *adj* severo; (*weather*) rigido; (*pain*) acuto; (*illness*) grave

sew [so] *v* (*pret* **sewed;** *pp* **sewed** or **sewn**) *tr & intr* cucire

sewage ['su·ɪdʒ] or ['sju·ɪdʒ] *s* acque *fpl* di scolo or di rifiuto

sewer ['su·ər] or ['sju·ər] *s* fogna, chiavica

sewerage ['su·ərɪdʒ] or ['sju·ərɪdʒ] *s* fognatura; drenaggio, rimozione delle acque di rifiuto

sew'ing machine' ['so·ɪŋ] *s* macchina da cucire

sex [sɛks] *s* sesso

sex' appeal' *s* attrattiva fisica, sex appeal *m*

sextant ['sɛkstənt] *s* sestante *m*

sextet [sɛks'tɛt] *s* sestetto

sexton ['sɛkstən] *s* sagrestano

sexual ['sɛk/u·əl] *adj* sessuale

sex·y ['sɛksi] *adj* (**-ier; -iest**) (coll) erotico; (coll) procace

shab·by ['/æbi] *adj* (**-bier; -biest**) (*clothes*) frusto; (*house*) malandato; (*person*) malvestito; (*deal*) cattivo

shack [/æk] *s* baracca

shackle ['/ækəl] *s* ceppo; (*to tie an animal*) pastoia; (fig) ostacolo; **shackles** ceppi *mpl*, manette *fpl* ‖ *tr* mettere in ceppi; (fig) inceppare

shad [/æd] *s* alosa

shade [/ed] *s* ombra; (*of lamp*) paralume *m;* (*of window*) tendina; (*for the eyes*) visiera; (*hue*) tinta, sfumatura; **a shade of** un po' di; **shades** tenebre *fpl;* ombre *fpl* ‖ *tr* ombreggiare; sfumare, digradare; (*a price*) ribassare leggermente

shadow ['/ædo] *s* ombra ‖ *tr* ombreggiare; (*to follow*) pedinare; **to shadow forth** adombrare, preannunciare

shadowy ['/ædo·i] *adj* ombroso, ombreggiato; illusorio, chimerico

shad·y ['/edi] *adj* (**-ier; -iest**) ombroso; spettrale; (coll) losco; **to keep shady** (slang) starsene lontano

shaft [/æft] or [/aft] *s* (*of arrow*) asta; (*of feather*) rachide *f;* (*of light*) raggio; (*handle*) manico; (*of wagon*) stanga, timone *m;* (*of motor*) albero; (*of column*) fusto; (*of elevator*) pozzo; (*in a mountain*) camino; (min) fornello; (fig) frecciata

shag·gy ['/ægi] *adj* (**-gier; -giest**) peloso, irsuto; (*unkempt*) trasandato; (*cloth*) ruvido

shag'gy dog' sto'ry *s* storiella senza capo né coda

shake [/ek] *s* scossa; stretta di mano; momento, istante *m;* **the shakes** la tremarella ‖ *v* (*pret* **shook** [/uk]; *pp* **shaken**) *tr* scuotere; scrollare; (*s.o.'s hands*) serrare; (*e.g., with a mixer*) sbattere; agitare, perturbare; eludere, disfarsi di ‖ *intr* tremare; (*to totter*) traballare, tentennare; scuotere; darsi la mano

shake'down' *s* estorsione, concussione; (*bed*) lettuccio di fortuna

shake'down' cruise' *s* (naut) viaggio di prova

shaker ['/ekər] *s* (*e.g., for sugar*) spolverino; (*for cocktails*) sbattighiaccio, shaker *m*

shake'-up' *s* cambiamento completo, riorganizzazione, rimaneggiamento

shak·y ['/eki] *adj* (**-ier; -iest**) tremebondo; traballante, zoppicante

shall [/æl] *v* (*cond* **should** [/ud]) *v aux* si usa per formare (1) il futuro dell'indicativo, per es., **I shall do it** lo farò; (2) il futuro perfetto dell'indicativo, per es., **I shall have done it** l'avrò fatto; (3) espressioni di obbligo o necessità, per es., **what shall I do?** che devo fare?, che vuole che faccia?

shallow ['/ælo] *adj* basso, poco profondo; leggero, superficiale

sham [/æm] *adj* falso, finto ‖ *s* frode *f*, contraffazione ‖ *v* (*pret & pp* **shammed;** *ger* **shamming**) *tr & intr* fingere

sham' bat'tle *s* finta battaglia

shambles ['/æmbəlz] *s* macello; confusione, disordine

shame [/em] *s* vergogna; **shame on you!** vergogna!; **what a shame!** che peccato! ‖ *tr* svergognare, disonorare

shame'faced' *adj* timido, vergognoso

shameful ['/emfəl] *adj* vergognoso

shameless ['/emlɪs] *adj* sfrontato, impudente, svergognato

shampoo [ʃæmˈpu] s shampoo m ‖ tr fare lo shampoo a

shamrock [ˈʃæmrɑk] s trifoglio irlandese

shanghai [ˈʃæŋhaɪ] or [ʃæŋˈhaɪ] tr imbarcare a viva forza ‖ **Shanghai** s Sciangai f

shank [ʃæŋk] s fusto; (of tool) codolo; (stem) gambo; (of bird) zampa; (of anchor) fuso; (coll) principio; (coll) fine f; **to ride shank's mare** andare col cavallo di San Francesco

shan·ty [ˈʃænti] s (-ties) bicocca

shan'ty·town' s bidonville f

shape [ʃep] s forma; **in bad shape** in cattive condizioni; **out of shape** sformato ‖ tr formare, foggiare; plasmare, conformare ‖ intr formarsi; **to take shape** prender forma

shapeless [ˈʃeplɪs] adj informe

shape·ly [ˈʃepli] adj (-lier; -liest) ben fatto, formoso

share [ʃɛr] s parte f; interesse m; (of stock) azione f; (of plow) suola; **to go shares** dividere in parti eguali ‖ tr (to enjoy jointly) condividere; (to apportion) ripartire ‖ intr partecipare, prender parte

sharecropper [ˈʃɛrˌkrɑpər] s mezzadro

share'hold'er s azionista mf

shark [ʃɑrk] s pescecane m; (schemer) piovra; (slang) esperto

sharp [ʃɑrp] adj affilato, acuto; angoloso; (e.g., curve) forte; distinto, ben delineato; (taste) pungente, salato; (pain) vivo; (words) mordace; (slang) elegante ‖ s (mus) diesis m ‖ adv acutamente; in punto, e.g., **at seven o'clock sharp** alle sette in punto

sharpen [ˈʃɑrpən] tr affilare; (a pencil) fare la punta a ‖ intr affilarsi

sharpener [ˈʃɑrpənər] s (person) affilatore m; (machine) affilatrice f

sharper [ˈʃɑrpər] s gabbamondo

sharp'shoot'er s tiratore scelto

shatter [ˈʃætər] tr frantumare; sfracellare; (health) rovinare; (nerves) sconvolgere; distruggere ‖ intr frantumarsi, andare in pezzi

shat'ter·proof' adj infrangibile

shave [ʃev] s rasatura; **to have a close shave** scapparla or scamparla bella ‖ tr (the face) radere, sbarbare; (wood) piallare; (to scrape) sfiorare; (prices) ridurre; (a lawn) tosare ‖ intr rasarsi

shaving [ˈʃevɪŋ] adj da barba, per barba, e.g., **shaving cream** crema da or per barba ‖ s rasatura; **shavings** trucioli mpl

shav'ing brush' s pennello da barba

shav'ing soap' s sapone m per la barba

shawl [ʃɔl] s scialle m

she [ʃi] s (shes) femmina ‖ pron pers (they) essa, lei

sheaf [ʃif] s (sheaves [ʃivz]) covone m; (of paper) fascio

shear [ʃɪr] s lama di cesoia; tagliatura; **shears** cesoie fpl ‖ v (pret **sheared**; pp **sheared** or **shorn** [ʃorn]) tr (sheep) tosare; (cloth) tagliare; **to shear s.o. of** privare qlcu di

sheath [ʃiθ] s (sheaths [ʃiðz]) guaina, coperta; (of a sword) fodero

sheathe [ʃið] tr rinfoderare, inguainare

shed [ʃɛd] s portico, tettoia; (geog) spartiacque m, versante m ‖ v (pret & pp **shed**; ger **shedding**) tr (e.g., blood) spargere, versare; (light) dare, fare; (feathers) spogliarsi di, lasciar cadere

sheen [ʃin] s lucentezza

sheep [ʃip] s (sheep) pecora; **sheep's eyes** occhio di triglia; **to separate the sheep from the goats** separare i buoni dai cattivi

sheep'dog' s cane m da pastore

sheepish [ˈʃipɪʃ] adj timido, goffo; pecoresco, pedissequo

sheep'skin' s pelle f di pecora; (parchment) cartapecora; (bb) bazzana; (coll) diploma m

sheer [ʃɪr] adj trasparente, fino, velato; puro; (cliff) stagliato ‖ adv completamente ‖ intr deviare

sheet [ʃit] s (for bed) lenzuolo; (of paper) foglio; (of metal) lamina; (of water) specchio; (naut) scotta

sheet' light'ning s lampeggio all'orizzonte

sheet' met'al s lamiera

sheet' mu'sic s spartito non rilegato

sheik [ʃik] s sceicco; (great lover) (slang) rubacuori m

shelf [ʃɛlf] s (shelves [ʃɛlvz]) scaffale m, scansia; (ledge) terrazzo, ripiano; banco di sabbia; **on the shelf** in disparte, dimenticato

shell [ʃɛl] s (of egg or crustacean) guscio; (of mollusk) conchiglia; (of vegetable) baccello; proietto, proiettile m; (cartridge) cartuccia; (of a cartridge) bossolo; (framework) armatura; (of boiler) involucro; imbarcazione da regata, schifo, iole f ‖ tr (vegetables) sgranare; bombardare, cannoneggiare; **to shell out** (slang) tirar fuori

shel·lac [ʃəˈlæk] s gomma lacca ‖ v (pret & pp **-lacked**; ger **-lacking**) tr verniciare con gomma lacca; (slang) dare una batosta a

shell'fish' ssg (-fish) frutto di mare; crostaceo; spl frutti mpl di mare; crostacei mpl

shell' hole' s cratere m

shell' shock' s psicosi traumatica bellica

shelter [ˈʃɛltər] s rifugio, ricovero; **to take shelter** rifugiarsi ‖ tr raccogliere, ospitare, dare rifugio a

shelve [ʃɛlv] tr mettere sullo scaffale; (a bill) insabbiare; mettere a riposo

shepherd [ˈʃɛpərd] s pastore m ‖ tr guardare, curarsi di

shep'herd dog' s cane m da pastore

shepherdess [ˈʃɛpərdɪs] s pastora

sherbet [ˈʃʌrbət] s sorbetto

sheriff [ˈʃɛrɪf] s sceriffo

sher·ry [ˈʃɛri] s (-ries) xeres m

shield [ʃild] s scudo; (for armpit) sottoascella m; (badge) scudetto; (elec) schermo ‖ tr proteggere; (elec) schermare

shift [ʃɪft] s cambio, cambiamento;

(*period of work*) turno; (*group of workmen*) operai *mpl* di turno, squadra di lavoro; espediente *m*, sotterfugio ‖ *tr* cambiare; spostare; (*blame*) riversare; ‖ *intr* cambiare; spostarsi; fare da sé; vivere di espedienti; (rr) manovrare; (aut) cambiare marcia

shift' key' *s* tasto maiuscole

shiftless ['ʃɪftlɪs] *adj* pigro, ozioso

shift·y ['ʃɪfti] *adj* (**-ier; -iest**) astuto; evasivo; pieno d'espedienti; (*glance*) sfuggente

shilling ['ʃɪlɪŋ] *s* scellino

shimmer ['ʃɪmər] *s* luccichio ‖ *intr* luccicare, mandare bagliori

shim·my ['ʃɪmi] *s* (**-mies**) (*dance*) shimmy *m;* (aut) farfallamento delle ruote, shimmy *m* ‖ *intr* ballare lo shimmy; vibrare

shin [ʃɪn] *s* stinco; (*of cattle*) cannone *m* ‖ *v* (*pret & pp* **shinned;** *ger* **shinning**) *tr* arrampicarsi su ‖ *intr* arrampicarsi

shin'bone' *s* stinco, tibia

shine [ʃaɪn] *s* splendore *m;* luce *f;* bel tempo; lucidatura, lucido; **to take a shine to** (coll) prender simpatia per ‖ *v* (*pret & pp* **shined**) *tr* pulire, lucidare ‖ *v* (*pret & pp* **shone** [ʃon]) *tr* (*e.g., a flashlight*) dirigere i raggi di ‖ *intr* brillare, luccicare, risplendere; (*to excel*) essere brillante, eccellere

shiner ['ʃaɪnər] *s* (slang) occhio pesto

shingle ['ʃɪŋɡəl] *s* assicella di copertura; (*to cover a wall*) mattoncino di rivestimento; (Brit) greto ciottoloso; (coll) capelli *mpl* alla bebé; **shingles** (pathol) erpete *m*, zona; **to hang out one's shingle** (coll) aprire un ufficio professionale ‖ *tr* coprire di assicelle or mattoncini; (*hair*) tagliare alla bebé

shining ['ʃaɪnɪŋ] *adj* brillante, lucente

shin·y ['ʃaɪni] *adj* (**-ier; -iest**) lucente, lucido; (*paper*) patinato

ship [ʃɪp] *s* nave *f*, bastimento; aeronave *f;* aeroplano; (*crew*) equipaggio ‖ *v* (*pret & pp* **shipped;** *ger* **shipping**) *tr* imbarcare; mandare, spedire; (*oars*) disarmare; (*water*) imbarcare ‖ *intr* imbarcarsi

ship'board' *s*—**on shipboard** a bordo

ship'build'er *s* costruttore *m* navale

ship'build'ing *s* architettura navale

ship'mate' *s* compagno di bordo

shipment ['ʃɪpmənt] *s* invio, spedizione

ship'own'er *s* armatore *m*

shipper ['ʃɪpər] *s* speditore *m*, spedizioniere *m*, mittente *m*

shipping ['ʃɪpɪŋ] *s* imbarco; spedizione; (naut) trasporto marittimo

ship'ping clerk' *s* speditore *m*

ship'ping room' *s* ufficio impaccatura

ship'shape' *adj & adv* in perfette condizioni

ship'side' *s* molo

ship's' pa'pers *spl* documenti *mpl* di bordo

ship'wreck' *s* naufragio; (*remains*) relitto ‖ *tr* far naufragare ‖ *intr* naufragare

ship'yard' *s* cantiere *m* navale

shirk [ʃʌrk] *tr* (*work*) evitare; (*responsibility*) sottrarsi a ‖ *intr* imboscarsi

shirt [ʃʌrt] *s* camicia; **to keep one's shirt on** (slang) non perdere la calma; **to lose one's shirt** (slang) perdere la camicia

shirt' front' *s* sparato

shirt' sleeve' *s* manica di camicia

shirt'tail' *s* falda della camicia

shirt'waist' *s* blusa da donna

shiver ['ʃɪvər] *s* brivido ‖ *intr* rabbrividire, battere i denti

shoal [ʃol] *s* secca, banco di sabbia

shock [ʃɑk] *s* urto, collisione; scossa; scossa elettrica; (pathol) shock *m* ‖ *tr* scuotere; (*to strike against*) urtare; scandalizzare, indignare; dare la scossa elettrica a; (fig) scioccare

shock' absorb'er [æb'sɔrbər] *s* ammortizzatore *m* di colpi

shocking ['ʃɑkɪŋ] *adj* disgustoso, scandalizzante

shock' ther'apy *s* terapia d'urto

shock' troops' *spl* truppe *fpl* d'assalto

shod·dy ['ʃɑdi] *adj* (**-dier; -diest**) scadente, falso

shoe [ʃu] *s* scarpa; (*horseshoe*) ferro da cavallo; (*of a tire*) copertone *m;* (*of brake*) ganascia, ceppo ‖ *v* (*pret & pp* **shod** [ʃɑd]) *tr* calzare; (*a horse*) ferrare

shoe'black' *s* lustrascarpe *m*

shoe'horn' *s* corno da scarpe, calzatoio

shoe'lace' *s* laccio delle scarpe

shoe'mak'er *s* calzolaio

shoe' pol'ish *s* crema or cera da scarpe

shoe'shine' *s* lucidatura, lustramento di scarpe

shoe' store' *s* calzoleria

shoe'string' *s* laccio delle scarpe; **on a shoestring** con quattro soldi

shoe'tree' *s* tendiscarpe *m*

shoo [ʃu] *tr* fare sciò a ‖ *intr* fare sciò

shoot [ʃut] *s* (*e.g., with a firearm*) tiro; gara di tiro; (*chute*) scivolo; (rok) lancio; (bot) getto, virgulto ‖ *v* (*pret & pp* **shot** [ʃɑt]) *tr* (*any missile*) tirare; (*a bullet*) sparare; (*to execute with a bullet*) fucilare; (*to fling*) lanciare; (*the sun*) prendere l'altezza di; (*dice*) gettare; (mov, telv) girare, riprendere; **to shoot down** (*a plane*) abbattere; **to shoot up** (coll) terrorizzare sparando a casaccio ‖ *intr* tirare, sparare; passare rapidamente; nascere; (*said of pain*) dare fitte; (mov) cinematografare; **to shoot at** tirare a; (coll) cercare di ottenere

shoot'ing gal'lery *s* tiro a segno

shoot'ing match' *s* gara di tiro a segno; (slang) tutto, ogni cosa

shoot'ing star' *s* stella cadente

shop [ʃɑp] *s* (*store*) negozio, rivendita; (*workshop*) officina; **to talk shop** parlare del proprio lavoro ‖ *v* (*pret & pp* **shopped;** *ger* **shopping**) *intr* fare la spesa; **to go shopping** andare a fare la spesa; **to shop around** cercare un'occasione di negozio in negozio

shop'girl' *s* venditrice *f*

shop'keep'er s negoziante mf
shoplifter ['ʃap‚lɪftər] s taccheggia-
tore m
shopper ['ʃapər] s compratore m
shopping ['ʃapɪŋ] s compra; (pur-
chases) compre fpl, shopping m
shop'ping bag' s sporta, shopping m
shop'ping cen'ter s centro d'acquisto,
ipermercato
shop'ping dis'trict s zona commerciale
shop'win'dow s vetrina
shop'worn' adj sciupato, usato
shore [ʃor] s costa, riva; spiaggia,
lido; (fig) regione; (support) soste-
gno, puntello || tr puntellare
shore' din'ner s pranzo di pesce
shore' leave' s (naut) franchigia
shore'line' s frangia costiera
shore' patrol' s polizia della marina
short [ʃɔrt] adj (in stature) piccolo,
basso; (in space, time) breve;
(scanty) scarso; succinto; (in quantity) poco, piccolo; (rude) brusco;
in a short time in breve; **in short** per
farla breve; **on short notice** senza
preavviso; **short of breath** corto di
fiato; **to be short of** scarseggiare di
|| s (elec) cortocircuito; (mov) corto-
metraggio; **shorts** (underwear) mutande fpl; (sports attire) calzoncini
mpl, shorts mpl || adv brevemente;
bruscamente; (com) allo scoperto,
e.g., **to sell short** vendere allo scoperto; **to run short of** essere a corto
di; **to stop short** fermarsi di colpo ||
tr (elec) causare un cortocircuito in
|| intr (elec) andare in cortocircuito
shortage ['ʃɔrtɪdʒ] s mancanza; (of
food) carestia; (from pilfering) ammanco
short'cake' s torta di pasta frolla; torta
ricoperta di frutta fresca
short'-change' tr non dare il cambio
giusto a; (coll) imbrogliare
short' cir'cuit s (elec) cortocircuito
short'-cir'cuit tr mandare in cortocir-
cuito; (coll) rovinare || intr andare
in cortocircuito
short'com'ing s difetto, manchevolezza
short'cut' s scorciatoia
shorten ['ʃɔrtən] tr raccorciare, abbre-
viare || intr raccorciarsi, abbreviarsi
shortening ['ʃɔrtənɪŋ] s raccorcia-
mento; (culin) grasso, strutto
short'hand' s stenografico || s steno-
grafia; **to take shorthand** stenografare
short'hand' typ'ist s stenodattilografo
short-lived ['ʃɔrt'laɪvd] or ['ʃɔrt'lɪvd]
adj effimero, di breve vita
shortly ['ʃɔrtli] adv in breve, breve-
mente; fra poco; bruscamente;
shortly after poco dopo
short'-range' adj di corta portata
short' sale' s vendita allo scoperto
short-sighted ['ʃɔrt'saɪtɪd] adj miope;
(fig) miope
short'stop' s (baseball) interbase m
short' sto'ry s novella
short-tempered ['ʃɔrt'tɛmpərd] adj irascibile
short'-term' adj a breve scadenza

short'wave' adj alle onde corte || s
onda corta
short' weight' s—**to give short weight**
rubare sul peso
shot [ʃat] s tiro, sparo; (cartridge) cartuccia; (for cannon) palla; (pellets
of lead) pallini mpl; (person) tiratore
m; (hypodermic injection) iniezione;
(of liquor) bicchierino; (phot) istantanea; (sports) peso; (mov) inquadratura; **not by a long shot** nemmeno
a pensarci; **to start like a shot** partire
come una palla da cannone; **to take
a shot at** tirare un colpo a; (to attempt to) provarsi a
shot'gun' s schioppo, fucile m da caccia
shot' put' s lancio del peso
should [ʃʊd] v aux si usa nelle seguenti
situazioni: 1) per formare il condizionale presente, per es., **if I should
wait for him, I should miss the train**
se lo aspettassi, perderei il treno;
2) per formare il perfetto del condizionale, per es., **if I had waited for
him, I should have missed the train**
se lo avessi aspettato, avrei perso il
treno; 3) per indicare la necessità di
un'azione, per es., **he should go at
once** dovrebbe andare immediatamente; **he should have gone immediately** sarebbe dovuto andare immediatamente
shoulder ['ʃoldər] s spalla; (of highway) banchina; **across the shoulder** a
bandoliera; **to put one's shoulders
to the wheel** mettersi a lavorare di
buzzo buono; **to turn a cold shoulder
to** volgere le spalle a || tr portare
sulle spalle; (a responsibility) addos-
sarsi; spingere con le spalle
shoul'der blade' s scapola
shoul'der strap' s spallina; (mil) tracolla
shout [ʃaʊt] s urlo, grido || tr urlare,
gridare; **to shout down** far tacere a
forza di strilli || intr gridare
shove [ʃʌv] s spintone m || tr spingere
|| intr spingere, dare spintoni; **to
shove off** allontanarsi dalla riva;
(slang) andarsene
shov·el ['ʃʌvəl] s pala || v (pret & pp
-eled or -elled; ger -eling or -elling)
tr spalare || intr lavorare di pala
show [ʃo] s mostra; apparenza; traccia; ostentazione; (mov, telv, theat)
spettacolo; **to make a show of** dar
spettacolo di; **to steal the show from**
ricevere tutti gli applausi invece di ||
tr mostrare, esporre; (a movie) presentare; dimostrare, insegnare; provare; (to register) segnare; (one's
feelings) manifestare; (to the door)
accompagnare; **to show in** fare entrare; **to show off** mettere in mostra
|| intr mostrarsi; presentarsi, appa-
rire; (said of a horse) (sports) arrivare terzo, piazzarsi; **to show off**
mettersi in mostra; **to show up** (coll)
mostrarsi; (coll) farsi vedere
show' bill' s cartellone m
show'boat' s battello per spettacoli teatrali

show' busi'ness s industria dello spettacolo

show'case' s bacheca, vetrina

show'down' s carte scoperte; chiarificazione

shower ['ʃaʊ·ər] s (of rain) acquazzone m; (shower bath) doccia; (e.g., for a bride) ricevimento cui i partecipanti devono portare un regalo; (fig) pioggia ‖ tr inaffiare; **to shower with** colmare di ‖ intr diluviare; fare la doccia

show'er bath' s doccia

show' girl' s ballerina, girl f

show'man s (-men) impresario teatrale; persona che ha molta scena

show'-off' s reclamista m, strombazzatore m

show'piece' s capolavoro, oggetto d'arte

show'place' s luogo celebre; **to be a showplace** (said, e.g., of a house) essere arredato perfettamente

show'room' s sala di mostra

show' win'dow s vetrina

show·y ['ʃo·i] adj (-ier; -iest) vistoso, sgargiante

shrapnel ['ʃræpnəl] s shrapnel m

shred [ʃred] s brano, brandello; ritaglio; (fig) granello; **to cut to shreds** fare a brandelli ‖ v (pret & pp **shredded** or **shred; ger shredding**) tr fare a brandelli; (paper) tagliuzzare

shrew [ʃru] s (woman) bisbetica; (animal) toporagno

shrewd [ʃrud] adj astuto, scaltro

shriek [ʃrik] s strido; strillo; risata stridula ‖ intr stridere; strillare

shrill [ʃrɪl] adj stridulo, squillante

shrimp [ʃrɪmp] s gamberetto; (person) omiciattolo, nanerottolo

shrine [ʃraɪn] s santuario, sacrario

shrink [ʃrɪŋk] v (pret **shrank** [ʃræŋk] or **shrunk** [ʃrʌŋk]; pp **shrunk** or **shrunken**) tr contrarre, restringere ‖ intr contrarsi, restringersi; ritirarsi

shrinkage ['ʃrɪŋkɪdʒ] s restringimento; (in weight) calo

shriv·el ['ʃrɪvəl] v (pret & pp -eled or -elled; ger -eling or -elling) tr raggrinzire; (from heat) raccartocciare; (to wither) avvizzire ‖ intr raggrinzirsi; accartocciarsi; avvizzire; **to shrivel up** incartapecorire

shroud [ʃraʊd] s sudario, lenzuolo funebre; (fig) cappa ‖ tr avvolgere

Shrove' Tues'day [ʃrov] s martedì grasso

shrub [ʃrʌb] s arbusto

shrubber·y ['ʃrʌbəri] s (-ies) arbusti mpl, cespugli mpl

shrug [ʃrʌg] s scrollata di spalle ‖ v (pret & pp **shrugged; ger shrugging**) tr scrollare; **to shrug one's shoulders** scrollare le spalle ‖ intr fare spallucce

shudder ['ʃʌdər] s brivido, fremito ‖ intr rabbrividire, fremere

shuffle ['ʃʌfəl] s (of cards) mescolata; turno di fare il mazzo; (of feet) strascichio; evasione ‖ tr mescolare; strisciare, strascicare ‖ intr fare il mazzo; scalpicciare; ballare di striscio; **to shuffle off** strascicarsi, scalpicciare; **to shuffle out of** evadere da

shun [ʃʌn] v (pret & pp **shunned; ger shunning**) tr evitare, schivare

shunt [ʃʌnt] tr sviare; (elec) shuntare; (rr) deviare

shut [ʃʌt] adj chiuso ‖ v (pret & pp **shut; ger shutting**) tr chiudere, serrare; **to shut in** rinchiudere; **to shut off** (e.g., gas) tagliare; **to shut up** tappare; imprigionare; (coll) fare star zitto ‖ intr chiudersi; **to shut up** (coll) stare zitto, tacere

shut'down' s chiusura

shutter [ʃʌtər] s (outside a window) persiana, gelosia; (outside a store window) serranda, saracinesca; (phot) otturatore m

shuttle ['ʃʌtəl] s spola, navetta ‖ intr fare la spola

shut'tle·cock' s volano, volante m

shut'tle train' s treno che fa la spola fra due stazioni

shy [ʃaɪ] adj (**shyer** or **shier; shyest** or **shiest**) timido; (fearful) schivo, ritroso; corto, a corto, e.g., **he is shy of funds** è a corto di denaro ‖ v (pret & pp **shied**) intr ritirarsi; schivarsi; (said of a horse) adombrarsi; **to shy away** tenersi discosto

shyster ['ʃaɪstər] s (coll) azzeccagarbugli m

Sia·mese [,saɪ·ə'miz] adj siamese ‖ s (-mese) siamese mf

Si'amese twins' spl fratelli mpl siamesi

Siberian [saɪ'bɪrɪ·ən] adj & s siberiano

sibilant ['sɪbɪlənt] adj & s sibilante f

sibyl ['sɪbɪl] s sibilla

sic [sik] adv sic ‖ [sɪk] v (pret & pp **sicked; ger sicking**) tr aizzare; **sick 'em!** va!; **to sick on** aizzare contro

Sicilian [sɪ'sɪljən] adj & s siciliano

Sicily ['sɪsɪli] s la Sicilia

sick [sɪk] adj ammalato; nauseato; (bored) stucco; **sick at heart** con una spina nel cuore; **to be sick and tired** averne sin sopra i capelli; **to be sick at one's stomach** aver la nausea; **to take sick** cader malato ‖ tr (a dog) aizzare

sick'bed' s letto d'ammalato

sicken ['sɪkən] tr ammalare; disgustare ‖ intr ammalarsi

sickening ['sɪkənɪŋ] adj stomachevole

sick' head'ache s emicrania accompagnata da nausea

sickle ['sɪkəl] s falce messoria, falcetto

sick' leave' s congedo per motivi di salute

sick·ly ['sɪkli] adj (-lier; -liest) cagionevole, malaticcio

sickness ['sɪknɪs] s malattia; nausea

side [saɪd] adj laterale ‖ s parte f, lato; (e.g., of a coin) faccia; (slope) versante m; (of human body, of a ship) fianco; **to take sides** parteggiare ‖ intr parteggiare; **to side with** schierarsi dalla parte di

side'board' s credenza

side'burns' spl basette fpl, favoriti mpl

side'car' *s* motocarrozzetta; carrozzino laterale (di motocarrozzetta)

side' dish' *s* portata extra

side' door' *s* porta laterale

side' effect' *s* effetto secondario

side'-glance' *s* occhiata di sbieco

side' is'sue *s* questione secondaria

side'line' *s* linea laterale; impiego secondario; attività secondaria

sidereal [saɪ'dɪrɪ·əl] *adj* siderale

side'sad'dle *adv* all'amazzone

side' show' *s* spettacolo secondario di baraccone; affare secondario

side'slip' *intr* (aer) scivolare d'ala

side'split'ting *adj* che fa sbellicare dalle risa

side' step' *s* passo laterale; scartata

side'-step' *v* (*pret* & *pp* **-stepped;** *ger* **-stepping**) *tr* evitare || *intr* farsi da parte; fare una scartata

side'track' *s* binario morto di smistamento || *tr* sviare; (rr) smistare

side' view' *s* vista di profilo

side'walk' *s* marciapiede *m*

side'walk café' *s* caffè *m* con tavolini all'aperto

sideward ['saɪdwərd] *adj* obliquo, a sghembo || *adv* verso un lato; di sghembo

side'ways' *adj* sghembo || *adv* di sghembo; di fianco

side' whisk'ers *spl* favoriti *mpl*

siding ['saɪdɪŋ] *s* (rr) diramazione, binario morto, raccordo ferroviario

sidle ['saɪdəl] *intr* andare al lato; muoversi furtivamente

siege [sidʒ] *s* assedio; (*of illness*) ricorrenza d'attacchi; **to lay siege to** cingere d'assedio, assediare

siesta [si'estə] *s* siesta; **to take a siesta** fare la siesta

sieve [sɪv] *s* vaglio, setaccio || *tr* vagliare, setacciare

sift [sɪft] *tr* (*flour*) abburattare; setacciare; (*to scatter with a sieve*) spolverare; (fig) vagliare

sigh [saɪ] *s* sospiro || *tr* mormorare sospirando || *intr* sospirare; **to sigh for** sospirare

sight [saɪt] *s* vista, visione; spettacolo, veduta; (opt) mira, traguardo; (mil) mirino, tacca di mira; (coll) mucchio; **a sight of** (coll) molto; **at first sight** prima vista; **at sight** ad apertura di libro; (com) a vista; **out of sight** fuori di vista; lontano dagli occhi; (*prices*) astronomico; **sights** luoghi *mpl* interessanti; **sight unseen** senza averlo visto prima, a occhi chiusi; **to be a sight** (coll) essere un orrore; **to catch sight of** arrivare a intravedere; **to know by sight** conoscere di vista; **to not be able to stand the sight of s.o.** not poter vedere qlcu nemmeno dipinto || *tr* avvistare; (*a weapon*) mirare || *intr* mirare, prendere di mira; osservare attentamente

sight' draft' *s* (com) tratta a vista

sight'-read' *v* (*pret* & *pp* **-read** [,red]) *tr* & *intr* leggere a libro aperto

sight'see'ing *adj* turistico || *s* turismo, visite *fpl* turistiche

sightseer ['saɪt ,si·ər] *s* turista *mf*

sign [saɪn] *s* segno; segnale *m;* (*e.g., on a store*) insegna, cartello; **signs** tracce *fpl* || *tr* firmare; ingaggiare; indicare, segnalare || *intr* firmare; fare segno; **to sign off** (rad, telv) terminare la trasmissione; **to sign up** iscriversi

sig·nal ['sɪgnəl] *adj* insigne, segnalato || *s* segnale *m* || *v* (*pret* & *pp* **-naled** or **-nalled;** *ger* **-naling** or **-nalling**) *tr* segnalare || *intr* fare segnalazioni

sig'nal corps' *s* (mil) armi *fpl* di trasmissione

sig'nal tow'er *s* (rr) posto di blocco

signato·ry ['sɪgnɪ ,tori] *s* (**-ries**) firmatario

signature ['sɪgnətʃər] *s* firma; segno musicale; (typ) segnatura

sign'board' *s* cartellone *m*

signer ['saɪnər] *s* firmatario

sig'net ring' ['sɪgnɪt] *s* anello col sigillo

significance [sɪg'nɪfɪkəns] *s* importanza; (*meaning*) significato

significant [sɪg'nɪfɪkənt] *adj* importante

signi·fy ['sɪgnɪ ,faɪ] *v* (*pret* & *pp* **-fied**) *tr* significare

sign'post' *s* palo indicatore

silence ['saɪləns] *s* silenzio || *tr* far tacere; (mil) ridurre al silenzio

silent ['saɪlənt] *adj* silenzioso, tacito

si'lent mov'ie *s* cinema muto

silhouette [,sɪlu'et] *s* silhouette *f*, siluetta

silicon ['sɪlɪkən] *s* silicio

silicone ['sɪlɪ ,kon] *s* silicone *m*

silk [sɪlk] *adj* di seta || *s* seta; **to hit the silk** (slang) gettarsi col paracadute

silken ['sɪlkən] *adj* serico, di seta

silk' hat' *s* cappello a cilindro

silk'screen proc'ess *s* serigrafia

silk'-stock'ing *adj* & *s* aristocratico

silk'worm' *s* baco da seta, filugello

silk·y ['sɪlki] *adj* (**-ier; -iest**) di seta; come la seta

sill [sɪl] *s* basamento; (*of a door*) soglia; (*of a window*) davanzale *m*

sil·ly ['sɪli] *adj* (**-lier; -liest**) sciocco, scemo

si·lo ['saɪlo] *s* (**-los**) silo || *tr* insilare

silt [sɪlt] *s* sedimento

silver ['sɪlvər] *adj* d'argento; (*voice*) argentino; (*plated with silver*) argentato || *s* argento || *tr* inargentare

sil'ver·fish' *s* (ent) lepisma

sil'ver foil' *s* foglia d'argento

sil'ver fox' *s* volpe argentata

sil'ver lin'ing *s* spiraglio di speranza

sil'ver plate' *s* vasellame *m* d'argento; argentatura

sil'ver screen' *s* (mov) schermo

sil'ver·smith' *s* argentiere *m*

sil'ver spoon' *s* ricchezza ereditata; **to be born with a silver spoon in one's mouth** esser nato con la camicia

sil'ver·ware' *s* argenteria

sil'ver·ware' chest' *s* portaposate *m*

similar ['sɪmɪlər] *adj* simile

similari·ty [,sɪmɪ'lærɪti] *s* (**-ties**) similarità *f*, somiglianza

simile ['sɪmɪli] *s* similitudine *f*

simmer ['sɪmər] *tr* cuocere a fuoco lento || *intr* cuocere a fuoco lento; (fig) ribollire; **to simmer down** (slang) calmarsi

simper ['sɪmpər] *s* sorriso scemo || *intr* fare un sorriso scemo

simple ['sɪmpəl] *adj* semplice

simple-minded ['sɪmpəl'maɪndɪd] *adj* semplicione, scemo

simpleton ['sɪmpəltən] *s* semplicione *m*

simulate ['sɪmjə‚let] *tr* simulare

simultaneous [‚saɪməl'tenɪ·əs] or [‚sɪməl'tenɪ·əs] *adj* simultaneo

sin [sɪn] *s* peccato || *v* (*pret & pp* **sinned;** *ger* **sinning**) *intr* peccare

since [sɪns] *adv* da allora, da allora in poi; da tempo fa || *prep* da || *conj* dacché; poiché, dato che

sincere [sɪn'sɪr] *adj* sincero

sincerity [sɪn'sɛrɪti] *s* sincerità *f*

sine [saɪn] *s* (math) seno

sinecure ['saɪnɪ‚kjur] or ['sɪnɪ‚kjur] *s* sinecura

sinew ['sɪnju] *s* tendine *m;* (fig) nerbo

sinful ['sɪnfəl] *adj* (*person*) peccatore; (*act, intention, etc.*) peccaminoso

sing [sɪŋ] *v* (*pret* **sang** [sæŋ] or **sung** [sʌŋ]; *pp* **sung**) *tr* cantare; **to sing to sleep** ninnare || *intr* cantare; (*said, e.g., of the ears*) fischiare

singe [sɪndʒ] *v* (*ger* **singeing**) *tr* strinare, bruciacchiare

singer ['sɪŋər] *s* cantante *mf;* (*in night club*) canzonettista *mf*

single ['sɪŋgəl] *adj* unico, solo; (*room*) a un letto; (*bed*) a una piazza; (*man*) celibe; (*woman*) nubile; (*combat*) corpo a corpo; semplice, sincero || **singles** *ssg* singolare *m* || *tr* scegliere; **to single out** individuare

single-breasted ['sɪŋgəl'brɛstɪd] *adj* a un petto, monopetto

sin'gle entry' *s* partita semplice

sin'gle file' *s* fila indiana

single-handed ['sɪŋgəl'hændɪd] *adj* da solo, senza aiuto altrui

sin'gle-phase' *adj* (elec) monofase

sin'gle room' *s* camera a un letto

sin'gle-track' *adj* (rr) a binario semplice; (fig) di corte vedute

sing'song' *adj* monotono || *s* cantilena

singular ['sɪŋgjələr] *adj & s* singolare *m*

sinister ['sɪnɪstər] *adj* sinistro

sink [sɪŋk] *s* acquaio; (*sewer*) scolo, fogna; (fig) sentina || *v* (*pret* **sank** [sæŋk] or **sunk** [sʌŋk]; *pp* **sunk**) *tr* sprofondare; infiggere; (*a well*) scavare; (*in tone*) abbassare; (*a boat*) mandare a picco; rovinare; investire; perdere || *intr* sprofondarsi; abbassarsi; (*said, of the sun, prices, etc.*) calare; andare a picco; lasciarsi cadere; (*in vice*) impantanarsi; (*said of one's cheeks*) infossarsi; (*in thought*) perdersi; **to sink down** sedersi; **to sink in** penetrare

sink'ing fund' *s* fondo d'ammortamento

sinner ['sɪnər] *s* peccatore *m*

Sinology [si'nɑlədʒi] *s* sinologia

sinuous ['sɪnju·əs] *adj* sinuoso

sinus ['saɪnəs] *s* seno

sip [sɪp] *s* sorso || *v* (*pret & pp* **sipped;** *ger* **sipping**) *tr* sorbire, sorseggiare

siphon ['saɪfən] *s* sifone *m* || *tr* travasare con un sifone

si'phon bot'tle *s* sifone *m*

sir [sʌr] *s* signore *m;* (Brit) sir *m;* **Dear Sir** Illustrissimo signore; (com) Egregio signore

sire [saɪr] *s* (*king*) sire *m;* padre *m,* stallone *m* || *tr* generare

siren ['saɪrən] *s* sirena

sirloin ['sʌrlɔɪn] *s* lombata, lombo

sirup ['sɪrəp] or ['sʌrəp] *tr* sciroppo

sis·sy ['sɪsi] *s* (**-sies**) effemminato

sister ['sɪstər] *adj* (*ship*) gemello; (*language*) sorella; (*corporation*) consorella || *s* sorella; (*nun*) suora, monaca

sis'ter-in-law' *s* (**sis'ters-in-law'**) cognata

Sis'tine Chap'el ['sɪstin] *s* Cappella Sistina

sit [sɪt] *v* (*pret & pp* **sat** [sæt]; *ger* **sitting**) *intr* sedere; posare; (*said of a hen*) covare; (*said of a jacket*) stare; essere in sessione; **to sit down** sedersi; **to sit in on** partecipare a; assistere a; **to sit still** stare tranquillo; **to sit up** alzarsi; (coll) essere sorpreso

sit'-down strike' *s* sciopero bianco

site [saɪt] *s* sito, luogo, posizione

sitting ['sɪtɪŋ] *s* seduta; (*of a court*) sessione; (*of a hen*) covata; (*serving of a meal*) turno

sit'ting duck' *s* (slang) facile bersaglio

sit'ting room' *s* soggiorno

situate ['sɪtʃu‚et] *tr* situare

situation [‚sɪtʃu'eʃən] *s* situazione, posizione; posto

sitz' bath' [sɪts] *s* semicupio

six [sɪks] *adj & pron* sei || *s* sei *m;* **at sixes and sevens** in disordine; **six o'clock** le sei

six' hun'dred *adj, s & pron* seicento

sixteen ['sɪks'tin] *adj, s & pron* sedici *m*

sixteenth ['sɪks'tinθ] *adj, s & pron* sedicesimo || *s* (*in dates*) sedici *m*

sixth [sɪksθ] *adj, s & pron* sesto || *s* (*in dates*) sei *m*

sixtieth ['sɪkstɪ·ɪθ] *adj, s & pron* sessantesimo

six·ty ['sɪksti] *adj & pron* sessanta || *s* (**-ies**) sessanta *m;* **the sixties** gli anni sessanta

sizable ['saɪzəbəl] *adj* considerevole

size [saɪz] *s* grandezza; quantità *f;* (*of person or garment*) taglia; (*of shoes*) numero; (*of hat*) giro; (*of a pipe*) diametro; (*for gilding*) colla; (fig) situazione || *tr* misurare, classificare secondo grandezza; incollare; **to size up** (coll) stimare, giudicare

sizzle ['sɪzəl] *s* sfrigolio || *intr* sfriggere

skate [sket] *s* pattino; (slang) tipo || *intr* pattinare; **to skate on thin ice** andare in cerca di disgrazie

skat'ing rink' *s* pattinatoio

skein [sken] *s* gomitolo, matassa

skeleton ['skɛlɪtən] *adj* scheletrico || *s* scheletro

skel'eton key' *s* chiave maestra

skeptic ['skɛptɪk] *adj & s* scettico

skeptical ['skɛptɪkəl] *adj* scettico

sketch [skɛtʃ] *s* schizzo, disegno; abbozzo, bozzetto; (theat) scenetta || *tr* schizzare, disegnare; abbozzare

sketch'book' *s* album *m* di schizzi; quaderno per abbozzi

skew [skju] *adj* obliquo || *s* movimento obliquo; (*chisel*) scalpello a taglio obliquo || *tr* tagliare di sghembo || *intr* (*to swerve*) deviare; (*to look obliquely*) guardare di sghembo

skew' chis'el *s* scalpello a taglio obliquo

skewer ['skju·ər] *s* spiedino || *tr* mettere allo spiedo

ski [ski] *s* (**skis** or **ski**) sci *m* || *intr* sciare

ski' boot' *s* scarpa da sci

skid [skɪd] *s* (*device to check a wheel*) scarpa; (*skidding forward*) slittamento; (*skidding sideway*) sbandamento; (aer, mach) pattino || *v* (*pret & pp* **skidded;** *ger* **skidding**) *tr* frenare || *intr* (*forward*) slittare; (*sideways*) sbandare

skid' row' [ro] *s* quartiere malfamato

skier ['ski·ər] *s* sciatore *m*

skiff [skɪf] *s* skiff *m*, singolo

skiing ['ski·ɪŋ] *s* sci *m*

ski' jump' *s* salto con gli sci; trampolino di salto

ski' lift' *s* sciovia

skill [skɪl] *s* destrezza, perizia

skilled [skɪld] *adj* abile, esperto

skilled' la'bor *s* manodopera qualificata

skillet ['skɪlɪt] *s* padella

skilful ['skɪlfəl] *adj* destro, abile

skim [skɪm] *v* (*pret & pp* **skimmed;** *ger* **skimming**) *tr* (*milk*) scremare; (*e.g., broth*) sgrassare; (*to graze*) sfiorare; (*the ground*) radere; (*a page*) trascorrere || *intr* sfiorare; **to skim over** scorrere

ski' mask' *s* passamontagna *m*

skimmer ['skɪmər] *s* schiumaiola; (*hat*) canottiera

skim' milk' *s* latte scremato or magro

skimp [skɪmp] *tr* lesinare || *intr* economizzare, risparmiare

skimp·y ['skɪmpi] *adj* (**-ier; -iest**) corto, scarso; taccagno

skin [skɪn] *s* pelle *f*; (*rind*) scorza; (*of onion*) spoglia; **by the skin of one's teeth** (coll) per il rotto della cuffia; **soaked to the skin** bagnato fino alle ossa; **to have a thin skin** offendersi facilmente || *v* (*pret & pp* **skinned;** *ger* **skinning**) *tr* pelare, spellare; (*e.g., one's knee*) spellarsi; (slang) tosare; **to skin alive** (slang) scotennare; (slang) battere in pieno

skin'-deep' *adj* a fior di pelle

skin'-div'er *s* nuotatore subacqueo, sub *m*; (mil) sommozzatore *m*

skin'flint' *s* avaro

skin' game' *s* truffa

skin·ny ['skɪni] *adj* (**-nier; -niest**) magro, scarno

skin' test' *s* cutireazione

skip [skɪp] *s* salto || *v* (*pret & pp*

skipped; *ger* **skipping**) *tr* (*a fence; a meal*) saltare; (*a subject*) sorvolare; (*school*) (coll) marinare || *intr* saltare, salterellare; (*said of typewriter*) saltare uno spazio; (coll) svignarsela

ski' pole' *s* racchetta da sci

skipper ['skɪpər] *s* capitano, comandante *m*

skirmish ['skʌrmɪʃ] *s* scaramuccia || *intr* battersi in una scaramuccia

skirt [skʌrt] *s* sottana, gonna; (*edge*) orlo; (*woman*) (slang) gonnella || *tr* orlare; costeggiare; (*a subject*) evitare

ski' run' *s* pista da sci

skit [skɪt] *s* (theat) quadretto comico

skittish ['skɪtɪʃ] *adj* bizzarro, balzano; timido; (*horse*) ombroso

skulduggery [skʌl'dʌgəri] *s* trucco disonesto

skull [skʌl] *s* cranio, teschio

skull' and cross'bones *s* due tibie incrociate ed un teschio

skull'cap' *s* papalina

skunk [skʌŋk] *s* puzzola, moffetta; (coll) puzzone *m*

sky [skaɪ] *s* (**skies**) cielo; firmamento; **to praise to the skies** portare al cielo

sky'div'er *s* paracadutista *mf*

sky'jack'er *s* pirata *m* dell'aria

sky'lark' *s* allodola || *intr* (coll) darsi alla pazza gioia

sky'light' *s* lucernario

sky'line' *s* linea dell'orizzonte; (*of city*) profilo

sky'rock'et *s* razzo || *intr* salire come un razzo

sky'scrap'er *s* grattacielo

sky'writ'ing *s* scrittura pubblicitaria aerea

slab [slæb] *s* (*of stone*) lastra, lastrone *m*; (*of wood*) tavola; (*slice*) fetta

slack [slæk] *adj* lento, allentato; negligente, indolente; (fig) fiacco, morto || *s* lentezza; negligenza; stagione morta, inattività *f*; **slacks** pantaloni *mpl* da donna; pantaloni sciolti || *tr* allentare; trascurare; (*lime*) spegnere || *intr* rilasciarsi; essere negligente; **to slack up** rallentare

slacker ['slækər] *s* fannullone *m*; (mil) imboscato

slag [slæg] *s* scoria

slake [slek] *tr* spegnere

slalom ['slɑləm] *s* slalom *m*

slam [slæm] *s* colpo; (*of door*) sbatacchiamento; (*in cards*) cappotto; (coll) strapazzata || *v* (*pret & pp* **slammed;** *ger* **slamming**) *tr* sbattere, sbatacchiare; (coll) strapazzare || *intr* sbattere, sbatacchiare

slam'bang' *adv* (coll) con gran rumore, precipitosamente

slander ['slændər] *s* calunnia, maldicenza *f* || *tr* calunniare, diffamare

slanderous ['slændərəs] *adj* calunnioso, diffamatorio

slang [slæŋ] *s* gergo

slant [slænt] *s* inclinazione; punto di vista || *tr* inclinare; (*news*) snaturare || *intr* inclinarsi; deviare

slap [slæp] *s* manata; (*in the face*) schiaffo, ceffone *m;* (*noise*) rumore *m;* insulto || *v* (*pret & pp* **slapped;** *ger* **slapping**) *tr* dare una manata a; schiaffeggiare

slap′dash′ *adj* raffazzonato, fatto a casaccio || *adv* a casaccio

slap′hap′py *adj* (*punch-drunk*) stordito; (*giddy*) allegro, brillo

slap′stick′ *adj* buffonesco || *s* bastone *m* d'Arlecchino; buffonata

slash [slæʃ] *s* sfregio; (*of prices*) riduzione || *tr* sfregiare; (*cloth*) tagliare; (*prices*) ridurre

slat [slæt] *s* travicello, regolo; (*for bed*) traversa; (*of shutter*) stecca

slate [slet] *s* ardesia, lavagna; lista elettorale; **clean slate** buon certificato || *tr* coprire con tegole d'ardesia; proporre la nomina di; (*to schedule*) mettere in cantiere

slate′ roof′ *s* tetto d'ardesia

slattern [ˈslætərn] *s* (*slovenly woman*) sciamannona; (*harlot*) puttana

slaughter [ˈslɔtər] *s* eccidio, carneficina || *tr* sgozzare, scannare

slaugh′ter·house′ *s* macello, scannatoio

Slav [slɑv] or [slæv] *adj & s* slavo

slave [slev] *adj & s* schiavo || *intr* lavorare come uno schiavo

slave′ driv′er *s* negriere *m*

slavery [ˈsleveri] *s* schiavitù *f*

slave′ trade′ *s* tratta degli schiavi

Slavic [ˈslɑvɪk] or [ˈslævɪk] *adj & s* slavo

slay [sle] *v* (*pret* **slew** [slu]; *pp* **slain** [slen]) *tr* scannare, uccidere

slayer [ˈsle·ər] *s* uccisore *m*

sled [slɛd] *s* slittino, slitta || *v* (*pret & pp* **sledded;** *ger* **sledding**) *intr* slittare

sledge′ ham′mer *s* [ˈslɛdʒ] *s* mazza

sleek [slik] *adj* liscio, lustro; elegante || *tr* lisciare, ammorbidire

sleep [slip] *s* sonno; **to go to sleep** addormentarsi; **to put to sleep** addormentare; uccidere con un anestetico || *v* (*pret & pp* **slept** [slɛpt]) *tr* dormire; aver posto a dormire per; **to sleep it over** dormirci sopra; **to sleep off a hangover** smaltire una sbornia dormendo || *intr* dormire; **to sleep in** dormire fino a tardi; passare la notte a casa; **to sleep out** passare la notte fuori di casa

sleeper [ˈslipər] *s* (*person*) dormiente *mf;* (*beam, timber*) trave *f*

sleep′ing bag′ *s* sacco a pelo

sleep′ing car′ *s* vettura letto

sleep′ing pill′ *s* sonnifero

sleepless [ˈsliplɪs] *adj* insonne; (*night*) bianco

sleep′walk′er *s* sonnambulo

sleep·y [ˈslipi] *adj* (**-ier; -iest**) insonnolito, sonnolento; **to be sleepy** aver sonno

sleep′y-head′ *s* dormiglione *m*

sleet [slit] *s* nevischio || *impers* **it is sleeting** cade il nevischio

sleeve [sliv] *s* manica; (*of phonograph record*) busta; (*mach*) manicotto; **to laugh in** or **up one's sleeve** ridere sotto i baffi

sleigh [sle] *s* slitta || *intr* andare in slitta

sleigh′ bells′ *spl* bubboli *mpl* da slitta, sonagliera da slitta

sleigh′ ride′ *s* passeggiata in slitta

sleight′ of hand′ [slaɪt] *s* gioco di prestigio

slender [ˈslɛndər] *adj* smilzo, snello; esiguo, esile

sleuth [sluθ] *s* segugio

slew [slu] *s* (coll) mucchio

slice [slaɪs] *s* fetta; (*of an orange*) spicchio || *tr* tagliare a fette; (fig) fendere

slick [slɪk] *adj* liscio, lustro; scivoloso; astuto; (slang) ottimo || *s* posto scivoloso; (coll) rivista stampata su carta patinata || *tr* lisciare, lustrare; **to slick up** (coll) acconciare

slicker [ˈslɪkər] *s* impermeabile *m* di tela cerata; (coll) furbo di tre cotte

slide [slaɪd] *s* scivolata, scivolone *m;* (*chute*) scivolo; (*landslide*) frana; (*for projection*) diapositiva; (*of a microscope*) vetrino; (*mach*) guida; (*of a slide rule*) (mach) cursore *m* || *v* (*pret & pp* **slid** [slɪd]) *tr* far scivolare || *intr* sdrucciolare, scivolare; (*said of a car*) pattinare, slittare; **to let slide** lasciar correre

slide′ fas′tener *s* chiusura lampo

slide′ projec′tor *s* diascopio

slide′ rule′ *s* regolo calcolatore

slide′ valve′ *s* (mach) cassetto di distribuzione

slid′ing door′ *s* porta scorrevole

slid′ing scale′ *s* scala mobile

slight [slaɪt] *adj* leggero, lieve; delicato || *s* noncuranza, disattenzione; affronto || *tr* fare con negligenza; (*to snub*) trattare con noncuranza, snobbare

slim [slɪm] *adj* (**slimmer; slimmest**) sottile; magro

slime [slaɪm] *s* melma; (*e.g., of a snail*) bava

slim·y [ˈslaɪmi] *adj* (**-ier; -iest**) melmoso; bavoso; sudicio

sling [slɪŋ] *s* (*to shoot stones*) fionda; (naut) braca; **in a sling** (*arm*) al collo || *v* (*pret & pp* **slung** [slʌŋ]) *tr* gettare; lanciare; (*freight*) imbracare; sospendere; mettere a bandoliera

sling′shot′ *s* fionda

slink [slɪŋk] *v* (*pret & pp* **slunk** [slʌŋk]) *intr* andare furtivamente; **to slink away** eclissarsi

slip [slɪp] *s* scivolone *m;* svista, errore *m;* (*in prices*) discesa; (*underdress*) sottoveste *f;* (*pillowcase*) federa; (*of paper*) pezzo; (*space between two wharves*) darsena, imbarcatoio; (*form*) modulo; personcina; (*inclined plane*) (naut) scalo d'alaggio; (bot) innesto; **to give the slip to** eludere || *v* (*pret & pp* **slipped;** *ger* **slipping**) *tr* infilare; liberare; liberarsi da; omettere; **to slip off** togliersi; **to slip on** mettersi; **to slip one's mind** dimenticarsi di, e.g., **it slipped my mind** me ne sono dimenticato || *intr* scivolare, scorrere; sdrucciolare; sbagliare; peggiorare; **to let slip** lasciarsi sfuggire; **to slip away** svignarsela; **to slip by** (*said of time*) passare, fuggire; **to slip out of s.o.'s hands** sgusciare dalle mani di qlcu; **to slip up** sbagliarsi

slip'cov'er *s* fodera
slip'knot' *s* nodo scorsoio
slip' of the tongue' *s* errore *m* nel parlare
slipper ['slɪpər] *s* pantofola
slippery ['slɪpəri] *adj* sdrucciolevole, scivoloso; evasivo; incerto
slip'shod' *adj* trasandato, mal fatto
slip'-up' *s* (coll) sbaglio
slit [slɪt] *s* taglio, fenditura || *v* (*pret & pp* **slit;** *ger* **slitting**) *tr* tagliare, fendere; **to slit the throat of** sgozzare
slob [slɑb] *s* (slang) rozzo, villanzone *m*
slobber ['slɑbər] *s* bava; sdolcinatura || *intr* sbavare; parlare sdolcinatamente
sloe [slo] *s* (*shrub*) prugnolo; (*fruit*) prugnola
slogan ['slogən] *s* slogan *m*
sloop [slup] *s* cutter *m*
slop [slɑp] *s* pastone *m;* (slang) sbobba || *v* (*pret & pp* **slopped;** *ger* **slopping**) *tr* versare, imbrodare || *intr* rovesciarsi, scorrere; (slang) perdersi in smancerie
slope [slop] *s* costa, pendice *f;* (*of mountain or roof*) spiovente *m* || *tr* inclinare || *intr* digradare, scendere
slop•py ['slɑpi] *adj* (**-pier; -piest**) fangoso; bagnato; (*slovenly*) sciatto; (*done badly*) abborracciato
slot [slɑt] *s* scanalatura; (*for letters*) buca; (*e.g., on a broadcasting schedule*) posizione
sloth [sloθ] *or* [slɔθ] *s* pigrizia; (zool) bradipo, poltrone *m*
slot' machine' *s* macchina a gettone
slouch [slaʊtʃ] *s* postura goffa; persona goffa; (coll) poltrone *m* || *intr* muoversi goffamente; **to slouch in a chair** sdraiarsi
slouch' hat' *s* cappello floscio
slough [slaʊ] *s* pantano; (fig) abisso || [slʌf] *s* (*of snake*) spoglia; (pathol) crosta || *tr*—**to slough off** spogliarsi di || *intr* sbucciarsi, cadere
Slovak ['slovæk] *or* [slo'væk] *adj & s* slovacco
sloven•ly ['slʌvənli] *adj* (**-lier; -liest**) sciatto, trasandato
slow [slo] *adj* lento; (*sluggish*) tardo; (*clock*) indietro, in ritardo; (*in understanding*) tardivo || *adv* piano || *tr* rallentare || *intr* rallentarsi; (*said of a watch*) ritardare
slow'down' *s* sciopero pignolo
slow' mo'tion *s*—**in slow motion** al rallentatore
slow'-motion projec'tor *s* rallentatore *m*
slow'poke' *s* (coll) poltrone *m*
slug [slʌg] *s* (*heavy piece of metal*) lingotto; (*metal disk*) gettone *m;* (fig) poltrone *m;* (zool) lumaca; (coll) colpo, mazzata || *v* (*pret & pp*

slugged; *ger* **slugging**) *tr* picchiare sodo
sluggard ['slʌgərd] *s* poltrone *m*
sluggish ['slʌgɪʃ] *adj* pigro, indolente; lento, fiacco
sluice [slus] *s* canale *m;* stramazzo
sluice' gate' *s* paratoia
slum [slʌm] *s* bassifondi *mpl* || *v* (*pret & pp* **slummed;** *ger* **slumming**) *intr* visitare i bassifondi
slumber ['slʌmbər] *s* dormiveglia *m*, sonnellino || *intr* dormire, dormicchiare
slump [slʌmp] *s* depressione, crisi *f;* (*in prices*) ribasso, calo || *intr* impantanarsi; peggiorare; (*said of prices*) ribassare, calare
slur [slʌr] *s* insulto, macchia; critica; (mus) legatura || *v* (*pret & pp* **slurred;** *ger* **slurring**) *tr* pronunziare indistintamente; (*a subject*) sorvolare; insultare, calunniare; (mus) legare
slush [slʌʃ] *s* poltiglia di neve; fanghiglia; (fig) sdolcinatezza
slut [slʌt] *s* cagna; (*slovenly woman*) sciamannona; troia, puttana
sly [slaɪ] *adj* (**slyer** *or* **slier; slyest** *or* **sliest**) furbo; insidioso; (*hiding one's true feelings*) sornione; **on the sly** furtivamente
smack [smæk] *s* schiaffo; (*of whip or lips*) schiocco; (*taste*) traccia, sapore *m;* (coll) bacio collo schiocco || *adv* di colpo, direttamente || *tr* dare uno schiaffo a; colpire; (*the whip or one's lips*) schioccare; schioccare un bacio a || *intr*—**to smack of** sapere di
small [smɔl] *adj* piccolo; povero; basso, umile; (*change*) spicciolo; (typ) minuscolo
small' arms' *spl* armi *fpl* portatili
small' busi'ness *s* piccolo commercio
small' cap'ital *s* (typ) maiuscoletto
small' change' *s* spiccioli *mpl*
small' fry' *s* minutaglia; bambini *mpl;* gente *f* di poca importanza
small' hours' *spl* ore *fpl* piccole
small' intes'tine *s* intestino tenue
small-minded ['smɔl'maɪndɪd] *adj* di corte vedute, gretto
small' of the back' *s* fine *f* della schiena, reni *fpl*
smallpox ['smɔl‚pɑks] *s* vaiolo
small' talk' *s* conversazione futile
small'-time' *adj* di poca importanza
small'-town' *adj* di provincia
smart [smɑrt] *adj* intelligente; scaltro, furbo; (*pain*) acuto; (*in appearance*) elegante; (*pert*) impertinente; (coll) grande, abbondante || *s* dolore acuto, sofferenza || *intr* bruciare; dolere; soffrire
smart' al'eck ['ælɪk] *s* saputello
smart' set' *s* bel mondo
smash [smæʃ] *s* sconquasso; colpo; collisione; rovina, fallimento; (tennis) smash *m*, schiacciata || *tr* sconquassare; sfracellare; rovinare; (tennis) schiacciare || *intr* sconquassarsi; sfracellarsi; andare in rovina; **to smash into** scontrarsi con
smash' hit' *s* successone *m*

smash'-up' *s* sconquasso
smattering ['smætərɪŋ] *s* infarinatura, spolvero
smear [smɪr] *s* macchia, imbrattatura; calunnia; (bact) striscio || *tr* imbrattare; spalmare; calunniare
smear' campaign' *s* campagna di vilipendio
smell [smɛl] *s* odore *m*; (sense) olfatto, odorato; profumo || *v* (pret & pp **smelled** or **smelt**) *tr* fiutare, odorare || *intr* odorare; (to stink) puzzare; profumare; **to smell of** odorare di; puzzare di
smell'ing salts' *spl* sali aromatici
smell·y ['smɛli] *adj* (-ier; -iest) puzzolente
smelt [smɛlt] *s* (ichth) eperlano || *tr* & *intr* fondere
smile [smaɪl] *s* sorriso || *intr* sorridere
smiling ['smaɪlɪŋ] *adj* sorridente
smirk [smʌrk] *s* ghigno || *intr* ghignare
smite [smaɪt] *v* (pret **smote** [smot]; pp **smitten** ['smɪtən] or **smit** [smɪt]) *tr* colpire; percuotere; affliggere, castigare
smith [smɪθ] *s* fabbro
smith·y ['smɪθi] *s* (-ies) fucina
smit'ten *adj* afflitto; innamorato
smock [smɑk] *s* camice *m*; (of mechanic) camiciotto
smock' frock' *s* blusa da lavoro
smog [smɑg] *s* foschia, smog *m*
smoke [smok] *s* fumo; **to go up in smoke** andare in cenere || *tr* affumicare; (tobacco) fumare; **to smoke out** cacciare col fumo; scoprire || *intr* fumare; (said, e.g., of the earth) fumigare
smoke'-filled room' *s* stanza da riunioni piena di fumo
smoke'less pow'der ['smoklɪs] *s* polvere *f* senza fumo
smoker ['smokər] *s* fumatore *m*; salone *m* fumatori; (rr) vagone *m* fumatori
smoke' rings' *spl* anelli *mpl* di fumo
smoke' screen' *s* cortina di fumo
smoke'stack' *s* fumaiolo
smoking ['smokɪŋ] *s* (il) fumare; **no smoking** vietato fumare
smok'ing car' *s* vagone *m* fumatori
smok'ing jack'et *s* giacca da casa
smok'ing room' *s* stanza per fumatori
smok·y ['smoki] *adj* (-ier; -iest) fumoso
smolder ['smoldər] *s* fumo derivante da fuoco che cova || *intr* (said of fire or passion) covare; (said of s.o.'s eyes) ardere
smooch [smutʃ] *intr* (coll) baciarsi, baciucchiarsi
smooth [smuð] *adj* liscio, levigato; (face) glabro; di consistenza uniforme; (flat) piano; senza interruzioni; tranquillo; elegante; (sound) armonioso; (taste) gradevole; (wine) abboccato; (sea) calmo; (style) fluido || *tr* lisciare, levigare; appianare, facilitare; calmare; **to smooth away** appianare
smooth-faced ['smuð‚fest] *adj* (beardless) glabro; liscio

smooth-spoken ['smuð‚spokən] *adj* mellifluo
smooth·y ['smuði] *s* (-ies) galante *m*
smother ['smʌðər] *tr* affoggare, soffocare
smudge [smʌdʒ] *s* macchia, imbrattatura || *tr* macchiare, imbrattare; (a garden) affumicare
smudge' pot' *s* apparecchiatura per affumicare
smug [smʌg] *adj* (smugger; smuggest) pieno di sé stesso; liscio, lisciato
smuggle ['smʌgəl] *tr* contrabbandare || *intr* praticare il contrabbando
smuggler ['smʌglər] *s* contrabbandiere *m*
smuggling ['smʌglɪŋ] *s* contrabbando
smut [smʌt] *s* sudiciume *m*; oscenità *f*; (agr) volpe *f*, golpe *f*
smut·ty ['smʌti] *adj* (-tier; -tiest) sudicio; osceno; (agr) malato di volpe
snack [snæk] *s* spuntino, merenda; porzione
snack' bar' *s* tavola calda
snag [snæg] *s* tronco sommerso; protuberanza, sporgenza; (tooth) dente rotto; (fig) intoppo, ostacolo; **to hit a snag** incontrare un ostacolo || *v* (pret & pp **snagged**; ger **snagging**) *tr* fare uno straccio a; (fig) ostacolare
snail [snel] *s* chiocciola, lumaca; **at a snail's pace** come una lumaca
snake [snek] *s* serpente *m*; (nonvenomous) biscia
snake' in the grass' *s* pericolo nascosto; (person) serpe *f* in seno
snap [snæp] *s* (sharp sound) schiocco; (bite) morso; (fastener) bottone automatico; (of cold weather) breve periodo; (manner of speaking) tono tagliente; (phot) istantanea; (coll) vigore *m*; (coll) cosa da nulla || *v* (pret & pp **snapped**; ger **snapping**) *tr* schioccare; chiudere di colpo; spezzare di colpo; (a picture) scattare; **to snap one's fingers at** infischiarsi di; **to snap up** afferrare; (a person) tagliare la parola a || *intr* schioccare; (to crack) rompersi di colpo; **to snap at** cercare di mordere; **to snap out of it** (coll) riprendersi; **to snap shut** chiudersi di colpo
snap'drag'on *s* (bot) bocca di leone
snap' fas'tener *s* bottone automatico
snap' judg'ment *s* decisione presa senza riflessione
snap·py ['snæpi] *adj* (-pier; -piest) mordente, mordace; (coll) vivo, vivace; (coll) elegante; **to make it snappy** (slang) sbrigarsi
snap'shot' *s* istantanea
snare [snɛr] *s* laccio, lacciolo; (of a drum) corda
snare' drum' *s* cassa rullante
snarl [snɑrl] *s* (of a dog) ringhio; groviglio; (of traffic) ingorgo; (fig) confusione || *tr* urlare con un ringhio; (to tangle) aggrovigliare; complicare || *intr* ringhiare; aggrovigliarsi; complicarsi
snatch [snætʃ] *s* strappo, strappone *m*; presa; pezzetto; momentino || *tr* &

intr strappare; **to snatch at** cercare di afferrare; **to snatch from** strappare a

sneak [snik] *s* furfante *m* ‖ *tr* mettere di nascosto; pigliare di nascosto ‖ *intr*—**to sneak in** entrare di nascosto; **to sneak out** svignarsela

sneaker ['snikər] *s* furfante *m;* scarpetta da ginnastica

sneak' thief' *s* ladro, topo

sneak·y ['sniki] *adj* (**-ier; -iest**) furtivo

sneer [snɪr] *s* ghigno ‖ *intr* sogghignare; **to sneer at** beffarsi si

sneeze [sniz] *s* starnuto ‖ *intr* starnutare; **not to be sneezed at** (coll) non essere disprezzabile

snicker ['snɪkər] *s* risatina ‖ *intr* fare una risatina

snide [snaɪd] *adj* malizioso

sniff [snɪf] *s* fiuto, fiutata; (*scent*) odore *m* ‖ *tr* fiutare ‖ *intr* aspirare rumorosamente; (*with emotion*) moccicare; **to sniff at** annusare; mostrare disprezzo per

sniffle ['snɪfəl] *s* moccio; **to have the sniffles** moccicare ‖ *intr* moccicare

snip [snɪp] *s* taglio; pezzetto; (*person*) (coll) mezza cartuccia ‖ *v* (*pret & pp* **snipped;** *ger* **snipping**) *tr* tagliuzzare

snipe [snaɪp] *s* tiro di nascosto; (orn) beccaccino ‖ *intr* sparare in appostamento; attaccare da lontano

sniper ['snaɪpər] *s* franco tiratore, cecchino

snippet ['snɪpɪt] *s* ritaglio, frammento; (fig) mezza cartuccia

snip·py ['snɪpi] *adj* (**-pier; -piest**) frammentario; (coll) corto, brusco; (coll) arrogante

snitch [snɪtʃ] *tr & intr* (coll) graffignare, sgraffignare

sniv·el ['snɪvəl] *s* moccio; singhiozzo, piagnisteo; falsa commozione ‖ *v* (*pret & pp* **-eled** or **-elled;** *ger* **-eling** or **-elling**) *intr* singhiozzare, piagnucolare; (*to have a runny nose*) moccicare, avere il moccio

snob [snɑb] *s* snob *mf*

snobbery ['snɑbəri] *s* snobismo

snobbish ['snɑbɪʃ] *adj* snobistico

snoop [snup] *s* (coll) ficcanaso ‖ *intr* (coll) ficcare il naso

snoop·y ['snupi] *adj* (**-ier; -iest**) (coll) curioso, invadente

snoot [snut] *s* (slang) naso

snoot·y ['snuti] *adj* (**-ier; -iest**) (coll) snobistico

snooze [snuz] *s* (coll) sonnellino ‖ *intr* (coll) fare un sonnellino

snore [snor] *s* russamento ‖ *intr* russare

snort [snɔrt] *s* sbuffo ‖ *intr* sbuffare

snot [snɑt] *s* (slang) moccio

snot·ty ['snɑti] *adj* (**-tier; -tiest**) (coll) snobistico; (coll) arrogante; (slang) moccioso

snout [snaut] *s* muso; (*of pig*) grugno; (*of person*) muso, grugno

snow [sno] *s* neve *f* ‖ *intr* nevicare

snow'ball' *s* palla di neve ‖ *tr* gettare palle di neve a ‖ *intr* aumentare come una palla di neve

snow'blind' *adj* accecato dalla neve

snow'bound' *adj* prigioniero della neve

snow-capped ['sno‚kæpt] *adj* coperto di neve

snow'drift' *s* banco di neve

snow'fall' *s* nevicata

snow' fence' *s* barriera contro la neve

snow'flake' *s* fiocco di neve

snow' flur'ry *s* neve portata da raffiche

snow' line' *s* limite *m* delle nevi perenni

snow'man' *s* (**-men'**) uomo di neve

snow'plow' *s* spazzaneve *m*

snow'shoe' *s* racchetta da neve

snow'slide' *s* valanga

snow'storm' *s* bufera di neve

snow' tire' *s* gomma da neve, pneumatico da neve

snow'-white' *adj* bianco come la neve

snow·y ['sno·i] *adj* (**-ier; -iest**) nevoso

snub [snʌb] *s* affronto ‖ *v* (*pret & pp* **snubbed;** *ger* **snubbing**) *tr* snobbare

snub·by ['snʌbi] *adj* (**-bier; -biest**) camuso, rincagnato

snuff [snʌf] *s* fiutata; tabacco da fiuto; (*of a candlewick*) moccolo; **up to snuff** (coll) soddisfacente; (coll) bene ‖ *tr* fiutare; tabaccare; (*a candle*) smoccolare; **to snuff out** spegnere; (fig) soffocare

snuff'box' *s* tabacchiera

snuffers ['snʌfərz] *spl* smoccolatóio

snug [snʌg] *adj* (**snugger; snuggest**) comodo; (*dress*) attillato; compatto; (*well-off*) agiato; (*sum*) discreto; (*sheltered*) ben protetto; (*well-hidden*) nascosto

snuggle ['snʌgəl] *intr* rannicchiarsi; **to snuggle up to** stringersi a

so [so] *adv* così; così or tanto + *adj* or *adv;* per quanto; **and so** certamente; pure; **and so on** e così via; **or so** più o meno; **to think so** credere di sì; **so as to** + *inf* per + *inf;* **so far** sinora, finora; **so long!** arrivederci!; **so many** tanti; **so much** tanto; **so so** così così; **so that** in maniera che, di modo che; **so to speak** per così dire ‖ *conj* cosicché ‖ *interj* bene!; basta!; così!

soak [sok] *s* bagnata; (*toper*) (slang) ubriacone *m* ‖ *tr* bagnare, inzuppare; imbevere; (coll) ubriacare; (slang) far pagare un prezzo esorbitante a; **to soak up** assorbire; **soaked to the skin** bagnato fino alle ossa ‖ *intr* stare a molle, macerare; inzupparsi

so'-and-so' *s* (**-sos**) tal *m* dei tali; tal cosa

soap [sop] *s* sapone *m* ‖ *tr* insaponare

soap'box' *s* cassa di sapone; tribuna improvvisata

soap'box or'ator *s* oratore *m* che parla da una tribuna improvvisata

soap' bub'ble *s* bolla di sapone

soap' dish' *s* portasapone *m*

soap' flakes' *spl* sapone *m* a scaglie

soap' op'era *s* (coll) trasmissione radiofonica o televisiva lacrimogena

soap' pow'der *s* sapone *m* in polvere

soap'stone' *s* pietra di sarto

soap'suds' *spl* saponata

soap·y ['sopi] *adj* (**-ier; -iest**) saponoso

soar [sor] *intr* spaziare, slanciarsi; (aer) librarsi

sob [sab] *s* singhiozzo ‖ *v* (*pret & pp* **sobbed**; *ger* **sobbing**) *tr* dire a singhiozzi ‖ *intr* singhiozzare

sober ['sobər] *adj* sobrio; non ubriaco ‖ *intr* smaltire la sbornia; **to sober down** calmarsi; **to sober up** smaltire la sbornia

sobriety [so'braɪ·əti] *s* sobrietà *f*

sobriquet ['sobrɪ‚ke] *s* nomignolo

sob' sis'ter *s* giornalista lacrimogeno

sob' sto'ry *s* storia lacrimogena

so'-called' *adj* cosiddetto

soccer ['sakər] *s* calcio, football *m*

sociable ['soʃəbəl] *adj* sociale, socievole

social ['soʃəl] *adj* sociale ‖ *s* riunione sociale

so'cial climb'er ['klaɪmər] *s* arrampicatore *m* sociale

so'cial con'tract *s* patto sociale

socialism ['soʃə‚lɪzəm] *s* socialismo

socialist ['soʃəlɪst] *s* socialista *mf*

socialite ['soʃə‚laɪt] *s* persona che appartiene all'alta società

So'cial Reg'ister *s* (trademark) annuario dell'alta società

so'cial secu'rity *s* sicurezza sociale

so'cial work'er *s* visitatrice *f*, assistente *mf* sociale

socie·ty [sə'saɪ·əti] *s* (**-ties**) società *f*; (*companionship or company*) compagnia

soci'ety ed'itor *s* cronista mondano

sociology [‚sosɪ'alədʒi] *or* [‚soʃɪ'alədʒi] *s* sociologia

sock [sak] *s* calzino; (slang) colpo forte; (slang) attore *m* di prim'ordine; (slang) spettacolo eccezionale ‖ *tr* (slang) dare un forte colpo a

socket ['sakɪt] *s* (*of eye*) occhiaia; (*of tooth*) alveolo; (*of candlestick*) bocciolo; (*wall socket*) (elec) presa di corrente; (elec) portalampada *m*

sock'et wrench' *s* chiave *f* a tubo

sod [sad] *s* zolla; terreno erboso ‖ *v* (*pret & pp* **sodded**; *ger* **sodding**) *tr* piotare

soda ['sodə] *s* soda

so'da crack'er *s* galletta fatta al bicarbonato

so'da wa'ter *s* soda, gazosa

sodium ['sodɪ·əm] *adj* sodico ‖ *s* sodio

sofa ['sofə] *s* sofà *m*, divano

so'fa bed' *s* sofà *m* letto

soft [sɔft] *or* [saft] *adj* molle; (*smooth*) morbido; (*iron*) dolce; (*hat*) floscio; (*person*) rammollito; (coll) facile

soft'-boiled' egg' ['sɔft'bɔɪld] *or* ['saft'bɔɪld] *s* uovo alla coque

soft' coal' *s* carbone bituminoso

soft' drink' *s* bibita

soften ['sɔfən] *or* ['safən] *tr* mollificare, rammollire; (fig) intenerire ‖ *intr* intenerirsi

softener ['sɔfənər] *or* ['safənər] *s* ammorbidente *m*

soft' land'ing *s* allunaggio morbido

soft'-ped'al *v* (*pret & pp* **-aled** *or* **-alled**; *ger* **-aling** *or* **-alling**) *tr* mettere in sordina; (coll) moderare

soft'-shell crab' *s* mollecca

soft' soap' *s* sapone *m* molle; (coll) adulazione

soft'-soap' *tr* (coll) insaponare

sog·gy ['sagi] *adj* (**-gier**; **-giest**) rammollito, inzuppato

soil [sɔɪl] *s* suolo, terreno; territorio; (*spot*) macchia; (*filth*) porcheria, lordura ‖ *tr* sporcare, macchiare ‖ *intr* sporcarsi, macchiarsi

soil' pipe' *s* tubo di scarico

soiree *or* **soirée** [swɑ're] *s* serata

sojourn ['sodʒʌrn] *s* soggiorno ‖ ['sodʒʌrn] *or* [so'dʒʌrn] *intr* soggiornare

solace ['salɪs] *s* conforto ‖ *tr* confortare, consolare

solar ['solər] *adj* solare

so'lar bat'tery *s* batteria solare

solder ['sadər] *s* saldatura; lega per saldatura ‖ *tr* saldare

sol'dering i'ron *s* saldatoio

soldier ['soldʒər] *s* (*man of rank and file*) soldato; (*man in military service*) militare *m* ‖ *intr* fare il soldato

sol'dier of for'tune *s* soldato di ventura

soldier·y ['soldʒəri] *s* (**-ies**) soldatesca

sold-out ['sold‚aut] *adj* esaurito; (*e.g., theater*) completo

sole [sol] *adj* solo, unico; esclusivo ‖ *s* (*of foot*) pianta; (*of stocking*) soletta; (*of shoe*) suola; (*fish*) sfoglia ‖ *tr* solare

solely ['solli] *adv* solamente

solemn ['saləm] *adj* solenne

solicit [sə'lɪsɪt] *tr* sollecitare; adescare, accostare

solicitor [sə'lɪsɪtər] *s* sollecitatore *m*; agente *m*; (law) procuratore *m*

solicitous [sə'lɪsɪtəs] *adj* sollecito

solicitude [sə'lɪsɪ‚tjud] *or* [sə'lɪsɪ‚tud] *s* sollecitudine *f*

solid ['salɪd] *adj* solido; (*not hollow*) sodo; (*e.g., clouds*) denso; (*wall*) pieno, massiccio; (*word*) con grafia unita; intero; unanime, solidale; (*good*) buono; (*e.g., gold*) puro, massiccio

solidity [sə'lɪdɪti] *s* solidità *f*

sol'id-state' *adj* transistorizzato, senza valvole

solilo·quy [sə'lɪləkwi] *s* (**-quies**) soliloquio

solitaire ['salɪ‚ter] *s* solitario

solitar·y ['salɪ‚teri] *adj* solitario; unico ‖ *s* (**-ies**) persona solitaria

sol'itary confine'ment *s* segregazione cellulare

solitude ['salɪ‚tjud] *or* ['salɪ‚tud] *s* solitudine *f*

so·lo ['solo] *adj* solo, solitario; (mus) solista ‖ *s* (**-los**) (mus) solo

soloist ['solo·ɪst] *s* solista *mf*

so' long' *interj* (coll) ciao!; (coll) addio!; (coll) arrivederci!

solstice ['salstɪs] *s* solstizio

soluble ['saljəbəl] *adj* solubile

solution [sə'luʃən] *s* soluzione

solvable ['salvəbəl] *adj* risolvibile

solve [salv] *tr* risolvere, sciogliere

solvency ['salvənsi] s solvenza
solvent ['salvənt] adj & s solvente m
somber ['sambər] adj tetro
some [sʌm] adj indef qualche; di + art, e.g., **some apples** delle mele; (coll) forte, grande || *pron indef* alcuni, taluni; ne, e.g., **I have some** ne ho
some'bod'y pron indef taluno, qualcuno; **somebody else** qualcun altro || s (**-ies**) (coll) qualcuno
some'day' adv qualche giorno
some'how' adv in qualche modo; **somehow or other** in un modo o nell'altro
some'one' pron indef qualcuno, taluno; **someone else** qualcun altro
somersault ['sʌmər,sɔlt] s salto mortale || intr fare un salto mortale
something ['sʌmθɪŋ] pron indef qualcosa; **something else** qualcos'altro || adv un po'; (coll) molto, moltissimo
some'time' adj antico, di un tempo || adv un giorno o l'altro, uno di questi giorni
some'times' adv talora, talvolta
some'way' adv in qualche modo
some'what' s qualcosa || adv piuttosto, un po'
some'where' adv in qualche luogo, da qualche parte; a qualche momento; **somewhere else** altrove
somnambulist [sam'næmbjəlɪst] s sonnambulo
somnolent ['samnələnt] adj sonnolento
son [sʌn] s figlio
sonar ['sonar] s ecogoniometro, sonar m
song [sɔŋ] or [saŋ] s canto, canzone f; **for a song** per un soldo
song'bird' s uccello canoro
Song' of Songs' s Cantico dei Cantici
songster ['saŋstər] s cantante m, canzonettista m
songstress ['saŋstrɪs] s cantante f, canzonettista f
song'writ'er s canzoniere m
son'ic boom' ['sanɪk] s boato sonico
son'-in-law' s (**sons'-in-law'**) genero
sonnet ['sanɪt] s sonetto
son·ny ['sʌni] s (**-nies**) figliolo
sonori·ty [sə'narɪti] or [sə'nɔrɪti] s (**-ties**) sonorità f
soon [sun] adv in breve, ben presto; subito, presto; **as soon as** non appena, quanto prima; **as soon as possible** quanto prima; **I had sooner** preferirei; **how soon?** quando?; **soon after** poco dopo; **sooner or later** prima o poi, tosto o tardi
soot [sut] or [sut] s fuliggine f
soothe [suð] tr calmare, lenire
soothsayer ['suθ,se·ər] s indovino
soot·y ['suti] or ['suti] adj (**-ier; -iest**) fuligginoso
sop [sap] s (*soaked food*) zuppa; (*bribe*) dono, offa || v (*pret & pp* **sopped**; *ger* **sopping**) tr intingere, inzuppare; **to sop up** assorbire
sophisticated [sə'fɪstɪ,ketɪd] adj sofisticato, smalizziato
sophistication [sə,fɪstɪ'keʃən] s eccessiva ricercatezza; gusti mpl raffinati

sophomore ['safə,mor] s studente m del secondo anno, fagiolo
sophomoric [,safə'marɪk] adj saputello, presuntuoso; ingenuo, imberbe
sopping ['sapɪŋ] adv—**sopping wet** inzuppato
sopran·o [sə'præno] or [sə'prano] adj per soprano, da soprano || s (**-os**) soprano mf
sorcerer ['sɔrsərər] s mago, stregone m
sorceress ['sɔrsərɪs] s maga, strega
sorcer·y ['sɔrsəri] s (**-ies**) stregoneria
sordid ['sɔrdɪd] adj sordido
sore [sor] adj irritato; indolenzito; estremo, grave; **to be sore at** (coll) aversela con || s piaga, ulcera; dolore m, afflizione; **to open an old sore** riaprire una ferita
sorely ['sorli] adv penosamente; gravemente, urgentemente
soreness ['sornɪs] s dolore m, afflizione
sore' spot' s (fig) piaga
sore' throat' s mal m di gola
sorori·ty [sə'rarɪti] or [sə'rɔrɪti] s (**-ties**) associazione femminile universitaria
sorrel ['sarəl] or ['sɔrəl] adj sauro
sorrow ['saro] or ['sɔro] s dolore m, cordoglio || intr affliggersi, provar cordoglio; **to sorrow for** rimpiangere
sorrowful ['sarəfəl] or ['sɔrəfəl] adj doloroso
sor·ry ['sari] or ['sɔri] adj (**-rier; -riest**) spiacente, desolato, dolente; povero, cattivo; **to be sorry** dolersi; dispiacere a, e.g., **he is sorry** gli dispiace || interj mi dispiace!, scusi!
sort [sɔrt] s tipo, specie f; maniera; **a sort of** una specie di; **out of sorts** depresso; ammalato; di mal umore; **sort of** (coll) piuttosto; (coll) un certo, e.g., **sort of a headache** un certo mal di testa || tr assortire; (*mail*) smistare
so'-so' adj passabile || adv così così
sot [sat] s ubriacone m
soubrette [su'brɛt] s (theat) soubrette f
soul [sol] s anima; **upon my soul!** sulla mia parola!
sound [saund] adj sano; solido, forte; valido, buono; (*sleep*) profondo; valido, legale; onesto || s suono; rumore m; (*of an animal*) verso; (*passage of water*) stretto; (surg) sonda; (ichth) vescica natatoria; **within sound of** alla portata di || adv profondamente || tr (*an instrument*) sonare; pronunciare; (e.g., *s.o.'s chest*) auscultare; (*praises*) cantare; (*to measure*) sondare || intr sonare; parere, sembrare; fare uno scandaglio; **to sound like** avere il suono di; dare l'impressione di, parere
sound' bar'rier s muro del suono
sound' film' s pellicola sonora
soundly ['saundli] adv solidamente; profondamente; completamente
sound'proof' adj a prova di suono || tr insonorizzare

sound' track' s (mov) sonoro, colonna sonora
sound' truck' s autoveicolo con impianto sonoro
sound' wave' s onda sonora
soup [sup] s zuppa, minestra
soup' dish' s piatto fondo
soup' kitch'en s asilo dei poveri che serve zuppa gratuitamente
soup'spoon' s cucchiaio (da minestra)
sour [saur] adj acido; (fruit) acerbo || tr inacidire || intr inacidirsi
source [sors] s fonte f, sorgente f
source' lan'guage s lingua di partenza
source' mate'rial s fonti fpl originali
sour' cher'ry s (fruit) amarena; (tree) amareno
sour' grapes' interj l'uva è verde!
south [sauθ] adj meridionale, del sud || s sud m, meridione m || adv verso il sud
South' Amer'ica s l'America f del Sud
South' Amer'ican adj & s sudamericano
southeast [ˌsauθ'ist] adj di sud-est || s sud-est || adv al sud-est
southern ['sʌðərn] adj meridionale
South'ern Cross' s Croce f del Sud
southerner ['sʌðərnər] s meridionale mf
South' Kore'a s la Corea del Sud
south'paw' adj & s (coll) mancino
South' Pole' s Polo sud
South' Vietnam-ese' [vɪ ˌetnə'miz] adj vietnamita del sud || s (-ese) vietnamita mf del sud
southward ['sauθwərd] adv verso il sud
south'west' adj di sud-ovest || s sud-ovest m || adv al sud-ovest
souvenir [ˌsuvə'nɪr] or ['suvəˌnɪr] s ricordo, memoria
sovereign ['savrɪn] or ['sʌvrɪn] adj sovrano || s (king) sovrano; (queen; coin) sovrana
sovereign-ty ['savrɪnti] or ['sʌvrɪnti] s (-ties) sovranità f
soviet ['sovɪ ˌet] or [ˌsovɪ'et] adj sovietico || s soviet m
So'viet Rus'sia s la Russia Sovietica
sow [sau] s porca, troia || [so] v (pret sowed; pp sown or sowed) tr seminare
soybean ['sɔɪ ˌbin] s soia; seme m di soia
spa [spa] s terme fpl
space [spes] adj spaziale || s spazio; periodo; after a space dopo un po' || tr spaziare; to space out diradare
space' bar' s barra spaziatrice, spaziatrice f
space' cen'ter s cosmodromo
space'craft' s astronave f
space' flight' s volo spaziale
space'man' s (-men') navigatore m spaziale
spacer ['spesər] s spaziatrice f, barra spaziatrice
space'ship' s astronave f
space'suit' s scafandro astronautico, tuta spaziale
spacious ['speʃəs] adj spazioso

spade [sped] s vanga; (cards) picca; to call a spade a spade dire pane al pane, vino al vino || tr vangare
spade'work' s lavoro preliminare
spaghetti [spə'gɛti] s spaghetti mpl
Spain [spen] s la Spagna
span [spæn] s (of the hand) spanna; (of time) tratto; (of a bridge) campata, luce f; (of horses) paio; (aer) apertura || v (pret & pp spanned; ger spanning) tr misurare a spanne; attraversare, oltrepassare; (said of time) abbracciare
spangle ['spæŋgəl] s lustrino || tr tempestare di lustrini; (with bright objects) stellare || intr brillare
Spaniard ['spænjərd] s spagnolo
Spanish ['spænɪʃ] adj & s spagnolo; the Spanish gli spagnoli
Span'ish-Amer'ican adj & s ispano-americano
Span'ish broom' s ginestra
Span'ish fly' s mosca cantaride
Span'ish om'elet s frittata di pomodori, cipolle e peperoni
Span'ish-speak'ing adj di lingua spagnola
spank [spæŋk] tr sculacciare
spanking ['spæŋkɪŋ] adj rapido; forte; (coll) eccellente, straordinario || s sculacciata
spar [spar] s (mineral) spato; (naut) asta, pennone m; (aer) longherone m || v (pret & pp sparred; ger sparring) intr fare la box
spare [spɛr] adj di riserva; libero, in eccesso; (e.g., diet) frugale; (lean) magro || tr salvare, risparmiare; perdonare; (to do without) fare a meno di, privarsi di; to have . . . to spare aver . . . d'avanzo; to spare oneself risparmiarsi
spare' parts' s pezzi mpl di ricambio
spare' room' s camera per gli ospiti
spare' tire' s ruota di scorta, pneumatico di scorta
spare' wheel' s ruota di scorta
sparing ['spɛrɪŋ] adj economico; (scanty) scarso
spark [spark] s scintilla; traccia || tr (coll) rianimare; (coll) corteggiare || intr scintillare
spark' coil' s bobina d'accensione
spark' gap' s (elec) traferro, intraferro
sparkle ['sparkəl] s scintilla; (luster) scintillio; allegria, vivacità f || intr scintillare; (said, e.g., of eyes) brillare, luccicare; (said of wine) frizzare, spumeggiare
sparkling ['sparklɪŋ] adj scintillante; (wine) frizzante, spumeggiante; (water) gassoso
spark' plug' s candela
sparrow ['spæro] s passero
sparse [spars] adj rado
Spartan ['spartən] adj & s spartano
spasm ['spæzəm] s spasmo; sprazzo d'energia
spasmodic [spæz'madɪk] adj spasmodico; intermittente, a sprazzi
spastic ['spæstɪk] adj & s spastico
spat [spæt] s litigio, battibecco; spats

ghette *fpl* || *v* (*pret* & *pp* **spatted;** *ger* **spatting**) *intr* avere un battibecco

spatial ['speʃəl] *adj* spaziale

spatter ['spætər] *tr* schizzare, spruzzare || *intr* gocciolare

spatula ['spætʃələ] *s* spatola

spawn [spɔn] *s* prole *f*, progenie *f*; risultato || *tr* produrre, generare || *intr* (ichth) deporre le uova

spay [spe] *tr* asportare le ovaie a

speak [spik] *v* (*pret* **spoke** [spok]; *pp* **spoken**) *tr* (*a language*) parlare; (*the truth*) dire || *intr* parlare; **so to speak** per così dire; **speaking!** al telefono!; **to speak of** importante, che valga parlarne; **to speak out** dire la propria opinione

speak'-eas'y *s* (**-ies**) bar clandestino

speaker ['spikər] *s* conferenziere *m*, oratore *m*; (*of a language*) parlante *mf*; (pol) presidente *m*; (rad) altoparlante *m*

speaking ['spikɪŋ] *adj* parlante; **to be on speaking terms** parlarsi || *s* parlare *m*, discorso

speak'ing tube' *s* tubo acustico

spear [spɪr] *s* lancia; (*for fishing*) arpione *m*; (*of grass*) stelo || *tr* trafiggere con la lancia

spear' gun' *s* fucile subacqueo

spear'head' *s* punta di lancia || *tr* condurre, dirigere

spear'mint' *s* menta romana spicata

special ['speʃəl] *adj* speciale || *s* prezzo speciale; treno speciale

spe'cial deliv'ery *s* espresso

spe'cial draw'ing rights' *spl* (econ) diritti *mpl* speciali di prelievo

specialist ['speʃəlɪst] *s* specialista *mf*

specialize ['speʃə‚laɪz] *tr* specializzare || *intr* specializzarsi

spe'cial part'ner *s* accomandante *mf*

special·ty ['speʃəlti] *s* (**-ties**) specialità *f*

spe·cies ['spisiz] *s* (**-cies**) specie *f*

specific [spɪ'sɪfɪk] *adj* & *s* specifico

specification [‚spesɪfɪ'keʃən] *s* specifica; (com) capitolato

specif'ic grav'ity *s* peso specifico

speci·fy ['spesɪ‚faɪ] *v* (*pret* & *pp* **-fied**) *tr* specificare

specimen ['spesɪmən] *s* esemplare *m*; (coll) tipo

specious ['spiʃəs] *adj* specioso

speck [spek] *s* macchiolina; (*of dust*) granello; (*of hope*) filo || *tr* macchiettare

speckle ['spekəl] *s* macchiolina || *tr* macchiettare, picchiettare

spectacle ['spektəkəl] *s* spettacolo; **spectacles** occhiali *mpl*

spectator ['spekتetər] or [spek'tetər] *s* spettatore *m*

specter ['spektər] *s* spettro

spec·trum ['spektrəm] *s* (**-tra** [trə] or **-trums**) spettro; (fig) gamma

speculate ['spekjə‚let] *intr* speculare

speech [spitʃ] *s* parola, parlata; (*before an audience*) discorso; (*of an actor*) elocuzione; **in speech** oralmente

speech' clin'ic *s* clinica per la correzione dei difetti del linguaggio

speechless ['spitʃlɪs] *adj* senza parole, muto

speed [spid] *s* velocità *f*; (aut) marcia || *tr* accelerare, affrettare || *intr* accelerare, affrettarsi; guidare oltre la velocità massima

speed'boat' *s* motoscafo da corsa

speeding ['spidɪŋ] *s* eccesso di velocità

speed' king' *s* asso del volante

speed' lim'it *s* limite *m* di velocità

speedometer [spi'dɑmɪtər] *s* tachimetro; (*to record the distance covered*) contachilometri *m*

speed'-up' *s* accelerazione

speed'way' *s* (*highway*) autostrada; (*for races*) pista

speed·y ['spidi] *adj* (**-ier; -iest**) veloce, rapido

spell [spel] *s* malia, incantesimo; fascino; turno; attacco; periodo di tempo; **to cast a spell on** incantare || *v* (*pret* & *pp* **spelled** or **spelt** [spelt]) *tr* compitare; scrivere in tutte lettere; voler dire; **to spell out** (coll) spiegare dettagliatamente || *intr* scrivere, sillabare || *v* (*pret* & *pp* **spelled**) *tr* rimpiazzare

spell'bind' *v* (*pret* & *pp* **-bound**) *tr* affascinare

spell'bind'er *s* oratore *m* abbagliante

spelling ['spelɪŋ] *adj* ortografico || *s* (*act*) compitazione; (*way a word is spelled*) grafia; (*subject of study*) ortografia

spell'ing bee' *s* gara di ortografia

spelunker [spɪ'lʌŋkər] *s* esploratore *m* di caverne

spend [spend] *v* (*pret* & *pp* **spent** [spent]) *tr* spendere; (*time*) passare

spender ['spendər] *s* spenditore *m*

spend'ing mon'ey *s* denaro per le piccole spese personali

spend'thrift' *s* sprecone *m*, spendaccione *m*

sperm [spʌrm] *s* sperma *m*

sperm' whale' *s* capodoglio

spew [spju] *tr* & *intr* vomitare

sphere [sfɪr] *s* sfera

spherical ['sferɪkəl] *adj* sferico

sphinx [sfɪŋks] *s* (**sphinxes** or **sphinges** ['sfɪndʒiz]) sfinge *f*

spice [spaɪs] *s* droga; spezie *fpl*; (fig) gusto, sapore *m* || *tr* drogare; dare gusto a, rendere piccante

spick-and-span ['spɪkənd'spæn] *adj* ordinato e pulito

spic·y ['spaɪsi] *adj* (**-ier; -iest**) drogato; piccante

spider ['spaɪdər] *s* ragno

spi'der·web' *s* ragnatela

spiff·y ['spɪfi] *adj* (**-ier; -iest**) (slang) elegante, bello

spigot ['spɪgət] *s* (*peg*) zipolo; (*faucet*) rubinetto

spike [spaɪk] *s* chiodo, chiodone *m*; (*sharp-pointed piece*) spuntone *m*; (rr) arpione *m*; (bot) spiga || *tr* inchiodare; mettere chiodi a; (*a rumor*) porre fine a; (coll) alcolizzare

spill [spɪl] *s* rovesciamento; liquido rovesciato; (coll) caduta || *v* (*pret* & *pp* **spilled** or **spilt** [spɪlt]) *tr* rovesciare, spandere; versare; (naut) sventare; (coll) far cadere; (slang) snocciolare || *intr* rovesciarsi; versarsi

spill'way' *s* sfioratore *m*, stramazzo

spin [spɪn] *s* giro; (*twirl*) mulinello; corsa; **to go into a spin** (aer) cadere a vite || *v* (*pret & pp* **spun** [spʌn]; *ger* **spinning**) *tr* far girare; (*e.g., thread*) filare; **to spin out** prolungare; **to spin a yarn** raccontare una storia || *intr* girare; (*said of a top*) prillare; filare

spinach ['spɪnɪtʃ] or ['spɪnɪdʒ] *s* spinacio; (*leaves used as food*) spinaci *mpl*

spi'nal col'umn ['spaɪnəl] *s* spina dorsale, colonna vertebrale

spi'nal cord' *s* midollo spinale

spindle ['spɪndəl] *s* (*rounded rod*) fuso; (*shaft, axle*) asse *m;* balaustro

spine [spaɪn] *s* spina; spina dorsale; (bb) costola; (fig) forza, carattere *m*

spineless ['spaɪnlɪs] *adj* senza spine; senza carattere

spinet ['spɪnɪt] *s* spinetta

spinner ['spɪnər] *s* filatore *m;* (*machine*) filatrice *f*

spinning ['spɪnɪŋ] *adj* filante || *s* filatura; rotazione

spin'ning mill' *s* filanda

spin'ning wheel' *s* filatoio

spinster ['spɪnstər] *s* zitella

spi·ral ['spaɪrəl] *adj & s* spirale *f* || *v* (*pret & pp* **-raled** or **-ralled;** *ger* **-raling** or **-ralling**) *intr* muoversi lungo una spirale

spi'ral stair'case *s* scala a chiocciola

spire [spaɪr] *s* (*of a steeple*) guglia, freccia; (*of grass*) foglia; (*spiral*) spirale *f*

spirit ['spɪrɪt] *s* spirito; valore *m*, vigore *m;* bevanda spiritosa; **out of spirits** giù di morale || *tr*—**to spirit away** portar via misteriosamente

spirited ['spɪrɪtɪd] *adj* brioso; (*horse*) superbo, vivace

spir'it lamp' *s* lampada a spirito

spiritless ['spɪrɪtlɪs] *adj* senza anima, senza vita

spir'it lev'el *s* livella a bolla d'aria

spiritual ['spɪrɪtʃu·əl] *adj* spirituale; (*séance*) spiritico

spiritualism ['spɪrɪtʃuə‚lɪzəm] *s* spiritismo; (philos) spiritualismo

spiritualist ['spɪrɪtʃu·əlɪst] *s* spiritista *mf;* (philos) spiritualista *mf*

spirituous ['spɪrɪtʃu·əs] *adj* alcolico

spit [spɪt] *s* sputo; (*for roasting*) spiedo, schidione *m;* punta; **the spit and image of** (coll) il ritratto parlante di || *v* (*pret & pp* **spat** [spæt] or **spit;** *ger* **spitting**) *tr & intr* sputare

spite [spaɪt] *s* dispetto, ripicco; **in spite of** a dispetto di, a onta di; **out of spite** per picca || *tr* far dispetto a; offendere; contrariare

spiteful ['spaɪtfəl] *adj* dispettoso

spit'fire' *s* persona collerica; (*woman*) bisbetica

spit'ting im'age *s* (coll) ritratto parlante

spittoon [spɪ'tun] *s* sputacchiera

splash [splæʃ] *s* schizzo, spruzzo; (*of mud*) zacchera; (*sound*) tonfo; **to make a splash** fare molto sci-sci || *tr & intr* sguazzare

splash'down' *s* (rok) ammaraggio, urto con l'acqua

spleen [splin] *s* cattivo umore, bile *f;* (anat) milza, splene *m*

splendid ['splɛndɪd] *adj* splendido; ottimo, magnifico

splendor ['splɛndər] *s* splendore *m*

splice [splaɪs] *s* giuntura || *tr* giuntare

splint [splɪnt] *s* stecca || *tr* steccare

splinter ['splɪntər] *s* scheggia || *tr* scheggiare || *intr* scheggiarsi

splin'ter group' *s* gruppo dissidente

split [splɪt] *adj* spaccato; diviso || *s* spaccatura; fessura; rottura, divisione; **splits** (sports) spaccato || *v* (*pret & pp* **split;** *ger* **splitting**) *tr* spaccare; dividere; **to split one's sides with laughter** scoppiare dalle risa || *intr* scindersi, dividersi; **to split up** separarsi

split' personal'ity *s* sdoppiamento della personalità

splitting ['splɪtɪŋ] *adj* che fende; che si fende; violento, fortissimo || *s*— **splittings** frammenti *mpl*

splotch [splɑtʃ] *s* macchia, chiazza || *tr* macchiare, chiazzare

splurge [splʌrdʒ] *s* ostentazione || *intr* fare ostentazione; fare una spesa matta

splutter ['splʌtər] *s* crepitio; (*utterance*) barbugliamento || *tr* barbugliare || *intr* crepitare; barbugliare

spoil [spɔɪl] *s* spoglia, bottino; **spoils** (mil) spoglie *fpl;* (pol) profitto, vantaggio || *v* (*pret & pp* **spoiled** or **spoilt** [spɔɪlt]) *tr* rovinare, sciupare; (*a child*) viziare; (*food*) deteriorare || *intr* guastarsi, andare a male

spoilage ['spɔɪlɪdʒ] *s* deterioramento

spoiled [spɔɪld] *adj* (*child*) viziato; (*food*) andato a male, passato

spoils' sys'tem *s* sistema politico secondo il quale le cariche vanno al partito vincitore

spoke [spok] *s* (*of a wheel*) raggio; (*of a ladder*) piolo

spokes'man *s* (-men) portavoce *m*

sponge [spʌndʒ] *s* spugna; **to throw in the sponge** (slang) gettare la spugna || *tr* pulire con spugna; assorbire; (coll) scroccare || *intr* assorbire; **to sponge off** (coll) vivere alle spalle di

sponge' bath' *s* spugnatura

sponge' cake' *s* pan *m* di Spagna

sponger ['spʌndʒər] *s* scroccatore *m*

sponge' rub'ber *s* gommapiuma

spon·gy ['spʌndʒi] *adj* (-gier; -giest) spugnoso

sponsor ['spɑnsər] *s* patrocinatore *m;* (*of a charitable institution*) patrono; (*godfather*) padrino; (*godmother*) madrina || *tr* patrocinare; (rad, telv) offrire

sponsorship ['spɑnsər‚ʃɪp] *s* patrocinio

spontaneous [spɑn'tenɪ·əs] *adj* spontaneo

spoof [spuf] *s* mistificazione; parodia ‖ *tr* mistificare; parodiare ‖ *intr* mistificare; fare una parodia ,

spook [spuk] *s* (coll) spettro

spook·y ['spuki] *adj* (-ier; -iest) (coll) spettrale; (*horse*) (coll) nervoso

spool [spul] *s* spola, rocchetto

spoon [spun] *s* cucchiaio; (*lure*) cucchiaino; **born with a silver spoon in one's mouth** nato con la camicia ‖ *tr* servire col cucchiaio ‖ *intr* (coll) limonare

spoonerism ['spunə͵rɪzəm] *s* papera

spoon'-feed' *v* (*pret & pp* -**fed**) *tr* nutrire col cucchiaino; (fig) coccolare

spoonful ['spun͵ful] *s* cucchiaiata

spoon·y ['spuni] *adj* (-ier; -iest) (coll) svenevole

sporadic(al) [spə'rædɪk(əl)] *adj* sporadico

spore [spor] *s* spora

sport [sport] *adj* sportivo ‖ *s* sport *m;* gioco; (*laughingstock*) zimbello; (*gambler*) (coll) giocatore *m;* (*person who behaves in a sportsmanlike manner*) (coll) spirito sportivo; (*flashy fellow*) (coll) tipo fino; (biol) mutazione; **to make sport of** farsi gioco di ‖ *tr* (coll) sfoggiare; **to sport away** dissipare ‖ *intr* divertirsi; giocare; farsi beffe

sport' clothes' *spl* vestiti *mpl* sport

sport'ing chance' *s* pari opportunità *f* di vincere

sport'ing goods' *spl* articoli *mpl* sportivi

sport'ing house' *s* (coll) bordello

sports'cast'er *s* annunziatore sportivo

sports' fan' *s* appassionato agli spettacoli sportivi, tifoso

sports'man *s* (-**men**) sportivo

sports'man·ship' *s* sportività *f*, spirito sportivo

sports' news' *s* notiziario sportivo

sports'wear' *s* articoli *mpl* d'abbigliamento sportivo

sports'writ'er *s* cronista sportivo

sport·y ['sporti] *adj* (-ier; -iest) (coll) elegante; (coll) sportivo; (coll) appariscente

spot [spat] *s* macchia; luogo, punto, posto; (*e.g., of tea*) goccia; **spots** locali *mpl;* **on the spot** sul posto; (*right now*) seduta stante; (slang) in difficoltà; **to hit the spot** (slang) soddisfare completamente ‖ *v* (*pret & pp* **spotted;** *ger* **spotting**) *tr* macchiare; spargere; (coll) riconoscere ‖ *intr* macchiare; macchiarsi

spot' cash' *s* pronta cassa

spot'-check' *tr* fare un breve sondaggio di; controllare rapidamente

spot' check' *s* breve sondaggio; rapido controllo

spotless ['spatlɪs] *adj* immacolato, senza macchia

spot'light' *s* riflettore *m;* (aut) proiettore *m;* **to be in the spotlight** (fig) essere il centro d'attenzione

spot' remov'er [rɪ'muvər] *s* smacchiatore *m*

spot' weld'ing *s* saldatura per punti

spouse [spauz] *or* [spaus] *s* consorte *mf*

spout [spaut] *s* (*to carry water from roof*) doccia; (*of jar, pitcher, etc.*) becco, beccuccio; (*jet*) zampillo, getto ‖ *tr & intr* sprizzare, zampillare; (coll) declamare

sprain [spren] *s* distorsione ‖ *tr* distorcere, distorcersi

sprawl [sprɔl] *intr* sdraiarsi

spray [spre] *s* spruzzo; (*of the sea*) schiuma; (*device*) spruzzatore *m;* (*twig*) ramoscello ‖ *tr & intr* spruzzare

sprayer ['spre·ər] *s* spruzzatore *m*, schizzetto, vaporizzatore *m;* (hort) irroratrice *f*

spray' gun' *s* pistola a spruzzo; (hort) irroratrice *f*

spray' paint' *s* vernice *f* a spruzzo

spread [spred] *s* espansione; diffusione; differenza; tappeto, coperta; elasticità *f;* (*of the wings of bird or airplane*) apertura; cibo da spalmare; (coll) festino; (journ) articolo di fondo o pubblicitario su varie colonne ‖ *v* (*pret & pp* **spread**) *tr* tendere, estendere; (*one's legs*) divaricare; (*wings*) spiegare; spargere, cospargere; (*the table*) preparare; (*butter*) spalmare; diffondere ‖ *intr* estendersi; spiegarsi; spargersi; spalmarsi; diffondersi

spree [spri] *s* baldoria, bisboccia; **to go on a spree** darsi alla pazza gioia

sprig [sprɪg] *s* ramoscello

spright·ly ['spraɪtli] *adj* (-ier; -iest) brioso, vivace

spring [sprɪŋ] *adj* primaverile; sorgivo; a molla ‖ *s* (*season*) primavera; (*issue of water from earth*) fonte *f*, polla; (*elastic device*) molla; elasticità *f;* (*leap*) salto; (*crack*) fenditura; (aut) balestra ‖ *v* (*pret* **sprang** [spræŋ] *or* **sprung** [sprʌŋ]; *pp* **sprung**) *tr* (*e.g., a lock*) far scattare; (*a leak*) aprire; (*a mine*) far brillare ‖ *intr* saltare; (*said of a metal spring*) scattare; scaturire, zampillare; nascere, derivare; esplodere; **to spring forth** *or* **up** sorgere

spring'board' *s* pedana, trampolino

spring' chick'en *s* pollo giovanissimo; (slang) ragazzina

spring' fe'ver *s* indolenza primaverile

spring' mat'tress *s* materasso a molle

spring' tide' *s* marea di sizigia

spring'time' *s* primavera

sprinkle ['sprɪŋkəl] *s* spruzzo, spruzzatina; (*small amount*) pizzico ‖ *tr* spruzzare; (*e.g., sugar*) spolverizzare ‖ *intr* spruzzare; piovigginare

sprinkler ['sprɪŋklər] *s* annaffiatoio; (*person*) annaffiattore *m*

sprinkling ['sprɪŋklɪŋ] *s* sprizzo, spruzzo; (*with holy water*) aspersione; (*with powder*) spolverizzamento; (*e.g., of knowledge*) spolvero, spolveratura; (*of people*) piccolo numero

sprin'kling can' *s* annaffiatoio

sprint [sprɪnt] *s* (sports) scatto, volata ǁ *intr* (sports) scattare

sprite [spraɪt] *s* spirito folletto

sprocket ['sprɑkɪt] *s* moltiplica; (phot) trasportatore *m*

sprout [spraʊt] *s* germoglio ǁ *intr* germogliare; crescere rapidamente

spruce [sprus] *adj* elegante, attillato ǁ *s* abete rosso ǁ *tr* attillare, azzimare ǁ *intr* attillarsi, azzimarsi

spry [spraɪ] *adj* (**spryer** or **sprier**; **spryest** or **spriest**) vegeto

spud [spʌd] *s* vanghetto, tagliaradici *m*; (coll) patata

spun' glass' *s* lana di vetro

spunk [spʌŋk] *s* (coll) coraggio, fegato

spur [spʌr] *s* sperone *m*; (rr) raccordo ferroviario; (fig) pungolo; **on the spur of the moment** lì per lì ǁ *v* (*pret & pp* **spurred**; *ger* **spurring**) *tr* spronare; **to spur on** spronare, incitare

spurious ['spjʊrɪ·əs] *adj* spurio

spurn [spʌrn] *s* disprezzo, sdegno; rifiuto ǁ *tr* disprezzare, sdegnare; rifiutare

spurt [spʌrt] *s* spruzzo, zampillo; (*sudden burst*) scatto repentino ǁ *intr* sprizzare, zampillare; scattare

sputter ['spʌtər] *s* barbugliamento; (*sizzling*) crepitio ǁ *tr* barbugliare ǁ *intr* barbugliare; crepitare

spu·tum ['spjutəm] *s* (**-ta** [tə]) sputo

spy [spaɪ] *s* (**spies**) spia ǁ *v* (*pret & pp* **spied**) *tr* spiare; osservare ǁ *intr* fare la spia; **spy on** spiare

spy'glass' *s* cannocchiale *m*

spying ['spaɪ·ɪŋ] *s* spionaggio

squabble ['skwɑbəl] *s* battibecco ǁ *intr* litigare

squad [skwɑd] *s* squadra

squadron ['skwɑdrən] *s* (*of cavalry*) squadrone *m*; (aer, nav) squadriglia; (mil) squadra

squalid ['skwɑlɪd] *adj* sordido; squallido, misero

squall [skwɔl] *s* groppo, turbine *m*; urlo ǁ *intr* gridare, urlare

squalor ['skwɑlər] *s* sordidezza; squallore *m*, miseria

squander ['skwɑndər] *tr* scialacquare, dilapidare, sperperare

square [skwɛr] *adj* quadrato, e.g., **two square miles** due miglia quadrate; di . . . di lato, e.g., **two miles square** di due miglia di lato; ad angolo retto; solido; saldato; (coll) onesto; (coll) diretto; (coll) sostanzioso; (slang) all'antica; **to get square with** (coll) fargliela pagare a ǁ *s* quadrato; (*small square, e.g., of checkerboard*) quadretto; (*city block*) isolato; (*open area in city*) piazza, piazzale *m*; (*of carpenter*) squadra; **on the square** ad angolo retto; (coll) onesto ǁ *adv* ad angolo retto; (coll) onestamente ǁ *tr* squadrare; dividere in quadretti; elevare al quadrato; quadrare; (*a debt*) saldare; **to square with** adattare a ǁ *intr* quadrare; **to square off** prepararsi, mettersi in posizione difensiva

square' dance' *s* danza figurata americana

square' meal' *s* (coll) pasto abbondante

square' root' *s* radice quadrata

square' shoot'er ['ʃutər] *s* (coll) persona onesta

squash [skwɑʃ] *s* spappolamento; (bot) zucca; (sports) squash *m* ǁ *tr* spappolare; spiaccicare; (*e.g., a rumor*) sopprimere; (*a person*) (coll) ridurre al silenzio ǁ *intr* spiaciccarsi

squash·y ['skwɑʃi] *adj* (**-ier; -iest**) tenero; (*ground*) fangoso, pantanoso; (*fruit*) maturo

squat [skwɑt] *adj* tozzo ǁ *v* (*pret & pp* **squatted**; *ger* **squatting**) *intr* accoccolarsi; stabilirsi illegalmente su territorio altrui; stabilirsi su terreno pubblico per ottenerne titolo

squatter ['skwɑtər] *s* intruso

squaw [skwɔ] *s* squaw *f*; (coll) donna

squawk [skwɔk] *s* schiamazzo; (slang) lamento stridulo ǁ *intr* schiamazzare; (slang) lamentarsi strillando

squaw' man' *s* bianco sposato con una pellerossa

squeak [skwik] *s* strido; cigolio ǁ *intr* stridere; cigolare; (*said of a mouse*) squittire; **to squeak through** farcela per il rotto della cuffia

squeal [skwil] *s* strido ǁ *intr* stridere; (slang) cantare, fare il delatore

squealer ['skwilər] *s* (slang) delatore *m*

squeamish ['skwimɪʃ] *adj* pudibondo; scrupoloso; (*easily nauseated*) schifiltoso, schizzinoso

squeeze [skwiz] *s* spremuta; stretta; abbraccio; **to put the squeeze on** (coll) far pressione su ǁ *tr* premere; spremere, pigiare; stringere ǁ *intr* stringere; **to squeeze through** aprirsi il passo attraverso; (fig) farcela a pena

squeezer ['skwizər] *s* spremifrutta *m*

squelch [skwɛltʃ] *s* osservazione schiacciante ǁ *tr* schiacciare

squid [skwɪd] *s* calamaro, totano

squint [skwɪnt] *s* tendenza losca; (coll) occhiata; (pathol) strabismo ǁ *tr* (*one's eyes*) socchiudere ǁ *intr* socchiudere gli occhi; guardare furtivamente

squint-eyed ['skwɪnt‚aɪd] *adj* guercio, losco; malevolo

squire [skwaɪr] *s* (*of a lady*) cavalier *m* servente; (Brit) proprietario terriero; (U.S.A.) giudice *m* conciliatore ǁ *tr* (*a woman*) accompagnare

squirm [skwʌrm] *s* contorsione ǁ *intr* contorcersi; mostrare imbarazzo; **to squirm out of** cavarsela da

squirrel ['skwʌrəl] *s* scoiattolo

squirt [skwʌrt] *s* schizzo; (*instrument*) schizzetto; (coll) saputello ǁ *tr & intr* schizzare

stab [stæb] *s* pugnalata; (*of pain*) fitta; **to make a stab at** (coll) provare ǁ *v* (*pret & pp* **stabbed**; *ger* **stabbing**) *tr* pugnalare, trafiggere ǁ *intr* pugnalare

stabilize ['stebəl‚aɪz] *tr* stabilizzare

stab' in the back' *s* pugnalata nella schiena or alle spalle

stable ['stebəl] *adj* stabile ‖ *s* stalla; (*of race horses*) scuderia

sta'ble·boy' *s* stalliere *m*

stack [stæk] *s* pila; (*of hay or straw*) pagliaio; (*of firewood*) catasta; (*of books*) scaffale *m;* camino; (coll) mucchio, sacco ‖ *tr* ammonticchiare, accatastare

stadi·um ['stedɪ·əm] *s* (**-ums** or **-a** [ə]) stadio

staff [stæf] or [staf] *s* bastone *m;* asta, albero; personale *m,* corpo; (mil) stato maggiore; (mus) rigo, pentagramma *m* ‖ *tr* dotare di personale

staff' of'ficer *s* ufficiale *m* di stato maggiore

stag [stæg] *adj* per signori soli ‖ *s* (*deer*) cervo; maschio; (coll) signore *m* ‖ *adv* senza compagna

stage [stedʒ] *s* fase *f,* stadio; tappa, giornata; (*coach*) diligenza; teatro; piattaforma; (*of microscope*) piatto portaoggetti; (theat) scena, palcoscenico; **by easy stages** poco a poco; **to go on the stage** diventare attore ‖ *tr* mettere in scena; organizzare

stage'coach' *s* diligenza

stage'craft' *s* scenotecnica

stage' door' *s* (theat) ingresso degli artisti

stage' fright' *s* tremarella

stage'hand' *s* macchinista *m*

stage' left' *s* (theat) la sinistra della scena guardando il pubblico

stage' man'ager *s* direttore *m* di scena

stage' right' *s* (theat) la destra della scena guardando il pubblico

stage'-struck' *adj* innamorato del teatro

stage' whis'per *s* a parte *m*

stagger ['stægər] *tr* far traballare; impressionare; (*troops; hours*) scaglionare ‖ *intr* traballare

stag'gering *adj* traballante; impressionante, stupefacente

staging ['stedʒɪŋ] *s* impalcatura; (theat) messa in scena

stagnant ['stægnənt] *adj* stagnante

staid [sted] *adj* serio, grave

stain [sten] *s* macchia; tinta; colorante *m* ‖ *tr* macchiare; tingere; colorare ‖ *intr* macchiarsi

stained' glass' *s* vetro colorato

stained'-glass window' *s* vetrata a colori

stainless ['stenlɪs] *adj* immacolato; (*steel*) inossidabile

stair [stɛr] *s* scala

stair'case' *s* scala

stair'way' *s* scala

stair'well' *s* tromba delle scale

stake [stek] *s* picchetto; (*e.g., of cart*) staggio; (*to support a plant*) puntello; (*in gambling*) puglia, giocata; **at stake** in gioco; **to die at the stake** morire sul rogo; **to pull up stakes** (coll) andarsene, traslocare ‖ *tr* picchettare; puntellare; attaccare a un palo; arrischiare; (coll) aiutare; **to stake out** picchettare; (slang) tenere sotto sorveglianza; **to stake out a claim** avanzare una pretesa

stale [stel] *adj* stantio; (*air*) viziato; (fig) ritrito

stale'mate' *s* (chess) stallo; **to reach a**

stalemate essere in una posizione di stallo ‖ *tr* mettere in una posizione di stallo

stalk [stɔk] *s* stelo; (*of corn*) stocco; (*of salad*) piede *m* ‖ *tr* braccare ‖ *intr* avanzare furtivamente; camminare con andatura maestosa

stall [stɔl] *s* (*in a stable*) posta; (*booth in a market*) bancarella; (*seat*) stallo; (*space in a parking lot*) spazio per il parcheggio ‖ *tr* (*an animal*) stallare; (*a car*) parcheggiare; (*a motor*) far fermare; **to stall off** eludere, tenere a bada ‖ *intr* impantanarsi; stare nella posta; (*said of a motor*) fermarsi; (*to temporize*) menare il can per l'aia

stallion ['stæljən] *s* stallone *m*

stalwart ['stɔlwərt] *adj* forte, gagliardo ‖ *s* sostenitore *m*

stamen ['stemən] *s* stame *m*

stamina ['stæmɪnə] *s* forza, vigore *m*

stammer ['stæmər] *s* balbuzie *f* ‖ *tr* & *intr* balbettare

stammerer ['stæmərər] *s* balbuziente *mf*

stamp [stæmp] *s* (*postage stamp*) francobollo; (*device to show that a fee has been paid*) timbro, bollo; impressione; carattere *m;* sigillo; (*tool for stamping coins*) conio; (*tool for crushing ore*) maglio ‖ *tr* timbrare, stampigliare, bollare; sigillare; coniare; (*one's foot*) battere, pestare; imprimere; caratterizzare; (mach) stampare; **to stamp out** spegnere; sopprimere ‖ *intr* battere il piede; (*said of a horse*) zampare

stampede [stæm'pid] *s* fuga precipitosa ‖ *tr* precipitarsi verso; far fuggire precipitosamente ‖ *intr* precipitarsi

stamp'ing ground' *s* (coll) luogo di ritrovo abituale

stamp' pad' *s* tampone *m*

stamp'-vend'ing machine' *s* distributore automatico di francobolli

stance [stæns] *s* posizione

stanch [stɑntʃ] *adj* leale; forte; a tenuta d'acqua ‖ *s* chiusa ‖ *tr* arrestare il flusso da; (*blood*) stagnare

stand [stænd] *s* posizione; resistenza, difesa; tribuna, palco; sostegno, supporto; (*booth in market*) posteggio; posto di sosta ‖ *v* (*pret & pp* **stood** [stʊd]) *tr* mettere in piedi; reggere, sostenere; sopportare, tollerare; (*one's ground*) mantenere; (*a chance*) avere; (*watch*) fare; (coll) pagare; **to stand off** tenere a distanza ‖ *intr* stare; essere alto; fermarsi; stare in piedi; trovarsi; aver forza; essere; (*e.g., apart*) tenersi; **to stand back of** spalleggiare; **to stand by** appoggiare; **to stand for** rappresentare, voler dire; appoggiare, favorire; tenere a battesimo; (coll) tollerare; **to stand in line** fare la fila or la coda; **to stand in with** (coll) essere nelle buone grazie di; **to stand out** stagliarsi, distaccarsi, risaltare; **to stand up** tenersi in piedi; resistere, durare; **to stand up to** affrontare

standard ['stændərd] *adj* (*usual*) normale; uniforme, standard; (*language*) corretto, preferito ‖ *s* standard *m;* (*model*) modello, campione *m;* (*flag*) stendardo

stand'ard·bear'er *s* portabandiera *m*

standardize ['stændər ˌdaɪz] *tr* standardizzare

stand'ard of liv'ing *s* tenore *m* di vita

stand'ard time' *s* ora ufficiale, ora legale

standee [stæn'di] *s* passeggero in piedi; spettatore *m* in piedi

stand'-in' *s* (mov) controfigura; **to have a stand-in with** (coll) essere nelle buone grazie di

standing ['stændɪŋ] *adj* (*jump*) da fermo; in piedi; fermo; (*water*) stagnante; vigente, permanente; (*idle*) fuori uso ‖ *s* posizione, rango, situazione; classifica; **in good standing** riconosciuto da tutti; **of long standing** vecchio, da lungo tempo

stand'ing ar'my *s* esercito permanente

stand'ing room' *s* posto in piedi

standpatter ['stænd'pætər] *s* (coll) seguace *mf* dell'immobilismo

stand'point' *s* punto di vista

stand'still' *s* fermata; riposo; **to come to a standstill** fermarsi

stanza ['stænzə] *s* stanza

staple ['stepəl] *adj* principale ‖ *s* articolo di prima necessità; elemento indispensabile; (*e.g., to hold wire*) cavallottino, cambretta; (*to fasten papers*) grappetta; fibra tessile ‖ *tr* aggraffare

stapler ['steplər] *s* cucitrice *f* a grappe

star [star] *s* (*any heavenly body, except the moon, appearing in the sky*) astro; (*heavenly body radiating self-produced energy*) stella; (*actor*) divo; (*actress*) diva, stella (*athlete*) asso; (fig, mov) stella; (typ) stelletta; **to thank one's lucky stars** ringraziare la propria stella ‖ *v* (*pret & pp* **starred;** *ger* **starring**) *tr* costellare, stellare; presentare come stella; (typ) marcare con stelletta ‖ *intr* primeggiare

starboard ['starbərd] or ['star ˌbord] *adj* di dritta, di tribordo ‖ *s* dritta, tribordo ‖ *adv* a dritta, a tribordo

starch [startʃ] *s* amido, fecola; (*in laundering*) salda; (coll) forza ‖ *tr* inamidare

starch·y ['startʃi] *adj* (**-ier; -iest**) amidaceo; (*e.g., collar*) inamidato; (*manner*) sostenuto, contegnoso

star' dust' *s* polveri *fpl* meteoriche; (fig) polvere *f* di stelle

stare [ster] *s* sguardo fisso ‖ *intr* rimirare; **to stare at** fissare gli occhi addosso a

star'fish' *s* stella di mare

star'gaze' *intr* guardare le stelle; sognare ad occhi aperti

stark [stark] *adj* completo; desolato; severo, serio; duro, rigido ‖ *adv* completamente

stark'-na'ked *adj* nudo e crudo

starlet ['starlɪt] *s* stellina, divetta

star'light' *s* lume *f* delle stelle

starling ['starlɪŋ] *s* storno, stornello

Stars' and Stripes' *s* bandiera stellata

Star'-Spangled Ban'ner *s* bandiera stellata

star' sys'tem *s* (mov) divismo

start [start] *s* inizio, principio; partenza; linea di partenza; (*sudden jerk*) sussulto, soprassalto; (*advantage*) vantaggio; (*spurt*) scatto ‖ *tr* iniziare, principiare; mettere in moto; dare il via a; (*a conversation*) intavolare; (*game*) stanare ‖ *intr* iniziare, principiare; mettersi in moto; incamminarsi; (*to be startled*) trasalire, sussultare; **to start + ger** mettersi a + *inf;* **to start + ger + again** rimettersi a + *inf;* **to start after** andare in cerca di

starter ['startər] *s* (*of a venture*) iniziatore *m;* partente *m;* (aut) motorino d'avviamento; (sports) mossiere *m*

starting ['startɪŋ] *adj* di partenza ‖ *s* messa in marcia

start'ing crank' *s* manovella d'avviamento

start'ing point' *s* punto di partenza

startle ['startəl] *tr* far trasalire ‖ *intr* trasalire, sussultare

startling ['startlɪŋ] *adj* allarmante, sorprendente

starvation [star'veʃən] *s* fame *f*, inedia, inanizione

starva'tion wag'es *spl* paga da fame

starve [starv] *tr* affamare; far morire di fame; **to starve out** prendere per fame ‖ *intr* essere affamato; morire di fame

starving ['starvɪŋ] *adj* famelico

state [stet] *adj* statale; ufficiale; di gala, di lusso ‖ *s* condizione; stato; gala, pompa; **to lie in state** essere esposto in camera ardente; **to live in state** vivere sfarzosamente ‖ *tr* dichiarare, affermare; (*a problem*) impostare

stateless ['stetlɪs] *adj* apolide

state·ly ['stetli] *adj* (**-lier; -liest**) maestoso, imponente

statement ['stetmənt] *s* dichiarazione, affermazione; comunicazione; (com) estratto conto

state' of mind' *s* stato d'animo

state'room' *s* cabina; (rr) compartimento privato

states'man *s* (**-men**) statista *m*, uomo di stato

static ['stætɪk] *adj* statico; (rad) atmosferico ‖ *s* disturbi *mpl* atmosferici

station ['steʃən] *s* stazione; rango, condizione ‖ *tr* stazionare

sta'tion a'gent *s* capostazione *m*

stationary ['steʃən ˌeri] *adj* stazionario

sta'tion break' *s* (rad, telv) intervallo

stationer ['steʃənər] *s* cartolaio

stationery ['steʃən ˌeri] *s* (*writing paper*) carta da lettere; (*writing materials*) cancelleria

sta'tionery store' *s* cartoleria

sta'tion house' *s* posto di polizia

sta'tion-mas'ter *s* capostazione *m*

sta'tion wag'on *s* giardinetta

statistical [stə'tɪstɪkəl] *adj* statistico

statistician [ˌstætɪs'trɪʃən] *s* statistico

statistics [stə'tɪstɪks] *ssg* (*science*) statistica; *spl* (*data*) statistiche *fpl*
statue ['stætʃu] *s* statua
statuesque [ˌstætʃu'ɛsk] *adj* statuario
stature ['stætʃər] *s* statura
status ['stetəs] *s* stato, condizione; condizione sociale
sta'tus sym'bol *s* simbolo della posizione sociale
statute ['stætʃut] *s* legge *f*; regolamento
stat'ute of limita'tions *s* legge *f* che governa la prescrizione
statutory ['stætʃuˌtori] *adj* legale
staunch [stɔntʃ] or [stɑntʃ] *adj*, *s & tr* var of **stanch**
stave [stev] *s* (*of barrel*) doga; (*of ladder*) piolo; (mus) rigo, pentagramma *m* ‖ *v* (*pret & pp* staved or stove [stov]) *tr* bucare; (*to smash*) sfondare; **to stave off** tenere a bada
stay [ste] *s* permanenza, soggiorno; (*brace*) staggio; (*of corset*) stecca di balena; sostegno; (law) sospensione; (naut) strallo ‖ *tr* fermare; sospendere; poner freno a ‖ *intr* stare; mantenersi; restare, rimanere; (*at a hotel*) sostare; **to stay up** stare alzato
stay'-at-home' *adj* casalingo ‖ *s* persona casalinga
stead [stɛd] *s* posto; **in his stead** in suo luogo; **to stand in good stead** esser utile
stead'fast' *adj* fermo, risoluto
stead·y ['stɛdi] *adj* (-ier; -iest) stabile, fermo; regolare, costante; abituale; calmo, sicuro ‖ *v* (*pret & pp* -ied) *tr* rinforzare; calmare ‖ *intr* rinforzarsi; calmarsi
steak [stek] *s* bistecca
steal [stil] *s* (coll) furto ‖ *v* (*pret* stole [stol]; *pp* stolen) *tr* rubare; involare; (*the attention*) cattivare ‖ *intr* rubare; **to steal away** svignarsela; **to steal out** uscire di soppiatto; **to steal upon** approssimarsi silenziosamente a
stealth [stɛlθ] *s* clandestinità *f*; **by stealth** di straforo, di soppiatto
steam [stim] *adj* a vapore ‖ *s* vapore *m*; fumo; **to get up steam** aumentare la pressione; **to let off steam** scaricare la pressione; (slang) sfogarsi ‖ *tr* (*a steamship*) guidare; esalare; esporre al vapore; (*e.g., glasses*) appannare ‖ *intr* dar vapore, fumigare; bollire; (*to become clouded*) appannarsi; andare a vapore; **to steam ahead** avanzare a tutto vapore
steam'boat' *s* vapore *m*
steam' en'gine *s* macchina a vapore
steamer ['stimər] *s* vapore *m*
steam'er rug' *s* coperta da viaggio
steam'er trunk' *s* bauletto da cabina
steam' heat' *s* riscaldamento a vapore
steam' roll'er *s* rullo compressore; (fig) rullo compressore
steam'ship' *s* piroscafo, vapore *m*
steam' shov'el *s* escavatore *m* a vapore
steam' ta'ble *s* tavola riscaldata a vapore per mantenere calde le vivande
steed [stid] *s* destriere *m*

steel [stil] *adj* d'acciaio; (*industry*) siderurgico ‖ *s* acciaio; (*bar*) stecca d'acciaio; (*for sharpening knives*) affilacoltelli *m*; (fig) spada, brando ‖ *tr* acciaiare; **to steel oneself** corazzarsi, indurirsi; armarsi di coraggio
steel' wool' *s* paglia di ferro
steel'works' *spl* acciaieria
steelyard ['stil ˌjɑrd] or ['stiljərd] *s* stadera
steep [stip] *adj* erto, scosceso, ripido; (*price*) alto ‖ *tr* immergere, saturare, imbevere
steeple ['stipəl] *s* campanile *m*; (*spire*) cuspide *f*, guglia
stee'ple·chase' *s* corsa ad ostacoli
stee'ple·jack' *s* aggiustatore *m* di campanili
steer [stɪr] *s* bue *m*, manzo ‖ *tr* governare, guidare; (aer) pilotare ‖ *intr* governare; **to steer clear of** evitare
steerage ['stɪrɪdʒ] *s* (naut) alloggio passeggeri di terza classe
steer'ing wheel' *s* (aut) volante *m*, sterzo; (naut) ruota del timone
stellar ['stɛlər] *adj* stellare; (*role*) da stella
stem [stem] *s* (*of pipe, of key*) cannello; (*of goblet*) gambo; (*of column*) fusto; (*of spoon*) manico; (*of watch*) corona; (*of a word*) tema *m*; (*of note*) (mus) gamba; (bot) peduncolo, stelo; (bot) gambo; **from stem to stern** da poppa a prua ‖ *v* (*pret & pp* stemmed; *ger* stemming) *tr* togliere il gambo a; (*to check*) arrestare; (*to dam up*) arginare; (*to plug*) otturare; (*the tide*) risalire, andare contro ‖ *intr* originare, derivare
stem'·win'der *s* orologio a corona
stench [stɛntʃ] *s* tanfo, fetore *m*
sten·cil ['stɛnsəl] *s* stampo, stampino; parole *fpl* a stampo ‖ *v* (*pret & pp* -ciled or -cilled; *ger* -ciling or -cilling) *tr* stampinare
stenographer [stə'nɑgrəfər] *s* stenografo
stenography [stə'nɑgrəfi] *s* stenografia
step [stɛp] *s* passo; (*footprint*) orma, impronta; (*of ladder*) piolo; (*of staircase*) gradino; (*of carriage*) montatoio; **step by step** passo passo; **to watch one's step** fare molta attenzione ‖ *v* (*pret & pp* stepped; *ger* stepping) *tr* scaglionare; **to step off** misurare a passi ‖ *intr* camminare, andare a passi; mettere il piede; **to step aside** scostarsi; **to step back** indietreggiare; **to step on it** (slang) fare presto; **to step on the gas** (coll) accelerare; **to step on the starter** avviare il motore
step'broth'er *s* fratellastro, fratello consanguineo
step'child' *s* (-children [ˌtʃɪldrən]) figliastro
step'daugh'ter *s* figliastra
step'fa'ther *s* patrigno
step'lad'der *s* scala a gradini or a libretto
step'moth'er *s* matrigna
steppe [stɛp] *s* steppa

step'ping stone' s passatoio, pietra per guadare; (fig) gradino
step'sis'ter s sorellastra
step'son' s figliastro
stere·o ['stɛrɪ ˌo] or ['stɪrɪ ˌo] adj stereofonico; stereoscopico ‖ s (-os) musica stereofonica; sistema stereofonico; fotografia stereoscopica
stereotyped ['stɛrɪ·ə ˌtaɪpt] or ['stɪrɪ·ə- ˌtaɪpt] adj stereotipato
sterile ['stɛrɪl] adj sterile
sterilize ['stɛrɪ ˌlaɪz] tr sterilizzare
sterling ['stʌrlɪŋ] adj di lira sterlina; d'argento; puro; eccellente ‖ s argento .925; vasellame m d'argento puro
stern [stʌrn] adj severo ‖ s poppa
stet [stɛt] v (pret & pp **stetted**; ger **stetting**) tr marcare con la parola "vive"
stethoscope ['stɛθə ˌskop] s stetoscopio
stevedore ['stivə ˌdor] s stivatore m
stew [stju] or [stu] s stufato, guazzetto ‖ tr stufare ‖ intr cuocere a fuoco lento; (coll) preoccuparsi
steward ['stju·ərd] or ['stu·ərd] s amministratore m, agente m; maggiordomo; (aer, naut) cambusiere m, cameriere m
stewardess ['stju·ərdɪs] or ['stu·ərdɪs] s (naut) cameriera; (aer) hostess f, assistente f di volo
stewed' fruit' s composta di frutta
stewed' toma'toes spl pomodori mpl in umido
stick [stɪk] s stecco; legno; bacchetta; bastone m; (e.g., of candy) cannello; (naut) albero; (typ) compositoio; **in the sticks** (coll) in casa del diavolo ‖ v (pret & pp **stuck** [stʌk]) tr pungere; ficcare, infiggere; attaccare; confondere; **to be stuck** essere insabbiato; essere attaccato; (fig) essere confuso; **to stick out** (the head) sporgere; (the tongue) cacciare; **to stick up** (slang) assaltare a mano armata, rapinare ‖ intr rimanere attaccato; persistere; (said of glue) appiccicarsi; (to one opinion) tenersi; stare; **to stick out** sporgere; **to stick together** rimanere uniti; **to stick up** risaltare; (said, e.g., of quills) rizzarsi; **to stick up for** (coll) stare dalla parte di
sticker ['stɪkər] s etichetta gommata; spina; persona zelante; (coll) busillis m
stick'ing plas'ter s cerotto
stick'pin' s spilla da cravatta
stick'up' s (slang) grassazione
stick·y ['stɪki] adj (-ier; -iest) attaccaticcio; vischioso; (weather) afoso, soffocante; (fig) difficile
stiff [stɪf] adj rigido, duro; forte; (price) alto; denso ‖ s (slang) cadavere m; **poor stiff** (slang) povero diavolo
stiff' col'lar s colletto duro
stiffen ['stɪfən] tr irrigidire ‖ intr irrigidirsi
stiff' neck' s torcicollo; ostinazione
stiff'-necked' adj testardo

stiff' shirt' s camicia inamidata
stifle ['staɪfəl] tr soffocare
stigma ['stɪgmə] s (-mas or -mata [mətə]) stigma m
stigmatize ['stɪgmə ˌtaɪz] tr stigmatizzare
still [stɪl] adj fermo, tranquillo; silenzioso; (wine) non spumante ‖ s calma; distillatore m; distilleria; (phot) fotografia singola ‖ adv ancora; tuttora ‖ conj tuttavia ‖ tr calmare ‖ intr calmarsi
still'birth' s parto di infante nato morto
still'born' adj nato morto
still' life' s (lifes') natura morta
stilt [stɪlt] s trampolo; (in water) palafitta; (orn) trampoliere m
stilted ['stɪltɪd] adj elevato; pomposo
stimulant ['stɪmjələnt] adj & s stimulante m, eccitante m
stimulate ['stɪmjə ˌlet] tr stimulare
stimu·lus ['stɪmjələs] s (-li [ˌlaɪ]) stimolo
sting [stɪŋ] s puntura; (of insect) pungiglione; (fig) scottatura ‖ v (pret & pp **stung** [stʌŋ]) tr & intr pungere
stin·gy ['stɪndʒi] adj (-gier; -giest) tirchio, taccagno
stink [stɪŋk] s puzza ‖ v (pret **stank** [stæŋk] or **stunk** [stʌŋk]; pp **stunk**) tr far puzzare ‖ intr puzzare; **to stink of money** (slang) aver soldi a palate
stinker ['stɪŋkər] s (slang) puzzone m
stint [stɪnt] s limite m; lavoro assegnato, compito ‖ intr lesinarsi
stipend ['staɪpənd] s stipendio; assegno di studio, presalario
stipulate ['stɪpjə ˌlet] tr stipulare
stir [stʌr] s agitazione, movimento; (poke) spinta; **to create a stir** creare una sensazione ‖ v (pret & pp **stirred**; ger **stirring**) tr mescolare; muovere; (fire) ravvivare; (pity) fare; **to stir up** eccitare, svegliare; (to rebellion) sommuovere ‖ intr muoversi, agitarsi
stirring ['stʌrɪŋ] adj commovente
stirrup ['stʌrəp] or ['stɪrəp] s staffa
stitch [stɪtʃ] s punto; maglia; (pain) fitta; (bit) poco, po' m; **to be in stitches** (coll) sbellicarsi dalle risa ‖ tr cucire; aggraffare ‖ intr cucire
stock [stɑk] adj regolare, comune; banale, ordinario; di bestiame; borsistico; azionario; (aut) di serie; (theat) stabile ‖ s provvista, scorta; capitale m sociale; azione f; azioni fpl, titoli mpl; (of tree) tronco; (of family; of anchor; of anvil) ceppo; razza, famiglia; materia prima; (of rifle) cassa; (broth) brodo; (handle) manico; (livestock) bestiame m; (theat) compagnia stabile; **in stock** in magazzino, disponibile; **out of stock** esaurito; **stocks** gogna, berlina; **to take stock** fare l'inventario; **to take stock in** (coll) aver fede in ‖ tr fornire; fornire di bestiame; fornire di pesci ‖ intr—**to stock up** fare rifornimenti
stockade [stɑ'ked] s staccionata
stock'breed'er s allevatore m di bestiame

stock′bro′ker s agente m di cambio

stock′ car′ s automobile f di serie; (rr) carro bestiame

stock′ com′pany s (theat) compagnia stabile; (com) società anonima

stock′ div′idend s dividendo pagato in azioni

stock′ exchange′ s borsa valori

stock′fish′ s stoccafisso

stock′hold′er s azionista mf

stock′holder of rec′ord s azionista mf registrato nei libri della compagnia

Stockholm [′stakhom] s Stoccolma

stocking ⟨′stakɪŋ] s calza

stock′ in trade′ s stock m; ferri mpl del mestiere

stock′ mar′ket s borsa valori

stock′pile′ s riserva, scorta ‖ tr mettere in riserva ‖ intr mettere in riserva materie prime

stock′ rais′ing s allevamento bestiame

stock′room′ s magazzino, deposito

stock•y [′staki] adj (-ier; -iest) tozzo, tarchiato

stock′yard′ s chiuso per il bestiame

stoic [′sto•ɪk] adj & s stoico

stoicism [′sto•ɪ‚sɪzəm] s stoicismo

stoke [stok] tr (fire) attizzare; (a furnace) caricare

stoker [′stokər] s fochista m

stolid [′stalɪd] adj impassibile

stomach [′stʌmək] s stomaco ‖ tr (fig) digerire

stone [ston] s sasso, pietra; (of fruit) osso; (pathol) calcolo ‖ tr lapidare; affilare con la pietra; (fruit) snocciolare

stone′-broke′ adj (coll) senza un soldo, senza il becco di un quattrino

stone′-deaf′ adj sordo come una campana

stone′ma′son s tagliapietra m

stone′ quar′ry s cava di pietra

stone′s′ throw′ s tiro di sasso; within a stone′s throw a un tiro di schioppo

ston•y [′stoni] adj (-ier; -iest) di sasso, sassoso, pietroso

stooge [studʒ] s (theat) spalla; (slang) complice mf

stool [stul] s sgabello, seggiolino; gabinetto; (mass evacuated) feci fpl

stool′ pi′geon s piccione m di richiamo; (slang) spia

stoop [stup] s curvatura, inclinazione; scalini mpl d′ingresso ‖ intr inclinarsi, piegarsi; degnarsi, umiliarsi

stoop-shouldered [′stup′ʃoldərd] adj con le spalle cadenti

stop [stap] s fermata, sosta; arresto; otturazione, blocco; cessazione; ostacolo; (of a check) fermo; (restraint) freno; (of organ) registro; to come to a stop fermarsi; cessare; to put a stop to metter fine a ‖ v (pret & pp stopped; ger stopping) tr fermare, cessare; arrestare, sospendere; tappare, otturare; (a check) mettere il fermo a; to stop up tappare, otturare ‖ intr fermarsi; arrestarsi; (said of a ship) fare scalo; (at an hotel) scendere; to stop + ger smettere di or cessare di + inf

stop′cock′ s rubinetto di arresto

stop′gap′ adj provvisorio ‖ s soluzione provvisoria; (person) tappabuchi m

stop′light′ s (traffic light) semaforo; (aut) luce f di stop

stop′o′ver s fermata intermedia

stoppage [′stapɪdʒ] s fermata, arresto; (of work, wages, etc.) sospensione

stopper [′stapər] s tappo, turacciolo

stop′ sign′ s segnale m di fermata

stop′watch′ s cronometro a scatto

storage [′storɪdʒ] s magazzinaggio; (place for storing) magazzino; (of a computer) memoria

stor′age bat′tery s (elec) accumulatore m

store [stor] s negozio; magazzino; (supply) scorta; in store in serbo; to set store by dare molta importanza a ‖ tr immagazzinare; to store away accumulare

store′house′ s magazzino, deposito; (of knowledge) miniera

store′keep′er s negoziante m

store′room′ s magazzino; (naut) dispensa

stork [stɔrk] s cicogna

storm [stɔrm] s tempesta, temporale m; (on the Beaufort scale) burrasca; (mil) assalto; (fig) scoppio ‖ tr assaltare ‖ intr tempestare; imperversare; (mil) andare all′attacco

storm′ cloud′ s nuvolone m

storm′ door′ s controporta

storm′ sash′ s controfinestra

storm′ troops′ spl truppe fpl d′assalto

storm′ win′dow s controfinestra

storm•y [′stɔrmi] adj (-ier; -iest) tempestoso, burrascoso; (fig) inquieto, violento

sto•ry [′stori] s (-ries) storia, racconto, romanzo; (plot) trama; (level) piano; (coll) storia, menzogna ‖ v (pret & pp -ried) tr istoriare

sto′ry-tell′er s narratore m, novelliere m; (coll) mentitore m

stoup [stup] s (eccl) acquasantiera

stout [staut] adj grasso, obeso; forte, robusto; leale; coraggioso ‖ s birra nera forte

stout-hearted [′staut‚hartɪd] adj coraggioso

stove [stov] s (for warmth) stufa; (for cooking) fornello, cucina economica

stove′pipe′ s tubo della stufa, cannone m; (hat) (coll) tuba

stow [sto] tr mettere in riserva; riempire; (naut) stivare ‖ intr—to stow away imbarcarsi clandestinamente

stowage [′sto•ɪdʒ] s stivaggio; (place) stiva

stow•a•way′ s passeggero clandestino

straddle [′strædəl] s divaricamento ‖ tr (a horse) cavalcare; (the legs) divaricare; favorire entrambe le parti in ‖ intr cavalcare; stare a gambe divaricate; (coll) tenere il piede tra due staffe

strafe [strɑf] or [stref] s attacco violento ‖ tr attaccare violentemente con fuoco aereo; bombardare violentemente; (slang) punire

straggle [ˈstrægəl] *intr* sbandarsi, sviarsi; sparpagliarsi, essere sparpagliato

straggler [ˈstræglər] *s* ritardatario

straight [stret] *adj* diritto, ritto; (*e.g., shoulders*) quadro; candido, franco; (*honest, upright*) retto; inalterato; (*hair; whiskey*) liscio; **to set s.o. straight** mettere qlcu sulla retta via; mostrare la verità a qlcu ‖ *s* rettilinea; (*cards*) scala ‖ *adv* dritto; sinceramente; rettamente; **straight ahead** sempre diritto; **straight away** immediatamente; **to go straight** vivere onestamente

straighten [ˈstretən] *tr* ordinare; raddrizzare ‖ *intr* raddrizzarsi

straight' face' *s* faccia seria

straight' flush' *s* (cards) scala reale

straight'for'ward *adj* diretto; onesto

straight' man' *s* (theat) spalla

straight' ra'zor *s* rasoio a mano libera

straight'way' *adv* immediatamente

strain [stren] *s* sforzo; fatica eccessiva; tensione, pressione; strappo muscolare; tono, stile *m*; (*family*) famiglia; tendenza, vena; (coll) lavoro severo; (mus) aria, melodia ‖ *tr* passare, colare; (*e.g., a rope*) tirare al massimo; (*one's ear*) tendere; (*a muscle*) strappare; (*the ankle*) slogare; (*e.g., words*) storcere, forzare ‖ *intr* colare, filtrare; tendersi, tirare; sforzarsi; fare resistenza; **to strain at** tirare; resistere a

strained [strend] *adj* (*smile*) stentato; (*relations*) teso

strainer [ˈstrenər] *s* scolatoio

strait [stret] *s* stretto; **straits** stretto; (fig) strettezze *fpl;* **to be in dire straits** essere nei frangenti

strait' jack'et *s* camicia di forza

strait'-laced' *adj* puritano, pudibondo

strand [strænd] *s* sponda, lido; (*of metal cable*) trefolo; (*of rope*) legnolo; (*of pearls*) filo ‖ *tr* sfilare; (*e.g., a rope*) ritorcere, intrecciare; (*e.g., a boat*) lasciare incagliato; **to be stranded** trovarsi incagliato

stranded [ˈstrændɪd] *adj* (*ship*) incagliato, arenato; (*e.g., rope*) ritorto, intrecciato

strange [strendʒ] *adj* strano; straniero; non abituato; inusitato

stranger [ˈstrendʒər] *s* forestiero; nuovo venuto, intruso

strangle [ˈstræŋgəl] *tr* strangolare; soffocare ‖ *intr* strangolarsi; soffocarsi

strap [stræp] *s* (*of leather*) correggia; (*for holding things together*) tirante *m*; (*shoulder strap*) bretella; (*for passengers to hold on to*) manopola; (*to hold a sandal*) guiggia; (*to hold a baby*) falda; (*strop*) coramella ‖ *v* (*pret & pp* **strapped;** *ger* **strapping**) *tr* legare con correggia *or* tirante; (*a razor*) affilare

strap'hang'er *s* (coll) passeggero senza posto a sedere

strapping [ˈstræpɪŋ] *adj* robusto; (coll) grande, enorme

stratagem [ˈstrætedʒəm] *s* stratagemma *m*

strategic(al) [strəˈtidʒɪk(əl)] *adj* strategico

strategist [ˈstrætɪdʒɪst] *s* stratego

strate·gy [ˈstrætɪdʒi] *s* (**-gies**) strategia

strati·fy [ˈstrætɪˌfaɪ] *v* (*pret & pp* **-fied**) *tr* stratificare ‖ *intr* stratificarsi

stratosphere [ˈstrætəˌsfɪr] *or* [ˈstretəˌsfɪr] *s* stratosfera

stra·tum [ˈstretəm] *or* [ˈstrætəm] *s* (**-ta** [tə] *or* **-tums**) strato

straw [strɔ] *adj* di paglia; di nessun valore; falso, fittizio ‖ *s* paglia; (*for drinking*) cannuccia; **I don't care a straw** non mi importa un fico; **to be the last straw** essere il colmo

straw'ber·ry *s* (**-ries**) fragola

straw'hat' *s* cappello di paglia; (*with hard crown*) paglietta

straw' man' *s* (*figurehead*) uomo di paglia; (*scarecrow*) spaventapasseri *m*

straw' mat'tress *s* pagliericcio

straw' vote' *s* votazione esplorativa

stray [stre] *adj* sbandato, randagio; casuale, fortuito ‖ *s* animale randagio ‖ *intr* sviarsi; (fig) sbandarsi

streak [strik] *s* stria; (*of light*) raggio; (*of madness*) ramo, vena; (*of luck*) (coll) periodo; **like a streak** (coll) come un lampo ‖ *tr* striare, venare ‖ *intr* striarsi, venarsi; andare come un lampo

stream [strim] *s* corrente *f;* (*of light*) raggio; (*of people*) fiumana, torrente *m*; (*of cars*) fila ‖ *intr* colare; filtrare, penetrare; (*said of a flag*) fluttuare

streamer [ˈstrimər] *s* pennone *m;* nastro; raggio di luce

streamlined [ˈstrimˌlaɪnd] *adj* aerodinamico; (aer) carenato

stream'lin'er *s* treno dal profilo aerodinamico

street [strit] *adj* stradale ‖ *s* via, strada

street'car' *s* tram *m*

street' clean'er *s* spazzino; (mach) spazzatrice *f*

street' clothes' *spl* vestiti *mpl* da passeggio; vestito da passeggio

street' floor' *s* pianterreno

street'light' *s* lampione *m*

street' map' *s* pianta della città; stradario

street' sign' *s* segnale *m* stradale

street' sprin'kler *s* carro annaffiatoio

street' walk'er *s* passeggiatrice *f*

strength [strɛŋθ] *s* forza; resistenza; (*of spirituous liquors*) gradazione; (com) tendenza al rialzo; (mil) numero; **on the strength of** basandosi su

strengthen [ˈstrɛŋθən] *tr* rinforzare; (fig) convalidare, rinsaldare ‖ *intr* rinforzarsi, ingagliardirsi

strenuous [ˈstrɛnju·əs] *adj* vigoroso; strenuo

stress [strɛs] *s* enfasi *f,* importanza; spinta; tensione, preoccupazione; accento; (mech) sollecitazione; **to lay**

stress on mettere in rilievo ‖ *tr* (*a word*) accentare, accentuare; (*to emphasize*) accentuare; (mech) sollecitare

stress' ac'cent *s* accento di intensità

stretch [stretʃ] *s* tiro, tirata; (*in time or space*) periodo; (*of road*) tratto, percorrenza; (*of imagination*) sforzo; (rr) tratta; (slang) periodo di detenzione; **at a stretch** di un tiro ‖ *tr* tirare; tendere, distendere; (*the imagination*) forzare; (*facts*) esagerare; (*money*) stiracchiare; (*one's legs*) sgranchirsi; (*the truth*) esagerare; **to stretch oneself** sdraiarsi ‖ *intr* estendersi; stiracchiarsi; distendersi; **to stretch out** sdraiarsi

stretcher ['stretʃər] *s* (*for a painting*) telaio; (*tool*) tenditore *m*, tenditoio; (*to carry wounded*) barella, lettiga

stretch'er-bear'er *s* portantino

strew [stru] *v* (*pret* **strewed**; *pp* **strewed or strewn**) *tr* spargere, cospargere; disseminare

stricken ['strɪkən] *adj* afflitto; ferito; danneggiato

strict [strɪkt] *adj* stretto, severo

stricture ['strɪktʃər] *s* aspra critica; (pathol) stenosi *f*

stride [straɪd] *s* passo; andatura; **rapid strides** grandi passi *mpl;* **to hit one's stride** avanzare a andatura regolare; **to take s.th in one's stride** fare qlco senza sforzi ‖ *v* (*pret* **strode** [strod]; *pp* **stridden** ['strɪdən]) *tr* attraversare a grandi passi; attraversare di un salto ‖ *intr* camminare a grandi passi; (*majestically*) incedere

strident ['straɪdənt] *adj* stridente

strife [straɪf] *s* discordia; concorrenza

strike [straɪk] *s* (*blow*) colpo; (*stopping of work*) sciopero; (*discovery of oil, ore, etc.*) scoperta; (*of fish*) abboccatura; colpo di fortuna ‖ *v* (*pret & pp* **struck** [strʌk]) *tr* colpire, percuotere; infiggere; (*a match*) strofinare; (*fire*) accendere; fare impressione su; incontrare improvvisamente; (*e.g., ore*) scoprire; (*roots*) mettere; (*a coin*) coniare; andare in sciopero contro; arrivare a; (*a posture*) prendere; (*the hour*) scoccare; cancellare, eliminare; (*sails*) calare; (*attention*) richiamare; **to strike it rich** scoprire una miniera; avere un colpo di fortuna ‖ *intr* dare un colpo; cadere; (*said of a bell*) suonare; accendersi; scioperare; (mil) attaccare; **to strike out** mettersi in marcia; (*to fail*) (fig) fallire, venir meno

strike'break'er *s* crumiro

striker ['straɪkər] *s* battitore *m;* (*clapper in clock*) martelletto; (*worker*) scioperante *m*

striking ['straɪkɪŋ] *adj* impressionante, sorprendente; notevole; scioperante

strik'ing pow'er *s* potere *m* d'assalto

string [strɪŋ] *s* spago, cordicella; (*e.g., of apron*) laccio; (*of pearls*) filo; (*of onions; of lies*) filza; (*row*) fila, infilata; (mus) corda; **no strings attached** (coll) senza condizioni;

strings strumenti *mpl* a corda; (coll) condizioni *fpl;* **to pull strings** usare influenza ‖ *v* (*pret & pp* **strung** [strʌŋ]) *tr* legare; allacciare; infilare; infilzare; (*a racket*) munire di corde; (*to stretch*) tendere; (*a musical instrument*) mettere le corde a; (slang) ingannare; **to string along** (slang) menare per il naso; **to string up** impiccare ‖ *intr*—**to string along with** (slang) andare d'accordo con

string' bean' *s* fagiolino

stringed' in'strument *s* strumento a corda

stringent ['strɪndʒənt] *adj* stringente; urgente; severo

string' quartet' *s* quartetto d'archi

strip [strɪp] *s* striscia; (*of metal*) lamina; (*of land*) lingua ‖ *v* (*pret & pp* **stripped**; *ger* **stripping**) *tr* spogliare; denudare; (*a fruit*) pelare; (*a ship*) sguarnire; (*tobacco*) togliere le nervature da; scortecciare; (*thread*) spanare; **to strip of** spogliare di ‖ *intr* spogliarsi; denudarsi; fare lo spogliarello

stripe [straɪp] *s* stria, striscia, riga, lista; tipo, qualità *f;* (mil) gallone *m* ‖ *tr* striare, filettare, rigare

strip' min'ing *s* sfruttamento minerario a cielo aperto

strip'tease' *s* spogliarello

stripteaser ['strɪp ,tizər] *s* spogliarellista

strive [straɪv] *v* (*pret* **strove** [strov]; *pp* **striven** ['strɪvən]) *intr* sforzarsi; lottare; **to strive to** sforzarsi di

stroke [strok] *s* colpo; (*of bell or clock*) rintocco; (*of pen*) tratto, frego; (*of brush*) pennellata; (*of arms in swimming*) bracciata; colpo apoplettico; (*caress*) carezza; (*with oar*) vogata; (*of oar or paddle*) palata; (*of a master*) tocco; (*of a piston*) corsa; (*keystroke*) battuta; (*of genius*) lampo; (*of the hour*) scocco; **to not do a stroke of work** non muovere un dito ‖ *tr* accarezzare

stroll [strol] *s* passeggiata; **to take a stroll** fare una passeggiata ‖ *intr* fare una passeggiata, andare a zonzo; errare

stroller ['strolər] *s* girovago; carrozzella; (*itinerant performer*) (theat) guitto

strong [strɔŋ] *or* [straŋ] *adj* forte, vigoroso; valido; acceso, zelante; (*butter*) rancido; (*cheese*) piccante; (com) sostenuto

strong'box' *s* cassaforte *f*

strong' drink' *s* bevanda alcolica

strong'hold' *s* piazzaforte *f*

strong' man' *s* (*in a circus*) maciste *m;* (*leader*) anima; dittatore *m*

strong-minded ['strɔŋ ,maɪndɪd] *or* ['straŋ ,maɪndɪd] *adj* volitivo

strong'point' *s* luogo fortificato

strontium ['stranʃɪ-əm] *s* stronzio

strop [strap] *s* coramella, affilarasoio ‖ *v* (*pret & pp* **stropped**; *ger* **stropping**) *tr* affilare

strophe ['strofi] *s* strofa, strofe *f*

struc'tural steel' ['strʌktʃərəl] *s* profilato di acciaio

structure ['strʌktʃər] *s* struttura; edificio || *tr* strutturare

struggle ['strʌgəl] *s* lotta; sforzo || *intr* lottare; sforzare, dibattersi

strum [strʌm] *v (pret & pp* **strummed;** *ger* **strumming)** *tr & intr* strimpellare

strumpet ['strʌmpɪt] *s* sgualdrina, puttana

strut [strʌt] *s* controvento, puntello, saettone *m;* incedere impettito; (aer) montante || *v (pret & pp* **strutted;** *ger* **strutting)** *intr* pavoneggiarsi, fare la ruota

strychnine ['strɪknaɪn] or ['strɪknɪn] *s* stricnina

stub [stʌb] *s (of tree)* coppo; *(e.g., of cigar)* mozzicone *m; (of a check)* matrice *f,* madre *f* || *v (pret & pp* **stubbed;** *ger* **stubbing)** *tr* sradicare; **to stub one's toe** inciampare

stubble ['stʌbəl] *s (of beard)* pelo ispido; **stubbles** stoppie *fpl*

stubborn ['stʌbərn] *adj (headstrong)* testardo; *(resolute)* accanito; *(e.g., resistance)* ostinato; *(e.g., illness)* ribelle; *(soil)* ingrato

stuc•co ['stʌko] *s* (-coes or -cos) stucco || *tr* stuccare

stuck [stʌk] *adj* infisso; attaccato; *(glued)* incollato; *(unable to continue)* in panna; **stuck on** (slang) invaghito di

stuck'-up' *adj* (coll) presuntuoso, arrogante

stud [stʌd] *s (in upholstery)* borchia; bottone *m* da sparato; *(of walls)* montante *m; (stallion)* stallone *m; (for mares)* monta; (archit) bugna, bugnato || *v (pret & pp* **studded;** *ger* **studding)** *tr* cospergere; *(with stars)* costellare; *(with jewels)* incastonare, ingioiellare

stud' bolt' *s* prigioniero

stud'book' *s* registro della genealogia

student ['stjudənt] or ['studənt] *adj* studentesco || *s* studente *m;* scolaro; *(investigator)* studioso

stu'dent bod'y *s* scolaresca

stud'horse' *s* stallone *m*

studied ['stʌdid] *adj* premeditato; *(affected)* studiato

studi•o ['studɪˌo] or ['stjudɪˌo] *s* (-os) studio

studious ['stjudɪ•əs] or ['studɪ•əs] *adj* studioso; assiduo, zelante

stud•y ['stʌdi] *s* (-ies) studio || *v (pret & pp* **-ied)** *tr & intr* studiare

stuff [stʌf] *s* roba, cosa; stoffa; materiale *m; (nonsense)* scemenze *fpl;* medicina; (coll) mestiere *m* || *tr* riempire, inzeppare; *(one's stomach)* rimpinzare; *(e.g., poultry)* farcire; *(e.g., salami)* insaccare; *(a dead animal)* impagliare; **to stuff up** intasare || *intr* rimpinzarsi

stuffed' shirt' *s* persona altezzosa

stuffing ['stʌfɪŋ] *s* ripieno

stuff•y ['stʌfi] *adj* (-ier; -iest) soffocante, opprimente; *(nose)* chiuso; pedante

stumble ['stʌmbəl] *intr* incespicare, inciampare; sbagliare, impaperarsi; **to stumble on** or **upon** intopparsi in

stum'bling block' *s* inciampo, scoglio

stump [stʌmp] *s (of tree)* toppo, ceppo; *(e.g., of arm)* moncherino, moncone *m; (of cigar, candle)* mozzicone *m;* dente rotto; tribuna popolare; *(for drawing)* sfumino; **up a stump** (coll) completamente perplesso || *tr* mozzare; lasciare perplesso; (coll) fare discorsi politici in

stump' speech' *s* discorso politico

stun [stʌn] *v (pret & pp* **stunned;** *ger* **stunning)** *tr* tramortire; (fig) sbalordire

stunning ['stʌnɪŋ] *adj (blow)* che stordisce; sbalorditivo, magnifico

stunt [stʌnt] *s* atrofia; creatura striminzita; bravata, prodezza; *(for publicity)* montatura || *tr* striminzire; arrestare la crescita di || *intr* fare delle acrobazie

stunt'ed *adj* striminzito

stunt' fly'ing *s* acrobazia aerea

stunt' man' *s* (mov) controfigura

stupe•fy ['stjupɪˌfaɪ] or ['stupɪˌfaɪ] *v (pret & pp* **-fied)** *tr* istupidire, intontire

stupendous [stju'pɛndəs] or [stu'pɛndəs] *adj* stupendo

stupid ['stjupɪd] or ['stupɪd] *adj* stupido, ebete, scemo

stupor ['stjupər] or ['stupər] *s* torpore *m,* stupore *m*

stur•dy ['stʌrdi] *adj* (-dier; -diest) forte; *(robust)* tarchiato; risoluto

sturgeon ['stʌrdʒən] *s* storione *m*

stutter ['stʌtər] *s* tartagliamento || *tr & intr* tartagliare

sty [staɪ] *s* (sties) porcile *m;* (pathol) orzaiolo

style [staɪl] *s* stile *m;* tono; *(mode of living)* treno || *tr* chiamare col nome di

stylish ['staɪlɪʃ] *adj* alla moda, di tono

sty•mie ['staɪmi] *v (pret & pp* **-mied;** *ger* **-mieing)** *tr* ostacolare, contrastare

styp'tic pen'cil ['stɪptɪk] *s* matita emostatica

Styx [stɪks] *s* Stige *m*

suave [swav] or [swev] *adj* soave

subaltern [səb'ɔltərn] *adj & s* subalterno

subcommittee ['sʌbkəˌmɪti] *s* sottocommissione

subconscious [səb'kɑnʃəs] *adj & s* subcosciente *m*

subconsciousness [səb'kɑnʃəsnɪs] *s* subcosciente *m,* subcoscienza

sub'deb' *s* (coll) signorina più giovane di una debuttante

subdivide ['sʌbdɪˌvaɪd] or [ˌsʌbdɪ'vaɪd] *tr* suddividere || *intr* suddividersi

subdue [səb'dju] or [səb'du] *tr* soggiogare, sottomettere; *(color, voice)* attenuare

subdued [səb'djud] or [səb'dud] *adj (voice)* sommesso; *(light)* tenue

subheading ['sʌb ,hedɪŋ] s sottotitolo; (journ) sommario

subject ['sʌbdʒɪkt] adj soggetto; **subject to** (e.g., a cold) soggetto a; (e.g., a fine) passibile di || s soggetto, materia, proposito; (of a ruler) suddito; (gram, med, philos) soggetto || [səb-'dʒɛkt] tr sottomettere

sub'ject cat'alogue s catalogo per materie

sub'ject in'dex s indice m per materie

subjection [səb'dʒɛkʃən] s soggezione

subjective [səb'dʒɛktɪv] adj soggettivo

sub'ject mat'ter s soggetto

subjugate ['sʌbdʒə ,get] tr soggiogare

subjunctive [səb'dʒʌŋktɪv] adj & s congiuntivo

sublease ['sʌb ,lis] s subaffitto || [,sʌb-'lis] tr subaffittare

sub·let [sʌb'lɛt] or ['sʌb ,lɛt] v (pret & pp -let; ger -letting) tr subaffittare

sub·machine' gun' [,sʌbmə'ʃin] s mitra m

submarine ['sʌbmə ,rin] adj & s sottomarino

sub'marine chas'er ['tʃesər] s cacciasommergibili m

submerge [səb'mʌrdʒ] tr sommergere || intr sommergersi

submersion [səb'mʌrʒən] or [səb-'mʌrʃən] s sommersione

submission [səb'mɪʃən] s sottomissione

submissive [səb'mɪsɪv] adj sottomesso

sub·mit [səb'mɪt] v (pret & pp -mitted; ger -mitting) tr sottomettere; presentare, deferire; osservare rispettosamente || intr sottomettersi

subordinate [səb'ɔrdɪnɪt] adj & s subordinato || [səb'ɔrdɪ ,net] tr subordinare

suborna'tion of per'jury [,sʌbər'neʃən] s subornazione

subplot ['sʌb ,plɑt] s intreccio secondario

subpoena or **subpena** [sʌb'pinə] or [sə-'pinə] s mandato di comparizione || tr citare

sub rosa [sʌb'rozə] adv in segreto

subscribe [səb'skraɪb] tr sottoscrivere || intr sottoscrivere; **to subscribe to** sottoscrivere a; (a magazine) abbonarsi a; (an opinion) approvare

subscriber [səb'skraɪbər] s sottoscrittore m; abbonato

subscription [sʌb'skrɪpʃən] s sottoscrizione; (e.g., to a newspaper) abbonamento; (e.g., to club) quota

subsequent ['sʌbsɪkwənt] adj susseguente, posteriore

subservient [səb'sʌrvɪ·ənt] adj subordinato; ossequioso, servile

subside [səb'saɪd] intr calmarsi; (said of water) decrescere

subsidiar·y [səb'sɪdɪ ,ɛri] adj sussidiario || s (-ies) sussidiario

subsidize ['sʌbsɪ ,daɪz] tr sussidiare, sovvenzionare; (by bribery) subornare

subsi·dy ['sʌbsɪdi] s (-dies) sussidio, sovvenzione

subsist [səb'sɪst] intr sussistere

subsistence [səb'sɪstəns] s sussistenza

subsoil ['sʌb ,sɔɪl] s sottosuolo

substance ['sʌbstəns] s sostanza

substandard [sʌb'stændərd] adj inferiore al livello normale

substantial [səb'stænʃəl] adj considerevole; ricco, influente; (food) sostanzioso; (e.g., reason) sostanziale

substantiate [səb'stænʃɪ ,et] tr provare, verificare; dare prova di, sostanziare

substantive ['sʌbstəntɪv] adj & s sostantivo

substation ['sʌb ,steʃən] s ufficio postale secondario; (elec) sottostazione

substitute ['sʌbstɪ ,tjut] or ['sʌbstɪ ,tut] adj provvisorio, interino || s (thing) sostituto, surrogato; (person) sostituto, supplente mf; **beware of substitutes** guardarsi dalle contraffazioni || tr—**to substitute for** sostituire (qlco or qlcu) a || intr—**to substitute for** sostituire, rimpiazzare, e.g., **he substituted for the teacher** sostituì il maestro

substitution [,sʌbstɪ'tjuʃən] or [,sʌbstɪ'tuʃən] s sostituzione; (by fraud) contraffazione

substra·tum [sʌb'strætəm] s (-ta [tə]) sostrato, substrato

subterfuge ['sʌbtər ,fjudʒ] s sotterfugio

subterranean [,sʌbtə'renɪ·ən] adj & s sotterraneo

subtitle ['sʌb ,taɪtəl] s sottotitolo; (journ) titolo corrente; (mov) didascalia || tr dare una didascalia a

subtle ['sʌtəl] adj sottile

subtle·ty ['sʌtəlti] s (-ties) sottigliezza

subtract [səb'trækt] tr sottrarre

subtraction [sʌb'trækʃən] s sottrazione

suburb ['sʌbʌrb] s suburbio, sobborgo; **the suburbs** la periferia

suburban [sə'bʌrbən] adj suburbano

suburbanite [sə'bʌrbə ,naɪt] s abitante mf dei suburbi

subvention [səb'venʃən] s sovvenzione || tr sovvenzionare

subversive [səb'vʌrsɪv] adj & s sovversivo

subvert [səb'vʌrt] tr sovvertire

subway ['sʌb ,we] s sotterranea, metropolitana, metrovia; sottopassaggio

sub'way sta'tion s stazione della metropolitana

succeed [sək'sid] tr succedere (with dat), subentrare (with dat) || intr riuscire; **to succeed to** (the throne) succedere a

success [sək'sɛs] s successo, riuscita

successful [sək'sɛsfəl] adj felice, fortunato; che ha avuto successo

succession [sək'sɛʃən] s successione; **in succession** in seguito, uno dopo l'altro

successive [sək'sɛsɪv] adj successivo

succor ['sʌkər] s soccorso || tr soccorrere

succotash ['sʌkə ,tæʃ] s verdura di fagioli e granturco

succumb [sə'kʌm] intr soccombere

such [sʌtʃ] adj & pron indef tale, simile; **such a** un simile, un tale; **such**

a + *adj* tanto + *adj*, e.g., **such a beautiful story** una storia tanto bella; **such as** tale quale, come

suck [sʌk] *s* succhio || *tr* succhiare; (*air*) aspirare; **to suck in** (slang) ingannare

sucker ['sʌkər] *s* lattante *mf;* (bot) succhione *m;* (mach) pistone *m;* (coll) fesso, pollo, minchione *m*

suckle ['sʌkəl] *tr* allattare; nutrire || *intr* poppare

suck'ling pig' ['sʌklɪŋ] *s* maiale *m* di latte

suction ['sʌkʃən] *s* aspirazione

suc'tion cup' *s* ventosa

suc'tion pump' *s* pompa aspirante

sudden ['sʌdən] *adj* subito, improvviso; **all of a sudden** all'improvviso

suddenly ['sʌdənli] *adv* all'improvviso

suds [sʌdz] *spl* saponata; schiuma; (coll) birra

sue [su] or [sju] *tr* querelare || *intr* querelarsi; **to sue for damages** chiedere i danni; **to sue for peace** chiedere la pace

suede [swed] *s* pelle scamosciata

suet ['su·ɪt] or ['sju·ɪt] *s* grasso, sego

suffer ['sʌfər] *tr* soffrire; (*e.g., heavy losses*) subire || *intr* soffrire, patire

sufferance ['sʌfərəns] *s* tolleranza

suffering ['sʌfərɪŋ] *adj* sofferente || *s* sofferenza, strazio, patimento

suffice [sə'faɪs] *intr* bastare

sufficient [sə'fɪʃənt] *adj* sufficiente

suffix ['sʌfɪks] *s* suffisso

suffocate ['sʌfə,ket] *tr & intr* soffocare

suffrage ['sʌfrɪdʒ] *s* suffragio

suffragette [,sʌfrə'dʒet] *s* suffragetta

suffuse [sə'fjuz] *tr* soffondere

sugar ['ʃugər] *adj* (*water*) zuccherato; (*industry*) zuccheriero || *s* zucchero || *tr* zuccherare

sug'ar beet' *s* barbabietola da zucchero

sug'ar bowl' *s* zuccheriera

sug'ar cane' *s* canna da zucchero

sug'ar-coat' *tr* inzuccherare; (*e.g., the pill*) addolcire

sug'ar ma'ple *s* acero

sug'ar-plum' *s* zuccherino

sug'ar spoon' *s* cucchiaino per lo zucchero

sug'ar tongs' *spl* mollette *fpl* per lo zucchero

sugary ['ʃugəri] *adj* zuccherino, zuccheroso

suggest [səg'dʒest] *tr* suggerire

suggestion [səg'dʒestʃən] *s* suggerimento; (psychol) suggestione; ombra, traccia

suggestive [səg'dʒestɪv] *adj* suggestivo; (*risqué*) scabroso

suicidal [,su·ɪ'saɪdəl] or [,sju·ɪ'saɪdəl] *adj* suicida

suicide ['su·ɪ,saɪd] or ['sju·ɪ,saɪd] *s* (*person*) suicida *mf;* (*act*) suicidio; **to commit suicide** suicidarsi

suit [sut] or [sjut] *s* vestito da uomo; (*of a lady*) tailleur *m;* (*of cards*) seme *m,* colore *m;* (*for bathing*) costume *m;* corte *f,* corteggiamento; domanda, supplica; (law) causa; **to follow suit** seguire l'esempio; (cards)

rispondere a colore || *tr* adattarsi (with *dat*); convenire (with *dat*); **suit yourself** faccia come vuole || *intr* convenire, andare a proposito

suitable ['sutəbəl] or ['sjutəbəl] *adj* indicato, conveniente

suit'case' *s* valigia

suite [swit] *s* gruppo, serie *f;* serie *f* di stanze; (*of furniture*) mobilia; (*retinue*) seguito; (mus) suite *f*

suiting ['sutɪŋ] or ['sjutɪŋ] *s* taglio d'abito

suit' of clothes' *s* completo maschile

suitor ['sutər] or ['sjutər] *s* pretendente *m;* (law) querelante *mf*

sul'fa drugs' ['sʌlfə] *spl* sulfamidici *mpl*

sulfate ['sʌlfet] *s* solfato

sulfide ['sʌlfaɪd] *s* solfuro

sulfite ['sʌlfaɪt] *s* solfito

sulfur ['sʌlfər] *adj* solfiero || *s* zolfo; color *m* zolfo

sulfuric [sʌl'fjurɪk] *adj* solforico

sul'fur mine' *s* solfara

sulfurous ['sʌlfərəs] *adj* solforoso

sulk [sʌlk] *s* broncio || *intr* imbronciarsi

sulk·y ['sʌlki] *adj* (-ier; -iest) imbronciato ||*s* (-ies) (*in horse racing*) sediolo, sulky *m*

sullen ['sʌlən] *adj* bieco, triste, tetro

sul·ly ['sʌli] *v* (pret & pp -lied) *tr* insudiciare, insozzare

sulphur ['sʌlfər] *adj & s* var of **sulfur**

sultan ['sʌltən] *s* sultano

sul·try ['sʌltri] *adj* (-trier; -triest) soffocante; infocato, appassionato

sum [sʌm] *s* somma; sommario; problema *m* di aritmetica || *v* (pret & pp summed; ger summing) *tr* sommare; **to sum up** riepilogare

sumac or **sumach** ['ʃumæk] or ['sumæk] *s* (bot) sommacco

summarize ['sʌmə,raɪz] *tr* riassumere

summa·ry ['sʌməri] *adj* sommario || *s* (-ries) sommario, sunto

summer ['sʌmər] *adj* estivo || *s* estate *f* || *intr* passare l'estate

sum'mer resort' *s* stazione estiva

summersault ['sʌmər,sɔlt] *s & intr* var of **somersault**

sum'mer school' *s* scuola estiva

summery ['sʌməri] *adj* estivo

summit ['sʌmɪt] *s* sommità *f*

sum'mit con'ference *s* riunione al vertice

summon ['sʌmən] *tr* convocare, invitare; evocare; (law) compulsare

summons ['sʌmənz] *s* ordine *m,* comando; (law) citazione || *tr* (law) citare

sumptuous ['sʌmptʃu·əs] *adj* sontuoso

sun [sʌn] *s* sole *m;* **place in the sun** posto al sole || *v* (pret & pp sunned; ger sunning) *tr* esporre al sole || *intr* prendere il sole

sun' bath' *s* bagno di sole

sun'beam' *s* raggio di sole

sun'burn' *s* abbronzatura || *v* (pret & pp -burned or -burnt) *tr* abbronzare || *intr* abbronzarsi

sundae ['sʌndi] *s* gelato con sciroppo, frutta o noci
Sunday ['sʌndi] *adj* domenicale ‖ *s* domenica
Sun'day best' *s* (coll) vestito da festa
Sun'day's child' *s* bambino nato con la camicia
Sun'day school' *s* scuola domenicale della dottrina
sunder ['sʌndər] *tr* separare
sun'di'al *s* meridiana
sun'down' *s* tramonto
sundries ['sʌndriz] *spl* generi *mpl* diversi
sundry ['sʌndri] *adj* vari, diversi
sun'fish' *s* pesce *m* mola, pesce *m* luna
sun'flow'er *s* girasole *m*
sun'glass'es *spl* occhiali *mpl* da sole
sunken ['sʌŋkən] *adj* affondato, sommerso; (*hollow*) incavato
sun' lamp' *s* sole *m* artificiale
sun'light' *s* luce *f* del sole
sun'lit' *adj* illuminato dal sole
sun·ny ['sʌni] *adj* (**-nier; -niest**) solatio, soleggiato; allegro, ridente; **it is sunny** fa sole
sun'ny side' *s* parte soleggiata; lato buono; **on the sunny side of** (*e.g., thirty*) al disotto dei . . . anni
sun' porch' *s* veranda a solatio
sun'rise' *s* sorgere *m* del sole; **from sunrise to sunset** dall'alba al tramonto
sun'set' *s* tramonto
sun'shade' *s* tenda; parasole *m*
sun'shine' *s* sole *m*, luce *f* del sole; **in the sunshine** al sole
sun'spot' *s* macchia solare
sun'stroke' *s* insolazione
sun' tan' *s* tintarella
sun'tan lo'tion *s* pomata antisole, abbronzante *m*
sun'up' *s* sorgere *m*, levare *m* del sole
sun' vi'sor *s* (aut) aletta parasole, parasole *m*
sup [sʌp] *v* (*pret* & *pp* **supped; ger supping**) *intr* cenare
super ['supər] *adj* (coll) superficiale; (coll) di prim'ordine, super ‖ *s* (coll) sovrintendente *m;* (coll) articolo di prim'ordine, super *m*
superabundant [,supərə'bʌndənt] *adj* sovrabbondante
superannuated [,super'ænju,etɪd] *adj* giubilato, pensionato; messo a riposo per limiti di età; antiquato
superb [su'pʌrb] *or* [sə'pʌrb] *adj* superbo
supercar·go ['supər,kɑrgo] *s* (**-goes**) (naut) sopraccarico
supercharge [,supər'tʃɑrdʒ] *tr* sovralimentare
supercilious [,supər'sɪlɪ·əs] *adj* altero, arrogante
superficial [,supər'fɪʃəl] *adj* superficiale
superfluous [su'pʌrflu·əs] *adj* superfluo
su'per·high'way *s* autostrada
superhuman [,supər'hjumən] *adj* sovrumano
superimpose [,supərɪm'poz] *tr* sovrapporre

superintendent [,supərɪn'tɛndənt] *s* soprintendente *m;* (*of schools*) provveditore *m*
superior [sə'pɪrɪ·ər] *or* [su'pɪrɪ·ər] *adj* superiore; di superiorità; (typ) esponente ‖ *s* superiore *m*
superiority [sə'pɪrɪ'ɑrɪti] *or* [su,pɪrɪ'ɑrɪti] *s* superiorità *f*
superlative [sə'pʌrlətɪv] *or* [su'pʌrlətɪv] *adj* & *s* superlativo
su'per·man' *s* (**-men'**) superuomo
supermarket ['supər,mɑrkɪt] *s* supermercato
supernatural [,supər'nætʃərəl] *adj* soprannaturale
superpose [,supər'poz] *tr* sovrapporre
supersede [,supər'sid] *tr* rimpiazzare, sostituire
supersensitive [,supər'sɛnsɪtɪv] *adj* ipersensibile
supersonic [,supər'sɑnɪk] *adj* supersonico
superstition [,supər'stɪʃən] *s* superstizione
superstitious [,supər'stɪʃəs] *adj* superstizioso
supervene [,supər'vin] *intr* sopravvenire
supervise ['supər,vaɪz] *tr* sorvegliare, dirigere
supervision [,supər'vɪʃən] *s* supervisione, sorveglianza, direzione
supervisor ['supər,vaɪzər] *s* supervisore *m*, sorvegliante *mf;* ispettore *m*
supper ['sʌpər] *s* cena
sup'per·time' *s* ora di cena
supplant [sə'plænt] *tr* rimpiazzare
supple ['sʌpəl] *adj* flessibile; docile
supplement ['sʌplɪmənt] *s* supplemento ‖ ['sʌplɪ,mɛnt] *tr* completare, supplire (with *dat*)
suppliant ['sʌplɪ·ənt] *adj* & *s* supplicante *mf*
supplicant ['sʌplɪkənt] *s* supplicante *mf*
supplication [,sʌplɪ'keʃən] *s* supplica
supplier [sʌ'plaɪ·ər] *s* fornitore *m*
sup·ply [sə'plaɪ] *s* (**-plies**) rifornimento, fornitura; provvista, scorta; (com) offerta; **supplies** rifornimenti *mpl*, vettovaglie *fpl* ‖ *v* (*pret* & *pp* **-plied**) *tr* fornire, provvedere; (*food*) vettovagliare
supply' and demand' *s* domanda ed offerta
support [sə'port] *s* sostegno, appoggio; puntello, rincalzo; mantenimento ‖ *tr* sostenere, appoggiare; puntellare; (*a cause*) caldeggiare; mantenere
supporter [sə'portər] *s* fautore *m*, sostenitore *m;* (*jockstrap*) sospensorio; giarrettiera; fascia elastica
suppose [sə'poz] *tr* supporre; ammettere; **suppose we take a walk?** che ne dice se facessimo una passeggiata?; **to be supposed to be** aver fama di essere; **to suppose so** credere di sì
supposed [sə'pozd] *adj* presunto
supposition [,sʌpə'zɪʃən] *s* supposizione
supposito·ry [sə'pɑzɪ,tori] *s* (**-ries**) suppositorio, supposta
suppress [sə'prɛs] *tr* sopprimere

suppression [sə'prɛʃən] s soppressione
suppurate ['sʌpjə,ret] intr suppurare
supreme [sə'prim] or [su'prim] adj supremo, sommo
Supreme' Court' s (in Italy) Corte f di Cassazione; (in U.S.A.) tribunale m di ultima istanza
surcharge ['sʌr,tʃardʒ] s soprapprezzo; soprattassa; sovraccarico; (philately) sovrastampa || [,sʌr'tʃardʒ] or ['sʌr,tʃardʒ] tr sovraccaricare
sure [ʃur] adj sicuro; **to be sure!** certamente!, senza dubbio! || interj (coll) certamente!; **sure enough!** (coll) difatti
sure-footed ['sjur'futɪd] adj dal piede sicuro
sure' thing' s (coll) successo garantito || adv (coll) certamente || interj (coll) di sicuro!
sure•ty ['ʃurti] or ['ʃurɪti] s (-ties) malleveria
surf [sʌrf] s frangente m
surface ['sʌrfɪs] adj superficiale || s superficie f || tr rifinire; spianare; ricoprire || intr emergere
sur'face mail' s posta ordinaria
surf'board' s tavola per il surfing
surfeit ['sʌrfɪt] s eccesso; sazietà f || tr saziare, rimpinzare || intr saziarsi, rimpinzarsi
surf'ing s surfing m
surge [sʌrdʒ] s ondata; fiotto; (elec) sovratensione || intr ondeggiare, fluttuare; (said, e.g., of a crowd) affluire
surgeon ['sʌrdʒən] s (medico) chirurgo
surger•y ['sʌrdʒəri] s (-ies) chirurgia; sala operatoria
surgical ['sʌrdʒɪkəl] adj chirurgico
sur•ly ['sʌrli] adj (-lier; -liest) arcigno, imbronciato
surmise [sər'maɪz] or ['sʌrmaɪz] s congettura, supposizione || [sər'maɪz] tr & intr congetturare, supporre
surmount [sər'maunt] tr sormontare; coronare
surname ['sʌr,nem] s cognome m; (added name) soprannome m || tr dare il cognome a; soprannominare
surpass [sər'pæs] or [sər'pɑs] tr sorpassare, superare
surplice ['sʌrplɪs] s cotta
surplus ['sʌrplʌs] adj eccedente || s sopravanzo, eccedenza
surprise [sər'praɪz] adj insperato, improvviso || s sorpresa || tr sorprendere
surprise' par'ty s improvvisata
surprising [sər'praɪzɪŋ] adj sorprendente
surrender [sə'rɛndər] s resa || tr arrendere || intr arrendersi
surren'der val'ue s (ins) valore m di riscatto
surreptitious [,sʌrep'tɪʃəs] adj clandestino, nascosto, furtivo
surround [sə'raund] tr circondare, contornare; (mil) aggirare
surrounding [sə'raundɪŋ] adj circostante, circonvicino || **surroundings** spl dintorni mpl; ambiente m

surtax ['sʌr,tæks] s sovrimposta, soprattassa; imposta complementare
surveillance [sər'veləns] or [sər'veljəns] s sorveglianza, vigilanza
survey ['sʌrve] s quadro generale, schizzo; indagine f; (of opinion) sondaggio; rapporto; rilievo topografico; perizia || [sʌr've] or ['sʌrve] tr fare un'indagine di; sondare; rilevare; misurare || intr fare un rilievo
sur'vey course' s corso di rassegna generale
surveyor [sər've·ər] s livellatore m, geometra m
survival [sər'vaɪvəl] s sopravvivenza
survive [sər'vaɪv] tr sopravvivere (with dat) || intr sopravvivere
surviving [sər'vaɪvɪŋ] adj superstite
survivor [sər'vaɪvər] s sopravvissuto, superstite mf
survivorship [sər'vaɪvər,ʃɪp] s (law) sopravvivenza
susceptible [sə'sɛptɪbəl] adj suscettibile, ricettivo; impressionabile; **susceptible to** (e.g., colds) soggetto a
suspect ['sʌspɛkt] or [səs'pɛkt] adj sospetto || ['sʌspɛkt] s sospetto || [səs'pɛkt] tr sospettare
suspend [səs'pɛnd] tr sospendere || intr essere sospeso; fermarsi; fermare i pagamenti
suspenders [səs'pɛndərz] spl bretelle fpl
suspense [səs'pɛns] s sospensione; sospeso; **in suspense** in sospeso
suspen'sion bridge' [səs'pɛnʃən] s ponte sospeso
suspicion [səs'pɪʃən] s sospetto
suspicious [səs'pɪʃəs] adj (subject to suspicion) sospetto; (inclined to suspect) sospettoso
sustain [səs'ten] tr sostenere, sorreggere; (with food) sostentare; (a conversation) mantenere; (a loss) soffrire; (law) confermare
sustenance ['sʌstɪnəns] s sostentamento
sutler ['sʌtlər] s (mil) vivandiere m
swab [swab] s (mil) scovolo; (naut) redazza; (surg) batufolo di cotone || v (pret & pp swabbed; ger swabbing) tr pulire con la redazza; spugnare; assorbire col cotone
swaddle ['swadəl] tr fasciare
swad'dling clothes' spl fasce fpl del neonato
swagger ['swægər] s spavalderia || intr fare lo spavaldo
swain [swen] s innamorato; (lad) contadinotto
swallow ['swalo] s (of liquid) sorso; (of food) boccone m; (orn) rondine f || tr & intr tranguiare, inghiottire
swal'low-tailed coat' ['swalo,teld] s frac m, marsina, abito a coda di rondine
swal'low-wort' s vincetossico
swamp [swamp] s pantano, palude f || tr inondare, sommergere
swamp•y ['swampi] adj (-ier; -iest) paludoso, pantanoso
swan [swan] s cigno
swan' dive' s volo dell'angelo

swank [swæŋk] *adj* (coll) elegante, vistoso || *s* (coll) eleganza vistosa

swan's-down ['swɑnz‚daun] *s* piuma di cigno, piumino; mollettone *m*

swan' song' *s* canto del cigno

swap [swɑp] *s* scambio, baratto || *v* (*pret* & *pp* swapped; *ger* swapping) *tr* & *intr* scambiare, barattare

swarm [swɔrm] *s* sciame *m* || *intr* sciamare; (fig) formicolare

swarth·y ['swɔrði] or ['swɔrθi] *adj* (-ier; -iest) olivastro, abbronzato

swashbuckler ['swɑʃ‚bʌklər] *s* spadaccino, rodomonte *m*

swat [swɑt] *s* colpo || *v* (*pret* & *pp* swatted; *ger* swatting) *tr* colpire; (*a fly*) schiacciare

sway [swe] *s* dondolio, ondeggiamento; dominio || *tr* dondolare, fare oscillare; influenzare; dominare || *intr* dondolarsi, ondulare; oscillare

swear [swɛr] *v* (*pret* swore [swor]; *pp* sworn [sworn]) *tr* giurare; (*to secrecy*) fare giurare; **to swear in** fare prestar giuramento a; **to swear off** giurare di rinunziare a; **to swear out a warrant** ottenere un atto di accusa sotto giuramento || *intr* giurare; (*to blaspheme*) bestemmiare; **to swear at** maledire; **to swear by** giurare su, avere certezza di; **to swear to** dichiarare sotto giuramento; giurare di + *inf*

swear'word' *s* bestemmia, parolaccia

sweat [swɛt] *s* sudata; sudore *m* || *v* (*pret* & *pp* sweat or sweated) *tr* sudare; far sudare; **to sweat it out** (slang) farcela fino alla fine; **to sweat off** (*weight*) perdere sudando || *intr* sudare

sweater ['swɛtər] *s* maglione *m*, golf *m*, sweater *m*

sweat' shirt' *s* maglione *m* da ginnastica

sweat·y ['swɛti] *adj* (-ier; -iest) sudato; che fa sudare

Swede [swid] *s* svedese *mf*

Sweden ['swidən] *s* la Svezia

Swedish ['swidɪʃ] *adj* & *s* svedese *m*

sweep [swip] *s* scopata; movimento circolare; estensione; curva; (*of wind*) soffio; (*of well*) mazzacavallo; **to make a clean sweep of** far piazza pulita di || *v* (*pret* & *pp* swept [swɛpt]) *tr* spazzare, scopare; percorrere con lo sguardo; (*eyes*) dirigere; travolgere || *intr* scopare; passare; estendersi; dragare

sweeper ['swipər] *s* spazzino; (*machine*) spazzatrice *f*; (nav) dragamine *m*

sweeping ['swipɪŋ] *adj* esteso; travolgente, decisivo || **sweepings** *spl* spazzatura

sweep'-sec'ond *s* lancetta dei secondi a perno centrale

sweep'stakes' *ssg* or *spl* lotteria abbinata alle corse dei cavalli

sweet [swit] *adj* dolce; (*butter*) senza sale; (*cider*) analcolico; **to be sweet on** (coll) essere innamorato di ||

sweets *spl* dolci *mpl*; (coll) patate *fpl* dolci || *adv* dolcemente; **to smell sweet** saper di buono

sweet'bread' *s* animella

sweet'bri'er *s* eglantina

sweeten ['switən] *tr* inzuccherare; raddolcire; purificare || *intr* raddolcirsi; purificarsi

sweet'heart' *s* innamorato; innamorata; caro, amore *m*

sweet' mar'joram *s* maggiorana

sweet'meats' *spl* dolci *mpl*, confetti *mpl*

sweet' pea' *s* pisello odoroso

sweet' pota'to *s* batata, patata americana; (mus) ocarina

sweet-scented ['swit‚sɛntɪd] *adj* odoroso, profumato

sweet' tooth' *s* debole *m* per i dolci

sweet-toothed ['swit‚tuθt] *adj* goloso

sweet' wil'liam *s* garofano barbuto

swell [swɛl] *adj* (slang) elegante; (slang) eccellente, di prim'ordine || *s* gonfiore *m;* onda, ondata; aumento; (mus) crescendo; (slang) elegantone *m* || *v* (*pret* swelled; *pp* swelled or swollen ['swolən]) *tr* gonfiare, ingrossare; aumentare || *intr* gonfiare, ingrossarsi; aumentare; (*said of the sea*) alzarsi; (*with pride*) montarsi

swelled' head' *s* borioso; **to have a swelled head** montarsi, essere pieno di sé

swelter ['swɛltər] *intr* soffocare dal caldo

swept'back wing' *s* ala a freccia

swerve [swʌrv] *s* scarto, sbandamento || *tr* sviare || *intr* scartare, sbandare

swift [swɪft] *adj* rapido || *s* rondone *m* || *adv* rapidamente

swig [swɪg] *s* (coll) sorso || *v* (*pret* & *pp* swigged; *ger* swigging) *tr* & *intr* (coll) bere a grandi sorsi

swill [swɪl] *s* imbratto; risciacquatura || *tr* tracannare, trincare || *intr* bere a lunghi sorsi

swim [swɪm] *s* nuoto; **the swim** (*in social activities*) la corrente || *v* (*pret* swam [swæm]; *pp* swum [swʌm]; *ger* swimming) *tr* traversare a nuoto || *intr* nuotare; essere inondato; (*said of one's head*) girare, e.g., **her head is swimming** le gira la testa

swimmer ['swɪmər] *s* nuotatore *m*

swimming ['swɪmɪŋ] *s* nuoto

swim'ming pool' *s* piscina

swim'ming trunks' *spl* mutandine *fpl* da bagno

swim'suit' *s* costume *m* da bagno

swindle ['swɪndəl] *s* truffa, imbroglio || *tr* truffare, imbrogliare

swine [swaɪn] *s* suino, maiale *m*, porco; **swine** *spl* suini *mpl*

swing [swɪŋ] *s* oscillazione; dondolio; curva; (*suspended seat*) altalena; alternarsi *m;* piena attività; (boxing) sventola; (mus) swing *m;* **free swing** libertà *f* d'azione; **in full swing** (coll) in piena attività || *v* (*pret* & *pp* swung [swʌŋ]) *tr* (*e.g., one's arms*) dondolare, oscillare; (*a weapon*) brandire; (*e.g., a club*) rotare; far girare; appendere; (*a deal*) (coll) riuscire ad ottenere ‖ *intr* dondolare, dondolarsi, oscillare; girare; essere sospeso; cambiare; (boxing) dare una sventola; **to swing open** aprirsi di colpo

swing'ing door' ['swɪŋɪŋ] *s* porta oscillante

swinish ['swaɪnɪʃ] *adj* porcino

swipe [swaɪp] *s* (coll) colpo forte ‖ *tr* (coll) dare un forte colpo a; (slang) portare via, rubare

swirl [swʌrl] *s* turbine *m*, vortice *m* ‖ *tr* far girare ‖ *intr* turbinare

swirling ['swʌrlɪŋ] *adj* vorticoso

swish [swɪʃ] *s* (*of whip*) schiocco; (*of silk*) fruscio ‖ *tr* (*a whip*) schioccare; ‖ *intr* schioccare; frusciare

Swiss [swɪs] *adj* svizzero ‖ *s* svizzero; **the Swiss** gli svizzeri

Swiss' chard' [tʃard] *s* bietola

Swiss' cheese' *s* groviera

Swiss' Guards' *spl* guardie *fpl* svizzere

switch [swɪtʃ] *s* verga; vergata; (*false hair*) posticcio; cambio, trapasso; (elec) interruttore *m*; (rr) scambio ‖ *tr* battere, frustare; (elec) commutare; (rr) deviare; (fig) girare; **to switch off** (*light, radio, etc.*) spegnere; **to switch on** (*light, radio, etc.*) accendere ‖ *intr* fustigare; cambiare; (rr) deviare

switch'back' *s* strada a zigzag; (rr) tracciato a zigzag

switch'blade knife' *s* coltello a serramanico

switch'board' *s* quadro

switch'board op'erator *s* centralinista *mf*

switch'ing en'gine *s* locomotiva da manovra

switch'man *s* (-men) deviatore *m*

switch'yard' *s* stazione smistamento

Switzerland ['swɪtsərlənd] *s* la Svizzera

swiv·el ['swɪvəl] *s* perno, gancio girevole ‖ *v* (*pret & pp* -eled or -elled; *ger* -eling or -elling) *intr* girare

swiv'el chair' *s* sedia girevole

swoon [swun] *s* deliquio, svenimento ‖ *intr* svenire

swoop [swup] *s* calata a piombo ‖ *intr* calare a piombo, piombare

sword [sord] *s* spada; **at swords' points** pronti a incrociare le spade; **to put to the sword** passare a fil di spada

sword' belt' *s* cinturone *m*

sword' cane' *s* bastone animato

sword'fish' *s* pesce *m* spada

swords'man *s* (-men) spadaccino

sword' swal'lower ['swɑlo·ər] *s* giocoliere *m* che ingoia spade

sword' thrust' *s* stoccata

sworn [sworn] *adj* giurato

sycophant ['sɪkəfənt] *s* adulatore *m*; parassita *mf*

syllable ['sɪləbəl] *s* sillaba

sylla·bus ['sɪləbəs] *s* (-bi [ˌbaɪ]) sillabo, sommario scolastico

syllogism ['sɪləˌdʒɪzəm] *s* sillogismo

sylph [sɪlf] *s* silfo; silfide *f;* (fig) silfide *f*

sylvan ['sɪlvən] *adj* silvano

symbol ['sɪmbəl] *s* simbolo

symbolic(al) [sɪm'bɑlɪk(əl)] *adj* simbolico

symbolism ['sɪmbəˌlɪzəm] *s* simbolismo

symbolize ['sɪmbəˌlaɪz] *tr* simboleggiare

symmetric(al) [sɪ'mɛtrɪk(əl)] *adj* simmetrico

symme·try ['sɪmɪtri] *s* (-tries) simmetria

sympathetic [ˌsɪmpə'θɛtɪk] *adj* simpatetico; ben disposto

sympathize ['sɪmpəˌθaɪz] *intr*—**to sympathize with** aver compassione di; mostrar comprensione per; (*to be in accord with*) simpatizzare con

sympa·thy ['sɪmpəθi] *s* (-thies) compassione, commiserazione; **to be in sympathy with** essere d'accordo con; **to extend one's sympathy to** fare le condoglianze a

sym'pathy strike' *s* sciopero di solidarietà

symphonic [sɪm'fɑnɪk] *adj* sinfonico

sympho·ny ['sɪmfəni] *s* (-nies) sinfonia

symposi·um [sɪm'pozɪ·əm] *s* (-a [ə]) simposio, colloquio

symptom ['sɪmptəm] *s* sintomo

synagogue ['sɪnəˌgɔg] or ['sɪnəˌgɑg] *s* sinagoga

synchronize ['sɪŋkrəˌnaɪz] *tr & intr* sincronizzare

synchronous ['sɪŋkrənəs] *adj* sincrono

sincopation [ˌsɪŋkə'peʃən] *s* sincope *f*

syncope ['sɪŋkəˌpi] *s* (phonet) sincope *f*

syndicate ['sɪndɪkɪt] *s* sindacato ‖ ['sɪndɪˌket] *tr* organizzare in un sindacato

synonym ['sɪnənɪm] *s* sinonimo

synonymous [sɪ'nɑnɪməs] *adj* sinonimo

synop·sis [sɪ'nɑpsɪs] *s* (-ses [siz]) sinossi *f;* (mov) sinopsi *f*

synoptic(al) [sɪ'nɑptɪk(əl)] *adj* sinottico

syntax ['sɪntæks] *s* sintassi *f*

synthe·sis ['sɪnθɪsɪs] *s* (-ses [ˌsiz]) sintesi *f*

synthesize ['sɪnθɪˌsaɪz] *tr* sintetizzare

synthetic(al) [sɪn'θɛtɪk(əl)] *adj* sintetico

syphilis ['sɪfɪlɪs] *s* sifilide *f*

Syria ['sɪrɪ·ə] *s* la Siria

Syrian ['sɪrɪ·ən] *adj & s* siriano

syringe [sɪ'rɪndʒ] or ['sɪrɪndʒ] *s* (*fountain syringe*) schizzetto; (*for hypodermic injections*) siringa ‖ *tr* schizzettare; iniettare

syrup ['sɪrəp] or ['sʌrəp] *s* sciroppo

system ['sɪstəm] *s* sistema *m*

systematic(al) [ˌsɪstə'mætɪk(əl)] *adj* sistematico

systematize ['sɪstəməˌtaɪz] *tr* ridurre a sistema

systole ['sɪstəli] *s* sistole *f*

T

T, t [ti] *s* ventesima lettera dell'alfabeto inglese; **to fit to a T** calzare come un guanto

tab [tæb] *s* (*strap*) linguetta; (*of a pocket*) patta; targa; (*label*) etichetta; **to keep tabs on** (coll) sorvegliare; **to pick up the tab** (coll) pagare il conto

tab·by ['tæbi] *s* (**-bies**) gatto tigrato; gatta; (*spinster*) zitella; vecchia pettegola

tabernacle ['tæbər‚nækəl] *s* tabernacolo

table ['tebəl] *s* tavola; (*food*) mensa; (*people at a table*) tavolata; (*synopsis*) quadro, prospetto; (*list or catalogue*) indice *m;* **to turn the tables** rovesciare la posizione; **under the table** ubriaco fradicio ‖ *tr* aggiornare, rinviare

tab·leau ['tæblo] *s* (**-leaus** or **-leaux** [loz]) quadro vivente

ta'ble·cloth' *s* tovaglia

table d'hôte ['tɑbəl'dot] *s* pasto a prezzo fisso

tableful ['tebəl‚fʊl] *s* (*persons*) tavolata; (*food*) tavola apparecchiata

ta'ble·land' *s* tavoliere *m*

ta'ble lin'en *s* biancheria da tavola

ta'ble man'ners *spl* maniere *fpl* a tavola

ta'ble of con'tents *s* indice *m* delle materie

ta'ble·spoon' *s* cucchiaio

tablespoonful ['tebəl‚spun‚fʊl] *s* cucchiaiata

tablet ['tæblɪt] *s* (*writing pad*) blocco; (*slab*) lapide *f;* (*flat rigid sheet*) tabella, tavoletta; (pharm) disco, pastiglia

ta'ble talk' *s* conversazione familiare a tavola

ta'ble ten'nis *s* ping-pong *m*, tennis *m* da tavolo

ta'ble·ware' *s* servizio da tavola

ta'ble wine' *s* vino da pasto

tabloid ['tæblɔɪd] *s* giornale *m* a carattere sensazionale

taboo [tə'bu] *adj & s* tabù *m* ‖ *tr* proibire assolutamente

tabulate ['tæbjə‚let] *tr* tabulare

tabulator ['tæbjə‚letər] *s* tabulatore *m*, incolonnatore *m*

tachometer [tə'kɑmɪtər] *s* tachimetro

tacit ['tæsɪt] *adj* tacito

taciturn ['tæsɪ‚tʌrn] *adj* taciturno

tack [tæk] *s* bulletta; cambio di direzione; (naut) virata; (sew) imbastitura ‖ *tr* imbullettare; attaccare; (naut) bordeggiare; (sew) imbastire ‖ *intr* virare; mutare di direzione

tackle ['tækəl] *s* attrezzatura; (mach) taglia, paranco; (*gear*) (naut) padiglione *m* ‖ *tr* attaccare, affrontare; (sports) placcare, bloccare

tack·y ['tæki] *adj* (**-ier; -iest**) appiccicaticcio; (coll) trasandato

tact [tækt] *s* tatto

tactful ['tæktfəl] *adj* pieno di tatto

tactical ['tæktɪkəl] *adj* tattico

tactician [tæk'tɪʃən] *s* tattico

tactics ['tæktɪks] *ssg* (mil) tattica ‖ *spl* tattica

tactless ['tæktlɪs] *adj* che non ha tatto, indiscreto

tadpole ['tæd‚pol] *s* girino

taffeta ['tæfɪtə] *s* taffettà *m*

taffy ['tæfi] *s* caramella, zucchero d'orzo; (coll) lisciata

tag [tæg] *s* etichetta; (*on a shoelace*) punta dell'aghetto; conclusione; (*last words of speech*) pistolotto finale; epiteto; frase fatta; (*of hair*) ciocca; (*in writing*) ghirigoro; (*game*) toccaferro ‖ *v* (*pret & pp* **tagged;** *ger* **tagging**) *tr* etichettare; (*to fine*) multare; aggiungere; soprannominare; accusare; stabilire il prezzo di; (coll) pedinare ‖ *intr* seguire da presso

tag' end' *s* (*e.g., of day*) fine *f;* estremità logorata; avanzo

tail [tel] *adj* di coda ‖ *s* coda; fine *f;* (*of coin*) croce *f;* **tails** falde *fpl,* frac *m;* **to turn tails** darsela a gambe ‖ *tr* attaccare; finire; (coll) pedinare

tail' assem'bly *s* (aer) impennaggio

tail' end' *s* coda, fine *f*

tail'light' *s* fanale *m* di coda

tailor ['telər] *s* sarto ‖ *tr* (*a suit*) tagliare, confezionare; (*one's conduct*) adattare ‖ *intr* fare il sarto

tailoring ['telərɪŋ] *s* sartoria

tai'lor-made' *adj* fatto su misura

tai'lor shop' *s* sartoria

tail'piece' *s* coda, estremità *f;* (mus) cordiera; (typ) fusello finale

tail'race' *s* canale *m* di scarico

tail'spin' *s* avvitamento

tail'wind' *s* (aer) vento di coda; (naut) vento in poppa

taint [tent] *s* macchia; infezione ‖ *tr* macchiare, infettare, corrompere

take [tek] *s* presa; (*of fish*) retata; (mov) presa; ripresa; (slang) incasso ‖ *v* (*pret* **took** [tʊk]; *pp* **taken**) *tr* prendere, pigliare; ricevere, accettare; portare; (*to get by force*) portar via; (*a nap*) schiacciare; (*a bath*) fare; (*a joke*) stare a; (*an examination*) sostenere; (*one's own life*) togliersi; (*to deduct*) cavare; (*a purchase*) comprare; (*to convey*) portare; (*time*) impiegare; (*a step, a walk*) fare; (*a subject*) studiare; (*a responsibility, role, etc.*) assumere; (*an oath*) prestare; (*root*) mettere; (*exception*) sollevare; credere; (*e.g., a photograph*) fare, scattare; (slang) fregare; **it takes** ci vuole, ci vogliono; **to take amiss** prendere a male; **to take apart** scomporre; smontare; **to take back** riprendere; **to take down** abbassare; smontare; prender nota di; **to take for** prendere per; **to take from** portar via a; **to take in** (*to admit*) ammettere, ricevere; (*to encompass*) includere; (*a dress*) restringere; (*to cheat*) ingannare; (*water*) fare; (*a point of inter-*

est) visitare; **to take it** accettare, ammettere; (slang) resistere; **to take off** (*e.g., one's coat*) togliersi; portar via; scontare, defalcare; (slang) imitare; **to take on** ingaggiare; assumere; intraprendere; accettare la sfida di; **to take out** cavare, togliere; (*e.g., a girl*) portar fuori; (*e.g., a patent*) ottenere; **to take over** rilevare; (slang) imbrogliare; **to take place** aver luogo; **to take s.o.'s eye** attrarre l'attenzione di qlcu; **to take the place of** sottentrare a; **to take up** cominciare a studiare; sollevare, tirar su; (*a duty*) assumere; (*time, space*) occupare || *intr* prendere; scattare; darsi; diventare; **to take after** rassomigliare a; **to take off** (coll) partire, andarsene; (aer) decollare, involare; **to take up with** (coll) fare amicizia con; (coll) vivere con; **to take well** riuscire bene in fotografia
take′off′ *s* parodia; (aer) decollaggio; (mach) presa di forza
tal′cum pow′der ['tælkəm] *s* talco
tale [tel] *s* storia, racconto; favola, fiaba; (*lie*) bugia, frottola; (*piece of gossip*) maldicenza
tale′bear′er *s* pettegolo
talent ['tælənt] *s* talento; persona di talento; gente *f* di talento
talented ['tæləntɪd] *adj* dotato di talento, dotato d'ingegno
tal′ent scout′ *s* scopritore *m* di talenti
talk [tɔk] *s* chiacchierata; discorso, conferenza; (*language*) parlata; (*gossip*) pettegolezzo; **to cause talk** originare pettegolezzi || *tr* parlare; convincere parlando; **to talk up** elogiare || *intr* parlare; discutere; **to talk on** discutere; continuare a parlare; **to talk up** parlare apertamente
talkative ['tɔkətɪv] *adj* loquace
talker ['tɔkər] *s* parlatore *m*
talkie ['tɔki] *s* (coll) parlato
talk′ing machine′ *s* grammofono
talk′ing pic′ture *s* film parlato
tall [tɔl] *adj* alto; (coll) stravagante, esagerato
tallow ['tælo] *s* sego
tal·ly ['tæli] *s* (-lies) tacca, taglia || *v* (*pret & pp* -lied) *tr* contare, registrare || *intr* riscontrare
tal′ly sheet′ *s* foglio di spunta
talon ['tælən] *s* artiglio
tambourine [,tæmbə'rin] *s* tamburello
tame [tem] *adj* addomesticato; docile, mansueto; mite || *tr* addomesticare; domare; (*water power*) captare
tamp [tæmp] *tr* pigiare, comprimere; (*e.g., ground*) costipare
tamper ['tæmpər] *s* (*person*) pigiatore *m*; (*tool*) mazzeranga || *intr* intrigare; **to tamper with** (*a lock*) forzare; (*a document*) manomettere; (*a witness*) corrompere
tampon ['tæmpɑn] *s* (surg) tampone *m* || *tr* (surg) tamponare
tan [tæn] *adj* marrone; (*by sun*) abbronzato || *v* (*pret & pp* **tanned**; *ger* **tanning**) *tr* (*leather*) conciare; ab-

bronzare; (coll) picchiare, sculacciare
tandem ['tændəm] *adj & adv* in tandem || *s* tandem *m*
tang [tæŋ] *s* sapore *m* piccante; odore *m* forte; traccia; (*of knife*) tallone *m*; (*sound*) tintinnio
tangent ['tændʒənt] *adj* tangente || *s* tangente *f*; **to fly off at a tangent** cambiare improvvisamente d'idea
tangerine [,tændʒə'rin] *s* mandarino
tangible ['tændʒɪbəl] *adj* tangibile
Tangier [tæn'dʒɪr] *s* Tangeri *f*
tangle ['tæŋgəl] *s* intrico; (coll) litigio || *tr* intricare || *intr* intricarsi; (coll) litigare
tank [tæŋk] *s* conserva, serbatoio; (mil) carro armato
tankard ['tæŋkərd] *s* boccale *m*
tank′ car′ *s* (rr) carro botte
tanker ['tæŋkər] *s* petroliera; (aer) aerocisterna
tank′ farm′ing *s* idroponica
tank′ truck′ *s* autocisterna
tanner ['tænər] *s* conciapelli *m*
tanner·y ['tænəri] *s* (-ies) conceria
tantalize ['tæntə,laɪz] *tr* stuzzicare con vane promesse
tantamount ['tæntə,maunt] *adj* equivalente
tantrum ['tæntrəm] *s* bizze *fpl*
tap [tæp] *s* colpetto, buffetto; (*in a keg*) spina, cannella; (*faucet*) rubinetto; (elec) presa; (mach) maschio; **on tap** alla spina; (coll) disponibile; **taps** (mil) silenzio || *v* (*pret & pp* **tapped**; *ger* **tapping**) *tr* battere; picchiare, picchiettare; (*from a barrel*) spillare; mettere il cannello a; (*resources*) usare; (*a telephone*) intercettare; (*water, electricity*) derivare; (mach) maschiare || *intr* picchiare
tap′ dance′ *s* tip tap *m*
tap′-dance′ *intr* ballare il tip tap
tape [tep] *s* nastro; (sports) striscione *m* del traguardo || *tr* legare con nastro; misurare col metro a nastro; registrare su nastro magnetico
tape′ meas′ure *s* metro a nastro; nastro per misurare
tape′ play′er *s* riproduttore *m* a nastro magnetico
taper ['tepər] *s* cerino || *tr* affusolare || *intr* affusolarsi; **to taper off** rastremarsi; diminuire in intensità; diminuire a poco a poco
tape′-re·cord′ *tr* registrare su nastro magnetico
tape′ record′er *s* magnetofono, registratore *m* a nastro
tapes·try ['tæpɪstri] *s* (-tries) tappezzeria || *v* (*pret & pp* -tried) *tr* tappezzare
tape′worm′ *s* verme solitario, tenia
tappet ['tæpɪt] *s* (aut) punteria
tap′room′ *s* taverna, osteria
tap′root′ *s* radice *f* a fittone
tap′ wa′ter *s* acqua corrente
tap′ wrench′ *s* giramaschio
tar [tɑr] *s* catrame *m* || *v* (*pret & pp* **tarred**; *ger* **tarring**) *tr* incatramare

tar·dy [ˈtɑrdi] *adj* (**-dier; -diest**) in ritardo; lento

tare [ter] *s* tara ‖ *tr* tarare

target [ˈtɑrgɪt] *s* segno, bersaglio

tar'get date' *s* data progettata

tar'get lan'guage *s* lingua obbiettivo, lingua di arrivo

tar'get prac'tice *s* esercizio di tiro a segno

tariff [ˈtærɪf] *s* (*duties*) tariffa doganale; (*charge or fare*) tariffa

tarnish [ˈtɑrnɪʃ] *s* ossidazione; (fig) macchia ‖ *tr* appannare ‖ *intr* appannarsi, perdere il lustro

tar'pa'per *s* carta catramata

tarpaulin [tɑrˈpɔlɪn] *s* telone *m* impermeabile incatramato

tarragon [ˈtærəgən] *s* dragoncello

tar·ry [ˈtɑri] *adj* incatramato ‖ [ˈtæri] *v* (*pret & pp* **-ried**) *intr* rimanere; ritardare

tart [tɑrt] *adj* acido, pungente ‖ *s* torta; (slang) puttana

tartar [ˈtɑrtər] *s* tartaro; cremore *m* di tartaro; (*shrew*) megera; **to catch a tartar** imbattersi in un muso duro

Tartarus [ˈtɑrtərəs] *s* Tartaro

task [tæsk] *or* [tɑsk] *s* compito, incarico; **to take to task** rimproverare

task' force' *s* gruppo formato per una missione speciale

task'mas'ter *s* sorvegliante *m;* sorvegliante severo

tassel [ˈtæsəl] *s* nappa; (bot) ciuffo

taste [test] *s* gusto, sapore *m;* buon gusto; (*sampling, e.g., of wine*) assaggio; esperienza; **to one's taste** a genio di qlcu ‖ *tr* gustare, assaggiare ‖ *intr* sentire, sapere; **to taste of** degustare; sapere di

tasteless [ˈtestlɪs] *adj* insipido; di cattivo gusto

tast·y [ˈtesti] *adj* (**-ier; -iest**) saporito; (coll) di buon gusto

tatter [ˈtætər] *s* brandello, sbrendolo ‖ *tr* sbrindellare

tattered [ˈtætərd] *adj* sbrindellato

tattle [ˈtætəl] *s* chiacchiera; (*gossip*) pettegolezzo ‖ *intr* chiacchierare; spettegolare

tat'tle-tale' *adj* rivelatore ‖ *s* gazzetta, chiacchierone *m*

tattoo [tæˈtu] *s* tatuaggio; (mil) ritirata ‖ *tr* tatuare

taunt [tɔnt] *or* [tɑnt] *s* rimprovero sarcastico, insulto ‖ *tr* rimproverare sarcasticamente, insultare

Taurus [ˈtɔrəs] *s* (astr) Toro

taut [tɔt] *adj* teso, tirato

tavern [ˈtævərn] *s* osteria

taw·dry [ˈtɔdri] *adj* (**-drier; -driest**) vistoso, sgargiante, pacchiano

taw·ny [ˈtɔni] *adj* (**-nier; -niest**) falbo, fulvo

tax [tæks] *s* tassa, imposta ‖ *tr* tassare; (*s.o.'s patience*) mettere a dura prova

taxable [ˈtæksəbəl] *adj* tassabile

tax'able in'come *s* imponibile *m*

taxation [tækˈseʃən] *s* imposizione, tassazione, contribuzione

tax' collec'tor *s* esattore *m* delle imposte

tax' deduc'tion *s* detrazione

tax'-ex·empt' *adj* esente da tasse

tax' evad'er [ɪˈvedər] *s* evasore *m*

tax·i [ˈtæksi] *s* (**-is**) tassì *m* ‖ *v* (*pret & pp* **-ied**; *ger* **-iing** *or* **-ying**) *tr* far rullare ‖ *intr* andare in tassì; (aer) rullare

tax'i·cab' *s* tassì *m*

tax'i driv'er *s* tassista *m*

tax'i·plane' *s* aeroplano da noleggio, aerotassì *m*

taxi' stand' *s* posteggio di tassì

tax'pay'er *s* contribuente *mf*

tax' rate' *s* imponibilità *f*

tea [ti] *s* tè *m;* (*medicinal infusion*) tisana; (*beef broth*) brodo di carne

tea' bag' *s* sacchetto di tè

tea' ball' *s* uovo da tè

tea'cart' *s* servitore *m*

teach [titʃ] *v* (*pret & pp* **taught** [tɔt]) *tr & intr* insegnare

teacher [ˈtitʃər] *s* maestro, insegnante *mf*

teach'ers col'lege *s* scuola magistrale

teach'er's pet' *s* beniamino del maestro

teaching [ˈtitʃɪŋ] *adj* insegnante ‖ *s* insegnamento, dottrina

teach'ing aids' *spl* sussidi *mpl* didattici

teach'ing staff' *s* corpo insegnante

tea'cup' *s* tazza da tè

tea' dance' *s* tè *m* danzante

teak [tik] *s* tek *m*

tea'ket'tle *s* bricco del tè

team [tim] *s* (*e.g., of horses*) pariglia; (sports) squadra, equipaggio ‖ *tr* apparigliare; tirare *or* trasportare con pariglia ‖ *intr*—**to team up** unirsi, associarsi

team'mate' *s* compagno di squadra

teamster [ˈtimstər] *s* (*of horses*) carrettiere *m;* (*of truck*) camionista *m*, autotrenista *m*

team'work' *s* affiatamento, collaborazione

tea'pot' *s* teiera

tear [tɪr] *s* lacrima; **to hold back one's tears** ingoiare le lacrime; **to laugh away one's tears** cambiare dal pianto al riso ‖ [ter] *s* strappo ‖ [ter] *v* (*pret* **tore** [tor]; *pp* **torn** [torn]) *tr* strappare; stracciare; (*one's heart*) squarciare; (*to wound*) sbranare; (*one's hair*) strapparsi; **to tear apart** rompere in due; separare; **to tear down** demolire; (*a piece of equipment*) smontare; **to tear off** staccare; **to tear to pieces** dilaniare; fare a pezzi; **to tear up** (*a piece of paper*) stracciare; (*a street*) scavare ‖ *intr* strapparsi, stracciarsi; **to tear along** precipitarsi; correre all'impazzata

tear' bomb' [tɪr] *s* bomba lacrimogena

tearful [ˈtɪrfəl] *adj* lacrimoso

tear' gas' [tɪr] *s* gas lacrimogeno

tear-jerker [ˈtɪr ˌdʒʌrkər] *s* (coll) storia lacrimogena

tear-off [ˈter ˌɔf] *adj* da staccarsi, perforato

tea'room' *s* sala da tè

tear' sheet' [ter] *s* copia di annuncio pubblicitario

tease [tiz] *tr* stuzzicare, molestare;

(*hair*) accotonare; (*e.g.*, *wool*) cardare

tea'spoon' *s* cucchiaino

teaspoonful ['ti ,spun ,ful] *s* cucchiaino

teat [tit] *s* capezzolo

tea'time' *s* l'ora del tè

tea' wag'on *s* servitore *m*

technical ['teknıkəl] *adj* tecnico

technicali·ty [,teknı'kælıtı] *s* (-ties) tecnicismo; dettaglio tecnico

technician [tek'nıʃən] *s* tecnico

technics ['teknıks] *ssg or spl* tecnica

technique [tek'nik] *s* tecnica

ted'dy bear' ['tedi] *s* orsacchiotto

tedious ['tidı·əs] or ['tidʒəs] *adj* tedioso, noioso

tee [ti] *adj* fatto a T ‖ *s* giunto a tre vie; (golf) piazzola di partenza ‖ *tr*— **to tee off** (slang) cominciare ‖ *intr*— **to be teed off** (slang) essere arrabbiato; **to tee off** (golf) colpire la palla dalla piazzola di partenza; **to tee off on** (slang) rimproverare severamente

teem [tim] *intr* brulicare; piovere a dirotto; **to teem with** abbondare di

teeming ['timıŋ] *adj* brulicante; (*rain*) torrenziale

teen-ager ['tin ,edʒər] *s* giovane *mf* dai 13 ai 19 anni

teens [tinz] *spl* numeri inglesi che finiscono in -teen (dal 13 al 19); **to be in one's teens** avere dai 13 ai 19 anni

tee·ny ['tini] *adj* (-nier; -niest) (coll) piccolo, piccolissimo

teeter ['titər] *s* altalena, dondolio ‖ *intr* dondolarsi, oscillare

teethe [tið] *intr* mettere i denti

teething ['tiðıŋ] *s* dentizione

teeth'ing ring' *s* dentaruolo

teetotaler [ti'totələr] *s* astemio

tele·cast ['telı ,kæst] or ['telı ,kɑst] *s* teletrasmissione ‖ *v* (*pret & pp* -cast or -casted) *tr & intr* teletrasmettere

telegram ['telı ,græm] *s* telegramma *m*

telegraph ['telı ,græf] or ['telı ,grɑf] *s* telegrafo ‖ *tr & intr* telegrafare

tel'egraph pole' *s* palo del telegrafo

Telemachus [tı'leməkəs] *s* Telemaco

telemeter [tı'lemıtər] *s* telemetro ‖ *tr* misurare col telemetro

telepathy [tı'lepəθi] *s* telepatia

telephone ['telı ,fon] *s* telefono ‖ *tr & intr* telefonare

tel'ephone book' *s* elenco or guida dei telefoni

tel'ephone booth' *s* cabina telefonica

tel'ephone call' *s* chiamata telefonica, colpo di telefono

tel'ephone direc'tory *s* elenco or guida dei telefoni

tel'ephone exchange' *s* centrale telefonica

tel'ephone op'erator *s* centralinista *mf*, telefonista *mf*

tel'ephone receiv'er *s* ricevitore *m*

tel'ephoto lens' ['telı ,foto] *s* teleobbiettivo

teleplay ['telı ,ple] *s* teledramma *m*

teleprinter ['telı ,prıntər] *s* telescrivente *f*

telescope ['telı ,skop] *s* telescopio ‖ *tr*

snodare; condensare ‖ *intr* essere snodabile; (*in a collision*) incastrarsi

teletype ['telı ,taıp] *s* telescrivente *f* ‖ *tr & intr* trasmettere per telescrivente

teleview ['telı ,vju] *tr* telericevere

televiewer ['telı ,vju·ər] *s* telespettatore *m*

televise ['telı ,vaız] *tr* teletrasmettere

television ['telı ,vıʃən] *adj* televisivo ‖ *s* televisione

tel'evision screen' *s* teleschermo

tel'evision set' *s* televisore *m*

tell [tel] *v* (*pret & pp* **told** [told]) *tr* dire; (*to narrate*) raccontare; (*to count*) contare; distinguere; **I told you so!** te l'avevo detto!; **to tell off** (coll) dire il fatto suo a ‖ *intr* dire; prevedere; avere effetto; **to tell on** (*s.o.'s health*) pesare a, e.g., **age was telling on his health** l'età pesava alla sua salute; (coll) denunciare

teller ['telər] *s* narratore *m*; (*of bank*) cassiere *m*; (*of votes*) scrutatore *m*

temper ['tempər] *s* indole *f*, temperamento; umore *m*; calma; (metallurgy) tempra; **to keep one's temper** mantenersi calmo; **to lose one's temper** perdere la pazienza ‖ *tr* temprare ‖ *intr* temprarsi

temperament ['tempərəmənt] *s* indole *f*, temperamento, carattere *m*

temperamental [,tempərə'mentəl] *adj* emotivo, capriccioso

temperance ['tempərəns] *s* (*self-restraint in action*) temperanza; (*abstinence from alcoholic beverages*) sobrietà *f*

temperate ['tempərıt] *adj* temperato

temperature ['tempərətʃər] *s* temperatura

tempest ['tempıst] *s* tempesta; **tempest in a teapot** tempesta in un bicchier d'acqua

tempestuous [tem'pestʃu·əs] *adj* tempestoso

temple ['tempəl] *s* (*place of worship*) tempio; (*of spectacles*) susta, stanghetta; (anat) tempia

tem·po ['tempo] *s* (-pos or -pi [pi]) (mus) tempo; (fig) ritmo

temporal ['tempərəl] *adj* temporale

temporary ['tempə ,reri] *adj* temporaneo, provvisorio, transitorio, interino

temporize ['tempə ,raız] *intr* temporeggiare

tempt [tempt] *tr* tentare

temptation [temp'teʃən] *s* tentazione

tempter ['temptər] *s* tentatore *m*

tempting ['temptıŋ] *adj* tentatore

ten [ten] *adj & pron* dieci ‖ *s* dieci *m*; **ten o'clock** le dieci

tenable ['tenəbəl] *adj* difendibile

tenacious [tı'neʃəs] *adj* tenace

tenant ['tenənt] *s* inquilino, pigionante *mf*; (*of land*) fittavolo

tend [tend] *tr* riguardare, governare; accudire (with *dat*), e.g., **he tends the fire** accudisce al fuoco ‖ *intr* tendere; **to tend to** propendere verso; (*e.g., one's own business*) attendere a; **to tend to** + *inf* tendere a + *inf*

tenden·cy ['tendənsi] *s* (-cies) tendenza, propensione

tender ['tɛndər] *adj* tenero; sensibile, dolorante || *s* offerta; (naut) nave *f* rifornimento; (naut) lancia; (rr) carboniera || *tr* offrire

tender-hearted ['tɛndər ,hɑrtɪd] *adj* dal cuore tenero

ten'der·loin' *s* filetto || **Tenderloin** *s* rione *m* della mala vita

tenderness ['tɛndərnɪs] *s* tenerezza

tendon ['tɛndən] *s* tendine *m*

tendril ['tɛndrɪl] *s* viticcio

tenement ['tɛnɪmənt] *s* appartamento; casa; casamento

ten'ement house' *s* casamento

tenet ['tɛnɪt] *s* dogma *m*, dottrina

tennis ['tɛnɪs] *s* tennis *m*

ten'nis court' *s* campo da tennis

ten'nis play'er *s* tennista *mf*

tenor ['tɛnər] *s* tenore *m*

tense [tɛns] *adj* teso || *s* (gram) tempo

tension ['tɛnʃən] *s* tensione

tent [tɛnt] *s* tenda; (*of circus*) tendone *m*

tentacle ['tɛntəkəl] *s* tentacolo

tentative ['tɛntətɪv] *adj* a titolo di prova; (*smile*) esile

tenth [tɛnθ] *adj*, *s* & *pron* decimo || *s* (*in dates*) dieci *m*

tenuous ['tɛnju·əs] *adj* tenue

tenure ['tɛnjər] *s* (*in office*) rafferma; (*permanency of employment*) inamovibilità *f*; (law) possesso

tepid ['tɛpɪd] *adj* tiepido

tercet ['tʌrsɪt] *s* terzina

term [tʌrm] *s* vocabolo, voce *f*; periodo, durata; termine *m*; (com) scadenza; **terms** condizioni *fpl*; **to be on good terms** essere in buone relazioni; **to come to terms** venire a patti || *tr* chiamare, definire

termagant ['tʌrməgənt] *s* megera

terminal ['tʌrmɪnəl] *adj* terminale || *s* (*end or extremity*) terminale *m*; (elec) morsetto; (rr) capolinea *m*

terminate ['tʌrmɪ ,net] *tr* & *intr* terminare

terminus ['tʌrmɪnəs] *s* termine *m*, fine *m*; (rr) capolinea *m*

termite ['tʌrmaɪt] *s* termite *f*

terrace ['tɛrəs] *s* terrazza, terrazzo; (agr) gradino, scaglione *m*

terra firma ['tɛrə 'fʌrmə] *s* terra ferma

terrain [tɛ'ren] *s* terreno

terrestrial [tə'rɛstrɪ·əl] *adj* terrestre

terrific [tə'rɪfɪk] *adj* terrificante; (coll) tremendo

terri·fy ['tɛrɪ ,faɪ] *v* (*pret* & *pp* **-fied**) *tr* terrificare, inorridire

territo·ry ['tɛrɪ ,tori] *s* (**-ries**) territorio

terror ['tɛrər] *s* terrore *m*

terrorize ['tɛrə ,raɪz] *tr* terrorizzare; dominare col terrore

ter'ry cloth' ['tɛri] *s* tessuto a spugna

terse [tʌrs] *adj* conciso, terso

tertiary ['tʌrʃɪ ,ɛri] or ['tʌrʃəri] *adj* terziario

test [tɛst] *s* prova, saggio; esame *m* || *tr* provare, saggiare; esaminare; (*e.g., a machine*) collaudare

testament ['tɛstəmənt] *s* testamento || **Testament** *s* Testamento Nuovo

test' ban' *s* interdizione degli esperimenti nucleari

test' flight' *s* volo di prova

testicle ['tɛstɪkəl] *s* testicolo

testi·fy ['tɛstɪ ,faɪ] *v* (*pret* & *pp* **-fied**) *tr* & *intr* testimoniare

testimonial [,tɛstɪ'moni·əl] *s* (*certificate*) benservito, referenza; (*expression of esteem*) segno di gratitudine

testimo·ny ['tɛstɪ ,moni] *s* (**-nies**) testimonianza

test' pat'tern *s* (telv) monoscopio

test' pi'lot *s* pilota *m* collaudatore

test' tube' *s* provetta

tetanus ['tɛtənəs] *s* tetano

tether ['tɛðər] *s* cavezza, pastoia; **at the end of one's tether** al limite delle proprie risorse || *tr* legare; incavezzare, impastoiare

tetter ['tɛtər] *s* eczema *m*, impetigine *f*

text [tɛkst] *s* testo; tema *m*

text'book' *s* libro di testo

textile ['tɛkstɪl] or ['tɛkstaɪl] *adj* & *s* tessile *m*

textual ['tɛkstʃʊ·əl] *adj* testuale

texture ['tɛkstʃər] *s* (*of cloth*) trama; caratteristica, proprietà *f*

Thai ['tɑ·i] or ['taɪ] *adj* & *s* tailandese *mf*

Thailand ['taɪlənd] *s* la Tailandia

Thames [tɛmz] *s* Tamigi *m*

than [ðæn] *conj* di, e.g., **he is faster than you** è più veloce di te; (*before a verb*) di quanto, e.g., **he is smarter than I thought** è più intelligente di quanto pensavo; che, e.g., **he had barely begun to eat than it was time to leave** non aveva appena cominciato a mangiare che era ora di andarsene

thank [θæŋk] *s*—**thanks** ringraziamenti *mpl*; **thanks to** grazie a, in grazie di || *tr* ringraziare || **thanks** *interj* grazie!

thankful ['θæŋkfəl] *adj* grato

thankless ['θæŋklɪs] *adj* ingrato

Thanksgiv'ing Day' [,θæŋks'gɪvɪŋ] *s* giorno del Ringraziamento

that [ðæt] *adj dem* (**those**) quel; codesto; **that one** quello, quello là || *pron dem* (**those**) quello; codesto || *pron rel* che, quello che, il quale; **that is** cioè; **that's that** (coll) ecco fatto, ecco tutto || *adv* (coll) tanto, così; **that far** così lontano; **that many** tanti; **that much** tanto || *conj* che

thatch [θætʃ] *s* paglia, copertura di paglia; (*hair*) capigliatura || *tr* coprire di paglia

thaw [θɔ] *s* sgelo || *tr* sgelare || *intr* sgelarsi

the [ðə], [ðɪ], or [ði] *art def* il; al, e.g., **one dollar the dozen** un dollaro alla dozzina || *adv*—**so much the worse for him** tanto peggio per lui; **the more . . . the more** quanto più . . . tanto più

theater ['θi·ətər] *s* teatro

the'ater·go'er *s* frequentatore *m* abituale del teatro

the'ater news' *s* cronaca teatrale

theatrical [θi'ætrɪkəl] *adj* teatrale

Thebes [θibz] *s* Tebe *f*

thee [ði] *pron pers* (Bib; poet) ti; te

theft [θɛft] *s* furto, ruberia

their [ðɛr] *adj poss* il loro, loro

theirs [ðɛrz] *pron poss* il loro

them [ðɛm] *pron pers* li; loro; **to them** loro

theme [θim] *s* tema *m*, soggetto; saggio; (mus) tema *m*

theme' song' *s* (mus) tema *m* centrale; (rad) sigla musicale

them·selves' *pron pers* essi stessi, loro stessi; si, e.g., **they enjoyed themselves** si divertirono

then [ðɛn] *adj* allora, di allora ‖ *s* quel tempo; **by then** a quell'epoca; **from then on** da quel giorno in poi ‖ *adv* allora; indi, poi; **then and there** a quel momento

thence [ðɛns] *adv* indi, quindi; da lì; da allora in poi

thence'forth' *adv* da allora in poi

theolo·gy [θi'ɑlədʒi] *s* (-gies) telogia

theorem ['θi·ərəm] *s* teorema *m*

theoretical [,θi·ə'rɛtɪkəl] *adj* teoretico

theo·ry ['θi·əri] *s* (-ries) teoria

therapeutic [,θɛrə'pjutɪk] *adj* terapeutico ‖ **therapeutics** *ssg* terapeutica

thera·py ['θɛrəpi] *s* (-pies) terapia

there [ðɛr] *adv* lì, là; **there are** ci sono; **there is** c'è; ecco, e.g., **there it is** eccolo

there'abouts' *adv* circa, approssimativamente, giù di lì

there'af'ter *adv* in seguito, dipoi

there'by' *adv* quindi, perciò, così

therefore ['ðɛrfor] *adv* per questo, quindi, dunque

there'in' *adv* lì; in quel rispetto

there'of' *adv* di ciò, da ciò

Theresa [tə'risə] or [tə'rɛsə] *s* Teresa

there'upon' *adv* su questo; a quel momento; come conseguenza

thermal ['θʌrməl] *adj* (*water*) termale; (*capacity*) termico

thermistor [θər'mɪstər] *s* (elec) termistore *m*

thermocouple ['θʌrmo,kʌpəl] *s* termocoppia

thermodynamic [,θʌrmodɑi'næmɪk] *adj* termodinamico ‖ **thermodynamics** *ssg* termodinamica

thermometer [θər'mɑmɪtər] *s* termometro

thermonuclear [,θʌrmo'njuklɪ·ər] or [,θʌrmo'nuklɪ·ər] *adj* termonucleare

ther'mos bot'tle ['θʌrməs] *s* termos *m*

thermostat ['θʌrmə,stæt] *s* termostato

thesau·rus [θɪ'sɔrəs] *s* (-ri [rɑi] or -ruses) tesoro, lessico, compendio

these [ðiz] *pl* of **this**

the·sis ['θisɪs] *s* (-ses [siz]) tesi *f*

Thespis ['θɛspɪs] *s* Tespi *m*

they [ðe] *pron pers* essi, loro

thick [θɪk] *adj* spesso, grosso; folto, denso; pieno, coperto; viscoso; stupido; (coll) intimo ‖ *s* spessore *m*; **in the thick of** nel folto di; **through thick and thin** nei tempi buoni e cattivi

thicken ['θɪkən] *tr* ispessire; ingrossare; infoltire ‖ *intr* ispessirsi; ingrossarsi; (*said of a plot*) complicarsi

thicket ['θɪkɪt] *s* boscaglia, macchia

thick-headed ['θɪk,hɛdɪd] *adj* indietro, stupido

thick'set' *adj* tarchiato; (*hedge*) fitto, denso

thief [θif] *s* (**thieves** [θivz]) ladro

thieve [θiv] *intr* rubare

thiever·y ['θivəri] *s* (-ies) furto

thigh [θɑi] *s* coscia

thigh'bone' *s* femore *m*

thimble ['θɪmbəl] *s* ditale *m*

thin [θɪn] *adj* (**thinner; thinnest**) (*paper, ice*) sottile; (*lean*) magro, smilzo; (e.g., *hair*) rado; (*air*) fine; (*excuse*) tenue; (*voice*) esile; (*wine*) leggero, annacquato ‖ *v* (*pret & pp* **thinned**) *ger* **thinning** *tr* assottigliare; (*paint*) diluire ‖ *intr* assottigliarsi; **to thin out** (*said of a crowd; one's hair*) diradarsi

thine [ðɑin] *adj & pron poss* (Bib & poet) tuo, il tuo

thing [θɪŋ] *s* cosa; **not to get a thing out of** non riuscire a capire; non cavare un briciolo d'informazione da; **of all things!** che cosa!; che sorpresa!; **the thing** l'ultima moda; **things** roba; **to see things** avere allucinazioni

think [θɪŋk] *v* (*pret & pp* **thought** [θɔt]) *tr* pensare; credere; **to think it over** ripensarci; **to think nothing of it** non darci la minima importanza; **to think of** (*to have as an opinion of*) pensare di, e.g., **what do you think of that doctor?** cosa ne pensa di quel medico?; **to think out** decifrare; **to think up** immaginare ‖ *intr* pensare; **to think not** credere di no; **to think of** (*to turn one's thoughts to*) pensare a, e.g., **he is thinking of the future** pensa al futuro; (*to imagine*) immaginare; **to think so** credere di sì; **to think well of** avere una buona opinione di

thinkable ['θɪŋkəbəl] *adj* pensabile

thinker ['θɪŋkər] *s* pensatore *m*

third [θʌrd] *adj*, *s & pron* terzo ‖ *s* terzo; (*in dates*) tre *m*; (aut) terza

third' degree' *s* interrogatorio di terzo grado

third' rail' *s* (rr) rotaia elettrificata di contatto

third'-rate' *adj* di terz'ordine

Third' World' *s* Terzo Mondo

thirst [θʌrst] *s* sete *f* ‖ *intr* aver sete; **to thirst for** aver sete di

thirst·y ['θʌrsti] *adj* (-ier; -iest) assetato, sitibondo; **to be thirsty** avere sete

thirteen ['θʌr'tin] *adj*, *s & pron* tredici *m*

thirteenth ['θʌr'tinθ] *adj*, *s & pron* tredicesimo ‖ *s* (*in dates*) tredici *m*

thirtieth ['θʌrtɪ·ɪθ] *adj*, *s & pron* trentesimo ‖ *s* (*in dates*) trenta *m*

thir·ty ['θʌrti] *adj & pron* trenta ‖ *s* (-ties) trenta *m;* **the thirties** gli anni trenta

this [ðɪs] *adj dem* (**these**) questo; **this one** questo, questo qui ‖ *pron dem* (**these**) questo, questo qui ‖ *adv* (coll) tanto, così

thistle ['θɪsəl] *s* cardo

thither ['θɪðər] or ['ðɪðər] *adv* là, da quella parte

Thomas ['taməs] s Tommaso

thong [θɔŋ] or [θɑŋ] s coreggia

thorax ['θɔræks] s (-raxes or -races [rə‚siz]) torace m

thorn [θɔrn] s spina

thorn·y ['θɔrni] adj (-ier; -iest) spinoso

thorough ['θʌro] adj completo, esauriente

thor'ough·bred' adj di razza; (horse) purosangue || s individuo di razza; (horse) purosangue mf

thor'ough·fare' s passaggio; **no thoroughfare** divieto di passaggio

thor'ough·go'ing adj completo, esauriente

thoroughly ['θʌroli] adv a fondo

those [ðoz] pl of that

thou [ðau] pron pers (Bib; poet) tu || tr dare del tu a

though [ðo] adv tuttavia || conj malgrado, sebbene; **as though** come se

thought [θɔt] s pensiero; **perish the thought!** (coll) nemmeno a pensarci!

thoughtful ['θɔtfəl] adj pensieroso, riflessivo; (considerate) sollecito

thoughtless ['θɔtlɪs] adj irriflessivo; sconsiderato; (reckless) incurante

thought' transfer'ence s trasmissione del pensiero

thousand ['θauzənd] adj, s & pron mille m; **a thousand or one thousand** mille m

thousandth ['θauzəndθ] adj, s & pron millesimo

thralldom ['θrɔldəm] s schiavitù f

thrash [θræʃ] tr battere; (agr) trebbiare; **to thrash out** discutere a fondo || intr agitarsi, dibattersi

thread [θred] s filo; (mach) filetto, verme m; **to lose the thread of** perdere il filo di || tr infilare; (fig) pervadere; (mach) filettare, impanare; **to thread one's way through** aprirsi il passaggio attraverso

thread'bare' adj frusto, logoro

threat [θret] s minaccia

threaten ['θretən] tr & intr minacciare

threatening ['θretənɪŋ] adj minaccioso; (e.g., letter) minatorio

three [θri] adj & pron tre || s tre m; **three o'clock** le tre

three'-cor'nered adj triangolare; (hat) a tre punte

three' hun'dred adj, s & pron trecento

threepenny ['θrɛpəni] or ['θrɪpəni] adj del valore di tre penny; di nessun valore

three'-phase' adj trifase

three'-ply' adj a tre spessori

three' R's' [ɑrz] spl lettura, scrittura e aritmetica

three'score' adj sessanta

three' thou'sand adj, s & pron tre mila mpl

threno·dy ['θrɛnədi] s (-dies) trenodia

thresh [θrɛʃ] tr (agr) trebbiare; **to thresh out** discutere a fondo || intr trebbiare; battere

thresh'ing machine' s trebbiatrice f

threshold ['θrɛʃold] s soglia

thrice [θraɪs] adv tre volte; molto

thrift [θrɪft] s economia

thrift·y ['θrɪfti] adj (-ier; -iest) eco-

nomo, economico; vigoroso; prospero

thrill [θrɪl] s fremito d'emozione; esperienza emozionante || tr emozionare || intr emozionarsi; vibrare

thriller ['θrɪlər] s (coll) thrilling m

thrilling ['θrɪlɪŋ] adj emozionante, thrilling

thrive [θraɪv] v (pret thrived or throve [θrov]; pp thrived or thriven ['θrɪvən]) intr prosperare, fiorire

throat [θrot] s gola; **to clear one's throat** schiarirsi la voce

throb [θrab] s battito, palpito, tuffo || v (pret & pp throbbed; ger throbbing) intr palpitare, pulsare

throe [θro] s agonia, travaglio, spasimo; **in the throes of** nel travaglio di; (e.g., battle) nel momento più penoso di

throne [θron] s trono

throng [θrɔŋ] or [θrɑŋ] s folla, stuolo || intr affollarsi

throttle ['θratəl] s (of locomotive) leva di comando; (of motorcycle) manetta; (of car) acceleratore m; (mach) valvola di controllo || tr soffocare; (mach) regolare

through [θru] adj diretto, senza fermate; **to be through** aver finito; **to be through with** farla finita con || adv attraverso; da una parte all'altra; completamente; || prep attraverso, per; durante; fino alla fine di; per mezzo di

through·out' adv completamente, da un capo all'altro; dappertutto || prep durante tutto, e.g., **throughout the afternoon** durante tutto il pomeriggio; per tutto, e.g., **throughout the house** per tutta la casa

throw [θro] s getto, tiro, lancio; gettata; coperta leggera || v (pret threw [θru]; pp thrown) tr gettare, tirare, lanciare; (a shadow) proiettare; (the current) connettere; (said of a horse) disarcionare; (wrestling) gettare a terra; (a game) (coll) perdere intenzionalmente; (coll) stupire; **to throw away** gettar via; perdere; **to throw back** rigettare; ritardare; **to throw in** (the clutch) innestare; (coll) aggiungere; **to throw oneself into** darsi a; **to throw out** sbatter fuori; (the clutch) disinnestare; **to throw over** abbandonare || intr gettare, tirare, lanciare; **to throw up** vomitare

thrum [θrʌm] v (pret & pp thrummed; ger thrumming) intr tambureggiare; (mus) far scorrere la mano sulle corde di uno strumento

thrush [θrʌʃ] s tordo

thrust [θrʌst] s (push) spinta; botta; (with dagger) pugnalata; (with sword) stoccata || v (pret & pp thrust) tr spingere; conficcare, configgere; **to thrust oneself** (e.g., into a conversation) ficcarsi

thru'way' s autostrada

thud [θʌd] s tonfo || v (pret & pp thudded; ger thudding) intr fare un rumore sordo

thug [θʌg] s fascinoroso

thumb [θʌm] *s* pollice *m;* **all thumbs** maldestro, goffo; **thumbs down** pollice verso; **to twiddle one's thumbs** girare i pollici, essere ozioso; **under the thumb of** sotto l'influenza di ‖ *tr* sporcare con le dita; (*a book*) sfogliare; **to thumb a ride** chiedere l'autostop; **to thumb one's nose (at)** fare marameo (a)

thumb' in'dex *s* margine *m* a scaletta

thumb'nail' *adj* breve, conciso ‖ *s* unghia del pollice

thumb'screw' *s* vite *f* ad aletta

thumb'tack' *s* puntina

thump [θʌmp] *s* tonfo ‖ *tr* battere, percuotere ‖ *intr* battere; cadere con un tonfo; camminare a passi pesanti; (*said of the heart*) palpitare violentemente

thumping ['θʌmpɪŋ] *adj* (coll) straordinario, eccezionale; (coll) grande

thunder ['θʌndər] *s* tuono; (*of applause*) scroscio; (*of a cannon*) rombo ‖ *tr* lanciare ‖ *intr* tonare, rombare; (fig) scrosciare

thun'der·bolt' *s* folgore *f*, fulmine *m*

thun'der·clap' *s* scroscio di tuono

thunderous ['θʌndərəs] *adj* fragoroso

thun'der·show'er *s* acquazzone *m* accompagnato da tuoni

thun'der·storm' *s* temporale *m*

thun'der·struck' *adj* attonito

Thursday ['θʌrsdi] *s* giovedì *m*

thus [ðʌs] *adv* così; **thus far** sino qui

thwack [θwæk] *s* colpo ‖ *tr* colpire

thwart [θwɔrt] *adj* obliquo ‖ *adv* di traverso ‖ *tr* contrariare, sventare

thy [ðaɪ] *adj poss* (Bib; poet) tuo, il tuo

thyme [taɪm] *s* timo

thy'roid gland' ['θaɪrɔɪd] *s* tiroide *f*

thyself [ðaɪ'sɛlf] *pron* (Bib; poet) te stesso; te, ti

tiara [taɪ'arə] or [taɪ'ɛrə] *s* (*female adornment*) diadema *m;* (eccl) tiara

tick [tɪk] *s* (*of pillow*) fodera; (*of mattress*) guscio; (*of clock*) ticchettio; (*dot*) punto; (ent) zecca; **on tick** (coll) a credito ‖ *intr* fare ticchettio; **to make s.o. tick** mandare avanti qlcu

ticker ['tɪkər] *s* telescrivente *f;* (slang) orologio; (slang) cuore *m*

tick'er tape' *s* nastro della telescrivente

ticket ['tɪkɪt] *s* biglietto; (*e.g., of pawnbroker*) polizza; (*slip of paper or identifying tag*) bolletta, bollettino; (*summons*) verbale *m;* (*e.g., to indicate price*) etichetta; lista dei candidati; **that's the ticket** (coll) questo è quello che fa

tick'et a'gent *s* bigliettaio

tick'et of'fice *s* biglietteria

tick'et scalp'er ['skælpər] *s* bagarino

tick'et win'dow *s* sportello

ticking ['tɪkɪŋ] *s* traliccio

tickle ['tɪkəl] *s* solletico ‖ *tr* solleticare; divertire ‖ *intr* avere il solletico

ticklish ['tɪklɪʃ] *adj* sensibile al solletico; delicato; permaloso; **to be ticklish** soffrire il solletico

tick-tock ['tɪk ˌtɑk] *s* tic tac *m*

tid'al wave' ['taɪdəl] *s* onda di marea; (fig) ondata

tidbit ['tɪd ˌbɪt] *s* bocconcino

tiddlywinks ['tɪdli ˌwɪŋks] *s* gioco della pulce

tide [taɪd] *s* marea; **to go against the tide** andare contro la corrente; **to stem the tide** fermare la corrente ‖ *tr* portare sulla cresta delle onde; **to tide over** aiutare; (*a difficulty*) sormontare

tide'wa'ter *s* marea; costa marina

tidings ['taɪdɪŋz] *spl* notizie *fpl*

ti·dy ['taɪdi] *adj* (-dier; -diest) pulito, ordinato ‖ *s* (-dies) cofanetto, astuccio; appoggiacapo ‖ *v* (*pret & pp* -died) *tr* rassettare, mettere in ordine ‖ *intr* rassettarsi

tie [taɪ] *s* laccio, nodo, vincolo; (*in games*) patta; (*necktie*) cravatta; (archit) traversa; (rr) traversina; (mus) legatura ‖ *v* (*pret & pp* **tied;** *ger* **tying**) *tr* allacciare, annodare; legare; confinare; (*a game*) impattare; (*a person*) impattarla con; **to be tied up** essere occupato; **to tie down** confinare, limitare; **to tie up** legare; impedire; (*e.g., traffic*) intasare ‖ *intr* allacciare; (*in games*) impattare

tie' beam' *s* catena

tie'pin' *s* spilla da cravatta

tier [tɪr] *s* gradinata; ordine *m*, livello

tiff [tɪf] *s* screzio, litigio

tiger ['taɪgər] *s* tigre *f*

ti'ger lil'y *s* giglio cinese

tight [taɪt] *adj* teso; stretto; compatto; impermeabile, ermetico; pieno; (*game*) (coll) serrato; (coll) tirato; (slang) ubriaco ‖ **tights** *spl* calzamaglia ‖ *adv* strettamente; **to hold tight** tenere stretto

tighten ['taɪtən] *tr* (*e.g., one's belt*) tirare; (*e.g., a screw*) stringere ‖ *intr* tirarsi; stringersi

tight-fisted ['taɪt'fɪstɪd] *adj* taccagno

tight'-fit'ting *adj* attillato

tight'rope' *s* corda tesa

tight' squeeze' *s*—**to be in a tight squeeze** (coll) essere alle strette

tight'wad' *s* (coll) spilorcio

tigress ['taɪgrɪs] *s* tigre femmina

tile [taɪl] *s* mattonella; (*for floor*) piastrella; (*for roof*) tegola, coppo ‖ *tr* coprire di mattonelle; coprire di piastrelle; coprire di coppi

tile' roof' *s* tetto di tegole

till [tɪl] *s* cassetto dei soldi ‖ *prep* fino a ‖ *conj* fino a che . . . non, fino a che, sinché . . . non, sinché ‖ *tr* lavorare, coltivare

tilt [tɪlt] *s* inclinazione; giostra, torneo; **full tilt** di gran carriera; a tutta forza ‖ *tr* inclinare; (*a lance*) mettere in resta; attaccare ‖ *intr* inclinarsi; giostrare; **to tilt at** combattere con

timber ['tɪmbər] *s* legno, legname *m* da costruzione; alberi *mpl;* (fig) tempra

tim'ber·land' *s* bosco destinato a produrre legname

tim'ber line' *s* linea della vegetazione

timbre ['tɪmbər] *s* (phonet & phys) timbro

time [taɪm] *s* tempo; ora, e.g., what time is it? che ora è?; volta, e.g., three times tre volte; giorni *mpl*, e.g., in our time ai giorni nostri; momento; ultima ora; ore *fpl* lavorative; periodo, e.g., **Xmas time** periodo natalizio; **for a long time** da lungo; **for the time being** per ora, per il momento; **in time** presto; col tempo; **on time** a tempo; a rate; (*said, e.g., of a bus*) in orario; **times** volte, e.g., seven times **seven** sette volte sette; **to bide one's time** aspettare l'ora propizia; **to do time** (coll) essere in prigione; **to have a good time** divertirsi; **to have no time for** non poter sopportare; **to lose time** (*said of a watch*) ritardare; **to make time** avanzare rapidamente; guadagnare terreno; **to pass the time of day** fare una chiacchierata; salutarsi; **to take one's time** fare le cose senza fretta; **to tell time** leggere l'orologio || *tr* fissare il momento di; calcolare il tempo di; (sports) cronometrare

time' bomb' *s* bomba a orologeria

time'card' *s* cartellino di presenza

time' clock' *s* orologio di controllo (delle presenze)

time' expo'sure *s* (phot) posa

time' fuse' *s* spoletta a tempo

time'keep'er *s* marcatempo; orologio; (sports) cronometrista *mf*

timeless ['taɪmlɪs] *adj* senza fine, eterno

time·ly ['taɪmli] *adj* (-lier; -liest) opportuno, tempestivo

time'piece' *s* orologio; cronometro

time' sig'nal *s* segnale orario

time'ta'ble *s* orario; tabella di marcia

time'work' *s* lavoro a ore

time'worn' *adj* logorato dal tempo

time' zone' *s* fuso orario

timid ['tɪmɪd] *adj* timido, pavido

tim'ing gears' ['taɪmɪŋ] *spl* ingranaggi *mpl* di distribuzione

timorous ['tɪmərəs] *adj* timoroso

tin [tɪn] *s* (*element*) stagno; (*tin plate; can*) latta || *v* (*pret & pp* **tinned;** *ger* **tinning**) *tr* stagnare

tin' can' *s* latta

tincture ['tɪŋktʃər] *s* tintura

tin' cup' *s* tazzina metallica

tinder ['tɪndər] *s* esca

tin'der·box' *s* cassetta con l'esca e l'acciarino; persona eccitabile; (fig) polveriera

tin' foil' *s* stagnola

ting-a-ling ['tɪŋə,lɪŋ] *s* dindin *m*

tinge [tɪndʒ] *s* sfumatura; pizzico, punta || *v* (*ger* **tingeing** *or* **tinging**) *tr* sfumare; dare una traccia di sapore a

tingle ['tɪŋɡəl] *s* formicolio, pizzicore *m* || *intr* informicolirsi, pizzicare; (*said of the ears*) ronzare; (*with enthusiasm*) fremere

tin' hat' *s* (slang) elmetto

tinker ['tɪŋkər] *s* calderaio, ramaio || *intr* armeggiare

tinkle ['tɪŋkəl] *s* tintinnio || *tr* far tintinnare || *intr* tintinnare

tin' plate' *s* latta

tin' roof' *s* tetto di lamiera di latta

tinsel ['tɪnsəl] *s* orpello, lustrino

tin'smith' *s* lattoniere *m*, stagnino

tin' sol'dier *s* soldatino di piombo

tint [tɪnt] *s* tinta, sfumatura || *tr* tinteggiare

tin'ware' *s* articoli *mpl* di latta

ti·ny ['taɪni] *adj* (-nier; -niest) piccino

tip [tɪp] *s* punta; (*of mountain*) vetta; (*of umbrella*) gorbia; (*of shoe*) mascherina; (*of cigarette*) bocchino; (*of shoestring*) aghetto; colpetto; (*fee*) mancia; informazione confidenziale; inclinazione || *v* (*pret & pp* **tipped;** *ger* **tipping**) *tr* mettere la punta a; inclinare, rovesciare; (*one's hat*) levarsi; dare la mancia a; toccare, battere; (*the scales*) far traboccare; **to tip in** (bb) inserire fuori testo; **to tip off** (coll) dare informazioni confidenziali a || *intr* inclinarsi; **dare la mancia**

tip'cart' *s* carro ribaltabile

tip'-off' *s* (coll) avvertimento confidenziale

tipped'-in' *adj* (bb) fuori testo

tipple ['tɪpəl] *intr* sbevucchiare

tip'staff' *s* usciere *m*

tip·sy ['tɪpsi] *adj* (-sier; -siest) brillo

tip'toe' *s* punta di piedi || *v* (*pret & pp* **-toed;** *ger* **-toeing**) *intr* camminare in punta di piedi

tirade ['taɪred] *s* tirata

tire [taɪr] *s* gomma, pneumatico; (*of metal*) cerchione *m* || *tr* stancare || *intr* stancarsi; infastidirsi

tire' chain' *s* catena antineve

tired [taɪrd] *adj* stanco, stracco

tire' gauge' *s* manometro della pressione delle gomme

tireless ['taɪrlɪs] *adj* infaticabile

tire' pres'sure *s* pressione (delle gomme)

tire' pump' *s* pompa (per i pneumatici)

tiresome ['taɪrsəm] *adj* faticoso; (*boring*) noioso

tissue ['tɪsju] *s* tessuto; tessuto finissimo, velina

tis'sue pa'per *s* carta velina

titanium [tai'teni·əm] *or* [tɪ'teni·əm] *s* titanio

tithe [taɪð] *s* decima || *tr* imporre la decima su; pagare la decima di

Titian ['tɪʃən] *adj* tizianesco || *s* Tiziano

title ['taɪtəl] *s* titolo; (sports) campionato || *tr* intitolare

ti'tle deed' *s* titolo di proprietà

ti'tle·hold'er *s* campione *m*, primatista *mf*

ti'tle page' *s* frontespizio

ti'tle role' *s* (theat) ruolo principale

tit'mouse' *s* (-mice) (orn) cincia

titter ['tɪtər] *s* risatina || *intr* ridacchiare

titular ['tɪtʃələr] *adj* titolare

TNT ['ti,en'ti] *s* (letterword) tritolo

to [tu], [tʊ] *or* [tə] *adv*—**to and fro** da una parte all'altra, avanti e indietro; **to come to** tornare in sè || *prep* a, e.g., **he is going to Rome** va a Roma; **he gave a kiss to his mother**

diede un bacio a sua madre; **she is learning** to sew impara a cucire; per, e.g., **he has been a true friend** to me è stato un vero amico per me; da, e.g., **there is still a lot of work** to do c'è ancora molto lavoro da fare; con, e.g., **she was very kind** to me è stata molto gentile con me; in, e.g., **we went** to **church** siamo andati in chiesa; fino a, e.g., **to see s.o.** to the station accompagnare qlcu fino alla stazione; in confronto di, e.g., **the accounts are nothing to what really happened** le storie non sono nulla, in confronto di quanto è realmente successo; meno, e.g., **ten minutes to seven** le sette meno dieci

toad [tod] *s* rospo

toad'stool' *s* agarico, fungo velenoso

to-and-fro [tu-ənd'fro] *adj* avanti e indietro

toast [tost] *s* pane tostato; (*drink to s.o.'s health*) brindisi *m*; **a piece of toast** una fetta di pane tostato ‖ *tr* tostare; brindare alla salute di ‖ *intr* tostarsi; brindare

toaster ['tostər] *s* (*of bread*) tostapane *m*; persona che fa un brindisi

toast'mas'ter *s* persona che annuncia i brindisi, maestro di cerimonie

tobac·co [tə'bæko] *s* (-cos) tabacco

tobacconist [tə'bækənɪst] *s* tabaccaio

tobac'co pouch' *s* borsa da tabacco

toboggan [tə'bagən] *s* toboga *m*

tocsin ['tɑksɪn] *s* campana a martello; scampanata d'allarme

today [tu'de] *s* & *adv* oggi *m*

toddle ['tadəl] *s* passo vacillante ‖ *intr* traballare, trotterellare

tod·dy ['tadi] *s* (-dies) ponce *m*

to-do [tə'du] *s* (-dos) (coll) daffare *m*, rumore *m*

toe [to] *s* dito del piede; (*of shoe*) punta ‖ *v* (*pret & pp* toed; *ger* toeing) *tr*—**to toe the line** filare diritto

toe'nail' *s* unghia del piede

together [tu'geðər] *adv* insieme; **to bring together** riunire; riconciliare; **to call together** chiamare a raccolta; **to stick together** (coll) rimanere uniti, stare insieme

togs [tagz] *spl* vestiti *mpl*

toil [tɔɪl] *s* travaglio, sfacchinata; **toils** reti *fpl*, lacci *mpl* ‖ *intr* travagliare, sfacchinare

toilet ['tɔɪlɪt] *s* toletta; gabinetto, ritirata; **to make one's toilet** farsi la toletta

toi'let pa'per *s* carta igienica

toi'let pow'der *s* polvere *f* di talco

toi'let soap' *s* sapone *m* da toletta

toi'let wa'ter *s* acqua da toletta

token ['tokən] *s* segno, marca; ricordo; (*used as money*) gettone *m*; **by the same token** per di più; **in token of** in segno di, come prova di

tolerance ['talərəns] *s* tolleranza

tolerate ['talə‚ret] *tr* tollerare

toll [tol] *s* (*of bell*) rintocco; (*e.g., for passage over bridge*) pedaggio; (*tax*) dazio; (*compensation for grinding grains*) molenda; (*number of victims*) perdite *fpl*; (telp) tariffa inter-

urbana ‖ *tr* (*a bell*) sonare a morto; (*the faithful*) chiamare a raccolta ‖ *intr* sonare a morto

toll' bridge' *s* ponte *m* a pedaggio

toll' call' *s* (telp) chiamata interurbana

toll'gate' *s* barriera di pedaggio; (*in a turnpike*) casello

toma·to [tə'meto] *or* [tə'mato] *s* (-toes) pomodoro

toma'to juice' *s* sugo di pomodoro

tomb [tum] *s* tomba

tomboy ['tam‚bɔɪ] *s* maschietta

tomb'stone' *s* pietra tombale, lapide *f*

tomcat ['tam‚kæt] *s* gatto maschio

tome [tom] *s* tomo

tomorrow [tu'maro] *or* [tu'mɔro] *s* domani *m*; **the day after tomorrow** dopodomani *m* ‖ *adv* domani

tom-tom ['tam ‚tam] *s* tam-tam *m*

ton [tʌn] *s* tonnellata; **tons** (coll) montagne *fpl*

tone [ton] *s* tono; (fig) tenore *m* ‖ *tr* intonare; **to tone down** (*colors*) smorzare; (*sounds*) sfumare ‖ *intr* intonarsi; **to tone down** moderarsi; **to tone up** rinforzarsi

tone' po'em *s* poema sinfonico

tongs [tɔŋz] *or* [taŋz] *spl* tenaglie *fpl*; (*e.g., for sugar*) molle *fpl*

tongue [tʌŋ] *s* (*language*) lingua; (*of bell*) battaglio; (*of shoe*) linguetta; (*of wagon*) timone *m*; (anat) lingua; (carp) maschio; **tongue in cheek** poco sinceramente; **to hold one's tongue** mordersi la lingua; **to speak with forked tongue** essere di due lingue

tongue' depres'sor *s* abbassalingua *m*

tongue'-lash'ing *s* sgridata

tongue' twist'er *s* scioglilingua *m*

tonic ['tanɪk] *adj* & *s* tonico

tonight [tu'naɪt] *s* questa sera, questa notte ‖ *adv* stasera; stanotte

tonnage ['tʌnɪdʒ] *s* tonnellaggio, stazza

tonsil ['tansəl] *s* tonsilla

ton·y ['toni] *adj* (-ier; -iest) (slang) elegante, di lusso

too [tu] *adv* (*also*) anche, pure; (*more than enough*) troppo; **too bad!** peccato!; **too many** troppi; **too much** troppo

tool [tul] *s* utensile *m*, attrezzo; (*person*) strumento; (*of lathe*) punta ‖ *tr* lavorare; (bb) decorare

tool' bag' *s* borsa degli attrezzi

tool'box' *s* cassetta attrezzi

tool'mak'er *s* attrezzista *m*

tool'shed' *s* barchessa

toot [tut] *s* (*of horn*) suono; (*of locomotive*) fischio; (*of car's horn*) colpo; (coll) gazzarra ‖ *tr* strombettare; **to toot one's own horn** strombazzare i propri meriti ‖ *intr* strombettare

tooth [tuθ] *s* (teeth [tiθ]) dente *m*

tooth'ache' *s* mal *m* di denti

tooth'brush' *s* spazzolino da denti

toothless ['tuθlɪs] *adj* sdentato

tooth'paste' *s* pasta dentifricia

tooth'pick' *s* stuzzicadenti *m*

tooth' pow'der *s* polvere dentifricia

top [tap] *s* cima, sommo, vertice *m*; (*upper part of anything*) disopra *m*;

(*of mountain, tree*) vetta; (*of box*) coperchio; (*beginning*) principio; (*of bottle*) imboccatura; (*of a bridge*) testata; (*of wagon*) mantice *m;* (*of car*) tetto; (*of wall*) coronamento; (*toy*) trottola; (naut) gabbia; **at the top of one's voice** a perdifiato; **from top to bottom** daccapo a piedi, dal principio alla fine; **on top of** in cima di; subito dopo; **the tops** (coll) il migliore, il fiore; **to blow one's top** (slang) dare in escandescenze; **to sleep like a top** dormire come un ghiro ‖ *v* (*pret & pp* **topped;** *ger* **topping**) *tr* (*a tree*) svettare; coronare; superare

topaz ['topæz] *s* topazio

top' bil'ling *s*—**to get top billing** essere artista di cartello; (journ) ricevere il posto più importante

top' boot' *s* stivale *m* a tromba

top'coat' *s* soprabito di mezza stagione

toper ['topər] *s* ubriacone *m*

topgal'lant sail' [ˌtap'gælənt] *s* (naut) pappafico, veletta

top' hat' *s* cappello a staio or a cilindro

top'-heav'y *adj* troppo pesante in cima, sovraccarico in cima

topic ['tapɪk] *s* topica, tema *m*

top'knot' *s* crocchia

topless ['taplɪs] *adj* (*mountain*) di cui non si vede la vetta, eccelso; (*bathing suit*) topless

top'mast' *s* (naut) alberetto

top'most' *adj* il più alto

topogra·phy [tə'pagrəfi] *s* (-phies) topografia

topple ['tapəl] *tr* abbattere, rovesciare ‖ *intr* rovesciarsi, cadere

top' prior'ity *s* priorità massima

topsail ['tapsəl] or ['tap ˌsel] *s* (naut) gabbia

top'-se'cret *adj* segretissimo

top'soil' *s* strato superiore del terreno

topsy-turvy ['tapsi'tʌrvi] *adj* rovesciato; confuso ‖ *s* soqquadro ‖ *adv* a soqquadro

torch [tortʃ] *s* fiaccola, torcia; **to carry the torch for** (slang) amare disperatamente

torch'bear'er *s* portatore *m* di fiaccola; (fig) capo, guida *m*

torch'light' *s* luce *f* di fiaccola

torch' song' *s* canzone *f* triste d'amore non corrisposto

torment ['tormɛnt] *s* tormento ‖ [tor-'mɛnt] *tr* tormentare

torna·do [tor'nedo] *s* (-dos or -does) tornado, tromba d'aria

torpe·do [tor'pido] *s* (-does) siluro ‖ *tr* silurare

torpe'do boat' *s* motosilurante *f*

torpe'do-boat destroy'er *s* torpediniera

torrent ['tarənt] or ['torənt] *s* torrente *m*

torrid ['tarɪd] or ['torɪd] *adj* torrido

torsion ['torʃən] *s* torsione

tor'sion bar' *s* barra di torsione

tor·so ['torso] *s* (-sos) torso

tortoise ['tortɪs] *s* tartaruga

tor'toise shell' *s* tartaruga

torture ['tortʃər] *s* tortura ‖ *tr* torturare

toss [tos] or [tas] *s* lancio, getto ‖ *tr* lanciare, gettare; (*to fling about*) sballottare; (*one's head*) alzare sdegnosamente; agitare; rivoltare; (*an opinion*) avventare; **to toss off** fare rapidamente; (*e.g., a drink*) buttar giù; **to toss up** (*a coin*) gettar in aria, gettare a testa e croce; (coll) rigettare ‖ *intr* agitarsi, dimenarsi; **to toss and turn** (*in bed*) girarsi; **to toss up** giocare a testa e croce

toss'up' *s* testa e croce; (coll) eguale probabilità *f*

tot [tat] *s* bambino, piccolo

to·tal ['totəl] *adj* totale; (*e.g., loss*) completo ‖ *s* totale *m* ‖ *v* (*pret & pp* **-taled** or **-talled;** *ger* **-taling** or **-talling**) *tr* ammontare a; (*to make a total of*) sommare

totalitarian [toˌtælɪ'tɛrɪ·ən] *adj* totalitario ‖ *s* aderente *mf* al totalitarismo

totter ['tatər] *s* vacillamento ‖ *intr* vacillare

touch [tʌtʃ] *s* (*act*) tocco; (*sense*) tatto; (*of an illness*) leggero attacco; (*slight amount*) punta; (*for money*) (slang) stoccata; **to get in touch with** mettersi in contatto con; **to lose one's touch** perdere il tocco personale ‖ *tr* toccare; raggiungere; riguardare; (*for a loan*) (slang) dare una stoccata a; **to touch on** menzionare; **to touch up** ritoccare ‖ *intr* toccare; **to touch down** (aer) atterrare

touching ['tʌtʃɪŋ] *adj* toccante, commovente ‖ *prep* riguardo a

touch'stone' *s* pietra di paragone

touch' type'writing *s* dattilografia a tatto

touch·y ['tʌtʃi] *adj* (-ier; -iest) suscettibile, permaloso; delicato, precario, rischioso

tough [tʌf] *adj* duro; forte; (*luck*) cattivo; violento ‖ *s* malvivente *m*

toughen ['tʌfən] *tr* indurire ‖ *intr* indurirsi

tough' luck' *s* disdetta, sfortuna

tour [tur] *s* gita, viaggio; (sports) giro; (mil) turno; (theat) tournée *f* ‖ *tr* girare; (theat) portare in tournée ‖ *intr* girare; (theat) andare in tournée

tour'ing car' ['turɪŋ] *s* automobile *f* da turismo

tourist ['turɪst] *adj* turistico ‖ *s* turista *mf*

tournament ['turnəmənt] or ['tʌrnəmənt] *s* torneo

tourney ['turni] or ['tʌrni] *s* torneo ‖ *intr* giostrare

tourniquet ['turnɪˌkɛt] or ['tʌrnɪˌke] *s* laccio emostatico

tousle ['tauzəl] *tr* spettinare

tow [to] *s* rimorchio; (*e.g., of hemp*) stoppa; **to take in tow** prendere a rimorchio ‖ *tr* rimorchiare

toward(s) [tord(z)] or [tə'word(z)] *prep* (*in the direction of*) verso; (*in respect to*) per; (*near*) vicino a; (*a certain hour*) su, verso

tow'boat' *s* rimorchiatore *m*

tow' car' *s* rimorchiatore *m*

tow·el ['tau·əl] *s* asciugamano; (*of paper*) salvietta; **to throw in the**

towel (slang) gettare la spugna ‖ v (*pret* & *pp* -**eled** or -**elled**; *ger* -**eling** or -**elling**) *tr* asciugare

tow′el rack′ s portaasciugamani m

tower ['tau·ər] s torre ƒ ‖ *intr* torreggiare

towering ['tau·ərɪŋ] *adj* torreggiante; gigantesco; eccessivo

towline ['to‚laɪn] s cavo di rimorchio

town [taun] s città ƒ; (*townspeople*) cittadinanza; **in town** in città

town′ clerk′ s segretario municipale

town′ coun′cil s consiglio comunale

town′ cri′er s banditore m municipale

town′ hall′ s municipio

township ['taunʃɪp] s suddivisione di contea

towns′man s (-**men**) cittadino; concittadino

towns′peo′ple spl cittadini mpl; gente ƒ di città

town′ talk′ s dicerie ƒpl, pettegolezzi mpl

tow′path′ s strada d'alaggio

tow′rope′ s corda da rimorchio

tow′ truck′ s autogru ƒ

toxic ['taksɪk] *adj* & s tossico

toy [tɔɪ] *adj* giocattolo; di giocattoli ‖ s giocattolo; (*trifle*) nonnulla m; (*trinket*) gingillo ‖ *intr* giocare; **to toy with** (*to play with*) giocare con; (*to trifle, e.g., with food*) baloccarsi con; (*an idea*) accarezzare; (*to flirt with*) flirtare con

toy′ bank′ s salvadanaio

toy′ sol′dier s soldatino di piombo

trace [tres] s traccia, vestigio; (*tracing*) tracciato; (*of harness*) tirella; (fig) ombra ‖ *tr* tracciare; (*e.g., s.o.'s ancestry*) rintracciare; (*a pattern*) lucidare

trac′er bul′let ['tresər] s pallottola tracciante

trache•a ['trekɪ·ə] s (-**ae** [‚i]) trachea

tracing ['tresɪŋ] s tracciato

track [træk] s (*of foot*) traccia, pesta; (*rut*) solco, rotaia; (*of boat*) scia; corso; (*course followed by boat*) rotta; (*of tape recorder*) pista; (*of tractor*) cingolo; (*of ideas*) successione; (*width of a vehicle measured from wheel to wheel*) (aut) carreggiata; (rr) binario; (*track and field*) (sports) atletica leggera; (*for horses*) (sports) galoppatoio; (*for running*) (sports) pista, corsia; **to keep track of** non perder di vista; **to lose track of** perder di vista; **to make tracks** (coll) affrettarsi; **to stop in one's tracks** (coll) fermarsi di colpo ‖ *tr* rintracciare, seguire le tracce di; lasciare tracce su; **to track down** rintracciare

track′ing sta′tion ['trækɪŋ] s (rok) stazione di avvistamento

track′less trol′ley ['træklɪs] s filobus m

track′ meet′ s incontro di atletica leggera

track′walk′er s (rr) guardialinee m

tract [trækt] s tratto, opuscolo, trattatello; (anat) tubo, canale m

traction ['trækʃən] s trazione

trac′tion com′pany s società ƒ di trasporti urbani

tractor ['træktər] s trattore m; (*of a tractor-trailer*) motrice ƒ

trac′tor-trail′er s treno stradale

trade [tred] s commercio; affare m; occupazione, mestiere m; (*people*) commercianti mpl, professionisti mpl; mercato; (*customers*) clientela; (*in slaves*) tratta ‖ *tr* mercanteggiare; cambiare; **to trade in** dare come pagamento parziale ‖ *intr* trafficare, commerciare; comprare; **to trade in** lavorare in; **to trade on** approfittarsi di

trade′mark′ s marca or marchio di fabbrica

trade′ name′ s ragione sociale

trader ['tredər] s trafficante m

trade′ school′ s scuola d'avviamento professionale, scuola d'arti e mestieri

trades′man s (-**men**) commerciante m; artigiano

trade′ un′ion s sindacato di lavoratori

trade′ un′ionist s sindacalista mf

trade′ winds′ spl alisei mpl

trad′ing post′ s centro di scambi commerciali; (*in stock exchange*) posto delle compravendite

trad′ing stamp′ s buono premio

tradition [trə'dɪʃən] s tradizione

traditional [trə'dɪʃənəl] *adj* tradizionale

traduce [trə'djus] or [trə'dus] *tr* calunniare

traf•fic ['træfɪk] s traffico, circolazione; commercio; comunicazione ‖ v (*pret* & *pp* -**ficked**; *ger* -**ficking**) *intr* trafficare

traf′fic cir′cle s raccordo a circolazione rotatoria

traf′fic court′ s tribunale m della polizia stradale

traf′fic is′land s isola spartitraffico

traf′fic jam′ s intralcio del traffico, ingorgo stradale

traf′fic light′ s semaforo

traf′fic man′ager s dirigente m del traffico; (rr) gestore m di stazione

traf′fic sign′ s segnale m di circolazione stradale, cartello indicatore

traf′fic tick′et s contravvenzione per violazione del traffico

tragedian [trə'dʒidɪ·ən] s tragico

trage•dy ['trædʒɪdi] s (-**dies**) tragedia

tragic ['trædʒɪk] *adj* tragico

trail [trel] s sentiero; (*track*) traccia, pista; (*of robe*) strascico, coda; (*of smoke*) pennacchio; (*left by an airplane*) striscia; (*of people*) codazzo ‖ *tr* strascicare; essere sulla fatta di; (*e.g., dust on the road*) sollevare; (*mud*) lasciar cadere ‖ *intr* strascicare; (*said, e.g., of a snake*) strisciare; (*said of a plant*) arrampicarsi; **to trail off** mutare; (*to weaken*) affievolirsi

trailer ['trelər] s traino; (*to haul freight*) semirimorchio; (*for living*) carovana, roulotte ƒ; (bot) rampicante m

train [tren] s (*of vehicles*) convoglio; (*of robe*) strascico; (*of thought*) ordine *m;* (*of people*) coda; (rr) treno ‖ *tr* addestrare, impratichire; (*a weapon*) puntare, rivolgere; (*a horse*) scozzonare; (*e.g., a dog*) ammaestrare; (*a plant*) far crescere; (sports) allenare ‖ *intr* addestrarsi; ammaestrarsi; (sports) allenarsi

trained' nurse' *s* infermiera diplomata

trainer ['trenər] *s* allenatore *m*

training ['trenɪŋ] *s* esercizio, esercitazione; (sports) allenamento

train'ing camp' *s* campo addestramento

train'ing school' *s* scuola di addestramento professionale; riformatorio

train'ing ship' *s* nave *f* scuola

trait [tret] *s* tratto, caratteristica

traitor ['tretər] *s* traditore *m*

traitress ['tretrɪs] *s* traditrice *f*

trajecto·ry [trə'dʒɛktəri] *s* (**-ries**) traiettoria

tramp [træmp] *s* lunga camminata; vagabondo; (*hussy*) sgualdrina ‖ *tr* attraversare; calpestare ‖ *intr* camminare a passi fermi; fare il vagabondo

trample ['træmpəl] *tr* calpestare; (fig) conculcare ‖ *intr*—**to trample on** or **upon** calpestare

trampoline ['træmpə‚lin] *s* trampolino di olona per salti mortali

tramp' steam'er *s* carretta

trance [træns] or [trɑns] *s* trance *f;* (*dazed condition*) estasi *f*

tranquil ['træŋkwɪl] *adj* tranquillo

tranquilize ['træŋkwɪ‚laɪz] *tr* tranquillizzare ‖ *intr* tranquillizzarsi

tranquilizer ['træŋkwɪ‚laɪzər] *s* tranquillante *m*

tranquillity [træn'kwɪlɪti] *s* tranquillità *f*

transact [træn'zækt] or [træns'ækt] *tr* sbrigare, trattare

transaction [træn'zækʃən] or [træns'ækʃən] *s* disbrigo, operazione

transatlantic [‚trænsət'læntɪk] *adj & s* transatlantico

transcend [træn'sɛnd] *tr* trascendere, sorpassare ‖ *intr* eccellere

transcribe [træn'skraɪb] *tr* trascrivere

transcript ['trænskrɪpt] *s* copia; traduzione; (educ) copia ufficiale del certificato di studi

transcription [træn'skrɪpʃən] *s* trascrizione

transept ['trænsept] *s* transetto

trans·fer ['trænsfər] *s* trasferimento; passaggio; (*pattern*) rapporto; (*of funds*) giro; (*of real estate*) compravendita; (law) voltura ‖ [træns'fʌr] or ['trænsfər] *v* (*pret & pp* **-ferred**; *ger* **-ferring**) *tr* trasferire, trasportare; (*funds*) stornare; (*a design*) rapportare; (*real estate*) compravendere ‖ *intr* trasferirsi; cambiare di treno

trans'fer tax' *s* tassa di successione; tassa sulla compravendita

transfix [træns'fɪks] *tr* trafiggere; paralizzare, inchiodare

transform [træns'fɔrm] *tr* trasformare; (elec) trasformare ‖ *intr* trasformarsi

transforma'tional gram'mar [‚trænsfər'meʃənəl] *s* grammatica trasformativa

transformer [træns'fɔrmər] *s* trasformatore *m*

transfusion [træns'fjuʃən] *s* trasfusione

transgress [træns'grɛs] *tr* trasgredire; (*a limit or boundry*) oltrepassare ‖ *intr* peccare

transgression [træns'grɛʃən] *s* trasgressione; peccato

transient ['trænʃənt] *adj* passeggero, temporaneo; di passaggio ‖ *s* ospite *mf* di passaggio

transistor [træn'zɪstər] *s* transistore *m*

transit ['trænsɪt] or ['trænzɪt] *s* transito

transition [træn'zɪʃən] *s* transizione

transitional [træn'zɪʃənəl] *adj* di transizione

transitive ['trænsɪtɪv] *adj* transitivo ‖ *s* verbo transitivo

transitory ['trænsɪ‚tori] *adj* transitorio

translate [træns'let] or ['trænslet] *tr* tradurre; convertire; (*to transfer*) trasportare ‖ *intr* tradursi

translation [træns'leʃən] *s* traduzione; trasformazione; (telg) ritrasmissione

translator [træns'letər] *s* traduttore *m*

transliterate [træns'lɪtə‚ret] *tr* traslitterare

translucent [træns'lusənt] *adj* traslucido; (fig) chiaro

transmission [træns'mɪʃən] *s* trasmissione; (aut) trasmissione

trans·mit [træns'mɪt] *v* (*pret & pp* **-mitted**; *ger* **-mitting**) *tr & intr* trasmettere

transmitter [træns'mɪtər] *s* trasmettitore *m*

transmit'ting set' *s* emittente *f*

transmit'ting sta'tion *s* stazione trasmettitrice

transmute [træns'mjut] *tr & intr* trasmutare

transom ['trænsəm] *s* (*crosspiece*) traversa; (*window over door*) vasistas *m;* (naut) specchio di poppa

transparen·cy ['træns'pɛransi] *s* (**-cies**) trasparenza; (*design on a translucent substance*) trasparente *m;* (phot) diapositiva

transparent [træns'pɛrənt] *adj* trasparente

transpire [træns'paɪr] *intr* (*to happen*) avvenire; (*to perspire*) traspirare; (*to become known*) trapelare

transplant [træns'plænt] or [træns'plɑnt] *tr* trapiantare ‖ *intr* trapiantarsi

transport ['trænsport] *s* trasporto; mezzo di trasporto ‖ [træns'port] *tr* trasportare

transportation [‚trænspor'teʃən] *s* trasporto; trasporti *mpl*, locomozione; biglietto di trasporto

trans'port work'er *s* ferrotranviere *m*

transpose [træns'poz] *tr* trasporre; (mus) trasportare

trans·ship [træns'ʃɪp] *v* (*pret & pp* **-shipped**; *ger* **-shipping**) *tr* trasbordare

trap [træp] *s* trappola, tranello;

(*double-curved pipe*) sifone *m;* (slang) bocca; (sports) congegno lanciapiattelli ‖ *v* (*pret & pp* **trapped;** *ger* **trapping**) *tr* intrappolare, accalappiare

trap′ door′ *s* trabocchetto, botola; (theat) ribalta

trapeze [trə'piz] *s* (sports) trapezio

trapezoid ['træpɪ‚zɔɪd] *s* (geom) trapezio, trapezoide *m*

trapper ['træpər] *s* cacciatore *m* di animali da pelliccia con trappole

trappings ['træpɪŋz] *spl* ornamenti *mpl;* (*for a horse*) gualdrappa

trap′shoot′ing *s* tiro al piattello

trash [træʃ] *s* immondizia, spazzatura; (*nonsense*) sciocchezze *fpl;* (*junk*) ciarpame *m;* (*worthless people*) gentaglia

trash′ can′ *s* portaimmondizie *m*

travail ['trævel] *or* [trə'vel] *s* travaglio; travaglio di parto

trav·el ['trævəl] *s* viaggio; traffico; (mach) corsa ‖ *v* (*pret & pp* **-eled** or **-elled;** *ger* **-eling** or **-elling**) *tr* viaggiare per, percorrere ‖ *intr* viaggiare; muoversi; (coll) andare

trav′el a′gency *s* ufficio turistico

traveler ['trævələr] *s* viaggiatore *m*

trav′eler's check′ *s* assegno viaggiatori

trav′eling bag′ *s* sacca da viaggio

trav′eling expens′es *spl* spese *fpl* di viaggio; (*per diem*) trasferta

trav′eling sales′man *s* (**-men**) commesso viaggiatore

traverse ['trævərs] *or* [trə'vʌrs] *tr* attraversare

traves·ty ['trævɪsti] *s* (**-ties**) parodia ‖ *v* (*pret & pp* **-tied**) *tr* parodiare

trawl [trɔl] *s* (*fishing net*) rete *f* a strascico; (*fishing line*) lenza al traino ‖ *tr & intr* pescare con la rete a strascico; pescare con la lenza al traino

trawling ['trɔlɪŋ] *s* pesca con la rete a strascico; pesca con la lenza al traino

tray [tre] *s* guantiera, vassoio; (chem, phot) bacinella

treacherous ['trɛtʃərəs] *adj* traditore, subdolo; incerto, pericoloso

treacher·y ['trɛtʃəri] *s* (**-ies**) tradimento

tread [trɛd] *s* (*step*) passo; (*of shoe*) suola; (*of tire*) battistrada *m;* (*of stairs*) pedata ‖ *v* (*pret* **trod** [trad]; *pp* **trodden** ['tradən] *or* **trod**) *tr* calpestare; (*the boards*) calcare; accoppiarsi con ‖ *intr* camminare; **to tread on** calpestare

treadle ['trɛdəl] *s* pedale *m*

tread′mill′ *s* ruota azionata col camminare; (fig) lavoro ingrato

treason ['trizən] *s* tradimento

treasonable ['trizənəbəl] *adj* traditore

treasure ['trɛʒər] *s* tesoro ‖ *tr* far tesoro di

treasurer ['trɛʒərər] *s* tesoriere *m*

treas′ure hunt′ *s* caccia al tesoro

treasur·y ['trɛʒəri] *s* (**-ies**) tesoreria; tesoro, erario

treat [trit] *s* trattenimento; (*something affording pleasure*) piacere *m,* diletto ‖ *tr* trattare; (*to cure*) curare, medi-

care; offrire un trattenimento a ‖ *intr* trattare; pagare per il trattenimento

treatise ['tritɪs] *s* trattato

treatment ['tritmənt] *s* trattamento; (*of a theme*) trattazione

trea·ty ['triti] *s* (**-ties**) trattato

treble ['trɛbəl] *adj* (*threefold*) triplo; (mus) soprano ‖ *s* (*person*) soprano *mf;* (*voice*) soprano ‖ *tr* triplicare ‖ *intr* triplicarsi

tree [tri] *s* albero

tree′ farm′ *s* bosco ceduo

tree′ frog′ *s* raganella

treeless ['trilɪs] *adj* spoglio, senza alberi

tree′top′ *s* cima dell'albero

trellis ['trɛlɪs] *s* traliccio, graticcio

tremble ['trɛmbəl] *s* tremito ‖ *intr* tremare

tremendous [trɪ'mɛndəs] *adj* tremendo

tremor ['trɛmər] *or* ['trimər] *s* tremito; (*of earth*) scossa

trench [trɛntʃ] *s* fosso, canale *m;* (mil) trincea

trenchant ['trɛntʃənt] *adj* mordace, caustico; vigoroso; incisivo

trench′ coat′ *s* trench *m*

trench′ mor′tar *s* lanciabombe *m*

trend [trɛnd] *s* tendenza, orientamento ‖ *intr* tendere, dirigersi

Trent [trɛnt] *s* Trento *f*

trespass ['trɛspəs] *s* (law) intrusione, violazione di proprietà ‖ *intr* entrare senza diritto, intrudersi; peccare; **no trespassing** divieto di passaggio; **to trespass against** peccare contro; **to trespass on** entrare abusivamente in; (*e.g., s.o.'s time*) abusare di; violare

tress [trɛs] *s* treccia

trestle ['trɛsəl] *s* cavalletto; viadotto a cavalletti; ponte *m* a cavalletti

trial ['traɪ·əl] *s* tentativo, prova; tribolazione, croce *f;* (law) giudizio, processo; **on trial** in prova; (law) sotto processo; **to bring to trial** sottoporre a processo

tri′al and er′ror *s* metodo per tentativo; **by trial and error** a tastoni

tri′al balloon′ *s* pallone *m* sonda

tri′al by ju′ry *s* processo con giuria

tri′al ju′ry *s* giuria civile or processuale

tri′al or′der *s* (com) ordine *m* di prova

tri′al run′ *s* viaggio di prova

triangle ['traɪ‚æŋgəl] *s* triangolo; (*in drafting*) quartabuono

tribe [traɪb] *s* tribù *f*

tribunal [trɪ'bjunəl] *or* [traɪ'bjunəl] *s* tribunale *m*

tribune ['trɪbjun] *s* tribuna

tributar·y ['trɪbjə‚tɛri] *adj* tributario ‖ *s* (**-ies**) tributario

tribute ['trɪbjut] *s* tributo; **to pay tribute to** (*e.g., beauty*) rendere omaggio a

trice [traɪs] *s* momento, istante *m;* **in a trice** in un batter d'occhio

trick [trɪk] *s* gherminella, inganno; trucco, tiro, scherzo; (*knack*) abilità *f;* (*feat*) atto; (*set of cards won*) presa; turno; (coll) piccola; **to be up to one's old tricks** farne una delle sue; **to play a dirty trick on** fare un brutto tiro a|| *tr* giocare, ingannare

tricker·y ['trɪkəri] *s* (**-ies**) gherminella, inganno

trickle ['trɪkəl] *s* gocciolio, filo || *intr* gocciolare; (*said of people*) andare or venire alla spicciolata; (*said of news*) trapelare

trickster ['trɪkstər] *s* imbroglione *m*

trick·y ['trɪki] *adj* (**-ier; -iest**) ingannatore; (*machine*) complicato; (*ticklish to deal with*) delicato

tried [traɪd] *adj* fedele, provato

trifle ['traɪfəl] *s* bazzecola, bagattella; (*small amount of money*) piccolezza, miseria; **a trifle** un po' || *tr*—**to trifle away** sprecare || *intr* gingillarsi; **to trifle with** giocherellare con; scherzare con; divertirsi con

trifling ['traɪflɪŋ] *adj* futile; insignificante, trascurabile

trifocal [traɪ'fokəl] *adj* trifocale || **trifocals** *spl* occhiali *mpl* trifocali

trigger ['trɪgər] *s* (*of a firearm*) grilletto; (*of any device*) leva di sgancio || *tr* (*a gun*) far sparare; (fig) scatenare

trigonometry [ˌtrɪgə'namɪtri] *s* trigonometria

trill [trɪl] *s* trillo, górgheggio; vibrazione; (*speech sound*) (phonet) vibrante *f* || *tr* gorgheggiare; pronunziare con vibrazione || *intr* trillare, gorgheggiare

trillion ['trɪljən] *s* trilione *m*

trilo·gy ['trɪlədʒi] *s* (**-gies**) trilogia

trim [trɪm] *adj* (**trimmer; trimmest**) lindo, azzimato || *s* condizione; buona condizione; (*dress*) vestito; (*of hair*) taglio, sfumatura; decorazione, ornamento; (*of sails*) orientamento; (aut) attrezzatura della carrozzeria || *v* (*pret & pp* **trimmed;** *ger* **trimming**) *tr* tagliare; (*an edge*) rifilare; adattare; arrangiare; (*Christmas tree*) decorare; (*hair*) sfumare; (*a tree*) potare; ordinare, assettare; (*a sail*) orientare; (aer) equilibrare; (mach) sbavare; (coll) rimproverare; (coll) bastonare; (*to defeat* (coll) battere, vincere

trimming ['trɪmɪŋ] *s* ornamento, guarnizione; (coll) battitura, batosta; **trimmings** guarnizioni *mpl;* (mach) sbavatura; (mach) rifilatura

trini·ty ['trɪnɪti] *s* (**-ties**) (*group of three*) triade *f* || **Trinity** *s* Trinità *f*

trinket ['trɪŋkɪt] *s* (*small ornament*) ninnolo, gingillo; **trinkets** (*trivial objects*) paccottiglia

tri·o ['tri·o] *s* (**-os**) terzetto

trip [trɪp] *s* viaggio; corsa; (*stumble*) inciampata; (*act of causing s.o. to stumble*) sgambetto; (*error*) passo falso; passo agile || *v* (*pret & pp* **tripped;** *ger* **tripping**) *tr* far inciampare, far cadere; fare lo sgambetto a; cogliere in fallo; (mach) far scattare || *intr* inciampare; fare un passo falso; avanzare saltellando, saltellare; **to trip over** inciampare in

tripartite [traɪ'partaɪt] *adj* tripartito

tripe [traɪp] *s* trippa; (slang) sciocchezze *fpl*

trip'ham'mer *s* maglio meccanico

triphthong ['trɪfθɔŋ] or ['trɪfθaŋ] *s* trittongo

triple ['trɪpəl] *adj & s* triplo || *tr* triplicare || *intr* triplicarsi

triplet ['trɪplɪt] *s* (*offspring*) nato da un parto trigemino; (mus, poet) terzina

triplicate ['trɪplɪkɪt] *adj* triplicato || *s* triplice copia || ['trɪplɪˌket] *tr* triplicare

tripod ['traɪpad] *s* (*e.g., for a camera*) treppiede *m;* (*stool with three legs*) tripode *m*

triptych ['trɪptɪk] *s* trittico

trite [traɪt] *adj* trito, ritrito

triumph ['traɪ·əmf] *s* trionfo || *intr* trionfare

trium'phal arch' [traɪ'ʌmfəl] *s* arco trionfale

trivia ['trɪvɪ·ə] *spl* banalità *f*, futilità *f*

trivial ['trɪvɪ·əl] *adj* insignificante, futile, banale

Trojan ['trodʒən] *adj & s* troiano

Tro'jan Horse' *s* cavallo di Troia

Tro'jan War' *s* guerra troiana

troll [trol] *tr & intr* pescare con la lenza al traino, pescare con il cucchiaino

trolley ['trali] *s* asta di presa, trolley *m;* carrozza tranviaria, tram *m*

trol'ley bus' *s* filobus *m*

trol'ley car' *s* vettura tranviaria, tram *m*

trol'ley pole' *s* trolley *m*

trollop ['traləp] *s* (*slovenly woman*) sciattona; (*hussy*) sgualdrina

trombone ['trambon] *s* trombone *m*

troop [trup] *s* truppa, gruppo; (*of animals*) branco; (*of cavalry*) squadrone *m;* **troops** soldati *mpl* || *intr* raggrupparsi; marciare insieme

trooper ['trupər] *s* soldato di cavalleria; poliziotto a cavallo; **to swear like a trooper** bestemmiare come un turco

tro·phy ['trofi] *s* (**-phies**) trofeo; (*any memento*) ricordo

tropic ['trapɪk] *adj* tropicale || *s* tropico; **tropics** zona tropicale

tropical ['trapɪkəl] *adj* tropicale

troposphere ['trapəˌsfɪr] *s* troposfera

trot [trat] *s* trotto || *v* (*pret & pp* **trotted;** *ger* **trotting**) *tr* far trottare; **to trot out** (coll) squadernare, esibire || *intr* trottare

troth [troθ] or [troθ] *s* promessa di matrimonio; **by my troth** affè di Dio; **in troth** in verità; **to plight one's troth** impegnarsi; dare la parola

troubadour ['trubəˌdor] or ['trubəˌdur] *s* trovatore *m*

trouble ['trʌbəl] *s* disturbo, fastidio; inconveniente *m*, grattacapo; disordine *m*, conflitto; (*of a mechanical nature*) panna, guasto; **not to be worth the trouble** non valere la pena; **that's the trouble** questo è il male; **the trouble is that** il guaio è che; **to be in trouble** essere nei guai; **to be**

looking for **trouble** andare a cercarsi le grane; **to get into trouble** mettersi nei pasticci; **to have trouble in** + *ger* durar fatica a + *inf;* **to take the trouble** incomodarsi ‖ *tr* molestare, disturbare; *(e.g., water)* intorbidare; dar del filo da torcere a; **to be troubled with** soffrire di; **to trouble oneself** scomodarsi

trouble' light' *s* lampada di soccorso

trou'ble-mak'er *s* mettimale *mf*

troubleshooter ['trʌbəl ʃutər] *s* localizzatore *m* di guasti; *(in disputes)* paciere *m*, conciliatore *m*

troubleshooting ['trʌbəl ʃutɪŋ] *s* localizzazione dei guasti; *(of disputes)* composizione

troublesome ['trʌbəlsəm] *adj* molesto; difficile

trouble' spot' *s* luogo di disordini, polveriera

trough [trɔf] or [traf] *s (to knead bread)* madia; *(for feeding pigs)* trogolo; *(for feeding animals)* mangiatoia; *(for watering animals)* abbeveratoio; *(gutter)* doccia; *(between two waves)* cavo

troupe [trup] *s* troupe *f*

trouper ['trupər] *s* membro della troupe; vecchio attore; tipo di cui ci si può fidare

trousers ['trauzərz] *spl* pantaloni *mpl*

trousseau [tru'so] or ['truso] *s* (**-seaux** or **-seaus**) corredo da sposa

trout [traut] *s* trota

trouvère [tru'vɛr] *s* troviero

trowel ['trau-əl] *s* cazzuola, mestola

Troy [trɔɪ] *s* Troia

truant ['tru-ənt] *s* fannullone *m;* **to play truant** marinare la scuola

truce [trus] *s* tregua

truck [trʌk] *s* autocarro, camion *m; (tractor-trailer)* autotreno; *(van)* furgone *m; (to be moved by hand)* carretto; verdura per il mercato; *(mach, rr)* carrello; *(coll)* robaccia; *(coll)* relazioni *fpl* ‖ *tr* trasportare per autocarro, autotrasportare

truck'driv'er *s* camionista *m*

truck' farm' *s* fattoria agricola per la produzione degli ortaggi

truculent ['trʌkjələnt] or ['trukjələnt] *adj* truculento

trudge [trʌdʒ] *intr* camminare; **to trudge along** camminare laboriosamente, scarpinare

true [tru] *adj* vero; esatto, conforme; legittimo; infallibile; a livello; **to come true** verificarsi; **true to life** conforme alla realtà

true' cop'y *s* copia conforme

true-hearted ['tru ,hartɪd] *adj* fedele

true'love knot' *s* nodo d'amore

truffle ['trʌfəl] or ['trufəl] *s* tartufo

truism ['tru·ɪzəm] *s* truismo

truly ['truli] *adv* veramente, correttamente; **yours truly** distinti saluti

trump [trʌmp] *s* (cards) atout *m;* (Italian cards) briscola; **no trump** senza atout ‖ *tr* superare; (cards) pigliare con un atout o con una briscola; **to**

trump up inventare, fabbricare ‖ *intr* giocare un atout or una briscola

trumpet ['trʌmpɪt] *s* tromba; *(toy)* trombetta; **to blow one's own trumpet** cantare le proprie lodi ‖ *tr* strombazzare ‖ *intr* sonar la tromba; strombazzare; *(said of an elephant)* barrire

truncheon ['trʌntʃən] *s* bastone *m* del comando; (Brit) manganello

trunk [trʌŋk] *s (of living body, tree, family, railroad)* tronco; *(for clothes)* baule *m; (of elephant)* tromba; (aut) bagagliaio; (archit) fusto; (telp) linea principale; **trunks** pantaloncini *mpl*

trunk' hose' *s* (hist) brache *fpl*

truss [trʌs] *s (to support a roof)* capriata, incavallatura; *(based on cantilever system)* intralicciatura; *(for reducing a hernia)* cinto, brachiere *m;* (bot) infiorescenza ‖ *tr* legare, assicurare

trust [trʌst] *s* fede *f;* speranza; fiducia, custodia; (com) trust *m*, cartello; (law) fedecommesso; **in trust** in deposito; come fedecommesso; **on trust** a credito ‖ *tr* fidarsi di; credere (with *dat*); *(to entrust)* dare in deposito a; dare a credito a ‖ *intr* credere; fidarsi, prestar fede; **to trust in** *(e.g., a friend)* fidarsi di; (God) aver fede in

trust' com'pany *s* compagnia fedecommissaria; banca di deposito

trustee [trʌs'ti] *s* amministratore *m;* fiduciario; *(of a university)* curatore *m; (of an estate)* fedecommissario

trusteeship [trʌs'ti ʃɪp] *s* amministrazione; (law) fedecommesso; (pol) amministrazione fiduciaria

trustful ['trʌstfəl] *adj* fiducioso

trust'wor'thy *adj* fidato, di fiducia

trust·y ['trʌsti] *adj* (**-ier; -iest**) fidato ‖ *s* (**-ies**) carcerato degno di fiducia

truth [truθ] *s* verità *f;* **in truth** in verità

truthful ['truθfəl] *adj* verace, veritiero

try [traɪ] *s* (**tries**) tentativo, prova ‖ *v* (*pret & pp* **tried**) *tr* provare; *(s.o.'s patience)* mettere a dura prova; *(a person)* (law) processare; *(a case)* (law) giudicare; **to try on** *(clothes)* provare; **to try out** provare; esperimentare ‖ *intr* cercare, tentare; **to try out for** cercare di ottenere il posto di; (sports) cercare di farsi accettare in; **to try to** cercare di

trying ['traɪ·ɪŋ] *adj* duro, penoso, difficile

tryst [trɪst] or [traɪst] *s* appuntamento

T'-shirt' *s* maglietta

tub [tʌb] *s* tino, bigoncia; vasca da bagno; *(clumsy boat)* (slang) carretta; *(fat person)* (slang) bombolo

tube [tjub] or [tub] *s* tubo; *(e.g., for toothpaste)* tubetto; *(of tire)* camera d'aria; (anat) tuba, tromba; (coll) ferrovia sotterranea

tuber ['tjubər] or ['tubər] *s* tubero

tubercle ['tjubərkəl] or ['tubərkəl] *s* tubercolo

tuberculosis [tju͵bɑrkjə'losɪs] or [tu͵bɑrkjə'losɪs] s tuberculosi f

tuck [tʌk] s basta ‖ tr ripiegare; **to tuck away** nascondere; (slang) fare una scorpacciata di; **to tuck in** rincalzare; **to tuck up** rimboccare

tucker ['tʌkər] s collarino di merletto ‖ tr—**to tucker out** (coll) stancare

Tuesday ['tjuzdi] or ['tuzdi] s martedì m

tuft [tʌft] s (of feathers) pennacchio; (of hair) cernecchio; (of flowers) cespo; (fluffy threads) fiocco, nappa ‖ tr impuntire; adornare di fiocchi ‖ intr crescere a cernecchi

tug [tʌg] s strattone m, strappata; (struggle) lotta; (boat) rimorchiatore m ‖ v (pret & pp **tugged**; ger **tugging**) tr tirare; (a boat) rimorchiare ‖ intr tirare con forza; lottare

tug'boat' s rimorchiatore m

tug' of war' s tiro alla fune

tuition [tju'ɪʃən] or [tu'ɪʃən] s (instruction) insegnamento; tassa scolastica

tulip ['tjulɪp] or ['tulɪp] s tulipano

tumble ['tʌmbəl] s rotolone m, ruzzolone m; (somersault) salto mortale; caduta; disordine m, confusione; (confused heap) mucchio ‖ intr rotolare, ruzzolare; cadere, capitombolare; gettarsi; rigirarsi; **to tumble down** cadere in rovina; **to tumble to** (coll) rendersi conto di

tum'ble-down' adj dilapidato

tumbler ['tʌmblər] s (acrobat) saltimbanco; (glass) bicchiere m; (in a lock) levetta; (toy) misirizzi m

tumor ['tjumər] or ['tumər] s tumore m

tumult ['tjumʌlt] or ['tumʌlt] s tumulto

tun [tʌn] s botte f, barile m

tuna ['tunə] s tonno

tune [tjun] or [tun] s (air) aria; (manner of speaking) tono; **in tune** intonato; **out of tune** stonato; **to change one's tune** cambiare di tono ‖ tr intonare; **to tune in** (rad) sintonizzare; **to tune out** (rad) interrompere la sintonizzazione di; **to tune up** (a motor) mettere a punto; (mus) intonare

tuner ['tunər] or ['tjunər] s (rad) sintonizzatore m; (mus) accordatore m

tungsten ['tʌŋstən] s tungsteno

tunic ['tjunɪk] or ['tunɪk] s tunica

tun'ing coil' or ['tunɪŋ] or ['tjunɪŋ] s bobina di sintonia

tun'ing fork' s diapason m, corista m

Tunis ['tjunɪs] or ['tunɪs] s Tunisi f

Tunisia [tju'niʒə] or [tu'niʒə] s la Tunisia

Tunisian [tju'niʒən] or [tu'niʒən] adj & s tunisino

tun·nel ['tʌnəl] s tunnel m, traforo, galleria; (min) galleria ‖ v (pret & pp **-neled** or **-nelled**; ger **-neling** or **-nelling**) tr costruire un passaggio attraverso or sotto a

turban ['tʌrbən] s turbante m

turbid ['tʌrbɪd] adj turbido

turbine ['tʌrbɪn] or ['tʌrbaɪn] s turbina

turbojet ['tʌrbo͵dʒɛt] s turboreattore m

turboprop ['tʌrbo͵prɑp] s turboelica m

turbulent ['tʌrbjələnt] adj turbolento

tureen [tu'rin] or [tju'rin] s terrina

turf [tʌrf] s zolla erbosa; (peat) torba; **the turf** il campo delle corse; le corse, il turf

turf'man s (-men) amatore m delle corse ippiche

Turk [tʌrk] s turco

turkey ['tʌrki] s tacchino ‖ **Turkey** s la Turchia

turk'ey vul'ture s (Cathartes aura) avvoltoio americano

Turkish ['tʌrkɪʃ] adj & s turco

Turk'ish tow'el s asciugamano spugna

turmoil ['tʌrmɔɪl] s subbuglio

turn [tʌrn] s giro; (time for action) turno, volta; (change of direction) voltata; (bend) svolta, curva; (of events) piega; servizio; inclinazione, attitudine f; (of key) mandata; (of coil) spira; (coll) colpo, sussulto; (aer, naut) virata; **at every turn** a ogni piè sospinto; **in turn** a tua (Sua, vostra, etc.) volta; **to be one's turn** toccare a qlcu, e.g., **it's your turn** tocca a Lei; **to take turns** fare a turno ‖ tr girare, voltare; (soil) rovesciare; (to make sour) coagulare; (to translate) tradurre; (e.g., ten years) raggiungere; (e.g., one's eyes) volgere; (on a lathe) tornire; (e.g., a coat) rivoltare; (to twist) torcere; (the wheel) (aut) sterzare; **to turn against** mettere su contro; **to turn around** rigirare; (s.o.'s words) ritorcere; **to turn aside** sviare; **to turn away** cacciare via; **to turn back** ricacciare; restituire; (the clock) ritardare; **to turn down** ripiegare; (the light) abbassare; (an offer) rifiutare; **to turn in** ripiegare; denunziare; rassegnare; **to turn off** (e.g., light) spegnere, smorzare; (gas, water, etc.) tagliare; (e.g., a faucet) chiudere; **to turn on** (e.g., light, radio, etc.) accendere; (e.g., a faucet) aprire; **to turn out** mettere alla porta; (animals) fare uscire dalla stalla; rivoltare; (light) spegnere; produrre, fabbricare; **to turn up** ripiegare in su, rimboccare; (on a lathe) tornire; tirar su; (a card) scoprire; trovare; (e.g., the radio) alzare ‖ intr girare; svoltare, e.g., **turn left at the corner** svolti a sinistra all'angolo; girarsi; cambiare; fermentare; cambiare di colore; diventare; (naut) virare; **to turn against** voltarsi contro; inimicarsi con; **to turn around** fare una giravolta; **to turn aside** or **away** sviarsi; **to turn back** ritornare; retrocedere; **to turn down** piegarsi in giù; rovesciarsi; **to turn in** piegarsi, ripiegarsi; tornare a casa; (coll) andare a dormire; **to turn into** sfogare in; trasformarsi in; **to turn on** voltarsi contro; girarsi su; dipendere da; occuparsi di; **to turn**

out riuscire; **to turn out to be** manifestarsi; riuscire ad essere; **to turn over** rotolarsi; rovesciarsi; **to turn up** voltarsi all'insù; alzarsi; apparire, farsi vedere

turn'buck'le s tenditore m

turn'coat' s voltagabbana mf; **to become a turncoat** voltar gabbano

turn'down' adj (collar) rovesciato || s rifiuto

turn'ing point' s punto decisivo

turnip ['tʌrnɪp] s rapa

turn'key' s secondino, carceriere m

turn' of life' s menopausa

turn' of mind' s disposizione naturale

turn'out' s (gathering of people) concorso; (crowd) folla; produzione; (outfit) vestito; stile m, moda; (in a road) slargo, piazzola; (horse and carriage) equipaggio; (rr) binario laterale

turn'over' s (upset) rovesciamento, ribaltamento; (of customers) movimento di clienti; (of business) giro d'affari; rotazione di lavoratori; (com) ciclo operativo

turn'pike' s autostrada a pedaggio

turn' sig'nal s (aut) indicatore m di direzione, lampeggiatore m

turnstile ['tʌrn‚staɪl] s tornello

turn'ta'ble s (of phonograph) piatto rotante; (rr) piattaforma girevole

turpentine ['tʌrpən‚taɪn] s trementina

turpitude ['tʌrpɪ‚tjud] or ['tʌrpɪ‚tud] s turpitudine f

turquoise ['tʌrkɔɪz] or ['tʌrkwɔɪz] s turchese m

turret ['tʌrɪt] s torretta

turtle ['tʌrtəl] s tartaruga; **to turn turtle** rovesciarsi, capovolgersi

tur'tle‧dove' s tortora

Tuscan ['tʌskən] adj & s toscano

Tuscany ['tʌskəni] s la Toscana

tusk [tʌsk] s zanna

tussle ['tʌsəl] s lotta, zuffa || intr lottare, azzuffarsi

tutor ['tjutər] or ['tutər] s istitutore privato, ripetitore m; (guardian) tutore m || tr dare ripetizione a || intr dare ripetizioni; studiare con un ripetitore

tuxe‧do [tʌk'sido] s (-dos) smoking m

twaddle ['twadəl] s sciocchezze fpl || intr dire sciocchezze

twang [twæŋ] s (of musical instrument) suono vibrato; (of voice) timbro nasale || tr pizzicare; dire con un timbro nasale || intr parlare con voce nasale

twang‧y ['twæŋi] adj (-ier; -iest) (tone) metallico; (voice) nasale

tweed [twid] s tweed m; **tweeds** abito di tweed

tweet [twit] s pigolio || intr pigolare

tweeter ['twitər] s altoparlante m per alte audiofrequenze, tweeter m

tweezers ['twizərz] spl pinzette fpl

twelfth [twɛlfθ] adj, s & pron dodicesimo || s (in dates) dodici m

Twelfth'-night' s vigilia dell'Epifania; sera dell'Epifania

twelve [twɛlv] adj & pron dodici || s dodici m; **twelve o'clock** le dodici

twentieth ['twɛntɪ‧ɪθ] adj, s & pron ventesimo || s (in dates) venti m

twen‧ty ['twɛnti] adj & pron venti || s (-ties) venti m; **the twenties** gli anni venti

twice [twaɪs] adv due volte

twice'-told' adj detto più di una volta; detto e ridetto

twiddle ['twɪdəl] tr—**to twiddle one's thumbs** rigirare i pollici, oziare

twig [twɪg] s ramoscello; **twigs** sterpi mpl

twilight ['twaɪ‚laɪt] adj crepuscolare || s crepuscolo

twill [twɪl] s diagonale m || tr tessere in diagonale

twin [twɪn] adj & s gemello

twine [twaɪn] s spago || tr intrecciare || intr intrecciarsi

twinge [twɪndʒ] s punta, dolore acuto

twinkle ['twɪŋkəl] s scintillio; batter m d'occhio || intr scintillare

twin'-screw' adj a due eliche

twirl [twʌrl] s giro, mulinello || tr girare; (slang) lanciare || intr girare rapidamente, frullare

twist [twɪst] s curva; giro; viluppo, intreccio; tendenza, inclinazione; (yarn) ritorno; (e.g., of lemon) fettina; (dance) twist m || tr intrecciare; torcere; (e.g., the face) contorcere; (the meaning) stravolgere, stiracchiare; girare || intr intrecciarsi; torcersi, divincolarsi; girare; serpeggiare; **to twist and turn** (in bed) girarsi e rigirarsi

twister ['twɪstər] s (coll) tromba d'aria

twit [twɪt] v (pret & pp twitted; ger twitting) tr ridicolizzare

twitch [twɪtʃ] s tic m; (jerk) strattone m; (to restrain a horse) torcinaso || intr contrarsi; tremare; **to twitch at** tirare

twitter ['twɪtər] s garrito, cinguettio; (chatter) chiacchierio; ansia, agitazione || intr garrire, cinguettare; chiacchierare; tremare d'ansia

two [tu] adj & pron due || s due m; **to put two and two together** arrivare alle logiche conclusioni; **two o'clock** le due

two'-cy'cle adj a due tempi

two'-cyl'inder adj a due cilindri

two-edged ['tu ‚ɛdʒd] adj a doppio filo

two'fold' adj duplice, doppio

two' hun'dred adj, s & pron duecento

twosome ['tusəm] s coppia

two'-time' tr (slang) fare le corna a

two'-way ra'dio s ricetrasmettitore m

tycoon [taɪ'kun] s magnate m

type [taɪp] s tipo; (typ) carattere m; (pieces collectively) (typ) caratteri mpl || tr scrivere a macchina; simbolizzare || intr scrivere a macchina

type'face' s stile m di carattere

type'script' s dattiloscritto

typesetter ['taɪp‚sɛtər] s (person) compositore m; (machine) compositrice f

type'write' v (pret -wrote; pp -written)
tr & intr dattilografare, scrivere a
macchina
type'writ'er s (machine) macchina da
scrivere; (typist) dattilografo
type'writ'ing s dattilografia, scrittura a
macchina; lavoro battuto a macchina
ty'phoid fe'ver ['taɪfɔɪd] s febbre f
tifoide
typhoon [taɪ'fun] s tifone m
typical ['tɪpɪkəl] adj tipico
typi·fy ['tɪpɪ,faɪ] v (pret & pp -fied)
tr simbolizzare

typist ['taɪpɪst] s dattilografo
typographic(al) [,taɪpə'græfɪk(əl)] adj
tipografico
typograph'ical er'ror s errore m di
stampa
typography [taɪ'pɑgrəfi] s tipografia
tyrannic(al) [tɪ'rænɪk(əl)] or [taɪ-
'rænɪk(əl)] adj tirannico
tyrannous ['tɪrənəs] adj tiranno
tyrant ['taɪrənt] s tiranno
ty·ro ['taɪro] s (-ros) principiante m
Tyrrhe'nian Sea' [tɪ'rɪnɪ·ən] s Mare
Tirreno

U

U, u [ju] s ventunesima lettera del-
l'alfabeto inglese
ubiquitous [ju'bɪkwɪtəs] adj ubiquo
udder ['ʌdər] s mammella
ugliness ['ʌglɪnɪs] s bruttezza
ug·ly ['ʌgli] adj (-lier; -liest) brutto
Ukraine, the ['jukren] or [ju'kren]·s
l'Ucraina f
Ukrainian [ju'krenɪ·ən] adj & s
ucraino
ulcer ['ʌlsər] s piaga, ulcera; (corrupt-
ing element) (fig) piaga
ulcerate ['ʌlsə,ret] tr ulcerare ‖ intr
ulcerarsi
ulterior [ʌl'tɪrɪ·ər] adj ulteriore; (motive) nascosto, secondo
ultimate ['ʌltɪmɪt] adj ultimo
ultima·tum [,ʌltɪ'metəm] s (-tums or
-ta [tə]) ultimato
ultimo ['ʌltɪ,mo] adv del mese scorso
ul'tra·high fre'quency ['ʌltrə'haɪ] s
frequenza ultraelevata
ultrashort [,ʌltrə'ʃɔrt] adj ultracorto
ultraviolet [,ʌltrə'vaɪ·əlɪt] adj & s
ultravioletto
umbil'ical cord' [ʌm'bɪlɪkəl] s cordone
m ombelicale
umbrage ['ʌmbrɪdʒ] s—to take umbrage at adombrarsi per
umbrella [ʌm'brelə] s ombrello, parac-
qua m; (mil) ombrello
umbrel'la stand' s portaombrelli m
Umbrian ['ʌmbrɪ·ən] adj & s umbro
umlaut ['umlaut] s metafonesi f;
(mark) dieresi f ‖ tr cambiare il
timbro di; scrivere con dieresi
umpire ['ʌmpaɪr] s arbitro ‖ tr arbi-
trare ‖ intr fare l'arbitro
UN ['ju'en] s (letterword) (United
Nations) ONU f
unable [ʌn'ebəl] adj incapace; to be
unable to essere impossibilitato a,
non potere
unabridged [,ʌnə'brɪdʒd] adj integrale, non abbreviato
unaccented [ʌn'æksentɪd] or [,ʌnæk-
'sentɪd] adj non accentato, atono
unacceptable [,ʌnək'septəbəl] adj
inaccettabile
unaccountable [,ʌnə'kauntəbəl] adj irresponsabile; inesplicabile
unaccounted-for [,ʌnə'kauntɪd,fɔr]

adj (e.g., failure) inesplicato; (e.g.,
soldier) irreperibile, mancante
unaccustomed [,ʌnə'kʌstəmd] adj (unusual) insolito; non abituato
unafraid [,ʌnə'fred] adj impavido
unaligned [,ʌnə'laɪnd] adj non impegnato
unanimity [,junə'nɪmɪti] s unanimità f
unanimous [ju'nænɪməs] adj unanime
unanswerable [ʌn'ænsərəbəl] adj per
cui non vi è risposta; (argument)
irrefutabile, incontestabile
unappreciative [,ʌnə'priʃɪ,etɪv] adj
sconoscente, ingrato
unapproachable [,ʌnə'protʃəbəl] adj
inabbordabile; incomparabile
unarmed [ʌn'armd] adj disarmato,
inerme
unascertainable [ʌn,æsər'tenəbəl] adj
non verificabile
unassailable [,ʌnə'seləbəl] adj inattac-
cabile
unassembled [,ʌnə'sembəld] adj smon-
tato
unassuming [,ʌnə'sumɪŋ] or [,ʌnə-
'sjumɪŋ] adj modesto, semplice
unattached [,ʌnə'tætʃt] adj indipendente; (loose) sciolto; non sposato;
non fidanzato
unattainable [,ʌnə'tenəbəl] adj inarri-
vabile, irraggiungibile
unattractive [,ʌnə'træktɪv] adj poco
attraente
unavailable [,ʌnə'veləbəl] adj non disponibile
unavailing [,ʌnə'velɪŋ] adj futile
unavoidable [,ʌnə'vɔɪdəbəl] adj inevitabile, ineluttabile
unaware [,ʌnə'wer] adj inconsapevole,
ignaro ‖ adv inaspettatamente; (unknowingly) inavvertitamente
unawares [,ʌnə'werz] adv inaspettatamente; (unknowingly) inavvertitamente
unbalanced [ʌn'bælənst] adj sbilan-
ciato, squilibrato
unbandage [ʌn'bændɪdʒ] tr sbendare
un·bar [ʌn'bar] v (pret & pp -barred;
ger -barring) tr disserrare il chiavistello di
unbearable [ʌn'berəbəl] adj insopportabile, insostenibile

unbeatable [ʌn'bitəbəl] *adj* imbattibile
unbecoming [ˌʌnbɪ'kʌmɪŋ] *adj* sconveniente, indegno; (*e.g.*, *hat*) disadatto, che non sta bene
unbelievable [ˌʌnbɪ'livəbəl] *adj* incredibile
unbeliever [ˌʌnbɪ'livər] *s* miscredente *mf*
unbending [ʌn'bɛndɪŋ] *adj* inflessibile
unbiased [ʌn'baɪ·əst] *adj* imparziale, spassionato
un·bind [ʌn'baɪnd] *v* (*pret & pp* **-bound** ['baʊnd]) *tr* slegare
unbleached [ʌn'blitʃt] *adj* non candeggiato, al colore naturale
unbolt [ʌn'bolt] *tr* (*a door*) togliere il chiavistello a; sbullonare
unborn [ʌn'bɔrn] *adj* nascituro
unbosom [ʌn'buzəm] *tr* (*a secret*) rivelare; **to unbosom oneself** aprire il proprio animo, sfogarsi
unbound [ʌn'baʊnd] *adj* sciolto, libero; (*book*) non rilegato
unbreakable [ʌn'brekəbəl] *adj* infrangibile
unbridle [ʌn'braɪdəl] *tr* sbrigliare
unbuckle [ʌn'bʌkəl] *tr* sfibbiare
unburden [ʌn'bʌrdən] *tr* scaricare; **to unburden oneself (of)** vuotare il sacco (di)
unburied [ʌn'bɛrid] *adj* insepolto
unbutton [ʌn'bʌtən] *tr* sbottonare
uncalled-for [ʌn'kɔld ˌfɔr] *adj* superfluo, gratuito; fuori di posto, sconveniente
uncanny [ʌn'kæni] *adj* misterioso, straordinario
uncared-for [ʌn'kɛrd ˌfɔr] *adj* negletto, trascurato
unceasing [ʌn'sisɪŋ] *adj* incessante
unceremonious [ˌʌnsɛrɪ'moni·əs] *adj* senza cerimonie
uncertain [ʌn'sʌrtən] *adj* incerto
uncertain·ty [ʌn'sʌrtənti] *s* (**-ties**) incertezza
unchain [ʌn'tʃen] *tr* scatenare, sferrare
unchangeable [ʌn'tʃendʒəbəl] *adj* immutabile
uncharted [ʌn'tʃartɪd] *adj* inesplorato
unchecked [ʌn'tʃɛkt] *adj* incontrollato
uncivilized [ʌn'sɪvɪˌlaɪzd] *adj* incivile
unclad [ʌn'klæd] *adj* svestito
unclaimed [ʌn'klemd] *adj* non reclamato; (*letter*) giacente
unclasp [ʌn'klæsp] *or* [ʌn'klasp] *tr* sfibbiare
unclassified [ʌn'klæsɪˌfaɪd] *adj* non classificato; non secreto
uncle ['ʌŋkəl] *s* zio
unclean [ʌn'klin] *adj* immondo
un·clog [ʌn'klɑg] *v* (*pret & pp* **-clogged;** *ger* **-clogging**) *tr* disintasare
unclouded [ʌn'klaʊdɪd] *adj* sereno, senza nubi
uncollectible [ˌʌnkə'lɛktɪbəl] *adj* inesigibile
uncomfortable [ʌn'kʌmfərtəbəl] *adj* scomodo, disagevole
uncommitted [ˌʌnkə'mɪtɪd] *adj* non impegnato
uncommon [ʌn'kɑmən] *adj* raro, straordinario

uncompromising [ʌn'kɑmprəˌmaɪzɪŋ] *adj* intransigente
unconcerned [ˌʌnkən'sʌrnd] *adj* indifferente, noncurante
unconditional [ˌʌnkən'dɪʃənəl] *adj* incondizionato
uncongenial [ˌʌnkən'dʒini·əl] *adj* antipatico, sgradito
unconquerable [ʌn'kɑŋkərəbəl] *adj* inconquistabile, inespugnabile
unconscionable [ʌn'kɑnʃənəbəl] *adj* senza scrupoli; eccessivo
unconscious [ʌn'kɑnʃəs] *adj* (*without awareness*) inconscio, inconsapevole; (*temporarily devoid of consciousness*) incosciente; (*unintentional*) involontario
unconsciousness [ʌn'kɑnʃəsnɪs] *s* incoscienza
unconstitutional [ˌʌnkɑnstɪ'tjuʃənəl] *or* [ˌʌnkɑnstɪ'tuʃənəl] *adj* incostituzionale
uncontrollable [ˌʌnkən'troləbəl] *adj* incontrollabile, ingovernabile
unconventional [ˌʌnkən'vɛnʃənəl] *adj* non convenzionale, anticonformista
uncork [ʌn'kɔrk] *tr* stappare
uncouple [ʌn'kʌpəl] *tr* sganciare, disconnettere
uncouth [ʌn'kuθ] *adj* zotico, incivile, pacchiano
uncover [ʌn'kʌvər] *tr* scoprire
unction ['ʌŋkʃən] *s* unzione; (fig) untuosità *f*
unctuous ['ʌŋktʃʊ·əs] *adj* untuoso
uncultivated [ʌn'kʌltɪˌvetɪd] *adj* incolto
uncultured [ʌn'kʌltʃərd] *adj* incolto, rozzo
uncut [ʌn'kʌt] *adj* non tagliato; (*book*) intonso
undamaged [ʌn'dæmɪdʒd] *adj* indenne, illeso
undaunted [ʌn'dɔntɪd] *adj* imperterrito, impavido
undeceive [ˌʌndɪ'siv] *tr* disingannare
undecided [ˌʌndɪ'saɪdɪd] *adj* indeciso
undefeated [ˌʌndɪ'fitɪd] *adj* invitto
undefended [ˌʌndɪ'fɛndɪd] *adj* indifeso
undefensible [ˌʌndɪ'fɛnsɪbəl] *adj* insostenibile
undefiled [ˌʌndɪ'faɪld] *adj* puro, immacolato
undeniable [ˌʌndɪ'naɪ·əbəl] *adj* innegabile, indubitato
under ['ʌndər] *adj* di sotto; (*lower*) inferiore; (*clothing*) intimo, personale ‖ *adv* sotto; più sotto; **to go under** affondare; cedere; (coll) fallire ‖ *prep* sotto; sotto a; (*e.g.*, *20 years old*) meno di; **under full sail** a vele spiegate; **under lock and key** sotto chiave; **under oath** sotto giuramento; **under penalty of death** sotto pena di morte; **under sail** a vela; **under separate cover** in plico separato; **under steam** sotto pressione; **under the hand and seal of** firmato di pugno di; **under the weather** (coll) un po' indisposto; **under way** già iniziato
un′der·age′ *adj* minorenne
un′der-arm′ pad′ *s* sottoascella *m*

un'der·bid' v (pret & pp **-bid;** ger **-bidding**) tr fare un'offerta inferiore a quella di

un'der·brush' s sottobosco

un'der·car'riage s (aut) telaio; (aer) carrello d'atterraggio

un'der·clothes' spl biancheria intima

un'der·consump'tion s sottoconsumo

un'der·cov'er adj segreto

un'der·cur'rent s (of water) corrente subacquea; (of air) corrente f inferiore; (fig) controcorrente f

underdeveloped [ˌʌndərdɪˈvɛləpt] adj sottosviluppato

un'der·dog' s chi è destinato ad avere la peggio; vittima; **the underdogs** i diseredati

un'der·done' adj non cotto abbastanza

un'der·es'timate tr sottovalutare

un'der·gar'ment s indumento intimo

un'der·go' v (pret **-went;** pp **-gone**) tr (a test) passare, sottostare (with dat); (surgery) subire, sottoporsi a; soffrire

un'der·grad'uate adj (student) non ancora laureato; (course) per studenti non ancora laureati || s studente universitario che non ha ancora ricevuto il primo diploma

un'der·ground' adj sotterraneo; segreto || s regione sotterranea; macchia, resistenza || adv sottoterra; alla macchia, segretamente

un'der·growth' s sterpaglia

underhanded [ˈʌndərˌhændəd] adj subdolo, di sottomano

un'der·line' or **un'der·line'** tr sottolineare

underling [ˈʌndərlɪŋ] s tirapiedi m

un'der·mine' tr scalzare, minare

underneath [ˌʌndərˈniθ] adj inferiore || s disotto || adv sotto, di sotto || prep sotto a, sotto

undernourished [ˌʌndərˈnʌrɪʃt] adj denutrito, malnutrito

un'der·pass' s sottopassaggio

un'der·pay' s (pret & pp **-paid**) tr & intr pagare insufficientemente

un'der·pin' v (pret & pp **-pinned;** ger **-pinning**) tr rincalzare

underprivileged [ˌʌndərˈprɪvɪlɪdʒd] adj derelitto, diseredato

un'der·rate' tr sottovalutare

un'der·score' tr sottolineare

un'der·sea' adj sottomarino || adv sotto il mare

un'der·seas' adv sotto il mare

un'der·sec'retar'y s (-ies) sottosegretario

un'der·sell' v (pret & pp **-sold**) tr vendere a prezzo minore di; (to sell for less than actual value) svendere

un'der·shirt' s camiciola, canottiera

undersigned [ˈʌndərˌsaɪnd] adj sottoscritto

un'der·skirt' s sottogonna

un'der·stand' v (pret & pp **-stood**) tr capire, comprendere; sottintendere; (to accept as true) constare, e.g., **he understands that you are wrong** gli consta che Lei ha torto || intr capire, comprendere

understandable [ˌʌndərˈstændəbəl] adj comprensibile

understanding [ˌʌndərˈstændɪŋ] adj comprensivo, tollerante || s (mind) intelletto; (knowledge) conoscenza; comprensione, intendimento; (agreement) intesa, accordo

understatement [ˌʌndərˈstetmənt] s sottovalutazione

un'der·stud'y s (-ies) (theat) doppio, sostituto || v (-ied) tr (an actor) fare il doppio di

un'der·take' v (pret **-took;** ger **-taken**) tr intraprendere; (to promise) promettere

undertaker [ˌʌndərˈtekər] or [ˈʌndərˌtekər] s impresario || [ˈʌndərˌtekər] s impresario di pompe funebri

undertaking [ˌʌndərˈtekɪŋ] s (task) impresa; (promise) promessa || [ˈʌndərˌtekɪŋ] s impresa di pompe funebri

un'der·tone' s bassa voce; (background sound) ronzio di fondo; tono; colore smorzato

un'der·tow' s (on the beach) risacca; (countercurrent below surface) controcorrente f

un'der·wa'ter adj subacqueo || adv sottacqua

un'der·wear' s biancheria intima

un'der·world' s (criminal world) malavita, teppa; (abode of spirits) ade m, averno; mondo sotterraneo; mondo sottomarino; antipodi mpl

un'der·write' v (pret **-wrote;** pp **-written**) tr sottoscrivere; (to insure) assicurare

un'der·writ'er s sottoscrittore m; (ins) assicuratore m

undeserved [ˌʌndɪˈzʌrvd] adj immeritato

undesirable [ˌʌndɪˈzaɪrəbəl] adj & s indesiderabile mf

undetachable [ˌʌndɪˈtætʃəbəl] adj non movibile

undeveloped [ˌʌndɪˈvɛləpt] adj (land) non sfruttato; (country) sottosviluppato

undigested [ˌʌndɪˈdʒɛstɪd] adj non digerito

undignified [ʌnˈdɪgnɪˌfaɪd] adj poco decoroso

undiscernible [ˌʌndɪˈzʌrnɪbəl] or [ˌʌndɪˈsʌrnɪbəl] adj impercettibile

undisputed [ˌʌndɪˈspjutəd] adj indiscusso, incontrastato

un·do [ʌnˈdu] v (pret **-did;** pp **-done**) tr sfare, disfare; rovinare; (a package) aprire; (a knot) sciogliere

undoing [ʌnˈduˌɪŋ] s rovina

undone [ʌnˈdʌn] adj non finito; **to come undone** disfarsi; **to leave nothing undone** non tralasciare di fare nulla

undoubtedly [ʌnˈdaʊtɪdli] adv indubbiamente, senza dubbio

undress [ˈʌnˌdrɛs] or [ʌnˈdrɛs] s vestaglia; vestito da ogni giorno || [ʌnˈdrɛs] tr spogliare, svestire; (a *wound*) sbendare ‖ *intr* spogliarsi, svestirsi

undrinkable [ʌn'drɪŋkəbəl] *adj* imbevibile, non potabile

undue [ʌn'dju] or [ʌn'du] *adj* indebito; immeritato; eccessivo

undulate ['ʌndjə‚let] *intr* ondulare

unduly [ʌn'djuli] or [ʌn'duli] *adv* indebitamente, eccessivamente

unearned [ʌn'ʌrnd] *adj* non guadagnato col lavoro; immeritato; non ancora guadagnato

un'earned in'crement *s* plusvalenza

unearth [ʌn'ʌrθ] *tr* dissotterrare

unearthly [ʌn'ʌrθli] *adj* ultraterreno; spettrale; impossibile, straordinario

uneasy [ʌn'izi] *adj* (*worried*) preoccupato; (*constrained*) scomodo; (*not conducive to ease*) inquietante, a disagio

uneatable [ʌn'itəbəl] *adj* immangiabile

uneconomic(al) [‚ʌnikə'nɑmɪk(əl)] or [‚ʌnɛkə'nɑmɪk(əl)] *adj* antieconomico

uneducated [ʌn'ɛdjə‚ketɪd] *adj* ineducato

unemployed [‚ʌnɛm'plɔɪd] *adj* disoccupato, incollocato; improduttivo ‖ **the unemployed** i disoccupati

unemployment [‚ʌnɛm'plɔɪmənt] *s* dismpiego, disoccupazione

unemploy'ment compensa'tion *s* sussidio di disoccupazione

unending [ʌn'ɛndɪŋ] *adj* interminabile

unequal [ʌn'ikwəl] *adj* disuguale, impari; **to be unequal to** (*a task*) non essere all'altezza di

unequaled or **unequalled** [ʌn'ikwəld] *adj* ineguagliato

unerring [ʌn'ʌrɪŋ] or [ʌn'ɛrɪŋ] *adj* infallibile; corretto, preciso

unessential [‚ʌnɛ'sɛnʃəl] *adj* non essenziale

uneven [ʌn'ivən] *adj* disuguale, ineguale; (*number*) dispari

uneventful [‚ʌnɪ'vɛntfəl] *adj* senza avvenimenti importanti; (*life*) tranquillo

unexceptionable [‚ʌnɛk'sɛpʃənəbəl] *adj* ineccepibile, irreprensibile

unexpected [‚ʌnɛk'spɛktɪd] *adj* insospettato, imprevisto

unexplained [‚ʌnɛk'splend] *adj* inesplicato

unexplored [‚ʌnɛk'splord] *adj* inesplorato

unexposed [‚ʌnɛk'spozd] *adj* (phot) non esposto alla luce

unfading [ʌn'fedɪŋ] *adj* immarcescibile; imperituro

unfailing [ʌn'felɪŋ] *adj* immancabile, infallibile; (*inexhaustible*) inesauribile; (*dependable*) sicuro

unfair [ʌn'fɛr] *adj* ingiusto; disonesto, sleale

unfaithful [ʌn'feθfəl] *adj* infedele

unfamiliar [‚ʌnfə'mɪljər] *adj* poco pratico; poco abituale, strano; non conosciuto

unfasten [ʌn'fæsən] or [ʌn'fɑsən] *tr* sfibbiare, sciogliere

unfathomable [ʌn'fæðəməbəl] *adj* insondabile

unfavorable [ʌn'fevərəbəl] *adj* sfavorevole

unfeeling [ʌn'filɪŋ] *adj* insensibile

unfetter [ʌn'fɛtər] *tr* sciogliere dalle catene

unfinished [ʌn'fɪnɪʃt] *adj* incompiuto; grezzo, non rifinito; (*business*) inevaso

unfit [ʌn'fɪt] *adj* disadatto; inabile

unfledged [ʌn'flɛdʒd] *adj* implume

unfold [ʌn'fold] *tr* schiudere; (*e.g., a newspaper*) spiegare ‖ *intr* schiudersi; svolgersi

unforeseeable [‚ʌnfor'si·əbəl] *adj* imprevedibile

unforeseen [‚ʌnfor'sin] *adj* imprevisto

unforgettable [‚ʌnfər'gɛtəbəl] *adj* indimenticabile

unforgivable [‚ʌnfər'gɪvəbəl] *adj* imperdonabile

unfortunate [ʌn'fɔrtjənɪt] *adj & s* disgraziato, sfortunato

unfounded [ʌn'faundɪd] *adj* infondato

un·freeze [ʌn'friz] *v* (*pret* **-froze**; *pp* **-frozen**) *tr* disgelare; (*credit*) sbloccare

unfriend·ly [ʌn'frɛndli] *adj* (**-lier; -liest**) *adj* mal disposto, ostile; sfavorevole

unfruitful [ʌn'frutfəl] *adj* infruttuoso

unfulfilled [‚ʌnfəl'fɪld] *adj* incompiuto

unfurl [ʌn'fʌrl] *tr* spiegare, dispiegare

unfurnished [ʌn'fʌrnɪʃt] *adj* smobiliato

ungainly [ʌn'genli] *adj* sgraziato, maldestro

ungentlemanly [ʌn'dʒɛntəlmənli] *adj* indegno di un gentleman

ungird [ʌn'gʌrd] *tr* discingere

ungodly [ʌn'gɑdli] *adj* irreligioso, empio; (*dreadful*) (coll) atroce

ungracious [ʌn'greʃəs] *adj* rude, scortese; (*task*) sgradevole

ungrammatical [‚ʌngrə'mætɪkəl] *adj* sgrammaticato

ungrateful [ʌn'gretfəl] *adj* ingrato

ungrudgingly [ʌn'grʌdʒɪŋli] *adv* di buon grado, volentieri

unguarded [ʌn'gardɪd] *adj* incustodito, indifeso; incauto, imprudente

unguent ['ʌŋgwənt] *s* unguento

unhappiness [ʌn'hæpɪnɪs] *s* infelicità *f*

unhap·py [ʌn'hæpi] *adj* (**-pier; -piest**) infelice, sfortunato

unharmed [ʌn'harmd] *adj* illeso

unharness [ʌn'harnɪs] *tr* togliere i finimenti a

unhealth·y [ʌn'hɛlθi] *adj* (**-ier; -iest**) malsano

unheard-of [ʌn'hʌrd‚av] *adj* (*unknown*) sconosciuto; inaudito

unhinge [ʌn'hɪndʒ] *tr* sgangherare; (fig) sconvolgere

unhitch [ʌn'hɪtʃ] *tr* sganciare; (*a horse*) staccare

unho·ly [ʌn'holi] *adj* (**-lier; -liest**) empio; terribile, atroce

unhook [ʌn'huk] *tr* sganciare

unhoped-for [ʌn'hopt‚fər] *adj* insperato

unhorse [ʌn'hɔrs] *tr* disarcionare

unhurt [ʌn'hʌrt] *adj* incolume, illeso
unicorn ['juni͟,kɔrn] *s* unicorno
unification [ˌjunɪfɪ'keʃən] *s* unificazione
uniform ['juni ˌfɔrm] *adj* & *s* uniforme *f* || *tr* uniformare
uni·fy ['juni ˌfaɪ] *v* (*pret* & *pp* -fied) *tr* unificare
unilateral [ˌjuni'lætərəl] *adj* unilaterale
unimpeachable [ˌʌnim'pitʃəbəl] *adj* irrefutabile; irreprensibile
unimportant [ˌʌnim'pɔrtənt] *adj* poco importante
uninhabited [ˌʌnin'hæbɪtɪd] *adj* inabitato, disabitato
uninspired [ˌʌnin'spaɪrd] *adj* senza ispirazione, prosaico
unintelligent [ˌʌnin'tɛlɪdʒənt] *adj* non intelligente; stupido
unintelligible [ˌʌnin'tɛlɪdʒɪbəl] *adj* inintelligibile
uninterested [ʌn'intristid] or [ʌn-'intə ˌrestɪd] *adj* non interessato
uninteresting [ʌn'intristiŋ] or [ʌn-'intə ˌrestiŋ] *adj* poco interessante
uninterrupted [ˌʌnintə'rʌptɪd] *adj* ininterrotto
union ['junjən] *s* unione; unione matrimoniale; (*of workers*) sindacato
unionize ['junjə ˌnaɪz] *tr* organizzare in un sindacato || *intr* organizzarsi in un sindacato
un'ion shop' *s* fabbrica che assume solo sindacalisti
un'ion suit' *s* combinazione
unique [ju'nik] *adj* unico
unison ['junisən] or ['junizən] *s* unisono; **in unison** all'unisono
unit ['junɪt] *adj* unitario || *s* unità *f*; (mach, elec) gruppo
unite [ju'naɪt] *tr* unire || *intr* unirsi
united [ju'naɪtɪd] *adj* unito
Unit'ed King'dom *s* Regno Unito
Unit'ed Na'tions *spl* Organizzazione delle Nazioni Unite
Unit'ed States' *adj* statunitense || **the United States** *ssg* gli Stati Uniti
uni·ty ['juniti] *s* (-ties) unità *f*
universal [ˌjuni'vʌrsəl] *adj* universale
u'niver'sal joint' *s* giunto cardanico
universe ['juni ˌvʌrs] *s* universo
universi·ty [ˌjuni'vʌrsiti] *adj* universitario || *s* (-ties) università *f*
unjust [ʌn'dʒʌst] *adj* ingiusto
unjustified [ʌn'dʒʌsti ˌfaɪd] *adj* ingiustificato
unkempt [ʌn'kɛmpt] *adj* spettinato; trascurato
unkind [ʌn'kaɪnd] *adj* scortese; duro, crudele
unknowable [ʌn'no·əbəl] *adj* inconoscibile
unknowingly [ʌn'no·iŋli] *adv* inconsapevolmente
unknown [ʌn'non] *adj* sconosciuto || *s* incognito; (math) incognita
Un'known Sol'dier *s* Milite Ignoto
unlace [ʌn'les] *tr* slacciare
unlatch [ʌn'lætʃ] *tr* tirare il saliscendi a
unlawful [ʌn'lɔfəl] *adj* illegale

unleash [ʌn'liʃ] *tr* sguinzagliare; (fig) scatenare
unleavened [ʌn'lɛvənd] *adj* azzimo
unless [ʌn'lɛs] *conj* se non che, salvo che
unlettered [ʌn'lɛtərd] *adj* ignorante; (*illiterate*) analfabeta
unlike [ʌn'laɪk] *adj* dissimile, differente; dissimile da, e.g., **a copy unlike the original** una copia dissimile dall'originale; (elec) di segno contrario || *prep* diversamente da, a differenza di; **it was unlike him to arrive late** non era cosa normale per lui arrivare in ritardo
unlikely [ʌn'laɪkli] *adj* improbabile
unlimber [ʌn'limbər] *tr* mettere in batteria || *intr* prepararsi a fare fuoco; (fig) prepararsi
unlimited [ʌn'limitɪd] *adj* illimitato
unlined [ʌn'laɪnd] *adj* (*e.g., coat*) non foderato; (*paper*) non rigato
unload [ʌn'lod] *tr* scaricare; (*passengers*) sbarcare; (*to get rid of*) liberarsi di || *intr* scaricare; sbarcare
unloading [ʌn'lodiŋ] *s* discarica; sbarco
unlock [ʌn'lak] *tr* aprire
unloose [ʌn'lus] *tr* rilasciare; sciogliere
unloved [ʌn'lʌvd] *adj* poco amato
unlovely [ʌn'lʌvli] *adj* poco attraente
unluck·y [ʌn'lʌki] *adj* (-ier; -iest) sfortunato, disgraziato
un·make [ʌn'mek] *v* (*pret* & *pp* -made ['med]) *tr* disfare; deporre
unmanageable [ʌn'mænɪdʒəbəl] *adj* incontrollabile
unmanly [ʌn'mænli] *adj* non virile, effeminato; codardo
unmannerly [ʌn'mænərli] *adj* scortese
unmarketable [ʌn'markɪtəbəl] *adj* invendibile
unmarriageable [ʌn'mærɪdʒəbəl] *adj* che non si può sposare; non adatto al matrimonio
unmarried [ʌn'mærid] *adj* scapolo; (*female*) nubile
unmask [ʌn'mæsk] or [ʌn'mask] *tr* smascherare || *intr* smascherarsi
unmatchable [ʌn'mætʃəbəl] *adj* impareggiabile
unmatched [ʌn'mætʃd] *adj* impareggiabile; (*unpaired*) spaiato, sparigliato
unmentionable [ʌn'mɛnʃənəbəl] *adj* innominabile
unmerciful [ʌn'mʌrsifəl] *adj* spietato
unmesh [ʌn'mɛʃ] *tr* disingranare || *intr* disingranarsi
unmindful [ʌn'maɪndfəl] *adj* immemore; incurante
unmistakable [ˌʌnmis'tekəbəl] *adj* inconfondibile
unmitigated [ʌn'miti ˌgetɪd] *adj* completo; assoluto, perfetto
unmixed [ʌn'mɪkst] *adj* puro
unmoor [ʌn'mur] *tr* disormeggiare
unmoved [ʌn'muvd] *adj* immoto; fisso, immobile; (fig) impassibile
unmuzzle [ʌn'mʌzəl] *tr* togliere la museruola a
unnamed [ʌn'nemd] *adj* innominato
unnatural [ʌn'nætʃərəl] *adj* contro natura, snaturato; innaturale, affettato

unnecessary [ʌn'nɛsə ˌsɛri] *adj* inutile

unnerve [ʌn'nʌrv] *tr* snervare

unnoticeable [ʌn'notɪsəbəl] *adj* impercettibile

unnoticed [ʌn'notɪst] *adj* inosservato

unobserved [ˌʌnəb'zʌrvd] *adj* inosservato

unobtainable [ˌʌnəb'tenəbəl] *adj* non ottenibile, irraggiungibile

unobtrusive [ˌʌnəb'trusɪv] *adj* discreto, riservato

unoccupied [ʌn'akjə ˌpaɪd] *adj* libero, disponibile; (*not busy*) disoccupato

unofficial [ˌʌnə'fɪʃəl] *adj* non ufficiale, ufficioso

unopened [ʌn'opənd] *adj* non aperto, chiuso; (*letter*) non dissuggellato; (*book*) intonso

unorthodox [ʌn'ɔrθə ˌdaks] *adj* non ortodosso

unpack [ʌn'pæk] *tr* spaccare, sballare

unpalatable [ʌn'pælətəbəl] *adj* di gusto spiacevole

unparalleled [ʌn'pærə ˌlɛld] *adj* incomparabile, senza pari

unpardonable [ʌn'pardənəbəl] *adj* imperdonabile

unpatriotic [ˌʌnpetrɪ'atɪk] or [ˌʌnpætrɪ'atɪk] *adj* antipatriottico

unperceived [ˌʌnpər'sivd] *adj* inosservato

unperturbable [ˌʌnpər't ʌrbəbəl] *adj* imperterrito, imperturbato

unpleasant [ʌn'plɛsənt] *adj* spiacevole; (*person*) antipatico

unpopular [ʌn'papjələr] *adj* impopolare

unpopularity [ʌn ˌpapjə'lærɪti] *s* impopolarità *f*

unprecedented [ʌn'prɛsɪ ˌdɛntɪd] *adj* senza precedenti, inaudito

unprejudiced [ʌn'prɛdʒədɪst] *adj* senza pregiudizio, imparziale

unpremeditated [ˌʌnprɪ'mɛdɪ ˌtetɪd] *adj* impremeditato

unprepared [ˌʌnprɪ'pɛrd] *adj* impreparato

unprepossessing [ˌʌnpripə'zɛsɪŋ] *adj* poco attraente, antipatico

unpresentable [ˌʌnprɪ'zɛntəbəl] *adj* impresentabile

unpretentious [ˌʌnprɪ'tɛnʃəs] *adj* modesto, senza pretese

unprincipled [ʌn'prɪnsɪpəld] *adj* senza principi

unproductive [ˌʌnprə'dʌktɪv] *adj* improduttivo

unprofitable [ʌn'prafɪtəbəl] *adj* infruttuoso

unpronounceable [ˌʌnprə'naunsəbəl] *adj* impronunziabile

unpropitious [ˌʌnprə'pɪʃəs] *adj* inauspicato

unpublished [ʌn'pʌblɪʃt] *adj* inedito

unpunished [ʌn'pʌnɪʃt] *adj* impunito

unqualified [ʌn'kwalɪ ˌfaɪd] *adj* inabile, inidoneo; assoluto, completo

unquenchable [ʌn'kwɛntʃəbəl] *adj* inappagabile, inestinguibile

unquestionable [ʌn'kwɛstʃənəbəl] *adj* indiscutibile

unrav·el [ʌn'rævəl] *v* (*pret & pp* -eled

or -elled; *ger* -eling or -elling) *tr* dipanare ‖ *intr* districarsi; chiarirsi

unreachable [ʌn'ritʃəbəl] *adj* irraggiungibile

unreal [ʌn'ri·əl] *adj* irreale

unreali·ty [ˌʌnrɪ'ælɪti] *s* (-ties) irrealità *f*

unreasonable [ʌn'rizənəbəl] *adj* irragionevole

unrecognizable [ʌn'rɛkəg ˌnaɪzəbəl] *adj* irriconoscibile

unreel [ʌn'ril] *tr* svolgere, srotolare ‖ *intr* srotolarsi

unrefined [ˌʌnrɪ'faɪnd] *adj* non raffinato, greggio; volgare, ordinario

unrelenting [ˌʌnrɪ'lɛntɪŋ] *adj* inesorabile, inflessibile; indefesso

unreliable [ˌʌnrɪ'laɪ·əbəl] *adj* malfido; (*news*) inattendibile

unremitting [ˌʌnrɪ'mɪtɪŋ] *adj* incessante, costante

unrented [ʌn'rɛntɪd] *adj* da affittare

unrepeatable [ˌʌnrɪpitəbəl] *adj* irripetibile

unrepentant [ˌʌnrɪ'pɛntənt] *adj* impenitente

un'requit'ed love' [ˌʌnrɪ'kwaɪtɪd] *s* amore non corrisposto

unresponsive [ˌʌnrɪ'spansɪv] *adj* apatico, insensibile

unrest [ʌn'rɛst] *s* agitazione

un·rig [ʌn'rɪg] *v* (*pret & pp* -rigged; *ger* -rigging) *tr* (naut) disarmare

unrighteous [ʌn'raɪtʃəs] *adj* ingiusto

unripe [ʌn'raɪp] *adj* immaturo

unrivaled or **unrivalled** [ʌn'raɪvəld] *adj* senza pari

unroll [ʌn'rol] *tr* srotolare

unromantic [ˌʌnro'mæntɪk] *adj* poco romantico

unruffled [ʌn'rʌfəld] *adj* calmo, imperturbabile

unruly [ʌn'ruli] *adj* turbolento; indisciplinato, insubordinato

unsaddle [ʌn'sædəl] *tr* (*a horse*) dissellare; (*a rider*) scavalcare

unsafe [ʌn'sef] *adj* malsicuro, pericolante

unsaid [ʌn'sɛd] *adj* non detto, taciuto; **to leave unsaid** passare sotto silenzio

unsalable [ʌn'seləbəl] *adj* invendibile

unsanitary [ʌn'sænɪ ˌtɛri] *adj* antigienico

unsatisfactory [ʌn ˌsætɪs'fæktəri] *adj* poco soddisfacente

unsatisfied [ʌn'sætɪs ˌfaɪd] *adj* insoddisfatto, inappagato

unsavory [ʌn'sevəri] *adj* insipido; (fig) disgustoso, nauseabondo

un·say [ʌn'se] *v* (*pret & pp* -said [sɛd']) *tr* disdire

unscathed [ʌn'skeðd] *adj* incolume

unscheduled [ʌn'skɛdjuld] *adj* non in elenco; (*event*) fuori programma; (*e.g., flight*) fuori orario; (*phase of production*) non programmato

unscientific [ˌʌnsaɪ·ən'tɪfɪk] *adj* poco scientifico

unscrew [ʌn'skru] *tr* svitare ‖ *intr* svitarsi

unscrupulous [ʌn'skrupjələs] *adj* senza scrupoli

unseal [ʌn'sil] *tr* dissigillare

unseasonable [ʌn'sizənəbəl] *adj* fuori stagione; inopportuno

unseasoned [ʌn'sizənd] *adj* scondito; (*crop*) immaturo; (*crew*) inesperto

unseat [ʌn'sit] *tr* (*a rider*) scavalcare, disarcionare; (*e.g., a congressman*) far perdere il seggio a, defenestrare

unseemly [ʌn'simli] *adj* disdicevole, sconveniente

unseen [ʌn'sin] *adj* non visto, inosservato; nascosto, occulto; invisibile

unselfish [ʌn'selfiʃ] *adj* disinteressato

unsettled [ʌn'setəld] *adj* disabitato; disorganizzato; disordinato, erratico; indeciso; (*bill*) da pagare

unshackle [ʌn'ʃækəl] *tr* liberare

unshaken [ʌn'ʃekən] *adj* inconcusso

unshapely [ʌn'ʃepli] *adj* senza forma, deforme

unshaven [ʌn'ʃevən] *adj* non rasato

unshatterable [ʌn'ʃætərəbəl] *adj* infrangibile

unsheathe [ʌn'ʃið] *tr* sguainare

unshod [ʌn'ʃad] *adj* scalzo; (*horse*) sferrato

unshrinkable [ʌn'ʃriŋkəbəl] *adj* irrestringibile

unsightly [ʌn'saitli] *adj* ripugnante, brutto

unsinkable [ʌn'siŋkəbəl] *adj* insommergibile

unskilled [ʌn'skild] *adj* inesperto

un'skilled la'bor *s* lavoro manuale; mano d'opera non specializzata

unskillful [ʌn'skilfəl] *adj* maldestro

unsnarl [ʌn'snarl] *tr* sbrogliare

unsociable [ʌn'soʃəbəl] *adj* insocievole

unsold [ʌn'sold] *adj* invenduto

unsolder [ʌn'sadər] *tr* dissaldare

unsophisticated [,ʌnsə'fisti,ketid] *adj* semplice, puro

unsound [ʌn'saund] *adj* malsano, malato; (*decayed*) guasto, imputridito; falso, fallace; (*sleep*) leggero

unsown [ʌn'son] *adj* incolto, non seminato

unspeakable [ʌn'spikəbəl] *adj* indicibile; (*atrocious*) innominabile, inqualificabile

unsportsmanlike [ʌn'sportsmən,laik] *adj* antisportivo

unstable [ʌn'stebəl] *adj* instabile

unsteady [ʌn'stedi] *adj* malfermo; incostante; irregolare

unstinted [ʌn'stintid] *adj* generoso, senza limiti

unstitch [ʌn'stitʃ] *tr* scucire

un-stop [ʌn'stap] *v* (*pret & pp* -stopped; *ger* -stopping) *tr* stasare

unstressed [ʌn'strest] *adj* non accentuato; (*e.g., syllable*) non accentato

unstrung [ʌn'strʌŋ] *adj* (*beads*) sfilato; (*instrument*) allentato; (*person*) snervato

unsuccessful [,ʌnsək'sesfəl] *adj* (*person*) sfortunato; (*deal*) mancato; **to be unsuccessful** fallire

unsuitable [ʌn'sutəbəl] *or* [ʌn'sjutəbəl] *adj* inappropriato

unsurpassable [ʌnsər'pæsəbəl] *or* [,ʌnsər'pasəbəl] *adj* insuperabile

unsuspected [,ʌnsəs'pektid] *adj* insospettato

unswerving [ʌn'swʌrviŋ] *adj* diritto, fermo, costante

unsympathetic [,ʌnsimpə'θetik] *adj* indifferente, che non mostra comprensione

unsystematic(al) [,ʌnsistə'mætik(əl)] *adj* senza sistema

untactful [ʌn'tæktfəl] *adj* senza tatto

untamed [ʌn'temd] *adj* indomito

untangle [ʌn'tæŋgəl] *tr* sgrovigliare

unteachable [ʌn'titʃəbəl] *adj* indocile; refrattario agli studi

untenable [ʌn'tenəbəl] *adj* insostenibile

unthankful [ʌn'θæŋkfəl] *adj* ingrato

unthinkable [ʌn'θiŋkəbəl] *adj* impensabile

unthinking [ʌn'θiŋkiŋ] *adj* irriflessivo

untidy [ʌn'taidi] *adj* disordinato

un-tie [ʌn'tai] *v* (*pret & pp* -tied; *ger* -tying) *tr* sciogliere; (*a knot*) slacciare, snodare ‖ *intr* sciogliersi

until [ʌn'til] *prep* fino, fino a ‖ *conj* fino a che, finché

untillable [ʌn'tiləbəl] *adj* incoltivabile

untimely [ʌn'taimli] *adj* intempestivo; (*death*) prematuro

untiring [ʌn'tairiŋ] *adj* instancabile

untold [ʌn'told] *adj* non detto, non raccontato; incalcolabile; (*inexpressable*) indicibile

untouchable [ʌn'tʌtʃəbəl] *adj & s* intoccabile *mf*

untouched [ʌn'tʌtʃt] *adj* intatto; insensibile; non menzionato

untoward [ʌn'tord] *adj* sfavorevole; sconveniente, disdicevole

untrammeled *or* **untrammelled** [ʌn'træməld] *adj* non inceppato

untried [ʌn'traid] *adj* non provato

untroubled [ʌn'trʌbləd] *adj* tranquillo

untrue [ʌn'tru] *adj* falso

untrustworthy [ʌn'trʌst,wʌrði] *adj* infido, malfido

untruth [ʌn'truθ] *s* falsità *f*, menzogna

untruthful [ʌn'truθfəl] *adj* falso, menzognero

untwist [ʌn'twist] *tr* districare ‖ *intr* districarsi

unusable [ʌn'juzəbəl] *adj* inservibile

unused [ʌn'juzd] *adj* inutilizzato; **unused to** [ʌn'justu] disavvezzo a

unusual [ʌn'juʒu·əl] *adj* insolito

unutterable [ʌn'ʌtərəbəl] *adj* impronunciabile; indicibile

unvanquished [ʌn'væŋkwiʃt] *adj* invitto

unvarnished [ʌn'varniʃt] *adj* non verniciato; puro, semplice

unveil [ʌn'vel] *tr* svelare; (*a statue*) scoprire, inaugurare ‖ *intr* scoprirsi

unveiling [,ʌn'veliŋ] *s* scoprimento

unvoiced [ʌn'vɔist] *adj* non espresso; (phonet) sordo

unwanted [ʌn'wantid] *adj* non desiderato

unwarranted [ʌn'warəntid] *adj* ingiustificato

unwary [ʌn'weri] *adj* incauto

unwavering [ʌn'wevəriŋ] *adj* fermo, incrollabile

unwelcome [ʌn'welkəm] *adj* malaccetto, sgradito

unwell [ʌn'wel] *adj* poco bene; **to be**

unwell (*said of a woman*) (coll) avere le mestruazioni

unwholesome [ʌn'holsəm] *adj* malsano

unwieldy [ʌn'wildi] *adj* ingombrante

unwilling [ʌn'wɪlɪŋ] *adj* riluttante

unwillingly [ʌn'wɪlɪŋli] *adv* a malincuore, a controvoglia

un·wind [ʌn'waɪnd] *v* (*pret & pp* -**wound** ['waʊnd]) *tr* svolgere || *intr* svolgersi; (*said of a watch*) scaricarsi; (*said of a person*) rilasciarsi

unwise [ʌn'waɪz] *adj* malaccorto

unwished-for [ʌn'wɪʃt,fɔr] *adj* indesiderato, non augurato

unwitting [ʌn'wɪtɪŋ] *adj* involontario

unwonted [ʌn'wʌntɪd] *adj* insolito

unworldly [ʌn'wʌrdli] *adj* (*not of this world*) non terrestre; (*not interested in things of this world*) non mondano; (*naïve*) semplice

unworthy [ʌn'wʌrði] *adj* indegno

un·wrap [ʌn'ræp] *v* (*pret & pp* -**wrapped;** *ger* -**wrapping**) *tr* scartare, svolgere, scartocciare

unwrinkled [ʌn'rɪŋkəld] *adj* senza una grinza

unwritten [ʌn'rɪtən] *adj* orale; non scritto; (*blank*) in bianco

unyielding [ʌn'jildɪŋ] *adj* inflessibile

unyoke [ʌn'yok] *tr* liberare dal giogo

up [ʌp] *adj* che va verso la città; diretto al nord; al corrente; finito, terminato; alto; su; (sports) pari; **to be up and about** essere in piedi || *s* salita; vantaggio; aumento; **ups and downs** alti e bassi *mpl* || *adv* su; in alto; alla pari; **to be up** essere alzato; (*in sports or games*) essere avanti; **to be up in arms** essere in armi; essere indignato; **to be up to a person** toccare a una persona; **to get up** alzarsi; **to go up** salire; **to keep up** mantenere; continuare; **to keep up with** mantenersi alla pari con; **up above** lassù; **up against** (coll) contro; **up against it** (coll) in una strettoia; **up to** fino a; (*capable of*) (coll) all'altezza di; (*scheming*) (coll) tramando; **what's up?** che succede? || *prep* su; sopra; fino a; **to go up a river** risalire un fiume

up-and-coming ['ʌpən'kʌmɪŋ] *adj* promettente

up-and-doing ['ʌpən'du·ɪŋ] *adj* (coll) intraprendente; (coll) attivo

up-and-up ['ʌpən'ʌp] *s*—**on the up-and-up** (coll) aperto; (coll) apertamente; (coll) in ascesa

up·braid' *tr* rimproverare, strapazzare

upbringing ['ʌp,brɪŋɪŋ] *s* educazione

up'coun'try *adj* all'interno || *s* interno || *adv* verso l'interno

up·date' *tr* aggiornare

upheaval [ʌp'hivəl] *s* sommovimento; (geol) sconvolgimento tellurico

up'hill' *adj* erto, scosceso; arduo, faticoso || *adv* in salita, all'insù

up·hold' *v* (*pret & pp* -**held**) *tr* alzare; sostenere; difendere

upholster [ʌp'holstər] *tr* tappezzare

upholsterer [ʌp'holstərər] *s* tappezziere *m*

upholster·y [ʌp'holstəri] *s* (-ies) tap-

pezzeria; (*e.g., of cushions*) imbottitura; (aut) selleria

up'keep' *s* manutenzione; spese *fpl* di manutenzione

upland ['ʌplənd] *or* ['ʌplænd] *adj* alto, elevato || *s* terreno elevato

up'lift' *s* elevazione; miglioramento sociale; edificazione || **up'lift'** *tr* elevare

upon [ʌ'pɑn] *prep* su, sopra, in; **upon** + *ger* non appena + *pp*, e.g., **upon arising** non appena alzato; **upon my word!** sulla mia parola!

upper ['ʌpər] *adj* superiore, disopra; (*town*) soprano; (*river*) alto || *s* disopra *m*; (*of shoe*) tomaia; (rr) (coll) cuccetta; **on one's uppers** ridotto al verde

up'per berth' *s* cuccetta superiore

up'per case' *s* (typ) cassa delle maiuscole, cassa superiore

up'per-case' *adj* (typ) maiuscolo

up'per classes' *spl* classi *fpl* elevate

up'per hand' *s* vantaggio; **to have the upper hand** prendere il disopra

up'per·most' *adj* (il) più alto; principale || *adv* principalmente, in primo luogo

uppish ['ʌpɪʃ] *adj* (coll) arrogante, snob

up·raise' *tr* alzare, tirare su

up'right' *adj* ritto, verticale; dabbene, onesto || *s* staggio, montante *m* || *adv* verticalmente

uprising [ʌp'raɪzɪŋ] *or* ['ʌp,raɪzɪŋ] *s* sollevazione, insurrezione

up'roar' *s* gazzarra, cagnara, fracasso

uproarious [ʌp'rori·əs] *adj* tumultuoso; (*noisy*) rumoroso; (*funny*) comico

up·root' *tr* sradicare

up·set' *adj* rovesciato; scompigliato; (*emotionally*) scombussolato; (*stomach*) imbarazzato || **up'set'** *s* (*overturn*) rovesciamento; (*defeat*) rovescio; (*disorder*) scompiglio; (*illness*) imbarazzo, disturbo || **up·set'** *v* (*pret & pp* -**set;** *ger* -**setting**) *tr* rovesciare; scompigliare; indisporre || *intr* rovesciarsi, ribaltarsi

upset' price' *s* prezzo minimo di vendita di un oggetto all'asta

upsetting [ʌp'sɛtɪŋ] *adj* sconcertante

up'shot' *s* conclusione; essenziale *m*

up'side' *s* disopra *m*

up'side down' *adv* alla rovescia; a gambe all'aria; a soqquadro

up'stage' *adj* al fondo della scena; altiero, arrogante || *adv* al fondo della scena || *tr* trattare altezzosamente; (theat) rubare la scena a

up'stairs' *adj* del piano di sopra || *s* piano di sopra || *adv* su, al piano di sopra

upstanding [ʌp'stændɪŋ] *adj* diritto; forte; onorevole

up'start' *s* arrivato, nuovo ricco

up'stream' *adv* a monte, controcorrente

up'stroke' *s* (*in handwriting*) tratto ascendente; (mach) corsa ascendente

up'swing' *s* (*in prices*) ascesa; miglioramento; **to be on the upswing** migliorare

up'-to-date' *adj* recentissimo; moderno; dell'ultima ora

up'town' *adj* della parte più alta della città || *adv* nella parte più alta della città

up'trend' *s* tendenza al rialzo

up'turn' *s* rivolta; (com) rialzo

upturned [ʌp'tʌrnd] *adj* rivolto all'insù; (*upside down*) capovolto

upward ['ʌpwərd] *adj* ascendente || *adv* all'insù; **upward of** più di

U'ral Moun'tains ['jurəl] *spl* Urali *mpl*

uranium [ju'rɛnɪ·əm] *s* uranio

urban ['ʌrbən] *adj* urbano

urbane [ʌr'ben] *adj* urbano

urbanite ['ʌrbə ˌnaɪt] *s* abitante *mf* di una città

urbanity [ʌr'bænɪti] *s* urbanità *f*

urbanize ['ʌrbə ˌnaɪz] *tr* urbanizzare

ur'ban renew'al *s* ricostruzione urbanistica

urchin ['ʌrtʃɪn] *s* monello, birichino

ure·thra [ju'riθrə] *s* (**-thras** or **-thrae** [θri]) uretra

urge [ʌrdʒ] *s* stimolo || *tr* urgere, sollecitare, spronare; (*to endeavor to persuade*) esortare; (*an enterprise*) accelerare || *intr*—**to urge against** opporsi a

urgen·cy ['ʌrdʒənsi] *s* (**-cies**) urgenza

urgent ['ʌrdʒənt] *adj* urgente; (*desire*) prepotente

urinal ['jurɪnəl] *s* (*receptacle*) orinale *m*; (*for a bedridden person*) pappagallo; (*place*) orinatoio, vespasiano

urinary ['jurɪ ˌneri] *adj* urinario

urinate ['jurɪ ˌnet] *tr* & *intr* orinare

urine ['jurɪn] *s* urina

urn [ʌrn] *s* urna; (*for making coffee*) caffettiera; (*for making tea*) samovar *m*

urology [ju'rɑlədʒi] *s* urologia

Uruguay ['jurə ˌgwe] or ['jurə ˌgwaɪ] *s* l'Uruguai *m*

Uruguayan [ˌjurə'gwe·ən] or [ˌjurə'gwaɪ·ən] *adj* & *s* uruguaiano

us [ʌs] *pron pers* ci; noi; **to us** ci, a noi, per noi

U.S.A. ['ju'ɛs'e] *s* (letterword) (**United States of America**) S.U.A. *mpl*

usable ['juzəbəl] *adj* servibile, adoperabile

usage ['jusɪdʒ] or ['juzɪdʒ] *s* uso, usanza; (*of a language*) uso

use [jus] *s* uso, impiego, usanza; **in use** in uso, in servizio; **it's no use** non giova; **out of use** disusato; **to be of no use** non servire a nulla; **to have**

no use for non aver bisogno di; non poter soffrire; **to make use of** servirsi di; **what's the use?** a che pro? || [juz] *tr* usare, impiegare, servirsi di; **to use badly** maltrattare; **to use up** consumare, esaurire || *intr*—**used to** translated in Italian in three ways: (1) by the imperfect indicative, e.g., **he used to go to church at seven o'clock** andava in chiesa alle sette; (2) by the imperfect indicative of **solere**, e.g., **he used to smoke all day** soleva fumare tutto il giorno; (3) by the imperfect indicative of **avere l'abitudine di**, e.g., **he used to go to the shore** aveva l'abitudine di andare alla spiaggia

used [juzd] *adj* uso, usato; **to get used to** ['juzdtu] or ['justu] fare la mano a, abituarsi a

useful ['jusfəl] *adj* utile

usefulness ['jusfəlnɪs] *s* utilità *f*

useless ['juslɪs] *adj* inutile, inservibile

user ['juzər] *s* utente *mf*

usher ['ʌʃər] *s* (*doorkeeper*) portiere *m*; (hist) cerimoniere *m*; (theat) maschera; (mov) lucciola || *tr* introdurre; **to usher in** annunciare, introdurre

U.S.S.R. ['ju'ɛs'ɛs'ɑr] *s* (letterword) (**Union of Soviet Socialist Republics**) U.R.S.S. *f*

usual ['juʒu·əl] *adj* usuale, abituale; **as usual** come il solito

usually ['juʒu·əli] *adj* usualmente

usurp [ju'zʌrp] *tr* usurpare

usu·ry ['juʒəri] *s* (**-ries**) usura

utensil [ju'tɛnsɪl] *s* utensile *m*

uter·us ['jutərəs] *s* (**-i** [ˌaɪ]) utero

utilitarian [ˌjutɪlɪ'tɛrɪ·ən] *adj* utilitario

utili·ty [ju'tɪlɪti] *s* (**-ties**) utilità *f*; compagnia di servizi pubblici

utilize ['jutɪ ˌlaɪz] *tr* utilizzare

utmost ['ʌt ˌmost] *adj* sommo; estremo; massimo || *s*—**the utmost** il massimo; **to do one's utmost** fare tutto il possibile; **to the utmost** al massimo limite

utopia [ju'topɪ·ə] *s* utopia

utopian [ju'topɪ·ən] *adj* utopistico || *s* utopista *mf*

utter ['ʌtər] *adj* completo, totale || *tr* proferire, pronunziare; (*a sigh*) dare, fare

utterly ['ʌtərli] *adj* completamente

uxoricide [ʌk'sɔrɪ ˌsaɪd] *s* (*husband*) uxoricida *m*; (*act*) uxoricidio

uxorious [ʌk'sɔrɪ·əs] *adj* eccessivamente innamorato della propria moglie; dominato dalla moglie

V

V, v [vi] *s* ventiduesima lettera dell'alfabeto inglese

vacan·cy ['vekənsi] *s* (**-cies**) (*emptiness*) vuoto; (*unfilled position*) vacanza; (*unfilled job*) posto vacante; (*in a building*) appartamento libero;

(*in a hotel*) camera libera; **no vacancy** completo

vacant ['vekənt] *adj* (*empty*) vuoto; (*position*) vacante; (*expression of the face*) vago

vacate ['veket] *tr* sgombrare; (*a posi-*

***tion*)** ritirarsi da; (law) annullare; **to vacate one's mind of worries** liberarsi dalle preoccupazioni || *intr* sloggiare; (coll) andarsene

vacation [ve'keʃən] *s* vacanza, villeggiatura; **vacanze** *fpl* || *intr* estivare, villeggiare

vacationer [ve'keʃənər] *s* villeggiante *mf*, vacanziere *m*

vacationist [ve'keʃənɪst] *s* villeggiante *mf*, vacanziere *m*

vaca'tion with pay' *s* vacanze *fpl* pagate

vaccinate ['væksɪ ,net] *tr* vaccinare

vaccination [,væksɪ'neʃən] *s* vaccinazione

vaccine [væk'sin] *s* vaccino

vacillate ['væsɪ ,let] *intr* vacillare

vacillating ['væsɪ ,letɪŋ] *adj* vacillante

vacui·ty [væ'kju·ɪti] *s* (-ties) vacuità *f*

vacu·um ['vækju·əm] *s* (-ums **or** -a [ə]) vuoto; **in a vacuum** sotto vuoto || *tr* pulire con l'aspirapolvere

vac'uum clean'er *s* aspirapolvere *m*

vac'uum-pack'ed *adj* confezionato sotto vuoto

vac'uum tube' *s* tubo elettronico

vagabond ['vægə ,band] *adj & s* vagabondo

vagar·y [və'gɛri] *s* (-ies) capriccio

vagran·cy ['vegrənsi] *s* (-cies) vagabondaggio

vagrant ['vegrənt] *adj & s* vagabondo

vague [veg] *adj* vago

va'gus nerve' ['vegəs] *s* (anat) vago

vain [ven] *adj* vano; (*conceited*) vanitoso; **in vain** in vano

vainglorious [ven'glorɪ·əs] *adj* vanaglorioso

valance ['væləns] *s* balza, mantovana

vale [vel] *s* valle *f*

valedictorian [,vælɪdɪk'torɪ·ən] *s* studente *m* che pronuncia il discorso di commiato

valence [.'veləns] *s* (chem) valenza

valentine ['vælən ,taɪn] *s* (*sweetheart*) valentino; (*card*) cartolina di San Valentino

valet ['vælɪt] **or** ['væle] *s* valletto

valiant ['væljənt] *adj* valoroso

valid ['vælɪd] *adj* valido

validate ['vælɪ ,det] *tr* convalidare, vidimare; (sports) omologare

validation [,vælɪ'deʃən] *s* convalida, vidimazione; (sports) omologazione

validi·ty [və'lɪdɪti] *s* (-ties) validità *f*

valise [və'lis] *s* valigetta

valley ['væli] *s* valle *f*, vallata; (*of roof*) linea di compluvio

valor ['vælər] *s* valore *m*, coraggio

valorous ['vælərəs] *adj* valoroso

valuable ['vælju·əbəl] **or** ['væljəbəl] *adj* (*having monetary worth*) prezioso; pregevole, pregiato || **valuables** *spl* valori *mpl*

value ['vælju] *s* valore *m;* importanza; (com) valuta, valore *m;* **an excellent value** un acquisto eccellente || *tr* stimare, valutare

value'-added tax' *s* imposta sul valore aggiunto

valueless ['væljulɪs] *adj* senza valore

valve [vælv] *s* (anat, mach, rad, telv)

valvola; (bot, zool) valva; (mus) pistone *m*

valve' gears' *spl* meccanismo di distribuzione

valve'-in-head' en'gine *s* motore *m* a valvole in testa

valve' lift'er ['lɪftər] *s* alzavalvole *m*

valve' seat' *s* sede *f* della valvola

valve' spring' *s* molla di valvola

valve' stem' *s* stelo di comando della valvola

vamp [væmp] *s* parte *f* anteriore della tomaia; (*patchwork*) rabberciatura; (*female*) vamp *f* || *tr* (*a shoe*) rimontare; rabberciare; (*to concoct*) inventare, raffazzonare; (*an accompaniment*) improvvisare; (*said of a female*) sedurre

vampire ['væmpaɪr] *s* vampiro; (*female*) vamp *f*

van [væn] *s* camionetta, autofurgone *m; (mil & fig)* avanguardia

vanadium [və'nedɪ·əm] *s* vanadio

vandal ['vændəl] *adj & s* vandalo || **Vandal** *adj & s* Vandalo

vandalism ['vændə ,lɪzəm] *s* vandalismo

vane [ven] *s* (*weathervane*) banderuola; (*of windmill, of turbine*) pala; (*of feather*) barba

vanguard ['væn ,gard] *s* avanguardia; **in the vanguard** all'avanguardia

vanilla [və'nɪlə] *s* vaniglia

vanish ['vænɪʃ] *intr* svanire

van'ishing cream' ['vænɪ ʃɪŋ] *s* crema evanescente

vani·ty ['vænɪti] *s* (-ties) vanità *f;* (*table*) toletta; (*case*) astuccio di toletta

vanquish ['væŋkwɪʃ] *tr* superare, vincere

van'tage ground' ['væntɪdʒ] *s* posizione favorevole

vapid ['væpɪd] *adj* insipido

vapor ['vepər] *s* vapore *m; (visible vapor)* vapori *mpl*

vaporize ['vepə ,raɪz] *tr* vaporizzare || *intr* vaporizzarsi

va'por lock' *s* tampone *m* di vapore

vaporous ['vepərəs] *adj* vaporoso

va'por trail' *s* scia di condensazione

variable ['vɛrɪ·əbəl] *adj & s* variabile *f*

variance ['vɛrɪ·əns] *s* divario, differenza; **at variance with** (*a thing*) differente da; differentemente da; (*a person*) in disaccordo con

variant ['vɛrɪ·ənt] *adj & s* variante *f*

variation [,vɛrɪ'eʃən] *s* variazione *m*

varicose ['vɛrɪ ,kos] *adj* varicoso

varied ['vɛrɪd] *adj* vario, svariato

variegated ['vɛrɪ·ə ,getɪd] **or** ['vɛrɪ- ,getɪd] *adj* variegato, screziato

varie·ty [və'raɪ·ɪti] *s* (-ties) varietà *f*

vari'ety show' *s* spettacolo di varietà

varnish ['varnɪʃ] *s* vernice *f* || *tr* verniciare; (fig) dare la vernice a

variola [və'raɪ·ələ] *s* (pathol) vaiolo

various ['vɛrɪ·əs] *adj* vari; (*varicolored*) vario, variegato

varsi·ty ['varsɪti] *adj* (sports) universitario || *s* (-ties) (sports) squadra numero uno

var·y ['vɛri] *v* (*pret & pp* **-ied**) *tr & intr* variare

vase [ves] or [vez] *s* vaso

vaseline ['væsə,lin] *s* (trademark) vaselina

vassal ['væsəl] *adj & s* vassallo

vast [væst] or [vɑst] *adj* vasto

vastly ['væstli] or ['vɑstli] *adv* enormemente

vastness ['væstnɪs] or ['vɑstnɪs] *s* vastità *f*

vat [væt] *s* tino, bigoncia

Vatican ['vætɪkən] *adj* vaticano || *s* Vaticano

Vat'ican Cit'y *s* Città *f* del Vaticano

vaudeville ['vodvɪl] or ['vɔdəvɪl] *s* spettacolo di varietà; (*theatrical piece*) vaudeville *m*, commedia musicale

vault [vɔlt] *s* volta; (*underground chamber*) cantina; (*of a bank*) camera di sicurezza; (*burial chamber*) cripta; (*of heaven*) cappa; (*leap*) salto || *tr* formare a mo' di volta; saltare || *intr* saltare

vaunt [vɔnt] or [vɑnt] *s* vanto, vanteria || *tr* vantarsi di || *intr* vantarsi

veal [vil] *s* vitello

veal' chop' *s* scaloppa, cotoletta di vitello

veal' cut'let *s* scaloppina

vedette [vɪ'dɛt] *s* (nav) vedetta; (mil) sentinella avanzata

veer [vɪr] *s* virata || *tr* far cambiare di direzione a || *intr* virare; (*said of the wind*) cambiare di direzione

vegetable ['vɛdʒɪtəbəl] *adj* vegetale || *s* (*plant*) vegetale *m*; (*edible plant*) ortaggio; **vegetables** verdura, erbe *fpl*, erbaggi *mpl*, ortaggi *mpl*

veg'etable gar'den *s* orto

veg'etable soup' *s* minestra di verdura

vegetarian [,vɛdʒɪ'tɛrɪ·ən] *adj & s* vegetariano

vegetate ['vɛdʒɪ,tet] *intr* vegetare

vehemence ['vi·ɪməns] *s* veemenza

vehement ['vi·ɪmənt] *adj* veemente

vehicle ['vi·ɪkəl] *s* veicolo

vehic'ular traf'fic [vɪ'hɪkjələr] *s* circolazione stradale

veil [vel] *s* velo; **to take the veil** prendere il velo || *tr* velare

vein [ven] *s* vena; (*streak*) venatura; (*of ore*) filone *m* || *tr* venare

velar ['vilər] *adj & s* velare *f*

vellum ['vɛləm] *s* pergamena

veloci·ty [vɪ'lɑsɪti] *s* (**-ties**) velocità *f*

velvet ['vɛlvɪt] *adj* di velluto || *s* velluto; (slang) guadagno al gioco; (coll) situazione all'acqua di rose

velveteen [,vɛlvɪ'tin] *s* vellutino di cotone

velvety ['vɛlvɪti] *adj* vellutato

vend [vɛnd] *tr* vendere; (*to peddle*) fare il venditore ambulante di

vend'ing machine' *s* distributore automatico

vendor ['vɛndər] *s* venditore *m*

veneer [və'nɪr] *s* impiallacciatura, piallaccio; (fig) vernice *f* || *tr* impiallacciare

venerable ['vɛnərəbəl] *adj* venerabile

venerate ['vɛnə,ret] *tr* venerare

venereal [vɪ'nɪrɪ·əl] *adj* venereo

Venetia [vɪ'niʃɪ·ə] or [vɪ'niʃə] *s* (*province*) Venezia

Venetian [vɪ'niʃən] *adj & s* veneziano

Vene'tian blind' *s* veneziana, persiana avvolgibile

Venezuelan [,vɛnɪ'zwilən] *adj & s* venezolano

vengeance ['vɛndʒəns] *s* vendetta; **with a vengeance** violentemente; eccessivamente

vengeful ['vɛndʒfəl] *adj* vendicativo

Venice ['vɛnɪs] *s* Venezia

venire·man [vɪ'naɪrimən] *s* (**-men**) membro di un collegio di giurati

venison ['vɛnɪsən] or ['vɛnɪzən] *s* carne *f* di cervo

venom ['vɛnəm] *s* veleno

venomous ['vɛnəməs] *adj* velenoso

vent [vɛnt] *s* sfiatatoio; (*of jacket*) spacco; **to give vent to** dare sfogo a || *tr* sfogare, sfuriare; mettere uno sfiatatoio a; **to vent one's spleen** sfogare la bile

vent' hole' *s* apertura di sfogo

ventilate ['vɛntɪ,let] *tr* ventilare

ventilator ['vɛntɪ,letər] *s* ventilatore *m*

ventricle ['vɛntrɪkəl] *s* ventricolo

ventriloquist [vɛn'trɪləkwɪst] *s* ventriloquo

venture ['vɛntʃər] *s* azzardo, avventura rischiosa; **at a venture** alla ventura || *tr* avventurare || *intr* avventurarsi, arrischiarsi

venturesome ['vɛntʃərsəm] *adj* (*risky*) rischioso; (*daring*) avventuroso

venturous ['vɛntʃərəs] *adj* avventuroso

vent' win'dow *s* (aut) deflettore *m*

venue ['vɛnju] *s* (law) posto dove ha avuto luogo il reato; (law) luogo dove si riunisce la corte; **change of venue** cambio di giurisdizione

Venus ['vinəs] *s* (*very beautiful woman*) venere *f*; (astr) Venere *m*; (myth) Venere *f*

veracious [vɪ'reʃəs] *adj* verace

veraci·ty [vɪ'ræsiti] *s* (**-ties**) veridicità *f*

veranda or **verandah** [və'rændə] *s* veranda

verb [vʌrb] *adj* verbale || *s* verbo

verbalize ['vʌrbə,laɪz] *tr* esprimere con parole; (gram) convertire in forma verbale || *intr* essere verboso

verbatim [vər'betɪm] *adj* letterale || *adv* parola per parola, testualmente

verbena [vər'binə] *s* (bot) verbena

verbiage ['vʌrbɪ·ɪdʒ] *s* verbosità *f*; (*style of wording*) espressione

verbose [vər'bos] *adj* verboso

verdant ['vʌrdənt] *adj* verde, verdeggiante

verdict ['vʌrdɪkt] *s* verdetto

verdigris ['vʌrdɪ,gris] *s* verderame *m*

verdure ['vʌrdʒər] *s* verde *m*

verge [vʌrdʒ] *s* orlo, limite *m*; bordo; (*of a column*) fusto; **on the verge of** al punto di; all'orlo di || *intr*—**to verge on** costeggiare, rasentare

verification [,vɛrɪfɪ'keʃən] *s* verifica

veri·fy [ˈvɛrɪˌfaɪ] *v* (*pret & pp* **-fied**) *tr* verificare, confermare

verily [ˈvɛrɪli] *adv* in verità

veritable [ˈvɛrɪtəbəl] *adj* vero

vermilion [vərˈmɪljən] *adj & s* vermiglio

vermin [ˈvɑrmɪn] *ssg* (*person*) persona abominevole || *spl* (*animals or persons*) insetti *mpl*

vermouth [vərˈmuθ] *or* [ˈvɑrmuθ] *s* vermut *m*

vernacular [vərˈnækjələr] *adj* volgare || *s* volgare *m*, vernacolo; (*language peculiar to a class or profession*) gergo

versatile [ˈvɑrsətɪl] *adj* (*person*) versatile; (*tool or device*) a vari usi

verse [vɑrs] *s* verso; (Bib) versetto

versed [vɑrst] *adj* versato

versification [ˌvɑrsɪfɪˈkeʃən] *s* versificazione

versi·fy [ˈvɑrsɪˌfaɪ] *v* (*pret & pp* **-fied**) *tr & intr* versificare

version [ˈvɑrʒən] *s* versione

ver·so [ˈvɑrso] *s* (**-sos**) (*of coin*) rovescio; (*of page*) verso

versus [ˈvɑrsəs] *prep* contro; in confronto a

verte·bra [ˈvɑrtɪbrə] *s* (**-brae** [ˌbri] *or* **-bras**) vertebra

vertebrate [ˈvɑrtəˌbret] *adj & s* vertebrato

ver·tex [ˈvɑrtɛks] *s* (**-texes** *or* **-tices** [tɪˌsiz]) vertice *m*

vertical [ˈvɑrtɪkəl] *adj & s* verticale *f*

ver'tical hold' *s* (telv) regolatore *m* del sincronismo verticale

ver'tical sta'bilizer *s* (aer) deriva

verti·go [ˈvɑrtɪˌgo] *s* (**-goes** *or* **-gos**) vertigine *f*

verve [vɑrv] *s* verve *f*, brio

very [ˈvɑri] *adj* (*utter*) grande, completo; (*precise*) vero e proprio; (*mere*) stesso, e.g., **his very brother** suo fratello stesso || *adv* molto, e.g., **to be very rich** essere molto ricco

vesicle [ˈvɛsɪkəl] *s* vescichetta

vesper [ˈvɛspər] *s* vespro; **vespers** vespri *mpl* || **Vesper** *s* Vespero

ves'per bell' *s* campana a vespro

vessel [ˈvɛsəl] *s* (*ship*) nave *f*, vascello; (*container*) vaso; (anat) vaso; (fig) vasello

vest [vɛst] *s* (*of man's suit*) panciotto, gilè *m;* (*of woman's garment*) corpino || *tr* vestire; **to vest** (*authority*) **in** concedere a; **to vest with** investire di || *intr* vestirisi; **to vest in** passare a

vest'ed in'terest *s* interesse acquisito

vestibule [ˈvɛstɪˌbjul] *s* vestibolo

vestige [ˈvɛstɪdʒ] *s* vestigio

vestment [ˈvɛstmənt] *s* (eccl) paramento

vest'-pock'et *adj* da tasca, tascabile

ves·try [ˈvɛstri] *s* (**-tries**) sagrestia; (*chapel*) cappella; giunta esecutiva della chiesa episcopaliana

ves'try·man *s* (**-men**) membro della giunta esecutiva della chiesa episcopaliana

Vesuvius [vɪˈsuviˌəs] *or* [vɪˈsjuviˌəs] *s* il Vesuvio

vetch [vɛtʃ] *s* veccia; (*grass pea*) cicerchia

veteran [ˈvɛtərən] *adj & s* veterano

veterinarian [ˌvɛtərɪˈnɛriˌən] *s* veterinario

veterinar·y [ˈvɛtərɪˌnɛri] *adj* veterinario || *s* (**-ies**) veterinario

ve·to [ˈvito] *s* (**-toes**) veto || *tr* porre il veto a

vex [vɛks] *tr* irritare, tormentare

vexation [vɛkˈseʃən] *s* fastidio, contrarietà *f*

vexatious [vɛkˈseʃəs] *adj* irritante, fastidioso; (law) vessatorio

vexing [ˈvɛksɪŋ] *adj* noioso, fastidioso, irritante

via [ˈvaɪˌə] *prep* via, per via di

viaduct [ˈvaɪˌəˌdʌkt] *s* viadotto

vial [ˈvaɪˌəl] *s* fiala, boccetta

viand [ˈvaɪˌənd] *s* vivanda, manicaretto

viati·cum [vaɪˈætɪkəm] *s* (**-cums** *or* **-ca** [kə]) (eccl) viatico

vibrate [ˈvaɪbret] *tr & intr* vibrare

vibration [vaɪˈbreʃən] *s* vibrazione

vicar [ˈvɪkər] *s* vicario

vicarage [ˈvɪkərɪdʒ] *s* residenza del vicario; (*office; duties*) vicariato

vicarious [vaɪˈkɛriˌəs] *or* [vɪˈkɛriˌəs] *adj* sostituto; (*punishment*) ricevuto in vece di altra persona; (*power*) delegato; (*enjoyment*) di riflesso

vice [vaɪs] *s* vizio

vice'-ad'miral *s* viceammiraglio, ammiraglio di squadra

vice'-pres'ident *s* vicepresidente *m*

viceroy [ˈvaɪsrɔɪ] *s* viceré *m*

vice versa [ˈvaɪsi ˈvɑrsə] *or* [ˈvaɪsə ˈvɑrsə] *adv* viceversa

vicini·ty [vɪˈsɪnɪti] *s* (**-ties**) vicinanze *fpl*, paraggi *mpl*

vicious [ˈvɪʃəs] *adj* vizioso; maligno, malvagio; (*dog*) cattivo, che morde; (*horse*) selvaggio; (*headache*) tremendo; (*reasoning; circle*) vizioso

victim [ˈvɪktɪm] *s* vittima

victimize [ˈvɪktɪˌmaɪz] *tr* fare una vittima di; ingannare; (hist) sacrificare

victor [ˈvɪktər] *s* vincitore *m*

victorious [vɪkˈtoriˌəs] *adj* vittorioso

victo·ry [ˈvɪktəri] *s* (**-ries**) vittoria

victuals [ˈvɪtəlz] *spl* vettovaglie *fpl*

vid'eo cassette' [ˈvɪdiˌo] *s* videocassetta

vid'eo sig'nal *s* segnale *m* video

vid'eo tape' *s* nastro televisivo

vie [vaɪ] *v* (*pret & pp* **vied**; *ger* **vying**) *intr* gareggiare; **to vie for** disputarsi

Vien·nese [ˌviˈˈniz] *adj* viennese || *s* (**-nese**) viennese *mf*

Vietnam [ˌvietˈnɑm] *s* il Vietnam

Vietnam·ese [vɪˌɛtnəˈmiz] *adj* vietnamita || *s* (**-ese**) vietnamita *mf;* (*language*) vietnamita *m*

view [vju] *s* vista; (*picture*) veduta; prospetto; esame *m;* punto di vista; **to be on view** (*said of a corpse*) essere esposto; **to keep in view** non perdere di vista; **to take a dim view of** avere un'opinione scettica di; **with a view to** con lo scopo di || *tr* guardare, osservare; considerare

viewer ['vju·ər] *s* spettatore *m;* (telv) telespettatore *m;* (phot) visore *m;* (phot) proiettore *m* di diapositive

view'find'er *s* (phot) traguardo, visore *m*

view'point' *s* punto di vista

vigil ['vɪdʒɪl] *s* vigilia; **to keep vigil** vegliare

vigilance ['vɪdʒɪləns] *s* vigilanza

vigilant ['vɪdʒɪlənt] *adj* vigilante

vignette [vɪn'jɛt] *s* vignetta

vigor ['vɪgər] *s* vigore *m*, gagliardia

vigorous ['vɪgərəs] *adj* vigoroso

Viking ['vaɪkɪŋ] *s* vichingo

vile [vaɪl] *adj* vile, malvagio; (*wretchedly bad*) orribile; disgustoso, ripugnante; (*filthy*) sporco; (*poor*) povero, basso

vili·fy ['vɪlɪ ˌfaɪ] *v* (*pret & pp* **-fied**) *tr* vilificare

villa ['vɪlə] *s* villa

village ['vɪlɪdʒ] *s* villaggio, paese *m*

villager ['vɪlɪdʒər] *s* paesano

villain ['vɪlən] *s* scellerato; (*of a play*) cattivo, anima nera

villainous ['vɪlənəs] *adj* vile, infame

villain·y ['vɪləni] *s* (**-ies**) scelleratezza, malvagità *f*

vim [vɪm] *s* vigore *m*, brio

vinaigrette [ˌvɪnə'grɛt] *s* boccetta dell'aceto aromatico

vinaigrette' sauce' *s* salsa verde

vindicate ['vɪndɪ ˌket] *tr* scolpare; difendere, sostenere; (*e.g., a claim*) rivendicare

vindictive [vɪn'dɪktɪv] *adj* vendicativo

vine [vaɪn] *s* (*climber*) rampicante *f;* (*grape plant*) vite *f*

vine'dress'er *s* vignaiolo

vinegar ['vɪnɪgər] *s* aceto

vinegarish ['vɪnɪgərɪʃ] *adj* acetoso; (fig) acre, mordace

vinegary ['vɪnɪgəri] *adj* acetoso; (fig) irritabile, irascibile

vineyard ['vɪnjərd] *s* vigna, vigneto

vintage ['vɪntɪdʒ] *s* vendemmia; vino di annata eccezionale; (fig) edizione

vintager ['vɪntɪdʒər] *s* vendemmiatore *m*

vin'tage wine' *s* vino di marca

vin'tage year' *s* buona annata

vintner ['vɪntnər] *s* produttore *m* di vino; vinaio

vinyl ['vaɪnɪl] or ['vɪnɪl] *s* vinile *m*

violate ['vaɪ·ə ˌlet] *tr* violare

violation [ˌvaɪ·ə'leʃən] *s* violazione

violence ['vaɪ·ələns] *s* violenza

violent ['vaɪ·ələnt] *adj* violento

violet ['vaɪ ˌəlɪt] *adj* violetto || *s* (*color*) violetto, viola; (bot) violetta; (*Viola odorata*) viola mammola

violin [ˌvaɪ·ə'lɪn] *s* violino

violinist [ˌvaɪ·ə'lɪnɪst] *s* violinista *mf*

violoncellist [ˌvaɪ·ələn'tʃɛlɪst] or [ˌvi·ələn'tʃɛlɪst] *s* violoncellista *mf*

violoncel·lo [ˌvaɪ·ələn'tʃɛlo] or [ˌvi·ələn'tʃɛlo] *s* (**-los**) violoncello

VIP ['vi'aɪ'pi] *s* (letterword) (**Very Important Person**) persona di maggiore riguardo

viper ['vaɪpər] *s* vipera; (*any snake*) serpe *f;* (*spiteful person*) vipera

vira·go [vɪ'rego] *s* (**-goes** or **-gos**) megera, donna dal caratteraccio impossibile

virgin ['vɑrdʒɪn] *adj & s* vergine *f* || **Virgin** *s* Vergine *f*

vir'gin birth' *s* parto verginale della Madonna; (zool) partenogenesi *f*

Virgin'ia creep'er [vər'dʒɪnɪ·ə] *s* vite *f* del Canada

virginity [vər'dʒɪnɪti] *s* virginità *f*

Virgo ['vʌrgo] *s* (astr) Vergine *f*

virility [vɪ'rɪlɪti] *s* virilità *f*

virology [vaɪ'rɑlədʒi] *s* virologia

virtual ['vʌrtʃu·əl] *adj* virtuale

virtue ['vʌrtʃu] *s* virtù *f*

virtuosi·ty [ˌvʌrtʃu'ɑsɪti] *s* (**-ties**) virtuosità *f*, virtuosismo

virtuo·so [ˌvʌrtʃu'oso] *s* (**-sos** or **-si** [si]) virtuoso

virtuous ['vʌrtʃu·əs] *adj* virtuoso

virulence ['vɪrjələns] *s* virulenza

virulent ['vɪrjələnt] *adj* virulento

virus ['vaɪrəs] *s* virus *m*

visa ['vizə] *s* visto || *tr* vistare

visage ['vɪzɪdʒ] *s* faccia; apparenza

vis-à-vis [ˌvizə'vi] *adj* l'uno di fronte all'altro || *adv* vis-à-vis || *prep* di fronte a

viscera ['vɪsərə] *spl* visceri *mpl*, viscere *fpl*

viscount ['vaɪkaunt] *s* visconte *m*

viscountess ['vaɪkauntɪs] *s* viscontessa

viscous ['vɪskəs] *adj* viscoso

vise [vaɪs] *s* morsa

visé ['vize] or [vi'ze] *s & tr* var of **visa**

visible ['vɪzɪbəl] *adj* visibile

Visigoth ['vɪzɪ ˌgɑθ] *s* visigoto

vision ['vɪʒən] *s* visione; (*sense*) vista

visionar·y ['vɪʒə ˌnɛri] *adj* visionario || *s* (**-ies**) visionario

visit ['vɪzɪt] *tr* visitare; affliggere, colpire; (*a punishment*) far ricadere || *intr* visitare; (*to chat*) fare un chiacchierata

visitation [ˌvɪzɪ'teʃən] *s* visitazione; punizione divina, visita del Signore

vis'iting card' *s* biglietto da visita

vis'iting hours' *spl* orario delle visite

vis'iting nurse' *s* infermiera che visita i pazienti a domicilio

visitor ['vɪzɪtər] *s* visitatore *m*

visor ['vaɪzər] *s* visiera; (fig) maschera

vista ['vɪstə] *s* vista, prospettiva

visual ['vɪʒu·əl] *adj* visivo, visuale

vis'ual acu'ity *s* acutezza visiva

visualize ['vɪʒu·ə ˌlaɪz] *tr* formare l'immagine mentale di; (*to make visible*) visualizzare

vital ['vaɪtəl] *adj* vitale; (*deadly*) mortale || **vitals** *spl* organi vitali

vitality [vaɪ'tælɪti] *s* vitalità *f*

vitalize ['vaɪtə ˌlaɪz] *tr* animare, infondere vita a

vi'tal statis'tics *spl* statistiche *fpl* anagrafiche

vitamin ['vaɪtəmɪn] *s* vitamina

vitiate ['vɪʃɪ ˌet] *tr* viziare

vitreous ['vɪtrɪ·əs] *adj* vitreo, vetroso

vitriolic [ˌvɪtrɪ'ɑlɪk] *adj* di vetriolo; (fig) caustico

vituperate [vaɪ'tupə ˌret] or [vaɪ'tjupə ˌret] *tr* vituperare

viva ['vivǝ] s evviva || *interj* viva!
vivacious [vɪ'veʃǝs] or [vaɪ'veʃǝs] *adj* vivace
vivaci·ty [vɪ'væsɪti] or [vaɪ'væsɪti] s (-ties) vivacità *f*, gaiezza
viva voce ['vaɪvǝ 'vosi] *adv* a viva voce
vivid ['vɪvɪd] *adj* vivido
vivi·fy ['vɪvɪ ,faɪ] v (*pret* & *pp* -fied) *tr* vivificare
vivisection [,vɪvɪ'sɛkʃǝn] s vivisezione
vixen ['vɪksǝn] s volpe femmina; (*ill-tempered woman*) megera
vizier [vɪ'zɪr] or ['vɪzjǝr] s visir *m*
vocabular·y [vo'kæbjǝ ,lɛri] s (-ies) vocabolario
vocal ['vokǝl] *adj* vocale; (*inclined to express oneself freely*) che si fa sentire, loquace; (*e.g.*, *outburst*) verbale
vocalist ['vokǝlɪst] s cantante *mf*; (*of jazz*) vocalist *mf*
vocalize ['vokǝ ,laɪz] *tr* vocalizzare || *intr* vocalizzarsi
vocation [vo'keʃǝn] s vocazione; professione, impiego
voca'tional educa'tion s istruzione professionale
vocative ['vakǝtɪv] s vocativo
vociferate [vo'sɪfǝ ,ret] *intr* vociferare
vociferous [vo'sɪfǝrǝs] *adj* rumoroso, vociferante
vogue [vog] s voga, moda; in vogue in voga, di moda
voice [vɔɪs] s voce *f*; (*of animals*) verso; in a loud voice a voce alta; in a low voice a voce bassa; to give voice to esprimere; with one voice con una sola voce || *tr* esprimere; (phonet) sonorizzare || *intr* sonorizzarsi
voiced [vɔɪst] *adj* (phonet) sonoro
voiceless ['vɔɪslɪs] *adj* senza voce; muto; (phonet) sordo, duro
void [vɔɪd] *adj* (*useless*) inutile; (*empty*) vuoto; (law) invalido, nullo; void of sprovvisto di || s vuoto; (*gap*) buco || *tr* vuotare; (*the bowels*) evacuare; annullare || *intr* andare di corpo
volatile ['valǝtɪl] *adj* volatile; instabile; (*disposition*) volubile, incostante
volatilize ['valǝtɪ ,laɪz] *tr* volatilizzare || *intr* volatilizzarsi
volcanic [val'kænɪk] *adj* vulcanico
volca·no [val'keno] s (-noes or -nos) vulcano
volition [vǝ'lɪʃǝn] s volontà *f*; of one's own volition di propria volontà
volley ['vali] s (*e.g.*, *of bullets*) scarica, sventagliata; (tennis) volata || *tr* colpire a volo || *intr* colpire la palla a volo
vol'ley·ball' s pallavolo *f*
volplane ['val ,plen] s planata || *intr* planare
volt [volt] s volt *m*
voltage ['voltɪdʒ] s voltaggio
volt'age divid'er [dɪ'vaɪdǝr] s divisore *m* del voltaggio
voltaic [val'te·ɪk] *adj* voltaico
volte-face [vɔlt'fɑs] s voltafaccia *m*

volt'me'ter s voltmetro
voluble ['valjǝbǝl] *adj* locuace
volume ['valjǝm] s volume *m*; to speak volumes avere molta importanza; essere molto espressivo
voluminous [vǝ'lumɪnǝs] *adj* voluminoso
voluntar·y ['valǝn ,tɛri] *adj* volontario || s (-ies) assolo di organo
volunteer [,valǝn'tɪr] *adj* & s volontario || *tr* dare or dire volontariamente || *intr* offrirsi; arruolarsi come volontario; to volunteer to + *inf* offrirsi di + *inf*
voluptuar·y [vǝ'lʌptʃu ,ɛri] *adj* voluttuoso || s (-ies) sibarita *m*, epicureo
voluptuous [vǝ'lʌptʃu·ǝs] *adj* voluttuoso
volute [vǝ'lut] s voluta
vomit ['vamɪt] s vomito || *tr* & *intr* vomitare, rigettare
voodoo ['vudu] *adj* di vudù || s (*practice*) vudù *m*; (*person*) vuduista *mf*
voracious [vǝ're ʃǝs] *adj* vorace
voracity [vǝ'ræsɪti] s voracità *f*
vor·tex ['vɔrtǝks] s (-texes or -tices [tɪ ,siz]) vortice *m*
vota·ry ['votǝri] s (-ries) persona legata da un voto; amante *mf*, appassionato
vote [vot] s voto; to put to the vote mettere ai voti; to tally the votes procedere allo scrutinio dei voti || *tr* votare; dichiarare; to vote down respingere; to vote in eleggere; to vote out scacciare || *intr* votare
vote' get'ter ['getǝr] s accaparratore *m* di voti; slogan *m* che conquista voti
voter ['votǝr] s elettore *m*
vot'ing machine' ['votɪŋ] s macchina per registrare lo scrutinio dei voti
votive ['votɪv] *adj* votivo
vo'tive of'fering s voto, ex voto, offerta votiva
vouch [vautʃ] *tr* garantire || *intr*—to vouch for (*s.th*) garantire; (*s.o.*) rendersi garante per, garantire per
voucher ['vautʃǝr] s garante *mf*; (*certificate*) ricevuta, pezza d'appoggio
vouch·safe' *tr* concedere, accordare || *intr*—to vouchsafe to + *inf* degnarsi di + *inf*
voussoir [vu'swar] s cuneo
vow [vau] s voto; to take vows pronunciare i voti || *tr* promettere; (*vengeance*) giurare || *intr* fare un voto
vowel ['vau·ǝl] s vocale *f*
voyage ['vɔɪ·ɪdʒ] s viaggio; (*by sea*) traversata || *tr* attraversare || *intr* viaggiare
voyager ['vɔɪ·ɪdʒǝr] s viaggiatore *m*, passeggero
vulcanize ['vʌlkǝ ,naɪz] *tr* vulcanizzare
vulgar ['vʌlgǝr] *adj* volgare; comune, popolare
vulgari·ty [vʌl'gærɪti] s (-ties) volgarità *f*
Vul'gar Lat'in s latino volgare
Vulgate ['vʌlget] s Vulgata
vulnerable ['vʌlnǝrǝbǝl] *adj* vulnerabile
vulture ['vʌltʃǝr] s avvoltoio

W

W, w ['dʌbəl ˌju] s ventitreesima lettera dell'alfabeto inglese

wad [wɑd] s (of cotton) batuffolo, bioccolo; (of money) mazzetta, rotolo; (of tobacco) pallottola; (in a gun) stoppaccio ‖ v (pret & pp **wadded;** ger **wadding**) tr arrotolare; (shot) comprimere; (fig) imbottire

waddle ['wɑdəl] s andatura a mo' di anitra ‖ intr scullettare

wade [wed] tr guadare ‖ intr guadare; avanzare faticosamente; sguazzare; **to wade into** (coll) attaccare violentemente; **to wade through** procedere a stento per; leggere con difficoltà

wad'ing bird' ['wediŋ] s trampoliere m

wafer ['wefər] s disco adesivo di carta per chiudere lettere; (cake) wafer m, cialda; (eccl, med) ostia

waffle ['wɑfəl] s cialda

waf'fle i'ron s schiacce fpl

waft [wæft] or [wɑft] tr portare leggermente or a volo ‖ intr librarsi, spandersi

wag [wæg] s (of head) cenno; (of tail) scodinzolio; (person) burlone m ‖ v (pret & pp **wagged;** ger **wagging**) tr (the head) scuotere; (the tail) dimenare ‖ intr scodinzolare

wage [wedʒ] s salario, paga; **wages** salario, paga; ricompensa; prezzo, e.g., **the wages of sin is death** la morte è il prezzo del peccato ‖ tr (war) fare

wage' earn'er ['ʌrnər] s salariato

wager ['wedʒər] s scommessa; **to lay a wager** fare una scommessa ‖ tr & intr scommettere

wage'work'er s lavoratore salariato

waggish ['wægɪʃ] adj scherzoso, comico, burlone

Wagnerian [vɑg'nɪrɪ·ən] adj & s wagneriano

wagon ['wægən] s carro, carretto; (e.g., Conestoga wagon) carriaggio; furgone m; carrozzone m; **to be on the wagon** (slang) astenersi dal bere; **to hitch one's wagon to a star** avere altissime ambizioni

wag'tail' s (orn) ballerina, cutrettola

waif [wef] s (foundling) trovatello; abbandonato; animale smarrito

wail [wel] s gemito, lamento ‖ intr gemere, lamentarsi

wain·scot ['wenskət] or ['wenskɑt] s pannello per rivestimenti ‖ v (pret & pp -scoted or -scotted) ger -scoting or -scotting) tr rivestire di pannelli di legno

waist [west] s vita, cintura; blusa, camicetta, corpetto

waist'band' s cintola

waist'cloth' s perizoma m

waistcoat ['west ˌkot] or ['wɛstkət] s corpetto, gilè m

waist'line' s vita, cintura; **to keep or watch one's waistline** conservare la linea

wait [wet] s attesa; **to lie in wait** atten-

dere al varco ‖ tr (one's turn) attendere ‖ intr attendere, aspettare; **to wait for** attendere, aspettare; **to wait on** servire; **to wait up for** (coll) aspettare alzato

wait'-and-see' pol'icy s attendismo

waiter ['wetər] s cameriere m; (tray) vassoio

wait'ing list' s lista di aspettativa

wait'ing room' s sala d'aspetto

waitress ['wetrɪs] s cameriera

waive [wev] tr (one's rights) rinunciare (with dat); differire; mettere da parte

waiver ['wevər] s rinuncia

wake [wek] s (any watch) veglia; (watch by a dead body) veglia funebre; (of a boat) solco, scia; **in the wake of** come risultato di; nelle orme di ‖ v (pret **waked** or **woke** [wok]; pp **waked**) tr svegliare ‖ intr svegliarsi; **to wake to** darsi conto di; **to wake up** svegliarsi

wakeful ['wekfəl] adj sveglio; insonne

waken ['wekən] tr svegliare ‖ intr svegliarsi

wale [wel] s segno lasciato da una frustata, vescica; (in fabric) riga, costa

Wales [welz] s la Galles

walk [wɔk] s (act) camminata; (distance) cammino; (for pleasure) passeggiata; (gait) andatura; (line of work) attività f, mestiere m; (sidewalk) marciapiede m; (in a garden) sentiero; (yard for domestic animals to exercise in) recinto; (sports) marcia; **to go for a walk** andare a fare una passeggiata ‖ tr (a street) percorrere; (a horse) passeggiare; (a patient) far camminare; (a heavy piece of furniture) abbambinare; **to walk off** (a headache) far passare camminando ‖ intr camminare; passeggiare; (said of a horse) andare al passo; (sports) marciare; **to walk away from** andarsene a piedi da; **to walk off with** rubare; vincere con facilità; **to walk out** uscire in segno di protesta; (coll) mettersi in sciopero; **to walk out on** (coll) piantare in asso

walkaway ['wɔkə ˌwe] s facile vittoria

walker ['wɔkər] s camminatore m; (to teach a baby to walk) girello

walkie-talkie ['wɔki'tɔki] s trasmettitore-ricevitore m portatile

walk'ing pa'pers spl—**to give s.o. his walking papers** (coll) dare gli otto giorni a qlcu

walk'-in refrig'erator s cella frigorifera

walk'ing stick' s bastone m da passeggio

walk'-on' s (actor) figurante m, comparsa; (role) particina

walk'out' s sciopero

walk'o'ver s facile vittoria, passeggiata

wall [wɔl] s muro; (between rooms; of a vein) parete f; (rampart) muraglia; **to drive to the wall** ridurre alla disperazione; **to go to the wall** perdere; fare fallimento || *tr* murare; **to wall up** circondare con muro

wall'board' *s* pannello da costruzione

wallet ['wɑlɪt] *s* portafoglio

wall'flow'er *s* violacciocca gialla; **to be a wallflower** fare tappezzeria

Walloon [wɑ'lun] *adj & s* vallone *mf*

wallop ['wɑləp] *s* (coll) colpo violento; (coll) effetto || *tr* (coll) dare un colpo violento a; (coll) battere completamente

wallow ['wɑlo] *s* diguazzamento; (*place*) brago, pantano || *intr* diguazzare; (*in wealth*) nuotare

wall'pa'per *s* tappezzeria || *tr* tappezzare

walnut ['wɔlnət] *s* (*tree; wood*) noce *m;* (*fruit*) noce *f*

walrus ['wɔlrəs] or ['wɑlrəs] *s* tricheco

Walter ['wɔltər] *s* Gualtiero

waltz [wɔlts] *s* valzer *m* || *tr* ballare il valzer con; (coll) condurre con disinvoltura || *intr* ballare il valzer

wan [wɑn] *adj* (**wanner; wannest**) (*face*) smunto, sparuto, smorto; (*light*) debole

wand [wɑnd] *s* bacchetta

wander ['wɑndər] *tr* vagare per || *intr* vagare, vagabondare; errare

wanderer ['wɑndərər] *s* vagabondo; pellegrino

Wan'dering Jew' *s* ebreo errante

wan'der·lust' *s* passione del vagabondaggio

wane [wen] *s* decadenza, declino; calare *m* della luna; **on the wane** in declino; (*moon*) calante || *intr* decadere, declinare; (*said of the moon*) calare

wangle ['wæŋgəl] *tr* (coll) ottenere con l'astuzia, rimediare; (coll) falsificare; **to wangle one's way out of** (coll) tirarsi fuori da . . . con l'astuzia || *intr* (coll) arrangiarsi

want [wɑnt] or [wɔnt] *s* bisogno, necessità *f;* domanda; miseria; **for want of** a causa della mancanza di; **to be in want** essere in miseria; **to be in want of** aver bisogno di || *tr* volere, desiderare; mancare; aver bisogno di || *intr* desiderare; **to be wanting** mancare, e.g., **three cards are wanting** mancano tre carte; **to want for** aver bisogno di

want' ad' *s* annunzio economico

wanton ['wɑntən] *adj* di proposito, deliberato; arbitrario; licenzioso, sfrenato; (*archaic*) lussureggiante

war [wɔr] *s* guerra; **to go to war** entrare in guerra; (*said of a soldier*) andare in guerra; **to wage war** fare la guerra || *v* (*pret & pp* **warred; *ger* warring**) *intr* guerreggiare; **to war on** fare la guerra a

warble ['wɔrbəl] *s* gorgheggio || *intr* gorgheggiare

warbler ['wɔrblər] *s* canterino; uccello canoro; (orn) beccafico

war' cloud' *s* minaccia di guerra

ward [wɔrd] *s* (*of city*) distretto; (*division of hospital*) corsia; (*separate building in hospital*) padiglione *m;*

(*guardianship*) tutela; (*minor*) pupillo; (*of lock*) scontro || *tr*—**to ward off** stornare, schermirsi da

warden ['wɔrdən] *s* guardiano; (*of jail*) direttore *m;* (*in wartime*) capofabbricato

ward' heel'er *s* politicantuccio

ward'robe *s* guardaroba *m*

ward'robe trunk' *s* baule *m* armadio

ward'room' *s* (nav) quadrato

ware [wɛr] *s* vasellame *m;* **wares** merce *f*

war' ef'fort *s* sforzo bellico

ware'house' *s* deposito, magazzino

ware'house'man *s* (**-men**) magazziniere *m*

war'fare' *s* guerra

war'head' *s* (mil) testa

war'horse' *s* cavallo di battaglia; (coll) veterano

warily ['wɛrɪli] *adv* con cautela

wariness ['wɛrɪnɪs] *s* cautela

war'like' *adj* guerresco, guerriero

war' loan' *s* prestito di guerra

war' lord' *s* generalissimo

warm [wɔrm] *adj* caldo; (*lukewarm*) tiepido; (*clothes*) che tiene caldo; (*with anger*) acceso; **to be warm** (*said of a person*) avere caldo; (*said of the weather*) fare caldo || *tr* scaldare, riscaldare; (*s.o.'s heart*) slargare; **to warm up** riscaldare || *intr* scaldarsi, riscaldarsi; **to warm up** (*said, e.g., of a room*) riscaldarsi; (*with emotion*) eccitarsi, accalorarsi; **to warm up to** prender simpatia per

warm-blooded ['wɔrm'blʌdɪd] *adj* (*animal*) a sangue caldo; impetuoso, ardente

war' memo'rial *s* monumento ai caduti

warmer ['wɔrmər] *s* scaldino

warm-hearted ['wɔrm'hɑrtɪd] *adj* caloroso, cordiale

warm'ing pan' *s* scaldaletto

warmonger ['wɔr,mʌŋgər] *s* guerrafondaio

war' moth'er *s* madrina di guerra

warmth [wɔrmθ] *s* calore *m*, tepore *m;* foga, entusiasmo

warm'up' *s* preparazione; (*of radio, engine, etc.*) riscaldamento

warn [wɔrn] *tr* avvertire, mettere in guardia; (*to admonish*) ammonire; informare; **to warn off** intimare di allontanarsi (da)

warn'ing *adj* di avvertimento || *s* avvertimento, ammonimento; (law) diffida

war' nose' *s* acciarino, testa

war' of nerves' *s* guerra dei nervi

War' of the Roses' *s* Guerra delle due Rose

warp [wɔrp] *s* (*of a fabric*) ordito; (*of a board*) svergolamento, curvatura; aberrazione mentale; (naut) gherlino || *tr* curvare, svergolare; (*a fabric*) ordire; falsare, alterare; (naut) tirare col gherlino || *intr* curvarsi; falsarsi, alterarsi; (naut) alare

war'path' *s*—**to be on the warpath** essere sul sentiero della guerra, prepararsi alla guerra; (*to be angry*) essere arrabiato, essere di cattivo umore

war'plane' *s* aeroplano da guerra

war' prof'iteer *s* pescecane *m*

warrant ['warənt] or ['wɔrənt] *s* garanzia; certificato; ricevuta; (com) nota di pegno; (law) ordine *m*, mandato || *tr* garantire; autorizzare

warrantable ['warəntəbəl] or ['wɔrəntəbəl] *adj* giustificabile, legittimo

war'rant of'ficer *s* sottufficiale *m*

warran•ty ['warənti] or ['wɔrənti] *s* (-ties) garanzia; autorizzazione

warren ['warən] or ['wɔrən] *s* conigliera; (fig) formicaio

warrior ['wɔrjər] or ['warjər] *s* guerriero

Warsaw ['wɔrsɔ] *s* Varsavia

war'ship' *s* nave *f* da guerra

wart [wɔrt] *s* verruca

war'time' *s* tempo di guerra

war'-torn' *adj* devastato dalla guerra

war' to the death' *s* guerra a morte

war•y ['weri] *adj* (-ier; -iest) guardingo

wash [waʃ] or [wɔʃ] *s* lavata; (*clothes washed or to be washed*) bucato; (*rushing movement of water*) sciacquio; (*dirty water*) lavatura; (*painting*) mano *f* di colore; (aer, naut) scia || *tr* lavare; (*dishes*) rigovernare; (*said of sea or river*) bagnare; **to be washed up** essere finito; **to wash away** (*soil of river bank*) dilavare; portar via || *intr* lavarsi; fare il bucato; essere lavabile; (*said of waves*) battere

washable ['waʃəbəl] or ['wɔʃəbəl] *adj* lavabile

wash'-and-wear' *adj* non-stiro

wash'ba'sin *s* conca, catinella

wash'bas'ket *s* cesto del bucato

wash'board' *s* asse *m* da lavanda; (*baseboard*) battiscopa *m*

wash'bowl' *s* conca, catinella

wash'cloth' *s* pezzuola per lavarsi

wash'day' *s* giorno del bucato

washed-out ['waʃt‚aut] or ['wɔʃt‚aut] *adj* slavato; (coll) stanco; (coll) abbattuto, accasciato

washed-up ['waʃt'ʌp] or ['wɔʃt'ʌp] *adj* (coll) finito

washer ['waʃər] or ['wɔʃər] *s* (*person*) lavatore *m*; (*machine*) lavatrice *f*; (*under head of bolt*) rondella, rosetta; (*ring to prevent leakage*) guarnizione

wash'er•man *s* (-men) lavatore *m*

wash'er•wom'an *s* (-wom'en) lavatrice *f*, lavandaia

wash' goods' *spl* tessuti *mpl* lavabili

washing ['waʃɪŋ] or ['wɔʃɪŋ] *s* lavata, lavaggio, lavanda; (*of clothes*) bucato; **washings** lavaggio

wash'ing machine' *s* lavabiancheria, lavatrice *f*

wash'ing so'da *s* soda da lavare

wash'out' *s* erosione; (aer) svergolamento negativo; (coll) rovina completa

wash'rag' *s* pezzuola per lavarsi; straccio di cucina

wash'room' *s* gabinetto, toletta

wash'stand' *s* lavabo, lavamano

wash'tub' *s* mastello, lavatoio

wash' wa'ter *s* lavatura

wasp [wasp] *s* vespa

waste [west] *s* spreco; (*refuse*) scarico, rifiuto; (*desolate country*) landa; (*excess material*) scarto; (*for wiping machinery*) cascame *m* di cotone; **to go to waste** essere sciupato; **to lay waste** devastare || *tr* perdere, sciupare, sprecare || *intr*—**to waste away** intristire, consumarsi

waste'bas'ket *s* cestino della carta straccia

wasteful ['westfəl] *adj* dispendioso; distruttivo

waste'pa'per *s* cartastraccia

waste' pipe' *s* tubo di scarico

waste' prod'uct *s* scarto; (*body excretion*) escremento

wastrel ['westrəl] *s* sciupone *m;* spendaccione *m*, prodigo

watch [watʃ] *s* orologio; (*lookout*) guardia; (mil) guardia; (naut) turno; **to be on the watch for** essere all'erta per; **to keep watch over** vegliare su || *tr* (*to look at*) osservare; (*to oversee*) vigilare; guardare; fare attenzione a || *intr* guardare; (*to keep awake*) vegliare; **to watch for** fare attenzione a; **to watch out** fare attenzione; **to watch out for** fare attenzione a; essere all'erta per; **to watch over** sorvegliare; **watch out!** attenzione!

watch'band' *s* cinturino dell'orologio

watch'case' *s* cassa dell'orologio

watch' charm' *s* ciondolo dell'orologio

watch' crys'tal *s* cristallo dell'orologio

watch'dog' *s* cane *m* da guardia; (fig) guardiano

watch'dog' commit'tee *s* comitato di sorveglianza

watchful ['watʃfəl] *adj* vigile

watchfulness ['watʃfəlnɪs] *s* vigilanza

watch'mak'er *s* orologiaio

watch'man *s* (-men) guardiano, sorvegliante *m;* (*at night*) guardia notturna, metronotte *m*

watch' night' *s* notte *f* di San Silvestro; ufficio religioso della vigilia di Capodanno

watch' pock'et *s* taschino dell'orologio

watch'tow'er *s* torre *f* d'osservazione

watch'word' *s* parola d'ordine, consegna; slogan *m*

water ['wɔtər] or ['watər] *s* acqua; **of the first water** di prim'ordine; (*e.g., a thief*) della più bell'acqua; **to back water** retrocedere; **to be in deep water** essere in cattive acque; **to fish in troubled waters** pescare nel torbido; **to hold water** aver fondamento; **to keep above water** (fig) tenersi a galla; **to make water** (*to urinate*) urinare; (naut) fare acqua; **to throw cold water on** scoraggiare || *tr* bagnare; dare acqua a; (*cattle*) abbeverare; (*wine*) annacquare || *intr* abbeverarsi; (*said of the mouth*) aver l'acquolina; (*said, e.g., of a ship*) fare acqua; (*said of the eyes*) lacrimare

wa'ter bug' s bacherozzolo
wa'ter car'rier s acquaiolo
wa'ter·col'or s acquerello
wa'ter-cooled' adj a raffreddamento ad acqua
wa'ter·course' s corso d'acqua
wa'ter·cress' s crescione m
wa'ter cure' s cura delle acque
wa'ter·fall' s cascata
wa'ter·front' s riva, banchina
wa'ter gap' s gola, passo
wa'ter ham'mer s colpo d'ariete
wa'ter heat'er s scaldabagno, scalda-acqua m
wa'ter ice' s granita
wa'tering can' s annaffiatoio
wa'tering place' s stabilimento balneare; stazione termale; (drinking place) abbeveratoio
wa'tering pot' s annaffiatoio
wa'tering trough' s abbeveratoio
wa'ter jack'et s camicia d'acqua
wa'ter lil'y s nenufaro
wa'ter line' s linea di galleggiamento or d'acqua; linea di livello
wa'ter main' s tubo di flusso principale
wa'ter·mark' s linea di livello massimo; (in paper) filigrana
wa'ter·mel'on s cocomero, anguria
wa'ter me'ter s contatore m dell'acqua
wa'ter mill' s mulino ad acqua
wa'ter pipe' s tubo dell'acqua
wa'ter po'lo s pallanuoto f
wa'ter pow'er s forza idrica
wa'ter·proof' adj & s impermeabile m
wa'ter·repel'lent adj idroripellente
wa'ter·shed' s spartiacque m, displuvio
wa'ter ski' s idrosci m
wa'ter sof'tener s decalcificatore m
wa'ter·spout' s (to carry water from roof) pluviale m; (meteor) tromba marina
wa'ter sys'tem s (of a river) sistema m fluviale; (of city) conduttura dell'acqua, impianto idrico
wa'ter·tight' adj stagno, ermetico; (fig) perfetto, inconfutabile
wa'ter tow'er s torre f serbatoio
wa'ter wag'on s (mil) carro dell'acqua; to be on the water wagon (slang) astenersi dal bere
wa'ter·way' s via d'acqua, idrovia
wa'ter wheel' s ruota or turbina idraulica; (of steamboat) ruota a pale
wa'ter wings' spl galleggiante m per nuotare
wa'ter·works' s impianto idrico; (pumping station) impianto di pompaggio
watery ['wɔtəri] or ['watəri] adj acquoso; lacrimoso; povero, insipido; umido, acquitrinoso
watt [wat] s watt m
watt'-hour' s (-hours) wattora m
wattle ['watəl] s (of bird) bargiglio
watt'me'ter s wattmetro
wave [wev] s onda; (of cold; of feeling) ondata; (of the hand) cenno; (of hair) onda, ondulazione || tr (a flag) sventolare; (the hair) ondulare; (the hand) fare cenno con; to wave aside fare cenno di allontanarsi a; (e.g., a

proposal) rifiutare || intr ondeggiare; fare cenni con la mano
wave'length' s lunghezza d'onda
wave' mo'tion s movimento ondulatorio
waver ['wevər] intr ondeggiare, oscillare; (to hesitate) titubare, tentennare; (to totter) pencolare
wav·y ['wevi] adj (-ier; -iest) (sea) ondoso; (hair) ondulato
wax [wæks] s cera; (fig) fantoccio || tr incerare; (a recording) (coll) registrare || intr aumentare; diventare; (said of the moon) crescere; to wax indignant indignarsi
wax' pa'per s carta cerata, carta oleata
wax'works' s museo di statue di cera
way [we] s maniera, modo; via; condizione; across the way di fronte; a good way un buon tratto; all the way fino alla fine della strada; completamente; all the way to fino a; any way ad ogni modo; by the way a proposito; in a way in un certo modo; fino a un certo punto; in every way per ogni verso; in this way in questa maniera; one way senso unico; on the way to andando a; on the way out uscendo; diminuendo, sparendo; out of the way eliminato; fuori mano; strano; irregolare; that way in quella direzione; per di lì; in quella maniera; this way in questa direzione; per di qui; in questa maniera; to be in the way essere d'impaccio; to feel one's way avanzare a tentoni; to force one's way aprirsi il passo a viva forza; to get out of the way togliersi di mezzo; to give way ritirarsi, cedere; (said of a rope) rompersi; to give way to cedere a, darsi a; to go out of one's way darsi da fare, disturbarsi; to have one's way vincerla; to keep out of the way stare fuori dai piedi; to know one's way around conoscere bene la via; (fig) sapere il fatto proprio; to know one's way to sapere andare a; to lead the way guidare, fare da guida; prendere l'iniziativa; to lose one's way perdersi; to make one's way avanzare; fare carriera; to make way for far largo a; to mend one's ways mettere la testa a partito; to not know which way to turn non sapere a che santo votarsi; to put out of the way togliere di mezzo; to see one's way to vedere la possibilità di; to take one's way andarsene; to wind one's way through andare a zig zag per; to wing one's way andare a volo; under way in moto; in cammino, avviato; way in entrata; way out uscita; ways modi mpl, maniere fpl; (naut) scalo; which way? da che parte?; in che modo?, per dove?
way'bill' s lettera di vettura
wayfarer ['we,fɛrər] s viandante m
way'lay' v (pret & pp -laid) tr tendere un agguato a; fermare improvvisamente
way' of life' s tenore m di vita

way'side' s bordo della strada; to fall by the wayside cadere per istrada; (fig) fare fiasco

way' sta'tion s stazione con fermata facoltativa

way' train' s treno omnibus

wayward ['wewərd] adj indocile, caparbio; irregolare; capriccioso

we [wi] pron pers noi; noialtri, e.g., we Italians noialtri italiani

weak [wik] adj debole

weaken ['wikən] tr indebolire, infiacchire || intr indebolirsi, infiacchirsi

weakling ['wiklɪŋ] s debolino, rammollito

weak-minded ['wik'maɪndɪd] adj irresoluto; scemo

weakness ['wiknɪs] s debolezza, fiacchezza; (liking) debole m

wealth [welθ] s ricchezza

wealth·y ['welθi] adj (-ier; -iest) ricco

wean [win] tr svezzare, slattare; to wean away from disavvezzare da

weanling ['winlɪŋ] adj appena svezzato || s bambino or animale appena svezzato

weapon ['wepən] s arma

weaponry ['wepənri] s armi fpl, armamento

wear [wer] s uso, servizio; (clothing) vestiti mpl, indumenti mpl; (wasting away from use) consumo, logorio; (lasting quality) durata, durabilità f; for everyday wear per ogni giorno || v (pret wore [wor]; pp worn [worn]) tr portare, avere indosso; (to cause to deteriorate) logorare, consumare; (to tire) stancare; to wear out logorare, strusciare; (a horse) sfiancare; (one's patience) esaurire; (s.o.'s hospitality) abusare di || intr logorarsi, consumarsi; to wear off diminuire, sparire; to wear out logorarsi; stancarsi; esaurirsi; to wear well essere di ottima durata

wear' and tear' [ter] s logorio

weariness ['wɪrɪnɪs] s fatica, stanchezza

wear'ing appar'el ['werɪŋ] s abbigliamento, articoli mpl d'abbigliamento

wearisome ['wɪrɪsəm] adj affaticante; (tedious) noioso

wea·ry ['wɪri] adj (-rier; -riest) stanco || v (pret & pp -ried) tr stancare || intr stancarsi

weasel ['wizəl] s donnola

wea'sel words' spl parole fpl ambigue

weather ['weðər] s tempo; maltempo; to be under the weather (coll) non sentirsi bene; (to be slightly drunk) (coll) essere alticcio || tr (lumber) stagionare; (adversities) superare, resistere (with dat)

weather-beaten ['weðər,bitən] adj segnato dalle intemperie

weath'er bu'reau s servizio meteorologico

weath'er·cock' s banderuola

weath'er fore'cast s previsioni fpl del tempo, bollettino metereologico

weath'er·man' s (-men') metereologo

weath'er report' s bollettino metereologico

weath'er strip'ping ['strɪpɪŋ] s guarnizione a nastro per inzeppare

weath'er vane' s banderuola, ventarola

weave [wiv] s tessitura || v (pret wove [wov] or weaved; pp wove or woven ['wovən]) tr tessere; (fig) inserire; to weave one's way aprirsi un varco serpeggiando || intr tessere; serpeggiare

weaver ['wivər] s tessitore m

web [web] s tessuto; (of spider) tela; (of rail) anima, gambo; (zool) membrana; (fig) rete f, maglia

web-footed ['web,futɪd] adj palmipede

wed [wed] v (pret & pp wed or wedded; ger wedding) tr sposare; (said of the groom) impalmare; (said of the bride) andare in sposa a || intr sposarsi

wedding ['wedɪŋ] adj nuziale || s sposalizio, nozze fpl, matrimonio

wed'ding cake' s torta nuziale

wed'ding day' s giorno di nozze

wed'ding invita'tion s invito a nozze

wed'ding march' s marcia nuziale

wed'ding ring' s fede f, vera

wedge [wedʒ] s cuneo; (of pie) spicchio; (to split wood) bietta; (to hold a wheel) scarpa || tr incuneare

wed'lock s matrimonio

Wednesday ['wenzdi] s mercoledì m

wee [wi] adj piccolo piccolo

weed [wid] s malerba, erbaccia; (coll) sigaretta; (slang) marijuana; weeds vestito da lutto, gramaglie fpl || tr sarchiare, mondare

weeder ['widər] s (agr) estirpatore m

weed'ing hoe' s sarchio, zappa

weed'-kill'er s diserbante m

week [wik] s settimana; week in, week out una settimana dopo l'altra

week'day' s giorno feriale

week'end' s fine-settimana m, fine f di settimana, week-end m || intr passare il fine-settimana

week·ly ['wikli] adj settimanale || s (-lies) settimanale m || adv settimanalmente

weep [wip] v (pret & pp wept [wept]) tr piangere; to weep oneself to sleep addormentarsi piangendo; to weep one's eyes out piangere a calde lacrime || intr piangere; to weep for joy piangere di gioia

weeper ['wipər] s piagnone m; (hired mourner) prefica

weep'ing wil'low s salice m piangente

weep·y ['wipi] adj (-ier; -iest) piangente, lacrimoso

weevil ['wivəl] s curculione m

weft [weft] s (yarns running across warp) trama; (fabric) tela, tessuto

weigh [we] tr pesare; (anchor) levare; (to make heavy) appesantire; (fig) soppesare, ponderare; to weigh down piegare || intr pesare; gravitare; to weigh in (sports) pesarsi; to weigh upon gravare a

weigh'bridge' s stadera

weight [wet] s peso; (fig) peso; to carry weight aver del peso; to lose weight diminuire di peso; to put on weight crescere di peso; to throw one's **weight around** far sentire la propria importanza || *tr* appesantire; (*statistically*) ponderare, dare un certo peso a

weightless ['wetlıs] *adj* senza peso, imponderabile

weightlessness ['wetlısnıs] *s* imponderabilità *f*

weight·y ['weti] *adj* (**-ier; -iest**) pesante; importante

weir [wır] *s* sbarramento; (*for catching fish*) pescaia

weird [wırd] *adj* soprannaturale, misterioso; strano, bizzarro

welcome ['welkəm] *adj* benvenuto; gradito; **you are welcome** (*i.e., gladly received*) sia il benvenuto; (*in answer to thanks*) prego; **you are welcome to it** è a Sua disposizione; **you are welcome to your opinion** pensi come la vuole || *s* benvenuto || *tr* dare il benvenuto a; accettare; gradire || *interj* benvenuto!

weld [weld] *s* saldatura autogena; (bot) guaderella || *tr* saldare || *intr* saldarsi

welder ['weldər] *s* saldatore *m;* (*machine*) saldatrice *f*

welding ['weldıŋ] *s* saldatura autogena

wel'fare' *s* benessere *m;* (*effort to improve living conditions*) beneficenza, assistenza; **to be on welfare** ricevere assistenza pubblica

wel'fare state' *s* stato sociale or assistenziale

well [wel] *adj* bene; in buona salute || *s* pozzo; (*for ink*) pozzetto, serbatoio; (*spring*) sorgente *f;* (*shaft for stairs*) tromba || *adv* bene; **as well** pure; **as well . . . as** tanto . . . come; **as well as** tanto come, non meno che || *intr* —**to well up** sgorgare || *interj* beh!; bene!; allora!, dunque!

well-appointed ['welə'pɔɪntıd] *adj* ben ammobiliato

well-attended ['welə'tendıd] *adj* molto frequentato

well-behaved ['welbı'hevd] *adj* beneducato; **to be well-behaved** comportarsi bene

well'-be'ing *s* benessere *m*

well'born' *adj* bennato

well-bred ['wel'bred] *adj* educato, costumato

well-disposed ['weldıs'pozd] *adj* bendisposto

well-done ['wel'dʌn] *adj* benfatto; (*meat*) ben cotto

well-fixed ['wel'fıkst] *adj* (coll) agiato, abbiente

well-formed ['wel'fɔrmd] *adj* benfatto

well-founded ['wel'faundıd] *adj* fondato

well-groomed ['wel'grumd] *adj* (*person*) curato; (*horse*) ben governato

well-heeled ['wel'hild] *adj* (coll) agiato, benestante

well-informed ['welın'fɔrmd] *adj* bene informato

well-intentioned ['welın'tenʃənd] *adj* benintenzionato

well'-kept' *adj* ben conservato; (*person*) benportante; (*secret*) ben mantenuto

well-known ['wel'non] *adj* notorio, ben noto

well-meaning ['wel'minıŋ] *adj* benevolo, benintenzionato

well-nigh ['wel'naı] *adv* quasi

well'-off' *adj* agiato, benestante

well-preserved ['welprı'zʌrvd] *adj* ben conservato; (*person*) benportante

well-read ['wel'red] *adj* colto, che ha letto molto

well-spoken ['wel'spokən] *adj* (*person*) raffinato nel parlare; (*word*) a proposito

well'spring' *s* sorgente *f*

well' sweep' *s* mazzacavallo del pozzo

well-tempered ['wel'tempərd] *adj* ben temperato

well-thought-of ['wel'θɔt ,av] *adj* tenuto in alta considerazione

well-timed ['wel'taımd] *adj* opportuno

well-to-do ['weltə'du] *adj* benestante

well-wisher ['wel'wıʃər] *s* amico, sostenitore *m*

well-worn ['wel'worn] *adj* (*clothing*) liso, consunto, trito; (*argument*) logoro, banale; portato con eleganza

welsh [welʃ] *intr* —**to welsh on** (*a promise*) (slang) mancare a; (*a person*) (slang) fregare || **Welsh** *adj & s* gallese *mf;* **the Welsh** il gallesi

Welsh'man *s* (-men) gallese *m*

Welsh' rab'bit or **rare'bit** ['rerbıt] *s* fonduta fatta con la birra servita su pane abbrustolito

welt [welt] *s* (*finish along a seam*) costa; (*of shoe*) guardolo; (*wale from a blow*) riga, sferzata

welter ['weltər] *s* guazzabuglio; confusione; (*a tumbling about*) rotolio || *intr* rotolarsi, guazzare

wel'ter·weight' *s* (boxing) peso welter, peso medio-leggero

wench [wentʃ] *s* ragazza, giovane *f*

wend [wend] *tr* —**to wend one's way** dirigere i propri passi

werewolf ['wır,wulf] *s* lupo mannaro

west [west] *adj* occidentale || *s* ovest *m,* occidente *m* || *adv* verso l'ovest

western ['westərn] *adj* occidentale || *s* western *m*

West' In'dies ['ındız] *spl* Indie *fpl* Occidentali

westward ['westwərd] *adv* verso l'ovest

wet [wet] *adj* (**wetter; wettest**) bagnato; (*paint*) fresco; (*damp*) umido; (*rainy*) piovoso; che permette la vendita delle bevande alcoliche || *s* umidità *f;* antiproibizionista *mf* || *v* (*pret & pp* **wet** or **wetted;** *ger* **wetting**) *tr* bagnare || *intr* bagnarsi

wet' blan'ket *s* guastafeste *mf*

wether ['weðər] *s* castrone *m*

wet' nurse' *s* nutrice *f,* balia

whack [hwæk] *s* (slang) colpo, percossa; (slang) prova, tentativo || *tr* (slang) percuotere

whale [hwel] *s* balena; **a whale of** (slang) gigantesco, e.g., **a whale of a lie** una bugia gigantesca; enorme, e.g., **a whale of a difference** una differenza enorme || *tr* (coll) battere || *intr* pescare balene

whale'bone' *s* osso di balena, fanone *m*

wharf [hwɔrf] *s* (**wharves** [hwɔrvz] or **wharfs**) molo

what [hwɑt] *adj interr* che; quale || *adj rel* quello . . . che; il . . . che, e.g., **wear what tie you prefer** mettiti la cravatta che preferisci || *pron interr* che; quale; **what else?** che altro?; **what if . . . ?** e se . . . ?; **what of it?** e che me ne importa? || *pron rel* quello che; **what's what** (coll) tutta la situazione || *interj* what a . . . ! che . . . !, e.g., **what a beautiful day!** che splendida giornata!

what·ev'er *adj* qualsiasi; qualunque || *pron* quanto; che; quello che

what'not' *s* scaffaletto

wheal [hwil] *s* vescichetta

wheat [hwit] *s* grano, frumento

wheedle ['hwidəl] *tr* adulare; persuadere con lusinghe; (*money*) spillare

wheel [hwil] *s* ruota; (*of cheese*) forma; (coll) bicicletta; **at the wheel** al volante; in controllo || *tr* roteare; portare in carrozzella || *intr* girare

wheelbarrow ['hwil‚bæro] *s* carriola

wheel'base' *s* passo

wheel'chair' *s* carrozzella

wheel' col'umn *s* (aut) piantone *m* di guida

wheeler-dealer ['hwilər'dilər] *s* (slang) grande affarista *m*

wheel' horse' *s* cavallo di timone; lavoratore *m* di fiducia

wheelwright ['hwil‚raɪt] *s* carradore *m*

wheeze [hwiz] *s* affanno; (pathol) rantolo || *intr* respirare affannosamente; (pathol) rantolare

whelp [hwɛlp] *s* cucciolo || *tr & intr* figliare, partorire

when [hwɛn] *adv & conj* quando

whence [hwɛns] *adv* donde, di dove || *conj* donde; per che ragione

when·ev'er *conj* ogniqualvolta, qualora

where [hwɛr] *adv & conj* dove

whereabouts ['hwɛrə‚bauts] *s* luogo dove uno si trova || *adv & conj* dove

whereas [hwɛr'æz] *conj* mentre; visto che, considerato che

where·by' *adv* per cui, col quale

wherever [hwɛr'ɛvər] *adv* dove mai || - *conj* dovunque

wherefore ['hwɛrfor] *s* perché *m* || *adv* perché || *conj* per cui, percome

where·from' *adv* donde

where·in' *adv* dove; in che modo || *conj* dove; nel quale

where·of' *adv* di che || *conj* di che; del quale

where·upon' *adv* sul che; laonde, dopodiché

wherewithal ['hwɛrwɪð‚əl] *s* mezzi *mpl*

whet [hwɛt] *v* (*pret & pp* **whetted;** *ger* **whetting**) *tr* affilare; (*the appetite*) aguzzare

whether ['wɛðər] *conj* se; **whether or no** ad ogni modo, in ogni caso; **whether or not** che . . . o che non

whet'stone' *s* pietra da affilare

whey [hwe] *s* scotta

which [hwɪtʃ] *adj interr* quale || *adj rel* il (la, etc.) quale || *pron interr* che; quale; **which is which** qual'è

l'uno e qual'è l'altro || *pron rel* che; il quale; quello che

which·ev'er *adj & pron rel* qualunque

whiff [hwɪf] *s* (*of air*) soffio; fiutata; (*trace of odor*) zaffata; **to get a whiff of** sentire l'odore di || *intr* soffiare; (*said of a smoker*) dare boccate

while [hwaɪl] *s* tempo; **a long while un bel pezzo; a while ago** un tratto fa; **to be worth one's while** valere la pena || *conj* mentre || *tr*—**to while away** passare piacevolmente

whim [hwɪm] *s* capriccio, estro

whimper ['hwɪmpər] *s* piagnucolio || *tr & intr* piagnucolare

whimsical ['hwɪmzɪkəl] *adj* capriccioso, estroso, stravagante

whine [hwaɪn] *s* (*of dog*) guaito; (*of person*) piagnucolio || *intr* (*said of a dog*) guaire, uggiolare; (*said of a person*) piagnucolare

whin·ny ['hwɪni] *s* (-**nies**) nitrito || *v* (*pret & pp* -**nied**) *intr* nitrire

whip [hwɪp] *s* frusta; uova *fpl* sbattute con frutta || *v* (*pret & pp* **whipped** or **whipt;** *ger* **whipping**) *tr* frustare, battere; (*eggs*) frullare; (coll) vincere, sconfiggere; **to whip off** (coll) buttar giù; **to whip out** tirar fuori rapidamente; **to whip up** (coll) preparare in quattro e quattr'otto; (coll) eccitare, incitare

whip'cord' *s* cordino della frusta; (*fabric*) saia a diagonale

whip' hand' *s* mano che tiene la frusta; vantaggio, posizione vantaggiosa

whip'lash' *s* scudisciata

whipped' cream' *s* panna montata

whipper-snapper ['hwɪpər‚snæpər] *s* pivello

whippet ['hwɪpɪt] *s* piccolo levriere

whip'ping boy' ['hwɪpɪŋ] *s* testa di turco

whip'ping post' *s* palo per la fustigazione

whippoorwill [‚hwɪpər'wɪl] *s* caprimulgo, succiacapre *m*

whir [hwʌr] *s* ronzio || *v* (*pret & pp* **whirred;** *ger* **whirring**) *intr* ronzare; volare ronzando

whirl [hwʌrl] *s* giro improvviso; corsa; mulinello; (fig) successione || *tr & intr* mulinare; **my head whirls** mi gira la testa

whirligig ['hwʌrli‚gɪg] *s* turbine *m*; (*carrousel*) giostra; (*toy*) girandola; (ent) ragno d'acqua

whirl'pool' *s* risucchio, mulinello

whirl'wind' *s* turbine *m*, tromba d'aria

whirlybird ['hwʌrli‚bʌrd] *s* (coll) elicottero

whish [hwɪʃ] *s* fruscio || *intr* frusciare

whisk [hwɪsk] *s* scopatina || *tr* scopare, spolverare; (*eggs*) sbattere; **to whisk out of sight** far sparire || *intr* guizzare

whisk' broom' *s* scopetta per i vestiti, spolverino

whiskers ['hwɪskərz] *spl* barba; (*on side of man's face*) basette *fpl*; (*of cat*) baffi *mpl*

whiskey ['hwɪski] *s* whisky *m*

whisper ['hwɪspər] *s* sussurro, bisbi- glio, mormorio; **in a whisper** in un sussurro || *tr & intr* sussurrare, bisbi- gliare, mormorare

whisperer ['hwɪspərər] *s* sussurrone *m*

whispering ['hwɪspərɪŋ] *adj* di maldi- cenze || *s* sussurro; maldicenza

whistle ['hwɪsəl] *s* fischio; **to wet one's whistle** (coll) bagnarsi l'ugola || *tr* fischiare || *intr* fischiare, zufolare; **to whistle for** chiamare con un fischio; *(money)* aspettare in vano

whis'tle stop' *s* stazioncina, paesetto

whit [hwɪt] *s*—**not a whit** niente affatto

white [hwaɪt] *adj* bianco || *s* bianco; **whites** (pathol) leucorrea

white'cap' *s* frangente *m*, cavallone *m*, onda crespa

white' coal' *s* carbone bianco

white'-col'lar *adj* impiegatizio

white' feath'er *s*—**to show the white feather** mostrarsi vile

white' goods' *spl* biancheria ḍa casa; articoli *mpl* di cotone; apparecchi *mpl* elettrodomestici

white-haired ['hwaɪt,herd] *adj* dai ca- pelli bianchi; (coll) favorito

white' heat' *s* calor bianco

white' lead' [lɛd] *s* biacca

white' lie' *s* bugia innocente

white' meat' *s* bianco, carne *f* del petto

whiten ['hwaɪtən] *tr* imbiancare, sbian- care || *intr* imbiancarsi, sbiancarsi; impallidire

whiteness ['hwaɪtnɪs] *s* bianchezza

white' plague' *s* tubercolosi *f*

white' slav'ery *s* tratta delle bianche

white' tie' *s* cravatta da frac; marsina, abito da cerimonia

white'wash' *s* imbiancatura; (fig) coper- tura || *tr* imbiancare, intonacare; (fig) coprire

white' wa'ter lil'y *s* ninfea

whither ['hwɪθər] *adv* dove, a che luogo || *conj* dove

whiting ['hwaɪtɪŋ] *s* (ichth) nasello; (ichth) merlango

whitish ['hwaɪtɪʃ] *adj* biancastro

whitlow ['hwɪtlo] *s* patereccio

Whitsuntide ['hwɪtsən,taɪd] *s* setti- mana di Pentecoste

whittle ['hwɪtəl] *tr* digrossare; **to whit- tle away** or **down** ridurre gradual- mente

whiz or **whizz** [hwɪz] *s* sibilo; (coll) asso || *v* (*pret & pp* **whizzed**; *ger* **whizzing**) *intr*—**to whiz by** passare sibilando; passare come una freccia

who [hu] *pron interr* chi; **who else?** chi altri?; **who goes there?** (mil) chi va là?; **who's who** chi è l'uno e chi è l'altro; chi è la gente importante || *pron rel* chi; il quale

whoa [hwo] or [wo] *interj* fermo!

who·ev'er *pron rel* chiunque

whole [hol] *adj* tutto, intero; sano, in- tatto; **made out of the whole cloth** completamente immaginario || *s* tutto; **as a whole** nell'insieme; **on the whole** in generale

wholehearted ['hol,hartɪd] *adj* molto sincero, generoso

whole' note' *s* (mus) semibreve *f*

whole'sale' *adj & adv* all'ingrosso || *s* ingrosso || *tr* vendere all'ingrosso || *intr* vendersi all'ingrosso

wholesaler ['hol,selər] *s* grossista *mf*

wholesome ['holsəm] *adj* (*beneficial*) salutare; (*in good health*) sano

wholly ['holi] *adv* interamente

whom [hum] *pron interr* chi || *pron rel* che; il quale

whom·ev'er *pron rel* chiunque

whoop [hup] or [hwup] *s* urlo; (pathol) urlo della pertosse; **to not be worth a whoop** (coll) non valere un fico secco || *tr*—**to whoop it up** (slang) fare il diavolo a quattro || *intr* urlare

whoop'ing cough' ['hupɪŋ] or ['hup- ɪŋ] *s* pertosse *f*

whopper ['hwapər] *s* (coll) enormità *f*; (coll) fandonia, bugia enorme

whopping ['hwapɪŋ] *adj* (coll) enorme

whore [hor] *s* puttana || *intr*—**to whore around** puttaneggiare; andare a put- tane

whortleber·ry ['hwʌrtəl,beri] *s* (-ries) mirtillo

whose [huz] *pron interr* di chi || *pron rel* di chi; del quale; di cui

why [hwaɪ] *s* (**whys**) perché *m*; **the whys and the wherefores** il perché e il percome || *adv* perché || *interj* dia- mine!; **why, certainly!** certamente!; **why, yes!** evidentemente!

wick [wɪk] *s* stoppino, lucignolo

wicked ['wɪkɪd] *adj* malvagio; (*mis- chievous*) cattivo; (*dreadful*) terri- bile, bestiale

wicker ['wɪkər] *adj* di vimini || *s* vi- mine *m*

wicket ['wɪkɪt] *s* (*small door*) portello; (*ticket window*) sportello; (*of a canal*) chiusa; (cricket) porta; (cro- quet) archetto

wide [waɪd] *adj* largo; esteso; (*eyes*) aperto; (*sense of a word*) lato || *adv* largamente; completamente; lontano; **wide of the mark** lontano dal bersa- glio

wide'-an'gle *adj* grandangolare

wide'-awake' *adj* sveglio

widen ['waɪdən] *tr* slargare, estendere || *intr* slargarsi, estendersi

wide'-o'pen *adj* spalancato; (*to a gambler*) accessibile

wide'-spread' *adj* (*e.g., arms*) aperto; diffuso

widow ['wɪdo] *s* vedova; (cards) morto || *tr* lasciar vedova

widower ['wɪdo·ər] *s* vedovo

widowhood ['wɪdo,hud] *s* vedovanza

wid'ow's mite' *s* obolo della vedova

wid'ow's weeds' *spl* gramaglie *fpl* ve- dovili

width [wɪdθ] *s* larghezza

wield [wild] *tr* (*e.g., a sword*) bran- dire; (*e.g., a hammer*) maneggiare; (*power*) esercitare

wife [waɪf] *s* (**wives** [waɪvz]) moglie *f*

wig [wɪg] *s* parrucca

wiggle ['wɪgəl] *s* dimenio; (*of fish*)

guizzo || *tr* dimenare || *intr* dimenarsi; guizzare

wig'wag' *s* segnalazione con bandierine || *v* (*pret & pp* -wagged; *ger* -wagging) *tr & intr* segnalare con bandierine

wigwam ['wɪgwɑm] *s* tenda a cupola dei pellirosse, wigwam *m*

wild [waɪld] *adj* (*animal*) feroce; (*e.g., berry*) selvatico; (*barbarous*) selvaggio; (*violent*) furioso; (*mad*) pazzo; (*unruly*) discolo, indisciplinato; (*extravagant*) pazzesco; (*shot or throw*) lanciato all'impazzata; **wild about** pazzo per || *s* regione deserta; **the wild** la foresta; **wilds** regioni selvagge || *adv* pazzamente; **to go wild** andare in delirio; **to run wild** crescere all'impazzata; correre senza freno

wild' boar' *s* cinghiale *m*

wild' card' *s* matta

wild'cat' *s* gatto selvatico; lince *f*; impresa arrischiata || *v* (*pret & pp* -catted; *ger* -catting) *tr & intr* esplorare per conto proprio

wild'cat strike' *s* sciopero non autorizzato dal sindacato

wilderness ['wɪldərnɪs] *s* deserto

wild-eyed ['waɪld ˌaɪd] *adj* stralunato; (*scheme*) pazzesco

wild'fire' *s* fuoco greco; fuoco fatuo; **to spread like wildfire** crescere come la gramigna; (*said of news*) spargersi come il baleno

wild' flow'er *s* fiore *m* di campo

wild' goose' *s* oca selvatica

wild'-goose' chase' *s* ricerca della luna nel pozzo

wild'life' *s* animali *spl* selvatici

wild' oat' *s* avena selvatica; **to sow one's wild oats** correre la cavallina

wild' ol'ive *s* olivastro, oleastro

wile [waɪl] *s* stratagemma *m*, inganno; (*cunning*) astuzia || *tr* allettare; **to wile away** passare piacevolmente

will [wɪl] *s* volontà *f*, volere *m*; (law) testamento; **at will** a volontà || *tr* volere; (law) legare || *intr* volere; **do as you will** faccia come vuole || *v* (*pret & cond* would) *aux* **she will leave tomorrow** partirà domani; **a cactus plant will live two months without water** una pianta grassa può vivere due mesi senz'acqua

willful ['wɪlfəl] *adj* volontario; ostinato

willfulness ['wɪlfəlnɪs] *s* volontarietà *f*; ostinatezza

William ['wɪljəm] *s* Guglielmo

willing ['wɪlɪŋ] *adj* volonteroso; **to be willing** essere disposto

willingly ['wɪlɪŋli] *adv* di buon grado, volentieri

willingness ['wɪlɪŋnɪs] *s* buona voglia, propensione

will-o'-the-wisp ['wɪləðə'wɪsp] *s* fuoco fatuo; (fig) illusione, chimera

willow ['wɪlo] *s* salice *m*

willowy ['wɪlo·i] *adj* pieghevole; (*slender*) snello; pieno di giunchi

will' pow'er *s* forza di volontà

willy-nilly ['wɪli'nɪli] *adv* volente o nolente

wilt [wɪlt] *tr* far appassire || *intr* appassire, avvizzire

wil·y ['waɪli] *adj* (-**ier**; -**iest**) astuto, scaltro

wimple ['wɪmpəl] *s* soggolo

win [wɪn] *s* vittoria, vincita || *v* (*pret & pp* won [wʌn]; *ger* winning) *tr & intr* guadagnare; **to win out** vincere, aver successo

wince [wɪns] *s* sussulto || *intr* sussultare

winch [wɪntʃ] *s* verricello; (*handle*) manovella; (naut) molinello

wind [wɪnd] *s* vento; (*gas in intestines*) vento; (*breath*) fiato, tenuta; **to break wind** scoreggiare; **to get wind of** subodorare; **to sail close to the wind** (naut) andare all'orza; **to take the wind out of the sails of** sconcertare; **winds** (mus) fiati *mpl* || *tr* far perdere il fiato a || [waɪnd] *v* (*pret & pp* wound [waʊnd]) *tr* (*to wrap up*) arrotolare; (*thread, wool*) dipanare, aggomitolare; (*a clock*) caricare; (*a handle*) far girare; **to wind one's way through** serpeggiare per; **to wind up** arrotolare; eccitare; finire, portare a termine || *intr* serpeggiare, snodarsi

windbag ['wɪnd ˌbæg] *s* (*of a bagpipe*) otre *m*; (fig) parolaio, otre *m* di vento

windbreak ['wɪnd ˌbrek] *s* frangivento

wind' cone' [wɪnd] *s* manica a vento

winded ['wɪndɪd] *adj* senza fiato

windfall ['wɪnd ˌfɔl] *s* frutta abbattuta dal vento; provvidenza, manna del cielo

wind'ing sheet' ['waɪndɪŋ] *s* lenzuolo funebre

wind'ing stairs' ['waɪndɪŋ] *spl* scala a chiocciola

wind' in'strument [wɪnd] *s* (mus) strumento a fiato

windlass ['wɪndləs] *s* verricello

windmill ['wɪnd ˌmɪl] *s* mulino a vento; (*air turbine*) aeromotore *m*; **to tilt at windmills** combattere i mulini a vento

window ['wɪndo] *s* finestra; (*of ticket office*) sportello; (*of car or coach*) finestrino

win'dow dress'er *s* vetrinista *mf*

win'dow dress'ing *s* vetrinistica; (fig) facciata, apparenza

win'dow en'velope *s* busta a finestrella

win'dow frame' *s* intelaiatura della finestra

win'dow-pane' *s* vetro, invetriata

win'dow sash' *s* intelaiatura della finestra

win'dow screen' *s* zanzariera

win'dow shade' *s* tendina avvolgibile

win'dow-shop' *v* (*pret & pp* -shopped; *ger* -shopping) *intr* guardare nelle vetrine senza comprare

win'dow sill' *s* davanzale *m* della finestra

windpipe ['wɪnd ˌpaɪp] *s* trachea

windproof ['wɪnd ˌpruf] *adj* resistente al vento

windshield ['wɪnd ˌʃild] *s* parabrezza *m*

wind'shield wash'er *s* lavacristallo

wind'shield wip'er *s* tergicristallo

windsock ['wɪnd‚sak] *s* (aer) manica a vento

windstorm ['wɪnd‚stɔrm] *s* bufera di vento

wind' tun'nel [wɪnd] *s* (aer) galleria aerodinamica

wind-up ['waɪnd‚ʌp] *s* conclusione

windward ['wɪndwərd] *s* orza, sopravvento; **to turn to windward** mettersi al sopravvento

Wind'ward Is'lands *spl* Isole *fpl* Sopravvento

wind-y ['wɪndi] *adj* (-ier; -iest) ventoso; verboso, ampolloso; **it is windy** fa vento

wine [waɪn] *s* vino || *tr* offrire vino a || *intr* bere del vino

wine' cel'lar *s* cantina

wine'glass' *s* bicchiere da vino

winegrower ['waɪn‚gro·ər] *s* vinificatore *m*, viticoltore *m*

wine' press' *s* torchio per l'uva

winer-y ['waɪnəri] *s* (-ies) stabilimento vinicolo

wine'shop' *s* fiaschetteria

wine'skin' *s* otre *m*

wine' stew'ard *s* sommelier *m*

winetaster ['waɪn‚testər] *s* degustatore *m* di vini

wing [wɪŋ] *s* ala; (*unit of air force*) aerobrigata; (theat) quinta; **to take wing** levarsi a volo; **under one's wing** sotto la protezione di qlcu || *tr* ferire nell'ala; **to wing one's way** volare, portarsi a volo

wing' chair' *s* poltrona a orecchioni

wing' col'lar *s* colletto per marsina

wing' nut' *s* (mach) galletto

wing'span' *s* (*of airplane*) apertura alare

wing'spread' *s* (*of bird*) apertura alare

wink [wɪŋk] *s* ammicco; **in a wink** in un batter d'occhio; **to not sleep a wink** non chiudere occhio; **to take forty winks** (coll) schiacciare un pisolino || *tr* (*the eye*) strizzare || *intr* ammiccare, strizzare l'occhio; (*to blink*) battere le ciglia; **to wink at** ammiccare a; far finta di non vedere

winner ['wɪnər] *s* vincitore *m*

winning ['wɪnɪŋ] *adj* vincente, vincitore; attraente, simpatico || **winnings** *spl* vincita

winnow ['wɪno] *tr* ventilare, brezzare; (fig) vagliare || *intr* svolazzare

winsome ['wɪnsəm] *adj* attraente

winter ['wɪntər] *adj* invernale || *s* inverno || *intr* svernare

win'ter·green' *s* tè *m* del Canadà; olio di gaulteria

win·try ['wɪntri] *adj* (-trier; -triest) invernale; freddo

wipe [waɪp] *tr* forbire, detergere; (*to dry*) asciugare; **to wipe away** (*tears*) asciugare; **to wipe off** pulire, forbire; **to wipe out** distruggere completamente; (coll) eliminare

wiper ['waɪpər] *s* strofinaccio; (mach) camma; (elec) contatto scorrevole

wire [waɪr] *s* filo metallico; telegramma *m*; (coll) telegrafo; **to pull wires** manovrare di dietro le quinte

|| *tr* legare con filo metallico; attrezzare l'elettricità in; (coll) mandare per telegrafo; (coll) telegrafare || *intr* (coll) telegrafare

wire' cut'ter *s* pinza tagliafili

wire' entan'glement *s* reticolato di filo spinato

wire' gauge' *s* calibro da fili

wire-haired ['waɪr‚herd] *adj* a pelo ruvido

wireless ['waɪrlɪs] *adj* senza fili || *s* telegrafo senza fili; telegrafia senza fili

wire' nail' *s* chiodo da falegname

wirepulling ['waɪr‚pulɪŋ] *s* manovra dietro alle quinte

wire' record'er *s* magnetofono a filo

wire' screen' *s* rete metallica

wire'tap' *v* (*pret & pp* -tapped; *ger* -tapping) *tr* (*a conversation*) intercettare

wiring ['waɪrɪŋ] *s* sistema *m* di fili elettrici

wir-y ['waɪri] *adj* (-ier; -iest) fatto di filo; (*hair*) ispido; (*tone*) metallico, vibrante; (*sinewy*) segaligno

wisdom ['wɪzdəm] *s* senno, sapienza, saggezza

wis'dom tooth' *s* dente *m* del giudizio

wise [waɪz] *adj* saggio, sapiente; (*decision*) giudizioso; **to be wise to** (slang) accorgersi del gioco di; **to get wise** (slang) mangiare la foglia; (slang) diventare impertinente || *s* modo, maniera; **in no wise** in nessun modo || *tr*—**to wise up** (slang) avvertire || *intr*—**to wise up** (slang) accorgersi

wiseacre ['waɪz‚ekər] *s* sapientone *m*

wise'crack' *s* (coll) spiritosaggine *f* || *intr* (coll) dire spiritosaggini

wise' guy' *s* (slang) sputasentenze *m*

wish [wɪʃ] *s* desiderio; augurio; **to make a wish** formulare un desiderio || *tr* desiderare; augurare; **to wish s.o. a good day** dare il buon giorno a qlcu || *intr* desiderare; **to wish for** desiderare

wish'bone' *s* forcella

wishful ['wɪʃfəl] *adj* desideroso

wish'ful think'ing *s* pio desiderio

wistful ['wɪstfəl] *adj* melanconico, pensoso, meditabondo

wit [wɪt] *s* spirito; (*person*) bellospirito; (*understanding*) senso; **to be at one's wits' end** non sapere a che santo votarsi; **to have one's wits about one** avere presenza di spirito; **to live by one's wits** vivere di espedienti

witch [wɪtʃ] *s* strega

witch'craft' *s* stregoneria

witch' doc'tor *s* stregone *m*

witch'es' Sab'bath *s* sabba *m*

witch' ha'zel *s* (*shrub*) amamelide *f*; (*liquid*) estratto di amamelide

witch' hunt' *s* caccia alle streghe

with [wɪð] or [wɪθ] *prep* con; a, e.g., **with open arms** a braccia aperte; di, e.g., **covered with silk** coperto di seta; **to be satisfied with the performance** essere contento della rappresentazione; da, e.g., **with the In-**

dians dagli indiani; **to part with** separarsi da

with·draw' v (*pret* **-drew;** *pp* **-drawn**) *tr* ritirare ‖ *intr* ritirarsi

withdrawal [wɪð'drɔ·əl] or [wɪθ'drɔ·əl] s ritiro, ritirata; (*of funds*) prelevamento

wither ['wɪðər] *tr* intisichire; (*with a glance*) incenerire ‖ *intr* avvizzire, intisichire

with·hold' v (*pret* & *pp* **-held**) *tr* trattenere; (*information*) sottacere; (*payment*) defalcare; (*permission*) negare

withhold'ing tax' s imposta trattenuta

with·in' *adv* dentro, didentro ‖ *prep* entro, entro di, dentro a, dentro di; fra; in; (*a time period*) nel giro di

with·out' *adv* fuori ‖ *prep* senza; fuori, fuori di; **to do without** fare a meno di; **without** + *ger* senza + *inf*, e.g., **without saying a word** senza dire una parola; **senza che** + *subj*, e.g., **she fell without anyone helping her** cadde senza che nessuno l'aiutasse

with·stand' v (*pret* & *pp* **-stood**) *tr* resistere (with *dat*), reggere (with *dat*)

witness ['wɪtnɪs] s testimone *mf;* **in witness whereof** in fé di che; **to bear witness** far fede ‖ *tr* (*to be present at*) presenziare; (*to attest*) testimoniare, firmare come testimone

wit'ness stand' s banco dei testimoni

witticism ['wɪtɪ,sɪzəm] s motto, battuta spiritosa, spiritosaggine *f*

wittingly ['wɪtɪŋli] *adv* consapevolmente

wit·ty ['wɪti] *adj* (**-tier; -tiest**) spiritoso, divertente

wizard ['wɪzərd] s mago

wizardry ['wɪzərdri] s magia

wizened ['wɪzənd] *adj* raggrinzito

woad [wod] s (bot) guado

wobble ['wabəl] s oscillazione, dondolio ‖ *intr* oscillare, dondolare; (*said of a chair*) zoppicare; (fig) titubare

wob·bly ['wabli] *adj* (**-blier; -bliest**) oscillante, zoppo, malfermo

woe [wo] s disgrazia, afflizione, sventura; ‖ *interj*—**woe is me!** ahimè!

woebegone ['wobɪ,gɔn] or ['wobɪ,gɑn] *adj* triste, abbattuto

woeful ['wofəl] *adj* sfortunato, disgraziato; (*of poor quality*) orribile

wolf [wʊlf] s (**wolves** [wʊlvz]) lupo; (coll) dongiovanni *m;* **to cry wolf** gridare al lupo; **to keep the wolf from the door** tener lontana la miseria ‖ *tr* & *intr* mangiare come un lupo

wolf'hound' s cane *m* da pastore alsaziano

wolfram ['wʊlfrəm] s wolframio

wolf's-bane or **wolfsbane** ['wʊlfs,ben] s (bot) aconito

wolverine [,wʊlvə'rin] s (zool) ghiottone *m*

woman ['wʊmən] s (**women** ['wɪmɪn]) donna

womanhood ['wʊmən,hʊd] s (*quality*) femminilità *f;* (*women collectively*) donne *fpl*, sesso femminile

womanish ['wʊmənɪʃ] *adj* femminile; (*effeminate*) effeminato

wom'an·kind' s sesso femminile

womanly ['wʊmənli] *adj* (**-lier; -liest**) femminile, muliebre

wom'an suf'frage s suffragio alle donne

woman-suffragist ['wʊmən'sʌfrədʒɪst] s suffragista *mf*

womb [wʊm] s utero; (fig) seno

womenfolk ['wɪmɪn,fok] *spl* le donne

wonder ['wʌndər] s (*something strange and surprising*) meraviglia; (*feeling*) ammirazione; (*miracle*) prodigio, miracolo; **for a wonder** cosa strana; **no wonder that** non fa meraviglia che; **to work wonders** fare miracoli ‖ *tr—* **to wonder that** meravigliarsi che; **to wonder how, if, when, where, who, why** domandarsi or chiedersi come, se, quando, dove, chi, perché ‖ *intr* meravigliarsi; chiedersi; **to wonder at** ammirare

won'der drug' s medicina miracolosa

wonderful ['wʌndərfəl] *adj* meraviglioso

won'der·land' s paese *m* delle meraviglie

wonderment ['wʌndərmənt] s sorpresa, meraviglia, stupore *m*

won'der-work'er s taumaturgo

wont [wʌnt] or [wɔnt] *adj* abituato, solito ‖ s abitudine *f*, costume *m*

wonted ['wʌntɪd] or ['wɔntɪd] *adj* solito, abituale

woo [wu] *tr* (*a woman*) corteggiare; (*to seek to win*) allettare; (*good or bad consequences*) andare in cerca di

wood [wʊd] s legno; (*firewood*) legna; (*keg*) barile *m;* **out of the woods** fuori pericolo; al sicuro; **woods** bosco, selva

woodbine ['wʊd,baɪn] s (*honeysuckle*) abbracciabosco; (*Virginia creeper*) vite *f* del Canadà

wood' carv'ing s intaglio in legno, statua in legno

wood'chuck' s marmotta americana

wood'cock' s beccaccia

wood'cut' s silografia

wood'cut'ter s boscaiolo

wooded ['wʊdɪd] *adj* legnoso, boschivo

wooden ['wʊdən] *adj* di legno; duro, rigido; inespressivo

wood' engrav'ing s silografia

wooden-headed ['wʊdən,hɛdɪd] *adj* (coll) dalla testa dura

wood'en leg' s gamba di legno

wood'en shoe' s zoccolo

wood' grouse' s gallo cedrone

woodland ['wʊdlənd] *adj* boschivo ‖ s foresta, bosco

wood'man s (**-men**) boscaiolo

woodpecker ['wʊd,pɛkər] s picchio

wood'pile' s legnaia

wood' screw' s vite *f* per legno

wood'shed' s legnaia

woods'man s (**-men**) abitatore *m* dei boschi; boscaiolo

wood'wind' s strumento a fiato di legno

wood'work' s lavoro in legno; parti *fpl* di legno

wood'work'er s ebanista *m*, falegname *m*

wood'worm' s tarlo

wood·y ['wʊdi] *adj* (**-ier; -iest**) boscoso, alberato; (*like wood*) legnoso

wooer ['wʊ·ər] *s* corteggiatore *m*

woof [wuf] *s* (*yarns running across warp*) trama; (*fabric*) tessuto

woofer ['wʊfər] *s* altoparlante *m* per basse audiofrequenze, woofer *m*

wool [wʊl] *s* lana

woolen ['wʊlən] *adj* di lana || *s* tessuto di lana; **woolens** laneria

woolgrower ['wʊl͵gro·ər] *s* allevatore *m* di pecore

wool·ly ['wʊli] *adj* (**-lier; -liest**) di lana; lanoso; (coll) confuso

word [wʌrd] *s* parola; **by word of mouth** oralmente; **to be as good as one's word** essere di parola; **to have a word with** dire quattro parole a; **to have word from** aver notizie da; **to keep one's word** essere di parola; **to leave word** lasciar detto; **to send word that** mandare a dire che; **words** (*quarrel*) baruffa || *tr* esprimere, formulare || **Word** *s* (theol) Verbo

word' count' *s* conto lessicale

word' forma'tion *s* formazione delle parole

wording ['wʌrdɪŋ] *s* fraseologia, dicitura

word' or'der *s* disposizione delle parole in una frase

word'stock' *s* lessico

word·y ['wʌrdi] *adj* (**-ier; -iest**) verboso, parolaio

work [wʌrk] *s* lavoro; (*of art, fortification, etc.*) opera; **at work** al lavoro, in ufficio; (*in operation*) in servizio; **out of work** senza lavoro, disoccupato; **to give s.o. the works** (slang) trattare male; (slang) ammazzare; **to shoot the works** (slang) scialare; **works** opificio; meccanismo; (*of clock*) castello || *tr* far funzionare; lavorare, maneggiare; (*e.g., a miracle*) operare; (*e.g., iron*) trattare; **to work up** preparare; stimulare, eccitare || *intr* lavorare; (*said of a machine*) funzionare; (*said of a remedy*) avere effetto; **to work loose** sciogliersi; **to work out** andare a finire; (*said of a problem*) sciogliersi; (*said of a total*) ammontare; (sports) allenarsi

workable ['wʌrkəbəl] *adj* (*feasible*) praticabile; (*e.g., iron*) lavorabile

work'bench' *s* banco

work'book' *s* manuale *m* d'istruzioni; (*for students*) quaderno d'esercizi

work'box' *s* cassetta dei ferri del mestiere; (*for needlework*) cestino da lavoro

work'day' *adj* lavorativo; ordinario, di tutti i giorni || *s* (*working day*) giorno feriale, giornata lavorativa

worked-up ['wʌrkt͵ʌp] *adj* sovreccitato

worker ['wʌrkər] *s* lavorante *m*, lavoratore *m*, operaio

work' force' *s* mano *f* d'opera

work'horse' *s* cavallo da tiro; (*tireless worker*) lavoratore indefesso

work'house' *s* carcere *m* con lavoro obbligatorio; (Brit) istituto dei poveri

work'ing class' *s* classe operaia

work'ing condi'tions *spl* trattamento, condizioni *fpl* di lavoro

work'ing girl' *s* ragazza lavoratrice

work'ing hours' *spl* orario di lavoro

working'man *s* (**-men**) lavoratore *m*

work'ing or'der *s* buone condizioni, efficienza

work'ing·wom'an *s* (**-wom'en**) operaia, lavoratrice *f*

work'man *s* (**-men**) lavoratore *m;* (*skilled worker*) operaio specializzato

workmanship ['wʌrkmən͵ʃɪp] *s* fattura; (*work executed*) opera

work' of art' *s* opera d'arte

work'out' *s* (sports) esercizio, allenamento

work'room' *s* (*for manual work*) officina; (*study*) gabinetto, laboratorio

work'shop' *s* officina

work' stop'page *s* sospensione del lavoro

world [wʌrld] *adj* mondiale || *s* mondo; **a world of** un monte di; **for all the world** per tutto l'oro del mondo; **in the world** al mondo; **since the world began** da che mondo è mondo; **the other world** l'altro mondo; **to bring into the world** mettere al mondo; **to see the world** conoscere il mondo; **to think the world of** tenere in altissima considerazione

world' affairs' *spl* relazioni *fpl* internazionali

world·ly ['wʌrldli] *adj* (**-lier; -liest**) mondano, secolare

world'ly-wise' *adj* vissuto

world's' fair' *s* esposizione *f* mondiale

world' war' *s* guerra mondiale

world'-wide' *adj* mondiale

worm [wʌrm] *s* verme *m* || *tr* liberare dai vermi; **to worm a secret out of s.o.** carpire un segreto a qlcu; **to worm one's way into** insinuarsi in

worm-eaten ['wʌrm͵itən] *adj* tarlato, bacato

worm' gear' *s* meccanismo a vite perpetua, ingranaggio elicoidale

worm'wood' *s* assenzio; (fig) amarezza

worm·y ['wʌrmi] *adj* (**-ier; -iest**) verminoso; (*worm-eaten*) bacato; (*groveling*) vile, strascicante

worn [worn] *adj* usato; (*look*) stanco, esausto

worn'-out' *adj* logoro, scalcinato; (*by illness*) consunto; (fig) trito

worrisome ['wʌrisəm] *adj* preoccupante; (*inclined to worry*) preoccupato

wor·ry ['wʌri] *s* (**-ries**) preoccupazione, inquietudine *f*; (*trouble*) fastidio || *v* (*pret & pp* **-ried**) *tr* preoccupare, inquietare; **to be worried** essere impensierito || *intr* preoccuparsi, inquietarsi; **don't worry!** non si preoccupi!

worse [wʌrs] *adj & s* peggiore *m*, peggio || *adv* peggio; **worse and worse** di male in peggio

worsen ['wʌrsən] *tr & intr* peggiorare

wor·ship ['wʌrʃɪp] *s* venerazione, adorazione; servizio religioso; **your Worship** La Signoria Vostra || *v* (*pret &*

pp -shiped or -shipped; *ger* -shiping or -shipping) *tr* venerare, adorare

worshiper or **worshipper** ['wʌrʃɪpər] *s* adoratore *m;* (*in church*) devoto, fedele *m*

worst [wʌrst] *adj* (il) peggiore; pessimo || *s* peggio, peggiore *m;* **at worst** alla peggio; **if worst comes to worst** alla peggio; **to get the worst** averne la peggio || *adv* peggio

worsted ['wustɪd] *adj* di lana pettinata || *s* tessuto di lana pettinata

wort [wʌrt] *s* mosto di malto; pianta, erba

worth [wʌrθ] *adj* che vale, da, e.g., **worth ten dollars** da dieci dollari; **to be worth** valere; essere di pregio; **to be worth** + *ger* valere la pena (di) + *inf*, e.g., **it is worth reading** vale la pena (di) leggerlo || *s* pregio, valore *m;* **a dollar's worth** un dollaro di

worthless ['wʌrθlɪs] *adj* senza valore; inutile; inservibile; (*person*) indegno

worth'while' *adj* meritevole, meritevole d'attenzione

wor·thy ['wʌrði] *adj* (**-thier; -thiest**) degno, meritevole || *s* (**-thies**) maggiorente *mf*

would [wud] *v aux* **they said they would come** dissero che sarebbero venuti; **he would buy it if he had the money** lo comprerebbe se avesse i soldi; **would you be so kind to** avrebbe la cortesia di; **he would spend every winter in Florida** passava tutti gli inverni in Florida; **would that . . . !** oh se . . . !, volesse il cielo che . . . !, magari . . . !

would'-be' *adj* preteso, sedicente; (*intended to be*) inteso

wound [wund] *s* ferita || *tr* ferire

wounded ['wundɪd] *adj* ferito || **the wounded** i feriti

wow [wau] *s* distorsione acustica di suono riprodotto; (slang) successone *m* || *tr* (slang) entusiasmare || *interj* (coll) accidenti!

wrack [ræk] *s* naufragio; vestigio; (*seaweed*) alghe marine gettate sulla spiaggia; **to go to wrack and ruin** andare completamente in rovina

wraith [reθ] *s* spettro, fantasma *m*

wrangle ['ræŋgəl] *s* baruffa, alterco || *intr* altercare, rissare

wrap [ræp] *s* sciarpa; mantello || *v* (*pret & pp* **wrapped;** *ger* **wrapping**) *tr* involgere; impaccare; **to be wrapped up in** essere assorto in; **to wrap up** avvolgere; (*in paper*) incartare; (*in clothing*) imbacuccare; (coll) concludere || *intr*—**to wrap up** imbacuccarsi, avvolgersi

wrapper ['ræpər] *s* veste *f* da camera, peignoir *m;* (*of newspaper*) fascia, fascetta; (*of cigars*) involto

wrap'ping pa'per ['ræpɪŋ] *s* carta d'impacco or d'imballaggio

wrath [ræθ] or [raθ] *s* ira; vendetta

wrathful ['ræθfəl] or ['raθfəl] *adj* collerico, iracondo

wreak [rik] *tr* (*vengeance*) infliggere; (*anger*) scaricare

wreath [riθ] *s* (**wreaths** [riðz]) ghirlanda; (*of laurel*) laurea; (*of smoke*) spirale *f*

wreathe [rið] *tr* inghirlandare; avviluppare; (*a garland*) intessere || *intr* (*said of smoke*) innalzarsi in spire

wreck [rɛk] *s* rottame *m*, relitto; naufragio; rovina; catastrofe *f*, disastro; (fig) rottame *m*, relitto || *tr* far naufragare; distruggere, rovinare; (*a train*) fare scontrare, fare deragliare; (*a building*) demolire

wreckage ['rɛkɪdʒ] *s* rottami *mpl*, relitti *mpl;* rovine *fpl*

wrecker ['rɛkər] *s* (*tow truck*) autogrù *f;* (*housewrecker*) demolitore *m*

wreck'ing ball' *s* martello demolitore

wreck'ing car' *s* autogrù *f*

wrecking' crane' *s* (rr) carro gru

wren [rɛn] *s* scricciolo

wrench [rɛntʃ] *s* chiave *f;* (*pull*) tiro; (*of a joint*) distorsione || *tr* torcere, distorcere; (*one's limb*) torcersi, distorcersi

wrest [rɛst] *tr* strappare, togliere a viva forza; (*to twist*) torcere

wrestle ['rɛsəl] *s* lotta, combattimento || *intr* fare la lotta, lottare

wrestler ['rɛstlər] *s* lottatore *m*

wrestling ['rɛslɪŋ] *s* lotta

wretch [rɛtʃ] *s* disgraziato, tapino

wretched ['rɛtʃɪd] *adj* (*pitiable*) misero, disgraziato, tapino; (*poor, worthless*) miserabile

wriggle ['rɪgəl] *s* (*e.g., of a snake*) guizzo; dondolio || *tr* dondolare, dimenare || *intr* guizzare; dimenarsi; **to wriggle out of** sgattaiolare da, divincolarsi da

wrig·gly ['rɪgli] *adj* (**-glier; -gliest**) che si contorce; (fig) evasivo

wring [rɪŋ] *v* (*pret & pp* **wrung** [rʌŋ]) *tr* torcere; (*wet clothing*) strizzare; (*one's heart*) stringersi; (*e.g., one's hands*) torcersi; **to wring the truth out of** strappare la verità a

wringer ['rɪŋər] *s* strizzatoio

wrinkle ['rɪŋkəl] *s* (*on skin*) ruga; (*on fabric*) crespa, grinza; (coll) trovata, espediente *m* || *tr* corrugare, raggrinzire; (*fabric*) increspare

wrin'kle-proof' *adj* antipiega, ingualcibile

wrin·kly ['rɪŋkli] *adj* (**-klier; -kliest**) rugoso, grinzoso

wrist [rɪst] *s* polso

wrist'band' *s* polso

wrist' pin' *s* spinotto

wrist' watch' *s* orologio da polso

writ [rɪt] *s* scritto; (law) ordine *m*

write [raɪt] *v* (*pret* **wrote** [rot];* *pp* **written** ['rɪtən]) *tr* scrivere; **to write down** mettere in iscritto; (*to disparage*) menomare; **to write off** (*a debt*) cancellare; (com) stornare; **to write up** redigere, scrivere in pieno; (*to ballyhoo*) scrivere le lodi di || *intr* scrivere; **to write back** rispondere per lettera

write'-in-vote' *s* voto per candidato il cui nome non è nella lista

writer ['raɪtər] *s* scrittore *m*

write'-up' *s* descrizione scritta, conto; stamburata, elogio; (com) valutazione eccesiva

writhe [raɪð] *intr* contorcersi, spasimare, dibattersi

writing ['raɪtɪŋ] *s* lo scrivere; (*something written*) scritto; (*characters written*) scrittura; professione di scrittore; **at this writing** scrivendo questa mia; **in one's own writing** di proprio pugno; **to put in writing** mettere in iscritto

writ'ing desk' *s* scrittoio

writ'ing mate'rials *spl* l'occorrente *m* per scrivere, oggetti *mpl* di cancelleria

writ'ing pa'per *s* carta da lettere

writ'ten ac'cent ['rɪtən] *s* accento grafico

wrong [rɔŋ] or [raŋ] *adj* sbagliato, erroneo; (*awry*) guasto; (*step*) falso; cattivo, ingiusto; **there is nothing wrong with him** non ha niente; **to be wrong** (*mistaken*) aver torto; (*guilty*) aver la colpa ‖ *s* torto; **to**

be in the wrong essere in errore; **to do wrong** fare del male; commettere un'ingiustizia ‖ *adv* male; (*backward*) alla rovescia; **to go wrong** andare alla cattiva strada; andare per la cattiva strada ‖ *tr* far torto a, offendere, maltrattare

wrongdoer ['rɔŋ,du·ər] or ['ran-,du·ər] *s* peccatore *m*, trasgressore *m*

wrongdoing ['rɔŋ,du·ɪŋ] or ['ran-,du·ɪŋ] *s* peccato, offesa, trasgressione

wrong' num'ber *s* (telp) numero sbagliato; **you have the wrong number** Lei si è sbagliato di numero

wrong' side' *s* rovescio; (*of street*) altra parte; **to get out of bed on the wrong side** alzarsi di malumore; **wrong side out** alla rovescia

wrought' i'ron [rɔt] *s* ferro battuto

wrought'-up' *adj* sovreccitato

wry [raɪ] *adj* (**wrier; wriest**) sbieco, storto; pervertito, alterato; ironico

wry'neck' *s* (orn & pathol) torcicollo

X

X, x [ɛks] *s* ventiquattresima lettera dell'alfabeto inglese

Xanthippe [zæn'tɪpi] *s* Santippe *f*

Xavier ['zævɪ·ər] or ['zevɪ·ər] *s* Saverio

xebec ['zibɛk] *s* (naut) sciabecco

xenon ['zinan] or ['zenan] *s* xeno

xenophobe ['zɛnə,fob] *s* xenofobo

Xenophon ['zɛnəfən] *s* Senofonte *m*

xerography [zɪ'ragrəfi] *s* xerografia

xerophyte [zɪrə,faɪt] *s* xerofito

Xerxes ['zɑrksɪs] *s* Serse *m*

Xmas ['krɪsməs] *s* Natale *m*

x-ray ['ɛks,re] *adj* radiografico ‖ *s* raggio X; (*photograph*) radiogramma *m*, radiografia ‖ *tr* radiografare

xylograph ['zaɪlə,græf] or ['zaɪlə,graf] *s* silografia

xylophone ['zaɪlə,fon] *s* silofono

Y

Y, y [waɪ] *s* venticinquesima lettera dell'alfabeto inglese

yacht [jɑt] *s* yacht *m*, panfilo

yacht' club' *s* club *m* nautico, associazione velica

yak [jæk] *s* yak *m* ‖ *v* (*pret & pp* **yakked;** *ger* **yakking**) *intr* (slang) ciarlare, chiacchierare

yam [jæm] *s* igname *m*; (*sweet potato*) patata dolce, batata

yank [jæŋk] *s* tiro, strattone *m* ‖ *tr* dare uno strattone a, tirare ‖ *intr* dare uno strattone, tirare

Yankee ['jæŋki] *adj* & *s* yankee *mf*

yap [jæp] *s* guaito; (slang) chiacchierio, ciancia ‖ *v* (*pret & pp* **yapped;** *ger* **yapping**) *intr* latrare, guaire; (slang) chiacchierare, ciarlare

yard [jɑrd] *s* cortile *m*; recinto; yard *m*, iarda; (naut) pennone *m*; (rr) scalo smistamento

yard'arm' *s* estremità *f* del pennone

yard' goods' *spl* tessuti *mpl* in pezza

yard'mas'ter *s* (rr) capo dello scalo smistamento

yard'stick' *s* stecca di una iarda di lunghezza; (fig) metro

yarn [jɑrn] *s* filo, filato; (coll) storia

yarrow ['jæro] *s* millefoglie *m*

yaw [jɔ] *s* (naut) straorzata; (aer) imbardata ‖ *intr* (naut) straorzare, guizzare; (aer) imbardare

yawl [jɔl] *s* barca a remi; (naut) iolla

yawn [jɔn] *s* sbadiglio ‖ *intr* sbadigliare; (*said, e.g., of a hole*) vaneggiare, aprirsi

yea [je] *s* & *adv* sì *m*

yean [jin] *intr* (*said of sheep or goat*) partorire

year [jɪr] *s* anno; **to be . . . years old** avere . . . anni; **year in, year out** un anno dopo l'altro

year'book' *s* annuario

yearling ['jɪrlɪŋ] *adj* di un anno di età ‖ *s* animale *m* di un anno di età

yearly [ˈjɪrli] *adj* annuale || *adv* annualmente

yearn [jʌrn] *intr* smaniare, sospirare; **to yearn for** anelare per

yearning [ˈjʌrnɪŋ] *s* anelo, sospiro ardente

yeast [jist] *s* lievito

yeast′ cake′ *s* compressa di lievito

yell [jɛl] *s* urlo || *tr* gridare || *intr* urlare

yellow [ˈjɛlo] *adj* giallo; (*newspaper*) sensazionale; (*cowardly*) (coll) vile || *s* giallo; giallo d'uovo || *intr* ingiallire

yellowish [ˈjɛlo·ɪʃ] *adj* giallastro

yel′low·jack′et *s* vespa, calabrone *m*

yel′low streak′ *s* (coll) vena di codardia

yelp [jɛlp] *s* guaito || *intr* guaire

yeo′man *s* (**-men**) (naut) sottufficiale *m*; (Brit) piccolo proprietario terriero

yeo′man of the guard′ *s* guardia del servizio reale

yeo′man's serv′ice *s* lavoro onesto

yes [jɛs] *s* sì *m*; **to say yes** dire di sì || *adv* sì || *v* (*pret & pp* **yessed**; *ger* **yessing**) *tr* dire di sì a || *intr* dire di sì

yes′ man′ *s* (coll) persona che approva sempre; (coll) leccapiedi *m*

yesterday [ˈjɛstərdi] *or* [ˈjɛstər‚de] *s & adv* ieri *m*

yet [jɛt] *adv* ancora; tuttavia; **as yet** sinora; **nor yet** nemmeno; **not yet** non ancora || *conj* ma, però, pure

yew′ tree′ [ju] *s* tasso

Yiddish [ˈjɪdɪʃ] *adj & s* yiddish *m*

yield [jild] *s* rendimento, resa; (*crop*) raccolto; (com) reddito, gettito || *tr* rendere, fruttare || *intr* rendere, fruttare, produrre; (*to surrender*) cedere, arrendersi; sottomettersi; cedere il posto

yodeling *or* **yodelling** [ˈjodəlɪŋ] *s* tirolesa

yoke [jok] *s* (*contrivance*) giogo; (*pair*, e.g., *of oxen*) paio; (*of shirt*) sprone *m*; (naut) barra del timone; **to throw**

off the yoke scuotere il giogo || *tr* aggiogare

yokel [ˈjokəl] *s* zoticone *m*

yolk [jok] *s* tuorlo

yonder [ˈjɑndər] *adj* situato lassù; situato laggiù || *adv* lassù; laggiù

yore [jor] *s*—**of yore** del tempo antico, del tempo in cui Berta filava

you [ju] *pron pers* Lei; tu; Le, La; te, ti; voi; vi; Loro || *pron indef* si, e.g., **you eat at noon** si mangia a mezzogiorno

young [jʌŋ] *adj* (**younger** [ˈjʌngər]; **youngest** [ˈjʌngɪst]) giovane || **the young** i giovani

young′ hope′ful *s* giovane *m* di belle speranze

young′ la′dy *s* giovane *f*; (*married*) giovane signora

young′ man′ *s* giovane *m*, giovanotto

young′ peo′ple *s* i giovani

youngster [ˈjʌŋstər] *s* giovanetto; (*child*) bambino

your [jur] *adj* Suo, il Suo; tuo, il tuo; vostro, il vostro

yours [jurz] *pron poss* Suo, il Suo; tuo, il tuo; vostro, il vostro; **of yours** Suo; **very truly yours** distinti saluti

your·self [jur'sɛlf] *pron pers* (**-selves** [ˈsɛlvz]) Lei stesso; sé stesso; si, e.g., **are your enjoying yourself?** si diverte?

youth [juθ] *s* (**youths** [juθs] *or* [juðz]) gioventù *f*, giovinezza; (*person*) giovane *mf*; **i giovani**

youthful [ˈjuθfəl] *adj* giovane, giovanile

yowl [jaul] *s* urlo || *intr* urlare

Yugoslav [ˈjugoˈslɑv] *adj & s* iugoslavo

Yugoslavia [ˈjugoˈslɑvɪ·ə] *s* la Iugoslavia

Yule [jul] *s* il Natale; le feste natalizie

Yule′ log′ *s* ceppo

Yuletide [ˈjul‚taɪd] *s* le feste natalizie

Z

Z, z [zi] *s* ventiseiesima lettera dell'alfabeto inglese

za·ny [ˈzeni] *adj* (**-nier; -niest**) comico, buffonesco || *s* (**-nies**) buffone *m*, pagliaccio

zeal [zil] *s* zelo, entusiasmo

zealot [ˈzɛlət] *s* zelante *mf*, fanatico

zealotry [ˈzɛlətri] *s* fanatismo

zealous [ˈzɛləs] *adj* zelante, volonteroso

zebra [ˈzibrə] *s* zebra

ze′bra cross′ing *s* zebre *fpl*

zebu [ˈzibju] *s* zebù *m*

zenith [ˈzinɪθ] *s* zenit *m*

zephyr [ˈzɛfər] *s* zefiro

ze·ro [ˈziro] *s* (**-roes**) zero || *tr*—**to zero in** (mil) aggiustare il mirino di || *intr*—**to zero in on** (mil) concentrare il fuoco su

ze′ro grav′ity *s* gravità *f* zero

ze′ro hour′ *s* ora zero

zest [zɛst] *s* entusiasmo; (*flavor*) aroma *m*, sapore *m*

Zeus [zus] *s* Zeus *m*

zig-zag [ˈzɪg‚zæg] *adj & adv* a zigzag || *s* zigzag *m*; serpentina || *v* (*pret & pp* **-zagged**; *ger* **-zagging**) *intr* zigzagare; serpeggiare

zinc [zɪŋk] *s* zinco

zinnia [ˈzɪnɪ·ə] *s* zinnia

Zionism [ˈzaɪ·ə‚nɪzəm] *s* sionismo

zip [zɪp] *s* (coll) sibilo; (coll) energia, vigore *m* || *v* (*pret & pp* **zipped**; *ger* **zipping**) *tr* chiudere con cerniera lampo; aprire con cerniera lampo; (coll) portare rapidamente; **to zip up** (*to add zest to*) dare gusto a || *intr* aprirsi con cerniera lampo; sibilare; (coll) filare, correre; **to zip by** (coll) passare come un lampo

zip' code' *s* codice *m* di avviamento
postale
zipper ['zɪpər] *s* cerniera or serratura
lampo
zircon ['zʌrkɑn] *s* zircone *m*
zirconium [zər'konɪ·əm] *s* zirconio
zither ['zɪθər] *s* cetra tirolese
zodiac ['zodɪ ˌæk] *s* zodiaco
zone [zon] *s* zona; distretto postale ||
tr dividere in zone
zoo [zu] *s* giardino zoologico
zoologic(al) [ˌzo·ə'lɑdʒɪk(əl)] *adj* zoologico

zoologist [zo'ɑlədʒɪst] *s* zoologo
zoology [zo'ɑlədʒi] *s* zoologia
zoom [zum] *s* ronzio; (aer) cabrata,
impennata; (mov, telv) zumata || *tr*
(aer) far cabrare, fare impennare;
(mov, telv) zumare || *intr* ronzare;
(aer) cabrare, impennarsi; (mov,
telv) zumare
zoom' lens' *s* (phot) transfocatore *m*
zoophite ['zo·ə ˌfaɪt] *s* zoofito
Zu·lu ['zulu] *adj* zulù || *s* (**-lus**) zulù
mf
Zurich ['zurɪk] *s* Zurigo *f*